MAYWOOD PUBLIC LIBRARY

3 1312 00183

W9-BLQ-508

West Africa

written and researched by

Jim Hudgens and Richard Trillo

this edition updated by

Nathalie Calonnec, Christopher Clarke, Katrine Green,
Emma Gregg, Brendon Griffin, Daniel Jacobs,
Katharina Lobeck, Adam Musgrave, Lone Mouritsen,
Sam Thorne and Richard Trillo

ROUGH
GUIDES

Maywood Public Library
121 S. 5th Ave.
Maywood, IL 60153

NEW YORK • LONDON • DELHI
www.roughguides.com

Canary Is.
Gran Canaria

MOROCCO

Tropic of Cancer

Dakhla

Moroccan-held Western Sahara

Berm Sand Wall

Polisario-held Western Sahara

Zouérat

Nouadhibou

Atar

1

MAURITANIA

MALI

NOUAKCHOTT

Aleg   Kiffa

Néma

Timbuktu

Niger

St-Louis

2

3

Senegal

DAKAR

SENEGAL

Kayes

Mopti

Douentza

BANJUL

4

6

Tambacounda

THE GAMBIA

5

7

Gambia

10

Ségou   San

BURKINA
FASO

Ziguinchor

GUINEA-
BISSAU

BISSAU

8

9

Niger

BAMAKO

OUAGADOUGOU

Labé

GUINEA

Bani

Sikasso

17

18

Boké

11

Kankan

Bobo-
Dioulasso

Black Volta

White Volta

CONAKRY

12

SIERRA
LEONE

CÔTE

19 Tamale

FREETOWN

Bo

13

Nzérékoré   Man

D'IVOIRE

16

GHANA

MONROVIA

LIBERIA

15

14

Bouaké

Yamoussoukro

Kumasi

ABIDJAN

21°

Sassandra

Takoradi

Tabou

Metres

4000
3000
2000
1500
1000
400
200
0

Unpaved road

0   200 km

Sal

ATLANTIC
OCEAN

St-Louis

CAPE VERDE
ISLANDS

DAKAR

PRAIA

BANJUL

at same scale

LIBERIA Countries thus labelled are not covered in this edition

All of West Africa is on Universal Time (also called Greenwich Mean Time or GMT) throughout the year, except Cape Verde (1hr behind) and Benin, Niger, Nigeria and Cameroon (1hr ahead).

ii

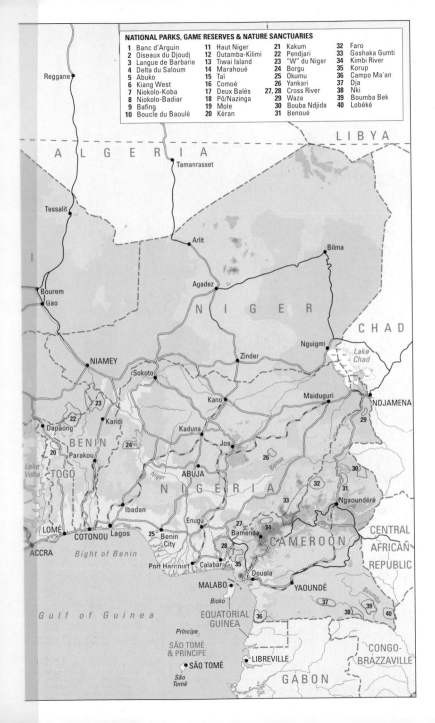

NATIONAL PARKS, GAME RESERVES & NATURE SANCTUARIES

1	Banc d'Arguin	11	Haut Niger	21	Kakum	32 Faro
2	Oiseaux du Djoudj	12	Outamba-Kilimi	22	Pendjari	33 Gashaka Gumti
3	Langue de Barbarie	13	Tiwai Island	23	"W" du Niger	34 Kimbi River
4	Delta du Saloum	14	Marahoué	24	Borgu	35 Korup
5	Abuko	15	Taï	25	Okumu	36 Campo Ma'an
6	Kiang West	16	Comoé	26	Yankari	37 Dja
7	Niokolo-Koba	17	Deux Balés	27, 28	Cross River	38 Nki
8	Niokolo-Badiar	18	Pô/Nazinga	29	Waza	39 Boumba Bek
9	Bafing	19	Mole	30	Bouba Ndjida	40 Lobéké
10	Boucle du Baoulé	20	Kéran	31	Benoué	

Introduction to
West Africa

The physical and cultural diversity of West Africa would be hard to exaggerate. Ranging from shifting sand dunes to dense and uncharted tropical forest, this is also one of the world's most complex regions in cultural and geo-political terms, comprising seventeen countries, from tiny Gambia to giant Nigeria, with a total area and population not far off that of the United States. Every country has distinctive attributes and attractions, and whether you get to know just one or travel widely across the region, West Africa offers opportunities for discovery and true adventure which are increasingly hard to find elsewhere.

Many West African countries are somewhat fragile entities, blocks of territory divided up by whim or convenience between the colonial powers of Britain, France, Germany and Portugal. With the exception of Liberia, none is more than two generations old as a modern nation state, and many are riven by traditional ethno-linguistic divisions that often set the interior apart from the more prosperous coastal regions. As well as one or more official languages, most have lingua franca trading languages and a multiplicity of tribal languages which often transcend borders and identify people before their identity cards. For behind the mosaic of modern states lies a more organic pattern – the West Africa of old nations built over hundreds of years, the societies the Europeans began to infiltrate in the sixteenth century and came to dominate by the early decades of the twentieth. This was the West Africa of the Mali and Songhai empires; the Yoruba city states and Hausa emirates of Nigeria; the Mossi

Fact file

West Africa's 17 nations cover a total **area** of 6.5million square kilometres – roughly the same area as the contiguous USA, minus Texas. The total **population** of the region is around 240 million people, equivalent to an average density of just 37 people per square kilometre, a little higher than the USA, but way below European or Asian averages. Nearly half of West Africa's people are Nigerians, and many of the smaller countries have populations no greater than a large metropolitan area in Europe or North America.

Most West Africans scrape a living from **subsistence agriculture**. West Africa has few **exports**: oil is the principal revenue earner for Nigeria; cocoa and gold are very important for Ghana; several countries have phosphate reserves; Sierra Leone's brutal civil war was about control of its diamond fields; Mali and Burkina rely on the cotton crop; Niger has uranium. Chronic **indebtedness** is common to the whole region, which owes a total of something over $50 billion to rich world lenders (again, the lion's share is Nigeria's, around $34 billion). Yet put in the global perspective, this figure – which averages out to more than $200 for every adult and child – is equivalent to less than two months of the USA's current defence expenditure. While West Africa has seen economic improvements in the 1990s, **living standards** have actually fallen over the last decade in Cameroon, Guinea-Bissau, Liberia, Niger, Nigeria, Sierra Leone and Togo – the same countries which have endured the worst periods of undemocratic rule since the early 1990s (although recent developments in Nigeria and Sierra Leone give cause for optimism). On the other hand, Benin, Cape Verde, Ghana, Mali and Senegal have led the way with relatively fair multi-party elections.

All West African countries except Cameroon are members of the Economic Community of West African states, or **ECOWAS**, whose military wing ECOMOG (the ECOWAS Monitoring Group), largely composed of Nigerian troops, is often called in to keep the peace – most notably in Sierra Leone and Liberia.

kingdoms of Burkina Faso and Ghana; the Asante empire in Ghana; the Wolof states of Senegal; the Muslim theocracy of Fouta Djalon in Guinea; the Bamiléké chiefdoms of Cameroon; and many more. From this older perspective, the countries of today, granted their independence between 1957 and 1975, are imposters, fixed in place by the European powers. Although the national borders are established and nationalism is a part of each country's social fabric, the richness and variety of West Africa only comes into focus with some understanding of its ancient past, and one of the aims of this guide is to bring that depth of culture to the fore.

Some of the biggest pleasures of West Africa, however, are the small things. You'll encounter a degree of good humour, vitality and openness which can make the relatively cold insularity of Western cultures seem absurd. Entering a shop or starting a conversation with a stranger without proper greetings and hand-shaking becomes inconceivable. If you stumble in the street, passers-by will tell you "sorry" or some similar expression of condolence for which no adequate translation exists in English. You're never ignored in West Africa; you say hello a hundred times a day.

This intimacy – a sense of barriers coming down – sharpens the most everyday events and eases the more mundane hardships. For travel, without a doubt, is rarely easy. Going by bus, shared taxi or pick-up van, you'll be crushed for hours, subjected to mysterious delays and endless halts at police roadblocks, jolted over potholes, and left in strange towns in the middle of the night. The sheer physicality never lets up. Cold water, dry skin and clean clothes take on the status of unattainable luxuries.

You can travel in more comfortable conditions, certainly, by hiring an air-conditioned car with driver, by flying whenever possible and by only staying in towns with good hotels. But whether you're paying a lot or a little, travel can often feel like one big breakdown interrupted by sporadic bursts of progress. In all this, the "real" West Africa might sometimes seem elusive.

However, the material hardships provide a background against which every experience and observation stands out with clarity. The sensuous impact of Africa is undeniable: the brilliance of red earth and emerald vegetation in the forest areas; the intricate smells of food cooking, charcoal smoke and damp soil; the towering clouds that fill the skies at the start of the rains; the villages of sun-baked mud houses, smoothed and moulded together like pottery; the singing rhythm of voices speaking tonal languages; and the cool half-hour before dawn on the banks of the Niger, when the soft clunk of cowbells rises amid a haze of dust from the watering herds. These are the images that stay, long after the horrendous journeys have become amusing anecdotes.

The geographical picture

With the exception of the extreme north of Mauritania and Mali, the whole of West Africa lies entirely in the tropics. Physically, the region consists predominantly of **savanna**, gently undulating plains of tree-scattered grasslands. As you head north, the vegetation thins and the patches of sand grow larger as you traverse the **Sahel** – an Arabic word meaning edge or coast, which here refers to the fringes of the Sahara desert. The **Sahara** accounts for much of the three northernmost countries of the region, Mauritania, Mali and Niger.

Topographically speaking, although most countries have their **highlands**, these are generally rugged hills rather than mountain ranges. The most mountainous parts of West Africa are Guinea's **Fouta Djalon**, Niger's **Aïr Massif**, and the highlands of eastern Nigeria and Cameroon, where Mount Cameroon peaks at a respectable 4000m and the summit, 500km from the equator, is usually icy. The big river of West Africa is the **Niger**, which flows in a huge arc from the border of Sierra Leone, through

The Niger River

The Niger – at 4030km Africa's third longest river after the Nile and the Congo – rises in the hilly country on the border between Sierra Leone and Guinea. Already a large river as it flows north through Guinea, it spreads in Mali into innumerable shallow watercourses to create a vast inland delta. The river then reaches the very fringes of the Sahara in northern Mali, where immense sand dunes rise on the riverbank behind snorting hippos, before turning south to flow determinedly through Niger and down to its true delta, the vast expanse of mangroves and creeks in southern Nigeria.

The Niger is the only West African river with a highly developed trading economy reliant upon its annual flood: much of Mali is utterly dominated by this seasonal cycle and during the short high-water season after the rains, the river is a pulsing artery between Bamako and Gao. Many visitors take the opportunity to travel on the river for a few days – an experience that is nothing if not memorable, and can be enchanting if you're lucky. Pressure on the upper reaches of the river and its tributaries, however, for irrigation and hydroelectricity, are having a serious impact on river transport, as it becomes too shallow to navigate.

Guinea and Mali and to the very fringes of the Sahara before turning south through Nigeria and into the Atlantic. Among other notable rivers are the **Bani**, the Niger's major tributary, on which the huge Sélingué hydro-electric dam has resulted in water levels so low that river transport is severely impeded; the **Senegal**, which separates that country from Mauritania and Mali; the **Gambia**, flowing through Senegal and The Gambia; the **Black Volta**, **White Volta** and **Oti/Pendjari**, which all flow into Ghana's vast artificial **Lake Volta**, behind the Akosombo dam; and the **Benue**, which flows down from northern Cameroon to join the Niger in central Nigeria.

As for the scenic environment, expectations of tropical forest are usually disappointed, at least to begin with. While the natural vegetation across the whole southern coastal belt is **rainforest** – with a gap in the Ghana–Togo area where grasslands come nearly to the coast – by far the commonest scene in the densely populated parts is a desolate, bush-stripped landscape where dust and bare earth figure heavily. True rainforest, however, is still present in parts of Ghana, Guinea, Sierra Leone, Liberia, Côte d'Ivoire, southeast Nigeria and much of southern Cameroon. Guinea also features beautiful savanna lands, as does Burkina Faso. Along the coast, creeks and mangroves make many parts inaccessible. The best **beaches** are in Sierra Leone and Côte d'Ivoire, though there is a danger of very strong currents, and you should be exceedingly wary of swimming if you haven't been assured it's safe.

Where to go

Choosing where to go is no easy task: the region offers so much and Africa is likely to confound many of your expectations and assumptions. In the main section of the guide, the individual country introductions and highlights boxes give an idea of what to look forward to. However, at the risk of reinforcing stereotypes, it's possible to make a few generalizations about the feel of the countries.

Of the eleven Francophone, **ex-French colonies**, the three nations most dominated by French culture and language are Senegal, Cameroon, and Côte d'Ivoire. These can also be the more expensive countries to travel in, and their relatively Westernized cities are inclined to be hustly. **Senegal** is an obvious choice as a base from which to launch travels: facilities are much better than in many parts of the region and the verdant **Basse Casamance** district has a network of village-based accommodation. **Cameroon** – which is English-speaking in the west – blends magnificent scenery and national parks with an extraordinary richness of culture, running the whole African gamut from "Pygmy" hunting camps to Arabic-speaking trading towns, and

Getting over culture shock

The desperate poverty of West Africa may come as a shock, especially if you fly in to a big city and have little experience of the third world: try to give yourself a day or two to start adjusting before plunging into exhausting travels. At the same time, try not to be disappointed by the tawdry banality of many of the cities: countless barefoot children in cast-off clothes (often bought from secondhand clothes merchants who sell the items donated to Western charities); urban roadsides ankle-deep in cheap plastic bags used to sell cold drinks in; everything worn out, dirty, confusing and inadequate, covered in a grimy paste of dust and diesel exhaust. But as you leave the city, be prepared to have your breath taken away: by traditional architecture, baobab trees and termite mounds; or by stands of rainforest resounding with bird calls and flecked with butterflies like showers of confetti; and by tantalizing side roads of red earth disappearing into the bush. At some point, you'll need to drive down one of those, or deliberately leave the bus if you're travelling by public transport, and explore off the beaten track. Once you get a few kilometres away from the main roads, a much more satisfying version of West Africa starts to appear, one in which people have plenty of time, the old ways are respected and traditional dress and culture are the norm. Every country has smaller ethnic groups who pursue lifestyles somewhat removed from modern society – see the individual chapters for details on visiting.

taking in the colourful kingdoms of the western highlands. **Côte d'Ivoire**, formerly the first choice in the region for French expatriate postings, but more recently traumatized by its civil war, provides a mélange of the traditional and modern, African and French.

Vast, land-locked **Mali** is blessed with the great inland delta of the Niger River and, again, striking cultural contrasts – the old **Islamic cities** of Gao, Timbuktu and Djenné (on, or near the river), and the magnificent **Dogon country** along the rocky Bandiagara escarpment. Other Francophone countries include the narrow strips of **Togo** and **Benin**, the latter being especially easy-going and fairly undeveloped as far as tourism is concerned; the laid-back, former revolutionary republic of **Burkina Faso**; and the remote and dramatic expanses of **Mauritania** and **Niger**. Perhaps the most impressive of the *pays francophones* is the republic of **Guinea**, with only a thin overlay of European culture, a low population density and superb landscapes.

Four of the West African countries are **former British colonies**, divided from each other by the

Religion

Although it's easy enough to observe that Islam, Christianity and "animism" – the original traditional religious practice – are the three religions of West Africa, the facts on the ground are more complicated. The structure of current belief systems in many parts of West Africa has Islam, or less often, Christianity, overlying the older religion, with elements of both incorporated into religious practice. The most devoutly Muslim countries are Mauritania, Senegal, The Gambia, Mali and Niger where declared adherence ranges from 85 to 99 percent. At the other extreme, in Ghana, Togo, Benin and Cameroon, Muslims make up around 20 percent or less of the population. Christianity has made the biggest inroads in Sierra Leone, Togo, Nigeria and Cameroon, where 30 to 40 percent are church-goers, and in Liberia, which is more than 60 percent Christian. Nigeria is the one country where fundamentalist Islam is gaining ground, several states in the federal republic having instituted sharia law, to the consternation of the federal government.

Traditional religious practice varies greatly between ethnic groups, but a distant supreme being is the norm, combined with a multitude of spiritual entities, represented by, or actually living in, parts of the natural world – animal and plant species, hills or caves, rivers and lakes. At the same time, people's ancestors are part of the community in a way that Westerners find hard to grasp. They have control over people's lives, and to ignore their needs – assuaged through regular sacrifices, celebrations and libations – is as risky as ignoring the requirements of a demanding elder.

speed of the French invasion in the nineteenth century. **The Gambia** is an easy place to set out from, a holiday destination that's small and personable enough to feel accessible for the least adventurous visitor. The distinctive personality of **Ghana** provides flamboyant cultural experiences: its splendid, palm-lined coast, dotted with old European forts, a handful of good wildlife sanctuaries and official encouragements to the tourist industry, make it one of West Africa's most promising countries to travel in. **Sierra Leone**, although hugely likeable, has always been a more demanding destination. It has some of the best beaches in the world – only minutes away from the raffish tumble of Freetown – but has only recently emerged from years of devastating civil strife. **Nigeria**, despite its democratic government, seems barely awake to its tourism potential. There are, however, big travel incentives inland – in the fine uplands of the plateau, the old cities of the north and the wildlife reserves in the east, to mention just three areas. It's a difficult country to come to terms with, but once you're away from Lagos with its unnerving reputation, there's no denying the overall ease and even tranquility which accompany travels here. The same cannot be said for **Liberia** – a former vassal state of the USA, nominally independent since 1847 – which is struggling to recover after 15 years of conflict, confusion and economic breakdown.

The **former Portuguese colonies** are West Africa's least-known destinations. The **Cape Verde Islands** are immediately beguiling, volcanic outcrops and desert islands in the mid-Atlantic, with a scenery and lifestyle that make them hard to leave. **Guinea-Bissau** has its own island highlights, the Bijagós – luxuriant green forests in the warm, inshore sea, as different from the Cape Verdes as it's possible to imagine.

What to eat – and what to avoid

West African food and drink is easy to get used to and mostly quite familiar. Rice or a root crop is the staple diet, eaten around the communal bowl, accompanied by vegetables and protein sources – fish, chicken, bushmeat – as available. Bushmeat is the term for the products of the hunt, and usually means cane rat (a large herbivorous rodent), gazelle, or monkey. Chillis are used quite widely and sauces can be awesomely hot, especially in southern Nigeria. Most of the tropical fruits you'd expect are widely available. For more on eating and drinking, see p.53.

In recent years, monkeys (and, in Cameroon, chimpanzees and gorillas) have been massively over-exploited as a ready market for dried and smoked bushmeat has emerged in the cities, and even overseas. Not only is improperly prepared monkey and ape meat a source of potentially lethal epidemics, but the pressure on primate populations and habitats, even within protected areas, is rapidly leading to a crisis over the future of a number of species. Just as you probably wouldn't buy ivory carvings, it is best to avoid consumption.

How far, how fast?

The first recommendation is to give yourself time. While it's easy to plan an optimistic itinerary covering a large part of West Africa in a few weeks, this is an immense region with poor communications, and you should always assume journeys will take longer than calculations might suggest. Moreover, the rewards become thinner the faster you go, and beyond a certain pace, the point of being there is lost in the pursuit of the next goal. While it may be hard to stop completely or limit yourself to a small corner, that is exactly the way to get the most out of your trip – and incidentally also gives you the chance to put something back in. In such a poor region, the idea of reciprocity is one worth keeping. Patience and generosity always pay off: haste and intolerance tend to lead to disaster.

By far the most satisfying way of visiting West Africa is overland, traversing the yawning expanse of the Sahara, arriving in the dry northern reaches of the Sahel – these days most likely in Mauritania – to the ravishing shock of an alien culture, and then adapting to a new landscape, a new climate and new ways of behaving. Then, a popular and viable route starts in Dakar or Banjul, heads east to Bamako (the road is now much easier than the increasingly chaotic railway) and turns south through Burkina Faso and Ghana to Accra for the flight home. If you don't intend to take in Senegal or The Gambia, allow a week to ten days from arrival on the west coast to arrival in Bamako and at least another two weeks to take in some of Mali – though three weeks would be more fulfilling. Allow at least two weeks extra for each country if you're flying out to the Cape Verde Islands or travelling in Guinea, Guinea-Bissau or Sierra Leone. Senegal, Burkina Faso and Ghana are relatively predictable and you can get anywhere in these countries in a couple of days. In Mauritania, Mali and Niger, visits to the desert need plenty of flexibility. Togo and Benin are straightforward enough, with main roads getting to most parts, as is Nigeria, which has a well-developed transport infrastructure. Finally, Cameroon is much more variable, with speedy travel and terrific delays quite possible on the same route, the latter particularly frequent if you head into the remote forest regions of the southeast.

If you're travelling alone – and it's really the best way if you want to get to know West Africa rather than your travelling companions – it may be useful to know about the main travellers' crossroads in the region, where you might team up for a while or swap experiences: these are Nouadhibou at the edge of the desert, Bamako and Mopti in Mali, Bobo-Dioulasso in Burkina Faso, Cotonou in Benin, and Busua or Accra on the Ghanaian coast.

Arts and crafts

There's a wide range of artisanal production in West Africa. Basket-making is a popular cottage industry all over the region, as is pottery. But textiles are perhaps the most pervasive craft: cotton is widely cultivated and is used, along with wool and imported threads, to produce a great variety of fabric. Weaving is a male craft, and you can often find young boys learning the skill, their hands flying to send the shuttle across, weaving narrow strips a couple of metres in length, which are then sewn together to form a sarong-type wrapper (*lapa* in pidgin English; *pagne* in French). Locally manufactured cloth is often died with indigo or red mud, both of which hold their colour remarkably well. Women who can afford to do so tend to dress in imported cloth wraps, manufactured in Europe. Look out for dramatically hued, geometrically patterned blankets and rugs, especially from Niger; for appliqué work from Ghana; and also for finely woven, high-status Ghanaian Kente cloth.

Certain ethnic groups perform masked dances, but the wooden carvings themselves are usually handed down, and only rarely fashioned anew for private use. The offerings at crafts stalls are generally much less impressive, though some centres (Ouagadougou for example) have excellent selections. Be prepared for serious bargaining and very high initial prices. Avoid buying anything that is of genuine antique value – a trade which has led people to sell their own doors and furniture, these ending up in New York apartments.

The lost-wax (or *cire perdue*) method of bronze-casting is used widely. Cameroon and Côte d'Ivoire produce a lot of small, sometimes comic or obscene statuary by this method, which involves making a basic form in clay, modelling the detail on top of that with wax, repeatedly dressing the delicate sculpture with clay "wash" and allowing it to dry, and then finally covering the whole thing with solid clay and firing it. The wax melts out and into the channel is poured the molten alloy. When that cools, the cast is broken and the work is done.

Look out for leather and silver (or nickel-silver) ware in the markets of the Sahel towns. Here, too, you'll find piles of neolithic arrow heads, stone knives and scrapers, collected from the dunes of the Sahara where they have lain since being abandoned by their makers and users in the last few hundred years. Small and beautifully worked, you can buy a pocketful for a few dollars. Also in the market stalls, you'll find glass trading beads, some old and Venetian, some of recent, local manufacture.

When to go

The big consideration is humidity and particularly the timing of the rainy seasons, rather than the heat: temperatures, in fact, only occasionally climb very much higher than you might experience in Europe and only rarely match the sheer hell of a hot day in Washington DC or Houston.

Broadly, the **rains** come mostly between April and October. Although travel is rarely out of the question during the rains, it's obviously not an ideal time as minor roads, which are usually just dirt tracks, can become quagmires, and transport may grind to a halt. You can be pretty sure of dry weather everywhere from mid-November to the end of January. However, it's as well to be aware of the unpleasant, dust-laden **harmattan** wind that blows southwest across the

Music

West Africa's musical traditions have become world-famous through the voices and CDs of Youssou N'Dour and Salif Keita. From Senegal's powerful *mbalax* and home-grown hip-hop to the soaring sound of the guitar bands of Mali and Guinea; from Ghana's sweet-natured highlife to Nigeria's percussion-based musical steam engines, *fuji* and *juju*, West Africa is a music

hothouse. This rich culture is not difficult to track down – relatively casual or domestic drumming for example is almost an aural constant, especially in rural areas. The role of *griot* or praise-singer is widespread, the professional musician caste always on the scene at parties, particularly weddings and funerals. All over the Mande cultural realm (in other words from Mali to southern Senegal and across most of Guinea and northern Côte d'Ivoire), the griot is known as jali or jeli, and plays the *kora*, a lustrous-sounding instrument in the harp family. You should also listen out for the *bala*, or *balafon*, a large wooden xylophone with gourd resonators. In the way of musicians the world over, the old repertoire of Mande *kora* songs has been modernized and expanded for guitar, drums and synth.

Late night in any city from Wednesday to Sunday, and especially at the end of the month when workers have been paid, you should be able to find clubs with live music, often starting after midnight. Dakar and Lagos are two of the most promising cities to explore, where you can see the stars on their home turf.

Wildlife

In general the central and eastern parts of West Africa have better game-viewing opportunities than the far west, but you won't see many of the large mammals typical of the African plains – such as elephants, rhinos, giraffe, buffalo and lion. They were fairly widespread until the early twentieth century, but today, with one or two exceptions, are to be seen only in

protected areas, where their survival is precarious. The primates (West Africa has two dozen species of monkeys and apes) are also threatened – by bushmeat hunting and habitat destruction – but you're bound to see monkeys at some point in your travels and there are districts where baboons are a common sight at the roadside. Gorilla-tracking, to see habituated groups in Nigeria and Cameroon, is just in the early stages of being established. Otherwise, big animal experiences include domestic camels, hobbled to stop them straying, which you'll soon grow accustomed to seeing all across the Sahel; hippos, which are quite noticeably dispersed in suitable habitats across the whole region; and, surprisingly perhaps, crocodiles, which you can see in every mainland country, either in sacred crocodile pools, where the reptiles are pampered and commonly believed to bring good luck, or on riverbanks, where you should beware them (and hippos). If the large wildlife is slightly thin on the ground, West Africa's birdlife is stunningly rich and rewarding. For more on the region's fauna and national parks, see p.000.

region, directly out of the Sahara, during the dry season, especially from November to March, and which can bring a miasma-like haze to the landscape for days on end.

Where the rainy seasons are very marked, the very end of the dry season is best avoided as it can be stiflingly humid. If you're planning extended travels of several months, the best time to leave is September. The introduction to each chapter contains climate details for that country.

Contents

Using this Rough Guide

We've tried to make this Rough Guide a good read and easy to use. The book is divided into four main sections, and you should be able to find whatever you want in one of them.

Colour section

The front colour section offers an **introduction** to West Africa. It aims to give you a feel for the region, with suggestions on where to go and boxed asides on topics such as West African food, wildlife, arts and crafts, religion, the Niger River and safe travel.

Basics

This section covers all the **pre-departure information** you need to plan your trip. This is where to find out about airlines, what paperwork you need, what to do about money and insurance, Internet access, accommodation, public transport and overland travel – in fact just about every piece of general information you might need.

Guide

This is the heart of the Rough Guide, divided into user-friendly chapters, each of which covers a country, from Mauritania in the northwest to Cameroon in the southeast, omitting Liberia and Côte d'Ivoire which were not safe to visit for this edition. Each chapter starts with a list of **highlights**, an **introduction** and **climate details**, to help you decide where to visit and when to go. The introduction prefaces the **country basics**, where specific practicalities are covered, followed by a look at the country's **history**, reviews of **books** for further reading and, in most cases, **music** and **language** sections. Then comes **detailed coverage** of the country, region by region, district by district: the introductions under each heading should help you plan your itinerary. Most town accounts start with information on arrival, general practical details and onward transport, followed by accommodation, then a tour of the sights, and finally reviews of places to eat and drink, and nightlife. Longer accounts also have a practical directory of general listings.

Index + small print

Apart from a full **index**, which includes maps as well as places and key subjects, this section also covers publishing information, credits and acknowledgements and includes Rough Guides' **contact details** for sending updates and corrections – and comments about how we can improve the next edition of the guide.

Contents

Colour section   i–xvi

Basics   9–87

Guide   89–1252

Map and chapter list

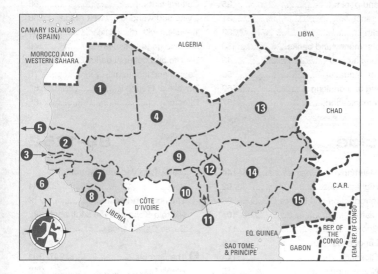

Index

1253–1274

Map symbols

Maps are listed in the full index using coloured text

▪▪▪▪	International boundary		🛆	Gardens
▪▪▪	Chapter division boundary		🕱	Windmill
▬▬▬	Motorway		⚑	Golf course
═══	Main paved road (regional maps)		Δ	Campground
═══	Minor paved road (regional maps)		◉	Accommodation
───	Unpaved road (regional maps)		▣	Restaurant
-----	Footpath		ⓘ	Information office
▬▬▬	Railway		⊠	Post office
─ ─ ─	Ferry route		①	Telephone
▬▬▬	River/canal		@	Internet access
-----	Seasonal river		⊞	Hospital
───	Dyke		🏊	Swimming pool
▮▮▮	Wall/fortifications		✈	Airport
⧫	Point of interest		★	Taxi/bus stop
⌣	Bridge		🅿	Fuel station
峠	Mountains		🕌	Mosque
▲	Peak		⚜	Church (regional maps)
𝍏	Cliff		✛	Church (town maps)
◉	Crater		▮	Building
🕈	Lighthouse		⊡	Cemetery
🚢	Shipwreck		⊻	Muslim cemetery
🌊	Waterfall		▦	Park
᷅	Escarpment		⋯	Beach
🛡	Fortress		◔	Dune
⚑	Museum		▭	Swamp
⊙	Statue/monument		⋰	Marshland
ⴲ	Shrine		▨	Mudflats

Map symbols

Basics

Basics

Getting there

The most straightforward – and usually the least expensive – way to get to West Africa is by air. If you have the time, though, making your way partly overland, either with your own vehicle or using any available transport along the way, gives rewards of its own – and an unbeatable introduction to the region.

Airline seasons for West Africa vary considerably from country to country but many fares, particularly discounted fares, don't vary with the time of year. Most student and youth fares, however, do have a seasonal structure to tie in with summer and Christmas holiday periods. Book as far in advance as you can: some routes are full to capacity at peak periods, especially Christmas, and discounted seats are often snapped up quickly.

You can often cut costs by going through a **specialist flight agent** – either a consolidator, who buys up blocks of tickets from the airlines and sells them at a discount, or a **discount agent**, who in addition to dealing with discounted flights, may also offer special student and youth fares and a range of other travel-related services such as travel insurance, rail passes, car rentals, tours and the like. Some agents specialize in **charter flights**, which may be cheaper than anything available on a scheduled flight, but again departure dates are fixed and withdrawal penalties are high.

For The Gambia, Senegal and Ghana, you may even find it cheaper to pick up a bargain **package deal** from a tour operator at home and then find your own accommodation when you get there. Separately, on pp.16–18, we've covered "overland tours", a catch-all which covers most of the organized holidays that *don't* feel like packages. Not all of them are overland the entire way – the "fly out, tour around by truck, fly back" option is increasingly popular.

You may be able to fly out to one destination and back from another (an "**open jaw**"), which costs more than a standard return ticket but less than two one-way fares. In rare cases, you may also be able to purchase a ticket *back* from West Africa, before you leave – useful if you're travelling out overland.

If West Africa is only one stop on a longer journey, you might want to consider buying a **Round-The-World** (RTW) ticket. West African cities don't normally feature in the standard itineraries of "off-the-shelf" RTW tickets but some travel agents will assemble an itinerary for you, tailored to your needs, at a price. Figure on at least £2000/$3000 for an RTW ticket including one or two West African cities.

Booking flights online

Many airlines and discount travel websites offer you the opportunity to book your tickets online, cutting out the costs of agents and middlemen. Good deals can often be found through discount or auction sites, as well as through the airlines' own websites.

Online booking agents

Ⓦ **www.cheapflights.com** Information on deals from the UK and Ireland. Scheduled and charter flights.

Ⓦ **www.cheaptickets.com** American discount flight specialists.

Ⓦ **www.expedia.co.uk** Discount scheduled airfares.

Ⓦ **www.lastminute.com** Offers good last-minute holiday package and scheduled flight deals. This UK site has links to partner sites in Europe, Australasia, South Africa and Japan.

Ⓦ **www.priceline.co.uk** Name-your-own-price website that has deals at around forty percent off standard scheduled fares. You cannot specify flight times (although you do specify dates) and the tickets are non-refundable, non-transferable and non-changeable. Departures from the UK (for the US Ⓦ www.priceline.com).

Ⓦ www.travelocity.com. Booking facility for car hire

and hotels as well as scheduled flights. Provides access to the travel-agent system SABRE, the most comprehensive central reservations system in the US.
Ⓦ www.travelshop.com.au Australian website offering discounted flights, packages, insurance and online bookings.

Flights from the UK and Ireland

The most reliable nonstop **scheduled flights** from London to West Africa are with British Airways, which serves Accra and Lagos, and with Virgin Atlantic, flying to Lagos and Port Harcourt. Ghana Airways, flying to Accra with connections to other cities, can be subject to overbookings. Nigeria Airways, which claims to connect London and Lagos, is presently barely functioning after years of corruption and mismanagement. Otherwise you'll need to fly via mainland Europe or an African air-travel hub. The airline with the busiest West Africa schedule is Air France, which serves the major Francophone cities, routing all flights through Paris. The French company Point-Afrique is a useful, cheaper alternative.

Most discounted return **fares** to West Africa fall somewhere between £350 and £500; one-ways are rarely less than £200. IATA one-month excursion fares to the region, quoted by airlines rather than travel agents, range from around £550 to £1000.

The only West African country served by regular **charter flights** from the UK is The Gambia, with services from London Gatwick, Bristol, Manchester and Glasgow. Fares range from £200–450, depending on the season and the length of stay. Special promotions are sometimes introduced to fill seats, and these can be really excellent value. All this makes The Gambia a useful, as well as low-cost, entry point to the region, from where you'll be within easy reach of Senegal, Mali, Guinea-Bissau, Guinea and Sierra Leone. The Gambia is also a good exit point: conveniently, you can buy one-way tickets for charter flights to London from specialist tour company Gambia Experience.

There are no direct flights from **Ireland** to West Africa: the best routings are via Paris on Air France, via London on British Airways or via Amsterdam on KLM (overnight stay sometimes required).

Airlines

Air France UK ☏ 0845/082 0162, Ⓦ www.airfrance.co.uk; Republic of Ireland ☏ 01/605 0383, Ⓦ www.airfrance.ie. Flights via Paris to Bamako, Conakry, Cotonou, Dakar, Douala, Lagos, Lomé, Niamey, Nouakchott, Ouagadougou, Port Harcourt (Nigeria) and Yaoundé.

Air Mauritanie France ☏ +33 1/825 825 496, Ⓦ www.airmauritanie.mr. Flights from Paris Charles de Gaulle to Nouakchott, with connections to Nouadhibou, Bamako and Dakar, plus a service from Las Palmas to Nouadhibou and to Nouakchott.

Air Sénégal International France ☏ +33 1/56 64 14 00, Ⓦ www.air-senegal-international.com. No service from London, but will take bookings for their flights to Dakar from Paris Orly, Marseille, Lyon, Las Palmas and Lisbon.

Air Togo France ☏ +33 825/825 587, Ⓦ www.airtogo.com. Flights from Paris Charles de Gaulle to Cotonou and Lomé twice a week (no service from London).

Alitalia UK ☏ 0870/544 8259, Republic of Ireland ☏ 01/677 5171, Ⓦ www.alitalia.co.uk. Flights via Milan to Dakar, Accra and Lagos.

Bellview Airlines UK ☏ 020/7372 3770, Ⓦ www.bellviewair.com. Nigerian airline flying from Amsterdam (with connections from London) to Lagos, Abuja and Port Harcourt, and on to Banjul and Freetown.

Britannia Airways UK ☏ 0800/000 747, Ⓦ www.britanniadirect.com. Charter flights to Banjul from London Gatwick and Manchester; usually Dec–April.

British Airways UK ☏ 0845/773 3377, Republic of Ireland ☏ 1800/626 747, Ⓦ www.ba.com. Direct flights from London to Accra and Lagos.

Cameroon Airlines UK ☏ 020/7727 9311. No flights from London, but will take bookings for their Paris–Douala service, with connections to Abidjan, Bamako, Cotonou and Lagos.

Condor Germany ☏ +49 1803/333 130, Ⓦ www.thomascook-flug.de. No service from London, but will take bookings for their charter flights to Dakar and Sal from cities in Germany, Belgium, Switzerland, Netherlands, Austria and Hungary.

EgyptAir UK ☏ 020/7734 2343 or 7734 2395, Republic of Ireland ☏ 01/370 011, Ⓦ www.egyptair.com.eg. Flights via Cairo to Abidjan, Accra, Kano and Lagos.

Ghana Airways ☏ 08707/707 117. Direct flights from London to Accra, with connections to Banjul, Conakry, Dakar and Freetown.

Iberia Airlines UK ☏ 0845/601 2854, Republic of Ireland ☏ 01/407 3017,

www.iberiaairlines.co.uk. Flights to Dakar via Madrid and Las Palmas.
KLM UK ☎0870/507 4074, ⊛www.klm.com. Flights via Amsterdam to Accra, Douala, Kano and Lagos.
Lufthansa UK ☎0845/773 7747, ⊛www.lufthansa.co.uk. Flights to Frankfurt with connections to Accra, Dakar and Lagos.
Point Afrique France ☎+33 820/000 154, ⊛www.point-afrique.com. Handy travel agency operating their own charter flights from France to West Africa, mainly in the winter. Routes include Paris to Atar (Mauritania), Bamako, Cotonou, Gao (Mali), Mopti (Mali), Niamey and Ouagadougou. They also have a convenient, inexpensive service for obtaining visas.
Royal Air Maroc UK ☎020/7439 4361, ⊛www.royalairmaroc.com. Flights from London to Abidjan, Bamako, Conakry, Dakar, Niamey and Nouakchott via Casablanca.
SN Brussels Airlines UK ☎0870/735 2345, ⊛www.brussels-airlines.com. Flights to Abidjan, Banjul, Conakry, Dakar, Douala, Freetown and Yaoundé via Brussels.
Swiss International Airlines UK ☎0845/601 0956, ⊛www.swiss.com. Services to Zürich for connections to Accra, Lagos, Douala and Yaoundé.
TACV Cabo Verde Airlines Cape Verde ☎+238/60 82 33, France ☎+33 825/358 357. Direct flights to Sal from Paris, Munich, Zürich and other European cities on a seasonal schedule (no service from London).
TAP Air Portugal UK ☎0845/601 0932, ⊛www.tap-airportugal.pt. Flights to Bissau, Dakar and Sal via Lisbon.
Virgin Atlantic UK ☎01293/747 747, ⊛www.virgin-atlantic.com. London Gatwick to Port Harcourt and London Heathrow to Lagos.

Flight and travel agents

UK

Africa Travel Centre ☎020/7387 1211, ⊛www.africatravel.co.uk. Helpful and resourceful Africa specialists offering flights, packages, overland tours, books, maps and advice.
Bridge the World ☎0870/444 7474, ⊛www.bridgetheworld.com. Specializing in RTW tickets, with good deals aimed at the backpacker market.
Co-op Travel Care ☎0870/902 0033, ⊛www.travelcareonline.com. Flights and holidays around the world.
Destination Group ☎020/7400 7045, ⊛www.destination-group.com. Good discount airfares.

Flightbookers ☎0870/010 7000, ⊛www.ebookers.com. Low fares on an extensive selection of scheduled flights.
North South Travel ☎01245/608 291, ⊛www.northsouthtravel.co.uk. Discounted fares worldwide – profits are used to support projects in the developing world, especially the promotion of sustainable tourism.
Quest Travel ☎0870/442 3542, ⊛www.questtravel.com. Specialists in RTW fares.
STA Travel ☎0870/1600 599, ⊛www.statravel.co.uk. Worldwide specialists in low-cost flights and tours for students and under-26s, though other customers welcome.
Trailfinders ☎020/7628 7628, ⊛www.trailfinders.com. One of the best-informed and most efficient agents for independent travellers.
Travel Bag ☎0870/890 1456, ⊛www.travelbag.co.uk. Discount flights worldwide.
Travel Cuts ☎020/7255 2082 or 7255 1944, ⊛www.travelcuts.co.uk. Specializing in budget, student and youth travel, and RTW tickets.

Republic of Ireland

Apex Travel ☎01/241 8000, ⊛www.apextravel.ie. Long-haul flight specialists.
Aran Travel International ☎091/562 595, ⊛homepages.iol.ie/~arantvl/aranmain.htm. Good-value flights to all parts of the world.
CIE Tours International ☎01/703 1888, ⊛www.cietours.ie. General flight and tour agent.
Joe Walsh Tours ☎01/676 0991, ⊛www.joewalshtours.ie. General budget fares agent.
McCarthy's Travel ☎021/427 0127, ⊛www.mccarthystravel.ie. General flight agent.
Trailfinders ☎01/677 7888, ⊛www.trailfinders.ie. Efficient agent for independent travellers.
usit NOW ☎01/602 1600, ⊛www.usitnow.ie. Student and youth travel specialists.

Tour operators

The Gambia is the best-known West African **package destination** from the UK. Most travel agents will have a choice of brochures which include it, and it's a good place to go if you're looking for a short winter holiday, with plenty of sun and a low-key African atmosphere that is not over-exploited. Most departures are scheduled for November to May but a few operators offer summer departures (during the rainy season), which are generally cheaper than the winter season.

The **Cap Skiring** coast in Senegal is as popular a package destination for the French as The Gambia is for the British; you can book through Club Med, if you can stomach the all-inclusive experience.

For information on adventure and other specialist tours organized by companies worldwide, see p.16.

UK

Cape Verde Travel ☎01964/536 191, ⦿www.capeverdetravel.com. Cape Verde specialists.

Club Med ☎08453/676 767, ⦿www.clubmed.com. All-inclusive stays at holiday villages in Senegal. Fun, if you speak reasonable French, and good for families, but very insulated from anything local or West African.

Cosmos ☎0800/093 3915, ⦿www.cosmos-holidays.co.uk. Offers a few packages to The Gambia from Gatwick and Manchester; not the cheapest.

First Choice ☎0870/750 0001, ⦿www.firstchoice.co.uk. Package holidays, including a few mid-price options to The Gambia.

The Gambia Experience ☎023/8073 0888, ⦿www.gambia.co.uk. Gambia specialist with a strong commitment to the country. Clear, honest brochure including far more Gambian hotels than any other operator and, uniquely, year-round departures from Gatwick, Manchester, Glasgow and Bristol.

Panorama ☎0870/759 5595, ⦿www.panoramaholidays.co.uk. Offers winter sun holidays in The Gambia, with a wider choice of hotels than most.

Thomas Cook ☎0870/752 2960, ⦿www.thomascook.com. Tours worldwide, including mid-price winter sun packages to The Gambia.

Thomson ☎0870/160 4529, ⦿www.thomson.co.uk. Offers winter sun packages to some of the better-quality Gambian tourist hotels at keen prices.

Flights from the US and Canada

Currently the only direct flights from North America to West Africa are from New York and Baltimore to Banjul or Accra with Ghana Airways, from New York to Sal with TACV Cabo Verde Airlines or South African Airways, plus South African's flights from New York to Dakar and Atlanta to Sal. There's not much to choose between the fares for direct flights and those routed through Europe – where the European national airlines connect to West African capitals. Typical return fares fall in the $1400–2000/Can$2000–2800 range.

If you do break your journey in Europe, remember that the "two pieces" luggage limit that applies on transatlantic flights becomes a 20kg (44lb) limit for the rest of the world.

Airlines

Air Canada ☎1-888/247-2262, ⦿www.aircanada.ca. Flights from Canada to Europe, with connections to West Africa with partner airlines.

Air France US ☎1-800/237-2747, ⦿www.airfrance.com; Canada ☎1-800/667-2747, ⦿www.airfrance.ca. Connects North American cities with Bamako, Conakry, Cotonou, Dakar, Douala, Lagos, Lomé, Niamey, Nouakchott, Ouagadougou, Port Harcourt and Yaoundé via Paris.

Alitalia US ☎1-800/223-5730, ⦿wwwalitaliausa.com; Canada ☎1-800/361-8336, ⦿www.alitalia.ca. Reasonably priced flights via Milan to Dakar, Accra and Lagos.

American Airlines ☎1-800/433-7300, ⦿www.aa.com. Flights to Europe, for connections to West Africa on partner airlines.

Bellview Airlines ⦿www.bellviewair.com. Nigerian carrier with flights via Amsterdam from New York to Lagos, Abuja and Port Harcourt, with connections to Banjul and Freetown.

British Airways US ☎1-800/247-9297, Canada ☎416/250-0880, ⦿www.british-airways.com. Flights to Accra and Lagos via London.

Continental Airlines ☎1-800/231-0856, ⦿www.continental.com. Flights to Europe, for connections to West Africa with KLM.

Delta Air Lines ☎1-800/241-4141, ⦿www.delta.com. Flights to Paris, to connect with Air France services to West Africa.

EgyptAir US ☎1-800/334-6787 or 212/315-0900, Canada ☎416/960-0009, ⦿www.egyptair.com.eg. Flights from New York (JFK) via Cairo to Abidjan, Accra, Kano and Lagos.

Ethiopian Airways ☎1-800/445-2733 or 212/867-0095, ⦿wwwflyethiopian.com. Flights from New York and Washington to Abidjan, Accra, Lagos, Douala and Yaoundé via Addis Ababa.

Ghana Airways ☎1-800/404-4262, ☎212/371-2800 or 410/694-6241, ⦿www.ghanaairways-us.com. Direct services from New York and Baltimore to Banjul and Accra, with onward connections to Dakar, Freetown and Conakry. Note that they can be prone to overbooking.

Iberia ✆1-800/772-4642, 🌐www.iberia.com.
Flights from New York, Chicago and Miami to Dakar
via Madrid and Las Palmas.
Lufthansa US ✆1-800/645-3880, Canada ✆1-
800/563-5954, 🌐www.lufthansa.com. Flights from
major North American cities to Accra, Dakar and
Lagos via Frankfurt.
Northwest/KLM Airlines ✆1-800/447-4747,
🌐www.nwa.com. Flights to Accra, Kano and Lagos
via Amsterdam.
Royal Air Maroc US ✆1-800/344-6726, Canada
✆1-800/361-7508, 🌐www.royalairmaroc.com.
Flights from New York and Montréal to Abidjan,
Bamako, Conakry, Dakar, Niamey and Nouakchott via
Casablanca.
South African Airways ✆1-800/722-9675 or
866/722-2476, 🌐www.flysaa.com. Direct flights
from New York to Dakar and Sal, and from Atlanta to
Sal.
Swiss International Airlines ✆1-877/359-
7947, 🌐www.swiss.com. Services from major US
cities to Zürich for connections to Accra, Lagos,
Douala and Yaoundé.
TACV Cabo Verde Airlines Cape Verde ✆+238/
60 82 33. New York to Sal, direct, once a week.
TAP Air Portugal ✆1-800/221-7370,
🌐www.tap-airportugal.pt. New York (Newark) to Sal
and Bissau via Lisbon.
United Airlines ✆1-800/538-2929,
🌐www.ual.com. Flights to Frankfurt connecting
with Lufthansa services to Accra and Lagos.
Virgin Atlantic Airways ✆1-800/862-8621,
🌐www.virgin-atlantic.com. Flights from major US
cities Lagos via London.

Flight agents and tour operators

For information on adventure and other specialist tours organized by companies worldwide, see p.16.
Airtreks.com ✆1-877-AIRTREKS, 1-877/247-
8735 or 415/912-5600, 🌐www.airtreks.com. The
website features an interactive database that lets you
build and price your own RTW itinerary.
Alken Tours ✆1-800/327-9974 or 718/856-
9100, 🌐www.alkentours.com. US company with a
specialist division for flights and trips to Africa,
including heritage, ecological and cultural tours, plus
bespoke itineraries.
Council Travel ✆1-800/2COUNCIL, 1-800/2268-
6245, 🌐www.counciltravel.com. Nationwide
organization that mostly specializes in
student/budget travel. Flights from the US only.
Educational Travel Center ✆1-800/747-5551
or 608/256-5551, 🌐www.edtrav.com.
Student/youth discount agent.

Spector Travel ✆617/338-0111,
🌐www.spectortravel.com. Well-connected travel
agency and flight broker, dealing only with Africa.
STA Travel ✆1-800/781-4040, 🌐www.sta-
travel.com. Worldwide specialists in independent
travel; also student IDs, travel insurance, car rental,
rail passes, etc.
TFI Tours ✆1-800/745-8000 or 212/736-1140,
🌐www.lowestairprice.com. Consolidator.
Travac ✆1-800/TRAV-800, 1-800/8728-800,
🌐www.thetravelsite.com. Consolidator.
Travelers Advantage ✆1-877/259-2691,
🌐www.travelersadvantage.com. Discount travel
club; annual membership fee required.
Travel Avenue ✆1-800/333-3335,
🌐www.travelavenue.com. Full-service travel agent
that offers discounts in the form of rebates.
Travel Cuts Canada ✆1-866/246-9762, US ✆1-
800/592-2887, 🌐www.travelcuts.com. Canadian
student-travel organization.
Worldtek Travel ✆1-800/243-1723,
🌐www.worldtek.com. Discount agency for
worldwide travel.

Flights from Australia and New Zealand

From Australia and New Zealand, you'll have
the most straightforward option if you fly to
Europe, and then connect with a flight to
West Africa. The only direct flights to Africa
on offer from Australia or New Zealand are
the Qantas or South African Airways flights
from Sydney or Perth to Johannesburg.
From there you can pick up connections to
West Africa.

Airlines

Air France Australia ✆02/9244 2100, New
Zealand ✆09/308 3351, 🌐www.airfrance.com.
Flights from Singapore to Paris, with connections to
West Africa.
Air New Zealand New Zealand ✆0800/737 000,
🌐www.airnz.co.nz. Flights from Auckland to
London, Singapore and Europe.
Alitalia Australia ✆02/9244 2400, New Zealand
✆09/308 3357, 🌐www.alitalia.com. Flights to
Milan or Johannesburg for connections to Accra,
Dakar and Lagos.
British Airways Australia ✆02/8904 8800, New
Zealand ✆0800/274 847, 🌐www.britishairways
.com. Flights to London with connections to Accra
and Lagos.
KLM Australia ✆1300/303 747, New Zealand
✆09/309 1782, 🌐www.klm.com. Flights to

Amsterdam via Kuala Lumpur, with connections to Accra, Kano and Lagos.

Qantas Australia ☎ 13 13 13, ⓦ www.qantas.com.au; New Zealand ☎ 09/357 8900, ⓦ www.qantas.co.nz. Flights to Europe or South Africa for connections to West Africa.

Singapore Airlines Australia ☎ 13 10 11, New Zealand ☎ 09/303 2129, ⓦ www.singaporeair.com. Flights from major Australian/New Zealand cities to Johannesburg for connections to West Africa.

South African Airways Australia ☎ 02/8826 3300, New Zealand ☎ 09/977 2237, ⓦ www.flysaa.com. Flights to Accra, Dakar, Lagos and Sal (Cape Verde) via Johannesburg.

Swiss International Airlines Australia ☎ 1800/883199, ⓦ www.swiss.com. Flights from Sydney to Accra, Douala, Lagos and Yaoundé via Zürich or Frankfurt.

Flight and travel agents

Backpackers Travel Centre Australia ☎ 029552 4544, ⓔ info@backpackerstravel.net.au.
Budget Travel New Zealand ☎ 0800/808 480, ⓦ www.budgettravel.co.nz.
Destinations Unlimited New Zealand ☎ 09/373 4033.
Flight Centre Australia ☎ 13 31 33 or 02/9235 3522, ⓦ www.flightcentre.com.au; New Zealand ☎ 0800/243 544 or 09/358 4310, ⓦ www.flightcentre.co.nz.
STA Travel Australia ☎ 1300/733 035, ⓦ www.statravel.com.au; New Zealand ☎ 0508/782 872, ⓦ www.statravel.co.nz.
Student Uni Travel Australia ☎ 02/9232 8444, New Zealand ☎ 09/300 8266, ⓦ www.sut.com.au.
Sydney International Travel Centre ☎ 02/9299 8000 or 1800/251 911, ⓦ www.sydneytravel.com.au.
Trailfinders Australia ☎ 02/9247 7666, ⓦ www.trailfinders.com.au.

Flights from the rest of Africa

Getting to each West African country from elsewhere in the region is covered in the Basics section of each chapter.

From **southern Africa**, South African Airways flies from Johannesburg to Abidjan, Accra, Dakar, Lagos and Sal; Cameroon Airlines flies from Johannesburg to Douala, connecting with their flights to Abidjan, Bamako, Bobo-Dioulasso, Cotonou, Dakar, Lagos and Ouagadougou.

From **East Africa**, Nairobi is the natural hub for flights, though even here, where discount ticket agents thrive, special fares to West Africa, apart from the odd Apex, are unknown. Kenya Airways has direct flights to Abidjan, Accra, Douala and Lagos. Ethiopian Airlines flies from Addis Ababa to Abidjan, Accra and – with a change of planes in Addis Ababa – connections to Abidjan, Bamako, Kano, Lagos and Lomé. Cameroon Airlines links Nairobi with Douala, via Kinshasa.

From **North Africa**, Royal Air Maroc connects Casablanca to Abidjan, Bamako, Conakry, Dakar, Niamey and Nouakchott; Tunisair has a weekly flight to Dakar and Nouakchott; and EgyptAir flies to Kano, Lagos, Accra and Abidjan.

South African discount agents

Africa Travel Centre Corner of Military Rd and New Church St, Cape Town 8001 ☎ 021/423-4530, ⓦ www.backpackers.co.za. Branch of the London-based Africa specialist.
STA Travel 27a Mutual Square, Rosebank, Johannesburg ☎ 011/447-5414, ⓦ www.statravel.co.za. Good youth and student fares, with branches all over South Africa.

Overland, adventure and specialist tours

The agents and tour companies in this section are listed by region, but since their packages generally **exclude flights**, it's normally possible to join their trips from any point on the globe. Note that as operators sometimes run trips "in association" with one another, the number of trips offered each year is actually quite small.

It can be worth investigating one of the more inexpensive (sometimes regrettably one-off) expeditions advertised in the travel pages of UK and European papers. These are often just private trips hoping to minimize costs by taking others. Scrutinizing their literature gives a good indication of their probable preparedness and real know-how. If their prospectus looks cheap or hasty, forget it.

As a destination for specialist **American Africa operators**, West Africa is little known in comparison with East and southern Africa. You will, however, find a few **"Roots" and African heritage tours** aimed directly at African-Americans.

Although West Africa is less well known for its wildlife than other parts of the continent, it's extremely attractive to ornithologists, who have a number of specialist **bird-watching trips** to choose from.

Tour agents and operators

UK

Adventures Abroad ☎0114/247 3400, Ⓦwww.adventures-abroad.com. Adventure specialists, with a good programme of small-group two- to four-week tours, which can be booked singly or combined. West African countries covered include Mali, Senegal, Ghana, Togo, Benin and Cameroon; prices for single trips are anything from £840 to £4500, excluding flights.

African Trails ☎01772/330 907, Ⓦwww.africantrails.co.uk. From the UK to Cape Town by truck in a seven-month camping safari, driving through Mali, Burkina Faso, Ghana, Togo, Benin, Nigeria and Cameroon.

Africa Travel Centre ☎020/7387 1211, Ⓦwww.africatravel.co.uk. Agent for several overland-tour companies.

Avian Adventures ☎01384/372 103, Ⓦwww.avianadventures.co.uk. Small-group bird-watching trips to The Gambia and Senegal.

Batafon Arts ☎01273/605 791, Ⓦwww.batafonarts.co.uk. Drumming- and dance-centred holidays in Guinea and The Gambia.

Birdfinders ☎01258/839 066, Ⓦwww.birdfinders.co.uk. Tours for bird-watchers, including one and two-week tours of The Gambia.

Bukima Adventure Tours ☎0870/727 2230, Ⓦwww.bukima.com. Seven-month trips across the African continent by truck, passing through West Africa on the way.

Dragoman ☎01728/861 133, Ⓦwww.dragoman.com. Personal and creative extended overland journeys in purpose-built expedition vehicles; shorter camping safaris too.

Encounter Overland ☎01728/862 222, Ⓦwww.encounter.co.uk. Long-established specialists in long trips by truck, offering a fourteen-week overland tour of North and West Africa, driving all the way south from London.

Exodus ☎020/8675 5550, Ⓦwww.exodus.co.uk. Environmentally and culturally aware adventure tour operator taking small groups on overland trips, including sixteen-day sojourns in Mali or Ghana.

Explore Worldwide UK ☎01252/760 000, Ⓦwww.explore.co.uk. Interesting selection of small-group tours, treks, expeditions and safaris, visiting Mali, The Gambia, Senegal, Cape Verde, Ghana,

Togo, Benin, Niger and Burkina Faso; less rugged in style than some of the more youth-oriented overland operators, with hotel accommodation rather than camping in most cases.

Guerba ☎01373/826 611, Ⓦwww.guerba.co.uk. One of the best adventure travel specialists, with a great deal of African experience; three- to ten-week truck safaris visit Togo, Ghana, Burkina Faso, Mali and Senegal.

Hidden Gambia ☎01527/576 239, Ⓦwww.hiddengambia.com. Customized Gambian tours.

The Imaginative Traveller ☎01473/667 337, Ⓦwww.adventurebound.co.uk. Adventure holidays, including a two-week tour of Mali.

Live Limited ☎020/8894 6104, Ⓦwww.live-travel.com. Tours to Mali, Ghana and Burkina Faso.

Nomadic Expeditions ☎0870/220 1718, Ⓦwww.nomadic.co.uk. Specializing in truck expeditions across North and West Africa, plus shorter cultural tours.

Nubian Travel Ⓦwww.nubiantravel.co.uk. Specialists in cultural tours aimed at travellers of African descent, but open to all. Programme includes a one- or two-week visit to The Gambia's International Roots Festival.

Ornitholidays ☎01794/519 445, Ⓦwww.ornitholidays.co.uk. Offers trips to renowned birding destinations, including The Gambia.

Responsible Travel Ⓦwww.responsibletravel.com. Trips and homestays that have been vetted for their sustainable-tourism credentials. Burkina Faso, Cameroon, The Gambia, Ghana, Mali, Niger and Senegal are among the countries covered.

The Travelling Naturalist ☎01305/267 994, Ⓦwww.naturalist.co.uk. Guided wildlife tours; programme includes an annual fifteen-day tour of Senegal and The Gambia.

Tribes ☎01728/685 971, Ⓦwww.tribes.co.uk. Highly respected organization offering small-group holidays run on fair-trade principles, including eight-day tours of The Gambia (from £480, plus flights).

US and Canada

Adventure Center US ☎1-800/228-8747 or 510/654-1879, Ⓦwww.adventure-center.com. Hiking and "soft adventure" specialists. Options include two weeks in Cape Verde ($1100) and fifteen days travelling from Dakar to Bamako via the Pays Dogon and Timbuktu ($1350). Prices exclude flights.

Adventures Abroad US ☎1-800/665-3998 or 360/775-9926, Canada ☎604/303-1099, Ⓦwww.adventures-abroad.com. Offers a good programme of small-group tours. Countries covered include Mali, Senegal, Ghana, Togo, Benin, Cameroon and Gabon; prices for single trips start at $1300 and climb to $7000 or so, excluding flights.

Africa Desk US ☎1-800/284-8796, Ⓦwww.africadesk.com. Cultural and adventure tours to several West African countries.

Bicycle Africa US ☎1-206/767-0848, Ⓦwww.ibike.org/bikeafrica. Easy-going small-group cycling tours that visit many West African countries between October and December.

Dreamweaver Travel US ☎715/425-1037, Ⓦwww.dreamweavertravel.net. Small community-based cultural- and adventure-travel company. West Africa offerings include trips to Niger, Cameroon, Mali and Togo.

Elder Treks Canada ☎1-800/741-7956, Ⓦwww.eldertreks.com. Small-group adventures for the over-50s, including a three-week tour of Mali and Burkina Faso.

Journeys International US ☎1-800/255-8735 or 734/665-4407, Ⓦwww.journeys-intl.com. Two-week guided tours of Mali for $2000–2500 excluding flights.

Mountain Travel Sobek US ☎1-888/MTSOBEK or 510/527-8100, Ⓦwww.mtsobek.com. Adventure travel specialists providing an original programme of trips which take you well off the beaten track, getting around by a mixture of 4WD, hiking, river and camel. Options include 16 days in Mali and Burkina Faso ($4000) and 25 days of desert driving and nomad culture in Niger ($5000). Prices do not include flights.

Trek Holidays Canada ☎780/439-9118, Ⓦwww.trekholidays.com. Agents for overland-tour companies.

Turtle Tours ☎888/299-1439, Ⓦwww.turtletours.com. Tours to many West African countries, with a focus on cultural events.

Wilderness Travel US ☎1-800/368-2794 or 510/558-2488, Ⓦwww.wildernesstravel.com. Specialists in worldwide hiking, cultural and wildlife adventures, offering a fifteen-day tour of Mali, including the Pays Dogon ($3500), with an optional side-trip to visit the Lobi and Gurunsi tribes of Burkina Faso. Also 23 days in Niger, exploring the desert by 4WD and camel ($4400).

Australia and New Zealand

Adventure Travel Company New Zealand ☎09/379 9755, Ⓦwww.adventuretravel.co.nz. Agent for several overland tour operators.

Adventure World Australia ☎02/8913 0755, Ⓦwww.adventureworld.com.au; New Zealand ☎09/524 5118, Ⓦwww.adventureworld.com.nz. Agents for a vast array of international adventure travel companies.

Africa Bound Holidays Australia ☎08/9361 2020, Ⓦwww.africabound.com.au. Travel consultant covering the whole of Africa.

Kumuka Expeditions Australia ☎1800/804 277 or 02/9279 0491, Ⓦwww.kumuka.com.au. Independent tour operator specializing in overland expeditions, as well as local and private transport tours.

Intrepid Travel Australia ☎1/300 360 667, New Zealand ☎0800/174 043. Agents for overland tour operators including Guerba.

Overlanding independently from Europe

From the Mediterranean coast, the Sahara is just a day's drive to the south – and a couple of days will see you well into the heart of it. Despite the troubles which have effectively closed the classic routes through Algeria to West Africa, overlanding from Europe is still feasible, **via Morocco** and into Mauritania. It's the best way to get to the region if you want to become fully immersed in the identities and landscapes of West Africa: as you finally arrive on the far side of the sea of sand and rock, the first sensations of another world are ones that endure.

If you're setting off on extensive travels, especially if you plan to hitch and use public transport, you should aim to be in North Africa in September and across the Sahara in October. Throughout most of the region, this gives you at least six months before you can realistically expect to be rained upon. You should also be careful to obtain the

---

Overlanding within West Africa

The practical information at the beginning of each country chapter has details on overland arrival **from that country's neighbours**, including transport availability, road conditions and the kind of treatment you might expect from border officials. As a general rule, borders close at dusk and often on public holidays. Very few are open 24 hours.

most up-to-date information about road conditions and political developments in the region. Talk to returning travellers and read the African news magazines.

Trans-Saharan routes

Even before the low-level civil war in Algeria broke out in 1992, the two main trans-Saharan routes through the country – the eastern Hoggar route through Tamanrasset to Agadez, and the western Tanezrouft route from Adrar to Gao in Mali – were becoming risky due to banditry. As the death toll spiralled into the tens of thousands and the north of the country became extremely dangerous, overland traffic all but dried up. At the time of writing – mid-2003 – there is no prospect of conditions changing sufficiently to make travel safe again; the kidnapping in 2003 of several groups of tourists northeast of Tamanrasset has emphasized the point. A third Algerian route, further west, to Tindouf and into the Polisario-controlled territory of Western Sahara, is formally closed to tourists.

However, the overland route **through Morocco** is now well established. Southbound traffic, following the **Atlantic route** that hugs the coast through southern Morocco, enters Mauritania by its northern border and proceeds towards **Nouadhibou**, the mineral port just inside the country. This a safe enough route; there's a minefield around the Mauritanian border (convoys used to lead vehicles past this) but as long as you stick to the well-worn tracks there should be no danger. Apart from a difficult section from Nouadhibou to Nouakchott along the coast – which can be avoided by putting your vehicle on the **ore train** heading from Nouadhibou inland to Choum, or driving alongside the railway track, then on to Atar for the road south – this route is relatively easy on vehicles, although scenically less impressive than the old Algerian routes.

Driving

Driving to West Africa isn't a difficult feat in itself, and many people complete the journey with unmodified road vehicles. Obviously, high ground clearance is important, as is good structural and mechanical condition.

Local mechanics are most familiar with Mercedes, Peugeot, Renault and Land Rover models, and spares for these are far more likely to be available than for other vehicles. Equipping yourself efficiently is essential; it's worth considering taking a GPS system.

All motorized travellers (whether on two, four or six wheels) agree that the comfort and independence of their own vehicle is a mixed blessing. It can, if you let it, insulate you from the life of Africa; it's a permanent security headache, especially in towns; and it says one thing – money – to everyone you meet along the way. You can feel like a travelling circus after a few weeks of this. Taking account of fuel, maintenance and insurance, it is a fairly expensive business, too. And unless you have someone aboard who knows the vehicle inside out (and even then), any serious breakdown can be immensely tedious and costly. Travelling in a **convoy** of at least two vehicles cuts down on the chances of getting stranded if disaster strikes.

The outstanding **advantages** of taking your own vehicle are that you can get off the beaten track (assuming the vehicle is sturdy enough) and visit areas that see a local vehicle only once in a toddler's lifetime. To a great extent, you can actually avoid towns and cities, or at least avoid staying overnight in them by driving out into the wilderness and camping.

One consideration can't be stressed enough – give yourself **time**. Rushing around in Africa is a bad enough idea using local transport. But to try to drive in your own vehicle with a fixed number of days and weeks is to court disaster. Allow a month to head in a leisurely fashion from the Mediterranean to sub-Saharan Africa. It's simply not worth the work, in any case, to rush through at a breakneck pace. The absolute minimum you're likely to need to make it from, say, London to Dakar is two weeks.

Good **books** for drivers heading to West Africa include *Africa By Road* by Charlie Shackell and Illya Bracht, and *Sahara Overland* by Rough Guide author Chris Scott (see also Scott's website ⓦ www.sahara-overland.com for useful, regularly updated information).

Selling your vehicle

A good way to cut the cost of overland travel to West Africa is to take a vehicle along with you for sale; all sorts of cars and jeeps are worth more in Africa. The UK, unfortunately, is not the best place to buy (prices are high and the steering wheel is on the wrong side).

If you intend to sell your vehicle in West Africa, your best investment would be a three-year-old left-hand-drive **Peugeot 505** *familiale* estate car or a **Mercedes saloon.** Most of these will end up in service as *taxis brousse*. **Mercedes commercial vans** are also much in demand. **Twin-cab pick-ups** sell like hot cakes and **4WDs** are also very popular.

Where you sell the vehicle can depend on how well it is still working. Selling the car earlier than planned and hitching a lift with other travellers is always an option.

In **Senegal, Mali, Burkina Faso** and most West African countries there is no problem selling a foreign car; any problems will be faced by the buyer when he registers it locally. In **Mauritania** the car's details are entered into your passport; if you sell the vehicle, it is vital to go with the buyer to the customs office to fill in the paperwork and pay the import duty that will allow you to leave the country without the vehicle. Some purchasers will suggest driving down to the Senegalese border at Rosso to evade Mauritanian duty: be suspicious. Rosso is a confusing border at the best of times and it is easy to get ripped off here; you'd be better off just driving across yourself and selling the vehicle without any customs hassle in Senegal. The worst countries in which to sell a car are **Ghana** and **Nigeria**, which require a carnet (see opposite). Bear in mind that as you near the coast you will start to compete with imports that arrive, rather less depreciated, by ship.

Vehicle documentation

Travelling by private vehicle drastically increases the red tape you'll have to deal with. First and foremost, you must be able to produce the vehicle's **carte grise**, an international registration certificate. Effectively making your car's logbook obsolete once in Africa, the *carte grise* states ownership, country of registration and the registration, chassis and engine numbers – all of which can be checked thoroughly at borders. In the UK, a *carte grise* can be issued by the AA or RAC on production of the vehicle's logbook and payment of a £4 fee. It's useful to carry a few photocopies of the *carte grise* as well. If you're not the owner of the car you're driving, you'll require a **notified document** (*attestation du propriétaire* in French) stating permission to use the car.

You'll also need an **international driving licence** – issued by your motoring organization at home. They will be able to advise whether the countries on your itinerary require you to have a particular format of licence. Spare copies can be useful, as it's the first thing police will confiscate in the event of a traffic offence and you won't get far without one.

A **carnet**, issued by the AA or the RAC in the UK, is also taken by many motorists. These documents allow you to temporarily import your car into a country without, in theory, paying import duties or a deposit. They're expensive, however, at £55–65, depending on how many pages you require, and you'll have to place a bank guarantee (usually twice the value of your car) or cash deposit before a carnet will be issued (though it's possible to take out insurance to cover this deposit). Most West African countries will issue a document that will allow **temporary importation** – in Senegal a *passavant*, in Mali a *laissez-passer*, while Mauritanian officials just write the car details in your passport. However there is almost always a fee to be paid for these documents, and a carnet also speeds your passage through borders. In West Africa only **Nigeria** and **Ghana** absolutely require a carnet. If you plan to **sell your car**, of course, a carnet is the last thing you need: if the vehicle isn't correctly stamped in and out of each country you'll lose your deposit.

Motor **insurance** is obligatory and varies in cost. Motorbike insurance costs approximately half that for cars, and commercial vehicles (including minibuses with eight seats plus driver) twice as much. Morocco is now covered by the European **"Green Card"** (often free; ask your insurance company), without which you will have to buy insurance at the border (about £30 for ten days). Both Mauritania and Senegal require drivers to buy into their national insurance schemes, but most other countries in West Africa are covered by a **carte brune**, an insurance policy that can be taken out in any ECOWAS member state (see ⓦ www.ecowas.int/brown-card).

Motoring organizations

UK and Ireland

RAC UK ☎ 0800/550 055, ⓦ www.rac.co.uk.
AA UK ☎ 0800/444 500, ⓦ www.theaa.co.uk.
AA Ireland Dublin ☎ 01/617 9988,
ⓦ www.aaireland.ie.

US and Canada

AAA ☎ 1-800/222-4357, ⓦ www.aaa.oom.
CAA ☎ 613/247-0117, ⓦ www.caa.ca.

Australia and New Zealand

AAA Australia ☎ 02/6247 7311,
ⓦ www.aaa.asn.au.
New Zealand AA New Zealand ☎ 09/377 4660.

Hitching and using local transport

If you're going to travel under your own steam, it's worth considering a cheap, one-way flight to Morocco or the Canary Isles to get started. Bearing in mind the possible cost of even a small number of days of travel through Europe, this can be a positive saving.

Of course, you can do it the hard way, if you have the stamina to keep **hitching** and are prepared to camp and to take on board the security risks that travelling this way can pose. Not a few Timbuktu-bound travellers have begun the trip hitching to a British channel port for the crossing to France and the unpredictable haul through Spain to

North Africa. Of the Mediterranean ferry ports, Algeciras is the cheapest and easiest embarkation point for Morocco with several ferries a day to Tangier and to the Spanish enclave of Ceuta on the Moroccan coast. Travelling like this, there's no reason you shouldn't get to the Mauritanian side of the Sahara at remarkably little cost.

The ease of hitching in much of Morocco compensates for the common misery of the roadside in southern Europe, though in the far southern regions of Morocco you will need to be lucky, as there's no public transport to the Mauritanian border. Travellers without their own transport here will have to find lifts with overlanders (free and often fun) or the occasional truck, which will generally charge. The final section of the **Western Sahara** will usually cost you to cross. Car sellers may have room for hitchers, but tourist vehicles are generally packed to the gills.

Cycling

If you have enough energy and time, it's quite feasible to consider mountain-biking through Europe in the summer, down through Morocco in the autumn, loading your machine aboard a lorry for the hardest part of the Sahara crossing and then cycling where your fancy takes you through the dry season.

It is of course possible to take a sturdy touring bike, or even use a locally bought roadster. A tourer is much faster on the main roads and a fit cyclist could expect to cover 120km a day or more. But you're likely to suffer more from broken spokes and punctures at unexpected potholes and you're much less free to leave the highways. Some routes and regions for which a mountain bike is ideal are beyond the scope of other bikes. More cycling practicalities are detailed on pp.48–49.

Red tape and visas

Visa regulations in West Africa are notoriously fickle and hard to pin down, though at the time of writing, eleven of the countries covered in this book – Mali, Niger, Burkina Faso, Cape Verde, Guinea-Bissau, Guinea, Ghana, Togo, Benin, Nigeria and Cameroon – require all non-West African visitors to have visas. Furthermore, all visitors to West Africa require a full ten-year passport, which should remain valid for at least six months beyond the end of the trip. Allow at least one blank page per country to be visited.

If you need to state your occupation when applying for a visa, try to avoid declaring yourself a journalist, photographer or anything that might be misconstrued as indicating curiosity in matters of state. Bear in mind also that a visa only constitutes "permission to apply to enter". This isn't mere pedantry. You can be turned away despite having a visa (for arriving on a one-way ticket, for example, in the case of Cameroon) and the length of **validity** of a visa may bear no relation to how long you're actually allowed to stay in the country when you arrive. It's almost always possible to **extend** a first stay; note that in several countries it can be a serious matter if you overstay without extending.

Further kinds of red tape which may entangle you on your travels involve currency declaration forms (see p.41), international vaccination certificates (see p.32), vehicle documentation if you're driving (see p.20) and photography permits (see the practical information in each chapter for more on this).

Getting visas before departure

If you're flying out to a limited number of countries on a short trip, you should apply for visas in advance. If you'll be away for longer, note that few visas remain valid beyond three months, and that certain countries, notably Nigeria and Cameroon, will generally only issue visas in the passport holder's country of residence, or at the nearest embassy representing that country. Although costly, it may make sense to obtain visas for these West African countries before you leave, let them expire, and then apply for

new visas later on at the relevant embassies in West Africa – often the presence of expired visas for these countries in your passport can be a help in getting new ones.

To get a visa in your home country you'll fairly often be asked to provide evidence of a return air ticket and occasionally have to show an invitation or a covering letter stating the purpose of your trip. **Tourist visas** and **business visas** are always distinct. The latter usually require a letter from your company and often a letter from an African contact. It may be worth asking for a **multiple-entry visa** (which often costs more) – it saves a lot of hassle should you need to re-enter one West African country from a neighbouring state. If you need a visa for a country which doesn't have a representative in your home country, note that personal applications made by mail to an embassy abroad can take several months to process.

West African diplomatic missions

UK and Ireland

Benin The Honorary Consul, 16 The Broadway, Stanmore, Middlesex HA8 4DW ☎020/8954 8800.
Cameroon 84 Holland Park, London W11 3SB ☎020/7727 0771.
Côte d'Ivoire 2 Upper Belgrave St, London SW1X 8BJ ☎020/7235 6991.
The Gambia 57 Kensington Court, London W8 5DG ☎020/7937 6316.
Ghana 104 Highgate Hill, London N6 5HE ☎020/ 8342 8686; 13 Belgrave Square, London SW1X 8PN ☎020/7235 4142, ⊛www.ghana-com.co.uk.
Guinea The Consul General, Churchill House, Suite 43–52, Brent St, London NW4 4DJ ☎020/8457 2902.

Mauritania 8 Carlos Place, London W1K 3AS
☎020/7478 9323.
Morocco 49 Queen's Gate Gardens, London SW7
5NE ☎020/7724 0719.
Nigeria UK: 56–57 Fleet St, London EC4
☎020/7353 3776. Republic of Ireland: 56 Leeson
Park, Dublin 6 ☎1/660 4366.
Sierra Leone Oxford Circus House, 245 Oxford St,
London W1D 2LX ☎020/7287 9884, ⓦwww.slhc-
uk.org.uk.

Mainland Europe

As Burkina Faso, Cape Verde, Guinea-
Bissau, Mali, Niger and Togo don't have their
own representation in the UK or Republic of
Ireland, we've listed their diplomatic mis-
sions in mainland Europe below.
Burkina Faso 159 bd Haussmann, 75008 Paris
☎01/43.59.90.63.
Cape Verde Burgemeester Patijnlaan 1930, 2585
CB The Hague, Netherlands ☎355-3651.
Guinea-Bissau 94 rue St-Lazare, Paris
☎01/45.26.18.51.
Mali 89 rue Cherche-Midi, 75006 Paris
☎01.45.48.58.43
Niger 154 rue de Longchamp, 75116 Paris
☎01/45.04.80.60.
Togo 8 rue Alfred-Roll, 75017 Paris
☎01/43.80.12.13.

US

Benin 2214 Kalorama Rd NW, Washington DC
20008 ☎202/232-6656; 222 Florence Ave,
Inglewood CA 90301 ☎310/754-2000.
Burkina Faso 2340 Massachusetts Ave NW,
Washington, DC 20008 ☎202/332-5577; 115 E
73rd St, New York, NY 10021 ☎212/288-7515
ⓦwww.burkinaembassy-usa.org.
Cameroon 2349 Massachusetts Ave NW,
Washington DC 20008 ☎202/265-8790; 147 Terra
Vista, San Francisco CA 94115 ☎415/921-5372.
Cape Verde 3415 Massachusetts Ave NW,
Washington DC 20007 ☎202/965-6820; 535
Boylston St, Boston MA 02116 ☎617/353-0014,
ⓦwww.capeverdeusa.org.
Côte d'Ivoire 2424 Massachusetts Ave NW,
Washington DC 20008 ☎202/797-0300; Pier 23,
San Francisco CA 94111 ☎415/391-0176.
The Gambia 1115 15th St NW, Washington DC
20005 ☎202/785-1399; 11718 Barrington Court
130, Los Angeles CA 90077 ☎310/274-5084.
Ghana 3512 International Drive NW, Washington
DC 20008 ☎202/686-4520, ⓦwww.ghana-
embassy.org; 19 E 47th St, New York NY 10017
☎212/832-1300.

Guinea 2112 Leroy Place NW, Washington DC
20008 ☎202/483-9420; 3505 S Side Blvd 5,
Jacksonville, FL 32216 ☎904/564-1628.
Guinea-Bissau 15929 Yukon Lane, Rockville
MD 20855 ☎301/947-3958; 211 E 43rd St,
Suite 604, New York NY 10017 ☎212/661-
3977.
Mali 2130 R St NW, Washington DC 20008
☎202/332-2249; ⓦwww.maliembassy-usa.org.
Mauritania 2129 Leroy Place NW, Washington DC
20008 ☎202/232-5700; 211 E 43rd St, New York
NY 10017 ☎212/986-7963, ⓦwww.ambarim-
dc.org.
Morocco 1601 21st St NW, Washington DC 20009
☎202/462-7979; 10 E 40th St, New York NY
10016 ☎212/758-2625.
Niger 2204 R St NW, Washington DC 20008
☎202/483-4224, ⓦwww.nigerembassyusa.org;
417 E 50th St, New York NY 10022 ☎212/421-
3260.
Nigeria 3519 International Court NW, Washington
DC 20008 ☎202/986-8400, ⓦwww
.nigeriaembassyusa.org; 020 Second Ave,
New York NY 10017 ☎212/808-0301, ⓦwww
.nigeria-consulate-ny.org.
Senegal 2112 Wyoming Ave NW, Washington DC
20008 ☎202/234-0540; 830 Westview Drive SW,
Atlanta, GA 30314 ☎404/614-5040.
Sierra Leone 1701 19th St NW, Washington DC
20009 ☎202/939-9261; 245 E 49th St, New York,
NY 10017 ☎212/688-1656.
Togo 2208 Massachusetts Ave NW, Washington
DC 20008 ☎202/234-4212.

Canada

Benin 58 Glebe Ave, Ottawa ON K1S 2C3
☎613/233-4429.
Burkina Faso 48 Chemin Range, Ottawa ON K1N
8J4 ☎613/238-4796, ⓦwww.ambaburkina-
canada.org.
Cameroon 170 Clemow Ave, Ottawa K1S 2B4
☎613/865-1664.
Côte d'Ivoire 9 Marlborough Ave, Ottawa K1N
8E6 ☎613/236-9919, ⓦwww.isa-africa.com/
AmbCiCa.
Guinea 483 Wilbrod St, Ottawa ON K1N 6N1
☎613/789-8444.
Mali 50 Goulburn Ave, Ottawa ON K1N 8C8
☎613/232-1501 or 232-3264.
Morocco 38 Range Rd, Ottawa ON K1N 8J4
☎613/236-7391, ⓦwww.ambassade-
maroc.ottawa.on.ca.
Nigeria 295 Metcalfe St, Ottawa ON K2P 1R9
☎613/236-0521, ⓦwww.nigeriahighcommottawa
.com.
Senegal 57 Marlborough Ave, Ottawa ON K1N 8E8

BASICS | Red tape and visas

☎613/238-6392, ⓦwww.ambassenecanada.org.
Togo 12 Chemin Range, Ottawa ON K1N 8J3
☎613/238-5916.

Australia and New Zealand

In either country, the only West African state with its own consulate is **Cameroon**, at 65 Bingara Rd, Beecroft, NSW 2119 (☎02/9989 8414, ⓦwww.camerooncon-sul.com). You can obtain visas for **Burkina Faso**, **Côte d'Ivoire**, **Mauritania**, **Senegal** and **Togo** from the French Consulate General, Level 26, St Martins Tower, 31 Market St, Sydney NSW 2000 (☎02/9261 5779, ⓦwww.consulfrance-sydney.org).

South Africa

Few West African consulates or embassies have opened here as yet. **Nigeria**'s consulate general is at 16 Rivonia Rd, Illovo, 2196 Johannesburg (☎011/442 3620, ⓦwww.nigeria.co.za). For **Mali**, go to Suite 106, Infotech Building, 1090 Arcadia St, Hatfield, 0083 Pretoria (☎012/342 7464). **Côte d'Ivoire** and **Ghana** also have representation in Pretoria (respectively ☎012/342 6913 and 342 5847).

Visa services

If you're in a hurry to secure a visa, or anticipate some kind of hassle getting one, it may be worth considering a commercial **visa service**. They will do all the legwork for a set fee, after you've signed the application forms and mailed them your passport. You still need to plan ahead of course – try to ascertain how long the agency will take to obtain the visa, and finish the paperwork suitably early. If you happen to be travelling with Point-Afrique (see p.13), note that they offer an inexpensive visa service to passengers.

Given the additional expense of using an agency, however, it makes sense to focus their services on obtaining those visas which you know you won't be able to obtain in West Africa itself. In that specific instance, however, note that you can sometimes avoid using an agency as it may be okay to organize your visa on arrival (this facility is more often available at the airport than to overland arrivals; see p.25).

UK

The Visa Service 2 Northdown St, London N1 9BG ☎020/7833 2709, ⓦwww.visaservice.co.uk. They charge £33 per visa, plus the cost of the visa itself and courier fees for overseas applications.

US

AAT Visa Services 3417 Haines Way, Falls Church VA 22041 ☎703/820-5612.
Embassy Visa Service 1519 Connecticut Ave NW, Suite 300, Washington DC 20036 ☎202/387-0300.
International Passports and Visas 205 Beverly Drive, Suite 204, Beverly Hills CA ☎310/274-2020.
Travel Agenda 119 W 57th St, Suite 1008, New York NY 10019 ☎212/265-7887.
Travisa ☎1-800/222-2589, ⓦwww.travisa.com. Offices in Washington DC, Chicago, San Francisco, Detroit and New York.

Getting visas along the way

On an **overland trip**, it would be simplest to pick up along the way the visas you need – were it not for the fact that some West African embassies in the region may occasionally refuse to issue visas to passport holders who could have obtained them in their home country. A further obstacle – though one that's steadily diminishing – is the lack of representation for a number of countries which have very few embassies. You'll need to take visa availability into account when planning your itinerary. Certain nationalities will have hassles getting some of these, so it's worth trying at the first opportunity. Take plenty of passport **photos** – allow three or four for each visa you expect to need.

In the country chapters of this guide, addresses for embassies and consulates have been given in the "Listings" section at the end of each capital city. Once you've located the embassy in question (where you've any choice, it's the consulate or consular section you need to go to), obtaining visas should be fairly straightforward in most cases and is often a good deal easier than sorting things out at home. Nevertheless, you ought to be prepared for an average wait of two to three days from application to delivery, and have a handy hotel address to use as your intended address in the country (nothing too slummy).

A **letter of introduction** from your own embassy is sometimes required (this can usually be provided on the spot, for a fee). Countries for which a letter of introduction is either helpful or mandatory include Mauritania, Guinea, Cameroon and Nigeria, but it's hard to generalize as rules and norms vary greatly from embassy to embassy. Ask about this in advance if you're unsure.

The person whose signature is required for the visa is invariably the **consul**. If you're being delayed or messed around, ask to see him or her in person. If you get stonewalled, or you're in a hurry and told to come back next week, try putting in an hour or two in the waiting room. This often has miraculous effects, especially combined with persistent whining.

Visa fees can be high (up to £40/$60 equivalent or more) and they sometimes vary mysteriously from one applicant to the next, not always depending on nationality. Visas are often issued with revenue stamps stuck in your passport, or a sum of money indicated in handwriting. The value should be what you paid. If it differs, it's worth complaining and asking for a receipt (there may have been an accidental overpayment).

In cities where there's no direct representation, visas for Mauritania, Senegal, Burkina Faso and Togo are often available from the **French embassy**; there's one in pretty well every country in the region. **British embassies** in Rabat and Dakar provide a similar service, in principle, for unrepresented Commonwealth countries in West Africa (including The Gambia, Ghana, Nigeria and Cameroon) though in practice this has often fallen into abeyance. High Commissions (as British embassies are known in Commonwealth countries) cannot do this. It's worth noting that Burkina Faso, Togo, Benin and Niger (and Côte d'Ivoire) have now instituted a system, **Visa Touristique Entente**, whereby you can buy a single visa (CFA25,000 – around £27/$40) from any of their embassies, which covers one entry to every country in the group.

A few West African countries issue (or have an official policy to issue – not the same thing) **visas on arrival** at the airport, particularly in cases where the passenger is arriving from a country with no embassy. Details are given in the relevant country chapters. Don't risk it unless you have to (and check that the airline won't refuse you boarding if you don't have the required visa), as it always delays the arrival formalities.

ℹ Information, websites, maps and books

Maps of countries and cities in West Africa are almost always expensive and hard to obtain in the region itself – buy those you need in advance of your trip. As for tourist offices, those few that exist outside the region are usually attached to embassies or airlines and rarely offer more than vague and outdated leaflets.

Useful websites

Government travel advice

Australian Department of Foreign Affairs Ⓦ www.dfat.gov.au.
British Foreign & Commonwealth Office Ⓦ www.fco.gov.uk/travel.
Canadian Department of Foreign Affairs Ⓦ www.dfait-maeci.gc.ca/menu-e.asp.
US State Department Travel Advisories Ⓦ travel.state.gov/travel_warnings.html.

News and general information

153 Club Ⓦ www.manntaylor.com/153.html. Club with useful quarterly newsletter for travellers to the "153" region (153 being the number of the old Michelin North and West Africa map).

Africa Centre ⓦwww.africacentre.org. American site with news and information from and about Africa.

Africa Confidential ⓦwww.africa-confidential.com. Fortnightly eight-page newsletter with solid inside information.

The Africa Guide ⓦwww.africaguide.com. Informative general-interest site covering the whole African continent.

Afrol ⓦwww.afrol.com. News and links.

AllAfrica ⓦallafrica.com. Excellent searchable database of news from the African press: the best African news site.

Contemporary Africa Database ⓦwww.africaexpert.org. Information about prominent Africans.

L'Intelligent ⓦwww.jeuneafrique.com. Hard-hitting French-language West African news and features from the publishers of *Jeune Afrique* magazine.

Travel Africa ⓦwww.travelafricamag.com. Features for travellers and armchair travellers alike; strong on wildlife and safari destinations.

West Africa Magazine ⓦwww .westafricamagazine.com. Long-established weekly news magazine with an emphasis on Anglophone countries.

West Africa Review ⓦwww.westafricareview .com. Features, essays and interviews.

African music and culture

AfricanCraft ⓦwww.africancraft.com. A showcase for African artists and craftspeople, mainly from West Africa, with articles to read and items to buy.

Africa on Roots World ⓦwww. rootsworld.com/ rw/africa.html. Features about the African music scene and audio clips from African musicians.

Libraries and resource centres

UK

Africa Centre 38 King St, London WC2E 8JT ☎020/7836 1973, ⓦwww.africacentre.org.uk. Houses a reading room with magazines and newspapers, and hosts exhibitions, music performances and language classes.

Commonwealth Institute Kensington High St, London W8 6NQ ☎020/7603 4535, ⓦwww.commonwealth.org.uk. Large centre offering library and resource services, a shop, exhibitions, workshops and a performance venue.

Royal Geographical Society 1 Kensington Gore, London SW7 2AR ⓦwww.rgs.org. Helpful

Expedition Advisory Service (☎020/7591 3030) provides a wealth of information, including maps and technical guides.

School of Oriental and African Studies Library Thornhaugh St, Russell Square, London WC1H 0XG ☎020/7637 2388, ⓦwww.soas.ac.uk/library. A vast collection of books, journals and maps.

US

Black Studies Library, Ohio State University ⓦwww.lib.ohio-state.edu/bslweb.

Boston University African Studies Center ⓦwww.bu.edu/africa.

Center for African Studies, University of Florida ⓦweb.africa.ufl.edu.

Herskovits Library of African Studies, Northwestern University ⓦwww.library.northwestern.edu/africana.

Howard University African Studies ⓦwww.founders.howard.edu/afroam2.htm.

Indiana University African Studies Program ⓦwww.indiana.edu/~libsalc/african.

Institute of African Studies, Columbia University ⓦwww.columbia.edu/cu/ias.

Michigan State University Africa Studies Center ⓦwww.lib.msu.edu/coll/main/africana.htm.

Schomburg Center for Research in Black Culture ⓦwww.nypl.org/research/sc/sc.html.

University of Illinois African Studies Center ⓦwww.afrst.uiuc.edu.

Maps and books

The single most useful item to take is the **Michelin map 741** *Africa North and West*. The newly revised edition of the old Michelin 953/153 map, it takes account of most new roads, showing water and fuel sources, roads liable to flood, ferry crossings and a mass of other details at a scale of 1cm to 40km (1 inch to 63 miles). It covers all of northwest Africa with the exception of southern Cameroon (which appears on their 746 *Africa Central and South*). The only serious competition is Kummerly & Frey's *Africa North & West* map – on the same scale but less detailed and altogether less user-friendly.

For individual countries, the **French Institut Géographique National** (ⓦwww.ign.fr) has maps for a number of West African countries. There's also a number of road maps of Nigeria, and good ones of The Gambia and Cameroon published by Macmillan.

As for **books**, while there's a substantial volume of reading material on West Africa, its subject matter and authorship is very unevenly distributed. By far the largest body of literature in English comes from Nigeria, with its hundreds of novelists and academics. By contrast, many of the Francophone nations have scant coverage other than in French. For pre-departure reading, probably the best foretaste is provided by West African fiction – much of which is available in paperback in Heinemann's **African Writers Series**.

Country-specific reading lists appear in the Basics at the start of each chapter. In the following general listings, o/p denotes a title that's likely to be out of print; books marked * are especially recommended. French works have been included only when there is little alternative in English – on which note, it's worth mentioning that **Jeune Afrique** and **Hachette** both do one- or two-country guides of a more practical nature, in French only, to most of the Francophone countries.

Series publications

African Historical Dictionaries If you're seriously looking to find out about a country, the Scarecrow series (⦿www.scarecrowpress.com) is what you need. They have titles on many African countries, covering names, places and events in detail.

* **Heinemann African Writers Series** AWS books are the vanguard of African publishing in English and add regularly to their list – over 200 titles, though kept erratically in print. See ⦿www.heinemann.com for more details.

Travel bibliographies

Louis Taussig Resource Guide to Travel in Sub-Saharan Africa Vol. 1 East and West Africa. The definitive guide to the guides and much more. Extraordinarily detailed country-by-country coverage of every published source and resource of interest to travellers or expatriates. Libraries will obtain it for you.

Travelogues and related literature

Peter Biddlecombe French Lessons in Africa. Like an uninvited travelling companion, businessman Biddlecombe rattles out his observations on Francophone West Africa so fast, it seems, there's barely the time to notice the stream of contradictions and inconsistencies. Funny, warm and light, and a good book for lone travellers to argue with.

* **Thomas Coraghassen Boyle** Water Music. Lengthy, meticulous – and at times outrageously funny – fictionalization of Mungo Park's explorations. Boyle's vision of the West Africa (and Britain) of two centuries ago is utterly captivating. Essential in situ reading for those long roadside waits: if you only take one book, take this.

Jens Finke Chasing the Lizard's Tail: By bicycle across the Sahara. Entertaining and insightful travelogue, recounting Rough Guide author Finke's journey from Morocco to a sudden end in The Gambia.

Blaine Harden Africa: Dispatches from a Fragile Continent. The Washington Post's former African bureau chief can't shake the arrogant pessimism American journalists seem to thrive on. Coverage of Ghana, Liberia and Nigeria.

Mark Jenkins To Timbuktu: A Journey down the Niger. Well-written and likeable – though admittedly macho – kayaking adventures.

David Lamb The Africans. This was a bestseller, but Lamb's fly-in, fly-out technique is a statistical rant couched in Cold War rhetoric – and, even when ostensibly uncovering a pearl of wisdom, he can be rebarbatively offensive.

Michael Palin Sahara. Amusing account of Palin's travels for the BBC-TV series. Features the photography of Basil Pao, which gives a wonderful flavour of Senegal, Mali and Niger (more of which is found in his own coffee-table book Inside Sahara).

Mungo Park Travels into the Interior of Africa. Absorbing account of the then youthful Scottish traveller's two journeys (1795–1797 and 1805) along the Niger.

Pamela Watson Esprit de Battuta: Alone Across Africa on a Bicycle. Muscular modern travelogue-diary, that takes the Australian author from Senegal to Cameroon and beyond – very strong on anecdotal highs and lows, and detailed documentation, less satisfying on insights.

History

Most histories cover the whole continent, and, inevitably, jump from place to place: Boahen, or Davidson, Buah & Ajayi are the easiest to follow, and are well complemented by various historical and cultural atlases.

The African continent

A.E. Afigbo et al The Making of Modern Africa,

Vol. 1 Nineteenth Century, Vol. 2 Twentieth Century. A detailed, illustrated guide, putting West Africa in the continental context up until the first big changes after independence.

Cheik Anta Diop *Pre-Colonial Black Africa.* First published in the 1950s, Diop asserts that the origins of Western civilization, as well as African, began in Africa. The work encouraged a whole generation to reinterpret the past from an African perspective.

Basil Davidson *Africa in History.* Lucidly argued and readable summary of Africa's dominant nineteenth- and twentieth-century events.

Christopher Hibbert *Africa Explored: Europeans in the Dark Continent, 1769–1889.* Entertaining read, devoted in large part to the "discovery" of West Africa.

West Africa

Adu Boahen et al *Topics in West African History.* An excellent introduction to basic themes in West African history, written in a clear and concise fashion by one of Ghana's most respected historians.

* Basil Davidson et al *A History of West Africa 1000–1800.* Clear, wide-ranging and readable.

J.B. Webster et al *West Africa since 1800: The Revolutionary Years.* An excellent companion to Davidson above.

Historical atlases

Brian Catchpole and L.A. Akinjogbin *A History of West Africa in Maps and Diagrams* (o/p). A remarkable and highly recommended encapsulation of the region's history from ancient times to the 1980s.

Colin McEvedy *Penguin Atlas of African History.* Useful for placing West Africa, and the whole continent, in context, and for getting to grips with some of the names and themes. Fifty-nine maps of Africa with facing text.

Land, people and society

Thomas D. Blakely et al (eds) *Religion in Africa: Experience & Expression.* Thorough examination of religion in Africa and the diaspora.

* R.J. Harrison Church *West Africa* (o/p). Formerly the standard geography reference – traditional in approach. Excellent and unexpectedly absorbing.

Betty Laduke *Africa: Women's Art, Women's Lives.* Laduke turns her worldwide focus on women's art to Africa to examine the pottery of Mali, Cameroon and Togo; bead-making in Cameroon; wall painting in Tiebele, Tiakane and Po in Burkina Faso; and textiles and leather-working in the Sahel.

Patrick R. McNaughton *The Mande Blacksmiths: Knowledge, Power, and Art in West Africa.* Accessible scholarship that deals with both the aesthetic qualities of ironworking and its social implications for Mande peoples.

Robert Farris Thompson *Flash of the Spirit: African and Afro-American Art and Philosophy.* "Art history to dance by" in the words of the *Philadelphia Inquirer*'s reviewer, and this is a unique book, illuminating the art and philosophy that connects the black worlds on both sides of the Atlantic. Big on Yoruba and Dan-Homey roots. Lots of illustrations.

Stephen Wright *African Foreign Policies.* A rare analysis of foreign policy in Africa that targets eleven countries across the continent. Interesting section on relations between Benin and Nigeria and the effects of changing domestic coalitions on their international strategies.

Claudia Zaslavsky *Africa Counts: Number and Pattern in African Culture.* A unique, extraordinary book, with a chapter on *warri* games (see p.87).

Arts

Stephen Belcher *Epic Traditions in Africa.* Elements of epic poetry described, followed by colourful narratives from across the continent in translation. Includes texts from the Sunjata and literary traditions of the Mande and Fula.

Margaret Courtney-Clarke *African Canvas.* Sumptuous colour photos bring out vivid details of exterior and interior house painting by women in a number of countries.

Susan Denyer *African Traditional Architecture.* Rewarding study, featuring hundreds of photos (most of them old) and a wealth of detailed line drawings.

Werner Gillon *A Short History of African Art.* A substantial study despite the name, though inevitably still very selective.

* Elian Girard et al *Colons: Statuettes Habillées d'Afrique de l'Ouest.* Fascinating illustrations of a little-known genre of sculpture: statues of Africans dressed in European clothes.

Thomas A. Hale *Griots and Griottes: Masters of Words and Music.* A comprehensive look at griots – male and female – of Niger, Mali, Senegal and The Gambia and their roles as historians, genealogists, diplomats, musicians and advisors.

Michael Huet *The Dance, Art and Ritual of Africa.* Remarkable photos of ceremonies and costume, captured with an exceptional clarity and power.

David Kerr *African Popular Theatre: From Pre-Colonial Times to the Present Day.* Includes sections on masquerade and concert party.

Esi Sagay *African Hairstyles.* What they're called, and how to do them; a wonderful little book.

Jan Vansina *Art History in Africa*. Readable theorizing by an interesting French anthropologist.
Frank Willett *African Art*. A cheaper, more accessible and better illustrated volume.
Geoffrey Williams *African Designs from Traditional Sources*. A designer's and enthusiast's sourcebook.

Music

Francis Bebey *African Music: A People's Art*. First published in French in 1969, this is an excellent and well-illustrated ethnomusicological survey, concentrating on Francophone Africa.
Wolfgang Bender *Sweet Mother: Modern African Music*. A cultural history of African urban music. Includes an extensive bibliography and discography.
* Simon Broughton, Mark Ellingham and Richard Trillo (eds) *The Rough Guide to World Music: Vol 1 Africa, Europe & the Middle East*. Detailed articles cover most West African countries individually, together with hundreds of potted artist biographies and CD reviews.
Samuel Charters *The Roots of the Blues: An African Search*. Charters' serendipitous journey (The Gambia, Senegal, Mali) aimed to find the blues' roots in West Africa. While he failed, his other discoveries make great reading.
John Miller Chernoff *African Rhythm and African Sensibility*. A travelogue and easy-to-read analysis of Ghanaian drumming, music's spiritual meaning and the place of art in African society. Beautifully written.
John Collins *Music Makers of West Africa*. First published in the 1980s, this is a collection of articles and interviews, mostly on highlife and its offspring, by a committed veteran of the Ghana music scene.
Graeme Ewens *Africa O-Yé!* One of the best Africa-only music books, with a mass of colour and black-and-white photos.
Chris May and Chris Stapleton *African Rock: The Pop Music of a Continent* (o/p). A highly readable account of the development of African music's many and diverse strands.
Michael E. Veal *Fela: The Life and Times of an African Music Icon*. Thorough profile of the phenomenon that was Fela Kuti, written by a Yale ethnomusicologist.
Christopher Alan Waterman *Juju: A Social History and Ethnography of an African Popular Music*. A detailed account of the origins, evolution and social significance of *juju*, tracing the roots back more than fifty years.

Food

Daniel K. Abbiw *Useful Plants of Ghana*. Unusual reference guide to plants, organized by use – as

food, fuel and medicine. Highly recommended for impoverished volunteers.
Jessica B. Harris *The Africa Cookbook: Tastes of a Continent*. Africa-wide collection of recipes for streetside samplings (bean cakes and fried plantains) and full-course meals.
* J.G. Vaughan and C.A. Geissler *The New Oxford Book of Food Plants*. Covers most of the fruit and veg that will come your way in West Africa.

Natural history

B. Bousquet *Guide des Parc Nationaux d'Afrique: Afrique de l'Ouest*. Coverage of the important national parks of Francophone West Africa.
T. Haltenorth and H. Diller *A Field Guide to the Mammals of Africa* (o/p).
W. Serle and G. Morel *A Field Guide to the Birds of West Africa*.

Map and book retailers

UK

African Books Collective ℡01865/726 686, ⊛www.africanbookscollective.com. Thousands of updated titles from over forty independent, state and university publishers in West Africa.
Blackwell's Map and Travel Shop 50 Broad St, Oxford OX1 3BQ ℡01865/793 550, ⊛maps.blackwell.co.uk.
Heffers 20 Trinity St, Cambridge CB2 1TJ ℡01223/568568.
The Map Shop 30a Belvoir St, Leicester LE1 6QH ℡0116/247 1400, ⊛www.mapshopleicester.co.uk.
National Map Centre 22–24 Caxton St, London SW1H 0QU ℡020/7222 2466, ⊛www.mapsnmc.co.uk.
Newcastle Map Centre 55 Grey St, Newcastle-upon-Tyne NE1 6EF ℡0191/261 5622.
Stanfords 12–14 Long Acre, London WC2E 9LP ℡020/7836 1321, ⊛www.stanfords.co.uk.
The Travel Bookshop 13–15 Blenheim Crescent, W11 2EE ℡020/7229 5260, ⊛www.thetravelbookshop.co.uk.

Republic of Ireland

Easons Bookshop 40 O'Connell St, Dublin 1 ℡01/858 3881, ⊛www.eason.ie.
Hodges Figgis Bookshop 56–58 Dawson St, Dublin 2 ℡01/677 4754, ⊛www.hodgesfiggis.com.

US and Canada

Adventurous Traveler.com US ℡1-800/282-3963, ⊛adventuroustraveler.com.

Distant Lands 56 S Raymond Ave, Pasadena CA 91105 ☎ 1-800/310-3220, ⊛ www.distantlands.com.

Globe Corner Bookstore 28 Church St, Cambridge MA 02138 ☎ 1-800/358-6013, ⊛ www.globecorner.com.

Map Link 30 S La Patera Lane, Unit 5, Santa Barbara CA 93117 ☎ 1-800/962-1394, ⊛ www.maplink.com.

Rand McNally US ☎ 1-800/333-0136, ⊛ www.randmcnally.com. Around thirty stores across the US.

The Travel Bug Bookstore 2667 W Broadway, Vancouver BC V6K 2G2 ☎ 604/737-1122, ⊛ www.swifty.com/tbug.

World of Maps 1235 Wellington St, Ottawa, ON K1Y 3A3 ☎ 1-800/214-8524, ⊛ www.worldofmaps.com.

Australia and New Zealand

The Map Shop 6–10 Peel St, Adelaide SA 5000 ☎ 08/8231 2033, ⊛ www.mapshop.net.au.

Mapland 372 Little Bourke St, Melbourne, Victoria 3000 ☎ 03/9670 4383, ⊛ www.mapland.com.au.

MapWorld 173 Gloucester St, Christchurch ☎ 0800/627 967 or 03/374 5399, ⊛ www.mapworld.co.nz.

Perth Map Centre 1/884 Hay St, Perth WA 6000 ☎ 08/9322 5733, ⊛ www.perthmap.com.au.

Specialty Maps 46 Albert St, Auckland 1001 ☎ 09/307 2217, ⊛ www.ubdonline.co.nz/maps.

Insurance

You'd do well to take out an insurance policy before travelling to cover against theft, loss and illness or injury. Before paying for a new policy, however, it's worth checking whether you are already covered: some all-risks home insurance policies may cover your possessions when overseas, and many private medical schemes include cover when abroad.

After exhausting the possibilities above, you might want to contact a specialist travel insurance company, or consider the travel insurance deal we offer (see box). A typical travel insurance policy usually provides cover for the loss of baggage, tickets and – up to a certain limit – cash or cheques, as well as cancellation or curtailment of your journey. Most of them exclude so-called dangerous sports unless an extra premium is paid. Many policies can be chopped and changed to exclude coverage you don't need – for example, sickness and accident benefits can often be excluded or included at will. If you do take medical coverage, ascertain whether benefits will be paid as treatment proceeds or only after return home, and whether there is a 24-hour medical emergency number. When securing baggage cover, make sure that the per-article limit – typically under £500/$750 – will cover your most valuable possession. If you need to make a claim, you should keep receipts for medicines and medical treatment, and in the event you have anything stolen, you must obtain an official statement from the police.

One thing to check: if you enter a country against the official advice of your government (see p.25), your policy may become invalid.

Rough Guides travel insurance

Rough Guide offers its own low-cost travel insurance, especially customized for our statistically low-risk readers by a leading British broker, provided by the American International Group (AIG) and registered with the British regulatory body, GISC (the General Insurance Standards Council).

There are five main Rough Guides insurance plans: **No Frills** for the bare minimum for secure travel; **Essential**, which provides decent all-round cover; **Premier** for comprehensive cover with a wide range of benefits; Extended Stay for cover lasting two months to a year; and **Annual multi-trip**, a cost-effective way of getting Premier cover if you travel more than once a year. Premier, Annual Multi-Trip and Extended Stay policies can be supplemented by a **"Hazardous Pursuits Extension"** if you plan to indulge in sports considered dangerous, such as scuba-diving or trekking.

For a **policy quote**, call the Rough Guide Insurance Line: toll-free in the UK ☎0800/015 09 06 or ☎+44 1392 314 665 from elsewhere. Alternatively, get an online quote at www.roughguides.com/insurance.

Health

There's no reason to expect to get ill in West Africa, but there are plenty of opportunities to do so if you're unlucky or careless. The most likely hazards are stomach problems and malaria. Health details for each country, with a brief rundown on local problems and issues, are given in each chapter.

The only officially required **international vaccination certificates** are for yellow fever and cholera. A **yellow fever** certificate is always a requirement – even if you're flying in direct from Europe – in Benin, Burkina Faso, Cameroon, Ghana, Niger, Sierra Leone and Togo. Several others require to see the yellow fever certificate if you're staying for longer than two weeks. All West African countries require the certificate if you've arrived by way of an area that's classified by the World Health Organization as infected – details online at ⓦ www.who.int/en. The **cholera** certificate is a bureaucratic rather than a health issue. Many doctors who keep up with tropical medicine advances don't recommend the cholera jab (see below). However, there have been cases of border officials demanding to see a cholera certificate, even though possession of one is not an entry requirement for any country. Some doctors will quite willingly provide a cholera certificate (while discreetly indicating on it that you haven't had the jab) – it seems to do the job at borders and airports.

If you lose a vaccination certificate, you can buy blank ones in many stationery stores. Explain your situation at a hospital or clinic and have it stamped and signed by someone (there'll probably be a small charge).

Vaccinations

Plan ahead: some inoculations need to be administered a few weeks in advance of your travels, and some can't be taken together.

A **yellow fever** jab is essential; there are no specific drugs to cure the disease, which takes a few days to develop into liver failure and kills about fifty percent of its victims. Though epidemics are very rare, there have been recent outbreaks in Senegal and Guinea. The jabs are good for ten years and confer high immunity. A yellow fever certificate becomes valid ten days after you've had the shot.

You shouldn't consider major travels without a **typhoid vaccination** (which lasts three years) or a **tetanus** booster. Nor is there any reason not to get Havrix shots which protect you for up to ten years against the common form of **hepatitis** ("A") spread by contaminated food and water. It's a lot nicer having the jabs than catching the disease, which seriously damages your liver and can leave it permanently scarred. The only problem with Havrix is its cost and the fact that you need to have the first shot at least two weeks before departure. Hepatitis "B", like HIV, is caught through unprotected sexual contact and through the transfer of blood products, usually from dirty needles.

The validity of a **cholera** inoculation, taken in two doses with a gap of two weeks in between, is a nominal six months, and it doesn't provide a great deal of protection against the disease. In fact the risks of contracting cholera are negligible unless you're in the middle of an epidemic.

Immunization against **meningitis** is a good precaution if you're planning extensive travels – outbreaks have occurred not long ago in Nigeria and Burkina Faso. **Polio** is now more or less eliminated in the region but it's still worth checking that you're covered.

Malaria

Malaria (*le paludisme* or "*palu*" in French) is caused by a parasite carried in the saliva of *Anopheles* mosquitoes, which can be distinguished by their rather eager head-down position. The parasite is transmitted to humans by the female mosquito, which prefers to bite in the evening. Malaria has a variable **incubation period** of a few days to several weeks, so you can become ill long after being bitten. If you go down with malaria, you'll probably know: the fever, shivering and headaches are something like severe flu and come in waves, usually beginning in the early evening. Malaria is not infectious but it can be dangerous, even fatal if not treated quickly.

Protection against malaria is absolutely essential in tropical Africa, where the disease is endemic below 1500m. As well as taking a few common-sense measures to **avoid being bitten** (see below), it's vital to be prepared with a course of **preventive tablets**. We've outlined below some of the drugs available, though it's important to discuss the various options with your doctor before deciding which one or combination to take. It's worth noting here that the strain of the malarial parasite commonly found in West Africa, **falciparum**, is both especially severe and often resistant to treatment with chloroquine. **Pregnant women** are at particular risk from the complications of falciparum malaria and need to explore the issue especially carefully with their doctor when planning a trip.

Antimalarial drugs

The range of antimalarial drugs available includes **chloroquine**-based tablets (such as Nivaquin, Aralen and Resochin), **proguanil**-based Paludrin and **pyrimethamine**-based Daraprim and Fansidar. Depending on where you live, you can buy some or all of these without a prescription at a pharmacy before you travel. In West Africa itself, they can be bought in small shops and from street drug stalls all over, though the drugs used with chloroquine-resistant malaria are only available in big towns. When taking any of these tablets to prevent malaria, it's important to keep a routine and cover the period before and after your trip with doses.

Mefloquine (sold as Lariam) is worth asking your doctor about as it's taken only once a week, though note that many people report neuropsychiatric side effects from its use. If you're not concerned about taking an antibiotic as a prophylaxis, you could consider **doxycycline**, which is effective against falciparum malaria. Taken daily, it's almost the only choice if you've left the decision to the last minute – the course is still effective if started just one day before you enter a malarial region. Another useful benefit is the protection it can offer against traveller's diarrhoea; on the downside, it can make your skin more susceptible to sunburn. Another option is **Malarone**, a relatively new drug, which can also be started a day before you travel and can be discontinued just a week after you leave the malarial zone. It's recommended by many doctors, but it's the most expensive option (the combination of chloroquine and proguanil is the cheapest). Note that the only completely safe antimalarial for pregnant women and infants is quinine, usually used as treatment.

Mosquito nets and repellants

Sleep under a **mosquito net** when possible – they're not expensive to buy locally – and burn **mosquito coils** (which you can buy everywhere, though don't use Cock Brand or Lion Brand as these are said to contain the insecticide DDT and are banned in many countries). Electric mosquito destroyers, which you fit with a pad every night, are less pungent than mosquito coils but more expensive – and you need electricity. Whenever the mosquitoes are particularly bad (and that's not often) cover exposed skin with a repellant. So-called "Neat Deet" (diethyltoluamide) works well, and you could try soaking wrist and ankle bands in the stuff, diluted 1:9 with water. Beware though, that Deet is corrosive and can chew through plastics and artificial fibres.

Treatment of malaria

If you think you might be getting a fever, the priority is to seek **treatment**. Delay is potentially risky; overly casual travellers die of the disease every year. Ideally, confirm your diagnosis by getting to a doctor and having a blood test to identify the strain. If you cannot get to a doctor, your options for self-medication will depend on which drugs you have, or can obtain. Take either four

Malarone tablets daily for three days; or 200mg of doxycycline daily for a week; or 20mg of Lariam per kilo of body weight in one or two doses (ie if you weigh 60kg, take 1200mg all at once or in two doses of 600mg). An alternative to these drugs is to take 600mg of quinine, twice a day for seven days, followed at the end of the course by three Fansidar tablets. It's very important to reduce the fever and drink plenty of clean water.

Be aware that the symptoms of malaria can be cyclic, and that after a day or two of improvement you may be knocked out again.

Bilharzia

Schistosomiasis – also known as **bilharzia** – is potentially very nasty, though easily curable. The disease comes from tiny flukes which live in freshwater snails and, as part of their life cycle, leave their hosts and burrow into animal or human skin to multiply in the bloodstream. The snails themselves favour only stagnant water, though the flukes can be swept downstream. While it's possible to pick it up from one brief contact, the risk of contracting bilharzia is fairly low unless you repeatedly come into contact with infected water. If infected, you'll get a slightly itchy rash an hour or two later where the flukes have entered the skin. Bilharzia is most prevalent in the Sahelian regions and particularly in artificial lakes. If you have severe abdominal pains and pass blood – the first symptoms occur after four to six weeks – see a doctor.

As regards avoiding the disease, the usual recommendation is never to swim in, wash with, drink or even touch lake or river water that's not been vouched for. On a long trip out in the bush though, this isn't always possible, particularly if you're drinking with local people. Snail-free water that's stood for two days, or has been boiled or chlorinated, is safe, as is brackish water.

Sleeping sickness

Sleeping sickness (**trypanosomiasis**) is mainly a disease of wild animals, but also affects cattle and horses and, to a much lesser extent, people. It's carried by tsetse flies that crowd streams and riverbanks in deep bush areas. They're determined, brutish insects with a painful bite, attracted to large moving objects such as elephants or Land Rovers. They tend to fly in the windows of vehicles driving through game parks.

Infection is extremely uncommon among travellers – fortunately, because the drugs used to treat it aren't very sophisticated. But a boil which suddenly appears, several days after a tsetse-fly bite, might indicate an infection you should get examined. Untreated, sleeping sickness results in infections of the central nervous system and drowsiness.

Digestive ailments

In many places in West Africa, the water you drink will have come from a tap and is likely to be clean. Since bad water is the most likely cause of **diarrhoea**, you should be cautious of drinking rain- or well-water. In truth, stomach upsets don't plague many travellers badly. If you're visiting for a short time only, it makes sense to be scrupulous – purifying tablets and/or boiling kills most bugs. If you want to be absolutely safe, **purification**, a two-stage process involving both filtration and sterilization, gives the most complete treatment. Portable water purifiers start from pocket-sized units weighing 60 grams.

For **longer stays**, and especially if you're travelling widely, think of re-educating your stomach rather than fortifying it. It's virtually impossible to travel around the region without exposing yourself to strange bugs from time to time. Take it easy at first, don't overdo the fruit (and wash it in clean, safe water before peeling), don't keep food too long and be very wary of salads. Ironically, perhaps, your chances of picking up stomach bugs are considerably reduced if you stick to inexpensive street restaurants serving one or two freshly prepared dishes (places popular with local people are a good bet) – at a minority of tourist restaurants with a range of dishes on the menu, careless thawing and refreezing of food is often the cause of digestive complaints.

If you do have a serious stomach upset, 24 hours of nothing but plain tea (or just boiled water) may rinse it out. The important thing is to replace lost fluids. You can make up a **rehydration mix** with four heaped teaspoons of sugar or honey and half a teaspoon of salt in a litre of water. Most stomach upsets resolve themselves, but if the diarrhoea seems to be getting worse – or you have to travel a long distance while stricken – any pharmacy should have name-brand antidiarrhoea remedies. These (Lomotil, codeine phosphate, etc) shouldn't be overused: a day's worth of doses is about the most you should take.

Antibiotics and antidiarrhoeal drugs shouldn't be used as preventives – this is potentially very dangerous – and you should also avoid jumping for antibiotics at the first sign of trouble. They annihilate what's nicely known as your gut flora (most of which you want to keep). By the time you're considering their use, you should really seek a doctor. If you've definitely got blood in your diarrhoea and it's impossible to see a doctor, then this is the time to take a course of the antibiotic metronidazole (Flagyl) – you'll have to get this on prescription before your trip.

If you use **oral contraceptives** (get your doctor to prescribe a supply), don't forget an alternative method to fall back on if you have a stomach upset or take a course of antibiotics, as either can leave you unprotected for the rest of the month.

Other diseases and complaints

Many people get a bout of **prickly heat** rash at first, before they've acclimatized. It's an inflammation of the sweat ducts caused by excessive perspiration which doesn't dry off.

A cool shower, **talcum powder** and cotton clothes should help.

On the subject of heat, it's important not to overdose on **sunshine** – at least in the first week or two. The powerful heat and bright light can mess up your system. A hat and sunglasses are necessities. Some people sweat heavily and lose a lot of **salt**; salt tablets, however, are unnecessary – simply sprinkle extra **salt** on your food. Even if you're not a great perspirer, it's important to keep a healthy salt balance. The body can't function without it and it's not uncommon to experience sudden exhaustion a few days after arrival in a hot climate.

Sexually transmitted diseases and AIDS

The only other real likelihood of your encountering a serious disease in West Africa is if it's **sexually transmitted**. Assorted venereal diseases are widespread, particularly in the larger towns, and the HIV virus which causes AIDS (SIDA in Francophone countries) is alarmingly prevalent and spreading all the time. **Condoms** are available from most pharmacies, or alternatively from some clinics and dispensaries, but they tend to be expensive or of dubious manufacture, so it's better to take some with you.

On the associated topic of receiving **blood transfusions** or injections in an emergency, you might want to carry a sterile emergency kit to be used by a doctor if you get into trouble. Usually, however, such treatment can only be offered in a hospital environment

Dental care

Make sure that you have a thorough **dental check-up** before leaving and take extra care of your teeth while in West Africa. Stringy meat, acid fruit and too many soft drinks are some of the hazards. Floss and brush at least once in the middle of each day. You could also get into the habit of using a fresh "toothbrush stick" cut from a branch, as many locals do. Some varieties (on sale at markets) contain a plaque-destroying enzyme. Get into the habit of chewing gum after eating – even sweet varieties quickly lose their sugar and are soon performing a useful function on your teeth.

If you lose a filling and aren't inclined to see a dentist locally, try and get hold of some **gutta percha**, a natural, rubbery substance available from some pharmacies; you heat it and then pack it in the hole as a temporary filling. Your dentist could get you some to take with you. **Emergency dental packs** are available from many vaccination centres.

where most staff are familiar with the need for sterile equipment and fresh needles.

Injuries and animal hazards

Take more care than usual over minor **cuts and scrapes** – the most trivial scratch can become a throbbing infection if you ignore it. As for animal attacks, West African **dogs** are usually sad and skulking and pose little threat though, like captive **monkeys**, they may carry rabies. **Scorpions** and **spiders** abound but are hardly ever seen unless you go turning over rocks or logs. Scorpion stings are painful but almost never fatal – and scorpions usually need considerable goading before they'll bring their tail into attack. Spiders are mostly quite harmless. The large, terrifyingly fast and active **solifugids** (also known as camel spiders or wind scorpions) do sometimes have a painful bite, but you're not likely to sit around and find out. **Snakes** are common but, again, the vast majority are harmless, and to see one at all you'll need to search stealthily – walk heavily and they obligingly disappear. For reassurance about larger beasts, see p.74.

Seeking medical treatment

If you need **medical treatment** in West Africa, you'll discover a frightening lack of well-equipped **hospitals**. In each country, we've tried to indicate which are the best and to give general practitioners and dentists in city "Listings". For serious treatment you're almost certain to want to come home. Blood and urine tests can be performed locally, but needles and other instruments might not be fresh from a sealed package. If in doubt, insist on paying for new ones.

Moderate injuries can be treated locally. In remote areas, there are Christian **missions** which may have a small clinic attached, and these are usually the first recourse. If you require treatment, it's normally proficient and the charges low, though comforts fairly rudimentary.

Travel health centres and resources

For a good **book** on health, get hold of the *Rough Guide to Travel Health* by Dr Nick Jones, or Dr Richard Dawood's *Traveller's Health*. If you're living in West Africa – especially if you need to treat yourself or others – the brilliant classic *Where There is No Doctor* by David Werner is well worth obtaining.

Websites

ⓦ **health.yahoo.com** Information on specific diseases and conditions, drugs and herbal remedies, as well as advice from health experts.
ⓦ **www.fitfortravel.scot.nhs.uk** UK NHS website carrying information about travel-related diseases and how to avoid them.
ⓦ **www.istm.org** The website of the International Society for Travel Medicine, with a full list of clinics specializing in international travel health.
ⓦ **www.tripprep.com** Travel Health Online provides an online-only comprehensive database of necessary vaccinations for most countries, as well as destination and medical service provider information.

UK

British Airways Travel Clinics 156 Regent St, London W1 (Mon–Fri 9.30am–5.15pm, Sat 10am–4pm, no appointment necessary; ☏020/7439 9584, ⓦwww.britishairways.com). Vaccinations, tailored advice from an online database and a complete range of travel healthcare products.
Communicable Diseases Unit Brownlee Centre, Glasgow G12 0YN ☏0141/211 1062. Travel vaccinations including yellow fever.
Hospital for Tropical Diseases Travel Clinic 2nd floor, Mortimer Market Centre, off Capper St, London WC1E 6AU (Mon–Fri 9am–5pm by appointment only; ☏020/7388 9600). A consultation costs £15, which is waived if you have your injections here. Their recorded Health Line (☏09061/337 733; 50p/min) gives hints on hygiene and illness prevention as well as listing appropriate immunizations.
Liverpool School of Tropical Medicine Pembroke Place, Liverpool L3 5QA ☏0151/708 9393 (walk-in clinic Mon–Fri 1–4pm). Appointment required for yellow fever, but not for other jabs.
MASTA (Medical Advisory Service for Travellers Abroad) Forty regional clinics (call ☏0870/6062782 or see ⓦwww.masta.org for the nearest). Also operates a pre-recorded 24hr Travellers' Health Line (UK ☏0906/822 4100, 60p/min), giving written information tailored to your journey by return of post.
Nomad Pharmacy 40 Bernard St, London WC1 (Mon–Fri 9.30am–6pm; ☏020/7833 4114 to book vaccination appointment). They give advice free if you go in person.

A medicine bag

There's no need to take a mass of drugs and remedies you'll probably never use. Various items, however, are immensely useful, especially on a long trip, and well worth buying in advance. If you're interested in herbal and other natural remedies, you'll find a wealth of natural cures in markets. You'll have to rely on intuition, common sense and persistent enquiries to judge whether they're worth trying.

Paracetamol Safer than aspirin for pain and fever relief.

Water purifying (chlorine) tablets or iodine tincture Both taste foul but do the trick, iodine more efficiently than chlorine (and iodine can double as an antiseptic). Ascorbic acid (vitamin C) can be used to neutralize the taste of iodine.

Antimalarial tablets Enough for prophylactic use, plus several courses of Fansidar and/or quinine tablets in case of attack.

Antibiotics Amoxil (amoxycillin) is a broad-spectrum antibacterial drug useful against many infections. Ciproxin (ciprofloxacin) can feel like a life-saver in a bowel crisis. Both should only be used as a last resort when you cannot see a doctor. Again these are normally prescription drugs only.

Antidiarrhoeal medication Codeine phosphate (prescription only) or Lomotil (co-phenotrope).

Antifungal powder Canestan, for example, for sweaty crevices.

Antiseptic Cicatrin is good, but creams in metal tubes invariably squeeze out messily sooner or later. Bright red or purple mercurochrome liquid dries wounds.

Alcohol swabs Paper Medi-swabs are invaluable for cleaning wounds, insect bites and infections.

Sticking plaster, steri-strip wound closures, sterile gauze dressing, micropore tape You don't need much of this stuff, and you can buy it in most capital cities.

Lip balm Invaluable in dry climates.

Thermometer Very useful. Ideally you'll be 37°C. A Feverscan forehead thermometer is unbreakable and gives a ready reckoning (from pharmacies).

Contact lens solution

Trailfinders Immunization clinics at 194 Kensington High St, London (Mon–Fri 9am–5pm except Thurs to 6pm, Sat 9.30am–4pm; ☏020/7938 3999; no appointment necessary). **Travel Medicine Services** PO Box 254, 16 College St, Belfast 1 ☏028/9031 5220. Offers medical advice before a trip and help afterwards in the event of a tropical disease.

Republic of Ireland

Dun Laoghaire Medical Centre 5 Northumberland Ave, Dun Laoghaire Co, Dublin ☏01/280 4996. Advice on medical matters abroad.
Travel Health Centre Department of International Health and Tropical Medicine, Royal College of Surgeons in Ireland, Mercers Medical Centre, Stephen's St Lower, Dublin ☏01/402 2337. Expert pre-trip advice and inoculations.
Tropical Medical Bureau Grafton Buildings, 34 Grafton St, Dublin 2 ☏01/671 9200,

ⓦtmb.exodus.ie. Provides a comprehensive vaccinations service.

US and Canada

Canadian Society for International Health 1 Nicholas St, Suite 1105, Ottawa, ON K1N 7B7 ☏613/241-5785, ⓦwww.csih.org. Distributes a free pamphlet, *Health Information for Canadian Travellers*, containing an extensive list of travel health centres in Canada.
Centers for Disease Control 1600 Clifton Rd NE, Atlanta, GA 30333 ☏1-800/311-3435 or 404/639-3534, ⓦwww.cdc.gov. Publishes disease outbreak warnings, suggested inoculations, precautions and other background information for travellers. International Travelers' Hotline on ☏1-877/FYI-TRIP.
International Association for Medical Assistance to Travellers (IAMAT) 417 Center St, Lewiston, NY 14092 ☏716/754-4883, ⓦwww.iamat.org; and 40 Regal Rd, Guelph, ON

N1K 1B5 ☎519/836-0102. A non-profit organization supported by donations, they can provide a list of English-speaking doctors in some West African countries, plus climate charts and leaflets on various diseases and inoculations.

International SOS Assistance Eight Neshaminy Interplex Suite 207, Trevose, USA 19053-6956 ☎1-800/523-8930, ⓦwww.intsos.com. Members receive pre-trip medical referral info, as well as overseas emergency services designed to complement travel insurance coverage.

MEDJET Assistance ☎1-800/863-3538, ⓦwww.medjetassistance.com. Annual membership program for travellers ($175 for individuals, $275 for families) that, in the event of illness or injury, will fly members home or to the hospital of their choice in a medically equipped jet.

Travel Medicine ☎1-800/872-8633, ⓦwww.travmed.com. Sells first-aid kits, mosquito netting, water filters, reference books and other health-related travel products.

Travelers Medical Center 31 Washington Square West, New York, NY 10011 ☎212/982-1600. Consultation service on immunizations and treatment of diseases for people travelling to developing countries.

Australia and New Zealand

Travellers' Medical and Vaccination Centres Australia: 27–29 Gilbert Place, Adelaide ☎08/8212 7522; 5/247 Adelaide St, Brisbane ☎07/3221 9066; 5/8–10 Hobart Place, Canberra ☎02/6257 7156; 2/393 Little Bourke St, Melbourne ☎03/9602 5788; Level 7, Dymocks Bldg, 428 George St, Sydney, NSW 2000 ☎02/922 1713. New Zealand: 1/170 Queen St, Auckland ☎09/373 3531; 147 Armagh St, Christchurch ☎03/379 4000; Shop 15, Grand Arcade, 14–16 Willis St, Wellington ☎04/473 0991. See ⓦwww.tmvc.com.au for details of additional locations in both countries, plus online travel health information.

Costs, money and banks

It's perhaps surprising to find that, in general, West Africa is an expensive part of the world. Mere survival can be dirt cheap, but anything like a Euro-American lifestyle costs as much, if not more, than in Europe or America.

In between these extremes you can use the cheapest transport, eat market food and spend nights either camping in the bush, staying with people or in budget hotels. Travelling like this, it's possible to get by on **£300/$450 a month** (though £600/$900 split between two gets you more value for money). It's clearly much harder to keep costs down in cities such as Dakar, where a panoply of tempting comforts and consumables is available in every direction and where it's hard to avoid staying in **hotels** – likely to be your biggest single expense.

As a very general guide, a twin room in a cheap hotel can usually be had for under £10/$15, often under £7/$10.50, but rarely under £5/$7.50. Long-distance **road transport** works out, on average, at about £1–3/$1.50–4.50 per 100km, though it varies with the quality and speed of the vehicle. **Train** travel, if it's an option where you are, tends to be cheaper, **river trips** more expensive. As for **food**, you can always fill yourself with calories for under £1/$1.50 if you eat street food or at a market or lorry park chop house.

At the other end of the scale, **international standard hotels** are predictably expensive in most cities, and **car rental** rates are some of the highest in the world (in a number of countries it's not difficult to work up bills of £130/$210 a day or more *without* taking the air-conditioned 4WD).

Bargaining

General stores, groceries and supermarkets invariably have **fixed prices**. Transport costs are usually subject to state control and almost always fixed, but baggage can be haggled over. Pretty well every other service (including budget hotel rooms in some countries) can and should be **bargained** over – it's the normal way of conducting business; moreover every time you pay an unreasonable price for goods or services you contribute to local inflation.

Bargaining is often just a case of showing reluctance to pay what you're told is the going rate, and in turn getting some sort of "discount". There's enormous flexibility around a few immutable rules. The most important is never to engage in bargaining if you've no intention of buying the item at any price. To offer what you thought was a silly price and then refuse to pay can cause grave offence. Nor should you embark on negotiations when you're in a hurry, or if you are feeling less than one hundred percent – it can be an exhausting business.

When negotiating, don't automatically assume you're in the clutches of a rip-off artist. Concepts of **honour** are very important, and stalls are often minded by friends and relatives with whom, if you're quick and convincing, you can sometimes strike real bargains.

Most importantly, men should make **physical contact** – hand-clasping (a prolonged handshake) is usually enough to emphasize a point. Be as jocular as possible and don't be shy of making a big scene – the bluffing and mock outrage on both sides is part of the fun. Women can't pursue these negotiating tactics in quite the same way,

except when buying from women – invariably much tougher anyway.

Getting down to figures, try to delay the moment when you have to name your price. When you hear "One hundred how much you pay?", say nothing. It's amazing how often the seller's price drops way below your expectation before you've made any offer, so forget the standard "offer-a-third-come-up-to-a-half" formulas. If you do arrive at an unbridgeable gap you can always drop the matter and come by later. With stalemates, a disinterested companion tugging your sleeve is always a help.

Currencies

Nine different currencies are used in the West African countries covered in this book. The currency of all the **Francophone countries** in West Africa, with two exceptions, is the **CFA franc**. There are in fact two types of CFA (normally pronounced "seffa", and standing for Communauté Financière de l'Afrique). Most of the Francophone West African states, except Mauritania and Guinea, are members of the Union Monétaire Ouest Africaine, and those countries use one variety of CFA franc, as does Guinea-Bissau, though not itself Francophone. Cameroon's currency is also CFA, but of a different regional grouping, the Communauté Economique et Monétaire Financière de l'Afrique Centrale – which includes Chad, the Central African Republic, Gabon, Equatorial Guinea and Republic of the Congo.

Exchange rates

As we go to press the following official exchange rates (approximate) apply:

	£1 =	€1 =	$1 =
CFA franc (both types)	930	656	600
Cape Verdean escudo	150	110	95
cedi	13,000	9000	8400
dalasi	40	27	25
Guinean franc	3100	2200	1950
leone	3400	2300	2000
naira	200	140	135
ouguiya	430	300	280

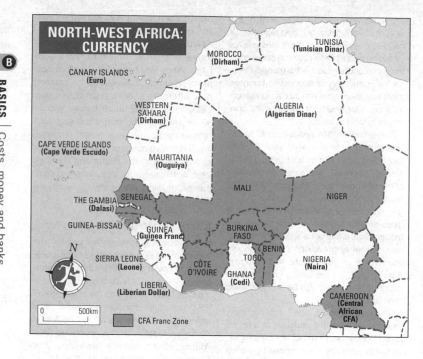

NORTH-WEST AFRICA: CURRENCY

CFA Franc Zone

CFA francs are guaranteed by the French treasury and have a fixed value of 655.957 against the euro. CFAs come in 1, 5, 10, 25, 50, 100 and 250 **coins** and **notes** of 500, 1000, 2500, 5000 and 10,000, making this easily the most convenient African currency. Although of equal value, the two types of CFA can't be spent outside their own region, and cannot be interchanged in any bank in the region either. Because of French backing, the CFA is a relatively hard currency – major banks in Europe will sometimes exchange CFA francs at their euro equivalent – and currency laws in the countries which use it are generally relaxed. In theory there are limits to the value of CFA you can export, even from one CFA state to another, but in practice these are very rarely enforced.

The countries **outside the franc zone** have their own, usually weaker ("soft") currencies. Mauritania uses the **ouguiya**; Cape Verde the Cape Verdean **escudo**; The Gambia the **dalasi**; Guinea the **Guinean franc**; Ghana the **cedi**; Sierra Leone the **leone**, and Nigeria the **naira.** The ECOWAS

member states – Ghana, Liberia, Nigeria, Sierra Leone, Guinea and The Gambia – are presently in discussion over the formation of a new monetary union, the West African Monetary Zone, with a common currency possibly anchored to the South African rand, but this is likely to be some years away.

Cash and traveller's cheques

If you're travelling widely in West Africa, you're best off carrying a large part of your funds in **euro traveller's cheques**. Apart from any commission on exchanging them for cash, if you're using them in CFA countries, you've already effectively made the exchange when you bought them. In the CFA zone you'll always know how much you've got in local currency and your funds won't vary in value as you travel. Hotels and some shops and traders will take euro traveller's cheques but it's essential also to have some **euros in cash** as a stand-by. You will get a better exchange rate for cash so it's worth weighing this up against the risk of losing the lot with no recompense when deciding how much to carry with you.

You generally end up better off if you have euros to convert to CFA, rather than going straight from, say, US dollars or pounds sterling to CFA, because the national banks of the CFA zone normally set their own rates of exchange with non-euro currencies. Indeed, in some towns in the CFA zone, banks will not deal in foreign currencies other than the euro.

Where CFA countries border non-CFA countries, your surplus CFA cash can't be changed in the banks, but it can generally be changed with ease on the black market, as it's commonly used by people crossing borders to buy goods (though note the details below on declaring your currency).

If you are heading directly for one of the **soft currency countries**, like The Gambia, Nigeria and Ghana, or are intending to spend most of your time there, then either **US dollars** or **pounds sterling** is probably the best currency to take. Again, carry some in cash – you'll often need it at borders and airports for your first food or transport. Note that in Nigeria, it's hard to find places that cash traveller's cheques.

Denominations of traveller's cheques and cash should be as small as you can manage, bearing in mind the bulk that a large sum of exchange will amount to. If you take mostly US$50 or €50 denominations for convenience, make sure you have plenty of US$10 and 20 or €10 and 20 as well. A small stash of really low-value hard-currency notes (US$1 and €5) is always useful.

The usual fee to buy traveller's cheques is one or two percent, though this fee may be waived if you buy the cheques through a bank where you have an account. Make sure to keep the purchase agreement and a record of cheque serial numbers safe and separate from the cheques themselves. Banks outside the major cities may not cash your cheque without the original receipt. In the event that cheques are lost or stolen, the issuing company will expect you to report the loss forthwith to their nearest office; most companies claim to replace lost or stolen cheques within 24 hours. In the CFA zone, the brand of traveller's cheque you carry isn't of much consequence. Outside the CFA countries, however, **American Express** and **Thomas Cook** are by far the most widely recognized brands and, should the need arise, also the fastest to supply replacements for lost cheques.

Banks and exchange

West African **banking systems** are generally slow and limited. The capital cities are by far the best, if not the only, place to change money. Even where sophisticated banking

Currency declarations

On arrival in some soft currency countries you'll have to make a **declaration** of the money you're carrying in cash and traveller's cheques. This may be accompanied by a search, varying from the cursory to the intimate. Mostly, you simply say what you've got and then show some of it.

You may also be issued with a **currency declaration** or **exchange control form**, which you retain until departure. This shows the money you imported and is supposed to be stamped and amended every time you change money at an authorized bank, hotel or bureau de change. In theory, when you leave any country, your currency declaration form is checked against the money you have on you and any discrepancy (which must have been exchanged unofficially, or lost, or given away . . .) has to be accounted for. In practice, forms are taken much more seriously on arrival than on departure. It's wise to assume, however, that your experience will turn out to be the exception.

None of this applies if you're travelling to, or within, **CFA zone countries** only. Here the fiscal arrangements commonly leave you feeling you're merely in an overseas French *département* and there's rarely any interest in the money you have on you, nor any currency declaration forms or concern about where you change your money.

systems operate you may not be able to change certain foreign currencies, and in some countries a parallel black market in hard currencies still thrives.

Always try to arrive early in the day and remember to bring your passport. Never start the transaction without checking the rate of exchange, the commission and any other charges. It's best to establish how much you'll expect to receive in advance, before the paperwork starts. In the **CFA zone** there can be marked differences in the rates offered by different banks: their scales of commission and rates are often well behind the latest American and European swings. In **non-CFA countries** it is also a good idea to check out the rate at the bureaux de change, which may be quicker than the banks, give you much less bureaucratic hassle and even offer a better rate.

Black markets

An unofficial, **parallel exchange rate** (the "black market") exists wherever there's a local demand for foreign hard currency that can't be met through official channels. **Outside the CFA zone**, you can't usually walk into a bank and buy dollars, sterling or other hard currency over the counter. Conversely, this means that hard currency can be exchanged for local money at **black market rates**, which can be anything from a few percentage points to several *hundred* percent better than the bank rate.

In the CFA zone, a parallel market of cross-border traders and businessmen flourishes in the main commercial centres, useful for those unwilling to pay the banks' commission rates (generally much higher than in non-CFA countries) and – since it is impossible to buy any of the softer currencies in the banks – for those crossing over into a non-CFA zone.

It may seem unfair on strangled economies to obtain cheap local currency on the black market and thus deprive the banks of foreign exchange. But on the other hand it's naive to hold exaggerated views of the benefit to local people of putting your hard currency into a bank rather than private hands. Sometimes the official exchange rate is simply set at an unrealistically high level

that makes the place swingeingly expensive. It's worth noting that most prices tend to adjust to black market levels and that some services (especially staying in hotels) may, in any case, have to be paid for in hard currency at the official rate of exchange.

Questions of altruism and morality apart, whatever else you do on your travels, *never change money on the street*. You run a high risk of being skilfully ripped off in public, even if the police informer scenario rarely comes to pass. Always take five minutes out to sit down in a shop or somewhere similar and count everything before handing over your cash.

Credit and debit cards

Credit cards are a very handy backup source of funds, and can be used either in ATMs or over the counter. Visa, American Express, MasterCard and Diners' Club are of some use in cities and large towns for tourist services such as upmarket hotels and restaurants, flights, tours and car rental. **American Express** has offices or agents in Mauritania, Senegal, The Gambia, Mali, Ghana, Togo and Nigeria. You can buy hard currency traveller's cheques with an Amex card – very useful. **Visa** and **MasterCard** have offices or agents in Senegal and Ghana.

Don't count on **cash advances** against credit cards outside the CFA zone, though it is possible in a few rare cases. Even in Francophone capitals you'll have to find the right local bank. Remember that all cash advances are treated as loans, with interest accruing daily from the date of withdrawal; there may be a transaction fee on top of this. It's more cost-effective to make withdrawals from ATMs – these are becoming easier to find in major urban centres – using a **debit card**, which is not liable to interest payments, and the flat transaction fee is usually quite small – your bank will able to advise on this. Make sure you have a personal identification number (PIN) that's designed to work overseas.

A compromise between traveller's cheques and plastic is Visa TravelMoney, a disposable pre-paid debit card with a PIN which works in all ATMs that take Visa cards. For more information, see Ⓦ international.visa.com.

Wiring money

Having money wired from home using one of the companies listed below is never convenient or cheap, and should be considered a last resort. Even faxed or telexed draft orders can take weeks to reach you at the counter – though the normal delay should be only four or five working days. When receiving money you should make sure that you have the money transfer **control number**; you may be told in your home country that this isn't necessary, but you risk being refused your money by West African banks without it. Note also that money is only paid out in the local currency and you probably won't be able to receive hard currency except in the CFA zone, and not necessarily even then.

It's also possible to have money wired directly from a bank in your home country to a bank in West Africa, although this is even less reliable because it involves two separate institutions. If you go this route, your home bank will need the address of the branch bank where you want to pick up the money and the address and telex number of the nearest head office, which will act as the clearing house; money wired this way normally takes two working days to arrive, and costs around £25/$40 per transaction.

Money-wiring companies

Thomas Cook US ℡ 1-800/287-7362, Canada ℡ 1-888/823-4732, UK ℡ 01733/318 922, Republic of Ireland ℡ 01/677 1721, Ⓦ www.us.thomascook.com.
Travelers Express Moneygram US ℡ 1-800/926-3947, Canada ℡ 1-800/933-3278, Ⓦ www.moneygram.com.
Western Union US and Canada ℡ 1-800/325-6000, Australia ℡ 1800/501 500, New Zealand ℡ 09/270 0050, UK ℡ 0800/833 833, Republic of Ireland ℡ 1800/395 395, Ⓦ www.westernunion.com.

Getting around

Private car ownership isn't common in West Africa, and most local people rely on public transport, lifts or walking to get around. While road transport is a good way to travel cheaply in the company of ordinary Africans you might not otherwise encounter, it can test your patience and powers of endurance. It's a mistake to set yourself a rigid timetable when planning extensive travels in the region, since delays on all modes of transport are commonplace and even flight bookings are not guaranteed.

What follows here is a general user's guide to West African transport. Information about transport conditions in each country is given in the "Getting around" section of the practical information at the beginning of each chapter.

Bush taxis

The classic form of West African public transport is the **bush taxi** (*taxi brousse* in French, plus numerous local terms). Bush taxis are nearly all licensed passenger vehicles, serving approved routes at fixed rates.

Many even have notional schedules, though these are never published and rarely adhered to.

The vehicle itself can vary from a reasonably comfortable Peugeot estate car (station wagon) seating five or six plus driver, to the same thing seating nine or ten in discomfort, to a converted **Japanese pick-up** with slat-wood benches and a canvas awning jammed with fifteen people or more. A basket of chickens stuffed under the bench, and maybe a goat or two tied to the roof are regular fare-paying additions. Larger French

box vans, increasingly replaced by Japanese and Korean **minibuses**, are no less zoo-like, though padded benches or seats help, as does the extra ventilation. Most vehicles have roof-rack luggage carriers and a more expensive seat or two at the front, next to the driver.

Peugeot taxis generally sell their places and drive straight from A to B, if possible without stopping. They often do the trip in half the time it takes a more beat-up bush taxi, which may drop people off and take fares en route. But the converted pick-ups (*bâchés* in French, after their tarpaulins) are often the only way to get to more obscure destinations, or to travel on the roughest roads; not surprisingly, they're cheaper. Beware of inadvertently **chartering** a bush taxi (a *déplacement* in French) – once you've done it, there's no way of avoiding paying for all the seats.

Given that It's rare to undertake any journey over 20km in West Africa without encountering a posse of uniforms at the side of the road, you should pay some attention to the condition of driver and vehicle before deciding to give him your custom. A neatly turned-out Peugeot with a well-tied load is likely to pause for a greeting and move on. Conversely, a bruised and shaken *camion bâché* (a covered pick-up) with nineteen passengers, no lights and the contents of someone's house on the roof may be detained for some hours.

Bush taxis are probably the most dangerous vehicles on the roads, so don't be afraid to make a very big fuss if the driver appears to have lost all sense. Ask and then shout at him to "Slow down!" ("*Ralentir!*" in French) and try to enlist the support of fellow travellers – though this is rarely forthcoming. In Peugeots it's nice to have a couple of cassettes for the stereo. In any vehicle, and in most parts of West Africa, sharing some kola nuts goes down well (see p.67). Lastly, if you're in a van with an engine mounted behind the front cab, be sure not to sit near it – you'll melt.

Taxi parks

Most towns have a **taxi park** ("garage", "motor park", "station", "stand", *gare routière*, *autogare*) where vehicles assemble to fill with passengers. Larger towns may have several, each serving different routes and usually located on the relevant road out, at the edge of town.

Practice varies slightly from country to country, but generally when you go to the taxi park, you'll find you're quickly surrounded by **taxi scouts** trying to get you into their vehicle. This can be trying and sometimes unnerving – when there's lots of competition and you're physically mobbed. It pays to behave robustly and to know exactly where you're going, and the names of any towns en route or beyond. It's often the case that your destination is not where all the vehicles are headed. You may have to change, or get out earlier. The ideal **time to travel** is early in the morning. By a couple of hours after sunrise the best vehicles have gone. In many parts there won't be another until the next day.

Before long on your travels, you'll run into a situation where you seem to be the only passenger in a vehicle you were assured was about to leave. It's true your presence will encourage others to join you – which is why they wanted you there in the first place. But sometimes it's better to forget over-ambitious travel plans (especially any time after noon) or to take a shorter journey with a vehicle that's nearly ready to go. Taxi parks are full of interest for up to an hour or so, but a half-day spent in one acting as passenger bait is a waste of time.

As for **fares**: in order to guarantee you'll stay and attract others, drivers, owners and scouts will often try to get you to pay up front. Again, practice varies from country to country. Your luggage tied on the roof generally ought to be sufficient sign of your good faith and, unless you see others paying, it's always best to delay. Make sure you pay the right person when you do. It's common for small offices or booths at the taxi park to issue tickets on behalf of one or more operators.

Overcharging to carry passengers is almost unheard of. It's your **luggage** that will cost you if you don't argue fiercely about how small, light and streamlined it is. Fellow passengers are just as likely to suffer but aren't in such a good position to create a scene. Shout, compare and contrast; tell the crowd how he's trying to kill you with his grasping ways. Make them laugh; make him happy to give you a good price. If you get nowhere, go to one side with him and be conspiratorial – this sometimes works because people like to show off business acumen and it draws attention again. You shouldn't have to pay more than **one third** (normally much less) of your fare for a backpack or large bag. Remember, you can argue forever about what you're *going* to pay, but once you've paid it, the argument is over.

During long waits it's a good idea to keep an eye on your luggage. Anything tied on the roof is safe, but taxi parks are notorious haunts for **thieves**, and bags sometimes get grabbed through open windows. Keep valuables round your neck. Don't worry unduly, however, if the vehicle, while waiting to fill, and with booked passengers scattered around, suddenly takes off with all your gear on top. While it's obviously a good idea to make a mental note of the vehicle registration, you should avoid causing offence by appearing anxious. Maybe nobody knows where they've gone (probably to fill up with fuel), but they'll be back.

Buses

Bus travel is usually more comfortable and less expensive than going by bush taxi, though certain manifestations are little better than gigantic bush taxis and not always much faster. Niger, Burkina Faso, The Gambia, Mali, Nigeria and Cameroon all have quite well-developed bus services. Ghana's state-run service is particularly good, and not expensive.

> Whether travelling by bus or bush taxi, it's worth considering your general direction through the trip and **which side to sit on** for the shadiest ride. This is especially important on dirt roads when the combination of slow, bumpy ride, dust and fierce sun can be horrible. If you're travelling on a busy dirt road with lots of other traffic, you don't want to be seated on the left of the vehicle in any case.

The big advantage of most buses is having your own seat (even Peugeot bush taxis usually sell more places than there are seats) and being able to buy tickets in advance for a departure at a set time. Having bought a ticket, leave a small item on a seat to reserve it and avoid having to wait inside the vehicle. There's still some room for discussion over the cost of transporting your luggage, but it's rarely a big issue.

Lorries and trucks

Although it's usually against the law, on all main routes – and in the remotest regions too – you'll be able to travel by **lorry**. Pick up a lift in small villages or along the road: because of its illegality, you'll rarely find a truck ride in a large town. You need to know the equivalent bush-taxi or bus fares and distances or you'll find yourself **paying** over the odds. Once aboard, you can expect the lorry to stop at every checkpoint to pay bribes – slow progress.

There's sometimes a spare seat or two in the cab, but more often space in the back. **Travelling in the back** of panelled vehicles is pretty miserable, but many older trucks are open at the back with wood-frame sides. When loaded with suitable cargo, these can be a delight to travel in. You get great views and even, on occasions, a comfortable ride in a recumbent position. Do bear in mind your safety however (look out for low branches) and avoid getting the driver in trouble with the police by being conspicuous or foolhardy.

Travelling in an empty goods lorry on bad roads can be close to intolerable. They go much faster unladen and you're typically forced to stand and clasp the sides as the vehicle smashes through potholes. Lorries often drive late into the night too – if you're being carried outside, be sure to have **something warm to wear** for later.

Hitching

The majority of rural people in West Africa get around by **waving down a vehicle**, but they invariably pay, whether in a truck or in a private car. Private vehicles are still comparatively rare and usually full. **Travelling for free** is often considered to be rather improper and most people will assume your car has broken down. There's some sense, however, in hitching in and out of large cities, especially if you can't find a bus or taxi. The kinds of drivers who respond positively are usually foreign-educated business types or expats.

Hitching **techniques** need to be exuberant. A modest thumb in the air is more likely to be interpreted as a friendly, or rude, gesture than a request. Beckon the driver to stop with your palm. You'll feel like a policeman but that doesn't matter. Always explain first if you can't – or won't – pay, and don't be surprised if you're left at the side of the road.

Best chances for conventional hitching are in Senegal, Niger and Nigeria. Hitching with overland tourists can be a good change of pace, and – if you're in the right vicinity – it can throw you in with people visiting game parks and other relatively inaccessible attractions.

Trains

For many (colonial) years there was a French plan to push a **railway** across the Sahara, linking Algiers with Dakar. Had it succeeded, it might have altered today's network, in which only two of the eight West African railway systems cross borders. And of those systems most are no more than single lines running from the coast to the interior.

In practice only three lines are much used by travellers: in Cameroon between **Yaoundé and Ngaoundéré**; the Océan-Niger line between **Bamako and Dakar**; and – until recent troubles – the line between **Abidjan and Ouagadougou**. Timed right, you could do a trip through Senegal and Mali taking as little as two or three weeks, substantially by train. Although other railway lines exist, not all of them are running and some are freight only. The ones marked on our map of the region in the colour section currently operate passenger services. Some offer student discounts, though these are usually intended for nationals.

Travelling by train in West Africa is usually slower than road and, while you can always get street food through the windows at stations, you should take your own drinking water for the duration. Toilets are rarely usable by the time you've left the city.

Ferries

There are hundreds of small, hand-hauled or spluttering diesel ferries pulling people and vehicles across the rivers of West Africa. But river transport upstream or down is very limited. The most interesting **ferry services** run on the Niger River in Mali, from the height of the rainy season to a couple of months after it finishes. Apart from the Ghanaian services on Lake Volta and The Gambian service across the mouth of the Gambia River from Banjul to Barra, there are few other significant car ferries operating in the region.

On the Niger, more or less anywhere between Kouroussa in Guinea and Niamey in Niger, you can usually negotiate a passage in a **pirogue** (a dug-out/plank canoe) or a **pinasse** (a larger, motorized freight-carrying vessel) at any time of year, but in parts of Mali this has now become prohibitively expensive.

There's virtually no scheduled regional **sea transport** except for ferries connecting the Cape Verde islands with each other (and occasionally Dakar), and minor shipping on the coasts of Senegal, Guinea-Bissau, Nigeria and Cameroon.

Flights

At the time of writing, the big West African interstate **airlines** are Ghana Airways, Cameroon Airlines and Air Sénégal International, which together more or less cover the region. Others (the larger of which operate interstate services) include Nigeria Airways, Air Burkina, Air Ivoire, Bellview Airlines, Air Mauritanie, TACV of Cape Verde and the new airline Afrinat. Airlines in a less certain state of health include Gambia International Airlines, Sierra National Airlines, TAGB of Guinea-Bissau and Air Guinée. Several "national airlines" are virtually defunct. Everywhere, with the new market-economic thrust of recent years, private entrepreneurs are setting up small airlines of light and medium-sized aircraft. Most flights on these airlines are operated on a charter basis, though sometimes with regularity, so you can buy a seat, in effect, from the charterer.

Flights **between West African countries** are expensive, and travel by air not automatically the quickest option. On several coast connections the combination of flying time, formalities and transfers to and from the airports are enough to obviate any advantage over fast road transport. You can expect domestic flights to **cost** around twice the surface transport rate. Beware of lower-than-expected baggage allowances on some internal flights.

The air ticket set-up in West Africa is quite different from that in Europe or North America. There's little unofficial discounting of fares; most tickets get sold at the approved rate, though some airlines operate anomalously, in which case you'll find it hard to discover what those fares are. If you possess an ISIC student card it's always worth requesting a **student reduction**.

Many domestic and regional flights in West Africa are heavily and permanently block-booked by government and not-so-government departments. Only when the actual number of required seats is notified to the airline can they open normal reservations to the public. In many cases notification comes, if at all, on the day of departure, in the airport. As a result, you can expect some problems in getting a reservation, further problems at the airport getting a boarding pass and (occasionally) problems yet again in exchanging the boarding pass for a seat.

There's little you can do about all this. Obviously, book as soon as you can and rebook if plans change, rather than wait until you're certain. This also gives you leverage in terms of personal recognition at the airline office, and bookings don't require a deposit as a rule. Be utterly sceptical of a "confirmed seat" until you're sitting in it. Arrive at the airport long before the flight if you've any doubt about your status, and use every angle and pull every string to improve your chances. Clearly this is a worst-case scenario, but even when there appears to be no problem and no question of not getting on, always **reconfirm your seat** in person two days before the flight.

Driving

Car rental is available in nearly every capital city, at most of the larger airports and in one or two provincial towns in a number of countries. Minimum age for renting a car varies from 21 to 25 (18 for Nigeria) with one or

two year's experience. You may be obliged to **take a driver** with the car, which inevitably puts the price up, though it isn't always a bad arrangement in itself – and can work out brilliantly. Whether you're driving or being driven, you should have an **international driving licence** with you (see p.20).

Don't automatically assume the vehicle is roadworthy. **Before setting off**, have a look at the engine and tyres and don't leave without checking water, battery and spare tyre (preferably two, with the means to change them) and making sure you've a few tools. Except on certain main highways, it's important to keep jerry cans of water and fuel on board. As for breakdowns, local mechanics are usually excellent and can apply creative ingenuity to the most disastrous situations. But spare parts, tools and proper equipment are rare away from the Michelin map's red highways – and not really common along them.

There are several other points to bear in mind. First, rented cars cannot as a rule be driven into **neighbouring countries**. In a number of countries, private self-drive car rental is a novelty and authorities feel uneasy about you driving out **beyond the city limits**. Some firms insist on **four-wheel-drive** (4WD) if you'll be departing from surfaced highways. The costs, especially for 4WD, can be astronomical and you may spend in a day what you would pay for a week's self-drive in Europe or North America.

An alternative is to consider simply **hiring a taxi** on a daily basis. Pay for the fuel separately and settle every other question – the driver's bed, board, cigarettes – in advance. However good the price, don't take on a vehicle that's unsafe, or a driver you don't like and can't communicate with.

Motorcycle rental is less common than car rental, but available in some cities. However, if you have some experience, it is well worth considering buying a machine in West Africa, avoiding the expense and paperwork of riding or shipping a bike all the way from Europe. In Mali, for example, reliable and economical Honda CG 125s are widely available and make ideal machines, if not overloaded (and you shouldn't find it too hard to find a buyer for your motorbike at the end of your trip).

Rules of the road

When driving, beware of unexpected rocks and ditches – not to mention animals and people – on the road. It's accepted practice to honk your horn stridently to warn pedestrians, though be cautious of doing so in built-up areas which may have local laws you'd quickly fall foul of.

All of West Africa **drives on the right**, though in reality vehicles keep to the best part of the road until they have to pass each other (fatefully positioned potholes account for many head-on collisions). Right- and left-hand **signals** are conventionally used to say "please overtake" or "don't overtake", but you shouldn't assume the driver in front can see. In fact, never assume anything about the behaviour of other drivers. Road death statistics are horrifying – Nigeria, famously, taking the lead in this respect.

You're unlikely to be kept for long by **police** or other security forces at the roadside, but you should *never* pass a checkpoint or barrier without stopping and waiting to be waved on. Nor should you ever drive anywhere without all your **documents** (see pp.20–21 for a discussion of these and for contact details of motoring organizations at home who issue them).

Car rental agencies

Avis UK ☏0870/606 0100, Republic of Ireland ☏01/605 7500, US ☏1-800/331-1084, Canada ☏1-800/272-5871, Australia ☏13 63 33, New Zealand ☏09/526 2847, ⊛www.avis.com. Offices in Senegal, Mali, Guinea, Burkina Faso, Ghana, Togo, Benin, Nigeria and Cameroon. Outlets are local licensed firms and, apart from being more expensive, not necessarily much different from others which don't have the international trademark.
Europcar UK ☏0845/722 2525, Republic of Ireland ☏01/614 2800, ⊛www.europcar.co.uk. Cover Cameroon and Ghana.
Hertz UK ☏0870/844 8844, Republic of Ireland ☏01/660 2255, US ☏1-800/654-3001, Canada ☏1-800/263-0600, Australia ☏13 30 39, New Zealand ☏0800/654 321, ⊛www.hertz.com. Countries covered include Senegal, Mali, Cameroon and Ghana.
National UK ☏0870/5365 365, US ☏1-800/227-7368, Australia ☏13 10 45, New Zealand

☏0800/800 115 or 03/366 5574, ⊛www.nationalcar.com. They have an office in Dakar.

Cycling

In many ways **cycling** is the ideal form of transport in West Africa, giving you total independence. A bike gives scope for exploring off the beaten track and getting round cities. Routes that can't be used by motor vehicles – even motorbikes – because they're too rough, or involve crossing rivers, are all accessible. With a tough bike, you can explore off the roads altogether, using bush paths – though remember to give ample verbal warning to people walking in your direction ahead of you, who may otherwise be seriously frightened by your sudden arrival behind them. You can camp out all the time if you wish, or take your bike into hotel rooms with you. When in rural areas you can often leave the bike unattended for a while if you're eating in a chop house or visiting a market – a crowd of onlookers will make sure no one touches it. If you get tired of pedalling, you've the simple option of transporting your bike on top of a bush taxi or bus (reckon on paying about half-fare) or even "cycle-hitching".

Depending on your fitness and enthusiasm, expect to cycle around 1000km a month, including at least two days off for every three on the road. During periods when you're basically cycling from A to B (often on a paved road, which is somewhat slow on a mountain bike), you'll find 40–50km in the early morning and 20–30km more in the afternoon is plenty.

Finding and carrying **water** is a daily chore on a long cycle trip. You'll need at least one five-litre container per person (more if you're camping out and want to wash) but you shouldn't often need to carry it full. Empty plastic oil jars and jerry cans, available all over North and West Africa, are convenient.

Bringing a bike with you

If time is limited, you can **fly your bike** to West Africa. To avoid paying excess baggage charges, you should write in advance to the ground operations manager of the airline, pack as many heavy items into your hand luggage as possible and arrive several hours before the flight to get to know the check-in staff. On scheduled flights it's rare that you'll be obliged to pay, though it's much harder to avoid excess fees on charter flights. Few airlines will insist your bike be boxed or bagged, but it's best to turn the handlebars into the frame and tie them down, invert the pedals and deflate the tyres.

Out on the road, you'll probably want to **carry your gear** in panniers. These are fiendishly inconvenient when not attached to the bike, however, and you might consider sacrificing ideal load-bearing and streamlining for a backpack you can lash down on the rear carrier; you'll probably have to do this anyway if you buy a bike locally. Using the kind of cane used for cane furniture, plus lashings of inner-tube rubber strips, you can create your own highly un-aerodynamic carrier, with room for a box of food and a gallon of water underneath.

With a bike from home, remember to take a battery **lighting system** (dynamo lighting is a pain) – it's surprising how often you'll need it. The front light doubles as a torch and getting batteries is no problem. It's also worth taking a U-bolt **cycle lock**: in towns, where you have to lock the bike, you'll always find something to lock it to. Out in the bush it's less important. Otherwise, improvise with a padlock and chain in a hose which you can buy and fix up in any market.

Apart from the commonest parts, **spares for mountain bikes** are rare in West Africa. But take only what you're sure to need – spare tubes, spare spokes and a good tool kit. If you need to do anything major, you can always borrow large spanners and other heavy equipment. Don't bother with spare tyres if you're going for under six months. On a long trip, it's worth talking to a reputable dealer before you leave so that, in an emergency, you can email for a part to be sent out by courier.

Buying and renting bikes locally

You can forgo any hassles associated with having an expensive bike by **buying** one of the heavyweight roadsters on sale locally. There are bike shops and market areas devoted to cycling in most large towns.

Ouagadougou in Burkina Faso has long been one of the cheapest places to buy, with a vast area devoted to bikes and good secondhand possibilities from about £40/$65. You should be able to get a new bike for under £100/$160. On busy roads a rear-view mirror is close to essential.

You can **rent bicycles and mopeds** in a number of places, including the Gambian coastal resorts, Basse Casamance (Senegal) and Ouagadougou. But they're not usually well-adapted for touring, although they often have carriers. Anywhere you fancy cycling, however, you can often make informal arrangements to lease a bike for a few days.

Walking and riding

Clearly, if you're hardy and not tied to any schedule, you can simply **walk**. All over the region, you'll come across local people walking vast distances because they have no money at all to pay for transport. If you're hiking for a few days you can fall in with them (if you manage to keep up), but they'll rarely speak any French or English. From a more recreational angle, we've covered a number of **hiking possibilities** throughout West Africa, mostly in upland and mountainous regions.

Using a **beast of burden** for your travels is an attractive idea. Unfortunately, **horses** succumb quickly in the more southern tsetse-fly regions and a horse in good shape is expensive. If you know what to look for and how to look after a horse, the most promising districts are sub-Sahelian – most of southern Mali, Burkina Faso, southern Niger, northern Nigeria and further south into highland Cameroon. If you ride south towards the coast, however, and sell your animal, it's likely to end up in a pot.

Mules are a lot tougher (they're used to long treks), cheaper and will happily go further south in the dry season. You'd need three mules between two with luggage, however. Then there are **camels** (dromedaries: *méharis* in Arabic or *chameaux* in French). It's not impossible to join a caravan in the desert or northern Sahel, though fewer and fewer such journeys are made these days. But buying, equipping and travelling with your own animals is not to be undertaken lightly even by the most qualified romantic.

Accommodation

There's not a huge diversity of accommodation options in West Africa. A good range of hotels is found only in the cities, and in several countries even hotels are rather uncommon outside the capital. Hostels of various kinds are usually an urban phenomenon, often permanently full and not to be relied upon, and there are no IYHA youth hostels. Campements, found in several of the French-speaking countries, are basically rustic motels, usually in the bush. The options of staying with local people or camping in the bush are usually there, depending on how you travel. Organized campgrounds are rare.

Hotels

In capitals and large towns, you'll want, and probably have, to stay in hotels. There tends to be a gap between the expensive places and the dives, and you sometimes need to look hard to find something good at a reasonable price. If you're splurging, there's usually a clutch of international establishments bookable from abroad. Local star ratings are not much used and, in any case, about as hopeless an indication of value for money as anywhere.

There's not much by way of Western-style hotels (with reception, bars, restaurant) except in countries with a mobile, salaried middle class. The few mid-range hotels are usually well-run and nice enough places to stay. But small-town hotels – and of course the cheapest joints in the cities – are usually equated with drinking and prostitution. Rooms are often taken for a few hours only, and there may well be a gang of women and toddlers permanently in residence. Don't be put off unduly. These can be fun places to stay – and by no means all are intimidating places for female travellers – though you may have to pick a room carefully (not easy) for anything like a quiet night.

Inexpensive hotels

In inexpensive hotels, always ask to see the room first and don't be surprised if it looks like a tornado's passed through, especially in the morning before it's been cleaned. Always ask for fresh clean sheets and towel if you're not happy with them. If you suspect bedbugs may lurk behind the plaster, pull the beds away from the wall; keeping the light on deters them.

Unless there's a proper tariff sheet, it's always worth **haggling** over the price of a room, and check there'll be no tax on top. If there's air conditioning or a fan but no electricity, ask for a discount. You usually pay on taking the room and may have to leave your passport with the person in charge if there's no registration card to fill out. Use discretion about leaving your keys with the management and, if your door locks by padlock, use your own and check the fixture. Finally, in highland regions or during the harmattan (the wind that blows in the Sahel region in December and January), it's normally expected you'll ask for a bucket of hot water to supplement the cold tap or well – but it may not be offered.

The following **abbreviations** have been used in accommodation reviews throughout this book:
a/c: air conditioning, air-conditioned
s/c: self-contained, with private shower or bath, and toilet
B&B: Bed and breakfast
HB: Half board, meaning dinner, bed and breakfast
FB: Full board, meaning all meals included.

Accommodation price codes

All accommodation prices in this book are coded according to the following scale. Prices refer to the rate you can expect to pay for a room with two beds. Single rooms, or single occupancy, will normally cost at least two-thirds of the twin-occupancy rate. Bear in mind that only the most expensive establishments have a set rate for every room and there's often a chance to negotiate a better deal. In most countries, for a simple but decent twin room with clean sheets, air conditioning and bathroom, expect to pay upwards of £10–15/$15–23. You can often get a fairly mediocre place, usually without air conditioning and certainly without hot water, for about £5–10/$8–15. The CFA countries generally have the cheapest hotels. Cape Verde is expensive and you'll find little below the ❸ bracket. The Gambia, Ghana and Nigeria fall somewhere in between.

❶ Under £5/$8.
❷ £5–10/$8–16.
❸ £10–15/$16–24.
❹ £15–20/$24–32.

❺ £20–30/$32–48.
❻ £30–40/$48–64.
❼ £40–50/$64–80.
❽ Over £50/$80.

Hostels, campements and resthouses

Although there are no internationally affiliated youth hostels in West Africa, you'll find **YMCA** and **YWCA hostels** in several Anglophone cities (notably Accra and Lagos) which are usually permanently full of students and single professionals. If you can get in, they're great places to meet people and, though they're generally run by slightly pious types, there are few limiting restrictions on what you do and when.

For non-camping travellers, alternative types of "hotel" accommodation are popular options in the rural areas. **Campements**, in French-speaking countries, have a fairly loose definition. They're certainly not campsites, though you can sometimes camp at them, but represent more the modern equivalent of a colonial caravanserai or "encampment" in the bush, often associated with game parks and areas of natural beauty. They tend to consist of huts or small room blocks made of local materials (often mud bricks and thatch) with shared washing and toilet facilities – at the top end they're effectively motels. At their most innovative, in Senegal, where some are known as CTRIs (*campements touristiques rurals intégrés* – "rurally integrated"), they are built with government loans by local villagers in order to host independent travellers.

In the English-speaking countries a network of government **resthouses**, for the use

of officials on tour, is theoretically at the disposal of travellers when rooms aren't occupied. There's a similar *réseau* of government villas in Guinea. In fact, these places are very often unused for long periods and need a good airing. Water and electricity are often turned off or disconnected. First, in any case, you have to find the caretaker to open up.

Lastly, there are the resthouses associated with aid, development and voluntary organizations, including the United States Peace Corps (some 1400 of whose graduate volunteers are on placements in thirteen West African countries at any one time) and, somewhat thinly these days, **missions**. If you're travelling extensively, you may find these alternatives helpful and generous. In some cases – a few of the Peace Corps resthouses, for example – there's a special tariff for "outsiders". But in general you'll be staying explicitly as a guest, using facilities intended for others. Where such arrangements are based on informal invitations and strictly word-of-mouth, we've usually kept them that way and not included them in this guide.

Camping

The few **campsites** that exist in West Africa are covered in the main country chapters. There are some in Mali, Mauritania, Burkina Faso and Niger, one or two on the coast in Togo and virtually no others. If you're bringing a tent, bring the lightest one you can afford; there are lots of good geodesic models around these days with snap-together aluminium frames. Or, if the prices put you off, consider making your own with ripstop nylon and fine nylon netting – not as hard to do as it sounds if you have any skill with a sewing machine.

Camping rough depends much on your style of travel. Clearly, if you're driving your own vehicle it's only necessary to find a good spot for the night. Don't assume you can always do this anonymously. A vehicle in the deep bush is unusual and noisy, and people will flock round to watch you. Bush camping is easier if you're cycling or walking. For safety's sake, always get right away from the main road to avoid being accidentally run over or exciting the interest of occasional motorized pirates. You may still be visited by delegations of machete-wielding villagers, especially if you light a fire, but satisfaction that you're harmless is usually their first concern. Some cigarettes or a cup of tea breaks any ice. If you're travelling by public transport, however, it's a lot harder to camp effectively night after night. Vehicles go from town to town and it's rare to be dropped off at just the right spot in between, all ready and supplied for a night under the stars. Walking out of town in search of a place to camp – it can be miles – is an exercise which soon palls.

In more heavily populated or farmed districts, it's usually best to ask someone before pitching a tent. Out in the wilds, hard or thorny ground is likely to be the only obstacle. Fill your water bottles from a village before looking for a site. During the dry sea-

sons, you'll rarely have trouble finding wood for a small fire so a **stove** isn't absolutely necessary, though one is very useful for wet or barren conditions. You can find *camping gaz* butane cartridges in most capital cities. Petrol stoves are more convenient once you've shelled out for them. If you're cycle-camping, a small kerosene lamp is perfectly feasible. Be sure to buy kerosene (*pétrole* in French) however, and not petrol/gasoline (*essence*). Wild animals pose little threat (see p.74); nighttime noises, especially in forest regions – some spectacularly eerie and sinister shrieks and calls – merely add to the atmosphere.

Staying with people

All over West Africa you'll run into people who want to put you up for the night. A warm, but more noticeably, a *dutiful* hospitality characterizes most of these contacts. The visitors most open to them are single travellers who get into conversation on public transport. Your hosts are typically a low-income family with ambitions whose son has been away and has brought you home. You'll be expected to correspond later and send photographs.

It's sometimes difficult to know how to repay such hospitality, particularly since it often seems so disruptive of family life, with you set up in the master bedroom and kids sent running for special things for the guest. While it's impossible to generalize, for female guests a trip to the market with the woman/women of the household is an opportunity to pay for everything. Men can't do this, but buying a sack of rice or a big bundle of yams (get it delivered by barrow or porter) makes a generous gift.

Eating and drinking

West Africa has little in the way of well-defined cuisines, in large part because supplies are erratic, recipes aren't written down, and no two meals ever taste quite the same. Nevertheless, there's a considerable variety of culinary pleasures and an infinite range of intoxicating drinks. Describing it all is complicated by the variety of terms used for common ingredients.

Where to eat

If you're lucky enough to be staying **with a family**, you're likely to experience consistently well-prepared and tasty food – though according to their means this may depend on how much you contribute. In homes, or when travelling on long-distance trucks or by trading canoe, people eat around a **communal dish** (in strictly Islamic regions always males at one, females at another – you generally finish in order of age, the eldest first). Because of this, restaurants, where someone goes and buys a meal for themselves, are not all that common.

It's wrong to assume you can't eat well at the cheapest **street food stalls** and roadside or market **restaurants**. The secret is to eat early – this means late morning (11am–noon) and dusk (5–6pm), when most people eat and food is fresh. Street food isn't usually a takeaway – there's often a table and benches, plastic bowls, spoons and cold water. Anything extra you want – soft drinks, instant coffee – can be fetched for you from nearby.

If you want to eat in more privacy, most towns, even the smallest, have at least one or two **basic restaurants** (sometimes called **chop houses** in the Anglophone countries). Much of the menu or blackboard is likely to be unavailable, however, and there's probably more cause for hesitation over what you eat in small restaurants where you can't be certain of the freshness or provenance of your food, than there is from street stalls where it all has to be cooked before your eyes.

Large towns have more restaurants and, in general, fewer street-food options. Dining on chop-house cooking at inflated prices in a silver-service restaurant seems odd at first, but can be a real treat. Throughout the guide, phone numbers for restaurants are given where **reservations** are advised. The eating-out alternative to African food, in cities, is usually **French** or vaguely **European**, **Chinese** or **Middle Eastern**. **Lebanese** fast-food joints are as common as burger franchises in the US, and serve up snacks and sandwiches, especially *chawarma* (sometimes *shawarma*) – which, like doner kebabs, consists of shreds of barbecued compressed mutton cut from a roll, then wrapped in a pitta bread or French bread.

Food

Most meals consist of a pile of the staple diet plus a sauce or stew often called "soup". The **staple** varies geographically. **Rice** predominates everywhere from Mauritania to Liberia and across the Sahel. **Root crops** (varieties of yam and cassava) and **plantains** figure heavily along the coast from Côte d'Ivoire through Nigeria to Cameroon. In the Sahara, **couscous**, tiny grains of durum wheat, is common.

Sauces can be based on **palm oil** (thick and copper-coloured, all along the coast from The Gambia south and eastwards); **groundnut paste** (peanut butter, found mostly in Sahelian regions); **okra** ("gumbo" or "ladies' fingers" – five-sided, green pods with a high slime content); various **beans**, and the **leaves** of sweet potatoes and cassava among others. All of them are usually heavily spiced, often with **chillies** – "hot pepper" – though it's rarely too much; only southern Nigeria is really dangerous territory for tender mouths. There's a multitude of names in different languages for the same few staples and vegetables – we attempt to clarify things a little on p.55.

Vegetarian West Africa

West Africa makes no concessions to vegetarians. Eating ready-prepared food, whether on the street or in any category of restaurant, is unrewarding: animal protein is the focus of most dishes, and even where it's apparently absent there's likely to be some meat stock somewhere (rice is often cooked in it, or animal fat is added to the vegetables). This means, if you're strictly vegetarian, you're mostly going to have to stick to market fruit and veg and any food you cook for yourself.

Groundnuts (peanuts) – found boiled as well as roasted – and locally made **peanut butter** are a good source of vegetable protein. **Milk** in various forms (and milk powder) and **hard-boiled eggs** are usually obtainable. Cheese is largely unheard of, except in its processed, foil-packaged variety. **Bread** and canned margarine are available everywhere.

Vegetarians who are the guests of African families have a hard time – with such status attached to meat, vegetarianism is regarded as an untenable philosophy. Avoiding meat is particularly trying if you consent to have eggs with every meal instead, as you can find yourself presented with six or more, specially prepared for you, every day.

The more expensive, or festive, "sauces" (often more like stews) have an emphasis on their animal protein content. **Fish** and **mutton** are probably the most common. **Beef** tends to be reserved for special occasions. **Chicken** is pricey, but a favourite meat for guests. **Pork** is very localized and hogs foraging at the roadside are a sure sign you're in a non-Islamic district. **Eggs** are rarely very popular (they're sometimes attributed with contraceptive powers) but they're always available. Various kinds of **"bush meat"** are widely eaten except in the most devoutly Muslim regions, and often bought and sold: in some areas monkeys and antelopes are becoming endangered as a result of this practice. Large, herbivorous rodents ("bush rat", "grasscutters", "agouti") are the commonest and usually delicious, but porcupines, antelopes, monkeys, even cats, dogs and giant snails are eaten in various parts of West Africa. Whatever else they consist of, sauces are made with **bouillon cubes**.

Although common, **bread** isn't a staple food in West Africa, but more of a luxury, often something to eat on long journeys. Different kinds tend to conform to the colonial recipes. In the Francophone countries it's a *baguette* – a French stick – though rarely as long or as crunchy as the real thing. In the Anglophone countries you have to search hard to find good bread. Mostly it's spongey white stuff, sometimes very sweet, and even dyed an unappetizing yellow or pink.

In the French-speaking countries you're likely to adopt the habit of eating **breakfast** in the street. Practice and adroitness vary, but in several countries you'll get excellent hot, whipped Nescafé with *pain beurre* (and real butter) for a set price of about 60p/$1. But be ready with appropriate French if you want your coffee black or – big shock to local people – without sugar. As coffee is sometimes made with sweetened condensed milk, white-no-sugar can be a problem.

Street food

Street food varies widely from country to country and regionally too, and is covered in more detail for each country. One snack that's pretty well universal is the **brochette** (*suya* in Hausa) – a tiny stick of kebabed meat. This is often eaten as a sandwich in a piece of French bread.

West African food plants

Besides the crops we discuss below, other common food plants include **onions** and **tomatoes** (available everywhere, even in the driest districts, but often tiny and sold in piles of four), **lettuces** (wash very carefully), short but tasty **cucumbers**, **avocados** (wonderful, huge specimens in Cameroon), tiger nuts (*chufa* – tiny coconut-flavoured tubers like shrivelled beans), **pigeon peas** (small, round, brown and white beans), **white haricot**, **lima** and **butter beans**, and various kinds of **gourd**, **pumpkin** and **squash**. Certain types of melon are good only for their large, oily seeds, commonly known by the Yoruba name, **egusi**, and widely used when crushed to flavour soups.

Aubergine/eggplant (*Solanum melongena*). Grown on garden plots all over and come in many shapes and colours (round, white, yellow, red) but rarely in the large, purple variety familiar in the West. Known variously as "garden eggs" or "bitter balls", they can be identified as aubergines by the star-shaped, leathery, leafy bits at the stalk end.

Cassava (*Manihot*; *manioc* in French). Spindly two-metre shrub from South America, with handlike leaves, seen growing all over. The tubers, which tend to have a bitter taste, are large and coarse and have to be boiled and then usually pounded in a mortar to reduce them to an edible glob of nearly pure starch (*fufu/foufou/eba*). Cassava leaves taste much nicer and are full of vitamins. They're finely shredded and used like spinach. *Gari* is cassava flour (from which tapioca is made), but the word gets used quite broadly for various types of flour.

Cocoyam (*Colocasia*). Tastier than yams or cassava, but easily confused. Grown mostly in wet forest regions, the plants have unmistakeably huge, heart-shaped, edible leaves. Tubers are rounded with a fleshy stalk and commonly known as "koko", "mankani", "taro", "eddo" or "dasheen". Similar names are often given to the introduced Tannia (*Xanthosoma*). This "new cocoyam" has giant arrow-shaped leaves and tasty, smaller, dark, hairy tubers.

Cowpeas (*Vigna*; black-eye beans). The commonest type of bean, cowpeas come in many varieties and are grown throughout the region. They're usually dried and stored for use, or made into flour, but you often see them freshly harvested in their long, pale pods. Mashed cowpeas are used for *akara* – "deep-fried balls" sold nearly everywhere. Common names include *wake* and *niebe*.

Groundnut (*Arachis*; peanuts, monkey nuts; *arachide* or *cacahouètes* in French). Groundnuts are grown widely to be used as the basis of sauces, and you'll see little dollops of peanut butter – on leaves or in plastic sachets – for sale in markets everywhere.

Maize (*Zea*; corn; sweetcorn; *maïs* in French). Grown a lot in forest region clearings, this is used widely on the cob as a stop-gap and a roasted or boiled snack. Maize flour is used quite extensively in some parts as a staple – in Ghana for fermented corn dough (*kenkey*) for example.

Millet (*Pennisetum*). *Gero* in Hausa, it looks like bullrushes with a maizelike stalk. It's grown mostly in the Sahel and is used for porridge, gruel and making beer.

Plantain (*Musa*). These mega-bananas are found all over the rainier southern part of West Africa. They're eaten cooked – fried when ripe, or boiled and sometimes pounded to a tasty *fufu* when hard).

Potatoes (*patate* in French). Unless specified as "Irish", these are always the *sweet* variety (*Ipomoea batatas*) with pink skins, known in the US, confusingly, as "yams". They're grown in mounds and ridges and have a mass of creeping vines. They tend to be something of a luxury, used to add flavour to stews and sauces. The leaves are edible and widely used. Regular, Irish potatoes (*Solanum tuberosum*) only grow in West Africa above an altitude of about 1200m.

Sorghum (*Sorghum*; *sorgho* in French). Tall plants (2–4m) similar to maize but with feathery, white- or red-grained flower heads. Also known as "guinea corn" and "giant millet", sorghum is grown mainly in the savanna zone, and is made into porridge. Sorghum beer – known as *bilibili*, *burukutu* and *pito* – is widespread.

Yam (*Dioscorea*; *ignames* in French). Massive tubers that grow singly beneath a climbing, vinelike plant with spade-shaped leaves, commonly seen in southern parts of the region, especially in Nigeria. They come in white and yellow varieties (the former is preferred) and are used like cassava to make pounded yam *fufu*, but they have a better flavour.

West African fruit and nuts

Perhaps the most satisfying eating in West Africa is **fruit**. There's a magnificent variety in the markets south of the Sahel, though even in the drier regions you'll find citrus most of the year, mangoes in season and the odd pawpaw. Besides the ones we've listed below, you'll also come across **star-fruit** (attractively shaped but tasteless), **cus-tard apples** or **soursops** (lovely pear-drop flavour in the roughly heart-shaped, green fruit) and **mangosteens** (amazing taste inside the small, round, brownish fruit with very thick skin). Towards the Sahara you get **dates** in all their different grades and, lastly, at certain times and places, quite a variety of **wild-collected fruit**, some of which (like the *ditak* in Senegal) is particularly good. **Sugar cane**, sometimes sold in markets, isn't actually a fruit; you simply strip off the shiny outside and chomp on the pith, which oozes sucrose.

Banana If you spend long in West Africa, you may never be able to face a banana again. But local varieties are often wonderfully flavoured compared to the imported, white-fleshed supermarket type. Look out for very thin-skinned dwarf bananas in huge bunches, and for very fat, squat varieties with pale orange flesh and sometimes red skins.

Cashew Not just a nut, the cashew also has a fruit attached. The arrangement of the nut at the apex of the cashew "apple" is hard to believe when you first see it. You can eat the apple, though the fibrous flesh can be bitter. In some parts the delicious, light juice is made into a potent hooch. Don't be tempted to feast off people's cashew trees – they only have a small number of valuable nuts each and owners get very upset.

Coconut The familiar brown "nuts" of coconut shies are contained within a thick husk and the whole thing is green and about the size of a football. Coconuts are very hard to open without a machete, but all along the coast (they won't grow easily above 500m) you'll have the opportunity to try them in several satisfying stages as the flesh changes from a thin jelly to a thick layer of coconut. They're not seasonal.

Grapefruit African varieties are often exceptionally sweet and big. Leave the segments to dry for a while and peel off the inner skins to reveal hundreds of little packets of grapefruit juice. A fine pleasure.

Guava Don't buy unripe ones – guavas should have a very strongly perfumed scent. The best ones have pink flesh.

Mango Available and rightly esteemed everywhere, mangoes come in hundreds of varieties. The mango season coincides with the end of the dry season and the first rains (roughly March–June depending on where you are). They're expensive at first and rapidly drop in price until they're two a penny (sometimes literally). Whole villages devote themselves to eating and selling the fruit. The very best, found in southern Cameroon, are long and narrow with bright green skins and very firm, orange, stringless flesh.

Oranges and tangerines Often bright green, even when perfectly ripe, these are the main juice fruits of West Africa. Oranges are always available for a few pence from girls and women with trays and sharp knives. The peel is shaved off, leaving the orange in its pith, then the top is lopped off and you squeeze the juice into your mouth and discard the emptied orange. You can easily go through a dozen or twenty in a day like this – diabolical for your front teeth.

Pawpaw Also known as papayas, pawpaws aren't regarded as worth selling in many parts of West Africa, where they grow as giant weeds, left for the children. If you don't see them for sale, approach the people of a house where they're growing in the compound and ask to buy one. The seeds – which taste like watercress – can be eaten as a tonic. They contain excellent supplies of invigorating minerals and vitamins, and are reckoned to help the healing process and to aid digestion. The smaller and more fragrant mountain varieties are delicious. Non-seasonal.

Pineapple Commonest in coastal districts of Ghana and eastwards to Cameroon. Available throughout the dry season.

Drinking

Probably the most widely consumed beverage in the region – after water – is **green tea** (in reality yellow). Rock sugar in huge lumps, China tea leaves and water are brought to the boil in a little kettle on a handful of coals, then poured out repeatedly to infuse and froth the brew. The tea has to be Green Gunpowder – a tin or packet of which makes a very good gift. In the Sahel, from Senegal to northern Cameroon, green tea is an essential part of every day and no long journey is completed without it. It's common further south, too, in all regions where Islam predominates. It's traditional to drink three glasses – strong and bitter, sweet and full-bodied, and sweet and mild.

Apart from Nescafé, **coffee** is less popular, and real coffee rare except in big hotels. Various **infusions** are locally common. One which has wide popularity in the western part of West Africa (as a base for mixing in a lot of *lait concentré sucré*) is *kenkeliba* (also spelled "quinceliba" and various other ways). *Kenkeliba* is mild and indifferently nutty when mixed with sweet milk or just on its own, but don't mistake it for water and have Nescafé added – the mixture has a revolting flavour.

When you can't get cold water, **soft drinks** – especially fizzy orange and lemonade and Coke – are permanent stand-bys and in remote areas any establishment with electricity is almost bound to have a fridge of battered bottles (bottles are always returned to the wholesaler, so *never* take the bottle away – this is serious theft!). Supermarkets and most general stores carry large bottles of **drinking water**. On the street, however, you'll often see locally made **fruit juices**, cold water and ices, in plastic bags, sold by children from buckets of ice. Ginger is refreshing, as too is the white sherbet made from baobab fruits. They're safe to drink in areas where you're already drinking the local water with no ill-effects (the same rule of thumb applies to locally bottled soft drinks).

Beer and spirits

The most noticeable drink in the region is **beer**, and almost every country has at least one brewery. Nigeria has many, and a whole host of competing brands. Only the Islamic Republic of Mauritania is dry. The beer usually comes in 35cl, half-litre or 70cl bottles and is mostly strong, gassy, sometimes quite bitter in flavour and, most of the time, cold (as is **Guinness**, brewed by local branches of European breweries).

However, bottled beer is extremely expensive for the majority of local people and it can therefore sometimes be difficult to find in smaller villages. As a convenient alternative, the local traditional **home-made beers** are well worth experiencing. Available under many different names, they're as varied in taste and colour as the ingredients used – basically a fermented mash of sugar and cereal (usually sorghum, maize or millet), sometimes with herbs and roots for flavouring. The results are cloudy, frothy and often

strong. Always made by women, home-made beer is usually drunk in the round, each person taking their turn with the dipper, from a central calabash.

In coastal parts, **palm wine** is produced from palm sap which, after tapping, ferments in a day from a pleasant, mildly intoxicating juice to a ripe and pungent brew with seriously destabilizing qualities. The flavour is aromatic and slightly acidic. The most common palms tapped are the stumpy, dark green oil palms, which also produce palm nuts for palm oil. Taller *borassus* and coconut palms can also be tapped, but rarely are.

Spirits distilled from beer, palm wine or sugar cane are locally much in evidence across the region (in Ghana, Cameroon, Burkina Faso, Nigeria and Cape Verde for example) and normally only alcoholically dangerous, rather than actually denatured with unknown toxic additives, as in other parts of Africa. But beware nevertheless.

Imported spirits are excessively expensive. **Imported beer**, too, is rarely worth the price. Cheap French **wine**, on the other hand, is fairly affordable in Senegal (unless you live in France, in which case it'll seem extortionate) where you can often buy it from ordinary general stores.

Communications

Mail and telecommunications have improved enormously over the last ten years or so. Ordinary letters sent from main post offices rarely go astray if they're carefully addressed, though receiving mail is a little more variable. As for phoning, all the West African countries are now on International Direct Dialling, and for mobile-phone users, international roaming agreements cover some regions. Specifics for each country are covered in the practical information at the start of the relevant chapter.

Mail

In French-speaking countries the post office is called the **PTT** (*Postes, Télécommunications et Télédiffusion*) or **Hôtel des Postes**, in English-speaking ones, the **GPO** and in Portuguese-speaking territories the Correio

or **CTT**. Post offices in Francophone countries usually have separate counters (*guichets*) for different services, so make sure you're in the right line. In Europe, allow two weeks for post sent to West Africa to be received and one week to ten days to receive mail from West Africa. Elsewhere, allow three days longer.

Sending mail

It's easiest and most secure to use **aerograms** for writing home – they're usually postage pre-paid, so you don't have to worry about weighing and handing over letters. Unfortunately, they're also often in high demand and forever going out of stock. **Postal rates** do vary widely, especially between CFA and non-CFA countries – the latter are often cheaper.

If you have **urgent mail** to send, the best place is usually not the main post office but the airport, from where mail is often sent on the next flight out. There may not be much of a post office, just a mail box. For similar reasons, if you're sending heavy or valuable items, it's worth doing so with a friend or contact who's flying.

Poste restante

To receive mail, It's not wise to have it sent anywhere except **capital cities**, not just in order to maximize your chances of getting it, but to speed up delivery (Kano, Nigeria, is an exception). Note, too, that some post offices only hold mail for a few weeks before returning it to the sender.

For clarity's sake, ask people to write your address in this form:

FAMILY NAME, Given Name
Poste Restante
PTT or GPO etc
City
COUNTRY

and to put their own address on the back.

To collect mail, write your name on a piece of paper as you'd expect it to appear on the letter, and go armed with your passport. Post office staff are often remarkably uncivil, so be prepared to smile and plead.

Alternatives to Poste Restante are your **embassy** or **high commission** (some of which will hold mail for up to three months) or **American Express** offices, all of which will hold mail for customers (including those who've merely bought their traveller's cheques). Local addresses for these are given throughout the book.

Telephones

Despite IDD, international phone calls from West Africa sometimes take a while to fix up. There might be someone "occupying" the line, or an operator in the ether somewhere. If you have to go through an **operator**, insist on a "station to station" (number-to-number) call if you know it'll be easy to get hold of the person you want; the alternative, a person-to-person call, costs more and will only connect you if the person you name is available.

In most areas, **phonecards** have replaced cumbersome counter procedures for making international calls and phone booths or telecentres are set up in many cities. Unfortunately, the cards, manufactured outside West Africa, are occasionally unavailable for months on end.

Reverse charge or collect calls ("PCV" – *pay say vay* – in French) are possible from most countries, though you may have some pleading to do. It's often easier, if you want to have a phone conversation, but aren't up to the very high likely cost, to arrange in advance to *receive* a call at a certain time and number.

Mobile phones

If you want to use your home mobile phone in West Africa, you'll need to check with your phone provider as to whether it will work abroad (you may then need to get international access switched on) and what the charges involved are. You are also likely to be charged extra for incoming calls when abroad. If you live in North America, you will need to have a GSM/triband cellphone for West Africa. A useful website is ⓦwww.gsmworld.com/roaming, showing coverage and roaming partners, country by country.

In some West African countries, it's possible to buy a **SIM card** and pay-as-you-go scratch cards in order to use your mobile phone on the local network. This saves money for you and your contacts if you're mainly expecting to use your phone to make and receive calls within the country itself. If your phone is programmed to be used exclusively on your home mobile network it will need to be unlocked – many West African mobile-phone shops offer this service.

Useful dialling codes

To **call home** from West Africa, you dial the international access code, which is usually 00, followed by your country code – see the list below – then the number you want in full, though you should omit any initial zero from the area code or cellphone number:

UK: 44
Ireland: 353
US and Canada: 1

Australia: 61
New Zealand: 64
South Africa: 27

West African IDD country codes

Benin 229 plus six-digit number
Burkina Faso 226 plus six-digit number
Cameroon 237 plus six-digit number
Cape Verde 238 plus six-digit number
The Gambia 220 plus five-digit number
Ghana 233 plus area code plus number
Guinea 224 plus six-digit number
Guinea-Bissau 245 plus six-digit number

Mali 223 plus area code and number totalling six-digits
Mauritania 222 plus area code and number totalling six digits
Niger 227 plus six digit number
Nigeria 234 plus area code plus number
Senegal 221 plus six-digit number
Sierra Leone 232
Togo 228 plus six-digit number

Internet access and faxes

In countries with a reasonably stable telephone service, major towns have at least one **cybercafé** or email service, though the state of the hardware and reliability of connections varies hugely.

Although Internet access is becoming more and more widespread in West Africa, it can still be very useful to have a **fax** number at home through which urgent messages can be relayed to friends or family. Faxing is more flexible than phoning – and usually works out cheaper. Every large town in West Africa has public fax offices at which you can send and receive messages (the cost of receiving a fax is nominal). Most large hotels have fax services, too, at slightly more expensive rates.

The media

There was a rebirth of the press in West Africa with the movement towards multiparty democracy in the early 1990s. Countries which formerly had almost no newspapers now have a thriving press, though critical and independent editors can still find themselves in serious trouble with governments – or government figures – uncomfortable with potential scrutiny of their policies.

Local press and broadcasting in West Africa isn't likely to give you much of an idea of what's going on in the rest of the world. The practical information at the beginning of each country chapter tries to uncover the best and most intrepid of the output. Some British and European newspapers, plus the *Herald Tribune* and *USA Today*, are often available in the lobbies of the more expensive big-city hotels, together with *Time*, *Newsweek* and *Jeune Afrique*. You'll find some of them, too, on sale a few days later from street vendors.

Radio and TV

National and local **radio stations** have blossomed in recent years, along with the print media. It's now common to have a few local stations, though, as with the press, they're frequently subject to all sorts of harassment. Most West African countries have **TV stations**, usually with a rather uninspired mix of deeds and words from government ministers and imported soaps and movies. Video rental and satellite television have swept across the region.

If you're travelling for any length of time, it's a good idea to invest in a pocket-sized short-wave radio. The **BBC World Service** is a real institution in parts of West Africa, and produces several excellent Africa Service programmes, including the morning magazine **Network Africa** and the vital **Focus on Africa**, broadcast in the afternoon and evening Monday to Friday. You can also listen to the BBC in French, Hausa and Portuguese. The best shortwave frequencies for the BBC are 6.005MHz (49m), 11.765MHz (25m) and 15.400MHz (19m) in the morning, and 17.830MHz (16m) in the afternoon and evening. BBC World Service can also be heard on FM in a number of cities, including Accra, Bamako, Cotonou, Dakar, Freetown, Lagos and Ouagadougou. For details of current schedules and frequencies, check ⓦwww.bbc.co.uk/worldservice. With a short-wave radio you can also pick up the **Voice of America** (ⓦwww.voa.gov) and other international broadcasters.

Public holidays and festivals

In addition to the main Christian and Islamic religious festivals, each country in West Africa has its own national holidays, listed in the practical information at the start of each country chapter. These are rarely as established as you would find, for example, in Europe. Some, commemorating no longer respected events, are quietly ignored. In one or two countries, the practice of mounting national celebrations for the president's birthday and similar anniversaries adds a bizarre and unfamiliar quality. Traditional, community festivals, connected either to annual agricultural cycles or to life-cycle events, are more attractive but less accessible. Details are given chapter by chapter wherever possible.

Islamic holidays

Each West African country, with the exception of Cape Verde, has a significant Muslim population. Islam is the dominant religion in most, but Mauritania is the only nation to dub itself an Islamic Republic. In other countries, Muslim holy days are variably observed – devoutly in strictly Muslim districts, perhaps only vaguely in the capital city.

The **Islamic calendar** dates from 622 AD, the "Year of the Hijra" (dates measured with respect to this are denoted AH), when the prophet fled from Mecca to Medina. It uses a lunar system, the Islamic year divided into twelve months of 29 or 30 days (totalling

354 days – thus the dates of Islamic festivals shift forward by around eleven days every year, relative to the Gregorian calendar).

The **principal events** of which to be aware are the ten days of the Muslim New Year which starts with the month of Moharem (**Ashoura** on the 10th of Moharem celebrates, among other events, Adam and Eve's first meeting after leaving Paradise), the **Prophet Muhammad's birthday** (known as Mouloud or Maulidi), the month-long fast of **Ramadan** and the feast of relief which follows immediately after (known as Id al-Fitr or Id al-Sighir), and the **Feast of the Sacrifice** or Tabaski, which coincides with

Islamic festivals

The Gregorian dates given below are approximate, as the Islamic months begin when the new moon is sighted. Muslim calendar dates are given in parentheses.

Beginning of Ramadan (1st of Ramadan)
Oct 16, 2004
Oct 5, 2005
Sept 24, 2006

Id al-Fitr/Id al-Sighir (1st of Shawwal)
Nov 14, 2004
Nov 4, 2005
Oct 23, 2006

Tabaski/Id al-Kabir (10th of Dhu'l Hijja)
Feb 1, 2004
Jan 21, 2005
Jan 10, 2006

New Year's Day (1st of Moharem)
Feb 22, 2004
Feb 10, 2005
Jan 31, 2006

Ashoura (10th of Moharem)
Mar 2, 2004
Feb 20, 2005
Feb 9, 2006

Mouloud/Maulidi (12th of Rabia el-Thany)
May 2, 2004
Apr 21, 2005
Apr 11, 2006

the annual hajj pilgrimage to Mecca, when every Muslim family with the means to do so slaughters a sheep.

The last of these festivals (known as the *fête des moutons* in French) can be a lot of fun. As for **Ramadan**, fasting applies throughout the daylight hours and covers every pleasure (food, drink, tobacco and sex). While non-Muslims are not expected to observe the fast, it's highly affronting in strict Muslim areas to contravene publicly. Instead, switch to the night shift, as everyone else does, with special soup to break the fast at dusk, and applied eating and entertainment through the night.

Christian holidays

Christmas and (to a much lesser extent) **Easter** are observed as religious ceremonies in Christian areas and, on a more or less secular, national basis, in every country. If you can't find a bank or post office open, you'll have no trouble finding street food and some transport.

Christmas and **New Year** are occasions for street parades and carnival festivities in a number of cities. On the downside, Christmas is a time to avoid contact, as far as possible, with people in uniform. This most applies to the police in the English-speaking countries, where a misappropriated tradition of "Christmas Boxes" – seasonal gratuities – survives and is relentlessly cultivated from mid-December to the middle of January.

Lastly, both Guinea-Bissau and Cape Verde have inherited and elaborated upon the Portuguese-Brazilian institution of **Carnaval** and host float parades and street festivals in February or March.

Crime and personal safety

It's easy to exaggerate the potential hassles and disasters of travel in West Africa. True, there's a scattering of urban locations, easily enough pinpointed, where snatch robberies and muggings are common. But most of the region carries minimal risk to personal safety compared to Europe and North America. The main problems are sneak thieving and corrupt people in uniforms. The first can be avoided; dealing with corruption (which is becoming less of a problem as democracy and accountability make inroads into the region) can become a game once you know the rules.

If you're heading for remote regions, to hike for example, it's worth leaving details of your trip with your embassy or the honorary consul.

Theft and scams

If you get mugged, it will be over in an instant and you're not likely to be hurt. But the hassles, and worse, that gather as soon as you try to do something about it, make it doubly imperative not to let it happen in the first place. Robbers and pickpockets caught red-handed are usually dealt with summarily by the crowd, so when you shout "thief" (*voleur* in French), be swift to intercede once you've retrieved your belongings.

Obviously, if you flaunt the trappings of wealth where there's urban poverty, somebody will want to remove them. There's less risk in leaving your valuables in a securely locked hotel room or, judiciously, with the management. If you clearly have nothing on you (this means not wearing jewellery or an expensive-looking wristwatch), you're unlikely to feel, or be, threatened.

Public transport rarely produces scare stories. Apart from the standard of driving, which is another matter, you haven't much

Big-city survival

Pickpocketing can happen anywhere – usually the work of pocket-high thieves, hanging around in markets or other crowded places. Make sure your valuables are secure. **Heavier attacks** usually take place in specific areas of the city – downtown shopping streets, docks and waterfront, city-centre parks and central markets. Don't feel unduly intimidated at transport parks – these are full of tough young men working as drivers or ticket sellers, and who tend to be on the lookout for threats to their passengers – or in the lower-income suburbs and slums away from the city centre, where people just aren't used to travellers.

When walking – assuming you have money or valuables on you – have a destination in mind and stay alert. Keep your hands to yourself. Loose hands are likely to be caught: in heavy places, a handshake from a stranger in the street, or a nick-nack pressed into your hand, or some murmured offer or suggestion can foreshadow a more aggressive act. If you want to give off strong defensive vibes, hands in pockets or round the straps of a backpack are effective.

Steer clear of creepy-looking street sharks in jeans and running shoes (every robbery ends in a sprint). And never allow yourself to be steered down an alley or between parked cars.

to worry about on the roads – except in Lagos, which is acquiring a certain notoriety for hold-ups (exaggerated, even so). Trains provide thieves with more opportunities, however. People fall asleep and robbers have been known to climb aboard and steam through the carriages. Establish a rapport with your fellow passengers as soon as possible.

If you're flying into West Africa, or arriving overland in your first big city, it's obviously wise to be particularly cautious for the first day or two. There's always a lot going on and it's important to distinguish harmlessly robust, up-front interaction (commonly part of the public transport scene) from more dangerous preludes. At the risk of sensationalism, the box above outlines some good strategies for big-city survival in Dakar, Lagos or Douala – the most difficult to deal with. Nouakchott, Banjul and Ouagadougou are more relaxed, while Lomé, Bamako and Niamey fall somewhere in between.

In one or two cities, **scams** which play on your conscience have begun to appear: a favourite is the "student agitator" routine, in which you get chatting to a friendly young person and either give him a little money, or exchange addresses. As soon as they have gone, a group of heavies arrives, claiming to be undercover police and informing you that you have been observed planning seditious activities for which you could be arrested,

though you can instead pay a fine now. Make a big fuss and insist on going to the police station with someone in uniform – they will disappear.

Don't feel victimized: every rural immigrant coming to the city for the first time goes through exactly the same process, and many will be considerably less streetwise than you. Finally, don't forget that fellow travellers are as likely – or as unlikely – to rip you off as anyone else.

Reporting crime

If you are the victim of crime, usually the first reaction is to go to the **police**. Unless, however, you've lost a lot of money (and cash is virtually irretrievable) or irreplaceable property, think twice about doing this. The police in West Africa rarely do something for nothing – even stamping an insurance form may cost you – and you should consider the ramifications if you and they set off to try to catch the culprits. If you're not certain of their identities, pointing the finger of suspicion at people is the worst possible thing to do. If they're arrested, as they probably will be, a night in the cells usually means a beating and confiscation of their possessions.

In smaller towns, or where you have some contacts, a workable alternative to police involvement is to offer a reward or enlist **traditional help** in searching for your stolen belongings. Various diviners and traditional doctors operate nearly everywhere. If the culprits get to hear of what you're doing you're likely to get some of your stuff back. Local people will often go out of their way to help.

Dealing with the police

West African **police forces** vary considerably from one country to the next. For example, in Guinea-Bissau they're not excessively corrupt but can be unnervingly conscientious and pedantic, while in Guinea they're outrageously on the make and seemingly unfazed by the question of upholding actual laws. Most police forces constitute a separate entity from the rest of the people: they have their own compounds and staff villages and receive – or procure – subsidized rations and services.

While it's wise to avoid the police as far as possible, the notion of "control" remains highly developed in the vast majority of West African countries, even where you're no longer obliged to check in at the local police station in every town. Checks on the movement of people (police and security services) and goods (customs, *douanes*) take place at junctions and along highways in most coun-

tries. Many capital cities have major checkpoints on their access roads.

If you have official business with the police, smiles and handshakes always help, as do terms of address like "sir", officer" or (in a French-speaking country) "*mon commandant*". If you're expected to give a bribe (see box, below) – as you often are – wait for it to be hinted at. Having said that, note that currency smuggling or drug possession can easily land you a large fine or worse, and possibly deportation. Don't expect to buy yourself easily out of this kind of trouble.

In **unofficial dealings**, the police, especially in remote outposts, can sometimes go out of their way to help you with food, transportation and accommodation. Try to reciprocate. Police salaries are always low and often months overdue, and they rely on unofficial income to get by.

Offences you might commit

Never go out without **identification**. You don't have to carry a passport at all times, but a photocopy of the first few pages in a plastic wallet is very useful. Not carrying an

Bribery

If you find yourself confronting an implacable person in uniform, you don't have to give in to tacit demands for gifts or money. The golden rule is to **keep talking**. Most laws, including imaginary ones about the importation of backpacks, the possession of two cameras or the writing of diaries, are there to be discussed rather than enforced. If you haven't got all day, a *dash* or **"small present"** – couched in exactly those terms – is all it usually takes to resolve matters, though you should haggle over it as you would any payment. The equivalent of a pound or dollar or two is often enough to oil small wheels.

If you can't, or won't, give gifts to officials, give words.

On extensive West African travels, you have literally hundreds of police, army, customs, immigration and security checkpoints to cross. You'll sail through ninety percent of them, and with patience and good humour, the other ten percent can be negotiated relatively painlessly too. When you know they know your "infraction" is bogus, keep joking, keep pleading and hang on. If you think you may be in breach of a law (or someone's interpretation of it) you might suggest paying the "fine" (*amende*) immediately, or "coming to an agreement" (*faire arrangement* or *s'arranger* in French).

If you're **driving**, you'll rarely be forced to pay sweeteners, except sometimes on entry to and exit from the country. Travelling by lorry or bush taxi, you'll note it's the driver who pays. If you're singled out, *remind them* it's the driver who pays. Avoid any show of temper – aggressive travellers always have the worst police stories.

ID (*carte d'identité*, *papiers* or *pièces* in French) is usually against the law.

Be warned that failure to observe the following points of **public etiquette** can get you arrested or force you to pay a bribe:

• Stand still on any occasion a national anthem is played or a flag raised or lowered. If you see others suddenly cease all activity, do the same.

• Pull off the road completely if motorcycle outriders and limos appear, or stand still.

• Never destroy banknotes, no matter how worthless they may be.

• And don't urinate in public.

Drugs offences

Grass (marijuana, cannabis) is the biggest illegal drug in the region, much cultivated (clandestinely) and as much an object of confused opprobrium and fascination as anywhere else in the world. Many social problems are routinely attributed to smoking the "grass that kills" and it's widely believed to cause insanity. In practice, if you indulge discreetly, it's not likely to get you into trouble. The usual result of a fortuitous bust is on-the-spot fines all round.

An altogether different state of affairs exists with **heroin** and **cocaine**, which are smuggled though West African airports en route to Europe (often inside hapless female "swallowers"). Some of the consignments get on to the streets of the capitals, together with the associated tensions and paranoia. Stay well clear: very long prison sentences and the death penalty are not unknown for those convicted of involvement in the trade.

Cameras and the state

At the risk of generalizing, West Africa is hostile to the camera's probing eye (for more on the subject of photography, see p.67). There are people, often teachers or civil servants, who may take it upon themselves to protect the state from your unwelcome inspection and ask you to stop taking pictures, or report you to the police. And there are the security forces themselves, who will often hassle you if they see you taking photographs – usually on the pretext that you are taking pictures of them.

This advice isn't intended to cause alarm, and plenty of travellers complete their trips with not a film confiscated or a camera opened. Nonetheless, disturbing encounters are not infrequent. You shouldn't take photos of anything that could be construed as **strategic** or **military** – including any kind of army or police building, police or military vehicles and uniforms, prisons, airports, harbours, ferries, bridges, broadcasting installations, national flags and, of course, presidents. Officially, this is seen as a "risk to state security", but some countries are specifically ill-disposed to tourists taking photographs of scenes reflecting poverty. With this kind of discretionary caveat, you can more or less rule out photography in the towns if you behave with rigid correctness. The Gambia, Senegal and Cape Verde are the least uptight about these subjects; Mali, Burkina Faso and Ghana are sufficiently familiar with tourists for it rarely to be an issue; Cameroon and Nigeria are notoriously touchy. One or two countries still require you to have "**photography permits**". Details are given in the practical information section for each country.

Finally, small **digital video** cameras generally attract less attention than SLR still cameras, especially if you shoot using a monitor rather than an eyepiece.

Cultural hints

You can't hope to avoid social gaffes on a West African stay, but humour and tolerance aren't lacking, so you won't be left to stew in embarrassment. Getting it right really takes an upbringing, but people are delighted when you make the effort.

Greetings

Greetings are fundamental – no conversation starts without one. This means a handshake followed by polite enquiries, even as you enter a shop. Traditionally, such exchanges can last a minute or two, and you'll often hear them performed in a formal, incantatory manner between two men. Long greetings help subsequent negotiations. In French or English you can swap something like "How are you?" "Fine, How's the day?" "Fine, How's business?" "Fine, How's the family?", "Fine, Thank God". It's usually considered polite, while someone is speaking to you at length, to grunt in the affirmative, or say thank you at short intervals. Breaks in conversation are filled with more greetings.

Shaking hands is normal between all men present, on arrival and departure. Women shake hands with each other, but with men only in more sophisticated milieux. Soul-brother handshakes and variations on the finger snap are popular among young males. Less natural for Westerners (certainly for men) is an unconscious ease in physical contact. Male visitors need to get used to holding hands with strangers as they're shown around the house, or guided down the street and, on public transport, to hands and limbs draped naturally wherever's most comfortable.

Social norms

Be aware of the **left hand rule**. Traditionally the left hand is reserved for unhygienic acts and the right for eating and touching, or passing things to others. Like many "rules" it's very often broken. Don't think about it then.

Unless you want a serious confrontation, never **point** with your finger. It's equivalent to an obscene gesture. For similar reasons, beckoning is done with the palm down, not up. **Hissing** ("Tsss!") is an ordinary way to attract a stranger's attention. You'll get a fair bit of it, and it's quite in order to hiss at the waiter in a restaurant.

Answering anything in the negative is often considered impolite. If you're asking questions, don't ask yes-no ones. And try not to phrase things in the negative ("Isn't the lorry leaving?") because the answer will often be "Yes . . . " (" . . . it isn't leaving"). Be on the lookout, too, for a host of **unexpected turns of phrase** which often pop up in West African English. "I am coming", for example, is often said by someone just as they leave your company – which means they're going, but coming back.

Don't be put off by apparent shiftiness in **eye contact**, especially if you're talking to someone much younger than you. It's fairly normal for those deferring to others to avoid direct looks.

Time-keeping

Although many people wear watches they're essentially jewellery: notions of time and duration are pretty hazy. Outside the cities, dusk and dawn are the significant markers. You'll soon find you, too, are judging time by the sun, and reckoning how long before dark.

People and things in West Africa are usually late. That said, if you try to anticipate **delays** you'll be caught out. Scheduled transport does leave on time at least some of the time. More importantly, transport may leave *early* if it's full. Even planes have been known to take off before schedule.

Note that in remote areas, if a driver tells you he's going somewhere "today", it doesn't necessarily mean he expects to *reach*

Kola nuts

Giving and receiving **kola nuts** is a traditional exchange of friendship. Kola nuts are the chestnut-sized fruit from the pods of an indigenous tree, cultivated widely all over the forest belt and traded on a grand scale throughout West Africa. Before the arrival of tobacco, cannabis, tea and coffee, kola was the main non-alcoholic drug of the region, an appetite depressant and a mild stimulant. It comes in dark red, pink and white varieties, of which the latter are the best and more expensive. Kola should be fresh and hard, not old and rubbery, and you chew it – don't swallow – for the bitter juice. Buy a handful for long journeys, as much to share among fellow passengers as to stay awake.

there today. Always allow extra time. There's no better way to ruin West African travel than to attempt to rush it.

Photographing people

West Africa is immensely photogenic but to get good pictures takes skill and confidence, and a considerable amount of cultural sensitivity. Photos from Africa are full of examples of people who didn't want to be photographed. That you might have taken some of their soul is not an explanation, but it's a good metaphor.

There are two options if you want to get **photos of people**. First, you can adopt a gleefully robust (or blithely arrogant) approach, take pictures before anyone knows it's happened and deal with the problems after the event. But this is the kind of crass behaviour that will almost inevitably get you into trouble and spread bad feeling in your wake.

Far better is to **ask people first**. Summoning the confidence and grace to ask to take people's portraits, and to accept refusal with equanimity, is at least half the affair. If they insist on posing, so be it. Try to come to terms with the reality of your position: you can't be a fly on the wall.

Be prepared to **pay** something or to send a print if your subjects have addresses. If you're motivated to take a lot of pictures of people, you should seriously consider lugging along an instant camera and as much film as you can muster, in order to offer a portrait on-the-spot – many people have never had a photo of themselves. A family you've stayed with is unlikely to refuse a photo session and may even ask for it. The same people might be furious if you jumped off the bus and immediately started taking photos, or worse, stayed on the bus and did it through the window.

Living and working in West Africa

Exceptions are noted in one or two places in the book, but in general there's no way you can work your way through West Africa. Direct, personal approach to the appropriate ministry might open some doors. But under-employment is a serious problem and work-permit regulations everywhere make your getting a wage nearly impossible without pulling strings. You usually sign a declaration that you won't seek work when you obtain the visa or fill in the arrival card.

Voluntary work is more likely. Bed and board in return for your help is sometimes available on development projects, in schools or through voluntary agencies, but such arrangements are entirely informal and word-of-mouth. Teachers and engineers have the best chances. Details of organizations to contact at home are given below. Note that you may need to involve yourself in fundraising activities in order to participate in some voluntary schemes.

As for furthering your education in West Africa, some universities which run courses in African studies offer **study-abroad progammes** to certain countries.

Useful contacts

UK and Ireland

AFS UK Ⓦ www.afsuk.org. Volunteer projects in a number of countries, including Ghana.
British Council ☎ 020/7930 8466. Produces a free leaflet which details study opportunities abroad. The Council's Central Management Direct Teaching (☎ 020/7389 4931) recruits TEFL teachers for posts worldwide (check Ⓦ www.britishcouncil.org/work/jobs.htm for a current list of vacancies), and its Central Bureau for International Education and Training (☎ 020/7389 4004) enables those who already work as educators to find out about teacher development programmes abroad. It also publishes a book, *Year Between*, aimed principally at gap-year students detailing volunteer programmes abroad.
Earthwatch Institute ☎ 01865/318 838, Ⓦ www.uk.earthwatch.org. Long-established international charity with environmental and archeological research projects worldwide (including Cameroon). Participation mainly as a paying volunteer (pricey) but fellowships for teachers and students available.

Field Studies Council Overseas ☎ 01743/852 150, Ⓦ www.fscoverseas.org.uk. Respected educational charity with over twenty years' experience of organizing specialized holidays with study tours visits worldwide. Runs short study tours in Ghana.
i to i International Projects ☎ 0870/333 2332, Ⓦ www.i-to-i.com. TEFL training provider operating voluntary teaching, conservation, business and medical schemes abroad. Contact Deirdre O'Sullivan. Countries covered include Ghana.
International House ☎ 020/7518 6999, Ⓦ www.ihlondon.com. Head office for reputable English-teaching organization which offers TEFL training leading to the award of a Certificate in English Language Teaching to Adults (CELTA), and recruits for teaching positions in Britain and abroad.
Raleigh International ☎ 020/7371 8585, Ⓦ www.raleigh.org.uk. This youth development charity organizes community and environmental work projects around the world. Ten 10-week expeditions are run every year, where project groups live in basic conditions in remote areas. Ghana is one of the countries included in the programme. If you're older than 25 and professionally qualified, you can join as volunteer staff overseeing the younger "Venturers".
VSO (Voluntary Service Overseas) ☎ 020/8780 7200, Ⓦ www.vso.org.uk. Highly respected charity that sends qualified professionals to spend two years or more working for local wages on projects beneficial to developing countries. Placements are available in The Gambia, Ghana, Nigeria and Cameroon. Teachers and health professionals are primarily in demand.

US and Canada

AFS Intercultural Programs ☎ 1-800/876-2377 or 212/299 9000, Ⓦ www.afs.org/usa; ☎ 1-800-361-7248, www.afscanada.org. Runs experiential programmes in many countries, including Ghana, aimed at fostering international understanding for teenagers and adults.

Association for International Practical Training ☎ 1-800/994-2443 or 410/997-2200, ⓦ www.aipt.org. Summer internships for students who have completed at least two years of college in science, agriculture, engineering or architecture; placements available in Ghana, Nigeria and Sierra Leone.

Council on International Educational Exchange (CIEE) ☎ 1-800/2COUNCIL, ⓦ www.ciee.org. They run summer, semester and academic-year programs in a number of countries worldwide, with West Africa figuring from time to time.

Earthwatch Institute ☎ 1-800/776-0188 or 978/461-0081, ⓦ www.earthwatch.org. International non-profit organization; volunteers work with research scientists each year on field research projects.

Experiment in International Living ☎ 1-800/345-2929 or 802/257-7751, ⓦ www.usexperiment.org. Summer programme for high-school students, including a five-week programme in Ghana.

Peace Corps ☎ 1-800/424-8580, ⓦ www.peacecorps.gov. Accepts applications from US citizens over the age of 18 for voluntary field work in some sixty areas of speciality. Postings are available in many developing countries, including most West African nations. Most commonly, they recruit people with a background in agriculture, education, engineering or health care, but volunteers with diverse experience in other fields also serve. The length of service is two years, following a three-month orientation.

School for International Training ☎ 1-800/336-1616, ⓦ www.sit.edu. Runs accredited college semesters abroad, comprising language and cultural studies, homestays and other academic work; programmes in Ghana and Mali.

Australia and New Zealand

Australian Volunteers International Melbourne ☎ 03/9279 1788, ⓦ www.ozvol.org.au. Postings for up to two years in developing countries.

Earthwatch Australia ☎ 03/9682 6828, ⓦ www.earthwatch.org/australia. International charity with research projects worldwide, on which volunteers work alongside scientists. At the time of writing their projects included two in Cameroon.

Travellers with disabilities

Although by no means easy, travelling around West Africa does not pose insurmountable problems for people with disabilities, and attitudes in the region to disabled people are generally good.

Government provision for disabled needs is almost completely absent, and facilities for wheelchair or frame users are non-existent (and wheelchairs virtually unknown) – though most hotels are single storey or have ground-floor rooms. Getting around in a wheelchair on half-paved or unpaved roads, or over soft sandy streets, is extremely hard work, while cabs are typically European or Japanese compacts. Intercity travel is even tougher, though in some countries the quality of long-distance buses can be well up to international standards. You'll at least have no problems recruiting local help and you can expect overwhelming consideration.

Visiting game parks and historical sites is problematic unless you have private transport. Historical and archeological sites are often barely maintained, or at least require some climbing of steps or hiking through a bit of bush. In the case of the parks, it's difficult not only to reach them, but to figure out how to get around them when you arrive. Guided tours in safari vehicles with good suspensions are rare: in Nigeria's Yankari Reserve, visitors are thrown in the back of a lorry with wooden benches for game-viewing.

Contacts for travellers with disabilities

UK and Ireland

Irish Wheelchair Association Blackheath Drive, Clontarf, Dublin 3 ☎01/818 6400, ⒻF01/833 3873, ⓌWwww.iwa.ie. Useful information provided about travelling abroad with a wheelchair.
Tripscope Alexandra House, Albany Rd, Brentford, Middlesex TW8 0NE ☎0845/7585 641, ⒻF020/8580 7021, Ⓦwww.justmobility.co.uk /tripscope. This registered charity provides a national telephone information service offering free advice on UK and international transport for those with a mobility problem.

US and Canada

Access-Able Ⓦwww.access-able.com. Online resource for travellers with disabilities.
Directions Unlimited 123 Green Lane, Bedford Hills, NY 10507 ☎1-800/533-5343 or 914/241-1700. Travel agency specializing in bookings for people with disabilities.
Mobility International USA 451 Broadway, Eugene, OR 97401 ☎541/343-1284, ⒻF343-6812, Ⓦwww.miusa.org. Information and referral services, access guides, tours and exchange programmes.

Annual membership $35 (includes quarterly newsletter).
Society for the Advancement of Travelers with Handicaps (SATH) 347 5th Ave, New York, NY 10016 ☎212/447-7284, Ⓦwww.sath.org. Non-profit educational organization that has actively represented travellers with disabilities since 1976.
Wheels Up! ☎1-888/389-4335, Ⓦwww .wheelsup.com. Provides discounted airfare, tour and cruise prices for disabled travellers; also publishes a free monthly newsletter and has a comprehensive website.

Australia and New Zealand

ACROD (Australian Council for Rehabilitation of the Disabled) PO Box 60, Curtin ACT 2605; Suite 103, 1st floor, 1–5 Commercial Rd, Kings Grove 2208; ☎02/6282 4333, TTY ☎6282 4333, ⒻF6281 3488, Ⓦwww.acrod.org.au. Provides lists of travel agencies and tour operators for people with disabilities.
Disabled Persons Assembly 4/173–175 Victoria St, Wellington, New Zealand ☎04/801 9100 (also TTY), ⒻF801 9565, Ⓦwww.dpa.org.nz. Resource centre with lists of travel agencies and tour operators for people with disabilities.

Sex and gender issues

Male egos in West Africa are softened by reserves of humour and women travel widely on their own or with each other, without the major problems sometimes experienced in parts of Asia and Latin America.

Much of what applies to women travellers in West Africa applies equally to men, though of course questions of personal safety and intimidation don't arise in the same way. It's common enough for women, and especially unmarried girls, to flirt with strangers. And many town bars and hotels are patronized by women who more or less make a living from **prostitution**. This is not the secretive and exploitative transaction of the West and pimps are generally unknown.

Unfortunately, **sexually transmitted diseases**, and the AIDS virus, are rife. Attitudes in West Africa have woken up to

this new reality, but you should be aware of the very real risks – and be prepared with condoms for the occasion – if you accept one of the many propositions you're likely to receive.

Women travellers

Travelling on your own or with another woman companion is by turns frustrating and rewarding. You'll usually be welcomed with generous hospitality, though occasionally you'll seem to get a run of harassment and hassles because of your gender. It's as well to know, if you're overlanding from Europe,

Sexual attitudes

Don't make any assumptions about puritanism on the basis of Islamic society in West Africa. It's the church which has successfully repressed sexuality. Otherwise, sexual attitudes are liberal (though you'll rarely see open displays of affection between men and women) and sex is openly discussed except in the presence of children. It's rarely the subject of personal hang-ups either, though sexual violence is surely as prevalent in families as it is anywhere. You'll be treated as a sexual person wherever you go. If you travel with a companion of the opposite sex, you'll find the relationship tends to insulate you – though not completely.

Gay life

Beyond the big cities, **homosexuality** is more or less invisible. People from a more traditional African background almost always deny it exists, find the notion laughable or childish, or describe it as a phase or a harmless peculiarity. As for the legality of gay sex, it's not *illegal* in Burkina Faso. Most countries, however, including all the Anglophone ex-colonies, inherited the laws of 1950s Europe and have hardly changed – though in practice prosecutions are almost unheard of. For gay male visitors, the only parts of the region you'll find like-minded company are the big capital cities and the resort areas. Gay women can't hope to find any hint of a lesbian community anywhere.

that the biggest difficulties will occur in North Africa – especially Morocco – and that Muslim regions south of the Sahara are altogether different.

On **public transport** a single woman traveller causes quite a stir and fellow passengers don't want to see you badly treated. They'll speak up on your behalf and get you a good seat or argue with the driver over your baggage payments. You can speak your mind, be open and direct, and nobody takes offence. Fellow male passengers always assume protective roles. This can be helpful but is sometimes annoyingly restrictive and occasionally leads to misunderstandings.

Women get offers of **accommodation** in people's homes more often than male travellers (and most of them without strings attached). And, if you're staying in less reputable hotels, there'll often be female company – employees, family, residents – to look after you.

Dress

The clothes you wear and the way you look and behave get noticed by everyone and they're more important if you don't appear to have a male escort. Your head and everything from waist to ankles are the sensitive zones, particularly in Islamic regions. Long, loose hair is seen as extraordinarily provocative, doubly so if blonde. Pay attention to these areas by keeping your hair fairly short or tied up (or by wearing a scarf) and wearing long skirts or, at a pinch, very baggy trousers.

In the heat it can be hard to be that disciplined, however, so if you have to wear shorts, try to make them long ones. If you find it's too hot to wear a bra, it's not going to interest anybody. Breasts aren't an important issue and topless bathing is tolerated by hotel pools and on tourist beaches. If you'll be travelling much on rough roads, however, you'll need a bra for support.

Dealing with propositions

Flirting is universal in West Africa and in order to avoid it you'd have to be perspicacious about where you go in towns. This is particularly true for white travellers; the fantasy inventory of black–white sexual relations tends to get played out whenever you find yourself in a bar, or on a dance floor. If a man asks you to "come and see where I live", he means you should come and see where he and you are going to sleep together. You'll have no shortage of offers. They're usually easy to turn down if you refuse as frankly as you're asked. Unwanted physical advances are rare. But it always helps to avoid offence and preserve a friendship if you make your intentions (or lack of them) clear from the outset. If you're not with a man, a fictitious husband in the background, much as you might prefer to avoid the ploy, is always useful – though it may well be met with such responses as "Tell your husband you have to go outside for some air."

If you're in a certain mood, all this can be fun. There's no reason you can't spend an evening dancing and talking and still go back to your bed alone and unharassed.

Meeting other women

It's often very difficult getting to know women in West Africa. Most contact is mediated, at least initially, through their male relatives, with whom you'll take on the role of honorary man, at least in the way you're

The status of West African women

Despite widespread paper commitments to women's rights, West Africa remains a powerfully male-dominated part of the world. Women do the large proportion of productive labour and most subsistence agriculture is in their hands, though this varies among different ethnic groups. **Matrilineal cultures**, which once held sway over large parts of the region, are on the decline, under joint assault by paternalistic Islam and Christianity. Matrilineal inheritance doesn't, in any case, necessarily imply *matriarchal* social structures but simply inheritance by a man from his mother's brother rather than his own father.

Women have the explicit support of government ministries (for what it's worth) in very few countries; in others there's often a non-governmental women's organization working to improve the lot of mothers, agricultural labourers and crafts workers. **Women's groups** flourish in some countries, occasionally under the aegis of a government ministry – though in several they've hardly taken off. Where they exist, they're concerned more with improvement of incomes, education, health and nutrition than with social or political emancipation. Professional market women usually run their own informal unions in the cities.

Current major women's **issues** in West Africa are primarily concerned with rights over women's bodies – contraception, abortion and the practices of genital mutilation. Few West African countries have successful **family planning** programmes; men are unwilling to cooperate by using condoms and women are pushed out-of-date pills at market stalls. **Abortion** is virtually a taboo subject in some parts, though abortions by traditional methods (and less traditional backstreet operations) are believed to be widely performed. Few governments permit abortion on demand.

Genital mutilation – known, in a classic bit of male "anthropologese" as "female circumcision" – is widespread and occurs to some degree in every mainland West African country. It's traditionally carried out by female practitioners on the occasion of a girl's initiation into womanhood. Today, although on the decline, it's also performed under anaesthetic in hospital and often at an early age. It varies from clitoridectomy to excision of the inner labia to excision of most of the outer labia as well (a major operation known as infibulation which, in West Africa, is nearly confined to Mali).

All these issues are complex. Both contraception and abortion (especially as encouraged by Rich World development agencies) are topics which can incense women as well as men, so be wary of crashing into conversation. In the case of genital mutilation, women campaigning to eradicate the practices have met resistance from traditionalist women. And mutilations can't be analysed just in terms of male sexual demands (a tighter vagina, loss of sexual response and consequent presumed fidelity). Unfortunately, it's an issue that many governments would prefer not to address.

Some advice for women travellers

- Carry pictures of your family to demonstrate your unavailablity.
- Beware of big men in small towns. Don't accept an invitation to the disco from the local commandant unless you're on very firm ground.
- Never meet someone as arranged if you're uncomfortable about it.
- Always lock your door at night.
- Take a supply of condoms. Don't tell yourself it will never happen. Be prepared, because he will never have any.
- And three useful French phrases for persistent clingers: *J'en ai marre de toi* (I've just about had enough of you), *Laisse-moi tranquille!* (Leave me alone!) or, in a crisis, *Va te faire foutre!* (Go and fuck yourself!).

treated socially. In the small towns and villages women are usually less educated than men and rarely speak English or French. They don't hang out in bars and restaurants either and are much more often to be found in their compounds working hard. Their fortitude as housewives is something to behold – always in total control of the family's food and comfort, from chopping wood to selling home-made produce in order to make ends meet. Even school-educated professional women dominate their household affairs and make sure everything runs smoothly. The extended family and the use of the younger girls as helpers is a major contribution. Men are away a great deal of the time.

For their part, West African women will try to picture themselves in your position, travelling around *your* homeland – a scenario that most find hard to imagine. Family obligations are everything. Conveying the fact that you, too, have a family and a home is a good way of reducing the barriers of incomprehension but, assuming you're over 15, explaining the absence of husband and children is normally impossible. You can either invent some or expect sympathy instead – and perhaps the offer of fertility medicine.

Wildlife and national parks

West Africa doesn't have the game reserves and wildlife concentrations of East or southern Africa, though it does offer a number of major national parks that are worth taking in if you're an enthusiastic naturalist. Outside these, too, it's possible to see a good variety of Africa's birds and mammals in habitats ranging from desert to swamp and floodland, savanna, dry woodland and dense, moist forest – both lowland and mountain.

Travelling by public transport, it always pays to spend a little more on a seat in the front. That way you can reckon on seeing a lot more creatures, mostly crossing or flying over the road.

Wildlife

The large animals you'll see most often out on the road, or in the bush, are **monkeys** and **baboons**. **Gazelles** and other small antelope are also quite common, especially in the Sahel. Larger grazing animals are localized and unusual sights. Along the Niger north of Niamey there are **giraffes**, and **buffalo** inhabit pockets of forest and bush thicket in various parts.

Elephants survive in dwindling numbers in a surprising number of countries – most in fact – but are in such a dire predicament that little international effort is being made to save those isolated pockets still hanging on in remote bush against the poachers. Park boundaries aren't always much of a safeguard. The **black rhino** has never inhabited more than the far east of the region: you can still see a few of them in Cameroonian parks.

None of these animals, even outside the confines of the parks, poses any threat to you as a traveller, even if you choose to camp out and hike or cycle. More threatening wildlife – the big cats, crocodiles, hippos – are very localized. You're extremely unlikely to see any large predators outside the parks. And even in a national park, seeing a **lion**, **cheetah** or **leopard** in West Africa is cause for some celebration. **Crocodiles** are hard to spot and are mercilessly hunted where they live (except in controlled village pools where they are the object of veneration in some countries) because they do occasionally

grab people at the water's edge. Be somewhat cautious by rivers and lakes. **Hippos**, too, deservedly have a dangerous reputation, especially when accidentally trapped on dry land or panicked in the water while dozing. You're quite likely to see them from a boat on the Niger in Mali, along the upper Gambia, or in Cameroon.

Another supposedly dangerous animal – the **gorilla** – is really very timid. It lives in the remote, southern forests of Cameroon and across the border in Nigeria in the Cross River National Park. **Chimpanzees** also survive here, as well as much further to the west, in patches of remote forest from Senegal to Côte d'Ivoire, but their existence is threatened by deforestation and the pet and laboratory trades.

Spiders, **scorpions** and various other multilegged invertebrates are less often encountered than you might expect, or fear. **Butterflies** – as many as a thousand different species in some districts – are extensive and colourful, especially in the lowland forests.

Lizards are common everywhere. You'll soon become familiar with the vigorous push-ups of the red-headed male **rock agama**. Some towns seem to be positively swarming with them, no doubt in proportion to the insect supply. Large lizards (all species are quite harmless) include the **monitors**, of which the grey and yellow Nile monitor grows to an impressive 2m. They live near water, but you can often see them dashing across the road. **Chameleons** too are often seen making painfully slow progress across the road – or wafer-thin, squashed on the tarmac. In some areas, at night, little house **geckos** come out like translucent aliens to scuttle usefully across the ceiling and walls in pursuit of moths and mosquitoes.

West Africa's **birdlife** is astonishingly diverse – nearly eleven hundred species ranging from the ostrich to the diminutive pygmy woodpecker. Characteristic sights are the urbanite pied crows of the Sahel and savanna; electric blue Abyssinian rollers, perched on telephone wires in the grasslands; the marvellous, lurching flight of hornbills swooping across the road in forest areas; and quite unmistakeable flocks of grey parrots in dense bush along the coast.

National parks

Most countries have some sort of national park network, though in several it consists of just the one park. The most important in the west are Mauritania's **Banc d'Arguin** (for sea and migratory birds) and Senegal's **Niokolo-Koba** (large savanna and forest mammals).

In central West Africa there's Ghana's surprisingly good **Mole Game Reserve**, Benin's **Pendjari** (excellent game-viewing), and the **Parc National du "W" du Niger**, which extends across the borders of Benin, Burkina Faso and Niger on a bend of the Niger River.

Nigeria and Cameroon have probably the best parks in West Africa. Nigeria's prime savanna reserve, **Yankari National Park**, has well-organized game-viewing and quantities of animals, while the new **Cross River National Park** is a remote rainforest gorilla refuge. Across the border in Cameroon are **Takamanda Forest Reserve** and **Korup National Park**. Cameroon's other parks include **Waza National Park** in the floodlands near Lake Chad, which for faunal diversity and herds of elephant is the best in West Africa.

Entrance fees, seasonality (many parks are closed during the rains) and **facilities** vary considerably. Of those included above, only Mole and Yankari are really accessible on a budget. Some of the smaller parks and reserves, however – in The Gambia and southern Senegal for example – are low-key enough to permit entrance on foot. Vital, if you're visiting parks, is a pair of good, light **binoculars**.

People and languages

Whether called peoples, ethnic groups, nations or tribes, West Africans have a multiplicity of racial and cultural origins. Distinctions would be simple if similarities in physical appearance were recognizable in those who speak the same language and share a common culture: the term "tribe" tends to imply this kind of stereotype. But tribes are rarely closed units: appearance, language and culture nearly always overlap and, even in the past, families often contained members of different language groups. Over the last fifty years or so, tribal identities have broken down still further, partly replaced by broader class, political and national ones.

The most enduring and meaningful social marker is, in fact, **language**. A person's "mother tongue" is still important as an index of social identity and a tribe is best defined as a group of people sharing a common first language. Many people speak two or three languages (their own plus French or English and sometimes a third or fourth regional lingua franca like Hausa, Bamana or Krio). And for a few, the old metropolitan languages – French, English or Portuguese – have become their first language. It's worth knowing something of the linguistic connections and differences

– apart from being fascinating in itself – if you want to get to grips with what can otherwise seem an unfathomable cultural region.

Language groups and names

West Africa is the most linguistically complex region in the world. There are dozens of **major languages** and literally hundreds of less important languages and distinct dialects. Some four hundred of these are spoken in Nigeria alone. Most of West Africa's languages are viable and thriving and very few are in any danger of extinction.

Most West Africans speak languages of one of three great groups – **"Niger-Congo"** (now renamed the Southern area of wider affinity – **Sawa**), **"Afro-Asiatic"** (the Northern area of wider affinity – **Nawa**) and **Mande**. African language classification (the attempt to assess the way the languages are presumed to have evolved from common ancestral languages) is immensely complicated and linguists have recently tried to get away from the notion of "families" of languages, as it may transpire they have elements in common through long association rather than shared ancestry.

For an outsider, the confusion is exacerbated by the fact that, until European colonization, almost none of these languages was written (today, many are written, the vast majority of them in the Roman alphabet, albeit sometimes with additional phonetic symbols). In the early days, even the language and ethnic **names** first recorded varied according to the nationality and ear of the researchers and the identity of the person asked. Often enough in West Africa, the name of the language and of the people who speak it are genuinely distinct. Often, too, the name in common usage in English and French may be different (for example Tukulor and Toucouleur) and the name by which a language group is known may depend on the linguistic context – analogous to *German*, *Deutsch* and *Allemand*.

We have tried to be as consistent and simple as possible in this book, without sweeping distinctions away. Generally,

we've used the **names** used locally (for example Malinké in Guinea, Mandinka in The Gambia). On the other hand, the variety of names for the widespread people and language often called **Fulani** is so diverse – Peul, Peulh, Fulfulde, Fulbe, Foulah, Pulaar, Fula and many more – that we've gone for simple **Fula** throughout the book except in Nigeria, where "Fulani" is in common usage.

Later in this section, we've given a broad and highly selective breakdown of West Africa's people and language groups into separate ethno-linguistic identities. These lists are intended to provide anchorages for the different names you're likely to encounter (and include every language or ethnic group mentioned in the book); the intention is to assist in working out who relates to whom, rather than to provide a scientific classification. Names in brackets are either alternative names for the same group or alternative spellings or pronunciations; additional names separated by commas are very closely related, distinguishable dialects. Names in inverted commas are major languages with closely related subgroups.

In trying to work out where everyone fits in, it helps to keep a flexible attitude to **spellings** (try pronouncing the word in as many ways as possible). Two sets of much interchanged sounds are the **p**, **b**, **v**, **f**, **w** set and the **d**, **gh**, **r**, **l** set. Anything spelled "qu" might just as well be spelt "kw" or, for that matter, "cou" or "kou". Likewise, "j" is commonly spelt "dy" or "di" in French transcription. The French were keen on apostrophes everywhere, too – see the singer Youssou N'Dour's name, for example. They don't usually mean any more than that someone found the word hard to pronounce. Finally, look out for prefixes or suffixes that may mean "people" ("Ba-" in the Bantu languages for example, or "-nke" in the Mande languages).

The southern area of wider affinity – Sawa

The **Sawa group** includes the four hundred **Bantu** languages that are spoken all over Central and southern Africa and in parts of

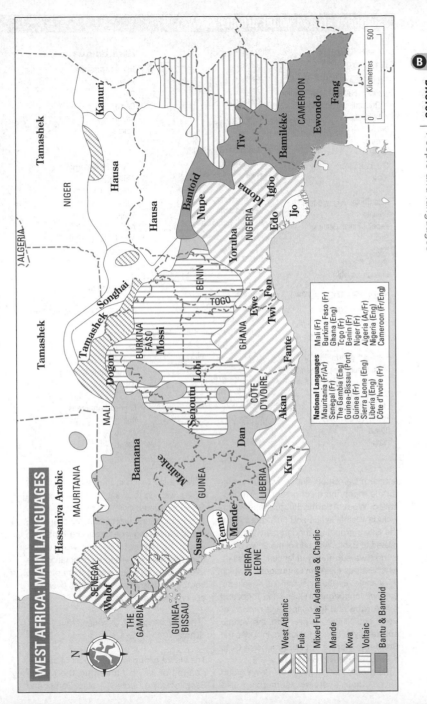

WEST AFRICA: MAIN LANGUAGES

National Languages
Mauritania (Fr/Ar)
Senegal (Fr)
The Gambia (Eng)
Guinea-Bissau (Port)
Guinea (Fr)
Sierra Leone (Eng)
Liberia (Eng)
Côte d'Ivoire (Fr)
Mali (Fr)
Burkina Faso (Fr)
Ghana (Eng)
Togo (Fr)
Benin (Fr)
Niger (Fr)
Algeria (Ar/Fr)
Nigeria (Eng)
Cameroon (Fr/Eng)

West Atlantic
Fula
Mixed Fula, Adamawa & Chadic
Mande
Kwa
Voltaic
Bantu & Bantoid

Southern area of wider affinity (SAWA)

West Atlantic languages

Fula (Fulfulde, Fulani, Peul, Peulh, Fulbe, Pulaar), Tukulor (Toucouleur), Bororo, Wodaabe
Wolof
Temne
Serer
Sherbro, Bulom
Kissi
Limba
Jola (Diola), Fogny, Banjal
Balante
Pepel, Manjak (Manjago)
Gola
Baga
Tenda, Basari
Bijago (Bidyago)

Voltaic languages

"Senoufo" group
Senoufo, Djimini, Karaboro
Minianka

"Grusi" group
Grusi (Gourounsi), Kassena (Kasem), Sissala
Dagara (Dagarti)
Lilse, Fulse (Kurumba)
Frafra (Fare-fare)
Builsa
Wagala

"Lobi" group
Loron
Nabe
Gan
Koulango

More (Mole)
Mossi
Dagomba (Dagbani)
Mamprusi
Wala

Gurma
Gourmantché
Bassari, Tchamba
Moba

Habe
Bobo, Bwaba, Kos, Siby

Dogon

"Tem" group
Tem (Kotokoli, Cotocoli)
Kabré (Kabyé), Logba, Tamberma, Lamba

"Bargu" group
Bargu (Bariba)
Somba (Betammaribe)
Yowa

Kwa languages

Kru languages
Bete
Dida
Grebo
Krahn
Bakwe
Bassa

"Twi" languages
Akan group
Twi (Asante)
Fante
Baulé
Agni
Abron
Akwapim
Guang

"Ewe" group
Ewe, Ang-lo
Fon, Adja, Xwala, Xuéda, Maxi
Ga-Adangme
Mina, Popo
Gun, Tofinu

Central Togo languages
Akposso

Lagoon languages
Abé
Ajukru
Abidji

southern Cameroon. Further west, the picture is much more complicated. The so-called **West Atlantic** languages, which include Wolof, Temne and Fula, are part of the Sawa grouping, though fairly distantly related to Bantu. Also part of the Sawa group is the **Kwa sub-family** of language clusters, which include the **Akan languages** (of which the Asante are the most famous speakers), the **Ewe languages** of Ghana and Togo, and the **Yoruba** and **Igbo** language groups of Benin and Nigeria. To the north, the **Voltaic sub-family** of language clusters includes the **Senoufo**, **More** and **Lobi** groups of Côte d'Ivoire, Ghana and Burkina.

Many of the languages in the Sawa group have **class systems** (something like

genders in French in that everything must agree) with up to twenty or more classes – Bantu languages, with their elegantly structured grammars, are the classic examples. Many Sawa languages, too, are **tonal** – in which the pitch of a spoken word determines its meaning – and extra notations are often necessary when writing them properly. Yoruba, with its mass of diacritics over vowels, is a good example.

The northern area of wider affinity – Nawa

The **Nawa group** includes most of the languages of North Africa and the Middle East, including Hebrew, Arabic, Berber and

Alladian
Assini, Nzima
Ebrie

"Edo" group
Edo
Bini (Benin)
Isoko, Urhobo (Sobo)
Kukuruku

"Igbo" group
Igbo (Ibo), Onitsha

"Yoruba" group
Yoruba, Oyo
Egba
Ijebu
Ekiti
Ife
Bunu
Itsekiri
Ana

"Nupe" group
Nupe
Igbira
Gwari, Koro

"Idoma" group
Idoma
Igala
Egede
Iyala

Eastern Nigritic languages

Adamawa
Fali
Massa
Mbum
Mundang
Namshi
Chamba
Longuda
Mumuye
Vere
Yungur

"Ijo" languages
Ijo (Ijaw)
Brass
Kalabari

Bantoid languages
Ibibio, Efik, Anang
Mada
Katab
Boki
Kamberi
Birom
Ekoi, Oban
Orri, Ukelle
Korup
Dukakari
Jerawa
Anyang
Basa-Kaduna

Yergum
Jukun
Ogoni

Macro-Bantu languages
Tiv
Jarawa
Mambila

Cameroon Highlands Bantu ("Semi-Bantu")
Bamiléké, Badjou, Bafang,
Bafoussam, Bamendjou,
Bangangté
Bamoun (Bamoum, Bamum)
Bafia
Banso (Bansaw)
Bali
Bafut
Bawidekum
Bafungom
Bandop
Tikar

North-Western Bantu
Bulu, Ewondo (Yaoundé)
Beti, Fang, Eton
Gbaya
Sango-Ngbandi
Bakundu
Duala (Douala)
Bassa, Bakoko
Batanga
Bakweri, Bimbia

Tamashek (the language of the Tuareg). The most important languages in the area as far as West Africa is concerned are known as "Chadic", the biggest of which is **Hausa**, spoken by some twenty million people as a first language. Nawa languages are mostly non-tonal and classless, though many have masculine and feminine genders.

Arabic dialects – Hassaniya cluster

Berabish, Imragen, Kunta (Kounta), Regeibat, Rehian, Tajakant, Arosien, Trarza, Zenaga, Chorfa, Tichit, Choa (Shoa)

Chadic languages

Hausa, Adrawa, Tazarawa

Angas
Bura
Kotoko (Longone)
Tangale
Mandara (Wandala)
Kapsiki (Margi)
Matakam (Mafa)
Mauri
Wakura
Toupouri (Tuburi)
Wajawa
Gude
Gerawa
Guizica, Mofou
Podoko
Bata
Mousgoum (Musgu)

Berber languages

Tamashek (Tuareg, Touareg)

Saharan languages

Kanouri (Kanuri, Beriberi)

Mande

The **Mande cluster of languages** doesn't belong to either area of wider affinity and, linguistically, it's on a classification level with both of them. The languages in this group are closely related and very old. Geographically, they're quite compact and appear to be centred in the Mali–Guinea border region – which, historically, was the heartland of the old Mande/Manding/Mali empire. From the linguistic point of view, the "nuclear Mande" family includes **Bamana**, **Malinké** (Mandinka), **Susu** and **Dyula**. This group is also known as "Mande-Tan" (after their word for "ten"). The languages of "Peripheral Mande" (or "Mande-Fu"), which deviate much more from the heartland languages, and from each other, include languages of Guinea, Sierra Leone and Liberia, such as **Mende**, **Dan-Gio** and **Vai**. Tones are important in this southern section, less so in the more mainstream Mande languages.

Nuclear Mande languages

Malinké (Mandinka, Mandingo)
Bambara (Bamana)
Soninke (Sarakolé)
Susu (Sousou)
Dyula (Dioula)
Kuranko
Diallonke (Yalunka)
Kasonke
Konyanke
Bozo
Kagoro

Peripheral Mande languages

Mende
Kpelle (Gerse)
Vai (Gallinas)
Dan, Gio (Dan-Gio), Mano, Guro
Loma (Toma), Buzi
Samo
Bussa (Busa)
Ngere (Guerze)
Kono
Sia
Loko
Gbande

Songhai

The **Songhai** of the middle Niger River are another old imperial people: their languages – Songhai (Sonray), Dendi and Djerma (Zerma) are quite distinct from any other in Africa.

Courses and other reading

There is little available on West African – or even African – languages in the sense of general background, but you will find various phrasebooks and some language-learning material.

Pierre Alexandre *Languages and Language in Africa* (o/p). Surprisingly entertaining tour of the arcane world of African linguistics, led by a magnificently enthusiastic French professor.

E.C. Rowlands *Teach Yourself Yoruba* and Charles H. Kraft and H.M. Kirk-Greene *Teach Yourself Hausa*.

US State Department Foreign Service Institute *Audio-Forum Basic Courses*. A number of self-instructional language courses available from ⓦ www.audioforum.com. Priced at $220–300, each one comes with a textbook and cassettes. Languages available include the Senegambian dialect of Fula, Hausa, Igbo, More, Twi and Yoruba.

Travellers' French

BASICS | Travellers' French

Apart from some specialized vocabulary, there's little that non-fluent speakers will find characteristic about West African French beyond the accent. As with English spoken as a second language, West African French has the rhythmic and tonal colouring of the speaker's mother tongue. It's generally a lot easier to understand than French as spoken in France, because it's more vigorously pronounced. And the French colonists encouraged the use of French far more than the British, so that, assuming you have at least some French, there are fewer language problems in the pays francophones.

Useful vocabulary

In the glossary at the end of this section, we've put together a mix of pertinent words and expressions, together with some French and West African street slang and a few historical terms, that have found their way into West African French.

Basic terms and phrases

today	aujourd'hui
yesterday	hier
tomorrow	demain
in the morning	le matin
in the afternoon	l'après-midi
in the evening	le soir
now	maintenant
later	plus tard
at one o'clock	à une heure
at three o'clock	à trois heures
at ten-thirty	à dix heures et demie
at midday	à midi
man	un homme
woman	une femme
here	ici
there	là
this one	ceci
that one	celà
open	ouvert
closed	fermé
big	grand
small	petit
more	plus
less	moins
a little	un peu
a lot	beaucoup
cheap	bon marché

expensive	cher
good	bon
bad	mauvais
hot	chaud
cold	froid

Talking to people

Excuse me	Pardon
Do you speak English ?	Vous parlez anglais?
How do you say it in French ?	Comment ça se dit en Français?
What's your name ?	Comment vous appelez-vous?
My name is . . .	Je m'appelle ...
I'm English/ Irish/ Scottish/ Welsh/ American/ Australian/ Canadian/ a New Zealander	Je suis anglais[e] irlandais[e] écossais[e] gallois[e] américain[e] australien[ne] canadien[ne] néo-zélandais[e]
yes	oui
no	non
I understand	Je comprends
I don't understand	Je ne comprends pas
Can you speak slower ?	s'il vous plaît, parlez moins vite?
OK/agreed	d'accord
please	s'il vous plaît
thank you	merci
hello	bonjour
goodbye	au revoir

good morning /afternoon	bonjour
good evening	bonsoir
good night	bonne nuit
How are you ?	Comment allez-vous?/ Ça va?
Fine, thanks	Très bien, merci
I don't know	Je ne sais pas
Let's go	Allons-y
See you tomorrow	à demain
See you soon	à bientôt
Sorry	Pardon, Madame/ je m'excuse
Leave me alone (aggressive)	Fichez-moi la paix!
Please help me	Aidez-moi, s'il vous plaît

Finding the way

bus	autobus, bus, car
car	voiture
boat	bâteau
launch/motorboat	chaloupe
plane	avion
What time does it leave ?	Il part à quelle heure?
What time does it arrive ?	Il arrive à quelle heure?
a ticket to . . .	un billet pour . . .
ticket office	vente de billets
how many kilometres ?	combien de kilomètres?
how many hours ?	combien d'heures?
on foot	à pied
Where are you going ?	Vous allez où?
I'm going to . . .	Je vais à . . .
I want to get off at . . .	Je voudrais descendre à . . .
the road to . . .	la route pour . . .
near	près/pas loin
far	loin
left	à gauche
right	à droite
straight on	tout droit
on the other side of	l'autre côté de
on the corner of	à l'angle de
next to	à côté de
behind	derrière
in front of	devant
before	avant

after	après
under	sous
to cross	traverser
bridge	pont

Other needs

doctor	médecin
I don't feel well	Je ne me sens pas bien
medicines	médicaments
prescription	ordonnance
I feel sick	Je suis malade
headache	J'ai mal à la tête
stomach ache	mal à l'estomac
period	règles
pain	douleur
it hurts	ça fait mal
chemist	pharmacie
bakery	boulangerie
food shop	alimentation
supermarket	supermarché
to eat	manger
to drink	boire
bank	banque
money	argent
with	avec
without	sans

Questions and requests

The simplest way of asking a question is to start with *s'il vous plaît* (please), then name the thing you want in an interrogative tone of voice. For example:

Where is there a bakery ?	S'il vous plaît, la boulangerie ?
Which way is it to Bobo ?	S'il vous plaît, la route pour Bobo ?

Similarly with requests:

We'd like a room for two	S'il vous plaît, une chambre pour deux
Can I have a kilo of oranges?	S'il vous plaît, un kilo d'oranges?
Where ?	où ?
How ?	comment ?
How many/ how much ?	combien ?
When ?	quand ?
Why ?	pourquoi ?
At what time ?	à quelle heure ?
What is/which is ?	quel est ?

Accommodation

a room for one/ two people	une chambre pour une/deux personnes
a double bed	un lit double
a room with a shower	une chambre avec douche
Can I see it ?	Je peux la voir ?
a room on the courtyard	une chambre sur la cour
a room over the street	une chambre sur la rue
first floor	premier étage
second floor	deuxième étage
with a view	avec vue
key	clef
to iron	repasser
do laundry	faire la lessive
sheets	draps
quiet	calme
noisy	bruyant
hot water	eau chaude
cold water	eau froide
breakfast	le petit déjeuner

Days and dates

January	janvier
February	février
March	mars
April	avril
May	mai
June	juin
July	juillet
August	août
September	septembre
October	octobre
November	novembre
December	décembre
Sunday	dimanche
Monday	lundi
Tuesday	mardi
Wednesday	mercredi
Thursday	jeudi
Friday	vendredi
Saturday	samedi
August 1	le premier août
March 2	le deux mars
July 14	le quatorze juillet
November 23	le vingt-trois novembre

Numbers

1	un
2	deux
3	trois
4	quatre
5	cinq
6	six
7	sept
8	huit
9	neuf
10	dix
11	onze
12	douze
13	treize
14	quatorze
15	quinze
16	seize
17	dix-sept
18	dix-huit
19	dix-neuf
20	vingt
21	vingt-et-un
22	vingt-deux
30	trente
40	quarante
50	cinquante
60	soixante
70	soixante-dix
75	soixante-quinze
80	quatre-vingts
90	quatre-vingt-dix
95	quatre-vingt-quinze
100	cent
101	cent-et-un
200	deux cents
300	trois cents
500	cinq cents
1000	mille
2000	deux milles
5000	cinq milles
1,000,000	un million

A traveller's glossary

amende	fine, penalty
atelier	workshop, studio
bâché	pick-up van, (lit. "tarpaulined")
balise	beacon or cairn, usually in the desert
banco	mud and straw mixture for building
barrage	road block, barrier

83

barraquer	to stop, rest awhile, camp
berline	saloon car
bic	disposable pen
biche	doe, gazelle, pet
bidonville	slum, shantytown
bonne arrivée	favoured greeting in Francophone Africa
bord	fortress (Arabic)
bordelle	prostitute, pick-up
borne	kilometre marker, "kilometre"
bouffer	to eat
break	estate car, station wagon
bricolage	the art of preserving equipment or making something out of nothing
brousse	countryside, the bush
buvette	outside bar, refreshments stall
cadeauter	to give a present; children may tell you, "*il faut me cadeauter*"
caféman	coffee, bread and omelette man
campement	budget motel or country guesthouse
canari	clay pot for storing cool water
carte d'identité	identity card
carte routière	road map
case	hut, small house
chef	boss, chief
chômer	to be unemployed
cinq cent quatre	Peugeot 504
climatisée	air-conditioned (room)
colon	a colonial
commander	ask someone to do something
contrôle	checkpoint
coupe-coupe	machete
coupers de route	roadside bandits
dancing	dance floor, disco
dépannage	breakdown service
depuis	a long time
devises	money or (hard) currency
discuter	to discuss, negotiate
doux	good (even a hot pepper soup, far from mild, can be *doux*)

eau potable	drinking water
en panne	out of order, broken down
escalier	washboard road surface
escroc	swindler, conman
exigé	required, demanded
faisable	feasible, doable
féticheur	religious man with a knowledge of the ways of the spirits
fiche	form, document to fill in
flic	cop, policeman
fréquenter	to go to school
fric	cash, dosh
fromager	silk-cotton (kapok) tree
garé	parked, not in use
gare routière	motor transport station
gare ferroviaire	railway station
gargote	cheap restaurant or chophouse
gaté	spoiled, broken, needing repair
gênant	bothersome, a hassle
gîte (d'étape)	boarding house, inn (staging post)
goudron	tar, tarmac
gri-gri	charm, amulet, juju
griot	traditional musician, storyteller, court minstrel
hivernage	rainy season
HLM	"low rent housing" (council flats)
Immeuble (Imm.)	Building
insh'allah	if Allah wills it (hopefully)
intéressant	good, enjoyable; eg a film or the food you're eating
lampe tempête	hurricane lamp, kerosene lamp
livres sterling	pounds sterling
machin	thingamajig, whatsitsname
mairie	town hall, city hall
maison de passage	boarding house used as a brothel
marigot	creek

marque	make or brand (eg vehicle or spare part)	sapeur	one who is well dressed-up, usually for discos and hanging out; from Sape, the fictitious Société des ambianceurs et per sons élégants
mec	guy, fellow		
moustiquaire	mosquito net/ mosquito screen		
occasion	a seat or place in a bush taxi		
ornières	wheel ruts		
paillote	straw hut, sun shade, thatched awning	sofa	Nineteenth-century Muslim cavalry
		source (d'eau)	spring, water source
palétuviers	mangroves	sous	money
palu/paludisme	malaria	sucrerie	mineral or soft drink
patron	boss, chief, mister	sympa/sympathique	nice, friendly
phacochère	warthog	tampon	rubber stamp
pièces	identity papers	tata	fortress (Mande)
pirogue	dugout canoe	tôle ondulée	corrugated iron, washboard
piste	track, trail		
préfet/sous-préfet	administrative prefect/assistant prefect (equivalent of District Commissioner and assistant)	tourner	to go out, go dancing, hang out
		triptyque	triptych; a document in three folds
quatre-quatre	four-wheel-drive	trop	more often means "very" than "too much"
récolte	harvest		
régler	to sort out, settle up, pay up	truc	thing, whatsit
		ventilée	"ventilated" – a room with a fan
renseignements	information, details		
route bitumée	surfaced road		

Directory

Addresses The postman never comes in West Africa. Mail is sorted into PO Boxes (BP in French, CP in Portuguese) or sometimes into Private Mail Bags (PMB). The lower the number, usually, the older the address – sometimes a useful indication of credentials when making bookings or enquiries. Street addresses are often buildings, or blocks – *Immeuble* in French, often abbreviated to *Imm*. Your address is likely to be much in demand – a stack of small address labels is very useful.

Beggars Beggars are part of town life, though not as much as you might realistically expect. Most are visibly destitute and many are blind, or victims of polio or accidents, or lepers, or homeless mothers and children. Some have established pitches, others keep on the move. They are harassed by the police and often rounded up. Many

What to take

- A **pocket dictionary** or phrasebook is extremely useful; Rough Guides publishes French and Portuguese dictionary phrasebooks.
- **Binoculars** (the small, fold-up ones) are invaluable for game- and bird-watching.
- A multipurpose **penknife** (remember to put it in your hold luggage when flying) is essential, but avoid ones with blades longer than a palm-width, which are sometimes confiscated.
- A **torch** (flashlight).
- A **padlock** – vital in cheap hotels where doors don't lock properly.
- **Plastic bags** are invaluable – bin liners to keep dust off clothes, small sealable ones to protect cameras and film.
- If driving or hiking in remote areas, take a **compass**.
- **Camping gas stoves** are light and useful even if you're not camping. The cylinders are sold somewhere in every West African capital city.
- A **sheet sleeping bag** (sew up a sheet) is essential for budget travel. A proper **sleeping bag** isn't much use since you'll sleep on top of it nine times out of ten anyway. If you do take one, get the best, most compressible bag you can afford – very useful for keeping film cool.
- If you shave, bring **disposable razors** (in West Africa they're available only at import supermarkets) or preferably an old-fashioned razor blade holder.
- **Tampons** are expensive and only available in big cities. Bring as many as you can be bothered with.
- Take the lightest, toughest, airiest **footwear** you can afford.

people give to the same beggar on a regular basis and, of course, alms-giving is a requirement of Islam, supposed to benefit the donor. Keep small change handy all the time for this purpose – it will hardly dent your expenses. There's no question of confusing real beggars with the incessant demands – in the more touristy parts of several of the Francophone countries – for "*cadeaux*", usually from children. These you simply have to devise strategies to deal with. Like heat and mosquitoes, they seem to trouble new arrivals most.

Clothes People in West Africa are generally very clothes-conscious. Ragged clothes and long hair on men don't go down well. Avoid absolutely any military-style, or army surplus, gear; camouflage prints are out. Cotton is obviously the best material to wear from a practical point of view. Dirty-looking colours are best and clothes should be tough enough to stand repeated hand washing. Mostly you'll want to wear the minimum, but pack at least one warm jacket or fleece. Though you can buy clothes as you go, they'll rarely be less expensive than at home.

Even "junk clothes" – "deadmen's clothes" shipped in bulk from Europe and the US – which you'll find in every town, may be less pricey bought nearer to source. If you fancy kitting yourself up in local style, both cloth and tailoring are inexpensive. However you dress, pack a set of "smart" clothes for difficult embassies and other important occasions. Forget about waterproofs: all that plastic and nylon is too hot. You won't go out in the rain, and if you do, you'll get wet anyway.

Electricity The mains supply is usually 220V AC 50Hz. Only top hotels have shaver points or outlets in the rooms. Note that it's common for electricity supplies to be restricted in West Africa, especially where hydro-electric power stations are responsible for providing power. The Akosombo Dam in Ghana, for example, supplies power across a wide region, but recent years of drought have reduced its generating capacity and power cuts are the order of the day, especially at the end of the dry season – the very time when air conditioning and cold drinks are most welcome.

Gifts It's very useful to have some tokens to give to people. Postcards of sights from home are appreciated by people who have little or no chance of possessing colour pictures. Pictures of you and your family are of tremendous value, too, while school kids are also delighted with ballpoint pens. However, you might consider visiting a school more formally, rather than just handing them out. Kola nuts (see p.67) are appreciated as gifts, especially by village elders.

Ivory Ivory is for sale in many West African cities, much of it carved in Hong Kong, and bracelets and bangles are widely touted. It seems it's still a viable way to earn a living and will likely remain so as long as ivory itself remains unstigmatized.

Laundry Washing is always done by hand, in a stream with flat rocks by preference. You won't find self-service laundries, but there are plenty of people willing to do the job. Even the smallest hotel can arrange it. If you have any choice, dry your clothes indoors. Avoid spreading them on the ground if you can – they may be infested by the tumbu fly which lays its eggs on wet clothes. Ironing kills the eggs.

Photography If you take a camera, make sure you've a dust-proof bag to keep it in, and take spare batteries, too. Film tends to be very pricey so bring all you'll need (or use a digital camera with as many memory cards as you can afford). Local print processing is available but tends to be hit and miss. The opportunity to process slides is rare. If you'll be away for some time, posting film home, or preferably sending it with someone flying back, is a good idea.

Student cards An International Student Identity Card (ISIC; ⓦ ww.isic.org) is no guarantee of cheap deals, but is worth waving for many payments (airlines, railways, museum entrance fees) you may make. If you're a student, it's useful also to have a rubber-stamped letter substantiating the fact.

Time Most of West Africa is on Greenwich Mean Time (GMT). Cape Verde is one hour behind while Benin, Niger, Nigeria and Cameroon are all one hour ahead. The 24hr clock is widely used in the French- and Portuguese-speaking countries. The 12hr system is usual in the English-speaking countries.

Toilet paper This is usually provided by the user of the facilities rather than the owner. Never run out – using a jug of water and your hand takes more time to get used to than most people have.

Warri Also spelt *wole*, *ouril* or *oware*, this ancient game for two is played all over Africa. It involves two opposing rows of holes, either on a wooden board or just dug in the sand, and a handful each of seeds, cowries or pebbles. The rules vary locally but the principle is always the same. Seeds are deposited in each hole and then the players take turns to pick up a pile from one of their holes and "sow" them, usually one by one, around the board. Depending on the rules, the hole the last seed is sown into determines the continuation of play, and, if it makes up a certain number of seeds in that hole, then they're captured. The player with the most seeds at the end, wins. It's a game that's devastatingly simple and, at the same time, mathematically highly complex in its endless chain of cause and effect – financial analysts love it.

Guide

Guide

Mauritania

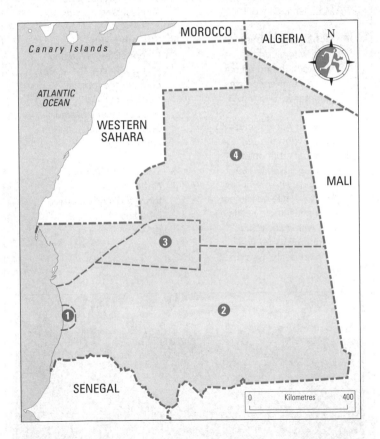

Mauritania highlights

✱ **Desert crocodiles**
Remarkably, small populations of Nile crocodiles survive in several remote oases. The easiest place to see them is near Moudjéria. See p.125

✱ **Tichit** Remote oasis town with elaborate architecture and an ethnic mix that epitomizes Mauritania. See p.126

✱ **Oualata** Ancient caravan town, worth the trek for its remarkable painted buildings. See p.129

✱ **Terjit** A fertile oasis near Atar, sheltered by cliffs and with a secluded campement and fine bathing pools. See p.132

✱ **Chinguetti and Ouadane** Ancient Saharan centres of learning, now boasting atmospheric ruins and some gorgeous landscapes. See pp.135–136

✱ **The ore trains** Immortalized in Michael Palin's Sahara, these are some of the longest trains in the world, and a popular means of transport between Noudhibou and the Adrar. See p.138

✱ **The Banc d'Arguin National Park** One of the world's great bird-breeding sites. See p.144

Introduction and Basics

Mauritania comes as a revelation to most travellers: pleasantly laid-back, spacious and physically comfortable because of its dry climate, scenically dramatic in several regions and culturally complex, with its rock paintings, medieval mosques and deep-rooted class structure.

The country's name comes from its dominant ethnic group, the **Moors**, who speak the **Hassaniya** dialect of Arabic and are traditionally nomadic. The Moors are broadly divided into "white" **Bidan**, who claim ancestors from Yemen and North Africa, and "black" **Haratin**, whose physical ancestry lies in Saharan and sub-Saharan Africa and who were subjugated and "Arabized" by the Bidan. Traditionally, the Haratin were vassals to the noble classes, but some Haratin elevated themselves into an independent caste which owed no tribute. The formal abolition of slavery in 1980 decreed that all "ex-slaves" (formerly called Abid) were henceforth to be known as "Haratin" – a source of offence to "real Haratin" and of confusion to outsiders.

This characterization oversimplifies the make-up of a very diverse and multifaceted population. **Social status** in Mauritania is considerably more than a question of skin colour. The white Moor community is divided broadly into Hassanes (noble families), Zouaya (or Tolba, the pious maraboutic caste) and Zenaga vassals (herders and cultivators). Status among black Moor families tends to be determined by their length of association and degree of intermarriage with white Moors, thereby blurring racial distinctions.

You can get an initial fix on the social complexities of Moorish society from the **position of women**, which is less rigidly defined than in most Arabic-speaking countries. Women may travel alone, drink tea with men, take an active part in male-dominated conversations and breast-feed their children in public; they rarely cover their faces, though they always cover their hair. The Berber and African heritage is apparent in these freedoms, which indicate the relative superficiality of the country's Arabic culture. In political matters, however, women's freedom to act is widely curtailed.

Outside the Moorish community, the remaining forty percent of the population are southerners – Soudaniens in Mauritanian phraseology – speaking **Fula** (Pulaar), **Wolof** or **Soninké**, and mostly farming and herding near the Senegalese and Malian borders. In Mauritania, the Fula-speakers of the Tukulor (Toucouleur) and Fula ethnic groups are known jointly as **Hal-Pulaar**.

In addition, Mauritania has a considerable population of African **immigrant workers**, from as far afield as Guinea and Nigeria. Some have come to work, while others are on their way north, fuelled by fictitious stories in their homeland of ships travelling direct to Europe from Mauritania. Many end up in Nouadhibou, hoping for a ticket to the Canary Islands, or passage into Morocco.

Facts and figures

The **République Islamique de Mauritanie** (often shortened to R.I.M.) covers over a million square kilometres, more than four times the size of the United Kingdom and nearly as big as California and Texas combined. With around 2.8 million people, the country has one of the lowest population densities in the world. That said, there's heavy migration to the towns, to the south, and abroad, while the eastern third of Mauritania is designated as *zone vide* (empty quarter). Mauritania's foreign debt is currently some £800 million ($1.2 billion; the price of two Stealth Bomber aircraft) – more than its annual GDP but a relatively minor figure in global terms. The government is led by President Maawiya Ould Taya and his Parti Républicain Démocratique et Social (PRDS).

Travel targets in Mauritania are easily pinpointed. Starting from Nouakchott and the coast, two roads cut across the country. The first leads to the central **Adrar region**, where a rugged landscape softened by rolling dunes shelters some ancient towns and oases – Atar, Terjiit, Chinguetti and Ouadane – and a rich archeological past, embodied in the stone tools and rock paintings found all over the region.

The other road is the desperate-sounding **Route de l'Espoir** (Road of Hope), which leads part of the way to the **Tagant region**, and the ancient towns of Tidjikja, Rashid and Tichit. The Route de l'Espoir also provides the easiest access to the colourful town of Oualata and the ruins of Koumbi Saleh, the latter once capital of the ancient Ghana empire.

Nouakchott, the capital, is a nearly inevitable but unremarkable transit point, while **Nouadhibou**, the second largest town, is the point of entry to West Africa for overland vehicles coming from Morocco and Europe, or for travellers arriving from the Canary Islands by air. The two-hundred-wagon iron-ore train linking Nouadhibou with central Mauritania makes for an unusual trip. Nouakchott and Nouadhibou, incidentally, both have **beaches** that seem to go on forever.

Wherever you go in Mauritania, you'll find a release from the freneticism of lands further south, and **travel conditions** generally more peaceful than elsewhere in West Africa. The worthwhile goals make travelling around attractive, and the desert journeys are a fair substitute for actually crossing the Sahara.

When to visit is conditioned more by burning temperatures than disruptive rainfall. The coast is cooled by sea breezes, but you'd probably want to avoid the interior between April and October (see the climate table for Atar, and remember these figures are averages: the thermometer often pips 50°C in the shade). The **southwest** gets oppressive humidity and occasional cloudbursts between July and October. At this time of year dirt roads can be cut – especially near the Senegal River – and transport off the paved highway can be very difficult.

Average temperatures and rainfall

NOUAKCHOTT
Temperatures °C

	Jan	Feb	Mar	Apr	May	June	July	Aug	Sept	Oct	Nov	Dec
Min (night)	14	15	17	18	21	23	23	24	24	22	18	13
Max (day)	29	31	32	32	34	33	32	32	34	33	32	28
Rainfall mm	0	3	0	0	0	3	13	104	23	10	3	0
Days with rainfall	0	1	0	0	0	1	1	3	3	1	1	0

NOUADHIBOU
Temperatures °C

	Jan	Feb	Mar	Apr	May	June	July	Aug	Sept	Oct	Nov	Dec
Min (night)	12	13	14	14	15	16	18	20	20	19	16	14
Max (day)	26	28	27	27	28	30	27	30	33	30	28	25
Rainfall mm	0	0	0	0	0	0	0	0	8	12	3	10

ATAR
Temperatures °C

	Jan	Feb	Mar	Apr	May	June	July	Aug	Sept	Oct	Nov	Dec
Min (night)	12	13	17	19	22	27	25	26	26	23	17	13
Max (day)	31	33	34	39	40	42	43	42	42	38	33	29
Rainfall mm	3	0	0	0	0	3	8	30	28	3	3	0

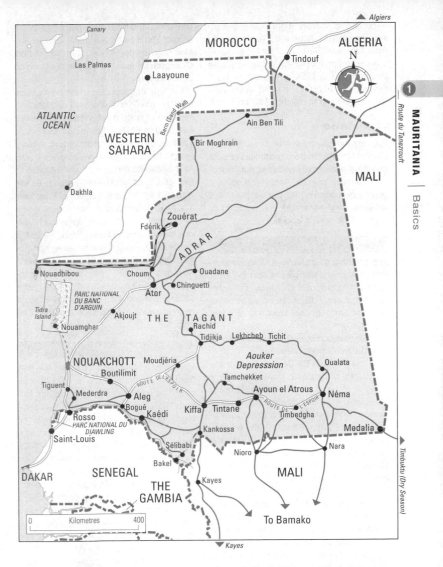

Getting there from the rest of Africa

Most of the international flights into Mauritania arrive in the capital, **Nouakchott**. There are numerous flights here from **Dakar** (around £85/$130 return) – take your pick from Air Sénégal, Tunisair or Air Mauritanie. The last of these also fly from **Cotonou** (£340/$500) via **Abidjan** (£200/$300) four times a week and from **Bamako** (3 weekly; £90/$135). Air France fly from **Conakry** in Guinea (3 weekly; £200/$300).

As for flights from North Africa, leaving from **Casablanca** you can choose from Royal Air Maroc, Air Mauritanie or Air Algérie, though if you wish to head back by this route as well, Royal Air Maroc's fares are keenest at £170/$250 return. There are also a couple of weekly flights apiece from **Algiers** with Air Algérie (£270/$400) and from **Tunis** with Tunisair (£230/$340).

Air Mauritanie operate flights from **Las Palmas** in the Canary Islands to both Nouadhibou (€250 for a return ticket valid for a month) and Nouakchott (€370).

Overland

Entering the country overland, you'll generally find Mauritanian **border officials** straight dealing, if occasionally pedantic, but seldom ostentatiously corrupt. Across the country, *postes de contrôle* may thoroughly check foreign drivers' paperwork and occasionally expect or demand a "*cadeau*".

From Morocco

The southbound route from Morocco, currently the only viable way of entering West Africa overland from North Africa, is straightforward, though distances between petrol stations are huge, so stock up at every opportunity.

Public transport is available as far south as **Dakhla** in Western Sahara and possibly even the village of **Bir Guendouz** near the Moroccan–Mauritanian border. The best place to find a lift from Dakhla is *Camping Moussaffir*, a favourite overlander's stopover located 500m before the first checkpoint to the north of town. Alternatively, wander around hotels and camp sites in Dakhla and ask who's going south. Two recommended places to stay in Dakhla are the *Hôtel Doubs* and the *Al Mouakouama*.

From Dakhla, the first ninety percent of the 450-kilometre road south to **Nouadhibou** is in reasonable condition, much of it hard-surfaced. Make sure you stock up with enough food and water (and, if you're driving, fuel) to last at least two days, just before you leave. Some travellers try to get from Dakhla to Nouadhibou in a day, but it is better to break the journey up as it can be

very tiring. There's a good place to stay for around 150 dirhams a night, 70km from the Moroccan border, or you can camp at **Fort Guerguarat** near the border itself, which closes at 6pm.

The tarmac comes to an end here as you enter no-man's-land, the road degenerating into 8km of rough bitumen interspersed with soft sand, surrounded by **mines**. Make sure you keep to well-marked tracks as the mines are still live; it's a good idea to hire a guide. At the Mauritanian border you will have to pay €10.00/UM1500 at the police post and €15.00/UM3000 at the customs. From here it is more or less a day's travel to negotiate just 50km of sandy track, dotted with various checkpoints and sand traps; the last of these is cleared a few kilometres north of Nouadhibou. For more detailed information on this route, see Ⓦwww.sahara-overland.com or Chris Scott's classic book *Sahara Overland*. Information on what to do once you arrive in Nouadhibou can be found on p.138.

From Mali

Routes into Mauritania from Mali are only **from the south**: there are no official border crossings on Mauritania's long eastern frontier. The principal crossing is Bamako–Nioro–Ayoun, with a less-used route running Bamako–Nara–Néma (or Timbedgha).

The Tuareg conflict in Mali (see p.330), though now over, has affected the southeast of Mauritania to some degree and there have been reports of banditry being a problem. Keep your ears open and don't proceed without being sure the route is safe. There's a lack of banks in eastern Mauritania, so you will have to change money unofficially one way or another (see p.98) – carry undeclared cash, either in euros or (preferably) dollars.

From Senegal

The main crossing point from Senegal is **Rosso**, near the mouth of the Senegal River. The car ferry regularly makes the five-minute crossing (but expect it to take up to an hour to load and unload) when the border is open. During the three-hour lunch break, the small currency-exchange booth on the Mauritanian side is also closed. If you're on foot, you can

For important practical information applying to all West African countries, covering health, transport, cultural hints and more, plus details on getting to the region from beyond Africa, see Basics, pp.9–87.

take a *pirogue* across when the border is open. The other major crossing, the **Diama barrage** road, is north of St-Louis and west of Rosso and requires a 4WD. Both these border crossings are open daily from 8am to noon and from 3pm to 6pm. Other, much less used, crossings, not open to vehicles, are at **Bogué**, near Aleg, and at **Gouray**, near Sélibabi; in both locations you'll need to take a *pirogue* across the river.

Red tape and visas

As regards **red tape**, note that alcohol is illegal except in licensed upmarket bars and hotels, and so can't be brought into the country. Note also that it's prohibited to take Mauritanian currency, the ouguiya, out of the country.

Visas to enter Mauritania are required by most nationalities except West Africans. In countries without Mauritanian representation, it is generally possible to obtain your visa at the French embassy or consulate – almost always easier than applying for one after you've left your own country.

To obtain a visa outside your country of residence, you may have to show a letter of introduction from your local embassy and an international air ticket. Some Mauritanian embassies will direct you to get a visa from the "country of embarkation" (in other words the one you'll be leaving immediately before entering Mauritania). Visa prices and durations vary considerably from embassy to embassy and even from one applicant to the next. Ask the price, get a receipt, and check what you've paid against the revenue stamps stuck into your passport. In several embassies, a little discussion about Mauritania's historic sites can break the ice.

Mauritania officials can be quite keen on health certificates and may ask you to show your **yellow fever certificate** at checkpoints or borders.

Mauritanian visas in Morocco

If you're planning to travel south into Mauritania along the Atlantic coast of Morocco, you're best advised to obtain your visa in your home country or in **Casablanca**, as this is much cheaper than getting a visa at the Mauritanian border.

The Mauritanian **consulate** In Casablanca is on 382 route d'el Jadida (☎022 257 373). To obtain a visa you'll need to bring your passport plus a photocopy of the key pages, as well as two photos and the visa fee (€10.00 for a one-month visa). If you bring these when the consulate is open in the morning (9–10.30am), you should be able to pick up the visa in the afternoon between 2pm and 4pm. Note that visas are actually valid from the day you apply, rather than your date of arrival in Mauritania.

Information, websites and maps

There are no Mauritanian tourist offices. Detailed guides (in French) to regions within Mauritania (the Adrar and the Tagant) are produced by the French Cultural Centre, and can be found in the larger hotels and bookshops in Nouakchott. If you read French and want an additional Mauritania-specific guide, consider Guides Arthaud's *Mauritanie*.

The Internet isn't overflowing with sites about Mauritania. That said, two portals worth a look are ⓦwww.inforim.mr and ⓦwww.mauritania.mr, both of which contain useful links; the latter is a safe info site with a strong official line.

The IGN 1:2,500,000 (1993) **map** of Mauritania has too small a scale to be useful for serious exploration, and isn't much better than the Michelin 741. However, the IGN 1:1,000,000 topographical surveys published in the 1960s are still available from their French headquarters (107 rue La-Boétie, Paris; ☎01 42 56 06 68, ⓦwww.ign.fr) and might be obtained, or ordered, through one of the map suppliers listed on p.29.

Costs, money and banks

Mauritania's currency is the **ouguiya** (or uguiya) Mauritanien (UM, Oug, Ug). Notes come in denominations of UM100, UM200,

UM500 and UM1000, with coins of UM1, UM5, UM10 and UM20. Banks are free to set their own **exchange rates** (typically UM430 = £1, UM280 = $1), so it can be worth shopping around when changing money.

Costs

Daily living costs in Mauritania are somewhat higher than in Senegal or Mali, and there's no avoiding high **transport costs** (see opposite). If you're staying in cheap hotels, eating in small restaurants and using public transport, you could survive on £10/$15 a day; if you want to stay in much more comfortable accommodation, eat well and rent a car (expensive in Mauritania), you could be looking at £100/$150 a day.

Banks and exchange

Although the export and import of ouguiya is prohibited, there's only a limited black market in the currency, more useful for convenience than profit. Outside of Nouakchott, **banks** are found in the larger towns, including Atar, Ayoune el Atrous, Boghé, Kaédi, Kiffa, Nema, Rosso, Sélibabi, Tintâne and Zouérat. **Bureaux de change** and even black-market street traders can also give official receipts for changed money, and are far quicker than banks.

The preferred currency is the **dollar**: best rates will be obtained for crisp $100 bills and if you change large quantities at a time. Note that the **CFA franc** is no longer a convertible currency and is not accepted by banks or hotels, though you may still be able to change CFA unofficially. Note also that towns in the interior are notoriously short of **small change**, and many shops or taxis cannot give change for an UM1000 note, so make sure you stock up on low-denomination notes (you can change UM1000s to smaller notes at the Banque Centrale de Mauritanie).

Traveller's cheques are accepted in most bureaux de change and some banks in the major cities, but you may have difficulty using them in the interior. **American Express** no longer have any representatives in Mauritania, so if you lose your traveller's cheques, or have problems cashing them, call Amex in the UK (☎+00 44 1273 57 1600). The major **credit cards** are accepted

by a few airlines and hotels in the capital, with bills written out in US$ but calculated at unfavourable rates. Credit-card cash advances can be arranged through certain travel agencies such as Secutour in Nouakchott (see p.122), though also at unfavourable exchange rates.

Health

The most critical feature of travel in Mauritania from a health aspect is the size of the country and the isolation of most towns and villages. You'll often be very far off the beaten track, and here, more than anywhere else in West Africa, you should have repatriation insurance in case of an accident or sudden illness.

Treat **water** with suspicion – reserves are usually low, and domestic animals depend on them too. It's good practice to carry a five-litre container and refill it at every opportunity. Fresh camel or goat's milk (*zrig*) is often offered to guests and it's probably best to limit your consumption: although tuberculosis is a very minor risk (even in the case of fresh Zebu cow's milk), brucellosis and hepatitis A can be contracted from infected milk.

The **malaria** risk is generally thought to be slight, except along the Senegal River, where it's as high as anywhere in West Africa. Roughly north of a line from Nouakchott to Tidjikja it's not reckoned to occur at all, but there are still plenty of mosquitoes about and it would be stupid to break your course of antimalarial pills for just a short stay in the country.

Hospitals and treatment facilities outside Nouakchott are strapped. The north, apart from Atar and Nouadhibou, has almost no public health provision, and although some of the southern towns have regional hospitals/health centres, these should be seen as a last resort. A much better option is to go to a private clinic – consultation fees start at around UM2000. **Pharmacies**, however, are a major growth industry in Nouakchott and in the interior, and these days they're often well stocked. Sanitary towels and disposable nappies are on sale in Nouakchott and upcountry.

Getting around

Most transport in Mauritania is by **4WD**, though bush taxis operate on the main highways. The **railway system** – a single line for the iron-ore train in the far north – is more of an adventure than an ordinary form of transport, but still a useful link between Nouadhibou and the rest of the country. Otherwise, **air travel** is not prohibitively expensive.

Road transport

The main form of long-distance public transport – between Rosso and Nouakchott, along the Route de l'Espoir, and Nouakchott to Atar – is a nine-seater **Peugeot 504** (otherwise known as a *taxi brousse*), though it is not unusual to have a choice of vehicles available. The best days to travel by bush taxi are Mondays, Thursdays and Saturdays. Few people travel on a Friday, so you may have to spend ages for a vehicle to fill up before you leave. Be prepared for long, dust-blown journeys, frequent breakdowns, lack of water, and no toilet stops. Road journeys **off the main routes** are arduous, with soft sand the recurring problem; conditions are detailed where relevant.

Fares are normally paid in advance. As a broad guide, expect to pay around £1.80/$2.70 per 100km on tarred roads and up to twice as much on dirt roads and desert tracks. Prices are fixed on what could be considered "scheduled runs", and you won't be overcharged; baggage, as usual, is another matter. If you want to get to out-of-the-way sites and towns, transport costs can quickly become exorbitant. The cheapest option is to wait for a vehicle that's going anyway.

Note that you normally pay for a particular **seat** in the vehicle, so choose carefully: try to work out where the sun will be during your journey and sit on the other side. Also avoid the seats over the back axle, which can be much higher, giving you a lot less headroom. Riding in the back of trucks, along these same routes, is slower and even less comfortable, but a good deal cheaper.

Given the lack of health-care provision in Mauritania, it's especially sensible to **avoid nighttime travel** – with its attendant risks of stray camels on the roads, oncoming vehicles with no lights, etc – and to be wary of **dangerous vehicles** being used for relatively rough desert and mountain passages. In the north and east, spare parts for vehicles are very hard to obtain and the scarcity of vehicles keeps many in use long after their safe life.

Road transport routes

Atar–Chinguetti Daily; 2–3hr; UM1500.
Atar–Choum 3–6 daily; 3hr; UM1600.
Atar–Ouadane 3–6 weekly; 4hr; UM2500.
Nouakchott–Aleg 3–6 daily; 3–4hr; UM1200.
Nouakchott–Atar Up to 12 daily; 5hr; UM2500.
Nouakchott–Ayoun el Atrous at least 1 daily; 15hr; UM4200.
Nouakchott–Kaédi Several daily; 6hr; UM2600.
Nouakchott–Kiffa 3–6 daily; 8–9hr; UM3200.
Nouakchott–Nouadhibou (4WD and trucks only) 2–6 weekly; 24hr; UM5000.
Nouakchott–Rosso Frequent; 3hr; UM1200 one-way.
Nouakchott–Sélibabi 1 or 2 daily; 18hr; UM6000.
Nouakchott–Tidjikja 1 or 2 daily; 10hr; UM5000.

Driving

Car rental is as expensive as you'd expect. Since there's pressure to take a driver at little extra cost, it's often indistinguishable from a personalized "safari" arrangement. Keep your fuel tanks and spare jerry cans full. **Fuel** costs about UM104 per litre for diesel and UM146 per litre for petrol. The further you go from Nouakchott, however, the higher the prices become, so stock up before you leave the city. Note that distances between towns are marked by kilometre posts (*piquets*); often a village or a turning will be referred to by the corresponding *piquet*, for example "PK70".

If you're **driving** yourself, you should treat Mauritania north of the Route de l'Espoir exactly as you would a trans-Saharan track; in many respects, because of the scarcity of other travellers, the routes are tougher and more dangerous. The track between the Tagant plateau and the Adrar (connecting Tidjikja with Atar), and the myriad tracks along the coast, are notorious for vehicles getting stuck. If you've no room to carry local people to guide you (they're never a problem to find), don't set off on little-trodden trails into the desert. The Mauritanians are not used to tourists' follies and nobody may think to prevent you from going – or search for you if you don't arrive. Lastly, avoid **night travel** – it is not uncommon to come across a stationary vehicle with its lights off in the middle of the road, or for camels to wander in front of your car.

Rail and air

If your point of arrival in Mauritania is Nouadhibou, the **train** from there to Zouérat is a good way into the country (see p.137), and you can hop off in Choum, only 100km short of the Adrar plateau, and take a *taxi brousse* direct to Nouakchott or Atar. You can take vehicles on this train at reasonable rates (details on p.138), but be prepared to lose days in transit.

Air travel makes sense if time is short (the longest flight is under 2hr). Air Mauritanie's fares are surprisingly reasonable; their typical schedule is as follows (prices quoted are one-way, with return fares costing double). Compagnie Mauritanienne des Transports Aériens provides slightly cheaper (though less frequent) flights between the capital and Nouadhibou and Sélibabi.

Domestic flights from Nouakchott

Ayoun el Atrous 1 weekly; UM12,600.
Kiffa 1 weekly; UM10,000.
Néma 1 weekly; UM15,000.
Nouadhibou 2 daily; UM14,000.
Sélibabi 2 weekly; UM12,000.
Tidjikja 1 weekly; UM7000.
Zouérat 2 weekly; UM15,600.

Accommodation

Mauritania's better hotels generally resemble Moroccan or Middle Eastern establishments, while cheaper lodgings offer shared rooms, generally designed for three people. The minimum price you can expect to pay for a room is about UM1000, less if you opt for a mattress only and sleep on the roof. The choice of hotels and *auberges* is very limited outside Nouakchott, Nouadhibou, Atar and Chinguetti.

Inexpensive hotels (❶–❷) typically offer a couple of thin mattresses on the floor with or without electric lighting, and rooms will not have air conditioning or private facilities. Rooms at **mid-range** establishments (❸–❺) have beds rather than mattresses, and also offer a fan and possibly en-suite bathroom. Above this price range there aren't many hotels to choose from, but those that exist have very comfortable rooms with TV, air conditioning and a small refrigerator. Whatever the price bracket, determined haggling can produce discounts, especially for longer stays.

Moorish hospitality being legendary, you may well be put up by taxi drivers and other casual acquaintances across the country. In this situation, never offer money as a gift – it may cause great offence, however poor the hosts. Instead, stock up on Swiss Army knives, watches, cigarettes, lighters, and bags of tea, sugar or instant coffee before you venture far from major towns.

The American **Peace Corps** may also put you up: several of their Regional Houses, in Atar, Ayoune el Atrous, Kaédi, Kiffa, Rosso and Sélibabi, are open to outsiders. You'll be charged slightly higher prices than volunteers (though rates are still extremely cheap), on the understanding that they aren't hotels and volunteers always have preference.

Accommodation price codes

Accommodation prices in this chapter are coded according to the following scale, whose equivalent in pounds sterling/US dollars is used throughout the book. Prices refer to the rate you can expect to pay for a room with two beds. Single rooms, or single occupancy, will normally cost at least two-thirds of the twin-occupancy rate. For further details see Basics, p.51.

❶ Under UM2200 (under £5/$8).
❷ UM2200–4300 (£5–10/$8–16).
❸ UM4300–6500 (£10–15/$16–24).
❹ UM6500–8600 (£15–20/$24–32).
❺ UM8600–13,000 (£20–30/$32–48).
❻ UM13,000–17,500 (£30–40/$48–64).
❼ UM17,500–21,500 (£40–50/$64–80).
❽ Over UM21,500 (Over £50/$80).

Camping out, as long as you have access to water, is always a fine option. A tent can be useful to keep off the desert wind, and a mosquito net is essential to keep out the creatures of the night.

Eating and drinking

Mauritania doesn't come up with much food that's memorable, but the variety is increasing. **Restaurants** don't exist much outside Nouakchott and Nouadhibou, though there are chop-house eating places in most towns, sometimes run by immigrants from other parts of West Africa.

Main meals are invariably **rice**- or **couscous**-based, and **bread** (French style) is usually in good supply. **Mutton**, **camel meat** and **chicken** are standard fare, as too is **fish**, usually dried and recooked. Outside influences are apparent in Mauritanian cuisine: you may be served Senegalese *chepbu-jen*, Lebanese-style grilled chawarma (pressed mutton slices), or Moroccan couscous dishes and *tajine* stews. If you eat with Mauritanians, **milk** (fresh, known as *zrig* – often diluted and sweetened, or curdled, can figure prominently.

Vegetarian travellers in Mauritania have quite a hard time of it. Quantities of **eggs** are served to non-flesh-eaters in homes and restaurants. Outside large towns, basic vegetables such as potatoes, carrots and onions can be found only in settlements with an adequate water supply. Nouakchott has many stalls with a good selection of local and European **fruit**, though you'll pay around UM250 per kilo for the former and UM400 per kilo for the latter. Otherwise, **fruit** is limited to **dates** – cheapest after the August and September harvest – and a small range of imports from Spain, Morocco, Senegal or Mali and what's grown in the far south of Mauritania itself.

Drinking is a serious business – not alcohol, which is illegal except at some licensed establishments in the major cities, but **tea**. Moors take their green tea often and seriously. Even more so than in Mali or Niger, a few small glasses of scalding, bitter-sweet yellow froth are part of the daily round. There's invariably a shortage of glasses:

pass yours back to the tea-maker as soon as you've drained it, and make sure you drain it well, because it can cause offence to Mauritanians if you leave the dregs behind. It's also not the done thing to leave before the third glass has been drunk – or to hang around after the glasses have been washed up and cleared away.

Opening hours and public holidays

The working week runs from Sunday to Thursday. Banks are open for changing money Sunday to Thursday, until noon; offices are usually open roughly between 8am and 1.30pm. Other businesses close at 2.30pm. Shops also open at 8am (except for groceries, often open as early as 7am), closing for a long break at lunchtime and opening again from the late afternoon until about 7.30pm.

Apart from those holidays decreed by the Islamic lunar calendar, Mauritania's **public holidays** are: January 1, February 26 (National Reunification Day), May 1 (Labour Day), May 25 (African Liberation Day), July 10 (Army Day), November 28 (National Day) and December 12 (anniversary of the 1984 coup). December 25 is a holiday for some businesses, though most shops stay open.

Communications

The main **post offices** are in Nouakchott and Nouadhibou, and most towns (except Chinguetti, Tichit, Ouadane and Oualata) have telephone shops. Poste restante is reliable but slow. Airmail delivery to and from Europe typically takes anything between a week and two and a half weeks; expect posting an ordinary letter this way to cost UM400.

Phoning or faxing abroad is reasonably efficient, and there is no trouble getting through to Mauritania from abroad. Note that Mauritanian phone numbers have **no**

Mauritania's IDD country code is ☎222.

area codes. Rates are roughly UM190 per minute to Francophone West Africa and the Middle East, UM220 per minute to the USA and UM270 per minute to Europe. In all cases, the cost between 3pm and 10pm is about twenty percent less than during the day, and from 10pm until 7am it's a third less than the daytime rate. On Friday, however, phoning at any time costs just a quarter of the daytime rate on other days of the week.

Mauritania is covered by two mobile-phone companies: Mattel and Mauritel. The latter has the widest coverage. You could also buy a local SIM card for UM3000 to make calls on the local network; a good place to do this is Mattel on avenue Charles de Gaulle in Nouakchott.

Internet cafés, charging around UM200 per hour, are springing up around the country, though note that connection speeds do vary considerably.

The media

Since free elections in 1992 the press has been liberalized and there are now a good dozen **daily papers**, most of which are in Arabic. Titles change with bewildering frequency, and though most papers tend to serve up the same bland mix of news and articles about drought and the doings of the elite, one or two are startlingly anti-establishment. The two papers produced by the official press agency are *Horizons* (in French) and *Chaab* (in Arabic). You'll find French-language newspapers and magazines around Nouakchott and Nouadhibou, and even a few English-language ones in the *Librairie Vents du Sud*.

The state-run Radio Mauritanie and TV Mauritanie network broadcasts in French and Hassaniya, with some programmes in Fula, Wolof and Sarakole/Soninké. **Television** has exploded in recent years, and even the current-starved *bidonvilles* around Nouakchott have battery-driven sets. The news and "cultural" programmes you'd expect are interrupted by the occasional French soccer match. Most hotels, even downmarket ones, have a satellite dish and can receive a variety of international channels.

Entertainment

Independent artistic expression is rather rare in Mauritania, in part a reflection of the nomadic culture, where crafts were generally the preserve of specific castes. Poetry was the only widespread artistic activity, and even then rarely written down.

Cinema has a couple of leading lights, one being the exiled director **Med Hondo**. His 1969 film *Soleil Ô* was a bleak and somewhat plodding mix of *cinéma vérité* and weird set pieces, dealing with African immigrants in France; more recently, with Burkinabe backing, he made the impressive historical epic *Sarraounia*, about a queen who resisted both the colonialists and the Muslims. More recently, the Moscow-trained **Abderrahmane Sissako** won the top award at FESPACO 2003 with *Heremakono*, about a Malian youth in Mauritania hoping to emigrate to Europe. **Theatre** is nonexistent, as is any accessible **literature** translated into English.

Music

The professional musical caste in Mauritania are called **igaouen** or *iggiw*. In the past they depended, like the *jelis*, on the patronage of big men and nobles. The more flexible modern *igaouen* repertoire includes complex songs of Middle Eastern character and others simple enough to be taken up in chorus by the audience. The music is based on a sophisticated modal system – known as the "black and white ways" – derived from Arab musical theory. If you are interested in hearing a local Pulaar band in Nouakchott, contact Gabreel Ba (☎632 81 07, ✉badjibril@yahoo.fr). A description of Pulaar instruments can be found opposite.

Khalifa Ould Eide and Dimi Mint Abba
Moorish Music from Mauritania (World Circuit).
Khalifa and Dimi, together with Dimi's two daughters, were the first Mauritanian group to tour in the English-speaking world, in the mid-1980s. This is a beautiful and evocative CD – note the flamenco-style hand-clapping.

Malouma *Desert of Eden* (Shanachie).
Malouma is in a league of her own, a hereditary ardin-playing griot and modern singer at the same time, who mixes the Senegalese mbalax style with her own Moorish traditions and, while singing

exclusively in the Hassaniya dialect of Arabic, shows no obedience to Moorish musical strictures. Compared with the recordings of most of her compatriots, this jazz-inflected debut CD is highly accessible. The ardin shines through to distinctive effect.

Tahra *Yamen Yamen* (EMI). Born in Nema in southeastern Mauritania in 1959, Tahra Mint Hembara is a hereditary griot (her aunt was the famous Lekhdera Mint Ahmed Zeidane, who has been steeped in Moorish musical tradition since the age of 10. This 1989 album, with Jean-Philippe Rykiel on synth, tested the stretchability of classic musical traditions on the world stage. An intriguing album of Mooro-tech.

Women travellers

Women travellers can expect a combination of chivalry and pestering, though not too much of the latter. Covering your hair is an effective way of cooling ardour: Moorish women never let their scarves slip. Also it is advisable to dress conservatively: exposing your legs and arms will bring out the knaves rather than the knights. Sex is openly discussed among women; if you find yourself among French-speaking Moorish women, or you speak a little Hassaniya yourself, the conversation can take remarkable turns.

It's natural that you'll spend a fair amount of time, like everyone else in Mauritania, lying on mattresses on the ground. It's useful to know, then, that lying either on your back or your stomach is considered highly suggestive; Moorish women invariably lie on their sides, supporting their head with a hand. It's also useful to know that it's difficult to get tampons outside Nouakchott, though pads are widely available.

Wildlife and national parks

Mauritania's wildlife has been depleted by hunting and the spread of the desert. Formerly, the south had a good cross-section of West African savanna animals, including elephants, hippos, giraffes, cheetahs, leopards, lions and several species of antelope. Now all that remain of these are a few leopards, though lions do still occasionally wander into southern Mauritania from Mali.

More common **desert species** include striped hyenas, jackals, fennec foxes, wild cats and wild sheep. Less common species found only in the south include gazelles, ostriches (near Néma), patas monkeys and baboons. You'll see plenty of camels, but these, like all of Africa's dromedaries, are domesticated. The uninhabited eastern desert is one of the last refuges of the endangered addax antelope. Another extraordinary survivor is the desert crocodile, found in scattered isolated pools hundreds of miles from the nearest permanent river (see p.128 for more). Nouadhibou, on the north coast, is the home of the world's largest colony of very rare Mediterranean monk seals.

For **bird-watchers**, the country's biggest potential attraction is the migratory birdlife of the isolated sandbanks and seashore in the Parc National du Banc d'Arguin (see p.144), south of Nouadhibou. The park is administered from Nouadhibou where there's a permit-issuing office for the suitably equipped. Another good place for seeing birds is the Diawling National Park on the north bank of the Senegal River (see p.123).

Traditional instruments of Moorish Mauritania

Ardin Ten- to fourteen-stringed women's harp, played with a calabash acting as a drum.

Daghumma Slender, hollowed-out gourd with a necklace, which acts as a rattle.

Tidinit Lute with two long strings on which the melody is played, and two short ones which give a fixed dronelike rhythm; played by men.

Tobol Large kettle drum, used by women in times of danger to warn men out in the fields or in the *palmeraies*.

Examples of some of these instruments can be seen in Nouakchott's museum.

Directory

Airport departure tax None.

Crafts and markets Mauritania is famous for stylishly refined carpets, woven in Nouakchott. Sadly these are impractical purchases for most travellers, as are the brass-fitted, dark-stained wooden chests and camel saddles (*rahla*). But there's quite a desirable selection of jewellery in silver and ebony, tobacco pipes and pouches, sandals and printed cotton cloth (good value). In the Adrar and Tagant, children and market sellers hawk neolithic stone arrowheads and tools. You can turn up medieval trading beads as well, though these are becoming internationally sought after and increasingly rare.

Names You'll quickly notice almost all Moors retain traditional names. Ould and Mint mean "son of" and "daughter of" in Hassaniya: hence Mokhtar Ould Daddah, Dimi Mint Abba.

Photography People tend to be suspicious of cameras and prefer not to have their pictures taken, but the reaction is not normally heavy. However, be careful in Nouakchott; check before snapping and avoid all broad street scenes – there's often an upset. In particular avoid the University area and the Ministries of av Abdel Nasser. There is no photography permit. Film in Nouakchott is expensive and unreliably stored.

Police and trouble Mauritania is report-to-the-police territory. Large towns have control posts on entrance roads where your particulars will be recorded. Smaller places don't, and it's up to you to find the man on duty and proffer your *pièce*. If you fail to do so, you could have an uncomfortable dressing-down when they apprehend you. To save time, particularly if you are in a group, it is a good idea to write your travel itinerary on a piece of paper with the names of all in your party, their passport numbers and nationalities. Make numerous photocopies of this and pass it on at each police checkpoint. If you're driving, you may in exceptional circumstances have your vehicle thoroughly searched; note that you're not allowed to bring alcohol into the country.

Sexual attitudes In the Moorish community, there is more openness than you might at first expect. Younger women are rapidly shaking off old values, if not always traditional costume. Urban men, too, are beginning to accept a realignment of sexual attitudes. Affairs, "love-marriages" and divorces are increasingly common in Nouakchott, and the bride price (paid to the woman or her family) is less often stipulated. Female circumcision is still practised, more in the far south. Male travellers aren't very likely to be hustled by prostitutes.

A brief history of Mauritania

Contemporary Mauritania doesn't coincide with the ancient "Mauretania Tingitana", a region confined to present-day Morocco and western Algeria, and annexed to the Roman Empire by Claudius in 42 AD. The events and processes that led to the creation of the République Islamique de Mauritanie are taken up below with the arrival of the first Europeans. Accounts of some of the little-known early history of the region are scattered throughout this chapter.

European contact

Direct contact with Europeans began in 1445, when **Portuguese explorers** under Nuno Tristão sighted a habitation at the Arguin Islands and promptly took 29 captives back to Portugal as slaves. At about the same time, the **Hassane Arabs** from upper Egypt were moving into the northern parts of the territory, subjugating the largely Berber-speaking population, spreading the use of the Hassaniya language, and creating the cultural complex that became **Moorish society**.

Early Portuguese efforts to conduct a trade in slaves and gold were not hugely successful. Instead, acacia-tree gum used in the manufacture of food and drugs (called "gum arabic" because it was originally exported to Europe by Red Sea Arabs) soon became the main item of commerce, most of it coming from the southwest region, near the mouth of the Senegal River.

When Portuguese commercial influence waned in the seventeenth century, the **gum trade** fuelled intense rivalry between French, Dutch and English trading houses. The Dutch pulled out in 1727, but Anglo-French competition (and war) continued until 1857, when the British withdrew from the region in exchange for the French ceding them Albreda Island in the Gambia River. Even alone, the **French** had to use force to impress their control over the gum trade on the Moors, in order to hold a profit.

Throughout the seventeenth and eighteenth centuries, the French had also been more successful than the Portuguese in whipping up the slave trade. From their main base at **St-Louis** at the mouth of the Senegal River, they sent foreign goods upriver, ensuring a supply of slaves from the feuding and rigidly class-stratified societies of the interior. Mauritania's involvement in this trade was heavy, and the class structure of the southern agricultural districts was set in aspic by the capture of non-Arabic-speaking peoples, who were sold down the river by their captors in exchange for firearms, cloth and sugar.

But the slave trade didn't account for the slow **decline in trans-Saharan commerce**. This came about through the increasing imposition of Arab (later Arab-Berber) rule throughout the territory during the seventeenth century. By 1800, most of today's Mauritania was divided into competing **"emirates"** – Trarza, Brakna, Adrar and Tagant – which were highly organized internally but had little in the way of constructive foreign relations, and were inimical to commercial links between their domains. The French at St-Louis were thus able to take advantage of the divisions, and actively promoted **civil war** in order to divert ordinary trade, as well as the slave victims of battle, in their direction.

French expansion up the Senegal River and gathering French interest in Morocco and Algeria led, towards the end of the nineteenth century, to the strategic penetration of the Mauritanian interior, with "protection"

Western Sahara and the Polisario war

The colony of **Spanish Sahara** was acquired by Spain in a succession of Franco-Spanish conventions between 1886 and 1912. The motivation for coveting this wedge of gravel plains and low hills (about the size of Britain) sprang from a desire to join in the "scramble for Africa", a sense of wounded imperialist pride at the loss of the South American colonies, and the proximity of the Spanish Canary Islands.

Villa Cisneros (Dakhla) and La Guera were the only Spanish bases until 1934, when the first foothold was established in the interior. However, Africa Occidental Española had no apparent economic potential and General Franco didn't waste money on it. By 1952 there were only 216 civilian employees, 24 telephones and 366 schoolchildren in the entire territory.

The Provincia de Sahara (as it became) with its capital El Ayoun (built in 1940), was ruled as a **military colony** where, as in Spain, independent political expression was ruthlessly crushed.

In 1966, the UN insisted on the right to **self-determination** for the colony. But a survey of Spanish Sahara's **phosphate reserves** in the early 1960s had indicated vast deposits of up to ten billion tonnes, and Spain was soon digging in. Although there had been armed resistance to Spanish occupation in the late 1950s in the wake of Morocco's independence, urban anticolonial demonstrations began only in June 1970, when troops fired on marchers in El Ayoun and hundreds more were arrested – and subsequently disappeared.

Polisario

The **Polisario Front** was born in Zouérat in Mauritania on May 10, 1973, spurred into existence by Spain's continued occupation and the threats posed by competing claims from Mauritania and Morocco. Meanwhile, Spain was planning a process of decolonization and independence to thwart Polisario's growing influence, with blueprints for limited self-rule, a referendum, and a state-sponsored Sahrawi National Unity Party of Sahrawi moderates. But King Hassan of Morocco put pressure on Spain to reconsider their plans and came to an agreement with Mauritania over partitioning Western Sahara. However, the International Court of Justice upheld the Sahrawis' right to self-determination. This was not enough to stop the **Green March** orchestrated by King Hassan of Morocco, involving 350,000 Moroccans marching, Korans in hand, into the Western Sahara to claim their country's so-called historical right to the territory.

After General Franco's death in 1975, Spain agreed to pull out of Western Sahara, leaving the territory to Morocco, Mauritania and the Spanish-installed Djemaa council – a body of conservative, urban Sahrawis through whom they had ruled. Although the UN continued to uphold resolutions on Western Sahara, a UN delegation in early 1976 decided that the prevailing turmoil in the territory was so great that there was no way the Sahrawis could be properly consulted. A guerilla war between Polisario and Morocco now began in earnest. More than half the population fled the country – old people, women and children to Algerian refugee camps around **Tindouf**, and men to

and "pacification" sounded as the keynotes to local people. The **assassination of Xavier Coppolani**, a French commander, at Tidjikja in 1905, ended a period of relatively peaceful expansion and brought down a five-year reign of terror in the territory. The Adrar was occupied in 1908, the Hodh (in the southeast) in 1911. The next year, France reached an agreement with Spain over respective spheres of influence in the western Saharan region, and in 1920 **la Mauritanie** became a colony of French West Africa. "Police actions" against nomadic guerilla resistance continued throughout the north up until 1933, when complete "pacification" was finally achieved.

join Polisario. The **Sahrawi Arab Democratic Republic** was proclaimed by Polisario – in exile in Tindouf – on February 27, 1976.

Mauritania at war

From the beginning Polisario concentrated on knocking Mauritania out of the picture, thus breaking the Morocco–Mauritania alliance. There were repeated, humiliating losses for Mauritania; the iron-ore railway was under constant threat; foreigners working at the mines were kidnapped; and twice, in June 1976 and July 1977, Polisario mounted daring raids on the outskirts of Nouakchott itself, shelling the presidential palace. Mauritania was crippled by debt, doubt and drought, and its war was an undignified fiasco. For President Ould Daddah, the situation had become untenable, and he was relieved of his post in July 1978. The new regime sued for peace with Polisario the following year.

Stalemate

In the 1980s, Morocco pulled back its front line to Dakhla and the northwest of Western Sahara (the so-called "useful triangle" containing the phosphate fields), while building immensely long, defensive, earthworks that now enclose almost ninety percent of the territory. The Tindouf refugee zone grew into a state-in-exile, a stable and, at first, relatively prosperous mini-republic which, though heavily dependent on international donations, managed to build a reputation for its agricultural efforts and welfare services.

In early 1991 a shaky **ceasefire** was agreed on the understanding that a referendum on the question of independence for the people of the territory would be held. But the UN-monitored process of identifying eligibility to vote has been lengthy and inconclusive. Moreover, Morocco has "West Banked" the sectors of the Western Sahara it holds, pumping resources – and 150,000 Moroccan **settlers** – into the region, in order to try to obviate a democratic solution for the indigenous people. Meanwhile, the three hundred UN peacekeepers have noted dozens of ceasefire violations by Morocco (against just a handful by the Sahrawis).

In 1997, Morocco was forced by a combination of US and UN pressure to accept face-to-face meetings with Polisario, brokered by UN Secretary-General Kofi Annan. As a result, an agreement was signed at the end of 1997 laying out the rules for registration to vote in the referendum. The process soon broke down, however, as tens of thousands made fraudulent claims of indigenous Sahrawi status, coached by Moroccan officials.

Prospects for Polisario are not good, with both the US and France encouraging Morocco and Algeria – Polisario's main backers – not to allow a regional war to flare up. Meanwhile, over a hundred thousand Sahrawis continue to languish in refugee camps in Algeria, where food is rationed and medical care is limited. The Moroccans are looking forward to a day when the UN troops might wearily depart – a *fait accompli* for the late King Hassan's colonial policy.

The path to independence

The French invested almost nothing in Mauritania's future, administering it as a part of Senegal and counting on nomadic conservatism to look after the population in traditional ways. Mauritania was used by the French as a buffer zone protecting their more valuable assets in Senegal and Soudan (Mali), and as a place of internal exile for political agitators from their other colonies.

In 1956, **Morocco** achieved independence, with King Hassan V's ruling group wanting to see the reconstruction of a "greater Morocco" that included much of Mauritania. The claims naturally had repercussions in Mauritania, where an extreme, Moorish, nationalist movement took shape, fighting to hive off part, if not all, of Mauritania to Morocco, which it believed was the true homeland of all Moors.

In the 1957 Territorial Assembly elections (the first with universal suffrage), the unaffiliated Union Progressiste Mauritanienne, Mauritania's first indigenous political party, won 33 out of 34 seats. **Mokhtar Ould Daddah**, a young, white Moor lawyer with considerable French support (he was de Gaulle's son-in-law), was elected vice-president of Mauritania's first governing council (the French governor was president). Like the Moroccans, he was territorially ambitious, calling on the people of the **Spanish Sahara** to unite with his own in a "great economic and spiritual Mauritania".

On November 28, 1958, Mauritania became an autonomous republic within the French community and the **République Islamique de Mauritanie** (the R.I.M.) was proclaimed. A national election held in 1959 gave Ould Daddah the post of prime minister, after his Parti du Regroupement Mauritanien won every seat in the new National Assembly, and on November 28, 1960, Mauritania became an independent nation-state, with Ould Daddah as president.

Ould Daddah's presidency

With the founding of the new capital of Nouakchott, the development of the Fdérik iron-ore mines and the completion of the railway to Nouadhibou in 1963, Mauritania's economic future looked fairly bright. But at the same time Ould Daddah set about eliminating **political opponents**, forming a one-party state run by his Parti du Peuple Mauritanien (**PPM**).

In the south and among the black, non-Arabic-speaking population, expectations raised by independence from France gave way to resentment and indignation. In 1966, Arabic was made the compulsory teaching medium in schools. Ensuing **riots** in Nouakchott were summarily suppressed and laws swiftly enacted to ban all discussion of racial conflict. The country had come close to civil war, but Arabization continued, with a 1968 law putting **Hassaniya** on a co-footing with French as dual official languages.

The government was intent on integrating the trade-union movement into the PPM, a move which angered **teachers** and **miners** particularly, and led to strikes and demonstrations in 1968, 1969 and 1971. For two months in 1971 there was a complete shutdown of iron-ore production. The force of government repression, and the determination of the ruling party to silence the opposition led to the creation of clandestine political movements and a simmering groundswell of anti-government feeling. Through much of this first decade of independence, however, foreign affairs issues served to dampen the opposition.

During the 1960s, support from the other Arab states for Morocco's claim over Mauritania had resulted in very few of them recognizing the R.I.M. But in 1969 came Morocco's formal recognition of Mauritania. Increasing Islamic radicalization, a slackening of ties with France coupled with growing links with Algeria, and a clear state socialist programme were the natural consequences. The huge iron-ore complex at Fdérik/Zouérat was nationalized and the country withdrew from the CFA franc zone to bring in its own currency, the ouguiya.

Spain's decision to withdraw its garrisons from the Western Sahara plunged Mauritania into a **war with the Polisario** (see box, pp.106–107). The war, over the small and economically worthless piece of territory ceded to Mauritania by Spain, proved the downfall of Ould Daddah.

The Lieutenant-Colonels

On the night of July 9, 1978, a quiet and bloodless **coup** ousted Mokhtar Ould Daddah. The coup's leaders dissolved the PPM and announced the formation of a **Comité Militaire de Redressement National** (**CMRN**) – "to save the country from ruin and dismemberment" – under the chairmanship of Chief of Staff Lt-Col **Moustapha Ould Salek**.

Ould Salek tried to bring Polisario and Morocco together for a negotiated settlement, but the terms suited neither party. When Polisario's kidnapping of a Mauritanian prefect pushed Mauritania into a **peace treaty** with Polisario in August 1979, Morocco immediately moved into the territory vacated by Mauritanian troops. Meanwhile, at home, Ould Salek was confronted by outbreaks of racial conflict, student agitation, and factional strife in the CMRN – upgraded, desperately, in April 1979, to the Military Committee for National Salvation (CMSN). Ould Salek resigned and was replaced as president by Lt-Col **Mohammed Louly**, whose prime minister, Lt-Col **Mohamed Khouna Haidalla**, in turn staged another palace coup in January 1980, to take control of government.

Haidalla's five years as head of state saw an overall improvement in foreign relations, but a deterioration in the domestic situation. Internally, Mauritania's most dramatic event – as far as the rest of the world was concerned – was the formal **abolition of slavery** in 1980. This may have been intended to forestall links between the Dakar-based black opposition and supporters of exiled white Moor groups in Paris, and also to divert attention away from the increasingly blatant racial discrimination against the Soudanien southerners, but the effect of the pronouncement was in fact to focus world attention on the brutal military Mauritania had become.

For a short time in 1980–81, President Haidalla experimented with **political relaxation**. He formed a civilian government led by prime minister Ahmed Ould Bneijara, and drew up a draft constitution recommending a democratic multiparty system. But rumours of a **Libyan-backed plot** (part of the ripple of Libyan-inspired insecurity that passed through West Africa at that time), and then a genuine **coup attempt** by the **Parti Islamique** of former government ministers operating from Morocco, shook the democracy idea apart. Having executed the coup leaders, the CMSN appointed a new prime minister, Lt-Col **Maawiya Sid'Ahmed Ould Taya**, and remilitarized the government.

Another military coup was foiled in February 1982, involving Ould Salek and the just-deposed Ould Bneijara. Severe **drought** in 1983 brought tens of thousands of famine-struck nomads virtually to the door of the Presidential Palace in Nouakchott; opposition groups continued to fight a war of words in France, Morocco and Senegal; and Haidalla's recognition of the Sahrawi Arab Democratic Republic early in 1984 brought further insecurity to the country as Morocco seemed more than ever determined to oppose any referendum in the Western Sahara – increasing the tension between Morocco and Mauritania. The prime minister, Ould Taya, who was already concerned about government corruption and inaction, deposed President Haidalla on December 12, 1984, in yet another palace coup.

Ould Taya: progress and reaction

With World Bank and IMF support, **President Ould Taya** adopted a programme of economic recovery with heavy emphasis on fishing and agriculture. Targets were set (and reached), and creditors were evidently impressed by Ould Taya's abandonment of some of the capital-intensive industrial schemes set up by Haidalla to the detriment of basic infrastucture and rural development. Iron ore remained a major source of foreign exchange, but in the late 1980s **fish** came to be seen as a more flexible resource, and was briefly the country's biggest earner.

But the government's agenda was set by political rather than economic concerns. In 1986, a tract in French entitled *Manifesto of the Oppressed Black Mauritanian: From Civil War to National Liberation Struggle, 1966–86* made the rounds among students and staff at the National Language Institute. It was the work of the Dakar-based **African Liberation Forces of Mauritania** (FLAM). Twenty prominent southerners were arrested and jailed on charges of "undermining national unity". Widespread rioting and destruction subsequently took place in Nouakchott and Nouadhibou, and thirteen of those involved were also jailed, in March 1987. Strict **Islamic law** was subsequently introduced.

In October 1987, 51 Fula-speaking Tukulor officers were arrested on charges of insurrection. Three of them were executed and 41 more were given long prison terms. This blow against the southerners was followed by a purge of Tukulor army officers, with over five hundred dismissals. Tension continued through 1988, with racial killings in Nouakchott.

The 1990 race riots

Events finally boiled over in April 1989, triggered by a minor incident on an island on the Senegal River, near Bakel, in which Mauritanian cows owned by Pulaars were supposed to have plundered Senegalese vegetable gardens owned by Sonninkés. The Senegalese Sonninkés crossed over into Mauritania, and during the ensuing dispute a Mauritanian border guard killed a Senegalese. Thirteen Senegalese were arrested and taken to Sélibabi in Mauritania, which led to attacks on Mauritanian shops in Bakel on the Senegalese side.

Within days, violence had spread to other Senegalese towns, resulting in the deaths of dozens of Mauritanians, while thousands more were driven out as their shops and homes were ransacked. In Dakar, the entire Mauritanian community sheltered in the Grande Mosquée and the Mauritanian embassy. In Mauritania there were even more savage attacks on Senegalese and other black Africans as security forces and lynch mobs of Haratins hunted for southerners. Both governments were quick to condemn killings by the other side, but neither took decisive action to control the violence.

A massive dual **air evacuation**, with international assistance, began as it emerged that up to two hundred Senegalese had died in Nouakchott. As the exodus from Mauritania went on (in the event, there was only a limited flight of Mauritanians from Senegal), it became clear that among those leaving were a large proportion of indigenous southern Mauritanians – whom the regime now routinely refers to as "Senegalese" but who are largely **Hal-Pulaar** (Fula-speakers) – many of whom were being forcibly expelled. The government was taking the opportunity to banish up to twenty thousand potential opponents, to reduce the impact of the returning Moors and to lessen the numbers of non-Moorish Mauritanians, who had been claiming for several years that they were in the majority. In November 1990 the government announced there had been a coup attempt, fostered by Senegal. Over three hundred southerners were picked up by the authorities, and never seen again. Most southerners remaining in any positions of responsibility in the civil service were sacked over the next few months.

The 1990–91 **Gulf War** drew the world's attention away from the horrors of Mauritania's human rights record. But Mauritania's military rulers had long been allies of Iraq (Iraqi military advisors are believed to have helped organize the pogroms against

Fula villages in the south), and the government stood behind Saddam Hussein throughout the conflict. This alliance put severe strains on Mauritania's relations with Morocco and, of more immediate economic consequence, France. Thus Ould Taya's pragmatic move to adopt a democratic constitution, when faced with the possibility of complete isolation, was hardly questioned: every other Francophone state in West Africa was undergoing the same process.

The multiparty era

Southerner political groups (and Muslim fundamentalists) boycotted the **referendum** on a multiparty constitution, arguing they hadn't been consulted in drawing up the document, which in practice banned political parties based on religion. Despite only a twenty percent turnout, the "yes" vote was carried into practice, Mauritania becoming a multiparty state on July 20, 1991, with a president as head of state and a prime minister running the country's affairs for him.

In 1992, the country's first "free" **presidential election** since 1960 was marred by fraud. The post of president was won by the former military leader, Ould Taya, despite the best efforts of his main rival, Ahmed Ould Daddah (half-brother of the country's first president) to have the results annulled by the supreme court. The general elections, later in the year, were boycotted by the opposition parties, and there was widespread vote-rigging, including leaving candidates' names off electoral lists.

In 1993, the government declared an amnesty for perpetrators of the 1989–90 racial violence. Officially, all seventy-thousand-odd **Mauritanian refugees** in Senegal were encouraged to return home, though in practice, few had any papers, job or land to return to. Mauritania has mended relations with **Senegal** and **Mali** and the three countries have been attempting to cooperate in their border areas to crack down on

banditry and smuggling. More than forty thousand Tuareg refugees who fled Mali during the Tuareg rebellion left their refugee camp in Mauritania to return home in 1997. However, relations with France, where the press often spotlights Mauritania's poor human rights record, are not good.

As for Mauritania's relations with **the rest of the Arab world**, these have been going through convulsions. After the isolation the country experienced during the Gulf War, especially from Morocco, Mauritania began a process of distancing itself from **Baghdad**. This was completed when the Iraqi ambassador was booted out of the country in October 1995, and a number of high-ranking Mauritanians – including both government and opposition MPs, army officers and a police commissioner – were arrested after rumours of a foiled coup plot, supported by Iraq, started circulating. There were a number of convictions, but the short prison sentences were commuted. Meanwhile, Mauritania's decision to enter into diplomatic relations with **Israel** led to a breakdown of relations with **Libya**, formerly an important source of economic assistance, but always an uncomfortably overbearing ally for Mauritania. The establishment of an Israeli Embassy in 2000, though widely unpopular with the Mauritanian people, is indicative of the government's pro-Western stance, emphasized when Mauritania withdrew from ECOWAS early in 2002 to concentrate on links with Morocco.

After legislative **elections in October 1997**, the Parti Républicain Démocratique et Social (PRDS) has 71 of the 79 seats in the Assembly. There is a handful of independent (non-aligned) legislators but only one opposition member of the Assembly, from Action pour Change (AC), a party formed mainly to lobby for the rights of the Haratin ex-slaves.

Slavery remains a sensitive issue, and excites some international attention. In early 1998, several human rights activists were arrested after their participation in a French TV documentary on the subject, and AC demonstrations to protest their treatment were met with police violence and more detentions.

Prospects

On the surface a certain stability is apparent, but the future for Mauritania is uncertain. Income from fishing has declined markedly and iron-ore output has dropped as the world market for it shrinks. However, offshore **oil** has recently been discovered, and exploration is currently underway to determine the extent of the reserves. At the time of writing, Ould Taya was expected to win the presidential elections in November 2003, having survived an attempted coup by disgruntled troops earlier in the year.

An alarming issue facing the country is **Islamic fundamentalism**. Despite the country's "Islamic Republic" label, and a legal system strongly influenced by the *sharia* (the body of Muslim doctrines), the government has been distancing itself from fundamentalism; the work of a number of Islamic groups in the country has been curtailed and Islamic leaders have been arrested for belonging to "secret foreign organizations". However, if the fundamentalists prove that they do indeed have widespread grassroots support, the crisis they are bound to precipitate will make the current status quo seem admirable in comparison.

Books

Literature in English on Mauritania is minimal, particularly as regards books focusing exclusively on the country. Titles marked o/p below are likely to be out of print.

Lauren Goodsmith *The Children of Mauritania*. Ex–Peace Corps volunteer writes a charming story about a Pulaar boy from the Senegal river valley, and a Moor girl from the Atar region, with excellent pictures.

Peter Hudson *Travels in Mauritania* (o/p). Tale of a two-month trek in 1988.

William Langewiesche *Sahara Unveiled*. Unsentimental account of a journey from Algiers to Dakar.

Odette du Puigaudeau *Barefoot in Mauritania* (1937; o/p). The author and her female companion took camels across "the land of death" – a ramble through a Mauritania that hardly knew it existed.

Language

Mauritania's most widespread language is **Hassaniya Arabic**, and although many people speak **French**, it is less popular – and slightly less widely acceptable – than formerly. Other languages are mostly concentrated in the non-Moorish regions of the far south and include **Fula** or Fulfulde, **Wolof** and **Soninké** or Sarakole. Few people speak English.

Hassaniya

Hassaniya, the sole language of the Moors, is a strongly Berberized form of Arabic. In 1991 it became, controversially, the official language of the country, usurping the less divisive French for many purposes.

Greetings and civilities

Moorish Mauritanians have an elaborate greeting ritual which they go through with resignation or enthusiasm depending on their mood. Farewells, on the other hand, are brief and free of sentiment. A phrase for "Please" is never used. "*Ski*" (with a short "i") is an expression of satisfaction, usually followed by a hand slap.

iyak la bas	hope nothing's wrong with you
la bas	nothing's wrong

The above is usually followed by numerous iyaks, eg

iyak mo a ve	hope you have no sickness

If you want to end the iyak sequence try

ma rahbeh	so be it
mah salaam	goodbye
sh'halak	an informal "How are you?"
ilhamdillah	praise be to God, often stuck on the end of sentences
salaam alaikum	peace be with you
alaikum salaam	and peace also with you
mash kuur	you (hardly used)

Other phrases

where is?	minayn?
where are you from?	anta min minayn?
what time is it?	waqt shin hoo?
that's ok/enough (if someone's serving you something for example)	kaavi
in the name of God (said before eating or starting something)	bismilah
yes	ahey
no	abdei
yes/by God	walahi
come here	wahai
tomorrow	subh
yesterday	yaames
today	ilyom
I am going to . . .	ana nymshee shawr . . .
I'm from . . .	ana min . . .
Australia	oostralia
Britain	bretanya
Canada	kanada
Ireland	irelanda
New Zealand	new zeeland
the US	amreeka
hotel	vondeg
do you have?	an dak?
is there?	khalig?
water	ilma'
food	lukeel
white person	nsara (pl. nasrani)
good	zaiyn
very good	zaiyn hatta
not good	maw zaiyn
how much is?	baash?
a little less? (to knockdown the price)	ingus shwei?
a little (or slowly)	shwei shwei
I am full	ana stuk fait
I am tired (male)	ana v'tran
I am tired (female)	ana v'trana
take it easy	beshawr

Numbers

1	wahid
2	ethnayn
3	athlath
4	arba'a
5	hamsa
6	setta
7	seb'a
8	thimayna
9	tesa'a
10	ashara

Glossary

Aftout Seasonal water course or flood zone.

Ain Spring.

Aklé Zone of jumbled, live dunes

Barkane Moving, crescent-shaped dune with characteristic "crest".

Barrad Teapot.

Birr Well.

Boubou Loose cotton shirt or cloak

Cheikh Elder respected for his knowledge.

Chemama Flood plain of the Senegal River.

Cherif Person who claims descent from the Prophet Muhammad.

Dar House.

Dahr/dhar Fault line (cliffs or escarpment).

Erg District of shifting ("live") sand dunes.

Girba Goatskin water bag.

Guelb Isolated mountain or peak.

Guelta Pond or small lake, sometimes augmented by a spring.

Guetna Date harvest (July & Aug).

Hal-Pulaar Fula-speaking people, including Fula and Tukulor

Hammada Vast stony plateau.

Houli Man's headscarf, turban.

Kas Drinking glass.

Kedia Long tableland, mesa.

Khaima Tent.

Ksar Fort.

L'msal Prayer ground.

Marabout Holy man from a marabout tribe.

Nsara Nazarene/Christian; white person (pl. *nasrani*).

Reg Flat gravel, windblown stony plain.

Rifi Hot wind from the north.

Sebkha Dry, salt plain.

Sirwal Loose, cotton pantaloons.

Tamourt Long, wooded depression, flooded during the rainy season.

Tabel Tea tray.

Tell Hill covering the ruins of a former settlement.

Tifinagh Ancient Libyan/Berber writing.

Tikit Temporary round hut constructed during the *guetna*.

Tishtar Dried meat.

Zrig Sweet, diluted milk given as a sign of welcome and supposed to cure many benign aches.

1.1

Nouakchott

Whipped by sandstorms for more than two hundred days a year, Mauritania's capital, **NOUAKCHOTT**, lives up to its Hassaniya name meaning "place of the winds". This is the biggest city in the Sahara, a sprawling place of almost a million inhabitants – more than a third of the country's population. Once you're settled in, it's hard to dislike; you can wander around more or less unhassled, and there's a certain ease in the wide, tree-lined streets bordered by drifts of sand.

The site of the new city of Nouakchott was nominated by Bidan elders in 1957, who chose to raise it near a French military post on the old imperial road. With funds limited and formal independence pressing, the city was hastily planned and constructed for an anticipated population of 50,000. It was already 20,000 by 1969, when the first great Sahel drought tipped the country into crisis. By 1980 the immigrant influx had pushed it past 150,000, and since then it has risen to over 900,000.

Arrival, transport and accommodation

The **layout** of Nouakchott can be confusing at first, and there are no heights from which to get your bearings. The city's main street, **Avenue Abdel Nasser**, runs east–west from just south of the Ksar district, through the centre, **La Capitale**, and out to the beach, 5km away. Cutting across this road at right angles are **Avenue Kennedy** and **Avenue Charles de Gaulle**, which connect the affluent, ambassadorial and expat quarter of **Tavrak Zeina** on the northern edge of La Capitale to the extensive commercial districts of the Cinquième Arrondissement in the south (Nouakchott is divided into numbered **arrondissements**, subdivided into alphabetical blocks called **îlots**). Most hotels, restaurants and shops are within a short walking distance of the Kennedy–Nasser intersection and this district is likely to be your main focus for the time you're in town.

The **airport** is in the Ksar district, northeast of the city centre. It's no longer necessary to complete a currency declaration on arrival, though some officials still try to play on this by asking you to declare your assets, then levying a €20.00 "tax"; politely refuse to fill in the form or pay, and move on. The airport has a small bank with worse exchange rates than anywhere else in town, a newsagent, a café, a bookshop and car rental available, but few other facilities. The official **airport taxis** charge around UM500 to the city centre, but if you can manage to lug your luggage as far as the large roundabout outside the airport, you'll easily find an ordinary taxi willing to take you to the town centre for only UM200.

Drivers arriving from Nouadhibou via the beach route are introduced to Nouakchott by the thatched cottages of *Terjit Camping*, separated from the city itself by 4km of waste-scattered dunes. Most **taxis brousse** arrive and leave from garages on the outskirts of Nouakchott, and the taxi fare from each to the centre shouldn't be more than UM400. Destinations along the Route de l'Espoir are served from the **gare routière** in the northeastern Ksar district; from here bush taxis go to Aleg (4hr; UM1200), Kiffa (9hr; UM3200), Tidjikja (10hr; UM5000), and Ayoune al

115

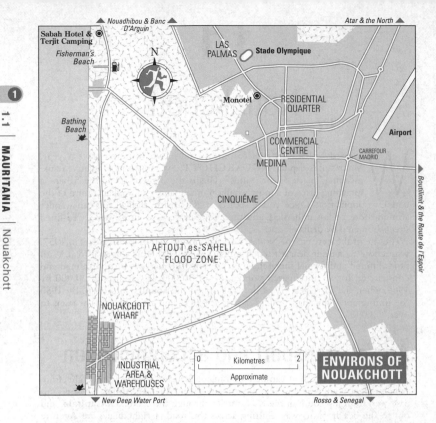

ENVIRONS OF NOUAKCHOTT

Atrous (13hr; UM4200). For Rosso (at least 3hr; UM1200) go to **Garage Rosso**, 7km south of town; for details of crossing into Senegal at Rosso, see p.124. **Garage Atar**, 2km north of the airport, serves Atar (6hr; UM2500), Choum (8hr; UM3500) and Zouérat (at least 12hr; UM5500). To get to Nouadhibou (24hr; UM5000), go to **Garage Nouadhibou** in the Cinquième district, southwest of the centre; also here is **Garage Cinquième**, serving Keur Macene and Ndiago (3hr; UM1500). For Kaedi (6hr; UM2600) and Sélibabi (18hr; UM6000), head to **Garage Sélibabi**, south of the centre, near the Moroccan mosque.

Ordinary **taxis** (normally Mercedes or Peugeots) will take you around town for UM200 and to the outskirts for UM300. Alternatively, you can travel along set routes using one of the battered old Renault **shared taxis** *(taxi toute droite;* UM50).

Accommodation

The range of accommodation available in Mauritania is much better than anywhere else in the country. Besides a decent range of hotels and hostels, there are worthwhile **apartments**, sleeping up to three, to choose from at *Semiramis Appartements,* at the end of Avenue Kennedy nearest the church (☎529 13 97, ⓦwww.semiramis.mr; UM15,000 per apartment) – especially good value if you hanker for your own kitchen and a lounge with TV. To **camp**, head to *Terjit Camping,* about 500m north of the Plage du Pêcheurs along the Nouakchott–Nouadhibou beach track (☎631 04 57 or 660 88 95), which you'll find adjacent to the *Hôtel Sabah.* Here there are charming, basic but clean three-person beach huts (UM3700) set among dunes, with fine views of the sea and fishing boats; camping is UM1200 per person. All the **hotels** and **hostels** reviewed below are in the Capitale area.

Auberge La Dune Opposite Air France on av Kennedy ☎525 62 74, ☎525 37 36. Homely hostel, with several delightful shady courtyards. Saïd, the Tuareg owner, is an expert guide and can manage most nooks and crannies of the country. Dorm beds UM2500, **❸**

Auberge Nomades Near the Naftec petrol station on av Charles de Gaulle ☎529 13 85, ☎525 11 61. Clean, friendly and well located right by the city's cheapest eating places. Accommodation is under a canvas awning or in simple rooms with a/c; parking is available in the large sandy courtyard. Dorm or tent bed UM1000, **❷**

Bivouac Paris Dakar Near the Saudi mosque ☎631 80 33, ℮etoiledetafarit@yahoo.com. Owned by a Frenchman and his Mauritanian wife, this is the overlanders' favourite, with space for parking and camping in a secluded courtyard shaded by large trees. UM1000 per person using their own tent. **❷**

Hôtel el Amane av Abdel Nasser ☎525 21 78,

℮elamane@toptechnology.mr. Probably the best downtown mid-range hotel in Nouakchott, with a pretty courtyard, charming staff and a good French restaurant serving alcohol. **❺**

Hôtel Halima Off av Charles de Gaulle ☎525 79 20, ℮reservation@hotelhalima.com. Homely establishment with a good coffee shop. Rooms in the main hotel are rather small, so ask to stay in the newer annexe where rooms are larger and newer. **❻**

Hôtel Mercure Nouakchott Marhaba av Abdel Nasser ☎529 50 50, ⊛www.mercure.com. The smartest hotel in the country and one of only three in the capital with a swimming pool. **❽**

Hôtel Oasis av Charles de Gaulle ☎525 20 11. Simple but pleasant, spacious, en-suite rooms with a/c; some also have TV and hot water. The best rooms are at the front of the hotel and have balconies. If the entrance to av Charles de Gaulle ic closcd, ontor through thc rcccption of the adjoining *Hôtel Houda*. **❸**

The Town

It's quickly apparent that Nouakchott doesn't spill over with things to see and do. There are, however, some very rewarding local **markets** and various **artisanal centres**, while the most obvious destination is the **beach**. In the centre itself, the national **museum** (Mon–Thurs & Sun 8am–3pm; UM300; ☎525 37 22), behind the *Marhaba* in the Maison du Parti du Peuple, is well worth a visit, though note that labelling is in French and Arabic. It contains a fine collection of beads, arrowheads and pottery, with the oldest artefacts to your left as you enter. Upstairs, past the huge elephant's tusk found near Zouérat, are ethnographical collections on nomads and their way of life.

The **silver market** (Foire Artisanale) is a taxi ride out of town on the Rosso road. Although the place is usually rather empty, there's an impressive array of silver-inlaid ebony chests, Tuareg earrings and bracelets, as well as wood carvings. Take a look behind the booths and you'll see craftsmen in small workshops making intricate jewellery out of silver and ebony. Don't forget to browse round the large building at one end of the market, as it has a good collection of ancient arrowheads and pottery, though you can buy similar items more cheaply in the Adrar (p.130).

The city's **general markets** are worth wandering around. The **Marché Capitale**, south of Avenue Abdel Nasser and between avenues Kennedy and de Gaulle, is the place to buy the flowing blue **dra'as** worn by men, or the women's **malahfas**, colourful body-length wraps. At the back of this market is a women's centre where the speciality is **embroidery**. Pushy souvenir sellers cluster between the Marché Capitale and the intersection of Avenue Abdel Nasser; if you don't wish to buy, just give a firm "no" and move on. Southwest of the centre, at the **Marché Cinquième**, you can shuffle along sandy lanes between tubs of home-made peanut butter and buckets of dried and fresh fish, and a wealth of good fabric, including exceptionally fine-weave lightweight muslin in attractive prints. A clutch of medicine and *gri-gri* sellers, with their displays of monkeys' and birds' feet and lizards' and turtles' heads, make for macabre browsing.

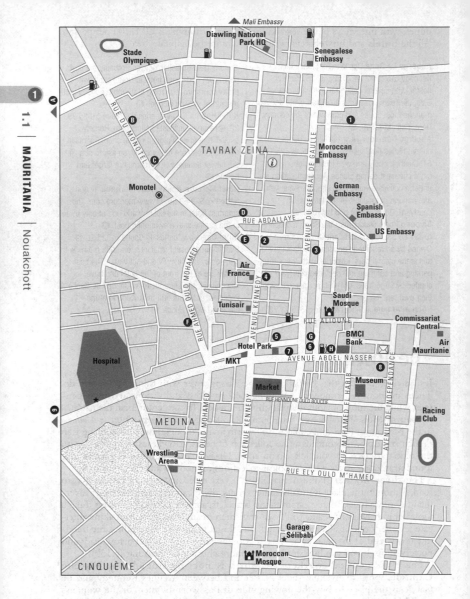

▲ *Mali Embassy*

Diawling National
Park HQ

Senegalese
Embassy

Stade
Olympique

Ⓐ

Ⓑ

Ⓒ

TAVRAK ZEINA

Ⓘ

❶

Moroccan
Embassy

Monotel

German
Embassy

Spanish
Embassy

Ⓓ

RUE ABDALLAYE

Ⓔ ❷

US Embassy

Ⓒ

Air
France

Ⓓ

Saudi
Mosque

Tunisair

Commissariat
Central

RUE ALIOUNE

Ⓕ

❺

Ⓖ

BMCI
Bank

Air
Mauritanie

Hotel Park

❼

❻

Ⓗ

MKT

AVENUE ABDEL NASSER

❽

Hospital

Market

Museum

RUE HENNOUNE OULD BOUCEIF

MEDINA

Racing
Club

Wrestling
Arena

RUE ELY OULD M'HAMED

Garage
Sélibabi

CINQUIÈME

Moroccan
Mosque

In the opposite direction from the centre, near the airport, is a relaxed boutique
selling souvenirs (☎525 14 29). Run by a Frenchwoman, Madame Sahuc, it offers
tie-dyed **batiks**, **wall hangings**, purses and so on, many of which are made by
local prisoners as part of their rehabilitation. To get there by car or taxi, head to the
airport roundabout and then take the road west heading towards the Boulevard
Péripherique; just before the next roundabout take a right turn down a tiny lane –
the boutique is in the garden of a private house, on your left. Further out, past the
airport roundabout on the road to Atar, opposite the entrance to the military air-

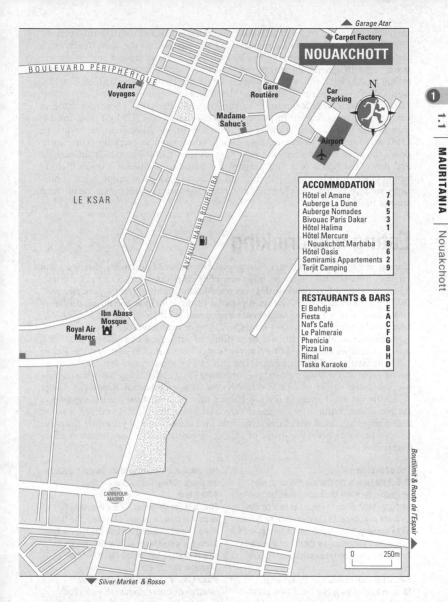

Garage Atar

Carpet Factory

NOUAKCHOTT

BOULEVARD PÉRIPHÉRIQUE

Adrar
Voyages

Gare
Routiére

Car
Parking

Madame
Sahuc's

N

Airport

LE KSAR

AVENUE HABIB BOURGUIBA

ACCOMMODATION

Hôtel el Amane	7
Auberge La Dune	4
Auberge Nomades	5
Bivouac Paris Dakar	3
Hôtel Halima	1
Hôtel Mercure Nouakchott Marhaba	8
Hôtel Oasis	6
Semiramis Appartements	2
Terjit Camping	9

RESTAURANTS & BARS

El Bahdja	E
Fiesta	A
Naf's Café	C
Le Palmeraie	F
Phenicia	G
Pizza Lina	B
Rimal	H
Taska Karaoke	D

Ibn Abass
Mosque

Royal Air
Maroc

CARREFOUR
MADRID

Boutilimit & Route de l'Espair

0   250m

Silver Market & Rosso

port (Direction de l'Air), is Matis, a **carpet factory** set up as a women's income development initiative. They produce finely woven camelhair **rugs and carpets** in subtle desert colours with rigorous geometrical patterns – sadly, these are out of range of most pockets.

The beach

The **beach** is the main event in Nouakchott. Once you've crossed the wasteland that separates the city from the sea, there's a solid phalanx of dunes, then an impressively straight sweep of fine sand stretching north and south to the horizon. The **Plage des Pêcheurs** is crowded and atmospheric all the time, mostly with Pulaar and Wolof fishermen, but the best time to visit is at around 5pm, when the boats come in against the setting sun, and there are cold-drink kiosks and stalls selling freshly fried fish with hot sauce. There are two popular bathing beaches, one a short walk north of the Plage des Pêcheurs opposite *Terjit Camping* and *Hôtel Sabah*, the other 500m south of the Plage des Pêcheurs. There's no shade so bring plenty of sunscreen. To get there, take a shared taxi (UM50) from the car park by the hospital west of the centre, or try to haggle an ordinary taxi down to UM300; to head on to the southern beach, you'll need to carry on 500m south down the coast road, towards the new port. Besides the 4WDs which thunder up and down the beach with little regard for bathers, occasional hazards include strong currents and stinging jellyfish, and it's best to ask local people what conditions are like before you plunge in. As muggings are not unknown, avoid these areas at night.

Eating and drinking

Eating in Nouakchott is better than anywhere else in Mauritania – there's a small range of international cuisine on offer, including Mexican, Moroccan and Lebanese. There are several **fast-food outlets** on rue Alioune, linking Avenue Kennedy with Avenue Charles de Gaulle. The most popular of these include *Snack Irak*, *Ali Baba's* and – best of all – *El Prince*, all serving *chawarma* for UM500, burgers, beans (*foul*), falafel and grilled chicken; most keep the TV on at maximum decibels.

Mauritania is officially dry, and **bars** don't advertise; the best places for a drink are the *Casablanca* and the *Taska Karaoke* (see below). Another option is the *Racing Club* on avenue de l'Independence, but this can be quite empty but for the occasional expat and is usually closed on Saturdays. For a distinctively Mauritanian tipple, ask a taxi driver to take you northwest to the *Democratic Republic of Congo Consulate*, off a side street in the Las Palmas suburb west of the Stade Olympique. Rather disconcertingly for anyone in search of a visa, this place is widely known as a drinking club, filled with local reprobates and the occasional prostitute. Seats are worn-out metal beds, the drink of choice is pastis and the conversation often emotional.

Restaurants

El Bahdja Next to the Catholic church on rue Mbdallaye. Excellent Moroccan *tajines* for UM1000–1400, though service can be a bit slow.
La Dune At *Auberge La Dune*, opposite Air France on av Kennedy. Typically one dish of the day, such as spaghetti bolognese, for UM800, or omelettes for UM400. They don't start serving until around 2pm though.
Fiesta Las Palmas ☎529 33 28. Authentic Mexican food, at the pricier end of things, in a homely atmosphere.
Hôtel El Amane av Abdel Nasser ☎525 37 65. Good, moderately priced French food and the best steaks in town.
Naf's Café rue du Monotel. Trendy café-bar with gateaux and good pancakes.
Le Palmeraie Next to the UN compound on rue Ahmed ould Hamed ☎525 73 44. Sophisticated French patisserie with a fine garden. The bread

and cakes are the best in town, though the pizzas are disappointing. Daily 7.30am–1pm & 4.30–11pm.
Phenicia rue Mamadou Konaté. Popular with locals and featuring a varied European and North African menu, including the best couscous in town. There is a secluded a/c room at the back for groups. Main dishes around UM1000–1500, omelettes UM500–800.
Pizza Lina rue du Monotel ☎525 86 62. Established pizzeria popular with expats and trendy Mauritanians. Serves alcohol (though not during Ramadan) and does good ice cream as well. The pizzas themselves will set you back around UM1300 each.
Rimal av Abdel Nasser, but difficult to find as the sign is almost completely obscured by vegetation. Long the restaurant of choice among gastronomes on a tight budget, with fish dishes and fried chicken, plus couscous and excellent *escalope cordon bleu*.

Taska Karaoke rue Mbdallaye, near the church ☏ 525 41 58. French-run restaurant which serves delicious seafood, though the portions are small.

Be ready later in the evening for soulful sing-alongs to French hits of the 1970s.

Listings

Airlines Air Algérie, av Abdel Nasser, next to Star Petrol Station ☏ 525 20 59; Air France, av Kennedy ☏ 525 39 16; Air Mauritanie, av Abdel Nasser east of the *Hôtel des Postes* ☏ 525 22 12; Air Senegal, c/o Agence Maghrebine de Voyage, av Charles de Gaulle ☏ 595 05 84; Compagnie Mauritanienne des Transports Aériens, av Kennedy ☏ 525 60 24; Royal Air Maroc, Immeuble SMAR, av Abdel Nasser, east of the *Hôtel des Postes* near the Palais de Justice ☏ 525 30 94; Tunisair, next to Librairie Vents du Sud on av Kennedy ☏ 525 87 62.

Airport Flight information on ☏ 525 83 19.

Banks The Banque Mauritanienne pour le Commerce International (BMCI) and the Banque Nationale de Mauritanie (BNM) can take ages to change money. They're open Mon–Thurs, Sat & Sun 7.30am–12.30pm. Out of hours, your best bet is to try one of the many bureaux de change along av Abdel Nasser. Alternatively, wander around the Marché Capitale and let the black-market money changers find you.

Bookshops Librairie Vents du Sud, av Abdel Nasser is the best. Scholarly works on Mauritanian culture and nature can be found at the French Cultural Centre, next to the French Embassy. Alternatively, check the *Marhaba's* more tourist-oriented offerings.

Car parts and mechanics Garage Express, bd Périphérique (☏ 525 75 48), is used by many aid agencies to fix their Toyotas. You could also try Adama Sow, an English-speaking mechanic who works for the US embassy (☏ 633 30 71). Parts for all the main 4WDs are on sale in the vicinity of the *gare routière* in the Ksar district.

Car rental Prices per day for the smallest town-car runabouts are around UM7300; expect to pay UM10,000 to head out of town. As for 4WD, Toyota Hiluxes go for around UM15,000 per day, usually including the services of a driver but excluding fuel. Rival operators Gazelle du Désert (☏ 525 06 69, ☏ 525 81 52) and Wefa (☏ 525 49 01, ☏ 525 50 09) face each other across bd Abdel Nasser; or check out Europcar for self-drive: they have an office in the *Mercure Marhaba* (☏ 525 11 36, ☏ www.europcar@mauritel.mr) and a branch at the airport terminal (☏ 525 83 20).

Cinemas The Oasis, dating from 1960, on av Charles de Gaulle shows Westerns, Bollywood and kung-fu flicks and occasional French and Egyptian movies for UM200–300. More upmarket is the Galaxy (☏ 638 4166) behind the Stade Olympique, which shows English movies every Saturday for UM500. The French Cultural Centre (☏ 525 25 46) shows French and Western movies three times a week for UM200.

Embassies and consulates Canada, av Charles de Gaulle ☏ 525 72 24; France, rue Ahmed Ould M'Hamed ☏ 525 17 40, ☏ ambafran@mauritel.mr; Mali, rue Palais des Congrès ☏ 525 20 78; Morocco, av Charles de Gaulle ☏ 525 14 11; Senegal, bd Périphérique ☏ 525 72 90; US, adjacent to the Presidential Palace ☏ 525 26 60; UK, c/o Honorary Consul, Sid Ahmed Ould Abeidna; ☏ 525 6172, ☏ 529 6493. The French embassy handles visas for Côte d'Ivoire, Burkina Faso, Togo and the Central African Republic.

Emergencies Police ☏ 17.

Hospitals and clinics West of the centre, the national hospital (Centre national l'hospitalier ☏ 525 85 13) is helpful, but you tend to come out with more illnesses than you went in with. Clinique d'Espoir on carrefour Madrid (behind the service station) has English-speaking doctors and nurses. Alternatively, try Clinique Chiva, off rue du Monotel (24hr; ☏ 525 80 80).

Internet access Nouakchott is not short of air-conditioned Internet cafés. A good place to look is along the bd Péripherique, between av Charles de Gaulle and rue du Monotel.

National Park offices Banc d'Arguin National Park (☏ 525 81 41, ☏ priba@mauritania.mr) has an office at av Abdel Nasser, near the hospital. The Diawling National Park office (☏ 525 69 22, ☏ pnd@opt.mr) is near the Senegalese embassy, just north of the bd Périphérique; book here to visit the park, though you pay at the park itself.

Post office The Hôtel des Postes is on av Abdel Nasser (Mon–Thurs & Sun 8am–4pm, or 9am–3pm during Ramadan). Collecting poste-restante mail depends on the availability of the bureau clerk but is otherwise efficient and costs UM110 per item. The city's main postbox is an unlikely-looking hole in the wall on the side of the building facing the *Marhaba*, with a drawing of an envelope above it.

Swimming pools There is a pool at the *Monotel Hotel* on rue de Monotel, open to non-residents (a week pass costs UM5000), and another at the *Marhaba* which you can use for free if you're dining there, otherwise you'll need to pay UM1500.

Telephones Calls abroad are most easily made from the numerous phone shops around town (from where you can also fax and make photocopies); a good place to find them is the intersection of av Charles de Gaulle and av Abdel Nasser. Make sure the shopkeeper sets the meter to zero before you begin.

Travel agents MKT, west of the av Abdel Nasser–av Kennedy intersection (☎529 12 55 or 641 74 38, ⊚www.mktours.net), are the biggest in Mauritania. They handle bookings for the *Keur Macene Lodge* near Rosso and the *Centre du Pêche Sportive* in Nouadhibou, and can arrange tours across the country. Adrar Voyages, at the Ksar end of bd Périphérique (☎525 17 17, ⊚adrarvoyages @toptechnology.mr), and ATV on av Charles de Gaulle (☎525 15 75, ⊚atv@compunet.mr) are both recommended, as is Secutour (☎525 23 82 or 642 69 00), next to *Rimal* restaurant.

Visas Visa "prolongation" is possible at the Commissariat Central, Lemine Sakho off av Abdel Nasser, east of the Hôtel des Postes. Besides your passport, bring two passport-sized photos, the UM10,000 fee, your passport and a photocopy of the relevant pages.

1.2

Southern Mauritania

S outhern Mauritania is the most densely populated part of the country, its major settlements connected by the 1099km Brazilian-built **Route de l'Espoir**. This *transmauritanienne* highway has certainly opened up the isolated southeast, bringing the far-flung regional capital of **Néma** within two days' drive of Nouakchott. There's a grim irony to the name, though. Instead of spreading wealth to the provinces, the "Road of Hope" has sucked them dry, offering swift escape from the parched countryside to the even less hopeful Nouakchott shanties – where the nomads and impoverished farmers can only sit and wait.

South of the Route de l'Espoir the population is largely non-Arabic-speaking, and the land is dry savanna and bush, with irrigated rice and millet lands near the river. The area around **Rosso**, on the north bank of the Senegal River, is of more than just passing interest, with a hunting lodge at **Keur Macene**, and rich birdlife at the **Diawling National Park**. North off the Route de l'Espoir itself is the fascinating upland region of the **Tagant**, containing the Moorish caravan towns of **Rachid**, **Tidjikja** and **Tichit**. **Oualata**, north of Néma, is also highly recommended for its unusual architecture, though you'll need plenty of time to get there.

For Bamako in **Mali**, various tracks drop down from the Route de l'Espoir: the one from Timbedgha to Nara passes near the site of **Koumbi Saleh**, probable capital of the ancient kingdom of Ghana.

Rosso and the southwest

ROSSO is one gateway to the rest of West Africa, offering the chance to cross into Senegal. If you're heading here in your own 4WD, you could deviate from the highway some 20km north of Rosso to visit **Mederdra**. An old gum-arabic centre at the heart of what was once the kingdom of Trarza, it's now renowned for wood and silver craftsmanship. The *gare routière* in Rosso itself is 500m out of town, an arrangement that seems to have been designed to allow the *calèche* drivers the opportunity of giving you a ride in their horse-drawn buggies (UM100). There's little to compel you to stay, though **rooms** with private facilities are available at the comfortable *Hôtel Al Asmaa* (☎556 90 29, ☎556 91 39; ❸), or the basic *Restaurant de Fleuve* (❶). You're unlikely to be stuck for **transport to Nouakchott** as *taxis brousse* leave until midnight, completing the run in three hours (UM1200) via a pleasant landscape of dunes and sand hills covered in acacias. To change money in Rosso, there's a bank just before the border gates, and bureaux de change between the border gates and the river.

Keur Macene and the Diawling National Park

Just south of *Hôtel Al Asmaa* in Rosso, directly opposite a building signed "Taamin", is the start of a track to the village of **KEUR MACENE** and the nearby **Diawling National Park** and the barrage at **Diama**, the track following the artificial dyke which separates the river from its flood plain.

The Keur Macene **lodge** (☎645 71 82), actually 9km from Keur Macene, doesn't feel at all like the rest of Mauritania – situated on the edge of a lake with large trees and a grassy lawn, it's a great place to relax after the stresses of the crossing from Senegal or visit as an excursion from Nouakchott, and the ideal base for a foray to the park.

Allow an hour and a half to reach the lodge from Rosso by public transport: a shared *taxi brousse* to the village costs UM500 per person, or you can hire the whole taxi for UM3000–4000. If you only manage to get as far as the village, ring the lodge to ask them to pick you up. Arriving from Nouakchott by 4WD, you can bypass Rosso using a shortcut at PK37, 37km north of Rosso and about 100km south of Nouakchott. **Accommodation** at the lodge itself consists of circular huts with bathroom and air conditioning (❼ including full board) and can be booked in advance at MKT Travel in the capital. If you're here between December and February, you may find you're sharing the place with parties of hunters from France who have come to shoot the numerous **warthogs** that roam the neighbouring swamps. This is also the best time for bird-watching at the **Diawling National Park** (see p.121 for park office details; entrance UM800), established in 1991 in the wake of the decimation of the environment of the lower Senegal delta, largely caused by the construction of two dams. To get there, go back to the dyke and turn right. Now that the pre-dam flood cycle has been restored (sluice gates have been installed to enable temporary flooding of the flood plain), there has been a massive increase in bird populations – the park now has significant numbers of wetland birds, including pelicans, black storks, spoonbills and flamingos. Local people have also benefited, with spectacular recoveries of fisheries and an improvement in grazing.

Crossing into Senegal

At Rosso, the **Senegal River** border crossing is open from 8am to noon and again from 3pm to 6pm. Foot passengers can opt to go by the car ferry that does the crossing every hour (UM50) or in one of the more frequent shared *pirogues* (UM100). Alternatively, south of Diawling, the 4WD track from Rosso continues to the barrage at **Diama**, another crossing into Senegal. If you're not taking a vehicle across the border, you could get a shared taxi from Nouakchott to the anonymous town of **Aleg**, from where you could get transport 60km down to the river and the Chemama (flood plain) town of **Bogué**. From here you can get across the river by *pirogue* to the Ile à Morfil in Senegal from here.

If you're driving your own vehicle, get your insurance for Senegal in Nouakchott (10 days, UM5700), rather than pay for it at the border, where it will be quite a bit more expensive. You'll have enough expenses to pay at the border anyway: it costs UM1000 to clear Immigration, UM2000 for Customs, UM500 in tax to the local commune, CFA4000 for the dam toll, and CFA2500 to clear Senegalese Customs. From here, it's another 30km to St-Louis.

The park headquarters are an hour's journey from the lodge, the drive taking you through most of the park – depending on the season, the vistas will be of vast flooded lakes or ponds. You can pay UM1200 per person to stay the night in the staff house, or the park's staff will put up a large Mauritanian-style six-person tent for UM3000. Whatever you decide, you'll need mosquito nets as the mozzies are very bad here. Meals can be arranged for UM300. From Diawling you can take a guide around the park, visit the beach (only 30km away) or ask a fisherman to take you out on the lake.

To Kaédi and Sélibabi

A less than engrossing two-hour drive from Nouakchott, **BOUTILIMIT** is the first major settlement along the Route de l'Espoir, a Moorish caravanserai with a large, permanent **market**. The religious capital of the country, Boutilimit is renowned for the collection of religious manuscripts housed at its Koranic school, whose library is among the richest and most important of its kind in Mauritania, and for its crafts – goat- and camel-hair rugs, and silverware.

KAÉDI, some 200km to the southeast (reached initially by a paved road beginning just before **Aleg**, then an eastward turn on to another paved road at **Bogué**), is Mauritania's fourth largest town, and a major market centre – it's a good place to buy cloth. A high percentage of Kaédi's people are settled, or semi-settled, Tukulor, whose white, long-horn zebu cattle can be seen roaming everywhere in the Gorgol and Guidimaka districts, to the southeast. For somewhere **to stay** in Kaédi, try the Base des Nations Unies way out on the eastern edge of town. It's officially intended for UN personnel, but if rooms are available (they have a/c and hot-water bathroom), they're worth angling for (❸). The cooking here is excellent and they have a swimming pool too. The *case de passage* of SONADER (Société National pour le Développement Rural; ❷) is nearer to the centre of town and has air conditioning, but you have to share facilities.

Heading east from Kaédi towards **Sélibabi**, Mauritania's southernmost and least typical town, is difficult in the dry season and usually impossible if it rains, although several *taxis brousse* try to maintain stages between one flooded river tributary and another. The journey is not made any easier by the impressive number of checkpoints along this "border" road, though the beautiful green valleys, stone hills and exotic bird-life compensate for these hassles. Alternatively, take the flights run by Air Mauritanie or the Compagnie Mauritanienne des Transport Aériennes.

The Tagant

The **Tagant** is a region of barren, stony plateaux, the remote location of some of Mauritania's oldest towns, some of which are notoriously hard to reach. It takes nine hours to get to **Tidjikja** from Nouakchott by 4WD, the road paved all the way except for a 45-kilometre stretch between Sangrafa and Letfatar, just west of Moudjéria. *Taxis brousse* run to Tidjikja from Nouakchott's *gare routière*, or you could catch a flight – there's a weekly service from the capital. The caravan route **north from Tidjikja** to **the Adrar plateau** – a journey of 470km – is best undertaken with high-clearance vehicles (two in preference) and – essential – an experienced guide; it's easier to go in this direction than the reverse, because you're travelling "with the sand".

If you're approaching from the west, the Tagant plateau first appears near **Moudjéria** (6hr from Nouakchott), with a short, steep climb to the top after you're past the town. At sunset, the panorama over Moudjéria and the sea of dunes beyond is nothing less than breathtaking. Another 20km further on is the **Tamourt En Na'aj**, one of the finest wooded valleys in Mauritania. The road crosses the valley by a small bridge – which turns into a ford during the brief wet season. To see a sliver of sub-Saharan Africa in the desert, turn right (south) just after the bridge as you approach from the west, and hire a local to guide you to the pools of **Matmata**. The track leads past several villages – beyond **Dar Es Salaam** (you'll recognize the village by the large boulders dotted among the houses), the track crosses a small palm grove and a sandy wadi before mounting a rocky platform. At the top of the platform you'll see numerous circular buildings, thought to be **granaries** dating back at least 2000 years. Continue on and take a left turn when you reach a junction; eventually the track leads down into a wadi strewn with large boulders dotted with seasonal pools during the autumn and winter. The rest of the journey down the wadi can only be done on foot. Look out for tracks of small **crocodiles** (see p.128) and **Nile monitor lizards** along the edges of the pools as you go along. As you descend, the wadi comes to an abrupt halt at the head of a large cliff forming the back of a stupendous horseshoe-shaped gorge. From here, look out for the crocodiles, which normally rest on a ledge on your right. You should also look out for **rock hyraxes** among the boulders, troops of **patas monkeys** playing on the sand dunes, and flocks of **grey hornbills** in the trees. During the rains the cliff becomes a massive waterfall tumbling down into the crescent-shaped muddy lake below.

Tidjikja and beyond

A 300-year-old bastion of conservative Bidan ideology, **TIDJIKJA** was founded by Moorish exiles from the Adrar, who planted the *palmeraies* for which it's still famous. The town subsequently prospered due to its position on the caravan trade route between Atar and Oualata.

As with other towns in the area, Tidjikja is split by a sizeable **wadi**, which runs wet for a few days at most each year. On the southwest of town, where you arrive, are most of the modern administrative blocks; the *gendarmerie*, where you should register your presence, is before the wadi on the right. The interest, though, lies up the slope in the **old town** on the northeast bank of the wadi, a fifteen-minute walk away, where it surrounds the Friday mosque, with palm groves and a jumble of houses spreading on either side. The houses, massively constructed out of dressed stone, cemented with and sometimes clad in clay, with flat roofs and palm-trunk waterspouts to drain storm water, display the ornamental *kefya* – triangular niches – that can be seen in various forms right across the Sahelian belt. Rooms are narrow, owing to the lack of long, strong beams, and focus inwards on interior courtyards.

The **airport** is a short distance west of town. Air Mauritanie has an office in a side-street off the market square (☎569 91 27). The only **accommodation** is the

Auberge des Caravanes (☎569 92 25 or 651 61 79, ☎569 92 25; ❷), located at the point where the paved road ends; the owner can arrange for the hire of a 4WD for UM15,000 per day. Other services in Tidjikja include a bank, a post office and a couple of Internet cafés.

Rachid

The first settlement on the route to the Adrar, **RACHID**, is only 38km northwest from Tidjikja, and is both more interesting and photogenic than Tidjikja itself. Several large rocky outcrops form an impressive backdrop to the town, best seen during sunrise or sunset. The deserted **old town**, on a hill separated from modern Rachid by a sandy wadi, was founded in 1723 as a Kounta Bedouin citadel, its piratical tradesmen preying on the caravans wending their way south from the Adrar to Tidjikja. At the foot of modern Rachid is the *Auberge Eraha*, a cosy place with a kitchen which guests can use, and secure parking for two vehicles (☎655 20 44 or 529 36 12; ❷, or UM1000 per person to sleep on the roof). The stone track that winds its way up from here offers a superb view of the old town.

Tichit

TICHIT is one of Mauritania's most interesting towns, dramatically located at the foot of the Tichit escarpment, and boasts some of the finest **Tagant architecture**, besides preserving the remnants of a complex ethnic division in its town plan. Only

The people of Tichit

Founded around 1150 AD, Tichit once had a population variously estimated at between six thousand and one hundred thousand. Today, however, the number of inhabitants has dropped to around five hundred, as more families leave each year and more houses are smothered by sand. Nevertheless, the basic ethnic divisions are still visible, encapsulating the ethnic complexity of Mauritania.

The biggest and most economically active group, who call themselves **Masena**, are concentrated on the south side of the town, towards the modern administrative quarter. They are probably descendants of the black peoples who lived all over the Sahara in earlier, more prosperous times, and who were pushed south into oases like Tichit (and Oualata) by the expansion of the desert – and by the Berbers. Wealthy Masena families used to keep slaves, known as **Abid** or **Ould Bella**, and most of these chose to hang on to their traditional way of life even after they were formally freed in 1982, working six days a week in their former masters' gardens or households, in return for their basic needs. Today the Abid form a separate group in Tichit, living in a ghetto in the east of the town. Many have mixed to some extent with Tichit's **Haratin** Moors, whose status as black freed slaves is much longer established, and who continue to enjoy a superior social status owing to their piety and long association with the Bidan Moors.

The Bidan Moors in Tichit are called **Chorfa**, a title indicating a claim to be descended from the Prophet Muhammad. Arabized Berbers who had established themselves in these parts by the ninth century, the Chorfa were originally part of the Zenaga group of Berber-speaking peoples. They are concentrated on the north side of Tichit, around the fourteenth-century mosque.

The final group are the **Rehian**, nomadic Bedouin Arabs who pass through the town to sell meat or take part in the date harvest. They move their tents around with the grazing, as much as 200km either way along the escarpment.

Despite this ethno-linguistic complexity, census returns from Tichit record 99 percent of the population as "Moor", meaning Hassaniya-speaking people – a reflection, perhaps, of the assumption that to identify oneself with any other ethnic group is politically suspect.

two or three dozen **houses** in the whole town are in reasonable condition, but these display a more elaborate and purer architecture than that seen in Tidjikja. Local stone of three different colours is used – greenish stone for the Chorfa quarter in the north; more crumbly, red stone used in the ruinous Masena quarter on the south side; and finely cut, hard, white stone, used only for the most prestigious buildings. The *kefya* ornamental niches are intricate, and the doors of a few of the old residences are still marvellously solid, with heavy, hobnailed bolts and latches made of wood from Mali. Sadly, the skills needed to maintain the buildings are fading, and few people are prepared to invest the time and energy needed.

The town's **museum** contains a few religious manuscripts and other interesting artefacts, including old doors and bits of weaponry. There are several *palmeraies* south of the town, between the houses and the **Aoukar depression** which, until about 1000 BC, was a vast reed-covered lake supporting a large population, though now dunes and saltpans cover the area, which is a haunt of the rare **addax** antelope. The salt from the saltpans here blows into the palm groves and coats the dates, making them inedible – so the people of Tichit have to spend the last two months of the ripening season painstakingly washing the crop with well-water. The joy of the actual harvest makes Tichit one of the best places to be at that time.

Travel practicalities

The route east from Tidjikja is clear enough to the Rehian stronghold of **Leckcheb** (a few windblown huts, some tents and a military post), but then the *piste* deteriorates. To the west of Tichit, the line of cliffs fades away and there's a sea of dunes in which to get stuck and lost. Eventually the track descends to the edge of the Aoukar depression, where it winds along the base of the scarp. Keep a lookout for **gazelles** on the way. You'd be lucky to get a lift here from Tidjikja; the alternative is to rent a vehicle from the *Auberge des Caravanes* – allow up to UM50,000 for the whole trip, but bargain furiously.

If you manage to reach Tichit without your own vehicle, you could be stranded here for several days. You couldn't ask for much more adventure – unless, that is, you're determined to go further and make a full circle by taking on the three days and 400km of *piste*-driving **from Tichit to Oualata** (see p.129). This represents a major desert crossing, and the police in Tichit will make sure you're part of a convoy of at least two vehicles and hire a guide. Mostly sandy, the *piste* follows the old caravan route around the Tichit and Oualata escarpments, with good wells at fairly regular intervals – Toujinet, Aratâne, Oujaf, Tagourâret, Hâssi Fouîni – and occasionally ascending the scarp to a kind of *Lost World* scene on top. You're unlikely to see other vehicles along the way. A less daunting forty-kilometre run east of Tichit leads to the nearly deserted and sand-swamped ruins of **Agrijit** – showing what Tichit itself is doomed to become.

The far southeast

East of the Route de l'Espoir's high point on the Tagant plateau – the Passe de Djouk – is the scrappy administrative town of **KIFFA**. The town has two **hotels**: the echoey *El Emel,* on the left past the *gendarmerie* just before you get to Kiffa (☎563 26 37, ☎563 26 38; ❹) and the *El Ghalgami* (☎563 23 45 or 641 53 23; ❹). If you book in advance you may get a place in World Vision's *Maison de Passage* (☎563 22 65; UM4000 single). Opposite the Commissariat de Police, Air Mauritanie (☎563 24 30) operate one flight a week to Nouakchott; the **airport** is just a few kilometres west of town.

The road from Kiffa to **Ayoun el Atrous** is very scenic by Mauritanian standards, with some fantastic **rock sculptures** just before Ayoun itself. If you happen to stop by a *guelta,* keep an eye open for small **crocodiles** disguised as logs and

Aoudaghost and the Ghana Empire

Aoudaghost (modern name Tegdaoust) was once a great trans-Saharan trade city on the edge of what was then grassland. Its inhabitants were probably speakers of a Mande language like Soninké. From perhaps 500 BC, caravans of horses and bullocks used to arrive from Marrakesh and the Roman Empire's Mediterranean shores. By the third centruy AD, the domestication of the camel had improved the viability of the trans-Saharan trade and Aoudaghost flourished on the commerce through most of the first millennium AD, in later years repulsing Berber Almoravid attempts to subjugate and convert it to Islam. The rapidly expanding empire of Ghana – focussed on Oualata and Koumbi Saleh – captured the town around 1050, but within a decade Ghana's Muslim western neighbour, **Tekrur**, helped the Berber Almoravids to invade and convert Ghana. By early in the twelfth century, the Berbers were leaving again, and over the next century both Tekrur and Ghana were swallowed up by the mightier empire of Mali to the east. Aoudaghost was rebuilt in the sixteenth and seventeenth centuries, and then finally deserted. Today, it's only as interesting as the most recent excavations, and not easily visited (being so hard to find), unless a dig is in progress.

groups of **baboons** scrambling over rocks. Those in search of the ruins of **Aoudaghost** (see box above) should take the track heading north off the road about 12km before Tintane. This leads to the town of **Tamchekket**, from where you will need a guide to take you to the ruins.

Ayoun el Atrous

AYOUN EL ATROUS is a more attractive town than most others along the road, its pink and red sandstone buildings set amid numerous small natural rock formations. If you're into collecting old trade beads, you'll enjoy the **market**. The town is also the starting point for one of the three principal *pistes* to **Mali**, a two-day trip to Bamako by *taxi brousse*.

There are weekly flights here from Nouakchott costing around UM12,750 one-way (Air Mauritanie here is on ☎515 13 78). Ayoun's **bank** should be able to change money, but may need to call Nouakchott to check the rate, the charge for which you might have to pay. The *Hôtel Aïoun,* on the right just before the *Garde Nacional* (☎515 14 62; ❹), has overpriced, en-suite air-conditioned rooms, though the view from the top storey is very fine. A cheaper alternative is to stay at the spartan *Auberge des Amis* (☎515 14 34; UM1500 per person in a tent) near the hospital,

The crocodiles of the Sahara

The writers of ancient Greece and Rome, including Herodotus and Pliny the Elder, mentioned the existence of crocodiles in the Sahara, but these accounts were not confirmed until the tantalizing discovery of fresh croc footprints in southern Algeria in 1864. Subsequently two more isolated populations were discovered, one in the Tagant Plateau of central Mauritania and the other in the Ennedi Mountains of southern Chad. The last Algerian desert crocodile was shot in 1924, and the Mauritanian population had been thought extinct since the 1930s. However, in the late 1990s Saharan crocodiles were rediscovered near Ayoun el Atrous.

These reptiles are **Nile crocodiles** (*Crocodylus niloticus*), though at under 2.5m in length, they're much smaller (and also less aggressive) than their counterparts which dwell in rivers and lakes. The Saharan crocodiles live in caves and burrows during the dry season, and migrate in search of water. Studies are under way to find out whether they are relicts of a bygone, wetter, era or have actually adapted to the climate of the southern Sahara.

100m north of the *Aïoun*. You can get a meal there or at *Restaurant Meilleur*, next to the *Aïoun*, which does chicken and peas for UM450.

Koumbi Saleh

The putative capital of the Ghana empire, **KOUMBI SALEH** is the most important medieval site in West Africa, though archeologists have barely scratched its huge extent, which unfortunately means that unless you've got a shovel there's not much to see. If you're bent on visiting the ruins, press on to **Timbedgha** (Timbedra) and then aim for the Malian town of Nara from there. The site is some 65km southeast of Timbedgha, close to the main route to Nara, and there's a chance of getting there by ordinary *taxi brousse* bound for the border, as long as you're prepared to pay a little extra for the diversion.

Koumbi Saleh is estimated to have had a population of about 30,000, which would have made it one of the largest cities in the world at the time. The Arab geographer Al-Bakri, writing in 1067, described a conurbation of two towns, a northern one with twelve mosques, and, 10km to the south, the royal town of **al-Ghala**, with huts arranged concentrically around a palace. Between the two, along the royal road, was a continuous "suburb" of houses. Curiously, although traces of the royal part of Koumbi Saleh have been found, the royal quarter doesn't appear to have been constructed in stone. The main part of town is more impressive, successive excavations having uncovered massive stone houses, an enormous mosque and flagstone floors covering a more ancient layer of buildings.

Néma and Oualata

The *transmauritanienne* ends with a whimper at the woebegone town of **NÉMA**, a cluster of shops and workshops surrounding a gritty wadi. The **old town** is worth a visit if you have time to kill, with some Oualata-style buildings, though without the paintings and in a worse state of repair. The basic *Auberge Moulaye Omar* behind the market offers simple rooms with breakfast included in the rate (℡650 34 89, ✉m.moulaye1@caramail.com; ❶).

There's **transport** to Nouakchott and Ayoun in the main *taxi brousse* garage at the western end of town, but for Oualata, you'll need to wander through the maze of streets north of the wadi and ask for the shop of Mohammed Lemine De'de, who drives to Oualata almost every evening around 5pm. He charges UM3000 in the front and half price to cling onto the goods at the back. It's a beautiful but bone-shattering four-hour ride from there to Oualata, and you'll need to wrap up if you're travelling in winter. There are two *pistes* leading south from Néma to Nara in Mali, but these should only be attempted in convoy.

Oualata

The glamour of **OUALATA** comes from the amazingly beautiful bas-relief ornamentation of its house walls. The decorations, of gypsum, white and red clay, and indigo, are designed and applied by the women, and although they're personal works, they share certain motifs and a thoroughgoing exuberance. Inside the houses, the effects created can be stunning; the doors are highly stylized as well, the best ones studded with copper and silver.

The town's origins go back to the eleventh century, to the heyday of the Ghana empire, when it was a Soninké town called Birou. It was destroyed in 1076 by the Almoravids, then re-founded in 1224 by Moorish merchants fleeing from Ghana's capital. It rose to fame equal to that of Timbuktu and Djenne, featuring in medieval European maps of Africa. At its zenith, skins, ivory, slaves, gold and kola nuts passed through to reach Arab markets in North Africa. The town faded with the decline in the great trans-Saharan commerce at the end of the seventeenth century, but it has kept its worldwide eminence as a centre of **Islamic scholarship**, the basis of long-term rivalry with Timbuktu. There are only twenty places in its Koranic school, creating a permanent waiting list of anything up to ten years.

You'll need to take a guide to see the interiors of houses; people will accost you to offer their services for half a day or a full day. One of the more interesting is that of Bati, the town's marabout, who traces his ancestry back 800 years to the founder of the town. His house is typical of many in Oualata, with a sculpted entrance leading to a small room with stone seats at either end, where business would have been transacted or children taught. This room opens onto a courtyard surrounded by several rooms, with steps leading up to more rooms and other compounds. The reception room, off one of the upper courtyards, has carpets spread on stick frames on both sides, instead of the mattresses used elsewhere in Mauritania. Note the fine white sand sprinkled deliberately on the floor and the numerous niches used for Koranic manuscripts and oil lamps.

If you're really into religious manuscripts, ask to see the **manuscript museum**, which has drawers full of 1569 ancient Korans and other books, the oldest dating back to the year 999. Don't forget to visit the **Maison des femmes**, where you can buy miniature replicas of an Oualatan house with its courtyard and rooms.

Opposite the *gendarmerie*, where you should register once you arrive, is the most comfortable **auberge** in town, the *Bon Accueil* (❸), which has a large parking area and proper toilets and showers. If more traditional accommodation is what you're after, head for the *Hôtel Oualata*, part of an original Oualata town house (❸); to find it, ask for the owner, Ba Ould Gemni. The cheapest option is the basic *Auberge de l'Amitié*, between the old mosque and the Cooperacion Espagnole office (❷). The owner, Mullai Ould De, does guided tours of the town (UM500 for a half day).

1.3

The Adrar

Breaking through the sands of the Sahara, the **Adrar plateau** is Mauritania's most outstanding region. Though nowhere higher than 1000m, the gaunt, brown scenery is strikingly clawed into deep **gorges** and sheer, cliff-edged mesas, surrounded by wind-carried **live dunes**. The town of **Atar**, plus a handful of villages, and the ancient settlements of **Chinguetti** and **Ouadane**, account for almost half the population; camels and oases of date palms determine the economy. The ubiquity of Neolithic stone tools – some remarkably small and fine – adds further interest to the area.

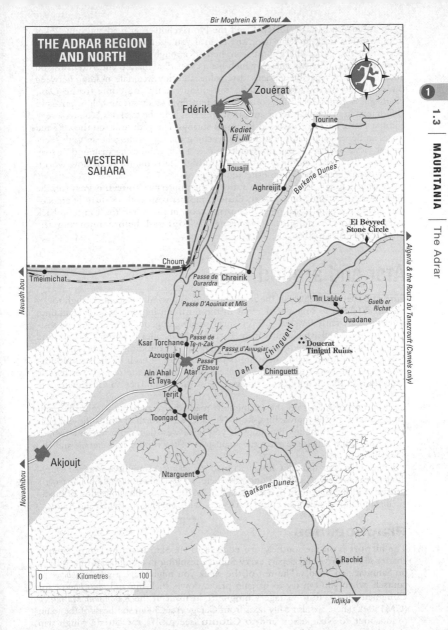

THE ADRAR REGION
AND NORTH

Bir Moghrein & Tindouf ▲

N

Zouérat

Fdérik

Kediet
Ej Jill

Tourine

WESTERN
SAHARA

Touajil

Aghreijit

Barkane Dunes

El Beyyed
Stone Circle

Choum

Passe de
Ourardra

Chreirik

Tin Labbé

Guelb er
Richat

▲ Algeria & the Route du Tanezrouft (Camels only)

Tmeimichat

Passe D'Aouinat et Mlis

Ouadane

◄ Nauadhibou

Ksar Torchane

Passe de
Te-n-Zak

Passe d'Amojjar

Chinguetti

Douerat
Tinigui Ruins

Azougui

Passe
d'Ebnou

Atar

D a h r

Chinguetti

Ain Ahal
Et Taya

Terjit

Toongad

Oujeft

Nouadhibou ◄

Akjoujt

Ntarguent

Barkane Dunes

Rachid

0   Kilometres   100

Tidjikja ▼

To Atar

The sealed Nouakchott–Atar road is efficient, taxis taking about six hours to complete the journey, usually stopping at the ancient copper-mining centre of **Akjoujt** on the way for food and petrol. With your own transport, you could overnight en

131

route at the lush oasis of **TERJIT**, off the Nouakchott–Atar road and only 25km from Atar. The track to Terjit is on the right if you are coming from Nouakchott, next to the first police checkpoint; from here it's a rough twelve-kilometre ride past foreboding cliffs until the village, which has a car park at the top end. After this you enter a world of vegetable gardens, date palms and tiny waterfalls nestling between the cliffs of a narrow gorge. After a ten-minute walk you come to the *Oasis Touristique de Terjit* (UM1500), consisting of tents by a sandy stream below a massive cliff draped in maidenhair ferns and stalactites. Past here the track leads on to several bathing pools, the lower two fed by warm springs. The path leads up the cliff and passes an upper cold-water pool before reaching the top of the plateau with spectacular views of Terjit. If you do decide to take a dip, avoid using shampoo or soap to reduce the impact on the environment. At night, look out for small glow worms by the stream between the campsite and the pools.

Continue a tough 35km further south via the impressive **Tourvine Pass** (off the Terjit–Atar track) and you come to **Oujeft**, another oasis with its share of archeological and paleontological relics, like many spots in the Adrar. You can loop back northwest to the delightful *palmeraie* of **Toungad** before rejoining the Nouakchott–Atar road.

Atar and around

From the edge of the plateau the road commences a winding ascent through rocky hills to **ATAR**, the largest settlement in the northern interior. Modern buildings and offices are fairly few, but this is a surprisingly energetic place, boosted by visitors arriving on charter flights from Paris and Marseilles between October and April. Although the town does have a maze of old buildings, a *palmeraie* and a mosque dating from 1674, there are better examples of each in the surrounding towns and villages, so most travellers use Atar as base for the several worthwhile excursions in the vicinity, or as a staging post on the journey to Chinguetti (see p.135).

The centre of Atar is on the Chinguetti road (the second right from the main roundabout if you're approaching from Nouakchott). North of this is the old Ksar quarter with its crumbling buildings. If you head west (left) from the roundabout you cross a dike which separates the main part of town from its *palmeraie* and the Séguélil wadi.

Between the Ksar and the Chinguetti road is a *quartier* of smiths who make everything from jewellery to saddle fittings; also here is a specialist leather shop. The town's **museum** (daily 9am–noon & 3–8pm daily; UM1000) has a fine collection of medicinal plants and Mauritanian cultural artefacts, with labelling in French and Arabic.

Practicalities

The **airport** is on the southeastern edge of town, 3km from the centre; French charter flights arrive and depart every Sunday, resulting in an influx of tour groups on Saturday and Sunday. The rest of the week you might have a whole *auberge* to yourself, when you can try to bargain prices down. Pick-ups and *taxis brousse* for Chinguetti depart from Garage Chinguetti, in front of the *Restaurant Marrakech* (UM1500). There are also daily taxis from Garage Atar, 300m southeast of the main roundabout, to Noaukchott and to **Choum** (see p.137), the latter a rough trip some 100km north, with beautiful scenery much of the way (3hr; UM1600). Once in Choum you can pick up the iron-ore train to Nouadhibou (see p.138) or Zouérat (see p.137); Choum taxi-drivers in Atar will ensure you get to the train on time. Before setting off for Choum, buy food for the journey, and take as much fresh water as you can – supplies on the train vary from limited to nonexistent and the water at Choum itself is unpalatably salty.

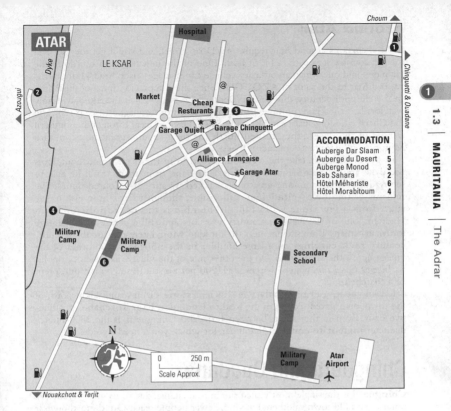

Accommodation and eating

Most accommodation will arrange **meals** for about UM1000 and breakfast for UM600, and on the road between the roundabout and the *Auberge Monod* are a number of inexpensive eating places where steak or chips can be had for UM500. Even cheaper Senegalese restaurants such as *Restaurant au bon coin* can be found in the sidestreets north of this road; a bowl of rice and fish will set you back around UM300.

Auberge Dar Slaam On the Choum road at the edge of town ☏546 46 22, ⓔcherif.dginde @caramail.fr. Simple rooms with a/c. Alternatively, two can pay UM2400 to stay in a *tikit*, one of the thatched huts used during the date harvest. ❷

Auberge du Désert On the eastern edge of town near the *Hotel El Waha* ☏546 46 35 or 631 06 17, ⓔmohdoua@yahoo.fr. Rooms and tents with mattresses on the floor. Staff are pleasant and there's Internet access too. Lone travellers pay half price for a double room outside weekends. ❷

Auberge Monod 250m east of the main roundabout ☏546 42 36. Besides a good location, this has a/c and private facilities and offers the best value of the mid-range establishments. ❸

Bab Sahara On the road to Azougui, past the wadi ☏647 39 66, ⓔjustusbuma@yahoo.com. Clean hostel with stone huts, several tents and a fine collection of old wooden doors. The owner, a Dutchman, speaks English. Vehicle owners have to pay UM300–500 to park. ❸ for a double in a stone hut, or ❷ in a tent

Hôtel Méhariste On the Nouakchott road ☏546 45 96. Comfortable s/c a/c rooms. ❹

Hôtel Morabitoun Just beyond the more northern of the two military camps southwest of the main roundabout ☏646 98 18, ⓔmourabitoune .hotel@caramail.com. Despite the air of gloom at this 1940s former French military mess hall, it does offer good value; rooms have private facilities, and some rooms also have a/c. ❷

Around Atar

Most excursions around Atar require 4WD or camel, and you'll get the best feel for the country if you try a bit of both. One of the best trips you can do in the vicinity – and one which an ordinary vehicle can manage – is to head 11km northwest of Atar to the ruins of **AZOUGUI**, once the Almoravid capital of the Adrar. In the eleventh century, this was the Berber base from which the Almoravid holy warriors launched raids on the Ghana empire town of Aoudaghost (see p.128), and the Ghana cities of Oualata and Koumbi Saleh. Having swept through the southern fringes of the desert, they turned north for their second great invasion, into Morocco and decadent Andalucian Iberia.

To get to Azougui, take the westbound road from the main roundabout, cross the dyke and *palmeraie*, ascend the Tarazi pass and from there you'll be able to see Azougui nestled among great cliffs banked by apricot-coloured dunes. The remains of the town's **citadel** are still visible, though there's little else to see apart from a few stone walls. Equally humble is the **necropolis** of Imam Hadrami, one of the eleventh-century warriors and still a centre of pilgrimage for Mauritanians. Both sites are near the mosque. More interesting are the seventh-century **rock carvings** on a large boulder in the northwestern corner of the village, across the sandy wadi. On the other side of the village, past the necropolis, is *Auberge Oued Illij*, which charges UM1200 per person to stay in a room, a tent or a thatched *tikit*.

Ten kilometres east of Atar there are ancient **stone circles**, and 20km north of the town, on a paved section of the road to Choum, is **Ksar Torchane**, an attractive oasis. Even further afield, between Terjit and Chinguetti, is the 1800-metre-diameter **meteorite crater** of Tenoumer, for which you'll need a guide.

Chinguetti and Ouadane

Chinguetti is the single most visited site in Mauritania, due to its mosque, ancient libraries and old town smothered in sand. Fewer people reach **Ouadane**, though it is more interesting and one of the most photogenic towns in the Sahara. Travel by *taxi brousse* to either town can involve a fair amount of waiting, and neither town has fixed telephones or mobile phone coverage.

From Atar to Chinguetti

It's about 120km from Atar to Chinguetti, the trip taking between two and four hours depending on your vehicle and which of the two routes you use. Heading east of town, you'll find the main road swings north to Choum; continue east, and the road forks after about 10km. The more straightforward route here is to keep right and you'll ascend the **Ebnou Pass**. About 1km from the top of the pass is a *gendarmerie*, and then it's another hour's driving on stony *piste* before you reach Chinguetti.

With your own 4WD, however, you can opt for the longer but more impressive route through the **Amogjar pass**: take the left branch of the fork and keep right on forks thereafter. After a steeply twisting series of hairpins, you reach the head of the Amogjar wadi, a gorge which gives onto a further incline and the Amogjar pass. In the interest of safety, it's standard practice for passengers to get out and walk the steepest ascents and descents. Among the sandstone massifs you'll see gun emplacements and the remains of military posts from the Polisario war. Up at the top squats the incongruous shell of "Fort Saganne", a fake built for the movie of that name in 1985. Up at around 800m, a couple of kilometres after the final climb, you pass a conical rock stack on the left, 50m or so in height. Under an overhang near the top of the stack there are some intriguing **rock paintings** of red lanky figures. Also look out for the fifty-centimetre-long **spiny-tailed uromastyx** (*dhub*), lizards which scamper into holes and crevices as you pass. Harmless vegetarians, they subsist between rains by drawing on reserves of fat in their spiky clublike tails, which they use to guard their tunnels.

Chinguetti

Whichever route you use to reach Chinguetti from Atar, you'll pass the turning for the upper route to Ouadane (see p.136), 10km before entering the "modern quarter" of **CHINGUETTI**. On this side of the town, the main building – in fact Chinguetti's most striking structure – is the former French Foreign Legion **fortress**, used in the movie *Fort Saganne*, starring Gérard Dépardieu, about the Legion's exploits in Algeria. The fortress doubled as set and film crew accommodation and is now a hotel; you can wander in and ask to climb the battlements for an excellent view of the town and the dunes that threaten to engulf it.

Cross the sandy wadi to the south and you come to old Chinguetti, a UNESCO World Heritage site. Once the most venerated town in Mauritania, it was a centre of learning, an assembly point for the pilgrimage to Mecca, and a city on the caravan route, with 11 mosques and 20,000 inhabitants. Its glory past, the town is now a small island of ruins in a sea of sand, dominated by a water tower. From the water tower, turn right, negotiating the dunes, to enter Chinguetti's most venerable quarter, dating at least back to the thirteenth century. Most of the buildings here are of stone, including the fine old **mosque**, off-limits to *nasrani*, though you can get fine views of it – complete with the five ostrich eggs atop its squat minaret, and much of the interior courtyard – from the dunes that have engulfed neighbouring alleys. The narrow alleys around the mosque are home to five ancient **Koranic libraries**, each of which typically charges UM500 entry; the Bibliothèque Ehel Hamoni is considered to have one of the best collections. The "*donnez-moi un cadeau*" brigade, who are out in some force in this area, will happily show you where the libraries are.

Relics of a much more ancient history can be bought in the **market**, near the *Hôtel Fort Saganne*. Extraordinarily fine, small **flint arrowheads** seem to be two a penny, as do the **barbs** that may have been used for fishing in a long-ago Adrar of forests and streams. These items are collected by children in the dunes, and you may come across a few yourself if you take a **camel ride** into the desert; Cheikh Ould Ahmar, owner of the *Auberge Rose des Sables*, can arrange this for UM4000 per day.

Practicalities

All *auberges* and hotels levy a UM200 tourist tax which is added to the rates they quote. All apart from *Fort Saganne* are in the old part of town. The phone numbers given below are for their representatives in Atar or Nouakchott. The *auberges* listed here provide meals, typically costing UM600 for breakfast, UM1000 for lunch or dinner; there's no reason why you can't stay in one *auberge* and eat in another.

Auberge du Maure Bleu East of the water tower ☎645 31 54, ✉sylviedesert@yahoo.fr. Tent accommodation (with rooms being built at time of writing), the best breakfasts in town and decent toilets. ❷
Auberge Echeylal East of the water tower ☎632 58 57, ✉echeylal@yahoo.fr. Pleasant garden surrounded by cosy stone rooms and tents. ❷
Auberge Fort Saganne Within the outer defence of the fort ☎525 63 08, ✉negib@toptechnology .mr. Much better value than the hotel on the same

site. Rooms have private facilities. ❷
Auberge La Vieille Ville Near the old mosque. Basic accommodation with parking. ❷
Hôtel Fort Saganne ☎525 63 08, ✉negib@toptechnology.mr. S/c rooms with a/c. ❹
Maison de Bien Être East of the water tower ☎630 12 38, ✉aubergevielleville@maktoob.com. Rooms surround a delightful terraced garden and retain various original features such as an *echeylaal* – a beam used for drawing water from a well – plus antique doors in one room. ❷

Ouadane and Tin Labbé

OUADANE was founded in 1147 by Berbers of the Ida-u-el-Hadj tribe. Its reputation, beyond the limits of the West African empires, as a **caravan crossroads** and trading centre for gold, salt and dates lasted nearly four hundred years. There was even a **Portuguese trading post** here as early as 1487, busily intercepting the trade for the main Portuguese base on the coast at Arguin Island. Ouadane's fortunes waned, unevenly, as it first succumbed to the onslaught of the sixteenth-century Saadian prince, Ahmed el Mansour of Morocco, who took control of the trans-Saharan trade and diluted much of the town's influence, and then lost its remaining economic power when the Alaouites invaded, also from the north, two centuries later.

The well-marked main route to Ouadane branches off the Atar–Chinguetti road, 10km west of Chinguetti, from where it's a couple of hours on stony *piste* through featureless desert before you arrive. There is also an eastern, lesser-used route to Ouadane, though this is a sandy, wadi-course for high-clearance 4WDs only. Guides are essential on the latter route due to the shifting nature of the dunes. If you can't find a vehicle going to Ouadane from Chinguetti, take a *taxi brousse* for Atar, then flag down any vehicles going in the opposite direction (tell your driver that you need to do this – the driver may even help); with luck, you'll find one heading to Ouadane rather than Chinguetti. If you haven't found any transport to Ouadane an hour out of Chinguetti, by which time you'll have reached the *gendarmerie* at the top of the Ebnou Pass, you may need to get off and wait by the road, though note that there may only be a couple of Ouadane-bound vehicles each day during the winter, and there may be hardly any at other times of year.

Once you're finally on the road to Ouadane, after several hours of dull stony desert you glimpse your destination clinging to a steep escarpment. The town is quite extraordinary, collapsing in ruins amid the jumble of rocks from which it was constructed eight hundred years ago. If you arrive in the middle of the day, with no shadows to define the buildings, you may not even notice them stacked along the scarp until you're almost upon them. Without doubt, the best time to arrive is in the evening when the setting sun bathes the ruins in pink light: no Saharan town is more spectacular than this.

Drivers using the main route approach the town along a wadi; on the left is *Auberge Weranei* (☎546 43 76, ✉mzmwarane12000@yahoo.fr; ❷), which has army-style tents, rustic **rooms** and an English-speaking owner. Further along at the foot of the escarpment is the efficiently run *Auberge Agouedir* (☎525 07 91, ✉agoueidir@yahoo.fr; ❷) with fine views of the old town. On the right, at the top of a rocky hill, is *Hôtel Palace*, with rooms with private facilities (❸). The track continues up the escarpment to reach the friendly *Auberge Vereny*, opposite the *gendarmerie* (where you should register), the only hostel in Ouadane itself (❷) and the nearest to the old town. All *auberges* provide a decent **meal** for UM1000 – the *Vereny* can even do savoury pancakes, which are a speciality of Ouadane. For a guided tour of the **old town**, west of the *gendarmerie*, ask for Khay ould Raajul, a local schoolteacher who speaks good English. The best approach is to start at the *palmeraie*, where you enter via the old town gate next to a fortified well, then work upwards. The ruins, with their modest wooden doors, granaries and ornamental niches, are still redolent of the prosperity this settlement had centuries ago.

Tin Labbé

Only 7km northwest of Ouadane, on the *piste* that curls round the mountain of Guelb er Richat, lies the semi-troglodytic village of **TIN LABBÉ**, where natural rock shelters and crevices have been incorporated into the cluster of stone and mud houses. If you've made it all the way to Ouadane, it would seem a shame not to walk up the wadi to see it. Among the tumble of huge boulders down by the vegetable gardens you can find rock paintings, and writing too, in both Arabic script and the archaic Tifinagh script of the Tuareg, a writing that traces its roots to a Libyan alphabet of the fourth century BC. If you don't fancy the trek to Tin Labbé, you can hire camels for the ride at *Auberge Agouedir* for UM1800 per day, plus UM2600 for the services of the camel driver.

1.4
The north

For travellers flying in from Europe or the Canary Isles, or arriving by land from Morocco, **Nouadhibou**, Mauritania's second city, comes as an unlikely first taste of West Africa. Isolated north and south by desert, and with no road connections with the rest of the country, it is far removed not just from Africa, but from the rest of Mauritania too. The main draw of this region for travellers is the immensely long **iron-ore railway** from **Zouérat** via **Choum**, which provides the best transport link to Nouadhibou. Intrepid birders could attempt a foray to the **Banc d'Arguin National Park**, south of Nouadhibou.

Choum and Zouérat

On the border with Western Sahara, **CHOUM** consists of a string of restaurants and crash-out houses where Nouadhibou-bound passengers snooze through the afternoon, waiting for the train. Arriving in Choum by taxi from Atar, leave your bags in the taxi; when the train arrives, you'll be driven alongside to meet the passenger wagon, right at the back. As the train may be over 2km long and often sets off within minutes, this is a taxi fare worth paying. If you're in your own vehicle, you can load it aboard the train by prior arrangement with the SNIM (see box, p.138).

Driving to Nouadhibou along the sandy route which runs alongside the tracks is not recommended without a guide (UM30,000), as half-buried cast-off lengths of track can cause terminal damage to your vehicle. The route crosses areas of sandy dunes, which a 4WD should be able to cover in two days. Avoid areas north of the railway line due to the mines along the border with Western Sahara.

Zouérat

The *route impériale*, the old military road, continues north from Choum to what is now the garrison town of **Fdérik**. East of Fdérik it's tarmac to **ZOUÉRAT**, the

The ore trains

The **iron-ore trains** carry on average 22,000 tons of crushed rock in a chain of wagons up to 3km long. **Schedules** depend partly on the speed of extraction at the mines, and on unpredictable hold-ups – damaged rails, engine failure and even, in the past, attacks by Polisario guerillas from Western Sahara – and travellers should realize that ore is the priority, not passengers.

In principle, three trains a day go from Nouadhibou to Zouérat (and vice versa), but the only one with a **passenger carriage** leaves Nouadhibou at 3pm and Zouérat at noon. These trains pass through Choum at 5.30pm or so from Zouérat, 2am from Nouadhibou. The usual journey time is around twelve hours from Choum to Nouadhibou, eighteen hours from Nouadhibou to Zouérat. In the passenger carriage, you could go for a **seat** or a **couchette** – given the length of the journey, taking the latter would be advisable. **Fares** are Nouadhibou–Zouérat UM1000/UM2200 seat/couchette; Nouadhibou–Choum UM800/UM2000; Choum–Zouérat UM400/1000. Riding the ore wagons is free – and you'll discover why, as the dust works its way into your soul. If you choose this option, buy flour-sacks from a local patisserie to protect your baggage, take a *houli* to wrap round your head, and have something warm for later in the night, when it can get remarkably cold.

Travellers with **vehicles** can sit inside them – in marginally more comfort – rocking on the flatbed wagons and held down with wire. The charge varies according to the size of the vehicle: from Nouadhibou to Zouérat it costs UM13,225 for an ordinary car, UM20,635 for a pick-up or minibus, and you'll need to contact Société Nationale Industrielle et Minière in Nouadhibou (☎574 29 75) at least 72 hours in advance to transport a vehicle. Their website, ⓦwww.snim.fr, has more background on the trains and may carry updated fares and schedules.

The journey generally passes without incident, with several stops to allow trains going the other way to pass. If you pick the right compartment you could find yourself sharing endless cups of tea and learning Hassaniya. The interest outside the carriage, even on a clear moonlit night, is minimal. For further information about taking the train from **Nouadhibou**, see opposite.

A **luxury train**, including a special observation carriage and cabins, but without the iron-ore wagons, also ploughs between Choum and Zouérat. For more details, contact SOMASERT (☎544 05 67) or check the Mauritania section of ⓦwww.cheminsdesable.com.

---

economic and political heart of the far north. If you're driving, you'll need to drive on the left on this section of road until the town boundary, then change to the right. Air Mauritanie runs two flights a week each way between Nouakchott and Zouérat. The iron-ore train from Nouadhibou and Choum gets in at 6am and departs at noon, arriving at Choum around 5.30pm and back to Nouadhibou around 6am. Tours of the spectacular **mining operations** can be arranged relatively easily from the *Hôtel Oasian* (☎544 06 05, ☎544 03 15; ❻), essentially a company resthouse – rooms have private bathroom and kitchen – with a restaurant serving food imported from the Canary Isles. A cheaper option is to stay in *Hôtel Tiris*, in front of the BMC bank (☎544 06 68, ☎544 01 57; ❹).

Nouadhibou

Set on the eastern side of the Cap Blanc peninsula, a finger of desert pointing into the sea, **NOUADHIBOU** ("Jackal's Well") is the first point of entry for overlanding West Africa travellers from Europe. It is a pale, flat, industrial city-satellite of Mauritania, where bars are permitted (or rather, alcohol is blind-eyed), and the mix on the streets add African, Mediterranean and Oriental traces to the predominant blue flowing robes of locals and of rural immigrants. Besides the busy **central market**, the area's wonderful **beaches** and extraordinary wave- and wind-formed **scenery**, on both sides of the peninsula, are the most obvious attractions.

Arrival and transport

Nouadhibou, like many desert cities, is spread out, and comes in three parts. The first is the new quarter of **Numerowat** in the north, with its mess of construction sites, fading into shantytown on the north side. This is where the majority of people now live. The various quarters of Numerowat are identified by *robinets* ("Premier Robinet", "Deuxième Robinet", etc) according to the nearest public water stand-pipe, which come at 500-metre intervals along the surfaced road to downtown Nouadhibou. Downtown is **ville**, with all the usual services and shops and the

Moving on from Nouadhibou

The **iron-ore train** for **Choum** (for taxis on to Atar) and **Zouérat** is described on the opposite page. If you intend to reach Atar and have your own vehicle, you can avoid the difficulties of the coastal track by loading your car on the train to Choum and then driving to Atar. Part of this route is tarmac (from the Adrar to Atar), but before this you'll have a wadi to cross and several patches of soft sand; without a 4WD, you should take a guide with you. Cars are loaded onto open flatbed railway wagons: start waiting at the station for vehicles (you'll come across it before you reach the passenger terminal) at 9am to stand a chance of getting loaded onto the 6pm freight-only train.

You can **fly** to Nouakchott with Air Mauritanie (2 daily) or Compagnie Mauritanien des Transport Aériens (5 weekly), or to Zouérat with Air Mauritanie. There are also Air Mauritanie flights to Las Palmas (2 or 3 weekly; UM71,000 return).

By road

Until construction of the southbound surfaced road is completed, the land route to the capital is a demanding **desert drive by convoy**. If you want to attempt it, you can follow Nouakchott-bound public transport, which leaves from Garage Nouakchott on the northern outskirts of Numerowat (UM100 by taxi from the town centre); passengers for the capital pay UM3000 to sit in the back of a pick-up, or UM5000 in a 4WD. Following these vehicles in your own car, you'll need to negotiate hard with the *chauffeurs*, who will try to charge a fat fee: leave it that you will pay on safe arrival and that you'll be charging them if they break down and require your help. A better option is to club together with a group of other overlanders and hire a guide, preferably one that has been vouched for: expect to pay him about UM50,000 for the trip. Travellers without vehicles who want to travel cheaply could always try to get a lift: hang around long enough – preferably speaking French – at *Chez Abba*, and if travelling light you're sure to get a ride with a Eurobanger vendor who hopes you can push, dig and position sand-ladders. By driving day and night, it's not uncommon to complete this trip inside 24 hours, but it makes much more sense to allow two to three days. The last third at least is along the shoreline and cannot be done at high tide, so you'll need to ask local fishermen about tide times, and plan your route accordingly. Be aware that you should seek permission at the *gendarmerie* to do this journey in your own car, and you will have to pay entry fees for the Banc d'Arguin National Park (see p.144).

Far fewer vehicles drive north between Nouadhibou and Moroccan-occupied Western Sahara than in the opposite direction. Citizens of the UK, US and most European nationalities don't need a visa for Morocco. Other nationalities can obtain one at the consulate in Nouadhibou (see p.143) or the embassy in Nouakchott (see p.121). Be aware of the dangers of **mines** south of the border until a little way beyond Fort Guerguarat in Western Sahara: stick to used tracks or hire a local guide.

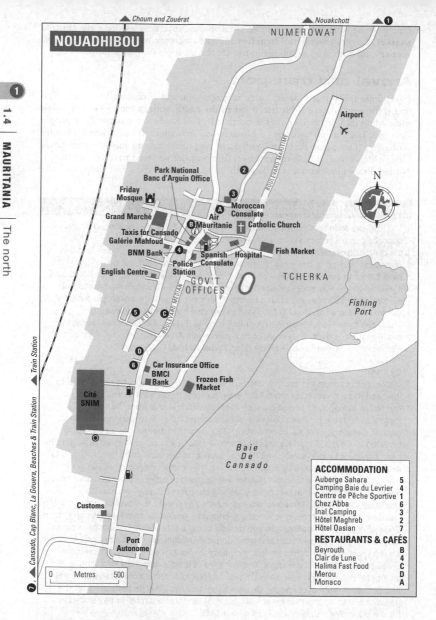

NOUADHIBOU

Choum and Zouérat

Nouakchott

NUMEROWAT

Airport

BOULEVARD MARITIME

Park National
Banc d'Arguin Office

Friday
Mosque

Moroccan
Consulate

Grand Marché

Air
Mauritanie

Catholic Church

Taxis for Cansado
Galérie Mahfoud

BNM Bank

Spanish
Consulate

Hospital

Fish Market

English Centre

Police
Station

GOV'T
OFFICES

TCHERKA

Fishing
Port

Car Insurance Office
BMCI
Bank

Frozen Fish
Market

Cité
SNIM

Baie
De
Cansado

N

Cansado, Cap Blanc, La Gouera, Beaches & Train Station   Train Station

Customs

Port
Autonome

0   Metres   500

ACCOMMODATION

Auberge Sahara	5
Camping Baie du Levrier	4
Centre de Pêche Sportive	1
Chez Abba	6
Inal Camping	3
Hôtel Maghreb	2
Hôtel Oasian	7

RESTAURANTS & CAFÉS

Beyrouth	B
Clair de Lune	4
Halima Fast Food	C
Merou	D
Monaco	A

city's main market. To the south, a full 10km from the city centre is the iron ore company's dormitory town of **Cansado** ("Sleepy" in Spanish). Since nationalization, this area has been almost entirely occupied by Mauritanians, and has the distinction of being the cleanest town in the country.

Arriving by **train**, the passenger wagon stops at the derelict rubbish-filled **station** on the way south out of downtown Nouadhibou. Wait by the road on the other side of the station to get a shared taxi to the town centre (UM100). The **airport** is northeast of the centre, from where it's a twenty-minute walk or a UM200 taxi ride to the centre – no shared taxis ply this route.

Car owners arriving from Morocco have formalities to undergo: these should be started as soon as possible after arrival in case any of the various offices decide to close early. If you didn't come across the **customs** (*douanes*) at one of the border posts, go to their office off the road south of the town centre to retrieve the car's *carte grise* registration document, which will have been retained by the border guards the previous night. Here you have your vehicle details entered into your passport, sign a bit of paper promising not to sell your car and pay the UM3000 (or €15.00) fee. Next, take a photocopy of your *carte grise* to the **insurance office** on the way back to the centre of town; it's directly opposite *Chez Abba* and marked "AGM". The minimum insurance period is ten days, with the rate depending on the engine capacity; expect to pay about UM4400 for a 4WD or UM3300 for a car. Don't scrimp on dates: your insurance will be frequently checked south of Nouakchott. Finally, drive to the middle of town to report to the **police** and get your passport stamped. Officials will then look at your passports for an hour before giving them back.

Standard fares apply for **shared taxis** around town – UM30 for any journey in the downtown area or up the tarmac to Numerowat; UM50 in the same areas, but going off-road; UM30 town to port or vice versa; and UM60 to anywhere in Cansado. Illogically, a shared taxi to the train station, which is between downtown and Cansado, costs UM100.

Accommodation

There's a decent range of accommodation in Nouadhibou, though in view of the town's reputation for vehicle theft, overlanders should place a priority on secure parking. The alternative is to camp out on the beach, which tends to be windy at night and baking hot by day.

Auberge Sahara West of bd Médian, downtown ☎574 62 16, ✉aubergechezmomo@yahoo.fr. Offering clean, quiet rooms, plenty of hot water, and access to a kitchen. There's also a roof-terrace barbecue where Berber *soirées* are arranged, a useful noticeboard giving information and advice on onward travel, and large garages and secure parking, which make the place popular with overlanders. The owner is helpful and well informed. Turn off bd Médian by the *Merou* restaurant and take the second right to find it: it isn't well signposted. ②

Camping Baie du Levrier bd Médian, downtown ☎574 60 18 or 574 65 36, ☎574 59 49. Good for overlanders with secure parking and a pleasant communal area. UM1000 per person to sleep under their tent. ②

Centre de Pêche Sportive 14km north of Nouadhibou at Baie de l'Etoile ☎644 73 75 or 574 61 67. Surf-casting is the big affair in this rustic fishing lodge, so come with a few yarns about "the one that got away". Good value though you're rather cut off without your own vehicle. Call or fax ahead to get picked up from the airport on arrival, or take a taxi (UM1000). ④

Chez Abba On bd Médian downtown, behind the colourful mural ☎574 98 96, ✉auberge.abba@caramail.com. Hostel offering double and triple rooms around a comfortable lounge area. The pleasant French owner, secure parking and friendly atmosphere help compensate for the often overstretched facilities and the sporadic hot water. Camping possible in guarded compound at the rear, and home-cooked Senegalese food is prepared on request. Recommended. Camping UM1000 per person in a car or tent. ②

Hôtel Maghreb Between bds Maritime and Médian, downtown ☎574 55 24. Quiet hotel with rooms arranged cloisterlike around a garden. Parking is available and there's a bar that can get lively (by local standards) at night. ③

Hôtel Oasian 10km south of town at Cansado, overlooking the bay ☎574 27 00, ☎574 09 53. The best hotel in Nouadhibou, but far from the action; if you reserve ahead, a courtesy bus will meet you at the airport. Rooms are en suite and have satellite TV, a/c and minibar, plus there's a bar and restaurant. ⑥

Inal Camping Next to the Moroccan Consulate, downtown ☎574 54 63, ☎ 574 64 69. Clean, cool, well-kept rooms with hot water and secure parking for vehicles, though a little run-down. ②

The Town and around

Nouadhibou's **Grand Marché**, open until 10pm daily, teems with cloth sellers, tailors and silver-smiths. Also worthy of exploration nearby is the wind-sculpted **table remarquable**, just east of the main airport runway, while down towards the sea from the fresh fish market, you can wander through what's left of the *village canarien*, once the Canary Islanders' settle-ment of **Tcherka** (aka Thiarka). To the south of the town, on the way to Cansado, is an atmospheric **ship's graveyard** of abandoned fishing hulks, scuppered for fraud-ulent insurance claims.

Further afield, 13km north of town, on the east side of the peninsula, there's delightful, shel-tered swimming in the almost enclosed **Baie de l'Étoile**. With your own transport (you could get a taxi from town for UM1000, in which case you'll probably want to arrange for it to come back for you later in the day), head east from Numerowat to the edge of the lagoon, then follow the track north past the place where camels are butchered, and continue, keep-ing to the left of the creek (a good place for bird-watching). The track leads you to the *Centre de Pêche Sportive*, the place to try your hand at surf-casting, fly fishing or night fishing, with boat excursions (UM8000) and rod rental (UM1500) available; their visitors' book is testimony to the produc-tivity of the waters. Also here is a hundred-metre-long pontoon from which boats can take you to the other side of the lagoon (UM900) to a lovely secluded beach with dunes. Avoid the beaches on the western side of the peninsula due to the mines hidden in the sand.

The Nouadhibou area is home to the world's largest colony of very **rare Mediterranean monk**

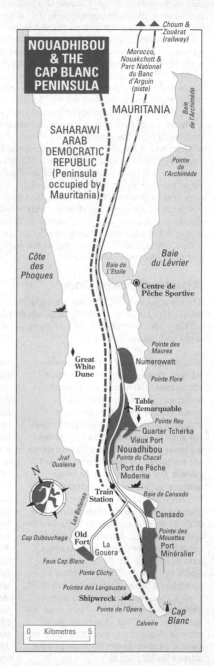

NOUADHIBOU & THE CAP BLANC PENINSULA

Choum & Zouérat (railway)

Morocco, Nouakchott & Parc National du Banc d'Arguin (piste)

MAURITANIA

SAHARAWI ARAB DEMOCRATIC REPUBLIC (Peninsula occupied by Mauritania)

Baie de l'Archimède

Pointe de l'Archimède

Côte des Phoques

Baie de L'Etoile

Baie du Lévrier

Centre de Pêche Sportive

Pointe des Maures

Numerowatt

Great White Dune

Pointe Flore

Table Remarquable

Pointe Reu

Quarter Tcherka

Vieux Port

Nouadhibou

Pointe du Chacal

Port de Péche Moderne

Jraf Oualeina

Train Station

Baie de Cansado

Cansado

Las Ballenas

Cap Dubouchage

Old Fort

La Gouera

Pointe des Mouettes Port Minéralier

Faux Cap Blanc

Ponte Clichy

Pointes des Langoustes

Shipwreck

Pointe de l'Opera

Calveire

Cap Blanc

0   Kilometres   5

Fishing rights

Mauritania, whose fish stocks in the rich cold seas off its shores have long been a magnet for fleets from Russia, Korea and Japan, has entered into an agreement with the European Union, under which the country receives some $81 million each year in licenses to allow unlimited fishing. The bizarre irony of the arrangement is that Mauritania is a big market for the sardines that form the bulk of the catch. Processed in the Canary Islands, the canned sardines end up for sale, at high prices, in the same communities that once caught the fish themselves. In this way, Mauritanians, with an average annual income of around $300, help pay the wages of the men of the EU fishing fleets, who earn at least a hundred times as much. Adding insult to injury, local fishermen say that their catches have at least halved since the foreign trawlers arrived.

---

seals (*phoques moines*), which you may see if you go down to the lighthouse at **Cap Blanc**. In appearance they resemble young elephant seals, growing to over two-and-a-half metres in length. Their valuable oil and skin has led to widespread extermination, but hunting them is now forbidden. To visit Cap Blanc, you'll need to get a permit from the Banc d'Arguin Park office (UM1200; see p.144). Park guides are available for UM3000 a day and taxis will take you there for UM2000. At Cap Blanc itself, you can ease yourself down the cliffs by using the fixed ropes provided, giving access to some fine beaches and the possibility of seal spotting.

Eating and nightlife

There's a fair number of cheap **restaurants** near the central market; standard lunchtime fare is rice and fish, with perhaps couscous and camel meat in the evening. In addition, there are a handful of cosy restaurants and cafés – even a burger bar. Several quite good **supermarkets** can be found along the main tarmac road, Boulevard Médian, and you can buy fish in the old fishing port area behind the stadium. The only **nightlife** that merits the term is *La Sirène* disco, in the traditional fishing port by the beach, which serves alcohol to foreigners.

Beyrouth The best of the basic restaurants, serving omelettes and *chep-bu-jen*.
Centre de Pêche Sportive Baie d'Étoile. Peaceful fisherman's retreat with a charming courtyard; see opposite for directions here. UM1000 for a burger and a drink, fish dishes UM1000–2000.
Clair de Lune Off bd Médian. The best place in town for breakfast and afternoon tea, serving French-style pastries and cakes. Also does takeaway pizzas, highly recommended for the hard

road south.
Halima Fast Food bd Médian. Hamburgers for UM400.
Merou bd Médian, near *Abba's Hostel*. Good, though not inexpensive, Korean and global cuisine with a wine list.
Monaco Opposite the Moroccan Consulate. One of the classier places in Nouadhibou with French food and a small bar tucked away at the back serving all kinds of spirits.

Listings

Airline offices Air Mauritanie, bd Médian ☎574 54 49 or 574 45 51; Compagnie Mauritanien des Transport Aériens, bd Médian ☎574 83 18.
Airport Flight information on ☎574 59 02.
Banks BMCI and BNM, both on bd Médian, usually give the best rates, though not as good as the bureaux de change.
Car rental SOGETRA Voyages, bd Médian ☎574 54 58.
Clinics Clinique Er Raja on bd Médian (☎574 90

95 or 636 25 12).
Consulates France, honorary consul at the Alliance Française ☎574 58 71, ⓔafm.mauritel.mr; Moroccan, off bd Médian, towards the *Hôtel Maghreb* ☎574 50 84.
Police ☎18 or 574 54 00.
Travel agents SOMASERT, next to the *Oasian* (☎574 90 42), is one of the biggest tourism enterprises in Mauritania, and offers a range of tours.

Banc d'Arguin National Park

Between Nouadhibou and the capital, the **Banc d'Arguin** is home to the **Imragen**, an isolated group of fisher people (see box, below). It's also one of the world's great **bird breeding sites**, with millions of water birds nesting and raising their chicks here from April to July and October to January. The migrants include flamingos, pelicans, white-breasted cormorants, several species of heron and egret, European spoonbills, grey-headed and slender-billed gulls, and several species of waders.

Regrettably for birders, the national park here is inaccessible and requires a major outlay to visit, though the entry fee itself is a reasonable UM1200 per person per day. Although the park has an office in Nouakchott (see p.121), it's easier to make arrangements at the head office on boulevard Médian in Nouadhibou (☎574 67 44), where guides are available. You'll still need your own 4WD vehicle to reach the area, calling at either of two Imragen villages: **Iouîk**, 200km south of Nouadhibou, or **Nouamghar**, about 250km south of Nouadhibou. To do actual bird-watching you'll need to rent a boat to go out among the shallow seas and sand shoals, which will cost you a further UM15,000. Almost every village provides limited camping facilities (without water), the campsite at **Tafarit** being especially recommended.

The Imragen

The Banc d'Arguin National Park contains the seven villages of the **Imragen**, whose survival on this barren shore is entirely dependent on an extractive economy; even water has to be trucked into the villages from Nouakchott or Nouadhibou. The traditional harvest of **yellow mullet** is caught in November, when huge shoals of fish spawn amid the sea grass in the warm shallows. By what appears to be a remarkable feat of cooperation between humans and animals, the catch is brought to shore with the assistance of dolphins. Summoned by the Imragen beating the water surface from the shore, the dolphins drive the fish to the beach, where the mullet provide a feast for them and a tremendous haul for the villagers. Recent research suggests that yellow mullet may actually like swimming underneath pods of dolphins, so that the only human intervention is to signal to the dolphins the fish trap that is at their disposal. In any event, it's an extraordinary occasion, a spectacular chaos of leaping fish, thrashing cetaceans and ducking fishermen. Other Imragen fishing methods are less successful: the Imragen aren't skilled boatbuilders and they only have a few small vessels. Another windfall is provided by the literally hundreds of ships scuppered offshore for insurance purposes, the vessels supplying fuel, building materials and occasionally more interesting bounty for the Imragen.

Senegal

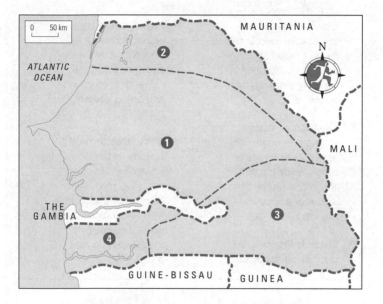

Senegal highlights

* **Dakar** Good restaurants and the vibrant music scene of Senegal's capital make up for all the hustle. See p.184

* **Ile de Gorée** Historic, UNESCO-protected island, whose pastel-coloured mansions and flower-draped alleys are particularly beautiful in the early morning. See p.199

* **The Saloum delta** Meander through mangroves in a *pirogue* or simply enjoy the quiet life on one of the Saloum's enchanting islands. See p.207

* **St-Louis** France's old colonial capital offers faded elegance in abundance, some great beaches, easy access to two national parks and an internationally renowned jazz festival to boot. See p.213

* **Pays Bassari** Little-visited corner of Senegal, where low hills and unspoilt villages make for great hiking and biking country. See p.226

* **Basse Casamance** Despite its troubles, Casamance remains easily the most seductive part of the country, with lush forests, sensational beaches and friendly people. See p.228

Introduction and Basics

Senegal is the most French-influenced of all West Africa's Francophone countries. In 1658 the island of St-Louis became the first part of the continent to be colonized by the French, and there's an enduring relationship between the two countries. Partly as a result of this pervasive Europeanism – and in recent years a growing American cultural influence – you could breeze through Senegal and hardly notice anything distinctive about it. It is one of West Africa's biggest holiday destinations, with a fair number of beach hotels and holiday clubs, and though the Casamance conflict has slowed the growth in tourism, it still attracts around half a million visitors a year.

As soon as you start scraping away the French skin, however, a far more fascinating creature is revealed. The **Muslim marabouts** (see p.174) wield exceptional power in Senegal, commanding bloc votes at elections and even directing the course of the economy by their injunctions to followers. Although Islam in Senegal is quite different from its North African counterpart, the idea of a future Islamic state doesn't seem wholly fanciful. The name of **Touba**, the holy city of one of the most powerful Muslim brotherhoods, is one you'll see all over the country, incorporated into numerous names and signs.

French style and deeply felt Islam coexist with extraordinary success, though both elements are relatively recent introductions to most of Senegal. Islam did not have a wide reach until the end of the nineteenth century, while the French, although long-established in key towns on the coast, finally subdued parts of the interior as recently as the 1920s.

From the travel and tourism perspective, Senegal is better organized than its neighbours: it's a country that's easy to get around, and one that's familiar with, and officially supportive of, independent travel. It is also one of West Africa's less expensive countries for visitors.

People

The people of Senegal are dominated by the biggest language group, the **Wolof**, who figure prominently in government and business and control the Mouride brotherhood. A clutch of Wolof kingdoms used to cover the heart of Senegal – an area now largely under fields of all-important **groundnuts** – in a highly stratified society based on class and caste differences.

The first Muslims were the **Tukulor** and the closely related **Fula** – people whose kingdom was in the northeast, which is still their heartland. The **Mandinka**, too, were widely converted to Islam before the Wolof. In the southwest, the **Serer** (Sérère) and **Jola** (or Diola) resisted Islam until the twentieth century – in parts they still do, preferring their indigenous religions – and they maintained more egalitarian, clan-based societies than the Wolof or the Muslim peoples. Christian missions have had a limited impact.

Today, most language groups are increasingly subject to **"Wolofization"** and a national Senegalese identity is emerging as people move to Dakar and other towns. More resilient have been the people of the south – the Jola of Casamance and scattered, largely non-Muslim, communities of Bassari, Bainuk, Konyagi and Jalonke.

Where to go

Senegal is one of the **flattest** countries in West Africa, rising to barely 500m in the Fouta Djalon foothills in the far southeast. Two main rivers, the Senegal and the Casamance, roughly mark the country's north and south limits, and the southern region is sliced through by The Gambia – the result of an asinine colonial carve-up in the 1890s. While there's some scenic variety to be sure, the country is most interesting at the cultural level.

The south, effectively screened from Dakar by The Gambia, provides the biggest

Fact file

La République du Sénégal has a **population** of over ten million people in an **area** of 196,000 square kilometres – roughly the size of England and Scotland combined, or half as big as California.

The country's **foreign debt** totals more than £2 billion ($3.2 billion), a colossal figure in the West African context, and more than three times the annual value of its exports – though not even one percent of the US's annual defence budget. Traditionally, the groundnut industry has formed the basis of Senegal's economy, but fishing, phosphate mining and tourism now rival it as the principal sources of foreign exchange.

Senegal's **political system**, a presidential democracy, is the longest established multiparty democracy in West Africa (since 1981). It is also one of the freest countries here, with one of the best human rights records in the region.

The Wolof have an apocryphal account of the **derivation** of the name Senegal, in which a witless explorer gestures across the Senegal River and asks some fishermen what it's called. "That? That's our boat" they reply – *li suñu gal le*. In fact the name probably derives from the **Sanhaja** Berbers who frequently raided the river region and were known by the early Portuguese explorers as *Azanaga*.

attraction for travellers. The forests and mangrove creeks of the **Basse Casamance**, and the exceptional **beaches** of the short southern coastline, are the biggest pull – these combined with the largely non-Muslim culture of the Jola. However, the conflict between Casamance separatists means that some parts of the region are now off-limits: you should keep abreast of the situation if you intend to travel there. In the southeast, the **Niokolo-Koba National Park** is one of the best game reserves in West Africa, and from here it is well worth the effort to push on into the remote southeast corner of the country with its rugged hills and traditional Bassari villages.

The attractions further **north** are round the edges: along the coast or up the Senegal River. **Dakar** – probably unavoidable, definitely two-faced – is a place to enter with some degree of caution. Yet for all its tough character, there are rewards in the city itself, and a number of good trips in the Dakar area. **St-Louis** is another ambiguous case, charged with atmosphere or depressingly run-down, as it strikes you. The upriver towns, small outposts along the Mauritanian border, are stopovers rather than ends in themselves.

When to go

Senegal's **climate** is one of the best in West Africa, with a short rainy season (*l'hivernage*) between June and September (October in the south) and a dry period between December and April. The winds tend to blow warm and humid from the southwest during the rainy season, then hot, dry and dusty from the northeast and the Sahara (a wind known as the harmattan) during the dry season. Early in the dry season, in December and January, Dakar and St-Louis can be surprisingly cool, especially at night. Through the rains, however, Dakar's combination of high humidity and city pollution can be pretty oppressive.

The weather needn't alter your travel plans as a rule, but you'll find some of the **national parks** closed during the wet season until tracks become passable again.

Getting there from the rest of Africa

Dakar is a common starting and finishing post for overland travels, and in many ways the city feels like a stepping stone between Europe/America and Africa.

The most useful flights from **North Africa** are from Tunis on Tunisair via Nouakchott and from Casablanca on Royalair Maroc or Air Sénégal International. There are direct flights to Dakar from almost every capital city in **West Africa**: daily or almost daily flights from Abidjan, Bamako, Banjul, Bissau and

Average temperatures and rainfall

DAKAR
Temperatures °C

	Jan	Feb	Mar	Apr	May	June	July	Aug	Sept	Oct	Nov	Dec
Min (night)	18	17	18	18	20	23	24	24	24	24	23	19
Max (day)	26	27	27	27	29	31	31	31	32	32	30	27
Rainfall mm	0	0	0	0	0	18	89	254	132	38	3	8
Days with rainfall	0	0	0	0	0	2	7	13	11	3	0	1

ZIGUINCHOR
Temperatures °C

	Jan	Feb	Mar	Apr	May	June	July	Aug	Sept	Oct	Nov	Dec
Min (night)	17	17	19	20	22	24	23	23	23	23	21	18
Max (day)	33	34	35	35	35	33	31	30	31	31	32	31
Rainfall mm	0	3	0	0	12	142	406	559	338	160	8	0

Conakry; and at least weekly from the other cities, including Praia on the Cape Verde Islands, which has several flights a week. From **Johannesburg**, South Africa Airways has a twice-weekly service to Dakar.

Overland

Senegal has for a number of years been a major **overland** terminus and departure point, as well as a crossroads for those using the Atlantic route across Mauritania. From **Nouakchott**, the Mauritanian capital, it's just over 200km of reasonable tarmac to the Senegalese border at **Rosso**, where a motor barge transports vehicles across the Senegal River. Other, less formal *pirogue* crossings from Mauritania are possible upriver at Kaédi or Gouray (for Sélibabi).

From Mali

Most people arriving overland **from Mali** do so on the **Océan-Niger train**. There are just two trains on the service: the Senegalese train has a restaurant and is marginally more comfortable than the Malian one, which has a limited buffet car (and was out of service at the time of writing). Departures from Bamako are scheduled for 10am on Wednesday and Saturday (the latter is the Senegalese train). Scheduled arrival time into Dakar is 4pm the following day (a journey time of 30hr), but the usual delays - which

can add the best part of a day to your journey - mean you're likely to arrive after dark. An alternative is to take the train from Bamako only as far as **Tambacounda** (where it should arrive at around 7am), from where it's a hot, uninteresting, but quicker journey **by road** to Dakar. Beware that **Muslim holidays**, particularly the Magal (see p.160), can alter train timetables.

Bamako–Dakar **fares** are around CFA25,500 2nd class, CFA34,000 1st class and CFA53,000 sleeper. Once you're on the train, it's possible to upgrade to **sleeper class** if there are berths available (double cabins only), but the protracted border formalities take place during the night and require you to disembark, so you don't get much sleep in any case. You can buy **street food** and drink from station vendors day and night.

Driving from Bamako to Dakar should become much quicker than the train once the new road from Bamako to Kayes via **Manantali** is finished. A sealed road from

For important practical information applying to all West African countries, covering health, transport, cultural hints and more, plus details on getting to the region from beyond Africa, see Basics, pp.9–87.

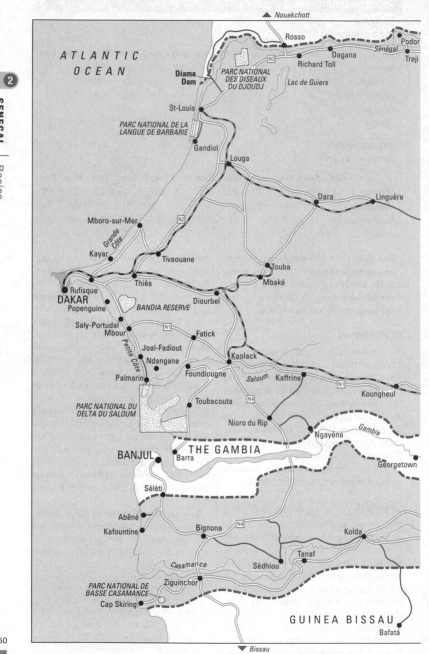

▲ *Nouakchott*

ATLANTIC
OCEAN

Rosso

Dagana
Richard Toll
Diama Dam
PARC NATIONAL
DES OISEAUX
DU DJOUDJ
Lac de Guiers
Sénégal
Podor
Treji

St-Louis

PARC NATIONAL DE LA
LANGUE DE BARBARIE

Gandiol

Louga

Dara
Linguère

Mboro-sur-Mer

Grande Côte

Kayar
Tivaouane
Touba
Mbaké

Thiès

DAKAR
Rufisque
Popenguine
BANDIA RESERVE
Diourbel

Saly-Portudal
Mbour
Fatick

Joal-Fadiout
Ndangane

Palmarin
Foundiougne
Kaolack
Saloum
Kaffrine
Koungheul

PARC NATIONAL DU
DELTA DU SALOUM
Toubacouta
Nioro du Rip

Petite Côte

THE GAMBIA
Ngayène
Gambia

BANJUL
Barra
Georgetown

Séléti

Abéné
Kafountine
Bignona
Kolda

Casamance
Tanaf
Sédhiou

PARC NATIONAL DE
BASSE CASAMANCE
Ziguinchor
Cap Skiring

GUINEA BISSAU
Bafatá

▼ *Bissau*

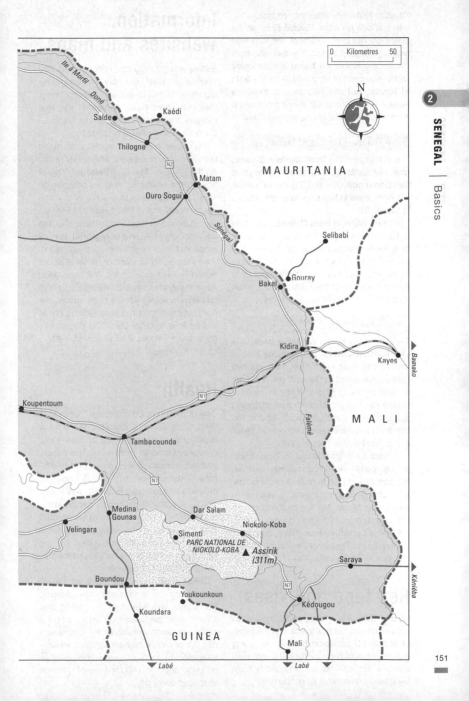

Kayes to Kidira has already been built, along with a bridge over the Falémé River on the Mali–Senegal border, where the ford was regularly deeply flooded. The old road from Bamako to Kayes via **Nioro** is notoriously sandy. You can put your vehicle on the **train** to Kayes, but the hassle and expense makes the *piste* a far more interesting proposition for suitably prepared vehicles.

From Guinea-Bissau and Guinea

The principal route **from Guinea-Bissau**, now fully surfaced, crosses into Senegal at **São Domingos**, direction Ziguinchor. Lesser crossings include Farim to Tanaf and Bafatá to Kolda.

Entering Senegal **from Guinea**, Koundara to Tambacounda is the usual route. A couple of spidery routes further east make the Labé–Kédougou crossing increasingly viable for suitable vehicles. You can expect daily transport except in the rainy season, when road problems will cause lengthy delays.

From The Gambia

Travelling from Banjul **to Dakar** involves a ferry ride to **Barra** on the opposite side of the Gambia River. From here, there are two buses a day direct to Dakar. If you don't get on one of these, the journey involves a couple of changes of bush taxi, including one short hop across no-man's-land at the border. The route is described in more detail in The Gambia chapter on p.296.

To head south from Banjul **to Ziguinchor**, you will need to take a bush taxi from the main taxi park in Serrekunda market to the border at **Séléti**, about an hour away, where there's usually little hassle. Make sure the Gambian officials stamp you in the right direction though – *Arrival* or *Departure*. From Séléti, bush taxis run regularly to Ziguinchor (2hr) and less often to Abéné and Kafountine (1hr).

Red tape and visas

US and Canadian citizens and EU passport holders do not need visas to visit Senegal. Most **non-EU passport holders**, including Australians and New Zealanders, do need visas, which can be issued quickly from Senegalese embassies or consulates.

Information, websites and maps

Before you go, you can collect maps and information from your nearest Senegalese embassy. As well as some tourist brochures, they may also have copies of the free monthly listings and adverts pamphlet *Le Dakarois*, also available in Dakar itself.

You're best advised to stock up on **maps** before you go to Senegal, where they're thin on the ground. The IGN **Senegal** map at 1cm:10km is useful, and its companion 1cm:100m **Dakar** is invaluable in the city; International Travel Maps also publishes a Senegal map at 1cm:8km. There are also some moderately useful **regional survey maps** that you'll only find in specialist shops.

An increasing amount of material about Senegal is available on the Web: two good general **websites** are ⓦ www.au-senegal.com and ⓦ www.senegal-online.com, which offer plenty of practical and cultural information, as well as links to other sites. The Senegalese government website ⓦ www.gouv.sn is also a useful resource.

Health

One of the most comfortable countries in West Africa, Senegal doesn't pose too many health problems to travellers. It's mostly dry, seasonally mild (at least along the coast), and has a relatively well-developed health-care infrastructure, with clinics and well-stocked pharmacies in cities and major towns. A yellow fever **health certificate** is required if you're arriving from an infected area, though there's sometimes a negotiable line between what's stipulated by the Ministry of Health and what's demanded by the official at the arrivals desk.

Dakar used to be the place to convalesce from the diseases of the interior. Nowadays, however, if you're getting over something, perhaps you should find a resting-up spot away from the city, which has the country's highest **typhoid** levels – attributed to exhaust fumes, industrial air pollution and the 1400 tonnes of garbage produced every day.

If you're basing yourself – or staying some time – in the Dakar area, especially during the cool, dry season from December to March, you may want to seek local advice about the necessity of **malaria** prophylaxis (see p.33 for more on the subject). Local doctors often insist it's more harmful than beneficial, and many expat residents don't bother. However, as soon as you move on, heading into the backcountry, especially in forested or watered areas, you expose yourself to risk again, a risk that is higher if you've broken your course.

Town **water** from taps is normally fine, though bottled water is widely available. From shops it's not too expensive, from hotels and bars usually much more. As in the other Sahel countries, seasonal drought means insufficient washing-water. Away from large towns, try to check on the provenance of the water used (if any) to wash your plate and glass in eating-houses.

Water-borne schistosomiasis (**bilharzia**) poses no threat in the brackish tidal waters of the lower Casamance, Saloum and Senegal rivers (though the lower reaches of the Senegal are much less brackish, and thus more dangerous, now that dams are in operation upstream). Make sure, nevertheless, that you're sufficiently downriver for it to be salty before plunging in.

Senegal has a higher than usual incidence of **diphtheria**. If you're not sure whether you were immunized as a child (possibly not if you were born after 1970), check with your doctor before leaving home.

Like much of West Africa, Senegal has become fully aware of the threat of **AIDS** and there's a massive anti-SIDA campaign. Needless to say, use prudence, and never have unprotected sex.

Costs, money and banks

Senegal's currency is the **CFA franc** (see p.39). Senegal isn't expensive: **accommodation** will cost you from around CFA10,000/day in Dakar (about £10/US$15), less outside the capital. Long-distance travel on **public transport**, when you've taken baggage into account, usually costs around CFA1500 per100km. An ISIC student card can be useful for reduced entry fees to sites and museums, and is worth trying for possible **discounts** on trains and planes.

Credit and debit cards are of more use than in other West African countries, with Visa and MasterCard the most widely accepted at banks and ATMs, as well as at car-rental companies and the smarter hotels, restaurants and shops. As in other CFA countries, it makes sense to carry some of your money in euro **traveller's cheques** for the security these offer, though changing them can be difficult in much of the country, so be sure to have a few dollars or euros on you outside of Dakar and the bigger cities. **Western Union** money transfers can be arranged at most banks and post offices.

The most ubiquitous **banks** in Senegal are SGBS, BICIS and CBAO, which have branches in most major towns and some smaller ones. SGBS and CBAO can arrange **cash advances** on Visa and MasterCard, BICIS on Visa only. Traveller's cheques can be bought using Amex through Senegal Tours in Dakar (see p.199).

Banks open and close early, and often have a long lunch break from around noon to 2.30pm. The only out-of-hours exchange facilities are the (usually exploitative) hotel desks, but 24hr **ATMs** can be found in large towns such as Dakar, St-Louis, Mbour, Thiès, Kaolack and Ziguinchor.

Getting around

Compared with many parts of West Africa, Senegal is easy to get around: bush taxis will get you nearly everywhere; plane, train and even boat are all viable options, and hitching is possible in some areas. Senegal has one of West Africa's better tarred **road networks**, with over 4000km of blacktop; for the rest, flat landscapes make for lots of passable, if monotonous and dusty, *pistes*.

Taxis brousse and buses

Most public transport is by **taxi brousse**. This may be (in descending order of price) a seven-seat Peugeot 504 (known as a *sept place*), a *car* (usually a white, ageing Mercedes minibus), a *camion bâché* (covered pick-up van) or a *car rapide* (blue and yellow minibus). You'll travel fastest and most comfortably in a 504, as long as you're not squashed in the back or too tall. Minibuses are better for shorter journeys and give more opportunity to soak up Senegalese life. In recent years, the Mouride brotherhood has started operating forty-plus-seater buses, known as **cars mourides**, on a few popular routes, usually leaving very early in the morning. Elsewhere, buses are not likely to figure much in your travels apart from in Dakar, where there's a decent bus system.

Autogares (or **gares routières**) are usually well organized, and the drivers (or their assistants) will always find you before you find them. Most of the motorable roads on the IGN map of Senegal get at least one vehicle of some description every day.

Routes

The busiest road in the country is the **Dakar–Kaolack–Ziguinchor** route, part of which forms the *transgambienne* highway. The route involves crossing The Gambia River between Farafenni and Soma, where you may have to wait for a place on the ferry. Droves of *taxis brousse* use this route (departure is early morning, journey time 7hr plus). The old route to **Ziguinchor via Barra and Banjul** (around 5 vehicles daily each way between 8am and 7pm; 30min) is much less important as a transit route.

Thiès, a little way east of the capital, is an important transport hub, with a constant stream of vehicles running up from Dakar (1hr) until late in the day. With a morning departure from Dakar you can also go straight through to **St-Louis** (at least 3hr) and **Rosso** (at least 5hr). St-Louis is the transport focus of the north, with departures all day for Rosso, **Richard Toll** and **Dakar**, though destinations further upriver are served only by a few early-morning departures and usually require vehicle changes.

A good number of vehicles make a living on the **Tambacounda** road, despite the train. You can easily make it there in a day

from the capital if you get down to the Dakar *autogare* early. Continuing to the **Kédougou** district in far southeastern Senegal, you'll be relying mostly on Tambacounda-based vehicles. The **Tambacounda–Ziguinchor** road is mostly quiet, so you'll need to make an early start.

Fares

Current **Peugeot fares** from Dakar are: Kaolack CFA2500; Karang (for Banjul) CFA4500; Kédougou CFA9000; Kolda CFA10,000; Mbour CFA1000; St-Louis CFA2850; Tambacounda CFA6800; Thiès CFA935; Touba CFA2350; Ziguinchor CFA6500. From Ziguinchor, expect to pay around CFA2000 for Séléti (for Serrekunda in The Gambia). Travelling in 12-seater minibuses is about fifteen percent cheaper; 25-seater minibuses are about 25 percent cheaper.

In Senegal it's usual to **pay** the bush taxi before the journey has finished, and often before it's even started. Don't pay, however, unless it's at least half full and other passengers have done so. It's also better to find out what the fare should be ahead of time, though if you are overcharged, it's more likely to be by way of a **baggage supplement**, which should be haggled over vigorously and knocked down to no more than ten percent.

Car rental

Car rental in Senegal is expensive and really only worth considering for special targets which might otherwise be inaccessible (national parks, for example), and even then most realistically for a group of three or four travellers. The **main agents** for Avis (the biggest), Hertz, National and Europcar provide the guarantee of a reputable name and the chance to pay by plastic, but the all-in cost for a Peugeot 205 or something similar, assuming 1000km and including fuel, will work out at a non-negotiable £450/$700 or so per week. Daily rates are fractionally more than pro rata, while a weekend's rental costs slightly less. These agents don't allow driving off the sealed highways, and require that you be at least 23 or so to drive. National driving licences, held for either one or two years, are sufficient, but don't be surprised if an international drivers' licence is specifically demanded if you're stopped.

If you're not insistent on going with a big-name firm, it's worth checking out some of the local car rental places, which are usually willing to negotiate, can be persuaded to give you unlimited mileage and aren't so fussy about off-road driving. They may work out less than half the price of the big agencies. A weekend is frequently the best deal, and a convenient length of time for many trips. Don't forget possible extras (*frais non-inclus*), such as collision damage waiver and twenty percent tax.

Trains

There's only one main railway line: the **eastern Océan-Niger service** via Thiès, Diourbel and Tambacounda (see p.149 for details), though it's unlikely you'd want to use this much as bush taxis are so much quicker. The **northern service**, which used to run daily between Dakar and St-Louis, remains indefinitely suspended. Dakar itself has its own commuter service (*le petit train bleu*; see p.188).

Hitching

Because of the number of private vehicles and expats in Senegal, and a relatively high volume of tourist traffic, **hitching** on some of the main routes is an option worth trying. Moreover, if you're stuck on a minor turn-off, trying to wave down passing vehicles is less frustrating than simply waiting for the day's *taxi brousse* service. As ever in West Africa, you may well be expected to pay, so enquire about the likely cost at the start – some drivers may ask for payment at a much higher rate than on public transport.

In decreasing order of feasibility, there are fair chances of lifts around the Dakar suburbs, to destinations on the coasts south and north of Dakar; and from Tambacounda to Dakar and into the Niokolo-Koba National Park. Before the unrest began, there were also reasonable hitching opportunities in Basse Casamance.

Flights

Air Sénégal International (@www.air-senegal-international.com) operates a few flights round the country from Dakar, but it's not a frequent enough service to be much competition for bush-taxi travel. There is a daily flight to **Ziguinchor**, two flights a week to **Cap Skiring** (Mon & Fri) and a flight to **Tambacounda** (Sat). Round-trip **fares** are CFA66,000 to Ziguinchor and CFA110,500 to Cap Skiring. Discounts are offered to groups over ten.

Boats

Pleasure boats ply the waters of the Saloum, Senegal and Casamance deltas; if you're interested, staying in the right hotels in those areas will give you rapid access. There's no steamer service higher up the Senegal or the Casamance rivers, though you can usually cross by *pirogue* and there's ample opportunity to arrange your own **river transport** locally. The Senegal is navigable all year by small boats as far as Kidira, the Casamance below Sédhiou.

The MV *Joola* **steamer** used to operate a twice-weekly overnight service between Dakar and Ziguinchor but it tragically sank in September 2002, with considerable loss of life (see box). The quicker *Kassoumay* catamaran was briefly introduced a few years ago to ply the same route but only operated for about a year before being suspended. The government has promised to provide a new boat to replace the *Joola* but at the time of writing, it was unclear when this would happen.

Other options

A characteristically Senegalese form of transport is the horse- or mule-drawn two-wheel buggy called a **calèche**, which you'll see all over the country. They're often used as town taxis in smaller places, ferrying goods and people from the *autogare*.

You can rent **bicycles** at various places along the Petite Côte, around St-Louis and in Casamance. Often they're not in particularly good condition, but they make a welcome change of pace. **Mopeds** and other leisure vehicles are also available for rent in some touristy spots, though you should be wary of shady dealers - and never pay up front.

The MV Joola disaster

Shortly before midnight on September 26, 2002, the **MV Joola** ferry capsized in stormy seas off the coast of The Gambia on its way from Ziguinchor to Dakar. Sixty-four people survived by clinging to the ship's overturned hull until local fishermen bravely picked them up, but most passengers perished after being trapped inside the ship when it flipped over. The official **death toll**, issued several months later, was 1863, exactly 350 more than died when the *Titanic* sank in 1912.

As news of the sinking came in, frantic **relatives** of the victims - most of whom came from the troubled Casamance region - rushed to Dakar's port and hospitals, and an angry crowd gathered outside the presidential palace, demanding to know who was responsible for the disaster. President Wade immediately promised **compensation** for the victims' families and launched an official inquiry into the disaster.

A report published a few weeks later concluded that a storm caused passengers and unattached freight to slide to one side of the vessel, tipping it over. The report blamed, among other things, the fact that the *Joola* was carrying double the number of passengers it was designed for. In the aftermath of the inquiry, Wade sacked his prime minister, **Mame Madior Boye**, as well as the head of the **navy**, which was responsible for operating the *Joola*.

By early 2003, there was still a great deal of anger and bitterness about the disaster, especially in Casamance, where many villages have been decimated by the tragedy. Most Senegalese are highly critical of the government's handling of the crisis, and the victims' families have complained about late and inadequate compensation. The government has responded by promising a new boat to replace the *Joola*, but even this gesture will do little to heal the country's wounds.

Accommodation

For the most part, accommodation in Senegal is sophisticated and wide-ranging. With the exception of youth hostels, most overnight options are available.

Hotels

Most large towns have several decent **hotels**. If you're arriving overland, you'll find Senegalese establishments on the whole plush and heavily Europeanized. In the higher price brackets, if they're not actually part of a chain, they're very often French- or Lebanese-owned or managed. And a surprising number of quite modest places turn out to have French hands behind the scenes.

The most basic lodgings (typically ❷–❸; the few ❶ places are likely to be brothels) may well be shabby and without air conditioning or private facilities. Mid-range places (❹–❻) offer unremarkable amenities at the lower end of the scale, though otherwise you can expect a clean, air-conditioned room with a shower and toilet, along with a restaurant and possibly a pool. Upmarket

places (❼ & ❽) will be very comfortable, offering a wider range of facilities. There is a **tourist tax** too, of CFA600 per person per night, sometimes included in the room charge, more often added to the bill afterwards.

Campements

Generally offering a little more character than the hotels are Senegal's ubiquitous **campements**, usually comprising a cluster of small huts or bungalows around a bigger bar/restaurant building. Originally, *campements* tended to offer a more basic alternative to hotels but many now offer mid-range or even luxury rooms.

An important and gratifying exception to the ordinary *campements* is the network of **campements touristiques rurals integrés** (CTRIs) in Casamance, introduced in the 1970s to bring tourist money to the rural economy (see box, p.236).

Camping

Senegal has no formal **campsites**, though a few *campements* have small areas set aside for tents. Camping out in the bush is

Accommodation price codes

All accommodation prices in this chapter are coded according to the following scale, whose equivalent in pounds sterling/US dollars is used throughout the book. Prices refer to the rate you can expect to pay for a room with two beds, including taxes. Single rooms, or single occupancy, will normally cost at least two-thirds of the twin-occupancy rate. Some resort hotels have two rates – high season from November to Easter, and low season roughly from May to October – in which case the price codes apply to the higher rate. For further details, see p.51.

❶ Under CFA4700 (under £5/$8).
❷ CFA4700–9000 (£5–10/$8–16).
❸ CFA9000–14,000 (£10–15/$16–24).
❹ CFA14,000–19,000 (£15–20/$24–32).
❺ CFA19,000–28,000 (£20–30/$32–48).
❻ CFA28,000–37,000 (£30–40/$48–64).
❼ CFA37,000–47,000 (£40–50/$64–80).
❽ Over CFA47,000 (£50/$80).

normally feasible, as the country has a fairly indulgent attitude to the eccentricities of foreigners; the French community has been doing it for years. Be sure, though, that you're out of any urban "zone of influence" where you might conceivably be putting yourself at risk of robbery. The Dakar region, and the towns in the groundnut basin – Thiès, Diourbel and Kaolack – are areas to avoid, as are the beaches.

Staying with people frequently comes out of efforts to camp on their land – even if it's not demarcated. Rewarding areas for such contacts lie throughout southern Senegal east of Ziguinchor – a region which, except for the Niokolo-Koba park, gets very few visitors, and virtually none who stay.

Eating and drinking

Senegal has some of West Africa's best food, giving opportunities for everything from serious dining to snacking on street food. Restaurants in the larger towns and main hotels incline towards French style, offering a *menu* (three courses or more, and usually a choice) and a *plat du jour* (main dish only). Predictably there's lots of tough steak and chips, heavy sauces and imported canned food. For a *menu* expect to pay CFA4500–6000, and upward of CFA1500 for the *plat*. There are some decent French restaurants, and a few other exotic eating houses as well, but with a few exceptions they're an unmemorable lot. More worthwhile – certainly in Dakar – are the cheaper local eating places, known as

gargotes, and distinguished by multicoloured ribbons over the doorways. Almost always you'll find a single Senegalese staple, and perhaps omelettes, on offer, which will cost you around CFA800. The better venues are covered in the chapter.

Most **indigenous Senegalese food** bears a heavy North African and Middle Eastern influence, with lots of seafood, mutton and Lebanese snacks. If you've been travelling elsewhere in West Africa you'll notice the near absence of plantains and root crops, and palm oil is used much less than in the southern coastal countries. The **basics**, though, as everywhere, are a staple – usually rice – and spicy sauces, though the key word is aroma rather than pungency.

Riz jollof – a mound of vegetables and meat in an oily tomato sauce on rice, named after the old Wolof kingdom – is common here, as it is all over West Africa. The national dish, eaten every day by millions of Senegalese, is **chep-bu-jen** (spelled variously as *cep-bou-dien* and *tiéboudienne*), Wolof for "rice-with-fish". This can be anything from plain rice with boiled fish and a few carrots to a glorious kind of paella with spiced rice and half a dozen vegetables. There's no fixed recipe, but it's virtually the only common meal that usually comes with vegetables.

Stuffed fish (**poisson farci**), which is an ingredient of the best *chep-bu-jen*, is associated with St-Louis and sometimes denoted *à la saint-louisienne*. Done properly, the result can be delicious. Mullet is usually

157

Wolof food terms

The list below will help you ask for and identify food in out-of-the-way places. For more Wolof, see p.180.

bey/sikket	goat	soow	sour milk
chep/maalo	rice	suukar	sugar
chere	couscous/millet	suuna	bulrush millet
chwi	stew	tomate	tomato
dom/garap	fruit	xiif	hunger
dugub	millet	xorom	salt
gejj	dried fish	yappa	meat
genar	chicken	yappi xar	mutton

gerte	groundnuts
jen	fish
jernat	sorghum millet
kaani	hot pepper
lem	honey
lemnad	soft drink
makka	corn
mar	thirst
mbaam	pork
mbum	boiled leaves
mburu	bread
meew	fresh milk
nag	beef
ndox	water
nen	egg
nex-na	good (referring to food)
nyam dunde	food
nyebe	beans
sangara	alcohol, spirits
soble	onions

There are various wild fruits, sold seasonally in the markets:

ditak	oval, pebblelike fruit, with thin, dry skin and aromatic, acid green flesh surrounding a fibrous seed, sometimes made into a drink; very common in Casamance
solom	brown, pea-sized berry, with furry (edible) skin and a black seed
cerise	tart, green "cherry"
nuul	fruit from oil nut palm tree
dimbu	medium-sized, green, soft fruit with a vegetable taste

used, filleted and flayed, leaving the skin whole; the flesh is then chopped finely, spiced and herbed, sewn up inside the skin and the whole package baked.

Varieties of **yassa** – a Casamançais dish – are characteristic of most menus too. Traditionally it uses **chicken**, but fish is also common, and any animal ingredient qualifies so long as it is marinated at length in lemon juice, pepper and onions.

Sauces include **mafé** and **domodah**, based loosely around tomatoes and groundnuts. The latter, so peanutty in The Gambia, is sometimes nut-less in Senegal. Both are best with beef or fish. **Soupe kanje** is a sauce made from okra with fish and palm oil.

You'll come across lots of places serving **couscous** (or basi-salete), though this is traditionally considered a festive meal and eaten at the Muslim New Year. Comprising steamed grains of millet flour with a smothering of vegetables, mutton and gravy, it's best by far when you're very hungry. **Méchoui**, a whole roast sheep, is one for Tabaski – the fête des moutons.

Away from the main growing areas in the south, **fruit** tends to be expensive: oranges imported from Morocco, Ivoirian pineapples and French apples. The best stuff is found in the Casamance, where you should look for unusual wild fruits.

Breakfast and snacks

The great French bequest is their **bread**, consumed in vast quantities. Pain beurre and café au lait is the ubiquitous **breakfast** and roadside snack, often with real butter. Be warned, though, that in some places the Nescafé is often made with **kenkeliba** (see p.56); specify "made with water" if you want Nescafé proper. Kenkeliba bars are known as **tangana** – which literally means "it's hot".

For **snacks** in towns you'll often end up in a **chawarma bar** – a dependable stand-by, and very cheap. Alternatives include *merguez* (spicy sausage), *kofta* (meat balls), *fataya* (mince and onion pies), *nems* (like a pancake roll made of vermicelli pastry) and **brochettes** of grilled meat.

In the suburbs and countryside the **dibiterie** takes over. Roadside or market stalls, *dibiteries* are really butcher's shops, where you can choose your flank of flesh which is then chopped and barbecued on the spot and served with a few slithers of raw onion. It's said that flies are attracted to the best cuts, so take their choice as a recommendation.

Drinking

Flag is Senegal's **beer**, and not at all bad. It comes in bottles of a third of a litre and two-thirds of a litre, and the price depends on where you buy it – any bar (there's no shortage of drinking places in large towns) that sells only the small size is going to be expensive. A quite acceptable alternative, assuming you're in need of refreshment rather than intoxication, is the less alcoholic Gazelle (large size only), which tends to be one of the cheapest bottled drinks you can buy.

Wine is available in groceries in most town centres, and tends to be about twice the French price. **Palm wine** costs next to nothing but to get some, you need to be in Casamance and friendly with the owner of a tree.

Non-alcoholic alternatives to bottled sodas and mineral water are plastic bags of **iced fruit drinks**: hibiscus syrup (*bisap*), ginger water, **bouille** (sherbety baobab juice) or tamarind juice. If you're interested in unusual tastes, seek out **njamban** – a concoction of tamarind juice, smoked fish, salt and cayenne pepper. Mellower are **thiacry**, a mixture of couscous, sour milk and sugar that's closer to a dessert than a drink, and **lakh** – millet, sour milk, sugar and orange water. Sahelian **tea** – tongue-liftingly strong and sweet – is another much loved refreshment just about everywhere.

Communications

Post offices (PTTs; typically Mon–Fri 7.30am–4pm plus Sat morning) operate with grinding, morose efficiency. Senegalese mail is expensive, and sending mail overseas from Dakar (where the central PTT has long hours) is slow. Getting mail at **poste restante** may require infinite patience: letters commonly take two to three weeks to find their box in the Dakar poste restante, and are then only held for a month.

Internet cafés are springing up all over the country, even in out-of-the-way places, reflecting the enthusiasm with which the Senegalese have taken to the Web. **Prices** in big cities such as Dakar, St-Louis and Thiès are a very reasonable CFA500 per hour, rising to CFA3000 per hour in smaller towns, where connection speeds are usually slower.

Phones and faxes

Centres téléphoniques, or *télécentres*, can be found just about everywhere, even in the smallest villages. Calls are made from a metered booth and paid for at the end – the **price** is measured in units and varies significantly from place to place (CFA75–100 per unit), so shop around. Note that Senegalese phone numbers don't have area codes. **Phoning home** costs around CFA600 per minute to Britain and Europe, a bit more to the US. **Fax machines** are also often available for receipt and transmission at the same *centres*.

Mobile phone coverage is very good in Senegal, especially in the more populated areas. The two GSM phone operators, **Sentel** and **Alizé**, have roaming agreements with most big foreign operators, though calls made this way are expensive. If you're going to be in the country for any length of time, it makes sense to hook up to a **local network**: you can buy SIM cards for Sentel's Hello network or Alizé for around CFA20,000 and prepaid cards from CFA5000.

Senegal's IDD country code is ☏221.

The media

The Senegalese **press** is relatively well developed, with a number of daily papers. *Le Soleil* – nominally independent but effectively the voice of government – has plenty of local news but not much international coverage; other dailies include *Walfadjri*, *Sud*, *Le Matin*, *L'Actuel* and *L'Info 7*. Since the papers are still all published in French – which many of the population can't read – newspaper reading remains very much city based.

If your French is up to it, *Le Cafard Liberé* (named after the Parisian satirical mag) is a weekly breath of fresher air. Paris-based weeklies available include *Le Temoin*, *Nouvelle Horizon*, *L'Intelligent Jeune Afrique* and *L'Autre Afrique*, as well as the monthly *Le Nouvel Afrique-Asie*, *Afrique Diagnostique* and *Economia*.

Language politics are reflected in Senegalese government **radio**. French is the official language but programmes, more or less, reflect the ethnolinguistic diversity of the country, with broadcasting in Wolof, Fula, Serer, Mandinka, Jola and Sarakolé/Soninké. The number of stations has increased considerably over recent years. Radio Sénégal (750MW) carries Dakar information and, on Friday afternoons, news about music and shows, and you can also pick up Sud-FM (98.5FM), Dakar FM (94FM), Nostalgie (playing French and African music from the 1970s and 1980s) and Walfadjri FM (99FM), a more recent addition and the most popular station. The BBC World Service is available in Dakar on 105.6FM.

TV, predominantly in French, is available all over the country. Apart from the government station, RTS, there are also pay-TV channels such as the local Canal Horizons, the French satellite channel TV5, CNN, C-Span and a host of Arabic channels.

Opening hours, public holidays and festivals

Shops are open from Monday to Friday between 8am and noon and again from 2.30pm to 6pm, while on Saturdays they're generally trading between 8am and noon. Banks follow roughly the same hours but close earlier in the afternoon. Most other offices are open from Monday to Friday between 7.30am and 4pm without a break. Many establishments, including some restaurants, close one day a week – museums usually on Monday.

Apart from Christian and Islamic holidays, during which time all official and most business doors will be closed (see p.61), Senegal also has holidays on April 4 (National Day, when independence as part of the Mali Federation was declared), May 5 (Labour Day) and June 20 (Independence Day).

There's also considerable unofficial disruption to normal hours and services at the time of **Magal** – the annual Mouride pilgrimage to Touba, which falls on the 18th of Safar, 48 days after the Islamic new year – ie around April 10, 2004, March 30, 2005 and March 20, 2006. Public transport all over Senegal is severely affected in the days before and after Magal, with many drivers preferring to do pilgrim business only.

Traditional festivals

One St-Louis and Gorée institution is the **Fanals** parade, featuring the decorated lanterns (*fanals*) that slaves used to carry in front of wealthy mixed-race women (*signares*) on their way to Christmas Mass. Competition developed between *quartiers* to produce the most elaborate lamp, the rivalry becoming so intense that the events were banned in 1953 after violence between the teams; it wasn't until 1970 that parades were revived in St-Louis. Impressive **pirogue races** also take place from time to time, notably in St-Louis.

Festivals in the south

In Basse Casamance and in the Bassari country beyond Niokolo-Koba park, a **seasonal cycle of festivals** and ritual events still dominates the cultural sphere, though to a diminishing extent. The events listed below are all worth checking out; most take place towards the end of the dry season.

Olugu (March). Jubilant entry of Bassari initiates who underwent *Nit* the previous year, signifying their re-integration as adults.

Fityay (March–April). Ritual appeasement of the spirit Beliba, supplicated to look after the people of Essil (the region around Enampore) through the dry months.

Nit (end of April). Ritual battle in the Bassari villages of Ebarak, Etiolo and Kote, with masked attacks on boys undergoing initiation.

Ufulung Dyendena (May). Throughout the kingdom of Essil, this ritual propitiation of rain spirits takes place before and after rice planting.

Synaaka (May). "Circumcision" of Jola girls, during which the initiates are instructed in retreat for a week; widespread partying.

Zulane (May & June). Festival of the royal priest of Oussouye.

Futampaf (May & June). This initiation of adolescent Jola boys into adulthood lasts two to three weeks, commencing and concluding with major celebrations.

Kunyalen (May & June). Three days of ritual performed to ensure Jola female fertility and the protection of newborn infants.

Ekonkon (June). Traditional dances in Oussouye.

Bukut (June). Initiation ceremony taking place in each Jola village roughly every twenty years.

Wrestling (June & July). In Tionk-Essil, the start of the rains is a traditional time for this.

Homebel (October). After the rains, girls' wrestling bouts around Oussouye.

Beweng or **Epit** (Nov & Dec). A two-day harvest festival in Basse Casamance, when the spirits are asked to sanction the transfer of the rice crop to the granaries. Each head of household donates a sheaf.

Ebunay (every two years). A festival in the Oussouye district involving all the women of the village; there are female (*bugureb*) dances in the first week, followed by the enthronement of a ritual priestess.

Entertainment

Unlike a number of countries where organized entertainments can be somewhat inaccessible to outsiders, Senegal has plenty of spectator sport, in addition to theatre and cinema – and Senegalese music is a revelation after the foreign imports heard in other countries. Major stadium gigs are held in Dakar, Ziguinchor and elsewhere, and you can pick up on even the big names in the Dakar clubs – the atmosphere is guaranteed to be electric, and tickets aren't expensive. For more on the music scene, see p.177.

Sport

Senegal's national sport is **la lutte** (wrestling; see p.299), a furious jostling of oiled and charm-laden poseurs trying to get each other down in the dust: it's fun to watch, best at a small venue. Casamançais style is less violent than the Wolof brawls.

If anything, **football** (soccer) is even more popular than wrestling, particularly since the Senegal national team unexpectedly and thrillingly reached the quarter-finals of the 2002 World Cup. Everywhere you'll see stickers, posters and T-shirts depicting Senegal's star players, and the locals avidly follow the French league, where most of the team play, on television.

Cinema

Senegal's film directors – notably **Ousmane Sembène** (see box, overleaf), **Pape B. Seck** (*Afrique sur Rhin*, 1984), **Djibril Diop Mambety** (*Touki Bouki*, a groundbreaking anti-modernization film from 1973; and *La petite vendeuse de Soleil*, released just after his death in 1999), and one of the continent's first women film-makers, **Safi Faye** (*Lettre Paysan*, 1975; *Mossane*, 1991) – struggle for funds and rely heavily on the state despite, in Sembène's, and to a lesser extent Faye's case, international critical acclaim.

Nevertheless, film-makers have attempted to diversify the image of African cinema through Le Collectif l'Oeil Vert, an association that aims at increasing co-operation between African film-makers and decreasing dependency on the state. The collective was founded by **Cheikh N'Gaido Bah**, who advocates a greater commercialization of film and who cast box-office draws like Jean-Paul Belmondo from France and Isaak de Bankolé from Côte d'Ivoire in *La Vie en Spirale*. Bah's film *Xew Xew* (1983) dealt with the popular culture of Senegalese music and featured well-known artists like Xalam and Youssou N'Dour.

Ousmane Sembène

A Marxist whose films are explicitly political, Ousmane Sembène (b. 1923) remains the "papa" of West African cinema. Since his debut in 1963, he has made over a dozen films, of which several are considered classics. Besides *Borom Sarret* ("Cart-driver", 1963) and *Mandabi* ("The Money Order", 1968), his most famous works are **Xala** (1974) – a satire that gets darker and darker about a corrupt Dakar bureaucrat who loses touch with the people and thereby becomes impotent – and the less accessible **Ceddo**, which deals with the three-way conflict in the nineteenth century between the jihadists, the traditionalists and the French.

The title character of Sembène's 1993 film **Guelwaar** is a political activist and baptized Catholic who, through a bureaucratic mix-up, gets buried in a Muslim cemetery. Sembène uses the community's attempts to rectify the situation to expose the petty jealousies and divisive religious dogmatism that bely contemporary politics. Like many of Sembène's works, the film was banned in Senegal when it was released and remains difficult to see abroad.

Sembène returned to the screen in 2000 with the deceptively light domestic drama **Faat Kine**, a masterful tribute to what he describes as the "everyday heroism of African women".

Senegalese film-makers were highly visible throughout the 1990s and into the new millennium. One of the most entertaining films of the past few years was by **Moussa Sene Absa**, whose coming-of-age film, *Ça twiste à Poponguine* (1993), is a breezy but insightful look at identity, dreams and the way cultures overlap. His *Tableau Ferraille* (1997) is more in the tradition of Sembène's *Xala* in its view of the ways that modernization erodes traditional culture and development, while *Ainsi Meurent les Anges* (2001) combines the lyricism of his first film with the acerbic social critique of his second.

Other well-known members of the new generation are **Amadou Seck** - whose *Saaraba* (1988), an indictment of a corrupt older generation, is something of a classic in the neorealist tradition - and **Joseph Gaï Ramaka**, director of *Karmen Gaï* (2001), a colourful reworking of the Carmen myth in contemporary Senegal.

Theatre

Theatre doesn't make much impression outside Dakar, where there is a small, active theatre community based around the Senegal National Theatre Company and the institutional Théâtre Daniel Sorano. Foreign cultural centres in Dakar, St-Louis and Ziguinchor may have something worth a look; where appropriate we've listed them in the chapter.

Crime and personal safety

Be **security-conscious** on first arriving in Dakar (see p.188 for more) – this is a city where too many new arrivals are robbed, usually in a snatch-and-run attack. The rest of the country is as safe as anywhere, though you should remain alert in the bigger towns – and it pays to keep tabs on the situation in Basse Casamance before heading there (see p.231 for more on this).

The **police** are of two main types – machine-gun-toting, brown-uniformed *gendarmes* and blue-togged *agents de police* who operate the occasional countryside road blocks. The latter, though generally not into bothering tourists, will pull you in if you're not carrying any identification, in which case you can be held for 24 hours and fined – this sort of thing happens, often. If you're out at night and would rather not take your passport, keep a photocopy and another piece of ID with you.

Directory

Crafts Senegal doesn't stand out as a country in which to buy handicrafts, but you'll find a number of hole-in-the-wall curio shops in Dakar, where some musty old relics can be unearthed and argued over. Officially sanctioned *centres artisanals* tend to be touristic set-ups, where you can see the stuff being made (carved statues and masks, model *pirogues*, paintings on glass, sand paintings) but where you might not want to buy it. Cloth *pagnes* are generally cheaper than in The Gambia, with Dakar's suburban markets being the best places for a good deal. Jewellery, in variety and notably in silver, is usually a good buy.

Emergencies Police ☎17, ambulance ☎18.

Photography Officially there are few problems: you can even take pictures of the presidential guards and palace, though you should ask first. But you'll certainly hurt people's feelings if you take their pictures without permission, and in many areas, high prices will be demanded. Film is easily available in cities and major towns; elsewhere, carry plenty to spare.

Sexual attitudes The Wolof tend to be exceptionally beautiful people, and unafraid of marrying out of their own communities, which tends to strengthen their already dominant position. Prostitution has a rather lower profile than, for example, in The Gambia. Gay attitudes seem relaxed, in Dakar at least: Avenue Georges Pompidou and Ngor beach to the north are well-known cruising areas for *gor-digen*.

Wildlife and national parks Senegal isn't well endowed with large animals. In the north, however, there may still be elephants along remoter parts of the river. In Niokolo-Koba National Park you can see western giant elands and quantities of crocs and hippos, plus, if you're lucky, elephants and lions, and chimpanzees at the northernmost point of their range. Senegalese birdlife is satisfying: the coast boasts some of the best spots in the world for watching palearctic migrants in the winter. For further information contact the Department of National Parks (BP 5135, Dakar; ☎832 23 09, ℻832 23 11, ℮dpn @sentoo.sn).

Women and the women's movement Dakar's fairly active women's movement is coordinated through the Fédération Sénégalaise des Groupements Féminins. Long-standing and continued French influence has been superficially helpful to women in terms of career opportunities. The central issue of institutional female genital mutilation – made illegal in Senegal in 1999 but still performed in some communities – is being tackled by a pan-African organization who have their headquarters in Dakar, the Commission Internationale pour l'abolition des mutilations sexuelles (CAMS).

Work and study Though by no means easy, Dakar is one place in West Africa where you could quite possibly find a job if you're prepared to settle in for a while. The most likely openings are English teaching (approach the British-Senegalese Institute; see p.198) and – if you have very good French – translating, secretarial and other office jobs, or working in upmarket stores. Most are strictly unofficial – making friends with the expat communities will help. It may be worth contacting Sénévolu (☎550 48 85, ℗www.senevolu.mypage.org), a Senegalese organization promoting community tourism, with homestay programmes whereby volunteers have the opportunity to gain work experience or attend culture and language classes in Senegal.

A brief history of Senegal

The earliest deducible history of Senegal, from about 1300 AD, comes from the oral accounts of the aristocracy of the Wolof kingdom of Jolof, in the centre of the country. Jolof fragmented into a number of small Wolof kingdoms which, together with Casamance, had frequent contacts with Portuguese traders after 1500. In 1658, the French settled on an island at the mouth of the Senegal River, which they named St-Louis, after Louis XIV. This account picks up the story from there. For the history of Islam in Senegal, see the section on the Muslim brotherhoods on pp.174–177.

French inroads

By 1659 the trading fort of **St-Louis** was properly established, buying in **slaves** and **gum arabic** – the first a product of upriver raids, the second a valuable extract from acacia trees, used in medicine and textile manufacture.

The permanent French presence at St-Louis stimulated the slave trade to a level at which it began to dominate the Senegal valley's economy, prompting a frenzy of warfare for profit in the region's indigenous states. Wolof rulers (the *damel*) and their warriors (the *ceddo*) were spurred to raid their own peasantry for slaves. In the 1670s a popular jihad by Muslim marabouts, rebelling against this social **cannibalism** of the traditionalist Wolof elite, was suppressed with the help of French soldiers and guns. Henceforth Wolof of all classes found themselves trapped between Islamic reformers and mercenary Europeans.

St-Louis in the eighteenth century

Throughout the eighteenth century St-Louis thrived and increasingly absorbed the Wolof people of Walo state, which occupied the area between Richard Toll and the coast. The Wolof had not been converted to Islam: on the contrary, the intermarriage of Wolof women and French Catholics created an exclusive miniature society, to a large extent run by the mixed-race matriarchs known as **signares**.

By the time of the French Revolution, St-Louis had a population of 7000, of whom a large proportion, including the mayor, were *métis* (mixed race). In deference to French blood – and also to post-revolutionary notions of the rights of man – the people of St-Louis and Gorée, the island near Dakar, were accorded most of the privileges of **French citizenship**, including, after 1848, the right to elect a deputy to the National Assembly in Paris – a right later extended to the mainland *communes* of Rufisque and Dakar.

Futa Toro and Omar Tall

In the interior, developments were under way that would shape the future of the modern state. In 1776 a league of **Tukulor marabouts** from north of the Senegal River overthrew the Fula dynasty of Denianke in **Futa Toro** on the south bank, a region the dynasty had ruled for more than 250 years. They were replaced by a reforming government of Muslim clerics (known as *almamys*) who, with fundamentalist zeal, dispatched warrior-missionaries to spread Islam across the western part of the subcontinent.

The greatest of these expansionists was **Omar Tall**. On his way to Mecca in the 1820s, Tall was initiated into the **Tijaniya brotherhood**, which was founded in Morocco in the late eighteenth century. He was appointed the Tijani chief khalif for the region and travelled extensively, gathering a huge following. By the early 1850s Tall had carved out a vast **empire** centred on **Ségou** in present-day Mali and stretching as far east as Timbuktu, though his ambitions to expand westwards to the coast were soon thwarted by the French.

French conquest

In the 1820s, after the **abolition of slavery**, Governor Baron Roger had tried unsuccessfully to develop agriculture upriver at Richard Toll with a view to French settlement. **Louis Faidherbe**, appointed governor in 1854, saw no mileage in that approach to imperialism. Instead he annexed the Wolof kingdom of **Walo** and brutally subjugated the Mauritanians of Trarza, who had long frustrated French ambitions to control the gum trade. To pay for the military campaigns, the first harvests of **groundnuts** were shipped to French soap and oil factories. In 1857 a deal was struck with the headman of the Lebu village of **Daxar** (Dakar) – which became the administrative capital of French West Africa for the next hundred years – and further settlements were established along the coast at Rufisque and elsewhere. He also strengthened the forts along the river at **Podor**, **Matam** and **Bakel**, which repulsed El Hadj Omar Tall's repeated attacks and provided bases for the French expansion across the Sahel. It was also Faidherbe who founded the **Tirailleurs sénégalais** (West African Infantry), the firepower behind France's "civilizing mission" across West Africa and as far afield as Madagascar.

Omar Tall was killed in 1864, besieged in the Bandiagara escarpment in present-day Dogon country, his empire still landlocked. His son **Amadu Sefu** continued his reign.

After Omar Tall's death, **Ma Ba**, a senior disciple, carried on the work of the Tijaniya with a clutch of Soninké (Sarakole) followers. They led and sponsored jihads against non-Muslim Mandinka along the Gambia river (see **"The Soninke-Marabout Wars"**, p.262), and also converted most of the Wolof kings to Islam, goading them into individual armed resistance against the French. But a united front of Wolof states proved impossible to achieve. In 1867 Ma Ba died in a battle with the **Serer**-speaking state of Sine, marking a temporary halt in the advance of Islam and leaving the Serer to a different evangelical fate with the Christian missions.

As Wolof leaders were converted, however, pushing their people – or sometimes pushed by them – into accepting Islam, so **conflict with the French** became, with increasing clarity, a conflict between Muslims and infidels. Humiliated by their 1871 defeat in the Franco–Prussian War, the French found new reserves of aggression. And despite the marabouts' powers of mobilization, the French grip on the territory grew tighter every year through the 1880s. The Wolof armies were defeated one by one, and the old authority structures – already weakened by the imposition of Islam – were dismantled as each kingdom was annexed to France.

Wolof capitulation

By now the French were irreversibly committed to making Senegal pay for itself and to administering directly the whole of their West African territory. **Lat Dior**, the ruler of **Kayor**, was ignored when he appealed to the French not to build the Dakar to St-Louis railway through his kingdom, and the railway was opened in 1885, despite sabotage by Lat Dior and his *ceddo*. The same year the **Berlin congress** divided the African spoils among the European powers, splitting Senegal with the creation of The Gambia and formally ratifying France's sovereignty over her possessions. Lat Dior was killed at Dekhlé the following year, and became one of the country's folk heroes.

Another Wolof *damel*, **Alboury Ndiaye** (Alboury of Jolof), at first allied himself with the French at St-Louis against Amadu Sefu's empire to the east, even undertaking to facilitate the building of the ambitious, and never-completed, railway to Bakel. But, along with his distant cousin Lat Dior, Alboury had been converted to Islam in 1864, and he was secretly in contact with Amadu Sefu. He later became violently opposed to French expansion, allying his kingdom with the Ségou empire, leading fanatical attacks and trying to expand Ségou even farther to the east. His own kingdom, whose capital was Yang Yang, was formally annexed by the French in 1889 – the last Wolof kingdom to lose its independence; Ségou fell in 1892, and Alboury died in exile in Dosso, Niger, in 1902.

French administration

As everywhere in the early years of Afrique Occidentale Française (AOF), the French stressed their **mission civilatrice** – their peaceful aim to bring French civilization to black Africa. It was only in Senegal that this was accompanied by any real manifestation of assimilationist ideals, and even here, it was only in the four *communes* that French citizenship was available. Through the rest of Senegal and AOF, most people had the status of *sujet* – subject – and were at the mercy of the hated **indigénat** "native justice" code, under which they were ruled by the local *commandant* – the equivalent of a district commissioner – who could impose summary fines and imprisonment. The *indigénat* and a mass of oppressive legislation, including tax provisions, compulsory labour and restrictions on movement, were mostly operated through *chefs de canton* ("district chiefs") nominated by, and answerable to, the *commandant*. The chiefs were frequently corrupt and almost always regarded as collaborators. The only legitimate leadership in the countryside came from the **marabouts** (see p.174).

Blaise Diagne and the marabouts

In marked contrast, Dakar, Gorée, Rufisque and St-Louis elected a territorial assembly – the **conseil général**, which controlled the budget for the whole of Senegal – and a deputy to the Paris National Assembly. In 1914 **Blaise Diagne**, a customs official from Gorée, became the first black deputy (previous deputies had been mixed race), a post he was to hold until his death in 1934.

The tone of Diagne's career was set early on when he offered to recruit Senegalese soldiers for the French war effort in exchange for legislation guaranteeing the political rights of the black *commune* residents – rights which the colonial administration was keen to erode. Laws were passed confirming that they were full citizens of France. As far as Diagne was concerned, only further **assimilation** could better the lot of the Africans. He saw Senegal's fate as inextricably linked to that of France.

Outside the *communes* the Senegalese still had hopes of redemption through their marabouts, but the warrior evangelists of the nineteenth century were gone. In their place, men like **Amadou Bamba** – founder of the Mouride brotherhood – and **Malick Sy** – leader of the biggest Wolof dynasty of the Tijaniya – bought their religious independence by coopting their followers in the colonial process, organizing recruitment drives and providing support to Senegalese politicians in the *communes*. Blaise Diagne's election owed much to support from the Mouride brotherhood, who counted on him to raise his voice on their behalf. The marabouts also encouraged the **cultivation of groundnuts**, a crop that quickly exhausted the soil, was totally dependent on the rains, forced farmers to buy food they would otherwise have grown for themselves and – as groundnut prices fell while others rose – led to falling living standards. In return the marabouts were given the administration's support in their land disputes with Fula cattle-herders. By the end of the 1930s a system of **reciprocal patronage** between marabouts and government was established, and two out of three *sujets* were growing groundnuts.

After Diagne

Diagne was succeeded as deputy by Galandou Diouf, a less enthusiastic assimilationist. His main rival was **Amadou Lamine Guèye**, Africa's first black lawyer, who came to prominence by demanding the extension of citizenship to the *sujets*. Already elected mayor of St-Louis in 1925, he forged strong links with the French Socialist party and, in 1936, founded the Senegalese branch of the Section Française de l'Internationale Ouvrière (SFIO), Africa's first modern political party. When the French Socialists came to power and conceded some limited rights to noncitizens – the right to form trade unions for example – he began organizing among *sujets* in the backcountry towns.

World War II

With the outbreak of **World War II**, political life virtually ceased as the citizens' rights in the *communes* were abrogated, the country was scoured for supplies and the social advances of the prewar government were swiftly negated. The Allies blockaded Vichy-ruled Dakar as Churchill and de Gaulle's **"Operation Menace"** attempted to rally the AOF to the war. Senegal was starved of imports, causing enormous suffering in the groundnut regions. Peasants were forced to switch to subsistence crops, and for the first time were encouraged by the colonial administration to do so.

After two years of Vichy control, the colonial administration turned to the Allies and for the rest of the war the country was an important logistical base for the Free French – though political rights were not restored until 1945. During the Allied occupation, an agricultural campaign – **"Battle for Groundnuts"** – was launched, which extracted more from the country, economically, than Vichy had.

Promises and blunders

The **Brazzaville Conference** of 1944 prepared the ground for major changes in France's relations with its colonies. A fairer deal for Africans, allowing them more administrative involvement, was the main theme, partly in recognition of the part played by them during the war, partly because France's credibility as a great and munificent nation was in question. The underlying aim was the reconstruction of postwar France and the incorporation of all its territories as integral parts of the Republic. The possibility of independence was explicitly ruled out. Yet there was a clear call for "Equal Rights for Equal Sacrifices", a reference to the 200,000 Africans who were recruited to the war, the 100,000 who fought and the 25,000 who died.

Events in Senegal brought citizens and *sujets* closer together. At the end of 1944 at **Camp Thiaroye**, outside Dakar, demobilized West African soldiers just returned from Europe refused to be transported to Bamako without their back pay. When a general was taken hostage, French soldiers were ordered to open fire. Forty Senegalese were killed, many more were injured and a number of survivors sentenced to long jail terms.

Then, in 1945, the **vote for women** was finally won in France, but in the four *communes* only white women were enfranchised, a discrimination that under Blaise Diagne's 1915 guarantee should have been impossible.

Although the women's-vote decision was shortly repealed, both these events sullied relations with France and added fuel to growing demands for radical reforms.

The rise of Senghor

To speak of independence is to reason with the head on the ground and the feet in the air; it is not to reason at all. It is to advance a false problem.

L.S. Senghor, Strasbourg, 1950

Early in 1945 a commission was set up to look into ways of organizing a new Constituent Assembly for the French colonies. One of the two black Africans to sit on it was a 38-year-old

Catholic Senegalese, **Leopold Sédar Senghor**, who was chosen because, despite having lived almost continuously in France since 1928, he was the first African to achieve the rank of *agrégé* (the highest teaching qualification), and was in addition a war veteran and a *sujet*. Moreover, he was a Christian Serer rather than a Wolof and had close contacts with the French administration.

In October 1945 **elections** were held to two electoral colleges of the Assembly, one for citizens and one for *sujets*. **Lamine Guèye**, now mayor of Dakar and seen as the most experienced black politician in AOF, successfully rallied various political groups to form a popular front and was elected to the first electoral college. **Senghor**, fresh back from France, was easily voted to the second college – even though few Senegalese knew who he was.

Reforms and advances

Though not without hindrance, **reforms** were rapidly pushed through: the *indigénat* was abolished, as was forced labour. Even more significant, Lamine Guèye succeeded in raising the status of all *sujets* to that of citizen.

Senghor meanwhile was emerging from Lamine Guèye's political tutelage within the SFIO, campaigning to extend the role of the peasants in the interior, for increased financial credits and improvements in health and education in the overseas territories, and supporting the 1947–48 **railway workers' strike** for non-racial pay differentials on the Dakar–Bamako line. In 1948 Senghor formed his own party, the **Bloc démocratique sénégalais** (BDS), and became leader of an association of African deputies – the Indépendents d'Outre-Mer.

The postwar reforms and the rise to power of the BDS in the early 1950s soon transformed Senegalese **politics**, even if the economy remained heavily dependent on the fickleness of the groundnut harvest. Senghor's party capitalized greatly on its leader's ex-*sujet*

status and the credibility this brought him with the newly politicized peasantry. Senghor also took advantage of maraboutic favour to impress on business interests his influence over the groundnut economy. The **marabouts**, formerly an important behind-the-scenes factor, were becoming political focal points themselves. Lamine Guèye's SFIO meanwhile struggled for support in the urban centres beyond the four *communes* and continued to ignore the countryside, to his party's cost.

The third political grouping, a loose association of **Marxist intellectuals**, trade unionists and students, tended to see the established politicians as too closely wedded to Paris. Their calls for independence were drowned by the clamour for fairer assimilation.

The **Loi Cadre** ("Blueprint law") of 1956 was a step in both directions. Self-government was instituted for each of the overseas territories. But there was not to be the widely desired **federation** of territories with a capital in Dakar. And defence, higher education and currency would still be issues debated in Paris.

This was transparently an attempt to **balkanize** French Africa. It's been argued, and was at the time, that it gave more Africans the chance to participate in government than would have been the case had they been answerable to Dakar instead of their own capitals. In that sense it was a device to cloud over the real issue – independence.

The UPS and the 1958 referendum

Senghor continued to build a power base, drawing his support from the marabouts, the business community and **Mamadou Dia**'s socialist movement. He also attempted to make an alliance with Felix Houphouët-Boigny's Rassemblement Démocratique Africain in Côte d'Ivoire, arguing the need for federation. When this was blocked by Houphouët, the BDS moved left and changed its name to Bloc populaire sénégalais, taking with it the

Mouvement autonome de Casamance – the regional independence movement for Casamance which had grown out of the final "pacification" in the region little more than a decade earlier. Mamadou Dia became prime minister in the new territorial government of 1957 after the defeat of Lamine Guèye's SFIO. His party subsequently merged with the BPS and the Union Progressiste Sénégalaise (UPS) was born.

The UPS was soon split by the coming to power of **de Gaulle** in 1958 and his intransigent offer of either immediate independence and severance from the French Union or continued self-government within the French Union. It was a critical choice and one that Senghor was unwilling to make. Mindful of French economic clout as well as his support among the marabouts and their mistrust of the party left wing, he ultimately sacrificed a section of young UPS radicals (who immediately formed their own party) and made sure that Senegal's vote to continue the Union was yes. With this Lamine Guèye and even Mamadou Dia were in accord. But trade unionists, intellectuals and Casamance separatists were mostly alienated and disappointed at the submission to de Gaulle. Modern opposition politics have their roots in the 1958 referendum.

Independence

Senghor still favoured an independent, Dakar-led federation of states. Working with the ex-territory of Soudan (now Mali) and others, the **Mali Federation** was formed to further this end. However, by the time it was constituted in April 1959, the federation's members were reduced to Mali and Senegal – an unworkable alliance given the influence of Dakar. But it was pursued nonetheless.

Lamine Guèye was now elected president of the new territorial assembly, Modibo Keita of Mali president of the Federal Government and Mamadou Dia vice-president. In September, inspired by Guinea's secession, the Mali Federation lobbied France for independence. In a *volte-face* that amazed most observers, de Gaulle conceded that total independence should not, after all, deny a country the right to remain within the French Union. On April 4, 1960 (now National Day), the principle of independence for the Mali Federation was declared, and on June 20, 1960, **independence** was proclaimed.

On August 20, 1960, the Mali Federation suddenly broke down over the election of a president. The Senegalese had insisted on Senghor for this role, having begun to distrust Bamako's rigorous Marxist policies. Senegal proclaimed its **independence from Mali** the same day, arresting Modibo Keita and sending him back to Bamako in a sealed train wagon. Mali refused to recognize the new **Republic of Senegal** and for three years the Dakar–Bamako railway was unused.

Senghor as president

Senghor took the presidency of the new republic, keeping Mamadou Dia as his prime minister. Senghor's formulation of **négritude**, Senegal's nationalism, blended with his motto "*Assimiler, pas être assimilés*", urging Africans to assimilate European culture, not be assimilated by it. On this foundation, Senghor and the UPS built the ideology of **African socialism**, which amounted to a tacit defence of the status quo in its emphasis on consensus. Dia, whose own politics remained to the left of Senghor, failed to find a balance between the business community and the radical left, and succeeded only in irritating the French. In 1962, Senghor had him arrested (he was sentenced to life imprisonment after an alleged coup attempt in which the army came to Senghor's rescue), and relations with France began to prosper.

The one-party state

The rest of the decade saw the government growing increasingly right-wing.

In 1963 a **revised constitution** was approved, strengthening the role of the president and effectively forcing radical opposition underground. Cheikh Anta Diop's Bloc des masses sénégalaises (BMS), the most powerful group the opposition could legally muster, was smashed by a massive and disputed UPS victory in the elections of that year. **Riots** in their aftermath were put down by troops, with many deaths – the first serious smear on Senegal's hitherto spotless reputation. The BMS was banned; the remaining opposition had by 1966 been forced into the UPS or harassed out of existence.

Farmers were badly hit by the abolition of French subsidies for groundnut prices in 1967, while most town dwellers were no better off than they had been before independence. In May 1968 **trade unionists** and **students protested** at the government's complacency, confronting it with the charge of neo-imperialism. Senghor confronted the protesters with the army. Further strikes were followed by some concessions, then the government tried to force the unions into its own muzzled national confederation of workers.

Repeated crises slackened at the end of the decade when Senghor revived the post of prime minister – given to Abdou Diouf in 1970 – and when, after further university unrest in 1973, banned the teachers' union and jailed some of the activists. The party was renamed the **Parti socialiste** (PS), a cosmetic alteration that convinced few.

Democratic reforms

In 1974, a cautious new liberalism was initiated with the release of ex-PM Mamadou Dia from twelve years in detention. Soon after, the **Parti démocratique sénégalais** (PDS), led by lawyer **Maître Abdoulaye Wade**, was allowed to register, and by 1976 various brands of liberal and social democracy were on offer, as well as a legal Marxist-Leninist party, which attracted a small number of radicals. A flood of political handouts and newssheets hit the streets. Anta Diop and Mamadou Dia were banned from forming parties, but not excluded from discussion.

By 1978, Senghor – now in his late 60s – was spending more time on poetry and the Académie française than running Senegal, and he began to groom **Abdou Diouf**, now vice-president, for leadership. Diouf was already taking responsibility for executive decisions and his status grew as he gained support from the major aid institutions for his austere management of the economy.

A sideshow in the late 1970s was the **militant Tijaniya dynasty** of Ahmet Khalif Niasse. Niasse went into exile in Libya allegedly intending to organize for an Islamic state in Senegal, which led to the cutting of diplomatic relations. The Libyan connection resurfaced across the border in The Gambia, where the "coup attempt" of October 1980 reportedly had the same roots. President Jawara invoked the two countries' historic relationship, and Senegalese troops were sent in.

Diouf in power

Senghor, the first African president to retire voluntarily, passed the presidency to Diouf on January 1, 1981. At first it was feared that Diouf's uncharismatic style would be insufficient to carry him, but **opposition groups** were hopeful he would lift remaining restrictions on political activities. Their hopes were soon fulfilled: Cheikh Anta Diop's Rassemblement national démocratique (RND) was legalized, and Dia founded the Mouvement démocratique populaire (MDP). Wade's PDS relinquished its role as the focal point of opposition and actually lost a few members in a purge of pro-Libyan sympathizers.

Diouf increased his popularity by launching an **anti-corruption drive** focusing on his own cabinet and by firing Senghor's "barons". And traditional supporters of the government – the moderate Muslim masses – were gratified to have a president at last who spoke Wolof as his mother tongue and peppered his speeches with Koranic references.

The July 1981 coup in **The Gambia** served as the most severe test of Diouf's nerve in his first year in office. President Jawara called him from London to ask Senegal to restore him to power, which the Senegalese army accomplished with considerable bloodshed. A Senegalese detachment stayed in The Gambia until the late 1980s. The spectre of an unfriendly and destabilizing power taking control in The Gambia galvanized Diouf to do something about the dormant **Senegambia confederation** (see p.264). In December 1981 an agreement was ratified and a Senegambian parliament met for its first session in 1983. The Gambia, with no army and little to offer Senegal except a headache and its river, was always likely to be the passive partner in a relationship that finally collapsed in 1989.

The **economy**, meanwhile, continued to decline. Although the state groundnut-buying monopoly was dissolved in 1980 after years of corruption and inefficiency, low prices and disastrous harvests that year and in 1984 meant no perceptible improvement for the peasant farmers. **Fishing** was pushed into first place as a foreign-exchange earner, with **tourism** second and groundnuts third.

The **1988 election** saw the first display of really serious political and social unrest during Diouf's presidency: an ominously quiet polling day was followed by violent riots in Dakar. Diouf declared a **state of emergency**; tanks and tear gas came onto the streets; a dusk-to-dawn curfew was in force for three weeks; and **Abdoulaye Wade**, who claimed to have been defeated by a rigged poll, was arrested. His trial and conviction on charges of incitement to subvert the state triggered further unrest, which was later quelled by his own, characteristically conciliatory, remarks.

Diouf, however, later withdrew any inference of a pact between him and Wade and set about making **changes to the electoral system**, ostensibly to guarantee fairer elections. In practice these adjustments delayed local elections and enraged Wade and the main opposition alliance, **Sopi** ("Change"), who accused Diouf of perpetuating the distortion of the democratic process by vested interests and vote buying.

Even the intense dissatisfaction with the political scene was overshadowed during the **Senegal–Mauritania crisis** of April 1989 to October 1990. Triggered by a land dispute on the border, local fighting flared into racial conflict as Mauritanian shopkeepers (the 300,000-strong mainstay of Senegal's retail trade) were hounded out of Senegal, hundreds killed and their stores looted. An international operation assisted refugees to return to Nouakchott, while Senegalese immigrants in Mauritania (who were even more violently and systematically attacked) returned to Senegal. Tens of thousands of Fula-speaking Mauritanians ("southerners" in Mauritanian parlance) also came – the Nouakchott government had taken the opportunity to expel them at the same time. The borders between the two countries closed, and a cloud of deep mutual mistrust hung over the two governments through much of the next decade.

The 1990s

On the political front, the dominant theme of the 1990s – viewed from Dakar, at least, if not from Ziguinchor (see box, p.231) - was a low-level, grumbling discontent with the inertia of the Parti socialiste, which several times boiled up into riots.

Like those of 1988, the **elections of February 1993** were again the subject of condemnation by Abdoulaye Wade over alleged photocopied registration papers, multiple voting and other ploys. In the presidential ballot Diouf won overall, though Wade came out in front in the main urban areas of Dakar and Thiès. Three months later in the national assembly elections, Wade's PDS obtained less than a quarter of the seats while the PS won more than two-thirds, on a turnout of well under half the electorate. Wade claimed that if the election had been conducted fairly, PDS would have been in the lead. Days after announcing the results the vice-chief of the electoral commission, **Babacar Sèye**, was assassinated. The perpetrators remain unknown (a previously unheard-of "Armée du Peuple" claimed responsibility) but it was Abdoulaye Wade and three associates who were arrested without charge. One of them, **Mody Sy**, was kept in jail for more than a year.

The **devaluation of the CFA franc** in February 1994 – supported by Diouf, and partly engineered by him – was particularly hard on the poor. Later that year, in a mass rally for democracy in Dakar, led by the **Tijaniya brotherhood**'s fundamentalist-leaning youth organization Daira al Moustarchidines wal Moustarchidates, militant protestors precipitated a riot and then rounded on the security forces, killing six policemen in a frenzied attack that left the country stunned.

Wade and six senior opposition figures on the march were among a group of 177 people arrested for incitement to violence, though most were eventually released. As a result, a new opposition alliance, Bokk Sopi Sénégal ("Uniting to Change Senegal"), was formed in September 1994 from Wade's PDS, **Landing Savané**'s communist And-Jëf–Parti Africaine pour la Démocratie et le Socialisme (AJ–PADS) and Mamadou Dia's Mouvement pour le Socialisme et l'Unité (MSU).

Despite their opposition status, in 1995 Wade and six PDS colleagues took **cabinet posts** in the national government on the invitation of Abdou Diouf – the better for Diouf to deal with the charismatic and outspoken Wade behind closed doors than across the barricades. This was not the first time that Wade had accepted a cabinet post, and his credentials as a man of the people – resigning from government to

campaign against Diouf at each election, then returning to the cabinet on Diouf's invitation after losing the poll – looked to be wearing thin.

In February 1998, the PS again won a resounding victory in national assembly elections, but there were signs that the party was running into trouble. Divisions started to emerge in late 1997, when **Djibo Laity Ka** and other senior figures within the party formed a breakaway faction called the Mouvement pour le renouveau démocratique (MRD); Ka was suspended from the party and a few months later he resigned, denouncing the PS for corruption and electoral fraud. In 1999, **Moustapha Niasse**, a former foreign minister, also broke ranks, criticizing Diouf and announcing his candidature for the 2000 presidential election; he was promptly expelled from the PS and formed his own party, the Alliance des forces de progrès (AFP).

The opposition, meanwhile, was also busy maneuvering for another attempt to dislodge Diouf. After once again resigning from government in 1998, Wade was nominated in March 1999 by a left-wing alliance of opposition parties to be their joint presidential candidate.

The 2000 presidential elections

As the 2000 presidential election approached, tensions were running high in Senegal, and the country seemed ripe for change. Young people in particular mobilized during the election campaign to work against Diouf, with students going on strike and returning to the regions to tell their elders how much they were struggling under PS rule. On election day, the talk on the streets was of possible civil war if the PS tried to rig the vote or Diouf somehow managed to win.

In the event, Diouf – with 41.3 percent of the vote – failed to win an overall majority, meaning that he proceeded to a **second round** of voting with the second-placed Wade (31 percent). A large part of the PS vote had gone to Niasse, who threw his weight behind Wade in the second round. Already supported by prominent left-wingers such as **Landing Savané** and influential members of the **Mouride brotherhood**, Wade went on to gain a substantial victory, garnering 58.5 percent of the second-round vote. Both the election itself, which was described as fair and transparent by international observers, and Diouf's gracious acceptance of defeat enhanced Senegal's reputation as one of the more stable and democratic countries in Africa.

The Wade era

Following his victory, Wade set about consolidating his position. Having rewarded Niasse for his support by making him prime minister, Wade went on to dismiss him in March 2001 and replaced him with the lower-profile **Mame Madior Boye**, Senegal's first female prime minister. Wade's mandate was strengthened further when his PDS-led **Sopi coalition** won a landslide victory in the April 2001 **parliamentary elections**.

Wade started his presidency positively, reaffirming his commitment to democracy

The Casamance conflict

The reawakening of separatist feeling in Casamance was signalled by sporadic **demonstrations** there throughout the 1980s, often put down at a cost of many lives and with hundreds in detention. In 1990, serious armed conflict erupted as the military wing of the **Mouvement des Forces Démocratiques de la Casamance** (MFDC) went into action. By 1993, in advance of the presidential and legislative elections (boycotted by the MFDC), there were five thousand troops in Casamance and the region was under military control. That year saw a ceasefire agreement and the release of many prisoners by the government, but hostilities flared up again in the southern districts at the end of 1994. Despite the establishment of a **Commission Nationale de Paix**, the army and air force retaliated with bombing raids and manhunts through the forest, in a sporadic, tit-for-tat war which has continued ever since.

The MFDC claim that Casamance existed as a separate territory before the French colonial era, and a large part of its membership wants independence from Senegal. The movement is split loosely into the Front Nord, based to the north of Baila and Bignona, and the more extreme Front Sud, focused on the villages along the Guinea-Bissau border. The MFDC's main leader is regarded as **Abbé Augustine Diamacouné Senghor**, though in recent years his influence has waned as the movement has disintegrated into various factions.

The violence in Casamance has severely damaged the **tourist industry**, on which the region is heavily dependent for foreign exchange, but it is ordinary villagers who have suffered the most as MFDC guerillas have abandoned their original aims. By the late 1990s it had become clear that banditry and control of the lucrative local **cannabis** crop were more important to most fighters in the bush than the political principles at stake. The MFDC began to turn on itself; retired or disenchanted guerillas were murdered by active units. Despite pleas from Diamacouné Senghor to desist, **mines** (smuggled in from Guinea-Bissau) were laid on minor roads and farm tracks, particularly between Ziguinchor and Cap Skiring, killing and maiming hundreds. Amnesty International accused both sides of terrorizing local people.

Hopes of a peaceful resolution to the conflict rose when President Wade came to power and launched negotiations in December 2000 with most of the MFDC faction leaders. A **provisional peace agreement** in which the MFDC modified its separatist position was signed in March 2001, but there has been little follow-up and the agreement's validity has been undermined by renewed clashes and by the MFDC's internal divisions.

by pushing through a revised **constitution** in January 2001, which reduced the presidential term of office from seven to five years and transferred some of the president's powers to the prime minister. He has cut an impressive figure on the international stage, leading Africa's response to the **September 11** attacks on America by calling for an African "pact against terrorism". A couple of months later, in December 2001, Wade led Senegal in mourning upon the death of its first president, Léopold Senghor.

Prospects and threats

Ironically, the wave of hope that swept Wade to power has turned out to be his biggest problem, as he and his government struggle to meet voters' unrealistically high expectations. At the start of the new century, Senegal's industry was in steep decline, relying heavily on imported raw materials; agricultural diversification was still needed; education was a shambles after years of class boycotts and strikes; and society was increasingly divided between employees of the state and their relatives – the state pays ten times the national average –

and those who have to rely for their income on the private sector or the informal and subsistence economy. Since coming to power, Wade has declared his commitment to liberalizing the economy, clamping down on **corruption** and developing **infrastructure** – a new international airport being one of his pet projects. But progress has been frustratingly slow, and as the role of the public sector has declined in line with Wade's reform programme, so **unemployment** has grown. The **Casamance** conflict has rumbled on (see box, p.231), despite Wade's promise to find a rapid solution when he took office.

The country's morale took a further blow with the **sinking** of the MV *Joola* in September 2002 (see p.156), in the aftermath of which Wade disbanded the cabinet and sacked several high-ranking officials, including Mame Madior Boye, replacing her with his close aide and PDS stalwart **Idrissa Seck**, who at 43 is regarded as Wade's heir apparent. Wade has not hinted at retirement, however, and some think that, health permitting, he may even run for a **second term** as president in 2007, when he will be 81.

Senegal's Muslim brotherhoods

Ligey si top, yala la bok
"Work is part of religion"

Amadou Bamba, founder of Mouridism

Any insight into modern Senegal requires an understanding of the country's extraordinarily influential Muslim brotherhoods. You won't stay here long without noticing – in the names on the bush taxis, the signs on the village shops and the flocks of multicoloured disciples – that something very unusual lies in the dusty heart of Senegalese society.

Origins

The Muslim **brotherhoods** are in conflict with original, Arabian, Islam, which

says everyone has a direct relationship with God. They resulted from the religion's spread to the Berber peoples of northwest Africa, the brotherhoods flourishing in these class-based societies where it was natural to think that certain men should be gifted with divine insight, able to perform miracles and bestow blessings.

One of the earliest dynasties of Moroccan Muslims to make permanent contact with the people south of the desert was the **Almoravid** (whence marabout: holy leader/saint) who, in the twelfth century, made conversions in the kingdom of **Tekrur** in northeast Senegal. In the fifteenth century, the **Qadiriya** brotherhood was introduced south of the Sahara and, by the end of the eighteenth century, was firmly based near Timbuktu. Stressing **charity**, **humility** and **piety**, Qadirism made no exclusive demands of its followers and recruited from all ethnic groups. A local Qadiri offshoot, the **Layen** brotherhood, was founded in the late nineteenth century as an exclusively Lebu-speaking order in the Cap Vert district near Dakar.

Another order, the **Tijaniya**, crossed the desert early in the nineteenth century and was spread over Senegal by the proselytizing warlord Omar Tall. Tijaniya laid less stress on humility than earlier orders. Indeed, its Moroccan founder Al-Tijani had claimed direct contact with the Prophet Muhammad and, as a consequence, his followers were forbidden allegiance to any other orders. The brotherhood rapidly recruited the mass of Tukulor speakers in northeast Senegal. Tukulor marabouts – notably the forefathers of the hugely influential **Sy** and **Mbacke** families – were largely responsible for the later conversion of the Wolof.

Marabouts and the French

The interplay between the brotherhoods and the French was complicated. Allegiances often cut through ties of birth and language, so that, typically, peasants found themselves in alliance with the marabouts against their own, traditional rulers who tended to conspire with the French. Moreover, "pacification" by the French often resulted in more fertile ground for the spread of Islam.

By the early 1900s, with the conversion to Islam of even the most resistant traditional rulers, a new establishment of **vested interests** had been founded, uniting the French and the marabouts. Although the Tijaniya traditionally had a core of fundamentalist, anti-French sentiment, the order soon adjusted to the material realities of colonialism. The latest and greatest brotherhood, the **Mouridiya** – exclusively rural and Senegalese – came, in practice, to be a bastion of the status quo.

Mouridism

The Mouridiya was founded in 1887 by **Amadou Bamba**, nephew of the Wolof king Lat Dior, and a member of the influential Mbacke family. An offshoot of the Qadiriya brotherhood, Mouridiya initially attracted many former anti-colonial fighters inspired by its discipline and dynamism, and by the charisma of Bamba.

Rumours of an armed insurrection from his court at Touba terrified the French ("We cannot tolerate a state within a state") and Bamba was twice exiled by the authorities – though these banishments served only to increase his standing at home. Mouride folk history places great emphasis on Bamba's anti-colonial credentials, but soon after his return to Senegal in 1907 (a return celebrated in the annual Magal pilgrimage), he was striking deals with the authorities and trusting in the slow wheels of political reform. He was also amassing a personal fortune.

One of Bamba's early disciples, **Ibra Fall**, though not a gifted Koranic student, was personally devoted to the marabout. Bamba gave him an axe and told him to work for God with that. Sheikh Ibra Fall went on to found the fanatically slavish **Baye Fall**. Today, these dreadlocked devotees in patchwork robes have their own khalif but are exempt from study and even from fasting at Ramadan.

The founding of Baye Fall signalled a radical shift in religious thought, making **labour** a virtue and bringing Mouridism into the very heart of contemporary life. Among Mourides (whose name means "the hopeful") there's a universal belief that hard work is the key to paradise. Bamba is credited with announcing "If you work for me I shall pray for you" and even the five daily prayers are less important than toiling in the groundnut fields. The colonial authorities and the Mouride marabouts – mostly from wealthy, landed families – soon found areas of agreement.

The brotherhoods today

With a few exceptions, the brotherhoods have rooted firmly in the safest political ground. The government, while insisting that the state and political process is strictly secular, lavishes publicity and patronage on the marabouts for delivering votes. In 1968 the chief khalif instructed Mouride university students to disobey the strike call, and for the next thirty years, **presidential elections** were heavily influenced by the usual maraboutic injunctions. It has long been an irony of Senegalese politics – and frustrating for the country's liberal movers and shakers – that Senegal, with its highly developed democratic structures, should find true democracy repeatedly brushed aside by the mass of its people in exchange for the grace of God.

Cooperation between the government and the brotherhoods has survived the transfer of power from the long-ruling Parti socialiste to Wade and his Sopi coalition (the Mouride brotherhood's endorsement of Wade was vital in helping him win). As the country enjoys its fifth decade of independence, there are few signs of the link between politics and the brotherhoods breaking down. Yet the relationship remains one of latent mistrust, and even if many of those involved profit through it, the potential for a reactionary and anti-secular revolt against the government has always been there, as the Mouride brotherhood is conservative and rigorously hierarchical.

Economically, the Mouride connection with groundnuts remains, on the whole, solid, with the religious elite supported by the harvest and the boundless offerings of their followers. Many senior and middle-ranking Mouride disciples today form a **new business class**. Even French-educated businessmen would rather become disciples of respected marabouts than short-cut the system. Over a dozen Mourides are multibillionaires in CFA francs (worth up to £100 million/$150 million) and Lebanese entrepreneurs find that business is increasingly out of their hands.

Trafficking has been profitable too, not least in the Mouride capital **Touba** itself, where the absence of government agents brought racketeering on a grand scale. All the hardware of Western consumerism, and even alcohol and arms, was widely available until the chief khalif, under pressure from Dakar, admitted that Mouridism was in danger of losing its soul, and allowed *gendarmes* into the holy city. The black market is clandestine again, but still funnels huge quantities of money and goods between Senegal and The Gambia.

The **Magal** pilgrimage to Touba has become the traditional occasion when the president reiterates his support for the Mourides and his appreciation of the benefits they have brought Senegal. In turn, the chief khalif is expected to emphasize to his millions of followers the sanctity of the groundnut harvest, the importance of not rocking the boat and their duty to support stable government. The implicit message is that a vote against the government would be a vote against the khalif, and therefore against God. The Tijaniya **Gamou** gatherings, in Tivaouane and Kaolack, are smaller-scale versions of the Magal, and similar back-slapping is the order of the day.

The **succession** to the position of chief khalif is a time of crisis in every brotherhood, since the relationship between the voters and the elected government hangs very heavily on the words of the marabouts. The current Mouride chief khalif, **Serigne Saliou Mbacke**, is considered to be less interested in worldly matters than his predecessor, and therefore less likely to throw his weight behind political campaigning. Since the death of the last Tijaniya chief khalif, Abdoul Aziz Sy, in 1997, there have been dynastic quarrels within that brotherhood, and the new Tijaniya chief khalif, **Serigne Mansour Sy**, has a reputation for independent thinking. These facts have worried successive governments, which remain concerned about the rise of a more **fundamentalist** strand of Islam in Senegal.

Music

While traditional **griots** are less and less to be seen, many Senegalese musicians are internationally known. **Youssou N'Dour** is the biggest star, but he's just one of many.

Folk music

Senegalese **folk music** is heavily influenced by the traditions of the Mande heartland to the east. You're most likely to hear Wolof, Fula, Tukulor (Toucouleur) and Serer music in the north and Mandinka, Jola and Balanta music in Casamance.

In the south, listen out for the huge double xylophones or **balo** of the **Balanta**, played by two people facing each other. You may hear them, but you'll have difficulty seeing them, because they're invariably surrounded by a jostle of whooping and clapping women.

The best-known **drums** are the Wolof **tama** and **sabar** (both used to great effect by Youssou N'Dour and his band). Drums of all shapes and sizes are in great abundance in Senegal and are the only instruments that can be played by absolutely anyone. Wrestling matches are fine opportunities to hear some first-class drumming – in snatches. The wrestlers bring their own drummers to support them and the drum teams jog and pace around the arena, competing with each other with cacophonous dedication.

Modern music

The **modern music** scene in Senegal has been dominated for many years by the soaring voice of **Youssou N'Dour**, backed by his band, the **Super Étoile de Dakar**. Youssou plays **mbalax**, a style rooted in the Wolof tradition, featuring frenetic rhythms with bursts of tama (battered by **Assane Thiam**) and complex time signatures. Of the many other superb musicians around, **Baaba Maal**, a conservatoire-trained Tukulor singer from Podor, is also internationally renowned.

In recent years, homegrown **rap** music, largely in Wolof, has been a huge phenomenon in Senegal. **Positive Black Soul** are the best known of the local acts, though there's a host of other names to check out, including **Daara J** and **Pee Froiss**.

The Rough Guide to the Music of Senegal and The Gambia (World Music Network). This compilation album features hits by stars such as Youssou N'Dour and Cheikh Lô, as well as several interesting works by lesser-known artists.

Streets of Dakar – Génération Boul Falé (Stern's). Gutsy, invigorating overview of the current scene, showcasing a wealth of emerging artists, from the earthy neotraditional sounds of Fatou Guewel and Gambian kora duo Tata and Salaam to rap and supercharged nouveau mbalax from Assane Ndiaye and Lemzo Diamono.

Youssou N'Dour

One of the outstanding African music stars of his generation, yet when in Senegal, Youssou still plays regularly at his club, *Thiossane*, in Dakar. Youssou's huge body of work, though patchy, is varied and fascinating, continually reworked to cater to the separate demands of his markets at home, in France and in the English-speaking world.

Etoile de Dakar Vols 1–4 (Stern's). The collected works of one of Senegal's seminal bands, featuring Youssou N'Dour. Near-essential.

The Guide (Sony/Columbia). Probably his most successful attempt at giving *mbalax* the big budget, international treatment. Containing many moods, it seems uncertain in places, but the single "7 Seconds" (with Neneh Cherry) certainly found an audience.

Immigrés (Earthworks). Homage to Senegalese migrant workers, this midperiod cassette, lovingly remastered for CD, has great warmth and an unusually open-ended feel.

The Rough Guide to Youssou N'Dour and Etoile de Dakar (World Music Network). Some of the strongest material by Youssou and his band.

Baaba Maal

One of the biggest stars of Senegalese music, Maal sings in the Tukulor language (a dialect of Fula), accompanied by guitarist Mansour Seck and electric band Dande Lenol (which means "The Voice of the People").

Djam Leelii (Palm Pictures). Playing acoustic guitar and singing with childhood friend Mansour Seck, Baaba Maal interprets the traditional tunes and themes of the Senegal River region where he was born. Music to be transported by.

Firin' in Fouta (Mango). An exciting slab of Afro-modernism. British producer Simon Emmerson finds Celtic resonances and enlists salsa hornmen and Wolof ragga merchants. A highpoint of its kind.

Lam Toro (Mango). One of the most personal of all Maal's albums, dedicated to his mother who died young but who remains the guiding spirit in all his art.

Missing You (Mi Yeewnii) (Palm Pictures). Recorded at one of Maal's homes, this richly atmospheric album adds influences from Mali and southern Senegal to his usual style.

Orchestra Baobab

Formed in 1971 by saxophonist Issi Cissokho and vocalist Laye M'Boup, Baobab were one of the first groups to use Wolof and Mandinka songs as the basis for electric music. The band broke up in 1982 but returned triumphantly twenty years later, winning the album of the year award for *Specialist in All Styles* at the 2003 BBC Radio 3 World Music Awards. If you find any old Baobab tapes, buy them; you won't be disappointed.

Pirate's Choice (World Circuit). Blissfully good 1982 set from the best Senegalese band of the 1970s. The *On Verra Ça* collection (also World Circuit) is almost as hot.

Specialist in All Styles (World Circuit, UK; Nonesuch, US). Old hits are reinvented and new songs introduced on Baobab's inspirational comeback album, featuring guest vocals from co-producer Youssou N'Dour.

Super Diamono de Dakar

Super Diamono go for a much harder sound with heavy bass and powerful kit drums, quite different from *mbalax*. The "people's band" of Dakar's proletarian suburbs, Diamono mixed reggae militancy, jazz cool and hardcore traditional grooves. Their influential early incarnations await some enterprising archivist: try to hear the early album, *Ndaxona*, which features the wailing vocals of Omar Pene.

Fari (Stern's). Two cassettes of material on one CD from the early 1990s when main man Pene had reformed the band with top Dakar session men. A bit smooth for some tastes, but the overall feel is deeply Senegalese.

Cheikh Lô

A member of the Baye Fall (the dread-locked guardians of Touba) and a some-time drummer with the band Xalam, Lô had to wait years before finally finding a chance with Youssou N'Dour's local studio.

Ne la Thiass (World Circuit, UK). Strong songs and a warm organic feel make for joined-up pop with real international appeal. Deservedly a huge hit.

Ismael Lô

Harmonica-player and guitarist, Lô was a member of Super Diamono during their early days in the late 1970s. "Super Diamono's manager asked if I wanted to join them and go with them on tour and I stayed with them for four years. My pay was a packet of cigarettes a day, and if you wanted something like shoes, you asked the boss."

Diawar (Stern's). Features one of Ismael Lô's best tracks, "Sophia", a 1989 interpretation of the song "On Verra Ça", previously recorded by Orchestra Baobab.

Books

There are several **books** by Senegalese writers in the Heinemann African writers series. Other, mostly academic, English-language works are only likely to be available in libraries or possibly over the Internet. In French, there's a very wide range of literature – by both French and Senegalese – and a steady output of glossy tomes to whet travellers' appetites. Books marked o/p below are out of print; those marked ⊞ are especially recommended.

Lucy C. Behrman *Muslim Brotherhoods and Politics in Senegal*. Fascinating, though dated, study with interesting statistical information about the marabouts at the start of the last century.

Michael Crowder *Senegal: A Study of French Assimilation Policy* (o/p). Concise, fairly unacademic look at how the French colonized African minds.

Donal B. Cruise O'Brien *The Murides of Senegal: the Political and Economic Organization of an Islamic Brotherhood* (o/p). The definitive text in English on the Mouride brotherhood.

Sheldon Gellar *Senegal: an African Nation between Islam and the West*. A condensed and very readable survey, though not updated since 1995.

⊠ **Mark Hudson** *The Music in My Head*. Energetic, constantly amusing and inventive "world music" novel, incorporating glowing passages of superb descriptive prose. If you're going to Senegal – sorry, "Tekrur" – this is the one for the beach.

Janet G. Vaillant *Black, French and African*. Biography of Léopold Senghor.

Novels and poetry

Mariama Bâ *So Long a Letter.* Dedicated to "all women and to men of good will", this is the story of a woman's life shattered by her husband's sudden, second marriage to a younger woman. Bâ's *The Scarlet Song*, published posthumously, eloquently traces the relationship between a French woman and a poor, Senegalese man.

Birago Diop *Tales of Amadou Koumba.* A collection of short stories based on the tales of a griot, and rooted in Wolof tradition.

Cheikh Hamidou Kane *Ambiguous Adventure.* The autobiographical tale of a man torn between Tukulor, Islam and the West. Recommended.

⭐ **Sembène Ousmane** (or Ousmane Sembène) *God's Bits of Wood; Xala; The Last of the Empire* and others. A committed, political and very immediate writer (and film-maker) who can also be very funny, as in *Xala*, the satirical tale of a wealthy Dakarois' loss of virility. The best of these, by far, is *God's Bits of Wood*, the story of the rail strike of 1947.

Leopold Senghor *Leopold Sédhar Senghor: Collected Poetry.* Works from the negritude era, including *Songs of Darkness and Nocturnes*.

Language

Though only twenty percent of the population has any fluency in the colonial tongue, communication is rarely a problem if you speak **French** to some degree. (English alone won't get you far.) You'll have a far better time, however, if you know some **Wolof**. It's not an easy language, but making the effort to say even a few simple greetings will gratify people out of all proportion to your ability.

Wolof is not the whole story. Important minority vernaculars include: **Fula**, spoken by the Tukulor and Fula; **Serer**, spoken by the partly Christianized people of the same name (we include a bit of Serer vocabulary on p.182); **Kriyol**, a Portuguese creole spoken by up to 50,000 people along the coast south of Dakar; **Jola**, spoken in various dialects in the Casamance region; the **Mande** languages (Mandinka/Malinké – see p.270; Bamana and Sarakolé/Soninké), spoken in scattered communities across the south and east; and the languages of the **Tenda** group – Konyagi, Bedik, Bassari. All are a major component of ethnic identity, especially so in the case of Jola (for a **Jola glossary**, see p.229).

Elementary Wolof

Wolof (sometimes Ouolof or Volof to the French) is understood by an estimated eighty percent of Senegalese. Perhaps half of these are ethnic Wolof, the rest being mother-tongue speakers of other languages, all of which are losing ground. Wolof is growing in importance all the time and there are regular calls for it to be adopted as the official national language.

Wolof is classified as a "West Atlantic" language, in the same large basket of "class languages" as Fula and Serer, quite different from the "non-class" Mande languages like Mandinka, Bambara and Dyula. The main criterion for this classification is the grammatical system of Wolof, which groups nouns into fairly arbitrary classes something like genders.

There's the usual confusion over **spellings** created by British and French transcribers using their own norms, but the following selection should be quite pronounceable. The letter *x* denotes a throaty "h" sound like the *ch* in "loch". A double vowel simply lengthens the same sound, while a double consonant makes it harder.

Greetings

All purpose greeting	**Salaam alekum**
...and response	**Alekum salaam**
How are you?	**Nanga def?**
I'm fine	**Mangi fii rek**
(lit. I'm here only)	
How are you? (lit. Do you have peace?)	**Jama ngaam?**
I'm fine (lit. Peace only)	**Jama rek** (can be used as the response to any greeting)
Thank God	**Alhamdoulila**
Good morning (lit. did you sleep well?)	**Jamanga fanaan?**
How are you all? (formal)	**Naka waa keur ga?**
How are your family /home/people? (very informal)	**Ana sa wa ker?**
They're fine	**Nyung fa**
Thank you	**Jerejef**
What's your name?	**Naka nga tudd?**
My name is Dave	**Mangi tudd Dave**
What is your surname?	**Naka nga santa?**
My surname is Warne	**Mangi santa Warne**
Goodbye (I'm off)	**Mangi dem**

General practicalities

I don't understand Wolof/ French	**Man deguma Wolof/Faranse**
Please repeat	**Wahat ko**
Yes	**Waaw**
No	**Deedeet**
Perhaps	**Xey na**
Where is . . .?	**Ana. . .?**
Where are you going?	**Fan nga dem nii?**
Where is the road to Dakar?	**Yoni Dakar fan la?**
Right	**Ndeyjoor**
Left	**Chamong**
Far	**Sori**
Slowly	**Ndanka**
Please (lit. If you want)	**Su la nexe**
I don't mind/ I don't care	**Ana sema yon**
When?	**Kan?**
No problem	**Anul sono**
Wife	**Djabar/sohna**
Husband	**Jeker**

Places

Market	**Marse**
Village	**Deuke ko**
House/Family compound	**Keur**
Room	**Neeg**
Bed	**Lall**
Field	**Toll**
Forest/bush	**All**

Days

Today	**Tey**
Saturday	**Aseer**
Sunday	**Dibeer**
Monday	**Altine**
Tuesday	**Telata**
Wednesday	**Alarba**
Thursday	**Alxemes**
Friday	**Ajuma**

Numbers

1	bena
2	nyar
3	nyeta
4	nyenent
5	jerom
6	jerom bena
7	jerom nyar
8	jerom nyeta
9	jerom nyenent
10	fuka
11	fuka bena (etc)
20	nyar fuka/nit
21 (etc)	nyar fuka bena
30	nyet fuka/fanver
40	nyenent fuka
50	jerom fuka
60	jerom bena fuka
70	jerom nyar fuka
80	jerom nyeta fuka

90	jerom nyenent fuka
100	temer
1000	june

Buying

Give me/sell me...	Mai ma/jai ma...
I want/I don't want...	Bognaa/boguma ...
Enough	Doi na
More, again	Dolili
A little	Tutti
Lots of	Yu bare
Full	Fes
That's all	Bah na
How much is that?	Bi nyata le?
It's too expensive	Dafa ser
It's much too expensive	Dafa ser torop
Cheap	Yombe na
Expensive	Ser
Not expensive	Serut
Money	Xalis
Lower the price (a little)	Wanil ko (tutti)
You're killing me!	Hey! Yangi ma rey!
Leave me alone, I'm fed up/tired	Baye ma, dama sona
Gift	Ndimbal

Other needs

Please give me some water	Mai man ndox bu la nexe
I'm hungry	Dama xiif
What would you like to eat?	Loo buga leka?
I'm sleepy	Dama neleew
I'm going to sleep	Mangi neleew
I'm going to sleep (and leave me alone!)	Mangi neleew waay!
Where are you going?	Fooy dem?
Are you going to the market?	Ndax marse ngay dem?
I feel ill	Dama feebar
I've got a stomach ache	Suma biir day metti
Show me the way to the post office	Won ma yonu post bi
What would you like?	Lan nga bugg?
Do you have a little bit of aspirin?	Amuloo tutti aspirin?
Do you smoke?	Ndax dingay toox?

Do you drink palm wine?	Ndax dingay naan sung?
I don't have any money	Amuma xalis
Someone's waiting for me	Am naa ku may xaar

Emergencies

Thief!	Sachee!
S/he's ill!	Dafa feebar!
Call the police/ a doctor quickly!	Woo wall police/medecin gewal legi legi!

Trees

Baobab	Gouigi
Silk-cotton (kapok)	Bentenki
Raffia palm	Bari
Locust bean	Tir
Mandingo	Jorut
Kola oil	Netetu
Palm	Tabu

Animals

Horse	Fas
Camel	Guelem
Goat	Bei
Pig	Mbam
Cow	Nak
Bull	Yek
Lion	Gawnde/daba
Leopard	Tenev
Monkey	Golo
Elephant	Nye
Hippopotamus	Leber
Large antelope	Koba
Hyena	Buki
Porcupine	Sav
Ostrich	Baa
Pelican	Jagabar
Crocodile	Jasik
Chameleon	Kakatar
Monitor lizard	Mbeutt
Gecko	Onka
Snake	Jan
Tortoise	Mbonat

Simple Serer

Hello	Nafio
I'm fine	Miheme
Does your family live in peace?	Fambina?

Yes, they have peace	Wamaha	Yes	Lo
		No	Ha a
Goodbye	Mereta	Coconut	Koko
Thank you	Dkoka djal	Rice	Tju

Glossary

Bana Bana Itinerant street vendor.

Baye Fall Zealous disciples of Mouridism, dressed in brilliantly coloured patchwork cloaks, often seen collecting money for their marabout.

Bolon(g) Mangrove creek (Casamance).

Borom Patron, chief, owner

Boubou Long gown worn by men and women.

Ceddo Traditional Wolof warrior caste.

Clando Clandestine bar.

Damel Pre-Islamic Wolof kings.

Dara Pioneering settlements of Mouride disciples.

Dibiterie Roadside butcher and barbecue artist.

Djigeen Woman.

Fatou Somewhat derogatory term (it's a woman's name) meaning domestic servant or "girl".

Filao Casuarina tree.

La Fleuve "The River" – the Senegal.

Fromager Silk-cotton tree (kapok).

Gewel Griot; praise singer, musician, storyteller.

Goor Man/Male.

Gue Ford, river crossing

Hajj The pilgrimage to Mecca; correspondingly El Hajj refers to someone who has been on the pilgrimage.

Herbe Qui Tu Cannabis.

HLM "Habitations à Loyer Modérés" – council flats, housing projects.

Jeu de Dames Draughts, checkers; a more competitive game than wure.

Keur/kerr/ker Place, home.

Magal Annual mass pilgrimage to Touba on the occasion of Cheikh Amadou Bamba's birthday.

Maquis Cheap place to eat.

Marabout Enormously powerful religious leader accredited with magical powers.

Mbalax Musical style, a modern expression of traditional roots rhythms.

Mouridiya One of the two most powerful Islamic orders, with its headquarters near Touba.

PDS Parti Démocratique Sénégalais, the ruling party under President Wade.

Planton Orderly, watchman, dogsbody.

PS Parti socialiste (though it has no socialist agenda), the long-time ruling party, now in opposition.

Radio Kankan Public rumour.

Sandarma *Gendarme*.

Sayisayi Playboy.

Talibe Disciple of a marabout.

Teranga Hospitality, generosity; sums up the Wolof code of behaviour to strangers

Tijaniya Numerically the largest Islamic brotherhood divided into dynasties, some of which are fundamentalist in nature; headquarters at Tivaouane.

Touba The holy city east of Dakar; also means "happiness".

Toubab Foreigner, usually white; from the Wolof "to convert"; you'll hear it a lot from kids.

Yamba Cannabis.

Dakar, Cap Vert and central Senegal

West Africa's westernmost point and one of its most westernized capital cities, **Dakar** wields a powerful influence. Its pull extends well beyond Senegal's borders, drawing in migrants from across the Sahel and expatriates from overseas – especially, still, France. The city swarms with newcomers caught up in the neocolonial whirlpool, and its attractions are tempered by all this hustle and by the sheer size of the place. But the physical setting is striking, and the city has undeniable style, epitomizing the residue of French colonialism in Africa.

Out of Dakar, the **Ile de Gorée** is a major draw, while the peninsula of **Cap Vert** offers beaches and out-of-town amusements. A more sheltered coast is the **Petite Côte** to the south of the city, which, beyond the dubious tourist magnet of **Joal-Fadiout**, merges into the bird-flocked creeks and islands of the **Sine-Saloum** region, adjoining the Gambian border.

Inland, the travel options from Dakar are harsher and the attractions scarcer, the focal points being the shady rail-network hub of **Thiès**, with its superb tapestry factory, and the much more distant Islamic hothouse of **Touba**.

Dakar

A giant of a city in African terms, with over two million inhabitants, **DAKAR** is hard work. The shock of arriving can be intense: it's incredibly dynamic, sophisticated and wretched in equal measure, and a test of will if your budget is tight. **French** influence is everywhere, especially in the downtown **Plateau** area, where the architecture and the whole feel of the place is more evocative of southern France than Africa. The results can be quite beautiful, without question. Between sprouting skyscrapers, the terracotta rooftops and shady, tree-lined avenues of the older quarters give Dakar an elegant maturity shared by few other African capitals.

Unfortunately some of the most attractive parts of the centre swarm with vendors, hustlers and hostile, hooting traffic, though this frenetic pace thankfully subsides on Saturdays, and on Sundays disappears altogether. At this time people hang out in shady shopfronts, kids play football in the streets and even the *colons* forsake their cars and taxis for a stroll out to Sunday lunch. During the week the **Ile de Gorée**, **Hann Park** and the beaches at **Ngor** and **Yof** all provide degrees of space and seclusion, and if, rather than retreat, you'd prefer a more human participation, most of Dakar's teeming **suburbs** are a lot more open and easy-going than experiences in the city centre might lead you to imagine.

Some history

The **Ile de Gorée** was first settled by European merchant adventurers in the fifteenth century, though the fortresslike peninsula of **Dakar** – the oldest European city in West Africa – was not established until 1857. The name Dakar was first used in the eighteenth century and is supposed to derive from the Wolof for tamarind tree – *daxar* – or refuge – *dekraw*.

The town's development really began towards the end of the nineteenth century, with the decline of St-Louis as a port, and the opening of the Dakar to St-Louis **railway** in 1885 (the first in West Africa), which gave a boost to groundnut farmers along its route. By the turn of the twentieth century the population numbered 15,000. With considerable dredging and port construction, Dakar became a **French naval base** in the early 1900s and the **capital** of Afrique Occidentale Française in 1904. It was also a calling port on the routes to South America and West and South Africa runs, and throughout the century of colonial occupation, Dakar's cosmopolitan reputation as the first call on "the Coast" went before it. On the opening of the Dakar–Bamako railway line in 1923, Dakar was easily the most important city in West Africa.

The original Lebu and Wolof inhabitants of the Plateau district were forced out to the new town of Medina in the early 1930s, when the Depression coincided with rent increases imposed to pay for improvements to their houses. Yet the white settlers who moved in were often poor – a rigorous colour bar prevailing over economic reality – and even today you'll see elderly French, some running small businesses, hanging onto very modest existences.

Orientation, arrival and information

Dakar is built on the twin-pronged **Cap Vert peninsula**. The southern spur contains the city's heart, with cliffs and coves along the ocean side and Cap Manuel, and the main port area along the sheltered eastern flank. The suburbs spread north and west towards the **airport** and the other prong of **Pointe des Almadies**, Africa's most westerly point.

Despite Dakar's size, the **city centre** is a relatively manageable two square kilometres of tightly gridded streets, with the **train station** to the south, the **museum** to the north, **Avenue Jean Jaurès** on the west, and the **Kermel market** and **PTT** to the east. In the middle of it all stands the big, sloping centrepiece of **place de l'Indépendance**, from where **Avenue Georges Pompidou** cuts the district into a northern, heavily commercial quarter and a southern, more affluent, residential one – the **Plateau**. Most of the grand buildings of state and several important embassies are south of this central district, where the street pattern breaks into graciously radiating avenues and looping clifftop corniches.

Arrival and information

Arriving by air, you emerge into the milling confusion of **Aeroport International Léopold Sedar Senghor** (☏820 07 80), 12km northwest of the city in Yof. Track down your luggage and hang onto it: the supervision of the arrivals hall is pretty relaxed, with lots of "porters" aiming to part you from your cash. You can change money in the airport at the CBAO **bank** (daily except Wed 8am–3pm & 5–11.30pm), which also has a 24-hour autoteller accepting Visa, MasterCard and Cirrus. Upstairs, you'll find a **business centre** (daily 8am–midnight) with a bureau de change, **Internet** access (CFA2000/hr) and **telephones**. There are also some SONATEL phone booths in the arrivals hall (cards available in shops upstairs). Information on flights can be had from the airport **information desk** and on **car hire** from the various agencies located opposite the exit.

Until 9pm, you can take a blue DDD **bus** (#8), which takes you through Yof Village and then the mishmash of Grand Dakar, past the University and right through the centre of the Plateau to the old Palais de Justice. Alternatively, **car rapides** pass about five minutes' walk away from the airport – cross the car park and turn left. They'll take you to the Marché Sandaga in Central Dakar for CFA100, and from here, a taxi across downtown Dakar shouldn't cost more than CFA500. Finally, a **taxi** to the centre officially costs CFA3000 in the daytime and

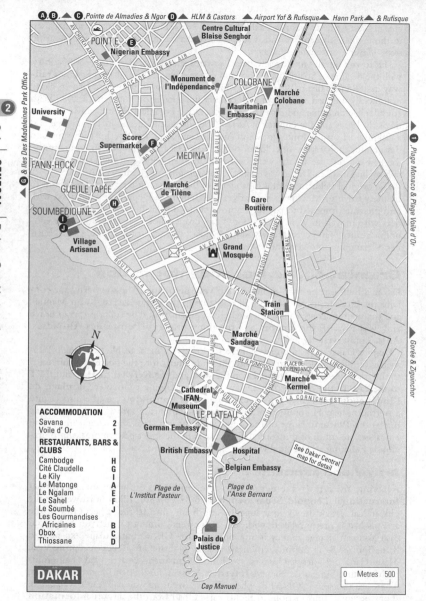

A, B, C Pointe de Almadies & Ngor D HLM & Castors Airport Yof & Rufisque Hann Park & Rufisque

1 Plage Monaco & Plage Voile d'Or

Gorée & Ziguinchor

& Îles Des Madeleines Park Office

POINT E

E Nigerian Embassy

Centre Cultural Blaise Senghor

Monument de l'Indépendance

COLOBANE

Marché Colobane

University

Mauritanian Embassy

Score Supermarket F

MEDINA

FANN-HOCK

GUEULE TAPÉE

Marché de Tilène

SOUMBEDIOUNE H

Gare Routière

I
J

Village Artisanal

Grand Mosquée

Train Station

Marché Sandaga

N

Cathedral
IFAN Museum

LE PLATEAU

Marché Kermel

PLACE DE L'INDÉPENDANCE

German Embassy

British Embassy

Hospital

See Dakar Central map for detail

Belgian Embassy

Plage de L'Institut Pasteur

Plage de l'Anse Bernard

ACCOMMODATION
Savana   2
Voile d' Or   1

RESTAURANTS, BARS & CLUBS
Cambodge   H
Cité Claudelle   G
Le Kily   I
Le Matonge   A
Le Ngalam   E
Le Sahel   F
Le Soumbé   J
Les Gourmandises
 Africaines   B
Obox   C
Thiossane   D

2

Palais du Justice

DAKAR

0   Metres 500

Cap Manuel

CFA3960 after midnight (rates are written on a sign over the taxi rank), though you'll probably still have to bargain hard.

Dakar is unusual in having just one main **gare routière**, Pompier, at the head of the *autoroute* that funnels suburban traffic into the city. It's fairly together, though not any less intimidating for that if you're not used to shouting in French at four people simultaneously while beggars pull at your clothing and the fumes from a

The obvious choices for moving on are **minibus** or **bush taxi**, for which you need the main *gare routière*, or **train**, with the latest details available at the station. Train tickets from Dakar **to Bamako** go on sale at 10am on Monday for the Wednesday morning Senegalese train and 10am Friday for the Saturday morning Malian train, though the latter was out of service at the time of writing. Second-class is always crowded. For full details, see p.313. If you're going **to Banjul** by public transport, check if the Gambian GPTC buses are running – the service used to leave from place Leclerc (just north of Marché Kermel) every afternoon but was indefinitely suspended at the time of writing. Failing that, your next best option is a seven-seat Peugeot 504 from the *gare routière*.

For a summary of **flight connections**, check the practical information at the beginning of this chapter. The main airlines are listed on p.197.

If the government has come good on its promise to replace the sunken MV *Joola* (see p.156), you may be able to take a **boat to Ziguinchor**; ask at the ferry terminal down by the Gorée wharf. At the time of its sinking, fares on the *Joola* were CFA3500 for hard seats, CFA6000 for comfortable seats, while a four-berth cabin cost CFA12,000 per person; prices are likely to rise if the service resumes.

hundred idling engines fill the air. From here it's a two-kilometre walk to the centre: much easier to take a taxi (CFA500–800) or a bus.

From the Art Deco **train station**, it's just five minutes' walk south to the closest budget hotels. The train from Bamako usually gets in after dark, so make sure you've looked at the map and know exactly where you're heading.

You may be able to glean some **tourist information** from the Ministry of Tourism on rue du Docteur Calmette, just off Boulevard de la République (BP 4049; daily 8.30am -1.30pm & 2.30-5pm; ☎821 11 26), which has some leaflets and, theoretically, some English-speaking staff. The free monthly **listings magazine** *Le Dakarois* contains some useful addresses; if you can't find it in hotels or restaurants, you can pick it up at the printers, Imprimerie St-Paul, on the corner of rue Sandiniéri and rue de Docteur Thèze (☎821 14 21).

City transport

One of Dakar's great pluses is its reliable **bus system**, run by DDD (Dakar Dem Dikk - literally "Dakar to and fro"). The easily recognizable blue buses are numbered and carry destination signs, run fairly frequently from dawn till late evening, and charge between CFA140 and CFA180. You can get to most places by bus, though during rush hours the squeeze – and the heat – are sapping. Where useful, we've included route numbers in the text.

Cars rapides – boxy Saviem or Mercedes buses, usually sporting marabout monikers ("Touba") – are a poorer, and mostly private, version. Destinations are shouted by the fare collector (CFA50–120), and although they're more erratic than the buses and confusing to newcomers, you're guaranteed an insight into the street life of Dakar. Big white ones leave from Avenue André Peytavin, near Marché Sandaga, for the route de Ouakam, Yof and Ngor, while slightly smaller yellow and blue ones jostle together up the nearby Avenue Emile Badiane for Grand Dakar, HLM and Colobane.

As for **taxis**, supply is ahead of demand so you can always argue about the fare. Most have meters, but nobody uses them, so agree the price up front. Daytime journeys in the town centre should cost no more than CFA500 and trips to the suburbs roughly CFA300 per kilometre; at night (from midnight to 5am) the tariff officially doubles, but more usually just increases by about twenty percent. Keep some change and small notes handy for drivers, who often deny having any.

Security in Dakar

The question of personal safety in Dakar is one you can't afford to be casual about, particularly when you first arrive. Decide quickly on an initial destination rather than wandering in hope. A few gangs of organized thieves operate with extraordinary daring and, burdened with luggage, you're an easy and valuable trophy. **Place de l'Indépendance** and **Avenue Georges Pompidou** are notorious trouble-spots, especially the *place* itself during banking hours – remain alert and keep valuables, purses and wallets completely out of sight. Don't be deflected or distracted by anything or anyone – keep a steady pace and get where you're going. Once you've found a base you'll soon make up your own mind about the relative safety of Dakar.

As a general rule, avoid carrying anything you'd hate to lose and never keep purses or wallets in outside or back pockets. Distractions, be they words or a touch, should always be ignored or treated with suspicion, however friendly they may seem - usually it's the overly friendly people who turn out to be the crooks. One group technique is to stop you by offering a bangle, hold your legs together from behind and grab your shirt sleeves. By the time you've realized what's happening, they're off down the street with your wallet. Another common trick is for hustlers to claim that they know you from your hotel before hitting on you for a "loan".

If you lose anything of personal value (as opposed to just money or expensive items), it's worth making a visit to the **market in Colobane** (the so-called *marché aux voleurs*), 500m east of the Monument de l'Indépendance, where, if you keep asking and manage to make the right connections, you may be able to buy it back.

The **train** isn't a very functional way of getting in or out of the city, although it is at least comprehensible. There's a commuter service to the suburbs of Tiaroye and Rufisque, both sometimes used by travellers as bases. Called *les petits trains bleus*, these trains run several times in the morning and evening in both directions (daily except Sun; 30min).

Accommodation

Dakar has dozens of **hotels**, which are generally of a decent standard but overpriced compared with the rest of the country. It's worth **booking** around the popular Christmas, New Year and Rally period (mid-Jan; see p.192), when finding a room can be difficult.

In the city centre, the majority of Dakar's budget options lie within a few blocks of place de l'Indépendance (though for the real bargains you're better off staying on Gorée; see p.199). Many budget places twin as **brothels** and can offer reasonable value, though the rooms can be shabby and the plumbing ropey – we've listed a few of the possibilities, where only particularly sensitive visitors will find the seediness uncomfortable. The **mid-price** establishments can be among the city's most pleasant lodgings, their neocolonial charm far more attractive than the range of more expensive, anodyne modern blocks. Most of the **top-bracket** (❽) hotels reviewed here charge at least CFA80,000 for a double room.

If you are planning a longer stay in Dakar, you may wish to consider **renting an apartment**. The first places to look are the free adverts and listings papers *Tam-Tam* and *L'Avis*, available at hotels and restaurants; *Tam-Tam* is the more comprehensive of the two, with a large section on apartments for rent in Dakar and on the Petite Côte. Failing that, you could try a real estate firm, such as Régie Immobilier Mugnièr et Compagnie, 11 rue Mohamed V (☎823 43 74 or 823 23 76). Some hotels below offer apartments, too, though these will be comparatively expensive. If your requirements are more modest, there are always unfurnished rooms available for around CFA20,000 a month in the Medina/Gueule Tapée quarters: knock on the doors of the larger buildings and ask "*Vous avez des chambres à louer?*"

All the hotels reviewed below are in **central Dakar**. A little further afield, the luxuriously landscaped *Hôtel Savana* at route de la Corniche Est (℡849 42 42, ⓦwww.savana.sn; ❽) is worth considering, the best place in Dakar to spend gratuitously in genuine comfort. Elsewhere we also review the region's top hotel, the *Hôtel Méridien Présidential*, out at Pointe des Almadies (see p.202); a couple of beachfront hotels nearer at hand (see p.194); and some pleasant options on the Ile de Gorée (see p.202).

Hotels

Around Marché Kermel and east of place de l'Indépendance

Du Marché 3 rue Parent ℡821 57 71. An old stand-by (albeit a brothel) near Kermel market, offering large, inexpensive s/c rooms with fans. ❸

Lagon 2 rte de la Corniche Est ℡823 60 31, ⓦwww.lagon.sn. Popular, French-run hotel right on the shore looking towards Gorée. No pool but has a private beach. ❽

Novotel av Abdoulaye Fadiga ℡823 10 90, ⓕ823 89 29, ⓦwww.novotel.com. Bland four-star highrise with recently refurbished rooms. ❽

Océanic 9 rue de Thann ℡822 20 44, ⓕ821 52 28, ⓔhotel-oceanic@sentoo.sn. Very pleasant old-style hotel, with clued-up owners and clean a/c, s/c rooms, plus four-bed apartments. ❺

Sofitel Teranga rue Colbert ℡889 22 00, ⓕ823 50 18, ⓦwww.sofitel.com. Dakar's priciest hotel – the preferred abode of visiting statesmen. Rooms from CFA100,000. ❽

On and north of Avenue Pompidou

Al Baraka 35 rue El Hadj Abdoukarim Bourgi ℡822 55 32, ⓕ821 75 41. Central place offering modern a/c rooms with TV and telephone. ❻

Continental 10 rue Galandou Diouf ℡822 10 83. One of the pleasanter budget choices, with basic mod cons. ❹

Farid 51 rue Vincens ℡823 61 23, ⓕ821 08 94. Great-value modern, clean rooms, with TV, fridge and showroom-like bathrooms and balconies. There's an excellent Lebanese restaurant downstairs. ❺

Indépendance place de l'Indépendance ℡823 10 19, ⓕ822 11 17. Dakar's earliest four-star

flagship tower block is overpriced, but does have a great view from the rooftop pool. ❽

Mon Logis 67 rue Galandou Diouf ℡821 85 25. Hard to find and depressing when you do, but just about the cheapest hotel in town, adequate as a last resort. Down an alley on av Lamine Gueye just past a blue-tiled mosque, left down a couple of steps and then right up the stairs. ❷

Provençal 17 rue Malenfant ℡ & ⓕ822 10 69. Cheap and popular hotel/brothel with a nice courtyard, just north of place de l'Indépendance. ❹

South of Avenue Pompidou

Al Afifa 46 rue Jules Ferry ℡889 90 90, ⓕ823 88 39, ⓔgmbafifa@telecomplus.sn. Slightly faded but comfortable hotel, with a pleasant pool and restaurant area out back, a bar and nightclub. ❼

Auberge Rouge 116 rue Moussé Diop, corner of rue Jules Ferry ℡823 86 61. Popular hotel with budget travellers, offering basic rooms with fans set around a courtyard. ❹

Ganalé 38 rue El Hadj A.A. Ndoye ℡821 55 70 or 821 58 54, ⓕ822 34 30, ⓔhganale@telecomplus .sn. One of central Dakar's more recent refurbishments, offering clean rooms with TV, some apartments and a popular bar/disco and restaurant. ❻

Miramar 25–27 rue Félix Fauré ℡849 29 29, ⓕ823 35 05. Slightly ageing s/c, a/c rooms with TV. Afro-kitsch spaceship decor in communal areas and the *Soninké Bar* downstairs add eccentric character. Good breakfast served. ❻

St-Louis Sun 68 rue Félix Fauré ℡822 25 70, ⓕ822 46 51. A charismatic choice, renovated in the *Louisienne* style with an attractive patio and restaurant and tidy a/c, s/c rooms with telephone. ❻

The City

Dakar is every inch a capitalist capital, with **consumption** as conspicuous and contradictory as you'd expect. Lepers, polio victims and various other beggars are a common sight, and you may find the contrasts repugnant. Once you've learnt to deal with the inevitable hassle, the two central markets of **Sandaga** and **Kermel** are worth a visit, and you'll find the irrepressible *commerçants* spilling out onto any traffic-free surface in the surrounding area. Of interest too are the superb and highly buyable offerings of the artisans at **Cour des Orfèvres**, a few minutes northwest of Sandaga.

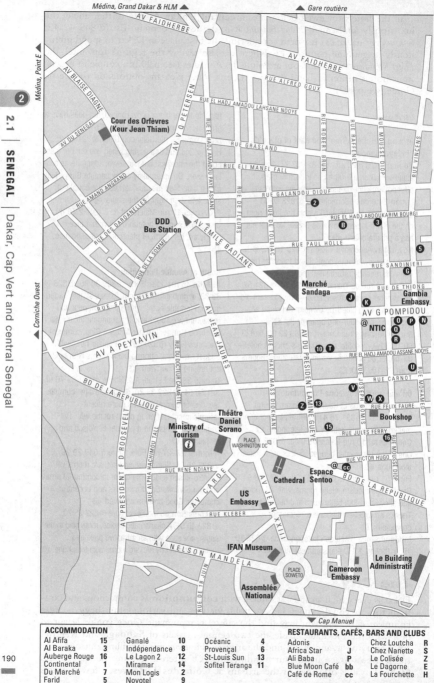

Médina, Grand Dakar & HLM ▲   **▲ Gare routière**

◀ Médina, Point E

◀ Corniche Ouest

AV FAIDHERBE
AV FAIDHERBE
RUE ALFRED GOUX
AV BLAISE DIAGNE
AV DU SENEGAL
RUE EL HADJ AMADOU LAHSANE NDOYE
RUE ROBERT BRUN
RUE RAFFENEL
RUE MOUSSE DIOP
RUE VINCENS
AV DU PETERSEN
Cour des Orfèvres (Keur Jean Thiam)
RUE GRASLAND
RUE AMAND ANGRAND
RUE EL HADJ AMADOU PAYE ASSANE
RUE ELI MANEL FALL
RUE DES DARDANELLES
RUE DE FLEURS
RUE GALANDOU DIOUF
2
RUE DE TOLBIAC
RUE EL HADJ ABDOUKARIM BOURGI
3
DDD Bus Station
B
AV EMILE BADIANE
RUE PAUL HOLLE
5
RUE DE LA SOMME
RUE SANDINIERI
RUE DE THIONG
Marché Sandaga
Gambia Embassy
RUE SANDINIERI
J
K
AV G POMPIDOU
AV A PEYTAVIN
@ NTIC
O P N
Q
R
AV JEAN JAURES
RUE EL HADJ AMADOU ASSANE NDOYE
10 T
U
RUE DU DOCTEUR CALMETTE
AV DU PRESIDENT LAMINE GUEYE
RUE CARNOT
BD DE LA REPUBLIQUE
RUE EL HADJ MASS DIOKHANE
RUE JOSEPH GOMIS
V
RUE MOHAMED V
W X
RUE FELIX FAURE
Théâtre Daniel Sorano
Z 13
Bookshop
Ministry of Tourism
i
15
RUE JULES FERRY
16
PLACE WASHINGTON DC
RUE RENE NDIAYE
RUE ALPHA HACHIMOU TALL
AV PRESIDENT F D ROOSEVELT
AV CARDE
Cathedral
RUE VICTOR HUGO
@ cc
Espace Sentoo
BD DE LA REPUBLIQUE
RUE MOUSSE DIOP
US Embassy
RUE KLEBER
AV JEAN XXIII
AV NELSON MANDELA
IFAN Museum
PLACE SOWETO
Cameroon Embassy
Le Building Administratif
RUE DE 18 JUIN
Assemblée National

▼ Cap Manuel

ACCOMMODATION					
Al Afifa	**15**	Ganalé	**10**	Océanic	**4**
Al Baraka	**3**	Indépendance	**8**	Provençal	**6**
Auberge Rouge	**16**	Le Lagon 2	**12**	St-Louis Sun	**13**
Continental	**1**	Miramar	**14**	Sofitel Teranga	**11**
Du Marché	**7**	Mon Logis	**2**		
Farid	**5**	Novotel	**9**		

RESTAURANTS, CAFÉS, BARS AND CLUBS			
Adonis	**O**	Chez Loutcha	**R**
Africa Star	**J**	Chez Nanette	**S**
Ali Baba	**P**	Le Colisée	**Z**
Blue Moon Café	**bb**	Le Dagorne	**E**
Café de Rome	**cc**	La Fourchette	**H**

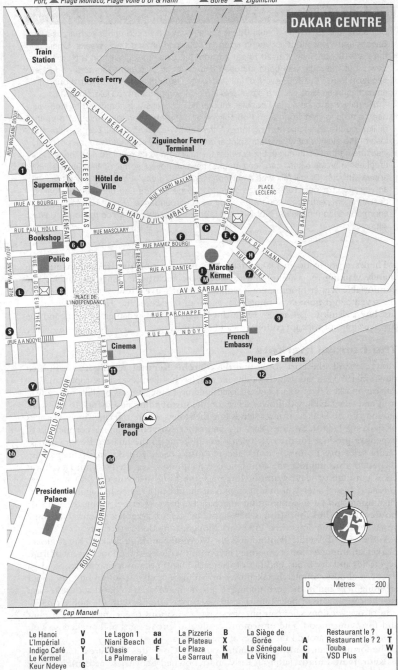

DAKAR CENTRE

Port, ▲ Plage Monaco, Plage Voile d'Or & Hann   ▲ Goreé   ▲ Ziguinchor

Train Station

Gorée Ferry

BD DE LA LIBERATION

Ziguinchor Ferry Terminal

❶

Supermarket

Hôtel de Ville

(RUE A K BOURGI)

RUE PAUL HOLLE

Bookshop

Police

PLACE DE L'INDEPENDANCE

❽

Ⓛ

Ⓢ

(RUE A A NDOYE)

Cinema

⓫

Ⓨ

⓮

bb

AV. LEOPOLD S SENGHOR

dd

Presidential Palace

RUE WAGANE DIOUF

BD EL H DJILY MBAYE

ALLEES R. DELMAS

RUE MALENFANT

RUE MASCLARY

BD EL HADJ DJILY MBAYE

RUE HENRI MALAN

RUE CAILLE

RUE RAMEZ BOURGI

RUE BERENGER FERAUD

RUE P MILON

RUE A LE DANTEC

Ⓐ

Ⓒ

Ⓕ

PLACE LECLERC

RUE DAGORNE

Ⓔ ❹

RUE DE THANN

AV DU BARACHOIS

Ⓗ

Marché Kermel

Ⓘ

Ⓜ

❼

RUE PARENT

AV A SARRAUT

RUE PARCHAPPE

RUE SALVA

RUE A A NDOYE

RUE MAGE

❾

French Embassy

Plage des Enfants

aa

⓬

Teranga Pool

ROUTE DE LA CORNICHE EST

N

0   Metres   200

▼ Cap Manuel

Le Hanoi	V	Le Lagon 1	aa	La Pizzeria	B	La Siège de		Restaurant le ?	U
L'Impérial	D	Niani Beach	dd	Le Plateau	X	Gorée	A	Restaurant le ? 2	T
Indigo Café	Y	L'Oasis	F	Le Plaza	K	Le Sénégalou	C	Touba	W
Le Kermel	I	La Palmeraie	L	Le Sarraut	M	Le Viking	N	VSD Plus	Q
Keur Ndeye	G								

The Dakar rally

Since the late 1970s the annual **Dakar Rally** (⦿ www.dakar.com) has torn across the Sahara and West Africa, covering up to 10,000km in around three weeks. Originally the Paris–Dakar Rally, it used to set off from the Champs Élysées on a New Year's dawn, but the route has been chopped and changed over the years and no longer begins in Paris. The 2003 event didn't even go to Dakar (it ended in Egypt), though the name has been kept and the organizers are planning to return to Dakar in 2004.

The rally was once hugely popular, though this success was tempered by frequent deaths among participants and onlookers, and the questionable ethics of a multi-million-pound spectacle hurtling through the poverty-stricken Sahel. Furthermore, the loss of the event's early amateur spirit and the necessary elimination of the politically insecure central Saharan sections, where the rally earned its reputation as the world's toughest trial for bikes, cars and trucks, have removed some of the Dakar's sex appeal, though it's still followed nightly on French TV. If you're in Dakar when the rally arrives, don't expect to see much more than huge crowds and champagne-soaked desert racers parading through the place de l'Indépendance. Watch out, too, for the enormous accommodation problems the rally brings to every town on the route, Dakar especially.

There's more to do in Dakar than shop, from visiting the IFAN **museum** to merely walking the avenues and exploring the backstreets, especially during the comfortable winter months. For a wonderful **bird's-eye view** of the city, go up to the seventeenth-floor swimming pool and roof terrace of the *Hôtel Indépendance* – just buy a drink to get access. From this height the old red-tiled quarters and the main avenues of dark green foliage stand out clearly.

The central markets

Down towards the port you'll find the **Marché Kermel**, rebuilt after it burned down in 1993 – a fate which, oddly enough, has befallen several metropolitan West African markets. The smart new market building houses a mass of stalls selling fish, fruit and vegetables, with flower sellers on the surrounding pavements. To the west, around rue Le Dantec, market stands line the streets where offerings include stacks of basketry, faddish fashions, carvings and other **souvenirs**, plus a cornucopia of expensive produce for the old-style *colons* still living in the quarter. Beware of dastardly sales psychology – don't accept "gifts" or, if you do, insist on paying. Repeated visits improve the atmosphere as the pushers get used to your face, but it takes courage to leave without buying something – if you do, you may hear "*libanais*" hissed after you in contempt. You should experience less aggressive merchandising, and far less interesting merchandise, below Kermel, along the portside **boulevard de la Libération**, where a grubby street market has operated for some years. Don't come down here after dark though, as it's dodgy territory.

At the end of Avenue Pompidou is the **Marché Sandaga**, Dakar's big *centreville* market, an unpretentious two-storey emporium with a tremendous variety of fruit, vegetables and dry foods, and lots of wonderful fish in the morning. Today, Sandaga has been almost completely taken over by Mouride traders. You can buy just about anything here and in the surrounding streets, from avocados to bootleg cassettes and attaché cases made of beer cans. The hassle can be intense, with the politest rejection of over-zealous salesmanship provoking accusations of racism; go in a patient and forgiving mood. The enormous crush also encourages pickpockets so you should take care around the fringes of the building.

The former Mauritanian silversmiths' yard, the **Cour des Orfèvres**, also known as **Keur Jean Thiam** (after an early and renowned Senegalese artisan), has long been located at 69 av Blaise Diagne, 500m downhill from Sandaga. Mauritanian artisans have been steadily returning to Dakar following the conflict of the early 1990s, and their superb **silver jewellery** and **wooden chests** (the latter are "authentic copies" no matter what story they spin you) are worth bargaining for; they can now also be seen all over the downtown areas, especially along rue Félix Fauré. Senegalese carved **wooden masks** and figures are also made and sold at Cour des Orfèvres – if you're serious about making a purchase, be prepared to discuss the matter over a couple of hours or, better still, a couple of visits.

Medina, Bène Tali and Castors

You can't miss the **Grande Mosquée**, a fifteen-minute walk to the northwest of Sandaga. Finished in 1964 and built after the style of the Mohamed V mosque in Casablanca, it's truly impressive, with seventy-metre minarets standing out above the low rooftops of the **Medina** quarter. Non-believers are strictly barred most of the time, so your only option is to peer in through the windows. The **Marché de Tilène**, a short distance north, brings you down to earth with its football-pitch-sized food market serving a massive array of **produce**. This is the place to come to absorb ordinary Dakar life.

Going a good deal further north, there's a vast array of **cloth** at the best possible prices in the market in the old African quarter of **Bène Tali** (buses #13, #20 from place de l'Indépendance), and more textiles at the less traditional **HLM V** (pronounced "ash-el-em-cinq" meaning "Council Flats 5") market in the middle-class suburbs out between Grand Dakar and the *autoroute* (buses #13, #20 again).

Lastly, if you go out further to the suburb of **Castors**, there's a humdrum general market (buses #13, #18, #20) where you can wander in complete tranquillity. A place to buy food, spices, traditional remedies, cheap cassettes, secondhand clothes and so on, it's somewhat cheaper than the central markets and easier to bargain.

The IFAN Museum and the Plateau

In truth, Dakar's cultural showpiece, the **IFAN** (Institut Fondamental d'Afrique Noir) **Museum**, on place Soweto in the southwest of the centre (Tues–Sun 8.30am–12.30pm & 2–6.30pm; ☎821 40 15, ✉bifan@telecomplus.sn; CFA200), does not make a great first impression. The permanent collection on the ground floor is basically thousands of objects from all over West Africa, many of them visibly decaying, pinned to the walls, lying in glass cases or draped over clay models with little in the way of background information. You can happily spend an hour here, however, longer if you're intrigued. The first floor, meanwhile, is given over to temporary exhibitions (CFA2000), which are a bit hit and miss but sometimes feature interesting works by contemporary artists.

On the left side of the main hall as you go in, look out for the **white man mask**, obviously modelled on a moustachioed colonial officer with a wrinkly neck. Carrying on to the left, you'll come to a selection of shell-encrusted **Dogon headdresses** from Mali, now a commonplace image of West African art, and next to the central staircase some ornate **wooden doors** from Côte d'Ivoire and a lovely **balafon**, also from Mali. On the right side of the hall, highlights include some beautifully carved **ceremonial drums** and **chairs** from Ghana and some fine **cattle and hippo masks** from Guinea-Bissau. In the far right-hand corner, some fierce-looking **Jola masks** from Casamance are sadly just about the only exhibits from Senegal.

Outside, an hour's wander around the Parisian quarter centered on place Soweto suffices to see all the main state buildings of the **Plateau**. On the *place* itself, across from the museum, is the **Assemblée Nationale**; along Avenue Courbet stands the appalling **"Building Administratif"**, a megablock of ministries crowned with scores of vultures; and then on the right, down Avenue Léopold S. Senghor, is the high-profile **Presidential Palace**, with its befezzed and unfazed presidential guards.

The corniches

Both the Corniche Est, from the end of Boulevard de la Libération to Cap Manuel, and the Corniche Ouest, from Avenue André Peytavin right up to Mermoz, are fine walks, mostly on the clifftop, with some stunning views. There are also beaches along here – on the Corniche Est, the pretty **Plage des enfants** and the deep cove at **Anse Bernard** (crowded with local kids at weekends); on the rougher Atlantic side of Cap Manuel, the **Plage de l'Institut Pasteur**. Note, however, that walking the corniches carries some **risk**, as both have reputations for bag snatching and various kinds of assault. Violent attacks are in fact rare, but you shouldn't carry valuables and it's better not to go alone.

The **Corniche Est** (4km) runs through dense vegetation, past the back gardens of various embassies and diplomatic residences and the front gate of the German ambassador's bizarre house, a kind of Sudanic-Teutonic construction. It then climbs to **Cap Manuel** via Dakar's most picture-postcard viewpoints over the city and Gorée. You pass the self-consciously tropical *Hôtel Savana* – a good place for a break and a drink – and from the forbidding yellow slab of the old **Palais de Justice** nearby you can bus back into town. As you go, look out for the beautiful **Aristide Le Dantec hospital** – Sudanic architectural influences in two shades of baby pink.

The eight-kilometre-long **Corniche Ouest** has a far less intimate feel – windswept, wave-ripped and racing with traffic and joggers. City tours come out here for the **Village Artisanal** on Soumbédioune bay, but it's frankly not up to much, with high prices and loads of pressure. However, it's fun to go down on the ant's-nest-busy **beach** to watch the world go by in **Lebu** style: from mid-afternoon it's full of returning Lebu **fishermen** and women selling a diverse catch. The Lebu are related to the Wolof, from whom they broke away at the end of the eighteenth century. Most belong to the Tijaniya brotherhood rather than the Mourides, but a few are Layen, a largely Lebu fraternity. Continuing north around Soumbédioune bay and beyond, you come to the suburb of **Fann**, featuring more diplomatic and expat residences with guard dogs and iron gates, and armies of Dakarois youth working out on the skyline – the **University** is nearby, and physical fitness is a big thing these days. Any time you get tired of walking, you can ride bus #10, which follows this whole route back to the centre.

Monaco and Voile d'Or beaches

The best town **beaches** are **Monaco** and **Voile d'Or** on the sheltered Pointe de Bel-Air, on the east side of the city, most easily reached by taxi. Unfortunately the whole of Bel-Air is a French military base, the only saving grace being that it makes the beaches as safe as you could wish (CFA500 entry fee). With the *militaires* on one side and chemical and groundnut plants fuming on the other, the scene could be prettier, but the sand and sea are clean enough, and palms and sunshades provide additional compensation. Monaco (formerly known as Tahiti) is the nearer and smaller of the two beaches; the adjoining Voile d'Or is definitely the better, stretching out to rocks at the point. Both beaches get crowded at weekends so come early, and bring a bite to eat and water – the bars here are fairly expensive. You can rent **windsurfers**, too, for around CFA5000 per hour, and jet skis for a lot more. The long-running *Monaco Plage* club has recently added some modern, good-value **rooms** (℡832 22 60; ❺) to its bar and unbeatable chill-out area under the palms. It's also possible to stay on Voile d'Or at the upmarket *Voile d'Or Hôtel* (℡832 86 48, ℻832 47 33; ❺).

Hann Park

One part of the city that doesn't yet appear to suffer the problems of the corniches – though you should be cautious nonetheless – is **Hann Park** (daily 10am–noon & 3–6.30pm; bus #12), eighty hectares of woodland and swamp with a zoo and a network of paths. It's a pleasant place for a stroll, full of joggers and keep-fit fanatics in the hour before dark, and a good complement to the beaches at Bel-Air. It's quite attractive to ornithologists, too, who can find several different habitats here. The **Parc Zoologique** (Tues–Sun 10am–noon & 3–6.30pm; CFA350), on the other hand, is not a happy place, a small collection of listless mammals and a large one of birds – not counting the vultures perching ominously on the trees outside. If you want to do it the Dakar way, go armed with sweets and groundnuts and feed everything – but it's probably best avoided.

Eating

Dakar has a blaze of **restaurants** to satisfy most tastes and budgets. If you're really short of cash, you could survive on streetside snacks and fruit for under CFA1000 a day. At the top of Sandaga market you'll find a very basic food hall selling the kind of nourishing breakfast foods sold around the suburbs of Dakar, like sour milk *thiacry* (*chagry*), with millet grains and sugar, or millet porridge *fondé*, all at about CFA50–100 a bowl. The cheapest sit-down meals are found in the **gargotes**, or for about the same price (around CFA800) you can get a *chawarma* or other Lebanese snacks from any of the **takeaway bars** found along Avenue Pompidou. Pay twice that and you'll get a tablecloth, less austere surroundings, service with a smile and a genuine choice; in the exotic or better African **restaurants** a meal costs from around CFA2000.

Central Dakar

Around Marché Kermel and east of place de l'Indépendance

Le Dagorne 11 rue Dagorne. Smart, ever-popular French restaurant that has been drawing them in for years with a great *menu*. Closed Mon.

La Fourchette 4 rue Parent ☎821 88 87. Close to the *Hôtel du Marché*, this features a French and Mexican menu, with an adjoining piano bar.

Le Kermel Opposite Marché Kermel. Bar-restaurant serving French and Senegalese food, with a very French atmosphere on Sun mornings.

Le Lagon 1 Near *Le Lagon 2 Hôtel*, rte de la Corniche Est. Great location, set on a small pier looking out to sea and popular with the French expat crowd. The seafood dishes are pricey, but the *menu* is always good value.

L'Oasis 8 rue Ramez Bourgi. Inexpensive restaurant/bar right by the Marché Kermel, offering *plats* such as *boudin* and chips, plus three-course meals and Flag beer. Closed Sun.

Le Sarraut av Albert Sarraut. Classy French restaurant a couple of minutes' walk east of place de l'Indépendance and popular with the expat community. An alfresco terrace cordoned by a thick herbaceous wall makes for a relaxing meal with *plats* and a *menu*.

Le Tacoma At the *Hôtel Océanic*, 19 rue de Thann. Excellent-value French food with a menu that changes every day. Closed Sun.

On and north of Avenue Pompidou

Adonis av Pompidou. Lebanese eat-in or takeaway. Fast service with great hummus and *baba ghanouge*.

Ali Baba av Pompidou. Good-value Lebanese fast food.

Farid At the *Hôtel Farid*, 51 rue Vincens. Dakar's best Lebanese restaurant, with dishes from CFA4000 and daily non-Lebanese specials for a little less.

L'Impérial (aka "*Robert's Bar*") place de l'Indépendance, corner of allée R. Delmas. Pleasant restaurant/bar retreat, away from *place* hustlers, serving pizza and fish dishes and a good-value *menu*.

Keur Ndeye Corner of rue Sandiniéri & rue Vincens ☎821 49 73. Upmarket Senegalese with *kora* minstrels; meals (including vegetarian fare and a wine list) are nicely served but contents much the same as in a *gargote*, for twice the price.

La Palmeraie 20 av Pompidou. Good-sized portions of tasty sandwiches and snacks, and noted for its wonderful cakes, coffee, hot chocolate and fruit juices. Newspapers and magazines, some in English, are available to read.

La Pizzeria 47 rue A.K. Bourgi ☎821 09 26. Franco-Italian pizza restaurant, catering mainly to expats and tourists.

Le Plaza 71 rue Raffenel ☎822 27 68. Varied menu featuring classic Italian pasta and seafood dishes plus a good selection of desserts.

South of Avenue Pompidou

Café de Rome bd de la République. Tasty international menu with daily specials, consumed in comfortable a/c premises or out on the shaded terrace.

Chez Loutcha 101 rue Moussé Diop ☏821 03 02. An exceptional Cape Verdean restaurant serving typically enormous meals. Wonderful tuna salad and an insurmountable three-course *menu*, including vegetarian options. Good breakfasts too. Closed Sun.

Chez Nanette rue Wagane Diouf. Portuguese-run bar with upstairs restaurant featuring a shaded terrace at the back and a couple of garrulous mynah birds.

Le Hanoi Corner of rue Carnot & rue Joseph Gomis. Vietnamese food at good prices, with a bar in the front and a shady patio out back. Closed Sun.

Indigo Café 26 rue Félix Fauré. Trendy new café opposite the *Miramar* hotel, offering breakfasts, mixed grills, plenty of desserts, cocktails and soul/salsa evenings.

Niani Beach rte de la Corniche Est ☏822 60 71. French cuisine and beautiful views – at the best tables you're sitting out over the waves.

Le Plateau 56 rue Félix Fauré. Popular and inexpensive, with a moderately smart interior offering full African meals.

Restaurant le ? ("*Le Point d'Interrogation*") 18 rue Mohamed V. Long menus of Senegalese food at outstanding value.

Restaurant le ? 2 rue El Hadj A.A. Ndoye. Run by the same family as *Restaurant le ?*, offering a similar, excellent range of Senegalese meals.

Touba Restaurant 95 rue Joseph Gomis. Busy, clean lunchtime eatery with generous helpings of Senegalese staples. Highly recommended *mafé* for CFA700.

VSD Plus rue Moussé Diop. Various good-value African dishes. From 9pm to 1am, it hosts the laid-back *Jazz Club*.

H5/Out from the centre

Cité Claudelle Out past Soumbédioune, near the University. A row of five or six good-value restaurants offering specialities from various African countries. Frequented by a good mix of mostly African diners.

Les Gourmandises Africaines rue 3, near rue A, Point E ☏824 87 05. Recommended for its Senegalese and other African dishes. Eat inside or in the leafy garden.

Le Matonge av Bourguiba, near the junction with av Cheikh Anta Diop and opposite the Ecole Normale ☏824 31 64. Excellent Congolese food.

Drinking, nightlife and entertainment

Despite the city's impeccably cosmopolitan credentials, Dakar's **nightlife** is less exotic than you might expect. If you want a fairly unpredictable night out, most of the bars and clubs we've listed will do the business. Most places tend to be pick-up joints for soldiers and all are pricey. The music played is generally a cosmopolitan mix of high- and low-energy Senegalese, Central African, Cuban and Western. For real action at a price, try one of the **big discos** or **music clubs**, which warm up around midnight (the "soirée"), but may also have an earlier session, from 7 to 11pm (the "matinée") that can be just as hot. If you're going to check out several places and move by taxi, anticipate spending at least CFA30,000 between two, and that's without many drinks – which may be as much as CFA2000–3000 after your first drink, included in the cover of CFA2000–5000. Going in a group works out cheaper and is more fun. Take IDs but leave all valuables behind.

For **theatre**, Théâtre Daniel Sorano (☏822 17 15, ✉sorano@sentoo.sn) on Boulevard de la République is the place, though shows – which sometimes feature big-name music stars – are not held nightly.

Bars

Blue Moon Café Corner of rue Victor Hugo & rue Mohamed V. Pricey, stylish bar where you can also play chess.

Cambodge Corner of rue 6 & bd de la Gueule Tapée, behind the cinema in Gueule Tapée. Try the courtyard here for a cheap drink in a relaxed African bar.

Le Colisée 70 av Lamine Guèye. Quiet, French family-style bar. Fairly expensive, but a regular setting-off point. An informal gathering of chess players meets here around 10pm on Tuesdays.

Le Sénégalou rue de Thann, near the PTT & Marché Kermel. Usually thronging with sailors and prostitutes, this lively bar does good French and continental food, with African nights at weekends.

Le Soninké At the *Hôtel Miramar*, 25–27 rue Félix Fauré. Colourful, cosy, happy-hour type of bar.

Le Soumbé Soumbédioune, in the Village Artisanal. This breezy bar is a great place to watch the return of the fishermen in Soumbédioune bay. At weekends, the Super Cayor salsa band pulls in a slightly older crowd than *Le Kily* (see below) next door.

Le Viking av Pompidou. Cool, comfortable pub-bar that provides welcome respite from the hustlers outside.

Clubs and discos

Africa Star Corner of rue Raffenel & rue de Thiong. Good dancing but very much a pick-up joint. Expensive.

Live music venues

These are the places to hit at weekends – or even around which to plan a stay in Dakar.

Le Kily Soumbédioune, by the Village Artisanal. Regularly packed out with a young crowd come to see Thione Seck and his formidable band, Raam Daan, who usually appear late on Wed, Fri, Sat & Sun.

Le Sahel Corner of av Cheikh Anta Diop & bd de la Gueule Tapée. One of the hottest clubs in town during the week and even livelier at weekends when Assane Ndiaye struts his stuff.

Le Ngalam bd de l'Est, Point E. Recorded music and expensive drinks.

Obox Ngor, next to the *Hôtel Diarama*. Caters more for a tourist crowd, with more Western music. If you're in the vicinity, well worth calling in on, otherwise the town clubs are better.

La Siège de Gorée Corner of allée R. Delmas & bd de la Libération, behind the Hôtel de Ville. A massive, packed open-air dance floor with mixed Western/African music and cheap beer. Free entrance, though go early – by 10pm – as the place quietens down at 1am and closes at 2am.

Stade Demba Diop Liberté. If there's a concert here at Dakar's major venue, the posters all over town will be pretty obvious. Get there on time, but be prepared for it to start two hours late and for gangs of robbers inside and out (take no valuables and get a taxi when you leave).

Thiossane SICAP rue 10; all the taxi drivers know it. Run by the legendary Youssou N'Dour, who usually plays late on Fri, Sat & Sun.

Listings

Airlines Air Algérie, 2 place de l'Indépendance ☎823 80 81; Air France, 47 av Albert Sarraut ☎820 81 21; Air Gabon, 5 av Pompidou ☎822 24 05; Air Guinea, 25 av Pompidou ☎821 44 42; Air Mali, 14 rue Sandiniéri ☎823 24 61; Air Mauritania, 2 place de l'Indépendance ☎822 81 88; Air Sénégal International, 45 av Albert Sarraut ☎842 41 00 or 823 62 29; Alitalia, 5 av Pompidou ☎823 31 29; Ghana Airways, 22 rue Ramez Bourgi ☎822 28 20; Iberia, 2 place de l'Indépendance ☎823 34 77; Royal Air Maroc, 1 place de l'Indépendance ☎849 47 47; Saudia, place de l'Indépendance, corner of rue Malenfant ☎823 72 42/5; SN Brussels Airlines, corner of rue Parchappe & rue Beranger Ferand ☎823 04 60; South Africa Airways, 12 av Albert Sarraut ☎823 27 60/2; TACV (Cape Verde Airlines), 103 rue Moussé Diop ☎821 39 68; TAP Air Portugal, 3 rue El Hadj A.A. Ndoye ☎821 01 13; Tunis Air, 24 av Léopold S. Senghor ☎823 14 35.

American Express The main agent is Senegal Tours, place de l'Indépendance (☎839 99 00), who will sell you traveller's cheques on your Amex card (which can be cashed in all banks except Citibank).

Banks and exchange Most of the bank head offices are on the west side of place de

l'Indépendance. There's a bit of a black market in currency around rue Raffenel and rue Sandiniéri.

Barbers Men can get their hair cut cheaply at the stalls on av Jean Jaurès (corner of av André Peytavin), though the barbers aren't too familiar with straight hair.

Books, newspapers and maps Librairie aux Quatre Vents on rue Félix Fauré, between rue Moussé Diop and rue Joseph Gomez (Mon–Sat 8.45am–12.30pm & 3–6.45pm), is probably the best bookshop in West Africa; they also sell a few books in English, a surprisingly rare commodity. Also try Clairafrique, 2 rue Sandiniéri, place de l'Indépendance, next to the Chamber of Commerce. The *Herald Tribune*, *Time* and *Newsweek* are available from newsstands along av Pompidou and the place de l'Indépendance end of Albert Sarraut. *West Africa* magazine is usually in by Friday. The best and cheapest large maps of Dakar and Senegal can be bought at the Direction des Travaux Géographique et Cartographique, Hann (☎832 11 82, ✉dtgc@sentoo.sn); head up the *autoroute* to the Hann exit, turn right after 1km and look for the sign for the nearby "Le Soleil". A smaller selection is available at the Librarie aux Quatre Vents.

Car rental Avis, 71 km 2.5 bd du Centenaire de la Commune de Dakar ☎849 77 57, airport ☎820 46 28; Europcar, bd de la Libération ☎822 06 91, airport ☎820 17 36; Hertz, 64 rue Félix Fauré ☎822 20 16, airport ☎820 11 74; National, av Abdoulaye Fadiga ☎822 33 66, airport ☎820 92 10. Local rental agents include Senecartours, at 64 rue Carnot (☎822 42 86, ⊛www.senecartours .com) and the airport (☎869 50 07); and the cheaper Assurcar at the Gorée wharf (☎823 72 50), where a Renault Clio costs CFA69,300 per week plus CFA110 per km, and a Suzuki 4WD costs CFA126,000 per week plus CFA200 per km; all credit cards accepted.

Cassettes and CDs Stacks of bootlegs are sold at stalls around Sandaga market and by street sellers in the vicinity. Beware of buying from the pavement cruisers down av Pompidou. Prices should be CFA1200-1500 for cassettes and around CFA5000 for CDs – if you buy home-made cassettes for CFA500 the quality will be dreadful. Legitimate recordings have a hologram on the box as the government supposedly cracks down on pirating. For browsing and listening in a more controlled and relaxing atmosphere, head out to a suburban market such as Castors.

Cinemas The Paris on place de l'Indépendance shows familiar American or European movies either *v.o.* (*version originale* with subtitles if not in French) or *v.f.* (*version française* with French soundtrack).

Crafts and curios For the real thing, visit El Hadj Traoré, rue Mohamed V, between rue Carnot and rue Félix Fauré – a fine musty collection. There are more further north on Mohamed V, on the left before av Pompidou. Avoid flashy "galleries" – unreasonably expensive and not special.

Cultural centres The library of the American Cultural Centre has moved out to the West African Research Centre in Fann-Residence (☎865 22 77). The British Council is at 34/36 bd de la République (☎822 20 15). The British–Senegalese Institute, 18 rue de 18 Juin, off av Courbet (Mon 3.30–6.30pm, Tues–Fri 9am–noon & 3.30–6.30pm, Sat 9am–noon; ☎822 28 70), caters to the small British community, and has a library and occasional film shows. The Centre Culturel Blaise Senghor, 6 bd Dial Diop (☎824 98 39), hosts arty events and concerts, shows movies and holds drumming classes. The French Cultural Centre, 36 rue El Hadj A.A. Ndoye (☎823 03 20), has a library, cinema and concerts, all in French, and a relaxing, inexpensive café in the garden. The Goethe Institute is at 2 av Albert Sarraut (☎823 04 70).

Clinics and hospitals If you need an emergency consultation try one of the following practitioners: Dr F. Coulibaly (Mme), 69 rue Moussé Diop ☎822 19 78; Dr Y. Diallo (gynaecologist), Clinique du Cap, av Pasteur ☎822 10 73 or 821 61 08; or Dr Djoneidi, corner of rue A & rue 1, Point E ☎825 75 03 (English speaker). For accidents, the Hôpital Principal is at the corner of av Nelson Mandela and Léopold S. Senghor (☎839 50 50), or try SOS Médecin, the private emergencies organization (☎821 32 13).

Embassies Burkina Faso, Lot 1, Liberté VI ☎827 95 09, ☏827 95 03; Cameroon, 157–159 rue Joseph Gomis ☎849 02 92, ☏823 33 96; Canada, 45 bd de la République ☎822 92 90, ☏823 87 49; Cape Verde, 3 av El Hadj Djily Mbaye, 13th floor ☎821 39 36, ☏821 06 97; Côte d'Ivoire, av Birago Diop, Point E ☎869 02 70; France, 1 rue El Hadj A.A. Ndoye ☎839 51 00, ☏839 53 59; The Gambia, 11 rue de Thiong ☎821 72 30, ☏821 62 79; Guinea, rue 7, Point E ☎824 86 06, ☏825 59 46; Guinea-Bissau, rue 6, Point E ☎824 59 22; Mali, 23 rte de la Corniche Ouest, Fann ☎824 62 50, ☏825 94 71; Mauritania, rue 37, Colobane ☎822 62 38, ☏822 62 68; Morocco, av Cheikh Anta Diop ☎824 38 36; Nigeria, rue 1, Point E ☎824 43 97, ☏825 81 36; South Africa, Lot 5, Ecole de Police, Mermoz-Sud ☎865 19 59, ☏864 23 59; UK, 20 rue du Dr Guillet ☎823 73 92, ☏823 27 66; USA, av Jean XXIII ☎823 42 96, ☏822 29 91.

Internet access Espace Sentoo, corner of bd de la République & rue Victor Hugo (daily 7.30am-11.30pm; CFA500/hr), has a fast connection, while NTIC-Center, 77 rue Joseph Gomis (24hr; CFA500/hr), is conveniently central.

Language courses Private and group courses in French and Wolof at the Alliance Franco-Sénégalaise, 3 rue Parchappe (☎821 08 22; CFA60,000 for 50hr), or Africa Consultants International, Baobab Training Center, 509 SICAP Baobab (☎825 36 37, ⊜aci@enda.sn; CFA2500-3000/hr).

Pharmacies Pharmacie Nelson Mandela, corner of rue Joseph Gomis & av Nelson Mandela (☎821 21 72), is open 24hr; or look in *Le Soleil* for a listing of after-hours pharmacies.

Police Commissariat Central, corner of rue de Docteur Thèze & rue Sandiniéri ☎823 71 49.

Post and telephones The main PTT is on bd El Hadj Djily Mbaye near the Marché Kermel (Mon–Fri 7am–7pm & Sat 8am–1.30pm). Large parcels can be sent from Colis Postaux office at place d'Oran, at the junction of av El Hadj Malick Sy & av Blaise Diagne. You can also call internationally at the PTT (Mon-Fri 8am–6pm, Sat 8am-1pm) and collect faxes for CFA1000 per fax (☎823 62 42).

Alternatively, go to one of the numerous *télécentres* located all over town; most places in the centre charge CFA100 per unit, though if you shop around you can find cheaper.

Supermarkets The city's biggest supermarket, Score, is at the Centre Commercial Sahm out on av Cheikh Anta Diop/bd de la Gueule Tapée. More convenient are the smaller Score supermarket at 31 av Albert Sarraut, and Le Supermarché Filfili just north of place de l'Indépendance.

Swimming pools Roof terrace at *Hôtel Indépendance* (officially CFA3000, but just buy a drink); Olympic-size and thoroughly tropical at the *Savana*, Cap Manuel (CFA5000, CFA8000 Sat & Sun); chic and popular behind the *Hôtel Teranga* (CFA4500); huge and inexpensive at the new national swimming centre in Point E (CFA1000).

Tailoring Good, reasonably priced tailors abound all over the centre and suburbs. The best bargains

are at Marché HLM, where they will often run something up for you while you wait.

Travel agents Try Senegal Tours, place de l'Indépendance (☏839 99 35, ☏823 26 44, ✉sngtours@sentoo.sn), or any of the following: SDV Voyages, 47 rue Albert Sarraut ☏839 00 00; Sénégambie Voyages, 27 bd de la République ☏821 68 31, ☏821 44 92, ✉sgv@sentoo.sn; or the established Nouvelles Frontières, 1 bd de la République ☏823 34 34, ☏823 65 54, ✉nouvelles-frontieres-senegal@sentoo.sn.

Wrestling *La lutte* can be seen all over the city, with regular Sun evening shows at the Stade Demba Diop attracting the big stars. Wandering around Medina and Grand Dakar at weekends you can find amateur – and kids' – bouts; around the Monument de l'Indépendance seems a popular venue. Wrestling is also televised on RTS every Sat afternoon.

Ile de Gorée and Iles des Madeleines

Just twenty minutes by *chaloupe* from Dakar lies the tiny **Ile de Gorée**, a mere 900m end to end and 300m across at its widest point. Its **slave-trading** history – which some historians now believe to have been exaggerated – has made it more or less a required visit and undoubtedly helped it win UNESCO World Heritage Site status, but it's a compelling retreat in any case, bristling with pastel-coloured old buildings and draped with bougainvillea. It's particularly beautiful in the early morning, when you may be the only visitor. Within similarly easy reach of the mainland are the **Iles des Madeleines**, which have been designated a national park and hold plenty of interest, particularly for naturalists.

Gorée

The first Europeans on Gorée were the **Portuguese**, who used the island as a trading base in the mid-fifteenth century. **Dutch** adventurers captured it in 1588 – naming it "Goede reede" (good roadstead) – but the Portuguese regained control before again losing the island, this time to the **French**, in 1678. This date marked the beginning of the golden age of the **signares** of Gorée; these daughters of white colonists and slave women wielded extraordinary power in a largely matriarchal, slave-worked society. Gorée was fought over by the French and the **English**, who repeatedly captured and recaptured Gorée from each other – the score for the eighteenth century being France 5, England 4. The island prospered despite the changes of ownership: by the 1850s there was a population of 6000 – six times the present figure. The first fortifications of Dakar in 1857 signalled the start of Gorée's slow, graceful demise.

The **Maison des Esclaves** (House of Slaves; Tues–Sun 10.30am–noon & 2.30–6pm; CFA500) is the sole survivor of a number of buildings reputedly used to store "pieces of ebony" before they were shipped to the New World. A visit could be anticlimactic, though – especially if you've ever seen film of weeping black Americans visiting it. Until a few years ago, the walls were festooned with the impressions of various showbiz and political luminaries felt-penned onto pieces of paper. Fortunately, the posters have been removed (though some scribblings by the museum's director survive), allowing the walls, dark chambers and slit windows to speak for themselves once again; there's little interpretation, so it's all left to your own imagination.

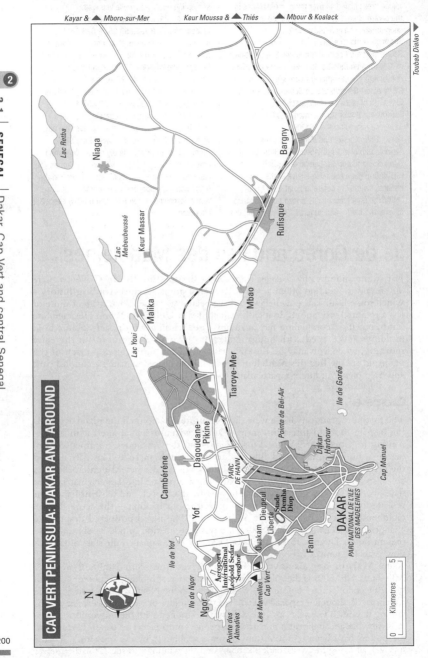

CAP VERT PENINSULA: DAKAR AND AROUND

Kayar & ▲ Mboro-sur-Mer   Keur Moussa & ▲ Thiés   ▲ Mbour & Koalack

Toubab Dialao ▶

Lac Retba

Niaga

Lac Mebeubeussé

Keur Massar

Bargny

Rufisque

Malika

Lac Youi

Mbao

Camběréne

Dagoudane-Pikine

Tiaroye-Mer

Ile de Gorée

Pointe de Bel-Air

Yof

PARC DE HANN

Dakar Harbour

Ile de Yof

Ouakam   Dieuppeul   Stade Demba Diop

Liberté

DAKAR

Cap Manuel

Ngor

Aeroport International Leopold Sedar Senghor

Les Mamelles

Cap Vert

Fann

PARC NATIONAL DE L'ILE DES MADELEINES

Ile de Ngor

Pointe des Almadies

N

0   5   Kilometres

Although Gorée is now thought to have been too small and impractical to have been a major holding area for slaves, the building stands as a mournful and numbing symbol of the first major phase in the European exploitation of Africa. Scarcely believable though it seems, the white traders lived in some style above the warehouse, where there are well-proportioned rooms, a balcony and a tiny reconstructed eighteenth-century Dutch kitchen.

Opposite, the **Musée de la Femme Sénégalaise** (Tues–Sat 10am–5.30pm, Sun 10am–5pm; CFA350) was opened in 1994 as a celebration of Senegalese women's role in the material and spiritual well-being of the family. Exhibits include textiles, baskets, kitchenware, jewellery and traditional dress, and some of the information is in English.

The cleverly designed **IFAN Historical Museum** (Tues–Sun 10am–1pm & 2.30–5pm; CFA200), at the northern end of the island in the horseshoe-shaped Fort d'Estrées, takes you on an instructive tour through Senegal's history to the present day. A few minutes' walk south, the **Museé de la Mer** (in theory Tues–Sun 10am–1pm & 2.30–6pm; CFA200) makes a more singular contribution,

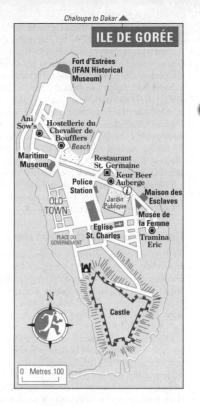

Chaloupe to Dakar ▲

ILE DE GORÉE

Fort d'Estrées (IFAN Historical Museum)

Ani Sow's
Hostellerie du Chevalier de Boufflers
Beach

Maritime Museum

Restaurant St. Germaine
Keur Beer

Police Station
Auberge
Maison des Esclaves

OLD TOWN
Jardin Publique

Musée de la Femme

Eglise St. Charles
Tramina Eric

PLACE DU GOVERNEMENT

N

Castle

0 Metres 100

being in large part devoted to the life cycle of the dogfish – note the human foot in a preserved fish stomach. In both museums, explanations are in French only.

In the town, dozens of flaking **houses** are virtually concealed from the street behind high walls and wrought iron, including a presidential villa (though Wade and his predecessor reportedly prefer to rest up in Popenguine). There's a cluster of fine and more easily viewed Gorée houses at the northern end. Gorée's oldest building is the seventeenth-century **police station**, believed to be built on the site of a Portuguese church dating from 1482. Apart from these, the island boasts the old **church** of St Charles Barromée and, at the southern end, a **castle** topping a warren of bunkers and underground passages from where there are superb views over the island and across to Dakar. The sheltered harbour **beach**, backed by a row of low-key **restaurants** and bars, is a draw in itself, but the real pleasure of the island is just wandering the sandy, quiet lanes and soaking the place up.

Practicalities

The *chaloupe* makes up to a dozen journeys daily from Dakar's Embarcadère de Gorée, off Boulevard de la Libération, between 6.15am and 11pm every one to two hours; a return ticket (valid for as long as you want to stay) costs CFA5000. With few exceptions, the return journeys from Gorée are thirty minutes later than departures from Dakar. For a day-trip from Dakar, it's best to take an early *chaloupe* to beat the crowds, and you should try to avoid weekends, especially in the high season; Mondays are quiet, but the museums are closed. Perhaps inevitably, pushy "guides" have found their way onto the island – their services are barely necessary, but if you do decide you want to be shown round, you're better off hiring an **official guide** from the island's *syndicat d'initiative* (in theory, daily 9am–6pm; ☎822 97 03) near the Maison des Esclaves.

There are a couple of high-quality commercial **accommodation** options on Gorée, usually heavily booked. The *Hostellerie du Chevalier de Boufflers* is the more established (☎ & ☎822 53 64; **⑤**), featuring classy rooms with fan and breakfast and a good but expensive seafood menu, while the modern *Keur Beer Auberge* (☎ & ☎821 38 01, ⓔkeurbeer@sentoo.sn; **⑤**) offers cool, comfortable rooms with fridge. A good alternative to the hotels is *Ani Sow's* (☎821 81 95; **③**), above the crafts shop Gallerie 3A, where you can rent three nicely furnished and comfortable **private rooms** set around a leafy courtyard. You should be able to find more private rooms by asking around town or at the many restaurants facing the jetty – the friendly *Tramina Eric* (☎821 19 31; **③**) has two available – or by accepting one of the many offers of assistance you'll receive from the moment you step off the ferry.

The **restaurants** are all pleasant, alfresco affairs with meals from around CFA3000. *Restaurant St Germaine* offers a particularly warm welcome, a *menu* from CFA6000 and several twin rooms (**③**).

Iles des Madeleines

Twenty minutes by motor *pirogue* from the mainland, the uninhabited **Iles des Madeleines** are home to a number of interesting **plants** – including a dwarf baobab and American wild coffee – and many species of indigenous and migratory **birds**: the tropic bird (*Phaeton aethereus*), recognizable by its bright red bill and immensely long pointed tail, is found nowhere else in Senegal. There's little in the way of coral to be found in the surrounding seas, but the clear waters harbour a rich variety of **fish**.

The island of **Sarpan** – the size of Gorée, and the only one at which a boat can anchor – is best visited between September and November, when the seas are not too rough and the anchoring point in the cove generally accessible. The **park office** (daily 7.30am–5pm) is just north of Soumbédioune bay on the Corniche Ouest, past the Terrou-Bi casino complex on the left. Here you can buy the obligatory park permit (CFA1000) and arrange for a **pirogue** to take you over (CFA3000 return for 1-3 people, less per person for bigger groups). You can stay on Sarpan all day - just tell the *piroguier* when you want to be picked up – so take food and drink as well as binoculars, and a snorkel and mask if possible.

The island slopes from thirty-metre cliffs at its northern end to a gentler southern shore where the boats moor. Although no one lives here (you'll almost certainly have the island to yourselves), it hasn't always been completely deserted, as occasional finds of **stone tools** indicate. More recently, however, it's acquired a malevolent reputation, and "L'ilot Sarpan" (named after a French soldier banished here) was soon corrupted to "L'île aux Serpents" – of which it has none. The Lebu traditionally believe that sea spirits live on the island; their own efforts to settle on it several centuries ago were met with odd weather and violent seismic effects and they chose Gorée instead.

North and east of Dakar

An easy and much-hyped trip out of town is the ride to the beaches of **Ngor** and **Yof**. From Dakar, white *car rapides* leave from near Marché Sandaga to take you up to Ngor past the two rounded hills of **Les Mamelles** and the turnoff to **Pointe des Almadies**, which manages not to be totally smothered by its *Club Med* holiday camp. The *Hôtel Méridien Présidentiel* here is the most expensive in the country (☎869 69 69, ☎869 69 24, ⓦwww.lemeridien.com; **③**) and is one of Africa's most important conference centres, with impressive facilities and standards if you can afford the CFA100,000-plus rooms. From Ngor, the *car rapides* continue on to Yof; if you want to bypass Ngor, bus #8 heads direct to Yof up the *autoroute*.

Public transport to **Lac Retba** and the monastery of **Keur Moussa** can be unpredictable, and in truth neither place need come high on your list. At the bottom of the list is **Kayar**, further up the coast; once a fishing village, it's now a tourist trap of the most oppressive kind, where groups are brought to see the fishermen coming in. You can see the same thing, less intrusively, all along the West African coast.

Ngor and Yof

NGOR has lost any charm it may once have had, with the hideous *Hôtel Ngor Diarama* invading the skyline (☎820 27 24 or 820 10 05, ℻820 27 23; ❽), and a rash of beach clubs, restaurants and sporting facilities between here and Yof airport. The hassles are obvious and tedious, and the only escape is to take a *pirogue* (CFA500 return) out to the **Ile du Ngor**, which is probably the best reason to come here. The island is mostly divided into small plots for private beach houses, pretty enough retreats between the casuarina trees, but hardly idyllic. An old military assault course adds nothing to the clifftops on the island's northern side. There's a couple of small beaches on the landward shore, but not much space when the tide comes in. **Accommodation** is sparse, though there are a few rooms at the *Hôtel Italienne*, better known as *Chez Carla* (☎820 15 86; ❹), and at the friendly *Chez Seck* (☎634 57 18 or 647 81 66; ❷), overlooking the bigger of the two beaches.

The village of **YOF** – a maze of houses, boats on the beach, children everywhere – has a sense of community that Ngor has lost. The beach is the start of a continuous strand that reaches to the mouth of the Senegal River. There's also a tiny island just offshore, given over mostly to goats but yours for the exploring: a *pirogue* will take you over, though at low tide you can almost wade across. *Campement Touristique Le Poulagou* (☎820 23 47; B&B ❸), right on the fishing beach, is a great place to stay.

Yof is also a focus for the **Layen** brotherhood, a Lebu fraternity whose most venerated shrine is the **mausoleum** of the founder Saidi Limamou Laye and his son Mandione Laye. For members of the brotherhood, this templelike building is the holiest of sites, and it attracts vast crowds at the end of Ramadan; if the festoon of vultures perched on its roof doesn't put you off climbing the steps, respect should. A nearby grotto containing perfumed sands is believed to be where Muhammad's spirit dwelt for a thousand years before being reincarnated as the sect's founder.

If you want to participate in something unusual – you won't be the only tourist on the scene – come to Yof to watch a **spirit possession dance** (*ndeup*). The dances are performed by traditional healers to treat the mentally ill, who come with their relatives from all over Senegal. There is an annual week-long ceremony in April or May, but the dances occur whenever the family of a mentally ill person asks (and pays) for a healer's help.

Lac Retba

The popular Dakarois picnic spot of **Lac Retba** – also known as Lac Rose, "Pink Lake" – is certainly a remarkable spectacle, but a trip out here is worthwhile as much for the opportunity to get right out of Dakar and see the beach, stretching all the way to St-Louis, as for the lake itself. The pinkness of the soda lake is caused by the action of bacteria that excrete red iron oxide; for maximum effect, watch the water as the sun goes down, when it turns from coral to mauve and violet. Women collect salt from the lake – almost as salty as the Dead Sea and just as hard to swim in – which is then packed into sacks by men at the far end. The shore is a beach of bleached shells, with banana plots and casuarina trees greening up an otherwise harsh landscape. Over the soft **dunes** to the north is the Atlantic, rough and swirling and definitely only for strong swimmers. Unfortunately the whole tourist area tends to be swarming with pickpockets and troublemakers.

To get to the lake, about 40km from Dakar, take a **bush taxi** to **Keur Massar** (not to be confused with Keur Moussa; see below) and then another to **Niaga**. The *campement* here – the *Keur Kanni* – has s/c concrete thatched huts and a nice atmosphere (☎836 55 17, ☎836 07 24, ✉keurkanni@sentoo.sn; ❸). It's a twenty-minute walk to the lakeside and several more *campements*.

Keur Moussa

The Benedictine monastery of **Keur Moussa**, up in the hills off the Thiès road 50km from Dakar, has acquired a reputation for its touristy *messes africaines* (African Masses) with koras, balafons and tam-tams, and plenty of stuff for sale afterwards, including rather good goat's cheese. Sunday morning Mass at 10am is the best. Without your own car, you'll need early transport towards Thiès and a drop-off at the junction 5km past Sebhikotane, from where it's another 5km to the monastery.

South of Dakar

Beyond the city centre, on the busy **coast road** heading southeast, there's still forty or more kilometres before the edges of the capital finally give way to open, baobab-dotted countryside. Road and railway go through the agglomeration of **Dagoudane-Pikine/Guediyawe**, a huge spillover of city workers and refugees from the interior: already larger in area than the rest of greater Dakar, the sprawl is fast encroaching on the shifting dunes of the north Cap Vert coast. At **Tiaroye-Mer**, 14km from Dakar, there's a pleasant small hotel just a kilometre from the beach on the route de Rufisque: *Chez Charlie* offers s/c twin rooms, some with air conditioning (☎834 07 42; ❷).

RUFISQUE – the Portuguese fifteenth-century Rio Fresco – is the last Dakar suburb, and already provincial in feel. A scruffy seafront town with a couple of hotels, it's more human in scale than anything closer to the city (you'll see *calèches* here, for example). Several wholesalers of **exotic birds** line the road – middlemen between the poverty-stricken peasants and a market in the west which will pay the equivalent of a year's labour for a parrot.

If you're beach-hunting, there's little difficulty in travelling along here by bush taxi, and it's one area where you might **hitch** successfully. It's worth making the slight extra effort to get to **Palmarin**'s near-deserted shore – especially if **Fadiout** to the north leaves a sour taste in your mouth. Before reaching Mbour, check out the "Serer pyramids" – burial mounds – in the **Bandia Reserve**, 63km from Dakar just off the main highway south to Kaolack.

The Petite Côte

At the small resort of Bargny, an hour or so from Dakar, the **Petite Côte** begins, and both road and railway turn inland to the junction for Thiès, Touba and St-Louis. You'll notice a Portuguese influence in some of the region's architecture, and a strong Catholic presence, not unlike parts of the Casamance.

Turning southeast onto the N1, 12km beyond Bargny, you pass several minor roads leading to **resort beaches** along the sandy, palm-fringed coastline. A new international **airport**, scheduled to open in 2007, is being built near here to bring yet more visitors to the already heavily touristed coast. Two of the nicest resorts on the Petite Côte are **TOUBAB DIALAO** and, just to the south, **POPENGUINE**, both around 10km off the N1 and reachable by bush taxi or hitching. The former is popular with Peace Corps volunteers and has a few low-key places to stay; at the latter, *Chez Ginette* is right on the beach and has a couple of roughly built rooms sleeping up to ten (☎957 71 10; CFA10,000 per room), with a choice between self-catering or home cooking. There's a fine restaurant, *L'Écho Côtier* (☎957 71 72), at

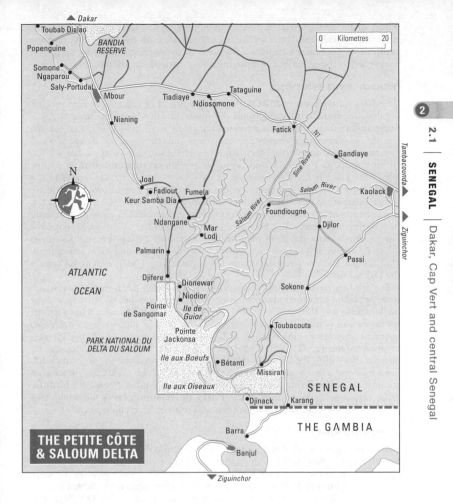

the southern end of the beach, which offers a *plat du jour* for CFA5000 and can arrange rooms locally (❸–❺).

Back on the N1, at the village of Nguekokh, a road leads southwest to the sea and the resorts of **Somone** and **Ngaparou**. A little further on, **SALY-PORTUDAL** (known simply as Saly) is a buzzing Mediterranean-style resort village with mostly extravagant lodgings, restaurants, bars and plenty of activities. If you fancy letting your hair down here for a couple of days, you can stay more cheaply just down the coast at **Saly-Niakhniakhale**, where you'll find the colourful *Auberge Khady* with modern rooms and a pool (☎ & ☏957 25 18; ❺), and, a kilometre further south, the *Ferme de Saly* (☎638 47 90, ⓦwww.farmsaly.sn; HB ❻), with comfortable s/c bungalows and a pleasant bar on the beach.

Away from the coastal swing of Saly, the scrub-and-baobab **Bandia Reserve** (daily 8am–6pm; CFA7000, plus CFA3500 for obligatory guide), to the east of the main highway to Kaolack (1km south of Sindia, 23km from the Thiès junction), contains an interesting archeological site; the **burial mounds** of the vanished Serer village of Tay, and a **burial baobab**, where Serer griots were once entombed. A collection of skulls and bones still lie at the baobab's small entrance. Don't miss the **replicas** of the burial huts which lie beneath the hardened earth mounds. The reserve also harbours various animals, including ostriches and lions.

Mbour and Nianing

The dusty fishing town of **MBOUR**, 80km southeast of Dakar, is an obvious base for this part of the coast, though not the most attractive. Since the town depends foremost on fishing, the **beach** is littered with fishy remains and associated odours, and the sea is uninviting anyway – usually calm and tending to weediness. Mbour's *gare routière* is on the northeastern edge of the centre, and the town has a PTT, Internet cafés and a BICIS bank with ATM. For **accommodation**, the most affordable place is *Les Citronniers* (☎957 24 57, 📠956 42 02; ❹), opposite the church, which has basic but clean s/c rooms and friendly, helpful owners. There are several alternatives in town, including the nearby *Coco Beach Hotel* (☎957 10 04, ⓦwww.coco-beach.com; ❺), a tired-looking tourist complex right on the shore next to the Préfecture, with a pool, tennis court, boules, bar . . . the lot. Mbour has a fair number of bars and small **restaurants**: *Restaurant d'Islam* is an old favourite, while *Le Djembe* is good for inexpensive Senegalese plates and turns into a lively club at night. For a treat, try *Le Massai*, *The Calabash* (aka *Chez Paolo*) or *L'Escale* on the Dakar road.

The road continues south towards **NIANING**, which has a cleaner beach and more appealing **accommodation** options. Two kilometres before Nianing, a sandy track leads to the *Warang Hôtel* (☎957 20 10, 📠957 01 21; ❻), which has a decent restaurant and pool in the dunes overlooking the sea. In the village itself are two excellent *campements* – the *Auberge des Coquillages* (☎ & 📠957 14 28, ⓦwww.tele-complus.sn/auberge; ❺), with a pool and a wonderful beachside position, and the cheaper *Ben'tenier* (☎957 14 20, 📠957 29 74, ⓦlebentenier.com; ❹), which has great food and a lovely garden. On the opposite side of the road, *Chez Annick* is an inexpensive **café** offering good-value fish and seafood dishes. Substantial **birdlife**, to be seen among the remains of the **Forêt de Nianing**, keeps the whole area pleasant, and the shore scene, with scattered palm trees, is certainly pretty.

Joal-Fadiout

From Nianing, the road bisects a couple of exclusive holiday villages – one for the French on the landward side and another for German packagers on the sands - on its way south to the next stop, **JOAL**, where Senegal's great statesman, Léopold Senghor, was born in 1906. Another former Portuguese settlement, with a few old houses still standing (including the Senghors'), it is today a fishing village. The hauling-in of the fish at the end of the day is as enjoyable to watch as anywhere.

But apart from a visit to Chez Senghor and a pat delivery of its history from the *gardien*, the big draw is a wander over the long wooden bridge to **FADIOUT**, the fishing village on the island in the estuary facing Joal. By virtue of a wicked combination of attractive features – proximity to the resorts up the coast, houses built of crushed shells, granary huts on stilts like a field of mushrooms, and a fishermen's cemetery on a neighbouring island – Fadiout has long been one of the biggest tourist traps in Senegal. Nevertheless, it's a fascinating place, a "shell midden" entirely composed of the refuse from centuries of shellfish consumption – it takes about an hour to trail around the houses and Serer cemetery. Fadiout used to be one of the most aggressive hustler haunts, too, but a *syndicat d'initiative* created a few years ago has succeeded in reducing the hassle to an extent. From their small office near the bridge (daily 8am-6pm), they arrange **guided tours** (CFA4000) and **pirogue trips** (CFA6000) round the village.

For **food and accommodation**, look to Joal. Next to the bridge are the tour-group oriented *Hôtel le Finio* (☎ & 📠957 61 12; ❸) and the somewhat preferable *Le*

Sénégaulois (☎ & 📠957 62 41; ❹), which has some neat s/c rooms and a pleasantly located restaurant overlooking the island. The best place in town, however, is the central and well-signposted *Relais 114* (☎957 61 78; ❷), run by a Guinean family and offering clean non-s/c doubles, a pleasant veranda with hammocks and hearty home cooking. If you want to stay in Fadiout, you're limited to *Les Paletuviers* (☎ & 📠957 62 05; ❹ including HB), a simple place on the water's edge at the far side of the island.

Palmarin

The **beaches** in Joal are too crowded, litter-strewn and hustly for abandonment to the sun, sea and sand: for that, you're better off continuing 20km south to **PALMARIN**. To get there, be prepared to wait a while and possibly to change vehicles at Keur Samba Dia. Going back again is harder, but there's always space when a vehicle comes, and if rains have washed the road out completely, you'll hear of it. On the road from Joal to Samba Dia, you'll pass what locals claim is the **biggest baobab** in Senegal - 32m in circumference and surrounded by souvenir sellers.

Palmarin - actually made up of four villages - has a good, if basic, **campement** right on the beach (📠665 87 89; ❸), an outpost of Casamance's system of CTRIs. A short distance from the first village you come to, Palmarin-Ngallou, it offers thatched, twin-bed huts among the palms, with electricity and shared bathrooms and full board available. Two much smarter, but fairly soulless, French-run *campements* lie a little further down the road, both with pools and aimed at package holidaymakers: *Gîte Touristique l'Eden* (📠668 79 68, 🌐perso.wanadoo.fr/gite_eden; ❺) and the newly opened *Djidjack* (☎ & 📠827 89 63, 🌐www.djidjack.com; HB ❻), where you can pitch a **tent** for CFA2500 a night.

The Saloum delta

Situated between Dakar and The Gambia, the delta of Senegal's third river – the **Saloum** – has become popular as a weekend destination from Dakar and a bird-watching and fishing district for foreign visitors. Within the delta, **Yayème**, near Ndangane (see p.208), and **Dionewar** and **Niodior** on the **Ile de Guior** are laid-back villages, little affected by the gradual advance of tourism. Niodior, in particular, is very alluring under its coconut trees, with really welcoming people. Nearer the Gambian border and inside the **Parc National du Delta du Saloum**, the **Ile aux Oiseaux** has variably interesting birdlife – early evening tends to yield better bird-watching, and palearctic migrants swell numbers from October to March. Turtles are common, too, and you might even see a dolphin.

Practicalities

Visiting the maze of islands and mangrove creeks by *pirogue* from the landward side – the usual way – can work out expensive (though you shouldn't pay more than about CFA20,000 for six hours' worth of boat and crew), but there are lots of choices, including organized trips with one of the tour operators in Dakar (see p.199).

A cheaper option is to organize your own *balade*, best done from the bustling fishing village of **DJIFERE**, 15km south of Palmarin. Djifere has a couple of **campements**, of which much the nicer is the friendly *Pointe de Sangomar* (📠835 61 91; ❹), with simple huts set in leafy grounds. Note, however, that if you want to swim, you're better off staying in Palmarin - Djifere's beach is filthy. From Djifere it may be possible to take a trading *pirogue* down to **Banjul**, which is the closest large town by boat; the voyage – 60km along the shore – involves an overnight stop on the **Ile de Bétanti**. *Pirogues* go several times a week and cost CFA3000 per person, plus about CFA2500 for the night's accommodation on the island. Alternatively, if you're on haggling form and unwilling to wait, you could rent your own *pirogue* for around CFA50,000 and get down there in about six hours.

Another departure point for the delta is **FOUNDIOUGNE**, west of Kaolack, 33km from the main highway at Passi, also accessible by road from Fatick and then a ferry (daily 7.30am until mid-afternoon; every 2hr). Here you'll find a handful of good places to stay, including *Le Baobab/Mer*, also known as *Chez Anne-Marie* (☎948 12 62, ☏948 12 63; ❹), a friendly Senegalese-run place; *Auberge les Bolongs* (☎ & ☏948 11 10, ⓦwww.lesbolongs.com; ❸), which offers African-style European comfort in a tranquil setting on the western outskirts of town; and, for a bit more luxury, B&B at the *Hôtel Foundiougne* (☎948 12 12, ☏948 10 12, ✉oudiougne@sentoo.sn; ❼). When you're moving on, it's useful to note that the first ferry from Foundiougne meets a minibus going straight to Dakar.

A convenient, but more expensive, jumping-off point is **TOUBACOUTA**, just 2km from the highway and 25km from the Gambian border. Toubacouta has two resort camps with pools, bars, restaurants and nightclubs: *Hôtel Keur Saloum* (☎948 77 15, ☏948 77 16, ⓦwww.keursaloum.com; HB ❽) and *Les Paletuviers* (☎948 77 76, ☏948 77 77, ⓦwww.paletuviers.com; HB ❽). Both organize expensive excursions, but you could try arranging cheaper ones through the souvenir stands outside the hotels. To the south of Toubacouta in the remote **MISSIRAH** is the *Gîte Touristique du Bandiala* (☎948 77 35, ✉gitedubandiala@sentoo.sn; HB ❺), while over the water is the exclusive *Ile des Paletuviers* (run by *Les Paletuviers*; ❽).

A final departure point from which to get *pirogues* to the delta is **Ndangane**. There's a good range of accommodation here, but it's a bit hustly, so you're better off taking a *pirogue* straight to the picturesque island of **Mar-Lodj**, a little downriver on the northern side of the delta, reachable from Joal or from the main highway east of Tiadiaye. Mar-Lodj has a string of pleasant, low-key *campements* along the riverbank. Try *La Nouvelle Vague* (☎634 07 29 or 936 39 76; B&B ❺), which has several smart little s/c huts with verandas; if you ring ahead, they will send a *pirogue* to collect you from Ndangane, though note there are no *pirogues* from Mar-Lodj itself to the delta.

Thiès and onward

The great garrison town and rail hub of colonial days, and now Senegal's second largest town, **Thiès** is close enough to Dakar (70km) to be an easy visit, and also lies en route if you're journeying by train to other parts of the country. If you're interested in local crafts, the **tapestry factory** here is an essential stop; the workmanship is the very finest, and few weaving centres – if any – in West Africa match Thiès for sheer impact.

Moving north, you might visit **Tivaouane** if you're gripped by the fascination of the Islamic brotherhoods. Or, heading east, you could go to **Diourbel** and on to **Touba**, the big Mouride stronghold with the country's most impressive mosque. From Touba there's the option of following the dusty N3 highway northeast, onwards via **Linguère** to Matam on the Senegal River. If, however, you're on the *transgambienne* highway or on the N1 to Tambacounda (see p.223), you might take time out to look at some of the Iron Age **stone circles** in the **Sine-Saloum region**. Independent transport is the best way to visit these places, though with the possible exception of the stone circles and Touba during *Magal*, you'll normally find public transport to the towns.

Thiès and around

THIÈS retains much of the character of a French town, with parks and wide shady avenues, solid brick and tiles, a remarkable old Sudanic-style cinema, and even the odd rampart from an earlier period of "pacification". Its history, even in recent times, has been punctuated by violent episodes, notably the 1947 strike by railway workers – "God's Bits of Wood" of Sembène Ousmane's novel, *Les Bouts de Bois de Dieu*.

The **Manufactures Sénégalaises des Arts Decoratifs** (Mon–Fri 8am–6pm, Sat & Sun 8am–noon & 3–6pm; ☎951 11 31), focuses the output of many of Senegal's artists and has an enormous influence on younger painters. Having work painstakingly redrawn and fabricated into glowing tapestries – many for exhibition and sale abroad – is an accolade providing a rare incentive. Since its foundation in 1966, the Thiès school has produced fewer than six hundred pieces: its annual output works out at around three hundred square metres, each tapestry produced in an exclusive edition of between one and eight. Prices are accordingly high – around £450/$700 per square metre. Common themes are village life, nature, history and myth, executed in dazzling, graphic style. Ask to see the design of the stunning *Rendezvous au Soleil* by Jacob Yacouba, a giant ten-metre version of which was pur-

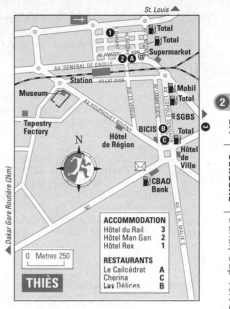

ACCOMMODATION
Hôtel du Rail   3
Hôtel Man Gan   2
Hôtel Rex   1

RESTAURANTS
Le Cailcédrat   A
Cherina   C
Les Délices   B

THIÈS

chased by Atlanta airport. It's interesting to see all the stages of work, from drawing up the original paintings to dyeing the wool and the rapid but careful process of weaving itself. However, if you turn up unannounced you will be allowed into the exhibition hall only, so it's essential to phone ahead - even then, you stand a better chance of gaining access to the factory if you are in a group. You should be allowed to take photos in the workshops, but not in the exhibition hall.

Around the corner is the town **museum** (Mon–Fri 9am–6.30pm, Sat & Sun by appointment; ☎951 15 20 or 540 33 98, ✉clacthies@jokkoo.sn; CFA500), located in the fort, built in 1879. It houses a number of interesting photos and a good deal of commentary on Senegalese history, as well as a fine collection of locally made muskets used against the French in the nineteenth century. Also inside the fort is a small library, a café and a very French-looking mansion in which a number of artists sell their paintings and sculptures.

Practicalities

Arriving by bus or taxi you'll almost certainly be left at the **gare routière**, 3km out of town (CFA350 to get into the centre); if you come by train, you'll be delivered straight to the *centreville*. The railway is still the pivot of much of the town's life, its rhythms adjusted to the comings and goings on the track.

The best **place to stay** is the centrally located *Hôtel Rex* (☎951 10 81, ☎951 48 89; ❷), which offers reasonable rooms, some with air conditioning, for about as cheap as they get in Thiès; otherwise, there's the *Hôtel du Rail* (☎951 23 13; ❸), 2km from the centre in Cité Balabé Thiès, with comfortable a/c, s/c rooms, or the *Hôtel Man Gan* (☎951 15 26, ☎951 25 32; ❹), where the rooms are adequate and the garden offers a quiet retreat.

Thiès's **restaurants** are mostly found along Avenue Léopold Senghor south of the tracks, in the town centre north of the station, or in the town's hotels. Try *Les Délices* for pastries and pizza or the *Restaurant Cherina* for tasty Lebanese food and a Senegalese *plat du jour* – both on Avenue Léopold Senghor. A good place to sit and watch the world go by is *Restaurant Le Cailcédrat* on Avenue Général de Gaulle;

meat, fish and Lebanese dishes cost CFA2000–5000. Just down the street, you'll find a 24-hour **Internet café**, *Bamba Ji* (CFA500/hr), which also serves food. BICIS, SGBS and CBAO all have branches with **ATMs** in Thiès.

Tivaouane and Mboro

TIVAOUANE, northeast of Thiès and 5km off the main N2 to St-Louis, is the seat of the **Sy** dynasty of the **Tijaniya** brotherhood, the largest in Senegal. The grand North African–style mosque is best seen during *Gamou*, the Tijani pilgrimage, or *Maulidi*, the prophet's birthday, when thousands of believers pour into the town. Accommodation, which seems pretty minimal at the best of times, is impossible to find during these periods.

Just north of Tivaouane, on the N2 highway, a road leads northwest 28km to the fishing village of **MBORO-SUR-MER** on what is known as the **Grande Côte**, a 150-kilometre unbroken sweep of sand linking St-Louis to Dakar, along which the Dakar Rally traditionally hurtles towards the capital. Despite the reforestation along this coastline, the *côte's* exposure makes it a far less popular holiday destination than the Petite Côte south of Dakar, which may be all the reason you need to come here. *Le Gîte de la Licorne* (☎ & ℱ955 77 88; HB ❺), 5km out of Mboro on the beach, offers great food and accommodation in several huts; it's best to book ahead.

Diourbel, Touba and on to Linguère

East of Thiès, **DIOURBEL**, with its beautiful huge domed mosque, is one of the principal saintly towns of the Mourides, and capital of the region of the same name, the heart of the groundnut basin. Fifty kilometres further east, following the Sine valley, lies **TOUBA**, the burial place of the founder of Mouridism, **Cheikh Amadou Bamba Mbacke** (1850–1927), and thus the high holy place of the brotherhood. The extraordinary 87-metre-high mosque – built over the family tomb in 1963 and visible for miles across the flat plain – is the largest and one of the finest in West Africa, and the most important religious shrine in Senegal.

Amadou Bamba's triumphal return home in 1907, after years of detention by the French, is celebrated annually in the festival of **Magal** (see p.160 for approximate dates). At this time, around half a million pilgrims flock here from all over Senegal and The Gambia, and public transport is virtually suspended on routes to and from Touba. If you're going there for Magal, expect to spend the night awake with the crowd of disciples: you'll almost certainly have found companions on the journey.

Senegalese authority is minimal here: the **maraboutic militia** is responsible for law and order, which includes absolute bans on tobacco and alcohol anywhere in the town precincts. Searches – especially of *toubabs* – aren't uncommon, and you will be fined and your drugs confiscated if found. Photography, too, isn't likely to please many. Despite this, Touba can be an irresistible challenge. Be warned, though, that **accommodation** is impossible to find in Touba if you don't get invited to stay at someone's house. There's a *campement* 10km away in **MBACKE**, a kind of secular counterpoint to Touba, where the maraboutic laws don't apply. You could get stranded there for the big night anyway, as Mbacke goes into partying hyper-drive, diverting attention from the devotions at Touba and increasingly reducing Magal to a Christmas-style commercialism.

If you're driving into Touba, you may end up jammed in pedestrian traffic or directed to leave your vehicle in a designated zone and walk. However you manage it, don't confuse piety with honesty; a nimble army of hustlers and pickpockets filters the crowds, particularly during Magal. You'll also need to be aware of cultural sensitivities: shorts are not acceptable round here and heads will need to be covered if entering the mosque. You're best off adopting a "local guide" to help with all the niceties.

To Linguère

With stamina you could continue by road from Touba or Mbacke to Linguère and from there on to Ouro Sogui and Matam. This route, the N3, goes right through the heart of the Fula **Réserves Sylvo-Pastorales**, a fragmented cluster of badlands (virtually tribal reserves) glumly conceded to the pastoralists and always under threat from the expanding Mouride groundnut enterprises. With improved irrigation and increases in population, agriculture encroaches on all sides except the east, where the Réserves de Faune du Ferlo-Nord and Ferlo-Sud – areas in which no grazing is permitted – create a barrier between the cattle herds and the potentially rich Senegal river valley.

LINGUÈRE is the main town of this region. Surrounded by the reserves and no longer accessible by train, it's a bit of a dead-end rarely used by travellers, though there is a *campement* here. If you've transport, or a dogged persistence coupled with a devotion to obscure archeological sites, you might move down the Ferlo river course from Linguère to the ruined **fortress** of Alboury Ndiaye, the last independent ruler of the Wolof kingdom of Jolof. The site is north of the road before the village of **Yang-Yang**, itself about 35km northwest of Linguère.

From Linguère a rough track to the Senegal River near Ouro Sogui follows the normally dry upper course of the Ferlo, between the faunal reserves. Transport is limited and vehicles depart early – you'll almost certainly be the only tourist on board.

Kaolack and east along the Gambian border

A big, noisy interchange town, hub of five road routes, **KAOLACK** is not likely to be a place you'll want to linger. The Niasse dynasty of the Tijaniya brotherhood – based here – is bent on founding an Islamic republic, a movement which is also reportedly funded by Libya. The **mosque** is the main sight of interest, a splendid creation paid for partly by Saddam Hussein. Kaolack also has a venerable and bustling **market**, one of the biggest covered markets in West Africa, and a craft market on the northern edge of town.

The **gare routière** for Dakar and all northern destinations is 1500m out of town to the north; for southern destinations, including The Gambia, Garage Nioro is on the southeastern corner of the town centre. The *gare routière ville* for bush taxis around town is next to the market. **Places to stay** include the decent *Hôtel de Paris* (☎941 10 19, ⊕941 10 17; ❻), southwest of the market; the better-value *Relais de Kaolack* (☎941 10 00, ⊕941 10 02; B&B ❺), a bit further out of the centre in a pleasant riverside setting, with a pool and tennis court; and the basic *Auberge Etoile du Sine* (☎941 44 58; B&B ❸), on Avenue Valdiodio Ndiaye, the main road out of town towards Tambacounda. You may also be able to find a bed at the *Mission Catholique* (☎941 25 26; ❷, dorm bed CFA2000), around the corner from the *Hôtel de Paris*.

Inexpensive street **food** is available around the market and *gare routières*. For a more varied menu, including pizza, fish, meat and salads, try *La Terrasse* (*Chez DuDu*) on rue des Ecoles, or *Le Brasero* (*Chez Anouar*), a couple of blocks north on Avenue Ndiaye – both busy in the evenings. Around the corner from *Le Brasero* on Avenue de Bugeaud is the buzzing *Blue Bird* **nightclub**, which also serves food, and an **Internet café**, Cadicom.sn (CFA500/hr).

Sine-Saloum stone circles

Part of the same cultural complex as the circles in The Gambia (see p.303), the **megaliths** scattered across the plain between Nioro du Rip on the *transgambienne* N4 and Tambacounda are vestiges of a prehistoric society about which virtually nothing is known. Including some unimpressive circles that you'd not glance twice at, they number approximately a thousand in this region. Associated with them are burial sites which have yielded a number of skeletons and a certain amount of weaponry, pots and copper ornaments. Seeming to date from before the twelfth century, they bear no sign of any Islamic impact.

Most impressive is the site known as **Djalloumbéré**, at **Ngayène**, hard against the Gambian border. Over eleven hundred individual pillars here make up 52 stone circles – some of them the sites of mass burials. It's virtually impossible to get here without your own transport – turn left 9km south of Nioro du Rip to Kaymor (17km) on a decent track, then continue southeast another 15km via Tène Peul and Keur Bakari to Ngayène. From here you can head straight back to the main road at Medina Sabak, 28km from Nioro. In the middle of this "circuit", 10km due south of Kaymor, is the village of **Payoma**, where stones from the local circles have been uprooted to support the buildings – including the mosque. Numerous other circles are visible at various points along these tracks.

Assuming you've got transport or you're using a *taxi brousse*, there are more sites along the Tambacounda highway, at **Malème Hodar** (right by the road) and **Keur Albé** and **Sali**, respectively 9km and 20km southwest of **Koungheul** on a minor road to The Gambia. This road crosses the border just north of Wassu: if you're enraptured by the circles and your papers are in order, you could cross over for further observations and stay in Kuntaur or Georgetown.

2.2
The north and east

Northern Senegal is the least populated part of the country, with few large towns and a landscape whose main interest derives from its harsh marginality. Northeast of Dakar stretches the **Sahel**, where the desert's southward advance is ever apparent. But there are two conspicuous attractions in the north: the **Senegal River**, forming the border with Mauritania and feeding a flood plain up to 30km wide; and the old French colonial capital of **St-Louis**, tucked behind the bar at the mouth of the river. Two **national parks** – the Djoudj and the Langue de Barbarie – are mainly visited by keen bird-watchers.

Should you be **heading north** to Mauritania and the Atlantic route across the Sahara, St-Louis is a natural break in the journey, a few hours by *taxi brousse* from Dakar. To follow the river, however, you have to be a little more determined and transport-hop your way inland to **Richard Toll**, **Ouro Sogui/Matam** and **Bakel**. Continuing south through the hills, you'll intercept the Dakar–Bamako train at **Kidira**, on the border, where there'll be a crush to find space on board. If you're approaching in the opposite direction, into Senegal from Mali, the river course is a marginally preferable route towards the coast: the alternative, following the direct line of the railway, has very little to detain you.

The main **ethno-linguistic groups** of north Senegal are **Wolof**, concentrated around St-Louis and along the lower reaches of the river, and **Tukulor** higher up, who speak a dialect of Fula. In the far east, around Bakel, there are **Sarakolé** (Soninké/Serahuli) speakers, while communities of semi-nomadic **Fula** live in the scorched region of Fouta Toro.

St-Louis and around

The oldest French settlement in West Africa and capital of Senegal and Mauritania until 1958, **ST-LOUIS** is something of a world apart. In later colonial times its *commune* status – shared with Gorée, Rufisque and Dakar – meant its inhabitants were considered citizens of France; today the town's crumbling eighteenth- and nineteenth-century European architecture and its white- and blue-draped Wolof and Moorish inhabitants maintain the culture clash. Like Gorée, St-Louis is a UNESCO-protected World Heritage Site. If decay, abandonment and the ghosts of slaves and fishermen attract you then you'll enjoy this town. Taking advantage of the Casamance's recent woes, beachside *campements* have sprung up along the Langue de Barbarie and, with its warm winters, dry summers and **national parks** nearby, it all adds up to a worthwhile few days' stay. An added attraction, if you happen to be in the area at the time, is the annual **St-Louis International Jazz Festival**, which takes place over a long weekend in May or June; artists come from all around the world to perform.

Arrival, information and accommodation

St-Louis' wonderfully ornate **train station**, which you're not likely to be using now that the regular service from Dakar has been suspended, is in the mainland quarter of **Sor**, close to the end of the iron Pont de Faidherbe; the **gare routière** is right by the tracks. It's a hectic area, thronged with stalls and child beggars. **Bush taxis** leave from here for Dakar (CFA3100; 4hr) and inland destinations along the Senegal River, including Rosso (CFA1550; 2hr), for the border crossing into Mauritania. The oldest part of St-Louis is the **island** of the same name, a ten-minute walk across the bridge (which, incidentally, spanned the Danube until 1897) from the *gare routière*.

For **tourist information**, the Syndicat d'Initiative et de Tourisme (Mon–Fri 9am–1pm & 3–6.45pm, Sat 9am–12.30pm & 3–6pm; ☎961 24 55, ⊛www.saintlouisdusenegal.com) at the end of the bridge has helpful staff, some English-speaking, who can assist you with tours and accommodation. There's an excellent bird's-eye view **sketch map** (CFA3000) of St-Louis and its environs - available from the *syndicat d'initiative*, some hotels and bookshops - which makes an informative companion for your wandering in and around town as well as a great memento when you leave.

Accommodation

St-Louis offers an excellent range of **accommodation** for its size, with the old colonial-era hotels situated on the island itself, a couple of places to stay on the mainland, and *campements* strung out along the spit of the Langue, south of the Guet Ndar quarter.

Auberge Café des Arts rue Adamson ☎961 60 78. Colourful and very friendly locally run place offering basic rooms and cheap, home-cooked meals. ❷

Auberge de Jeunesse l'Atlantide North end of av Jean Mermoz, corner of rue Bouet ☎961 24 09. Best place in town to lodge cheaply and commune with other travellers. There are segregated dorms and twins – with fans, shared ablutions and a modest breakfast included. Also offers *plats* for CFA2000–3000, has bikes for hire and organizes trips to the national parks. Dorm beds CFA5500, ❸

Auberge de la Vallée rue Blaise Diagne ☎961 47 22, ☎964 10 92. Clean bright dorms with mosquito nets and some twins. Dorm beds CFA5000, ❸

Campement Langue de Barbarie 20km down the spit. Comfortable, established *campement* run by the *Hôtel de la Poste*, who will drive you down there (4WD only). Offers lots of beach activities, plus *pirogue* and fishing excursions. ❹

Hôtel de la Poste By Pont Faidherbe on the waterfront ☎961 11 18, ☎961 23 13. The island's definitive colonial-era hotel with splendid rooms

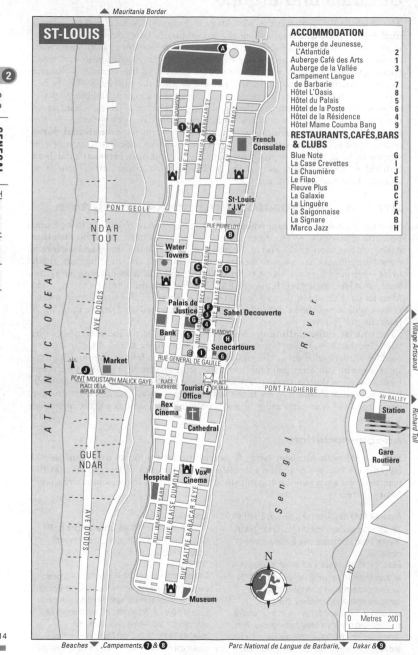

ST-LOUIS

▲ Mauritania Border

2.2 | SENEGAL | The north and east

ACCOMMODATION

Auberge de Jeunesse, L'Atlantide	2
Auberge Café des Arts	1
Auberge de la Vallée	3
Campement Langue de Barbarie	7
Hôtel L'Oasis	8
Hôtel du Palais	5
Hôtel de la Poste	6
Hôtel de la Résidence	4
Hôtel Mame Coumba Bang	9

RESTAURANTS, CAFÉS, BARS & CLUBS

Blue Note	G
La Case Crevettes	I
La Chaumière	J
Le Filao	E
Fleuve Plus	D
La Galaxie	C
La Linguère	F
La Saigonnaise	A
La Signare	B
Marco Jazz	H

French Consulate

St-Louis "J.V"

PONT GEOLE

NDAR TOUT

ATLANTIC OCEAN

AVE DODDS

Water Towers

RUE ADANSON
RUE DE FRANCE
RUE KHALIFA ABABACAR SY
AV JEAN MERMOZ
RUE PIERRE LOTI
RUE BLAISE MARIE PARSINE

Palais de Justice
Sahel Decouverte

Bank
RUE BLANCHOT
RUE ABDOULAYE SECK MARIE DIAGNE

Senecartours

RUE GENERAL DE GAULLE

Market

PONT MOUSTAPH MALICK GAYE
PLACE DE LA REPUBLIQUE
PLACE FAIDHERBE

Tourist Office
PLACE DE LILLE
PONT FAIDHERBE

Rex Cinema

Cathedral

GUET NDAR

AVE DODDS

Hospital

RUE IBRAHIMA SARR
RUE BLAISE DUMONT
RUE MAITRE BABACAR SEYE

Vox Cinema

Museum

River

Senegal

Station
AV BALLEY
Gare Routière

N2

Village Artisanal ▶
Richard Toll ▶

N

0   Metres   200

Beaches ▼, Campements, ❼ & ❽   Parc National de Langue de Barbarie, ▼   Dakar & ❾ and ambience, and a hunter-themed bar. All the usual excursions are on offer, including day runs down the beach to their *campement* on the Langue (see p.217). **❻**

Hôtel de la Résidence rue Blaise Diagne ☎961 12 60, ℱ961 12 59, ℯhotresid@sentoo.sn. One of the town's most comfortable hotels, with clever colonial details and a great rooftop terrace. Bicycles available for hire. **❻**

Hôtel du Palais rue Ababacar Sy ☎ & ℱ961 17 72, ℮www.hoteldupalais.net. Friendly, co-operative and least expensive of the old-style hotels, offering clean a/c, s/c rooms, which were being gradually renovated at the time of writing. Adjacent café/patisserie has good croissants and

coffee. Inexpensive excursions organized to regional attractions. **❹**

Hôtel Mame Coumba Bang Bois des Amoureux, 6.5km south of town on the mainland next to turnoff for Gandiol ☎961 18 50, ℱ961 19 02, ℮www.hotelcoumba.com. Ageing luxury tourist hotel including a pool, an excellent restaurant and trips into the surrounding countryside. **❻**

Hôtel L'Oasis 4km south of Guet Ndar ☎ & ℱ961 42 32, ℮hoteloasis.free.fr. One of a clutch of decent *campements* that have recently opened on the spit, *L'Oasis* has a choice of pleasant grass huts with shared ablutions and smarter en-suite rooms, but the main attraction is its proximity to

The Town

Most of the town's hotels, as well as local travel agents (see p.216), offer **tours and excursions** all around St-Louis, as well as to the national parks and over the border into Mauritania. The *Hôtel de la Poste* offers an especially good calèche tour of the town and can also take you down to the beach in the morning and pick you up at the end of the day – at a price.

The **mainland** area of St-Louis, **Sor**, is on the whole an anonymous district, though there are some old buildings, and there's a lively African feel by night which the weary island can't match. The population here swells with every downward cycle of drought in the interior. On the route de Corniche at Sor's northern end is the **Village Artisanal** where you might pick up a wider and less expensive range of Senegalese and Mauritanian artefacts than those you'll be offered outside the island's better hotels.

The island

You can walk round the **island** – *ndar* in Wolof – in about an hour and a half. Shuttered windows, occasional balconies and flaking yellow paint are the abiding impressions. Some of the best houses – which, as in Gorée, tend to conceal their interiors from snooping strangers – are around and just north of the hotels, especially along rue Blanchot and rue Pierre Loti. Maurel et Prom was a slave market, and the *Hôtel de la Poste* started as a gum-arabic warehouse. The old houses characteristically have interior courtyards, warehouses on the ground floor (mostly now converted) and first-floor, inward-facing living quarters. Don't miss the **Palais de Justice**, on rue Blanchot, with its massive, palm-shaded staircase.

At the place de Lille, named after St-Louis' twin city, notice the plaque commemorating the town's most celebrated citizen, Mbarick Fall, who as **Battling Siki** became the first world professional boxing champion in 1925. Heading south round the corner from here, beneath a wonderful old silk-cotton tree, you come to the **place Faidherbe**, centering on a bust of the eponymous French governor, and surrounded by government and military buildings.

At the southern tip of the island, the **museum** is worth a look (daily 9am–noon & 3–6pm; ☎961 10 50; CFA500). The first floor has displays on the great marabouts and politicians of Senegal and the historic personalities of St-Louis, together with local ethnographia from neolithic times to the coming of the *colons*. Temporary exhibitions are held on the second floor.

Ndar Tout and Guet Ndar

Across the other arm of the river on the spit of the Langue de Barbarie, the scene is much more animated. Turn right across either of the bridges and you're strolling on

Avenue Dodds, main drag of the **Ndar Tout** quarter. With its tall, gracious houses rising behind the pavement palm trees, it's easy to picture this as the Champs Élysées of the local *signares* set, at a time when there were four thousand French *colons* and military based in St-Louis. At the far north end, ruination sets in – skeletal buff and red remains of French army buildings and then a marker pillar designating the **Mauritanian frontier** (not an official border crossing).

Action in Ndar Tout focuses on the **market** and sandy **place de la République**, which gives out straight onto the Atlantic down Avenue Servatius, itself ankle deep in sand. From here you can walk south along the shore into the fishing quarter of **Guet Ndar** – rewarding, if odoriferous in the late afternoon – and down as far as the Islamic fishermen's cemetery, a net-and-stake graveyard with the familiar and disquieting vulture retinue.

Eating, drinking and nightlife

St-Louis has a few reliable and economical **places to eat** around the main centre on the island. A good spot for cheap street food is around place de la République on Ndar Tout; for greater expense and quality take your pick from the restaurants at the better hotels, such as the *Poste* or *Résidence*.

The hotels are probably your best bet for **drinking**, though there's also a classy **nightclub**, *La Chaumière*, in Ndar Tout, owned by the *Hôtel de la Poste* (closed Mon). Charging around CFA1500-3000 at the door (but free to guests at the *Poste*) and with ordinary bar prices, it only gets into gear after midnight. For a taste of the **jazz** scene that St-Louis is famous for, check out *Marco Jazz*, a couple of blocks north of the *Hôtel de la Poste*, or the more lugubrious *Blue Note* on rue Abdoulaye Seck, both of which have regular sessions. Alternatively, simply cut east across the Servatius bridge to the mainland and let your ears track down the action: community events are easily located.

Restaurants

La Case Crevettes rue Abdoulaye Seck. Cosy little place done out to resemble a grass hut, specializing in prawn dishes and other tasty Senegalese fare for around CFA2500-3000.

Le Filao (aka *Ker Gaya*) rue Abdoulaye Seck. Basic daily specials of fish and chicken for CFA1000-2000.

Fleuve Plus rue Blaise Diagne. Popular restaurant with an extensive Senegalese menu; main courses for CFA1500-3000 and tasty juices – try the tamarind.

La Galaxie rue Abdoulaye Seck. About the best deal in town: friendly service and, for once, a pleasant interior, plus entrees for CFA800.

La Linguère Next to *Auberge de la Vallée*, rue Blaise Diagne. Good food at around the CFA1500 mark.

La Saigonnaise North end of av Jean Mermoz. Elegant Vietnamese restaurant on the northern tip of the island.

La Signare rue Blaise Diagne. A plush non-hotel French option. Closed Wed.

Listings

Bank BICIS, corner of rue de France & rue Blanchot (Mon–Thurs 7.45am–12.15pm & 1.40–3.45pm, Fri 7.45am–1pm & 2.40–3.45pm), is able to change cash and traveller's cheques. There's a 24hr ATM outside which takes Visa cards.

Car rental Ask at your hotel, or try Senecartours, rue Blaise Diagne (☎961 38 12); plan ahead as vehicles are transferred from Dakar on request.

Cinemas Kung-fu flicks, Indian epics and soft-core erotic films, all dubbed into French, are shown at the open-air Rex. The Vox is more comfortable, has a roof and shows mostly US action films, also dubbed into French.

Internet café *Ch@mps Elysée*, rue Général de Gaulle (daily 8am-midnight; CFA500/hr), is the biggest Internet place in town and also serves tasty fruit juices.

Travel agents Try Sahel Decouverte (☎961 42 63, ℮kine-sahel@sentoo.sn) or St-Louis "J.V." (☎961 51 52), both on rue Blaise Diagne.

The Langue de Barbarie

South of town, you can drive down the **Langue de Barbarie** as far as the national park, dodging the waves and hundreds of thousands of crabs as you go. The drive (4WD required) to the Langue de Barbarie starts in Guet Ndar, passing the remains of the **Hydrobase**, the seaplane centre used as a staging post by the early airmail service between Europe and South America. The first South Atlantic crossing took off from here in 1930; the *Hôtel de la Poste* in town is full of mementos. Many of the casuarina trees planted here by Governor Faidherbe when the Langue was called La Piste des Cavaliers, have since perished, and it's an often melancholy beachscape populated by a string of new *campements*.

The tip of the spit lies within the **Parc National de la Langue de Barbarie**, which covers twenty square kilometres of estuarine islands and waterways around the southern end of the Langue. There's a good chance of seeing cormorants, pelicans and turtles here. To **visit the park**, you need to buy a permit (CFA2000) from the park office (daily 7.30am–5pm), 20km south of St-Louis on the landward side of the estuary after the village of **Gandiol** - accessible by bush taxi from the Sor *autogare*, through **tours** organized by the main hotels in town or, if you're feeling energetic, by bike. From the park office, you can arrange **pirogue trips** into the park (CFA7500 each for 1-3 people, CFA2500 for 4 or more). The quantity of birds depends on the time of year – from November to August the park is a breeding site for terns, gulls and egrets – and on an element of luck: flamingos and pelicans are the obvious species, but rarer ones require more patience. About halfway along the road to Gandiol, you'll pass the **Réserve de Guembeul** (daily 7.30am–6.30pm; CFA1000), where you can see warthogs and, in a huge fenced enclosure, several tortoises and a herd of deer gifted by King Juan Carlos of Spain. There's a place to **stay**, *Zebrabar*, 500m from the Langue de Barbarie park office (☎638 18 62, ⓦcome.to/zebrabar; ❸). This laid-back *campement* has a range of comfortable huts, good-value meals, kayaks, windsurfers and a fabulous look-out rising above the palm trees; camping is also possible (CFA2500 per person).

Parc National des Oiseaux du Djoudj

Situated in the heart of the Walo delta of the Senegal River, and considerably bigger than the Langue de Barbarie park, the **Parc National des Oiseaux du Djoudj** (Nov–April daily 7am–7pm; CFA2000, cars CFA5000) is Senegal's ornithological showcase, its estimated 100,000 **flamingos** and 10,000 **white pelicans** among the world's largest concentrations. It's rated the third most important **bird reserve** in the world; if you're at all into birds and are here during the palearctic migrants' season between October and April, you should make the effort to get in. January is probably the ideal time to visit, with the migrants in residence but the water levels already receding. Flamingos prefer the high alkalinity – and the reduced water surface tends to concentrate the birds, making them easier to spot. Crowned cranes are among the park's more ostentatious inhabitants. You should also keep a lookout on the water surface for the eyes and snouts of **crocodiles**, especially visible in the dry season.

The track into the park is signposted to the left off the Rosso/Richard Toll road near the village of Ndiol. Those without their own transport can arrange **trips to the Djoudj** with most of St-Louis' hotels for around CFA15,000 per person, which includes entrance fees, a two-hour *pirogue* ride and unlimited stops en route. Taxis can also be persuaded to spend the day taking you there and back, but you'll pay at least CFA20,000 per taxi (plus fuel and entrance fees) and you've little room to protest if the trip is cut short.

Once you're in the park, restricting yourself to the tracks gives just half the picture; only by taking a *pirogue* across the shallow expanses can you get really close to the wildlife. You can buy tickets for **pirogue trips** at the park entrance (CFA3000 per person from the village shop next to the park office and CFA3500 per person from the *hostellerie* - see p.217), from where it's another few kilometres' drive to the *pirogue* jetty. At the park entrance, you can **stay** at the *Hostellerie du Djoudj* (☎963 87 02, ☎963 87 03; ❹), which offers overpriced s/c huts and smarter en-suite rooms grouped around a pool. If you ask nicely, you may be allowed to lodge more cheaply at the research station just inside the park gates.

Along the Senegal River

From St-Louis there is frequent **transport upriver** to **Rosso** (for Mauritania) and **Richard Toll**. Thereafter, vehicles from St-Louis are scarcer, so you'll have to hop your way along the highway from town to town. As the heat rises noticeably inland it can be a long slog in the back of a crowded *bâche* to **Kidira**, two long days and nearly 600km from St-Louis. There's little of interest to see along this route other than glimpses of the Senegal River and rural, upcountry communities getting on with life, although you'll find the former trading outpost of **Bakel**, just north of Kidira, a charismatic stopover. If you have a little more time, however, you could make things more exciting by travelling up the river by *pirogue*; trading boats ply the waters between Matam, Bakel and Kayes in Mali.

The Lower River

Between St-Louis and Richard Toll, the scene varies sharply with the time of year: in the dry season from November to May, you'll see the oblong wicker huts of migrant Fula herders who've moved from the higher, drier lands of the interior. Signs of human habitation include the practice of planting old car tyres in the mud to stake a land claim – common all over West Africa.

Around the turnoff to Rosso, and all along the six-kilometre causeway road to it, you see thousands of hectares of rice, along with **sugar cane**, intended not only to feed domestic sugar consumption but also, eventually, to produce fuel alcohol to offset the high cost of oil imports. In the irrigation ditches, **Nile monitor lizards** abound, growing enormous – up to 2m long – on a diet of insects, frogs and rodents.

Rosso

On the frontier with Mauritania, **ROSSO** (about 1hr 30min from St-Louis by minibus) is bustling with black marketeers trading ouguiya, the Mauritanian currency. If you're heading for Mauritania you're likely to be offered ouguiya at about ten percent above the going rate.

As you approach the town the road curls through desperate shacks and official buildings to a tongue of land from where a barge regularly ferries vehicles across the brown flow to **Rosso–Mauritania** (see p.124). If you're **crossing the river** – and there's little point in coming up here if you're not – you'll need to get your passport stamped out of Senegal at the first flagpoled white building on the left, just after the minibus stop. You can get across the river easily enough using *pirogues* for about CFA250 per person, but avoid going between noon and 3pm, when both the *piroguiers* and the barge crew shut down for lunch. The border opens at 8am and closes at 6pm.

Richard Toll

Meaning "Richard's Field", the unremarkable **RICHARD TOLL** is named after the ambitious regional development planned by the French planter Claude Richard in the 1820s. The town's only notable building is Baron Jaques Roger's **colonial mansion**, built on an island in the Taouey River – which flows into the Senegal on

△ Palais de Justice, St-Louis

the east side of town. It's surrounded by the remains of his ornamental park – now a dusty and overgrown jungle and nothing special.

For **accommodation** you've two options: directly north of the *gare routière* is the *Gîte d'Etape* (T & F963 32 40; ❺), a great spot to rest up if you've had a tiring few days, with its lovely riverside setting, restaurant and, most usefully, a swimming pool (CFA2500 for non-residents). Otherwise, there's the overpriced *Hôtel La Taouey* (T963 34 31; ❹), a few hundred metres west behind the first of two Shell stations. Along the town's long main drag you'll spot plenty of **street food** snack bars and a CBAO **bank**. If you're moving on east and there's nothing remotely full in the *gare routière*, you might prefer to take a *calèche* the couple of kilometres to the edge of town (CFA150), and wait there for a passing vehicle.

Lac de Guiers

Protected from the Senegal River's brackish contamination by a dam in the Taouey River at Richard Toll, the **Lac de Guiers** supplies much of Dakar's drinking water, which is purified at Gnit on the western shore and piped 300km to the capital. The lake, some 30km southwest of Richard Toll, is a wild area swarming with most of the birds present in the Djoudj, with the exception of flamingos. Warthogs are common and if you find a way to get out on the water you might even see **manatees** – strange, aquatic mammals which hold on to a precarious existence here. **People** of the area include Tukulor and Black Moor fishermen, and Fula herders at certain times of year.

You can't get right round the lake – it's best seen from the village of **Mbane**, on the eastern shore. The reedy western shore is accessible only from the St-Louis–Dakar road or a track which leads off south from the N2, 10km west of the Rosso junction – both unsignposted. If you don't have your own transport, you can arrange **tours** to the lake with most of the St-Louis hotels.

The Middle River

Beyond Richard Toll, the road rises out of the valley bypassing the town of **Dagana** – an old gum-arabic entrepôt on the Senegal, with colonial buildings and a semi-intact nineteenth-century fort. Just east of town you get a tempting flash of the river (a good spot for lunch, but stay out of the water) and from here you leave traditional Wolof country. East of here most of the people you'll see are **Tukulor** or **Fula**, and the atmosphere is more laid-back, with commerce no longer quite such a feature.

Moving upriver you pass various villages – some traditional mud and grass affairs, others agglomerations of concrete blocks. At the spartan settlement of **Treji** you can change into a clapped-out Peugeot 504 for the 24-kilometre run north (CFA375) to **PODOR**, Senegal's northernmost town right by the river. Despite the town's notable history – the name comes from its gold (*or*)-trading past and there's the remains of an 1854 French fort – and the fact that it's singing star Baaba Maal's home town, there is little to recommend a diversion off the highway. If you end up **staying**, your best bet is the basic *Gîte d'Etape Le Douwayra* (❷), close to the *gare routière* but not clearly signed.

Podor is situated on the western tip of the **Ile à Morfil** (Island of Ivory), a long slug of floodlands (120km by 10km) between the main course of the river and the meandering Doué. The Ile à Morfil lay at the heart of the **state of Tekrur** (whence "Tukulor" and the misleading French spelling "Toucouleur"), which was at its most powerful in the eleventh century, when it became a major sub-Saharan trading partner with the Almoravid Arabs of North Africa. The Tukulor claim, as a result, that they were the first West Africans to adopt Islam, and went on to evangelize, among others, the Fula – with whom they share a common language and much else. Their own state was annexed by ancient Ghana, with its power base to the east at Koumbi Saleh, in present-day Mauritania. When the Almoravids attacked Ghana, Tekrur helped the invaders, only to fall shortly afterwards to the Mali empire.

At one time the island had a large population of **elephants**, supported by the covering of dense, silt-fed woodland. It's still a good wildlife district, with monkeys, crocodiles and a proliferation of birdlife, but elephants haven't been regularly seen since the 1960s and it's doubtful if any survive. There's a fair number of villages with Sudanic-style **mosques** scattered along the island's one main track as far as **Salde**, the furthest east, where you can ferry back to the main road 90km short of Matam. If you can find transport the length of the island, it's a far preferable alternative to following the main N2, which is unremittingly dull.

The Upper River

Further inland, the next town of note is **Ouro Sogui**, the biggest settlement along the *haute fleuve* and around 200km (and a hot and dusty six hours) by minibus from Treji, shorter if you can catch a Peugeot 504. If you're coming from St-Louis you'll need to make a dawn start as you'll have to make a couple of vehicle changes. Along the way various routes to the river give access **into Mauritania** at Kaédi; branching north at **Thilogne**, 50km before Ouro Sogui, is the best bet. From Kaédi, there's regular transport around southeast Mauritania, and up to Nouakchott. Travellers frequently mistake the large highway town of Ouro Sogui for the former Tukulor slave-trading station of **Matam**, a fading town 10km northeast of the highway, and still featured as the larger settlement on most maps.

At **OURO SOGUI**, turning south at the roundabout by the Shell and Total petrol stations leads 1km along the main street to the town centre and market, passing two cheap eating places, *Restaurant Teddungal* and the adjacent *Dibiterie Islam*, on the left. A few hundred metres further on, keep an eye out for the two-storey *Auberge Sogui* (☎966 11 98; ❷) on the right, the town's best-value **accommodation**, with large fan or a/c rooms, some s/c, and *plats* in the restaurant from CFA2000, if you let them know you're coming. There's also a rooftop terrace on which to rest when the harmattan isn't tearing in from Mauritania. Back on the main road, just west of the roundabout, are two new, bigger and smarter options: the *Hôtel Oasis du Fouta* (☎ & ☎966 12 94; B&B ❹), which has a good bar, and the posher but pretty anonymous *Hôtel Auberge Sogui* (☎966 15 36, ⬥www.hotel-sogui.sn; ❹). There's a BICIS **bank** underneath the latter and a CBAO next door at the Shell station. The **gare routière** is a couple of hundred metres north of the roundabout; you'll want to get there early in the day for the run on to Bakel and Kidira.

Bakel

South of Ouro Sogui, the roads are much improved, and you can expect a fairly smooth ride all the way to Tambacounda. Tucked in a bend in the river among a knot of hills, **BAKEL**'s narrow streets and colonial architectural relics make it perhaps the only place to linger a couple of days in the northeast. The hills around evoke a sense of isolation similar to the dunes surrounding Timbuktu – indeed René Caillié stayed here and later took the post as prefect of Bakel on his return from the legendary city. The old French **fort** overlooks the river, where *piroguiers* ply for fish, onto an uncharacteristically verdant corner of Mauritania. As home to the town *préfecture*, the fort is officially closed to visitors, but if you ask politely at the gate, you'll probably be allowed to look round.

Bakel's **gare routière** is a few minutes' walk from the town centre, where the cheapest **place to stay** is the rather shabby but very friendly *Hôtel d'Islam* (☎983 90 29; ❶), with some a/c rooms (the ones without a/c have no fans either, and are stiflingly hot), plus mat space on the roof terrace. There's a **restaurant** here, too, serving good, cheap dishes for about CFA400; otherwise you could try the various fast-food places along the main street. For a bit more comfort, check out the a/c rooms in the *Hôtel Ma Coumba* (☎983 52 80; ❸), on the riverbank a little north of town; or, along the way at the end of the tarmac road, the *Campement Jikke* (☎983 90 52; ❷), with ordinary little s/c huts and a lively weekend dance scene in the *Jikke* nightclub in the grounds.

In common with a number of other settlements in the area, Bakel is twinned with a French town (Apt), and the whole district is surprisingly full of émigré money: many of the Soninké villagers from here live in France, remitting savings which are put towards impressive houses. The villages of **Golmy**, **Kongany** and **Ballor** are all to the north, ideally visited with your own transport. You can also get a *pirogue* to the Mauritanian village of **Gouray**, or to the Malian village of **Guthurbé**. Most of the Soninké villages organize *journées culturelles* every year or two, during which traditional Soninké ways are dusted off and presented to the community – occasions well worth planning around.

Kidira

From Bakel's *gare routière*, bush taxis and a Mouride bus leave daily for the sixty-kilometre run to **KIDIRA** (1hr) and on to Tambacounda (see opposite; 4–5hr). On arrival in Kidira, you'll be delivered to the *sûreté* at the west end of town, where you should get stamped out of Senegal if heading for Mali. Whatever time you arrive, you'll have to spend some time here, as both the east- and west-bound **trains** come through on Wednesday and Saturday evenings around midnight, if running and not too badly delayed. Unfortunately the town has little to offer the visitor apart from some street food by the Kidira railway crossing, but the Falémé River (follow the tracks 1km east) is a good place to pass the time and maybe catch up on your washing.

Those passing through Kidira **by road** will find a newish bridge spanning the Falémé River just south of the rail bridge, while a good sealed road leads southwest 180km to Tambacounda. The road on the Malian side has also been surfaced and passes through light baobab woodlands to Kayes, just over 100km to the east.

2.3

Niokolo-Koba and the southeast

S enegal's number one **national park** and the flag-bearer for the country's conservation policies, **Niokolo-Koba** covers 8000 square kilometres – a little smaller than the area of The Gambia – of savanna, forest and swamp. It's an undulating wilderness, straddling the Gambia River and two major tributaries in the gentle uplands of **Sénégal Oriental**.

Aside from the park, which itself is only visited by around two thousand people a year, **southeast Senegal** is little affected by tourism. You'll find strongly traditional ways enduring, although hunting as a livelihood took a severe blow when the park opened, displacing a large, scattered population of Mandinka, Bassari and

Fula. Tourist excursions to **Bassari country**, beyond the park, have been running in a small way from the regional centre of **Tambacounda** for some years and more recently from **Kédougou**, but to reap the high rewards of this part of the country, you must be prepared to hike, bike or make your own arrangements by 4WD.

Tambacounda

Getting to Niokolo-Koba can be difficult: it's feasible without your own transport only if you're prepared to put in considerable time waiting for a ride, probably at **TAMBACOUNDA**, 80km from the park entrance. The town is eastern Senegal's major transport hub, the big station on the Dakar–Bamako railway after Kayes in Mali. Situated in the flat, dreary scrub, 180km from the Malian border and 460km from Dakar, the town has little of interest to detain you, but if you're using public transport you will almost inevitably have to spend time here.

Practicalities

The centre of Tamba is bunched around the station, where **trains** from Bamako are due around 7am on Thursdays and Sundays, and those from Dakar around 7pm on Wednesdays and Saturdays – although they are invariably extremely late. Trains are usually packed by this stage, whichever way you're going, so don't expect a seat or bearable toilets. In theory, there are fourteen seats reserved for passengers embarking in Tamba: book ahead the day before if possible. The train is supposed to take twenty hours to Bamako, thirteen hours to Dakar.

The main **gare routière** – for services to Dakar (quicker than the train), Kédougou, Ziguinchor (see p.231 for details), Guinea and Guinea-Bissau – is located in the town's southwestern corner. There is also a daily Mouride bus to Dakar, which leaves early from near the train station. A second *gare routière* – for services to Kidira, Mali and northeast Senegal – is located about 1km along Boulevard Kandioura Noba. The **airport** is a little way south of town.

Routes into Guinea

Travellers heading for Guinea by **public transport** should try hard in Tambacounda to find something going the whole way rather than setting off on a series of bush-taxi hops – transport via Niokolo-Koba into Guinea is fairly hit and miss. Keep an eye out for the all-terrain Russian lorries heading for **Mali**, a small town in northern Guinea, 120km south of Kédougou.

The **main route** from Tambacounda into **Guinea** parts from the Tambacounda–Ziguinchor road where it scrapes the Gambian border. From here the route goes via **Medina-Gounas** (a devout community of the Tijaniya brotherhood, where the women are veiled) to the Senegalese post at **Boundou**, whence an extremely rough *piste* leads 55km to Koundara on the Guinean side.

The first of two possible **minor routes** passes west of **Kédougou**, and heads up into the Fouta Djalon highlands, a ride you won't forget in a hurry and from which even experienced 4WD drivers have turned back. Eventually this ends up at the major town of **Labé**, as does the alternative route east of Kédougou, which winds for over 200km. You might be lucky with transport on the first route, which is also by far the most scenic. On the second, the Gambia River crossing in Guinea is particularly uncertain. Both are supposed to have Guinean entrance formalities on the border itself, but expect to have to check in again at Mali or Labé. With your own vehicle, you might prefer the less arduous crossing to the Guinea town of **Youkounkoun**, 100km west of Kédougou.

If you're heading for the park, stock up on **supplies** in Tamba, as there's really nothing but a handful of restaurants in the park itself. There are a couple of well-stocked *épiceries* and pharmacies along Avenue Léopold Senghor, the main street, along with a shop selling camera film. The SGBS **bank** here (Mon–Thurs 7.45am–noon & 2.15–3.45pm, Fri 7.45am–noon & 2.45–4.15pm) should be able to cough up a Visa or MasterCard cash advance. Next to the bank is a small place where you can access the **Internet**. The **PTT**, another pharmacy and a **market** are grouped around boulevard Demba Diop, near the station. At the **national park office** (daily 7am–6pm; ⊙ & ⊕981 10 97), 1km out of town on the Mali road, you can buy entry permits for Niokolo-Koba in advance.

Accommodation and eating

Accommodation choices have increased over recent years. Down Avenue Léopold Senghor and east of the main *gare routière* you'll find the *Hôtel Niji* (⊙981 12 50, ⊕981 17 44; ❹), which offers a good selection of fan, a/c and s/c rooms, as well as organizing *soirées folkloriques* (CFA50,000, minimum five people) and *piroguing* along the Gambia River (CFA60,000). The comfortable *Hôtel Asta Kebé* (⊙981 10 28, ⊕981 12 15; ❸), signed another 200m down the main road,

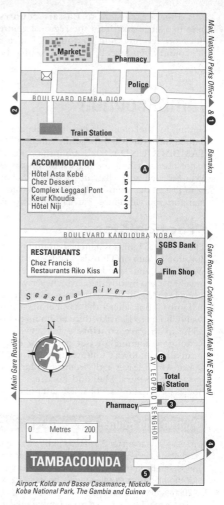

gives you the works, including a pool; while the charmingly off-the-wall *Chez Dessert* (⊙559 97 79; ❷), next door to the carpenters opposite the *Hôtel Asta Kebé* sign, has bed or floor space and even meals with advance notice. Two reasonable *campement*-style places are the *Complexe Leggaal Pont*, 1km out of town on the Mali road (⊙981 17 56, ⊕981 17 52; ❸), with bar, restaurant and nightclub; and in the opposite direction, *Keur Khoudia* (⊙981 11 02, ⊕981 90 49; ❹), past the Mobil fuel station a few hundred metres on the way out of town, and part of the same set-up as the *Simenti Hôtel* in Niokolo-Koba (see p.226).

You can **eat** cheaply at several restaurants on Boulevard Demba Diop, on either side of the train station, as well as at the *Restaurant Riko Kiss* on Avenue Senghor, which has a nice terrace out back. South down Avenue Senghor, *Chez Francis* has an even better terrace and serves a good steak and chips. The *Niji* does a *menu* for CFA4500, the *Asta Kebé* for CFA5500.

Parc National de Niokolo-Koba

Parc National de Niokolo-Koba is officially open only during the December to June dry season (exact dates fixed according to the weather), when animals gather along the watercourses, though in fact you can visit at any time of the year. Among the commoner large species here are buffalo, hartebeeste (*bubale*; uniquely ugly with their long faces and hooked horns), shaggy Defassa waterbuck (*cobe defassa*), timid and fast-moving bushbuck (*antilope harnaché* or *guib*; beautifully white-marked on russet coat), warthogs (*phacochère*), of course, and crocodiles in the rivers. **Hippos** are sometimes visible from the authorized halts along the Gambia River, and you can see them in many areas where the water is deep enough all year round. Look out also for the large, maned **roan antelope** (*hippotrague*) and especially for the huge and very uncommon **western giant eland**, which stands a couple of metres at the shoulder. Baboons and other monkeys, notably vervet and red patas, are also common. The park's **chimpanzees** are exceedingly rare, but can occasionally be seen east of Assirik, the most northerly chimpanzee outpost in Africa.

Sighting **lions** is also rare; with patience, though, you might see them in pockets of deep shade at the base of trees, or in hollows, especially around the confluence of tracks known as Patte d'Oie – "Crow's foot". **Elephants** are said to gather in a broad zone around Mont Assirik, and in the months before the rains (March–May) are sometimes found in the south of this area – a drive between Bangaré ford and Worouli could be successful. **Leopards**, like lions, can range outside the park's confines and are probably Africa's most under-counted large predator; very rarely seen, they are most likely to be spotted high in a tree.

Practicalities

The easiest way of visiting the park is to take an **organized excursion** with one of the Tambacounda hotels, though cost is a major drawback. A two-day safari costs CFA35,000 each for a group of at least ten people with the *Hôtel Asta Kebé*, while a day's chauffeured 4WD is CFA50,000 each for two or three people plus fuel and entrance fees. The *Hôtel Niji* offers less expensive day-trips at CFA75,000 between five people, though it's worth paying more to spend at least one night in the park. One possibility for a free lift to the park from Tamba is to hang around by the pool at the *Asta Kebé* or at the *Niji* bar, where there's often a contingent of tourists about to make their way there.

Travelling independently, you can get to the park **entrance** at **Dar Salam** in a Kédougou-bound **taxi brousse** from Tamba, though you'll almost certainly have to pay the full Kédougou fare (CFA3500) and you may find it hard to continue into the park from there. Four people simply sharing a taxi from Tamba all the way to the park **headquarters** at Simenti can expect to pay around CFA5000 each. Alternatively, you can always find a **taxi** driver who's willing to spend the day – possibly even longer – driving you round. The advantage is the price – negotiable down to realistic levels of CFA25,000–30,000 per taxi per day (excluding fuel, entrance fees and guide hire). But be sure the driver knows what he's about, that the vehicle is sound and has spares, and that you pay for fuel separately, otherwise your game-viewing is going to be limited indeed. Note that the park's tracks are pretty rough, and that you'll definitely need a 4WD if it's wet or if you're planning a trip to Mont Assirik; on the plus side, good signposting ensures you won't have much trouble finding your way around. Note also that driving isn't allowed after dark.

Your chances of seeing wildlife will be greatly improved if you **hire a guide** (CFA6000 per day), either at the park entrance or Simenti; all the guides speak French, but are unlikely to speak English. The park **fee** per day is CFA2000 per person, plus CFA5000 per car. At the park entrance you can buy entry permits and booklets with maps for CFA5000, and there's also a reasonable *campement*

(☎981 25 75; ❷). **Accommodation** within the park at the main centres of **Simenti** and **Niokolo-Koba** is slicker, the *campements* almost indistinguishable from hotels, with restaurants, swimming pools (non-guests can pay a fee for a swim) and fuel supplies. The *Simenti Hôtel* (☎982 36 50; ❷) has some simple huts and more comfortable, en-suite rooms, plus an excellent location above the Gambia River and a good game-viewing **hide**; meals are available for CFA5000, half-day game drives for CFA6500 per person and pick-ups from Dar Salam for CFA15,000. Eight kilometres east of Simenti is *Campement du Lion* (❷), a much more basic set-up in one of the park's most tranquil spots, also overlooking the river. You can **camp** for free at Badi (where another *campement* was being built at the time of writing), Malapa, Damantan, Badoye, Dalaba, Wouroli and Bafoulabé. For up-to-date information contact the **national park office** (see p.224).

Kédougou and the Pays Bassari

Set in Senegal's verdant and rarely visited southeastern corner, the **Pays Bassari** is an area of low hills watered by the run-off from the Fouta Djalon highlands to the south and the perennial Gambia River. This is the least known part of the country, ethnically diverse and very different from the Wolof-Franco Senegal to the north and west. Living in hill villages at the foot of the Fouta Djalon mountains, the ancient Bassari people have stood against the tide of Islam that over the centuries has swept around them on the plains. Matrilineal and divided into age groups, they traditionally subsist on farming and hunting (though some still pan for gold). Major initiation ceremonies are held every year, and there's an annual **festival** before the rains in April or May, notably at the village of **Etiolo**, a few kilometres from the Guinean frontier.

KÉDOUGOU is the only major settlement, once a bit of a dead-end to all but the very few pushing on to Guinea or Mali but now more easily accessible – and a viable alternative base for the Niokolo-Koba park – thanks to the good-quality surfaced road from Tambacounda. The town's *campements* offer a range of **excursions** to Bassari, Beduk and Fula villages in the region, along with the spectacular **waterfall** near Dindefelo and traditional gold mines, plus tours to Niokolo-Koba (though these are no cheaper than in Tamba).

If you've just turned up from Mali or Guinea, get your passport stamped at the **police** post, 500m up the Tamba road just past the phone box. Kédougou has a post office, pharmacies, fuel and Internet access, as well as several **accommodation** options. The best-value are *Chez Diao's campement* (☎985 11 24, ☎985 10 07; ❷), 100m east of the *gare routière* in the town centre, and *Chez Moise* (☎985 11 39; ❷), north of the *gare routière*; both offer comfortable huts with showers. For a bit more comfort try *Le Relais*, perched high above the river at the west end of town (☎985 10 62, ☎985 11 26; ❸), or its annexe, *Hippo Safari Lodge*, 5km east of town on an even more picturesque bend of the river. They're both popular with tour groups and the *Relais* has a good pool, which you can use if you eat there. The *campements* are the best places for **food**, the only other options being the fast-food restaurants at the *gare routière*. Around the *gare routière* you can also rent bikes, motorbikes and mopeds, though the mopeds in particular are unlikely to be in good enough condition to tackle the rough tracks in the surrounding countryside.

From Kédougou, Land Rovers serve **Saraya**, 60km to the northeast, and occasionally continue another 70km along a maze of minor bush tracks to **Kéniéba** in **Mali** (a rough half-day to two days' drive). This is not a regular route and is dependent on demand as well as the depth of the Falémé River which denotes the unmanned frontier – it's usually fordable from January until the rains come. Expect to pay at least CFA6000 – if the car is full – for this unusual and rarely-used back route into Mali. You can also cross into **Guinea** near Kédougou, though note that public transport is best caught in Tambacounda; see p.223 for routes and transport details.

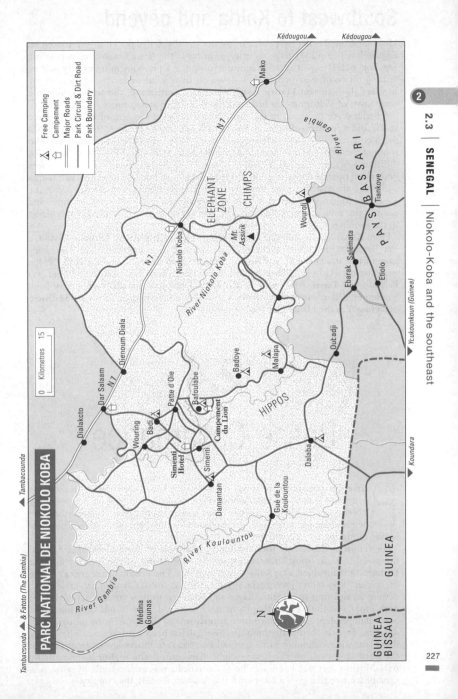

PARC NATIONAL DE NIOKOLO KOBA

Tambacounda▲ & Fatoto (The Gambia)

▲ Tambacounda

Kédougou▲   Kédougou▲

Legend:
△ Free Camping
⌂ Campement
═ Major Roads
── Park Circuit & Dirt Road
── Park Boundary

0   Kilometres   15

Mako

N7

ELEPHANT ZONE

CHIMPS

Mt. Assiirik ▲

Niokolo Koba ⌂

N7

River Niokolo Koba

Wouroli △

P A Y S   B A S S A R I

Tiankoye

Ebarak   Salémata

Etiolo

▶ Ycukounkoun (Guinea)

Dienoum Diala

Dar Salaam ⌂

N7

Dialakoto

Patte d'Oie

Bafoulabe

Badoye △

Malapa △

Outadji

Badi △

Wouring

Campement du Lion ⌂

Simenti Hotel ⌂

Simenti

Damantan

HIPPOS

Dalaba △

▶ Koundara

Gué de la Koulountou

River Koulountou

Médina Gounas

River Gambia

GUINEA

GUINEA BISSAU

N

River Gambia

Southwest to Kolda and beyond

Heading from Tamba by public transport for the full-day's ride (CFA6800) to Ziguinchor (see p.231) – the security situation in the Basse Casamance permitting (see box, p.231) – you want to be sure you catch a pre-8am minibus or you'll be waiting till noon. Few people slow down on their southwesterly way through the increasingly luxuriant **Haute** and **Moyenne Casamance**, and to be honest the small town of **Velingara** has little to offer other than a *campement*.

A better place to break up the journey is the regional centre of **KOLDA**. Here you'll find **accommodation** at the *Hôtel Moya* (☎996 11 75, ✆996 13 57; B&B ❸), a cosy nest of en-suite chalets with huge beds, located by the riverside 400m south of the bridge and Total station; and the *Hôtel Hobb* (☎996 11 70, ✆996 10 39, ✉diahobbe@sentoo.sn; ❹), a couple of blocks further south near the *gare routière*, with more upscale rooms, a pool and Internet access. For something to **eat**, there's a cheaper alternative to the hotel restaurants: two blocks west of the *Moya*, the *Restaurant Moussa Molo* serves a heap of *tieboudienne* for CFA700 at lunchtime, and meat in the evenings for CFA1250. The **bar** at the *Moya* is a centre for socializing in the evenings.

From Kolda a daily minibus takes a minor *piste* to **Bafatá** in **Guinea-Bissau**, a four-hour journey which includes border formalities – expect to have your baggage turned inside out by the Bissau customs – and a walk across a rickety bridge spanning the Rio Gêba. There's also a more direct bush taxi option to Bissau (via Farim) from **Tanaf**, 70km west of Kolda. At Tanaf you can also take a ferry from Sandenièr, 10km northwest of town, across the Casamance River to **Sédhiou** (*campement*) in the Haute Casamance region.

2.4

Basse Casamance

B asse Casamance – the lower reaches of the Casamance River – is the most seductive part of Senegal. Wonderfully tropical, with dense forest, winding creeks, rice fields and quiet backroads shaded by massive silk-cottons, the region seems to have little in common with the Senegal of Islamic brotherhoods, groundnuts, cattle and dust.

For centuries the mostly **Jola**-speaking population of Basse Casamance resisted the push of Islam (most successfully on the south bank of the river), while the Portuguese maintained a typically torpid presence. The ceding of the region to the French in 1886 didn't precipitate any great social shifts. Changes are under way, despite an isolation in which villages and language groups are cut off even from each other, but there's a resolve to maintain some degree of self-determination. Since independence, the **Casamance question** and the apparent threat to Wolof-speaking, French-abetted metropolitan Senegal, has been a prickly one. The charge that Casamance continues to be ignored because it produces less groundnuts than the north and can't muster heavyweight marabouts – the region is substantially non-Muslim – is not baseless. The Casamançais resent the snub, because it is Casamance rice that goes a substantial way towards feeding the country.

The Jola

The people of Basse Casamance are predominantly **Jola** (or Diola; no relation to the Diola/Dyula of Côte d'Ivoire) – broadly divided by the river into Buluf and Fonyi on the north bank and Huluf (or Fulup) on the south. From around the sixteenth century they gradually displaced earlier Casamance inhabitants called the Banyun, who used to be great traders and still live among them. Where the Jola came from nobody seems to know, but their dialects are closely related to the Manjak spoken in Guinea-Bissau, and indeed the Jola generally claim to come from the south. They never developed a unified state, and their fragmentation has resulted in some **Jola dialects** being mutually unintelligible. In fact the idea of a Jola "tribe" is mostly a colonial one: only contact with outsiders has given the term any meaning for the people themselves. The word is supposed to derive from the Manding *jor la* – "he who avenges himself".

A distinctive style of **wet-rice farming** has been practised for at least six hundred years in the reclaimed land between the creeks. **Dykes** are built around new fields so that the rains will flood them and leach out the sea salt, which runs away through hollow tree trunks in the dykes while the fields lie fallow. Once the field is flooded, the drains are blocked and the rice plants brought out from the nurseries and planted, one by one, in the mud. After three or four months of weeding and dyke care by the men, the women gather the **harvest** in November or December. For the first half of the year, though, there's little work in the rice fields and increasingly this is a time when young people drift away to Ziguinchor, The Gambia or Dakar. Many don't return for the next season. Later in the year, you'll see villagers walking to the fields early in the morning with the amazingly long, iron-tipped hoes called **kayendos**.

Traditionally, rice was never sold. Having huge numbers of granaries full of it, often for years, brought the kind of **prestige** every Jola man wanted. Consequently, conflicts over **land rights** have always been close to the surface and still occasionally erupt. Islam has made little headway among the Jola, but an erosion of traditional values has been brought about by **groundnuts**. Introduced to the region in the early nineteenth century, the crop provided a commercial alternative to rice that could earn ready money, with relatively little labour, on land that had hitherto been unplanted bush. Now grown on raised ground all over the region, the groundnut crop has resulted in deforestation, soil degradation and reliance on imported food. "He who wears a *boubou* can't work in the rice fields" goes the Jola saying, ironically excusing the way things increasingly are in terms of Islam.

Jola word list

Jola is a diverse language, comprising several dialects: the following words and phrases could be helpful in Basse Casamance, but may not all provoke immediate recognition.

Kassoumay?	Hello, welcome	*Ounomom*	Sell me
Kassoumaykep	Universal Response to kassaoumay (peace only)	*le dadat*	This is good
		le diacoutte	This is not good
		Katenom	Stop (leave me alone)
Aow	Yes		
Oolat	No	*Joom*	Stop (in a car)
Safi	Bonjour, hello	*Sinangas*	Rice
Oukatora	Goodbye	*Siwolassou*	Fish
Karessy boo?	What is your name?	*Bunuk*	Palm wine
Karessom...	My name is...	*Bulago bara . . . ?*	Which way to ...?
Oubonkatom	Please	*Boussana*	Pirogue
Emitakati	Thank you	*Sibeurassou*	Trees
Bunu kani?	How is it? Ça va?	*Karambak*	Forest
Iman jut	I don't understand	*Falafou*	River

229

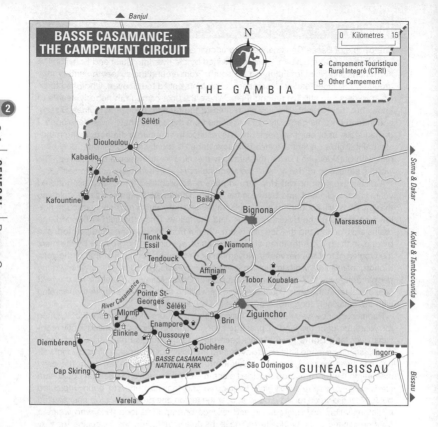

▲ Banjul

**BASSE CASAMANCE:
THE CAMPEMENT CIRCUIT**

N

THE GAMBIA

| 0 | Kilometres | 15 |

⚑ Campement Touristique Rural Integré (CTRI)
⌂ Other Campement

Séléti

Diouloulou

Kabadio

Abéné

Kafountine

Baila

Bignona

Marsassoum

Tionk Essil

Niamone

Tendouck

Affiniam

Tobor Koubalan

River Casamance

Pointe St-Georges

Mlomp

Séléki

Enampore

Elinkine Oussouye

Diembéreng

Brin

Ziguinchor

Diohère

Ingore

Cap Skiring

BASSE CASAMANCE NATIONAL PARK

São Domingos

GUINÉA-BISSAU

Bissau

Varela

Soma & Dakar

Kolda & Tambacounda

Furthermore, without the Casamance's full participation in national affairs, the issue of *rapprochement* with The Gambia – an even more troublesome thorn in Senegal's side – will never be resolved.

Despite the ongoing **separatist conflict** (see the box opposite for a consideration of the security issues, and the box on p.173 for the historical background), now is in some ways a good time to travel to Basse Casamance: for one thing, **prices** are incredibly low, and the local people - especially in the most run-down villages - are all the more welcoming and appreciative of anyone who makes the effort to visit.

Getting to and around Basse Casamance

There are three **main roads** to Basse Casamance: from **Banjul**; from **Dakar** on the faster *transgambienne* route; and from far-off **Tambacounda** in the east. If you're coming from Mali on the train, this third route makes a much better introduction to Senegal than an after-dark arrival in Dakar. Several minibuses and Peugeots depart daily from Tambacounda for Ziguinchor, most leaving early; a late start will probably mean changing in **Kolda**, making a full day on the road. At the time of writing, there were frequent army checkpoints on all main roads in and around Basse Casamance - you'll have to show your passport but otherwise you won't be hassled - and roads were closed after dark.

Security in Basse Casamance

At the time of writing, sporadic **conflict** was continuing in the Basse Casamance between the Senegalese government and the various, disunified factions of the MFDC separatist movement (see p.173). As a result, both the British Foreign Office and the US State Department were advising visitors against travel to the region. In practice, while some parts of the region were still **no-go zones** because of rebel activity and/or land mines - notably the forests south of the Kolda-Ziguinchor-Cap Skiring road, including the Basse Casamance National Park, and a couple of stretches along the Gambian border - other areas hadn't seen any armed conflict in years, if ever.

Much of Casamance's dangerous reputation has come from intermittent **road ambushes** by rebels turned bandits. These hold-ups have occasionally turned violent, but have rarely involved tourists and had died down by 2003, when the main roads were generally considered safe during the day, thanks to numerous army roadblocks. Once inside Ziguinchor, Cap Skiring and other villages traditionally popular with tourists, the security risks were virtually non-existent - certainly much smaller than being mugged in Dakar, for example.

Of course, things could deteriorate or improve during the lifetime of this edition, so you should check the latest security situation **before you go**. Most people in other parts of Senegal will be full of dire warnings about Casamance, but unless they've actually been there, they won't really know what they're talking about. You can get a more reliable account of the situation from the **bush-taxi drivers** who travel to Ziguinchor every day, or by calling one of the Ziguinchor hotels. Alternatively, you could take one of the cheap, frequent **flights** (or a boat, if it's operating) from Dakar to Ziguinchor or Cap Skiring and make up your own mind when you get there.

Getting around Basse Casamance is generally simple. **Ziguinchor** is the main transport hub with daily transport to most sites of interest. You can **rent bikes** in Ziguinchor, Oussouye and Cap Skiring, making cycling around the popular southern part of Basse Casamance a practical option. Unless you have lots of time, it's perhaps best to rent in Oussouye, where there's an excellent bike shop, or Cap Skiring, rather than Ziguinchor, as in that case you'll probably spend your first day cycling straight to Oussouye anyway – not the most exciting bike ride in the area. If you're going anywhere on your own, you should always consult first with locals, who will take care not to let you get close to any trouble. If you're unhappy about travelling by road, note that you can reach pretty much anywhere you want in the region by **pirogue**. Hiring a **guide** to show you round for a few days is cheap and also worth considering.

Because Basse Casamance is so affected by tides, no two **maps** of it ever look the same: much of what appears to be virtually underwater on some maps is actually firm ground most of the time.

Ziguinchor

Something of **ZIGUINCHOR**'s appeal comes through in its exotic name, pronounced "Sigichor" by most Jola. There's a luxuriant sense of repose here, found in no other Senegalese town of its size, and life here is a good deal cheaper than in Dakar or The Gambia. Surprisingly, you need reminding that Ziguinchor is on the river: its colonial trading houses don't stand out, and the river port isn't likely to figure prominently in your meanderings. It's a town of trees and avenues, roosting birds, orchestral crickets and fluttering bats at dusk, with a strong flavour of the Guineas. Less pleasant is the attention lavished by local mosquitoes from March to October – and sporadically by highly persistent hustlers, vendors and hangers-on.

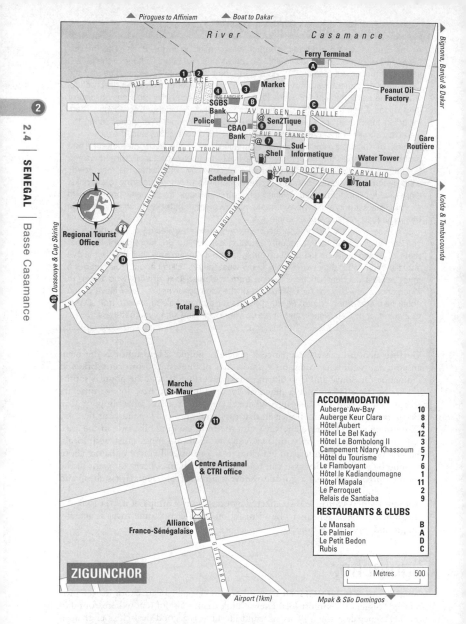

Pirogues to Affiniam ▲   ▲ **Boat to Dakar**

River *Casamance*

Bignona, Banjul & Dakar ▶

Ferry Terminal

Ⓐ

RUE DE COMMERCE

❶❷

❹ RUE FARGUES

SGBS
Bank

Police

CBAO
Bank

❸ Market

Ⓑ

AV. DU GEN. DE GAULLE

Ⓒ

Peanut Oil
Factory

@ Sen2Tique
❻ ❺

RUE DE FRANCE

RUE DU LT. TRUCH

@ ❼

Shell

Sud-
Informatique

Gare
Routière

Water Tower

AV. DU DOCTEUR G. CARVALHO

Cathedral ✝   Total

Total

Kolda & Tambacounda ▶

N

Regional Tourist
Office

ⓘ

Ⓓ

AV. EMILE BADIANE

AV. IBOU DIALLO

❽

AV. BACHIR AIDARA

❾

Oussouye & Cap Skiring ▲

AV. EDOUARD DIATTA

Total ❿

Marché
St-Maur

⓬ ⓫

Centre Artisanal
& CTRI office

Alliance
Franco-Sénégalaise

AV. LYCÉE GUIGNABO

ZIGUINCHOR

Airport (1km) ▼   Mpak & São Domingos ▼

ACCOMMODATION

Auberge Aw-Bay	10
Auberge Keur Clara	8
Hôtel Aubert	4
Hôtel Le Bel Kady	12
Hôtel Le Bombolong II	3
Campement Ndary Khassoum	5
Hôtel du Tourisme	7
Le Flamboyant	6
Hôtel le Kadiandoumagne	1
Hôtel Mapala	11
Le Perroquet	2
Relais de Santiaba	9

RESTAURANTS & CLUBS

Le Mansah	B
Le Palmier	A
Le Petit Bedon	D
Rubis	C

0   Metres   500

Arrival, information and accommodation

The old part of town is a comprehensible one-by-half-a-kilometre grid of streets extending south of the river to **Avenue du Docteur Gabriel Carvalho** on which the **rond-point** (roundabout) is situated. Within this area you'll find the banks, post office, main hotels and other services as well as the small portside

market, good for fresh fruit, vegetables and early morning fish. South of the *rond-point*, Avenue Ibou Diallo leads past the **cathedral** a kilometre or two to the more animated quarter of town around the **Marché St-Maur**.

If boats from Dakar are running again (see p.187), coming into Ziguinchor up the river is the best approach; the **ferry terminal** is right in the heart of the town, a few minutes from the main hotels. Arriving by road from the north or from Tambacounda, you'll be dropped at the **gare routière**, 1km east of town, just south of the bridge. If you've come up from Guinea-Bissau, you may be dropped off on the wide, sealed road, just east of the Marché St-Maur and close to a few cheap accommodation options. If you arrive by air you're a kilometre further south of the Marché St-Maur.

You can get advice on travel and accommodation in the region from the helpful **regional tourist office** on avenue Edouard Diatta (Mon–Fri 8am–1.30pm & 2.30–5pm; ☎991 12 68) as well as the excellent **website** ⓦwww.casamance.net, run by the owner of the *Flamboyant* (see below).

Accommodation

Ziguinchor offers an excellent and inexpensive range of **accommodation** – basic, central rooms, *campement*-style set-ups, and a few plusher alternatives at knock-down prices. This last category has suffered badly from the drop in tourist numbers since the early 1990s, though the better establishments have remained popular – always a good sign.

Old Ziguinchor

Campement Ndary Khassoum rue de France ☎991 11 89. Centrally located and with a shady courtyard, but the rooms – all with huge bathrooms and some with toilets – are a bit dingy. ❷
Le Flamboyant rue de France ☎991 22 23, ☏991 22 22, ✉lamboyant@casamance.net. Spotless, well-run hotel offering comfortable s/c, a/c rooms with satellite TV, and a pool. A bargain. ❹
Hôtel Aubert rue Fargues ☎938 80 20, ☏991 54

54. The only luxury hotel to successfully survive the tourism crash of 1993, and deservedly so, with immaculate, recently renovated rooms with all mod cons, a pool open to non-residents and a new sports centre over the road, painted a garish tangerine. B&B ❺
Hôtel du Tourisme rue de France ☎991 22 23, ☏991 22 22. Since its owners opened the glamorous *Flamboyant* opposite, this old colonial-era favourite seems to have been somewhat

---

Moving on from Ziguinchor

There's a daily **Air Sénégal** (☎991 10 81) flight to **Dakar** (CFA37,500). You may be able to get a **boat** to Dakar if the government fulfils its promise to replace the MV *Joola* (see p.156). Before it sank, the *Joola* left once a week for the seventeen-hour voyage. Prices were CFA3500 for a hard seat, CFA6000 for a comfy one and CFA18,000 for a cabin to yourself, but prices are likely to go up if a new ship arrives. The ticket booth is down at the ferry terminal.

From the *gare routière*, there are frequent **bush taxis** to **Oussouye** and **Cap Skiring** and at least one **minibus** a day to many smaller villages, including **Enampore** and **Elinkine**. A cheap, regular **pirogue** service for **Affiniam** leaves from the jetty by *Le Perroquet* on Monday, Wednesday and Friday at 3pm. At other times you can try to reach an agreement with the *piroguiers* on the waterfront. This is a good way of starting a tour round the north-bank region of **Buluf**, as an alternative to taxiing straight out of Ziguinchor.

For **Guinea-Bissau**, the Senegalese border post is at **Mpak** (18km); the Guinea-Bissau post is at **São Domingos** (25km). Plan for an early start from the *gare routière*. You can get Guinea-Bissau **visas** from the consulate, next to the *Hôtel du Tourisme* (Mon–Fri 8am–2pm); all you need to take is a passport photograph. All visas are processed on the spot; a one-month double-entry visa costs CFA5000 and a three-month multiple-entry CFA15,000.

neglected, but it still offers reasonable s/c rooms and a good restaurant. **2**

Hôtel Le Bombolong II rue Fargues ☎991 80 01, ℻991 11 46. Owned by the *Kadiandoumagne*, the *Bombolong* offers good-value s/c, a/c rooms, though they don't have much ambience. Home of the *Bar Americaine* and, on a good night, the town's best nightclub (free to guests). **2**

Hôtel Le Kadiandoumagne rue de Commerce ☎991 80 00, ℻991 16 75. Very smart colonial-style hotel on the riverfront, with all mod cons, a fine restaurant and a beautiful garden. **5**

Le Perroquet rue de Commerce ☎991 23 29, ✉perroquet@sentoo.sn. Along with the *Flamboyant*, this riverside French-run establishment offers the best value in town, with neat s/c, fan rooms around a garden and a bar/restaurant popular with the owners of the bobbing yachts just offshore. **3**

Out from the centre

Auberge Aw-Bay Signed 2.5km down the Oussouye road ☎936 80 76. Offers clean rooms and a pleasant, shady courtyard – a reasonable option if you have your own transport. *Pirogue* excursions offered for around CFA9500. **2**

Auberge Keur Clara Off av Ibou Diallo. Set in a quiet side-street with basic singles or s/c twins and a fabulous terrace upstairs, where you can put down a mat for the night for CFA1000. The terrace used to be a restaurant/bar, but this has now been moved down the road so guests won't be kept up by its thrice-weekly jazz sessions. **2**

Hôtel Le Bel Kady Just south of Marché St-Maur ☎991 11 22. Popular budget option run by a friendly bunch of youths. Faintly bordello-ish with non-s/c rooms and dubious ablutions but a good-value restaurant. **1**

Hôtel Mapala Opposite *Le Bel Kady* ☎991 26 27. Basic, s/c doubles with fan, plus a cheap restaurant and bar. **2**

Relais de Santiaba Qtr Santiaba ☎991 11 99. Decent-value *chambres de passage* up on the roof; plain but not rough, with decent, shared ablutions. Also some s/c rooms, a bar/restaurant and mountain bike rental. **2**

The Town

There's not a great deal to keep you in Ziguinchor, but just hanging out is pleasure enough. In the old quarter of the town centre, there's a string of public gardens, heavily shaded, with park benches and – sign of a non-Muslim region – rootling piglets. Pelicans and storks congregate in the trees, however, making this a some-times noisy and unpredictable place to relax.

Both the **Marché St-Maur-des-Fossés** (named after the southeast Paris suburb with which Ziguinchor is twinned) and the **Centre Artisanal** just to the south are relatively hassle-free and well worth visiting. The municipal St-Maur, divided into merchandise zones, heaves with activity, while the *arti-sanal*, where the stall holders really are working at their crafts, is a relaxing place to get all your souvenirs in one go and offers real bargains for hardened hagglers.

For a bit of an excursion, you can take a *pirogue* via the Ile aux Oiseaux to **Dilapao** on the north side of the river and continue up the serpentine Marigot de Bignona to Affiniam (see p.244). At Dilapao, there's a two-storey mud-brick house owned by a local artist and decorated with sculptures (CFA500 to look round), while Affiniam's large *case à impluvium* (see p.238) is one of the oldest and nicest *campements* in the rural *integré* circuit. Most Ziguinchor hotels and the *Mansah* restaurant offer this popular day-trip; prices start around CFA10,000 each for a motor *pirogue* for two people, usually less per person with a group, but can vary wildly from place to place. Ask around at the cheaper *campements* or hotels.

Eating, drinking and nightlife

With a few exceptions noted below, food in Ziguinchor is unremarkable. **Street food** is generally limited to fruit and nuts (cashews make a pleasingly inexpensive treat) or portside bread and coffee stalls. You'll find numerous nondescript **restau-rants**, offering a low-priced daily *plat*, on the way to Marché St-Maur along

Avenue Lycée Guignabo, south of the Total station; there's more sophisticated eating in town, especially at the hotels.

Hôtel du Tourisme See p.233. Charming restaurant offering excellent Franco-Senegalese three-course menus for CFA4500 and pricier à la carte options.

Hôtel Le Bel Kady See p.234. A good place for an inexpensive meal, with *plats* for under CFA1500 as well as drinks and beers.

Hôtel Le Kadiandoumagne See p.234. Top-quality seafood restaurant on a jetty overlooking the river.

Le Mansah rue de Capitaine Javelier. Right in the town centre and well worth a visit for great-value Senegalese dishes and delicious *brochettes*. Check out the huge carved masks up on the walls too – they're the real thing.

Le Perroquet See p.234. Franco-Senegalese meals for around CFA2500. Great location, but bring some mosquito spray.

Le Petit Bedon av Emile Badiane. Serves delicious fish and European/French cuisine for CFA3000–5000 for a main dish. Closed Mon.

Restaurant Le Palmier rue de Commerce. Cheap and cheerful place down by the port, serving tasty Senegalese fare.

Drinking and nightlife

After dark, Ziguinchor smoulders. *Le Bombolong* and *Rubis Nightclub* (formerly well established as *Kathmandu*) have been *the* places to visit for a number of years, both repaying the entrance fees of around CFA1500 with hot music – lots of *zouk* – and as many chance encounters as you want. *Le Bombolong* is more exclusive and scores highly with the French community, as well as passing *toubabs*, while *Rubis* has a greater head of steam and a largely local crowd; the patio behind is a vital cooling-off area. Expect the drinks at *Le Bombolong* to be pricier than those at *Rubis*.

Listings

Banks Of the six banks in town, the CBAO (Mon–Thurs 7.45am–3.45pm, Fri 7.45am–1.15pm & 2.45–3.45pm) and the SGBS (Mon–Thurs 7.45am–noon & 2.15–3.45pm, Fri 7.45am–noon & 2.45–4.15pm) are your best bets for foreign exchange, getting cash advances on Visa or MasterCard and changing traveller's cheques. SGBS also has a 24hr ATM round the back on rue Fargues.

Bike rental The *Relais de Santiaba* has one-speed bikes available for rent for CFA2500 a day and mountain bikes for CFA5000 per day. If you give them advance warning, they'll get the bikes serviced before you pick them up. Try to arrange a weekly rate.

Clinic Dr Simon Tendeng (by appointment only: Mon–Fri 8.30am–2.30pm & 6–8pm, Sat 8.30am–2.30pm; ☎991 13 85, emergency ☎991 17 75; CFA5000); 50m east of the *rond-point* down av du Docteur Gabriel Carvalho on the left.

CTRI office At the Centre Artisanal, for *campement* reservations (☎991 35 14).

Cultural centre The Alliance Franco-Sénégalaise, south of the *centre artisanal*, puts on exhibitions and concerts, but it's worth visiting simply for its beautifully ornate building – a modern variation on a *case à impluvium* – and shady garden. There's a cheap café here, too.

Internet access Try *Cyber Café Sen2Tique* (Mon–Sat 8am–11pm, Sun 5.30–10pm; CFA1000/hr) or *Sud-Informatique* (Mon–Fri 8am–1pm & 3–8pm, Sat 8am–1pm & 4–8pm; CFA1000/hr), both on rue Javelier near the CBAO bank.

Police ☎991 10 13, or ☎17 in an emergency.

The southern Basse Casamance

Between Ziguinchor and the coast lies the heart of the **southern Basse Casamance**, a district of tall hardwood forest and rice fields cut by three major creeks and their fringes of mangrove flats. As the longest distance between significant places is just 34km, this is an ideal region for **cycling**, though the problems of the last decade have meant that certain areas are now off-limits (see p.231). You can

"Rurally integrated" campements

Casamance's network of **campements touristiques rurals integrés** (CTRIs) was introduced by the Ministry of Tourism in the 1970s to cater for people with small budgets wanting a change from mainstream accommodation. Built by villagers with loans from central funds, often in a traditional architectural style, the *campements* theoretically bring tourist money into parts of the rural economy that don't usually benefit.

Facilities at the CTRIs – also known as *campements villageois* – are basic but include cold running water, kerosene lighting, three-course meals, and cold drinks from a gas fridge. They provide mosquito nets and foam mattresses and sheets. For the same charge you can always camp outside. **Prices** are the same at all CTRIs and you can pay for accommodation only, or as many meals as you want. At the time of writing, costs were as follows: FB at CFA9800; bed only CFA3000; breakfast CFA1800; each meal CFA2500.

In recent years, the CTRIs have taken a severe beating from the drop in tourism caused by the Casamance conflict. Many have closed, been occupied by the army or fallen into disrepair, but some still struggle on, often keeping one or two rooms open in the hope that tourists will one day return. We have indicated where *campements* were closed at the time of writing, but the situation can change - and even if the *campement* isn't open, it will usually be no problem to find a room somewhere in the village.

For more information, or to book a room, contact the **regional tourist office** or the **CTRI office** in Ziguinchor (see p.233 & p 235).

rent bikes at **Oussouye** or **Cap Skiring** – or mopeds at the latter, which is Senegal's foremost holiday resort (and one of the top few in West Africa). Apart from needing a water bottle and devising a way to carry your gear, there are no special practical problems in cycling around.

Ziguinchor to Enampore and Oussouye

Climbing the gentle valley out of Ziguinchor, the road passes through the remains of the **forest** that once covered the entire area. The magnificent thirty- or fortymetre trees, strung with vines, are inhabited by large numbers of birds and small animals – though you'll only see monkeys where the trees are close enough together to form arboreal highways. About 4km out of town, you'll come to **DJI-BELOR**, where the signposted **crocodile farm/orchard** (Mon–Sat 8am–6pm; CFA1000) is well worth a visit. The orchard comprises several hectares of fruit trees – you can buy the fruit at the entrance – and flowers, among which fenced enclosures and sheds house about a thousand Nile crocodiles of various sizes. **BRIN**, 6km further, has its own small, basic *Campement Filao* (❶) right by the Enampore track, where the *taxi brousse* will drop you off.

Enampore and Séléki

It's a thirteen-kilometre, four-hour walk to **ENAMPORE**, best done in the cool of the early morning – at this time there is also a chance of getting a lift with some village-bound transport – passing Essil after 6km. The CTRI at Enampore is one of the best preserved, a beautiful *case à impluvium* wonderfully constructed and a pleasure just to be in, especially during the hot hours of the day. However familiar you become with the region's *impluvium* architecture, the simplicity and calm of Enampore are memorable. It's possible to rent a *pirogue* in Enampore to take you to the superb *Campement Les Bolongs* (see p.238) just to the east of Oussouye.

SÉLÉKI, a couple of kilometres further on from Enampore, also has its own pleasant CTRI (closed for repairs at the time of writing). From here you can continue across the **dykes and rice fields** to Etama and then – if you've plenty of

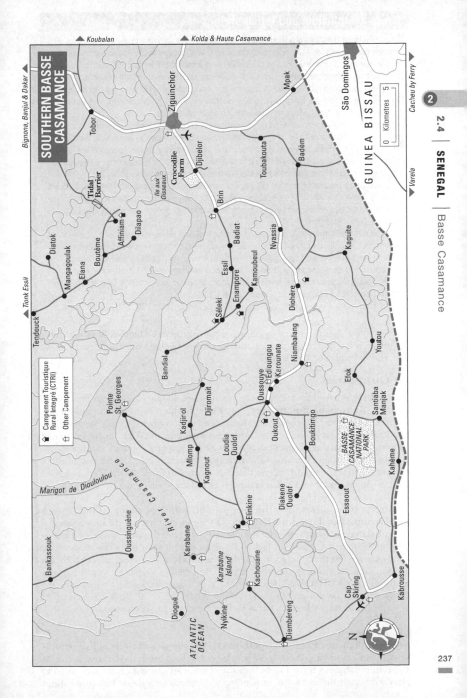

Cases à impluvium and fetish shrines

The traditional Jola **case à impluvium** translates as "rain reservoir hut", a somewhat demeaning term that tells only half the story. The design is doughnut-shaped, with entrances into a shared, circular courtyard and internal doors into private rooms that are built as individual units. There's a stunning quality to the light reflected off the clean-swept courtyard floor to illuminate the living space. The thatched, saddleback roof circling above the living quarters is built like a funnel to allow rain to drain into a central reservoir, from where it runs outside through a drain.

In the past the *impluvium* was good insurance in times of war or drought, but since pure water wells have been dug all over, few *impluvium* houses are being built these days. Yet they make wonderful homes, and undoubtedly more Jola families would build new *cases à impluvium* if they could afford to – but the increasing nuclearization of families means that few can find the necessary money or labour.

Although it's often written that the only other examples of *impluvium* architecture are found in New Guinea, similar houses were traditional in Guinea-Bissau and parts of southwest Côte d'Ivoire, and also in parts of southern Nigeria, where they were square in plan.

In the bush around, you'll also come across isolated miniature huts in the briefest of clearings. Often just a forked stick under a thatched roof, these are **fetish shrines**, the earthly visiting rooms of spirits that hold power over rain, fertility and illnesses. They are consulted less frequently than in the past, but there are still matters about which many Jola feel the traditional spirits know more than modern science or medicine. You should be careful not to disturb them or take photos.

---

time – on to Bandial (a 15km round trip from Enampore). There's interesting architecture en route, and as the people don't get many foreign visitors out on the mud flats, they'll be pleased to see you.

To Oussouye

Back at Brin, the road from Ziguinchor turns south, looping away from the river to cross the **Kamobeul Bolong** creek on a new bridge. Oussouye, the next major focus, is 34km from Ziguinchor, across scrub, open mangrove flats and more scrub – good for birds west of the bridge, otherwise unenthralling. The rurally integrated *campement* at **Diohère**, signposted 14km from Brin, is rarely visited and was occupied by the military at the time of writing. For mountain-bikers, the eastward route back to Ziguinchor from Diohère through farms and forest to the Ziguinchor to Guinea-Bissau road is idyllic, but had been closed for several years because of possible land mines.

Another 10km down the main road to Oussouye you come to the **Case à Impluvium chez Theodore Balousa** (❶), signposted left a little after a sign for **Niambalang**; go 400m along the track and it's just after the well. A *case à impluvium* built in 1980, it has a lived-in feel and is a lot livelier than most *campements*. The family charge less than the going rate for the two rooms offered, although they'll need advance warning if you want a meal. Just before Oussouye you'll pass the small village of **EDIOUNGOU**, with a winding track leading to its pleasant *Campement Les Bolongs* (☎993 10 41 or 936 90 18, ☎936 90 10; ❸), which offers great creek-side views from its bar as well as the customary excursions.

Oussouye

Another kilometre brings you to **OUSSOUYE**, the seat of a line of Jola **priest-kings**, and occupying the largest patch of dry land around. Royalty is not as much in evidence as it used to be, but the town is still an important and growing place. Although the market here is pretty dull, there are one or two good shops and an excellent **craft centre**, Le Métissage, housed in an intriguing wooden building on the road out to Cap Skiring, a fine example of Jola architectural innovation. Also based in Oussouye, behind the post office, is Casamance VTT (℡ & ℱ993 10 04, ✉casavtt@telecomplus.sn), which is the best place in the region to **rent bikes** and organizes recommended guided excursions into the surrounding countryside.

A track from the roundabout in the middle of town leads to three **campements**, the first of which is the small and exceptionally friendly *Auberge de Routard* (℡993 10 25; ❷), run by Gouho Diatta – his wife prepares great food and a vat of palm wine is passed around afterwards. Just behind the *Routard* is the newer *Gîte d'Afrique*, or *Campement Emanaye* (℡ & ℱ993 10 04; ❷), which offers decent s/c rooms, and bike and canoe excursions. Continuing another 600m up the track you may see men hanging beneath the crowns of the palm trees tapping the wine for the day. Oussouye's unusual two-storey mud-brick CTRI (under reconstruction at the time of writing) is on the left, the biggest in the network.

The road leading from the roundabout back towards Ziguinchor has a couple of inexpensive **restaurants**. Check out *Chez Rachel*, where you eat whatever's in the pot, always good value.

Moving on from Oussouye, there are a few bush taxis a day to Mlomp and Elinkine, while Cap Skiring- and Ziguinchor-bound vehicles pass through town more frequently.

Mlomp and Pointe St-Georges

From Oussouye the road swoops through the forest to **MLOMP**, notable for its pair of two-storey *banco* **cottages** with their amazing grove of silk-cotton trees. Two-storey buildings are uncommon in traditional African architecture, and nobody knows why Mlomp should have them; they're reminiscent of Ashanti houses from Ghana and it's possible that the earlier Banyun traders of Casamance brought the innovation back from their travels. The family who live there will show you round one of them (CFA500 donation), and a postcard from your home is much appreciated: many already adorn the walls.

From the village a sandy footpath leads directly north to **Pointe St-Georges**, the Casamance River's last elbow before it reaches the sea. There's not much to the place – it's just a flat, densely wooded stretch of land – but the Pointe does have its own *campement*, built after the upmarket *Village-Hôtel* was burned down by the MFDC in 1992. Access remains a problem, however, as the only driveable track (and 4WD at that) starts from the village of Kagnout, 5km west of Mlomp.

Elinkine and Karabane Island

Beyond Kagnout, the turning to Pointe St-Georges, several stands of huge silk-cottons give way to monotonous, open country as a flat, straight route leads to the fishing village of **ELINKINE**, 10km from Mlomp. Little more than a tiny naval base and a collection of creek-side buildings, Elinkine makes an enjoyable stopover, with two decent *campements*. The more secluded is the CTRI, 700m to the right as you enter the village from the east. A spacious set-up by a sandy beach, it has become a bit run-down but still offers a tropical-postcard view through the palms across the creek. Alternatively, transport from Ziguinchor stops right outside the *Campement Le Fromager* (❷) in the town centre, a smaller and more animated *case à impluvium* – recently rebuilt after a fire – with energetic hosts. Styling themselves as the village's *centre nautique*, they have canoes for rent, offer *pirogue* trips to Karabane, fishing, and so forth; they can also take you by boat to Kachouane (see p.242) for CFA7500 or all the way to Cap Skiring for around CFA15,000 if you don't fancy the circuitous road trip via Oussouye.

Karabane Island

At Elinkine the done thing is to take a trip to the history-laden island of **Karabane** in the river mouth. A public *pirogue* leaves every day at 3pm (CFA500 one-way) for the thirty-minute voyage; going the other way, the boat leaves Karabane at 10am. If you hire your own *pirogue*, expect to pay around CFA7500.

Karabane, or rather its headland, was an early offshore trading base with the interior, and the first French toehold in the Kasa Mansa – the kingdom of the Kasa, one of the ancestral Jola peoples. Slaves, ivory, gum and hides were exported from here, paid for with cloth, alcohol and iron bars. There's a large Breton-style **church**, partly in ruins, dating back to the earliest days of the Holy Ghost Fathers, and a number of crumbling merchant houses. The beach is beautiful, with 10km of salty Casamance River in front and coconuts behind, but in truth, on a short visit, the whole place can feel slack with isolation and irrelevance. However, once everyone else has left and you can walk along the beach in peace, Karabane quickly becomes a place that's hard to leave. The *campements* of *Chez Amathe* (or *Le Barracuda*; ☎659 60 01; ❷), nearest the jetty, and the more atmospheric *Chez Badji-Kunda* (☎553 10 54 or 991 14 08; ❷), a few hundred metres along the beach and owned by a painter, are both preferable to the *Hôtel Karabane* between the two (☎633 17 82; ❹), a dull mission money-earner.

Cap Skiring and around

CAP SKIRING offers most of the tourist facilities you'd expect of a big holiday resort, with lots of souvenir shops and restaurants, plus a handful of bars and nightclubs – as well as a *Club Med*, whose enormous, fenced-off grounds harbour a golf course. The village itself has little to recommend it, but the sands are undeniably pretty – spectacular, even, along the more deserted stretches – and the sea is warm and safe. This is hedonistic territory and lacks much of deeper interest; bronzing and bathing are the main daytime occupations in Cap Skiring, and you can rent **jet skis** and **windsurfers** from the more expensive hotels – there's almost always a good breeze.

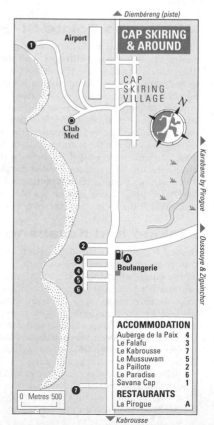

Arrival, accommodation and eating

From the T-junction at the western end of the Oussouye road, Cap Skiring village is 1km to the north, and the cheaper accommodation opportunities are a few hundred metres to the south; *La Paillote* hotel is directly ahead here. If you are arriving **by air**, you will be flown practically into the heart of the village. The **gare routière** is centrally located; frequent bush taxis leave from here for Ziguinchor throughout the day.

Accommodation options are plentiful. You won't be faced with gleaming white high-rises, either; Cap Skiring's luxury hotels are modest constructions, while budget lodgings are low-key affairs, variations to a greater or lesser extent on the CTRI theme. Right on the junction is *La Pirogue* **restaurant**, which offers a high-quality alternative to hotel and *campement* meals.

Auberge de la Paix Just south of the T-junction ℡ 993 51 45. Offers the same great views and beach as its neighbours, good food and a choice of plain rooms, some s/c. ❶

Le Falafu ℡ 993 52 63, ⓦ www.welcome.to /falafu. Colourful *campement* with a pleasant bar and flower-filled garden. The garden-facing rooms are nothing special but the three spacious, en-suite ocean-facing rooms, each with a balcony, are probably the best-value mid-range rooms in Cap Skiring. ❷

Hôtel Savana Cap 2.5km north of Cap Skiring village ℡ 993 51 52/86, ⓕ 993 51 92. The Cap's beautifully landscaped five-star jewel offers it all – at a cost. ❽

Le Kabrousse 2km south of the T-junction ℡ 993 51 26, ⓕ 993 51 27. Plush hotel with cabins set in landscaped greenery, similar to *La Paillote*, and with a pool, mini-golf, driving range and the beach just a stone's throw away. HB ❸

Le Mussuwam ℡ 993 51 84, ⓕ 993 51 25. Established *campement* owned by Ziguinchor's *Bel Kady* with a good range of a/c, s/c rooms. Also offers several excursions. ❶

La Paillote Opposite the Oussouye road junction ℡ 993 51 51, ⓕ 993 51 17, ⓦ www.paillote.sn. Luxurious beachside huts, plus a fine restaurant, souvenir shop and a wide range of excursions. You can also rent bikes here from Casamance VTT (see below). B&B ❸

Le Paradise ℡ 993 51 29, ⓦ perso.libertysurf.fr /pecheparadise. Decent *campement* with a *case à impluvium* alternative to its neighbours and various excursion options. ❷

Excursions from Cap Skiring

To get out from Cap Skiring, you'll find a couple of places in the village renting out **4WDs** (from around CFA25,000 per day), quad bikes and mopeds, but you'll probably get more value out of renting a **mountain bike** from Casamance VTT at *La Paillote* (see above; CFA7500 per day).

Day-trips to **Karabane Island** (see p.240), arranged by most hotels in Cap Skiring, leave from the creek behind the village and cost around CFA15,000 from *Le Paradise* and CFA25,000 from *Mussuwam* and *La Paillote*. Trips normally take in Elinkine (see p.239), Karabane, the Ile des Feticheurs, and an Ile aux Oiseaux or two. That's a lot of messing around on the river among low mangroves, which cast little shade, so make sure you wear a hat. It's not a bad way, incidentally, of getting to Elinkine.

Diembéreng and beyond

An ideal excursion from Cap Skiring, **DIEMBÉRENG** lies deep behind the dunes, 8.5km north. By bike you can easily get up to Diembéreng in an hour or two along the beach at low tide when the sand is firm; the main motorable track through the bush is a sandy 8km (allow at least an hour). You may get the odd dirty look weaving through the sunbeds in front of the *Club Med* and *Savana Cap* hotels, but the beach is a public right-of-way. If you don't want to walk or cycle, you could use the daily minibus, about 6pm, returning to Cap Skiring in the morning – but you'll get to see little of Diembéreng by day.

Past the *Savana*, there's one last jumble of low rocks to negotiate before a magnificent sweep of sand. Shortly after this point there's what looks like an open-air mosque built into the cliffside. Diembéreng is a traditional village, its economy based on fishing and livestock, and by no means dependent on tourism. The most striking thing about the place is the hill that rises from its centre, a steep and ancient dune crowned and stabilized by a grove of venerable silk-cotton trees. It's no more than 30m high, but in Basse Casamance it looks like a mountain, and there's no escaping the strong and mysterious sense of place.

On your left as you come into town along the *piste* from Cap Skiring is the first of three **places to stay**, all struggling badly from a lack of tourists: the *Asseb* *campement* (❷) is nothing special but the only one that's accessible by car. You'll need the help of the boys who hang out under the mother of all *fromagers* (silk-cottons) opposite to search out the other two accommodation options. The *Campement Aten-Elou* (closed for repairs at the time of writing), named after a local priestess, is situated at the top of the hill, just past a fallen tree trunk. Closer to the beach along a maze of fencebound footpaths is *Albert's campement* (❶), a *case à impluvium* set on the far side of the village, and probably the best place to stay (albeit with basic ablutions), undercutting CTRI rates and just ten minutes' walk over the dunes to the sea. Just off the beach, a new and much smarter *campement* was under construction at the time of writing.

If you're craving true isolation, you could walk or cycle – again, preferably at low tide – north to **Nyikine**, a village at the very mouth of the Casamance. It's a place of coconuts and seclusion, recommended by some of the boys hanging around in Diembéreng, and possibly worth visiting in their company. Another option is to head 7km northeast to **KACHOUANE**, a highly picturesque village set on a palm-fringed channel of the Casamance opposite Karabane Island. There's an excellent **restaurant** here, *Chez Paul Bocuse* (warn the chef you're coming on ☏534 93 15), popular with tour groups from Cap Skiring, and a private *campement*, which was nearing completion at the time of writing and was due to charge CTRI rates.

Kabrousse and around

South of Cap Skiring, the road turns through the village of **KABROUSSE**, a scattered community of farmers. There are three last tourist hotels here (including *Le Kabrousse*; see p.241), but nothing in the way of *campements*. Kabrousse is famous as the birthplace of Alinsitoé, a Jola visionary who led a major anticolonial rebellion during World War II. Aged only twenty, she spearheaded a revolt provoked by the tax burden placed on the Jola peasantry by the government. After a vicious battle at Efok, near the present-day Basse Casamance National Park, Alinsitoé was arrested and exiled to St-Louis, then to Timbuktu, where she died. Her name is evoked whenever the question is raised of Casamance secession from northern Senegal.

From Kabrousse, it used to be possible to follow a blissfully peaceful forest path 22km east to the Basse Casamance National Park, but at the time of writing this was unsafe because of land mines and rebel activity in the area. **Santiaba Manjak** was the largest village you passed through before the park gate; 2km further, a right turning leads off to the Alinsitoé battle village of **Efok** (5km) and equally isolated **Youtou** (10km).

Parc National de Basse Casamance

The **Parc National de Basse Casamance** has been closed since 1993. As a result it's impossible to say which animals survive in the park, a forty-square-kilometre area of streams, marshy savanna, and partly untouched primary forest. Large mammals such as forest buffalo, leopard, hippo and bushbuck were rarely seen here anyway, but there used to be wonderful **monkey-spotting** from several of the paths and lookout towers (*miradors*), **crocs** in the creeks, and, in the deep forest, species of **birds and insects** that couldn't be found anywhere else in Senegal. If by any chance the park does reopen, the best time to visit is well into the dry season, when, even in this relatively moist part of the country, waterholes dry up and sources become good spots to watch animals. There used to be a *campement* at the park entrance but this was trashed a long time ago, so your best bet would probably be to base yourself in Oussouye and arrange a visit from there.

Northern Basse Casamance

Coming over the border **from The Gambia** at **Séléti** is a straightforward business – many tourists visiting The Gambia take the plunge into Casamance for a few days and are rewarded by a more leisurely pace of life, reasonable transport, and some idyllic and inexpensive lodgings. It's a short taxi ride from Séléti to **DIOULOULOU**, the first Senegalese town, where you swap vehicles to head for the as yet unspoilt resorts of Abéné and Kafountine. Diouloulou has a good *campement* in the shape of *Relais Myriam* (☎936 95 91; ❶), a short way north of the main roundabout on the Gambia road, with helpful management.

The potholed N5 continues southeast across the tidal mud flats to Ziguinchor 80km away, passing through the underwhelming regional centre of **Bignona**, a two-kilometre string of roadside stalls at which point the N5 joins the *transgambienne* N4. In this area various tracks lead southwest into the often overlooked **Buluf** district of the northern Basse Casamance, served by a couple of CTRIs. Still less visited is the **Yassine** region to the east, sandwiched between the Soungrougrou and Casamance rivers.

Abéné and Kafountine

Southwest of Diouloulou a road heads seaward to unbroken beaches running down to the spit of the **Presqu'île aux Oiseaux**, at which point the coastline breaks up into mangrove inlets and the mouth of the Casamance. The sealed road passes the village of **Kabadio**, near which a couple of good *campements* have sprung up, and shortly afterwards a turnoff to the village of **Abéné** (18km) before continuing south to the small town of **Kafountine** (24km). Waiting at the roundabout in Diouloulou for transport may take an hour or two, less in the high season.

From the main road a track leads 2km to **ABÉNÉ**, a sandy-laned village situated 2km from the sea with a charmingly isolated and relaxed feel, a lively **folklore festival** (in Dec; ⊛www.alnaniking.co.uk/festival), and a number of accommodation options. The best place to stay in the village itself is *La Belle Danielle* (☎936 95 42/24; ❷), which offers simple rooms, an inexpensive restaurant, excursions and bike rental; it's a couple of hundred metres down a side track to the nearby village of **Diana**. Continuing down the main track to the sea, you'll find a cluster of *campements*. At a small crossroads just before the *Samaba CTRI* (closed at time of writing), a right turn leads to the delightful *Le Kossey*, a superior, dunebound *campement* offering s/c huts set in a lovely garden with HB or FB options (❸) – this is the place to head if you're looking for beachside seclusion rather than company. Turning left at the crossroads will bring you instead to *Casamar* (☎994 86 05 or 991 18 65, ⓔcasamar@sentoo.sn; ❸), which offers a similarly pleasant garden but less attractive rooms. Up the coast, 2km from Abéné village, the altogether different *Village Hôtel Kalissai* is beautifully sited right by the beach with a landscaped mangrove creek (☎994 86 00, ☎994 86 01, ⓔkalissai@sentoo.sn; ❻). Even at the price, this beats much of what's on offer in the fast lane at Cap Skiring, but it's not exactly *integré*. There are a few places to **eat** in the village, but most people take full board at the *campements*.

Kafountine

Continuing south down the sealed road another 6km brings you to the fishing village of **KAFOUNTINE**, served by daily minibuses to and from Ziguinchor via Diouloulou. More animated than sleepy Abéné – and with a reputation as the hip alternative to Cap Skiring – Kafountine has a decent range of accommodation, a market, shops, bike, moped and car rental outfits and several **restaurants**: just north of the market, *Café Couleur* and, opposite, *Le Baobab*, offer inexpensive and wholesome Senegalese dishes. Like Abéné, Kafountine hosts a colourful **festival** of music, dance and local culture, every February.

Most **accommodation** is ranged up and down the coast, about 1km west of town. Just south of the market, a sandy track leads west to the *Sitokoto CTRI* (☎994 85 41), one of the best-maintained CTRIs in the network, in a tranquil, beachside location. A couple of hundred metres before the CTRI, you'll pass the other top

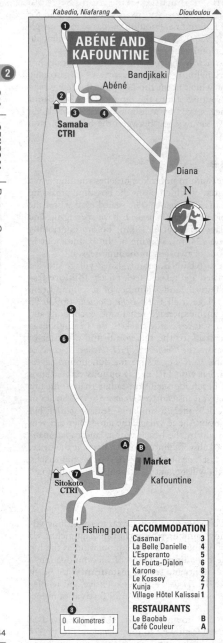

ABÉNÉ AND KAFOUNTINE

Kabadio, Niafarang ▲   Diouloulou ▲

Bandjikaki
Abéné
Samaba CTRI
Diana
N

Sitokoto CTRI
Market
Kafountine

Fishing port

ACCOMMODATION

Casamar	3
La Belle Danielle	4
L'Esperanto	5
Le Fouta-Djalon	6
Karone	8
Le Kossey	2
Kunja	7
Village Hôtel Kalissai	1

RESTAURANTS

Le Baobab	B
Café Couleur	A

0   Kilometres   1

budget choice, the *Kunja* (❷), a very pleasant, privately run *campement*, offering simple rooms and good home cooking. A couple of kilometres north along the coast are the best of the mid-range options, both fairly new: *Le Fouta-Djalon* (☎936 94 94; ❹) and, 500m further on, *L'Esperanto* (☎936 96 08, ☎936 94 94, ✉speranto@arc.sn; ❺). Both offer elegant, comfortable bungalows at very reasonable prices with HB and FB available, but *L'Esperanto* just edges it for its beautifully designed bar/restaurant overlooking a seasonal lake. The resort area is extending in the other direction as well, with a couple of bland new developments opening along the track to the south of the fishing port. At the end of the track, 2km south of the port, is Kafountine's most luxurious hotel, the *Karone* (☎994 85 25, ☎994 85 75, ✉lekarone@sentoo.sn; ❻), which offers secluded huts in landscaped grounds, beachside *paillotes*, a gleaming new pool, lots of motorized toys – including a small hovercraft – and a plush restaurant/bar.

Affiniam and Koubalan

Southeast of Diouloulou, the pot-holed road continues across a *marigot* or two to the village of **BAILA** with its welcoming CTRI (☎936 95 16), set in a grove of mango trees at the village's northern end. Between Baila and Bignona several tracks lead southwest into the **Buluf district**, a wooded region of mango groves as well as orange and palm trees and rice fields. Passable tracks, as well as several minor, cycleable routes, lead to all the villages, with a CTRI (occupied by the military at the time of writing) at the southern end of the laid-back settlement of **Tionk Essil**.

Southeast of Tionk, along a rough track, the peaceful village of **AFFINIAM** is regularly visited by *pirogue* excursions from Ziguinchor; there are also regular departures for Ziguinchor on Monday, Wednesday and Friday at 9am. Spread out among the silk-cotton trees among webs of sandy tracks, the village has a strong Catholic presence and boasts one of the most appealing CTRIs in the network (☎936 96 19). Situated south of the village, this large-diameter, galvanized *case à impluvium* is one of the best spots in the region to rest up for a few days.

Ten kilometres south of Bignona and 3km north of Tobor on the N5, a large sign marks the track leading to the CTRI at **KOUBALAN** (☎936 94 76). While not situated in an especially scenic spot, overlooking a cleared mangrove swamp, the *campement*'s cavelike interior is cool, the welcome warm and the food excellent. South of Tobor the woodlands end as the N5 crosses the dreary tidal expanse of Casamance to the river itself and the bridge leading into Ziguinchor.

The Gambia

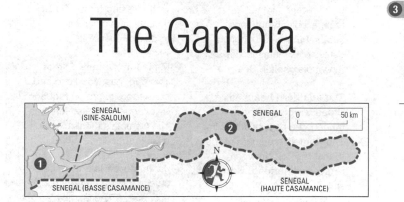

Gambia highlights

✳ Arch 22 Banjul's monument to President Jammeh's regime looks pretty monstrous, but the top-floor balconies give fantastic views of the whole capital. See p.275

✳ The southern beaches Broad, empty and palm-fringed, the best beaches in The Gambia are south of the tourist resorts, between Brufut and Kartong. See p.294

✳ Tanbi Wetlands Best explored by small boat, the mangrove-lined saltwater creeks at the mouth of the Gambia River offer superb bird-watching and angling. See p.290

✳ Juffureh The upcountry village made famous by Alex Haley's novel *Roots* is well worth visiting for its small but thought-provoking slave-trade museum. See p.295

✳ Makasutu Culture Forest This park has woodland and creeks to explore on foot and by *pirogue*, and also features The Gambia's most luxurious bush lodge. See p.293

✳ Janjanbureh Island Once a crucial trading centre, this is now one of The Gambia's emerging ecotourism destinations, and a great base for river trips. See p.302

✳ Wassu stone circles Mysterious relics of ancient Senegambian culture, these stones are the most impressive of The Gambia's prehistoric sites. See p.303

Introduction and Basics

The Gambia could easily be dismissed as an inconsequential little tourist trap. A tiny and frail country, eking out its existence along the banks of the Gambia River, it relies heavily on the October to April influx of British and European visitors taking a step beyond Spain and the Canaries. Out of season most of the beach resort hotels go to sleep or close down, and Gambians turn their attentions inland to the peanut harvest. The feeling of nothing much happening can be acute, and if you've already travelled widely in West Africa, The Gambia isn't going to wow you.

But after a major overland trip, The Gambia is a congenial enough place to rest up. Equally, it's an easy access point from which to embark on more extensive African wanderings, with the flight from Europe taking less than six hours. Should you want to stay put, you can spend a week or two here in package-holiday style for less than what you'd pay in many European resorts – and of course you can do it in midwinter. The beaches are good – though they get a lot better the further you go from the hotels – and the sea is usually warm.

The Gambia's surest appeal lies in its smallness: even the largest settlements have an overgrown-village atmosphere, and there's a rapidly acquired feeling of knowing everyone. Pomp and exclusivity are hard to maintain and you can find yourself in conversation with government ministers without even realizing it.

Where to go

While a surprising drabness characterizes the capital **Banjul**, and organized excursions can seem a little superficial, West Africa does reveal itself if you make an effort to leave the crowds and visit the interior. Dominated by the daily cycle of tides and the annual swing of flood and drought, the **Gambia River** has a compelling life of its own. Once you get beyond **Brikama**, the upcountry villages and main centres of Soma, Farafenni, Janjanbureh, and Basse are little affected by the coast's tourism. Animal and birdlife is diverse and exotic (ornithologists will recognize many wintering migrants from Europe); there are coconut trees, rice fields and mangrove swamps, and creeks plied by dugout canoes. And the country's borders need not limit your explorations: encircling Senegal is vast in comparison.

Fact file

The country is officially designated *The* Gambia, a device that has a certain cachet but only tends to emphasize the fact that the Gambia River is all there is to it. The Gambia's **population**, over 1.5 million and rising steadily, lives in a strip of only 11,300 square kilometres of riverbank, making it one of the smallest and most densely populated countries in Africa. The majority ethnic group is the Mandinka (and upcountry, Mandinka is the lingua franca), but in the coastal region Mandinkas are outnumbered by Wolofs. Other ethnic groups represented include the Fula, Jola, Manjago, Serahule and Serer.

From independence in 1965 until 1994, the country's leader was Sir Dawda Jawara – head of the ruling People's Progressive Party and president of a nominally multiparty democracy (there were regular elections, but no other party had ever held power). In 1994 a coup brought in a military government led by Lieutenant (later Captain) Yahya Jammeh, who went on to become the country's second elected president in 1996. Jammeh and his party were returned to power in the elections of 2001/2.

The Gambia's **national debt** is approximately £375 million ($600 million), nearly twice the value of its annual exports of goods and services.

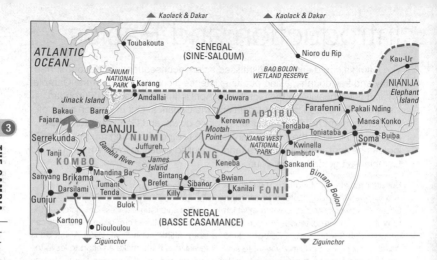

When to go

Deciding when to go is governed, for most people, by the **rainy season**. If you're going on a package you'll quickly see that there's a much reduced choice of hotels from May to October, the period when The Gambia gets up to 1300mm of rain – about fifty percent more than Britain's annual average. However, there is a degree of regional variation. On the coast the rains don't begin in earnest much before July, but inland they can start in May; upriver they may finish by the end of August, down at Banjul often not until October. August is usually the wettest month, making north-bank roads impassable for days on end.

The period from March to May is normally rainless, but dust and wind from across the Sahara can be a torment, and the haze can even block out the sun. Although year-round

tourism has been promoted since the early 1990s, and going in the low season can feel less touristy, the ideal period for a visit is December or January, when you can expect dry, hot days and mild – even cool – nights.

Getting there from elsewhere in Africa

There are flights from several cities in the region, and all other West African capitals have connections to Banjul via Dakar. From Dakar, Air Guinée, Air Sénégal and Gambia Airlines operate regular flights, with Air Guinea also flying from Conakry. Ghana Airways has flights from Accra, while the Nigerian company Bellview Airlines operate services from Abuja, Freetown, Lagos and Port Harcourt. Sierra National Airlines run a service from Freetown. There are no direct

Average temperatures and rainfall in Banjul

Temperatures °C

	Jan	Feb	Mar	Apr	May	June	July	Aug	Sept	Oct	Nov	Dec
Min (night)	15	16	17	18	19	23	23	23	23	22	18	16
Max (day)	31	32	34	33	32	32	30	29	31	32	32	31
Rainfall mm	3	3	0	0	10	58	282	500	310	109	18	3
Days with rainfall	0	0	0	0	1	5	16	19	19	8	1	0

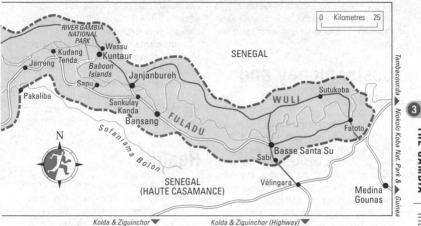

Kolda & Ziguinchor ▼   Kolda & Ziguinchor (Highway) ▼

flights from elsewhere in Africa, though from South Africa you could fly with South African Airways to Dakar and continue to The Gambia overland. Royal Air Maroc fly to Dakar via Casablanca.

Overland

Whichever way you travel overland, you'll arrive first in **Senegal**. From **Dakar**, there are bush taxis from the main *gare routière* to take you to the border post at Karang, where you change for another vehicle for the short hop to the Gambian border post at Amdallai. Here you have to change again for onward transport to Barra, where you can catch the ferry to Banjul. Expect routine, everyone-out baggage searches by customs at both border posts. From **Ziguinchor**, a batch of Peugeot 504 bush taxis runs every morning to **Serrekunda** (outside Banjul), and the border is less of a hassle.

From **Mali**, the direct route **from Bamako**, entering The Gambia at its eastern end, is more enjoyable than the dreary highway through Senegal to Dakar, though there's little to choose between them in terms of journey time or cost. On the direct route, break your journey at Tambacounda, then make your way to Velingara and pick up a bush taxi to Basse via the Gambian border post at Sabi. From Basse, you can take a bus to Banjul (2 daily), bush-taxi-hop your way down the river, or, by prior arrangement, join a river cruise by tourist boat to Janjanbureh (see p.302).

Red tape and visas

Most Commonwealth and European Community passport holders don't require a visa. French, Swiss, US and Japanese nationals are among those who do – in theory. In practice, if nationals of these countries fly in without a visa, they're routinely given a visitor's pass at the airport, but they may then be required to obtain a visa from the Immigration Office in Banjul. If you're simply traversing the country, from northern to southern Senegal or vice versa, visas aren't required by any nationality.

All visitors require a **full passport**, valid at least six months beyond your stay. You will only be asked for a yellow fever vaccination certificate if you are visiting other countries in the region. On arrival, you'll normally be given permission to stay for up to 15 days. If you're staying longer, ask for the maximum of 28 days; extensions cost D200 per month (for up to three months, after which you'll need to get a residence permit) from the Immigration Office in Banjul.

For **onward travel** from The Gambia, you can obtain visas in Banjul for Mauritania, Senegal, Ghana, Guinea-Bissau and Guinea. Visas for Nigeria may be available too, if harder to obtain. Full details are given on p.288. There's no French embassy, only a French honorary consul, who doesn't issue visas for Francophone countries in the region.

Costs, money and banks

Gambian currency is the **dalasi** (D), divided into 100 **buluts** (approximately £1 = D40, US$1 = D25). Notes come in denominations of D5, D10, D25, D50 and D100, with coins of D1, and 5, 10, 25 and 50 buluts. Bear in mind that Gambian dalasis aren't officially convertible abroad, so go easy and only change what you think you'll need. There is no currency declaration form.

Costs tend to be somewhat lower than in northern Senegal, and overall rather higher than in the Basse Casamance region of southern Senegal. But the two countries aren't really comparable: away from Banjul and the coast there simply isn't much to spend your cash on. Ordinary market produce and grocery-store fare isn't going to break the bank. If you're staying on the coast, you'll soon discover which hotels charge D40 for a beer and where you can find one for less than half that. Beer and soft drinks get pricey upriver and away from main centres. Note that **inflation** is rampant in The Gambia, and there are regular price hikes for most commodities, particularly fuel (in mid-2003, D15/litre).

There is normally no commission for currency exchange at banks or exchange bureaux. There are **banks** in Banjul, Bakau, Serrekunda, Kololi, Brikama, Farafenni and Basse (usually open Mon–Thurs 8am–1pm & Fri 8–11am; some open in the afternoon or early evening too). Some of the **forex bureaux** in the tourist areas will cash personal cheques on British bank accounts with a cheque guarantee card, sometimes charging a commission. You will get at least five percent more than the bank rate for cash on the **parallel market**, with the moneychangers at the airport, Westfield Junction in Serrekunda, or in most Gambian markets (but be aware that the Gambian police have begun to clamp down on the moneychang-

ers). Avoid changing money at the hotels, who do a brisk trade with their captive clients at poor rates.

Credit cards (notably Amex, Visa and MasterCard) are handy if you're staying in one of the main beach hotels, but they're not of much use anywhere else in the country. Cash advances can only be obtained from Standard Chartered banks (branches in Banjul, Bakau, Serrekunda, Kololi).

Health

The Gambia poses no special health risks beyond the usual ones applying to the region. Many doctors will recommend nothing more than antimalaria tablets, though you should certainly consider a hepatitis jab if your travels are likely to take you off the beaten track.

Given the prevalence of chloroquine-resistant malaria in the region (see p.33 for more on the subject), you should take **antimalaria tablets** even if you're holidaying for a week. That said, while Banjul and the river are mosquito-prone all year round, the hotel areas on the Atlantic coast are mostly free by the middle of the season (Christmas), and the mosquitoes aren't often a persistent menace.

As for health care, treatment costs are minimal, but hospital facilities are limited and over-stretched. The Gambia's principal hospital is the Royal Victoria in Banjul, and there are also hospitals upcountry in Bwiam, Farafenni and Bansang. If you're seriously ill, ask your hotel to arrange a visit from a private-sector health professional or, upriver, the nearest dispensary or foreign-aid worker. Emergency services are rudimentary. Of a range of **private clinics**, the Lamtoro clinic (see p.289) is conveniently close to the Senegambia hotel area and good if an overnight stay looks necessary (though more expensive than the other options). Otherwise, the Momodou Musa Memorial Clinics in Banjul and Serrekunda are recommended.

Water in The Gambia is considered safe when it comes from taps or pumps. You needn't hesitate to drink tap water in your hotel, but plastic bottled water is very widely available. If you buy it, get it in bulk from one of the supermarkets at a fraction of the hotel price.

Information, websites and maps

It's worth visiting a **Gambia National Tourist Office** before you leave. The London office (at the High Commission; see address in Basics, p.22) is friendly enough, but only has basic information on packages, flights and the rest. In The Gambia, there are no official tourist offices, though resort-hotel representatives are a good source of information.

There are quite a few **websites** focusing on the Gambia that are worth a look. Among these, **Gambia Tourist Support** (⊛www.gambiatouristsupport.com) is a good place to start, with excellent general information on the country from a committed charitable organization. **Gambia Net** (⊛www.gambianet.com) is a Gambian news portal, with a few oddities such as traditional Gambian recipes; **Asset** (⊛www.asset-gambia.com) is run by The Gambia's Association of Small Scale Enterprises in Tourism, with features on responsible tourism, including coverage of non-mainstream hotels; and Gambia Tourism Concern (⊛www.subrosa.uk.com/tourism) contains news from a campaigning organization supporting sustainable tourism in The Gambia.

Maps can be bought in hotel shops: the best general map, available in The Gambia and overseas, is Macmillan's 1:400,000 *The Gambia Travellers' Map* (1996), but roads have been improved and extended since its publication.

For detailed **maps**, you need to visit the Department of Lands and Surveys in the Offshore Marina area of Banjul, near Arch 22, open weekday office hours. The 1:250,000 sheet (1980) covers the country but there's also a nice 1:50,000 series (1982) based on aerial photographs that show all major roads, tracks and streams. They're all hard to obtain outside the country, and they're badly out of date, but an update is under way. Some maps may have to be copied up for you, which takes time and isn't cheap.

Getting around

The Gambia has no rail routes or scheduled domestic flights, and its river is barely a significant means of transport; there are ferry services across it, but no regular river transport system. What ought to be viewed as an asset is seen as a hindrance to north–south communications.

There's one main, hard-surfaced **road** from Banjul to Basse, along the south bank of the river. It's in excellent condition only as far as Brikama, deteriorating soon after this and becoming really appalling as far as Soma. East of Soma the road is quieter, and the surface not too bad. At the time of writing, the worst stretches of the south-bank highway are being resurfaced, but progress is slow. There's new tarmac from the airport to Kololi in the resort area, and from Fajara, south down the Atlantic coast

Organized trips

Many visitors to the resort area explore the country further on organized excursions, including bush safaris, village visits, and trips to upcountry bush lodges; details are available from hotel reps. Local tour operators (see p.289) will help plan itineraries and provide transport with a driver and an expert guide. You can also make more ad hoc arrangements for local visits and longer trips with the uniformed and badged Official Tourist Guides who work in the resort area.

Among the more unusual ways to see the country, there are one- to four-day package trips travelling by double-decker **pirogue** and taking in Tendaba, Janjanbureh, Basse and Fatoto, operated by Gambia River Excursions (details on p.290). It's also possible to arrange tours and **flights** (for example, to Tendaba or Janjanbureh) departing from the small light-aircraft base at Banjul International Airport.

to Kartong. North-bank roads are made entirely of laterite, mud, sand or rock, apart from the short stretches from Barra into Senegal and from Barra to Kerewan.

The principal **car ferry crossings** are Banjul to Barra and Yelitenda to Bambatenda (the trans-Gambian highway crossing between Soma and Farafenni). Both these crossings are fairly reliable. Further east, there are vehicle ferries at Basse and Fatoto and two from Janjanbureh (north and south). Other ferries are for passengers only.

Buses and taxis

The main **GPTC** (Gambia Public Transport Corporation; ☎390103 for timetable information) bus route, along the **south-bank highway** between Kanifing bus station (near Serrekunda) and Basse, has only two services daily, departing between 8.30am and 10am. On the **north bank**, GPTC services run between Barra and Dakar (but not in the opposite direction due to an ongoing dispute with the Senegalese transport authorities) twice daily.

Privately operated **bush taxis** known as "cars", "*gelle-gelles*" or "*tanka-tankas*" (mostly Japanese vans, pick-ups, a few saloons and goods trucks), run long-distance services covering the entire country. You'll find them at "garages" – the equivalent of *gares routières* in the Francophone countries. Bush taxis also operate locally – in which case they're yellow saloons with green stripes, or minibuses – running along set routes and cramming in as many pas-

sengers as they can at D3–5 per person per hop. Alternatively, the yellow cars can be privately chartered for a "town trip" direct to your destination (from D25 for a short hop). Another option around the touristy parts are **tourist taxis** (see p.272).

Car and bike rental

Car rental is undeveloped, with only one recommended local operator and one international agency represented – and often preferring to provide drivers. Self-drive deals are generally only available in the Banjul/resorts area (see p.288), and start from around £17/$25 per day all-in, in the low season. Petrol costs from £0.38/$0.60 a litre for "Super".

Motorbikes (of variable quality) can be rented in the coastal hotel area, as can **bicycles**; The Gambia is quiet, safe and offers very flat terrain for a first try at cycling in Africa, with ample opportunity for leisurely sidetracking to the river. In the dry season, a complete circuit of the country (inland on the south bank, back to Banjul on the north) would take a couple of weeks, assuming about 75km a day.

Accommodation

The vast majority of visitors have hotels pre-booked for the duration of their stays, which works out relatively cheaply. Some of the tourist hotels are block-booked by tour operators, but the others are worth

---

Accommodation price codes

Accommodation prices in this chapter are coded according to the following scale, whose equivalent in pounds sterling/US dollars is used throughout the book. Prices refer to the rate you can expect to pay for a room with two beds. Single rooms, or single occupancy, will normally cost at least two-thirds of the twin-occupancy rate. The resort hotels have two rates – high season roughly from the end of October to Easter, and low season roughly from Easter to October. Where seasonal rates are indicated, you can expect the low-season rate to give a more accurate reflection of facilities. For further details see Basics, p.51.

❶ Under D200 (under £5/$8).
❷ D200–400 (£5–10/$8–16).
❸ D400–600 (£10–15/$16–24).
❹ D600–800 (£15–20/$24–32).

❺ D800–1200 (£20–30/$32–48).
❻ D1200–1600 (£30–40/$48–64).
❼ D1600–2000 (£40–50/$60–80).
❽ Over D2000 (over £50/$80).

considering if you arrive by independent means and feel the urge to splurge (or even just the need for some decent comfort, which is all that most of them offer). The outlay is likely to be heavy in package hotels (typically ⑥–⑧) unless you turn up a special deal or visit out of season. The hotels ignored by the tour operators are of course more affordable, and there are a small but growing number of tourist lodges and local hotels upriver. Options at the budget end ❶–❸) are limited to simple guesthouses at least 1km from the beach.

Camping makes a lot of sense. There are virtually no campsites as such, but, away from the coastal resorts, pitching a tent is unproblematic if you have your own transport; despite a fairly high population density, you're likely to find secluded spots off the main road where you can peg out for a night and enjoy the bush. If you're using public transport, you're going to have to ask to camp on people's land – which will often lead to invitations to stay with them instead.

Eating and drinking

International-style **restaurants** abound in the coastal area, with fast-food places opening – and then closing down – regularly along the main thoroughfares. Upriver, you will find virtually no restaurants (as opposed to shops serving *afra* – barbecued meat – and **chop houses**, found in urban areas and upcountry towns) except in tourist hotels, which are thinly scattered. Europeanized food upcountry is usually restricted to chicken, or omelette, and chips.

Gambian dishes tend to be spicier than Senegalese. The tourist hotels' Gambian "standard" is **yassa chicken**, delicious when prepared well, but often just casseroled fowl with a searing sauce of lemon, chilli and onions. **Domodah**, if you like groundnuts, is invariably good (the thicker the better), usually with chicken, sometimes beef, always rice. **Mafe** is another peanutty variation. The best feature on the coast is quantities of fresh **seafood**: shrimps, ladyfish (like sole), barracuda if you're in luck, and excellent chowders and bisques in a few places.

Jollof rice is usually served with beef (or sometimes fish), tomato puree and vegetables – sweet peppers, aubergine, carrots and squash. **Benachin** is like the *tieboudienne* you get in Senegal, essentially fish and rice, sometimes with vegetables. **Plasas** (also called palava sauce) is an okra and palm-oil sauce with dried fish and sometimes meat.

You'll find quite good French-style **bread** (chewy *tapalapa* and the airier *senfour*) all over. **Pies** – resembling Britain's Cornish pasties but fried like samosas – seem to be a leftover of colonial influence; found in meat and fish varieties, they are often surprisingly tasty. **Fruit** you can get just about everywhere – bananas and papayas at any time (though the latter aren't often sold and you'll have to ask in the countryside), and mangoes, guavas, avocados, watermelons and oranges in season – the last often imported from Morocco.

Drinking

For **drinking**, you'll have to get used to The Gambia's **lager** – JulBrew – which is fairly

Mandinka food and drink terms

bread	*mburo*	onion	*jaboo*
rice	*maano*	aubergine	*patansay*
meat	*suboo*	orange	*lemuno*
barbecued meat	*afra*	watermelon	*sarro*
fish	*nye*	water	*jio*
millet (grain)	*nyo*	hibiscus cordial	*wonjo*
groundnut (peanut)	*teo*	green tea	*attaya*
groundnut paste	*degee*	soft drink	*lemnato*
groundnut oil	*dulino*	palm wine	*tendolo*
palm oil	*tulusay*	alcohol	*doloo*

strong but not one of West Africa's better-tasting beers, and **softs** – fizzy drinks – from the same enterprise. Imported beers are increasingly common in the resorts. Bottled Guinness is a colonial relic, sold quite widely, but rarely cold and perhaps verging on the medicinal in the eyes of most Gambians. Plastic-bottled "spring" or "mineral" water is widely available, but it can be a pricey way of avoiding contamination (D40 per litre). Tap water is generally very healthy and attacks of "Banjul belly" that affect so many are more easily attributed to the assaults of heat and unusual food – or sometimes to incautious freezing and reheating in hotel kitchens.

If you're drinking tap water, try the home-made plastic-bag **juices**, or ices, which are popular because they're so cheap, and on sale all over. Tasty but sticky sweet, they come in three main kinds – white, brown and red – made from baobab fruit (*bwi*), ginger and hibiscus-like *wonjo* sorrel pods. Breakfast-time coffee from roadside stalls isn't quite as common as in the French-speaking countries except at transport stops. Green tea is fairly widespread though, especially in Fula areas upriver.

Palm wine – which of course you'll be told is a Gambian speciality – is pretty well universal; the speciality lies in getting the tourists plastered on it during "bush and beach" excursions. As everywhere, it varies considerably in taste and strength depending on when it was tapped and what it's been stored in. As usual, too, it's tolerated but not strictly legal.

Communications

Keeping in contact with home is relatively easy. Aerograms are the cheapest way of writing, if the Banjul GPO has any, and ordinary post isn't expensive, though if you plan on posting souvenirs home, it's worth knowing that there is no surface mail from The Gambia; the airmailing of large items can be very expensive. Poste restante facilities at Banjul are not especially efficient compared to, say, Dakar, and there's a small charge.

Post offices are generally open daily except Sunday from 8am until noon, and also from around 2pm to 4pm Monday to Friday.

Phoning home, on West Africa's best international telecom system, is good value, especially to the UK. You can dial from Gamtel offices and private telecentres (both daily 8am–10pm) and pay in cash afterwards, or buy a Kachaa **phonecard** (the most cost-effective option, available from Gamtel or a supermarket) which gives you an access code with which to make calls from any landline. The international access code is ☎00 (though for Senegal, dial ☎01 and then the number, ie no country code is needed). Reverse charge (collect) calls can be made by dialling ☎00044 for the UK and asking for the operator, or ☎00111 for the US. Note that Gambian phone numbers don't have area codes.

Mobiles are rapidly becoming essential accessories for urban Gambians, and cell-phone coverage is generally excellent in most Gambian towns, though the signal drops off sharply to zero on the fringes of urban areas. At the time of writing, there were no international roaming agreements in place, though Gambian SIM cards (costing around £7.50/$12) and pay-as-you-go scratch cards (various denominations from D50) can be bought from either Gamcel or Africell, the country's two rival GSM networks. You'll automatically have the benefit of voicemail that's retrievable from any Gambian landline – useful when you're out of mobile range.

All Gamtel offices around the coastal district have public **fax** machines, also very cheap to use. You can receive faxes at these public machines for a nominal fee.

Internet cafés have started to spring up around the coastal area. Charges are reasonable (from under £1/$1.60 per hour) but vary a great deal from place to place, as does the quality of the hardware and the speed and reliability of the service. It's much harder to find public Internet access upcountry.

The media

Gambian **newspapers** are a little hard to track down, but include the *Daily Observer*, *The Point*, *The Independent*, *The Gambia*

The Gambia's IDD country code is ☎220.

Daily (thrice weekly) and the leftish sheet *Foroyaa*. "Political" papers are banned by the AFRC government. British papers are available in several of the supermarkets on Kairaba Avenue (the road linking Serrekunda to Fajara) and from vendors at tourist hotels. *Time* and *Newsweek* are obtainable, though often late. A local magazine covering topics of interest to tourists, *Mango News*, is sold by reformed bumsters in the resort areas.

The state-owned **Radio Gambia**, part of Gambia Radio and Television Services (GRTS), broadcasts in English and the main national languages on 648 AM and 91.4 FM. It offers news, announcements ("Will all members of the national football squad please get in touch with the coach . . .") and endless request shows – it sometimes seems there can be very few Gambians who haven't said hello to everyone who knows them. **Radio 1 FM** (101.2 FM), based in Fajara and flourishing, is one of the most popular stations, with an excellent selection of reggae and ragga, the favourite music of young Gambians. **Radio Syd** (909 AM), a long-established commercial station, specializes in good music and mundane adverts. **West Coast** on 95.3 FM blasts out of many local bars and hangouts, playing mostly reggae, soul and R&B, plus chat shows.

Gambia TV, also part of GRTS, covers Gambian news (with plenty of coverage of presidential goings-on), as well as relaying CNN, various sports programmes and British comedy series.

Opening hours, public holidays and festivals

Government offices are open from Monday to Thursday between 8am and 3pm or 4pm, and on Friday and Saturday from 8am to 12.30pm. **Shops** and **businesses** are open Monday to Thursday from 8am to 5.30pm (sometimes later, and sometimes with a break for lunch) and on Friday and Saturday from 8am to noon. Supermarkets have longer hours, which may include Sundays. Daily markets are generally open from 8am till dusk.

The Gambia is predominantly Muslim and, with the exception of tourist services, everything comes to a halt on **Muslim holidays** (see p.61). Christmas and Easter are also observed, with banks, offices and most shops closed around Banjul and the coast and a few other places. Otherwise, the principal annual days off are January 1, February 18 (Independence Day), May 1 (Labour Day) and July 22 (Revolution Day or Anniversary of the Second Republic, commemorating the 1994 coup).

Crime and personal safety

The Banjul/resorts area is very **safe** on the whole, but very occasionally there are muggings at night, and pickpocketing and bag slashing in the markets. Avoid dark alleys, and hold on tight to your possessions, and you should be fine. The most trouble you're likely to encounter is with **"bumsters"**, professional hustlers of tourists, whom you might fail to shake off and who later expect payment for the services you didn't want. Tell them you're not going to pay at the very beginning and they'll soon give up.

Trouble with the **police** – who are unarmed and among the nicest in West Africa – is unusual, though overlanders with vehicles occasionally report problems over vehicle import duty, which strictly speaking you're not liable to pay. If you're going to smoke grass (*djamba*), be extremely discreet as there have been some hefty fines and prison sentences recently.

Women travellers

Sexual hassles in the resort areas are generally not a problem, though you may find the frank scrutiny unnerving. And of course sexual interest is by no means exclusively one-sided – which can make life harder for women not in search of adventures. If you find your freedom is being seriously compromised by the ubiquitous presence of "bumsters", one strategy is actually to give in – to *one* of them; you may need to be ruthless in your choice and should be frank about your

The Gambian women's movement

The Women's Bureau, located in Marina Offshore near Arch 22 in Banjul (☎228730), is the main organ of the Gambian **women's movement**. It's concerned primarily with establishing financial stability for women and developing non-traditional income sources, especially crafts co-operatives. Emancipation is a long way off, with polygamy still the norm and six children commonly planned (even in middle-class marriages). **Contraception** is free and campaigning for family planning quite extensive, but few people take notice. Clitoridectomies, performed at the Royal Victoria Hospital in Banjul, are common.

intentions. He'll act as your chaperone and, if you occasionally tip him or offer the odd souvenir from home, may become a real friend for the duration.

While **topless bathing** is fine by hotel pools and on their beaches (not on fishing beaches), women should not appear elsewhere less than well-covered; unlike in many predominantly Muslim countries, uncovered shoulders are acceptable, but showing your thighs is considered very provocative. Long baggy shorts are fine in coastal urban areas but short, tight ones are only appropriate within hotel grounds. Upcountry, foreign women travelling alone are a rare sight and can arouse enormous curiosity; here, women should wear longer dresses, skirts or trousers. Disappointingly, your contacts with Gambian women may not prove any more fruitful if you're travelling alone than if you were to travel in male company.

Wildlife and national parks

The Gambia is wonderful for **bird-watchers**: around 560 bird species have been recorded here, and the country contains a remarkable variety of habitats within its small area, many easily accessible on foot. It's not a destination for anyone hoping for **big game**, however: the faunal heritage has been diminishing for many years. But monkeys and baboons are common enough; there are a few hippos upriver and small crocs in the streams; warthog are common but overhunted; hyenas, aardvarks and leopards are nocturnal, their status uncertain. Many southern Senegalese animals occasionally range towards the river.

The tiny **Abuko Nature Reserve** 8km from Serrekuna is the premier reserve, with great bird-watching and monkey-viewing opportunities. **Bijilo Forest Park**, very near the resort hotels, is a good place to see monkeys, and there is an excellent variety of bird habitats at the **Tanji River Karinti Bird Reserve** which includes The Gambia's only offshore islands, the Bijol Islands, a breeding colony for seabirds.

At **Kiang West National Park**, further upcountry, you can witness a completely different habitat with wild baboons and bush pig, and across the river from here is **Bao Bolon Wetland Reserve**, a large isolated area of salt marshes and mangrove creeks. Some of the country's most beautiful riverine forest is found further upcountry in the **River Gambia National Park (Baboon Islands)**, part of which is a rehabilitation centre for chimpanzees which is closed to the public but can be passed by boat for distant views of the chimps. On the north bank of the river near Banjul is **Jinack Island**, part of the Niumi National Park and noted for its untouched stands of mangroves. For further information on these reserves, contact the Department of Parks and Wildlife Management, Abuko (☎472888; ✉wildlife@gamtel.gm).

For important practical information applying to all West African countries, covering health, transport, cultural hints and more, plus details on getting to the region from beyond Africa, see Basics, pp.9–87.

Entertainment and sports

While entertainment means the hotel formula-mix of "folkloric dance troupes" and home-style discos for the majority of visitors, it's easy enough to escape the dross and find real Gambian musical entertainment. To be fair, the hotels do sometimes host worthwhile **gigs** – the country's *kora* players have all played to tourist audiences. The best time to be in the Banjul area for live music is the end of the month, when people can afford tickets for the bands that occasionally visit from abroad (usually Senegal). There are normally two or three gigs – the first a more expensive **"dance"** (D80 or more, starting around 11pm and going on until 3 or 4am) and the next night a more proletarian **"show"** (tickets from D25) – all at the big Bakau stadium. Arrive early to get a seat or you'll never see the musicians.

Most Gambian groups gravitate inevitably to Dakar, if not to Europe, as soon as they reap a measure of success and, musically, Dakar is The Gambia's real nerve centre. Currently the biggest vogue is for **reggae and ragga**, which a number of local groups play. The Gambia however is more distinguished for its Mandinka-speaking **kora musicians**. The most famous talents – **Dembo Konteh**, his brother-in-law **Kausu Kouyaté**, **Foday Musa Suso**, **Jaliba Kuyateh**, **Malamini Jobarteh**, **Ebrima Jobarteh**, **Tata Din Din** and junior **Pa Jobarteh** – are as likely to be playing in a British folk festival or with American musicians, as in a compound in Brikama or at a wedding in Serrekunda. **Wolof drummers** often perform at "private" functions too. Keep your ears open and drop in politely. Stars of **ndaga** (a distinctive style of the Senegambian region), such as **Maudo Sey**, **Mam Tamsir Njai** and **Mass Lowe** play at the Bakau stadium when they're not performing internationally.

The Gambia's biennial **International Roots Festival** (10–14 days in June; ⓦwww.rootsfestival.gm), an ambitious programme of events celebrating Gambian culture and heritage, is without a doubt the best opportunity to experience Gambian music. Other festivals, including national holidays and community celebrations, are marked by spirited drumming, dance and masquerades.

If you're into the idea of musical **participation**, rather than merely being part of the audience, see the listing on p.289. And for pre-departure inspiration, there's a growing list of Gambian *kora* CDs available, including most of the artists above. *The Rough Guide to World Music* has good coverage.

Lastly, with no national film industry (though of course imported kung fu, Hindi movies and the like are enjoyed on video and screen all over) and theatre non-existent, **spectator sports** are the other principal entertainment in the country. **Football** is very popular and even cricket gets played once in a while. Officially, **wrestling** is The Gambia's national sport, but it's been gradually fading over the last decade or so with the universal onset of football fever. President Jammeh is keen to keep the sport alive, and the large arena at Kanilai (see p.299 for details and for a discussion of the rules) is one of the few places where major matches are still held, albeit irregularly. Events at The Gambia's other main arena, in Serrekunda, are far more occasional, a result of the sport getting over-commercialized, with wrestlers spending more time touting for tips than actually wrestling, and popular interest drying up.

Directory

Airport departure tax Intercontinental departure tax of £12.50/$20 is payable in hard currency. The departure tax will have already been included for most flights – you'll need to check your ticket.

Emergencies Ambulance ☏16; fire service ☏18; police ☏17.

Gay life Since even the straightest Gambian men customarily dance together and walk hand in hand, gay men may feel quite at home. Although there's nothing in the way of a gay scene as such (and The Gambia's laws on homosexuality are the fossilized edicts inherited from the British at independence in 1965) there's a broad acceptance of gay male visitors and several very low-key haunts in the resort area. Lesbian women won't find the same.

Photography Be sure to ask before photographing anyone. Around the tourist areas you may be asked to pay for the privilege. Video cameras can arouse hostility as people feel they are perhaps being exploited for commercial purposes. The "security" angle is rarely played up by police – though, as usual, you should avoid photographing them without their permission, or snapping anything to do with "the state". Upcountry attitudes vary from clear hostility to enthusiasm. There's good-quality colour processing in Banjul and Serrekunda, and you can also buy slide film (though you can't get it developed locally).

Shops and crafts The crafts tradition isn't spectacular; Banjul, the Kombo district and Brikama are the only areas where you're likely to find much worth buying. "Ebony" and mahogany carvings rarely are, and the trade encourages deforestation. At crafts markets (*bengdula*), it's best to go for cheaper softwood carvings, gaudy cloth (including batik clothing), jewellery, leather and basketwork.

Tipping It's a bit of a problem in the resorts to know when and how much you should give in recognition of services: you somehow have to reconcile what you give a waiter or tour guide with the fact that many staff will only be paid a wage of £1–2/$1.50–3 per day, while those in business for themselves, such as taxi drivers (no tipping required), might make ten times as much. D10 is a decent tip, while D25 or D50 would be very generous. Holiday reps are always good at suggesting how much you should give hotel staff at the end of a stay.

A brief history of The Gambia

The earliest people of the Gambia valley may have been the Jola, who by tradition keep very limited oral history. By the fifteenth century, most of the valley was under the control of small Mandinka kingdoms founded by immigrants from the Mali empire. The first European settlers of the late fifteenth and sixteenth centuries were mostly Portuguese and tended to set themselves up in partnership with headmen of the locality, marrying their daughters and trading cloth for slaves. The descendants of mixed unions became important go-betweens in the slave trade.

From the mid-seventeenth century, English, Dutch, French and Baltic merchant adventurers shared and fought over trading rights from the restricted, neighbouring bases of Fort James Island and Albreda. The British won lasting influence after the Napoleonic wars, declaring a Protectorate along the river in the 1820s and in 1888 establishing a **Crown Colony** that comprised Banjul Island, the district of Kombo St Mary and MacCarthy Island. In the same year, the territory ceased to be governed from Freetown (Sierra Leone) and was given its own government.

Colony and protectorate

In the second half of the nineteenth century, while the British hesitated and focused their attentions elsewhere, the French were battling their way deep into the Soudan (the inland areas of West Africa), actively engaged in a mission to conquer (see the Senegal chapter). From 1850 to 1890 the whole of the Gambia region was in a state of social chaos as the **"Soninké–Marabout Wars"** repeatedly flared up (see box, p.262), eventually forcing the British to consolidate in the region or else lose it to France.

The Gambia's acquisition by Britain, which was formally agreed at the Paris conference of 1889, stemmed less from commercial ambitions than **imperial strategy**. The intention was later to pawn the country off in exchange for some better French territory; Gabon was one chunk favoured by the British – they'd already turned down the offer of the Ivory Coast coastal forts. But the temporary expedient of holding the river became permanent when, having failed to agree on an exchange, the British succeeded merely in delimiting a narrow strip of land on each side of The Gambia, into the heart of French territory. Yet Britain wasn't really reconciled to its responsibilities along the Gambia River until after World War I – thus The Gambia's era of effective colonialism lasted little more than forty years.

The imposition of **British hegemony** wasn't impressive. Beyond the limits of the colony, the country's headmen and chiefs, some of whom were appointed by the Crown, were allowed to rule their people little disturbed by the two "travelling commissioners" to whom they were answerable. Two or three African representatives from Bathurst (the future Banjul) were nominated to the Legislative Council after 1915, but there was no representation of the 85 percent of the population who lived in the Protectorate, the upcountry areas outside the Crown Colony.

Two-thirds of the Gambia's revenue was accounted for in the salaries of the

The Soninké–Marabout Wars

Mandinka civil war along both banks of the Gambia River began in the 1850s. Local **marabouts** – influenced by the great Muslim expansionist Omar Tall – called for the overthrow of the traditional Mandinka kings known as **Soninkés**, whose adherence to Islam was greatly tempered by indigenous religion and alcohol. The marabouts aimed to install a puritanical Islam and to capture local states (best described as manors) and trading networks.

Most of the "wars" consisted of battles, skirmishes and feuds between villages, which disrupted trade and agriculture year after year. Serer and Jola mercenaries were bought in on both sides to bulk out the limited armies. The main areas of unrest were **Kombo**, south of the tiny British enclave at Bathurst, where a wild young marabout called **Fodi Kabba** spread serious anarchy; **Baddibu** and **Niumi** on the north bank, where a renegade Soninké-turned-marabout, **Ma Ba**, caused massive destruction; and **Fuladu**, upriver on the south bank, where **Fula marabouts** from the southeast, right outside the region, swept the local Mandinka aside with great savagery.

By the mid-1870s, the whole of the Kombo district was under maraboutic control. Religious imperatives had been forgotten as purely political and economic considerations pitted one leader against another. Acting under financial constraints laid down in London, the **British** avoided interference whenever possible, refused requests for protection from besieged Soninké leaders and only went into battle to defend the Colony or British subjects. Only when there seemed to be a risk that the fighting might jeopardize British commercial interests did the governor try to impose a truce.

But in the **1880s**, the British were unable to avoid being drawn into the conflicts. In Baddibu the wars had now become an internal affair between competing marabouts, and spilled over into French-occupied Senegal. The French, in hot pursuit on behalf of their Sine-Saloum chiefs (the French were much more actively involved in protection than the British), chased the marabout army back into "British" territory as far as Barra. The British were forced to arrest the marabout in question, **Said Mati**, to forestall any further French advances. Mati's removal led to a power vacuum in Baddibu, which the French began to fill with their own appointees. The British had no choice but to enter into binding protection agreements with as many Gambian chiefs as possible.

A period of relative peace broke out, but in the Kombo and Foni regions Fodi Silla and Fodi Kabba kept up **continued resistance** against the now-expanding British. With the country's borders fixed and support at last from London, the British moved against **Fodi Silla** in 1894, occupying all the towns of Kombo – Gunjur, Sukuta, Brikama – and pushing Silla into Senegal, where he was captured and exiled to St-Louis.

Fodi Kabba pursued the struggle, killing a travelling commissioner and his entourage at Sankandi on the border in 1901. The British and French moved swiftly and in concert, "pacifying" the region in imperial style and killing Fodi Kabba, a campaign which marked the end of the Soninké–Marabout Wars.

colonial administration. The remainder was insufficient to develop the country's infrastructure, education or health systems. "Benign neglect" is about the best that can be said of the administration's performance. It started to improve only after World War II, though the government was gravely embarrassed by the financially disastrous **Yundum egg scheme**, which parasites made an unredeemable fiasco costing £500,000. **Groundnuts** (peanuts) have been the country's main export crop since the middle of the nineteenth century – The Gambia is a classic monoculture – and until the 1970s it was also self-sufficient in food. There were minor advances in education and medical services: by 1961 for example, the country had five doctors and there were 37 upcountry primary schools.

Financial pressures on the Colonial Office in the 1950s and mounting international demands for decolonization were as much instrumental in **the push to independence** as Gambian nationalism. Britain was at least as anxious to rid itself of the financial liability as the country's own senior figures (they were barely yet leaders) were to take power. From Britain's point of view, there was no reason to delay the country's return to independence – except, perhaps, a measure of concern over the fate of such a small and unprotected nation. Colonial civil servants were in broad agreement that The Gambia would be forced to merge with Senegal, but chose to defer the move.

The road to independence

The progression to independence was not a heroic one. In a manner similar to that of many other countries in West Africa, the men who led The Gambia into the neocolonial era were not so much nationalists as pragmatic and ambitious politicians.

Although the **Bathurst Trade Union** had been founded in 1928 and struck successfully for workers' rights, the first **political party** wasn't formed until shortly before the Legislative Council elections of 1951. Through most of the 1950s, the Gambian parties were reactive, personality-led interest groups rather than campaigning, policy-making, issue-led organizations. The Rev. John Fye founded the **Democratic Party** as a vehicle for the civic ambitions of his Bathurst coterie; I.M. Garba-Jahumpa founded the **Muslim Congress Party** in an attempt to align religious consensus behind a political movement; and Pierre S. N'Jie founded his largely Catholic **United Party**, which maintained close relations with upcountry chiefs. All these early-1950s parties were Wolof- and Colony-based and highly sectional. The Gambia had to wait until 1960 before a party with a genuine grassroots programme emerged. This was the Protectorate People's Party, quickly relabelled **People's Progressive Party (PPP)**, led by an ex-veterinary officer from the MacCarthy Island Division, **David Jawara**. The PPP looked to the Protectorate for support, but was distinctly anti-chief. It spoke for the rural Mandinka and others in their resentment against corrupt chiefdoms, and for disenfranchised and younger Wolof subjects of the Colony.

The administration overhauled the constitution in 1951 and finally, after consultation with senior Gambian figures, produced a complicated new constitution in 1954. This gave real representation to the Protectorate peoples for the first time, but precipitated sharpened demands for greater responsibility for Gambian ministers in the government. It also put extraordinary power in the hands of the chiefs, who were, for the most part, supporters of the colonial status quo. To avoid a crisis, another constitution was formulated in 1959 which abolished the Legislative Council and provided for a parliament – the House of Representatives.

In the run-up to the **1960 elections**, the Democratic and Muslim Congress parties merged as the **Democratic Congress Alliance (DCA)**, but couldn't shake off the popular impression that their nominees were all puppets of the administration. As a result the DCA took only three seats, while the United Party of P.S. N'Jie (with whom the governor had recently fallen out) and David Jawara's PPP took eight seats each. The governor, in a move to placate the Protectorate chiefs, offered the post of prime minister to P.S. N'Jie, to the consternation of Jawara, who became education minister. But the 1959 constitution was bound to give rise to further indecisive election results. More talks resulted in yet another constitution, providing for a 36-seat House of Representatives with

32 elected seats and just four chiefs nominated by the Chiefs' Assembly.

The balance of power now shifted against the United Party. Jawara and the Democratic Congress Alliance found room for co-operation and, in the **1962 elections** – which were to determine the political configuration for full self-government – the two parties contested seats in concert to squeeze out the UP. The results of this electoral alliance were highly successful for the PPP, who won 17 out of the 25 Protectorate seats and one of the 7 Colony seats. The DCA, however, managed to gain only one seat in the Colony, and couldn't shift the UP from its urban power base. As a result, with the support of the DCA's two elected members, Jawara had an absolute majority in parliament and his party remained in control until the coup of 1994.

Subsequently, Jawara entered into a coalition with the experienced P.S. N'Jie to form the first fully independent government. Independence Day came on February 18, 1965, with **The Gambia** admitted to the Commonwealth as a constitutional monarchy, with the Queen as titular Head of State.

Independent Gambia

In 1966 N'Jie took his United Party out of government to lead the opposition. Four years later, on April 24, The Gambia became a **republic** and prime minister Dawda Jawara (now using his Muslim name), president. At every election, the PPP continued to win the vast majority of seats, and at every election P.S. N'Jie claimed that the vote was rigged. The PPP, however, despite its roots in the Mandinka villages, managed to establish credible support across the country.

The first fifteen years of independence were peaceful, and the groundnut economy fared better than expected thanks to high prices on the world markets. But by 1976 prospects for the government were less favourable. Two

new opposition parties had formed: the somewhat Mandinka-chauvinist **National Convention Party (NCP)**, led by dismissed vice-president Sherif Mustapha Dibba, and the more left-wing **National Liberation Party** of Pap Cheyassin Secka. And as groundnut prices fell in the late 1970s, The Gambia experienced a string of disastrous harvests.

The economic recession that ensued, and political opposition to the government – which was perceived increasingly as incompetent and corrupt – partly account for the conditions that led to the formation of two new **Marxist groupings** in 1980 and an **attempted coup** in October of that year. Senegalese troops were flown in under a defence agreement and the leaders of the **Gambia Socialist Revolutionary Party** and the transnational **Movement for Justice in Africa-Gambia** (MOJA-G) were arrested and their organizations banned.

A far more **serious coup attempt** on July 30, 1981 (while Jawara was in London), resulted in a force of 3000 Senegalese troops arriving with a group of SAS soldiers from Britain, to put down sporadic, bloody fighting and disorder around Banjul. The trouble lasted a week and cost up to a thousand lives. **Kukoi Samba Sanyang**, the self-styled revolutionary who led the plot – "we do not believe in elections, we wanted a radical transformation of the entire socio-economic system" – escaped to Guinea-Bissau and thence to Libya.

The Senegambia Confederation

The insurrection shook the government and immediate steps were taken to maintain Senegal's support. The **Senegambia Confederation** was ratified on December 29, 1981, assuring The Gambia of Senegal's protection while ostensibly assuring Senegal of The Gambia's commitment to political union. **Treason trials** in the wake of the attempted coup led to long terms of imprisonment but, with the increasingly important tourist industry to consider, there were no executions.

A popular **presidential election** in 1982 gave Jawara a personal vote of 137,000, more than double that of Sherif Mustapha Dibba, who was in detention at the time. With Dibba released, the NCP mounted a serious challenge at the 1987 general and presidential elections. However, it was a new opposition grouping, the **Gambia People's Party** (GPP), led by the respected former vice-president **Hassan Musa Camara**, that made the most impact on the government. Though Jawara's party's share of the vote was also reduced, the PPP still managed to win 31 of the 36 elected seats in the House, with the NCP holding the remaining five. Supporters of the GPP, particularly in its Fula- and Serahule-speaking strongholds upriver, were left frustrated, as were supporters of the new socialist party, the **People's Democratic Organization for Independence and Socialism**, a party with close ties to the banned MOJA-G.

Another **coup plot** – really a long-running, conspiratorial rumble – was uncovered a year after the elections, in February 1988. The conspiracy involved both Gambian leftists and Casamance separatists from Senegal. It was suggested at the trials that the Senegalese opposition leader, **Abdoulaye Wade**, had been involved in planning it, along with Kukoi Samba Sanyang, but attempts to implicate Libya directly were treated with scepticism abroad.

In 1985, the government embarked on an **Economic Recovery Programme** designed to encourage aid donors. The privatization of various state enterprises, a public expenditure squeeze and cutbacks in subsidies to farmers led to increasing hardship in the countryside.

Throughout the end of the 1980s and the first years of the 1990s, with the Economic Recovery Programme still grinding through its measures, the country faced widespread malnutrition, insufficient schools for enrolled students, and mounting evidence of high levels of corruption and mismanagement. President Jawara routinely "cleaned out" public offices, but accountability was not enforced with tough sanctions, and a prevailing sense of stagnation and recycled rhetoric hung over Banjul.

On the broad economic front, the liberalization of the groundnut trade removed the GPMB's monopoly and allowed farmers to sell their harvests to the highest-bidding private trader. Although this risked forcing *down* the price in remote areas, the net effect was to keep more of the crop from being smuggled to high-paying Senegal. Tourism benefitted, too, from the sale of the state's hotel interests and an increased profile abroad. But the wider future was marred by the breakdown of the Senegambia Confederation (officially dissolved on September 30, 1989), as a result of Senegal's frustration at the slow pace of moves towards union. Senegal, facing conflict with Mauritania (see p.110), withdrew its troops from The Gambia, saying they were needed at home.

The end of the Senegambia Confederation left a huge question mark over The Gambia. It had been the national controversy for the best part of a decade, supported by the mostly urban Wolof but generally mistrusted by the Mandinka, whose dominant position in the country was always threatened by a powerful Senegal. For The Gambia's opposition parties and minorities of all ethnic groupings, the prospect of a greater Senegambia was always a provocative one which left many doors open. Those doors were now closed.

Attention was focused in 1990 on **Liberia**, with numbers of Liberian refugees making their way to The Gambia, and Jawara sending a small detachment of Gambian troops to support the West African ECOMOG forces trying to maintain the peace in Liberia.

Administrative failures resulted in the soldiers not being paid and a dangerous confrontation was narrowly averted when they returned to Banjul. The chief of the armed forces resigned, admitting he'd lost the confidence of his men, and was replaced by a Nigerian officer. It was a warning of changes to come.

President Jawara was re-elected for a sixth term in April 1992, after being persuaded to stand, despite his wish to retire. He polled 58 percent of the vote; his nearest rival Mustapha Dibba 22 percent. Jawara softened his stance against MOJA-G and the Gambian Socialist Revolutionary Party, announcing an amnesty for all members of the previously proscribed organizations. He also began again to make noises about corruption in public life.

Military rule

In April 1994 there were protests in Brikama – the country's third largest town, close to the coast but not benefitting from tourism – over the unaffordable cost of public utilities. Then, on July 22, after returning ECOMOG soldiers had been offended by Nigerian commanding officers at Banjul airport, their widespread anger and demands for unpaid salaries coalesced into a successful **coup** led by **Lt Yahya Jammeh**, with the support of a hastily assembled **Armed Forces Provisional Ruling Council (AFPRC)**. Jawara and some of his cabinet fled to the sanctuary of an American ship, coincidentally docked at Banjul, and received asylum in Senegal. Others were arrested.

Jammeh, a young and uncharismatic figure in regulation dark glasses, made a poor impression on the international community. Casual observers had long harboured the illusion that Jawara's Gambia was one of the few admirable political cultures in West Africa. Indeed, it appeared hard at first to find an altruistic justification for a coup in The Gambia. Though the country's human rights record was not unblemished, the fundamental fairness of its multiparty system had not seemed open to question. Opposition parties were consistently frustrated at elections but the evidence for vote-rigging was limited: Jawara won because he commanded a popular following, albeit also a largely Mandinka one.

However, the AFPRC managed to convince sceptics that, fair or not, the political system was shoring up a Gambian state riddled with **corruption** from bottom to top: President Jawara himself was said to have spent the equivalent of the annual health-care budget on a six-day shopping trip to Switzerland just weeks before the coup. Jammeh insisted his administration, which included some civilian members, would seek the return of stolen state property.

However, Jammeh's announcement that the AFPRC would not step down to an elected civilian government until 1998 was greeted with disbelief. After an unsuccessful counter-coup, in which several soldiers were killed, and a reported threat by Jammeh to the safety of citizens of any countries that might be planning the forcible reinstatement of Jawara, the British government warned tourists the country was unsafe to visit. Nearly all the tour operators and charter airlines pulled out and **tourism plummeted** to twenty percent of normal levels, precipitating a genuine crisis. The response was pragmatic: Jammeh brought the date of transition forward to July 1996, which led to the withdrawal of the British Foreign Office's travel advisory notice and the tour operators' resumption of bookings for the winter 1995–96 season.

Jammeh's first few months in office convinced him he had considerable grassroots support: most Gambians noticed no downswing in their fortunes since his coup, and the country at large anticipated some results from the AFPRC's efforts to return looted Gambian funds. They were to be disappointed: rumours circulated that the

AFPRC itself was not squeaky clean, ministers previously sacked by Jawara for corruption were given posts by Jammeh, and the story quickly spread that Jammeh had engineered the counter-revolt himself in order to eliminate potential rivals. Throughout 1995, there was a rash of accusations and counter-accusations of corruption and theft from the public purse on a grand scale. The finance minister died in suspicious circumstances; a new secret police service, the National Intelligence Agency, was created, with sweeping powers of arrest and interrogation; and the death penalty was reinstated.

The Second Republic

Jammeh's first real test came in 1996. With the electorate beginning to realize that an elected government would almost certainly be headed by Jammeh himself, in civilian clothing, a **constitutional review commission** was established to hear the views of Gambians and to usher in a new republic. It was manipulated by the AFPRC to give Jammeh and his coterie every advantage over all opposition elements: the age for presidential candidates was set at 30–65, thus making the youthful Jammeh eligible and ruling out many senior politicians of the Jawara era; political parties which had been active in the Jawara era were all banned from competing; and the timing of the elections was set such that Jammeh's opponents had virtually no opportunity to campaign, while the AFPRC had effectively been on the campaign trail throughout the country since soon after coming to power.

The **presidential election**, which eventually took place on September 26, 1996, was flawed in every respect. Jammeh's 22 July Movement, which was to be dissolved, was replaced by a new party, the aptly acronymic **Alliance for Patriotic Reorientation and Constuction** (APRC) – the AFPRC out of uniform. The Gambia's new TV station almost entirely neglected the opposition while the military breathed down the necks of the minor parties. Jammeh took 55 percent of the vote, Ousainou Darboe of the **United Democratic Party** 35 percent. In the **legislative elections**, which took place in January 1997, the severely limited resources of most of the opposition meant they could only field candidates in a proportion of the country's 45 constituencies. The vote itself, however, was observed to be fairer than the presidential poll, with less intimidation of rival candidates. Jammeh's party took 33 seats, five of them unopposed, while the opposition was lucky to secure twelve seats spread among three parties and two independent MPs.

Early parliamentary sessions in the **Second Republic** were undignified affairs, with opposition members prevented from asking difficult questions by the Jammeh-appointed speaker of the house, and repeated complaints that the president seemed unable to abide by the country's new constitution in his dealings with parliament. **Unrest** rose to the surface in 2000 when twelve people were shot dead during student demonstrations in protest at the alleged torture and murder of a student by police the previous month. A few weeks later, opposition leader Ousainou Darboe and twenty of his supporters were charged with the murder of an APRC activist; they were released on bail. The arrests continued: shortly after this, nine people, including several soldiers, were charged with treason in connection with an alleged plot to overthrow the government, just one of a series of **conspiracies and attempted coups**.

In October 2001, Jammeh won a second five-year presidential term, with a landslide victory over Ousainou Darboe. Despite rising tension beforehand, the polls were given a clean bill of health by foreign observers. However, the opposition boycotted the parliamentary elections in January 2002, claiming that presidential elections had been fraudulent and marred by APRC harassment of UDP candidates. Amid widespread voter apathy, the APRC scooped a victory. Ousainou Darboe and **Yankuba Touray**, Tourism Minister, APRC Mobiliser, and one of Jammeh's right-hand men since the 1994 coup, continued to lock horns, and in November 2002 new amendments to the Criminal Procedure Code were drafted, denying bail to anyone on a murder charge, and allowing Darboe to be re-arrested.

Jammeh's themes are **development**, **agricultural reform** and **foreign investment**; he has been at pains to cultivate the image of a model Muslim president in order to successfully attract donations from the Arab states. In February 2003 he spent two weeks attending countrywide rallies, during which his primary message was that Gambians should "get back to the land" and re-invest time and resources in farming. He was often greeted by rapturous crowds, suggesting that his upcountry power base is growing steadily.

Jammeh appears keen to promote the interests of Gambians over those of foreign residents: a new **alien registration scheme** introduced in 2003 requires all foreign residents – many of those affected are Senegalese – to pay around £25/$40 (a considerable amount in local terms) per family member per year. This has resulted in the exodus of a large section of the work force, leaving some industries, such as small-scale fishing, teetering on the brink of collapse. Matters weren't helped when fighting between Senegalese and Gambian football fans in June 2003 in Dakar led to serious disturbances in the Banjul area, including attacks on Senegalese residents and the trashing and looting of Senegalese businesses. Hundreds of Senegalese fled home and the border was temporarily closed.

The optimism and energy generated by projects such as long-overdue road, school and hospital construction disguises a growing sense of wariness, particularly in Banjul and the Kombos, and among journalists and non-APRC politicians. Clumsy attempts at **censorship** have included the closure and hypertaxation of radio stations and the arrest of newspaper staff. Undisguised corruption, **harassment of the opposition** and government disputes with the **supreme court** are the most public displays of insecurity and incompetence within the Banjul government. With inflation now spiralling out of control, The Gambia is beginning to exhibit all too many signs of a country in serious financial trouble, and there's little indication that Jammeh's youthful and inexperienced government has the ability to avert a crisis.

Books

The choice of general books on The Gambia and fiction by Gambian writers, is very limited (and several titles reviewed below are likely to be out of print, denoted o/p). If you're after a more detailed guide to the country than given in this book, consult the *Rough Guide to The Gambia*.

Mark Hudson *Our Grandmothers' Drums*. Rich, absorbing story of Hudson's stay in the village of "Dulaba" (Keneba) in the Kiang National Park area.

Arnold Hughes and David Perfect *A Political History of The Gambia, 1816–1994*. The most up-to-date history of the country.

Rosemary Long *Under the Baobab Tree* and *Together Under the Baobab Tree* (o/p). Chatty autobiographical accounts of a Scottish writer's new life in The Gambia, married to a Gambian.

Berkeley Rice *Enter Gambia: the Birth of an Improbable Nation* (o/p). A digestible work, but marred by an unpleasantly derisory tone.

Patience Sonko-Godwin *Ethnic Groups of the Senegambia* (o/p). A brief and graspable social history of the region.

Bamba Suso et al *Sunjata*. In Mande culture "Sunjata" is the big one, the legend of the founder of the Mali empire. This new Penguin edition presents two strikingly different Gambian versions of the epic.

Fiction

William Conton *The African* (o/p). A classic rags-to-premiership story by a writer from the colonial era, heavily influenced by his Sierra Leonean upbringing.

Ebou Dibba *Chaff in the Wind* (o/p). Highly accomplished author, now living in Britain, describing lives and loves in the 1930s. *Fafa* (o/p) tells of goings-on at a remote trading post on the Gambia River.

Alex Haley *Roots*. A reasonably entertaining American saga to read on the beach, though only the first few chapters are set in Kunta Kinte's semi-mythical Gambian homeland.

Natural history

Clive Barlow et al *Field Guide to the Birds of The Gambia and Senegal*. Excellent, authoritative work, the bird bible for the region.

Stella Brewer *The Forest Dwellers*. The story of Brewer's chimpanzee rehabilitation project, within the River Gambia National Park.

Rod Ward *A Birdwatchers' Guide to The Gambia*. Detailed information on some of the country's prime ornithological sites, accessibly presented.

Language

The Gambia's official language is **English**, fairly widely spoken in Banjul and the resorts, but often not understood outside the metropolitan areas or upriver. **Krio**, a creole still spoken by the descendants of freed slaves who moved from Freetown, is heard less and less. The African language you'll most often hear around Banjul is **Wolof** (see p.180 for some words and phrases), but the language with the strongest claim to be the country's traditional tongue is the Mande tongue, **Mandinka**, which is very widespread upriver, especially on the south bank.

There's a large **Fula**-speaking contingent also, particularly on the north bank. Other languages you may come across include **Jola** towards the Casamance in the south; **Serahule**, originally from far to the northeast; **Serére**, spoken by fishermen along the coast on the north bank; and **Manjango**, the language of the palm-wine tappers, mainly in the Kombos area. Around the Bakau and Fajara resort areas many young people are Senegalese and speak **French**, while in the tourist resorts, young men may speak a smattering of German, Swedish and Dutch.

Mandinka

The Mandinka of The Gambia is a fairly mainstream dialect of the large **Mande** language group. As usual in languages of Islamic peoples, it includes a scattering of Arabic.

Mandinka is not difficult to get your tongue round. A characteristic of spoken Mandinka is the omitted final vowel, lending a "clipped" quality to the language. A double vowel spelling, however, lengthens the sound. The "kh" sound is the "ch" of loch.

Greetings and useful phrases

How are you? (do you have peace?)	Khaira be?
How are you all?	Al be khaira to?
I'm well (I've peace)	Khaira dorong
How is everyone in the compound?	Suu molu ley?
They're well	Ibi jay
All OK? (general, further greeting)	Kortanante?
All OK	Tanante
How's the work? (if you're passing by)	Ih nimbara? (pl. Al nim baraa?)
The work's OK	Nimbara, nimbara
Thank you	Abaraka
Is Musa at home?	Musa ley?

Yes (I'm here)	Naam
What's your name?	Ito ndi?
My name is Kaba	Nto mu kaba leti
Where do you come from?	I bota min to ley?
Sit down	Si jang
White person	Toubab
Black person	Moo fingho
Where are you going?	Ih kata min?
I'm going to Basse	Nkata Basse
Let's go	Ali nghata
Goodbye (sing./pl.)	I si kontong/Al si kontong
Clear off! (to cheeky children)	A cha!
I'll beat you! (beware!)	Mbe bute la!
I want some bananas	Banano san nye
Five dalasis	Dalasi lulu
Too much!	Alcoleata!/ Ada jaweata!
Lower the price!	Atalat!/ A jaweata!

Numbers

1	kiling
2	fula
3	saba
4	nani
5	lulu
6	woro
7	worowula

8	sei	20	moang
9	kononto	35	tang saba ning
10	tang		lulu
11	tang ning kiling	100	keme

Glossary

This list includes Wolof and Mandinka terms and a number of suffixes used in place names.

APRC Alliance for Patriotic Reorientation and Construction.

Alkalo Village elder.

Ba Big, as in *tenda-ba* (big wharf).

Bantaba Men's communal siesta platform in every village and in many compounds.

Banto faro River floodlands.

Bengdula Craft market.

Bitiko Small shop.

Bolon Creek.

Bumster Beach boy, hustler.

Car Minibus.

Duma Lower.

Fode Teacher/marabout.

Garage Bush-taxi park.

Ghetto Unofficial palm-wine bar.

Kafoo Traditional "youth club".

Kankurang Mandinka masquerade dancer.

Kerr/Keur Place or compound.

Koriteh Eid (the end of Ramadan).

Koto Old.

Kunda Place.

Kuta New.

Lumo Weekly (or regular) rural market.

Nding Small.

Santo Upper.

Su Home.

Tenda Port, wharf.

3.1

Banjul and around

Banjul and the Kombo districts (Banjul's hinterland), fronted by 50km of beaches, are all that most visitors to The Gambia ever see, and virtually all the country's hotels are located here. A large and increasing proportion of the population of The Gambia lives in this district, but Banjul itself, sited on a flat island jutting into the mouth of the **Gambia River**, is sleepy and unfocused, and increasingly a daytime city only. At dusk, workers by the minibus-load pour back over Denton bridge and down the highway to the relative metropolis of **Serrekunda** and the leafier districts around Bakau, behind the hotels. Banjul is not attractive in the conventional sense, and apart from a few noteworthy attractions such as the National Museum, an excellent market, and an interesting architectural heritage, there's little here that could hold you longer than a day. Arriving overland from Senegal, however, or flying in to start a trip through West Africa, the capital is likely to figure to some extent in your plans, though you may prefer to mingle with the sun-worshippers out by the hotels and travel into town only when necessary.

The **beaches** are the big attraction, but some stretches in the resort centres at **Bakau**, **Fajara**, **Kotu** and **Kololi** are suffering, to varying degrees, from natural tidal erosion that has stripped away sand and toppled palm trees. As you head south, however, you can still find some spectacular strands. Inland, in Kombo North, Kombo South and Kombo Central districts, there are dozens of small, backcountry villages set in the random patchwork of forest, savanna and farmland, all accessible on foot, or by bicycle or rented car, bush taxi or bus.

For **naturalists**, and especially ornithologists, the region is a rewarding one. The **Tanbi Wetlands**, the maze of mangrove-festooned **creeks** behind Banjul and the justly popular **Abuko Nature Reserve** have great appeal, and even walks in the bush near the hotels can yield delightful discoveries – monkeys, parrots, chameleons and tortoises. There is more wilderness to explore beyond the bustling, musical town of Brikama, at **Makasutu Culture Forest** and the ecotourism camp at **Tumani Tenda**.

One of the most popular (but not necessarily the most rewarding) excursion destinations is the area around **Juffureh** on the north bank, made famous by Alex Haley's novel *Roots*, and accessible either by river cruise from Banjul, or by crossing by ferry to the north-bank town of **Barra** in order to continue overland. Also on the north bank and less than an hour away from Barra is **Jinack Island**, the coastal strip of Niumi National Park, quiet and excellent for bird-watching.

For **transport** between Banjul, Serrekunda and the resorts, you've got the choice of **tourist taxis** or **bush taxis**. A clutch of tourist taxis – dark green with a white diamond on their bodywork – can usually be found outside every hotel, or group of hotels, with fixed **fares** to various local points displayed (as an indication, expect to pay D200 from the airport to Kololi, D100 from Fajara to Bakau and D200 from Fajara to the *Senegambia* hotel). Note that a tourist-taxi trip costs around three times as much as the equivalent "town trip" in a bush taxi, and that tourist-taxi drivers pay a premium to be allowed to work in the tourist areas – confrontations may result if you persuade a bush taxi to carry you *from* a tourist-taxi zone. At the same time, it's worth noting that competition among the tourist-taxi drivers, especially in the high season, means that some may be prepared to offer you better prices than the fixed rates displayed.

Banjul

At no time of year is little **BANJUL** a prepossessing place. Its tarmac streets seem to pump out heat in the dry season, and its alleys become a chaos of red mud and puddles during the rains. The dilapidated assemblage of corrugated iron and peeling paint, and a lattice of open drains deep in the backstreets, with no slopes to drain them, complete a somewhat melancholy picture.

As a national capital, Banjul (or Bathurst as it was known to the colonial British) was doomed to failure by its site. It was acquired by Britain in 1816 to defend the river from slavers and to control trade with the interior, but its size was restricted to the area of land that could be kept free of flooding from the creeks and swamps behind. Kankujeri Road (formerly Bund Road) dykes the city on its present small patch, and further expansion is impossible. Hot, confined and seething with mosquitoes, Banjul is not a town where many choose to live. The exodus after business hours is understandable, and nightlife all but nonexistent.

If you have to be here, compensations are scant. To be won over by Banjul you need a little patience, and perhaps a specialist interest in West African history or architecture: more than any other Gambian town, the capital conveys a strong sense of the country's colonial past. However, with a population of barely 50,000 and shrinking, Banjul is too small to offer any of the ordinary facilities and diversions of a capital – though at least whatever you need to accomplish can usually be done in reasonable safety, and on foot. Walking gets you anywhere and the paranoia of some West African capitals is absent.

Arrival, information and transport

The new, modern terminal building at **Banjul International Airport** is 24km south of Banjul and 18km from the resorts. There's a **Trust Bank** exchange counter here (Mon–Fri 9am–5pm, Sat 9am–1pm), but you'll get better rates from the calculator-wielding moneychangers who make themselves conspicuous. There's also a **post office** (Mon–Sat 8am–4pm or until after the last flight), an **Internet café**, public telephones and an outlet for mobile phone SIM cards and scratch cards. Other facilities in the main hall of the terminal include a **Gambia Tourism Authority** office which offers sketchy tourist information such as lists of hotel phone numbers (they can't offer much advice) and a Hertz vehicle-rental desk (see Listings, p.288).

Moving on from Banjul and Serrekunda

The **Banjul–Barra ferry** across the mouth of the Gambia River is scheduled to depart Banjul or Barra daily from 7am to 11pm, hourly on the hour in each direction (vehicles D145, foot passengers D5). You can contact the Port Authority on ☏228205 for the latest information, though note that the ferry is subject to frequent delays. Large *pirogues* cover the same route, but they have an unsafe reputation. Note that because the riverbed badly needs dredging, the end of the dry season in May and June can see the river too shallow for the ferry at low tide. From Barra, there are two **GPTC buses** daily to **Dakar** which wait for passengers on the 7am and 9am ferries from Banjul. Buy your ticket (D150) from the GPTC office in Kanifing, Serrekunda, to avoid the rush for seats in Barra. Alternatively, estate-car **bush taxis** leave from Barra's bush-taxi garage (next to the ferry terminal) for Dakar when they are full. Expect all-out baggage checks at **Amdallai**, the Senegalese border crossing, and **Karang**, the first Senegalese village.

GPTC buses **upcountry** from the main bus station in Kanifing are discussed on p.254. Taxis and minibuses (no buses) to **Casamance** in southern Senegal commence in Serrekunda, at the "Main Garage" behind the market.

If you're arriving on a package deal you'll be driven straight to your hotel by complimentary coach. Fixed **taxi** fares from the airport are posted on a board outside the arrivals area – D200 is the rate for either Banjul or the resorts with a tourist taxi (green) – but you might be able to negotiate a lower rate with a local taxi (yellow). Otherwise it's a three-kilometre walk to the main road where, during the day, you can pick up a **bush taxi**, either straight into Banjul or just as far as Serrekunda, from where you can get another to the beach resorts.

If you're coming from Senegal, you'll arrive on the north bank of the Gambia River, at the small port of **Barra** (see p.296). From here the regular ferry brings you straight to the **wharf** in Banjul town centre. Banjul has two **bush-taxi garages**: vehicles arriving from the resorts, Serrekunda and Brikama use the garage off Freedom Lane near the Gamtel tower; while Bakau minibuses use the garage outside the National Museum.

Despite its compactness, Banjul's layout can initially be confusing as all the streets look much the same. To add to the confusion, most of the street names in Banjul were changed in the late 1990s, in a move towards further divorcing the city from its colonial past, but local people and businesses still occasionally use the old names. Most of your movements are likely to be centred around **July 22nd Square** – once known as MacCarthy Square but renamed on the day of the 1994 coup to commemorate the takeover – and down by the **waterfront** on Liberation Avenue (formerly Wellington Street), where you'll find **Albert Market**, the post office and banks. Traffic into and out of town uses the **Banjul–Serrekunda Highway** northwest of the centre.

Accommodation

The Gambia's capital city has only two tourist-class **hotels**, both very well known: the *Atlantic*, which is also one of The Gambia's best business hotels, on the beach near the town centre, and the *Palm Grove*, a beach hotel out of town on the Banjul–Serrekunda Highway. There's also a clutch of fairly down-at-heel hotels and **guesthouses** in the centre of Banjul, catering mainly for travelling Africans; the best of these are a little shabby, while the worst rent out rooms by the hour, but for a low-cost experience of Banjul some of these are worth investigating.

Apollo Hotel Tafsou Ebou Samba St ☎228184. A characterless place, but a reasonable choice if you're looking for something vaguely resembling an international-style en-suite room, on a budget; however, the *Carlton* offers more atmosphere for very similar prices. ❸

Atlantic Hotel Marina Parade ☎228601, ⓦwww.corinthiahotels.com. Recently renovated, large and comfortable establishment. The grandly proportioned bar and restaurant areas are popular with local movers and shakers. Most rooms have views of the pool, the ocean, the flower gardens, or a jungly bird garden. You can parasail or jetski with The Gambia Watersports Centre, based here (see p.289). ❽

Banjul Ferry Guest House Liberation St ☎222028. The best choice in this price range, near the Barra Ferry terminal, with a communal balcony great for watching the incessant activity in the street below. It looks unpromising from the outside, but the rooms (some s/c with a/c) are well kept and a good size. ❷

Carlton Hotel Independence Drive ☎228670, ⓕ227214. Old-fashioned hotel with decently furnished s/c rooms, with optional a/c. Some just about have views of Arch 22. ❸

Duma Guest House Jallow Jallow St ☎228381. Friendly guesthouse in a residential quarter; the rooms (some s/c) have seen better days but are good value. ❶

Palm Grove Hotel Mile 2, Banjul–Serrekunda Highway ☎201620, ⓦwww.gambia-palmgrove hotel.co.uk. Tourist hotel with a pleasant location next to a lagoon and a quiet stretch of beach. Unfortunately, it's way outside the town centre, and guests mostly have to rely on tourist taxis to get around – it's difficult to flag down bush taxis outside the hotel. It's an attractive place to spend time, though; the decor includes works by local artists. ❻

Princess Diana Hotel Independence Drive ☎228715. Small hotel with plain, s/c rooms with fans or a/c. Clean and adequate, but a little soulless. ❷

The Town

The **National Museum** on Independence Drive (Mon–Thurs 8am–4pm, Fri & Sat 8am–1pm; D25) though small, poky and badly lit, contains some gems – you just have to be patient to find them. A great deal of mouldering ethnographia – mostly the remains of private collections and not all of it Gambian – and a lot of old anthropological "type" photos are the main displays. Kids used to interactive displays will be yawning within minutes at the yellowing notices against the exhibits; they might pause at the traditional musical instrument collection, but just for long enough to discover that you're not allowed to touch anything – unlike at the Tanje Village Museum (see p.294), where playing the instruments is positively encouraged. But if you take time to peer into some of the dark corners, you can come across excellent *warri* boards, fascinating maps and documents, and generally informative stuff about the wars and migrations of the Senegambia region. There's an impressive array of palm-wine tapping and drinking equipment too, an early Iron Age wood drill with its modern-looking bit, and a natural-resources display interesting to those unfamiliar with the flora and fauna of the region.

About half a kilometre to the east, **Albert Market** (Mon–Sat), a relatively laid-back and rather sanitized version of what you find everywhere in West Africa, is one of Banjul's big pluses. The highly enjoyable **tourist market** is deep inside the general market – take a pocketful of dalasis and argue your head off. While you're busy bargaining for D5 bangles you can eye up the better merchandise and come back later if it appeals. There are some great bargains, especially in cloth and clothing: Chinese-made garments are especially inexpensive. If you're not into parting with money at all, then you're likely to feel uneasy – and free gifts of the very thing you didn't want to buy are all part of the wearing-down process. Go in a bright mood. For more on craft shopping in the locality, see p.288.

West of the National Museum, Independence Drive is graced with the impressive, boat-shaped Court House. The road is spanned at its far end by **Arch 22** (daily 8am–10pm; D25), a cream-coloured monstrosity that greets you as you enter the capital. Built to commemorate the coup of July 22, 1994, the arch was completed in 1996 at a cost of $1.15 million, but was a technical disappointment – one of its lift shafts is unusable due to the twisting of the structure as it settled into the soft ground. However, the arch does house a **museum** of traditional textiles and tools where, incongruously, you can view the seat Yaya Jammeh was sitting on when he announced his takeover of The Gambia, and, halfway up, a **restaurant** and **bar**, where you can eat your snacks in a breeze while watching the Banjul traffic. The best views of the town, however, are afforded from the **balcony** right at the top. To the north, Marina Parade is one of Banjul's pleasanter and shadier streets, fringed with somnolent government buildings and terminating, after the *Atlantic Hotel* and the hospital, at the guarded gates of **State House**.

Eating, drinking and nightlife

Banjul suffers from a serious shortage of **restaurants**, particularly in the evenings, but there is first-class simple food to be had from local eating places and fast-food joints in the daytime. For rice and sauce, there's plenty of choice among the stalls in the Albert Market, where all the traders eat, and you'll find itinerant traders everywhere – especially around July 22nd Square – with fruit, fritters, frozen juices and peanut brittle. There's not much **nightlife**, either, in the conventional sense: at the time of writing the last club in town had closed, and the only option was the plush air-conditioned disco at the *Atlantic Hotel* (nightly till 3am). For the most happening nightclubs, you'll have to travel out to the tourist resort areas and Serrekunda. You could also check if anything watchable is showing at the Capital **cinema** on Imam Omar Sowe Avenue – it shows mostly action movies.

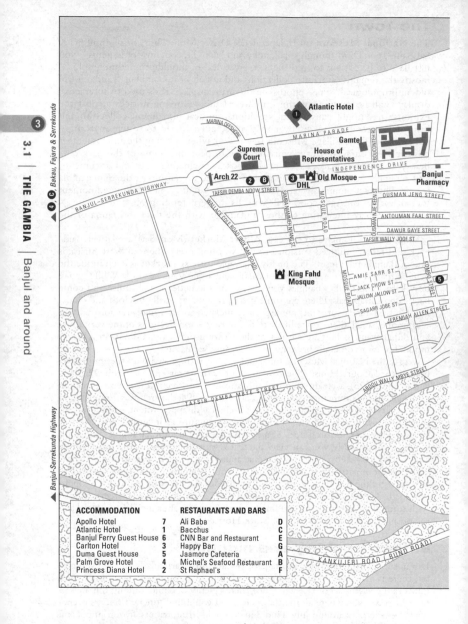

ACCOMMODATION

Apollo Hotel	7
Atlantic Hotel	1
Banjul Ferry Guest House	6
Carlton Hotel	3
Duma Guest House	5
Palm Grove Hotel	4
Princess Diana Hotel	2

RESTAURANTS AND BARS

Ali Baba	D
Bacchus	C
CNN Bar and Restaurant	E
Happy Bar	G
Jaamore Cafeteria	A
Michel's Seafood Restaurant	B
St Raphael's	F

Restaurants and bars

Ali Baba Nelson Mandela St. Lebanese place that's popular and highly recommended, even though it's nothing much to look at. Decent snacks, sandwiches and main meals, including first class falafel, and juicy burgers, plus mango and guava juice and fresh fruit smoothies. Mon–Sat 9am–5pm.

Bacchus Beach Bar & Restaurant Mile 7, Banjul–Serrekunda Highway ☎227948. Situated on the lagoon behind what used to be the *Wadner Beach Hotel* (now derelict), this

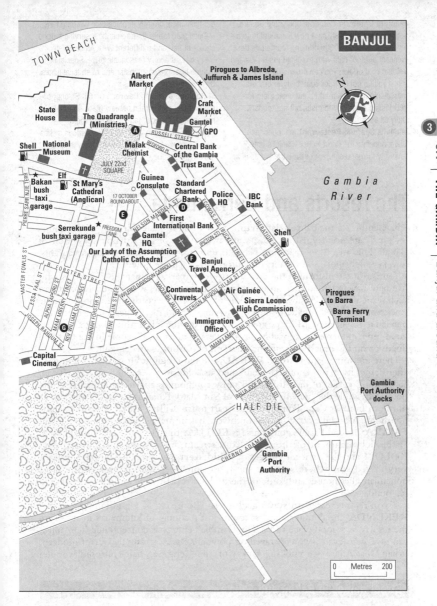

popular but slightly overpriced bar/restaurant serves tourist standards like steak and barracuda.

CNN Bar & Restaurant Rene Blain St. Serving *chawarma* , chicken and chips, this is a bit grimy and, despite the name, doesn't have a TV. Open

24hr and more likely to be busy late at night (it can be near-deserted by day).

Happy Bar Rev William Cole St. A tiny hole-in-the-wall drinking place with a very local atmosphere, in a quiet street where kids play table football on the corner.

Jaamore Cafeteria Corner of July 22nd Square, near Albert Market. Giving a new lease of life to a lovingly preserved 1930s drinking fountain is this pleasant outdoor café with excellent meat pies and hot and cold drinks; you can order simple meals, too, if you've got time for somebody to buy the ingredients from the market and cook them for you. Visited mostly by tourists, but not touristy. Daily till 8pm.

Michel's Seafood Restaurant Independence Drive, opposite the Court House. Banjul's only relatively formal restaurant outside the hotels is an old-fashioned, brightly lit place with whirring fans – functional, rather than romantic – serving a good choice of fish and a different West African dish every day, at a very reasonable price. Specialities include tiger prawns, lobster and fresh local juices. Daily 8am–late.

St Raphael's Wilfred Davidson Carroll St, opposite the Catholic cathedral. Low-key place that feels rather like a Catholic family drawing room. *Benachin*, *domodah*, and other West African dishes such as *chew-kong* (catfish) and *fufu* with soup are all good value.

The resorts and Serrekunda

The Gambia's principal **tourist strip**, which accommodates virtually all the country's package holidaymakers, covers just over 10km of the Atlantic coast west of Banjul. This area is an appealing place to unwind, with its easy-going restaurants, low-key nightspots, and clusters of clifftop and beachside hotels.

Tourism has transformed the area utterly. It's remarkable that the Gambians who live here have retained such an equable regard for visitors who generally pay them such scant attention. As always where the poor world meets the holidaying rich, the stories of locals who made good by marrying abroad fuel hopes and dampen the inevitable resentment. More positively, there's considerable enthusiasm for having a good time and it's not impossible for travellers to meet local people in the bars and discos or on the beach without the question of patronage creeping in.

There are four main **resorts**. **BAKAU**, the most significant coastal community after Banjul itself, is the longest-established, its "old town", east of Sait Matty Road, a swarming village of dirt streets and noisy compounds and home to many of the hotel staff, while the "new town", west of Sait Matty Road, is more affluent, and its northern limit, at Cape Point, becomes part tourist village, part well-to-do neighbourhood. Along the coast to the southwest, Bakau merges with the more affluent **FAJARA**; beyond Fajara's golf course is **KOTU**, with a clump of established hotels, at the debouchment of the small Kotu stream. Finally, further south, there's **KOLOLI** and the adjacent villages of **Bijilo**, **Kerr Serign** and **Manjai Kunda**, a very mixed area where some of the most upmarket hotels, some of the most bohemian guesthouses and some of the trashiest tourist traps in the country are to be found.

If you're interested in staying close to the heart of Gambian life, **SERREKUNDA**, the country's largest town, just a couple of kilometres inland from the resorts, is a good place to be. The Gambia's energy is concentrated here and it can give you (even if you're travelling nowhere else) a strong flavour of modern, urban West Africa – a choking racket of diesel engines, half-collapsed wooden

Street names in Bakau and Fajara

As in Banjul, a number of roads in Bakau carry the burden of more than one name. Atlantic Road, Atlantic Avenue and Atlantic Boulevard are all the same; Garba Jahumpa Road is still also called New Town Road; Kairaba Avenue used to be known as Pipeline Road, and often still is. The main road from Kairaba Avenue to Kotu and Kololi, sometimes referred to as Hotel Road or Badala Park Way, has been officially renamed Bertil Harding Highway; beyond Bijilo it becomes the Kombo coastal highway.

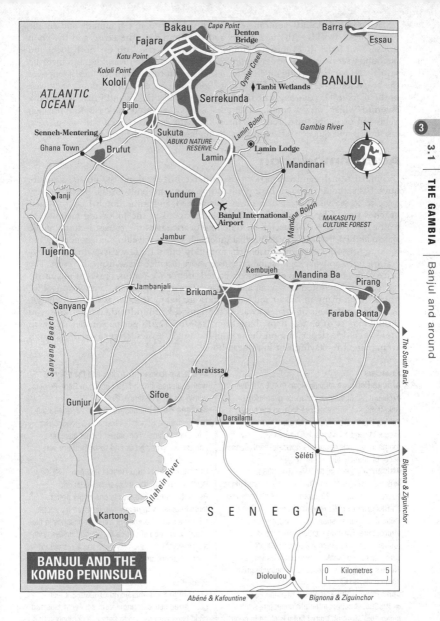

ATLANTIC
OCEAN

Bakau
Cape Point
Denton
Bridge
Barra
Essau
Fajara
Kotu Point
Kololi Point
Kololi
Bijilo
Serrekunda
Tanbi Wetlands
BANJUL
Oyster Creek
Gambia River
N
Senneh-Mentering
Ghana Town
Brufut
Sukuta
ABUKO NATURE
RESERVE
Lamin
Lamin Bolon
Lamin Lodge
Mandinari
Tanji
Yundum
Banjul International
Airport
Mandina Bolon
MAKASUTU
CULTURE FOREST
Jambur
Tujering
Jambanjali
Brikama
Kembujeh
Mandina Ba
Pirang
Sanyang
Faraba Banta
Sanyang Beach
Gunjur
Marakissa
Sifoe
The South Bank
Darsilami
Séléti
Bignona & Ziguinchor
Allahein River
S E N E G A L
Kartong

BANJUL AND THE KOMBO PENINSULA

0   Kilometres   5

Dioloulou

Abéné & Kafountine ▼   ▼ *Bignona & Ziguinchor*

trolleys, bricollaged stalls selling a riot of dust-covered imports, and music blaring from the hundreds of cassette players and radios. The focus of all this is the town's central garage and market. It's a lot of fun, and not unsafe, to wander round here, though avoid dangling your valuables and keep your bag under your arm. Serrekunda's residential neighbourhoods and suburbs, such as Kanifing, Latrikunda and Sukuta, see few tourists.

Staying in Serrekunda, you can get to the beach resorts in ten minutes and get the best of both worlds – the beach bars and restaurants on the coast, and the chop houses and local dives in Serrekunda. The town is the hub for both local and upcountry services: buses to Basse run from the bus station in Kanifing, and there are several taxi garages serving different routes. The main **taxi stand** for local services to the beach resorts of Kotu and Kololi is at "London Corner", a five-minute walk west of the market. The thoroughfare that links Serrekunda, Bakau and Fajara is **Kairaba Avenue**, which, only a couple of decades ago, was a rutted track running through fields and orchards. Today, Kairaba's three-kilometre length is lined with shops, bars, restaurants and offices, and commands the highest rents in the country.

Accommodation

By international standards most of the **tourist hotels** along the coastal strip are quite basic, though they all have pools. While many are built on the beach, or very close to it, sea views are by no means guaranteed, and some hotels have had their beaches ruined by coastal erosion (a problem noted in the following reviews). In season, the Kotu–Kololi stretch becomes the heartbeat of the tourist industry, while Bakau and Fajara hotels are somewhat quieter. If you're travelling independently and looking for somewhere reasonably cheap to flop out for a few days, you'll find several friendly, non-package establishments a short distance away from the coast. The price codes below, unless otherwise indicated, are for s/c rooms, breakfast included.

If you are interested in staying as a house guest in a Gambian compound (something which many in Bakau and Serrekunda are happy to offer as they can charge, daily, the equivalent of a week's wages), then just ask around and take pot luck; you should expect to be asked anything from D100 to D200 per person per day, with meals included, depending on the season. It's usually easiest to turn up this kind of arrangement by staying first in a cheap hotel.

Bakau

African Heritage Atlantic Road ☎ 496778. Two excellent s/c upstairs rooms, one overlooking Bakau market, the other overlooking the busy fishing beach. Both rooms have the use of a fridge, TV, and a lovely small garden. Four new rooms in an annexe provide down-to-earth budget accommodation. ❶

African Village Atlantic Road ☎ 495384, ✉ europrop@qanet.gm. Conveniently located in the heart of Bakau, this 73-room tourist hotel perched on Bakau's low cliffs is a little scruffy but good value and recommended for its warm, Gambian atmosphere. Accommodation with fans is in roundhouses, crammed tightly into a leafy compound, and blocks, some with sea views. There's a very reasonable restaurant with great Atlantic views. ❸

Cape Point Hotel Kofi Annan St, Cape Point ☎ 495005, ✉ capepointhotel@qanet.gm. A little faded, this 35-room tourist hotel is close to good beaches and there's a tiny pool. Some rooms have a/c, all are spotless. ❹

Jabo Guest House Old Cape Rd ☎ 494906, ⊛ www.jabo-enterprises.com. A down-to-earth, reasonably priced place which feels more like a family compound than a guesthouse, with six

simple, s/c rooms with fridge, and the use of a well-equipped kitchen. The beach at Cape Point is within walking distance. ❷

Romana Hotel Atlantic Rd ☎ 495127, ℗ 496042. Unpromising exterior, but inside is a good, basic, small urban hotel. The eleven rooms have fans, and the easy-going bar and restaurant are very reasonable. ❷

Sunbeach Hotel and Resort Kofi Annan St, Cape Point ☎ 497190, ✉ sunbeach@gamtel.gm. Recently refurbished, this is one of the better tourist hotels, with nearly two hundred a/c rooms with satellite TV, on one of the best beaches in the resort area. A good choice for young families, with an excellent pool and play area and a restaurant serving European meals. ❽

Fajara

Croc John's Off Atlantic Rd ☎ 496068. Clean, good-sized self-catering apartments with fans and good beds with mosquito nets in a compound that feels homely, secure and un-touristy. Popular with volunteers and long-term visitors as well as independent travellers who don't need the facilities of a tourist hotel. ❹

Fajara Golf Apartments Off Kairaba Ave ☎ & ℗ 495800. In a pair of compounds enlivened by the work of a local artist, these eight self-catering apartments are spotless, spacious and very well equipped, with useful extras like CD and cassette players and free mountain-bike rental. Recommended. ❹

Fajara Guesthouse Signposted off Kairaba Ave, near the golf club ☎ 496122, ℻ 494365. A peaceful haven offering small, simple, clean rooms with fans, around a bright white-pillared courtyard. ❸

Leybato Guesthouse Off Atlantic Rd ☎ 497186, ℻ 497562. Known and loved for its beach bar and hammocks, *Leybato's* has a few basic guest rooms – good if you want to be on the beach, but there are better-value places elsewhere. ❸

Ngala Lodge Atlantic Rd ☎ 494045 or 497429, ⓦ www.ngalalodge.com. A former ambassador's residence, converted into a hotel with six luxurious suites, plus a small swimming pool and a superb restaurant. Likely to appeal to anyone with a sense of the unusual looking for somewhere secluded and serene. Worth every penny. Bookings through The Gambia Experience (see p.14) only. ❽

Safari Garden Hotel Off Atlantic Rd, near the golf club ☎ 495887, ⓦ www.safarigarden.com. Very good value and thoroughly recommended, this un-touristy, independent hotel is a gem. Besides a dozen simple rooms around a colourful garden courtyard, it boasts a small but excellent pool, a good restaurant, and extremely friendly staff. Pleasantly situated in a quiet neighbourhood of sandy residential streets, within walking distance of the beach. ❸

Kotu

Badala Park Hotel Kotu Stream Rd ☎ 460400, ℻ 460402. Popular with young independent travellers and bird-watchers, this is one of the cheapest package hotels. Some of the two-hundred-plus rooms, with optional a/c, are shabbily furnished – the ones furthest from reception are quieter. There's a path to a pleasant beach a short walk away. ❹

Bakotu Hotel Kotu Stream Rd ☎ 465555, ℻ 465959. An attractive, though rather cramped, tourist hotel, a couple of minutes from the beach, with a small swimming pool; the best rooms are upstairs, away from the road and with a balcony. They also have eight small self-catering apartments – they're a little tired, but have private balconies with fabulous views over Kotu Stream, excellent for bird- and monkey-watching. Rooms ❻, apartments ❼

Bungalow Beach Hotel Kotu Stream Rd ☎ 465288, ℮ bbhotel@qanet.gm. Self-catering tourist hotel, right on a reasonable beach, with friendly staff and a loyal clientele, mostly of retired Europeans and young families. The 110 mini-apartments are well-equipped, with optional a/c, but they're a little on the small side; better-value options exist elsewhere. ❼

Kombo Beach Hotel Kotu Stream Rd ☎ 465466, ℮ info@kombobeach.gm. Popular with young European package tourists, this is a lively hotel with plenty of activities, set on a reasonable stretch of beach. Mass-market atmosphere, with block after block of rooms (250 in all) designed to a familiar international formula; huge crowds congregate in the bar to watch football on satellite TV. ❼

Palm Beach Hotel Kotu Stream Rd ☎ 462111, ℻ 460402. Sister hotel to the *Badala Park*, and with a similar atmosphere – much more Gambian than the other places in Kotu – but more upmarket. The rooms (with TV and a/c) are in villas packed into jungly gardens, close to the good beach. ❻

Sunset Beach Hotel Kotu Stream Rd ☎ 496397 or 463876, ⓦ www.sunsetbeachhotel.gm. Newly refurbished tourist hotel in a good location on a well-kept stretch of beach, relatively secluded for Kotu. Most of the rooms are in utilitarian bungalows in regimented rows, but the place is clean and well-furnished. ❻

Kololi: around the Palma Rima and Senegambia hotels

Kairaba Hotel ☎ 462940, ⓦ www.kairabahotel .com. The Gambia's top large hotel – and prime honeymoon territory – with wide-ranging facilities including a choice of good restaurants. Pleasant rooms, 140 in all, with direct-dial phones, excellent bathrooms, safes, TV – the lot. Loyal customers return again and again. Unfortunately, the once-splendid beach is now practically nonexistent, but the pool and grounds are good compensation. ❽

Kololi Beach Club ☎ 464897, ⓦ www.kololi.com. Started life as a timeshare, but now operates as a hotel, with accommodation in self-catering villas in well-tended grounds, including a small golf course, and a pleasant pool edged by low palms. Extremely expensive. ❽

Palma Rima Hotel Bertil Harding Highway ☎ 463380 or 463381, ℻ 463382. A brash, mega-touristy resort hotel, famous for its huge swimming pool, a short distance back from the beach. Packed entertainment programme, a choice of restaurants and bars, and a tame but busy club (the *Moon Light Disco*) that cranks out the Europop every night. ❻

Paradise Suites Hotel ☎ 463429, ℻ 463415. North of the main Senegambia area, and set in small but beautifully planted gardens, this self-catering accommodation is comfortable and well-furnished. Attractive options from small apartments to large villas. ❹

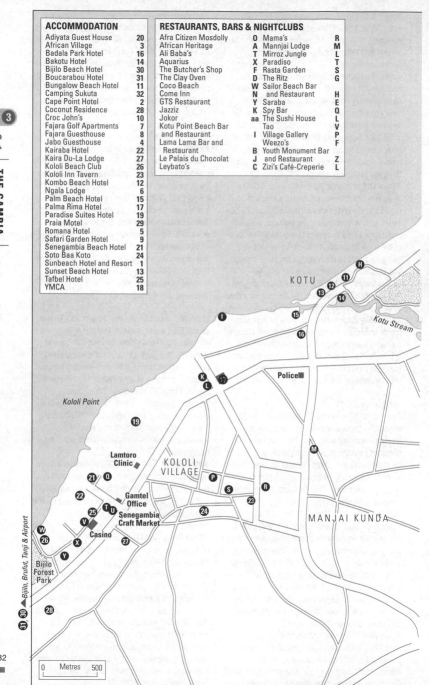

ACCOMMODATION

Adiyata Guest House	20
African Village	3
Badala Park Hotel	16
Bakotu Hotel	14
Bijilo Beach Hotel	30
Boucarabou Hotel	31
Bungalow Beach Hotel	11
Camping Sukuta	32
Cape Point Hotel	2
Coconut Residence	28
Croc John's	10
Fajara Golf Apartments	7
Fajara Guesthouse	8
Jabo Guesthouse	4
Kairaba Hotel	22
Kaira Du-La Lodge	27
Kololi Beach Club	26
Kololi Inn Tavern	23
Kombo Beach Hotel	12
Ngala Lodge	6
Palm Beach Hotel	15
Palma Rima Hotel	17
Paradise Suites Hotel	19
Praia Motel	29
Romana Hotel	5
Safari Garden Hotel	9
Senegambia Beach Hotel	21
Soto Baa Koto	24
Sunbeach Hotel and Resort	1
Sunset Beach Hotel	13
Tafbel Hotel	25
YMCA	18

RESTAURANTS, BARS & NIGHTCLUBS

Afra Citizen Mosdolly	O	Mama's	R
African Heritage	A	Mannjai Lodge	M
Ali Baba's	T	Mirroz Jungle	L
Aquarius	X	Paradiso	T
The Butcher's Shop	F	Rasta Garden	S
The Clay Oven	D	The Ritz	G
Coco Beach	W	Sailor Beach Bar	
Come Inn	N	and Restaurant	H
GTS Restaurant	Y	Saraba	E
Jazziz	K	Spy Bar	Q
Jokor	aa	The Sushi House	L
Kotu Point Beach Bar		Tao	V
and Restaurant	I	Village Gallery	P
Lama Lama Bar and		Weezo's	F
Restaurant	B	Youth Monument Bar	
Le Palais du Chocolat	J	and Restaurant	Z
Leybato's	C	Zizi's Café-Creperie	L

KOTU

Kotu Stream

Police

Kololi Point

Lamtoro
Clinic

KOLOLI
VILLAGE

Gamtel
Office

Senegambia
Craft Market

MANJAI KUNDA

Casino

Bijilo
Forest
Park

Bijilo, Brufut, Tanji & Airport

0 Metres 500

Sukuta, Brufut ▼ & ㉜

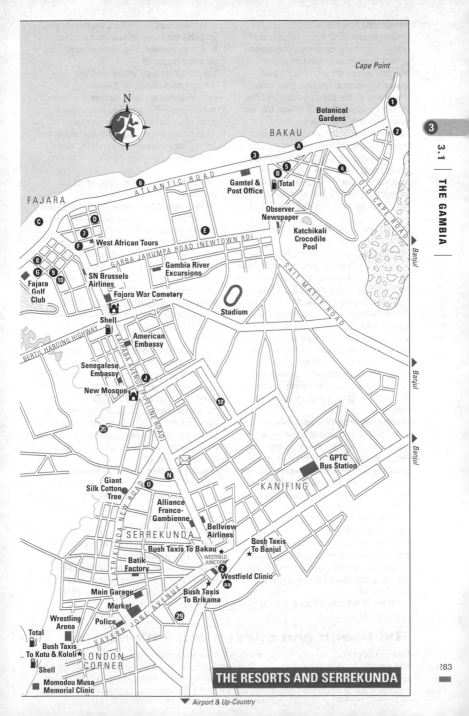

Cape Point

Botanical Gardens

BAKAU

FAJARA

ATLANTIC ROAD

Gamtel & Post Office

Total

Observer Newspaper

Katchikali Crocodile Pool

OLD CAPE ROAD

SAIT MATTY ROAD

Banjul

West African Tours

GARBA JAHUMPA ROAD (NEWTOWN RD)

Gambia River Excursions

SN Brussels Airlines

Fajara Golf Club

Fajara War Cemetery

Stadium

Shell

BERTIL HARDING HIGHWAY

KAIRABA AVENUE (PIPELINE ROAD)

American Embassy

Senegalese Embassy

New Mosque

GPTC Bus Station

KANIFING

Giant Silk Cotton Tree

Alliance Franco-Gambienne

Bellview Airlines

SERREKUNDA

Bush Taxis To Bakau

Batik Factory

WESTFIELD JUNCTION

Bush Taxis To Banjul

Westfield Clinic

Main Garage

Market

Bush Taxis To Brikama

Wrestling Arena

Police

Total

SAYERR JOBE AVENUE

Bush Taxis To Kotu & Kololi

LONDON CORNER

Shell

Momodou Musa Memorial Clinic

THE RESORTS AND SERREKUNDA

KANIFING NEW ROAD

N

Banjul

Banjul

283

Airport & Up-Country

Senegambia Beach Hotel ☎462717, ⊛www.senegambiahotel.com. Gigantic tourist hotel, recommended for its impressive tropical gardens (great for bird-watching but dusty between February and the rains), and good service. The rooms are cool and clean; some are newly furnished but others are rather tired. Like the *Kairaba*, its neighbour, it's suffered from the devastation of the beach. ❽

Tafbel Hotel ☎460510, ⊜tafbel@qanet.gm. Unpretentious tourist hotel, with a good pool in an attractive central courtyard. A reasonable choice, but the rooms (with optional a/c) are pretty shabby, with uncomfortable beds; unless you manage to fly in on a special offer, there are better-value places in other areas. ❺

Kololi Village, Ker Serign and Bijilo

Bijilo Beach Hotel Bertil Harding Highway, Bijilo ☎426706, ⊜bijilobeach@airtip.gm. A new tourist hotel with mini-apartments and double rooms with optional a/c, all small but bright and finished to a high standard, European-style. ❹

Boucarabou Hotel Kerr Serign Njaga, midway between Kololi Village and Bijilo ☎463363, ⊜ovl.caputh@t-online.de. An innovative hotel known for arranging music and dancing lessons and sessions (see p.289) as well as offering simple accommodation, with twin rooms with fans and large, clean, shared washrooms, in a delightful environment of gardens, orchards and vegetable plots. ❹

Coconut Residence Bertil Harding Highway, Kerr Serign ☎463377, ⊜coconut@qanet.gm. A luxurious hotel with 36 dreamily decorated suites: some have four-poster beds, all have huge bathrooms. For total seclusion there are two villas with private pools tucked away in gardens behind the main buildings. The atmosphere is suave, and the restaurant one of the best in the country. Hardly the "real" Gambia, but a very appealing place to indulge. ❽

Kaira-Du-La Lodge Kololi Village ☎460529, ⊜kaira.du.la@qanet.gm. Smartly equipped self-catering apartments in roundhouses set in a small, well-kept garden; each has a living room and a small patio. ❸

Kololi Inn Tavern Kololi Village ☎463410,

⊜460484. Budget option that's frayed round the edges but still a good place to unwind in cool, African surroundings; the garden compound has a bar and barbecue. ❷

Soto Baa Koto Kololi Village ☎460399, ⊜renate-thomas@web.de. Budget accommodation in shabby but appealing thatched roundhouses with a shared cooking area, in a dusty, shady garden. You'll need your own mosquito net. The two-storey bamboo-and-thatch *bantaba* bar/restaurant is worth visiting even if you're staying elsewhere. ❷

Serrekunda, Kanifing and Sukuta

Adiyata Guest House Well-signposted off Kairaba Ave, Latrikunda ☎395510 or 925537. An excellent choice if you want to experience a villagey neighbourhood of Serrekunda, away from the bustle of Kairaba Avenue. Simple rooms with large beds, nets and fans in six characterful roundhouses around a small courtyard planted with trees and shrubs. ❷

Camping Sukuta Bijilo Rd, Sukuta ☎917786, ⊛www.campingsukuta.de. Well-signposted from Bertil Harding Highway and from Serrekunda, this camping site and lodge is very popular with European overlanders taking a breather on their way to or from Senegal and beyond. There's plenty of shade to park and camp, accommodation in simple huts, and good shared kitchen and washing facilities. If you've crossed the Sahara by vehicle and are thinking of selling up and flying off, this is a good place to be put in touch with potential buyers. The much-travelled owners are also a prime source of information on overland routes and travel issues. ❶

Praia Motel 3 Mam Youth St, Serrekunda ☎394887. A modest but comfortable Gambian-owned place in a quiet backstreet of Serrekunda with secure parking. Rooms are s/c, with TV and either fan or a/c. ❷

YMCA Off Kairaba Ave, Kanifing ☎392647, ⊜ymca@ymca.gm, ⊛www.ymca.gm. Adequate and well-managed hostel accommodation with single and double rooms with fans, some s/c. Features table-tennis tables and a restaurant (daily 9am–midnight, cheap meals), plus a computer centre with Internet access next door. ❶

The beach and coastal attractions

Before venturing into the **sea** you should make sure your patch is safe – every year sees several swimmers swept out. Cape Point (also known as Cape St Mary) has some of the area's most attractive beaches, but, with its cross-cutting tidal and river currents, it's a notorious blackspot, as is the rocky area by *Leybato Beach Bar* in

Fajara. The rollers that sometimes sweep in further south can also bring a dangerous undertow. Many of the hotels use red flags to warn swimmers when the sea is unsafe, and it's wise to observe them.

Unfortunately, **coastal erosion** is a big problem in West Africa and the Gambian beaches have taken a battering over the last few years. One of the worst affected stretches in the resort area is Kololi, where what little visible sand remains gets completely submerged at high tide. Ill-fated attempts to counter the natural progress of the erosion – and stop the ocean eating away at the hotel gardens – have ruined the beaches outside the *Kairaba Hotel* (known, in happier times, as the *Kairaba Beach Hotel*) and the *Senegambia*. For the best part of a decade, these beaches have been scarred with hideous, toppling sandbags and concrete blocks, while experts puzzle over a suitable remedy. During particularly high tides you may get your feet wet while eating at *Paradise Beach Bar* on Kotu Strand. The beaches south of the tourist area, such as Sanyang, Tujering and Gunjur don't suffer quite so much.

Beach bars are a colourful part of the Gambian beach scene, and some visitors spend their whole stay moving happily from one to the next, or just setting up camp at one for the duration. They provide a laid-back alternative to the inland tourist restaurants and bars, with reggae on the sound system and local live music from time to time; many also serve excellent fresh food, notably prawns, grills, and fish baked in foil. Gambian beaches are simply too hot to lie out on for long periods, so beach bars provide a shady haven. You have to allow time to enjoy the experience, as food tends to be prepared to order. Opening times can be unpredictable, although some stay open at night and during the rainy season. All along the beach you'll also find **fruit stalls**, and **juice-pressers' stands** where you can buy freshly squeezed juices – few bars sell these.

Coastal attractions

There's a lot you can do with wheels of your own (see p.288 for details of car and bike rental): trundle down the coast in search of better beaches, explore the back-country between the coast and the airport, visit Serrekunda for the shopping – even get across to the north bank of The Gambia.

The small **botanical garden** in Bakau is a rather beautiful, though neglected, hideaway just off the main road, greenest and most impressive after the rains. Note the fairy-tale teak tree and the specimens of ancient cycads. The **crocodile pool** of Katchikali is just a ten-minute walk from here in the heart of Bakau, a path leading almost straight to it from the junction of Atlantic and Old Cape roads. Local children will show you the way. There's usually a small payment to visit the poolside to see the crocodiles – none too big and strangely white among the dense covering of lilies. No one fears these crocs: you can approach quite close even when they're out of the water and they are believed to have a magical effect on the pool, ensuring pregnancy for women who wash in it – not that there's very often much water. Every few seasons it's necessary to call a work party together to dig a little deeper, and sometimes to introduce new crocodiles.

Bijilo Forest (daily 8am–6pm; D25) is a half-square-kilometre reserve at the south end of Kololi beach, accessible from opposite the *Kololi Beach Club*. Containing one of the country's last remaining stands of striking **rhun palms**, it's managed by the Gambian–German Forestry Project. Within the reserve there are good chances of seeing red colobus and vervet monkeys, squirrels, large monitor lizards and a galaxy of birds. Trails are marked clearly, with a choice between long and short circuits of the park.

Eating, drinking and nightlife

In addition to the **bars** and **restaurants** of the main hotels (some of the best of which are found at the *Coconut Residence*, *Kairaba*, *Ngala Lodge* and *Safari Garden* hotels, all open to non-residents), there are plenty of independent, international-style places aimed at tourists and expats, many around the hotel zones, others distributed through the urban areas. For local **chop houses** and *afra* places, you need to head for the backstreets of Bakau and the market area of Serrekunda. A number of bar/restaurants have happy hours, and become nightclubs by night. In season, the after-dark action can be lively along the tourist strip, with hotel nightclubs pumping out international chart music, but don't be afraid of trying strictly Gambian nightspots. For night-time mobility, unless you have your own vehicle, you'll need to rely on **taxis**. You could get a group together and rent one for the whole evening, and you may even get a taxi driver who's willing to be a guide, sharing his local knowledge and the fun. Taxi drivers and local guides often know about live music events which aren't advertised elsewhere. If you want to hold your own party, there's palm wine for sale by the grove of tall palm trees on the landward side of Fajara golf course.

Bakau

African Heritage 114 Atlantic Rd. A quiet, pleasant place to stop, serving good-value light meals including African and Danish specialities, and freshly squeezed lime juice, with a great gallery shop to browse. Mon–Sat 10am–6pm.
Lama Lama Bar and Restaurant Off Atlantic Rd. Live music nightly, with a busy local vibe. Daily 8.30am–12.30am.
Saraba Off Newtown Rd. A low-key place, tucked away in a quiet neighbourhood, serving top-notch *afra* to in-the-know locals, with fresh *tapalapa* from the next-door bakery. Nightly 7pm–3am.

Fajara and Kairaba Avenue

Alliance Franco-Gambienne Kairaba Ave. The garden bar at the back of the centre serves excellent-value French and Senegalese-style lunches.
The Butcher's Shop 130 Kairaba Ave ☏ 495069. This superb deli has an equally superb restaurant on the decking at the front: chic by day and romantic by night, with above-average prices, but excellent value juices. Mon–Sat 8am–late.
The Clay Oven Near VSO and MRC, signposted off Atlantic Rd ☏ 496600. The Gambia's best Indian restaurant takes itself extremely seriously – and prices are high. Daily noon–3pm and 7pm–late.
Come Inn 17 Kairaba Ave. Beer garden with an African twist, popular with a mixed crowd of Gambian and tourist regulars, this place serves steaks, fish, pizza and German fare, plus probably the best draught JulBrew in the country.
Leybato's Beach Bar Off Atlantic Rd. Long-established beach bar, with hammocks strung over the sand. It's a great place to catch the sunset, or sample home-style African cooking or tourist standards. Not a place to choose if you're in a hurry.
Le Palais du Chocolat Kairaba Ave. Authentic French-style café with excellent coffee; the

pastries are good and the calorific cakes are well worth a splurge. Tues–Sat 8am–9pm, Sun 8am–1pm & 5–9pm.
The Ritz Near *Safari Garden Hotel*, off Atlantic Rd ☏ 924205. A friendly, casual place in a small courtyard, catering for tourists wanting a change from more formal hotel restaurants, and best-known for steak. Daily 10am–late.
Weezo's Kairaba Ave ☏ 496918. Casual but upmarket, Fajara's most stylish restaurant serves contemporary European dishes at lunchtime; by night it's part cocktail bar, part Mexican restaurant, part gourmet restaurant. Expensive but outstanding. Restaurant Tues–Sun 11.30am–3pm & 7–11pm; bar open till late. Closed Mon.

Kotu

Kotu Point Beach Bar and Restaurant Kotu Point, near the *Palma Rima*. One of the best beach bars in the resort area, and one of the simplest, on a quiet stretch of good sand where you can eat the freshest fish around; beer, soft drinks and palm wine are good value too. Daily 9am–late, happy hour Sun 5–7pm followed by a barbecue with live drum show.
Sailor Beach Bar and Restaurant Kotu Beach, next to Fajara Craft Market. One of the better beachside restaurants, but not expensive, and good for fish, plus freshly squeezed juice. Daily 10am–11.30pm; live music every evening except Thurs.

Kololi: around the Palma Rima Hotel

Jazziz Palma Rima Rd ☏ 462175. Ground-floor bar/restaurant and live-music venue beneath *Calabash* nightclub, with jazz, blues, Afro-beat and highlife on Fridays, and salsa and reggae on Saturdays. Recommended.
Mirroz Jungle Farida's Arcade, Palma Rima Rd. Masks and spears adorn this sleek little bar, very good for cocktails, and with lager on draught.

The Sushi House Farida's Arcade, Palma Rima Rd. An atmospheric Asian-American restaurant serving sushi, grills (*teppanyaki*, *teriyaki*), seafood *tempura*, and *shabushabu* fondue; there's also a good wine list. Recommended. Above-average prices.

Zizi's Café-Creperie Farida's Arcade, Palma Rima Rd. Creperie and coffee bar in a class of its own, with excellent sweet and savoury crepes, salads, good wine, fresh juices and great coffee. Open till late: Mon, Thurs & Fri from 11am, Tues & Wed from 5pm, Sat & Sun from 10am.

Kololi: around the Senegambia Hotel

Ali Baba's Corner of Senegambia Rd. The Lebanese-run terrace bar and restaurant is a perennially popular hangout, though the cooking's not great – the garden restaurant behind (also *Ali Baba's*, entrance round the corner) is a much better option, with a good house band every night. Daily till 1am; band 9pm–11.30pm.

Aquarius Near the casino ☎460247. Sleekly international cocktail bar and disco. Just about big enough to dance; popular with tourists and smart young Gambian business. Daily till 3am.

Coco Beach *Kololi Beach Club.* A cut above most beach restaurants, with light European-style options for lunch and a more elaborate and expensive evening menu. Recommended.

GTS Restaurant Senegambia Rd. On the edge of the Senegambia action but definitely worth seeking out, this characterful restaurant has a relaxed atmosphere and good simple food (African and European) at extremely reasonable prices.

Paradiso Senegambia Rd. This ordinary-looking place on the tourist strip serves the best pizzas in The Gambia, plus the usual standards – steak, chicken, seafood, pasta – at keen prices. They do take-aways – perfect for pizza on the beach.

Spy Bar Near the *Senegambia Hotel*. Once the Senegambia's most happening venue, presently in decline after increasing hassle from hustlers. House, garage and West African music; occasional live music sessions. Daily 9pm–4am, entry fee at weekends.

Tao Senegambia Rd. The Gambia's only Thai restaurant, with pan-Asian influences. It's very popular with tourists, but flavourings are a little heavy-handed, and the staff tend to be brusque. Daily 7.30–10.30pm.

Kololi Village and Manjai Kunda

Mama's Kololi Village. An excellent local restaurant with a cheerful, shaded roadside terrace, serving simple food (omelettes, yassa chicken, great breakfasts and buffets) at low prices. Not to be confused with *Mama's* in Fajara.

Mannjai Lodge Manjai Kunda ☎463414. The courtyard bar at this hotel is occasionally the venue for live music sessions featuring big names from the Gambian and Senegalese scene, drawing an upmarket Gambian crowd. The sound system isn't great, but there's a mellow, appreciative atmosphere to the place.

Rasta Garden On the main road through Kololi Village. Synonymous in the area with rastas, reggae and ragga, this popular open-air club with occasional live music is a great place to dance under the stars or just chill out with the locals. Entrance fee at weekends.

Village Gallery Kololi Village. The garden courtyard outside this interesting art gallery is a restaurant, serving simple and cheap but good daily specials such as grilled chicken or fish.

Serrekunda

Afra Citizen Mosdolly Mosque Rd. Cavelike *afra* shop run by Mauritanians; the setting may look medieval but their barbecued lamb is as good as it gets. Daily, evenings only till late.

Jokor Westfield Junction. The best club and live-music venue in the area, primarily a hangout for fast-living Gambians, but friendly and relaxed – visitors rarely feel out of place. The mood is different every night, depending on whether they're playing African, Caribbean or European music; you dance under the stars in a garden with trees laced with fairy lights. Nightly till late.

Youth Monument Bar and Restaurant Westfield Junction. Unlikely location, at one of The Gambia's busiest road junctions – but this casual, low-key place is excellent for a beer, a simple cheap meal (good kebabs and grills) or a coffee. Open all day, and busy as a pre-club venue for *Jokor*, nearby.

Banjul and area listings

Airlines Air Guinée, 17 OAU Boulevard, Banjul ☎227585; Air Sénégal International, Ecowas Ave, corner of Mandela St, Banjul ☎202117; Bellview

Airlines, 16 Kairaba Ave, Kanifing ☎373606; Gambia International Airlines, Satellite House, Banjul ☎223702 & Midway Centre, Kairaba Av,

Kanifing ☎374100; Ghana Airways, 10 Nelson Mandela St, Banjul ☎226913; Sierra Leone National Airlines, ☎397551; SN Brussels Airlines, 97 Kairaba Ave, Fajara ☎496301

Airport For details of flight arrivals and departures, call ☎473000.

American Express Gamtours Kanifing Industrial Estate, Serrekunda ☎392259 or 392505 (Mon–Fri 9am–5pm)

Banks and exchange Standard Chartered, 8 ECOWAS Ave, Banjul; Senegambia area, Kololi; Kairaba Ave, Serrekunda; Atlantic Rd, Bakau. IBC Bank, Liberation Ave, Banjul; Atlantic Rd, Bakau; Sayerr Jobe Ave, Serrekunda. Trust Bank, 3–4 ECOWAS Ave, Banjul; Sait Matty Rd, Bakau; Banjul International Airport, Yundum; Sayerr Jobe Ave, Serrekunda.

Bike rental You can rent bikes at around D80/half-day, D120/day from stands in each hotel zone. You can also buy them in town, but they're expensive at D1500–4000. You can forgo the benefits of exercise under a hot sun by renting a quad bike: Quest Quad Trekking, on Palma Rima Road (between *Abi's Restaurant* and *Churchill's Pub*; ☎981074) offers self-drive or bush and beach safaris with a qualified instructor on 125cc Yamaha Breezes.

Bird-watching Bird guides sometimes meet and wait for clients on the Kotu Stream Bridge, Kotu; another common meeting place is the Education Centre at Abuko Nature Reserve (see p.291). The Gambia Birding Group (ⓦwww.gambiabirding.org) is a good source of information and advice on guides and other ornithological matters. Birds of The Gambia (☎936122, ⓔbirdsofthegambia@hotmail.com) offer private bird-watching safaris for specialists and keen beginners, run by the renowned British ornithologist Clive Barlow, author of the region's most authoritative field guide. The following are also highly experienced in guiding: Mass Cham, c/o *Senegambia Hotel* (☎462717); Wally Faal, Serrekunda (☎372103); and Solomon Jallow, based at *Lamin Lodge* (☎907694, ⓔhabitatafrica @hotmail.com).

Books Timbooktoo, Kairaba Ave, Fajara, on the corner of Garba Jahumpa Rd, is the most useful general bookshop; it also has a branch at Banjul International Airport. There are small selections of books for sale at supermarkets and hotel shops.

Car rental AB Rent a Car (☎460926, ⓦwww.abrent-gambia.com; Mon–Fri 8am–6pm, Sat 8am–12.30pm), is the most reputable of the independent agencies, with an office near the *Senegambia Hotel*; rates are reasonable, with reductions for longer periods. Drivers are D250 per

day. Hertz, Banjul International Airport ☎473156; Bakoteh ☎390041 – rates are high, from $73/day for a Toyota saloon to $145/day for a Toyota Land Cruiser; drivers are D100–150 per day. West African Tours ☎495258 or 495532, ⓦwww.westafricantours.com, hire out Land Rovers with drivers and guides.

Couriers DHL, Independence Drive, Banjul (☎223899). Alternatively, take your items, unwrapped, to Banjul International Airport the day before a flight to London; call ahead on ☎472405. Fedex, c/o Saga Express, Kanifing ☎472405 or 472301.

Crafts and souvenirs Good *bengdulas* include the one on Atlantic Road, where you can watch craftsmen at work, and the one on the corner of Bertil Harding Highway, Kololi, good for bespoke leather items. Also along Atlantic Road are tourist-oriented clothing shops and stalls selling West African-style dresses, trousers and skirts, and batik hangings. For more batik and tie-dye, there's Serrekunda's famous "batik factory", Musu Kebba Drammeh's place in Dippa Kunda, signposted off Mosque Rd, and a workshop, Gena Bes, near the old Katchikally Cinema in Bakau (☎495068), where you can see the whole process in action, and even join a one-day workshop to do it yourself. There are crafts, curios and textiles from all over West Africa at the highly recommended African Living Art Centre, Garba Jahumpa Rd, Bakau; the African Heritage Gallery, Atlantic Rd, Bakau; and, close together on Sayerr Jobe Ave, Serrekunda, Bamboo, Samory, and the African Art Collection. The Village Gallery, Kololi Village, sells contemporary West African art. Finally, there's a drum factory in Manjai Kunda where craftsmen make and carve drums; prices start at under £10/$15 and can go up to £100/$150 for something very special.

Cultural centres The Alliance Franco-Gambienne, Kairaba Avenue (☎375418). French cultural-exchange centre with live music sessions, also art exhibitions, a library (daily 10.30am–6.30pm), a recording studio, French language classes, and English and French film nights.

Dentist Swedent, signposted off Bertil Harding Highway on the opposite side from *Palma Rima Hotel* ☎461212 (Mon–Fri 9am–6pm, Sat 10am–1pm).

Embassies and consulates France, Ecole Française, Atlantic Rd, Kairaba Ave end ☎495487; Germany, Independence Drive, Banjul ☎227783; Ghana, 18 Mosque Rd, Latrikunda ☎391599; Guinea, 78 Daniel Goddard St, Banjul ☎226862; Guinea-Bissau, Atlantic Rd, Bakau, near the Standard Chartered bank ☎494854;

Mali, consul c/o VM Company Ltd, Cherno Adama Bah St, Banjul ☎226942 (though visas can't be issued here); Netherlands, c/o Shell Company, Macoumba Jallow St, Banjul ☎227437; Nigeria, 52 Garba Jahumpa Rd, Bakau ☎495803; Senegal, Off Kairaba Ave, Fajara ☎373752; Sierra Leone, OAU Blvd, Banjul ☎228206; USA, Kairaba Ave, Fajara ☎392856, 392858, 391971; UK, 48 Atlantic Rd, Fajara ☎495133 or 495134 or 495578.

Emergencies Banjul police station ☎223146; Bakau police station ☎495739; Kotu police station ☎463351, fire service ☎18. For medical emergencies, see "Hospitals" below.

Film processing Saffideen, Photo Star and Photo Express have labs in Banjul and Serrekunda. You'll pay around D300 per 36-exposure film; the quality is variable.

Hospitals and clinics The Lamtoro Clinic (☎460934), near the *Senegambia Beach Hotel*, is highly rated but pricey; the Royal Victoria Hospital, Banjul (☎228223 or 228227) has outpatient facilities. Westfield Clinic, Westfield Rd, Serrekunda ☎392213 and the Momodou Musa Memorial Clinic (Banjul ☎224320, Serrekunda ☎371683) are recommended for malaria treatment. The Medical Research Council, Fajara (☎495442) has a British nurse on duty. The British High Commission nurse, Sheelagh Fowler (☎495133, mobile ☎994785), runs a clinic Mon & Wed 8–10am & 4.30–5.30pm, Tue & Thurs 8–10am, Fri 10am–noon only.

Internet access There are plenty of Internet cafés in the resort area, with new ones springing up all the time.

Music lessons One way to become involved in Gambian culture is to spend time with a *jali* or *griot* – a traditional musician – learning the art of playing the *kora*, *balafon* or drums (such as the *djembé*), or singing and dancing. The following contacts, all based in or near the resorts, can provide lessons, or put you in touch with musicians. Alagi M'Bye (☎950030), the *kora* player who runs Maali's Music School in Nema Kunku, between Serrekunda and Sukuta, offers *kora* lessons to visitors; the music school itself is a ground-breaking project whereby the children of local non-*jali* families have the opportunity to learn music. Foday Suso (☎934760) is a talented and charismatic musician running a new residential music project in Brufut on the coast just southwest of Bijilo. The *Boucarabou* guesthouse in south Kololi (see p.284, or book through Cool Running Tours ✺www.cool-running-tours.de) specializes in setting up music and dance workshops and jam sessions for individuals and groups, while the

Safari Garden Hotel (see p.281) can recommend good *djembé* and dance teachers in Fajara and has a weekly Gambian dance-aerobics session. Residential music workshops or individual *djembé* tuition in Bakau, with a UK-based musician, can be arranged through Drum Doctors (UK ☎01373 /831171, ✺www.realafrica.net); drum lessons can also be arranged at the drum factory in Manjai Kunda (see "Crafts and souvenirs", p.288). Otherwise, the town of Brikama (see p.292), home to many talented *jalis*, is a good place to make enquiries, especially about *kora* lessons; you may be able to stay in your teacher's family compound.

Pharmacy Banjul Pharmacy has Banjul outlets on Independence Drive (☎227470) and Liberation Ave (☎227648), plus further afield at Sayerr Jobe Rd, London Corner, Serrekunda (☎391053) and on Kairaba Ave (☎390189). Kairaba Pharmacy is on Independence Drive, Banjul (☎225787) and at London Corner, Serrekunda (☎290839).

Post offices and telephones The GPO, Russell St, Banjul (Mon–Fri 8.30am–noon & 2–4pm, Sat 8.30am–noon) is the country's main post office and the best place to have mail sent to you poste restante. There are other post offices on Atlantic Rd, Bakau, and off Kairaba Ave, Serrekunda. There are Gamtel offices on Russell St, Banjul; Atlantic Rd, Bakau (opposite the *African Village Hotel*); at the bottom of Kairaba Ave, Serrekunda; and near the *Senegambia Hotel*. Private telecentres are widely scattered around the urban area.

Sports and outdoor activities The Fajara Club has an 18-hole golf course (daily 7am–7.30pm; ☎495456). Greens fees are D200 per player per day, plus clubs and caddies if required. Temporary membership (D100/day, D400/week) gives access to their clubhouse, swimming pool, tennis courts and other facilities. The Gambia Watersports Centre at the *Atlantic Hotel* in Banjul (☎765765) offers jet-ski hire, parascending, waterskiing and various boat rides. Lama Barry (☎776689) can arrange horse riding along the Kombos beaches for D250/hr.

Supermarkets The resort area has supermarkets and minimarkets selling imported food, toiletries, wine and spirits, household goods and newspapers, along Kairaba Ave, at Cape Point, and in Bakau, Kotu and the Senegambia area, Kololi. Most open Mon–Sat 8.30am–7.30pm, Sun 10am–2pm; some close later, especially in the hotel zones. Many petrol stations also have minimarkets. Banjul has no supermarkets as such, just a couple of small grocery stores.

Travel agents and tour operators The Gambia Experience at the *Senegambia Hotel*, Kololi

(☎463867), act as agent for charter flights to the UK. For other flight bookings and general flight information, try Banjul Travel Agency, ECOWAS Ave, Banjul (☎228813); IPC Travel, 16 Kairaba Ave (☎375677, ✉ipctravel@qanet.gm); or Continental Travels, 70B Daniel Goddard St, Banjul (☎224058).

There are plenty of Gambian tours available – considering just the areas around Banjul and the resorts (see pp.290–297), there are offerings like "Gambian Safari" (Abuko Nature Reserve), "Bush and Beach" (the coast west of Kololi) and "Roots" (Juffureh). To book yourself on an organized trip, ask at the excursions office if you're staying at a resort hotel, otherwise you could contact the following firms: African Adventure Tours (☎497313, ✉adventure@gambianet.gm) includes an unusual "Roots by Land" trip in its itineraries; Gambia River Excursions (☎497603,

🌐www.gre.gm) specialize in upriver boat trips, including cruises between Tendaba and Fatoto, and mangrove creek boat trips; Paradise Tours (☎494088 or 920201, ✉trawallyfoday @hotmail.com) arrange visits to *Madiyana Lodge* on Jinack Island, by *pirogue*; West African Tours (☎495258, 🌐www.westafrican tours.com) is a well-established and reliable firm, an ideal first port of call for bespoke trips as well as offering many popular excursions in the Kombos and upcountry. Also worth trying, with a good range of options, are Discovery Tours (☎495551, 🌐www.discoverytours.gm); Gambia Tours (☎462601, 🌐www.gambiatours.gm) and RM Tours (☎462226, 🌐www.rmtours.gm).

Visa extensions Immigration office, 21 OAU Boulevard, Banjul ☎228611

Around Banjul and the resorts

While many hotel guests end up on organized excursions to the places detailed in this section (see above for some recommended operators), it's easy enough and considerably more satisfying to take off on your own explorations in the coastal region.

The Tanbi Wetlands

Southwest of Banjul, the **mangroves** of the **Tanbi Wetlands** are beautiful, eerie and surprisingly tall – up to 20m – and their birdlife is prolific and fairly spectacular. Fiddler **crabs** beckon maniacally on every mudbank, gathering in silent, jostling droves as the boat approaches. The quicksilver, dun-coloured hopping things are **mud-skippers** – fish seemingly intent on becoming terrestrial – which always seem to have gone by the time you've noticed them. Occasional, and odder, inhabitants of the mangrove creeks are **monkeys**, bounding through the foliage, presumably taking refuge from persecutors on the farm plots inland. Hippos, incidentally, don't circulate this far downstream – though this isn't because the brine interferes with their buoyancy control (hippos live in salt water off the coast of Guinea-Bissau), but because of over-hunting in the past.

Lamin Lodge, reached up the snaking Lamin *bolon* – a tributary of the Gambia River – is the usual destination for boat trips to the wetlands. It's a large, triple-storey wooden pile built over the water at the creek head, which does food and refreshments for visitors – though if you arrive unexpectedly this may take some time to prepare. *Lamin Lodge* is a fine place to come by road, too, early in the morning, when you can watch the comings and goings of bird and human life in the *bolon*, and perhaps rent a *pirogue* by the hour to nose round the waterways. Besides the lodge, another, more distant, destination is the village of **Mandinari**, situated near rice fields and seasonally lush jungle foliage, jewelled with a mass of birdlife that makes the creek look dead in comparison. Mandinari has one or two small shops where you can get soft drinks and something to eat.

Practicalities

In the high season half-day **boat trips** in the Tanbi Wetlands can be arranged in just about any hotel lobby for around £20–25/$32–40 per person. The cheapest way of arranging the trip is to get a group together and fix up boat rental yourself with the fishermen on the shore close to the **Barra ferry terminal** in Banjul, or with the boat owners at **Denton Bridge**, the bridge that carries the Banjul–Serrekunda highway across Oyster Creek, connecting Banjul to the mainland. Prices depend on demand and what the boatmen reckon they could earn from a day with the nets, but don't expect much of an outing for less than D300 per person, maybe substantially more in the high season. While it's always useful to have a guide acting as intermediary, try to establish exactly what is going to be provided and make sure the crew know what they're about. Being stranded up a dead-end *bolon* at low tide, miles from anywhere, in the middle of the day – or worse, with the sun going down – may give you more of the mangrove experience than you want. Take plenty of water and food, clothes and hats to cover up with, and binoculars.

By road, *Lamin Lodge* is signposted down a two-kilometre dirt track off the main airport–Banjul road at the village of **Lamin**, close to Abuko Nature Reserve. Bush taxis run from Banjul to Mandinari, which is about 10km from Lamin and the main road.

Abuko Nature Reserve

Certainly one of The Gambia's best bits, the celebrated **Abuko Nature Reserve** (daily 8am–6.30pm; D31.50) is less than two square kilometres in extent, but within its carefully protected confines it preserves one of the last surviving examples of tropical riverine forest (also known as gallery forest) in the country. Whether you're an overlander or a Gambia holiday-maker, it's a must, and it's easily explored on foot.

Lamin stream (the tip of Lamin *bolon*) and its stunning necklace of forest was noticed in 1967 by Eddie Brewer, father of The Gambia's conservation movement, and was fenced the following year. The barrier is there to keep domestic animals, hunters and woodcutters out, rather than anything in – Abuko's three-hundred-odd bird species and dozens of varieties of small mammals and reptiles need no encouragement to stay.

Apart from pond dredging, path clearing and hide building, the reserve is left more or less as it was found. While the reserve includes forest and Guinea savanna, the strongest impression is created by the magnificent **gallery forest trees**, spiralling up from the webbed fingers of their buttress roots through a canopy of intertwined trailing creepers and epiphytes to create dark cathedrals of evergreen vegetation.

The park

The whole walk around the marked trail through the reserve takes a couple of hours, but it could easily turn into half a day depending on your interest in the various bird species (more often heard than seen) and your curiosity about the more bizarre life forms on the forest floor. Early morning and late afternoon tend to yield the most wildlife sightings, as creatures take refuge from the midday heat.

You can expect to see **patas**, **vervet monkeys** and **western red colobus**, as well as a high number of – harmless – **monitor lizards** which dart across the paths and claw their way through the undergrowth. Most are small, but they can grow as long as two metres. With patience, it's normally also possible to spot **crocodiles** at the Bambo pool from the lookout at the Education Centre. Watch for two distinct species: the larger, pale Nile crocodile, and the small, darker dwarf crocodile, which is critically endangered. **Snakes** are infrequently observed: the reserve boasts green mamba, puff adder, royal and African rock python, forest and spitting cobras, among others.

At the top of the circuit is the unprepossessing **Animal Orphanage**, a rehabilitation centre set up by the Department of Parks and Wildlife Management in 1997. Primates and parrots form the vast majority of animals taken in, and those

Abuko birdlife

Well over **three hundred species of birds** are the chief fauna delight of Abuko. This is the closest patch of tropical forest to Europe, and each winter it attracts thousands of bird-watchers as well as a host of **palearctic migrants** (willow warblers, chiff chaffs, black caps, melodious warblers) to swell the numbers of its native species. Most obvious are the water birds – a couple of photo hides overlooking the stream and pools are usually occupied by murmuring birders. Look out for **kingfishers** (blue-breasted, Senegal, malachite and pied), the "umbrella fishing" **black heron** and two great bird-watcher's sights – the **painted snipe** (the male incubates the eggs) and the stunning **red-bellied paradise flycatcher**, with its thirty-centimetre tail feathers. You can generally see **hammerkops** around the pool at the start of the trail; in flight, their swept-back crest of feathers and pointed beaks make them look exactly like miniature pterodactyls, and their huge nests, courtship displays and trumpet calls are remarkable. In the clearings, wait to see **fanti roughwinged swallows** and the occasional **shikra** darting through the light and, above the forest canopy, **hooded vultures**, **black kites**, swooping **bee-eaters** and **rollers**, and maybe **palm nut vultures**.

unsuitable for release are on display to the public alongside the orphanage's other permanent residents – lions, hyenas and baboons.

Practicalities

The excursions organized by tour operators, sometimes more than thirty people at a time, are to be avoided if you're keen to get the most from your visit: shouting guides and chattering crowds shatter the tranquillity of the place. The reserve is situated right by the main road from Serrekunda to Brikama, and you can take a **bush taxi** bound for Abuko, Lamin or Brikama from Banjul or Serrekunda to the reserve's front gate easily enough. The **office** by the front gate has some good booklets and leaflets about the trees and wildlife, and you can leave bags or bicycles safely. Take something to eat and drink if you intend to stay for a while; alternatively, the café near the Animal Orphanage serves snacks and soft drinks. Bring mosquito repellent to the reserve, especially during the rains.

Brikama

If you leave the Serrekunda conurbation on the south-bank road into the interior, the first town you hit is The Gambia's third largest, **BRIKAMA**, a divisional capital and a gateway to the upcountry provinces. It's famous for its rich musical heritage – many Gambian traditional musicians come from here – and its woodcarvers' market, a routine stop on tourist excursions to the area. It also has the beginnings of a vibrant club and gig scene: a new sister club to *Jokor*, the legendary Serrekunda club, is pulling in crowds from all over the Kombos.

The only regular lodgings in Brikama are at the *Domorr Deema Mini Hotel* on Mosque Road (☎903302; ❷). A simple place with a local feel, it has four very small rooms with fan and shared shower; it's clean but can be noisy. There's also a small restaurant where you can sit at the streetside table and eat omelettes, chicken, steak, or rice and sauce at low prices, but for simple food you're better off heading for the fast-food places and chop houses scattered around the main road and market. The best place to eat is *Kambeng Restaurant*, which is excellent value for grilled fish and other standards. It's outside *Jokor*, Brikama's swish new **nightclub**, on the main road into town from the Serrekunda highway. There are two **bars** to quench your thirst: *Big Ens Bar and Restaurant*, Gunjur Road, an echoey, garagelike space that's open 24 hours a day, and *Bantang Bantaba* at the Methodist Mission, Sanyang Road, serving *wonjo*, sandwiches and snacks in the

daytime; tour groups sometimes stop here, so local kids
hassle visitors.

Further south, there's a
fifteen-kilometre track from
Brikama down to the
Senegalese **border** at Darsilami,
while the main road to
Senegal branches off right at
Mandinaba, a small place
distinguished by a large, four-
towered mosque.

Makasutu Culture Forest

Five kilometres east of
Brikama (turn left at the
totem pole after the Botrop
School and follow the roads
around to the right until you
find it), **Makasutu Culture
Forest** is a private forest park
(daily 8am–dusk; D350 half-
day, D400 per day if arriving
independently). Run by a
couple of English entrepreneurs, it's The Gambia's best-
known ecotourism project.
The forest edges a beautiful
bolon, and groups of tourists
visit for the day for organized

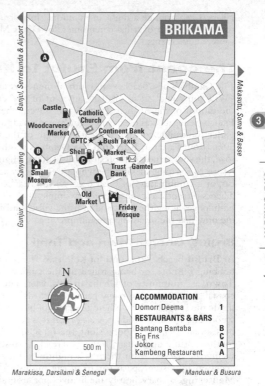

BRIKAMA

Banjul, Serrekunda & Airport

Makasutu, Soma & Basse

Sanyang

Gunjur

Castle
Catholic Church
Woodcarvers' Market
Continent Bank
GPTC
Bush Taxis
Shell
Market
Small Mosque
Trust Bank
Gamtel
Old Market
Friday Mosque

N

ACCOMMODATION
Domorr Deema   1
RESTAURANTS & BARS
Bantang Bantaba   B
Big Fns   C
Jokor   A
Kambeng Restaurant   A

0   500 m

Marakissa, Darsilami & Senegal

Manduar & Busura

bird-watching, canoe trips and forest walks, with a break in the middle of the day
for lunch in an impressively designed restaurant area, while local Jola women put
on a spirited show of drumming and dancing. Day-trips from the resort hotels,
including transport, entrance and a visit to Brikama, typically cost £29/$47.

There's a sizeable new luxury bush lodge, *Mandina Lodge* (book through
Ⓦwww.gambia.co.uk; ⑧), on the far side of the site, which is opening in stages.
Stunningly situated and designed, this is without a doubt The Gambia's most attractive place to stay, with a gorgeous, curvy swimming pool and accommodation for
just eight guests, in two lodges built on stilts over the *bolon*, and two more floating
like anchored houseboats on the water.

Tumani Tenda

Around 20km east of Brikama, **TUMANI TENDA**, a Jola hamlet next to Kafuta
bolon, has an enterprising community-run ecotourism project based on the *campement* system in Senegal. A visit to, or stay at, *Kachokorr Camp* (☎462057 or 903662,
Ⓔtumanitenda@hotmail.com; ②), is a great experience for those seriously interested in immersing themselves in village life. The clean and very simple accommodation is outside the village, near the creek, in thatched huts. Some visitors come
here just to enjoy the complete peace – the camp itself has no electricity or phone
and vehicles seldom come anywhere near here. There are plenty of activities to
choose from, though (D200 per group per activity), including guided tours of the
school, plantations and vegetable gardens, on foot or by cart; walking in the community forest, where medicinal plants are gathered; exploring the mangrove creeks
by dugout canoe; oyster gathering; batik making and tie dying. In the evening, the

villagers can arrange a night of traditional Jola drumming and dancing, including the re-enactment of tribal ceremonies, for D500. Meals are provided using locally sourced ingredients.

The coast from Brufut to Kartong

The Gambia's best beaches are south of the resort area. Given transport, preferably 4WD, you could get to virtually any part of **the coast** between Cape Point and the mouth of the Allahein (San Pedro) River, where Anglo-Gambia finishes and Franco-Senegal takes over. And if you're equipped for a few days' self-sufficiency, it's perfectly possible to walk the entire length of the Gambian coastline – less than 50km from Fajara to **Kartong**, The Gambia's southernmost village. A new tarmac road, the southern extension of Bertil Harding Highway, runs all the way from the resorts to Kartong, making the whole area quickly accessible by bicycle, taxi, rented car, or a combination of bush taxis: all the beaches are within 3km of the road. There's presently a scattering of very simple, appealing beach lodges, beach bars and bush lodges along the coast and near the villages inland, and the options are increasing now that the infrastructure is improving.

Brufut, Ghana Town and Tanji

At **Brufut** beach, 7km south of Kololi, you'll see brightly-painted fishing *pirogues* bobbing offshore, or being rolled up the sand. Next to Brufut village is **Ghana Town**, a community of Ghanaian fish driers and smokers, not an uncommon coastal phenomenon in many parts of West Africa. If you're curious you can stoop inside the long, low huts where the racks of blackening fish cure over smouldering wood. The finished product – *bonga fish* (basically kippers, and often good) – can be seen all over the region. Along the forested and palm-planted stretch of track south of Brufut and Ghana Town, you're likely to see several species of monkeys – saving the harvest from them is a nightmare for farmers. Above the beach and accessed by a steep path (or from the highway) is the holy site of **Senneh-Mentering**, a marvellously meditative spot around a craggy old baobab tree on the clifftop, the air wafting with incense burned by the incumbent marabout. Local people come here for cures, consultations and peace, and it's a good place to visit at sundown.

Just north of the busy fishing beach at **TANJI** (also spelt Tanje), 12km southwest of Kololi, is the **Tanji River Karinti Bird Reserve** (daily 8am–dusk; D31.50), The Gambia's only gazetted bird reserve, with a rich combination of habitats including mangrove, woodland and lagoons. The reserve includes the Bijol Islands, the country's only offshore islands, and a breeding colony for seabirds, which can be visited by arangement with the Department of Parks and Wildlife Management at Abuko (Oct–Mar only; D200 per person; ☏375888). Highly recommended is a visit to the **Tanje Village Museum** (daily 9am–5pm; D25), by the highway south of Tanji village and fishing centre, which gives interesting insights into traditional Gambian village life and the workings of the family in an authentic traditional compound, along with displays of traditional foods, dyes and pesticides, and a nature trail. The museum also has a few basic roundhouses (☏371007; ❷) for those interested in participating in the goings-on at the museum, which include traditional music, weaving and metalworking sessions. Also in Tanji village is the area's most comfortable bush lodge, the *Paradise Inn Lodge* (☏922444 or 912559, ⓦwww.tanji.nl.paradise; ❸), which has roundhouses scattered in woodland next to the Tanji River, and is very popular with bird-watchers. Alternatively, deeper in the backstreets of Tanji village is the *Kairoh Garden Guest House* (☏903526, ⓔkairohgarden@hotmail.com; ❷), a peaceful retreat with simple rooms (some s/c), about 5km from Tanji beach. *Nyanya Safari Lodge* (☏394759 or (☏797251; ❷), on the beach and overlooking the mouth of the river, has a few basic rooms and is a scenic place to enjoy big platefuls of Gambian stews.

Tujering, Sanyang and Gunjur

TUJERING, about 7km south of Tanji and some 4km inland, is a pleasant old village that owes nothing of its character to tourism or colonialism: whitewashed mudstone houses and a central crossroads with meeting place, mosque and market.

The long beach nearest the village of **SANYANG**, 12km from Tanji, is one of the best in the area, and is sometimes called Paradise Beach – a broad, smooth sweep of firm sand backed by coconut palms, with a few mellow beach bars. North of the fishing boats is *Osprey Beach Bar*, which caters for tourist groups as well as independent visitors. South of here is the brightest enterprise is the *Rainbow Beach Bar*, which serves excellent fish, has a beach shower, and sometimes lights a campfire in the evening. In bushland about 2km inland from here is *Sanyang Nature Camp* (☎945730; ❷), a quiet, friendly lodge with small but attractive rooms in thatched roundhouses in a huge, dusty garden compound.

Continuing south, you approach the biggest focus of Kombo South District, **GUNJUR** beach – a messy, active seafront where fish are more important than tourists and you'll probably be ignored. On the point north of the fishing boats is *Sankule Kunda Beach Hotel* (☎486098), a relaxing bar/restaurant with a beautiful beachside garden, and accommodation planned, that's a good place for impromptu drumming sessions. To the south is another drummers' hangout, *Kaira Kunda Bar and Restaurant*, a friendly shack-type beach bar serving cheap drinks and couscous or barbecued fish. In a wonderful bay to the south is *Rasta Kunda* (✉www.rastakunda.com; ❷), with simple rooms in huts and a large beachside bar playing non-stop reggae.

Kartong

Right on a glorious stretch of beach 2km north of the village of **KARTONG** is *Boboi Beach Lodge* (☎776736, ✉www.gambia-adventure.com; ❷), with a few very basic roundhouses and room to camp in a small palm-shaded compound. Nearby, in the bush on the inland side of the highway, the **Gambian reptile farm** (✉www.gambianreptiles.bizhosting.com; D35) is run as a small education and research centre, open to visitors – you can get close to a good representation of Gambian snake species here. Closer to the village, high on a hill overlooking the the sand dunes, is *Kartong Folonko Rest House* (❷), which has a couple of guest rooms and cooks up good spaghetti and espresso. The attractions of the village itself include a crocodile pool, similar to the Katchikali pool at Bakau, though a good deal more atmospheric and sacred-looking (there's no money to pay for a start), set in a deep, shady grove. There are reputed to be a fair number of crocs, though why they stay in this lily-choked swamp is hard to imagine. Women from both Kartong's communities – Muslim Mandinka and Christian Karoninka (Karoninka is a Mandinka dialect) – visit to pray and ask favours on Monday and Friday mornings. The woodland and dunes on this side of the village are great for bird-watching.

If you have your own transport, you'll be able to drive **south of Kartong** to the last extremity of Gambian territory, a police checkpoint near the mouth of the Allahein River. A short drive from the checkpoint, you can turn right towards Kartong's isolated fishing beach, and left towards the riverside smokehouses where shark meat is laid out to dry.

Barra, Albreda, Juffureh and James Island

The visit to **Juffureh** used to be an inevitable business, when the *Roots* industry was at its peak and thousands of African-Americans made the pilgrimage to see the village they believed **Alex Haley** had been describing in his book. So convincing was the hype that the author himself seems to have believed the same thing – pictures of Haley with an elderly Kinte descendant are part of the myth of modern Gambia, used to boost the small country's respectability on the world stage. As an excuse for a trip to the **north bank**, the visit to the supposed birthplace of Kunta Kinte is still an enjoyable day out, but unless you do one of the organized *Roots* tours you'll find **transport** long-winded. Cycling is a possibility, but the seventy-odd kilometres there and back can be hard work, despite the flat earth roads, and well-nigh impossible if the roads are wet (if you rent a car, be sure it's 4WD if there's any chance it's going to rain). There are only a few bush taxis a day from Barra to Juffureh (D15).

If you're travelling under your own steam, your initial target is the slow 7am or faster 8am **ferry** from Banjul to Barra (see box, p.273), a wonderful crossing at this time of day, with dolphins often plunging in the bow-wave. **Barra**, the old capital of the Mandinka kingdom of the same name, no longer has much of interest except for the squat hulk of **Fort Bullen**, neglected on the grassy shore. There's only one hotel hereabouts, the *Barra* by the ferry dock (☎795134; ❶).

Albreda and Juffureh

Albreda, also known as Albadarr, is down on the shore, and still has its old trading house with dangerously leaning walls and an immovable cannon pointing fiercely out over the river. **JUFFUREH**, a short walk away from the river and Albreda's immediate neighbour, isn't distinguished by any such monuments and, apart from a very basic sign, looks much like any other Mandinka village – a gathering of thatched, mud-brick cottages, *bantabas* and goat pens. It's hard to understand why this particular Juffureh (a widespread place name) or the local Kintes (a common Mandinka family name) should have been chosen by Haley as his roots. According to the book, the griot he met here told the same story as the one passed down through his family – but it was a simple and familiar history. It seems Haley had already written his Africa passages when he came here, and his account of Juffureh appears to be unrelated to the location of today's village. In the book, Kunta Kinte is surprised by a slave-raiding party, yet Juffureh is only a few hundred metres from the Gambia River and close by the sites of the trading stations of Albreda and Fort James, which would have been there throughout his childhood. On the other hand, villages can move, and ten generations or so have passed since the young Kunta Kinte went out to collect firewood and never came back. You can't be sure who is taking whom for a ride – the story has been a winner for both Haley and the Juffureh griots – but it's worthwhile participating in the pretence if you've read, and were moved by, the novel.

Most visitors to Juffureh come on an organized tour, on which they are escorted across the village and introduced to members of the Kinte family, believed by Alex Haley to be his distant cousins. If you arrive independently, people will assume you want the same, so make clear right away if you don't. First you pay a few dalasis to the guardian of the Juffureh maintenance fund and make a visit to the *alkalo*. Accompanied by a gang of children, you then proceed on a brief tour, winding up at the **Kintes' compound** to meet whoever's in, usually the senior lady, Binta Kinte, and various sons, daughters and grandchildren. Photos are allowed, but you pay for the right to take them, and to do just about anything in this village. The **Exhibition of the Slave Trade** at the local museum (Mon–Thurs & Sat 10am–5pm, Fri 10am–1pm; D35) is probably the most interesting part of the visit. It mostly consists of display boards, with lots of reading to do, but you'll come away with a good insight into what slavery was all about in this part of the world. There's simple **accommodation** next to the museum at the *Juffureh Rest House* (☎710276 c/o Juffureh Museum; ❶), which is sometimes used as a base for Gambian music workshops organised by the French-run Kunta Kinte Association.

James Island

Less questionable history is out mid-river on **James Island**, though the very ruined ruins of **Fort James** are probably only for enthusiasts; the *pirogue* ride from the shore should cost no more than D50 per person, return. Originally constructed in 1651 by agents of the Duke of Courland (now Latvia and Lithuania), Fort James rode the usual roller coaster of occupations, routings, sackings, desertions and rebuildings. It was seized by **Britain** in 1661 when, in Britain's first imperial exploit in Africa, the Royal Adventurers Of England Trading Into Africa bundled out the Baltic occupants and set themselves up under the Royal Patent of Charles II, buying gold, ivory, peppers, hides and, of course, **slaves** for the American colonies. In one mercantile guise or another, the British and the **French** fought over the fort for more than a century. France held the trading "factory" of Albreda on the shore and continued slaving long after the British had opted for a new role as anti-slavers at the end of the eighteenth century. After 1779 James Island was rarely inhabited, and today the remains of the old walls and the strewn cannon are dominated by a grove of large baobabs.

Jinack Island

North of Barra, **Jinack Island** is part of The Gambia's Niumi National Park, which in turn adjoins the National Parc du Delta du Saloum in Senegal. Together, the parks protect one of the last remaining untouched stands of mangroves in West Africa and, inland, an area of dry woodland and grassland savanna. The shallow off-shore waters provide excellent feeding for terns, gulls and other fish-eating birds, and the park is the stopping-off point and feeding site for seventeen species of war-bler. Other wildlife in the park includes the elusive West African manatee, dolphins, green turtles, hyenas, endangered clawless otters and leopards.

Occasional bush taxis serve Jinack from Barra (D15), dropping you a short *pirogue* ride away from the village of **Jinack Kajata**, on the opposite side of the island from *Madiyana Safari Lodge*, the best place **to stay** on Jinack (book through Paradise Tours, see p.290; ❹). On the seaward side of the island, the lodge is a comfortable and relaxing beach hideaway with fine food and good nature-watching opportuni-ties nearby. The easiest way to get there is to make arrangements with the owners to take you, usually by boat from Banjul: it takes about an hour to cross the estuary and sail up the coast by motorized *pirogue*. On the south side of the village, *Coconut Lodge* has bright, clean, colourful rooms (☎954814 or 908456; ❷), solar electricity, and hammocks slung under the gingerbread-plum trees.

3.2

Upriver Gambia

To travel **upcountry** is to travel upriver: the **Gambia River** is the national life-line and the country's very definition. With its headwaters 500km from Banjul in the Fouta Djalon highlands of Guinea, it snakes down in typically West African fashion, heading any direction but seawards most of the way. While you might expect a frontier feel along the length of the country, there are plenty of short side-tracks off the main road, which quickly get you into districts of creeks, bushland and villages where traditional customs are preserved, more or less intact.

The river's course is paralleled by the **Senegalese frontier**, which was drawn by compass at a cannon-shot's distance from the river bank. Inland, this extraordinary artificiality is madly apparent. Senegal, never more than 10km from the south-bank highway – the only tarred road going upcountry – breathes all around the country, creating an increasing osmosis of Francophone language, customs, food and music. At one point the Dakar–Ziguinchor highway cuts clean across the country, a traverse that, but for border formalities, would take only twenty minutes. Whether the Gambians like it or not, Senegal's influence looks set to increase.

The principal towns of Soma/Mansa Konko, Bansang and Basse are all on the **south bank**, linked by the highway. **Janjanbureh** (previously known as Georgetown) is on Janjanbureh Island, mid-river. The **north bank** is altogether bushier, with no hard-surface roads apart from the two that cross the country into Senegal, little transport or electricity, and only a couple of important centres at **Kerewan** and **Farafenni**. If you've time to explore, it's interesting territory, with much to be discovered and bearable walking distances. The site most often visited on the north bank is **Wassu**, with its strange **stone circles**, reached easily from Janjanbureh and the south-bank highway.

Travel practicalities

Unless you're heading for Tambacounda and the Niokolo-Koba National Park in Senegal, or else down into eastern Guinea, the interior of The Gambia is a bit of a cul-de-sac. Still, it's a relatively easy – and easy-going – district, and if you're just starting your travels in West Africa, not a daunting introduction to the region. As for **river transport**, while the steamers of colonial times are long gone, you can currently book a long-distance excursion by rustic but comfortable *pirogue* from Tendaba, Janjanbureh, Basse or Fatoto, lasting one to four days and including meals, nights on board sleeping under mosquito nets on mattresses on deck, and local visits en route (details from Gambia River Excursions; see p.290).

Road travel up the main tarred route along the south bank is the only other straightforward option. The road is in a decrepit state until you reach Soma (it's decent tarmac from there to Basse), but bush taxis still bomb along at high speeds; there are also two GPTC buses daily in each direction. Renting a car for a few days will get you just about anywhere, though you'll need 4WD to get off the highway during the wet season. Otherwise, to do any sort of diversion you have to hope for an occasional bush taxi, cycle, or walk.

Central Gambia

As you move eastwards from Banjul and the Kombo peninsula, the large concrete-block and corrugated-iron houses that set the scene on the coast are increasingly replaced with more attractive straw thatch and mud-brick compounds. Tripod water pumps – supplied by Saudi Arabia over German bore-holes – become a familiar sight in every village too. In the wet season or after the rains, brilliant emerald **rice fields** mark the shallow wooded valleys inland, and at the end of the growing season in August and September, anti-monkey watchtowers are dotted among the rows of groundnuts and bush on the ridges between.

The ruins at **Brefet**, mentioned in some tourist literature, are all but obscured by vegetation much of the year, and there's nothing to see of the "long-abandoned European trading post" which supposedly exists. Local people know of the site, but they'll be pretty surprised if you make the six-kilometre effort down the sandy track (turn off about 30km from Brikama) to look for it. More ruins at **BINTANG** (turn off at Killy, about 45km from Brikama) are equally invisible, although you can stay overnight, if you don't mind forgoing some comforts. *Bintang Bolon Lodge* (☎929362; ❷) here used to be an enchanting place, built on stilts over the creek, but now looks ready to collapse into the mud; it has a few very basic rooms which are still (just) habitable. The main attraction here is the large *bantaba* restaurant, operating informally. Given a little notice, the staff will prepare a meal from whatever's available locally (fish is, of course, abundant); they can also make arrangements for you to explore Bintang Bolon by canoe. Getting to Bintang can mean a five-kilometre walk from the highway with little chance of a lift, unless you have your own transport or catch one of the two bush taxis which leave Brikama in the early afternoon.

Kanilai

The Jola village of **KANILAI**, 95km southeast of Serrekunda and 6km from the south-bank highway, is the birthplace of President Yahya Jammeh. It's mysteriously hard to find on most pre-1994 maps of The Gambia, but, since Jammeh took control of the country in that year, Kanilai's fortunes have changed radically. What was once an obscure upcountry village with little to distinguish it now has a good access road, a luxury lodge, a large wrestling arena, a game park stocked with imported wildlife, good healthcare facilities, an electricity supply – and a vast presidential palace. The Game Park and Zoo (daily 7–10am & 5–7pm; D25) visitable only by vehicle, won't detain you long – animals are hard to spot in the long grass – but the village is well worth visiting at festival times or during wrestling championships, and is the venue for two days of exuberant celebrations and tribal rituals during The Gambia's biennial International Roots Festival (see p.259).

There's an attractive and upmarket place to **stay** on the edge of the village, *Sindola Safari Lodge* (☎483415, ✉sindola@gamtel.gm or c/o *Kairaba Hotel*, Kololi, see p.278, ❾), with landscaped gardens, a swimming pool and a good restaurant; this is an ideal place for peaceful relaxation, or to use as a base for trips. The lodge can organize fishing and bird-watching excursions, and village visits.

Wrestling

Watching traditional **wrestling** (*lutte traditionelle* in Francophone countries), which goes back to the thirteenth century, is a favourite pastime of the Jola in general, and of President Jammeh in particular. Wrestling teams themselves comprise members of a single tribe, and the Jola are renowned for winning most of the time – for some years the Gambian champion was a native of Kanilai – and for losing with good grace, a sure sign of a true sportsman in Gambian society.

Drumming and whistling teams keep up steady competitive rhythms as the action builds slowly, the first few wrestlers pacing around the court flexing their muscles and psyching themselves up. The referee starts whistling the men into order and gradually the opponents pair off to start their bouts. The **object** is to land the opponent on his back as cleanly as possible. Dust flying, bodies bound with *gris-gris* – powerful amulets – and slicked with sweat and charmed potions to weaken the opponent's grip, this usually takes a few seconds, though bouts can last for several minutes, as contestants bluff and threaten, facing each other with backs bent and hands trailing in the dust to make for a good grip. Contestants are evenly matched, it being forbidden for small wrestlers to take on bigger men, however much the crowd roars its approval. The winner of each bout takes a triumphal turn around the edge of the arena, accompanied by his drum team, and counting on collecting a few tips as he goes (take a pocketful of small change).

Visitors are welcome at wrestling matches, which comprise dozens of bouts in the course of an afternoon; there's a small entrance fee. If you want to take **photos** there's no problem – it's expected – but you'll need a telephoto lens and fast film to capture the excitement as the contest develops and the sun goes down.

Kiang West National Park

The south-bank road turns north over the head of Bintang *bolon*, passing the **Kiang West National Park** (daily 8am–6.30pm; D31.50) to the west. This is one of the wildest, least-explored regions in the country, 110 square kilometres mainly comprised of dry deciduous woodland and Guinea savanna, but also containing mangrove creeks and tidal flats. Bounded to the north by the Gambia River and dissected into three areas by the Jarin, Jali and Nganinkoi *bolons*, the park is one of the most important reservoirs of wildlife in The Gambia, harbouring representatives of most of the remaining mammal species, including sitatunga, bushbuck and duikers, clawless otter, warthog and spotted hyena. West African manatees and dolphins are occasionally seen at Jarin *bolon*. The area also possesses an impressive range of over three hundred bird species, including the threatened brown-necked parrot, 21 birds of prey, all ten species of Gambian kingfisher and the booming ground hornbill.

The park's headquarters are at **DUMBUTO**, where there is guest accommodation in plain, comfortable s/c bungalows (for enquiries and to arrange to be picked up by vehicle, if there's one available, contact the Department of Parks and Wildlife office at Abuko on ☎472888; ❶). The most established base for visits to the park, however, is *Tendaba Camp* (☎541024 or 911088; ❸), in the village of **TENDABA** to the east. Standard excursions from the camp are a jeep safari (enjoyable but dusty and a non-starter for wildlife-watching), and trips in a *pirogue* across the River Gambia to the creeks of Bao Bolon Wetland Reserve, designated a wetland of international importance, and excellent for bird-watching. *Tendaba* was the first upcountry camp to open, in the 1970s, and has well-maintained s/c chalets with mosquito netting. Rooms are sprayed every evening because, as the staff's T-shirts declare: "One million mosquitoes can't be wrong – *Tendaba Camp* is fantastic!" Without your own wheels, you could walk the 5km from Kwinella on the main road, but if you ask around you can probably arrange for a local donkey cart to take you. If you have to hang around at Kwinella for a while, you could look for a group of silk-cotton trees in the village which is the habitual roost and nesting site of hundreds of **pelicans** – cacophonous and an extraordinary sight close up.

An alternative Kiang West base is *Kemoto Hotel* (☎990031 or 460606, ℻460252; ❹), near the village of **Kemoto** at Mootah Point, on an isolated meander of the river at the far western end of a track through the park. This pleasantly laid-back hotel has panoramic views of the river and is located close to some of its most interesting creeks. Rooms are clean and comfortable, and there's a swimming pool.

Toniataba, Soma and Farafenni

Before the trans-Gambian highway's halfway mark at **Soma/Mansa Konko**, you pass the unremarkable village of **TONIATABA**: unremarkable that is, except for the enormous, grass-thatched circular house in the compound of Fatikunda ("Fati's place"). Fatikunda is the home of the Fati family, and the family head, Alhaji Fodali Fati, is one of the district's most senior religious leaders, or marabouts. First constructed in the nineteenth century by Fodali's father Sheikh Othman, the house is believed to be one of the largest traditional homes in The Gambia, at around 60m in circumference. It's not exactly unknown, but nor are the Alhaji's family or his house a tourist attraction, and unless you speak Mandinka you'll probably feel more at ease with a guide to introduce you. Take your shoes off if you're invited in, and come with some gifts – the marabouts expect payment for any kind of consultation. The old man is generally delighted to get visitors. The house itself is of unusual design, its outer wall surrounding an interior house divided into separate rooms. In the middle is an inner sanctum, a private area reserved for family prayers.

A few minutes further down the road you're hit by the trashy, sprawling contrast of **SOMA**, about 160km from Brikama, where there's the opportunity to turn either left over the river into northern Senegal for Kaolack and Dakar, or south into the Casamance district. You can also escape southwards further upriver, but this is the furthest point at which you can easily turn north into Senegal. Soma is just a bustling truck stop, a charmless string of fuel stations, inexpensive restaurants, bars and shops where you can get all sorts of Senegalese imports. Buses stop here, and bush taxis whirl up the dust, collecting passengers for the short ride down to the ferry crossing for the north bank and Farafenni. **Mansa Konko** ("King's Hill"), a couple of kilometres away, is the administrative quarter, quiet and uncommercial in exact proportion to Soma's racket. The best **accommodation** in central Soma is at the headquarters of the Soma Scout Group: the *Kaira Konko Lodge* (☎531453; ❶), on the Serrekunda road, with five breezy rooms, secure and spotlessly kept, though unfortunately there's no generator. The other option in town is *Moses Motel* on the Serrekunda/Trans-Gambian highway junction (☎531462 or 919542; ❶), a Rasta-run place attracting a mixture of Gambians and shoestring travellers. It has a dozen scruffy rooms crammed round a courtyard, and a bar/restaurant and large yard where live music events are occasionally held. At **Pakali Nding**, the hamlet 3km north towards the river, the highly recommended *TransGambia Highway Lodge* (☎531402; ❶) is quiet and a favourite of locally-based NGOs. The large compound provides secure parking, good simple food can be provided on request, and there's a generator. Central Soma is a busy transport stop so there are plenty of chop shops and coffee stands in town.

Across the river is **FARAFENNI**, whose big day is Sunday, when the *lumo* is held. *Eddy's Hotel* is the best-known place to sleep here (☎735225; ❷), with a courtyard that's a pleasant place for a drink, and decent-sized rooms (s/c, some with a/c), though the place badly needs an overhaul. An alternative that's more basic but in better condition is the unpretentious *Ballanghar Motel* (☎735431; ❶). There are a few chop houses on the main street – *Sunn Yai* does great chicken and chips – and the best bar is the unmarked *Assane's*, near the post office, serving Gambian Guinness and cold Senegalese Gazelle beer.

Eastern Gambia

The condition of the south-bank road improves dramatically east of Soma, from potholed oyster-shell mix to hot, black macadam, as it passes through a fairly wild stretch of bush where baboons and other monkeys can be seen. If you're on the water, you can start looking out for **hippos** from this point on, as the estuarine part of the river ceases and the mangroves peter out, allowing them to come ashore at night to graze. The no longer appropriately named Elephant Island in mid-stream appears to be the hippos' lowest grazing ground.

The village of **Buiba** is the site of a long-established traditional curing centre for the mentally ill, but the first real punctuation in the new upriver scene is **PAKALI BA**, 50km from Soma, a village by the Sofaniama *bolon*. It's an attractive place, marked by a ridge of small rocky hills that are surprising in the undulating savanna. Pakali Ba is the source of a fable about a crocodile hunter called Bambo Bojang, who learned to control the Sofanyama crocodiles after being attacked by them; he's now the patron saint of the crocodile (*bambo* in Mandinka), and his descendants live in the area.

As the road heads on through mostly flat and open grasslands, the only place you might want to stop off is at **Jarreng**, 12km further on, where people make an impressive – and very cheap – range of palm beds, chairs and other furniture. The wharf at nearby **Kudang Tenda**, 3km down a sidetrack, is the end-point of the popular boat trips which sail downstream from Janjanbureh, passing the River Gambia National Park on the way.

There's a convenient and particularly comfortable place to stay in this area – the National Agricultural Research Institute (NARI) **resthouse** (☎ & ☎678073; ❸) at **Sapu**, on the riverbank some 110km from Soma and 3km down the slope which lies 2km east of the road village of Brikama Ba. With air conditioning, fans, a kitchen and only seven rooms in the three houses, it often gets booked up.

A few kilometres downstream is the **River Gambia National Park**, also known as **Baboon Islands**. There's a rehabilitation centre on three of the islands, where rescued chimpanzees have been reintroduced to the wild, and are now breeding successfully. Landing on the islands is not permitted, but if you're passing by boat, you may see some of the chimps in the dense foliage at the water's edge.

Janjanbureh Island

The town of **JANJANBUREH**, known in its colonial days and up until recently as Georgetown, is located mid-stream on Janjanbureh Island (previously MacCarthy Island). During the steamboat era, Georgetown was The Gambia's second town, a relatively thriving administrative outpost and a major upriver trading centre. The prestigious Armitage High School is still in business, but dismiss any notions of nostalgic, tropical languor conjured up by the colonial names: backwaters don't come much further back than this, and indeed Janjanbureh town remains the site of the country's main prison. On the north side of the island, there's a whole quarter of the town that's like an open museum of the old trading days, with tiled floors and ornate plasterwork disintegrating behind an onslaught of tropical vegetation. The big roofless barn usually labelled a "slave house" was probably no such thing, more likely a warehouse for perishable goods.

Much of Georgetown's significance was lost in the 1970s after the completion of the main south-bank highway and its fate was sealed by the closure of the riverboat service. Judging by the closed shops and clubs, it's obvious that the islanders are continuing to leave. The main reason to visit is not for the town, but for the river environment – it's a peaceful place, rich in birds and good for river fishing, and it's fast becoming one of The Gambia's foremost **ecotourism** destinations. It's also a good base for visits to the Wassu stone circles.

Practicalities

The southern arm of the river, barely 100m wide, is crossed by a hand-hauled ferry from the south bank, and there's a corresponding ferry from the town, on the north side of the island, to the north-bank mainland. Janjanbureh's useful mix of **accommodation**, all either on or very close to the river, makes it a viable and laid-back place to unwind. *Janjang Bureh Camp* (☎676182; ❸; c/o *Dreambird Camp*, or book through Gambia River Excursions, see p.290) is a charming and friendly lodge built in a beautiful grove of trees at Lamin Koto on the north bank of the river facing the island, and has excellent bird-watching opportunities. Boat trips are available and the camp's launch shuttles guests to and from *Dreambird* jetty on the island for free. In secluded woodland at the westernmost tip of the island, away from the town, *Bird Safari Camp* has safari tents on the riverbank (☎676108, ✪www.bsc.gm; ❹), plus rooms in huts, and is the only place on Janjanbureh with a pool. Lodgings in the town itself include the Divisional Forestry HQ resthouse (☎676198; ❶), with attractive self-catering accommodation in a lush, wild garden by the river, intended for visiting researchers, but open to others when there's room. There's also *Baobolong Camp* (☎676133; ❷), a quiet lodge with spotless rooms; *Alakabung Lodge* (☎676123, ✉alakabung@qanet.gm; ❷) on the main street, a basic but decent budget option; and, almost opposite, *Dreambird* (☎ & ☎676182; ❸), which has a good bar, more rooms and more character.

Guests at *Janjang Bureh Camp* and *Bird Safari Camp* invariably make their lodgings their base for **eating** and **drinking**, and non-residents may visit these camps for meals, but there are also a few local-style options in town. *Bendula Bar and Restaurant* (daily 7am–late) serves cold JulBrew, soft drinks, some spirits and Gambian food. Also open late for decent Gambian meals and drinks is *Roadside Pop*, near *Alakabung Lodge* and *Dreambird Camp. Tida's Bar*, a very local drinking place in

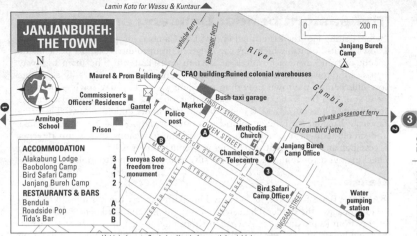

the residential part of town, is run informally by Janjanbureh's Methodist head-mistress, in her compound. There's also a clutch of simple eating and drinking places around the *badala* (wharf area) where the passenger ferries land and the bush taxis wait.

Wassu stone circles

WASSU (daily 8am–sunset; D25), a village 20km northwest of Janjanbureh, is The Gambia's prehistory lesson, but it's no Stonehenge, so adjust your expectations accordingly. The hardened laterite pillars here, clustered in loose rings, vary from mere stumps to veritable menhirs weighing several tonnes and standing three metres high. They were apparently levered into place and then jammed upright with packed earth, hence their tendency to fall out of the circle. The burial places of senior personages, they have obscure cultural origins. Carbon dating has pin-pointed some of them to 750 AD, but recent research indicates that the burials had taken place long before the circles were erected, suggesting the sites themselves were sacred. You're not likely to illuminate the mystery by asking local people – the migration of the local Mandinka clans into this area post-dates the stones, and their oral history contains no clues. It's considered good form to leave rocks on top of the pillars, though again, no one knows why.

The white huts at Wassu are a small museum, with models and illustrations of how the circles and graves were made. If you're captivated by the antiquity of Wassu, you may want to go on to explore **other stone circle sites** on the north bank. There are stones on each side of the road at Niani Maru, the largest stones (up to ten tonnes) at Njai Kunda, and nine circles of pillars, including a bizarre V-shaped one, at Kerr Batch. And you could also pursue the quest for the stones into the Sine–Saloum region of Senegal (see p.211).

The easiest approach to the Wassu stone circles is from **Lamin Koto**, opposite the island on the north bank, and connected to Janjanbureh town by the vehicle ferry and the hand-paddled boats that take foot passengers across. From the north-bank landing, bush taxis to Kau-ur or Farafenni will drop you in Wassu a few hundred metres from the stones (this route is busiest on Mondays, the day of Wassu's *lumo*); alternatively arrange your own taxi for around D300 return. If you're heading to Wassu by river boat, disembark at **Kuntaur**, just a few kilometres away, from where you can reach the stone circles by bush taxi or on foot.

The eastern bends: Bansang and Basse

Before getting into the eastern tail end of The Gambia, you pass **BANSANG**, best known for its hospital, which was the only one in upcountry Gambia prior to the recent opening of new hospitals at Bwiam and Farafenni. The main highway bypasses the town, which is located on a magnificent bend, with easily accessible low hills behind the town providing excellent views. If you're staying the night here, your best bet is the friendly *Carew's Bar*, offering basic accommodation in a few thatched huts (☎674290; ❶) near the bus stop in the middle of town. The bar, a favourite hangout for foreign volunteers posted at the hospital, serves cold drinks and simple food all day, and hosts occasional music sessions; there's also Internet access. Bansang's **silversmiths** have a good reputation for making to order – worth checking out if you're in the market for silver and know what to look for.

Basse

BASSE – Basse Santa Su, in full – is The Gambia's last town, only 20km from Vélingara across the border. The town is a surprisingly animated centre that gets its energy from its proximity to Senegal: its shops tend to be full, and there are banks, bars and hotels, and a produce market that's particularly lively and colourful during the harvest (Jan–June). *Traditions*, a crafts centre-cum-café housed in the 1906 trading post on the river (daily except Tues 9am–6pm; ❽www.traditionsgambia.com), next to the vehicle ferry, sells West African arts, crafts and traditional textiles; it's a great place to meet people, have a snack and watch life on the river from the veranda.

Most **accommodation** choices in Basse are simple or run-down, or both, but have character nonetheless. *Basse Guest House* (☎668283; ❶) is the best of the cheap options, with a central location and a balcony overlooking the busy street below. The rooms are basic, with grubby shared washing facilities. About 1km south of town in the administrative suburb of **Mansajang**, the *Government Rest House* is roomy, with an old-fashioned atmosphere (☎668262; ❷). *Jem Hotel* (☎668356; ❷), on the southeast side of town and notorious for the eccentricity of its owner, has large but near-bare rooms off a pretty courtyard that would be quiet if not for the generator. Basse's upmarket option is, in theory, *Fulladu Camp* (☎917007; ❸); it's in a great riverside location, on the north bank (there's a boat to shuttle guests across), and quite pretty, but running water is intermittent except when there's a big group staying and the pump's running.

The possibilities for eating and drinking include *Traditions*, *Fulladu Camp* and *Jem Hotel*, plus *Fatou's* in Mansajang, which is good for burgers and *brochettes*. There's an unmarked palm wine "ghetto" in the centre of town. As a busy transport hub, Basse is great for chop shops, street food and *afra*, one of the best chop houses being *Ebrima Ceesay, International Coffee Maker*, near the palm wine "ghetto".

Beyond Basse, it's just dirt track to **Fatoto**, with its derelict trading station on the higher than usual riverbank. Tambacounda in Senegal (see p.223) lies to the east, three or four hours' journey by bush taxi via Vélingara. Here there's a passenger **ferry** to the north-bank road along which you could make the return loop to Banjul by whatever transport you can find – this might take several days.

Mali

Mali highlights

✳ Bamako's National Museum
One of West Africa's best museums is inspired by the smooth lines of Djenné's architecture, and houses an informative and well-displayed collection. See p.346

✳ The Bamako music scene
The home of international stars such as Salif Keita and Toumani Diabaté still provides great live music opportunities at weekends. See p.348

✳ The train through the Manding Highlands A beautiful landscape of dramatic rock formations, best enjoyed at dawn. See p.351

✳ Mopti Mali's biggest river port teems with trading activity and colour. See p.364

✳ Djenné's Grande Mosquée A masterpiece of Soudanic

architecture, this huge Friday mosque is dominated by its towers and characteristic protruding beams. See p.371

✳ The Niger River Travel downstream from Gao by *pirogue*, inches above the water surface, brushing past bird-filled reed beds and herds of hippos. See p.400

✳ Trekking in Dogon country The best time for this is early morning, when the sandstone cliffs glow in the sun and echo to a peaceful symphony of birdsong, cocks crowing, and locals greeting each other on the footpaths. See p.383

✳ Hombori Mali's highest elevations consist of sheer mesas and unfeasibly needlelike spikes of rock. See p.398

Introduction and Basics

Historically, geographically and from the point of view of the traveller, Mali is West Africa's centrepiece. Long a bridge between the north and the south, the area outlined by the butterfly shape of the present country formed the meat of three great empires, the oldest of which was ancient Ghana, which flourished as early as the third century. The region's location on the main caravan routes and the banks of the Niger River later fuelled the rise of the powerful Mali and Songhai states, which lasted until the sixteenth-century invasion by Morocco. The political stability and unity of previous centuries was never recovered thereafter.

Reminders of Mali's great past are remarkably intact. Camel caravans still make their way from salt mines in the Sahara to **Timbuktu**, where you can visit a fourteenth-century mosque built when the town was one of the world's most prestigious centres of learning and culture. Wooden *pinasses* continue to carry their cargo along the river from here to **Djenné** – a great commercial town that spawned numerous technical innovations including the Sudanic style of architecture now common throughout the region. Boats also ply the river to the Sahelian town of **Gao** – formerly the capital of the Songhai Empire and final resting place of the **Askia** kings.

The outstanding geographical feature of Mali is the **Niger River**. Known to the Greeks and Romans (who called it Nigris, a conflation of *niger* – "black" – and a Berber expression, *gher nigheren*, meaning "river of rivers"), the Niger long fascinated Europeans. But it took them nearly 2000 years – until the nineteenth-century exploits of Mungo Park, Gordon Laing, René Caillié and Heinrich Barth – to figure out its source and the place where the river emptied into the ocean. Today, 1300km of the river, from Koulikoro in the west to Gao in the north-east, is navigable at least for a few weeks of the year (though the Sélingué dam, upstream from Bamako on a tributary of the Niger, has considerably reduced the water level), and most of the population lives on or near the Niger's banks.

Despite the presence of the Niger, and the headwaters of the **Senegal River** which flow through the western tip of the country, much of Mali lies in the **Sahara**. The extreme north is desert, empty except for a few stranded oases and Tuareg camps. Between the desert and the river stretches the **Sahel zone**, mostly flat plains with scruffy bush and thin trees that are especially resistant to the arid climate.

Fact file

The largest country in West Africa, the **Republic of Mali** spreads across nearly 1,240,000 square kilometres, an area five times the size of the UK and three times as big as California, with a **population** of around twelve million. The country was known as **Soudan Français** – the French Sudan – during the colonial period; the name Mali was chosen for its historical resonance and significance for the Mande-speaking peoples of the region.

The country's president is Amadou Toumani Touré ("ATT"), elected in 2002. A military man, he has no official party affiliation, and with the two main political parties represented in his government, he has no real opposition.

In 2001, Mali's crippling **foreign debt** stood at in excess of US$1.4 billion – more than six times the value of its annual exports of goods and services (though not much more than a single day's expenditure for the US defence budget). Livestock rearing, cotton production and – of relatively recent importance – gold mining are the three largest areas of economic activity.

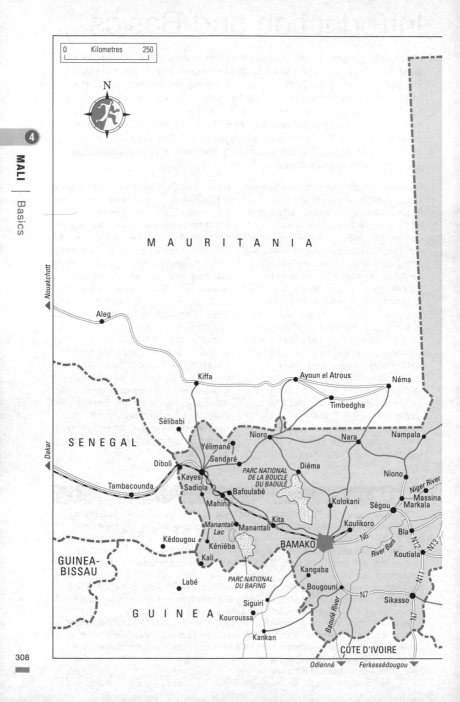

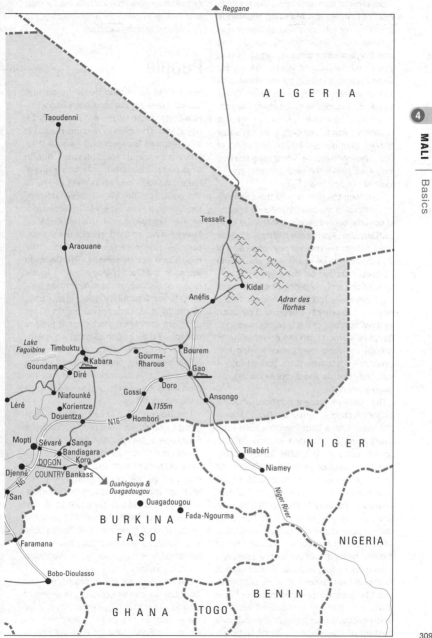

Only a few ripples interrupt the overall impression of flatness across the country. West of Bamako, the **Manding Highlands** provide a rare hilly spectacle as they rise to heights of 500–1000m, and the **Bandiagara escarpment**, which winds across the landscape east of Mopti for some 200km, is striking for the sheer cliffs that drop some 300m to the plain. Other formations include the gaunt mesa-like outcrops and dramatic pinnacles of the **Hombori** a little further east, towering sheer to heights of nearly 1200m, and north of Gao, the inaccessible **Adrar des Iforhas** mountains astride the trans-Saharan chariot route of classical times.

Tempering the romance of the country's opulent past is the more immediate spectre of **poverty**, evident even in the shabby capital, **Bamako**. Apart from a little gold, Mali lacks substantial mineral resources and is almost wholly dependent on its animal and agricultural production (especially its important cotton crop), rendering its **droughts** all the more devastating. In the early 1980s harvests failed almost entirely, and as much as three-quarters of the livestock was lost. People swarmed from the countryside to already crowded towns and, having lost everything, nomads were forced into a sedentary lifestyle and a cruelly inadequate wage economy.

The country's present position, while no longer precarious, remains difficult. Mali is still faced with a large national debt and, every year, the Sahara creeps further south, converting arable land, barely twenty percent of which is cultivable, to dust. On the positive side, a 1996 peace deal intended to assuage the conflict over **Tuareg autonomy** in the north and east has been adhered to, and there has been reasonable economic growth in recent years, subject as ever to the vagaries of the international market for the country's main crop, cotton. In 2002, France agreed to cancel forty percent of Mali's debt to it, and Mali's economy – and prospects for tourism in general – received another much-needed boost through the country's hosting of the African Cup of Nations, which brought soccer fans to the country in their tens of thousands. Throughout the country, roads and hotels were upgraded or built from scratch – it's now easier than ever before to get around the country and find decent accommodation.

People

Numbering more than three million, the Mande-speaking **Bamana** (also known as Bambara) are the largest linguistic community in Mali. Though they're concentrated in the region of Bamako and Ségou, their influence spreads much further, due in large part to their language, which is one of the most widely spoken in West Africa. To the west, from the Manding Highlands to the Senegal River, the **Malinké** share a similar language and customs. Many Malinké have retained traditional religions, despite Islam's early penetration in the region and repeated jihads. The **Senoufo** live near the Côte d'Ivoire border in the region of Sikasso. In the sixteenth century, they formed small kingdoms at Kong, Korhogo and Odienné (now in Côte d'Ivoire), and when the Songhai Empire collapsed they began expanding northward. Their social structure is strongly influenced by the *poro* – an initiation rite that lasts 21 years, during which time the men learn the secrets of Senoufo religion and philosophy.

The **Dogon**, who speak a Voltaic language related to Senoufo, occupy the Bandiagara escarpment east of Mopti. There's reason to believe these people may have originated from the Nile Valley, but migrated to the isolated cliffs near the Burkina Faso border in the twelfth century. Here, they kept at bay the waves of Muslim invasions that swept through Mali over the centuries and, thanks to their tight social and religious organization, have been remarkably successful at maintaining ancient traditions.

Several peoples live in the north. The **Songhai** are concentrated in the region of Gao to which they migrated in waves after the seventh century, probably from northern Benin. The **Fula** – after the Bamana, one of the most populous groups in Mali – traverse the country but are concentrated in the delta region between the Niger and the north-western border with Mauritania – a historical region known as Masina (Massina is the contemporary town). The **Tuareg**, of Berber origin, were pushed southward into present-day Mali after the Arabs came to North Africa from Arabia. The Tuareg mixed with sub-Saharan peoples and formed numerous independent, and often warring, clans. They still cling to their nomadic traditions, though droughts and conflict with the state in the 1980s and early 1990s (not just in Mali, but also in Niger and southern Algeria) have forced many Tuareg to settle. They speak Tamashek, as do their former slaves, the **Bella**. Mali is also home to a sizeable population of **Moors**, localized in the north between Timbuktu and Nioro. They too are of Berber origin, but adopted the Hassaniya Arabic language through their contact with the Moroccans.

Where to go

Mali breathes the very essence of West Africa, and has more good reasons to visit than any other country in the region. Remarkable visual and cultural contrasts in close proximity are Mali's hallmark. The **Niger River** is magnificent (unforgettably so

at dawn) and offers the chance to make the last great river journey in West Africa, while the old cities – notably **Djenné** and **Timbuktu** – carry their ragged history with immense grace. Hiking through the fractured **Dogon country** – where traditional, non-Islamic culture has survived to a remarkable degree – is a goal of most travellers. If you approach it carefully, it's possible to get right inside this fascinating district and experience one of West Africa's most interesting civilizations.

Mali's **musical output** – which continues to stoke the pistons of the international record industry with the likes of Salif Keita and Ali Farka Touré – is another major attraction and enough on its own to draw music lovers. Mali is also the country best placed for onward travel to virtually anywhere in the region – by rail to Dakar, by road to the south-facing coastal states or northwest to Mauritania and thence to North Africa.

When to go

Without taking into account seasonal variations, it's tempting to sum up Mali's climate in two words – gaspingly hot. Rains generally last from June to September in the southwest. In the northeast, they may arrive

Average temperatures and rainfall

Bamako

	Jan	Feb	Mar	Apr	May	June	July	Aug	Sept	Oct	Nov	Dec
Temperatures °C												
Min (night)	16	19	22	24	24	23	22	22	22	22	18	17
Max (day)	33	36	39	39	39	34	31	30	32	34	34	33
Rainfall mm	0	0	3	15	74	137	279	348	206	43	15	0
Days with rainfall	0	0	1	2	5	10	16	17	12	6	1	0

Timbuktu

	Jan	Feb	Mar	Apr	May	June	July	Aug	Sept	Oct	Nov	Dec
Temperatures °C												
Min (night)	13	14	19	22	26	27	25	24	24	23	18	13
Max (day)	31	34	38	42	43	43	39	36	39	40	37	32
Rainfall mm	0	0	3	0	5	23	79	81	38	3	0	0
Days with rainfall	0	0	1	0	2	5	9	9	5	2	0	0

at any time during that period, either for a prolonged wet season or in a few unpredictable cloudbursts. The dry season takes over for the rest of the year. Between October and February the harmattan can blow for days at a time and it can be chilly in the couple of hours before dawn. Climatewise, this is probably the best time to plan a trip, and it's also the period when the Niger is most easily navigable.

Getting there from the rest of Africa

Mali is positioned at the heart of West Africa, and its links with other countries in the region are improving. Apart from various flights to Bamako, there's a weekly rail service from Dakar in Senegal, several decent new highways from Burkina Faso, and a good road from Côte d'Ivoire. Land connections with Mauritania, Algeria and Niger remain rough and unpredictable.

Flights

Flights into **Bamako** from other African cities are handled by a number of different West African airlines, with quite a few services routed via **Abidjan**, from where there are at least daily services. There are also plenty of flights from **Ouagadougou** and from **Dakar** (with Air Sénégal flying via **Banjul** weekly, on Sunday at the time of writing). A couple of Bamako flights leave each week from **Accra** (with Ghana Airways), **Conakry** (Air Guinée), **Douala** (Cameroon Airlines), **Lagos** (Air Guinée), **Kano** (Ethiopian Airways) and **Nouakchott** (Air Mauritanie). Rounding off the picture are four flights a week from **Cotonou** (two apiece with Trans Air Benin and Air Mauritanie) and from **Niamey** (two apiece with Air Sénégal and the Libyan Afriquiyah Airways).

For important practical information applying to all West African countries, covering health, transport, cultural hints and more, plus details on getting to the region from beyond Africa, see Basics, pp.9–87.

As for flights to Bamako from other parts of Africa, Royal Air Maroc has three weekly nonstop flights from **Casablanca**; Air Algérie three flights a week from **Algiers**; Ethiopian Airlines two services a week from **Addis Ababa** via **Ndjamena** (Chad) and Kano; Air Guinée weekly flights from **Kinshasa**; Trans Air Benin two flights a week from **Brazzaville**; Afriquiyah two weekly flights from **Tripoli** via Niamey and Dakar. From **Johannesburg**, South African Airways covers the route to Abidjan weekly, from where you can pick up a connecting flight to Bamako.

Overland

The **Tanezrouft route** from **southern Algeria** ends in eastern Mali at Gao on the Niger River, from where a paved road leads all the way to Bamako. See p.19 for more on trans-Saharan journeys, in particular on the **security issues** affecting travel through Algeria.

From Niger

From **Niamey**, the main route to Mali follows the Niger River to Ayorou (where the tarmac ends) and continues through numerous villages and increasingly frequent patches of soft sand to Gao. SNTV in Niger and Askia Transport, plus a few minor companies in Mali, all provide a bus service (a converted truck) between Niamey and Gao; SNTV vehicles leave Niamey on Monday and Thursday at 8am (CFA8620 one-way). The wait for enough passengers to gather before departure is a standard cause of delay, and breakdowns en route are common. Border formalities on both sides are often protracted, and you're almost certain to be asked to pay some fictitious extra fee – ask for a receipt, and they generally back down.

Alternatively, there are Niamey–Bamako buses which travel **through Burkina Faso**, via Fada-Ngourma and Ouagadougou.

From Burkina Faso

The quickest routes **linking Burkina and Mali** originate in **Bobo-Dioulasso**. From here, you can travel either to **Sikasso** (tracks are extremely rough on the Burkinabe side, especially during the rains) or to **Ségou** via Faramana and Koutiala on a surfaced road (Sogebaf-run buses leave daily at 2pm). Direct transport also leaves from Bobo-Dioulasso to **Mopti** via **San**.

A rewarding way to enter the **Dogon country** is by using the new, partially surfaced route there from Burkina – setting out from **Ouahigouya** and passing through **Koro** on the way to **Bankass**. Sogebaf buses to Bankass depart from Ouahigouya and Ouagadougou daily.

Some Burkinabe border posts close at dusk, but the main **Faramana crossing** north of Bobo-Dioulasso is usually open 24 hours.

From Côte d'Ivoire

At the time of writing, the border with Côte d'Ivoire was closed due to the civil war in that country. In more peaceful times, the main point of entry from Côte d'Ivoire is along the road from **Ferkessédougou** to **Sikasso**, linked by daily buses. The stretch of sealed highway from the Pogo/Zégoua border to Sikasso has been resurfaced and is in good condition. Traffic between **Odienné** and **Bougouni** (from where a good paved road continues to Bamako) is far less frequent.

From Guinea

After the Niger has swelled with seasonal rains (roughly Aug–Dec) it's theoretically possible to travel down the Milo – a tributary of the Niger – by **barge from Kankan** to Bamako. However, this service has been suspended for years, originally due to falling water levels (see box, p.588). If, by some miracle, the boat is running again, the 385-kilometre trip will take you past Niandakoro, where the Milo joins the Niger, and Siguiri, before terminating some five days later at Bamako. This is an adventure, but it's no pleasure cruise: you sleep on mats and share mediocre toilets; food is provided.

The main alternatives are by **bush taxi** from Kankan or **Kouroussa**, the latter an especially pretty route. Malian formalities are less of a hassle than Guinean.

From Senegal and The Gambia

Most overland travellers used to arrive from Senegal on the **Océan-Niger train** from **Dakar**. But the twice-weekly service, using one Senegalese train and one Malian one, has been allowed to deteriorate by both countries, and the Malian train has not been in operation for several years. A departure from Dakar is still scheduled for Wednesday at 9.15am, arriving Bamako Thursday at 2.30pm. In reality, it's usually more like a 36-hour journey and it has been known to take up to fifty hours. You should reserve seats at least a day in advance, and longer if possible, for what is a pretty gruelling journey – one of the last great train rides in Africa. At the time of writing, mid-2003, the service appears to have ceased operating entirely.

Assuming the trains continue to run, the latest fares to Bamako are CFA25,480 2nd class, CFA34,320 1st class and CFA53,145 sleeper (wagon lit). Second class is not very dissimilar from first, and it's worth paying the difference only if you want more legroom and fewer companions. Once you're on the train, it's possible to upgrade to **sleeper** class assuming there are berths available (double cabins only), but the protracted border formalities take place during the night and you have to disembark, so you don't get much sleep in any case. Don't count on any facilities, food or water: you can buy street food from station vendors around the clock. Thieving is rife: keep an eye on your bags at all times.

Part of the reason for the demise of the rail service is the huge improvement in the road from Dakar to Bamako, which is now paved all the way to Kayes. You could catch the straightforward local train – the **Autorail** – from Kayes to Bamako (see p.352). A new paved road from Kayes to Bamako via Manantali is nearing completion and will cut costs and travel times further.

From Mauritania

The main overland route from Mauritania to Bamako starts at **Néma** and passes through Nara and Kolokani. The tracks between Néma and Nara may be impassable during the rainy season.

From **Ayoun el Atrous**, you may be able to get transport to Nioro, from where you can continue to Bamako, or to Kayes along difficult *pistes*. Again, rains can make this route impassable and even in other seasons the frequency of vehicles may not add up to much. Another option is to get down to **Sélibabi**, just 60km from the Mali border, from where you can try to make your way to Kayes.

Red tape and visas

Everyone needs a visa for Mali; for addresses of Malian embassies outside Africa, see pp.22–24. You may need to show your yellow fever certificate when you apply. If you're arriving in Mali on a scheduled flight, you can use the services of a visa agency. In the UK, an alternative to using a visa agency is to get a temporary (five-day) visa faxed to you from Bamako, which can be converted to a proper visa once you arrive in the capital. The procedure involves paying a fee of around £50. If you're flying in from Paris on the French charter airline Point-Afrique, note that the airline routinely obtains low-cost visas for its passengers (see p.13).

If you're arriving **overland**, it's advisable to pick up your visa en route from a Malian embassy in a neighboring country, as visas are usually issued with less fuss and sometimes less expensively than visas issued outside Africa. If you arrive without a visa you're likely to be refused entry: you might be permitted to obtain one at the nearest préfecture (this most likely means Sikasso, Kayes or Bamako) but there is no guarantee. **Drivers** will need Malian insurance and a "tourist visa" (carnet or *laissez-passer*) for their vehicle, and will need to get this extended at customs in Bamako unless driving straight through the country.

Mali was once notorious for its red tape, and tourists were subject to the scrutiny and control of the dramatically named SMERT tourist organization – now defunct. Official hassles such as photography permits and tourist cards have since been abolished, and you no longer need to report to the police and get your passport stamped in towns north and east of Mopti (the **zone securité** designated during the Tuareg rebellion). However, until all of Mali's police force becomes aware of this change, they may give you grief if you don't have a stamp; to counteract this, local tourist offices stamp passports free of charge. This is especially recommended in tourist zones such as Mopti and Timbuktu where the police are sometimes known to trouble tourists in order to make a little extra cash. The government office of tourism and hotels (OMATHO) is adamant that any police irregularity should be reported to them, in line with their ambitious plans to boost tourism.

Costs, money and banks

Mali's currency is the **CFA franc** (£1=CFA930, US$1=CFA600). The country is one of the region's more expensive destinations for travellers, especially if you choose to stay in comfort and eat at the better restaurants. You'll manage most cheaply on the main highways, and especially in Bamako and around, where you can easily get by on CFA20,000 per day (CFA30,000 for two travelling together), but locations where goods have to be transported by 4WD or portered in, for example parts of the Dogon country and the north, can see some prices doubling. In these areas, you should budget an extra CFA10,000 per person per day for guiding fees and supplementary transport costs. Conversely though, these areas often have very inexpensive, basic accommodation.

There are **banks** in most large towns throughout the country – and many different ones at that – but not all change foreign currency, and many that do will only process foreign-exchange transactions before noon, though the Banque Nationale de Développement Agricole (BNDA) does it all day. Almost all banks change euros, and most branches of the Banque de Développement du Mali (BDM) and BNDA change dollars. The bank rate for euros and dollars is generally the same as on the street, the street being a lot faster and friendlier. On the **street** you may also be able to change traveller's cheques, which is worth considering as the bank commission for these is an outrageous CFA2300 (BNDA) or CFA5000 (BDM), plus various taxes. You can also change money at the **major hotels**; they charge a commission similar to those of the banks, but the rates are often lower.

Visa cards can be used at some of the larger hotels. However, there was only one working ATM at the time of writing, at the Banque Internationale pour le Commerce et Industrie au Mali (BICIM) in Bamako, though more are being installed. Most other large branches of the BDM, BNDA and Banque Internationale pour le Mali (BIM) give cash advances on Visa cards for a fee of CFA5000. Unfortunately this process depends on the phone system, which in some remoter towns can be unreliable, and it may take a couple of days before you get your cash. Don't be fooled by the presence of Visa stickers everywhere, as these often represent wishful thinking rather than real facilities.

Health

The only vaccination certificate normally required to enter Mali is for yellow fever. Outbreaks of cholera occur from time to time, in which case this certificate may be necessary too. Chloroquine-resistant malaria is a serious problem – see p.33.

Bilharzia is another disease that remains all too common, especially in rural areas with slow streams and brackish water. Don't swim in such areas, especially if they're bordered by grass. Even stretches of the Niger can be dubious, notably in the dry season when the low waters become stagnant in many places. Elsewhere, swimming in the river is generally safe – you'll see people bathing, doing their washing and bringing their animals to drink. But if you come to a place where no one from the area goes into the water, it pays to do likewise.

Tap **water** is heavily chlorinated and drinkable in Bamako and other big towns. In distant villages, wells and river water are commonly used for drinking and the purity may be suspect. Bottled water is available very widely, even in remote places like the Dogon country. Expect to pay CFA500–1500

for a 1.5-litre bottle (the price varies depending on how far the water has been transported). Iodine tincture, purifying tablets or filters are a cheaper alternative.

Hospitals tend to be underequipped and overcrowded. For a serious problem, your best bet is either the Hôpital du Point G (☎222.50.02 or ☎222.50.03) or the Hôpital Gabriel Touré (☎228.27.38), both in Bamako.

Information, websites and maps

There are no Mali tourist offices abroad. In Bamako, the most useful function of the **Office Malien du Tourisme et de l'Hôtellerie** (OMATHO; ⓦ www.le-mali.com /omatha; see p.344) seems to be the policing of local guides and the establishment of tourist offices and guide associations around the country. So far offices have opened in Kayes, Ségou, Mopti, Timbuktu and Gao, and recognized guide associations exist in Ségou, Timbuktu, Gao, Bandiagara and Sangha. The number of **independent travel agencies** has also increased significantly in recent years, mainly in Bamako and Mopti; many of these firms have websites and can usually provide leaflets. They're principally concerned with offering excursions along the Niger River, into the Manding Highlands northwest of the capital and out to the country's primary tourist attractions – the Dogon country and Timbuktu.

Recommended websites

ⓦ **www.afribone.com/en/index.html** General information and news from Mali – with many useful links, mostly in French.

ⓦ **www.malinet.ml** Mali's most informative website, with a little bit about everything – news, sport, culture, tourism. In French.

ⓦ **www.friendsofmali-uk.org** Lively new London based organisation.

ⓦ **www.malipages.com** Useful "yellow pages" site with a bit of everything.

Maps

The best **map** of the country is IGN's 1:2,000,000 map of Mali, published in 1993. Still rare in the country, save for the capital, it's a covetable item to some border guards – keep it out of sight. More detailed information is available from the IGN 1:200,000 maps, which are difficult to get hold of, but indispensable when travelling in the desert. The 1:1,000,000 IGN series are good for general topography but, now forty years old, no longer useful for roads and towns.

Getting around

The longest navigable stretch of the Niger flows through Mali and, for a short season each year, it's possible to travel by boat virtually from one end of the country to the other, stopping along the way at historic towns like Ségou, Mopti, Timbuktu and Gao. The regular boat service is almost unique in West Africa and is an exciting – if at times tiring and uncomfortable – way to see the country. Otherwise, there is a regular train service from Bamako to Dakar, plus flights linking the main towns and, of course, buses and bush taxis. Car rental is available from a few outlets, but is very costly.

Bush taxis and buses

Most Malians rely on bâchés (over short distances), taxis brousse and minibuses (short to medium distances) and buses (long distances) to get around the country. Bâchés are furnished with tightly packed rows of hard wooden benches filled to the brim with passengers, goods, and anything else that needs transporting, and are extremely uncomfortable for protracted journeys – which is probably why they generally only do short trips. Bush taxis and minibuses are more comfortable, though not quite as plush as in some neighbouring

countries, and fares, usually fixed, are relatively high: CFA1750 from Sevaré to Bandiagara for example, a sixty-kilometre journey. In addition, drivers tend to charge quite steeply for baggage and you'll have to bargain hard.

Mali's growing privately-run bus network provides a reasonably comfortable and practical means of travelling between major towns. Most companies run a one-person, one-seat system (often including an extra row sitting on stools down the aisle) and it's always a good idea to buy tickets in advance, and to claim a seat as soon as possible. The fare should cover one piece of luggage in the hold. Bittar Trans, Somatra, Somatri and YT all run a decent service, though its worth checking around the smaller companies too, to compare schedules and costs. As a general indication of prices, the fare from Mopti to Bamako is in the CFA6000–8000 range.

A final note of warning: on some imported air-conditioned buses the windows are not designed to be opened. If the air conditioning doesn't work, you're in for an uncomfortable ride to say the least: get a seat at the front.

Trains

One weekly Senegalese-run train operates on the rail line from Dakar to Bamako, described on p.343. There are also slow Autorail trains – making twice as many stops as the international service – from Bamako to Kayes.

The line to Koulikoro, the upper terminus of the Niger River boats, is currently served only by freight trains. Student reductions apply on train fares at the beginning and end of term.

Domestic rail fares from Bamako

	First class	Second class
Kayes (express train)	CFA16,200	CFA11,500
Kayes (local Autorail)	CFA11,700	CFA7000
Kita (express)	CFA6400	CFA4600
Kita (Autorail)	CFA4600	CFA2900
Mahina (express)	CFA12,500	CFA8800
Mahina (Autorail)	CFA9050	CFA5500

River boats

It's possible to travel over 1300km along the Niger River, between Koulikoro (60km downstream from Bamako) and Gao. Such a trip can only be made, however, in the period during and just after the rains – roughly from August to November between Koulikoro and Gao, or from August to January/February downstream between Mopti and Gao – when waters are high enough for the steamers. The exact dates vary each year with the timing and volume of the rains. Aim for months in the middle if you want to be sure of travelling by boat.

Three boats, in theory, ply the waters: the *Kankou Moussa* (operating since 1982, it's the largest and newest of the vessels) is possibly the most comfortable, followed by the *Tombouctou* and the *Général A Soumaré*. Note, however, that only one boat was operating in the 2002 season, and that comfort levels are at best rudimentary – by the end of a voyage, especially towards the end of the season, you may be glad to disembark. Reservations for the trip can be made through the Compagnie Malienne de Navigation (**COMANAV**) in any of the port towns, while their Bamako office can help with information (☏222.38.02).

Boat schedules

The entire journey takes six days downriver from **Koulikoro** to **Gao**, and seven days back again. However, the official schedule applies only if at least two out of the three vessels are operable, which is not often. According to the schedule, one boat leaves weekly from Koulikoro on Tuesday at 10pm. Every third departure (ie the *Kankou Moussa*) sails only as far as Timbuktu, returning upriver from there on Sunday at 2pm. The other departures go all the way down to Gao, returning on Monday at 8pm. En route, sailings from **Mopti** to **Korioumé** (the actual port for the now high-and-dry port town of **Kabara**, and Timbuktu's nearest port) should depart on Thursday evening and arrive Saturday morning. In the other direction, boats should leave Korioumé Wednesday evening and reach Mopti Friday afternoon. In practice, the only fairly predictable elements of the service are the approximate journey times between ports, assuming no delays.

Fares and facilities

There are five **classes** of accommodation: **luxe**, a single or double cabin with (sometimes nonfunctioning) extras like a fridge, a/c and hot showers; **first class**, a double cabin with WC located just outside the cabin; **second class**, four people to a cabin with two bunks and shared washing facilities; **third class**, rather cramped cabins for eight to twelve people, according to the vessel, and no frills, though some cabins do have fans (third-class passengers generally have access to the second-class showers and toilets); and a basic **fourth class** which provides no accommodation, only access to the lower deck.

From Koulikoro, first-class **fares** are around CFA57,000 to Mopti, CFA101,000 to Timbuktu and CFA147,000 to Gao; from Mopti, expect to pay CFA46,000 to Timbuktu. Third-class fares are about forty percent of these prices, while travelling fourth class costs only about a tenth of the corresponding first-class fare. Third class is probably the best option if you're on quite a tight budget.

Food is served three times a day in separate dining rooms for each class, and the price is included in luxe, first, second and third class. Each boat has a bar. Only in the luxe, first- and second-class dining rooms can you get **bottled water**.

Pirogues and pinasses

Anywhere along the Niger, and virtually year-round, you can find local **pirogues** to get you from A to B; details are given throughout the chapter. These canoelike vessels are rowed – or poled much of the time – and sometimes venture quite long distances with large consignments of rock salt or other goods. As for fares, after protracted negotiations you can expect to pay CFA3000–5000 per person per day (50–100km) with shared food. They provide the most rewarding, if basic, means of seeing the Niger – from a few inches above its surface.

Along certain stretches of the river, it's also possible to get **pinasses**, large handmade motorized boats covered with a type of matted overhang. They can be privately rented for longer journeys (from Mopti to Timbuktu, say, expect to pay CFA300,000–400,000 for a boat carrying twenty people) with mattresses for you to sleep on board, and food provided. Alternatively, you can pay for a seat in a public *pinasse* that primarily carries goods; it will be moored every night and you sleep on the riverbank nearby. Costs (including a share of the communal rice bowl) are CFA10,000–15,000 or so for Mopti–Timbuktu or Timbuktu–Gao.

Despite the basic conditions, this sort of travel has been operating for centuries along the Niger and retains a nostalgic attraction. However, the experience can be either very worthwhile or gruelling and never to be repeated, depending on the vessel, the route, the goods on board and the crew. Be prepared for frequent delays: your journey can take twice as long as expected if the *pinasse* is heavily laden and if water levels are so low that the boat gets stuck. You'll need snacks, water-purifying equipment or tablets, plenty of reading matter and infinite patience.

Domestic flights

Air Mali only operate a twice-weekly flight from **Bamako** to **Timbuktu** via **Mopti**, and three flights a week from the capital to **Kayes**. **Société Avion Express** (SAE) supplement this with flights from Bamako to **Mopti** and **Timbuktu** (2 weekly), **Kayes** (2 weekly), **Yélimané** (2 weekly), **Nioro** (1 weekly) and **Kéniéba** (1 weekly). Lastly, **Société de Transport Aérién** (STA; ⓦwww

.sta-airlines.com) run a thrice-weekly service from Bamako to Kayes. There were no internal flights to Gao at the time of writing.

One-way **fares** from Bamako are approximately CFA60,000 to Mopti, CFA100,000 to Timbuktu and CFA65,000 to Kayes, Yélimané or Nioro. The departure tax for internal flights is CFA3500. Note that schedules are frequently affected by delays or cancellations.

Accommodation

In 2002 Mali hosted the African Cup of Nations football tournament, which provided a dramatic boost to the array of accommodation available across the country. Smaller towns have at least one place with hot water, air conditioning and TV, while larger towns usually have at least one luxury address. If you're on a tight budget, you'll also find a good range of options, including simple *campements*, sleeping on the roof in hotels or *auberges*, or, in many cases, the option of putting up a tent. Note that the "Rail" hotels in railway towns tend to be operated on a half-board basis, including dinner and breakfast in the rate.

In budget accommodation (price codes ❶–❸), you'll generally find dorm beds, some provision for camping on site or sleeping on the roof (mattress and sometimes mosquito net not provided), and basic rooms, sometimes s/c. Rooms in mid-range establishments (❹–❻) are s/c, with fan or air conditioning and sometimes a TV, and they are quite comfortable at the upper end of the range; hotels in this bracket occasionally

---

Accommodation price codes

All accommodation prices in this chapter are coded according to the following scale, whose equivalent in pounds sterling/US dollars is used throughout the book. Prices refer to the rate you can expect to pay for a room with two beds. Single rooms, or single occupancy, will normally cost at least two-thirds of the twin-occupancy rate. Note that all rooms are subject to a CFA500 tourist tax per person per night, which we've included when determining the price code.

❶ Under CFA4700 (under £5/$8).
❷ CFA4700–9000 (£5–10/$8–16).
❸ CFA9000–14,000 (£10–15/$16–24).
❹ CFA14,000–19,000 (£15–20/$24–32).
❺ CFA19,000–28,000 (£20–30/$32–48).
❻ CFA28,000–37,000 (£30–40/$48–64).
❼ CFA37,000–47,000 (£40–50/$64–80).
❽ Over CFA47,000 (£50/$80).

have their own restaurant and even a swimming pool. The expensive hotels (**7** & **8**) have all the mod cons and luxuries you'd expect.

Eating and drinking

Mali's main staple is **rice**, often eaten with a thin beef broth mixed with tomatoes – *riz gras*. There are numerous regional variations on this common stand-by. In the Dogon country, **millet** (*petit mil*) provides the basis of nearly every meal and is prepared in hundreds of ways. Most commonly, it's served in a boiled mush called **tô**, and eaten with sauce, often made from local onions. For breakfast it's fried in small round patties known as *beignets de mil*. The Senoufo consume rice and millet dishes less than other peoples, and tend more towards tubers (**yams** and **cassava**).

Food in Djenné has retained a strong Moroccan flavour. A type of **couscous** is eaten here, as is a noodlelike dish known as **kata**, which is accompanied by meat. **Nempti** is a type of *beignet* mixed with hot peppers, while **fitati** is a kind of thin pancake. During special celebrations the people make a pastry called **tsnein-achra** from rice flour and honey. The Tuareg, too, make a variant of couscous from a wild grain known as *fonio* or "hungry rice".

All along the river, of course, people eat **fish** – one of the most common varieties is *capitaine* (Nile perch), a boney little creature that's quite good when deep fried in oil or grilled over coals. In the northern regions of the Fula herders, **beef**, **mutton** and **goat** outsell fish, although for many people red meat is still a luxury. Just about everywhere in Mali, *gargote*s and street-food sellers charcoal-grill marinated meat **brochettes** (kebabs), served with French bread and hot sauce.

Drinking

Beer is expensive relative to other countries in the region, at CFA900 for a large bottle or CFA500 for a small one, rising to CFA1500 for a large beer in the remoter north and east, including parts of the Dogon country (where soft drinks, called **sucrerie**, can also be pricey at around CFA750 per bottle). The main Malian beer is **Castel**. **Home-brewed beer** made from corn or millet is common to many different peoples – especially non-Muslims like many Dogon and Senoufo – and is known variously as *konjo*, *dolo* or *chapalo*. Lastly, sweet, green China **tea** is drunk all over the country, but with particular devotion in the north, and above all by the Tuareg.

Communications

If it weren't for the mushrooming of Internet cafés across the country, contact with Europe and the rest of the world would be slow, even out of Bamako. Though inexpensive to send, **letters** usually take their time arriving: estimate two weeks from the capital, and as much as a month from the provinces. That said, the Office Nationale des Postes (ONP) in Bamako has a poste-restante service which works relatively well.

You can make IDD calls from private, metered booths in **télécentres**, which are reasonably common in commercial centres; you pay afterwards for the units used. It takes a while to get through, though, and it's often easier (if more expensive) to call from the big hotels, where queues tend to be long and obstructions many. Alternatively you can use one of the many card phones spread across the country. Sotelma, the Malian telecom company, sells cards of fifty units for CFA5000, which can be used for both national and international calls (price per minute is CFA100 for local calls, CFA400 for national calls and CFA1500–2000 to Europe, with discounts in the evening and at weekends). Note that Malian phone numbers do not have area codes.

At the time of writing, Mali's **mobile phone services** were a little behind the regional average, with the coverage offered by Malitel – one of two domestic mobile operators – limited to small areas around Bamako, Ségou, Mopti, Sikasso and Kayes. A new French network, Ikatel, was expected to start operations soon.

Prices for **Internet access** can vary enormously, from CFA500 per hour at some

Mali's IDD country code is ☎223.

places in Bamako to several times this where there's only one outlet in town. Connection speeds also vary; they're usually best at Internet cafés operated by Sotelma. Note also that many premises with computers advertise Internet access even when they don't yet have it.

The media

The Malian **press** is improving. There's a rash of daily French-language tabloid newspapers, of which *L'Essor* is the most respected. Other widely-read titles include *L'Indépendant*, *Les Echos*, *Le Soir de Bamako*, *Informatin* (the main opposition paper) and the outspoken *Nouvel Horizon*. *Nyéléni* magazine, published monthly in French, covers women's issues, and there's a music magazine, the bimonthly French-language *Starflash*, with features on new and traditional music. You might come across several dozen other occasional magazines, any of which is worth checking out to get a feel for what's going on in the country.

National TV (ORTM) is broadcast from about 6pm to midnight on weekdays and from 10am to midnight on Friday and Saturday; international **satellite TV** is becoming increasingly common, especially in hotels. Government-controlled **radio** goes out in nine languages (though not in English). The big development, as everywhere in the region, is a plethora of small **FM music stations** operating from various quartiers in Bamako and other towns. Radio France Internationale (98.5FM), BBC Bamako (88.9FM; a 24-hour relay of the BBC African Service) and Africa No. 1 (the Libreville-based station, 102FM) are also available.

Opening hours, public holidays and festivals

Businesses, including banks, tend to open from Monday to Thursday between 8am and noon, and then from 2pm to 5pm, while on Friday they're open between 8am and noon. Many business are also open on Saturday afternoons. **Government offices** are open from Monday to Thursday between 7am and noon and between 2pm and 4.30pm; on Friday they open from 7am to noon.

Muslim holidays are celebrated with fervour in Mali, and during the month of Ramadan virtually everything closes down during the daytime – though nighttime feasts redress the balance. See p.61 for approximate dates. Christian celebrations – Christmas Day and Easter – are also public holidays, as are New Year's Day and Labour Day (May 1). During Christmas and New Year it's on the nights of *la veille* (Dec 24) and *le trente-et-un* (Dec 31) that Malians really let their hair down. Secular holidays include the Fête de l'Armée (Jan 20), the Fêtes de Martyrs (March 26), Africa Day (May 25) and Independence Day (Sept 22).

Entertainment and sports

Mali is world-famous for its **music**. The singer Salif Keita and guitarist Ali Farka Touré stand out, but other musicians such as Oumou Sangaré and Habib Koité also enjoy international recognition. There's a wealth of live music and dance on offer in Bamako; elsewhere, your best chance of hearing traditional music is to happen to be around for a festival. Two towns which are particularly famous for their musical traditions are **Kita** and **Kela**, both of which have an unusually high population of *jalis* (or griots) who may be willing to give lessons or private performances. The **Festival au Désert**, a unique Tuareg music event, has taken place each January since 2001 (see p.382). For more on the Mali music scene, see p.332.

Traditional **wrestling** (*la lutte*) is still popular in Mali but, with football on the ascendant, traditional bouts no longer command the crowds and excitement of even a decade ago. Since Mali hosted the African Cup of Nations in 2002, **football** has assumed a high profile in the country, and most towns have regular games. Bamako's Djoliba AC, Stade Malien and Cercle Olympique are the big teams to watch out for.

Cinema

Malian **cinema** is also thriving: two of the most famous names in Malian cinema are Souleymane Cissé, who made his international name with the memorable *Yeelen* (1986), and Cheick Oumar Sissoko, whose *La Genèse* opened the 1999 Panafrican Film Festival in Ouagadougou.

Apart from Souleymane Cissé, two other early Malian film-makers also received their training in the USSR – **Djibral Kouyaté** and **Kalifa Dienta**. Kouyaté was the first Malian to make a fiction film, *Le Retour de Tiéman* (1970) – the story of a young agriculturalist who runs into the resistance of traditionalists when he tries to implement modern methods in his village. Dienta is best known for his feature *A Banna*, in which the main character, Yadji, takes his new bride from Bamako to meet his family in the village. The clash between urban and rural values comes into focus as Yadji's wife has to contend with everything from the authority of the griot to

old-fashioned divisions between men and women.

Alkaly Kaba was another pioneer, best known for films portraying the conflict between Western and African worlds. Early films in this vein from the 1970s include *Wallanda* and *Wamba*.

Sega Coulibaly comes from a new generation of film-makers whose experiences are rooted in post-independence society. Born in 1950, he briefly studied film in Paris before returning to Mali where he helped Kaba shoot *Wamba*. Coulibaly's first feature, *Mogho Dakan* (1976), follows a city teacher stationed in a village, whose success with women (because of his status), backfires when one of them gets pregnant. His second film, *Kasso Den*, is all action, a prisoner wrongly jailed seeking vengeance on the men who framed him.

Issa Falaba Traoré gained recognition for *An Be Nodo* (1980), the story of a promising student. Too poor to continue her studies, she brings shame on her family

Souleymane Cissé

Souleymane Cissé, like Senegal's Ousmane Sembène (see p.162), was trained at the famous Moscow film school. Since the early 1970s, he has been as prolific as Sembène and has made a good number of films which have gone on to commercial and critical success in Africa and Europe. Unlike Sembène, however, his craft always leads his message, not the other way round.

In addition to well-known early works like *Cinqs jours d'une vie* (1972) and *Baara* (*The Porter*; 1977) – a full-length look at the relationship between workers and patron in a textile factory – he has made perhaps the two best films to come from Africa. In the first, the Bamana-language *Finyé* (*The Wind*; 1982), about the overweening pressures of seniority on youth, the wind symbolizes a new generation of post-independence youth, struggling against the repression of the military government. It was an international success, and was presented at Cannes, Carthage and Ouagadougou, where it won first prize. The second, *Yeelen* (*Brightness*; 1986), at last saw his recognition as a major film-maker. Through the conflict between the main character, Nianankoro – an initiate possessed of magical powers – and his father, the film looks at the conflict of generations in Africa and gives non-African moviegoers a spine-tingling insight into traditional values. With its deft visual impact and atemporality – and a deliberate ambiguity about the level of reality at which the images operate – the metaphysical world of the old West Africa comes alive and is as real as any drought or slave trade. For this lyricism – which made the film an art-house hit in the West – Cissé inevitably ran into criticism from those who would prefer a more realist cinema talking about exploitation, colonialism and repression. *Yeelen* went on to win the Grand Prix du Jury at the 1987 Cannes Film Festival.

Cissé's most recent film, *Waati* (1994), is the epic story of Nandi, a South African girl living under apartheid. In her quest for freedom, she leaves her homeland and heads on a quest that takes her to Namibia, Mali and Côte d'Ivoire. As she passes from childhood to adulthood she discovers a continent in search of an identity.

when she drops out of school and becomes pregnant.

Cheik Oumar Sissoko emerged in the late 1980s as a new film-maker in the social realist tradition. An early documentary, *Rural Exodus* (1984), considered the plight of peasants displaced by drought, while *Nyamanton* ("Garbage Boys", 1986) focused on the condition of urban children. Sissoko gained international recognition for *Finzan* (1989), a fictional piece that uses the theme of genital excision to address wider social issues of women's rights and the struggle for freedom. Titles at the beginning of the film remind the viewer that women do two-thirds of the world's work, receive only one-tenth of the reward and only one percent of the property. Sissoko won the best picture award at the 1995 FESPACO for *Guimba*, the tale of a chief whose obsession with power drives him to make a pact with the devil. Sissoko describes the film as an allegory about the downfall of Malian president Amadou Traoré. His 1999 movie, *La Genèse* (*Genesis*) is a visually stunning retelling of the biblical story of the house of Abraham, in which Salif Keita plays the lead role of Esau. At the time of writing, his most recent movie is *Battu* (2000), filmed in Dakar and revolving around the relationship between government and beggars in African cities. Sissoko was elevated to the post of Malian Minister of Culture in 2002.

Another name to emerge in recent years is **Draba Adama**, whose *Taafe Fanga* (*Skirt Power*; 1997) used a Dogon folk tale as a vehicle to poke fun at gender roles while making a serious comment about the status of African women.

Directory

Airport departure tax CFA3500 domestic flights, CFA9000 for flights within Africa and CFA14,000 for intercontinental departures.

Emergencies Police ☎017, fire ☎018.

Guides In Mali, far more than in most West African countries, it is common for young men to work full time as tourist guides. A guide who's touting for work will do his best to convince you that it's essential to be accompanied when travelling in Mali. With the exception of the Dogon country, this is certainly not the case, but a good guide can smooth your path and open your eyes to a lot of things you would otherwise miss. The usual rules apply: don't immediately hire the first guide to approach you, try to get personal recommendations, trust your instincts, ask searching questions, and bargain hard. Expect to pay around CFA3000–5000 per day for a guide around town, and about the same – but reckoned per person in the group – for trekking guides. Additionally, you could negotiate over the guide's language skills or for an extra-long day, and it's good to offer the incentive of CFA500–1000 extra if you're particularly happy with the day. Local tourist offices have lists of qualified guides (with official guide association badges or ID cards). When taking on a guide for more than a day or so, make sure it's clearly understood for what length of time you will need them, where you want to go during this time, and who will be responsible for what expenses. Then draw up a contract in writing and if possible have it approved at a local tourist office and signed in their presence. As a rule of thumb, the further your guide is from home, the less likely they are to know much about a place, so if you're planning extensive travels it's well worth considering employing a series of guides as you go along.

Names The same ones crop up all the time and it doesn't mean everyone is related; these are great clan branches incorporating many strands, and complex class and caste-like hierarchies. Classic Manding names are Diabaté/Jobarteh and Traoré (which are historically related); Keïta (with its royal associations); Kanté/Konté/Kondé; and Kouyaté. Fula names include Bari/Barry, Diallo/Jalo, Sidibé and Cissé; and typical Songhai names are Maïga and Touré. Many people have at least one Arabic name – Fatima, Moussa, Ali, etc.

Photography Photo permits are not required in Mali, but as elsewhere discretion and good sense should be used before snapping away. In certain areas, such as the Dogon country, there are still many taboos associated with taking pictures.

Wildlife Mali's vast expanses of bush and swamp used to provide a major sanctuary for West African wildlife, with large predators and many other mammals present in significant numbers. Unfortunately, due to massive over-hunting, the numbers have seriously declined. Hippos are, however, still relatively common all along the course of the Niger, and Mali's elephants also appear to be surviving and even increasing in numbers. There are herds in the region of the Parc Nationale de la Boucle du Baoulé and a separate population of 600 or more range seasonally across the dry lands between northeast Burkina and the Gourma district around Gossi, west of Gao. These latter "desert elephants" are protected in part by the presence of the Tuareg, who traditionally don't hunt them. Their migration cycle is regular and, if you have time, it's not difficult to find them, though you need to have (or hire) a four-wheel-drive vehicle. Mali's main national park, the Parc National de la Boucle du Baoulé, suffers from inaccessibility and a lack of infrastructure and is not much visited.

Women's issues Women travellers don't find Mali a special hassle. In the West African context, there's a good deal of proud, feminine freedom in the country, coupled paradoxically with the highest incidence of initiatory genital mutilation, including the brutal practice of infibulation. Ninety-four percent of women are affected, and although healthcare organizations, such as PLAN International, run community education projects to increase awareness, progress is arduous. Other statistics are equally depressing: a third of deaths among Malian women of childbearing age are pregnancy-related, and one in ten women die during childbirth or as a result of an unsafe abortion. Mali has the second highest birth rate in the world (surpassed only by neighbouring Niger), and the eighth highest infant-mortality rate. Only 25 percent of girls receive more than four years of schooling and it's normal for them to be married by the age of 16, with ninety percent married before 20.

A brief history of Mali

The outstanding features of Mali's history are the old empires. Much of the modern country was part of the old Mali (or Manding) empire during its maximum extent (ranging from Kita to Djenné and Timbuktu) in the thirteenth and fourteenth centuries. When the Moroccans crushed the Askia dynasty of the **Songhai Empire** in 1591, they left the region in a political vacuum, partially filled from time to time by the rapid rise and fall of mini-empires. The first was the kingdom of **Ségou** (written "Segu" in many histories), founded in the early eighteenth century and almost immediately eclipsed by the Fula jihad that spread from Masina (Macina). This kingdom was founded in 1818 by Cheikou Ahmadou Hammadi Lobbo – a religious zealot inspired by Dan Fodio's religious war that had spread from Sokoto in present-day Nigeria. And from Senegal, the Tukulor marabout El Hadj Omar Tall launched his own holy war, setting out in 1852 to conquer animist Mandinka districts to the east.

Arrival of the French

The Tukulor cavalry spread across the Niger belt with lightning speed, carving out an empire headquartered at Ségou that extended from Masina to Bandiagara. Increasingly, it came to be seen as a threatening obstacle to the designs of French colonials in St-Louis, Senegal, bent on commercial and military penetration into the Soudanese interior.

The governor of Senegal, **General Louis Faidherbe**, opted in the first instance for a diplomatic response to Tukulor expansion and sent an expeditionary mission to Ségou. Arriving in 1868, the French signed a treaty with the new ruler **Ahmadou**, son of Omar who had been killed in battle in 1864. By 1880, the French were back to renew the treaty, but, although Ahmadou was increasingly suspicious of their motives and this time had the emissary locked up, it was too little too late. **French forces** had now advanced as far east as Kita and brought with them the parts of an armed gunboat which they assembled and launched at Koulikoro. They thus managed to control the river as far down as Mopti. But the Tukulor Empire based at Ségou refused to cede. Finally, the capital fell in 1890 and the other towns in the interior toppled like dominos in their turn – Djenné and Bandiagara in 1893, and, after fierce Tuareg resistance, Timbuktu in 1894.

Tieba and Samory

Meanwhile, resistance was fomenting in the Senoufo country around Sikasso. The Malinké chief **Samory Touré** had been carving out his own small empire since 1861 and had taken the Senoufo strongholds of Kong, Korhogo and Ferkessédougou. He ran into conflict with **Tieba**, king of Sikasso. Samory attacked Sikasso in 1887 and beseiged it for fifteen months, but the town resisted. The French, under Lieutenant Binger, watched the rivalry with close attention and eventually allied themselves with Tieba, helping him reinforce his regional power.

Tieba died in battle in 1893 and was replaced by his son **Ba Bemba**. The new king, however, mistrusted the French and refused to follow through on the kingdom's commitment to help the colonials destroy Samory's influence. In May 1898 the French attacked and took Sikasso. The king committed suicide, escaping the fate of Samory, who was captured in September as he dashed southwest towards Liberia, hoping to get more weapons from the British. The same year, El Hadj Omar's son Ahmadou died in exile in Sokoto. France was now the sole power in the region.

The French Soudan

Confident of eventual victory, the French had already declared the **Soudan** an autonomous colony in 1890. Later it was incorporated into the colony of **Haut Sénégal-Niger**, of which **Bamako** was made the capital in 1908. The railway had been extended from Dakar to Koulikoro in 1904 and, with the creation of the Office du Niger – a national agricultural agency based in Ségou – the French hoped to turn Mali into the breadbasket of West Africa and even make the colony turn a profit through the production of cash crops like groundnuts and cotton. *Pistes* were traced through the interior to facilitate the transportation of crops and, in 1932, a dam was built near Ségou in the hope of turning hundreds of thousands of square kilometres into irrigable land.

From the beginning, however, these ambitious designs were frustrated. In the first place, the colonial authorities soon ran into a shortage of labour which they solved by forcibly recruiting volunteers from neighbouring countries, notably the region of the Upper Volta (Burkina Faso). In addition, much of the soil in the Soudan turned out to be too poor to support cotton production and rice was substituted. Finally, the Office du Niger had restrictive financial limitations. As a result, only a small fraction of the territory destined to become an agricultural miracle was ever exploited. Not that it made much difference to Malians at the time, since the production was almost exclusively destined for export to France.

World wars I and II

Of all the colonies in the **AOF** (Afrique Occidentale Française), Mali paid the highest price with the outbreak of World War I. The Bambara, especially, were recruited in large numbers to fill the ranks of the famous **Tirailleurs sénégalais**. These infantry soldiers experienced European war as early as 1908 when they had been used by France to "pacify" Morocco. After 1914, tens of thousands of Africans were sent to Verdun, where one in three died in the muddy war of attrition. Back in the Soudan, uprisings to protest the draft of native soliders for a foreign war were brutally suppressed by the French authorities.

As if the price wasn't high enough, when the war was over, the new colonial governor, Just Van Vollenhoven, began mobilizing civilians in the Soudan to develop agricultural production and the regional infrastructure. It was a move he deemed necessary to make the colony profitable after the stagnant period during the war.

Parallel to this, the French made minimal concessions to give Africans an extended role in the **politics** of their countries. By 1925, Africans could be elected to sit on the governors' advisory councils, although this of course gave them no direct political power. From the 1930s, laws were made to facilitate access to **French nationality** – a status considered by the government to be a great honour despite the sacrifices Africans had made during the war. But by 1937 only some 70,000 people in the entire AOF had been granted French citizenship and the vast majority of these were Senegalese.

Postwar political developments

Though World War II had the effect of nipping political and social development in the bud, it also acted as a catalyst that gave rise to a new political consciousness in Africa and a determination to achieve political rights. Independence was still only envisaged by a very few, and de Gaulle himself ruled out this possibility at the 1944 **Brazzaville conference**, although he did say France was willing to make concessions, including greater African involvement in the respective governments.

In the aftermath of Brazzaville, three **political parties** were formed in Mali: the Parti Soudanais du Progrès (PSP), headed by **Fily Dabo Cissoko**; a Soudanese affiliate of the Section Française de l'Internationale Ouvrière (SFIO) with **Mamadou Konaté** at the helm; and the Parti Démocratique du Soudan (PDS), founded by French Communists living in Mali. Though Cissoko came out ahead in elections to a constituent assembly in 1945, the first year of government was characterized by infighting among the parties – notably the PSP and the SFIO.

In 1946, Bamako hosted the **Rassemblement Démocratique Africain (RDA)** – a vast political convention that brought together over eight hundred delegates from Senegal, Côte d'Ivoire, Guinea, Benin, Togo, Cameroon, Chad and Mali. For the Soudan to have a single voice within the RDA, the three political parties agreed to form a single Union Soudanaise within the RDA (USRDA) – to the surprise of everyone. But within a couple of days, Cissoko announced that a bloc with what he called "unrepentant communists" was impossible and he reformed the PSP.

The Soudan swings left

The next decade saw an intense **rivalry** between the PSP and the USRDA but, by 1957, the latter had clearly won the upper hand. This was in large part because the USRDA had more effectively distanced itself from Paris and had better grass-roots organization in Mali. After the elections of 1959, in which the PSP fared badly, they were constrained to join forces with the USRDA. On the eve of independence, there was no effective opposition to this party.

Changes had occurred within the USRDA when Konaté died in 1956. A moderate voice on the left, Konaté had advocated union of all the peoples of Mali. The void he left in the party ranks was quickly filled by more radical elements headed by **Modibo Keita**.

In the same year, the **Loi Cadre** drafted in Paris had opened the door to semi-autonomous governments in each

of the territories of the AOF. This led to divisions in the formerly united RDA between leaders like Sekou Touré of Guinea and Léopold Senghor of Senegal – who advocated the maintenance of a federal government in Dakar – and those such as Houphouët-Boigny of Côte d'Ivoire, who advocated the maximum autonomy for each of the territories.

Federalists and federation

Modibo Keita stood firmly in the camp of the Federalists, mainly because, as a poor country, the Soudan had a lot to gain from uniting itself with other territories (many of the country's colonial projects had been financed by AOF funds that originated outside Mali). Senghor's motives were more ideological, and he pleaded for a politically united West Africa that would maintain good relations with France. It became more pressing to decide on the pros and cons of a federation after the **1958 referendum** where AOF nations voted to continue self-government within the French Union.

Sekou Touré was the only African leader who, for better or worse, had the courage to storm out of the French Union. Guinea was thereby excluded from any West African federation as well. Côte d'Ivoire was also out, since Houphouët-Boigny had stated loud and clear that he wouldn't have his country become the "milk cow" to feed the mouths of hungry neighbours.

In January 1959, the four remaining members of the former AOF – Soudan, Senegal, Upper Volta and Dahomey – met in Dakar and drew up the constitution for a **federation** of their territories. Under pressure from Côte d'Ivoire, Upper Volta eventually backed out of its commitment and Dahomey followed suit. Hopes for a broad-based political union in the region had been pared down to two nations, but it was still an important step for pan-African ideals. The **Mali Federation** of Mali and Senegal was born.

Unhappy union with Senegal

From the beginning, the alliance was uneasy. Keita was eager that Mali be granted independence. Senghor was more methodical, less hurried. De Gaulle himself helped sort out this problem by recognizing in 1959 that it was possible for the federation to be granted **independence** while staying in the French Community. The Mali Federation did, in fact, become independent – on April 4, 1960 – but the honeymoon between Senghor and Keita lasted barely two months.

Although numerous social and economic inequalities existed between the two former territories (which without doubt had an adverse effect on the union), the most glaring divergences were political and symbolized by the **clash of personalities** of the two leaders. Keita championed a Marxist approach to "African socialism". He was a man of (often admirable) principles who liked decisive action and who was unused to compromise. Senghor's approach was more measured and tended to favour dialogue and diplomatic action. He was especially cautious and pragmatic in his attitude to France which he hoped to keep as a friend and ally.

The stand-off between the two men – and as a consequence the territories they presided over – came to a head during the 1960 elections for President of the Federation, a powerful office that the Soudanese were wary of Senghor occupying. Senegal ruled out any alternative nominee and the brief federal arrangement collapsed.

Birth of the Mali Republic

After the failure of the Federation, Keita set about creating the basis of the independent Malian state – a task of Promethean proportions at such short notice. He was helped, however, by the wave of **nationalist pride** and unity that swept the country, now destined to stand alone. Even Keita's former opponent, Cissoko, threw his support behind the USRDA in the name of the national cause. In September 1960, a special congress of the USRDA announced the implementation of a **planned socialist economy**. Shortly afterwards, Keita closed French military bases in Mali. He then set up state enterprises, starting with SOMIEX, which had a monopoly on all imports and exports of primary products – an advantage French companies operating in the country hardly appreciated. In 1962, Keita pushed his country further into **isolation** by taking it out of the franc zone and creating a national currency, the Franc Malien. In the same year, a **Tuareg revolt** in the Adrar des Iforhas mountains northeast of Gao was savagely repressed by the army

It was a difficult start, made even worse by the fact that Senegal stopped trains to Bamako for three years after the rupture and closed its borders with Mali. As Keita continued down his radical path (and he was sincere in his belief that Mali could be the spearhead of a new brand of "African socialism", though his conception of what this meant differed from that of other regional leaders) he distanced himself from other African nations. And the West, too, turned an icy shoulder as, in the middle of the Cold War, he chose to ally his country with the Soviet Union. Opposition mounted grimly at home as the business community saw their economic privileges being eroded into state assets.

By the **mid-1960s**, Keita had created a heavy state machinery that dragged mercilessly on the nation's already fragile economy. The situation was characterized by numerous national enterprises (almost all of them running a deficit), a plethora of civil servants clogging the administrative machinery, a soaring balance-of-trade deficit and foreign debt, and a rapid weakening of the currency. Inflation soared and wages were frozen – a combination that wasn't calculated to enthuse Malians. By 1967, taking his cue from Peking, Keita was engaged in a **"cultural revolution"** to purge the nation of enemies within. He was supported in this by radical students, some of the unions, and by some lower grades in the civil service who resented the corruption of senior officials and business profiteers. But in the same year, Keita was obliged to devalue the Malian franc by fifty percent. The public outcry was immediate; the government's entire direction came under attack from all sides.

Keita seemed not to notice that opposition was sprouting up all around him. Believing the monumental role he'd played in his country's development absolved him from criticism by a populace faced with a deepening economic crisis, he was apparently surprised and aggrieved when a group of young military officers staged a **bloodless coup** in 1968.

The Traoré years

The **Comité Militaire de Libération Nationale (CMLN)** was quickly formed, headed by a 32-year-old lieutenant, **Moussa Traoré**. Keita and senior members of his government were arrested and the former president died in prison ten years later.

The military recognized the need to correct certain errors committed by the previous regime, to bring new order to the management of the economy and to boost production. To this end, Traoré continued to rely on Soviet and Chinese technical aid. However, the first years of military rule brought little relief to the country. Overnight revival of the economy was impracticable, and the military didn't challenge the nation's socialist orientation.

The **drought** that ravaged the nation in 1973 and 1974 had a disastrous effect on agriculture. Industrial development didn't fare much better, and the 1974 **border war** with Burkina Faso put an extra drain on human and financial resources. Despite discouraging signs in

the political and economic spheres, the military drew up a new constitution in 1974 that was approved in a plebiscite by what the government claimed was 99.7 percent of the population.

The new constitution, however, didn't go into effect until 1979, when a single party, the **Union Démocratique du Peuple Malien (UDPM)**, was charged with running the country. Traoré remained at the head of government. This symbolic transformation to civilian rule was accompanied by a softening of the rigid socialist philosophy. The trend was accelerated after a second drought devastated the country from 1983 to 1985. In an effort to assure continued foreign aid, Traoré worked hard to improve relations with the West, notably with France. Most of the state organizations and companies that were a tremendous financial burden were privatized in an effort to dynamize the economy. Additionally Traoré brought Mali into the CFA fold in 1985, a move which encouraged investment.

Democracy and the Third Republic

Through such steps Traoré thought he could bring his country out of the quarter-century of political and economic isolation into which it had retreated after the so-called Balkanization of French West Africa on the eve of independence, and especially after the final rupture with Senegal. But, intentionally or otherwise, he also opened Mali to the **pressure for democratic reform** which was sweeping the region by 1990 and which was increasingly a condition of foreign aid.

At first, Traoré tried to contain the pressure within the party framework. Opposition leaders from the Alliance pour la Démocratie au Mali (**Adema**) wanted more, and published an article in one of the new newspapers, *Les Echos*, calling for a national conference to draft a new constitution and lead the transition to multiparty politics. Soon after, a series of independent parties came into being, including the Comité National d'Initiative Démocratique (CNID) and the Union Soudanaise –Rassemblement Démocratique Africain (US-RDA), the re-formed pre-independence party.

By December 1990, dissent was trickling down to the streets: the government tried to evict street vendors from downtown Bamako, provoking a **mass demonstration** that coincided with the anniversary of the Universal Declaration of Human Rights. On New Year's Eve, a pro-democracy demonstration attracted 15,000 marchers and, on January 8, 1991, a **general strike** for better wages was called – the first in Mali since independence. **Student protestors** jumped into the fray, organizing a demonstration that was brutally suppressed by the police and resulted in a number of deaths.

The government wasted no time in demanding that political parties and student organizations cease all activity. It closed the country's schools, and deployed heavy weapons on the streets of Bamako. In the **mass arrests** which followed, Amnesty International reported widespread torture in the prisons, sometimes of schoolchildren as young as 12.

Malians barely had time to recover from these incidents when a more concerted round of **rioting** broke out in March. In three days of intense fighting, police and gendarmes killed some 150 people and injured nearly a thousand. Wave after wave of protestors continued to swell through the city, however. In the face of a failed policy of violent suppression, coupled with international disapproval and complete disruption of the economy, Traoré made plans to flee, but promised elections, and said shortly after that he would not resign and that his troops were loyal.

The new era

The military responded by arresting Traoré. The **coup** leader, Lt-Col

Amadou Toumani Touré dissolved the government, suspended the constitution and abolished the UDPM. Within days, a multiparty committee had been formed to oversee the democratization of Mali. **Soumana Sacko**, a former finance minister sacked by Traoré when he tried a little too diligently to crack down on corruption, was appointed interim prime minister. More arrests followed, with ex-government ministers charged with corruption and murder. An unsuccessful **counter-coup** mounted by officers loyal to the ex-president was easily quashed, a jubilant crowd swarming through the streets of Bamako when it was learned the putsch had failed.

The people seemed less enthusiastic at voting time, however. The hero of the democratic revolution, **Amadou Toumani Touré**, or "ATT" to his millions of admirers, did not seek a permament role in power and, in the first free municipal and presidential elections in 1992, barely a fifth of eligible Malians bothered to vote. The Adema party secured a large majority, however, and their man, the academic **Alpha Oumar Konaré**, was sworn in as president of the Third Republic on June 8, 1992.

In 1993, Traoré and several members of his disgraced government were convicted of murder. They were subsequently sentenced to death, sentences which were later commuted to life imprisonment (Mali has had no judicial executions since 1980).

Konaré was not an instinctive politician, and although his self-effacement earned him broad respect, it also made his first term in office somewhat difficult and unproductive. It was only in 1994 that he established a proper working relationship with the brusque, though effective, **Ibrahim Boubacar Keita**, who was his prime minister until February 2000. Meanwhile, the students, not surprisingly, quickly switched from backing the democrats to opposing the government that was formed, and the new order provoked rather than

The roots of the Tuareg rebellion were put in place after France's abortive attempt to form a Tuareg state – "Azaouad" – in 1958, on the eve of independence. The revolt began in 1990 with an attack on a military post at Ménaka, 300km east of Gao, followed up by a much bigger attack in September on Bouressa, which left at least 300 dead on both sides. The rebellion coincided with the return from Algeria of **drought refugees** who were unhappy with their reception in Mali, and was framed in terms of overthrowing Moussa Traoré and improving development aid to their regions. But as the democracy movement in Bamako took hold and Traoré was deposed, the Tuareg rebellion made more specific demands for, at the very least, greater autonomy for the desert regions. Ultimately the issues boiled down to one: **race**. The Tuareg viewed themselves, and were viewed as, "whites" and former lords (or oppressors), while the sedentary population considered themselves "blacks", newly enfranchised by democratic reforms.

A ceasefire agreement was signed in Tamanrasset in Algeria in January 1991. The rebels' signatory was **Iyad Ag Galli**, leader of the Azouad Popular Movement (MPA), whose agenda listed a better deal for the Tuareg above greater autonomy and specifically excluded the ideal of independence for a Tuareg state.

The accord was rejected by other Tuareg militia, which continued a campaign of armed attacks, usually by small groups of rebels, on police stations and government buildings. These attacks were invariably followed by brutal military reprisals on the most obvious Tuareg target in the district. Tens of thousands of refugees, mostly Tuareg, fled the affected areas to southern Algeria and Mauritania.

A second peace agreement – the **national pact** – was signed in April 1992, with a new umbrella organization of the Tuareg in Mali, the Unified Fronts and Movements of the Azouad (MFUA). During the course of the year, 600 ex-rebels were integrated into the Malian army, 300 given civil service posts, and joint Tuareg-army patrols were instituted.

But the MFUA began to disintegrate, with several factions at war with each other. As for the MPA, with its demands for full Tuareg integration into Malian national life, it was accused of a sell-out. Additionally, there were clashes between regular soldiers of the Malian army and "integrated" Tuareg troops.

Resentment at the Tuaregs' comparative success at achieving their aims through violence led to the formation of various ethnic vigilante groups. The most menacing was a Songhai resistance militia, **Ganda Koi** ("Owners of the Land"), which launched vicious attacks on Tuareg camps. Despite the widespread violence, the Bamako government remained committed to a peaceful solution and, encouraged by positive talks in January 1995 between the Tuareg and Ganda Koi representatives in Bourem, a series of community meetings was launched, followed by a lengthy tour of northern Mali and of Tuareg refugee camps in Algeria and Mauritania. The government's programme to reinstall civilian local government and to improve education and healthcare provision in the conflict areas gave the predominantly young Tuareg fighters reasons to engage in civilian life, and rapidly led to the disarmament of rebel fighters.

A **repatriation scheme** to bring back tens of thousands of Tuareg refugees from Algeria, Mauritania, Burkina and Niger was launched in October 1995, and a final **peace agreement** was signed in 1996. There was a burning of weapons in Timbuktu in March 1996, which marked the end of the six-year rebellion, since when the Tuareg have reintegrated with Malian society. Many former Tuareg fighters have joined Mali's armed forces, and prospects for the Tuareg in Mali appear significantly better than for their kin in Algeria and Niger.

satisfied their demands. There were violent protests in Bamako in 1994 over the devaluation of the CFA franc, a policy popularly interpreted as neo-colonial. Konaré's government was condemned by Amnesty for its frequently heavy-handed response to ordinary criticism from leading lights in the opposition – ad hoc imprisonment, harassment and detention were regular occurrences – and for not doing enough to eradicate the use of torture in prisons.

In the country's **second elections**, which rolled for several tedious months through the rainy season of 1997, President Konaré got nearly 96 percent of the vote in the presidential election, while his Adema party took 130 seats out of parliament's total of 147 in the national assembly elections. In both cases, however, there was a widespread opposition boycott and a very low turnout (twenty percent across the country, but down to twelve percent in Bamako). The opposition did more than accuse Adema of cheating; they accused the electoral commission itself of malpractice and demanded the entire electoral process be rescheduled. In the event both elections were simply rerun. To the dismay of many in his Adema party, Konaré's response to the landslide result was typically conciliatory, and he offered concessions to the opposition, including a fairer distribution of public money to opposition campaign funds.

Mali at the turn of the century

As the twentieth century came to an end, Mali's political life was dominated by the issue of the Adema party's firm grip on power. The Adema leadership was more willing to drive democracy forward than many of its rank-and-file supporters, and has frequently been cited as being in the vanguard of democratic reform in Africa. Behind the steady turmoil of Bamako party politics, the legacy of the old order continues to haunt the new Mali. The country's first success in recovering **looted public money** came in 1997, when several Swiss banks agreed to repay to Konaré's government more than £1.5million/US\$2.4million of state funds stolen by the former head of the national tobacco and match company. However, the return of two billion dollars estimated to have been stolen by former dictator Moussa Traoré may take longer. The economic crimes committed by Traoré and his cronies were not brought before the courts until 1998 when, to the disgust of many Malians, the sums he was accused of embezzling amounted to only fifteen percent of his estimated total scoop. He received another death sentence, which Konaré commuted to life imprisonment in 1999.

The biggest single issue faced by Konaré's government in the 1990s was the **Tuareg rebellion** (see box, opposite). At the conflict's peak, an estimated 160,000 people had fled to refugee camps in Algeria, Mauritania and Burkina Faso. Two-thirds of the country – everywhere north and east of the Bamako–Mopti road – was too dangerous to travel through, and the region's towns were transformed into besieged garrisons in the wilderness. The Tuareg fighters pursuing the war probably numbered no more than several hundred. But every new atrocity dug each side into a deeper hatred of the other. The fact that Konaré's government and the Tuareg faction leaders resolved this bitter and bloody dispute with little third-party assistance is one of the better chapters in post-colonial African history.

ATT back in power

Konaré, having failed to convince his people or international observers of his determination to crack corruption, appears to have set himself on a course to improve his reputation after retiring. Recognizing the splits within his Adema party, he gave tacit support in the 2002 presidential elections to Mali's *éminence grise*, the charismatic **Amadou Toumani Touré** ("ATT"). ATT's campaign aimed to build links to all the parties – though allying with none – as well as civil rights groups. Twenty-four candidates stood for the election, but his two main opponents were Soumaïla Cissé (Economy and Finance Minister under Konaré, and the official Adema candidate) and the Prime Minister until 2000, Ibrahim Boubacar Keita. After an inconclusive first round of voting, in which ATT was narrowly ahead of his two main rivals, Keita decided to side with ATT, whose resulting victory, on a very low turnout, came as no surprise, though it took a month for the constitutional court to validate the results after numerous murmurings of fraud. The election result appeared to signal the end – or at least the chance of a re-birth – for Adema, which had been beset by internal strife for years. ATT's non-partisan "anti-politics" ticket, stressing reconciliation and economic probity, brought him plaudits at home and internationally (he has good contacts at the UN and in the US).

The crisis in Côte d'Ivoire hit Mali's emigré workers particularly hard, and the tens of thousands who fled home added to the country's economic difficulties. Meanwhile, opposition to ATT is mounting, led by younger activists in the Espoir 2002 coalition, who have no representatives in ATT's government despite forming the largest body in the National Assembly. They are frustrated at ATT's willingness to toe the IMF line, which causes considerable hardship. Nevertheless, ATT appears to be well in control and up to the job, and is likely to run with the reform programme that his professorial predecessor Konaré never got much beyond the paper stage.

Though not all Malians would accept that democracy has brought significant benefits, the prospects for the economy and for inward investment are better now than they have been since independence, and better here than in most of Mali's neighbours.

Music

Mali's music is steeped in tradition. Even in the country's modern popular music, featuring wide-ranging international influences, the musical roots run deep. The music of the Bamana and Malinké, the Fula, the Songhai and the Dogon have all helped to give today's Malian music its flavour and colour.

Manding music: the *jeli* tradition

Largely untouched by Western influences, "Manding" music is about sweet melodies and hypnotic rhythms, a style to which you can either dance or day-dream. You'll find this broad genre from The Gambia to Mali and down through Guinea, in an area roughly corresponding to the spread of the Mande languages – in Mali, this is the region west of Bamako.

Manding musicians are easy enough to track down. The members of certain families – notably Konté, Kouyaté /Kuyateh and Diabaté/Jobarteh – carry the title of **jeli** (**griot** in French), hereditary musician. The *jelis* have been around since at least the thirteenth-century origins of the Mali empire, based in the northeast of what is now Guinea, under Emperor **Sundiata Keita**. Traditionally, most instruments, including the **kora** – West Africa's distinctive harp-lute – are restricted to them.

A *jeli*'s reputation is built upon humility and correct behaviour as well as his (or her) knowledge of history and family genealogies – originally, the role was to do with the preservation of oral

Manding instruments

Kora 21- to 25-stringed harp-lute made with a large decorated half-gourd covered with a skin. The strings – which used to be twisted leather, but tend now to be various gauges of fishing line – are attached with leather thongs to a rosewood pole put through the gourd. The top of the body has a large sound-hole that doubles as a collection point for money from the audience.

Bala (or *balafon*) Rosewood xylophone with between 17 and 20 keys, known to have been around since the fourteenth century.

Kontingo Small, oval lute with 5 strings.

Bolom (or *bolombato*) Lute with 3 or 4 strings and an arched neck that used to be played for warriors going into battle. It's now an instrument played by men who are not of a *jeli* family.

history. Mostly, this meant singing the praises of the noble and wealthy (no occasion – a wedding or child-naming ceremony for example – would be complete without a *jeli*), but now they're just as likely to have business or civil service patrons. *Jelis*, moreover, are personalities who have the ears of the people and any corrupt politician or civil servant has to reckon with them.

Jelis call on a great **repertoire of songs**. If you have the chance to hear a number of artists, however, you'll start to recognize lyrical variations on common melodic themes. Old classics like "Sundiata Faso", "Tutu Jara", "Lambang", "Koulanjan", "Duga", "Tara" and "Sori" are heard time and again, interspersed with songs from this century, often with a regional flavour, such as "Kaira". A griot's skill lies in the improvised flourishes and ornamentation – the *birimintingo* – that he brings to the recurrent theme or core melody, called the *donkili*.

In Mande-speaking society **men** always play the instruments. **Women artists** are considered the better singers and often receive extraordinary gifts – even planes and houses aren't unknown. Even at ordinary live performances, people in the audience, moved by a particular song, just shed their jewellery on them there and then.

Traditional Manding music is a lasting influence on Mali's modern music. **Mory Kanté** and **Salif Keita** both derive artistic sustenance from it, and a popular band like **Bembeya Jazz** reinterprets Manding songs.

Toumani Diabaté

A brilliant *kora* virtuoso, Toumani Diabaté is also an ambitious and highly creative artist.

Kaira (Hannibal). Solo *kora* music at its finest.

New Ancient Strings (Hannibal). Extraordinary artistry is evident on this collaboration with cousin and fellow *kora* master Ballaké Sissoko.

Kandia Kouyaté

"La dangereuse" has a stunning stage presence and has been Mali's top female *jeli* singer for the past two decades. Her forceful voice and choral arrangements and her working of traditional social and court music has earned her huge wealth and a status unequalled by any other female artist from Mali.

Kita Kan (Stern's). Kandia's first international release. The *kora*, *ngoni*, guitars and *balafon* just keep on rolling and there are enough lush studio effects – and even full orchestral backing – to qualify *Kita Kan* for any number of radio playlists.

Contemporary Manding sounds

After **independence**, there was a renaissance of popular music in Mali. The bands, who had for many years been playing latin styles, became aware that people wanted to hear music from their own cultures. The government supported this search for roots and a number of groups received state sponsorship. Orchestras were at last able to afford modern instruments.

One of the most famous venues in Mali is the *Buffet Hôtel de la Gare* in Bamako, a venue which emerged from the hotel's quest for financial salvation. The director of Mali's state railway in the 1960s, **Djibril Diallo** was a big music fan and decided to create a station orchestra. The **Rail Band**, as they became known, mixed plaintive vocal styles over traditional Manding rhythms played with electric instruments. Showcased at the *Hôtel Buffet de la Gare*, the band rapidly acquired legendary status, and the venue became the hottest spot in Bamako. The band is still going today, and over the years has provided a launch pad for many talented musicians, including **Salif Keita** and **Mory Kanté**.

Salif Keita

An albino, Salif Keita started out singing in bars for loose change, evidently to the disgrace of his family. In 1970 he joined the Rail Band, which gave him an opportunity to modernize traditional songs. After being ousted from the *Buffet Hôtel* by the then *balafon* (xylophone) player Mory Kanté, Salif joined Les Ambassadeurs – who had immediate success with hits like "Primpin" – and recorded three albums for Safari Ambience. In 1978 he moved to Abidjan and, with Kanté Manfila, formed Ambassadeurs Internationaux, who recorded the wonderful song "Mandjou" – dedicated, ironically, to the despotic ruler of Guinea, Sekou Touré. Then he left for Paris and international stardom.

Soro (Stern's in the UK; Mango in the US). Released in 1987, this would become one of the biggest selling African recordings ever – outside the

continent – and one of the greatest successes of world music. Breathtaking and seamless high-tech arrangements of Manding music with contributions from guitarist Ousmane Kouyaté and French keyboard player Jean-Philippe Rykiel form the perfect backdrop to some extraordinary vocals.

The Mansa of Mali ... a Retrospective (Mango). Includes highlights from his three Mango releases, plus the all-time 1978 hit with Les Ambassadeurs, "Mandjou".

Moffou (Universal). A return to form, asserting Salif Keita's position as a truly inspired musician and songwriter, *Moffou* reflects his own roots, swaying between melancholy and bursts of energy.

Habib Koité

A popular singer-songwriter, the *jeli* Habib Koité goes well beyond Bamana praise songs to include traditions from across Mali.

Muso Ko (Contre Jour). Koité's first album was a sensation, winning him the prestigious Radio France International African Discovery award for hisanti-smoking "Cigarette Abana".

Ma Ya (Putumayo). Koité's acoustic guitar is to the fore here, rounding off a subtle, highly melodic album.

Baro (Putumayo). Another good example of Koité's talent on acoustic guitar, although traditional instruments are present in abundance, the backing as ever served up by his band Bamada.

Kasse Mady Diabaté

Arguably the best contemporary Mande voice, Kasse Mady Diabaté rivals Salif Keita for beauty and lyricism, while being rooted in the *jeli* tradition.

Kela Tradition (Stern's). Kela is a Malinké village in western Mali, almost entirely inhabited by *jelis* of the Diabaté family. This is an almost entirely acoustic studio-produced album, featuring *ngoni* and *balafon* as well as guitars and Jean-Philippe Rykiel on keyboards. Includes expansive and gorgeous versions of Mande classics like "Koulandjan" and "Kaira".

Ali Farka Touré

Not from one of the traditional families of hereditary musicians, Ali Farka Touré started playing purely for his own pleasure and did so in a style which resonates with American blues affinities – although he had never heard the blues until he was already firmly established. He still spends most of his time (and most of his money) on his farm at Niafounké, on the Niger near Timbuktu.

Talking Timbuktu (World Circuit). A collaboration with Ry Cooder, this is a record out of left field that actually sounds like people playing together in a room.

Radio Mali (World Circuit). Beautifully produced compilation of radio recordings made in 1970–78, a decade or more before he achieved international recognition.

Niafunké (World Circuit). A determined return to roots in every sense, allowing the world to hear Ali doing his wonderful stuff almost literally in his own backyard.

Amadou et Mariam

Both blind, Amadou et Mariam (often written with an "&" for *et*) have been acclaimed one of the best modern acts in Mali. Amadou Bagayoko formerly played together with Manfila Kanté and Salif Keita in the legendary Ambassadeurs, while Myriam Doumbia started playing with him in Côte d'Ivoire where they made their first five albums between 1988 and 1993.

Sete Djon Ye (Sonodisc). Their first album made back in Mali, an eclectic affair with influences from reggae and salsa.

Tiè Ni Muso (Universal). Another wonderful mix, featuring Portuguese *cavaquihino*, a dash of Bengali violin, plus some reggae and jazzy piano.

Rokia Traoré

Born in 1973, Rokia Traoré is the voice of young women in Mali, and her songs are about the place of women in society, while her roots are firmly grounded in the *jeli* and *kora* tradition. On her recordings her soft voice is accompanied by electric guitars, *ngoni* (a lutelike instrument, the precursor of the banjo) and *bala* (see p.333). The result is mesmerizing.

Wanita (Indigo). A bit more assertive than her debut *Mouneissa*, though as subtle and enchanting as ever.

Modern Fula sounds – Wassoulou

There are Fula communities all over Mali – Fula herders dominate the flat floodlands of the inland delta region for example – but it's the **Wassoulou** region of southwest Mali that has been musically the most important for Fula artists over the last two decades. The people of Wassoulou do not have griots, and their music is based on an ancient tradition of hunters' songs, with pentatonic (five-note) melodies. This tended in the past to be viewed as teenage music, and only a few decades ago such songs were regarded as slightly subversive, and forbidden by the elders.

The Wassoulou Sound: Women of Mali and **The Wassoulou Sound: Vol. 2** (Stern's). Excellent compilations featuring a range of female voices and Wassoulou styles, including the pioneers of "Wassoulou electric", Kagbe Sidibé and Coumba Sidibé. Buy the CDs as a set – the notes were written for both.

Oumou Sangaré

Oumou Sangaré is the best-known exponent of the Wassoulou sound, whose passionate style ("I sing of love, not praises") shook up the musical status quo in Mali, a country previously dominated, musically, by fat-cat *jelis* and the Paris-based elite.

Ko Sira (World Circuit). A breath of fresh air from a young woman singer whose impact on traditional musical culture could hardly have been greater, wielding her voice like a weapon, and deploring, as she put it, the male-dominated status quo. Beautifully produced, this is Wassoulou music at its best.

Worotan (World Circuit). Here Sangaré defies tradition with her lyrics ("Marry you? Why?!"), custom with her musical arrangements (Pee Wee Ellis and others adding funky horn grooves), and stereotyping with her range.

Tuareg music

Although Tuareg men and women both make music, they traditionally have separate forms and styles. Women's songs include **tinde nomnas** (praise songs), **tinde nguma** (songs of exorcism) and **ezele** (dance songs). The **tinde**, used to accompany women's songs, is a drum made from a goatskin stretched over a mortar. Other instruments used by women include the **assakhalebo** water drum, made from a half-gourd floating upside down in a bowl of water, and the **tabl** – a kettledrum (traditionally a battle drum) with a broad camel-skin top. There's also an end-blown flute, called the **sarewa**, constructed from a sorghum stem in which four holes are made, with leather thongs tied round its body for ornamentation and protection.

The men's songs, or **tichiwe**, are, in striking contrast to the women's, essentially lyrical. They sing about the beauty of the women they love or celebrate some happy event. The songs are performed by soloists – whose virtuosity lies as ever in improvisation – either with or without an accompaniment. This is usually provided by a single-stringed fiddle, the **inzad**, which consists of a half-gourd, goatskin-covered resonator and a horsehair string stretched over a bridge in the form of a small wooden cross.

Tinariwen

Tinariwen were formed in a Tuareg refugee camp in southern Libya in the 1980s and claim the influence of Dylan and Bob Marley on a ragged, repetitive sound which they initially used to promote the goal of Tuareg independence (getting them banned from the tape shops in Mali). Several members saw action during the Tuareg rebellion before the 1996 peace accord.

The Radio Tisdas Sessions (Wayward). Rough-and-ready first international release from one of the few Tuareg groups on the world stage, recorded in a radio station in remote Kidal. The electric guitars and percussion plus vocal improvisation don't quite match the live performance, but it's a gutsy display nonetheless and every track breathes a harsh desert spirit. If you can't make it to Le Festival au Désert (see p.382), this is the stay-home alternative.

Books

There's not a great deal of accessible writing in English from, or about, Mali. Malian literature in French – we've listed a couple of recommendations – repays the effort, though a few titles are sporadically translated into English. Titles marked ⊡ are especially recommended.

Ibn Battuta *Travels in Asia and Africa.* Selections from the writings of the great fourteenth-century wanderer, including his travels along the Niger.

Walter E.A. van Beek and Stephanie Hollyman *Dogon: Africa's People of the Cliffs.* A photographic collection showing Dogon society engaged in daily work and sacred ritual.

Banning Eyre *In Griot Time: An American Guitarist in Mali.* Musician, writer and broadcaster, Eyre brilliantly captures the flavour of modern Mali through its music, in this account of a sojourn spent studying Malian guitar styles under Djelimady Tounkara.

Jean Marie Gibbal *Genii of the River Niger.* The French author's personal account of travels by *pirogue* through eastern Mali. Some of the more interesting passages depict healing ceremonies, which revolve around the river.

Mark Jenkins *To Timbuktu: A Journey down the Niger.* By turns macho and self-deprecating, Jenkins' account of his 1970s journey, and 1990s return (with kayaks) is a readable, if sometimes fanciful, travelogue, interwoven with the stories of the nineteenth-century explorers.

⊡ **Lieve Joris** *Mali Blues.* Four accounts of travel and conversation in Senegal, Mauritania and Mali. The main story is a kind of extended on-the-road interview with the Malian singer and guitarist Boubacar Traoré, exploring the pervasive and unsettling spiritual dimension of Africa – though never quite following through to confront or enter it.

Seydou Keïta *Seydou Keïta: African Photographs.* An extraordinary collection of black-and-white studio photos of Bamako people from the 1950s to the 1970s – a testament to the richness of African urban culture.

Mamadou Kouyaté (translated by G.D. Pickett) *Sundiata: An Epic of Old Mali.* Slim and fascinating transcription of a griot's history of Mali.

William Seabrook *The White Monk of Timbuctoo.* First published in the 1930s, this is the biography of Père Yakouba, a white priest who married a Timbuktu woman and changed his vocation.

Bettina Selby *Frail Dream of Timbuktu.* Selby's account of her bicycle journey from Niamey to Bamako is beautifully written and covers much more than just the journey – with interest-filled deviations and asides.

Fa-Diga Sissoko (translated by John William Johnson) *The Epic of Son-Jara.* A recent translation – and a new spelling for Sundiata/Sunjata – of the 800-year-old story of the Mali empire's founder.

Fiction

Seydou Badian *Caught in the Storm.* A tale of culture clash, set within a rural family during French colonial rule.

Maryse Condé *Segu.* An epic historical novel – already a Francophone classic before its translation into English – by a Guadeloupan author of Bamana descent, that paints a mesmerizing and unsettlingly graphic portrait of the Ségou empire from 1797 to the middle of the nineteenth century.

Amadou Hampate Ba *Fortunes of Wangrin.* Hampate Ba, born in Bandiagara, was a Fula academic and transcriber of oral literature (he died in 1991). In this novel, an administrative interpreter tells of the colonial period from 1900 to 1945, and his successful collusion with it.

Chukwuemeka Ike *The Naked Gods.* A comical tale of the clash between conservatives and progressives at a fictitious Malian university, by a Nigerian author.

Bokar N'Diaye *La Mort des Fétiches de Sénédougou.* Traumas from changes to the traditional way of life during the colonial era.

⭐ **Yambo Ouologuem** *Bound to Violence.* This treatment of

brutality and deceit in an invented African empire, Nakem, insists that West African society rests on foundations as bloody and self-destructive as any other. By the only Malian writer to have achieved international recognition, the book screams for a new, rehumanizing look at the liberal romantic version of black history – a position that upset the earnest negritude movement.

Mamby Sibidé *Contes Populaires du Mali.* Captivating stories and legends from the oral tradition of different Malian ethnic groups.

Languages

French is the official language in Mali and the one you'll have to deal with for all administrative preoccupations, though only a small percentage of the population speaks it fluently. The most widely spoken national language is **Bamana** (more commonly spelt **Bambara**), which is similar to Malinké and used throughout the country, especially in the region around Bamako. Other languages include Pulaar (Fula), Senoufo, Songhai, Tamashek and Dogon.

Basic Bamana

Compare the words and phrases below with those in the Mandinka section in the Gambia chapter, p.270.

Greetings

Hello	A ni tié (Kosèbè)/ N-bifo
Good morning	Ani sogoma
Man's response	M-ba
Woman's response	Oun sé
Good afternoon	Ani woula
Good evening	Ani sou
How's the family?	Somo go bédi?
They're fine	Toro té
How's it going?	I ka kènè wa?/ Hèrè bé?
Everything's fine	Toro si té
See you later	Ka an bé sogoma/Kanbé

Numbers

1	kèlèn
2	fila
3	saaba
4	naani
5	douru
6	wooro
7	wolonwula
8	seguin
9	kononton
10	tan
20	mugan
25	mugan ni douru
30	bi sabi
40	bi nani
50	bi douru
100	kèmè
120	kèmè ni mugan
150	kèmè ni bi dourou
200	kèmè fila

5 franc piece	dorem		
10 francs	dormè fila		
25 francs	dormè dourou		
50 francs	dormè ta		
75 francs	dormè tan ne dourou		
100 francs	dormè muga		
200 francs	dormè bi nani		
300 francs	dormè bi woro		
400 francs	dormè bi segui		
500 francs	dormè kèmè		
700 francs	dormè kèmè ni bi nani		
1000 francs	dormè kèmè fila		
2000 francs	dormè kèmè nani		

Useful expressions

How much?	Joli?
It's lovely	A kaï
I'll take it (give it to me)	A di yan
It's too expensive	A songo ka guèlè
Do you know of a cheap restaurant?	I bi resitoran da duman don wa?
Where's the bank?	Bank bé voro djimé?
Show me the way	Sila jira kan na
Where are you going?	I bi taa min?
I don't know	N'ta lou
I don't understand	N'ma fahamuya
Excuse me/Sorry	Ya fan ma
What did you say? (please repeat)	Aw kodi
Yes/No	Awo/Aï
Thank you (very much)	I ni tié (kosèbè)

Glossary

ADEMA Alliance pour la démocratie au Mali. The largest political party.

Azalaï Desert caravans that formerly dominated Saharan trade. They continue today in small numbers, notably between the salt mines of Taoudenni and Timbuktu.

Banco Clay or mud-brick.

Bogolan Literally "mud cloth", cotton strips with a batik print.

Cadeauter Transformation of the French word *cadeau*, meaning "gift", into a verb. Sometimes used by children in the expression "il faut me cadeauter", meaning "give me something".

Dourou-dourouni *Camion bâché*, pick-up or bush taxi.

Ghana In the historical context, usually refers to ancient Ghana, the earliest Mande-speaking kingdom (precursor of Mali), the ruined capital of which, Koumbi Saleh, is located in southeast Mauritania. The name "Ghana" was the title used by its Soninké rulers.

Hogon Dogon priests who live in isolation. These elderly men represent the highest spiritual authority in the Dogon country.

Mali An old empire (based southwest of Bamako) as well as the modern state, "Mali" is synonymous with "Manding", just as the language Malinké is basically the same one as Mandinka. Mali in Malinké means "hippo".

Masina Historically, the Fula empire centred on the town of Massina northeast of Ségou.

Oued Pronounced "wed"; French version of the Arabic word *wadi*, designating a rocky riverbed, dry except in the rainy season.

Pinasse Large wooden boat originally invented in Djenné to carry cargo. Though the basic covered design hasn't changed over the centuries, motors are added today.

S(o)udan Former colonial name for the territory encompassing Senegal, Mali and Burkina Faso. The term is sometimes used today to refer to this same basic area. Sudanic architecture has nothing to do with the modern state of Sudan, referring in fact to the style that originated in Djenné.

4.1

Bamako

Although **BAMAKO** has grown quickly since independence, evidence of modernization is only slowly penetrating the dusty city centre. Here, the mix of day-long crowds, hostile traffic and sludge-filled sewers adds up to an oppressive combination for visitors just in from the *brousse*, although arrivals from Dakar welcome the fact that Bamako's hustlers are less aggressive – debilitated, presumably, by the perennial heat. At dusk the dust settles down like a pink fog as the centre expels its torrid activity into the suburbs where the conspicuous aid community reposes in air-conditioned comfort.

Architecturally, ostentatious modern developments like the Saudi-built **Pont du Roi Fahd** and nearby, the neo-Sudanic **Tour BCEAO** – the city's stunning showpiece – emerge from amid the medieval sanitation and dreary Soviet-funded blocks of the early 1960s. Compared with Mali's undeniable rural attractions, the capital is just too hot, dirty and crowded to be immediately appealing, and for most the few days taken to obtain the next visa, go to the supermarket, write a few letters or wait for transport connections will be long enough. However, while you're here, don't miss out on the great nightlife and the music scene.

Some history

As rock paintings (notably at the **Point G caves**) attest, Bamako is the site of ancient settlements, peopled as early as the African Paleolithic and Neolithic ages. Oral history traces the roots of the present town back to **Seribadian Niaré**, who sought refuge in the Bamana empire after being chased from the region of Nioro du Sahel in the seventeenth century. Upon arrival in the capital town of **Ségou**, Niaré married the sister of the king, **Soumba Coulibaly**. The couple had a son, **Diamoussadian Niaré**, and moved to the region around the present capital of Mali. A hunter of heroic dimensions, the son eventually killed a giant crocodile that had long terrorized the people of the area, thus fulfilling a prophecy and laying the basis for the establishment of a dynasty (also prophesied) that would grow up on the site. The Niarés thereby became rulers of the chiefdom at Bama-ko (crocodile-river). An alternative tale recounts how a hunter from Kong in Côte d'Ivoire, Bamba Sanogo, killed an elephant here on the north bank of the Niger and received permission from the local lord to found a town, which he named Bamba-Kong after himself and his city of origin. As he left no heirs on his death, the post of town chieftain went to Diamoussadian Niaré.

Whichever its origin, Bamako grew to be a prosperous trading centre. By the time the Scots explorer **Mungo Park** arrived in the early nineteenth century the population had grown to about 6000. By 1883 the French had built a fort here and soon afterwards colonized the region. In 1904 the railway line was pushed through from Kayes and in 1908 the town was made capital of the colony of **Haut Sénégal–Niger**. When independence was returned to the country in 1960, Bamako became the Malian capital. At the time, the town's population was some 160,000, but in the following years of rapid growth that figure has risen nearly six-fold.

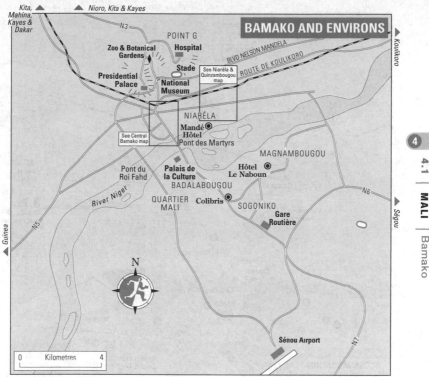

Kita, Mahina, Kayes & Dakar

Nioro, Kita & Kayes

N3

POINT G

Zoo & Botanical Gardens

Hospital

Presidential Palace

Stade

National Museum

BLVD NELSON MANDELA

ROUTE DE KOULIKORO

See Niaréla & Quinzambougou map

Koulikoro

NIARÉLA

See Central Bamako map

Mandé Hôtel
Pont des Martyrs

MAGNAMBOUGOU

Pont du Roi Fahd

Palais de la Culture

Hôtel Le Naboun

N6

BADALABOUGOU

River Niger

QUARTIER MALI

Colibris

SOGONIKO

Gare Routière

Ségou

N5

Guinea

N

Kilometres

Sénou Airport

N7

Bougouni & Côte d'Ivoire

Orientation, arrival and transport

Although Bamako's compact centre makes it an easy town to walk around, orientation can be difficult as one market-thronged street can look very much like another, especially at night. To get your bearings, the prominent *Hôtel de l'Amitié* and bat-eared **Tour BCEAO** serve as useful reference points: they are by the river and either side of the main thoroughfare which leads from the **Pont des Martyrs** to **Square Lumumba**, with the large French embassy and airline offices alongside. The **Avenue du Fleuve** (or **Avenue Modibo Keïta**), leading north from this square to the **place de la Liberté**, is one of the town's main streets, lined with banks, restaurants and stores. If you follow this street all the way to the end, you'll reach the junction with the **rue Baba Diarra**, which runs parallel to the railway tracks. Turning right along this street, you'll pass the **train station** and American embassy before arriving at the **Boulevard du Peuple**, where another right turn takes you past the **Centre Artisanal** and the **Grande Mosquée**, then back down to the Square Lumumba. These three streets form a triangle within which you'll find Bamako's commercial centre, including one of the city's principal (if incidental) attractions, the **street market**.

If you arrive by **bush taxi** or **bus**, chances are you'll be let off at or near the **gare routière de Sogoniko**, about 7km from the centre on the south side of the

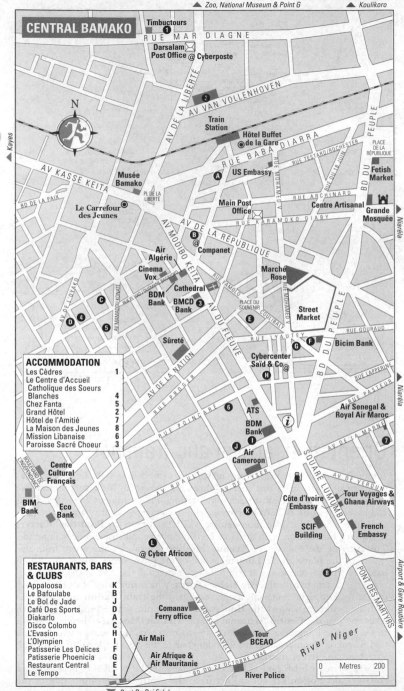

CENTRAL BAMAKO

▲ Zoo, National Museum & Point G   ▲ Koulikoro

RUE MAR DIAGNE

Timbuctours ❶

Darsalam ✉
Post Office @ Cyberposte

AV VAN VOLLENHOVEN

❷

Train
Station

Hôtel Buffet
de la Gare

RUE BABA DIARRA

AV DE LA LIBERTÉ

Musée
Bamako

PL DE LA
LIBERTÉ

Ⓐ   US Embassy

RUE MOHAMED V

RUE TESTARD/ROCHESTER

RUE DU 18 JUIN

RUE ARCHINARD

PLACE DE
LA RÉPUBLIQUE

BD DU PEUPLE

Fetish
Market

AV KASSE KEITA

BD DE LA PAIX

Le Carrefour
des Jeunes

AV DE LOYADO

Main Post
Office

RUE KARAMOKO DIABY

Centre Artisanal

Grande
Mosquée

Niaréla ▲

AV MODIBO KEITA

Air
Algérie

Cinema
Vox

BDM
Bank

AV DE LA RÉPUBLIQUE

Ⓑ   Companet

RUE FAMOLO

Cathedral

BMCD
Bank ❸

Marché
Rose

RUE MOHAMED V

PLACE DU
SOUVENIR

Street
Market

BD DU PEUPLE

AV MAMADOU KONATE

RUE EL HADJ OUSMANE BAGAYOKO

Ⓒ

Ⓓ ④   ⑤

AV DU FLEUVE

Ⓔ

RUE GOURAUD

Sûreté

AV DE LA NATION

RUE LYAUTEY

Ⓖ Ⓕ   Bicim Bank

RUE LAPPERINE

Cybercenter
Saïd & Co @

Ⓗ

RUE PASTEUR

Niaréla ▲

AV PROGER

RUE POINCARÉ

⑥

ATS

BDM
Bank Ⓘ

ⓘ

Air Senegal &
Royal Air Maroc

AV DE LA MARNE

Ⓙ

Air
Cameroon

SQUARE LUMUMBA

Ⓚ

Côte d'Ivoire
Embassy

AV DE VERDUN

Tour Voyages &
Ghana Airways

AV RUAULT

AV DE L'YSER

SCIF
Building

French
Embassy

Centre
Cultural
Français

BOULEVARD DE
L'INDEPENDANCE

BIM
Bank

Eco
Bank

Ⓛ @ Cyber Africon

⑧

PONT DES MARTYRS

Airport & Gare Routière ▲

ACCOMMODATION
Les Cèdres	1
Le Centre d'Accueil Catholique des Soeurs Blanches	4
Chez Fanta	5
Grand Hôtel	2
Hôtel de l'Amitié	7
La Maison des Jeunes	8
Mission Libanaise	6
Paroisse Sacré Choeur	3

RESTAURANTS, BARS & CLUBS
Appaloosa	K
Le Bafoulabe	B
Le Bol de Jade	J
Café Des Sports	D
Diakarlo	A
Disco Colombo	C
L'Evasion	H
L'Olympien	I
Patisserie Les Delices	F
Patisserie Phoenicia	G
Restaurant Central	E
Le Tempo	L

Comanav
Ferry office

Air Mali

Air Afrique &
Air Mauritanie

AV MOUSSA TRAVELE

Tour
BCEAO

BD DU 22 OCTOBRE 1946

River Police

River Niger

0   Metres   200

▼ Pont Du Roi Fahd

Moving on from Bamako

Bush taxis (covering short distances) and **long-distance buses** leave from or near the **Sogoniko gare routière**. The larger bus companies all have their own well-organized terminals within the *gare routière* itself or on the road leading to it. Kénédougou Voyages (☎262.07.19) run services to Sikasso; Somatra (☎222.38.96) go to Ségou, Koutiala, Sikasso, Sévaré and Mopti, and Bobo-Dioulasso in Burkina (Tues–Thurs); Somatri buses (☎249.02.76) head to Ségou and Sikasso; Bani Transport (☎221.44.83) go to Gao, Mopti, Sévaré and Koutiala; Bittar Trans (☎220.15.05) has buses to Sikasso, Ségou, Gao, Mopti Sévaré and Koutiala, as well as Bobo-Dioulasso and to Cotonou in Benin. Finally, Gana Transport (☎243.07.21) serves Koulikoro, Kati, Diré, Ségou, Bla, San, Mopti, and Sévaré. You can be sure to find at least one daily departure to the main towns. For Timbuktu, change at Ségou, Mopti or Douentza (take a Gao bus for Douentza). There are also **two smaller autogares** in Bamako: one, serving Nara and Nioro, is behind the Grande Mosquée; the other, below Point G, is used by bush taxis to Kati and Koulikoro.

By train

The Senegalese **train to Dakar** is scheduled to leave Bamako on Saturday mornings at 9.15am. It's wise to book the day before, and to be there at 7am on the day of departure, to ensure your reserved seats aren't then assigned to someone else. For more on the Bamako–Dakar trains, see p.313.

Daily Autorail trains also leave for **Kayes** at around 7.30am daily except on Wednesday and Saturday. Stopping at many stations en route, including **Kita** and **Mahina**, the trains can take up to double the scheduled time (12hr). Kita is also served by a slow train which leaves daily at 3.30pm (taking 5hr if you're lucky). Fares are shown on p.316; stop by the station for the latest schedules and prices, or contact the Régie du Chemin de Fer du Mali (RCFM), Avenue Kasse Keïta (☎222.59.67).

By boat

The Gao ferries operate from **Koulikoro** when the rains swell the river to a suitable level, roughly from late July or early August until November (for further details, see p.317). To reach Koulikoro (and thus get around the rapids which make it impossible to travel directly by water from the capital), catch a bus or a bush taxi from Point G – the hill in the north of the city – or from the Route de Koulikoro. For reservations (get them early, especially for second and third class) and up-to-date information on departures, contact the office of the Compagnie Malienne de Navigation (COMANAV; ☎222.38.02; Mon–Fri 8am–4pm), Avenue Moussa Travélé, behind the Tour BCEAO. You could also try calling the head office in Koulikoro on ☎226.20.94. If the **barges to Guinea** resume, COMANAV would also be the people to contact for information.

By air

Theoretically, Mopti/Sévaré, Timbuktu and Kayes are served by at least one Air Mali **flight** a week, though these are frequently delayed or cancelled, and schedules should be taken with a pinch of salt. Departures for Timbuktu, via Mopti/Sévaré, are currently timetabled for Tuesday and Saturday in the morning, returning the next day; for Kayes, flights leave Monday, Thursday and Saturday in the morning, returning the same day. STA has flights to Kayes on Monday, Thursday and Saturday, returning the same day. SAE has flights to Kayes on Monday and Friday; to Yélimané on Monday and Thursday; to Timbuktu (via Mopti/Sévaré) on Tuesday and Saturday, returning the next day; and to Nioro on Thursday. They also have a Saturday-morning Bamako–Kéniéba–Bamako flight. **Fares** on all three airlines are roughly the same, as discussed on p.318. For airline telephone numbers, see p.349.

Niger River. From here you can take a taxi into town, or catch a northbound bus for a fraction of the cost, or hop on a Peugeot *bâché*. Whichever way you proceed, you'll cross the overworked **Pont des Martyrs** which spans the Niger. Arriving by **train**, you'll find the station lies within walking distance of a few good accommodation options.

Bamako's **airport** is 15km south of town at **Sénou**. If you have a booking with one of the city's top hotels, there should be a minibus waiting to take you straight there. Otherwise you'll have to catch a taxi to town, as no bus service exists; the cost shouldn't exceed CFA5000–6000 in the daytime and CFA10,000 at night. If you're coming from Mopti or beyond by **river boat** you'll get only as far as **Koulikoro**, the port 60km east of Bamako, which is linked to the capital by buses and bush taxis heading to Route de Koulikoro and Point G north of the centre.

There's an efficient, private **bus service** in Bamako, run by Tababus. They run on fixed routes with fixed stops and fares (usually CFA150 per hop).

Information and accommodation

For **tourist information**, the Office Malien du Tourisme et de l'Hôtellerie (OMATHO; Mon–Sat 7.30am–4pm; ☎222.56.73, ✆www.tourisme.gov.ml) is on rue Mohamed V, just north of Square Lumumba. Staff here rarely have any maps to give away but can recommend guides and approve their contracts before you sign. In line with the new tourism promotion strategy, they insist on helping out in case of any sort of trouble and will even accompany you to the police if you need them to.

Unless you are prepared to put up with something very basic, **accommodation** in Bamako is likely to carve a large chunk out of your budget during your stay in the city. Although many options are centrally located, most of the better-quality hotels are located in the relatively prosperous **Niaréla district**, 3km east of the centre.

Central Bamako

Les Cèdres (aka *Chez Georges*) Route de Darsalam, a 15min walk from the train station ☎ & ✆222.79.72. Good-value hotel in a quiet administrative quarter of Bamako. Rooms are all s/c and some have a/c. Some Friday nights there are live bands in the front courtyard bar-restaurant. ❸

Le Centre d'Accueil Catholique des Soeurs Blanches Corner of rue 130 (El Hadj Ousmane Bagayoko) and rue 133 ☎ & ✆222.77.61. Bamako's best budget option. The nuns here accept travellers if there is space (being a lone woman helps) and offer commendably clean s/c rooms with mosquito nets, peace and quiet, and a key to the gate (key deposit CFA5000). New arrivals need to turn up before nightfall to gain entry; at busy times you may only be allowed to stay for a couple of nights, and there's always a limit of four nights. Note that Malian/tourist couples have been turned away in the past. Dorm beds CFA3000. ❶

Chez Fanta A small two-storey building close to the *Centre d'Accueil des Soeurs Blanches*. It's unsigned, but people in the area know Fanta's friendly family home, where there are two basic dorms. Bathroom and toilets are in the courtyard. Dorm beds CFA4000.

Grand Hôtel av Van Vollenhoven ☎222.24.92, ✆www.grandhotel.cefib.com. International-standard affair just north of the station, with two swimming pools, tennis courts, and a business centre with Internet access. It also houses the city's best bookshop and a high-quality restaurant. ❼

Hôtel de l'Amitié av de la Marne ☎221.43.21, ✆222.36.37. Ugly Soviet-built landmark currently under renovation and planned to reopen in 2004. Pool, golf course, business centre, fine restaurant and pricey rooms. ❽

La Maison des Jeunes Three-storey complex near the Pont des Martyrs ☎222.23.20. Lowest rates in the centre and a good place to meet people. Friendly enough, but security is far from guaranteed – the compound is not locked at any time, and muggings have occurred in the vicinity (so avoid unlit shortcuts at night). Choose between dorms of six to ten beds or basic one-, two- or three-bed rooms, some of which have a/c, though mosquito nets are not provided; some of the communal bathrooms are more bearable than others. Camping is possible in the yard (CFA1500). There's a cheap Internet café in the building (CFA500/hr), and *La Buvette Kanava* across the

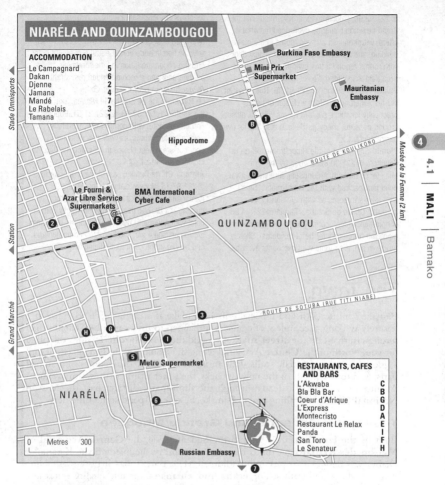

NIARÉLA AND QUINZAMBOUGOU

ACCOMMODATION

Le Campagnard	5
Dakan	6
Djenne	2
Jamana	4
Mandé	7
Le Rabelais	3
Tamana	1

Stade Omnisports

ROUTE DAFAKA

Burkina Faso Embassy

Mini Prix Supermarket

Mauritanian Embassy

Hippodrome

ROUTE DE KOULIKORO

Musée de la Femme (2 km)

4.1 | MALI | Bamako

Le Fourni & Azar Libre Service Supermarkets

BMA International Cyber Cafe

Station

QUINZAMBOUGOU

Grand Marché

ROUTE DE SOTUBA (RUE TITI NIARE)

Metro Supermarket

NIARÉLA

RESTAURANTS, CAFES AND BARS

L'Akwaba	C
Bla Bla Bar	B
Coeur d'Afrique	G
L'Express	D
Montecristo	A
Restaurant Le Relax	E
Panda	I
San Toro	F
Le Senateur	H

N

0   Metres   300

Russian Embassy

yard is a good live-music venue (Fri & Sat). Dorm beds CFA2000, ❷

Mission Libanaise (aka *Mission Père Français*) rue Poincaré, 200m west of av du Fleuve (no phone). Scruffy but quiet, friendly and secure haven with a few stuffy twin bedrooms with fans and nets, and use of a shared bathroom. Off-street parking and a pleasant garden with camping possible. ❶

Paroisse Sacré Coeur Just south of the cathedral ☎222.58.42. A very central two-storey colonial building with single rooms – and one double, plus a five-bed dorm, all on the upper floor. Breakfast is included. Dorm beds CFA5000, ❸

South of the river

Colibris South of the river, 3km from the center

on av de l'OUA (Sogoniko) and near the Sogoniko *gare routière* ☎222.66.37, ✉colibris@spider .toolnet.org. Good-value hotel with swimming pool, quiet s/c rooms with a/c and TV. There's also a popular bar-restaurant and Internet access on the premises. ❺

Le Naboun A 10min walk from the *gare routière* Sogoniko, in Magnambougou ☎277.38.01. Small hotel with good-sized s/c rooms, some with a/c, all with balconies. There's a decent rooftop bar-restaurant with a first-rate view and friendly management. ❸

Niaréla, Cité du Niger and Quinzambougou

Le Campagnard Off the rte de Sotuba, on the second floor above the Métro supermarket

☎221.92.96, ⓔlecampagnard@afribone.net.ml.
Brand new hotel, slightly overpriced for what it
offers, with smallish s/c, a/c rooms in the main
building, and a more spacious annexe next door
with rooms around a tiny swimming pool.
Breakfast is included. ❼
Dakan Niaréla district ☎221.91.96. This pleasant,
old-fashioned hotel offers a cluster of twenty
practically identical, s/c, a/c rooms with TV, all set
around peaceful shady gardens. It also has its own
bar-restaurant. ❺
Djenne Southwest of the Hippodrome, off rte de
Koulikoro ☎221.30.82. Owned by the former
Minister of Tourism, an unusual Soudanese-style
hotel jam-packed with Malian artefacts. Small
well-kept s/c rooms all with a/c and TV. ❺
Jamana Off rte de Sotuba, Niaréla ☎221.34.56,
ⓔhojamana@cefib.com. Next to the *Métropolis*
nightclub (free entry for hotel residents). Slightly
rundown s/c, a/c rooms with discounts available

for stays of more than a night or two. ❺
Mandé Cité du Niger, on the north bank of the
river 2km east of Pont des Martyrs ☎221.19.93,
ⓦwww.hotelmande.com. Beautiful riverside hotel
offering accommodation in little rondavels, a
pristine pool and a recommended restaurant, *Les
Pilotis*, built out over the river. ❼
Le Rabelais rte de Sotuba, in Niaréla, 3km east of
the station ☎221.52.98, ⓕ221.21.51. Popular
French-run hotel with comfortable, tastefully
decorated a/c rooms, as well as a relaxing
pool/bar area. Best choice in its category. Rate
includes breakfast. ❼
Tamana Off rte Dafaka, east of the Hippodrome
☎221.37.15, ⓦwww.datatech.toolnet.org
/tamana/index.htm. A stone's throw from the
buzzing *Bla Bla* bar, this is a friendly family-run
hotel with minimalist decor and smallish, very clean
a/c rooms, some s/c. Food is prepared on demand
and served in the communal dining area. ❺

The Town

Bamako's bustle, filth and especially its heat make it a tiring place to enjoy at a
leisurely walking pace unless, of course, you happen to thrive in sub-Saharan urban
settings. In that case the **street market** around the new **Marché Rose** is the place
for you. North of the **Centre Artisanal** along the Boulevard du Peuple, you'll find
a good selection of **fetish stalls** with an impressive array of decomposing animal
parts. And to the north of the railway tracks, the other main north–south avenue –
Avenue de la Liberté – leads through the diplomatic district past the **Musée
National**: if you do nothing else in Bamako, be sure to spend some time here.

The Centre Artisanal and Grande Mosquée

Built by the French in the 1930s in the Sudanic style, the **Centre Artisanal** or
Maison des Artisans (at the corner of Boulevard du Peuple and rue Karamoko
Diaby) was designed to promote traditional Malian art. Today it houses an abundance of shops and stalls selling **crafts and curios** of variable quality – leatherwork, fabric, silverware, masks, carvings, bronze figurines and musical instruments –
as well as artisans' **workshops** where you can watch woodcarvers, silversmiths,
drum makers and other craftspeople at work. Prices are reasonable.
   A little to the east of the crafts market, the **Grande Mosquée** was a gift to
Bamako from Saudi Arabia. It's not one they can have been too enthralled by – an
imposing twin-minareted dome lacking the grace of the country's indigenous
Sudanic architecture.

The museums

North of the centre, at the junction of Boulevard Nelson Mandela and Avenue de
la Liberté, Bamako's **Musée National** (Tues–Sun 9am–5.30pm; CFA500 including
tour) is housed in a low-rise building inspired by the smooth lines of Djenné's
architecture and contains some remarkable masterpieces of African art. Turn right
after the new fly-over (courtesy of CAN) on to Boulevard Nelson Mandela, and
the entrance is on your left. Inside, objects are beautifully displayed, with photographs discreetly lining the walls, putting the exhibits in a broader context. Lighting
is subtle and the museum comfortably air-conditioned – in short, it's a good deal

more than you might expect. All the labels are in French, but some of the well-informed guides speak English and they do some excellent tours.

Something of a pioneering institution, the museum is engaged in efforts to repatriate some of the vast treasure-store of artefacts taken abroad in colonial times, as well as periodically rounding up materials from different parts of the country. Part of the museum concentrates on domestic objects, including those used in **forging** and **weaving** – and a large, particularly strong, section is dedicated to the techniques involved in making some of the many types of **cloth** for which the region has a wide reputation. A separate section displays religious objects from Mali's various ethnic groups. Highlights include the stylized antelope **tyiwara** (chiwara) masks of the Bamana; various examples of **Senoufo statuary**; and, of course, the world-renowned antique **Dogon sculptures and masks**. The museum extends across the road into a series of caves with prehistoric relics and an exhibition about evolution, apparently intended for children.

Away to the northeast of town is the small but interesting **Musée Muso Kunda**, or Musée de la Femme, in Quartier Korofina (officially Tues–Sun 9am–6pm, though call ☏224.06.21 to check as these aren't followed strictly). The museum is devoted to the traditional customs and dress of women from the various ethnic groups that make up Mali's population, with displays on clothing, jewellery, hairstyles and marriage trousseaux. There are also some artisans' workshops with quality *bogolans* and crafts for sale, and a good restaurant.

Bamako's **regional museum** on place de la Liberté sits in a new building that has been ready for some time now, with a museum signboard at the front and grounds filled with horrid fibreglass sculptures of animals from the region – but it's empty; at the time of writing there were no plans to begin setting up displays inside the building.

The zoo and botanical gardens

Bamako's **zoo** was a good idea whose time has passed. In theory, the cages and enclosures are designed to resemble closely the animals' natural habitats, but it's run-down and neglected, and the range of creatures is limited. While gazelles are kept in a quite large open space, monkeys, lions, birds and others are not so lucky. The surrounding **botanical gardens** are vast and, with a little attention, could provide a beautiful retreat from the city.

From the National Museum and zoo, you can walk up to the **north of the city** and to the hill known as **Point G**, the location of the main hospital. There are wonderful views from here, and some abandoned cliff dwellings featuring old **rock paintings**.

Eating, drinking and nightlife

Bamako features some of the country's best dining – if you've made your way here from the northeast, you'll be pleasantly surprised at the range of French, Italian, Lebanese, Chinese and fancy Malian fare on offer, while if you've arrived from Dakar, it's the affordability of eating out here that impresses. Most of the town's better **restaurants** – almost all French – are in the hotels (the ones at the *Rabelais*, *Mandé*, *Le Campagnard* and *Grand* have good reputations, as do *l'Amitié*'s three restaurants, which were shut during time of writing for refurbishment). **Street food** is abundant in central Bamako, and it's worth noting the locations of the better roadside stalls or *cafémen*, who serve Nescafé, baguette-and-omelette breakfasts as well as meat-based snacks during the day. A popular area to check out is the square off Avenue Modibo Keita next to Cinema Vox, but pretty much every neighbourhood has its own collection of stalls.

Bamako has first-rate nightlife, though the action only really gets going late. **Rue Dafaka**, near the Hippodrome east of the centre, is abuzz with life throughout the weekend, and worth seeking out; it's known locally as place Pigalle (after the liveliest area of Paris), and lined with bars and restaurants.

Restaurants, cafés and snack bars

Central Bamako

Appaloosa rue 311, off av de l'Yser. Tex-Mex place with steak- and burger-type dishes and decor so convincing (not to mention waiters in cowboy hats) that you forget where you are. Ask about their karaoke nights when it's a hoot watching the expat community making fools of themselves.

Le Bafoulabe Off av Modibo Keita at the place de la Liberté. Cheap and friendly Senegalese restaurant on a quiet first-floor terrace, serving *riz gras* and other specialities from the area at rock-bottom prices. It's in the same building as Companet Internet café, a convenient combination if you need to satisfy both hunger and the urge to fire off some emails.

Le Bol de Jade av Ruault. Well-established restaurant just west of Square Lumumba offering Chinese and Vietnamese dishes, and a good-value set menu.

Café Des Sports rue 133, opposite the Catholic hostel. Friendly little shack whose affable owner offers good breakfasts and *riz gras* at very reasonable prices.

Diakarlo Across from the train station. Inexpensive pizza place that also does first-rate sandwiches, with a 24hr take-away service, in a quiet corner of an otherwise hectic neighborhood.

L'Olympien av Ruault, next to *Bol De Jade*. A popular pizza place, this one a lot more pricey than the rest, serving a few select French dishes as well.

Patisserie Les Delices rue Famolo Coulibaly. Welcoming, inexpensive patisserie/restaurant with an irresistible display of cakes and pastries, plus ice cream, drinks and a long menu of light meals including omelettes, pizzas, burgers and salads. Choose between the sun-shaded terrace or the air-conditioned interior. Mon–Fri 6.30am–midnight, Sat till 1am. ☎223.35.02 for pizza delivery.

Patisserie Phoenicia rue Mohammed V. Lebanese-owned teahouse and snack bar, serving fresh croissants and other pastries as well as drinks, snacks and delightful Lebanese meals.

Restaurant Central rue Loveran. Well-established formica-and-vinyl place with a small terrace outside and reasonably priced daily *plats* as well as burger and spring roll (with pork) specialities. Open late in the evening for meals or drinks.

Niaréla and Quinzambougou

L'Akwaba rte Dafaka ☎221.06.45; reservations recommended at weekends. Reliably good French/African food, with live traditional music at weekends.

Coeur d'Afrique rte de Sotuba opposite Shell station, Quinzambougou. Cheap meals in a courtyard, very popular with Peace Corps volunteers and something of an institution.

L'Express rte de Koulikoro, near the Hippodrome. Upmarket French and Lebanese snacks. Daily till late.

Restaurant Le Relax rte de Koulikoro ☎222.79.18. Airy patisserie/restaurant with a bright terrace; popular with the expat community. Fresh croissants and juice for breakfast, snacks and specialities such as *Capitaine a la Bamakoise* (Nile perch with plantain) at any time of day. Recommended.

Panda Off rte de Sotuba, near *Hôtel Jamana*. Good-value Chinese food served indoors in a/c premises, or out on the porch or garden terrace.

San Toro rte de Koulikoro. Refined Malian cuisine from the owners of the nearby *Djenné Hôtel*. The interior is decorated with authentic Malian artefacts and there's a pleasant garden; musicians often play live. No alcohol.

Nightlife

The now rather grubby *Hôtel Buffet de la Gare* used to be the town's most famous nightspot, a showcase for the **Rail Band** (see p.334), who still play here occasionally (when they do, it generally happens on Saturdays). Among the **hotel discos**, *Le Village* at the *Grand Hôtel* draws the largest crowds and features a good mix of music. One highly recommended club, *Le Hogon* (☎223.07.60), is some distance west of central Bamako in the N'Tomikorobougou quarter, off the N5 road to Guinea (taxi drivers know it). A welcoming outdoors place with a lot of expat regulars and a low cover charge, it's owned by *kora* star Toumani Diabaté, who plays here on Fridays when he's in town.

Bars, clubs and music venues

Atlantis rue 221, off av OUA, Badalabougou Est. Lively club at weekends. Look out for the dance band GB5 who play here Saturdays.

Bla Bla Bar rue Dafaka. One of the hottest haunts in town, with a busy terrace bar and dancing until the early hours. Nearby the *Byblos* disco next to *Le Relax* restaurant is equally happening, and *Montecristo*, a bit further out off the Koulikoro road, draws a similar large crowd at the weekend.

Carrefour des Jeunes av Kasse Keïta. You're more or less guaranteed live music every weekend at this community youth centre; there's an upstairs terrace bar where you can enjoy a beer under the stars while listening to Malian blues, Afro-Cuban dance music or reggae.

Disco Colombo Off av Mamadou Konaté. A sleazy joint though no less fun for that, with Malian bands on Friday and Saturday nights, and street food and taxis outside – the latter is a good option as muggers around here prey on the inebriated and, increasingly, on the wide awake.

L'Evasion Slap bang in the centre, just off av du Fleuve. An upmarket disco, a packed weekend venue for hardcore zouk.

Métropolis Niaréla district, in the same building as the *Jamana* hotel. Laser-lit disco that's a favoured hangout for young Bamakois and French volunteers.

Le Sénateur Off rte de Sotuba, Niaréla. A lively outdoor bar hosting live bands playing Malian music or reggae at the weekend.

Le Tempo av Moussa Travélé. Salubrious and expensive, with a garden bar and an indoor dance floor and bar/restaurant. Like everywhere else, it's busiest on Fridays and Saturdays, but the music is different every night of the week: regular sessions include a good choice of Senegalese, Cuban and Malian music. There's also a monthly salsa night.

Listings

Airlines Air Algérie, corner of av Modibo Keïta and rue 324 ☎222.31.59; Air Burkina, Immouble Sonavie, near *Hôtel de l'Amitié* ☎221.01.78; Air France, Immeuble SCIF, Square Lumumba ☎222.22.12; Air Guinée, rue Carron ☎221.31.50; Air Ivoire, av de l'OAU ☎223.95.59; Air Mali, Immeuble SCIF, Square Lumumba ☎222.94.00 or ☎222.93.94; Air Mauritanie, Immeuble Air Afrique ☎222.58.02 or ☎223.87.38; Air Sénégal, *Hôtel de l'Amitié* ☎221.82.87; Cameroon Airlines, av de l'Yser ☎223.82.85; Ethiopian Airlines, Immeuble SCIF, Square Lumumba ☎222.60.36; Ghana Airways, at Tam Voyages, Square Lumumba ☎221.90.05; Point-Afrique, Immeuble ex-USAID, av de l'Yser ☎223.54.70; Trans Air Benin, av Modibo Keita ☎223.14.97; Royal Air Maroc, *Hôtel de l'Amitié* ☎221.61.05; Société Avion Express (SAE), rte de Sotuba ☎223.14.65; Société Transport Aérién (STA), av de l'Yser ☎222.33.33. **Airport** ☎222.27.01.

American Express ATS (Afric Trans Services), av Modibo Keïta ☎222.44.35, @ats@malinet.ml.

Banks BDM, av du Fleuve ☎223.18.72; BIM, bd de l'Indépendance/av de la Nation ☎222.50.89, does Western Union money transfers; BICIM, on av du Peuple ☎223.33.70; BNDA, av du Mali ☎229.64.64. At the time of writing, the BICIM above had the city's only working ATM, taking Visa cards.

Bookshops There's a decent stock of books, fiction, travel guides, as well as French-language newspapers and magazines at the *Grand Hôtel*. *Hôtel de L'Amitié*, under renovation at the time of writing, used to have a well-stocked bookshop which is due to reopen along with the hotel.

Car rental Djennó, at the *Grand Hôtel* ☎222.24.94; Malienne de l'Automobile (Hertz representative), rte de Koulikoro ☎224.67.68 or 224.28.56, ☏224.12.41.

Cinemas The most comfortable cinemas are the Babemba, near Place de Point G north of the centre, and those at Palais de la Culture (on the south side of the Niger) and at the *Hôtel de l'Amitié*; all three screen recent Hollywood releases, dubbed into French. For Asian action movies, head to Vox, off av Modibo Keïta.

Cultural centres The Centre Cultural Français, bd de l'Indépendance, has a café-bar and a good library with French newspapers and magazines. They also organize exhibitions, film screenings and concerts. Similar activities are arranged at USIS, the American cultural centre on the south bank, Badalabougou Est; they have American magazines and newspapers plus a few good books about Mali.

Embassies and consulates Algeria, rte Aéroport, Daoudabougou ☎220.45.72, ☏222.93.74; Burkina Faso, rue 224, north of the rte de Koulikoro ☎221.31.71, ☏221.92.66; Canada, rte de Koulikoro ☎221.22.36, ☏221.43.62; Côte d'Ivoire, Square Lumumba ☎221.22.89, ☏221.13.76; European Union, av OUA, Badalabougou Est

☎222.20.65, ℉222.36.70; France, Square Lumumba ☎221.31.41 or ☎221.29.51, ℉222.31.36; Germany, av OAU, Badalabougou Est ☎222.32.99, ℉222.96.50; Guinea, bd de Peuple, Medina Coura ☎221.08.06; Mauritania, rte de Koulikor ☎221.48.15, ℉221.49.08; Morocco, av OUA, Badalabougou Est ☎222.21.23, ℉222.77.87; Nigeria, south of the Pont des Martyrs, Badalabougou Est ☎222.57.71, ℉222.52.84; Senegal, 341 rue 287, av Nelson Mandela; ☎221.82.73, ℉221.17.80; UK, Liaison office at Canadian Embassy ☎277.67.37, ℮belo@afribone.net.ml; USA, rue de Rochester/rue Mohammed V ☎222.56.63 or ☎222.54.70, ℉222.37.12.

Internet access Many of the bigger hotels have business centres with Net access, though these are generally more expensive than the Internet cafés dotted around town, of which the most reliable are: BMA, behind *Le Relax* restaurant, rte de Koulikoro (daily 8am–10pm; CFA1000/hr); Cyber-Africon, behind the *Tempo* nightclub (Mon–Fri 7am–8pm, Sat 7am–5pm; CFA500/hr); Cybercenter Saïd & Co, rue Mohamed V (Mon–Sat 8am–8pm; CFA2000/hr); Cyberposte, av de la Liberté (post office hours; CFA1000/hr); and Companet, off rue de la République (daily 8am–8pm; CFA1000/hr). There's also an Internet café at *La Maison des Jeunes* (see p.344; Mon–Sat 8am–4pm; CFA500/hr).

Maps The Direction Nationale de Cartographie, off av de l'OAU, Badalabougou Est, is the place to go for 1:200,000 survey maps. They also have a few country and town maps.

Post and telephones The *poste centrale* (Mon–Fri 7.30am–5.30pm, Sat 8am–noon) is on rue Karamoko Diaby, not far from the market. There's a reliable poste restante service here (CFA300 to collect a letter). Scattered around town are payphones which take phone cards (Sotelma's cards are cheapest: CFA5000 for 50 minutes of local calls) sold on the street at most junctions.

Alternatively, calls can be made (at higher rates) from any of the *télécentres* – there are plenty in the area around the main post office.

Supermarkets The eastern end of the city, where most of the expat community live, is a good place to find these. The Metro is along rte de Sotuba, in Niaréla, next to the Shell station, and the Fourni and Azar Libre Service are a similar distance from the centre along the rte de Koulikoro, near *Le Relax* restaurant. Nearby is also the new Mini Prix, on route Dafaka, not far from the *Bla Bla Bar*.

Swimming pools The pools at the *Grand* are small, but okay for cooling off (CFA2500); the one at the *Mandé* has the best setting (CFA3000); *Le Rabelais* charges the same as the *Mandé* and has a popular poolside bar.

Travel agents It can be useful to talk to a travel agent if you're looking to rent a 4WD vehicle and driver, or to join an organized tour; common destinations are Djenné, Mopti, Timbuktu and the Dogon country, though some companies also offer visits to Ségou and the Manding Highlands, and cruises on the Niger. Among the better firms are: ATS, av Modibo Keïta ☎222.44.35, ℮ats@malinet.ml; the Tuareg-run Azawad Voyages, specializing in the Gao and Timbuktu region ☎221.98.69, ℮azawadvoy@hotmail.com; Bani Voyages, at the *Grand Hôtel* ☎223.26.03, ℮bani@afribone.net.ml; TAM Voyages, Square Lumumba ☎222.05.47 or 222.30.69, ℮tamvoyage@cefib.com; Timbouctours, next door to *Hôtel Les Cèdres* ☎223.35.65, ℮tbt@cefib.com; Saga Tours, 659 rue 802 ☎220.27.08, ℗www.sagatours.com; and the helpful West African Air Services, 27 rue 283, Hippodrome ☎224.81.57, ℗www.africa-ata.org/mali.htm.

Visa extensions At the Sûreté Nationale, av de la Nation (Mon–Thurs 8am–2pm, Fri & Sat 7.30am–12.30pm).

4.2

Kayes and the west

Often ignored by travellers because of its poor transport connections, rough roads and inaccessibility during the rainy season, **western Mali** contains some of the country's most beautiful scenery and easily rewards travellers with their own robust vehicles, or footloose adventurers with time and patience on their hands. Fortunately, roads in this region are in the process of being upgraded and, on a good day, it's possible to travel by car between Bamako and **Kayes**, the regional capital, in less than twelve hours. It's a region of remote villages, wooded escarpments and rivers where the Baoulé, Bakoye and Bafing rivers rush from the **Manding Highlands** through the hilly landscapes of the **Malinké country** before joining forces to form the **Senegal River**. It's also the best place to encounter some of Mali's **wildlife**: warthogs, baboons and iridescent blue kingfishers prosper in this isolated district, and there are even small numbers of lions in the vicinity of Kéniéba. The region is also historically significant, for it was the heartland of the thirteenth-century **Mali kingdom** which expanded into a vast empire incorporating Djenné, Timbuktu and distant Gao.

The Senegal flows through the realm of the Fula-speaking **Tukulor** people, which extends west from Kayes, an isolated commercial centre of 90,000 people serving the region's mining ventures. The old *piste* from Kayes to Bamako passes through the town of **Nioro du Sahel** close to the Mauritanian border, after which it deteriorates still further as it swings south for the capital. South of Kayes, **Kéniéba** is a remote outpost serving local gold-mining activities, and a dead end unless you plan to undertake the infrequently used backcountry crossings into Guinea or Senegal.

Kayes and south to Kéniéba

An agreeable riverside town (and the first major town if you've come by road from Dakar), **KAYES** was once the capital of the Haut Sénégal-Niger colony, until the seat was transferred to Bamako early last century, when the train line pushed through from Dakar. Today it has the dubious honour of being Africa's hottest town, with afternoon temperatures between March and May crackling into the high forties Celsius. Kayes is of most use as a transportation hub, with a daily train to Bamako which slowly crosses the scenic west Manding Highlands in daylight. It is also the best place to seek out transport into parts of the region not served by the train and a viable (if adventurous) departure point, via Kéniéba, for northern Guinea and southeast Senegal.

If you're stuck here for a few days, the **French Fort** in **Médine**, 12km southeast of Kayes on the Senegal River, is easily reached and a good distraction. Built by the French in 1855 to protect their commercial interests in the area, it withstood a siege by the Tukolor jihadist El Hadj Omar in 1857 and became a base for French troops in 1878. The most scenic way of getting here is by *pirogue* – you can rent one near the new bridge in Kayes. It's a peaceful picnic and camping spot, and guides can easily be found in Kayes and Médine.

Practicalities

The **train station** is about 1km southeast of the town centre and several taxis greet the arriving trains. Kayes has a post office, airstrip (west of the train station at the time of writing, though a new airstrip is being built north of the river), several pharmacies and three banks: BDM, BIMSA and Bank of Africa. Visa and MasterCard can be used to get cash advances at the BDM main branch, near the post office on the road along the river's south bank but, as the phone connection is often poor, it may take days before you get your money. Changing on the black market (in the central market) gives you a worse rate than the banks. A reliable **Internet** place is Sotelma, next to the post office and open daily (CFA1500/hour).

Accommodation

Kayes has few accommodation options. The *Khasso* offers the best rooms, but if you're on a tight budget, the *Centre d'Acceuil* is probably the best value.

Relais de Centenaire About 300m west of the hotels *Khasso* and *Logo* ☎ 252.18.97. Most of the rooms here are dorms – without fans or mosquito nets – though there are a few doubles with fans or a/c. The dorms can get murderously hot. Dorm beds CFA2500. **②**

Centre d'Accueil de la Jeunesse Just 300m from the station (head towards town and take the first left after *Hôtel du Rail*) ☎ 252.12.54. Good-value cheapie that was refurbished for the African Cup of Nations. The rooms – eight in all – are split between two bungalows, each with two toilets and a shower. You can also camp on the roof or in the courtyard for CFA2000 per person. **②**

Le Khasso Near the waterfront on av Macdeoura ☎ 253.16.66. The fourteen small, tidy chalets with a/c are the best in town and it's sometimes full. The bar-restaurant is a popular venue. **⑤**

Le Logo Across the road from the *Khasso* ☎ 252.13.81. A few a/c rooms with bath, and there's a bar-restaurant serving reasonable food. **④**

Hôtel du Rail Directly opposite the station ☎ 252.12.33. Long past its colonial-era heyday, this still offers a certain faded splendour with spacious s/c rooms and suites. There's a decent enough bar-restaurant and another bar set in the peaceful garden out front. **⑤**

Moving on from Kayes

The obvious form of transport out of Kayes is the **train to Bamako**. Heading to **Senegal**, you'll find that road improvements on both sides of the border make going by road an increasingly attractive option. You can get a bus from Kayes all the way to Dakar (Wed & Sat at 5pm; CFA13,000), a relatively painless trip of fifteen hours. Bush taxis to the border town of **Diboli** leave constantly (CFA3000; 2hr), passing through light baobab woodland en route to the border, where a road bridge spans the Falémé River and leads straight into the flyblown Senegalese town of **Kidira**.

Because of the lamentable state of the "old northern route" between Kayes and Bamako **via Nioro du Sahel**, few people make this journey by bush taxi, but the route is occasionally tackled by adventurous travellers on motorbikes. The **direct road to Bamako** via Diamou, Bafoulabé, Manantali and Kita, following the railway line part of the way, was being upgraded at the time of writing, and will shorten the travel time substantially to less than nine hours. The road from Kayes to Yélimané has been upgraded as well and is good. For details of the route south from Kayes to Senegal and Guinea, see opposite page.

If **Mauritania** is your destination, ask around in Kayes Ndi market (on the north side of the river) for vehicles heading for **Sélibabi**, just 160km to the northwest, or **Kiffa** on the Nouakchott highway.

In theory at least, three weekly Air Mali **flights** serve Kayes: on Monday and Friday mornings and on Thursday afternoon there's a flight from Bamako to Kayes which returns to Bamako within an hour. STA (☎ 672.58.97) has four flights a week to Bamako while SAE (☎ 672.93.96) has two, with an optional stop at Yélimané.

Eating and nightlife

Budget **restaurants** are thin on the ground in Kayes. The two best value are *L'Eclosion*, at rue du 22 Septembre, which does good breakfasts and main meals, and *Damou*, a shack next door to the *Centre d'Accueil*, which does exceptionally cheap rice and stew. The alternative is **street food** at the large market or train station. Otherwise the hotels all have restaurants – *Khasso*'s is the best. **Nightlife** in Kayes isn't exactly hectic: *La Détente*, on the road between the railway and the town centre, is a spacious beer garden with TV; *La Paillotte,* by *Hôtel du Rail,* does chilled beer (and excellent *brochettes*); and for a spot of clubbing, check out *Le Mamery* at *Le Khasso* (Fri–Sun).

To Kéniéba and beyond

South of Kayes, a corrugated *piste* follows the **Falaise de Tambaoura** for 240km to the small town of **Kéniéba**, caught in a suntrap by a bend in the Tambaoura's picturesque, towering cliffs. This is the start of a possible (but arduous) route from western Mali to **Labé**, in Guinea's highland Fouta Djalon region. It also provides an interesting, if time-consuming, entry point to the extreme southeastern corner of Senegal.

Transport to Kéniéba leaves Kayes from Avenue du 22 Septembre around the *L'Eclosion* patisserie, in the town centre. Trucks and minibuses leave in the late afternoon or early evening and take up to twelve hours (CFA5000); 4WD vehicles leave early morning and take eight hours (CFA7500). An alternative is to ask around in Kayes for trucks making the bumpy, eight-hour journey every day. You'll have to pay, but if you're lucky enough to be offered a front seat, you'll enjoy some fine views on the way down.

The road is straightforward only as far as **Sadiola** (a third of the way to Kéniéba), a stretch maintained by the mining companies. The women in the Sadiola district have collected **gold** from the bush for centuries – local legends tell of their ostensibly destitute husbands having amassed several kilos of the metal each during a lifetime. These days, Sadiola houses West Africa's most important gold mine, and South African technicians have arrived en masse.

Kéniéba and on to Guinea and Senegal

The frontier-town isolation of **KÉNIÉBA**, and its proximity to the Senegalese and Guinean borders, make it something of a smuggling entrepôt for cigarettes and alcohol coming in from Guinea, just a few kilometres away. You can **stay** at the basic, none too clean *La Casa Ronde* (❶) with an okay restaurant. Down here you'll find a post office, some stores and a small **market**. The town also has a regional hospital and a couple of petrol stations.

If you're looking for transport to **Guinea**, ask around in town; trucks are said to leave regularly from the *centre transportique* opposite the post office for some illicit trading at **Kali** on the Guinea border. If you head this way expect the unexpected on the Guinean side and have money, *cadeaux* and time to spare. Alternatively you can rent a **motorbike** (plus rider; ask for the mechanics near the market) to Kali (CFA7500) and catch a vehicle on from there.

Rides to **Kédougou in Senegal** are dependent on there being enough passengers to fill up a Land Rover, and on the depth of the Falémé River (usually crossable from January until the rains resume), which marks the unstaffed frontier. If nothing turns up after a couple of days' wait, again renting a motorbike is the alternative (CFA15000). Although twice the price of a shared 4WD, it's a memorable, no less uncomfortable six-hour ride along winding bush tracks into Senegal's Pays Bassari region.

From Kayes to Bamako

In the dry season, the northern route to Bamako via **Nioro**, close to the Mauritanian border, is less travelled and less direct than the southern route via **Kita**, and both routes, particularly the one via Nioro, are frequently impassable in the rainy season. The upgrading of the road via Manantali and Kita will reduce still further the traffic via Nioro.

Via Kita

The Kayes–Bamako rail line passes through a scenic area of hills and wooded escarpments, a welcome change from bleak plains if you've arrived from Senegal. The west-flowing **Bakoye** and **Senegal rivers** run parallel to the tracks for a good part of the journey, thrashing into rough rapids at several points along their courses. The lowest of these rapids are the **Chutes de Felou**, just 10km east of Kayes, though slightly disappointing since a hydroelectric dam was built by the French further upriver. The more spectacular **Chutes de Gouina**, 65km further upstream, towards Bamako, is a popular swimming and picnic spot, but can be hard to get to even with a 4WD.

The Bafing and Bakoye rivers converge about 130km east of Kayes to form the Senegal at **BAFOULABÉ**, whose main attraction is its large hippo population. The town, 3km north of **Mahina** where the train stops, also has a small market and basic accommodation next to the river at *Les Cases Provinciales du Khasso* (❷). An interesting detour 80km to the south is **MANANTALI** (this will soon be on one of the main roads to Bamako), perched on the northern point of a vast lake formed by the damming of the Bafing to power a huge hydroelectric plant. The scenic lake is favoured by development workers as a place to swim and hippo-watch, and you can still see the remains of submerged trees and buildings beneath the surface. There's good food and accommodation in well-kept a/c cabins available at *La Cité des Cadres* (❶), run by the dam company; the guard will help you to get the keys from the head office. *La Paillotte* (❷) nearby is also competently run and has a good restaurant.

Leaving Bafoulabé, drivers share the long rail bridge across the Bafing River and continue 200km east to Kita. Just east of Bafoulabé are the **Chutes de Kale**, followed in turn by the **Chutes de Billy**, 270km short of Bamako. Unfortunately, none of these rapids is visible from the train, and you do need your own transport to get off the road that crisscrosses the railway line to get near them. If you're travelling by rail, you'll welcome the food stop at **Toukoto**, 67km short of Kita, where plenty of cooked and fresh food is brought to the train.

Kita

Roughly two-thirds of the way from Kayes to Bamako, **KITA** is one of the former capitals of Sundiata Keïta's medieval Mali empire, and if you're into Malian **music** it's a good place to stop over a night or two, as many traditional griots hail from around here. **Mont Kita Kourou**, with caves decorated with rock paintings, rises impressively to the west of the town. There are several **places to stay** in town. *Hotel Dieudonne* (❷), on the Manantali road, has rooms with fans, decent food and cold beer, and is the place to find lifts for Manantali. A good alternative is the *Relais Touristique* (☎257.30.94; ❷), 200m down the road from the railway station, with clean and comfortable s/c rooms (some with a/c and TV) in a pleasant garden compound that includes a restaurant, a small bar-nightclub, and a (seldom filled) pool. Kita's best budget option, often full, is the *campement* (❶), next to *Relais Touristique*, with basic fanned rooms. For good inexpensive **food** try *L'Oasis* (*Chez Issa*), in the centre, which offers basic meals on the terrace, or *Restaurant Appia*, on the station road, a seedy late-night brothel-type place, which does serve excellent rice and sauce.

The **train** to Bamako passes through Kita every afternoon or evening (depending on delays); there's also a local train which starts its journey here at 6.45am and arrives in Bamako anything between five and eight hours later. If you're **driving** from Kita to Bamako, expect some confusion in correctly locating the main *piste*, especially when entering and leaving small villages with their various secondary tracks.

Bafing National Park

For the adventurous and independently mobile, a deteriorating track leads 140km southwest of Kita to the rarely visited **Parc National du Bafing**, close to the Guinean border. Wildlife is scarce here, due to intensive hunting, with few monkeys and very few chimpanzees (not seen for a long time), and today the park is mainly visited for its flora. The park can also be reached from Manantali via Makindougou, where you can find the reserve office and get permission to visit and camp. They'll also help with a much-needed guide (even to find the reserve itself).

Via Nioro

Between Kayes and Nioro lies a great region for exploration in your own (suitably equipped) vehicle. The whole district is beautiful, roamed by Fula herders and with impressive baobabs. But the rough bush tracks are mostly in a state of advanced disrepair and any kind of transport and facilities almost nonexistent.

In recent years, there has been an emerald rush in the area of **Sandaré** (144km east of Kayes on the main *piste*), with hundreds of hopeful miners flocking to the area of Angoulá, living in improvised camps near the mines. You are certain to be offered emeralds for sale here. The most worthwhile diversion, however, is to **Yélimané**, turning left off the main *piste* 83km east of Kayes, and driving 68km north, on a newly graded *piste* easily recognized as the best in the region. Ten kilometres or so before Yélimané, there's a marshy area called **Goumbogo**, highly recommended if you're interested in wildlife, especially migratory birds. West of Yélimané, you can make a 45-kilometre trip to the **Mare de Toya**, a spectacular geological rift and lake forming part of the Mauritanian frontier. There are morning Bamako–Yélimané–Bamako flights (Mon & Thurs), with SAE (Yélimané agency ☏252.22.62) if you want to reach civilization quickly.

From Yélimané, enquire about the condition of the 134-kilometre direct route onwards to Nioro, as it's often impassable during the rains. Back on the main Kayes–Nioro *piste*, it's 168km from the Yélimané junction to Nioro, via Sandaré.

Nioro du Sahel and beyond

NIORO DU SAHEL is a seventeenth-century town – one of the old royal capitals of the Bamana kingdom of Kaarta – built on a plateau and famed for its **mosque**, which is one of the most important in Mali. Nioro has a police and customs post, petrol stations, a bank, a pharmacy, a hospital and an airstrip (flights to and from Bamako on Thursday morning with SAE; ☏221.22.46) but **accommodation** is limited to two frugal *campements* (CFA2000 per person). The one in the administrative quarter is a little more bearable than the one by the war memorial statue, and has a restaurant with simple food and cold beer.

Nioro is a common departure point for **Mauritania**, but traffic along the 212-kilometre *piste* to Ayoun el Atrous is thin at the best of times and can dwindle to nothing in the rainy season between July and October. Check for trucks around the marketplace. If you're driving to Bamako, you can bypass Nioro and save nearly 100km by forking east at Sandaré for **Diéma**, though ask at Sandaré about road conditions first.

There is a significant deterioration in the road for the last 430km from Nioro to the capital, and if you are in a low-clearance vehicle expect plenty of deviations and some digging. Twenty kilometres after Diéma, the *piste* passes through the **Vallée du Serpent**, named for the **Baoulé River**'s tortuous course as it snakes down from the Manding Highlands. The route marked on the Michelin map from Diéma to Didjéni can be very difficult, and you may need to go via Dioumara, 80km to the east of Diéma.

The route of the Baoulé River forms the northern borders of the **Parc National de la Boucle du Baoulé** – 3300 square kilometres of wooded savanna and forest, which once harboured a significant animal population, including elephants, antelope, buffalo, warthogs, giraffe and even lions. Today, practically all the wildlife has been hunted out of the park and the best reason to visit the park (assuming you have a 4WD vehicle) is for its many **archeological remains**: there are more than two hundred sites of rock paintings, ancient tombs and burial grounds. The park's infrastructure is extremely limited, but there are three *campements* in the southern district, the main one being at the village of Baoulé, at the southeast entrance to the park, north of Négala. You can get the latest information at the park's headquarters, inside the botanical gardens in Bamako (see p.347).

4.3

Ségou and around

Between Bamako and the Delta Region lies a broad expanse of territory where numerous kingdoms rose to power after the demise of the Songhai Empire. Most important were the **Bamana Empire** of Ségou and the **Kénédougou Empire** in the **Senoufo country**, with **Sikasso** its capital. Although they were eclipsed almost as quickly as they sprang up, these towns have remained important commercially thanks to their positions on well-travelled routes, and all are interlinked with daily bus or bush-taxi services.

Ségou and around

The fourth largest town in Mali, **SÉGOU**, 240km northeast of Bamako, makes a very pleasant stopover between Bamako and Mopti. Reminders of the colonial period still stand out in graceful administrative buildings in the neo-Sudanic style, especially at the west end of town. Traditional Bamana architecture is still mostly successful in holding its own against modern cement buildings, and today whole quarters of this quiet tree-lined town are filled with rust-coloured *banco* houses. Away from the busy **market** (the main day is Monday), much of the modern activity focuses on the banks of the **Niger**, with its *pirogues* and crowds. The town also has a thriving community of artisans, including cotton weavers, *bogolan* artists, rug makers and potters.

Bozo fishermen live in permanent camps on both sides of the Niger near Ségou, and have done so since the seventh century, long before the town was founded. It's possible to take a guided trip by *pirogue* or *pinasse* to visit their **riverbank villages**. The Ségou area is also renowned for its pottery: **Kalabougou**, forty minutes upstream by *pirogue*, is a picturesque potters' village where you can see the women at work. Renting a *pirogue* to Kalabougou costs around CFA20,000 for a day. Balanzan Tours (☏232.02.57), near *L'Auberge* (see p.360), can make arrangements

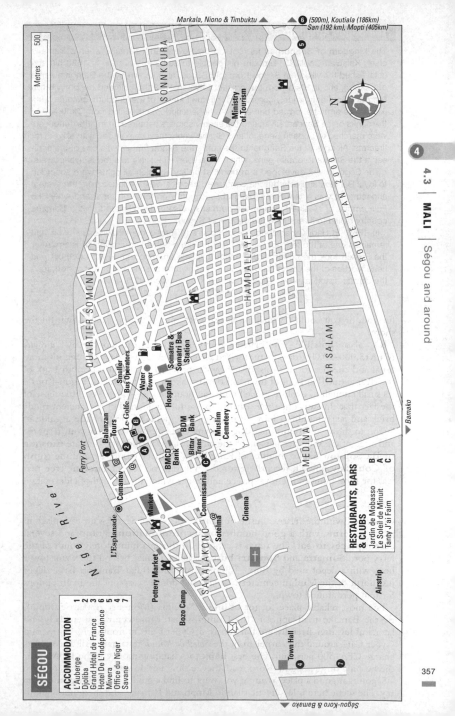

SÉGOU

ACCOMMODATION
L'Auberge 1
Djoliba 2
Grand Hôtel de France 3
Hotel De L'Independance 6
Mivera 5
Office du Niger 4
Savane 7

RESTAURANTS, BARS & CLUBS
Jardin de Mobasso B
Le Soleil de Minuit A
Tanty J'ai Faim C

Markala, Niono & Timbuktu ▲ ▲ **6** (500m), Koutiala (186km)
San (192 km), Mopti (405km)

SONNKOURA

QUARTIER SOMONO

Ministry of Tourism

ROUTE L'AN 2000

HAMDALLAYE

DAR SALAM

Smaller Bus Operators

Balanzan Tours

Le Golfe

Water Tower

Somatra & Somatri Bus Station

Hospital

BDM Bank

BMCD Bank

Bittar Trans

Muslim Cemetery

MEDINA

Ferry Port

Comanav

L'Esplanade

Market

SAKALAKONO

Sotelma

Commissariat

Cinema

N i g e r   R i v e r

Pottery Market

Bozo Camp

Town Hall

Airstrip

▶ Bamako

▼ Ségou-Koro & Bamako

0   Metres   500

N

357

The Ségou kingdom

The **kingdom of Ségou** had its roots in the seventeenth century, when a Bamana chief, Kaladian Coulibaly, brought his people to settle in the area. In 1620 his son established the village of Ségou-Koro (old Ségou, also known by the Bambara name of Sékoro), about 10km from the present town. In 1712 the able and despotic **Biton Mamary Coulibaly**, widely considered the true founder of the kingdom, became *fama* (king). The army he formed carved out a huge kingdom stretching from Timbuktu to the banks of the Senegal River, and the enemy soldiers captured during the conquests were marched to ports in Senegal and Ghana where they were traded with slavers for firearms. Along with the Songhai to the north, the Ségou Empire was one of the earliest in the Sahara to obtain guns, which were used effectively to subdue rival powers.

The Ségou rulers developed a **nationalist policy** in which all rights were accorded to loyal Bamana subjects but the conquered peoples were excluded from the system altogether. It was a tenuous situation based purely on force of arms, and when the Fula empire of Masina arose in the northeast, disgruntled elements in the Bamana country rallied to it, assuring the demise of Ségou.

In 1861, El Hadj Omar conquered Ségou and forced the inhabitants – who had remained one of the few non-Muslim groups in the Sahel – to convert to Islam. After the French took the city in 1892, Ségou became an important French outpost and headquarters of the Office du Niger. For a captivating description of this period, read the classic historical novel *Segu* by Maryse Condé (see p.337).

---

for you, or you could try striking a deal with one of the *piroguiers* down on the shore.

It's also possible to cruise upriver to **Ségou-Koro** by *pirogue* (CFA15,000–20,000/day) or motorized *pinasse* (CFA25,000/day); though it's more usual and cheaper to visit this village by car or *mobylette*; it's on the south bank of the river about 10km out of town, off the Bamako road. The scale of Ségou-Koro – it's small enough to explore in well under an hour on foot – gives you little sense of the fact that this was once the seat of a powerful kingdom, but the ancient mud-brick and *banco* buildings have an unmistakable grace. It's best to hire a guide in Ségou to show you round the village (in any case you'll have to pay your respects, and a fee of CFA500 per person, to the chief). Sights include the delicate **mosque of Ba Sounou Sacko**, mother of King Biton Mamary Coulibaly, and the **tomb of Coulibaly** himself, recently restored. Look out too for the **ancient tree** that was the focal point of the royal palace and under which the council of elders sat.

Practicalities

Compared with the relative hustle of Bamako or Mopti, Ségou is an easy place in practical terms, with a good number of **accommodation** options and several decent **places to eat**. The town is centred on the area immediately south of the ferry port. **Somatra** and **Somatri buses** have a terminal behind the water tower here, with a depot used by Binke Transport opposite; Bittar Transport has a depot just north of the Muslim cemetery. *Bâchées* and donkey carts are the main options for transport around town.

The most reliable place to **get online** is Sotelma (Mon–Fri 7.30am–5.30pm), on the Bamako road opposite the Commissariat. More central, open daily and later, but less user-friendly, are Balazan Tour Cyber Café, in front of *L'Auberge*, and Cyber Café, around the corner from the *Soleil de Minuit* restaurant. All three places charge CFA1500 per hour. The best **bank** for changing money is the BDM, near the hospital on the Ségou–Koro road; they're slow, but do Visa cash advances.

Ségou is as good a place as any, if you want to find a guide for the **Dogon country**. The scene here is less hectic than in Mopti and Bamako, and the guides (ask to

The bus operator Somatra (☎232.02.66) have a daily 5am departure for **Bamako**, and services at 9am and noon for **Mopti**, via San and Sévaré. Bittar Transport has an hourly departure to Bamako, and four buses going to Mopti every day. Fares are roughly CFA2500 to Bamako and CFA4500 to Mopti. Binke Transport, on top of regular departures to Mopti and Bamako, have services to distant **Gao** (daily at 8am, 11am and noon; CFA9000) via Douentza and Hombori. There are minibuses to **Djenné** on Saturday and Sunday, leaving at around 4.30pm from the area around the water tower (CFA4500), or you could charter a vehicle there.

Somatra and Somatri (☎232.05.91) buses leave for **Sikasso** daily between 8am and 9am (CFA3500). There is a Somatra bus to Bobo-Dioulasso in **Burkina Faso** (daily at 11.30am; CFA6000); an alternative route is to take a bus to San or Koutiala and pick up a connection there. For **Côte d'Ivoire**, make for Sikasso where, if the border is open, you can change for onward transport south.

In the rainy season, you can of course travel **by boat** to **Koulikoro** (for Bamako) or all the way up to **Gao**. The COMANAV ferry office (☎232.02.04) overlooks the jetty in Ségou. For more information on the river boats, see p.317.

Driving the back road to Timbuktu

During the dry season, it's possible to zigzag from here all the way across the Niger delta to **Timbuktu** by a network of tracks. Although this involves tackling long stretches of tortuous *piste* and occasional muddy river crossings, it allows you to take in fascinating scenery along a little-travelled route. This short account assumes you'll be using your own 4WD vehicle, though given time you could achieve this with available local transport such as the weekly truck-cum-bus from Bamako to Timbuktu that supposedly passes this way, but is seldom actually seen (enquire at Ségou's bus station for details).

From Ségou, take the northern road towards **Niono**, and then turn east beyond **Markala** to **Massina**, 105km on. This route passes through the old city of **Sansanding**, "the great marketplace of the Western Sudan" according to the nineteenth-century scholar, Heinrich Barth. From Massina, you can make an interesting side-trip, 44km to **Diafarabé**, a small village located on one of the narrowest points of the Niger (see box, p.360, for details of the annual cattle crossing here).

From Massina, tracks lead north towards **Nampala**, also accessible directly from Ségou via Niono, passing lush green fields of irrigated rice. It's 90km from Nampala to **Léré**, a small village with a Friday **livestock market** that unites herders from all over the region – and another 136km across mud-cracked lagoons to the town of Niafounké, whose most famous resident, virtuoso musician Ali Farka Touré, owns the town's only hotel (CFA6500). A ferry crosses the river at Niafounké, making it possible to connect with the road leading to **Korientze** and back south to Mopti. Alternatively, you can continue 90km northeast to the Songhai town of **Goundam**. An increasingly sandy track requiring 4WD then leads over the remaining 100km to the dunes surrounding **Timbuktu**.

see their badges or a "cartes de Guide" before agreeing to anything) are members of a new association who, besides covering the Dogon country, can arrange some excellent trips around the Ségou area. The Ministry of Tourism southeast of the centre has a list of official guides, or you could head to *Le Golfe* (see p.360) restaurant, the unofficial headquarters of the guides.

Accommodation

Ségou has a growing range of places to stay, though several are away from the town centre.

L'Auberge ⊕232.01.45, ⊛www.promali.org/aub-ind. Very central, almost by the river, and offering very pleasant s/c, a/c rooms with satellite TV. Lebanese-owned and popular with expats, it has a pricey restaurant and a shady garden with a pool. ❹

Djoliba Next to the *Auberge* ⊕232.15.72, ⓔzarth@afribone.net.ml. Immaculate, German-run establishment with smartly equipped s/c rooms which, when the remote control for the a/c is removed, become cheaper ones with fan. CFA4000 to sleep on roof, ❺

Grand Hôtel de France Right in the middle of town ⊕232.03.15. Named thus by the Francophile owner rather than being the venerable colonial pile you might imagine, this has nets and fans in the s/c rooms, and even some with a/c. It's a bit of a whorehouse, but perfectly okay, and about the cheapest place in the town centre. ❷

Hôtel De L'Indépendance Some 5km east of the centre, down the Mopti road ⊕232.04.62, ⊛www.promali.org/aub-ind. Owned by the same owners as *L'Auberge*, this place is quiet and comfortable and has good-sized a/c rooms with TV. The only drawback is the distance from the centre. ❹

Mivera Around 5km east of the centre near the *Indépendance* ⊕232.03.31, ⓔsosafi-ol @hotmail.com. Free parking, s/c rooms with TV and fan or a/c – but no more charm than motels worldwide. ❸

Office du Niger (aka *Centre d'Accueil–Hôtel Delta*) A little way down a side road leading south off the Bamako road at the western end of town, 3km from the bus terminals ⊕232.03.72. Pretty much the default option in its price bracket, this is quiet, with a few s/c rooms with fan (more with a/c), free parking and a spacious camping area (CFA3000 per person). ❸

Savane About 200m south of *Office du Niger* ⊕232.09.74, ⓔsavane@spider.toolnet.org. A peaceful place with a range of well-kept s/c rooms with fan, plus a dorm and some more expensive a/c rooms and bungalows, all with TV. Dorm beds CFA5000, ❸

Eating and nightlife

For inexpensive **meals** fresh from a spotless kitchen, the best choice is *Le Soleil de Minuit*. Across the road, the *Djoliba*'s bar-restaurant is slightly more expensive, with draught beer and an open-air pizza evening on the rooftop every Saturday. The food at *Le Golfe* nearby isn't outstanding, but it's popular nonetheless for inexpensive sandwiches and as a drinking spot. At the Bittar Trans depot, *Tanty J'ai Faim* is a good bet for hefty servings of basic stodge. As for **nightlife**, the *Jardin de Mobasso*, east of *Le Golfe*, a lively garden bar/grill, sometimes hosts live music during weekends, and *Le Rivage* nightclub at the *Esplanade* hotel packs in the crowds at weekends, but doesn't open until 11pm.

Zinzana, Bla, San and Koutiala

If you're travelling southeast from Ségou in your own vehicle, you might want to stop overnight some 40km from the town at **ZINZANA**, where the excellent *campement* (❹) at the agricultural research station is a haven of peace and tranquility, with spotless sheets, a vine-shaded terrace, cold beer and good food.

The Diafarabé cattle crossing

In December, **Fula herders** descend en masse on the village of **Diafarabé**, on the north bank of the Niger 60km northwest of Djenné and 190km northeast of Ségou. Here, and at several other crossing points in the vicinity, they lead their cattle from the northern Sahel grazing ground to the southern banks of the river to await the return of the rains in May or June. The spectacle of thousands of **cattle** crashing into the water and swimming to the other side as herders prod them along is memorable indeed. Music and festivities accompany the event, but there's no set date. Ask around in Ségou if you think you might be there around the right time.

Diafarabé has an interesting old quarter between the market and the river, with an attractive, modern, Sudanic-style mosque. There's a small **ferry** here, and you can **stay** at the basic *campement* (CFA2500 per person).

Southeast of Zinzana, the main road divides at the junction town of **BLA**, with the N6 continuing northeast to San and Mopti and the N12 heading south to Koutiala and Sikasso. Drivers often make a stop at Bla to eat at one of the roadside *gargotes*, and there's very basic accommodation here at *Le Refuge* bar (CFA5000).

SAN is an important commercial crossroads, and a major departure point for Burkina and Côte d'Ivoire. The town **market**, best on Monday, is the largest in the region, trading in everything from livestock to imported goods. There's no real reason to spend time here on any other day, but if you need to **stay**, try the rooms at the *Campement Teriya* (☎237.21.07; ❷), which is better known for its good restaurant; the reception is 2km down the road from the *campement*. Basic **food** can also be had at the *Bon Coin*, just outside town on the road to Ségou.

The cotton-growing town of **KOUTIALA** is, like San, an exit point for travellers to Bobo-Dioulasso, and is also a staging post between Sikasso and Ségou or Mopti. There's a bank here, and if you overnight it, you can stay comfortably at *Motel La Chaumière* (☎264.02.20; ❸), which has good-value s/c rooms with fan or a/c, all with TV.

Sikasso and around

Mali's southernmost and second-largest town, **SIKASSO** is an evergreen place, traditionally largely Senoufo, with a humid tropical languor in which tea, cotton and market garden produce flourish. The town grew to become a colonial outpost, as the decaying administrative buildings from that era attest, and its gentle, welcoming atmosphere and verdant surroundings give it an appeal unique in Mali. Sissoko's proximity to Côte d'Ivoire has until recently assured a good deal of international activity, but at the time of writing, the ongoing crisis across the border had made the town's prospects uncertain.

Sikasso was the last capital of the **Kénédougou Empire**, a kingdom founded by Dioula traders in the seventeenth century. A warrior named **Tieba** became ruler of the mini-empire in 1876, and he transformed Sikasso – his mother's birthplace – from a tiny agricultural village, based around the sacred Mamelon hill, into a fortified capital, expanding his empire and developing trade. On the top of the hill, **Tieba** had a two-storey house built to receive royal guests. During the same period, however, the Malinké warlord **Samory Touré** was expanding his influence in the region, and came into conflict with the Senoufo, destroying the town of Kong, as well as Senoufo strongholds like Korhogo and Ferkessédougou, in present-day Côte d'Ivoire. Samory laid siege to Sikasso in 1887 but fifteen months later the city had not fallen and, soon after, Tieba received support from a new invasion force, the French, under Binger. Tieba died in battle in 1893, leaving his son, Babemba, as ruler. But Babemba fell out with the French and they attacked and routed Sikasso in 1898, symbolically planting the tricolor flag on top of the Mamelon. Babemba committed suicide; his erstwhile enemy, Samory Touré, was captured by the French and sent into captivity in Gabon, where he died.

The town still gravitates around the **Mamelon**, a thirty-metre hillock which was once believed to host a spirit protecting the town (now it houses a water tower and an antenna); and the **market**, impressive on any day of the week but enormous on Sundays, and outstanding for its fruit and vegetables. The Mamelon is an easy climb that offers the best views of Sikasso, but apart from that and the market, the town has few obvious sights, though you can still see remnants of the fortifications – known as **tata** – that, despite their impressive size, couldn't hold out against the onslaught of the French. One other place that is worth a visit is the **Galerie Kéné Arts**, an artisans' co-operative selling jewellery, fabrics, leatherwork, masks and carvings, located behind the Bank of Africa.

Practicalities

From the roundabout by the Mamelon, a road heads south across the Lotio River to the **autogare**, used by all the bus companies; it's 1500m south of the town centre on the road to Ferkessédougou in Côte d'Ivoire. Near the Mamelon roundabout you'll find a **post office** and five **banks** – Bank of Africa, BNDA, BIM, BDM and a new branch of BCEAO, but none of them give Visa cash advances, even if they advertise the fact; BIM and BDM change traveller's cheques. Sikasso has three **Internet cafés**: the reliable *Sikanet*, on the Bamako road across from the Elf station (daily until 9.30pm; CFA1500/hr during the week and CFA1000/hr at the weekend), with a branch next to the *Sowlait* café (same hours and prices), and the post office Internet café (post office hours). There is 24-hour fuel at the Total garage on the Bamako road.

Accommodation

Sikasso has plenty of places to stay, though tourist traffic here is minimal – with the civil war in Côte d'Ivoire, the hotels here have been busy putting up journalists and Malian returnees. If you want a comfortable night and aren't too concerned about the price, go straight to the *Wassoulou*; if you're on a budget, try the *Tata*.

Lotio On the Bamako road near the centre ☎262.10.01. A grubby, slightly seedy bar, but friendly enough; rooms come with fans and shared facilities. **②**

Le Mamelon Close to the market ☎262.00.44 & ℻262.04.40. Plain s/c, a/c rooms with TV, and a good restaurant. **④**

Motel Le Wassoulou On the new Koutiala road north of town ☎262.04.24 & ℻262.04.44. The best hotel in Sikasso, well known for its restaurant. Rooms are in chalets with a/c and TV, and you can also pitch your tent in the peaceful garden. **⑤**

Soundiata Off the Bamako road next to the Marché Médine, west of the centre ☎262.19.48. A fairly new place with good-sized s/c rooms with

fan or a/c, free parking and a good restaurant (though no alcohol). **③**

Tata In the town centre, in front of the *Soundiata* ☎62.04.01. Unexceptional rooms in a variety of conditions, plus a basic restaurant. **②**

Le Touban On the north side of town on the Old Koutiala Road ☎262.05.34, ℮panierkone@cefib .com. Reasonable-value, secure, comfortable s/c rooms with a/c, TV. Breakfast is included in the rate, and the place is right next to a well-stocked supermarket, too. **④**

Zanga Near the *autogare* ☎262.04.31. A few rooms with fan (but no mosquito protection) and shared facilities, and overpriced s/c, a/c rooms. Don't be seduced by the pool, which positively glows with green algae. **③**

Moving on from Sikasso

Buses to **Bamako** are operated by various bus companies. The local firm Kénédougou Voyages (☎260.07.19) has many daily buses to Bamako via Bougouni (5–6hr), as do Somatri (☎262.01.39) and Somatra (☎262.17.05); expect to pay CFA4000 for the trip. Kénédougou Voyages and Somatri go to **Mopti** (Sévaré) via Koutiala (daily at 7pm; CFA5000; 9hr). Somatra and Bani voyages have departures to **Gao** via Mopti and Douentza once and twice a week respectively (Thurs & Sun 4pm for Bani; Sun 7pm for Somatra; 13hr plus; CFA11000). All the bus companies go to **Ségou** via Koutiala and Bla, and have a daily 9am or 10am departure (CFA3500). It shouldn't take more than five hours but there are often delays, especially with Kénédougou, who have a reputation for piling in more passengers, goods and animals than there's room for.

For **Bobo-Dioulasso** (4hr; CFA3500) or **Ouagadougou** (9hr; CFA10,000), there are services with Kénédougou and YT (☎262.08.27 or 672.54.53), which each have two daily departures at 8am and 5pm via Zegoua; YT continues to **Niamey** (CFA22,500), **Lomé** (CFA22,500) and **Cotonou** (CFA25,000). At the time of writing, the daily buses operated by Kénédougou and CTB to **Yamoussoukro** (CFA8500) and **Abidjan** (CFA9000) in Côte d'Ivoire had been suspended.

Eating and nightlife

For French and Malian **food** served in a pleasant garden, full of nesting weaver birds, the restaurant at *Le Wassoulou*, on the new Koutiala road, is highly recommended: arrange a return taxi if you plan on making the trip out from the centre (CFA400 each way). Less upmarket but also a good bet is the *Bar-Restaurant Chez Les Amis*, a quiet, friendly place serving excellent staples such as *couscous*, *capitaine*, and *poulet kedjenou* (an Ivoirian speciality) in a shady garden; it's off the old Koutiala road, about 200m from *Hôtel Le Touban*. *La Vieille Marmite*, on the Bamako road near *Hôtel Lotio*, is also a good place to go for African dishes. The Sowlait dairy outlet, by the Mamelon roundabout, has fresh milk and delicious yogurt at CFA250, and an excellent streetside terrace. There are several basic eating places near the *autogare* and on the Bamako road, but the pick of the bunch is the central, small and friendly *Restaurant Kassonke*, which serves inexpensive rice and sauce as well as grilled meat. The best **supermarket** is Le Panier de la Ménagère, attached to *Le Touban* hotel, clearly signposted from the town centre. **Nightlife** is not thrilling in Sikasso, but there are two *boîtes* (both Thurs–Sat; CFA1250 entrance): *Angara* next to the hospital, and *Vision* behind the small market.

Around Sikasso

About 12km southwest of Sikasso, inside a cathedrallike limestone outcrop jutting up from the plain, are the **Grottes de Missirikoro**, also known as Faramissiri (Stone Mosque) in Bambara. The sacred grotto is said to be inhabited by guardian spirits that Kénédougou kings used to consult before an expedition – and is home to colonies of bats, some tribal relics, and a few latter-day cave-dwellers. It's still used as a place of worship and sacrifice by animists, Muslims and Christians alike, each using one of the three different natural entrances. You can clamber up the outcrop itself by means of ladders and chains for a 360-degree view of the surrounding wooded plains. A taxi to the caves and back should cost around CFA7000 including waiting time. Take a torch to illuminate the gloomy recesses, and some kola nuts to offer to the caves' residents.

The **Chutes de Farako**, 30km east of Sikasso (on the road to the Burkina border), are particularly impressive in the rainy season and can be visited in a day. There are smaller but equally picturesque waterfalls some 15km south of town, which are a favourite retreat of Sikasso's Peace Corps volunteers; the pool here is deep enough to swim in.

4.4

Mopti and the delta region

T he Niger's extraordinary **inland delta** is one of the most compelling parts of West Africa, and bound to leave a lasting impression. As the Niger and its major tributary, the Bani, slow and meander out across the plain into hundreds of channels and lagoons, they pass near the medieval towns of **Djenné** and **Timbuktu** – once renowned as centres of commercial prosperity and Islamic piety, and still worthy magnets for travellers. Although the allure of Timbuktu's fabled reputation is undeniable, Djenné is undoubtedly the more impressive destination and much easier to reach. Today, the economic importance of both towns has been overshadowed by **Mopti** and its satellite town, **Sévaré**, together the joint hub of Mali's tourist industry and the country's major route intersection.

A rewarding, if by no means luxurious, way to travel through the region is by **river boat**. When you travel along the river, the ports become your *gares routières*, and your arrival at any port will be amid a rush of activity as merchants from throughout Mali scramble to buy whatever goods are available before the boat pulls out and continues its ponderous journey. The boats operate only after the rains, though for the seven or so months that the river boats are out of commission, it's possible to explore the river routes – or simply travel from A to B – by chartered *pirogue* or *pinasse*. For more on the general practicalities of boat travel on the Niger, see p.317; for details of trips from Mopti, see p.368.

Dotting the riverbank are small towns and villages, consisting mostly of ground-hugging mud-brick buildings towered over by traditional **Sudanic-style mosques**, such as the impressive one at **Quaddaga**, about 20km downstream from Mopti, or the two large mosques at **Koa**, 100km upstream. Although Fula and Tuareg nomads still lead their flocks and herds through the region, vegetation is relatively sparse and the landscapes often flat and barren. Occasionally, fields of rice and other cereals can be seen – evidence of government attempts to irrigate large portions of the delta before they are irretrievably claimed by the advancing Sahara.

Mopti and Sévaré

Built on three islands connected by dykes, the riverside town of **Mopti**, with its reputation for hustlers, isn't immediately attractive to every visitor. The old town lacks aesthetic harmony, the new town isn't particularly modern, and the whole place, hemmed in on three sides by the waterways at the confluence of the Niger and the Bani (the "Venice of Africa" is a common sobriquet) can feel a little crowded and oppressive, especially down on the busy and odoriferous shores of the port. If you're arriving direct from Europe on Point-Afrique's winter charter flight, or even by bus straight in from the bush, you can experience a strong dose of culture shock. Don't be scared off wandering around, though: as your face becomes known, and especially if you have a guide to look after you, so the port and the busy canals begin to work their magic. Mopti pulls together all the peoples of Mali – Bamana, Songhai, Fula, Tuareg, Moor, Bozo and Dogon – and its buoyant pace and mix of cultures add to the charm. If you can arrange it, aim to be here on market day, Thursday.

Mopti offers little choice in accommodation, virtually nothing at the budget end. In many ways, **Sévaré**, 12km southeast on the main Bamako–Gao road, is a preferable base, used increasingly by overnighting tourists. A blander and more functional place, Sévaré is a main pick-up point for onward travel and the location of Mopti's **airport**, and it's easy to make short trips down the causeway to Mopti itself – *bâches* ply between the two towns from around 7am to 8pm (15min; CFA200).

Mopti Town

Originally a cluster of islands inhabited by **Bozo fishing people**, **MOPTI** became an important site early in the nineteenth century when, with the jihad proclaimed by the Fula scholar and ascetic **Cheikou Ahmadou Lobbo**, it gained strategic significance as an outpost of his Masina Empire, centred on Djenné and the surrounding Fula pasturelands. Mopti was later captured by the Tukulor warmonger **El Hadj Omar**, who turned the settlement into his principal military base, from where he launched attacks against his Fula rivals. A small town grew up around the site, but Mopti remained largely overshadowed by Djenné.

It wasn't until the beginning of the twentieth century that the town found commercial importance – at first with the export of white egret feathers to the *belle époque* couturiers of Paris. Indeed, economic development was largely due to the French, who exploited Mopti's position at the confluence of the Bani and the Niger and its accessibility from the main overland routes. When the railway line connecting Bamako to Dakar was built, Mopti became the largest river port in the French Soudan. Its population has grown steadily and today, with more than 100,000 people, it rivals Sikasso as Mali's second town.

The harbour

Most of the sights in Mopti, built on three islands connected by dykes, centre around Mopti's *raison d'être*, the **harbour**, built by the French in the early part of

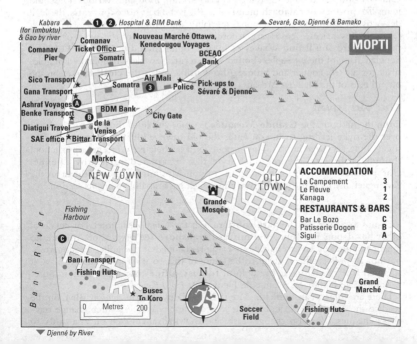

the last century. Large, traditional *pinasses* with their canvas covers and colourful flags waving in the breeze tie up regularly to unload cargo and passengers, while *pirogues* taxi people back and forth from different points on the islands that make up the town. The terrace at *Bar Le Bozo*, a restaurant right on the riverfront, provides an excellent and breezy vantage point from which to take in all the activity in the harbour, and watch the invariably beautiful sunset.

A **fish market** occupies the southern edge of the port near *Bar Le Bozo*. Behind it is a large open-air workshop where craftsmen build the *pinasses* from large planks imported from the south. On the northern shore of the harbour, Moorish traders mill around stacks of marblelike **salt slabs**, brought by camel caravan from the desert to Timbuktu and then transported by boat to Mopti. Formerly one of the desert's great riches, salt is still a precious commodity for herders who need it for their livestock.

The harbour is the place to get boats to see the Bozo and Tuareg communities nearby. These trips are ultimately rather voyeuristic and artificial experiences, but the boat ride is enjoyable and gives an interesting perspective of the town. The **Bozo** are fishing people who, during the rainy season when the catch is most prolific, build circular thatched huts around Mopti, clustered in small *campements*. If you take a *pirogue* to one of these, you'll see them repairing their boats and nets. The **Tuareg** "camp" is nothing more than a few huts where women sell **crafts** – bracelets, necklaces and leather goods – at elevated prices, but beyond, there is a "beach" where you can swim during the dry season. Kids in Mopti will find you and propose the trip (just hang around the *Bar Le Bozo*); their brothers or uncles are inevitably **boatmen** who will give you a "special rate" – the going rate is around CFA1000 an hour per boat, though the first price will be many times this.

The new town

North of the harbour in the new town, the **nouveau marché Ottawa**, a Canadian-sponsored building, is a good place to find food, plus various household items like **pottery** or **calabash** utensils. Nearby is the best place for **crafts**, the Hall des Artisans. **Blankets** are a regional speciality and Mopti has a wide selection at relatively low prices – costs vary according to the quality of the wool or cotton threads. Here you'll find weaves of local peoples including Dogon, Fula and Songhai. Each of these peoples also has characteristic jewellery handcrafted in gold, silver (or nickel), copper and bronze. Also worth a visit is the **cloth** market on the outer limits of the Hall des Artisans.

The old town

From the harbour, the **Grande Mosquée** is easily visible to the east. As you cross over the dyke leading to it, you enter the old town with its narrow traffic-free streets and grey *banco* houses. The mosque itself is a relatively recent construction, though faithful to the regional style that originated in nearby Djenné. Unfortunately, the interior is off limits to non-Muslims. To the southeast in the Komuguel district is the **grand marché**, which has a small handicrafts section.

Practicalities

Pick-ups to Sévaré use the **gare routière** near the *Campement* hotel. For details of other bus depots in Mopti, and **onward transport**, see box, p.368. You are no longer required by law to have your passport stamped at the police headquarters, but not all police officers seem to be aware of this, so it's a good idea to have it stamped free of charge at the helpful **tourist office** (Mon–Fri 8am–noon & 2–4pm; ☎243.05.06), on Avenue du Fleuve past *Hotel Kanaga*.

There are three main **banks** in Mopti: BCEAO, by the *gare routière*; BIM, on the road to the *Hôtel Kanaga*; and BDM, west of the city gate. All three change traveller's cheques; BIM also changes cash, and BDM advances cash on Visa cards. To

Travel agents and Dogon tours

There are several **travel agents** in Mopti's new town near the BDM bank, all offering tours of the main tourist circuits, including Dogon country treks and excursions to Timbuktu; most can also arrange land-cruiser rental. The firms include: Ashraf Voyages (☎243.02.79, ✉ashraf.voyages@malinet.ml), Bambara African Tours (☎243.00.80, ⟲www.bambara.com) and Diatigui Travel (☎243.02.73, ✉diatigui_travel @hotmail.com). Mali-Voyages, in the *Campement*'s compound, specializes in river travel (☎243.08.02, ✉youssoufditgole@hotmail.com).

Mopti itself is straightforward enough not to require the assistance of a **guide** (and if you don't want one, you need to be firm with the persistent and sometimes aggressive candidates), though you might opt to hire one for the Dogon country. Although most of the guides turn out to be quite well informed and hard working, there are no guarantees: you may discover your guide knows little about the area, or that he can't arrange to get you to places he promised. Whatever the outcome, it will cost you a fraction of organized excursions. You normally **pay** the guide's transport there and back plus a negotiable daily fee (CFA3000–4000 per person per day is a fair budget, though you should anticipate extra for porterage, meals and accommodation en route). It's wise to agree a payment for your trip before setting out; pay part before leaving and the rest when you return, and, if possible, sign a contract with your guide at the Mopti tourist office, which has a list of recommended guides – though these are likely to be the same as the ones you meet in the street.

get **online**, head to *Cybercafé Librairie Papeterie de la Venise*, opposite *Patisserie Dogon* (CFA2000/hr).

Accommodation

Besides trying the places reviewed below, you could also consider **staying with people**, in which event you'll get either a room to yourself in their house, or a mat on a rooftop terrace. Though the practice is officially forbidden, the prices (negotiable) are usually reasonable. Make sure you can lock your valuables away when you go out.

Le Campement Near the police headquarters and the *gare routière* ☎243.00.32. Smallish but tidy s/c, a/c rooms in a new building, and large s/c rooms with fans in the old colonial-style edifice. The restaurant serves good-value basic European-style meals, and there's a backyard where you can pitch your tent (CFA2500). Overnight parking CFA2000. ❸

Doux Rêves Southeast of the old town on rue 540, next to the CAN football stadium ☎243.04.97. With a variety of clean s/c rooms, a bar and the occasional band, this is great value – Mopti's best budget option. Shared taxi rides from the new town run about CFA150 or less. Dorm beds CFA4000, ❷

Le Fleuve Two pink new buildings behind *Kanaga* ☎ & ☎243.02.46. Good-sized s/c rooms, most with a/c. You can also sleep under the stars on the roof (CFA2500), next to a rooftop bar-restaurant with a fabulous view of the river. ❸

Kanaga Near the waterfront on the north side of the new town ☎243.05.00, ✉kanaga@bambara.com. Mopti's best hotel (Michael Palin stayed here when filming his Sahara programmes for the BBC) with comfortable s/c, a/c rooms, satellite TV, a pool and a bar under a thatched awning, with live traditional music every weekend. The restaurant is also the best in town. Mountain bikes can be rented at reception for CFA4000 a day, while non-residents pay a hefty CFA3500 to use the pool. ❼

Eating

The *Bar Le Bozo* is a famous haunt for a sundowner and, while there's nothing particularly fancy about the rice and fish dishes, it's good value, and a great place to watch the waterfront traffic and commerce. It's also a hangout for tourist touts, but there's usually a security man on duty. The *Restaurant Le "Doun Ka Fa"* at the *Hôtel Kanaga* gives you the option to splurge with your credit card on carefully prepared

African specialities and a decent wine list. *Sigui*, Avenue du Fleuve, on the waterfront, also provides upscale fare – European, African and Asian dishes – and has tables both inside and outside in a courtyard. **Street food** is plentiful, especially around the harbour and the transport parks, and stalls are open mornings and evenings for omelettes and bread; a popular and inexpensive little restaurant is *Baramuso*, near the Somatra office. *Patisserie Dogon*, next to BDM bank, gets plenty of custom for its cakes and sandwiches.

Sévaré

SÉVARÉ hasn't got its neighbour's atmosphere, but its location, on the main road between Bamako and Gao, makes it unavoidable if you're travelling by road. Boasting plenty of decent hotels and restaurants, and a generally better nightlife than in Mopti, Sévaré is a convenient base for exploring the Dogon country and the rest of the region.

Moving on from Mopti and Sévaré

From the airport in Sévaré, Air Mali operates **flights** four times a week to Timbuktu and Bamako (on the return leg). If you're in town during the late dry season, this may be the easiest way to get to Timbuktu. Schedules tend to change quite a lot, so contact the airport (☎242.01.08) or the Air Mali office at the *Campement* in Mopti (☎243.00.32) for current details. In the winter there are weekly flights to Marseilles and Paris with Point-Afrique (☎242.07.89).

River boats

From August to January or February (depending on the rains), you can travel down the Niger to **Gao**. During this period, boats also provide the quickest link to **Korioumé**, the port of call for **Timbuktu**. Upriver, to **Koulikoro** (for **Bamako**), the boats usually stop running in mid-November due to the low waters. Mopti–Timbuktu fares are CFA20,000 third-class, CFA33,000 second, CFA46,000 first and CFA86,000 *luxe*; for Koulikoro, the corresponding fares are CFA25,000 third, CFA42,000 second, CFA58,000 first and CFA110,000 *luxe*. Tickets and schedules are available from COMANAV, near the port (☎232.00.06).

Pirogues and pinasses

For a general picture of the practicalities of travel by *pinasse* and *pirogue*, see p.317. From Mopti, a seat on a non-motorized goods *pinasse* or *pirogue* to **Korioumé** costs around CFA10,000, but even these don't operate much after February. The journey varies from spellbinding (when you push off at dawn) to alarmingly uncomfortable (early afternoon out on the river), and the romance can wear thin given the restricted space and potential for delays: the trip should take three to five days, but voyages of up to ten days aren't unheard of, on an overloaded *pinasse* repeatedly running aground on sandbanks. But, in retrospect at least, it's a wonderful adventure, and birdlife is prolific and hippos easily seen. You might prefer to charter a *pinasse* to yourself, for around CFA400,000, but you can put quite a few travellers on board and still have room. Motor *pinasses* also operate up the Niger to **Ségou**, a three-day journey; a five-person *pinasse* with everything included will cost you around CFA450,000.

Besides being the major port of call on the Niger, Mopti is the most convenient springboard for trips up the Bani to **Djenné**. *Pinasses* are most likely to leave Sunday afternoons (around CFA3000–4000) to arrive in the morning in time for Djenné's Monday market, but ask at the port for other possible departures. Chartering a motor *pinasse* for your group, count on about CFA100,000 for a day-trip, using a boat with *two* engines (an important point, if you're not going to end up spending the night on

The town **centre** is the big crossroads where the Mopti–Bandiagara road crosses the Bamako–Gao highway. The **gare routière** is on the Bandiagara road 500m east of the crossroads; all buses in or out of Mopti stop there. The **airstrip** is 2km southeast of town. Mopti *bâchées* depart from just west of the main crossroads. An interesting souvenir shop, selling leatherwork and traditional jewellery, with a little bead museum upstairs, is the Musée Bijoux, next to the *Cyber Café* on the Bamako road. The best-stocked supermarket is the small Mini Prix, opposite the **post office** on the Mopti road. A bit further along, the BNDA **bank** changes traveller's cheques. The helpful Tellem Voyages travel agency is located about 500m from the power station.

Accommodation, eating and nightlife

Sévaré has, surprisingly perhaps, some of the best-value and nicest **accommodation** in Mali, and it can be hard to choose between the best two – *Mac's Refuge* and

board); non-motorized charters go for as little as CFA40,000, but it can take up to three days to pole and paddle to Djenné.

By road

Nearly all transport in and out of Mopti and Sévaré stops in both towns (though some long-distance transport on the Bamako–Gao route doesn't make the trip right down to Mopti). Bush taxis to **Djenné** leave from Mopti's *gare routière* via Sévaré, and normally take about three hours for the 130-kilometre trip. Your best chance of finding taxis is on Sunday and early morning on Monday (Djenné's market day). At other times there may be nothing at all, or transport only as far as the Djenné turn-off, where you'll have to find another bush taxi for the remaining 35km – a matter of luck and patience. During the rains the overland route may be out altogether.

The main bus companies for **Bamako**, **San** and **Ségou**, can be found in Mopti in the streets around the waterfront and near *Bar Le Bozo*. If you're starting from Sévaré, it's a good idea to find out which company has the next departure (depending on when they arrive from Mopti or Gao) before you buy your ticket. Bus operators include Bittar Transport (☎678.10.42), Bani Transport (☎242.01.85), Sico Transport, Somatra, Somatri (☎243.02.76), Gana Transport and Binke Transport; all operate at least one daily departure to Bamako (CFA6000–7000), San (CFA2000) and Ségou (CFA4500) from Sévaré's *gare routière*.

For **Sikasso**, Kénédougou Voyages has a daily departure at 4pm (CFA5000) originating from the Ottawa market in Mopti. Transport to **Bobo-Dioulasso** in Burkina Faso leaves daily, early in the evening from behind *Bar Le Bozo* (CFA6500), arriving the following morning.

For the **Dogon country**, Bani Transport has a twice-weekly bus via Douentza to Hombori (CFA4000). Otherwise you can get a *bâché* to Bankass (CFA2500) and Koro (around CFA4000) from Mopti's port or Sévaré's *gare routière* every morning. *Bâchés* and bush taxis to Bandiagara (around CFA1750) and Bankass (around CFA2500) also leave from just outside the *gare routière* in Sévaré.

For **Gao**, Bani Transport has two departures every evening except on Sunday – and Bittar has one departure every other day (CFA6000). Both companies stop late in the day at Douentza, from where you can usually catch transport on to **Timbuktu** the following day. Additionally, you can make the journey there by 4WD (at least 14hr); vehicles depart from the Timbuktu *gare routière* behind the Palais de Justice in Mopti, at the place du Syndicat, also known as the place de Timbuktu. Expect to pay CFA15,000 (more for the front seats) and note that vehicles will not make the trip unless there are at least seven or eight passengers (failing which you may want to pay extra for the remaining places).

Makan Tè. It's worth calling or emailing ahead to reserve rooms, as they're often full. Most of the town's hotels are found on or near the Bamako road, just about within walking distance of the main crossroads.

Street **food** is easy to come by in Sévaré. On the Bamako road you'll find plenty of breakfast spots and grilled-meat stalls, and nearby, set in a beautiful flowery garden, restaurant *Makan Tè* (owned by the hotel), which does tasty *brochettes de capitaine* and mince-meat sandwiches. During weekends this is also the place to head to for all-night **dancing** in the large garden *paillote*. The *Byblos* Lebanese restaurant off the Bamako road is also popular, and becomes a lively nightclub at weekends.

Hotels

Le Byblos Signposted off the Bamako road ☎243.04.57, ✉cbyblos@hotmail.com. A Lebanese restaurant primarily, but with a few tidy s/c, a/c rooms in the back garden, and more in an annexe nearby. ❹

Mac's Refuge Signed 500m west of the Bamako road ☎672.90.97, ✉malimacs@yahoo.com. Owned by a Malian-American former missionary (son of the Reverend McKinney – see p.385) whose reputation for hospitality and local fixing and guidance grows year by year, *Mac's* is renowned for superb meals and delightful staff – a true refuge from heat, hustle and stodge, and a great place to recoup before or after a Dogon trek or river trip. As well as limited accommodation in the house, there's a clutch of purpose-built, s/c rooms in the yard, with a/c or fan, each named after an ethnic group whose artefacts decorate the room. The dining room has a refectory table where excellent meals are served at set hours.

There's a good selection of French- and English-language videos, a book exchange and, most surprising of all, a small but immaculate swimming pool. Sleeping on the roof costs CFA4500, otherwise ❹ .

Makan Te Signed off the Bamako road ☎242.01.93, ✉makante@gmx.de. Relaxed and homely, this small hotel is run by a sociable German woman who'll help arrange trips in the region. Housed in two adjoining well-maintained villas, it has comfortable a/c rooms, some with shared facilities. ❹

Motel Sévaré On the Bamako road ☎ & ℱ242.00.82. Forty good-sized s/c rooms, some with fans, the rest with a/c and TV, around a huge courtyard, and a restaurant serving a varied menu. ❹

Teranga Bamako road. Clean double and triple rooms with fans and shared facilities, with a popular garden restaurant. Sleeping on the roof costs CFA2500. ❷

Djenné and around

DJENNÉ, on a meander in the Bani River, is unquestionably the most beautiful town in the Sahel and, despite the incessant attention of unnecessary guides, a unique place to visit. On an island for most of the year, the buildings are shaped in the smooth lines of the Sudanic style, moulded from the grey clay of the surrounding flood plains. In the main square, the famous **Grande Mosquée** dominates the townscape. People from throughout the region gather in town for the festive market day on Monday – the best day to plan a trip (transport to or from Djenné on other days can be difficult). If you can ignore the multitude of visitors here doing the same, you can imagine what life in the Sahel must have been like a hundred years or more ago.

Originally a **Bozo settlement**, Djenné was founded around 800 AD, according to the *Tarikh es-Soudain* – one of the earliest written records of the Sahel. The original site was at a place called Djoboro, but it may have moved to the present location as early as 1043 (other sources put the date two centuries later). In the thirteenth century, during the reign of the Soninké king **Koï Kounboro**, Djenné converted to Islam: the king himself dutifully razed his palace to make room for the town's first mosque. Djenné became a way-station for gold, ivory, lead, wool, kola nuts and other precious items from the south. Merchants had their main depots here, and sold their wares from outlets they operated throughout the region, notably in Timbuktu. They developed a large flotilla of boats – some up to 20m long – capable of transporting tens of tonnes of these goods to Timbuktu, from where they made their way to the north.

In 1325, Djenné was incorporated into the **Mali Empire** under which it enjoyed a period of stability and continued prosperity. In 1473 it was conquered by the **Songhai Empire**. The intellectual and commercial exchanges with Timbuktu were reinforced during this period until, in 1591, Djenné fell to the Moroccans, under whose dominion it remained until the nineteenth century. The town went into a slow decline that successive invasions were powerless to stop. **Cheikou Ahmadou** – a religious zealot from Masina – ousted the Moroccans in 1810, and destroyed Djenné's famous mosque. The **Tukulor Empire** briefly swallowed up the town in 1862, but held it only until 1893 when **French troops** arrived and took control. Djenné was classified as a UNESCO World Heritage Site in 1988.

The Town and around

Arriving by road, you'll see Djenné's **Grande Mosquée** from some distance as you travel over the dyke leading to town. This architectural masterpiece dates only from 1905, but was built in the style of the original mosque constructed in the reign of the Koï Kounboro. The rounded lines of the facade are dominated by three towers, each 11m high and topped with an ostrich egg. Protruding from the edifice, the beams serve more than an aesthetic function; like scaffolding, they are essential for the upkeep of the building. Each year rains wash away the building's smooth *banco* outer layer and the townspeople work to restore it in the dry season. Inside is a forest of pillars connected by sturdy arches. The mosque is said to hold up to five thousand worshippers – not bad when you consider that Djenné's total population is barely double that number. Regrettably, due to abuses of the site by insensitive visitors, the fascinating interior and rooftop are now off limits to non-Muslims, though you can get a fairly good exterior view from the roof of the house opposite for CFA500 (ask kids to show you the way). Two hundred metres behind the mosque is the **Tombeau de Tapama Djenepo,** the grave of a Bozo girl who, according to oral tradition, was sacrificed by the founders of Djenné to protect its buildings from collapse.

The weekly **market** is a fascinating experience, and it's worth making every effort to time your trip for a Monday when traders from throughout the region make a commercial pilgrimage to town. They spread their wares on the main square in front of the mosque in much the same way that French explorer **René Caillié** described in the nineteenth century in his *Travels through Central Africa to Timbuktu*. There are few (if any) markets as animated, as colourful and as *rich* – those colossal swaying earrings are solid gold – as Djenné's on a Monday morning. After you've finished at the market it's satisfying to leave the crowds and wander through the dusty streets on your own, taking in the architecture and the way of life.

Djenné-Djeno

In 1977, a team of American archeologists discovered an ancient village 2km from Djenné at a spot now called **Djenné-Djeno** (old Djenné), near the entrance to town off the road to Mopti. The foundations of buildings they uncovered here, along with terracotta statues, utensils and jewellery, date back as far as the third century BC and prick holes in a blanket of ignorance about archaic Africa – a highly developed, commercial society (the town counted over ten thousand inhabitants) that existed long before the arrival of Islam. For reasons still unclear, the town went into decline in the early Middle Ages and was abandoned by the fourteenth century. You're supposed to get permission from the police to visit the site, although guides will sometimes agree to take you there; in practice you can just turn up. Keep your eyes on the ground and you'll see the pottery sherds everywhere.

Villages around Djenné

There are several **villages** around Djenné, built on small elevations in the flood plains. One of the most interesting is **Sennissa** – peopled mainly by Fula and just

△ Tellem architecture, Youga-Dogourou, *pays Dogon*

4km from Djenné as the crow flies (take a guide). The village boasts two beautiful **mosques** and an abundance of artisans working along the small streets, lined with single-storey *banco* homes. You're likely to see women here wearing the huge gold heirloom earrings that were once common in the region. The biggest ones may be the size of a rugby ball and hang down to the woman's breasts; some are so heavy they have to be strung from a cord that passes over the head.

Further afield lies **Kouakourou**, a Bozo village about 45km north of Djenné on the banks of the Niger. Its original architectural style, known as *saou*, is unique to the Djenné region. Of special interest are the dwellings for unmarried men whose walls are decorated with geometric forms. Market day is Saturday. You can get here by *pinasse*, or overland in the dry season.

Practicalities

As you enter town, you will be asked to pay a CFA1000 tourist tax (ask for a receipt) as a contribution to help maintaining Djenné's fragile buildings. The small **gare routière** in front of the Grande Mosquée is used by all road transport. **Guides** are not necessary to get around town, but CFA1000–2000 will give you a companion with some knowledge for a few hours, allow you to explore unhesitatingly, and keep the others away. If you need to change money in Djenné, you'll have to do so at a hotel – there's no bank. There is a central post and telephones office, across from the Palais de Justice, but there was nowhere to get online at the time of writing.

For **food**, all the hotels serve more or less similar dishes, with couscous, chicken and chips, spaghetti and fish (if you are lucky) on all menus. Try the *Kita-kourou*, south of the post office, for inexpensive pancakes and the traditional local speciality *tiaom-tiaom*, made with ground, dried onions and fish sauce.

Accommodation

There are several **accommodation** options in Djenné. Children or guides will also offer to put you up on their family roof terraces, but you can end up paying more than for sleeping on a hotel's roof, and possibly with less comfort and security.

Chez Baba On a side street near the Palais de Justice Dorms with mattresses on the floor and fan. Alternatively, you can sleep on the terrace for CFA2000, including mattress and mosquito net. *Baba*'s friendly but overpriced restaurant becomes a bar/disco later in the evening. ❶
Le Fleuve Near the *gare routière* and before the mosque. Rooms around a courtyard and a roof terrace with mattresses and mosquito netting provided. The restaurant does cheap, filling breakfasts. ❶
Le Maafir 200m behind the mosque ☏242.05.41. New and stylish, this is the best hotel in town, owned and designed by a former tourist minister. It has eleven agreeable s/c rooms with fan and mosquito nets, arranged around a

Moving on from Djenné

Road transport to and from Djenné uses the ferry across the Bani, 6km southeast of town; there's a paved road from the landing stage on the right bank to the *route nationale* 29km away. **Taxis** and **minibuses** run to **Sévaré** and **Mopti** (CFA1750) on Monday afternoons when Djenné's market closes down. There are buses for **Bamako** every Monday at 2pm, Tuesday at 9pm and Thursday at 8am (CFA6000). On Mondays at 2pm, there's a bus to **San** (CFA2500) and **Sikasso** (CFA6000).

An alternative exit from Djenné when the Bani is high enough is by motorized *pinasse*; these leave Djenné early Tuesday morning and arrive in Mopti in the evening (CFA3000), transporting goods in time for Mopti's Thursday market. Any child in town can take you to their dock, whose location moves with the river level, though most of the year they use the ferry landing stage.

courtyard. The hotel's restaurant has a set menu and doesn't serve alcohol. Rate includes breakfast. ⑤

Tapama Djenepo Next to the *Maafir* and near the tomb of the same name, this is a quiet, reasonably priced and secluded haven. All the rooms, some s/c, have fan and mosquito protection. The view from the roof is fantastic. ③

Timbuktu (Tombouctou)

If I told you why it is mysterious then it would not be mysterious.

Former Minister of Sports, Art and Culture

Is that it?

Bob Geldof, after looking around during his Live Aid visit

Long associated with mysterious beauty, learning and, above all, wealth, **TIMBUKTU**, "the forbidden city", has always fascinated outsiders. From the time of the crusades, it was one of the main entrepôts through which came the West African **gold** on which European finance relied. From the fourteenth century, when Mansa Musa, Emperor of Mali, passed through Cairo on his way to Mecca (stunning the city with his fabulous entourage and selling so much gold that its price slumped for decades), to the sixteenth, when Leo Africanus from Granada in Spain visited and described Timbuktu's opulent royal court, to as late as the nineteenth century when a lemming-like "explorers' rush" broke out to settle the enigma of the city roofed with gold, Timbuktu has achieved a near-legendary reputation. "Going to Timbuctoo" is still synonymous with going to the ends of the earth – or to hell – and only in the last few years has a more prosaic recognition forced itself into popular awareness.

Of course the town couldn't live up to the myths which disguised it so long and any illusions of grandeur you harbour are bound to be frustrated. As long ago as 1828, René Caillié wrote:

I found it neither as big nor as populated as I had expected. Commerce was much less active than it was famed to be . . . Everything was enveloped in a great sadness. I was amazed by the lack of energy, by the inertia that hung over the town . . . a jumble of badly built houses . . . ruled over by a heavy silence.

This frank assessment rings true today. Though the entire town was formally declared a UNESCO World National Heritage site in 1988, as you walk the sandy streets, lined with pale grey stucco-covered mud-brick houses, you're more likely to be struck by the poverty than by historical monuments evoking a prouder past. There is now another reason to visit the Timbuktu region, for the **Festival in the Desert**, an annual celebration of Tamashek and Malian music and culture (see p.382).

Some history

Towards the end of the eleventh century, a group of **Tuareg** who came to the Niger to graze their herds discovered a small oasis on the north bank where they set up a permanent camp. When they went off to pasture their animals, they left the settlement in the care of an old woman named Tomboutou – "the woman with the large belly button". However, other tales have it that Tin or Tim Buktu was the well belonging to a woman named Buktu, while it's also possible that Buktu or *bouctou* may derive from the Arabic for "dune", while *tim* in Berber signifies "place of".

Whatever the origins of its name, the camp quickly developed into an important commercial centre where merchants from Djenné set up as middlemen between the salt caravans coming down from the north (and general dealers from the other side of the Sahara) and the river traffic bringing goods downriver from the grasslands and forests of the south. Although the Tuareg herders didn't live permanently in the town, they continued to control it, levying heavy and arbitrary taxes from the increasingly wealthy traders. Eventually, in response, the inhabitants invited the great Mali ruler **Mansa Musa** to liberate the town from Tuareg domination and he annexed it in 1330. To commemorate the occasion, the king visited Timbuktu and built a palace and the **Djinguereber mosque**.

Under the hegemony of the **Mali Empire**, Timbuktu enjoyed a period of stability and prosperity, but as the kingdom declined in the fifteenth century, the town again slipped into Tuareg control. Extortions began again, and in 1468 the merchants turned for help to the Songhai emperor **Sonni Ali Ber**, of Gao, who chased the Tuaregs west to the desert post of Oualata, in present-day Mauritania. Sonni Ali laid the foundations of the **Songhai Empire** which grew under the impetus of **Askia Mohammed**. Timbuktu reached its zenith at this point and became one of the Sahel's principal centres of commerce and learning. Reports of unimaginable wealth trickled back to Europe. The **Moroccan invasion** of 1591, however, when firearms were used in the Sahel for the first time, was a catastrophe for Timbuktu. The expedition's Andalucian leader, Djouder Pasha, had a number of senior scholars executed, exiled most of the others to Fez, and caravanned out the bulk of the city's wealth. Under the descendants of marriages between the invaders, who included conscripted Scots, Irish and Spanish soldiers and Songhai women – a group who came to be known as the **Arma**, after their guns – Timbuktu went into a steady decline that lasted throughout the seventeenth and eighteenth centuries. At different times it was attacked by the Mossi, the Fula, the Tukulor and the Tuareg. Subjected to pillage and oppression, the townspeople retreated behind the heavy, metal-studded wooden doors characteristic of Timbuktu houses. These were one of the few symbols of the city's former wealth that endured until the final arrival of the Europeans in the nineteenth century.

The European explorers

On the strength of a few translated books and a skein of rumours, Europeans set about uncovering Timbuktu's fabled riches. Between the late sixteenth century (by which time the city was, unknown to them, already nearly destitute) and 1853, at least 43 travellers attempted to reach it, of whom just four succeeded. The race really began in 1824, when the Geographical Society of Paris offered a prize of 10,000 francs to the first explorer to return with a verifiable account of the city. The earliest firsthand account by a non-Muslim, however, had already been given, not by an explorer, but by an illiterate American sailor, **Robert Adams**, who had been sold into slavery after his ship was wrecked off Mauritania, and who almost certainly spent several months in Timbuktu in 1811. But the story he related to the British Consul in Morocco in 1813 wasn't given much credibility, as Adams wasn't aware of the mystique surrounding the city and his dreary description was too flat to be believed – except by Moroccan Muslims who themselves had been there. Whether or not Adams did get to Timbuktu is still a matter of some argument.

The first explorer to succeed conclusively – a prudish Scot named **Gordon Laing** – reached Timbuktu on August 13, 1826, after a hazardous desert crossing from Tripoli in which he was slashed almost to death by Tuareg robbers. The squalid slaving town was a bitter disappointment, but Laing was apparently greeted warmly by the sheikh of Timbuktu and by the townspeople. On hearing of the arrival of a Christian, however, the Fula sultan who claimed authority over the town ordered Laing to get out on pain of death. Worried for his guest's safety, the sheikh sent Laing off towards Ségou (he was hoping to reach Sierra Leone) with an armed guide. Unfortunately, the latter turned out to be in the service of the sultan, and Laing and most of his servants were killed one night, 50km out of Timbuktu. One trailed back to Tripoli with Laing's notes and letters, two years later.

The first European to return from Timbuktu to write about the adventure himself was a Frenchman named **René Caillié**, whose fantastic journey started on the west coast on the Rio Nunez (now in northwest Guinea). Prior to taking off for Timbuktu, Caillié had lived in a Moorish village further north, learning Arabic and immersing himself in Muslim culture. Amazingly, he was sponsored by no government or association, and set off alone to the unexplored interior, disguised as an Egyptian. After making his way through the Fouta Djalon hills, he reached the Niger at Kouroussa, then continued to Tiémé (Côte d'Ivoire), where he fell gravely ill. After recovering, he pushed on to Tangrela and then to the devoutly Muslim town of Djenné where he made a deep and favourable impression on the sheikh – who would instantly have had him executed had his disguise been discovered. Caillié arrived in Timbuktu on April 20, 1828, and was received by a rich and pious merchant, Sidi Abdallahi Chebir. Two weeks later, the adventurer joined a camel caravan and headed across the Sahara to Tangiers. In eighteen months, he had crossed 4500km, alone.

Caillié's book wasn't considered the last word on Timbuktu, however, and in Britain, especially, it was initially judged to be bogus. The person who finally convinced the world was the German polyglot and explorer **Heinrich Barth**, who left Tripoli in 1850 on an expedition financed by the British government. He survived the desert crossing to Agadez, in present-day Niger, then worked his way down to the Hausa country, his two companions dying en route. With delays and long residences in various towns, including diversions into Dogon country, he finally made it into Timbuktu on September 7, 1853. Like Caillié, he originally disguised himself as an Arab, but it didn't take long for the townspeople to discover he was Christian, after which his life was in danger. Barth, phlegmatic and undeterred, stayed eight months under the protection of Sheikh El Backay and collected the most detailed information known at the time. El Backay was virtually beseiged by his Fula overlords and only after long negotiations was Barth at last able to escape, following the river back east to Gao before continuing to Sokoto, Kano and on to Lake Chad. From here, he again set out across the Sahara, arriving in Tripoli in 1855. His explorations had lasted nearly six years and had taken him over 16,000km; the five-volume book he published at last overturned some of the myths.

Apart from a lucky young German, **Oskar Lenz**, who skipped through Timbuktu in 1880 and apparently had a wonderful time, the next European visitors were French: they came through the 1890s, little doubting success, to conquer and colonize.

Recent times

In the 1990s, Timbuktu yet again suffered the traditional depredations of the Tuareg who, threatened by the continuing suppression of their nomadic lifestyle, and increasingly supportive of a movement to create their own state from parts of Mali, Niger and Algeria, rebelled against the agents of Bamako. At one point history repeated itself as the Tuareg held the town in a state of virtual siege; it was their disruption which contributed to the dictator Moussa Traoré's fall and to subsequent reforms. Peace was finally cemented in March 1996 with the burning of three thousand Tuareg and government arms in a ceremonial pyre commemorated by the **Flamme de la Paix** monument in the northern part of town. Since then troubles have mainly been limited to incidents of banditry in the area north of Gao, and Timbuktu is once again a safe and intriguing travel destination.

Arrival, information and transport

Timbuktu's inaccessibility comes as no surprise, but unless you arrive by road, you'll still need transport to get to the town itself. Niger **river transport** docks at **Korioumé**, 19km south of town and connected to Timbuktu by a fast, paved road (CFA500–1000 by *bâché*). The **airport** is 5km south of town, off the Route de Korioumé.

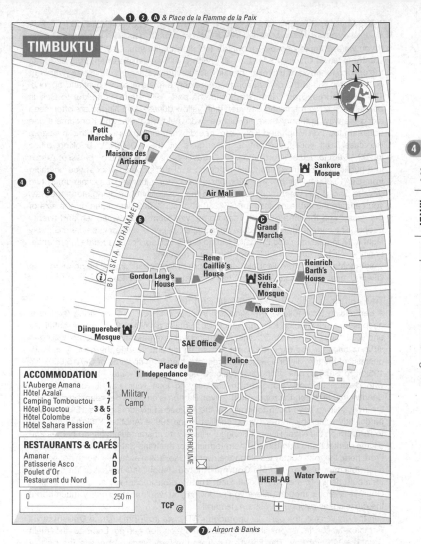

It's no longer necessary to register with the police upon arrival and even the unpopular CFA5000 tourist tax, which formerly permitted free entry to the museum and the Djinguereber mosque, has been abolished. You can allegedly still be stung for this, however, if you visit the police. If you want a Timbuktu stamp in your passport (this may even prove useful if you encounter police who appear to have forgotten the tax has been abolished), either of the **tourist offices** – the one at the airport or the one in town near the Djinguereber mosque (Mon–Sat 7.30am–4pm; ℡292.20.86)– are happy to oblige, free of charge. While at the tourist office you might ask about **guides** (see p.322 for general advice on hiring one) – this is a town where their services are not only useful but almost necessary if you don't want to be pestered constantly.

If you weren't impressed by Timbuktu's isolation during your stay, you will be when you try to leave. Unless you're travelling with your own vehicle or an organized tour, the options for **onward travel** in the rainy season are pretty much limited to river craft or the plane, and in the dry season there are only a few alternative overland options. The **river journey** from Timbuktu (Korioumé port, 19km from Timbuktu) to Gao is beautiful – the Niger snaking between high yellow dunes – and hippos are often seen along the way. In theory there should be two weekly boats leaving Korioumé – one upstream towards Mopti and Koulikoro, one downstream to Gao – but this is seldom the case, and your best bet is to enquire at the COMANAV booking office (☏292.12.06) for latest information. River travel can also be done by *pinasse*. A seat in a public *pinasse* (most likely balancing on sacks of goods) will cost you anything from CFA10,000 upwards – including basic food – for a journey of a minimum of two days to Gao. If you want more comfort and the possibility of stopping along the way, you can hire the entire *pinasse* for CFA250,000 to 300,000 depending on the size of the vessel and the time of year. They come with room for between ten and twenty people. The current **flight schedule** consists, on paper, of a Wednesday and Sunday flight to Mopti (Sévaré) and Bamako, but no flights to Gao. For up-to-date information, check at Air Mali (☏292.10.91) near the *grand marché*.

Note that a *bâché* from Timbuktu to the port, or vice versa, should be no more than CFA500, even with luggage – about half of what you'll be asked.

The pistes to Gao, Douentza and Ségou

A demanding *piste* follows the Niger's north bank 425km to **Gao**. Along the route, deep sandy ruts winding through acacia bush make a 4WD or trail bike essential. As unofficial cargo, merchants travelling overland will take passengers who are willing to sit atop baggage, be exposed to the desert winds and tolerate the general precariousness of the trip, all for a negotiated fee (anything from upwards of CFA15,000). It's 195km to **Bamba**, one of the first major villages along the route – a difficult stretch with deep soft sand, along which it's easy to lose your way if you're driving. Sandwiched between the road and the river, Bamba is an oasis between the *piste* and the river, said to have been founded by the Moroccan invaders of the 1590s. It was particularly vulnerable in the Tuareg conflict of the 1990s. Another 135km brings you to **Bourem** on the Niger River, a Songhai village with characteristic *banco* homes and a large market – and also the southern terminus of the trans-Saharan Tanezrouft route. From here, the road continues along the river to Gao, 95km away. It's worth noting that a feasible route also exists from **Gourma-Rharous** (about 110km east of Timbuktu on the south bank), to the Gao–Mopti road. There's a basic car ferry across the river at Gourma-Rharous, though unless you're driving you won't need to worry much about the crossing, as *pirogues* cross on demand.

In the dry season, the partially upgraded 4WD *piste* from Timbuktu to **Douentza** via Bambara-Maoundé is possibly the easiest option for getting back to the main Bamako–Gao highway. The 250km trip from the ferry landing opposite the port of Korioumé to Douentza takes around four to six hours by 4WD and costs from CFA15,000 for a seat. The northern part of this *piste*, as far as a few kilometres short of Bambara-Maoundé, is slow going – treacherously sandy and even hilly in places – but the second half of the route is firm and fast on the newly graded *piste*. Once in Douentza you can catch a ride with one of the bus companies plying the road between Bamako, Sévaré and Gao, but if you arrive late you should be prepared to spend the night there (see p.394).

Lastly, in the dry season converted bus-trucks ply the road to Bamako via Goundam, Léré and Niono to Ségou, a two-day journey stopping overnight in Léré on the way north, and Niono on the way south (CFA12,500). Note that the state of the road varies enormously from season to season, and cancellations and long delays are common.

Just like town guides, offers to take you on **desert excursions** by camel are almost unavoidable once you arrive in Timbuktu. Everybody has a brother, an uncle or a cousin willing to take you into the desert at a rate much better than his competitors' prices. The tourist office's guide association should, in principle, minimize the risk of anything going wrong and ensure that you get what you pay for. Potential guides are given training – in first aid and cookery, among other subjects – before being awarded an official tourist guide photo ID. Trips into the desert, usually ranging from two hours to a couple of days, are magical and unforgettable. Prices vary but half a day should cost around CFA7500 and an overnight trip starting mid-afternoon around CFA20,000; this includes camel and guide and relevant meals. Part of the trip normally includes a visit to a Tuareg settlement for tea and a rest: if you choose to take photos of people, don't forget to leave a small *cadeau*. It's also possible to visit the desert by 4WD, with prices running from at least CFA50,000 a day, excluding fuel, driver, and whatever food and drink you want to take. The tourist office can supply agency contacts with relatively reliable vehicles. Whichever way you choose to take a trip out of Timbuktu, prices quoted will initially be at least double what you should aim to agree on.

Timbuktu's **banks** (as usual the BNDA is the one to use for foreign exchange), **post office** and **Internet centre** (CFA2000/hr) are all located several hundred metres down the Route de Korioumé. There are **telephone centres** scattered around the town.

Accommodation

Reasonably priced **accommodation** in Timbuktu has long been a problem. Cheaper alternatives are slowly appearing, but if you can afford it, you might relax your budget here for a night or two. Alternatively, most hotels with suitable roofs will allow you to sleep on them. A lavish new place, the *Hendrina Khan*, was set to open on the south side of town in 2004.

L'Auberge Amanar On the north side of town, near the *Sahara Passion* ☎ & ☏ 292.12.85, ✉ amanar@dromadaire.com. A small place affiliated to the restaurant of the same name just up the road. Good rooms, all of which are s/c, some with fan and some with a/c. ❹

Hôtel Azalaï On a low rise on the western edge of town ☎ & ☏ 292.11.63. Overlooking a permanently dry wadi, this is the best option in town (though only just), and considerably more expensive than any other hotel. They offer reasonable a/c rooms (with power from their own generator if necessary) but no mosquito nets and a complete lack of atmosphere. There's a restaurant with pricey but decent French food. ❻

Hôtel Bouctou Western edge of town ☎ 292.10.12. A traditional Moroccan-style structure with good views of the dunes, the *Bouctou* has s/c rooms with mosquito nets and a/c or fan, either in the main building or the nearby annexe. There are also some cheaper rooms with fans and shared facilities, and you can pay

CFA6500 to sleep on the roof. Meals here tend to be basic and not particularly cheap. ❹

Camping Tombouctou About 1km out of town on the rte de Korioumé ☎ 292.40.32. For camping in Timbuktu, this is your best bet; they also have a few basic rooms. CFA2500 per person to camp, ❷

Hôtel Colombe bd Askia Mohammed ☎ 292.14.35. A fairly new hotel with a/c, s/c rooms, a good position and a fine roof terrace. Tends to be patronized by a more local clientele than the *Azalaï* and the *Bouctou*. ❺

Pâtisserie Asco rte de Korioumé. A few very basic rooms. ❷

Restaurant Poulet d'Or The restaurant's new extension behind the cemetery has some basic rooms. ❷

Hôtel Sahara Passion av de la Paix, on the north side of town ☎ 292.13.94, ✉ spassion @malinet.ml. Not far from the Flamme de la Paix monument, and next to the *Amanar* restaurant, this is possibly the best-value place in town, offering a range of clean, basic rooms (some with a/c, some s/c). CFA5000 to sleep on the roof, ❹

The Town

There are no obvious starting points to a sightseeing trip round Timbuktu, but most people will find themselves down on the Route de Korioumé fairly soon after arrival, and there's a good opportunity for a grand view of the town from the top of the **water tower** (*château d'eau*) near here. For another good view of Timbuktu – in silhouette – climb one of the town's **dunes** at dawn to watch the sun rising above the town. The easiest dunes to reach are a short walk north of the Flamme de la Paix monument.

There are two main **markets** in Timbuktu – the **grand marché**, for which a new multistorey site was under construction when this edition was researched, and the **petit marché**, which was large and busy at last check, but which will become smaller when the new market opens. Close to the *petit marché* you'll find the **Maison des Artisans**, where you can browse a good variety of crafts without undue pressure to buy. With a bit of effort you'll get good prices on nicely worked knives, leatherwork, and Tuareg silver (or nickel) crosses, bracelets and rings. Look out for delicately fashioned neolithic arrowheads and stone axes, knives and scrapers from the Sahara's relatively recent past: these can still be found in the dunes in more remote districts of the desert.

Mosques and the museum

The key sites in Timbuktu are the mosques, the oldest and most famous of which is the Friday **Djinguereber mosque** on Boulevard Askia Mohammed. It was first built in 1327 by El Saheli – an Andalucían architect and poet whom Mansa Musa met in Cairo during his pilgrimage to Mecca – who is credited with the invention of mud bricks, before which time all building had been done using mud and straw, slapped on a wooden framework. Appropriately covered up and respectful, you can enter the newly restored mosque (entry fee CFA2500) and you can also usually climb onto the roof here – but permission isn't always granted unless you're visiting the town with a guide. Timbuktu's other two main mosques, a little way east, are barred to non-Muslim visitors. The **Sankore** dates from the fifteenth century and, during Timbuktu's golden era, it doubled as a **university**, specializing in law and theology, and renowned throughout the Muslim world – up to 25,000 students were studying here in the sixteenth century. The **Sidi Yahya** mosque was first constructed in 1400 by a marabout named El-Moktar Hamalla and was intended to serve a saint whose imminent arrival had been prophesied. Four decades later, Sherif Sidi Yahya crossed the desert and asked for the keys to the mosque. He was declared imam, and is today one of the most revered of the town's 333 saints.

Opposite the Sidi Yahya is the town's new **Ethnographic Museum** (daily 8am–4pm or later if accompanied by a guide; CFA1000). With its centrepiece, the Bouctou well that the town supposedly developed around, the museum focuses on the lifestyles and customs of the main ethnic groups in the area. Musical instruments and games as well as personal decorations of the Tuareg, Songhai and Bella are exhibited in simple and well-composed displays, unfortunately with very little labelling. A bonus is a section devoted to the ancient rock carvings at Tin-Techoun.

Timbuktu's houses

Though Timbuktu's mosques and museum are the main sights, it's also rewarding to spend some time walking through the confusion of narrow streets to take in Timbuktu's unique **architecture**. The finest homes – usually owned by Moorish merchants – are made of carved limestone brought from a desert quarry. Again, the basic design of these homes may date, like that of the Djinguereber, to El Saheli; the columns of square pilasters that decorate the facades are reminiscent of those in Egyptian temples, an element he may have picked up in Cairo. The small shuttered windows and heavy wooden doors with geometric ironwork designs also bear an

Arabic stamp, though they seem to hark back to the Moroccan invasion of the late sixteenth century.

Plaques still mark the homes where **Laing**, **Caillié** and **Barth** stayed during their exploits in Timbuktu. The first two are near neighbours in the Djinguereber district and any kid can point them out to you. Heavy rains occasionally reduce one or other of the houses to rubble, but they're regularly repaired again for the sake of Timbuktu's precarious tourist industry – building in mud guarantees an authentic, weathered, historical look. Barth's old house, now a private home that doubles as a small library/museum assembled in his honour, is the only one you can go inside (for a negotiable CFA500–1000). More modest houses are made of *banco* in a style that originated in Djenné. Along the streets you'll also notice dome-shaped **clay ovens** where women bake round loaves of bread, a speciality of the town, traditionally made from wheat grown near Lake Faguibine and easily recognized by the crunchy, sandy crust.

Institut des Hautes Études de Recherche Islamique

One of the greatest remaining legacies of Timbuktu's former glory is the wealth of Islamic literature that was produced here. Traditionally, families wrote their histories in **chronicles** known as *tarikh* – one of the most important of which was the *Tarikh es-Soudan*, written by El Sadi in the seventeenth century. These and other related writings have provided invaluable information about the scientific, legal and social practices of the seventeenth, eighteenth and nineteenth centuries throughout the region, and indeed the entire Muslim world. In addition, they've helped trace Mali's history back to the empire of ancient Ghana. Countless volumes remain in private family collections, where, exposed to damp, dust and insects, the works (some of which may be 400 years old or more) could soon be lost for ever. Timbuktu's **Institut des Hautes Études de Recherche Islamique – Ahmed Baba** (IHERI-AB, formerly known as the Centre des Recherches Ahmed Baba, or CEDRAB) is trying to persuade reluctant families to part with these priceless documents, at least long enough for them to be restored and digitized. To date, more than twenty thousand manuscripts have been collected, about eighty percent of them written in Arabic and most of the rest in Songhai. The centre is near the water tower on the south side of town, down the airport road and left after the post office. It's very much worth a visit but it's a good idea to make an appointment first, even to visit during their normal hours (Mon–Fri 9am–noon; CFA1000 is a standard donation). Ask the staff to show you some of the older, handwritten documents, the most beautiful of which contain geometric artwork and gold lettering. Buying and exporting manuscripts is illegal but you can sometimes obtain souvenir copies of the originals.

Close to the Institute, the private **Mamma Haidara Memorial Library** has recently been opened by one of the CEDRAB's former employee-researchers, and is also worth a look inside. Its displays are more accessible than the IHERI-AB's slightly chaotic presentation, and possibly a better bet if you're interested in the content of the manuscripts. Again, you're expected to leave a donation.

The outskirts

Around most of the outskirts of Timbuktu are scattered clusters of circular straw huts, the homesteads of Tuareg, Bella and Fula nomads; walk out past the *Azalaï* hotel in the west to see them. Also near the *Azalaï*, a district of photogenic **terraced gardens** challenges the intense heat. Resembling little amphitheatres, they're each built around a large crater dug deep into the earth, at the bottom of which stands a pond of brackish water.

On the northern outskirts of town is the **Abaradio district** where the *azalaï* or camel caravans formerly arrived in great numbers (even when the first European explorers arrived, as many as sixty thousand camels a year unloaded their goods here).

Apart from goods from North Africa and the Mediterranean, the Sahara's biggest prize was salt from the ultra-remote oasis of **Taoudenni**, 700km due north of Timbuktu. Taoudenni is famous for its salt mines – and was until 1989 a Malian Siberia where the former president Modibo Keita was detained until his death and political undesirables were banished. Caravans of salt slabs still come down here from Taoudenni.

Eating

Eating options in Timbuktu have been on the increase during recent years, and you no longer need to stick to the main hotels if you want a decent meal, although they all have reasonable, if overpriced, restaurants, none of which depart much from the staples of rice, couscous or potatoes accompanied by chicken or beef. The market itself doesn't offer a great deal, making self-catering a difficult option.

Pâtisserie Asco rte de Korioumé. Good Western and local dishes, but their pastries aren't great.
Poulet d'Or Near the *petit marché*. Serves standard Western dishes, most often chicken, at tables outside. They have an annexe a few hundred metres to the north which sometimes stays open after the main restaurant has closed.
Restaurant Amanar On the north side of town, facing the Flamme de la Paix monument (and separate from the *auberge* of the same name). This, the new hit in town, does European and local dishes at reasonable prices and has a very popular pavement bar.
Restaurant du Nord At the northeast corner of the *grand marché*. A good coffee-and-omelette breakfast spot.
Restaurant Salama Within the Maison d'Artisans. Simple and affordable dishes.

Around Timbuktu

One hundred kilometres west of Timbuktu is **Lac Faguibine**, once of the largest natural lakes in West Africa and varying greatly in size with the seasons, though it has been completely dry since the late 1980s. The approach is via **Goundam**, an important agricultural town in the middle of a region considered to be the bread-basket of Mali. Rice, millet, corn and – remarkably – wheat, are all grown in the area. Situated on the much smaller **Lac Télé**, Goundam has a *campement* (❷) and is linked to the river by a 34-kilometre road from Diré, a sizeable port on the Niger, 100km upstream from Timbuktu. From Goundam, continue to Lac Faguibine via the *piste* that passes through the village of Bintagoungou.

To get to these places using local transport you'd need luck to make much head-way, or money to rent a vehicle. Most people visit in their own 4WD or on a pri-vately organised excursion.

The Festival in the Desert

Since 2001, Mali has hosted an annual **Festival in the Desert** in January – a celebra-tion of Tuareg and Malian music and culture, grafted onto a traditional Tuareg gather-ing and coordinated and publicized by Efès and Aïtma, two Tuareg associations, and by committed individuals in Belgium, Britain, France and the USA. In 2003 the location was **Essakane**, a remote oasis 65km northwest of Timbuktu, and future events are likely to take place in the same area (2004's festival is scheduled for January 9–11 in Essakane) and to see increased promotion for what has been billed as the most remote festival in the world. On the bill in 2003 were the guitar band Tinariwen, the folkloric Ensemble Tartit and a number of other Tuareg and Songhai groups, plus Ali Farka Touré, Afel Bocoum and numerous other Malian artists, not to mention overseas guests Robert Plant, Justin Adams, Lo'Jo and the Navajo band Blackfire from Arizona.

Essakane has just a couple of hundred inhabitants and virtually no supplies or facilities, so everything – from generators to stage equipment and all food and supplies– has to be trucked in. Although you may be able to pick up information locally and make your own arrangements to attend (tickets are inexpensive) you're rec-ommended to get details in advance at ⓦ www.festival-au-desert.org.

4.5

The Dogon country

Until the end of the colonial era, the **Dogon** were one of the African peoples who had most successfully retained their culture and traditional way of life, remaining largely non-Muslim. This was in large part due to the isolation of their territory in the remarkable and picturesque **cliffside villages** they built along the **Bandiagara escarpment** south and east of Mopti – a 200-kilometre-long wedge of sandstone, pushed up by movements of the earth's plates in prehistoric times and running from Ouo in the southwest to the Hombori Mountains in the northeast. Dogon villages are scattered over three distinct areas: the plateau, the escarpment (*falaise*) itself, and the sandy Gondo-Seno Plain which stretches out from the foot of the cliffs towards the southeast and Burkina.

The Dogon remain dogged defenders of their customs, religion and art, but in more recent years they have become the object of a fairly intense **tourist industry**. Although much of the Dogon country (*pays Dogon*) can only be visited on foot or at best with a donkey- or ox-cart (a *charette*), some of the more accessible villages on the paved roads or 4WD routes can be swarming with tourists, especially over Christmas. With patience and plenty of time, you can still manage to get more or less off the beaten track, but don't be disappointed not to be the first to have done so.

It can't be overemphasized that as a visitor to the *pays Dogon*, you are a guest in a fragile community. As long as tourists continue to respect the Dogon people's culture and environment, and their right to privacy, there is no reason for relations to become strained. Try to behave conservatively and be careful to avoid widening the generation gap between the more cosmopolitan young and their exclusively Dogon-speaking elders. If you want to give presents, it's worth carrying a small supply of kola nuts which are much appreciated by village elders. The Dogon are rightly celebrated for their artistic heritage but, tragically, much of their art and furniture has been sold overseas – their richly symbolic carved doors, windows and meeting-house pillars in particular. Resist buying any artefacts that look remotely old; there are plenty of items for sale that have been made expressly as souvenirs and the quality of workmanship is often extremely good. *La Gallerie Antique*, across from the mayor's office in Bandiagara, is well-stocked with Dogon artefacts, all okayed by the local *mission culturelle*.

Dogon history

Archeological research has uncovered caves dating to around the third century BC dug into the cliffs around the Dogon town of Sanga. The Dutch scientists who discovered these caves called the people who made them the **Toloy**, but there seems to be a rather large gap between this culture and the next known inhabitants of the escarpment, the **Tellem**, who arrived in the eleventh century. The Tellem were small people, often said to have been "pygmies", although they probably weren't related to the contemporary Central African people of small stature. They built distinctive, cellular houses in sheltered crevices and beneath overhangs on the cliffside – places where sun and rain were least able to penetrate. Their architecture is still visible today, strikingly similar to that of the ancient cliff dwellings of the southwestern USA. It is generally thought that the Tellem shared the escarpment for a couple of centuries with the **Dogon**, who arrived in the fifteenth

The Dogon believe in a single God, **Amma**, who created the sun, moon and stars. According to Dogon legend, after this he created the earth by throwing a ball of clay into space. The ball spread to the four points of the horizon and took on the shape of a woman with an anthole for her vagina and a termite mound for her clitoris. Alone in the universe, Amma attempted to make love to the earth, but the termite mound blocked his path and he tore it out. Because of this violence, the earth could not bear the twins that would have resulted from a happy union and instead gave birth to a jackal.

Amma again had intercourse with the earth, and a pair of twins resulted, known as **nommo**. They were born of divine semen, the precious water found in everything in the universe. Green in colour, their upper bodies were human and their lower bodies like snakes. Living in the heavens with their father, the *nommo* looked down on their mother and, seeing her naked, made a **skirt** into which they wove the first **language**. Thus the earth was the first to possess speech.

Meanwhile, the jackal was running loose. His mother was the only woman, and he raped her. The earth bled and became impure in the sight of Amma. It is for this reason that today, menstruating women are considered impure in Dogon society (as they are in nearly all African cultures). When he forced himself upon the earth, the jackal also touched her skirt and thus stole language.

Having turned from his wife, Amma decided to create a human couple from clay. The couple had elements of both sexes – the foreskin being the feminine part of the man, and the clitoris the masculine part of the woman. Foreseeing that problems would arise from this ambiguity, the *nommo* circumcised the male and later an invisible hand removed the clitoris from the woman (circumcision of men and clitoridectomy of women is still an important step into adulthood for the Dogon). The couple was thus free to procreate and produced eight children, the original **Dogon ancestors**. After creating eight descendants of their own, the ancestors were purified and transformed into *nommo*, and then went to join Amma in the sky. But before his ascension, the seventh ancestor was charged with giving the **second language** to humans. Using his mouth as a loom, he spat out a cotton strip from which the new speech was transmitted to humanity.

The eight ancestors didn't get along with Amma and the *nommo* and were eventually sent back to earth. On the way, the eighth ancestor came down before the seventh, who was angry as a result. He turned himself into a snake and set about disturbing the work of the other ancestors. They told the people to kill the snake – which they did. But this seventh ancestor – whose name was Lebe – held the **third language**, needed for mankind, since the second wasn't adequate. The oldest of the eight original descendants thus had to be sacrificed and was buried with the head of Lebe the snake. Humans then received the third language in the form of a drum.

To this day, Dogon **dances** symbolize this creation story. **Masks** are an important element of the dances and the Dogon use over eighty different varieties according to the celebration. The biggest ceremony is the **Sigui**, celebrated every sixty years (the next should be in 2027) to commemorate the passing of a generation. The frequency of Sigui is calculated by the periodicity of an invisible moon of Sirius, a satellite which remained unknown to western astronomers long after it was mentioned to Marcel Griaule, the first westerner to study Dogon culture. Sirius itself appears brightly between mountain peaks exactly when expected, suggesting a level of astronomical knowledge which has long baffled outsiders. The Sigui serves to venerate the Big Mask, made in the shape of a serpent in reference to **Lebe**, who is credited with leading the Dogon to the Bandiagara escarpment as well as bringing them speech and, simultaneously, death.

century. Some time around the seventeenth century, the Tellem were pushed out of the Dogon country and migrated to the area that is now Burkina Faso.

The Dogon may originally have come from the region of the Nile, but before moving to the Bandiagara escarpment they lived in the Mandé country to the west. Determined to preserve their traditional religion in the face of Muslim expansionism and religious jihads, they migrated to the safety of the *falaise* in the fifteenth century. Even with this natural shelter as a homeland, they had to fight off numerous aggressors over the centuries. In the 1470s the country was invaded by the **Songhai**, and in the early eighteenth century it was attacked by the **Ségou kingdom**. Much later, in 1830, the Fula from **Massina** marched on the region and, in 1860, the Tukulor ruler **El Hadj Omar** brought his holy war to the escarpment, making Bandiagara his capital; he died in Deguembere near Bandiagara. The **French** occupied the region of Sanga in 1893, but it wasn't until the battle of Tabi in 1920 that the colonial army finally "pacified" the Dogon people.

In the 1930s the Reverend Francis McKinney, an American, established the first Christian mission in Sanga. Several years later **Marcel Griaule**, a French anthropologist, came to the same town to study traditional Dogon religion and customs. He spent a quarter of a century living in Dogon country, helping them set up dams for irrigation and introducing the onion crop that's now one of the only exports of the region to the rest of Mali and Burkina. Respected by the Dogon, he also helped open the eyes of the rest of the world to the complexity and integrity of a civilization that had long been regarded by Muslim and Christian invaders as merely primitive.

Travelling around Dogon country

Many people use Mopti or Sévaré as an **initial base** for exploring Dogon country, but viable alternatives, now that the roads have been improved, are Bandiagara, Sanga, Douentza or Bankass. **Bandiagara** offers the most trekking options, the quickest access to **Sanga** and the most popular treks; **Bankass**, convenient if you're arriving from Burkina Faso, takes you straight to the southern *pays Dogon* and **Douentza** to the northern districts. All over Dogon country there are rewarding sights and experiences at any time of year, but it's fair to say that the Sanga area is the most heavily developed for tourism, with lots of small hotels and *auberges* and swarms of visitors over Christmas and holiday periods, while the northern and southern ends of the escarpment are more remote and undeveloped.

A trip to the Dogon country can involve hours of **trekking** in the sweltering sun, and usually entails climbing up and down the three-hundred-metre escarpment and walking over a great deal of rocky terrain. Depending on your inclinations and those of your guide, you're likely to pass through about three villages a day this way. You'll want to travel light; ideally you should leave all but the essentials behind before making the trip. Most of the better lodgings and hotels will guard your luggage for a small fee while you're away, or, if you're not returning, you can always have the bulk of your luggage carried by porter or *charette* (a donkey- or ox-cart).

Much of Dogon country is rough, and while it's true that special **footwear** is not essential, a good pair of walking boots is a big asset, especially if you're going to be walking for several days and plan to move up and down between the plain and the plateau – which, unless you suffer from vertigo, or really can't manage the occasional scramble over rocks, is surely the whole point. If you aren't going to climb, it is possible to stay on the plain, and you'll still get some stunning views of the cliffs. It's worth noting that the precise **locations of villages** can be confusing, as most "villages" consist of between two and five separate hamlets, usually scattered from the plateau to the clifftop, then down to a midway point and onto the plain.

The heat can be intense, and you will certainly need a light and comfortable **hat**. Bring a **water bottle** or canteen for the long stretches between villages, most of which have no running water. You'll be drinking water from local wells or pumps (or buying bottled water, which is widely available). It's not essential to filter the water,

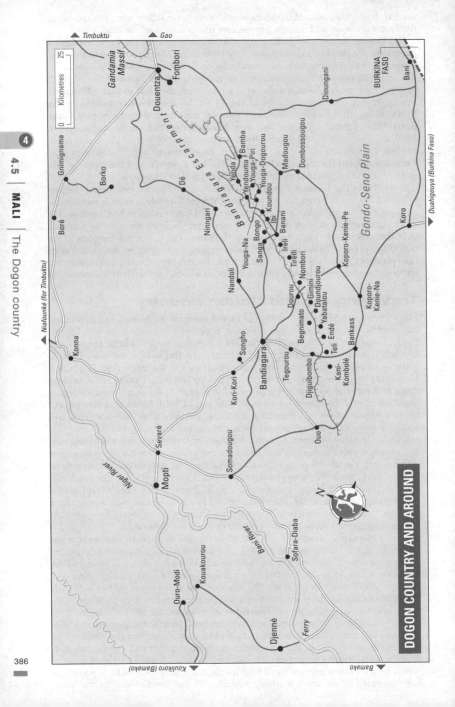

DOGON COUNTRY AND AROUND

but it's a good idea to purify it. If you're here in the middle of the hot season, **rehydration salts** are also not a bad idea. You may also want to take some fruit or snacks with you to supplement the generally basic food you'll be eating in the villages.

It's normal practice to start walking as early as possible, say 6.30 or 7am and stop by 11am for lunch and a long rest during the hottest part of the day, leaving no earlier than 3pm. Note that few Dogon villages have electricity, and where there is a supply, it's likely to come from a small solar panel or, in wealthier places, a generator (*groupe*).

For greater flexibility and a speedier pace, you could travel by **mobylette** (moped), **moto** (motorbike), or **4WD**, though you should bear in mind that once you're off the paved road the routes can be extremely challenging. Travelling by *mobylette* or *moto* is an invigorating way to discover the region, but few rented bikes go really well even in the best conditions. Around here you'll spend all your time fixing your bike, and then, when you return it to the owner, arguing about who should pay for the necessary replacement parts. If you have your own vehicle and it's not a 4WD, you're best off leaving it behind.

Guides and costs

Notwithstanding your experiences in Mali's other towns, **guides** are essential in Dogon country, and you'll be expected to have a local escort in every community you visit. Guides are useful for locating villages and the quickest or most rewarding footpaths between them, for figuring out market days (every five days in most villages) and harvest fetes (many around early December and also an interesting batch in April), and making arrangements for sleeping and eating in isolated places. Moreover, without a guide, you'll have real problems just communicating: many older people don't speak French and, even more so than elsewhere in Mali, the manner in which people greet each other is elaborate, and a very important element of any social exchange. There are also a number of taboos, often specific to certain villages, and without the assistance of a clued-up guide you risk making cultural faux pas at every turn. Finally, a good guide should also be able to fill you in on the history of the places you visit, and the significance of the various elements that make up each village.

As a rough indication of **trekking costs**, you should expect your guide to charge a basic CFA4000–5000 per day per person. On top of that you generally pay, per person, CFA3500 per day for three meals (sometimes prepared by the guide, sometimes bought by him on your behalf) and CFA1500 per night (invariably sleeping on the roof, accessed by a tricky, notched tree-trunk staircase, at a basic village *campement* or *auberge*, or camping in your own tent if you prefer), which includes use of shower and toilet facilities. Unless you're travelling very light, you'll want a porter to take your bags, usually by *charette*, by the most direct route between your night stops, and the charge for that will be around CFA4000 per day to carry the bags of two people and their guide. In addition, most villages charge a village tax for visitors, payable to the chief – usually CFA1000 per person.

It is standard practice for your guide to work out a complete price for the trip from start to finish and take a down payment, followed by instalments. A daily price per person of between CFA10,000 and CFA15,000 is thus what you should expect to pay. The only extras will be drinks and any transport that has to be rented to get you into, or out of, Dogon country. A 4WD vehicle and driver will generally cost CFA75,000–80,000 per day plus fuel charges (including fuel to get the vehicle back again) of around CFA100/km. (Diesel, or *gasoil*, costs CFA350–400 per litre, but there is always a safe markup for the vehicle owner.) If there's just one or two of you, plus the guide, then renting *mobylettes* to get to the relevant trailhead is perfectly feasible, and will save you at least half the cost of a 4WD. But accidents are very common: drive slowly.

A word of warning: an unfortunate by-product of the Dogon country's popularity as a tourist destination is the problem of inexperienced and unreliable **rogue guides**. It isn't essential for your guide to be Dogon (there are some excellent guides, personally known all over the region, who are not), but it is often a good start. Ideally you should choose a guide through one of the Ministry of Tourism endorsed

A few words of Dogon

Many Dogon speak little or no French, so a few words in the Dogon language are bound to help communication. The words and phrases below are intended as a guide but there are differences in dialect (sometimes major ones) between villages.

Standard greetings
(Often people will run through the entire sequence)

Hello/how's the work going?	*Po*
Good morning as above but addressing a group	*Poiye*
Good morning/ evening (north village)	*Agapoyeh/Ey Wahna*
Good morning/evening (south village)	*Agayamwe/Eli Waleh*
How are you?	*Seyoma?*
– Fine	*Seyo*
How's the family?	*Gineh Seyom?*
– Fine	*Seyo*
How's your father?	*Deh Seyom?*
How's your mother?	*Na Seyom?*
How are the children?	*Ulumo Seyom?*
Everything's OK/Thanks	*Awa/Popo*
See you later	*Yemeh Ehso/Bolanee Jeh/Pinan Segeramo*
Yes/No	*Aha/Eye-ee*
Thank you	*Gana*
Village chief	*Emiru/ Amiru*
Chief's wife	*Emeri Ana*
Boy	*Ah*
Girl	*Ñe*
God	*Amma*

1	*Ti*	6	*Kuray*
2	*Loy*	7	*So*
3	*Tahnu*	8	*Sira*
4	*Nay*	9	*Tuwa*
5	*Noonay*	10	*Peo*

And, of course, millet beer – *konjo*.

endorsed guide associations (ask for their guide association membership card) and better still by personal recommendation. If this isn't possible, make sure you quiz your guide carefully before agreeing to an itinerary. As ever, it's a good idea to draw up a contract before you go, stating your itinerary and a list of all your expenses and even, if there's a large group of you, having it stamped at a police station.

Bandiagara and around

Although commercial tours are convenient if you want a perfunctory overview of Dogon territory, you may prefer less organization and the flexibility of following your own plans and pace. In that case it's usually best to head directly to **BANDIAGARA**, on the banks of the Yamé River, a 63-kilometre taxi ride on a fine paved road from Sévaré and 25km from the closest escarpment-edge trailheads at Djiguibombo or Dourou (Sanga is 45km away). A flat, dusty, sizeable administrative town, Bandiagara is nothing like more traditional villages in the region, although the population is sixty percent Dogon. There's a good deal of commerce by Dogon standards, with a lively market on Mondays and Fridays, plus a hospital, mission and police headquarters. It's a convenient point of entry to the Dogon region, and a pleasant enough town, but brace yourself for hopeful guides swarming around you from the minute you arrive, offering their services.

Practicalities

The Association des Guides Bandiagara, near the centrally located **gare routière**, has a number of registered **guides** and a price list. To ensure that your guide has the right experience for your trip, it's a good idea to discuss your requirements in the presence of the association's president (if there's no one at the association's office-shack when you turn up, you can get in touch with them c/o the *Hôtel Village*). The Mission Culturelle off the Sévaré road behind *Le Village* hotel is also recommended for advice on guides. It was set up to ensure that the Dogon's precious cultural artefacts don't leave the region and encourage villages to establish museums instead, an initiative that has already been very successful. Finally the *Kambary* hotel houses an alternative independent association of guides who also organize hiking trips into the region at fixed rates, and arrange vehicle rental.

Accommodation and eating

A guide may be able to offer you **accommodation** in Bandiagara in his family compound, on negotiable terms. If that doesn't happen, or doesn't appeal, try one of the places listed below. Assuming you order well in advance, basic spaghetti-and-stew-type **dishes** are available at all the town's cheaper hotels, and *Le Cheval Blanc* at the *Kambary* Hôtel offers a pricier, Swiss-inspired *carte*, a relic of the former Swiss proprietor. Otherwise, inexpensive basic food and cold drinks are available at *Restaurant Le Petit Coin* and *Restaurant Ogotunga* near the *gare routière*, both popular hangouts for potential guides.

Auberge Kansaye Near the bridge over the river ✆242.04.87 A basic place popular with travellers, with a shady garden and a lively bar. CFA3000 to sleep on the roof, ❷

Kambary Well signposted off the Sévaré road ✆ & ℱ242.03.88. Vaguely upmarket, an atmospheric complex with dome-shaped stone buildings like those featured in *Star Wars*. It's well worth visiting even if only for a drink or meal. ❺

Satimbe Near the *gare routière*. Easy-going place with four basic rooms, two with two double beds, and shared facilities outside. CFA3000 to sleep on the roof, ❷

Toguna About 4km north of town on the Sévaré road ✆242.01.59. The *Toguna* has a pleasant campsite as well as a few simple rooms, some s/c. CFA3000 to camp, ❷

Le Village Near the Mission Culturelle, on the Sévaré road ✆242.03.31. Decent, clean rooms with shared facilities, a peaceful garden of *neem* trees – and cool beer. CFA2000 to camp, ❶

Pays Dogon market days

It's not only useful in itself to know when markets are taking place, but also because the days often determine availability of local transport – usually heading towards the market in the morning, and back again mid-afternoon.

7-day week market days	5-day week market days
Monday: Bandiagara (Dogon market), Madougou	Day 1: Dourou, Ibi, Tirelli
Tuesday: Bankass	Day 2: Nombori
Wednesday: Djiguibombo	Day 3: Yendouma-Sogol
Thursday: Kani-Kombolé	Day 4: Sanga, Banani
Friday: Bandiagara (Tukulor market)	Day 5: Ireli
Saturday: Bamba, Koro	
Sunday: Douentza, Endé	

Around Bandiagara and the southern pays Dogon

Once you've reached Bandiagara, you can choose between making the town your base while you make short trips to visit other villages (Songho, Sanga, Dourou and Djiguibombo can each be visited in a half-day round trip by car *moto* or *mobylette* from Bandiagara), or setting off on a longer trek, sleeping in villages as you go.

Anatomy of a Dogon village

Dogon villages are frequently divided into **twin parts** – as in Sanga, which incorporates Ogol-du-haut and Ogol-du-bas – signifying the original twin ancestors. Many villages are further divided into distinct **quartiers** according to the religion of the inhabitants. The Christian quarter may include a simple church, while the Muslim quarter is, naturally, marked by its mosque (the mosque at Kani-Kombolé is particularly impressive). The Muslim quarters tend to be large, Islam being the dominant religion, though the Dogon in fact resisted it for many years, and even now Muslim practices are generally grafted onto animist practices rather than adopted to the exclusion of traditional rites. In the animist *quartier*, the external walls of houses contain niches for fetishes that allude to primitive ancestors, and you will see small rocks, mounds or clay pilasters that serve as altars.

Village walls and buildings are collectively built, using dry stones or sun-fired mud bricks plastered with *banco*, which the Dogon make by hand from a sludge of straw, rice husks and clay. Walls often have graceful geometric patterns pressed into them. The roofs of the granaries and the elders' meeting place are thatched with millet stalks and waterproofed with *banco* mixed with karité oil. Everything has to be rebuilt, or at least repaired, at the end of each rainy season.

A Dogon village is in theory laid out to a symbolic plan in which different areas represent different parts of the **body**, with the forge and the *togu-na*, or elders' meeting place, at the head (the northernmost point); the house of the *ginna bana* – the head of a *ginna*, that is, an extended family or lineage – in the chest area (the centre); one or two *maisons des règles*, where women stay during menstruation, representing the hands (at east and/or west); and sacrificial altars at the feet (south). In reality this pattern isn't always strictly followed, but there is nonetheless a symbolic purpose in the positioning and layout of every structure in every village.

Togu-na (or *case à palabres*) This open-sided construction is the meeting place where village elders (strictly men only) gather to discuss village affairs, or to socialize and swap stories. The Dogon have an extremely rich oral tradition (reading and writing is not widespread), so the village *togu-na* is effectively a cultural treasure-house. The *togu-na* is built according to strict rules. The roof is supported by eight wooden pillars, which represent the eight Dogon ancestors and are often decorated with carvings; there are particularly beautiful examples at the villages of Dombossougou and Madougou. The roof is low, both to give maximum shade and also to help defuse any arguments before they get out of hand, the idea being that if people can't stand up, they can't come to blows.

House of the ginna bana A *ginna* (pronounced "gheena") *bana*'s house tends to be more impressive than an average dwelling, and contains an altar where the founders of the village are honoured. On the outside of the front wall of the house there may be ten rows of eight niches representing the eight Dogon ancestors.

Family compounds A compound is shared by a family unit made up of adults and young children: at the age of 7–9 years, children leave home to live communally in a *maison des jeunes*. The family compound consists of a courtyard, rooms and granaries, linked by stone walls. Rooms are normally square with flat roofs on which millet and other produce is left out to dry in the sun. Inside, houses are constructed according to a standard layout, symbolizing a seated man. There are specific guidelines as to which domestic duties take place where in the interior, and the system even runs as far as specifying where and in what position a couple should make love.

Songho

The village of **Songho** is spectacularly situated on the plateau, some distance from the *falaise*, between two craggy rock formations, and can easily be seen in a couple of hours (a guide can be found at the *campement* on the way into the village). To get there from Bandiagara, take the five-kilometre sandy track that turns off to the north side of the Sévaré road, about 10km outside Bandiagara. Although Songho is a Muslim village, the villagers keep their animist traditions

Granaries The pepperpot-shaped granaries give Dogon villages their distinctive fairy-tale quality. Tall and thin, they stand on stone legs to protect them from vermin. The interior of each granary is divided into compartments according to a pattern that represents the cosmos; these are used to store grain, obviously, but women also use their own granary to store their private possessions (jewellery, cloth, money).

Maison des règles While they are menstruating, women (referred to as "women who want a baby") are excused their domestic duties, and are isolated together in a round hut, overseen by a wise woman who offers them natural remedies for any ailments. The Dogon are renowned for their medical skills and their practices have recently become the subject of Western medical research.

Sanctuaire du binou This templelike building, decorated with *boummon* (ritual painting) in animal blood and *bouillie de mil* (millet porridge), is a place where the *hogon* (spiritual leader of the village) conducts sacred ceremonies dedicated to the *binou*, an ancestral spirit. It's often a rectangular house with rounded corners and towers and a low door blocked by rocks. Over the door is a forked iron hook which symbolizes the mythical ram's horns on which clouds are caught to bring rain. Only the *hogon* knows the meaning of the symbols and totemic objects inside the sanctuary.

Altars Sacrificial altars are sometimes no more than small earth mounds or pilasters marked with traces of animal blood and *bouillie de mil*. It is thought that when the rain washes the blood and *bouillie* away, the *nyama* (vital power) that these carry is transferred to the fields to restore the equilibrium of the earth and ensure a good harvest. Chickens and goats are the usual sacrificial victims but special occasions may call for the sacrifice of a more valuable animal.

Tellem houses The Tellem pygmies built cavelike dwellings high up in the cliff face. It's a mystery how these diminutive people managed to scale the *falaise* but it's thought that they did so either by weaving rope ladders out of baobab bark or other vegetation, or by climbing the large trees that used to grow right up to the foot of the cliff until the Dogon cleared the plain to grow millet. Some Tellem houses still contain ritual objects. Many are now used by the Dogon to keep livestock, store belongings, or bury dead.

Hogon house The isolated dwelling near the village ritual sites is where the *hogon* lives, either temporarily or permanently, guarding the village's sacred bones and relics. The walls of this dwelling are painted in totemic symbols in the ritual colours of red, black and white: red for sacrificial blood (a sign of peace) and the blood of the *hogon*; white for purity of heart and for the light of day; black for the skin of the *hogon* and for the night.

Ritual sites The most important ritual sites of a Dogon village are often outside the village itself; in the *falaise* villages they are generally situated on an isolated platform or ledge high up on the cliff face. It is here that circumcision ceremonies take place once every three years. The act of circumcision is performed on a designated blood-blackened rock, and the walls of the site are decorated with paintings in red, black and white. Each initiate adds his own personal symbol to those of his predecessors, and while older symbols follow traditional stylized patterns, more recent additions may reflect modern interests (a car, a plane). The cave paintings at Songo are particularly fine. The walls of some ritual sites (notably at Teli and Yabatalou) are hung with monkey skulls, totems in the Dogon farmers' war against the pests that steal their crops.

very much alive, as testified by the freshness of the cave paintings at the village **circumcision site** – a large ledge 100m up the crag. Your guide will point out the rocks where the participants sit for the ceremony, and the painted targets, which are the winning posts for the running race which takes place immediately after the ceremony. The newly circumcised complete a three-kilometre circuit and the winner is presented with a sack of millet – and the wife of his choice. You may also be shown the vertiginous platform where dances take place, and the cave in which ceremonial musical instruments are stored.

From Bandiagara to Djiguibombo

A 25-kilometre stretch of new paved road separates Bandiagara from Djiguibombo at the edge of the *falaise*. This relatively flat road over the plateau passes through sparse vegetation of bush savanna with the occasional baobab rising up to dominate the rocky landscape. After about 12km you pass the village of **Tegourou**, near which are a dammed stream and the terraced fields of the Dogon's famous onions. Before continuing the trip down the escarpment, most guides will stop at **Djiguibombo**, a charming and friendly place in an extremely rocky area near the cliff; a stone wall surrounds it and many of the houses use stone in their construction.

Along the plain from Kani-Kombolé to Teli

A couple of kilometres south of Djiguibombo, you finally arrive at the edge of the plateau, from where there's a sweeping vista over the plains below. For those on foot, although the cliff drops suddenly, your guide will lead you along walkable paths down it, and the 300-metre descent poses no special problem. On the plain, **Kani-Kombolé** – with a beautiful mosque, a Thursday market, a reasonable little restaurant and somewhere to stay if you need it – isn't too far off. This is where the new paved road ends and becomes a *piste*, to Bankass.

Following the foot of the cliffs eastwards, you come next to **Teli**, a four-kilometre walk over a flat, sandy stretch bordered by millet fields. If you don't manage to get to Sanga (see opposite), Teli is a satisfying, less-visited substitute, with some of the most spectacular **cliffside houses** along this part of the escarpment and, in the rainy season, waterfalls nearby. Some guides are better than others at getting you permission to climb up to the cliff-dwellings.

Endé to Bandiagara via Dourou

From Teli, you could either return to Bandiagara by retracing the route described above, or continue east across the plain to **Endé**, where there are three *campements*, the best belonging to the village chief who's quite accustomed to putting up travellers. You can pay to have meals of chicken and rice prepared, and wash it down with home-brewed millet beer. There's a market every Sunday, and in the rainy season you can swim in the waterfall pool near the village.

After Endé, the dirt road continues through a number of villages. One of the more picturesque is **Doundjourou**, known for its spectacular homes carved in the cliff. Still following the base of the escarpment northeastwards, you next come to **Konsagou**, and finally **Guimini**. After this village, you can climb back up the *falaise* and walk along the edge of the plateau to **Dourou**, which has one of the most important **markets** so close to the escarpment edge, and is also on a motorable road to Bandiagara. Every five days, vehicles arrive here from Bandiagara and Sévaré bringing traders and goods to the heart of Dogon country. In addition to the ubiquitous Dogon onions, grown nearby and sold in large quantities, you'll find cereals, Fula milk and rough cotton weaves of indigo-dyed material, a common element in Dogon dress. If you time your visit to coincide with market day, you can hope to get a ride back to Bandiagara, 25km to the north. There's good accommodation at the new *Campement Teriya* (❶, CFA1000 to sleep on the roof) with six double rooms and a restaurant serving the usual spaghetti stew and cold beer.

ILDS

Intersystems Library Delivery Service
Routing Label

Do not remove this label until item reaches destination

Send to:

_____

From:

_____

Circle destination library's ILDS address:

ALS-4	LCLS-5	SHLS-6
Augustana-4	Loyola U-1B	SIUC-6
Bradley U-3	LTLS-3	SIUE-5
Chicago PL-1A	MLS 1-A	SIUM-3
DePaul U-1B	Neastern U-1B	SWIC-6

The Rough
Guide to
West Africa
916. 6/HVD

Centuries of Greatness
966/KOS
966.2/KOS

A wonderful diversion from Dourou is to **Begnimato**, spectacularly situated under castlelike rock formations up on the plateau. The two *campements* here – *Chez Daniel* and *Chez Michel* – are next to each other and run by two brothers.

Sanga and the central pays Dogon

Much has been written about **SANGA**, a striking example of a classic Dogon village with traditional homes and granaries, sited on the plateau above the escarpment. Now more a small town than a village, this is where the Reverend McKinney set up the first mission in the Dogon country in the 1930s and where, soon after, Marcel Griaule lived and studied. Overflowing down the cliffs of the Bandiagara escarpment, the town was too picturesque to go unnoticed for long and some of the best and most popular **walking tours** through Dogon country start here. As a consequence, in the high season, it sometimes feels as if the tourists outnumber locals here by about two to one.

Sanga is a conglomeration of hamlets, the most useful of which is **Ogol-du-haut**, where you'll find the *gendarmerie* and *Campement Hôtel La Guina* (℡242.00.92; ❹) on the former site of Marcel Griaule's home, and somewhat overpriced despite the views and the cold beer served on the terrace. The alternative is the *Gîte de la Femme Dogon* (❷, CFA2500 to sleep on the roof), which is more basic but has clean rooms and decent food. Accommodation is cheaper a bit outside town at *Hôtel Guryamoin* (❷), and good **food** can be had at the *Kastor Restaurant*. Sanga is a good place to find a **guide** if you've arrived without one – the Sanga Association des Guides (℡242.00.92) is near the town's main junction or the people at the *campement* will offer advice – and also to hunt out **souvenirs**.

Tours around Sanga

You'll be offered three different **day-trips** from Sanga, ranging from seven to fifteen kilometres in length. The first includes a tour of Sanga and a seven-kilometre round-trip trek to **Gogoli**. The ten-kilometre tour continues from Gogoli to **Banani** (see p.397), located partly on the *falaise* near Sanga and partly on the plain below. The descent from the plateau takes you through a strange tunnel carved into the cliff near the village of Bongo where a former guide has opened up a small hotel (CFA3000 per person). All along the escarpment, you'll see caves – originally used by the Tellem as granaries or for defence in case of attack – cut into the rocky face. The fifteen-kilometre tour extends the loop to include **Tirelli**, another particularly pretty village stretching from the cliff to the plain. These treks last roughly between three and ten hours, and you can also arrange longer walking trips that last anything up to a week.

Dogon country from the south

One alternative to the normal route from the north into Dogon country bypasses Bandiagara altogether, entering the Dogon region via **BANKASS**, reached from the road that passes through Somadougou, south of Mopti. From this direction you start the trek from down on the plains, approaching the escarpment from below. Bankass is a small market town with a mixed population, and makes for a less busy departure point, although organized trips from Burkina Faso, via Bankass, are on the increase. Hiking access to the foot of the *falaise*, where the villages of Kani-Kombolé, Teli and Endé are located, is a fifteen-kilometre slog across the plain, but you can find transport by 4WD or *mobylette* in the dry season, and by donkey- or ox-cart all year round.

Moving on from Bankass and Koro

Now that the road between Bankass, Koro and Burkina Faso has been upgraded, transport to the **Burkinabe border** is not a problem. There are few direct departures from Bankass to Burkina but there are many daily departures to Koro (1hr; CFA1000), from where SOGEBAF buses for Ouagadougou (CFA5000) leave every afternoon at 2pm, a journey of around six hours. Additionally, minibuses leave constantly for the border town of Tiou.

There are two routes from Bankass to **Bandiagara** – one via Ouo, which is mostly good paved road but follows a very roundabout route; and one via Kani-Kombolé which, as far as that village, can be a difficult dirt road, especially during the rains. There is little scheduled transport from Bankass to Kani-Kombolé (best bet is on a Thursday, Kani-Kombolé's market day). From Kani-Kombolé, a good paved road climbs the *falaise* and runs north to Bandiagara, with frequent minibus departures.

Accommodation in Bankass covers a range of budgets. *Campement Hogon* (❷) offers rooms equipped with fans and mosquito nets, while *Camping Hogon*, on the road leading out of town (❷), merits a visit if only to appreciate the *togu-na* on the premises (accommodation is in roundhouses with traditional outside showers). *Camping Seno* (❷), next to the water tower, has clean rooms with shared outdoor facilities, an interior garden with a good bar, and a hallway decorated by the owner's private collection of masks and Dogon art. *Hôtel Les Arbres* behind the Centre des Impôts (☎228.66.42; ❷, CFA3500 to sleep on the roof, camping CFA2500 per person), offers overpriced a/c rooms with mosquito nets, and cheaper, very basic rooms. Camping is also available at *Hôtel Les Arbres*, and on the roof terraces of *Camping Seno* and *Campement Hogon*.

Camping Hogon organizes excursions along the *falaise* and you can get good guides here as well. If you don't have your own transport, ask about the possibility of renting a *mobylette* or *charette* to Kani-Kombolé. Once there, you can visit other villages along the escarpment by following the routes described on p.392.

Bankass is also the commonest entry point for the *pays Dogon* if you're arriving from Burkina Faso on the newly upgraded road from **KORO**. Koro has a large Saturday **market** and beautiful **mosque**, but is a little too far from the heart of the Dogon country to be an immediate springboard for a trek. The lone and rather sad-looking *campement* (❶) serves as a liaison for tours setting out from Bankass.

Douentza and the northern pays Dogon

DOUENTZA, stretched out beneath the towering cliffs of the **Gandamia massif**, 167km east of Sévaré on the main highway to Gao, has a good Sunday **market** and an impressive mosque, and is becoming an increasingly important local tourism hub. If you're looking for information about the elephants of Gourma (the Service de la Conservation de la Nature here (☎245.20.29) can recommend guides. Douentza is also a good base for visiting the northern Dogon country. Although access to the *pays Dogon* is a little more difficult from here, this is repaid by friendly villages with a less commercial atmosphere than those around Sanga. The *Auberge du Gourma* (see below) is the base for a local tourist guide association, and the little office can arrange just about anything.

Douentza itself is strung out uneventfully along the highway, with an older quarter to the south of the road. **Accommodation** options include the fairly new and under-patronized *Hôtel Falaise* at the western end of town, with comfortable s/c fanned (CFA10,000) and a/c (CFA12,500) rooms, and the well-run and more soulful and popular *Auberge du Gourma* (☎245.20.31; CFA2500 per person), at the

For **Gao**, Bani Transports comes through Douentza late evening, daily except Sunday, and Bittar Trans makes the run every other day. Both companies stop at **Hombori** and **Gossi**. The same companies make the journey in the opposite direction, to **Sévaré**, **Mopti**, **Ségou** and **Bamako**, usually arriving in Douentza from Gao between mid-morning and mid-afternoon.

South of Douentza towards **Dogon country** and Burkina, the main "road" is a diffi-cult track to follow (and can be treacherous in the rainy season) and there's no sched-uled transport, though one or two bush taxis normally go on market days to **Bamba** (Sat) and **Madougou** via Bamba (Mon).

For **Timbuktu**, a fast, newly graded gravel road heads north from Douentza as far as the desolate outpost of **Bambara-Maoundé**, roughly halfway there, to be succeeded by a difficult sandy track winding through thorn scrub that's strictly 4WD territory and can be very arduous in the rains. Normally, you can reach Bambara-Maoundé in under two hours, but the total journey time for the 220-odd-km trip, assuming there are no delays, is around six hours. There's no regular transport from Douentza, but put your intentions about and you're likely to find someone heading up to Timbuktu early the next morning – so long as there are enough passengers. Most drivers will want at least CFA50,000 for the trip, which means that three passengers paying CFA15,000 each (the notional "fare") isn't quite sufficient, while with four you have a green light.

eastern side of town, with basic rooms and roof, camping in the pleasant, shady yard, and a good restaurant. Both are on the main road. If you're looking for **food and drink** beyond your hotel, the *Restaurant Sénégalais*. at the roadside in the middle of town, serves quick and reasonable food and cold drinks to passing trav-ellers: further east, beyond *Auberge du Gourma*, on the south side of the road, the *Restaurant Mediterranée* usually has good food and loud music, but the service can be erratic.

The northern pays Dogon

The northern districts of Dogon country are on the whole less affected by tourism than the centre and south. You can see the evidence of that in the carved doors and windows and traditional *togu-na* pillars that are still happily to be seen in many vil-lages, where elsewhere they have been sold to overseas collectors and dealers – check the fancy furnishing stores in New York and Paris. There are various options for **Dogon trekking** out of Douentza. The most straightforward, and pricey, option is to rent a 4WD vehicle and driver to get you down to Bamba, about two hours' drive south, and then trek from here to Sanga over three or four days. On Bamba's market day, Saturday, you can also get to Bamba by battered Peugeot 404 *taxi brousse*. If you're thinking of driving this route yourself, the track you want is signposted to Koro off the main highway, just east of Douentza. But drivers should beware: the track is very difficult (with taxing stretches of soft sand and boulders) and it's hard to follow its endless branches across the plain. If you were planning on trying to get lifts to some of the villages below, note that infrequent vehicles link them on market days.

Borko

An alternative to heading straight down to Bamba is to explore some of the plateau Dogon region southwest of Douentza. Here, the most alluring destination is the extraordinary crocodile village of **BORKO**, an exceptionally beautiful and verdant Dogon village that's well worth a half-day trip out of Douentza, or a serious side track if you have your own 4WD vehicle.

Borko is a tough 22-kilometre drive by 4WD from the Douentza–Sévaré road, accessed most directly from Douentza by turning left (south) at an unmarked track by the name-board for the highway village of **Gnimignama** (also spelt Nimignama), 46km west of Douentza. Allow an hour and a half to get to Borko and bring somebody who knows the way, or else be prepared to stop frequently to ask anyone you see on the track. You'll know you're almost there when you cross a ford and reach a village checkpoint (*comptoir routier*) and the track begins to climb steeply. The village lies at the head of a valley, right at the end of a five-kilometre oasis of greenery wedged into a continuation of the Gandamia massif. Verdant fields of onions and garlic, irrigated by a network of ditches (*marigots*), and dotted with groves of mangos and *doum* palms, create a vivid carpet of green, even in the dry season. The centre of the village is a shady area with the local government office and meeting house. Borko has a distinguished mosque, and soft drinks are usually available, but there are no other services as such.

Borko's inhabitants have an old respect for, and relationship with, the small **crocodiles** that live in the ditches and ponds all around the village and surrounding fields. There are certainly dozens – people say hundreds – of crocodiles in this well-watered neighbourhood, and they come, almost scampering, at the first sight of a crowd of people, which signals tourists and goat meat. If you're not accompanied by a guide, you'll need to spend some time introducing yourself, finding the old butcher responsible for feeding the crocs – the *maître des cäimans* – and negotiating a price for a few kilos of goat scraps and offal. Most visitors will be making the whole trip accompanied by a guide who can make this process straightforward, but either way you'll spend at least CFA5000. The spectacle of crocodiles, some a couple of metres long, advancing from all directions on your group, is one that sticks in the mind – as does the pestering of them by the village children (a number of crocodiles have lost eyes). Accidents are said to be unheard of, but you should be extremely careful nevertheless.

Bamba and the trek to Sanga

To go trekking from Douentza, there are several options: you can walk to **Fombori**, 3km south of Douentza, with its Tellem cemetery and little Dogon **museum** (run like a pawnshop for Dogon artefact donors); and then to Ewerle/**Everi**, on a high mesa (4km further).

Alternatively, if you start off by vehicle, your most likely first night stop will be **BAMBA**, about one and a half hours from Douentza by 4WD and a good place to start walking, as most of the soft sand is behind you by then. Crouched at the foot of the escarpment and spilling onto the plain, Bamba's numerous hamlets add up to a thriving small commercial centre, with a highly recommended Saturday market that draws in head-loaded columns of traders, clapped-out bush taxis and donkey- and ox-carts from miles around. If you stay for the market, note that it really doesn't get going till midday. There are one or two little *auberges* in Bamba, including the pleasant *Auberge Chez Soumaila Guindo* (❶).

Some 14km west of Bamba, after a twisting route across the plain via **Yenda**, **YENDOUMA** is a clutch of five hamlets, dotted up the cliffs. Hike up to **Yendouma-Atô**, the prettiest of the quintet and a twenty- to thirty-minute walk from the plain, to pay a visit to a locally famous artist, Alaye Atô. Alaye, who lost his left hand in a shooting accident at a funeral, will sell you his book *Alaye Atô – Dessinateur Dogon* (Eds Adeiao, Paris, 1999), full of phantasmagorical Dogon imagery, mostly in felt pens donated by visitors. Down at **Yendouma-Sogol**, Yendouma's chef-lieu and the location of the school, dispensary and market, the obvious place to stay is the lively *Auberge Guina Dogon* (*Chez Youssouf Nango*; ❶).

From Yendouma, you can follow the track southwards, directly to Koundou, or, more interestingly, strike out east towards the Youga Plateau, a separate chunk of escarpment that rises over the plain. An hour of soft sand (make an early start) sees you to the foot of the cliffs and a fine climb up over boulders and beneath baobabs, to the first of the **YOUGA** villages, the cliff hamlet of **Youga-Piri**, with weavers at work and close-up views of Tellem houses. Above Youga-Piri, you reach the plateau itself, a lunar landscape of black rock, cut through by crevasses bridged by makeshift wooden spans, or simply stepped across – cautiously. Descending again from the plateau, you pass a hogon's burial site and a small trekker's café, and more fabulous Tellem architecture, and then reach **Youga-Dogourou** (sometimes spelt Dourou), the village where the **Sigui** (see p.384) originated. If you've seen film of this spectacular, masked dance, you'll recognize the boulder-bounded sandy square.

Finally, down on the plain, the main Youga village of **Youga-Na**, whose people decamped here in 1992 from the abandoned houses you can see a little futher up, has places to stay, crafts for sale and, usually, other tourists. *Chez Akougnon Doumbo* is a pleasant midday or night stop, patrolled by its helpful, wheelchair-bound owner. Or you can continue to **KOUNDOU**, a largely non-Muslim village just 4km further south along a reasonable track, and stay at *Auberge Koundou* (*Chez Assama Dara*) or the larger and fancier *Campement Amitié* (**❶**).

Koundou is barely 10km from Sanga as the crow flies, and you can get there easily enough along the track. But it's much more rewarding to climb up onto the main plateau again, passing through pretty areas of grassland, huge baobabs and broken rocky scenery, including a dramatic rock arch, to descend again towards **IBI**, a straggling large village on the plain with several simple *auberges*, just an hour's walk short of Banani at the foot of the escarpment at Sanga.

BANANI, with its busy market area, small shops and crafts booths – and a surprising amount of gentle hustling to buy or at least inspect the wares – signals your imminent return from the wilds to something like metropolitan Mali. *Campement Hogon* has dispensed with tree-trunk staircases and provides built-in concrete ones, real showers and toilets (though the primitive versions in the remoter villages are invariably cleaner and nicer to use) and multiple options for sleeping in rooms or on rooftops. Banani also has a paved road snaking up the escarpment to Sanga, but a much preferable walking route takes you high above Banani and up through a steep cleft – almost a tunnel – carved in the rock, to emerge on the flat plateau a half-hour from **Sanga** (see p.393).

4.6

Northeastern Mali

A rid and inhospitable, northeastern Mali would not be habitable but for the Niger River, along which life in the area concentrates (the exception being the Tuareg nomads, who thrive in the desert). The riverside town of **Gao**, the largest in the northeast, was formerly the capital of a great kingdom, and is now the administrative and commercial centre of Mali's Seventh Region, and easily accessible by a decent paved road from Mopti (allow a full day) and Bamako (allow two days). The Mopti–Gao stretch runs through the dramatic, towering landscapes of the **Gandamia Massif** and **Hombori**, encompassing Mali's highest elevations. From Gao you can strike out to **Kidal** in Mali's remote Eighth

Region, or follow the river south to **Niamey** (in Niger) along a difficult but scenic *piste* leading through small fishing villages. Alternatively **the river** itself can serve as your highway, certainly a more memorable way to travel – providing you time your travels to coincide with the immediate aftermath of the rains, when the water levels are high enough for the river boats to make a few weekly voyages downstream to Gao.

From Mopti to Gao

Initially, the journey from Mopti (Sévaré) to Gao is uneventful. Around 55km from Sévaré, you reach **Konna**, a market town close to the river, at the turning for the difficult road traversing the Niger inland delta to Timbuktu via Niafounké (requiring a ferry crossing at Niafounké and impassable during the rains). The next settlement of note, **Boré** (50km beyond Konna), boasts an exceptionally large and beautiful **mosque** for such a small place. Some 20km further, if you have 4WD, you can turn off the road at Gnimignama and follow a sometimes elusive track to the crocodile village of **Borko** (see p.395).

Hombori and around

East of **Douentza** (see p.394), the scenery shifts from neutral into top gear, with more than twenty huge sandstone mesas and needlelike rock formations rearing up from the plains to the north and south. Tourist offices like to refer to the whole area as *Le Monument Valley de Mali*, and the comparison is justified. The pinnacles culminate in the spectacular shape of **La Main de Fatima**, also known as Gami Tondo – or the *Aiguilles de Gami* (Needles of Gami) – which is said to resemble the hand of the prophet Muhammad's daughter, with outstretched thumb and finger (Fatima's Hand is a protective symbol in Islamic tradition).

The small, strikingly situated town of **HOMBORI** is 11km east of the Main de Fatima, straddling the highway. The newer districts lie to the north of the road, while the old stone town on the south side straggles up over the rocky apron of **Hombori Tondo** – a massive flat-topped mesa rising to 1155m – the highest point in Mali. The unusual architecture of Old Hombori makes for a highly recommended afternoon stroll: most of the houses are built of rock, and the narrow alleys between become tunnels beneath second storeys in several places. You'll certainly be tailed by a gaggle of children, but choose a couple of older boys to accompany you and the rest will leave you in peace (don't forget to tip your guides). You can return back to the main road via a series of palm-tree-shaded wells at the foot of the village.

For **accommodation** you can choose between the sweetly informal and relaxing rooftop, rooms and huts at *Camping Kaga Tondo/Chez Lélélé* (❶), on the north side of the road near where the buses stop, and the less welcoming, though better equipped, *Campement Mangou Bagni/Chez Kolly Cissko*, a few minutes' walk further east along the road, which offers rooms at the back with mosquito nets (❶). *Mangou Bagni* has a fridge and electricity, cold beer, a menu of sorts, and an occasionally busy roadside bar-restaurant. *Kaga Tondo*, on the other hand, will prepare good food to order – and you can always send for cold drinks from *Mangou Bagni*. Hombori's market takes place on Tuesday.

Climbing and hiking at Hombori

Even non-climbers can see the massive appeal of the awesome stone spires and walls around Hombori. With accessible sheer faces rising between 100m and 600m from the rocky plain, this is one of Africa's premier technical **rock-climbing** areas, and draws experienced climbers from around the world, especially in the winter. There is, however, virtually no infrastructure for climbers and, beyond guides and some ropes (ask at the *campements*), you'll find little help, so keen climbers are advised to bring their own gear. Guides charge around CFA5000 per day per person. The district's climbing possibilities and mesas are all sketch-mapped at ⓦwww.alpinisme.com/fr/topo/mali, which also offers some useful local advice. If you want to visit the Main de Fatima, informal *mobylette* rental is available in Hombori for around CFA6000 per day: ask at the *campements*. You pay a visit fee of CFA1500 at the foot of the rock formation, and note that, apart from the two needles (the smaller is **Kaga Pamari** and the larger **Kaga Tondo**), the rest of the sacred massif is largely off-limits to outsiders.

If you aren't suitably equipped, resist the temptation to free-climb any part of the Hombori rock faces: needless to say, there's no emergency service here. Instead, pursue the wealth of hiking opportunities, the most obvious of which are the lower reaches of **Hombori Tondo** and its neighbour, the pyramid-shaped **Cle de Hombori** (Hombori's Key) rising up behind the town. It takes roughly ninety minutes, half of it jumping from boulder to boulder, to reach the col between the Cle and the main mesa, where a superb tennis-court-sized rock platform gives you a panoramic view over the yawning plain to the south and the empty wastelands of northern Burkina. Directly below you lies the village of **Tondourou**. From the col, you can scramble to the summit of the steep, rocky spine of the Cle – another forty minutes to an hour – but it's not for the faint-hearted. A few hundred metres to the east, the sheer walls of the western end of Hombori Tondo rise like some lost world, completely unscalable without ropes. This hike requires around four to five hours away from Hombori town, and, although the sun rises behind Hombori Tondo, so you'll be in shade most of the morning if you make an early start, you'll still need a couple of litres of water per person.

There are a number of other good hikes you can do further west, towards the domes of **Kissim** and **Fada Tondo**, and the whale-shaped mesas of **Barkoussou** and **Ouari** which rise (in that order from east to west) southwest of the town. The main footpath to this area runs from the old quarters of Hombori between the loaflike Fada Tondo and the broad mesa of Barkassou, and as you climb closer you'll see the spike of **Aiguille de Xoussi** between them.

In contrast to boulders and climbing, the formation of steep **red dunes** that rises to the northeast of the town, about forty minutes' walk away, is a wonderful area to visit before sunset. For a spot of dune-skiing, *Campement Mangou Bagni* rents out skis and toboggans, which go reasonably well.

Gossi and Doro

GOSSI is the next small Songhai and Bella town along the road, 85km northeast of Hombori. It's a kilometre north of the highway, on the shore of a muddy lake, the Mare de Gossi, and is the site of a sizeable reforestation and agricultural project headed by a Norwegian church fund. It also has **elephants**: a herd of some six hundred – known as the elephants of Gourma – migrate towards the end of the year from northern Burkina through the **Réserve du Gourma**, as the vegetation from the summer rains begins to diminish, and they can quite often be seen at waterholes north of the road between Hombori and Gossi, and especially near the Mare de Gossi itself. In February or March they begin to trek west through the **Réserve de Douentza** and then south again, usually crossing the road to the west of Hombori. The elephants' numbers may be increasing as the traditional Tuareg resistance to hunting them offers partial protection. But many Tuareg are making the uneasy transition to a sedentary lifestyle in this area, and their crops are threatened by the *elouan*. If the herd isn't near Gossi, you can make a 4WD trip to see them, driving more or less cross-country, but 4WD availability is a bit thin on the ground in this area and the elephants can be elusive, so you might end up paying quite a lot for many hours of bumpy trail-bashing, to little avail. Both reserves have very limited infrastructure and no formal system of entry fees. The usual target is the Tuareg village of **I-n-Adiattafene**, 80km west of Gossi, well out in the bush.

Gossi has sandy streets, a few small shops and one "hotel", *Le Campement* (**❶**), with utterly basic rooms. Nevertheless, the town is a pleasant place to stop off for a lukewarm drink and a bite to eat. Reasonably priced grilled meat is sold in large quantities at the market. Monday is the highlight, with the largest cattle market in the region.

The later stages of the Mopti road are dull, thorny country, with long stretches of monotonous Sahelian landscape. Some 62km from Gossi you arrive at **Doro**, a small settlement in a region where lions are said to exist. If the reports are true, you'd have to follow tracks a good 40km south of town to have any hope of seeing them. Ask in Doro if any have been spotted recently and enquire about the possibility of taking someone along as a guide.

The final approach to Gao necessitates a short ferry ride across the Niger (last ferry 6pm) followed by a seven-kilometre causeway above the river channel to the town itself.

Gao

In the repertoire of trans-Saharan campfire talk, **GAO** was always one of the most romantic cities. As you arrived from Algeria and the void of the Sahara, it seemed like a miracle of civilization emerging from the wasteland. Once you'd passed the last stretch of soft sand thrown up by the desert around the town, and entered its dusty tree-lined avenues of mud-brick shops and houses, thronging with crowds, the physical sensations of admission into a new world were powerful and enchanting. Traditionally, desert-crossers would celebrate their arrival in West Africa by heading straight to the *Hôtel Atlantide* – a tatty colonial pile that might as well have been the *Ritz* out here – and downing a few cold beers. Behind the hotel (which these days is very run-down and invariably beer-less) lies the source of all the vigour, the **Niger River**, tangibly and magically connecting Gao with the whole of West Africa.

If you've flown in from Paris, the early morning arrival can still be pretty exhilarating as you sweep low over glinting expanses of river. But if you've come up from Mopti on the main road, you may have rather different first impressions of Gao. The river, which from this direction is neither new nor unusual, is unlikely to stir special excitement, while the town itself resembles any other Sahelian city, bigger than most, but neither beautiful nor unusually dynamic.

Some history

The original founders of Gao, known in its early days as Kawkaw, were **Sorko fishermen** who migrated from Benin between the sixth and eleventh centuries. They mingled with the rural Gabili peoples living along the banks of the Niger, and eventually this mixture evolved into a people known as the Songhai. The first **Songhai** monarch at Gao was Kanda, who founded the **Za (or Dia) dynasty** in the seventh century. He quickly opened the town to trans-Saharan trade and to Berbers who wanted to settle there for commercial reasons.

A later king of Songhai, Za Kossoi, converted to **Islam** in 1009. The town prospered to the point where it rivaled all the great regional trading centres in power and wealth, even surpassing the capitals of ancient Ghana and later Mali. Rulers of the Mali Empire coveted Gao's success and potential and annexed the town in 1325, although the Songhai princes managed to flee from their clutches. One of them, **Ali Golon**, went on to found the **Sonni dynasty**, still based at Gao. The greatest of the Sonni rulers was the despotic Sonni Ali Ber, or **Ali the Great**. It was he who, towards the end of the fifteenth century, expanded the kingdom at Gao to the dimensions of an empire (see box, opposite). The capital continued to

The Songhai empire

By the second half of the fifteenth century, the influence and power of the Mali Empire had diminished greatly and the stage was set for **Sonni Ali Ber** – nineteenth ruler in the Sonni dynasty and the effective founder of Songhai as an empire (emperor from 1464 to 1492) – to embark on his great conquests. A shrewd administrator, Ali was also a brilliant and ruthless strategist, and it is said he never lost a battle. A half-hearted Muslim, Ali quickly set about terrorizing the Fula and Tuareg nomads, his bitter enemies in the region. His expansionist designs were greatly facilitated in 1468 when he was invited by the governor of **Timbuktu** to liberate that town from Tuareg domination.

Historians of the period reported that Ali's conquest of Timbuktu was brutal, and many townspeople who had longed for the Songhai "liberation" fled west to Oualata for fear of persecution. After an initial period of purging religious leaders who stood in his path, however, Ali brought stability to the town which once again prospered under his rule. At the same time, he managed to neutralize the **religious influence** of Timbuktu's powerful marabouts, who exercised considerable political power over the entire region.

Ali next turned his sights on **Djenné**, which proved a harder target. The Sonnis are said to have besieged the town for seven years, seven months and seven days before it finally fell in 1473. Rather than wreaking vengeance on the ruling class as he had in Timbuktu, Ali married his fortunes with those of Djenné by taking the queen mother to be his wife. **Massina** was his next objective, and he conquered this Fula stronghold shortly afterwards.

All the chief strategic points of the Niger and the delta region were now under Songhai control. The nation's military strength was founded in its **navy** and Ali depended so heavily on his flotilla that, at one point, he envisaged digging a canal from the port town of Râs el Mâ on Lac Faguibine to the desert oasis of Oualata, in order to attack the Tuareg there. Although work started, the plan was eventually abandoned as Ali extended his control south and east to the villages of Bandiagara, Bariba and Gourma.

After he died, Sonni Ali was succeeded by his son Bakari, but the new king followed his father's example of keeping a distance from the faith and thus incited religious disapproval. He was overthrown by Mohammed Torodo, the governor of Hombori, who formed a new dynasty known as the **askia** or "usurper". Though he had no hereditary claim to the throne, Askia Mohammed legitimized his rule through religious channels, soliciting the backing of powerful marabouts. He received the ultimate benediction to his rule after making the pilgrimage to Mecca with 500 horsemen and 1000 footsoldiers in 1493. There he was granted the title of khalif for the entire Soudan. Returning to Mali, he set about expanding his empire into Mossi country, in present-day Burkina, then pushed eastward to Hausa-land and into the Aïr (in what's now Niger) as far as Agadez.

While away on a campaign, Mohammed was forced out of power in 1528. Internal intrigue followed and a number of *askias* succeeded one another until the reign of **Ishak I** who ruled from 1539 to 1549 – a decade which marked the Songhai Empire's apogee. The country now extended from Senegal to the Aïr mountains and from the Taghaza salt mines in the desert to the Hausa-land in what today is Nigeria.

Meanwhile **Morocco** far to the north was in a period of crisis. Ejected from Andalucía and hemmed in to the east by the Turks, the Moroccan sultan turned his sights towards the south, where he sought to gain control of the salt and gold trades. In 1591 he sent an army to wrest the Soudan from Songhai control. Thanks to a combination of Moroccan firearms and the disarray of the *askia* rulers, the sultan's army won a decisive battle at **Tondibi**, 60km north of Gao; Gao, Djenné and Timbuktu all fell soon afterwards.

El Sadi, writing in the *Tarikh es-Soudan*, described the invasion in these terms: "Everything changed after the Moroccan conquest. It signalled the beginning of anarchy, theft, pillage and general disorganization". And indeed the entire Sahelian region suffered a blow to its prestige and independence from which it never recovered.

flourish under the reign of the **askias**, founders of a new dynasty that lasted throughout the sixteenth century. At the time, Gao had 70,000 inhabitants and in the busy harbour were crowded more than a thousand war boats from the *askias'* flotilla, four hundred barges and thousands of *pirogues*.

With the **Moroccan invasion** of Songhai in 1591, the empire collapsed and Gao was virtually razed. The town never recovered and when the German explorer **Heinrich Barth** arrived in 1854, he described the once ostentatious city as "a desolate abode with a small and miserable population". Much of the town's present look dates to the beginning of the twentieth century. The **French** built up the port, traced new streets (which explains the rather uniform grid layout) and established an administrative district with characteristic colonial buildings still used by the present government. With a population of some 38,000, Gao still hasn't returned to its former grandeur and, in its current economic and political predicament, it is struggling.

The Town

In physical terms, Gao has few reminders of its glorious past. The **mosque** in the centre of town near the police station was initially built by Kankan Moussa after he annexed the town in the fourteenth century but, its origins apart, it's unimpressive compared even with those in Timbuktu and certainly in comparison with the mosque at Djenné. Following the principal Boulevard des Askias to the northeast brings you in fifteen minutes to the **askia tomb** – the *Tombeau d'Askia Mohamed* or *Tombeau des Askias*. You can visit this mosque – a smaller women's side, used only on Fridays, and a large men's side – and climb the odd-shaped, fifteenth-century *banco* mausoleum (CFA2000, plus CFA2500 to use a camera) with wild wooden crossbeams sticking out porcupine-style from the facade. From the top, you get a good view of the town and the river. The tomb was built in 1495 by the first *askia*, in the style of a pyramid, after his return from Mecca to perform the hajj. He died in 1539 and is interred inside. Every two years the pyramid has to be resurfaced, and the workmen use the beams to climb – the oldest of which are said to have been brought back from Mecca. Outside, in the graveyard within the precincts of the mosque, are buried ten of his descendants.

Considering the centuries of history through which Gao has played a leading role, the **Musée du Sahel** (Tues–Fri & Sun 8am–12.30pm & 3–6pm; CFA1000) on the north side of town, behind and a few streets on from the hospital, is disappointingly small, dedicated to the different **peoples of the Sahel**, with displays of their art and domestic implements. You'll see farming and fishing tools (some rather impressive harpoons), musical instruments, and household items used by the **Tuareg**, **Fula**, **Chamba** and **Arma** (the last of these being the descendants of Moroccan–Songhai marriages). Guided tours are included in the entrance fee – extra donations are not declined – and the guides extremely enthusiastic. Boards explain the exhibits in French and English, so you can easily go it alone.

In the town centre, Gao boasts two good **markets**. The *grand marché*, just opposite the *Hôtel Atlantide*, and undergoing redevelopment on last checking, has long had an entire section devoted to **crafts**, for which the region is well known. The most common items are Tuareg **leather boxes**, knives and swords; on sale too are numerous examples of **Sahelian sandals** – flat and wide to facilitate walking on the sands. Some pairs incorporate intricate weaving and green- or red-dyed leather in the design. Fula and Tuareg **jewellery** can also be a good buy here, but vendors generally set astronomically high starting prices: bargaining tends to be more of a headache than the good-humoured exchange you're perhaps used to. A more laidback place to buy crafts, jewellery and other souvenirs is the Maison des Artisans in Château district, just beneath the water tower.

Behind the crafts section, women bunch around desert wares – anonymous spices, dollops of peanut butter, sour milk, fish and meat, pyramids of miniature tomatoes, onions, peppers and lettuces carefully washed (in the river) – and, in season if you're lucky, the full range of tropical fruits and vegetables. The **petit marché**, or Marché Washington, near the police station, specializes in **cloth**. Dozens of tailors – all men of course – treadle ancient sewing machines and will take orders if you want to have loose-fitting Sahelian clothes made to measure. Another market, primarily selling foodstuffs, takes place at night: **le marché de nuit**, by the *gare routière* for Bourem, Kidal and Timbuktu east of the centre and behind Boulevard des Askias.

Another of Gao's attractions is **La Dune Rose**, visible from the top of the *askia* tomb, a picturesque sand dune that glows pink and orange at dawn and dusk. Askia Mohammed was born in a village near the dune and, after he was deposed, lived there until he died. It's a three-hour *pirogue* trip away (CFA10,000 there and back).

Practicalities

The paved road from Mopti and Bamako gives out a few hundred metres short of the crossing point over the Niger, a narrow stretch of water running past a causeway reaching across from the left bank, about 7km south of Gao. The **ferry** operates from dawn to dusk, but public transport to Gao always arrives in the early hours, so passengers have to sleep on the riverbank (kids will rent you a mat for the night). There are plenty of food stalls for breakfast.

The occasional flight into Gao (often just the weekly winter charter from Paris and Marseilles with Point-Afrique) lands at the rudimentary **airport** 8km southeast of town near the Niamey road. Formalities are usually very swift and customs informal. A ride into town along Route de l'Aeroport (there are usually several *taxi brousse* drivers on the prowl for customers) costs CFA1000–2000 per person, though you might be able to tag along for free with a tour operator's minibus.

The main **gare routière** in Gao is on the place de l'Indépendance. There are two **banks**: BDM (Mon–Fri 8am–noon for exchange), halfway between *Hôtel Atlantide* and Marché Washington, who change traveller's cheques at poor rates, and don't change cash; and the better option of BNDA (Mon–Thurs 7.30am–5pm & Fri 7.30am–12.30pm), next to the *gare routière*, who change euros, dollars and traveller's cheques at higher rates. International **phone calls** can be made 24 hours a day from SOTELMA or nearby at the **post office** (Mon–Fri 8am–noon & 1.30–4pm); Gao's poste restante is notorious for its delays. **Internet** access was established in Gao in 2003.

Since peace between Tuareg and government forces was cemented with the symbolic burning of arms in Timbuktu in 1996, travelling in the Gao region is no longer considered dangerous, and you no longer need to register with the police upon arrival. However, a few police officers have been slow to catch on, so to avoid the risk of police hassle, it's now a possibility to have your **passport** stamped at the newly established **tourist office** (Mon–Fri 8am–12.30pm & 1.30–6pm) behind Marché Washington. The staff can also help with travel advice in the region.

Accommodation

Most of the best-value accommodation options in town are located to the south of the town centre, past the hospital on the way out of town on the Route de l'Aeroport, in **Quartier Château** (location of the water tower). Centred around a small mosque and a Shell station, it's a thirty-minute walk from the central *gare routière*. Catching a taxi to this quarter can be difficult as there are only seven taxis in Gao, and frequent fuel shortages, resulting in ludicrous prices (the normal fare is CFA500 per person). A *charette* (donkey-cart) may be an alternative, but when taxi prices go up, so do *charette* rates. With heavy bags, you'll find it's still a fair walk from most of the hotels from the main road at the Shell station. The *Hôtel Atlantide* (☎282.01.30), Gao's traditional first choice, close to the river in the town centre and the best bet unless you were counting every penny, was barely functioning at the time of writing in mid-2003, though a future upsurge in trans-Saharan traffic might change that.

At the time of writing, Air Mali had stopped all its **flights** to and from Gao, and the only planes leaving the airfield were the weekly Point Afrique (☎282.02.24, ⓦwww.point-afrique.com) flights to Marseilles and Paris, operating only in the winter.

By river

During and after the rains, you can take advantage of the **boats** that pass along one of the most interesting stretches of the **Niger** between Gao (their terminus) and Mopti. In addition to the main August–November boat, most of the year it's possible to use smaller river craft for transport. Upstream, poled *pirogues* set off for **Bourem** (all day and half the next), **Bamba** (3–4 days), **Gourma-Rharous** (4–5 days) and **Timbuktu** (one week). Downstream, *pirogues* rarely go much beyond **Gargouna** (one day away; Tuesday market) or **Ansongo** (two days away; splendid Thursday market). This latter trip, below Gao, is especially rewarding from a natural history viewpoint, as the boats crush through marvellous deep reed beds harbouring a wealth of **birdlife**, and then break onto open water where they regularly pass several herds of snorting **hippos**. *Pirogue* fares have increased enormously in recent years, but a place on a *pinasse* shouldn't cost you more than CFA7000 per day, including communal rice and fish.

By road

Getting from **Gao to Bamako** is easy on the fast paved road, but you need to cross the river 7km south of Gao, by a ferry service operating roughly from dawn to dusk. Regular buses leave Gao for **Mopti** and **Bamako** from the central *gare routière*. There is a daily bus for Mopti (7hr; CFA5000) taking roughly seven hours. Allow at least sixteen hours to reach Bamako with one of many daily buses or minibuses (CFA10,000).

Travelling overland in any other direction can be a trying experience and will require lots of time. The Nigerien SNTV bus, based near the Musée du Sahel (☎282.03.95), leaves Gao for **Niamey** (CFA8700) twice a week, on Wednesday and Saturday. You're allowed onto the bus in the order you book, so it's wise to book several days in advance, as you want to avoid the bumpy back seats at all costs. If things go according to plan, the bus leaves Gao sometime after 7am and gets into Niamey early evening on the same day, but note that during the rainy season there are many delays. The *piste* is notoriously difficult (for some stretches there is effectively no visible track, and the bus can get stuck for days) and this, added to protracted border formalities and the endless customs checks on the Niger side, makes it a challenging journey. Bring plenty of water. Askia Transports also have scheduled departures for Niamey every Friday morning, but their buses are even shoddier than SNTV's. Two other companies, Airfagosse and Ham Kouma, make the journey as well, but are exceedingly slow and continually get stopped at checkpoints. They leave from the *gare routière* behind the *marché de nuit*.

To track down the exceedingly rare vehicles heading direct to **Timbuktu**, check at hotels, with guides, and at the *gare routière* behind the *marché de nuit*. If you get fed up waiting, take a vehicle to Bourem (from the same *gare routière*) and try waiting there: some traffic crosses the desert as far as Bourem and turns west to Timbuktu. It's a lot easier to take one of the Bamako or Mopti buses as far as **Douentza**, where you can buy a seat in a 4WD heading north.

The route **north across the Sahara**, is generally considered safe as far as **Kidal** (you will find trucks going here at the *marché de nuit* and occasional buses with Bani Transports and Binke Transports), but consult the authorities in Kidal for the latest news about travelling further north. Kidal has three hotel-restaurants – *Motel Krutel*, *Campement les Dattiers/Chez Mathias* and *Gîte Amazar* – and an excellent website ⓦwww.kidal.info.

Auberge/Escale Saneye A few hundred metres from *Camping Bongo*. Dorms with fans, rooftop camping and two small Songhai rondavels. At weekends, this place fills up with traditional live music and dancing. CFA5500 per person, CFA3000 camping on the roof.

Bon Séjour Quartier Château, secteur 1 ☎ 282.03.30. A decent place with a bar and menu and a range of accommodation, from pricey air-conditioned rooms to good-value rooms with fan to cheap roof or camping spaces. Prices are negotiable and depend on the size of your party. Recommended. ❷

Camping Bongo Septième Quartier, signposted off the east side of the rte de l'Aeroport. Basic rooms with shared facilities in a *banco* building with a flat roof – excellent to sleep on – or, for the same price, an exotic Songhai tent in the courtyard. The energetic proprietress, Hawa, also makes excellent meals. CFA2000 per person to sleep in a room, on the roof, or in Songhai tent, CFA1000 to camp.

Camping Tizi-Mizi Quartier Château, secteur II, well outside town, on the rte de l'Aeroport ☎ 282.01.94. *Tizi-Mizi* offers s/c rooms, some with a/c, and also a number of unappealing, scorching hot bungalows (without fans). On the plus side, it has a large, safe parking area and a pleasant garden bar. Showers cost CFA1000 for non-residents. Camping CFA3500, ❸

Hôtel Askia Quartier Château ☎ 282.00.87. An easy-going place consisting of a large converted family house with a range of rooms – some s/c with a/c – and a small dorm and traditional Songhai tents in the garden. CFA7500 per tent for up to five people, dorm beds CFA4000, ❷

Hôtel le Bel Air Quartier Château, a 10min walk from the *Sahara Passion* ☎ 282.04.27. A mishmash of small rooms with fans, some s/c. A block further east, Bel Air's annexe has larger rooms (same price), a roof for camping (CFA2000) and a bar with a small stage hosting sporadic gigs. ❸

Hôtel Sahara Passion Quartier Château, secteur IV, clearly signposted off the rte de l'Aeroport ☎ 282.01.87, ⓦ www.sahara-passion.com. This is probably the best accommodation in town, run by a Swiss-Tuareg couple, offering a traditional flat-roofed *banco* building with a few rooms sharing facilities and some better s/c, a/c rooms. They also run a travel agency and organize trips in the desert. The restaurant, not the cheapest place in Gao, usually offers a choice of meals, sometimes very good, but quality varies. Camping CFA5000, ❹

Eating

Gao doesn't boast very classy **restaurants**, but has a few friendly and unpretentious places not to miss. The very central and inexpensive *Source du Nord*, in front of *Hôtel Atlantide*, is the best and most popular place with locals and tourists alike. The menu offers European and African dishes and they cook a delicious *couscous arabe* on Saturdays. *Restaurant Koundjido*, a few streets behind the *gare routière*, to the north, has good local cuisine including the regional yam stew – *ragoût d'igname*. *Auberge Saneye* and *Camping Bangou* also have good-value restaurants with an easy-going atmosphere. Cheaper still is a string of basic eating houses on the road running parallel to the Boulevard des Askias – two blocks east as you walk away from the river. And be sure to sample Gao's delicious, long spicy sausages – always a reliable evening street-food fallback.

South to Niamey

Although only 443km separate Gao and Niamey, the trip involves at least a very long day's drive, and as much as a week in the rains, or if you take it easy and stop off at the numerous fishing villages. The road hugs the banks of the **Niger** through some memorable scenery with palms, river views and dunes. It's a well-travelled route, but full of sandy pitfalls and thorn trees whose spines work their way through hot, soft rubber.

The initial 95km as far as **Ansongo** – a picturesque village with an important Thursday **market** – present few problems. The town is essentially Songhai, but you'll also see numerous Tuareg who make their way through the region. South of Ansongo, the road becomes progressively worse, with stretches of treacherous sand that may become impassable during the rains. Despite the difficulties, it's a beautiful stretch that the government has officially classified as a protected natural area. You have a good chance of seeing **hippos** at some point along the river: in many instances they come quite close to the villages and the areas where people swim. Several species of **gazelle** can occasionally be seen, and a small herd of **giraffe** also roam through the region, though you're unlikely to spot them from the *piste*.

The road continues tortuously until you arrive at Labbezanga, 191km from Gao, the Mali–Niger **border post** where you'll be subjected to protracted formalities. There's a bar near the customs post. It's another 44km to **Ayorou**, a large market town where you pass through Niger customs and the surfaced road begins, then a further 200km to Niamey via **Tillabéri**.

5

Cape Verde

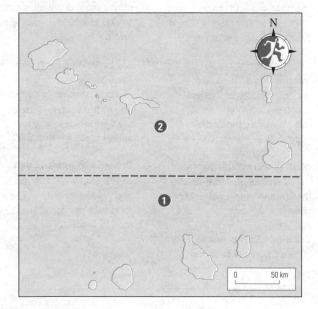

Cape Verde highlights

* **Cape Verde's music**
  Deliciously, impossibly sad; its echo will remain with you long after you've left the islands. See p.432

* **Cidade Velha** Picture-postcard streets and world heritage architecture in Cape Verde's oldest settlement. See p.446

* **Mount Fogo** The otherworldly beauty of this volcano will leave you as breathless as the ascent. See p.452

* **Fajã d'Agua** Cape Verde's most stunningly located and horizontally laid-back village. See p.456

* **Hiking in Santo Antão**
  There's scenery to make your head spin – and *grogue*-heavy hospitality to make it spin even more. See p.467

* **Pedra de Lume, Sal** The atmosphere of a Wild West movie set and the cinematic sweep of a hidden salt lake. See p.476

* **Santa Maria Beach, Sal** Cape Verde boasts many glorious beaches, and this is one of the best, with azure seas and excellent watersports facilities. See p.477

* **Driving around Boa Vista** Check your 4WD is sound and preferably take a guide for a truly remote off-road tour. See p.483

The Cape Verde Islands

From a traveller's viewpoint, and indeed a West African one, the Cape Verde Islands are barely on the map. If you ever hear of them, it's usually as an off-shore supplement to the grim process of desertification on the African main-land, 450km away. An Atlantic world apart, the archipelago falls in more neatly with the Azores, or even the Canary Islands.

The Cape Verdes consist of nine main islands in two groups, the **Barlaventos** (Windwards) and the **Sotaventos** (Leewards). Six of them – **Santiago, Fogo, Brava, São Nicolau, São Vicente** and **Santo Antão** – are volcanic and inspiringly scenic, while the three to the east – **Maio, Boa Vista** and **Sal** – are flat and sandy. Although the islands are isolated, they're not difficult to get around, with good ferries and an internal air service. There's usually some-where to stay, a small hotel or *pensão*, and prices are reasonable. Despite the **cost** of flights to the Cape Verdes, the islands are, emphatically, worth the hassle.

The Cape Verdes were uninhabited until first colonized by the **Portuguese** in 1462. The first Portuguese immigrants, who in the sixteenth century made the islands an Atlantic victualling station and entrepôt for the trade in African produce and **slaves**, were a mixed population of landless peas-ants, banished malefactors, adventurers and exiles. The islands were soon being culti-vated by the slaves and freed slaves who rapidly made up the bulk of the population.

But while the mixed race population that emerged was considered "assimilated" – accepted as Portuguese by Lisbon – the islanders suffered in various degrees from oppressive and racist policies. In Cape Verdean society there was great emphasis on skin colour, the criterion by which "real Portugueseness" was measured.

Commercial planting was mostly of cotton, woven into the *panos*, lengths of distinctive, banded blue-and-white cloth prized along the Guinea coastlands. But catastrophic **droughts** brought despair and neglect; for nearly the whole of their colonial period the islands remained a largely ignored back-water of the Portuguese empire. Over the last 150 years, tens of thousands of Cape Verdeans have left the islands for São Tomé, Guinea-Bissau, Senegal, Europe and the USA. The **New England connection** is especially strong, with *americanos* remitting the hard currency which the island families need.

The **feel** of the Cape Verde Islands is unplaceable – not quite African, scarcely European, but Portuguese mannered and

Fact file

The islands' name, **Cabo Verde** in Portuguese, derives from their position off Cap Vert, the Dakar peninsula of Senegal. Their total **land area**, just 4000 square kilome-tres, is about the same size as Kent or a little larger than Rhode Island. Less than 400,000 Cape Verdeans (under half the total population) now live on the islands, with the remainder living or working abroad.

In January 1991, Cape Verde was one of the first countries in the region to see democratic elections, with a peaceful transition from the PAICV single-party regime to the Movimento para a Democracia (MPD). Although the PAICV have since regained power, the multiparty system remains. Cape Verde's **foreign debt** is a severe test of its resources, yet at about £190 million ($300 million) in 2001, it's less than half its annual gross domestic product of about £400 million ($650 million).

Maize is the islands' staple crop, and cultivation of cassava, sugar cane, potatoes, bananas and papayas is also important, though viable agricultural land is in such short supply that a significant proportion of the food consumed is imported. Tourism is the fastest growing sector of the economy.

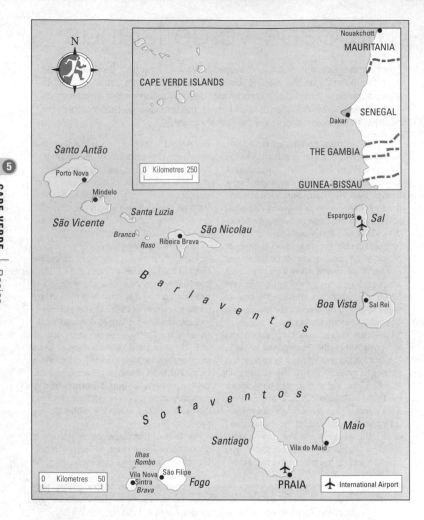

Kriolu-speaking (an African/Portuguese creole). The islands are no tropical paradise – banish any Caribbean associations. The most recent **drought**, which lasted from the early 1970s to 1985, brought malnutrition and hardships which only worsened the country's economic plight in the first decade of independence. But some good rainy seasons in recent years have seen the islands increasingly green – especially on their northern windward slopes. Several have interiors resembling anything but deserts, with towering, cloud-drenched peaks and ravines choked with vegetation. The **coasts** vary from white sands against metallic, azure blue to full-tempered Atlantic seas on black cliffs. Inland, the **roads** are for the most part steep, winding and cobbled, as if harking back to pre-motor days; **trees** are baobab, silk-cotton and breadfruit, coconut and date palm. **People** distil *grogue* from sugar cane, fish for huge tuna, and strum out mournful *mornas* on the right occasions. Rip-offs and hustle seem almost unknown. In the few small, tidily colonial-style **towns**, each clustered around a central square – the *praça* –

you'll find restless teenagers perched on mopeds, widows in black going to Mass and potted plants on the window ledges. The towns on most of the islands are referred to simply as *povoação* – "the town". Except on Santiago island, which has several towns, there could be no confusion.

Where to go

Where to go in Cape Verde is a fairly simple matter – in a few weeks you can get to most of the islands and see a good deal of each one. If you've any choice in the matter try to allow for unplanned delays. Some islands – **Santiago** for its size, **Santo Antão** and **Fogo** for their stunning scenery, **Maio** and **Boa Vista** for their beaches – may hold you longer than others, but they're all small enough to be quickly graspable.

When to go

The best time to visit Cape Verde is probably **October and November**, when the vegetative results of a successful rainy season are truly verdant, the islands' name suddenly no longer ironic. The first five months of the year before the anticipated July to October summer rains are not ideal because of the dry, dusty conditions. From April to June, the higher reaches of the mountainous islands are often blanketed in cold fog. If the rains come, splendid thunderstorms and torrents of water across the roads are the norm, though they shouldn't hinder your travels if you're visiting during this season. Between December and March it can be unpleasantly windy, especially in the northeast part of the archipelago, as harmattan winds blow across from the Sahara.

Exceptions to the above guidelines would be special visits to São Vicente, either for the annual Mindelo *Carnaval*, a riot of Rio-style floats, costumes and small-scale street entertainment which takes over the town every February, or for the August music festival.

Getting there from the rest of Africa

With no ferry services running from the African coast, **flying** to the islands is the only way of reaching them – unless you have an ocean-going yacht. Most flights from the African mainland are to the capital, Praia, on Santiago island. Flights from **Dakar to Praia**, operated by Air Sénégal and TACV, are usually full and routinely overbooked; both companies fly three times a week in both directions. The cheapest official round-trip fare is CFA160,000 (£170/US$270), though Air Sénégal offer students and over-65s an impressive 45 percent discount. TACV offer students (and seamen) a 25 percent discount. Make a reservation as soon as you can and be sure to reconfirm your seat a couple of days before – or to make a strong impression in the office in Dakar. Although the introduction of an upgraded reservations system should mean that in theory things should run smoothly, "confirmed" seats on a ticket purchased in Europe are no guarantee. Check again when you get to Dakar.

The exception to the rule that flights from Africa land at Praia are the handful of flights to **Sal** from **Johannesburg** with South African Airways. There are currently no flights to Cape Verde from Guinea-Bissau and The Gambia.

Average temperatures and rainfall											
PRAIA											
Temperatures °C	Jan	Feb	Mar	Apr	May	June	July	Aug	Sept	Oct	Nov	Dec
Min (night)	20	19	19	20	21	22	23	23	24	23	22	20
Max (day)	27	28	29	29	30	30	30	30	31	31	30	27
Rainfall mm	2	0	0	0	0	1	8	76	102	30	10	2

For important practical information applying to all West African countries, covering health, transport, cultural hints and more, plus details on getting to the region from beyond Africa, see Basics, pp.9–87.

TACV run a weekly flight to Sal from **Las Palmas** in the Canary Islands; this operates in both directions on Sunday and costs CV$34,000 return (around £210/$325). If you're in Las Palmas, you might check around the **yachts** for anyone headed to the Cape Verdes. During the east–west transatlantic crossing season, roughly from October to March, hundreds make the journey and they invariably call at the "Verdes". Even without experience, it's possible to get a berth in exchange for some basic crewing and boat chores. Expect to pay the skipper around $15 per day for your keep.

Red tape and visas

All nationalities require **visas** to visit Cape Verde. There are few Cape Verdean consulates and no diplomatic representation in Britain. The easiest place in Europe to get a visa is the embassy in Lisbon (Av do Restelo 33; ☎+351 3019521, ☎3015308). In West Africa the only consulate is in Dakar in Senegal (see p.198).

Once you've found a consulate, visas are no problem. In Dakar, you should be able to get one in a matter of hours, with three passport photos. Be sure to check when you're supposed to come back, as the office may keep slightly irregular hours. If you arrive on the islands without a visa, experience suggests you're unlikely to be turned away, as your immediate point of departure probably had no Cape Verde consulate in any case (airlines in cities with consulates will normally ask to see your visa before issuing a ticket). If you fly in on an unusual route, or arrive by sea, you can invariably obtain a visa relatively simply at the immigration desk for CV$2500, though you may need to wait if quite a few people have arrived visa-less. Should your onward travel within Cape

Verde require a really tight connection, it's best to try to get a visa in advance.

The easiest solution for **UK residents** is to contact the extremely helpful and well-informed specialist Cape Verde Travel, 10 Market Street, Hornsea, HU18 1AW (☎01964/536 191, ☎www.capeverdetravel .co.uk). If you use their services, they will fax your details ahead to Sal to simplify the issue of a visa on arrival, though as ever, allow a reasonable interval for this to happen if you're planning to catch a connecting flight to another island.

A further point to note is that, frustratingly, visas are normally only valid for a week. If you're planning on staying longer, you'll have to get your **visa renewed** at either the Direcção de Imigração e Fronteira in Praia (see p.445 for contact details) or any local police station.

On **duty-free allowances** of alcohol and tobacco, there's a simple rule: none. But the principle is not adhered to and, in practice, reasonable personal quantities are fine. There's rarely much of a customs check anyway.

Costs, money and banks

Cape Verde's currency is the Cape Verdean **escudo** (CV$). On the islands, it's usual to put the dollar sign after the number of escudos – thus 500$00 means 500 escudos; centavos account for the zeros. You'll frequently encounter 200 and 500 escudo notes, and coins of 100, 50, 20 and 10 escudos (with the occasional 200 escudo coin). A **conto** is 1000 escudos.

Cape Verde is not a cheap destination, though your **outlay** will very much depend on how and how much you travel between islands. The flight network is not inexpensive and travel costs can quickly break into even fairly generous budgets (see p.414 for more on this and information on **air passes**, which must be bought abroad). Ferries are cheaper but don't offer the same flexibility. Road travel is inexpensive but the cost of exploring those islands which don't have much public transport can soon mount up.

A basic room in the very cheapest type of *pensão* will cost upwards of £6/$10 and a straightforward three-course meal goes from about £3/$5, with individual dishes in fancier establishments costing about the same.

Visiting half a dozen islands in three weeks, keeping flights to a minimum, staying in the cheapest *pensões* and restricting yourself to one restaurant meal a day, you'd likely spend £35/$55 a day, somewhat less if you're sharing rooms and much less if you spend any time hiking and camping. **Prices** are much lower outside the few main towns, but noticably higher where there are international connections or a whiff of tourism (Sal, Praia itself, São Vicente, Fogo, Boa Vista). Save for any dealings with the ubiquitous Senegalese traders, you won't save much by **bargaining** either. This is hard to accept at first, if you've grown accustomed to West Africa's noisy exchanges of mock outrage, but it makes life more relaxed and seems entirely appropriate in Cape Verde's almost hassle-free environment.

At the time of writing, it looks likely that the government will introduce **VAT** at a rate of around fifteen percent in April 2004.

Banks and exchange

The escudo is pegged at a fixed **exchange rate** with the euro, CV$110 = €1 and is fairly stable against other currencies: CV$160 = £1, CV$110 = US$1. Escudos are not convertible outside Cape Verde so buy currency upon arrival. There's a bank at Sal airport but not at Praia's, so if you're arriving at Praia, have low-denomination dollar or euro notes to pay for a taxi ride into town.

The Banco Comercial do Atlântico is the most useful bank, with branches in most towns and all island capitals. They normally take traveller's cheques in all major currencies and service is reasonably efficient. Larger hotels also accept traveller's cheques with commission charges pretty standard at around CV$1000. The limited **black market** isn't worth bothering with; at most you'll add a few percent to your spending power as the rates are normally exactly the same as the bank's. Western Union money transfers are handled by branches of Caixa Económica.

Credit cards

Credit cards don't help much on the islands. The big tourist hotels in Santa Maria, on Sal, usually take Amex, Visa and MasterCard, but they're about the only establishments that will. You'll be routinely charged around CV$500 for most transactions. Local ATMs do not accept foreign cards, although banks pay cash advances on credit cards at a cost of CV$1000 per transaction.

Health

Arriving direct from outside Africa, you don't need any inoculations. Coming from the mainland, cholera and yellow fever certificates are routinely demanded, though you may get away without a yellow fever certificate if you're connecting straight through to São Vicente, Sal, Maio or Boa Vista.

One of the health successes of Cape Verde has been the virtual elimination of **malaria**. Until the nineteenth century a posting to the islands from Portugal was viewed as one step short of a death sentence. Now, all planes arriving from Africa get insect-sprayed before any passengers are allowed off and all visitors are issued with a health card asking them to report any fever they get on the islands. Only parts of Santiago have a malaria risk and few people use anti-malaria pills. If you're on Cape Verde for a short time only, however, and planning to return to the mainland, you shouldn't break your course.

Water from the tap is almost always safe but water shortages mean that you'll sometimes be drinking water that's been stored or sold, so beware (eighty people died of **cholera** in Mindelo in 1995). And be sparing too: islanders pay for tap water, which is metered, and big price increases are common during droughts. Bottled brands are widely available.

Health care on the islands isn't bad and while infant mortality is still high, life expectancy, at 70, is very impressive. **Leprosy** is still a big problem on Fogo, but not one that will affect your own health. Surprisingly few people **smoke** – though it's a habit enjoyed in pipes by elderly ladies in rural Santiago. Litter bins and enjoinments to social responsibility are features of urban life and Praia is a refreshingly clean capital.

There are **hospitals** in Praia and Mindelo with adequate facilities for ordinary problems. Dispensaries, cottage hospitals and pharmacies (*farmácia*) exist in most towns or, failing these, *postos venda medicamentos* (health posts) should fulfil basic needs. If, on your travels, you had the misfortune to get ill, Cape Verde would be a good place to **convalesce**. Low humidity, sea breezes and clear skies are the norm.

Information, websites and maps

Cape Verde has no tourist offices abroad and the few embassies and consulates have either nothing or the most limited leaflets.

Websites

ⓦ **www.umassd.edu/specialprograms /caboverde** Plenty of useful links to CapeVerde–related information at this excellent (if not always up-to-date) site hosted by the University of Massachusetts at Dartmouth.

ⓦ **www.caboverde.com** An Italian tourist-oriented site, although many descriptions are in English; not bad for pictures of places to stay around the islands.

ⓦ **www.caboverde24.com** A decent portal and search engine, great for up-to-the-minute news and weather. It also features lists of both recommended and new sites.

ⓦ **www.cvmusicworld.com** Slick site dedicated both to documenting the islands' musical history and supporting current artists.

ⓦ **www.caboverdeonline.com** Features some insightful articles written by ordinary Cape Verdeans and useful introductions to the island's history, politics, demographics etc.

Maps

There's an increasing number of reasonably priced good-quality **maps** coming onto the market from Germany. Freytag & Berndt publish a general 1:80,000 sheet of the archipelago while a more professional 1:150,000 map is produced by Reise Know-How. Superior 1:50,000 hiking maps of both Santo Antão and São Nicolau, complete with photos and marked routes, are produced by Goldstadt Wanderkarte. In Cape Verde itself, Promex/Tectoplaca-produced maps of Santiago, Sal and São Vicente are fairly easy to get hold of. They include detailed town plans of Praia, Mindelo and Santa Maria, and are usually available from the Promex kiosks for CV$300 each or direct from Tectoplaca, 14 rua do Tejo, Mindelo (☎ & ℱ32.22.18).

Getting around

The most important inter-island connections are by **plane**, with **ferries** providing a good alternative if you have more time. Except on Santiago, **road transport** on the islands is fairly limited.

Domestic flights

All the inhabited islands are linked by **internal flights** run by Transportes Aereos de Cabo Verde (TACV); details are given later in this chapter. Fares range from CV$4000–9000 one-way (£25–60/$40–95). It's worth considering a **Cabo Verde Air Pass**, which must be purchased abroad in conjunction with a TACV ticket to the islands. The pass is valid for 22 days and comprises anything from two flight coupons (£115/$185) to ten flight coupons (£320/$510), with child (67 percent) and infant (10 percent) rates.

It's important to reserve seats as far ahead as possible, as flights are usually full; always reconfirm your seat if it's been booked for more than 24 hours. It's often possible, even when there's no direct flight, to get where you want to on the same day with a little island hopping. Note however that international arrivals delayed into Sal airport can sometimes knock the whole domestic service out of joint, as domestic planes may be delayed for connecting passengers.

Ferries

Three German-built **ferries**, *Barlavento*, *Sotavento* (currently out of action) and the new *Praia D'Aguada* run weekly services through the islands, though schedules are variable and difficult to pin down precisely. From its home port of Mindelo on São

Vicente, the *Praia D'Aguada* sails to São Nicolau, Sal, Praia, Fogo, Brava and back to Mindelo or, in the other direction, to Praia, Sal, São Nicolau and back to Mindelo. Some weeks, however, this ferry travels from Mindelo to Praia, Fogo and Brava before heading back to Mindelo. In theory, the *Praia D'Aguada* departs Mindelo on Monday and returns there on a Friday or Saturday.

The *Barlavento* and *Sotavento* sail from Brava to Praia and back, via Fogo most of the time; some weeks they also make forays out to Maio and Boa Vista. While the short hop between Brava and Fogo takes around an hour and a half, the crossing between Fogo and Praia comes in at roughly fifteen hours. Exact timings for all three ships always depend on cargo requirements, however (the vessels are primarily supply ships), and, of course, on the weather. The big question is which itinerary is operating in any given week. If you want to plan ahead before arriving in Cape Verde, the Companhia Nacional de Navegação Arca Verde (see p.439 for contact details) can provide the latest details, but even they may not know which itinerary will be in force more than a month in advance. Agenamar (the Fogo ferry travel agency), meanwhile, have usually got an up-to-date (in theory) timetable of ferries running from Fogo to Brava and Praia posted on ⓦ www.caboverde.com.

Other principal services

The **Ribeira de Paúl** and **Mar Novo** sail at least daily between Mindelo (São Vicente) and Porto Novo (Santo Antão), the crossing taking about one hour. The former leaves Mindelo at 7.30am and Porto Novo at 10.30am every day except Sunday when there's no sailing; the latter departs Mindelo at 8am and Porto Novo at 10.30am every day except Sunday when the times are 9am and 5pm respectively. In Mindelo, tickets for the *Mar Novo* can be purchased from Somatrans (see Mindelo "Listings", p.445, for address) while in Porto Novo, both Somatrans and Silva & Silva (the company who run the *Ribeira de Paúl*) have offices near the harbour. Prices are CV$500 one-way and CV$1000 return.

Practicalities

Deck berths are cheap (roughly CV$1000–3000) and insalubrious. Cape Verdeans are surprisingly poor sailors and the seas usually rough, leading to results which keep the crew occupied with mops and buckets (it may be worth your while taking seasickness tablets). Available at just under twice the price of a deck berth are comfortable four-berth **cabins**, with sinks and secure lockers. You'll find that cabin berths are often left unsold, giving you a private cabin and, in effect, a budget cruise. With a little planning you can spend the days visiting islands and nights aboard the pitching, rolling vessel. This kind of travel doesn't give you much time ashore, but its great advantage is cheapness and – assuming you can handle the seas – an unexpected degree of luxury.

A few considerations: there's not much **food** for sale on board (though you can usually buy cold beers from the tiny bar area), no safe **drinking water** (bring your own in case the bar's supply runs out) and **no showers** save for a communal shower on the smarter *Praia D'Aguada*, so be inventive with the hand basins.

Buses, taxis and hitching

Compared with getting between them, **getting around each island** is relatively straightforward: the longest land journey is less than 100km, on Santiago, and in practice most trips take under an hour. On some islands, however, transport is infrequent to and from outlying villages.

Minibuses called **carrinhos** (but usually known simply as "Hiace" after the popular Toyota vehicles) and trucks with bench seating in the back (occasionally with a tarpaulin over them but usually open to the elements) have replaced nearly all the large buses that used to cover the islands. These vehicles operate wherever there's sufficient demand and usually carry a sign in red marked **aluguer** – "for hire". They're very inexpensive (rarely more than CV$200) although you'll normally have to wait until the vehicle is full before the journey begins; in practice this rarely takes more than half an hour.

Carrinhos are also available for private hire which is much more expensive – reckon on CV$40 per kilometre, the rate rising to CV$50 at night. Unsurprisingly, many drivers are usually very keen on this arrangement, especially when dealing with tourists. In more rural areas in particular, they'll try and tell you the public services have finished for the day. While this may be true, don't take their word for it. Tell them explicitly you want a **coletivo** (public bus) and be prepared to walk away or hang around for a bit in the hope that they change their tune.

A ride in a **particular** ("private") **taxi** or car costs about the same as hiring a *carrinho* privately. For an extended charter, however, (often referred to as a **deslocação**), expect to pay CV$3000–4000 per half-day; this can be a viable option for inaccessible places on the smaller islands.

Hitching, when there are any vehicles, is easy and drivers *simpatico* – though habitually reckless. The lack of traffic gives some drivers a vivid sense of immortality, but the combination of tortuous bends and precipices with cobbled roads is perilous. Be confident in saying "*devagar*" ("slow down"). It's normal to pay for lifts when hitching, though it won't always be expected – agree in advance.

Car rental and cycling

The **car rental** business in Cape Verde is small but growing in line with tourism. This is especially noticeable on Sal where international companies like Hertz and Avis have moved in. Outside of Sal, the largest choice of outlets is in Praia and Mindelo; the small local operations on the more outlying islands are not very impressive, but at least they're

not overpriced. Deposits are normally around the CV$20,000 mark, occasionally as much as CV$30,000 (in cash). Credit card guarantees aren't required. **Fuel costs** are standardized at CV$100/litre for petrol (gasoline) and CV$60/litre for diesel fuel.

Cape Verde is wonderful **cycling** territory for the fit and fanatical and, in view of the gradients, not to mention the cobblestone roads, obviously suited to mountain bikes.

Accommodation

Putting your head down for the night is a simple business. You will usually find a Portuguese-style *pension* (**pensão**, plural **pensões**) or **residencial** (plural *residencias*) offering clean, down-to-earth accommodation – often with a fan, though bathrooms are usually shared – for CV$1000–1500 for a room.

Ask to see several rooms and perhaps ask "*Tem um quarto mais barato?*" ("Do you have a cheaper room?") Full-scale hotels – with hot water, private bath, air conditioning and restaurants – are increasingly common, with rooms starting from around CV$2500 and rising to CV$8000 or more in a few establishments.

It is often assumed that you'll know about the twelve o'clock **checkout** rule, sometimes applied quite ruthlessly. Hotels, especially, will try hard to make you pay an extra half- or whole day if you haven't vacated on time. That said, many people will allow you to leave your bags behind the desk for a few hours if your onward travel is later in the day.

In smaller towns you may have to ask to locate your accommodation: everyone

---

Accommodation price codes

All accommodation prices in this chapter are coded according to the following scale, whose equivalent in pounds sterling/US dollars is used throughout the book. Prices refer to the rate you can expect to pay for a room with two beds. Single rooms, or single occupancy, will normally cost at least two-thirds of the twin-occupancy rate.

❶ Under CV$750 (under £5/$8).	❺ CV$3000–4500 (£20–30/$32–48).
❷ CV$750–1500 (£5–10/$8–16).	❻ CV$4500–6000 (£30–40/$48–64).
❸ CV$1500–2250 (£10–15/$16–24).	❼ CV$6000–7500 (£40–50/$64–80).
❹ CV$2250–3000 (£15–20/$24–32).	❽ Over CV$7500 (£50/$80).

knows where the lodgings are, and sign-posting is often absent. This may apply particularly in the case of the local *pousada municipal* – the town resthouse – where you may need to track down the landlord for the key. Such places are usually very basic and cheap.

Cape Verde has no youth hostels or campsites. Surprisingly perhaps, truly wild country suitable for camping – as opposed to marginal agricultural land – isn't plentiful. Still, as an eccentric foreigner you'll be happily tolerated if you camp in the neighbourhood. You're likely, anyway, to have an opportunity to ask permission when you collect water.

Eating and drinking

It would be surprising if Cape Verde had an extensive and flourishing cuisine: with severe malnutrition and famines that killed tens of thousands in living memory, the question of food has tended to concentrate on the number of calories – and in respect of variety most mainland countries can do a lot better than the islands. Still, the dishes on offer are a wholesome and always filling selection, probably little changed since the sixteenth century.

Apart from the big hotels in Sal, Praia and Mindelo, and a handful of restaurants where you'll get a decent variety of unremarkable international fare as well as local dishes, the choice is always strictly limited. In smaller towns the *pensões* usually serve meals somewhere in the building, but a **casa de pasto** (dining room/diner) is the standard, and often unmarked, place to eat. You eat what they have, the *prato do dia* (dish of the day), which as often as not will be *cachupa* (see box, overleaf), the national dish, the name of which is believed to derive from the same African term that resulted in "catsup/ketchup".

Staples include rice, potatoes (ordinary and sweet), beans, maize, squash, pork and – inevitably – tuna. Meals often start with a solid vegetable broth and finish with fruit, occasionally *pudim* (crème caramel).

Unfortunately, **vegetarians** will have to make do with omelette and chips most nights. On the plus side, eggs are wholly free-range and usually delicious, as are the home-made chips. As an alternative, you can risk the *cachupa*; just ask if it contains any meat. Also, in large towns like Mindelo and Praia you can vary your diet with some quality pizza.

Drinking

When it comes to drinking, Cape Verdeans usually think first of **grogue** or *canna* (sugar cane distillates known collectively with other spirits as *aguardente*), which get consumed – and apparently made at home – in large quantities. A cautious approach is recommended when trying a *copa* (glass): liquor often comes from anonymous bottles and sacking-wrapped jars and you're never quite sure what the effect will be. There are "new" (*novo*) and "old" (*velho*) varieties and different degrees of smoothness. It's usually clean, but even so can be quite deadly, gasping stuff. "Punch" (*ponche*, *panche*) – a concoction of dark rum, honey and lemonade – is, like *aguardente*, often on sale over the counter in rural shops. It's not an ideal midday thirst quencher.

Beer (*cerveja*) is still largely imported from Portugal – Sagres, and to a lesser extent, Superbock – but Praia has a brewery (Ceris) and bottles of very malty Coral are now available in the bars and cafés. Some establishments serve the above beers on draught but they are often slightly flat – ask for a *cleps* (a glass of beer). Ceris also makes soft drinks. For juices ask for **sumo** – *de laranja*, *limão*, etc.

Wine has some potential on the islands as a significant industry, but the remarkably heavy, spicy, red product of Fogo's volcanic slopes doesn't inspire much enthusiasm just yet. Reasonably inexpensive **imports** of Portugal's favourites can be found in most bars and groceries.

Coffee is by and large of a fair standard and usually freshly brewed. At breakfast it's usually served with a pitcher of hot milk but beware of the awful concoctions served in some of the cheapest *pensões*. Angola once supplied a lot, but Fogo's own more recent contribution isn't that great; it's often stale or mixed with chicory. Santo Antão, meanwhile, produces some wonderfully mellow beans which you can purchase direct from the villages.

Portuguese and Kriolu food terms

English	Portuguese/Kriolu	English	Portuguese/Kriolu
Beans	*Feijões*	Carne de vaca	Beef
Bread	*Pão*	Coelho	Rabbit
Bread roll	*Bolho*	Espadarte	Swordfish
Butter	*Manteiga*	Feijoada/	Beans and salt
Cheese	*Queijo*	Feijão Congo	pork
(usually goat)		Frango	Chicken
Coffee	*Café*	Langosta	"Lobster"; strictly
Eggs	*Ovos*		cray fish
Fish	*Peixe*	Lapas	Tiny mussels,
Food	*Comida*		usually in
Jam/marmalade	*Marmelade*		a spicy sauce
Maize/corn	*Milho*	Licuda/linguiça	Sausage
Meat	*Carne*	Linguado	Sole
Menu	*Ementa*	Polvo	Octopus
Milk	*Leite*	Prato do dia	Dish of the day
Pork	*Carne de porco*	Tubarão	Shark
Potatoes	*Batatas*		
Rice	*Arroz*	**Terms**	
Salt	*Sal*	Assado	Roasted
Shellfish	*Mariscos*	Bife	Steak or cutlet,
Soup/broth	*Sopa*	Bife de Atum	as in
Squash	*Abóbora*	Cozido	Boiled
Sugar	*Açúcar*	Frito	Fried
Tea	*Chá*	Molho	Sauce
Tuna	*Atum*	Piri piri	Hot sauce
Vegetables	*Legumes*		
Water	*Agua*	**Fruit and snacks**	
Yams	*Inhames*	Banana	*Banana*
		Guava	*Goyaba*
Dishes		Orange	*Laranja*
Cachupa	A mash of beans	Mango	*Manga*
	and maize,	Watermelon	*Melancia*
	sometimes	Melon	*Melão*
	with bacon and	Pawpaw	*Papaya*
	sausage, eaten	Dates	*Tâmaras*
	primarily at	Grapefruit	*Toranja*
	breakfast	Breadfruit	*Frutapão*
Cachupinha	Similar to	Fish cakes	*Croquetes*
	cachupa,	Dessert/sweet	*Doce*
	with green bits	Ice cream	*Gelado*
Caldeirada de	Fish stew	Yoghurt	*Iorgurte/Yaourt*
peixe		Pies	*Pasteles*

Communications

Post in Cape Verde is run by the **CTT**, or simply Correio, while telecommunications are handled by **Cabo Verde Telecom**. There's at least one **correio** (post office) on each island, usually open Monday to Friday 8am to noon and 2.30pm to 5.30pm. **Post**, both outgoing and incoming, is generally efficient and honest though not especially swift. For poste restante have your mail marked "Lista da Correios".

If you have **urgent mail** for home to post from one of the more isolated islands, apply the appropriate postage and try taking it to the local airstrip for the next flight to Sal, or even ask at the local TACV office if someone could give it to the pilot – people are usually understanding.

Telephoning locally has become much more significant now that there are solar-powered cardphone boxes (which don't take coins) in most towns and villages. IDD is now available to most countries; dial ⊕00 then the country code. Phones are often out of order, however, while some booths (in Sal Rei, Boa Vista, for instance) have had the phones removed completely. **Phone cards** are available from CV Telecom offices (there is one in every large town; Mon–Fri 8am–noon & 2.30–5.30pm) as well as Shell garages and certain shops, bars and restaurants in values of CV\$250 and CV\$750.

If you are calling abroad, a single phone card won't pay for more than a few minutes, so it's more convenient to use the public phones available in most post offices. You pay the clerk after finishing the call but be aware that costs are fairly high. Off-peak rates (8pm to 7am and all weekend) are CV\$144 per minute to the US, Canada and Europe, CV\$192 to other Portuguese-speaking countries, and CV\$242 per minute to most other countries. The international operator is on ⊕111. You can't normally make reverse charge/collect calls.

Mobile phones are as popular in Cape Verde as they are elsewhere, and the operator CVMovel has many roaming partners. Local SIM cards can be bought from the CV Mobiles office at Sal airport as well as in most of the larger towns.

Online services are relatively abundant in Cape Verde with at least one Internet café in every large town and two or three in places like Praia and Mindelo. The cost is usually CV\$250 per hour although some places may want you to pre-pay for fifteen- or thirty-minute periods.

The media

Radio and TV are important in Cape Verdean culture, with the national Rádio Televisão de Cabo Verde handling both formats. The TV arm broadcasts an eclectic mix of Brazilian soap operas, European football and right-on documentaries while the radio broadcasts on FM (in Portuguese and Kriolu) with an enlightened playlist. There's also the government-run Voz de São Vicente, and the Portuguese-run cable-TV channel RTP Africa is ubiquitous.

The **press** consists of two weekly newspapers: the privately owned *A Semana* and the state-run *Horizonte*. There's also the weekly, Mindelo-based *O Cidadão* and a decent arts and culture publication, *Artiletra*. Portuguese is easier to read than to speak, which is just as well, as foreign papers are virtually unobtainable.

Entertainment

There's little in the way of an organized leisure industry – less than a handful of cinemas in Praia and Mindelo and no theatre to speak of. Portuguese bullfighting was never established. The game of *orzil* or *oril* (see p.87) is popular everywhere, as is draughts or chequers.

The commonest entertainments are home-spun – births, baptisms, confirmations, marriages and funerals providing occasions for gathering together. In the evenings it's quite the thing for young people to meet in the town square (*praça*) with a guitar or two.

Cape Verdean **music** (see p.432) is becoming increasingly well known abroad, with an increasing number of CDs available generally – notably those by **Cesaria Evora**. The islands have a number of nightclubs (*boites*), a clutch of which are regular venues for live music (*musica ao vivo*), as are certain restaurants. More often than not, however, you'll stumble spontaneously upon the best music in the most unlikely and out-of-the-way places. Most towns also have a decent **record shop**; CDs are priced in the CV\$1,500–2,000 range.

Opening hours, public holidays and festivals

Most shops and businesses are open from about 8am to noon and again from 3 to 7 or 8pm, Monday to Friday; on Saturday they close at noon for the weekend. Lunch hours are long and lazy and *everything* closes, even – curiously and frustratingly – many bars and cafés.

Cape Verde follows the main **Catholic holidays** (Dec 8, Immaculate Conception; Jan 1, Circumcision of Our Lord; Aug 15, Assumption; Nov 1, All Saints' Day), with some local additions: National Heroes' Day (Jan 20), Labour Day (May 1), Independence Day (July 5). There's a whole host of other days off – including any number of saints' days and a major **Carnaval** every February in Mindelo, emulated in the same month by Praia.

In addition, **annual festivals** with horse and mule races, discos, bands and more than the usual *grogue* consumption take place on many islands, including Boa Vista (June 24), Brava (June 24), Fogo (April 20), Maio (early May), Sal (Sept 15), Santo Antão (early June), São Vicente (May 3, June 13 and August – the last of these is a three-day music festival; see p.467). They generally last about a week.

Crime and personal safety

It's hard to imagine getting into any **trouble** in Cape Verde, where etiquette has grown out of the combination of Latin manners and West African social convention that you'd expect. You're just as unlikely to be a victim of **crime**. While theft is not unknown, the islands are one of the safest places in the world for absent-minded travellers. Even long-term expatriates agree on this, which must say something – though they tend to single out Praia as an exception.

Though Cape Verde is a largely tolerant country, **drug use** carries a strong stigma in the close-knit island communities and doesn't go unnoticed. While quite a few youngish men smoke home-grown weed, you could expect a barrel-load of trouble if seen doing so by the wrong people. **Nudity** and **topless bathing** are pretty well out of the question and particularly ill-advised for unaccompanied women.

Women's issues

Women travellers will find the Cape Verde Islands relaxed after mainland West Africa.

While **sexual attitudes** do contain an element of machismo, it's normally expressed as nothing much stronger than winks, whistles, stares and strong expectations that you *will* dance. It can also come across as almost absurdly innocent: heavy sexual pestering is unusual. Younger women, travelling without men, may find that their "unmarried condition" gives them almost adolescent social status, which can be frustrating. But, with the possible exception of Praia, the towns are too small for problems to last long.

As for the lives of **Cape Verdean women**, little seems to have changed despite the government's commitments to reducing sex discrimination and promoting their rights and welfare. Yet there are good reasons why change is needed: the continued emigration involves mostly men, and there are now 108 women for every 100 men, leaving many households where rural women are the de facto heads. The Organizão das Mulheres de Cabo Verde (Rua Unidade Guiné-Cabo Verde, Praia; ☎61.24.55) is quite active and the main contact-making body.

Directory

Airport departure tax Included in the ticket price.

Contraceptives You can get condoms (*preservativas* or, more colourfully, *camisas de vênus*) from most pharmacies and *postos venda medicamentos*.

Emergencies Police ☎132; medical emergencies require a hospital: ☎130.

Photography When taking pictures of Cape Verdeans, ordinary courtesy is your only restraint: you'll rarely be asked for payment.

Place names On the islands, Cape Verde is called Cabo Verde (Cáu Berde in Kriolu), the people Cauberdianos. It's not uncommon on Santiago, however, to hear people referring to "Cabo Verde" when they mean Santiago, as if it was the mainland, while referring somewhat dismissively to the other Cape Verdes as "as Ilhas" – the islands. Many towns and villages are called Ribeira something, which just means River – understandable where fresh water is so important. Tarrafal is another common name; every island seems to have its Tarrafal – which makes it useful to know which one's being referred to. There's a good deal of rivalry between the islands, with competition between the people of the Barlaventos – who see themselves as more urbane and metropolitan – and the Sotaventos where, in Santiago particularly, a larger proportion of the population are descended from slaves. There are subtle cultural variations from island to island too, with differences in the local form of Kriolu. Look out too, as you travel, for the characteristic women's headscarf style – tied differently on each island.

Religion Cape Verdeans are mostly Catholic, although American Protestant churches have made some headway since independence. There's probably quite a lot to be learned about the process of Islam's arrival and spread in West Africa from the fact that it's completely unknown in the Cape Verdes. It's likely that Islam hadn't made much impression in the African peasant communities from which slaves were commonly taken between the fifteenth and eighteenth centuries.

Tampons Usually available from larger general stores, but not easily outside the main towns.

Water sports There's some good snorkelling in places and exciting diving in a number of wreck-strewn shallows, notably off Boa Vista and Sal. Cape Verde's windsurfing is some of the ocean's most challenging. The big centre (though not, in fact, big at all) is Santa Maria on Sal island (see p.477). Sal Rei on Boa Vista is now growing in importance.

Wildlife Cape Verde's native fauna is a meagre show, with no large mammals and few outstanding birds. There are monkeys on Santiago and Brava. Herpetologists are excited by Tarentola giganta (the giant gecko) and the Cape Verde Island skink (another relative giant) but disappointed at the total absence of snakes. Bird-watchers might want to go out of their way to spot the Razo Island lark, though non-specialists will find it fairly uninteresting. The seas are more rewarding, with good chances of seeing dolphins, whales, turtles and amazing flying fish.

A brief history of Cape Verde

The Cape Verde Islands blew out of the Atlantic in a series of volcanic eruptions during the Miocene period some 60 million years ago – though Maio, Sal and Boa Vista may be a geological extension of the African mainland. The islands were uninhabited (so far as is known) until 1462, making the country unique in West Africa. In the gloriously clumsy eloquence of Adriano Moreira, Portugal's Overseas Minister from 1961–62, the Cape Verdes were "islands asleep since the eve of time, waiting to be able to be Portugal". After five centuries of such paternalism, the turn of recent events has been remarkably peaceful.

Discovery and colonization

Although African sailors may have visited the islands in earlier centuries, it was a Genoese navigator, **Antonio da Noli**, working for Prince Henry of Portugal, who discovered and first documented Santiago (which he called São Tiago – St James) and four other islands, some 500km off Africa's Cap Vert, in 1455. Three more in the northwest (Santo Antão, São Nicolau and São Vicente) were reached by Diogo Afonso in 1461. Santiago, by far the biggest prize, was split between the two navigators, who were granted a captaincy each: da Noli set himself up at **Ribeira Grande** in the south and Afonso made his headquarters in the northwest. Slaves were brought from the African mainland to work the parcels of land allotted the handful of immigrants, and in the capital, Ribeira Grande, work began on a cathedral. The Portuguese crown viewed the new extension of empire – 2500km from Lisbon – with indifference: the archipelago could serve as a stepping stone to exotic riches, and it would certainly do as a penal colony.

Fogo was settled in the 1480s and its western region was singled out as one of the most likely productive areas on the islands – rolling, partly wooded country, with substantial rainfall in most years.

But Fogo islanders were forbidden to trade with foreign ships – a right reserved by Santiago – and the island was considered a hardship post for the Portuguese officials sent there. By the end of the sixteenth century its population had barely reached two thousand and there were appeals to Lisbon for more settlers – petitions which were met with the arrival of convicts and political undesirables (*degredados*) from Portugal and the internal banishment, from nearby Santiago, of certain offenders.

The tiny volcanic pimple of **Brava** attracted its first colonists in the early 1540s. They kept much to themselves: climatically the island was one of the easiest to survive on, yet it was very remote. It was only when large numbers of families escaped here from Fogo in 1680, after volcanic eruptions and an earthquake, that Brava became heavily populated. It has had the densest population of the islands ever since.

The big island of the far northwest, **Santo Antão**, got its first inhabitants in 1548 but its large size, with remote and rugged interior valleys and craters, and its distance from the main shipping lanes, kept it very isolated and little known for at least two hundred years. Among its settlers were Jewish families fleeing the Inquisition and subsequent European persecutions. The village of Sinagoga is a reminder.

São Nicolau offered fewer opportunities to adventurous migrants and only

The Cape Verdean slave trade

As the New World opened across the Atlantic in the sixteenth century, the **trade in slaves** gathered momentum and the Cape Verde Islands – by then important stepping stones to Brazil and the Caribbean – became an emporium for their **transshipment** and taxation.

Although they were more expensive, slaves at **Ribeira Grande** on Santiago (the main entrepôt; now called Cidade Velha – see p.446) were better value than those bought directly on the Guinea coast: they tended to be healthier, as the sick had already perished; they spoke some Portuguese and some had even been baptized (the Portuguese were keen on finding religious justifications for their slave-trading, safeguarding the captives from purgatory). And for the slave ships, buying at Ribeira Grande was a much safer option than sailing directly into the creeks of Guinea to barter for slaves.

Roughly between 1600 and 1760 (the peak years), anything from a few dozen to several thousand slaves were sold annually through Ribeira Grande, most of them exported to the Spanish West Indies and Colombia. Large numbers were shipped off in years of bad drought on Santiago, when planters would sell their farm slaves to traders when they couldn't afford to feed them. This was prohibited in law: the only slaves supposed to be exported from Cape Verde were those just imported from the coast under licence.

From the earliest years of the colony, Lisbon had passed a succession of laws governing trade in slaves and other products. This was to ensure that as much of the profit and tariffs as possible accrued to the crown, even if that meant relegating much business to the status of smuggling – from which the crown received nothing. Besides ruling that the resale of slaves and foreign trade partnerships were illegal, Portugal obliged contract holders in the trade to buy the limited range of goods for resale and barter offered by the state supply monopoly. Between 1512 and 1519, crushing (though unenforceable) edicts were issued outlawing the much-in-demand Indian and Dutch cloth from the islands, banning the commissioning of *lançado* adventurers to trade on the mainland, and ruling that all legally contracted slave ships bound for the Americas should first detour to Lisbon – because Ribeira Grande could not be trusted to extract duty honestly.

Successive **governors** of the islands, who generally viewed their postings with misgivings if not actual horror, succumbed to the inevitability of corruption (if they survived malaria and other diseases long enough to care). Some succumbed too enthusiastically for the likes of the islands' clergy, aldermen, court and treasury officials – whose own commercial interests they threatened – but most governors managed to amass reasonable wealth while leaving space for smaller operators to do business.

Lançados, tangomaus, grumetes and ladinos

As well as bona fide licensed contractors waving charters from Lisbon or Madrid, the people involved in the complex mesh of buying, selling and bartering for slaves and other goods included:

• *Tangomaus* (dragomans): Cosmopolitan Africans, familiar with Portuguese ways; they traded in the Guinea interior and did much of the initial negotiating for slaves.

• *Lançados* ("sent outs"): Originally white or part-white Cape Verdeans who had familiarized themselves with African ways on the mainland and had settled in African communities to trade and transport goods along the coast. They eventually became indistinguishable from *tangomaus*. The bane of Lisbon, the *lançados* eventually became totally estranged from Portugal and even at times from Santiago. Once fully acculturated in Guinea, and unable to return to Portugal (on pain of death), they had no need to worry about the trade rules and could deal with the Dutch, English and French boats which sailed around the Atlantic in growing numbers. In this way they kept a good selection of merchandise for purchasing slaves and other African goods.

• *Grumetes*: African or mixed-race deckhands and carriers working for the traders.

• *Ladinos*: Slaves or other Africans who could speak Portuguese or Kriolu.

its northwest valleys – even these with uncertain rainfall – made colonization viable in the middle of the sixteenth century. The town of Ribeira Brava became an important literary and ecclesiastical centre and was the seat of the Cape Verdean bishopric from the end of the eighteenth century until the beginning of the twentieth.

São Vicente, one of the driest islands, was virtually uninhabited until the start of the nineteenth century, when the sheltered bay at Porto Grande (the best harbour in the islands) was chosen as the site of a British coal bunkering station for steamships on the Brazil and East Indies runs.

The "flat islands", **Boa Vista**, **Maio** and **Sal**, were also late in being fully colonized. Maio and Boa Vista had small numbers of herders and poor farmers, most of them freed or escaped slaves, and Maio eventually became the virtual private fiefdom of a freed slave family, the Evoras.

The development of trade

An early plan, conceived by Genoese merchant adventurers, was to create a major **sugar** industry on Santiago, following its success in Madeira. With the conquest and colonization of tropical lands, Europe could begin to grow the crop for itself instead of relying on expensive imports. But the Cape Verdean climate proved unsuitably dry and, although the **rum** which normally came as a by-product of sugar production was found to be useful for **slave trading** along the Guinea coast, the sugar farms at Ribeira Grande never really took off. By the late sixteenth century their output was already eclipsed by the vast quantities being produced in Brazil.

Instead, the Cape Verde Islands found themselves in the middle of a growing network of **trade routes** – between Europe and India, between West Africa and the Spanish American colonies and between Portugal and Brazil. They took on the function of **victualling stations** for the trading vessels, supplying fresh water, fruit, salted and dried meat, and carrying on a trade of their own in commercial goods – salt, hides, cotton *pagnes* and slaves.

With the break-up of the union between Portugal and Spain in 1640, business went into the doldrums for a number of years. Several governors were denounced to Lisbon after they monopolized what trade there was or even started applying the rule of law in order to confiscate and penalize foreign trading ships for their own gain. The islands were at a severe disadvantage because international demand for slaves had saturated the Guinea coastlands with **iron bars**, the principal currency, causing huge increases in the price of slaves. Portugal, which produced very little iron and forbade its export, was unable to compete.

Cotton, though, had become Cape Verde's main commercial crop, grown especially on the estates of Fogo. Slave women spun it; men wove it into strip cloth, dyed it with cultivated indigo and native *orchilla*, and sewed the strips together into *pagnes*. Some of the material found its way to Brazil but most was traded – generally for more slaves – on the Guinea coast. From the sixteenth century until some way into the eighteenth century, Cape Verdean cotton **panos**, in a multiplicity of inventive designs, were the prized dress material of the West African coast. They were traded as far east as Accra (until slave trading began to be threatened by abolitionists) and were as valuable as iron bars in many districts. The value of Cape Verde cloth became so universal in the region that it was also the usual currency of the archipelago: administrative officials were commonly paid with it and accumulated vast hoards of the stuff.

The Crown Monopolies

In the second half of the seventeenth century, after the split with Spain, the private contracts system fell out of use. Portugal's African territory and trade routes were seriously depleted and for some years only the most recklessly optimistic merchants had been willing to purchase the expensive rights on slaving in those parts. With wily Cape Verdeans stealing the trade from under their noses and the price of slaves going up all the time, it was difficult to make contracts pay.

Instead, in 1675, the first of the **Crown Monopolies** – the Companhia de Cacheu – was set up, reserving for itself sole rights to trade in foreign goods with the coast and outlawing (again) the transshipment of slaves through Santiago. Cape Verdeans were only allowed to export their own produce, a state which aroused bitter feelings in Santiago.

When a new company, The Company of the Islands of Cape Verde and Guinea, was formed, and bought a fat contract to supply four thousand slaves a year to the Spanish West Indies, the governor of the islands was placed on the company payroll. With their governor now effectively playing for the opposition, the islanders were more disgruntled than usual. And true to form, the new company did nothing for their prosperity, stockpiling goods to inflate prices, undersupplying vital commodities and levying high freight charges for their meagre exports. However, with the **War of the Spanish Succession** (1701–13), into which Portugal was pulled against Spain and France, the company's valuable slaving contract was lost and in 1712, Ribeira Grande itself was comprehensively sacked and plundered by a French force. The **cathedral**, a century and a half in the building, had only been completed nineteen years earlier. About this time, serious attention began to be given to creating a new and better fortified capital at Praia. Ribeira Grande was in steep decline from the middle of the eighteenth century and **Praia** was eventually dedicated as the seat of island government in 1774.

The eighteenth century

The first half of the eighteenth century had witnessed a great **relaxation of trade embargoes**. But Lisbon's persistent and neurotic attempts to prevent the trans-shipment of slaves and the sale to non-Portuguese of Cape Verdean cloth mystified foreign traders, especially English and Americans, who broke the laws without compunction. Apart from its triumphant (but peaking) textiles industry, the archipelago was in a state of **economic ruin**.

With the foundation in 1757 of the **Companhia de Grão Para e Marnahão**, which had the sole purpose of providing slave labour to the states of the new Brazilian empire, a twenty-year era of unparalleled cruelty and hardship began for the islands. The annexation of political control which had begun with the last company was taken to its logical conclusion, so that the Company now effectively *owned* the islands; while in Lisbon, a clique of English gentlemen maintained discreet but weighty capital interest in its enterprises.

Apart from the utter destitution which the enforced bypassing of trade brought to the archipelago, a severe **drought** struck from 1772 to 1775. By this point in the islands' history the population had grown too big to be able to survive such disasters on whatever came to hand – as they had during the famine of 1689 in Santiago when they ate horses and dogs. In the face of **starvation** throughout the islands, the Company was implacable – it held back food supplies, pushed up prices and milked the islanders of every last resource. In return for food, hundreds were abducted abroad and forced into slavery by English and French traders. Smuggling, of course, had never been so essential nor so profitable. The famine left an estimated 22,000 dead – out of a total population of less than 60,000. By the time the rains returned in 1777, the Company's charter had expired and it went into merciful liquidation.

The nineteenth century

At the beginning of the **nineteenth century** the Cape Verdes faced a quite different future. The harsh Company regime had battered the textile industry with enforced low prices, while drought had extinguished the cotton crop as well as many of the field slaves and textile workers. The emergence of the newly independent **USA** as a major economic power began to be more important than the distant historical links which tied the islands to Portugal. Lisbon, in any case, was too distracted by Napoleonic strife at home, and tail-and-dog upsets with Brazil about who ruled who, to be much concerned with the insignificant islands and their irrepressible flouting of trade laws. Moreover, Angola and Mozambique held far more promise.

New England whalers began calling at the Cape Verdes from the end of the eighteenth century, to take on supplies and crew and to do a little trading. Goatskins were a profitable sideline back in the States and, once the practice had become established, the Americans arrived each year with holds full of merchandise. Brava, Fogo and São Vicente were the main islands of contact and from these a steady trickle of impoverished Cape Verdeans escaped to New England through the closing decades of the nineteenth century.

Slavery in the nineteenth century was contained by the British and (ironically) by the American presence. While the trade in slaves from the Guinea coast was forbidden from 1815, slaves were still sold, by weight, well into the 1840s. Only with the end of the American Civil War and with pressure from Britain (to whom Portugal owed a debt going back to the Napoleonic era) was an abolition process set up on the islands. Slaves were not formally emancipated until 1869 and even then they had to work for their ex-owners as indentured labourers for a further ten years.

Famine and emigration

A series of disastrous **famines** hit the islands during the nineteenth century. In the first of these, from 1830–33, an estimated 30,000 people died. No relief of any kind came from Lisbon, but America, on this and several other occasions, sent large consignments of relief aid, though towards the end of the century it was generally wealthy émigré Cape Verdeans who organized it.

While the dispossessed of the Sotaventos moved to Praia or tried to emigrate, the poor of the Barlaventos headed to the new "city" of **Porto Grande** (Mindelo) on São Vicente to find work at the British-run **coaling station** or in the shops, bars and bordellos.

At the peak of its importance at the end of the nineteenth century the port of Mindelo was servicing over 1300 ships every year – and tens of thousands of sailors. The latter industry had a far-reaching effect on the culture of the islands, introducing even more of a racial mixture and enriching Kriolu with words like *ariope* (hurry up), *fulope* (full up) and *troba* (trouble).

Meanwhile, Portugal's first efforts at "humanitarian relief" took place during the drought of 1863–65 (with a death toll of some 30,000). It seemed an ideal time to profit from the availability of labour eager for food by engaging the people in civil engineering projects. The islands' first **cobbled roads** date from this famine, when peasants were rounded up to work for starvation wages.

A more sinister method of dealing with famine was **enforced migration** to the "Cacao Islands" of São Tomé and Principe. For a number of reasons, the abolition of slavery in São Tomé and Principe led to serious labour shortages. In the Cape Verdes the shortages were of land. Offered apparently huge bonuses by the recruiting agencies when (and if) they returned, thousands of poverty-stricken Cape Verdeans were persuaded to "go south" over the next ninety years to a system of equatorial plantation labour that was little better than ordinary chattel slavery. Like the monopoly companies of a century before, Portugal's **cocoa industry** found drought on the Cape Verdes was easily turned to its advantage.

The twentieth century

Right from the first use of the enforced migration system, measures were taken to limit the number of Cape Verdeans emigrating to the USA: a heavy departure tax was imposed, beyond the means of those who desperately needed to go, and travel permits and passports were made almost impossible to obtain. Nevertheless, the trickle of emigrants to New England became a flood between 1910 and 1930, when an estimated 34,000 people left the islands. This mass exodus was to become enormously significant after World War II, when the emigrants were able to send back substantial **remittances** to the islands, and after independence, when the economy became largely dependent on them. The USA, however, began to make literacy a condition for emigration from 1913 and, after 1922, the door to new immigrants was progressively closed.

Drought continued to be the single most important factor shaping the lives of Cape Verdeans in the twentieth century, with big crises in 1902–4 (15,000 dead), 1920–22 (17,000), 1940–43 (25,000) and 1947–48 (21,000 lives lost). The drought of World War II was probably the worst catastrophe in Cape Verde's history. Brava and Fogo suffered appallingly when they had to cope with a surge of re-emigrants returning from the American depression, the "rainy" years of the Thirties having lulled islanders into a false sense of security. And during the war years remittances from American relatives dried up completely. Only following the drought of 1959–61 were genuinely compassionate measures taken to alleviate the suffering, and these seem likely to have been initiated mostly by international outrage at the colonial labour migration policies.

Agitation for independence

A small number of Cape Verdeans emigrated to **Guinea-Bissau** – not out of destitution, but with ambitions. Following the opening of *liceus* (the colleges of São Nicolau in 1866 and São Vicente in 1917), about two-thirds of mainland Portuguese Guinea's teachers and civil servants had been Cape Verdeans. It was principally from their ranks that organized **resistance to Portuguese rule** first germinated. In response to what they described as a "wall of silence" around the islands, a group of mostly Cape Verdean intellectuals led by **Amílcar Cabral** – and including Luiz Cabral and **Aristides Pereira** – met secretly in Bissau in 1956 to form the **PAIGC** (Partido Africana para Independência da Guiné e Cabo Verde).

When peaceful representations to the colonial government were met with indifference and more repression (culminating in the massacre of striking dockers in Bissau – see p.500), the PAIGC began planning for a **guerilla war** on the mainland, with the declared aim of liberating both Guinea-Bissau and Cape Verde. After four years of preparation and fairly continuous efforts to negotiate a peaceful alternative, war began in 1963. The Cape Verdes became a massive Portuguese military base, swarming with Portuguese troops drafted to the front in Guinea-Bissau – and in Angola and Mozambique, where wars of independence had also begun.

On the Cape Verdes themselves, the question of a violent uprising was purely academic. The small, barren and isolated islands are unpromising ground for guerilla warfare. Yet the island government and police force (with help from the military and the PIDE) were acutely sensitive to the possibility of open revolt: every subversive indication was examined and squashed, and activists sent to Tarrafal on Santiago, or

The slave estates had varied in size from small landholdings run on paternalistic lines, where landlord and slave led similar lives, to extensive plantations (especially on Santiago) where wealth differences were extreme. The traditional **morgadio** system of land tenure, in which inheritance was strictly by primogeniture (inheritance by the eldest son), produced a growing population of landless aristocrats and tenant farmers on marginal land. Under the system, land could not be bought or sold. The estate slaves were often tied closely to the landlord's family, occasionally by blood. Over the centuries, intermarriage blurred the distinction between slaves and share-cropping peasants, the only practical difference being that the sharecroppers were always in debt to the landlords, a life in many ways as arduous as slavery. Freedom for slaves – an act of "charity" periodically undertaken by some landlords, or else an economic necessity when food supplies were exhausted in a famine – was no release from the cycle. If they ran into debt as sharecroppers, freed slaves lived on the sufferance of the landlord.

This, together with the fact that the islands are too small to offer much refuge, meant that slave rebellions were rare and provoked only by the most savage treatment. Among the landed families there were real fears, principally because they themselves were divided (the *morgadio* system created bitter feuds) and sometimes engaged in fierce vendettas with their rivals. At one time many slaves were armed by their masters, and gangs of pistol-toting slaves are known to have clashed on occasions, even in Praia. There was a certain insecurity about what might happen if the arms were turned against the elite. In the Santiago interior there was a large underclass of freed and escaped slaves, the *badius*, partly independent of the estates. And on Santiago, relations were less paternalistic and the estates often owned by absentee landlords. A group of slaves did organize a stand against their particularly oppressive landlord in 1822 and there was an aborted general slave revolt in Santiago in 1835 (given passive encouragement by the administration's ragged armed forces). But that was about the extent of resistance, and it was largely brought about by anticipation in the run-up to the abolition of slavery.

As for political resistance which might eventually culminate in an independence movement, there isn't a great deal of early evidence for that either. Conditions on the estates in the twentieth century became worse. With the old *morgadio* system discredited and abandoned, and the landlords themselves in debt to the National Overseas Bank, much of the land was bought up by a new class of absentee landlords, often returned United States emigrants. Coaling labourers mounted strikes for increased pay at Mindelo in 1910, and again in 1911, but they were defeated.

Opportunities for dissent on the islands in the fascist "New State" of Portugal's prime minister Salazar (1932–68) were limited to the private publication and distribution, among a small intellectual circle, of poetry and subtly nationalistic Kriolu literature. Organized demonstrations of opposition were impossible, and even further ruled out by the chronic plight of the islands during the famine years of World War II and the labour migrations of the early Fifties. Debtor peasants were treated as criminals and could claim nothing from the state until their debts had been repaid. Political dissidents found themselves imprisoned in the notorious detention centre at **Tarrafal**, alongside victims ejected from Portugal, and interrogated by the Gestapo-modelled PIDE political police.

To make the possibility of grassroots resistance even less likely, Cape Verde has an **alcoholism** problem going back to the earliest years of the sugar industry. Never viable as a major export, cane was still grown in vast quantities for distilling *grogue*, on land that could otherwise have provided food crops. The national addiction to *grogue* was such that, in the drought years of the 1960s, sugar was imported to satisfy demand.

worse places in Angola. On Santiago, a *badiu* religious cult movement, known as the **rebelados**, was labelled communist for criticizing the corrupt, state-run Catholic church, advocating the hands-together system of community help (the *juntamão*) and resisting outside interference, especially the anti-malaria campaign, which tried to spray members' homes. The movement virtually deified Amílcar Cabral. Its leaders were brutally interrogated and deported to other islands, though their threat was no more politically coordinated or potentially subversive than that posed by the **Nazarene church**, whose American-led, Puritan-inspired clergy were also subject to repression for their denunciations of the Salazarist church.

Cultural opposition was the only kind available and cultural repression the inevitable response. **Kriolu**, virtually unintelligible to ordinary Portuguese-speakers, was considered subversive in itself and its use banned from state property.

On the mainland, the war was drawn-out but successful. Only the **assassination of Amílcar Cabral** at his headquarters in Conakry on January 20, 1973 (partly inspired by jealousy of the Cape Verdean role in Guinea-Bissau's revolution) deflected it from a well-planned and predictable course. In September 1973, with most of Portuguese Guinea controlled by the PAIGC, the party proclaimed de facto independence. Portugal **withdrew from Bissau** the following year after the overthrow of the dictatorship in Lisbon on April 25, 1974.

Independence for Cape Verde

On the islands, the pre-coup government continued in office, though in less than a week, the clandestine fragments of Cape Verde's own PAIGC cells had coalesced, and a **public meeting** was held in Praia on May 1. The Tarrafal detainees were released and the PAIGC took its message around the islands, agitating semi-legally for the independence

that was almost at hand. The "wall of silence" had caved in. Other parties, hatched and nurtured by the administration, tried to promote the idea of some kind of "shared independence" between the islands and Portugal, but none of them convinced many islanders.

Lisbon sent a new governor in August 1974, charged with asserting **Portuguese continuity** in Cape Verde. He was shouted out of Praia and back to Lisbon within a month. Another arrived with a heavier hand, his troops shooting into a demonstration in Mindelo in September. But with Guinea-Bissau already independent, the **demonstrations** only grew larger. By October, with "continuity" sounding increasingly hollow, the Portuguese were negotiating with PAIGC leaders. In December, a meeting in Lisbon agreed on a transitional government consisting of three PAIGC members and two Portuguese representatives. The Portuguese conceded a general election the following June. With a landslide of votes, **Aristides Pereira**, took office on **July 5, 1975**, as president of the new Republic of Cape Verde. The PAIGC party also monopolized power in Guinea-Bissau, and while that territory retained a separate constitution from the islands, the long-term aim was to unify the two into one country.

The split with Guinea-Bissau

Amílcar Cabral had been obsessive about the importance of **Cape Verde–Guinea unity** and Aristides Pereira continued to emphasize it. But the most significant political event in the first twenty years of Cape Verdean independence was the 1980 coup in Bissau which overthrew **President Luiz Cabral**, Amílcar's half-brother, and led to the formal separation of the two countries.

After the liberation war there had been lingering unease within the PAIGC in Guinea-Bissau. Luiz Cabral, though a close friend of party leader Aristides Pereira, was not a statesman of the same rank, and he became an increasingly isolated figure, mistrustful of his own ministers and – it seemed to them – unwilling to discuss economic and social questions outside a clique in which Pereira figured too prominently. Suspicions grew that policy in Guinea-Bissau was being constructed by the two presidents in secret and that Cape Verde, which had achieved independence relatively painlessly – though at the cost of Guinean lives – was seeking to dominate the union. Furthermore, while Cape Verdeans had been instrumental in starting the independence movement, they had also formed a large proportion of the colonial civil service in Guinea-Bissau, most of whom had passively collaborated with the Portuguese. The charge of **neocolonialism** didn't have to be made explicit.

Against Pereira's advice, Cabral modified the Guinea-Bissauan constitution to give himself more power and his nationalistic prime minister, **Nino Vieira**, less. It was Vieira who subsequently led the coup of November 14, 1980, putting himself in the Bissau presidency. Pereira, in condemning the coup, pointed out that the party constitution provided the means for dealing with factional problems. On January 20, 1981 (the eighth anniversary of the assassination of Amilcar Cabral), the Cape Verdean arm of the party renamed itself the **PAICV** and, at a summit in Maputo in 1982, a formal division of the two countries' assets ratified the split.

The PAICV era

After 1981, with the union of the two countries a fast fading dream, Cape Verde at least had a chance to address purely **national problems**. The question of the very habitability of the islands was raised, but the **economy** was made viable, a result of careful and sensitive development and a remarkable absence of corruption.

The PAICV government answered OAU demands that it apply the sanctions policy on South Africa, and refuse refuelling rights to South African Airways on Sal, with the response that it could not afford to commit suicide by solidarity. It also increased the level of **aid** coming into the country and used it on local projects of direct utility. Non-governmental aid, channelled through the National Development Fund, matched foreign interests to Cape Verdean requirements. By leaving the door open for *americanos* to return, it encouraged **private investment** and maintained goodwill among the vast majority of the Cape Verdean diaspora, whose remittances continued to be the number one economic pillar.

One hundred percent **adult literacy** as well as free and compulsory **primary education** are goals that the PAICV pretty well achieved. **Agrarian reform** was patient, seeking to avoid alienating landlords and always to avoid damaging the country's overseas image of independence and openness. The worst effects of **drought** and flash floods were combated with tree-planting programmes on all the islands, dyke building and better terracing.

Health was a priority for the PAICV government, which reckoned to spend three times as much per person as the average developing country. High-profile Mother and Child Protection and Family Planning programmes were operated by the PAICV at a community level, with theatre shows and public demonstrations organized to mobilize people on the issues – including breast-feeding, contraception and nutrition. The off-loading of unwanted First World drugs, so common in under-developed countries, was avoided by setting up a national pharmaceuticals industry.

Even under one-party rule, the **legal system** in Cape Verde was one of the most progressive in Africa. There were no political prisoners – indeed there are still few of any kind – and there is no death sentence.

Despite the successes, there remained several lurking problems which would not fade away. **Alcoholism**, especially in the rural areas, has been an ongoing problem for centuries. At root a strictly male issue, it is triply destructive where it not only wastes productive land on sugar cane but hard earnings as well, and reduces the workforce.

A more pointed issue in the late 1980s was the battle between church and state over the issue of **abortion** on demand, which the PAICV supported. Although the majority of children are brought up in mother-only families, the position of **women** in Cape Verdean society has never had as much attention focused on it as the male-formulated charter of the Organization of Cape Verdean Women – OMCV – would suggest. The division of views was by no means straightforward: there were OMCV members among those taking part in the anti-abortion campaign.

Good **rainy seasons** in the late 1980s broke a drought that had persisted on some islands virtually throughout the years of independence. But the PAICV was not equipped to ride out the inevitable wave of rising expectations that came with better harvests and the end of the Cold War. It never properly examined its own renewal mechanisms, thus allowing the ex-guerillas of the party to grow old and stagnant together.

The democratic era

At the PAICV party congress in 1988, there were discussions led by younger members about ending its status as the country's sole political party. The new **Movimento para a Democracia (MPD)**, led by lawyer Carlos Veiga, held its first meeting in June 1990, and demands were made for sweeping reforms to Cape Verde's "revolutionary" constitution and the established political culture in which the PAICV held such sway.

Under a tide of mounting pressure, especially from the church, the prime minister Pedro Pires took over as PAICV party secretary from Aristides Pereira (who saw himself as state president, outside politics), in preparation for the introduction of a **multiparty system**. In January 1991, the MPD swept to power in Portuguese-speaking Africa's first ever multiparty legislative elections, taking more than two-thirds of National Assembly seats. **Carlos Veiga** was subsequently elected prime minister and former supreme court judge **António Mascarenhas** won the presidential election, soundly defeating Pereira. The MPD also won most of the seats in local council elections held later in the year, with PAICV wins only on the home islands of PAICV dignitaries.

Economically, the MPD government put great efforts into making the country **investor-friendly**, with emphasis on its tourism and fishing potential. The scrapping of the PAICV's last major initiative, the agrarian reform laws, was popular at home, and was judged to have signalled the right messages to overseas investors. The civil service payroll was reduced by half and embezzlement of state funds by former PAICV officials were investigated.

Yet despite the peaceful and widely approved transition to multiparty politics, there remained widespread **dissatisfaction** with lack of progress and the slow rate of economic improvement on the islands. The MPD was subsequently torn by splits, resignations and defections. One ex-MPD official, Eurico Monteiro, formed a new party, the Partido da Convergência Democrática, and gained a seat in the 1995 elections.

Further internal disputes led to the sacking of two government ministers and the Secretary of State for Decentralization in one fell swoop in late 1999, while the MPD performed poorly in municipal elections in early 2000. Veiga himself was to resign later that summer with the intention of standing for the presidency.

Into the twenty-first century

The PAICV emerged anew and went on to secure a majority in the legislative elections of 2001. The president of the PAICV, **Jose Maria Neves**, became prime minister while **Pedro Pires** scraped the narrowest of victories (by twelve votes) in the presidential election; the result was so close it had to be scrutinized by the Supreme Court.

Back in power, the PAICV vowed to improve the precarious financial situation they had inherited, committing themselves to a healthy macroeconomic policy and prudent fiscal management. While they've since succeeded in balancing the budget and reducing inflation, the IMF has obliged them to go further and implement the kind of conservative policies, including privatization, which they wouldn't have dreamed of twenty or thirty years earlier. In addition to this burden, their relatively slim majority in the national assembly has put a brake on their ability to effect change. **Unemployment** is running at around 25 percent, and for those families not in receipt of overseas remittances, life is still desperately hard.

On a brighter note, **tourism** is beginning to yield results. There are ongoing plans for the expansion of Praia airport as well as the introduction of a catamaran to enhance sea travel. Partnerships between the state and the private sector are seen as the way to finance these projects.

With the US's African Growth and Opportunity Act paving the way for countries like Cape Verde to gain duty-free access to the American market, foreign investors are being seen as key to the establishment of light manufacturing industry geared towards export; a number of duty-free zones have been set up to facilitate this. In tandem with this, more and more elderly emigrants are returning to the islands and investing in their homeland.

Prospects for Cape Verde look reasonably healthy – at least in West African terms – assuming the occasional good rainy season and continued foreign investment. The danger for the government is that expectations in the poor, rural heartlands of the most heavily populated islands of Santiago, Santo Antão and Fogo will outstrip its ability to deliver.

Music

The most widely known Cape Verdean forms are guitar and fiddle songs – the **morna**, a mournful lament reminiscent of Portuguese *fado*, and the more upbeat and very danceable **coladeira**, music with a wonderful muscular rhythm. Many songs are love songs – addressed to the islands – and powerfully sentimental. **Cesaria Evora**, The "barefoot diva", has released a number of superb CDs and is the foremost musical emissary of the isles, now based in Paris. Working hardest for the cause of Cape Verdean music inside Cape Verde itself are **Simentera**, an ensemble dedicated to preserving and rekindling interest in the islands' various musical traditions.

In the past, in smaller towns and rural areas, you might have heard someone playing the **cimbó** or the **berimbau**, old one-stringed instruments of African origin producing plangent, ancient sounds – either with a bow on the former, or plucked and resonating in a sound box, or the mouth, with the latter. Both have virtually fallen into the realm of folklore, though in parts of Santiago you might still be lucky.

To whet your appetite, we've compiled the following brief list of recommended CDs, most of which are available outside the islands, but Cape Verde's musical legacy is rich and there are always new discoveries to be made.

Têtê Alhino *De-Cor-a-som* (available locally). The pick of the Simentera singer's solo albums, this has a wonderfully sensual, Brazilian flavour.

Bau *Cape Verdean Melancholy* (Doçura/Lusafrica). A choice selection culled from the master guitarist/violinist's four instrumental albums.

Cesaria Evora *Café Atlântico* (BMG). Her best album, an irresistible combination of windswept *mornas* and Cuban instrumentation. Alternatively, go for the obvious *Best of Cesaria Evora* (BMG).

Raíz di Djarfogo *Traditions of the Fogo Island* (Ocora). Beguiling roots music from perhaps Cape Verde's most beguiling island. Full of vibrant *coladeiras*, composed in the tradition of Fogo's strident social criticism.

Simentera *Cabo Verde en Serenata* (Piranha). Simentera have both an uncannily intuitive feel for tradition and the vision to take the music forward. Includes the powerful "Dor Di Amor".

Various artists compilations

Afropea 3: Telling Stories to the Sea (Luaka Bop). A vibrant sweep of Afro-Portuguese music from David Byrne's label. Includes Cesaria's definitive "Sodade".

Cape Verde: Anthology 1959–1992 (Buda Musique). If you want to educate yourself properly, this is the place to start. Includes extensive sleeve notes and photos.

Evocação de Amílcar Cabral No Folclore Cabo-Verdiano (A. Rui Machado/Sons D'Africa). Beautifully packaged tribute to national icon Amílcar Cabral, with incredible 1970s recordings from the likes of Tony Lima and Nhô Balta. Essential.

Rough Guide to Cape Verde (World Music Network). Another good entry point for the beginner, with the emphasis on modern releases.

The Soul of Cape Verde (Lusafrica). Another outstanding collection featuring hauntingly atmospheric 1960s tracks from Humbertona & Piuna, Bana and Voz de Cabo Verde alongside newer material. A peerless introduction.

Books

Cape Verde is one of the least documented countries in the world. Sources of information in English are few, and most are technical, research-based studies that you'll find only in university libraries. Books marked ⊞ are especially recommended; those marked o/p are likely to be out of print.

Basil Davidson *The Fortunate Isles – a Study in African Transformation*. A positive and not unduly critical survey, mixing impression with historical accounts.

⭐ **A.B. Ellis** *West African Islands* (o/p). First published in 1885, this covers adventures from Madeira to Ascension, with a couple of lively chapters on "St Vincent" and "San Antonio". Entertaining stuff.

Marilyn Halter *Between Race and Ethnicity, Cape Verdean American Immigrants 1860–1965*. An exhaustive study of a fascinating subject, one that cuts to the heart of the unique relationship between the land and its people.

Richard Lobban *The Historical Dictionary of the Republic of Cape Verde.* Great for dipping into, with a wealth of useful information on Cape Verde's roots, as well as sections on ethnomusicology, linguistics, etc. The same author's *Crioulo Colony to Independent Nation* is a comprehensive overview of Cape Verde's five-hundred-year history, with the emphasis on twentieth-century politics and economic development.

Archibald Lyall *Black and White Make Brown: An Account of a Journey to the Cape Verde Islands and Portuguese Guinea* (o/p). Worth trying to find for its vivid account of Cape Verde prior to the disastrous drought of the World War II era.

★ **Joe Würfel** *Cabo Verde West of Africa.* A fascinating and original collection of contemporary monochrome photography documenting the diversity of Cape Verde's populace.

Language

The day-to-day language of Cape Verde is **Kriolu** (Creole), quite distinct in structure and in much of its vocabulary from the official language, Portuguese: the two are not mutually intelligible. Kriolu contains many elements of Fula and Mandinka and a wide range of adopted vocabulary from archaic seafaring Portuguese and other European languages, including English.

If you speak **Portuguese** – and it's one of the easiest languages to pick up, particularly if you're familiar with Spanish or Italian – you'll find you can get by easily everywhere. Even in rural areas everyone speaks some: papers, signs and radio are all in Portuguese and education is largely conducted in it. Learning Kriolu is another matter: Cape Verdeans tend to slip in and out of Kriolu and Portuguese, and Kriolu takes some time to tune into.

While a little Portuguese goes a long way, if you don't have any you may just be able to get by in **French,** which a surprising number of Cape Verdeans speak relatively well and which – even more surprisingly perhaps – they seem to enjoy doing. **English** is a different matter; many people seem somewhat shy of speaking the little English they know. In most places, though, you'll run into younger people who've learned both languages at school, as well as returnee emigrants from Europe, Senegal and especially the USA who speak them fluently.

Useful vocabulary

Basic terms and phrases

Hello	**Bon dia**
How are you?	**Kuma ño sta?**
I'm fine	**N sta ben**
What's your name?	**Kali e bo nómi?**
[or more formally]	
What is your (masc./fem.) name?	**Kal e nómi di?**
My name is Caroline	**Ña nómi é Caroline**
Do you have...?	**Ño ten...?**
Is there any...?	**ño/di ña...?**
Goodbye	**Bon dia/te lóg**
See you soon/ sometime	**Te lóg/te dipos di mañan**
God go with you	**Deus ta kunpaño-lo**
Please	**pur fabor**
Thank you	**brigod**
Today	**oshi**
Tomorrow	**mañan**
Yesterday	**ónti**
Before	**ántis**
After	**dipos**

Near	pértu
Far	lonzi
Here	li
There	la

Travelling

I'd like some water	N kre agu
How do I get to Tarrafal?	Kma N pode bai pa Tarrafal?
Is this the bus stop for Tarrafal?	Undi e paraza di otukaru pa Tarrafal?
What time does the plane leave/arrive?	Ki óra avion ta sai/tchga?
Where are you (masc./fem.) going?	Undi ño/ña ta bai?
We're going to Praia	Nu ta bai pa Praia
How much is it?	Kal e presu?
Change (money)	Troco
Is there a cheap hotel near here?	Ten penson li pértu?
I'd like a room for one person /two people	N kreba kuartu pa un psoa/dos psoa
Is there a toilet/ bathroom?	Ten kasa di bañu li?
What is it?	Kuse e es?
I don't know	N ka sabe
We don't speak Kriolu	Nu ka ta papia kriolu
Open	abert
Closed	fetchod
Where?	undi?

Numbers and days

1	un
2	dos
3	tres
4	kuatu
5	sinku
6	sais
7	séti
8	oitu
9	nóvi
10	dés
11	ónzi
12	dozi
13	trezi
14	katorzi
15	kinzi
16	dizasais
17	dizaséti
18	dizóitu
19	dizanóvi
20	vinti
21	vinti y un
30	trinta
40	korenta
50	sinkuenta
60	sasenta
70	satenta
80	oitenta
90	novénta
100	sén
101	sén-t y un
200	duzéntus
500	kiñéntus
1000	mil
Monday	segunda-feira (2ªF)
Tuesday	terça-feira (3ªF)
Wednesday	quarta-feira (4ªF)
Thursday	quinta-feira (5ªF)
Friday	sexta-feira (6ªF)
Saturday	sábado (S)
Sunday	domingo (D)

Glossary

Aluguer Shared taxi-van or pick-up truck (the public transport of the islands).

Americano Cape Verdean living in America.

Badiu Peasant from rural Santiago descended, according to tradition, from runaway slaves.

Bairro Suburb, outskirts of town.

Boite Nightclub.

Branco White – or wealthy – person.

Camâra Town hall.

Cidade City, town.

Conto One thousand escudos.

Criança Child.

Crise Drought, community crisis.

Deslocação Private taxi trip.

Festa Feast, festival, party.

Funco Round, stone, thatched house.

Grog, Grogo, Grogue Sugar-cane firewater, *aguardente*.

Igreja Church.

Lenço Traditional headscarf worn differently by women of each island.

Liceu Secondary school.

Mercado Market.

Morabeza Kindness, gentleness, considered to be a peculiarly Cape Verdean quality.

Morna The heavy-hearted music of the islands, sweet-sounding, nostalgic and very characteristic.

MPD Movement for Democracy.

PAICV African Party for the Independence of Cape Verde.

Pano Cloth, *pagne*.

Paragem Bus stop.

Pelourinho Pillory, the slave auction post.

Povoação "Town", the local town.

Praça Square, *place*.

Praia Beach.

Quinta Estate, owned by a landlord; rare today.

Quintal Courtyard of a house.

Ribeira Stream, river or rivercourse.

Seca Drought.

Sobrado A Portuguese-style house of two or more floors, particularly opulent examples of which were built in Fogo's capital, São Felipe.

Sodade A defining term of Cape Verdean identity, signifying longing for homeland, yearning.

Vila Town.

5.1

The Sotaventos

Santiago, **Fogo**, **Brava** and **Maio** make up the **Sotaventos**, the leeward group of islands, with two-thirds of the population, more of the rainfall (which arrives from the south) and a good deal of the wealth.

If you're coming from Dakar, your first port of call on the islands may well be **Praia** on **Santiago island**, Cape Verde's capital and the nation's largest town. It's a pleasant enough place but there are no gripping reasons to spend time here: if you're stuck for a few days, your time is better spent enjoying one of the easy and satisfying short trips out of town. The rest of Santiago offers more enticing attractions in the mountainous **central region** and the beaches in the northwest, though Santiago's scenery doesn't compare with that of the Barlavento islands of São Nicolau and, outstandingly, Santo Antão.

Fogo island is a vast, semi-active volcano, rising to nearly 3000m above sea level, whose last eruption was in 1995. There's a magnificent road tracking along the lava-covered eastern slopes, fine walking country in the gentler western parts, and fascinating and very feasible hiking up in the old crater itself, now a domain of citrus orchards and vineyards.

The smallest of the inhabited islands is **Brava**. Cape Verdeans often rate it the most beautiful island and it's still somewhat hard to visit as there are no scheduled flights and the sea journey is rough and unpredictable. Brava is certainly the most cultivated island, with a relatively benign climate – and it's long been a sanctuary for those families who could afford to flee the droughts on other islands.

Maio, one of the *ilhas rasas* or "flat islands", is duller and drier. Locally famous for its cattle, which provide the country's limited milk supply, it has some deserted, desert island–style beaches. Attempts to drum up interest in it seem a little desperate, however. As one Portuguese brochure of 1970 put it: "The desolation of its landscape contrasts with the warm welcome of its people and the fine flavour of its fresh lobsters". So there you have it.

Santiago

With half the cultivable land and half the population, **SANTIAGO** is the **agricultural backbone** of Cape Verde. Unusually among the islands, it's large enough that it takes a few hours to get from one end to the other, switchbacking through the mountains or along the jagged eastern coast.

Santiago's main focus is the capital, **Praia**, at the southern tip. From Praia, one main road snakes through the interior, sending secondary roads like suckers down to the coast; another forks off it to the northeast to link up the east-coast fishing villages before meeting with the main route again at **Tarrafal** in the northwest – site of the best beaches. The village of **Ribeira Grande** (Cidade Velha), west of Praia, was the first settlement on the islands and remained the effective administrative centre until early in the eighteenth century when Praia took over the role of capital. Today, Cidade Velha is one of Santiago's principal tourist attractions, with its

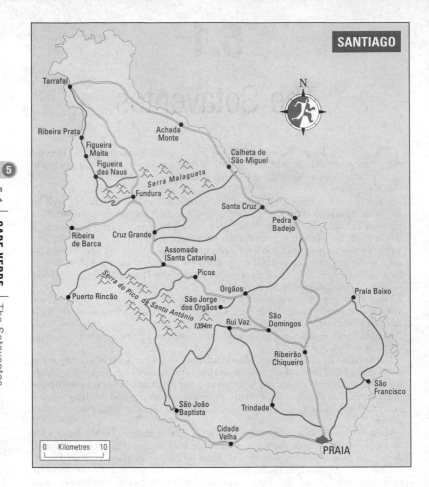

handful of picturesque streets, indomitable hilltop fort (now a museum) and assorted ruins in various stages of restoration.

There are dozens of hamlets and villages scattered across the island, and any number of hidden coves and *ribeiras*. A few of the travel possibilities are covered in the next few pages, but Santiago, in common with all the islands, is still little explored by outsiders. Most of your discoveries will be very much your own.

Praia and around

Cape Verdeans – and foreign residents too – tend to complain that **PRAIA** is soulless, thinks of nothing but money and has no *joie de vivre*. If you're already tuned to Cape Verde's gentle sensibilities this may be relatively true. But if you fly in from Dakar, it all comes as a welcome drop in tension and the nicest possible culture shock. The presence of a couple of power-generating windmills rotating on the brown hills across the *ribeira*, the layout of the little town on its small proud plateau, indeed everything about Cape Verde you can see, is going to be quite different. Though Praia has almost nothing to offer in terms of sights or entertainment, it is a capital where just being here is enjoyable: the streets are friendly; the *praça* has benches and a bandstand where visiting naval bands sometimes play on Sundays; and there are good views from the edge of the plateau, particularly from the *pensão* on the western side.

Arrival, information and transport

The downtown part of Praia is all concentrated on the fortresslike slab of the **Platô**, a neat grid of streets 800m long and 300m wide, which overlooks the expanding suburbs and is simplicity itself to get around. Off the Platô to the north-west is the **Fazenda** district; to the southwest is **Várzea**, with the impressive new ministries' building, the Palácio do Governo; beyond is **Achada do Santo António** (Achada Sto António) where many international organizations have their headquarters; while further south, facing the islet of Santa-Maria, is the embassy and smart hotels district of **Prainha**.

The best way to arrive at Praia – and by far the most likely – is by plane. Until the much-vaunted new international airport opens, you'll land at **Francisco Mendes airport**, 1500m northeast of town, which has a small terminal building with a little café/bar (usually open 24hr) and toilets; there are no money-changing facilities. You walk from the arrivals hall to the front gate and out onto the forecourt. Below is the manageable muddle of the capital, five minutes away by taxi – about CV$300 to the Platô and CV$500 to Prainha. The taxi drivers are very laid-back, though if you've flown in from Senegal, you may find it hard to persuade your driver to accept CFA francs; dollars or euros would almost certainly be acceptable, or just ask him to wait till you've changed some at the end of your trip (you could even ask him to stop at a bank en route to your destination). Drivers often don't have change, so it's worth being prepared. Many people head for one of the more modest *pensões*, but unless you're loaded down with luggage you might just ask for the main *praça* in Platô – **Praça Alberquerque** – and hop out when you get there – it tends to be cheaper than naming a specific destination.

Arriving by sea, you dock at the **pier** roughly beneath the end of the airport runway. Again, it's a five-minute taxi ride northwest to town, barely 2km if you walk.

The only real **tourist information** on offer in Praia is from the tiny Promex kiosk on the northeast side of the *praça* on the plateau. They have ferry timetables, maps, postcards and one or two friendly staff. Transcor **buses** ferry people from the Platô out to the suburbs and back again for fares of around CV$50. **Taxis** aren't marked as such, but you'll have no problem finding one – or being found by the drivers, who honk their horns at foreigners in the hope of getting a fare.

Accommodation

Although the budget accommodation – mainly consigned to the Platô (see map, p.442) – is limited, there's a decent range of mid-range and upmarket options, and you're unlikely to find yourself without a bed.

Moving on from Praia

TACV (☎60.82.00) operates **flights** to Boa Vista (Tues, Thurs & Sun; 50min), Fogo (daily; 30min), Maio (Mon, Wed & Fri; 20min), Sal (several daily; 45min), Santo Antão (Ponta do Sol; Tues & Fri; 1hr 20min), São Nicolau (Tues, Fri & Sun; 40min) and São Vicente (at least 1 daily; 1hr).

Private Hiace minibuses run to out-of-town destinations from the depot next to the main Sucupira market, though **aluguers** to **Cidade Velha** go from a parking area in Terra Branca, southwest of the Platô. Arca Verde (Companhia Nacional de Navegação Arca Verde) at 153 Rua 5 de Julho in Platô is the main **ferry-ticket** office (☎61.54.97, ☎61.54.96), though you can also try the Agencia Nacional de Viagens on Rua Serpa Pinto, Platô (☎61.31.02, ☎61.21.62).

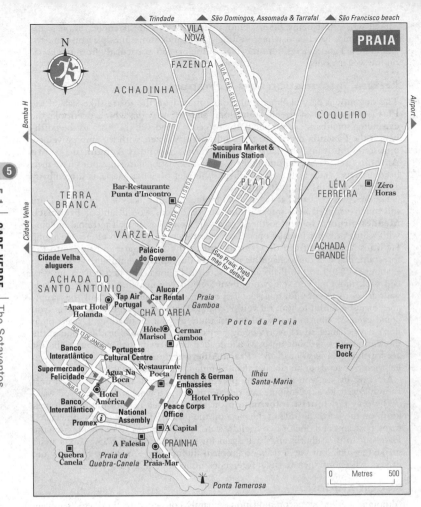

Platô

Hotel Felicidade Rua Serpa Pinto, though the main entrance is on the adjacent Rua Andrade Corvo ☎61.55.85, ℻61.55.84, ℮felicidade @cvtelecom.cv. Previously a popular budget choice, the *Felicidade* has undergone a makeover and repositioned itself in the mid-range market. All rooms come with TV, fridge, a/c and spotless bathrooms, although some rooms are windowless. Same price for single occupancy as double; good value if you're sharing. B&B ❺

Pensão Paraiso Rua Serpa Pinto ☎61.35.39. Clean if slightly poky rooms set around an open courtyard. Somewhat overpriced, although the

balcony rooms (#3 and #9) offer better value, and hot water is available. ❹

Residencial Anjos Rua Serpa Pinto ☎61.43.37, ℻61.57.01. A mixed bag of rooms (some with balconies) with a/c, hot water and a communal TV room. ❺

Residencial Praia Maria Rua 5 de Julho ☎61.85.80, ℻61.85.54. An oasis of calm from the heat and bustle below with a bright reception and some gloomy (inward-facing) though very comfortable rooms; the only sunny, street-facing room is the suite (no. 101). Laundry, Internet access and B&B. ❻

Residencial Rosymar 32 Rua Tenente Valadim

℗61.63.45. Down a narrow side-street at the northern end of the plateau, this has bright and quiet, if slightly musty, s/c rooms with hot water. B&B ❹

Residencial Sol Atlântico Unmarked entrance at 24 Av Amílcar Cabral ℗61.28.72. The oldest place in town, and one of the cheapest, the *Atlântico* offers spartan rooms with character, some s/c. There's no hot water but the lived-in colonial feel makes up for it. Room 1, despite being hot and noisy, is recommended for its window/balcony overlooking the square. ❹

Elsewhere in Praia

Apart Hotel Holanda Achada Sto António ℗62.39.73, ℗62.37.10, ℗hotelholanda @mail.cvtelecom.cv. Run by a Dutch/Cape Verdean couple and boasting a decidedly orange colour scheme, *Holanda* has decent, non-s/c rooms around an open courtyard, and an atmospheric old bar. ❸

Hotel América Achada Sto António ℗62.14.31,

℗62.14.32. Located opposite the offices of the EC and next to the *Agua Na Boca* restaurant, this friendly hotel is fitted out in beautiful dark-wood furniture with the requisite a/c, TV and fridge. Recommended. B&B ❻

Hotel Marisol Chã de Areia district ℗61.34.60, ℗61.25.35, ℗mago@marisol.cv. Slightly faded establishment, and somewhat gloomy, though the seafront rooms are brighter and it's mostly well maintained. ❼

Hotel Praia-Mar Prainha district ℗61.37.77, ℗61.29.72. With a reputation somewhat inflated by its airy, seafront position, this place is seriously overpriced for s/c rooms that are fraying around the edges. The renovation and extension of the premises, under way at the time of writing, may put a noisy dampener on your stay. ❽

Hotel Trópico Prainha district ℗61.42.00, ℗61.52.25, ℗hotel.tropico@mail.cvtelecom.cv. Praia's most expensive hotel, with luxurious, tasteful and spacious rooms set around a large freshwater pool. ❽

The Town

While several dilapidated colonial buildings on the Platô are being renovated, much of Praia is new and drab, the scrawny suburbs crawling up boulder-strewn gulches away from the centre. Such action as there is on the Platô itself tends to focus around the **market**, refurbished in 1999, which, despite its small size, brings in country women from all over Santiago and, in a good harvest year, can pack surprising variety and colour: papayas, bananas, watermelons, potatoes and cassava, goat cheeses, piglets trussed in baskets, dried beans, slabs of red tuna, even potted palms. **Sugar** products are much in evidence. For the Portuguese in the sixteenth and seventeenth centuries, the islands were strategic in their efforts to dominate Atlantic trade routes: rum in particular – distilled from cane sugar – was enormously useful in the **slave trade**, commanding high prices along the Guinea coast. Cane, which grew well enough in lusher valleys on several islands, was never produced in the kind of quantities that would have led to huge commercial success. But Cape Verdeans continue to distil plenty of *grogue*, *canna* and *aguardente* (all variants on the same theme), and to make irresistible sweets. Various kinds of sickly fudge, often made with coconut, and cuplike moulds of brown molasses crystal, are always on sale in Praia.

The few large public buildings around town hold no special interest, though the **Catholic Cathedral** is quite an imposing block of a place with its potted plants and figurines. Formerly, if you wanted a glimpse of the interior courtyard and gardens of the then Office of the Prime Minister, now the **Praia Municipal Council headquarters**, you needed the excuse of visiting to see if they were holding any unwanted seats on flights. With the advent of democracy, you can nowadays walk freely around the council building's pretty grounds and the perimeter of the presidential palace itself, the **Palácio da República**, which overlooks the beach. The **statue of Diogo Gomes**, the Portuguese explorer who was one of the first to visit the islands, stands here.

There are a couple of **museums** that are worth a look, though note that labelling is in Portuguese. In a nicely restored colonial building with a poorly marked entrance at the north end of the plateau, the **Museu Etnográfico da Praia** on Rua 5 Julho (Mon, Wed & Fri 10am–noon & 3–6pm, Tues 10am–1pm;

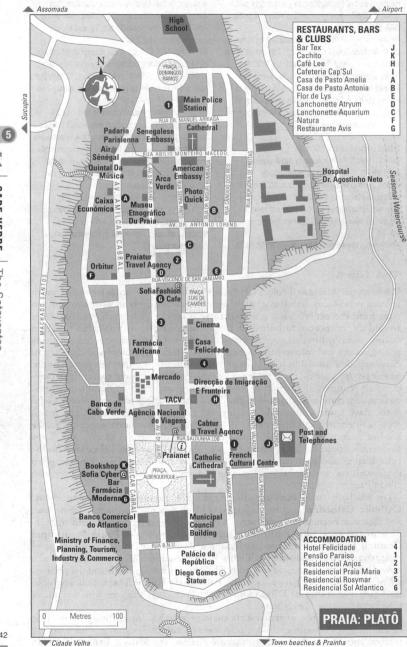

5.1 | CAPE VERDE | The Sotaventos

N

High School

PRAÇA DOMINGOS RAMOS

1 Main Police Station

RUA DR. MANUEL ARRIAGA

Padaria Parisienna   Senegalese Embassy   Cathedral

Air Sénégal

RUA ABILIO MONTEIRO MACEDO

Quintal Da Música

Arca Verde   American Embassy

Caixa Ecunómica   **A** Museu Etnográfico Du Praia   Photo Quick   **B**

AV. DR. ANTÓNIO LORENO

C

Praiatur Travel Agency   **2**

Orbitur   **F**   **D**   **E**

RUA VISCONDE DE SAN JANUARIO

SofiaFashion   **G**   @ Cafe   PRAÇA LUIS DE CAMÕES

3

Cinema

Farmácia Africana   Casa Felicidade

4

Mercado

TACV   Direcção de Imigração E Frunteira   **H**

Banco de Cabo Verde

Agência Nacional de Viagens

@   RUA SALDUNHA LOB

Cabtur Travel Agency   **5**

i   Praianet

PRAÇA ALBERQUERQUE

Catholic Cathedral   French Cultural Centre   **I**   **J**

Post and Telephones

Bookshop   **K**
Sofia Cyber @ Bar
Farmácia Moderna   **6**

Banco Comercial do Atlantico

Municipal Council Building

Ministry of Finance, Planning, Tourism, Industry & Commerce

RUA B.N.U.

Palácio da República

Diego Gomes Statue

Hospital Dr. Agostinho Neto

Seasonal Watercourse

AV. MACHADO SANTOS

AV. AMILCAR CABRAL

AV. 5 DE JULHO

RUA SERRA PINTO

RUA DR. MIGUEL BOMBARDA

RUA CANDIDO DOS REIS

RUA BORJONA DE FREITAS

RUA TENENTE VALADIM

RUA CESARIO LACERDA

RUA NEVES FERREIRA

RUA PINHEIRO CHAGAS

RUA ANDRADE CORVO

RUA GENERAL BARROS (closed)

RESTAURANTS, BARS & CLUBS	
Bar Tex	J
Cachito	K
Café Lee	H
Cafeteria Cap'Sul	I
Casa de Pasto Amelia	A
Casa de Pasto Antonia	B
Flor de Lys	E
Lanchonette Atryum	D
Lanchonette Aquarium	C
Natura	F
Restaurante Avis	G

ACCOMMODATION	
Hotel Felicidade	4
Pensão Paraiso	1
Residencial Anjos	2
Residencial Praia Maria	3
Residencial Rosymar	5
Residencial Sol Atlantico	6

PRAIA: PLATÔ

0   Metres   100

CV$100) has a deliciously cool interior housing displays of traditional domestic artefacts and blue-and-white *pano* weaving; in the basement you'll find coins, vases, cannonballs and other items salvaged from shipwrecks. Another fascinating collection is on show at the **Centro de Restauração e Museologia** on Rua Alfândega, Chã de Areia (Mon–Fri 9am–noon & 3–6pm), which has coins, guns, ivory and other artefacts salvaged by Portuguese firm Arqueonautas Worldwide (Ⓦwww.arq.de describes their work) from shipwrecks littering the seabed around Cape Verde.

Despite the name Praia (meaning **beach**), the one or two small coves near the town are none too great. The grey strip beneath where the road snakes off the end of the Platô – Praia Gamboa – is a possibility (and the site of a music festival in May – worth checking out if you're in Praia at the right time), though it tends to be used by exercising soldiers, and the pair of small crescents on either side of the *Hotel Praia-Mar*'s peninsula are nothing special. You'll do much better, if you can find transport, going out to São Francisco, 13km east of Praia (see p.446).

Eating

Praia has a decent variety of **restaurants** ranging from workaday eating house *casas de pasto* (CV$400–600) to more upmarket places (from CV$1000). The cheapest places are mostly away from the Platô area. Note that many establishments close on Sunday. If you want to save money, use the market or one of the **supermarkets** (the Supermercado Felicidade in Achada Sto António is the biggest shop in Cape Verde, and there's a branch beside the hotel of the same name on the plateau) and put together your own picnics. The friendly Parisienne bakery at the northern end of the plateau is a good place to stock up on cakes.

Restaurants and cafés

Platô

Cachito Av Amílcar Cabral. Chic, friendly and funky little café with great, freshly brewed coffee, draught beer, and a range of cakes and savoury snacks. Also a handful of terminals for inexpensive Internet access.

Café Lee Rua Andrade Corvo. Hole-in-the-wall local favourite with a *prato do dia* and a selection of tempting cakes.

Cafeteria Cap'Sul Centro Cultural Francês, Rua Andrade Corvo. Pleasant outdoor retreat. Mon 2.30–7pm, Tues–Fri 9am–noon & 2.30–7pm, Sat 10am–1pm.

Casa de Pasto Amelia Av Amílcar Cabral. Long-established and justly popular with townspeople and a scattering of foreign workers and volunteers for its reliable set meals (for around CV$600) and generous glasses of wine.

Casa de Pasto Antonia Rua Dr Miguel Bombarda. Basic, Kriolu-speaking place with one dish a day. Cheap, friendly, filling.

Flor de Lys Rua Cândido dos Reis. Restaurant with tiny adjacent bar popular with locals. Large helpings of freshly prepared food from a limited menu. Good value with main courses in the CV$600–700 range.

Lanchonette/Bar Aquarium Rua Serpa Pinto.

Very pleasant and lively place to eat and drink, with tropical fish on display and a selection of sandwiches, plus scrambled eggs, omelettes and soups all priced around CV$200. Daily except Sun 7am–9.30pm.

Lanchonette Atryum Rua Visconde de San Januário. Established restaurant and bar with good-value set lunches and inexpensive snacks.

Natura Rua Visconde de San Januário. Snug little pine-furnished café connected to the health-food shop of the same name. Serves treats like locally produced yoghurt and some tasty snacks. Mon–Fri 5–7pm.

Restaurante Avis Av 5 de Julho. Long-established and reliable café/bar, open on Sundays, with snacks and one or two dishes.

Restaurante Panorama Rua Serpa Pinto, on the *Hotel Felicidade* rooftop ☎61.41.00. Though its lofty position is perhaps the main attraction, this rather upmarket place does perhaps the most delicious omelettes in Cape Verde, cooked to perfection and beautifully presented. Daily except Sun 11am–3pm & 7pm–12.30am.

Elsewhere in Praia

Agua Na Boca Rua Union Europa, Achada Sto António ☎62.14.37. Up next to the *Hotel América*, this pleasant, pastel-shaded restaurant offers a very respectable range of pasta dishes alongside the usual fish and meat choices.

Bar-Restaurante A Falésia Rua 19 de Maio, Prainha district ☎61.77.76. Run by a friendly Portuguese couple, with terrace right above the beach. They serve Portuguese *bacalhau* (cod), a surprising range of salads and irresistible home-made cakes. Daily 11am–12.30am.

Bar-Restaurante Punta d'Incontro Av Cidade de Lisboa, west of the Platô. Popular with hip locals, this Italian establishment does quality pizza and exquisite Catalonian-style desserts, plus there's a pleasant thatched-roof terrace on which to enjoy them. Recommended. Open in the evenings from 7pm.

Cermar Gamboa Chã d'Areia district ☎61.44.08. Tasteful restaurant, very popular with well-heeled families and tourists from the nearby hotels.

Expensive, with lobster coming in at a whopping CV$2,800. Brazilian specialities at weekends. Daily noon–5pm & 7pm till late.

Hotel Marisol Chã d'Areia district ☎61.34.60. Has a deserved reputation and is correspondingly expensive, but the pleasantly situated terrace (good sea views) is a perfect spot for a lunchtime drink and a huge serving of the mouth-watering *sopa alentejana*, a Portuguese speciality made with garlic, coriander, chunks of bread and poached egg.

Quebra Canela Praia Quebra Canela ☎62.42.86. Out on a limb on the promontory above Quebra Canela beach, this well-appointed restaurant specializes in seafood. Closed Sun.

Restaurante Poeta Achada Sto António ☎61.38.00. Bland, upmarket establishment with reasonable international-style food. The sea views are undeniably good.

Drinking and nightlife

At nights the Platô is all but deserted by about 10pm, when even the kiosks in the *praça* are stacking up their chairs and battening down their hatches. The *praça* is a little livelier earlier in the evening, especially on Sunday evenings when the brass band occasionally fires up.

It's the wonderful **Quintal da Música** on Avenida Amílcar Cabral which keeps the flag flying for the Platô. One of the best places in Cape Verde to watch a performance of traditional music (in the evenings, usually free), it's an arts centre, recording studio, Internet café and record shop all rolled into one, the open-air seating contributing to the atmosphere.

The **nightclub** scene is limited: none have opened in the restrictive streets of the Platô, though there are a number of friendly **bars** here. Clubs are mostly scattered across the suburbs and never get going until around midnight. Music is generally a sweaty mixture of chart-topping European and American sounds and Cape Verdean *coladeira* and *funana* dance styles. Weekend admission charges are pretty uniform at CV$500. Offerings at the Platô **cinema** on Rua Serpa Pinto are rarely interesting.

Bars

Apart Hotel Holanda Achado Sto António. The vintage bar here, frequented by expats and worldly locals, has long played host to up-and-coming local musicians.

Bar Tex Rua Cesário Lacerda, Platô, opposite the post office. Great little subterranean bolthole (unmarked entrance) where local musicians often take to the tiny stage. Nightly except Sun.

Casa de Pasto Amelia Av Amílcar Cabral, Platô. You'll usually find a good atmosphere here – if you're simply into knocking back a few *copas*.

Flor de Lys Rua Visconde de San Januário, Platô. Like the *Amelia*, a popular local hangout.

Hotel Marisol Chã de Areia district. Attractive outdoor bar.

Lanchonette/Bar Aquárium Rua Serpa Pinto,

Platô. Friendly atmosphere, beer on tap and English-speaking boss. Mon–Sat 7am–11pm.

Restaurante Poeta Achada Sto António. A better place to drink than eat, with a pleasant bar.

Clubs

A Capital Part of the *Hotel Praia Mar* complex, Prainha. Attracts a smart, 30-something-and-up crowd (dress code enforced). Open from 10pm.

Bomba H On the road to Cidade Velha, about 1km from the intersection where the Cidade Velha *aluguers* ply their trade. The hippest place in Praia, with a playlist geared towards younger clubbers.

Zero Horas Achada Grande, between the port and the airport. An open-air affair with perhaps the most cosmopolitan musical mix of any of Praia's big clubs.

Listings

Airlines TACV, Rua Serpa Pinto, Platô ☎60.82.00, airport ☎63.39.82; Air Sénégal, Av Amílcar Cabral, Platô ☎61.75.29; TAP Air Portugal, Chã D'Areia, near the Palácio do Governo ☎61.58.26. There's no official airport information service but the TACV office in town knows as much as anyone.

Banks Branches of Banco Comercial do Atlântico, the national Banco de Cabo Verde and a Caixa Económica are all situated on Avenida Amílcar Cabral. Banco Interatlântico have a couple of branches on either side of *Hotel América* up in Achada Sto António.

Bookshop The best – nearly the only one – is the Instituto da Biblioteca Nacional on Avenida Amílcar Cabral, Platô, under the *Sofia Cyber Bar* (together, they make up the Palácio da Cultura) which has a limited stock of books in Portuguese. There are a few imported publications but nothing in English.

Car rental Alucar, Chã de'Areia, south of the plateau (☎61.73.24, ☏61.49.00), is the largest local firm; Hertz operate from *Hotel Trópico* in Prainha (☎61.82.60, ☏61.82.61). Both offer reasonable Japanese saloons for between CV$3900 and CV$6500 per day, inclusive of 80–100km travel. Taxis can be rented by the hour for around CV$1000.

CDs Head for the Instituto da Biblioteca Nacional (see above) where you'll find a good stock of Cape Verdean sounds as well as a decent Brazilian selection. In theory the little shop inside Quintal da Música stocks CDs from around the globe, although the shelves looked a bit bare at time of writing.

Cultural centres The Centro Cultural Francês is at Rua Andrade Corvo, Platô (Mon–Fri 8am–noon & 2.30–6.30pm, Sat 10am–1pm; ☎61.11.96, ☏61.12.60, ⊛ccf-praia.com). They have a French-language library and run a programme of film nights, exhibitions and concerts. Next to the Portuguese embassy, the Portuguese Cultural Centre at Achada Sto António (Mon–Fri 9am–noon & 2–6pm; ☎62.30.30, ☏62.30.58, ⊜cult.portugues@cvtelecom.cv) also has a library and screens Portuguese films.

Embassies and consulates Most consuls, including the UK's, reside in Mindelo (see p.466). In Praia, the French (☎61.55.91) and German

(☎61.20.76) embassies are located together in Prainha (Mon–Fri 8.15–11am & 2.30–3.15pm); the French embassy issues visas for Burkina, Côte d'Ivoire, Mauritania and Togo. The American embassy is at Rua Abilio Monteiro Macedo, Platô (Mon–Sat 8am–5pm; ☎65.16.56), and is generally helpful to Anglophone travellers. Senegal has an embassy at Rua Abilio Monteiro Macedo, Platô (Mon–Fri 8.30am–12.30pm & 2.30–4.30pm; ☎61.56.21).

Film and developing Photo Quick, Rua Serpa Pinto, is a busy place, but no cheaper than anywhere else. To develop and print a 24-exposure roll costs CV$1150.

Hospitals The Agostinho Neto Hospital at the northern edge of the plateau (☎61.45.36) is adequately equipped.

Internet access Sofia Fashion Cafe, above the Instituto da Biblioteca Nacional on Av Amílcar Cabral, and the stylish Sofia Cyber Bar on Rua Serpa Pinto have a good number of computers with Internet access for CV$300 per hour; both places also serve a range of drinks. Also worth trying are Cyber Quintal (inside Quintal da Música), Praianet (on the north side of the *praça*) and Cachito.

Pharmacies Farmácia Moderna and Farmácia Africana, on Avenida Amílcar Cabral, Platô, are both well stocked.

Post and telephones The post office on Rua Cesário Lacerda, Platô (Mon–Fri 8am–12pm & 2–5.30pm; ☎61.10.49), has an express service if you need to rush a letter back home, with collections on Mon, Wed and Fri. Poste restante is available and there's also a public telephone service in the same building.

Travel agents Travel agents such as Cabetur, Rua Serpa Pinto, Platô (☎61.55.11); Orbitur, Rua Roberto Duarte Silva, Platô (☎61.57.37); and Praiatour, Av Amílcar Cabral, Platô (☎61.57.46); tend to specialize in Brazilian package holidays, although they can organize flights, accommodation and excursions around Santiago for foreign visitors.

Visa extensions At the Direcção de Imigração e Fronteira on Rua Serpa Pinto (☎61.18.45), near the TACV office.

Around Praia

All the following trips from Praia are feasible within a day, or even half a day. The **São Francisco** area of beaches northeast of Praia has been earmarked as a tourism development zone. West of Praia, **Cidade Velha** is just about Cape Verde's only historical site and, while the ruins are interesting in their own right, the old village streets are among the prettiest in Cape Verde.

There's no great reason to visit **SÃO DOMINGOS**, about 20km north of Praia, but it's worth it for the pretty **journey** – only half an hour from Praia by Hiace – which takes you rapidly from the trashy outskirts of the capital into the heartland of rural Santiago. The minibus plunges into deep valleys where straight-backed women grind corn with a boulder against a flat rock (a *pilão*), pigs root at the roadside, and be-satchelled children walk home from school. São Domingos itself is one of the earliest settlements on the island, over 450 years old; its church has a famous boat-shaped pulpit. Drake ventured this far inland in 1585 and, find-ing the settlement abandoned like Ribeira Grande, thought better of continuing into the wild interior. On the way into town from Praia, there's a craft sales co-operative on the right, with a limited selection of pottery, weaving and ornaments, at sensible prices. There is a **pousada** here where you can stay, the somewhat imposing cream-and-orange *Bela Vista* – which might open for your visit, on demand. It's a delightful place, in the floor of the valley and surrounded by irri-gated cultivation.

São Francisco beaches

The string of coves at **SÃO FRANCISCO**, about 13km northeast of Praia, is worth the effort required to get there, to escape the odd bit of pollution and occasional hassles at the town beaches. There's no scheduled transport, but hiring a taxi from Praia, allowing you two hours at the beach before returning, will cost around CV$2000–3000. Otherwise, head in the direction of the airport, turn left just over the bridge, walk through the *bairro* and try hitching – which is most likely to be successful on a Saturday or Sunday morning. The track from Praia has been scraped across the island's steep and rocky southern corner, and tips you out onto a flat sandy plain by the sea, where there are several **beaches** to choose from. The first you reach on the track is the biggest, dotted with palms and a couple of villas built further back, but the furthest to the south is the best, with steps for the arthritic ex-President Pereira to climb down for his swims. There's clean sand and good waves, though take food and drink, as there's nothing at the beach.

Cidade Velha

Heading west out of town for 10km in the opposite direction brings you to the old capital – **Ribeira Grande** – now known simply as **CIDADE VELHA**, "Old City". After the hot, dry moors on the way from Praia, you round the last bend and the village is down below. The setting is everything – a living, moving sea, awash with foam, thundering against the black crags.

Nowadays Cidade Velha is a village of fishing people and farmers living among the ruins of sixteenth- and seventeenth-century Portugal. As one bit of local tourist literature pointed out a few years back: ". . . one can find valuable patrimonial wit-nesses still in ruins, thus deserving restoration, good keeping and consolidation". Fortunately, it looks as if this sage advice is finally being heeded. The ruins of the cathedral are now home to archeologists and restorers – as well as the occasional tourist – while Cidade Velha itself has been designated a UNESCO World Heritage site.

Down in the town *praça* stands Cidade Velha's most famous relic, the **pelourinho** or pillory, where captives were shackled on display. The most notable building is the **cathedral**, finished in 1693, a century and a half after the foundation of the dio-cese; it's located on the hillside to the right as you arrive from Praia. The large fleet of red fishing boats on the beach indicates more activity than you'd at first think, though many young people have moved to Praia. Today the village is increasingly popular with both Cape Verdean and foreign tourists, most of whom seem to retire to the thatch-roofed beach bar after a hard day's sightseeing. Should you wander into the tiny "tourist office"/craft shop off the main square in fruitless search of

The rise and fall of Ribeira Grande

Ribeira Grande was the site of the **first Portuguese base** in Africa, founded to create a slave-trading entrepôt, selling labour to the Spanish West Indies. With a relatively good anchorage (there was nothing any safer in Madeira or the Azores), Ribeira Grande rapidly became the main mid-Atlantic victualling point for European merchant vessels in the sixteenth century. The *ribeira* almost never dried up and was dammed at its mouth to provide a permanent pool of **fresh water**. The town became a "city" in 1533 when a papal bull made it the seat of a diocese extending along half the West African coast.

In Atlantic trading circles Ribeira Grande's reputation soon spread. The English sea dog **Sir Francis Drake** caught the scent in 1585 and attacked the settlement with a force of 1000. The assault was more than just piracy – the union of Spain and Portugal meant that Cape Verde was considered enemy territory by the English – and it was well planned. Drake landed at Praia to sneak overland and attack Ribeira Grande from behind, only to find the town deserted: the inhabitants had sensibly fled inland. Drake's crew stayed a fortnight, plundering what little there was and foraying into the interior without reward. One of the force was killed and mutilated by African slaves and Drake torched Ribeira Grande in reprisal, sparing only the hospital – the Casa Misericorde – whose ruins are still visible to the right as you descend into the centre of the present-day village.

Ribeira Grande's eventual defeat by a French force in 1712 led to a rethink on the part of the Portuguese and the more considered development of the new capital of Praia. The cathedral was already falling apart by 1735 and, when a new bishop was appointed in 1754, he quickly left Santiago and spent the rest of his life on Santo Antão.

glossy brochures, you may well find yourself pleasantly waylaid with a game of *ouril* and a few glasses of *grogue*.

It's worth going down to the *ribeira* west of town and up the other side, through cane and corn and under mango trees, to further, less explored ruins – the church of **Nossa Senhora do Rosário** which served as a cathedral in miniature when the diocese was first created, and the Capuchin **Monastery of São Francisco** higher up the valley, neither of which should take more than twenty minutes to reach on foot. Once up there, you can admire the palm-filled valley and muse on what five centuries of Portuguese rule have brought, and taken from, the islands. When the first buildings were put up the treeless scene must have had much the barren cast of a tropical Iona: all the trees have been established since that time. Today, you're likely to come across sugar-cane presses and *grogue* stills as you climb through the jungly allotments – the aroma is unmissable.

Alternatively, hike back up the road into town from Praia and cut back to the left, to look over the extensive remains of the **Fortaleza Real de São Filipe** (CV$100), which dominates the whole of Cidade Velha from on high. The fort has weathered the years incredibly well and offers stunning views of the *ribeira* and, behind, of the Serra do Pico de Santo António.

Practicalities

Aluguers from Praia leave regularly from Sucupira and from the parking area in Terra Branca, southwest of the Platô. Getting back to Praia can be a little problematic, though you can easily pass the time waiting for the next *aluguer* by drinking *grogue* with the elders down in one of the village stores. If you want to **stay** the night, there are a couple of earthy B&B rooms for rent (CV$2500) in one of the old thatched cottages on Rua Banana. Ask in the craft shop or just ask around for the owner, Abel Borges (☎67.13.74).

North and east Santiago

The main reason to go north is to visit **Tarrafal**, a beautiful fishing village that makes an ideal spot to rest up for a few days. It's right at the opposite end of Santiago from Praia, and there are two different minibus routes that go there – one over the rugged spine of the island, the other along the indented east coast. The journey can make a very satisfying round trip.

The mountain route

The mountain route goes straight across an unexpectedly fairy-tale interior – peaks and rocky needles, soaring valleys, narrow terraces and ridges – a fine journey, especially during or after the rains. There are steep climbs and some great views before Assomada, then higher passes in the Malagueta range, rising to over 1300m.

The highest point of the island, the 1394-metre Pico de Santo António – with some of the few monkeys in Cape Verde on its slopes – rises above the town of **São Jorge dos Orgãos**, a few kilometres south of the main road.

Shortly before you reach Assomada from the south, you come to the small town of **Picos** perched on a crag on the right, next to a huge basaltic outcrop looking out over a wide, deep valley. In season, the blooms of jacaranda and frangipani bubble around the small *praça* and church. The town is the site of the INIDA, the National Institute of Agrarian Research and Development, which has a *miradouro* (panoramic viewpoint) overlooking the plantations, and a flourishing Botanical Garden where you can see Cape Verdean flora and birdlife.

Assomada

ASSOMADA, also known as Vila de Santa Catarina, is the second largest town on the island – a lively place by Cape Verdean standards, with a large market and some quaint architecture. On market days it can be very hot and hectic, not the kind of place you want to be carrying heavy or bulky baggage around between bus rides. If you have only an hour or two, take a short walk north out of town and a turning right, then a steep path down into the *ribeira* to see what must be a contender for the biggest **silk-cotton tree** in the world (though it's always referred to locally as a "baobab"); ask for **Boa Entrada**, the neighbouring village, tucked in the *ribeira*. You can't fail to see the tree standing on the slope across the valley: it's a monster. The trunk – over fifty metres round at the base – is a maze of contorted buttresses, and it would stand out anywhere, but in Cape Verde, land of limited leafiness, it's a fantastic sight. The tree must be as old as the first generation of settlers. In 1855, according to a Rev. Thomas, chaplain to the African Squadron of the US Navy, it was "forty feet in circumference" and had been "standing where it now stands when the island was first discovered".

There's no shortage of **accommodation** options in Assomada, the best-value of which is the smart *Paris 2000* round the corner from the BCA bank in the centre of town (☎65.35.02; ❹). Slightly cheaper is the modern but neglected *El Mundo* on the edge of town next to the Shell garage (☎97.54.38; ❸). For snacks, *Café Central* off the main square is a cool retreat offering quality coffee, ice cream and cakes. Cheap Internet access – and quite possibly Cape Verde's biggest pool table – is available at the improbably named *Ciber Buggs Bilhar*, five minutes' walk from the main square on the main road out of town.

The east coast route

Heading north by the **east coast route**, you follow the same road out of Praia as for the mountain route, then cut right at the Ribeirão Chiqueiro junction, with the village of **Praia Baixo** 7km away on the coast. There is direct transport to Praia Baixo from Praia's Sucupira depot, but you're likely to be the only visitor if you come outside the weekend. The village is reached down a long, low *ribeira* of partially deserted smallholdings, the road to it passing over concrete flood crossings. The beach is safe, in a deep, sheltered bay, with beach shades on the sands, one or two holiday villas behind, and at least one functioning beach bar. Men do some fishing by boat, but it's very quiet and, with the graffitied evidence of frustration with the former government (A Baixa MPD – "Down with MPD", and so on), it all has a rather depressing air.

The first village you come to on the main road is **PEDRA BADEJO**, with a magnificent **coconut** grove marking the entrance to the settlement and gigantic bananas on sale – if you're lucky. You can see *pedreiros* making cobbles here, each shaded under a banana leaf on the clifftop. It's all very floral and pleasant, with good beaches and caves. There are even a couple of interesting places to stay. The *Tiara* (T94.38.20; ❹) is a strange, almost apocalyptic-looking concrete block looking out to sea at the edge of town, with reasonable, pine-furnished rooms, a restaurant and even a disco. Even more eccentric, and certainly more charming, is the nameless white villa owned by Frenchman Francis Laresche (T69.17.71; ❹). Great value if you're looking to chill out for a while, it has a wonderful location right on the edge of town with a view of uninterrupted desert and ocean. For meals, try the friendly, compact *Joyce*, up the hill on the first left as you head out along the main street.

Calheta de São Miguel, the next stop, has a big old church on the hilltop. The dependence on rainfall in the Cape Verdes comes home to you as the road repeatedly drops to cross stony *ribeiras* where women wash clothes in the narrow streams: when water is about, the flanks of the gulches are dense with crops – bananas, papayas, cane and cassava – and heavy rains can also bring floods that smash the cobbles in many places.

Tarrafal

TARRAFAL doesn't look much at first. You have to go right through the small town to discover the wonderful, clean white **beach** below its gentle cliffs. Once the site of a political prison under the Portuguese, Tarrafal's main claim to fame is now this beach. The town has an attractive hibiscus-filled *praça* with church and marketplace set around. There are palms and discreet beach houses to one side and a working, fishing-beach atmosphere on the other. Once installed in Tarrafal it's easy to pass a few days – or even much longer – swimming and lounging, drinking cold beers, eating slabs of fresh tuna and watching the fishing boats coming in and the children playing. Except at weekends, when Cape Verdean tourists and expatriate beach hunters zone in, it's fairly peaceful, and with the mountainous interior of the island looming behind, the place can seem incredibly isolated. Yet a boy shooting down the cobbled hill on his shiny new American mountain bike is a reminder of close and important ties with the outside world.

If you fancy something more active than sunbathing, try the dive centre, Blue Adventure (T66.18.80), right on the beach. Walk south and you come to **further beaches** – of black sand – and more coconuts. Head north and a fine **coastal path** leads up over the cliffs above the crashing surf for as far as you like, with terrific views. There are some tiny coves along here, with great, natural swimming pools.

In stark contrast is the former concentration camp just outside town. Now a **museum** (daily 7am–6pm; CV$100), this intimidating place was used to incarcerate Portuguese communists during the 1940s, and was re-opened by the Portuguese authorities in the 1960s to house prisoners from the wars of independence in the various African colonies. Nowadays the only inmates are a few wandering goats, although the ruined barracks and solitary confinement tanks retain an oppressive atmosphere. A chalet has been built outside the perimeter walls to house a fascinating collection of documents and photographs (including a great shot of the prisoners rushing ecstatically towards their families on the day of the camp's closure). To reach the museum, head out of town on the Assomada road for about 2km and you'll see the white stone entry portal on your right.

Practicalities

The town's attractive hibiscus-filled *praça* has a church and marketplace set around, together with a Banco Comercial do Atlântico and a **post office**. **Accommodation** is easily arranged. The best-value **beach** option is the *Solmarina* (℡66.12.19; ❸), a colourful, funky little budget place with balconies, a roof terrace and some mountain bikes for rent (CV\$1400 for 3–4hr). *Baía Verde* has well-equipped, palm-shaded chalets by the beach (℡66.11.28, ℻66.14.14, ✉baia.verde @mail.com; ❺) while the *Hotel Tarrafal*, also on the beach (℡66.17.85, ℻66.17.87, ✉htltarrafal@cvtelecom.cv; ❼), is suitably gleaming and luxurious, and has its own pool and Internet facilities. In town itself, among a number of *pensões*, your best bet is the bright and clean *Tátá* (℡66.11.25).

At the market, the *Casa de Pasto Sopa de Pedra* and *Graciosa* are cheap, basic places to **eat**. For dinner, you might want to try the pleasant but pricey terrace restaurant at *Baía Verde*, which occasionally hosts live music.

Fogo

The first impression of **FOGO** is of its tremendous mass – a brooding volcanic cone rising forbiddingly 2829m out of the sea, its steep peaks rising above the clouds. Flying from Praia, sit on the right of the plane for the best views. The arrival at the capital **São Filipe**, on the west coast, involves the plane dipping low over the rough ground to touch the runway, perched high on the dunnish cliffs. Below the airport, a striking beach of baking black sand drops straight into an ultramarine sea. If you arrive by ferry, you dock at the tiny port of **Vale da Cavaleiros**, 3km north of São Filipe.

Although all the islands have their own distinguishing marks, it's Fogo which stands out as the great character of the Cape Verdes – it's impossible to forget you're on a **volcano** here. Fogo – which means "fire" – last had an eruption in 1995, when deluges of molten lava streamed into the main caldera, and four thousand people were evacuated. On the west side of the island, the land is gentler, with better soil, low trees, farms and plantations. The ancient volcanic base in this district is undisturbed by fresh eruptions and after rain it's often cloaked beneath a pastoral blanket of wild flowers.

Transport on Fogo depends on *aluguers* and the odd private vehicle; the southern road between São Filipe and Mosteiros in the northeast is the only one on which there's any real traffic. People on Fogo are often startlingly kind, accommodating hikers, showing you directions miles out of their way and doing everything possible to help.

São Filipe and around

SÃO FILIPE has an orderly civility which sits oddly with its steeply sloping clifftop location, high above the black beach. The streets link a number of small squares and gardens and a promenade along the cliffs, while a number of the town's pretty *sobrados* (colonial houses) have been exquisitely restored to their former glory. Others lie in various states of disrepair but the architecture is never less than captivating – it's fair to say that São Filipe stands as one of Cape Verde's most attractive towns.

Although it has an unhurried bustle during the day, after dark everyone's inside, apparently watching TV: through every open doorway there's a blue glow and a stack of silhouetted backs. All in all, it's a significant improvement on the 1930s when an English visitor, Archibald Lyall, reported a community in the grip of diabolical poverty, isolated from Praia, let alone Lisbon, and totally without electricity or transport – small, shaggy horses were the only way to get about.

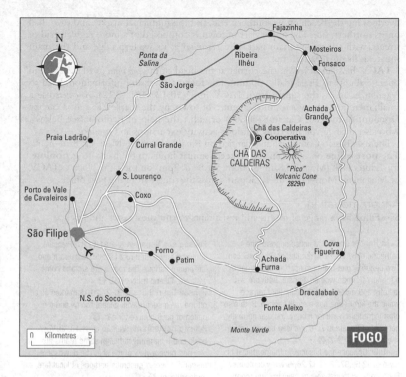

The Town and around

There's little to do around town, but strolling through the cobbled streets has its own quiet satisfaction: there are several small *praças* to sit in, while the tiny **market**, with an all-purpose selection, is worth a visit. You might also care to drop by the **Casa da Memória** (Wed–Fri 10am–noon or by appointment), a restored nineteenth-century house on the block immediately north of the church on the south side of town; it holds an interesting collection of photos and artefacts documenting Saõ Filipe's history.

For a recreational walk, head up the airport road a couple of kilometres south of town and then scramble down the cliffs, past the ruins of a tiny church to a *ribeira*, where you can join a path to the beach and some fish-processing works. The **beach** itself is great if you're in the mood: a steep shelf of black sand – ferociously hot – with big waves breaking, seemingly without any fetch, directly onto it. You dive into them from the shore. Heading back to town, take the fishermen's path and look out for the building with arms hanging out between bars – São Filipe's **prison**, on the cliff's very edge. You'll be told off by the guards if you engage in shouted exchanges of greetings with the prisoners across the gully. It's a mournfully picturesque spot to be jailed, with vistas out across the channel to Brava and the Atlantic.

Practicalities

The town's small **airport** is located 2km to the southwest, from where you can get an *aluguer* or taxi into the centre. The town itself – divided roughly into upper and lower parts (Bila Riba and Bila Baxo) by an imposing stone wall – is compact and it's fairly easy to find your way around the largely nameless cobbled streets. The small, irregular grid of streets in the lower part is bordered by a promenade overlooking the beach on its southern end, and the municipal market and town hall on its northern side. The upper part of town is composed of a more regular grid of streets, with the town's main park (the *pracinha*) at its western edge and the main square at its northeastern tip.

TACV have an office on the corner at the head of the *pracinha* (℡81.12.28), and operate flights to Praia (daily; 30min). For **ferry** tickets and information, head to Agenamar, across the square from TACV (℡81.10.12, ℻81.13.12). *Aluguers* use a small, mercifully shady *praça* in the centre of town, by the market. To rent a car, try Discount Auto Rent Car (℡81.14.80) or enlist the help of Ecotour (see below), who also arrange volcano trips, outdoor-activity excursions and the like.

There's a Banco Comercial do Atlântico on Rua do Hospital (Mon–Fri 8am–3pm). The **post office** on the main square keeps similar hours to the bank. To get **online**, try Eduteca Alf (Mon–Fri 8am–8.30pm, Sat 8am–2pm) on the same block as TACV, or Megabyte (Mon–Fri 8am–10.30pm), across the square from the post office.

Accommodation

São Filipe has a range of rooms and restaurants to suit most tastes and pockets.

Casa Renate Unmarked house opposite the cathedral ℡81.25.18, ✉renatefogo@hotmail.com. Two beautiful one-bedroom apartments let out by a friendly German woman, Renate. Both are s/c, tasteful and modern with a communal terrace, while the larger one has a small kitchen. Both also offer incredible value for money. You can normally get hold of Renate in *Le Bistro* (see below), which she also owns. ❹ & ❺

Ecotour Opposite the hospital, in the northeast of town ℡92.69.97, ℻81.17.26, ⓦwww.ecotour.cv. Fogo's official tourist agency have inviting rooms and apartments to let. ❺

Pensão Fatima ℡81.13.59. On the other side of the cathedral, this is a decent place with s/c rooms and a rooftop terrace. ❹

Pensão Las Vegas ℡ & ℻81.12.81. Pleasant, light and airy, with a roof terrace, restaurant and ice-cream parlour. The rooms are s/c and come with a/c, TV and fridge. B&B ❹

Pensão Open Skies ℡81.27.26. Unmarked place off the main square with decent rooms and the option of paying more for a/c. ❹

Pensão Restaurante Vulcão ℡81.18.30. Very basic and a bit grimy although some rooms are airy and have a view of the sea. The downstairs restaurant serves generous portions of local fare (order ahead). ❸

Pousada Bela Vista ℡81.17.34. Up near the TACV office, this offers good value for money with clean, very pleasant rooms in a graceful, colonial building. ❹

Eating, drinking and nightlife

Boite Hexagonal/Café Katen Tádju Opposite the *Pensão Las Vegas*. The *boite* (club) kicks in on Friday and Saturday nights and special occasions, while the rooftop bar/café is open daily 7am–11pm for beers, wine, *grogue* and a small range of snacks.

Esplanada Nhácanda Sunny little terrace up from the market with a wonderful view of Brava on a clear day. Serves beers, sodas and small fish pastries.

Le Bistro ℡81.25.18. Brightly painted, slightly arty little German-run restaurant with a great terrace. As well as meat and fish dishes there are

are simple but surpisingly tasty options for vegetarians who've overdosed on omelette – the soups are especially recommended (try the pumpkin). A deserved first choice for foreign tourists. Open all day, all week, with breakfast served from 7am and dinner from 5pm.

Restaurant Seafood ℡81.31.42. Located in a prime position above the beach at the bottom of town, this is a popular place with good lobster at a decent price (CV$700) and a fine terrace.

Tropical Club A bar rather than a club, popular as an evening meeting place where people gather for beer and cocktails on the leafy terrace.

Exploring the volcano

The **volcano** is a dominant and potentially time-filling lure. At the caldera rim you may be lucky and have the whole eight-kilometre-wide bowl of the Chã das

Caldeiras ("Field of Boilers") – the huge **collapsed crater** that was created by the island's formative eruption – spread clearly before you, or it may be blotted out by thick cloud. It's an extraordinary, unearthly, black-lava landscape and nothing can quite prepare you for the strange thrill of witnessing it for the first time, even if the scanty vineyards and other cultivation soften it a little. There are in fact a number of families on the upper reaches of the road to the crater who brew their own wine, and who will be only too glad to offer a tasting.

The cobbled road winds through the crater like a causeway. The small, oblong houses are built of lava stone and crouch low against the ground. It's hard to imagine what keeps people here, or how they make ends meet in this inhospitable environment, but you'll see a variety of livestock, and the vineyards are relatively successful. Many families in this district trace their descent from a Duc de Montrond who is said to have fled France in the nineteenth century after a duel – and thoughtfully brought some vines with him. You may well find the people of the crater among the friendliest and kindest in Cape Verde, in stark contrast with the harshness of the landscape and despite their obvious grinding poverty.

The Pico de Fogo

The moonscape of lava and scattered mini-craters is dramatically surmounted by the main cone, the **Pico de Fogo**, which rises in a cindery, pyramid-shaped heap on the east side, about a thousand metres above the caldera floor. This cone has been dormant since the eighteenth century, but volcanic activity continues in a big way deep below the surface and once in every few decades, as in 1995, new "mini-cones" are blown up within the caldera. You may be reassured to know that vulcanologists monitor the activity and local people now get good warning of impending eruptions.

To **climb the Pico**, you should aim to make an early start. If you set off much after 7am, you'll find you're still out there in the midday sun, instead of back down in the village having a celebratory drink. It's an exhausting three-to-four hour scramble to the summit, up a two-steps-forward-one-step-back slope of fine volcanic scree. There are several guides in the village who will happily accompany you – without one of them you won't easily find the best route, which changes sporadically. Companions are a good idea, anyway, as a fall in a remote place like this can be dangerous. When you reach the top, don't be tempted to try to ascend to the very highest point – it's an unstable and tricky little climb which has resulted in accidents in the past. There are routes down into the deep, red and yellow, egg cup-shaped crater of the peak itself. But few people feel like tackling them at this stage in the day – it's much more tempting just to sit and absorb the views, especially down towards the eastern side of the island. Here, tens of thousands of years ago, during a heightened period of seismic activity, a cataclysmic landslide removed a huge part of the eastern side of the island, taking the original crater edge with it into the Atlantic and leaving the crater exposed on its eastern flank.

Coming down, in contrast to the climb, is like a free fairground ride, as you simply gallop down through the scree of the forty-degree slope in big bounds, and reach the floor of the caldera in little over an hour.

Practicalities

It can be hard to reach the caldera if you try to set off at the wrong time of day. You can take a vehicle to the village of **Chã das Caldeiras**. There are **aluguers** most mornings from São Filipe (2hr; about CV$500) but they are not super-abundant. If you ask taxi drivers about hiring a *particular* you'll usually get quoted at least CV$4000 and as much as CV$6000 for the one-hour-plus trip. If you've got the time, an alternative plan would be simply to set off with water and supplies and **walk up**. The main staging post in this case is the straggling village of **Achada Furna** on the south side of the caldera, about 15km from São Felipe. From here, the caldera rim is about 6km as the crow flies, but it's a steep climb and a good three-hour hike up the road that twists for 9km up the mountainside. Before you set off from São Filipe, make sure you have suitable snacks and drinking water. And if you plan to climb the peak itself, it's best to have hiking boots.

When arriving in Chã das Caldeiras, arrange to be dropped at the house of a guide in the first part of the village; most *aluguer* and taxi drivers will do this anyway. The standard rate for a guide to the peak is CV$1500. The only formal **accommodation** in the village is *Pousada Pedra Brabo* (☎61.89.40, ☎81.29.04; ❹), a basic yet tastefully constructed (partly from local materials) guesthouse run by a hospitable Frenchman. You could quite easily spend a few days here, sunning yourself in the courtyard and marvelling at the Pico looming up behind the walls. Delicious meals are also available and breakfast is included in the price. Alternatively, you can go local and opt for dinner, bed and breakfast in a private house; the going rate is CV$1000 and you can fix this up at the Cooperativa (see below). While facilities are basic, you'll be made very welcome; more importantly, you'll be contributing towards a much-needed source of income for the villagers. You can also pick a spot anywhere on the black cinders and camp, but you should count on bringing your **food** requirements with you – there are no real shops in the caldera.

Even if you aren't organizing a homestay, at some point during your visit you should pop in to the **Cooperativa**, the community's principal social venue, where you can buy bottles of the fearsomely robust local red, plus mouth-wateringly fresh goat's cheese and basic provisions. You'll also be able to buy the ubiquitous model houses which the locals fashion from volcanic rock, matchsticks and straw; they make great presents. It's surprising how often the Cooperativa band sets up for a Cape Verdean jam – guitar, violin, *cavaquinho*, keyboard, scraper – behind the bar. If you are lucky enough to hear music up here, it'll very possibly be the rawest, most visceral and emotional you'll hear anywhere in Cape Verde. The gas storm-lamps (there's no mains electricity) only add to the atmosphere, but take care if you've been indulging in the wine: the lack of any streetlighting whatsoever can mean a potentially hazardous stagger home as you negotiate the low lava-brick walls.

It's hard to get **public transport** back to São Filipe after finishing the climb or indeed if you've merely overslept. Most vehicles leave around 6am, so you're likely to have to stay in Chã das Caldeiras a second night. If you have to get back for a flight, you're at the mercy of whatever a vehicle-owner wants to charge you. Alternatively, you could hike out down to Achada Furna (14km), where you should have more luck with transport, or hitching. If you aren't pressed for time, it's a beautiful descent – on foot or in a vehicle – from Chã das Caldeiras down the exposed eastern side of the volcanic massif to Mosteiros.

From Mosteiros to São Filipe

From **Mosteiros** ("Monastery"), where there's a solitary *pensão*, *Christine & Irmãos* (☎81.28.54; ❹), transport on to São Filipe shouldn't be too much of a problem, although, as usual, most *aluguers* leave early in the morning. Otherwise, you'll probably have to walk a couple of kilometres to **Igreja** ("Church"), which is the nearest thing to a town centre in this part of the island. The fare to São Filipe shouldn't be more than CV$700, but a *particular* could cost ten times as much.

Heading **anticlockwise** out of Mosteiros, there's a breathtaking road up to the hamlet of **Ribeira Ilheu**, terrifyingly steep if you're in a vehicle. Scarcity of lifts aside, this is really worth the walk – allow a day to climb the 15km – which rewards you with stunning views, sheltered and overgrown little valleys, and a village where your arrival will cause a minor sensation. Once committed, you'll probably have to continue on foot, covering the worst portion of the round-island road, another 10km or so, as far as São Jorge, where you should find transport on to São Filipe, some 17km further south. There's a good beach at Ponta da Salina, a short walk from São Jorge.

Travelling clockwise, you climb quickly from Mosteiros and skirt beneath the crater walls over a battlefield of strewn lava. The road runs high in places and, with a fast driver, it's not a journey you'll ever forget: the cobbled highway traverses the cinder slopes in an unnerving series of undefended loops hundreds of metres above the waves. The isolated **settlements** of lava-block houses have a temporary look about them – there's a menacing slag-heap darkness here. It's high up on this eastern side that most of Fogo's famous **coffee** is grown.

Once the road curves **west**, the countryside opens out to more relaxing dimensions; a mellow, rolling landscape of maize and agave takes over and there's a surprising amount of tree cover, mostly acacias. In the pockets of fertile volcanic soil that haven't been rainwashed away, there are beans growing around the maize stalks, with squash, sweet potatoes and cucumbers between. Bananas (a Santiago speciality) are much scarcer.

Brava

BRAVA, the smallest inhabited island, has always been the most isolated of the Cape Verdes, only properly settled at the end of the seventeenth century after a major eruption on Fogo, in 1675. Its capital, **Vila Nova Sintra** (Vila) – named after the royal resort of Sintra outside Lisbon – is one of the archipelago's loveliest towns, sedately arranged in a long-extinct crater high above the coast. The island's stone walls overflow with lobelia and vines, and clouds drift through even when the rest of the archipelago is parched with drought. Although its name means "wild", the island has long enjoyed a remarkable degree of domestication, with virtually all the land under neatly tended cultivation, supporting the archipelago's highest population density. Bravans have a long seafaring tradition: the American **whalers** called at this island more than any other, and the largest contingent of *americanos* comes from Brava. Sadly, much of Brava's infrastructure was destroyed in 1982 by Hurricane Beryl, and not all has been rebuilt.

Small enough to walk all over, but precipitous too, Brava is worth the few days' visit you'll have to devote to it between ferry or plane connections. There haven't been any flights from Praia for a good few years now (the airstrip on the west coast is so short, and so often very windy, that pilots were having to return to Praia without having landed) and the situation doesn't look like changing any time soon. Even if there were flights, the road from the airport is in such a state of disrepair it's positively dangerous. Although there should be about two crossings a week, **ferry** connections are inconvenient and you'll have to work around whatever timetable Arca Verde are operating at the time you plan to travel (see p.414). The channel between Fogo and Brava is notoriously rough: you may well need seasickness pills and the voyage, even in "normal" conditions, can be quite frightening; there are moments

when you seriously have to hang on. On many trips, everyone and everything gets drenched. The boat docks at the tiny port of **Furna** (where you can buy tickets for your return journey if necessary), five winding kilometres below Vila.

Vila Nova de Sintra

Vila is tiny – a five-minute walk from one side to the other. There's little to do in town: the market has nothing to offer, and there's no real sightseeing or shopping to do (the late-opening Shell station shop on the east side of town probably has the best selection of groceries). Music lovers, however, are better served, Vila Sintra being another excellent place to catch some authentic local sounds.

There's a Banco Comercial do Atlântico on the road north of the square, a post office on the square's east side and a TACV office (℡85.11.92) just off to the right of the main road at the square's western end. **Accommodation** is a straightforward matter: stay at the clean and quiet little state-run *Pousada Municipal* (℡85.16.97; ❸; if there's nobody about, ask for keys in the Camara Municipal). Alternatively, check out the *Pensão Paulo Sena* (℡85.13.12; ❸), which, though run-down and seriously in need of refurbishment, has a good reputation; the owner's effusive welcome and the large survey map of Brava on the wall are two other reasons you might call in, and Paulo also does good food to order, with his restaurant/front room pretty busy most nights.

The *Por Sul* bar/restaurant on the main *praça* is dedicated to showcasing what it terms *tocatina*, basic but captivating acoustic music played on guitar, *cavaquinho* and occasionally violin. You might be lucky enough to hear a spontaneous warm-up in the tiny bar (where the barman, José, speaks English with a New Jersey accent) but failing that, a full band plays in the restaurant on weekend evenings. Even if you haven't ordered one of the generous portions of seafood (from CV$500), you can go through and watch the band. Also in Vila, a nightclub, *Kananga*, fires up at weekends.

Around the island

Fajã d'Agua, on the west coast, is one of the most idyllic villages in Cape Verde, worth at least a day of your no doubt limited time in Brava. As for the rest of the island, it's small enough to explore simply by **walking**: there are fine hikes and strolls everywhere, and even from coast to coast won't take more than a day. Be aware, however, that distances on the winding roads are always longer than they look on the map. There's a superb three- to four-kilometre walk from Vila Nova

Tavares, writer of mornas

A native of Brava, Eugénio Tavares (1867–1930) is a romanticized figure in Cape Verdean lore. A journalist and civil servant for most of his life, he was the country's best-known writer of the **morna** song form, the distinctive Cape Verdean music. Like Portugal's *fado*, the *morna* has a minor-key melody and both may have originated in the Portuguese slave islands of São Tomé. But the heart of a *morna* is its lyric. *Mornas* evoke an unmistakeably Cape Verdean feeling of *sodade* – yearning, longing, home-sickness – and the classic examples are all by Tavares, who achieved his huge popularity through his use of the Kriolu language rather than Portuguese.

Tavares' *mornas* deal with the pain of love and loss. One of his best-known is "O Mar Eterno", inspired by his affair with an American woman visiting Brava by yacht. Her disapproving father set sail one night and the two never met again. Another famous composition, "Hora di Bai" ("The Hour of Leaving"), was traditionally sung on the dock at Furna as relatives boarded America-bound ships. You can hear a set of his songs on a CD entitled *Saozinha Canta Eugenio Tavares* by the singer Saozinha (MB Records, US).

Sintra down to **Santa Barbara** and the fountain at **Vinagre**, and another beautiful short walk from **Nossa Senhora do Monte** to nearby **Cova Joana**. From Cova you can ask directions for the steep path down to Fajã; it's a bit hairy in places and will take a few hours, but the vistas are wonderful. Your view of Fajã is obscured until the very end; to emerge from the tangle of greenery at the bottom of the Ribeira and suddenly be confronted with the stunningly situated village is one of the highlights of Cape Verde. There's also a good one-hour trail from Campo Baixo down to the beach at **Tantum**, 2km south of Portete; and a fine, easy walk from Vila Nova to the impressively sited village of **Mato Grande**, perched out on a promontory high above the east coast.

Fajã d'Agua and Portete

From Vila, you can walk to **FAJÃ D'AGUA**, two hours down an incredible switchback of a road, or take an *aluguer* (one or two drivers make the trip regularly enough) for CV$200 in a *coletivo* (locals pay only CV$50: a rare example of tourist profiteering) or CV$800 if you charter the vehicle. Fajã's setting is unforgettable, a pretty hamlet strung out along the shoreline, dotted with palm trees, hemmed in by imposing, sun-baked mountains and backed by a steep, lush *ribeira*. People here are very friendly and you'll quickly feel part of its tightknit community. It has possibly the best budget **hotel** in Cape Verde, *Burgo's Pensão* (☎85.13.21; ❷), or, to give it its full name, *Bar Dos Amigos Campo Ocean Front Motel and Bar Restaurant*. Three pretty s/c double rooms, with a shared balcony, perch above the family's own accommodation and the little bar/restaurant below. Alternatively, if you manage to track down Danny Pereira (☎85.14.18), you may be able to rent his sister Julia's house (❸). With two bedrooms, a living room, kitchen and bathroom, it offers great value, but its best feature is a perfectly positioned balcony where you can watch the moon shimmer over the bay. More upmarket but still great value for money is *Sol Na Baia* (☎ & 🖷85.20.70; ❺), with three bright, beautifully furnished rooms, a dining room with French cuisine and a lovely garden. Seven more rooms are planned along with a library and Internet facilities.

The locals spend the days drinking *grogue* and drifting from group to group along Fajã's single street, a round of ceaseless but harmonious socialising which you'll soon find yourself drawn into. It's utterly peaceful but you can always work up an appetite for the hearty meals (courtesy of *Bar Coqueiro*, where you can also play bingo under the thatched awning) by hiking up the terraced *ribeira* or out to the wind-whipped, deserted airstrip, a couple of kilometres to the south. On Saturday nights, the tiny sweatbox of a club splutters into haphazard life and continues until everyone's finally had enough (usually Sunday afternoon). You may also be treated to the highly entertaining sight of local lads shimmying up vertigo-inducing palm trees in sixty seconds flat. If the coconuts are ripe you won't taste anything sweeter in Cape Verde.

If you want to swim, go beyond the airport to the neat little black-sand beach at **Porteto**, about an hour's walk in total from Fajã. You should take a companion from Fajã the first time you go, to get on the right path. At Porteto you'll meet the odd fisherman, and sometimes a couple of children, but it's otherwise deserted.

Maio

MAIO was first sighted on May 1, 1460 – hence its name – but there's really nothing very springlike about it. Early on, slaves were taken there to look after the livestock surplus of landowners on Santiago, but historically, Maio was important as a **salt collecting** island: vast quantities of evaporated sea salt – "huge heaps like drifts of snow" by Francis Drake's account – were available for the cost of the labour needed to load it on board ship. As that was often paid in old clothes or other

△ Chã das Caldeiras, Fogo

unwanted items, the trade was a lucrative one. The English were largely in control of it and for a period Maio was, by Portuguese default, in English hands.

Today, Maio is a godforsaken place, poor in agriculture and a neglected neighbour of weighty Santiago, where most of its young people soon migrate. Surprisingly, more than a few people on the little twin prop plane are likely to be tourists these days, although the place is hardly geared up for them. If you do take the **flight** from Praia (5 weekly; 20min) or arrive by **ferry**, you'll find a place with a very distinct flavour. It's perhaps the least European of the Cape Verdes, with a relatively wooded, savanna-esque interior and long, white, desolate beaches.

Once you've explored the main town, **VILA DO MAIO** (the pretty white nineteenth-century colonial church overlooking the main square

is practically the only "sight" of real interest), you can take a stroll along the desert island-style beach where there's nothing but the occasional fisherman, impossibly blue water and blinding white sand as far as the eye can see.

The **airport** is situated 3km north of Vila do Maio. Ferries dock centrally at the town pier. It's surprising to find that at least one of the limited **accommodation** options is so good: *Hotel Marilú*, on Rua 3 De Maio northeast of the main square (☏55.11.98, ☏55.13.47; ❸; discounts in low season), has very pleasant rooms in a rustic kind of way and a good **restaurant** with excellent breakfasts. On the west side of the square, the rooms at *Hotel Bom Sossego* aren't too bad (☏55.13.65, ☏55.13.27; ❹), though the service in the downstairs restaurant is almost comically awful, with lazy, disinterested and downright arrogant staff. If you fancy a cold beer, the little shop on the corner of the square has a jovial owner who'll set a couple of battered stools on the cobbles for you. As for facilities, there's a Banco Comercial do Atlântico on the square, a post office up on the hill, a TACV office (☏55.12.56) and limited Internet access (Mon–Fri 9.30am–1.30pm) at the *Casa de Juventud* off the main road into town.

If you fancy seeing the rest of Maio, rent one of the rudimentary bicycles from Agemoto (they quote CV$600 per day, though don't be surprised if they then try to charge something higher) and set off up either flank of the island. Taking the western route, there's an extended salt pan reaching more than halfway up the coast to **Morro**, site of another paradisical beach, where *Hotel Bela Vista* (☏56.13.88, ⊛www.terra.es/personal/hawaii; ❻) offers a number of lovely, semi-detached stone chalets to rent. They also have a tennis court, swimming pool and car rental, and they run jeep safari tours around the island.

5.2

The Barlaventos

nternationally – at least in the English-speaking world – it's the **Barlaventos** that have drawn most attention to the Cape Verde Islands. Among them, **São Vicente** stands out, the location of a British coal-supply depot for over one hundred years. Its capital, **Mindelo**, is now the travel hub of the Barlaventos and focus of much of what's happening culturally in the Cape Verdes. While the interior of the island is relentlessly barren, the town has a self-contained appeal that draws a good deal on its evident cosmopolitanism, and its rivalry with Praia for civic pre-eminence.

To see the Cape Verde Islands at their most naturally glorious, hop across the channel from Mindelo to **Santo Antão**, the most northerly isle, for restorative **hiking** among the magnificent canyons (*ribeiras*). Santo Antão is a splendid massif, comparable to Fogo but no longer volcanically active, with an awesomely rugged interior.

São Nicolau is like a poor relation of Antão. Its four hundred years of human habitation seem to have been a dirge of destitution and fruitless toil, and yet its town has the oldest educational and literary tradition in the country. It also offers breathtaking scenery, as well as opportunities similar to Santo Antão's for determined walkers.

Sal, the aptly named "Salt" Island, is now the site of Cape Verde's main international airport, and the focus of ninety percent of the country's tourist industry, all located along one glorious beach, Santa Maria. The last of the windward islands is **Boa Vista**, a large and flat island in the east of the archipelago that's beginning to vie with Sal as a target for water-sports enthusiasts. It also has exhilarating desert travel opportunities.

São Vicente

It's hard to avoid identifying **SÃO VICENTE** with its main town and, indeed, there's not a lot on the island that matters outside **Mindelo**. The music festival at Baia das Gatas every August is a major event (see p.467), but unless your visit coincides with this or February's carnival, the one or two unexceptional things to do are best achieved by striking out from the town – there are no other significant centres of population on this small hunk of moonscape.

The **British**, as the operators of the **coaling station** at Mindelo, had a long and influential connection with the town. From 1838 until the 1950s, Mindelo – or rather Porto Grande as the town was then called – grew from nothing to a major supply depot on the East Indies and South America shipping runs. With the opening of the Suez Canal in 1869, the eastbound shipping diminished and diesel eventually took over from coal. But by the end of World War II, the hundred years of British presence had made some impact on the cultural life of the island. A number of English words were adopted into São Vicente Kriolu, including *blaqyefela* (blackfellow), *trôsa*, *ovacôte* (trousers and overcoat), *boi* (boy), *ariup* (hurry up), *djob* (job), *ovataime* (overtime) and, under American influence, *sanababiche*. English influence is still discernible in the architecture of some of the larger mansions. The British also introduced **cricket**, and though the game no longer figures very prominently, a team still plays occasionally.

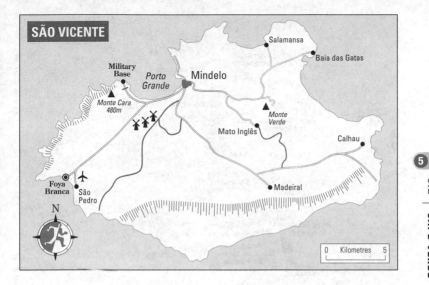

Mindelo

A sense of identity has never been a problem for **MINDELO**. "Taken as a whole," thought Major A.B. Ellis of the First West India Regiment in 1873, "it is, perhaps, the most wretched and immoral town that I have ever seen." He stayed in the *Hotel Brasiliero* where a notice over the door proclaimed "Ici on parl Frances, Man spreucht Deutsch, Man spiks Ingleesh, Aqui se habla Español, Sabe American"; and where his room was invaded by a French farce of characters during the night. By the second half of the nineteenth century, Mindelo's importance as a coaling and victualling station was at its peak, and less reputable ancillary industries were in top gear.

Today, while only the faintest traces of the bawdiness remain, this is the liveliest town in the Cape Verdes – and no longer especially wretched. Relatively well-provided with hotels, restaurants and bars, it buzzes contentedly after dark, its *praça* a noisy hangout zone, its streets cheerfully animated. Although it's a small town, don't be surprised to find the atmosphere here tainted with hustle around the edges: yachts and cruise ships are intermittent and not infrequent callers (even the QE2 makes a stop once or twice a year) and the boys on the waterfront are still making escudos out of naive travellers in time-honoured ways.

Arrival, transport and information

The **airstrip** is 11km from town on a bleak flat at São Pedro. For a hefty CV$700, a taxi gets you to Mindelo (*aluguers* are hard to come by at the airport, though on your way back you can take one from Mindelo to São Pedro and get them to drop you off) past brave acres of **reafforestation** where windswept acacias struggle for a foothold. With a stand of windmills – stark, whirling sentinels on the hillside, generating the island's electricity – and a strong ambience of desert desolation, Mindelo initially gives rise to fairly bleak impressions. Yet these soon recede as you get into the town with its Portuguese buildings, restored pink governor's residence and palm-tree-lined esplanade. Arriving **by boat**, it's a ten-minute walk south along the seafront to the town centre.

The main **taxi** ranks are in the obvious centre of town near the church (*igreja*). Rates are reasonable for journeys within town (CV$50–100 in the centre;

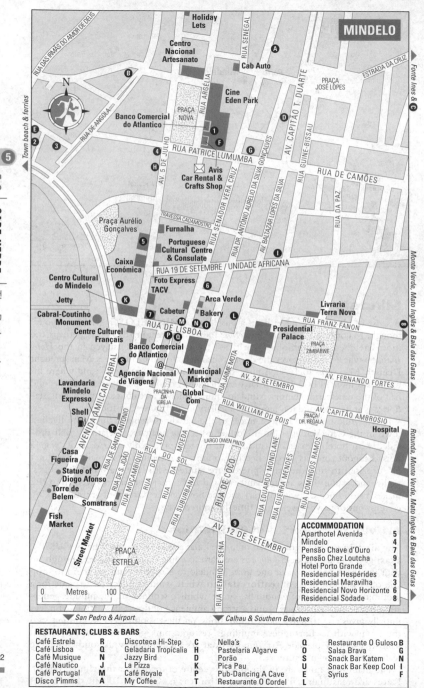

MINDELO

Holiday Lets

Centro Nacional Artesanato

Cab Auto

RUA SENEGAL

ESTRADA DA CRUZ

Fonte Ines & C

RUA DAS IRMAS DO AMOR DE DEUS

PRAÇA JOSÉ LOPES

Cine Eden Park

RUA ARGÉLIA

AV. CAPITÃO T. DUARTE

RUA GUINÉ-BISSAU

Town beach & ferries

PRAÇA NOVA

RUA DE ANGOLA

Banco Comercial do Atlantico

RUA PATRICE LUMUMBA

RUA DE CAMÕES

RUA DA PAZ

RUA 5 DE JULHO

Avis Car Rental & Crafts Shop

RUA SENADOR VERA CRUZ

RUA DR ANTONIO AURELIO DA SILVA

AV. BALTAZAR LOPES DA SILVA

TRAVESSA CADAMOSTRO

Praça Aurélio Gonçalves

Furnalha

Portuguese Cultural Centre & Consulate

Caixa Económica

RUA 19 DE SETEMBRE / UNIDADE AFRICANA

Centro Cultural do Mindelo

Foto Express TACV

Arca Verde

Livraria Terra Nova

RUA FRANZ FANON

Jetty

Cabetur

Bakery

Presidential Palace

PRAÇA ZIMBABWE

Cabral-Coutinho Monument

RUA DE LISBOA

Centre Culturel Français

Banco Comercial do Atlantico

RUA JAIME MOTA

Agencia Nacional de Viagens

Municipal Market

AV. 24 SETEMBRO

AV. FERNANDO FORTES

Lavandaria Mindelo Expresso

PRACINHA DA IGREJA

Global Com

RUA WILLIAM DU BOIS

AV. CAPITÃO AMBROSIO

PRAÇA DR. REGALA

Shell

AVENIDA AMILCAR CABRAL

RUA DE SANTO ANTONIO

RUA DA LUZ DO SOL

RUA DA MOEDA

LARGO OWEN PINTO

Hospital

Casa Figueira

RUA DE S. JOÃO

RUA MOÇAMBIQUE

RUA DE COCO

RUA EDUARDO MONDLANE

RUA GUERRA MENDES

RUA DOMINGOS RAMOS

Statue of Diogo Afonso

Torre de Belem

Somatrans

RUA SUBURBANA

Fish Market

Street Market

PRAÇA ESTRELA

AV. 12 DE SETEMBRO

RUA HENRIQUE SENA

San Pedro & Airport

Calhau & Southern Beaches

Monte Verde, Mato Inglês & Baía das Gatas

Rotunda, Monte Verde, Mato Inglês & Baía das Gatas

0 Metres 100

ACCOMMODATION

Aparthotel Avenida	5
Mindelo	4
Pensão Chave d'Ouro	7
Pensão Chez Loutcha	9
Hotel Porto Grande	1
Residencial Hespérides	2
Residencial Maravilha	3
Residencial Novo Horizonte	6
Residencial Sodade	8

RESTAURANTS, CLUBS & BARS

Café Estrela	R	Discoteca Hi-Step	C	Nella's	Q	Restaurante O Guloso	B
Café Lisboa	Q	Geladaria Tropicalia	H	Pastelaria Algarve	O	Salsa Brava	G
Café Musique	N	Jazzy Bird	D	Porão	S	Snack Bar Katem	N
Café Nautico	J	La Pizza	K	Pica Pau	U	Snack Bar Keep Cool	I
Café Portugal	M	Café Royale	P	Pub-Dancing A Cave	L	Syrius	F
Disco Pimms	A	My Coffee	T	Restaurante O Cordel			

Moving on from Mindelo

TACV has an office on Avenida 5 de Julho (☎32.15.24, ☏32.37.19). Flights go to Praia (at least 1 daily; 1hr); Sal (at least 2 daily; 50min); São Nicolau (Wed & Sun; 25min). Availability on flights to Sal and Praia, notably those connecting with international departures, is often very tight.

The main office for the **ferries** *Praia D'Aguada*, *Barlavento* and *Sotavento* is Arca Verde, 12 Rua Senador Vera Cruz (☎32.13.49, ☏32.49.63). Somatrans, 95 Rua S. João (☎32.40.67, ☏32.40.68), runs the daily Mindelo–Porto Novo (Santo Antão) ferry.

As for transport on the island itself, regular **aluguers** to San Pedro, Baia das Gatas and Calhau (all around CV$80) leave from the far end of Praça Estrela.

CV$150–200 to the suburbs). A limited array of **tourist information**, including maps of other islands and Mindelo itself, is available from the small kiosk on the far corner of Praça Aurélio Gonçalves.

Accommodation

In keeping with its cosmopolitan image, Mindelo boasts a good range of accommodation; while budget travellers are adequately catered for, the best-value options are the mid-range establishments.

Aparthotel Avenida Av 5 de Julho ☎32.11.76, ☏32.23.33. Old, fairly stylish apartment-style hotel with a/c and TV. Some rooms have balconies and views of the bay. Also acts as an agent for local lets. ❻

Hotel Porto Grande Praça Nova ☎32.31.90, ☏32.31.93, ✉pgrande@cvtelecom.cv. Although it can't compete with the *Mindelo* in the luxury stakes, this place definitely has more soul. Front rooms have a great view over the *praça*, but can be very noisy, especially at weekends. Good-sized fresh-water pool. ❽

Mindelo Hotel Av 5 de Julho ☎32.88.81, ☏32.88.87, ✉mihotel@cvtelelcom.cv. A new establishment with all the facilities you'd expect from a top-flight, corporate hotel. Delicious pizza, pasta and *calzone* is to be had in the busy downstairs restaurant which is frequented by well-dressed locals as well as guests. ❽

Pensão Chave d'Ouro Av 5 de Julho ☎ & ☏32.70.50. The "Golden Key" is a Mindelo institution and a long-established budget focus. It's undoubtedly a bit run-down, but its colonial charm and the quaint officiousness of the staff (all dressed in sober black and white) make for a memorable stay. There are tiny, inexpensive top floor attic-style rooms and big airy rooms on the first floor, all with shared facilities. Breakfast extra. ❸

Pensão Chez Loutcha Rua do Coco ☎32.16.36, ☏32.16.35. While the rooms are a bit hit-and-miss (some are dark and musty; the better ones have balconies) for the price, there's a popular restaurant and regular live music. ❺

Residencial Hespérides Alto S. Nicolau district, bottom of Rua de Angola, near the seafront ☎32.86.88, ☏32.73.72, ✉isabel097@aol.com. Modern, s/c rooms arranged around a communal living room, and with an equally unconventional naming system (Annette, Max, Lola, etc). Upper rooms have balconies overlooking the bay. Good value. ❹

Residencial Maravilha Alto S. Nicolau, up and round the corner from the *Hespérides* ☎32.22.03, ☏32.22.17, ✉Gabs@mail.cvtelecom.cv. With gorgeous, very tastefully fitted rooms and an interior decorated with rustic materials such as *pano*. A bargain in low season. ❻

Residencial Novo Horizonte 62 Rua Senador Vera Cruz ☎32.39.15. Clean if worn-out guesthouse, somewhat dark and stuffy. Very reasonably priced for B&B. ❸

Residencial Sodade Rua Franz Fanon ☎30.32.00, ☏31.40.10, ✉residencialsodade @hotmail.com. Friendly place with English-speaking staff. The cheapest rooms (a bit dark) are on the bottom floor with more expensive lodging upstairs, with a/c and TV. Its big selling point is the great view from the rooftop restaurant. ❹

The Town

Mindelo is the town that Cape Verdeans resident abroad always go on about – perhaps because so many Cape Verde expatriates come from here – and compared with

Praia it does have a more animated, less official feel. Helped along by the bay with its twin headlands, its esplanade and its clutter of backstreets, Mindelo feels like a holiday. The **carnaval** in February tends to infect the town for the entire year, so it never entirely stops partying.

Exploring it for yourself is the main daytime pursuit and the seafront provides an obvious anchor point. The unusual eagle-topped **monument** near the jetty commemorates the first Lisbon–Rio air crossing, in 1922, by aviators Cabral and Coutinho, who spent a number of days recuperating in Mindelo after their 80mph leg from the Canaries in the flying boat *Lusitania*. Away to the south, the curious ornate little castle is the **Torre de Belem**, a copy of the tower of the same name outside Lisbon; the latter was built in the early sixteenth century, the Cape Verdean replica in the 1920s. For many years the Torre at Mindelo was the seat of the Portuguese administrator of São Vicente, but even before independence it had been abandoned. For decades, the shored-up and rat-infested structure looked as if it had been deliberately ignored; it's currently being renovated and not for the first time. Back in town a short way, the old **Presidential Palace** has been well looked after and was recently restored in pale pink some years back. Now the headquarters of São Vicente island council, it's clearly the object of considerable civic pride.

Mindelo's **beach**, the Praia da Lajinha, is a kilometre out of town on the north side. Backed by a rumbling industrial plant, the dark yellow sands are clean, nonetheless, the sea is warm and clear, and there are a couple of beach bars on the other side of the road. Continuing northwards in the same direction, you can walk or drive up to the **Fortim del Rei**, a deserted hilltop fortification – one-time prison – overlooking the city and the bay.

The closest you'll come to a museum in Cape Verde is a visit to the **Centro Nacional Artesanato** on the north side of Praça Nova (Mon–Fri 8am–noon & 2–6pm; CV$100). The place is divided into a display area and a shop, and there's also a workshop at the back where you're generally allowed to nose around the weaving looms: doubtless this depends on the behaviour of the last batch of cruise passengers or shore-leave sailors. The knick-knacks on sale aren't hugely appealing, but the items on display, particularly some of the musical instruments, rugs and home-made toys, do seem old and of genuine interest. If you're drawn to **crafts and paintings**, you should pay a visit to a couple of other addresses. The arts and crafts shop on the corner opposite Praça Nova is one of the few places to buy the colourful woven wall hangings you see in some hotels and restaurants. Be warned, though, they don't come cheap at around CV$35,000. Casa Figueira, near the Torre de Belem, is a private gallery of canvases by a father-and-son team.

For more routine shopping, Mindelo is at least as well-equipped as Praia. There's a scattering of small **supermarkets**, a lively **fish market**, and a fine, newly restored **municipal market**, running to two floors, bang in the centre of town, which contains a good number of small retail enterprises. There's also an *azulejo*-tiled little **market village** on the far side of Praça Estrela with stalls manned by both West Africans and Cape Verdeans. Some of the back walls depict sculpted scenes of toil from Mindelo's past.

Eating and drinking

There are more than a few decent restaurants and snack bars – though it's well to remember that many of them close once a week, usually on a Sunday. Ironically, many of them also close over lunch at the weekend.

Café Estrela Av Fernando Fortes, by the palace. Limited range of top-value meals and snacks.
Café Lisboa, Café Portugal and **Café Royale** Facing each other on Rua de Lisboa. Established downtown cafés – unfussy, fast places where locals of every strand congregate, business types read *A Semana*, and much coffee, beer and *aguardente* is consumed. The cracked panes and peeling paint of the *Royale* give the impression it closed down years ago, but be assured it is open for business.

Geladaria Tropicalia Av 5 de Julho. Good ice cream and snacks.

La Pizza Av 5 de Julho. Sandwiched between the *Centro Cultural* and *Club Nautico*, this kiosk is great for feasting on cheap, tasty pizza and watching the sun set over the bay.

My Coffee Rua de Sto António. Dowdy but inviting local café-bar with comfy sofas and *cachupa* for CV$180.

Nella's Restaurant/Bar Rua de Lisboa ☎31.43.20 Up above *Café Lisboa*, this trendy bistro deals in French-influenced Cape Verdean cuisine with the menu chalked up on a blackboard. Main courses start at around CV$600.

Pastelaria Algarve Rua de Lisboa. Snacks and cakes, with a bar.

Pica Pau Rua de Santo António ☎32.82.07. The "Woodpecker" is another Mindelo institution, a tiny restaurant, largely unchanged for twenty years, though now festooned with the multilingual testimonials of happy eaters. There's great-value seafood, especially the piping hot and tasty *arroz mariscos* (CV$800) or lobster (CV$1300), with wine and beer from the even tinier bar to wash it down. Reserve ahead: it's usually full.

Restaurant Chave d'Ouro Av 5 de Julho. Upstairs in the *pensão* of the same name, this huge, antique dining room has good food, bags of atmosphere and a loyal local clientele. It's open for lunch (noon–3pm) and dinner (7–11pm) while breakfasts are served from 8am in the equally atmospheric little bar along the corridor.

Restaurante O Cordel Av Baltazar Lopes da Silva ☎32.29.62. One of Mindelo's best, longest-established restaurants, with multilingual staff and Mediterranean-influenced dishes from about CV$700.

Restaurante O Guloso Rua Angola ☎31.70.66. Engagingly eccentric place where you definitely need to reserve ahead to get any food at all. English-speaking owner guarantees to provide food fit for the "gourmand" of her establishment's name.

Snack Bar Katem Rua de Lisboa. Cheapest of the local hangouts, this shady café is crammed with characters and usually has a display of photos from the *carnaval*.

Snack Bar Koop Cool Rua 19 de Setembro. Popular café, sometimes known as the *Unidade Africana*, serving an inexpensive *prato do dia*.

Nightlife

After dark, social gravity sooner or later draws most people down to Praça Nova, where there's always some excitement and a lot of rather Mediterranean courting and flirting going on, accompanied by huge volumes of noise. Although the town's youth are steadily deserting the town for Praia and further, Mindelo still holds a racy and sophisticated reputation for the young people of the Barlavento country hamlets. Sitting in the square really is fun: you'll quickly find yourself in some kind of conversation, tuning in to the evening grapevine. There's also a cinema here showing the usual Hollywood guff, although they sometimes screen big international football games.

Mindelo has a number of **boites** (down-to-earth nightclubs), generally discos rather than live-music venues. Apart from Cape Verdean *morna*, *coladeira* and *funana*, you're most likely to come across variants of zouk, often with Senegalese influences. Not surprisingly, successful singers and bands don't wait long before flying out to Lisbon, Paris, Holland or New England, where Cape Verdean audiences (and certainly the market for CDs) can be larger than in Mindelo itself.

Clubs and bars

Argentina Rua 5 de Julho, beneath the *Chave d'Ouro*. Earthy watering hole.

Café Musique Rua de Lisboa, upstairs above the *Katem* snack bar. Stylish bar and live venue rolled into one. European tourists and male yachting types flock to this place, both to witness the abundance of local musical talent and to congregate on the balcony and shout to the girls below.

Club Náutico Rua 5 de Julho. Bar/club with a maritime theme, an open courtyard and views of the port.

Disco Pimms Rua Senador Vera Cruz. Always hot and crowded, although at present it's only open during the summer months. CV$300 entry charge.

Discoteca Hi-Step Fonte Inés, just off Estrada da Cruz, east of the town centre. A good midweek bet; busy on a Thursday when you'll pay CV$200 (CV$300 at the weekend).

Jazzy Bird Rua Patrice Lumumba. Brilliantly named little backstreet bar with good sounds but no live music.

Porão Av da República. Trendy, cavernous

warehouse conversion–style bar by the waterfront, with live music nightly Wed–Sat.

Pub-Dancing A Cave Alto S. Nicolau district, opposite the *Maravilha*. Long-established subterranean club with a dedicated older crowd. Admission is CV$500 (with one free drink). It starts to swing around 1.30am.

Salsa Brava Rua Patrice Lumumba. Vaguely stylish pre-club bar where women get in free but

men, for their sins, must consume CV$100 worth of drinks.

Syrius Situated below the *Porte Grande*, this is the most desirable disco in town, a great place to discover that, sweetly enough, Cape Verdean men and women dance *together*, even if the soundtrack happens to be hip-hop. Weekends and every night in summer. CV$300 cover charge.

Listings

Banks Branches of Banco Comercial do Atlântico in the old building on Rua de Santo António, south of Rua de Lisboa and in front of the *Hotel Porto Grande*. Caixa Económica is on Avenida 5 de Julho.

Bookshops You could try the Livraria Terra Nova on Rua 19 de Setembro, but it rarely has anything but a limited range of foreign-language dictionaries and evangelical works in Portuguese. Otherwise try the Centro Cultural do Mindelo (see below) or Furnalha (see "Internet access"), which has a very limited stock.

Car Rental São Vicente is a good place to explore for a day by car. Half-daily or daily rates are around CV$2000 or CV$4000. One of the best is Cab Auto, CP 117 Largo Medina Boé, behind the *Hotel Porto Grande* (T & F 32.28.12). A CV$10,000 deposit is required. More expensive is Avis (T 32.71.71, F 32.31.93), in front of the *Hotel Porto Grande*.

CDs There's a fairly decent music shop in Furnalha (see "Internet access").

Cultural centres Culturel Culturel Français/Alliance Française, Rua de Lisboa (Mon–Fri 10am–12.30pm & 3–7pm, Sat 10am–12.30pm; T 32.11.49), is worth visiting for books, mags, movies and Internet access. The Centro Cultural Português do Mindelo is at Av 5 de Julho (T & F 31.30.40, @ ccpmindelo @cvtelecom.cv), next door to the Portuguese embassy. Worth a visit is the Centro Cultural do

Mindelo, opposite the *Chave D'Ouro* (T 32.58.40), a long-established locally run institute promoting Cape Verdean culture; it has a good Portuguese-language bookshop, a gallery and a lively theatre, always in use.

Consulates The British honorary consul is Mr. Antônio Canuto, at *Shell Cabo Verde* on Av Amílcar Cabral (T 32.66.25, F 32.66.29, @ antonio.a.canuto@scv.sims.com).

Film Foto Express, 14 Av 5 de Julho, charges CV$1350 to process a roll of 24.

Internet access Furnalha is a mini-shopping mall on Avenida 5 de Julho (daily 9am–midnight) where online services are in fact the main attraction. Also worth trying are Global Com (daily 7.30am–11pm), up around the corner from *Café Royale*, or the French cultural centre (see above).

Laundry Lavandaria Mindelo Expresso, 24 Rua de Sto António (Mon–Fri 8.30am–7.30pm, Sat & Sun 8.30am–1.30pm), is cheap, friendly and efficient. Pay by weight.

Post and telephones Inside the CV Telecom office on Rua Patrice Lumumba (Mon–Fri 8am–noon & 2.30–5pm). You can also make international calls and buy phonecards here.

Travel agents Cabetur, 57 Rua Senador, Vera Cruz T 32.38.47, F 31.38.42; Agencia Nacional de Viagens, off Rua de Sto António T 31.33.33, F 32.14.45; Agência Albino dos Santos, 49 Rua de Sto António T 32.18.95, F 32.18.98. The latter is an agent for TAP Air Portugal.

Around São Vicente

If you don't venture beyond Mindelo you'll not be in a minority. Away from Mindelo, the rest of the island is desperately arid, for the most part treeless, and largely uninhabited – all but a couple of thousand of the island's 50,000 inhabitants live in the *povoação*.

Baia das Gatas and Monte Verde

For a break, and really quite a nice **beach**, the twenty-minute drive to **Baia das Gatas** is a good trip. Baia, as it's commonly known (the reason for the *gatas* – cats – is unknown), is protected by a concrete mole and black boulders to break the

Live at the Bay of Cats

The **Baia das Gatas Music Festival** has become Cape Verde's major summer attraction, with thirty thousand people attending for the three days at the end of August. People camp out (it never rains in August), sleep in cars on the dunes, or occupy the weekend chalets around the bay. Cape Verdean emigrants time their summer vacations on the islands to coincide with the festival, and the crowd is full of reunited families and long-unseen friends bumping into each other. Inter-island flights are all heavily booked at this time and hotel rooms in Mindelo hard to find, while public transport between town and bay may involve some waiting — and inflated prices.

The event is now in its third decade, and national radio and TV cover it nonstop. In 2002, Cesaria Evora, Luís Morais and Tabanka Djazz (from Guinea-Bissau) headlined, though the quality of the music varies from year to year and indifferent overseas groups are sometimes booked for local youth appeal, while top local acts can be disappointingly absent. For details, contact the organizers on ⊕32.52.37 or visit ⓦ www.festivalbaiadasgatas.cv.

thrashing surf. In the **lagoon**, the water is calm and delightfully transparent, though even with a mask there's not a lot to see. Beyond the lagoon's confines, the sea is more challenging and the combination of urchin-covered rocks and the threat of sharks should be enough to put you off. There's a Sunday beach bar, weekend bungalows and, in August, a major international **music festival**.

The road to Baia climbs steeply past the junction for **Monte Verde**, the dark mass commonly wreathed in clouds that rears up behind Mindelo, and the island's highest point. This too is worth an outing but you'll probably have to take a taxi (CV\$1,000) and you'll need to set aside a full morning or afternoon. The last section on the Mato Ingles branch gets right to the summit. It is, truly, a "green mountain", covered in the once commercially important *orchil* lichen, used to produce brilliant scarlet and purple dyes. The views down over Mindelo and Baia can be stunning, but they're not to be counted on, as the summit area is often wreathed in cloud.

Southern beaches

A difficult road leads southeast from Monte Verde to **Calhau** (the direct route from Mindelo is easier), a deliciously tranquil (at least during the week) village full of empty holiday homes where there's a good beach and a couple of restaurants: *Hamburg*, open daily year-round, is a colourfully painted, slightly eccentric place where you can lounge in the courtyard all afternoon without seeing a soul, while *Chez Loutcha* (a branch of the Mindelo hotel/restaurant) is open Sundays only when townies head for the seaside. Another road heads south to Madeiral and the island's most dramatic and isolated region, a fifteen-kilometre ridge (altitude 500–700m) paralleling the southern coast at a distance of just two or three kilometres, from which *ribeiras* plunge down to the sea.

Another worthwhile beach, somewhat easier to get to, lies just beyond the airport at **Praia de São Pedro**. This is the location of the island's only tourist development, *Foya Branca* (⊕30.74.00, ⊕30.74.44; ❻), an oddly bleak but upmarket villa-style set-up. Across the bay, the scruffy, but colourful, little village of San Pedro has a certain charm but offers nothing beyond an excuse for a walk along the shore.

Santo Antão

SANTO ANTÃO, the second largest of the Cape Verdes, is rugged and exciting – a tortoise shape cut into deep, arcing **ribeiras**, with the savage grandeur of a much bigger landmass. The island is also the last to suffer whenever a prolonged drought ravages the country, the northern slopes and valleys retaining a perennial verdure which is hard to believe after the desolation of Santiago and São Vicente. In times not so long past, Mindelo got almost all its drinking water from Santo Antão – a lucrative trade that dried up with the withering of the coaling industry on São Vicente and the opening there of a water-desalination plant.

Getting here today, you can fly from Praia and Mindelo to the airport at Ponta do Sol, near the island's capital, **Ribeira Grande**. Much cheaper are the ferries – the *Ribeira de Paúl* and the *Mar Novo* – across the deep, shark-infested channel from Mindelo to **Porto Novo**. A single **highway** now snakes up over the barren south-facing slopes on the island's eastern tip, then edges between the peaks and abysses to Ribeira Grande on the north coast. In the past, however, communications were difficult. The story goes that Bishop Jacinto Valente visited Santo Antão from Santiago in 1755, and set off to cross the island on foot. Having been hauled up several precipices dangling from a rope, he eventually lost his nerve and had to stay put between a cliff and a chasm. The islanders went on ahead, sent him back a tent and supplies, and began to construct a road for his rescue. Even as late as 1869, three hundred years after it was first colonized, the Portuguese minister of colonies remarked that Santo Antão had "the appearance of an island that had only been discovered months ago".

Porto Novo and on to Ribeira Grande

Porto Novo itself used to be an uneventful place subsisting on the daily contact with Mindelo across the channel, but in recent years, development funds have seen considerable growth. A crowd is always down on the quay to welcome the boat, and there's a **tourist office** on the pier which organizes its opening hours around the ferry. A huge fleet of **minibuses** also meets the ferry, usually tailing back way up the hill; most head over the island's spine to Ribeira Grande (1hr–1hr 30min; CV$300); try to get a front seat on the right for the most heart-stopping views.

If you need **rooms** in Porto Novo, the best place is the very pleasant, great value *Residencial Antilhas* (☎22.11.93, ☎22.17.58; ❷), right above the port, with s/c rooms, hot water and a separately run bar/restaurant on the ground floor. Many rooms also have balconies overlooking the channel to Mindelo. It's also right on

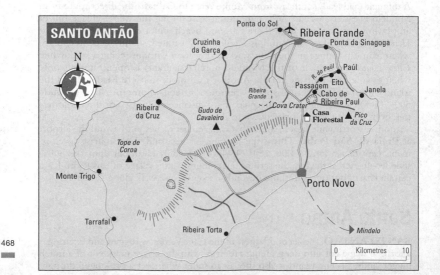

the edge of town whence, if you want to stretch your legs, you can hike eastwards along the coast until the path peters out and you're faced with nothing but baking brown rock, wind and sea. Less attractive, more expensive and less conveniently located, a couple of minutes' walk inland from the clifftop is the *Girassol* (☎22.13.83, ℉22.18.91; ❹), where the rooms are non-s/c, but breakfast is included in the rate. *Residencial Pôr Do Sol*, a huge blue-and-yellow edifice a minute's walk off to the right of the main street, past the bank (☎22.21.79, ℉22.11.66, ℮por-dosolpn@cvtelecom.cv; ❺), is a newly built mid-range place located down in the main part of town with sleek, spotless, good value s/c rooms with TV and air conditioning. Finally, there's the cheap and cheerful *Sabura* (☎22.13.05; ❷), an unmarked place across from the bank, also in the main part of town; ask in the supermarket next door.

You can **eat** quite well, and catch up with European football on the TV, at the *Sereia*, a bar perched on the clifftop whose terrace fills up quickly after the ferry has docked. Alternatively, the *Pôr Do Sol* has a sunny rooftop **restaurant** (main dishes from CV$600; try the delicious *pudim do queijo* if they have it – it's a variation on *pudim* with cheese in place of milk, and is vaguely reminiscent of cheesecake) with fine views to São Vicente.

The road to Ribeira Grande

As you head north out of Porto Novo, the haul up the south slope of the island presents a bleak picture to begin with: the neat, cobbled road snakes steeply through a lifeless mountain desert of tumbled volcanic rocks, bleached pale in the sun. Temperatures drop and views over Porto Novo become dramatic as the vehicle climbs; if it's a clear day, you can see São Vicente – a black mountain sitting, strangely, below the horizon.

But save your enthusiasm and your film for the descent down the northern side of the island. As you approach the crest, the road's contours relax as groves of coniferous trees and low herbage make an appearance. The **Casa Florestal** (forest station) is a sort of halfway house, a convenient place to hop out, where people will try to sell you large quantities of goat's cheese. Continuing by minibus to the *povoação*, you sweep over the island's twisted spine and skirt the magnificent circumference of **Cova crater**. Clouds drift below the road, and over the houses and sugar-cane plots patched into the crater's colossal scoop. From this point on, the bus repeatedly veers past steep terraced slopes and chasms of hundreds of sheer metres. Bishop Valente's vertigo was understandable: even Cape Verdeans gaze down – and cross themselves – at the hairpins. Glimpsing the sea through the crags, it seems impossible the road can get down to Ribeira Grande in such a short distance.

Ribeira Grande

With fortresslike cliffs and narrow streets, **RIBEIRA GRANDE** feels like a mountain town lost in a huge range, its slightly forbidding, singular atmosphere quickly compelling and not quickly forgotten. The town perches at the mouth of the *ribeira*, a cluster of closely bunched and shady houses hemmed in by cliffs rising behind and by the dark sea lashing a shingly beach. A broad *praça* fronts the **Igreja de Nossa Senhora do Rosário**, the formidable church intended, at one time in the eighteenth century, to be the cathedral of Cape Verde.

On the square, the **TACV office** (Mon, Wed & Thurs 8am–3pm, Tues & Fri 11am–3pm; ☎21.11.84) works its opening hours around the flights from Ponta do Sol to São Vicente (Tues & Fri; 25min) and Praia (Tues & Fri; 50min). There's also a Banco Comercial do Atlântico, a **post office** and a small **Internet café**, *Cyber-cafe Internet.com* (daily 8am–10pm), where you'll be charged by the minute, though it works out no more expensive than average; the antiquated 1970s plywood panelled interior makes for an interesting contrast with its hi-tech purpose.

Finding a **place to stay** is simple enough, even if none of the trio of inexpensive *pensões* is particularly inviting. The options are the gloomy, neglected *Residencial 5 de Julho* (℡21.13.45; ❷) with a few s/c rooms; the cheap, charmless and really rather grim *Residencial Aliança* (℡21.12.46; ❷); and the good-value, carefully looked-after rooms let out by Dona Bibi (❷), down an alley opposite the *5 de Julho*. You can find Dona Bibi working in a little grocery, the *Mercearia Nascimento*, next door in the same alley. Breakfast (CV$140) is served around a communal table in the dining room downstairs. There's also a solitary mid-range place, *Residencial Tropical* (℡21.11.29, ℻21.21.26; ❺), which is situated a minute's walk from Dona Bibi's place and offers immaculate, if slightly dark, rooms with TV, a/c and hot water.

The town has little to offer foodwise. The *Tropical* is your best bet for a **meal** with a nice little patio dining area, attentive service and main dishes in the CV$600 region. The *5 de Julho* serves breakfast and basic meals like *feijoada* and *cachupa* (CV$500) in an unattractive little dining room, while the *Aliança's* menu sometimes includes pizza.

Ponta do Sol

As an alternative to staying in Ribeira Grande – and even for a semi-decent meal – you could take an *aluguer* ten minutes up the coast (a fairly continuous stream of vehicles makes the four-kilometre journey; CV$50) to **PONTA DO SOL**, a more spacious little town with the island's tiny airport (just outside town, with transport to Ribeira Grande for CV$500), where tourism and the accompanying range of accommodation options has mushroomed over the past few years. In comparison with Ribeira's claustrophobic feel and chronic lack of facilities, this is a pretty, laid-back town with a leafy *praça* and picturesque little shorefront.

If you're heading in by road, the first place you'll encounter is the imposing but pleasant *Casa Azul* on your left at the top of the hill (℡25.12.95; ❹). Again on your left a little further down is *Pension Chez Louisette* (℡25.10.48, ℡25.11.15, ✉che-zlouisette@cvtelecom.cv; ❹), with clean, graceful s/c rooms and breakfast included. The similarly priced, garishly painted *Residencial Ponta do Sol* (℡25.12.38, ℻25.12.49; ❹) is a minute beyond on the right, a newish hotel with sparkling s/c rooms, some with balconies. There's also a sun-baked rooftop bar/restaurant with mains starting at CV$600.

Down in the main part of town, the upmarket *Hotel Bluebell* (℡25.12.15, ℻25.13.08, ✉bluebell@telecom.cv.com) boasts a friendly English-speaking owner, luxurious, good-value rooms with minimalist furniture and a smart ground-level restaurant; a rooftop restaurant is planned. Directly opposite, *Bar-Restaurante Lela Leite* (℡25.10.56; ❷) offers local dishes and cold drinks (call 2hr ahead from Ribeira Grande to order a meal), and basic, dirt-cheap rooms. The popular, family-run *Pensão Dona Dedei* (℡25.10.37, ℻25.14.37; ❸) is an unmarked green house in the street behind *Bluebell* which offers reasonable B&B rooms, some with hot water. *Pasquinha* (℡25.10.91; ❸) is another unmarked (grey painted) house round the corner from *Dedei* offering similar facilities.

Much more interesting is the fresh and funky, French-owned *Por do Sol* down on the harbour (℡25.13.70, ✉blaisecv@yahoo.fr; ❷). With a handful of pastel-shaded rooms upstairs (complete with log beds) and a craft shop/workshop (where you can see young local artists beavering away through the back) down below, this is a vibrant and memorable place to stay. By the time you read this there should be a full restaurant service with food available all day. For a secluded afternoon drink try the eccentric and really quite wonderful *Bistro Housi's Place*, an ancient, leafy and very peaceful courtyard with a few rickety tables; marked with a tiny wooden sign, it's located off the main street down towards the harbour. For something more substantial, the *Restaurant Esplanada Nova Aurora* on the square should be able to sort you out. Fish and meat dishes here start at CV$700 and the patio tables allow views to the mountains behind.

Tarrafal

If you fancy really getting away from it all, you might want to strike out for the remote west-coast settlement of **Tarrafal**. You should be able to find an *aluguer* headed there among the throng on Porto Novo's pier. The journey is a long one by Cape Verdean standards and the road isn't the best, but there's wonderfully peaceful, friendly accommodation to be had at the idyllic *Mar Tranquilidade* (T27.60.12, Wwww.martranquilidade.com; ❸), courtesy of a German/American couple, Susi and Frank. They have a series of stone-walled, thatch-roofed cottages right on the beach. The little town is sheltered by mountains from the winds which buffet many parts of Cape Verde and there are miles of secluded, black-sand beaches to escape to. A few rooms (❶) are also available from José Almeida Delgado (T22.31.05), who can provide breakfast and dinner at extra cost.

Hiking around the island

The most compelling activity here is **hiking**, with routes all over the island. It's very helpful to have a decent **map**; the *Goldstadt Wanderkarte* hiking map (see p.414) is perfect. Also worth looking out for is the huge, though somewhat out of date, 1cm:250m island map on the wall of a small, nameless bar on the south side of Ribeira Grande's main street.

One option for a hike, a particularly dramatic route in its later stages, heads from Ribeira Grande to Ponta do Sol, thence to the precarious village of **Fontainas** and on to **Cruzinha da Garça** via a cliff-face footpath that is at times barely half a metre wide. With several days to spare, you'll have the chance to explore the three big **ribeiras** of eastern Santo Antão – Grande, Paúl and Janela ("Big", "Swamp" and "Window"). The hike up the **Ribeira Grande**, a solid morning's work, requires an early start and a good supply of drinking water. If you're heading back to Porto Novo for the day's ferry, in the dry season you should take an *aluguer* up the *ribeira* for a few kilometres: the route has to be rebuilt nearly every year after the rains. If you get a *particular* to meet you at the head of the Ribeira, expect to pay upwards of CV$3000. You might also want to hire a guide for the day – CV$1800 is a fair price. If you're lucky you will see the *ribeira* cloaked in green, but unfortunately it can't be guaranteed.

Ribeira do Paúl

Ribeira do Paúl is the most beautiful and densely planted of the three canyons. Get there by *aluguer*, 10km along the coast road – again, a busy enough route (CV$50). Your starting point is the village of Vila das Pombas, basically one long street lashed by Atlantic waves and watched over by a Rio de Janeiro-style Christ statue. It's peopled by a memorable array of characters and prone to spontaneous outbursts of music making, so keep your eyes and ears peeled. There's a solitary accommodation option, the basic *Residencial Vale do Paúl* (T23.13.19; ❷), which has a reasonably priced restaurant with amazing views; get your order in a few hours beforehand. A steep kilometre or so inland, through the first tresses of deep, sugar-plantation verdure, you come to the hamlet of **Eito**, where the *Casa Familial Sabine* (T23.15.44; ❷), situated 50m south of the road from the two-storey orange house (turn left if walking inland), offers slightly eccentric, beautifully located accommodation. The cobbled road up the *ribeira* (there's not much transport along here) climbs far inland, snaking through a fantastic riot of vegetation and at one point skirting an almost vertical wall of rock dizzying in its height and immensity. Equally dizzying is the local *grogue*, sold in the little shops and bars along the way and produced by sweaty, soot-blackened men at stills along the route; they'll normally let you look round and take photos. Some 4km from Paúl, at **Passagem**, the path fetches up at a kind of tropical garden with a swimming pool and café open at weekends. At times the landscape, with its robustly constructed stone path and vertiginous, neatly ordered terracing is reminiscent of Peru, albeit on a smaller scale.

In the upper reaches of the valley is the hamlet of **Cabo de Ribeira Paúl**, where you can stay at *Chez Simon* (☏23.10.39; ❶), with two very basic but wonderfully situated rooms; Simon is available for hire as a guide if needed, and can prepare traditional food given notice. The village is also home to Sandr'Arte, a little craft shop selling various permutations of *grogue* and *ponche* (which you may well be invited to sample) as well as coffee beans from the surrounding hills.

As a fine and arguably even more scenically spectacular alternative to hiking up, you can walk down the Ribeira do Paúl by getting dropped off on the main trans-island road above the Cova crater (CV$1700 if you're hiring privately, a fraction of that if you leave early on one of the morning runs to Porto Novo or Ribeira Grande). Ask your driver to point out the initial stretch and you can't go far wrong.

Santa Luzia, Ilhéu Branco and Ilhéu Razo

Three desert islands line up in the lee of São Vicente. The biggest, **Santa Luzia**, had a bit of a population towards the end of the eighteenth century – mostly destitute farmers from São Nicolau – but successive droughts and an impossibly harsh terrain expelled them. A more recent inhabitant was the "Governor of Santa Luzia", Francisco Antonio da Cruz, who fled there from his wife and eighteen offspring and lived as a hermit for a number of years. It's now deserted again and, unless you make special efforts by boat, out of reach. Charles Darwin called here in the *Beagle*; herpetologists know Santa Luzia as the only habitat of a large, herbivorous lizard – though it seems likely that it's extinct.

Ilhéu Branco is more of a rock than an island, white (hence the name) from the guano deposits of generations of seabirds, and rising sheer from the sea in a shape supposed to resemble a ship at anchor. Ships stay well clear of its dangerous approaches. If you're sailing between Mindelo and São Nicolau, you're likely to get a good view of the **dolphins** which frequent this leg. **Flying fish** are common too – skittering things the size of a seagull which streak above the surface for several seconds at amazingly high speed.

By the time you reach **Ilhéu Razo**, you can see the jagged, cloud-protected silhouette of São Nicolau. Razo is famous – among ornithologists and conservationists – for the **Razo Island lark**, a dun, ordinary-looking lark that, perversely, nests only on this barren slab, making it an exceedingly rare species. The Razo lark has an extra strong beak for digging up the drought-resistant grubs it feeds on. It should survive until population pressure and a solution to the problem of drought bring the first human colonists to the island.

São Nicolau

Like the peaks of a submerged mountain, **SÃO NICOLAU** rises from the ocean between São Vicente and Sal. There's no doubt about its **beauty** – an elegant, hatchet-shaped trio of ridges meeting in spectacular summits above the hidden capital of **Ribeira Brava**. But the cruelly desolate slopes (this is the driest of the "agricultural" islands) testify to a history of extraordinary hardship – eternal isolation, migration and desertion. The problem, as ever, is water, or chronic lack of it. Over the last decade, efforts have been made to tap the deep underground water table – notably with the help of French *cooperants* (paid "volunteers") – but the legacy of centuries of neglect lives on, and the drift away from the island is continuous. However there have been a few good rainy seasons in the last decade; maize, planted every year, actually grows to maturity some seasons, and water has flowed again from village pumps.

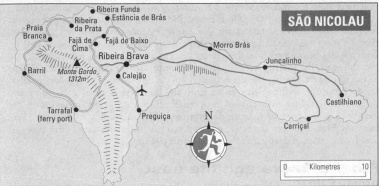

Arriving **by ship** at **Tarrafal**, the island's main port, you should aim to get the first transport up to Ribeira Brava. Shared *carrinhos* charge about CV$300, chartered taxis about CV$2500, and the journey time is about an hour. The **airstrip** is just 4km from Ribeira Brava (midway between the town and the minor port of Preguiça), and you're likely to be able to find a taxi into town (CV$250).

São Nicolau is a good place to have **transport** of your own. If, as is likely enough, you haven't – and don't have unlimited time on the island either – you should make efforts to fix something up straight away; there's very little public transport. One of the few available Land Rovers is sometimes rented out (with owner) for around CV$5000 per day: it's almost worth the expense for the pleasure of being able to offer lifts to dozens of foot-weary Nicolauans as you go.

Tarrafal and the northwest

At **Tarrafal**, straggling along the southwest coast, none of the island's meld of destitution and scenic splendour is immediately obvious. The shallow bay gives on to the largest district of relatively gentle terrain on São Nicolau, from where the spectacle of the interior isn't apparent.

Tarrafal's main activity is **tuna fishing**, supplying an important canning plant. While you can see the great beasts being hauled up on many a Cape Verdean beach, at Tarrafal the evening business seems to yield some particularly spectacular specimens, many as big as a person, and people are quite happy to have you watching as the fish are wheeled into the co-op on wagons. You can also join the kids on the **swimming beach**, the hot, grey sands of which are said to be good for rheumatism. A few kilometres further north, towards Barril, there are much better beaches, safe and good for snorkelling, among them the little white-sand cove of Praia das Francêses.

If you get stuck at Tarrafal, you'll soon locate the good *casa de pasto* at *Pensão Alice* (☎36.11.87), along the shore to the north, where the welcome is warm and the meals generous. **Rooms** are also available (❷). The sparkling white *Residencial Natur* (☎ & ⓕ36.11.78; ❸), located in the same general direction, is another good option, with breakfast CV$250 extra. There's also limited accommodation at the more upmarket *Pensão Aquário* (☎ & ⓕ36.10.99; ❺), where tuna is the culinary speciality. A couple of decent bars and restaurants complete the picture; *Patchê* has main courses around the CV$500/600 mark.

Over the island's spine

The 26km of nearly deserted cobblestone between Tarrafal and Ribeira Brava is another of Cape Verde's scenically outstanding routes. After a steady and satisfying pull away from the broad, southwest bay and up to around 800m, the road takes a sudden and breathtaking swing to the west and within seconds is skating above the fractured bowl of the island's north side. Going by foot from here is a good plan: there's a steep track down to the town, an hour or two's knee-wobbling on foot or, with the day before you, take the gentler descent along the main road, incised into the cliff, with the soaring needle peaks of **Monte Gordo** dominating the skyline to the southwest. During the late summer months this valley, the Fajãs, can be fabulously beautiful, spilling with green from the concerted efforts of farmers and hydrologists, dashed with colour from briefly flowering plants, spiked with the strange shapes of drought-resistant **dragon trees**. The enchanting road, about 15km from the peaks down to the town, winds down past the hamlets and farm plots via a swerving series of deep rents along the north coast.

Ribeira Brava and the east

RIBEIRA BRAVA, facing out to sea on the north side, is firmly Portuguese in feel. A delightfully pretty mesh of narrow streets and whitewash, nestled deep between towering crags, it was established in the seventeenth century, about as far inland as possible, in order to resist the attacks of pirates. The attractions are all rather obscure perhaps, but they're central to the town's appeal: Ribeira Brava, once the flourishing centre of academic and literary life in Cape Verde, quickly establishes its remote, insular identity and is a rewarding place to stay for a few days.

The big, sky-blue **parish church** here, the Igreja Matriz, was the Cape Verdean see until the twentieth century. It's supposed to hold a small museum of religious bits and pieces, among them a valuable and unusual sixteenth-century golden chalice, but it rarely seems to be open. Prospects are better at the **seminary**, a little way up the *ribeira*, which once provided a classical education for students from all over the islands. Here there's a library and reliquary attached to the chapel, and you should be able to persuade the priest to let you in. Back in town there's a fine *praça* and a town hall with neatly tended gardens in front, the site of the birthplace in 1872 of José Lopes da Silva, a leading Cape Verdean poet. Down on the bank of the *ribeira* a shady, second *praça* hides a café and tables for serious draughts playing and *grogue* imbibing.

Out of town, a very pleasant day is to be had **hiking** up the *ribeira*, where you'll meet an array of colourful locals and at least one donkey buckling under a load of water or firewood. Look out too, for the discarded dragons and other papier-mâché monsters from the carnival (the biggest outside Mindelo) which often turn up in the strangest of places. There's a *grogue* distillery about halfway up on the left-hand side; they may let you look around if you ask politely. A little church is perched right at the top, keeping a sentinel-like watch over the valley below.

Looking **east**, the long axis of the island stretches 30km, narrowing at one point to less than 3km across. There are two principal tracks – a "ridgeway" and a north coast path – which meet high above the harbour of **Carriçal** to the east. You'll need to be fit and determined to hike out here – supplies are very few and far between.

Practicalities

The town musters a **TACV office** (☎35.11.61), bank, post office, a small *mercado* and two or three basic general stores. You may even stumble across a workshop manufacturing cups and utensils – functional and miniature – out of bamboo: a tiny part of a tiny souvenir industry. It's not enough to keep many younger people here and the drift to Mindelo, Praia and abroad is unceasing.

For **accommodation**, if you're counting the escudos, check out the large but rather scruffy *Pensão da Cruz* (☎35.12.82; ❷) or the basic but good-value *Residencial Jumbo* (☎35.13.15; ❷); don't bother with the breakfast, however – stale bread and dishwater coffee. The third option, if you want a clean, comfortable room and B&B, is the beautifully located *Pensão Residencial Jardim* (☎35.11.17, ☎35.19.49;

♦). Rooms #201 and #202 have the best views, while the compact little restaurant (order a few hours beforehand) offers reasonably priced traditional fare (including *modje*, a hearty local stew of meat, potatoes, onions and maize) and incredible vistas over the town below. By the time you read this, the *Pensão Santo Antão* should be open, a strikingly pretty renovated colonial town house with lovely s/c rooms, TV and a/c. It's the work of local entrepreneur Manuel Conceição, who's also conceived a highly original cellar bar/club, *A Caverna*, where he plans to showcase traditional musicians on a nightly basis.

Ribeira Brava has several small **casas de pasto**. Chief among these is the *Bela Sombra "Dalila" de Netinha Santos* (☎35.15.18) – try the tasty tuna steaks, though as ever it's as well to order in advance. Another decent place is *Bar Restaurant Sila* where you'll find good, filling fare and an old, but still functioning, pool table.

Sal

SAL, the "island of salt" – a piece of Sahara in the middle of the ocean – is the least inviting of the archipelago. It was one of the last islands to be colonized, early in the nineteenth century, when the Portuguese began to exploit its **salt** ponds properly and introduced purification techniques. In earlier centuries, vast heaps of salt could be loaded onto ships for the cost of the labour alone, though since it was full of donkey dung it was considered low-grade even then. Sal's salt was picked up by trawlers from England on their way to North Atlantic fishing grounds, and exported to the Newfoundland fishing towns, and later to Brazil for beef preservation.

There's a high chance you'll sample Sal sooner or later, whether you fly in from Europe or pass through on a boat or plane connection. Relentlessly windy and mostly flat, Sal is a good location for Cape Verde's main international **airport**. The majority of islanders seem to be involved with this in some way – or in the military base nearby – and the old salt-based economy looks pretty defunct. Attractions are simple to list – one beautiful white **beach** and burgeoning associated water sports, which you're recommended to aim for without delay. Save for the magnificent **salt pans** at **Pedra de Lume**, there's almost nothing else worth a pause. On a positive note, if Sal is your first stop in Cape Verde, you can at least be sure that everywhere else you go will be more interesting.

The tourist hotels and water sports – especially windsurfing, for which the island has a first-class reputation – are down at the beach at **Santa Maria**, at the southern tip of the

island. **Espargos**, the capital, is the business end of things, with the bulk of its budget accommodation.

Arrival on Sal

Surprisingly modern as the **airport** is, it only bursts into life when an international flight is in. If your **visa** has been arranged in advance, you'll need to pay for it (in local currency CV$2500). For a group of travellers, it's simplest if one person queues at the **bureau de change** while the others wait at the police counter for the passports to be returned. There are **domestic flights** to Boa Vista (daily; 20min), Fogo (Tues; 1 hour), Praia (several daily; 45min), São Nicolau (daily except Fri; 35min) and São Vicente (at least 1 daily; 45min). If you're catching a connecting flight, ask if your **bags** will be checked right through, though even then you'll still have to clear customs and then check in again. **Airline offices** – South African Airlines (℡41.36.95), TAAG Angolan Airlines (℡42.10.51), TAP Air Portugal (℡41.12.55) and TACV (℡41.12.68) – are scattered around the tarmac, and for **car rental**, Hertz (℡41.37.02) and Rental Auto (℡41.35.19) have offices in here too. There's an efficient and helpful **baggage store** where you can leave bulky items (CV$100 per 24hr), if you want to spend a few hours unencumbered down at Santa Maria.

Espargos is less than 2km north up the road from the airport – you could probably walk there in twenty minutes. **Taxis** charge CV$200 into town, with a thirty percent surcharge at night; the tariff is CV$700 *deslocação* to get to Santa Maria, though you might well get a free lift if you walk out to the Espargos–Santa Maria road. Arriving **by sea**, you enter a drab grey bay – **Palmeira harbour** – 4km from Espargos, and will have to wait for a lift, which shouldn't be too long in coming.

Espargos and Pedra da Lume

Little **ESPARGOS** may be uninspiring but it's always buzzing with activity. You can make a jaunt out of town quickly (and perhaps illicitly, so don't stop to ask anyone) by climbing to the summit of the **telecommunications hill** just five minutes' walk from the main square. From up there behind the dishes you have a good view of the entire, drab island; to the north a number of old volcanic hills; southwards the bleak brown wastelands fading away to the fringe of white beach at Santa Maria. On the east coast of the island, about 6km from Espargos, are one of the highlights of Cape Verde (and perhaps Sal's saving grace), the salt pans at **Pedra da Lume**.

Espargos itself has a **post office**, Banco Comercial do Atlântico, Internet access (*Com Cyber Space* in the street behind *Paz e Bem*), a few bars and a *praça* which, on occasional Saturday nights, the entire population seems to squeeze into. The **aluguer** park is at the southern end of town.

An increasing number of tourists are choosing to take advantage of Espargos' **accommodation**, which is cheaper than that in Santa Maria. The plain and simple s/c rooms at the *Casa Ângela* (℡41.13.27; ❹) are your best bet, some with hot water. The unmarked (ask in the main supermarket on the square) *Residencial Central* (℡41.13.66, ℻41.16.10; ❹) has an antiquated, lived-in feel, although water (and it's not hot) can be a problem. The more modern *Pensão Paz e Bem* on the side-street off the northeastern corner of the square (℡41.17.82, ℻41.17.90; ❹) is better value, with breakfast included in the rate. Opposite the *aluguer* park, the slightly more upmarket *Hotel Atlântico* (℡41.10.58, ℻41.15.22, ℮hotelatlantico @mail.cvtelecom.cv; ❺) has the sort of ho-hum, airport-style facilities you'd expect; TACV sometimes lodge passengers here when connections are overbooked. Built and run by the brother of the inimitable proprietor of the *Casa*, the *Residencial Santos* (℡41.19.00, ℻41.35.99, ℮residencialsantos@hotmail.com; ❹) up by the post office offers modern, spotless s/c rooms although there are only double beds, no twin rooms; a room with two double beds costs CV$4000.

For **eating**, options are a bit more limited; if you've gone down to Santa Maria for the day, you're advised to have dinner before returning. The amiable, Portuguese-run *Restaurant Salinas* halfway along Rua 5 de Julho (☎41.17.99) is your best bet, with fish and meat dishes from around CV$600. Both the food and service at *Restaurant Sivvy*, on the northwestern corner of the square, are rather sour, while *Esplanada Bom Dia* (opposite the *Atlântico*) is good for snacks.

Pedra da Lume

Aluguers heading to **PEDRA DA LUME** are few and far between, although it's a pleasant enough – if windy – walk. The village itself is a desolate, haunting place comprising a row of old miners' cottages, a lonely white church, a picturesque if tiny harbour too shallow for any but the smallest vessels, and an ancient, towering set of wooden pulleys and loading equipment. There's also a (barely functional) ship repair yard, while the harbour is home to a bizarre ship runway used to haul out small boats for loading.

Follow the creaking overhead pulley system uphill for a kilometre and you come to a tunnel gouged through the hillside. Aim for the shaft of light at the end and you suddenly emerge blinking onto the rim of a gigantic, shallow crater, vast in extent. In its floor is a patchwork of salt pans, squared off by paths and channels, and tinted various shades of the spectrum by the mineral wealth within. People will tell you it's all still in use, but it certainly doesn't look that way. A neat row of white plastic sun loungers at the far end adds an utterly incongruous and rather surreal touch, a reminder that large tour groups now frequent the place; make sure you arrive either early in the morning or late in the evening to fully appreciate the crater's singular atmosphere and avoid the ridiculous sight of tourists wallowing in the pans en masse. Also rather incongruous is the smart new restaurant, *Ca'da Mosto* (☎42.22.10), on the beach front, a place which caters to the tour groups and serves undeniably fine, good-value pizza (around the CV$500 mark).

Santa Maria

SANTA MARIA DAS DORES (St Mary of Sorrows) was practically a ghost town only a few years ago. Ruined timber buildings in ornate style were scattered across the flats, linked by the twisted remains of narrow-gauge rail track which once shifted tuna for the Portuguese and ran out to the end of the thoroughly unsafe jetty. Now it is the engine room of Cape Verdean tourism, helping to power the archipelago's economy. Its simple draw is the stunning flex of white sand dipping into blue-green waves of scintillatingly clear water, and the heady shade of the hotels by the beach. The old town, still slightly ragged around the edges, is rapidly taking on the mantle of a bona fide holiday resort, with a main drag, various restaurants with different themes, and enough vacationing Europeans – a hard core of them globetrotting windsurfers – to give the place a gentle buzz. Happily, that rickety jetty is still there, now tastefully fortified, but still wobbly enough to make it fun. And the local boys still leap from the end of it into three fathoms of transparent water.

Arrival and transport

The short trip from the airport or Espargos (you can catch an *aluguer* from the latter) down to the south coast is a journey through a real desert. Goats are about the only animals you'll see: their introduction in the seventeenth century, before any significant human settlement, began a process of **soil destruction** which is now virtually complete. Nothing really grows, wild or cultivated – the whole scene looks as if it was scoured by bulldozers earlier in the day.

The long, narrow grid of Santa Maria runs in an east–west direction parallel to the beach with its main street, Rua Amílcar Cabral, linking with the Espargos road. The other principal streets are Rua 1 de Junho, one block south, which gives on to the main square Marcelo Leitão halfway along, and Rua 15 de Agosto, one block south again and which extends to the quieter eastern beach. At the western edge of town, a new road runs out parallel to the busy beach for a couple of kilometres, along which are bunched the upmarket resort hotels. A cobbled pedestrian **causeway** also runs out along the sand in the same direction for a few hundred metres or so, the main route for the resort guests to head into the town centre.

For out-of-town trips, **aluguers** gather at the western end of town on the corner opposite the bank; **taxis** also ply their trade from this area. While they run between Espargos and Santa Maria all day, *aluguers* can be thin on the ground at night, so be prepared for a bit of a wait.

Accommodation

There's a huge range of **places to stay** for such a small, compact town, from the affordable to the super-expensive, although genuine budget accommodation is sorely lacking. Besides the clutch of hotel and resort rooms, there are self-contained **apartments** with open-plan kitchen and dining room, double bedroom and bathroom at *Ilha do Sol* (T42.16.31, F42.16.33; ⑥), next to the *Pousada da Luz* (see below). *Baía Village*, Baía da Murdeira (T41.16.04, F41.16.04, ⓔturismal @mail.cvtelecom.cv), is a development set around a natural bay with a dusting of fairly unenticing sand, and rows of identical terracotta-roofed **bungalows** (some actually quite funky inside and sleeping up to four people; CV$8400). Roughly halfway between Espargos and Santa Maria, it also has a diving centre and decent bar/restaurant with sweeping Atlantic panorama.

Hotels and resorts

The Town

Aparthotel Santa Maria Beach Out on the eastern stretch of Rua 15 de Agosto T42.14.50, F42.14.78, ⓔsantamariabeach@yahoo.br. Pleasant airy rooms, some with balconies. ⑤

Hotel Central Rua das Salinas T42.15.03, F42.15.30, ⓔcentralhotelcv@hotmail.com. Clean, reasonable if unremarkable s/c rooms at the back of town, with a/c and TV. ⑥

Hotel Sobrado On the road to Espargos, before the Shell garage T42.17.20, F42.17.15, ⓔhotelsobrado@hotmail.com. Out on the wind-scoured fringes of town with a brightly turned-out facade and spare, spotless B&B rooms. Prices negotiable. The restaurant is bright and airy and does a CV$1000 buffet. Quad bikes for rent. ⑦

Pensão Les Alizés Off Rua Amílcar Cabral T42.14.46, F42.10.08, ⓔlesalizes @cvtelecom.cv. Run by a French father-and-daughter team and housed in a traditional *sobrado* with very bright, tasteful and comfortable rooms (all with balconies), and an exquisite roof terrace. Recommended. ⑥

Pensão Nha Terra Rua 1 de Junho T42.11.09, F42.15.34, ⓔnhaterra@hotmauil.com. Sunny, clean and good-value rooms within striking distance of the beach. Located on what passes for Santa Maria's busiest intersection at the western

end of town, it has a fine seafood restaurant with an extensive menu (many dishes under CV$1000). ⑤

Pousada da Luz T42.11.38, F42.10.88. Out of the way at the back of town, this place has reasonable rooms set around a courtyard with a small swimming pool and restaurant. Overpriced for what it is, although breakfast is included, and a free meal is thrown in if you pay in cash. ⑥

Residencial Alternativa Rua Amílcar Cabral T42.12.16, F42.11.65. The cheapest and most central option in Santa Maria. The B&B rooms are clean and homely if a little gloomy. ④

The beach

Aparthotel Leme Bedje Far eastern edge of town, a stone's throw from the beach T42.11.46, F42.16.84, Ⓦwww.lemebedje.com. Rooms, bungalows and apartments fitted out in upmarket but rustic style using local art and materials. Besides offering reasonable value and a quiet location, it also has mountain bikes for rent. ⑦

Hotel Belorizonte/Novorizonte The first of the big hotels on the westbound road T42.10.45, F42.12.10, ⓔhborizonte@cvtelecom.cv. Considering the price, this place – used by European tour operators – has a disappointing holiday-camp atmosphere. It comprises two parts. The *Belorizonte* has standard upmarket rooms with facilities such as a Jacuzzi and swimming pool; it's comfortable enough, but the rooms are none too big and many face inland. The *Novorizonte* has pleasant wooden cabins with space for two adults and two children. Seasonal rates apply. ⑧

Hotel Morabeza Start of the causeway on the beach ⓣ42.10.20, ⓕ42.10.21, ⓦwww.hotel morabeza.com. Not a cheap place to stay but a fine resort. Rooms, starting at CV$11,000, vary greatly in size: the best value are the sea-facing ones numbered in the 300s. There's also a good

restaurant, scuba diving centre and popular disco. ⑧

Hotel Odjo d'Agua Off Rua 15 de Agosto, near the Municipal Market at the eastern end of town ⓣ42.14.14, ⓕ42.14.30, ⓦwww.odjodagua.com. An undeniably attractive and charmingly situated hotel, right on the beach. The restaurant is pricey but has a wooden walkway where you can watch the waves crashing against the rocks below. The foyer has some great old black-and-white photographs of Cape Verde. Worth the money. ⑧

Eating, drinking and nightlife

Many of the places to stay have their own **restaurants**, the best of which have been mentioned in the reviews. These, together with the places listed below, provide Sal with possibly the most varied and cosmopolitan range of food you're likely to encounter anywhere in Cape Verde. Most of the restaurants serve lunch from noon until three, are closed in late afternoon and begin serving dinner in the early evening. With most hotels laying on all kinds of entertainment to keep their clients on the premises at night, the centre of Santa Maria is often disappointingly quiet. There's nevertheless a scattering of bars and at least one nightclub. Many of the restaurants have regular live music, though some of it can be of the tacky cabaret variety.

The Town

Bar Aonda A nautical-themed Italian *gelateria* next to *Bar Disco Pirata* with beer on tap and delicious ice cream.

Bar Disco Pirata On the Espargos road right on the corner, this perennially popular, piratical-themed club gets going in the early hours.

Café Krioulu Small, atmospheric bar sandwiched between Rua Amílcar Cabral and Rua 1 de Junho, whose alfresco tables are seemingly occupied by tourists (and a scattering of locals) all day and night. Serves tapas-style snacks.

Calema A lively bar at the west end of Rua 1 de Junho, *Calema* has long been a fixture of Santa Maria's nightlife, particularly with the windsurfing/surfing crowd.

Casa Amarela ⓣ94.15.12. A very yellow establishment tucked away on the edge of town behind *Hotel Sobrado*. The Italian fare features a little more imagination than usual; try the fish ravioli.

Cultural Café With patio tables (carved in the shape of each of the islands) on the square, this place draws flocks of tourists for drinks at dusk. Foodwise, the emphasis is on traditional, locally sourced fare.

Pastelaria Relax Rua Amílcar Cabral ⓣ42.11.83. A favourite with tourists and locals alike, serving delicious cakes, yoghurt, fruit, sandwiches and pizza downstairs (great for breakfast or brunch) while the upstairs restaurant opens at night. They

also have some rooms available in the summer season.

Restaurant Américo's Rua 1 de Junho ⓣ42.10.11. Near *Praça Marcelo Leitão*, this is a long-established seafood place with an enclosed cobbled courtyard.

Restaurant Ceu Azul Shawarma Rua Amílcar Cabral. If you really must have your end-of-evening kebab, this late-night gathering spot for locals is the place.

Restaurant Macau Rua 1 de Junho ⓣ95.10.48. Chinese restaurant with a Cape Verdean twist. Open every day, noon until midnight.

Tam Tam Modern, comfortable African-themed bar on the main drag with enticing little booths.

Vulcão de Fogo Opposite the *praça*, the *Vulcão* serves reasonable if pricey fish dishes (CV$700 upwards). Quiet during the day, the place perks up with live music at night.

The beach

Barracuda Spanish-run patio-style restaurant near the pier with great-value tortillas (CV$350) although the *bruschetta* (fashioned from white hamburger-style buns, proceesed cheese and ketchup) is best avoided. Great place to watch the sun go down over a cold Sagres.

Crêtcheu Beginning of the beach causeway on western edge of town ⓣ42.12.66. Quality seafood, pasta and pizza cooked by an Italian chef, with main dishes from around CV$600.

Funaná Out on the beach near the start of the causeway ☎ 42.12.38. Fish dishes start at CV$680. You might be tempted by the house speciality, conch-shell stew.

Restaurant Aquarium Beach location and menus in English featuring oddities like *gazpacho* and octopus salad. You'll no doubt be desperate to try the "Cape Verde sweaty lobster".

Listings

Bank Banco Comercial do Atlántico (Mon–Fri 8am–3pm) is on the corner at the head of Rua Amílcar Cabral.
Car rental Hertz, *Hotel Crioula* ☎ 42.16.61; Alucar, *Hotel Morabeza* ☎ 42.11.87. Local operators like Cartour Lda (☎ 42.17.00) and Hifacar (☎ 42.12.41) have 4WD vehicles for around the CV$5500 mark.
CDs The Centro de Artesenato at the eastern end of Rua 1 de Junho has has a well-chosen couple of shelves (as well as a large stock of good-quality but tourist-oriented souvenirs; Visa cards accepted), although your best bet is the record shop in the airport.
Diving Sal is a major centre for diving, with one of the most experienced establishments being the Stingray Dive Centre (☎ 42.11.34), based in *Hotel Odjo d'Agua*. On the beach at the western end, the well-equipped Technosea/Scuba Team Cabo Verde (☎ 42.10.20) offer a variety of PADI courses; a single dive (with gear) comes in at CV$3700.
Fishing It could be you landing one of the whoppers on the pier: Max Dias (94.29.22) is the man to sort you out, whether you're after tuna, wahoo or marlin, big game or bottom fishing. Expect to pay CV$27,500 per half-day for a group of four or five with a boat and skipper provided.
Internet access It costs a pricey CV$400 per hour to get online at *Cyber Café*, on the western end of

Rua 1 de Junho (daily 8.30am–11pm).
Police ☎ 41.11.32.
Post office Towards the northeast end of town (Mon–Fri 8am–noon & 2–5pm).
Travel agents Oceanis at the western end of the main drag (☎ & ☎ 42.13.35) organize jeep safaris around Sal, quad bike hire, shark-watching trips and tours to other islands. CVTS, at the west end of Rua 1 de Junho (☎ 42.12.20), offers similar packages as does Planeta (☎ 42.15.7, ☎ 42.16.19, ✉ planeta.cvt@cvtelecom.cv) near the *Leme Bedje*.
Windsurfing/Kitesurfing Sal being the windsurfing capital of Cape Verde, there are very good facilities: Planeta (☎ 95.34.86) have friendly centres on both ends of the beach with a day's hire at CV$4500 and a one-hour private lesson at CV$3900. Kitesurfing is also available although lessons are pretty much obligatory for beginners (a tryout session is CV$4400) and they won't rent equipment unless they know you can handle it. The similarly priced Club Mistral on the western end of the beach (☎ 92.54.64, ☎ www.club-mistral.com) are also very good, although they're geared towards pre-booking (you can do this through the website), which warrants a ten percent discount. Finally, Fun System are a small but friendly operation on the beach in front of *Hotel Albatross*.

Boa Vista

Boa Vista is said to have been productive at one time; at present it is almost a desert. Its people, of whom there are four thousand, are almost always hungry, and the lean cattle, with sad faces and tears in their eyes, walk solemnly in cud-less rumination over grassless fields. In the valleys there is some vegetation. Fishing, salt-making and going to funerals are the chief amusements and employments of the people.

Life was not easy when the Reverend Charles Thomas went to **BOA VISTA** in the 1850s, but things have improved a little, at least for the cattle. The rains of recent years have made the hillocky pancake of an island greener than in living memory, though it still retains large areas of spectacular shifting **sand dunes**, notably in the west. The island has a captivatingly desolate interior, and a necklace of spectacular white **beaches** all around (the one at Santa Monica is the most beautiful). It's a great island to explore in a rented Suzuki, with a clear enough route right round the island, though *aluguers* tend to be very scarce – less than 5000 people live on the island, eight out of ten of them in **Sal Rei**. If you make the effort to get into the parched and peaceful countryside, you'll find the few people graciously welcoming, with a high proportion of English-speakers who've spent years at sea. The traditional *mornas* (folk songs) of the island are rated the most cheerful and upbeat in Cape Verde.

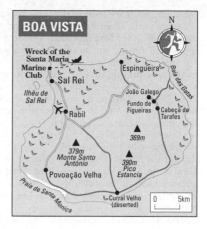

The island's struggling economy long depended on salt, but that industry has died out and now date farming – there are large palm groves near the airstrip – supplemented by fishing and some livestock grazing provide the main alternatives to emigration. Tourism is beginning to have an impact, too, with the more adventurous windsurfing aficionados barely pausing at Santa Maria these days before heading straight to Boa Vista. Italian visitors are by far the most prominent. Boavistans themselves seem to have made best use of the island's famous **shipwrecks**; vessels frequently came to grief in the treacherous rocky shallows on the north and northeast coasts – and still occasionally do, since navigation charts for the seas around Boa Vista are inaccurate, in some cases by several hundred metres. There are judged to be about a hundred wrecks, some of them quite old.

Turtles were grist to the Boavistan mill as well, and unfortunately still are – there are precious egg-laying sites on many beaches. **Humpback whales** are also regularly seen in waters around Boa Vista, specifically in the bay southwest of Sal Rei. This is the most important breeding site for this small population only now recovering from centuries of hunting. Unfortunately, their future recovery cannot be taken for granted, with proposed tourist developments posing a threat. While the whales are often visible from the beach, you may be able to persuade local fishermen to take you out for a closer look.

Flights arrive at the **airport**, 5km south of Boa Vista's capital, **Sal Rei**, near the old village of Rabil. The fare into town depends on the number of passengers and the mood of the driver; you'll often be quoted a price of CV$600–700 but it's possible to bargain them down to half that. On your return journey, it may be difficult to find any vehicle, never mind an inexpensive one, so start looking down on the square well before your check-in time. **Ferries** come close to the port, in the heart of the little town, and passengers come ashore by lighter.

To **get around** the island under your own steam, any of the main hotels will arrange for a Japanese 4WD to be parked outside ready for you first thing (CV$5500 for 24hr; CV$10,000–30,000 deposit). To rent a vehicle independently, head to the Santa Monica travel agency on the north side of the square (☎ & ℗51.14.45), which also runs day-long excursions to the "Norte" villages and the beach near Rabil for around CV$2500, including guide and insurance. Alternatively, you can rent **mountain bikes** at *Hotel Dunas* (see p.483; expect to pay about CV$1500 a day).

Sal Rei

SAL REI has a gentle buzz: there are always people knocking around the central square, usually boisterous teenagers, while the row of African market stalls beyond the square's northern edge are suitably animated. The town beach is at its liveliest on weekends, and if your visit coincides with a football match at the Sal Rei "stadium" you'll see most of the male population in one go. If you can find a boat, a trip out to the **Ilhéu de Sal Rei**, an islet opposite the town, is interesting: it holds the ruins of an old **fort** (Fortaleza Duque de Braganza) and the waters are good for snorkelling. Around the month of August you may even see turtles here.

If you want to be active, Sal Rei can offer a number of diversions, including **mountain biking**, **diving** and, of course, **windsurfing**. There are currently a couple of places you can get your sea wings: Happy Surf (in conjunction with *Hotel Dunas*) offers an hour's hire for around CV$1800; a full eight-hour beginners' course is CV$6000 and they also hire kitesurfing equipment. The smaller, friendlier Boavista Wind Club (sometimes known as Os Alisios; T51.10.36, Wwww.boavistawindclub.com) is comparable on price and boasts a small, shaded wooden terrace with hammocks, a great place to chill and play chess after a hard day on the waves. **Diving** is another popular diversion; the Submarine Dive Centre (T92.48.65) can provide equipment and lessons from beginner to advanced and its Brazilian owner, Atila, is a certified PADI instructor. All of the above firms are to be found next to one another on the beach at the southeastern edge of town.

Mountain biking is more fun than it might at first appear: head south out of town, turning immediately left opposite the Enacal petrol station to join the cobbles of the old road, the **Via Pittoresca**, down to the airport and **Rabil** village; the route undulates through a veritable forest of palm trees for several pretty kilometres before rejoining the main road. Considerably more taxing is the Boa Vista **Ultramarathon**, a gruelling annual desert race over 75km or 150km (the latter in two stages; for more info, see Wwww.runnersplanet.it).

With a 4WD vehicle, it's possible to get right down to the wreck of the **Cabo de Santa Maria**, 8km northeast of Sal Rei. The Spanish freighter has been rusting off the beach since 1968, when its cargo of car parts, garlic, rosemary and pornographic magazines was seized and rapidly traded across the island. From Sal Rei, drive out towards the Marine Club, then leave the road before the hotel entrance and head across country to the east, following the tracks for a few hundred metres until you reach a little church in a large, white-walled plot. From here, continue generally uphill and over the crests until you emerge above the island's northern coast with a clear view of the wreck a couple of kilometres away. A driveable track goes down to the beach and tyre marks lead you the whole way there.

Practicalities

The town is simplicity itself to navigate, with a huge, rather bare central square ringed by acacia trees and flanked by two main streets, Avenida Amílcar Cabral and Rua Dos Emigrantes, running roughly north–south. There's a Banco Comercial do Atlântico right on the square, while both the **post office** and **TACV** (T51.11.86) office are up the slope of Rua Dos Emigrantes. The latter operate flights to Praia (Tues & Thurs; 35–45min) and Sal (at least 1 daily; 20–25min). To get **online**, try the Centro Informático Municipal, a small stone edifice in the middle of the square (daily 10am–1pm & 4–9pm).

Aside from the hotels, there are few places to eat, drink or shop in Sal Rei. The best (and busiest, so book ahead) restaurant by a mile is *Riba D'Olte* (T51.15.63; 6–10pm daily, closed Wed) housed in a garish pink building opposite; the food is delicious – try the Spaghetti a Pomodora. The lively patio **bar** – usually called the *Esplanada* – behind the jetty, a stone's throw from the *Hotel Dunas* is another obvious target; there's cheap pizza to be had here although it's not great. *Bar Naida* on the main square has a good reputation for local fare. For a pleasant afternoon beer you can drop by *Gelateria Criola* (T51.13.73, @scaramellipier @cvtelecom.cv) on the beach. You might also make arrangements to eat in Rabil, at the *Sodade di Nha Terra* – a prepared-to-order-only restaurant run by an excellent cook.

Hotels and pensões

Estoril Beach Resort On the south side of town
☎ 51.10.78, ⓕ 51.10.46, ⓔ hotelestoril@mail
.cvtelecom.cv. Italian-run, this is similar in feel to *A
Paz* but rates are much heftier. There's a nice
upstairs restaurant serving, unsurprisingly, quality
Italian fare. **❼**

Hotel Dunas On the seafront ☎ 51.12.25,
ⓕ 51.13.84, ⓔ dunas@bws.cv. Pleasantly informal
and welcoming establishment with fine, bright
rooms, some of which offer incredible vistas
across the bay. They also run the expensive
beach restaurant, *Tortuga*, located next to Happy
Surf. **❽**

Pousada Boa Vista ☎ 41.15.03, ⓕ 51.14.23,
ⓔ pousadaboavista@cv.telecom.cv. Bright,
unremarkable rooms, all with fridge and fan, and
some with balconies. There's a decent if rather
pricey seafood restaurant (main dishes from
CV$750) with an antiquated lurid green interior.
Group discounts available. **❻**

Residencia A Paz Off the square's southern end
☎ 96.53.71, ⓦ www.a-paz.com. Offering incredible
value, with s/c rooms fitted out with lots of natural
fabrics and a wonderful roof terrace. You're assured
of a hearty welcome from the Italian owner. **❺**

Residencial Boa Esperança One block east of
the south side of the square ☎ 51.11.70. Some
rooms are s/c but there's no hot water; the
breakfast (inclusive) is good for the price. **❷**

Residencial Santa Isabel On the square
☎ 51.12.52, ⓕ 51.16.25. Arguably the best-value
budget option; rooms have their own facilities and
hot water. **❸**

Driving round the island

A highly recommended day can be spent **circumnavigating Boa Vista** with your own transport, though ensure you have sufficient drinking water and a good spare. And don't go alone either: either take a companion or hire a guide – if you have an accident out here (and Suzukis have been prone to roll), you may have a long wait for the first *aluguer* to come by.

The road south of Sal Rei goes through wiry little **Rabil**, then descends to a seasonal watercourse to cross through palm trees; take the left fork and you'll find yourself on desolate open road heading across the central and northern part of the island. After 45 minutes you reach **João Galego**, the first of three tiny hamlets comprising the small, inhabited district known as "Norte" (pretty much the only populated part of the island apart from Sal Rei and Rabil and a small town in the southwest, Povoação Velha). A couple of kilometres further is **Fundo de Figueiras**, with a little surrounding farmland, whence a six-kilometre off-road diversion down a gentle shelving valley takes you to the splendidly wild and remote beach of **Baía das Gatas**. You'll find turtle bones and even the occasional dolphin skeleton here. Back at the "main road", the southernmost Norte settlement is **Cabeça de Tarafes**, and at this point the cobbled surface ceases abruptly and the real adventure begins. The track (easy to follow even though you're now unlikely to see another human being for a couple of hours) scales the gentle, brown rocky slopes of the depopulated eastern part of the island, crawling across the little ravines of seasonal watercourses, and speeding up over the hilltops. As you finally descend to reach the **southern coast**, near a deserted palm-tree oasis, and turn right to follow the shore, you'll need that four-wheel-drive as the track meets soft sand, and at the right time of year, even mud. You can drive straight down to a marvellously empty strand from here.

Curral Velho, an abandoned settlement at Boa Vista's southern extremity, is 28km beyond Cabeça (about 2hr). Don't try to continue direct to Praia de Santa Monica from Curral Velho – the rough track deteriorates as you leave the old settlement behind and rapidly becomes impossible. Instead, as you arrive in Curral Velho from the east, turn right at the first large wall leading off inland and start to follow it north, and you can pick up a clear track which leads across the great, bare back of the island, more or less north or northwest, to rejoin the Norte road after about an hour. This track is mostly firm going, with some soft sand: keep the distinctive cone of Mount Santo António in view to your left and you can't really go wrong.

Guinea-Bissau

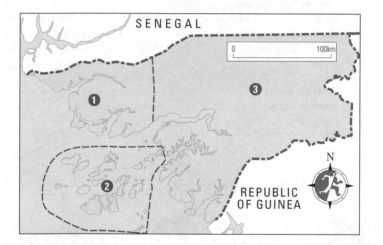

Guinea-Bissau highlights

* **Varela** A beach to rival Senegal's Cap Skiring coast just across the border. **See p.516**

* **Bolama town** Decaying colonial buildings, crumbling monuments and leafy scenery all make this a worthwhile offshore destination. **See p.518**

* **Praia da Bruce** On the island of Bubaque, a postcard-pretty beach with hardly a soul in sight. **See p.522**

* **Orango** This Bijagós island not only features pristine tropical beaches but is home to unusual wildlife too – a population of saltwater-dwelling hippos. **See p.523**

* **Bafatá** Nestling in the forests of the interior, a small, pretty town with an intriguing feel and a complement of red Portuguese-style houses. **See p.525**

Introduction and Basics

One of the smallest and least-known countries in West Africa, Guinea-Bissau isn't on the region's tourist trails. But if you're driven by a taste for adventure and discovery, you will spend an unforgettable time here – the opportunities to explore little-visited districts are always available.

Guinea-Bissau only gained its independence from Portugal in 1974 after a long and painful **war of liberation**, which contributed to the overthrow of the dictatorship in Portugal and turned the nation into a highly charged symbol of colonial repression. Until the end of the 1970s, the country's struggle for national survival inspired progressive movements in Europe and North America, as Nicaragua did in the 1980s. But political rigidity set in with economic failure, and enthusiasm for the revolution waned both in Guinea-Bissau and overseas. A military takeover in 1980 and subsequent lurch into a flawed democratic system brought little improvement. Long-standing rifts within the armed forces, fuelled by economic desperation, were the cause of the 1998/99 **military uprising** which ousted the elected government. The country is slowly recovering from the civil war which ensued, and remains cripplingly poor.

The **Guinea-Bissauans** are renowned for being very laid-back company, and the country is refreshingly free of hassle. The sense of personal security which travellers experienced prior to the fighting has returned, but the fragility of the current peace shouldn't be underestimated; it's especially important to keep tabs on the situation while planning a trip.

People

For its small size, Guinea-Bissau features a great diversity of ethnic groups. Most numerous are the **Balante**, mainly concentrated in the southern coastal creeks and forests. Much of the area under rice cultivation has been cleared by them over the centuries. In the northwest, the smaller population of **Fulup** (part of the Jola group from southern Senegal) are also great rice farmers. **Pepel** and **Manjak** farmers from the Bissau region are heavily dependent on the city as a market, and operate a more diverse economy. In contrast, the **Bijagó** people, who inhabit the islands, are mostly self-sufficient (principally through fishing and palm-nut gathering), though men increasingly find work on the mainland or abroad. Numbering fewer than 40,000, the Bijagó have been under little pressure to change over the last 200 years. They've resisted Islam and Christianity, and remain attached to traditional ways. Women have relatively greater economic power than is usually the case, as traditionally they are the owners of houses.

Most of the **Mandinka** live in the north, along the Senegalese border. The **Fula** inhabit the northeast and, as ever, they are powerful players in local politics: their conservative, feudal roots can't be ignored by whoever governs the country.

Fact file

La Republica da Guiné-Bissau covers 36,000 square kilometres, barely half the size of Scotland or Maine. The population is around 1.5 million, with a slower rate of growth than most African countries. The country's **foreign debt** amounts to some £600 million ($960 million), nearly twenty times the value of the country's annual exports of goods and services. It seems a massive figure until compared with the bill for the construction of London's Millennium Dome – some fifty percent more.

Just before this went to press, the ineffectual president, Kumba Yala, was overthrown in a bloodless coup. At the time of writing, the country was peaceful.

A large proportion of Guinea-Bissauans are mixed-race **Kriolu**-speakers, the majority of whom are Cape Verdean by descent, though some are descendants of the small number of Portuguese settlers and traders. There still exists a fragmented Portuguese settler community and a growing population of French expatriate workers.

Where to go

The country is spread across a region of low-lying jungle and grassland, mangrove swamp, estuarine flats and meandering rivers. The most worthwhile destination is the **Bijagós archipelago**, a scattering of immaculate and admirably languid islands. Thanks to their distance from the mainland, these islands have preserved a unique culture, and have escaped the worst consequences

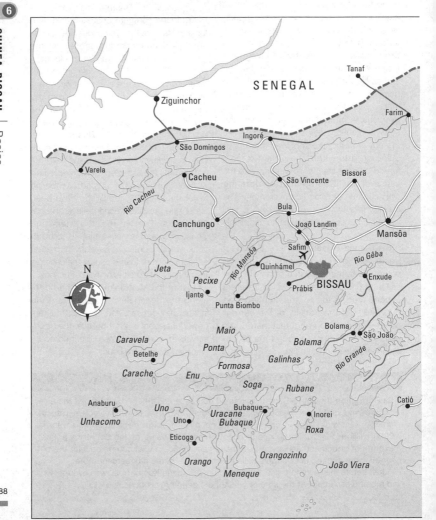

of the unrest that has troubled the country. They're a short boat ride from **Bissau**, which is strangely low-key for a capital city. Most visitors pass through Bissau on the way to the islands, though the city is an excellent place to relax and admire Portuguese-influenced colonial architecture.

With its abundance of greenery and a handful of gorgeous beaches, the country's **mainland** has some appeal, but travel there requires patience (most journeys require at least one ferry ride), and you should be prepared for the stark poverty and inadequate facilities you'll encounter in rural areas.

When to go

The best time to visit is December and January, when the islands are really pleasant. The *carnaval* season in Bissau (February) is a good time to be in the capital.

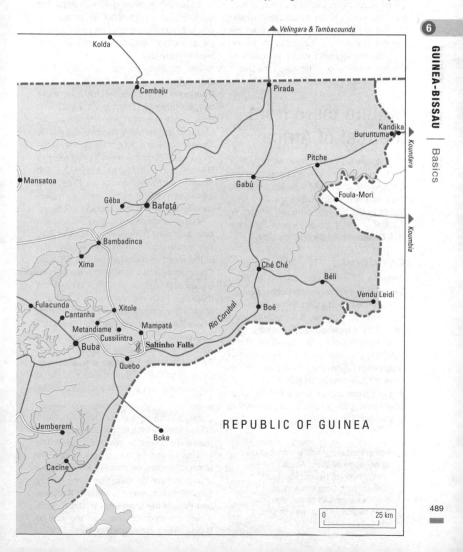

▲ *Velingara & Tambacounda*

▶ *Koundara*

▶ *Koumbia*

REPUBLIC OF GUINEA

0   25 km

Average temperatures and rainfall

Bissau

	Jan	Feb	Mar	Apr	May	June	July	Aug	Sept	Oct	Nov	Dec
Temperatures °C												
Min (night)	18	19	20	21	22	23	23	23	23	23	22	19
Max (day)	32	33	34	34	33	31	30	29	30	31	32	30
Rainfall mm	2	2	7	1	45	200	850	900	390	180	40	5

Bad times, particularly in Bissau itself, are the nerve-fraying run-up to the rains in April and May when you can hardly breathe, and the end of the rains in November, when the sun evaporates the moisture into the leaden air. In the five very wet months, from June to October, the air is dripping wet all the time – whether it's raining or not.

Getting there from the rest of Africa

Most visitors to Guinea-Bissau either fly in or cross the border from Senegal, though a few European yachts make it down here from the Canaries. Even before the civil war, **flights** to Bissau were extremely limited. At the time of writing, the only regular flights are from **Dakar** with Air Sénégal (6 weekly).

Overland

Because of limitations on flights from Europe, many visitors fly into Dakar or Banjul and continue overland to Bissau by public transport. The journey is straightforward despite its complicated appearance on the map, though note that, because of the enduring civil conflict in the Senegalese Casamance region (see p.173), travelling this route still bears a certain risk. If you're setting out **from Dakar**, you'll find Peugeot 504s heading direct to Ziguinchor and Kolda in southern Senegal. You have to overnight

in either town, and take another bush taxi on to Bissau in the morning. From **Banjul**, the trip to Bissau via Ziguinchor can be made in one long day, though you may prefer to plan for an overnight stop in Ziguinchor and continue the next day.

The closest border crossing from Ziguinchor into Guinea-Bissau is at **São Domingos** (daily 8.30am–6pm), from where onward travel to Bissau is via Ingoré and Bula, involving a short ferry crossing at São Vincente (check first if the ferry is currently functioning). From Bula, bush taxis take the route east along the newly tarred road to Bissora, then on to Mansôa and Bissau. The direct, southward route from Bula, also served by public transport, involves a passenger-only ferry at Joaõ Landim.

Alternative routes into Guinea-Bissau have become more popular as a result of São Domingos' closure during the civil war, and in the event of disturbances in the Basse Casamance, it can be safer to enter Guinea-Bissau east of Ziguinchor. You may well find that bush taxis will take you to **Tanaf** and from there across the border to **Farim**, where it's easy to find a taxi to Bissau. It's also possible to travel from **Kolda**, 70km east of Tanaf, to **Bafatá** in central Guinea-Bissau, and from **Velingara** in southeastern Senegal to **Gabú**. Both Bafatá and Gabú have several daily connections to Bissau.

From Guinea

Driving **from Guinea** in your own vehicle, you have a choice between two main routes. The first takes the tarmac road to **Labé** via Mamou, battles on north to **Koundara** (a stretch that can be reasonable during the dry season), then crosses the border at **Kandika**, and follows the bush track to **Gabú**, from where it's smooth tarmac all the way to Bissau. This is normally a two-day trip.

For important practical information applying to all West African countries, covering health, transport, cultural hints and more, plus details on getting to the region from beyond Africa, see Basics, pp.9–87.

The second route goes from Conakry north to Boké, through **Koumbia** and **Foula-Mori**, then takes the ferry crossing at the border and joins the main road to Bissau at Pitche. Normal driving time between the capitals in the dry season is not much less than 22 hours on this route. With a dawn start from Conakry in a 4WD you might just make it to the border in time to catch the ferryman at dusk, and thus arrive in Gabú or Bafatá late at night, but planning on a two-day journey is much more realistic.

There's **public transport** on both the above routes. Taxis never do the trip in less than two days, which means spending at least one uncomfortable night en route.

The third, more obvious-looking route **following the coast** is an arduous trek, not recommended unless you have bags of time. From **Boké** it goes via a bridge and Sansalé to Buba in Guinea-Bissau, thence to Enxude and by *pirogue* to Bissau. It's a route hardly anyone travels, and there's no public transport.

Red tape and visas

Visas, generally easy to obtain, are required by nearly all nationalities apart from West Africans. If you're flying into Bissau from one of the many countries with no Guinea-Bissau embassy or consulate, you can usually get a visa at the airport in Bissau.

At the consulates in Banjul, Ziguinchor and Conakry, visas are cheap and normally issued while you wait. The embassies in Dakar and Abidjan are more formal. The consulate in Ziguinchor, Senegal, issues thirty-day **single-entry visas** on the spot. If you travel into Guinea-Bissau from Guinea, note that border officials ask for a small administration fee (FG2500) to give you the necessary *laissez-passer*.

Extending your visa, once in the country, isn't difficult, but allowing it to expire and over-staying can lead to serious problems if detected. For onward travel, don't count on getting many stamps in Bissau, as many embassies that closed during the civil war haven't returned. At the time of writing, Nigeria, Senegal, The Gambia, Mauritania and Guinea were the only West African states with diplomatic missions (details on p.515).

Information and maps

Tourist information on Guinea-Bissau in English is almost nonexistent. There are no official tourist offices, nor much of an organized government department dealing with this minor industry. If you want to exhaust all possibilities, you could pay a direct visit to the Ministério do Comércio e Turismo, off the Avenida Pansau Na Isna in Bissau (☏20 21 95 or 20 60 62).

The 1:500,000, 3615 series IGN **map** of the country, updated in 1993, is reasonable – and the only one available.

Health

Healthcare in the country is very basic. Unsurprisingly, the main **hospital** in Bissau is the best equipped, and Bafatá, Canchungo, Bolama, Bubaque and Gabú have some limited medical services, but pharmacies are few and far between, and out on the remote islands and in the south, your health problems are largely your own to deal with.

Always keep your **yellow fever** certificate in your passport while travelling, in case you're asked for it. **Bilharzia** is a menace on sluggish inland waters, but the rivers are tidal far into the interior (the Rio Gêba as far upstream as Bafatá, the Cacheu past Farim and the Corubal as far as the Saltinho falls) and the schistosome worms can't survive in brackish water.

Costs, money and banks

Guinea-Bissau uses the **CFA franc** (£1 = CFA930, US$1 = CFA600; see p.39). Though public transport is inexpensive, petrol is fairly costly, a factor to be taken into account even if you're not using your own vehicle, as this has an impact on accommodation prices, since hotels run their own generators. There are few really inexpensive places to stay in the capital, where the majority of hotels charge at least £16/$25 a night for a double room. Outside the capital, there's very little to spend your money on, and accommodation is a little cheaper, except for a smattering of resorts on the islands.

Banks and exchange

Changing money in **banks** is a generally inefficient process – go early in the day, and don't be surprised if it takes all morning. The only official exchange bureaux are in Bissau's top hotels, with unlicensed moneychangers at the Central Market and in one or two shops selling imported goods. Outside of Bissau, the only banks with exchange facilities are in **Canchungo**, **Bafatá** and **Gabú**, though their services may be unreliable; you're better off changing funds before you travel inland or out to the islands.

Credit cards are virtually useless in Guinea-Bissau. There are no ATMs, and even Bissau's top hotel wasn't accepting cards at the time of writing. There's also no guarantee that banks will accept your **traveller's cheques**. All of this means you should arrive with sufficient cash, though you can have funds transferred to Guinea-Bissau via Western Union should you run out.

Getting around

There used to be regular **flights** from the capital to Bubaque and, when there was enough demand, to Gabú and Catió, but these were out of service at the time of writing. This being a compact country, getting around by **road** is usually easily manageable.

Most travel in Guinea-Bissau is ruled by the **tides**: on the coast there's a tidal range of over five metres, more than twice the world average. Several communities are cut off except at high tide when boats can reach them.

The operations of the former state-owned ferry company Rodofluvial are currently suspended. At the time of writing, **Afripesca** provided the only regular boat service to the islands, to **Bubaque**, leaving Bissau on Friday and returning on Sunday (5hr;

CFA2500 one-way). An extra charge might be levied for bicycles and large items of luggage.

In addition, there are dozens of small hand-hauled ferry bridges and **canoa** (*pirogue*) services around the country. As a rule of thumb, it's not recommended to use the *pirogues* or to hitch a ride in one of the local fishing boats, as these vessels aren't well maintained and aren't equipped for emergencies. That said, we've mentioned *pirogues* in the text where there are few alternatives to using them.

By road

The **bush taxi** network is improving all the time, and a large number of new **minibuses** (referred to as **toko toko**) have been imported since the end of the war. You generally have to be out and about first thing in the morning to get anywhere though, as taxis and buses tend to leave early. Later departures can take forever to fill up. As an indication of fares, expect to pay CFA1500 from Bissau to Bafatá, a journey of about three hours. In the south of the country, you might occasionally find yourself getting a ride in one of the **banana wagons** which transport the fruit to market; negotiate a fare with the driver.

Hitching might seem a hopeless task, but it's fairly safe and you might find it preferable to waiting in the taxi park (**paragem**) of some distant village. Guinea-Bissau's main routes enjoy a regular traffic flow, but as soon as you venture off the beaten track, transport becomes a problem. Passing vehicles carrying NGO workers and volunteers will often oblige, and it's always worth asking fellow guests at your hotel if they happen to be heading in your direction.

Car and bike rental

There are no **car rental** firms in Guinea-Bissau, though if you ask at Conakry hotels about private arrangements, they will usually come with a vehicle and driver. Expect to pay at least US$60 a day, plus **fuel** (CFA570 per litre for petrol, CFA360 per litre diesel). Fuel is a lot more readily available than it used to be – every major town now has a petrol station.

Cycling through Guinea-Bissau, so long as you choose your season, is an attractive option. The five-hundred-odd kilometres of sealed road are pleasantly quiet and flat or gently undulating, and often flanked by dense foliage and grass pouring over the road. With a week or two to spare you could explore the south and east quite extensively this way. Renting a bike privately in Bissau isn't too difficult. You should also try to do this if you're visiting the islands as, with the exception of Bubaque, transport on them is hard to come by.

Accommodation

There are few hotels in Guinea-Bissau, and inexpensive rooms aren't plentiful, even in rural areas, and especially in Bissau itself. Such **budget** places as exist (often in the ❸ bracket) are usually very basic affairs, though better value is on offer at a few upcountry establishments. Facilities vary widely among **mid-range** places (❹–❻) – some are hardly better than the cheap hotels, while a few do actually offer a decent level of comfort. The only international-class establishments (❼ & ❽) are in the capital.

During *carnaval* in February and possibly also during football's Amílcar Cabral Cup Final in May, you'll have trouble finding a room. An alternative to regular hotels is the *pensão* (plural *pensões*) – a family-run establishment along Portuguese lines. In most of the older, Portuguese-built towns – Canchungo, Bafatá, Gabú – you'll find a couple of adequate accommodation options, but in more out-of-the-way places basic, sleazy, bar-restaurant establishments with a few rooms are the norm. All but the cheapest hotels and guesthouses have their own **generators**, which tend to be turned on from early evening until late.

Camping is tolerated, and a tent is particularly helpful on the islands. There are no campsites, however. Food and water supplies may be a problem if you're camping far from any village or town.

It's not uncommon for travellers to find **private lodging** with Guineans they have met on their travels. This can be a rewarding experience, but given the incidence of poverty, most people appreciate a contribution in cash or in kind towards the evening meal.

Eating and drinking

In a small country as poor and battered as this, it's no surprise to find little attention paid to gastronomy. White rice is the staple diet of nearly everyone and, for the majority, something to accompany it once or twice a week is the best they can expect.

This is unlikely to be your diet, at least not in Bissau itself. Restaurants in the capital make the most of **seafood** and whatever else is available, and hotel dining rooms usually manage to produce enormous four-course meals in rustic **Portuguese style**. Rice soup, fish, chicken, tough beef or pork and potatoes are standard fare with, invariably, a banana to finish.

If you're used to eating **bananas** all day, then Guinea-Bissau will be less of a shock to your system. Together with oranges, cashew nuts and small loaves, they're obtainable just about everywhere. Although

---

Accommodation price codes

All accommodation prices in this chapter are coded according to the following scale, whose equivalent in pounds sterling/US dollars is used throughout the book. Prices refer to the rate you can expect to pay for a room with two beds. Single rooms, or single occupancy, normally costs at least two-thirds of the twin-occupancy rate.

❶ Under CFA4700 (under £5/$8).
❷ CFA4700–9000 (£5–10/$8–16).
❸ CFA9000–14,000 (£10–15/$16–24).
❹ CFA14,000–19,000 (£15–20/$24–32).

❺ CFA19,000–28,000 (£20–30/$32–48).
❻ CFA28,000–37,000 (£30–40/$48–64).
❼ CFA37,000–47,000 (£40–50/$64–80).
❽ Over CFA47,000 (£50/$80).

small supermarkets and corner shops exist, they carry less of a range of produce than you'd find in, say, Ziguinchor or Conakry, and you'll turn to the markets for basic food requirements.

There are few Guinea-Bissauan **specialities** but some dishes to try are *kalde de manjara*, a peanut stew; *kalde de chebeng*, crushed palm-nut stew; *kalde branco*, fish in white sauce; and *galinha cafriella*, a chicken dish. *Cachupa*, a beans, corn and pork dish characteristic of the Cape Verde Islands, is a meal for special occasions. **Monkey meat** (*carne de mono*) is common everywhere except in the Muslim North, though monkey-hunting poses a threat to many species. If you find yourself eating it, be certain it's well cooked to avoid the possibility of catching a dangerous virus. Seafood is good in Bissau. Delicious **gambas** – king prawns – are the stock in trade of the European-style restaurants. **Oysters** and other shellfish are often on Bissau menus too.

Locally made **palm and cashew wine** is the national brew. Both are usually tasty and sweet, but beware that their alcohol content can be anything from virtually zero to pretty potent. And make sure you don't ask for the cashew liquor **cana** by mistake – it's a lethal brew made from cashew apples. (Incidentally, if you are given unshelled cashew nuts, do not try to crack them open with your teeth: the shell contains an intense irritant that will inflame your mouth for days.) There are a few imported **beers** – including Sagres from Portugal – and soft drinks are available. Local juices (lime, lemon and the wonderful **cashew juice**) can all be found for about CFA50–100 a bottle. Cashews and groundnuts are very widespread (something like forty percent of export earnings comes from cashew nuts). Together with the magnificent mangoes, they help to make the end of the dry season bearable.

Communications

Guinea-Bissau's **mail** service isn't particularly efficient or reliable. Sending or receiving parcels is best not attempted, as many get tampered with or simply don't arrive. The Guinea-Bissau's IDD country code is

☎245.

main post office is in Bissau, and **poste restante** letters should be marked Lista da Correios, CTT, Bissau. There are functioning branch post offices in provincial towns, but you should be prepared for considerable delays if you send letters from them.

The telephone system is generally reliable, though calls are pricey (except to Portugal). Telecentres have sprung up in recent years, mainly concentrated in the capital. You can phone Guinea-Bissau direct from abroad, and IDD calls aren't difficult. Note that reverse-charge (collect) calls can be made to Portugal only. Guinea-Bissauan phone numbers don't have area codes.

Getting online is steadily becoming easier, though be prepared for very slow connections. Internet cafés were mainly confined to the capital at the time of writing.

The media

Radio is the most important form of broadcast media. Programmes are generally in Portuguese, although Radio Mavegro (100 FM) transmits the BBC World Service news in English most hours. Mavegro is one of several private stations, the other main ones being Radio Bombolon and Radio Pidjiguiti. As for **television**, the national station RTGB broadcasts every evening from 7pm. In Bissau, the Portuguese channel RTP International is widely available, though reception gets harder the further inland you go, and there are very few TV sets outside of Bissau.

Looking to **the press** for news, you might be able to get hold of the state-run *No Pintcha*, as well as the privately owned *Diario de Bissau* and *Gazeta de Noticias*. Foreign papers are notoriously hard to obtain.

Entertainment and sport

The main cultural event of the year is the **carnaval** in February. Guinea-Bissau's **cinema** output revolves around one major figure, **Flora**

Gomes, whose films span three decades. In his most recent film, the deeply symbolic musical comedy *Nha Fala* ("My Voice", 2003), the central character emigrates to Paris while bearing the family curse that kills all who sing. Gomes' vibrant work (*Nha Fala* was shortlisted at Fespaco 2003) is constrained by conditions at home and, unsurprisingly, no other filmmakers have matched his career. The music scene (see p.507) shows much more promise, and the capital's nightclubs are in full swing.

The big sport is **football**, encouraged by the cultural ties with soccer-mad Portugal and Brazil. There are even two women's teams. Village football is often played at dusk, but the most exciting games take place at the impressive stadium outside Bissau. The Amílcar Cabral Cup Final in May is the major national sporting event.

Opening hours, festivals and public holidays

There is very little consistency in **opening hours**. A long lunch break is common, however, usually from 11.30am or noon to 3pm.

The following **public holidays** are observed: New Year's Day, Heroes' Day (Jan 20, marking the assassination of Amílcar Cabral), International Women's Day (March 8), National Day (Aug 3, Pidjiguiti Massacre), Independence Day (Sept 24, commemorating the proclamation of the republic in the liberated zone of Boé in 1973), Redemption Day of the Republic (Nov 14, marking the 1980 coup that brought the PAIGC to power), Christmas Day and December 26 (a family occasion in Bissau). The **Islamic calendar** is observed throughout the northeast, where a few closures and Muslim holidays aren't likely to have much noticeable effect on your travels. The weekend before Shrove Tuesday (Feb or March) is when Bissau celebrates **carnaval** (see p.512).

Crime and personal safety

Guinea-Bissau is currently calm and largely trouble-free. It's safe to stay out late at night, particularly in the company of local people. Crime isn't a particular problem, though it pays to be discreet about carrying valuables, as pickpockets and muggers aren't unheard of. The only checkpoints are in border areas and on the main road out of Bissau.

The laws on **drug possession** are very tough: possession of a few joints normally leads to deportation, and quite often only after a spell in jail. The maximum sentence for this offence is 25 years.

If you're out on the street at 8am or 6pm, when the official flag-raising and -lowering takes place, accompanied by a bugle, you are required to stand still in silence. The same rule applies when VIP convoys pass you on the road, or when a funeral procession goes by.

Directory

Airport departure tax None.

Crafts A couple of spots in Bissau sell woodcarvings: the main one, the Centro Artístico Juvenil (see p.514), is rather good. Most vendors take a fairly relaxed approach, and you can mull over a fair range of items without being hassled. Animal skins, such as crocodile, python, even leopard and serval, are openly displayed too. The government applies no effective sanctions, though the problem is a small one at present.

Electricity In 2003 there was no mains electricity, the lack of which leaves Bissau pitch black at night, except for the candles of traders and for establishments with their own generator – all but the cheapest hotels and guesthouses, some restaurants, and the always brilliantly lit Portuguese Embassy. Generators get rarer and nights darker the further upcountry you venture.

Photography Officialdom is fairly suspicious of cameras. In Bissau, avoid the port, presidential palace and most other places with your camera. Don't take pictures of people, unless you have asked permission. In country areas, people aren't much concerned and may even ask you to take pictures of them. Photography on the islands is relaxed. Video, and photography in general, is much easier if you're part of an aid project, or connected to one, rather than a tourist.

Wildlife Much of the indigenous wildlife was hunted out during the war years of the 1960s and early 1970s, or lost its habitat to defoliants or subsequent land clearance. Still, for such a small country, the fauna can be rewarding. The best areas to look are the hilly southeast, parts of the forested centre, and the outer islands. Guinea-Bissau has a number of national parks, notably the Cacheu and Cantanhez national parks, and the Bijagós, where the island of Orango is a park in its own right. Though the large terrestrial mammals are seldom found, the many species of monkeys and antelopes and some unusual coast dwellers – manatees, saltwater-dwelling hippos in the Bijagós islands, and large sea turtles – compensate for this, and reptile life is prolific.

Women travellers and women's status
For women travellers, Guinea-Bissau is one of the most relaxed countries in West Africa, one where men and women can mix freely without their association carrying sexual connotations. Guinean women fought in the war of independence, and their presence in the ranks of the revolutionary cadres made a lasting impression in the traditionally conservative and Islamic parts of the country. The women's movement, the União Democrática das Mulheres (UDEMU) still has a lot of work to do, with the literacy rate among women running at a third of that for men.

A brief history of Guinea-Bissau

From the thirteenth to the fifteenth centuries, large areas of West Africa, including some of what is now Guinea-Bissau, were under the control of the **Mali empire**, established by the legendary Mande leader Sundiata Keita. When Mali began to decline in the mid-fifteenth century, these states joined together to become the kingdom of Kaabu.

Ruled from its capital **Kansala**, Kaabu became one of the most powerful states in the region. The kingdom was to last until the mid-nineteenth century, when war broke out between Mandinka-led Kaabu and the neighbouring Fula empire of Fouta Djalon, during which Kaabu's last ruler, Janke Wali, was defeated.

Kriolu society

Guinea-Bissau was first visited by Europeans in 1456, when Cadamosto, an Italian navigator working for the Portuguese crown, sailed as far as the Rio Mansôa and the Bijagós islands looking for the gold which figured so hugely in the trans-Saharan trade. Other sailors settled on the uninhabited Cape Verde Islands over the following decades. By 1500, these communities had sprouted subcolonies on the Guinean mainland: groups of Portuguese or mixed-race immigrants, partly absorbed into African society, trading with the interior and looking to the ocean. More about this early history of European contact is detailed in the Cape Verde chapter.

While the export of gold was significant during the first half of the sixteenth century, subsequently much of what is now Guinea-Bissau was drawn into the **slave trade** linking West Africa with Europe, the Caribbean and the Americas via Cape Verde. **Cacheu** was the headquarters: by 1600 it had as many as a thousand Kriolu (mixed-race) slave traders and employees. Portugal established a military garrison in 1616 in order to guarantee the maximum revenue to the crown, charging duty on exported slaves and sending cargos on to the Cape Verdes where they paid further duty. Other towns were established at Farim, Ziguinchor and, later, Bissau and Bolama. But despite Portugal's efforts, the benefits of trade tended to bypass Lisbon; French and English ships could offer better trade goods and more choice. Repeated efforts by the Portuguese government to enforce **trading monopolies** in their area of influence simply pushed traders into illegal commerce.

The **slaves** tended to come from the least stratified ethnic groups of farmers, fishers and hunters; Fulup and Jola, Manjak and Pepel. The main **slavers** were Mandinka and, later, Fula. The Bijagó were notorious slave-hunters too, launching lethal canoe raids against the mainland. Yet who was slave and who slaver depended much more on economic strength or vulnerability and on family contacts and position, than on "tribal identity". It wasn't unusual for a king or headman to sell off people under his own rule, such was the attraction of cloth and other imported goods. **Firearms** were available from the early eighteenth century to those who could afford them.

With the general **abolition of slavery** in the early nineteenth century, the slave trade from Guinea continued illicitly, given new life by the needs of Cuba's plantations. Domestic slavery (which was not abolished) was commonly used as a cover. The last big shipments crossed the Atlantic in the 1840s.

Meanwhile, the local use of labour rather than its sale became significant with the introduction of **groundnuts**, first grown along the Gambia River at the end of the eighteenth century. Phillip Beaver's attempt to start an English colony of groundnut planters on Bolama had been a disaster (see box on p.520), but local Kriolu landowners had more success. Agreements were made with Bijagó elders on Galinhas and Bolama, from where the crop was spread to the shores of the Rio Grande on the mainland. On the islands, the plantations used slaves; on the shores of the Rio Grande they called them contract labourers, with tools, transport, food, clothes and accommodation charged to the plantation workers out of their share of the crop, usually leaving nothing for wages. Portugal, however, benefited little from the exploitation of its colonies. As much as eighty percent of the crop was sold to French trading concerns.

In 1879, Portugal's Guinean territory was separated from Cape Verde administration. The French had occupied Ziguinchor and, following a brief British occupation, **Bolama** became the **first capital** of "Portuguese Guinea".

The Portuguese province

The **partition of Africa** after 1885 left Portugal with a scattering of territories, of which Guinea-Bissau was perhaps the least promising. Unlike the British and the French, however, Portugal did not make any great effort to develop these colonies. Portuguese settlers weren't interested in going there for fear of the climate, and there appeared to be no attractive natural resources. Then, Fula-led jihads against non-Muslim plantation workers and raids on the foreign-run *feitoria* groundnut stations along the Rio Grande led to a slump in the only viable export. With the region now formally annexed to Portugal, only Bolama and the fort towns of Bissau, Cacheu, Farim and Gêba were in any sense under colonial rule.

Military campaigns of "pacification" took fifty years to subdue the state of general **revolt** that ensued in the 1890s. In that time there was precious little attention paid in Lisbon to the administration of the African territories. The republican government in Portugal, wracked as it was by one military intervention after the other, and by the costly involvement in World War I, virtually ignored Guinea-Bissau.

Hut taxes were imposed and labour conscripted to help maintain the colony with as little support from Portugal as possible. Almost the entire African population was classified as **indígena** – disenfranchised, second-class non-citizens. Opportunities for education were very limited, and in practice most urbanites with prospects were Cape Verdeans, or the descendants of Cape Verdean marriages. They, together with Kriolus and a tiny proportion of **assimilado** mainlanders, formed the bulk of the civil service as government agents and tax collectors. Cape Verdeans held many professional posts as well.

It was from this small middle class that the first calls for political reform were heard. Before World War I, a political group called the **Liga Guineense** campaigned for the interests of small traders and landowners, highlighting the abuse of power by government agents and calling for a change in the laws favouring the big commercial enterprises. The Liga was outlawed in 1915 without making much impact, but it provided a background – the only indigenous political example – for the radical demands of the PAIGC that emerged forty years later.

The **groundnut trade** began to pick up after about 1910, though it crashed again in 1918 when a law came into force prohibiting peasant farmers from trading their crop to foreign buyers. The law was repealed, and by the 1920s, the central parts of the country, particularly the region around Bafatá, had become the groundnut heartland.

Despite the heavy exploitation and inequalities, there was a looseness in governing the overseas territories that failed to suppress freedom of expression completely. The paternalistic idea of **"colonial trusteeship"** was taken seriously by some: Portuguese culture allowed a vague and distant respect for Africans stemming partly from its own infusion of African culture during the medieval Moorish occupation. But these sentiments were smothered after 1926.

Guinea under the Portuguese "New State"

In 1926, a military takeover turned Portugal into a violent dictatorship that was to last until 1974, holding Portugal back and crippling her overseas territories. **António de Salazar**, a monetarist economics professor, was prime minister from 1932 until 1968. He promulgated the Estado Novo, or **"New State"**, and ran Portugal on strictly authoritarian lines. The "Province of Guinea", along with the other parts of "Overseas Portugal" were brought to heel. The last pockets of resistance to the colonial invasion were finally "pacified" in 1936 and any chinks of progressive light from republican days were blacked out by the quasi-fascist curtain now drawn across the country.

Guinea was forced into becoming one giant groundnut and oil palm plantation with **compulsory planting and purchases**. Small traders were banned from dealing in cloth and alcohol, while Portuguese commercial agents tried vainly to interest the people in Portuguese wine and cotton clothing.

Economic repression, passbook laws and a continuation of forced labour came with an unwieldy and over-staffed **bureaucracy**. All potential sources of opposition were organized into officially sanctioned associations, from within which their members could be scrutinized by the PIDE, Salazar's political police force. For over four decades, there was an almost total suspension of political life.

In the 1950s, **Amílcar Cabral**, an agronomist of mixed Cape Verdean and Guinean parentage, was working in the colonial service, conducting agricultural censuses across the country. He analysed his remarkably detailed land-use surveys in Marxist terms of modes of production. His conclusions convinced him that mechanization, collectivization, a rejection of the groundnut mono-culture and a return to mixed farming could transform Guinean society and set the country on a path to socialism. His reputation as a subversive assured, he quit the service and left the country.

The war of liberation

A small coterie of African tradesmen and Lisbon-educated civil servants resident in Bissau (capital since 1941) began gently to agitate for independence from Portugal. On September 12, 1956, Cabral, briefly back from work in Angola, and five others met secretly and formed the Partido Africano para Independência da Guiné e Cabo Verde (**PAIGC**). With painstaking discretion and patience, they recruited people to their ranks. Within three years they had about fifty members.

The spark for armed conflict came with a **dockworkers' strike** for a living wage in 1959. On August 3, police confronted the strikers on the **Pidjiguiti** waterfront in Bissau (see box, overleaf). When they refused to go back to work the police opened fire at point-blank range, killing fifty men and wounding more than a hundred. The massacre and subsequent police interrogations convinced Cabral and the party leadership that peaceful attempts to bring about independence would be fruitless. Cabral, his half-brother Luiz, and Aristides Pereira went to Conakry (the capital of the Republic of Guinea, newly independent from France) to set

Jose Emilio Costa worked for the Bissau Port Administration when this report was first published. In 1959 he took part in the Bissau dockworkers' strike that ended in a bloody massacre.

Most of us worked for the big Casa Gouvea company, either on the dock or on boats taking goods to and from company shops all over the country. But with our low wages, life was becoming more and more difficult. The basic wage was only ten escudos [approximately 15 pence/23 US cents] a day. In 1959, after much discussion in the club and at work, we finally decided to ask for higher wages.

The manager was Antonio Carreia, who had just left his post as colonial administrator to work with Gouvea. Well, he refused even to listen. Of course, this was the first time in Guinea's history that workers united to confront their boss. So, Rafael Barbosa and Augusto Laserde said that we had to go on strike and show them we were serious.

On 3 August we all gathered at Pidjiguiti, about 500 men. Nobody worked, neither on the dock nor on the boats. Carreia came down and shouted and swore, but we just looked at him without moving. At about 4.30 in the afternoon several trucks of armed police arrived. First they sealed off the gate to the street, then they ordered us back to work. When no one obeyed, they began moving slowly down the pier, now packed with striking workers.

This old captain friend of mine, Ocante Atobo, was leaning against the wall of the office shed. When the line of police reached the spot where he was, an officer suddenly raised his gun and shot him point-blank in the chest. Ocante collapsed in a pool of blood. For a split second everyone froze – it was as if time stood still. Then hell broke loose. The police moved down the pier, shooting like crazy into the crowd. Men were screaming and running in all directions. I was over by my cousin Augusto Fernandes' boat, the *Alio Sulemane*. Augusto, who was standing next to me, had his chest shot wide open; it was like his whole inside was coming out. He was crying: "Oh God, João kill me, please". But it wasn't necessary; when I lifted his head from the ground he was already dead.

up a party headquarters and training school. In Guinea-Bissau, others began to prepare clandestinely for **social revolution** and a **war of liberation** against the Portuguese.

Other nationalist groups were forming at the time, both inside Bissau and in Senegal. Their ideologies tended to be less well-honed than the PAIGC's. They were prepared to accept a transfer of political power without a transformation in the economy, and they didn't work on behalf of the Cape Verde Islands. Nor did they approve of the Cape Verdean intellectuals who characterized PAIGC's executive. These other groups coalesced into the Front for the Liberation and Independence of Portuguese Guinea (FLING), based in Dakar under Leopold Senghor's sponsorship.

There had been scattered attacks by the PAIGC from 1961, but military action began in earnest in January 1963. Senghor and Touré reluctantly allowed the guerillas to launch operations from Senegal and the Republic of Guinea. In Europe, the Scandinavian countries voiced their solidarity. Internally, the most enthusiastic insurgents were the brutally exploited, rice-planting **Balante** of the southwest, though coordination of their sabotage attacks with PAIGC strategy was often tenuous. At the other extreme, many **Fula** communities in the north and east, long established in a feudal framework which had Islamic sanction, and positively supported by the Portuguese, resisted subversion, or tried to prevent their peasants from being politicized.

As large stretches of bush and

Now all the men were running for the end of the pier. The tide was out so all the boats and *pirogues* were resting on the beach. To hide there, however, was impossible since the police, standing high up on the dock, were shooting right into them. One officer was kneeling on the edge firing at those trying to get away in the water. All around me people were shouting "Run, run!", but I stayed beside my dead cousin. "No, if they want to kill me, let them do it right here".

I don't know how long this lasted when a PIDE inspector named Emmanuel Correia arrived and ordered the firing to stop. The last one to die was a boatman hiding in the mud under his *pirogue*, out of sight of the police. A Portuguese merchant, however, spotted him from his apartment window and shot him in the back with his hunting rifle just after Correia had arrived. One Portuguese, Romeo Martins, always a friend of the Africans, had been trying to keep the police from shooting, but all by himself he couldn't do much.

When the massacre finally ended I saw dead and wounded men all over: on the dock, on the beach, in the boats, in the water – everywhere. Among the dead were Caesare Fernandes and Jose de Pina who had worked for the Party. Afterwards we were taken to the police for interrogation. For three straight days I had to report to the administrator, Guerra Ribeiro, who wanted to know who had organized the strike. My answer was always the same: "We all organized it; our wages were so bad we had no choice". Later, when Ribeiro had finished his enquiry, the wage went up to 14 escudos a day.

Soon after the massacre a message from Amílcar Cabral was secretly circulated among us. It said that August 3 would never be forgotten and that now we had to organize to win our independence from Portuguese colonialism. Since then we never looked back. Many other workers and I joined the Party and started the difficult work of political mobilization here in Bissau. With experience of Pidjiguiti behind us, we knew that we had to accept the risks and sacrifices of an armed revolution to win freedom for our people.

Reprinted from *Sowing the First Harvest:
National Reconstruction in Guinea-Bissau* (1978), LSM Press, California.

countryside, then the first few towns, became liberated, the guerillas of the PAIGC became consolidated into an effective, mobile army, clearing the way for a network of "people's stores", new schools, medical services and political institutions. Portugal attacked their bases with weaponry purchased from **NATO**. Napalm was used in fighting that was at times as intense as in Vietnam. In retaliation, the guerrilla army – the People's Revolutionary Armed Forces (FARP) – persuaded the Soviet Union to deliver arms on a regular basis.

While the war continued with relentless success for the liberationists, the first **internal cracks** were being felt in their upper ranks. All PAIGC decisions were now being taken in Conakry by the Cape Verdean leadership. The need

to co-ordinate a national policy came increasingly into conflict with democratic imperatives. Although Cabral enjoyed enormous support and trust, his growing stature as a world leader physically distanced him from his half-million followers. In many liberated areas, there were very few democratically elected representatives between the top leadership and the people. Only at the village level were local committees elected, and then only to discuss how to implement party strategy, not to consider the strategy itself. Beyond the villages, the exigencies of war stalled and diverted elections. Party cadres with regional responsibilities were often unaccountable.

Cabral was conscious of these difficulties. In 1970, the war could have been won in a few months, as heavy armaments had just been delivered from Eastern Europe. But Cabral decided to hold off the final assault on Bissau because only Soviet-trained Cape Verdeans knew how to use the weapons, and he did not want such a display to reinforce the unpopular high profile of Cape Verdean power-holders. After seven years of fighting, however, all the indications were that the mass of the people were fed up with the war and popularity would have been more likely to follow a swift end to it.

External factors intervened. In November 1970, an invasion force of Portuguese troops and African collaborators set off from Soga island in the Bijagós to attack Conakry, with the intention of assassinating President Sekou Touré and Amílcar Cabral. They failed, and retreated in chaos. But a more carefully planned action in Conakry, involving PAIGC traitors who sought a deal with the Portuguese dictatorship, led to the **assassination of Amílcar Cabral** on January 20, 1973.

Portugal's plan to install a puppet "liberation government" in Guinea-Bissau had no chance of success. The PAIGC, nurtured for so long by one of Africa's most radical and humane political thinkers, did not disintegrate. Nonetheless, the damage to morale was serious and the leadership vacuum plain to see. Aristides Pereira took over as party chief and Luiz Cabral as president-in-waiting.

Major weaponry (heat-seeking missiles) came straight into play after the assassination; one aircraft after another was shot down. The Portuguese, based in military camps across the country, were increasingly besieged by a confident People's Army under the general command of **João "Nino" Vieira** (later to succeed Luiz Cabral as president). In four months, through the end of the dry season of 1973, the Portuguese lost the war. With their air force demoralized and growing discontent among their conscripted troops, rumbles of revolution began in Portugal itself.

On September 24, 1973, in the liberated village of Lugajole in the southeast, the People's National Assembly declared the **independence** of Guinea-Bissau. It only remained to kick out the enemy. Around the world, dozens of countries recognized the new republic and the United Nations passed a resolution demanding Portuguese withdrawal. The **military coup in Lisbon** on April 25, 1974, made withdrawal inevitable. Portugal and the PAIGC signed a treaty on September 10, and the last Portuguese troops were gone within a month. **Luiz Cabral** became the new head of state, while the party leader and senior ideologue, Aristides Pereira, became president of the new sister republic of Cape Verde.

The early years of independence

The colonial bequest to the newly independent country was dismal. Guinea-Bissau had only a handful of graduates and doctors, and not more than two percent of its population were literate. Its industrial base consisted of one brewery – there was no other manufacturing plant – and there was almost no energy production. Earnings from exports barely covered a tenth of the cost of imports, and the Portuguese had left a colossal national debt.

The PAIGC took over a centralized and autocratic administration. Far from Amílcar Cabral's optimistic ideas of a decentralized state, **Bissau**, by far the largest and most developed city of the country, became the main governmental centre. The urgency of the takeover, the shortage of material and human resources, and the refugee problem in the capital all led to government by crisis-management. The peasants of the liberated zones, who had supported the party and the war for so long and at such cost, were hardly consulted: nor were the minor-ranking party cadres who now expected to receive the fruits of independence.

Apart from national reconstruction, there was **political work** to do in Bissau. Compared with the peasants of the liberated zones, some of whom had lived under PAIGC government for ten years, Bissau's inhabitants were more cosmopolitan, the best educated and the most cynical. Now that the PAIGC was in control, they had to come to terms with it, but did not necessarily support it down the line.

There were national **"elections"** in 1976, with voting consisting of a "for" or "against" to candidates nominated to the Regional Councils (who themselves elected the members of the National Assembly). There were no alternative candidates. Results showed the widest dissent in the traditionally anti-PAIGC northern and eastern regions, a fifteen percent opposition in Bissau, but over ninety percent support everywhere else.

The broad approval seems surprising in light of the **difficulties** the party was having in delivering on its independence promises to build a new society. Bissau city, for example, received over half the country's resources – justified by Luiz Cabral in terms of attracting foreign-aid agencies (who poured funds into the country between 1976 and 1979) and investors. **Drought** damaged the prospects of new agricultural projects and efforts to become self-sufficient in food made no progress. A joint fisheries enterprise with Algeria was a flop. The ludicrous N'Haye car-assembly plant was a grotesque waste of money, as was the over-massive and never finished agricultural processing plant at Cumeré near Bissau. Salaries in the state sector were eating away (in fact *exceeded*) the national budget. The currency was kept overvalued, and inflation soared, while in real terms agricultural production and exports declined. In a remarkable echo of the fascist "New State" policy, the government tried to control the marketing of produce, setting prices at levels too low to be worth selling at and perforce encouraging a black-market economy. People in the rural areas could no longer afford basic imported goods like soap and matches. The persistent street rumour was that all this was the fault of the Guinea-Bissauans of Cape Verdean origin who, in many cases, had kept civil-service positions since Portuguese times. Many of the "people's stores" were run by them, too, and often corruptly. But it was their visibility, as part of the self-interested and irrepressible middle class, that made them popular scapegoats for a **failing economy**.

In November 1980, an extraordinary session of the National Assembly discussed the unification of Guinea-Bissau and Cape Verde. Luiz Cabral, having increasingly isolated himself, refused to temper his support for the idea. Four days later came the largely bloodless **coup of November 14**, which toppled his government. The Commissioner for the Armed Forces, **Nino Vieira**, revoked the constitution and took control of the country. Luiz Cabral was detained on Bubaque, then allowed to fly to Cuba.

The 1980s

Despite popular anti-Cape Verdean sentiment, the new "Provisional Government", formed in 1981, looked much like a rearranged version of Luiz Cabral's. Several of Cabral's Cape Verdean ministers had fled, but Vieira was adamant in his speeches that Cape Verdeans were welcome in Guinea-Bissau, and that the two countries' destinies remained linked.

One of the first announcements of the new government was the disclosure of a series of **mass graves**, containing up to five hundred bodies, in the Oio region northeast of Bissau. The story was taken up by the foreign press. Vieira's intention was to point out the summary justice meted out by his predecessor's government to dissidents and those who had collaborated with the Portuguese. But there were counter-claims from a furious **Aristides Pereira** (the president of Cape Verde), who believed Vieira had sabotaged any chance of unification, that Vieira had known about the murders and was even implicated. Cape Verde set up its own party, and broke relations.

Coup attempts, allegations of plans for coup attempts and widespread repression characterized the early 1980s. In 1984, however, there was a shift to a freer climate with new elections, a rewritten constitution and a return to civilian government, though the country was still a one-party state and Vieira remained president. Still, the plots continued. An attempted coup in 1985 led to the execution of vice-president **Paulo Correia** and five co-accused in July 1986. Six more of those accused of involvement were said to have died in prison.

None of this, of course, helped the government to run the country effectively. Although the IMF and the World Bank had given loans, the **austerity measures** on which they were conditional were hardly followed through and, despite debt rescheduling, the country's economic plight continued to worsen. In August 1986, however, the government finally agreed to the **abolition of trade laws** that had reserved all import and export licences for state monopolies. The *peso* was massively devalued, knocking the life out of the black market and encouraging potential investors. Support for Vieira's government was suddenly stronger as exports rose impressively and the economy began to revive. Within a year, Guinea-Bissau was entering into long-term agreements with the IMF and World Bank to **restructure the economy**, prune the state payroll by a third, reduce fuel subsidies and boost agriculture, fisheries and technical training. Although the countryside still lagged behind Bissau, the economic future began to look a little brighter. **Cashew nuts** continued to be the most valuable export, and many farmers were paid for their cashew crop in rice. The negative side-effect of this policy was a serious alcohol problem from the widespread distillation of cashew juice

from the fruits, which have no other use.

The advent of multiparty politics

In the late 1980s and into the early 1990s, political opposition to the one-party state increased. The banned **Movimento Bafatá**, with offices abroad, upped the pressure in 1990 with demands that the PAIGC should hold talks with it or face unspecified consequences. At the same time, and in common with other African partners of the World Bank and IMF, Guinea-Bissau was asked to reform its political institutions as a condition of further aid.

By the beginning of 1991, Vieira had set a schedule for **multiparty elections**. He also cut the link between the PAIGC and the **military**, which had supported the party in its early years. The army had long felt betrayed by the years of independence from which it had received so little benefit, but this event marked the start of the slow crisis of relations between the government and the military. Increasingly, soldiers turned to making a living from regional cannabis smuggling and arms trading to the rebels in Senegalese Casamance.

Over a dozen small **political parties** were formed and recognized between 1991 and 1994. Among the most important were the Partido para a Renovação Social (**PRS**), headed by former teacher Dr Kumba Yala, and the Resistência da Guiné-Bissau–Movimento Bah-Fatah (**RGB-MB**), formed from the previously outlawed Bafatá movement. In addition, **FLING**, the old Frente da Luta para a Libertação da Guiné (banned for thirty years and exiled in Senegal until 1992) made a comeback. Safeguards in the registration process ensured that none of the new parties had an entirely ethnic or regional basis, though the PRS, for example, was dominated by the Balante, while the RGB-MB began as a movement of business interests with

Mandinka and Fula support, opposed to the Marxist rhetoric of the PAIGC in the 1980s. However, once the PAIGC had shed every vestige of socialism from its agenda, it was hard to see how it differed from the RGB-MB except in the ethnic constituents of its membership.

The brief election campaigns mounted by the parties were mostly personality-led and ignored the big issues facing the country. At least Kumba Yala's PRS campaigned for the restoration of state property held in private hands – an open threat to the PAIGC elite about whom they were remarkably phlegmatic. The **elections**, when they were finally held in July 1994, were surprisingly trouble-free, and the results widely judged to reflect a fair poll. The PAIGC won just under half the votes for seats in the National Assembly (which, however, gave it 64 of the 100 seats), while Nino Vieira, the incumbent president and leader of the PAIGC, won a similar proportion of votes for president. To win, Vieira needed an outright majority, which he obtained a month later in a run-off against his closest rival, **Kumba Yala**.

Yala, Guinea-Bissau's most charismatic and trenchantly outspoken politician, complained, not unreasonably, that the PAIGC had been able to use the resources of the state, particularly in the remotest areas, to weigh the dice in Vieira's favour. Tactics included heavy-handed campaigning among largely illiterate communities and the denial of seats to Yala's poll-observers on the only helicopter flying to outlying islands. Nevertheless, Yala's acceptance of his defeat seemed to bode well for the future stability of the country.

Guinea-Bissau's **economic plight** continued to worsen, however. The PAIGC government seemed powerless to halt the slide (and was, in the view of many observers, complicit in it) and appeared immune, too, to the scathing reproaches of the opposition and the majority of the electorate, whose only viable course of action was mass protest.

Entry to the **CFA franc zone** in April 1997 added further to the miserable lot of most Guineans, as inflation spiralled.

The civil war

But it was the deteriorating situation in Senegal's Casamance region (see p.173) on Guinea-Bissau's northern border which finally tipped the country into civil war. A Casamance-bound arms cache was discovered at a military barracks and the chief of staff, Brigadier **Ansumane Manè** (a Jola, born and raised in The Gambia, and with close connections to the Casamançais), was sacked and went into the bush with his supporters.

When news emerged in June 1998 that Vieira was planning to halve the army to ten thousand men, a group of **rebel troops**, led by Manè, seized strategic locations around the capital, including the airport, and demanded Vieira's resignation and immediate elections. Dakar and Conakry sent troop reinforcements to shore up the Vieira regime, and **war** broke out in and around Bissau. Diplomats and expats were evacuated, a quarter of a million residents fled the capital for the countryside and towards the Senegalese border, which was promptly closed. Virtually the entire army joined Manè's forces. Efforts by President Jammeh of The Gambia to bring the sides together came to nothing, as his partiality in the conflict was widely suspected.

Cape Verde eventually brokered talks between the government and Manè's side, and a grudging **stalemate** was reached in December 1998, when Manè and Vieira agreed to a power-sharing arrangement. The Senegalese troops withdrew in early 1999, while the contingent from Guinea and smaller forces from other West African nations sustained serious losses before also pulling out.

There was an **international dimension** to the Bissau conflict: since Guinea-Bissau's adoption of the CFA franc, it had been clear that Vieira was aiming for closer cooperation with Francophone West Africa and Paris. These trends were viewed with great unease by the Portuguese, as well as by Kumba Yala and many others in the opposition, who traditionally looked for support from the Casamance and The Gambia, and who received sympathetic coverage in the Portuguese media.

A fragile peace

Finally, in May 1999, remaining loyalist troops surrendered to Ansumane Manè after fierce fighting in Bissau, and Vieira was granted political asylum by Portugal. Ansumane (now General) Manè installed the former leader of the national assembly, **Malam Bacai Sanka**, as acting president. Elections followed in January 2000, in which **Kumba Yala** gained an overwhelming victory, winning over seventy percent of the vote. In November of that year, General Ansumane Manè rejected President Yala's senior army appointments as ethnically biased, and attempted to declare himself head of the army. A few days later he was killed in a shoot-out with government troops. His removal from the scene simplified regional politics: Manè and Yala had been allied to opposing factions of the rebel movement in the Casamance, and Manè had also enjoyed support from President Jammeh of The Gambia.

Since his election, President Kumba Yala has consistently dismissed members of the government and other figures in authority who have voiced doubts about his policies. In January 2001, the RGB pulled out of the ruling coalition, claiming that it hadn't been consulted about a cabinet reshuffle. Only two months later, Prime Minister Caetano Intchama was replaced. Kumba Yala dismissed the head of the Supreme Court in September 2001, accusing him of having overturned a presidential decision, and several judges and journalists were arrested shortly after. The sacking of "rebellious" ministers continued into early 2002, and in November 2002, Kumba Yala dissolved parliament and replaced the entire cabinet. All ministries were sealed off and for several days the country was effectively without a functioning government. This move resulted from a long-standing conflict with the prime minister, who is rumoured to have powerful connections to the army, which could potentially result in yet another coup.

At the time of writing, the country was heading towards financial collapse. Civil servants hadn't been paid for months, schools had been closed for over a year since teachers weren't willing to work without pay, and public life had practically come to a halt. Kumba Yala's long-promised elections, repeatedly deferred, were cancelled again in June 2003. Yala's record shows scant evidence of any ability to govern the country with judgement and foresight, and there seems tragically little prospect that Amílcar Cabral's promise that the people of Guinea-Bissau would "live better and in peace, to see their lives go forward" will quickly be realized.

Another coup

On 14 September 2003, Kumba Yala was overthrown in a bloodless coup by the army chief of staff, General Verissimo Correia Seabre, who declared himself president and said he would remain in charge until elections could be organized.

Music

Guinea-Bissau's special music is **gumbe**. Always sung in Kriolu, it's a creative amalgamation of local musical traditions with contemporary sounds, a true expression of Guinea-Bissau's Kriolu culture. It has a slight Latin feel to it, and has been compared to samba, though it's much more polyrhythmic. In Bissau you may encounter youngsters entertaining themselves by playing *gumbe* beats on spoons, empty plastic containers and calabash drums (*tina*).

The many musical styles that echo in popular *gumbe* all continue their independent existences: each of the country's ethnic groups has its own musical tradition, and especially in the non-Muslim regions of the country, there are plenty of opportunities to see local groups perform during ceremonies or for their own enjoyment.

An absolute treat is the *broxa* dancing of the Balante people, which is frequently accompanied by the gentle plucking of the *kussunde* (lute). Other regional traditions include the wild acrobatics and haunting flute of the Fula, the Mandinka *kora* (which has its origin in the area) and the drumming and masked dances of the Bijagós.

Though *gumbe* is the archetypal music of the country, the most widely played genre, however, is *zouk*, ubiquitous in Bissau's nightclubs.

For some outrageously sexy dancing, you should try to see the performance of a **kuduru** troupe. *Kuduru*, the latest trend coming out of Angola, sounds like a slightly crazed African form of house coupled with ragga, soca and other Latin beats.

Guinea-Bissau has brought forth some fantastic singers, and though many in the current crop have left to take up residence in Portugal (or, more rarely, France), few have made much of an impact on the international stage. Their music is generally smooth as honey, blending *gumbe*, *zouk* and a wagonload of other influences (from Arabic to ragga) into a sugary concoction.

José Carlos Schwartz

This soulful singer, who died in the 1970s, is regarded as the "father" of modern Guinea-Bissauan music. His outspoken lyrics gave a powerful voice to the people in pre- and post-independence days, and have made him a national hero.

Flema Di Corçon (available in Guinea-Bissau). Subdued, moving, guitar-based material, containing plenty of evergreen songs that today's musicians are reworking.

Dulce Neves

Virtually the only female professional singer of the country, Neves is very outspoken about women's rights. She apparently divorced four times, unable to find a husband who could tolerate her career.

Balur di Mindjer (Maxi Music). Produced by Manecas Costa, this is probably the best of her albums to date, a well-executed, accessible blend of *gumbe* and *zouk*.

Kaba Mané

Mané is one of the few Guinea-Bissauan musicians whose albums you might actually find in the West, though he's not much of a figure at home. A master of a variety of styles, he learned the *kora* when young and actually plays electric guitar in a *kora* style.

Best of Kaba Mané (Mélodie). Tasty compilation of the best material from two earlier albums.

Manecas Costa

Having for years carved out a career for himself at home, Manecas Costa now has an international deal with a BBC label.

Paraiso di Gumbe (Late Junction). A masterpiece of semi-acoustic Guinean music, that lets his exceptional guitar skills truly shine and subtly interweaves a number of local styles, such as *broxa*.

Zé Manel

A long-established artist, formerly with Mama Djombo, Manel has maintained a highly politicized stance throughout his career.

Maron di Mar (Mélodie). An enjoyable album that reworks some of his biggest hits with jazz-tinged arrangements.

Super Mama Djombo

Mama Djombo, who put *gumbe* music on the map, were favourites of the first independent government, but soon fell out with them. Their 1980s recordings still sound remarkably fresh.

Super Mama Djombo (Cobiana). A great retrospective of a key Bissau band, including tracks from the five albums recorded in Lisbon in 1980 at the height of their popularity.

Bidinte

Guitarist and singer-songwriter Jorge da Silva Bidinte was born in Bolama, and began composing music for singer Maio Coopé when he moved to Bissau to attend secondary school. He later emigrated to Europe and was drawn to flamenco.

Kumura (Nubenegra). Subtle and distinctive music reflecting a multiplicity of influences, from David Byrne (who was present through most of the recording) to flamenco, with a melting blend of guitar and Kriolu lyrics – nowhere better than on the effortless "Ke cu minino na tchora?" (Why does the child cry?) with its sadly apposite lyrics by José Carlos Schwartz.

Books

Works in English specifically about Guinea-Bissau are extremely sparse, and there's no Guinea-Bissauan literature in translation. Books likely to be out of print are marked o/p below; those marked ▣ are especially recommended.

Amílcar Cabral *Unity and Struggle* (o/p). Speeches and writings from the father of the revolution – and he did speak, and write, well. Such was his immense popularity, there seems little doubt his assassination marked a point of turning back for the country, and for the whole of Africa.

Patrick Chabal *Amílcar Cabral: Revolutionary Leadership and People's War*. The biography if you're a committed student, and Chabal does a good job of contextualizing Cabral's thinking.

Basil Davidson *No Fist is Big Enough to Hide the Sky: The Liberation of Guiné and Cape Verde*. Enthusiastic, quirky account of the war of liberation and its aftermath. The late Davidson's close and sympathetic involvement with the liberation fighters, particularly Amílcar Cabral himself, gives a rosy picture, tarnished by subsequent events.

Rosemary E. Galli and Jocelyn Jones *Guinea-Bissau: Politics, Economics and Society*. A well-researched, rather gloomy survey published in 1987, which found parallels between the independent governments and the fascist New State regime in their alienation of the rural people.

Walter Rodney *A History of the Upper Guinea Coast 1545–1800* (Monthly Review). An Afrocentric history covering the region from the Casamance to Sierra Leone, dealing in depth with the area the Portuguese moved into and providing a mass of fascinating material on its social complexity.

Toby Green *Meeting the Invisible Man*. Story of a surreal journey with a Senegalese photographer – much of it through Guinea-Bissau – in search of magic powers. Green's descriptive writing is elegant and sparse and his transliteration of dialogue impeccable as he leads the reader through a universe that flips unnervingly between dusty banality and a parallel world of magic and spells.

Language

Although the official language of Guinea-Bissau is **Portuguese**, the widely used, street-friendly vernacular is **Kriolu** (or Crioulo). An old amalgam of seafarers' Portuguese with various African languages, Kriolu becomes semi-intelligible if you speak Portuguese, and is very similar to Cape Verdean Kriolu (see p.434). Just about every Guinea-Bissauan speaks Kriolu, often next to one or two other local languages. Among the most common tongues are **Mandinka** (see p.270), **Fula** (see p.556), **Balante**, **Manjak**, **Pepel**, and **Bijagó** (see p.518), spoken on the islands of the same name.

Glossary

Assimilado In colonial times, an indigenous Guinean who, through education and connections, had achieved the status of Portuguese citizen.

Bairro Suburb.

Cana Cashew alcohol.

Canoa *Pirogue*.

Feitoria "Factory", in the historical sense of a trading post.

Fermanza Local name for the dry, dusty harmattan wind from the north.

Kirintim A fence of woven brushwood (like wattle) often surrounding and identifying a bar.

Navetanes Seasonal migrant workers.

Paragem Taxi park or, more generally, transport stop.

Praça Square.

Ponta Small land concession or trading post in Portuguese Guinea.

Tabanka Rural village.

Toko toko Public minibus.

6.1

Bissau and the northwest

The majority of overland travellers approach the relaxed capital, **Bissau**, from the north, using one of several overland routes from southern Senegal to travel for a day or so through **northwest Guinea-Bissau**. The northwestern region has little to offer apart from the vast beach along the coast at **Varela** – one of the best reasons to come to the country.

Bissau

BISSAU itself isn't a sightseeing city, though there are a couple of visits worth making, and the city is not without architectural interest in its narrow nineteenth-century houses with their wrought-iron balustrades. More memorable, however, is the city's absence of tension and clamour, which will come as a relaxing surprise if you have arrived from one of the adjacent Francophone countries. The impact of the civil war is obvious wherever you go: at night, it can be hard to find your way around due to the lack of electricity, and by day war damage is all too evident, notably at the bombed-out French Cultural Centre and the ruined presidential palace. Though still one of the most impoverished West African capitals, Bissau is on the move again: imported cars dodge the rusting shells of abandoned vehicles and a few new offices sprout cautiously between derelict buildings.

Arrival, information and city transport

The **airport** at Bissalanca is only 11km from the centre. Private charter taxis meet all flights, but you can also get shared transport or walk down to the main Safim–Bissau road and pick up a ride there. There's one main road into the capital, and if you arrive by bush taxi, you'll be dropped at the *paragem* west of the town centre, from where a taxi into the centre costs around CFA500.

For **tourist information**, visit the Ministério do Comércio e Turismo (☎20 21 95 or 20 60 62), off Estrada de Santa Luzia, north of the centre. Ask to see the Secretaria de Estado do Turismo (Secretary of State for Tourism), who may be helpful. The best way to get around the compact centre of Bissau is by **shared taxi**, in one of the blue-and-white cabs which follow a circular route. Simply hail a taxi that is heading in the direction you wish to go, and you'll be dropped off at the front door. Expect to pay around CFA250 a short ride, twice that if you're going across town. There are also a growing number of buses, but you may well have to wait longer for one to show up than it would take to walk to your destination.

Accommodation

The choice of **accommodation** in Bissau offers little of good value, and if you're travelling on a budget, you'll find you spend more on lodgings here than you're accustomed to. See the map on p.513 for locations of central establishments.

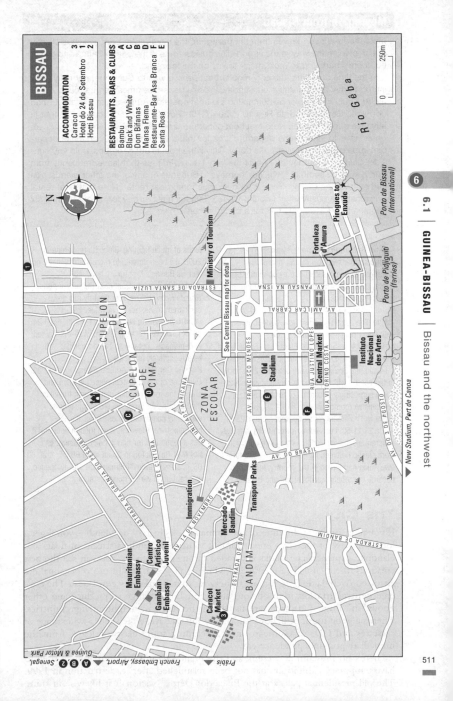

BISSAU

ACCOMMODATION
Caracol	3
Hotel do 24 de Setembro	1
Hotti Bissau	2

RESTAURANTS, BARS & CLUBS
Bambu	A
Black and White	C
Dom Bifanas	B
Mansa Flema	D
Restaurante-Bar Asa Branca	F
Santa Rosa	E

Rio Gêba

Porto de Bissau (International)

Porto de Pidjiguiti (ferries)

Pirogues to Enxude

Fortaleza d'Amura

Ministry of Tourism

ESTRADA DE SANTA LUZIA

See Central Bissau map for detail

AV PANSAU NA ISNA

AV AMILCAR CABRAL

CUPELON DE BAIXO

CUPELON DE CIMA

AV DA UNIDADE AFRICANA

ZONA ESCOLAR

AV FRANCISCO MENDES

Old Stadium

RUA JUSTINO LOPES

Central Market

RUA VITORINO COSTA

Instituto Nacional des Artes

AV DO 3 DE AGOSTO

AV DE CINTURA

AV DO BRASIL

Transport Parks

Mercado Bandim

AV 14 DE NOVEMBRO

Immigration

ESTRADA DE BOR

BANDIM

ESTRADA DE BANDIM

ESTRADA DA GRAÇA DE LISSIRE

Mauritanian Embassy

Centro Artístico Juvenil

Gambian Embassy

Caracol Market

▶ New Stadium, Port de Canoa

◀ Prabis

▲ B 2 ▲ A 1 ▲ French Embassy, Airport,

Guinea & Motor Park, Senegal,

N

0 250m

6

Moving on from Bissau

Most road transport leaves from the **paragem**, the main motor park, which is slightly out of town on the way to the airport. The busiest route is the one to Bafatá and Gabú, but there's transport to most major towns on the mainland.

At the time of writing, the only regular boat service was to **Bubaque**, normally leaving on Friday and returning on Sunday. Precise departure times can be found out at the Pidjiguiti harbour, or by contacting the boat operator, Afripesca, in Bissau at Chão de Papel, Continuação da Rua 10 (℡20 47 75). Tickets (CFA2500) can be bought in advance or on the boat. Note that boat departure times change with the tides; indeed, boats have to stick to the departure time for that day, as the tides can make departure impossible in the event of a delay. Only if the boat is out of order should you consider doing the journey by one of the very basic *pirogues* that leave frequently from Port de Canoa south of town. For journeys to Bubaque or any of the other islands, you can contact the *Casino Galeon*, who arrange motorboat rental. Note that boat rental is invariably a costly affair (around £120/$190 plus fuel per day for a boat holding six people or £60/$100 plus fuel for a boat for four).

Casino Galeon Praça Che Guevara ℡20 15 48. Restaurant/bar with few rooms, one of the cheapest, cleanest, safest and most central places to stay in Bissau. The staff can arrange motorboat trips to the islands. ❹

Hotel Caracol Av Caetano Semedo, west of the centre. The usual run-down, low-budget option with water supplied in a bucket. ❸

Hotel do 24 de Setembro Estrada de Santa Luzia ℡22 10 33/34, ℗22 10 02, ℮hotel24setembro @bissau.net. Spacious luxury complex 2km north of the centre, with a pool, car rental agency, and some surprisingly decent rates for the most inexpensive rooms. ❺

Hotel Hotti Bissau Av 14 de Novembro ℡25 12 51, ℗25 11 52. Located 4km from town, this ugly concrete block was traditionally where contracts were signed between flights – a focal point for everything happening in the country. In 1998, it became the rebels' headquarters and thus the

focus of much fighting. Since its reopening in 2000, it's been striving to regain the cachet it once had, as Bissau's first luxury hotel. ❻

Jordani In a quiet street near the now-defunct *Grande Hotel* ℡20 17 19. Slightly run-down backstreet place, not great value. ❼

Lobato Av Pansau Na Isna ℡21 35 48, ℗20 24 05, ℮lobato@mail.aguitel.com. Well-maintained, well-managed hotel with TV and minibar, with an Internet café close by. ❽

Pensão Centrale Av Amílcar Cabral ℡20 12 32. Once one of the cheapest places in town and among the most popular places with travellers, though rates for its basic, s/c rooms aren't especially competitive these days. It's as charmingly run-down as ever, though note that it has a reputation for things going missing. ❹

Sol Mar Rua Victorino Costa ℡20 60 04, ℗20 60 05, ℮solmar_apth@hotmail.com. Newly opened, pleasant hotel with a good restaurant. ❼

The City

If you're in Bissau at the time of the **carnaval** – February or March – you'll get a lopsided view of the city's entertainment value, as an endless stream of floats and elaborate papier-mâché masks is paraded through the streets. You can see the best creations (there's usually a theme, and winners) all year at the Instituto Nacional des Artes, on Avenida do 3 de Agosto. Otherwise, there's little to see in Bissau. The covered **central market** is an obvious attraction, but its range of produce and other goods isn't huge and prices are usually higher than in neighbouring countries. There's a good music stall, however, run by Tafa Ndiaye, which sells a wide range of cassettes and CDs of Guinean music, including some classic releases from the immediate post-independence era.

There's no museum at present, and the French Cultural Centre, which used to have temporary exhibitions, has not been relaunched after its destruction in 1999. The old presidential palace at the Praça dos Hérois Nacionais is likewise in ruins,

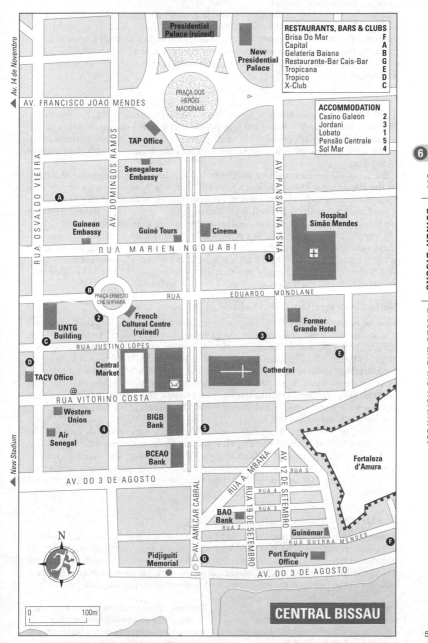

RESTAURANTS, BARS & CLUBS

Brisa Do Mar	F
Capital	A
Gelateria Baiana	B
Restaurante-Bar Cais-Bar	G
Tropicana	E
Tropico	D
X-Club	C

ACCOMMODATION

Casino Galeon	2
Jordani	3
Lobato	1
Pensão Centrale	5
Sol Mar	4

◄ Av. 14 de Novembro

AV. FRANCISCO JOAO MENDES

Presidential Palace (ruined)

New Presidential Palace

PRAÇA DOS HERÓIS NACIONAIS

TAP Office

RUA OSVALDO VIEIRA

AV. DOMINGOS RAMOS

Senegalese Embassy

AV. PANSAU NA ISNA

Hospital Simão Mendes

A

Guinean Embassy

Guiné Tours

Cinema

RUA MARIEN NGOUABI

1

B

PRAÇA ERNESTO CHE GUEVARA

2

RUA

EDUARDO MONDLANE

UNTG Building

French Cultural Centre (ruined)

Former Grande Hotel

C

RUA JUSTINO LOPES

3

D

TACV Office

@

Central Market

Cathedral

E

RUA VITORINO COSTA

Western Union

BIGB Bank

5

Air Senegal

4

BCEAO Bank

Fortaleza d'Amura

AV. DO 3 DE AGOSTO

AV. AMÍLCAR CABRAL

RUA A. MBANA

AV. 12 DE SETEMBRO

RUA 5

RUA 4

RUA 19 DE SETEMBRO

RUA 3

BAO Bank

RUA 2

Guinémar

F

◄ New Stadium

N

Pidjiguiti Memorial

G

Port Enquiry Office

RUA GUERRA MENDES

AV. DO 3 DE AGOSTO

0   100m

CENTRAL BISSAU

but still worth a look, with a substantial monument in front dedicated to the heroes of the independence struggle.

Down by the port, you won't miss the impressive **Pidjiguiti Memorial** to the striking dockers massacred here on August 3, 1959 (see p.500). Regrettably, the imposing **Fortaleza d'Amura** is still a military barracks and there's no way you'll get in to look around. The **mausoleum** of Amílcar Cabral is located within, but even Guineans only get to pay their respects on rare occasions – reportedly on September 24.

Crafts

There's been an enormous resurgence of **strip-woven cloth** in the last few years, produced mainly by Pepel and Manjak people. You'll find a decent selection at the Mercado Bandim, with prices for a single *pagne* at around CFA5000, perhaps twice as much for heavier weaves. Popular patterns include *kassave* (a check) and *volta de Bissau* (bands).

You'll usually find a spread of **carvings** and similar souvenirs opposite the bank by the *Pensão Centrale* and on Praça Che Guevara, and there are always one or two stalls of artefacts at the central market. However the recommended place to browse is the **Centro Artistico Juvenil** (also known as the Centro Padre Batista; irregular times), located 3km from the centre on the north side of Avenida do 14 de Novembro. The centre produces carvings of varying quality but there is some fine craftsmanship here and many pieces have real flair. Look out for telling family statuary – woman supporting kids and husband – and beautiful, cowrie-inlaid stools. Watch the carvers for as long as you like: there's no pressure to buy although prices are reasonable and there's a mass of small items as well.

Beaches around Bissau

You can explore beyond Bissau if you have transport; renting a bicycle from a private owner is a good plan and not difficult for the nearer beaches – or if you can afford it, rent a car and driver or negotiate charter of a taxi. Don't bother struggling to get to the beach unless you know you'll be there at **high tide** – ask at the port for tide tables. The nearest **sea swimming** is at **Perfilis**, where there's a bit of artificial beach; it's 18km from Bissau near Prabis, and reached by following the road past the new stadium. **Quinhámel** (39km; follow the airport road) has a fine beach, on the Rio Mansôa creek shore. **Punta Biombo** (22km further) has a nice, tiny beach on the open sea.

Heading out on these short trips west of the city centre, you pass through the intensively farmed lands of the **Pepel**, a curious landscape, the road winding like an English country lane in a deep trough between fenced and carefully tended raised fields. The Pepel (one of the country's smaller ethnic groups, numbering about sixty thousand) are famous for their artisanal skills, especially their iron- and leatherwork.

Eating

Street food is poor in Bissau, limited to ubiquitous oranges, bananas and groundnuts, with doughnuts a treat at CFA50 apiece. If you're in search of cafés with no names and basic meals, head for the Bandim quarter, where Avenida de Cintura meets the main airport road. Unbeatable is the Senegalese *riz gras* sold by local women. In the centre, there are a couple of well-established restaurants.

Restaurants and cafés

Brisa Do Mar Av do 3 de Agosto. A cheap and popular eating and drinking place for local fare.
Dom Bifanas Near the French embassy. A delicious selection of European and African dishes.

Gelateria Baiana Praça Che Guevara. A place to be seen, where you can write postcards over croissants and coffee. Members of the government are sometimes to be found here, sipping early-morning coffee.

Restaurante-Bar Asa Branca Rua Justino Lopes. Upmarket Portuguese and African fare.
Restaurante Bar Cais-Bar Av do 3 de Agosto. Near the port, this place serves simple meals and snacks – *chawarma* and sandwiches.
Santa Rosa Bar & Grill West of the old stadium. Cheap snack bar specializing in *chawarma* sandwiches, and which proudly claims to serve the best chicken in the country.

Guinea-Bissau's best musicians can often be heard here for free.
Sol Mar Rua Victorino Costa. The restaurant at this hotel is a tranquil, Portuguese-run place serving tasty – not to mention gigantic – lobsters and prawns. Reasonably priced too.
Tropico Rua Justino Lopes. Meals in the evening and snacks during the day in a pleasant atmosphere.

Drinking, nightlife and entertainment

Guineans describe their capital as a 24-hour fiesta, and it's certainly the case that from Thursday to Sunday in particular, Bissau is alive with bars and music. Occasionally, impressive street parties are organized, at which you can watch (and even participate in) *zouk* and *gumbe* dance contests. If you intend to spend an evening trawling the city's clubs, you might consider **chartering a taxi** for the duration (CFA3000 or so), best done early as cabs become scarce after midnight.

There are several **nightclubs** with reasonable admission (around CFA2000). Cape Verdean, Guinean and Antillean *zouk* is the music that dominates all of Bissau's dancefloors. It's slower and easier to learn than *salsa*, and arguably sexier too – don't hesitate to plunge right in. For a popular, unpretentious and very youthful disco check out the *Tropicana* on Rua Justino Lopes, which occasionally hosts bands. Other vibrant clubs frequented by locals are the *Bambu*, a little further out on Avenida 14 de Novembro, and the *Black and White*, an unpretentious *bairro* club off Avenida de Cintura. Rather more stylish is the *Capital*, which is also the most expensive place with the widest selection of music. The *X-Club* on Rua Osvaldo Vieira is a plush club with costly drinks, Latin music, and an almost entirely Portuguese clientele.

The best place to hear **live music** is the enduring though slightly scruffy *Mansa Flema* bar, situated in the lively district of Cupelon de Cima. A DJ spins local music from around 10pm and live gigs tend to start around midnight. *Santa Rosa*, west of the old stadium, doesn't have quite the same vibrancy but is worth visiting on weekend nights. Music festivals tend to take place in the *carnaval* season, during the summer holidays and in December, and may well be staged in Bissau's **cinema**, off Rua Marien Ngouabi.

Listings

Airlines Air Sénégal, Rua Osvaldo Vieira ☎ 20 24 09; TACV, Rua Osvaldo Vieira ☎ 20 12 77; TAP Air Portugal, 14 Praça dos Héróis Nacionais ☎ 20 13 59.
Banks and exchange Both BAO, Rua Gurra Mendes, and BIGB, on Av Amílcar Cabral, change cash, but may be reluctant to accept traveller's cheques. You can also approach the street moneychangers outside the main post office or at the central market, or try the Mavegro supermarket (see overleaf).
Bookshops Pama Papeleria, at the south end of Av Domingos Ramos, sells books and magazines, though only in Portuguese, plus maps, postcards and an excellent range of stationery.
Car rental Try the *Hotel do 24 de Setembro* or *Hotti Bissau*, or talk to Guiné Tours on Av Amílcar

Cabral, who can help you find a private car with driver to hire.
Embassies and consulates Most embassies shut during the civil war and had not reopened at the time of writing. Currently represented are: France, Av 14 de Novembro ☎ 20 13 12, ℗ 20 12 85; The Gambia, Av do 14 de Novembro ☎ 25 10 99; Guinea, Rua Marien Ngouabi ☎ 21 26 81; Mauritania, near the Centro Artístico Juvenil in Chapa ☎ 20 36 96; Nigeria, Av Francisco Mendes ☎ 20 10 18; Portugal, 6 Rua de Lisboa ☎ 21 12 61, ℗ 20 12 69; and Senegal, near the Praça dos Héróis Nacionais ☎ 21 29 44. The British, US and Canadian embassies in Dakar (see p.198) deal with enquiries relating to Guinea-Bissau, though at the time of writing there was an honorary British Consul in Bissau (☎ 20 12 24 or 20 12 16, ℗ 20 12 65).

Hospital Hospital Simão Mendes, av Pansau na Isna, just north of the defunct *Grande Hotel*.

Internet access One of the most central places to get online is on the Rua Vitorino Costa, near the central market; alternatively, there's a well-equipped cybercafé right next door to the *Lobato* hotel.

Post office The main post office is on the corner of Av Amílcar Cabral and Rua Vitorino Costa.

Supermarkets Mavegro, Rua Eduardo Mondlane, has a wide variety of imported foods and other goods, and also changes money.

Travel agents Guiné Tours, on Av Amílcar Cabral (☎21 43 44, ✉guine-tours@sol.gtelecom.gw), can help with general information and car rental. Another efficient agency is the Agencia de Viagem et Turismo at the *Hotti Bissau* hotel (☎21 37 09, ✉odyssetours@sol.gtelecom.gw). Other agencies you might want to try are Surire Tours, Rua Angola (☎21 41 46); A.V.T. Expresso, Rua Cabo Verde 7 (☎20 42 17); and Agencia de Viagens Sagres (☎21 37 09).

Visa extensions The immigration office is near the Mercado Bandim; visa extensions are usually quick and hassle-free.

Western Union They have a representative on Rua Vitorino Costa (☎20 53 43; Mon–Fri 8.30am–5pm).

The northwest

With the exception of the beautiful beach at **Varela**, the northwest of the country is little visited except by travellers passing through on their way from Senegal to Bissau; **São Domingos** is the country's principal entry point from its northern neighbour. Now that the ferry from São Domingos to **Cacheu** has stopped operating, the old route south to Bissau – via **Canchungo** – is rarely used; most travellers instead take the tarred road via Ingoré and Bula. Note that the infrastructure of the northwest has been badly affected by the civil war.

Canchungo and Cacheu

CANCHUNGO is a sleepy place, enlivened on weekends by a couple of nightclubs. You can get here by hopping on a direct *toko toko* from Bissau, or you could change at **Bula**. The fine avenue of trees running into town gives a favourable first impression, and the central *praça*, a renascent market area with sellers of boiled starch and oranges, is alive with people waiting for transport. Just off the square are a few places where beer, meals and rooms are available.

CACHEU, 100km from Bissau, has nothing much to offer in itself, though you may want to visit the nearby **Parque Natural de Tarafes de Cacheu**, established to protect the area's extensive mangrove swamps. Rather than bank on there being staff to guide you, it's better to contact the Ministry of Tourism in Bissau before venturing out (see p.510). As for Cacheu, it is the site of a sixteenth-century fort, the whitewashed substance of which (only 20m square) is still in place, along with its guns, and more ruins to the right, down on the shore. Notice the unusual material used on the roads in Cacheu: broken oil-palm kernel pits which are very hard-wearing, like vegetable gravel. Cacheu has no restaurants, little in the way of shops or food, and just one hotel, closed at the time of writing, though you should have no problems finding locals willing to put you up in exchange for a small fee. A traditional "fair" or market is held every eight days.

São Domingos and Varela

São Domingos is mainly a transit point to the beach at **VARELA**, 50km to the west. Few people overnight in São Domingos, but if it can't be helped there's a restaurant where they always rustle up a decent meal, and staff here may be able to suggest accommodation. Varela beach is stunning, arguably outdoing Cap Skiring across the Senegalese border, with gorgeous swimming, pine trees and low cliffs. As a place to come for the weekend, Varela is a favourite among locals and Guinea-Bissau's small expatriate community, though relatively quiet, thanks to the difficulty of **access**, requiring a slow, bumpy journey along the dirt road – very muddy after rain – from São Domingos. It's easy enough to get a bush taxi to São Domingos from the *paragem* in Bissau, but you'll have to hitch or negotiate a ride in a local vehicle to Varela. You may well see hunters en route with monkey carcasses slung over their shoulders. **Accommodation** is available at the *Jordani Hotel* (⑤; enquire with the *Jordani* in Bissau), which offers pleasantly tiled a/c, s/c rooms on the stepped cliffside, and good, moderately priced food. If your budget won't stretch to that, you'll find *Chez Helene* a pleasant enough place to stay (⑨), or you could camp in the vicinity.

6.2

The Bijagós islands

The largest island group along the West African coast, the **Bijagós archipelago** is made up of more than forty islands, only some of which are inhabited or used for fishing. Not all the islands are accessible, but if you rent a speedboat and have at least a week to spend here, you should be able to see **Bubaque**, the principal island, **Bolama**, **Galinhas**, **Rubane** and maybe even **Orango**. At the moment, the islands are pretty much devoid of tourists, competitive anglers accounting for the majority of the hotel guests.

Now declared a UNESCO Biosphere Reserve, the islands are mostly covered in dense forest, with large stands of oil palm and cashew groves, patches of cultivation and necklaces of white sand or mangroves along the seashore. The islanders, predominantly Bijagó-speakers who've lived surrounded by these calm, warm waters for centuries, are remarkably autonomous. Quite a few communities remain matriarchal societies, and you'll still see women in traditional short palm-fibre skirts (*saiya*). Many of the more remote islands felt little impact from the centuries of Portuguese presence in the region (several were never, officially, "pacified" at the end of the nineteenth century when the rest of the country was being shot into line). And several still have only the most tenuous of links with whoever happens to be in government in Bissau, or with the outside world.

Although the Bijagós are truly idyllic, **island-hopping** is unfortunately harder than you might hope, with no regular boat services, though motorboats and *pirogues* can be rented on Bubaque. Travel between the islands depends always on the **tide**, so make sure you're punctual for your boat's departure, and don't try to cram too many excursions into a short space of time. You should also be prepared for an almost complete lack of facilities outside the two small towns of Bubaque and Bolama, and even those two had no banks at the time of writing, so bring sufficient funds to cover your stay. Bubaque is the usual destination for the **boat from Bissau**, and the only island equipped with a choice of hotels and restaurants – use it as a base to organize other trips.

Bolama

A warped sliver of jungle and farm plots, 25km long by 5km wide, pressed in on most sides by dense mangroves, **Bolama** is the island closest to the mainland. In

Bijagó dialects don't vary much. The phrases below, some of them recognizably Kriolu in derivation, are from Orango. Accented letters are stressed syllables.

How are you?	Ména?	1	Mudíge
I am fine	Ñekagobo	2	Asóge
Thank you/		3	Oñyóko
expression of		4	Ngoyagáne
agreement	Eséyta	5	Modevokóko
Yes	Eng	6	Modevokóko na
No	Ñidóku		mudíge
What is your name?	Amenáwe?	7	Modevokóko na
My name is John	Aynáme John		asóge
White person	Ororá	8	Modevokóko na
Black person	Utúngko		oñyóko
Where are you	Mindánewe?	9	Modevokóko
going?			na ngoyagáne
See you later	Ñibóy	10	Muranáko
Rice	Omán	(with a handclap)	
Fish	Ngokáto	Numbers after 10 are expressed with a	
Water	Ño	combination of claps and the numbers	
Good, beautiful	Ngoséney	1 to 9.	
Bad, ugly	Odéyney		

the past it exercised the imaginations of the British as well as the Portuguese, and was the subject of a protracted colonial dispute in the nineteenth century. Today, the town of Bolama makes for an interesting historical and architectural excursion, and if you're equipped with a bicycle, it's straightforward to head off to the island's most beautiful beaches, on the southern coast.

Curiously, the first colonial adventure attempted on Bolama was conducted by the **British** in 1792 (see box, p.520) and they tried again in 1814. But the agreements with local Bijagó elders on which these incursions were based were no more binding than the treaties the Bijagó had also signed with the **Portuguese**. And it was the latter – particularly the mixed-race Cape Verde islanders – who survived both Bolama's fevers and the Bijagó warriors long enough to establish a real community. Throughout the nineteenth century the British returned periodically to claim sovereignty by pulling up the Portuguese flagpoles, shouting at the settlers and shipping their domestic slaves off to liberation in the colony of Sierra Leone. But they made no serious efforts to settle permanently, or to take charge of the island, until 1860, when Bolama was annexed to Sierra Leone, hundreds of miles to the south. The Portuguese, desperate to preserve their stake in the slave trade which the British were busy trying to abolish, had formally lodged their own claim in 1830 and, by the time the British annexed the island, there were seven hundred loyal Portuguese subjects living there. The dispute wasn't settled until 1870, when a commission headed by United States President Ulysses S. Grant found in favour of Portugal. Grant's efforts were rewarded with a statue in the town square.

Bolama town

The town of **BOLAMA** is on the landward side of the island, facing the mainland barely 2km away. Partly deserted, it echoes with the past grandeurs of the Portuguese empire. Solid mansions attest to a century of trading in ivory and forest products and the opening up of the West African groundnut industry, but ever since the capital of Portuguese Guinea was transferred to Bissau in 1941, Bolama has been steadily

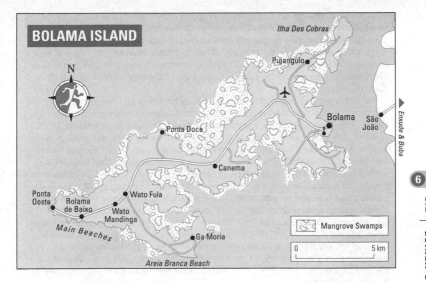

BOLAMA ISLAND

Ilha Des Cobras

Pujangulo

N

Bolama

São
João

Ponta Doce

Canema

Ponta
Oeste
Bolama
de Baixo
Wato Fula

Wato
Mandinga

Main Beaches

Ga Moria

Areia Branca Beach

Mangrove Swamps

0   5 km

Enxude & Buba

crumbling away. The town is still the seat of government of Bolama Region, which includes most of the islands and a little chunk of mainland, and has its own regional president, a hospital, a nurses' school and a teacher training college.

Walking around the town will take you all of forty minutes. Down by the port you'll not miss the ugly **sculpture** bestowed on the island by Mussolini after an Italian seaplane crashed here in 1931 (Bolama used to be a "hydrobase" on the Rome–Rio de Janeiro seaplane route). The solid construction of the monument means it hasn't fallen victim to the tide of nationalism which knocked Ulysses Grant off his pedestal near the bandstand in the overgrown main *praça*, a few minutes' walk from the seafront. The grandest buildings in town surround this main *praça*, and include the colonnaded **Governor's Palace**, the **post office** and the abandoned, Manueline-style **Hotel de Turismo**. This upper part of town reeks of post-colonial decay, though in fact most of the buildings are still in use. The only reminder of Britain's ephemeral presence on Bolama is down to the left behind the church: the reddish two-storey ruin almost throttled by rank undergrowth is the **Casa Inglesa**, a monstrous edifice built entirely of corrugated iron. Architecturally, at any rate, the Portuguese deserved to win the island.

There's a pleasant evening stroll out of town past the secondary school and down an attractive, sandy avenue of trees, with compounds set back on both sides – surely a colonial conception, but one that's endured. Out this way too, at the start of the avenue on the left, there's a rather Gothic graveyard which is worth a look: a curious assembly of souls, including a number of middle Europeans and even one or two Britons. Brown snakes shimmer out of the way as you walk.

Around the island

Fork right at the end of the avenue out of the town and you soon find yourself on a delightful, narrow lane, twisting through cashew groves. There are no beaches down here, but you do pass a **cashew jam factory** which is open a few days every year – they make more deadly cashew wine rather than jam (out of the fruits, not the nuts) – and a cloth manufacturing plant that evidently hasn't been open from the day the looms were delivered. Passing through the hamlet of Pujangulo, the path becomes a muddy track through the mangroves at low tide, at which time it

Beaver's colony

If the **British expedition to Bolama** had resulted in a successful colony, the map of West Africa might today be radically different. **Phillip Beaver**, 26, set sail from Gravesend in England on April 4, 1792, with 274 prospective settlers. Included among them were a ready-made Legislative Council and Governor, chosen in the *Globe Tavern*, London.

The first deaths occurred through smallpox before they had reached the Isle of Wight, and by the time the two ships, *Hankey* and *Calypso*, were nosing through the Bijagós islands six weeks later, half the passengers had malarial fever. Bolama, at first, seemed perfect and uninhabited, and those colonists who were well enough went ashore to chase elephants and butterflies, lie in the sun and collect oysters. Beaver was irritated at their lack of industry. They saw a Bijagó war canoe, but Beaver insisted "the inhabitants were thought to be of peaceable disposition, well-inclined towards the English culture". A week later the warriors attacked, surprisingly well-armed with muskets and Solingen swords, killing and wounding a dozen people and kidnapping several women and children. The settlers' cannons had never even been unpacked.

The colony looked doomed from then on. Although the captives were released when Bolama was "bought" for £77 worth of iron bars from a pair of local headmen, over half the emigrants chose to continue to Sierra Leone in the *Calypso* in July. As the rains set in, the remaining 91 died of malaria at a remarkably even rate, until by the end of the year there were only thirteen survivors. A typically laconic entry in Beaver's journal reads:

Sun 2nd Dec. Killed a bullock for the colony. Died and was buried Mr. Webster. Thermometer 92. Three men well.

Beaver and five others survived the rains of the following year and he and a companion sailed back to England in May 1794. "An ill-contrived and badly executed, though well intended expedition", he mused. The timing, arriving at the start of the rains, could not have been worse. His book was entitled *African Memoranda: Relative to an Attempt to Establish a British Settlement on the Island of Bulama on the Western Coast of Africa in the year 1792, with a Brief Notice of the Neighbouring Tribes, Soils, Productions Etc., and some Observations on the Facility of Colonising that part of Africa with a View to Cultivation; and the Introduction of Letters and Religion to its Inhabitants but more particularly as the means of gradually Abolishing Slavery*. Published in 1805, it's hugely readable and worth scanning the antiquarian bookshops for.

joins the main island to the **Ilha das Cobras** – an uninhabited islet. It's exciting stuff, but watch out for snakes on the other side and don't get stranded by the tide. The walk or ride is about 15km there and back.

There are other, shorter walks you could do in the peninsula immediately south of Bolama town. But the main interest lies further south across the island where, unless you're prepared to set off early with food and water sufficient for a couple of days, you're really going to need transport. The dirt road cuts through pretty forest, farm and plantation lands, following the central ridge of the island (maximum elevation just 26m), never far from the sea. The people you'll meet are mostly Bijagó; for rural Bijagó, tourists are a sensational novelty and you'll occasionally find children for whom such a meeting is a first.

Hamlets and clusters of compounds are, in many cases, named after ethnic groups. Some 17km from Bolama you turn left at Wato Fula and plunge into a tunnel of cashews. **Areia Branca beach** is a further 7km down here, a narrow lip of white sand dipping beneath the coconuts into a milky blue sea. There are other beaches along the southern coast, but this is said to be the best spot, and you're unlikely to find it anything but deserted. This corner of the island is very sparsely populated and you can nose around for hours completely alone. Remember, however, if you're tempted to knock off a few coconuts for their milk and flesh, that all the trees are individually owned.

Practicalities

In the absence of a regular ferry service, you might consider taking a *pirogue* (Mon & Fri–Sun only; CFA1500) from **Port de Canoa**, in the south of Bissau. From the point of safety and convenience, however, it's much better to rent a motorboat from the *Casino Galeon* in Bissau or one of the hotels in Bubaque (see overleaf). If you feel adventurous, you can take the long route to the island via **Enxude**, which faces Bissau on the mainland: to get there, take a *pirogue* from Limpar port east of Bissau's centre. Once at Enxude, catch a Buba-bound bush taxi and get off at the junction to hitch the final 20–25km to São João, from where *pirogues* ply the short journey across the channel to Bolama.

Facilities for visitors on Bolama are very limited. There's one **hotel** (rooms have fan and shared bathroom; ❸) and a **restaurant** by the harbour, where you have to order in the morning for your meal in the evening. You can normally spend a night or two here under a *paillote*, on the understanding you buy the odd meal. A local woman runs another, cheaper, restaurant in her house; ask anyone around town where to find her. Should you have problems finding somewhere to stay, you may come across aid workers or missionaries willing to put you up. A good idea is to bring your own **tent**, and a better plan still is to bring some wheels of your own. It's really worth renting a **bicycle** in Bissau and bringing it with you. Exploring the island otherwise means a lot of footwork. There's no more than a handful of vehicles here.

On the question of **food**, the only shops are in Bolama itself, and they don't amount to much at all. There's a limited market (in a large, walled marketplace) where a small selection of fruit and vegetables, fish, peanut butter and bread is usually available. Bring with you what you can from Bissau. What you don't use will find eager recipients.

Bubaque

In Guinea-Bissau, tourism begins and ends in **BUBAQUE**. In colonial days the island was a Portuguese favourite, and after independence Swedish aid provided a hotel and a tarmac road to the beach. Trips were arranged here from The Gambia in the 1970s, later to be replaced by regular visits from French tourists, flying in for the renowned game fishing of the waters nearby.

Unless you're flying to Bubaque on a charter from Dakar (see below), you will probably get here on the weekly boat, which leaves Bissau on Friday, returning Sunday (5hr; CFA2500). One weekend is hardly enough time for a visit, however, so you might allot at least a week to venture out to some of the other islands. One alternative is the *Ten A Manha*, a well-maintained motorized **pirogue** that goes from Port Bandim near Bissau. However, the small *pirogues* that leave regularly from Port de Canoa are old, unstable, overloaded and feature no safety provisions, and you'll be sharing them with goats, pigs, and a whole lot of merchandise – definitely not a recommended way to travel.

On the outward voyage from Bissau, until you have cleared the **Ilha das Galinhas**, a sea as flat as a millpond is the normal vista in the dry season. But as you approach the isle of Rubane, the mood improves. The intense tropicality of the green, horizontal islands leaves a strong sense of place, reinforced as you enter the channel between Bubaque and Rubane and see the red tin roofs of Bubaque with its high pier. By this stage of the voyage, it will be low tide. The scene – children picking in the mud, the viridescent foliage of the two islands tumbling to the water, the tranquillity after the racket of the diesel and what seems like bustle in Bissau – is magic.

Bubaque town

Bubaque offers a number of **places to stay**. The *Pensão Cadjoco*, run by a friendly Franco–Italian couple, has rooms with fan (➋) or inexpensive tents, both with full board as an option. Other budget bases include *Chez Dora* (➋) and the highly recommended *Chez Titi* (➋), run by a welcoming and helpful Senegalese manager and with an excellent cook. Reasonable and very comfortable is the *Hotel Calypso* (☎82 11 16; ➍), a friendly French-run place equipped with swimming pool, a restaurant that serves good pizzas, and which rents out motorboats, cars and bicycles. The bikes are cheap to rent (CFA2500 a day), but boat hire can be expensive, depending on the distance covered and the fuel needed. There are also a couple of more expensive *campements* (both ➍) which offer a good degree of comfort – *Maiana Village* (☎+874 762 28 12 42) and *Le Club des Dauphins* (☎+871 761 28 29 64). Both offer angling holidays (at CFA650,000 for six days), as well as individual angling and tourist excursions by motorboat. They can also arrange for you to fly here from Dakar (CFA200,000 return), or to travel to and from Bissau by speedboat (CFA150,000).

As for **something to eat**, there are good and varied restaurants at *Calypso*, *Chez Titi* and the *Pensão Cadjoco*. Also try *Julio* for good local food and a lively bar, and the inexpensive and friendly *Chez Raoul*, which serves the best Senegalese food on the island.

Looking around Bubaque village is nice in the early morning and late afternoon. Immensely picturesque seascapes flicker through the mango boughs; oil palms in massive stands are covered in the nitlike nests of weaver birds, and resound with their chatter; lizards and butterflies dart everywhere; and mambas are occasionally seen. In the village, a **produce market** sets up every morning and a growing number of **shops** sell all sorts of things. The **post office**'s reliability is uncertain but you can make international phone calls easily enough. **Nightlife** in Bubaque is pretty much restricted to the *Tatumi*, which has a surprisingly good sound system and plays the usual mix of Guinean and Cape Verdean music for locals and tourists.

Praia da Bruce

Don't miss out on a trip to **PRAIA DA BRUCE**, 15km away on the south coast. It's very appealing: the beach offers shady cashew trees, as much clean sand as you could wish for, and an isolation that's palpable – though one or two fishermen may come by, stationing themselves in the waves to catch a garnish for the evening rice. If you only have a weekend on the island, you might even consider staying at the newly renovated *Hotel Epicuro* (☎+871 763 09 48 35; ➎), an appealing, Italian-run *campement* that proudly sports a handful of tastefully decorated *paillotes*. The hotel sits on a low cliff right behind the beach, from where a short run downhill takes you within minutes to your morning swim.

Most of the Bubaque hotels can arrange a trip here. Alternatively, you could rent a bike and venture out on a beautiful ride along Bubaque's straight, flat road, which is lined by thick forest and passes by the occasional village. Make sure you leave early in the morning, as the heat becomes unbearable around midday. Try to get to the beach when the tide is high, and bring drinking water – lots of it.

Other islands

If you think Bubaque is beautiful, the **other islands** will truly take your breath away. Getting there may be hard, and living conditions rough, but it's worth it.

Bubaque is the place to rent **speedboats** at one of the bigger hotels – be prepared to pay anything from CFA20,000 to CFA50,000 per person per day, including fuel, for a four-passenger boat, excluding the driver. You may also find a reasonably priced **pirogue** at the port or through your hotel, but make sure it's in a good state. The larger hotels have radio equipment you can take with you to contact them in the event of an emergency. Alternatively, you can arrange boat trips with one of Bissau's hotels, though this will invariably cost a bit more.

Recognized **accommodation** on **Rubane** consists of two French-run *campements* specializing in angling holidays, *Club Acaja* and *Tubaron* (both ⑥) – if you're not an angler, you might find it hard to join in the conversations. On **Galinhas**, there's a highly recommended Guinean bungalow development, *Hotel Ambancana* (☎21 55 55; ❷), and on **Orango**, the Italian resort *Chez Frédérico* (⑥). Apart from these possibilities, you're at the mercy of Bijagó hospitality – usually profound. There is little experience of tourism out here and any generosity you show is unlikely to be exploited. The Bijagó have very severe sanctions in cases of stealing.

Central and northern isles

Rubane and **Soga** (the latter being the island from which the 1970 Portuguese invasion of the Republic of Guinea was launched) are close to Bubaque and not hard to get to. **Punta Biombo**, 60km west of Bissau, is a reasonable place to get a *pirogue* (CFA500–1000) to the relatively populated and forested **Formosa** island, 30km away. Ask to be dropped at **Nago** in the creek between **Maio** island and Formosa.

On the archipelago's northwest periphery the string of stunning beaches and crystal-clear water surrounding **Caravela** are the jewel in the Bijagós' crown: the island is a traditional stop-off point for cruises from Senegal and The Gambia.

Southern and western isles

The wilder, and most beautiful, islands are on the archipelago's seaward, southwestern edge and require a concerted effort to reach, with the probability of several days' wait for a return passage. All make Bubaque look cosmopolitan by comparison and offer tremendous rewards to adventurous and flexible travellers. You'll find no shops, police or *pensões*, almost no motor vehicles and negligible outside influence. The tenuous **missionary presence** succeeds only superficially in subduing the islanders' traditional values: clandestine **initiation ceremonies** incorporating the use of *irãn* (fetishes) combine freely with Christian beliefs and practices. You're almost certain to witness the rich cultural life of the islanders, expressed through drumming and dancing.

The marine and terrestrial **wildlife** on these remoter islands is extraordinarily prolific. Exploratory walks through the bush will reveal hornbills, monkeys and even green mambas; sharks and stringrays patrol the shallows. While the mamba's bite has no remedy (just don't get bitten), a ray's excruciating sting is soothed by the islanders with a slice of fresh papaya and a few cow-hornfuls of *cana*.

ETICOGA, the principal settlement on **Ilha de Orango**, has an unusual population of saltwater-dwelling **hippos** in the creek east of town. The hippos are able to swim between the islands, and are held in some fear by the islanders owing to their penchant for ruining crops and exhibiting menacing behaviour in defence of their young. Orango also used to be the seat of the ancient Queen Pampa, whose life is celebrated in legends. Artefacts dating back centuries have been found here and the island has been designated a national park in itself. Further to the east, the remote **João Viera** is famous for its marine turtles, which frequently attract researchers and conservationists.

If you wish to visit **Roxa** (also known as **Canhabaque**), the most traditional of the islands, it's best to take a guide from Bubaque with you – any hotel should be able to put you in touch with one. A guide is essential, above all, to indicate sacred sites that should not be walked upon. On arrival you'll be taken to meet the local chief, whom you present with rum and other gifts in exchange for permission to visit the island.

The islands of **Uracane** (with its colony of flamingos outnumbering the residents a hundredfold), **Uno** and **Unhocomo** take some getting to. On the outside of the furthest island, Unhocomo, the seas become rough Atlantic swell, traversed by the sea route to the main settlement, **Anaburu**.

6.3
The south and east

R eserves of enthusiasm for the **Bissau interior** – a patchwork of low ridges, divided by the country's creeks and rivers – run pretty low once you've visited the capital and the islands. From the travel perspective, the rest of the country divides into two: the **south**, a relatively inaccessible and little-known region, fronting up against the Republic of Guinea; and the **east**, hardly explored by travellers either, though Guinea-Bissau's main road runs out this way, with a number of large towns and villages along the line of travel.

The south

Before the civil war, the south – with its impressive areas of rainforest – was just beginning to open up, with considerable improvements in both roads and public transport. The gateway to the region is **Enxude**, across the Rio Gêba from Bissau and accessible by *pirogue* or by bush taxi. From Enxude, there are always bush taxis waiting to take you to Tite, Fulacunda and Buba. Banana wagons are a popular form of transport around the region.

The main town and transport hub of the south, **BUBA**, is situated around a pretty natural harbour. It has a few small places to stay, of which *Buba Hotel* (☎61 11 20; ❹) is the most popular. Nearby there are swimming beaches and waterfalls along the Rio Corubal, which separates the south from the rest of Guinea-Bissau. These are most easily reached via **Bambadinca** (117km east of Bissau) and the tarmac road down from there to Buba (111km). The falls (mere rapids in the dry season) are at **Saltinho**, near **Mampatá**, the only bridge over the Corubal. A French-run *campement*, *Samba Loba* (❸), is located on the north bank of the Corubal, 5km from Mampatá (signposted), down a track. Beautifully situated, it's usually packed to the gills at weekends and school holidays, but it's a fair bet you'd have it to yourself at other times. The only potential drawback is the fact that you are more or less obliged to eat there too (generous and excellent French cooking). **Cussilintra**, a dozen kilometres downstream and closer to **Xitole**, was a colonial beauty spot, like Saltinho, and is still a popular weekend excursion with good swimming nearby.

To the south of Buba, the village of **Jemberem** is part of the **Parque Natural de Cantanhez** (still very much in its developing stages), an area of fairly unspoilt tropical rainforest, offering the chance to spot chimpanzees, elephants and other wildlife. To get there from Bissau, take a bush taxi as far as **Catió**, then hitch.

Alternatively, banana wagons can take you directly there (ask at the banana-wagon station near the airstrip).

East of Buba, along a track which skims the Guinean border, the town of **Boé** is famous as the first place to be liberated from the Portuguese by the PAIGC back in 1967. Its reputation is undeserved, though, as the first town to be liberated was in fact in Boé *district*, a place called **Lugajole** in the deep southeast; a small plaque and hut there commemorate the occasion. Strange, hilly landscapes around Lugajole – the outliers of the Fouta Djalon – make a change from the maze of mangroves and mud nearer the coast.

The east

The two main towns of the interior, **Bafatá** and **Gabú**, are located along Guinea-Bissau's one main highway. You'll find **transport** fairly easily along here, with several daily *toko toko* and taxi departures between both towns and Bissau.

It's a good road most of the way, with unremarkable scenery of tall grass and charcoal-burning villages. Before Mansôa, the road forks: right for the east, and left (north) over the Rio Mansôa for the town. **Mansôa**, at the centre of fighting in 1998, has no hotels, but you should be able to find rooms for rent and there are a couple of restaurants. Mansôa is home to a Balante community, and if you happen to be here during the season of their initiation ceremonies, you might encounter one of the brilliant Balante **broxa** dance troupes moving from village to village here. With their warriorlike dress – fantastic head-shaving patterns, sea-shell adornments strapped on arms and legs, metal chains draped around their necks, and other accoutrements including turtle shells, body paint and sometimes army helmets and red berets, the *broxa* dancers are an impressive sight. If you get to watch a show, hold on to your things, as some groups specialize in comedic thieving routines, and you'll have to buy back the small items they take off you during their dance.

The road on to **Farim** and the Senegalese border town of **Tanaf** is decent enough, with two bush taxis making the journey each day. Plenty more bush taxis operate between Farim and Bissau.

Bafatá and Gêba

East of the old trading river, the Rio Gêba, **Bambadinca** marks the start of the road south to Xitole. The nearby port of **Xime** is the furthest into the interior that ferries (at least 2 monthly) run from Bissau. Some 30km northeast of Bambadinca, **BAFATÁ** comes as a surprise, its street lights offering an optimistic welcome, its brick factory apparently turning the red dust that smothers everything into the tiled Portuguese-style houses that make up the centre. The town is the birthplace of Amílcar Cabral, and a statue near the small market pays tribute to this Guinean hero.

Perched on a low rise, Bafatá is an orderly, appealing town, as placid as the river that winds its graceful course below the town to the west where time seems to be standing still. It's definitely worth spending a couple of days in the area, and you'll find good **accommodation** in the pleasant and comfortable *Maimouna Kape* (☎41 15 93; ❸), right in the centre of town. Its outdoor bar is a popular stopover for travellers to and from Bissau, and you stand a good chance of hitching a lift with one of them. The Portuguese hotel manager organizes hunting trips as well as wildlife tours around Bafatá. If you prefer to be close to the antelopes and monkeys that inhabit the surrounding forest, the *Campement Kape* is a great place to stay (❹), sharing management with the *Maimouna Kape* (enquire here; they'll drive you out to the *campement*) and offering bonuses such as a swimming pool, *paillotes* and good views. If both hotels are too expensive for you, try asking at the *paragem* for guesthouses, and you'll stand a good chance of finding a cheap room for the night. For **food**, try the Portuguese café *Ponto de Encontro*, serving enormous portions of chicken. There are a few other restaurants where food needs to be ordered in advance, though they serve drinks all day.

The most thriving upcountry trading post of the Portuguese province of Guinea in the late nineteenth century was **Gêba**, 12km west of Bafatá down a side road off the highway on the Bissau side of town. Gêba is now virtually a ghost town, and the overgrown **ruins** are worth a look if you're drawn to such places. You can charter a taxi in Bafatá for the trip.

Northeast of Bafatá, there's a well-maintained dirt road to the **Senegalese border** at **Pirada**, while a fork crosses a rickety bridge and continues along a deteriorating track to the frontier at Cambaju and on to **Kolda** on the Ziguinchor–Tambacounda road. From Bafatá to Gabú, unusual tall stands of bamboo flank the road.

Gabú

The most significant eastern town, **GABÚ** is also the country's Fula and Muslim capital. If you are familiar with the Fouta Djalon – the Fula heartland of the Republic of Guinea – you'll instantly recognize the cultural similarities between both regions, which have strong historical ties. Until the nineteenth century, Gabú lay at the heart of the Kaabu empire and was home to a mixed population of animist Mandinka, from whom the rulers of the empire were drawn, and Muslim Fula, who represented a substantial minority. When religious and ethnic conflicts mounted, the Fula called upon the neighbouring Fouta Djalon empire for support. The Fula army occupied the land, overthrowing the Mandinka ruler Janke Wali, and worked towards the Islamization of the region. Today, Gabú is an animated commercial centre, prospering from triangular trade with Senegal and Guinea, and bearing little evidence of the battles fought here in the past. Though not of great architectural interest, the town is worth strolling around in the early evening when the seemingly endless street market really comes to life, featuring an abundance of merchandise from bread and oranges to colourful fabric and cassettes.

Gabú is a convenient stopping place en route to or from Tambacounda in Senegal, or Foula-Mori or Koundara in Guinea, and there's a small selection of decent, decently priced **hotels**. The *Hotel Visiom* in Bairro 14 (☎51 14 14; ❷) is a popular, safe and comfortable place with running water, electricity, good local food and a bar that becomes busy on weekends. The *Medina Boé* (☎51 15 42; ❷) is another excellent place to stay, about twenty minutes' walk from the centre, with nicely decorated huts scattered around a large, tree-lined garden area, and a nightclub, restaurant and video lounge. Only slightly cheaper is the dire and depressing *Oasis* on the southwestern edge of town – not worth considering, though their affiliated restaurant in the centre offers a good selection of African and European **food**. Some of the best and cheapest food in town can be had in the numerous street cafés, serving large bowls of rice, plus sandwiches and coffee. For **nightlife**, Gabú has the surprisingly slick club *Jomav*, featuring one of Guinea-Bissau's most powerful sound systems and a good selection of music. Given the town's location, the ubiquitous *zouk* mixes here with Senegalese and Guinean beats, plus a wide selection of global sounds. Late on Saturday night is best, when the club gets packed out.

Gabú has good **transport** connections with all points along the road to Bissau, and vehicles heading for Senegal, The Gambia and Guinea pass through with some regularity. You have to get to the *paragem* early in the morning (around 8am), though, or you risk waiting for hours for a taxi to fill up and leave. The northern route out of Gabú to Pirada and Tambacounda is a reasonable, maintained track, where you may even have luck hitching.

Into Guinea

The surfaced highway continues east from Gabú to **Pitche**, from where the main road into Guinea is a rough earth track winding and bumping its way through the bush – chokingly dusty in the dry season, barely passable in the rains. Direct bush taxis bound for **Koundara** via Pitche, Kandika and Saréboïdo leave Gabú almost daily (around CFA15,000), and Sareboïdo's Sunday market generates commercial traffic. It's best to expect the unexpected on this route (east of Pitche the road is truly appalling), and bear in mind that the Guinea-Bissau frontier post at **Buruntuma** closes for lunch. Most drivers bound for Conakry prefer to take the route **south into Guinea** via **Foula-Mori** (further details on p.535), an exciting journey that involves an unsurfaced road through woodland, use of a hand-hauled ferry over a small river and the traversal of sandy troughs. Taxis leave almost daily from Gabú, charging CFA35,000 to Conakry.

Guinea

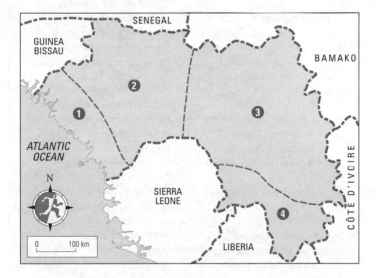

Guinea highlights

* **The Iles de Los** A short boat ride off the coast from Conakry, this attractive cluster of islands offers some of Guinea's best and most accessible beach destinations. **See p.565**

* **Conakry nightlife** Conakry's nightlife is one of its saving graces – you can often watch famous Guinean bands rehearsing for a major gig. **See p.567**

* **Pita to Télimélé** One of the finest 4WD and hiking trails in West Africa, this route offers a great range of magnificent scenery and warm encounters with local people. **See p.578**

* **Parc National Niokolo-Badiar** An exciting development on the Senegalese border that's home to a wide variety of animals, including antelopes, monkeys and lions. **See p.583**

* **La Voile de la Mariée** Named for their resemblance to a bridal veil, these spectacular waterfalls drop for 60m over a cliff amidst a pretty green landscape near Kindia. **See p.574**

* **Kankan Market** The vast *marché central* in this historic Haute Guinée university town is one of the country's best. **See p.586**

* **Case de Palabre** Dating from the 1930s, this former Fula chiefs' assembly hut boasts an inscribed floor, elaborate ceiling decorations and exceptional wall carvings. **See p.577**

Introduction and Basics

Between 1958, when it reclaimed its independence and effectively cut itself off from France, and the death of dictator Sekou Touré in 1984, the Republic of Guinea was an isolated and secretive country. Only in the late 1980s did it begin, hesitantly, to open its borders to tourists.

Despite immense cultural and natural riches (it holds the world's third-largest bauxite reserves, for instance), Guinea is one of the **poorest countries** in West Africa. For visitors this means that there is hardly any semblance of a functioning tourist industry, and travel around the country is as rough as it is exciting.

Guinea's people display a wide cultural diversity. No single language predominates and there's considerable regional variation. **Susu**, spoken mainly in the coastal region, is the language of the capital, Conakry, as well as most of Lansana Conté's government. An easy-to-learn Mande tongue, it's related to **Kouranko** and **Malinké**, the languages of Haute Guinée, to the trading lingua franca known as **Dyula**, and more distantly to the minority languages of the highland forests – Kpelle and Loma. Thanks to the business activities of the **Fula**, markets all over Guinea tend to resound with the guttural tones of their language, otherwise primarily spoken in the Fouta Djalon region.

Where to go

At the moment, Guinea seems to be living in a state of permanent suspense. The conflicts in neighouring Liberia, Sierra Leone and Côte d'Ivoire have destabilized the entire region, and though Guinea has so far escaped severe problems, mainly due to the relative strength of its military, future developments are far from certain, with fears that the country will plunge into turmoil once the ailing president Lansana Conté goes – check the political situation carefully before you visit.

Despite its troubles, Guinea holds great appeal as a place to **travel**, sprawling in a great arc of mountains and plains from the creeks and mudbanks of the mangrove coast to the forests on the border with Côte d'Ivoire. The great rivers of West Africa – the Gambia, the Senegal and the Niger – all rise in Guinea, while the Michelin map shows more green-bordered scenic routes in Guinea than any other country – always a promising indication.

Guinea's best-known attraction is the **Fouta Djalon** highlands, a plateau region dramatically dissected into myriad hills and valleys which spouts waterfalls like a colossal rock garden. On the plains of **Haute Guinée** to the east you feel the cultural echoes of the Niger valley's medieval empires, while to the south, another great highland region, **Guinée Forestière**, comprises a zone of wet forest and remote peoples, where liana bridges cross the rivers and pre-Islamic traditions survive. It's sometimes hard to be positive about Guinea's capital, **Conakry**,

Facts and figures

The **République de Guinée** is often called Guinea-Conakry, to distinguish it from other Guineas. The population is just under eight million, around ten percent of whom live in Conakry. Guinea's land area (246,000 square kilometres) is about the same as Great Britain or Oregon. Guinea has a colossal foreign debt, estimated to be more than £2 billion ($3.6 billion), which is more than four times its annual earnings from the export of goods and services, yet roughly equivalent to only a month's expenditure by the British Ministry of Defence. At the time of writing, the ruling party was still the Parti de l'Unité et du Progrès (PUP) of the ailing President Lansana Conté (in power since 1984). It currently holds 71 of the 114 seats in the national assembly. There are around a dozen other significant political parties.

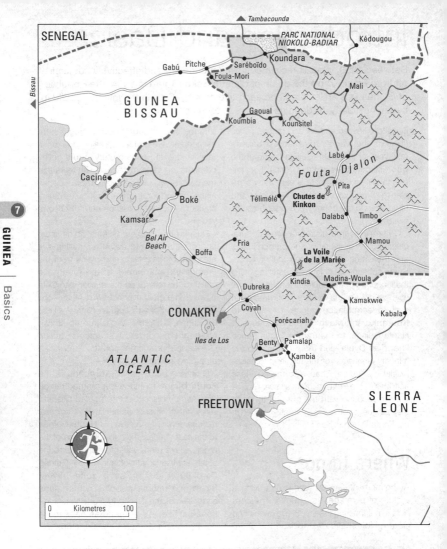

but its treasure islands – the **Iles de Los** – and nightlife are good compensations for aggressive vendors, police roadblocks and pollution.

When to go

When you visit Guinea and where you go is likely to be determined largely by the **seasons** – overall, the **easiest time to travel** in Guinea is from late November to March. Away from the country's limited network of surfaced highways, much of the remote countryside is isolated during **the rains**, mainly concentrated between June and October, during which flooding can leave many minor routes completely impassable for days or weeks. Be prepared for plans to go awry, though you may find that the spectacular storms, gushing waterfalls and abundance of greenery are more than adequate compensation.

The weeks following the rainy season are the best time to visit the **Fouta Djalon**, which

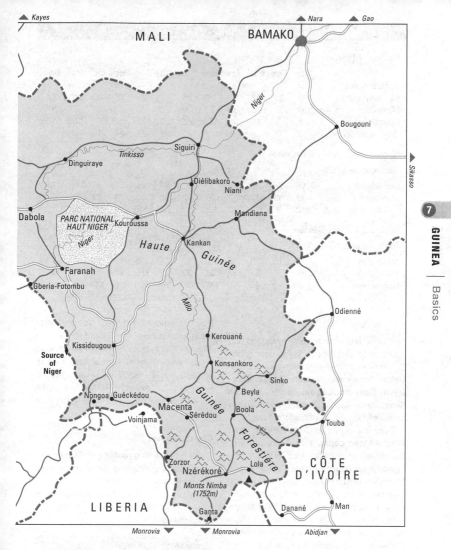

has a very agreeable climate all year round. Hot during the day, temperatures can plummet at night: you'll need warm clothes and perhaps a sleeping bag. As the **dry season** progresses, travel in Fouta Djalon and (especially) in the Malinké plains of **Haute Guinée** becomes increasingly dusty and hot. The harmattan winds from the north can bring dry haze and dust as early as December, and by April you'll find travel around the region of **Kankan** almost impossibly stifling. **Conakry** has an insupportable climate at the best of times, with humidity rarely below eighty percent and July delivering the heaviest month's rainfall anywhere in West Africa.

Getting there from the rest of Africa

Guinea is well connected **by air** to neighbouring countries. If you're not planning to fly in, there are **overland routes** into Guinea from all surrounding countries.

Average temperatures and rainfall

Conakry (coast)

	Jan	Feb	Mar	Apr	May	June	July	Aug	Sept	Oct	Nov	Dec
Temperatures °C												
Min (night)	22	23	23	23	24	23	22	22	23	23	24	23
Max (day)	31	31	32	32	32	30	28	28	29	31	31	31
Rainfall mm	3	3	10	23	158	559	1298	1054	683	371	122	10
Days with rainfall	0	0	1	2	11	22	29	27	24	19	8	1

Kouroussa (Haute Guinée)

	Jan	Feb	Mar	Apr	May	June	July	Aug	Sept	Oct	Nov	Dec
Temperatures °C												
Min (night)	14	17	22	23	23	22	21	21	21	21	19	15
Max (day)	33	36	37	37	35	32	30	30	31	32	33	33
Rainfall mm	10	8	22	7	135	246	297	345	340	168	33	10

Mamou (Fouta Djalon)

	Jan	Feb	Mar	Apr	May	June	July	Aug	Sept	Oct	Nov	Dec
Temperatures °C												
Min (night)	13	15	18	19	20	18	19	19	19	18	17	13
Max (day)	33	34	35	34	31	29	27	25	28	29	30	31
Rainfall mm	8	10	46	127	203	257	335	401	340	203	6	8

Flights

Air Guinée has been recently revitalized and now has several weekly flights connecting Conakry and other places in Guinea with **Dakar**, **Monrovia**, **Abidjan**, **Banjul**, **Freetown**, **Bamako**, **Lagos**, **Accra** and even **Kinshasa** (via Lagos). Be prepared for lengthy delays and frequent cancellations though.

There are flights to Conakry from most **West African capitals**. Air Ivoire provides the widest range of services, with nonstop flights from **Abidjan** (twice weekly) and **Bamako**, **Douala**, **Libreville**, **Dakar** and **Cotonou** (weekly), although the most regular and reliable connection to Dakar is provided by Air Sénégal (four weekly). TACV flies twice weekly from Cape Verde to Conakry, while Ghana Airways has twice-weekly flights from both **Accra** – one via **Abidjan** and **Freetown**, the other via Abidjan only – and from Dakar via **Banjul**.

> For important practical information applying to all West African countries, covering health, transport, cultural hints and more, plus details on getting to the region from beyond Africa, see Basics, pp.9–87.

Both Paramount and West Coast Airlines leave twice a week from Freetown. Gambia Airways and Nigeria Airways leave at least twice weekly from Banjul and **Lagos** respectively. Air France has several services weekly to Conakry from **Nouakchott**, while SN Air Brussels has two weekly flights from Dakar.

Overland

There are **overland routes** into Guinea from all surrounding countries. Most of these are endurance tests of one sort or another, but many also provide fine scenery and glimpses of wild, little-travelled districts along the way.

From Mali

From Bamako, there are regular bush taxis to both **Siguiri** and **Kankan**. Be prepared for a long and tiresome journey, though the border itself is usually hassle-free. Direct taxis only operate a few times a week, but if you're prepared to travel in stages, you can leave any time of the week. When the Niger River is high enough and the boat in working order, the **ferry to Siguiri and Kankan** provides a second option – this usually runs from August to January.

From Guinea-Bissau

Bissau to Conakry is one of the region's toughest international journeys, liable to be cut by floods and mud pools during the rains; public transport along the various sections of the route, especially in the border region, is tenuous. The direct coastal route to Conakry, over the creeks **from Buba and Cacine to Boké**, is really not a viable option and is hardly covered by public transport. The usual route follows the tarmac inland through Guinea-Bissau via **Gabú** and **Pitche** (in Guinea); thence via **Koundara** and back onto tarmac at **Labé.** Bush taxis for Koundara leave Gabú two or three times a week; the road between Pitche and the border is little more than a bush track and can be empty of passing transport as far as Saréboido (in Guinea), though Saréboido's Sunday market generates commercial traffic. From Koundara there are daily departures for Labé, through the beautiful northern Fouta Djalon. Note that officials at Koundara will try to persuade you to change money with them, but their rates are poor. Change a note or two only.

You can also cross the border into Guinea **between Pitche and Foula-Mori**, connected in the dry season by a passable, though rough, 30km track and a hand-hauled ferry over the Koliba River – transport on this route can be limited except on Mondays, Pitche's market day. You go through Guinea-Bissau formalities at the ferry and Guinea formalities at the friendly Foula-Mori post. Although not marked on the maps, this is a recognized border crossing, and worth the trip just to see Alfa Yaya's birth hut (see p.582). **Koumbia**, 80km further on, is the first town of any size and from here there's regular transport to the coast or up into the Fouta Djalon. If you're heading to Conakry, it's a rocky, dusty journey to Boké, from where a beautifully smooth tarmac road leads all the way to Conakry.

Driving yourself, in good conditions you can do the trip from Koumbia to Conakry in under twelve hours; public transport can take up to two days. Travel times invariably depend on the ferry crossing over the Fatala River at Boffa. The ferry usually closes around 9pm, and late arrivers are obliged to spend a night in mosquito-ridden Boffa.

From The Gambia and Senegal

The choice is between two main routes. Firstly, there's the fairly straightforward bush taxi route to **Koundara**. Taxis go from **Basse** in The Gambia or **Diaobé** in Senegal via the border posts at Dialadiang (Senegal) and Missira (Guinea). The journey from Diaobé to Koundara takes roughly six hours. Secondly, there's the more interesting but very tough route from **Kédougou** in Senegal up into the Fouta Djalon to the village of **Mali** and on to **Labé** (for route details, see p.223). The large trucks which ply this route take up to three days to cover the 120km of boulder-strewn *piste*, while taxis also travel the route; you're not advised to use your own transport unless you own a tough 4WD.

From Sierra Leone

At the time of writing, two buses a week were running along the relatively busy main route from **Freetown** via Kambia and Pamelap to **Conakry**. This is a day's journey if things go well, though extensive checkpoints on the Guinean side of the border and lengthy searches and interrogations of passengers without valid ID can extend the journey up to two days. It's generally quicker to go by **bush taxi**, even though you'll have to change either at the ruined border town of Pamelap in Sierra Leone or in pretty Forécariah on the Guinean side.

All other routes between Guinea and Sierra Leone are less-travelled and riskier. A second route leads from the former rebel centre of **Koindu** in Sierra Leone's eastern highlands to **Guéckédou**, a town that has been completely destroyed in the conflict. A third route runs from northern Sierra Leone via **Kabala** to **Faranah**, though there's very little transport on this route. A fourth possibility is to find transport heading north from **Kamakwie** to **Madina-Woula**, and from here to Kindia or Mamou.

There's also a **ferry service from Freetown** to Conakry. Ferries leave three times a week from Waterwharf in Freetown, usually at around 8pm, reaching Conakry early the next morning. It isn't exactly a luxury cruise, though you can at least get some sleep and avoid the checkpoint hassles of the road journey.

From Liberia

There's a range of border crossings along the watershed frontier between Liberia and Guinea, but given the amount of smuggling that goes on here and the two countries' longstanding mutual distrust (not to mention the more recent refugee problem resulting from the Liberian civil war), it's no surprise that these borders can be troublesome to negotiate – always seek local advice. The **main frontiers** are at Foya–Guéckédou, Voinjama–Macenta, Ganta–Diécké and Yekepa–Yalézou/Bossou (for Nzérékoré).

The **ferry service from Monrovia** to Conakry is currently suspended.

From Côte d'Ivoire

There are three main routes from Côte d'Ivoire to Guinea, though with the conflicts in Côte d'Ivoire, and the growing numbers of Ivoirian refugees, getting across them has become more problematic. The first, from **Odienné** to **Kankan**, is better than it looks on most maps, but it's still an extremely tough drive and customs checks at the border are rigorous. The second route is from **Odienné to Sinko** and then Beyla. There's a huge market in Sinko (Guinea) on Friday, for which vehicles leave Odienné early Thursday morning.

The third main route is the lovely forest road from **Danané** to **Nzérékoré**. You'll sometimes find taxis along here, and there's always transport on a Tuesday for Nzérékoré's big weekly market. The road is normally passable throughout the year, but it can be surprisingly difficult to find transport to **Gbapleu** – where Ivoirian formalities are conducted – and from there on to the Guinean frontier near **Nzo**.

Red tape and visas

Visas are required by everyone except West Africans. Once notoriously difficult to obtain, they are now obtainable in a number of African cities, and officials in Guinea are generally welcoming to tourists. Depending on where you apply for a visa, you may simply be required to present your passport with a photocopy of the ID pages, photos and a fee of around CFA20,000. The embassies at **Accra**, **Banjul**, **Bissau**, **Bamako**, **Dakar** and **Freetown** normally issue visas within 48 hours; there are also embassies in **Monrovia** and **Lagos**. Three-month single-entry visas are the norm, but you can get an extension for FG80,000 at the Direction Nationale Police Aire et Frontières in the district of Coléah in Conakry. If you want to stay for longer than six months, you may wish to apply for a *carte de séjour*, available for the hefty sum of up to FG750,000 (or less, if you're a skilled negotiator) from the same office.

It's possible to pick up **visas for onward travel** in Conakry for all neighbouring countries, plus Ghana, Morocco, Nigeria, Togo and Cape Verde. See p.569 for a full list of addresses.

The only **health certificate** formally required is yellow fever but it's best, as usual, to have a cholera certificate too. You will have to show your vaccination certificate at the airport, and may frequently be asked for it at Guinea's notorious checkpoints. You no longer need a **photography permit**, but you should still be very discreet.

Checkpoints

Checkpoints can make travel around the country bothersome. Every larger town has an army barricade at its entry and exit, and Conakry's main roads get blocked off after 11pm. Checkpoints are staffed by a mix of military, police, anti-gang units, customs and gendarmerie. They exist for the sole purpose of maintaining the officials who operate them, and some will try anything to find a fault with your passport, visa or, if nothing works, your vaccination papers. Put on a stony face, don't accept their made-up reasons as to why you're in breach of the law (such as claiming that passports aren't valid after midnight), and you won't have to pay. If nothing helps, FG1000 is a sufficient bribe, though with around fifteen stops on the road to Labé alone to negotiate, paying for being left alone can get expensive. The stops near the border to Sierra Leone,

Liberia and Côte d'Ivoire are more trouble-some, as are Conakry's night barricades. You're not advised to venture out alone in Conakry at night, and definitely not to argue with drunken military. Always **carry your passport** and **vaccination certificate** with you.

If you intend to travel the entire country, you're strongly advised to apply for an **ordre de mission** from the Ministry of Tourism. This is a signed and stamped official paper that will get you past checkpoints without any difficulty (you won't even need to show your passport). Both the Ministry and Office de Tourisme (see p.561) are usually happy to issue you with an *ordre* (free), and it's certainly worth waiting for it for a couple of days in Conakry, as it will hugely smooth your travels.

Information, websites and maps

It's a good idea to get reliable advice before heading into the country's interior. In Conakry, the **Office de Tourisme** (see "Listings", p.561) is very helpful and can suggest itineraries and help you get an *ordre de mission*. In the regions, it's always worth trying the local **radios rurales**, which are generally well-informed about local attractions and culture. Two **Internet resources** are also worth checking out: Ⓦwww.guinee.net has detailed information on Guinean history, culture and politics; Ⓦwww.boubah.com is the most comprehensive source on current affairs and politics, and also contains some tourist information, plus links to the homepages of Guinea's national papers and other related sites.

As for **maps**, the IGN map of Guinea (published 1992) is definitely worth obtaining before you go, and vital if you intend doing any hiking. For long stays in Conakry, the IGN map of the capital (published in 1982) is out of date, but still worth getting hold of.

Health

Guinea provides some of West Africa's roughest travelling and it's this, rather than

any intrinsic unhealthiness, which can lead to problems. Out in the wilds, the basic health infrastructure is too limited to be a safety net.

Guinea is largely mountainous, and **temperatures** drop quickly after dark in the higher parts. Travelling by public transport, it makes good sense to keep something warm close at hand: your vehicle may roll for hours into the night with your luggage stowed in some inaccessible corner.

Water, as usual, is a major consideration. You may be offered water originating from pumped boreholes, which is usually safe, though not as safe as using bottled water or using purifying tablets (bottled Coyah water is increasingly available in the provinces). Try to avoid wading through slow-flowing waters and dry-season pools, since there's a high incidence of **bilharzia**.

Malaria is a major health risk throughout the entire country, and you are strongly advised to take precautions. **Yellow fever** has become an increasing problem, and large vaccination missions are undertaken to combat the disease.

Costs, money and banks

Guinea uses its own currency, the **Franc Guinéen** (FG). With the abolition of Sekou Touré's syli currency, the Guinean franc was reintroduced at the same value as the CFA franc. It has slipped to a rate of FG16,200 to CFA5000. In mid-2003, the official exchange rates were $1 = FG2000 and £1 = FG3200.

You'll need to make sure you've got enough cash on you before travelling upcountry, since if you run out, you'll have to rely on an expensive Western Union transfer or return to Conakry. The **Banque Internationale pour le Commerce et l'Industrie de la Guinée** (BICIGUI) is the country's main bank, with (generally efficient) branches in Conakry, Boké, Fria, Kankan, Kamsar, Kissidougou, Labé, Macenta and Nzérékoré. All these will probably change dollars and pounds sterling cash, though only the branch in Conakry cashes traveller's cheques and has an ATM. Don't count on finding banks anywhere else. The lack of banks may force you to change money unofficially. In most towns, the **black market** generally flourishes around markets and the *gare voiture*. You'll get a far better rate than at the banks, but you're advised to go with a local friend, if possible, to avoid getting ripped off or robbed. **Credit cards** can only be used in a few of the larger hotels, and to pay for car rental and air tickets.

Costs

Guinea may be poor, but visiting isn't cheap. Cheap **hotels** outside Conakry charge FG10,000–20,000 a room. Rice and sauce are usually around FG1000, and you can get several pieces of most kinds of fruit for FG50 or FG100. **Conakry**, by contrast, is much more expensive than the provinces, particularly for accommodation – you'll be lucky to get a basic room for FG40,000.

Transport costs can also be high, especially if you're renting a car or travelling in your own vehicle. A litre of petrol costs FG1400–1600. Seat prices on taxis are fixed on the main routes. Fares are cheap (FG18,000 from Conakry to Labé, for instance), but you'll be squeezed inside a heavily overloaded vehicle. If you prefer a little comfort, you can always pay the double rate and enjoy the luxury of having the front seat all to yourself.

Getting around

Most travellers find Guinea the toughest country to get around in West Africa. Apart from internal flights, there's no alternative to travelling by road: journeys are frequently long and often follow tedious waits while seats are being filled.

Only a few overgrown tracks remain of the once-famous Conakry–Kankan **railway line**, and there hasn't been a passenger rail service for years.

Bush taxis, trucks and buses

Transport on Guinea's main routes is usually by **bush taxi**, usually crammed Peugeot 504s – the front seat is always shared by at least two people (avoid the space above the gearshift, unless you feel like getting very close to the driver). On more remote byways, you might find all sorts of vehicles, anything from relatively new minibuses to converted goods vehicles and lorries. There are occasional **bus services** run by private companies. Most of these are restricted to the Fouta Djalon, and all originate in Conakry. Never be tempted to climb on the back of a **truck** (*gros camion*), as they regularly break down, overturn, and are generally renowned for having dodgy brakes.

Before you step into any vehicle, have a look to see what sort of condition it's in and (if you have a choice) opt for the one least likely to break down or kill you (cars get driven until they fall to pieces). The **fare** is usually payable before the trip. On regular routes, you can generally rely on the price given, and you'll be handed a ticket. Travel by bush taxi is relatively cheap: the equivalent of £10/$15 will get you from Conakry to Kankan (for example), though prepare for much higher rates if you're travelling between small villages, as you'll often have to rent the whole car. The price of **baggage**, by contrast, is negotiable; bargain hard to avoid being ripped off.

A comfortable and entertaining alternative to travelling by taxi is the **post service**, whose well-maintained minibuses link the central post office in Conakry with all major cities. Prices are a little cheaper than for a taxi, and you get a whole seat to yourself. Journeys are leisurely, with halts at every local post office (though you'll rarely be stopped at checkpoints). Tickets have to be bought in advance by contacting the post office in Conakry (see "Listings", p.568).

Routes and frequencies

The road from **Conakry to Mamou** is the busiest in the country, with bush taxis running until early afternoon. The trip to Mamou takes five hours along a smooth, well-surfaced road. **Mamou to Labé** (3hr) is also busy, and the road is in good condition. **Mamou to Faranah** is fairly quiet, with few local vehicles. The road from Mamou to **Kankan** is riddled with potholes as far as **Kouroussa**, where a brand new, perfectly straight and flat road takes you the rest of the way. You are not advised to travel from

Kankan to Nzérékoré via Kerouané unless equipped with a sturdy 4WD and exceptionally good off-road driving skills – not even Guinea's taxi drivers use this route, as breakdowns are almost unavoidable, and you might wait days for help to arrive. Expect long waits for bush taxis along any of the non-tarmac roads between the country's smaller towns: the more remote your destination, the less frequent transport will be. Your best (sometimes your only) chance of finding a taxi in small villages is on the local **market day**; ask locally for information.

Domestic flights

Guinea's **domestic air service** has recently experienced a revival, with Air Guinée now flying several times weekly to all the country's major domestic airports: Sambailo (Koundara), Boké, Labé, Kankan, Siguiri, Nzérékoré and Kissidougou. Most tickets cost around FG100,000. There are also less frequent domestic flights operated by Paramount Airlines. Details are given on p.570 and in "Moving on" boxes throughout the chapter.

Car rental

Car rental rates are extortionate. It's not unusual to pay FG100,000–200,000 per day for a 4WD, the high costs reflecting the damage wrought by Guinea's road system. There are some Hertz outlets in Conakry city, at the airport and the *Novotel* (see p.564), but none upcountry. There are always people in town along Avenue de la République offering private car-hire deals, while the Centre Culturel Franco-Guinéen (see p.569) may also be able to set you up

with some informal car hire, but this won't be much cheaper than through more formal outlets. You always have to hire a driver along with the car. If bought from a pump, **essence** (petrol/gasoline) costs around FG1600/litre, while **gasoil** (diesel) is FG1300/litre. Both can be bought by the jerrycan from market traders in cheaper but diluted form.

Other forms of transport

Guinea is wonderful territory for **hiking**, **cycling** and **motorbiking**. Reliable guides for hiking trips around the Fouta Djalon can be found at the *Tangama* hotel in Dalaba or the *Tata* hotel in Labé. It's also worth contacting the Office de Tourisme or Mondial Tours in Conakry (see p.569). You'll need to be self-sufficient and well-equipped, with a tent, cooking equipment, water bottles, spares if you're cycling, and as much time as possible.

Guinea also has several **canoeing** rivers – the upper Niger (see p.585) is probably the best.

Accommodation

There's been a recent boom in **hotel** building in Conakry, while facilities in the provinces are also slowly being improved. The Fouta Djalon has the best hotels outside Conakry. In the remotest parts of the country, you'll have to content yourself with fairly basic lodgings. There are hardly any hostels or campsites.

Cheap places (❶) are usually primitive: electricity is sporadic and water generally

---

Accommodation price codes

Accommodation prices in this chapter are coded according to the following scale, whose equivalent in pounds sterling/US dollars is used throughout the book. Prices refer to the rate you can expect to pay for a room with two beds. Single rooms, or single occupancy, will normally cost at least two-thirds of the twin-occupancy rate. For further details see Basics, p.51.

❶ Under FG16,000 (under £5/$8).
❷ FG16,000–32,000 (£5–10/$8–16).
❸ FG32,000–48,000 (£10–15/$16–24).
❹ FG48,000–64,000 (£15–20/$24–32).

❺ FG64,000–96,000 (£20–30/$32–48).
❻ FG96,000–128,000 (£30–40/$48–64).
❼ FG128,000–160,000 (£40–50/$64–80).
❽ Over FG160,000 (over £50/$80).

comes in buckets (though it may sometimes be warmed for you). In smaller towns and villages you can always ask to see the *sous-préfet* (district officer) with a view to spending a night at the **villa** (accommodation for visiting government employees). Not all of them are welcoming, and you'll have to bargain. **Cheaper mid-range places (❷–❸)** are usually modest hotels, normally with self-contained rooms and a choice of fan or a/c; moving up the price scale there are also some reasonable business and tourist-class hotels (❹–❺) with self-contained a/c rooms and a restaurant. At the **top end** of the scale (❻–❽), there are a few luxury establishments with pool and other special features.

As for **private accommodation**, Guineans are very hospitable, and once it's understood that you need a roof, you'll repeatedly be offered places to stay in people's compounds. Don't forget to pay and contribute to meals.

Camping, in the bush, shouldn't be a problem. Doing so near large towns is bound to cause suspicion, and you might end up having to bribe someone to avoid hassle.

Electricity and water

Guinea's **electricity supplies** are very erratic and depend strongly on the season. During the rainy season and shortly after, when reservoirs are full and hydro-electric stations running properly, you might occasionally be treated to 24 hours of electricity. In the dry season (Dec–March), electricity is usually only supplied at night, while 24-hour cuts can occur. Luxury hotels have their own generators, while smaller hotels and guest-houses are more likely to rely on state provision, or only switch on their generators at night. Remote villages aren't connected to any electricity services. Wherever you are, always have a torch and a few candles handy.

Don't expect to find **running water** outside established hotels. Many cheap places, especially in the interior, only have bucket water drawn from a well. Just like electricity, water supplies dwindle with the dry season. If you're staying with locals, be aware that each bucket of water you use may be precious.

Eating and drinking

Guinean food is based on three main ingredients – rice, leaves and groundnuts – but there's a terrific variety of delicious flavours. Hotel restaurants all over the country serve **European food** – you can always rely on them for chicken and chips if all else fails. **Street food** is a serious business, with big pots of rice, sauces, chipped yams, potatoes and bananas – but keep a careful eye on hygiene. If you're not alone, order for one person at a time and share – servings are on the gigantic side. Every region also has its own **local specialties**. Fish and spicy food are most common in Conakry and near the coast. The Fouta Djalon's classic meals are **fonio** (millet couscous) and sauce, or **lacciri e kosan** (sweetened or salted maize couscous served with sour milk). **Tori**, a steamed cassava stodge, and **yams** are a staple of the diet in Haute Guinée, while Guinée Forestière has the best **aloko** (plantains) and **atiéké**, a grated cassava dish that originated in Côte d'Ivoire.

The consistently delicious – and usually meatless – **sauce de feuilles** is best made with the finely chopped leaves of young cassava, sweet potato or aubergine. **Bouillon** is usually a beef or mutton stew made with offal. **Mafé** is the standard term for rich, usually meaty, groundnut sauce, and fish or meat **brochettes** (little kebabs) are common everywhere. **Bush meat** of various kinds is mostly found in Guinée Forestière: bush rats are tasty; if it's monkey, make sure it's been very well cooked or you risk being poisoned.

There's an abundance of delicious **fruits** all year round. **Bananas** in various shapes and sizes are sold everywhere, but are particularly good around Nzérékoré. Kindia is **mango** heaven from April to May, though heavy mango trees line streets all over the country. **Papayas** reach gigantic sizes, are very sweet and are available most of the year. **Oranges** are the biggest fruit crop; in the Fouta Djalon they're abundant from November to April and cheap enough to buy all day as a drink. The Fouta is also the place to come for huge **avocados**.

Beer drinkers can choose between locally brewed Skol (FG1000 for a half-litre) and Guiluxe, Guinea's "national beer". **Palm**

wine is common in non-Muslim areas such as Guinée Forestière and some coastal regions. The most popular **spirits** are pastis, whiskey and gin. Guinea being a predominantly Muslim country, bars are usually hidden behind grimy plastic curtains and generally only visited by men and prostitutes. People do drink (often lots) in nightclubs, but tend to exercise discretion.

There are all the usual bottled **soft drinks**. White **coffee** (Nescafé/*café au lait*) is served as a rule with *pain beurre*, not drunk on its own. For black coffee order a **petit café noir**, and you'll get a strong espresso made from ground coffee beans rather than instant powder. Guinea's *kinkeliba* herbal tea is healthy and worth a try. **Sour milk**, laced with sugar, is more of a meal than a drink.

Communications

Guinea's **telecommunications** network is disastrous: there are public telecentres everywhere, but you're never guaranteed a line beyond Conakry, while phoning the capital from the provinces can take days. Calls to Europe cost FG4000 per minute, though street hustlers offer clandestine connections for FG1000–1500. Several operators compete for **mobile phone** business, but Guinea only has coverage in the immediate environs of Conakry.

The **post service** isn't guaranteed either. Things do occasionally go missing, either by theft or in the general disarray of the central post office. If you're expecting something valuable, it's better to have it sent to your embassy or consulate. Post office opening hours vary (Mon–Sat 8am–5pm in Conakry, 7.30 or 8am–4pm in Kankan and Nzérékoré). There are other main post offices at Boké, Kindia, Labé and Faranah – you can (theoretically at least) phone or fax abroad from any of these offices.

Internet access is steadily spreading all over Guinea, but the country is still more poorly provisioned than the West African average, and it's still the case that the first

Guinea's IDD country code is ☏224.

Internet café in any town invariably exploits its monopoly: be sure to ascertain the exact tariff before sitting down – it shouldn't ever exceed FG5000 per hour.

The media

All Guinean **TV and radio** is state-controlled, which means that TV programmes are full of government propaganda and radio is dominated by Guinean music, though the music of other African countries and Cuba also gets a look in (unlike European and American music). Radiodiffusion-Télévision Guinéenne (RTG) broadcasts radio programmes in French, Susu, Malinké and Fula and puts out evening TV in French with news in six Guinean languages. Cultural programming is a priority, and the **Radios Rurales** in Kankan, Kindia, Labé, Nzérékoré, Mamou and Faranah broadcast mainly traditional music. A short-wave radio is worth having in order to keep up with the BBC, VOA or other foreign stations.

The national **press** used to consist only of *Horoya*, a weekly rag of inspired awfulness carrying limited African news. These days there are several other newspapers, and you'll find that the press is far more critical of state and government than radio or TV. The main independent papers are *L'Observateur*, *la Lance*, *L'Enqueteur*, *L'Indépendant* and *Le Lynx* – the last is a satirical weekly that is equally scornful of the government and the opposition. If you're famished for overseas news, foreign papers and magazines are increasingly available in Conakry. Try the large supermarkets, street vendors in town or bookshops.

Entertainment

The best place to check up on the latest **cultural events** is the Centre Culturel Franco-Guinéen in Conakry (see p.569). They have regular exhibitions, concerts and films, and are generally well-informed about events in and around Conakry. **Theatre** is getting some encouragement, and there are several young groups that do great stuff, though they suffer from a lack of decent venues. Try to catch one of the regular rehearsals (actual performances are rare) of the historical ballet troupe **Ballets Africains**, founded by Keita Fodeba in the early 1960s, and still one of the most renowned dance troupes of West Africa. Equally enticing are the shows of the young **Circus Baobab**, West Africa's first aerial circus, which merges traditional dancing and drumming with hip hop and experimental performance. The troupe rehearses every day at the Imprimerie Patrice Lumumba. If you go there on a Saturday morning, you'll be able to witness a rehearsal by the Ensemble Instrumental, one of the country's famous traditional ensembles, at the same time.

For more on **Guinean music**, see p.552.

Cinema

A lack of resources means that **cinema** has never been a major cultural force in Guinea. Even so, some fine films have come out of the country, notably *Naitou* (1982) by **Diakité Moussa Kemoko**. Featuring the Ballet National de Guinée, the film recounts an African folk tale exclusively through music and dance – a radical, and universally comprehensible, attempt to deal with the issue of the appropriate language for African cinema.

Among the newer film-makers, **Mohammed Camara**, who trained as an actor, made an impressive entry at the 1993 FESPACO with the short film *Denko*. Camara tackles his difficult subject with sensitivity: a mother commits incest to restore sight to her blind son and reveals the hypocrisy of society through her transgression. Diving deeper into controversy, Camara's *Dakan* (1997) was the first film in sub-Saharan Africa to treat the subject of male homosexuality; filming was often interrupted by protests. **David Aschkar** also created a stir with his 1991 experimental documentary *Allah Tanto* – the story of the director's father, Maroff Aschkar, who was Guinea's ambassador to the United Nations until his imprisonment and death in one of Sekou Touré's infamous political prisons.

In a totally different vein, film historian and critic **Manthia Diawara**'s documentary *Rouch in Reverse* (1995) is an interesting analysis of one of the most influential ethnographic film-makers ever, and provides a rare look at European anthropological stud-

ies from an African perspective. **Cheick Doukouré**'s first feature – *Paris Selon Moussa* – won the Human Rights prize at the 2003 FESPACO for its touching tale of a farmer sent to Paris to buy a water pump for his farming co-op. Check the Centre Culturel Franco-Guinéen (see p.569) for films by the French film-maker **Laurent Chevalier**. His documentary of *djembe* player Mammadi Keita and his cinematic realization of Camara Laye's *L'enfant Noir* are both worth watching. The Centre Culturel Franco-Guinéen can also direct you to films by Guinea's young generation of directors.

Football

Guineans are not such big **football** fans as their neighbours in some other West African countries, partly because the lack of stadiums and slow media development has held the game back. Look out, nonetheless, for recent league champions Satellite FC and Horoya AC, as well as cup winners AS Kaloum Stars and Hafia FC (all from Conakry).

Directory

Airport departure tax Usually included in the price of your ticket.

Cassettes Guinea's street and market vendors offer the best music deal in West Africa – about FG2000 for cassettes, FG1000 for pirate copies.

Photography People are particularly averse to having their photos taken by strangers, and you're likely to cause a scene if you get out your camera and start snapping away – while if you're unlucky enough to get any military personnel or checkpoints in the picture, chances are your camera will be confiscated and you'll have to pay a lot of money to get it back. Be very careful with your camera in Conakry's inner city, near the port, and in the markets.

Public holidays Aside from New Year's Day, May 1 (Labour Day) and the usual shifting Islamic calendar, the principal Guinean holidays are April 3 (anniversary of the 1984 coup) and October 2 (Independence Day). Christian holidays are observed more haphazardly, mainly by large businesses and government offices.

The commemoration of other significant moments in Guinea's history depends on more ephemeral political considerations. Dates include May 14 (the anniversary of the founding of the PDG party); September 28 (the anniversary of the "No" vote; see p.546); March 8 (International Women's Day); and August 27 (the day in 1977 when the market women revolted and forced Sekou Touré to change tack).

Regional and local non-Islamic festivals were attacked as sectarian and unproductive during the Touré dictatorship, and for many the generation-long repression destroyed their viability. You might still come across one if you're well-placed and well-timed – January to March is the most propitious season.

Religion As usual, the pig is a fair indication of the boundaries of Islam. You won't see many between the jungles of the northwest and the hilly forests in the southeast. Islam continues to consolidate and displace the indigenous religions, and its international dimension is increasingly important in shaping Guinean society. The vast majority of practising Muslims (more than three-quarters of the population) are members of the Tijaniya brotherhood, though the Wahabiya school is increasingly gaining ground. Christianity is a minority religion, only significant locally around Conakry and in Guinée Forestière.

Sexual attitudes Polygamy is common and prostitution is widespread, but homosexuality is frowned upon – be discreet.

Toilet paper Hard to obtain except in major towns.

Trouble Guinea is a military state, and though you're unlikely to have any problems, you should be aware of this state of affairs – if you're confronted with trumped-up accusations, you will usually have to resolve them with a "voluntary donation". Driving in your own vehicle, you will experience repeated efforts at extortion from the police and military, ranging from mildly humorous (and irritating) to hysterical (and contemptible). Treat the police with caution, force out some humour, defuse them with cigarettes and never argue with them – they will happily keep you hanging around for hours.

Wildlife Guinea has two national parks: the Parc National Haut Niger (see p.585), near Kouroussa, and Parc National Niokolo-Badiar (see p.583) along the Guinea-Bissau border at Koundara. There are also a large number of *forêts classées*, designed to help preserve the environment. Guinea is one of the few West African countries that has preserved a diverse indigenous fauna. Most large species – including chimpanzees, hippos, elephants, lions and buffalo – survive, unprotected and rarely seen. It's been forty years since any field surveys were carried out and the current position is hazy. Hunting appears to be as much of a threat as environmental destruction. Regionally, outside the parks the best wildlife zones are the hilly acacia savanna in the northeast, between the Tinkisso River and the Malian border; the undulating bush and grassland between Mamou and Faranah where the Fouta Djalon slopes down to Sierra Leone; and the southeast highlands, particularly east of the Macenta–Nzérékoré road.

Women travellers Women travellers have a reasonably easy time in Guinea, sheltered from some of the hassles of Mali, Senegal or Côte d'Ivoire by the lack of tourists. So long as your French is adequate, you'll find quick access to people's homes and lives wherever you go. Be prepared for low-key sexual harassment, and respond to roadside hassle firmly and unambiguously, and you'll be left in peace. You might prefer to describe yourself as something other than a tourist, which carries slightly pejorative connotations. Remember that you're in a Muslim country, so don't wear provocatively short skirts or tiny tops in the street. Sexy wear is perfectly passable, even expected, in nightclubs, but will make you look like easy prey during the day.

A brief history of Guinea

Some of West Africa's most influential **old empires** stretched across the area covered by present-day Guinea. It was on Guinean soil in the early thirteenth century that the sorcerer-king Soumaoro Kanté was defeated by **Sundiata Keita** – Sundiata subsequently established the Mali Empire, which stretched at its height all along the Niger from today's regions of Mali and Guinea to Mauritania. Its capital was at Niani, today an insignificant little town in Haute Guinée.

In 1725, Muslim **Fula** fought the first of many West African jihads, establishing a flourishing Muslim theocracy in the Fouta Djalon, which survived until the late nineteenth century, when infighting between the Muslim leaders prevented them putting up any unified resistance against the French.

The French occupation

The first French expeditions into the hinterland of the Guinea coast took place from Boké, a creek-head base whose population had been in contact with Europeans – mostly Portuguese – since the fifteenth century. Following the expansion initiated by Colonel Faidherbe across the Sahel, and to prevent the British linking The Gambia with Sierra Leone, the French commanders in "the rivers of the south" (as the Guinea region was known) forced protection treaties with dozens of small rulers through the middle of the nineteenth century. In the 1880s they came up against the first serious resistance in the shape of the guerilla army of the **Almamy Samory Touré**. Once Samory had been deported to Gabon in 1898, there was only relatively minor resistance to the French. The forest communities put up a fight, and were aided by the hilly jungle in which the French couldn't use cavalry, but their political organization was weak and the villages submitted one after another in the years leading up to World War I.

In the early colonial days, wild **rubber** was Guinea's main crop. By 1905 the commerce was supporting a 700-strong Lebanese community in Conakry. But the export declined after 1913 as plantation markets opened in Southeast Asia. By 1914, the French had driven a **railway** over 600km through mountain terrain to the river port of Kankan, linking Conakry with Bamako by rail and river. This, however, was a strategic railway rather than a commercial one. Apart from limited gold and diamonds, Haute Guinée didn't appear to offer much return. Better prospects lay in the forest regions to the south, where coffee and other tropical crops were developed on French-owned plantations, and near the coast and southern foothills of the Fouta Djalon, where bananas flourished. The French largely neglected Guinea's biggest prize, however: **bauxite** (aluminium ore). The country still possesses a third of the world's reserves, but it wasn't until the 1950s that the French began to exploit these systematically.

French **rule** in Guinea followed standard patterns except that, more so than elsewhere, the opportunities to become a privileged *evolué* were desperately few: until 1935 there was no secondary **education** in Guinea and, on the eve of independence, only 1.3 percent of Guinean children were receiving even primary schooling. With one singular exception, almost all the prominent Guineans before independence came from wealthy families who had sent them to the Ecole Normale William Ponty near Dakar.

The rise of nationalism

Ahmed Sekou Touré, a Malinké speaker from Faranah, first came to attention as a disruptive and perspicacious

The rise of the jihad state

The original inhabitants of the highlands were Jalonke, Baga and Nalo – all of whom coexisted in relative harmony, herding on the hills and farming the valleys. The region was known then as **Jallonkadugu**, after its dominant inhabitants. The first **Fula immigrants** arrived in the fifteenth century from Tekrur on the Senegal River and Djenné on the Niger River in search of pasture for their herds of cattle. Their numbers increased when **Koli Tengela** and his followers settled in the north of the Fouta, looking to establish an area free of Muslim influence. This relatively peaceful state of affairs began to change when the first Muslim Fula arrived in the late seventeenth century from Macina in Mali and Fouta Toro in Senegal. They began spreading Islam, and in 1725 started West Africa's first *jihad* under the leadership of **Karamoko Alfa Barry**, who won a breakthrough military victory against the animist populations at Talansan in 1730.

The **Muslim Theocracy of Fouta Djalon** emerged as a result of this victory, with Karamoko Alfa Barry as its leader, or *almamy*, and its capital at **Timbo**. Karamoko's nephew, Ibrahima Sory, took power when his uncle went insane in 1767 and the kingdom was divided into nine provinces, one of which, **Labé**, became a noted centre of learning. There were **conversions** among the animists, but many fled. Throughout the nineteenth century, Labé drew apart from Timbo, and by the 1890s its territory extended over most of northwest Guinea, making Labé as powerful a state as the Timbo-based kingdom of Fouta Djalon itself. With the arrival of the French, separate treaties were entered into with both realms. Today, both **Alfa Yaya**, the great-grandson of Karamoko Alfa Barry and the last ruler of Labé, and **Bokar Biro**, the last ruler of Timbo, are considered folk heroes.

schoolboy in the late 1930s, and then as founder of Guinea's first union, the Post and Telecommunications Workers, in 1946. In 1947, Touré and others formed the Guinean section of the Rassemblement Démocratique Africain (RDA; a broad alliance of French West African political groupings) and named it the **Parti Démocratique de Guinée** (PDG).

Guinea made huge strides after the war, with major investment in the bauxite industry and a rapidly urbanizing workforce. Touré, meanwhile, was making his name as a politician and unionist. He was a delegate to the 1947 Communist French Trade Unions (CGT) Congress in Dakar and, with support from the French Communist party, he backed several **strikes** in the early 1950s and produced the labour newspaper *L'Ouvrier*. The most trenchant strike was the ten-week action in 1953 over the demand for a twenty-percent wage rise to accompany a reform in the labour laws – this made a lasting impression on the Guinean public and across French West Africa.

Sekou Touré's rise to power

By the time of the strike, Sekou Touré was the territorial assembly member for Beyla. From this platform, he and other trade unionists began a campaign to disaffiliate and Africanize the Guinean sections from the parent French unions.

In 1955, at the age of 33, Touré became **mayor of Conakry**. A year later, he also became first secretary of the **African Federation of Labour Unions** (UGTAN), created after the break of the Guinean unions from the French. Uniquely in West Africa, Touré now succeeded in marrying the PDG party with the labour federation. In 1957, Sekou Touré became vice-president of the new **Territorial Council of Government**, a post that made him effectively prime minister of Guinea under the low-profile Governor Jean Ramadier. Touré firmly advocated an independent West African federation of states and denounced Senghor of Senegal and Houphouët-Boigny of Côte d'Ivoire as puppets for wanting to consolidate the French connection.

One of Touré's first major acts was the **abolition of chiefs** and their replacement by party cadres. The move was particularly resented in the Fouta Djalon, where chiefdoms had some traditional legitimacy. It was accompanied by some bloody settling of scores: the groundwork for the Guinean state security network was being prepared. With **de Gaulle's return to power** in France, Sekou Touré was soon given the chance to wield full power. The new constitution of the French Fifth Republic was unacceptable to him, and the idea of a free federation of completely independent states wasn't acceptable to de Gaulle – who insisted on their giving up some of their sovereignty to the federal government.

De Gaulle's visit to Conakry to put his case was a waste of time. He would "raise no obstacles" in Guinea's path if the country chose to "secede" from the community of French states, but he would "draw conclusions". Sekou Touré replied, "We prefer poverty in freedom to riches in slavery", and the two leaders snubbed each other at every opportunity for the rest of the visit. "Good Luck to Guinea", sneered de Gaulle on his departure.

Guinea under Sekou Touré

While other Francophone leaders thought he was bluffing, Sekou Touré prepared his country to go it alone. On September 28, 1958, there was a 95 percent "No" vote to the referendum on staying in the French community. On October 2, **independence** was declared.

The example of Ghana under Nkrumah was an inspiration, while the swift reaction of the French in Guinea – flight with the booty, sabotage of the infrastructure, burning of files and cancellation of all cooperation and invest-

ment – was made to seem like good riddance by the party, though the severity of the withdrawal was a vindictive blow. The country had virtually no technical expertise and a total of six graduates. It started work from scratch, with aid from Czechoslovakia, the Soviet Union and seven other Eastern-bloc countries, and solid support from the European and Third World left. Morale was high and the PDG organization initially effective.

France excluded Guinea from the CFA franc zone of the newly independent Francophone nations. Guinea adopted its own franc (and later the syli) which isolated it further from neighbouring states, and hindered what little (non-French) trade remained, but at least stemmed the drain of capital to France. Despite Nato fears that Guinea might become a West African Cuba, United States President Eisenhower waited six months before even sending an ambassador to Conakry, for fear of offending de Gaulle. In 1962, a substantial American **aid package** was finally worked out and the Peace Corps went in. Revolution aside, American aid and investment, particularly in the profitable bauxite industry, have been firm ever since.

Poverty in slavery

As the first few years of independence unrolled, Sekou Touré, the Pan-African ideologue and co-author of the OAU charter, began to be seen in a less glamorous light as his extreme policies started to bite and the popular enthusiasm of 1959–60 sloughed away. A planned economy without planners was taking shape (or rather not), state enterprises were extended, private business curtailed and a small but growing middle class was reaping illicit benefits from mismanagement and fraud.

The results of the first **three-year plan** weren't encouraging. Critics in the PDG complained the party was out of its depth in trying to control the market economy, and mistaken in extending power to the illiterate masses.

Sekou Touré scolded them in a twelve-hour speech designed to weed out the party faithful from the conspirators. He wrote later: "Everything became rotten, the elite enjoyed riding in cars and building villas."

There was a massive **market crackdown** in November 1964, with widespread harassment of traders and confiscation of assets. Limits were set on the number of traders allowed outside the state sphere, and arrests, interrogations and arbitrary punishments grew in frequency. The party was moulded in Touré's image and political life stagnated. The very freedoms that lay at the heart of party policy (on paper anyway) were savagely suppressed. Thousands fled the country.

In 1965 a group of opposition exiles, the **Front pour la Libération de Guinée** (FLING), began to organize outside the country with tacit support from Senegal and Côte d'Ivoire and less discreet help from France. The **"traders' plot"** of 1966 – an apparent attempt to install a liberal government with capitalist leanings – resulted in the complete rupture of diplomatic relations with Paris.

The Terror

Guinea now entered a dark period of isolationism and widespread terror. At the end of 1967 the eighth party congress had radicalization of the revolution at the top of the agenda. To shore up its bankrupt ideology, the party formally adopted a path of **"Socialism"**. Local revolutionary authorities were set up in every village – ostensibly to allow power to flow from the base up; in reality to extend the security blanket to every corner of the country. And as China was promulgating its bloody Cultural Revolution, Guinea, one of China's biggest African aid recipients, started its own campaign against "degenerate intellectuals".

The elaborate and cruelly anti-human security apparatus continued to grow. The army was kept under constant surveillance by a network of junior officers. Early in 1969 came the first big **purge** of figures close to the party leadership – Fodeba Keita, Minister of Justice, met his death in Camp Boiro, the notorious prison camp he himself had helped construct. There was an assassination attempt on Touré and more arrests in Labé the following year.

The invasion and after

Although Sekou Touré had been predicting an "aggression" with more than customary conviction, the country was unprepared for the **invasion** of November 22, 1970. Four hundred troops landed from ships at night and attacked Conakry and the peninsula. This was supposed to trigger a general uprising of Guinean dissidents and the overthrow of Sekou Touré. But although three hundred defenders were killed, and a number of prisoners released by the attackers, none of the key targets (the presidential palace, radio station or airport) was taken. When the invaders' ships moved away 48 hours later, they left behind large numbers of stranded troops who were rounded up and subjected to people's justice.

Reactions to the invasion proved a crucial test of party loyalty and provided the military victory over the "forces of imperialism" that Sekou Touré had always craved. It was, he wrote, "one of those sublime moments of exaltation and patriotism: the affirmation of collective dignity." A United Nations fact-finding mission ascertained that most of the force had been composed of Guinean exiles of FLING and loyalist African soldiers from Portuguese Guinea, commanded by Portuguese officers from the Caetano fascist regime, with West German logistical support. The real aim of the invasion was to destroy the base in Guinea of the **PAIGC guerillas** fighting for independence from Portugal. It was to the lasting humiliation of the Guinea-Conakry opposition that their alliance with Caetano's fascist forces failed.

The purge which followed was predictably brutal. Ninety-one people were sentenced to death and hundreds of others imprisoned and tortured. The hundred-strong German technical mission was expelled and dozens of Europeans spent time in jail in the aftermath.

But the popular rage whipped up by the party against imperialist aggression obscured the **mass violations of human rights** – torture, disappearances, summary executions and detention without trial – that ravaged Guinea through the early 1970s. Tens of thousands of Guineans, particularly Fula-speakers, continued to flee the country every year. As the internal and external pressures against his regime mounted, Sekou Touré resorted to increasingly desperate measures. As there was nothing to encourage farmers, **food shortages** became increasingly common. Obstinately, Touré authorized the local revolutionary authorities to handle all the production and marketing of commodities. Then, early in 1975, came the banning of all private trade and, at the same time, the setting up of agricultural production brigades. The borders were closed and Touré declared a "holy war" against smugglers, who were shot if caught. In the north of the country, the Sahel drought added to deteriorating prospects.

Guinea struggled for two-and-a-half years, going through another purge in 1976 in response to the **"Fula Plot"** (see box below). Meanwhile, the exodus from Guinea continued: by the end of the 1970s, as many as a million Guineans were believed to be living abroad.

The turnaround

In August 1977, **market women** in Conakry and other towns spontaneously rose up against the intolerable trade situation, which made it impossible for them to afford the produce of their own harvests. It was a turning point. Riots flared across the country and several provincial governors were killed. Sekou Touré's resolve collapsed. He began a slow process of **economic liberalization**, as well as adopting a more pragmatic approach

---

The permanent plot

The idea that there was a permanent, **anti-Guinea plot** obsessed the party hierarchy. The first plots had been exposed even before independence, but the climate of conspiracy thickened until virtually any action could be read as suspicious. At the height of Guinea's isolation, "citizen" and "suspect" became virtually synonymous.

For the first decade of independence, most of the "plots" originated outside the country and the party skilfully manipulated them to maintain control, timing announcements to co-ordinate with national events. Internal dissent was simply annihilated wherever it first breathed, usually before any chance of genuine conspiracy. In 1969, however, the focus was shifted squarely to **internal opposition**, and the Fula came under increasingly harsh attack. Touré was convinced that the densely populated Fouta Djalon was trying to secede, with the help of Senegal. Army units at Labé were purged and, after the Portuguese invasion of 1970, it was the Fula who bore the brunt of his revenge.

In 1973, Sekou Touré announced the discovery of a "fifth column active in all walks of life". Again, the Fula came under concerted attack with waves of arrests, executions and disappearances. This ethnic repression culminated in 1976 with the announcement of the **"Fula Plot"** and Touré's declaration that the Fula-speaking peoples were "racist" and "enemies of socialism". Diallo Telli, a Fula, and the first OAU secretary general, was accused of leading a CIA-backed conspiracy. He was arrested and starved to death. If there was any real "permanent plot" during Sekou Touré's tyrannical rule, it would appear to have been his own genocidal one against the Fula. For the present regime of Lansana Conté, as unevenly Susu as Touré's was Malinké, the rehabilitation of Fula confidence remains a priority.

to government, reducing revolutionary rhetoric and making cosmetic improvements in democratic practices and human rights.

In his last few years, Touré left the running of the party and state more and more to a leading clique of ministers while devoting himself to the cultivation of an image as the grand old man of Pan-Africanism – 1982 saw the grotesque spectacle of Touré in Washington being hailed by President Reagan as "a champion of human rights".

Progressive ideas were forgotten, however, as Touré forged close links with **King Hassan** of Morocco (whose side he took in the dispute over Western Sahara), and other bastions of the rigid right. Hassan provided the money desperately needed by Touré to tide him over after the collapse of IMF negotiations in 1983, and arranged with conservative Arab states for Guinea to be the largest recipient of **petro-dollar aid** in sub-Saharan Africa.

In January and February 1984, groups of soldiers were arrested near the Senegalese border and accused of plotting against the government. At the time of **Sekou Touré's death** on March 26, 1984, in a private clinic in Cleveland, it appears that sections of the army had indeed been planning a coup d'état.

The new regime

Colonels **Lansana Conté** (president) and **Diara Traoré** (prime minister) waited several days after the lavish funeral before announcing, after an almost peaceful takeover, the dissolution of the constitution and the party, the freeing of political prisoners, the unbanning of trade unions and the reopening of Guinea to private investment. Judicial reforms began and French was reintroduced as the official language of education. Most of the old party structures swiftly disintegrated. Asked why the military hadn't acted years earlier, Conté said: "the spirit of the Guinean was such that he would not think. Some Guineans behaved like imbeciles. They were remote-controlled."

The **Comité Militaire de Redressement National** was given an enthusiastic welcome and ministers went on foreign tours to introduce the new Guinea and cultivate aid donors. But apart from a general liberalization, it was hard to pinpoint the direction of the new government. There was soon a split with prime minister Traoré, and his post was abolished. Predictably, perhaps, Traoré and fellow Malinké officers attempted a coup against Conté in July 1985. Two years later, it was announced that those involved, together with a number of detainees from Sekou Touré's government – sixty people in all – had been given secret trials and were to be executed. It was widely presumed, however, that most of them had died extra-judicially long before and Conté was merely setting the record straight.

On the **economic front**, Conakry was soon full of French technical advisors and business people. One of the IMF's structural adjustment programmes was put in operation which, coupled with general austerity, state sector job losses, and widespread civil

Achievements

In retrospect, the first quarter-century of independence was a tragic waste. Yet there were one or two significant achievements which can't be overlooked. Touré's radical anticolonial stance has meant that many Guineans have a freedom of political thought that isn't found in the same way in other countries of francophone West Africa, and there's a genuine national pride among people that has so far succeeded in uniting the country's distinct ethnic groups and prevented serious rifts between individual peoples. Sekou Touré also encouraged artistic expression in Guinea and nurtured the creation of a modern musical tradition that inspired many surrounding countries.

service corruption and ostentation, was not warmly received. Conakry boiled over in January 1988 with **street riots** over price rises – which, yet again, had outstripped wage increases. The riots forced the government to back down, and commodity prices were reduced.

The 1990s

The initiative Conté had lost after abolishing the post of prime minister and the subsequent coup attempt was recovered when he increased **civilian representation** in the government, though some of his rivals were banished from Conakry in the process. Malinké speakers have been particularly under-represented since the demise of the old regime and they, together with the Fula, are regarded as the unofficial opposition to Conté's predominantly Susu leadership.

By the end of 1990, serious protests were emerging from schools and the university in Conakry against conditions, educational standards, and the slowness with which democratic reforms were being instituted. A number of students were killed by police or army gunfire during demonstrations. Conté maintained his slow pace, setting up the **Comité Transitoire de Redressement National** (CTRN), which he ensured had some recently departed members of his own cabinet sitting in it. Meanwhile, demonstrations and strikes continued.

In 1991, **Alpha Condé**, long-exiled Malinké opposition leader and Secretary General of the Rassemblement du Peuple Guinéen (RPG), briefly returned home, but fled soon after when the security forces fired on a crowd of his supporters. Despite this setback, the RPG was formally registered in April 1992, with Condé returning once more to Guinea.

Lansana Conté himself formed a puppet party as a front for the CTRN. Called the **Parti de l'Unité et du Progrès** (PUP), it focused on the parts of the country where the CTRN was providing development funds. Despite intimidating the opposition and operating with state support and government money, Conté's PUP was insufficiently confident of its electoral strengths to stick to the election dates scheduled for the end of 1992. The CTRN deferred the presidential and legislative elections for another year, during which Guinea saw some of the most savage political violence of the post-Touré era.

In the **presidential election**, finally held in December 1993, Conté polled just over 51 percent, while the votes from two massively anti-Conté (and pro-Condé) prefectures, Kankan and Siguiri, were disallowed for reasons of the RPG's "malpractice". As it became clear that the opposition had been cheated, there were chaotic scenes at polling stations. Several Guinean embassies, acting as polling stations for Guinean émigrés in other parts of West Africa, were ransacked.

As "democratic" presidential elections in West Africa go, Guinea's first effort was blatantly dishonest and unimpressive. In its wake, Condé's RPG and the Parti pour le Renouveau et le Progrès (PRP), led by a former journalist on *Jeune Afrique* magazine, **Siradiou Diallo**, formed an alliance to contest the legislative elections. In response to this and other signs of opposition, the government disenfranchised Guineans overseas, thus excluding some three million potential voters. Meanwhile, there were rumours of a coup attempt, and arrests in May 1994.

The **multiparty general elections** to the legislative assembly were finally held on June 11, 1995. In the run-up to them, opposition rallies throughout Guinea were disrupted by the security forces. Condé and Diallo, having earlier said they would not boycott the elections despite the PUP's flagrant rigging, ultimately pulled out on the day. Although the coalition won about a quarter of the seats (28 out of 114 seats to the PUP's 71) they boycotted the national assembly.

Late pay increases was the provocation that led part of the army to **mutiny** in February 1996. The incident – which came close to toppling Conté, when various units seized the airport and radio and TV stations, and shelled the city centre – was defused when Conté, banged up in his palace, offered an immediate 100 percent pay increase and no prosecutions, in exchange for his freedom. True to form, he reneged on the deal soon afterwards and a ragged series of trials and hearings ran for the next two years.

In the (once again, openly rigged) **elections of December 1998**, Conté's PUP scored 56 percent against a divided opposition. Alfa Condé, the country's most high-profile opposition leader, had bided his time in exile in Paris – his personal safety in Guinea always in doubt – until days before the election, arriving finally to a hero's welcome in Conakry. Soon after his arrival, he was arrested and accused of being a threat to state security.

Guinea today

Since the late 1990s, Guinea has been on a downward political and economic spiral. In addition to internal problems of state oppression, poverty and corruption, the country has become increasingly embroiled in the conflicts raging in neighbouring countries. Between September 2000 and March 2001 there were repeated attacks by **Liberian** and **Sierra Leonean rebels** at the frontiers, while in the same period **Guinean rebel groups** appeared on the scene, some believed to be soldiers who quit the army at the time of the 1996 mutiny – 1500 Guinean civilians are said to have died in the confrontations that left the town of Guéckédou completely ruined. The conflicts in Liberia and Sierra Leone have also caused huge numbers of refugees to seek sanctuary in Guinea. By the end of 2000, refugee numbers were estimated at 500,000, and though many Sierra Leoneans are now returning home, numbers have again risen since 2002 with the arrival of refugees from the civil war in Côte d'Ivoire.

Guinea suffers further from insecurity over its political future. In November 2001, President Lansana Conté staged a referendum on constitutional changes to allow him to stand for another term, whilst increasing the length of the presidential term from five to seven years and abolishing the age limit of 70. Not surprisingly, this move created strong opposition, and marches from Kankan and Labé to Conakry were blocked by the military, and all opposition leaders temporarily put under arrest. A united opposition alliance, **CODEM**, called for a boycott of the referendum – which produced the inevitable governmental success.

At the time of writing, September 2003, Conté is terminally ill and has returned to his home village – it is unlikely he will be fit to stand for election in December 2003. There is no obvious successor to Conté, and it is expected that the military will once again take power after his death. The uncertainty over the future, aggravated by fears that the conflict in Liberia will spill over into Guinea, has created a climate of anxiety, while water and electricity shortages, fuel price rises and subsequent increases in transport costs caused serious student rebellions in early 2003. Similar protests have been boiling for years, with Kankan, Mamou and Conakry at the centre of student action.

With almost limitless agricultural potential, plus its bauxite, iron and other mineral reserves, Guinea has the potential to become the most prosperous state in West Africa and the region's dominant Francophone nation, yet the next few years are unlikely to bring the relief, justice, and forward-thinking government the country needs so badly.

Music

Guinea's four geographical regions correspond roughly to four population zones, which all have their own forms of **traditional music**. In the lowland coastal area of the west, the **Mande**-related music of the Susu dominates with the sound of the *bongo* lamellaphone and the **balafon** (xylophone) which originated in Susu culture but has become an essential element of Mande music all over West Africa.

Public performances are more difficult to find in the strongly Islamic, **Fula**-inhabited Fouta Djalon highlands, though weddings, baptisms and other community celebrations give visitors the chance to enjoy the breakneck acrobatics and passionate flute playing and drumming of the hugely entertaining *nyamakala* performers.

The eastern savanna of Haute Guinée is mainly occupied by the **Malinké**, whose cultural domain spreads into eastern Mali. The Mande griots are without doubt the leaders of the Guinean music scene, stunning audiences with their refined vocal and instrumental skills and historical knowledge. Guinea's most typical sound – the intricate polyrhythms of **djembe** drumming ensembles – also comes from Haute Guinée.

In Guinea's southeast highland forest region, the **Kissi**, **Toma**, **Guerzé** and **Kono** have nurtured musical traditions which have more in common with the music of Central Africa than the rest of West Africa, dominated by polyphonic cow-horn ensembles, single- and double-headed drums, slit-drums and xylophone-drums. Mask dances are also more common here than elsewhere in Guinea, a legacy of the region's strong animist traditions.

Modern Guinean music

Guinea was once West Africa's most influential musical nation. With independence in 1958 and Sekou Touré's *authenticité* campaign, the government encouraged the creation of a modern sound that married the country's traditional roots with the electric tones, jazz, Cuban and Congolese influences of the big bands. The revolutionary style created during that time still resounds in the latest Guinean releases, and has

influenced the music of most neighbouring countries.

The era's most famous band was the mighty **Bembeya Jazz**, but there were also a bunch of similar orchestras including Les Amazones, the all-female army orchestra; Tele-Jazz de Télimélé, from the Fouta Djalon; Balla et Les Balladins; Keletigui et ses Tambourins; and the forest band Orchestre Nimba Jazz. Their recordings were originally released on the state-owned Syliphone label of the Touré era, and have now been largely re-released on the Paris-based Syllart label.

During the post-Touré years of the mid-1980s, Guinean popular music became increasingly influenced by Antillean *zouk*, which retains its powerful hold over Guinean pop to this day. In addition, reggae, hip hop and techno have gradually merged with Guinean sounds in the work of younger musicians. These days, it's no longer big orchestras, but individual performers who are favoured. Some of the biggest artists include the unrivalled Sekouba Bambino Diabaté, the charming Oumou Dioubaté and her daughter Missia Saran, and Mory Kanté, the "techno griot".

Compilations

The Rough Guide to Mali & Guinea (World Music Network). A fine selection of Guinean tracks from Balla et ses Balladins, Sekouba

Bambino, Bembeya Jazz, Jali Musa Jawara and the late Momo Wandel Soumah.

Les Ballets Africains

West Africa's foremost musical ensemble, created in 1952, have made many international tours and perform a spectacular live show.

Héritage (Buda). Recorded in Germany in 1995, this production ranges across the country's cultural heritage – from the mythical origin of the *balafon* to family totems – to create a richly woven sound tapestry.

Bembeya Jazz

Formed in 1961, Guinea's greatest band of the post-independence era mixes Malinké praise songs with Congolese musical threads and Islamic traditions with Cuban styles. The death in 1973 of their celebrated lead singer Aboubacar Demba Camera robbed Africa of one of its greatest vocalists. The band is now led by lead guitarist, Sekou "Diamond Fingers" Diabaté, and is currently enjoying a revival in its fortunes after a period of near complete silence.

Live – 10 Ans de Succès (Bolibana, France). Atmospheric recording from 1971 of Guinea's most famous band at their finest. Wild solos from Diabaté alternate with the unforgettable voice of Aboubacar Demba Camera.

Bembeya Jazz National (Sonodisc/Esperance, France). Bembeya in the mid-1980s with their classic recording of "Lanaya", featuring the romantic voice of Sekouba Bambino.

Bembeya Jazz (Marabi). This 2002 release of the re-awakened giants makes for entertaining listening, but doesn't measure up to the classic earlier Bembeya releases.

Balla et ses Balladins

One of Guinea's best ever bands, who have superbly modernized classic Malinké songs.

Reminiscin' in tempo with Balla et ses Balladins (Popular African Music). Compilation of greats with the classic Guinea-rumba sound of the 1960s and 1970s, including two stunning versions of one of the greatest Mande love songs, "Sara".

Sekouba Bambino Diabaté

Once Bembeya Jazz's youngest lead singer, Bambino is now Guinea's best-loved artist, gifted both with an ethereal voice and an uncanny instinct for heart-rending melodies, as well as a taste for the experimental.

Kassa (Syllart). A daring album featuring the beautiful ballad "Damanseya".

Sinikan (Sonodisc) African music that isn't afraid to look forward, this is Bambino's most fully realized album to date and sees him experimenting with a wide range of styles, all perfectly executed.

Kade Diawara

Guinea's finest female singer in the Mande tradition.

L'Archange du Manding and **L'Eternelle Kade Diawara** (both on cassette). Wonderful old ballads and love songs from a superb voice.

Oumou Dioubaté

A griotte of the dancefloor from Kankan, and one of the country's most successful artists, based in Paris since the 1980s, Dioubaté earned the soubriquet "La Femme Chic-Shoc" for her style and confrontational approach.

Wambara (Stern's, UK). Stunning melodies, irrepressible beats and great guitar work mark a set of fine songs from a real individual.

Kaloum Star Felenko

Founded in 1969 by Maître Barry, Kaloum Star from Conakry were the last state-run band to be set up during the rule of Sekou Touré.

Felenko (Buda). Fine, well-developed songs: the title track carries a strong flavour of Fela Kuti's Afro-Beat.

Jali Musa Jawara

Mory Kanté's *kora*-playing half-brother leads an excellent acoustic ensemble.

Yasimika (Hannibal, UK). A classic of Mande acoustic music from 1983, never since matched by him, with Jawara's soaring vocals and luscious choruses from Djanka Diabaté and Djenne Doumbia over guitar, *kora* and *balafon*.

Mory Kanté

Mory Kanté started playing music at the age of seven, later joining the Rail Band in Bamako before embarking on a hugely successful solo career playing what he describes as "kora-funk". Loathed by purists, his music has a global village feel that makes him a star of the world stage.

Akwaba Beach (Barclay). Kanté's breakthrough album, with his world-wide hit conversion of the traditional "Yeke yeke" – high-tech *kora* music for the dancefloor.

Tatebola (Arcade/Missliin). Still driven by techno rhythms but in slightly more mellow mode, with a lovely version of the classic kora song "Alla l'aa ke".

Tamala (Arcade/Missliin). Mory Kanté at his best, though the sugary duet with Shola Ama takes some getting used to.

Famoudou Konaté

A master of the *djembe*, the ever-popular, egg-timer-shaped drum of western West Africa, who formerly toured with the Ballets Africains. He now fronts his own Ensemble Hamana Dan Ba.

Guinée: Percussions et Chants Malinké (Buda). A series of immaculate set-piece renditions of traditional songs.

Kanté Manfila

The guitar wizard of the Ambassadeurs, Kanté Manfila (aka Manfila Kanté) is one of Africa's most innovative guitarists.

Tradition (Celluloid). Gorgeous rolling acoustic melodies from Kankan with guitars and *balafon*, and *kora* accompaniment by cousin Mory Kanté.

Diniya (Celluloid). Some fine melodies buried underneath a full-blown, high-tech production.

Kankan Blues (Popular African Music). Probably the best of the acoustic offerings on PAM.

Momo Wandel Soumah

Momo Wandel Soumah was a conservatoire-trained saxophonist who studied jazz and performed with the Orchestre Kélétigui during the Sekou Touré era. He died in 2003.

Guinea: "Matchowe" (Buda). A rich voice to complement a strongly flavoured union of jazz and Guinean music.

Books

There's little published in English, though a hunt through libraries may turn up some of the following.

Manthia Diawara *In Search of Africa.* Diawara, best known for his books on film, returns to Guinea to shoot a documentary on Sekou Touré, and pens a moving analysis of the state of Africa forty years after the independence movement.

Alioum Fantouré *Tropical Circle.* A novel about Guinea between the end of World War II and the reign of terror. The build-up to independence is a muddle but the second half is illuminating, despite a dire translation.

★ **Camara Laye** *The African Child.* One of the best-known books by an African writer, these sweet-scented memoirs of a privileged rural childhood are a homage to the author's parents. Other translations of works by Laye include *The Radiance of the King, A Dream of Africa* and *The Guardian of the Word.*

Various *Politique Africaine, Guiné: L'après Sekou Touré.* A useful collection of articles (in French) looking at political and economic changes in Guinea since the death of Sekou Touré in 1984.

Language

French is the official language, and is spoken to some degree by most people who've had a school education. In villages you may have difficulties communicating in any other language than the local tongue. **English** is rarely spoken other than by refugees from Sierra Leone or Liberia. The most important Guinean languages are **Susu** (mainly spoken in the capital), **Fula** (spoken in the Fouta Djalon), and **Malinké** (spoken in Haute Guinée; see the Bamana language section on p.338).

Simple Susu

Susu, the main language in Conakry, is more straightforward in many respects than Fula and relatively easy to learn. It bears comparison with Bamana and Mandinka (see p.270).

Greetings

Hello (to one person)	Inwali
(two or more people)	Wo inwali
Good day	Wo mamabé
Good morning (literally, "did nothing bad happen in the night?")	Tana mokhi?
Good afternoon/ evening	Tana mogegné
How's the family?	Tana modinbayama?
See you later/ good bye	Won je segué

Numbers

1	keren
2	firin
3	sakhan
4	nani
5	suli
6	senné
7	soloferé
8	solomasakham
9	solomanani
10	fu

20	mokhein
25	mokhein nu suli
30	tongosakhan
40	tongonani
50	tongosuli
60	tongosenné
100	kémé
200	kémé firin

Useful expressions

How much?	Yéri?
I'll take it (give it to me)	A sun nyi
It's too expensive	Asaré khorokho
Show me the way	Kira ma sembé
I don't know	M'ma kolon
I don't understand	M'ma fahamukhi
Excuse me	Diyema
Please repeat it	Nakhadi
Where's the bank?	Banque na mindé?

Fundamental Fula

Fula (also called Pulaar) is one of the most difficult West African languages: it has an immensely rich vocabulary, an unusual and complex grammatical structure, and guttural tones that are hard to pronounce – and there's little instructional material in English. Note that the following is based on the Fula of Fouta Djalon; the Fula spoken in other parts of West Africa – Senegal, Mali, Nigeria and Cameroon – differs markedly.

Greetings

How are you?	On djaarama
Are you fine?	Tana alaa ton?
[response: fine]	Djam tun
How's the family?	Bengure no edjam?
[response: fine]	Bengure no edjam
How's the work?	Gollere nden?
[response: fine]	No marsude or No jokka
Sorry	Achanee lan hakke
Nevermind	Hakke alaa

Conversation

Do you speak Fula?	A wawi Pulaar? or A nani Pulaar?
Yes	Hi-hi
No	O-o

I don't know	Mi andaa
I don't understand	Mi famaali
What did you say?	Kohundun wi'idha?
Welcome!	Ko tooli!
Nice to meet you	Mi weltikke fii ma
What's your name?	Ko hundun inettedha? or Inde ma?
My name is Michael	Ko Michael me wi'ete
Where are you from?	Ko huntu djeedha? or Ko huntu iwurudha?
I'm from England	Ko Angleterre mi iwri

Travel

Where are you going?	Ko huntu yahataa?
Where is Dalaba?	Ko huntu woni Dalaba?
Straight ahead	No yeeso
Right	Sengo nyaamo
Left	Sengo nano
Far away	No woddhi
Village	Fulawaa
Big	No njandi
Small	No fandi
Hill	Fello
Waterfall	Djurnde
Mosque	Julirde

Shopping and food

It's too expensive	No satti!
Please reduce a little.	Duytanan seedha, fii Allah
Won't you reduce it?	A duytantaalan seedha?
Where's the bank?	Ko huntu bank woni?
How much?	Ko jelu?
Food	Nyaamete
Rice	Maaro
Potatoes	Pute
Meat	Tewu
Milk	Bira
Sour milk	kosan
Water	Ndiyan
Tea	Dute
It's excellent (food)!	No moyy'i!
I'm full	Mi haari (tef)

Numbers

1	goo

2	dhidhi	9	jeenay
3	tati	10	sappo
4	nay	11	sappo e goo
5	jowi	20	nogay
6	jeego	25	nogay e jowi
7	jeedhidhi	100	teemedere
8	jeetati	200	teemede dhidhi

Glossary

Alfa King (Fula).

Bowe Eroded Fouta Djalon hill (plural *bowal*).

CTRN Transitional Committee for National Redress.

Dougou Place (Mande languages).

Foté, Porto White person (corruption of "Portuguese").

Gara Indigo (and indigo cloth).

Koro Old (as in Dabolakoro – old Dabola).

Lumo Market held weekly (or sometimes every four or five days).

PDG Democatic Party of Guinea, the party of the old regime.

PUP Unity and Progress Party, the ruling party of Lansana Conté.

Sofa Malinké soldier (nineteenth century).

Syli Elephant (and defunct Guinean currency).

Villa Administration guesthouse, often usable by travellers.

Woro Kola (Mande languages).

7.1

Conakry and around

CONAKRY, once known as "the Paris of Africa", is a city of few graces. A continuous sprawl of urbanization claws its way off the peninsula and up into the hills behind the city centre. This elongated conurbation is animated but morbidly dirty; heavy with the raw noise and choking exhaust fumes of lines of jammed vehicles trying to get from one end of town to another. Although central Conakry is gradually becoming a more pleasant place to visit, with lively restaurants and cafés opening everywhere, it's relatively expensive and too full of shady street vendors and stifled by pollution to allow for a peaceful stay. You may spend much of your time here planning your escape to the fabled hills and grasslands of the interior.

On the positive side, it's absolutely worth visiting Conakry's markets, especially the vast **Marché de Madina** and the slightly smaller **Marché de Niger**: both are bountiful, constantly expanding, and have become much safer over the last two years. The city also boasts a first-rate **nightlife**, while the strikingly pretty **Iles de Los** nearby offer an easily accessible retreat.

Some history

Conakry was originally an island – as you can still see from the narrow causeway between the Palais du Peuple and the motorway bridge. For many years known as **Tumbo**, the island provided safe haven for slavers and merchant vessels trading along the Guinea coasts. The Portuguese adventurer Pedro da Sintra first set foot here around 1460 and named it Cap de Sagres, after Prince Henry the Navigator's residence in Portugal. At this time the inhabitants of Conakry were idol-worshipping, skin-wearing farmers, cultivating indigenous African dry-land rice and millet. By the sixteenth century, the Portuguese had began to use the deep waters on the southeast side of the island as an anchorage, and over the succeeding centuries they and the Dutch, English and French all took turns to occupy the site and trade in slaves, transforming the Iles de Los into an entrepôt for the transfer of slaves from smaller coastal vessels to ocean-going merchant ships.

Yet by the time Britain ceded rights over the fledgling colony to France in 1887, Tumbo island still only had four tiny settlements – Bulbinay and Konakiri and the non-native African toeholds of Krootown and Tumbo – with just a few hundred inhabitants. A road into the interior was started and the channel between Tumbo and the Kaloum peninsula on the mainland was filled in. By the time Britain handed over the Los islands in 1904, Conakry – the new capital of Guinée Française – had acquired its present grid pattern and a population of ten thousand. The **railway** to Kankan was completed in 1914 and bananas from Kindia became the country's biggest export. Major developments came in the postwar colonial period, and concentrated on improving the port for the shipping of newly discovered iron ore and bauxite. The last twenty years have seen massive growth: the city, whose population numbers well over a million, now covers almost the entire peninsula.

Arrival, information and city transport

Conakry is built twenty kilometres out to sea on a **promontory**. Most of what you'll want in the way of banks, embassies and restaurants is right at the end, in

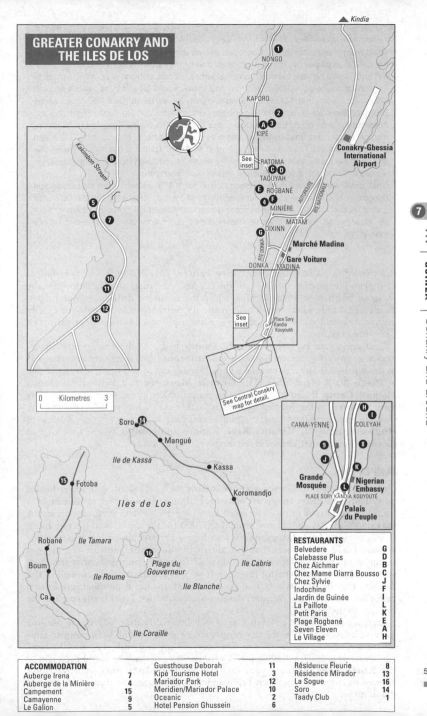

GREATER CONAKRY AND THE ILES DE LOS

Kindia

NONGO

KAPORO

KIPÉ

See inset

RATOMA

TAOUYAH

ROGBANÉ

MINIÈRE

MATAM

DIXINN

DONKA

MADINA

Marché Madina

Gare Voiture

Place Sory Kandia Kouyouté

See inset

See Central Conakry map for detail.

Conakry-Gbessia International Airport

RTE NATIONALE

AUTOROUTE

RTE DONKA

Katimbon Stream

Soro

Mangué

Ile de Kassa

Kassa

Koromandjo

Fotoba

Iles de Los

Robané

Boum

Ile Tamara

Ca

Ile Roume

Plage du Gouverneur

Ile Blanche

Ile Cabris

Ile Coraille

0   Kilometres   3

CAMA-YENNE

COLEYAH

Grande Mosquée

Nigerian Embassy

PLACE SORY KANDIA KOUYOUTÉ

Palais du Peuple

RESTAURANTS	
Belvedere	G
Calebasse Plus	D
Chez Aichmar	B
Chez Mame Diarra Bousso	C
Chez Sylvie	J
Indochine	F
Jardin de Guinée	I
La Paillote	L
Petit Paris	K
Plage Rogbané	E
Seven Eleven	A
Le Village	H

ACCOMMODATION					
Auberge Irena	7	Guesthouse Deborah	11	Résidence Fleurie	8
Auberge de la Minière	4	Kipé Tourisme Hotel	3	Résidence Mirador	13
Campement	15	Mariador Park	12	La Sogue	16
Camayenne	9	Meridien/Mariador Palace	10	Soro	14
Le Galion	5	Oceanic	2	Taady Club	1
		Hotel Pension Ghussein	6		

Apart from a few main roads, Conakry's streets are numbered, rather than named. In the centre, **avenues** run from east to west and **boulevards** from north to south; "1ère av" and "4ème bd" are the common local abbreviations, and are used here, though in English-language publications you may see these names given as 1st Avenue and 4th Boulevard. Note that 10ème av is also known as av de la Gare, 8ème av as av Tubman, 6ème av as av de la République (which leads into Route du Niger and the Autoroute), 6ème bd as bd Telly Diallo, and 3ème bd as bd du Commerce. There are also two important **"bis" avenues**: 9ème av bis and 7ème av bis, not to be confused with 9ème av and 7ème av, which run next to them. Things are complicated by the fact that the locals themselves are rarely aware of road numbers, and locations are usually only identified by the nearest well-known landmark.

All street names have officially been altered to **"KA" numbers** – the old boulevards becoming odd-numbered KA numbers (with "1ère bd" changing to "KA 001", for example) and the old avenues becoming even-numbered KA numbers (so that "1ère av" changes to "KA 004"). We've shown both the old and new street names on our map of central Conakry.

the two square kilometres of the **city centre**, arranged on an easy-to-follow grid plan. The northern *quartiers* of the centre – Almamya and Kaloum – are the focus of business and bureaucracy, while the southern districts – Manquépas, Boulbinet, Sandervalia – are mostly made up of tight-packed, single-storey city compounds and still have a village-like atmosphere of brush-swept yards and open-fire cooking.

Landwards, past the huge **Palais du Peuple** and over the strategically narrow causeway onto the mainland, you hit the **Autoroute** (not a motorway or freeway in the usual sense, since all vehicles and pedestrians use it) and pass under the bridge at **Place du 8 Novembre**. The **Grande Mosquée** and, behind the Donka Hospital, **Camp Boiro** (the main Touré-era prison camp) are over on the left. The **gare voiture**, in the Madina quarter, is further out, while stretching above the shore to the north, you hit the rapidly expanding and more affluent districts of **Rogbané**, **Taouyah**, **Ratoma**, **Kipé**, **Kaporo** and **Nongo**, where a number of Conakry's best hotels, clubs and restaurants can be found.

Arrival

Conakry's open-plan Gbessia **airport** is fairly well organized, with fewer hassles now than even just a couple of years back, though it's still best to be met by a friend or hotel staff in order to avoid lengthy price debates with taxi drivers. A **taxi** into Conakry should cost around FG7000 for the *déplacement* (private hire). If you prefer a little luxury, it's easy to hire a private, air-conditioned car for around FG25,000. Alternatively, walk to the autoroute outside the airport entrance and wave down a taxi (FG300–750 depending on the distance travelled; you may be charged extra for luggage). If your flight arrives early enough in the day, you may be able to leave Conakry and head upcountry immediately. In that case, take a taxi towards the *gare voiture* in Madina, which should cost you half the full fare to the centre.

Arriving at Conakry **overland**, taxis will invariably drop you at the Madina **gare voiture**, 6km from the city centre, where you can find *déplacements* to anywhere in Conakry, regular taxis to most destinations, and bush taxis into the interior. Note that when travelling into Conakry you may have to spend the night at the **Km36 checkpoint** if your taxi arrives after 11pm, since vehicles aren't allowed to enter town between 11pm and 5am. Delays are the norm here, even in the daytime.

Although people may tell you that Conakry is a den of thieves, in comparison with, say, Dakar, it's relatively peaceful. Although you should certainly be on your guard for pickpockets and the like, the real hassles come from the police, who can be quite inventive in trying to extract a bribe. Carry your passport and vaccination certificate at all times.

Information

The **Office du Tourisme**, av de la République, next to Ecobank (℡45.51.63, Ⓦwww.mirinet.com/ont), can give you general information, has maps and guidebooks for sale, and, most importantly, can help you get an *ordre de mission* to facilitate travel into the interior. Mondial Tours (see p.569) are also usually helpful. The free monthly "what's on" magazines, **Djeli** and **Tam Tam**, are available in the Centre Culturel Franco-Guinéen on Espace Sory Kandia Kouyaté (see p.569) and at various bookstalls and supermarkets.

City transport

There are three forms of public transport in Conakry: battered yellow taxis, crammed minibuses, and a small number of buses. **Shared taxis** run along four main routes: "Route Donka" (north side of the peninsula), "Autoroute" (Autoroute bridge to the airport), "Route du Niger" (joining with "Autoroute"), and "Route du Madina". To hail a taxi, you need to point your thumb in the direction of your destination and wave your arm impatiently (imitate what other people are doing). **Fares** in shared taxis work according to a zone system, with a fixed fare of FG250 per leg (or FG150 along the Autoroute). Rip-offs are very rare.

If you don't feel like squeezing into a tiny taxi with five other passengers and a bunch of chickens – or if you want to go somewhere off the main shared taxi routes – it's possible to hire a taxi for your own exclusive use: a so-called **déplacement**. Simply hail any empty taxi and negotiate a price, though be aware that you'll have to bargain ruthlessly – from town to Kipé and other nearby suburbs shouldn't cost more than FG2000.

Magbanas (minibuses) are a little cheaper than taxis, but slower, more uncomfortable and less frequent. Each leg costs FG150. Forget about the city's **buses**, which are too infrequent, unreliable and cover too few destinations to be useful to tourists.

Accommodation

Accommodation options in Conakry are very limited if you're on a tight budget: there are no **hostels**, and anything under FG40,000, even for a single room, is likely to be a brothel. Electricity and water are both unreliable and the really cheap places are usually in a disgusting state. Conakry does, however, have an increasing number of mid-range and expensive **hotels**. If you don't mind commuting to the city by boat, you could stay on the Iles de Los (see p.565).

City centre

The following places are marked on the map overleaf.

Hôtel Centrale Next to the *Patisserie Centrale*, off av de la République ℡43.12.50 or 43.11.40, Ⓕ43.11.30, Ⓔhotelcentralgn@yahoo.fr. Fairly clean and comfortable French-run hotel in a very central location with large, fully equipped rooms. ❹

Hôtel Galaxie 5ème av, near l'UGAR ℡45.10.03 or 22.21.33. Well-furnished rooms with satellite TV

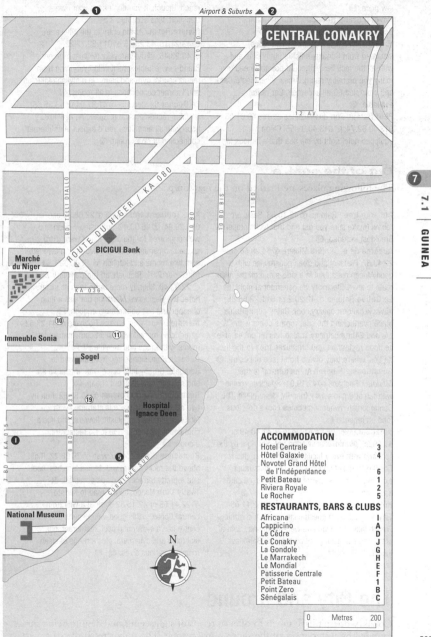

9 BD
10 BD
11 BD
12 AV
10 BD BIS
11 BD

BD TELLI DIALLO

ROUTE DU NIGER / KA 080

BICIGUI Bank

Marché
du Niger

KA 036

⑩

Immeuble Sonia

⑪

Sogel

⑲

9 BD / KA 033

KA 031

8 BD / KA 015

7 BD / KA 015

Hospital
Ignace Deen

❶

❺

CORNICHE SUD

National Museum

N

ACCOMMODATION

Hotel Centrale	3
Hôtel Galaxie	4
Novotel Grand Hôtel de l'Indépendance	6
Petit Bateau	1
Riviera Royale	2
Le Rocher	5

RESTAURANTS, BARS & CLUBS

Africana	I
Cappicino	A
Le Cédre	D
Le Conakry	J
La Gondole	G
Le Marrakech	H
Le Mondial	E
Patisserie Centrale	F
Petit Bateau	1
Point Zero	B
Sénégalais	C

0   Metres   200

– all in a central location and for a comparatively low price. ⑤

Novotel Grand Hôtel de l'Indépendance Boulbinet ☎ 41.50.21, ⓕ 41 16 31, ⓔ novotel@sotelgui.net.gn. Stylish place, insulated from Conakry's fickle utility cuts and with all the facilities you could possibly need (and many you probably don't). Amex, Visa, MasterCard and crumpled FG all accepted. Car rental available. ⑦

Petit Bateau Port de Plaisance ☎ 013.40.61.06 or 013.40.62.74, ⓕ 013.40.91.55. Clean, well-equipped hotel right by the sea that's famous for its seafood restaurant and boat club. It's hard to reach, though, if you don't have your own transport. Visa accepted. ④

Riviera Royale At the entry to the city centre ☎ 43.24.15, 43.25.15 or 011.22.17.22, ⓕ 43.23.45, ⓔ rivieraroyalhotel@usan-gn.net. Brand-new establishment with everything from tennis courts, gym and sauna to a stylish nightclub and Internet connections in all rooms. ⑦

Le Rocher Sandervalia ☎ 41.37.04 or 43.55.55, ⓔ hotel_rocher@yahoo.fr. Sparkling new luxury hotel with all amenities you'd expect, and Internet connection in every room. ⑦

Out of the centre

The following places are marked on the map on p.559.

Auberge Irena Ratoma ☎ 42.10.63. Basic a/c rooms (make sure you get one that locks properly). Breakfast included. ③

Auberge de la Minière Minière ☎ 54.28.56 or 22.43.67. Pleasant and clean guesthouse with a good African restaurant in a side-street off the main route to town. Electricity via generator at night. ③

Le Galion Ratoma ☎ 42.20.2 or 011.22.66.85, ⓦ www.galion-conakry.com. Calm, comfortable place overlooking the sea; rooms come with TV, a/c and 24hr electricity. It also has an unbeatable seafood restaurant and organizes trips to the Îles de Los, where they own a hotel (see opposite). ④

Guesthouse Deborah At the turn-off to the *Meridien*, Rogbané ☎ 42.19.01. Spacious rooms with fan or a/c in a very friendly, clean place. The Cameroonian owner sometimes cooks delicious food on request. ③

Hôtel Camayenne Camayenne ☎ 41.40.49 or 41.29.95, ⓔ info@camayenne.net. Set right by the sea, and with every facility you'd expect, this is Conakry's most famous – and one of its most expensive – hotels. Car rental available. All cards accepted. ⑦

Hôtel Pension Ghussein Ratoma ☎ 42.11.03. Tiny, very pleasant guesthouse run by a charming French lady. It's clean and well-maintained with a pretty terrace looking out on the sea. Breakfast included. ③

Kipé Tourisme Hotel Kipé ☎ 22.08.99 or 011.29.94, ⓕ 46.90.42. Surprisingly clean and well-organized for the area. If you want extra space and comfort, there's a two-floor maisonette with two rooms and kitchen for FG80,000. ③

Mariador Park Taouyah, off the *Carrefour Transit* ☎ 22.97.40. Slightly more basic than its sister hotel, the *Résidence Mariador*, but also a little cheaper and still comfortable enough. ③

Meridien/Mariador Palace Rogbané ☎ 41.27.52, ⓔ meridien.mariador@mirinet.com. Immaculate rooms with fridge and satellite TV. ⑦

Oceanic Kipé, signposted from the road to Bambeto. Grubby little place with unreliable a/c and no running water, but cheap. ②

Résidence Fleurie Coleyah ☎ 46.58.89. Run by two old ladies, this place is crammed with pictures, statues and plastic flowers, and has a cute country house feel to it. No restaurant, though. ④

Résidence Mariador Taouyah ☎ 26.06.22. Right above the rocky shore, with tennis facilities, pool and a pretty terrace. All cards accepted. ④

Taady Club Nongo, on the road to Kaporo ☎ 22.41.58 or 42.15.82. A bit of a way from central Conakry, this good-value sports and leisure centre has a swimming pool, restaurant, bar, nightclub and cybercafé, plus a range of clean rooms of various sizes. ③–④

The City and around

Conakry doesn't have much to offer in terms of sightseeing, and despite being surrounded by water, most of the shore is inaccessible. The only stretch of coast with any pretensions towards trying to be a beach is at **Rogbané**, about 5km up the peninsula from the city centre, which has been cleared by local youths to provide an area for beach football. It's a good place to people-watch and enjoy the sunset, though the sand isn't very clean.

You could spend an unexceptional hour or so at the city's **National Museum** (Tues–Sun 9am–6pm; FG1000), in the Sandervalia quarter off the Corniche Sud. The permanent collection consists of masks and other carvings, instruments and a few weapons. In the yard, you can admire a few colonial statues and a reconstruction of the hut of explorer Olivier de Sanderval, who used to live in some of the buildings in which the museum is now housed.

For shopping, don't miss a stroll around the infamous **Marché de Madina**, where you can buy anything from fine African fabrics to cassettes, carvings, clothes and food. The market is a massive maze of narrow alleyways lined by makeshift market stalls, always full of people and ringing with the noise of beeping cars, shouting drivers, screaming vendors and haggling customers. Madina used to be almost a no-go area due to its high crime rate, but has become a lot safer now, although you're still advised to keep money and possessions secure, and don't bring any big bags – and be cautious of bogus street vendors aiming to distract and rob you. To get to the market, catch a shared taxi on the "Autoroute" route.

For cassettes and videos try the **Marché du Niger** in the city centre or the box container at **Taouyah** junction. Downtown, you'll find several trendy **boutiques** selling Western clothes and shoes at high prices, and a few **arts and crafts** stalls. The big craft stall in Camayenne, a few kilometres north of the city centre, is one of the better ones. For **drums** and other musical instruments you can try the drum maker on the main road in Coleyah, near Camayenne, or contact the Centre Culturel Franco-Guinéen (see p.569) for advice.

The Iles de Los

Just a few kilometres offshore from Conakry, the **Iles de Los** are well worth a visit and have become quite a magnet, especially at weekends, when half the expatriate community of Conakry seems to head out to Ile Roume. The islands have a colourful past, and were inhabited from the earliest times by idol-worshipping farmers, which earned them the Portuguese label "*idolos*", transmuted by the French into Iles de Los. Roume itself – a lavishly picturesque pair of jungle-swathed hillocks joined by a sandy-shored isthmus – was once a slaving base, the site of the execution in 1850 of the notorious slaver Crawford, whose name the island carried until the end of the nineteenth century. Tales of Crawford's buried loot are supposed to have inspired Robert Louis Stevenson's *Treasure Island*.

There are various ways of **getting to the islands**. You can hire *pirogues* through Conakry's major hotels, including the *Camayenne* (FG14,000 per person for the whole day), *Galion* (FG10,000) or *Petit Bateau* (FG12,000). Alternatively, you can charter a *pirogue* at Port Boulbinet, not far from the *Novotel* hotel. The price will depend heavily on your negotiating skills, but you should be able to hire a boat for FG30,000 per day. There are also **public pirogue** services from Port Boulbinet, although travel by these is usually slower, since services don't leave until they're full, while massive overcrowding and non-existent safety measures make for an uncomfortable and potentially dangerous journey. Public *pirogues* leave from Port Boulbinet to Kassa village and Koromandjo on Ile de Kassa (about FG500 per person), and Ile Roume (FG1000). On Sundays there are also usually *pirogue* services to Soro beach (FG1000) on Ile de Kassa. There's also at least one *pirogue* daily to Fotoba on Ile Tamara (FG1000).

Ile de Kassa

Ile de Kassa is home to the sandy, palm-fringed **Soro beach**, the largest on the islands, though its popularity means that it gets extremely crowded on Sundays in the dry season; there's an access fee to the beach of FG1000. There are also a couple of **hotels** here: *Soro* (❸; open dry season only); while a little further away is the swanky *Magellan* (❹), run by the owners of *Le Galion* in Conakry, where you can arrange bookings and *pirogue* trips.

Spending a few days on eight-kilometre-long Kassa gives you the opportunity to explore the secluded beaches along the west shore, and the settlements which dot its lovely forests. It only takes an hour or so to walk to **Kassa village** from Soro beach and you're likely to see monkeys and birds along the way.

Ile Roume and Ile Tamara

The small **Ile Roume** is best on weekdays, when it's very quiet. It has always been favoured by the expatriate community and is the most expensive island to visit, with pricey accommodation on the south shore at the *Hôtel le Sogue* (reservations through Karou Voyages, see p.570; ❼; open early Oct to June), which has its own, sheltered and private **Plage du Gouverneur**. There's an extensive public beach on the north shore. You may find cheaper accommodation by staying in a private house – ask the locals.

Ile Tamara – also known as Ile Fotoba – used to be a penal colony and was for many years off limits. The old penitentiary near Fotoba village is worth visiting if you're on the island, but as on Roume and Kassa, the main attractions are the forests and seashore. There's a *campement* if you want to spend the night.

Eating, drinking and nightlife

Street food, such as grilled fish and plantains and huge plates of rice, is served everywhere, while **fast-food joints**, specializing in *chawarma*, burgers and chicken, are opening all the time. Conakry has a good selection of **restaurants**, ranging from fairly cheap places to others which are ridiculously overpriced.

City centre

The following places are marked on the map on pp.562–563.

Africana Behind the Anglican Church, city centre ☏41.35.18. A quiet, friendly and unassuming place that serves excellent African and European food at very reasonable prices, and has a delicious selection of homemade juices. If you come around lunchtime, you may be treated to live *kora* music.

Cappicino Opposite the port, city centre. Snack, *chawarma* and sandwich place.

Le Cédre Almamaya, city centre. Small, intimate Moroccan restaurant, popular with expats at lunchtime.

Le Conakry 4ème av, by the Ministry of Finance, city centre. Solid, Guinean business-class restaurant, with a French chef, a lunchtime *menu* (FG8000), and à la carte (dishes FG6000 plus). Closed Sun.

La Gondole av de la République, city centre. Very expensive patisserie, with excellent ice cream and freshly brewed coffee; there's also a pizza and *chawarma* place attached.

Le Marrakech Next to the *Hôtel Galaxie*, city centre. Nice Moroccan restaurant, with good food in a quiet atmosphere.

Le Mondial Behind av de la République, city centre. Patisserie-restaurant serving snacks, cakes and light meals all day. A good place to take a break from the Conakry bustle.

Patisserie Centrale av de la République, city centre. Serves the best croissants in town, and has a good selection of snacks, cakes and ice cream. Something of a Conakry landmark and a cult place with expats.

Petit Bateau At the *Petit Bateau* hotel, Port de Plaisance. Expensive restaurant overlooking the sea, popular with well-to-do Guineans.

Point Zero 10ème av, city centre. Cheap Guinean food in the centre of town.

Sénégalais Corner of 10ème av and 7ème bd, city centre. Delicious rice and fish *mafé*, *poulet yassa* and *steak frites* for around FG1500.

Restaurants: out of the centre

Belvedere Dixinn, near the Bellevue roundabout. Large, landmark Lebanese restaurant near the coast – though the food isn't as flashy as the surroundings.

Calebasse Plus Taouyah. Lively bar–restaurant with live music by the talented Ba Cissokho trio three times a week.

Chez Aichmar Kipé, next door to the *Climax* nightclub. Calm restaurant that serves delicious grilled fish; there's sometimes live music at weekends.

Chez Mame Diarra Bousso Taouyah. One of the cheapest and best Senegalese restaurants in town, with gigantic plates of *riz gras* or *yassa poulet* for FG1000–1500. Also serves delicious home-made *bissap* sorrel juice. Highly recommended.

Chez Sylvie Camayenne. Huge plates of rice and *atiéké* for FG5000 from early evening till late at night in this popular eaterie.

Indochine Minière ☎ 42.21.44. Classy Vietnamese/Thai restaurant, with excellent Asian food at top prices served up by Guineans draped in Far Eastern outfits.

Jardin de Guinée Coleyah. One of Conakry's longest-running restaurants, serving reasonably priced food in the evening; also has a late-opening bar.

La Paillote Near Place Sory Kandia Kouyaté. Evenings see regular rehearsals by the likes of Bembeya Jazz or Les Amazones, while you can treat yourself to a plate of rice and meat in the shade of a mango tree. The food is basic and can take a long time to come, but the beer is good, and the ambience great.

Petit Paris Coleyah. Popular bar-restaurant that's currently expanding to host regular cabaret and music events. Serves solid African food at lunchtime (noon to 3pm), and at other times if ordered in advance.

Plage Rogbané Rogbané beach. Serves drinks all day and food most evenings; a good place to watch the sun go down.

Seven Eleven Kipé, on the road to Bameto. Lebanese *chawarma* place.

Le Village Coleyah. Delicious African food (evenings only) in a quiet, green setting.

Nightlife

Conakry **nightlife** is enjoyable and ever-changing, with everything from purely African clubs to the hottest hip-hop joints – the places listed below are just some of the most popular venues, and a trip around Conakry will reveal small dance clubs on every corner. Unfortunately, going out is made a bit difficult by the roadblocks that are put up after 11pm, and the usually drunken state of the officers by the time you want to go home. Never go out at night without your passport, or you're in for trouble, and try to have some FG1000 bills handy to avoid unpleasant debates that can spoil the fun of going clubbing. Club prices differ from day to day, and usually double on national holidays, but usually run around FG1000–5000.

Nightclubs

Albatros Route Nationale. Upmarket club catering to a slightly older generation – ministers, businessmen and the like tend to come here with their girlfriends (or, more rarely, their wives), and move gently to salsa or Guinean rhythms.

L'Atlantique At the *Riviera Royale* hotel. Expensive and classy place with a good sound system.

Bataclan Shiny new club in Taouyah that plays a wide range of music, but is particularly good on African pop.

Le Cheval One of several clubs at the Carrefour Transit in Taouyah, which vibrates with the bass frequencies of several nightclubs at weekends. Specializes in techno and hip hop.

Le Climax Kipé. One of Conakry's most popular venues, attracting a young, stylish crowd with the latest in hip hop and ragga, though African music gets a look-in too.

Mistral Club 7ème av, city centre. Cheap and seedy Chinese-run place with occasional karaoke nights.

Millenium Trendy place in the city centre playing a broad mix of music.

Nelson Taouyah. Up-and-coming place which now rivals the *Climax* in popularity, with a good atmosphere and a great mix of American, African and reggae music.

L'Oxygene Ratoma. Tiny but vibrant place that's always packed at weekends.

Zambezi Route Nationale (all the taxi drivers know it). Very popular and smart club with an eclectic mix of people and music. It's a place to dress up, and you're usually expected to show up as a couple.

Live music

Guinea may be famous for its music, but suffers from a lack of decent live venues. The **Palais du Peuple** is Conakry's most famous and prestigious live spot, though a rather soulless affair. Don't be surprised if concerts everywhere turn out to be playback performances, with the artist miming to a recording, or if sound systems cut out unexpectedly, and enjoy the vibe anyway. You could also check the Ancien Imprimerie Patrice Lumumba in Coleyah for rehearsals (proper performances are rare) by Circus Baobab and the Ensemble Instrumental. You'll be able to find out there where the famous Ballets Africains are currently practicising, and walk into one of their rehearsals for a real treat of drumming and dancing.

Bembeya Club On the corner of av Tubman and 4ème bd. Long-established place which still hosts regular performances by Bembeya Jazz.

Calebasse Plus Taouyah junction Small bar-restaurant which is home to the upcoming Ba Cissokho trio.

Centre Culturel Franco-Guinéen Place Sory Kandia Kouyaté, just north of the city centre. One of the city's most interesting places for live music. On Wednesdays, Conakry's up-and-coming artists compete for attention in the Café Concerts, which always attract crowds of young people. At weekends, Guinean and foreign artists often perform acoustic African music, jazz and other styles. Usually a treat.

Les Copains d'Abord Taouyah. Spacious bar-restaurant with loud (and often trashy) live music at weekends. Popular with expats and tourist-hunting prostitutes.

La Paillote Near Pont de 8 November. One of Guinea's most vibrant venues during the days of

Sekou Touré, this place now exudes nostalgia, and many of Guinea's former star orchestras, such as Les Amazones, Bembeya Jazz and Keletigui et ses Tambourins, rehearse here during the week in the early evening. Actual concerts are rare, but you'll always meet a couple of old bandmembers telling stories of days past over a glass of beer.

Palais du Peuple Just north of the city centre. This huge, Chinese-built edifice hosts all of Guinea's main music events, including performances by Guinea's music stars and frequent festivals. Check the radio and posters around town for announcements.

Relax Small nightclub in Dixinn that currently hosts regular, informal performances by Fode Kouyaté, one of Guinea's best-loved singers. Kouyaté often performs on Saturdays, but check with the locals first.

Stadium Dixinn Hosts occasional big concerts and festivals. Check *Djeli* magazine, posters and the radio for announcements.

Listings

Airlines Unless otherwise noted, the following are all clustered along av de la République: Air France ☎41.30.96; Air Guinée ☎44.46.14; Air Ivoire, c/o Air France ☎41.30.96; Air Sénégal, Imm. Sonia Route du Niger ☎41.38.96; Gambia Airways, opposite Imm. CBG, bd du Commerce ☎44.30.00; Ghana Airways ☎45.48.13; Nigeria Airways ☎44.40.82; Paramount Airlines ☎45.46.69; Royal Air Maroc, Imm. Sonia ☎41.58.98; SN Air Brussels ☎41.34.40; West Coast Airlines ☎45.38.01.

American Express No representative. The *Novotel* may help.

Banks and money-changing The reasonably efficient BICIGUI, on av de la République (Mon–Thurs 8.30am–12.30pm & 2.30–4.30pm, Fri 8.30am–12 pm; ☎41.50.11), is the main bank for foreign exchange in Conakry. They accept traveller's cheques and are the only bank in the city with an

ATM that accepts Visa cards. You'll get a much better rate on the black market at Madina market, near the airport or in town – moneychangers will approach you constantly in all these places, but go with a local friend to avoid being ripped off.

Car rental Expect to pay a minimum of FG70,000 for a standard car, and FG100,000–200,000 per day for a 4WD. You can rent vehicles at the Hertz outlets on av de la République (☎43.07.45) and at the *Novotel* hotel (☎41.50.21, ✉sas-hertz@mirinet.net.gn), or at *A Tout Service* at the *Hotel Camayenne* (☎011.21.50.60 or 013.40.70.80, ✉mail atout@afribone.net.gn). Alternatively, you can always rent informally with drivers waiting along the av de la République, but you won't get a much better deal. You always have to hire a driver along with the car – just as well really, given the state of the roads.

Cassettes and CDs Guinea is West Africa's pirate cassette capital, although most of the cheap cassettes on offer start disintegrating after you've played them about ten times. The Marché du Niger is a good place to pick up some nice cassettes along with tapes of the latest films. The vendor at Taouyah junction also has a good variety of music on offer, while most of the stalls in town specialize in pirate CDs of the latest R&B and hip hop. Original cassettes cost FG2000, while pirate versions can be picked up for FG1000–1500.

Cinemas Try the Centre Culturel Franco-Guinéen, Place Sory Kandia Kouyaté, for showings of African films and art movies. Directly opposite the centre, the Cinema Liberté shows a mixture of Bollywood and Hollywood movies, though rarely the latest releases, as does the Cinema Rogbané, near Taouyah junction.

Crafts and curios The city's top-end hotels usually have a selection, but they're expensive. Visit the markets and check out 4ème bd between av de la République and av de la Gare, near the post office. In addition, the craft stall in Camayenne often has a few interesting pieces on offer.

Cultural centres The Centre Culturel Franco-Guinéen, Place Sory Kandia Kouyaté, just north of the city centre, hosts exhibitions, theatrical and music events, and also has Internet access and serves coffee, sandwiches and soft drinks during the day. The American Cultural Center on the Corniche Sud, near the Autoroute bridge, has a library with periodicals, English- and French-language movies and American satellite TV.

Embassies, consulates and honorary consuls include: Canada, near Cité Douanes, Corniche Sud, Matam ☎41.23.95; Cape Verde, Minière ☎42.11.37; Côte d'Ivoire, bd du Commerce, Boulbinet ☎45.10.82; France, bd du Commerce, entry on 8ème av, city centre ☎41.16.05 (also issues visas for Burkina and Mauritania); Ghana, Matam, Coleyah ☎44.15.10; Guinea-Bissau, rte de Donka ☎46.21.36; Mali, Matam, between the Autoroute and rte de Niger, after the Total station ☎41.15.39; Morocco, Boulbinet, Cité des Nations Villa 12, ☎41.36.86; Nigeria, Corniche Sud, Coleyah ☎41.43.75; Senegal, Corniche Sud, Coleyah ☎46.28.34; Sierra Leone, Bellevue ☎44.50.99; Togo, Matam, Madina ☎46.47.72; UK, bd du Commerce, opposite the French embassy, city centre ☎45.58.07, ⓔbritcon.ggft@biasy.net; USA, rue KA038 ☎41.15.20, ⓦwww.usembassy.state.gov/conakry.

Internet access Internet cafés have sprung up all over town, and connections are now reasonably fast in most places. Particularly recommended are Cyber Ratoma, on the road to Kipé, and Dixinn Gate, on the junction to the Corniche. Most places in the city centre have slower connections and are less comfortable, with the possible exception of ATI, off the av de la République, and the Business Centre on the ground floor of the UK consulate. Most places charge FG1500 for 30min.

Medical/dental attention For emergencies, go to the Hôpital Ignace Deen (☎44.20.53, 41.43.36 or 44.20.78) or the Hôpital Donka (☎44.19.33). For further information about doctors and medical services in the city, email the International Medical Centre at ⓔCMI@eti-bul.net.

Pharmacies Check a copy of *Djeli* or *Tam Tam* for *pharmacies de garde* (the out-of-hours pharmacy rota).

Photography Photo permits aren't required, though money-hungry military may occasionally ask you to present one. Be careful taking pictures, though: it's not usually welcome, and downright dangerous in busy markets, where you might either be threatened or have your camera stolen (or both), and near governmental or military buildings and checkpoints. There are photo labs all over town; try the one in the city centre opposite the *maison d'impôts*, rte de Niger, or the one opposite the Dixinn end of Madina market. Both also repair cameras.

Post and telephones The main PTT (Mon–Thurs 8am–4pm, Fri & Sat 8am–12pm) is just off the av de la République. Poste restante is neither stunningly secure nor organized, so avoid having anything of value sent to you by post. The Sotelgui telephone section opposite the post office stays open until 8pm. International calls cost FG4000 per minute. Sotelgui is usually more expensive, but also more reliable, than the private telecentres that you'll find on every corner. The cheapest international calls can be made from clandestine operators, where you'll be charged FG1500 for an illegal call.

Supermarkets The big ones are Superbobo, rte de Donka, Camayenne (which sells English-language newspapers and magazines); A-Z Supermarket, Bellevue, next to the Sierra Leone embassy; and Leaderprice, on 5ème bd in Almanya in the city centre.

Travel agents Airline offices (see opposite) often also act as general travel agents. One of the most reliable and best-organized travel agents is Mondial Tours, on av de la République (☎41.46.25, ⓔmtg@mirinet.net.gn); they can book tickets, organize car rental, and run interesting tours into the interior. Other agents

Flights to the interior are mainly handled by Air Guinée (☎44.46.14); you can buy tickets from the Air Guinée office next to the French embassy on bd du Commerce in the city centre, and through travel agents. UTA and Paramount Airlines also operate occasional flights. Air Guinée flies to Labé on Mondays, Kankan and Siguiri on Wednesdays, Kissidougou and Nzérékoré on Thursdays, Sambailo (Koundara) and Labé on Fridays, and Nzérékoré, Kankan and Siguiri on Saturdays.

All upcountry **road transport** leaves from the Madina *gare voiture*. SOGETRAG **buses** are no longer running, and though there are a few irregular private bus services, you're far better off travelling by **bush taxi**. The standard Peugeout 504s leave to all major towns from Madina. If you get there before 9am, you stand a good chance of leaving quickly; it tends to take a long time for later departures to fill up, and taxis never leave until every seat is sold.

Leaving Conakry, the smog-laden road to Coyah heads out through the oily squalor of the city immigrants' highway-side *ateliers*, manufacturing every conceivable kind of item, before reaching the tedious **checkpoint** at Kilometre 36 that marks the official exit of Conakry – an outlandish scene of strutting and loafing khaki-clad officials where delays are commonplace.

worth trying include Karou Voyages, av de la République (☎43.19.63, ✉karouvoyagegn @yahoo.com), who specialize in booking flights; Dunia Voyages, av de la République (☎45.48.48), who operate some tours inland;

and Guinée Voyages (☎45.19.92, ✉guinee.voy@mirinet.gn).
Visa extensions FG80,000 for three months; available from the Direction Nationale Police Aire et Frontières in Coleyah.

Around Conakry

DUBREKA is just off the road to Boffa, which forks (north) from the main high-way at Km36. The town is surrounded by mangrove swamps, which you can visit on motorized *pirogues*, available for hire (along with knowledgeable guides) at the Soumba port – though you'll have to bargain hard. Dubreka's most famous attraction is the **Cascades de la Soumba**, a pretty waterfall that you can bathe in, except at the end of the dry season. The falls lie off the road to Boffa, around 10km from Dubreka, and there's a small *campement* if you want to spend the night. For hiking excursions, there's **Mount Kakoulima** (1013m), the closest large mountain to Conakry. Locals will point out the rock formation known as **Le Chien Qui Fume** (smoking dog), though it's really not as impressive as it's sometimes made out to be.

Further up the coast, **BOFFA** is mainly known for its mosquito swarms, and the town itself doesn't have much to offer apart from a depressing choice of grubby guesthouses. About 40km beyond Boffa lies **Bel Air**, one of Guinea's most beautiful beaches. It's popular with foreign aid workers and locals, and well worth a visit. There isn't any accommodation near the beach, but you shouldn't have any problems camping, and you can always rely on helpful locals.

COYAH, 18km beyond the Boffa turning at Km36, is surrounded by dense green forest and plantations. **South of Coyah**, pale, dramatic cliffs rise from a broken plain of bush and palms, forming isolated tablelands crowned with greenery, and apparently uninhabited on top. If you're interested in hiking up onto the table-lands, stop at the village of **Tabili** and follow the left bank of the Badi upstream between the cliffs as it runs off the plateau.

△ Kouroussa children

7.2

The Fouta Djalon

Covering the greater part of the western interior, the **Fouta Djalon highlands** are Guinea's major attraction. Cut into innumerable, chocolate-bar plateaux, the sandstone massif is the source of hundreds of rivers, including the Gambia and Senegal, major tributaries of the Niger and a lattice of streams running down to the Guinea coast – after the rains, waterfalls spume everywhere. Populated by **Fula** herders and the remnants of the indigenous agricultural groups in whose territory they settled hundreds of years ago, the region has a fascinating ethnic history, as well as an extraordinary variety of **landscapes**. Lushly cultivated or jungle-filled valleys rise – sometimes with sheer cliffs – to scrubby high ground, bare and rocky wastelands or lightly wooded plateaux. Wherever the contours are gentle enough to retain the soil, swaths of grassland roll in the wind. It's fabulous country and needs only time, and average determination, to explore.

Kindia

The gateway town to the Fouta Djalon, **KINDIA** (135km from Conakry) developed following the construction of the railway line in the early 1900s and is now a bustling, workaday place dramatically located beneath the hulk of Mont

Hiking, biking and related practicalities

The Fouta Djalon is one of the best regions in West Africa for serious **off-the-beaten-track travel**. There are hundreds of kilometres of sometimes optimistically labelled "motorable tracks" and footpaths throughout the region (see p.578 for an account of cycling along one of them). For serious **hiking**, it's best to get hold of the IGN map of the country (the Michelin 741 isn't sufficient). **Mountain bikes** are ideal, and on the main routes you'll have little trouble loading them onto vehicles whenever your enthusiasm for pedalling wanes. **Motorbikes**, preferably trail bikes, are also fine. **Cars and off-road vehicles** however – even 4WD ones – will run into repeated difficulties on steep, rugged terrain and narrow footpaths, and you'd need the most agile and powerful machine to negotiate less-travelled minor routes. If you're cycling or on a motorbike, take obsessive care: roads which seem relatively good can turn a bend and disappear without warning into a river, or lose themselves in a jumble of rocks and gullies. Have purifying tablets for water – which often comes straight from the local stream – and carry some back-up rations for emergencies.

This is the most densely populated part of the country. The **people** of the Fouta Djalon are, in general, wonderfully kind and show a disinterested concern for the welfare of wayward *portobhe* (white people). There's a growing population of English-speaking refugees from the wars in Liberia and Sierra Leone, too. People will nearly always get water for you when you need it. The highlands, moreover, are a major citrus-growing area and during the early dry season you'll be able to rely on oranges in their hundreds as a cheap source of fluid. Remember, of course, to stock up on **essentials** like toilet paper and batteries, which don't grow on trees, and also bear in mind that temperatures at night can drop below 10°C, so you'll need something warm.

Gangan and shaded by innumerable mango trees (Kindia is a wonderful place for mangoes in season, boasting many different varieties: *chocolat, fini pas,* and so on). The railway barely functions any more and there aren't any obvious attractions in town apart from the huge **market** – a large section of which is devoted to local cloth – where the vendors shout to be heard over the whirring of sewing machines.

Practicalities

Kindia offers a good choice of **accommodation**, though the most exciting place to stay is without doubt the *campement* at the Voile de la Mariée falls, 18km further east (see p.574). There are a few budget spots in the centre of town, such as the *Buffet de la Gare* (℡61.10.20; ❶), which is shabby, but still inhabitable, though it also incorporates the *La Paillotte* nightclub, so can get noisy. A short distance from the town centre are the basic *Mont Gangan* youth hostel (❶), and *Phare de Guinée* (℡61.05.31; ❷), which has clean rooms with fan or a/c, and the equally acceptable *Cabane Bambou* (61.08.39; ❷). *Le Flamboyant* (℡61.02.12; ❸) is a lot more elegant, and has a swimming pool, plus TV and a/c in all rooms. A short drive along a dirt road from the edge of Kindia lies a small cluster of stylish hotels. The *Kanya* (℡011.29.29.81; ❸) is a brand new place with spacious, spotless rooms and a nice terrace. The adjacent *Bungalow* (℡011.29.84.49; ❸) is built on a mango patch, and houses guests in good-value, modern a/c huts. It's also home to Kindia's best **nightclub**, the *Linsan*, whose powerful sound system and renowned musical selection attracts clubbers from Conakry every weekend. Other popular clubs in Kindia include the *Bananier, King Kindy* and *Christina*.

Kindia's **eating** options are quite diverse, and you can get *atiéké* on the street, always served with fish. The restaurant at the *Le Mont Gangan* is pleasant, with African dishes and a surprisingly extensive French menu. For a broadly international menu of chicken, fish and steak dishes, the *Buffet de la Gare* or *Le Bananier* will provide, though it's wise to order in advance to be sure of getting what you want.

Kindia is a good place to go shopping, especially for **cloth** (*tissus*). A pair of batik *pagnes* (2m lengths of printed cloth) go for FG10,000–12,000, indigo dyed cloth (*gara*) for not much more, and beaten damask (*lepi*) for around FG30,000 a pair. There's a large covered area devoted to cloth – the *marché aux tissus* – in the main market. Various beads and leatherwork are sold across the street. You could also visit the woodworkers near the old station: expect to be offered ivory as well as woodcarvings. Kindia has a **post office**, but no bank.

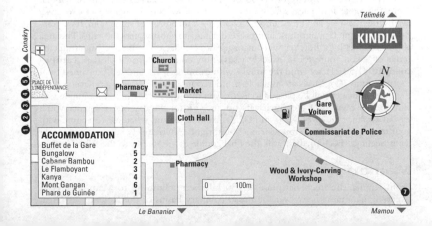

KINDIA

Télimélé

Conakry

Church

Pharmacy

Market

Place de l'Indépendance

Cloth Hall

Gare Voiture

Commissariat de Police

Pharmacy

Wood & Ivory-Carving Workshop

ACCOMMODATION
Buffet de la Gare	7
Bungalow	5
Cabane Bambou	2
Le Flamboyant	3
Kanya	4
Mont Gangan	6
Phare de Guinée	1

0   100m

Le Bananier

Mamou

7.2 | GUINEA | The Fouta Djalon

Moving on from Kindia

The main road out of Kindia heads northeast to **Mamou**. Plenty of taxis leave the *gare voiture* in Kindia towards Mamou; the earlier you arrive, the less time you're likely to have to wait. A minor route winds north out of Kindia to **Télimélé**, from where you could continue to **Pita** and the far north. There's a handful of vehicles each day and the road condition is kept up fairly well. For travellers heading for **Sierra Leone**, Kindia has occasional bush taxi departures for **Madina-Woula**, from where it's possible to reach the area around the Outamba–Kilimi National Park and Kamakwie.

Around Kindia

There are several worthwhile day-trips in the Kindia area: **Mont Gangan**, rising above the town 10km to the north; **Pastoria**, the birthplace of TB immunization; and the **Voile de la Mariée falls**, where you might even be tempted to stay a few days.

Mont Gangan

The massif of **Mont Gangan** is one of the highest peaks (1117m) in the southern Fouta Djalon and is relatively easy to climb. The big plateau halfway up offers brilliant views over Kindia, especially after the rains. You can arrange hiking tours at the *Flamboyant* in Kindia (see p.573), or venture out on your own, but be careful not to stroll through the military camp on the way.

Pastoria

Three kilometres up the road to Télimélé from Kindia is **Pastoria**, the "Institut Pasteur". The institute was founded in 1925 as a primate research centre, principally with the aim of developing various vaccines for human use – we have their consumptive chimps to thank for the BCG (Bacillus Calmette-Guerin) antituberculosis jab. The Pasteur Institute in Paris later charged Pastoria with the collection of snake venom for antivenin preparations. They used to have a large collection of primates and reptiles, of which only a few snakes and a couple of unhappy crocodiles have survived. The institute is still open for visitors, but doesn't hold much attraction beyond the architectural layout of the place itself. If you want to visit, you'll have to *déplace* a taxi or walk.

La Voile de la Mariée

The best known of Kindia's local excursions is to **La Voile de la Mariée**, the "Bridal Veil" falls, a five-kilometre diversion off the road to Mamou, 13km from Kindia. Here, the Santa River leaps from a black and yellow cliff in two streams to crash against the rockface and break into a broad fan – a total drop of some 60m. It's a year-round phenomenon, but most impressive during and shortly after the rains. The area is looked after by a hotelier who manages fifteen spacious concrete huts (built by order of Sekou Touré for his weekly visits), now converted into a pleasant **campement** (☎41.50.21), set amid the jungle, with camping space and self-contained twin rooms in huts (**❸**). Meals are available if ordered in advance. If you stay several days, the hotel manager will be pleased to escort you into the nearby hills for a jungle trek and bird's-eye views of the district. If you just visit for the day out of Kindia, you'll pay an entrance fee of FG1000, an FG2500 parking fee and whatever you agree with your taxi driver (FG8000 round-trip is about right). Alternatively, take a *taxi brousse* as far as Segueya (FG400), then walk the final couple of kilometres to the falls.

Mamou

From Kindia, the steep, hairpinning 130-kilometre climb up to Mamou offers a sweeping panorama back over the broad tributary basins of the Kolente (or Great

Scarcies) River, which marks the border with Sierra Leone. If you're coming by taxi from Conakry, you're likely to take a short break in the village of **LINSAN**, some 50km before Mamou – a lively market town where you can find a cheap plate of rice, *brochettes*, and calabashes full of sweetened sour milk (*kosan*). Some 25km before Mamou, a 5km detour leads to the village and falls of **KONKOURÉ**. There's an old sacred wood here, containing remnants of the ancient forest that once covered large parts of the Fouta Djalon.

MAMOU, piled up on the hillside, strikes a surprisingly low-key note. Before the building of the railway, the religious and political centre of the Fouta Djalon was **Timbo** – now just a village 50km northeast of Mamou. Despite considerable local opposition, the French decided to bypass Timbo and set up a new railway halt and fuel depot at the hamlet of Mamou. The Fula chieftaincy was transferred and, until the end of World War II, Mamou served as the chief administrative centre for much of the highlands. Today, the old railway station offers an overgrown reminder of Mamou's former glory, though it's now better known for its agricultural college and meat-processing industry.

Accommodation has improved in recent years, with the opening of a number of new hotels. *Hôtel Luna* (**2**) is the most central place to stay, though also the least impressive, with thirty self-contained rooms overlooking a large courtyard. The nicer places are all grouped around the road out of town to Labé. The *Rama* (☎68.04.30; **2**) is basic but cheap, while the new *Hôtel Africana* (☎68.01.43; **2**) offers cleaner rooms, better service, and a nice terrace restaurant for about the same price. About 1km further out of town, the *Balys Hôtel* (☎68.02.52; **3**) is one of the country's best mid-range hotels, with clean, brand-new rooms and good service. A large underground nightclub is currently under construction here, which may transform *Balys* into Mamou's liveliest party spot. Mamou has plenty of **street food**, grimy **bars** hidden behind dirty plastic curtains, and a few good **restaurants** – try the *Pergola* for large plates of African or European food, the *Luna* for more basic meals, or any of the unnamed eateries around the centre of town.

Mamou is such a major transport hub that **moving on** is rarely a problem. The town's three taxi and bus parks are hives of activity from dawn to dusk. The two in the town centre handle the **Conakry–Faranah** route; the one on the road out of town towards Labé handles **Fouta Djalon** traffic, and transport on the less busy routes to **Timbo**, **Dabola** and **Dinguiraye**.

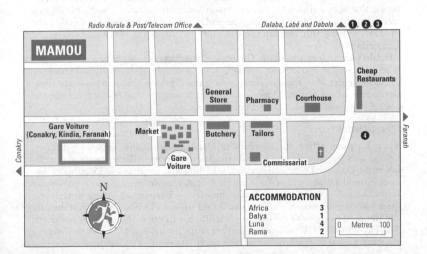

Mamou to Faranah

Southeast of town, the rough road from **Mamou to Faranah** (see p.584) drops down from the highlands through forest and hilly bush before reaching the plains below, where the road runs through monotonous elephant grass and bush savanna for the rest of the journey to Faranah, at times running within a dozen kilometres of the Sierra Leone border – this area is one of the richest areas for fauna in Guinea, and your chances of seeing large wild animals are quite high.

Timbo

The surfaced road from **Mamou to Dabola** (see p.584) cuts through impressive scenery, with sheer rocky outcrops and forest populated by chimpanzees and other primates. Cradled between forest-covered mountains 50km along the road, **TIMBO** is the old capital of the Fula *almamys*, or religious leaders, and a worthwhile day's excursion from Mamou (taxis leave every morning from Mamou's *gare voiture*). You can pay tribute at the **tombs** of two former Islamic leaders, have a look at the restored eighteenth-century **mosque** (though only from the outside) and soak up the village's unusual air of religious devotion. You'll also come across traditional Fouta Djalon **houses**: fine conical beehive structures, with solid tiers of thatching to exclude the cold.

The central Fouta Djalon

The central Fouta Djalon – including the ancient settlements of **Dalaba**, **Pita** and **Télimélé** – offers some of Guinea's most beautiful countryside. About 15km out of Mamou, the eastward-flowing stream you cross is the Bafing, the first headwater of the Senegal; its source is in the hills a few kilometres off the road to the west. The road steepens after **Bouliwel** (which has a Saturday market), then drops to enter Dalaba, hidden in a conifer-carpeted valley.

Dalaba and around

DALABA has a beautiful setting in the hills at 1200m, and the town's agreeable climate (though with very cool nights during the dry season) and pretty green scenery make it ideal for extended walks. The French considered the site so therapeutic that they built a sixty-room sanatorium, now in ruins. The South African jazz singer Miriam Makeba spent time in Dalaba during her period of exile from the USA in the 1970s, and you can still visit her large white house near the ruined sanatorium.

Dalaba's layout is easy to grasp. The limited **market** – greatly enlarged on Sunday, when it hosts the district *lumo* (market) – and a couple of streets around comprise the town centre, with a row of cheap eating and drinking places on the street along the bottom of the market. Market produce includes, from the end of December to March, cultivated strawberries – a colonial bequest.

Practicalities

There's a **post office** but no bank in Dalaba. Staff at the *Tangama* hotel (see below) can put you in touch with the local **tourist office**, where the well-informed Daimou Diallo can arrange bike hire and organizes sightseeing excursions around Dalaba and as far away as Pita. A ten- to fifteen-minute walk away across the valley is the administrative quarter of **Etaconval** – rural in feel, and spread among the woods – where you'll find some of Dalaba's nicest **restaurants** and the only two **places to stay** it currently has to offer. The formerly luxurious *SIB Hotel* (☎69.71.10; ❸) now smells a little mouldy, but it's still well worth enjoying a meal or drink on its terrace, from where there's a stunning panoramic view of the surrounding hills. It's more pleasant however to stay at the small *Hôtel Tangama* (☎69.11.09; ❶) – a clean and friendly place which also has an excellent restaurant. For good Senegalese **food**, try the unnamed but easy to find Senegalese family place near the junction leading to the *Tangama* hotel (order in advance). *Chez Kofi*, also known as *L'Auberge*, offers a wide selection of African and European food. At weekends, Dalaba's youth usually gathers in the popular *Le Kouratier* **nightclub**.

Moving on **from Dalaba to Pita** by public transport can sometimes prove difficult: most vehicles either arrive full from Mamou en route to Labé, or vice versa. An early start might get you a ride without having to pay the fare the whole way to Labé.

Around Dalaba

A five-kilometre walk through the forest from the *Hôtel Tangama* (ask at the hotel for directions) takes you to the old colonial Villa Jeannine and the **Case de Palabre**, a former assembly hut for Fula chiefs built in the 1930s and boasting an inscribed floor, elaborate ceiling decorations and exceptional carving on its interior walls. Two other worthwhile walks (though you'll need a guide) offering good views go to **Pont Tangama** and **Mont Diaguissa**. Five kilometres outside Dalaba on the right, a steep road leads to Tinka and **Le Jardin de Professeur Chevallier**, an ornamental garden constructed in 1908 as a botanical experiment designed to prove that European plants can grow in West Africa. It's still just about kept up, and is worth a visit. From November to May, you can also visit the **Jardin de Fraises** in Dounkimania, where strawberries are grown by the local population; a small basket costs FG2500. If you're interested in local **arts and crafts**, Daimou Diallo can take you to the villages of **Ponké** and **Sebhory**, where local women have established a collective that manufactures the woven wall hangings (*beddo*) and baskets typical of the Fouta Djalon region – prices are cheap, and you can watch the women at work.

There are a couple of impressive **waterfalls** off the main road from Dalaba to Pita. The **Pont de Dieu**, around 10km outside Dalaba, is a pretty little waterway that snakes its way over and under rocks resembling a natural bridge. Some 30km further towards Pita are the famous **Ditinn** waterfalls, an eighty-metre-high cascade, dropping from a perfectly vertical cliff – very impressive when there's sufficient water (usually best Oct–Dec), and you can also swim in the plunge pool. Other falls are more easily seen from a distance than reached, such as the **Bomboli** falls, about 15km before Pita, which are very difficult to get to, though clearly visible, several kilometres over on the right.

Pita and around

PITA isn't as restful as Dalaba, but has a lively and appealing atmosphere. Market day is Thursday, when locals visit the town to buy sticks of delicious white **bread** – the town is home to some of Guinea's best bakeries. The town boasts one fading **hotel**, the *Hôtel Kinkon* (❶), in a quiet area near the school on the northwestern edge of town –very basic but just about adequate, and warm water can be ordered for the self-contained washing cubicles. It's also possible to stay at the Centre d'Acceuil, the imposing complex near the *commissariat*, which has spotless, very reasonably priced rooms (❶). There's a **nightclub**, *Le Koubi*, a short walk or drive from town, and big-screen action at the Cinéma Rex, with daily showings of American and Indian movies.

The pretty and well-known **Chutes de Kinkon** are 10km from Pita, an easy cycle ride or a more taxing walk; you'll need to get permission (*laissez-passer*) to visit the falls from the *commissariat* on the north side of town – this is issued on the spot and is usually free (depending on the whim of the policeman you deal with). To reach the falls, go past the checkpoint at the exit from town on the road to Labé and take a left at the sign to the falls. After a mostly downhill 7km you arrive at a control post where you hand in your *laissez-passer*. From here, it's 500m down to the right if you want to inspect the unimpressive dam across the lake (the reason for the *laissez-passer*) and about a kilometre left for the main falls. You can stand directly on the **rock platform** above the falls which – before the dam was built – would have surged with water. There's evidence of colonial safety measures in the broken stumps of cliff-edge railings, but nothing to stop present-day visitors plunging dramatically to their deaths – take care, as the flow is powerful. Behind, on the cliffs, is a scrappy but just about legible list of various heads of state, with the dates of their visits.

Far more impressive, though only reachable after a very strenuous walk, are the gigantic **Chutes de Kambadaga**, which gush down over two steep rock terraces. It's best to take a local guide to visit the falls, in order not to get lost in the wilderness surrounding Pita. If your thirst for waterfalls still isn't satisfied you could visit the small but pretty **Mitty** waterfalls near the village of **Maci**, a few kilometres outside Pita on the road to Dalaba. The turning to Maci is indicated by a sign; the falls are a short walk off the main road from here.

Pita to Télimélé

Exceptionally beautiful in parts, the **Pita–Télimélé road** is a relatively straightforward drive and ideal for **motorbikes** or **4WDs** (count on eight hours plus from Pita to Télimélé), **mountain bikes** (two days) or **hiking** (four to six days). The Paris–Dakar rally came this way in January 1995, but it's still little used by public transport. The route in reverse is considerably less attractive as the rewards are mostly westwards (eastbound you face a continuous thirty-kilometre climb from Léi-Mîro to Dongol-Touma). If you're cycling or hiking, you may want to deviate from the road to take short cuts in the company of local people. One walking route follows, roughly, the course of the Fétoré River, which flows westwards, a few kilometres to the north of the road. Alternatively, you might try to get a lift as far as the village of **Dongol-Touma**, where the thrills begin. There's transport from Pita to Dongol-Touma at least once daily, though you'll probably have less of a wait if you go to the junction 3km north of Pita, where vehicles from Labé, as well as Pita and Mamou, turn off westwards towards Télimélé.

The people of the area, who live in immaculate mud-moulded compounds, are happy to bring visitors water from their wells or the local stream, and will just as soon give you handfuls of oranges and bananas as sell them.

Over the bowe

A signpost 3km up the Pita–Labé road marks the turn-off to Télimélé, which at first brings you to a confusion of tracks. Bear right where another sign points left to the Chutes de Kinkon (see above; given an early start, you could easily visit the falls as part of the journey). The correct track soon starts bucking and twisting unmistakeably, with many descents to narrow streams and many wearing climbs to short, level ridges. There are usually a fair number of Fula people about, invariably surprised to see any strangers, let alone foreign travellers. The track heads northwest, southwest, east and south before establishing a more or less westerly course along a barren hogback of rocky land discernible on the IGN map. This part of the journey, across the **bowe** – the Fula name for these high, sere plateaux – isn't scenically enthralling. In December smoke from burning grass obscures any views and the hazy dust brought by the harmattan wind normally fogs the horizon between January and April.

The path runs over unrelenting bare rock in places, then begins to descend gently, with occasional wooded intervals. The village of **Timbi-Touni** has an enormous mosque, while an hour's walk further west brings you to **Combouroh**, home to a remarkable country market every Tuesday during which hundreds of Fula women converge to share news, sell and shop – their assortment of hairstyles and print patterns is stunning, and typical. At the end of the *bowe*, you reach the strung-out village of **Dongol-Touma**, 55km from the Pita junction, and site of a Wednesday *lumo*. If you see the *sous-préfet* you'll likely be able to **stay the night** in Dongol's *villa*, superbly sited on a high bluff with a 270-degree panoramic view.

Downhill to the Kakrima River

The road snakes out of Dongol-Touma and starts a **steep descent**, with inspiring sweeps of Fouta Djalon visible through the trees. If you're cycling or motorbiking, the only effort you'll need to make for 26km is to keep the brakes on. Driving a car or truck, exercise extreme caution: parts of the route are likely to have succumbed to erosion and you could turn a bend and run into a jumble of boulders and bedrock. When you're not watching the surface ahead, however, this is a breathtaking ride, zigzagging down a long spine, with striking views of the bush country to the south, the fortress-like hills rising in a ridge to the west, and plunging valleys below. Streams, flecked with butterflies and patrolled by parrots and hornbills, cut across the road, while giant leaves litter the ground and lianas tangle overhead. Occasionally a hunter or a woodcutter emerges – usually to stand still, nonplussed, on seeing you. Monkeys, the hunters' main targets, are common.

At last the gradients relax and the road unwinds, through more cultivated country, towards the Kakrima River. The village of **Djounkoun** leaves little impression, but **Léi-Mîro**, 4km east of the river, is the second large settlement along the route. You'll find rice and other street food if you turn up early enough, or bread and sandwich ingredients if not. Léi-Mîro's *lumo* takes place every Thursday.

The winch-ferry across the **Kakrima River** has an engine, but it's not far across (either hauling the ferry's line or renting a *pirogue*) in the event of breakdown. **Koussi** is just beyond, where people know a good short cut, useful if you're walking to Télimélé. The main route beyond Koussi is hard work on a bicycle, mostly flat – and sandy in parts – with tall elephant grass blocking any view. Sixty-one kilometres beyond Dongol-Touma the route hits the broad, red sweep of the Kindia–Télimélé road, where you should find a lift easily enough. The final gruelling 15km to Télimélé up the soaring flank of **Mont Louba** are noted for gut-churning accidents on the hairpins.

Télimélé

A pleasing, well-kept town, perched as if to admire its grand views, **TÉLIMÉLÉ** sees very few visitors. Nearby lies **Gueme Sangan**, the ruined fortress of the fifteenth-century Fula warlord Koli Tengela (see p.545). Télimélé is a town of pine trees, citrus orchards and fresh air, surrounded by imposing mountain flanks and trench-like valleys. There are two adequate **hotels**: the *Hôtel de l'Indépendance* (①) and the slightly more attractive *Petit Palais* (②).

When you're ready to leave Télimélé there are two or three jeep or Land Rover departures each week to **Gaoual**, 130km along a beautiful route to the north. The road down to **Kindia** isn't too bad and transport is reasonably frequent, but it's worth investing a little extra for a place in a Peugeot rather than one of the minibuses. Stay awake for the last half-hour before Kindia; there are some outstanding tabular massifs, rearing like lost worlds across the valley.

Labé and the northern Fouta Djalon

Heading north from Pita, the **road to Labé**, 38km away, loops across a mellow, pastoral landscape of undulating grass, scattered with boulders and copses of oak-like *koura* trees, and fringed with lines of forest along the watercourses. The district, one of the highest in the Fouta Djalon, is a watershed between the streams that flow west and the Gambia and Senegal tributaries pouring off northwards.

Labé

Strategically situated in the middle of the highlands lies **LABÉ**, the historic strong-hold of the Fula and capital of the Fouta Djalon. It's now the largest town in the region, and a good place to check your emails, make phone calls, and enjoy the nearest thing this part of Guinea has to a real city. Labé's appeal arises from its status as the Fouta Djalon's largest market town and the area's main artisanal centre. **Tata** district, a kilometre or so to the left as you head out to the airport, is home to the yards of a couple of **weaving** guilds. You might do well to enlist someone to guide you to the weavers (*tisserands*) if you're interested in seeing them at work. Also on the way to the airport, you pass the National Apiculture Centre, with local potted **honey** for sale.

For something a little more substantial in the way of food, the **market** in the town centre – huge, vibrant and teeming – is one of Labé's strong points, though a tight squeeze to walk around. There's a remarkable variety of groundnut pastes on offer, and all the usual Fouta Djalon profusion of produce. Look out for exquisite **gara** cloth, made from Czech damask, tie-dyed with local indigo and beaten with clubs to a shine; it's sold, as usual, in pairs of *pagnes*. Inside the market, you can also watch **shoemakers** at work manufacturing the colourfully ornamented leather sandals the region is famous for; a pair will cost around FG5000–7000 depending on your negotiating skills. Labé also has a pretty little **museum** in a bright new building slightly away from the town centre; exhibits include various historical items, examples of traditional arts and crafts, musical instruments and the like.

Labé is a good base for excursions into the surrounding countryside – indeed, if you hire a taxi and get an early start, you could get all the way to Mali-ville and back in a day. The *Hôtel Tata* has a couple of knowledgeable guides, who will take you on **hiking trips** around the region (fees negotiable); alternatively, you could always venture out on your own. One of the Fouta's most impressive waterfalls, the **Chutes de la Saala**, lies 40km north of Labé. Follow the road to Koundara, then turn off near the road to Lélouma and follow the unpaved road until you reach the falls. A day's taxi hire at the *gare routière* should cost FG35,000–40,000 plus petrol. Take stout shoes so you can climb around the falls (there are good views of the multiple cascades from all sides) and swimming gear to bathe in the plunge pool, plus some food for a picnic, and be careful on the cliff edges.

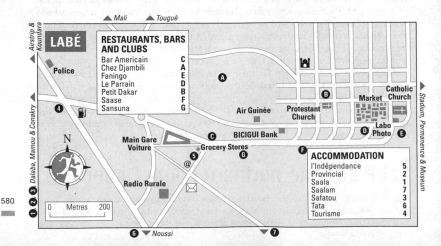

△ Old Fula meeting house in Dalaba

Practicalities

Arriving from Pita, you enter Labé past the dominating hulk of the *Hôtel de Tourisme* (☎51 09 10; ❷), a once grand establishment in a vaguely Swiss-chalet style, but now, despite its newly painted exterior, somewhat decrepit. Still, there's hot running water and the **rooms** are very reasonably priced, the large bar-restaurant serves meals all day and the *Tinkisso* club downstairs comes alive with a young crowd at weekends. A better alternative is the clean and very friendly *Hôtel de l'Indépendance* (☎51.10.00; ❶) at the lower end of the *gare voiture*. The pleasant *Hôtel Tata* (☎51.05.40; ❷) is the favoured gathering place for European NGO workers and Peace Corps staff, and also has the best pizzas in Guinea in its good restaurant. The only other hotel in town is the *Hôtel Salaam* (☎51.24.72; ❷), in Kouroula district – a clean, still fairly central place. If you have transport, you might prefer to stay in one of the hotels on the south side of town. *Hôtel Saala*, 2km from the town centre, is a pretty place with spacious rooms and a very good restaurant. A little further out is the *Provincial* (☎51.61.37; ❷), which has few rooms, but is best known as the home of one of Labé's more stylish nightclubs. The *Safatou* (☎51.11.09; ❸) is Labé's most reputable place, with large rooms equipped with TV and fridge, though it's a little far from the centre, and isn't the best value for money. Its nightclub is the town's place to be seen.

The market offers a wealth of food, and the town's **restaurants** are equally well-stocked – being at the centre of Guinea's potato-cultivating region, Labé is the place to eat home-made fries and potato salad. Besides the *Restaurant Tata* and the *Tinkisso* at the *Hôtel de Tourisme* (see above), try the *Bar Americain* near the *Hôtel de l'Indépendance* for snacks and drinks. The sociable *Petit Dakar* serves drinks and sandwiches, and is the main meeting spot for Labé's youth. Well hidden in the *quartier* Mairie is the informal *Chez Djambili*, where a local woman prepares delicious *atiéké*, meat sauce, salad and grilled fish at a corner outside a popular bar – a great place to eat, drink and meet the locals, if you can find it.

Moving on from Labé

Labé is something of a cul-de-sac as far as regular **taxi brousse** and **bus transport** goes. Plenty of Peugeot 504s run down the Fouta Djalon spine to Pita, Dalaba, Mamou and Conakry every morning; all these destinations are served from the main *gare voiture*. Northbound traffic is a lot less dense; most services leave from the *gare voiture*, though you may find some vehicles bound for Mali-ville along the road out of Labé or near the market in town. A second main *gare voiture* – the *gare* Dakar – to the right of the road out to the airport, handles *taxi brousse* and truck traffic for Koundara and Senegal (taxis to Dakar take a full day and night).

Air Guinée operates **flights** to Conakry, Banjul and Dakar twice a week. The fare to Conakry is around FG60,000, to Banjul FG100,000 and Dakar FG150,000 one way.

Discos in town include the popular *Faningo*, which gets massively crowded at weekends; *Saase*, a teenage place; and *Le Parrain*, which attracts a mixed crowd. Labé has several **live-music** venues: you could try the seedy *Sansuna*, which has a local dance band at weekends, but mind the drunkards and prostitutes and be prepared to find yourself the constant centre of attention. The **Radio Rurale** (☎51.03.05) is a useful source of information on music events, and will also have information on any upcoming concerts of traditional music or other special events.

Labé boasts the only **bank** in the Fouta Djalon, a branch of the BICIGUI (Mon–Fri 8.30am–12.30pm & 2.30–4pm), as well as a **post office** (Mon–Sat 7.30am–4pm) and an **Internet** café, next to the *Hôtel de l'Indépendance*.

The northern Fouta Djalon

If you've come up to Labé from the south, the most obvious onward option is to continue, off-tarmac, to the towns of **Mali** (or Mali-ville) and **Koundara**, from where it's possible to continue to Kédougou in Senegal. You can reach Koundara via Mali, or directly from Labé – the latter route is much easier, but still a full day's journey by bush taxi even in the dry season, and virtually impossible in the rains. If you're heading east towards **Kankan** (see p.586), it's better to head back to Mamou and follow the main route from there.

The fabulously picturesque route from **Labé to Gaoual** is an alternative if you're heading for Guinea-Bissau and Senegal's Basse Casamance region. On this route you're almost certain to have to take a Koundara vehicle and change at **Kounsitel**, from where local vehicles head to Gaoual, Koumbia and north to Guinea-Bissau. **GAOUAL** itself is a friendly little town, with a wide avenue of trees and an old colonial PTT, though it gets extremely hot here in the dry season. The *Fromagier* (❶), little more than a small hut in a family compound, is a nice (in fact the only) **place to stay**, and the lady of the house will be happy to cook for you.

Right on the border with Guinea-Bissau, the town of **FOULA-MORI** is home to the birth hut of legendary Fula leader **Alfa Yaya** (see box on p.545). The impressively well-kept hut is maintained by Alfa Yaya's descendants, who will show you around for a small tip; exhibits include the shards of Alfa Yaya's war drum, his bed and a few other items. Officials at the friendly border post can put you in touch with locals who can provide lodgings for a night or two.

Mali

The route from Labé to the small town of Mali switchbacks through the loftiest sections of the Fouta Djalon, with a number of fair-size villages on the way. Fourteen kilometres north of Labé, **Tountouroun** still has beautiful Fula houses, while just a kilometre or so further the road crosses a small stream running east – this is the **Gambia River**, whose source is nearby to the west. Further villages include **Sarékali** at 35km; the pretty hamlet of **Pellal** off to the left at 65km; and **Yambéring**, the largest, at 74km.

At 1460m, **MALI** is the highest settlement in the Fouta Djalon, renowned for its low temperatures (down to 3°C) and magnificent views. These are particularly good from the summit of **Mont Loura** (1538m), the highest peak in the Fouta Djalon, which lies 7km northeast of the village. On its eastern flank you can spot the **Dame de Mali**, a cliff eroded into a feminine profile.

Mali has two **places to stay**: the small and primitive *La Dame de Mali* (●) and the slightly better *Auberge Indigo* (●). A new hotel was under construction at the time of writing. If you're trying to get **from Mali to Koundara**, Mali's market day, Sunday, offers the best chance. Otherwise, you might have to wait days for a vehicle. Be prepared for a diabolical road with one-in-four gradients, some dangerous hairpins and several skeletal bridges.

Koundara and the Parc National Niokolo-Badiar

KOUNDARA, 50km from the Senegalese border, is the jumping-off point for excursions to the **Parc National Niokolo-Badiar**, which lies on the border adjoining Senegal's Parc National Niokolo-Koba. Visitors stand a good chance of seeing wild animals including lions, leopards, antelopes, monkeys and hippos. Facilities for visitors are still basic, but the staff in the park head office in **SAMBAILO** (reachable by taxi from Koundara, with regular flights from Conakry) are helpful and can help arrange car hire, which is the only way to get around the park. The park is closed during the rainy season, when it's virtually impossible to get from Labé to Koundara in any case. You can **stay** in the park itself at the *campement* or else base yourself in nearby Koundara: try the reasonable *Hôtel du Gangan* or the *Mamadou Boiro* (both ●).

7.3

Haute Guinée

The great plains of the east, known as **Haute Guinée**, stretch immensely vast and flat over more than a hundred thousand square kilometres. In this huge expanse, the few towns – **Kankan**, **Kouroussa**, **Faranah** and **Siguiri** – seem lost amid yellow grass, thorn trees and termite spires. In contrast to the Fouta Djalon to the west and the rainforest-covered highlands further south, the population is sparse: most people live along the meandering **tributaries of the Niger** which pull together in a fan in the most populous part of the region around Kankan and Kouroussa.

Without your own **transport** you're mostly restricted to the clutch of main routes (a mix of surfaced roads and dirt tracks) which traverse the region. Away from the main routes, distances between settlements are often too far for comfortable walking or cycling – indeed even on the main roads you can go miles without seeing a soul. In addition, Haute Guinée gets blisteringly hot and painfully dry during the dry season.

Dabola and Kouroussa

DABOLA grew up after 1910 as a staging post, and it retains a slightly Wild West feel, hemmed in by gaunt plateaux rising directly behind the town and making a living by keeping those passing through well fed and entertained. It's not an unattractive place, with neat compounds surrounding the small commercial centre. There are also a couple of very decent **hotels**. The upmarket *Hôtel Tinkisso* (❸), set in large grounds, has comfortable self-contained rooms with showers and a large bar-restaurant with satellite TV. Equally comfortable, but cheaper, is the more intimate *Hôtel Mont Sincery* (❷), whose cute lobby doubles as a TV lounge bar.

Just outside town, the **Tinkisso Falls** are worth a short detour. A gentle six-kilometre climb along the road to Mamou brings you to a track on your left, which drops over the railway line through a teak plantation and, forking right, to the top of the **dam** and a mass of birdlife (an alternative route follows the power lines from town straight to the falls). The **falls** themselves – which must have been impressive indeed before the dam was built – cascade over rocky shelves (except at the end of the dry season, when there's no water). Determined hikers might want to extend the walk into a circular trek by following the path from the falls which descends steeply to the power station. Continue on the same footpath downstream and you reach an immaculate Fula village and, eventually, the Dabola–Faranah road. The circular walk makes a good day's excursion, whether or not the falls are in spate, for the landscape and birdlife.

From Dabola, you can also arrange transport to **DINGUIRAYE**, a tough 100-kilometre drive further north, which is home to Guinea's most famous **mosque**, a huge and well-maintained construction dedicated to the legendary **Al Haj Omar Tall**, a Fula religious leader who made mass conversions throughout West Africa in the nineteenth century. The *Hôtel de l'Amitié* (❶) has reasonable rooms at reasonable prices.

Kouroussa

KOUROUSSA is little more than a place to spend the night if you can't make it all the way from Dabola to Kankan in a day, though it's in a beautiful area, and, thanks to the new road from Dabola, it's easy to reach. Kouroussa was also the birthplace of Guinea's best-known author, **Camara Laye**: the Laye family house is near the station and easily found if you want to pay homage. The town is pleasant and leafy, though its **accommodation** is dire. Try any of the bars at the market, such as *Bar La Baobab* and the *Chateau D'eau* near the *gare voiture* for information on rooms. You can get food at the friendly *Café Savane*, near the market.

Faranah and around

Until independence in 1958, **FARANAH** was an unimportant village on the old road from Dabola to Kissidougou. **Sekou Touré** pumped money into his native village, building a large mosque, as well as the Cité du Niger conference centre in

---

Moving on from Dabola

Dabola has daily transport connections to Mamou, Faranah, Kouroussa and Kankan. The 110-kilometre earth road to **Faranah**, which descends gradually from Dabola before running past irrigated rice fields and along the stripling Niger valley into Faranah, is in rough condition. The journey from Dabola to **Kouroussa** takes less than three hours, but the Kouroussa to **Kankan** stretch is still tough going – an uncomfortable five hours by Peugeot 504.

1981 and a massive block of a villa for himself, which unfortunately is now closed. Today, Faranah seems to be steadily slipping back towards its original state as a sleepy village, its selection of restaurants and hotels diminishing year by year. It's a town you're likely to pass through, and although it's still adequate for most practical needs, there's little of interest to hold you. If you're visiting the Parc National Haut Niger, you can get information at their office in town (☎81.04.82).

Accommodation is very limited. Try the relatively decent *Hôtel Bati* (❶) or ask in the popular *Bantou* bar next door for a bed in one of Faranah's informal guest-houses. In the town centre, cheap **eateries** compete at one end of the main *gare voiture*, serving high-quality street food all day, and – at least some of them – at night too.

Parc National Haut Niger

The **Parc National Haut Niger** is the second national park to open in Guinea in recent years. The park's headquarters are in the village of **SIDAKORO**, 45km from Faranah, where you can also spend the night in the very basic *campement*. There's no public transport to Sidakoro, so you'll need your own vehicle to get to and around the park (you can rent a vehicle and driver for a day-trip at Sidakoro for around FG60,000), and you may be able to spot buffaloes, chimpanzees, water-bucks, hippos and elephants, among other wildlife, though the animals tend to scatter after the rains. An alternative tour of the park can be had from the waters of the **Niger River**: hiring a *pirogue* and guide for the day will cost around FG10,000 – unless you fancy having a boat made to order – see the box below.

Canoeing down the Niger

If you're looking for adventure, and have a full life-support system (tent and cooking equipment essential), Faranah is a good place to acquire a boat and **canoe down the Niger**, either as far as Kouroussa, or all the way to Bamako in Mali. A four-metre plank boat, adequate for one, can be made to order for about FG100,000. A six- or seven-metre boat, big enough for two, will cost up to FG350,000. The wood is the main expense, and while a plank boat is slightly more expensive than a dugout, it is lighter, faster and more manoeuvreable. You don't need to be an experienced canoeist for the trip, but you will need to take sufficient **food** (rice and canned food) to last the whole journey, as you cannot rely on the occasional fishing camps having food for sale (there are no villages in the Faranah to Kouroussa section). Money and precious items need to be protected in waterproof bags, as you're almost certain to capsize sooner or later.

The 350-kilometre trip from **Faranah to Kouroussa** should take between ten and fourteen days. The river winds through **forest** which looms out from the banks, and there are several sections of **rapids** along the way, though only two difficult sections – any local fisherman will give you advice. **Wildlife** is abundant and interesting: you'll see beautiful birds, monkeys and baboons, antelope, warthogs, snakes, small crocodiles and several groups of hippos. Because they are hunted, hippos tend to stay well clear of boats but you should give them a wide berth anyway, as they can be dangerous. There are some larger crocodiles (up to four metres) but you are very unlikely to see them, and you're safe in a boat. Bilharzia is not a problem and the swimming, hippos permitting, is fine nearly everywhere. **Downstream from Kouroussa**, the riverscape opens out, running through farmland and savanna – the channel is well over a kilometre wide in places. There are plenty of villages to restock your supplies along this stretch, but the journey is less interesting, with no rapids, no crocs and few hippos. Kouroussa to Bamako is roughly a two-week trip of about 400km.

The **best time** to do the trip is after the rains (they usually finish in October) and before the end of the dry season (March–April). At the end of the dry season, parts of the river are very shallow, making progress slow, and the rainy season is a bad time because the water level fluctuates and camping on the banks is unsafe.

> ### Moving on from Faranah
>
> Vehicles bound for **Mamou** and **Kissidougou** cluster at the main *gare voiture* below the market. It's easy to reach Conakry, Labé, Kankan or Nzérékoré in a day, though it's worth noting that the highway from Faranah to Kissidougou is in bad shape. The *gare voiture* for **Dabola** and **Kouroussa** is at the opposite end of town, its only land-mark being a blue house.
>
> Some 15km west of Faranah, a big sign on the left saying "Direction Sierra Leone" points the way across the border to **Kabala**. Since the civil war in Sierra Leone, bush taxis rarely take this route, and you are advised to use the main route via Pamalap on the main road between Conakry and Freetown instead.

⑦ Kankan

The name alone is alluring: **KANKAN** may be mostly very ordinary, but there's a sense of place here and a depth of history that knocks spots off every other place in the country. The spell it casts arises largely from the fact that Kankan is one of the oldest and biggest Malinké towns anywhere in West Africa – in fact, the town is actually made up of a loose federation of villages which have grown into each other over time, a fact which goes some way to explaining its very laid-back and open atmosphere. At the height of the dry season, however, Kankan is so unbearably hot that you may decide to abandon visiting the region altogether.

It was Muslim warrior-traders, the **Soninké**, who are credited with the foundation of a mini-empire centred on Kankan. They arrived at the end of the seventeenth century and set themselves up in a dozen villages stretched out along the banks of the Milo River, including the embryonic – and at that time non-Muslim – Kankan. This trading empire was known as **Baté** (the village of Baté Nafadj, 40km north of Kankan, is a reminder). Kankan grew to become its capital, and by 1850 had grown to a considerable size and acquired protective walls, while its fleets of *pirogues* plied the Milo and Niger rivers as far as Gao in Mali. Caravans arrived from the Sahel and the desert, and from the highland forests in the south, which it largely controlled, came kola nuts, palm oil and slaves. Another reason for Kankan's ascendancy was gold, from the Bure goldfields, which extended from north of Siguiri to far up the Milo.

Kankan's apogee didn't last long: Samory Touré (see p.544) smashed the hegemony of the city in 1879 after a ten-month siege, and twelve years later the French were in occupation.

The Town

Kankan has a beguiling ambience, with a spacious layout and long, mango-shaded avenues; a woman on a bicycle is a rare sight in most of West Africa, common enough here. There's a university and *lycées* and lots of students (this is where many of Guinea's student unrests have started), two hospitals and a considerable, scholarly, Islamic presence. The vast **markets** are well worth a visit. The covered **Marché Central** sells mostly clothes: a lot of trashy imports, but also brilliantly coloured local confections that look great (but would require lots of guts to wear), plus myriad selections of *pagnes* and items imported from Mali and Niger, mostly rugs and blankets. There are also a couple of stalls specializing in old bits of carving, *gris-gris*, amulets and mystical substances. If you're interested in receiving some supernatural aid, then Kankan is the place to ask: **marabouts** here are considered some of the most powerful in West Africa and inscriptions and potions can be obtained easily, for a fee – you don't have to be a Muslim.

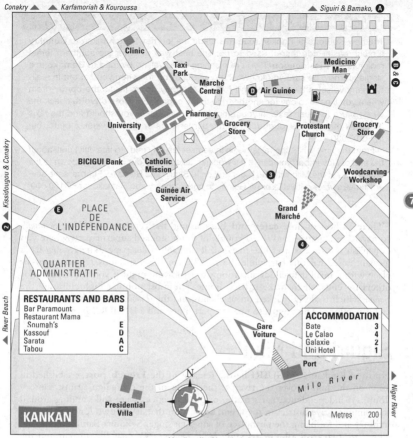

Clinic

Taxi
Park

Marché
Central

Ⓓ Air Guinée

Medicine
Man

Pharmacy

University

Ⓐ

Grocery
Store

Protestant
Church

Grocery
Store

BICIGUI Bank

Catholic
Mission

Guinée Air
Service

Woodcarving
Workshop

Ⓔ

PLACE
DE
L'INDÉPENDANCE

Ⓑ

Ⓒ

Grand
Marché

Ⓒ

QUARTIER
ADMINISTRATIF

RESTAURANTS AND BARS

Bar Paramount	B
Restaurant Mama	
Soumah's	E
Kassouf	D
Sarata	A
Tabou	C

Gare
Voiture

ACCOMMODATION

Bate	3
Le Calao	4
Galaxie	2
Uni Hotel	1

Port

Milo River

N

KANKAN

Presidential
Villa

0   Metres   200

If you're in Kankan in the **mango** season (March to April) you're in for a real treat – the town is full of mango trees.

Practicalities

The main **gare voiture** is a shady patch of dust down by the river at the edge of town, but you may well find yourself dropped off at one of the minor taxi parks near the town's access roads. The main budget **accommodation** is the *Hôtel Galaxie* (☎71.21.08; ❶), in the southwest of town near the *briquetterie*, which has reasonable self-contained rooms and decent meals on request. *Hôtel Bate* (☎71.23.68 or 71.26.86; ❸) is the town's most popular option for well-heeled tourists and business travellers; it has a good restaurant and bar and comfortable, albeit expensive, a/c rooms. An equally good and much cheaper option is the *Hôtel Le Calao* (☎71.27.97; ❷), right next to the market, which has spotless carpeted rooms with TV, plus a good restaurant and a small arts and crafts shop in a quiet courtyard. The *Uni Hotel* (☎71.06.28; ❸), built on university land, offers similarly well-equipped self-contained rooms, but don't consider staying here if the university students are engaged in one of their frequent strikes – these always lead to violent clashes between military and students.

The new Kouroussa–Kankan road has made the journey from Kankan to **Conakry** a much easier ride than it used to be. The best way to enter the southern forest region is via **Kissidougou**. If you're planning on travelling by road to **Bamako** in a single journey, be sure you know what you're paying for when you set off: in reality, many vehicles allegedly bound for Bamako only go as far as the border, from where you'll have to pay for another ride to the capital. For **Côte d'Ivoire** check the *gare voiture* for bush taxis. If you're not going to Bouaké, you should find the *taxis brousses* that run the rough road to the border once or twice a week a better bet at FG10,000.

From the time when the rains begin in earnest (usually mid- to late July) until about the end of November, you can, if it's working, take a **ferry** out of Kankan, down to the confluence of the Milo with the Niger and on to Siguiri and Bamako. **Flights** leave several times a week with UTA or Air Guinée to both Conakry and Bamako for FG100,000.

There's a host of little **cafés and bars** around the centre – try *Mama Soumah's* courtyard restaurant – and also a couple of thinly stocked supermarkets where you can splash out on luxuries like marmalade and soft toilet paper. The *Kassouf* has a pleasant raised balcony bar, while the *Bar Paramount* is a spacious, relaxed open-air place with a small dancefloor and rooms to let for the night if you're too drunk or otherwise engaged to make it back home. The most popular nightclubs are the *Sarata*, which is always packed on weekends, and the *Tabou*, a large disco with several dancefloors. The town also boasts a post office and a BICIGUI **bank**.

Siguiri and Niani

North of Kankan at **SIGUIRI** lie the remains of the **French post**, established in 1888 on the hilltop over the river, at the height of the campaign against Samory Touré. At independence, parts of the original defences were still standing around the administrative district of the town. Apart from that, it's known for its goldsmith industry and for being the birthplace of superstar singer Sekouba Bambino Diabaté. There are two basic **places to stay**: *Hôtel Tamtam* (**❶**), near the airstrip, and the *Hôtel de la Paix* (**❶**). Air Guinée operates direct **flights** to Conakry (FG100,000), as well as an indirect one via Kankan.

NIANI is a village on the Sankarani River (which forms the border with Mali), 80km on a very rough track southeast of Siguiri. Nowadays, Niani doesn't look any different from your average north Guinean town, but it was here that **Sundiata Keita** (also known as Mari-Djata; 1205–1255), the legendary founding king of the Mali Empire, installed his capital. Mande griots have transmitted the legends of his reign for generations, though only excavations among the baobabs have convinced Western historians of the truthfulness of their claims, with the uncovering of the sites of foundries and cemeteries dotted around the town.

Kérouané and Beyla

South of Kankan, the direct route to Guinée Forestière runs alongside the gaunt whaleback of the **Chaîne du Going** ridge to the town of Kérouané and then up into the remote and rugged region beyond Beyla. This is a richly historical route. On the way down to Kérouané you pass **Bissandougou**, the recruiting point and eventual capital of **Almamy Samory Touré**'s first empire; people in your vehicle will point it out to you. Whether the small cemetery with its *banco* wall surround is still there, is hard to tell, but the nineteenth-century fort has definitely returned to the soil.

Samory signed a treaty with the French at Bissandougou in 1887, hoping to keep them confined to the left bank of the Niger, but new French commanders swept the agreements aside and moved on Kankan and Bissandougou in 1890. Samory adopted scorched-earth tactics and retreated south, burning villages in his path. At Kérouané he had a fort constructed on the hilltop and from here his forces harassed the French while the warrior planned his next move (for more on Samory, see p.544).

Today, the small prefecture of **KÉROUANÉ** barely hints at its place in history. The remains (and very little remains) of the **Tata de Samory fortress** on a low hill are now the site of the "Villa" – the administrative quarter. Archeologically the interest is thin: a huge block of laterite bricks – part of the massive old wall of the fort which measured 170m across – and what looks like a gate house: a hollow hut like a honey pot near the entrance. Inside, you're supposedly able to see the stone-enshrined profile of a pregnant woman whom Samory enclosed in the wall before his withdrawal. Alongside, on the new wall, there's a faded portrait of Samory.

With table-top hills rising around and the steep, bluish ridge of Going soaring to over 1300m, it's a fine setting. Kérouané is surprisingly lively and, although the attractions are hard to pinpoint, it does have a certain appeal. Because of the transport situation, you may well end up **staying the night** here in *chambres de passage* – very basic rooms without electricity or running water. For **meals and food**, there's a large market and some good rice and sauce in the street leading away from the police station. Nice *café fort* and *thé vert* can be had at a couple of licensed cafés up here on the left, with pleasant patios to loaf around and meet people. From here during the dry season you can watch the progress of bushfires on Mont Going – a sombre spectacle on December and January nights as giant orange tongues leap from its flanks.

Beyla

South of Kérouané lies **BEYLA**, founded in the thirteenth century by Mande-speaking kola traders, and favoured by the French in colonial times. If you've a tough vehicle of your own, the Beyla region is unquestionably one of Guinea's most worthwhile – a number of tracks run through the Kourandou mountains, just northeast of town. For **accommodation**, the grubby *Hôtel Simadou* (①) is your only option.

Moving on from Kérouané

There's normally a truck or two and the occasional *taxi brousse* out of Kérouané to **Nzérékoré** early each morning, though you only undertake this journey if you're willing to spend an entire day in a vehicle trying to negotiate one of the country's toughest routes, and be prepared for any eventuality – such as spending several days in the bush while the driver tries to get his vehicle out of a ditch, waits for help, or abandons all efforts in favour of finding a wife in a nearby village.

From **Konsankoro**, south of Kérouané, there's a highly rated but extremely rough hundred-kilometre track over the ranges to **Macenta**, through rarely visited **diamond-mining country**. The road is beautiful, though you may be too busy praying for safe arrival and long life to enjoy the sight of massive granite sugarloaf mountains and mesas pushing up from the bush.

7.4

Guinée Forestière

Piled up in the fractured border region where Guinea meets Sierra Leone, Liberia and Côte d'Ivoire, the highland chains of the southeast – commonly known as **Guinée Forestière** – provide inducements to match or surpass the Fouta Djalon. Although the region lacks the Fouta Djalon's towering cliffs and waterfalls, the highlands of Guinée Forestière weigh in with rainforest-covered ridges, challenging routes and a largely non-Islamic ethnic make-up. **Climatically** this is perhaps the most appealing part of the country, even if travel can be stubbornly difficult between April and November. Altitude and clouds keep it mild or warm most of the year, and while the rains are torrential, storms are accompanied by impressive electrical phenomena. There also tends to be a drier spell in the rainy season, between the end of April and mid-June. The forest harbours significant numbers of **wild animals**, including chimpanzees, leopards, forest elephants and buffalos, as well as hippos and crocs in the rivers.

Ethnically, this is singular territory. The region's predominant **Kissi**, **Loma** and **Guerzé** inhabitants are linguistically diverse and resolutely independent. Ancestor worship, totemism and *forêts sacrés* ("sacred forests": usually a clearing within the forest where rituals are performed) are all important cultural elements. Islamic influences are far less pronounced than elsewhere and the impress of colonialism is light. Colonial subjugation – a gruelling village-by-village war of invasion – wasn't complete until 1920, having persisted bloodily since Samory's demise in 1898. Most of the **towns** in the forest region are recent creations, dating back no further than the first French post at a suitable source of food, water and labour. Once victorious, the French maintained a thin and rather miserable presence. During the reign of Sekou Touré, many Guineans sought refuge in the relatively unpoliticized highlands, and tens of thousands more fled the country from here, especially to Côte d'Ivoire.

Sadly, this is not only Guinea's most beautiful, but also its most troubled region. In 2000 and 2001, the **civil wars** of Liberia and Sierra Leone spilled over into the region, and severe clashes between rebel troops and the Guinean army left some places, such as Guéckédou, in ruins. During the crisis years, Guinée Forestière also had to cope with large numbers of Sierra Leonean refugees, who have gradually started returning home, only to be replaced by new truckloads of people escaping the fighting in Côte d'Ivoire in 2002 and 2003. The region itself was peaceful at the time of writing, but there have been reports of occasional rebel activity from Liberia. British Foreign Office advice is not to leave the main routes, and to avoid solo travel. Check with your embassy or consulate in Conakry, if possible, and consult locals. The region's recurring troubles have also meant that the **roads** are in poor condition, and travelling around the region is harder than in any other part of the country.

Kissidougou

The gateway to Guinée Forestière, **KISSIDOUGOU**, comprises three no longer easily distinguishable villages. **Kenéma Pompo** is the oldest, a Kissi village which goes back to the eighteenth century, when it was tucked in its sacred forest. The second, **Hérèmakono** (which means roughly "Home Sweet Home"), is the administrative and commercial district built away from the forest. The third, **Dioulabou** (the "Dyula town"), lies on the east side and was established by Samory's vanquished lieutenants in 1893. Kissi Kaba Keita, the ruler of the town at the time of French penetration, put up a notional resistance. Today, Kissidougou borders the largest zone of **forest** in West Africa and the sense of transition is apparent in the patches of tropical woodland around the town. The town is also notable as the centre of Guinea's main coffee-growing area.

Spacious and unusually flat, the town doesn't seem such a bad place after one of Haute Guinée's arduous taxi rides. A tiny **museum** (free), opposite the Commissariat de Police Centrale, contains two or three dozen local objects of interest, including various bits of Kissi and Kouranko ethnographia and some contemporary domestic items. Fading black-and-white photos show scenes from French colonial days. The daily **covered market**, in the quarter behind the central silk-cotton tree, is worth exploring. You'll find a fair selection, at fair prices, of the kind of imported stuff (Sierra Leone country cloth, Malian blankets, printed *pagnes*) that's found in greater quantities at the international markets of Nzérékoré and Kankan. Goods from Mali for example, often inflated in markets there, are offered at knockdown prices. Kissidougou's **football stadium** hosts national league matches, watched by hundreds of spectators, some of whom stand on lorries and buildings to catch a glimpse of the action.

An interesting trip leads out to Kissidougou's **pont artisanal**, a liana bridge about 2km east of the town centre off the road to Kankan. Take the second turning on the right after the roundabout and keep walking towards the water supply building, often to be seen emitting smoke.

Practicalities

Kissidougou has a surprising selection of **places to stay**. A very decent option is the slightly distant *Hôtel Savannah* (☎98.10.40; **❷**), with well-appointed a/c rooms and others with fan. It's the only hotel that provides reliable electricity, and also houses a good nightclub. In town, the new *Hôtel Mantise* (☎98.12.13 or 98.13.47) is a good alternative: this consists of the more luxurious *Palace Madina* (**❸**) and the more basic but still very adequate *Résidence Madina* (**❷**). Both have a choice of rooms with a/c or fan. The basic but charming *Hôtel Béléfé* (**❶**) is run by an old

The Kissi

The **Kissi** are a long-established indigenous people who live across the wide swath of territory from the southern Niger headwaters to the foothills of the southeast highlands. Adroit farmers (it's their swamp rice which you'll see along the Kissidougou–Guéckédou road), they traditionally worship their ancestors, on whose benevolence they believe they depend for the success of their crops, and maintain strong beliefs in witchcraft. Until recently, nearly all Kissi villages had their own witch-hunters (the *wulumo*), whose skills were called upon to divine the evil-minded whenever misfortune struck.

Kissi people still venerate small stone figures, each imbued with the spirit of an ancestor. These sculptures, usually in soapstone and called **pomdo** ("the dead"), are dug up in the fields, or found in the forest, but never carved today. The Kissi traditionally believe the sculptures are the physical essence of their ancestors, but their origin is an enigma. Like the *nomoli* of Sierra Leone, they were certainly carved by an ancient culture, probably before the fifteenth century, though it's not certain that they were produced by the ancestors of the people who now revere them.

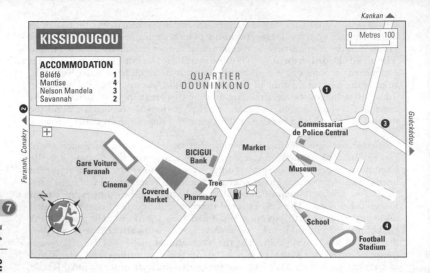

KISSIDOUGOU

ACCOMMODATION

Béléfé	1
Mantise	4
Nelson Mandela	3
Savannah	2

QUARTIER
DOUNINKONO

Commissariat
de Police Central

Market

BICIGUI
Bank

Museum

Gare Voiture
Faranah

Cinema

Tree

Covered
Market

Pharmacy

School

Football
Stadium

forestier, who will be happy to switch on the generator for you, thereby attracting the whole neighbourhood for TV evenings in the lounge. It's signposted off the main road into town. Lastly, the *Hôtel Nelson Mandela* (☎98.13.05; ❷) is fairly acceptable and has a nice restaurant.

The Faranah road has the largest selection of **street food**, including huge servings of delicious fried plantain and *atiéké*. There are few proper **restaurants** in town – although you could try the *Escale Cosmos* near the banks – but plenty of enjoyable, usually unnamed bars along the roadside. Kissidougou has both a **post office** and BICIGUI **bank**, which face each other across the curve of the main street, as well as a hospital.

Moving on from Kissidougou, the road surface to **Faranah** has been improved, reducing the journey time to a couple of hours. The roads to **Kankan** are less well-surfaced, but still possible. A scenic place to stop on the way to Kankan is **TOKOUNO**, crowded beneath a mountain escarpment. There's a hotel here, eating places and a *balafon* workshop, where you can buy the instruments and watch them being made.

The source of the Niger

If you've a couple of spare days, an adventurous but not too difficult trip leads from Kissidougou to the **source of the Niger** (there are no hotels en route, so you'll have to either stay with locals or camp). First base is the village of **Bambaya**, northwest of Kissidougou, accessible up a road signposted "Kobikoro" off the Kissi–Faranah highway; you'll need to *déplace* a taxi to reach Bambaya. There's a Friday market at **Baleya**, 3km from Banbaya. Second base is **Kobikoro**, 12km further on, where the *chef* and *sous-préfet* are both welcoming – in theory you need the *sous-préfet*'s permission to visit the source. From here on the route gets tough for walkers and the scenery interesting as you head up to third base, **Forokonia**, 20km further on. There are magnificent forest trees up here, though they're being logged. Forokonia has a Thursday market. On reaching Forokonia you'll need a guide (ask around the village) to show you the actual source, a three- or four-hour walk away. The **source** – at 9° 5' north, 10° 47' 14" west – itself isn't impressive, but the surrounding scenery is beautiful.

Kissidougou to Nzérékoré

The road from Kissidougou into the deeper regions of Guinée Forestière leads via Guéckédou to Macenta and Nzérékoré. **GUÉCKÉDOU** used to be a flourishing centre, attracting a vibrant mix of Sierra Leonean, Ivoirian, Liberian, Guinean and Malian traders to its lively market. Unfortunately, much of the fighting between the Guinean army and rebels from Sierra Leone and Liberia in 2000–2001 was concentrated here, and has left the town completely in ruins. Though some cautious efforts at rebuilding had begun at the time of writing, most of the town was still full of wrecked houses, with walls covered in shell and bullet holes, and makeshift homes pieced together with the help of UN blankets and sheets of corrugated iron.

The route southeast from Guéckédou to Nzérékoré is rough and exciting. The ribbon of the road buckles and falters for much of the way, tunnelling through towering green jungle and sometimes pitted with lorry-deep holes. A new tarmac highway was being built from Guéckédou to Nzérékoré in the 1990s, but work stopped at Sérédou when the region became the entry point into Guinea of rebels from neighbouring countries.

Macenta and around

Once out of Guéckédou, the serious forest starts with the climb on the road from the bridge over the Makona, just beyond **Bofossou** – a large village and military post dating back to 1905. It's a steep haul up what's known, somewhat mysteriously, as the *descente des cochons*. Whether pigs or nefarious humans are being referred to, you do indeed begin to see small hairy swine poking around at the roadside – signs of a strong non-Muslim presence.

Around 44km from Guéckédou the route passes through **Niagézazou**, tucked in the forest near a liana bridge over the Makona. Then, some 5km beyond the road bridge over the Makona River, you might check out the village of **Niogbozou** up a side track shortly after the old mission centre of Balouma. Built on a rocky platform and apparently encircled with lianas, Niogbozou used to have a famous troupe of acrobats, dancers and stilt walkers who toured Europe several times before independence.

> ## The Toma
>
> The oldest inhabitants of the Macenta district, the **Toma**, earned respect from the French "pacification" troops for their resilience despite raid upon raid on their isolated villages. Of all the highland peoples, it was the Toma who most harried the French invaders. Their last stronghold, the fortified village of Boussedou, was attacked by two French expeditions and numerous cannon before it finally succumbed in 1907.
>
> Once battered into submission, the Toma found favour with the French for being good scouts and solid soldiers, utterly at home in the forest. They're fairly small people and they may have distant pygmy ancestors: oral history in the forest regions recounts stories of ancient inhabitants of small stature who were decimated by the taller invaders from the north. What's certain is that the Toma lost ground to the Malinké and ultimately mixed with Dyula Malinké to form the Toma–Manian. Today, their language – **Loma** – is a Mande tongue, related to Malinké.
>
> You should look out for highly impressive **dancing** while you're in the Toma region, but you'll be lucky indeed to have the opportunity to witness one of the major lifecycle **celebrations**. Traditionally at circumcisions, marriages, births and funerals, "bird men" – the *onilégagi* – danced, dressed in feathers and painted with kaolin; *lanebogué* pranced and hopped on their stilts; and *akorogi* swirled and bounded in their raffia-leaf costumes and haunted masks. Similar dances take place in Côte d'Ivoire, but generally with your attendance and money in mind.

Passing from Kissi country into the lands of the Toma you arrive in **MACENTA**. This used to be the most important town in the highlands, chosen for its central position as a supply base for the "pacification columns" sent to the remote areas. Free Liberian troops attacked Macenta in 1906 but were fended off, and it was only in 1908 that the limits of the two territories were set. The French tried to grow tea in Macenta, but not with much success. They had much more luck with **coffee**, which remains important, though much of the crop is smuggled out of the country. The biggest indigenous cash crop is **kola**.

Today, Macenta is a pleasing, moderate-size town set amid a tumble of hills with fine views all around, and still composed of hundreds of thatched, roundhouse compounds. If you find yourself **staying** in town, you have the choice between the pretty *Palm Hôtel* (**①**) in the centre, the very basic *Hôtel Magnetic* (**①**) near the *gare voiture*, or the fairly upmarket *Bamala* with clean a/c rooms, slightly further from the town centre (**③**). There are several decent **places to eat**: the best is the unnamed Senegalese place next to the central petrol station.

Out of Macenta through the Malinké quarter, there's the wild **route to Kérouané** (see box, p.589) and, ultimately, Kankan.

Sérédou to Nzérékoré

As you burrow through the jungle and over the ridges, there's a string of minor but interesting stop-offs if you have your own transport. One place where trucks and Peugeots often stop to stock up on palm wine or food is **SÉRÉDOU**. At 800m it straddles a col through the moist, jungly Ziama hills and most vehicles need the rest by the time they've got here. Church bells are heard ringing here: it's an old mission and quinine research station. The roadside cafés serve delicious bush-rat stew to passing drivers and daring tourists.

The stretch of road **from Sérédou to Irié** is renowned for its lepidoptera, including the giant swallowtail *Papillio antimachus*, Africa's largest **butterfly**, with a wingspan of up to 23cm. The males are occasionally seen around the treetops and, very rarely, sipping moisture at muddy puddles; female giant swallowtails, however, are extremely elusive.

NZÉBÉLA is a traditional music centre, though whether you will have much chance of hearing *divogi* drums and *pouvogi* trumpets is hard to tell. Shortly after the village of **SAMOÉ**, a path leads left to a small hamlet where a group of **sacred tortoises** are kept by the community. Different groups of people throughout the forest region identify with a wide range of animals; the tortoise is a simple and popular totem. If you can't find them, you could try asking the White Fathers in Samoé.

Nzérékoré

With a very large Wednesday market and an atmosphere of thriving commerce, **NZÉRÉKORÉ** is the big town of Guinée Forestière. Set amid the forest and traced through by tributary streams which feed the Mani River border with Liberia, the town's shack-lined dirt streets straggle stylelessly over hillocky ground. Yet for a backwoods agglomeration with no discernible centre, so far from anywhere (it's closer to Monrovia and even Abidjan than to Conakry), Nzérékoré is really rather an enjoyable place to be.

Nzérékoré just has to be visited on **market day**. From the permanent market, stalls overflow onto the main street and the activity stretches from the hospital to the roundabout. Liberians and Ivoirians are prominent; women show off their best wraps and the atmosphere vibrates with the racket of trade – everything from multifarious qualities of palm oil and a riot of local produce to clothes (some cotton shirt bargains), Liberian plastic trinkets, prints and indigo *gara*. Crafts, unless you count fabrics, are fewer, but there are good lines in leather sandals, wallets and

The Guerzé

The people of the Nzérékoré district and eastwards are **Guerzé**, or **Kpelle** – related by language and some cultural elements to the Toma, and distantly to the other Mande-speaking ethnic groups. They are profoundly animist by tradition and rather resistant to Islamic influence; their mythic ancestor descended from the sky, married a local woman and settled east of Nzérékoré. Tradition relates that a man called **Yegu**, with a number of followers, populated the Nzérékoré district late in the nineteenth century, and these headmen were the ones in power at the time of the French arrival. It's hard to unravel the veracity of stories like these – they can easily be read as apologetics for subsequent French actions – but it seems more likely that the Guerzé had been around for rather longer than the French wanted to believe, and that colonial chiefs were not often pre-invasion notables.

There's no doubt about the **Guerzé revolt** in 1911, abetted by free Guerzé forces from Liberia, which was put down by a Captain Hecquet. His life was abruptly ended during the campaign by a poisoned arrow.

some beautifully worked and relatively inexpensive silver. And of course you can add to your cassette collection. Lastly, and by no means unique to Nzérékoré, but unmissable if you've not seen them before, are the traditional **pharmacists** who set up on market day with a festoon of graphic boards, illustrating their range of treatments for complaints ranging from worms to impotence.

Practicalities

There are a few **places to stay**. The Vietnamese-run *Bar Hanoi* (**①**), out on the road to Yomou, is clean and safe and has a well and generator. The *Pension Bohema* (turn left off the Macenta road) has comfortable, excellent-value rooms (**④**) and a good restaurant, as does the *Case Idéale* (☎91.08.73; **④**), though its noisy nightclub will keep you awake at weekends. The popular *Banarama* (☎91.13.37; **②–③**) has decent rooms, while the *Maison Blanche* (☎91.15.52; **②**) in the Quartier le Sud is very nice, clean and friendly. In the same *quartier* lies the luxury *Mont Nimba* (☎91.15.57; **④**), owned by President Lansana Conté, with all mod-cons including a/c, satellite TV, a casino, swimming pool and a fabulous nightclub – all quite a surprise in the rainforest so far from urban Conakry.

There's a BICIGUI **bank** by the market (Mon–Fri 8.30am–12.30pm & 2.30–4pm), though it doesn't change traveller's cheques, and a **post office** (Mon–Sat 8am–4pm), a couple of minutes' walk south of the market.

The Monts Nimba and around

Assuming you feel confident about the security situation, you can visit an interesting corner of Guinea near the point where it meets Liberia and Côte

Moving on from Nzérékoré

Until Côte d'Ivoire and Liberia have become more stable, the only advisable route out of Nzérékoré is the one back to Conakry. In peacetime, you can go east via **Lola** and the foot of the Monts Nimba to the **Côte d'Ivoire border** and **Danané**. Make an early start or you'll get stuck in Lola. There are several **routes to Liberia**: southwest towards Yomou, then on to Diécké and Ganta at the border; east along the reasonably fast Lola road, 6km out of Nzérékoré (signposted), which a number of taxis use to Yekepa and Sanniquellie; or along the track from Bossou to Yekepa.

Flights to Conakry (FG80,000) with Air Guinée leave on Thursday and Saturday.

d'Ivoire, though at the time of writing, the places covered below were **off limits**.

East of Nzérékoré, the scenery along the way is nothing special until you reach **Nzo**, from where you start to get good views of the **Monts Nimba** – at 1752m, Guinea's highest point. The road tunnels through impressive thickets of **giant bamboo** and tracks over precarious wooden bridges in the forest. If you have time, or your own transport, you could visit the village of **Bossou** (turn right 5km east of Lola at Gogota, then continue 15km south), where "sacred chimpanzees" are under research by Japanese and Guinean primatologists. Ask in **Lola** if you'd like to visit.

Lola is also the place to get permission to visit the **Monts Nimba Reserve**, which you should be able to reach without much hassle from the *préfecture*. The reserve entrance is at **Gbakoré**, some 15km from Lola on the way to Côte d'Ivoire, where your permit (FG5000) is stamped by the *chef du village*. There's a **research project** based halfway up, between the reserve entrance and the peaks area, that can sometimes offer transport from Gbakoré, but if you don't find any vehicles, you may have to hike there (a two-hour walk). You can sleep at the research station (a small apartment with kitchen; ❷). From here, the ridge formed by the Monts Nimba peaks – all above 1600m, which is above the tree line – can be reached in a further two hours. There are some fine views from up here on a clear day. The summit, straddling the Ivoirian border 8km to the south, is a further two- to three-hour hike.

Sierra Leone

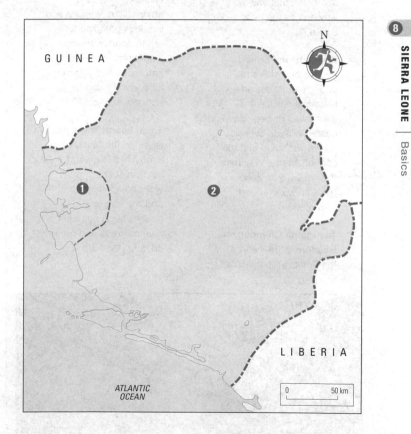

GUINEA

❶

❷

LIBERIA

ATLANTIC OCEAN

0   50 km

N

Sierra Leone highlights

* **River No. 2 Beach**
Among the irresistible beaches of the Freetown peninsula, River No. 2 offers crocodile-spotting excursions up the narrow creek that snakes its way across the beach. See p.637

* **Bunce Island** Bunce houses one of Sierra Leone's most important historical relics – the ruins of an ancient slave castle. With its overgrown walls and antique cannon scattered across the area, it's an eerie place to walk around. See p.638

* **Tacugama Chimpanzee Reserve** In the heart of the Freetown peninsula, this affords protection to many chimps, which you can observe at play. See p.639

* **Outamba-Kilimi Nature Reserve** The park's uninhabited savanna and jungle is paradise for ornithologists, though elephants, monkeys, antelopes and pygmy hippos may also be spotted. See p.640

* **Tiwai Island** This small island in the Mano River is covered in colourful tropical scenery, rings with the noises of birds and the forest, and houses large numbers of chimpanzees and other animals. See p.644

Introduction and Basics

Having emerged from a ten-year civil war that devastated the entire country and forced over a third of the population into exile, Sierra Leone is slowly returning to normality. The country has been calm since the official end of the war in 2002, but it's a fragile peace that is easily threatened by the weak economy, the displacement of communities and the potential repercussions to the war crimes trials that began in 2003. Furthermore, Sierra Leone lies at the heart of a volatile region, and disorder in nearby Liberia, Guinea and Côte d'Ivoire constitutes an ongoing threat to its stability and security. With the continuing volatility, you should not enter the country without weighing up the current security situation, and if you do go, it's wise to register with your diplomatic representation upon arrival.

If Sierra Leone returns to normality, it will resume its place among West Africa's most attractive tourist destinations. With long stretches of white, sandy beaches, lush green forests and extensive nature reserves, the country has an intrinsic appeal surpassing that of many neighbouring nations.

People

Sierra Leone's **ethnic configuration** is unusual. Two language groups dominate: the **Temne**, who speak one of the idiosyncratic West Atlantic languages, are concentrated in the central north, inland from Freetown; the **Mende**, whose language is distantly related to the rest of the large Mande group, are strongest more to the southeast, especially around Bo and Kenema. The Mende are a many-sided group, incorporating the Komende, the Gbamende (which just means "different Mende") and the Sewa. In addition, both Temne and Mende have culturally absorbed many of the less populous groups around, often through the powerful influence of their flourishing **secret societies**. Along the coast, for example, the **Bullom** and **Sherbro**, who once spoke the same language (Bullom), now tend to speak Temne north of Freetown and Mende to the south. Smaller inland groups like the **Loko** (around Port Loko) and the Limba have moved into close association with the Temne, while in the east and southeast, the **Kono** and **Kissi** have moved towards Mende culture. In the far north, the **Susu** (northwest), **Koranko** and **Yalunka** (northeast) have remained closer to their Mande roots. In the north

Fact file

Sierra Leone's **area**, about 72,000 square kilometres, is a little smaller than Scotland or Maine. The country has a relatively high **population** density, with just over five and a half million people.

Sierra Leone's **foreign debt** was estimated in 2000 to be around £850 million ($1.3 billion), which compares to the insignificant sum of £40 million ($65 million) earned from the export of goods and services. President Ahmad Tejan Kabbah was reconfirmed as head of state in the elections of May 2002.

The **name** "Sierra Leone" (Salon in Krio) has various etymologies. The idea that the first Portuguese visitors were referring to the Freetown Peninsula as "Lion-like Mountain" when they called the country Serra Leão, seems unlikely, as nothing in the topography resembles the shape of a lion, and suggestions to do with the sound of roaring surf seem equally fanciful. The possibility that the area swarmed with lions in the fifteenth century is the most likely.

and east there's also a fair scattering of Fula communities – many of them exiles from Guinea.

But what's remarkable about Sierra Leone is the influence of the **Krios** (Creoles) – ex-slaves of diverse origins who were already in positions of power before the interior was carved onto Britain's plate. Numerically, they have always been a small group, confined mostly to the Freetown Peninsula. With the invasion and "protection" of the interior, they lost their influence with the colonial government to British-appointed tribal chiefs, whose descendants have mostly run the country since independence. The Krio language, partly derived from archaic English, has made a lasting and widespread imprint on Sierra Leonean society.

Where to go

Geographically, Sierra Leone is diverse. A steep indented coast at the capital, **Freetown**, and shallow sand banks and mangrove swamps elsewhere are backed by tidal creeks that penetrate far inland and make a mess of the road system in the south and west. Further upcountry, the land rises through dense forest (most of it now cleared) to rolling savanna hills, rocky outcrops and mountains. The remaining patches of **rainforest**, mostly in the far southeast, beyond the Moa River, are nowadays islands in a sea of secondary growth and shifting agriculture. Most of central Sierra Leone is covered by dry open plains (*bolylands*). In colonial days, these lands used to be intensively cultivated, but these days, they are farmed on a household or community basis, though cultivation remains restrained by lack of tools, seeds and labour. Swamp rice still covers much of the lowlands.

In **Freetown**, hotels, restaurants and other services are functioning more or less normally, many embassies and high commissions are open, and external telecommunications work reasonably well. Most visitors tend not to venture beyond the mountain-flanked Freetown Peninsula and its beautiful shoreline. During the week, the beaches are largely deserted, while weekends see them packed with aid workers and UN peacekeepers who currently make up a large percentage of Freetown's population. The small tourist industry that had been established along the coast by the British and French in the 1980s is only slowly recovering. Like the British colonials, the winter vacationers extended their interests little beyond the Peninsula, leaving the interior of the country ripe for exploration by adventurous travellers. **Outamba-Kilimi National Park** in the north, **Tiwai Island Nature Reserve** in the south and some unusually high hills and mountains in the east (including the spectacular **Mount Bintumani**) are all worthy goals, though at the time of writing (late 2003), you're advised to defer independent travel into the interior: visits to the former centres of conflict – Makeni and Kabala in the north and Kenema and Koidu in the east – still carry some risk.

When to go

From **May to November**, most of the country gets drenched in heavy and prolonged **monsoon rain**. Only in the extreme south, around Sulima, is there a short break in the rains during July or August. While temperatures aren't extremely high, humidity is usually excessive, above all along the coast. The lowest nighttime temperature ever recorded in Freetown (19°C) is actually the *highest* record minimum temperature for any African country – indication of Freetown's altogether very uncomfortable climate much of the year.

The risk of visiting in May or November is repaid, if you're lucky, with brilliant collages of green, wonderful skies and tolerable road conditions; but between these months, travel off the hard-surfaced routes varies from slow and gruelling to impossible.

In the **dry season**, a harmattan wind from the northeast can bring slightly cooler, dusty weather even to the coast. It's very difficult to predict clear blue skies and good visibility.

Average temperatures and rainfall

	Jan	Feb	Mar	Apr	May	June	July	Aug	Sept	Oct	Nov	Dec
Freetown												
Temperatures °C												
Min (night)	24	24	25	25	25	24	23	23	23	23	24	24
Max (day)	29	30	30	31	30	30	32	31	32	29	29	29
Rainfall mm	13	3	13	56	160	302	894	902	610	310	132	41
Days with rainfall	1	1	2	6	15	23	27	28	25	23	12	4
Bo												
Temperatures °C												
Min (night)	20	21	21	22	22	21	21	21	21	21	21	20
Max (day)	32	34	35	34	32	31	28	28	30	31	31	31
Rainfall mm	8	16	76	130	252	368	406	436	419	325	170	38
Sefadu												
Temperatures °C												
Min (night)	14	17	19	20	21	20	20	20	20	20	19	17
Max (day)	32	34	35	34	33	31	29	29	31	32	31	31
Rainfall mm	10	20	96	160	228	282	269	411	401	292	145	41

Getting there from the rest of Africa

Practically all visitors arrive in Sierra Leone by air. International flights arrive at Sierra Leone's main Lungi International airport, across the Sierra Leone River estuary from the capital. From **Banjul**, there are flights operated by Gambia International Airlines (2 weekly), West Coast Airlines (3 weekly), Sierra National Airlines (1 weekly) and Bellview (3 weekly). Bellview also connect **Lagos** with Freetown three times a week. From **Conakry** and other Guinean airports, there are daily flights with Paramount Airlines, West Coast Airlines or Air Guinée. Ghana Airways operates four flights a week from **Accra** and **Abidjan**, with a couple more flights a week from the latter with SN Brussels Airways. From **Dakar**, you can reach Freetown with Paramount Airlines, Gambia Airlines or West Coast Airlines, each of which operate two services a week on this route.

> For important practical information applying to all West African countries, covering health, transport, cultural hints and more, plus details on getting to the region from beyond Africa, see Basics, pp.9–87.

Overland

You're unlikely to want to travel overland **from Liberia** given the turmoil in that country, though if you do, the main route from Monrovia arrives in the southeast of Sierra Leone, near Sulima. From **Guinea**, the principal **Conakry-Freetown** route is via Pamelap and Kambia. By private vehicle or bush taxi, assuming no border delays, this route, mostly on tarred road, is about seven hours' drive. By bus, usually involving a change of vehicle on the Guinean side of the border as well as tiresome waits at Guinea's numerous military checkpoints, the journey takes at least a day.

Less-trodden, and hardly recommended routes into Sierra Leone include the track off the Conakry–Mamou road east of Kindia, to Madina-Woula for access to the Outamba-Kilimi National Park and Kamakwie (an extremely tough route, even with a 4WD); the ferry crossing from Nongoa to Koindu wharf in the far east; and the very little-used route from Faranah to Falaba in the northeast, on which there's a good chance you'll have to walk the ten no-man's-land kilometres in the middle.

Freetown has an overnight **ferry** link with **Conakry** (3 weekly), leaving between 8pm and 10pm.

Red tape and visas

Visas are required by all nationalities except for ECOWAS (Economic Community of West African States) nationals. The validity of visas varies, but stays of longer than a month are rarely granted in advance, though you can extend your stay at the immigration office on Rawdon Street in Freetown. Upon arrival in Sierra Leone, you should register with your diplomatic representation (if your country doesn't have its own embassy in Freetown, it's worth finding out in advance which embassy looks after your national interests). You are required to show a certificate for yellow fever and cholera **vaccinations** on entering Sierra Leone.

In West Africa, Sierra Leone has embassies, high commissions or representatives in Dakar, Banjul, Conakry, Accra, Abidjan and Lagos. The status of Sierra Leonean representation at British embassies and consulates is unclear, though they are still a good starting point for enquiries in countries with no Sierra Leonean representation.

Once in Sierra Leone, you can obtain visas in Freetown for all West African countries except Guinea-Bissau, Benin and Cameroon.

Visitors to Sierra Leone are allowed to carry up to $5000 in **foreign currency** without declaring it. Otherwise, it's advisable to ask for a declaration form at the airport to avoid hassles on departure.

Health

Schistosomiasis (bilharzia) and river blindness are both common in the countryside. But apart from a high incidence of malaria (for more on prophylaxis and treatment, see p.32), Sierra Leone's main health problems for travellers revolve around water supplies. The lack of clean water is especially acute towards the end of the dry season in the north. Even piped water may come straight from an open tank. Freetown's water supplies come from a huge dam up in the hills of the Freetown Peninsula, and though it is equipped with a purification system, it is old and breaks down occasionally. It's best to drink bottled water or use purification tablets.

Medical treatment in Sierra Leone is best avoided, but in an emergency, contact one of the organizations listed on p.635. There are some pharmacies in Freetown (see p.635).

Costs, money and banks

Sierra Leone's currency is the **leone** (£1 = Le3400; $1 = Le2200). Notes of Le50, Le100, Le500, Le1000 and Le5000 are in circulation. Rather confusing for travellers going upcountry is the northern habit of referring to "**pounds**" rather than leones, a pound being Le2 (historically, this stems from the fact that when leones were introduced in 1964, they were valued at Le2 to UK£1).

Having only recently emerged from a civil war and currently housing large numbers of UN soldiers and NGO workers, Freetown is relatively expensive. Modest hotels charge £20–50/$33–80 for a twin room, though you can only expect something really decent at the upper end of the price scale. A twin room in one of the more established hotels costs from £75. Basic chop-house meals can be had for the equivalent of £0.65/$1, though many Western-style restaurants charge Western-style prices. Because of the steady decline in the value of the leone, some prices in this chapter are given in pounds sterling or dollars.

Credit cards and traveller's cheques weren't accepted anywhere in Sierra Leone at the time of writing, so it's best to bring ample sums in cash. You can change money either at the main **banks** (see "Listings", p.634) or in one of the **exchange bureaux** around Freetown's Siaka Stevens Street or Lumley Beach Road, which usually have a better rate. There's also a small black market centred around Siaka Stevens Street.

Information, websites and maps

The best place to get tourist information is the **National Tourist Board** in Freetown (see p.625 for addresses). They have leaflets, maps (including the Shell map – see below) and up-to-date information on travel and accommodation. Two fairly useful brochures that they carry, with information on hotels, bars and basic travel advice, are *Green White and Blue* published by Sierra National Airlines, and the board's own *Visitors' Guide to Sierra Leone*. Otherwise, you can also rely on the British High Commission to have up-to-date information for travellers. If you're intending to travel upcountry to visit Sierra Leone's nature reserves, it's really worthwhile contacting the **Conservation Society** in Freetown (see p.608).

The government **website** ⊛www.state-house-sl.org features the latest on the activities of the president and vice-president, and some useful links. Much more interesting is ⊛ww.sierra-leone.org, containing a cornucopia of news and historical articles, recipes, derivations of local place names, not to mention a slew of Krio proverbs – with helpful explanations – and a collection of handy Mende phrases.

Obtaining up-to-date **maps** of Sierra Leone is difficult – about the best you'll find is the 1:560,000 map of the country published by International Travel Maps. Shell Sierra Leone publish the only tourist map of the country (1:396,000), with a fanciful rash of tarmac roads, and reliable Freetown street plans on the reverse. It can be bought at the National Tourist Board.

Getting around

West Coast Airlines operates flights to Bo and Kenema from the domestic airport, **Hastings**, southeast of the capital. Paramount can charter helicopters to groups of travellers to any destination (though naturally this doesn't come cheap).

Heading upcountry by road requires a lot of patience. **Bush taxis** and **poda podas** (minibuses) connect Freetown with major towns in the interior, including Port Loko, Bo, Makeni, Kenema, Pamelap and Kabala, with at least daily services, though as ever it pays to arrive early at the garage. It's much harder to explore smaller villages upcountry, and once you leave the main arteries, long waits may be required to find transport.

If you aim to spend much time in the interior, and have sufficient funds, you may want to try **renting a car** in Freetown for flexibility (see p.634 for firms to contact). Be prepared to pay up to £250/$350 per day to travel upcountry, or £65–130/$100–200 to get around the Peninsula. The driver's fee will be included in the rate, though petrol (gasoline), at around £1.60/$2.40 per gallon, isn't.

Hitching is pretty easy in and around Freetown, and not too difficult elsewhere; private drivers are usually sympathetic. Much of the time you'll be expected to pay.

Accommodation

Freetown and the Freetown peninsula have a growing number of relatively pricey places to stay, though few inexpensive lodgings. Until the war engulfed the country, Bo, Makeni, Kenema and Koidu all had a handful of basic boarding houses, and one or two more comfortable addresses, but nothing luxurious. At the moment, accommodation in the interior of the country is scarce, and is completely unavailable in many provincial towns.

If you happen to arrive at dusk in a strange village, it's best to ask to see the **chief** and explain to him your "mission" and your needs. Custom dictates that you should be accommodated somewhere, but since the war destroyed entire communities, many people are still living in overcrowded and impoverished conditions and may not be able to put you up. **Camping** is not recommended (people aren't accustomed to the practice and nerves are still fragile, especially after dark), unless you are heading out to nature reserves and are able to link up with conservation staff on-site.

Eating and drinking

Freetown has a good selection of **restaurants** that serve (mainly European) food at prices compared to what you'd pay in the West. There are also inexpensive **chop houses** serving variations of rice and palm-oil-based meals during lunchtime, and rarely have anything left by the afternoon. For quick snacks, fried-chicken places are the most popular option – you can't fail to spot their colourful frontages.

The capital (and upcountry towns, to some extent) boasts a good range of **street food**: rice *akara* (rice cake), fried dough (doughnuts), roast meat, egg sandwiches, boiled cassava, yams, plantains and sandwiches. A popular snack is the "steak

---

Accommodation price codes

All accommodation prices in this chapter are coded according to the following scale, whose equivalent in pounds sterling/US dollars is used throughout the book. Prices refer to the rate you can expect to pay for a room with two beds. Single rooms, or single occupancy, normally costs at least two-thirds of the twin-occupancy rate.

① Under Le16,000 (under £5/$8).
② Le16,000–32,000 (£5–10/$8–16).
③ Le32,000–48,000 (£10–15/$16–24).
④ Le48,000–64,000 (£15–20/$24–32).
⑤ Le64,000–96,000 (£20–30/$32–48).
⑥ Le96,000–128,000 (£30–40/$48–64).
⑦ Le128,000–160,000 (£40–50/$64–80).
⑧ Over Le160,000 (£50/$80).

Krio food and drink terms

agidi	corn stodge	*kabej*	cabbage
airish petehteh	potato	*kasada*	cassava
akara	rice and banana cake	*kek*	cake
		kenda	seasoning
aweful	kind of fish	*kohn*	corn, maize
behni	sesame seed	*kondo*	basic chop
bia	beer	*krain-krain*	slimy leaf sauce
bif	meat, animal	*letu*	lettuce
binch	beans, peas	*lif*	leaf
biskit	biscuit	*magi*	Maggi cube
bita	bitter leaf for sauces	*mampama*	palm wine
		okroh	okra
bolgoh	bulgar wheat	*omole*	liquor, hooch
bonga	dried fish	*orinch*	orange
bota	butter, margarine	*oriri*	seasoning
brefos	breakfast	*pamai*	red, banga nut oil
brefrut	breadfruit	*panapul*	pineapple
buli	jug for palm wine	*pap*	porridge
bush bif	game	*petete*	sweet potato
chak	drunk	*pia*	pear (avocado)
egusi	squash seeds used in sauces	*plantan*	plantain
		plasas	(palava) sauce
fis	fish	*plet*	plate
fohl	chicken	*pongki*	pumpkin
fud/chop/yil	food	*popoh*	pawpaw, papaya
fresh	new palm wine	*rehs*	rice
frut	fruit	*sawa-sawa*	*plasas* made of sour leaves
funde	millet		
gari	cassava meal	*sof*	soft drink
golik	garlic	*sol*	salt
granat	groundnut	*stek*	beef
grepfrut	grapefruit	*slu*	stew
grin	greens, used in *plasas*	*suga*	sugar
		sup	soup
jibloks/kobokobo	aubergine	*tamatis*	tomato, tomato purée
jolof	rice in tomato paste served with beef, goat or fish stew		
		ti	tea
		yabas	onion
		yams	yam

sandwich" – slivers of kebab with palm oil in bread, known as *rosbif* in Krio. Be sure your sandwich really is steak, unless you like grilled tripe: at night, it can be hard to see what's cooking.

The commonest **sauce** is *plasas* ("palava sauce"), made with finely shredded leaves of sweet potato or cassava, okra, dried fish and hot pepper, all cooked in palm oil. There are numerous variations on *plasas* – a version based on groundnuts is most common in the north – and it's often served with

meat. You may also get *egusi* sauces or soups, based on crushed squash seed. Along the coast, fish stew is very common.

Stay long in Sierra Leone and you'll begin to appreciate significant differences in taste and texture between the **rice** of different regions. Upland "hill rice" is the more traditional short-grain variety; the red-speckled Mende kind is the best and can be delicious. **Plantains** are commonly used as a staple in place of rice. **Fufu** (fermented, mashed cassava stodge) and **agidi** (heavy, maize-meal stodge) are also eaten as the main meal, though not often prepared in chop houses.

If you're far off the beaten track, you won't find chop for sale. In these areas, it's quite acceptable – and quite the custom – to carry rice, palm oil, Maggi stock cubes and other ingredients around with you and ask local people to cook meals for you, in exchange for some of the food (the family meal is usually prepared late afternoon), or perhaps for some leones.

Yebe is a good and popular breakfast dish, a kind of stew made of potato, cassava or mangoes when in season. You buy it by the ladle in markets and truck parks between 6.30 and 8am. *Pap*, a sweet rice broth, is also nice for chilly, early starts.

Sweet bread (sugar-laden) and ordinary bread (a basic, non-sweet, white bread) are sold almost everywhere; specify which kind you want, otherwise the seller will probably give you sweet.

Of the wide variety of **fruit** you'd expect, oranges are probably the cheapest; in the north, in season, they'll cost you a penny each. Mandarins, misleadingly, are called lemons in Krio.

Drinks

As for drinking, it all comes down to Star **beer**, one of West Africa's best and also reasonably priced. Imported beer costs about twice the price of Star. **Palm wine** is socially and commercially very important, and a pleasant way to while away an afternoon. Sierra Leonean liquor from Freetown distilleries, on the other hand, is a more self-destructive commodity; Daddy Kool gin and Man Pickin rum are names to be wary of. Non-alcoholic, home-made ginger beer is popular in Freetown and normally sold in small plastic bottles.

Lastly, while Sierra Leone is more or less outside the green-tea zone, **coffee**, which is quite often freshly ground (and invariably served with Peak evaporated milk), can be a pleasant surprise.

Communications

The Sierra Leone **postal system** (run by Salpost) usually takes seven days between Sierra Leone and the UK, and ten days to the USA. Aerograms are fastest and safest. Upcountry, the mail – incoming as well as outgoing – is unreliable, though letters posted from Freetown don't usually go astray. There's a **DHL** office in the capital (see p.635).

Internet access is slowly improving, and Internet cafés are opening up, mainly in Freetown, at the time of writing. Connections tend to be slow, however.

Phones

Sierra Leone's telephone system is surprisingly reasonable, better than that of neighbouring Guinea. You won't have trouble finding a telecentre in the capital. The main telephone provider is **Sierratel**. Overseas calls are best made from Sierra Leone External Telecommunications (SLET) in Freetown. The charge for calls to the US or Europe is Le6000 (approximately £5/$8) for three minutes. SLET is also the place to send and receive **faxes**.

Of the three **mobile phone** providers, Celtel, Millicom and Mobitel, only Celtel has coverage extending beyond Freetown to Bo and Kenema. It's best to bring your own mobile and buy a SIM card from one of the many dealers in the centre of Freetown.

Sierra Leone's IDD country code is ☎232.

The media

There are twelve weekly **papers**, most of which are in English (the *Daily Mail* and the *Concord Times* publish twice a week). *West Africa* magazine is usually on sale in Freetown the week after its Friday publication in the UK. The state television station **SLTV** broadcasts local football games, cheap imported documentary fillers, news and movies. All large hotels are equipped with satellite TV either in the rooms or the public bar. Apart from the Sierra Leone Broadcasting System (**SLBS**) on 99.9FM, radio stations include Radio FM 98.1, VOH FM 96.2, SLAJ and KISS FM 104, which feature a mix of music and chat. The BBC World Service can be heard in Freetown on 94.3FM.

Entertainment and sport

Sierra Leone has a rich variety of **music** and the influence of Freetown over the last 200 years has been large. But today, while cheaply produced gospel cassettes sell by the wagonload, there's no real recording industry and few places to hear live music. The most popular musician at the time of writing is **Jimmy B**, who has recorded Sierra Leonean-style house/ragga/hip-hop in South Africa. He has his own studio in the capital, where he produces other, lesser-known local artists.

Afro-Nationals *CD Classics 1 & 2* (H&R Enterprises, US). Afro-Nationals wereby far the most popular Sierra Leonean band of the 1970s, featuring the sweet lead guitar, trademark brass and live percussion that epitomized the era.

Ngoh Gbetuwai *Biza Body* (H&R Enterprises, US).From Moyamba, Ngoh Gbetuwai are the most promising of the new generation of home-based Sierra Leonean artists. Given the circumstances in Freetown under which this album was recorded, its very existence is little short of miraculous.

SE Rogie *The Palm Wine Sounds of SE Rogie* (Stern's). The doyen of Sierra Leonean musical entertainers developed an effortlessly sensual style of palm-wine guitar playing and had hits in the 1960s all along the West African coast. He emigrated to the US and died in the UK in 1994.

Various *Sierra Leone Music* (Zensor). Compilation of Krio and up-country tracks, recorded for the radio in Freetown in the Fifties and Sixties. Including tracks by the Krio singer Ebenezer Calender, who played guitar and trumpet and wrote all his own songs, this is a real collector's item with an excellent accompanying booklet.

Cinema and theatre

Cinema is, no surprise, dormant if not extinct; miserable imported movies and videos are all you'll see. Film could perhaps be great in Sierra Leone, if the country's record in the field of drama is any indication – Freetown has a remarkable tradition of popular theatre. Quite a few theatrical groups are currently functioning, and all of them write their own plays or self translate scripts.

The 1979 banning of *Poyotong Wahala*, about high-level corruption, led to routine censorship of plays. In their attempts to outwit the censors, playwrights have moved increasingly from concert party – musical variety show – to exuberant farce and satire. Shows are uproarious, even rowdy. There's a strong blend of comedy and social comment in these Krio plays.

Three of the main professional groups are Spence Productions, Freetown Players and Kailondo Theatre. The best plays tend to be performed at the British Council Library in Freetown. Forthcoming events are usually well advertised; look out for banners, especially around Freetown's Cotton Tree and Law Courts.

Sport

Football is popular all over the country, but most of the big action is concentrated around Freetown, where Mighty Blackpool, East End Lions, FC Kallon and Wellington People are some of the clubs you might watch.

Opening hours and public holidays

Most offices, banks and embassies are open Monday to Friday (rarely Saturday morning) 8am to 5pm, though some tend to close for an hour at lunchtime. Shops usually close by 5pm, but are open Saturday morning. Many restaurants and other establishments are closed all day Sunday.

The somewhat unpredictable secular **holidays** include Republic Day (April 19) and Independence Day (April 27). The Islamic calendar only affects business and office openings at the end of Ramadan.

If the north is safe, don't miss the New Year's Day "outing" in Kabala (see p.641). If you're in the Freetown area around that time, go to Lumley Beach, Goderich Beach or River No. 2 on Boxing Day or New Year's Day, when literally thousands of people come to dance, swim and party.

Crime and personal safety

Though Sierra Leone is generally calm at the time of writing, that stability is fragile and problems may erupt unexpectedly. When registering with your embassy on arrival, it's worth asking about the security situation. Carry your passport with you at all times.

In general, Freetown and the peninsula are likely to be relatively safe, though it's advisable to avoid the East End of Freetown, especially after dark. Avoid the Liberian border area and the Moa River region: the smuggling of Sierra Leone's biggest asset – **diamonds** – is a major problem and your presence may not be welcome.

As for drugs, grass (*dhambi, yamba*) is widely smoked, but not in public. Police entrapments are more likely to lead to a bribe than the pressing of charges.

Women travellers

With the exception of Lumley Beach, where beach boys of all descriptions gather, Sierra Leone is in peace time probably one of the friendliest, least hassley countries for female travellers. Women in shorts and T-shirts don't raise too many eyebrows.

Settle in one place to stay, or work, though, and you're bound to be persistently irritated by inflamed egos. "When can we meet to do some loving?" is the kind of question that Sierra Leonean women have to field all the time, though the perceived cultural gap and your potential as a source of funds, too, make you more vulnerable. It's possibly unfair in individual cases, but broadly true, to expect more posturing in the north and less arrogant attitudes in the south.

In the wider field of **sexual attitudes**, public displays of affection are more acceptable in Sierra Leone than in many other countries in the region, though in certain Krio quarters of Freetown, conservative "Victorian values" are still prevalent. Female genital mutilation is widely practised within the framework of the traditional women's Sande society (see p.644). Power for women in the provinces tends to be determined by ethnic affiliation. While there are a number of women paramount chiefs in the Mende chiefdoms, a Temne female paramount chief would be unheard of.

Wildlife and national parks

Sierra Leone's **fauna** still includes elephants (in the Outamba-Kilimi National Park), chimpanzees (also in the park, and widely if thinly dispersed across the whole country) and pygmy hippos, which are so solitary and secretive that it's hard to know what their status is.

There are several important faunal reserves. The big one is the **Outamba-Kilimi National Park** in the north, which was well on its way to becoming a fully operational park with visitor facilities and an active research program when the Peace Corps workers based there left the country. The other is the **Tiwai Island Primate Reserve**, a jungle-covered island in the Moa River near the Liberian border. Its population of chimps and endangered monkey species has been strongly reduced by the war, but you should still be able to spot some primates. Facilities are currently being rebuilt.

If you're an enthusiastic naturalist, you'll want to visit the **Conservation Society of Sierra Leone** in Freetown (2 Pike St; ☏022/22.97.16, ✉cssl@sierratel.sl). They can advise on travel routes, accommodation, worthwhile destinations and security concerns, and may be able to find you a reliable guide.

Directory

Airport tax US$25, payable in hard currency.

Chiefs If you travel widely in Sierra Leone you're likely to meet quite a few chiefs. These men – and women – will often be your introduction to a small town or village. Local government in the three Provinces (Northern, Southern and Eastern) is organized around the 169 paramount chiefdoms, which have the status of local councils. These were consolidated – and invented where necessary – by the British. They are not structured according to strict ethnic divisions, though most of them have a dominant group. Beneath the paramount chiefs come section chiefs and village chiefs.

Appointments are by somewhat arbitrary popular vote. The Western Area of Freetown and the peninsula have district councils rather than chiefs. The national museum has an impressive exhibition of chiefs' portraits on display.

Crafts Sierra Leone's best buys are cloth (indigo tie-dyed *gara*, rusty red and black block-printed *ronko*, soft and heavy strip-woven country cloth – single-weave *barri* and double-weave *kpokpoi* – and batik); leather goods (especially slot-together neck bags and purses); masks connected with the secret societies (but the made-for-tourists ones are over-priced and often crude, while the real thing is seriously expensive and requires the museum's permission to export); and *nomoli* soapstone figurines (see p.632, strictly speaking these cannot be exported if they're authentic).

Electricity Power is rationed in Freetown, with only a quarter of the town receiving electricity at any one time. Upcountry the situation can be even more unreliable, and small towns may not have any mains supply at all.

Photography Freetown itself has a tough attitude to cameras, and you're advised to be careful. There's no permit necessary, however, and so long as you avoid getting uniforms, banks and government buildings in the viewfinder and apply due respect, you'll find that most of the country is easier than usual for photography. Often enough, people will line up enthusiastically for group portraits ("Mek yu snap wi"). Colour print film is available in Freetown, and you can get your pictures developed at reasonable prices.

Religion Krio influence has given a broadly Christian colouration to the whole country, especially the south and west, but most deeply ingrained in and around Freetown. You'll see more mosques around the northern and eastern fringes. Indigenous religion, however, is deep-rooted and widely practised, with the powerful secret societies (see p.644) playing a major role in keeping it alive.

Units of measurement Most measurements in Sierra Leone are still given in old Imperial units – yards, feet and inches, pounds and ounces, gallons (100 fluid ounces) and pints (20 fluid ounces). Where distances are given on signposts, they are usually only in miles. To convert from miles to kilometres, multiply by eight and divide by five.

A brief history of Sierra Leone

Sierra Leone has one of the longest "modern histories" of any West African nation. It was in the 1560s that, in effect, Sir John Hawkins started the American slave trade, at the watering station by the present site of the King Jimmy Market in Freetown. Inland, at Port Loko, Afro-Portuguese *lançado* traders settled and flourished through the seventeenth century. Early British colonists gravitated to the slaving "factory" of Bunce Island (downriver from Port Loko) and the coasts of Sherbro and the other islands further south. Here, the more adventurous married into local royalty and seeded new, Creole dynasties. At the end of the eighteenth century, the first free black settlers arrived to establish themselves on the Freetown Peninsula.

The Province of Freedom

There were tens of thousands of **freed slaves** in the English cities of Bristol, Liverpool and London in the late eighteenth century. After the outbreak of the American War of Independence in 1775, many slaves deserted to the British side from their southern plantation owners, and later made their way to London. And as early as 1772, a legal test case had ruled that, once freed, a slave could not be returned to captivity.

In 1787, the first settlers arrived in Sierra Leone from Britain. They were a group of 411 people, mostly "black poor" immigrants but including some sixty deported white women – "wives" for the freed slaves. Their patron, Granville Sharp, declared the mountainous shore of the Peninsula "The Province of Freedom". The expedition was nearly a disaster. Sierra Leone had been chosen on the recommendation of a botanist, Henry Smeathman, who'd lived there for some years and whose private intention had been to set up plantations – using slave labour. He died before the expedition set off, but many of the putative settlers had second thoughts at the last minute and backed out. The expedition was badly managed and much delayed, so that the ships finally arrived just before the onset of the rains. The colonists had tents, and built makeshift huts, but within three months of living through the rainy season on the sodden hillside, a third of them were dead, of malaria or other diseases.

They bought the area of what's now Freetown from King Tom, a Temne headman and tributary of King Naimbama. But Naimbama hadn't been consulted and the area had to be bought again from him (the treaty can be seen at the Public Archives in Fourah Bay College). Tom was succeeded by King Jimmy, who resented and harassed the Bunce Island slave-trading operation that was still going on. A British naval vessel, which had by coincidence arrived with new supplies for the flagging colony, torched one of Jimmy's towns – with the approval of the settlers, who had also been in dispute with him.

And there ended the "Province of Freedom". King Jimmy **evicted the settlers** from their homes and burnt their little colony to the ground. Those who remained (it was now 1790) were absorbed into surrounding Temne villages.

Nova Scotians and Maroons

A new consortium, the **Sierra Leone Company**, was formed to take over the assets of the defunct Province of Freedom and make a second attempt to establish a colony. Its members were Granville Sharp (the driving force), the liberal lord William Wilberforce, and a young radical, Thomas Clarkson.

They soon found a new group of colonists – some twelve hundred **"Nova Scotians"** – for their philanthropic experiment. These were freed slave refugees from the United States whom the British had fobbed off with a dead-end resettlement scheme in the Canadian colony. One of them went to London, where Sierra Leone was suggested to him as an alternative. The small hill farms the new settlers were allocated to were not much of an improvement on Canada, but the Nova Scotians formed a viable community. They brought strong churches, and some of them became Company administrators. French Revolutionary forces caught the ill-defended British off-guard in 1794 and ransacked Freetown. But the Nova Scotians rebuilt. The **colony of Sierra Leone** (as it became in 1808) owed its existence to them.

In 1795, five hundred escaped Asante slaves – the **Maroons** – who had set up an independent state in the mountains of Jamaica, were tricked into negotiations, leading to their capture and deportation, once again to Nova Scotia, and then eventually to Sierra Leone. The Maroon settlers arrived at Freetown in 1800, just as a group of Nova Scotians, in an attempt to form their own government, were in the middle of Sierra Leone's first rebellion. The Maroons, and a detachment of soldiers accompanying them, came to Governor Thomas Ludlam's rescue. The Nova Scotian rebels were captured; two were hanged and the rest banished. From the beginning of the nineteenth century, the settlers were given no voice in the government of Sierra Leone, Britain ruling directly.

Temne defeat

Pushing home their new strength, the Sierra Leone Company refused to countenance claims by members of the Temne ethnic group that a new treaty be negotiated whenever there was a new Temne king as landlord. For the governor, the treaty of 1788 was good in perpetuity. To make the point, the British garrison built a stone fort, now part of State House. The Temne, led by a new King Tom and encouraged by a partisan Nova Scotian named Wansey, attacked it in November 1801 and were quickly repulsed. In a counteroffensive, the British ousted the Temne and their Bullom relatives from most of the peninsula and carried out savage punitive raids on many villages in King Tom's dominion.

While the Temne prepared a new plan, a Susu ally of theirs arrived with his retinue to settle in Freetown. This sell-out turned the tide against the Temne, who gave up the peninsula.

The Crown Colony and the recaptives

On January 1, 1808, the Sierra Leone Company, by now deeply in debt, handed over the running of the settlement to the British government, and Sierra Leone became a **Crown Colony**. In the same year, Westminster passed the **Abolition Act** and the antislavery movement at last had some teeth, although the last slave ships weren't intercepted until 1864. Bunce Island ceased slave trading and the Temne country inland turned to timber (another non-renewable resource) to maintain its economic strength.

Freetown had a naval base, charged with intercepting slave ships and "recapturing" the slaves. It soon became clear that few of them could be returned to their original homes, and they were simply released at Freetown to found new villages. Between 1808 and 1864, some 70,000 **"recaptives"** were resettled in the Sierra Leone colony. Leicester was founded by Wolof and Bambara people, Kissy by freed slaves from the Scarcies River district and

Congo Town by Congolese recaptives. In the 1820s, in war-torn Yorubaland (Nigeria), thousands of slaves of war were shipped west, in Cuban, Brazilian or American vessels, many of them to be quickly recaptured by the Freetown frigates. The "Aku", as they were called, formed the first significant Muslim community in the colony. Slave trading also continued along the southern coasts of the Sierra Leone region. Many of the recaptives here, far from being complete strangers to the region, had roots in the territory that later became Sierra Leone the country.

After peace was achieved with the French in 1815, many of the **African soldiers** who had served in British regiments were pensioned off to the colony, where they founded villages with pugnacious names like Waterloo, Hastings and Wellington. From the interior came determined Fula and Mandinka traders who settled in Foulah Town. And much of the town's heavy labour was done by the Kru (or Kroo), who came to the coast on long residences from their homes in southeast Liberia.

In this melting pot of people, many of them traumatized by their experiences, the **Church Missionary Society** made headway through the early decades of the nineteenth century. Many who felt that the Bible had saved them from slavery were converted to Christianity. The Nova Scotians were an example, African and yet European in their ways: prosperous, literate, worldly and Christian. Many recaptives adopted European names and, with intermarriage and the inevitable breakdown of many ethnic barriers, there was the gradual moulding of a new configuration – the Creoles, or **Krios**.

In the **interior**, the British paid kings and headmen annual stipends to try to guarantee peace between peoples whose economies had been damaged by the termination of the slave trade. Centuries of dependence upon it had left many Temne families, and whole districts, in disarray; while the farming peoples, like the Limba and the Loko, whom the Temne had exploited for so long, were now attacked and harassed by them. By the 1820s, the Temne had emerged as the dominant language group northeast of Freetown.

On the **peninsula**, recaptives began moving to Freetown from their villages. Captured cargos of European goods for slave trading were auctioned off and a number of recaptive traders took advantage, selling inland, even setting themselves up in business in the interior, under the patronage of village headmen, who called them "white men". The timber trade declined with the introduction of iron steamships and a more easily undertaken trade in wild-collected **palm nuts**, for the burgeoning industries of Europe and the USA, spread across the country.

Further afield, the first **recaptive missionaries** began to follow the traders, not just inland from Freetown, but along the coast, and especially to Nigeria. From the 1850s onwards, the advent of steamships made Freetown the hub of the whole West African coast. With the return of peace in Yorubaland, large numbers of Krios headed back there and went on to colonize the coast of Cameroon.

Expansion and consolidation

Expansion of the Freetown colony in the 1860s took in parts of Sherbro Island and the southern coast. Treaties were signed by local chiefs, who were forced to choose the lesser evil of British overlordship, when French traders made clear their designs on the region. Inland from the peninsula, a minor incident was used to force the "leasing" (in reality annexation) of the low-lying Koya Temne farming district around Songo – about as far inland as present-day Mile 38. Loko and Mende mercenary allies of the British helped clear the area of recalcitrant Temne.

The end of the slave trade in 1865 was in fact just the cessation of

transatlantic shipments. Slaves continued to be traded in the interior of the country, for domestic work and for labour on export crops. As the pace of trade and competition increased, the British in Freetown made no effort to control slavery beyond the border of the Freetown colony, if anything recognizing its usefulness and the danger of upsetting the chiefs who profited from it.

Alongside these developments, missionaries, in particular those of the American United Baptist Church, aimed to create conditions in the interior that would result in the gradual dismantling of traditional ways. They spread the gospels, of course, and set a lot of store in conversions. But more significantly, they taught new economic practices in their boys' schools and offered substantial credit to their graduates to set them up as traders. As more and more traders left the colony to trade outside the British customs area, so Freetown Krios, complaining of unfair competition and price wars, demanded an extension of British control to annex the whole coast. London, however, explicitly prohibited any further annexations. Indeed a parliamentary committee of 1865 had already laid out a general principal of eventual withdrawal and self-government for the West African colonies.

In 1882, the borders of separate spheres of influence with Liberia and France were settled along the coast, and Britain found itself operating a **customs area** that extended from the Great Scarcies in the north to the Mano River in the south. The purely exploitative nature of this arrangement, in which no responsibility for internal affairs was taken by the British, led to the beginning of a draining of Krio confidence in the colonial government. One incident that incensed them was the execution of William Caulker in 1888 for the murder of his half-brother, the disputed king of Shenge (the coast between Freetown and Sherbro). Although the king had the govern-

ment's support for his succession, his enthronement had been unpopular. Krio opinion had it that such affairs could be avoided if Britain were to annex and administer the whole country, rather than simply extract duty.

The creation of the new customs area also coincided with a general recession in trade in the 1880s and repeated confrontations and battles between the trading chiefdoms along the coast and in the interior. A number of statelets, which managed to stay on the right side of the British, emerged supremely powerful in Mende country – among them Senehun, under Madam (Mammy) Yoko; Panguma, under Nyagua; Pujehun, run jointly by Momo Ja and Momo Kai Kai; and, in the east, Kailahun, a new Mende-Kissi confederation under Kai Lundu.

Partition

With the recognition of Freetown's importance as a coaling station for British shipping, and a sense of urgency in Europe's attitude to Africa, a new pragmatism overcame the colonial government in the closing years of the nineteenth century. The French were chasing Samory Touré's giant *sofa* army (which was supplied with weapons from Freetown) across territory in the British zone of influence. A war between Britain and France in the region couldn't be discounted.

Hastily, the British began formulating exclusive friendship treaties with as many chiefs as would entertain them, hoping to set up a buffer zone of allies between the French and Freetown. Boundary agreements were signed with the French in 1895, a partition that forced the British to accept the **Protectorate of Sierra Leone**. The domineering governor Frederic Cardew initiated a system of **indirect rule** through local chiefs under European District Commissioners – a system that was later followed in northern Nigeria. All kings and queens became **paramount chiefs** (under

Queen Victoria) and their sovereignty over their peoples strictly limited to whatever their district commissioner considered appropriate. The "treaties of friendship" they'd signed were reinterpreted as surrenders of power in the new Protectorate.

Cardew's decision to build a **railway**, based on the need to encourage trade, and the requirement that the Protectorate's administration should not be paid for by the colony, led unavoidably to the invention of ways of paying for it. It was the first ever built and run by the British government: all previous lines had been private. Trading licences were introduced and a tax imposed of five shillings per year on every house in the Protectorate. Payments had to be forced out of people. The undisciplined **Frontier Police** (initially mainly Krio, later largely upcountry men) smashed their way across the country, effectively robbing the people to pay for the administration they had never asked for. People of the Protectorate regarded the white man's **"hut tax"** as an inversion of the proper order of things, which should have had them extracting payment from the newcomers. They assumed they were being charged rent on their houses, which had been stolen from them.

The Hut Tax War and the Mende Revolt

In the north, the Loko chief **Bai Burreh** resisted demands for the hut tax and fought a protracted guerilla war against better-equipped but untrained Caribbean troops. There was support for Bai Burreh's action from the Krio, whose views about taxes concurred with his and who detested Governor Cardew's arrogance.

At the beginning of the rainy season in 1898, there was a massive organized **uprising**, planned through secret society meetings. Hut tax and trading licences were the main grudges, but decades of resentment were released in unprecedented violence directed against "every man in trousers and every woman in a dress". Hundreds of administrators, traders and missionaries were hacked and bludgeoned to death. Atrocities were widespread and few escaped; the Krio traders in the Protectorate suffered most. Although there was panic in Freetown, the colony was not invaded.

Pro-British chiefs helped the government resume control in the Protectorate, although there were fierce skirmishes in several districts. Over 200 arrests were made and 96 people were hanged. Many others, including, eventually, Bai Burreh, were deported to the Gold Coast. A new West African regiment having replaced the West Indians, Cardew followed the crushing of the resistance with a military victory tour around the country. The Krio community was sickened. The hut tax was not repealed.

A new authoritarianism

The beginning of the twentieth century saw a new, more complex Sierra Leone. The Krios were demoralized, being ignored by the government and mistrusted by the people of the Protectorate. The Protectorate people had been defeated by the government and now found themselves paying allegiance (and corruptly inflated taxes in many cases) to increasingly alienated chiefs in the pay of the British. At least the Frontier force was disbanded. Chiefdom "court messengers" were given the job of policing the Protectorate.

British policy in general moved right away from the benevolence of a century earlier. In concordance with the new authoritarian order, **racial discrimination** became policy. Blacks – whether "natives" or "creoles" – were kept in subordinate positions no matter how highly qualified. Social mixing between the races became rare and, with the discovery that mosquitoes transmitted malaria, a new whites-only suburb was created on the high ground above Freetown, Hill Station, served by its own railway. Once malaria became less of a deterrent, more and more European companies came to trade in Sierra Leone, buying out the less prosperous Krio traders and bringing venture capital with them.

But it was the arrival of **Lebanese traders** in the 1890s (many, it's said, brought by unscrupulous ships' captains who told them West Africa was America) which really did for the Krio traders at the smaller end of business. World War I and the influenza epidemic, and the food shortages that followed, stalled the political advances that might otherwise have taken place. Predictably, perhaps, the Lebanese (who never seemed to go short) were accused of hoarding and profiteering. Anti-Lebanese demonstrations took place and their shops were looted.

Railway workers went on strike in 1919 and again in 1926, but their demands for improved pay and conditions were not met. Although an increased quota of Africans was nominated to the Sierra Leone Legislative Council, only three were elected, and then only by restricted suffrage for the literate and propertied. The voices of Africans were timid and restrained. The **abolition of slavery** as an institution came only in 1927, when the outrage from abroad became impossible to ignore. Slave-owners lost little, as most slaves preferred to stay with them as employees.

Apart from an isolated Islamic resistance movement led by a marabout, Idara (who was killed near Kambia in 1931, and his followers jailed), there wasn't much motion on the political scene. But the radical propaganda of **I.T.A. Wallace-Johnson** represented a break from conservative reformism. Organizing a mass consciousness nationalist movement in the Gold Coast and Sierra Leone, he formed the West African Youth League and outspokenly denounced the government of Sir Douglas Jardine. Wallace-Johnson's use of Krio, a language more widely understood than English, was especially provocative. He was imprisoned on a charge of criminal libel, followed by years of detention through World War II, on the spurious pretext of his threat to security.

The road to independence

Only World War II broke the numbing spell of repression which had settled on the country since partition. By the time peace was declared in Asia and the black veterans of the Burma campaign and RAF were coming home to Sierra Leone, it was clear that profound changes could not be held off much longer.

To begin with, the colour bar was removed, opening senior civil service posts to Africans. And there was a major change in budgetary policy too, with British taxpayers now funding colonial development. Independence at some point in the future was explicitly stated to be the goal. The **new constitution** of 1947 gave the Protectorate fourteen seats on the Legislative Council, and the Colony just seven, which was still a gross under-representation of Protectorate interests, despite Krio complaints that the Colony should have held a majority of seats. Wallace-Johnson bitterly opposed the new order and reminded the government of the 1865 proposals to allow for self-government in the Colony, now being swept aside.

Surprised at the vehemence of the Krio attacks, the government stalled in implementing the new constitution. In the Protectorate, meanwhile, the **Sierra Leone People's Party** (SLPP) was being formed, the country's first. It was led by **Milton Margai**, a doctor (the first Protectorate man to receive a medical qualification) from a Bonthe business family, related to the powerful and pro-British Banta Mende chiefdom. His brother, **Albert Margai** (the first lawyer from the Protectorate), and **Siaka Stevens**, a Vai-Limba man with a union background, were also founder members. The SLPP insisted on the introduction of the new constitution. Elections held in 1951 gave them a huge majority over the **National Council of Sierra Leone**, the Krio-based party.

The People's Party gradually took over power from colonial appointees. Margai became Chief Minister in 1954, but was in no hurry to form a government to run the country independently. "It will come," he said, "but we are not ready yet. We have not got the men to run it. We want our friends to go on helping us for some time to come."

Throughout the 1950s prosperity and confidence grew. The **diamond fields** in the east were opened to private licensees and there was considerable investment in health and education, as well as general infrastructure. There were also signals of rumbling discontent at the way political reforms lagged behind growth. In 1955, price riots in Freetown and anti-chief demonstrations throughout the north drew little response from Margai, whose conservative and parochial leanings were becoming increasingly apparent.

The creation of a House of Representatives (the Sierra Leonean parliament) in 1956 replaced the Legislative Council. There was a **general election**, in which all tax-paying men were eligible to vote, in 1957, which returned the SLPP to power with a slightly reduced majority.

Independence

Albert Margai and Siaka Stevens, unhappy with Milton (Sir Milton in 1959) Margai's record, left his cabinet to form opposition parties. Although a brief, ritualistic, all-party unity was on show in the United Front for the **independence talks** held in London in 1960, there was a rapid fission of interests in the final, faster-than-expected lead-up to independence. Stevens

formed the All-Peoples' Congress (APC); Sir Milton Margai, now the prime minister, refused his demands for a general election before independence and went further by detaining Stevens and several others for over a month, throughout the transition, on the pretext that they posed a risk to the country's stability. Sierra Leone's **Independence Day** came on April 27, 1961. A general election held the following year, under **universal suffrage** for the first time, reaffirmed SLPP dominance, but also confirmed mass opposition support for the APC.

Dissatisfaction with the SLPP was spreading, but the death of Sir Milton Margai in 1964, and the return to the fold of his brother Albert (soon Sir Albert) increased popular resentment of the government, especially in the north. The party appeared to be squandering the foreign funds that were poured into the country. It still showed scant concern to reform the corrupt and antiquated system of local government by chiefs, and too much interest in its own, Mende, power base. In Freetown, however, important developments were under way. Siaka Stevens was elected **mayor** from 1964 to 1965 and he built up solid support among the disenchanted Krios, for whom independence had so far been disappointing. The general election in 1967 was a turning point. It ousted the SLPP and ushered in a period of intense instability, which arguably has persisted to the present day.

The coups and Siaka Stevens

As soon as Siaka Stevens (elected leader of the victorious APC) had been sworn in as prime minister, a chauvinistic army brigadier, David Lansana — an eastern Mende whom Albert Margai had been grooming in a push for regional dominance — attempted a coup to retain Margai. The following day, Lansana's own officers usurped him and seized power, eventually succeeding in nominating Andrew Juxson-Smith to chair their army-and-police National Redemption Council (NRC).

Stevens went into exile in Guinea, with his senior supporters. At first, they had to restrain him from launching an armed invasion of Sierra Leone, with the help of Sekou Touré (the Guinean president). He waited a year in exile, while the NRC's popular promises to restore the flagging economy, clean up corruption and return the country to civilian rule came to nothing. In April 1968 a mutiny in the lower ranks led to the arrest of the members of the NRC and Stevens' return to power.

Stevens in power

Stone wey dey botam wata, no no say wen rain de cam.
A stone under the water doesn't know when it's raining.

– Krio proverb

Siaka Stevens' first decade in power was characterized by a growing alienation from his political roots and the jettisoning of virtually all objectives with the exception of "national unity". Publicly, he quickly ceased to be the champion of Freetown's interests. His former outward adherence to socialist principles was ploughed under by the need constantly to retain his power base. At the same time, he was careful to shed those of his supporters who became dangerously close. He avoided clear ethnic affiliation, using his mixed background to adopt a succession of tribal identities. And all the time, he continued to accumulate a massive personal fortune.

Early after the return to civilian rule, senior ministers in Stevens' government – Mohammed Forna and Ibrahim Bash-Taqi – resigned to form the **United Democratic Party** (the UDP, banned in 1973). A coup attempt by the army commander, John Bangura, and two assassination attempts on Stevens, all led to executions and to the arrival of detachments of Guinean troops to protect Stevens from his own military.

Repeatedly, too, states of emergency were imposed. Sierra Leone became a **republic** in 1971, with Stevens, now president, replacing Queen Elizabeth as head of state.

Such was the political climate by 1972 that there was no further effective opposition for nearly five years. The House of Representatives became a discussion forum for APC members, in which the pronouncements of Pa Siaka (old man Siaka) were aired and approved. A bomb explosion in April 1974 at the home of the finance minister gave Stevens an opportunity to smash home his dominance. Eight opponents of the regime, including the ex-APC members Forna and Bash-Taqi, were hanged in public and their bodies desecrated.

The general election of 1977 came in the wake of student-led demonstrations across the country, amid mounting economic disarray. Despite vote-rigging, and violence that resulted in more than a hundred deaths, the SLPP gained fifteen seats at the expense of Siaka's supporters and, for a short period, the opposition was bolstered with new confidence. This lapsed again with Siaka's announcement that he was "obliged" to hold a referendum on the question of a **one-party state**, to save Sierra Leone from tribalist chaos. The results of this poll (officially, more than 97 percent in favour) led to the absorption of the SLPP into the ranks of the APC and the formalization of one-party rule.

To seal his control, Siaka was lavish with his political patronage. But his appointment of the chief of the armed forces, Major General Joseph Momoh (from the minority northern Limba-speaking group), to the House of Representatives and the Cabinet itself as president-in-waiting was a strategic bequest to the country. His two vice-presidents, Francis Minah and Sorie Koroma, were ignored.

The hosting of the 1980 **OAU conference**, which cost an estimated US$100 million, marked the end of the era of stagnation and corruption. Food shortages, price rises and non-payment of salaries led to huge and general discontent in the towns, while in the rural areas production was depressed by, among other factors, low prices paid to producers. The black economy was tolerated, and even thrived under the bankrupt official system. A government handbook to mark the OAU conference remarked that "the nation's aims of self-sufficiency and country-wide prosperity are now on the verge of achievement". By 1985 Sierra Leone's economy was apparently on the verge of total collapse – where it was to teeter for four years.

Momoh in power: "The New Order"

Siaka Stevens retired in November 1985. (He died, in his mansion overlooking Freetown, on May 29, 1988, after a long and painful illness.) The transfer of power to Major General Joseph Momoh was peaceful, the new man welcomed with enthusiasm after seventeen years of Siaka's hollow rhetoric. Elections in 1986 saw many of the old guard lose their seats and some 150 new APC members installed in the House of Representatives. A number of political prisoners were released, including twelve convicted after the bomb attack of April 1974.

Momoh's economic strategy was to cut back on public spending, in line with IMF-imposed financial conditions. Fearful of the results of austerity measures in the already hard-pressed towns, however, he declined to follow through with a full implementation that might have satisfied the IMF. In **agriculture**, a "Green Revolution" was promulgated but, from lack of consultation with subsistence farmers, it never had much chance of success. Farmers were deserting their plots for diamond and gold prospects in the east. And, despite an economy dominated, in human terms, by rice farms, self-sufficiency in rice

was far from being achieved. Escalating prices resulted, early in 1987, in student-led demonstrations, riots and several deaths, sparked by those on government bursaries with not enough money for food. Three colleges at Bo were closed, and government-funded students were dismissed and told to reapply.

The causes of growing public disillusion with the new government were easy to fathom. While the "New Order" tag was lauded, there was no clean sweep; a number of Stevens' old cabinet cronies were retained in senior positions. Corruption blazed in all corners of society. The government's economic measures bit deep, yet apparently had little effect, as Momoh still fell out with the IMF for refusing a comprehensive devaluation of the leone and insisting on retaining the petrol subsidy. Sierra Leone was working itself into a deep mire.

By the end of 1987, all other problems were overshadowed by the treasury's predicament in finding itself quite unable to pay the salaries of government employees, due to the hoarding of money and a consequent severe shortage of currency in the banks. Declaring a state of **economic emergency**, Momoh beefed up border controls, announced severe measures against diamond and foreign currency smugglers, slapped limits on the amounts of Sierra Leonean currency that could be privately held, and gave Sierra Leoneans a deadline to deposit their cash in the banks.

The emergency measures, notably efforts to get leones back in the banks, had some success. But economic performance hardly altered: indeed it continued to decline. By the end of 1988, the economy seemed to have bottomed out.

In March 1991, a serious threat to national security emerged from the east of the country. Here the forces of the then Liberian warlord, **Charles Taylor** (who subsequently became Liberian president), and the Revolutionary

United Front (RUF) – a Sierra Leonean rebel army under the leadership of an ex-army corporal, **Foday Sankoh** (supported by Taylor and his own backer, President Blaise Compaoré of Burkina Faso) – began taking control of the diamond areas. They proved to be too strong a force to be submerged by the undersupplied and underpaid army.

Later that year, Momoh finally announced that he was accepting a constitutional commission report recommending a return to **multiparty politics**, raising hopes about impending elections. They never took place, as the government was **overthrown** by the military a few months later.

The NPRC

The coup of April 29, 1992 was not unexpected – and it was certainly not unwelcome. A group of exasperated young officers led by Captain Valentine Strasser, 26, stormed into the president's office to claim back-pay and demand more support for the war. Momoh then broadcast messages intended to be reassuring from the SLBS station, while Strasser, speaking on 99.9 FM, claimed he was in charge of the country and, to a backing of "Ain't No Stopping Us Now, We're On The Move!" made a string of pronouncements about the price of foodstuffs, unpaid company taxes and the cancelling of diamond-export licences. Strasser's National Provisional Ruling Council (NPRC) took control, and the whole country seemed to be cheering while Momoh went into exile in Guinea.

The honeymoon for the coup-leaders was relatively brief. Sober behaviour soon gave way to high living and excess, and popular cynicism set in just as quickly. As the ebb and flow of the war in the provinces gradually turned more and more against the government troops, now led by Strasser, Foday Sankoh's RUF rather than Liberian rebels were identified as the main enemy. But the war fronts became increasingly complex, as the anti-Taylor **ULIMO** forces in Liberia and a new rebel group, the National Front for the Restoration of Democracy (**NAFORD**) who fought to reinstate Joseph Momoh, entered the conflict. Rebel forces, the *kamajors* (members of the traditional hunter societies who generally supported the army), "sobels" – soldiers turned rebels and the national army supported by the Military Observer Group (**ECOMOG**) of ECOWAS, clashed in an increasingly tangled war that was primarily fuelled by the desire to control the nation's extensive diamond fields, and largely fought by teenage, even child, soldiers.

The civil war

In January 1996, the Strasser government was overthrown in another military coup led by General Julius Maada Bio. Elections held the following month resulted in a clear victory for Alhaji **Ahmed Tejan Kabbah**, leader of the SLPP. The RUF, however, did not participate in the elections. The conflict continued. A special UN envoy was sent to assist in the negotiations of a peace agreement (the Abidjan Accord) between government and RUF in November 1996. It proved unsuccessful. On May 25, 1997, the government was ousted in yet another coup perpetrated by junior soldiers and RUF units who formed a ruling junta called the Armed Forces Revolutionary Council (AFRC) under the leadership of Major General Johnny Paul Koroma. President Kabbah went into exile in Guinea, and Sierra Leone descended deeper into a chaotic, brutal guerilla war. UN-led attempts to persuade Koroma's junta to step down failed. Sierra Leone was suspended from the Commonwealth, and an oil and arms embargo was put in place, secured by **ECOMOG** troops. Plans for a ceasefire, drawn up in October 1997, remained ineffective, despite initial verbal claims by the junta to accept its terms. By 1998, the war had engulfed almost the entire country. Thousands of people had been mutilated or killed, and even more forced into exile.

In February, the Nigerian-led ECOMOG forces (almost a quarter of the entire Nigerian army was deployed in Sierra Leone at the time) launched a military attack that led to the collapse of the junta. ECOMOG was supported by imports of arms funnelled through a British company, Sandline, technically breaking the UN embargo and causing severe embarrassment to the British Foreign Office – who either hadn't known, or had chosen to look the other way. Large numbers of rebel forces fled the capital, only to regroup in less accessible parts of the country. ECOMOG managed to consolidate control over Freetown, and on March 10, 1998, President Kabbah made a triumphant return to Freetown. The UN Security Council terminated the oil and arms embargo, and hope for a peaceful future was in the air, yet stability could not be secured. The rebel alliance once again took territory in the interior, eventually gaining control over more than half the country. In December 1998 the RUF and its allies began a brutal offensive to retake Freetown, which culminated in **"Operation No Living Thing"**, a carefully planned assault, supported by South African mercenaries, in which over six thousand lost their lives. All UN personnel were evacuated and much of Freetown's East End was left ruined. Though ECOMOG troops retook the capital later that month, it became clear that dialogue with the RUF would have to be sought in order to bring the enduring war to an end. The RUF had become an organization of killers and mutilators, kidnapping and co-opting children into its ranks, forcing families to execute each other, and routinely hacking off the limbs of those not murdered.

Negotiations between government and rebel units began in May 1999, and on July 7 the unhappy **Lomé agreement** was signed, which gave Foday Sankoh the powers of a vice-president and control over diamond production. It was never put into practice.

With the agreement, the UN Security Council authorized the formation of a much larger UN mission to Sierra Leone – the United Nations Mission in Sierra Leone (**UNAMSIL**). Six thousand military personnel were sent over in October 1999, a contingent which was eventually stepped up to 17,500, making it the largest, and most expensive, peacekeeping mission in the UN's history. However, clashes between army and rebels continued, and UN forces were increasingly drawn into the hostilities. Sankoh and another rebel leader, Sam Bokari, disputed the UN's presence in the country, and the peacekeeping forces found themselves under attack in some areas, their mission blocked in others.

In April 2000, another crisis – the abduction of three hundred UN troops – tipped the balance of power. They were released the following month when Foday Sankoh was finally captured, and his rebel troops forced onto the defensive by a vigorous assault of unilaterally deployed **British forces**, operating under the protection of the UN contingent. Following this success, the British brought in military trainers to strengthen the Sierra Leone Army, a police inspector to run the civil police force, and numerous other specialists to work alongside the faltering Sierra Leonean civil service. There were calls from some quarters in Sierra Leone for the country to become a British trusteeship – not a serious option for the Blair government, but a stark reminder of how low the country had sunk.

In August 2000, the UN agreed to pursue the rebels through an **international tribunal**, and efforts to put a special court, composed of Sierra Leonean and international representatives, in place began in July 2001. Sporadic clashes with rebel forces were finally halted in February 2002 with the disarming of remaining troops by UN forces. The war was officially declared over.

Peaceful **elections** followed in May 2002. President Kabbah won convincingly, and with the RUF as a party garnering little support, there was cautious optimism for a new era of stability.

Prospects

At the time of writing Sierra Leone appears relatively stable, though concerns are continually raised as Liberia is still embroiled in conflict, and there are fears that Guinea may face a military coup should President Conté succumb to his long illness. A new UN court for the prosecution of **war crimes** began its work in 2003, with Charles Taylor, former president of Liberia, one of the first to be indicted. The court's work is a delicate task, as figures who still hold influential positions in Sierra Leone may have to face the consequences of their actions. Two of the accused rebel leaders, Bokari and Koroma, escaped trial by fleeing the country, though Bokari was shot dead in Liberia in April 2003; Koroma is thought to be hiding in Liberia; and Foday Sankoh died in jail in July 2003.

Sierra Leoneans joke that when God created the world, he endowed the country with such a wealth of natural resources that the angels protested it was unfair on other countries. "Don't worry", God replied " just look at the people I've put there!" The country does have exceptional natural resources: diamonds and gold are the most obvious, but iron ore, titanium ("rutile"), chrome, coffee and cocoa, palm oil and rice could all create the conditions for a country as prosperous as any in West Africa. With the war apparently behind it, with UN and British support, with a functioning democracy, and with international controls over conflict diamonds at last stemming that traffic, there has to be a better chance now for Sierra Leone, than for decades. But what happens beyond its borders and out of its control may ultimately decide the future.

Books

Sierra Leone has never had as much literary or scholarly attention as Ghana or Nigeria, though there are books to be found if you search. Titles marked ⊠ are especially recommended.

Sylvia Ardyn Boone *Radiance from the Waters: Ideals of Feminine Beauty in Mende Art.* Circumspect account of the Mende women's Sande society by an art historian who promised not to reveal all.

Greg Campbell *Blood Diamonds.* If you want to understand the impulses behind Sierra Leone's descent into anarchy, you have to get to the diamond trade – the economic driver that finances the conflicts in neighbouring countries, and now props up al-Qaida. Campbell traces a sticky web of corruption and brutalization that links impoverished diamond collectors with the arms trade and the ring on your finger.

Syl Cheney-Coker *The Last Harmattan of Alusine Dunbar.* American-educated professor's first novel – a black comedy of life in a neo-colonial state.

Mariane C Ferme *The Underneath of Things.* A sensitive and thoughtful ethnography of the Mende. Subtitled *Violence, History and the Everyday in Sierra Leone*, it shows how the secret societies have both served to foster the country's bloody chaos and at the same time provided a means of coping with it.

Aminatta Forna *The Devil that Danced on Water.* Subtitled *A Daughter's Quest,* Forna's deeply affecting account of her return to the Sierra Leone she lived in until the age of 10, and where her politician father was hanged for treason, is tender and excruciatingly painful, as she assesses the chaos of today and its roots in the 1960s.

Graham Greene The Heart of the Matter. Set in Freetown during World War II and touching on the racism and repression then present in the colony, Greene's novel uses the town as a seedy web in which his protagonists struggle. Greene's atmospheric *Journey without Maps,* narrating his progress towards the Liberian border in 1935, is still worth reading.

Gail Haddock *What for Chop Today?* Recollections of a young volunteer doctor in Sierra Leone in the early 1990s, mostly delivered through warm and witty dialogue. Good, light preparatory reading – with dark undertones.

Yulisa Amadu Maddy *No Past, No Present, No Future.* Three Sierra Leonean boys in Europe make up for, and make the most of, their different backgrounds.

People's Educational Association *Fishing in Rivers of Sierra Leone.* A major collection of oral literature – stories and songs – from thirteen Sierra Leonean language groups, with hundreds of photos of the performers in action.

Teun Voeten *How de Body?* Dutch photojournalist Voeten visited in 1998 on assignment to photograph child soldiers. The result is harrowing and occasionally funny, though perhaps not as illuminating as you might hope.

Languages

The most useful thing you can do to keep in touch with events around you in Sierra Leone is learn some **Krio**. Unless you have lessons, however, this isn't as easy as it might appear: Krio isn't a pidgin, so you can't guess it.

Krio is written phonetically. Although many words look familiar (and numbers are the same as in English), it's a different matter to get them right in speech, and to structure your sentences correctly. Remember, too, that even with reasonable Krio, you'll still be speaking a foreign language to the nine people out of ten who are more likely to speak Mende or Temne.

A little Krio

Aw di bohdi?	How are you?
No bad, bohdi fine	Not bad, fine
Mohnin-o!	Good morning!
Ivinin-o!	Good evening!
Kushe-o!	Hello
A no sabi tok Krio	I don't speak Krio
Usai yu kohmot?	Where are you from?
A kohmot . . .	I'm from . . .
Wi go si bak	Goodbye/ see you again
Dehn geht hotel	Is there a hotel in

na dis tohn?	this town?
A ebul slip naya?	Can I sleep here?
Dehn get chop os naya?	Is there a chop house here?
Wetin na yu nem?	What's your name?
A nem . . .	My name is . . .
Usai yu de go?	Where are you going?
A de go na . . .	I'm going to . . .
Wan naya!/ Lef me naya	Let me off!/ Drop me here
Tap!	Stop!
A wan wata/ Gi mi wata	Can I have some water

Ohmos foh di panapul?	How much is the pineapple?
Ten-ten lion	Ten leones
(Duya) lehs mi smohl	(Please) lower your price a little
Ustehm wi de go?	When are we leaving?
Wi de go jisnoh	We're going now
Bai gohd in powa	By the grace of god/Insh'allah
Aw foh du?	What can a person do? (rhetorical)
Nafoh bia nomoh	Just bear it, nothing can be done

Some Mende

Mende, one of the Mande languages, is related to Susu and Mandinka. It's somewhat "tonal", so that meaning varies with the pitch of voice.

Buae! (pl.)/ Wuae! (sing.)	Hello there! (response the same)
Bisye! (sing.)/ Wusye! (pl.)	Thanks, greetings (said as you pass through the village)
O bi gahui?	How are you? ("Your bones?")
Kaye Ngewo ma	Response ("God can't be blamed")

Ngi ya le	I am leaving
Mm, ta mia, ma lo-o	Yes, OK, see you again
Bi lei?	What's your name?
Nya la a . . .	My name is . . .
Pelei ji a li mi?	Where does this road go?
A li . . .	It goes to . . .
Sao	No
Li lele!	Go slowly!
Gbe jongo lo a ji?	How much is this?
Na bagbango, ba mayeilo?	It's too much, can you lessen it?
Kulungoi	All right
1	Yila
2	Fele
3	Sawa
4	Nani
5	Lolu
6	Woita
7	Wofela
8	Wayakpa
9	Talu
10	Pu
15	Pu mahu lolu
20	Nu yila gboyongo
	(lit. "one man finished"; ie ten fingers and ten toes)

Glossary

Alagba Bigwig, personage.
Ambohg "Humbug"; to bother or pester someone.
Bafa Shelter made of thatch or leaves.
Bohboh Small boy.
Bruk To wash clothes.
Bundu Generic term for secret societies.
Cora Lebanese or Syrian, after the coral they used to sell.
Gara Indigo; usually refers to dyed cloth.
Johnks Used clothes, "deadmen's clothes".
Kola Can mean a tip or inducement, not always of kola nuts.

Lorry Often a minibus or converted pick-up.
Pikin Child.
Poda poda Minibus.
Porto European, white person.
Pumwe European (Mende).
Salone Sierra Leone.
Siraman Lebanese, or other white.
Titi Small girl.
Turntable Roundabout, traffic circle.
Wetman "White man"; can apply to anyone with a European lifestyle.

8.1

Freetown and around

An aged and crumbling tumble of sagging streets, clapboard and cement-block buildings, with a population now in excess of half a million, **FREETOWN** fills the level areas and spreads up the steep hillsides of the otherwise vegetation-flanked Freetown Peninsula. Before the war, Freetown used to be charmingly dilapidated, but today, urban decay and the scars of war have eaten so deeply into the fabric of the town that it seems as though only a strong breeze would bring the wood-panelled houses down. Granted, there are some newer, multistorey buildings, but rot and collapse are ubiquitous among the palms and mango trees, and the prevailing sense is one of teetering on the edge of chaos.

If you fly in fresh from Europe, the impact of so much mutant tropicality can shock temperate sensibilities. Yet, if you're arriving from almost anywhere else in West Africa, Freetown's overall effect is still enchanting. The town (and it feels like a town, not a city) gurgles with twice as much atmosphere as any other West African capital. The hilly relief gives constantly changing points of view and there are photogenic street prospects in every direction.

Architecture and a real depth of history have much to do with it. Run-down, pastel-painted Creole houses, with rusty-red tin roofs, often propped up on posts against steeply scaling streets, are preserved even in the town centre. The anonymous apartment blocks and broad thoroughfares of many cities are largely absent from Freetown. After dark you catch domestic glimpses, through the burglar bars and tatty curtains, of murky interiors lit by dim light bulbs – or kerosene lamps; Freetown's electricity supply is far from stable, and power is distributed under a rotation system, with only 25 percent of town receiving electricity at any one time.

Walking or driving through the town in the heat of the day is best avoided. You'll find yourself surrounded by maddening chaos, or spending hours in unmoving traffic jams, which usually don't dissolve until late at night. There's a fair choice of places to stay and eat, though, and the business and embassy districts are compact and central. Sierra Leone's best **beaches** are all nearby on the **Freetown Peninsula** – far enough away to ensure clean sea and tranquillity, but still an inexpensive taxi ride from the town and exceptionally beautiful.

Orientation, arrival and information

Freetown's wonderful hilly layout is sprawling and confusing at first, and its north-facing aspect curiously disorientating. The town begins in the east at **Wellington**, and stretches into the poor residential areas of **Kissy**, **Cline Town**, **Fourah Bay**, **Kossa Town** and **Foulah Town** (together known as **East End**). The East End "towns" were originally mostly developed by immigrants from the interior and from neighbouring parts of West Africa (Temne, Mende, Limba, Kissi, Fula, Yoruba and Bamana). Some arrived in the nineteenth century looking for commercial opportunities, but many, like the Kissi and the influxes of Muslim Yoruba from Nigeria, were recaptured slaves, saved from the Atlantic crossing. The character of this side of the town thus has a less creolized flavour. Many of its founding families were traders, and a great deal of trade still goes on in the East End. The East End was also hit hardest by the fighting in 1999, when most of its already dilapidated houses were left in ruins. Today, it's deeply impoverished, chaotic, and gripped by traffic jams throughout the day.

The half square kilometre of the main **commercial and business district** roughly coincides with the historical centre. The oldest and most established blocks are roughly within a triangle formed by **Siaka Stevens Street** (the town's major thoroughfare), Pademba Road and Waterloo Street. This triangle, at its apex the famous, huge **Cotton Tree**, was home to the freed-slave Nova Scotians and the Maroons from Jamaica. The unfortunate English immigrants of 1787 settled a few hundred metres to the north of here on the peninsula of **Kingtom**. It's no longer possible to differentiate quarters of the town centre according to the origins of their inhabitants.

West of the centre, through a jungle of ravines, streams and sprawling shanties, stretch the more residential, less commercial areas of **Congo Town**, **Murray Town**, **Wilberforce** and other nineteenth-century freed-slave settlements. Down by the shore near the centre, **Kroo Town** is an area still largely inhabited by Kru fishing people from Liberia. Wilkinson Road and Aberdeen Road cut west out of the town, down the steep hillside to the sea and over a bridge to the Aberdeen Peninsula, on the far side of which lies the five-kilometre sweep of **Lumley Beach** and the head of the road that runs south along the peninsula shore. The West End is where most NGOs have their premises, and their employees their homes. There aren't many reasonable guesthouses or hotels outside the West End and Lumley Beach, and Wilkinson Road is where you'll find most of the supermarkets and the better restaurants.

Arrival and information

Sierra Leone's international **airport** at Lungi is cut off from the capital by the mouth of the Sierra Leone River. Paramount Airlines run a helicopter service ($20 one-way, included in the price of some flights) from there to Freetown, the schedule tying in with the arrival of flights. The journey by ferry is slower and much cheaper: ferries cross from Tagrin Point Ferry Terminal, 16km from Lungi, to the old Kissy Ferry Terminal about 4km east of the centre (Le1500 or £0.40/$1). The journey from the airport to the town centre this way takes a minimum of ninety minutes and can easily stretch to three hours depending on the state of the ferry.

There's only one main road into Freetown. Most taxis, minibuses (*poda poda*) and lorries have drop-off/pick-up points in the centre or east of town. The main location for those serving the north of the country (Makeni and Kabala) is **Ashoebi Corner**, on Blackhall Road at the Upgun turntable (roundabout), a taxi ride from the centre. Vehicles for Bo and Kenema use the **Dan Street bus park** (just off Kissy Road to the west of Upgun turntable). Upcountry vehicles also use the Shell petrol station in Kissy on the new road to Waterloo. Conakry vehicles park in Free Street, a couple of hundred metres west and uphill from PZ turntable, at the eastern end of the town centre.

For tourist information, contact the **National Tourist Board**, whose main office is at Room 100, *Cape Sierra Hotel*, Aberdeen Hill (☏022/27.25.20, ℗27.20.96, ℮ntbinfo@sierratel.sl). They have a less well-equipped branch off Lumley Beach.

City transport and accommodation

There's no bus service in town, but you can generally walk between most points in the centre – indeed the permanent traffic jams in the heart of town may convince you to do so, or simply spend the day at the beach away from town. For slightly longer trips, wave down one of the shared **minibuses** or **route taxis** (unmetered, with yellow licence plates) going in your direction. These vehicles run on agreed

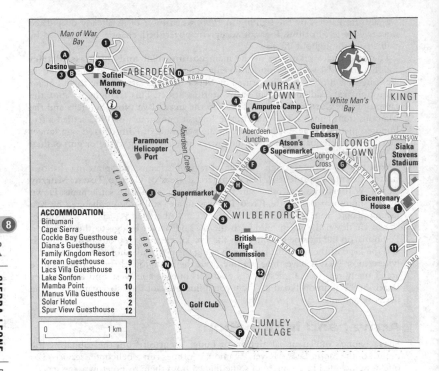

routes, dropping off and picking up anywhere (expect to pay the equivalent of £0.10/15¢ for short hops). You can always charter a taxi if you manage to wave down an empty cab; a trip from the centre of town to Lumley beach shouldn't cost more than £2.50/$4 this way, though you might end up paying double if you don't bargain effectively. Alternatively, try hitching a ride, especially if you're heading out to the beaches; many drivers will oblige. You can offer to pay (reckon on twice the shared-taxi seat fare), but you'll often get free lifts. Siaka Stevens Street at the Cotton Tree roundabout is a likely spot.

Accommodation

Inexpensive lodgings are hard to find in Freetown. The cheapest places are in the East End of town, but it really isn't a good idea to stay in this poor, crime-ridden area. Practically all the accommodation reviewed below is **west of the centre**, including a handful of places on Lumley Beach, though at the time of writing the *Mammy Yoko* here was still used as the headquarters of UNAMSIL forces, and not open to the public. There are also a couple of places to stay on the southern beaches, reviewed on pp.637–638.

Electricity ("light") is the limiting factor at most hotels. Often enough, you'll have to put up with power cuts that last most of the night, ruling out electric fans and air conditioning, and necessitating kerosene lamps or candles for lighting.

Bintumani Lumley Beach Rd ⊕022/27.27.78, ⊕27.33.77. Once Freetown's top hotel, this was used as the RUF rebel HQ during the war, and was completely destroyed in the fighting. Rebuilt by Chinese investors, it has once again become a

stylish luxury complex with all the facilities you would expect. A charming Chinese influence is present in decorations, bilingual signs and the menu. ⑧

Cape Sierra Hotel Lumley Beach

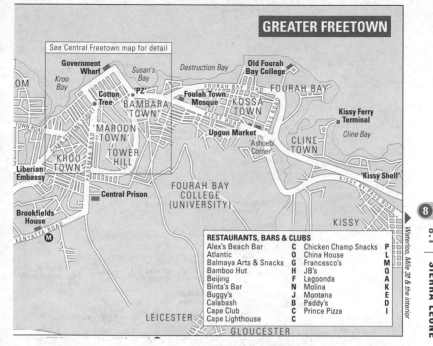

GREATER FREETOWN

RESTAURANTS, BARS & CLUBS

Alex's Beach Bar	C	Chicken Champ Snacks	P
Atlantic	O	China House	L
Balmaya Arts & Snacks	G	Francesco's	M
Bamboo Hut	H	JB's	Q
Beijing	F	Lagoonda	A
Binta's Bar	N	Molina	K
Buggy's	J	Montana	E
Calabash	B	Paddy's	D
Cape Club	C	Prince Pizza	I
Cape Lighthouse	C		

☎022/27.22.72. Comfortable though slightly sterile international establishment. ⑧

Central Guest House Regent St. Run-down place with just about acceptable, ventilated rooms and, as the name suggests, it's right in the heart of Freetown. Keep an eye on your belongings here. ②

Cockle Bay Guesthouse Aberdeen Rd. Basic, s/c rooms at outrageous rates. ⑥

Diana's Guesthouse 19 Mudge Farm, off Aberdeen Road ☎022/23.33.91. Trying-to-be-English B&B, and quite reasonable, though a little scruffy. ⑤

Family Kingdom Resort Lumley Beach Rd ☎022/27.31.33, ℱ22.27.63, ℮fkingdomresort@yahoo.com. With its playgrounds, shallow pool, open-air stage and mini-zoo, this looks more like a theme park than a hotel. It's evidently child-friendly, and has comfortable a/c rooms. ⑦

Korean Guesthouse 24 Lower Pipe Lane, off Wilkinson Rd ☎022/23.10.16. Spacious, a/c rooms, tiled floors, pretty decor and an outstanding Korean restaurant at one of Freetown's best-value options. ⑥

Lacs Villa Guesthouse 3 Cantonment Rd ☎022/24.07.14, ℱ23.50.64, ℮lacs@sierratel.sl.

From the carpets to the breakfast menu, a very English B&B hidden in a quiet leafy courtyard. There's a good restaurant too. ⑧

Lake Sonfon Sequeen Drive, 119 Wilkinson Rd ☎076/63.82.66. Scruffy B&B-type establishment, with unenthusiastic staff. ⑤

Mamba Point Wilberforce ☎022/23.25.27. One of Freetown's most popular lodgings with clean a/c rooms and a lively bar. ⑧

Manus Villa Guesthouse 52 Charles St ☎022/22.39.58. Basic, clean guesthouse with a small number of a/c rooms. ⑤

Solar Hotel 66 Cape Rd, Man of War Bay, Aberdeen ☎022/27.25.31. This is trying hard to be a top-class hotel. While the rooms aren't top-notch, they're not bad at all, and cheaper than some of the dingy guesthouses. There's a good bar and swimming pool. ⑥

Spur View Guesthouse 26C Spur Rd ☎022/23.33.91. Sharing management with, and of a similar standard to, *Diana's Guesthouse*. ⑤

YMCA 32 Fort St, in the centre ☎022/22.36.08. Freetown's cheapest option is also little more than a dingy dive only recommended to hardy travellers. Bathrooms are shared and there's no electricity. ②

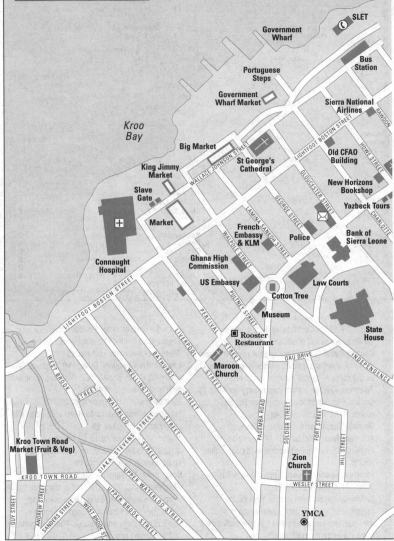

CENTRAL FREETOWN

Government
Wharf

SLET

Bus
Station

Portuguese
Steps

Government
Wharf Market

Sierra National
Airlines

*Kroo
Bay*

LIGHTFOOT BOSTON STREET

RAWDON

Big Market

Old CFAO
Building

HOWE STREET

WALLACE JOHNSON STREET

St George's
Cathedral

King Jimmy
Market

New Horizons
Bookshop

GLOUCESTER STREET

GEORGE STREET

Slave
Gate

Yazbeck Tours

CHARLOTTE

Market

LAMINA SANKOH STREET

French
Embassy
& KLM

WALPOLE STREET

Police

Bank of
Sierra Leone

Connaught
Hospital

Ghana High
Commission

US Embassy

PULTNEY STREET

Cotton Tree

Law Courts

LIGHTFOOT BOSTON STREET

Museum

State
House

PERCIVAL STREET

LIVERPOOL STREET

Rooster
Restaurant

OAU DRIVE

INDEPENDENCE

WEST BROOK STREET

WELLINGTON STREET

BATHURST STREET

Maroon
Church

PADEMBA ROAD

SOLDIER STREET

FORT STREET

Kroo Town Road
Market (Fruit & Veg)

WATERLOO STREET

SIAKA STEVENS STREET

Zion
Church

HILL STREET

KROO TOWN ROAD

UPPER WATERLOO STREET

WESLEY STREET

GUY STREET

ANDREW STREET

SANDERS STREET

WEST BROOK ST

UPPER BROOK STREET

YMCA

Conservation Society

The Town

Wandering around Freetown is generally easy, though it can be murderously
uncomfortable outside the cooler season, and you may not delay long before
migrating out to the beaches. The town's decrepitude conceals a few sights to see,
including a museum and, remarkably, nearly a hundred churches and mosques.

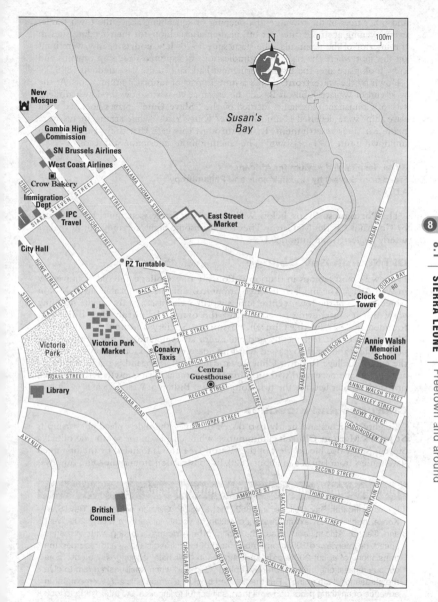

An obvious place to start a walking tour, and Freetown's most famous landmark, is the **Cotton Tree**, a magnificent silk-cotton older than the town itself and as tall as any of its buildings. Beneath the tree's younger branches, slaves were once sold and, in 1787 in the same place, the first colonists from England are supposed to have gathered – a group of "Black Poor" immigrants and sixty white women who had been deported to Sierra Leone. Notice the large bats hanging in the Cotton Tree and other trees in the town centre, sleeping or squabbling above the town traffic: every evening at sunset, they set off, in dramatic fashion, for their feeding sites in the interior of the peninsula. The statuesque 1920s **law courts** nearby were built on the spot where the trials and adjudications of captured slave-ship captains and crew took place after the British parliament had banned the slave trade in 1808.

Down by the **waterfront**, there's a meagre pair of historical monuments. At the west end of Wallace Johnson Road, the entrance to what's now the lower dispensary of Connaught Hospital is formed by the **"Slave Gate"**. Slaves liberated from slave ships were detained behind it in the "King's Yards" while arrangements were made for their resettlement. It was through this gate that they walked to an unknown future in "Free Town". The sanctimonious inscription still reads:

Royal Hospital and Asylum for Africans
Freed from Slavery by British Valour and Philanthropy
A.D. 1817

The **Portuguese Steps**, below Wallace Johnson Street, were built the same year by Governor Charles McCarthy. They're a handsome flight, certainly, but nowadays utterly neglected and unnoticed.

Old Fourah Bay College

Freetown's most famous institution is **Fourah Bay College**, the oldest university in West Africa. The modern (though atrophied) university is located up at Mount Aureol, south of the town centre, and is worth a visit itself, partly for the stunning view. But it's interesting to go and see the **original Fourah Bay building**, founded in 1827 by the Church Missionary Society, and now a half-ruined Magistrate's Court. It makes a good excuse for an exploration of one of the town's poorer, older and much-bypassed East End quarters. The old four-storey building at the end of College Road in Cline Town dates from 1845, and is made of red laterite bricks and decorated with iron fretwork. Samuel Adjai Crowther, the college's first student, later became the first home-grown Bishop of West Africa.

Churches and mosques

Of eighty churches and nearly two dozen mosques, the oldest place of worship is **St John's Maroon Church**, a diminutive white chapel on the south side of Siaka Stevens Street two blocks west of the Cotton Tree. It was founded by the first freed slave settlers from Jamaica in about 1820. In construction around the same time was

The Reverend Koelle and his Polyglotta Africana

It was at Fourah Bay College, in 1852, that a young German pastor, the Rev. S.W. Koelle, published an extraordinary collection of vocabularies from nearly 200 West and Central African languages, the **Polyglotta Africana**. Working with immense speed, he interviewed 205 informants – most of them freed slaves – and recorded the translations of about 300 words and phrases in their natal languages. He got some curious replies: one man apparently replied "Gud-bai" when Koelle asked him to give the phrase for "I am going". But the finished book is a remarkable achievement, far in advance of anything produced until then, still useful to linguists and interesting to look through today; there are copies in the Fourah Bay College library and recent editions available abroad.

Apart from giving clues about the relatedness of different West African languages, the *Polyglotta* also gives interesting cultural information. Less than a third of the informants, for example, could come up with words in their mother tongues for "butter" or "ink" and there were problems too with "book", "hell" and "soap". Missionaries must have found the blanks provocative.

the colonial high temple of **St George's Cathedral** on Lightfoot Boston Street, completed in 1828 and dedicated in 1852. Memorial plaques inside commemorate British administrators and traders who didn't survive the "White Man's Grave" to return home. The **Zion Church** on Fort Street is one to check out during a service. The Catholic community, much smaller than the reforming churches, has its relatively modest Sacred Heart Cathedral on Siaka Stevens Street, on the corner of Howe Street. Sunday is the day when you can't fail to notice the importance of Freetown's churches, as thousands of people, and especially the Krio community, dress in their Sunday best – classically, men in dark suits and homburgs, women in frocks and creative hats, boys in sailor suits and girls in virginal white frills. Services are long and enthusiastic.

The oldest mosque is the **Foulah Town Mosque** on Mountain Cut, just off Kissy Road in the East End. It's surprisingly churchlike in its design, possibly in deference to the concerns of colonial and Creole ruling groups in the mid-nineteenth century – there was considerable opposition to Islam from Christian freed slaves. The freed Yoruba slaves from Nigeria (known as "Aku" or "Oku") were predominantly Muslims. In 1832, a British lawyer, William Henry Savage, was persuaded by his Aku servant to press for the release of a group of Aku who had been jailed for practising "Muhammedanism". In gratitude, several took the name Savage, and a mosque was built near his house, in the street now called Savage Square. Encouraged by this, other Aku built the **Foulah Town Mosque** a kilometre further west. But opposition to Islam, and a low-key conflict between the Creoles and the Aku (who came to be considered "Muslim creoles") has kept mosques out of the commercial town centre – a quarter containing no less than sixteen churches – to this day.

Sierra Leone museum

The newly refurbished **museum** (Mon–Fri 10am–4pm; entry by donation) was, until 1929, a railway terminus ("Cotton Tree Station") at the foot of the "Hill railway" up to Wilberforce and Hill Station. The diminutive white building then saw

---

Freetown markets

Freetown as a whole resembles one big, colourful, noisy market, and though most of the merchandise available comprises mundane household goods and cheap clothes, you can spend an enjoyable time just browsing. For specific purchases, try the following:

King Jimmy Market (Tues & Thurs). Fruit, vegetables and fish.

Government Wharf Market (daily). General goods, from pomade to potato peelers.

Big Market ("Basket Market"; daily). A covered market for a range of crafts, tourist bric-a-brac, traditional medicines and mystical materials. There are good baskets (*shuku*, *blai*), some nice musical instruments and rather a lot of small animal skins, but you need to spend some time at the stalls to discover interesting bargains that you'd actually want to take home.

Victoria Park Market Can be fun, but keep your wits about you: a lot of people are after your custom. This is the best market in Freetown for Sierra Leonean "country cloth" and locally tailored dresses and shirts.

Kroo Town Road (daily). Fruit and vegetables.

East Street/Kissy Road Market (daily). A place of some commotion, with a good fruit and veg market, and some small stores trading in cloth and other merchandise.

Upgun/Kennedy Street Market On the left, 1500m further east down Kissy Road from the East Street Market, immediately before the Upgun roundabout.

Bombay Street Market In Kossa Town, the old Bamana (Bambara) quarter, not far from the shore.

service as a school, a soft-drinks factory and a telephone exchange before becoming the repository of Sierra Leonean cultural heritage in 1957. The collections are emphatically worth a visit: this is Sierra Leone's only museum. There aren't many visitors and you're likely to get a guided tour of some kind.

The **Ruiter stone** replica takes pride of place in the museum. This 1664 rock graffito, scratched by bored Dutch sea captains during a lull in a military expedition against the English, was discovered in the course of drainage work on the waterfront in 1923. It's the oldest archeological evidence of a European presence on the peninsula. A rubbing of the names and date ("M.A. Ruiter, I. C. Meppell, Vice Admiralen, Van Hollant en Westfriesland, AD 1664") was made and the stone was then reburied "six feet below the ground just above the high water mark at King Jimmy Market, to protect it from the weather". Potentially more interesting is another stone, yet to be uncovered, but referred to by Richard Burton in 1862, which is supposed to carry the initials of Francis Drake and Richard Hawkins.

The museum's main interest, though, lies in the ethnographic pieces from around the country. There's an interesting **mask** corner where some of the regalia from Sierra Leone's still lively **secret societies** is fearlessly displayed. Look out for the figure of "Mammy Wata", the transmogrifying Medusa-like sea goddess (a widespread coastal icon) who can assume serpentine or human form and act for good as well as evil. Notice too, some excellent and rather rare examples of Sierra Leonean home-made country cloth, instruments of music and war, and a fine old *warri* board.

The statue of **Bai Burreh** is dressed in the nineteenth-century Temne guerilla leader's own clothes and holds the cutlass with which he fought in the Hut Tax War of 1898. Bai Burreh was captured and taken to the Gold Coast to rot in jail, but was allowed to return in 1905 to end his years in his old kingdom. The "bullet-proof" *ronko* cloth he wore can still be bought today in Kabala, Northern Province.

Upstairs, there's an impressive photo exhibition of Sierra Leone's chiefs, by Vera Viditz-Ward in collaboration with the Smithsonian Institute. The large images capture the regional leaders in their traditional regalia. Other displays include minerals, prehistoric stone tools and Mende **nomoli** – small, rather arcane soapstone figurines, first identified from a pair dug up on Sherbro Island in the 1880s and later found in huge numbers in farmland right across the centre of the country. The Mende don't claim any connection with them, though they traditionally revered them and believed they protected the fertility of the land. Like the *pomtan* (singular *pomdo;* see p.591) of the Kissi country in eastern Sierra Leone and Guinea, they were almost certainly carved by earlier peoples as ancestor figures. The most likely artists are thought to be the **Sherbro**. Now mostly living on the island of the same name, they were displaced from the interior by the Mende around the fifteenth century. Early Portuguese sources suggest they were the best artisans in the region. Much larger figures – life-size heads from Mende and Kono country known as *mahen yafe* ("spirit of the chief") – have also been found. As with the *nomoli* and *pomtan*, the best ones are mostly in private collections or museums abroad.

Lumley Beach

Though the least appealing of the beaches of the Freetown Peninsula, **Lumley Beach** is handily close to Freetown. From downtown, you can share a taxi from the Cotton Tree to take you the 5km to the junction for Lumley village/Aberdeen (marked by a busy petrol station), from where there are slightly cheaper shared vehicles to Aberdeen and the beach. But unless the heat is overpowering, it's worth walking some of the way, at least from the junction onwards. It's about an hour's walk in the unlikely event of your not getting a lift.

At Lumley Beach's first roundabout, the *Hotel Bintumani* is up on the right. Continue west and the entrance on the right leads to the small, sheltered, north-facing beach of **Man-O-War Bay** and some beach bars and restaurants. On the left is the *Mammy Yoko* (named after the powerful nineteenth-century queen), currently used as UNAMSIL headquarters. A second roundabout to the right sends you up to Cape Sierra and the hotel of the same name, to the headland lighthouse, and to the *Lagoonda* entertainment complex, with its bright lights glittering across Man-O'-War Bay after sunset. In front of you starts the great sweep of Lumley Beach, dotted with the odd coconut tree, but backed mostly by scrub and grass. In season, there's a cluster of beach bars and snack restaurants, detailed below. The beach here is pleasant, sloping gently, with little undertow and, on occasions, half-pint waves. Late in the afternoon, the beach road from the hotels down to Lumley village makes a nice walk, and, if you've got the gear, an equally good run or cycle ride (it's exactly 5km from Lumley Beach north to Lumley centre). A lift back again should be easy to find.

Bars and restaurants on Lumley Beach thrived before the war, and are gradually getting back to business. Besides the bunch of **beach bars**, two of Freetown's major nightclubs (*Lagoonda* and *Buggy's*) are found on Lumley Beach. They're reviewed overleaf.

Eating, drinking and nightlife

Freetown is well endowed with eating places. While a number of them are heavily dependant on resident volunteers and aid workers, there are also some good Lebanese establishments and chop houses, and unsurprisingly there are numerous fried-chicken places too. Many restaurants close on Sunday, and some of the more established places only tend to open in the evening. Note also that many of the listed hotels have good restaurants open to the public, and that there are several decent restaurants and bars out at Lumley Beach.

Snacks and fried food

British Council Café Tower Hill. Snacks and light meals.

Chicken Champ Snacks 34 Freetown Rd, Lumley. Cheap fried chicken, sandwiches and the like served on a terrace bar overlooking the Wilkinson Rd/Spur Rd roundabout.

Crown Bakery Wilberforce St. This has long been a major meeting place in Freetown, clean, a/c, and well run, with the best pastries in town and decent food for lunch – fried chicken, sandwiches, pizza. Open daytime only.

Prince Pizza Wilkinson Rd. A modest selection of smallish pizzas from Le5000.

Rooster Restaurant Electricity House, Siaka Stevens St. Slightly grubby fast-food joint with great fried chicken and sandwiches.

Restaurants

Balmaya Arts and Snacks 32 Main Motor Rd, Congo Cross ☎022/23.00.55. Airy terrace restaurant offering tasty, reasonably priced snacks and drinks. Popular with NGO workers. The attached gallery is worth a look if you're interested in buying crafts.

Bamboo Hut Wilkinson Rd ☎022/23.04.62. This small, understated place serves reliable African and European meals, at prices that are much more reasonable than most places in the area.

Beijing 112 Wilkinson Rd ☎022/23.06.95. Popular Chinese restaurant. Daily noon–11pm.

Francesco's Jomo Kenyatta Rd ☎022/24.19.86. Recently opened restaurant offering large servings of European cuisine.

Golf Club Lumley Beach ☎022/27.29.56. Popular for brunch on Sundays.

Korean Guesthouse 24 Lower Pipe Lane, off Wilkinson Rd. Delicious Korean food and a laid-back ambience. Dishes from Le10,000.

Molina 152 Wilkinson Rd ☎076/60.31.12. One of the best restaurants in town, serving a wide range of delicious Lebanese and European fare from 6pm till late. If you stop by on a Fri or Sat night, you might be treated to some live Lebanese music.

Montana Wilkinson Rd. Stylish place with a pretty terrace and steepish prices. Especially well known for its ice cream, though it also does more than passable sandwiches and salads.

Nightlife

After years of curfew-enforced early bedtimes, Freetown's **nightlife** is quickly recovering. The spacious, open-air entertainment complexes are famous far beyond the country's borders, and certainly worth a visit. Unlike other nightclubs, they allow you to swing on and off the dancefloor, chill at the bar, play a game of snooker or simply withdraw to the quieter corners and observe the crowds. Francophone West Africa loves Freetown's nightlife for its American-style swagger, and you'll get to hear plenty of hip hop and R&B in addition to a cross-section of African music.

Live-music venues, however, are rare, and good live bands even rarer. The groups you'll see perform at places like *Buggy's* or *China House* tend to be mediocre local cover bands, though you may stumble across the occasional gem. Though you can't call to book a taxi, you should have no problems finding a taxi at night, as long as you don't leave it too late (and it's not a good idea to walk around Freetown alone at night).

Alex's Beach Bar 64 Cape Rd, Man-O-War Bay, Aberdeen ☎022/27.21.55. Overlooking the lagoon, this smart bar is where you'll find many off-duty NGO and UN personnel on the weekend. Good for on-screen football.

Atlantic Lumley Beach ☎022/27.23.00. Popular bar/restaurant on the would-be tourist stretch that is Lumley Beach. Good for drinks and light meals on the beach.

Binta's Bar Lumley Beach. One of several bars/snackhouses along the beach road. Does delicious fried chicken.

Buggy's Lumley Beach. One of Freetown's most popular nightclubs, a spacious open-air place where you can move lazily between dancefloor, bar, snooker corner, restaurant and the people-watching benches along the sides.

Calabash Lumley Beach ☎022/27.20.02. Pretty beach bar with a relaxed ambience and occasional live music.

Cape Club Man-O-War Bay, Aberdeen. Another beach bar – with tasty grills and fish dishes – amid the cluster of drinking spots around Man-O-War Bay. Same is true of the nearby *Cape Light House*.

China House King Harman Rd, Brookfields. Bustling inner-city bar, popular with locals. It doesn't hurt to pop by on Fridays to catch the occasional dodgy live act.

JB's Hill Station. Bustling city club, popular mainly with local youth. The usual staple diet of hip hop, R&B and African sounds.

Lagoonda Run by, and near the main compound of, the *Cape Sierra Hotel*, Lumley Beach ☎022/27.24.81. Freetown's slickest entertainment complex, housing a casino, restaurant, nightclub and the only decent cinema in town. Open day and night, it really comes to life on weekend nights.

Paddy's Sir Samuel Lewis Rd, Aberdeen. Open-air all-round entertainment complex with a good selection of hip hop and R&B. This used to be the only place to go just after the war, and it's still extremely popular with locals, NGO members and UN soldiers alike.

Listings

Airlines Bellview, UMC Building, Lightfoot Boston St ☎022/22.73.11; Ghana Airways, 15 Siaka Stevens St ☎022/22.48.71; Paramount Airlines, *Mammy Yoko*, Aberdeen ☎022/27.20.06; SN Brussels Airlines, 14 Wilberforce St ☎022/22.60.75; Sierra National Airlines, 13A Lightfoot Boston St ☎022/22.45.47; West Coast Airlines, Wilberforce St ☎022/22.75.61.

Banks Standard Chartered Bank Sierra Leone, 9/11 Lightfoot Boston St ☎022/22.50.22; Sierra Leone Commercial Bank, 29/31 Siaka Stevens St ☎022/22.52.64; Rokel Commercial Bank, 25/27 Siaka Stevens St ☎022/22.23.50. Banking hours are usually 9am–2pm.

Car rental The big international agencies aren't represented. Try Global Development Four, 58c Wilkinson Rd (☎022/23.08.06). Alternatively, travel agents IPC and Yazbeck, and established hotels such as *Cape Sierra* and *Bintumani*, will also be able to arrange private hire for you. Cars are always rented along with a driver.

Cinemas The only cinema currently worth seeking out is at the Lagoonda entertainment complex at *Cape Sierra Hotel*, Lumley Beach (☎022/27.24.81).

Courier DHL, 15 Rawdon St ☎022/22.52.15, 🖷22.90.76.

Cultural centres The British Council is a massive building at Tower Hill (☎022/22.22.23, 🖃info.enquiry@sl.britishcouncil.org), with a well-equipped library and a theatre.

Dentists Dr Dennis Wright, 47 Percival St ☎022/22.25.40; Dr Rekab, Rawdon St ☎022/22.26.71.

Embassies and consulates France, Honorary Consul, 1 College Rd, Cline Town ☎022/22.05.44; The Gambia, 6 Wilberforce St ☎022/22.51.91, 🖷22.68.46; Ghana, 13 Walpole St ☎022/22.34.61, 🖷22.70.43; Guinea, 6 Wilkinson Rd ☎022/23.25.84; Ireland, Honorary Consul, 8 Rawdon St ☎022/22.71.01; Liberia, 10 Main Motor Rd ☎022/23.09.91; Mali, Honorary Consul, 40 Wilkinson Rd ☎022/23.17.82; Nigeria, 37 Siaka Stevens St ☎022/22.42.02; Senegal, Honorary Consul, 9 Upper ECOWAS St ☎022/29.48; UK, 6 Spur Rd, Wilberforce ☎022/23.29.61, 🖷22.81.69; USA, Walpole St ☎022/22.64.81, 🖳freetown.usembassy.gov.

Hospitals and doctors The main hospitals are T. Choithram Memorial Hospital on Hill Station (☎022/23.25.98); Connaught Hospital, Percival St (☎022/22.44.05); Marie Stopes, Adelaide St (☎022/24.16.07); or Netland Nursing Home, College Road Congo Cross (☎23.01.35). Dr Anthony Williams has a surgery at 33 Goderich St (☎022/22.50.87). Others include Dr W.A. Renner, 8 Pultney St ☎022/22.45.55; Dr Patrick Coker ☎022/22.22.25; Dr Aboud, Rawdon St ☎022/22.48.98.

Internet access There's an Internet café on Wilberforce St near the *Crown Bakery*, and there are several other places to get online hidden away on various streets in the middle of town.

Newspapers and magazines The British Council has some of the London dailies, as does the British High Commission. *West Africa* magazine is fairly widely available and should be sold for the price printed on the cover. Copies of *Time* and *Newsweek* are sometimes available too.

Pharmacies Bahsoon Pharmacy, 2 Regent Rd ☎022/22.38.38); Capital Pharmacy, 15 Siaka Stevens St ☎022/22.67.51; New Chemist Limited, 30 Wallace Johnson St ☎022/22.41.45.

Police The headquarters is on George St (☎022/22.30.01).

Post office The main post office is on the corner of Siaka Stevens St and Gloucester St (Mon–Fri 8am–5pm).

Supermarkets With the large number of NGO workers and UNAMSIL forces in the country, supermarkets are doing good business in Freetown. Some of the main ones include Atson's, 16 Wilkinson Rd; Freetown Supermarket, 137D Wilkinson Rd; and Monoprix, 4C Wilkinson Rd.

Travel agents Yazbeck Tours, 22 Siaka Stevens St (☎022/22.20.63, 🖷22.54.57), are the best-known firm. A spin-off of theirs is IPC Travel, 10 Siaka Stevens St (☎022/22.14.81, 🖷22.74.70, 🖃ipc@sierratel.sl). Karou Voyage, 10 Lamina Sankoh St (☎022/23.30.73), are particularly useful for travel to Guinea.

Visa extensions The Immigration Office is on Rawdon St (☎022/22.71.74, 🖷22.47.61).

Western Union c/o Union Trust Bank, Lightfoot Boston St (☎022/22.69.54 or 22.27.92).

Around Freetown

The **beaches** of the Freetown Peninsula are arguably the finest in West Africa, and certainly only those in western Côte d'Ivoire offer any competition. Single women should beware of nimble-fingered bag snatchers and irritating beach boys. Bring nothing of value, and your camera only if you're going to take pictures. Ideally, go in a group. Two of Sierra Leone's handful of beach resorts are to be found here, nestling on the strands south of Lumley.

Much mentioned but less often visited than the beaches (and strangely omitted on most maps), **Bunce Island** in the Sierra Leone River is definitely worth a visit for its old slave fort. Elsewhere on the peninsula there are a handful of minor attractions, among them the **chimpanzees** of the Tacugama reserve.

The southern beaches

For committed sun-and-sand devotees, the southern reaches of the peninsula harbour some spectacular shores. The sand of every beach is a different colour, from dazzling white to golden yellow. The best way to take in the beauty of the shoreline is by boat. You can arrange **canoe rental** with *Pierre's Beach Resort* on Lakka

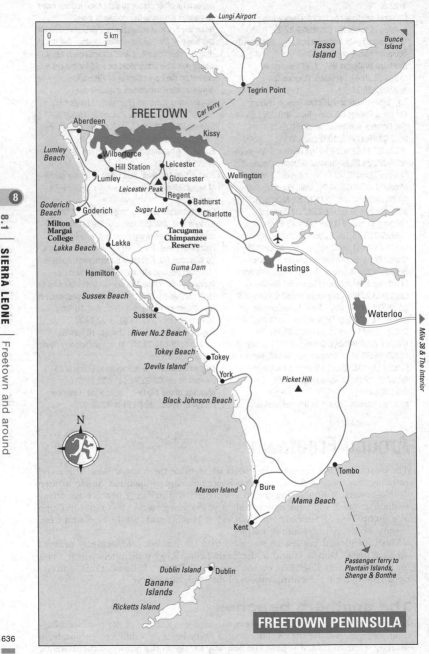

(see below) and devote a whole day (or more) to a leisurely coastal tour. Take some food and drink with you and settle down for a picnic on one of the deserted beaches. Fresh coconut juice is delicious, and easily obtained by paying a few local kids to pick some coconuts.

It's useful to have wheels of your own to get around the peninsula, though you can get around using public transport, hitching or muddling along in whatever "public" transport comes your way. *Poda podas* head down this way several times a day, as far as York. You're more likely to score a lift at the roundabout in Lumley village with weekenders or expatriates. On weekdays, the sand lorries that scour some beaches for Freetown's building requirements often give lifts. Be prepared for some walking; it's a badly maintained road, but pretty for most of its length. Road signs, distances and directions aren't always clear: those included below, unless indicated otherwise, are road distances from Lumley roundabout.

If you go as far as Tombo, there may be an occasional **ferry** south via the Plantain Islands to Shenge, which is an attractive means of heading on down the coast.

Goderich, Lakka and Sussex beaches

Out of Lumley village, past the quaint red-brick St Mary's Church, and Siaka Stevens' distant mansion perched high above, you cross Lumley creek, then come to the somewhat cluttered Juba Beach, and then **Goderich** (3km from Lumley and 1km off the road). This beach is a perfectly good place to see an archetypal West African event late every afternoon – the return of the fishing boats – but not one to go out of your way for otherwise. Goderich village sits behind the kilometre of steeply shelving yellow sand.

From here on, the coast road steadily deteriorates. In places, the tar surface gives up completely; if you're driving, beware some dastardly potholes and virtually invisible speed bumps. A sign (4km) for the "Milton Margai Training College" indicates one means of access to the first really wonderful beach, **Lakka**, which consists of a pair of long, gently shelving bays punctuated by a minuscule, rocky peninsula, two-thirds of the way along. At the far north end the bay curves to face the south, beneath a riot of vegetation. Beyond the rocky promontory, the second bay crescents down towards Hamilton, with a cascade of coconut jungle behind it.

Lakka has one of the country's functioning **beach resorts**, and a very pleasant one at that, *Pierre's Beach Bar and Resort* (☎030/20.78.35; ❻). Here you can rent a spacious wooden bungalow with a beach view (discounts can be arranged for longer stays), wake up to the sound of the sea and revel in glorious sunsets from the beach bar. The friendly resort has a fabulous restaurant (try their delicious "Lobster in Love"), a lively bar and a nightclub, *Voodoo Lounge*, a mask-decorated affair that plays a good selection of British, American and African beats on weekends. Pierre can arrange *pirogue* rental for excursions to the adjacent beaches.

Following the fairly unappealing fisherman's strand of Hamilton, that abuts Lakka to the south, you reach **Sussex beach**, another inviting shoreline. Be careful if you choose to take a dip though, as the sea is deep, and the current here can be strong depending on the tide. There's a pleasant little guesthouse, *Frankel's* (❻), which is separated from the beach by a narrow river during high tide.

River No. 2 and Tokey beaches

Most people who reach Sussex head on, close to the shore, to **River No. 2** (19km) and the much-hyped beach of the same name. This is magnificent country, dense, green jungle hills rising steeply behind a beach of brilliant white sand, through which the River No. 2 (or Guma River) slices in an ever-changing course. If you're patient and lucky, you might spot pygmy crocodiles and other animals in the clear river water. Hiking upriver, you'll come to a small waterfall which can be stunning in the rainy season, or unimpressive when dry. Appealing though No. 2 beach is, it doesn't offer brilliant conditions for swimming, as the current is strong and there's a very steep shelf. A small **guesthouse** here has fairly inexpensive rooms (❹). On weekends in season and on public holidays, the beach gets busy with "car park attendants", plus food stalls and even crafts, set up among the village houses behind.

At low tide you can get across the river to the much longer stretch of **Tokey Beach**; you're then stuck until the next low tide, unless you walk the 3km or so to Tokey village to find the track up to the main road. The beach is usually deserted and absolutely stunning, with fine sand and a background of luscious forest. A small gateway of clear water separates Tokey Beach from Devil's Island, which is reputed to be a meeting place of male Poro society members. Unfortunately, with the once-fabulous beach resort *Africana* now in ruins, Tokey Beach was without any accommodation or eating places at the time of writing.

York and Black Johnson Beach

Four kilometres beyond Tokey junction, you come to the village of **York** (31km) at the mouth of Whale River creek. There's an old fort on the other side of the village, with glorious views. The coast bends in a smooth arc, and forest-covered mountains rise steeply behind the narrow shoreline.

From here south, all semblance of a surfaced road ceases, and transport becomes very difficult. If you're fairly self-sufficient, and don't expect to get back anywhere the same day, you could walk on to **Black Johnson Beach** (36km) on Whale Bay, five hilly kilometres round the creek from York. You might also find a boat to take you the relatively short distance across the creek. Palm-fringed, remote and quite undeveloped, with clear sea, Black Johnson is an excellent area for snorkelling or diving.

Kent, Bure and Mama beaches, and the Banana Islands

At the southern extremities of the peninsula, and off the main dirt road, are **Bure** (48km) and **Kent** (52km), both of which have postcard-perfect beaches several kilometres long. The forested **Maroon Island**, just 300m from the shore, lies between Bure and Kent beaches. Near the village of Kent you'll see a series of fairly large caves, some of which were used to hold slaves before they were shipped across the Atlantic.

East of Kent, on the peninsula's south-facing coastline, there's a chain of coves and small bays with a tourist/weekender base at **Mama Beach**. Heading back to Freetown or Lumley Beach from this far south, it's quicker to make for **Waterloo** (20km past the turn-off for Bure and Kent), where you can pick up the reasonably surfaced highway into Freetown.

The main point of coming down to Kent Beach, though, is to find a boat across to the **Banana Islands** 5km offshore; prepare yourself for some vigorous bargaining. Dublin Island and Ricketts Island are joined by a causeway and have villages of the same names at opposite ends connected by an eight-kilometre footpath. Dublin has a couple of small beaches (limpid water and some coral) on its northwest coast; Ricketts is steeper (233m high) and more densely forested. You can camp here, but neither has any real facilities, so take supplies. Mes-Meheux, an uninhabited island, lies southwest, just off Ricketts' shore.

Bunce Island

Transport to **Bunce Island** is a little tricky. Yazbeck's sometimes offers day-trips in the winter season, and the Conservation Society (see p.608) may be able to offer help in getting here. You might also be lucky on the ferry quay at Kissy and find a motorboat willing to make the voyage. But in view of the distance – over 20km – you should make sure the vessel is seaworthy and the fuel, shade and water supplies sufficient. If you're very patient and adventurous, you can try to get the regular boat from **King Jimmy Point**, west of Government Wharf in Freetown, which goes every Tuesday, Thursday and Saturday to **Pepel**, from where Bunce lies a couple of kilometers offshore. It's easier to reach Pepel by road via Port Loko, a journey of 160km from Freetown. From Pepel, negotiate a *pirogue* with the local fishermen (expect to pay Le5000–10,000), and they'll happily take you to Bunce and back. On the island, you'll probably be welcomed by the old employee of the National Museum who lives here, waiting for the occasional visitor to whom he can relate his anecdotes of the island's history in a strongly accented Krio.

Situated on the small island are the ruins of a massive **slave fort**, built here in 1670 by the British. Attacked by the Portuguese, and reclaimed by the British, the fort was rebuilt several times, and remained in use until 1807. During those years, an estimated fifty thousand slaves were sold from this fortress. In the 1780s, Fort Bunce was supplying an average of three thousand slaves a year from the interior to Danish traders alone, who sold them to the new American rice plantations of South Carolina.

Though protected as a national historic monument under the Monuments and Relics Act of 1947, the old fort's remains haven't been effectively preserved. The ruins are still impressive, though, being almost entirely overgrown, covered in creepers and fig trees and rather eerie to wander around. Old British cannon still lie scattered around the entrance and lookouts, and the nearby cemetery contains the tombstones of several British slave traders who died here.

Regent's Village and the Chimpanzee Reserve

A short, rewarding excursion on the peninsula itself is a tour through the mountains to **Regent's Village** and the adjacent Tacugama Chimpanzee Reserve. To reach the village, simply follow the road into the peninsula's interior at Hill Station. With your own transport, you can leave your vehicle before reaching the village and take a diversion to **Leicester Peak**, one of the highest points on the peninsula, from where you get a good view all over the area. Regent's Village itself is famous mainly for its **St Charles Church**, one of the oldest churches in West Africa. The small, pretty church lies up a steep hill from the village centre.

The road winds its way through forest and greenery, past the villages of Gloucester and Bathurst, beyond which there's a sign indicating the **Tacugama Chimpanzee Reserve** (®www.tacugama.com). A brief walk up a very steep hill takes you to the reserve, established as a refuge for chimpanzees that were either ill, in danger, or had been kept as pets by residents of Freetown. Beautifully laid out, it now holds more than fifty chimps that can be observed leaping around the trees of the expansive reserve during the day.

8.2

The interior

While Freetown and surrounding districts have experienced up to two centuries of Creole history, this influence has hardly rubbed off on the upcountry towns, chief among which are **Makeni**, **Kabala**, **Bo**, **Kenema** and **Koidu**. All of these grew from small seeds in the early part of the last century, though with the exception of the diamond centre **Koidu** (also known as Koidu-Sefadu or Kono), they reached some sort of zenith of development shortly after independence, subsequently increasing in size but not in stature.

The north

The Northern Province's top attraction is **Outamba-Kilimi National Park**. Pressed around the foot of the Kuru Hills, and hard up against the Guinean border, the park is the only one in this part of the country and worth the effort to visit. To the southeast, on wonderful mountainous backroads beyond **Kabala**, there are a couple more adventurous possibilities, the beautiful **Lake Sonfon** and the trail to the top of **Mount Bintumani**.

The diversions en route from Freetown are limited, though **Port Loko** is a pleasant stop, split by tumbling streams and positioned on steep slopes above Port Loko creek. Once the site from which Loko slaves were shipped to Bunce Island, it was a strategic town in the eighteenth century, when there was a significant Portuguese-speaking community. For ornithologists with their own transport, the creeks and flats to the west offer exceptional birding.

The provincial capital of the north, **MAKENI**, is easily reached by bush taxi from Freetown. The town boasts a famously good market, though, like Sierra Leone's other provincial centres, it can make few credible touristic claims. Makeni was once the terminus of the northern branch railway line, and quite a boomtown in the 1920s. Before the war, it was still a busy trading centre, and its market still attracts vendors and buyers from the whole region. There are two basic **guesthouses** (❶–❷), one right next to the police station.

Outamba-Kilimi National Park

The **Outamba-Kilimi National Park** was set up in 1980 after the International Union for the Conservation of Nature and Natural Resources singled the region out for urgent protection. Much of the region was formerly occupied by the **Tambakha chiefdom**, named after the Tamba – "leader" – of a successful nineteenth-century slave revolt. Slave-owning Susu were massacred by their captives, who moved to this region and set up their own, very mixed, kingdom, in which Susu, the slaves' customary language, was retained. Sensitive work with the people of the Tambakha chiefdom (or at least with their paramount chief) led to agreements to cede land for the park and give up hunting rights. For over a decade, there was steady progress, with major Peace Corps involvement and the Worldwide Fund for Nature supporting the energetic work of the people on the ground. The Peace Corps have now left and the park is vulnerable to poaching.

The park's thousand-odd square kilometres cover two great slabs of untouched, undulating **savanna and jungle**, in the basins of the Great and Little Scarcies rivers. There's a rich diversity of animal species, including elephants and most of the other large West African savanna mammals (lions and giraffes excepted), as well as a solid population of chimpanzees and twelve other primates, among them red colobus, black-and-white colobus and sooty mangabey. In the deepest sections of forest there are rare and scattered bongo antelope – magnificent, heavily built animals – and in the overgrown water margins you may spot pygmy hippos. Over 150 different bird species make the park a particular attraction to ornithologists.

The nearest town, which has one guesthouse (❶), is **Kamakwie**, 15km south of the site. At the park itself, a visitors' camp with rudimentary facilities was being established at the time of writing. Be prepared for very basic lodging without running water or electricity, and come equipped with sleeping bag, torchlight and provisions.

Kabala

Northeast of Makeni, the architectural interest improves, with small, steeply conical houses of the Temne pattern, topped with an extra tuft of thatch and an entrance lobby at the front. Muslim praying circles are to be seen all over, though sometimes, as reserved areas, they're used for drying rice or other grain.

The Koranko

More than most of Sierra Leone's ethnic groups, the Koranko of the northeast have maintained a fairly distinct cultural integrity. Koranko is a Mande language, very close to the most mainstream Mande tongue, the Malinké of Guinea and Mali, and only distantly related to the more peripheral Mende of southern Sierra Leone. The Koranko are great **rice farmers**, filling the valleys with an emerald green carpet, and they grow a fair amount of cotton, too, for their famous *ronko* cloth.

The Koranko are also hunters of some repute (and have always supplied most of the troops for the Sierra Leone armed forces). Traditionally, they belonged to totemic clans, known as "houses", each called by a "surname" and symbolized by taboo animals that were never eaten. For example, the Fona clan's totem was the royal python, the Mensereng had the monitor lizard and the lion, the Kamara's were the hippo and the chimpanzee, the Kagbo's and Sise's was the crocodile and the Mara's (the most distinguished) was the leopard – not that all these animals were commonly eaten by members of other clans.

Today, an increasing contingent of the Koranko community is Muslim, and the old clan divisions are less significant. But the Bundu society initiations (*biriye* in Koranko) are still important for young people in rural areas, with girls in seclusion for a few weeks' instruction during the rains and boys going off in the dry season. Circumcision and clitoridectomy usually take place at the same time. Another pre-Islamic activity that's pursued with enthusiasm is the making of *kamakuli* – bamboo wine. It's not always available, but you should try to get a taste if you're in the territory for a few days; talk to the youth of the village rather than the big men.

Cursory Koranko

Greetings, thanks, goodbye	*N-weli*	Yes	*Ohn* (pronounced like the French *non*)
Greetings (pl)	*Wa-n-wali*		
Good morning	*Tanamase*	No	*Oh-oh*
Good day	*Tanamatale*	Thank you	*Kubaraka*
Good evening	*Inoor-agh*	Bamboo wine	*Kamakole*
		What's your name?	*Eh tu kama?*

Ringed by a circle of hills, the highest of which leap, bold and bare, right above it to the west, **KABALA** is an attractive highland town. It splits roughly into two: on the way in from Makeni, the town centre is dominated by the Koranko people; across the stream on the northwest side of town, the district is more Limba. Try to buy some *ronko* cloth if you're here: made by the Koranko, it's a deep rusty-red country cloth, patterned in black block prints, sewn together from narrow strips. Soft yet durable, it's claimed by some to have bullet-proof powers. If you have to spend the night here, there's little choice but the *Gbawuria Guest House*, which has reasonable rooms (❶).

Kabala is famous throughout Sierra Leone for the **New Year's Day** mass picnic that normally takes place on the gaunt inselberg summit at the edge of the Wara Wara range, west of town. Several thousand people spend the day up there, eating, drinking and dancing. It's a steep climb, but not difficult or long; other than on New Year's Day, the heights are usually deserted.

Lake Sonfon

Lake Sonfon is Sierra Leone's largest inland lake, cradled in the picturesque landscape of the Sula mountains. It's worth the effort getting there if you're happy to spend a couple of days in perfect solitude amid stunning scenery, though it should be said that the environment has suffered a little from the gold mining in the area, and that hunting has taken its toll on the wildlife that once inhabited the hills.

The lake is extremely difficult to reach, and the trip should only be attempted if you are travelling in a sturdy 4WD. From **Kabala**, 35km to the north as the crow flies, head towards **Makakura** on the Kabala–Makeni road, where you turn off and continue towards Alikalia, where you can ask someone to show the way to the lake. If heading up from the south, make for **Bendugu**, 20km from the lake, then take the just about passable road towards **Benekoro**, from where you can start walking towards the lake. You'll have to stay with locals here, unless you wish to camp closer to the lake. To explore the area, hook up with a local guide in Bendugu.

Mount Bintumani

Midway between Kabala and Koidu in the east, **Mount Bintumani** in the Loma Mountains is the highest peak in Sierra Leone, and the highest mountain in West Africa west of Mount Cameroon. The mountain is best climbed at the beginning or end of the rainy season (either in April/May or October/November); dry season dust limits visibility. Whenever you go, it can get very cool at night near the summit (1945m) and you should take some warm clothes, as well as a sleeping bag.

There are no tarred roads nearby, and climbing Bintumani of necessity involves some trekking from the end of the nearest motorable road. **Kabala** is probably the easiest base from which to go if you're using public transport. The aim is to reach **Firawa** (51km from Kabala), from where a five-day hike will get you to the top and back again. There are usually several people in Firawa who know some English and who will be more than willing to hike up the mountain with you. The small town of **Koinadugu** (28km from Kabala) is the most likely destination of vehicles heading this way. Koinadugu's hill-top location and venerable silk-cotton trees make it a great place to stay. **Yirafilaia Badala** (36km) is another nice village, located above a rocky bend of the Seli River. There's a sandy beach here, wonderful for swimming, fishing and washing clothes. Just beware of the current if you're here at the height of the rains. If you have your own transport or a sturdy rental car, an even better option is to head for the village of **Yifin**, east of Alikalia and 15km from the peak, where the local chief resides. Yifin has a missionary compound where you can stay.

If you're taking a couple of weeks or more to climb Bintumani, you may even want to walk the whole way from Kabala. All the villages along the Bintumani trail are **Koranko** (for whom the mountain is Loma Mansa – King of the Lomas) and you'll find charming hospitality. If you want to stay in a village, ask to speak to the headman, who'll arrange overnight accommodation for you. It's important to carry some basic provisions – rice, palm oil, onions, salt and pepper – as supplies along the way can be short, especially in the "hungry season" before the rice harvest (August and September). Don't worry about cooking, as this will be fixed for you; naturally you'll be expected to share some food. Take a supply of the freshest **kola** you can find, as well. This is the traditional gift in return for hospitality, though you can give leones instead. For snacks on the move (don't forget most people only cook once a day) take fruit and groundnut cakes from Kabala.

After Firawa or Yifin, you'll need a guide to find your way along the maze of footpaths to **Banda-Karafaia**, about 20km distant from both. This day's hike is where the trip becomes exciting and the scenery spectacular. At Banda-Karafaia, you have to sign the headman's register of people climbing the mountain. A cash gift is expected for this service; while there's no fixed fee, it will be made clear if it's too small. About 13km further is **Yalembe**, a small village at the foot of the mountain, where you hire a guide for the final ascent.

The south

The frustrating thing about the geography of southern Sierra Leone, as of much of West Africa's southwest-facing shores, is that the coast itself tends to be indistinct and often miles from the nearest road. The sea lies beyond vast expanses of mud, marsh and mangroves, only accessible down narrow ridges of slightly higher ground between the maze of creeks. The coast here seems to be separating entirely from the mainland and, indeed, **Sherbro** (with its town of **Bonthe**) and the Turtle Islands are already adrift in the Atlantic. Southeast of Sherbro, the surf hits a tremendous, unbroken beach, which stretches 110km to the little port of **Sulima** on the Liberian border. Backed by small fishing villages, this is a highly recommended week-long walk, assuming you can confirm that security is adequate.

Inland, much of the south is sticky, palm- and bush-specked grassland, which makes for uninspiring travel. But the higher forest areas are another matter. In the southeast, the hills come to within 50km of the sea and here, south of the provincial capital, **Bo**, there are opportunities for some of the country's most rewarding explorations. The trip to **Tiwai Island Primate Reserve**, blanketed in rainforest in a crook of the surging Moa River, used to be hugely impressive before the war.

Bo

Long established as the most important town in the colonial "Protectorate" of upcountry Sierra Leone, **BO** was overtaken in size some years ago by the burgeoning diamond-fed Koidu conurbation in the northeast. Bo holds a big, spread-out population of fifty or sixty thousand people, mostly Mende, but with a heavy Krio presence. Though it has suffered during the war, it hasn't been hit as badly as Freetown, and gives you an idea of what the East End of Freetown may have looked like before the war. It's a vibrant trading centre, where plenty of **diamond traders** have their businesses. Don't get tempted into purchasing any stones, though, as you're likely to be cheated or to run into difficulties on leaving the country. The town's best-known institution, the "Chief's School" (now Bo School) north of the old railway yards, was founded in 1906 for the education of chiefs' sons from the Protectorate. It was a curious amalgam of English public school and extended traditional instruction, intended to lend weight to the position of the chiefs, through whom the British ruled the country. The boys, divided into "houses" of Liverpool, Manchester, London and Paris, were expected to wear the customary dress of their fathers, learn improved farming and building methods, adopt "good manners" and speak "good English". The use of Krio was forbidden.

Bo is easily reachable by taxi from Freetown, with several cars leaving every morning. There's a choice of several basic **guesthouses** that exude a certain charm in their scruffiness. *Madam Wokie Hotel* is the most basic (❸); the *Sir Milton Margai Hotel* offers a little more comfort, with reliable air-conditioning, TV, and slightly cleaner rooms (❹). **Nightlife** in Bo is concentrated around one spot, the *Black and White Bar* near the *Sir Milton*; it gets loud and lively on weekend nights.

Tiwai Island Nature Reserve

The **Tiwai Island Project** – run by Njala University College and the Peace Corps until the war engulfed the district – transformed an island in the Moa River into a national park. Although only covering about twelve square kilometres, the largely pristine, forest-cloaked island shelters an extraordinarily rich fauna, including chimps and ten other primate species (though war has greatly diminished numbers), pygmy hippos, red river hogs, crocodiles and electric fish. In the background is the dim rush of the **rapids** on the river, where it splits to roar around Tiwai through rocks and channels.

Tiwai is currently being renovated and all of the tracks are being re-cut. To get there, head for the island office at **Kambama**, 17km northeast of the small town of **Potoru**, which is an hour's drive southeast of Bo. Before the war came to this region, the chief would arrange the river crossing and the visitors' facilities on the

The Mende and secret societies

There is a thing passing in the sky; some thick clouds surround it; the uninitiated see nothing.

Opaque Mende proverb

The **Mende** are skilled and very long-established farmers, to whom trading and hunting are low priorities. Rice, sorghum and millet, root crops, oil palms and kola are the big crops. Women fish the streams, too, with circular nets, as much for relaxation as for the meal. The Mende **language** – the biggest group in Sierra Leone – is supposed to have arrived from the northeast, either with people fleeing the chaotic conditions in sixteenth-century Songhai, or perhaps before the creation of the Mali empire in the thirteenth century. Ptolemy's second-century map even indicates *Purrus Campus* in roughly the place where the ancient Mende might have had a "Poro Bush" – a secret society grove.

Along classic "divide and rule" principles, the British split the Mende kingdoms into dozens of "paramount chiefdoms", introducing a new tribal identity. The Mende chiefs came to see themselves as natural successors of the British, in competition – or association – with the powerful Temne. But the upper-class Krio families of Freetown had the same idea. The most serious of the anti-tax revolts, in Mende country in 1898, resulted in the deaths of hundreds of Krio traders and deepened a rift, never completely bridged, between the indigenous Protectorate peoples and the non-native Krios of the Colony. The Bo School for chiefs gave an incentive to Protectorate ambitions. Later, Mende politicians from a pro-British family of Bonthe – Milton Margai and his brother Albert – became the country's first and second prime ministers. Krio opponents attributed much of the second Margai's attachment to power to membership of the secret **Poro** society.

You can't spend more than a week in the country without hearing mysterious rumours about the **secret societies**, which still dominate life in Sierra Leone. They're followed in almost all communities, as secret brotherhoods and sisterhoods, cutting across the family and clan divisions, maintaining stability and marking life-cycle events. Christians don't exclude themselves from membership, and Islam, while other side were well established. Today, you have to rely on small boats which can be rented from the locals. The Conservation Society has a few guides in the area, who can point you to campsites and even to accompany you to the Mape and Mabesi lakes on the coast midway between Mano and Sulima.

Sulima and the south coast

SULIMA was a trading station in the nineteenth century. The first Englishman here was John Myer Harris, a Jewish trader who arrived in 1855. Harris soon creamed off much of the Moa River trade, which had previously been controlled by the Liberian government, thus effectively pushing the frontier back to the Mano River. A number of the old colonial buildings are still standing and there's a freshwater lagoon, where you can swim and wash. Sulima used to gather a community of holidaying NGO volunteers every Christmas, building *baffas* (shelters) and sitting round fires on the beach; now, there are thousands of Liberian refugees in the area.

In theory it's possible to follow the unbroken **beach** west from Sulima (110km) in a walk that takes from five days to a week without strain. This is **Turner's Peninsula**, a strip of land ceded to the British as long ago as 1825. The people are Vai, Krim and Sherbro but, increasingly, everyone speaks Mende first, Krio second and English a poor third. Houses are made from entirely natural materials – woven palm-frond walls with thatched roofs.

opposing them, makes no purist insistence. Society graduates are sworn to secrecy and the arcane details remain hidden. Among older or more traditional Mende people, enquiries get a hostile response, and the few books on the subject tend to disappear from libraries.

The general name for the societies is **Bundu**, a Krio word. **Poro** is the men's society (the same name is found elsewhere in West Africa, for example among the Senoufo in Côte d'Ivoire) and is by far the most powerful; the women's is called Sande. Poro and Sande provide the framework for traditional instruction to adolescents about sex, adult behaviour and folk knowledge. Traditionally, too, the period of seclusion and endurance in the bush was when circumcision and clitoridectomy were performed. Boys of the same age group go through the school in the dry season, girls in the rains. Beyond the teenage rites of passage, membership of Poro proceeds by different stages. In addition to Poro and Sande, there's a kind of high Poro society called **Wunde**, and a number of other societies, some operating as professional associations of medical, psychiatric and social welfare specialists – Humo, Toma, Njaye – and some of entertainers and conjurers, the Njoso.

Heavy black Bundu **masks** worn by women in the Sande society (called Sowo by the Mende) are the most visible signs of the societies' active existence. Carved by men, they reveal a lot about Mende ideals of feminine beauty – high-domed foreheads, elaborately braided hair, fine-pointed features, eyes that see nothing, mouths closed. As an outsider, you should beware of "No Entry" signs in the bush, indicating a society grove, and fenced compounds outside villages. It's acceptable to witness youngsters with whitened faces, however, celebrating their new names and status.

"Animal societies" – "Baboon" (chimpanzee), "Boa" (python), "Alligator" (crocodile) and "Leopard" – were always uncommon, though sensationalized. Their members would mount attacks in the guise of wild animals, the aim being to obtain human organs for witchcraft. These societies tended to die out along with the animals imitated: nobody would believe a chimpanzee murder in Bo any more, though witchcraft remains another matter.

Most of Turner's Peninsula is backed by low scrub, but towards the western end, coconut palms start to appear. The most attractive stretches of coast, however, are on Sherbro and the nearby **Turtle Islands**. The latter is a small cluster ideal for swimming and snorkelling, and which has in the past boasted one or two small tourist developments. *Pierre's* on Lakka Beach (see p.637) rents out boats for trips to the islands.

Sherbro Island

Though very much in ruins these days – it was attacked several times during the war – **BONTHE**, the main settlement on Sherbro Island, is one of Sierra Leone's most appealing towns. When Frederick William Hugh Migeod (Colonial Service, retired) visited in 1924 while writing his *View of Sierra Leone*, he found "about forty Europeans there, including those on York Island, and a big gathering at tennis every evening". The atmosphere has changed somewhat in the intervening years, but Bonthe is still very pleasant. Wide sandy lanes cross the town, and some of the great old run-down buildings of the glory days are still upright. The secondary school is magnificent and the people of Bonthe are charming.

Eastern Province

Diamonds and cross-border trade have made **Eastern Province** the country's most densely populated region, with **KOIDU** the biggest provincial town. **Sefadu** is another official alternative name for it, but most locals refer to **Kono** (the district of which it's capital) when they mean the town. The old settlement was called Sembehun, so New Sembehun is a fourth possibility. More than 100,000 people live in the district, the one place in the country where it's possible to make money without connections – through hunting for diamonds in the alluvial deposits. Even the town centre is pitted with water-filled diggings and you see people everywhere sifting gravel. Formerly a busy trading centre with luxury goods in the stores, street lighting and tightly guarded villas humming smugly with air conditioning, Kono has been trashed. It was ransacked by all sides during the war, and services and facilities at the time of writing were extremely limited. In better times, it would be a good jumping-off point for Mount Bintumani (see p.642) and, closer but rather inaccessible, the Tingi Mountains and the source of the Niger.

Sakanbiaiwa, in the Tingi Mountains, is Sierra Leone's second highest peak (1709m) – a botanical sanctuary for its **orchids**, especially at the end of the dry season, but more remote and much less visited even than Bintumani. First step in getting there is transport to **Jegbwema**, 18km east of Koidu, where you turn left into the mountains. The village to head for is **Kundundu** (38km from Jegbwema), along a really rough road.

Koindu

KOINDU (not to be confused with Koidu) was originally a Kissi settlement, but it's been swelling for decades with immigrants from a wide reach and was the RUF rebels' base during the war. The town is a sort of tradesman's entrance to Sierra Leone, where everything from rice and sugar to diamonds and human sacrifices is available, or rumoured to be – and most of the rumours are verifiable on a Sunday, market day. There's locally made cloth in the market (cotton is sown in with the local rice crop and harvested afterwards), along with excellent silversmiths who specialize in filigree earrings and pendants. And you can still buy "Kissi pennies" here, the regional currency of pre-Protectorate days, that continued to be used until World War II – pieces of twisted iron rod, about 30cm long, with the ends flattened out into a T-shape.

Kenema

KENEMA is busy, but only worth the visit if you're keen on seeing diamond diggers at work. Originally a Mende settlement, it grew fast on the strength of the railway and burst into development after the discovery, in 1931, of diamonds a few kilometres to the east, and the opening up of the Tongo diamond field to the north. Kenema's original industries, however, were logging and carpentry – it only evolved as a major centre of diamond trade after the industries around Koidu and Sefadu ran into difficulties. If you really want to observe miners at work, you're bound to be hassled by the authorities guarding the area, and once you get to a mine you'll see little more than impoverished workers sieving sand again and again in search of precious stones.

There are two **guesthouses**, which are signposted off the main road when you enter town. Both are basic (❶–❷), but offer reasonably clean rooms, cold beer and fried chicken to the tired traveller. If they're full and you're really stuck for a place to stay, try approaching the Catholic Mission, who are likely to help you out.

Burkina Faso

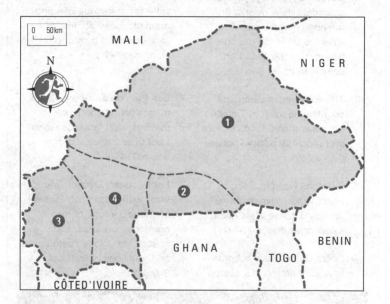

Burkina Faso highlights

* **FESPACO and SIAO** Ouaga comes alive during these vibrant, internationally renowned festivals. See p.660

* **Gorom-Gorom** Dynamic and colourful village market on the edge of the Sahara, where turban-clad merchants ride in from the desert on camels to trade. See p.692

* **Tiébélé** Deep in Guorounsi country, the town of Tiébélé boasts wonderful architecture and intricately painted houses. See p.703

* **Balafons** Head to Bobo to hear the addictive rhythmic sounds of these West African xylophones. See p.704

* **Dafra** Dafra village is home to a giant catfish in a sacred pond, though the real reason for coming here is the stunning surrounding scenery. See p.709

* **Banfora** The region around Banfora boasts a scenic waterfall, a tranquil lake and dramatic rocky domes, all easily reached by moped along sandy tracks. See p.711

* **Les Pics de Sindou** Isolated, magnificent golden rock formations, with fabulous views from their craggy summits. See p.714

* **Lobi country** Quench your thirst with a calabash (or two) of *chapalo* in one of the numerous cabarets, and absorb the unique customs and traditions of the Lobi. See p.715

Introduction and Basics

Few countries are as unlucky as Burkina Faso. But for a twist of administrative fate in colonial times, it would never have existed. It is desperately, and famously, poor, with an almost total lack of raw materials or natural resources. And although it shares its landlocked predicament with Niger and Mali, unlike them it lacks direct access to the important trans-Saharan routes. From the traveller's point of view the country also suffers from several superficial disadvantages: it's unremittingly flat, and offers little of the natural spectacle and traditional cultural colour of its neighbours, while its image problem in the foreign press acts as a further deterrent.

Despite all this, however, most visitors really enjoy Burkina. Poverty here is no more apparent than in neighbouring countries, and there's an increasing range of places to stay. The numerous military checkpoints that once littered the country are now less evident, and the soldiers and customs agents who you do meet treat you with respect, venturing a "Bonne arrivée, ça va?" while verifying your passport. Improvements to the country's basic infrastructure and the provision of services such as medicine, water and electricity through the 1990s has given the country a climate of youthful optimism, backed up by a vital popular culture. Despite the repressive political climate and the fact that getting business done is perhaps no easier here than anywhere else in the region, as a place to travel, or simply hang out, Burkina leaves a good taste with most visitors.

People

With some sixty different language groups, Burkina has the usual West African ethno-linguistic mosaic. But most Burkinabe (Burkinabè is also used, but not Burkinabé) speak languages of the large Voltaic group, and the country is unusual in having an overwhelming majority of a single people, the More-speaking **Mossi**, who live in the central plains around Ouagadougou, and make up over half the population. They are related to the **Gourmantché**, who live in the east around Fada-Ngourma, and less closely to the Grusi or Gourounsi from around Pô and Léo.

Fact file

The country's official name, Burkina Faso, is a hybrid of a More word meaning dignity-nobility-integrity and a Dioula word meaning homeland. The name, changed in 1984 from Haute Volta (Upper Volta), and commonly abbreviated to Burkina, means roughly "Land of the Honourable". With an area of 275,000 square kilometres, the country is slightly larger than Great Britain and slightly smaller than the state of Nevada. Nearly all flat, most of it is swathed in semi-arid grasslands. The further north you go, the drier things become, until you arrive at the denuded Sahelian landscapes of the extreme north. Only in the southern regions of Banfora and the Lobi country will you find much greenery. Although the Volta Blanche, Volta Rouge and Volta Noire rivers all rise in Burkina, only the Volta Noire flows in the dry season. The three meet up much further south in Ghana where they form the navigable river which the Portuguese called Rio da Volta, or "River of Return".

Burkina's population numbers some twelve million people, just over a million of whom live in the capital, Ouagadougou. Since 1991 it has had a constitutional democracy, in theory at least, if not always effectively in practice. On the economic front, Burkina's foreign debts total some £940 million ($1.5 billion), over double the value of its annual exports of goods and services – though it's still a piffling amount in international terms, less than the cost of an aircraft carrier, for example.

9

BURKINA FASO | Basics

651

The main peoples of the north include the **Fula**, the **Hausa** and the **Bella** (Tamashek-speaking former slaves of the Tuareg). Near the northwestern border with Mali live small enclaves of **Dogon**, **Samos** and **Pana**. In the south, different **Bobo** peoples – Bwaba, Kos and Siby – populate the area around Bobo-Dioulasso. The **Senoufo** occupy the southwestern tip near Côte d'Ivoire and Mali, while the **Lobi**, towards the border with Ghana, remain one of the most isolated peoples in the country.

Burkina's population has suffered greatly over the last two or three generations. It was from the Upper Volta region that the French recruited much of the **labour** to work plantations in their Côte d'Ivoire colony, and the Burkinabe continue to look south for work, as the land at home becomes impoverished – although many returned to Burkina after civil war broke out in Côte d'Ivoire in 2002. Burkina has been one of the countries most blighted by the recurrent Sahel droughts, and it remains a major focus of many aid and development agencies.

Where to go

Specific targets for travel include the second city, **Bobo-Dioulasso** ("Bobo"), which is unquestionably one of the most attractive cities in West Africa; the hilly and prettily wooded **Banfora region** in the southwest; and the remote and fascinating **Lobi country** in the south, with its mysterious stone ruins. The appeal of the capital, **Ouagadougou** ("Ouaga"), isn't especially strong, but you'll get more out of a visit here if you have some background knowledge of the venerable **Mossi kingdoms**, of which Ouagadougou was formerly one of several in the central region. Ouagadougou also has a major attraction in the FESPACO festival of African film, which is held every odd-numbered year (2005, 2007) in February.

When to go

Burkina's climate is characterized by two main seasons. The **rains** last from June to October; violent storms gather quickly, inundate everything, then blow away, leaving clear blue skies behind. Many of the country's *pistes* are impassable during this period, and except on the main routes, you can have trouble getting around the country. The **dry season** lasts from November to May. This is when the **harmattan** blows across the country, whipping up dust and smothering everything in a dreary ochre haze. At night it can get quite chilly, especially in the north. The **best period to travel**

Average temperatures and rainfall

	Jan	Feb	Mar	Apr	May	June	July	Aug	Sept	Oct	Nov	Dec
Ouagadougou												
Temperatures °C												
Min (night)	16	20	23	26	26	24	23	22	23	23	22	17
Max (day)	33	37	40	39	38	36	33	31	32	35	36	35
Rainfall mm	0	3	13	15	84	122	203	277	145	33	0	0
Days with rainfall	0	1	1	2	6	9	12	14	11	3	0	0
Bobo-Dioulasso												
Temperatures °C												
Min (night)	18	21	23	24	24	22	21	21	21	21	20	18
Max (day)	33	34	35	35	34	31	30	29	31	32	34	32
Rainfall mm	3	5	28	54	119	124	253	310	219	65	18	0
Gorom-Gorom												
Temperatures °C												
Min (night)	12	17	22	26	28	26	25	23	25	25	18	15
Max (day)	32	35	38	42	41	38	36	33	38	38	35	32

is from December to February – after the rains have finished, but before the ground gets hot and temperatures reach oppressive levels.

Getting there from the rest of Africa

Burkina is a great West African travel crossroads, with main highways from Niger, Benin, Togo and Ghana converging in Ouagadougou, and roads from Mali and Côte d'Ivoire meeting at Bobo-Dioulasso. **Road transport** along these axes is relatively good, but **air links**, apart from the regular services from Abidjan, are poor.

Air Burkina (VH) flies daily to Ouagadougou from **Abidjan**, usually via Bobo-Dioulasso; from **Lomé** and **Niamey** twice a week; and from **Dakar**, **Bamako** and **Cotonou** three times weekly. Bobo-Dioulasso also has connections with all these cities, often via Ouagadougou, with weekly flights from Lomé and Cotonou and daily flights to Abidjan. There are also Sunday flights from Dakar to Bamako. Ghana Airways provides a twice-weekly link from **Accra** (Wed & Fri) to Ouagadougou, while Air Ivoire flies from Abidjan to Ouagadougou three times a week.

There are no direct flights to Ouagadougou from Banjul, Bissau or Conakry: in most cases Abidjan offers the best connection. There are no direct flights from east and southern Africa: again, the best connections are via Abidjan. From South Africa, Cameroon Airlines fly twice weekly from **Johannesburg** via Yaoundé.

Overland

The following border crossings are some of the most travelled and straightforward in the region, although most close from 6pm to 7am.

> For important practical information applying to all West African countries, covering health, transport, cultural hints and more, plus details on getting to the region from beyond Africa, see Basics, pp.9–87.

From Niger

A 499-kilometre surfaced road links **Niamey** with Ouagadougou via Fada-Ngourma. *Taxis brousse* regularly make the trip in about twelve hours; fares range from around CFA7000–10,000, depending on the vehicle. There's also a comfortable weekly SOTRAO bus from Niamey as far as Fada-Ngourma.

From Mali

The main route from Mali to southwest Burkina is via **Koutiala**; the busy 24-hour border crossing at **Faramana** is generally straightforward, and the Burkinabe formalities efficient. Another alternative from Bamako is via **Sikasso**, although the Sikasso to Bobo stretch (168km) is very rough *piste* in parts, and gets periodically washed out during the rains, when you'll need to make a big detour north via Koutiala (345km). The best service is on the comfortable **TCV bus**, which runs daily from Bamako to Ouaga (CFA13,000) via Bobo (CFA8000). Alternatively, **taxis** run regularly along both these routes, taking some twelve hours in good conditions. They're slightly cheaper than the buses, but far less comfortable.

It's also possible to come down through Dogon country via **Koro**. On the Malian side up to Koro, you'll have to rely on *taxis brousse*, but from there onwards you can pick up the daily SOGEBAF service to **Ouahigouya** (CFA2500), from where there are plenty of connections on to Ouaga. You can't rush this approach, but it gives an interesting first perspective on Burkina through Ouahigouya and the historic Yatenga region.

From Côte d'Ivoire

At the time of writing (mid-2003), the border with Côte d'Ivoire had been closed for nearly a year. The following details should apply when it reopens.

The French-run **train service** from **Abidjan** to Ouagadougou via Bobo-Dioulasso is meant to take about 26 hours, but often runs late; sleeping cabins are available. Trains leave Abidjan around 10.30am, crossing the border in the middle of the night and arriving at Ouagadougou the following early afternoon.

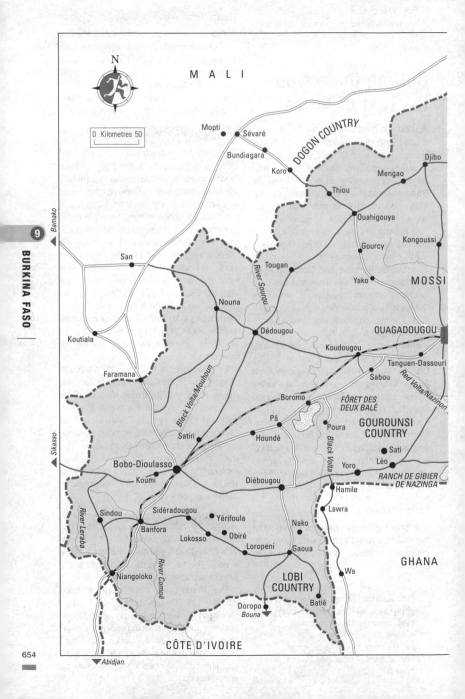
9

BURKINA FASO

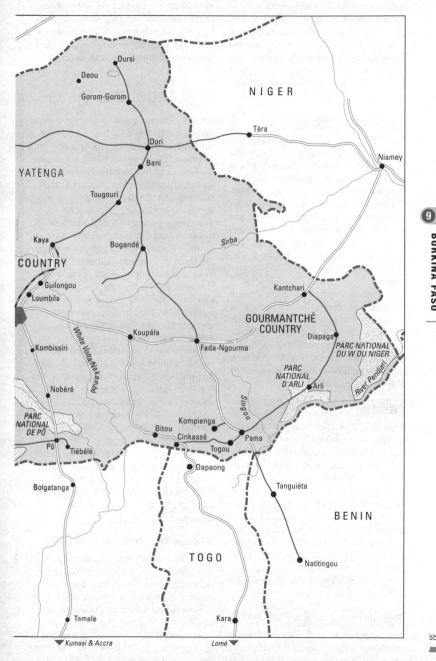

Bus and bush taxis are generally a little faster, and the 1224-kilometre road is in reasonable condition. Bush taxis arrive and depart for Abidjan from **Ouagarinter** *gare routière* in Ouaga (CFA14,000). Note that the routes through the Lobi country in the northeast are very lightly trafficked and transport there mostly depends on markets on five-day cycles.

From Ghana

Ghana State Transport Corporation buses run to Ouagadougou from **Accra** (CFA10,500), departing at 6pm on Mondays and Saturdays and returning to Accra on Monday, Wednesday and Friday mornings. The entire 977km of road between Accra and Ouagadougou is in good condition, and the journey takes eighteen to twenty hours, assuming there are no hitches. The Burkinabe company SKV runs a twice-weekly bus (equipped with a/c and TV) from **Kumasi**.

An alternative route from Ghana crosses the border at **Hamile**, though transport is scarce on both sides of the border. From Hamile, one or two *taxis brousse* leave daily (before 9am) for both Ouagadougou (CFA9000) and Bobo (CFA3500) – the latter journey is a gruelling ten-hour-plus run along *piste* via Diébougou.

From Togo

Bush taxis ply regularly between **Lomé** and Ouagadougou (around CFA14,000), taking about twenty hours to cover the 967 kilometres. As usual, you'll save money by changing vehicles between countries (in this case about CFA5000), but you'll have to spend the night in **Dapaong**. The surfaced road is in generally good condition as far as the Burkina border, from where it's a lot rougher until you reach Koupéla. SKV run a good service between Ouaga and Lomé (CFA12,500, or CFA15,000 with a/c); alternatively, try the weekly SOGEBAF service (CFA13,000).

From Benin

The journey from **Cotonou** to Ouaga is increasingly easy, with a good tarred road as far as Natitingou, and major improvements under way on the remaining section via Tanguiéta to the border. On the Burkina side of the border, the road via Pama and Fada-Ngourma is tarred and in excellent condition. TCV run a twice-weekly service from Cotonou to Bobo (CFA25,000) via Ouaga.

Red tape and visas

Visas for Burkina are required by everyone except nationals of ECOWAS countries. Burkinabe embassies are few and far between, but in many countries where Burkina lacks representation, the French embassy can process the application, charging CFA16,400 for a single-entry visa. Burkinabe embassies in West African countries charge around CFA15,000 for a three-month multiple-entry visa, but often demand payment in CFA. Visas can also be obtained on arrival at Ouagadougou airport, and at most of the country's major land borders. However, you may not be able to obtain a visa at less frequently used entry points such as Hamile, so if you plan on entering Burkina at one of its more obscure border crossings, it's best to get a visa in advance.

If you're flying into Burkina on a scheduled service, you can use the services of a **visa agency** (see p.25). The French charter airline Point-Afrique can often arrange cheap visas for their passengers (see p.13).

Burkina Faso is also part of the **Visa Touristique Entente** scheme. This visa costs CFA25,000 and allows a single entry into Burkina, Côte d'Ivoire, Togo, Benin and Niger, and so makes financial sense if you're travelling to more than one of these countries. The visa is obtainable (in theory, at any rate) from any of these countries' embassies.

Visas for onward travel

There are relatively few diplomatic missions in Ouagadougou. The French embassy handles visas for several West and Central African countries, including Togo and Mauritania (see p.25), though they don't take care of visas for Benin, Niger, Cameroon or Guinea, none of which have representation in Ouagadougou. For **Benin**, 48-hour visas are obtainable at the border (CFA10,000), and are easily extended for CFA12,000 in Natitingou or Cotonou. Visas for **Ghana** and **Mali** are easily obtained at their respective embassies in Ouaga. The consulate in the Canadian embassy may be able to issue visas for **The Gambia**. The Visa Touristique Entente (see above) is currently difficult to obtain in Ouaga; try the Côte d'Ivoire embassy.

Information, websites and maps

Burkina Faso doesn't have any overseas **tourist offices**; in the country itself, there are potentially helpful branches of the Office National du Tourisme Burkinabe (ONTB) in Ouagadougou and Bobo-Dioulasso.

The best **map** of the country is the IGN *Carte Touristique* (1:1,000,000), most recently published in 1994 and available in good map shops in Europe. In Ouagadougou, the Institut Géographique du Burkina (open Mon–Fri; ⓦwww.igb.bf) has good **city maps** of Ouaga and Bobo.

On the **Internet**, the best Burkina-related website is ⓦwww.primature.gov.bf, which provides a range of practical information, plus historical and socioeconomic background. ⓦwww.ouaganet.com has general information and a public forum for Burkina-related subjects.

Health

Chloroquine-resistant **malaria** is a serious problem in Burkina (see p.32). You'll need a **yellow fever** vaccination certificate, as elsewhere in West Africa. During outbreaks of **cholera**, you may (unpredictably) need that certificate too. **Tap water** is treated in Bobo-Dioulasso and Ouagadougou; it smells of chlorine, but is drinkable. In the bush, progress has been made on water purity, but some supplies are still dubious. If you have any doubts, use purifying tablets. The only other real worry is **bilharzia**, and except around Bobo, where there are several bodies of clean water, you should be careful of swimming, especially where the water is stagnant or grassy.

Costs, money and banks

Burkina Faso is part of the **CFA zone**. At the time of writing, **exchange rates** were roughly CFA930 to £1, and CFA600 to US$1. **Banks** in Ouagadougou and Bobo-Dioulasso will readily change **traveller's cheques** (providing you can show the original purchase receipt; American Express are the most widely accepted) and **cash** (euros, dollars and sterling are all fine). In other towns, banks will usually only change cash euros, while banks in small towns in the extreme north may refuse to change even these, so plan ahead and change enough money in the major towns to see you through your travels. Bank **opening hours** vary: they're typically Monday to Friday 7.30–11.30am and 3.30–5.30pm.

Credit cards are not widely accepted, though you'll find Visa and Amex of some use to pay for expensive hotels and travel services in Ouagadougou and, to an even more limited extent, Bobo-Dioulasso. In the major towns, including Ouaga, Bobo and Koudougou, the Banque Internationale pour le Commerce, l'Industrie et l'Agriculture de Burkina (BICIA-B) has **ATMs** which accept foreign Visa cards. Elsewhere, it's very difficult to get a cash advance on Visa, while MasterCard is even more difficult, and most banks, even in the larger cities, no longer accept it. If you get in a fix, try the major hotels.

Costs

Compared to neighbouring Francophone countries, prices in Burkina are reasonable, and even Ouagadougou isn't too expensive (although if you've come from Ghana, costs may seem very high). **Accommodation** in budget hotels around the country costs from CFA3000 to CFA6000, rising to CFA10,000 to CFA20,000 in mid-range places, while eating street **food** you can fill up on *riz sauce* or *tô* for as little as CFA300. **Transport** costs are also reasonable, ranging from CFA7 to CFA20 per kilometre (rarely more), depending on whether the road is paved or *piste* and the type of vehicle.

Getting around

A decent **road system** connects Ouaga with most places in the south of Burkina, and even the route to Diébougou and down to Gaoua in the Lobi country has been vastly improved recently. Access to certain areas north of Ouaga, such as Ouahigouya, is also much better these days, though reaching the remote northern village of Gorom-Gorom remains a challenge, especially in the rainy season.

Bush taxis, trucks and buses

Bush taxis are usually 504 *breaks* (estate cars/station wagons) or 404 *bâchés* with boarded-up back ends. The latter are cheaper and, given the level of comfort, rightly so. You won't see much of the countryside in them unless you pay a small supplement to sit in the cab.

A far better option are the numerous **private bus companies** which have been springing up in Burkina Faso over the past few years, and which offer competitive prices, less hassle at highway checkpoints and greater comfort (some even have a/c). The ones you'll come across most frequently are STMB, SOGEBAF, STAF, TRANSMIF, SKV, Rakieta, TCV, Sans Frontières and SOTRAO – each usually has its own separate bus station, and all are fairly reliable.

Routes, frequencies and sample fares

There's plenty of traffic along the main **route nationale** axis Banfora–Bobo–Ouaga–Fada-Ngourma, and frequent enough vehicles north to Ouahigouya and Dori and south to Pô. It's only when trying to get to more remote northern towns – or to other isolated areas such as the Lobi country – that you might experience long waits for vehicles (sometimes even days).

Ouaga–Bobo (360km): CFA5000, hourly (6hr).
Ouaga–Fada-Ngourma (234km): CFA3000, 1 daily (4hr).
Ouaga–Gaoua (385km; mostly paved): CFA5000, daily (6–7hr).
Ouaga–Gorom-Gorom (300km; paved as far as Dori): CFA4000, twice weekly (8hr).
Ouaga–Ouahigouya (182km): CFA2500, daily (3hr).
Ouaga–Pô (142km): CFA1500, daily (3hr).

Car and bike rental

You'll find **car rental** agencies in Ouagadougou and Bobo-Dioulasso (see the "Listings" for those towns), and they are not excessively expensive. However, it's more economical, and potentially much more satisfying, to rent a **bicycle**, **mobylette** (moped) or **motorbike**. This is an excellent way to see the sights around Ouagadougou, Bobo-Dioulasso and Banfora: you'll find people around the market places who rent out machines, and you can even transport them on the roofs of *taxis brousse* if you get bored with riding.

Trains

The Ouagadougou–Abidjan Express runs three times a week (in theory at least, though services are often disrupted) via **Koudougou**, **Bobo-Dioulasso**, **Banfora** and **Niangoloko** – the Burkinabe border post. Trains depart from Ouaga on Tuesdays, Thursdays and Saturdays at 8.30am, arriving in Bobo at 2.30pm (CFA5800 second class) and Banfora at 4.12pm (CFA7400 second class). They return from Abidjan the following day (Wed, Fri and Sun). You might want to check with Sitarail in Ouagadougou (☎31.07.35) to see whether services have been affected by the current unrest in Côte d'Ivoire. Another line runs north from Ouaga to **Kaya**, with departures every Saturday at 8am.

Domestic flights

Air Burkina flies most days between **Ouagadougou** and **Bobo**, often en route to or from Abidjan, Bamako, Cotonou or Lomé.

Accommodation

Ouagadougou and Bobo-Dioulasso have their fair share of international-class **hotels**, which are invariably full during the big festivals (see p.660). But in any town smaller than Koudougou, the country's third largest, accommodation is much more basic. In smaller towns, especially in the extreme north, **electricity** and **running water** become more sporadic. Hotel rates usually carry a "tax pour la commune", a minimal amount of CFA500 per hotel star per stay.

In terms of **room rates**, anything under around CFA5000 is likely to be very rudimentary – often a *chambre de passage* rented to the average guest by the hour. Above CFA5000 you'll get a basic hotel with simple amenities, usually self-contained with fan (or a/c, at higher rates). Mid-range establishments (roughly CFA14,000 and upwards) are usually reasonable business- or tourist-class hotels, while above CFA40,000 you're looking at a comfortable, first-class hotel, with good facilities.

A network of **auberges populaires** has been set up by the Ministry of the Environment and Tourism. These very basic hotels at least ensure that there's somewhere to stay in each of Burkina's thirty main towns. Off the few beaten tracks, **staying with people** is a viable and recommended option. In the bush, so too is **camping**.

Eating and drinking

Despite its drought-stricken reputation, most towns in Burkina have an array of **street food**; and throughout the country you'll find women selling bean or banana fritters, yam chips, fried fish and *brochettes*. The staples in Burkina are **rice** and **millet**. After grinding, the rice or millet is boiled and made into a mush known as **tô**, often eaten with a sauce made from cassava (manioc) leaves with palm oil, fresh fish and seasonings. **Gumbo** (okra) is another common sauce base.

Drinking

Nationally brewed **beers** include SOBRA, Brakina and Flag. You may be offered the unopened bottle to see if it's cold enough. Different home-made drinks are enjoyed in the various regions. A national favourite is **chapalo**, locally made millet beer, also known as *pit* or *dolo*. The deadly African gin, known in Burkina as **patasi** or "qui me pousse", is cheap. Around Banfora, you'll find a lot of palm wine, **banji**, which you can order by the (beer) bottle in most small bars (cabarets). Sweet and frothy, it goes down easily and has the added advantage of being cheap.

Throughout the country (especially in motor parks), you'll find **lemburgui**, thirst-quenching home-made ginger beer and purple *bisap* juice, frozen in small plastic bags. Lafi **mineral water** is available across the country in 1.5 litre bottles, not too expensive at around CFA450.

Communications

You can make direct-dial **international phone calls** from Burkina to the UK, North America and most of Europe. **Mobile (cell) phone** connectivity through Celtel Burkina is increasing rapidly and the take-up among local people is noticeably on the increase. Your mobile will work in Ouaga and Bobo, around several other large towns and along some main highways, though connections can be tenuous.

Ouagadougou's **poste restante** works well, although you should be careful to have your letters addressed with the exact name that appears in your passport – which you'll have to produce to claim your post. There's also a poste restante service at Bobo-Dioulasso.

Accommodation price codes

All accommodation prices in this chapter are coded according to the following scale, whose equivalent in pounds sterling/US dollars is used throughout the book. Prices refer to the rate you can expect to pay for a room with two beds, including taxes. Single rooms, or single occupancy, will normally cost at least two-thirds of the twin-occupancy rate. For further details, see p.51.

❶ Under CFA4700 (under £5/$8).
❷ CFA4700–9000 (£5–10/$8–16).
❸ CFA9000–14,000 (£10–15/$16–24).
❹ CFA14,000–19,000 (£15–20/$24–32).

❺ CFA19,000–28,000 (£20–30/$32–48).
❻ CFA28,000–37,000 (£30–40/$48–64).
❼ CFA37,000–47,000 (£40–50/$64–80).
❽ Over CFA47,000 (over £50/$80).

For **Internet** access, you'll find a good selection of cybercafés in Ouaga and Bobo, and even smaller towns such as Banfora and Ouahigouya now have places where you can get online. Prices range from CFA800 to CFA1500 per hour.

> Burkina Faso's IDD Country code is ☎226.

The media

The **national press** consists of a government French-language daily, *Sidwaya* ("Truth"), and the independent dailies *Le Pays* and *L'Observateur*. The weekly *Journal du Jeudi* attempts a satirical treatment of current events and is worth a look. Other weeklies that have sprung up in the "democratic" era include *L'Opinion*, *San Finna*, *Bendre* and *L'Indépendant*.

Listening to **Radio Burkina**, the government radio (in sixteen Burkinabe languages, on 747 AM) or watching **TV** (one channel, with very limited transmission and audience) aren't likely to be major leisure activities. For something a bit livelier, there are various commercial stations including **Canal Arc-en-ciel** (96.6FM), **Radio Energie** (103.4FM), **Horizon FM** (104.4FM in Ouaga and 102.7FM in Bobo) and **Radio Bobo-Dioulasso** (92.0FM). The BBC World Service can be heard in the capital on 99.2FM.

Entertainment

Burkina has a thriving **football** culture, with a first division of a dozen clubs, the most notable being Étoile Filante (Oauga), Racing Club de Bobo, and Union Sportive des Forces Armées (USFA). There's an equally thriving, though severely underfunded, popular-culture scene in Burkina. In Ouaga and Bobo, **live music** is a nightly occurrence, and even isolated villages periodically come alive with the sounds of impromptu *balafon* bands. (For more on the country's music, see p.668). During the major **festivals**, Burkina's international stars can be counted on to make appearances. But Burkina is best known as the capital of African **cinema**: you have a better chance of catching an African movie here than in any other country in the region, especially during the huge **FESPACO film festival** (see below). For more on Burkinabe cinema, see p.669.

Burkinabe **drama** has received a boost in recent years and now has over a dozen drama troupes giving regular performances, whilst the major towns (Ouagadougou, Bobo-Dioulasso, Koudougou) all have well-equipped theatres. You can check out what's going on by calling in at the French cultural centres in Ouagadougou or Bobo. If you're really keen, be sure to catch the **Festival du Théâtre** (see opposite).

Festivals

Burkina has a growing reputation for major **arts festivals**, of which the best known is the big African filmfest, FESPACO. It's well worth timing a trip around one of these.

The **Festival Panafricain du Cinéma** (FESPACO) is held in Ouagadougou every odd-numbered year at the end of February. FESPACO was founded in 1969 and is dedicated to promoting African film-makers throughout the world. Thrusting Burkina to the forefront of African cinema, the festival now attracts tens of thousands of people. If you happen to be here at the time, you won't find a hotel room unless you've booked in advance, as the city fills with an international crowd of film-makers and movie hacks flocking to the ten-day extravaganza. Rooms in private homes help mop up the overflow; enquire at the festival's headquarters, not far from the Place des Nations Unies, or at the information centre in the *Hôtel Indépendance*.

In theory, the event is open to all, and a CFA10,000 **ticket** allows you entrance to all the myriad films showing simultaneously in the capital's many theatres. You can also purchase individual tickets at the respective cinemas (about CFA1000) – if you have the stamina, you could easily take in thirty or more African films in the course of the event. This is undoubtedly the most star-studded event you'll see in West Africa: celebrities from throughout the African diaspora increasingly make the pilgrimage, and the energy is electric. Local bands play everywhere, as people crowd the streets stopping for a drink or to browse at the countless booths for traditional crafts and FESPACO merchandise. Organization is excellent: **schedules** are posted throughout town; a free daily festival paper lists each day's events; and hotels provide free shuttles. For more information, contact FESPACO (01 BP 2505, Ouagadougou ☎30.75.38 or 33.20.66, ◍www.fespaco.bf).

SIAO

Another biennial event (held in October in even-numbered years), the **Salon International de l'Artisanat de Ouagadougou** (SIAO) is touted as the largest crafts meeting on the African continent. The SIAO attracts over 100,000 visitors, including buyers from throughout the world. The entire city centre fills with exhibitors' booths and stalls, with the focus around the **SIAO village**, a purpose-built structure on the outskirts of town. While the objectives – to promote African crafts as cultural expression while stimulating the industry – is serious, the atmosphere is festive, with music, food, fashion shows, and performances of dance and theatre on every street corner. For information, contact the Secrétariat Permanent, SIAO (01 BP 3414, Ouagadougou ☎37.32.56, ◍www.siao.bf).

Festival du Théâtre

Ouagadougou's biennial **Festival du Théâtre** (late November in even-numbered years) hosts national troupes performing works as diverse as Greek tragedy and modern African comedies. For information, contact the Secrétariat du Festival (☎30.73.89).

Semaine Nationale de la Culture

The **Semaine Nationale de la Culture** is another biennial event (February/March in even numbered years), this time held in Bobo-Dioulasso. The town turns into a fair for the event, with dance and percussion troupes from throughout the country performing nonstop. You can also catch demonstrations of traditional wrestling and archery, while booths everywhere display national crafts and regional cooking and music is played all over the town. For information, contact the Secrétariat in Bobo on ☎98.02.30.

Directory

Crafts Crafts are an important industry in Burkina, ranging from those intended for everyday use (pottery, basketwork, wooden utensils) to those used in ceremonies (masks, statues) or as tourist fodder or decoration. Bronze statues, cast using the lost-wax method, were traditionally made for the royal court, but are now widely available in Ouagadougou. Pottery is the most widespread craft in Burkina and is used everywhere. Look out for leatherwork, too, an offshoot of the country's large livestock industry.

Opening hours Businesses open 8am–12.30pm and 3–6pm on weekdays; many are open Saturday mornings too. Government offices operate 7am–12.30pm and 3–5.30pm on weekdays only.

Photography In theory, before taking any pictures in Burkina you need to obtain a (free) photo permit at the ONTB tourist office in Ouagadougou (see p.673) – this is issued on the spot. Obtaining the permit is definitely advised if you want to use your camera in the capital, but you'll rarely be checked for the permit except in Ouagadougou and possibly Gorom-Gorom. The ONTB tourist office has a long list of scenes and places of which photos are prohibited.

Public holidays Office holidays include all the usual Muslim and Christian celebrations. Additional Christian holidays include Ascension Thursday, Pentecost and Assumption. New Year's Day is also a bank holiday. The principal national holidays are January 3 (1966 Revolution), May 1 (Labour Day), August 4 (Revolution Day), August 5 (Independence Day) and December 11 (Proclamation of the Republic).

Wildlife and national parks Burkina's flat, overgrazed and relatively overpopulated lands offer poor refuge for the country's natural savanna fauna. A conscientious conservation programme does exist (with controlled tourist hunting as part of its policy), though its best chances of success lie with the Burkinabe ethic stressing community before individual – hippo and crocodile "pools" are recognized tourist assets. Encouraging reports indicate a relatively large elephant population in the Burkina sector of the Parc National du "W" and in the Parc National d'Arli (both in the remote southeast) and in the Ranch de Gibier de Nazinga/Parc National de Pô, south of Ouagadougou. For information on the game reserves contact the ONTB tourist office (T31.19.59, Wwww.ontb.bf) or the office of the Nazinga reserve (T30.84.43, Eranch.nazinga@cenatrin.bf), both in Ouagadougou.

A brief history of Burkina

The **Mossi empires** dominated the Volta region's politics until the French usurped the independence of their states in the 1890s. For two decades the colonials simply merged their new territory with the Colonie du Haut-Sénégal Niger, and it wasn't until 1919 that they divided this huge mass into two separate colonies – Soudan Français and **Haute Volta** (Upper Volta) – the latter comprising present-day Burkina Faso. In 1932, commercial considerations (primarily a need for manual labour in neighbouring colonies) led the French to divide Upper Volta again, annexing half the colony to Côte d'Ivoire and dividing the rest between the French Sudan and Niger. It wasn't until 1947 that Upper Volta re-emerged as an entity.

Independence

Maurice Yaméogo, a prominent figure in pre-independence politics, founded the **Union Démocratique Voltaïque** – the UDV, a local section of Félix Houphouët-Boigny's Rassemblement Démocratique Africain – shortly after World War II. By 1958, Upper Volta had become an autonomous territory, and Yaméogo its prime minister. When full independence was granted on August 5, 1960, he was elected the country's first president.

Yaméogo had inherited a desperate situation – the French had done little to give Upper Volta an infrastructure capable of spurring economic development – but the new president did little to reverse the trend, and outside of Ouagadougou the country continued to lack all but a few roads and communications systems. As the economic situation deteriorated, Yaméogo introduced austerity measures, making him increasingly unpopular with disgruntled workers and civil servants. In the face of rising opposition, he banned political parties apart from the UDV and adopted an autocratic style. He was ousted, on January 3, 1966, in a coup led by the army chief of staff, **Sangoulé Lamizana**.

The 1970s

The army, with Lamizana at its head, ruled the country during a four-year period in which the nation was ostensibly being prepared for a **return to civilian rule**. Parties were formed and a new constitution was drafted. In 1970, a semi-civilian government was elected, with the UDV winning a majority of the seats in parliament. The UDV's leadership was split, however, with a rivalry developing between **Joseph Ouédraogo** and **Gérard Ouédraogo** (unrelated, though both of Mossi origin). After a period of political infighting, it was agreed that Gérard would serve as prime minister and Joseph as president of the National

Assembly. Lamizana remained in office as head of state and the army retained real power.

By the early 1970s, drought had struck the country and the economic outlook was bleaker than ever. As parts of the north were faced with the prospect of starvation, a scandal erupted with the discovery of **food aid embezzlement** by members of the government distribution committee – confirming rumours of widespread administrative corruption. The government suffered a further crisis in 1973, when conflict developed between civilian leaders and the militant teachers' union, and a **general strike** swept through the public sector. As the situation deteriorated, the National Assembly refused to pass further legislation until the prime minister stepped down. Gérard Ouédraogo refused to do so, and on February 8, 1974, the army took control of the country once again, dissolving the assembly and suspending the 1970 constitution.

A new crisis hit Upper Volta in 1975, when **war** broke out with Mali over the Agacher Strip. Their rival claims to this 150-kilometre-wide border strip in the desolate northern regions of the Sahel – believed to be rich in mineral deposits – were based on legal documents dating back to when Upper Volta had been divided and redivided between Côte d'Ivoire, the French Sudan (Mali) and Niger. Before the dispute was settled with OAU mediation, a new generation of popular military heroes had arisen, including a young officer, **Thomas Sankara**.

The rise of Sankara

Under pressure from the labour unions, elections were once again held in 1978, and on May 28 of that year, the **Third Republic** was proclaimed. Lamizana was elected president, but his UDV party didn't have an overall majority in parliament and his tenure was habitually challenged by the students and trade unions (at the time, an unusually powerful force,

since half of all wage earners belonged to one of the four national unions). He was overthrown in a quiet palace coup on November 25, 1980, by **Colonel Saye Zerbo**, who became head of the new "Military Committee for Recovery and National Progress" (CMRPN).

The coup was initially supported by the unions, but they quickly became disgruntled after the CMRPN's **banning of political activity**. Relations deteriorated utterly when the Military Committee withdrew the right to strike in 1981. Serious cleavages began to become apparent within the Military Committee, and in 1982 Sankara – whose popular appeal was growing – was removed from his influential position in the Ministry of Information.

Unrest quickened, and a **coup d'état** followed. On November 7, 1982, a group of military officers forced out Zerbo and set up the "Provisional People's Salvation Council" (CSP) with an army doctor named **Jean-Baptiste Ouédraogo** at its head. The new regime let fire a volley of denunciation at Zerbo's corrupt and repressive government and took a radical pro-union position, championing the right to strike. In January 1983, Sankara was named prime minister.

By early 1983, it was clear that the new government was divided between **traditionalists** – led by the army chief of staff, Colonel Gabriel Somé – and **radicals**, headed by Sankara. The two factions came into open conflict when Sankara invited Colonel Gaddafi to Upper Volta in May 1983. The day after the Libyan leader's departure, Ouédraogo ordered Sankara's arrest on the grounds that he had dangerously threatened national unity.

The arrest of the prime minister triggered a rebellion in Sankara's commando unit at Pô, a small town near the Ghanaian border. The commandos, led by **Captain Blaise Compaoré**, believed the move to have been instigated by Somé and encouraged by France. They took control of Pô and refused orders from the capital until

Sankara was unconditionally released. But Ouédraogo refused to dismiss Somé and gradually the rebellion spread to other commando units in the country. On the eve of the 23rd anniversary of independence – August 4, 1983 – Sankara seized power. Ouédraogo had lasted less than a year as head of state.

The Sankara reforms

Sankara settled in as president of the new governing body, the Conseil National de la Révolution (CNR), and as head of state; Compaoré was nominated minister of state to the president; and the country was renamed **Burkina Faso**. With the logistic help of the previously underground "Patriotic Development League" (LIPAD), the CNR quickly set about reorganizing the administrative regions of the country and ousting traditional rulers from their positions of power and influence. Revolutionary **"people's courts"** were established to try former public officials charged with political crimes and corruption. One of the first to be tried was Lamizana, who was acquitted. But several former ministers were convicted and sentenced to prison, as were ex-president Zerbo (who was also ordered to repay US$200,000 in public funds) and Gérard Ouédraogo, former UDV leader.

Only 34 years old when he came to power, Sankara symbolized a new generation of leaders with innovative ideas, but his popularity went beyond his ability to compose revolutionary music on his guitar or eloquent denunciations of capitalism and imperialism. Sankara may have had a penchant for facile rhetoric, but he could also transform words into action. He waged war on desertification, women's inequality and children's diseases (creating a "vaccination-commando"). When foreign investors refused to finance a railway line to magnesium deposits in the north of the country, he launched the *bataille du rail* – encouraging peasants to build the tracks themselves (although critics said his recruitment methods were haunt-

ingly reminiscent of French *travaux forcé*). But perhaps his greatest achievement was the virtual elimination of **corruption** and government waste, proving his commitment to the cause by having himself chauffeured around in the back of a Renault 4, rather than the customary black Mercedes. In another popular move, Sankara early in his term announced **free housing** for all Burkinabe and called a moratorium on rents (an incautious decision from which he later had to retreat). But even though the young president seemed to prove himself as a capable, if unpredictable leader, he was gaining a long list of enemies.

Detractors – at home and abroad

By early 1984, there was growing **opposition** to Sankara's radical style, and in May of that year a plot to overthrow the government was uncovered. The leaders were hastily arrested and tried. Unlike the people's courts, these proceedings took place in secrecy and the penalties were severe. Seven of the alleged plotters were executed and five others sentenced to hard labour.

In light of these events, **relations with France** soured, and Sankara accused the French government of supporting exiled political rivals. Other Western nations also viewed the new regime with scepticism, though the fact that Sankara made efforts to distance his government from Libya and the Soviet Union was interpreted as an encouraging sign. Gradually, the "revolution" came to be identified less with Marxist ideology and was seen more as a means of unifying a wide cross-section of society. The success of the CNR and the genuine popularity of the movement hinged primarily on the dynamic personality of its founder.

War with Mali flared up again in late 1985. Over fifty people were killed and the better-armed Malians did major damage in Burkina. In December 1986, the International Court of Justice in

The Hague divided the disputed Agacher Strip between the two countries and peace was restored. But relations were also deteriorating with other West African neighbours – especially **Côte d'Ivoire** and **Togo**. Close ties between Sankara and Jerry Rawlings of **Ghana** were regarded suspiciously by these conservative nations – especially after 1986 when the two socialist neighbours decided to work towards political integration by the late 1990s. Relations with Togo were nearly broken off after an attempted coup in Lomé shook President Eyadema's regime in September 1986. Both Ghana and Burkina were accused of involvement and of harbouring Togolese dissidents. Despite a 1987 visit to Ouagadougou by François Mitterrand, France continued to treat Burkina with reserve – a wait-and-see attitude generally shared by Western powers.

At home, Sankara was frequently criticized by intellectuals, labour unions and business leaders, though he had a charismatic knack for diffusing enmity from all these groups. Even salary cuts for civil servants and the military were accepted on the grounds that they were necessary to raise the level of social services among the poor. In the absence of serious opposition from traditional political forces, it was a growing lack of consensus within the governing CNR and resulting rifts that ultimately proved Sankara's downfall.

The new regime

On October 15, 1987, Thomas Sankara was killed in a botched and bloody coup. It was precipitated by a group of soldiers loyal to Blaise Compaoré (Sankara's companion in arms and partner in the government), who opened fire on Sankara after arresting him. The precise nature of the overthrow is still shrouded in mystery. It did not, at any rate, take a planned course and it doesn't seem likely that Compaoré intended to come out of it looking like a murderer. He later said "Thomas confiscated the revolution and brought untold suffering to the people", and it's clear at least that Sankara had allowed himself to become fatally isolated. But Compaoré's image as a West African leader with the blood of a brother on his hands has never been erased.

Sankara's death sent shock waves through the region and chilled progressive movements round the world. For even if his methods were often open to question (something he never denied), he had demonstrated sincerity in his aims and proved himself a credible friend of the people. Most importantly he had managed to instil **national pride** and create a realistic sense of hope in one of West Africa's most impoverished countries. Most West African, and not a few Western governments seemed relieved with the change, but the Burkinabe people's response varied from mournful to muted – not a good sign for the new president.

The basis of the revolutionary system Sankara set in place remained intact, although Compaoré quickly announced that "rectification" would be made, signalling a willingness to conform to the inevitable pressure of World Bank and IMF loan negotiations. The early years of the new regime were characterized by the almost continuous rumble of rumour and incident within the Front Populaire (high-level disagreements, coup attempts and a number of subsequent executions). Though by 1990 the party had been purged, by death or desertion, of all members of the original 1983 revolution, events suggested considerable latent support of Sankara and serious threats to the survival of the new leadership. Compaoré therefore sought to bring disenfranchized political groupings into the fold and to achieve peace with the powerful unions.

Towards this end, a new constitution was drafted in 1990, which called for a multiparty **electoral system**. Political parties mushroomed, and a transitional government was set up with Compaoré as head of a council of ministers that contained a smattering of opposition leaders. But conflict arose quickly at a conference to discuss the constitution's implementation. The new parties decried the fact that their input was merely consultative and there was to be no sovereign national conference such as those taking place elsewhere in West Africa. Soon after, opposition leaders resigned their government posts to protest Compaoré's intransigence on the issue.

The Fourth Republic

As the presidential elections approached, opposition parties united under the banner of the **Coordination des Forces Démocratiques** (CFD) and collectively pushed for a sovereign national council. Popular demonstrations in support of opposition demands occurred throughout the second half of 1991, and, as the outcomes tended increasingly towards violence, the government banned political rallies. By the end of the year, it was clear there would be no council and no opposition: "opposition" candidates withdrew from the presidential race and called for an election boycott. Compaoré was left as the only candidate and, naturally enough, won the election, although three out of four voters stayed away from the polls. He was sworn in as president of the **"Fourth Republic"** on December 24, 1991, but was probably no closer to having obtained wide public support than he was after the unpopular coup of 1987.

Even as the president called for **national reconciliation** following the elections, he became increasingly mistrusted when opposition leaders were attacked. One, Clément Oumarou Ouédraogo, was assassinated just outside the Hôtel Indépendance as he left a CFD meeting. Although Compaoré condemned the murder, there was general public cynicism, and angry crowds stoned the minister of defence when he showed up at Ouédraogo's funeral. Still, with some deft political manoeuvring, the president managed to persuade much of the opposition to participate in the upcoming **legislative elections**. By the polling date in May 1992, almost half of the nation's 62 political parties had decided to contest.

Although Compaoré's party, the Organisation pour la Démocratie Populaire Mouvement du Travail (ODP-MT) won a majority of the parliamentary seats, the president's image suffered as a result of the popular belief that the elections had been rigged. In keeping with the theme of reconciliation, the new cabinet contained some opposition leaders – though mostly relegated to the least important posts.

In the early years of the Fourth Republic, Burkina Faso was most often in the headlines as a sponsor of various rebel forces in West Africa and as a mediator of regional conflicts. Compaoré actively supported Charles Taylor in the civil war in **Liberia**, supplying arms and troops to Liberian forces and to rebel militias in Sierra Leone, as well as involving Burkina in the diamond trade. Compaoré also played a key role in negotiating a settlement of the **Tuareg crisis** that gripped Mali and Niger – partly because Burkina was one of the countries most affected, with 50,000 refugees sheltering there at the height of the conflict. Burkina's relationship with France grew warmer following the election of Jacques Chirac in 1995.

At home, Burkina's economy experienced the fastest growth of any country in West Africa at the end of the 1990s – a performance that bolstered Compaoré's chances of keeping his seat as his first term drew to a close. More importantly, there was no real alternative to his candidacy. As the **1998 elections** neared, the main opposition parties again called for a boycott, but this time voters seemed weary of complaints about the electoral process, and the boycott gathered only a lacklustre following. More than fifty percent of the voters participated in the elections and gave Compaoré a resounding victory, making him the first president since independence to survive a first term and be re-elected.

The Zongo scandal and after

Compaoré barely had time to bask in the glow of his victory, however, when a scandal erupted that had far-reaching political implications. In December 1998, four charred bodies were found in a vehicle that had apparently crashed near the village of Sapouy. One of the victims was **Norbert Zongo**, editor of the *L'Indépendant* newspaper and president of the Private Press Association in Burkina. Zongo had been investigating the business dealings of Compaoré's younger brother François, as well as the suspicious circumstances surrounding the death of François' chauffeur, whom Zongo alleged had been tortured to death by the Régiment de Sécurité Presidentielle, the president's own security forces. **Demonstrations** in Ouagadougou called for an investigation into Zongo's death, which the public widely believed to be murder, and Compaoré set up an independent commission to look into the matter.

The commission's report, returned in May 1999, was damning to the presidency: "Norbert Zongo was assassinated for purely political motives because he practiced investigative journalism. He defended a democratic ideal and had chosen to become involved, with his newspaper, in the struggle for the respect of human rights and justice, and against the poor management of the public sector and impunity."

Protestors flooded the streets of Ouagadougou, setting up barricades and burning tyres as they marched to the Ministry of Justice. Security forces met them with tear gas and, as unrest spread to the university, police raided dormitories and arrested students. The rest of the country was not spared from the violence. In Koudougou – the birthplace of Zongo – rioters burned private residences and destroyed public property. The key opposition leader and MP, Herman Yaméogo, was accused of inciting the rioters, and arrested.

Although Compaoré denounced the commission's findings, the damage was already done. It was a huge blow to his attempts to reinvent himself as a legitimately elected democratic leader and it rekindled opposition. In the aftermath of Zongo's death, an umbrella organization of the Sankarist opposition was formed by members of the Presidential Guard. At the same time, the president lost a friend and political ally in the region when Niger's head of state, **Ibrahim Mainassara**, was assassinated in Niamey. At the start of 2002, Compaoré's standing was shaken again when Amnesty International claimed there had been over a hundred extra-judicial **executions** since the launch of an anti-banditry campaign in November. The incidence of armed robbery and rural violence grew, along with other alarming indicators of internal unrest, while students at Ouaga University suspected of harbouring leftist sympathies were harrassed by the president's ruthless security network.

Burkina Faso today

Burkina's **legislative polls** in May 2002 gave renewed impetus to democracy in Burkina Faso. Compaoré's party, renamed the Congrès pour la Démocratie et le Progrès, which had previously held 107 of the 111 seats in the National Assembly, was reduced to just 57, with opposition parties holding 54. These results briefly inspired the hope that Compaoré might even retire earlier than anticipated, though it now appears that he is preparing to run for a third term at the presidential elections in 2005, boosted by recent rises in Burkina's GDP and a $45 million grant to help reduce poverty from the World Bank. Problems loom, however: in 2002 there were further trade union strikes in support of pay rises, while civil strife in Côte d'Ivoire threatens Burkina's export and labour markets. Given these uncertainties, Compaoré's fate in the elections of 2005 might hang on how far he is prepared to move towards genuine democracy.

Music

Despite the amount of local music on offer in Burkina Faso, very few artists have reached a wide African or international audience. Yet the country has a rich musical heritage. *Balafons*, combined with complex drumming, characterize much Burkinabe music. A few traditional groups have made tours of Europe. Dance is an important part of their acts, so they tend to get booked at outdoor festivals.

The best-known artists outside the country are the brilliantly watchable percussion group **Farafina** and the very exciting **Les Frères Coulibaly**. Other national artists rising to prominence include the rapper **Black Soul** and female vocalist **Amity Meria**. All are based, when at home, in **Bobo-Dioulasso**, the town to head for if you want to get to grips with Burkinabe music. The big **Semaine National de la Culture** festival held each even-numbered year in February or March offers a tremendous spectacle for dance and percussion enthusiasts, and is attracting increasing interest from drummers around West Africa.

Farafina

The musicians of Farafina have been touring Europe and America since the mid-1980s, getting audiences on their feet with complex but clearly structured polyrhythms. Apart from the *balafon* they also use the *djembe*, *tama* (the Wolof hourglass drum), *bara* (calabash drums) and flutes. They have collaborated and recorded albums with Brian Eno, composer and trumpeter Jon Hassell, the jazz musician Malcolm Braff, and were invited to perform with the Rolling Stones in "Continental Drift", on their *Steel Wheels* album. They have also recorded three albums of their own. For more details, see Ⓦ www.farafina.com.

Kanou (2002, L'Empreinte Digitale). Their latest album, featuring the enchanting voice of Fatoumata Dembele, the first female addition to the band.

Faso Denou (Real World). Feel the percussive power of the two *balafons* (xylophones), *bara*-skinned open calabash, *doumdou'ba* tall drums and voluble *djembe*.

Les Frères Coulibaly

The Coulibaly griot family belongs to the Bwa people living in the north of Burkina. Brothers Souleyman, Lassina and Ousséni lead a standard percussion orchestra with *djembe*, *bara*, *tama* and *kenkeni* drums, *barafile* rattle, *balafon* xylophone and *kamele ngoni* harp-lute. In 2001 they released their latest album, *Senwie*, and they continue to tour in America and Europe.

Musiques du Burkina Faso & du Mali (Musiques du Monde/Buda). Features brother Lassina Coulibaly with his traditional acoustic group Yan Kadi Faso. Beautiful *kora* playing is the standout, but there's also a great *balafon* duet, "Massoum pien".

Various

La Vedette Voltaïque and Le Chanteur Voltaïque (Sonodisc). Two albums by Hamidou Ouédraogo, one of the nation's better-known stars. A Fula-speaker from the region of Dori, Ouédraogo moved to Ouagadougou in the 1970s and formed the group l'Orchestre Super Volta.

Haute Volta (Agence de Coopération Culturelle et Technique). Good compilation of Mossi, Fula, Bamana, Lobi and Gan music.

The Art of the Balafon (Arion). Various artists, with a sound similar to

Farafina, featuring music from six ethnic groups including the Lobi, Gan and Dagara.
The Balafons of Bobo-Dioulasso – Sababougnouma (Playasound).

Powerful *balafon* and *djembe* ensemble, featuring mainly Djola and Senoufoi rhythms, and using the pentatonic, as opposed to the heptatonic, *balafon.*

Cinema

The government of Burkina Faso has long been active in promoting the cinema in West Africa – the country nationalized movie theatres in 1979, the first nation besides Guinea to do so. In its early days, the national film company helped finance mainly educational films, as well as producing **Djim Mamadou Kola**'s *Le Sang de Parias* (1971), the first national feature. Kola is still an active film-maker; his award-winning *Etrangers* was released in 1993.

In 1981, a private businessman, Martial Ouédraogo, invested in **CINAFRIC** – a production company with 16mm and 35mm cameras. The only private film company of its kind in Africa, CINAFRIC has been criticized as "Hollywood on the Volta", yet despite its commercial intent, it has helped free local film-makers from dependence on the West. Within a year, CINAFRIC produced its first feature, *Paweogo* (1981), and thus launched one of the country's most prolific film-makers, **Sanou Kollo**.

Burkina Faso was thrust into the spotlight by **Gaston Kaboré**, who won a French César in 1985 for *Wend Kuuni* – a rural tale which demonstrates how traditional values can heal a modern African state. A prominent figure in Burkinabe, and indeed in pan-African cinema (he is currently director of the Pan-African Federation of Film-makers), Kaboré has gone on to make numerous features including *Zan Boko* (1988) – about the problems of urbanization, its impact on people and their relationship to the environment – and *Rabi* (1991). His film *Buud Yam* (1996), a sequel to *Wend Kuuni*, won the grand prize at the 1997 FESPACO.

Idrissa Ouédraogo is probably the country's best known film-maker in the West. *Yaaba* (1988), *Tilai* (1990) and

Samba Traoré (1992) are strongly rooted in the African rural experience, while *Kini and Adam* (1997) was a co-production shot on location in Zimbabwe with the collaboration of Zimbabwean and South African crew and cast – a type of cross-continental collaboration that is becoming increasingly common.

Today, the government continues to be supportive, and new film-makers continue to emerge. **Drissa Touré** was widely acclaimed for his first feature *Laada* (1991), while **Pierre Yaméogo**'s *Wendemi* (1992) received several awards at the 1993 FESPACO, after which he went on to direct *Silmande* ("Whirlwind"; 1998) and *Moi et Mon Blanc* ("Me and My White Friend"; 2002), which was shortlisted at FESPACO 2003. The son of a griot, **Dani Kouyaté** weaves the epic adventure of Soundjata with the present-day education of a young boy in *Keita* ("The Heritage of the Griot"; 1995), while his more recent *Sya, Le Rêve du Python* (2000), met with huge acclaim at FESPACO in 2001.

Female film-makers are also beginning to emerge. In 2001, **Fanta Regina Nacro** won first prize for best short film at FESPACO with *Close-up of Bintou*, which explores the survival of a downtrodden housewife against the odds.

Books

There's next to nothing published in English on Burkina – and nothing very digestible in French either. A handful of locally published French-language novels are available in Burkina.

Thomas Sankara *Thomas Sankara Speaks*. Collection of the revolutionary's speeches – worth dipping into to see where the revolution was supposed to be going.

Lars Engberg-Pedersen *Endangering Development: Politics, Projects and Environment in Burkina Faso*. From a development perspective, the Danish author critically examines non-governmental organizations' development practice in Burkina.

Pierre Englebert *La Révolution Burkinabé*. Thorough look at the country's modern history by a political scientist.

Ben O. Nnaji *Blaise Compaoré: The Architect of the Burkina Faso Revolution*. Unashamedly propagandist offering, with some general information on the country.

Robin Sharp *Burkina Faso: New Life for the Sahel*. Published by Oxfam and showing the depth of the country's difficulties without being patronizing.

Malidoma Patrice Some *Of Water and the Spirit*. The autobiography of a Dagari man, born in southern Haute Volta in the late 1950s, who fell into the hands of Jesuit missionaries when he was four and didn't return to his roots until adulthood. Some's descriptions of his initiation and, to put it mildly, unusual experiences back in the Dagari community are recounted with a lucidity and persuasiveness that invite comparison with Carlos Castaneda – and inevitably risk the same criticism of exaggeration. Some is now a cult speaker on the US men's-movement circuit.

Languages

French is the official language of Burkina, although it's estimated that only fifteen percent of the population actually speak it with any degree of fluency – that percentage is noticeably higher in the large towns. The most widely spoken African language is **More**, mother tongue of the Mossi and spoken by over half the population. Other widely spoken languages are **Pulaar**, spoken by the Fula herders of the north, and **Dioula** (Dyula), which has become the major commercial lingua franca spanning most of the borders in this part of West Africa.

A little More

Greetings

Good morning (early)	Neyibeogo
Response	Yibeoog soab yeaala
Further response (men)	Naaba
Further response (women)	Eyn
Good day	Neywindaga
Response	Windg soab yeaala
Good evening	Neywungo
Response	Yung soab
How are you?	Yibeoog yaa laafi?/ Lafi beeme?/ Laafi bala?

Response	Lafi bala		Monday	Fene

Response	Lafi bala		Monday	Fene
Goodbye	Wend na tasse		Tuesday	Falato
See you later	Wend na kodnin daare		Wednesday	Arba
			Thursday	Lamusa
See you tomorrow	Wend na kodbeo go		Friday	Arzuma
Response	Wend na kodbeo go/Ammi		Saturday	Sibri
			Sunday	Hado

Basics

			Numbers	
Excuse me	Ysugri			
Sorry	Ykabre		1	Aye
Thank you	Barka		2	Ayiibu
Yes	Nye		3	Ataabo
No	Ayo		4	Anaase
How much?	Wanwana?		5	Anu
I have no money	Ligidi kabay		6	Ayoobe
Water	Koom		7	Yopoe
			8	Anii
Days			9	Awe
Today	Dunna		10	Piiga
Tomorrow	Beoogo		100	Koabga
Yesterday	Zaame		1000	Tusri
This evening	Zaabre			

Glossary

Américain General term for a missionary, regardless of nationality or religious affiliation. Early missionaries in the region were anglophone Protestants.

Brousse Common West African term for bush or countryside, but to the Mossi it means anywhere outside the Mossi country, especially outside the purlieu of Ouagadougou. Thus someone who has gone to study in Côte d'Ivoire or France is said to be *en brousse*.

Burkinabe (or Burkinabè). A person from Burkina Faso; there is no masculine or feminine form.

Cabaret A rural bar (especially in Lobi country).

CDR (Comités pour la défense de la Révolution). First established by Sankara to implement government policy and organize local affairs on a regional level.

Ghanéenne A popular term for a prostitute, equally insulting to Ghanaian women and to barmaids (most of whom are Ghanaian).

Koure Mossi funeral ceremony.

Kwara Gourounsi chief's sacred insignia, equivalent of a staff of office.

Marabout Muslim holy man who may use his spiritual powers for divination.

Mogho Naba Also spelled Moro Naba; traditional leader of the Mossi people who resides in Ouagadougou. Mogho signifies the traditional cultural realm of Ouagadougou.

Naba King of a Mossi state, and also village chief.

Nassara Common appellation for white people and other foreigners (from "Nazarene").

Ouédraogo The most common surname in Burkina, it's derived from the More *ouefo* (horse) and *raogo* (male). It is the Mogho Naba's name and that of other important political and cultural leaders.

Zaka Round house in the countryside with *banco* walls and thatched conical roof. The plural is *zaksé*.

9.1

Central and northern Burkina

L ying plumb in the centre of Burkina, **Ouagadougou** is an inevitable stop-off point for visitors to the country and a pleasant place to rest up for a few days before heading off to more isolated outposts. Though relatively small for a capital city, it offers a satisfying amount of commercial and cultural activity. Main roads head from here to all major destinations. West of Ouaga, the route to Bobo-Dioulasso is lined with small Mossi towns and villages such as **Sabou**, famed for its sacred crocodile pond, while a branch road leads off to **Koudougou** – the nation's third-largest town and a centre of Burkina's textile industry. The eastern route to Niamey in Niger passes through the **Gourmantché country** and the important market town of **Fada-Ngourma**. Another busy junction along this route is **Koupéla**, where the highway to Dapaong in neighbouring Togo starts its southern course.

Possible trips to **northern Burkina** include the impressive market town of **Gorom-Gorom**, near the point where Burkina, Mali and Niger meet, and through the old **Yatenga state** to the historic town of **Ouahigouya** – an obvious overnight stop if you're heading for the Dogon country in Mali.

Ouagadougou

On the surface, **OUAGADOUGOU** – pronounced "Wagadougou", and routinely abbreviated to "Ouaga" – has little to offer. Capital of one of the world's poorest countries, it seems more like a shambling provincial town than the centrepiece of a nation. Yet despite its unpromising appearance, Ouaga is exceptionally animated. Over the last twenty years, drastic measures have been taken to try to improve the city's image. New roads have been paved, more efficient sewerage systems are being laid and the government has encouraged people to clear the streets of garbage and goats, both of which had become permanent fixtures. As the town modernizes, a number of building projects have materialized, including the enormous BCEAO Bank, whose distinctive tower has even inspired a modernist local style of haircut.

Ouaga is the traditional capital of the **Mossi empire**, but all the country's major ethnic groups, religions and languages coexist here with remarkable harmony. A good number of international organizations, and the nation's only university, are also based in Ouaga. Life moves at a brisk pace, and as a visitor you'll find that contact with the people is as immediate as in any West African city.

Some history

Mossi oral literature traces the beginning of the **Mogho** or **Moro** (the Mossi empire: *Mogho* literally means "the world") to the thirteenth century and a chief named Gbewa or Nédéga who ruled over Pusiga in present-day Ghana. In the course of a battle, Gbewa's daughter, a horsewoman named **Yennenga**, was separated from the clan when her horse took fright and fled into the Bitou woods. She chanced upon the forest's one inhabitant, an elephant hunter named **Rialé** (a corruption of the More words *ri*, "to eat", and *yaré*, "anything", since bush-dwellers ate anything they found). The couple eventually returned to Gambaga and had a baby, which they named **Ouédraogo**, after Yennenga's steed – from *ouefo*, "horse", and *raogo*, "male".

But the territory of Pusiga became overpopulated and Ouédraogo set off with a company of his father's cavalry to conquer the northern territories. He established a kingdom at **Na Ten Kudugo** (Tenkodogo). Much later, Ouédraogo's grandson **Oubri** sought to conquer new territories and founded the statelet of **Oubritenga**, later known as Wogodogo. A grandson of Oubri broke off to form another small state, **Yatenga**, with Ouahigouya as its capital.

The autonomous Mossi states or kingdoms remained remarkably stable for over four centuries, but by the end of the nineteenth century, the French, Germans and British were pressing in on the region. In 1898, the French occupied Wogodogo (which they spelled Ouagadougou), and within a short time subjugated the surrounding empires, which they integrated into their colony of **Haut-Sénégal Niger**. Today, there are still four Mossi kings, whose authority is applied in parallel with that of the Burkinabe state in the kingdoms over which they hold sway.

Arrival and information

Ouagadougou spreads across a considerable area, though the centre is fairly compact. It's officially divided into thirty *secteurs* (like the *arrondissements* of Paris), though you're likely to spend time only in the few at the centre.

The **international airport** is only a couple of kilometers southeast of the central market. Collecting your baggage and going through **customs and immigration** is normally an untraumatic experience, but you'll be asked your place of residence; just say the *RAN Hôtel* or any other that comes to mind. There's a small **bureau de change** at the airport. To **get into town** you'll need to catch a taxi – fares are marked up outside the airport, but double check with the driver. A quick zip up Avenue Yennenga gets you to the centre in a matter of minutes and costs around CFA250 in a shared taxi, or CFA1000 if you hire the entire vehicle.

Arriving **by train** is even more straightforward – the **station** is just a stone's throw from Avenue de la Nation and the *zone commerciale* in the heart of the city. There are several hotels within walking distance of the station, though taxis aren't expensive – worth bearing in mind if you've got a lot of luggage. The main *gare routière*, commonly known as **Ouagarinter**, is some 6km south of the city on the Route de Pô. Again, you'll have no problem finding a shared taxi (around CFA400) to take you into the centre. **Long-distance buses** arrive at the various company terminals dotted around the city – see the map overleaf.

The **Office National du Tourisme Burkinabe** (ONTB) is on Avenue Frobenius, opposite *Oscars* (Mon–Fri 7.30–11.30am & 3–5.30pm; ☎31.19.59, Ⓦwww.ontb.bf). They have a variety of brochures, but are more useful as a place to pick up a photography permit (free).

Orientation and city transport

All major roads in Ouaga seem to start from the **Place des Nations Unies**, with its ironwork globe sculpture. To the east, Avenue de l'Indépendance leads through the **administrative quarter** down to the *style coloniale* **Palais Présidentiel**. The Avenue d'Oubritenga leads off to the northeast, past the **hospital** and on to the **Zone du Bois** (formerly the Bois de Boulogne). This road then joins the main route to Niamey. West of the Place des Nations Unies, Avenue de la Nation passes through the **zone commerciale** and continues to the semi-modern **Maison du Peuple** and **Place de la Révolution** where political gatherings take place. To the

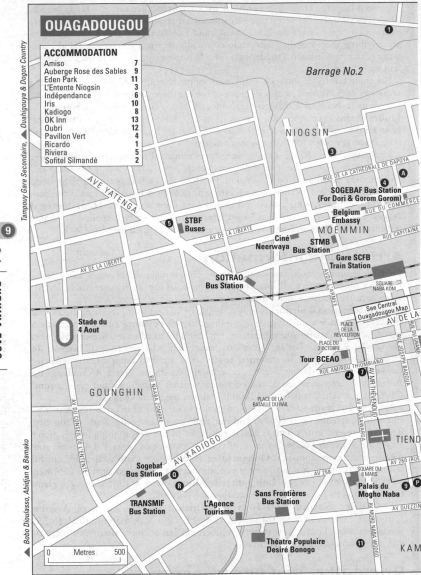

OUAGADOUGOU

ACCOMMODATION

Amiso	7
Auberge Rose des Sables	9
Eden Park	11
L'Entente Niogsin	3
Indépendance	6
Iris	10
Kadiogo	8
OK Inn	13
Oubri	12
Pavillon Vert	4
Ricardo	1
Riviera	5
Sofitel Silmandé	2

Tampouy Gare Secondaire, ▲ *Ouahigouya & Dogon Country*

Barrage No.2

NIOGSIN

AVE YATENGA

RUE DE LA CATHEDRALE DE DAPOYA

SOGEBAF Bus Station
(For Dori & Gorom Gorom)

Belgium
Embassy

RUE DU COMMERCE

STBF
Buses

AV DE LA LIBERTE

MOEMMIN

RUE CAPITAINE

Ciné
Neerwaya

STMB
Bus Station

AV DE LA LIBERTÉ

Gare SCFB
Train Station

AV DE LA LIBERTE

SOTRAO
Bus Station

AV DE L'ARMÉE

SQUARE
NABA KOM

See Central
Ouagadougou Map

AV DE LA

○ **Stade du**
4 Aout

PLACE
DE LA
REVOLUTION

PLACE DU
2 OCTOBRE

Tour BCEAO

RUE AMIROU THIOMBIANO

RUE DU GRAND

RUE JOSEPH BADOUIA

AV MR THEVENOUD

GOUNGHIN

BD NABA ZOMBRE

PLACE DE LA
BATAILLE DU RAIL

AV BASSAWARGA

TIEND

AV OUI CONSEIL DE L'ENTENTE

AV KADIOGO

AV 258

SQUARE DU
8 MARS

AV 260 RUE

Bobo Dioulasso, Abidjan & Bamako ▲

Sogebaf
Bus Station

TRANSMIF
Bus Station

L'Agence
Tourisme

Sans Frontières
Bus Station

Palais du
Mogho Naba

AV MORO NABA WOBGO

AV QUEZZIN

KAM

Théatre Populaire
Desiré Bonogo

0	Metres	500

▼ *Ouaga Camping, Ougarinter (gare routière), Leo, Pô and Ghana*

south, Avenue Kwame Nkrumah runs parallel to Avenue Yennenga. This latter is one of the most animated streets in town, running past the **Grande Mosquée** in a neighbourhood of small *commerçants* before ending near the **airport**.

The town also has distinctive *quartiers*, each with its own flavour. North of the train station, **Moemmin** is the traditional Muslim neighbourhood, home to Ouaga's grand imam and its first mosque. Further north, **Niogsin** is a residential area known

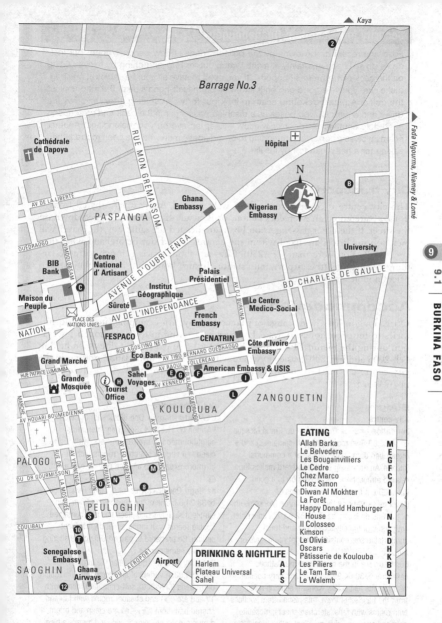

▲ Kaya

Barrage No.3

Cathédrale
de Dapoya

Hôpital

N

▶ Fada Ngourma, Niamey & Lomé

AV DE LA LIBERTÉ

PASPANGA

RUE MON GREMASSOM

Ghana
Embassy

Nigerian
Embassy

University

OUEDRAOGO

AV DIMDOLOBSAM

BIB
Bank

Centre
National
d'Artisant

AVENUE D'OUBRITENGA

Palais
Présidentiel

BD CHARLES DE GAULLE

C

Institut
Géographique

Maison du
Peuple

Sûreté

AV DE L'INDEPENDANCE

French
Embassy

Le Centre
Medico-Social

AV DU BURKINA

PLACE DES
NATIONS UNIES

NATION

FESPACO

6

RUE AGOSTINO NETO

CENATRIN

Côte d'Ivoire
Embassy

Eco Bank

D

AV TIBO

AV BAOUL

BERNARD OUEDRAOGO

FOLLEREAU

Grand Marché

RUE PATRICE LUMUMBA

Sahel
Voyages

E G

F

American Embassy & USIS

I

Grande
Mosquée

i **H**
Tourist
Office

K

AV KENNEDY

AV BLAISE OUEDRAOGO

L

ZANGOUETIN

MARCHE

KOULOUBA

AV HOUARI BOUMEDIENNE

PALOGO

RUE DE

AV YENNENGA

AV DE OUIDIN

AV N'KRUMAH

AV LEO FROBENIUS

AV DE LA RESISTANCE DU 17 MAI

DU DR GOURMISSON

M

LA MOSQUEE

O

N

8

PEULOGHIN

S

COULIBALY

10

T

Senegalese
Embassy

Ghana
Airways

AV DU LAEROPORT

Airport

SAOGHIN

12

DRINKING & NIGHTLIFE

Harlem	**A**
Plateau Universal	**P**
Sahel	**S**

EATING

Allah Barka	**M**
Le Belvedere	**E**
Les Bougainvilliers	**G**
Le Cedre	**F**
Chez Marco	**C**
Chez Simon	**O**
Diwan Al Mokhtar	**I**
La Forêt	**J**
Happy Donald Hamburger House	**N**
Il Colosseo	**L**
Kimson	**R**
Le Olivia	**D**
Oscars	**H**
Pâtisserie de Koulouba	**K**
Les Piliers	**B**
Le Tam Tam	**Q**
Le Walemb	**T**

for its metalworkers, many of whom still work here in small *ateliers*. East of here, **Paspanga** has reputedly the city's best *dolotières* (women who make millet beer, or *dolo*) – bars and small *cabarets* are common here. In the centre, the Avenue Yennenga passes through **Tiendpalogo** and **Peuloghin** – the latter is a Fula neighbourhood with Muslim-style homes and Koranic schools. **Zangouetin**, at the eastern end of Avenue Boumedienne, is a Hausa neighbourhood with a similar feel to Peuloghin.

675

Security and scams in Ouagadougou

Following recent crackdowns by the police, Ouaga is now generally **safe**, but incidents do still happen, mainly at night. Watch out for **bag-snatching** by thieves riding on the back of *mobylettes* (mopeds). If you need to have all your valuables in one bag, make sure you've a good grip on it and walk on the left-hand side of the road against the traffic. A **pick-pocketing** scam to look out for when sharing a taxi involves the driver and a partner, who poses as a disabled passenger in the back and pretends to need help shutting his door or window – keep an eye on your belongings. Another scam involves a con artist pretending to be a diabetic man who has been robbed, then asking for a hefty loan to buy insulin.

City transport

The city centre is compact enough to walk around. Alternatively, shared **taxis** – usually battered green Mercedes saloons or Renault 4Ls – can be flagged down on the street. If the other passengers on board are headed the same way, the driver will pick you up. Prices are fixed within the centre, so find out beforehand what they are (usually not more than CFA250). Fares are about twice as much to more far-flung destinations (the airport, train station, luxury hotels and outer suburbs), and prices double after midnight.

Accommodation

Ouagadougou has a wide range of **places to stay**, from camping sites and dormitories to four-star hotels. Beware, however, of arriving in town without a reservation during the biennial FESPACO film festival (see p.660; next due to be held in Feb 2005 and Feb 2007), as everywhere will be full. Accommodation options in the city centre are marked on the map opposite; others are marked on the map on pp.674–675.

Budget
City centre

Fondation Charles Dufour rue du Grand Mosque ☎30.38.89. Two rooms (not self-contained) and a fifteen-bed dorm, plus the use of a communal kitchen. An appealing small courtyard makes for a relaxed atmosphere, and profits go to a good cause. Dorm beds CFA2500; rooms ❷

Hôtel de la Paix av Yennenga, three blocks south of the Grande Mosquée ☎33.52.93. Friendly hotel with some of the city's cleanest and most comfortable self-contained budget rooms (a/c or fan). ❷

Les Lauriers In the gardens of the Catholic cathedral ☎30.64.90, ☎31.65.90. Very popular with tourists (especially women) seeking refuge from the hassles of town, this place offers spotless twin rooms with fans, starched sheets, mosquito nets and showers, plus excellent-value breakfasts and dinners. ❷

Pension Guigsème av Yennenga, south of the Grande Mosquée. Very basic, cleanish rooms with shared bathroom grouped around a pleasant courtyard – but not cheap enough to make this good value. ❷

Out of the centre

L'Entente Niogsin One block east of av de l'Armée ☎31.55.51. Set in an interesting neighbourhood of bronze-workers, with clean – if slightly shabby – rooms with fan or (more expensive) a/c and private bathroom. ❷

Kadiogo One block west of av de la Résistance ☎33.24.63. One of the cheapest in town, this simple if slightly jaded place has self-contained double rooms with fan in a friendly, pleasant setting. Be prepared to pay extra if you're sharing with the same sex. ❶

Oubri av de la Mosquée, near the airport ☎30.64.83. A variety of accommodation including dorm beds (CFA4800), self-contained rooms with TV and a/c (❸) and cheaper rooms with fan and shared bathroom (❷) – all are clean and bright, if a bit cramped and overpriced, and there's a nice airy terrace.

Pavillon Vert av de la Liberté ☎31.06.11, ⓔ pavillonvert@liptinfor.bf. Popular place with a pleasant courtyard and a range of options, from rooms with shared bathroom to apartments with a/c and private bathroom. The congenial

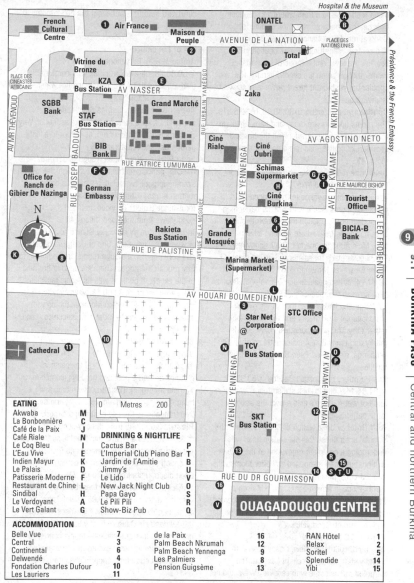

EATING

Akwaba	M
La Bonbonnière	C
Café de la Paix	J
Café Riale	N
Le Coq Bleu	I
L'Eau Vive	E
Indien Mayur	K
Le Palais	D
Patisserie Moderne	F
Restaurant de Chine	L
Sindibal	H
Le Verdoyant	A
Le Vert Galant	G

DRINKING & NIGHTLIFE

Cactus Bar	P
L'Imperial Club Piano Bar	T
Jardin de l'Amitie	B
Jimmy's	U
Le Lido	V
New Jack Night Club	O
Papa Gayo	S
Le Pili Pili	R
Show-Biz Pub	Q

OUAGADOUGOU CENTRE

ACCOMMODATION

Belle Vue	7	de la Paix	16	RAN Hôtel	1
Central	3	Palm Beach Nkrumah	12	Relax	2
Continental	6	Palm Beach Yennenga	9	Soritel	5
Delwendé	4	Les Palmiers	8	Splendide	14
Fondation Charles Dufour	10	Pension Guigsème	13	Yibi	15
Les Lauriers	11				

atmosphere and setting make up for the distance from the centre. ❷

Riviera av Yatenga, near the STBF bus station ☎30.65.59, ℱ30.66.81. Attractive round huts and decent rooms with fan, a pleasant courtyard and nice management. Basic meals available. ❷

Mid-range and expensive
City centre

Belle Vue Corner of av Nkrumah and rue de Palistine ☎30.84.98, ℱ33.00.37. Comfortable, lively and centrally located hotel with slightly shabby self-contained a/c rooms with TV. Also has a rooftop terrace from where you can look over central Ouaga as you drink or dine. ④

Central rue de la Chance ⓣ30.89.24, ⓔh.central@cenatrin.bf. Great location in the heart of the town and a range of comfortable rooms, though some are slightly scruffy. The popular bar-restaurant (great pizzas and cocktails) is always busy. ⑥

Continental av Loudun ⓣ30.86.36, ⓕ30.69.19. The rooms upstairs are dingy and bare, although many have balconies overlooking the bustling commercial centre. Also has a popular dining room. ③

Delwendé rue Lumumba, half a block west of Grande Marché ⓣ30.87.57, ⓔhoteldelwende@yahoo.fr. Over-priced self-contained rooms (some with a/c), no better than the budget hotels, though the streetside rooms have balconies from where you can take in the busy life around the market. The balcony restaurant is a popular place for salads and grilled meat. ③

Palm Beach av Nkrumah ⓣ31.09.91 or 30.87.74, ⓔhotel.palmbeach@liptinfor.bf. Rooms here have all the mod-cons, including a/c, satellite TV, fridge and IDD phone, though the overall atmosphere's a bit dreary and the rooms look rather tatty. The pool (nonguests CFA1500) is murky and uninviting. A sister hotel on av Yennenga, also called *Palm Beach*, has similar facilties. ⑥

Les Palmiers rue Joseph Baddua ⓣ33.33.30, ⓕ31.84.44. Comfortable, stylish rooms with a/c and hot water; there's also a pool the size of a large bathtub. ⑥

RAN Hôtel av de la Nation ⓣ30.61.06. Once the colonial era's finest, this old station hotel was undergoing a complete renovation at the time of writing, but when re-opened will offer rooms with all mod-cons, plus a pool. ⑦

Relax av de la Nation across from Maison du Peuple ⓣ31.32.31, ⓕ30.89.08. Centrally located, upmarket hotel with swimming pool, nightclub, bar and restaurant. Good value. ⑧

Soritel 370 av Nkrumah ⓣ33.04.78, ⓔsoritel@liptinfor.bf. New, classy hotel with friendly staff and an excellent location. The carpeted rooms come with satellite TV, a/c and hot water. ⑦

Splendide av Nkrumah ⓣ31.24.54, ⓔsph@fasonet.bf. Second only to *Silmandé*, this newish hotel offers well-equipped and stylish accommodation, plus a large pool. ⑧

Yibi rue du Gourmission ⓣ30.73.23, ⓔypi@cenatrin.bf. Upmarket hotel in the heart of things. Rooms are immaculate (though the decor's dated) and there's a nice pool in a courtyard setting – but avoid the noisy rooms at the front. ⑥

Out of the centre

Amiso 198 av Thevenoud ⓣ30.86.74, ⓕ30.86.78. Ultra-smart hotel, with comfortable tiled rooms with TV, a/c, phone and hot water – spotless, but sterile. ⑦

Auberge Rose des Sables Saint Leon ⓣ31.30.14, ⓔla.rose.des.sables@fasonet.bf. Very clean rooms, with fan or a/c, next door to a leafy garden bar and restaurant. ④

Eden Park av Moro Naba Wodgo ⓣ31.14.87, ⓔeden_park@cenatrin.bf. Luxury high-rise with swimming pool, nightclub, restaurants and a rooftop terrace. Comfortable though dated furnishings (colour TV, video, minibar) and some good views from the upper floors. ⑥

Indépendance av de la Résistance ⓣ30.60.60, ⓦwww.hotelinde.com. One of Ouaga's top hotels and very popular, although rooms are beginning to fray around the edges. There's a popular bar next to the excellent pool, as well as tennis facilities. ⑥

Iris av Yennenga ⓣ33.00.53, ⓦwww.hotel-iris.com. Smartish and comfortable rooms with spacious bathrooms – most with balconies – and a/c. ⑤

OK Inn About 6km south of the centre, near Ouagarinter and Route de Pô ⓣ37.00.20, ⓕ37.00.23. Relaxing place set in spacious grounds around a pool and gardens (complete with 12-hole mini-golf). The attractive rooms and bungalows come with a/c, colour TV, and there's free transport to the city centre and airport. ⑥

Ricardo 3km north from the city centre ⓣ30.70.72. It's a shame this hotel is so far from the centre, because the comfort and friendly reception are worth the effort of getting there. Good disco, restaurant and pool. ⑥

Sofitel Silmandé 3km northeast of the centre, near the reservoir ⓣ35.60.05, ⓔhotelsilmade@fasonet.bf. One of the few high-rises in town, the *Silmandé* is Ouaga's luxury base, with total comfort and lots of facilities – tennis courts, pool, disco – at prices far in excess of anywhere else. Great views and photo opportunities from the roof. ⑧

Camping

Ouaga Camping Route de Pô, 500m from Ouagarinter and 6km from the centre (it's signposted from the *gare routière*) ⓣ30.48.51. Unfriendly set-up, run-down facilities including hideous communal toilets, but their scruffy courtyard is the only camping option in town. CFA1500 per person.

The City

Ouaga has few sights, though the lure of the **Grand Marché** – once it's rebuilt – will probably draw you back for more than one visit. The small **Musée Nationale** is also worth a look, and when you're through with sightseeing, the shopping possibilities are endless. A satisfying way to get to know Ouaga is to settle at a *café terrasse* and simply observe the town's life as it passes by your table. Once you become known you'll find it easy to make contact with other *habitués*, who always have time for a chat.

The Grand Marché and crafts markets

Sankara razed the old market in 1985, and its replacement, the **Nouveau Grand Marché "Rood Woko"**, was the most modern marketplace in West Africa until it was gutted by fire in May 2003. At the time of writing it's still not clear what the city's plans for its future are, though Ouaga's importance as a trading centre means that the market will always be a huge attraction. The variety of stock ranges from Chinese bicycles to American beauty products and local *gris-gris*. This is by far the best place to shop for fresh **fruit and vegetables**, meat and poultry (live), and cereals. Basketry (of which Burkina produces some of the region's best), like the round multicoloured **baskets** with leather-wrapped handles, are sold beside Asian-made enamel bowls, commonly used for eating throughout Africa. Much of the market is reserved for **fabric sellers**, who sit by stacks of much-prized Holland wax prints, made in the Netherlands, and the slightly less revered "Manchesters", made in England. They also sell quite decent, and substantially cheaper, prints made down the road in Koudougou and Côte d'Ivoire, plus a good selection of indigo tie-dyed cloth from Guinea and Mali. Tailors work inside the market to the hum of lovingly tended, foot-operated sewing machines, and will make clothes to order. They're adept at European styles (shirts, trousers, dresses) if you don't think you'll get much wear out of more African designs. But the best way to get what you want, as always, is to take along a garment to be copied.

A good place to start shopping for **crafts** is at the state-operated **Centre National d'Artisinat d'Art**, 3 av Dimdolobsom (Tues–Fri 8am–noon & 3–6pm, Sat 9–11.30am & 3.30–5.30pm), near the main BIB Bank on the north side of the city centre. The quality of the bronze castings, carvings and weavings is quite good, and prices are fixed, while Burkinabe artists have mastered the exotic **batik** form better than any others in the region, mixing beautiful colours with striking village scenes. Come to get an idea of how much items should be before heading off to bargain in the **Grand Marché** or at the **Vitrine du Bronze**. These latter operators sell from a specially constructed centre on Avenue de la Nation, opposite the French Cultural Centre. Despite signs to the contrary, they don't deal in antiques, but do offer one of the widest selection of **bronzes** in town in addition to other crafts. **Masks**, imported from the Côte d'Ivoire and Mali, may be treated in workshops in Laglin or Dapoya to give them an ancient look, which is often aesthetically effective if nothing else. Other wooden objects include **Senoufo chairs** and **Dogon carvings**. You'll also find jewellery – desert crosses and terracotta beads from Niger for example, and the ubiquitous old glass trade beads.

Some 5km out of town on the Boulevard des Tengsoba next to SIAO, the new **Village Artisanal** is open daily and has a wide selection of crafts on sale in a hassle-free atmosphere. The boutique at the front offers a taste of the quality, at fixed, but very high, prices – far more interesting are the craftsmen working in their shops in the main part of the building.

Try too, the **Centre de Formation Féminine et Artisanale** at the exit of town on the Bobo road (Gounghin district). This is a religious-sponsored organization, where women make a variety of crafts such as Tuareg-inspired **woollen rugs** and less compelling tablecloths and napkins embroidered with African motifs. For **leather goods**, there's the **Centre du Tannage**, 4km from the city centre on the

Fada road opposite the prison; or look out for the Tuareg vendors selling leather boxes and other wares, usually roaming along Avenue de la Nation, particularly in front of *Hôtel Relax*. The Galerie Art et Emballage, 51 av Yennenga, offers a good selection of **masks** and **wooden statues**; a bigger selection, including paintings, carved tables, jewellery and antiques can be found at the Galerie des Arts, 4 av Oubritenga. Finally, **Nuances**, opposite the Zaka Centre in the city centre, is an excellent boutique and gallery selling top-quality arts and crafts in a relaxed atmosphere.

The Musée Nationale

Ouaga's **Musée Nationale** (Tues–Sat 7.30am–12.30pm & 3–5.30pm; CFA1000) is still situated in the Maison du Peuple on Avenue de la Nation pending the construction of its new building on Avenue Charles de Gaulle, due for completion in 2003/2004. Primarily an **ethnographic collection**, it holds various Burkinabe household utensils, tools and weapons. There are numerous **clay pots** on display, including ones made specifically to store clothing, jewellery or grain. Among the most interesting are the magic pots used for keeping medicines – their potency was protected with sacrifices. **Basketmaking** and **weaving exhibits** from around Burkina are complemented by **regional costumes**, including a Mossi **chief's regalia** – compare it with what the Mogho Naba wears on a Friday morning at the *Nabayius Gou* ceremony. A good part of the display is dedicated to sculptures in wood, including **ancestral statues** of the Bobo, Mossi, Lobi and Gourounsi. These are accompanied by carved stools and sceptres (*kwara*) symbolizing the authority of chiefs, and a fantastic collection of **masks** showing different regional styles: abstract and geometric in the north; exaggerated animal shapes in the Senoufo country; cylindrical helmets used by the Mossi; and horizontally shaped *masques papillon* ("butterfly masks") common among the Bobo-Bwa. Depending on the progress of the new building, some of the museum's artefacts may be in boxes ready for transit.

Sankara's grave

After Sankara's assassination (see p.665), his body was relegated to an **unmarked grave** outside the centre. Martyrdom made the leader an international symbol of hope, and people from throughout the continent still make the pilgrimage to his burial site. The route to the grave follows much the same path that the body took –

The Nabayius Gou

Ouagadougou's answer to Buckingham Palace's Changing of the Guard, the **Nabayius Gou** is a re-enactment, every Friday at 7am by the western side of the Mogho Naba's palace, of events that took place in the early eighteenth century, in the reign of Ouarga, the twentieth **Mogho Naba**. During this period, the kingdom's frontiers were under threat by raids from Yako. The Mogho Naba's favourite wife had obtained his permission to visit her family, but she hadn't returned on the agreed date. Heartbroken, he prepared to set out and find her, but his courtiers, fearing war, begged him to stay. With a heavy heart, the king agreed that his duty to his subjects came before personal concerns and, dismounting from his horse, he returned to his palace.

The present-day ceremony reaffirms the Mogho Naba's commitment to his people. The present-day Mogho Naba comes out of his palace, dressed in red for war. His courtiers surround him, begging him to stay, and eventually he heeds their pleas and returns to the palace, to re-emerge in white. This rather solemn affair isn't a spectacle put on for tourists, and needs to be approached with some respect. Nonetheless, it's a fascinating ceremony, and well worth getting up early for. The taking of photographs isn't usually allowed, but you may be able to get special permission by applying (in advance, with a normal photo permit) to the Naba's secretariat.

from the presidential palace, head east along Boulevard Charles de Gaulle for 2.5km, turn right at the Tagui petrol station and head straight on for 1km. To the left, you'll see a large tree behind a row of *banco* houses. Fifty metres east of the tree is a row of white-washed tombs, bearing only the name and rank of those killed in the 1987 coup – among them, Thomas Sankara. Despite the site's isolation, it's not uncommon to find mourners paying their respects, or leaving scribbled notes on the grave.

Eating

Finding good, reasonably priced **places to eat** is no problem in Ouaga. The town is full of small **café terrasses** separated from the dusty streets by brightly painted fences. A host of such places along Avenue Yennenga all serve similar food – spaghetti, rice and meat sauce, couscous, potato stew. Most of them also do large bowls of home-made **yoghurt** – delicious, especially at breakfast when it's freshly made.

The more upmarket restaurants – and there are some very good ones, serving a range of international cuisines – are usually good value, but where the city really excels is at **street food**. In the evenings, the streets fill with **brochette vendors** gathered around the glow of their charcoal fires. You can get beef and lamb, beautifully cooked, but if you want to savour the smoky flavour, be sure to ask for *sans piment*. Kerosene lamps light the tables of *les cafémans* who also emerge in the morning to whip up omelettes and sticky Nescafé concoctions. Finally, Ouaga's **patisseries** are wonderfully lively places to sit eating fattening cakes while watching the world go by.

City centre

All the following are shown on the map on p.677.

Budget

La Bonnnière City centre, av de la Nation. Still the most popular (and pricey) pastry shop in Ouaga, and a great breakfast address. Fresh and flakey croissants to go with juices and yoghurt. The apple turnovers and meat pies are also excellent – but watch out for hassle from the street vendors outside.

Café de la Paix av de Loudun. Mostly African food, with baked chicken a speciality.

Café Riale av Yennenga, one and a half blocks south of the Grande Mosquée. The best of the countless *café terrasses* in the area, with a more extensive menu than most.

Les Lauriers At *Les Lauriers* hostel. Run by the sisters of the Catholic cathedral, this restaurant serves a daily set meal of solid, home-style food with soup, veg, meat and dessert (under CFA1500; servings at noon and 7pm). Book ninety minutes in advance and turn up punctually.

Patisserie Moderne City centre, rue Patrice Lumumba. Well-known bakery – don't be put off by the shabby appearance – and *the* spot for breakfast if you're staying at the *Delwendé* next door.

Sindibal av de Loudun. Set in an attractive thatched outdoor seating area, this is a great spot for snacks like burgers and *chawarmas* at reasonable prices.

Moderate to expensive

Akwaba av Kwame Nkrumah. Excellent African dishes prepared by an Ivoirian cook; a bit on the pricey side, but worth it. Closed Sunday.

Le Coq Bleu av Kwame Nkrumah ☏ 30.01.93. One of the best places in town, this chic restaurant serves excellent French cuisine (mains CFA4000–6000). Closed Tuesdays.

L'Eau Vive av Kwame Nasser ☏ 30.63.03. The most famous restaurant in Ouaga, this is an appealing place where the waitresses (who are also nuns) pause mid-service to belt out *Ave Maria*. More international than French, the menu shifts daily between African, European and American specialities (from CFA3000–5000). There's an attractive shop attached selling clothes and handicrafts; proceeds help fund an orphanage. Closed Sundays.

Indien Mayur av Thevenoud. Reputedly the only Indian restaurant in Ouaga, offering freshly cooked food made with spices imported from the subcontinent (mains CFA4000 plus). Eat in the a/c restaurant or outside in a white canvas tent.

Le Palais 100m southwest of the Place des Nations Unies. Popular and friendly place with a West African menu and Senegalese specialities.

Restaurant de Chine Junction of av Loudun and av Boumedienne ☏31.18.60. Excellent Chinese restaurant with a/c and attractive decor. Expensive but worth it (mains around CFA4000). Closed Tuesday.

Le Verdoyant av Dimdolobsam ☏31.54.07. Unbelievably popular restaurant serving fantastic pizzes, pastas and ice cream in a stylish open-air setting. Prices are moderate (from CFA2200) and the food is excellent value. Make sure you reserve at weekends. Closed Wednesdays.

Le Vert Galant rue Patrice Lumumba ☏30.69.80. This expensive and hugely popular French restaurant features fish and meat dishes accompanied by salads and soups, crêpes and sorbets, plus a small wine list. Around CFA5000 and up for a main course. Closed Sundays and Mondays.

Out of the centre

All the following are shown on the map on pp.674–675.

Budget

Le Cedre av Kennedy. Inexpensive Lebanese restaurant, offering more *chawarmas* and *steak-frites*.

Chez Simon av Kwame Nkrumah. Popular new spot for a variety of snacks (great *chawarmas*, pizzas and burgers), pastries and ice cream.

Happy Donald Hamburger House Peuloghin, av Nkrumah, opposite *Chez Simon*. Serves up reliably tasty and cheap snacks – pizzas, omelettes, sandwiches, burgers and chips – 24 hours a day.

Oscars av Frobenius. Popular with both expats and locals, serving the best ice cream in town, plus a good selection of cakes. You'll struggle to find a seat some evenings.

Pâtisserie de Koulouba av de la Résistance (closed Sun afternoons). Second only to *La Bonbonnière* in popularity, with great pastries, ice cream, sandwiches and omelettes.

La Rose des Sables At the *Auberge Rose des Sables*, St Leon. A sign on av Bassawarga (two blocks north of av Coulibaly) points the way to this popular restaurant, which serves good and inexpensive European food in a sheltered courtyard.

Moderate to expensive

Allah Barka av de la Résistance. Moderately priced African and European specialities (another Ivoirian cook) served in an a/c dining room or in a shaded outdoor eating area. Lunchtimes only; closed Sundays.

Le Belvedere av Raoul Follereau ☏33.64.21. One of Ouaga's fancier restaurants, with a shaded terrace, a/c dining room and a well-established reputation for pizza and other Italian food, complemented by African and Lebanese dishes. Evenings only; closed Tuesdays.

Les Bougainvilliers av John Kennedy ☏31.48.81. Stylish wining and dining with great pizza and pasta in a cosy indoor restaurant or attractive outdoor terrace. Meals from CFA3000.

Chez Marco 12 av Dimdolobsam ☏30.70.83. Good, moderately priced French cuisine which you can eat either on the charming outdoor terrace or in the stylish dining area inside.

Diwan Al Mokhtar av du Burkina ☏33.57.75. Delicious Lebanese dishes plus a range of other European offerings served up by super-attentive staff.

La Forêt av Bassawarga, down a small drive opposite the Groupe Hage building ☏30.72.96. This is a place where well-heeled Ouagalais head for lunch, with good African food – try the *poulet yassa* – served in the seclusion of a pleasant wooded courtyard. There's a private swimming pool attached (CFA1000).

Il Colosseo av Houari Boumedienne ☏25.67.39. Friendly pizzeria with a proper pizza oven heated by an open fire. Evenings only; closed Mondays.

Kimson Off av Quezzin Coulibaly ☏34.03.08. Small and informal Vietnamese restaurant with a sound reputation and popular with expats. Closed Tuesdays.

Le Olivia rue Tibo Bernard Ouedraogo ☏33.58.71. The most expensive place in town, this classy and pretentious restaurant serves impeccably prepared French cuisine, and you can watch your food being cooked in the open-fire oven. Closed Mondays.

Le Piliers Zone du Bois. Out of town and difficult to find, but worth the trek to sample the excellent (and expensive) Italian cuisine with delicious pasta dishes.

Le Tam Tam av Kadioga next to the SOGEBAF station ☏34.71.03. Dishes up a range of Austrian specialities – sauerkraut, sausages, breaded veal and cordon bleu – you never dreamed of seeing in Burkina, all well prepared and not overly pricey. Occasional live music performances in the outdoor courtyard.

Le Walemb Off av Coulibaly, behind the *Hôtel Iris*. Set in a large walled courtyard, and with some of the best African food in town – try the *poulet yassa* or *atieké au poisson*.

Nightlife

One of the few Sahelian towns that's predominantly non-Muslim, Ouagadougou's **nightlife** has a rewarding mix of trendy clubs, lively bars and a good range of cinemas and music venues. Avenue Kwame Nkrumah throbs with packed **clubs** and **bars**, while weekend **live music** and dancing is an added bonus. Cover charges for clubs are never more than CFA4000, but pricey drinks can make for an expensive night out.

As a direct result of FESPACO, Ouaga is full of cinephiles and boasts some great movie theatres, showing some of the very best in new African **cinema**. For **theatre**, it's worth checking out the Théâtre Populaire Desiré Bonogo on Avenue Coulibaly in the southwest of town, which also hosts a biannual theatre **festival** in late November. You might also catch a show at the French Cultural Centre (see p.684) or the Théâtre de la Fraternité (☎36.59.42). You can find out about live music and theatre performances from the noticeboard outside the Zaka Cultural Center on Avenue Yennenga.

Clubs and bars

Cactus Bar City centre, av Nkrumah. Plush a/c bar with Western music, pool tables, pinball, cocktails and burgers.

Harlem rue Henn Guissou, Dapoya Secteur, north of av de la Liberté, Moemmin. Outside courtyard with *paillotes*. Occasional live music and nightly disco sounds. No cover.

L'Imperial Club Piano Bar City centre, av Nkrumah. Piano bar like no other, with red and black loungy decor, and a dimly lit, seedy atmosphere. Live music on Fridays and Saturdays. No cover, but expensive drinks.

Jardin de l'Amitie City centre, near Place des Nations Unies. Very popular garden bar, with live music every night and traditional drumming on Sundays. CFA500 entrance at weekends.

Jimmy's City centre, av Kwame Nkrumah, corner of rue Gourmission. One of the best-established and most popular discos in Ouaga, usually packed out on weekends. CFA2500 entrance at weekends and pricey drinks thereafter. Open from 11pm.

Le Lido City centre, half a block south of *Hôtel de la Paix*. Great location for a drink in a sprawling open-air courtyard with loud music and a vibrant atmosphere. Daily from 10am till late.

New Jack Night Club City centre, av Nkrumah. Linked to the next door *Cactus Bar*, this classy new club is popular with expats. CFA3000 entrance.

Papa Gayo City centre, av Nkrumah, in the same building as *Jimmy's*. Similar to *Jimmy's*, but aimed at an older clientele. Watch out for the Friday night specials, including the occasional foam nights.

Le Pili Pili City centre, av Kwame Nkrumah next to *Jimmy's*. Popular bar in a good position for preclub drinks. Beers are reasonably priced, and they serve pizza.

Plateau Universal Near the *Auberge Rose des Sables*, St Leon. Local drinking bar, with a friendly atmosphere which picks up at night. Simple, cheap meals also available.

Sahel Peuloghin, av Loudun. Vibrant hot spot for live music and dancing, and crowded nightly.

Show-Biz Pub City centre, av Nkrumah. Smart a/c bar with red leather decor and a range of spirits, cocktails and fast food. Occasional karaoke, dancing and video nights.

Cinemas

Ciné Burkina City centre, near the Grande Mosquée. Modern a/c theatre with bar and the newest films. Also try the lively *Zoodo* bar inside.

Ciné Neerwaya Off av de l'Armée, Cité An III. The city's newest a/c theatre, with a big screen and screenings of some African films.

Ciné Oubri City centre, rue Lumumba near the Grand Marché. Outdoor theatre, low prices and generally older films.

Ciné Rialé City centre, rue Lumumba. Another inexpensive indoor theatre showing a variety of films.

Kadiogo Gounghin Nord, near the Lycée St Jean. Indoors, but no a/c. Foreign or "B" films.

Listings

Aid agencies If you want to contact any of the agencies, there's a central bureau for all the NGOs in Burkina, the Secrétariat Permanent des ONG, on ☏36.09.95.

Airlines Air Algérie, av Kwame Nkrumah ☏31.23.01 or 31.23.02, ℉31.56.61; Air Burkina, av de la Nation ☏31.47.05 or 30.76.76, ℉31.31.65; Air France, 493 av de la Nation ☏30.63.65; Air Ivoire, rue Badoua at rue Lumumba ☏30.11.95; Ghana Airways, av Nkrumah near av du l'aéroport ☏30.41.46; Point-Afrique, c/o *Hôtel Pavillon Vert*, av de la Liberté ☏33.16.20.

American Express No official representation, though the BICIA-B Bank on av Kwame Nkrumah will replace lost or stolen cheques if you present receipts.

Banks and exchange The fastest service tends to be at the BIB on av Dimdolobsom off place des Nations Unies, which offers good exchange rates, but you'll have to show receipts for traveller's cheques. BICIA-B, av Kwame Nkrumah, a block east of Ciné Burkina, give Visa cash advances and accept traveller's cheques at their first-floor exchange counter. Finally, Ecobank (open until 4.30pm with no break for lunch) change cash with no commission. If you want to change cash when the banks are closed, and are willing to accept a lower rate, try the counter at the Marina Market on av Yennenga (dollars and euros only) or the bureau de change at the *Hôtel Indépendance*. Try to get the smallest denominations possible when changing money, as change is hard to find in town.

Bicycles and mobylettes The best place to try is the bicycle/moped market next to the cemetery on av Houari Boumedienne, two blocks west of av Yennenga. A new bike costs about CFA115,000, or you can get one secondhand for around half that. You can rent, too – rates are open to negotiation, but range between CFA3000 and CFA6000 per day.

Books and magazines The premier place for books is the Diacfa Librairie on the rue du Marché at the northwest corner of the market. They have a large selection of French titles and a good sampling of the foreign press, plus some maps and travel guides. Also check out the bookshops at the *Indépendance* or the *Silmandé* hotels.

Car rental In Ouaga, typical rates are CFA25,000 per day for a small car, plus around CFA100 per km and an eighteen percent road tax. Chauffeurs, particularly when travelling outside of town, are usually obligatory (CFA5000 per day), although if you pay for insurance (CFA5500 per day) and stay in the city, you may be able to travel without one. All this adds up to about CFA40,000–50,000 per day if you drive 100km or so, but negotiate hard – for longer periods rates can drop to as low as CFA25,000 per day for everything. The two main rental agencies are Burkina Auto Location, at the *Hôtel Indépendance* (☏30.68.11) and Car Location, at the *Hôtel Silmandé* (☏35.60.05). Other agencies include DEZ Auto Location on av Yennenga (☏30.64.56); Ets Derme Abdoulaye (☏30.66.81) and Ada Location next to *Palm Beach Yennenga* (☏33.12.97, ℉33.12.97). Alternatively, **taxis** can be rented in town for about CFA20,000 per eight-hour shift.

Cultural centres The American Cultural Centre (USIS), on av Kennedy near av Houari Boumedienne (Mon–Fri 7.30am–noon & 1–4.30pm; ☏30.17.13), show videos of recent ABC and CBS news along with various films, as well as staging other events. You can pick up a schedule here or at the library (which also has copies of major international newspapers) located across the street from the US Embassy on av Kennedy (Tues–Thurs 9am–noon & 1.30–5pm). The French Cultural Centre (Centre Culturel George Méliès) is on av de la Nation (Tues–Sat 9.30am–noon & 3.30–7pm; ☏30.60.97, ℮ccf@fasonet.bf). With a vast library, exhibition space, open-air theatre, indoor cinema and shaded café featuring live broadcasts of French television and occasional live music, this is the most active cultural centre in Ouaga and an excellent source of information. You can pick up their schedule of events at the big hotels and Marina Market. Finally, the Zaka Cultural Centre, av Yennenga (☏31.53.12 or 31.42.41, ℮zaka@fasonet.bf), has live music nightly, and both open-air and indoor restaurants plus a bar.

Embassies and consulates Canada (handles the affairs of nationals of Commonwealth states in Burkina), av Agostino Neto, west of av de la Résistance ☏31.18.94 or 31.18.95, ℉31.12.00; Côte d'Ivoire, av Raoul Follereau, across from the American Embassy ☏31.36.20 or 31.82.28; France (issues visas for Togo and Mauritania; ℗www.france-burkina.bf), bd de la Révolution, ☏30.67.74, ℉31.41.66; Ghana, av d'Oubritenga ☏30.17.01 or 30.76.35, ℉30.69.60; Mali, av Bassawarga ☏38.19.22 or 30.05.35; Nigeria, av d'Oubritenga ☏30.66.67 or 36.10.87; Senegal, off av Yennenga (at *Hôtel Iris*, go south, turn right at the first street, and it's one-and-a-half blocks on the left) ☏31.28.11, ℮spe@fasonet.bf; UK,

Honorary Consulate, *Hôtel Yibi* ⑦ 30.73.23,
ⓔ ypi@cenatrin.bf; USA, av Raoul Follereau, three
blocks east of av de la Résistance ⑦ 30.67.23 or
31.63.60, ⓕ 31.23.68.

Horse riding The French-owned Cheval
Mandingue (⑦ 34.35.00), on the Bobo road on the
right just before the police barrier, can arrange
riding in the countryside and horseback trips in the
Dogon country in Mali.

Hospital and medical treatment Hôpital Yalgado
Ouédraogo, av d'Oubritenga ⑦ 31.16.55,
ⓕ 31.18.48. The best place for a consultation is Le
Centre Medico-Social de l'Ambassade de France
off bd du Faso (⑦ 30.66.07, ⓔ cms.fr@fasonet.bf).

Internet The best place in town is CENATRIN
(Centre National de Traitement de l'Information) at
876 Boulevard du Faso (CFA200 per 15min). A
more central option is Star Net Corporation, on av
Yennenga (open 24hr; CFA1000 per hour).

Maps The Institut Géographique du Burkina, av de
l'Indépendance (⑦ 32.48.23 or 32.48.24,
ⓦ www.igb.bf), has a variety of decent maps,
including outdated (1991) city maps of Ouaga and
Bobo (CFA1500 each), plus a good, more recent
national map with routes (CFA3250), and detailed
topographic maps (CFA3250) – useful if you're
heading off the beaten track.

Pharmacies Two central pharmacies are
Pharmacie de Yennenga (⑦ 37.03.37) and
Pharmacie du Sud (⑦ 30.65.37), both on av
Yennenga.

Photography Many places in the centre develop
black-and-white or colour film – some offer a
same-day service, including Photo Olympia on av
Loudun, across from Ciné Burkina. To buy film, try
Photo Vision, opposite the *Hôtel Central*; Photo
Optique, off av Loudun one block west of Ciné
Burkina; or Photo Lux, on av Lumumba across
from the Ciné Oubri. Photography permits are
obtainable from the Office National du Tourisme
Burkinabe (ONTB) on av Frobenius, opposite
Oscars (Mon–Fri 7.30–11.30am & 3–5.30pm;
⑦ 31.19.59, ⓦ www.ontb.bf), a process which
normally takes no more than five minutes and
costs nothing.

Post office The main PTT is on av de la Nation,
just west of Place des Nations Unies (Mon–Fri 7am
to noon & 3–5.30pm, Sat 8am to noon).

Supermarkets The Marina Market (open daily
until at least 9pm), on av Yennenga across from
the Grande Mosquée, is probably the best stocked
in town. Cobodium, on av de la Nation across from
the Maison du Peuple, and Scimas, where av
Yennenga meets rue Lumumba, are also well
stocked.

Swimming pools One of the cheapest is at *La
Forêt* restaurant on av Bassawarga (CFA1000;
Mon–Fri 9am–6pm). Of the hotels, the
Indépendance's pool is central and clean
(CFA1500); if you're prepared to trek out to
Ricardo's, they also have an excellent and good-
value pool and terrace (CFA1500). The best and
most expensive (CFA2500) pool is at the *Hôtel
Sofitel Silmandé*.

Telephones The ONATEL–Agence building, three
doors down from the main post office on av de la
Nation (daily 7am–5pm), sells magnetic *télécartes*
which can be used in booths outside the building,
as well as in the *Hôtel Indépendance* and Ciné
Burkina. You can also send telexes and faxes from
ONATEL (Mon–Fri 7am to noon & 3–5pm).

Travel agents Besides national excursions to
places like the Lobi country, the southern Sahel
and the reserves, larger operators arrange
interesting treks to the Dogon country and
Timbuktu in Mali, to Togo, Côte d'Ivoire, Ghana and
Benin. The major ones are: Vacances OK Raid, av
Nkrumah ⑦ 37.00.20; L'Agence Tourisme, av
Coulibly ⑦ 34.13.20,
ⓔ agence.wbtourisme@cenatrin.bf; Globe
Voyages, av Loudun next to BICIAB ⑦ 30.58.98,
ⓕ 30.87.94; Kenedia Travel, 1029 av Kwame
Nkrumah ⑦ 31.59.70, ⓕ 31.59.70; Sahel Voyages,
608 av de la Résistance in the RDC building
⑦ 31.53.45, ⓕ 31.35.04; Savanna Tour
⑦ 33.73.01; Meycom Voyages ⑦ 33.09.83,
ⓔ meycom@fasonet.bf.

Visa extensions Visa extensions are processed at
the Service Passport (most taxi drivers know this)
at the Immigration Services on the road to Bobo
(7am–noon & 3–5pm; ⑦ 34.26.43). They cost
CFA10,000 for up to three months, CFA20,000 for
up to twelve months.

Western Union Money transfers can be made at
the main PTT on av de la Nation and at most major
banks in town.

From Ouaga to Koudougou

Just west of Ouaga, the road to Koudougou passes through the small town of
Tanguen-Dassouri, which has a lively market every three days. From here a
piste leads 6km north to **BESOULÉ**, a friendly village renowned for its sacred

Buses

Various bus companies provide services from Ouaga to every conceivable national and international destination (though at the time of writing the border with Côte d'Ivoire had been closed since October 2202). Major companies are:

Sans Frontières av Coulibaly, across from the Théâtre Populaire in Bilbalogho district ☏32.20.18 or 30.46.75. Services, currently suspended, are due to resume in 2003 with new buses. It's intended to run three buses daily to Abidjan via Yamassoukro – quicker than the train, unless you don't manage to clear customs by midnight and have to sleep in your seat at the border (not unheard of). They also plan three daily buses to Bobo (CFA5000), and two daily to Ouahigouya (CFA2500) and Kaya (CFA1500). A Djibo-bound bus will leave daily (CFA4000).

SOGEBAF av Kadiogo at bd Naaba Zombre in Gounghin district ☏34.42.55. Buses leave for Bobo-Dioulasso (9 daily; CFA5000), Banfora (5 daily; CFA5500), Ouahigouya (7 daily; CFA2500) and Cinkansé (2 daily; CFA4000). Buses for northern destinations such as Dori (2 daily; CFA4000) and Djibo (7 daily; CFA4000) and Gorom-Gorom (1 weekly departing Wed; CFA5000) leave from a separate station, between av de la Liberté and rue du Commerce.

STC av Houari Boumedienne ☏30.87.50. The Ghanaian State Transport Corporation provides three coaches a week to Accra (CFA10,500) with stops at Pô, Bolgatanga, Tamale and Kumasi (although you have to pay the full fare for either Kumasi or Accra). Book your tickets in advance. Departures are at 8.30am (Mon, Wed and Fri); buses depart from Ouagarinter *gare routière*.

STBF av Yatenga ☏31.27.95. Buses depart for Bobo-Dioulasso (4 daily; CFA5000), Bamako and Mopti in Mali (2 daily; CFA14,500), and Abidjian (2 weekly; CFA18,000).

STMB between rue de Commerce and av Cpt. Ouedraogo (☏31.13.63, ⓦwww.stmb2000.com). Perhaps the most reliable company, with six daily buses (two a/c) to Bobo (CFA5000–7000), plus services to Ouahigouya, Dori, Gorom-Gorom, Pô, Banfora, Fada and other locations. STMB also run a metered taxi-service (you can call one on ☏30.89.90), though these are more expensive than ordinary taxis.

Other useful bus companies include: **SOTRAO**, bd Charles de Gaulle ☏30.42.96 (buses to Gaoua, Pô and Djibo); **STAF**, rue Joseph Baddua ☏30.19.21 (Ouahigouya); **TRANSMIF**, av Kadiogo ☏34.29.35 (daily to Gaoua via Diébougou); **TCV**, av Yennenga, south of *Palm Beach Yennega* (Bobo and Bamako, Fada-Ngourma, Koupela and

crocodiles. You'll be expected to pay a small fee (around CFA2000; be prepared to bargain) and the cost of a chicken; in return, you'll be shown where the crocodiles (*caïmans*) live – the chicken is used to lure the crocodiles onto land, and the prospect of food apparently keeps them from taking bites out of visiting tourists. After sacrificing the chicken, you can touch and photograph the reptiles (the oldest male is the most docile). There's no public transport from Tanguin-Dassouri to Besoulé, and the place is much less visited than **SABOU** – about 90km further down the main road towards Bobo – whose **crocodile pool** is a staple destination for tour operators. Sabou has become a ghastly tourist trap, although at least it's in a pleasant setting and has a modest *campement* (CFA4000).

West of Sabou, you may see **elephants** – your chances are greatly increased if you have your own transport and time to turn off the main highway. They're to be found in the vicinity of the **Deux Balés National Park**, named after the Petit Balé and Grand Balé rivers. The best opportunities are around POURA, reached down a dirt road leading south off the highway about 25km east of the small town of **Boromo** (itself 90km west of Sabou). At the Poura junction there's a small huddle of roadside stalls and businesses where you may well find a guide. Alternatively, ask in Boromo itself, where you can stay at the very basic *Relais*

Cotonou); **Rakieta**, rue de la Palistine ☎31.40.56 (Bobo and Banfora); **SKV**, av de Loudun ☎31.22.61 (Gaoau and Lomé); and **KZA**, av Nasser ☎30.03.47 (Koudougou).

Official taxi brousse stations

Taxis from the **Ouagarinter gare routière** leave for Lomé (CFA12,500), Niamey (CFA8100), Abidjan (CFA14,000), Dapoang in northern Togo (CFA7500) and Bolgatanga in Ghana (CFA4000). Ouagarinter also serves most destinations in Burkina.

Northern towns like Djibo and Ouahigouya are served by the **Tampouy gare secondaire** on Avenue Yatenga, just north of the railway tracks and 4km from the city centre. You can even get to Bobo, Kaya and Dori from here.

Unofficial taxi brousse stations

There are also several **unofficial stations** in town, which are subject to closure by the police (not that the vehicles themselves are in any way illegal). There's a fairly well-established station at the **Total station** near the Zaka Cultural Centre, southwest of Place des Nations Unies. Taxis collect fares here for Lomé and to the eastern towns on the road to Fada. For some unknown reason, Lomé taxis are about thirty percent cheaper from this station than from Ouagarinter. Also check at the service station across the road for other destinations.

If you're heading to Bobo, Diebougou, Gaoua and Léo it's worth checking the station on **Avenue Kadiogo** at Avenue de l'Entente (across from the Elf station).

Trains

The French-run company Sitarail (☎31.07.35, ☎30.77.49) runs trains **to Abidjan** in Côte d'Ivoire via Koudougou, Bobo, Banfora. Services depart on Tuesdays, Thursdays and Saturdays at 8.30am, arriving in Bobo at 2.30pm (CFA5800 second class) and Banfora at 4.12pm (CFA7400 second class), returning from Abidjan the next day. Trains are comfortable, but often late. There's also a service **to Kaya**, departing once a week on Saturday around 8am. Schedules change, however, so check at the station.

Planes

Air Burkina (☎31.47.05, ✉de2j@fasonet.bf) operates flights **to Bobo** five times a week, every day except Mondays and Wednesdays; the 40–50-minute flight costs CFA31,900.

Touristique (☎53.80.84; ❷). The impressive *Campement Touristique Le Kaïcedra* (☎21.26.91; ❹), 7km away, is a better option.

Koudougou

Before reaching Sabou, the main road to Bobo branches in the direction of **KOUDOUGOU**, Burkina Faso's third-largest town. It's a quiet place with wide tree-lined avenues, though a certain degree of liveliness is assured by the presence of the country's largest textile factory, **Faso Fani**, and no less than three secondary schools (*collèges*). Koudougou was also the hometown of the first president of Upper Volta, Maurice Yaméogo.

The **market** is especially good for its fruit – mangoes, pineapples, avocados, bananas – as well as vegetables and cereals. There's a reasonable selection of **handicrafts**: woven goods (hats and baskets), leather (handbags, wallets and shoes) and pottery (jugs and bowls of all sizes). You'll find ready-to-wear outfits made from locally hand-woven and embroidered cloth. At the time of writing the central market was being renovated and wares were temporarily being sold from stalls along the Ouaga road. There's a superb **bronze maker** in

Koudougou – seek out Gandema Mamadou's shop in Secteur 7 if you're interested in buying.

Practicalities

Koudougou boasts a variety of **places to stay**. The centrally located *Oasis*, near the market, is the newest and one of the cheapest options, with bare rooms with fans or a/c (②); whilst the relatively pleasant *Relais de la Gare* (☏44.01.38; ②), 100m from the train station, houses a decaying bar with a blaring TV and clean self-contained rooms with fans. The friendly *Yelba Central* (☏44.09.89; ②), on the same street as the old mosque, has clean rooms (some with a/c) with shared bathrooms, but is looking a little run-down. A step up and a much smarter option is *Toulourou* (☏44.01.70; ③), down a dirt track across from Ciné Yam, which has comfortable self-contained rooms, some with a/c, plus a European-style restaurant serving good, reasonably priced African and continental meals. *Photo-Luxe*, on the eastern edge of town by the junction with the road to Ouaga (☏44.00.88; ③), has seen better days but still has clean self-contained, a/c rooms and a good bar, restaurant and nightclub (open Sat; entrance CFA1500). If you don't mind the trek, there are two good hotels further out on the road to Ouaga, the *Bonne Sejour* (☏44.46.80; ②) and *Hôtel Denver* (☏44.18.83; ②), both with clean, attractive, self-contained rooms in quieter settings than the more central hotels. Finally, 1.5km out on the other side of town past the lake, on the Dégoudou road, *Esperance Plus* (☏44.05.59; ①) offers great-value clean rooms with showers and sinks.

Apart from the hotel restaurants, there's plenty of **street food** near the market or at the train station. A Koudougou speciality is *pintade* (guinea fowl) which you see being grilled on roadside braziers in the evening. Also worth a try is the array of cheap local food at the *Jardin d'Eden*, set back from the road across from Ciné Yam, at *Wend n Guudi* near the KZA bus station, and *Del-Wende's* near the train staion.

For evening entertainment, you could catch a Burkinabe film at the **Ciné Yam**, north of the market near the mosque. The town also boasts an impressive **théâtre populaire** out west beyond the Palais de Justice. Koudougou has its own troupe that puts on periodic performances (mostly in More) at the theatre – worth seeing if you're in town at the right moment. On other nights, the theatre doubles as an open-air **cinema**. Good **discos** in town include the popular *Leader Bar Dancing* on the Ouaga road, which also serves African food; and the equally lively and colour-fully painted *Au Joie du Peuple*, set around a courtyard in the north of town. For a daytime or evening drink, try *La Bache Bleue* on the main road to Ouaga.

Changing money is far easier in Bobo or Ouaga. The Koudougou BICIA-B changes cash (euros only); the BIB requires you to provide a local address (not a hotel), and even then they will only change American Express. There are several **Internet** cafés around town, and a **post office**, near the STKF station west of the market.

Moving on, a **train** leaves Koudougou on Tuesdays, Thursdays and Saturdays for Bobo and on Wednesdays, Fridays and Sundays for Ouaga. **Bush taxis** for Ouaga and the north leave from near the market, although for Ouaga it's better to take one of the frequent **buses** operated by STKF, which leave from just west of the market, or Rayi's and KZA, who depart from stations east of the market near the mosque. Bush taxis to Bobo and the Côte d'Ivoire leave from the *autogare* near the train station; Rayi's have a bus service to Bobo twice a day.

From Ouaga east to Fada-Ngourma

The route to Niamey runs from Ouagadougou through the **Gourmantché coun-try**. The first town of any size on this road is lively **KOUPÉLA**, on the main road to Togo. The town has a large daily **market** renowned for its pottery (which is concentrated around the southern end). There's also a small *centre artisanal* at the junction of the Ouaga and Togo roads, with a very limited selection of leather and weaving by artisans with disabilities. There's a BICIA-B **bank** opposite the *centre artisanal*, though there's no guarantee that they'll change traveller's cheques.

If you want to **stay the night** in Koupéla, there are several options. The *campement* (☎70.01.33; ❷) on the main Ouaga road has a bar, restaurant and basic self-contained rooms, some with a/c. Better value is the *Calypso* next door (☎70.03.50; ❶), which has very clean rooms with showers and grubby communal toilets – if you can stand the noise from the adjoining bar. Other options include the clean and good-value *Wend Waogo* near the BICIA-B bank (☎70.01.64; ❶), and the *Hôtel de la Gare*, opposite the *gare routière* (☎70.03.52; ❶). If you want to escape the constant activity and noise of town, the best option is the *Mission Catholique* in the Centre Zacharie Nikiema behind the church (☎82.24.35; ❷), which has spotless doubles with showers (some also have a/c).

Food is no problem. Countless vendors line the streets waiting for taxis and buses to roll in. Buy a grilled *pintade*, take it to the *Amicale Bar* on the eastern edge of the market, and wash it down with a cold Brakina, or buy good grilled fish from just outside the *campement* and eat it in the bar there. On the same road, there's a couple of bar-restaurants – *Neeb Nooma* and *Welcome* – right next to each other, and both serving local dishes; *Café Copa Cabana*, next to *Hôtel de la Gare*, is a lively bar.

Fada-Ngourma and beyond

Midway between Niamey and Ouagadougou, **Fada-Ngourma** is another of Burkina's junction towns, the eighth largest in the country. The town was founded by Diaba Lompo, who is variously claimed to be the son, maternal uncle or cousin of Ouédraogo. Fada is a pleasant, tranquil place, and hosts a colourful **market** with a wealth of goods from across the Sahel region. The beautifully woven **blankets** and **rugs** on sale are invariably better buys here than in Ouagadougou. The town was originally called Bingo, meaning a slave settlement, but Fada-Ngourma is a Hausa appellation, mysteriously meaning "The place where you don't pay tax". It happens to be twinned with Epernay, the champagne capital of France – a more unlikely match would be hard to imagine.

Practicalities

For **places to stay**, *Auberge Liberté*, conveniently located not far from the STMB bus station on the Niamey road, has cheap and grubby rooms with shared bath (☎81.02.17; ❶). A step up is the *Auberge Yemmamma* (☎77.00.39; ❷), again not far from STMB and nearer the market, which has clean, plain – though slightly overpriced – rooms with fan or a/c, plus a good restaurant serving the likes of grilled chicken and chips. Out on the road to Niamey some 800m from the market, the *L'Avenir* offers clean and comfortable self-contained rooms and a courtyard bar and restaurant (☎77.04.09; ❷). On the same road you'll find *Panache*, the newest and smartest place to stay in town with a/c rooms with TV and phone (☎77.03.73; ❹). For **eating and drinking**, *Caraibes*, in front of the *Panache*, is a popular and lively drinking spot, serving simple meals. The best place in town is the *Restaurant de l'Est*, some 200m from here as you walk towards town, set inside a quiet walled courtyard and serving European dishes for around CFA2000. If you're in the mood for **dancing**, try *Le Kasalak's*, near the *L'Avenir* (Fri–Sun; entrance CFA1000).

The BIB **bank** will change cash euros and traveller's cheques (if you can show purchase receipts). You'll find the small **autogare** on the main road near the modern, particularly strange-looking cathedral; there are direct, frequent departures for Ouagadougou and Niamey, and less regular vehicles for Pama. STMB buses (☎77.06.94) leave for Ouaga five times a day and for Kantchari and Diapaga once a day; TCV have daily services to Ouaga and Pama; and SOTRAO run to Niamey on Fridays and Tanguiéta (Benin) on Sundays.

From Fada, a decent road heads to the Benin border past the worthwhile **Parc National d'Arli** (open mid-Dec to mid-May; CFA5000), home to a variety of wildlife including lions, hippos and elephants. You can **stay** at the village of **PAMA** at the central and characterful *Campement Bonazza* (aka *Safari Bonazza*), an ex-Italian colonial set-up, where the house is adorned with impressive hunting memorabilia, including black-and-white photos of the ex-proprietor's prize lion kills. The pool's empty and there's no electricity, but the rooms (**❶**) are spotless and great value, and you can also camp here. Some 15km west of Pama in the town of Kompienga, *La Kompienga* (**☎**31.84.43, **🖰**www.agence-tourisme.com; **❺**) is an upmarket option with its own pool and tennis courts. An attractive alternative is the *Auberge de l'Ile* at Tagou (about 14km west of Pama; **❺**; open mid-Dec to mid-May only), with great lake views, a pool and restaurant.

Both SOTRAO and TCV run **buses** to Pama from Ouaga, stopping at Fada en route, but onward transport south from Pama is extremely sporadic unless you coincide with the Sunday TCV service to Cotonou. If you're **driving** – and there's really no other way of exploring the park – you might do better to continue on the Ouaga–Niamey road to **Kantchari** and then skirt south through **Diapaga** – where there's a hunting lodge (*campement de chasse*; **❹**) – to **Arli** village and the *Safari Hôtel* (**☎**31.84.43, **🖰**www.agence-tourisme.com; **❹**), which is the base for game-viewing trips around the park.

Northeast from Ouaga to Gorom-Gorom

Until recently the 300 kilometres of dirt roads and tracks separating Ouaga from the remote outpost of **Gorom-Gorom** in the **Sahel** took a considerable time to cover, even in the dry season. Now the road is paved as far as **Dori**, making it a relatively easy journey from the capital. Along the way you'll notice a change in the peoples as Mossi-speakers give way to northerners – principally Fula, Tuareg and Bella – and the Muslim influence becomes more predominant. The vast majority of the people of the north are farmers and herders, whose livelihoods are especially sensitive to the drought conditions that continue to threaten the country.

From Ouagadougou to Kaya

The route to Kaya passes a couple of villages which have important roles in Mossi tradition. Whenever the Mogho Naba dies, a **blacksmith** is sent to the Muslim fief of **Loumbila**, and confined there for three years in order to cast a bronze effigy of the deceased ruler. Since the death of Ouédraogo, thirty-six sets of five statues (each representing the Mogho Naba, one of his wives, a servant and two musicians) have been cast, and are carefully guarded in the chief's compound. The other village, nearby **Guilongou**, marks the spot where, according to Mossi legend, pottery was first invented. It's still an important industry here.

Kaya

KAYA, 98km from Ouaga, is the last major Mossi town on the road north. The flourishing **market** here sells many of the **crafts** for which the region is known; there are weavers and tanners in town, and more pour in from neighbouring villages to sell their wares. This is the place to buy leatherwork.

From Kaya a weekly **train** leaves for Ouagadougou on Saturday afternoons; STMB and SOGEBAF **buses** stop here en route to and from Dori, while Sans Frontières (when it reopens in late 2003) also operate two daily buses between Kaya and the capital.

Market days in the Burkinabe Sahel

Market days north of the Djibo–Dori road follow a predictable weekly pattern – useful to know whether you're interested in coinciding with a market or if you simply want to use bush taxis, which usually only run on market days.

Monday Markoye, Tongomayél
Tuesday Bani, Yalogo
Wednesday Djibo, Ti-n-Akof
Thursday Gorom-Gorom
Friday Dori
Saturday Aribinda, Déou, Falagountou
Sunday Oursi, Assakana

From Kaya to Dori and Djibo

Sixty-eight kilometres beyond Kaya, the town of **Tougouri** marks the northern limits of the Mossi country. A short distance further on is **Yalogo**, a Fula village with a large Tuesday **market**. Another 60km brings you to the Islamic stronghold of **Bani**, whose solid, large mud-brick mosque stands out among the numerous other minarets that push against the side of a hill; there's also an important regional market here every Tuesday.

Dori

Despite its small size, **DORI** is an important administrative centre. The BIB **bank** near the market changes euros and traveller's cheques, and there's an **Internet** café, Cyber Contact Service, right next door. The town also boasts a few **accommodation** options. The most popular is the *Sahel Hébergement* (☎46.07.04; ❶), 2km east of the town centre, which has rooms with or without bath (all with fan) plus a lively bar with satellite TV. Not far from here is the more upmarket *Oasis du Sahel* (☎46.03.29; ❹), originally built to house Italian workers building the road from Ouaga; however, the "villas" with a/c and hot water are rapidly declining, and the whole place lacks atmosphere. Some 600m west back towards the centre of town, *Accueil Bunbon* (☎46.02.66; ❶) is a good standby with basic but clean rooms (shared bathrooms); food is available on request. Most locals, however, will point you to the more central and well-known (but less appealing) *Auberge Populaire* (☎46.07.11; ❶), which has fanless huts in a scruffy compound. If you do want to stay out of town, the Fomtugol Association, based at the youth cultural centre not far from the SOGEBAF station, can help arrange homestays with Peul families (CFA7500) and excursions to nearby Sahelian villages. If you time it right, you might also catch a rehearsal by **Fomtugol**, an internationally acclaimed dance and theatre troupe.

Dori's **market day** is Friday and, just as reported by the German explorer Heinrich Barth – who passed through in July 1853 – it's really good for blankets. They have a variety of styles and prices, those woven from camel hair being the most expensive. Also worth a visit is the Artisanal Groupement Féminin, 200m from *Sahel Hébergement* – a huge array of napkins, tablecloths, aprons and bags, which are said to be sold as far afield as France.

Djibo

From Dori, a rough but pretty route runs across a barren landscape to **DJIBO**, about 180km west. Founded in the sixteenth century, the town became capital of the Peulh (Fula) kingdom of Djilgodji, then, in the nineteenth century, came under the control of the Muslim state of Masina, in present-day Mali. Little evidence of this past remains, however, outside the handed-down memories of a few old men and women. Djibo today is a livestock market, at the mercy of the encroaching desert. The *Auberge Populaire* (**①**), 1km out of town on the Ouaga road, serves food and has bare rooms with standing fans in a large scruffy compound. The only other option is the overpriced *Hôtel Massa* (☎55.10.06; **①**) in the centre of town, which has basic doubles with shared facilities. For **eating**, there's inexpensive chicken and rice at *215* and *La Causette*, both of which are near the market in the town centre. *Mimi-Laiterie Kosam*, near *La Causette*, serves good fresh yoghurt.

STMB have a **bus** service linking Djibo with Dori on Tuesday and Thursday mornings at 9am (roughly 6hr). Djibo is also accessible on the twice-daily STMB bus from Ouahigouya (☎55.00.59), and on the twice-daily SOGEBAF service from Ouaga (☎55.07.31) – the latter route travels along a newly improved *piste* via **KONGOUSSI**. If you want to break the journey here, the central *Ambiance* (**①**) has basic rooms with shared bathroom; while the nicer *Hôtel Bar-du-Lac*, a five-minute walk from the centre near the lake, has rooms with fan or a/c (**①**) and the liveliest bar-restaurant in town.

Gorom-Gorom

Fifty-three kilometres of lousy earth road separate Dori from **GOROM-GOROM**, a large Sahelian village with a **market** – one of the biggest in the north – that draws a vast array of northern peoples. Tuareg, Fula and Bella nomads trek into the mostly Songhai-run market on Thursday, the main trading day. In addition to foodstuffs, you'll find a variety of leather goods, jewellery and textiles, all produced locally (though it's possible that the main market will be moved into a modern new concrete building in the next few years). A short distance away, camels, goats, sheep and donkeys are bought and sold at the **animal market**. The village itself remains a picturesque blend of *banco* houses and narrow dusty streets dotted with numerous mosques.

Practicalities

Upon arrival in Gorom-Gorom, tourists should theoretically visit the police station to register and pay their *touristique tax* (CFA1000 per person per day) and – so long as you have the necessary photography permit from Ouaga – an extra CFA5000 camera fee must be paid at the Mairie (if you don't have the permit from Ouaga, you're technically not supposed to take any photos). Some visitors adhere to this system; others don't, and appear to suffer no problems as a result.

The most popular **place to stay** is the *Auberge Populaire* (☎46.94.18; **②**) at the entrance to town on the road from Dori, which has cleanish accommodation (no fans) set around a busy courtyard where locals eat, drink and watch TV, especially on the eve of market day. The homely *Mission Catholique* (☎46.92.57), opposite the church behind the square, offers beds in fan-less dormitories (CFA2500 per person). The recently opened *Campement Tondikara* (CFA3000), a ten-minute walk from the main drag, is a decent option; rooms have showers and mosquito nets, and there's a shared kitchen. Nearby you'll find the tragically deteriorating *Campement l'Hôtel* (no electricity; CFA6500), once "the cornerstone of a different kind of tourism based on dialogue and exchange" modeled on a Sahelian village, but now the dilapidated dormitory and rooms are very over-priced. Directly opposite, a spanking new, upmarket establishment is currently under construction – this is likely to be the best accommodation in town when it opens in 2004, with plush a/c rooms and a pricey restaurant. *Le Kawar* is a recommended locals' **restaurant** opposite the old cinema, serving tasty and inexpensive fare like macaroni and *riz gras*.

Numerous self-appointed "guides" will try to convince you to take a **camel trek** out to the surrounding villages, with a night's camping out in the sands. It's an enjoyable experience, although one that can be expensive. The starting price for a guide is CFA15,000 per person including food, plus a guiding fee of CFA10,000 for the group. Alternatively you can do a shorter, three-hour camel

△ Small bar, Gaoua

trip to the village of Menegou, some 12km from Gorom-Gorom (CFA8000 per person plus CFA5000 guiding fee per group). All fees are highly negotiable. If you've got your own 4WD transport, it's worth driving to the sand dunes at **Oursi**, a two-hour drive from Gorom – or you could rent a 4WD vehicle and driver for the day (CFA45,000 including a guide, but excluding fuel). The **Mare d'Oursi**, near the dunes, is a vast watering hole which attracts herders and livestock from throughout the region – an amazing sight in such a dry and barren region. The dunes themselves offer a picturesque foretaste of the Sahara. Ask any of the small kids from Oursi village for directions.

SOGEBAF **buses** leave from the *gare routière* for Ouaga via Dori and Kaya on Thursdays (10am & 2pm) and Mondays (11am & 4pm); STMB also depart for Ouaga on Thursdays (10.30am). For details of routes on **into Niger** see p.970; *taxis brousse* also head off for **Mopti** in Mali.

Ouahigouya and the Yatenga state

Bone dry but historically important, **Ouahigouya** (pronounced "Weegooya") is the capital of northern Burkina. It was founded in the eighteenth century as capital of **Yatenga**, the northernmost Mossi kingdom, which had broken away from Ouagadougou some three hundred years before. It's a relaxed and pleasant place to mooch around, perhaps dallying in its large market, or taking in some of the 37 picturesque mosques. Most of Yatenga's sights, however, lie outside the city in the villages: its former capitals at **La** and **Gourcy** in the south; the burial sites of many of its *nabas* at **Somniaga**; and the region's most impressive mosques at **Ramatoulaye** to the west, and **Yako** to the south. All these places are worth a look, but you'll be back in Ouahigouya by sunset if you value cold beer and music.

The **Yatenga region** is an arid, undulating plateau, barren for most of the year. The rains in May cover the earth in a green carpet that lasts until October, during which time the region's main crops – particularly millet and sorghum, but also maize, cotton, groundnuts and indigo – are sown and harvested. Outside this season, Yatenga reverts to a scrubby savanna of tree-dotted thornbush – shea-nut, *neré* (carob) and false mahogany trees – with tamarind and types of plum (*nobega*) and fig (*kankanga*) among the wild fruits. The animal life is unimpressive (there was still the odd lion in the region fifty years ago, but you'd be lucky to see as much as a gazelle today), but **birds** are much in evidence – especially vultures, which seem even more overbearing here than in the rest of Burkina. A good deal more agreeable are the electric-blue **Abyssinian roller birds**, perched on telegraph wires in the barren landscape, like travellers' heralds.

Ouahigouya

OUAHIGOUYA's wide streets and low buildings impart a lazy feeling of space, especially after the dust and shimmering heat of day. The market sprawls, the *auto-gare* sprawls, the main square sprawls: you can't rush about here. The town's lack of specific sights belies its significant **history** – most important buildings were destroyed in the nineteenth-century Yatenga civil wars. Ouahigouya was founded in 1757 – the last of Yatenga's capitals – and marked the northern limit of that state's expansion. **King Kango**'s summons to the chiefs of Yatenga to pay him homage gives the town its name (from *Waka yuguya!* – "Come and greet!"). Unfortunately, the great palace where this took place was destroyed in 1825 during one of the struggles for the throne, in which the city was razed to the ground.

Kango may originally have built Ouahigouya as a salt depot; he certainly had his eye on trans-Saharan commodities (gold and kola for example), and hoped to make money by channelling more of their trade through Yatenga. Another motive in building the town could have been to escape from the power of the Mossi aristocracy which had always resented his rule and may well have been responsible for usurping him in the first place. At any rate, Kango populated the new city with captives and ethnic minorities, from whose number he chose many of his officials.

As well as the dynastic struggles of the 1820s and 1830s, Ouahigouya suffered serious damage in the later wars between Sons of Sagha and Sons of Tougouri (see box, pp.696–697). By the time the French managed to secure their stooge Boulli on the throne at the end of 1896, it was half in ruins again, but they needed a base for eastward conquest and "pacification" of Yatenga, and so constructed a fort and rebuilt the town as the regional capital.

Accommodation

Ouahigouya's **hotels** are mainly basic, although there are a couple of more luxurious options.

L'Amitié 1km from the centre on av de Mopti ☎55.05.21 or 55.05.22, ✉amitié@fasonet.bf. Long-established hotel with a range of rooms to suit every budget. The older block has the cheaper options, including basic and bare rooms with fans (❶). The new, upmarket extension opposite offers classy self-contained rooms (❺) with hot water, fridge, satellite TV and IDD phone, plus a restaurant and pool.

Auberge Populaire av de Mopti near to the cinema ☎55.06.40. Large, simple rooms with fan, shower and grubby walls. Can be very noisy thanks to the attached bar and adjacent road. ❶

Bamb-Yam 2km south of the centre ☎55.00.88. Clean, simple self-contained rooms with fan or a/c in a pleasant courtyard, though there are no taxis around and it's a long trek to town, but just about worth it. ❷

Colibri 1km northeast of town, just off av de

OUAHIGOUYA

▲ Koumbri, Bani & Douentza (Mali)　　　Djibo, Dori & Gorom-Gorom ▲

ACCOMMODATION
de l'Amitié	4
Auberge Populaire	3
Bamb-Yam	6
Colibri	1
Dunia	2
de la Liberte	5

0　Metres　200

Yatanga Naba's Compound

CDP Building

Tomb of Naba Kango

Hospital

Market

STAF Bus Station

Mairie

Alimentation Chaine-Avion (Supermarket)

RUE DE POUYTENGA

Market

Excel Petrol Station And Supermarket

STMB Bus Station　Cinema

BICIB-B Bank

Commissariat

AVENUE DE MOPTI

Lycée Yadega

Autogare/ SOGEBAF Buses

Sports Ground

Gendarmerie

AVENUE DE CHAMBERY

RUE DE PARIS

RUE DE LA SUISSE

DE LAHNSTEIN

◀ Barrage (1Km), Dogon Country & Mopti (Mali)

Séguénéga & Kaya ▶

Yako & Ouagadougou ▶

EATING
Caiman's	E
Ciné Restaurant	D
Faso Benie	B
Hawai Café Express	C
Salon de Thé Faso Beni	A

▼ Tougan & Bobo Dioulasso

The history of Yatenga

The first great Mossi conqueror, **Naba Rawa**, eldest son of Ouédraogo, founded the kingdom of **Zandoma** around 1470. His great nephew Ouemtanango, son of Oubri, perhaps jealous of Rawa's success, expanded his father's Oubritenga kingdom (later Ouagadougou) to the north, moving its capital from Tenkodogo to **La**.

The kingdom of Yatenga was probably founded around 1540 on the death of the fourth Mogho Naba, **Nasbire**. Nasbire's son and heir, **Yadega**, who was away, heard about his father's death and rode straight to La to claim the kingdom. He arrived, however, to find that his brother **Kumdumye** had taken power and moved south to Ouagadougou. Yadega followed, but found Kumdumye's authority already well established. He returned angrily to La, where he was soon followed by his sister Pabre, who'd managed to seize the **royal amulets** embodying the Mogho Naba's power. With these, Yadega declared a new kingdom and had himself enthroned at La. His new state was known after him as **Yatenga** (from *Yadega tenga*, "Yadega's land"). A legacy of the dispute is the continued mutual avoidance of the holders of the offices of Mogho Naba and Yatenga Naba, who to this day refuse to set eyes on each other.

Oral history is a bit confused on some of these points. Ouagadougou tradition inserts a fifth Mogho Naba between Nasbire and Kumdumye, making the latter the sixth Naba, and also claims that the royal amulets were recovered from Pabre – though Yatenga tradition says they got nothing more than her horse's droppings. It's possible that Nasbire had named Kumdumye his heir in any case. But why Yadega was away from La, and where he was, are also disputed, as is his relationship to Kumdumye, who may have been his cousin. The date of Yatenga's foundation could have been as much as four hundred years earlier.

The rise of Yatenga

At first the Yatenga statelet was the runt of the Mossi litter. Consisting of the towns of **La**, its first capital, and **Gourcy**, its second, plus a few surrounding villages, it lay sandwiched between Zandoma to the north and Oubritenga to the south. When Yadega's brother Kouda jumped on the bandwagon and set up his own kingdom of Risiam, to the southeast (independent until the nineteenth century), it was bigger than Yatenga. What changed this balance a tradition of conquest and expansion that commenced with the activities of the ninth Yatenga Naba, **Vanteberegum**. He moved the Yatenga capital to **Somniaga**, extending the kingdom to do so, and his son set out on a campaign of aggrandisement that gobbled up most of Zandoma and established Yatenga as the second most powerful Mossi kingdom. However, it was the twenty-fifth *naba*, **Naba Kango**, famous for his cruelty as much as his conquests, who really fixed Yatenga in the oral histories.

Deposed almost as soon as he took power in 1754, Naba Kango returned after three years, aided by the formidable advantage of **firearms**, to retake power with an army of mercenaries. He then built a new capital and an enormous palace at **Ouahigouya** and summoned all Yatenga's chiefs (including the *naba* of Zandoma) to pay homage to him there. Those who failed to do so received a visit from his troops, who then went on to invade neighbouring territories, leading to a vast expansion of Kango's kingdom. Within it, he maintained an impressive unity, largely by burning down any villages that defied his authority. He had criminals publicly burnt to death and even massacred his own Bamana troops when they misbehaved. He was

Chambery ☎ 55.07.87. Big, clean self-contained rooms with fan or a/c; basic but pleasant. **②**
Dunia rue de Paris, 1.5km east of the centre ☎ 55.05.95, ⓕ 55.00.07. Boasts a great atmosphere, a pool and luxury a/c rooms (**④**),

plus cheaper rooms with fans (**②**).
La Liberté 100m off av de Mopti, follow the signs ☎ 55.05.72. Quiet location, with small rooms, some with private bathroom, a/c and TV. Also has dorm beds (CFA2500). Food available on request. **①**

succeeded in 1787 by his nephew, **Naba Sagha**, but the large kingdom was growing unwieldy, and within forty years Yatenga had plunged into the series of civil wars that were to destroy it.

Civil war and dissolution

The wars concerned the succession of Sagha's 133 sons, the first of whom, **Tougouri**, managed to succeed him in 1806. Following his death in 1825, war broke out between those of Sagha's sons who were next in line. Only after 1834 was there a lull in the strife. On the death of Naba Yende, in 1877, however, the dynastic conflicts flared up once more. This time the dispute was between Sagha's grandsons. The sons of his first-born and successor, Tougouri, claimed that they alone were entitled to rule. The sons of Tougouri's brothers and successors disagreed, pointing out that the intended *naba*'s mother had been a concubine, and that in any case, each branch of Sagha's family should take a turn. The two groups formed opposing parties called **Sons of Tougouri** and **Sons of Sagha**.

When two Sons of Sagha were successively enthroned as *nabas*, the Sons of Tougouri went to war against them. Baogo, the incumbent *naba*, turned to the **French** – who, although new on the scene, had just taken Bandiagara, and were hovering on Yatenga's borders. **Desteneves**, the leader of the French expeditionary force, offered only to mediate. Undeterred, Baogo went into battle against the Sons of Tougouri in 1894 and was killed.

All other eligible branches of Sagha's family having had their turn, the kingdom now returned to Tougouri's family. His senior son, Naba Boulli, took the throne but predictably the Sons of Sagha refused to accept him and set up a rival *naba* in **Sissamba**. Boulli turned to the French, who this time seized the opportunity and, on May 18, 1895, declared Yatenga a protectorate, thus usurping its independence.

The French sacked Sissamba, but the Sons of Sagha successfully recaptured Ouahigouya as soon as they had left. The French bailed out Boulli and put him back on the throne twice more, by which time half Ouahigouya was in ruins. The rebellion of the Sons of Sagha wasn't put down until 1902, and violent incidents in connection with it continued until as late as 1911.

Modern Yatenga

French military occupation ended in 1909, when Yatenga passed to civilian colonial rule, and the region was generally quiet during the 1916 anti-conscription rebellion. With the 1932 division of Upper Volta, Yatenga became part of the French Sudan until the re-creation of Upper Volta in 1947. The 1930s and 1940s saw the rise of **Hammalism**, a reformist Muslim cult which the French considered anticolonial (it was). The movement was largely responsible for the spread of Islam in Yatenga (hitherto strongly resisted because of its association with hostile empires, especially the Songhai to the north). This in turn became the base for opposition to the traditionalist, chief-led Union Voltaïque in the region. A UV breakaway, the MDV (Mouvement Démocratique Voltaïque), carried Yatenga in the 1957 election with a base of Muslim support.

Since independence, Yatenga has been a *département* of Burkina, divided into four *cercles*: Ouahigouya, Gourcy, Séguénéga and Titao. Yako lies outside it in the *département* of Koudougou.

The Town

By day, Ouahigouya lends itself to gentle meanderings. The only sight as such is **Naba Kango's tomb**, an imposing white edifice between the Mairie and the present Naba's compound. According to popular legend, anyone who walks all the way round it will die soon after. The **Yatenga Naba's compound** lies on the old site of Kango's palace. With luck, you may even get to meet the Naba, who's said to be an expert on Yatenga history – as well he would need to be to justify his position. On the way back, you could check out the **market**, always worth a wander. Ouahigouya also boasts no less than 37 **mosques**, built in a pretty and distinctive style. Not to be overlooked either is the attractive lake formed by the **barrage** 1km west of town – the desert blooms around here, and you can stroll across the *barrage*. To reach the *barrage*, take the track on the left just before *Hôtel L'Amitié* and then the second turning on the right.

Eating and other practicalities

Hotel food in Ouahigouya is good; the *L'Amitié* serves up satisfying meals, and the *Dunia*'s excellent French-Middle Eastern food makes it the first choice of local expats. Smaller places, where you pay for the food – rice, yam, pasta, soup, chicken, liver, beans and salad – rather than the service, include the *Ciné Restaurant* and the *Faso Benie*. The latter is not to be confused with *Salon de Thé Faso Beni* next to the STMB station, which has a small selection of delicious pastries. Another great spot for breakfasts and fresh yoghurt is the *Hawai Café Express* on Avenue de Mopti. If you're near *L'Amitié*, *Caiman's* is popular with locals, offering the likes of *steak-frites* and spaghetti. For **picnic supplies**, the best place is *Alimentation Chaine-Avion* opposite the Lycée on Avenue de Mopti.

In the evenings, there's a pleasant atmosphere with fires burning and food being prepared along the roadside. For **drinking**, there's cold beer at the *Auberge Populaire* or under the thatch *paillote* at the *Military Bar* (around the corner from *Colibri*) until midnight. If you want to keep going even later, *Dancing de L'Amitié*, next to the hotel of the same name, is the main weekend **nightspot** in Ouahigouya (Fri & Sat only; CFA1000).

The BICIA-B **bank** changes cash euros and American Express euro traveller's cheques only; the BIB bank changes nothing.

Around the Yatenga district

Most of Yatenga's sites of interest are spread around the villages. Its first capital, and the Mossi capital before Yatenga's secession, was La, now called **La-Todin**, beyond the borders of modern Yatenga, 22km west of Yako. The fourth Yatenga Naba, Guéda, moved his capital north to **Gourcy**, where you can see the **sacred hill** on which his successors are still enthroned. Here, too, are the royal amulets stolen by Pabre on behalf of her brother Yadega. In the civil wars of the 1890s, the Sons of Sagha kidnapped the amulets, thus preventing the French from crowning Naba Boulli until they were returned at the end of 1897. Gourcy is on the main Ouagadougou–Ouahigouya road, 42km south of Ouahigouya.

The kingdom's third and penultimate capital, **Somniaga** was seized from the kingdom of Zandoma by Naba Vanteberegum as part of his campaign to enlarge Yatenga. Seven kilometres south of Ouahigouya on the Ouaga road, it makes an

---

Moving on from Ouahigouya

There are plenty of **buses** heading to **Ouaga**: SOGEBAF (℡55.07.31) depart eight times daily; STMB (℡55.00.59) five times daily; and STAF (℡55.02.51) three times daily. The road is now paved the whole way to Ouaga; allow three hours for the trip. You should also be able to find transport to **Djibo** (STMB and SOGEBAF both leave twice daily), and **Bobo-Dioulasso**, weather permitting (SOGEBAF eight times daily; STMB three times daily). If you're heading to **Mali**, transport is scarcer; you'll have to take the daily bus to **Koro** (SOGEBAF; 10am daily) and change there. The *piste* to Koro is passable in the dry season, but be prepared for tough travelling conditions.

The main ethnic group in Yatenga is the **Mossi**, who had settled here by the end of the 1330s, when they sacked Timbuktu. It's probable that the Mossi took power in the region in the second half of the fifteenth century, though some claim that this happened several centuries earlier. The Dogon, then living in the north of the region, fled up to the Bandiagara escarpment in Mali, while the Samos, based in the east, stayed on and have now more or less assimilated with the Mossi.

The principal state was run by the **Kurumba**, or Fulse, who claim to have come from the region of Say and Niamey some two hundred years before the Mossi to establish the Kingdom of Lurum, whose last capital was at Mengao, now in Djibo district. Just as the Dogon hadn't resisted the Kurumba invasion, so the Kurumba hardly opposed the Mossi, and the two communities have merged into the dual sociopolitical system, still largely operational today, in which the **Mossi** hold political power (as "masters of the sky") while the Kurumba have authority over agriculture and the land (the "masters of the earth"). Each village has a Kurumba "earth chief", whose functions complement those of the Mossi *naba*.

There's a third element in this system, the **blacksmiths** (*saaba*), who never marry out, usually live in their own wards (*zaka*) inside Mossi villages (though they have one or two villages of their own, like Séguénéga) and have special ceremonial duties such as performing circumcisions. Only men can be blacksmiths; women are generally potters. Within this same system are the **captives** (*Yemse*). Descendants of prisoners of war, and loyal to the Yatenga *naba*, they live in their own section of town called the *bingo*. Ouahigouya's *bingo* consists of half the city and captives form more than half its population. Village chiefs and court dignitaries are often descendants of captives.

The **Peulh** (Fula) are the region's other main group. Although based in Djibo and outside the Mossi–Kurumba system, they've often played a major role in Yatenga's history. The **Silmi-Mossi**, descendants of unions between Fula and Mossi (which are considered somewhat disreputable), live in their own villages, mainly isolated in the south and southeast of the region. Lastly, members of three Islamic trading nations, the **Songhai**, **Bamana** and Mande-speaking **Yarse**, also live in Yatenga. The Mossi themselves, despite having resisted the advances of Islam for so long, are nowadays mostly Muslim too.

easy walk first thing in the morning (but don't forget to carry a few litres of water), or you can hitch. Most of Yatenga's *nabas* are buried here in the **royal cemetery** (*nayaado*) and looked after by the Yaogo Naba, the man to find if you want to see it. One quaint Yatenga burial custom was the interment of the *nabas*' court jesters – alive – with their dead king.

Of the capitals of neighbouring traditional states, **Yako** is the easiest to visit. Some 70km south of Ouahigouya, it is now accessible by paved road. The most striking first impression is of its **mosque**, but its main claim to local fame goes further. Capital of a kingdom founded by Naba Yelkone – son of the same Kumdumye who split with Yadega over the question of the Mossi throne – it was a perpetual object of Yatenga–Ouagadougou rivalry, generally a fief of the latter. Naba Kango managed to force it into submission. The French also found Yako a tough nut to crack. More recently, **Thomas Sankara** was born here; with some discretion, you may be able to get someone to show you exactly where.

Zandoma, the region's very first Mossi capital, is now a tiny village some 40km southwest of Ouahigouya, northwest of Gourcy. The chief still claims descent from **Naba Rawa**, whose tomb can be seen close to his compound.

Other places of interest in and around Yatenga include: **Ramatoulaye**, 25km east of Ouahigouya on the road to Rollo, with another impressive **mosque**, a major centre of Hammalism (see p.697) in colonial days; **Lago**, some 30km south of Ouahigouya (but 41km by road from Zogoré), **burial site** of the first Yatenga *nabas*; **Sissamba**, 11km southwest of Ouahigouya and en route to Lago, where the Sons of Sagha installed their pretender to the throne on Naba Boulli's accession in 1894 and which the French sacked the following year; and **Mengao**, 82km northeast of Ouahigouya on the road to Djibo (27km further), which was the last capital of the kingdom of Lurum and is still the home of the **Kurumba paramount "earth chief"**, the counterpart of the Yatenga Naba – the Mossi paramount sky chief.

9.2

The Gourounsi country

The area around Pô on the Ghanaian border **south of Ouagadougou** is dominated by the **Gourounsi**, or Grusi (a group who are usually said to include the Kassena, the Nouna and the Sissala from around Léo), whose distinctive architecture provides the region's main attraction. Gourounsi country also boasts a couple of national parks – difficult to get to without your own transport – and some interesting archeological remains near Léo.

The Gourounsi build their **houses** from mud in smooth, sandcastle shapes, often painted with striking diamond patterns. Larger compounds may consist of whole labyrinths of submerged rooms and doorways through which people weave and duck. Buildings are not expected to last more than a few seasons and new houses are built around the foundations of older dwellings, resulting in a characteristic organic appearance. Also typical are the forked and notched logs, leant against the walls, which are used as ladders to the flat roofs where grain is commonly dried, out of the reach of goats. Women gather here to chat and smoke during the day, the whole family often sleeps here, and all sorts of stuff is stored. Village chiefs usually

The Gourounsi country

How long the people known as **Gourounsi** (originally a Mossi term of denigration) have lived in the region isn't clear, but Mossi tradition claims they were pushed back across the Red Volta River by the thirteenth Mogho Naba, Nakiem, at the end of the seventeenth century. Never united, the various strands of Gourounsi speakers have long existed in a state of near-permanent village war. Their lack of central government has always made them vulnerable to attack from more organized groups, especially the Mossi, who often made raids into the area for slaves. Many Mossi dissidents set themselves up as chiefs in Gourounsi-land, and their families continue to live here. Gourounsi chiefs possess sacred objects called *kwara* – insignia of office – which are handed down from generation to generation.

At the end of the nineteenth century, the Gourounsi were the targets of Djerma Muslim zealots from the Niamey region, who stormed down on horseback and engaged in heavy slave-raiding under the pretext of a jihad. They converted the son of the chief of Sati and set up shop there, almost decimating the lands of the Sissala, Nouna and Kassena, before being defeated by a Gourounsi–French alliance in 1895.

have the largest and most impressive compounds – though not necessarily the prettiest. You can often tell the status of a family from the height of its walls.

On the way to **Pô**, the region's main town, from Ouagadougou, you pass through **Kombissiri**, 40km south of the capital. This town became a Muslim centre following the settlement here of a community of **Yarse** (Mande-speaking traders) in the eighteenth century. Its religious status was developed by the pro-Muslim 25th Mogho Naba, Sawadogho, who ruled from 1825 to 1842 and had the mosque built. It's 4km east of the town: follow the *piste* from the police checkpoint at the northern end of Kombissiri.

Pô

PÔ lacks traditional architecture, but has plenty of fountains with revolutionary names – "Nelson Mandela", "Enver Hoxha", "Les Trois Luttes". Coming from Ghana, Pô is a gentle introduction to some of French Africa's more tiresome aspects – higher prices and an obsession with *papiers*. The Pô police are fond of asking for these and you can expect a fair number of spot checks, but like most of the townspeople they're friendly enough and there's no big hassle. Pô is also a garrison town with a chequered history – though the soldiers don't obtrude.

Some history

According to legend, Pô was founded around 1500, by a Mossi man, **Nablogo**, son of Mogho Naba Oubri. He started cultivating a field (*pô*) but got into a land rights dispute with Kassena neighbours. About this time, a certain **Gonkwora** from Kasana near Léo turned up here, having left his village after being disinherited of his rightful chiefship. He brought three magic bracelets with him (still looked after by his descendants in Pô) and fell in with Nablogo, who helped him, and in whose dispute with the Kassena he interceded. Gonkwora's brother – the ancestor of Pô's present chief – then arrived from their home village with the village *kwara*. Gonkwora meanwhile married Nablogo's daughter and they all lived happily ever after. Gonkwora's tomb is supposed to be under a sacred baobab in the Kasno quarter of town.

More recent and less halcyon history has also been made in Pô. In 1976, **Thomas Sankara** set up the Centre Nationale d'Entrainement here, taken over by Blaise Compaoré in 1982. The following year the Ouédraogo regime arrested Sankara and fellow officers. Pô became a radical focus for students, young workers and academics, who came to join the commandos. In August 1983, the coup that toppled Ouédraogo, fired the revolution and put Sankara in power, was launched here. And

---

The Gourounsi language

If you learn no other Gourounsi, at least learn to say *Din le*, the all-purpose greeting, which means "Thank you". The following sampler comes from "Kassem", the main dialect of Gourounsi, spoken by the Kassena.

Good morning	*Tim paga*	8	*Nana*
Good evening	*Tim dadan*	9	*Nogo*
1	*Kalo*	10	*Fuga*
2	*Inle*	20	*Finle*
3	*Nto*	50	*Finnu*
4	*Nna*	100	*Bi*
5	*Unu*	500	*Bi yennu*
6	*Trodo*	1000	*Moro*
7	*Tirpai*		

it was from Pô that Compaoré planned a second takeover in 1987, that led to Sankara's untimely death and put Compaoré in power.

Practicalities

Accommodation in Pô is pretty basic, but as a frontier town, there is at least some choice. The friendly and brightly painted *Auberge Agoabem* on the main road (℡39.01.42; ❶) has running water, clean rooms (shared bathroom), and a decent restaurant and bar in the grounds. For a little more luxury, you could check out the *Hôtel Mantora* (℡39.00.25; ❶), behind the *cité* (housing development) north of the town; the 24 aid workers' houses here, built by Sankara, are looked after by an elusive caretaker, and the clean fanned rooms (some with showers) are set around an attractive courtyard. The newest and most expensive option is *Hôtel Lido* (℡39.02.41; ❷), which is overpriced but still the nicest in town, with comfortable rooms with fan and private bathroom.

For street **food**, try near the market and around the cinema. Every evening, there's good fried fish from the Black Volta, *brochettes*, guinea fowl, roast mutton and plenty more. There's a variety of sit-down places, too, dishing up couscous, sandwiches, omelettes, rice, spaghetti, *tô* and *brochettes*. Pô bursts into life in the **evenings**, despite the fact that electricity is mainly confined to the north end of town (and goes off periodically during the night); the restaurant and bar at the *Lido* serves ice-cold beer and mediocre food for around CFA2000, and has music till midnight – if you've got the stamina, try the new indoor club just down the road. The *Auberge Agoabem* serves cheaper, decent food at roadside tables. *Nion et Frères* (aka *Sounoogo*), next door, is another popular drinking spot.

The banks in Pô don't **change money**, but people in the market or around the *autogare* will change Ghanaian cedis, euros, dollars and (if you're lucky) sterling for CFA francs.

Around Pô

The best of the Gourounsi country is to be found outside Pô and in the smaller villages along the roads parallel with the frontier on both sides. The Gourounsi traditional capital, **Tiébélé**, has the finest architecture, and the highest volume of visitors. The declining **Parc National de Pô** lies across the road from Ouaga to Pô and, south of **Nobéré**, you may see representatives of the district's elephant herd – one of the few places in West Africa where "Elephants on Road" is a delightful

---

Moving on from Pô

Frequent *taxis brousse* to **Ouagadougou** (taking anything from two to five hours) leave from the *autogare* in front of the police station. You're less likely to be held up at police checkpoints if you travel on one of the official bus companies: **Rakieta** (℡39.00.42) go to Ouaga four times a day, whilst **STMB** (℡39.01.10) do the route twice daily. Heading south into **Ghana**, there are taxis to Paga and even as far as Bolgatanga, especially on Friday (market day in Bolga). Alternatively you could hitch from the customs post just south of town. La Société Colombe du Faso, based near the *autogare*, runs a service three times a week to Kumasi, whilst the STC Ouaga–Accra bus also halts in Pô and is scheduled to roll into town on Monday, Wednesday and Friday morning – though you may struggle to get a seat.

Transport to **Tiébélé** and **Léo** is much easier to find on market days (held every third day in Tiébélé, and on Sundays in Léo). On other days, and to other destinations such as the wildlife reserves, you may have to make private arrangements with taxi drivers or car or moped owners, though taxis are expensive if you want to do a *déplacement*. To rent, ask around the *autogare* or market, or see if your hotel proprietor knows anyone.

possibility. Finally, if you can find transport from Pô (tricky except on Sundays, which is Léo's market day), you could make the 126-kilometre trip to the Djerma-Gourounsi ruins near **Léo**.

Tiébélé

TIÉBÉLÉ, the traditional Gourounsi capital, 31km east of Pô, is something of a tourist attraction, and worth a visit. The chief here is the most important *chef de canton* in Gourounsi country and his **compound** – a magnificent maze of mud-pie huts – is the town's main attraction. Coming into town from Pô, you'll pass the excellent *Restaurant Titantic*, soon after which the road bends to the left. Follow the track to the right here for about 400m, past the football field, to reach the chief's compound. You're bound to be met by one of the guides from the Association pour le Dévelopement de Tiébélé, asked to sign the visitor's book and pay CFA1500 to visit the compound. The interesting tour lasts some thirty minutes – ask to scale the refuse heap by the entrance, which has excellent views of the compound and the town.

Tiakané

TIAKANÉ, 7km west of Pô, is more laid-back. Its houses aren't as striking as those in Tiébélé but you'll feel more like a visitor and less like a punter. The **Cave du Binger** in the chief's compound is a mini underground labyrinth where the villagers hid the nineteenth-century French explorer Binger from a party of Mossi who were out to kill him – Binger went on to become governor of Côte d'Ivoire. His family have evidently not forgotten Tiakané: they recently sent funds from France to build a village school. The chief provides a guide to show you round Binger's hide-out and both will expect a reasonable tip. Tiakané makes a nice early-morning walk from Pô, especially after it's rained.

The Ranch de Gibier de Nazinga and Parc National de Pô

There are two **reserves** near Pô, but you'll need your own transport or hired vehicle to reach them. The **Ranch de Gibier de Nazinga** (open Dec–July), south of the Léo road (its north boundary runs along the road from about 15km to about 40km west of Pô), is easily reached and offers good chances of spotting game. Set up by Canadians to study wildlife resource management, the place is (comparatively) bursting at the seams with elephants, and also harbours several species of monkeys, baboons, antelopes, gazelles, warthogs and, rather surprisingly, lions. There's **accommodation** in the *Camp de la Touristique de Nazinga*, which offers basic bungalows with electricity but no fans (❸), dormitory rooms (CFA5000 per person) or camping (CFA3000 per head). There's also a **restaurant** serving sporadic meals (from CFA2000). At the reception (☎41.36.17) you'll have to pay your entrance (CFA8500), camera (CFA1000) and guide fees (CFA2000). A ranger will accompany you around the reserve; if you don't have your own transport, you can hire vehicles at the reception (CFA15,000 per trip), although the two on offer are regularly booked up. It's even possible to do an unofficial tour on foot, though you do so at your own risk. For more information, either contact the reserve's reception or visit their helpful office in Ouaga on rue du Travail (☎30.84.43, ✉ranch.nazinga@cenatrin.bf).

The **Parc National de Pô** (open Nov–May) is in severe decline and has been virtually inaccessible to tourists for some time. The park *pistes* are in poor shape, there's no accommodation, and rangers have been advising people to stay away. You can check to see if the situation has improved at the park office (☎39.02.29), behind the old PTT in Pô, near the police station. The park's main gate is 31km north of Pô, 5km south of the bridge over the Volta Rouge; baboons and antelope are the most obvious inhabitants; there are also elephants, buffalo and warthog, though they're more difficult to spot.

Léo and the Djerma-Gourounsi ruins

A small border town with a couple of hotels, **LÉO**'s main attraction is the nearby **ruins** in the villages of Satí and Yoro. They date from the period of the **Djerma invasions** at the end of the nineteenth century, when the Djerma made alliances with Gourounsi Muslim chiefs. Satí became the capital of a Djerma mini-state and Yoro was fortified as a holding place for slaves and booty acquired in raids on the local "infidel" Gourounsi. Later, the Gourounsi Muslim leaders had a change of mind about their Djerma business partners and revolted – a resistance which eventually involved collusion with a Djerma renegade called Hamaria, who successfully enlisted French support to defeat the Djerma. French involvement led, as everywhere, to a colonial sell-out and the formal "protection" of the Gourounsi.

SATÍ, 22km northwest of Léo, should still have the remains of fortifications and battlements, especially on the eastern side, while a kilometre to the south, the chief's personal mosque and compound may still be visible. Seven kilometres back down the road to Léo are the ruins of more fortifications – including triangular loopholes and a well, used by the Djerma while besieging Satí. **YORO**, 32km west of Léo on the way to Diébougou, still preserves a long stretch of wall, part of the Djerma treasure house. Admittedly, none of these remains are very impressive, but the search for the ruins makes a good excuse to poke around the area. If you have your own transport, Léo is a reasonable night stop en route from Gourounsi to **Lobi country** (see p.715); for accommodation try *Auberge de Leo* (☎41.32.32; ●) or *Bar Cosmopolis* (☎41.30.19; ●).

9.3

Bobo, Banfora and the southwest

F ed by the **Comoé** and other lesser rivers, the southwest is the hilliest and most densely forested region in Burkina, and a pleasant change from the relentless grasslands which cover most of the country. Rich vegetation camouflages a wealth of natural sites, ranging from **waterfalls** and lakes to striking cliff formations. But the southwest also contains important urban centres – **Bobo-Dioulasso** and **Banfora** – that grew up on the Abidjan train line in a productive agricultural region.

Bobo-Dioulasso and around

Burkina's second city, with around 350,000 inhabitants, **BOBO-DIOULASSO** ("Home of the Bobo and the Dioula") was long the country's economic capital, a position which has only in recent years been usurped by Ouagadougou. Yet life moves at a slow pace here, and Bobo has style and a great atmosphere. Sweeping avenues roofed by the foliage of cool mango trees, colonial buildings in the *style soudanais* and a rich mixture of peoples give it a unique character that makes it one of the most inviting places to unwind anywhere in West Africa. It's also a traditional music centre, with *balafon* orchestras and electric bands adding night-time action to the town's many bars. As Burkina's principal tourist destination, Bobo's only drawback is the hassle of dealing with countless guides and vendors constantly touting for business.

Some history

Bobo was founded in the fifteenth century, when it was known as **Sya**, or "island". According to tradition, a man named Molo Oumarou came here and, after founding villages in Timina and Sakabi, built a house in a clearing of the woods by a stream called the Houët. A village of Bobo-Fing and Bobo-Dioula people grew up around this original home. The French arrived in the late nineteenth century, and set up their first administrative headquarters here in 1897. In 1928, Pépin Malherbe broadened the town limits as Bobo awaited the arrival of the **railway line** from Abidjan. The RAN pushed through in 1934, two decades before the line was extended to Ouaga, and a large colonial town grew up around the station, a short distance from the original settlement (the graceful, Sudan-inspired architecture of the *gare routière*, market and Palais de Justice dates from this period). Bobo thus gained a large economic headstart on Ouaga, which helps to explain its commercial importance today. On the main routes to Mali and the Côte d'Ivoire, too, the town has acquired an international flavour, with numerous foreign workers and students.

Information and accommodation

For **tourist information**, contact the Office National du Tourisme Burkinabe (OTNB; ℡97.19.86, ℻ 97.19.87, ✆ontb@cenatrin.bf), on Avenue de l'Unité just south of the train station. The staff can answer questions about nearby excursions and provide some useful brochures. **Lodgings** in Bobo range from dormitory beds to a/c hotels with pools. In between, there's a good number of inexpensive *auberges*, lacking in luxury but usually well maintained.

Accommodation

Budget

Algouta Secteur 5, off av Louveau, 1km from the centre ℡98.07.92. Cosy little place in a quiet residential area, with a terrace restaurant; tasteful rooms and large bathrooms. ❷

Casafrica Off av de l'Indépendance near the Brakina Brewery ℡98.01.57, ⓦwww.casaafrica.multimania.com. The best budget option in town, this French-owned place has clean rooms arranged around a delightful shady courtyard (where you can also camp very cheaply). An ideal place to relax and escape the hassles of town, and there's an excellent restaurant to boot. ❶

Hamdalaye rue Alpha Moi, near SOGEBAF ℡98.22.87. Nice management and very clean, self-contained rooms with fans. Bike rental available. ❷

Meridien av de l'Unité ℡98.03.42. Friendly place with clean, good-value rooms (some self-contained) with fan. ❶

Okinawa Accart Ville district, Secteur 9, on the way to the stadium ℡97.05.97. Simple rooms without fan but clean and friendly. The attractive courtyard hosts a (noisy) disco on Saturday nights and there's a restaurant serving reasonably priced meals. ❶

Pacha rue Malherbe, 2km from the centre ℡98.09.54. French-owned restaurant and hotel (with camping facilities) set in attractive gardens. Rooms (with fan or a/c) are spotless, and the communal bathrooms are clean. The hotel pizzeria offers excellent, though expensive, dishes from CFA2500. ❶

Renaissance av de la République ℡98.23.31. Excellent location in the very heart of town. Rooms, grouped around an attractive courtyard, are clean and have fans and mosquito nets. ❷

Teria 2129 av Diawara ℡97.19.72. Comfortable and calm place with an ideal location near the market, a very nice, leafy courtyard, and friendly staff. ❷

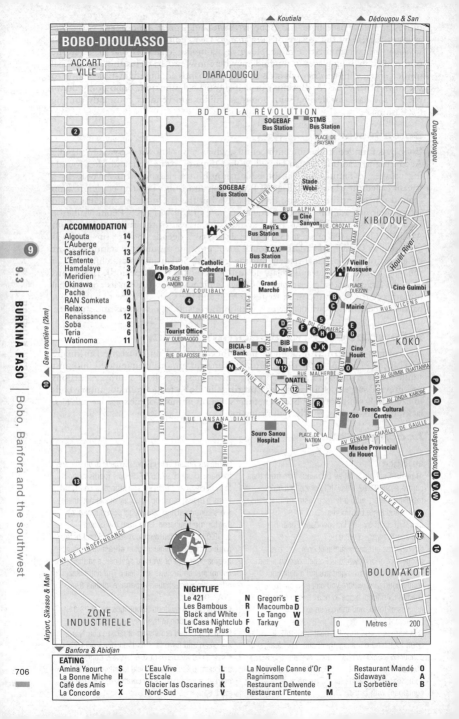

BOBO-DIOULASSO

ACCART VILLE

DIARADOUGOU

▲ Koutiala ▲ Dédougou & San

BD DE LA RÉVOLUTION

SOGEBAF Bus Station

STMB Bus Station

PLACE DE PAYSAN

Stade Wobi

SOGEBAF Bus Station

AVENUE DE LA LIBERTÉ

RUE ALPHA MOI

Ciné Sanyon

Rayi's Bus Station

T.C.V. Bus Station

RUE JOFFRE

KIBIDOUÉ

RUE CROZAT

AV IMAM SAKIDI SANOU

AV SAKIDI SANOU

Vieille Mosquée

Houët River

Ouagadougou ▶

PLACE OUEZZIN

Ciné Guimbi

Train Station

Catholic Cathedral

PLACE TIÉFO AMORO

Total

Grand Marché

Mairie

KOKO

RUE VICENS

ACCOMMODATION

Algouta	14
L'Auberge	7
Casafrica	13
L'Entente	5
Hamdalaye	3
Meridien	1
Okinawa	2
Pacha	10
RAN Somketa	4
Relax	9
Renaissance	12
Soba	8
Teria	6
Watinoma	11

AV COULIBALY

RUE MARÉCHAL FOCHE

Tourist Office

AV OUEDRAOGO

BICIA-B Bank

RUE DELAFOSSE

BIB Bank

Ciné Houët

RUE DU COMMERCE

AVENUE DU PÈRE NADAL

AVENUE CLOZEL

AVENUE DE LA NATION

RUE MALHERBE

ONATEL

AV DIAWARA

French Cultural Centre

Zoo

AV DE LA CONCORDE

AV GUIMBI OUATTARA

AV ZINDA KABORÉ

DE L'UNITÉ

RUE LANSANA DIAKITÉ

AV FAIDHERBE

Souro Sanou Hospital

PLACE DE LA NATION

AV GÉNÉRAL CHARLES DE GAULLE

Musée Provincial du Houet

AV OUYEAU

Ouagadougou ▶

AV DE LA RÉVOLUTION

BOLOMAKOTÉ

AV DE L'INDÉPENDANCE

N

ZONE INDUSTRIELLE

NIGHTLIFE

Le 421	N	Gregori's	E	
Les Bambous	R	Macoumba	D	
Black and White	I	Le Tango	W	
La Casa Nightclub	F	Tarkay	Q	
L'Entente Plus	G			

0   Metres   200

▼ Banfora & Abidjan

EATING

Amina Yaourt	S	L'Eau Vive	L	La Nouvelle Canne d'Or	P	Restaurant Mandé	O
La Bonne Miche	H	L'Escale	U	Ragnimsom	T	Sidawaya	A
Café des Amis	C	Glacier las Oscarines	V	Restaurant Delwende	J	La Sorbetière	B
La Concorde	X	Nord-Sud	V	Restaurant l'Entente	M		

◀ Gare routière (2km)

◀ Airport, Sikasso & Mali

Moderate to expensive

L'Auberge 685 av Ouédraogo ☎99.14.26, ⓕ97.21.37. Central, upmarket hotel with luxurious, attractive rooms with hot water, satellite TV, fridge and a/c. There's a fantastic pool in the shaded courtyard, billiards in the bar, and the *terrasse* is a popular place for drinks. Try to get a room with a balcony. The restaurant, serving French cuisine, can be rather hit and miss, however. ❻

L'Entente Corner of rue du Commerce and av Binger ☎97.12.05. Good self-contained rooms with fans and nets or a/c. Also has Land Rovers for rent. ❷–❹

RAN Somketa Near the train station ☎97.09.00, ⓕ97.09.12, ⓔhot.ran@fasonet.bf. Three-star hotel

with bright, well-equipped rooms with all mod-cons and a pool, though the place lacks atmosphere and is beginning to look a little dated. ❻

Relax av Diawara ☎97.22.27 or 97.00.96, ⓕ97.13.07. Well-located hotel with a good pool (CFA1500 for non-guests); the self-contained rooms have good facilities but lack style. ❻

Soba av Gov. Clozel ☎97.10.12. Colonial-style place, with spacious rooms, some with a/c and TV, and a pleasant patio garden. ❸

Watinoma Corner of rue Malherbe and av Binger ☎97.20.82, ⓕ97.57.30. Popular hotel set in a pleasant courtyard, with self-contained rooms with a/c, hot water and satellite TV. They also have an excellent restaurant with European food and speciality pizzas. ❺

The Town

Situated in the heart of Bobo, the **Grand Marché** has been renovated by the City Council over the past few years and is now once again the town's bustling centre-piece, with traders selling all manner of foodstuffs. And despite the constant hassle of would-be guides outside the market, few will pester you once you're inside, and the atmosphere is generally relaxed. The **Vieille Mosquée** (sometimes referred to as the Grande Mosquée) – a *banco* construction originally built in 1880 – is located in Bobo's **old town** in the **Kibidoué** district. You're not allowed in the mosque, but you can take photos from outside. Here, you'll be asked to buy a ticket (CFA1000) and assigned a **guide** to show you around the historic core of town. First on their list of worthy sites is the "Konsa", the **oldest house** in town, said to date from the fifteenth century. As you follow them through the narrow streets of the ancient neighbourhoods, they'll point out **traditional artisans** – mostly black-smiths and weavers – and finish the tour with a stop at the **sacred fish pond** – the murky backwaters of the Houët stream where oversize mudfish peer up for food. There's no telling what makes them sacred: fishy totems are a Bobo speciality.

In the midst of your meanderings, don't miss the **Marché de Poterie**, two blocks north of the mosque, where demand is still high for earthenware vessels from remote villages like Dalgan, Tcheriba and Sikiana. Pots vary in size and shape depending on their function, but they're all quite reasonably priced, and there are striking examples of unusual water jugs painted in bright colours and bold designs.

Lastly, it's worth making time to see the **Musée Provincial du Houët**, on the Place de la Nation (Tues–Sat 8.30am–noon & 3.30–6pm, Sun 8.30am–noon; CFA500). This small museum boasts an interesting collection of **ethnographic artefacts** such as Bobo wooden statues and Senoufo funeral masks, as well as regional clothing worn by the Fula, Senoufo and other peoples. Outside in the grounds of the museum you can stroll through examples of Burkinabe housing styles – Bobo, Fula and Senoufo – beautifully decorated and furnished.

Bobo's **zoo**, on Avenue de la Révolution, is a pretty sad collection of half a dozen beasts, none faring too well in captivity. Don't bother with it.

Eating

Quite apart from the consistently good hotel restaurants, Bobo has plenty of fine **places to eat**, many of them serving up the especially delicious local **beef**.

Amina Yaourt av Fairherbe. The best yoghurt in town – and popular with a young, hip crowd

La Bonne Miche av Binger at av Ouédraogo.

Popular patisserie and the best *pain au raisin* in the country.

Café des Amis av Binger. Basic snacks, and fresh

yoghurt daily – a pleasant place to sit, eat and watch the world go by, despite the lack of atmosphere.

La Concorde av Louveau. Classic French cuisine served at courtyard tables set around a dance-floor – a favourite local haunt with a lively atmosphere.

L'Eau Vive rue Delafosse across from the *Relax Hôtel* ℡ 97.20.26. Sister restaurant to the *L'Eau Vive* in Ouaga, with similar international specialities, waitressing nuns, and themed nights with food from around the world. Meals for around CFA4000.

L'Escale Secteur 5 cité CNSS, off av Charles de Gaulle, 2km from the centre ℡ 97.44.15, ℮ lescale@hotmail.com. The classiest place in town, with tables set around a great pool (CFA2000) in a pleasant courtyard and pricey drinks and meals (from CFA3000). Closed Mondays.

Glacier les Oscarines Part of the *Hôtel Oasis*. Sister café to *Oscars* in Ouaga, and with a similar selection of delicious ice cream and other snacks.

Nord-Sud 1883 av Charles de Gaulle, 1km from the centre. New, attractive bar-restaurant with a small pool. Meals for around CFA3500.

La Nouvelle Canne d'Or Off av Charles de Gaulle, 300m from the French Cultural Centre

℡ 98.15.96. New, plush restaurant, beautifully decorated with local art and craft work and serving French cuisine, excellent seafood and fantastic deserts.

Ragnimsom (aka *Chez Augustin*) av Faidherbe. New, Burkinabe-run restaurant serving French cuisine for around CFA1500, including succulent *steak sauce bordelaise*.

Restaurant Delwende (aka *Chez Tanti Abi*) opposite the *Relax Hôtel*. Ultra-friendly locals' joint serving inexpensive local dishes with great fish soup, rice sauce and salads.

Restaurant l'Entente rue Delafosse ℡ 97.03.96. Attractive terrace restaurant with African and European meals for less than CFA2500. The attached courtyard bar gets lively from 9.30pm, with loud music and dancing.

Restaurant Mandé av de la Révolution ℡ 98.28.42. Popular, mid-range restaurant with pleasant outdoor seating serving European meals for around CFA2000.

Sidawaya Near the train station. Bar-restaurant set in pleasant gardens and serving a wide range of European dishes for around CFA2000.

La Sorbetiére av Binger. Rivals *La Bonne Miche* as the town's best patisserie, serving delicious pastries, including fantastic *pain au chocolat*.

Nightlife

Like the Ouagalais, the people of Bobo are great night-timers. The percussionist **Coulibaly Twins** and **Mahama Konaté**, the founder of Farafina, are from Bobo and regularly play the town clubs when home from Paris. Some restaurants are worth a visit, including *La Concorde* and *L'Entente* (see above). There's also a wealth of **traditional music** in the Bon Makote district just south of the city centre – including *balafons* and calabash drums at *dolo* bars – by far the cheapest entertainment in town.

Le 421 In the *Hôtel Sobur-Tours (421)*, rue Malherbe at av du Gouverneur Faidherbe. Dark indoors bar, very frenetic and usually full despite the high cover charge.

Les Bambous av Binger, 200m from Place de la Nation ℡ 81.58.12. Named after the resident pet monkey, this French-owned restaurant and music venue is set in attractive gardens and hosts live music every night from 9pm, regularly featuring top-class musicians (CFA600 entrance).

Black and White av Binger at rue du Commerce. The restaurant is bad (limited menu, dreadful service), but the nightly disco is fine, with good music and plenty of sweaty bodies.

Gregori's av de la Révolution. Kicking club playing African and European music nightly. CFA3000 cover at weekends.

La Casa Nightclub rue Alwata Diawara.

Happening club across from *Hôtel Teria*; busy at weekends. Also serves mediocre food.

L'Entente Plus av de la Révolution, next to *Gregori's*. Open-air bar-dancing with attractive *paillotes* in the courtyard and nightly disco sounds. A lot of people, and hustlers can be a hassle.

Macoumba av de la République. Central and popular club with music nightly from 10.30pm (except Tues), CFA2500 cover charge at weekends.

Le Tango rue 435 off av Charles de Gaulle, zone des Ecoles. Out of the centre, but well known by taxi drivers. Energetic drinking and dancing, with seating under thatched umbrellas, and local meals.

Tarkay Off av Charles de Gaulle, not far from the French Cultural Centre. Lively bar and dancing, popular with the older generation. Open, and often busy, all day.

Listings

Airlines The Air Burkina office is on av du Gov. Clozel next to *Hôtel Soba* ☎ 97.13.48, ☏ 97.06.97 (for details of their flights, see p.687).

Banks BIB on av de la République is best for changing traveller's cheques, providing you can show receipts. If you can't, BICIA-B on av Ouédraogo may be able to help, though at a higher rate of commission. Other banks in the centre include Ecobank, which changes both cash and traveller's cheques, and the Bank of Africa, which changes cash (though at a high commission) but not traveller's cheques.

Bike/mobylette rental Easy to find around the Grand Marché, especially at the west end towards the train station; CFA2500–5000 per day.

Books, newspapers and maps International press, mostly French, is available at the French Cultural Centre or *L'Auberge* hotel. Bookshops in the market area include Diafca, where you can also buy city maps.

Car rental Faso Auto-Location has an office on av de la Nation (☎ 23.55.68), or try Avis on av Binger (☎ 97.12.46).

Cinemas Cine Sanyon, on av de la République across from the stadium, is new, comfortable and air-conditioned. Less state-of-the-art venues include Ciné Houët, av de la Révolution, and Ciné Guimbi, off rue Vicens.

French Cultural Centre Junction of av Général Charles de Gaulle and av de la Concorde, just east of the river ☎ 97.39.79, ✉ ccfhm@fasonet.bf. The centre has a good library and outdoor reading area, with magazines and newspapers. African, European and American films on Tuesdays, Thursdays and Saturdays (CFA500), and occasional concerts as well.

Hospital Hôpital Souro Sanou, av Lansana Diakité ☎ 97.00.44 or 97.26.89, ☏ 97.26.93.

Internet Info Elec, next to the *Hôtel Oasis*, is central but expensive at CFA750 for thirty minutes; alternatively, try Cyber Space which is cheaper, opposite *Macoumba*.

Post office av de la Nation at av de la République (Mon–Fri 8am–1.30pm & 2.30–5.30pm, Sat 8am–1.30pm). Poste restante service. International calls can be made from the ONATEL office nearby on rue Malherbe.

Supermarkets Marina Market and AGB (Alimentation Generale du Burkina) are the best in the centre of town.

Swimming The *Auberge* and *Relax* allow non-residents to use their pools for CFA1500, while the *RAN* charges an extortionate CFA2500; the best pool, however, is at *L'Escale* (CFA2000). If you're eating at *Nord-Sud* you can use their pool for free.

Theatre Check the schedule at the Théâtre Amitié, on av Général Charles de Gaulle. Also ask at the French Cultural Centre.

Western Union Money transfers possible at the Bank of Africa or the SGBB Bank, both on av Ouédraogo.

Around Bobo

There are some rewarding side-trips within easy distance of Bobo. If you haven't got a car, the best way to see them is by renting a bicycle or moped (see "Listings", above). The best of these excursions is to a swimming hole called **La Guinguette**, 18km west of town in the **Kou Forest**. You can splash around in bilharzia-free waters, though it's sometimes crowded, especially at weekends. To get here, take the road to Sikasso as far as **Koumi,** interesting in itself, with characteristic pseudo-fortified Bobo architecture – check with the chief if you want to take pictures (whether you've a permit or not). In the village you'll see a sign to the Guinguette pointing right; follow this path, passing through two villages to reach a fork, then turn right and go straight ahead till you reach the entrance gate (CFA1000).

DAFRA, 8km southeast of Bobo, boasts a **pool of sacred fish** in beautiful surroundings, much more interesting than the underwhelming mud hole in Bobo. Chickens are sacrificed to the enormous catfish, who are the symbol of Bobo and reproduced on the Mairie (town hall) wall in town. **To get to Dafra** from Bobo, you can either take a taxi most of the way or walk along the path from the junction of the Ouaga road and Avenue du Gouverneur Général Eboué, right on the edge of town – it's tricky to follow, however, and you'll probably need a guide (kids en route will no doubt oblige for the customary *cadeau*) but it's worth it for the scenery. Set off early and take water.

In addition to domestic destinations, Bobo is a springboard for Mali (Mopti, Bamako) and – assuming the border is open – Côte d'Ivoire. You can get fuller details on buses and flights from Bobo's travel agents: try Egi Voyages on rue Delafosse. Note that to reach Gaoua in the Lobi country, it's better to go via Pa and Diébougou, where the route is now paved for virtually the whole distance, than via Banfora.

Trains

Ouagadougou–Abidjan trains run three times a week (departing Bobo at 2.30pm on Tuesdays, Thursdays and Saturdays), and offer one possible means of reaching **Banfora** (1hr 30 min). The train returns Wednesdays, Fridays and Sundays, departing Bobo for Ouaga at 10.30pm (7hr). For more information contact Sitarail (℡98.15.71) or check at the station – and buy your tickets in advance.

Bush taxis and buses

The main *gare routière* for *taxis brousse* is on the west side of town. This is the quickest means to points in **Mali** (punishing *piste* as far as Sikasso or reasonable tarmac to Ségou) and **Côte d'Ivoire** (good sealed road), as well as to Ouagadougou and Dédougou, Banfora and Boromo.

There are several private bus stations coveniently located in the city centre, all of which are fairly reliable: **Rakieta** has buses to Ouaga, Banfora and Gaoua (all 2 daily), and Niangoloko (3 daily); **SOGEBAF** (℡98.02.44) buses leave for Ouaga and Banfora every hour from their depot off rue Alpha Moi, near Hamdalaye, and for destinations in the Côte d'Ivoire from their main station on bd de la Révolution; **STMB** (℡97.08.78, ℻97.38.78) have buses to Banfora (2 daily) and to Ouaga (5 daily), from where they have connections across the country. For international destinations try the excellent **TCV**, on rue Crozat (℡97.10.53), who have a daily service to Bamako, a twice-weekly service to Cotonou, and a weekly service to Lagos; or **STBF** (℡97.09.81), who have buses to Bamako (2 daily), and Abidjan, Niamey, Lomé and Cotonou (all three daily) as well as Ouaga.

Flights

Air Burkina (℡97.13.48) currently has flights most days from Bobo to **Ouagadougou** (40–50min; CFA31,900), as well as flights to **Abidjan** (Tues, Thurs, Sat; 1hr 10min; CFA78,400).

Unfortunately, there have been some recent muggings, so don't take any valuables. Remember, too, not to wear anything red – it's prohibited at this sacred place.

Another popular attraction, the **hippo lake** (*mare aux hippopotames*), is located some 60km from Bobo, near Satiri on the road to Dédougou and Ouahigouya. It's a little far to do on a moped, especially given the difficult tracks (even in the dry season), so take a Dédougou-bound taxi from the main *gare routière*, or head to the *gare de Satiri*, at the intersection of Boulevard de la Paix and Avenue Général Merlin, and catch a taxi to Satiri. The Satiri taxi stops in small villages along the way – many of them featuring picturesque **Sahelian-style mosques** – and takes up to three hours (as opposed to less than two for the Dédougou-bound taxi) to cover the scenic route. To get to the lake from Satiri, you could try to catch a lift with passing tourists at weekends; alternatively, you could probably find someone to take you on the back of a bike. Fishermen at the lakeside will take you out by *pirogues* for as close an inspection of the hippos as you're likely to want. Agree a fee in advance – they appreciate aspirins and cigarettes as a tip. If you're extremely lucky, they say, you may even spot elephants.

Banfora and around

Although the town of **Banfora** lacks the spark of Ouaga and Bobo, it lies in a beautiful region of cliffs and forests – you'll notice the vegetation getting denser as you approach from Bobo, with the sight of streams and waterfalls from the roadside. Today, the region's economic importance springs from the vast **sugar cane** projects that have made Burkina a net exporter of manufactured sugar.

Banfora

With a population of some 50,000, **BANFORA** is Burkina's fifth-largest town, developed during colonial times due to its position on the railway line. Banfora's only paved road is its main street – the centre of the town's limited commerce. There are few distractions in town and wandering about won't turn up much apart from the **traditional drinking places** scattered about the backstreets, where you can guzzle *banji* (palm wine) and *chapalo*. To kill an hour or two in the afternoon, a ten-minute walk along the Sindou road takes you across the tracks to the **palm wine sellers**. Join the old men and women under the mango trees for a calabash or two. In the **evening**, you could take in a film at the Nerigab cinema or head to one of the many open-air nightclubs with garden seating and large dance areas.

Banfora has a BICIA-B **bank**. There's **Internet** access at the *Restaurant Calypso*, which is fast but pricey, and at the cybercafé next to *McDonald's*.

Accommodation

Since the area around Banfora has become a major attraction in Burkinabe terms, enterprising young people have started **renting rooms** in their homes (you may be approached and offered rooms at the motor park upon arrival). A bed and bucket shower at these places usually costs less than CFA2000. There are a few reasonable official places too, and smarter new hotels are beginning to open.

Belna Up a dirt track near Yankadi, off the road to Bobo. The cheapest hotel in town (though it feels like it's only been partially completed), with basic rooms (some self-contained) with fan. **②**

Canne à Sucre Near the train station ☎88.01.07, @ hotelcanneasucre@fasonet.bf. Traditionally Banfora's top hotel, and popular amongst expats, with a variety of good accommodation: luxury a/c apartments (**⑤**), a/c rooms (**④**), and cheaper but stylish self-contained thatched huts (**③**). The pool is for the exclusive use of apartment guests, unless they're vacant. The restaurant dishes up

excellent international cuisine – a good place for a splurge.

Comoé On the southern edge of town ☎88.01.51. No-frills budget accommodation with rooms (some with private bath and a/c) around a shaded courtyard that serves as restaurant and bar. **②**

Fara Behind the *autogare* ☎88.01.17. Set in a huge empty compound with spartan self-contained rooms with fan. **②**

La Paix Centre of town, just north of the Mairie ☎88.00.16. Six basic and dingy rooms with

Market days in Western Burkina

Market days west of Bobo follow a predictable weekly pattern which can be useful in itself and for ensuring you don't get stranded somewhere remote without transport: most small villages only have *taxi brousse* connections with main towns on market days.

Monday Koloko, Kotoura, Samorogouah, Sindou, Soukouraba

Thursday Mahon

Friday Kangala

Saturday Oroda

Sunday Banfora, Gaoua

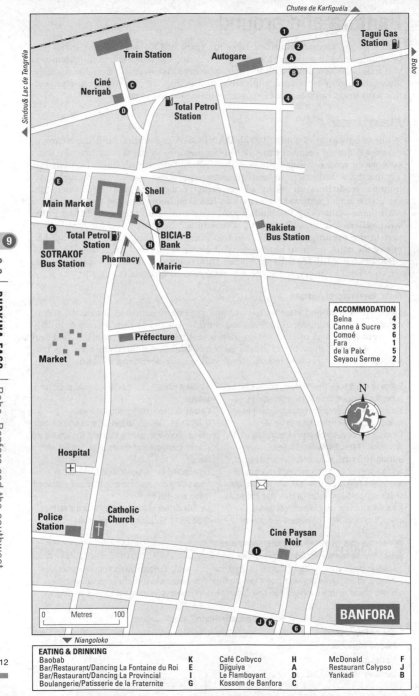

Chutes de Karfiguéla ▲

Train Station

Autogare

Tagui Gas Station ⬛

▶ Bobo

◀ Sindou& Lac de Tengréla

①
②
Ⓐ
Ⓑ
③
④

Ciné Nerigab **Ⓒ**
Ⓓ
Total Petrol Station 🅿

Ⓔ
Main Market

Shell ⛽
Ⓕ
⑤
Rakieta Bus Station

Ⓖ
Total Petrol Station 🅿
SOTRAKOF Bus Station
Pharmacy
Ⓗ **BICIA-B Bank**

Mairie

Préfecture

Market

N

ACCOMMODATION
Belna	4
Canne à Sucre	3
Comoé	6
Fara	1
de la Paix	5
Seyaou Serme	2

Hospital ✚

Police Station
Catholic Church ✝

Ciné Paysan Noir

Ⓘ

0 — Metres — 100

BANFORA

Ⓙ Ⓚ
⑥

▼ Niangoloko

EATING & DRINKING

Baobab	**K**	Café Colbyco	**H**	McDonald	**F**
Bar/Restaurant/Dancing La Fontaine du Roi	**E**	Djiguiya	**A**	Restaurant Calypso	**J**
Bar/Restaurant/Dancing La Provincial	**I**	Le Flamboyant	**D**	Yankadi	**B**
Boulangerie/Patisserie de la Fraternite	**G**	Kossom de Banfora	**C**		

mozzy nets, and communal sit-down toilets.
There's a decent restaurant attached. ❷, including
a basic breakfast.
Seyaou Serme Near the *autogare* ☎88.08.62.

New, upmarket establishment, with rooms inside
round huts with white-tiled floors, private
bathrooms, a/c, TV and phone. There are also
plans for a restaurant, bar and pool. ❹

Eating, drinking and nightlife

Baobab Southern edge of town, near *Hôtel
Comoé*. Generous portions of basic European food
served up in an attractive low-key set-up with
seating indoors or out, under roadside thatched
paillotes.
Bar/Restaurant/Dancing La Fontaine du Roi
Just west of the main market. Bar and dancefloor
(CFA500) which gets lively on Friday and Saturday
nights.
Bar/Restaurant/Dancing La Provincial Next
door to the old Ciné Paysan Noir. A large rambling
place, set in pleasant gardens, with the usual
inexpensive selection of fish, chicken, rice or
couscous, plus a bar and an indoor dancefloor
which opens up on Saturday nights.
Boulangerie/Patisserie de la Fraternité Near
Sotrakof station. Open 6am–8pm. A useful address
for tea, coffee, croissants and other pastries.
Café Colbyco Opposite the Mairie. Pleasant little
place – especially good for breakfasts – with

yoghurt, omelettes, tea and coffee. Open from
7am.
Djiguiya Across from the *Yankadi*. Pricey menu,
including fish and chicken dishes (CFA3000 plus),
and crepes, served up in a large attractive outdoor
set-up.
Le Flamboyant Opposite the Ciné Nerigab.
Restaurant-terrasse with inexpensive meals and
nighttime dancing (Thurs–Sat; CFA1000).
Kossom de Banfora Across from Ciné Nerigab.
Delicious milk and yoghurt served all day.
McDonald Near the *Hôtel de la Paix*. Extremely
popular place with really good food, superb *filet
de Capitaine* and fresh fruit juices. Closed
Wednesday afternoon.
Restaurant Calypso Near the *Hôtel Comoé*.
French-owned place serving excellent food for
CFA1000–3000 in a pleasant garden courtyard.
Yankadi On the road to Bobo. Basic and clean,
with an extensive menu of European dishes.

Around Banfora

To see the region **west of Banfora** – which is richly endowed with sites of scenic
beauty – it's best to rent a *mobylette* from near the market (around CFA3500 per
day), or a slightly faster moped (CFA4500, excluding petrol). The **Lac de Tengréla**
and **Chutes de Karfiguéla** can be difficult to find (numerous tracks lead through
a tall growth of sugar cane most of the year), so you might consider taking someone
from town along with you.

Lac de Tengréla

Some 7km from Banfora, the **Lac de Tengréla** makes a great excursion. Take the
Banfora–Sindou road west out of town; after about 6km, a sign points left to the
lake, along a track which runs for 1km to the hamlet of **Tengréla**. Just beyond the
village, you can stop and refresh yourself with a cool drink at the *Campement
Farafina*, near the lake (☎24.46.21, ✉soloisa6@hotmail.com; ❶), which has food
and basic accommodation in round thatched huts with mosquito nets and bucket
showers; you can also camp here. The owner, Souleymane, also leads a traditional
dance and drumming school, and if you stay here you will probably be treated to an
energetic live performance.

At the lake itself, you'll have to pay an entrance fee of CFA1000, or CFA2000
including a *pirogue* ride. It's occasionally possible to spot the **hippos** that live in the
waters here. At the edge of the lake, an abandoned cement house provides an ideal
place for **camping** if you've got your own tent, although mosquitoes are a problem.

Chutes de Karfiguéla

The **Chutes de Karfiguéla** waterfalls, located in a beautiful, verdant setting, are
about 12km from the lake, though the route there is difficult to find (ask the fishermen

or people in the vicinity to point you to the *chutes* or *cascades*). They are probably easier to reach direct from Banfora, as the route is signposted most of the way – make sure you turn left at the barrier, along the side of the rice fields, and then make another ninety-degree left turn shortly afterwards. Note that the river has been dammed, and in the dry season (Nov–May) the falls are a disappointing trickle. During the rains, however, they swell to thunder impressively over the solid rock formations. From the car park and entrance, where you pay CFA1000 plus a nominal parking fee, you approach the falls by means of a narrow path bordered with huge mango trees. If you're tempted to swim, be aware that bilharzia is a risk here. You can continue upstream from the falls to reach a number of less spectacular but still attractive falls. About half-way between Banfora and the Chutes, the *Baobab Campement* is a good place to rest up en route and has drink and food (European and African) as well as accommodation in attractive round huts (❷).

Around 3km from the falls are the **Domes de Febedougou** (entrance CFA1000) – an oddly shaped cluster of rock formations created by water erosion. Climbing to the top is relatively easy and gives you a great view over the far-stretching fields of sugar cane. Bring plenty of water. The Domes are relatively easy to find from the falls – return to the main track and turn left alongside the cane fields. At the crossroads turn left and follow the signs.

Sindou

SINDOU derives its fame from **Les Pics de Sindou**, a three-kilometre-long chain of sculpted crags which form a dramatic backdrop to the village, particularly at sunset. The sandstone has been eroded by the elements into spectacular pancake towers and 50-metre-high needles, often topped with precarious rocky crowns. It's an excellent place to spend a day or so exploring or rock climbing. There's an entrance fee of CFA1000, payable at the roadside by Les Pics, where you'll also be assigned a mandatory guide, although the post is frequently unmanned – in which case just ask someone in Sindou to show you the easiest route to scramble up to the top of the rocks. Despite the area's natural beauty, Sindou remains little visited. Mango trees line the main street of conically thatched *banco* houses, yet to be replaced by corrugated iron shacks. Bring lots of film.

Getting to Sindou is tricky. Although it lies on a back route into Mali, few vehicles make the fifty-kilometre run from Banfora. Without your own transport, you have two equally feasible options: hitching with occasional local traffic (Sindou's market day is Monday), or renting a *mobylette* or bike in Banfora. The two-to-three-hour ride on a rough road is tiring, but rewarding. **Supplies** are limited to street food and a couple of tiny restaurants. There is some relief, however, with tepid beer at the **bar** which also has ultra-basic *chambres de passage* (❶) – if you have your own equipment, it's much better to camp out among *les pics*.

If you get stranded in Sindou, you can try hitching a ride with the enormous Sofitex cotton trucks which occasionally head for Banfora.

9.4

The Lobi country

Nestling between the Ghanaian and Ivoirian frontiers, the green and pleasant **Lobi country** is a favourite travellers' destination and an interesting diversion en route from Bobo and the southwest into Ghana. The area is all hilly, tree-scattered savanna, and rich enough in wildlife for the elephant stories to be just about credible. Although the lively town of **Gaoua** and the strange ruins of **Loropeni** are the region's only real tourist draws, the welcoming Lobi themselves, with their well-preserved traditions and *cabaret* drinking bars, make their corner of the country one of the best to visit, especially now that good, mainly tarred roads connect Ouagadougou with Gaoua via Pa and Diébougou.

Food in the Lobi country is generally of the rice and sauce variety, though there are other staples, such as fish and guinea fowl, if you look for them. More typically Lobi is millet *tô* with a sauce of baobab leaves, shea nuts or *néré* fruit.

Gaoua and around

Though the principal reasons for coming to Lobi country are to see the **ruins** and bustling **market** at **Loropeni**, the region's main town is **Gaoua** – absolutely shaking with *cabarets* – and it's here that you'll probably want to base yourself.

Lobi traditions

The Lobi believe in maintaining their **traditions**. Lobi men, for example, still hunt with bow and arrows for hares, guinea fowl and gazelles, and it's common to see men carrying these weapons – traditionally poison-tipped – as they walk along the road. Another notable aspect of Lobi culture is the cutlery embedded in gravestones: the Lobi are buried with their fork, spoon, plate and saucepan. Every seven years, too, the new generation of young people take part in the **djoro** initiation ceremony. Some customs, however, are disappearing. Few Lobi women nowadays wear the disc plugs through their lips which used to be so admired. And the old-fashioned, all-in-one method of house building is giving way to easier mud-brick construction.

The traditions the Lobi maintain best are the ones with widest appeal – booze, music and markets. No Lobi town or village would be complete without its **cabarets** – not nightclubs, but places where *chapalo* and *qui-me-pousse* or *patasi* (home-brewed firewater) are consumed in serious quantities and **traditional music** is often played. Many *cabarets* brew their own *chapalo*, and it's so much cheaper than bottled beer that you could afford to shout the whole place a drink for the same price as a bottle of Brakina in a bar. Many *cabarets* keep a drum and a *balafon* handy in case anyone feels like playing, which they often do. Even in the unlikely event you don't acquire a taste for *chapalo* and Lobi music, *cabarets* are the best places to go and mix with the locals – who are always very welcoming. The region's **markets** are traditionally held on a five-day cycle, though now increasingly on the same day every week.

Gaoua

GAOUA is almost certainly the best place to get acquainted both with *chapalo* and traditional roots music, though obviously the sounds in Bobo-Dioulasso are more refined. The main draw in town though, apart from the *cabarets*, is the magnificent Sunday **market**, a maelstrom of colour and activity. Look out for the leatherworkers just north of the market, spread out under a tree west of the mosque. You could also visit the town's sacred grove, **Bafuogi**, which is easily identified by the masses of plucked feathers from sacrificed chickens. The grove is about 1km south of town on the edge of a small hill – head south up the hill towards the hospital office; you'll spot the large water tower on top from a distance. There are great views across town from the grove, too. You're supposed to have a guide, who will tell you spine-tingling tales about the pythons living in the caves.

Up the hill in the administrative quarter, the **Musée de Poni** (CFA1500 including tour) is set in an old colonial-style house and has exhibits of traditional art, Lobi lifestyles and homes typical of local ethnic groups, together with interesting photographs from the colonial period.

Practicalities

Gaoua has very limited **accommodation**. The *Hôtel de Poni*, next to the market (☎87.02.00; ❶), has cheap and grubby rooms with equally grim shared toilet facilities – choose a room away from the noisy bar. Alternatively, people in town can point you (there are no signs) to the informal and incredibly basic *Eberge Campement* – CFA2000 per person, for a mattress on the floor and an open-air bucket shower. The *Hala*, a pleasant 1.6km walk out on the Diébougou road (☎87.01.21, ℱ87.02.66; ❹), offers much better but somewhat overpriced accommodation, with comfortable a/c rooms with sit-down toilets; they also have a laundry service.

Food-wise you'll find plenty of stalls doing roast meat and fried fish, especially around the mosque, and several of the bars (see below) serve food too. Try the established *Café Chez Francoise*, in front of the Poni Cinema, though the frozen yoghurt here is more of a draw than the plates of kidney, liver and heart. The *Cafétariat* and the *Salon de Thé Royal*, both north of Shell, are alternative spots for

---

Limited Lobi

The simplest Lobi greeting is *Me foaré* ("Hello"), to which the normal response is *Monicho?* ("How are you?") and the reply to that *Michor* ("Fine thanks"). "Thank you" is *Ferehina foaré*.

Food		Numbers	
Water	*Ñyoñi*	1	*Biel*
Chicken	*Yolo*	2	*Yenyo*
Egg yolk	*Pala*	3	*Yetter*
Meat	*Nuni*	4	*Yena*
Maize	*Wologyo*	5	*Yamoi*
Millet	*Gyo/di*	6	*Maado*
Yam	*Puri*	7	*Makonyo*
		8	*Makotter*
Times		9	*Nuor biri pero*
Today	*Ni*	10	*Nuor*
Tomorrow	*Kyo*	20	*Kpuele*
Day after tomorrow	*Gye ale*	50	*Kpalanyo nuor*
Yesterday	*Daoule*	100	*Tama*
		1000	*Bulani*

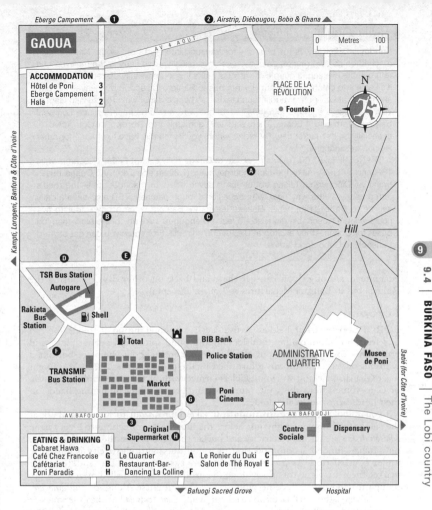

couscous, omelettes, tea and coffee. *Restaurant-Bar-Dancing La Colline*, near Rakieta, serves up simple meals of rice and chicken, as do *Poni Paradis* and *Le Quartier*. At weekends, *Poni Paradis* also opens up its indoor a/c dancefloor (CFA1000). The *Hala* hotel has a limited range of Lebanese, African and French cuisine – mediocre and over-priced, though the portions are gigantic – and breakfasts (CFA2000). **Drinking** is mainly a *cabaret* sport: *Cabaret Hawa* stays open late, or until the *chapalo* runs out, and has sporadic live music. There are dozens of other places, such as the *Le Ronier du Duki*, east of the *Cafétariat* – follow the noise.

For **telephone** calls, ONATEL, on the hill, is as cheap as anywhere else. There is a BIB **bank** in the centre of town, which should change euro cash, but nothing else.

Around Gaoua

Due west of Gaoua, **Loropeni** has a colourful market and some intriguing ruins nearby – it's an easy excursion from Gaoua on market days, when transport is

Sunday (market day) is the best day for transport into or out of Gaoua. **Nako** is best reached on its own market day, when vehicles usually leave early in the morning and return in the evening; a couple of vehicles make this journey daily. To reach **Loropeni**, it's easiest to catch the 7.30am Rakieta bus to Banfora (a second bus leaves at 2pm) and get off at Loropeni; irregular bush taxis also head out that way. To return to Gaoua, your best bet is again to join the Rakieta bus, which returns back through Loropeni between 1pm and 1.30pm. There's usually something to **Doropo** in Côte d'Ivoire, especially on its market day, Thursday, where you'll probably have to change for other Ivoirian destinations.

TRANSMIF (☎87.00.10) has a service to **Ouaga** daily except Friday (7.30am), while TSR and SALIMA make the same journey daily (7.30am and 7am). All Ouaga buses travel via Diébougou, taking about six to seven hours to reach Ouaga – the road's tarred nearly all the way now, with occasional rough patches. TSR also have a daily service to **Bobo** (3pm), while Rakieta leaves for Banfora twice a day – four to five hours along a reasonable dirt road. To reach **Diébougou**, take any of the early-morning buses for Ouaga – they all stop at Diébougou en route. From here you can get onward transport to Bobo and Hamile.

guaranteed, although you can get there and back on other days too, using the Rakieta bus to Banfora (departures at 7.30am and 2pm).

Loropeni

LOROPENI's **market**, held every five days, is a bustling throng of colour. You can buy fruit, hot food, chillies, multicoloured ground spices and peanut paste, and watch flip-flops being made out of old tyres, and enamel bowls being re-bottomed with bits of vegetable-oil tins ("furnished by the people of the USA"). You might meet Ghanaians selling worming tablets (armed with lurid photographic displays), or Gan women from the west, often wearing brown string mourning bands on their heads, arms, necks and ankles.

If you're looking for **accommodation**, take the road out to Kampti and ask at the *buvette* (bar) on your right, just before the mosque, for directions to a very basic *Maison de Passage* (❶; no electricity and bucket showers). Across the road from here, new Italian-funded accommodation in round huts with electricity is currently under construction. Apart from the *riz-sauce* **restaurant** in the middle of the market, there are plenty of *tabliers* along the main road doing grilled meat and soup, though tea and coffee become quite scarce after breakfast. Alongside the *autogare*, *Don Hai* serves the usual rice and spaghetti, while *Club Yemsafa* has cheap servings of rice and cold drinks – you'll see a sign to it as you walk to the *Maison de Passage*. Drinks are also available at the *buvette* behind the *autogare*.

The ruins

To get to Loropeni's enigmatic **ruins** (entrance 1500CFA), head out of town on the Banfora road. After 3.5km you come to a small hill, at the top of which a track leads off to the right. Follow it for 500m to the ruins. Though not massively impressive, the Loropeni ruins are among West Africa's very few stone remains, rising up out of the scrub like some lost temple in a Hollywood movie. Unlike the great stone ruins of East Africa and Zimbabwe, they don't get many visitors, and since their origin and the identity of the people who built them are still mysteries, your ideas about them are as good as anyone else's. The ruins are more or less rectangular, around 50m long by 40m wide, and would originally have stood 6–7m high. They lack any doors or windows. Inside, the ruins are divided into two enclosures, one large and one small, connected by a door, and each subdivided into further chambers.

If you don't have transport, you can usually persuade somebody to let you hire their *mobylette* or bicycle to visit the ruins, as well as the Gan village of **OBIRÉ**, 8km northwest of Loropeni, which is remarkable for its round thatched huts (a thatching style very different from Lobi houses) and for its life-size **mud statues** of ancestral kings (entrance CFA1500). If you prefer, a local will also happily guide you there for a *cadeau*.

The **Gan country** a few kilometres north and west of Loropeni harbours more archeological oddities if you can organize transport. There are ruins near **Yerifoula**, others near **Oyono** and **Lokosso**, and some large relics at **Loghi**.

Diébougou and Hamile

Lying outside the Lobi country proper, **DIÉBOUGOU**'s people are mostly Lobi-Gan and Dagara (Dagarti). There's not a lot to see here, but it's a friendly place, and the intricate system of underground defence tunnels nearby – known as **La Grotte** – add some interest. These underground defence tunnels were commissioned by a French army in 1900 and built using local labour. The tunnels are an easy fifteen minutes' walk out of town along the Bobo road in Diébougou Forest; get directions at the *Relais La Bougouriba* and take a torch.

DIÉBOUGOU

Bougouriba River & Lycée

Gare Routière

Market

Original Supermarket

Market

RED LIGHT DISTRICT

Catholic Mission

Commissariat de Police

Protestant Mission

BIB Bank

Shell

Hospital

Bobo Dioulasso & La Grotte

Crocodile Swamp ▶ Ouessa (for Ghana) & Léo

▼ Gaoua

0 Metres 200

ACCOMMODATION	
Campement L'Hôtel	2
Relais La Bougouriba	1

EATING & DRINKING	
Café Flambeau	C
Macoumba Night-Club	B
Restaurant Walem	A
La Source	D

During the wet season (June–Oct) **crocodiles** collect in the swamp at the eastern end of town – they're best observed around dawn.

Practicalities

There are a few **accommodation** options in town, the most convenient of which is in the courtyard of the *gare routière*, where there are some surprisingly pleasant rooms, despite the grubby exterior (❶). *Campement l'Hôtel* (☎86.01.60; ❶), which also serves as a bar and pick-up joint, has very basic rooms with fan and rather mucky communal showers and toilets. The nearby *Relais La Bougouriba* (☎86.02.80; ❷) is slightly smarter and cleaner, with a shower and fan in every room. For **eating and drinking**, *La Bougouriba* has a bar and restaurant offering rice, guinea fowl and steak, while *La Source* (almost next door) has basic fare and some pleasant seating outside. *Café Flambeau* does breakfasts with coffee, tea, omelettes and so forth, as does the small eaterie inside the bus station. In addition, there's a run of food stalls around the market and lots of *cabarets* to slake your thirst. **Nightlife** revolves around the *Macoumba Night-Club*, which has drinking, dancing and simple food. The BIB **bank** changes euro cash only.

TSR and TRANSMIF **buses** coming from Gaoua stop here en route to Ouaga (9am), a five-hour journey along a good road. TSR and TRANSMIF buses leave for Gauoua (90min) daily between noon and 1pm from the *gare routière*. The *pistes* to Hamile (5hr plus) and Bobo are in a terrible condition, and transport is limited to occasional private minibuses.

Hamile and into Ghana

A busy border town and the main crossing point into Ghana from Bobo-Dioulasso, **HAMILE** has little to offer – nowadays people pop across the border to the Ghana side for cheaper beer, and it never goes dry. If you're looking for a place to drink and sleep, *Mandou* (❶) has basic but pretty clean rooms; better value than those on the Ghanaian side.

Cedis are available at the ordinary (poor) border rate, a rate beaten just about everywhere else in Ghana. Almost all **transport on the Ghanaian side** goes to Lawra and Wa, although be prepared for a long wait as transport is very infrequent along this rough *piste*. From Wa, there are onward connections to Tamali, Kumasi and Accra.

Ghana

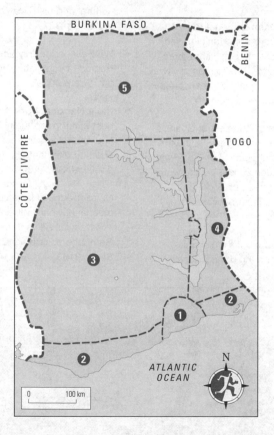

Ghana highlights

* **Cape Coast Castle** Among the most impressive of the forts along the coast, sympathetically restored and housing evocative displays on the slave trade. See p.776

* **Kakum National Park** A superb opportunity to see the rainforest, with a three-hundred-metre rope walkway high up in the forest canopy to traverse. See p.777

* **Busua** The best of Ghana's fine coastal resorts, a wonderful place to chill out, with golden sands, inviting water and fresh seafood, fruit juices and pancakes available. See p.784

* **Nzulezo** It's a glorious canoe trip through lush creek vegetation to reach this destination, a community living in stilt houses beside the water. See p.785

* **Kumasi** Hectic, bustling Asante city, with a strong cultural and historical identity. See p.787

* **Wli Falls** In the hilly Volta Region, a captivating waterfall. See p.803

* **Mole National Park** The best safari opportunity in the country: relax and unwind spotting elephants from the poolside. See p.809

* **Nakpanduri** An isolated, traditional northern village with spectacular views from the Gambaga escarpment. See p.816

Introduction and Basics

From a traveller's point of view, Ghana has a lot to commend it. Compared with the other Anglophone countries in West Africa, Ghana offers a transport and accommodation infrastructure that's second to none; a cultural mix that's every bit as rewarding as Nigeria's (without that country's immense size or intimidating reputation); and better beaches than The Gambia. Moreover, the Ghanaian government has an enthusiastic commitment to tourism with a number of regional tourist offices set up and plenty to engage visitors.

Ghana was the first modern African country to retrieve its **independence**, in 1957. At the time it was one of the richest nations on the continent – the world's leading **cocoa** exporter and producer of a tenth of the world's **gold**. But after Kwame Nkrumah's optimistic start it suffered a hornet's nest of setbacks. For years, coups, food shortages and sapping corruption combined to make Ghana a place to be avoided.

However, since the near economic collapse of 1979, conditions have improved almost out of recognition and the country is back on its feet. Politically Ghana is increasingly viewed as a good example of an African **democracy**, having undergone a peaceful transition in 2000 from benign dictatorship; that said, Ghanaians still complain, justifiably, about continued inefficiency and corruption.

The country has a distinctive personality and perhaps more claim to a **national** character than any other in the region. School education has had a major impact, going back four generations now, and there's an inventiveness with language – both written, on signs and in the press, and spoken, in repartee – that hints at a creativity as yet barely unleashed in Africa. Ghanaians are hospitable and generous to a fault, and there's more warmth to be experienced in Ghana than in either of its coastal neighbours.

As regards the **terrain**, Ghana has few highland regions, with the exception of the striking **scarp system** curving through the country – from the Gambaga escarpment in the northeast round to the Wenchi scarp west of Lake Volta, and southeast as the Mampong scarp through the forest. There are some attractive rolling green landscapes and, in the central regions, away from the **cocoa** plantations and the **goldfields**, several large districts of dense **rainforest** with

Facts and figures

Known as the **Gold Coast** during the colonial era, **Ghana** took its present name – for symbolic reasons – from that of the former West African empire which was located in present-day southeast Mauritania. With around twenty million people and an **area** of 239,000 square kilometres (about the same size as Britain or Oregon), divided into ten administrative units called "regions", Ghana is one of the region's most densely populated states.

Ghana has a directly elected president overseeing a national assembly of two hundred members of parliament. Having pursued a course of IMF rehabilitation, the country receives debt relief under the Heavily Indebted Poor Countries Initiative, though in 2001 its **foreign debt** still stood at around £3.7 billion ($6 billion), nearly four times annual earnings from the export of goods and services (though less than a week's spending by the US military). Agriculture accounts for forty percent of the domestic economy, with cocoa and gold among the main exports.

Ghana has traditionally been known for a relatively high level of **education**. There's a high level of literacy and four **universities** – the University of Ghana, near Accra; the University of Science and Technology, Kumasi; the University of Cape Coast; and the University of Development Studies, Tamale.

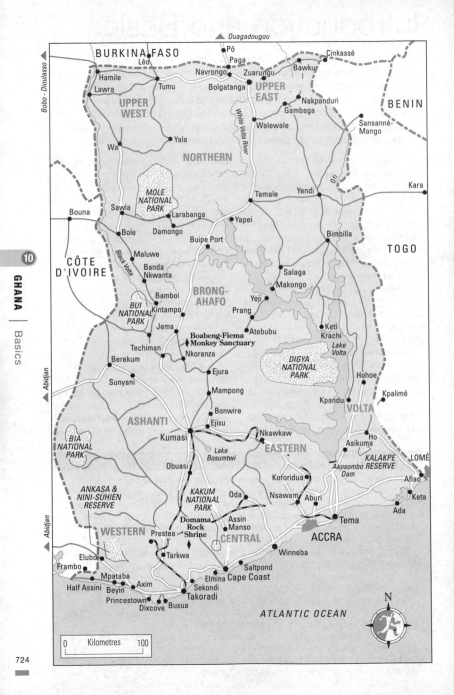

giant hardwoods and palms vying for space. The biggest impact, however, is made by the enormous stretch of **Lake Volta**, an artificial lake created in the wooded savanna in 1966, which has totally changed the anatomy of the country – not to mention the lives of the thousands of rural dwellers its waters displaced. In the eastern Volta region, between the lake and the Togolese border, the hills of the **Akwapim range** roll across the landscape to create a district of verdant green valleys and gentle peaks.

The **Accra district** and much of the surrounding bushy, **coastal plain** is surprisingly dry – almost desolate in places, partly the result of an unusual local subclimate – but the coastal road to the west runs within striking distance of the shore for much of its length, and the beaches themselves are alluring. The coast has a special dimension, too, in its European **forts and castles**, some dating from the fifteenth century, which were built as trading posts for gold, ivory and, later, slaves. The beaches of the far southwest are backed by lowland forest and patchy jungle agriculture in a scene similar to most of the Ivoirian coastline over the border.

People

Of the myriad ethnic groups that people Ghana, the **Akan** – including the **Fante** and **Asante** (also spelled Ashanti) – predominate. The Asante occupy the central forest, and in pre-colonial days their empire stretched into the regions of present-day Côte d'Ivoire and Togo. The **Ga-Adangme** and **Ewe**, who probably came from Yorubaland in Nigeria, settled mainly in the east and south. The major peoples of the north are all speakers of Voltaic languages and have much in common, culturally, with the Burkinabe over the border in Burkina Faso. They include the southern Mossi kingdoms of **Mamprusi** and **Dagomba** in the northeast, the **Wala** and **Dagarti** in the northwest, the **Gonja** and other Grusi peoples – **Kassena**, **Frafra**, **Sissala**, **Builsa** and **Talensi** – near the Burkinabe border.

Islam is widespread among the northerners, some of whom migrated south from Muslim communities in Mali. **Christianity**, of course, spread with European involvement in the Gold Coast, but pantheistic beliefs and ancestor veneration remain the most widely practised religions in the country.

Where to go

After decades of neglect, **Accra** is beginning to look the part of a capital once again. It's manageable and friendly enough, though unless you're drawn to the nightlife, and your visit coincides with some weekend live shows, you'll only want to spend a few days here before getting out along the coast or into the interior. The **west coast** is exceptional, and the European **castles**, most of which can be visited, provide excellent focuses for beach-hopping. Slightly inland, the protected rainforest of the **Kakum National Park** is one of the country's major natural attractions. To the east, the lush hills and waterfalls of the **Volta region** are also currently generating great interest among travellers. **Kumasi**, in the centre of the country, has a strong sense of identity, and the forest region of which it is capital is scenically and culturally Ghana's most appealing area. The **north** is quite different, both in landscape and people, but its climate is more tolerable and, if there's not a lot that demands to be seen as you pass through – apart from **Mole National Park** – there's plenty of interest in its ethnographic history if you have more time in the area.

When to go

Ghana has a lot more **climatic variation** than most of West Africa. **Central and southern Ghana** – south of Tamale – is unusual in having two distinct rainy seasons, the first lasting roughly from March to June and the second from September to October. The **far southwest** gets heavy rains, but in **Accra** the rains tend to be light, and it's uncommon to experience day after day of torrential downpour. The **central rainforest** regions tend to be wetter and (although you wouldn't know it because of the high humidity) slightly cooler. The **north** is basically hot

Accra

	Jan	Feb	Mar	Apr	May	June	July	Aug	Sept	Oct	Nov	Dec
Temperatures °C												
Min (night)	23	24	24	24	24	23	23	22	23	23	24	24
Max (day)	31	31	31	31	31	29	27	27	27	29	31	31
Rainfall mm	15	33	56	81	142	178	46	15	36	64	36	23
Days with rainfall	1	2	4	6	9	10	4	3	4	6	3	2

Tamale

	Jan	Feb	Mar	Apr	May	June	July	Aug	Sept	Oct	Nov	Dec
Temperatures °C												
Min (night)	21	23	24	24	24	22	22	22	22	22	22	20
Max (day)	36	37	37	36	33	31	29	29	30	32	34	35
Rainfall mm	3	3	53	69	104	142	135	196	226	99	10	5
Days with rainfall	1	1	1	6	10	12	14	16	19	13	1	1

and dry most of the year, with a climate much like that of Ouagadougou in Burkina, and a single rainy period from June to October.

Getting there from the rest of Africa

Ghana is one of the most popular countries for independent travel in West Africa, its good transport links and central location making it an excellent starting point for longer travels.

All international flights arrive into Accra. Ghana Airways makes two long treks west up the coast twice a week, calling at **Banjul**, **Conakry**, and **Dakar** before returning to Accra; there are also several weekly flights from **Monrovia** and **Freetown**. Ghana Airways and Air Ivoire operate flights from **Abidjan**, though the volatile situation in Côte d'Ivoire means these are liable to be suspended at short notice.

From the other direction, Ghana Airways operate nonstop flights from **Cotonou** (1 weekly) and **Lagos** (several weekly). Flights

For important practical information applying to all West African countries, covering health, transport, cultural hints and more, plus details on getting to the region from beyond Africa, see Basics, pp.9–87.

from **Lomé** are run by Air Togo and by Ethiopian Airlines twice weekly.

Inland, **Bamako** is linked with Accra by twice-weekly flights on both Air Ivoire and Ghana Airways; **Ouagadougou** is connected by Ghana Airways twice a week. Flights from other cities in West Africa require a change of plane, though you'll find it well nigh impossible to get a convenient connection from Nouakchott, Bissau, the Cape Verde Islands or Niamey.

From South Africa, South African Airlines fly four times a week from **Johannesburg**. Ethiopian provides a link from East Africa with a flight from Addis Ababa four times a week, while Kenya Airways serves Accra from Nairobi twice weekly. EgyptAir has flights from **Cairo** to Accra twice a week.

Overland from Burkina Faso

Coming **from Ouagadougou**, you can either take a **bush taxi** or **bus** to the border at Paga, or get transport through to Navrongo, Bolgatanga or Accra. You'll make better time on the road by bush taxi, but the buses are more comfortable and generally get through the border and various checkpoints more quickly. If you're lucky with connections, it can sometimes work out cheapest and fastest to change transport at the border, which is generally an amicable process – though note that it closes at 6pm. The direct STC bus leaves Ouaga for Accra three times a week, and is by far the most comfortable of all the options (around ₵90,000 or CFA10,500).

Other crossings include the one between Léo and Tumu and the one at Hamile. Transport is patchy on both sides of the border, and there's no direct through transport to speak of in either case – your prospects are best by far on market days.

The **fast route to Accra** goes via Tamale, Kintampo and Kumasi; the more easterly route, involving a Lake Volta ferry or canoe crossing between Makongo and Yeji, is extremely rough.

Overland from Togo

The Lomé–Accra road is surfaced. The quickest way between the two capitals is by **bush taxi** but you'll save the hassle of sitting through vehicle searches if you first get to the border on the western outskirts of the city of Lomé, cross on foot to Aflao in Ghana, and then continue by bush taxi or bus – a journey of about three hours. You can also take one of the Intercity STC buses which depart Aflao three times a day to Accra (₵17,000), and which are more comfortable than bush taxis, but take slightly longer. The border is open daily from 6am to 10pm, although watch out for hassle and scams on both sides of the border.

Other possible crossing points are at the village of Wli near **Hohoe**, at Tatali east of Yendi, and at Pulimakum east of Bawku in the far northeastern corner of the country (Togolese border formalities take place in Cinkassé as there is no official post in Pulimakum). All involve rough travel and lengthy delays due to a lack of transport, which is much easier to find on respective market days.

Overland from Côte d'Ivoire

The coastal stretch of road between Abidjan and Accra is in good condition, and intercity STC and STIF **buses** – not to mention fleets of **bush taxis** – connect the two capitals in around fourteen hours. Buses leave from the Treichville *gare routière* in Abidjan. There's also a fast route direct to Kumasi via Abengourou – also a day's journey – from Abidjan's Adjamé *gare routière*. At the time

of writing, timetables were subject to frequent change due to instability in Côte d'Ivoire.

Red tape and visas

Visas are required by most non-ECOWAS nationals visiting Ghana. Single-entry (£30 in the UK, $20 in the USA) and multiple-entry visas (£40/$50) are available, though note that upon entering the country, you will be stamped with a sixty-day limit. Extensions are, in practice, only available in Accra and are painfully slow to obtain (see p.767).

If you're carrying more than $5000 or the equivalent in foreign currency into the country, you'll need to make a currency declaration upon arrival. Officially you're not allowed to take more than ₵5000 of Ghanaian currency out of the country, though this is rarely checked.

Information, websites and maps

Virtually no official tourist information is supplied outside the country. The **Ghana Tourist Board** has offices in Accra and all the regional capitals throughout the country (Cape Coast, Takoradi, Kumasi, Tamale, Wa, Bolgatanga, Ho, Koforidua, Sunyani). Services are as yet uneven across regions, with little communication between them; they are most useful in tourist areas such as Cape Coast.

You can get a feel for Ghanaian current events and culture through the detailed coverage provided by *Ghana Review International* (ⓦwww.ghanareview.com). A couple of other websites worth a look are ⓦwww.ghana.co.uk, containing a miscellany of news, music reviews, recipes and other Ghanaian information; and ⓦwww.ghana-classifieds.com, a useful directory of Ghanaian businesses and institutions, including Web links.

Maps

The International Travel Maps 1:900,000 map of Ghana is reasonably up to date. In

GHANA | Basics

Accra, the best place to find detailed regional and basic national maps is at the Survey Office on Giffard Road, (☎021/77.71.01), near the airport. They sell **town maps** for a number of places outside the capital, as well as an **Accra city map**. Also look out for the country map produced by KLM and Shell, which has an Accra map on the reverse. In theory it's available at the KLM office on Ring Road in Accra, at Shell stations and from some supermarkets.

The Ghana Wildlife Division produces a useful map of all the country's **national parks**, and there are maps of the individual parks at ⓦ www.wildlife-ghana.org.

Health

Yellow fever jabs are in theory required for entry, but certificates of vaccination are rarely checked at the airport, more so at land borders. Cholera epidemics can occur, especially in isolated regions with limited sources of clean water. Bilharzia is another concern – Lake Volta is a notorious risk; in general, stay away from stagnant ponds or slow-running streams, especially in savanna areas. Chloroquine-resistant malaria is also a serious issue (see p.32).

In large towns, **tap water** is usually drinkable. In smaller places, and villages, the well or stored rainwater isn't always the purest and you may want to try some combination of boiling (not always practical), filtering or purifying tablets. Except in the remotest areas, bottled water is available at around ₵4000 for a 1.5-litre bottle.

The main **hospitals** are in Accra and Kumasi. Smaller hospitals and clinics can be found in towns throughout the country, but for a major medical problem you may prefer a private clinic. Your embassy may be able to recommend a suitable practice.

Ghana has a surging **AIDS** problem, as much as any other country in the region, with thousands of cases reported and hundreds of thousands of HIV carriers. Fortunately, there is a growing acknowledgement of the problem, as demonstrated by emerging radio and television broadcasts and several recent health awareness campaigns.

Costs, money and banks

Ghana's currency is the **cedi** (₵; pronounced *see-dee*). Formerly, one cedi was divided into 100 pesewas, but inflation long ago rose well past the point at which pesewas had any value. There are ₵50, ₵100, ₵200 and ₵500 coins; notes come in denominations of ₵5000, ₵10,000 and ₵20,000. The official **exchange rate** is around ₵14,000 = £1; ₵8750 = $1. Note that because of the continuing decline in the value of the cedi, **inflation** is a big issue in Ghana, and cedi prices may well have risen substantially by the time you read this, though in hard-currency terms prices remain fairly constant. With the largest-denomination note only worth around £1.50/$2.25, Ghanaians carry money in huge plastic bags, and you'll find yourself walking around with **wads of money** that don't add up to much. Don't casually destroy any; a tourist was once fined and jailed for a month for lighting a cigarette with a ₵100 note.

Costs

Cedi devaluations and inflation – currently at around ten percent per year – make it difficult to gauge **costs**, but in hard-currency terms they are falling all the time. **Accommodation** in Ghana is inexpensive: a simple, decent hotel costs as little as £3/$5 a night for a double room, and can be cheaper still upcountry. **Transport** is also cheaper in Ghana than surrounding countries – roughly half the cost of travel in Burkina or Côte d'Ivoire – especially if you travel by intercity State Transport Corporation (STC) buses. Although Ghanaians find even street **food** expensive on their wages, it will seem cheap enough to you, as you can usually eat heartily for under ₵5000 (£0.40/$0.60), while dining at a decent restaurant will typically set you back ₵40,000 (£3/$4.80) for a main course.

Businesses which rely heavily on customers wielding foreign currency (which of course includes the more expensive hotels and restaurants, imported-goods outlets and so on) tend to keep a close eye on the exchange rate and adjust their prices accordingly. Often they actually quote prices in dollars, though they'll accept payment in some other hard currency, with the exchange rate skewed in their favour, or in cedis. Note that a 12.5 percent **value added tax** is always added to your bill at hotels and restaurants; check the prices quoted to see if it's already included.

With an **ISIC card** (the only recognized student card), you will get a discount (typically fifty percent) on admission at most of Ghana's tourist attractions. **Volunteers** with NGOs are also eligible for discounts at many attractions, though you may have to produce a staff card or other proof of your status to claim the reduced rate.

Changing money

You'll find **foreign exchange (forex) bureaux** in Accra, Kumasi and other major towns, and new ones springing up all over the country. Shop around for the best rates, which are always to be had for large-denomination foreign notes. The forex bureaux offer slightly better rates for cash than the banks, but note that it can be difficult to change traveller's cheques at forex bureaux, and Thomas Cook cheques are particularly unwelcome on account of their perceived forgeability.

For changing **traveller's cheques**, **banks** are a better option, and this is generally more straightforward than in Ghana's Francophone neighbours. Barclays and Standard Chartered have branches in all the main towns, and offer the best rates without charging commission. Other banks which may be able to help include the Ghana Commercial Bank (which has over a hundred branches throughout the country) and the Agricultural Development Bank. **Banking hours** are Monday to Friday 8.30am to 3pm.

Credit cards and wiring money

Credit cards are accepted in major hotels in Accra and Kumasi and at some travel agencies. Outside the main cities they won't get you far, except at some upmarket hotels. Barclays handles Visa cash advances at a reasonable exchange rate, but subject to a two percent fee. With credit cards or Visa

debit cards, you can obtain cash through ATMs at most branches of Barclays and Standard Chartered Banks. The withdrawal limit is ₵800,000 per transaction, and you can withdraw cash up to three times a day.

You can have **money wired** to you easily enough at the Bank of Ghana, High Street, Accra (PO Box 2674; ☎021/66.93.62). In the UK you can do this through the Ghana International Bank, 69 Cheapside, London EC2P 2BB (☎0207/2480191). You can also transfer money using **Western Union**, who despatch funds to Agricultural Development Banks across the country.

Getting around

The government has made real improvements to the transport system, resurfacing roads, buying new rolling stock for the railway system and expanding the country's now highly efficient bus service. Buses are, in fact, the most convenient means of travelling around the country and you'll find them a real luxury after the battered bush taxis you may have grown accustomed to using elsewhere.

Buses

Buses operated by the government-run State Transport Corporation (**Intercity STC**) provide a cheap, hassle-free way to get around the country, with a minimum of waiting at roadside checkpoints. The buses run on fixed schedules to all towns of any size and are fast and comfortable. It's always a good idea to book seats in advance, especially if you're heading for popular destinations like Accra, Kumasi or Tamale. You will need to get your luggage weighed and paid for too, if you want to get your gear into the hold.

In some parts of the country you'll also find Omnibus Services Authority (**OSA**), **Kingdom**, and **City Express** buses, all of which are in general slower than those of STC. All these firms prohibit smoking on their buses.

Sample bus fares

Accra–Cape Coast ₵12,000 (3hr).
Accra–Kumasi ₵28,000 normal, ₵40,000 a/c (4–5hr).

Accra–Takoradi ₡20,000 (4hr).
Accra–Tamale ₡48,000 (12hr).
Accra–Wa ₡60,000 (14–16hr).
Kumasi–Wa ₡40,000 (10hr).
Tamale–Bolga ₡9000 (2hr).

Shared taxis and tro-tros

Tro-tros (minibuses) and **shared taxis** (which have a characteristic orange stripe) are less comfortable than the coaches, but they leave more frequently and are marginally cheaper – and you can ask to be let off ("drop") at any point you choose. They're notoriously overloaded, though, and if you're out to enjoy the ride, should be used only if you're not going far or can't get on a bus. Worse than the shared taxis are **lorries**, or mammy wagons, which you'll only want to consider as a last resort. These squeeze as many people as can possibly fit onto wooden planks in a boarded-up truck. You'll see nothing on the way and collect lots of bruises to boot.

Transport **within cities and towns** generally involves *tro-tros* or shared taxis running on set routes, though things may appear chaotic if you've just arrived. Fares shouldn't exceed ₡2000 for a short hop.

You can **charter a taxi** for private use – drivers of long-distance and town vehicles are often amenable to being hired. Expect to pay around ₡25,000 per hour, possibly a little more in touristed areas, excluding fuel, and make sure to agree the price before setting off. You might need to pay the driver a little extra if your journey involves traversing any rough dirt roads.

Trains

Trains are the cheapest way of travelling and, since the government bought new rolling stock in the 1980s, they're actually quite comfortable. Of the three main lines, the most used is the stretch linking **Kumasi to Takoradi** (12hr), connecting the Asante country to the coast. There's a daily sleeper train, and a slower passenger service three times a week. Only one of the other two lines, **Accra–Takoradi** (1 slow, overnight train every other day) is operating, although unfortunately the line runs well inland; in terms of scenery the coast road is better.

Check at stations to see if the **Accra–Kumasi** train has restarted. As a guide to fares, Accra–Takoradi costs ₡15,000, Kumasi–Takoradi ₡10,000 (or ₡17,000 for the sleeper).

Domestic flights

National air carriers open and shut down sporadically. At the time of writing, flights within Ghana are run only by **Sobel Air** (☎021/78.28.14), flying between Accra and Kumasi (4 or 5 weekly; 40min; $45 one-way) and Accra and Tamale (3 weekly; 1hr 15min; $100). Schedules can be obtained in Ghana directly at the airports or Sobel Air offices, or check the Ghana Civil Aviation Authority website ⓦwww.gcaa.com.gh/sobel_schedule.htm.

Volta ferries

You can cover part of the country by boat, as a Lake Volta **ferry service** links the southern town of Akosombo (100km north of Accra) with Yeji once a week, via Kpandu and Kete Krachi. Apart from this "scheduled" passenger service, vessels also ply this route and venture further north – as far as Buipe, southwest of Tamale (except at the end of the dry season), a voyage which can take up to three days, depending on stops en route. The scenery is not as exciting as you might expect – long stretches of dead tree trunks sticking up through flooded landscapes, but it is a peaceful alternative to *tro-tro* travel. For more details, see the box on p.798.

Driving and cycling

Outlets for **car rental** are limited, though Accra has a number of possibilities, including some licensed outlets representing the big international agencies. Note that car rental in Ghana normally means paying for a vehicle and driver. **Fuel** is relatively cheap at about ₡2310 per litre (₡10,500 per gallon).

Outside of Accra, Ghana is a good country for **cycling**, being of a manageable area (two to three weeks from north to south) and offering immense scenic variety. You don't need to be super-fit: the hilly zones are fairly restricted. You can tour along the coast, slog up to Kumasi, then take the switchback route back to Accra – again a perfect trip for two to three weeks.

Accommodation

Major Ghanaian towns have quite a few decent hotels to choose from. Since the Tourist Development Plan started in 1996, most former state-owned hotels have been privatized, and many new mid-range hotels have been built in the major towns. There has also been an effort to develop more four- and five-star outfits in major tourist cities. Furthermore, accommodation in Ghana is remarkably inexpensive. There are plenty of **budget** hotels (**❶**–**❸**), basic and tolerable at the lower end of the scale but surprisingly comfortable at the pricier end, with TV, hot water and air conditioning often available. **Mid-range** hotels (**❹**–**❻**) offer excellent value, including all mod-cons, slick decor and a good level of comfort. Expensive hotels (**❼** & **❽**) are found mainly in the cities and in a few resorts, and feature international standards of comfort and service.

Running water and air conditioning can be had in most places, and should be reliable in Accra and Kumasi, though they may prove sporadic elsewhere. Special mention should also be made of the handful of coastal **forts**, sections of which have been converted into basic resthouses (see p.770).

Ghanaians are generally curious to meet travellers, and if you're on your own, you may be surprised how many offers you get to **stay with people**. It can be rewarding, but you should be extremely conscious, when accepting such offers, of the expense your stay imposes; even for salaried government workers a bottle of beer may be a rare luxury. Be as generous as your host; pay at the cinema, bars or discos, and, if you go to the market together, pay for the food. Ghana's cost of living is incredibly high relative to local wages and most people are barely scraping by, and generally doing so outside the official economy.

For **organized homestay** accommodation, try Friendly Homes of Ghana (FHOG), an organization of Ghanaian families and individuals who open their homes to visitors for an arranged fee (PO Box 0621, Osu, Accra; ☎027/54.47.05, ☎021/23.23.07). Community-based ecotourism projects sometimes also offer homestay accommodation, which we've detailed in the accounts later in the chapter.

Camping

Camping is feasible in the bush. In practice it's most pleasant in the north, beyond the damp forest zone. If you arrive in a village you can ask the chief if and where you can spend the night, and he'll make the arrangements. Camping **gas** is very hard to find in Ghana; stock up in Francophone countries where it's readily available.

Eating and drinking

Plantains are used a lot in Ghanaian cooking and, together with beans, groundnuts, rice, fresh and dried fish, guinea fowl (especially in the north) and grasscutter (the large, tasty

---

Accommodation price codes

Accommodation prices in this chapter are coded according to the following scale, whose equivalent in pounds sterling/US dollars is used throughout the book. Prices refer to the rate you can expect to pay for a room with two beds. Single rooms, or single occupancy, will normally cost at least two-thirds of the twin-occupancy rate. Value added tax of 12.5 percent will be added to your bill, included in our price codes. For further details, see p.51.

❶ Under ₵65,000 (under £5/$8).
❷ ₵65,000–130,000 (£5–10/$8–16).
❸ ₵130,000–195,000 (£10–15/$16–24).
❹ ₵195,000–260,000 (£15–20/$24–32).
❺ ₵260,000–390,000 (£20–30/$32–48).
❻ ₵390,000–520,000 (£30–40/$48–64).
❼ ₵520,000–650,000 (£40–50/$64–80).
❽ Over ₵650,000 (over £50/80).

rodent, also known as bush rat, hunted mainly in the south), supply the basis of one of West Africa's best national cuisines. If you're adventurous, there are other flavours, including clay-baked **lizard** (in Dagomba country; the skin comes off with the clay) and giant forest **snails** – even bat, rat, cat and dog in various parts of the country. Note, however, that organophosphate-laced bait has resulted in scores of deaths and hospital cases – so you might want to ask local people to recommend somewhere to try bush meat, rather than heading for the nearest chop house.

In southern Ghana, the most common staple is **kenkey** – fermented maize-flour balls, steamed and wrapped in maize leaves. You'll see it in markets everywhere. The sour taste takes a while to acquire, and you don't often get much sauce to help it down – just a splash of ground tomatoes, onions, peppers and deep-fried fish. But it does, eventually, taste good. In the north, **tozafi** (or TZ) takes over – a mush made from millet (occasionally maize) flour, and commonly eaten with palm nut or okra soup.

As for **foreign cuisine**, in Accra and Kumasi you'll find restaurants serving Chinese, Lebanese, Indian, Italian or other European fare, and some American-style fast-food places. Further afield, the most common alternative to local staples is Chinese-style dishes, invariably sweet-and-sour or black-bean-sauce stir-fries, and fried rice.

Bread, as you would expect, reflects the taste and style of the British former rulers and is usually soft, white and plastic bagged, available in "tea", "sugar", or "brown" varieties. Baguette-style bread sticks and wholemeal loaves are becoming more widely available.

The country's outstanding fruit is the **pineapple** (notably along the coast), cheaper in Ghana than anywhere else in West Africa. **Coconuts**, too, are incredibly cheap.

Ghana has a lot of good **chocolate**, available everywhere and not expensive for tourists, though beyond the reach of the average Ghanaian. Kingsbite chocolate is high in cocoa and is available across the

Ghanaian food terms and dishes

Abenkwan	Palm nut soup (Akan)	Koko	Corn or millet porridge with milk and sugar
Aduane	Food (Akan)		
Akawadu	Banana (Akan)	Kokonte	Cassava meal (Akan)
Akokoh	Chicken (Akan)	Kontumbre	Cocoyam leaves
Amadaa	Fried, ripe plantain (Ga)	Kyinkyinga	Beef with vegetable sauce (Hausa)
Ampesi	Plantain and yam		
Banku	Corndough, good with groundnut soup	Momone	Sun-dried fish (Akan)
		Nsuomnam	Fish (Akan)
Bodie (kokoo)	(Ripe) plantain (Akan)	Nuhuu	Cocoyam porridge (Akan)
Boflot	Doughnut (north)		
Borodo/Panu	Bread (Akan)	Ode	Yam (Akan)
Ekwei bemi	Boiled, sweetened corn kernels	Omo tuo	Mashed rice balls with soup or stew, usually served Sundays only (also written Emo or Amo tuo)
Enam	Meat (Akan)		
Fufu	Yam mash		
Gari	Cassava grated and dried		
		Rice water	Rice pudding, often for breakfast
Gari foto	Gari dish, mixed with palm oil and other ingredients	Shito	Pepper soup (Ga)
		Suya	Small shish kebab
Kelewele	Spicy fried ripe plantain with stew	Tatare	Ripe plantain, pounded and fried
		TZ (Tozafi)	Millet mush (north)
Khosay	Bean cakes (north)	Waachi	Rice and red beans
Klaklo	Ripe plantain dough, deep-fried		

country, sometimes in lemon, orange and coffee flavours.

Finally, Accra-made **Fan** ice cream and frozen yoghurt products, including Fan-ice, Fan-yogo and Fan-choco, have become something of a phenomenon, and can be found in neighbouring countries as well. Sold by young men with ice-boxes on a bike or on their heads, the frozen sachets are very inexpensive and the ice cream in particular is delicious.

Drinking

Ghana was the first West African country to possess a brewery and now has a wide range of **beers**. The most popular are Star and Club, with Gulder and ABC also on sale – all come in 750ml bottles or smaller "mini" bottles. Bottled Guinness is also very popular. Voltic mineral water is widely available, as is "pure water" – sachets of filtered water – and Fan's Tampico, a sugary orange drink. **Minerals**, as fizzy soft drinks are referred to locally, include the usual Coke and Fanta varieties, as well as Malta Guinness, dark and sugary with a burnt caramel flavour.

Home-made drinks include **taka beer**, a ginger drink; and **ice kenkey**, sweetened, fermented maize flour in water, a taste you may not acquire. **Pito** is the millet-based beer commonly drunk, from shared bowls, in the north; it varies greatly but is quite likeable. In the south, the favourite local brews are naturally fermented **palm wine** (known in Akan as *ntunkum* when it's fresh and low in alcohol, and *nsa* when it's winey) and **akpeteshie**, a potent firewater distilled from palm wine, also called "VC10" or "Kill-me-quick".

Communications

Ghana's **postal services** are inexpensive and relatively efficient to Europe and America. Letters take a week to ten days to reach Britain, slightly longer to North America, although to neighbouring West African countries they can take up to two

Ghana's IDD country code is ☎233.

months. Accra's poste restante is free and reliable.

Telephones are improving all the time and card-operated public phones in the major towns provide international direct dialling. Phonecards can be bought from petrol stations and roadside kiosks. AT&T's World Traveler service can be accessed on ☎0191. **Reverse-charge calls** are expensive from a hotel or a telecentre (called a "communication centre" locally). Note that some communication centres allow **"reception"** – basically, you make a quick call to let your family or friends know where you are, then they call you back at the telecentre, for which you pay a small fee based on the duration of this call.

Mobile phones can be used in all of Ghana's major towns through the Scancom network, including towns in the far north such as Bolga and Wa, and within a wide radius of Accra.

Internet access is easily available in the major cities and towns, and connections are improving all the time. Expect to pay ₡6000 or so for half an hour.

The media

Ghana has an established and respected press, with an enthusiastic readership. Press freedom is a fact of everyday Ghanaian life and there are dozens of weekly papers and periodicals.

The main **newspapers** are the *Daily Graphic* (⊛www.graphic.com.gh), the *Ghanaian Times* – both state-owned – and the Kumasi-based *Pioneer*. Though they stick fairly close to the government line (*Pioneer* can be more critical), their coverage of national and regional events can be quite interesting. Other papers, mainly serving as mouthpieces for different political parties, include *The Ghanaian Voice*, *New Nation*, the *Weekly Spectator* and the *Statesman*, which together have a circulation of over 800,000 a week. Most are unsophisticated in their layout and tend more towards editorializing than hard journalism.

As for the **foreign press**, there's normally a reasonable selection of British and American papers available at Accra airport and the posher hotels, as well as in expatri-ate areas, such as along the main Cantonments Road in Osu, Accra. *West Africa* magazine is always on sale.

TV comprises three channels: the state-owned GTV, which transmits CNN and BBC World at certain times; Metro TV, partly state-owned, and the private TV 3. These are all competitive and constantly improving in their programming. DSTV, a satellite sub-sciber service, is increasingly available in mid-range and top hotels, and includes M-Net, a channel featuring international pro-gramming. Ghana also has several **radio** stations, the most popular of which are music stations, including Gold FM (90.5), Choice FM (102.3), Atlantic FM (the only jazz station), Vibe FM (91.9) and Groove FM (106.3). Joy FM (99.7) is the most highly respected, carrying a mix of music and news, including the BBC's *Focus on Africa* at 3pm daily. BBC World Service is available in Accra on 101.3 FM. The state-owned **GAR** FM (95.7) covers news and the social scene and plays current pop. Radio Canada and Radio France are also available on FM all day in some areas.

Opening hours, public holidays and festivals

Government offices are open Monday to Friday from 8am to 12.30pm and from 1.30pm to 5pm. Most **businesses** operate Monday to Friday from 8am or 9am until noon and between 2pm and 5.30pm. Many shops open also on Saturday, from around 8am to 1pm. Shops are closed on public holidays, without exception – it's the law.

The main Christian and Muslim **holidays** are celebrated in Ghana, the impact of Islam being strongest in the northwest. Shops and businesses also close down for Fourth Republic Day (Jan 7), Independence Day (March 6), Revolution Day (June 4), Republic Day (July 1) and Farmers' Day (first Fri in Dec). While the Anniversary of the Second Revolution (Dec 31) is not a public holiday, it is celebrated on New Year's Eve, which is.

Though not a public holiday, **Emancipation Day** (Aug 1), commemorat-ing slavery and its legacy, is observed with much ceremony in Accra, Cape Coast and Assin Manso (on the Cape Coast–Kumasi road). On July 31 wreaths are laid in Accra at the DuBois Center, the George Padmore Library and the Nkrumah Memorial Park. That evening a candlelight procession walks the streets of Cape Coast to the castle, ready to welcome the dawn. On August 1 itself a procession (*grand-dubar*) gathers in Assin Manso, to lay wreaths on the graves of slaves from Jamaica and the USA, whose remains were repatriated to Ghana when Emancipation Day was first marked here in 1998.

Festivals

In addition to the official public holidays, many **regional celebrations** or festivals (*afahye* in Twi) animate the country through-out the year. The selective listing below covers most of the country but there are very many more. Note that dates are approximate in most cases and, in some, the local name of the occasion just means "festival".

January

Kwafie (early in the month). In Berekum.
Ntoa Fokuokese (Jan 10). Nkoranza, west of Ejura, Asante Region.
Kpini-Kyiu (Jan 22). Wa, Upper West Region.
Danso Abaim Afahye (end). Techiman, 130km north of Kumasi.
Tengbana Tongo, Upper East Region.
Jimbenti Tumu (Sissala people). A period of purification and pacification of the gods, this all-day festival ends at sunset when burning sticks are thrown into the eastern sky to scare away unknown demons.
Adae Kese Asante festival culminating in the purification of the ancestral stools. Kumasi and other Asante towns.

February

Damba Wa, Upper West Region.
Amu Harvest festival including ritual Asafo dances and other cultural displays. Vane Avatime near Ho, Volta Region.

March

Kotokyikyi (first Fri). Senya Beraku, west of Accra.

Kyiu Sung (March 7). Throughout Upper West and Upper East.

Golgu (around Easter). Bolgatanga.

Lalue Kpledo (March 10). Prampram, east of Accra.

Ogyapa (end March, early April). Senya Beraku.

Sigi Sheep and chickens are slaughtered and *pito* offered to God through the ancestors in a thanksgiving and harvest celebration that includes drumming and dancing. Navrongo.

April

Dam and Bugum festivals. Tamale and around.

Godigbeza Celebrations to commemorate migration from the Ewe ancestral lands at Notse (Togo) include drumming, dancing, ceremonial costumes. Aflao.

Aboakyer (late April/early May). Often known as the Deer Hunting Festival, this famous event actually involves two hunting groups competing to bring back a live antelope. The first to present it to the chief and elders is proclaimed champion. Winneba, Central Region.

May

Don (May 14). Wa, Bawku and Bolgatanga.

Sallah Tamale and Tumu.

Chimisi Bawku, Upper East Region.

June

Dzimbenti or Bugum (June 11). Throughout Upper West and Upper East Region.

Apiba Senya Beraku, west of Accra.

Fire festival Tamale and Bawku.

Dongu Wa, Upper West Region.

July

Bakatue Festival (first Fri). Elmina, coast.

Damba (last week of July or early Aug). Dagomba people, Northern Region.

Yam Festival Tamale.

Edjodi Senya Beraku, west of Accra.

Bugumlobre Bongo, Upper East Region.

Jimbanti Tumu, Upper West Region.

Dzumbanti Wa, Upper West Region.

August

Asafotufiiam (first week). Ada, coast east of Accra.

Akumasi (second week). Senya Beraku, coast west of Accra.

Damba (Aug/Sept). Tamale and surrounding region.

Bontungu Five days of drumming and dancing in which villagers clear all superfluous or undesirable objects from their homes and ask God for good health and prosperity in the coming year. Anomabu, near Saltpond, west of Accra.

Homowo (Aug/Sept). Traditional festival of the Ga people including street processions of twins and offerings of ceremonial *kpokpoi* food to the gods. Accra, Prampram and surrounding districts.

September

Odwira Thanksgiving festival held any time in September. Held throughout the Asante country and also marked by most Akan people.

Yam Festival (all month). Volta Region.

Oguaa Fetu Afahye (first Sat). A big, dressy occasion lasting several days. Cape Coast.

Black Stool Festival (Sept 25). Seikwa, north of Berekum.

Yam Festival (last week or early Oct). Effiduasi, Asante Region.

October

Daa (Oct 1–12). Tongo, Upper East Region.

Sabre dance (Oct 9). Lawra, Upper West Region.

Akonedi (Oct 9–13). Larteh, 56km north of Accra.

Kobina (Oct 15). Lawra.

Boaram (Oct 28). Tongo.

Yam Festival Ejura and Effiduasi, Asante Region.

Fijyiiyna/Monomene Bayere Afahye Nkoranza, west of Ejura.

November

Atweaban (second week). Ntonso, northeast of Kumasi.

Yam Festival Ejura, northeast of Kumasi.

Afahye Agogo, 100km east of Kumasi.

Yango Bawku, Upper East Region.

Boaram Tongo, Upper East Region.

Hotbetsotso Commemoration of the Anlos' migration from a tyrannical kingdom to their homeland. Anloga, on the coast southwest of Keta.

December

Fao (Dec 1). Navrongo, Upper East Region.

Kwafie (over the New Year). Berekum.

Kpini guinea fowl festival Dagomba and Gonja people.

Crime and personal safety

Muggings aren't too much of a problem in Ghana, not even in Accra – though there have been reports of muggings in Black Star Square. Ordinary pickpocketing is probably worst in Kumasi market, while theft is a problem on the Accra beaches. Police sometimes stop travellers (and Ghanaians) and pretend to be really angry about a minor offence (such as jaywalking, which is illegal at certain places including Kwame Nkrumah Circle in Accra); customs and immigration officers employ similar tactics. They are almost certainly angling for "dash" (a small present or bribe), and you may have to pay up, though politeness and smiles also help alleviate the situation.

At the time of writing in mid-2003, a night-time **curfew** (from 10pm) was in place in Tamale and Yendi, following civil unrest in the wake of the murder of the paramount Dagomba chief in Yendi (see p.804). The area remains potentially unstable, so it's best to check with your embassy in Accra for the latest on the situation before deciding whether to travel there.

Entertainment and sports

Ghana has a satisfying cultural life, with the-atre, cinema and especially music all accessible. If you're in Accra in June, you'll catch notice of the annual Entertainment Critics and Reviewers Association of Ghana awards. Every two years or so, somewhere between the end of July and November, you will find the Panafest music and arts festival in progress (www.panafest.org), with some events tied in to Emancipation Day (see p.734).

Theatre

Accra's fine, Chinese-built **National Theatre** and the **Greater Accra Centre for National Culture** are the capital's two main theatre venues. The **School of Performing Arts** at Legon University also stages occasional pro-ductions in Accra. In the country as a whole, **"concert party"**, a traditional, lightly satirical musical-comedy-drama, is the theatrical form you're most likely to come across. A high degree of audience participation is the norm, with akpeteshie the accompanying

drink, and the "party" typically goes on all night. You might get a taste, if you can't attend a show, by tracking down a concert party cassette, like the one by the stand-up comic "Waterproof" (on the local "Q" Production label).

Cinema

Ghanaian **cinema** has a wealth of unex-plored potential (there's talent in the wings, held back by financial constraints), but you're still more likely to get a helping of Bond or Stallone than something from top Ghanaian director **Kwaw Ansah**. In Accra, the GAMA Film Company (see p.766) exclu-sively shows Ghanaian and African films. Video shows, in any case, are fast taking over from fleapit cinemas. There's more on Ghanaian film on p.750.

Music

While Ghana is famous for the urban good-time dance music known as **highlife**, the country has an active tradition of **rural music and dance** that continues to influ-ence urban sounds. Look out for folkloric gigs and events.

Although "big-band highlife" declined in the 1970s with the frequency of coups, cur-fews and power cuts, these technical prob-lems didn't really affect guitar highlife, which can still be heard all over. Concert parties and **gospel highlife** took off in the 1970s and are still thriving. With the advent of the Charismatic Christian Church, gospel has boomed tremendously, artists such as **Daughters of Glorious Jesus**, **Tagoe Sister** and **Stella Dugan** benefiting from the trend. So popular is the music now that even secular musicians record gospel albums to appeal to the emerging market.

Following the 1970s, many "name" stars migrated to Europe, and more went to Nigeria, where they've kept the highlife flame burning. Those currently based in Ghana include **Kwame Ampadu and the African Brothers**, still one of the nation's top electric guitar bands after nearly three decades, and the irrepressible **Alex Konadu**. Newer artists like **Kojo Antwi**, **Nana Achampong**, and **Charles Kojo Fosu (Daddy Lumba)** – the threesome formerly known as the **Lumba Brothers** – have focused on their solo careers, once in a while recruiting session musicians for live performances.

Musicians playing traditional African music include the great traditionalist **Mustapha Tetteh Addy** who, with his **Obunu drummers**, incorporates African drums and xylophones into his music, and **Nana Danso Abeam and his Pan African Orchestra**. Rather than using Western-style batons to conduct his orchestra, Nana uses traditional African instruments. There's a more detailed exploration of Ghana's musical culture, on pp.747–750.

For concert dates in Accra, get hold of a copy of the listings mag *Ghanascope* and see the *Daily Graphic*'s "Entertainments" page every Saturday.

Sport

Soccer is the most popular sport in Ghana and a number of Ghanaians play overseas, including Tony Yeboah and Abedi Pele. Through the mid-1980s and early 1990s, Kumasi Asante Kotoko were consistently the best team, and won the Africa Cup three times. More recently, Accra Hearts of Gold have gained the top spot, winning the national league several years running.

Wildlife and national parks

Ghana's native fauna is not in as desperate a position as you might expect. The current wave of interest in new national parks and the attraction they hold for travellers and tourists are positive signs for the future of Ghana's flora and fauna. On the downside, much of the rainforest was felled decades ago, never to return. Along the coast, the British RSPB and the government's Ghana Wildlife Division (℡021/66.46.54, ℻66.64.76, ℠www.wildlife-ghana.org) have been effective in helping to curb the killing of **sea birds** for sport and food – especially the very rare and now protected **roseate tern**, which migrates to these shores every winter from northern Europe. Ghana **Friends of the Earth** is an active group, one of the few such in Africa.

The Ghana Wildlife Division is in the process of opening up several of its parks to exploration. However, while Ghana's largest and longest-established park, **Mole National Park**, is functioning and well stocked with the full complement of bush-savanna mammals, most of the newer parks don't yet provide facilities and some tracks are not maintained. This means you are limited to what you can see on foot, though the park rangers are typically very enthusiastic and helpful in organizing excursions. Apart from Mole, the **Kakum National Park** in the south of the country, just 35km from Cape Coast, is easily accessible and has been a popular target for tourists for some years.

Listen on the travellers' grapevine to find out if there have been any developments in the **Digya National Park**. Bordering the western edge of Lake Volta, this is one of Ghana's larger parks, harbouring elephants, various antelopes, hippo, waterbuck and a wide range of other species. It's also worth checking the latest developments at **Bia National Park** in the rainforests of the west near the Côte d'Ivoire border. With the help of Raleigh International, facilities for visitors have rapidly improved, with several camps and trails already established. Check with the Protected Areas Development Programme (℡031/25322, ℻25327, ℠padp@africa online.com.gh) in Takoradi for the latest developments. Further north, the **Bui National Park** straddles tributaries of the Black Volta in a protected woodland, and has very basic chalet accommodation and camping facilities.

In the Western region, the twin reserves of **Ankasa** and **Nini-Suhien** near the Ivoirian border now have tourist facilities including visitor centre and restaurant, and a limited range of accommodation options.

In the Volta region, **Shai Hills Reserve**, home to over 160 bird species, a few monkeys and a bat colony, is a popular day excursion from Accra. Several large species inhabit the scenic **Kyabobo Resource Reserve**, including various elephant, lion, leopard, buffalo and antelope species. The **Kalakpe Resource Reserve**, 15km southwest of Ho, has a proliferation of birdlife, along with buffalo, antelope and many varieties of monkeys.

Women travellers

There are few special problems for women travellers – indeed, many rate Ghana one of the most hassle-free countries in West Africa.

Ghana is further advanced than other African countries in actively encouraging women to become more involved in business and other areas of public life, and many **women's organizations** have sprung up in recent years. The 31 December Women's Movement (DWM), for example, led by the former First Lady, Nana Konadu Agyemang, has made considerable advancements – such as providing day-care centres for children throughout the country. If you're interested in making contact with women's groups, write to the Ghana Assembly of Women (PO Box 459, Accra) or the Federation of Ghanaian Women (PO Box 6326, Accra).

Interestingly, the **matrilineal** system of inheritance (in which men inherit from their maternal uncles rather than their fathers) practised by the Akan-speaking people has, if anything, had a negative impact on women's status. There is firm government pressure against this form of inheritance.

Directory

Drugs *Wee* (marijuana) is illegal, though widely available. The main areas of production are around Ejura in the Asante region and Nsawam north of Accra. It's generally looked upon more as a bad habit than a dangerous drug, and consumers aren't likely to run into big trouble, though discretion is always advisable.

Ecotourism An increasing number of ecotourist projects – some of which we've covered in the *Guide* – have been established across the country, designed to maximize the benefits of tourism for local communities involved. With the help of the Peace Corps, accommodation and other facilities have been set up, while official prices for the attractions have been set.

Gold You'll be hard pressed to find much sign of the precious metal (except during major festivals, notably the Ogua Fetu Afahye in Cape Coast) away from the big goldfields around Tarkwa and Obuasi, southwest of Kumasi. The Ashanti Goldfields Company in Obuasi is the best set up to receive visitors (see p.794).

Photography You don't need a permit to take pictures in Ghana, though the usual regulations against snapping military installations and strategic points are rigorously enforced. Especially sensitive is Osu Castle in Accra, the seat of government. Taking pictures anywhere in the vicinity could, in theory, lead to the confiscation of camera and film, if not arrest.

Shopping Ghana has a huge variety of arts and crafts, still widely made for local consumption. The Asante region is a prolific producer of textiles and well known for its *kente* and *adinkra* cloths. These can be bought in villages around Kumasi or at the town's cultural centre. The region is also famed for its carvings – especially of stools made in Ahwiaa. The north specializes more in leather goods, rough cotton weaves and basketry, all of which are found at the Bolgatanga market. Perhaps the best selection is in Accra where art from all over the country – and from throughout West Africa – comes together at the crafts market. If you buy antiques, or anything in substantial quantities, you may have to obtain an export permit – declaring the item has no historical value – from the Ghana Museum and Monuments Board. Take your purchases to their office in the Centre for National Culture or the National Museum and they'll sell you a certificate on the spot.

Voluntary work Besides the organizations mentioned in Basics, p.68, two Ghana-based groups are worth mentioning here. The Save the Earth Network (PO Box CT 3635, Cantonments, Accra; ☎021/66.77.91, ⓕ021/66.96.25, ⓔebensten@yahoo.com) run volunteer programmes lasting at least four weeks. The range of work on offer includes reforestation projects, staffing orphanages, and building schools and libraries in rural communities, and organized stays with host families are provided. The Suntaa-Nuntaa project, a tree-planting initiative, aims to provide local women with regular supplies of fruit and fuel wood. They're based in Wa, Upper West Region (PO Box 207; ☎0756/22215, ⓔsuntaa@africaonline.com.gh).

A brief history of Ghana

The earliest reasonably clear movements of present-day peoples in Ghana took place at the beginning of the second millennium AD, when the Ntafo, early ancestors of the Akan-speaking peoples, moved south to the parkland west of Gonja, in northern Ghana. By the fourteenth century, successive generations were gradually spreading further south, in three waves, consisting of the Guan, Asante and Fante peoples.

Early **trading** relations existed with much of West Africa, particularly with the western Soudan (the region which is now Mali). Gold and kola nuts were important products which poured out of the region, across the Sahara and into North Africa. Mande peoples from the Niger bend greatly influenced the economy and culture of northern Ghana as they established numerous trading centres alongside existing towns.

European arrival

European involvement in the region provoked a shift in the emphasis of trade away from the northern routes to the southern ports. Searching out new trade routes and a way to obtain the gold of the trans-Saharan caravans closer to source, the first **Portuguese** ships came to Ghana in 1471. By 1482 they had returned to build a fort at **Elmina** ("the mine"), using a mixture of persuasion and threats to gain the consent of the local ruler. The region turned out to be rich in gold, ivory, timber and skins, and other Europeans followed the Portuguese. Over the next four hundred years, sea powers like the Dutch, Danes and British competed heavily for the trade. With the European colonization of America, this expanded to include **slaves**, in exchange for which the Europeans brought hard liquor and manufactured goods like **clothing** and **weaponry**. Guns eventually helped the **Asante** – the principal traders with the foreigners – to expand their influence over the region's interior and to apply pressure to the **Fante** middlemen through whom they'd been dealing with the British since the 1600s.

The British colony

By the early nineteenth century the Gold Coast interior had developed a complicated network of northern states – Gonja, Dagomba, Mamprusi and Nanumba – and, in the south, smaller confederations (the Fante for example) and statelets (Ga, Ewe, Nzima). In the central region, the Asante confederation was rapidly mushrooming. Given time, the Asante empire might have conquered and assimilated most of the smaller political units in the surrounding territories which were later to come under French rule.

Such a scenario, however, was thwarted by the colonial experience. By the early nineteenth century, the British had emerged as the strongest foreign power on the **Gold Coast**. In 1807, they abolished the slave trade in the region and began looking for other exploitable resources. Over the next hundred years, palm oil, cocoa, rubber, gold and timber were developed as exports. These products drew the British – hitherto content to remain in their coastal forts – increasingly into the hinterland.

The stage was set for the outright **conquest** of the interior when the Asante invaded the Fante confederation in 1806. The Fante had long been able to resist the attempts of their powerful northern neighbours to dominate them, thanks in large part to their role as preferential trading partners with the Europeans. Now the British rallied to the aid of their Fante "allies", even offering them protection in one of their coastal forts.

Hostilities flared and **tenuous treaties** were reached between the two Akan factions throughout the first half of the century. But, as competition increased for the control of trade, the British decided there could be only one victor. They ultimately found the excuse they needed to invade the interior when war again broke out between the Fante and Asante in the 1870s. The British sacked the Asante capital, Kumasi, in 1874. Subsequent **Asante wars** followed in 1896 and 1900, when the ruling Asanthene was finally exiled (see box, p.790).

By that time Germany, France and Britain had already agreed on borders for the areas they would control. The British introduced elements of **indirect rule** in their new colony, even allowing the Asante confederation to be re-established under the Ashanti Confederacy Council – a government agency – in 1935. After World War I, part of German Togoland was integrated into the British colony.

The rise of nationalism

Nationalist movements were created early in the colonial period, with one – the Aborigines' Rights Protection Society – dating as far back as 1897. Other parties sprang up during the 1920s and 1930s and, by 1946, concessions to African demands for representation had led to an African majority in Ghana's Legislative Council, although the executive branch – and effective rule – was still in the hands of the British Governor.

In 1947, **J.B. Danquah** formed the United Gold Coast Convention (UGCC), a party which favoured the principle of a gradual shift to self-government and independence. The same year, the party invited **Kwame Nkrumah** to join its ranks as party secretary in an effort to broaden a base that consisted mainly of the educated elite – civil servants, lawyers, businessmen and doctors.

In the aftermath of the 1948 **Accra riots** (see p.754) Nkrumah lost patience with conservatives in the UGCC and split from it to form his own party, the Convention People's Party (**CPP**) – campaigning slogan, "Self-government now". He gained prominence among the masses as a result and the British detained him when he called for a national strike in 1950. The CPP, meanwhile, won the Legislative Assembly election of 1951, and the governor, Sir Charles Arden-Clarke, prudently released Nkrumah and invited him to help form a government. Thus, in 1952, Nkrumah became the first African prime minister in the Commonwealth. He went on to win the elections of 1954 and 1956 – a period during which his CPP party shared power with the British. On August 3, 1956, the Legislative Assembly passed a unanimous motion calling for complete independence.

Independence: Ghana under Nkrumah

When **independence** was ultimately realized on March 6, 1957, the future looked bright for the first African country to break colonial bonds. Ghana was then the world's leading cocoa exporter and produced a tenth of all the world's gold. Other valuable resources, of which the country had many, included bauxite, manganese, diamonds and timber. Perhaps Ghana's greatest asset was a high percentage of educated citizens who seemed well qualified to run the new nation (a quarter of the population was literate, compared, for example, to an estimated one percent in Portugal's colonies).

Nkrumah became a larger than life figure, respected throughout Africa and the African diaspora and highly regarded in the West. He was an eloquent advocate of **pan–Africanism** and the **non–aligned movement**. His economic principles looked sound, too, as he sought to create an industrial base that would reduce dependence on foreign powers while improving social services throughout the country (hospitals and clinics, universities and schools were part of his legacy). The port city of **Tema**, with its smelting and other industrial plants, was constructed at this time as was the ambitious **Akosombo Dam**, built to supply hydro-electric power.

Nkrumah's economic strategy was, however, extremely costly, and with hindsight it seems painfully clear that his biggest mistake was to emphasize **prestige projects** at the expense of a solid agricultural base. Worse still, many of the projects held no prospect of any economic return: Accra's showy conference centre – designed to be the headquarters of the Organization of African Unity, which based itself instead in Addis Ababa – and symbolic monuments like Black Star Square and the vainglorious State House were the dizzy results of a belief in the invincible rightness of Nkrumah's ideals. Foreign currency reserves dwindled at a frightening rate and the country accumulated a debt running to hundreds of millions of pounds.

As the economic situation turned suddenly bleak, political discontent rose. Government suppression of a 1961 workers' strike had already seriously alienated Nkrumah from the working class, and the educated elite had long been disillusioned with his expensive brand of scientific socialism. When the world price of cocoa plummeted in the mid-1960s, Ghana's hopes for economic self-sufficiency – and long-term stability – were dashed.

By 1964, Ghana was legally a **one-party state.** As the CPP tried measures to stamp out opposition, the government increasingly arrested those it feared under the Preventive Detention Act which allowed for "enemies" of the regime to be held for up to five years without trial. Public gatherings were strictly controlled, press censorship became commonplace and an extensive network of informants was developed by the party central committee. Such measures were effective in crushing opposition, or at least in driving it deeply underground, but Nkrumah still had to contend with the **military**. Suspicious of the army's loyalty, he lost his nerve and made policy decisions that were bound to antagonize officers – placing limits on recruitment and hedging military procurement procedures with elaborate safeguards. Isolating himself still further from the support of the military, he formed an independent **presidential guard**, accountable only to himself.

In the light of such developments, Western nations increasingly criticized governmental corruption and the personality cult surrounding Nkrumah, who was forced to abandon his non-alignment and turn to the Soviet bloc for support. By then he had totally lost the backing of the military and almost every other element of society. Only a blind sense of impunity could have allowed him to travel abroad. On February 24, 1966, while on a visit to China, he was **overthrown** in a bloodless coup by British-trained officers. He died in exile in Conakry in 1972.

Coups and "kleptocrats"

Following Nkrumah's departure, Lieutenant-General **Joseph Ankrah** was appointed head of the National Liberation Council (**NLC**) that ruled until 1969. The conservative junta went on a witch-hunt, arresting left-wing ideologues, banning the CPP and harassing its leaders. The junta's **economic direction** seemed promising to the West, however, as they privatized many state enterprises and broke off relations with the Soviet Union and its allies. But for all the promises made to better the economy, life for most people without special connections grew steadily worse.

From its inception, the NLC viewed itself as a provisional government and much of its period of rule was spent preparing for a return to civilian democracy. A bill of rights was drawn up, and safeguards were implemented to ensure the independence of the judiciary and prevent the reconstitution of an autocratic one-party state. In May 1969, political parties were legalized. The **Progress Party**, headed by Kofi Busia – an Akan who represented the traditional middle-class opposition to Nkrumah's rule – was counterbalanced by the **National Alliance of Liberals** led by Komla Gbedemah, an Ewe and one-time associate of Nkrumah who had broken with the leader and gone into exile.

In September 1969, Ghanaians gave democracy another try, and elected **Dr Kofi Busia** prime minister. But the new leader struggled to wade through the economic mess. Cocoa prices dropped again in 1971, sparking a new crisis and, at the same time, mismanagement and racketeering led to shortages in food production, supplies and foreign exchange. Under mounting pressure, Busia took the necessary but politically dangerous step of **devaluing the cedi**. Massive price increases followed and the public enthusiasm that had ushered in the new regime faded almost immediately. Busia was overthrown on January 13, 1972.

Kleptocracy

From 1972 to 1979, Ghana was led by a series of juntas with remarkably **corrupt generals** at the helm. One of the most flagrant offenders was **General I Acheampong**, who headed the National Redemption Council (NRC) from 1972 to 1975 and then the Supreme Military Council until 1978. During his period in office, Ghanaians coined the term "kleptocracy" – rule by thieves – as the official economy moved closer and closer to complete collapse. The **black market** thrived, meanwhile, as basic goods like bread and eggs became unattainable for the poor. Production declined even further and the few agricultural goods produced

were smuggled abroad to Togo and Côte d'Ivoire, where they fetched higher, hard-currency prices. The educated elite – doctors, teachers, lawyers – led a brain drain to Nigeria and overseas where they had some chance of supporting themselves.

The basis of Acheampong's economic policy was **"self-reliance"**, symbolized by programmes such as "Operation Feed Yourself", launched in 1972. Moderate successes were achieved in the early years of the NRC, but by the mid-1970s the economic outlook was so grim that the professional middle class, and especially the Ghana Bar Association, demanded a return to party politics. Acheampong sought a compromise by proposing a **"union government"** where power would be shared between civilians, the armed forces and – radically – the police. The opposition viewed this as a mechanism to keep the military in power and reacted cynically when Acheampong pushed his idea through on the back of a trumped-up referendum held in 1978.

As criticism grew, so did **repression**, and hundreds of opposition leaders were jailed without trial. Viewed increasingly as a tyrant, Acheampong withdrew into isolation. He was quietly deposed in a coup led by **General William Akuffo** on July 5, 1978. Akuffo established the "Supreme Military Council II" and eventually set a date for elections in June 1979, but little else changed and widespread discontent in the country now spread to the ranks of the military.

Rawlings Mark I

There can be no peace where there is no justice – and there will be no justice unless everyone can be made to answer for his conduct.

Jerry Rawlings, 1979

On May 15, 1979, there was a bungled uprising of junior ranks in the army, led by a 32-year-old flight lieutenant of mixed Scottish–Ghanaian parentage – **Jerry Rawlings**. He was captured and imprisoned but freed by fellow soldiers and they made a second, successful, attempt to take power on **June 4, 1979**.

Rawlings made it clear that his coup would be different, that he was out to eliminate corruption and restore national pride to an economic order neglected in fifteen years of waste. The title of his governing **Armed Forces Revolutionary Council (AFRC)** set the tone – Rawlings envisaged a "moral revolution" based implicitly on socialist principles of an economy for need rather than profit. He took a hard line, sending high-ranking officers to the firing squad (including Acheampong and Akuffo) and approving a purge of public figures under suspicion of fraud. At the same time he pledged that the AFRC would work quickly to restore order and return the reins of power to a civilian government.

The world community noted little more than another coup d'état in Ghana, but, in a remarkable departure (no African military ruler had ever voluntarily relinquished power before), the promise was kept. Following elections held on June 18, 1979, the newly elected president, **Dr Hilla Limann**, took office in September and the soldiers returned to their barracks barely three months after leaving them.

Limann rode in on a wave of popularity at home and in the West where his conservative politics won respect. But despite his best intentions, the economy continued to slide – production dropped further, the cedi remained overvalued (fearing unpopularity, the president refused to devalue the currency and thereby cost his country a major IMF loan) and the country's infrastructure became hopelessly eroded. And despite the moral high ground captured by the Rawlings clique, and Rawlings' own shadowy behind-the-scenes presence, **corrupt practices** had been re-established by the end of 1980 in virtually every sphere of public life.

Rawlings' second coming

On December 31, 1981, Rawlings led a **second successful coup**, toppling the Limann government, abolishing the entire "democratic" framework, and placing the government in the hands of a **Provisional National Defence Council (PNDC)**. As before, he justified the action by the urgent need to halt corruption and put Ghana's wrecked and abused economy in order. This time, however, no plans were made to restore the country to civilian rule. Rather, the PNDC decided to put into practice the leftist populist principles of the original coup. Early moves were made to democratize the decision-making process and to decentralize political power. This was done through **People's Defence Committees (PDCs)**, which replaced district councils and were intended to increase local participation in the revolution while raising political consciousness at the grassroots level.

Like Thomas Sankara, who arrived on the scene in Burkina Faso two years later, Rawlings initially enjoyed huge popularity among the masses fed up with government lies and excesses. With his battle cry of "accountability", he proved sincere in the **war against corruption** and, although the economy continued to slide during his first years, he soon managed to produce a turnaround (by 1984, the economy was showing a five percent growth rate, the first upswing in ten years). Despite Rawlings' penchant for revolutionary rhetoric, his early friendship with the Libyan leader Colonel Gaddafi and his ties with Cuba and Eastern Europe, his pragmatic economic approach – including taking the risky political step of drastically devaluing the cedi – earned him high marks with the IMF, which started once again to provide sizeable loans to the country.

The political orientation of the second revolution proved too much for large sections of the army, particularly northerners, and there were several **coup attempts** in 1982 and 1983, including one mounted from Togo.

Relations with **Burkina Faso** were extremely close while Sankara was alive, and at one point the countries even envisaged a common currency. Predictably, more conservative regimes were less receptive to Rawlings' style of government. Relations with **Britain**, **Côte d'Ivoire**, and especially **Togo** were, at best, cool. All three countries harboured Ghanaian exiles, some of whom have maintained links with **dissident opposition** groups in Ghana. In 1983 this secret opposition came dangerously close to toppling the government as they infiltrated Accra from Togo and took over the GBC broadcasting station before being apprehended. (The January 1994 coup attempt against Togo's President Eyadéma triggered new tension between the two countries: the rebels were said to have entered Lomé from Ghana, and the border was frequently closed throughout the 1990s.)

By the end of the 1980s, Rawlings had made much of what seemed a hopeless situation. But he had not always had an easy time straddling diverse elements in society. Although most rural dwellers and many wage earners remained loyal, he had suffered scrapes with the ambitious middle class, who loathed his socialist rhetoric and raised the banner of human rights. Many students and academics, on the other hand, charged him with selling out to the IMF, saying he presided over a neocolonialist state. Still, the performance of the economy (Ghana recorded the highest consistent rates of economic growth in Africa throughout much of the 1980s) seemed to shield the president from pressure to liberalize the government, whether it came from disgruntled nationals, or Western donors.

The 1990s

Ghana entered the 1990s against the background rumble of the **Quarshigah**

Affair – Major Courage Quarshigah and six other officers were sentenced for their connection with an alleged plot to murder Rawlings and overthrow the PNDC. One of them was found hanged in his cell, and Amnesty International adopted the others, denouncing what they claimed was imprisonment for political dissension. Ghanaians rallied around the affair, demanding the abolition of a number of laws, particularly those relating to detention, and an end to the ban on political parties. Foreign pressure to democratize also increased.

Rather than entrenching, Rawlings surprised many when, in July 1990, he formed a **National Commission for Democracy** to review decentralization and consider Ghana's political future. Though opponents criticized the commission for being too close to the ruling party, changes took place quickly. By 1991 the commission was recommending a new constitution and presidential and legislative elections – recommendations approved by the PNDC which, contrary to all expectations, endorsed the restoration of a **multiparty system**. In addition to the completion of the new constitution and the unbanning of political parties, the following year saw the emergence of a **free press** and three new human rights organizations, plus the release of remaining political detainees.

As the November **presidential election** drew near, opposition parties – especially the New Patriotic Party (**NPP**), an Asante-based group in the Danquah-Busia tradition, headed by Professor Albert Adu-Boahen – seemed confident of success in the polls against Rawlings' National Democratic Congress (**NDC** – the party formed from the PNDC). Dr Hilla Limann, who had been overthrown in Rawlings' second coup, returned to the political arena as candidate for the People's National Convention (**PNC**).

The opposition euphoria faded fast after the elections: Rawlings took 58 percent of the vote (compared with 30 percent for Adu-Boahen). As the stunned opposition claimed, some **voting irregularities** undoubtedly did take place, though the margin of victory was large enough to have ensured Rawlings' win even under fair conditions. In the eyes of many Ghanaians, however, Rawlings had held onto power without a clear popular mandate. The subsequent **opposition boycott** of the ensuing legislative elections assured victory to the NDC and its affiliates, the NCP and the EGLE party, and denied the new **Fourth Republic** (based on the constitution devised by the National Commission for Democracy) the legitimacy it might otherwise have had. As a result, the post-democracy government looked oddly like the military dictatorship that had preceded it, and rather than usher in a new era of optimism, the elections poisoned the political atmosphere which had seemed so promising at the beginning of the 1990s.

But there were encouraging signals. In his first address to Parliament, Rawlings offered an olive branch to opposition parties, inviting them to dialogue with the legislature from which they had excluded themselves. Also encouraging was the role of the **press** in providing a platform for opposition. Before and during the elections, Rawlings was generally credited with exercising restraint towards the slew of publications that emerged when the press ban was lifted, especially since many bolstered sales with the type of president-bashing articles still considered treasonous throughout much of Africa. Although the "Culture of Silence" appeared to have ended for newspapers, soon after the elections the NPP charged that the state was **censoring television**. Their complaint came after the current affairs programme *Talking Point* abruptly went off the air just as an NPP spokesman was launching into an attack on Rawlings' economic policy. The Supreme Court agreed that the government acted unconstitutionally, the ruling sending a reassuring signal that the judiciary would not be a rubber stamp.

An elusive economic dawn

Important as political issues were, success or failure for Rawlings' government was dependent ultimately on the **economy**, as it tried to juggle policies that maintained foreign approval while not further alienating Ghanaians at home. The IMF talked about Ghana in glowing terms, and recommended an Asian-style growth strategy.

Despite the rapid expansion of the country's new **stock market** and populist programmes including rural electrification and road building, the poor and the wage-earners paid a heavy price for economic reform. Equally troublesome was the fact that much of the expansion had been fuelled by a boom in gold mining rather than new economic initiatives.

The first signs that the population at large had reached breaking point came in May 1995, when parliament introduced **Value Added Tax** at a rate of 17 percent. With a rallying cry of *kume preko* ("Why not just kill me?"), tens of thousands of protestors demonstrated on the streets of Accra. Five people died in the melee, including at least two killed by unidentified gunmen. It was the most serious display of popular oppostion to date and was seized upon by detractors – many in exile – who deplored Ghana's human rights record.

With **elections** on the horizon in 1996, the government was forced to rescind the tax. Against its defensive posturing, a group of opposition parties found room for agreement. The NPP, PCP (People's Convention Party) and NDM (New Democratic Movement) formed the **Alliance for Change**, with NPP member **John Kufuor** – a Danquah Busiaist lawyer from Kumasi – as its candidate. This initially provided Rawlings with a serious challenge, but Kufuor let the momentum of the VAT resistance slip away, and couldn't compete with Rawlings on personal charisma or party organization. Rawlings won 57 percent of the vote at the December elections.

Renewed from his election victory, Rawlings once again was hailed in the west as a champion of constitutional democracy with a wise free-trade policy. Economic prospects seemed less fortuitous from within the country itself, where the years right after the election were characterized by budget deficits, debt servicing burdens and slow aid disbursements. The percentage of people living below the poverty line had barely decreased since the preceding decade; social services were all but non-existent; and in many areas the only available health care was from mission-run clinics. Poor rains in the late 1990s led to lower than expected agricultural production, and just as importantly, reduced the Akosombo Dam's capacity to keep pace with the country's need for energy. The resulting rationing of water and electricity was hard on the populace and precipitated a slowdown in industrial growth. The same period saw the world price of gold plummet, and with it much of Ghana's foreign earnings.

To the present

By the end of the 1990s, the depressing economic outlook had been coupled with accusations against the NDC leadership of mismanagement, corruption and intimidation. This reputation gained credibility at the grass roots and even within the NDC itself. In January 1999 this internal disillusion was vividly expressed by Goosie Tanoh – long-time friend and political ally of Rawlings – and his collaborators, when they formally broke away to create the **Reform Movement** (**RM**). Rawlings, having served two terms, the maximum allowed by the constitution, thrust **John Atta Mills** forward as the NDC's presidential candidate. The elections of late 2000 were closely fought, with a result emerging on the second round of voting: in a peaceful transfer of power, **John Kufour** of the NPP was sworn in as president in January 2001.

Excessively expansionary policies prior to the 2000 elections led to accelerating inflation in early 2001. That year, a depressed cocoa market and continued weak growth in exports other than the country's usual commodities did not alleviate matters.

In 2002, Ghana was granted **debt relief** under the Heavily Indebted Poor Countries (HIPC) programme. But despite IMF assertions that this would allow the Ghanaian government to increase spending on education, health and agriculture, in reality, the NPP's efforts to qualify for debt relief have led to a decline in economic growth and commerce, while water and electricity prices have soared at a time when most Ghanaians are poorer than they were 25 years ago.

Rawlings, seemingly unable to tear himself away from the political arena, is poised to exploit any chink in the armour of the present government. He was quick to denounce the government's internal security apparatus after **civil unrest** in the Northern Region in March 2002, when a militant group beheaded the powerful king of the Dagombas, **Ya-Na Yakubu Andani**, and killed 25 of his supporters in the town of Yendi. A surge of violence followed and the government announced a state of emergency in the north, establishing a nightly curfew that was still in force at the time of writing. In a similar vein, the NDC accused Kufour of **economic mismanagement** in August 2002, when he considered taking a huge $1 billion loan (from the obscure International Finance Consortium) which would have increased the country's foreign debt to some $6 billion and triggered inflation.

In the light of growing discontent within the NPP, John Atta Mills – still in close alliance with Rawlings – is priming the NDC for the **2004 presidential election**. However, Ghanaians still harbour many bad memories of nineteen years under strict and overbearing NDC leadership. Consequently, though Kufour is considered to lack both the common touch and the oratorical skills of his predecessor, and was not the popular choice in the poorest regions, he has the backing of many who simply want a clean break from the past. His standing was re-affirmed in January 2003 when he was elected chairman of ECOWAS.

However, the **National Reconciliation Commission**, established in 2003 to look at human rights violations under Rawlings, may yet precipitate a crisis if Rawlings himself is asked to testify in public. His influence continues to be deeply felt, especially in the north and east, and he is given to making inflammatory pronouncements. But his health is failing, and whether he could count on the support of the military – many of whom are nowadays considered loyal to the constitution – if he tried to organize a third comeback, and whether Ghanaians would tolerate another coup if Kufuor's NPP government is seen to have failed, are questions that are likely to dominate Ghana's political scene for some years to come.

Music

Ghana's "town music" is well known abroad, but the country has a strong tradition of rural music, which is still commonly performed and continues to influence urban sounds.

Traditional music

The main types of music are **court music** played for chiefs, **ceremonial music** and **work songs** – and of course music for its own sake. In **northeastern Ghana**, you'll find mostly fiddles, lutes and wonderful hourglass talking-drum ensembles. It's customary for musicians to perform frequently for the local chief – in the Dagomba country each Monday and Friday. In towns like **Tamale** and Yendi professional musicians, although attached to chiefs, regularly perform for the general public. Dagomba drummers are always a great spectacle, their flowing tunics fanning out as, hands flying, they dance the *takai*.

In the **northwest**, the main instrument of the **Lobi**, **Wala**, **Dagarti** and **Sissala** is the xylophone – either played alone or with a small group of drums and percussion instruments. Finger bells and ankle bells are often worn by the dancers.

The music of the **Ewe** of **eastern Ghana** is closer to the traditions of Togo and Benin than to that of other Ghanaian peoples, and with their enthusiasm for music associations and dance clubs they've developed many different kinds of recreational music. In the **southern** part of central Ghana the **Akan** peoples, notably the **Asante** and **Fante**, have an elaborate court music using large drum ensembles and groups of horns. Another great spectacle is that of the huge log xylophones played in **asonko**, a form of recreational music.

Ghanaian instruments

Northeast
Gonge One-stringed fiddle.
Kologo Two-stringed lute.
Donno Talking drums, in an ensemble.

Ewe
Sogo and **kidi** Drums.
Atsimewu Master drum.
Axatse Rattles.
Gankogui Double bells.

Asante
Atumpane Sets of twin drums.
Ntahera Ensemble of ivory horns.

Palm-wine music

"Palm-wine" is the generic name for the popular music of the Asante. Primarily solo, good-time guitar music, it originated in the palm-wine "bars" – usually under a big tree. A musician would turn up with his guitar and play for as long as people wanted to buy him drinks. Such palm-wineists tend to be comedians as well as parodists of the local scene.

Palm-wine guitar music is dying out, partly because musicians are being enticed into guitar bands. In any town someone will be able to point you in the direction of a palm-wine player but you may have to find an instrument for him to play on. Buy the man a drink and you may well find your name included in the current song.

Ghanaian highlife

Highlife originated in Ghana and Sierra Leone and has proved to be one of the most popular and enduring African styles. Originally a fusion of traditional percussion and melodies, with European influences like brass bands, sea shanties and hymns, it started in the early 1920s with the growth of major ports along the West African coast. The term itself is no more than a reference to the kind of European-derived evening of dressing up and dancing (the "highlife") to which new immigrants to the towns of West Africa between the wars were quite unaccustomed – but which they soon made their own.

The first 78rpm records were released in the 1930s and highlife's international reputation started to grow. There are about a dozen different styles of highlife but the two main ones are the guitar-band and dance-band styles. **Guitar-band highlife** is basically a more organized form of palm-wine music, and became known as **concert party** when exponents added other elements – dance routines and comic turns. **Dance-band highlife**, in its extreme form, was all top hats and tails and as much brass as possible. There's a wonderful highlife variation in "gospel highlife" – do everything possible to hear something recorded by the **Genesis Gospel Singers**.

Various *The Rough Guide to Highlife* (World Music Network). A wonderful mix of Nigerian and Ghanaian numbers from the Sixties and Seventies, including Ghanaians E.T. Mensah, Alex Konadu, George Darko, Jerry Hanson and the Ramblers, and Nana Ampadu and the African Brothers.

Various *I've Found My Love* (Original Music). Guitar-band highlife from the 1950s and 1960s. Relaxed shuffles based on the prototype highlife tune, "Yaa Amponsah".

E.T. Mensah

The "King of Highlife", Mensah had a musical childhood and developed his skills on the guitar, organ, sax and trumpet. During World War II he came into contact with British and American styles like calypso, swing and cha-cha, and in 1948 he formed the Tempos Band, then the only professional dance band in Ghana. After a string of hits, the group went international with frequent tours of West Africa – a golden age of highlife. Soon there were hundreds of bands imitating their style. Mensah's popularity declined during the 1970s, but he made a comeback towards the end of the decade. He died in 1996.

All For You (RetroAfric). All the classics from the 1950s are here, including the wacky "Inflation Calypso", "Sunday Mirror" and the title track. Never mind the crackles, everyone likes it.

African Brothers International Band

Formed in 1963 by Nana Kwame Ampadu, and still one of the country's most innovative and enduring guitar groups. Always a group to mix street wisdom with thinly veiled political comment (they had their earliest and one of their best-loved hits in 1967 with "Ebi Tie Ye", a plea for democracy in the dark days following the fall of Nkrumah), they never let this interfere with good music, and are forever trying something new. During the 1970s they experimented with a variety of styles including reggae, rumba and what they called Afro-hili, a James Brown–inspired beat which was a challenge to Fela Kuti's Afrobeat.

Agatha (available in Ghana). A West African hit in 1981, this was perhaps their best album – although their singles of the mid-1960s and late 1970s would give any band a run for their money.

King Bruce & the Black Beats

King Bruce (1922–77) was a major figure of the classic highlife era, a trumpeter who formed the Black Beats, the first of a string of successful dance bands in Accra, in the early 1950s.

Golden Highlife Classics from the 1950s and 1960s (RetroAfric). Superb introduction to the sound of Ghana nearly half a century ago – all laid-back grooves and claves and slightly pear-shaped horns.

Koo Nimo (Daniel Amponsah)

Guitarist who has done as much as anyone to enrich and preserve Ghana's traditional guitar music. He still performs regularly at concerts and festivals with his all-acoustic Adadam band and commands huge respect among Ghanaians at home and abroad.

Osabarima (Adasa/Stern's). Originally recorded in 1976, his only commercial recording to date.

A.B. Crentsil's Sweet Talks

One of Ghana's most successful highlife bands in the 1970s, the group gained national popularity after a string of hit albums.

Hollywood Highlife Party (Popular African Music). An out-and-out classic, recorded in the USA in 1978, here re-issued with bonus tracks.

Osibisa

Taking their name from *osibisaba*, a proto-highlife rhythm, the band were formed in London by three Ghanaians: Teddy Osei, Mac Tontoh and Sol Amarfino. Three of their Afro-rock singles, "Dance the Body Music", "Sunshine Day" and "Coffee Song", rose to the British top ten. Perhaps they were five years too early: by the time Sunny Ade was making headlines with undiluted *juju*, they had melted away.

Fire – Hot Flashback Vol 1 (Red Steel). All the hits are here from "The Coffee Song" to "Sunshine Day". If you're too young to remember what all the fuss was about, move heaven and earth for this collection.

Alex Konadu

Today the uncrowned king of guitar-band highlife, Konadu plays music firmly rooted in Ghanaian traditions and has enjoyed massive sales all over West Africa. He claims to have played in every town and village in Ghana.

One Man Thousand Live in London (Akuboat). The master of sweaty, good-time music – infectious tunes that come back to you months later.

Hip-life

In 1992, the rap duo Talking Drums exploded onto the country's music scene with **hip-life**, a hybrid of American hip-hop and Ghanaian highlife. Despite initial scepticism from the critics, hip-life immediately connected with the youth of Ghana. A Ghanaian creation, its appeal was that it spoke to people in languages they could understand, a style which young people could identify with. Hip-life is now the biggest selling brand of music in Ghana, and is played in nightclubs and bars across the country, and particularly in Accra. Hip-life artists to look out for include Sidney, Reggie Rockstone, Lord Kenya, T.H.4 Quages, Bukbak and Abrewa Nana.

Cinema

The wave of productivity that swept the Francophone countries generally bypassed the English-speaking states, only two of which – Ghana and Nigeria – have gone beyond government-sponsored documentaries to create an independent cinema. In Ghana, independent film-makers began producing features that combined comedy and melodrama.

That said, the government branches of the film industry have left their mark on some of the country's top film-makers. The documentary style of the former state-run Ghana Film Industry Corporation (now GAMA Film Company), for example, has influenced such well-known directors as **Sam Aryete** (*No Tears for Ananse*, 1968), **King Ampaw** (*They Call It Love*, 1972; *Kukurantumi*, 1983; *Juju*, 1986), **Kwate Nee Owo** (*You Hide Me*, 1971; *Struggle for Zimbabwe*, 1974; *Angela Davis*, 1976), and **Kwaw Ansah** (*Love Brewed in the African Pot*, 1981).

Ghana's modern film industry isn't reliant on state funding and some of the best-known film-makers finance their projects through local and international backing. Kwaw Ansah, for example, produced his *Heritage Africa* – which won the grand prize at FESPACO in 1989 – with the backing of Ghanaian banks and other financial institutions. The films of these more independent directors have produced a good box-office return both in and outside Ghana. *Love Brewed in the African Pot*, for example, conveys its narrative through musical performances, wedding ceremonies and sports events – all popular with African audiences – and drew record attendances not only in Ghana, but also in Sierra Leone, Liberia, Kenya and Nigeria.

Since the late 1980s, Ghana has increasingly seen film production become **video production**: the equipment is relatively affordable and the results on VHS instantly marketable. It's estimated that around fifty feature videos a year are produced in this way with local actors and even amateurs. The subject matter is always relationships, and tends to revolve around love and death, jealousy and illness, morality and honesty, polygamy and Christian monogamy, and often incorporates ghosts and the power of the ancestors – beliefs woven deep into the fabric of all Ghanaian communities. Popular hits of recent years have included *Ghost Tears* and *Fatal Decision*.

October 1999 saw the first **Ghana Film Awards**, now an annual event, symbolizing the country's growing awareness of the importance of the film industry. The charity Scriptnet has also been established recently to address the need for film and television training.

Books

Ghana has an established literary tradition, with a number of widely available works. Out-of-print titles are denoted o/p below; especially recommended books are marked ★ .

Mike Adjei *Death and Pain: Rawlings' Ghana, the Inside Story* (o/p). Highly critical look at the Rawlings regime, cataloguing alleged political murders.

Peter Adler and Nicholas Barnard *Asafo! African Flags of the Fante.* Affordable and striking photo collection of Asafo flags and details.

Maya Angelou *All God's Children Need Travelling Shoes.* The story of American black activist Angelou's emigration to newly independent Ghana and her growing sense of disillusion, picked out in dialogue.

F.K. Buah *History of Ghana.* A basic text, with a fair amount of illustration.

Gracia Clark *Onions Are My Husband: Survival and Accumulation by West African Market Women.* Insightful portrait of Kumasi market women.

Paul Nugent *Big Men, Small Boys and Politics in Ghana.* Subtitled *Power, Ideology and the Burden of History*, this is the best account of the Rawlings years, simultaneously academic in approach and accessible.

★ **Thierry Secretan** *Going into Darkness: Fantastic Coffins from Africa.* A coffee-table book about a bizarre art form – the model coffins (in the form of a boat for a fisherman, a Merc for a market woman, etc) of the Ga in Ghana.

Fiction

Ama Ata Aidoo *The Dilemma of a Ghost* and *Anowa.* In the former, Aidoo, one of Africa's relatively few female writers, deals with the unusual theme of a black American girl married into a Ghanaian family; in the latter title, the subject is a Ghanaian legend about a girl who refuses her parents' chosen

suitors. Also available is the short-story collection *No Sweetness Here*, most of whose tales handle the theme of conflict between traditional and urban life in Ghana.

Ayi Kwei Armah *The Beautyful Ones Are Not Yet Born.* Politics, greed and corruption in newly independent Africa, seen through the life of a railway clerk. Armah beautifully captures the sense of frustration and crisis that befell Ghana after the fall of Nkrumah. A compulsive historical novel, Armah's later *The Healers* is set in the Asante empire at the time of its demise. His most recent book, *Osiris Rising: A Novel of Africa, Past, Present and Future* tells the compelling and complex story of an African-American scholar who travels to Africa seeking inspiration and love.

Akosua Busia *The Seasons of Beento Blackbird.* The author, the daughter of a former Ghanaian prime minister, created quite a stir with this debut. Here she deals with the condition of the African diaspora through the story of one man, loved by three women (one from the Caribbean, one from America and one from Africa), exploring the contrasting emotional, sexual and cultural forces they embody.

Joseph Casely-Hayford *Ethiopia Unbound.* Generally considered the first West African novel (it appeared in 1911), this treats a theme that later became familiar in African literature: the student who goes to study in London, and returns home to find he's a stranger.

Amma Darko *Beyond the Horizon.* Provocative story of a Ghanaian woman's prostitution in Germany. *The Housemaid*, a later work, addresses gender politics in modern Ghana.

Languages

Ghana's official language is English, which you can use without much trouble throughout the country, although you'll likely need a period of adjustment before completely understanding the broader **pidgin** accents. If English is not your first language, you might be misunderstood.

The two main language "families" into which Ghanaian languages fall are Kwa in the south and Voltaic in the north. The great **Twi group** of Kwa languages and dialects includes the **Akan languages** like **Asante-Twi**, spoken by the Asante and Fante; **Ewe** and its associate dialects (spoken in the southeast – see p.838), and **Ga**, or Ga-Adangme, the traditional language of the Accra region. Important **Voltaic languages** include the large **More** (or Mole) cluster – among them **Dagomba** and **Mamprusi** – and various **Grusi** tongues, such as **Frafra** and **Nunumba**.

A number of Ghanaian languages have long been written with unfamiliar **orthography** and you'll see satisfyingly exotic-looking spellings used in many hand-painted ⑲igns: ɔ (pronounced "o" as in "cost"); ɜ (pronounced "e" as in "men"); ŋ (pronounced "ng" as in "sing"); and ɤ (pronounced as a very soft "h").

Twi

Twi, pronounced somewhere between "Twee" and "Chooi", is the name commonly given to the language of the Asante and Fante people. It's a difficult tongue to master, with a complex tonal system, but a few words and phrases in Twi always go down well. Note that it's usually written with the somewhat impenetrable orthography mentioned above, but we've opted for a simple transliteration that should sound OK.

Greetings

Hello, you are welcome	A kwaaba; response Yaa
Good morning	Mma ache
Good afternoon	Mma aha
Good evening	Mma adjo; response response Ye muu
Anyone home?	Ebi wo fie?

Basic conversation

How are you?	Wo o te sen?
I'm fine	Me ho ye
Come here (to children)	Bra
Go away (to children)	Koh
Yes	Aan
No	Dabe
Please (lit. "I beg you")	Me pawocheo
What's your name?	Ye ferew sen?
My name is . . .	Ye fere me . . .
Where do you come from?	Wo fri he?
I come from . . .	Me fri . . .
Thank you	Meda ase
Response (you're welcome)	Mme enna ase
Do you speak English (lit. "white language")?	Wote Borofo anna?
I don't understand	Mnta se
I'm married	Ma ware
(Please) give me water	Ma me nsuo
I want/like . . .	Me pe . . .
I'm not well	Me nti apoh
I'm hungry	E komdeme

Travel

I'm going	Me ko
We're going	Ye ko
Today	Enne
Tomorrow	Echina
Yesterday	Enrah
Tonight	Annajoh
Lorry	Lore
Bus stop	Bossogy inabea

Numbers

1	biako
2	abieng

3	abiesa	40	aduanang
4	anang	100	oha
5	anum	200	ahannu
6	asia	300	ahasa
7	asong	400	ahannang
8	awotwe	500	ahannum
9	akrong	600	ahansia
10	du	700	ahansong
11	dubiako	800	ahangwotwe
20	aduonu	900	ahangkron
30	aduasa	1000	apem

Glossary

Adinkra Cotton funeral cloth with printed black symbols worn by Akan mourners.

Agbada Large embroidered robe, usually white, worn on special occasions.

Akan The language that includes dialects spoken by the Fante and the Asante.

Asafo Military-style "company" of the Fante.

Asante Standard spelling of the Kumasi-based ethnic group.

Ashanti Popular European spelling and name of the administrative region.

Burglar Means rip-off artist in general, including con-merchant.

Chop Food, or "to eat".

Colo Ingratiating, "colonial" behaviour.

Concert party Popular entertainment that started in the villages. When people couldn't afford to go to clubs, they began "concert parties", a theatrical performance – usually humorous – accompanied by highlife music.

Dash From Portuguese for "to give", it means a gift or bribe. It can also function as a verb, as in "How much you dash me?"

Drop In the context of public transport, this can mean either "to disembark" (as in "Where do you want to drop?") or "chartered" (as in the phrase "dropping taxi").

Durbar Not the horse rally of northern Nigeria, this is the occasion that climaxes traditional festivals, when chiefs receive distinguished guests.

Highlife "Big Band Highlife" is Ghana's best-known dance-music form, but Ghanaians use the term to refer to a much broader range of music which is no more homogenous than, say, rock.

How be? Common greeting meaning "How are you?"

Kalabule Corruption and palm greasing.

Kente Multicoloured, woven strip fabric, sometimes silk, made by the Akan and Ewe.

Kotoko Porcupine, symbol of the Asante. The animal's countless sharp quills stand for boundless Asante bravery, reflected in the saying *kotoko wokum apem, apem beha* (kill a thousand porcupines and a thousand more will come).

Obruni/Bruni Akan word for white man, often chanted by children.

Obroni wawu Imported secondhand clothes (lit. "a white man has died").

Oware The game of pebbles and holes (see p.87).

Paa "Very", for example "It's expensive, paa", very expensive.

Posuban Shrines made by Asafo companies.

Silly Pejorative term implying an insult to one's intelligence – stronger term than in US or Britain.

Stool The royal throne of Akan-speaking peoples. "Stooling" means enthronement.

Wee Marijuana.

Weeding, or Weeding-off, is the collective grave-tending ceremony that takes place some time after a funeral.

10.1

Accra and around

F lat, sprawling and for the most part nondescript, the cityscape of **ACCRA** is still blighted by heavy concrete stacks harking back to the Soviet-inspired early years of independence. Belying first impressions, though, Accra is an exciting city making a rapid comeback. Soulless concrete blocks are offset by some attractive tree-lined avenues and glitzy, modern hotels, the vibrancy of which is matched by the energy of the people, including a good number of foreigners attracted to one West African capital that can look ahead with some confidence.

With a population of 2.2 million (unofficial estimates put the figure much higher), Accra is one of Africa's biggest cities, and though its trees make it exceptionally green, it hasn't been spared from traffic, noise or overcrowding. Rush hours are dynamic, the streets thronged with a racket of vehicles and people, while after dark, Accra's club scene is one of the liveliest in West Africa.

Some history

Accra's **Ga founders** arrived in the region some time before 1500, setting up their capital at Ayawaso ("Great Accra") some 15km inland, and building a "Small Accra" on the coast for trade with the **Portuguese**, who put up a fort here in the sixteenth century. Trade – of slaves, gold and palm oil for guns – increased over the next hundred years with the building of the Dutch **Fort Ussher**, the Danish **Christiansborg** and the British **Fort James**.

Accra originally consisted of **seven quarters** – the Ga quarters of Asere, Abola, Gbese, Sempe and Akunmadzei; Otublohu, the Akwamu quarter; and Alata, which later became the core of the British-protected area of Jamestown. Other quarters placed themselves under Dutch protection and became Usshertown. Much later, in 1840, the chief of Abola was chosen as the military leader (Ga Mantse) for the whole city, and treated by the British as the Ga king; nowadays he is considered the Ga paramount chief.

Akwamu expansion from the north led to victory over the Ga in 1660 – Chief Okai Koi, defeated by treachery, put a curse on Accra that it should remain disunited against its enemies ever after – and to the destruction of Ayawaso, now just a tiny village. But the Ga regained much of their independence in 1730, when Akwamu fell to the Akim state of Akwapim, which now took over control of the **"notes"** (documents issued by African rulers giving Europeans the right to trade) for the Accra forts. These "notes" later passed to the Asante, who gained control of the area at the beginning of the nineteenth century, but gradually lost it in a series of wars with the British. Battle was averted in 1863 when British and Asante armies were both struck by dysentery and too ill to fight, but a decisive victory in 1874 led to the British taking over and setting up the Gold Coast Colony with its capital at Accra after 1877.

Since then the city has expanded considerably, despite serious earthquakes in 1862 and 1939. After the introduction of **cocoa**, Accra became a major export port, also shipping out gold, palm oil and rubber and, from 1933, boasting West Africa's first brewery (Club). The municipality, set up in 1896, was expanded east to include Christiansborg and, in 1943, to encompass the ancient, walled, farming and salt-producing village of Labadi. On February 28, 1948, major **anticolonial riots** in the city centre followed British police shootings at a demonstration at the junction of Rowe, Castle and Christiansborg roads. Twenty-nine protestors died and 237 were wounded in an outburst that caused £2 million worth of damage.

Orientation and arrival

Despite the urban sprawl, downtown Accra is neatly contained by the **Ring Road**. The core of Accra stretches from the banking district of **High Street** near the waterfront to the **Makola market** – a colourful hive of activity that overflows into the surrounding streets. In between, the ample proportions of the stately colonial **Old Parliament House** and **Supreme Court** give an idea of the importance the British placed on their Gold Coast Colony.

Lined by shops and commercial and business premises, two main thoroughfares – Nkrumah Avenue and Kojo Thompson Road – run through the city centre south to north from the old districts of **Usshertown** and **Jamestown** to **Kwame Nkrumah Circle** (known simply as "Circle"). Shady **Independence Avenue**, sprinkled with embassies and business headquarters, also leads north, past East Ridge and North Ridge and Ringway Estate to **Sankara Circle** in the northeast and on out to the airport. **Cantonments Road** runs from the coast near **The Castle** (the seat of government) northeast through the frenzied district of **Osu**, seething with fast-food restaurants, hotels and supermarkets, to **Danquah Circle**, and then on through the Cantonments district to the airport. Cutting east to west through the city centre are the main arteries of Castle Road, Liberia Road and Kinbu Road. The **beaches** lie not far from town: the nearest is La Pleasure beach, 5km east.

Moving on from Accra

Bookings for internal **flights** to Kumasi or Tamale on Sobel Air (☎021/78.28.14) can be made either through the airline or with M&J Travels and Tours (☎021/77.34.98 or 70.60.81). As for **trains**, there are very slow passenger services from Accra to Takoradi (1 overnight train every other day; ₡15,000; tickets at the station itself).

Buses and tro-tros

STC buses for the **west and north** depart from the STC station. **Kumasi**-bound STC buses (some of which are a/c) leave roughly hourly, from dawn until 6pm or so, taking up to five hours. Air-conditioned STC buses also run direct to **Abidjan** once daily, and to **Ouagadougou** twice a week (₡90,000) – but be prepared to spend the night at the Bolga bus station since you will arrive slightly after the Burkina border closes at 6pm. Alternative routes to Ouaga are either to change in Kumasi and spend the night there, or to take an STC bus to Bolga (3 weekly; 14hr) or Paga (2 weekly; 15 hr) and find a car heading across the border. STC also runs a direct service to **Wa** (2 weekly; 14–16hr). STC buses for the **east** go from the transport park along Kinbu Road, between Tudu Crescent and Barnes Road, serving **Ho** and **Hohoe**, as well as **Aflao** on the Togolese border.

Buses operated by other firms follow roughly the same division, with north- and westbound buses operating out of a transport park just to the west of Nkrumah Circle and eastbound buses departing from Kinbu Road.

Tro-tros pretty much follow the bus pattern – with less organization. Greater Accra and the coast are their main areas of operation. For the northern and eastern suburbs including Tema and Aburi, get a seat at the Tema Station. For Ada Foah, Keta and towns in eastern Ghana go to Tudu Station near Makola market. For the western suburbs and towns north of Accra, including Kumasi, go to Nkrumah Circle. Finally, for the western coast, at least as far as Takoradi (though you really have to want to save money to go so far by tro-tro), go to Kaneshie.

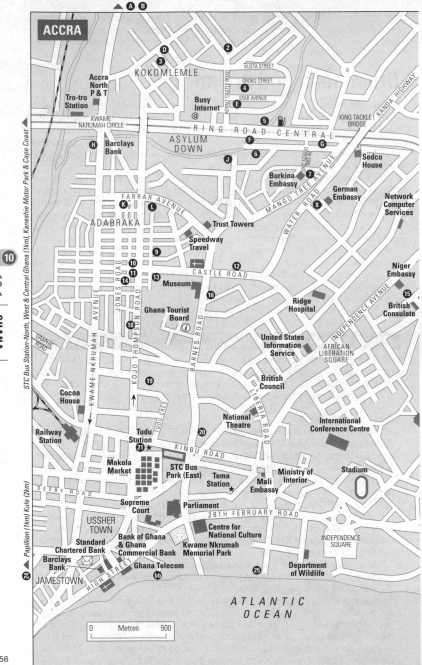

ACCRA

KOKOMLEMLE

Accra North
P & T

Tro-tro
Station

KWAME
NKRUMAH CIRCLE

KUSTA STREET

OROKO STREET

STAR AVENUE

Busy
Internet
@

Barclays
Bank

ASYLUM
DOWN

RING ROAD CENTRAL

KING TACKLE
BRIDGE

Sedco
House

Burkina
Embassy

German
Embassy

Network
Computer
Services

FARRAR AVENUE

ADABRAKA

Trust Towers

Speedway
Travel

CASTLE ROAD

Niger
Embassy

British
Consulate

Museum

Ridge
Hospital

Ghana Tourist
Board

United States
Information
Service

AFRICAN
LIBERATION
SQUARE

Cocoa
House

British
Council

National
Theatre

International
Conference Centre

Railway
Station

Tudu
Station

KINBU ROAD

Makola
Market

STC Bus
Park (East)

Tema
Station

Mali
Embassy

Ministry of
Interior

Stadium

DERBY ROAD

Supreme
Court

Parliament

28TH FEBRUARY ROAD

INDEPENDENCE
SQUARE

USSHER
TOWN

Standard
Chartered Bank

Bank of Ghana
& Ghana
Commercial Bank

Centre for
National Culture

Kwame Nkrumah
Memorial Park

Barclays
Bank

JAMESTOWN

Ghana Telecom

HIGH STREET

Department
of Wildlife

ATLANTIC
OCEAN

0   Metres   500

STC Bus Station–North, West & Central Ghana (1km), Kaneshie Motor Park & Cape Coast

Papilion (1km) Kule (2km)

GRAPHIC ROAD

KWAME NKRUMAH AVENUE

JONES ROAD

KOJO THOMPSON ROAD

BARNES ROAD

LIBERIA ROAD

INDEPENDENCE AVENUE

WATER ROAD

MANGO TREE AVENUE

KANDA HIGHWAY

ROYAL CASTLE ROAD

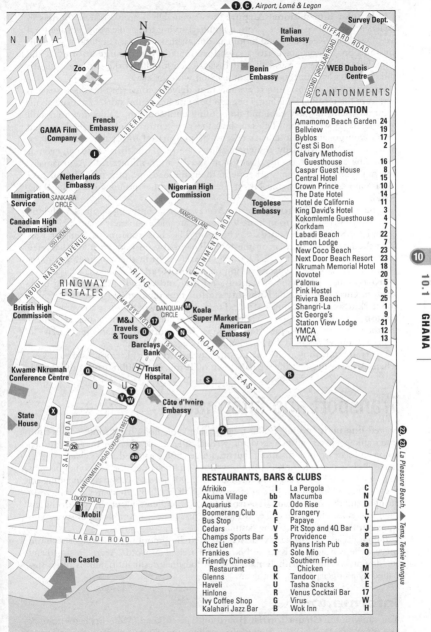

ACCOMMODATION

Amamomo Beach Garden	24
Bellview	19
Byblos	17
C'est Si Bon	2
Calvary Methodist	
Guesthouse	16
Caspar Guest House	8
Central Hotel	15
Crown Prince	10
The Date Hotel	14
Hotel de California	11
King David's Hotel	3
Kokomlemle Guesthouse	4
Korkdam	7
Labadi Beach	22
Lemon Lodge	7
New Coco Beach	23
Next Door Beach Resort	23
Nkrumah Memorial Hotel	18
Novotel	20
Paloma	5
Pink Hostel	6
Riviera Beach	25
Shangri-La	1
St George's	9
Station View Lodge	21
YMCA	12
YWCA	13

RESTAURANTS, BARS & CLUBS

Afrikiko	I	La Pergola	C
Akuma Village	bb	Macumba	N
Aquarius	Z	Odo Rise	D
Boomerang Club	A	Orangery	L
Bus Stop	F	Papaye	Y
Cedars	V	Pit Stop and 4Q Bar	J
Champs Sports Bar	5	Providence	P
Chez Lien	S	Ryans Irish Pub	aa
Frankies	T	Sole Mio	O
Friendly Chinese		Southern Fried	
Restaurant	Q	Chicken	M
Glenns	K	Tandoor	X
Haveli	U	Tasha Snacks	E
Hinlone	R	Venus Cocktail Bar	17
Ivy Coffee Shop	G	Virus	W
Kalahari Jazz Bar	B	Wok Inn	H

At **Kotoka International Airport** there's generally a crowd of KIA porters in boilersuits (inscribed "Porter", with a number) trying to handle your luggage for a fee of ₵10,000. Keep cool and nominate one, or make it clear you'll do it yourself. Customs procedures are pretty straightforward. You can **change money** at the forex bureau in the arrivals hall, which stays open for all but the late-night flights, and their rates are not too bad in comparison with the city.

There's no airport bus into town and **taxi drivers** converge on you as soon as you leave the terminal building. They can be quite heavy and stories circulate about menacing demands; stay cool and do nothing until someone calms down enough for you to go with them. The fare into the city centre should be clearly agreed before you go, and although it's easy to be pressurized into paying ₵25,000 or more, the fare to virtually anywhere should be no more than ₵15,000, even at night. The city centre is only about 8km away – a ten-minute ride. Alternatively, you can walk out of the airport zone to the main road, and pick up a **shared taxi** for around ₵800 to Kwame Nkrumah Circle, or other points around the Ring Road.

If you're **arriving by road**, entering Accra can be a confusing business, with little in the way of landmarks to indicate where you are and a generally chaotic cityscape of dust (or mud) on the outskirts. The main STC **bus station**, handling arrivals from the north and west, is on the Ring Road between Nkrumah and Lamptey circles (☎021/22.14.14, 📠22.19.45). STC arrivals from the east, including Ho, Hohoe and Aflao, use a separate station on **Kinbu Road** near Makola Market.

Tro-tros use a number of stations. *Tro-tros* (and shared taxis) arriving from Western Ghana head to the **Kaneshie station** near the market of the same name, about 2km west of Nkrumah Circle. From eastern towns, *Tro-tros* arrive in **Tudu station** near Makola Market, while *Tro-tros* from northern centres such as Kumasi use the station just west of Nkrumah Circle. *Tro-tros* from Aburi and Tema arrive at Tema Station between Kinbu Road and 28th February Road.

The **train station** is in the heart of the city, a short taxi ride from just about anywhere. Accra's **port** is at the separate town of **Tema**, some 30km east of the capital.

Transport and information

Shared **line taxis** (around ₵600–1500 per hop) roll along fixed routes, often from one traffic circle to another, servicing virtually the whole city. For these, flag down a taxi and state your destination; tourists are generally assumed to be chartering, so make it clear if you're not. If you do want to charter a taxi for a specific journey, expect to pay ₵5000–12,000 in town and ₵15,000 for the outskirts, depending on the distance. Confirm the price before setting off, and note that fares may increase at night and during the rain. **Tro-tros** are slower and cost about thirty percent less than line taxis. The *tro-tro* driver works with his "mate", a conductor of sorts, who leans out the door shouting the destination.

Tro-tros drivers and some taxi drivers use a circling motion of the finger to mean the vehicle is headed to Kwame Nkrumah Circle. The word "Accra" is shorthand for downtown Accra, with Tema Station as the final destination, and is often signalled by a finger pointing in the air.

Information

You can visit the **Ghana Tourist Board** on Barnes Road (Mon–Fri 8am–noon & 1–4.30pm; ☎021/23.18.17, 📧gtb@africaonline.com.gh), but most of the information they provide – including a directory of hotels, restaurants, travel and car-rental agencies – can be found at various hotels and bookshops. If you'll be spending a lot of time venturing into national parks, you may want to drop by the **Wildlife Department**, near Independence Square (☎021/66.46.54), although they provide limited information and maps. For those planning to spend some time in the capital, the second edition of the excellent *No More Worries – The Indispensable Insider's Guide to Accra*, is a useful directory of businesses and services, available at an extortionate ₵225,000 from the ATAG shop in the Trade Fair Centre (see p.763) and from some Mobil stations; handy listings can also be found at ⊛www.ghanacityguide.com.

Accommodation

Accommodation in Accra is relatively cheap and varies from absolutely basic dorm space for those counting every penny to luxury hotel rooms. Problems with power cuts and water shortages are diminishing. The majority of the city's **inexpensive hotels** are to be found within a two-kilometre belt stretching from Adabraka, just north of the centre, through Asylum Down and up to Kokomlemle north of the Ring Road. The nearest **campsite** is at Coco Beach, about 10km east of the centre on the Tema road (around ₵20,000 per person); beware of theft in the area.

Hostels and student rooms

Accra Polytechnic Opposite *Novotel*, on Barnes Rd ☎021/66,29.39. Basic and very inexpensive accommodation outside term-time (ie around Christmas and Easter, and also over the northern hemisphere summer). Dorm beds ₵15,000.

YMCA Castle Rd ☎021/22.47.00, ☎021/22.62.46. Basic, fanless dormitory rooms, but central, and some of the cheapest accommodation in town. Good place to meet Ghanaians. Dorm beds ₵10,000.

YWCA Castle Rd, near the intersection with Kojo Thompson Rd ☎021/22.05.67, ☎ywca@ghana.com. Cleaner and more pleasant than the men's version, with dorm beds and one excellent-value s/c room with a kitchenette. Dorm beds C/10,000. ❷

Hotels and guesthouses

Inexpensive

Amamomo Beach Garden Set right on the seafront 3km west of Jamestown; you'll find the *Amamomo* signposted down a dirt road on the left, off the old Winneba Road ☎024/64.87.03. If you're on quite a tight budget and want to escape the city centre, this is where to head; here you can stay in simple and attractive non-s/c wooden chalets and learn traditional drumming and dance in the leafy garden. ❶

Bellview Tudu Crescent, off Kojo Thompson Rd, behind Accra Polytechnic, Adabraka ☎021/66.77.30, ☎021/22.58.38. Good budget hotel, with s/c rooms with fan – choose carefully though, as some are a lot nicer than others – in a

convenient location, and there's a well-liked restaurant to boot. ❶

Calvary Methodist Guesthouse Opposite the National Museum, Barnes Rd, Adabraka ☎021/23.45.07. Good value, carpeted s/c rooms, some with balconies with attractive views. ❶

C'est Si Bon Royalt Castle Rd ☎021/22.90.04. Reasonable singles and doubles, with fan or a/c and private bath. ❶

Crown Prince Kojo Thompson Rd, ☎021/22.53.81. The a/c rooms with shared facilities are quite good value, but the noise from the busy road never stops, and the water supply is sporadic. ❷

The Date Hotel Adama Ave, Adabraka ☎021/22.82.00. One of the best-value places, with spacious, clean rooms, a good bar area and a great restaurant for *fufu* and groundnut soup. ❶

Hotel de California Junction of Kojo Thompson Rd and Castle Rd, Adabraka ☎021/22.61.99. Long a popular haunt with travellers, but now a good prospect for that reason only – the rooms, with fans and shared facilities, are scruffy; thankfully much-needed renovations are under way. ❶

Kokomlemle Guesthouse Oroko St, Kokomlemle ☎021/22.45.81. If you're heading there by taxi, tell the driver it's near the ATTC (Accra Technical Training College). Excellent value, with cleanish s/c rooms, friendly staff and a relaxed atmosphere in the lively bar and restaurant. Popular with visiting NGO workers and travellers. ❶

Korkdam 18 2nd Crescent, off Mango Tree Ave, Asylum Down ☎021/22.32.21, ⊛www .korkdamhotel.com. Range of rooms from s/c singles with hot water and fridges to "executive suites" with the works (phones, TV, a/c). ❸

Lemon Lodge 2nd Crescent Road, off Mango Tree Ave, Asylum Down ☎021/22.78.57. In a quiet, leafy neighbourhood, this offers good value and is usually full. Rooms have fans and are generally clean. ❶

Nkrumah Memorial Hotel Kojo Thompson Rd, Adabraka ☎021/25.46.88. Walls are thin, but the place is kept clean and the location is great. ❶

St George's Amusudai Rd, opposite Methodist School, Adabraka ☎021/22.46.99. In a restored colonial home, this has charm and posh s/c, a/c rooms, with fridge, phone and TV. Clean and comfortable, with a great location near the museum. ❸

Station View Lodge Kinbu Rd, next to the lorry park. Good for the bustling location, but the rooms, with fans, are very basic. ❶

Mid-range

Caspar Guest House 30 North Ridge ☎021/22.02.73, ☏22.18.04. Opposite the German consulate, this is a luxurious though homely set-up, offering bed and breakfast in a quiet residential area. Twin or double rooms with TV, fridge and hot water, plus a small restaurant in the grounds. ❺

King David's Hotel Near Nkrumah Circle, Kokomlemle ☎021/22.52.80, ☏66.59.60. Small, very clean hotel with friendly staff and large rooms. Good restaurant too. ❹

Next Door Beach Resort On the La Pleasure Beach–Teshie Nungua Rd, some 4km beyond *Labadi Beach Hotel* ☎021/71.39.47, ✉info@nextdoor.com. Charming accommodation with great views. The tasteful chalets are made of wood or stone, all with TV and fridge; some are s/c with hot water and a kitchenette. A pretty constant flow of *tro-tros* plies the La–Teshie Nungua Rd in both directions. ❺

Paloma Hotel and Suites C137/2 Ring Road Central ☎021/22.87.00, ☻www.africa online.com.gh/Paloma. Comfortable rooms including new stylish chalets; all mod-cons. Good central position. ❻

Pink Hostel Opposite the American Chamber of Commerce, Asylum Down ☎021/25.67.10, ☏25.67.10, ✉pinkhostel@ghana.com. This establishment is reviewed here by virtue of its excellent student and volunteer discounts. Rooms are s/c and feature a/c and minimalist decor, phone and optional TV. Rates include breakfast. An overpriced ❼, though the student rate is equivalent to ❹

Riviera Beach Marine Drive, midway between Independence Square and the Centre for National Culture ☎021/66.29.90, ✉aimsgh@ghana.com.

The name suggests something exotic, but the s/c, a/c rooms are run-down. That said, there's an excellent terrace bar and restaurant overlooking the sea, worth a detour even if you don't sleep here. ❹

Expensive

Byblos 11th Lane/Embassy Rd, adjacent to *Venus Cocktail Bar*, Osu ☎021/78.22.50/60, ☻www.bybloshotels.com. Ideal location for those drawn to the perpetual energy of Osu. The rooms are stylish and equipped with TV, fridge, a/c and phone line, and there's a ground-floor restaurant serving a Middle Eastern and European menu. ❼

Central Hotel Osu Avenue ☎021/70.10.60, ✉centralhotel@ghana.com. On a quiet road, this is a popular new hotel with good-value s/c rooms with satellite TV, minibar and a/c; there's a small pool too. ❼

Labadi Beach La Pleasure Beach, 5km east of the centre ☎021/77.25.01, ☏77.25.20, ☻www.labadibeach.com. Opened in 1991, this is Ghana's most expensive (doubles cost around $250 a night) and well-appointed hotel. Amenities include a health club, gym, pool and beautiful garden, and a huge breakfast buffet. Happy hour in the bar Wed 6–7pm. Accepts most cards. The adjoining *La Palm Royal Beach Hotel* (☎021/77.17.00, ☻www.goldenbeachhotels.net) offers similar facilities at similar prices. ❽

New Coco Beach 10km east of the city in the suburb of Nungua and near Coco Beach ☎021/71.72.35, ☏71.72.39, ✉newcocobeach@yahoo.com. An increasingly popular option, much more affordable than other hotels in this bracket, and good value. Local bands play reggae and highlife every weekend on the poolside stage. ❽

Novotel Barnes Rd, north of Kinbu Rd ☎021/66.75.46, ☏66.75.33, ☻www.novotel.com. Accra's first international establishment still has an antiseptic feel. Free airport shuttle for guests; non-guests are welcome to partake of their great buffet breakfast. Major credit cards accepted. ❽

Shangri-La 1500m from the airport, ☎021/77.75.00, ☏77.48.73, ✉shangri@ncs .com.gh. More intimate and much less expensive than others in this bracket, though not lacking in facilities like tennis courts and a swimming pool. The local feel makes it deservedly popular with expats. You can dine on great pizzas and "pastabilities" at reasonable prices, either inside or in the pleasant gardens. Accepts all major credit cards. ❽

The City

Accra doesn't especially lend itself to scenic walks and, by day, there's not much in the way of things to see. The main diversion is simply absorbing the energy of an African urban centre. Even the coast and lagoons aren't shown off to any real advantage and, from most places in town, you're barely aware that Accra lies right on the seafront – Jamestown is an exception. A visit to the interesting **National Museum** is recommended, as is a quick trip to the **WEB DuBois Memorial Centre**, and perhaps a look at the gradually improving **zoo**, on Kanda Avenue, past the Ring Road (daily 9.30am–5.30pm). Near the seafront, the **crafts market** offers a vast selection from all over the region, though not necessarily at the best prices.

The National Museum of Ghana

The **National Museum of Ghana**, on Barnes Road near the junction with Castle Road (☎021/22.16.33; daily 8.30am–4.30pm; ₵10,000 and ₵5000 for cameras), houses one of West Africa's best ethnographic, historical and art collections, with exhibits from Ghana and across the continent. You could conceivably visit the entire museum in a morning or afternoon, but because of the variety and eclecticism of the exhibits, it's perhaps best to pop in several times to avoid cultural fatigue. The exhibits are well displayed, though poorly explained – and in some cases in need of a dusting.

The museum is dedicated in large measure to still-thriving **local crafts**. There are numerous examples of clay water-coolers, bowls and lamps, calabash drums, iron clappers and wooden zithers, ornamental brass pots and implements, while complementary exhibits show the **technology** of the cottage industries. You can see displays showing how iron is forged (still common in the north), how brass weights, once used for weighing gold, are cast, and how glass beads are manufactured.

Interesting, too, are the **ceremonial objects** so common among the Akan and other peoples of the country. Gilded umbrella tops, carved royal stools, metal swords of state and intricate *kente* cloth are charged with a social and religious significance that the displays help illuminate. Upstairs, dusty **archeological relics** trace the country's history back to the late Stone Age.

The National Theatre and the Greater Accra Centre for National Culture

The **National Theatre**, on the corner of Liberia Road and Independence Avenue, is a striking construction, designed and funded by the Chinese. The lobby houses four huge drums and two evocative carvings, specially commissioned for this site; the drums are played only on auspicious occasions (which included the transfer of government in 2000). To arrange your obligatory guided tour (₵10,000), visit the PR Unit in room 310 on the second floor.

Downtown on 28th February Road, the **Centre for National Culture**, more commonly known as the Arts Centre, is a concrete showpiece dedicated to promoting the arts. Inside is a large gallery for exhibitions by national painters and sculptors. The building also contains theatres to showcase national dance and theatre troupes and periodic live-music shows. A schedule of activities is posted outside.

Monuments and other central sights

Jamestown, a bustling centre of small commerce at the heart of the colonial town, is worth a wander, though not **Fort James** itself – it's a prison. You can, however, visit the nearby colonial-era **lighthouse** for scenic town views, although the caretaker may insist on a heavy "dash" for the privilege. East of here, opposite the Parliament building on High Street, the **Kwame Nkrumah Memorial Park** (daily 10am–6pm; ₵5000 plus ₵3000 for cameras) pays homage to the pan-African pioneer and nation builder who became Ghana's first president; it was here, formerly the site of a polo ground, that Kwame Nkrumah first declared Ghana's independence. Built in the 1990s, the monument to him is a throwback to 1960s triumphalism, but the surrounding gardens provide a peaceful refuge from the mayhem of the city.

To the east again, **Independence Square** (also known as Black Star Square) is worth a wander, but be aware of possible muggings and theft at night. The **Triumphal Arch** here, an Nkrumah-era monument of heroic dimensions built to herald African liberation, looms west of **Osu Castle** (no photos allowed), the former Danish Christiansborg, today the seat of government and referred to simply as "The Castle". All surrounding streets are somewhat barricaded, so you can't get too near to this historical curiosity. Independence Square itself is a giant parade ground, site of the Eternal Flame of African Liberation, lit by Nkrumah. Nearby are the ministries and **National Stadium**, north of which is the impressive **International Conference Centre**, built in record time to house the 1991 conference of non-aligned nations. A few hundred metres to the northeast of the square stands the first president's proudest legacy, the monumental **State House** and adjoining **Kwame Nkrumah Conference Centre**, built in 1965 to serve as headquarters of the Organization of African Unity.

The WEB DuBois Memorial Centre

In the northeast of the city, the house where **W.E.B. DuBois**, the black American champion of pan-Africanism, died in 1963 and is buried has been turned into the WEB DuBois **Memorial Centre for Pan-African Culture** (Mon–Fri 8.30am–4.30pm, Sat 11am–4pm & Sun 2–4pm; tour ₡5,000, camera ₡2,000, video ₡5,000). Located on 1st Circular Road (off Giffard Road, opposite the Midwives Association), it's a highly informative and inspiring monument to pan-Africanism and its vanguard, and features a research library and gallery full of manuscripts and other DuBois memorabilia. Photographs and brief biographies of other black world leaders line the walls of his living room and study. The centre contains facilities for lectures – keep an eye out for these if you're around in the summer – and other educational and cultural programmes. On auspicious occasions, the commemorative wreaths from devotees – including reggae dancehall greats Shabba Ranks and Buju Banton – are brought out of storage and once again laid at his tomb.

Markets and crafts shops

The vast **Makola Market**, along Kojo Thompson Road, is where you feel the city centre's retail pulse most strongly. These days it contains just about everything in the food and domestic line, including cheap glass beads. The **Kaneshie Market** by the motor park on Weija Road is also huge and an excellent place for rummaging.

Spreading out around the Centre for National Culture on 28th February Road is the **crafts market**, a huge depot for works from throughout West Africa. On the whole, buying here isn't as satisfying or cheap as searching out such goods in the regions where they're manufactured, but if you've got no time or just like one-stop shopping, this is the place. You'll find everything from **Asante sandals** and **kente cloth** to **leatherwork** from the north, woven cotton fabric and glass beads, any of which can easily be bought more cheaply elsewhere. The wood crafts – **masks**, **carvings** and **boxes** – and the **brasswork** are somewhat harder to find. Expect heavy pressure to buy; bargaining tends to be a battle of wits here and not a great deal of fun. A more relaxed place to buy is from the craftsmen around **Tetteh Quarshie Circle** on the outskirts of town, past the *Shangri-La Hotel*. The quality and selection here is similar to that of the crafts market, but you'll do less bargaining to get a good price. Further afield, the town of Aburi (see p.767), an hour's drive north of Accra, is renowned for its crafts, particularly its drums, and is a pleasant environment to shop in.

The **ATAG** (Aid To Artisans Ghana) **Crafts Shop** (Mon–Fri 8am–6pm, Sat 10am–4pm; ☎021/77.13.25, ✉atag@ataggh.com) in the International Trade Fair Centre, just north of the *Labadi Beach Hotel* at La Pleasure Beach, is less overwhelming if you're not up to speed with your bargaining skills, and is packed with good-quality, though pricey, crafts. The **Loom Gallery**, at the top end of Kwame Nkrumah Avenue, also has a good selection of crafts and jewellery.

Finally, in Nungua, some fifteen minutes' drive east of central Accra on the coast road to Tema, you'll find the **Artists' Alliance** (daily 7am–7pm; ☎ & ☎021/71.23.50), an art gallery/shop selling artefacts, modern art, cloth, pottery and jewellery. All the goods are high quality, and there's no pressure to buy, but most prices differ little from what you'd expect to pay for Africana in a shop at home. The most compelling items are the samples of old *kente* cloth (see p.796), which surpass anything else you're likely to come across. This is cloth with soul, and very dear – ₵650,000–2,500,000 a piece – and you can't help wondering how it came to be here.

For **batik cloth**, try Betdove Batik Factory (pronounced bet-dow) on the La road (☎021/77.23.89), 200m after La Polytechnic on the left-hand side. It's a five-minute drive by line taxi from Danquah Circle; asked to be put off at the adjoining *Jokers* nightclub. Fabrics here cost ₵12,500–15,000 a yard, and you can also watch the fascinating dyeing and waxing process in the open-air factory. The fabrics they sell are less likely to fade and are more keenly priced than those you find on the roadside as you wander around Osu. For batik designs of superb quality, try Mercy Asi Ocansey and Sons Dyeing Enterprise in Osu (☎021/77.78.35), just off Cantonments Road and beside *Frankies* on 4th Lane, opposite the police hospital – though the fabrics here are much more expensive (around ₵18,000 a yard).

Beaches

The best area for sea swimming in Accra is **La Pleasure Beach** (formerly Labadi; ₵5000 entrance fee), directly below the International Trade Fair site. Unusually for Ghana, there are lifeguards stationed here, occasionally called upon to rescue swimmers swept out by the strong undertow. This is *the* place to be on weekends when Accra's young people turn out for beach parties – and just to see and be seen. Several bars and restaurants line the beach, and you may be plagued by hangers-on trying to sell something or play music for a "dash". Taxis and *tro-tros* run here from Nkrumah Circle. To relax in a less hassley environment, Coco Beach, a fifteen-minute drive further east, is a better bet. You can also take a dip below the *Riviera Beach Hotel*, but take nothing of value (and be seen to have nothing of value).

Eating, drinking and nightlife

In addition to the places listed below, cheap **street eats** are available in the motor parks, markets and in certain districts – Adabraka, for example. If you're staying in one of the neighbourhood's inexpensive hotels, you'll find numerous *kenkey* and fish vendors in back streets running between the *Date* and the *Hotel de California*. Mid-priced restaurants (₵20,000–50,000 for a main course) offer more varied cuisine, with a good variety of Asian restaurants and several high-quality Middle Eastern and European-style establishments, as well as a number of very classy African places. Prices at the most expensive eating houses, which include hotel restaurants not mentioned here, run to about ₵60,000 a head.

Inexpensive

In most of the following establishments you can eat a hearty one-course meal for ₵10,000–25,000 – standard international fast food in most of them, with salads and some Ghanaian dishes also featuring.

Bus Stop Ring Road Central, opposite *Paloma Hotel*. Eat at pavement tables from a varied menu of snacks (sandwiches, kebabs) and European specialities. Popular after dark.

Edvy Restaurant At the Ghana National Museum gate, Barnes Rd. Excellent Ghanaian food served at lunchtime only, though note that it can be closed sporadically. Nice Wednesday buffet – eat all you can for ₵20,000.

Odo Rise Kokomlemle. Winner of the Best Chop Bar award in 2001, this serves cheap Ghanaian and European dishes for less than ₵9000. Heaving at lunchtimes. Indoor and outdoor seating available.

Papaye Cantonments Rd, Osu. Another fine example of Accra's growing fast-food culture, with excellent charcoal-grilled chicken (around ₵25,000) which you can eat out on the breezy first-floor balcony or indoors in an a/c area. Try to catch the cultural dance performance on the forecourt every Sat night. Daily 9am–midnight.

Southern Fried Chicken Danquah Circle. Fried, flamed and charcoal-grilled chicken by the bucket. Also serves Indian, and Lebanese food, and vegetarian pizzas. Daily 8am–11pm.

Tasha Snacks and Fast-foods Star Ave, Kokomlemle. Cosy, laid-back café with a great breakfast menu, including pancakes and full English breakfast.

Wok Inn Nkrumah Ave near Circle. Perennially popular Chinese place, serving good-value meals in dimly lit premises. The specials are particularly good. Call ☏021/23.72.09 to order take-away.

Moderate and expensive

African

Afrikiko Liberation Rd, near Sankara Circle ☏021/76.10.27. An expat hangout with moderately priced African and European dishes with tables set around a pleasant garden. Good chicken and salads. There's often live music and dance at weekends, including salsa. Daily 9am–midnight.

La Pergola Airport Rd, near the *Golden Tulip Hotel*. Togolese restaurant serving African and Western food in a pleasant setting, with some open-air seating and a friendly owner. With costs coming in around ₵35,000 a head, it's one of the best places to eat in town in its price bracket.

Providence Cantonments Rd, just off Danquah Circle. Very good, reasonably priced Ghanaian food. Open for lunch only, until 5pm.

Asian and Lebanese

Cedars 3rd Lane, off Cantonments Rd, Osu ☏021/78.22.36. Attractive, café-style restaurant serving excellent Lebanese snacks and meals – *charwarmas*, hummus and other specialities – and some European dishes. Around ₵30,000 per head.

Chez Lien Osu. Excellent Vietnamese restaurant.

Friendly Chinese Restaurant Off Cantonments Rd, Osu ☏021/78.23.68. Unpretentious establishment serving reasonably priced Thai and Chinese food.

Haveli Osu. Popular Indian restaurant with a large variety of tandoori, rice, vegetable and curry dishes. Daily noon–3pm & 7–10.30pm.

Hinlone Off Ring Road East. Well-established Chinese restaurant, with wonderful fresh selections of premium-quality vegetables, meat and seafood. Daily 11.30am–3pm & 6.30–10.30pm.

Tandoor Angola Rd, Kaku Hill behind State House ☏021/77.87.60, ✉tandoorgh@yahoo.com. Well worth seeking out for excellent Indian food in stylish surroundings. Expect to pay ₵55,000 or more per head. Daily noon–3pm & 6–11pm.

European

British Council Restaurant (aka *Kesal Katering*) Liberia Rd, just off Independence Ave ☏021/68.30.68. Good standard of food at affordable prices (from ₵12,000–26,000 a plate). They do a variety of meats cooked over the open-air grill in the adjacent garden, plus a selection of European and Ghanaian dishes. It's a popular spot, particularly at lunch, and BBC News 24 is often showing on the TV. Mon–Fri 9.30am–4pm.

Frankies Cantonments Rd, Osu ☏021/77.35.67. Quickly becoming an Accra landmark, this family-owned complex includes a *boulangerie* with fresh baguettes and pastries, and the best (Italian) ice cream in town. There's also a fast-food take-away, and a second-floor restaurant which, despite the plastic chairs and tables, does serve excellent beef burgers, plus pizzas and Lebanese *chawarmas*. Extremely popular with expats and tourists. Daily 7am–11pm.

Ivy Coffee Shop Ring Road Central, between the Lufthansa and Alitalia offices ☏021/22.84.49. Pricey café with great sandwiches and salads, an unusually good range of French cheeses, and a choice of magazines and papers to read.

Le P'tit Paris Café Ground floor of Sedco House, south of Ring Road Central behind Mobil. Expensive French bakery, selling fresh bread, pastries and sandwiches. One of the few places in town serving freshly brewed coffee. Very popular among expats.

Orangery Crepe and Salad Bar Farrar Ave, Adabraka ☎ 021/23.29.88. Swanky restaurant with a veranda overlooking a lively part of town. French-influenced seafood, pastas and crepes as well as great desserts, all from ₵20,000.

Pit Stop and 4Q Bar Asylum Down,

☎ 021/22.29.44. Unusual set-up, attached to a garage and, for those in the know, a popular spot for full English breakfasts, fish and chips, and delicious steak sandwiches. Daily 8.30am–midnight, Sat until 4pm.

Sole Mio Opposite *Byblos Hotel*, Osu. Italian restaurant with antipastos, pasta, meat and fish dishes – and European prices. Daily noon–3pm & 6.30–11pm.

Nightlife

Nightlife in Accra is an ever-evolving scene, one of the hottest in West Africa. Many of the venues we've listed serve food and may even present themselves as restaurants some of the time, just as certain restaurants sometimes offer live music – anything to get the punters in. The big nights out are Thursday to Sunday; from Monday to Wednesday the action – if it happens at all – starts late, though there are one or two "ladies' nights", usually Wednesday, when women get free admission. Wednesday is also when the La Pleasure Beach party (₵5000) takes place, drawing Accra's youth to drink and dance the night away under the stars. At weekends you can party most of the daytime, too, in some venues. Cover charges are very moderate by international standards – ₵20,000 is about the most you'll pay, if anything at all.

Akuma Village Signposted off High St. Attractive courtyard bar and restaurant overlooking the sea, with seating under thatched roofs. Occasional live music at weekends.

Aquarius Off Cantonments Rd, south of Danquah Circle. Supposedly a German pub (it feels anything but), with pool tables. Expensive, but a popular starting point for a night out.

Boomerang Club Caprice Building, north of Nkrumah Circle. Up three flights of stairs, this popular club has an unpretentious feel, featuring highlife and other African sounds Thurs and Sun, plus R&B and hip-hop. Cover around C25,000.

Champs Sports Bar Ring Road Central, set within the *Paloma Hotel* complex. Canadian-owned sports-oriented bar, with screens showing big sports fixtures and serving pricey Mexican and North American food.

Glenns Farrar Ave, Adabraka. Happening disco playing mostly funk and reggae music, with a highlife special on Sun. Open Wed & Fri–Sun.

Kalahari Jazz Bar Caprice Building, 800m north

of Nkrumah Circle. Ultra-swanky new bar with wicker furniture, a resident band, and occasional artists from the US, playing a range of jazz. Admission ₵20,000. Open Wed–Sun.

Macumba Ring Rd East, near Danquah Circle. The oldest and best-known club in town, still very popular – as well as a well-known pick-up joint.

Next Door In Teshie-Nungua on road to Tema ☎ 021/71.39.47. Open-air weekend hot spot for quality live African music in a cliffside setting by the sea, with great views. Highly recommended.

Ryans Irish Pub Off Cantonments Road in Osu. Popular expat hangout with good Guinness, and live music every Sat. Happy hour Fri 5.30–8pm.

Venus Cocktail Bar Embassy Rd, Osu. Trendy new bar with great cocktails and themed music nights – Latino, jazz and reggae are just some of the sounds featured.

Virus Saleem St, off Cantonments Rd, Osu. *The* place to be at the time of writing, with a varied selection of movies on Sun and Mon, karaoke on Wed, and a jam night on Fri and Sat.

Listings

Airlines Air Ivoire, Cocoa House ☎ 021/24.14.61; Air Mali, 23 CFC, Taesano ☎ 021/22.22.11; American Airlines, Valco Trust House ☎ 021/23.18.04; Alitalia, Ring Road Central ☎ 021/22.98.13; British Airways, corner of Kojo

Thompson Rd and Liberia Rd ☎ 021/24.03.86/7; EgyptAir, Ring Road East, just south of Danquah Circle, Osu ☎ 021/77.35.37; Ethiopian Airlines, Cocoa House ☎ 021/66.48.56; Ghana Airways, Cocoa House ☎ 021/22.10.00; KLM, 86 North

Ridge Crescent, Ring Rd Central ☎021/24.15.60; Lufthansa, Fidelity House, Ring Rd Central ☎021/24.38.93; Nigeria Airways, Danawi Building, D631/4 Kojo Thompson Rd ☎021/22.37.49; South African Airlines, Pyramid House, Ring Rd Central ☎021/23.07.22; Swiss, E.45/3 Pegasus House, Independence Ave ☎021/23.19.18/9.

American Express Represented by Afro Wings in the shopping centre of the Trust Towers, Farrer Ave ☎021/23.54.20.

Banks and exchange The head branches of the major commercial banks are on High Street near the intersection of Bank Lane and include Barclays Bank ☎021/66.49.01; Ghana Commercial Bank ☎021/66.49.11; and Standard Chartered Bank ☎021/66.45.91. Forex bureaux are widespread, with several on Kojo Thompson Rd offering good rates.

Books and newspapers Riya's Bookstore, near the Côte d'Ivoire Embassy off Cantonments Road (☎021/78.10.05) has an excellent selection of new books, as does Arabisco Enterprise Payless Books in Naktan House on Ring Road East (☎021/76.09.75), opposite the US Embassy Chancery Section. There's a good selection of secondhand books at Books For Less, 17th Lane, off Cantonments Rd (☎021/77.07.70). Overseas newspapers, mostly British, can be bought at the *Labadi Beach* and other upmarket hotels. Alternatively, you can read them at the British Council's library.

Car rental Avis, c/o Speedway Travel and Tours, 5 Tackie Tawia St, Adabraka ☎021/22.77.44 or 22.87.60; Hertz, Hertz International House, 37 Hospital ☎021/22.33.89; Marriot Cars, Aviation House, Aviation Rd ☎021/78.41.10. The big hotels can usually help arrange car rental as well.

Cinemas The best places to see Ghanaian and other African films are the GAMA Film Company, north of Sankara Circle near the French Embassy (☎021/22.86.97), and the Rex, on Barnes Rd behind Parliament House, both of which have screenings every night from 6.30pm. For the latest European and American releases on DVD, try Busy Internet on Ring Rd Central on weekend evenings (₵10,000), or *Champs* on Sunday nights (no cover).

Couriers DHL, near KLM on North Ridge Crescent ☎021/22.16.47, ⬤www.dhl.com/gh. To ship goods, EWALD are reliable agents (34 North Ridge; ☎021/22.89.94, ✉services@ewaldgh.com).

Cultural centres The British Council, Liberia Rd, just off Independence Ave (Mon–Wed & Fri 9am–4pm, Thurs 9am–6pm, Sat 9am–1pm; ☎021/68.30.68, 🖷021/68.30.62,

✉info@gh.britishcouncil.org), has an excellent library, stocking British newspapers, and regularly hosts musical and theatrical events. The Alliance Française, Liberation Link Rd, Airport Residential Area (☎021/77.31.34, ✉alliance@ghana.com), does the same in French. The USIS (☎021/22.98.29 or 22.91.79) on Independence Ave and the German Goethe-Institut on Kakramadu Rd, East Cantonments (☎021/77.67.64, ✉goetheil@ncs.com.gh) also run active programmes.

Embassies and consulates Australia, c/o Canadian High Commission; Benin, 3 Switchback Lane, Cantonments ☎021/77.48.60; Burkina Faso, 772/3 Asylum Down, off Mango Tree Ave ☎021/22.19.88; Canada, 42 Independence Ave ☎021/22.85.55 or 22.85.66; Côte d'Ivoire, 9 18th Lane, off Cantonments Road, Osu ☎021/77.46.11; France, 12th Liberation Ave ☎021/77.44.80; Guinea, 161A 4th Norla St, Labone ☎021/77.79.21; Mali, Liberia Rd near the junction with Kinbu Rd ☎021/66.32.76 or 77.51.60; Netherlands, 89 Liberation Rd, Sankara Circle ☎021/25.31.75; New Zealand, c/o British High Commission; Niger, E 104/3 Independence Ave ☎021/22.49.62; Nigeria, 5 Josif Tito Ave ☎021/77.61.58/9; South Africa, Plot 10, Klottey Crescent, North Labone ☎021/76.45.00; Togo, Cantonments Circle ☎021/77.79.50; UK, 1 Osu Link, off Abdul Nasser Ave ☎021/22.16.65; USA, Ring Road East near Danquah Circle, Osu ☎021/77.53.48.

Hospitals The best in town is the Nyaho Clinic, a small hospital in Airport Residential Area (☎021/77.53.41, 🖷77.75.93). The Trust Hospital in Osu (☎021/77.71.37), next to *Dynastys* restaurant, is open 24hr and does fast laboratory tests.

Internet access Busy Internet on Ring Road Central has fast connections (☎021/25.88.00; ₵4000 for 30min). Also fast are the two Cyberia Internet cafés in Osu, charging ₵3000 for 15min. Finally, try Network Computer Services' (NCS) cybercafé at no. 7, 6th Ave, near Immigration Services and KLM.

Photos If you want decent-quality passport photos, the quickest place is a first-floor digital camera service at Max Mart Shopping Centre (☎021/78.37.50) near the *Golden Tulip* hotel on Liberation Rd, where the process takes a matter of minutes; expect to pay around ₵25,000. Otherwise head to a studio (there's a 24hr one on the corner of Kojo Thompson and South Liberia roads and another at Danquah Circle). Finally, you can get fuzzy wooden-box photos done outside the Ghana Immigration Office near Sankara Circle.

Post and telephones Post restante is available free of charge at the GPO in Usshertown (Mon–Fri 8am–4.30pm). As for phone calls, there's no shortage of communication centres and phone booths.

Supermarkets Many supermarkets have sprung up to the south and west of Danquah Circle. Koala is expat heaven, with fresh cheese, meat and French bread. Others nearby include Quick Pick and Afridom. The newest and probably biggest supermarket is Max Mart (℡021/78.37.50) near the *Golden Tulip* hotel; next door, the Bacchus Wine Shop has by far the best selection of wine in town. Petrol-station shops have become very popular for bottled water, bread, cheese and ice cream.

Swimming pools The best pool for the money is at the *Shangri-La*, which non-guests can use for ₵20,000. There are also pools at the *Labadi Beach Hotel* and *La Royal Palm*. Canadian nationals can use the bar and pool at their High Commission.

Travel agents Speedway Travel and Tours, 5 Tackie Tawia St, Adabraka (℡021/22.77.44 or 22.87.99) and Tropical Sun Travel and Tours, 393/2 Tackie Tawia St (℡021/22.48.95) are both near the Trust Towers in Adabraka, and are very helpful for a range of organized tours in the country. M&J Travels and Tours, Embassy Rd, Osu, are also reputable (℡021/77.34.98 or 70.60.81).

Visa extensions The Immigration Office is on Independence Ave, near Sankara Circle (Mon–Fri 8am–1pm). They expect two photos and proof of a return air ticket to extend a visa, and will usually retain your passport for around two weeks while this is done, so if you might need to change traveller's cheques, do so beforehand.

Western Union At branches of Agricultural Development Bank, the most central of which is in Adabraka on Kojo Thompson Road.

Around Accra

Getting out of the city for a while, especially at the hottest and most humid times of the year, from January to June, can be a relief. To the north, **Aburi**, a former hill station whose large gardens are still well maintained, offers the best escape from the heat. Slightly further inland, there are wildlife-spotting opportunities at the **Shai Hills Reserve**. Another easy-day-trip from Accra is **Kokrobite**, 30km to the west, an ideal spot for relaxing on the beach (see p.769).

Legon, Aburi and Shai Hills

LEGON, 14km north of Accra, is the headquarters of the **University of Ghana**, described by the Ghana Tourist Board as "a showpiece of Japanese architecture". There's a good bookshop but less opportunity to meet students than you might wish. You can visit the university's botanical garden in the grounds, but there are older, more interesting and extensive gardens at **ABURI**, on Akwapim Ridge, 23km further north, with potentially magnificent views north over the forest and south to the city when the air is clear. Aburi, several hundred metres above the plain, was a colonial hill station and site of a sanatorium (now a hotel), and the gardens (₵10,000) still bear the well-tended hallmarks of landscaped colonial taste, with hundreds of tree specimens from all over the tropical and sub-tropical regions. There are two restaurants in the grounds: *Roses Plot* is a no-frills place with basic fare, while the *Royal Gardens Restaurant* is smarter with fantastic views, though the food and service are mediocre. The rooms and s/c bungalows at the *Aburi Gardens Rest House* (℡0876/23037; ₵54,000) are in decline, but there's an excellent alternative in the *Olyander Hotel* (℡0876/22058; ❶), which has very homely carpeted rooms. *Sweet Africa Guest House* (℡0876/22069; ❶) has clean, non-s/c rooms and is owned by a Liberian professor who, alongside writing poetry, is enthusiastically manufacturing corn-husk wares. The upmarket choice is the *Little Acre* (℡0876/22103; ❸), out of town on the road to Accra, which has an expensive restaurant and attractively furnished, tiled rooms with TV and fridge. The surrounding forest has cycle routes which you can explore by renting a bike from Aburi Bike and Hike Tours, by the south gate of the Botanical Gardens (Mon & Thurs–Sun 9am–6pm; ℡024/26.73.03, ✉aburibike@email.com)). A final point of interest in town is the impressive structure near *Sweet Africa* with the Lions of Judah at the gates – this is in fact a top-notch recording studio established by Rita Marley, wife of the reggae legend.

Tro-tros from Tema station run frequently to Legon, taking half an hour or so, and **buses** from the same station take about an hour to Aburi (the last one back to Accra leaves at about 6.30pm, not at 6pm as taxi drivers may tell you). If you're driving to Aburi, you continue past the airport to Tetteh Quarshie Circle, then take the Akosombo road until it forks right; take the left-hand fork and start climbing.

Some 60km to the northeast of Accra is the **Shai Hills Reserve** (¢15,000). Troops of baboons and parrots are the most likely sights here, though kob antelope and ground hornbills can also be seen. There are also some extensive bat-populated caves which can be visited. These were used as sites of worship by the Shai people until they were moved out by the British in colonial times; nowadays the Shai return annually to perform ceremonies.

The main gate to the reserve is on the Akosombo road, and the reserve's location makes it a better staging post than Aburi if you're en route to Akosombo or Ho. The easiest way to get here by public transport from Accra is by changing in the small town of **Ashaiman**, served by *tro-tros* from Accra's Tema station. You can **stay** here at an old office block/camp near the rangers' office in very basic dorms (¢10,000 per person) and staff are available to take you around the reserve (¢5000/hr). The *Midway Spot*, opposite the reserve gates, is an alternative to the dorms, with fanless cell-like rooms (❶). Nearby, the *Shai Hills Resort*, still under construction at time of writing, will offer much more comfortable accommodation.

10.2

The coast

The scenic coastline stretching **west from Accra** to the Côte d'Ivoire border is one of the most obvious tourist targets in West Africa. The big attractions are the densest concentration of European **forts and castles** anywhere on the continent – 29 of them, some over 500 years old – and innumerable, unspoiled Fante **fishing villages** tucked between links of sandy, coconut-backed beaches. It's an irresistible combination, and not one you'll be alone in discovering. You'll have to come on a weekday or out of season to have much hope of finding your own isolated paradise. Nevertheless, few places are ever more than quietly humming with tourist business. As for the coast **east of Accra**, there are watersports resorts at **Ada Foah** and **Keta**, popular with Ghanaians.

East of Accra

Prampram, 40km east of Accra, is reputed to be one of Ghana's best beaches, and is distinguished by the French **Fort Vernon**. Further east, the village of **ADA FOAH** (often shortened to Ada) attracts tourists drawn by the golden beaches of the Volta rivermouth, 120km from Accra. To reach Ada from Accra, take a bush taxi from the Tudu station (₵5000) direct to the village, or change at the Kasseh/Ada junction. If you have private transport, follow the main Accra–Lomé road and branch off at this junction. The most popular accommodation here is at *Cocoloko Beach Camp Resort*, a collection of basic though comfortable reed huts built on the sands near the beach, about 2km west of the town centre (❶). The *Garden's Club Annex* (☎0968/22262; ❶) near the market offers acceptable rooms with fan. The cheapest place in town is the *New Grove Seaview Cottage* (☎0968/22401; ❶), with basic huts, some on stilts, located near the lorry park – ironically there's no longer a sea view. The upmarket choice is the *Manet Paradise Beach Resort* (☎0968/22398, ✉manet@ghana.com; ❼), which has jet-skis, sailing dinghys, windsurfing and a pool. For local Ghanaian dishes (₵20,000) in a cheerful garden setting, try the *Brightest Spot*, off the main road. Ada has an unofficial tourist office – basically a travel agent – on the main road (daily 9am–6pm), where you can book yourself onto an excursion or ferry ride up the Volta.

The serene golden sands and unbelieveably blue shores at **KETA**, out on the Volta delta 175km from Accra (and served by *tro-tros* from Tudu station), were once among the nicest in Ghana. Unfortunately, a lot of the village, built on sand, has been destroyed by the sea – leaving a ghost-town feel; a recent multi-million-dollar sea defence project has not improved Keta's appeal. Despite these misfortunes, the fishing village is still inviting, with a welcoming local community, and the *Keta Beach Hotel* (☎0966/42288; ❶), off the main road, is a pleasant surprise, with excellent-value clean, quaint rooms, and a garden restaurant. *Agblor Lodge* (☎0966/42379; ❶) is equally popular though staff can be miserable, while the plush *Lorneah Lodge* (☎0966/42162, ✉42160; ❺), back in the village of Tegbi, offers bland, good-value rooms with all mod-cons. You can also get a *tro-tro* to **Fort Prinsensten** at the east end of town for a brief tour (a ₵5000 tip to the caretaker is appreciated). Both Ada and Keta offer first-class **bird-watching**.

To reach the **Togolese border** from Keta, take a shared Land Rover from the Keta lorry station (₵5000; 40min). Your vehicle will have to traverse the beach for a stretch, as the road has been completely washed away.

From Accra to Cape Coast

West of Accra, the highway at first stays well inland, running through scrubby bush and farming country, hot and unyielding. Just 30km west of Accra is the first break, at the beach resort of **KOKROBITE**. Dance and music lessons are offered here by the Academy of African Music and Arts Ltd (look out for the "AAMAL" sign on the main road; ☎021/66.59.87). The internationally renowned Ga master drummer Mustapha Tettey Addy is the leader of the group and joint owner of the establishment, which doubles as a hotel (❷) and bar. There are wonderfully dynamic drumming and dance displays on weekend afternoons between 2pm and 6pm (non-guests ₵5000). You can reach Kokrobite directly from Accra by *tro-tro* from Dansoman station in the Kaneshie motor park (about ₵1300). Coming from the west, disembark at the junction for Kokrobite at the police barrier, and either charter a taxi for around ₵12,000 or wait for a passing *tro-tro*.

The **accommodation** at the academy is beginning to decline and is no longer good value for money. The **restaurant** is excellent however, providing a foretaste of the grilled seafood that abounds further along the coast. Next door, *Maajoa Beach Front* has just three rooms, all clean and well furnished (☎024/20.45.59; ❷); camping is also permitted at ₵15,000. Another good place to stay is *Big Milly's Backyard* (✉bigmilly2000@hotmail.com; ❷), an incredibly successful set-up that's popular with the backpacker crowd, with fifteen charming huts in a pretty compound beside the beach. The bar and restaurant here are excellent and always lively. Nearby, you can enjoy pizza and pasta at the Italian-run restaurant *Kokrobite Gardens* (✉fsavastano@yahoo.com), a hidden gem which also has some attractively rustic

The forts

Soon after the Portuguese found the maritime routes to the Gulf of Guinea in the fifteenth century, they began setting up trading posts. Rumours of the vast wealth of the region filtered back to Europe and it wasn't long before other nations established themselves on the coast, building sturdy **fortresses** to protect their interests in the trade of gold, ivory and, later, slaves. By the end of the eighteenth century, thirty-seven such forts dotted the coastline, eight of which have since been completely destroyed.

After independence several forts started taking in travellers – it's now theoretically possible to sleep at the **resthouses** (denoted "RH" below) in at least four of them. They offer exceptionally cheap and characterful accommodation – in basic rooms with fan and shared facilities – though they have limited space so are often full in high season. The museum at Cape Coast may be able to help with bookings.

Recent restoration work – including the whitewashing of slave cells – has enraged African-American visitors, who argue they have a right to a say in how these relics of their history are to be preserved. They complain that the Ghanaian Ministry of Tourism is trampling on their history for profits, sanitizing the crumbling slave forts at the behest of funding bodies like the "white" Smithsonian Institution and USAID. Limited catering facilities at one or two forts have had to close after vigorous protests.

Along the coast from east to west, sites with **major forts** include:

• **Prampram** East of Accra, Fort Vernon was built in 1756 by the French and taken by the British in 1806.

• **Accra** Christiansborg was built by the Danes in 1659. Earlier a Swedish fortress, which at one time had probably belonged to the Portuguese, stood on the same spot. Ussher Fort was built by the Dutch in 1642. Ten years later it was taken by the French and named "Fort Crevecoeur", then passed through the hands of the Dutch and finally the British, who rebuilt it in 1868. James Fort was built by the Portuguese in the mid-sixteenth century, taken by the English, and rebuilt in 1673.

• **Senya Beraku** (RH). The last fort built by the Dutch, Fort Good Hope was erected in 1702 and extended in 1715.

• **Apam** (RH). Fort Leydsaemheyt was built in 1698 by the Dutch. Occupied by the British (who named it Fort Patience) in 1782 and retaken by the Dutch three years later, it was abandoned around 1800.

lodgings, in lush gardens (❶). East of *Big Milly's*, *Andy's Akwaaba Lodge* (☎024/27.72.61; ❶) offers a quiet refuge in a spacious grassy compound, with German specialities in the restaurant.

The village of **GOMOA FETTEH**, 15km or so from Kokrobite, is the site of two attractive resorts and an increasingly popular destination on this stretch of coast. The *Tills No. 1 Hotel* here has neat and comfortable rooms and an appealing location looking down onto a stretch of clean, private beach (☎027/550480, ✉tillsbeach@web.de; ❻, camping $7 per person). The rather more auspicious *White Sands Beach Club* (☎027/55.07.07, ℻77.40.64, 🌐www.whitesandsbc.com; ❽) has a unique set-up where guests have to use a motor boat to travel from the reception area and stunning "mainland" restaurant out to the hotel's beach (₵20,000 non-guests) and funky *Barefoot Bar*. The accommodation, in a separate location five minutes' drive away, is in charming, luxurious villas with their own kitchenette and lounge.

The first fort along this stretch is **Fort Good Hope** at **SENYA BERAKU**, 5km west of Gomoa Fetteh. To get here from Accra, take a bush taxi to Awutu junction (not Senya junction, from where you won't easily get onward transport). From there, you can get another taxi down to the coastal village, 10km away. The village is dull, but the setting is scenic, and the trip interesting mainly for the fishing activities of the Fante inhabitants (note, however, that the Fante don't fish on Tuesdays).

- **Anomabu** A Dutch lodge was founded here in the seventeenth century and taken by the British in 1665. Fort Charles was built on its site in 1674, expanded in the 1730s and renamed Fort William.

- **Mouri (Moree)** Fort Nassau was built by the Dutch in 1598. It went back and forth between the British and Dutch until it was finally abandoned in 1815. It is now in ruins.

- **Cape Coast** The original castle was founded by the Swedes, then taken by the Danes and passed to the hands of the Dutch before finally being taken by the English in 1662. After a French bombardment in 1757, it was entirely reconstructed in 1760 when it lost its original design.

- **Elmina** St George's Castle, the oldest European monument in sub-Saharan Africa, was built by the Portuguese in 1482 with dressed stones brought from Europe. The original castle was expanded by the Dutch in 1637. Fort São Lago (RH), which faces it, dates from the seventeenth century and was taken by the Dutch in 1683.

- **Komenda** Fort Vredenburg was built by the Dutch in 1688, taken by the English in 1782 and abandoned three years later. Fort English, in the same town, was founded by the English in 1663. Both forts are now in ruins.

- **Shama** Fort Sebastian was founded by the Portuguese around 1560 and occupied by the Dutch in 1640.

- **Sekondi** Fort Orange was built by the Dutch in 1640; it became British after 1872.

- **Dixcove** Fort Metal Cross was built by the English in 1691, and occupied by the Dutch from 1868 to 1872.

- **Princestown** (RH). Grossfriedrichsburg was built in 1683 by the German Brandenburgers and taken by the Dutch and later British. In ruins at independence, the fort has since been restored.

- **Axim** Fort Santa Antonia (Fort St Anthony), built in the fifteenth century, was the second Portuguese fort on the coast. Taken by the Dutch in 1642, it was rebuilt on several occasions.

- **Beyin** (RH). Fort Apollonia was built by the English Committee of Merchants in 1756.

You get sweeping panoramic views from the fort (☎021/30.44.88), which hangs over the sea, where you can **stay** the night in one of their rooms (❶) and have a delicious plate of chicken and chips prepared on request. Senya Beraku is the site of a number of **festivals** throughout the year (see p.734).

Winneba and Apam

The main town in these parts, **WINNEBA** is perched on raised ground between the Muni and Oyibi lagoons. It's easily reached from Accra: transport leaves from Kaneshie station for Swedru junction (aka Winneba junction), 6km away on the main coast highway, from where shared taxis continue to Winneba. Although it is beginning to acquire a reputation for its **pottery**, Winneba is most famous in Ghana as the site of the Aboakyer or **"deer-hunting festival"** which takes place at the end of April or early May (see p.735). At other times of year, there's little to do in the town itself apart from watching canoes at work and fish being smoked, and enjoying the noise and bustle of dusk. The newest and best **accommodation** in town is *Lagoon Lodge* (❶), down a sandy track near the lagoon, with spotless s/c doubles with fans and tiled floors, while not far away, the modest *Winneba Resthouse* (aka *Armed Forces Resthouse*) is another reasonable option, with airy rooms looking out to the sea (☎0432/22208; ❶). More upmarket options can be found 3km from

Like other Akan states, the Fante maintain a highly formalized military institution known as **Asafo** (from *sa*, "war", and *fo*, "people"). The original function of the Asafo was the defence of the Fante state. Although that role largely disappeared after the colonial invasion, Asafo companies still thrive and exercise considerable political influence. They enstool chiefs – and can destool them in certain instances – and act as royal advisors.

The companies put on at least one major festival each year and also provide community entertainment in the form of singing, dancing and drumming.

A Fante town typically has between two and twelve Asafo companies, each identified in a military fashion by number, name and location (for example Number 5 Company, Brofu-mba, Cape Coast), with members in ranks, easily identifiable as general, senior commander, divisional captain and so on. Asafo membership is patrilineal (in contrast to the chieftaincy, which is matrilineal, passing to the next man through the line of his maternal uncle).

As well as their military-ceremonial duties, the Asafo are active in the arts. In every Fante town there are painted cement **Asafo shrines**, known as **posuban**, for each of the town's companies. Rich with symbolism, the *posuban* evokes proverbs proclaiming one company's superiority over its rivals. The shrine of No. 3 Company, Anomabu, for example, is guarded by two life-size cement lions, recalling the saying "A dead lion is greater than a live leopard". The rival No. 6 Company boasts a warship-shaped shrine, symbolic of its military prowess.

Similar symbolism carries over into the vibrantly coloured, appliqué **Asafo flags** made and paraded by each company. These can be seen flying over shrines or, more often, displayed throughout a company's area during town festivities. They have recently acquired serious value in European and American galleries and private collections – a phenomenon that, more than anything else, threatens to unravel the social fabric of the Asafo companies.

the centre off the Winneba–Agona Junction road at the excellent *Hunter's Lodge* (❸), with some budget rooms and stylish doubles with satellite TV, fridge and hot water. or *Windy Lodge* (℡0432/22479; ❶), both. Out on the beach you can watch **drag fishing**, with music and singing, and fifty men hauling the net rope. For meals, *Hut D'Eric* off the Accra road near Swedru junction serves a few Continental and Ghanaian dishes for around ₵25,000, including fantastic spring rolls. Back in the centre, *Halo Halo* is the *in* bar. For Internet access, try *Big Nana's Cyber Café* near the Ghana Telecom building.

Some 20km west of Winneba is **APAM**, where you can stay at **Fort Patience**. Getting here from Accra requires taking a taxi or *tro-tro* to the Apam junction and changing. It's about 8km down to Apam – too far to walk in the heat of the day. At the entrance to town is an imposing *posuban* shrine, a three-storey affair topped by a white Jesus and decorated with colourful statues of Africans mounted on horseback. Fort Patience is beautifully sited above the town and has spartan rooms and well water for washing (₵40,000). A more comfortable place to stay is the *Lynnbah Guesthouse* (℡021/30.72.08; ❶), a homely establishment set around an attractive, leafy courtyard, and which once hosted Stevie Wonder. Eating here is an option if you order in advance; otherwise food in town is limited pretty much to the market.

Saltpond, Anomabu and Biriwa

The next town to the west is **SALTPOND**, 42km west of Apam junction (you may have to change buses at Mankessim, 35km west of Apam junction), which offers precious little reason to call in (a bypass skirts the town) though it vies with Winneba for importance. If you fetch up here for the night, try the gently decaying

△ Wli falls

Palm Beach (☎031/46683; ❷). A better plan is to go another 6km west to **ANOMABU**, which has some excellent accommodation options and a superb beach nearby. On the western side of town, the *Anomabu Beach Resort* (☎042/33801, ✉anomabu@hotmail.com; ❹) offers comfortable chalets in a sandy compound, an excellent and attractive restaurant overlooking the palm-fringed golden beach, and camping opportunities right on the sands ($16 to hire a tent). *Weda Lodge* (❹) is an unmissable structure, formerly a private mansion, perched on top of a hill nearby; it offers five spacious, simplistic and stylish rooms with balconies and unbelievable views. At the other end of town, the *Mariesabelle* (☎042/33734; ❶) is recommended for clean, carpeted rooms, while the *Ebenezer Rest Stop* (☎042/33673; ❷) is of a similar standard. Anomabu's fort, Fort William, is a prison, so no photos are allowed – and in any case there is little to admire. But do look out for the *posuban* shrines dotted around town – Dontsin No. 3 shrine, near *Ebenezer's*, is particularly intricate.

The last place of note on this stretch is the idyllic crescent of sand and coconuts at **BIRIWA**, 3km west of Anomabu. It's right beneath the main highway, which makes it both accessible and a little too popular at weekends. Time was it sheltered various semi-resident hippies in wooden shacks at the village end of the beach, but those days have passed and there's now a fair-sized crowd on the beach at weekends. There's also an excellent if somewhat pricey restaurant at the German-run *Biriwa Beach Hotel* on the hill behind the strand (☎042/33333, ⓦwww.biriwabeach.com.gh; ❻). If the comfortable s/c chalets with TV, a/c and minibar are beyond your budget (room 101 has the best views), you could opt to camp here, for a small charge. Supplies are available in the village above the rocky bluff.

Cape Coast

British capital of the Gold Coast until 1876, **CAPE COAST** is a relatively large town with a solid infrastructure, the site of the nation's first university and major secondary schools. The major attraction is the seventeenth-century **Cape Coast Castle** and museum, but there are no recommendable beaches nearby.

Arrival and information

Through traffic doesn't go via the town, but round its north side on a **bypass**, off the frame of our map. Kotokuraba **tro-tro station**, near the market of the same name, is used by transport from and to surrounding towns such as Takoradi, Anomabu and Twif Prasso (via Kakum); Accra has its own station, from where you can also get transport to Kumasi. **STC** (located west of the Pedu junction at the Goil station) runs four daily services to Accra and two to Kumasi (fewer services on Sun); for Takoradi you can join one of the numerous buses passing through from Accra every day; and for the north, the service leaves between 8 and 9am on Monday, Wednesday and Friday, calling at Tamale, then Bolga. Shared taxis heading for Elmina – along the nicest stretch of the coastal highway, where it runs directly above the beach through endless swaying coconut trees – leave from both the junction of Jackson and Commercial streets in town, and from a small station just off the Inner Ring Road.

The **Cape Coast Tourist Board** (☎042/32062, ✉ccgtb@yahoo.co.uk) is located in the SIC building off the Cape Coast–Takoradi highway on the outskirts of town. Heritage House (formerly the governor's home) in the centre of town contains a number of useful offices: on the first floor, the **Ghana Wildlife Society** has information on ecotourism sites in the region (☎042/36350), and next door is a **Tourist Information Centre**, though it's not always manned. **Kakum HQ** (☎042/30265) are up on the second floor and can help you book guided tours at the park. The organizers of **Panafest** (ⓦwww.panafest.org), the biennial arts and

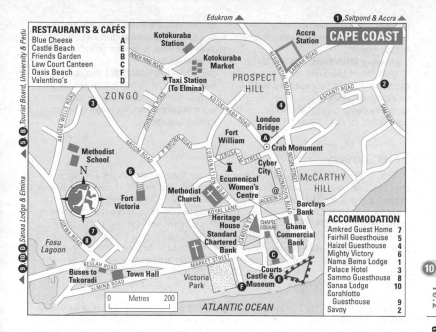

RESTAURANTS & CAFÉS

Blue Cheese	A
Castle Beach	E
Friends Garden	B
Law Court Canteen	C
Oasis Beach	F
Valentino's	D

ACCOMMODATION

Amkred Guest Home	7
Fairhill Guesthouse	5
Haizel Guesthouse	4
Mighty Victory	6
Nama Bema Lodge	1
Palace Hotel	3
Sammo Guesthouse	8
Sanaa Lodge	10
Sarahlotto Guesthouse	9
Savoy	2

culture festival that takes place during odd-numbered years at the end of July and the start of August, have an office on the ground floor; they also organize celebrations for Emancipation Day.

Standard Chartered and Barclays **banks** are both centrally located and have very similar exchange rates, with ATMs outside; Barclays also give cash advances on Visa and MasterCard. Cyber City, on Commercial Road one block south of the Crab monument, offers slick **Internet** connections.

Accommodation

Cape Coast has a good range of hotels to choose from, and if you're on a tight budget, it's worth trying Cape Coast's university hostels (¢15,000 per person) – Adehye Hall, at the entrance to the main campus on the western side of town, is your best bet.

Amkred Guest Home Behind *Sammo Guest House* ☏ 042/32868. Great new place, with a range of s/c rooms with hot water and fan or a/c. Food available on request. ❶

Fairhill Guesthouse Off the main Accra–Takoradi highway, in the northern part of Ola district ☏ 042/33322, ℻ 33323. Homely and down-to-earth choice in this price range. Excellent-value rooms with all the amenities – TV, video, fridge and a/c, make up for the inconvenient location. ❸

Haizel Guesthouse Residential Rd, south of the Accra lorry station ☏ 042/32044. Despite the hideous three-storey exterior, this is a good, clean, central option with no frills. ❶

Mighty Victory Hotel Aboom Rd, close to Fort Victoria ☏ 042/30135, ⊛ www.hometown .aol.com/gh72. Spotless, comfortable rooms with TV and hot water. Good location. ❷

Nama Bema Lodge Sam's Hill, off Sarbah Road ☏ 042/32103, ℻ 32616, ℮ bemahotel@yahoo.com. Plush and stylish hotel in an elevated position – with a fabulous 360-degree view of Cape Coast. ❹

Palace Hotel Aboom Rd ☏ 042/33556. One of the cheapest lodgings in town with acceptable non-s/c rooms. ❶

Sammo Guesthouse ☏ 042/33242. Well maintained and deservedly popular. There's a ground-floor restaurant serving Ghanaian cuisine, and a rooftop bar with fabulous views and some European fare. ❶

Sanaa Lodge Off the Elmina Rd ☏ 042/32570, ☏ 32898. Still the town's best, though beginning to fray around the edges. Comfortable and stylish a/c, s/c rooms with minibar. ❼

Sarahlotte Guesthouse 183 Ola Estates ☏ 042/32871. Located in Ola, on the outskirts of

town on the road to Elmina – thankfully, shared taxis run by frequently. A small, homely place with six well-furnished rooms, most s/c and some with TV and fridge. ❶

Savoy Ashanti Rd ☏ 042/32805. Best value in town and often full: rooms are clean, with fan, and the hotel is centrally located near the beachfront on the east side of town. The restaurant serves middling food. ❶

The Town

A World Heritage Site since 1979, **Cape Coast Castle** perches on a rocky ledge that juts out over the ocean. Originally a Swedish and then a Danish fort, it was taken in 1665 by the British and was their Gold Coast headquarters until 1876. In the nineteenth century, the building was enlarged to its present dimensions. A guided tour (₵40,000; half-price for self-guided tours; cameras ₵5,000, videos ₵10,000; student discounts available) takes you through the maze of damp, suffocating **dungeons** where slaves were held before being shipped to Europe through the "door of no return". The **castle museum** contains a thought-provoking exhibition documenting Ghana's history, exploring issues such as the conditions endured by slaves and its legacies, including the lives of black Americans after the diaspora.

The new Centre for National Culture on the road to the University is worth seeking out – it houses a **Gramophone Records Museum** that's a must for serious devotees of mid-1960's and early 1970's highlife music and students of early West African recordings. The collection includes 15,000–20,000 recordings representing 700 artists dating back to 1900. Also worth a visit is the **Ecumenical Women's Centre** (Mon–Fri 9am–5pm) opposite Barclay's Bank. Dedicated to the education and development of women in the area, the centre runs a batik vocational training school, where seamstresses make a wide range of batik cloths and clothing which are sold at very reasonable prices at the first-floor shop. Bespoke orders are accepted at no extra cost, and all proceeds go to funding the centre.

Eating and drinking

One central and unusual place to grab a bite is in the Law Court's canteen, which is open to all (Mon–Sat 7am–7pm). *Cape Café*, inside the Ecumenical Women's

---

The Oguaa Fetu harvest festival

Of many harvest festivals held in the region, one of the biggest is Cape Coast's **Oguaa Fetu Afahye**, which takes place on the first Saturday in September, when traditional chiefs from throughout the surrounding districts parade in sumptuous *kente*-cloth togas and bedecked with gold crowns and medallions. The most important rulers are carried in canoe-like stretchers balanced on the heads of four manservants and shaded by huge parasols. They're accompanied by the queen mothers, wearing bracelets, necklaces and rings of solid gold, with more gold ornaments in their beehive coiffures. Fetish priests dance through the procession dispensing good fortune and collecting payment; palm wine flows freely. The parade lasts most of the day, terminating in **Victoria Park** for speeches by the chiefs and government representatives. Later, the streets fill up again and the party continues through the night with brass bands, music and dancing. This carnival atmosphere reigns for a couple of days and is worth making a detour for – arrive early and book a hotel in advance, as most are crammed solid for the duration.

Centre (daily 8am–8pm) serves delicious pancakes, juices and milkshakes. *Oasis Beach* and *Castle Beach Restaurant*, unsurprisingly, both have attractive coastal settings and offer good and varied food for less than ₵25,000. *Oasis* also has a musical or other cultural performance every Saturday night. For fresh grilled tilapia you can't beat the *Blue Cheese*, a buzzing evening hangout on Kotokuraba Road; another lively spot for a drink, with a small indoor restaurant, is *Friends Gardens*, up the Jukwa road. Heading out of town across Fosu lagoon, you can't miss *Valentino's*, offering loud music, grilled food and cheap beer until the early hours. And lastly, for something different, as you hit the Elmina side of the lagoon, you'll find *Asasse Pa* (Mon–Sat 6am–8pm), a "health and wellness" resort serving only vegetarian dishes and fruit juices in a quiet, scenic location.

Kakum National Park and around

The superb **KAKUM NATIONAL PARK** (entry ₵500), 35km north of Cape Coast, consists of 360 square kilometres of protected forest, harbouring monkeys, elephants and antelopes. Park facilities have greatly improved over the past few years, and there's an attractive and adequate restaurant (daily 7.30am–3.30pm), in addition to a museum and main **visitor's centre** at the park HQ just outside the village of **Abrafo** (☎042/32583). **Tro-tros** are fairly frequent from the Kotokuraba station in Cape Coast to the visitor's centre near Abrafo.

The highlight of Kakum is the hugely popular three-hundred-metre **aerial walkway** through the rainforest canopy, 30m above the forest floor. Although it costs a steep ₵60,000 to use (students and NGO volunteers ₵30,000), it's still a must, just to mingle with the birds, butterflies and squirrels among the towering trees. Get there early morning or late afternoon to avoid the rush.

Down on the forest floor, **trail hikes** to see the animals, medicinal plants and variety of butterflies cost ₵20,000 for the first hour (₵5000 for each subsequent hour) with a mandatory guide. The very early morning or late afternoon are the best times to avoid the daytime heat; if you arrive at midday, they'll take you on a shorter trek to point out the wide range of flora, explaining the names and various medicinal and domestic uses of the different trees and shrubs. It's possible to camp in the park at a site fifteen minute's walk from the visitor's centre, sleeping on roofed platforms, with toilet and shower facilities (₵40,000 per person with your equipment, ₵80,000 without). Note that the restaurant in the visitor's centre closes at 3.30pm, so bring your own food for the night. Arrange for a guide to meet you for a night or early morning walk, when you're most likely to see wildlife, though the chances of coming across large mammals are very slender. Alternatively you can spend the night on the atmospheric **Masomagor Tree Platform**, 10m up in the forest canopy. You need to book in advance at the visitor's centre in **Masomagor village** on the eastern side of the park (☎042/33041, ✉cighana@ghana.com), and bring your own food and equipment. The platform is an hour and a half's walk from Masomagor, where you shouldn't miss seeing the **Bamboo Orchestra**, a fantastic percussion group who will perform for a fee of ₵100,000.

Another place you could consider staying is 23km south of the park on the Cape Coast–Kakum road, at the oddly named *Hans Cottage Botel* (☎042/33621, ℱ33623, ⓦwww.hansbotel.com; ②), which boasts a terrace restaurant on stilts over a crocodile pool. The crocs are usually difficult to see except at feeding time, but the bird-watching is good. It's a great place for a late breakfast after an early-morning park trip, or for a late-night drink in the double-decker thatched restaurant/bar overlooking the pond. There's a variety of rooms to suit most budgets, Internet access and a small swimming pool; camping is also allowed.

Domama Rock Shrine

Some 26km further on from Kakum, an eerie array of giant boulders, known as the **Domama Rock Shrine**, is becoming an increasingly popular tourist destination, largely through the efforts of a community-based ecotourism project. Although the spiritual importance of the shrine seems to have waned somewhat and the rocks are not spectacular in themselves, the site is set incongruously in dense jungle and still makes for a good excursion, the walk to reach the rocks being a highlight in itself. A visit to the shrine, 7km from the village of **Domama** (where you pay the ₵8000 admission fee and are assigned a guide) along a terrible dirt track, is usually followed by a 45-minute canoe tour of the Pra River (₵12,000), though the latter isn't permitted on Wednesdays when activity on the river is taboo. Occasional direct **tro-tros** leave for Domama from Kotokuraba station in Cape Coast (market days, Tuesdays and Fridays, are your best bet), or you can take a Twifo Praso-bound car and get off at the junction at Ankaako – either way you may in be for a long wait. You may be able to find a taxi to charter, though expect to pay a phenomenal rate. There's a very basic **guesthouse** with no electricity or running water (❶) in Domama, and simple Ghanaian food can be prepared on request.

Elmina and around

A small but active fishing town, **ELMINA** ("the mine" in Portuguese) was one of the first European toe-holds on the West African coast. The principal attractions remain the **Portuguese castle and fort**, although the slow pace makes Elmina a rewarding place to relax and absorb the rhythms of a coastal town. But it's not all calm – when the fishing boats come in, Elmina can be spectacularly vibrant – and the town's unusual layout is arresting, counterposing the ocean against the lagoon and the two castles against each other. With a number of interesting *posuban* shrines to boot, this is one of the most rewarding places for photographers along the coast.

The castle and fort

One of the oldest buildings still standing in West Africa (and now a World Heritage Site), the castle of **St George El Mina** was built by the Portuguese in 1482 – ten years before Columbus discovered America – although the original stockade was barely half the size of the present structure. It served as the **Portuguese headquarters** in West Africa for over 150 years until it was captured by soldiers of the Dutch West Indies Company in 1637. By that time, St George had grown roughly to its present size. Finally, in 1872, the British bought the castle, along with the other Dutch possessions on the Gold Coast.

In the courtyard, you'll notice a **Catholic church** built by the Portuguese. The protestant Dutch transformed this place of worship into a mess hall and **slave market** – an onerous image that poignantly drives home the barbarity of the trade. Today the church houses a fascinating exhibition documenting Elmina's history, people and culture. Given its age, the castle has held up well, and some restoration work has taken place using funds from USAID. Extremely good **tours** of the castle run daily from 9am till 5pm, every hour on the hour (₵40,000 plus ₵5,000 for cameras and ₵10,000 for videos; student discounts available). Alternatively you can simply walk around on your own, communing with the baffling past, for half the price.

Across from the castle atop a steep, partly artificial hill, **Fort St Jago** (São Iago) was built by the Dutch in 1666 to protect the castle from future attacks. Formerly a guesthouse offering fine vistas of the ocean and sprawling town below, the fort was declared a World Heritage Site in 1992 and closed for renovation, though a dispute lingers with UNESCO as to whether the site should operate simply as a museum or a guesthouse, or both. For now, you can visit the site daily from 6am to 6pm

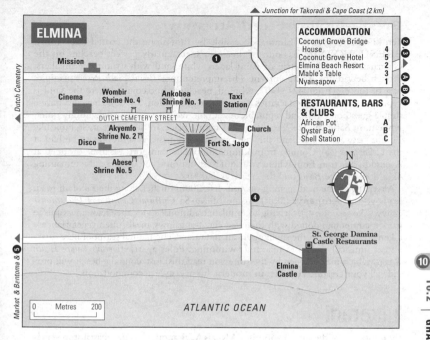

ELMINA

ACCOMMODATION

Coconut Grove Bridge House	4
Coconut Grove Hotel	5
Elmina Beach Resort	2
Mable's Table	3
Nyansapow	1

RESTAURANTS, BARS & CLUBS

African Pot	A
Oyster Bay	B
Shell Station	C

Mission

Cinema

Wombir Shrine No. 4

Ankobea Shrine No. 1

Taxi Station

DUTCH CEMETERY STREET

Akyemfo Shrine No. 2

Church

Disco

Abese Shrine No. 5

Fort St. Jago

N

◀ Dutch Cemetery

◀ Market & Bentoma & 5

St. George Damina Castle Restaurants

Elmina Castle

0   Metres   200

ATLANTIC OCEAN

(and watch the sun rise and set from the tower) at no fixed fee, though donations are gratefully received and duly recorded in the log.

Practicalities

New **hotels** are emerging around Elmina, but at the budget end of the scale the choice is still limited. The *Nyansapow* has good-value, clean accommodation set around a lovely courtyard (☎33955; ❶). Located opposite the castle is the *Coconut Grove Bridge House* (☎042/34557, ℱ033646, ⒲www.coconutgrovehotels.com; ❺), whose stone exterior looks incongruous amid the shabby fishermen's quarters. Rooms here are s/c and have all mod-cons. For a plush resort right on the coast, try *Coconut Grove Beach Resort* on the Western outskirts of town (☎042/33648, ⒲www.coconutgrovehotels.com; ❺), or *Elmina Beach Resort* on the eastern side (☎042/33105, ⒲www.gbhghana.com; ❷). Further afield, about 3km from town on the road to Cape Coast, a couple of options are signposted on the right: *One Africa Guest House* offers six delightful thatch bungalows with sea views (☎ & ℱ042/33710, ⒲www.oneafrica-ghana.com; ❹), and almost next door, *Mabel's Table* (☎042/33598, ℮haveli@ighmail.com; ❸) has accommodation of a similar style and standard.

All of the above places to stay have decent **restaurants** attached. The castle itself contains an attractive place to dine up on the ramparts. The *Oyster Bay Hotel*, 2km out on the road to Cape Coast, serves reasonable Western food with fine sea views (though the rooms are rapidly declining); opposite you'll find *African Pot*, a popular restaurant with a rooftop bar, offering variety and good prices. A good place to unwind is the *Shell Station* close to *Oyster Bay*, where there are outdoor tables and music playing nightly. Finally, at the weekend try the exclusive *Ngwa Nightclub* at *Elmina Beach Resort* (cover charge ₵20,000 Fri & Sat, free to get in Sun) – on Sundays they spin jazz recordings from 7pm till midnight.

Brenu-Akyinim and Ampenyi

Ten kilometres west of Elmina, accessible by foot along the coastal track (3hr), **BRENU-AKYINIM** has one of the most spectacularly perfect beaches on the Ghanaian coast, a long strip of palm-laden white sand with swimmable breakers, though beware the strong current. The unpretentious *Brenu Beach Resort* occupies part of the beach (☎042/33907, ✉brenu_beach@yahoo.co.uk), where the sand is kept clean and changing facilities are available (admission ₵3000). They also have a simple guesthouse (**②**) and reputable restaurant. Weekdays can be delightfully quiet, while most Saturdays see "beach parties" taking place. In the village itself, built like Elmina between the sea and the lagoon, there are basic, clean rooms to be had at the *Celiaman's* (**①**). Coming from Elmina on public transport, ask to be dropped at Ayensudo junction, from where your quickest option is to take a taxi the remaining 4km down to the *Brenu* and the beach (₵5,000).

Alternatively, the next turning on your left, 200m further along the Takoradi road, leads you to **Ampenyi** (5km), home of *Ko-Sa Cultural Centre and Guesthouse* (**❤**www.ko-sa.com; **②**). Striving to emulate traditional styles, they have an exquisite garden compound dotted with thatched clay bungalows; meals, often vegetarian, are taken communally in the small open-air restaurant. The natural sea-pool here guarantees unusually safe and relaxing swimming. Poles apart, *Alberta's Palace Beach Resort* (which may be open by the time you read this) just along the beach will provide all your creature comforts in modern, luxury-style accommodation.

Takoradi

By no stretch of the imagination is **TAKORADI** another scenic coastal stop – primarily an industrial centre, it has few redeeming features though, as home of the nation's second **port**, it does have a certain vitality. A convenient springboard for places as far afield as Abidjan, or as near as Dixcove, Takoradi is often referred to as Sekondi-Takoradi, **Sekondi** being the naval base 10km to the east which existed before Takoradi's harbour was built.

Practicalities

The **main market**, completely encircled by an enormous roundabout, is Takoradi's nerve centre. Liberation Road leads from Market Circle south towards Takoradi harbour, where the **GPO**, hospital and **train station** are all located; shared taxis ply the route. Leaving, you may want to take the train to Kumasi: the slow passenger train departs at 2pm (Tues, Thurs and Sat), and there's a nightly train at 8.30pm with sleepers. The night train to Accra leaves at 7.15pm, every other day. **STC** buses (info on ☎031/23351, 23352 or 23353) use the station on Axim Road, from where there are services to Accra (10 daily), Bolga, via Tamale (Mon, Wed, Fri at 8am) and Kumasi (daily at 5.30am and 1pm). Three **lorry stations** line the Axim Road north of the STC yard. Accra and Aflao have their own depot; the remaining two stations are slightly further north, with Axim and Tema transport leaving from the more easterly station near Hayford Road, and vehicles to Abidjan, Beyin and Kumasi leaving from the depot on the northern side of Axim Road. Cape Coast transport leaves from a separate yard off the Cape Coast road. To get to Busua, you can take *tro-tros* from Takoradi to Agona junction (40min), then pick up a shared taxi to Busua – if you can't stand the wait, charter a taxi for around ₵7,000. **Shared taxis** around town operate from a station on John Sarbah Road.

All the major **banks** are represented on Liberation Road (though to change traveller's cheques you need to visit the branches on Axim Road near the hospital). The **Tourist Board** (☎031/22357, ☎23601) can be found on the third floor of the SIC building near the Harbour roundabout, and can provide you with information on

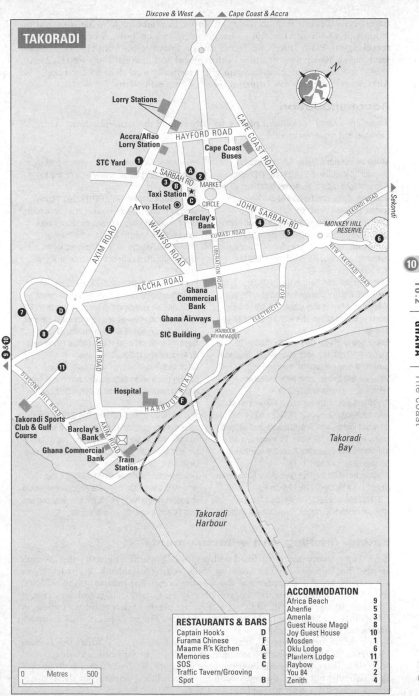

TAKORADI

Dixcove & West ▲   ▲ Cape Coast & Accra

Lorry Stations

Accra/Aflao
Lorry Station

Cape Coast
Buses

STC Yard ●1

HAYFORD ROAD

J. SARBAH RD
●3 Ⓑ MARKET
Ⓐ ●2
Taxi Station ★
Arvo Hotel ◉ Ⓒ CIRCLE

Barclay's
Bank

JOHN SARBAH RD
●4
●5

KUMASI ROAD

MONKEY HILL
RESERVE
●6 ▲ Sekondi

CAPE COAST ROAD

SEKONDI ROAD

NEW TAKORADI ROAD

AXIM ROAD

WIAWSO ROAD

LIBERATION ROAD

ACCHA ROAD

Ghana
Commercial
Bank

Ghana Airways

SIC Building

HARBOUR
ROUNDABOUT

ELECTRICITY ROAD

●7
Ⓓ
●8
Ⓔ

AXIM ROAD

●11

Hospital
Ⓕ

HARBOUR ROAD

DIXCOVE HILL ROAD

▲9&10

Takoradi Sports
Club & Gulf
Course

Barclay's
Bank

Ghana Commercial
Bank

AXIM ROAD

✉

Train
Station

Takoradi
Bay

Takoradi
Harbour

0   Metres   500

RESTAURANTS & BARS

Captain Hook's	D
Furama Chinese	F
Maame R's Kitchen	A
Memories	E
SOS	C
Traffic Tavern/Grooving	
Spot	B

ACCOMMODATION

Africa Beach	9
Ahenfie	5
Amenla	3
Guest House Maggi	8
Joy Guest House	10
Mosden	1
Oklu Lodge	6
Planters Lodge	11
Raybow	7
You 84	2
Zenith	4

travel in the Western Region. There are **forex bureaux** on John Sarbah Road on either side of the market; none changes traveller's cheques. A centrally located **travel agent**, Esam Travel and Tours, can be found across from *Amenla Hotel* on John Sarbah Road; they organize both regional and national tours (☏031/24540, ☏24117, ☏sam4tt@africaonline.com.gh). Practically next door to the hotel, J.W. Andrews offers a fairly fast **Internet** service (daily 8am–9pm).

Accommodation

There are several convenient **places to stay** around the triangular town centre, all passable but none outstanding.

Africa Beach Hotel Beach Rd, 1km west of Takoradi Sports Club ☏031/25148, ☏21666, ☏giraud@ghana.com. Upmarket hotel with all the amenities, a nice circular pool (₵20,000 non-guests) and good views. ❻

Ahenfie Hotel Corner of John Sarbah and Kumasi roads ☏031/22966, ☏info@ahenfiehotel.com. Well-established mid-range option with a popular restaurant and disco (Fri & Sat night; ₵20,000), plus an Internet café. ❷

Amenla Hotel John Sarbah Rd ☏031/22543. Well-kept, highly recommended hotel in the heart of Takoradi, offering very clean, non-s/c and s/c rooms with fans or a/c. The four s/c rooms fill up fast. ❶

Guest House Maggi Off Axim Rd ☏031/22575 or 22852, ☏30183, ☏www.ghmaggi.com. Peaceful location, a range of tasteful rooms all with TV, a/c, hot water and fridge, some with attractive balconies. Breakfast included. ❸

Joy Guest House On the beach 600m west of Takoradi Sports Club ☏031/30347, ☏27418, ☏crjoy@hotmail.com. Small, private and informal; rooms are s/c with hot water, TV, fridge and a/c, and attractively decorated. There's a worthwhile Chinese restaurant on site. ❷

Mosden Hotel On the first floor of the Mankessim White House Building, 77A/10 Axim Rd ☏031/22266 or 22872. On the roadside and adjacent to the STC station, therefore convenient

while noisy. The rooms, though slightly drab s/c affairs, are good value, mostly with TV and fridge. ❷

Oklu Lodge Monkey Hill ☏031/22767. Mainly used by Ghana Telecom workers, this guesthouse offers excellent value with s/c, carpeted rooms, some with TV and a/c. It's set in the tranquil Monkey Hill Reserve, only a 15min walk from the town centre. Best to book in advance as it's often full. ❶

Planters Lodge ☏031/22233, ☏22230, ☏planters@africaonline.com. Ghanaian-owned outfit with six chalets in attractive grounds. The *Palava Hut*, an open-air restaurant beside the pool, does a good range of Western dishes. ❻

Raybow International Hotel Off the roundabout on Axim Rd ☏031/22072, ☏23960, ☏info@raybowhotel.com. Very plush up-and-coming place with pristine suites and chalet-type accommodation, as well as a stylish thatched outdoor restaurant. ❺

You 84 Hotel Market Circle ☏031/22945. Great-value accommodation at prices to suit a variety of budgets. Rooms are a little cramped, but all are s/c with hot water and phone, and most also have TV and a/c. ❶

Zenith Hotel Califf Ave ☏031/22359. If the *Amenla* is full, try the not quite so spruce selection of budget rooms here, which are spacious and s/c, with TV and fridge. ❶

Eating, drinking and entertainment

If you fancy combining some **food** with a spot of physical activity, try the Takoradi Sports Club, opposite *Planter's Lodge*, an idyllic setting for a drink or a snack, looking over the green golf course and down to the ocean. The only snag is the ₵4,000 guest fee per head; for this, though, you have access to table-tennis and darts plus, at extra cost, snooker and golf. Otherwise, there are plenty of decent dining options in Takoradi, a selection of which are reviewed below. For groceries, there's a **supermarket** at the *You 84 Hotel*.

For a **drink**, try the ever-popular *Stomach Care Gardens*, as the bar at the *Harbour View Hotel* is known, which has stunning views of the harbour and an attached disco (₵10,000 entrance). Also worth considering are the *Traffic Tavern* and *Grooving Spot*, two adjacent street-side bars on John Sarbah Road across from the taxi station, which offer a great atmosphere for a beer.

Restaurants

Captain Hook's Just off the Axim Rd roundabout ☎031/27085. German-owned and highly recommended for its huge variety of tantalizing dishes, from seafood to steaks, pizzas and the occasional Chinese stir-fry. The attractive outdoor beer garden is a pleasant spot where you can relax in wicker chairs. Be prepared for a bill as imposing as its reputation (₵50,000 for a main course). Restaurant daily from 5pm, beer garden daily except Mon from 10am.

EFFE'S *Hotel Arvo* ☎031/21530. Pleasant, low-key restaurant serving Ghanaian and simple European dishes on request. Also a safe bet if you are struggling to find an omelette for breakfast.

Furama Chinese Adjacent to the *Harbour View Hotel* ☎031/23556. Clean and unpretentious; dishes around ₵25,000 each.

Maame B's Kitchen 22/5A Collins Ave, across from *Grooving Spot* ☎031/30540. The menu is a little brief, but the portions of local and European dishes are generous and prepared to a high standard. Daily 9.30am–midnight.

Memories Axim Rd ☎031/24765. Good food, both Ghanaian and European, at great prices (all plates less than ₵18,000). Indoor and outdoor seating.

SOS Corner of Market Circle and Ashanti Rd ☎031/25064. Fast-food outlet serving burgers, kebabs and fried rice to eat in or take away for around ₵12,000. The balcony has great views of the market.

You 84 Market Circle ☎031/22945. Two restaurants within the hotel of the same name. Both have an identical menu, an extensive selection of Ghanaian and European dishes. The ground floor restaurant is the more popular, with an upbeat atmosphere. Mon–Sat 9am–9pm.

Dixcove and Busua

Sheltering behind Ghana's southernmost headland, Cape Three Points, the twin villages of **Dixcove** and **Busua** have long been a favourite overlanders' hideaway. There are two principal attractions: first the cute, whitewashed hilltop **Fort Metal Cross** at Dixcove, overlooking the exceptionally animated fishing village and its deep, forest-bound, circular bay; and the long strand of **Busua beach**. Dixcove and Busua are no longer isolated retreats, though, the highway between Ghana and Côte d'Ivoire making it easy to visit them as a small diversion en route, and the area draws people from Abidjan as well as Accra.

If Busua does get a little crowded at weekends (particularly in season, Dec–Feb), it doesn't detract much from the area's intrinsic appeal – the quintessential Ghana **beach scene**. More disappointing is the dying coconut forest all around, attacked by a morbid blight that has reduced it to a miserable cemetery – there are plans, however, to replace the trees with resistant varieties at some stage. A multitude of short **walks** are possible in the area, either west to Cape Three Points, 5km beyond Dixcove, or east along Busua Beach, cutting over the headland and down to **Butre**, just a kilometre beyond the beach, which used to have a fort of its own – Fort Batenstein – now completely in ruins.

If you're on public transport, alight at the Agona junction on the main Takoradi highway and either charter a taxi (₵7,000) or wait for a shared taxi. With your own transport, after turning south towards the coast at the Agona junction, you'll come to a fork 6km down the road: head left for Busua or right to Dixcove. It doesn't matter greatly which you decide to take, as the two are connected by a twenty-minute walk through the coastal bush.

Dixcove

DIXCOVE is home to **Fort Metal Cross**, built by the English between 1692 and 1698. Though currently owned by the Ghana Museums and Monuments Board, the fort has been leased to a company that plans not only to carry out renovations, but to erect a luxury hotel in front of the fort. More promisingly, this may mean that the fort's four rooms with erratic water supplies and electricity may soon be functioning as a guesthouse. The fort's site is otherwise marred by a monolithic block of flats of surpassing ugliness – ironically the Chief's Palace – right in front of it. A fee of ₵10,000 allows you entry to the fort and a brief tour.

The *Ebenezer Guesthouse* (also known by its old name, *Quiet Storm*) is the only place to stay in Dixcove (☎024/644140; ●). If you're more intent on lazing in the sun and swimming, however, you'll need to be on Busua Beach.

Busua

You can walk to **BUSUA** from Dixcove via the bush-farm footpath that leads northeast from behind the fort. Once you climb the rise, you can practically see Busua. There's a small tidal river as you descend the hill, which you may have to wade through to reach Busua village. Though a very pleasant walk, several muggings have been reported, and locals will virtually insist you take a guide with you. With police already intervening, there's hope that the situation will improve quickly. The beautiful sands and clean waters of Busua are a very big plus, but watch out for the strong current.

For a modest village, Busua is bursting with **accommodation** options, all not far from the junction where taxis drop you. Homestays here are becoming increasingly popular, and *Elizabeth's*, *Sabina's* and *Peter's Place* (all ●) each provide simple accommodation adjacent to family compounds. *Elizabeth's* has the edge, with cheery rooms and delicious pancake breakfasts served on the first-floor balcony. **Camping** is allowed but, because of thieving, not encouraged.

Busua Beach Resort (☎031/21210, ℱ21858; ●), once the most extravagant place to stay in town, is now rivalled by the *African Rainbow* (☎031/32149, ⌨africanrainbowresort@yahoo.ca; ●), a three-storey block which offers kayak rental and sailboat charter. More reasonably priced is *Dadson's Lodge* (●), where the rooms are comfortable and airy, and some are s/c; there's also a great little restaurant off the courtyard. *Bliss Joy Lodge* has just four neat rooms, all s/c and carpeted, some with TV (☎031/22823; ●).

All of the above places serve **food**. Alternatively, the village is full of itinerant food vendors: "Dan the pancake man", near *Sabina's*, prepares a range of reasonably priced meals and delicious pancakes, and you're bound to meet "the lobster man" too. A visit to *Black Mamba Corner* is highly recommended – you'll see the entrance as you leave Busua walking to Dixcove – where delicious pizzas are the speciality.

Princestown and west to the Ivoirian border

The principal attractions on the westernmost stretch of Ghana's coast are **Princestown** and **Axim,** the latter served by most buses along the main road towards Côte d'Ivoire. Both have fine castles, magnificent views and great stretches of beach. Inland from **Beyin**, which lies on the coast 45km west of Axim, you'll also find the traditional stilt village of **Nzulezo**.

Princestown

In 1681, Prince Friedrich Wilhelm of Brandenburg sent an expedition to the area of what is now **PRINCESTOWN** (aka Prince's Town) in an effort to break the seventeenth-century Portuguese, British and Dutch hold over West African trade. This led to the founding of **Fort Grossfriedrichsburg**, within whose walls the Brandenburgers soon fell victim to malaria and repeated attacks by the Dutch and British. They abandoned the citadel in 1708, turning it over to the Ahanta-Pokoso chief **Johnny Konny**, who earned the dubious title "Last Prussian Negro Prince".

The Dutch stormed the fort in 1748 and renamed it Hollandia; around 1800, the fort was finally abandoned.

Direct transport to Princestown from Takoradi or Agona Junction is possible, but slow to fill, even on market days. It may be quicker to drop at the junction for Princestown on the main highway, some 15km west of Agona Junction, though you still may have a wait for onward transport down the rough eighteen-kilometre track to the village. The fort has been restored since independence and offers spectacular **views** (daily 6am–6pm; ₡5000). You can spend the night in one of the very basic rooms at the resthouse (❶); the caretaker is very helpful. The nearby beaches are beautiful, and for real isolation you can take a canoe trip across the Kpani river.

Axim

Now in the small town of **AXIM**, **Fort San Antonio** was built by the Portuguese, probably in the fifteenth century, and taken by the Dutch in 1642. Until recently the fort housed government offices, but it has now been taken over by Ghana Museum and Monuments Board, who have plans to renovate. You can still visit the fort (days 8am–6pm; ₡5000,) which is very run-down but offers excellent views.

Arriving by road transport, you'll be dropped at the **station** just east of the castle. The only decent place to stay in Axim itself is the *Frankfaus Hotel*, on the road into the centre (☎0342/22291; ❶), with clean rooms, running water and an excellent restaurant. Some 5km from Axim and 800m off the main coastal highway, the *Ankobra Beach Hotel* (☎0342/22400, ☏22398; ❷) is also a cultural centre hosting African music, dance, and craft workshops and performances. There are wooden chalets set back from the beach in the worker's compound, but more interesting is the accommodation modelled on the round huts of northern Ghana, featuring stone interiors (and a more substantial price tag; ❹). If you can't afford to stay here, it is worth visiting just for a drink on the spectacular palm-lined beach (though watch out for the rocks). *Ankobra* arranges transport to a variety of nearby villages, including **Nzulezo** (₡100,000; see below), and to the Ankasa and Nini-Suhien reserves (₡130,000; see overleaf). The other upmarket option near Axim is the *Axim Beach Hotel* (☎0342/22260, ☏22706, ☝www.aximbeach.com; ❹), perched on a hilltop on the eastern side of town and thus offering fantastic views of golden sand from its chalet rooms. Bikes, boogie boards and fishing gear are available to rent.

Onward travel **into Côte d'Ivoire** is simple from Axim. There are daily buses through to the border a little way inland at **Elubo**, where, if you don't cross directly, you can stay in s/c accommodation with the friendly people at the *Hotel Cocoville* (☎0345/22041; ❶), near the motor park. It's a comfortable place with a/c and fan rooms, some with TV. You can change money at the big new branch of the Ghana Commercial Bank in **Half Assini**, though this entails a detour on the coastal road west of Beyin.

Beyin and Nzulezo

By the village of **BEYIN**, **Fort Apollonia** (daily 7am–5pm; ₡5000) is the last of the forts along the Ghana coastline and has rudimentary accommodation (❶), although renovations are planned which will turn the entire fort into a museum. Alternative lodgings can be found right on the beach near the fort, with Robinson Crusoe-style bamboo huts built on stilts (❶). Unless you charter a taxi, transport to Beyin from Axim is painfully slow, and you may have to change vehicles at Esiama, west of Axim. Arriving from Elubo, you proceed via **Mpataba** and **Tikobo I** village before heading eastwards along the coast to Beyin.

Beyin is the departure point for the stilt village of **NZULEZO** on the

Amansuri lagoon. Tradition has it that the inhabitants of the village originally came from Mali and moved to the lagoon for protection from enemies, led by a snail to their current place. You can arrange to visit Nzulezo by canoe at the Ghana Wildlife Society Visitors Centre on the Western edge of Beyin; the trip (₵30,000, students ₵18,000, camera ₵5000) takes two to four hours depending on the season. The canoe trip is a highlight in itself, traversing jungle-fringed banks of the lagoon before arriving at Nzulezo, where you must show your receipt and sign the visitor's book. The office in Beyin can also arrange **homestays** in very basic, fanless rooms in the stilt village (❶).

Ankasa and Nini-Suhien reserves

Near the border town of **Elubo**, the adjoining rainforest **reserves** of **Ankasa** and **Nini-Suhien**, run as one park, are rapidly becoming tourist-ready, with a visitors' centre and an attractive restaurant about to open at the park gates, and basic accommodation inside the perimeter. With forest elephants, monkeys, leopards, an abundance of birds and butterflies, and some unique plant species, the area boasts a rich biodiversity which arguably surpasses that at Kakum.

To get to the park gates, some 6km north of the main coastal highway on a rough dirt road, your best bet is to take a *tro-tro* from Axim to **Aiyanasi**, the nearest town to the park, and then charter a taxi from there to the main gates. Alternatively you could ask to be dropped at the Ankasa junction (signposted) and walk the remaining 6km – bring plenty of water. After paying the park entrance (₵40,000) and vehicle fees (₵10,000 for a two- to five-seater), you can take informative guided tours of the forest along well-marked trails (₵15,000 per hour).

The best way to imbibe the forest experience is to **stay** the night in one of four sites. *Nkwanta Camp*, 7km from the park entrance, and *Elubo Camp*, are the most developed, with chalet-style huts with solar electricity, outside toilet and shower and basic cooking facilities (❸).

10.3

Kumasi and central Ghana

The **central part of Ghana** is one of the country's most attractive regions. The road from Accra, skirting past the northeast fringe of the old **Asante heartland**, is scenic and hilly. Around the great hub of **Kumasi** itself, a clutch of different routes radiate through steep scarp and forest country. Much of this has long been under cultivation – especially **cocoa**, which brings a dark, gloomy silence to the woods – but plenty is still jungle-swathed, stacked with impressive, buttress-rooted forest giants, and scattered with hillside villages. These settlements, misty grey-green in the chilly mornings, sticky and brilliantly coloured in the afternoons, are the key elements in an area to savour. Travel is easy, and the cultural heritage as rich as anywhere.

Kumasi

KUMASI still oozes with the traditions and customs of the **Asante**, one of the most powerful nations in West Africa at the end of the nineteenth century. Additionally, the town has remnants of colonial architecture, a reminder of half a century of British domination. The combination of the old order and hectic modernity makes this extremely active commercial centre one of Ghana's most satisfying cities. Kumasi is also a good place to base yourself for trips into the surrounding countryside (see p.794): within easy reach are a handful of natural attractions, including three **national parks**; several villages known for their **crafts**; and other potential excursions – including the **gold mines** of Obuasi.

Arrival and information

Even in its early days, Kumasi was an imposing capital. Today it spreads widely over the hills, and is home to over a million people. The heart of the downtown district is marked roughly by **Kejetia Circle**, and nearby, the **central market** – the largest in Ghana and one of the very biggest in Africa – spills over the railway tracks to fill a hollow in the city centre. Just west of the market, the **Adum district** is the commercial centre where you'll find major banks, supermarkets, department stores, the post office and most forex bureaux too. Up the hill northwest of Adum, **Bantama district**, site of the expansive **Ghana National Cultural Centre**, takes over.

The **airport** is 6km east of town, from where taxis charge around ₵12,000 to the centre. Sobel Air (☎051/30197) have regular **flights** to Accra. The **train station** is half a kilometre south of Kejetia Circle. There's a daily sleeper service down through the forest to Takoradi (12hr), leaving at around 8.30pm. A daytime train does the same route, departing at 8.30am on Mondays, Wednesdays and Fridays. There are several major **lorry parks**, used by bush taxi and *tro-tro*; these include **New Tafo park**, in the north, used by vehicles to and from Tamale, Bolgatanga, Navrongo and Yendi; **Asafo park**, by the Asafo market, for Lake Bosumtwi, Koforidua, Accra, Cape Coast and Takoradi; and **Kejetia park** for Mampong, Sunyani, Berekum, Wenchi and Abidjan.

STC buses use the station on Prempeh I Street, around the corner from the *Presbyterian Guest House*. There are services to Accra (4–5hr), Takoradi (5hr), Cape Coast (3–4hr), Tamale (8hr) and Bolgatanga (10hr). Most of these destinations have twice-daily service, though runs are often cancelled at the last minute. Less frequent are buses to Ouagadougou (2 weekly) and Abidjan. Buses to and from Wa use the **Alaba station**, east of the central market. **SKV**, a Burkinabe company, run a twice weekly service to Ouaga (most with a/c and TV), departing from the **Citilink station** near the STC station (₵85,000).

The **Ghana Tourist Board** (☎ & ₣051/26243), adjacent to the museum in the Ghana National Cultural Centre, has friendly and enthusiastic staff, and guides to hotels, restaurants and sights in the Asante Region, plus large-scale Kumasi city maps. To access the **Internet**, try the central Harrods Office World on Prempeh II (☎051/27972), Hekminks System Limited (24hr; ☎051/39195) near the *Sanbra Hotel*, or *Internet Ghana Internet Café* above the Shell garage on Harper Road (☎051/21563). The **British Council** has premises on Bank Road (☎051/23462, ⓔbckumasi@bcghk.africaonline.com.gh).

Accommodation

Although Kumasi lacks any really luxurious **accommodation**, inexpensive lodgings abound, getting cheaper the further you move from the centre. Outside term time, the university halls of residence 7km from the centre are often open to travellers; the pleasant **Unity Hall**, for example, has gardens and no lack of company.

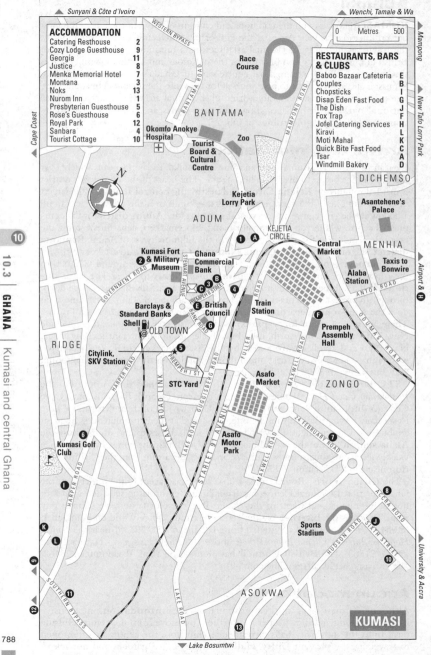

▲ Sunyani & Côte d'Ivoire   ▲ Wenchi, Tamale & Wa

ACCOMMODATION

Catering Resthouse	2
Cozy Lodge Guesthouse	9
Georgia	11
Justice	8
Menka Memorial Hotel	7
Montana	3
Noks	13
Nurom Inn	1
Presbyterian Guesthouse	5
Rose's Guesthouse	6
Royal Park	12
Sanbara	4
Tourist Cottage	10

RESTAURANTS, BARS & CLUBS

Baboo Bazaar Cafeteria	E
Couples	B
Chopsticks	I
Disap Eden Fast Food	G
The Dish	J
Fox Trap	F
Jofel Catering Services	H
Kiravi	L
Moti Mahal	K
Quick Bite Fast Food	C
Tsar	A
Windmill Bakery	D

WESTERN BYPASS

Race Course

BANTAMA

Okomfo Anokye Hospital

Tourist Board & Cultural Centre

Zoo

DICHEMSO

Kejetia Lorry Park

ADUM

Asantehene's Palace

KEJETIA CIRCLE

Central Market

MENHIA

Kumasi Fort & Military Museum

Ghana Commercial Bank

Taxis to Bonwire

Alaba Station

Barclays & Standard Banks
Shell
@ OLD TOWN

British Council

Train Station

Prempeh Assembly Hall

Citylink, SKV Station

ZONGO

STC Yard

RIDGE

Asafo Market

Kumasi Golf Club

Asafo Motor Park

Sports Stadium

ASOKWA

KUMASI

0   Metres   500

Mampong ▶

New Tafo Lorry Park ▶

◀ Cape Coast

Airport & H ▶

University & Accra ▶

▼ Lake Bosumtwi

Catering Resthouse Just off Government Rd ☎051/26506, ⓔ kcrhouse@yahoo.co.uk. Unpretentious and good value for money; some rooms have phone and a/c. Convenient for downtown. ❹

Cozy Lodge Guesthouse Mango Tree Lane, Nhyiaeso, 3km from the centre ☎051/27030, ⓕ27031, ⓔ cozygardens01@yahoo.com. Stylish rooms in a quiet, leafy setting, with a 24hr fast-food restaurant, newly opened jazz club and a bar on the grounds. ❺

Georgia Southern Bypass just off Harper Rd, Adiebieba ☎051/24154. Stylish hotel with friendly management, a pleasant bar in the gardens, a pool and nicely furnished rooms with TV and a/c. Used to be one of Kumasi's best, but is now somewhat in decline. ❼

Justice Accra Rd ☎051/22525. Monolithic structure with slightly dingy rooms. Set on a busy road – avoid the rooms at the front. ❶

King's Hotel Ahodwo district ☎ & ⓕ051/24490. Small hotel in a quiet residential neighbourhood with a rustic feel. Rooms are s/c, with a/c, phone and fridge, and there's a car park, bar and restaurant. ❷

Menka Memorial 24th February Rd ☎051/26432. Large, and very dilapidated, hotel about 2km from the centre; s/c and non-s/c rooms with fans, and there's a lively bar and restaurant. Rooms at the front are noisy. ❶

Montana Adum ☎051/32389. Slightly run-down place located within easy walking distance of points of interest downtown. The rooms are dimly lit and have fans; facilities are shared. ❶

Noks Asokwa district ☎051/24162. One of the better hotels, with comfortable s/c rooms, some with a/c, and efficient service. Also has a restaurant, bar and parking. ❸

Nurom Inn Adum. Besides an excellent location, this has clean, spacious non-s/c rooms and pleasant communal areas. ❶

Pink Panther ☎ & ⓕ051/38340. Small hotel in quiet location out of town. The rooms are comfortably kitted out, with VCRs and CD players as well as the usual mod-cons, and there are palatial suites as well. There's an attractive thatched bar and restaurant in the small, landscaped grounds. ❼

Presbyterian Guest House Mission Rd, near the STC station and British Council ☎051/23879. "The Presby" offers comfortable twin rooms in an imposing colonial building once used as the missionary's residence. The best budget place in town – an excellent place to meet fellow travellers – with a low-key atmosphere that's hard to tear yourself away from. You can camp on site if the rooms are full. ❶

Rose's Guest House 4 Old Bekwai Rd ☎051/24072, ⓔ oasis@ghana.com. An intimate place with very comfortable, tidy s/c, a/c rooms, complete with satellite TV, in a pleasant garden setting. ❹

Royal Basin 10km from the centre off the Accra Rd ☎051/60144 or 60169, ⓔ rbasin@ghana.com. Kumasi's fanciest hotel, with a jazz bar with live music (Thurs–Sun), car rental, restaurant, business centre with Internet access, and a (disappointingly small) pool. ❼

Royal Park Old Bekwai Rd, just beyond the Southern Bypass ☎051/39353, ⓕ25584. Chinese-run, unpretentious establishment with an excellent restaurant. Rooms are stylish and have all mod-cons. ❼

Sanbra Paul Sagoe Lane, Adum ☎051/31257 or 31258, ⓕ31259, ⓔ sanbra@yahoo.com. Classy new establishment right in the heart of town. Excellent value s/c rooms with hot water, a/c, satellite TV and fridge are complemented by a restaurant and cocktail bar. ❸

Tourist Cottage In Asokwa, not far from the stadium ☎051/25219. A bit hidden away, but worth the search. Pleasant good-value rooms in a quiet setting. Recommended. ❶

The Town

Kumasi is one of the rare West African towns where you can go **sightseeing** in the formal sense. In addition to the **museums**, other historic points of interest, like the **palace** of the Asante king, dot the cityscape, and you could easily spend a few days just checking them out. The enormous **central market** alone merits a couple of trips to search hidden corners for unusual finds – though avoid the terrible "**zoo**", north of Kejetia Circle, like the plague. The main attraction at the large **University of Science and Technology** off the Accra road is its Olympic-sized swimming pool, open to the public.

The central market

Despite the tumbledown appearance of rambling, rusty, corrugated-iron-clad stalls,

The Asante trace their **origins** to the northern regions of the savanna belt. Along with other Akan peoples, they came to this region around the eleventh century and settled in the area of **Lake Bosumtwi**, carving farms from the wild rainforest. These districts contained rich goldfields and trade in the metal gradually developed, at first to the north, supplying the Saharan caravans. By the fifteenth century, however, the Akan also had commercial links with the Portuguese and, by the seventeenth century, they were organized into dozens of small states, each vying for control of the mines and the slave-supplying districts in the far interior where European merchants hadn't ventured.

The founding of the Asante nation

In the 1690s, **Osei Tutu** – the first great **Asante king**, or Asantehene – brought together a loose confederation of states into a single nation under his rule. **Kumasi** was chosen as the site of the new capital on the advice of Osei Tutu's most trusted adviser, **Okomfo Anokye**, an extremely powerful fetish priest. Okomfo planted the seeds of two *kum* trees in separate locations, one of which sprouted, indicating where the Asante seat was to be established (*kum asi* means "under the *kum* tree"). Having received this sign, the priest evoked the **Golden Stool** from the heavens. This "throne" descended from the clouds to alight upon Osei Tutu, and thereby became the single most important symbol of national unity and the authority of the king. The Asante nation was born.

Expansion and consolidation

Osei Tutu set about expanding his empire. One of his most important early victories was against the Denkyira king, **Ntim Gyakar**, under whom the Asante had traditionally lived as vassals. They captured, tried and killed Ntim Gyakar in 1699. Other rival powers fell in their turn, each conquered state left intact, but owing allegiance and taxes in goods and labour to the Asante. Gradually the kingdom grew to include most of present-day Ghana and Côte d'Ivoire, with only the **Fante** states of the coast putting up realistic resistance, using European allies to their advantage.

The sheer size of the Asante kingdom spawned a royal **bureaucracy** and **judicial system**. Administrative functions were transferred from the hereditary nobility to a new class of appointed functionaries controlled by the king. Even **commoners** could fill lower court offices, among them linguists and commissioners or governors sent to oversee vassal states. In the matrilineal system, the Asantehene himself was chosen from the king's brothers or his sisters' offspring by the queen mother, who consulted

the **central market** is a fantastic place to explore, and the largest market (certainly in terms of acreage) in West Africa. The traders come from all the surrounding countries, and beyond, to buy and sell here. You can while away hours browsing the stalls of fruit and vegetables, provisions, plastic imports and car spare parts (if you need the latter, incidentally, Magazine, in the north of the city, is a separate, vast district entirely devoted to spares). You can also search out the "zones" filled with every kind of **Asante craft** (beads, sandals, leather goods, pottery) and, most importantly, **cloth**.

This is probably the best place in Ghana to buy *kente* cloth and it's worth paying a child to take you to the row of stalls where it's actually stored – a dedicated lane in the northwest of the market, near Kejetia lorry park – as they're easily missed otherwise. Prices are high and depend on whether you're buying single- or more expensive double-weave *kente*. To add a further complication, there's *kente* woven from imported rayon and real silk. You can sometimes buy just a small piece, or even a souvenir strip.

with advisers before making her decision. Though his power was nearly absolute, an unworthy Asantehene could be "destooled" – removed from the throne – by the royal family.

War with the British

The Asante empire had reached its apogee by the year 1800 when **Osei Bonsu** ascended to the throne. The borders of the country now extended well beyond the present-day borders of Ghana, and Kumasi was a capital with a population of 700,000. In the vast market in the heart of town, trade was so healthy that the king's servants periodically sifted the sand to collect loose gold dust. Despite the prosperity, **rebellion** was fomenting among Asante refugees who took shelter in the Fante confederation of the coast. In 1806, Osei Bonsu launched a full-scale attack against the Fante and invaded their lands. The attack marked the beginning of the last phase of the great conquests.

The coastal **Fante** had traditionally traded directly with the British, and Osei Bonsu's invasion thus led to direct conflict between the British and the Asante. In 1824, on the death of Osei Bonsu, the British were anxious to squash this main obstacle to the control of Gold Coast trade. Hostilities, which were to simmer throughout the nineteenth century, erupted in the **First Anglo–Asante War**. War broke out again in 1826 when the Asante were heavily defeated and Britain assumed the role of "Protector" along the coast and as far as 130km inland. A third war, in 1863, was inconclusive, though Asante history relates it as a victory, with a strong invasion force from Kumasi holding the British back for a few years. After some preparation, the British marched on Kumasi in the **Fourth Anglo–Asante War** (1874), but found the palace empty since the Asantehene and his retinue had fled to the forest. The British troops took whatever treasure they could find in the palace (most of which was later auctioned in London) and then blew it up. The rest of the city was razed to the ground.

By the end of the nineteenth century, the British had annexed the Asante country as part of their Gold Coast colony. They sought to humiliate and demoralize the nation by publicly arresting the young Asantehene, **Prempeh**, and exiling him to the Seychelles. The final slap in the face came in 1900 when the new colonial governor, Sir Frederick Hodgson, demanded the Golden Stool be handed over for him to sit on. Having foreseen such a scenario, astute royal court members had made a fake golden stool and concealed the real one, which was only discovered by accident much later, in the 1920s. Nobody, not even the Asantehene, had ever sat on it. To do so would have violated national unity.

Prempeh II Jubilee Museum and the National Cultural Centre

West of the zoo, in the grounds of the **Ghana National Cultural Centre**, the small **Prempeh II Jubilee Museum** (Tues–Sun 9am–5pm; ₡4000) holds a rich collection of Asante artefacts. They're housed in a reproduction of a traditional Asante regalia house, few examples of which remain since the nineteenth-century wars with the British. Such buildings served both as palaces and **shrines** – note the characteristic mural decorations on the lower walls. The designs, like those found on the **adinkra cloth** for which the region is famous, symbolize proverbs commenting on Akan moral and social values.

Among the many historical articles inside the museum is the **silver-plated stool** that the Denkyira chief Nana Ntim Gyakari was supposedly sitting on when captured in a surprise attack by the Asante in 1699. This victory marked the expansion of the Asante empire and the stool, with its intricate carving and design, became an important symbol of liberation and power. Also on display is the fake **golden stool**, designed at the beginning of the nineteenth century to deceive the British, who demanded that the most sacred of all Asante symbols be handed over to them. The real one remains guarded in the Asantehene's palace east of the central market, and is only brought out for special occasions.

Note, too, a treasure bag on display that was presented to the Agona king by the fetish priest Okomfo Anokye. No one knows what the leather sack contains, for according to tradition to open it would bring about the downfall of the Asante nation. Other articles include examples of traditional dress, jewellery, furniture and musical instruments.

In addition to the museum, the grounds of the cultural centre contain a model Asante village, a cocoa farm, a palm-wine "factory", performance facilities for music and dance, and a **crafts centre** where you can see how **kente** and **adinkra fabrics**, traditional sandals, brass weights and pottery are produced. Prices are fixed and seem fair. Don't miss the centre's small **library** with numerous works dedicated to Asante civilization.

The Okomfo Anokye Sword

Just up the hill from the National Cultural Centre, the **Okomfo Anokye Teaching Hospital** contains another sacred Asante symbol in its grounds (Mon–Sat 9am–5pm, Sun 11am–2pm; ₡5,000). The symbol in question is the Okomfo Anokye **sword** that Osei Tutu's fetish priest planted on the spot shortly after choosing Kumasi as the Asante capital in around 1700. According to the legend, the day this sword is pulled from the ground, the Asante nation will collapse. The deteriorating state of the heavy metal blade seems an ominous portent, but locals swear that bulldozers have tried and failed to budge it – though they don't explain why. At the hospital's main entrance take the small door in the wall on the right-hand side – in the courtyard behind you'll spot the building housing the sword by the *adinkra* symbols on its walls.

Fort Kumasi and the military museum

West of central market, the **military museum**'s collections, housed in a British-built fort dating from around 1900, have a heavy emphasis on modern **weaponry** captured by Ghanaian troops in World War II's East Africa and Asia campaigns. Far more interesting, but less extensive, are the exhibits documenting the **Anglo–Asante wars**, with period photographs and mementoes. **Fort Kumasi** itself (Tues–Sat 8am–5pm) is an intriguing structure where, as part of the obligatory guided tour, you'll be locked in a dark dungeon, to experience briefly the manner in which the British dealt with rabble-rousers. Those who went in rarely came out alive, and a few seconds is plenty to impart a sense of the terror the condemned must have felt.

The Manhyia Palace Museum

The present **Asantehene's palace** is glaringly modern, and security will see you off before you get close enough for a proper look. Just behind is the former palace, opened as a **museum** in 1995 (daily 9am–noon & 1–5pm; ₡15,000). There are obligatory guided tours (45min) with no fixed fee but a "dash" is gratefully received. The former palace was built by the British in 1925 to serve as the residence of Nana Prempeh I when he returned from exile. It was then home to two subsequent kings until the late Otumfuo Opoku Ware II moved to his new palace next door in 1972. The tour of the former royal home gives insight into the curiously colonial lifestyle of the Asantehene, typified by his desk, gramophone, coffee table and dresser. Even more eerie are the life-size effigies made at Madame Tussauds, London, of the kings and their queen mothers.

Eating and drinking

Kumasi is a fine place for **street food**, which you'll find throughout town, notably in the motor parks and markets where numerous **chop bars** serve rice dishes, *fufu* or plantains with sauce. Streetside coffee men whip up two-egg omelettes with Nescafé and sweet Ghana bread at breakfast time.

Besides the bars at some of the **restaurants** below, there are numerous other **drinking spots**. Popular ones include the lively open-air *Timber Gardens*, 6km south of town; *Goil Rest Spot* at the Santase Roundabout, for the over-30s crowd; and the slick *Moves Pub*, near *Chopsticks*, for the smarter Kumasi set. *BB Spot* across from Asafo Market serves cheap beer and is popular at the weekends.

Restaurants

Baboo Bazaar Cafeteria (aka *Vic Baboo's Café*) Prempeh II Rd, Adum. Vast menu with good pizza, falafel, spring rolls and burgers. Extremely popular with travellers.

Couples Second floor of the CEDEP building off Prempeh II St. European and Ghanaian dishes for under ₵25,000, consumed at the smart indoor restaurant or out on the balcony overlooking the town.

Chopsticks Harper Rd, near the golf club ☎051/34176. Chinese restaurant which also happens to do excellent pizzas. The relatively high prices reflect the place's popularity.

Disap Eden Fast Food Just off Bank Rd. Inexpensive, cosy restaurant serving mainly Ghanaian dishes, plus burgers and chicken.

The Dish 6th St, off Hudson Rd ☎051/30355. Subdued place serving mainly Chinese dishes, and some Ghanaian fare, for around ₵25,000 per dish. The adjoining bar is a lively spot and has pool tables.

Jofel Catering Services Airport Rd, Asokwa, 6km from the centre ☎051/21213. Swish establishment serving a variety of Ghanaian and Continental dishes. There's also an attractive bar outside, underneath the trees. Mon–Fri 8am–10pm, Sat & Sun 8am–midnight.

Kentish Kitchen At the Cultural Centre. Tasty, moderately priced Ghanaian dishes. Closed eves.

Moti Mahal Up a dirt track off the southern bypass, Nyiaeso district ☎051/29698. Attached to the *OAU Hotel*, this serves fantastic Indian cuisine. Expect to pay ₵40,000–60,000 for a main course.

Quick Bite Fast Food Prempeh II Rd, Adum. Small, low-key restaurant in the heart of town, with a limited menu, including great chicken and chips. Popular with locals and often full at lunchtime. Healthy portions.

Royal Garden Chinese Restaurant *Royal Park Hotel* ☎051/39353. Arguably the best in town for Chinese cooking, with the opportunity to sample frog's legs. More refined, though no more expensive, than *Chopsticks*.

Ryans Irish Pub Old Bekwai Rd ☎051/24072. Sharing premises with *Rose's Guest House*, the bar here is somewhat seedy, but there's also a pleasant restaurant serving excellent European meals for around ₵26,000.

Windmill Bakery and Snack Bar Down an alley opposite Barclays Bank in Adum. Inexpensive Ghanaian and European fare including excellent toasted cheese sandwiches, real wholemeal bread and great almond cake.

Nightlife and entertainment

Keep your eyes and ears open for **live music** in Kumasi; shows take place irregularly at the main hotels. The Cultural Centre hosts programmes of music, dance,

Akan names

The Akan are named according to the day of the week on which they are born.

	Girls' names	Boys' names
Monday	Ajoa	Kojo
Tuesday	Abena, Aba	Kwabena, Kobina
Wednesday	Akua	Kweku
Thursday	Yaa	Yao, Ekow
Friday	Efua	Kofi
Saturday	Ama	Kwame, Kwamena
Sunday	Esi	Kwesi

poetry and drama, as well as occasional **live concerts** – often of highlife – and less recreational **choral evenings** with church choirs. Also watch out for live jazz at the weekends at the *Royal Basin* and *Cozy Lodge*.

Among the **clubs**, *Tsar* near Kejetia Circle is the *in* place, with a cocktail bar and pool tables, playing hip-hop, R&B and highlife. Other popular nightspots include *Kiravi*, a spacious disco in Nhyiaesco district, and *Foxtrap* in Bompata, which has pool tables, a big screen and dancing.

On Sunday afternoons it's worth checking if there's a **soccer match** at the Sports Stadium; tickets are very inexpensive. The home team is Kotoko (meaning porcupine, the Asante symbol). The best **cinema** is the Rex near the Prempeh Assembly Hall, showing a good mix of movies, from mainstream Hollywood flicks to kung-fu thrillers and even the occasional Ghanaian film.

Around Kumasi

In the rainforest hills around Kumasi, numerous villages offer a less urbanized glimpse of Asante lifestyles. Many of these settlements – **Bonwire** to the northeast, and **Pankronu**, **Ahwiaa** and **Ntonso** along the road to Mampong – are known for the **traditional crafts** industries for which the entire region is famous, and best treated as day-trips. You may want to spend a night in the resthouse at the **Boabeng-Fiema Monkey Sanctuary** to the north, 100km or so from Kumasi. **Lake Bosumtwi**, too, offers a variety of accommodation and makes a good retreat. If you have your own transport, even a bicycle, **the road past Mampong** to the shore of Lake Volta – once the main route through Ghana, but now very much a back road – offers some exciting travel.

A more obvious excursion – though one seldom embarked on – is to the gold mines at **OBUASI**, 50km southwest of Kumasi, a relatively easy trip (*tro-tros* head there from Kejeita motor park). The Obuasi district is an interesting – though hardly a scenic – place to visit: the whole area is scarred into a lunar landscape by the open mining pits. The Ashanti Goldfields Company is establishing a tourist centre to organize both underground and surface tours ($10–20; book in advance on ☎0582/404309). There are several budget hotels here, and one of the many English and Italian expatriates may be able to advise on accommodation.

Kumasi is also a good base for the Bia, Bui and Digya **national parks**. **Digya** is one of the country's largest, with elephants, antelopes and hippos among its animal population, though there are no facilities for travellers, so be prepared to camp if you visit. **Bui**, spanning the Black Volta River and adjacent to the Ivoirian border, is notable for its large population of hippos. To get there, head to **Wenchi**, 35km northwest of Kumasi, from where a daily *tro-tro* makes for the village of Bui, passing the ranger base. Campsites and trails have been developed at **Bui** – check with the Wildlife Department in Accra (☎021/66.46.54) for the latest on the accommodation and transport situation. From Kumasi, it's a long *tro-tro* ride to the park headquarters at New Debiso, via Bibiani.

Along the Accra road

In **Ejisu**, twenty-five minutes' drive from Kumasi, the **Nana Yaa Asantewaa Museum** (daily; ₵5,000) was opened in 2000 as a dedication to this "heroine of Asante resistance", the queen mother who led the revolt against the British in 1900. It's a beautiful reminder of traditional architecture, made of striking orange clay and adorned with huge black wooden *adinkra* symbols. The spartan rooms inside, containing the belongings of the Asantewaa or modern replicas – clothes, beads and sandals, are a little disappointing however. To get to Ejisu from Kumasi, you can charter a taxi for about ₵15,000, or take a *tro-tro* from Asafo motor park. Just a couple of kilometres further on is the **Ejisu-Besease Shrine** (Tues–Sun

8am–5pm; ₵6,000). In the town of the same name, a couple of kilometers further along the Accra road, it's another fine example of Asante heritage, built in 1850 and recently renovated with help from UNESCO. To get here, take the last turning on your right before the speed bumps which signal that you're leaving town.

The **Bobiri Reserve** lies about another 12km along the Accra road, an idyllic tract of forest that is home to 350 species of butterfly. With a small arboretum to visit and a charming guesthouse (❶) as well, it makes an ideal retreat if you're prepared to make the effort to get here. From Kumasi, take a *tro-tro* from Asafo lorry park heading for **Konongo** and alight at Kubease. Transport can drop you at the large archway marked "Akwaaba" – head through it and remain on the path for at least 1km, then take the branch to your right. Continue straight on for another 2km and you'll arrive at the guesthouse. Alternatively, charter a taxi direct from Kumasi (₵50,000) or take a *tro-tro* to Ejisu and charter a taxi for the final leg only.

Lake Bosumtwi

Only 35km south of Kumasi, **Lake Bosumtwi** is the largest natural lake in Ghana, filling a crater 8km in diameter. Surrounded by steep hills that rise nearly 400m above sea level, the lake lies in the midst of lush greenery, a superbly relaxing scene in which to unwind. Traditional boats are still used to fish the lake, propelled by fishermen with calabashes cupped in their hands to serve as paddles. Formerly, the spirit of the lake forbade other forms of transport but, as one villager commented, "People used to be scared, but we don't believe in that nowadays" – clearly not, with expats and rich kids from Kumasi coming to water-ski and motorboats buzzing over the lake. Government-run one-hour boat trips cost a very pricey ₵150,000, or you may be able to find some locals to take you out on a motorboat for a cheaper price. Swimming is fine – the waters are free of bilharzia.

You can get here from Kumasi by taking a Benz **bus** or **tro-tro** from the Asafo lorry park to the town of **Kuntanase** (a half-hour drive that costs almost nothing); from there you can either catch another vehicle (ask for the "Abono/Lake" car, though expect a long wait) or walk the remaining 5km to the village of **Abono** on the lakeshore. There are a few places to **stay** in the vicinity. In Kuntanase, the *Lake Bosumtwe Tourist Lodge* (✉Bosomtwilake@yahoo.com; ❶) is set in quiet, attractive grounds. The *Government Guesthouse* (aka *BAKDA Guesthouse*) on the Kuntanase–Abono road offers fantastic views and comfortable rooms (❷). Down on the lake shore, the *Lake Bosumtwe Paradise Resort* is the upmarket choice, with twenty stylish s/c rooms with a/c, satellite TV and fridge (☎051/20164; ❺).

Bonwire

A frequent target for tourists, **BONWIRE** is a traditional Asante village. It's also the principal home of **kente cloth**, which dates back to the early days of the Asante empire and still the usual dress of Asante people on special occasions. Along the streets in town you can still see weavers working hand-operated looms to turn out the long strips of intricately patterned material. Because of its importance and its complex design, *kente* remains very expensive – especially here.

Bonwire is just over 20km northeast of Kumasi, southeast of Ntonso on the road to Effiduasi. **Taxis** go to the town regularly from the Kejetia motor park. The quickest route if you're getting there under your own steam is down the Accra road, then turn left near Kumasi airstrip.

Boabeng-Fiema Monkey Sanctuary

An increasingly popular target, about 100km north of Kumasi, the **Boabeng-Fiema Monkey Sanctuary** (entrance ₵20,000) is a remarkably successful experiment in community conservation. The villagers of Boabeng and Fiema have a traditional veneration for the large numbers of monkeys living in the small patch of

Kente cloth

The dazzling **patterns** of *kente* are intended to enhance their owners' status as kings, queens and nobles. Court designs took the name of the clan or individuals by which they were commissioned: a common pattern known as *mamponhema*, for example, derives its name from the Queen of Mampong, while *asasia* designates a pattern and type of cloth worn only by the Asantehene.

Like most African cloth, *kente* is woven in narrow strips, later sewn together. The highest-quality pieces are made entirely of silk threads. In former times these were unavailable to the Asante, so to satisfy the demands of royalty, craftsmen unravelled imported silk fabric and rewove the threads into *kente* patterns. In addition to the name denoting their owner, the most valuable cloths bore another name – *adwe-neasa* – a technical term indicating that the already complicated pattern contained an additional inlaid design. The word means "my skill is exhausted", indicating that the weaver had made his supreme effort.

forest nearby. This sacred grove, just 4.5 square kilometres in size, complete with a monkey cemetery, has been set aside under their guardianship. The forest has one of the highest densities of monkeys of any forest in West Africa, the inhabitants including **Lowe's mona monkey** and the strikingly beautiful **black and white colobus**; they're best seen in the early morning or late afternoon and you need be accompanied by a guide only on your first walk.

You can reach Boabeng by taking a bush taxi from Kumasi to **Techiman**, a shared taxi from there to **Nkoransa**, and finally another shared taxi from Nkoransa for the remaining 12km to Boabeng. There are also *tro-tros* from the race-course lorry park near Kejetia Circle in Kumasi (it's the same station as for Techiman taxis) direct to Nkoransa. The villagers run the friendly **guesthouse** at the sanctuary itself, which has no electricity or running water yet, and prepare simple but delicious meals (❶).

The Mampong road

Within a short distance of Kumasi, the small towns along the Mampong road have developed reputations for artwork and handicrafts; it's feasible to charter a taxi and visit all three within the same day. The first you come to is **PANKRONU**, just 5km away, a village known for its **pottery**, which is traditionally produced by the women; they'll do a demonstration for a small donation.

The next stop along the road is the town of **AHWIAA**, which specializes in decoratively carved wooden tables, statues and games, but the **carved stools** you'll see being sculpted stand out among the wares. Commonly the first gift a father would give to his child was a stool, which his soul was believed to occupy until death. To this day, stools still represent one of the most important elements of a chief's regalia and symbolize his office. When he dies, a good chief's stool is blackened with ash and smeared with the yolk of an egg, and this **black stool** is preserved in a special house in memory of the late owner. The stools carved in Ahwiaa today are mostly made with an eye for tourism – note the lacquers and shoe-polish dyes that give them a tawdry finish – though they do contain many intricate traditional symbols. They're expensive, reflecting high tourist demand and the fact that they take an age to make. It's worth avoiding the more expensive hardwoods – not just for the sake of the forests, but because softer wood is lighter, cheaper and more authentic.

Further down the Mampong road, **NTONSO** is the famed home of **adinkra cloth**. Not quite as prestigious as *kente*, it's made of cotton material – often a deep red colour – covered with black patterns which are produced with stamps carved from bits of calabash and dipped in a tree-bark dye. Some stamps have geometric patterns, others stylized representations of plants or animals, but most use symbols

Ntonso dye stamps	

Nyame biribi wo soro na ma :
  embeka mensa
	"God, there is something in the sky, let me
	  reach it"

Gye Nyame:	"God must be part of everything we do" or "Alone we can do nothing unless God helps us"
Dwonnin ye asise a ode *n'akorana na ennye ne mben:*	"The heart, not the horns, leads a ram to bully"

reflecting an Asante saying. A cloth incorporating all such symbols in its pattern was known as the **adinkrahene** and was reserved for the Asante king; equally a ruler may have worn a cloth marked by a single symbol that reflected a specific message he wanted to convey to the people. These cloths are still worn by Ashantis today, notably at funerals.

Mampong and northeast to Lake Volta

MAMPONG itself is surprisingly large and busy, perched on the lip of the impressive **Mampong escarpment**. A good place to stay is the *Midway Hotel*, a welcoming establishment with basic, clean non-s/c rooms on the outskirts of town (❶). Beyond Mampong, the road north curls down through formidable forest to the deep valley of the Afram River and then steeply, in a series of hairpins, up the other side to **Ejura**. The scenic beauty of this road is matched by the pleasure of being relatively off the beaten track. **Atebubu**, the next settlement, is a small, smoky town at the savanna's edge. Beyond, there's only the villages of **Prang** – which on this road, once tarred, now ragged asphalt and dirt, could hardly have a more appropriate name – and then **Yeji**, on the bleak Volta shore, where small boats irregularly make the crossing to **Makongo**, 150km short of Tamale.

10.4

The southeast: Akosombo, Ho and Hohoe

Formerly part of German Togoland, **southeastern Ghana** has periodically provided a bone of contention between the governments of Ghana and Togo and those who favour the reunification of the **Ewe** people, who live here and in Togo. Traditionally engaged in agriculture and fishing, the Ewe primarily grow maize and yam. The administrative capital of the region is at **Ho**, a large town in the middle of an agricultural area rich with cocoa plantations. The mountains add to the beauty of the fertile landscapes, but the outstanding geographical feature of these parts is artificial – the vast body of **Lake Volta**, created when the dam and hydro-electric plant were built at **Akosombo** in the mid-1960s.

This region provides an interesting alternative **route to northern Ghana**, either through the remote eastern border region via **Hohoe** or straight across the great lake to **Yeji** by ferry. The forest and hills – Ghana's highest – are rapidly becoming a major draw for travellers, and transport and facilities are steadily improving, at least as far as Hohoe.

Akosombo

Nkrumah's pet hydro-electric project – the giant **Akosombo Dam** – once provided electricity for the greater part of Ghana, with some left over for export to neighbouring countries, but today Ghana's economy has grown beyond its capacity. Indeed, in recent years the diminishing levels of **Lake Volta** – the largest artificial lake in the world – prompted power rationing throughout the country. Amid the landscape of hills and water, the general interest of the once insignificant village of **AKOSOMBO** lies more in the **scenic beauty** than in the traditional lifestyle of the employees here, who come from all over Ghana.

Note that both the Akosombo Dam and the Atimpoku Bridge are considered strategic installations and it's therefore technically illegal to photograph them. Now that tours are available of the site, so many people have done so, however, that few officials seem concerned any more.

Atimpoku district

Five kilometres south of Akosombo on the main Accra road, the bustling district of **Atimpoku** runs parallel to the river, in the shadow of the large bridge spanning

Crossing Lake Volta

Transport on Lake Volta has been erratic and timetables unreliable for years, a fact which deters many travellers, but the trip is a highly enjoyable one. If you're setting out from Akosombo, there'll usually be some kind of vessel in a day or two.

The official **ferry** is the *Yapei Queen*, which plies between **Akosombo** and **Yeji** once a week. Departures from Akosombo have in recent years been Monday afternoons (around 4pm), stopping at **Kete Krachi** around twelve hours later before finally arriving in Yeji at around 6pm the following day; meals are available on board. Ferries return from Yeji to Akosombo on Wednesdays at 4am, again calling in at Kete Krachi before arriving at noon on Thursdays. If you're after first-class tickets (about ₵70,000), make sure you book well in advance as there are only three cabins available. Both second class (₵35,000) and third class (₵30,000) provide a limited number of benches on which to spend the journey. Midweek, the vessel is supposed to run a shuttle between Kete Krachi and **Kpandu**, though unfortunately this often doesn't operate. Note that the ferry dock in Kete Krachi is a ten- to fifteen-minute walk from the centre of this isolated town: there is nothing at the dock itself in the way of services or food. If you must spend a night or two in Kete Krachi awaiting the ferry, you can stay at the well-hidden *Administration Guesthouse* overlooking the lake (C50,000), but you'll need to find a vehicle to take you there.

When the passenger ferry isn't running, **cargo barges** – the *Volta Queen* and *Buipe Queen* – also make the trip, but rarely run on fixed schedules. They sometimes go as far upriver as **Buipe**, on the course of the Black Volta, usually stopping en route at **Kpandu**, Kete Krachi and Yeji. The voyage to Buipe takes between one and two days (and nights) and you sleep on the deck. You should stock up on **food** for the trip: water and cooking facilities are provided.

For more details, enquire at the Volta Lake Transport Company at Akosombo port (☎0251/20686, ✉akoport@ghana.com) or in Accra (☎021/66.53.00).

the Volta River. Taxis run regularly from here to the lower part of Akosombo town proper. Atimpoku has most of the **cheap accommodation** in the area. Right by the noisy central roundabout, the *Adomi* offers rather bare rooms with decent toilets and showers (❷). The *Benkum*, 300m south of the roundabout (❶), looks very basic from the outside, but has good-value, comfortable rooms out back. Just north of the roundabout, the *Aylos Bay Garden Lodge* (☎0251/20901, ✉aylosbay@hotmail.com; ❷) has a beautiful setting among the palm trees and five comfortable, stylish chalets overlooking the water.

Street food abounds in Atimpoku: oyster kebabs and smoked shrimp to go with *abolo*, the slightly sugary, but not unpleasant, dumpling commonly eaten in the region. For more formal meals, try *Aylos Bay* for excellent Continental dishes.

Akosombo town

Shared taxis and *tro-tros* run between Atimpoku and **AKOSOMBO** during day-light hours. Akosombo consists of two communities, both of which emerged in the 1960s when workers flooded here to fill demand for labour. The first perches on a hillside, commanding a magnificent view of Lake Volta and the mountains around. The spot was too scenic for developers to resist putting in luxurious expat and executive villas, a yacht club and the swish *Volta Hotel* (☎0251/20731 or 66.26.39, ✉voltahl@africaonline.com.gh; ❽), with a bird's-eye view of the lake and dam, modern, comfortable a/c rooms, tennis courts, swimming pool and golf facilities. At least have a drink in the terrace **restaurant** overlooking the lake – the views are terrific. The second community, in the valley below, is a neighbourhood for employees of the Volta Power Authority. There's a **lorry station** here (though note that it's easier to get onward transport from Atimpoku), a Ghana Commercial Bank and several bars. On a lane behind the lorry station, the *Zito Guesthouse* (☎0251/20474; ❷) is pleasant and quiet and serves decent food.

To visit the **dam** itself, contact the Visitor's Reception Centre (☎0251/20550) by the Ghana Commercial Bank to book one of the hourly **tours** (Mon–Sun 9am–3pm; ₵8000) . For a more relaxing and slightly touristy view of the Volta, you can take a pleasure **cruise** on the *Dodi Princess* out to the attractive Dodi Island on the lake (every Sun at 10.30am, returning at 4pm; ₵40,000). There's live music on board and a plunge pool for children.

Ho and around

Despite its prestigious designation as the Volta Region's capital, **HO**, 50km north-east of Akosombo, remains a quiet, rural community, and is an excellent base for exploring the Volta region. Set in a green valley dominated by **Mount Adaklu**, the town is graced with a tidy tracing of narrow paved roads winding through the trees, and the interesting **Volta Regional Museum** (daily 8am–5pm; ₵5,000) – some surprise in a rather remote corner like this. Well presented and little frequented, the museum is worth a visit to see exhibits of ceremonial objects (Akan "spokesmen" staffs and swords), traditional **musical instruments**, and carved **stools** from vari-ous regions. **Colonial relics** complement the ethnic displays, including some dating to the district's German Togoland period.

Practicalities

The road leading from Aflao, on the coastal border with Togo, constitutes the main street in town. It heads from the Shell garage in the south, past the Ghana Commercial Bank and up to the **STC station**, from where there's an early morn-ing bus to Accra. Shared taxis and *tro-tros* to a variety of destinations, including Accra, Hohoe and Amedzofe, leave from the **lorry park** in the northeast of town.

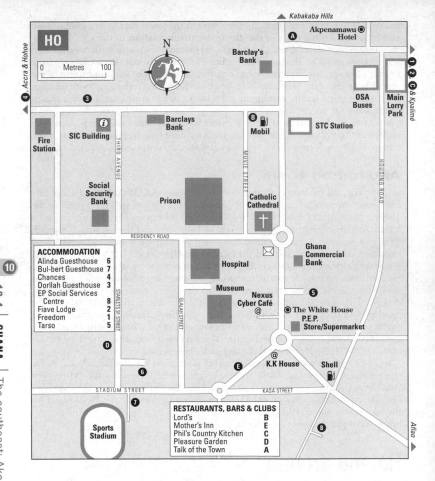

Opposite here is a station used by OSA buses to Kumasi and the capital. There's a branch of Barclays Bank along the Accra road, and a **post office** near the large roundabout on the Aflao road.

The **Ghana Tourist Board** is on the third floor of the SIC Building, on the Accra road (Mon–Fri 8am–5pm; ☎091/26560, ✉gtb@africaonline.com.gh), and offers helpful information for the entire Volta region. For **Internet access**, Nexus Cyber Café, up the dirt track across from the *White House* restaurant, has a pretty fast service; or try K.K. House, a stone's throw south.

Accommodation

Ho has a good choice of inexpensive **accommodation**, though there's little to tempt you upmarket.

Alinda Guesthouse Off Starlets 91 St. Basic inexpensive accommodation, with a pleasant courtyard. A bit run-down. ❶
Bul-bert Guesthouse Next to the stadium

☎091/26678. New establishment where some rooms have TV, fridge and hot water. There's also a bar and a large car park attached. Good value. ❶

Chances 4km out on the Accra Rd ☎091/28344, ℻27083, ✉chanceshotel@hotmail.com. Ho's most upmarket hotel, with stylish chalets as well as more sparsely decorated rooms in the three-storey main block. Set in pleasant landscaped gardens with the Kabakaba Hills as a backdrop, the hotel also has a small pool, Internet facilities and a good restaurant. ❺

Dorllah Guest House Across from the SIC Building ☎091/26141. Homely budget option (the name is pronounced "dollar"); rooms and facilities feel well cared for. ❶

EP Social Services Centre 1km from the centre at the Ewe Presbyterian Church headquarters ☎091/26670. Very clean rooms, some s/c, and

dorms for next to nothing. The canteen does good, inexpensive food. Highly recommended. Dorm beds ₵12,000, ❶

Fiave Lodge Off the Kpalime Rd, 800m from the lorry park ☎091/26412. Clean and quiet, an intimate retreat with friendly management. ❶

Freedom Hotel On the Kpalime Rd ☎091/28151, ✉freedomh@africaonline.com.gh. Well-established hotel with good facilities, though the restaurant is merely average. Something of a social focus, so often noisy, but clean and well located. ❶

Tarso Hotel Up the main street from the Ghana Commercial Bank ☎091/26732. Pleasant place with s/c rooms. ❶

Eating and entertainment

Street food is readily available near the main lorry park: a traditional Ewe dish is cat, often advertised rather graphically. The *White House* restaurant attracts a lot of travellers, serving decent foreign and local dishes with cheap beer; *Mother's Inn* is another reliable option for inexpensive food or a drink in a lively atmosphere. *Talk of the Town*, along the road from the *Akpenamawu Hotel*, offering the likes of fried rice and chicken, or tilapia with *banku*. On the Kpalime road, *Phil's Country Kitchen* (24hr) prepares generous portions of mainly Ghanaian food; nearer the centre, *Lord's* serves more of the same at reasonable prices. For drinking, the *Pleasure Garden*, on Starlets 91 Street, is a popular **bar** in an attractive setting. In the evenings several places show **videos**, notably Eliatta Video Theatre, behind the YMCA on Muvie Street.

Around Ho

About 15km southwest of Ho at **Abutia Kloe**, the **Kalakpe Resource Reserve** has an abundance of birdlife, monkeys and antelope. The Wildlife Office in Abutia Kloe will point you in the direction of the reserve, where the rangers will – for a dash – give you a tour of the park.

Some 12km due south of Ho, you'll find the village of **Helekpe** at the foot of **Mount Adaklu** – it's a challenging two- to three-hour hike to the summit (₵15,000). There's a range of accommodation available: a room in the guesthouse (₵20,000), a homestay in the village, or you could camp if you've got the gear.

For an isolated retreat on the banks of Lake Volta, head out to **XOFA Eco-village**, southwest of Ho (☎021/51.49.89, ⊛www.xofa.org). The staff can arrange a range of activities including canoe trips on the lake, bird-watching and nature hikes, and drumming and dance workshops. Accommodation is in stone, thatched huts with camp beds and mosquito nets (₵50,000 per person), and the staff can arrange activities including trips on the lake. To reach the village, take a *tro-tro* to Asikuma Junction, and then a taxi to Dodi Asantekrom, from which you can walk or rent a canoe to take you the last stretch to the village.

North of Ho

In addition to the verdant slopes of some of Ghana's highest hills, the road **north** towards Hohoe passes traditional Ewe cemeteries shaded by groves of white, pink and yellow frangipani. However, the chances of explorations off the main road are limited if you don't have your own transport.

Relatively easy to get to by public transport from Ho (although virtually impossible from Hohoe) is the village of **Amedzofe**, 30km north of Ho and just

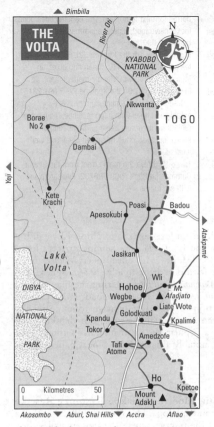

THE VOLTA

▲ Bimbilla

River Oti

N

KYABOBO NATIONAL PARK

Nkwanta

TOGO

Borae No 2

Dambai

Yeji ◄

Kete Krachi

Poasi   Badou

Apesokubi

Lake Volta

Jasikan

DIGYA

Wli

Hohoe   Mt Afadjato
Wegbe
Liate Wote

NATIONAL

Kpandu   Golodkuati   Kpalimé
Tokor

PARK

Tafi Atome   Amedzofe

Ho   Kpetoe

0   Kilometres   50

Mount Adaklu ▲

Atakpamé ►

Akosombo ▼   Aburi, Shai Hills ▼   Accra   Aflao ▼

east of the road at the base of **Mount Gemi**. At the community-run **visitor's centre** (☏0931/22037) you pay the fee – ₵15,000 for the village's namesake waterfall, ₵7,000 for Mount Gemi – and are assigned a guide. A guide is very helpful when seeking out the **waterfall**, as it's difficult to find on your own and is accessed by a steep leaf-strewn path, but is much less so when walking the straightforward path up Mount Gemi. At the summit you'll find a tall iron cross erected as a transmitter by German missionaries in the 1930s, but more striking are the vistas stretching in every direction. From up here, the Volta stands out shimmering beyond the Biakpa hills. There's a modest **government resthouse** in Amedzofe with sporadic electricity and water from an outside tap. The bungalows (❶) have large bedrooms and living rooms, a lush setting and wonderful views from the terraces. Another option is to stay in a private home. This can be arranged at the visitor's centre, but if you arrive late at night the most obvious house is Matilda's (aka Daria; the *tro-tros* drop you almost outside her home, on Corner House Square), a very welcoming and comfortable place with electricity but no running water (❶).

From the main road, you could branch westward, 25km north of Ho, towards **Tafi Atome**, a town known as a refuge for various species of **monkey**. Early in the morning, they romp unhindered through the streets and courtyards looking for scraps. Later in the day, they retreat to the surrounding bush and you'll have to rely on a guide to find them. With the help of the Peace Corps, the villagers have set up a visitor's centre, from where you can arrange **guided tours** to see the monkeys in the jungle (₵7,000 plus an entrance fee of ₵20,000) and either a **homestay** with a local family (mosquito nets included, meals upon request; ❶) or a room in the guesthouse (❶). Evenings can be lively with drumming, dancing and story-telling sessions.

Hohoe and around

A town of no sights of specific interest, **HOHOE** ("ho-hoy") is both restful and convenient as a base for treks to nearby waterfalls, or as a stopping point on the eastern route to the north. The main **motor park** is south of the centre on the Ho road. Vehicles leave here for points north (including Nkwanta and Bimbilla) as well as for **Ho** and **Accra**. Bush taxis also go direct to Kpalimé in **Togo**. There are two daily STC buses for **Accra** from the main intersection in town, near the post office.

Barclays Bank, a couple of minutes' walk from the centre on the road to Wli, changes both cash and traveller's cheques, and there's also a **forex bureau** near the post office. You can get **online** at Index Computer Services; to find it, head along the back street across from the Bank of Ghana.

Hohoe has a reasonable choice of places to **stay**, reviewed below. For a sit-down **meal**, the hotel restaurants are your best bet – *Taste Lodge*, *Geduld* and the *Grand* all serve reliably good food at reasonable prices. For cheap eating, the area around the post office abounds with street stalls. Across the road from *Hotel de Mork*, *Kitcut* serves mainly Ghanaian food and has a pleasant seating area outside for **drinking**. An alternative place for a beer is the *Tanoa Gardens*, a small relaxed place with comfy chairs and a TV; it's off the main road near Ghana Commercial Bank.

Accommodation

De Mork 2km out on the main Accra Rd in Kpoeta ☎0935/22082. Clean rooms at this hotel make up for the concrete bunker of an exterior and the inconvenient location. Good value. ❶

Evergreen Lodge Off the Jasikan road, past the *Matvin* ☎0935/22254. By far the town's best accommodation, in a lush, tranquil location. The s/c rooms with a/c, satellite TV and hot water are very smart and excellent value. ❹

Geduld Hotel Near the *Pacific Guesthouse* ☎0935/2177. Good-value s/c rooms, some with TV and a/c, set in an attractive courtyard south of the centre. Lack of taxis means a hike to the town centre. ❷

Grand Hotel On the main street opposite the Bank of Ghana ☎0935/22053. Bright rooms and a courtyard bar and restaurant serving good food. ❶

Matvin Hotel Signposted off the Jasikan Rd, a 15min walk north from the post office ☎0935/22134. A range of accommodation is on offer here, from a/c chalets with fridge and TV to non-s/c rooms with fan. Though the pricier rooms don't offer great value and the whole place is in need of a lick of paint, it does have a reasonable restaurant and bar, and some fine views over the Danyi River. ❶

Pacific Guest House Signposted off the Helu road beyond *Taste Lodge*, 600m south of the post office ☎0935/22146. Quiet and clean with a communal lounge/TV area. ❶

Taste Lodge Off a dirt track on the Helu road ☎0935/22023. Small, very clean rooms with fridge, TV, a/c and private porch, in a relatively quiet garden setting. Excellent restaurant with reasonable prices. ❷

Wli Falls and on to Togo

The most obvious target for sightseeing around Hohoe are the **Wli Falls**, 20km to the east. Relatively frequent *tro-tros* from the Hohoe motor park head out to the village of **Wli** (pronounced like "vlee"), nestling at the foot of the hills forming the Togolese border. You'll be shown to the Game & Wildlife Office to pay a ₡26,000 fee (students and NGO volunteers ₡8000, cameras ₡2000) and be assigned a (largely unnecessary) guide. The path to the lower falls crosses and re-crosses a winding brook over eleven log bridges. The cascade itself, set in a coomb where thousands of bats nest, plunges 30m into a pool just deep enough for swimming. With your own gear you can **camp** by the falls, where the tranquillity is disturbed only by kids shooting the bats with home-made flintlocks and locally manufactured shot. They'll gladly sell you their catch, should you be interested in sampling it, and even cook it up for you. If you're feeling fit, you can undertake the two-hour hike to the top of the lower falls (there are upper falls which are barely visible from the ground), for which a guide is essential (₡20,000). The walk is extremely steep and at times a little dangerous, and thus only permitted in the dry season – bring plenty of water.

En route to **Togo**, Ghanaian border formalities are casually carried out at the eastern end of Wli. From there, you must walk the half-kilometre to **Yipa-Dafo** for the Togo crossing. Transport onwards from here heads either to Dzobégan or Kpalimé, both routes tracing the scenic curves of the Danyi plateau.

Liati Wote and Mount Afadjato

Southeast of Hohoe, the village of **Liati Wote** is near the base of Ghana's highest peak, **Mount Afadjato** (968m). *Tro-tros* head to the village from Fodome station in Hohoe, near the post office. Upon arrival, seek out the visitor's centre who can arrange guided tours to either the **Tagbo Falls** (¢12,000) or the summit (¢8,000) or both (¢15,000). It's an easy one-hour walk to the falls, through dense bush full of bright flowers and butterflies, and fields of cocoa and coffee. They appear without warning as they flow off an almost circular cliff formation covered with moss and ferns, into a pool beneath. Equally satisfying are the views from Afadjato, across the border to the Togolese mountains; it's a manageable one-hour trek to the top. The **guesthouse** in Liati Wote, adjacent to the visitor's centre, has basic rooms with mosquito nets (❶) and inexpensive food can be prepared on request; plus there's the possibility of a warm beer at *Stella's Inn*.

West and north of Hohoe

Off the Kpandu road, 10km west of Hohoe, the "seven-stepped cascade" **Tsatsudo Falls** (¢10,000) provide another opportunity for exploration. Stop at the village of **Alavanyo Abehenease** to visit the chief for permission and pick up a guide.

Ethnic conflict in the north

A setback for Ghana that was not widely foreseen was the outbreak of an **ethnic war** between the Konkomba and Nunumba people in the northeastern Bimbilla region in 1994. In the space of a few days,the conflict flared from a marketplace brawl over a chicken to widespread carnage costing the lives of over 2000 people, leaving another 150,000 homeless in refugee camps, destroying or badly damaging as many as sixty villages and small towns and paralyzing much of northern Ghana for months.

The roots of the conflict lie in the tensions between the Konkomba, who have no traditional system of chiefhood, and the chieftancy-organized Nunumba. The Nunumba have always assumed a dominant stance in areas where both groups live, claiming that the Konkomba are "newcomers" from Togo who pay them tribute in the form of work, crops and livestock, in return for the use of Nunumba land. The Konkomba retort that the Nunumba invaded their lands from the north centuries ago and have never had any rights over it. The oral histories of most ethnic groups in the region tend to support the view that the Konkomba are the "indigenous" local people.

In 1995, the government created a **Permanent Peace Negotiating Team** (**PPNT**) made up of religious leaders, NGO representatives and Council of State members, to help resolve the continuing tensions. In 1996 the PPNT held highly publicized "peacemaking" ceremonies, with leaders on both sides pledging to solve their differences through negotiations.

The focus of the dispute shifted from land to the issue of chieftancy. While Nunumba chiefs have traditionally held sway in the Northern Region House of Chiefs and have some key figures in government, there has been no equivalent role for Konkomba leaders. The Konkomba have thus been marginalized when government spending plans are put into effect.

In 2002, the **murder of the Ya-Na** (king) of the Dagombas, in the royal palace in Yendi, 100km east of Tamale, arose from a **chieftancy dispute** rather than from ethnic strife. Dozens of members of two rival families were killed amid accusations that the Accra government was biased – some of President Kufuor's security advisers are from the area and the dead Ya-Na was a former supporter of Rawlings. The local MP and the Northen Regional minister both resigned and a state of emergency was declared. At the time of writing, there is a continued ban on firearms in the Northern Region and the northern part of the Volta Region.

As the route to Bimbilla continues north, cultivation declines and the road narrows noticeably. Between Jasikan and Poasi, it deteriorates into deep ruts and channels dug out by the overloaded yam lorries that ply the route. Arriving at Nkwanta, you can branch left towards **Dambai** to catch a fifteen-minute ferry or canoe across the lake (boats leave several times daily) or you can continue north over the flat, open landscapes that lead directly to Bimbilla. En route is the **Kyabobo National Park**, home to several large animals including lions, leopards and elephants, but as yet undeveloped.

BIMBILLA provides a convenient place to break up the long trip from Hohoe to Tamale. **Accommodation** can be found here at the central and friendly *Work and Happiness Guesthouse* (❶). For **food**, you're pretty much limited to the chop bars and street food around the old market, or try the *Pito Bar* near the clinic. From Bimbilla, buses leave for **Kete Krachi** (Mon, Wed & Fri between noon and 3pm; change here for Akosombo ferries). Daily buses to **Tamale** leave between 5am and 6am via Yendi, or you can try to grab a seat on the Wulensi bus, which passes through Bimbilla around 9am. The daily bus to **Accra** via Hohoe leaves at 11am and arrives in the late evening.

10.5

Northern Ghana

Coming either from the coast and Kumasi, or up the country's eastern fringe, you'll be struck by the changing landscape, as the central forests give way to arid, low-lying **grasslands**. Due to the harsher, unpredictable climate and the legacy of the slave trade (from which the inhabitants of the open plains and plateaux lacked natural protection), the region remains sparsely populated, characterized by traditional **compound agriculture**. The few urban centres like **Tamale** or **Bolgatanga** seem more subdued than their counterparts to the south.

The main peoples of the Upper West, Upper East and Northern regions include the More-speaking **Dagomba**, with their capital at Yendi, and the **Mamprusi** people, based around Nalerigu. The **Gonja**, with their capital at Damongo, are formed partly of the remnants of sixteenth- and seventeenth-century Mande-speaking migrant invaders from Songhai in the north, and partly of local Voltaic-speaking peoples. As a result, the Gonja, who are mostly Muslim, speak different languages according to their class – the nobles using a dialect of Akan known as Guang, the commoners speaking Wagala. **Sudanic influences** have been important in this region, reflected in architecture, customs and dress – *boubous* (body-length, embroidered gowns) or *fugus* (long, woven shirts) for the men and long veils for women, draped over their heads. In short, the north is a completely different world and – with the exception of the popular **Mole National Park**, which is easily visited and well set up for relatively inexpensive stays – remains a region where you're unlikely to run into throngs of fellow travellers.

It's worth noting that in the northeast, ethnic conflict and local chieftaincy disputes have led to outbreaks of violence in recent years (see opposite), and that it's possible that you will encounter curfews in some towns.

Tamale

Capital of the **Northern Region**, **TAMALE** is a large commercial town, at the junction of the main roads from Burkina Faso in the north, Togo in the east and Accra and Kumasi in the south. Despite its size and importance, it lacks the slightest cosmopolitan spark, and you're not going to want to spend an inordinate amount of time here. Still, if you are stopping over en route to other destinations, you'll find a reasonable number of hotels and diversions. Note that the water is a constant problem in Tamale, with the taps often dry.

Arrival and information

The centre of town wraps around the **motor park** – used by taxis and *tro-tros* – and the **STC bus station**, easily recognized by the towering telephone transmitter which juts up next to it and can be seen from almost anywhere in town. The **central market** (good for locally woven cloth) and major **banks** are an easy walk away. If you arrive at the airport, some 20km north on the Bolgatanga road, you can charter a taxi into town (around ₵30,000).

The **Ghana Tourist Board** has an office in the Regional Co-ordinating Office (RCO) on the eastern fringes of town (Mon–Fri 8am–5pm; ☏071/24835). In addition they run an office in the Goil garage, opposite the STC station in the town centre. Both are relatively helpful, offering advice on regional attractions. For the **Internet**, the only two central options are I.B. Dot Com just west of the telephone tower, or Second Sight next to Standard Chartered Bank.

Accommodation

There's an increasing range of accommodation in Tamale, a few more upmarket hotels having opened recently. The central *Al-Hassan Hotel* has long been something of an institution among travellers but is a noisy, grimy affair – you could do much better elsewhere, though it's worth dropping by at its restaurant, which remains something of a social focus (see p.808). Most of the places reviewed here are outside the centre, but all are easily reached by shared taxi from the central local-taxi station.

Atta Essibi Hotel St Charles Rd ☏071/22569. Clean, comfortable rooms with fans, some s/c, on the southern side of town. ❶

Catholic Guest House Gumbehini Rd, off the Bolgatanga Rd 1km north of the centre

☏071/22265. Pleasant garden setting, s/c rooms with fan or more plush a/c rooms with TV. Often full. ❶

Gariba Lodge 4km from town on the Bolgatanga Rd ☏071/23041/42/43, ℮garibalodge@hotmail.com.

Moving on from Tamale

As the north's major city, Tamale is the springboard for **Burkina Faso** via **Bolgatanga**, and the road north is in excellent shape. Heading south, the road is paved to **Kumasi** and **Accra**, and passes through **Yapei**, where you cross Lake Volta. On the west side of the lake, a road for **Sawla** in western Ghana, via **Damongo** (for the Mole National Park) splits off from the Accra highway. STC and OSA **buses** head out in all these directions, as do *tro-tros* and taxis. There is also one daily bus at 11am from Tamale to **Yendi** and **Bimbilla**, where you can continue to Accra via eastern Ghana.

The nearest **ferry** link with Akosombo and the south is at **Buipe port** (*tro-tros* head there from Tamale's motor park), where cargo vessels sporadically take passengers. Full ferry details are given on p.798.

There are Sobel Air **flights** to Accra (Mon, Wed & Fri), bookable through the *Gariba Lodge*.

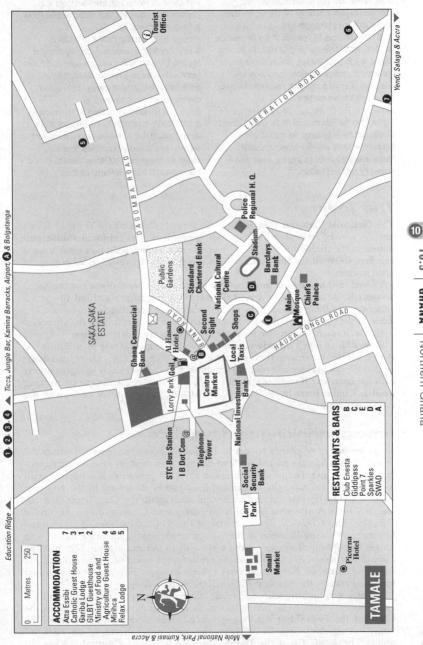

TAMALE

▲ Education Ridge

▲ Tics, Jungle Bar, Kamina Barracks, Airport, Ⓐ & Bolgatanga

① ② ③ ④ ▲

ACCOMMODATION
Atta Essibi	7
Catholic Guest House	3
Gariba Lodge	1
GILBT Guesthouse	2
Ministry of Food and Agriculture Guest House	4
Mirihca	6
Relax Lodge	5

N

Metres
0   250

RESTAURANTS & BARS
Club Enesta	B
Giddipass	C
Point 7	E
Sparkles	D
SWAD	A

DAGOMBA ROAD

SAKA-SAKA ESTATE

LIBERATION ROAD

BANK ROAD

HAUSA ZONGO ROAD

Tourist Office ⓘ

Ghana Commercial Bank

Al Hasan Hotel

Lorry Park Goil

STC Bus Station

I B Dot Com @

Telephone Tower

National Investment Bank

Central Market

Local Taxis

Standard Chartered Bank

Public Gardens

Police Regional H. Q.

Stadium

National Cultural Centre

Barclays Bank

Second Sight

Shops

Main Mosque

Chief's Palace

Social Security Bank

Lorry Park

Small Market

Picorna Hotel

⑤

⑥

⑦

▲ Yendi, Salaga & Accra

▲ Mole National Park, Kumasi & Accra

⑩

807

Tamale's most expensive place to stay. Rooms are rather sterile but have all the facilities – a/c, international phone, satellite TV. The slightly dull restaurant serves European food. **6**

GILBT Guesthouse Signposted off the Bolgatanga Rd, 2km north of the centre ℡071/22341 or 23709, ✆kgh-gillbt@sil.org. Run by the Ghana Institute for Literacy and Bible Translation, this offers lots of small bungalows, containing spotless rooms with kitchen facilities. **2**

Ministry of Food and Agriculture Guest House Across from the Tamale Institute for Cross Cultural Studies, off the Bolgatanga Rd ℡071/22923. Small-scale place with four large s/c double rooms, offering a/c, fridge and hot water, with a shared TV area and kitchen. **2**

Mirihca Hotel Off Liberation Rd ℡071/22935. Ten well-cared-for rooms with satellite TV, set in a pleasant leafy courtyard, with attractive tiled floors in the pricier rooms. **1**

Picorna Hotel Kaladan Park ℡071/22672, ✆picornahotelgh@yahoo.com. Slightly cramped but smart s/c, a/c rooms with hot water and a nice garden. There's also a reasonable bar and restaurant in the grounds, plus a large outdoor cinema screen and stage area. **3**

Relax Lodge Northeast of town off Dagomba Rd ℡071/24981, ✆relax@africaonline.com. Highly recommended, Indian-owned hotel and restaurant set in a leafy, attractive courtyard. Spacious, stylish s/c rooms have hot water, satellite TV and fridge. Accepts Visa and MasterCard. **6**

The Town

The **National Cultural Centre**, near the central market off the Yeji road, is in a horrific state of repair, but holds sporadic performances of **regional music and dance**; in the afternoons, you can sometimes catch a rehearsal. You can watch some excellent **football** on Sunday afternoons, when major Ghanaian teams play at the main stadium.

A paved road leading out from the west of the market heads down past the Social Security Bank and a small market before arriving at a large **classified forest** – a rather unusual thing to find in the middle of an important administrative town. The shade of the teak trees makes for an excellent place to retreat from the afternoon heat, which reaches oppressive levels on the exposed avenues downtown.

It's possible to rent a **bicycle** in town (hotels can help) and ride up to Education Ridge, off the northwesterly road out of town; there's a fine ride commencing behind the polytechnic and running for about 8km through lovely villages, coming back the same way. If you need to cool down afterwards, check out the **swimming pool** at Kamina barracks (℡071/22707; ₵10,000), about 5km out of town on the Bolgatanga road.

Eating, drinking and nightlife

There are plenty of **places to eat** in Tamale, including the hotel restaurants. All around the Goil garage after about 6pm there's a mass of street food on offer, especially guinea fowl. The new restaurant at the Goil garage itself is popular with locals, serving fantastic chicken and chips. *Sparkles Restaurant* in the National Cultural Centre does decent sandwiches and salads, while the *Crest Restaurant* at *Al-Hassan's* does good-value, no-frills Ghanaian and Chinese dishes for under ₵20,000. The *Giddipass Bar*, southeast of the STC bus station, is a perennial favourite, with a similar menu to the *Crest* at nearly double the price, though you do get the option of dining on the terrace or in the rooftop bar. Out past the *Catholic Guesthouse*, *SWAD* has a more sophisticated menu of seafood, pizzas and some Indian dishes. For an upmarket option serving Chinese, Continental and Indian cuisine, try the excellent *Kitchen 2000* at *Relax Lodge*.

You may well find **nightlife** in Tamale affected by a 10pm curfew, though local establishments seem to be taking this in their stride. Across the street from the *Giddipass*, the *Point 7* **bar** is a long-standing favourite for cold beers, or try the dingy but cheerful *Club Enesta* down the road, which livens up on weekend nights. The *Jungle Bar* at the Tamale Institute for Cross Cultural Studies, on Gumbehini Link off the Bolgatanga road, 1km north of the centre, is an excellent place to relax and unwind in comfy seats on the breezy terrace, and also does American-style burgers and hot dogs. Southwest of the centre, *Picorna Hotel*'s disco is a happening place on Saturday night and serves up great kebabs, or you can catch an evening film there (Mon & Fri–Sun 8.30pm) or at any of the other **video** theatres throughout town – look out for the street-corner blackboard announcements.

Mole National Park

Set in the savanna country west of Tamale, the 5000-square-kilometre **MOLE** (pronounced "moh-lay") **NATIONAL PARK** (₵15,000, students and NGO volunteers ₵3000) protects a wide variety of fauna – including elephants, lions, leopards, buffaloes and numerous species of antelope, monkeys and birds – in an environment which varies little but for the Konkori escarpment, which runs northeast to southwest. Christmas is the best time to visit, when animals are most visible and the mosquitoes least oppressive (at other times it's vital to have repellant).

Park practicalities

Although the concentration of animals isn't as high as in some other West African parks, Mole's striking advantage, if you don't have your own transport, is **ease of access**. An OSA bus leaves daily from the transport yard in **Tamale** (officially at 3pm but frequently late – check at the station to be sure; 5–7hr; ₵8000) and takes passengers all the way into the park, dropping them off at the *Mole Motel* (the last stop). Alternatively you can catch the 6am OSA bus from Tamale to Wa, and disembark in **Larabanga** (see overleaf) to make your own way into the park on foot or by bicycle. Be sure to purchase tickets early in the morning to ensure a space, as the bus is always crowded. Reservations for the return bus to Tamale must be made the night before departure at the motel. Approaching from any other direction – most obviously Bouna in Côte d'Ivoire or Wa – you can connect with one of these buses at **Damongo** (any other transport is extremely rare), where they stop before continuing into the reserve, although be warned that they are very often full. Driver and bus stay the night in the reserve, and depart again for Tamale at 5am or 6am, so you will really need to stay at least two nights in the park in order to see any animals.

A network of **tracks** crisscross the park; in the dry season, you can cover a lot of ground in an ordinary car. The only mode of transport that can be easily rented at the park are the rangers' **bicycles** (₵10,000 per day).

Accommodation

At the park's entrance, the *Mole Motel* (☎0717/22045) perches on a bit of a hill dominating two artificial water holes where animals gather to drink in the dry season. **Accommodation** here ranges from rooms in a dorm to twin-bed spacious chalets with large bathrooms and screened verandas overlooking the water hole (❷, dorm beds ₵34,000). Electricity and water are fairly reliable and there's also a swimming pool and **restaurant** – though you have to order in advance. If you're arriving by bus in the evening, eat before leaving or bring your own food: you won't get anything much here until next morning's breakfast. The motel turns its electricity off from 1am to 6am. You can **camp** near the motel buildings in your own tent (₵11,000 per person) or in one of the hotel's tents (₵22,500 per person), using the dorm washing facilities.

In addition to the motel, three **camps** are operational (no provisions, so bring your own bedding and food). **Nyanga** is right in the centre of the park on the Mole River, while closer to *Mole Motel* are **Lovi** (30km) and **Brugbani** (9km). It's feasible to walk to Brugbani, but you'll need your own vehicle to reach the other two sites.

In the dry season – especially during weekends or holidays – you should be sure to **reserve** in advance as accommodation is often fully booked. During the rains, this doesn't seem to be much of a problem. Reservations for any of the above sites can be made by contacting the *Mole Motel* itself or through their Accra office (☎021/76.58.10).

Around the park

When you check in at the motel, book a place on one of the **walking safaris** (6.30am & 3.30pm). The official hourly fee of ₵5000 is well worth it as the guides are generally quite helpful and know where to find what's around. Your chances of seeing **elephant**, **antelope** and **buffalo** at dawn near the motel water hole are relatively good. To have any real chance of seeing other large animals, such as lions, you'll need a vehicle. In the absence of other transport, you might try your luck with other park visitors. Even with your own transport, for safety reasons you're obliged to take a ranger to help in the quest for animals.

Larabanga

Only 4km from the park gates, **LARABANGA** was once merely a village which tourists speedily passed through en route to Mole. Thanks to the efforts of a community-based tourism project, it has become a regional attraction in its own right. The principal point of interest is the mud-and-stick Soudanese-style mosque, reputedly the oldest in Ghana. A tourist centre has been established where you pay a fee for a tour of the village (₵5000, plus a ₵2000 obligatory donation to the imam), visiting the **mosque** (though note that the interior is off-limits to non-Muslims) and the **mystic stone** – a large boulder on the outskirts of the village – where you receive an explanation of the role it played in the origins of Larabanga. A simple **guesthouse** here, run by the Salia brothers, founders of the project, has five rooms, some of which have fans; alternatively you may sleep up on the roof beneath the stars (❶). They also have **bikes** (₵10,000) and binoculars (₵10,000) for Mole available to rent. The OSA bus stops right outside the guesthouse on both the inward and outward journeys.

Wa and the Upper West Region

Capital of the Upper West Region, **WA** is predominantly Muslim as the many **mosques** dotting the townscape attest. Although it's noticeably poorer than towns in the south, shortages of food and other goods no longer pose the problems they did twenty years ago. Though a number of office workers have come from outside to work in local administrative posts, Wa feels very remote from Accra – Tamale seems positively metropolitan in comparison.

Wa is home of the **Wala** people who migrated from Mali and, upon arrival in Ghana, chased the resident Lobi population to the west and converted the Dagarti inhabitants to Islam. The **traditional chief**, the Wa-Na, formerly lived in a large white **palace** built in the Soudanese style. However since the death of the last Wa-Na in 1998, a chieftaincy dispute between four rival factions has not been resolved, and the palace has remained unoccupied since. You can visit the palace (located behind the government transport yard), although you're not officially allowed inside as the building is considered unsafe. The small Wa museum would be worth visiting if there was anything in it: it's just a shell.

Practicalities

The small **STC bus station** is on the town's central roundabout, and is also used by City Express buses. The main **lorry park** 400m west of here is used by *tro-tros*

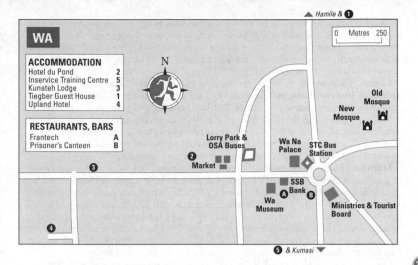

WA

0   Metres   250

ACCOMMODATION

Hotel du Pond	2
Inservice Training Centre	5
Kunateh Lodge	3
Tiegber Guest House	1
Upland Hotel	4

RESTAURANTS, BARS

Frantech	A
Prisoner's Canteen	B

N

Old Mosque

New Mosque

Lorry Park & OSA Buses

Wa Na Palace

STC Bus Station

❷ Market

❸

SSB Bank

Ⓐ Ⓑ

Wa Museum

Ministries & Tourist Board

❹

and shared taxis for surrounding towns such as Lawra, Hamile and Wechai, as well as OSA buses. STC buses leave for Accra only, departing at 2pm on Tuesdays and Thursdays. For Bolga, City Express have a daily service (10am), and for Tamale and Sunyani, OSA provide daily services. For all other destinations, including Kumasi, go to the main lorry park.

Located in block B of the town's administration buildings (known locally as "Ministries"), the **Ghana Tourist Board** (℡0756/22431) can offer information on nearby sites. The *Kunateh Lodge* (℡0756/22102; ❶), a ten-minute walk from the lorry park, has the best-value **accommodation** in town, with clean comfortable rooms and an upbeat atmosphere, but get there early since it fills up fast. A fall-back budget option is the clean *Hotel du Pond* west of the lorry park (℡0756/20018; ❶). The *Inservice Training Centre*, just over 1km from the centre on the Dorimo road (℡0756/22469, 🖷22581; ❷), has spotless accommodation and an affordable restaurant. The *Tiegber* (meaning "stretch your leg") *Catholic Diocesan Guest House* (℡0756/22375; ❶) is on the outskirts of town, 3km from the centre, has extremely clean rooms, a garden bar, and a good restaurant run by the friendly nuns. The upmarket option in Wa is the *Upland Hotel* west of the centre (℡0756/22180; ❷), also with a garden bar and restaurant.

The **restaurant** at *Tiegber* is probably the best choice for Ghanaian and Western dishes; slightly more expensive and with a wider range of European fare is the restaurant at the *Upland*, also highly recommended. For budget meals, *Frantech*, behind SSB Bank, serves up simple meals, as does the *Inservice Training Centre*. Otherwise meals are pretty much limited to the usual **chop bars** located around the market and transport park. Cold beers can be had at the *Prisoner's Canteen*, a popular weekend spot for volunteers in the area.

Around Wa

Wechai Community Hippo Sanctuary, west of Wa on the Burkinabe border, offers a good opportunity to see hippos in the wild – September to May is the best time of year. The sanctuary is some 20km from **Wechai** village, itself 4km from Wa, and has two basic lodges in Telawona and Tankara to house visitors. The admission fee of ₡70,000 includes land and river guides as well as lodging, but you'll need to bring your own food. Alternatively you could spend the night in Wechai village in a homestay (₡25,000) and see the Wechai-Na's palace. You can get the morning *tro-tro* to Wechai but you'll need to get to the station early, as you'll have to charter a taxi if you miss it (₵100,000–200,000, depending on your bargaining skills). From there, you can rent bikes to do the final leg to the sanctuary – it's a hard cycle down a rough track, or again you can try to charter a taxi, though some drivers may refuse to attempt the rough track.

Lawra, 80km north of Wa on the road to Hamile, is well known locally for its **musical instruments**, notably *balafons*, and also hosts the culmination of the important northern harvest festival of **Kobine**. Dancing and percussion teams come from throughout the north to take part in this nationally televised event, which usually takes place in mid-October. **Accommodation** is available at the *District Assembly Guest House* (☎0756/22805; ●), which rarely sees tourists despite having spacious, comfortable rooms with running water and electricity.

Hamile, in Ghana's far northwest corner, 35km north of Lawra, is a regular crossing point for Burkina. The only half-decent place to **stay** is near the lorry park, the unsigned *By the Power of God Resthouse* (₵20,000), which has noisy videos in the courtyard every night until midnight – worth a visit just to see the number of people they manage to cram into a tiny space. Hamile's market is held on the second day of the six-day cycle. It's easy to visit Burkina briefly, whether you have your passport or not (much less your visa): Ghanaian and Burkinabe officials are unlikely to mind if you want to pop across the border for a few hours.

On the Kumasi road south of Wa, there are interesting mosques at **Sawla**, **Maluwe**, and especially at **Bole** and **Banda Nkwanta** (one of the oldest in the district). They all date from the sixteenth-century Gonja conquest.

Navrongo and around

NAVRONGO is the first Ghanaian town south of Ouagadougou on the main highway. In the middle of a vast but undeveloped **agricultural region** (where crops include rice, millet and yams), it is the second town of the Upper East Region (Bolgatanga being the first). The people here are mostly **Kassena** farmers.

Navrongo enjoys a reputation in the north as a centre of education because of its large secondary school. It was also one of the first towns in the region to have a church built, in around 1920, which has had a grotto in the grounds since 1934, said to be an imitation of Lourdes. The church, now a **cathedral**, was done in the traditional style with *banco*, and the interior decorations reflect regional art and cultural values. Today it's one of the few "sights" in town and definitely worth a visit (Sundays especially) – though it may soon be overshadowed by the new two-storey cathedral being constructed close by.

Practicalities

Your most likely point of arrival is the **lorry park** in the heart of town. Shared cars and *tro-tros* leave regularly, either north to Paga, from where you can continue on to Ouagadougou; or east to Bolgatanga. Heading west to Wa, the daily 6am City Express bus from Bolgatanga stops at Navrongo but is often full.

Navrongo has very limited facilities, which make it less convenient as a stopping point than Bolgatanga, though the lively *Catholic Social Centre* (☎0742/22161; ●), just across from the cathedral, does have good, clean s/c **rooms** and prepares food on request. *Hotel Mayaga*, a large cream-and-orange building set back from the road to Wa (☎0742/22327; ●), offers a variety of tired rooms (renovations pending), some with a/c. The only other choice is the *St Lucion Guesthouse* (☎0742/22707; ●) inside the lorry park, with neat, carpeted, recently renovated rooms. They also have a pleasant **restaurant** serving simple inexpensive dishes – fried rice, fish and *banku*; or else try the numerous **chop houses** and bars crowded around the market and the motor park, either side of the Bolga road. *Pito* bars are also plentiful. In the evenings you have a choice of several **video theatres** showing "action" and "brutal" films or – if you've timed it right – the monthly disco at *St Lucion*.

Around Navrongo

Some 6km from Navrongo (₵15,000 in a dropping taxi), down a turning off the Tumu road, are the Irrigation Company of the Upper East Region's residences and *Guesthouse* (☎0742/22629; ❷), built within comfortable walking distance of **Tono Lake**. Sometimes referred to as the "Akosombo of the Upper Region", the lake resulted from a dam designed to create a massive irrigation project for sugar, rice and tomato production. Though the guesthouse has seen better days, the lake is still a scenic spot for bike rides, bird-watching or a picnic.

Twenty kilometres further west, beyond **Chuchiliga**, are the **Chiana-Katiu caves**, 1km out of **Chiana** village. They feature natural rock formations that appear, eerily, to be of human construction – though no one seems to know much about them. Any *tro-tro* on the Tumu road can drop you in Chiana.

Five kilometres north of Navrongo on the Burkina border, the **sacred crocodile pools** at **PAGA** have been developed into an ecotourism project. After you pay the fee of ₵17,000, which includes the cost of a live chicken, the crocs are lured onto land by throwing the chicken into the shallows and general splashes in the water. You pose for snaps holding their tails or squatting lightly on their backs, until finally the chicken is fed to them. The Chiefs' Crocodile Pond is the most regularly visited, on the northern side of the village and within sight of the border post. You can also visit the Paga Pio's Palace (₵8000), in which case it pays to have kola nuts on hand in case you are introduced to the chief.

Bolgatanga and the Upper East

Capital of the Upper East Region and of the Grusi-speaking **Frafra** people, **BOLGATANGA** (aka Bolga) is much larger and busier than Navrongo. If you're entering the country from Burkina, it's a good place – far better than Navrongo – to take care of business, change money or find decent accommodation. The large town **market** has some decent local **handicrafts**, especially leather, and there are a number of interesting sites to explore in the vicinity.

Arrival and information

From Bolgatanga's central intersection, the **Navrongo road** runs approximately northwards, the **Zuarangu road** eastwards, and the **Tamale road** southwestwards. Most of the town's places to stay and other facilities lie northeast of the central intersection. Five hundred metres away is the **STC bus station** on the Tamale road. **OSA buses** use a station a short distance up a minor road which branches east off the Zuarangu road about 1500m east of the centre, as the Zuarangu road veers southeast. The main **lorry park**, used by shared taxis and *tro-tros* as well as by City Express buses, is 250m north of the southern end of Bazaar Road. STC (☎072/24669), OSA (☎072/22372) and City Express all have daily services to Accra via Tamale and Kumasi, at around 4pm. Additionally, STC depart for Ouaga (Sun 6am) and Bawku (daily 6.30am); OSA leave for Hamale (Mon & Fri 7am); and City Express for Wa via Tumu (daily except Sun 6am). Shared taxis and *tro-tros* serve the surrounding towns plus destinations further afield such as Ouaga, Tamale, Kumasi and Accra. The main **taxi station** for town transport is on the north side of the Zuarangu road, a couple of minutes' walk east of the central intersection.

The **Ghana Tourist Board** has a helpful regional office (Mon–Fri 8am–12.30pm, 1.30–5pm; ☎072/23416) on a small road which leads west off the

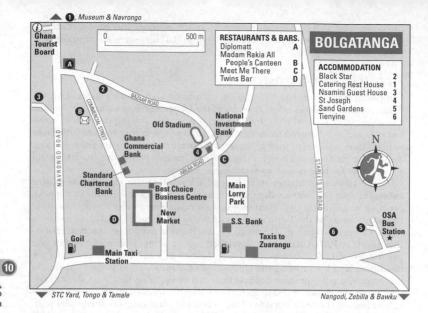

Navrongo road 1500m north of the central intersection. You can change both cash and traveller's cheques at the **Standard Chartered Bank** on Commercial Street, 500m north of the Zuarangu road. The bank is located at the intersection with Abilba Road, which runs east here along the north side of the market; a short walk along brings you to the Best Choice Business Centre on the south side of the road, with **Internet access** seven days a week. There's a **bike rental** outlet at the southern end of Commercial Street.

Accommodation

There's plenty of accommodation to choose from in Bolga, most of it at the budget end of the scale, with new lodgings popping up all the time.

Black Star Hotel Bazaar Rd, just east of where it meets Commercial St ☎072/22346 or 23042, ✉ghandaa@yahoo.com. A reasonable standby – the rooms are unimpressive for the price and due for renovation, but the shared bathrooms are surprisingly clean. Decent restaurant attached. ❷

Catering Rest House Off the Navrongo road, 3km north of the centre ☎072/22399. Chalets with TV, fridge and a/c. Feels very dated. ❷

Catholic Social Centre Off the Bazaar Rd ☎072/23216. Clean, non-s/c rooms or dorm accommodation; a bit on the scruffy side and not good value for money. Simple restaurant attached. ❶

Hotel St Joseph On a dirt track behind National Investment Bank, 700m from the southern end of Bazaar Rd ☎072/23214. A hideous exterior and a

mix of middling accommodation, with s/c rooms, some with a/c, TV and fridge. ❶

Nsamini Guest House Off the Navrongo Rd ☎072/23403. Friendly atmosphere and six spotless, non-s/c rooms, all with fan, set around a welcoming courtyard. ❶

Sand Gardens Hotel Up a lane leading north from the OSA bus depot ☎072/23464, ✉sandgardens47@yahoo.com. An increasingly popular choice – consider reserving – with a wide range of good-value rooms, some s/c. TV, a/c and fridge available in some rooms. ❶

Tienyine Hotel Starlets 91 Rd, north off Zuarangu Rd about 1200m east of the central intersection ☎072/22355. Attached to the well-established *Comme Ci Comme Ca Restaurant* in a quiet location. Very clean rooms with a/c, TV, phone and fridge, though lacking something in style. ❸

The Town

The main feature downtown is the newly renovated central **market**, where many goods, including leather items, superb basketwork and clothes, are still made by hand. There are beautiful examples of hand-made smocks, sewn from locally woven material and commonly worn by men throughout the region. The main market day is on a three-day cycle.

Bolgatanga has a **museum** (daily 8am–5.30pm; C7000), in the administrative block behind the library off the Navrongo road; to find it, take the road leading east off the Navrongo road about 300m beyond the northern end of Bazaar Road. Housed in two small rooms here is a permanent exhibition on the region's cultural, historic and ethnographic heritage. Though not a big draw, it's an interesting way to spend an hour or two, with displays of stools, pots and musical instruments, and there are some temporary pieces on issues of contemporary interest.

Eating and nightlife

Both the *Sand Gardens* and *Tienyine Hotel* have highly recommended restaurants, with a wide selection of dishes for less than C20,000. More centrally, the *Diplomatt* (inside SSNIT House) is a pleasant enough place with Western and local cuisine; it's open from 7.30am for breakfasts too. *Madam Rakia All Peoples' Canteen*, on Commercial Street, has *banku*, *plantain* and *jollof* rice; omelette stands are scattered along this street at night. In among the houses behind the *Black Star Hotel* and Commercial Street you'll find a few chop stands. The favourite local dish is TZ, often eaten with *kino* sauce made from bitter green leaves. A more specialized Bolga taste is hot **dog**, available as very spicy kebabs from stalls at the lorry park.

Meet Me There on Bazaar Road and *Twins Bar* – local shorthand for two adjacent bars, *Midway* and *Street View* on Commercial Street – both guarantee a pretty good **drinking** atmosphere. On Saturdays, try *Old Timer's* at the *Black Star Hotel* (C8,000) – a popular **disco** that draws a mixed crowd.

Around Bolgatanga and the Upper East Region

Sambrungo, 8km out of town on the Navrongo road, has a **night market**, offering an atmospheric – romantic even – stroll through the lanterns in the cool, evening air. Some 15km north of Bolga, the village of **Bongo** is the starting point for hikes through the attractive Bongo Hills. Notable here is **Bongo Rock** which, when thumped, makes an appropriately resounding boom that can be heard all over the district. *Tro-tros* leave regularly for Bongo from Bolga's main lorry park.

Eastwards to Bawku

The road **east from Bolga** takes you through the villages of **Nangodi** (20km away), with sacred fish and a gold mine (though only small-scale mining continues today); **Zebilla** (40km from Bolga), with beautifully decorated houses (people are supremely hospitable if you're invited in); and on to the market town of **Bawku**, right on the Burkinabe border and only 30km from Togo. Apart from smuggling, now on the wane, Bawku is a centre for the manufacture of *fugu* shirts, the north's characteristic costume. The hospital **guesthouse** offers four very comfortable rooms (℡0734/22345; ❶). Across the street from the Mobil garage, regular *tro-tros* leave for Bolga (up to 2hr) and an STC bus departs daily for Accra (4pm). Alternatively you could head east into Togo, or to Burkina, both via Cinkassé.

The area between Bolga and Bawku, the **Red Volta Valley**, has been identified as a prime location for eco-tourist projects; it may be worth asking at Bolga's tourist office about canoe trips and wildlife treks in the area.

History in the Upper East

The Upper East Region is the traditional domain of the More-speaking peoples. Their history goes back to a thirteenth-century chief named **Gbewa** who founded a kingdom at **Pusiga**, east of Bawku on the Togolese border (where his tomb can still be seen). His sons fought over their inheritance and founded a number of mini-states in the region which grew from the fourteenth century and remained essentially intact until the nineteenth – **Mamprusi**, founded at Gambaga, **Dagomba**, and the other "Mossi" kingdoms mentioned in the Burkina Faso chapter. These nations are now the names of distinct ethnic groups speaking dialects of More. Dagomba's first Ya Na (king), founded a capital at **Yendi Dabari** (Dipali), north of Tamale, where ruins were unearthed in 1962. That capital was abandoned for **Yendi** (100km east of Tamale) after the sixteenth-century Gonja invasions; the Ya Na's palace is still there. At **Bagale**, in the remote country south of Gambaga, is the Dagomba kings' mausoleum. The house built over it is the abode of the spirits of all departed Ya Nas.

Tongo and around

Southeast of Bolga, the hills around the Talensi village of **Tongo** make for an interesting and scenic day-trip. The best time to visit the area would be for the **Sowing Festival** around Easter or the **Harvest Festival**, usually in September or October. Both reflect a curious blend of old and new – iron-bangled dancers shaking radios, tennis racquets and rubber dolls. However, the principal attraction in the area is the **Tengzug shrine**, a famous religious site in a rocky cavern. The British destroyed it in 1911 and again in 1915, but couldn't prevent people from going there. The shrine is a twenty-minute walk from the village of Tengzug, a steep climb with a mountain of feathers – the by-product of sacrificial offerings – at the entrance to the shrine. There are good views over the village and the surrounding area. It costs ₵15,000 to enter the village and another ₵15, 000 to see the shrine; note that both sexes are required to enter the holy site topless.

Tro-tros run sporadically to Tongo every day from Bolga's main lorry park, though the journey's easiest on market day (the market here follows the same cycle as Bolga's). With your own means of transport, head 9km down the Tamale road, then take the clearly signposted turning off to your left to Tongo; from here it's another 4–5km up a winding track to Tengzug. A **guesthouse** and visitor's centre are being constructed in Tongo as part of an ecotourism project. Several kilometres north of Tongo, the village of **Bare** features a sacred **bat tree**, making for a change from crocodile pools and holy fish ponds.

The road from Walewale to Nakpanduri

South of Bolga, **Walewale** is the site of a venerable mosque, the Nakora. **Gambaga**, 50km east of here, is famous for its scarp, stretching out towards the Togolese border and up to 300m high in places. The town is also the **ancient Mamprusi capital** and the site of current excavations investigating the origins of the Mamprusi kingdom (see box above). The modern Mamprusi capital is **Nalerigu**, 8km east of Gambaga, home of a highly regarded mission hospital. Here you can see the palace of the Mamprusi kings, as well as remains of the defensive walls built around the town when it was founded in the seventeenth century.

NAKPANDURI, 30km further east, is an unspoilt village situated high on the scarp. The **government resthouse** here is superbly sited, with a magnificent view north and some inspiring hikes nearby through rocky outcrops (₵25,000). Eating options in town are severely limited to the odd chop bar, but you may use the resthouse kitchen. Vehicles run here from Bawku (early departures from the market around 6am), and though traffic is slow outside the market day (a three-day cycle), the relaxed and scenic atmosphere makes it worth a detour.

Togo

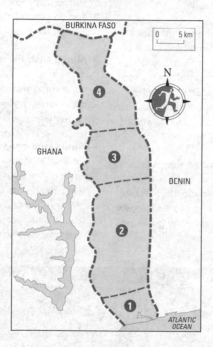

Togo highlights

* **Lomé** Despite political problems, the friendly capital still has a genuine appeal and is an attractive place to hang out and enjoy an exceptional range of bars and restaurants. See p.840

* **Agbodrafo and Lac Togo** Set on the southern shore of idyllic Lac Togo, the relaxing town of Agbodrafo offers various watersports, as well as *pirogue* trips over the lake to the historic voodoo town of Togoville. See p.852

* **Mont Klouto** A dramatic, winding road leads to the village of Kondo, from where you can climb Mont Klouto for fabulous views and go hiking in the surrounding jungle-strewn hills, which boast an amazing abundance of beautiful butterflies. See p.858

* **Akloa Falls** A fantastic walk through dense forest brings you to this stunning waterfall, and you can also swim in the pool at the base. See p.862

* **Aledjo** Near the dramatic site of the Faille d'Aledjo, this welcoming village offers impressive views across barren landscape. See p.868

* **Tamberma country** Living in fortresslike houses in the far north of the country, the isolated Tamberma continue to preserve their fascinating and unique architecture and customs. See p.875

Introduction and Basics

Togo – French-speaking West Africa's smallest nation – is still comparatively little known outside the region, and has been through heavy political weather in the last two decades. In the post-independence years of the 1960s and 1970s it attracted investors, expatriates and trans-Saharan tourists, while in 1975 it hosted the Lomé Convention, forever linking the country's capital with co-operation in development. If it wasn't democratic – well, few other countries in West Africa were.

The country's reputation for stability and prosperity carried it into the 1980s, when opposition protests began to mount. Despite a commitment to democracy – on paper – the government's political repression repelled visitors through most of the 1990s, and Togo's fortunes have plummeted. The economy struggles and infrastructure is in decline.

The enormous influence of "The Guide" – as President Gnassingbe Eyadéma is known – is noticeable throughout the country. His ample presence on photos, posters, TV and radio is ubiquitous and overbearing. People are usually jumpy when the conversation turns to politics, which it rarely does, and almost never in public places. The farcical nature of Togo's democracy is increasingly apparent – the EU didn't even bother sending observers to the most recent elections.

The mood of despondency is not so pervasive, however, that it completely overshadows Togo's attractions. The country has a wonderful climate and good food, and also boasts a vigorous **culture**, with over a dozen linguistic and ethnic groups. It also packs a satisfyingly diverse range of **scenery** into a small space, ranging from the dense forest and rolling hills of the cocoa triangle in the southeast to the savanna and barren landscapes of the north. In addition, the nation's political problems mean that there's a refreshing lack of tourists, and the Togolese themselves remain welcoming and friendly.

People

The big groups in Togo are, in the south, the Ewe (often spelled Ewé or Evé, and pronounced midway between "Ehveh" and "Eyway"), and in the north, the Kabyé (Kabyié, Kabré, Kauré). The **Ewe**, who are divided into a multiplicity of local and district communities – the Mina-speakers are one of the biggest – are traditionally the most powerful ethnic constituency in the country. They have linguistic and cultural affinities with other Twi-speaking peoples like the Akposo in central Togo, the Asante and Fante in Ghana, and the Fon in eastern Togo and Benin. The Ewe diaspora – especially in

11

Fact file

The **République Togolaise** is a strip of a country with a 56-kilometre coastline and an area of only 57,000 square kilometres – less than half the size of England or New York State. The name Togo means "Upon the hill" in Ewe. The **population** is officially estimated at 5.2 million, with some 700,000 living in the capital, Lomé, although hundreds of thousands of refugees fled to Ghana and Benin during the upheaval of the early 1990s. Togo has a **foreign debt** of about £950 million ($1.5 billion), a relatively small sum even by modest West African standards, yet still amounting to four times the annual value of its exports. The **government** is theoretically democratic, although President **Gnassingbe Eyadéma** has been in power for more than thirty years, and (having adjusted the constitution) was re-elected in 2003 for a third successive term after elections of breathtaking iniquity. Most of his support is in northern Togo.

France and Ghana – is a source of firm opposition to Eyadéma, while the Ghanaian border, which splits the Ewe traditional homeland into two regions, is the butt of considerable frustration. The Togolese Ewe, particularly the Mina, are the producers of much of Togo's export earnings, through coffee and cocoa.

The **Kabyé** and related **Tamberma** peoples are mostly poor subsistence farmers who have tended to unite behind the president's regional development plans (he himself is a Kabyé). Other Voltaic-speaking northerners include the Tchamba and Bassari, and the Kotokoli, one of the nation's most populous groups, whose people also count among the country's most influential traders.

Where to go

The country's small size makes getting around relatively easy. The main **Route Nationale**, which shows off the country's cultural and geographical variety, runs from Lomé north to Dapaong, near the Burkinabe border, and even the most isolated villages lie within 100km of its path.

The capital, **Lomé**, feels for the most part like a provincial town, tuned to the shuffling pace of crowded narrow streets, where goats and chickens share space with the occasional taxi. During the worst periods of the military madness, tens of thousands of people fled Lomé, leaving it like a ghost town. Many refugees have returned, and although the heyday of the late 1980s – when Lomé was one of *the* places to be in West Africa – has gone, the capital is still a friendly place to relax and enjoy some creature comforts before or after a trip to the country's rural areas.

The **coast** is also worth savouring, not just for the palmy villages rustling between the lagoons and the Atlantic, but also for **voodoo**. The fetishes, shrines and festivals of **Togoville**, **Aného** and **Glidji** reveal a lot about a religion no less bizarre than the **Catholicism** with which it is strikingly interwoven. Followers are usually open about *vaudau* and willing to discuss it with interested travellers – surprising in view of the

secrecy under which traditional religions are usually shrouded.

Northwest of Lomé stretches the mountainous and fertile **plateau region**. Although they never exceed 1000m, the peaks of this area feel higher, especially when you're climbing the twisting roads to **Badou**, **Kpalimé** or **Atakpamé**. These three towns delineate the **coffee and cocoa** triangle – the richest agricultural district in the country, characterized by thick woodland studded with fruit orchards and palm plantations.

In the **central region**, Sokodé and Bafilo are Muslim strongholds, while Bassar and Kara have retained predominantly traditional religious beliefs. Mango and Dapaong, located in the semi-arid savanna region of the **far north**, already evoke the Sahel and the spectre of drought. For wildlife viewing, the country's only option is at the **Parc National de Fazao-Malfakassa**, west of Sokodé – Togo's other parks have vanished as most of the large mammal species were poached. The president's hometown, **Kara**, has benefited from a number of industrial and other development projects that have catapulted it into "second city" status.

When to go

Togo's pleasant **climate** has always been a factor in its popularity with visitors. The **rainy seasons**, which vary from north to south, need not be an overriding factor in deciding when to go. Lomé and the southern region has its "long rainy season" from March to June and a period of short rains some time between September and November. Sokodé and the north get a single, and less predictable, rainy season between April and September. Note, though, that there's not a lot of rain, even in the south (the baobab, that archetypal dry-country tree, grows right down to within 10km of the coast) and the table given opposite for Lomé is an average of wet and dry years. Except in small villages off the paved road, notably in the Tamberma country or the areas around Bassar and Tchamba – where steep muddy tracks can be demanding – the weather won't greatly hamper your travels.

Average temperatures and rainfall

Lomé

Temperatures °C	Jan	Feb	Mar	Apr	May	June	July	Aug	Sept	Oct	Nov	Dec
Min (night)	23	24	25	24	24	23	23	22	23	23	23	23
Max (day)	31	31	32	31	31	29	27	27	28	30	31	31
Rainfall mm	15	24	52	118	145	224	71	8	35	61	28	10
Days with rainfall	1	2	4	8	9	12	5	1	5	9	2	1

Getting there from the rest of Africa

Since the troubles of the early 1990s, Togo has not been a common target for travel. On a more positive note, the border with Ghana – closed frequently in the early 1990s – is now usually open, and if you're entering Togo by road, you'll find all the main highways paved and in good condition.

Flights from other African countries

There are flights most days from **Abidjan** on Air Ivoire, whilst Air Gabon and Air Togo both fly twice a week from Abidjan to Lomé. Air Togo and Air Burkina fly twice weekly (and Trans Air Benin weekly) to Lomé from **Cotonou**. Air Togo fly twice weekly from **Accra**, while Air Burkina fly three times weekly from **Ouagadougou** and also offer twice-weekly flights from **Bamako** and **Dakar** via Ouaga. Air Gabon have five flights weekly to **Libreville** in Gabon, and also fly from **Douala** in Cameroon three times weekly.

From **East Africa**, Ethiopian Airlines fly from **Addis Ababa** twice a week, which has onward connections to **South Africa**.

Overland from Burkina Faso

The road from Ouagadougou is sealed most

> For important practical information applying to all West African countries, covering health, transport, cultural hints and more, plus details on getting to the region from beyond Africa, see Basics, pp.9–87.

of the way to Lomé, apart from a rough stretch between Koupéla and the border on the Burkina side. The border is open from 6am to 6pm, and formalities are straightforward. Coming from Ouaga by **bush taxi**, you can save money by going as far as **Dapaong** and changing vehicles there. By **bus**, SOGEBAF provide a weekly service from Bobo (CFA18,000) via Ouaga (CFA13,000), while SKV has air-conditioned services (CFA15,000) once a week.

Overland from Ghana

The chaotic main border crossing with Ghana is a few kilometres west of Lomé city centre and is open from 6am to 10pm (although there are currently plans to extend this to 24hr). The taxis from Ghana that go all the way to Lomé's Grand Marché auto-gare charge a big premium for the few extra kilometres. It's cheapest to get transport to the Ghanaian border town of **Aflao**, from where you can walk to a number of good hotels located near the border. Alternatively, you can cross the border on foot and then take a taxi or zemidjan for the final 2km to the centre, though you'll have to contend with the border's aggressive and rapacious taxi drivers (don't pay more than CFA1500) and moneychangers. You may prefer to walk a few hundred metres from the border to escape these hassles, and then flag down a taxi.

There's a less stressful border crossing between Ho and Wli in Ghana and Kpalimé in Togo. Alternatively, there are less frequented crossings west at **Badoudjindji**, a few kilometres west of Badou; at **Tatali** between Yendi and Kara; and at **Pulimakum**, between Bawku and Cinkassé in the far north of the country – there's no

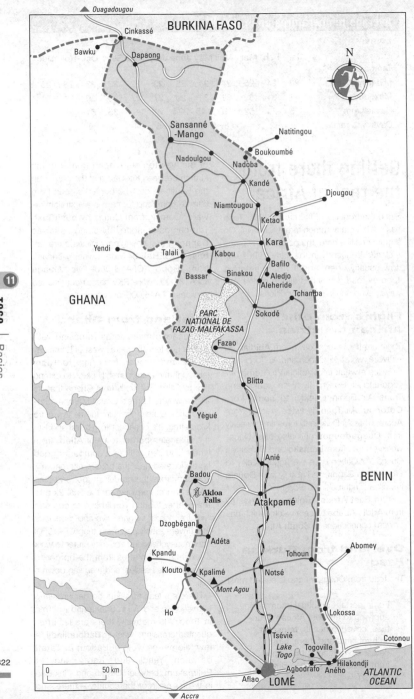

official post on the Togolese side at the Pulimakum crossing, so you'll have to go to Cinkassé to be formally stamped into the country.

Overland from Benin

The main border crossing between Togo and Benin is at **Hilakondji**. The post is open 24 hours a day and is relatively hassle-free. Regular bush taxis and a once-daily STIF bus ply the *route internationale* between Cotonou and Lomé, which is in good condition. Less used border crossings can be found at **Tohoun**, 53km due west of Notsé; **Kemerida**, just east of Kétao (which leads to Djougou); and – perhaps the most difficult of all – at **Nadoba** in the Tamberma country, where you cross from Boukoumbé.

Red tape and visas

Visas for Togo are required by everyone except nationals of ECOWAS countries. Where Togo has no diplomatic representation, you can usually get one at the French consulate. Visas are also issued at the country's **major border crossings**: Aflao, Cinkassé and Hilakondji (CFA10,000). These are valid for one week only but can be extended in Lomé (see p.851). The **Visa Touristique Entente** (see p.25) is valid for entry into Togo.

Whether you enter by air or overland, customs and immigration officials usually give you little hassle. You may sometimes be asked how much money you're carrying, but the amount is rarely verified. The only other piece of paper you'll need is a **yellow fever certificate**.

For **visas for onward travel**, Lomé has only a limited number of West African embassies and consulates (see p.850). Visas for some Francophone countries, including Burkina Faso, are issued from the French consulate. Benin has no embassy, but 48-hour visas are issued at the Hilakondji border (CFA10,000) and can be extended in Cotonou. Ghana's embassy will issue single-entry visas (CFA10,000) with minimal fuss, but Nigerian visas are issued to Togolese residents only. The Niger consulate issues one-month visas in 24 hours

(CFA22,500) and can also issue a Visa Touristique Entente (CFA25,000), which covers you for one entry into Burkina, Benin, Niger and Côte d'Ivoire.

Information, websites and maps

The best **map** of Togo is the large 1cm:5km sheet produced by the French IGN, although it's badly out of date (the last edition was published in 1991). Alternatively, try the more up-to-date ITMB map of Togo and Benin (1:864,000; published 2001) or the Michelin 741 which, although far less detailed, is still useful. In Lomé, the Togolese survey office, the Direction de la Cartographie Nationale, is responsible for large-scale (1:200,000 and 1:50,000) mapping. Whether they will sell you any sheets is another matter.

North Americans can get tourist information from the **Togo Tourist Information Office** at the Togolese embassy. In Europe, you can try writing to the Togolese embassy in France (see p.23). The best Togo **Internet** site is ⓦ www.republicoftogo.com, which mainly covers the latest political and economic news, but also has a range of country information.

Health

In common with most of West Africa, a **yellow fever vaccination certificate** is compulsory, though rarely checked. **Malaria tablets** are essential. Towns and large villages have either a hospital or, more likely, a **dispensary**, but these are characteristically overcrowded and lack adequate supplies. If you get seriously ill, it's best to get to your embassy (or telephone if you are upcountry) or one that speaks your language. They'll be able to refer you to a specialist or decide if you wouldn't be better off flying back home to get the help you need.

Costs, money and banks

Togo is part of the CFA zone (£1=CFA930; US$1=CFA600). If you're arriving overland, you're likely to have some CFA; if you're arriving by air from Europe, it's a good idea to bring some euros, which are widely accepted as payment for taxis, services and hotels.

Changing other major **international currencies** (whether traveller's cheques or cash) is no problem in Lomé, Kpalimé, Kara and Sokodé, although banks will virtually always demand to see purchase receipts if you're changing traveller's cheques. In smaller towns, **banks** are likely to accept euros only. Banking hours are short and inconvenient (usually Mon–Fri 7.30–11.30am & 2.30–4.30pm). Outside of Lomé, banks shut on Mondays but open on Saturday mornings from 7am to 1pm instead. **Credit cards** are accepted in major hotels, while in Lomé you can get Visa cash advances at the UTB Bank. BTCI banks in major towns, including Lomé and Kara, have ATMs which accept Visa cards.

The black market

Lomé has the biggest currency **black market** in West Africa, most visible in Lomé around the BIA bank and along the aptly named rue du Commerce – and also near the old Cotonou taxi station and Grand Marché. The quarter is notorious throughout the region, and the black market operates here quite openly. You can buy Nigerian naira and Ghanaian cedis here, as well as CFA (useful if you get caught short when the banks are closed) and other international currencies. Though you're not breaking any Togolese law by changing money here, bear strongly in mind the fact that cedis and naira may not legally be exported or imported.

Streetwise **moneychangers** are very adept at sleight-of-hand tricks, so go with a friend, pay attention, and only carry the money you want to change. In general, it's advisable to avoid the sharks on the street who'll perform magic before your eyes, and deal with one of the bigger bosses at a shop, doing the actual exchange inside. Don't hand anything over until you've checked the money you've been given note by note. Much more relaxed exchanges can often be done with resident expatriate money-dealers, who have legal currency businesses and will give better-than-bank rates if you're buying CFA. Ask around.

Costs

The **cost of living** in Togo is substantially lower than that in West Africa's other Francophone countries, though if you plan on living and eating *à l'européen*, you'll pay dearly for imported goods that would be cheap at home. Budget **hotel rooms** start from around CFA3000 in the countryside (slightly more in Lomé), while mid-range hotels start at around CFA8000. Ready-cooked **street food** and market produce is very cheap, especially in the productive southwest. **Restaurants** serving European food generally do meals for about CFA2000, although expensive eateries abound in Lomé, and often charge over CFA5000 for a main course. Beer and soft **drinks** are very inexpensive and cost the same price in local bars countrywide (CFA425 for a large beer, CFA350 for large soft drinks), although big hotels and tourist hangouts knock prices up, as you'd expect. **Petrol** costs about CFA450 per litre for super, though you often find it sold more cheaply all over the south in jerry cans along the roadside.

Getting around

Getting around Togo is now only possible by road, since the railway service in the south has been discontinued and there's no domestic air service. The good news is that Togo has generally well-maintained roads, while Lomé is linked by tarmac highways to all neighbouring capitals.

Given the lack of alternatives, you're likely to do most of your travelling in Togo by **bush taxi**. These are traditionally Peugeot 504s, though every year Japanese vans – comfortable Nissans and Hiaces – gain ground. You'll normally be asked to pay extra for your **luggage**; this should never be more than CFA100–300, according to the length of the journey and the size of your bag. Routine **police checks** along roads are more prevalent in Togo than in neighbouring countries and can severely lengthen your journey, particularly in the south of the country, although there are far fewer north of Atakpamé.

There are no internal **bus** services in Togo, although you could feasibly catch the Burkina-bound SOGEBAF or SKV buses from Lomé and get off along the way (although you'll have to pay the full fare). In Lomé and all other towns, **zemidjans** (moped taxis) are common and convenient, if a little dangerous, since no helmets are provided. Lomé has a few **car rental** agencies, but prices are prohibitive.

Accommodation

Except in Lomé, Togo has little in the way of luxury accommodation, although it does have an adequate number of more modest lodgings, either privately owned or government-run. Accommodation is usually good value compared with neighbouring Francophone countries, although amenities like air conditioning, TV and phones are less common.

Basic **budget hotels** (❶–❷) start at around CFA3000 and range from rudimentary *chambres de passage* to decent self-contained rooms. **Mid-range** places (❸–❺) in modest business- or tourist-class hotels typically offer self-contained rooms with a/c and often amenities like TV and phone, plus an in-house restaurant. Top-end hotels (❻–❽) are only found in Lomé.

Togo has no youth hostels and little in the way of mission accommodation, though the **Affaires Sociales** government resthouses will always put you up cheaply if they have a room free. There's a handful of organized **camping** sites east of Lomé and a limited number of other sites throughout the country. Some hotels allow campers to pitch a tent on their grounds for CFA2000–3000 a night. If you have your own transport and are out in the bush, you can pull off the road discreetly and camp for the night; it's advisable though – not to mention polite – to let local people know who and where you are first.

Officially, **staying with people** is frowned upon unless you have made a declaration at the town *préfecture*. However, Lomé is big enough for you to be able to skip this formality, and it seems that, even outside the capital, the authorities don't bother too much with it nowadays.

Eating and drinking

Togo has a deserved reputation for some of the best cooking in West Africa, and small restaurants and street stands as far afield as Niamey, Bamako and Abidjan are often run by Togolese women. The secret of their success lies in their sauces, which tend to be less oily than usual and contain more vegetables. Not that you'll necessarily love Togolese food; some of it may seem unappealing at first (slimy gumbo, or okra, can be a real turn-off) and all of it is guaranteed to be heavily laced with hot peppers.

Staples vary across the country. In the south, **cassava** (manioc) predominates, along with **palm oil** and **maize**. Cassava is often grated and steamed as *atiéké*. In the plateau region, the diet contains more tubers – **yams**, **cocoyams** and **sweet potatoes** – boiled, grilled, steamed or fried. **Plantains** are another favourite staple, commonly pounded into **fufu** (which can also be made with cassava or yams). In the north, **sheanut oil** is more commonly used than palm oil. Likewise, **rice**, **millet** and **sorghum** (any of them can be ground, boiled and served as a mash) are eaten more frequently in the north than towards the coast. **Pâte** – also found in

---

Accommodation price codes

All accommodation prices in this chapter are coded according to the following scale, whose equivalent in pounds sterling/US dollars is used throughout the book. Prices refer to the rate you can expect to pay for a room with two beds, including taxes. Single rooms, or single occupancy, will normally cost at least two-thirds of the twin-occupancy rate. For further details, see p.51.

❶ Under CFA4700 (under £5/$8).
❷ CFA4700–9000 (£5–10/$8–16).
❸ CFA9000–14,000 (£10–15/$16–24).
❹ CFA14,000–19,000 (£15–20/$24–32).

❺ CFA19,000–28,000 (£20–30/$32–48).
❻ CFA28,000–37,000 (£30–40/$48–64).
❼ CFA37,000–47,000 (£40–50/$64–80).
❽ Over CFA47,000 (over £50/$80).

Benin – is the generic term for pounded starch based on cassava, yam or sweet potato.

Vegetables include tomatoes, gumbo, aubergines (small and yellowish), squash and beans. These are used in **sauces** with cassava, baobab or taro leaves and mixed with fish, shellfish, meat or poultry. Common **spices** are ginger, peppers, anis, garlic, basil and mustard.

The south and plateau region have the most **fruit**, although even in the extreme north you'll find a good variety. **Pineapples, mangos, papayas**, all the **citrus fruits, avocados** and **guava** are plentiful in the markets (depending of course on the season) and especially cheap in the south.

Supplements to the basics include "**agouti**" (the large and tasty herbivorous rodent known in Ghana and Nigeria as "bush rat" or "grasscutter") and **koliko** (deep-fried yam chips). Togo's best-known dishes are **moutsella** (a spicy fish and vegetable dish), **adokouin** (shellfish with a prawn sauce known as *azidessi*), **djek-oumé** (chilli chicken), and **gboma** (a spinach and seafood based dish). You're most likely to sample these at an important private gathering, or as part of the *Cuisine Togolaise* menu in one of the more expensive restaurants.

Togo has great **street food** and, even in the smaller **village markets**, women sell exotic as well as fairly familiar food by the portion, from basins. The variety is huge. In addition, all large towns have restaurants serving **European food**, mainly French dishes, though these tend to be fairly expensive. In Lomé, you'll also find a limited range of Chinese, Lebanese, Italian and Spanish restaurants; again, these tend to be expensive.

Finally, you'll find a shop selling inexpensive **Fan Products ice cream** and frozen **yoghurt** in most large towns.

Drinking

Togo has its share of local drinks, similar to the other common intoxicants of West Africa. **Palm wine** is big in the south: the juice that flows from the trunks is already fermented and ready to drink, its frothiness indicating its freshness (if it's flat it will be high in alcohol). A hard liquor can be produced by distilling it. Though illegal, this highly potent "African gin", or **sodabi**, flows freely in the coastal region. Northern Togo specializes in millet beer, known locally as **choucoutou** – a taste somewhat reminiscent of dry cider. Filtering it produces **chacbalo**, which is clear and slightly sweeter than *choucoutou*.

Togo's **beer** is excellent and cheap. Bière du Bénin (referred to as BB, "Bé-Bé") produces both "Lager" and "Pils", along with the slightly more expensive Flag and the more potent Eku. Guinness is also available, served cold. There's also a wide range of **soft drinks**, including good Lion Killer lemonade, soda water, tonic, and the splendidly fruity, carbonated "Cocktail de Fruits". These come in large and small bottles and are all refreshingly inexpensive.

Communications

Post isn't too expensive: CFA450 for letters to Europe and CFA500 to the US. Postcards are slightly cheaper. Parcels can only be sent air mail and are very expensive. If you want to **phone** home, reverse-charge (collect) calls are only possible to France, and normal calls are pretty expensive (CFA1500 per minute to America and most of Europe, CFA1000 to France). There are now some phonecard-operated IDD telephone booths in Lomé and other major towns.

Internet access is still fairly limited, and cybercafés are only found in large towns such as Lomé, Atakpamé, Kara and Dapoang. Costs are low, however, averaging around CFA500 per hour, while connections are relatively good compared to neighbouring countries.

Mobile phones (cellphones) can be used in Togo through the Togotel network; the coverage is relatively good. Your mobile phone will work in the southwest of the country from Lomé to Kpalimé, and in towns including Atakpamé, Sokodé, Kara and even Dapaong in the far north, although connections can be tenuous at times.

Togo's IDD country code is ☏228.

The media

The country's only readily available **newspaper** is the state-owned *Togo Presse*, published daily in French, with Ewe, Kabyé and even English pages; its international coverage is sketchy, but local news items are often interesting. A vigorous free press developed in the early 1990s, but bombings and other intimidation have dampened the enthusiasm of most publishers. Look out for *Tribune du Peuple* and *Combat du Peuple*. You'll find international **English-language papers and magazines** like *The Herald Tribune*, *Time* and *Newsweek* (as well as French and German magazines and papers) at the airport and the big hotels.

Radio Togo, the national station, broadcasts news in French, Ewe, Kabyé and English (endless reports of the president's activities followed by a wrap-up of West African events). **Radio France Inter** (91.5FM) is better, with more comprehensive international news coverage (although this has currently been suppressed by the government). There are also numerous **private stations** (Zephyr, Metropolys and Nana FM are the most popular), although their news coverage is not of a very high standard.

The national **TV** company, Television Togolaise, broadcasts every evening – news in French and local languages plus old movies. The pay-per-view Media Plus channel broadcasts various foreign programmes.

Festivals and public holidays

Muslim and Christian holidays – including Catholic festivals like Pentecost, Ascension and Assumption (the former two are variable; the latter is on August 15) – are celebrated in Togo, along with New Year's Day. National holidays are: January 13 (National Liberation Day); April 27 (Independence Day); May 1 (Labour Day); June 21 (Martyr's Day); September 24 (Anniversary of the failed attack on Lomé) and November 1 (All Saints Day). There are also a few days in July on the occasion of Evala which, with so many Kabyé employees granted leave, is increasingly considered a public holiday.

Traditional festivals take place in the regions, many with ancient ethnic roots and corresponding celebrations in Ghana and Benin. The following are the most notable.

July

Evala Initiation celebration in the Kabyé country with wrestling matches (*lutte traditionelle*). The tournaments in Kara are now televised nationally and attended by the president, who is himself said to be a former champion.
Akpema Kabyé young women's initiation ceremony.

August

Kpessosso Harvest festival of the Gun (an Ewe group), celebrated in the region of Aného and marked by traditional dances (Adjogbo and Gbékon).
Ayize Bean-harvest festival celebrated by the Ewe, particularly in the region of Tsevié.

September

Agbogbozan Festival of the Ewe diaspora celebrated on the first Thursday in September and especially colourful in Notsé.
Yékéyéké or Yakamiakin Week-long festival starting on the Thursday before the second Sunday in September, in Glidji near Aného.
Dipontre Yam festival celebrated around the first week of September in Bassam.

Entertainment and sport

Togo's **music** scene isn't especially vivacious, and nightlife in Lomé has been severely disrupted over the years by periodic violence and nighttime curfews. No **film** industry ever developed here and in the current climate of media censorship, there's little incentive.

Football, however, is a little more promising, with seventeen players based in overseas teams and the national squad regularly reaching the group stage of the African Cup of Nations. A sport in complete contrast, traditional **wrestling** receives official patronage from Eyadéma's government (see p.872).

Directory

Airport departure tax None.

Crafts There are numerous places throughout the country where crafts are plentiful. The principal market in Lomé is the Rue des Sculpteurs: a small alley next to the *Hôtel du Golfe* where art vendors sell sculptures, bronzes, jewellery and textiles from across West Africa. In Kpalimé, the Centre d'Enseignement Artistique et Artisanal gives traditional forms of pottery, calabash decoration and woodcarving a modern, more commercial flavour. Kpalimé is also a good place to buy *kente* cloth (see p.796), which is woven in the town's streets. Traditional cloth is also woven in Bafilo and can be purchased directly from the Groupement Essovale Dégbembia, the weaver's co-operative in the town centre. An unwelcome footnote is the presence of ivory in Lomé's craft shops and a flourishing ancillary trade in fake ivory bangles.

Opening hours Offices and most businesses are open from 7.30am to noon and from 2.30pm to 5.30pm. Banking hours vary slightly from one institution to the next, but are roughly 7.30–11.30am and 2.30–4.30pm. Note that in Lomé, these hours apply Monday to Friday, but outside of Lomé, banks are closed on Mondays and often open on Saturday mornings instead. The more modern "journée continue" hours (roughly 8am–2pm, with no closure) are increasingly common.

Photography No photography permit is required in Togo, though the usual restrictions apply to taking pictures of military installations and strategic points. People generally tend to be less camera-shy here than in other parts of the region.

Soccer A popular sport, with particularly fierce competition between Semassi, the team from Sokodé, and Gomido, from Kpalimé.

Wildlife parks Most of Togo's former game reserves and national parks have been closed down, and the largest park, Parc National de la Kéran, has reverted to farmland, as most of the game has been killed off. The only park which is still functioning is the Parc National de Fazao-Malfakassa, west of the main north–south highway near Sokodé. Closed for rehabilitation for many years after much of its wildlife was also decimated, it has been taken over by the Fondation Franz-Weber and is now open for visitors. Although the chances of seeing larger wildlife are slim, it's set in stunning scenery and offers good odds of seeing monkeys and a variety of birdlife.

Women Tradition, in rural areas especially, dictates a strict sexual division of labour. Women have considerable economic clout, however, particularly in the south where well-organized women merchants – known in Lomé as the *Nanas Benz* after their favourite cars – are a political force of consequence. The government recognizes the Union Nationale des Femmes Togolaises. Women have access to all administrative functions and professions, but the reality is that education, though compulsory in theory for all children, is less likely to be given to girls than boys, and there are few women in high-level positions in government or business.

A brief history of Togo

For centuries, Togo has been on the fringes of several empires – Mali, Asante, Benin, Mossi – but the centre of none. The country, which formed part of what was once called the Slave Coast, came into contact with Europeans in the fifteenth century as the Portuguese made their sweep of the African continent. Porto Seguro (Agbodrafo) and Petit Popo (Ainého) evolved to become important trading posts where slaves were exchanged for European goods. By the end of the nineteenth century, trade had shifted to "legitimate" products – principally palm oil, used in soap manufacture in Europe. French and German companies competed along the coast in their dealings with the Mina people.

The colonial period

In 1884, **Gustav Nachtigal** sailed into Togo and signed a treaty with a village chief that made the country a **German protectorate**. In the following years, **Togoland** developed into the Reich's "model colony" as the Germans tried to force the country to produce economic miracles. Railways and roads were laid, and forests cleared for coffee and cocoa plantations. A direct radio link with Berlin was established and wharves were built.

The beginnings of an ill-defined educational system tried to create Christians and wage labourers out of reluctant farmers and fishermen. It took the Germans until 1902 to "pacify" the people of Togo, relying on forced labour and other repressive measures to push through their progress.

Despite the colony's economic importance, German military presence in Togoland was weak. When World War I broke out, the British and French easily overran the territory, forcing the Kaiser's soldiers to capitulate at **Kamina** on August 26, 1914. The tiny village was thus the site of the Entente Powers' very first victory. After the war, a **League of Nations mandate** placed a third of the territory under British administration and two-thirds (corresponding to the present country's borders) in the hands of the French.

The way to independence

Both **France and Britain** showed only half-hearted interest in their new acquisitions, which technically were not colonies. The British quickly attached western Togo (the present-day Volta Region in Ghana) to the Gold Coast, but the French administered eastern Togo as an entity separate from its other holdings in West Africa. Thus several of Togo's peoples – the Adele, Konkomba and especially **Ewe** – suddenly found their communities divided by a border. Reunification was an early political theme, but one the European powers looked on unfavourably. A "pan-Ewe" vision, championed by early nationalist leaders like **Sylvanus Olympio**, was dealt a severe blow in 1956 when the people of West Togo voted in a referendum to amalgamate with the Gold Coast, then preparing for independence.

At the same time, the French were grooming eastern Togo for independence. In 1956, Togo became an autonomous republic, with **Nicolas Grunitzky** as prime minister. Two years later, Olympio took over the role and, when Togo became fully independent on April 27, 1960, he was elected the nation's first president.

A shaky start

Olympio aspired to the ideals of early nationalists such as Nkrumah, Touré and Senghor, although he never achieved their stature. In any case, even as he ushered in a new era, the stage was set for his own demise. In a scenario all too common to the former colonies, the

Germans, and later French, had groomed a class of coastal peoples to be civil servants and the educated elite. After independence, these peoples inherited political power and, as a consequence, economic advantages. It was a formula guaranteed to result in ethnic tension in countries where unity should have been of primary importance.

In the case of Togo, Olympio, an Ewe from Aného, represented the **elite minority**. He tended to put reunification with the Ewe in Ghana ahead of Togolese national unity and was openly contemptuous of the northern Togolese, whom he called *petits nordistes*. Increasing repression and disregard for the poor north didn't help to broaden his already narrow political base. Meanwhile **Nkrumah** of Ghana, who had supported Olympio's efforts for Togo's independence, had apparently intended the territory to be integrated with Ghana and, that objective thwarted, actively harassed Olympio's new government with border closures and trade sanctions.

In 1963, returning **Togolese soldiers** who had fought for France in the Algerian war of independence, were prevented by Olympio from joining Togo's national army, since in his eyes they had betrayed the African liberation movement. For these troops, mainly Kabyé men from the north, it was a humiliating snub and seeming proof that Olympio was determined to exclude northerners from participation in the new nation.

On January 13, 1963, a group of these disenfranchised soldiers, including a young Kabyé sergeant named **Etienne Eyadéma**, staged the first coup in independent Africa. They stormed the president's home and, according to the official version, shot and killed Olympio while he was trying to escape by scrambling up the wall from his residence and into the grounds of the American embassy where he had hoped to seek refuge.

The soldiers set up a civilian government and placed Grunitzky, who had returned from exile, at its head. The new president lasted four ineffectual years and, as the country's increasing problems outstripped his competence to deal with them, he was replaced in a **bloodless coup** by Eyadéma – staged (in a symbolic style that became his hallmark) on January 13, 1967, four years to the day after Olympio's assassination.

The early Eyadéma years

After his second coup, Eyadéma seized power "at the insistence of the people", suspended the constitution, dissolved political opposition and set about protecting his political future through the powerful mechanism of the single party he himself controlled – the Rassemblement du Peuple Togolais (RPT). By 1972, he was secure enough to hold a referendum on his future as president, in which voters held up one colour card to indicate a "yes" vote and a different colour for "no" as soldiers guarded the booths. A landslide 99 percent of the population thus expressed its desire for Eyadéma to remain the national leader.

Two years later, the president profited from a bizarre series of events that seemed to give supernatural backing to the demonstration of popular support. It started in 1974 with what has gone down in Togolese political legend (actively encouraged by the president) as the **"Three Glorious Days"**. On **January 10**, Eyadéma announced that a 51 percent share of the French-operated phosphate mines (one of the country's principal resources) would be nationalized. Exactly two weeks later, on **January 24**, the president's private plane crashed over **Sarakawa**, but Eyadéma walked away from the wreck virtually untouched. An international plot was suspected, and, without any real proof, the world was led to believe this was a classic case of capitalist meddling – an assassination attempt on the man who had dared to liberate his country's economy.

After recovering, the president made a drawn-out journey from Kara to Lomé, and throngs of people came to look at the man who had become a myth. On **February 2**, Eyadéma made his **triumphal return** to the capital and announced that the phosphate industry was henceforth one hundred percent in Togolese hands.

The incident turned into a political windfall that made Togo look like the mouse who roared. Eyadéma's **anti-imperialist record** was enshrined in myth. He began an **"authenticity"** campaign, modelled closely on Mobutu's in the former Zaire, abolishing French names (and renaming himself Gnassingbe) and introducing Kabyé and – with a little shrewdness – Ewe into the schools as languages of instruction. Phosphate money helped construct a few modern buildings in Lomé and Kara along with ambitious projects like an oil refinery, steel plant (both now closed) and cement factory near Lomé. But rather than creating jobs, these simply lost money, forcing the country to bend to IMF pressure to denationalize as the economy slumped badly in the 1980s. The irony of Togo's position ever since Sarakawa is that it became one of the most pragmatically **pro-Western** countries of the Cold War era.

International affairs

Despite economic decline, Eyadéma managed to keep a high diplomatic profile and created a new larger-than-life image for himself as **West African peacemaker**. At one point he served as an intermediary between combatants in the Chadian war and helped smooth over relations between Nigeria and the Francophone countries that had backed Biafra. More recently he provided another African platform for **Israel**, with which Togo opened diplomatic relations in 1987.

On an economic level, Eyadéma has championed ECOWAS (the West African common market, known in French-speaking countries as the CEDEAO). Along with Nigeria, Togo was a major sponsor of the organization, established in 1975 when fifteen regional nations signed the Treaty of Lagos. But his proudest achievement was hosting the meeting that resulted in the signing of the **Lomé Convention**, giving Third World nations in Africa, the Caribbean and the Pacific preferential treatment from the EC and linking the name of Lomé with cooperation in development policy.

Cross-border relations

Relations with **Ghana** have traditionally been rocky, partly as a result of the pan-Ewe movement, which dates from the colonial era and continues in a more subtle form today. The ideological opposition of Rawlings' and Eyadéma's regimes also led to serious tensions between the two neighbours. During Thomas Sankara's period in power, Togolese relations with **Burkina Faso** also chilled, but improved rapidly after Compaoré's assumption of power in 1987. Eyadéma was the first African head of state to recognize the new Burkinabe government, and he did so just hours after Sankara was overthrown.

Ideology has also been a source of conflict with **Benin** – a country periodically charged by Togo with giving refuge to politically active exiles. During the 1980s, the Togo–Benin border was frequently closed.

At home: increasing opposition

Eyadéma, who orchestrated two coups and has been witness to numbers of others in the states neighbouring his own, has been careful to nip **opposition** in the bud. Active underground dissent has long existed, and it rises to the surface in periodic eruptions of violence.

In 1984, when the papal visit focused international attention on Togo, a series of **bombings** rocked Lomé. A **coup attempt** occurred in a 1986 shoot-out with armed rebels who got perilously close to the presidential residence. The attempted takeover was blamed on an exiled movement led by Gilchrist Olympio (son of the former president) who was subsequently sentenced to death *in absentia*. The date of the aborted uprising – September 24 – is today celebrated as a national holiday.

In 1990, the government was again shaken when members of the **Convention Démocratique des Peuple Africains du Togo** (CDPA-T), an opposition group which had been based in Côte d'Ivoire until ousted by Houphouët-Boigny in 1989, were arrested for distributing anti-government literature. The ensuing trial led to massive demonstrations in Lomé which left many dead or injured.

Subsequent protests forced Eyadéma to **legalize political parties**, but student unrest again erupted in April 1991. Fatalities were reported in Lomé when security forces dispersed demonstrators who demanded Eyadéma's resignation. Afterwards, mutilated bodies began surfacing in Lomé's brackish Bé district lagoons. Twenty corpses were discovered, and the opposition blamed the brutality on the military. Anxious to dispel the idea that army thugs now publicly perpetrated the types of **human rights abuses** they had long been suspected of carrying out behind prison walls, Eyadéma ordered an investigation. But the opposition persisted and called a **general strike**, again demanding Eyadéma's resignation. More protests followed, and in June 1991 the government was constrained to agree on the mandate for a **national conference**, similar to the one that had brought sweeping reform to Benin.

In July 1991, delegates of newly legal political parties and the government convened and, with lightning speed, the conference proclaimed itself sovereign and suspended the constitution. By August, Eyadéma had been stripped of most of his power and the RPT had been outlawed. In an act of defiance, the president suddenly changed course and suspended the conference.

Opposition leaders refused to disband and proclaimed a **provisional government** under the leadership of **Joseph Kokou Koffigoh**, a lawyer and leader of the Ligue Togolaise des Droits de l'Homme. To stave off further unrest, Eyadéma consented to recognize Koffigoh. But within weeks of being instated, the new prime minister woke up to find soldiers had seized his house, captured the radio and television stations, and surrounded his office with tanks. Troops returned to the barracks on Eyadéma's orders, but in the following months, repeated popular protests led to bloody clashes with security forces. In November, the army **arrested Koffigoh** and demanded the transitional government be disbanded.

In prison, Koffigoh "reconsidered" his stance and consented to Eyadéma's euphemistically titled **"government of national unity"** which paved the way for the RPT's re-entry into the political scene. Although he spared the transitional government and allowed Koffigoh to remain as head, Eyadéma padded the council of ministers with close associates. With a tight grip on the council, the president allowed the appearance of reform to continue and laid plans for **new elections**.

Early 1992 was marked by repeated delays in the transitional process and by resulting protests. Trouble intensified when Olympio was shot while campaigning in Eyadéma's northern stronghold. The security forces were implicated in the **assassination attempt** and evidence even pointed to the president's son, Captain Ernest Gnassingbé. While Olympio recovered in Paris, a massive two-day general strike paralyzed Lomé as demonstrators once more flooded the streets.

Undaunted, the president cautiously took back all the power he had ceded to the national council in 1991. The sham of democratization was further highlighted in October 1992 when security forces stormed the parliament and held forty MPs hostage until the speaker pushed through a bill returning frozen funds to the RPT. In November, another **general strike** was called as opposition parties and union members demanded the creation of a politically neutral security force, a new government, and free and fair elections.

The promised elections still hadn't materialized by January 1993 and the strike dragged on. A French and German delegation arrived in Lomé to help mediate the crisis, but their efforts were thwarted when security forces fired on a crowd of opposition supporters, killing at least twenty according to the French minister of cooperation who witnessed the atrocity. After two security officers were found murdered on January 30, the army went on a retaliatory **shooting and looting spree** which left hundreds dead at the hands of the military.

The new wave of violence led to a **mass exodus**, and forty thousand refugees streamed over the borders to Ghana and Benin, straining Togo's already dismal international relations. President Jerry Rawlings of Ghana condemned Eyadéma's continued denial that security forces were responsible for the slaughter and seemed to advocate sending ECOWAS troops to Togo to prevent it from becoming "another Liberia". While both Ghana and Benin mobilized troops along their borders to protect the refugees, the United States, France and Germany suspended aid to Togo.

New elections and more of the same

Against such a troubling backdrop, Eyadéma announced that **presidential elections** would be held in August. Opposition leaders objected, demanding a recomposition of the Supreme Court and a postponement of the election date as preconditions for participating. They also called for a revised voter register and the issuing of new voters' cards. Eyadéma rejected the requests and furthermore denied the candidature of Gilchrist Olympio on the grounds that his medical examination was invalid.

The team of international observers monitoring the elections denounced the polls as undemocratic, and US and German observers withdrew from the process. Candidates **Edem Kodjo** (Union Togolaise pour la Démocratie, UTD) and **Yao Agboyibo** (Comité d'Action pour le Renouveau, CAR) pulled out of the race in protest and called for a **national boycott**. On a turnout of only 36 percent, Eyadéma garnered 96 percent of the vote and proclaimed himself victorious. The following day, fifteen CAR members, who had been arrested for allegedly tampering with electoral material, died in prison.

On January 5, 1994, gunfire once again erupted near Lomé's Tokoin military base where President Eyadéma normally sleeps. Simultaneous **rocket fire** blasted a presidential motorcade, striking Eyadéma's bulletproof Mercedes and sending it skidding off the road. Soon after, the government issued a communiqué saying that the city was under a **commando attack**, but that the president and prime minister, who were in a private meeting far away from the motorcade at the time of the incident, were unscathed.

Fighting continued for four days as Loméans remained locked in their homes. When the dust had settled, Eyadéma announced that government forces had defeated the insurgents which he claimed had infiltrated the capital from Ghana. Official reports put the death toll at 69, mostly members of the commando forces. Some estimates, however, ran as high as 300–500 victims, including many civilians.

The nation was shocked and demoralized as **legislative elections** were held in February. In a tight race, Agboyibo's CAR won 36 seats in the

81-member parliament, while Kodjo's UTD won 7 and the RPT 37. Though the RPT thus formed the minority in parliament, Eyadéma gained leverage by appointing Kodjo to the premiership – a move that gave the appearance of benevolence to the opposition, while effectively dividing it, since Agboyibo naturally felt he had claims to the post.

As a result, CAR members refused to sit in the cabinet of ministers, which was quickly padded out with Eyadéma supporters, and the party began a parliamentary boycott. This was called off in 1995 after Eyadéma offered guarantees for a fairer approach to future elections, and CAR resumed its representation in parliament. But even with a majority there, the opposition couldn't get a grip on governance, and Kodjo complained that he was increasingly left out of the decision-making process, as in 1996, when the president called **by-elections** designed to pad out RPT seats in the assembly. Angered at the fact that the president refused to live up to his earlier promises and appoint an international monitoring committee to oversee the elections, CAR refused to participate. The RPT and allied parties gained enough seats to have a majority and Kodjo was swiftly replaced by **Kwassi Klutse**, a more conciliatory technocrat and former minister. The opposition was left out of the cabinet completely.

The continuing slide from democracy

In 1997, as he celebrated thirty years as head of state – and his survival through six years of political upheaval and the economic ruin of his country – Eyadéma was firmly back in control. Noticeably absent from the military parade and lavish government ceremonies marking the anniversary were foreign dignitaries, both regional and international, who were reluctant to endorse the nation's slide from democratic rule. The EU, especially Germany (one of whose embassy staff was shot

dead at a roadblock in May 1996), remained highly critical of the regime and refused to renew much-needed financial aid.

With control of the presidency, parliament and courts, Eyadéma was accused of wielding his power to repress genuine opposition and secure another five-year term in the elections scheduled for 1998. Reports of **human rights abuses** were legion by 1997, and the president's security forces were charged with extrajudicial killings, beatings and arbitrary arrests that the government neither investigated nor punished. Intimidation restricted freedom of speech and the press; police and RPT youth groups harassed streetside sellers of private publications like *Crocodile* and *Le Kpakpa désenchanté*, seizing copies of critical newspapers, beating or arresting the vendors and smashing their stalls. In January 1998, a **student strike** to protest against the non-payment of study grants ended abruptly when *gendarmes* raided Lomé's Université du Bénin. In the ensuing mêlée, the president of the Union Nationale des Étudiants Togolais – who had refused to sign a government communiqué ordering students to return to classes – "fell" from a second-storey window, fracturing his spine. Eleven other students were arrested.

Trade unions fared no better. Despite the economic slump of the late 1990s and the fact that government salaries often went unpaid, the Union Nationale des Syndicats Indépendants (UNSI) could do little to improve working conditions, complaining that it operated under "extreme difficulty". The government promised reprisals for even modest strike action; in 1998, the deputy secretary of the UNSI was assassinated in his Lomé home. No one was charged in connection with the killing.

The mood was thus sombre as the **presidential elections of 1998** took place. Olympio and Agboyigbo, along with four other opposition candidates, courageously contested the elections. The establishment of a **National**

Election Commission (NEC) to oversee the voting was a positive sign, but members were packed with supporters of the RPT and refused to act on the recommendations of international observers. The government ban on political rallies, conveniently ignored by the RPT, was widely viewed as an attempt to limit the opposition's ability to recruit supporters. And the state-owned radio and television gave little coverage to opposition candidates, despite constitutional guarantees of equal access.

Voting proceeded without incident in June 1998, at least in pro-Eyadéma precincts. But stations in opposition strongholds, such as Lomé and Sokodé, opened late or not at all; many voters were turned away because they hadn't been issued registration cards; while the army confiscated ballot boxes in many precincts and refused to let the NEC preside over the counting of votes. The chair of the commission resigned rather than declare Eyadéma the winner, stating that members of the NEC had been the victims of "pressure, intimidation and threats". That left the counting to the government, which interrupted television programming the following day to announce that Eyadéma had been re-elected, having received 52 percent of the vote and an outright majority. From Ghana, Olympio, who received 34 percent by official accounts, claimed that he had been robbed of the victory and many international observers believed he was right. Days of protests and strikes followed the elections, but the government would not budge on the results, which the Supreme Court dutifully ratified.

Completely demoralized, and with no hope of a better outcome for the **legislative elections** planned to follow in July 1999, the opposition called for a **boycott** of them. In its mind, the government was illegal anyhow. As the crowning achievement of Eyadéma's return to absolute supremacy, the RPT took all the seats but one in the assembly.

Having silenced the critics at home, Eyadéma decided in May 1999 to take on his international detractors, and hired a French lawyer to sue Amnesty International over allegations that large numbers of people were killed by security forces before the presidential elections of 1998. More than 100 bodies had been washed ashore in Benin's coastal villages, many of them found handcuffed. French president Jacques Chirac's visit in July 1999 coincided with confirmation from the Benin League for the Defence of Human Rights that **mass executions** of hundreds of people had taken place and their bodies had been dumped at sea. However, Chirac's surpise visit seemed to pay dividends when he gained assurances that Eyadéma would step down before the 2003 elections – which he was constitutionally obliged to do in any case, having served the maximum two terms.

Eyadéma . . . again

Despite the agreement with Chirac, further tampering with the democratic system soon followed. In September 2001, Prime Minister Agbeyome Kodjo – an Ewe from the south – postponed that year's **legislative elections** with talk of constitutional change (he himself was sacked in June 2002, apparently for harbouring presidential ambitions). The elections, finally held a year later, were boycotted by the opposition. Not surprisingly, the RPT gained 73 of the 81 seats in the National Assembly. Two months later, the National Assembly pushed through an amendment to the 1993 constitution abolishing the restriction that allowed presidents to serve only two terms, thus allowing Eyadéma to stand once more. The amendment also stated that all presidential candidates had to be resident in the country for twelve months prior to the elections, meaning Eyadéma's main rival, the exiled Gilchrist Olympio, could not stand. The remaining six candidates suffered intimidation and harassment in the run-up to the **2003 presidential election**, while political broadcasts were censored and rallies interrupted by pro-Eyadéma activists. There were also concerns over the new voters' roll, which appeared to have been massively falsified to Eyadéma's advantage, whilst people in pro-opposition areas were not issued with voters' cards. Given these factors, the EU decided not even to bother sending international observers to the 2003 elections – a clear signal that EU aid (suspended since 1993) would not restart.

The elections went ahead in June 2003 in an atmosphere of tension and unrest. Dozens were killed and wounded in clashes between opposition and government supporters. Eyédema received 57 percent of the vote, whilst his nearest challenger, **Bob Akitani**, behind whom Olympio had thrown his support, received 34 percent. By the time the results were officially declared,

the government was hailing the result as "a victory for democracy in Togo", while Akitani was forced into hiding due to fears for his safety.

After three decades in power, Eyadéma had managed to cling to power once again, and no one at home or abroad is likely to forget the catastrophic 1990s when he governed through intimidation and force. He stands little hope of restarting Togo's crippled economy, and even less of persuading the gaping pockets of resentment in Togolese society that he represents their best interests. In the present international climate, with the world's attention focused on fears of terrorism and rogue states, Eyadéma seems to be assuming the world will take little notice of another minor African dictatorship, while his personal friendship with French president Jacques Chirac offers another example of France's often unhelpful involvement in West African affairs.

Music

Traditional music tends to split into two: Kabyé in the north; and "Ghanaian Folk Music" and Ewe/Mina in the south. The **Kabyé** have a rich musical culture. Some of the most interesting instruments are only used for special celebration, like the *picancala*, a xylophone-like instrument made of stones and rocks – a "lithophone" – and the unusual water flutes. There's also music played on horns, flutes and whistles and even a trumpet – the *xokudu* – made from the fruit of the baobab tree. There's an excellent selection on *Togo: Music from West Africa* (Rounder Records, released in 1992), which has a good mixture of traditional and modern styles, and features some nice acoustic guitar songs from Ali Bawa.

Modern music in Togo has not thrown up any great stars and most of the few singers seem content to imitate foreign styles. Togo's urban music was greatly influenced by Congolese styles during the 1960s and 1970s and reggae, soul, highlife and Latin music have all dominated the local scene at some time or other. **Bella Bellow** was the leading

singer in the late 1960s and dominated the music scene until her death in 1973. She toured Europe and America and made an album, with the help of Manu Dibango, *Album Souvenir* (Safari Ambience). More recent Togolese stars who have gained fame throughout West Africa include Nimon-Toki Lala from Kara, Fifi Rafiatou, Afia Mala and

Jimmy Hope – the last is one of Togo's biggest stars, a rock and blues musician with a huge following who often plays around Lomé.

King Mensah

Mensah Ayaovi Papavi has performed on stage since he was nine years old. A singer with Les Dauphins de la Capitale, he is also a storyteller, has been part of the Ki-Yi M'Bock Theatre in Abidjan, and is today the most popular musician in Togo. Since 1996 he has released four albums – his latest, *ELOM*, was released in 2002 on KMD. For more information on discography and photos of performances, see his website ⓦwww.kingmensah.com.

Madjo (Bolibana). Driven by powerful percussion deeply rooted in African traditions, King Mensah's music, moving from Afrobeat to reggae, is also strongly influenced by jazz and jazz-rock.

Books

Very little devoted to Togo has ever been published in English. Books marked ▣ are especially recommended.

David Ananou *Le Fils du Fétiche*. Intended to combat the racism of its time by a portrayal of a typical Togolese family, the effort is confounded by Ananou's rejection of traditional beliefs for the "lofty" tenets of Christianity.

Yves-Emmanuel Dogbé *La Victime*. A treatment of the interracial theme in West Africa: a white girl's parents come to recognize the error of their prejudice, but too late.

★ **Fauziya Kassindja** *Do They Hear You When You Cry?* This powerful book describes Kassindja's own experiences, first fleeing Togo at the age of seventeen to escape a forced marriage and genital circumcision ceremony, then her attempts to claim political asylum in the USA, where she spends several years in detention centers and prisons while her landmark case was being fought.

Tete Michel Kpomassie *An African in Greenland*. The narrative of a Togolese explorer on a whimsical journey among the Inuit. Never quite transcends the basic oddity of its theme, and begs a few questions along the way, but entertaining nonetheless.

George Packer *The Village of Waiting*. An informative book, recounting the experiences of a Peace Corps volunteer.

Comi M. Toulabor *Le Togo sous Eyadéma*. A solid discussion of 1980s politics – and about the only one to appear.

Languages

The official language of Togo is **French**, which is widely spoken. Due to commerce with Ghana and Nigeria, many traders also speak rudimentary **English**, especially in the area around Lomé.

There are some fifty African languages and dialects in Togo, the most widely spoken being **Mina** and **Ewe**. Mina is spoken by thirty percent of the population in the coastal region. **Kotokoli** – the language of Sokodé and environs (see box on p.869) – is also prevalent, whilst **Kabyé** (also known as Kabré or Kauré), President Eyadéma's mother tongue, is widely spoken in the region around Kara. Other languages include **Bassari**, in the area around the town of Bassar, **Tchamba** in the east, **Moba** around Dapaong and scattered communities of **Hausa**, **Fula** and **Mossi** in the extreme north.

Minimal Mina and essential Ewe

Mina is spoken by about a third of the population in Togo, making it the most common language in the country. You'll run into it mostly along the coast, as well as in parts of Ghana and Benin. Unlike **Ewe**, to which it's closely related, Mina is not written. Both languages are tonal, so that meaning varies (as in Chinese for example) with the pitch of the voice ("ò", for example, denotes a descending tone). They're therefore rather hard languages for speakers of European tongues to come to grips with. The following words and expressions are only a very rough guide to pronunciation.

Mina greetings and basics

Good day	Sobaydo
Reply	Dosso
How are you?	O foihn?
Reply ("fine")	aaaaa (as in cat)
Thank you	Akpay
Thank you very (very) much	Akpaykaka (kaka)
Have a nice day	Nkekay anenyo
Yes	Aaaaa
No	Ow
Come here (to a child)	Va
See you later	Sodé or Sodaylo
Until we meet again	Mia dogou/ mia dogoulo
See you tomorrow	Ayee'soh

Numbers

1	Dekaa
2	Amevé
3	Ametòn (low tone)
4	Amené
5	Ametón (high tone)
6	Amadé
7	Ameadrreh
8	Ameni
9	Amesidiké
10	Amewo

Ewe greetings and basics

Good morning	Nngdi
Good afternoon	Nngdo
Good evening	Fie
Good night	Do agbe
Welcome	Woe zo
How are you?	E foa?/ Ale nyuie?
I'm fine	Mefo/Meli nyuie
Pleased to meet you	Edzo dzi nam be medo go wo
I don't understand	Nye mese egome o
Goodbye	Hede nyuie
I'm a stranger	Amedzro menye
Please	Taflatse
What is your name?	Nko wode?
My name is . . .	Nngkonyee nye . . .
I am leaving Ewe land	Mele Evegbe srom

Ewe numbers

1	Deka
2	Uhve
3	Etoh
4	Enah

5	Atoh	12	Weuhve, etc
6	Adee	20	Blave
7	Aderen	30	Blatòh (low tone)
8	Enyee	40	Blana
9	Asiekee	50	Blatóh (high tone)
10	Ewo	60	Bladee, etc
11	Wedekee	100	Alohfa deka

Glossary

Anasara In the northern parts, a white, derived from Nazarene, or Christian.

Authenticité Programme initiated by Eyadéma to instil pride in "authentic" roots, requiring French names to be exchanged for African and proficiency in Ewe, Mina or Kabyé for all school children.

Auto-suffisance alimentaire Food self-sufficiency – which, in non-drought years, Togo had nearly obtained before the unrest of the early 1990s.

Evala The annual wrestling matches in the president's hometown of Kara.

Soukala A compound of round huts connected by a wall, found in the north.

Vaudau/Vodu Generic names for the spirit children of God – *Mawu-Lisa* in Ewe.

Yovo White person (Mina).

11.1

Lomé and the coast

The pace of **Lomé** falls far short of the frenzied tempo of West Africa's other big cities, with most of its activity centred around the bustling market and surrounding commercial district – a pleasantly archaic area laid out by the French. The mix of urban sophistication and rural informality once combined to make Lomé West Africa's most enticing capital: for overlanders a popular respite from the rigours of travel in the bush; for the large expat community working in finance, development or as volunteers, an important centre of operations. But the strikes and violence of the 1990s hit Lomé badly, and the city's spark is still struggling to return.

East of the city, there are just fifty kilometres of coastline, wedged between the Ghanaian and Benin borders. The surf is notoriously rough, even dangerous at times, yet the whole **Atlantic shorefront** is picture-postcard perfect, with its coconut groves, white-sand beaches and fishing villages – none more than an hour's journey from the capital. The towns of **Togoville**, **Aného** and **Glidji**, with their fetishes, shrines and festivals, offer interesting insights into local voodoo customs.

These towns also served as the spearhead for the German colonial invasion which began in 1884 – the year when Gustav Nachtigal landed in Togoville and signed a treaty placing the chief under the Kaiser's "protection". Soon after, Aného became capital of German Togoland. Today, the coastal villages are full of colonial vestiges, in varying states of dilapidation, which stand in sharp contrast to the dominant voodoo culture.

Lomé

Although **LOMÉ** spreads widely, the city's population of around 700,000 is hardly enough to push it into the major metropolis category. The heart of the downtown district sweeps around the crowded old **Grand Marché**. In the immediate vicinity, throngs of **shoppers and street vendors** press through a maze of narrow avenues and sandy streets lined with two-storey colonial buildings – the domain of Lebanese shopkeepers and small import-export businesses. The whole area is dominated by the **beach** and pervaded by ocean breezes. Only along **Boulevard 13 Janvier** (previously named – and still frequently referred to as – Boulevard Circulaire) do you encounter the broad streets and high-rises that attest to the city's one-time status as West Africa's financial capital. The city's factories are out of sight, about ten kilometres east beyond the port.

Some history

Lomé was founded by Ewe people fleeing a tyrant ruler in their homeland of Notsé in the eighteenth century. By the end of the nineteenth century, the Germans had moved the **capital** of their newly declared colony from Aného to Lomé. Reminders of their rule – like the **neo-Gothic cathedral** and the **old wharf** near the Grand Marché – are still visible. Lomé remained the capital of the French protectorate after World War I, but Togo had lost its former importance, and development was minimal compared with other colonies.

Much of the infrastructure of the old part of town dates from the colonial period and has proved inadequate in coping with rapid growth. **Development** has been concentrated elsewhere. The first part of the city to be modernized was the **administrative centre** west of the Grand Marché. Wide tree-lined avenues were laid out here, and the capital's first skyscraper – the **Hôtel du 2 Février** (or *Corinthia Hôtel du 2 Février*, as it's now officially named) – erected. Built in the middle of nowhere, this 37-storey marble-and-glass tower was part of Eyadéma's bid to have the Organization of African Unity's headquarters transferred to Lomé. The plan failed and, despite government PR, the hotel – one of the most luxurious in Africa – was for many years virtually empty for most of the time. Further expensive symbols were built to promulgate the glory of Eyadéma and Togo's entry into the twentieth century – the **Palais de Congrès** (formerly the convention hall of the RPT) and the **ministries** with their gold-tinted glass.

Development of the city's northern and eastern fringes came to a virtual standstill when the troubles started. The Avenue Jean Paul II and the Boulevard Général Eyadéma lead to neighbourhoods that may still have a future of economic activity – if Lomé ever regains its position as a magnet of regional trade. For the moment, however, the Nouveau Marché, the Lomé 2000 conference centre and the new *gare routière* at Agbalepedo and Akodessewa still feel isolated from the city centre.

Arrival

Lomé's **airport** is about 6km northwest of the centre and, although small, is one of the most modern in West Africa and still relatively hassle-free (customs and immigration are thorough, but not intimidating). There's a **bureau de change** (daily 8.30am–8pm) plus a branch of the Union Togolaise de Banque (closed Sun), which changes cash (but not traveller's cheques) at slightly poorer rates. There's also a branch of **Union Tours** (☎226.42.28, ✉uniontour@infrance.fr) who, amongst other services, arrange car rental. There's no airport bus service, so you'll have to rely on taxis; fares to various destinations are posted up outside in the car park – it's around CFA3000 to the town centre. During the day, you can often flag down collective taxis on the main road outside the airport a few hundred metres from the arrivals hall.

Coming in by *taxi brousse*, from **Benin** or **Nigeria**, you're most likely to be deposited at the *gare routière* at **Akodessewa**, about 3km east of the city centre. From here, you can take a shared or private taxi into town, most easily to the **Grand Marché autogare** (sometimes known as **Holando Gare**), right in the middle of things, from where you're within walking distance of a number of hotels (at least if you're not piled down with luggage). This is where vehicles from Aflao and Aného terminate, and some international vehicles from Accra and Cotonou are now also using this *autogare*.

From **Ouagadougou** and **northern Togo**, most vehicles terminate at the *gare routière* in the **Agbalepedo** neighbourhood, a good 10km north of the centre. To get to the centre of Lomé, either hire a cab (around CFA1000) or pile into one of the collective taxis (CFA200–300) which ply between the *gare routière* and the Grand Marché *autogare*. Arriving **from Kpalimé**, you'll wind up (unless your driver continues to the centre) at the large *gare de Kpalimé* just off the route de Kpalimé, about 5km northwest of the central market. Again, there are collective taxis waiting to take you into town.

Security

Crime rates in Lomé rose sharply during the 1990s, and although things have improved over the last few years, certain areas of the city should be avoided. Muggings, some at knifepoint, are common along the beach and bd de la République, whilst the area around the Grand Marché should also be avoided after dark. Walking anywhere at night with valuables is inadvisable.

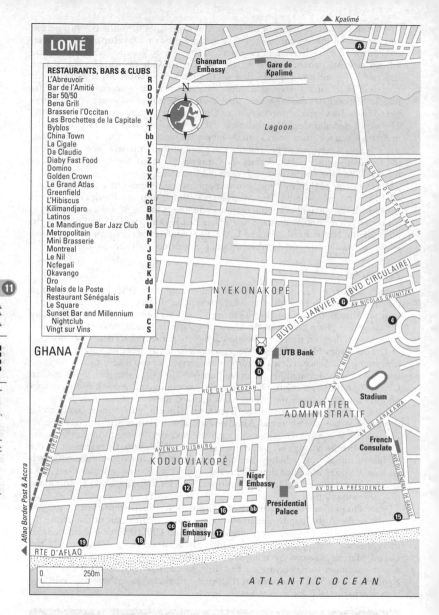

LOMÉ

RESTAURANTS, BARS & CLUBS
L'Abreuvoir	R
Bar de l'Amitié	D
Bar 50/50	O
Bena Grill	Y
Brasserie l'Occitan	W
Les Brochettes de la Capitale	J
Byblos	T
China Town	bb
La Cigale	V
Da Claudio	L
Diaby Fast Food	Z
Domino	Q
Golden Crown	X
Le Grand Atlas	H
Greenfield	A
L'Hibiscus	cc
Kilimandjaro	B
Latinos	M
Le Mandingue Bar Jazz Club	U
Metropolitain	N
Mini Brasserie	P
Montreal	J
Le Nil	G
Ncfegali	E
Okavango	K
Oro	dd
Relais de la Poste	I
Restaurant Sénégalais	F
Le Square	aa
Sunset Bar and Millennium Nightclub	C
Vingt sur Vins	S

GHANA

NYEKONAKOPÉ

QUARTIER ADMINISTRATIF

KODJOVIAKOPÉ

ATLANTIC OCEAN

Orientation

Getting around Lomé isn't difficult if you think of the Grand Marché as the hub from which all the major roads shoot out like spokes. Hotels, restaurants, banks and shops are within walking distance. The big SGGG supermarket (the Société Générale du Golfe du Guinée – pronounced "S-trois-jay"), 500m northwest of the Grand Marché, is also something of a landmark in the town centre.

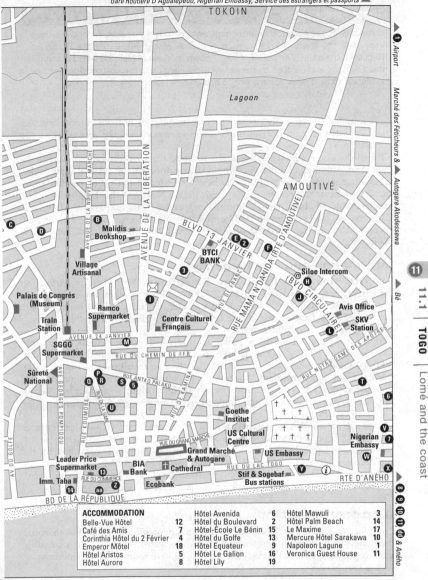

ACCOMMODATION

Belle-Vue Hôtel	12	Hôtel Avenida	6
Café des Amis	7	Hôtel du Boulevard	2
Corinthia Hôtel du 2 Février	4	Hôtel-École Le Bénin	15
Emperor Môtel	18	Hôtel du Golfe	13
Hôtel Aristos	5	Hôtel Equateur	9
Hôtel Aurore	8	Hôtel Le Galion	16
		Hôtel Lily	19

Hôtel Mawuli	3
Hôtel Palm Beach	14
Le Maxime	17
Mercure Hôtel Sarakawa	10
Napoleon Lagune	1
Veronica Guest House	11

The city's residential areas and commercial centres fan out from here in concentric semicircles, the first of which is hemmed in by the **Boulevard 13 Janvier**. Beyond the **Quartier Administratif** and west of this artery, the **Kodjoviakopé** neighbourhood was hardly more than a fishing village thirty years ago and still moves to a slower rhythm than the city centre. Many travellers opt to stay at one of the beachfront hotels here. To the northeast, the **Amoutivé** neighbourhood – the home of the traditional chief of Lomé, a descendant of the

Street names

Lomé has its fair share of street names surplus to requirements. Among the more important, the Boulevard 13 Janvier is almost always known as the Boulevard Circulaire; the route d'Amoutivé is also known as Avenue Mama N'Danida; and the main seafront avenue goes by the names Boulevard de la République, Boulevard de la Marina, route d'Aflao, route d'Aného and *route internationale*.

city's founder – is presently one of the busiest quarters in town. Streets here are more crowded at night than in other neighbourhoods and the area throbs with commerce.

Bé, to the east, is another lively neighbourhood that was formerly a village in its own right. Although it's still a stronghold of **voodooism**, the external signs of the religion are increasingly rare. Flagpoles bearing a white banner in certain homes in the area indicate the presence of a fetish priest. North of **the lagoon**, another semicircle unfolds. Important institutions such as the CHU hospital, the Université du Bénin and the Lycée are situated beyond this natural barrier among the unpaved streets and vacant lots of the essentially residential **Tokoin** district, accessible both via the Atakpamé and the Kpalimé roads.

Information and city transport

The **Direction de la Promotion Touristique** (Mon–Fri 7am–noon & 2.30–5.30pm; ☎221.43.13 or 221.56.62), in a small courtyard off rue du Lac Togo, just east of *Bena Grill*, has a few leaflets on offer, the most helpful being a small booklet entitled *Passport pour le Togo* (available in English and French), featuring tourist highlights across the country.

In the absence of a bus system, public transport in Lomé is in **taxis**, either *taxis collectives* (about CFA200 per short hop), or chartered for a specific journey (about CFA600 for the average hop around town), collective **minibuses** (about CFA100 per short hop), or **zemidjans** "moped taxis", which will take you right to your destination for CFA150. These are especially useful at night, when they're easier to find than taxis, though not all the moped drivers are very good, and you won't be protected by a helmet.

Terminals for *collectives* are scattered around the vicinity of the Grand Marché: those for Kodjoviakopé, Tokoin and Agbalepedo are located west of the market; those for Amoutivé and Lomé 2000 are to the north on Avenue Mama N'Danida; those for Bé and Ablogamé are to the east. *Collectives* run on fairly fixed routes – for example up and down the main radial thoroughfares from the Grand Marché to Boulevard Circulaire, or clockwise around Boulevard 13 Janvier to Bé and back again.

Accommodation

Lomé has dozens of hotels, and although most people head to the **beachfront**, there are plenty of good options away from the seafront as well. The **camping sites**, beyond the port to the east of the centre all have rooms and/or bungalows, as well as tent pitches.

Budget

Café des Amis 26 rue des Mauve, off bd 13 Janvier ☎221.06.18, ⓔcocozza23@hotmail.com. This small pizzeria has some well-kept, self-contained rooms (fan or a/c), all spotlessly clean and attractively furnished. ❷

Emperor Môtel 635 rte d'Aflao, Kodjoviakopé ☎222.13.14. Grubby but cheap rooms (some with

a/c) set on a busy road near the border, with pleasant sea breezes. ❶

Hôtel Aurore 90 rue du Lac Togo, behind *Krimas Hôtel* on the rte de Aného ☎ & ⓕ221.05.17. Spacious and spotless rooms, and there's a pretty garden out back. ❷

Hôtel du Boulevard bd 13 Janvier, just west of av Mama N'Danida ☎221.15.91. A bit run-down, but still quite comfortable and friendly. Rooms are basic but clean, and there are great views from the roof. ❶

Hôtel Le Galion rue des Camomilles, off rte d'Aflao, Kodjoviakopé ☎222.00.30, ⓔhotel.galion@cafe.tg. Popular option, with stylish design, attentive staff and spacious, immaculate rooms in a refurbished home with a landscaped courtyard. Excellent value. ❷

Hôtel Lily rte d'Aflao ☎222.14.36. Lively hotel on the seafront. The self-contained rooms (fan or a/c) are clean but very bare, and can get noisy thanks to the lively bar downstairs. ❷

Hôtel Mawuli 21 rue Maoussas northeast of the main post office ☎222.12.75. Bright, pink building, with simple but well-maintained rooms and a friendly, homely atmosphere within the small courtyard. ❷

Le Maxime rte d'Aflao, near bd 13 Janvier ☎221.74.48. Homely, French-run hotel and restaurant near the beach, with bright, comfortable rooms (with fan or a/c), some of which have small balconies. The restaurant is very popular, and serves good – but expensive – European food. ❸

Moderate

Belle-Vue Hôtel (formerly the *Hotel California*) Kodjoviakopé, behind the German embassy ☎949.27.27. Set on a quiet road near the beach, with fine views from the balcony, this spotless, recently restored hotel offers rooms with a/c, TV, fridge and plentiful hot water. ❸

Hôtel Avenida 30 rue d'Almeida, just off bd 13 Janvier ☎221.46.72, ⓔavenida@cafe.tg. Large hotel in a good position. It's not particularly stylish, but the staff are friendly and the rooms (with a/c) are good value, with TV and IDD phone. ❸

Hôtel-École Le Bénin On the seafront, corner of av du Général de Gaulle ☎221.24.85, Ⓕ221.61.25. This training hotel is now looking a bit tatty round the edges, though it still offers a good atmosphere, location and competitive prices, and promised renovations should smarten things up. ❺

Hôtel Equateur 102 rue Litimé, off bd 13 Janvier ☎221.99.92. A gem of a place, with tasteful decor, a peaceful atmosphere and an attractive first-floor restaurant. Rooms come with fan or a/c, TV and hot water. ❸

Hôtel du Golfe rue du Commerce ☎221.02.78, Ⓕ221.49.03. Set in an extremely central location, this older establishment has seen better days. The more expensive rooms (❹) have a/c and phones (some also have TV), and there's a cheaper block with rooms with fan (❸).

Napoleon Lagune 3km northeast of the centre, off bd de l'Oti ☎227.56.66, ⓦwww.woezon.com /napotogo. Set on the banks of the lagoon, the rooms here are stylish, clean and excellent value for money, and there's a small pool. ❺

Expensive

Corinthia Hôtel du 2 Février Place de l'Indépendance ☎221.00.03, ⓔcorinthia_hotel2fevrier@yahoo.fr. This glitzy landmark skyscaper is the country's most expensive hotel, with stylish rooms with all mod-cons, plus a pool, tennis courts, several restaurants and a nightclub. The views from the upper floors are fantastic. ❽

Hôtel Aristos rue Aniko Palako, near *Vingt sur Vins* ☎222.97.20, ⓔharistos@ub.tg. Quiet, despite the central location, and with modern, attractive rooms – good value for creature comforts without chain-hotel sterility. ❻

Hôtel Palm Beach 1 bd de la République, corner of rue Koumore ☎221.85.11, Ⓕ221.87.11. High-rise hotel overlooking the beach. The swanky, comfortable rooms come with all mod-cons, and there's also a pool, nightclub and casino. ❽

Mercure Hôtel Sarakawa 3km east of the centre ☎227.65.90, ⓔH2102@accor-hotels.com. Arguably the best of the top-end hotels, set in 25 acres of tropical gardens, with a fabulous 50m pool, three tennis courts and horse-riding facilities. Rooms are luxurious and stylish, with IDD phone, satellite TV, and hot water. ❽

Veronica Guest House bd du Mono, just off rte de Aného ☎222.69.07 or 222.96.98, ⓔveronicagh@bibway.com. New, international-standard hotel. The rooms are beautifully tiled and tastefully decorated, and come with phone, fridge, hot water and a/c. It's tiny and very popular – best to book in advance. ❻

Camping

There are three beaches near Lomé where you can camp; **rates** are around CFA1000 per person at all three, and they also have rooms. Unfortunately, the immediate vicinities of the beach camping sites are now notorious for armed **robbery**. Take precautions if you're carrying valuables and be especially careful after dark. If you don't have your own transport, collective taxis can get you out to the campsites for about CFA300.

Chez Alice 14km east of the centre near the village of Baguida, 300m from a dirty beach ☎227.91.72, ©chezalicetogo@hotmail.com. Something of a roadside holiday camp, with rooms (❶–❷) of varying standards, as well as tent pitches. The good restaurant and bar make this a favourite overlanders' haunt, and the live music every Wednesday (8pm) is a big added draw.

Le Ramatou 10km east of the centre ☎227.43.53, ℱ222.02.72. This place is OK, but nothing special, with rather ugly views of the port and a general sense of dilapidation. As well as tent pitches, there are also some rooms with fan or a/c, plus a fairly expensive restaurant. ❷–❸

Robinson Plage 10km east of the centre, next to *Le Ramatou* ☎947.00.17. Lomé's nicest camping options, with tent pitches plus self-contained rooms (fan or a/c) and a good but expensive seafood restaurant, though some people are less than impressed by the service and the squalid mini-zoo attached to the site. ❷–❹

The City

Lomé has few specific sights, but there's plenty to take in as you wander through town. At some stage in your stay, try and have a look at the **Hôtel du 2 Février**, built to commemorate the president's miraculous escape and "Triumphal Return" after his plane crashed near Sarakawa. On clear days, you get a splendid panoramic view of Lomé, Ghana and the coastline from the top-floor restaurant and bar, though even a small drink costs a packet.

If you're looking for a **beach** to lie on in town, you're limited to the stretch of shore in front of *Hôtel-Ecole Le Bénin*, although it's dirty and prone to crime, while the sea has a fearfully strong undertow. Out of town past the port, *Robinson Plage* draws a large weekend crowd, and the fact that it's a private beach means it's safer, although again the sand and sea are not particularly inviting. The best place to try is the *Lomé-Rivage* resort, about 1km past the *Mercure Hôtel Sarakawa* (see p.845), on a dirt track off the roundabout. The private beach here offers the best swimming, and there are body-boards to hire as well.

The Grand Marché

The focal point of the city, the **Grand Marché**, takes up a full city block near the ocean. Business here has picked up considerably after the strikes of the early 1990s, and though the market is not the regional draw it once was, there's a wide range of goods – this is about the only place you need to go for provisions, presents, or purchases of any kind whilst in the city. Commerce spills over into all the surrounding streets as traders (mostly girls and women between the ages of 3 and 103) zigzag through the crowd to hawk everything from rat poison to greeting cards.

The **ground floor** of the unattractive market building is filled with a mish-mash of cosmetics, bags, clothes and food – canned food, fruit and vegetables, meat, poultry, fish and staples like yams, rice, cassava and pasta, spices and peanut butter. Sellers have a flare for display, and fruit and vegetables are invariably arranged in eye-catching pyramids. Quality is generally high, though if you're cooking it's best to buy meat first thing in the morning, for obvious reasons.

Up on the **first floor**, the celebrated, and extravagantly proportioned, **"Nana Benz"** (which, roughly translated, means "Mercedes Mamas", a reference to the cars they often drive) lounge around fanning themselves in a decadent style befitting their reputation as some of the richest and most adept businesspeople in Africa. They monopolize the sale of **cloth** and journey as far as Europe and Saudi Arabia to assure a stock that attracts buyers from the whole region. "Made in Holland" Dutch wax prints are their most expensive and prestigious wares, but you'll also find English and African prints, hand-woven *kente* cloth from Ghana, Ewe strip cloth, naturally dyed indigo wraps from Guinea and Mali, and rough cotton weaves from the Sahel.

Generally you'll have to buy in relatively large quantities here (the rue du Commerce is the place for single cloths), though after recent lean years the Mamas have begun to make exceptions. Material is traditionally sold by *la pièce*, *une pièce* being six *pagnes*, and a *pagne* roughly equal to an arms' spread – or about 1.8m, the length of a wrap. The smallest length you can traditionally buy in the market is a *demi-pièce* or three *pagnes'* worth, the cost of which varies according to the method and place of manufacture. Prices are marked and, although you may be able to get the vendor to come down slightly, bargaining never gets you very far.

The **second floor** at the top is a hodgepodge emporium of goods – everything from bicycle tyres to wigs, envelopes and Chinese enamel basins to plastic dolls (white as well as black). Mountains of cosmetics – lotions, shampoos, make-up – swamp an entire section.

Handicraft markets

Crafts from all over West Africa filter into Lomé and there are several locations in town to look for them. The main venue is the **Rue des Sculpteurs**, a small alley next to the *Hôtel du Golfe*, where you'll find a large selection of carvings, batiks, sculpture and other handicrafts. The majority come from Nigeria, Cameroon, Ghana and even Kenya; there's little in the way of typically Togolese art. Beware of "antiques", which almost never are. Prices are steep and the pressure to buy can be unpleasant, but the urgency of the vendors gradually gives way to something more bearable if you hang on for a few minutes, especially if you make a purchase, even of something small.

You can pick up comfortable and sturdy handmade **sandals** on the streetside near the cathedral on Avenue de la Libération. The kind with the cushioned soles and toe loop go for about CFA3000 and are worth every franc. On the same street, you'll also find **cloth**; you can easily buy short lengths of one or two *pagnes* here.

Look out for the brilliantly patterned **blankets** – mainly from Mali and Niger, sold on rue Koumore, just north of Immeuble TABA. These are handmade and expensive, but patient bargaining gets results. Something big enough to cover a double bed or look huge and striking on a wall should ultimately cost somewhere between CFA20,000 and CFA30,000, though price is determined to some extent by the state of the market, the time of year and the number of profligate punters in town.

The friendly and hassle-free **Village Artisanal** (Mon–Sat 7am-5.30pm), on Avenue de la Nouvelle Marché, 400m north of Ramco Supermarket, is well worth a visit. You can watch local craftsmen creating batik, wood sculptures, pottery, jewellery, sandals and baskets – you could even have an outfit made to order. Work is of a high standard, and prices are reasonable.

The Musée National

The **Musée National** (Mon–Fri 8am–noon & 2.30–5.30pm, Sat 9am–3pm; CFA1000) has been relegated to a small room in the Palais de Congrès (formerly the party headquarters) for over a decade, and the pickings are decidedly slim. Musical instruments and religious objects (statues, masks and ceremonial dress) give the merest glimpse into the material cultures of various ethnic groups such as the Kabyé, Mina and Ewe. One room is dedicated to the colonial period, tracing it from Nachtigal's landing in 1884, through the division of Togoland between the French and British in 1914, and ploddingly on to independence, with a succession of pictures of moustachioed governors puffing out their bemedalled chests.

Akodessewa fetish market

The **Marché des Féticheurs** at Akodessewa is a popular draw for visitors and Loméans alike, despite being some 8km from the city centre. West Africa's largest fetish market, it has myriad stalls displaying animal skulls, rotting bird carcases, statues, bells, powders and all the imaginable and unimaginable ingredients of **traditional medicine and religion**. Though fetishers won't hesitate to make a quick sell, at times giving the feeling of a fleecing operation, it's a serious profession, still handed down jealously from generation to generation. The reputation of the Togolese for their spiritual gifts is widespread. The powers of the *féticheurs* are sought after by all classes, while the reputation of Akodessewa attracts people from all over West Africa, and from as far away as Gabon and Congo. In Togo, the overwhelming majority still practises traditional ("animist") religions, and even the Christian and Muslim minorities commonly incorporate traditional practices into their beliefs. A little time spent here listening to tales of supernatural healing and therapy will sow seeds of doubt in the most rational mind.

Guides will pounce on you the moment you approach and demand very expensive entrance fees – CFA15,000 for a tour with video camera, CFA10,000 for a still camera and CFA5000 just to visit the market, with a guide to explain its "secrets". If you just want to browse (no photos or guide), you may be able to pay a reduced amount – but only after a lot of haggling. You'll find disarmingly inexpensive talismans to ensure safe travel or success in love, as well as more ghoulish items like scorpions and dead snakes, which are used to make potions for ailments such as arthritis and rheumatism.

There are two ways of **getting to the market**. The first is to head out on the Nouvelle rue de Bé or the rue Notre Dame des Apôtres, which converge by the old **Forêt Sacré** ("Sacred Forest", on the left) and pass the former site of the fetish market at Bé. The forest is a remarkable little jungle, surrounded by buildings, but out of bounds to non-believers. Alternatively, you can go the more boring way, by taking the route d'Aného along the coast, past the *Hôtel Sarakawa*. At the *rond-point du port*, 6km from central Lomé, turn left and follow the paved road for a kilometre and a half. If you're getting to Akodessewa by private taxi, expect to pay over the odds for the distance. A *zemidjan* all the way there shouldn't cost you more than CFA400–500.

Eating

Lomé has an excellent choice of **restaurants**, including a particular abundance of expensive (mainly French) establishments – all the big hotels serve French cuisine at elevated prices. There's also a decent selection of cheap places, while cheap **street food** can be found – during the day only – mainly around the different markets in town. At the Grand Marché, women serve delicious salads from stands directly opposite the taxi park. They'll throw anything that strikes your fancy onto the bed of lettuce – tomatoes, macaroni, avocados, even grilled chicken or Guinea fowl – and top it off with a tangy vinegar sauce. It's an excellent meal, so long as your system is acclimatized. Behind these stalls, women sell *fufu*, or *akoumé* (fermented white corn mash) with different sauces and meat (beef, goat, chicken). Similar food can be found in the Amoutivé and Bé markets.

At **breakfast**, keep your eye out for *les caféman*, scattered about town, who serve cheap omelettes with Nescafé and bread.

Budget

Bar de l'Amitié Off bd 13 Janvier near *Sunset*. Local, inexpensive food with no pretentions – choose from four or five gigantic pots of sauce with fish or meat and rice. Very popular at lunchtimes.

Les Brochettes de la Capitale bd 13 Janvier. A local institution, this place has huge barbecues which turn out an endless supply of juicy meat kebabs in crusty bagettes. You can eat at tables on the sand under the stars, though you'll struggle to find a seat at weekends.

Diaby Fast Food rue de la Gare, across from the BIA bank. Centrally located, serving sandwiches,

burgers and snacks in an indoor café.

Le Grand Atlas bd 13 Janvier, across from *Les Brochettes de la Capitale*. Tiny café serving superb fruit juices, milkshakes and snacks such as burgers, omelettes and chips.

Metropolitain bd 13 Janvier, next to *Bar 50/50*. Looks like a bar-cum-kiosk from the road, but behind there's a small outdoor seating area where you can tuck into inexpensive dishes like rice and sauce or spaghetti.

Ncfegali 229 bd 13 Janvier. Delicious fresh African cuisine served in a relaxed and friendly atmosphere.

Restaurant Sénégalais rue du Commerce. This basic restaurant with blaring TV serves up healthy portions of spaghetti, couscous and salad with a few Senegalese specialities.

Moderate

Bena Grill (formerly the *Marox Restaurant*) 24 rue du Lac Togo ☎222.41.38. German-run place which does a big trade in sausages and meat dishes with fries and salads (from around CFA2500). There's always a crowd in – mainly expat and showy Togolese.

Le Galion At *Hôtel Le Galion*, off bd de la République. Good food at moderate prices, including pasta, fish and some Vietnamese specialities, and there's live music on the terrace Wednesday to Saturday evenings.

Kilimandjaro bd 13 Janvier, near av de la Nouvelle Marché. Excellent restaurant serving authentic Spanish specialities, including excellent tapas (CFA1000 each).

Montreal 211 bd 13 Janvier. Flash new bar-restaurant with three TVs. It's great for snacks salads, burgers and sandwiches, all for under CFA2400 – and reasonably cheap draught beer. Daily from 6pm.

Relais de la Poste av de la Libération. Despite the dismal decor, this long-established place has a lively and friendly atmosphere and an excellent reputation for first-rate French food at reasonable prices – the chocolate mousse is something else.

Expensive

Brasserie l'Occitan 220 bd 13 Janvier, near rte d'Aného ☎221.42.75. Classy new brasserie-style restaurant with excellent French cuisine, plus Senegalese and Togolese specialities, prepared by a chef from Toulouse. Closed Sunday.

China Town bd 13 Janvier, near bd de la République. Friendly and unpretentious Chinese restaurant – though not the smartest place in town. Mains with rice from CFA4500.

La Cigale bd 13 Janvier, 250m north of bd de la République ☎221.99.30. Lavish set-up with European dishes from CFA4000 to CFA10,000, plus pizzas. Also does take-aways.

Da Claudio 298 bd 13 Janvier ☎904.03.37. Formal and expensive Italian dining with mains from around CFA4000; you're guaranteed a good atmosphere, and the small dining room is often packed out. Evenings only; closed Wednesday.

Golden Crown bd du Mono, around the corner of bd 13 Janvier and route d'Aného. First-class Chinese–Vietnamese restaurant with wonderful dishes, mains from CFA4000.

Greenfield rue Akati, just east of the rte de Kpalimé. Set in a leafy courtyard, complete with wacky decor, where the chef slaps pizzas together and the overworked waitresses try to cope with hordes of customers. Special nights include DVD films on Tuesdays, candlelight meals on Fridays, and occasional live jazz music at weekends.

L'Hibiscus Kodjoviakopé, behind the German embassy ☎222.74.99. Set in an extension of the owner's beautiful home, this new, small French restaurant already has a solid reputation for excellent food and service.

Okavango bd 13 Janvier, next to the post office ☎221.05.78. Expensive French cuisine. Choose between outdoor seating in a lovely garden courtyard, complete with tame antelope, or the stylish a/c restaurant inside.

Le Square Just off bd de la République near *Hôtel du Golfe* ☎222.02.20. Smart, but not too pretentious, French restaurant with main courses for around CFA5000. Evenings only; closed Sundays.

Vingt sur Vins rue Aniko Palako ☎221.08.82. Cosy, Canadian-owned restaurant with a variety of European cuisines; mains cost around CFA5000. Closed Sundays.

Nightlife

Nightlife has picked up considerably since the early 1990s, when people tended to keep indoors after dark, but sections of town are still considered dangerous when the sun goes down, notably anywhere along the beach road or around the Grand Marché. There's a range of **discos**, running the gamut from popular spots where you pay no entrance and drinks are hardly more expensive than in daytime bars, to flashy joints with complicated light shows and DJs.

If you're after **live music**, *Chez Alice* (see p.846) hosts live traditional African music and dance on Wednesdays from 8pm.

Bars, clubs and discos

The area at the northern end of rue de la Gare is often referred to as the **Bermuda Triangle**, marked by three of the oldest and most notorious night haunts –

Domino, *Mini-Brasserie* and *L'Abreuvoir*. Locals say that once you enter you can easily become disoriented and led astray.

L'Abreuvoir rue de la Gare, near SGGG. Lively bar, popular with travellers, with European and African music.

Bar 50/50 Popular choice, not too touristy, and a good place to kick the evening off.

Byblos bd 13 Janvier, near *De Claudio*. Playing mainly African music, this club has a good atmosphere and is popular with the wealthy Togolese youth, though entrance is expensive (CFA5000) and drinks are pricey.

Domino rue de la Gare, opposite *L'Abreuvoir*. Popular, dimly lit and very seedy nightspot which hots up after 11pm. Expensive drinks.

Latinos av 24 Janvier near av de la Libération. Classy bar, which gets lively after 10pm, when dancing takes over.

Le Mandingue Bar Jazz Club 8 rue Koketi, just off rue de la Gare. Top-quality live music from Wednesday to Sunday (from 9pm & 7pm on Sundays). Mostly jazz, but with good blues and rock 'n' roll as well. No cover, but pricey drinks. There's a happy "hour" for the whole of Wednesday night.

Mini Brasserie 42 rue de la Gare. Longstanding and popular Western-style bar, with slot machines and red leather stools.

Le Nil av Nicolas Grunitzky, just off bd 13 Janvier. Smart new club (CFA4000 cover) with Arab-style decor, playing variety of music including African, Arabic and European tunes, plus live jazz on Fridays. Open Tues–Sun from 10pm.

Oro rue de Litime, east of bd 13 Janvier. French-owned club playing a variety of African and European music. CFA3500 cover; open from 10pm; closed Tuesday.

Privilège At the *Hôtel Palm Beach*. No longer the place to be seen, but still popular on Friday and Saturday nights (cover CFA3000).

Sunset Bar and Millennium Nightclub bd 13 Janvier, corner with rte de Kpalimé. Not the most sophisticated of set-ups, but a range of people come here for the table football, pool and slot machines, and the varied music in the dingy adjoining club.

Listings

Airline offices Air Burkina, rue de la Gare, ☏220.00.83; Air France, Immeuble TABA, 2 rue du Commerce ☏221.69.10, ℱ222.01.78; Air Gabon, Immeuble TABA, 2 rue du Commerce ☏221.05.73; Air Togo, Immeuble TABA, 2 rue de Commerce ☏220.01.03; Alitalia, c/o Equinox Holiday Club, rue du Grand Marché ☏222.01.08; Ethiopian Airlines, Immeuble TABA, 2 rue du Commerce ☏221.56.91; Ghana Airways, Immeuble TABA, 2 rue de Commerce ☏221.56.91; Trans Air Benin, at the airport ☏226.17.95.

American Express No official representation.

Banks Ecobank (Mon–Fri 7.45am–4pm, Sat 9am–2pm), 20 rue du Commerce, change cash and traveller's cheques with no commission. BIA, on the corner of rue du Commerce and rue de la Gare (Mon–Fri 7.30–11.30am & 2.30–4pm), changes cash and traveller's cheques, providing you can show proof of purchase; UTB, bd 13 Janvier (Mon–Fri 7.45–11.30am & 2.45–4.30pm) change cash and traveller's cheques, but service is very slow. BTCI, bd 13 Janvier (Mon–Fri 7.30–11.30am & 2.30–4.30pm), give cash advances on Visa.

Books and magazines You'll sometimes find *Time*, *Newsweek* and even *West Africa* magazine hawked around town. Malidis bookshop, off av de la Libération, has a good selection of books and

foreign newspapers, occasionally in English. Librairie Bon Pasteur, on the corner of rue du Commerce and av de la Libération, has a wide selection of French papers and mags plus fiction and non-fiction. For secondhand books in English, try the hawkers along the rue du Commerce.

Car rental Union Tours, at the airport (☏226.42.28, ℯuniontour@infrnace.fr), charge around CFA35,000 for a day's car rental for around Lomé, including driver. Alternatively try Elite Car, bd 13 Janvier (☏221.44.79, ℱ222.05.00); Avis, 252 bd 13 Janvier (☏221.05.82, ℱ221.17.36), who can arrange to have a car waiting for you at the airport; or *Hotel Napoleon II*, which also rents out vehicles.

Clinics and hospitals Lomé's main hospital is the Centre Hospitalier Universitaire (☏225.47.39), in the north of town in Tokoin. Alternatively, try the Clinique de l'Union in Nyekonakpoe.

Embassies and honorary consulates Democratic Republic of Congo, 325 bd 13 Janvier ☏221.42.33; France (Consulate), rue Charles de Gaulle ☏221.81.94; Gabon, Tokoin Super-Taco ☏226.75.63, ℱ226.75.61; Ghana, Tokoin-Kondomé ☏221.31.94; Niger, rue de Dahlias, Kodjoviakopé ☏222.43.31; Nigeria, av Eyedéma, ☏221.34.55; UK, Honorary Consul, Mrs J.A. Sayer, British School, Cité du Bénin ☏226.46.06,

ⓕ221.49.89; USA, 15 rue Kouenou ⓣ221.29.91; ⓕ221.79.52.

Emergencies Police ⓣ171 or 117; fire service ⓣ118.

Gym Power Star Gym, bd 13 Janvier (ⓣ905.69.30), has a good range of equipment and charges CFA2500 per day.

Internet access Cyber Montreal, bd 13 Janvier, next to *Brochettes de la Capitale* (Mon–Sat noon–1am), has fast service in a quiet environment, whilst across the road is Siloe Intercom (closed Sundays). Both places charge CFA500 per hour.

Libraries and cultural centres The American Cultural Center at the corner of rue Caventou and rue Vauban has a free library with American magazines and papers (Mon–Fri 9am–12.30pm & 3–6pm, Sat 9am–noon), ABC TV news and free movies every Friday afternoon at 3pm and 6pm respectively. The Centre Culturel Français on rue 24 Janvier is the most active of the cultural centres with theatre, dance, music, library and videos. The German equivalent, the Goethe Institut, hosts shows and events.

Maps Direction de la Cartographie Nationale, inside the Ministère des Travaux Publiques (ⓣ221.03.57). In theory, survey maps of the whole country at 1:50,000 and 1:200,000 are available.

Mechanics Garage Turbo on rue de la Kozoh, Kodjoviakopé (ⓣ222.16.02), offers a professional and reliable service.

Pharmacies For information on pharmacies which are open out of hours (*pharmacies de garde*), ring ⓣ242.

Phones There's a telephone and fax service behind the PTT. Calls can also be made from major hotels (more costly), communication centres, and from an increasing number of phone boxes.

Photos and film For passport photos, Photoland in Immeuble TABA charges CFA1500 for a one-hour service. Magic Photo, rue du Commerce, offers more expensive one-hour development and on-the-spot passport photos.

Post office The main PTT (Mon–Fri 7am–5.30pm, Sat 8am–noon) is on av de la Libération. Stamps for letters cost CFA450 for Europe, CFA500 for the US and Australia. Poste restante is helpful and reliable.

Supermarkets The best stocked are SGGG, which has several stores at the corner of rue Koumore and rue de la Gare; Leader Price, on rue du Commerce; and Ramco, on av de la Nouveau Marché.

Swimming pools The best pool by far is at the *Mercure Hôtel Sarakawa* (CFA3000 for non-guests); the *Corinthia Hôtel du 2 Février* is equally expensive, but not as good.

Travel agents Amongst the more reliable operators are: Togo Voyages, 13 rue du Grand Marché (ⓣ221.12.77); Ocean Travel, Immeuble TABA (ⓣ221.65.30), who mainly deal with flights; and Union Tours, based at the airport (ⓣ226.42.28, ⓔuniontour@infrance.fr), who arrange both flights and tours.

Visa extension The chaotic Service des Etrangers et Passports (7.30am–noon & 2.30–6pm; ⓣ250.78.56) is based at the Ministère de la Défense Nationale, some 10km from the centre and adjacent to the enormous GTA building (most taxi drivers will know this landmark). Extensions are free (apart from a small fee for the form) and take at least 48 hours to process. You'll need three passport photos.

Moving on from Lomé

The main **gare routière** is in **Agbalepedo** district, 10km north of the centre; this handles northbound traffic to Atakpamé, Sokodé, Kara, Dapaong and Ouagadougou. For Kpalimé and towns along the Kpalimé road, head to the gare de Kpalimé in the **Kondomé** neighbourhood, about 5km from the centre off the route de Kpalimé. Most taxis for Aflao, Aného, Cotonou and Lagos depart from the old **downtown** *gare routière* near the Grand Marché, but the *nouvel autogare* at **Akodessewa** also handles transport on the coastal routes, including direct taxis to Accra, Cotonou and Lagos.

A good **bus** service is provided by STIF (ⓣ221.38.48), which has a station on bd de la République, about 400m west of the junction with bd 13 Janvier. They have a daily service to Abidjan (CFA17,000) and Accra (CFA4000) departing at 4pm, and a daily service to Cotonou (CFA3000) at 8.30am. The Burkinabe company SOGEBAF uses the same station, and has once-weekly service to Bamako (CFA26,000) in Mali via Ouagadougou (CFA13,000) and Bobo-Dioulasso (CFA18,000) in Burkina. Alternatively, SKV buses depart from their station on bd 13 Janvier for Ouagadougou (CFA12,500, or CFA15,000 for a/c).

East of Lomé

The short drive from Lomé to the Benin border passes along the coastal highway, with alternating views of the Atlantic and **Lac Togo**, a large, bilharzia-free lake which provides a scenic retreat from the city and has become a popular weekend destination thanks to its sandy shores and clean water for swimming and watersports. The villages along this stretch are peopled by Mina and Gun (or Guin), who migrated from Ghana at the beginning of the nineteenth century. Today, they make their living principally from fishing, coconut planting and small-scale cultivation.

On the lake's south shore, the village of **Agbodrafo** has an excellent range of hotels and is where you're most likely to stay. It's also the departure point for *pirogues* to the town of **Togoville** on the northern bank of the lake, interesting both for its history and voodoo shrines, though it's disappointingly touristy. Further east along the coastal highway is the crumbling former colonial capital of **Aného**, whilst the nearby village of **Glidji** has a variety of interesting fetish shrines and hosts the annual Yékéyéké festival.

Agbodrafo

Only 30km from Lomé, **AGBODRAFO** was formerly known by its Portuguese name, Porto Seguro, and was the site of a small coastal fort similar to those in Ghana. It's now ruled by one **Apeto Eneke Assiakoley V**, who keeps the royal sceptres, thrones and weapons that have symbolized his family's authority in the region for 150 years. There's a number of **accommodation** options in the village, although little choice if you're on a tight budget. Right on the lakeshore, the *Hôtel Le Lac* (☎331.60.19, ℻331.60.09; ⑥) is the most expensive and luxurious, with comfortable self-contained a/c rooms with satellite TV, as well as a pool (CFA2000 for non-guests) and jet skis for hire on the private beach. Not far away and next to the main jetty for *pirogue* rides, the *Hôtel Swiss Castel* (☎904.15.08; ②) is a step or two down, with slightly shabby rooms (fan or a/c) set around an attractive courtyard. A hidden gem is the Swiss-owned *Hôtel Safari* (☎902.65.13; ②), set 1km from the lake and only 300m from the sea. The excellent-value, stylish rooms (some with a/c) are built around a beautiful courtyard, and there's a good restaurant as well. Just around the corner, you can't miss the *Maison Blanche* (☎331.60.14; ⑤), an incredibly grandiose building with ten stylish and comfortable self-contained rooms with hot water and an enormous restaurant. Finally, about 3km along the road to Lomé, a track to the right leads to the *Auberge du Lac* (☎904.72.29, ✉auberge-du-lac@hotmail.com; ②), which offers thatched, self-contained bungalows in idyllic surroundings on the sandy lakeshore; it also has windsurfers and sailing dinghies for hire.

Pirogues ply regularly between Agbodrafo and **Togoville**, leaving from a lagoon landing about 100m from the highway near the *Hôtel Swiss Castel*. You can rent a *pirogue* by negotiating a fare for the round trip (aim for about CFA2000 per person) and arranging to be picked up in Togoville at a specified time. Alternatively, you can simply wait for the boat to fill up with market women, though you'll have a hard time convincing the *piroguier* to take you for the normal collective fare, and you may have a lot of hanging around on both shores. The simplest option is to visit the *Hôtel Le Lac*, who can organize a *pirogue* for around CFA2500 for the return trip.

Togoville

Once you dock in **TOGOVILLE**, you will no doubt be approached by one of the semi-obligatory **guides** who wait on the shore. They may claim to be from the Association de Jeune de Togoville Tourism, and try to charge an obligatory fixed fee of around CFA2500 per person for a tour of the town. However, until the organization is formalized and an official fee and ticket established, you can refuse their demands. If you want a guide, it's best to agree a price up front; if not, you should be able to eventually shake them off.

It was in Togoville that the treaty was agreed which made the Germans protectors of the region (at which time the town was known simply as Togo). The contract signed by **Mlapa**, the chief of this tiny village, was the basis on which the colonial government laid claim to all of present-day Togo and part of Ghana. In the past it was necessary to visit the **village chief**, who was thought to be a direct descendant of Mlapa, although the last chief of Togoville, Mlapa V, was de-stooled in 2001 due to a political disagreement with the government and now lives in exile in Europe. (There's also currently an ongoing dispute between two families in the village, with each claiming to be rightful heirs to the chieftancy.) Despite this, you can still visit the **Maison Royale**, where you'll be shown memorabilia, including old photographs and copies of the famous document signed with the Germans. You'll also be asked to sign the scruffy notebook labelled "Livre d'Or", and a small gift is expected at this point.

Wandering around town, you'll easily spot the imposing **Catholic cathedral**, near the lakeside, which was built in 1910 by the Germans. Notice the interior murals of African martyrs being burned at the stake, and a shrine to the Virgin, who was allegedly seen walking on the lake in the early 1970s. This miracle reportedly inspired the 1985 visit of Pope Jean Paul II to Togoville – he stayed in the *Hôtel Le Lac* in Agbodrafo before arriving by *pirogue* at a specially constructed jetty in town. Celebrations are still held every year on November 7 to commemorate the Virgin's appearance. Despite the work of the Catholic church, Togoville remains essentially animist. Walking through the narrow backstreets, you'll be shown several fetishes, including two **fertility shrines** – one of a formidably endowed man and the other of a well-rounded woman with spikes protruding from her body. Photographs are permitted provided you leave a small offering. Beyond the small market, on the north side of town, a modern **statue** marks the centenary of the Germano-Togolese treaty, celebrated in 1984. Set under a thatched roof between the main jetty and the cathedral, the **Centre Adanu Cooperative d'Art et d'Artisanat**, has a limited choice of wooden carvings and other crafts for sale.

There's excellent **accommodation** at the *Hôtel Nachtigal* (⊕333.70.76; ❷), near the market, which offers spotless, tiled rooms and has a pool and tennis court. The only other option in town are the ultra-basic rooms with bucket showers at the *Auberge QG* (⊕905.25.30; ❶). If you don't fancy the *pirogue* ride, or want to avoid the would-be guides who wait at the jetty, you can reach Togoville by **taxi** from Aného, a 30-minute drive along a dirt road. If you're planning to take a *pirogue* back to Agbradrafo, be warned that you'll be quoted extortionate prices for the one-way trip.

Aného

Of all Togo's towns, the colonial presence is most strongly and most eerily felt in **ANÉHO**, 10km from Agbodrafo and only 2km from the border with Benin. The Portuguese were the first to come to the spot – a pleasing natural setting with sea and lagoon vistas – which soon developed as a major slave market. Current African family names like de Souza and the light skin of the people are surprising reminders of this "Brazilian" period, further reflected in the history and culture of Ouidah in Benin (see p.913).

Many buildings bear witness to the days when "Anecho" was the capital of Kaiser Wilhelm's prize African possession, among them the **Peter and Paul Church** (1898), close to being washed away by the ocean, the thick-walled **préfecture** near the bridge, the interesting **German cemetery**, and the finely restored **Protestant church** (1895) on the route de Lomé. Other buildings offer a reminder of the French presence, including a number of grandiose

villas used by colonial administrators when Aného was capital of the protectorate.

Aného has been in a slow decline for decades. Walking the streets, there's a feeling
that residents are too entrapped in their daily routines of farming, fishing and trade
to have any illusions of grandeur – or much opportunity to bring the old town to
life. It's a small community, completely overshadowed by Lomé, all of which is a
source of frustration for the young, most of whom migrate to the capital to seek
their fortunes. But they leave Aného a satisfyingly moody place for travellers. The
main **market** is on Tuesday, and has a small fetish selection featuring monkey
heads, crabs (dead and alive) and various skulls.

In contrast to the crumbling reminders of European occupation, Aného's **voodoo
culture** thrives. Fetish priests are highly respected members of the community and
are often more trusted than doctors practising Western medicine. Sacrifices are
offered to shrines guarding many of the homes, and regular festivals are dedicated to
the cult. For some background on "voodooism" and the *vodu*, see the box on p.914
in the Benin chapter.

Practicalities

It isn't hard to find your way around Aného since virtually the whole of the town
stretches along the **route de Lomé/Cotonou**. The market, post office, bank, *préfecture* and most shops can be found along this street between the Protestant church
and the bridge. Across the bridge in the east of town lies a more residential neighbourhood which is home to the *autogare* and some of the town's **hotels**. The
cheapest place to stay is the friendly and reasonably comfortable *Auberge Elmina*
(℡949.02.94; ❷), on the seafront about 80m east of the Peter and Paul Church.
Sandwiched between the lagoon and the main road, just east of the bridge, is
L'Oasis (℡331.01.25, ✉oasisaneh@hotmail.com; ❷), which has somewhat dated
self-contained rooms with fans or a/c, and the best views of the sea and lagoon in
town. Even if you don't stay, have a drink at the thatched terrace restaurant and
watch the fishermen cast their nets into the shallow lagoon waters. More upmarket
is the *Môtel le Relais de l'Union*, not far from the *autogare*, with slightly overpriced
but spotless self-contained a/c rooms (℡331.02.38; CFA15,300). *Le Becca*, on the
route de Lomé/Cotonou west of the market (℡331.05.13; ❷), is a newer establishment with a grandiose exterior and spotless self-contained rooms, some with a/c.
The town's fanciest accommodation is at the *First Hotel-Nightclub* (℡331.10.04; ❷),
on the western edge of town on the route de Lomé/Cotonou, which has excellent
a/c rooms with hot water, phone, satellite TV and tiled floor, as well as some
cheaper – though poor value – rooms with fan. There's also a good pool (CFA500
for non-guests), tennis facilities, and the best **nightclub** in town (Saturdays only;
CFA3000).

The market is the place for cheap **eating**; or try *Anastasia* just opposite, a lively
café serving up omelettes, sandwiches and light meals. *Café Delice*, on a road behind
Le Becca, is a great breakfast joint for tea, coffee and omelettes, whilst across the
autogare, *Pago Pago* is a lively bar which also serves spaghetti, couscous and other
basic meals. Otherwise try one of the hotels listed above. For **drinking**, check out
the *Bar Amite de la Gare*, opposite the SGGG supermarket and near the market,
which has a shady thatched *paillotte*, and *brochettes* in the evenings.

Moving on from Aného

The main *autogare* in Aného is across the lagoon in the east of town towards the Benin
border at Hilakondji. **Bush taxis** run direct from here to Cotonou and Lomé. It's also
possible to flag down taxis to Lomé if you stand on the main road near the market.
There are less frequent taxis to Togoville; if you don't want to wait for the vehicle to
fill, you could charter the entire vehicle for around CFA3000 one way.

Because of its historical and religious pre-eminence, Glidji is the site of the **Yékéyéké festival**, celebrated annually on the Thursday before the second Sunday in September. Delegations arrive from all the major Mina and Gun centres to make offerings to the deities and to be blessed by the priests. Animals are sacrificed, but the climax of the ceremonies occurs when the colour of the **sacred stone** is revealed. This stone determines the fortune of the coming year. For example, a blue stone indicates abundant rain. If your stay in the area coincides with the festival, these are four days of celebrating not to be missed, but note that room availability is very tight.

Glidji

On the surface, **GLIDJI**, 4km north of Aného, looks just like any other Mina village. You'll notice the same *banco* huts with thatched roofs and the same narrow sandy streets found all along the coast. Yet the town is symbolically important, since the present chief is a direct descendant of **Foli–Bebe** – the first ruler of the region and the man responsible for the political organization of the Gun and Mina into independent chiefdoms after these peoples migrated from the Accra area in the early seventeenth century. Before starting off through town, you should pay a **visit to the chief**. To do so, you have to fill out a request at the royal secretariat. If the chief is around, and not otherwise occupied, he will receive you.

Glidji is also important from a religious perspective, since all the major sanctuaries to the principal **voodoo deities** are found in this town. You won't have trouble finding a boy to take you around to visit the different fetish shrines and voodoo meeting places. Ask to see the **temple of Egou**, the deity who is the traditional protector of the Mina people. Your only option for **accommodation** in the village is the *Auberge Alpha & Omega* in the Adamage area (☎331.05.40; ❷), which has six slightly grubby self-contained rooms, some with a/c. To get to Glidji from Aného, it's easiest to take a *zemidjan* (around CFA300).

11.2

The plateau region

Some of the country's most beautiful and fertile rural backcountry is located in the **plateau region** in the southwest corner of the country along the Ghanaian border. This is Togo's most agriculturally significant district, with lush plantations of coffee, cocoa and fruit crops, but it also contains wilder areas, with mountain vistas, vine-strewn forests and streams leaping in cascades from ragged clifftops – just how you always imagined the jungle should look, especially if you've been brought up on Tarzan-type images.

Given that it's just a few hours from Lomé, the whole area is wonderfully accessible too, as well as being ethnically diverse and full of hiking opportunities. The **coffee and cocoa** triangle, hemmed in by the towns of **Kpalimé**, **Badou** and

Atakpamé, is home to several ethnic groups who came here from Ghana and the coast. Kpalimé and surrounding villages retain essentially Ewe populations, but Badou and Atakpamé are melting pots of agricultural peoples.

Kpalimé and around

Capital of the *pays cacao* – the **cocoa country** – and of the entire fruit-growing region, **KPALIMÉ**'s unusually busy market is the first hint of its economic importance. Early on in their brief rule, the Germans recognized the agricultural potential of this mild and attractive district. Once the plantations were established, they wasted no time in driving a railway through the forested hills to the town, and since that time Kpalimé (pronounced "Pal-ee-may"; the *k* is silent) has never been long out of the news in Togo. It was a stronghold of Olympio support in the early days after independence, and even now is considered to be anti-Eyadéma.

There's enough to see and do around Kpalimé to keep you busy for a couple of days – and longer if you're into **trekking** in the nearby mountains. But the town is small and, if you have less time, you can still get a good feel of the place in a day.

Arrival and orientation

The **gare routière**, where **bush taxis** arrive, is on the eastern side of town. There are two **banks** just north of the market (UTB is better than the BTCI for changing money), whilst **shops** and cheap **restaurants** line the streets that box in the market area. The **post office** is on the main road in town, across from the Shell garage. If you've just arrived from (or are heading to) Ghana, **moneychangers**, who hang around the *gare routière*, convert cedis to CFA and vice versa – but try to get an idea of the correct street rate in advance.

Accommodation

Kpalimé has a good choice of hotels, and you can also find accommodation amidst the beautiful scenery around the pretty nearby town of **Klouto** (see p.858), though you're likely to feel stranded there if you don't have your own car.

Auberge l'Aurore 1km north of the centre on the Atakpamé road ☎441.04.08, ✉aubergeaurore @yahoo.fr. Four spotless self-contained rooms – not much space, but well-maintained and good value – set around an attractive courtyard with trees and a small thatched bar. ❶
Auberge Bafana Bafana 100m west of the post

office, near the church. A great budget option, with cheap drinks at the terrace-bar and simple rooms set around a pleasant courtyard out back – they're spartan, but comfortable and quiet. ❶
Chez Fanny 2 km south of town opposite *Hôtel du 30 Août* on the road to Lomé ☎441.00.99,

---

Ewe names

As in the Asante country in Ghana, Ewe people usually take at least one name after the day of the week on which they were born.

	Girls' names	Boys' names
Monday	Adzo	Kodjo
Tuesday	Abla	Komla
Wednesday	Aku	Kokou
Thursday	Ayawa	Yao
Friday	Afi	Koffi
Saturday	Ami	Komi
Sunday	Kosiwa or Essi	Kossi

@hotelchezfanny@yahoo.fr. Homely place with six spotless and well-furnished self-contained rooms with a/c. There's also an excellent, cosy restaurant serving up European dishes including great pizzas, a range of desserts, and French cheese to finish. ❸

Hôtel Cristal 100m northwest off the Atakpamé road ☎ 441.05.79. Large, new hotel with a range of rooms – they're not particularly stylish, but most are well-equipped and come with a/c, TV, fridge and hot water. The cheaper rooms are very cramped, but good value. ❷–❸

Hôtel Domino Close to the centre, just off the Texaco roundabout ☎ 441.01.87. Old favourite in a great location offering basic accommodation (fan or a/c) and the bonus of an attractive garden out the back. ❶

Hôtel Le Geyser On the road to Mt Klouto, 2km from the town centre ☎ 441.04.67,@ hotelle geyser@hotmail.com. Attractive, quiet place with a pool (CFA1000 for non-guests) and spacious, clean (if slightly overpriced) rooms. ❷

The Town

Kpalimé's **market** is the town's most compelling attraction, and one of the region's best markets for produce. Among the citrus fruit you'll find beautiful oranges, grapefruit and mandarins, all green-skinned, juicy and sweet – street vendors squeeze them into plastic mugs to make a delicious juice for next to nothing (make sure to tell them not to add water if you don't want it). Avocados as big as boats sell for a pittance, and bananas, pineapples and lesser-known fruits are all available in abundance. You'll also find woven *kente* cloth and other fabric for sale. Kpalimé is known for its weavers and the quality of the material is very good – it's said President Eyadéma's official ceremonial wrap was made here. It was also in Kpalimé that, on August 30, 1971, the president announced the founding of what was then the nation's only political party, the RPT. A giant statue of Eyadéma was erected to commemorate the event just south of the market, but was toppled in the riots that followed the 1991 coup attempt. Now a stronghold of anti-Eyadéma sentiment, thousands of refugees passed through the border here into Ghana during the upheaval of the early 1990s. Just off the market square, the **train station** (now disused) stands on a hilltop, giving views of mountains rising in all directions around you. To the east, a TV tower marks the summit of **Mont Agou** (986m), Togo's highest peak.

On the eastern side of town, the towering steeple of the **Église Catholique** dominates the skyline. Built by the Germans in 1913, the church looks like it's jumped straight out of the Bavarian countryside, and exudes an incongruous beauty and calm. Down near the stadium, **weavers** work foot-operated looms in a shack by the roadside and are happy to chat, though without ever breaking the rhythm of their

KPALIMÉ

▲ ❶ & Kpimé Falls

Texaco
Gare Routière
Fan Milk Shop
Eglise Catholique
Shell
UTB Bank
BTCI Bank
Main Market
Train Station (disused) & Old Rail Line
Taxi Station for Mont Agou
Stadium
Weavers

Centre D'Enseignement Artistique et Artisanal & Mont Klouto ◀

▶ Mont Agou

0   200m

▼ ❻ & Lome

ACCOMMODATION		RESTAURANTS & CAFÉS	
Auberge l'Aurore	1	Amical Bon Café	D
Auberge Bafana Bafana	5	Cafetariat La Patience	E
Chez Fanny	6	Maquis 2000	F
Hôtel Cristal	2	Regency Palace	C
Hôtel Domino	4	Restaurant Le Fermier	A
Hôtel Le Geyser	3	Restaurant Macumba	B

movements during conversation. It's not hard to appreciate the time involved in making cloth and why it's so expensive. You can order directly from the weavers, but you'll have to wait several days (or even weeks) for bespoke products.

There's further local craftsmanship on display at the **Centre d'Enseignement Artistique et Artisanal** (Mon–Fri 9am–noon & 3–5.30pm, Sat 9am–3pm) on the route de Klouto, a couple of kilometres from the town centre. This state-run school for crafts has two boutiques where all items manufactured at the school – batiks, clothes, bags, ceramics and wooden carvings – are exhibited for sale. Prices are fixed and slightly higher than on the street, but there's an excellent range to choose from, the quality is high, and it's a relaxed environment to shop in. Visitors are welcome to watch the students and professors at work, but ask permission at the office first.

Eating and drinking

There are lots of good cheap **food stalls** in the market. For **drinking and nightlife**, try *Maquis 2000*, an outdoor bar set in a scruffy courtyard on the main road just south of the post office; or the trendy *Imperial Nightclub* at the *Hôtel Cristal* (open Friday and Saturdays from 10pm; cover CFA3000, free for guests).

Amical Bon Café Long-standing, tiny café serving up a good range of dishes including chicken and chips, omelettes, couscous and *riz gras* at inflated prices.

Cafetariat La Patience This dilapidated shack south of the Texaco roundabout does decent omelettes with baguettes, coffee and tea – a good place for a cheap breakfast.

Regency Palace One of the town centre's classier options, specializing in Lebanese and Italian dishes. Mains cost around CFA2000–3000.

Restaurant Le Fermier 1km northwest of the centre, just off the road to Klouto. A good range of European dishes, as well as good ice cream, which you can eat either in the café (which has the added attraction of table football) or in the a/c restaurant.

Restaurant Macumba 1km northwest of the centre, just off the road to Klouto. The best place in town, with friendly service and outstanding value for money – it's a pain to find, but well worth the effort for the delicious meals including steaks, chicken and fish dishes for around CFA2000.

Mont Klouto and Mont Agou

Some 12km northwest of Kpalimé, **KLOUTO** (also spelled Kloto) is a mountain retreat and site of an old **German hospital** built before World War I. The views from the summit of Mont Klouto are stunning, and the area around offers good opportunities for hiking, with dense forest, streams and waterfalls, as well as boasting a huge variety of **butterflies**. The road up here from Kpalimé is spectacular. Carved out by the Germans, it snakes up steep slopes through cocoa plantations and burrows through the dense **Missahohé Forest**, where tree branches form a complete tunnel over the road in certain areas. A few kilometres before Mont Klouto you'll see the entrance to the **Chateau Viale** – a medieval-looking stone fortress built during World War II by a French lawyer, Francois-Raymond Viale. It became state property in 1971 and is now used by the president, so you can forget about visiting it, and photography is forbidden.

Moving on from Kpalimé

Taxis run from Kpalimé's *gare routière* to **Lomé** (2hr) and **Atakpamé** (2hr) via a pretty route skirting the Danyi plateau. They also go to **Sokodé** (5hr), **Kara** (7hr) and **Dapaong** (12hr) in the north, and along a rough road to **Ho** (1hr 30min) in **Ghana**. Shared taxis for **Mont Agou** leave from a tiny station next to the stadium, just south of the market.

Overcrowded collective **taxis** (CFA250–300) run fairly regularly from the Kpalimé *gare routière*. If you don't want to wait for a taxi to fill up (your best chances are on market days on Tuesdays and Saturdays), it costs around CFA2000 to charter a taxi one-way. You'll be dropped in the village of **KONDA**, just 1km short of **Mont Klouto**. You can **stay** here at the *Auberge Papillons* (📧prosnyanu @yahoo.fr; ❶), run by local celebrity butterfly-collector Prosper, which offers simple, fanless rooms (no running water) arranged round a *paillote* and set in fledgling jungle. Prosper organizes guided bushwalks and *safaris papillon* ("butterfly safaris") in the surrounding area, visiting small waterfalls, explaining the uses of local plants and trees and looking at butterflies – there are more than five hundred different types hereabouts (best seen from September to February). It costs CFA6000 per person for the day (lunch included), or CFA3000 for a shorter, two-hour trek. Just outside the village, the Association Découverte Togo Profond (📞441.08.17, 📧adetop@caramail.com; they're known in town as ADETOP) has six clean though basic double rooms (❶) and also offers similar guided walks at similar prices to Prosper. Less rudimentary lodgings can be found near the summit of Mont Klouto, set amidst rolling hills and forest, where the old colonial buildings of the German hospital have been turned into the government-owned *Campement de Klouto* (📞913.17.69; ❷), providing a rustic retreat with pretty views in every direction. Even if you don't sleep here, it's worth stopping at the large *paillote* for something to eat or drink.

From the *campement*, a path bordered by huge mango trees leads to the top of **Mont Klouto** (741m). Before you set off, you'll be asked to pay a CFA500 fee by the guides at the *campement*, who keep the paths clear. From the mountain, you can see across into Ghana and may even be able to make out the shining, artificial expanse of the dammed **Lake Volta**, 35km away to the west. Guides at the *campement* will offer to take you on hikes through the forest – these are similar to those organized by Prosper, but more expensive at CFA5000 for half a day.

On market days, it's also possible to catch taxis from Kpalimé to various villages on **Mont Agou** and hike around its 1000-metre peaks. Taxis in Kpalimé leave from a small station next to the stadium; you'll have to set off at dawn and return early, or you risk missing the last taxi back to Kpalimé. If you have your own car, a good road leads all the way to Mont Agou's 986-metre summit.

From Kpalimé to Atakpamé: the Danyi plateau

The road from Kpalimé to Atakpamé runs along the base of the sheer cliffs of the **Danyi plateau**, rising up to the west. About 10km out of Kpalimé in the village of Kpimé-Seva you can see the **Kpimé falls** on the left, signposted from the roadside (the driver or other passengers will point them out if you're in a taxi). It's an easy 1km walk along a good path to the entrance of the falls, where you'll have to pay the CFA500 entrance fee. The results of the hydro-electric dam built in the late 1970s haven't done much for the site's aesthetic appeal and in the dry season the falls are little more than a trickle, but during or after the rains, they tumble rewardingly a hundred metres down off the cliffside. It's possible to walk to the top of the falls and visit the dam, a 90-minute walk from the falls' base.

It's a picturesque drive to Atakpamé, passing through numerous Akposso villages where you could easily stop and have a look around if you have your own transport. A kilometre outside the town of **DZOGBÉGAN** (turn off the road at Adéta, 30km from Kpalimé, from where it's a further 20km), the **Benedictine monastery** features an unusual chapel built entirely of local materials – teak, iroko, mahogany, bamboo. The real interest here is gastronomic, however: the monks run an orchard and produce jams from the exotic fruit, as well as coffee, honey and other comestibles not so often found in these regions. The *soeurs bénédictines*, who run a convent closer to the village, sell some of the same items. It's possible to **stay** at the monastery in simple rooms with shared facilities, but make sure you book in advance (✆abdzog@cafe.tg; CFA5000 per person for full board).

Atakpamé and around

Situated in the mountains, **ATAKPAMÉ** has historically been a place of refuge. The **Ewe** were the first to arrive, from Notsé, in the seventeenth century. They were followed by the **Ana** – a people related to the Yoruba who came from the east in the nineteenth century – and then by the Akposso, who came down from the surrounding mountains in the early part of this century to farm the fertile plains. Today, Atakpamé's road links with Lomé, Badou and Kpalimé and the industry in the area – a nearby textile works, the new hydro-electric power station and a sugar refinery 20km to the north in Anié – have all helped it maintain its status as a regional hub and ethnic melting pot.

Arrival and orientation

The most scenic approach to Atakpamé is from Kpalimé via Hihéatro, a couple of kilometres west of the town. After this village, vehicles wind their way up one last steep hill and, before you were aware the town was anywhere nearby, turn a bend to pull into the *autogare* near the main market. If you're coming from Lomé, you'll probably be dropped in the suburb of **Agbonou** on the Route Nationale, from where you can easily get a shared taxi into town (4km). From Sokodé or any town in the north, you'll arrive at a different station on the Route Nationale, about 1km north of the junction near *Le Sahelien*; again, there are plenty of *zemidjans* or shared taxis to take you to the centre.

The town's hilly topography and scattered environs are confusing. The town centre is 3km northwest of the Route Nationale. The major thoroughfare, the Avenue de la Libération, runs northwest–southeast and turns into the route de

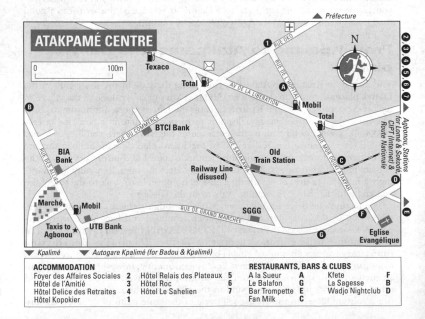

ACCOMMODATION				RESTAURANTS, BARS & CLUBS			
Foyer des Affaires Sociales	2	Hôtel Relais des Plateaux	5	A la Sueur	A	Kfete	F
Hôtel de l'Amitié	3	Hôtel Roc	6	Le Balafon	G	La Sagesse	B
Hôtel Delice des Retraites	4	Hôtel Le Sahelien	7	Bar Trompette	E	Wadjo Nightclub	D
Hôtel Kopokier	1			Fan Milk	C		

Lomé to meet the Route Nationale. The PTT and most hotels are along this street, whilst **banks** (BIA, UTB and BTCI) and **shops** cluster around the market on the west side of the centre. The **market** is located on the western edge of town; on Friday – market day – the commotion is sensational. For **Internet** access, head to CIPI (Mon–Fri 7am–8pm, Sat & Sun 3–8pm; ☎440.12.73) on the route de Lomé opposite the Shell garage, which has fast connections for CFA600 per hour.

Accommodation

Most of the **places to stay** listed below are on the route de Lomé, between the centre and the Route Nationale.

Foyer des Affaires Sociales rte de Lomé near the Shell garage ☎440.06.53. Clean but spartan rooms and dorm beds, dorm beds CFA1000. ❶

Hôtel de l'Amitié Agbonou, set back 100m from the Route Nationale, 200m north of the main junction ☎440.06.25. Located well out of the town centre, this quiet place has a family feel and clean self-contained rooms (fan or a/c), plus a bar and a good restaurant. ❶

Hôtel Delice des Retraites (formerly the *Hôtel Miva*) rte de Lomé near the Route Nationale junction, 3km from the centre ☎440.04.37. Friendly place offering some of the cheapest accommodation in town, with clean but very basic, cell-like rooms, all with fan and shared facilities. ❶

Hôtel Kopokler At the junction of rue de l'Hôpital and rue Oke ☎440.02.84. Set in an excellent location, this well-established hotel has five spacious, self-contained rooms with a/c or fan. ❶

Hôtel Relais des Plateaux rte de Lomé by the Commissariat de Police ☎440.11.05. Not too far from the centre, this well-maintained place has clean and comfortable self-contained rooms, with good views across town from the balconies. ❶

Hôtel Roc Up a steep drive near the Shell garage, off the rte de Lomé ☎440.02.37. Set on a hill overlooking the entire town, this government-run hotel is the town's most expensive, though it's looking increasingly dated and tatty. The self-contained a/c rooms are still comfortable though, and the views are great. ❸

Hôtel Le Sahelien Route Nationale, 1km north of the main junction ☎440.12.44. Very inconveniently located and right on the busy Route Nationale, but the self-contained rooms with a/c and TV are excellent value for money, and there's a great rooftop bar/restaurant. ❷

Eating, drinking and nightlife

Atakpamé's **bars** and **restaurants** are mostly workaday places, but there's a decent number to choose from. If you're after something more swish, head to one of the hotel restaurants – the rooftop setting at *Le Sahelien* is probably the best choice for food, whilst *Hôtel Roc* offers great views from their terrace while you dine.

A la Sueur rue de l'Hôpital. Despite its dilapidated appearance, *A la Sueur* – "By the sweat (of my brow)" – is still just about functioning, with cheap beer and a lively atmosphere at weekends.

Le Balafon Near the Église Evangélique. Hugely popular and lively bar with cheap beer and loud music – you'll struggle to get a seat at the outside tables.

Bar Trompette West of the centre off rue du

Moving on from Atakpamé

Taxis for **Badou** (2hr) and **Kpalimé** (2hr) leave from the *autogare*, just south of the market. For **Lomé** (2hr 30min), vehicles depart from a station in the suburb of Agbonou near the main junction, whilst the station for transport to **Sokodé** (3–4hr), **Kara** (5–6hr) and other northern towns is on the Route Nationale some 1km north of the junction near *Le Sahelien*. To get to these latter stations, you can either charter a taxi or *zemidjan* from the centre; shared taxis for Agbonou leave from a small station near the Mobil garage.

11 | 11.2 | TOGO | The plateau region

861

Grand Marché. Lively drinking spot where dancing takes over on Friday and Saturday nights.

Fan Milk rue Atakpah. Good ice cream and yoghurt.

Kfete rue du Grand Marché, near the Église Evangélique. Decent range of European and Togolese snacks and meals, and open 24hr.

La Sagesse rue des Alliés, near the market. Friendly, brightly painted place that serves up solid meals including couscous and *poulet frites*, though there's not much choice.

Wadjo Nightclub rue du Grand Marché, opposite the BTD Bank. The small and quiet restaurant upstairs serves decent European dishes for around CFA2000. The music downstairs gets going on Saturday nights (CFA1000 cover), with a selection of mainly modern Togolese tunes.

Badou and around

Located 79km west of Atakpamé, and less than 10km from the Ghanaian border, **BADOU** is the smallest, most isolated and most distinctly rural of the three towns of the coffee and cocoa triangle. Most of its people are cash-crop farmers and, despite the small size of the average farm, cocoa and coffee have brought a measure of prosperity to the people of the region. In neighbouring Akrowa they've even managed to pay for all their streets to be paved. But there have been setbacks in recent years with the falling price of cocoa on the world market, while recent gluts of both crops have wreaked economic havoc in the quiet forest districts around Badou, and many young people are pinning their hopes on salaried jobs in the towns.

Badou is most easily reached from Atakpamé, a spectacular drive around hairpin bends through the hilly peaks.

Practicalities

Arriving from Atakpamé, you'll be dropped at one of two stations: either **Tomegbé Gare**, at the entrance of town by the junction of the Atakpamé and Tomegbé roads, or **Dayconta Gare**, nearer the centre. At the latter, you'll find the first **accommodation** option in town, *La Cascade Plus*, which has basic, self-contained rooms with standing fans (⊕443.00.96; ➊), as well as the liveliest **bar** in town. To get to the **market** from here, turn right down the road that leads to Ghana, across a small bridge. Further along this same thoroughfare, you'll come to a road junction marked by the *Carrefour 2000 bar/dancing* (⊕443.00.47; ➊), another lively place at night, which also offers basic and bare rooms with shared facilities. Turning left at this junction, you pass the **post office** en route to the government-run *Hôtel Abuta* (⊕443.00.16; ➋), Badou's fanciest accommodation, though it feels totally dead and has dated and dusty a/c rooms. You can also **camp** in the grounds here for CFA1500 per person. There's a **pharmacy** just behind the hotel. There's nowhere to change money in town.

Young boys like to earn a few francs by showing visitors round their town and its surrounds. Although Badou itself doesn't merit this treatment, you might want someone to take you to nearby hamlets. They'll sometimes even offer lodgings *en famille*, a cheaper and more enjoyable option than staying in town.

Around Badou

One of the main attractions around Badou is the spectacular **Akloa Falls**, 11km south of the town. To reach the falls, you first need to take a taxi from the Tomegbé *gare* to the village of **Akloa** (Akrowa on some maps). Shared taxis and pick-ups can take a while to fill – if you're short of time you can charter a vehicle for about CFA2000. At the entrance to the village, you'll see a hand-painted sign advertising the falls. This is the official starting point for the hike to the falls, and the place where you pay CFA500 for a ticket and are assigned an obligatory guide.

The **climb** to the falls is strenuous, but requires determination rather than fitness. In any case, there's no rush; it's hard to resist dawdling through the cool,

△ Tamberma country

dark underbrush of the forest. After some thirty minutes of hiking through the dense vegetation, you arrive at the falls – a drop of over thirty metres from the granite cliff. You can swim in the pool at the base of the falls and it's said the waters are therapeutic. Ask the guide to tell you about **Mamy Wada** – the spirit that guards the water – or about the numerous other supernatural forces in the forest. Two generations ago this whole area was sacred and off-limits to the uninitiated.

11.3

Sokodé and the central region

In the semi-daze of a long and comfortless taxi ride, you could miss the many signs indicating the shifts in peoples and lifestyles as you move from the balmy south of Togo to the central and northern regions. Gradually, however, you take in the change from the traditional square buildings of the south to the round, thatch-roofed **banco huts** of the interior. Around these are fixed silos of baked earth, used to store millet and corn. North of the coffee and cocoa zone, **subsistence farming** is the major economic activity, and along the roadside the earth is pushed up into small mounds planted with yams, groundnuts and cassava. Traditional **African religions** retain a tight hold on the inhabitants of **Bassar** and **Tchamba**, two major towns in the region. The place of the church in southern Togo, however, is increasingly taken by **Islam** as you head north. And by the time you reach **Sokodé**, a long day's travel from Lomé, the whole environment – natural, cultural, social – has changed.

The predominant ethnic group of the central region is the **Kotokoli**, a people who migrated south from Mali in the late eighteenth or early nineteenth century. They brought Islam with them and Sokodé is now the most devoutly Muslim town in the country. Numerous **mosques**, in faded pastel colours and crowned with the star and crescent moon, attest to their faith. So, too, does **dress style**, especially the flowing *boubous* (embroidered gowns) and skullcaps commonly worn by men. Women don't wear veils, but they do drape a long, transparent scarf over their heads, wrapping it around their necks and letting it fall over their backs to flap on the ground when they walk. In accordance with the strict code of manners, people bow to one another in greeting and children even go down on their knees when greeting parents or elders.

Sokodé

In terms of numbers, **SOKODÉ** is easily Togo's second largest town, with around 100,000 inhabitants. Development has been slow in coming, but several roads are now paved, including the Lomé–Dapaong Route Nationale and the road to Bassar, both of which run through the centre. Sokodé's position at the crossroads of these routes assures it a certain vitality, despite the government's obvious lack of interest in stimulating the local economy. A good number of homes in the heart of town are still made of *banco* and thatch, and most of the people are involved in trade and subsistence farming.

Arriving in Sokodé, you'll be dropped at the *gare routière* in the centre, just west of the market.

Accommodation

Sokodé has a number of **places to stay**, but note that rooms can fill up quickly during the town's festivals.

La Bonne Auberge About 2km from the centre on the rte de Kara ☎550.02.35. Good-value accommodation in spacious rooms (fan or a/c) with comfy beds and tiled floors, but ask for a room at the back to avoid the noise from the main road. There's also a good restaurant and an attractive bar under a thatched roof. ❶

Le Campement Tchaoudjo Off rte de Lomé, near the *préfet*'s residence ☎550.15.57. Set in an old colonial building on a wooded hill overlooking the town, this place hasn't been well kept up, but the modest rooms with standing fans are amongst the cheapest in town, and you can also camp on the grounds. ❶

Cercle de l'Amitié rte de Kara, next to the BTCI bank ☎550.09.06. Funky hotel and restaurant

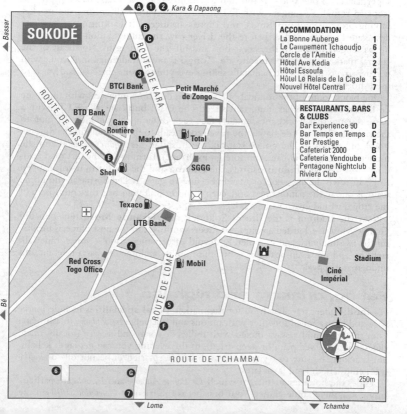

SOKODÉ

▲ Bassar

ROUTE DE KARA

ROUTE DE BASSAR

BTCI Bank

BTD Bank

Gare Routière

Market

Petit Marché de Zongo

Total

Shell

SGGG

Texaco

UTB Bank

Red Cross Togo Office

Mobil

Ciné Impérial

Stadium

ROUTE DE LOMÉ

ROUTE DE TCHAMBA

▲ Bé

▼ Lomé

▼ Tchamba

▲ A, ❶, ❷, Kara & Dapaong

ACCOMMODATION	
La Bonne Auberge	1
Le Campement Tchaoudjo	6
Cercle de l'Amitie	3
Hôtel Ave Kedia	2
Hôtel Essoufa	4
Hôtel Le Relais de la Cigale	5
Nouvel Hôtel Central	7

RESTAURANTS, BARS & CLUBS	
Bar Experience 90	D
Bar Temps en Temps	C
Bar Prestige	F
Cafeteriat 2000	B
Cafeteria Yendoube	G
Pentagone Nightclub	E
Riviera Club	A

N

0   250m

with an African theme and clean and comfortable rooms, though it's set right on the main road, so can be noisy. ❶

Hôtel Ave Kedia Signposted off the rte de Kara 2km from the centre, then 100m up a dirt track ⍟ 550.05.34. Inconveniently located, but very quiet and with well-furnished rooms (fan or a/c). Also has a bar, restaurant, and a small but well-stocked shop. ❶

Hôtel Essoufa On a side-road off the rte de Lomé, near the Red Cross office ⍟ 550.09.89. This place has a variety of options, ranging from rooms with fan and shared facilities to a carpeted a/c room with satellite TV. All are spotless and good value, and there's also a bar and restaurant. ❶

Hôtel Le Relais de la Cigale rte de Lomé ⍟ 550.00.19. Clean and colourfully decorated rooms with fan and shared facilities. The restaurant has a good choice of European meals. ❶

Nouvel Hôtel Central rte de Lomé ⍟ 550.01.23. Dated but comfortable and friendly hotel, with self-contained a/c rooms or bungalows with hot water set in attractive, leafy grounds. There's also a pleasant restaurant and bar, and tennis facilities. ❸

The Town

The international highway that runs through Sokodé – known as the **route de Lomé** on the south side and the **route de Kara** on the north – is the town's main street. Numerous bars and restaurants jostle for custom along this two-kilometre thoroughfare, while in the middle of it all, Sokodé's centre of gravity is defined by a major roundabout and the large, two-storey **market building**. On the same roundabout – an independence monument at its centre and the SGGG supermarket to one side – is the filling station where every taxi passing through stops to refuel. Passengers with five minutes to spare mill around the market buying presents and provisions, and there's an incessant barking from hawkers desperate to sell their gear before the driver pays the filling station *pompiste*, yells his passengers back into the sweat-box and hits the road again. Northeast of the central market, the **Petit Marché de Zongo** is more traditional in flavour, with narrow streets full of thatched stalls selling everything from charcoal and yams to used shoes and clothing.

One block south of the roundabout, the route de Lomé intersects with the route de Bassar, Sokodé's other important street. The UTB **bank** and the **PTT** (with a poste restante that works, incidentally) face each other at this junction. Turning to the right up the route de Bassar, the paved road leads to the Tchaoundja neighbourhood and passes by the police station, the hospital, *Les Affaires Sociales* and the modern-looking BTD bank (no foreign exchange). Turning left, the dirt road leads down to the town's main **mosques**, the **cinema** and the **stadium**. If you happen to be in town during a soccer match, be sure to get a ticket: **Semassi**, the home team, is one of the nation's best and, even if soccer isn't your bag, the enthusiasm of the crowd would give anyone a buzz.

Near the stadium is the site of Sokodé's new **Grande Mosquée**. The old Grande Mosquée, located a couple of streets southwest of the post office, is beautiful for its simplicity, and completely devoid of ornamentation – you could walk right by and not even notice it – but the humble architecture has a tolerant and undogmatic appeal.

Eating, drinking and nightlife

For **food**, budget travellers head for the market. **Local specialities** include *watche* (rice and beans boiled together with onions and hot peppers), *kadadia* (mash made from finely ground cassava mixed with millet or corn) and *wagassi* (locally made cheese either served plain or deep-fried). In the evening you can get lamb kebabs. For snacking, be sure to try *kosse* (bean batter deep-fried in peanut oil) or *koliko* (yam chips), both local favourites.

Besides the hotel restaurants, of which *La Bonne Auberge* and *Essoufa* are particularly good, there's little choice. Your best bet is the friendly *Cafeteriat 2000* on the

Festivals in Sokodé

Sokodé is well known for its **festivals**, most of which revolve around Muslim religious holidays – during these occasions, the town breaks from its normal slow pace to become surprisingly animated. One of the most important festivals is that marking the **end of Ramadan** (see p.61 for dates), when the city's entire male population – decked out in embroidered *boubous* – gathers at the stadium for collective prayers, before returning to town for feasting and dancing.

The **Fête du Tabaski** – celebrating Abraham's sacrificing the lamb in place of his son – takes place two months later. Several days prior to this festival, the streets in town begin filling with sheep and goats, which are slaughtered en masse on the day of Tabaski, then roasted and shared out among the community.

The **Knife Festival**, or Adossa (about three months after Tabaski), mixes Muslim elements with a custom which pre-dates the introduction of Islam into Kotokoli society and has many parallels in other West African societies. On this occasion – marking Muhammad's birthday – the men drink a potion specially prepared by a marabout which supposedly renders their skin impenetrable. In public dances, they then proceed to cut one another with knives. It's even said that babies who have been administered the potion are rolled over broken bottles with no harm coming to them.

route de Kara, a 24-hour café which serves up generous portions of the usual staples including chicken and chips, spaghetti and couscous. *Cafeteria Yendoube* on the route de Lomé is another 24-hour option serving similar food, whilst just up the road, *Bar Prestige* has more limited options of rice, spaghetti or couscous with sauce, but serves cheap large beers.

Nightlife

The town has a few lively **bars and clubs** which stay open until the early hours. Two bars to start the evening off are *Bar Temps en Temps* and *Bar Experience 90*, very close to each other on the route de Kara. The *Riviera Club* (cover CFA1000), 2km from the centre on the route de Kara, gets going at weekends, playing a variety of Togolese, American and European music, and has a ladies' night on Fridays. The only other option for dancing till late is at *Pentagone Nightclub* (cover CFA1500), on the route de Bassar.

Around Sokodé

The mountainous scenery and good roads around Sokodé provide opportunities for some easy excursions. West of Sokodé, the **Parc National de Fazao-Malfakassa** is set in stunning mountainous scenery and offers a good chance of seeing some wildlife. North of Sokodé, the Route Nationale passes near the **Barrage d'Aleheride**, an old reservoir which is now home to several hundred crocodiles, before winding between the dramatic rocks of the **Faille d'Aledjo**. Not far from here, the friendly village of **Aledjo** offers spectacular views.

Moving on from Sokodé

Taxis brousse from Sokodé head in all directions from the *gare routière* in the town centre, including Bassar (1hr), Lomé (7–8hr), Kpalimé (5–6hr) and Kara (1–2hr). There are no direct taxis to **Ouagadougou**, and vehicles coming up from Lomé are already full. You'll have to take a taxi to Cinkansé (7–8hr) on the border, or alternatively go to Dapaong (6–7hr) and stop there for the night before picking up an onward connection.

The Parc National de Fazao-Malfakassa

The **Parc National de Fazao-Malfakassa** (open Nov–May) has now reopened under the management of the Fondation Franz-Weber (office in Sokodé: ☏550.02.96, ✉fazapo@hotmail.com), and with the demise of the Parc National de la Kéran further north, represents your only real chance of going on safari in the country. The park is home to some fifty elephants, but you're more likely to see monkeys and a variety of birdlife.

There are two entrances to the park: from the northern edge at the rangers' camp at **Binakou**, 38km from Sokodé on the road to Bassar; and the main entrance at the village of **Fazao**, accessible by a dirt road which turns off the Route Nationale at Adjengré, some 45km south of Sokodé, and leads 32km to the park gates. Driving **tours** of the park take place in the mornings or early evenings to avoid the heat of the day, and you'll be accompanied by an obligatory guide. **Entrance fees** are CFA10,000 per vehicle, plus CFA3000 per person. If you don't have your own transport, you can hire the hotel's car, in which case the tour costs CFA18,000 for one person (CFA13,000 per person for 2–3 people, CFA9000 for 4–6) inclusive of entrance fees. Entrance fees are charged per day, so if you're planning on staying the night, you'll have to pay twice. The only **accommodation** option is the *Hôtel Parc Fazao* (❺), which you'll see as you approach the village of Fazao. The hotel has 25 comfortable, a/c bungalows, plus a bar and restaurant, though there are rumours that the hotel may close due to a lack of tourists – check with the office in Sokodé. Alternatively you can camp in the park for CFA5000 per person, but you'll need to bring your own gear.

North of Sokodé

The road to **Bafilo** runs through striking scenery, and there are several reasons not to rush this stretch. Roughly halfway between Sokodé and Bafilo, the **Barrage d'Aleheride**, the old reservoir which used to supply water for Sokodé, reportedly contains over two hundred **crocodiles** – the best times to visit are early mornings or late afternoons. To get there, turn right off the Route Nationale at the village of **Aleheride** (pronounced "Alla-heary") down a dirt track past the mosque for about 1.5km. You'll see a signpost for the *barrage*, where you'll need to get permission to visit from the caretaker – the reservoir is just behind the caretaker's office. Make sure you ask for the *ancien barrage*, otherwise you may be taken to the new reservoir which is being constructed several kilometres further along the track.

Back on the Route Nationale, the scenery becomes more dramatic as you continue north to the famous **Faille d'Aledjo** – a dramatic chasm, dynamited out of the cliff, through which the highway passes. Pictures of it help keep the Togolese postcard industry alive. Skull and crossbones warning signs line the twisting and looping road as it works its way over the mountains: if you're driving, the wrecked vehicles strewn in the valleys below are evidence they should be taken seriously. If you're a bush-taxi passenger, tell the driver *allez doucement!*

At the top of the pass, about one kilometre north of the Faille d'Aledjo, you'll come to **Kpéwa** village, where a dirt track on the right leads 6km to the village of **ALEDJO**. Set high on a ridge which runs parallel to the Route Nationale, the village offers panoramic views in every direction. It's best to ask the chief for permission to visit – his compound is on the left as you enter the village, past the hospital – and he'll probably send a boy with you to show you around. You'll be taken to see the derelict *campement* at the far end of the village, built on a rocky summit from where there are stunning views, then to the other side of the village and the rocky outcrop known as the **Rocher de la Morte** – the views are again fantastic, and the sheer cliff face dauntingly high. Local boys will tell you how evil sorcerors were once thrown off the cliff, and will probably also show you the tree which the executioner was tied to in order to prevent him being pulled off as well.

To get to Aledjo, take any vehicle heading along the Route Nationale and get off at Kpéwa. You may have a long wait for shared transport from here to Aledjo, so you might prefer either to walk the 6km or try to charter a car.

Bafilo and around

Surrounded by mountains, **BAFILO** is the Kotokoli's second largest town, and famous for its hand-weaving industry. It's also another Muslim fief – you'll see the town's large white **mosque** some time before you arrive. Bigger than any of the mosques in Sokodé, it was paid for by a single **alhadji** (one who's been to Mecca), a wealthy merchant and native son.

The town's main dirt road leads from the *gare routière* down to the mosque. About 100m before the mosque, a small road to the right leads up to the **weavers' co-operative** known as the Groupment Essovale Dégbembia. Look for the single-storey cream building – you can hear the knocking of their looms as you approach. If you can't find them, ask someone to take you *chez les tisserands*. The quality of their work has earned them national fame, but prices, depending on your bargaining skills, are as low here as anywhere. They sell either strips of woven cloth, complete *pagnes* or ready-made clothes direct from their boutique next door, and you can wander into the main workshop to see the sixteen or so looms packed into the room. You'll be asked to sign the visitors' book and offer a small donation.

Bafilo has just one **hotel**, the friendly *Maza Esso* ("I thank God"; ❶), on the route de Kara. Although it looks attractive from the outside, the rooms are increasingly run-down, particularly the cheaper rooms with fan and shared facilities; the a/c rooms are better value. There's also a good bar and restaurant – but make sure you order well in advance.

A little Kotokoli

Welcome	*Nodé*
Good morning (5–8am)	*Nyavinakozo* (pl. *Mivinekozo*)
Good day (8am–4pm)	*Nawsé* (pl. *Minawose*)
Good evening (4–7pm)	*Neda nana* (pl. *Minadananga*)
Good night	*Esofesi*
("May God wake you well")	
See you tomorrow/later	*Blabtcheri* or *blabtesi*
Thank you (for a gift)	*Eesobodi Natimaré*
(for help or work	
completed)	
Yes	*Mmm*
No	*Ay*
How are you?	*Alafyaweh?*
("Are you in health?")	
Fine ("fit")	*Mumumum*
Fine ("The work is fine?")	*Kokani*
How much?	*Ngyinidé?*
Money	*Lidé*
Five	*Byé*
Ten	*Byefu*
Twenty-five	*Tchente*
One hundred	*Alfa*
Two hundred	*Alfa nolé*
One thousand	*Milé*

Bafilo Falls

The **Bafilo Falls**, some 5km from town, are the main local attraction. Before you set off, it's best to visit the chief of Bafilo to ask permission, especially since he has a key which you'll need if you want to visit the higher falls – his compound is on the right as you leave Bafilo heading towards the waterfall. To reach the falls, continue down the main road past the mosque for about 2km, then turn right along a footpath through the fields of corn, groundnuts and beans and head for the mountains. There are usually villagers around to offer directions; ask for *la cascade*, which you should soon be able to see in the distance. Alternatively, you can take a *zemidjan* the whole way, although the last 2km along the footpath is very bumpy. A concrete staircase leads to a gate (which you unlock using the key) at the top of the falls, which are slightly disappointing in the dry season, especially now that swimming isn't allowed in the small dam. Nevertheless, the walk to the falls is worth doing in itself, and the whole trip makes for a pleasant excursion.

There are a couple of other waterfalls located a bit further from town, several kilometres further on from Bafilo Falls; the hotel can give you directions, or ask someone in town.

Bassar

Culturally, the **Bassari** (no relation to the people of southeast Senegal) are worlds apart from the Kotokoli – and linguistically they belong to another cluster of Voltaic languages, **Gurma**, while the Kotokoli speak a **Tem** language. Unlike the Muslim Kotokoli, they maintain traditional religious beliefs, and they are known for their many festivals and powerful fetishes. Traditionally the Bassari were the iron smelters for the region – in Africa, indication enough of their special status – and traces of their smelting furnaces can still be seen in some of the villages neighbouring the town of **BASSAR**. The Bassari **fire dance** is still celebrated in the town and surrounding villages. Staged versions are sometimes organized by the hotel in town, but only spirits can determine the dates for the real thing by speaking through a member of the community, who enters the arena in trance.

Practicalities

The paved road coming in from Sokodé runs right up to the town **marketplace** – where it suddenly stops. A dirt road runs in a ring round the market and functions as the town's high street. To the right where the tarmac ends is the *école centrale* and, just after, the Total garage with the **autogare** and **PTT** behind. Continuing, you pass the CAI garage and the old SGGG, before coming to a huge carbuncled **baobab**, revered by the Bassari, and thus tolerated bang in the middle of the street. Beyond it there's not a lot – unless you count a couple of small bars – until you get back to the paved road, having by now completed the circle. Note that there is no bank in town.

The town's best **accommodation** option is the *Auberge Kibetankpeou* (☎663.00.24; ❶), 1km out of town on the route de Gipato, which has reasonably new, clean rooms with fan or a/c, and a good restaurant. The *Hôtel de Bassar* (☎663.00.81; ❶) seems perennially dead, though its self-contained a/c rooms are comfortable enough, and it's nicely sited on the hilltop overlooking the town. The cheapest option is the grubby *Campement de Bassar* (❶), with fanless cells for rooms – it's off the paved road in the Kebedipou neighbourhood, near the *préfecture*.

For cheap **eating**, the market provides the best sources of tasty food, while two nearby **bars** – *Le Palmier* and the quieter *Bar Tchin Tchin* (aka *Centre Culturel de Bassar*) – usually run spirited discos (small entrance charge). The first is 100m down the dirt road that runs left out from the market as you enter from the Sokodé direction; the second is by the *gare routière*.

11.4

Kara and the north

Relatively harsh geography and climate make **the north** Togo's poorest region, and one where you're unlikely to spend a great deal of time. Much of the area is open savanna, where the ochre grass of the dry season suggests the drought conditions of the Sahel, just a few hours' travel to the north. During the rains, however, green shoots quickly cover the hilly countryside, briefly lending a lush appearance to the region.

The region's people, mainly small farmers of the Voltaic language group, including Tamberma, Lamba, More and Kabyé, grow staple crops of millet and, in isolated areas, rice. Cotton – an important cash crop – is grown around Dapaong. The only town of any size north of Sokodé is **Kara**, which is gradually becoming the nation's administrative centre. The **Kabyé country** spreads over a rocky, mountainous area centred around Mont Kabyé, some 20km north of Kara; its people have acquired a reputation as skilled agriculturalists, despite the hostile setting. The Kabyé country is the homeland of President Eyadéma – who, not unexpectedly, has made great efforts to develop his district and to transform its humble city, Kara, into the capital of the north.

Despite a feeling of stagnation, the north offers a number of interesting places to visit. The principal attraction is the **Tamberma country**, in the valleys around **Kandé**, which is famous for its architecture, each home being built like a small fortress. In addition, this region remained quite isolated until very recently, and as a result the traditional folklore, festivals and customs of the Tamberma people have changed little over time. **Niamtougou**, 28km north of Kara, hosts a lively Sunday market and is home to a co-operative of disabled artisans who produce good-quality crafts, whilst in the far north, **Dapaong** is a worthy stop-off en route to Burkina.

Kara

KARA doesn't impress as a major metropolis and, seeing the town for the first time, you start to realize why the hype about "Togo's second city" is so necessary. But even if the town retains a provincial, not to say rustic, flavour, it has come a long way in the past three decades, since its days as a rural village called Lama-Kara. Crucial political considerations – it was the nearest village of any size to Eyadéma's birthplace, and home town of his most ardent supporters – have led to Kara acquiring favoured status, and in the space of a few years it has become the nation's second most important centre for administration and manufacturing industries. Now incontestably the main town of the north, Kara has been boosted by the arrival of new regional industries, including the Brasserie du Bénin brewery, which have been the driving force behind the city's expansion. Some of the institutions here are worthy of a city of international pretensions, including the four-star *Hôtel Kara*, the imposing Banque Centrale, the sophisticated radio station and, especially, the grandiose **Maison du RPT** – the party headquarters. The town also boasts more paved roads than anywhere outside Lomé, and flashy illuminated road signs just like those in Paris.

Kara also has a lot going on. Every July, the **Evala** initiation celebrations and wrestling contests take over the town. Traditionally a strictly Kabyé affair, Evala is now a national event, televised across the country, and of huge importance to the town's economy. Competitions start as neighbourhood bouts, then move on to competitions within villages, and finally competitions between villages. Champions from the first, second and third year of initiation face each other for the supreme bouts. Greased with sheanut butter (to prevent their opponent getting a firm grip), they try to grab their opponent's arms or legs to topple him over and pin him in the dust. Bouts rarely last longer than a minute or two but the atmosphere among the rival spectators is feverish.

Arrival and accommodation

The centre of town is occupied by the **Grand Marché** and the adjoining **Gare du Marché**. Most of the town's shops and bars are near here, and there's an SGGG supermarket on the corner of the market on Avenue du 13 Janvier. The main **gare routière** is some 2km to the south of town on the Route Nationale, next to the Total station. This is where you're most likely to arrive, and there are plenty of taxis and *zemidjans* waiting to take you into the centre.

Your best bet for changing money and traveller's cheques is the UTB **bank** on Avenue Eyedéma, 2km north of the centre. The BIA bank next to the SGGG changes cash euros only, whilst the BTCI bank near the UTB has an ATM, but

▲ *Dapaong & Ouagadougou* ▲

KARA

0   500m

► *Kétao*

UTB Bank
BTCI Bank

RUE DU COLLÈGE CHAMINADE

A

AV. EYADÉMA

Palais de Justice
Banque Centrale
Stadium

B

2

AV. MAMA N'DANDA

4   **3**

Lufthansa Complex
BTD Bank

RUE DE L'HÔTEL KARA

Mairie

AV. DU 23 SEPTEMBRE

5   **D**
E **6** **7**
9

8

Shell

Grand Marché & Gare du Marchée

F
G   **10**
H 11

Total
SGGG

Fan Milk Depot

BTA Bank

I

Kara River

ROUTE NATIONALE

N

ACCOMMODATION
Auberge de la Détente   11
Centre Communautaire
  des Affaires Sociales   3
Hôtel La Concorde   8
Hôtel La Fayette   10
Hôtel de France   1
Hôtel Le Jardin   7
Hôtel Kara   5
Hôtel La Providence   4
Hôtel Le Relais   2
Hôtel Sapaw   9
Hôtel Le Sourire   6

RESTAURANTS, BARS & CLUBS
Bar Cascade   D
Bar La Détente   H
Bar Idéal   E
Café Muset   C
Centre Grill   A
Le Château   F
Chez Navi   G
Mini-Rizerie   B
La PJ Café Express   I

Gare Routière

▼ *Sokodé & Lomé*

doesn't change cash. At weekends, you may be able to change money at the *Hôtel Kara*'s reception desk. There's good, cheap **Internet** access at the cybercafé on the first floor of the Lufthansa Complex, near the BTD bank.

Accommodation

There's a good range of **places to stay**, though they fill up quickly for Evala in July.

Auberge de la Détente One block south of av du 13 Janvier ☎660.14.22. Good location in the centre of town, with clean, secure rooms with fan or a/c. The rooms in the new block are cleaner and better value. **①**

Centre Communautaire des Affaires Sociales av Mama N'Danida ☎660.61.18. Private rooms (some with a/c) and inexpensive dorm rooms with clean showers and baths. The restaurant serves inexpensive European dishes and good continental breakfasts. Dorm beds CFA1500, rooms **①**

Hôtel la Concorde Off av du 13 Janvier, near the post office ☎660.19.00, ✉rokpatcha@voila.fr. Friendly place in a good position and with a range of rooms, from swanky a/c rooms (**③**) with satellite TV, fridge and phone, to disappointing cheaper rooms (**①**) with shared facilities and fan. There's also a good rooftop bar.

Hôtel la Fayette av du 13 Janvier, east of the market ☎660.00.69. Brand-new accommodation in a central location, with great views across town from the rooftop. Rooms are spotless, comfortable and excellent value, and come with TV, phone and hot water. **②**

Hôtel de France Off rue du Collège Chaminade, north of the centre ☎660.03.42. A range of clean, well-furnished rooms, either with a/c or fan, and a good restaurant. **①**

Hôtel le Jardin Just off rue de l'Hôtel Kara, opposite the BTD bank ☎660.01.34,

✉le.jardin@bibway.com. Best known for its French-style garden restaurant, but also has four comfortable a/c rooms out the back – though they're a bit overpriced. **②**

Hôtel Kara rue de l'Hôtel Kara ☎660.05.17, ✆660.62.42. A bit of a dated concrete eyesore. The rooms all have a/c, satellite TV, phone and hot water, and there are also some more expensive and stylish bungalows, plus three tennis courts and a small, clean pool (CFA1000 non-guests) – a good place to beat the heat. **⑤**

Hôtel la Providence Off av Mama N'Danida, east of the centre ☎660.17.42. A bit far from the centre, but with clean rooms in a pleasant garden. Food available. **①**

Hôtel le Relais Off av Mama N'Danida ☎660.01.88. A 2km trek from the centre and slightly difficult to find, but set in a quiet courtyard with *paillotes* and exotic plants. The spacious self contained rooms, with fan or a/c, are tiled and spotless, and there's a pleasant bar as well. **①**

Hôtel Sapaw On a dirt track off rue de l'Hôtel Kara ☎660.14.44. One of the oldest and cheapest places in town, but rooms are still clean and comfortable, if a little pokey. There's also a cheap, popular bar and a restaurant. **①**

Hôtel le Sourire Just off rue de l'Hôtel Kara ☎660.03.48. In a good location near bars and amenities, but not too noisy, and with a variety of budget rooms (some a/c) set around a flowery courtyard. **①**

Eating, drinking and nightlife

Despite Kara's rapid modernization, the town still has many traditional features like the old **streetside restaurants** – the majority of these can be found around the Gare du Marché and the market. At the northern end of the market, stalls under corrugated-iron roofs have been set aside as *fufu* bars – this is where you'll get the best calorie-to-money ratio in town, though if you want something a bit more exciting, women nearby sell rice, beans, macaroni and so on, while *choucoutou* is served in calabashes by women at the Gare du Marché. If you're after **ice cream**, the ground floor of the Lufthansa Complex near the BTD bank has a fantastic ice-cream parlour; the Fan-Milk depot, south of the market near *Auberge de la Détente*, offers a cheaper alternative.

Café Muset rue de l'Hôtel Kara. Open 24 hours, this place does excellent cheap breakfasts and cheap meals like couscous, spaghetti and chips.

Centre Grill av Eyadéma. Popular, German-owned place with a vast selection of pizzas (CFA1000–3000), salads, pastas and American specialities, and you can watch CNN while you dine. It's also home to the town's best-stocked supermarket, as well as tennis courts and a children's playground.

Le Château Near the market. Run by the people who manage *Centre Grill*, and with an identical menu. Food is served at tables on a terrace overlooking one of the town's liveliest streets.

Chez Navi Opposite the market. The best in town for inexpensive but tasty Togolese cuisine, with rice or *pâte* served with spicy sauces from huge pots.

Hôtel Le Jardin Just off rue de l'Hôtel Kara,

opposite the BTD bank. The best of the hotel restaurants, with excellent French and Chinese specialities. Even if you don't eat here, it's worth coming for a drink on the garden terrace.

Mini-Rizerie Near the Palais de Justice. This old favourite has a good range of dishes, including European and Chinese, and a *menu du jour* for around CFA6000.

La PJ Café Express Down a dirt road opposite *Hôtel Kara*. Classy, upmarket bar which also serves a limited selection of European meals for up to CFA4500.

Drinking and nightlife

After dark, there's a limited number of good **bars** to choose from. *Bar Cascade*, next to *Café Muset*, is a popular choice, while *Bar Idéal*, across the road, has cheap beer and a few slot machines. *Bar la Détente*, just off Avenue du 13 Janvier and near Fan Milk, is another lively place with cheap beer. More expensive entertainment can be found at the *Lafeve Nightclub* (Saturdays only; cover charge CFA1000) at the *Hôtel Kara*. The glitzy *Nondwou Discotheque Kara* (CFA1000 entrance) at the *Hôtel de l'Union* is the town's only other nightclub; it's popular on Friday and Saturday nights with a younger crowd.

North of Kara

The route north from Kara leads through the **Kabyé country**, dotted with characteristic *soukala* – round *banco* houses covered with conical thatched roofs, called *tatas* by the French. The picturesque road, with its striking mountain vistas, passes through the town of **Niamtougou** before continuing as far as **Kandé**, the departure point for travel in the **Tamberma country**. After Kandé, it passes through the farmland that once was the **Kéran National Park** and the village of **Nouboulou**, former site of the reserve's lodgings, now abandoned. Finally it reaches **Dapaong**, the last major town before Burkina Faso.

Just north of Kara, a deviation in the road takes you around **Pya** – the president's birthplace. Look out for an odd building on a distant hilltop, with monumental dimensions that might lead you to mistake it for a modern cathedral. That's the general's humble abode and the reason why you're making a detour.

North of Kara, the first town of any size is **NIAMTOUGOU**, home to the Co-operative des Handicapés de Niamtougou (CODHANI), on the Route Nationale at the southern entrance to town. The co-operative produces a variety of clothes and crafts and you can wander around the workshops and watch batik being made. Items made here can be bought at the co-operative's shop – prices are high, but the quality is good and profits go back to this worthwhile cause. They also have pleasant

---

Moving on from Kara

Kara's *gare routière* is the largest in the north and has departures to any point between **Lomé** (7–8hr) and **Dapaong** (5hr), including **Kandé** (1hr 30min). If you're heading to **Bassar** (2hr), there are direct taxis from the Gare du Marché which travel along a good *piste*, saving you the trouble of changing in Sokodé. The road to **Benin** is good as far as Kétao and the border, but deteriorates after that until you arrive in **Djougou** (regular taxis from Kara), from where it's paved all the way to Parakou. The road to **Ghana** is also good on the Togo side.

accommodation in well-furnished, thatched huts with fans and shared facilities (☎665.00.30; ❶).

Kandé and the Tamberma country

KANDÉ (also spelled Kanté), 55km north of Kara, would surely have faded into obscurity had it not been on the Route Nationale. There's not much of anything in this tiny town of the Lamba people, and the surrounding countryside is hardly conducive to cultivating more than the bare staples of millet and yams. There's a small *gare routière* at the Unipetrol garage on the southern side of town on the Route Nationale, with vehicles mostly to Kara. Some 800m north, off a dirt track just west of the main road, the modest *Campement* (☎667.00.73; ❶) has an adequate **restaurant** and **accommodation** in spartan rooms with fans, although you're likely to be the only guests. At the southern entrance of town, the more atmospheric *Oxygène Plus* (☎667.01.19; ❶) has basic but comfortable self-contained rooms with fan.

Kandé would be easily overlooked if it weren't the starting point for excursions into the **Tamberma country**. The region was settled by the Tamberma (closely related to the Somba across the border in Benin) in the seventeenth century, as they sought refuge from the king of Abomey in present-day Benin, who raided far and wide in his quest for slaves to trade with the Portuguese. This explains the amazing fortresslike construction of Tamberma houses and their deep-rooted suspicion of outsiders.

Because these people have lived so long in isolation, their customs have remained largely unadulterated by outside influences. For that reason, if you get the chance to visit one of the villages, it can be a fascinating experience. On the other hand, this region is no longer a secret and the Tamberma country has long figured on the route of tour buses driving up from Lomé. This in turn has whetted the community's appetite for tourist money and reduced their fear of foreigners. You may be invited into a Tamberma home only to find, as soon as you enter, the women pulling off their tops, inserting bones through their lips, lighting up pipes and grinding millet. Meanwhile the men are rounding up bows and arrows, clay pipes, carvings and anything else that looks like something a tourist might buy. It's all about as spontaneous as a circus performance, and probably not as traditional, but you can take pictures – as long as you pay, of course.

These reservations apart, however, the **homes** are indeed remarkable, self-sufficient settlements, both aesthetic and functional, built some distance from each other with millet fields planted around each one. Their large central entrances were originally designed to store animals in case of attack, while grain was stockpiled in the towers and everything necessary for preparing and cooking food kept inside the house. The roof doubled as a lookout post, with rooms for sleeping built into those towers not being used as silos. With **fetishes** dotted around the house and built into the walls, the Tamberma had everything necessary in their homes to allow them to withstand long sieges. While the threat that led to the creation of such fortresses no longer exists, their architectural style has remained unchanged.

Practicalities

Unfortunately, unless you have your own vehicle, **getting to the Tamberma country** can be mighty difficult. One possibility is to walk, though the first village is over 20km from Kandé through raw bush, and hotels and even *buvettes* are unheard of. The alternative is to find a **taxi** in Kandé, but drivers will charge as much as they can get away with and are unlikely to take you at all for much under CFA10,000. Much cheaper are the collective taxis which run on market day (Wednesday) to **Nadoba**, 26km from Kandé and only 5km short of the Béninois border. The *Tata Bar* (☎667.20.10; ❶) in the village centre has basic **rooms** (no electricity or running water), a bar-restaurant and a small "museum" (actually a handful of objects in a room the size of a cupboard).

With your own vehicle, follow the *piste* from Kandé, which leads east off the main road just before the *gare routière* and heads all the way to **Natitingou** in Benin – although at times it's hard to tell if you're still on the road or in the middle of a millet field. If you see people walking along the road, don't hesitate to stop and give them a lift. It could lead to a friendship with someone who'll invite you to a village. Kids flagging down cars along the roadside are invariably looking for tourists – if you stop, they'll show you inside their homes and expect you to pay. It's a cringing notion, perhaps, but the easiest way to see inside a home and, as long as vast sums aren't laid out, doesn't do the Tamberma economy any harm.

Dapaong

Togo's last town in the north, **DAPAONG** (also spelled Dapaongo and Dapango) is home to a mixture of peoples of whom the **Gourma**, immigrants from the Burkina region, are the most numerous. This is a farming district, with cotton and rice the most important crops, while cattle ranching is also prevalent, owing to the presence of a sizeable Fula (Peulh) population, who came down from the Mossi country in Burkina in the mid-nineteenth century. Not many travellers show up in these parts, but Dapaong is a very pleasant town and a reasonable enough place to stop over on a journey north or south.

Arrival and orientation

The Route Nationale bypasses the centre, curving in a semicircle to the east. The **gare routière** is at the southern entrance to Dapaong some 2km south of the centre, where a road leads off the Route Nationale, goes through the centre of town, and rejoins it north of the centre. Normally, you'll be dropped off in the town centre; if you do get dropped at the *gare routière*, either walk north into town or get a *zemidjan* to the centre. **Taxis brousse** coming into the centre usually stop where the road forks around the *douane*, right by the Pharmacie le Soleil, with the Hôtel de Ville and hospital off to the west. From here, it's an easy walk to many of the town's hotels.

The **market** (main market days Wednesday and Saturday) is just southeast of the *douane*, down the dirt road opposite the Hôtel de Ville. Besides the usual bric-a-brac, you'll find handmade farm tools, pottery and cheap woven gear, including the broad-rimmed hats that are so common in the region – and there's no shortage of *choucoutou* bars where you can pause. Around the market square are several small shops and the old SGGG, now the Institut Tchakala, which houses a surprisingly good **Internet** café and bookshop; there's more expensive Internet access at *Cyber Espace*, near the Affaires Sociales building. The **post office** is by the central roundabout in town. The nearby **Musée Regional des Savanes** (Tues–Fri 9am–12.30pm & 3–6.30pm; CFA500) isn't particularly interesting, but is worth a look if you've got time to kill. The UTB **bank** on the hill behind the market is the only place in town to change money.

Moving on from Dapaong

Heading south, you can get taxis to Kara (5hr), Sokodé (6–7hr), Atakpamé (9–10hr) and Lomé (12–13hr) from the *gare routière*. Note that if you want to get off before Kara (for example in Mango, Niamtougou or Kandé), you'll still have to pay the full fare to Kara. Many people up from Lomé heading for **Ouagadougou** change taxis in Dapaong because it's cheaper than going direct (you'll save about a third on your fare). You'll almost certainly wait several hours, however, for a Ouaga-bound vehicle – if not a day or two – which tends to cancel out any saving. A better alternative to waiting in Dapaong is to take a taxi to the border town of **Cinkassé**, nominally in Burkina (though much of it spreads into Togo), from where you have a better chance of finding transport to Ouagadougou. Shared taxis leave from the station in the Zongo quarter of Dapaong, although even these aren't particularly regular, except on Cinkassé's market day (Sunday). If you're in a hurry, try to cross the border on foot to avoid the long queue of vehicles waiting to get through customs, and pick up onward transport from on the far side. If you get stuck, there's basic accommodation in the Togo side of town at the *Relais du Prince* (☎716.00.87; ①) in the main *gare*. Whatever option you take, be sure to leave early, as this stretch is notorious for its many checkpoints, which often make the journey to Ouagadougou a ten- or twelve-hour affair.

It is also possible to cross the border into **Ghana** from Cinkassé, heading for the town of **Bawku**, some 30km to the west. Again, the best day to find transport on this little-travelled route is on the market day of Sunday. There's no border post on the Togolese side, so you'll have to go to the officials at the Togo–Burkina crossing in Cinkassé to be officially stamped out of the country, before entering Ghana at Pulimakum, several kilometres west of Cinkassé.

Accommodation

There is nowhere luxurious to stay in Dapaong, but several pleasant and inexpensive hotels compete for custom.

Auberge CNTT 3km north of the centre on the Route Nationale ☎770.81.61. Upmarket lodgings with very clean rooms (a/c or fan) with private bathrooms, plus a reasonable restaurant. ①
Centre des Affaires Sociales Off the rte de Burkina, 1km north of the market. Typical of Affaires Sociales throughout the country, with clean dorm beds and self-contained rooms, some with a/c. It's all a bit grubby, but cheap. Dorm bed CFA1000, rooms ①
Hôtel Le Campement 300m south of the market on the main road into town ☎770.80.55. The best and most expensive accommodation in town, set in a colonial-style building with well-furnished, attractive rooms with a/c or fan. The courtyard bar and restaurant, with giant carved elephants, serves excellent but expensive French food. ②
Hôtel Lafia 1km south of the market on the main

road into town ☎946.22.41. Clean and friendly place with comfortable a/c rooms with bathroom, or less expensive lodgings with shower and fan. Try for a room with a balcony. ①
Hôtel Le Sahelien On the market square ☎770.81.84. An old favourite in the heart of town, but not too noisy and with good-value self-contained rooms with a/c or fan. ①
Hôtel la Tolérance Dapaong Off the Route Nationale 3km north of the centre ☎770.89.48. New hotel on the outskirts of town, with nicely decorated, comfortable rooms (fan or a/c) set around a small courtyard, and a good rooftop restaurant. ①
Hotel Le Verger Off the Route Nationale, 2km north of the centre. Set around a leafy courtyard with well-maintained and good-value rooms with fan – don't be put off by the run-down exterior. ①

Eating, drinking and nightlife

There's plenty of the usual street **food** around the market, including coffee and omelettes in the morning, but a dearth of more sophisticated places to eat. *Le Bon Samaritain*, near the *douane*, serves tasty and filling meals like chicken and chips. Out of town by the *gare routière*, the *Restaurant Sonu-Bé* opposite the Shell garage looks pretty scruffy from the outside but offers a good range of European-style meals for under CFA2000. *Bar La Rosse* on the main roundabout is popular for **drinking**. For **nightlife**, the *Pharaon Nightclub* (CFA1500), just off the Route Nationale north of town and near *Hôtel Le Verger*, gets going on Friday and Saturday nights from 10pm, while if you can stand the seedy atmosphere, you could try *Ca Coule Nightclub*, near the *Restaurant Sonu-Bé*, which plays mainly African music on Fridays and Saturdays (CFA500). A final, classier alternative is the *Oasis Night-club*, 50m behind *Hôtel Le Sahelien*.

Benin

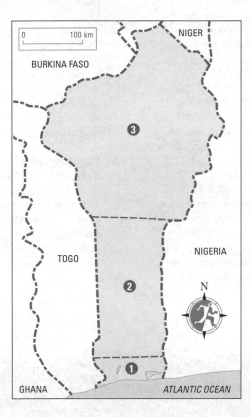

Benin highlights

✻ **Ganvié** Fascinating fishing village built on stilts on the lagoon north of Cotonou. See p.912

✻ **Ouidah** A former slave town and now centre of voodoo; retrace the tragedy of the Route des Esclaves, leading down to the beach and the Door of No Return. See p.913

✻ **Grand Popo** An ideal spot for relaxing on golden sands, with several great resorts nearby. See p.917

✻ **Porto Novo** Benin's official capital boasts crumbling colonial buildings in shades of orange and brown, dominated by a beautiful multicoloured mosque. See p.919

✻ **Abomey** Explore the history of the Dan-Homey kingdom through its palaces, now partially restored and vividly evoking its past grandeur – and cruelty. See p.922

✻ **Tata-Sombas** The fascinating, fortresslike homes of the Sombas; there's a particular concentration near the remote village of Boukoumbé. See p.931

✻ **Parc National de la Pendjari** One of the best reserves in West Africa, with hippos and crocodiles widespread in the Pendjari River. See p.933

Introduction and Basics

The world's lack of awareness of **Benin** – the Gulf of Guinea's least-known nation – is partly the result of two reclusive decades of struggle through one of West Africa's least successful and most repressive revolutions. Then, in 1991, the revolutionary rhetoric was thrown out, and Benin adopted a multiparty democracy and a liberal economic system. The government's long wariness of **tourism** changed rapidly, and Benin is now a popular and pleasant place to travel, with a steadily improving tourist infrastructure.

Benin's years of seclusion have left it an intriguing country, considerably more open than you might suspect. Several factors distinguish the country. First, a number of sophisticated indigenous states developed here, the largest and most urbane of which was the Fon kingdom of **Dan-Homey**, whose capital, in the heartlands of the southern savanna, was **Abomey**. Second, this well-organized and prosperous kingdom was one of Africa's biggest centres of the slave trade from the sixteenth to the nineteenth century. The trade wasn't finally ended until 1885, when the last Portuguese slave cargo steamed out of Ouidah, bound for Brazil. By then, a considerable amount of imported wealth had been amassed in the country. Lastly, it was in the French colony of Dahomey – as Benin was known – that Catholic **mission schools** were most influential in the old empire of Afrique Occidentale Française. Thousands of highly qualified students graduated from its secondary schools and taught all over West Africa, giving the country a dynamic intellectual reputation that has coloured its personality deeply.

The ancestors of the **Béninois** of today come from many different areas and arrived in the territory of the present country after several centuries of migrations, a fact that explains the variation in social organization and cultural practices. Most Béninois adhere to traditional African **religious beliefs**. Along the coast, **voodooism** is common, particularly among the Ewe-speakers. **Islam** was brought from the north by Arab, Hausa and Songhai-Dendi traders. It extended as far south as Djougou, and even into the Yoruba country. Perhaps as much as fifteen percent of the population are Muslim. **Christianity** came with the Europeans and spread principally along the coast – where it was soon integrated into voodoo – and over the central plateau.

Fact file

Known as **Dahomey** during the colonial period (after the Fon kingdom, Dan-Homey), the **République du Bénin** adopted the name of the old West African kingdom (located in present-day southern Nigeria) after the 1972 coup led by northerner Mathieu Kérékou. The **population** is around 7 million, a good tenth of whom live in Cotonou, the de facto capital. The **official capital** remains Porto Novo, a much smaller coastal town that served as the colonial administrative centre. Benin's area is 113,000 square kilometres, approximately the size of Louisiana, or slightly smaller than England. The **national debt** is around £726 million ($1.18 billion), less than, for example, France's annual state subsidy for the arts.

In 1990 Mathieu Kérékou's dictatorship collapsed and the nation began converting to a **multiparty democracy**. Nicéphore Soglo became president when democratic elections were held in 1991, though Kérékou returned to power in the 1996 elections, retaining his presidency in 2001 after disputed elections. The next elections are scheduled for 2006.

Where to go

Benin is mostly thinly wooded savanna, part of the **open country** that penetrates south more or less to the coast between the rainforests of Nigeria and Ghana and which partly accounts for the different shifts of history that have taken place here – easier travel and trade, more successful armies and faster conquests.

A flat sandy plain runs the whole length of the **coast**, broken up by a string of picturesque **lakes and lagoons**. The coast offers little enticement in the sea (rough and terrifyingly dangerous) but the **old towns** – including **Porto Novo**, Benin's crumbling capital, and the old Brazilian quarters of **Ouidah** – have a certain flaked-out appeal, and are full of interest in their museums and markets. The over-exploited stilt village of **Ganvié** is the coastal site of which you're most likely to catch a (tourist's-eye) glimpse, while grubby, post-revolutionary **Cotonou**, the country's only city, makes a poor first impression.

Inland, the improvement is rapid, as a gentle **plateau** slopes gradually north to spread over the entire centre of the country in a rich patchwork of agriculture. Coffee, cotton and oil-palm **plantations** collide with small fields of **subsistence crops** – maize, millet, rice, yams and cassava. The most interesting town is **Abomey** – capital of the Dan-Homey kingdom and site of its surviving royal palaces and museum.

In the northwest, the sheer cliffs and abundant greenery of the **Atakora Mountains** rear up in a long, dramatic ridge that stands in impressive contrast to the plains and provides a striking backdrop for one of the country's most interesting and inaccessible cultures – that of the **Somba**, who lived in relative isolation until the 1970s. On the border with Burkina, the **Parc National de la Pendjari** is rated one of West Africa's most interesting faunal reserves; while in the extreme north, the Gourma plains roll up in sweeping grasslands to the **Parc National du "W" du Niger** – not at all easy to get to without your own transport – which spreads across the borders into Niger and the southeast tip of Burkina Faso.

When to go

Although roads are improving, the weather can have a very adverse effect on travel, particularly if you intend to travel off the main highways. It's best to avoid the rainy seasons, which can be prolonged and oppressive. In the **south**, there are two **rainy seasons** (a long one from April to July and a short one in October and November) and two **dry seasons** (a short one, August and September, and a long one from December to March). Temperatures fluctuate little throughout the year.

In the **north**, the year divides simply into the rainy season, which lasts from late May to October, and the dry season, which lasts from November to early May. In parts of the Atakora region – Natitingou, for example – the rain falls virtually unabated from April to November. Temperatures vary more dramatically than in the south, and when the northerly harmattan wind blows in December, nights can be quite cool.

Getting there from the rest of Africa

Despite being so centrally placed in the region, Benin is not a country to which many

Average temperatures and rainfall

Cotonou

	Jan	Feb	Mar	Apr	May	June	July	Aug	Sept	Oct	Nov	Dec
Temperatures °C												
Min (night)	23	25	26	26	24	23	23	23	23	24	24	24
Max (day)	27	28	28	28	27	26	26	25	26	27	28	27
Rainfall mm	33	33	117	125	254	366	89	38	66	135	58	13
Days with rainfall	2	2	5	7	11	13	7	3	6	9	6	1

travellers make initial flights into West Africa. All international flights operate to and from **Cotonou**, with most of the direct flights from neighbouring countries handled by Trans Air Benin. They fly from **Abidjan** to Cotonou three times a week, with additional flights on this route operated by Air Ivoire, Air Sénégal and Air Mauritanie. Trans Air Benin, Air Togo, Air Ivoire and Air Burkina all offer flights from **Lomé**. From **Ouagadougou** to Cotonou, Air Burkina provide a service four times weekly, while Inter-Air fly weekly, and there are a similar number of flights each week from **Douala**, either with Air Ivoire or Cameroon Airlines. Air Sénégal fly weekly from **Dakar**, while from **Bamako** Trans Air Benin provide a weekly service. There are a couple of flights a week from **Accra**, one with Ghana Airways and one with Air Ivoire, and also a couple of flights each week from **Pointe Noire** in the Republic of the Congo, with Trans Air Benin.

From South Africa, Cameroon Airlines fly three times a week from **Johannesburg**. There are no direct links or convenient connections to Cotonou from Lagos, Conakry, Banjul or Bissau.

Overland

Béninois customs and immigration rarely present any special problems, but at most border posts you must state where you plan on staying. All border posts now operate around the clock and can issue 48-hour **transit visas** (Mon–Fri 8am–12.30pm & 3–6.30pm, Sat 8am–12.30pm).

From Nigeria

The commonest point of entry has traditionally been via the **Badagri** coastal road from Lagos to **Kraké** on the Benin side. This border crossing is always crowded and it may take some time to get through the formalities. Your bags will be given a perfunctory search, but it's not likely your Nigerian currency declaration form will even be checked. Previously, when the Badagri route was sometimes closed, travellers have used the border crossing from **Idiroko** in Nigeria to **Igolo** in Benin, a little way north of Porto Novo. Roads on both routes are surfaced and in reasonable shape.

From Niger and Burkina Faso

The road is tarred the whole way from **Niamey** to Cotonou.

The road from **Fada-Ngourma** in Burkina Faso is tarred to the border on the Burkina side, from where a stretch of rough *piste* down to Natitingou via Porga is undergoing major improvements. There's a twice-weekly TCV bus (Tues & Sat) from **Bobo-Dioulasso** via **Ouagadougou** and **Fada-Ngourma** to Cotonou, and a daily service to Pama, from where infrequent transport runs to the border at Porga, where you can change for Tanguiéta or Natitingou.

From Togo

Taxis speed along the coastal highway from **Lomé** to Cotonou all day long. Although there's no Béninois embassy in Togo, **visas** are issued on the spot at the border post of **Hilakondji**.

From the north of Togo, a paved road leads from Kara to the border post at **Kétao**. The *piste* leading on to Djougou in Benin is well maintained, if a bit slippery when wet. Alternatively, if you have your own vehicle, you could take a very minor *piste* that branches off the main road at Kandé and heads through the **Tamberma country**. Little traffic uses this route and you're not likely to be aware that you've crossed the border until you get to the main road to Natitingou. When you arrive at this latter town, go to the police and customs to get your passport stamped.

Red tape and visas

All nationalities, apart from those from ECOWAS member states, need a visa to enter Benin. Single- and multiple-entry visas can be obtained from Benin's embassies. If you're flying in on a charter with the French

> For important practical information applying to all West African countries, covering health, transport, cultural hints and more, plus details on getting to the region from beyond Africa, see Basics, pp.9–87.

company Point-Afrique, note that they routinely obtain visas for their passengers (see p.13).

All **border checkpoints** issue 48-hour transit visas, requiring no photos and costing CFA10,000. Visa extensions (CFA12,000 for up to three months, though in practice the length of the extension awarded can vary) are easily obtained both in Cotonou at the immigration office and in Natitingou at the Police Nationale Commissariat. For details of embassies in Benin, see p.911.

Information, websites and maps

Benin has no overseas tourist offices. In Cotonou, the **Direction du Tourisme et de l'Hôtellerie** has very limited material and is of little practical help. On the **Internet**, ⓦwww.benintourisme.com has general information on Benin's culture, arts and government, as well as facts on accommodation and transport for visitors to the country. For the latest news and general info on Benin in English, try ⓦwww.beninpost.com. A good online paper, in French, is ⓦwww.lematinalonline.com.

The best **map** of Benin is published by IGN (1:600,000), and includes detailed *pistes* and topographical material, and is especially useful in the confusing lagoon areas along the coast. They also produce a detailed, although slightly outdated, map of Cotonou (1:15,000). Alternatively there's the ITMB map of Togo and Benin (1:864,000). The Institut National de Cartographie in Cotonou (see p.911) has reasonable maps – their Cotonou map is excellent.

Health

Yellow fever is currently the only vaccination required for travel to Benin. Malaria is widespread and, as in neighbouring countries, increasingly resistant to chloroquine-based drugs (see p.32).

Except in Cotonou, some sort of **water purification** is highly recommended, unless you're sticking to the widely available mineral water Possotomé. You should avoid swimming in streams and lakes in the lagoon regions of coastal Benin, and don't walk barefoot in the grass surrounding them. These areas are almost invariably infested by schistosome parasites which transmit **bilharzia**. **Hospital facilities** throughout the country are meagre, with drugs and equipment in short supply. Cotonou has more reliable places, while Tanguiéta's Hôpital Saint Jean de Dieu is the best hospital in the north. Major towns have a sprinkling of **pharmacies**.

Costs, money and banks

Benin is part of the **CFA zone** (£1 = CFA930, $1 = CFA600). You can get by on £8/$13 a day if you're staying in inexpensive hotels and eating street food; reckon on at least £15/$25 if you want to stay in midrange places and enjoy one decent restaurant meal a day.

The major **banks**, including Ecobank, Financial Bank, Bank of Africa and the Banque Internationale du Bénin (BIB), have branches in most towns. Bank opening hours are usually Monday to Friday 8am–12.30pm & 3.30–7pm, with the exception of Ecobank which conveniently stays open from 8am to 5.30pm with no break, and is open Saturday mornings. The Financial Bank usually offers the best service and good exchange rates, and they also give cash advances on **Visa cards**. Note that MasterCard in Benin will get you nowhere. Euros are by far the best currency to bring; dollars and sterling can only be changed in the major towns. As for **changing traveller's cheques**, all the banks will insist on seeing receipts and your passport before any transaction.

Getting around

Benin's **road network** has improved dramatically since the early 1990s. The **rail** network, on the other hand, is down to one line between Parakou and Cotonou. There are no scheduled **domestic flights**.

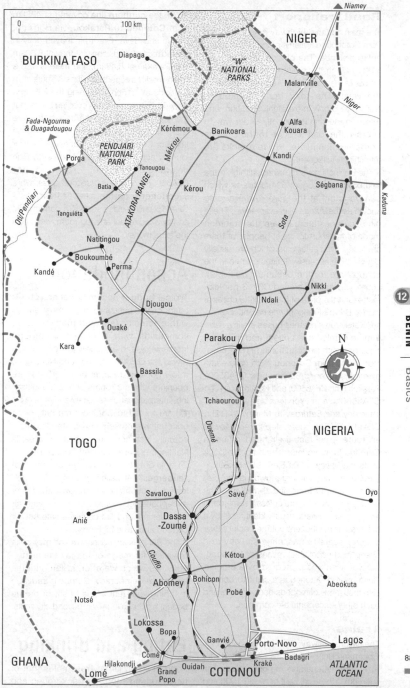

Road transport

The main **national highway** runs for 742km from Cotonou to Malanville and is paved the entire distance. The other main road runs 114km along the coast from the Nigerian border in the east to the Togolese border in the west. The road from Parakou to Natitingou is now in excellent condition, and major engineering is currently under way to improve the road through to the Burkina border via Tanguiéta. Police checks are refreshingly infrequent.

The Béninois have remained faithful to the **taxi brousse**, Peugeot 504 *familiales* which can be found at the *gare routière* (also known as the *autogare*) in every town. These nine-seater estate cars are the common mode of transport for most people, or there are faster, five-seater cars which are usually slightly more expensive (prices quoted in the chapter are for the cheapest possible). Journeys work out around CFA13 per kilometre, and the price of fuel is a little cheaper than in Benin's Francophone neighbours.

Privately-run Africalines **buses** are invariably a more comfortable option, and most are equipped with air-conditioning. They cover four routes **from Cotonou**, with daily early-morning services to Savalou (5hr; CFA3500), Parakou (7hr; CFA6500) and Natitingou (10hr; CFA8500), and services on Tuesday, Thursday and Saturday to Malanville (12hr; CFA11,000). The buses stop in most towns en route – contact their head office in Cotonou for more information and to book seats in advance (℡30.85.85, ℻30.85.89).

Public transport in large towns is the preserve of **shared taxis** and **zemidjans**. The latter (pronounced, more or less, "zemi-john") are *mobylette* drivers, usually identifiable by a coloured shirt, who rent out the back of their scooter seats to passengers. They're a cheap (and negotiable) means of transport, but you won't be protected by a helmet. Rush hour in Cotonou is a sight to behold, with thousands of mopeds dodging cars and each other – accidents are common.

Trains

The national **railway** company, l'Organisation Commune Bénin-Niger des Chemins de fer et Transports, operates the only railway line still running in Benin. Built between 1900 and 1939, the **northern line** covers the 438km from **Cotonou to Parakou**, via Bohicon, Dassa and Savè. One train leaves daily in each direction, departing Cotonou at 8.30am and Parakou at 8.42am, and there is also a twice-weekly sleeper train (Tues & Thurs from Cotonou at 7.15pm, returning the following day). The whole trip takes over ten hours, but many Béninois still take the train as the fare is slightly lower than the same route by bush taxi. For Cotonou–Parakou one-way (a 10hr journey according to the schedule, though delays are frequent), expect to pay CFA5600/CFA4000 first/second class, while a **couchette** on the sleeper train costs CFA7150. First-class seats are comfortable and give you reasonable leg-room, well worth the extra money.

Accommodation

Typical **budget** accommodation (❶–❸) offers quite pleasant rooms, almost always with electricity, fans and running water, sometimes with a private bathroom. Increasingly, and especially in well-travelled towns like Ouidah, Abomey and Natitingou, a few good **mid-range** hotels (❹–❻) are opening, with s/c rooms and air conditioning. International-class establishments (❼ & ❽) are limited to Cotonou; the only place upcountry approaching this standard (and actually featuring much cheaper rates) is Natitingou's hotel in the ACCOR chain.

Look out for the French-run chain of **"auberges"**. All called *"Auberge de…"* followed by the name of the town, they offer exceptionally clean rooms, some with air conditioning, and are usually a safe bet for comfort and value for money.

The Béninois are hospitable and may invite travellers for meals or to stay the night – activities which were forbidden until the advent of democracy. *Camping sauvage* (pitching your tent in the bush, or on the beach) has been legalized beyond city limits.

Eating and drinking

Food in Benin largely resembles that of neighbouring Togo: for background and

Accommodation price codes

Accommodation prices in this chapter are coded according to the following scale, whose equivalent in pounds sterling/US dollars is used throughout the book. Prices refer to the rate you can expect to pay for a room with two beds. Single rooms, or single occupancy, will normally cost at least two-thirds of the twin-occupancy rate. For further details, see p.51.

❶ Under CFA4700 (under £5/$8).
❷ CFA4700–9000 (£5–10/$8–16).
❸ CFA9000–14,000 (£10–15/$16–24).
❹ CFA14,000–19,000 (£15–20/$24–32).

❺ CFA19,000–28,000 (£20–30/$32–48).
❻ CFA28,000–37,000 (£30–40/$48–64).
❼ CFA37,000–47,000 (£40–50/$64–80).
❽ Over CFA47,000 (£50/$80).

details on local staples and popular dishes, refer to the food section in the previous chapter. Cotonou has no particular gastronomic reputation in West Africa, but there is a growing variety of top-quality restaurants serving French, Lebanese and Chinese food. Outside of Cotonou, cuisine is pretty much limited to French or African cuisine.

Many hotels, even less expensive ones, have their own restaurant. In the provinces, eating houses are usually small **buvettes** specializing in rice, **pâte** (the generic term for pounded starch based on cassava, yam or sweet potato), **moyo** (like wheat semolina) or macaroni served with sauce.

Street food is very inexpensive, and you can easily eat your fill for less than CFA1000. Mid-range restaurants charge between CFA1000 and CFA3000 for a main course – although in Cotonou there's little in the lower end of this scale.

One of Benin's leading industries is the Société Nationale des Boissons which produces the national beer, **La Béninoise**, and a variety of carbonated soft drinks. The mineral water Possotomé is widely available in 1.5-litre bottles. Along the coast, **palm wine** is plentiful, as is the lethal African firewater known as **sodabi**. In the north, **home-made beer** made from millet, known as *chapalo* or *tchacpalo*, is more common.

Communications

Cotonou is the only reliable place to receive post. The main PTT here is fairly efficient

Benin's IDD code is ☎229.

and the poste restante service good. Parcels can only be sent air mail, which is very expensive.

International phone calls can be made either from PTTs in most towns or from any other telecentre. Expect to pay CFA1850 per minute to France, CFA2400 to elsewhere in Europe, CFA1850 to the USA and CFA3500 to Australia. As for domestic calls, note that Benin numbers don't have area codes.

Cellphones are increasingly popular in Benin, especially due to the poor landline system. You can use your mobile in the major towns and in a wide radius of Cotonou through the GSM 900 Spacetel network, although connections are often sporadic.

Internet access is available in the major towns. Connections are relatively good and cost anything from CFA500 to CFA1000 per hour.

The media

Although not as visible as the press in other countries, there are two daily **newspapers** – *Le Matin* and *La Nation* (the government-owned paper) – and dozens of small weekly, fortnightly or monthly sheets. None has a big circulation. The best for a political-economical analysis are *Le Point*, *Matinal* and the weekly *Gazette Du Golfe*.

The state-run Office de Radiodiffusion et de Télévision du Bénin (**ORTB**) puts out **radio** broadcasts in French, English and eighteen national languages, and several hours of **television** from the afternoon onward. There are many privately owned radio stations, and a commercial TV station,

12

BENIN | Basics

LC2. BBC World Service can be heard in Cotonou on 101.7 FM.

Opening hours, public holidays and festivals

Most businesses are open from Monday to Friday between 8am and 12.30pm, and again from 3.30pm until 7pm; government offices open and close half an hour earlier in the afternoons.

Christian holidays and New Year's Day are public holidays. Muslim celebrations are less formally observed, though everything shuts down in the north for them. Ramadan, however, isn't conspicuously disruptive. In addition the following holidays are observed: Martyrs' Day (January 16), Labour Day (May 1), Independence Day (August 1), Assumption (August 15), Armed Forces' Day (October 26), All Saints' Day (November 1), National Day (November 30) and Harvest Day (December 31). An annual festival centered around Ouidah is held on January 10, celebrating the importance of the **voodoo** religion in Benin. In 1996 this was designated as a national public holiday and is known as **Vodoun** or Traditional Day, now celebrated throughout the country.

Ouidah was also an important focus for the **Festival International Gospel et Racines**, first held in late October and early November of 2002, and also celebrated in Cotonou and Porto Novo. Commemorating slavery and celebrating reconciliation, it hosts a series of live concerts of gospel and African music, featuring well-known musicians from around the world, and is expected to become an annual event.

Entertainment and sport

Musical culture is well-developed in Benin, but global sounds continue to exert a strong influence on local musicians. For a short account of musicians and CDs, see p.898.

Theatre has never been a significant part of cultural life in Benin, and Béninois cinema has long been in the doldrums. Béninois and French cinéastes recently tried to jump-start the industry with an annual (January) film festival in Ouidah – Quintessence – with support from one of the country's best-known young directors, Jean Odoutan, whose first and most successful feature film, the darkly comic *Barbecue-Pejo* (2000), recounts the disastrous purchase of a European's Peugeot car by an impoverished farmer. *Si-Gueriki* ("The Queen Mother"), a film by another Béninois director, Idrissou Mora Kpai, was shortlisted at FESPACO 2003.

In the sphere of **sports**, the dismal performance of the national **football** team, Les Écureuils (the "Squirrels") for many years suppressed the game's profile in Benin. However, there were successes in 2002 and 2003 against Tanzania, Niger, Burkina and Zambia, and at the time of writing, mid-2003, football was enjoying a renaissance as the country looked forward to participating in the African Cup of Nations in Tunisia in 2004. Key local teams to look out for are Buffles de Borgou, Énergie Sport and Mogas 90 de la Sonacop.

Directory

Airport departure tax CFA2500, if not already included in the ticket.

Crime and personal safety Benin for the most part is an exceptionally safe country to travel in. However, in recent years there have been a number of armed robberies after dark on the northern highways, and local people say that it is inadvisable to travel in the north at night. The road from Malanville to Kandi has been known to be closed at night for extended periods.

Emergencies Police ☎17, fire service ☎18.

Photography You need no official permit to take pictures in Benin, but photographing people can be a sensitive issue. It's wise to ask permission first, especially in areas such as Somba country. People in touristic areas like Ganvié and Ouidah are likely to demand money, and snapping away without permission can, as usual, lead to problems.

Voodoo Voodoo is the religion of the coast, especially among Ewe-speakers. In many ways, Ewe practices are similar to those of the Yoruba and Fon: all believe in a single supreme God who created the universe (Mawu in Fon). On earth, lesser divinities are charged with power over thunder (Xebioso or Shango), iron and war (Ogun or Gu), land and disease (Sakpata or Cankpana), and so on. They possess or "mount" the bodies of their devotees and their help can be solicited through the work of fetish priests. See the box on p.914 for more details.

Wildlife Benin's northern regions, although densely farmed and populated in their southern parts, spread into a broad zone of thinly populated savanna and uplands – one of West Africa's best game-viewing areas. There are significant concentrations of wildlife, especially in the Pendjari and "W" du Niger national parks, including several hundred – possibly a thousand – elephants.

Women's issues The position of women in Benin has been little improved by the revolutionary 1970s and 1980s, or by democratization. In fact it appears they have even less involvement in politics and decision-making than elsewhere in West Africa. From the traveller's point of view, there's relatively little sexual harassment.

A brief history of Benin

The earliest history of the territory that is now Benin is obscure. The far north was under thrall to the Niger River's Songhai empire by the end of the fifteenth century. Meanwhile, in the south, having built the fort at Elmina in Ghana in 1482, the **Portuguese** continued along the coast and began trading with local rulers from the 1520s. Porto Novo and Ouidah developed through the sixteenth and seventeenth centuries into important commercial centres where slaves were traded for European cloth and guns.

The British, Dutch and French, seeking labour for their American colonies, soon joined the Portuguese in the traffic, establishing their own coastal forts and commercial depots during the seventeenth century. By the 1690s, some twenty thousand slaves were being shipped annually out of Ouidah and lesser ports.

The Slave Coast

By as early as the beginning of the eighteenth century, the **Dan-Homey kingdom** (a vassal of the great Yoruba **Oyo empire** to the east) dominated the politics of the region. One of Dan-Homey's rulers, **Agadja** (in power 1708–40), subjugated the districts south of his capital Abomey, and finally took Ouidah itself. With access to the coast, his empire was now poised to control international trade – primarily in slaves. But he had exceeded the terms of his licence with Oyo and a protracted conflict ensued which resulted in Oyo's definitive conquest of Dan-Homey. There followed a period of desperate slave-hunting as the Dan-Homey king **Tegbesu** tried to rebuild his country's war-shattered economy (see p.924).

After the French Revolution, however, a wave of **antislavery sentiment** began to sweep Europe. In France, the *Decret du 16 pluviôise an II* of February 4, 1794, abolished the trade, though it was later reinstated by Napoleon. In 1802, Denmark became the first European nation to abolish the slave trade permanently. Britain followed in 1807 and from 1819 to 1867, British ships patrolled the coast, arresting slave ships and resettling the captives in Freetown, Sierra Leone. France definitively outlawed the trade in 1818.

These moves coincided with a severe shortage of slaves in the region, in large part because of excessive human sacrifices in Abomey. A Brazilian mulatto, **Francisco Felix de Souza**, entered into a blood pact with the young **Prince Ghezo** of Dan-Homey and supplied the guns for him to overthrow the incumbent of the stool (throne) in Abomey in 1818, in return for which he was granted a monopoly over the slave trade (and became the "Viceroy of Ouidah"; see p.924).

By the 1830s, however, the nature of most commerce in the region had fundamentally changed and **palm oil** became the primary export. The French soon gained the upper hand in the regional trade when representatives from Marseille soap-making companies arrived in Ouidah in 1843 and travelled to Abomey, where they signed a contract with the Dan-Homey king, the same Ghezo, granting them trading rights at Ouidah. In 1861, Lagos became a British colony. **King Toffa** of Porto Novo had claims on the town of Badagary which the British now controlled. Worried that their influence would spread westward, Toffa called on the French for support and, in 1863, Porto Novo became a **French protectorate**. In 1868, the new **King Glele** of Abomey ceded rights to Cotonou to the French, who had by now established themselves as the most prominent European power along Benin's coast.

French conquest

Good relations between France and the Dan-Homey kingdom had soured by the end of the century. In December 1889, a new sovereign, **Behanzin**, was enstooled. He adopted a more combative attitude to the French, who were beginning to look less like trading partners and more like a force of occupation. Behanzin refused to recognize French rights over Cotonou and was angered that the foreigners had allied themselves with Toffa, one of his bitterest enemies. After funeral ceremonies for his father Glele, Behanzin ordered an **attack on Cotonou**. On March 4,

1890, some five to six thousand Dan-Homey warriors marched on the city and withdrew only after inflicting numerous casualties. A month later, the army surrounded Porto Novo and clashed with the French at Atchoukpa on the northern outskirts of the city.

Other skirmishes followed and in April 1892, Behanzin sent the following message to French authorities: "I warn you that if one of our villages is touched by the fire of your cannons, I will march directly to crush Porto Novo and all the villages belonging to Porto Novo. I would like to know how many independent French villages have been overtaken by me, King of Dan-Homey. I request you to keep calm and do your business in Porto Novo. That way, we can remain in peace as it was before. But if you want war, I am ready. I will not finish it. It will last a hundred years and will kill 20,000 of my men."

The threat was taken seriously by the French, who knew that Behanzin possessed more than 5000 modern firearms and was still being supplied by the Germans and the British. The government in Paris sent a distinguished commander to handle the situation, **Colonel Dodds**, a mulatto from St-Louis in Senegal. In August 1892, Dodds began his northern march to conquer Abomey. Accompanied by Senegalese and Hausa infantry, the French went to the Oueme River and followed its course. Although the army was sporadically engaged by Dan-Homey troops, including divisions of **Amazons** – skilled female warriors specially trained to use the new Martini-Henry rifles – it was the Dan-Homey which received the heaviest casualties in the clashes. By November 1892, when the French arrived at Cana – the village where Dan-Homey kings were traditionally buried – Behanzin's army had lost 4000 dead and twice as many wounded.

The king prepared himself for a **last stand**. He recruited every warrior capable of carrying a gun, including the massed ranks of his Amazons, and got the nation's slaves to join the battle, promising them freedom in return. But the effort was in vain; the army was defeated and Behanzin was forced to retreat with meagre reserves. On November 16, 1892, Dodds marched on Abomey to find the city already in flames, torched by the retreating army. It took another two years for the French to track down and capture Behanzin (betrayed by the newly French-enstooled Fon king) and he was transported to exile in Martinique.

The colonial era

Their main rival in the region at last conquered, the French went on to subdue the north of the country, which they now called **Dahomey**. Colonial frontiers were drawn up in agreement with Britain to the east and Germany (which held Togo) to the west. In 1901, the present borders were fixed and, in 1904, Dahomey became part of AOF (French West Africa).

French policy in Dahomey was partly shaped by the influence of Catholic missions, which sent large numbers of envoys into the territory in the 1920s and 1930s. Catholic seeds had been sown from a very early period, with the arrival in the eighteenth century of influential **Brazilian** families and Christian **freed slaves**. Moreover, the climate, open country and dominant voodoo religion of the south were not strongly antithetical to missionary activity. The result was that early in the colonial period, Dahomey acquired a reputation for mission-educated academics and administrators. By the 1950s, many middle-ranking posts in the French colonial service right across West and Central Africa were occupied by Dahomeyans, most of whom were Fon or Yoruba from the relatively prosperous south.

With few mineral resources (no gold or other precious metals), Dahomey's economy depended very heavily on its **oil-palm plantations**. In addition, there were close commercial relations with Nigeria, both legal trade and illicit smuggling.

Independence

No single, national leader rose to pre-eminence during the fifteen-year post-war period on the road to independence. Instead, an ethnic and regional competition developed in which three prominent figures jockeyed for political prominence. They were **Hubert Maga**, representing the north, **Migan Apithy** of the southeast, and **Justin Ahomadegbe** from the southwest. On the eve of independence, the three managed to form a coalition, the Parti Progressiste Dahoméen, but unity was superficial. Each commanded the loyalties of about one-third of the country's population and distrusted the others. After some seventy years of French rule, the **Republic of Dahomey** became independent on August 1, 1960.

Elections were held in December 1960, which Maga's Parti Dahoméen de l'Unité won. The northerner became the nation's first president. But an uneasy dissatisfaction prevailed in the south where supporters of Apithy and Ahomadegbe suspected the new leader was trying to consolidate his position and eliminate his two most formidable rivals. By 1963, unrest had led to **political riots**, as students and workers took to the streets of Cotonou. Truckloads of angry northerners descended on the town to confront the protestors.

Years of instability

The situation had got out of hand and it was clear that serious violence would ensue if Maga stayed in power. At the same time, it also seemed possible that the north would try to secede if either of Maga's rivals took over the presidency.

The impasse was resolved in October 1963 when Maga was deposed in a **military coup** led by **Colonel Christophe Soglo**. The takeover was not a sudden or unexpected event, however. For two days prior to the coup, Soglo met with Maga and Apithy (who was vice-president) and members of the trade unions and the army. His ascent to power seemed the only way to maintain order. Soglo never mobilized the army and no shots were ever fired. After taking over the leadership, he immediately set about restoring civilian rule. A new constitution was adopted and, in January 1964, transparently undemocratic **"elections"** took place. The coalition party formed by **Apithy and Ahomadegbe** during the four months of military rule received 99.8 percent of the vote.

Maga had meanwhile been jailed on charges of conspiracy to assassinate the two southern leaders. Apithy thus became the new president and Ahomadegbe took on the job of prime minister. Under a guise of unity, the two men worked against one another, each trying to consolidate his own position within the party. The **exclusion of the north** from the political process led to more riots and bloodshed in the northern town of Parakou and there were more political detentions for conspiracy to overthrow the government. But what brought the two southern leaders to loggerheads was a law concerning the appointment of members to the Supreme Court – Maga happened to be on trial at the time – which placed the judiciary in conflict with the government. Ahomadegbe, with the party behind him, demanded President Apithy's resignation. The president refused. Chaos within the party was coupled with widespread public discontent from outside its ranks, which reached fever pitch with the announcement of a 25 percent salary cut for civil servants to try to reduce the country's burgeoning deficit. In its distress, the government was virtually unable to act and normal administration began to break down. The military again intervened, and Colonel Soglo forced both Apithy and Ahomadegbe to step down.

A provisional government, headed by **Tahirou Congacou**, who was president of the National Assembly, released Maga from prison and set about writing a new constitution with the joint consultation of all three leaders. Elections were to be held in January 1966, but campaigning never began as, still posturing for position, Maga and Apithy allied themselves against Ahomadegbe in a move which triggered trade union protest. On December 22, 1965, Soglo intervened for a third time, on this occasion assuming power as the head of a **military regime**. Maga, Apithy and Ahomadegbe exiled themselves in Paris.

Soglo remained head of state for two years, but his term soon met with criticism. He was accused of mishandling Dahomey's affairs and of presiding over a military structure that was rife with **corruption**. In 1967, workers went on strike to protest against intolerable economic conditions. The subsequent and predictable ban on union activity led to yet another, equally predictable **coup**, led by **Major Maurice Kouandété**, and supported by junior officers including one Captain Mathieu Kérékou.

Continuing coups

After protracted disputes and negotiations, the army chief of staff **Alphonse Alley** took over as head of state, with Kouandété his prime minister. The military government had a strongly northern cast. Kouandété drew up another constitution and scheduled new elections for May 1968. Many politicians were banned from participating, however, including the elder statesmen Maga, Apithy and Ahomadegbe. The trio, reunited in their exclusion, called for a boycott, and on the day of the elections, only 26 percent of the eligible voters turned out. An unknown doctor, **Basil Akjou Moumuni**, won the presidency, but the elections were immediately annulled, and the military instead conferred the presidency on the low-profile former Foreign Minister, **Emil Derlin Zinsou**.

In December 1969, sixteen months into his term, Zinsou was himself overthrown by the same man who had put him in power, Kouandété. The newest coup was spurred by divisions within the military and seemed to have more to do with corruption and personality differences than with ethnic tensions; there was no special crisis to justify the military takeover. It was the first time force had been used. Zinsou's car was sprayed with bullets in downtown Cotonou, but the president escaped with his life.

Fellow officers prevented Kouandété taking power himself. Instead, a **Military Directorate** was established with Lieutenant-Colonel **Paul Emile de Souza** in charge. Once more, elections were set and this time the three old-guard politicians were allowed to participate. Maga was set to win in his loyal Atakora region, but not to receive a majority over Apithy and Ahomadegbe combined. De Souza cancelled the Atakora poll. Declaring that the north would secede if the Military Directorate refused to accept his presidency, Maga pushed the country to the brink of civil war. Apithy upped the stakes by stating his region would attach itself to Nigeria if Maga was instated. In a last-ditch compromise to save Dahomey from self-destruction, a **Presidential Council** was formed in which the three men would rotate power every two years. Maga was the first to serve as president, replaced in 1972 by Ahomadegbe.

The system seemed to be working when, in 1972, internal rivalries within the army triggered two mutinies at the Ouidah military camp. Though these were put down, more than twenty high-ranking officers were arrested, six of them – including Kouandété – sentenced to death. That move prompted one last coup, led by a man who, like Kouandété, was a northerner from Natitingou – **Major Mathieu Kérékou**, a soldier who had served with the French army.

Stability – and a step to the Left

At the time of Kérékou's takeover on **October 26, 1972**, Dahomey had suffered nine changes of government in twelve years. Administration had grown used to the notion of government by crisis control and the nation had struggled with no clear lead and almost continual uncertainty.

Although remarkable **stability** marked the next phase in the country's history, it seemed at first that the pattern of biennial coups might continue. In **1973**, the national radio, "The Voice of the Revolution", reported that top-ranking military officers had been arrested for trying to overthrow the government. Later that year, some 180 student organizations were banned following demonstrations and strikes.

1975 was another bleak year for the government. Finance Minister Janvier Assogba was arrested after it was disclosed he had documents allegedly linking the president and other important government members in a financial scandal. In March, former president Zinsou was sentenced to death *in absentia* (he had been living in Paris where he headed the outlawed Parti Démocratique Dahoméen) for allegedly planning to assassinate Kérékou. And in May, Captain Aikpe, the Minister of the Interior, was shot to death by a Kérékou bodyguard when the president allegedly caught him *in flagrante delicto* with Mme Kérékou.

In **1977** there was another dramatic **coup attempt** when a group of **mercenaries** landed at Cotonou airport and, after trying to shell the presidential mansion, were forced to retreat (events on which some of Frederick Forsyth's thriller *The Dogs of War* are said to have been based). Most of the mercenaries, led by the notorious thug Bob Denard, were French and, afterwards, already dismal Franco-Béninois relations sank to a new low. Morocco, Gabon and the Mouvement de la Rénovation du Dahomey – an exiled political party based in Brussels – were all implicated. A personal experience of the events is described by Bruce Chatwin, in typically laconic fashion, in "A Coup" (in *Granta 10: Travel Writing*; ⊛www .granta.com).

Kérékou's revolution

Kérékou weathered all the storms. Two years after his coup, the new leader announced that Dahomey would engage in a **popular revolution**, embarking on a socialist path based on Marxism-Leninism. The country established relations with the People's Republic of China, Libya and North Korea, and received the blessing of Sekou Touré of Guinea. Benin also moved closer to the Soviet Union and its tributary states.

Also in 1975, Kérékou changed the country's name from Dahomey to the **République Populaire du Bénin** (after the old city-state in neighbouring Nigeria) and launched the single political party, the Parti de la Révolution Populaire du Bénin (PRPB). The new course instigated significant changes. Schools were nationalized, the legal system was reorganized and committees were established round the country to stimulate participation in local government. In 1977, a *Loi Fondamentale* established new political structures including the Assemblée Nationale Révolutionnaire. In 1979, the assembly's 336 members were selected by the party and approved by 97 percent of the voters. Later in the year, the party selected Kérékou as the sole presidential candidate and the assembly unanimously elected him in February 1980.

It would be hard to assert that Kérékou was ever a committed Marxist. Certainly it was a late conversion which only became clear after he took power and which was only defined in 1974. While the **centralized economy** hardly produced miracles for the nation, the revolutionary stance was a major contributing factor in maintaining stability in the 1970s. In the first place, it significantly reduced the

regional disputes that continuously brought down early governments, by shifting political argument from ethnic loyalties to issues of social and economic ideology. It also helped to appease Benin's radical intelligentsia. For a long time, Benin's dissatisfied intellectual elite (the French called the country the "West African Latin Quarter") were unable to find work in the stagnant economy. Their calls for radical reforms in the early days of independence were popular with unions and student groups and helped to topple more than one president.

Liberalization

While rhetorically supporting the revolution, Kérékou began gradually to embark on a path of **liberalization**. By 1982 the government was busy selling off or reforming its unproductive and corrupt state-run companies and *sociétés*. Under IMF and World Bank pressure, Cotonou also began retraining officials and adopting measures to encourage private investment. In 1985, the government asked the IMF for assistance – a policy, it said, designed to "exploit the positive factors of capitalism".

The former leaders Maga, Apithy and Ahomadegbe had been released in 1981 and many other political prisoners were pardoned (though those implicated in the bitterly resented "mercenaries invasion" of 1977 remained behind bars). The country also began fostering **relations with the West**. The relationship with France improved after the French Socialists came to power in 1981, especially following President Mitterrand's official visit to Benin in 1983. Three years later, Kérékou made a series of trips to Western Europe urgently seeking more aid and better debt terms. He also moved closer to conservative African nations, repairing old rifts with Togo, Côte d'Ivoire, Cameroon and Gabon.

Most of the policy reforms of the early 1980s were prompted by the deteriorating state of the economy and a scramble to find new sources of foreign aid. **Oil**, discovered off the coast, began to be exploited in 1982. It provided some relief to the government as the country was able to produce sufficient to export small quantities. Bright prospects, however, turned gloomy as the world price of oil dropped and ambitious plans for increased exploration and drilling were scrapped. With few other viable resources, the economy was still heavily reliant on the agricultural sector – cotton and, especially, palm oil.

Economic woes had already forced the government to devise extreme austerity measures, announcing in 1985 that it would no longer guarantee **jobs to graduates**. That decision sparked bloody rioting and widespread arrests. Kérékou quickly removed the Minister of Education, who was a Fon, thereby isolating himself from that ethnic community. When the border with Nigeria closed that year and relations with Benin's powerful neighbour deteriorated, resentment also grew among the Yoruba-speaking communities in the southeast, diminishing still further Kérékou's political stock. His resignation from the army seemed to impress no one.

The democratic era

There were **demonstrations** in **December 1989**, unprecedented since Kérékou's coup of 1972, as they involved public demands for his resignation, for the adoption of a multiparty system and for a complete purging of entrenched, corrupt economic practices. Students and civil servants hadn't received allowances or pay for months, absenteeism had reached epidemic proportions and the country was in a state of muddle, discontent and stagnation not witnessed since the 1960s. Because of the **fear of coups**, most of the armed forces were no longer armed and, for several days in December 1989, anti-riot police stood by in Porto Novo and Cotonou as tens of thousands of protesters roared for Kérékou's downfall. In the middle of all this, Kérékou decided to go on a walkabout in the poor quarters of Cotonou. He got a mixed response, state radio reporting his progress at one stage as taking place "amid ovations and stone-throwing".

The events were inevitably compared to similar scenes being played out in **Eastern Europe**, and certainly the Béninois were encouraged by the limited news from there that filtered through. But it had been abundantly clear for many years that Benin's wasteful command economy was not working and that the human resources at the country's disposal – some of the best-trained **administrators and teachers** in West Africa – were being squandered by a top-heavy and grossly inefficient bureaucracy.

After the events of December 1989 – which coincided with an agreement by the IMF and World Bank to bale out Kérékou one more time, and pay some of the salary backlog – the Marxist-Leninist ideology was dropped: this was a condition of French economic support. By March 1990, a **national conference**, at which fifty-two different political groups were represented, had been held to establish a framework for the country's future – and to decide what role Kérékou might play. The conference declared itself sovereign, reduced the powers of Kérékou to that of a figurehead, and appointed a new cabinet headed by **Nicéphore Soglo**, a former official of the World Bank.

So wide-reaching were the reforms and so effective was the transitional government in replacing members of the military regime with civilian administrators, that Benin was quickly dubbed the first country in West Africa to experience a "civilian coup". Independent newspapers flourished; Amnesty International commended Benin for releasing all its political prisoners. A giddy sense of renaissance swept the country. With the referendum of August 1990 overwhelmingly supporting the conference's draft multiparty constitution, the way forward seemed optimistic and when Soglo soundly beat Kérékou in the **presidential elections** of 1991, the nation's mood was ecstatic.

Despite the new lines of credit, Western-imposed structural adjustment hit wage-earners especially hard, reducing Soglo's popularity. Labour unrest continued through the early years of his administration with strikes and demonstrations causing occasional havoc in Cotonou, and several coup attempts were reported in the early 1990s. Approval for Soglo had already begun to drop in 1994, after he accepted a regional agreement for the devaluation of the CFA, a move widely interpreted as bending to Western insistence on painful **economic remedies**.

Soglo, never a man of the people, was accused of "duvalierism" because of the way he transformed the government into a family affair: his wife Rosine was a member of parliament; his brother-in-law Desiré Vieyra was minister of defence; and his son Liadi was in charge of military affairs at the presidency. But more troublesome to most were the rising prices and high levels of unemployment at a time when aid was arriving. There was a feeling that money was being squandered, and Soglo was blamed.

In the run-up to legislative elections in March 1995, Soglo formed, and became leader of, the **Parti de la Renaissance du Bénin** (RB), which soon merged with another new party, the Pan-African Union for Democracy and Solidarity. At the elections, 31 parties fielded over 5000 candidates for just 83 deputies' seats. The majority went to the opposition alliance, with the Front de l'Action pour le Renouveau et le Développement (FARD) capturing a commanding 18 seats. Though FARD was led by barrister and long-time political activist from Porto Novo, **Adrien Houngbédji**, the job of speaker of the assembly went to the head of a smaller opposition party, **Bruno Amousso**, who was voted to the position with the help of ministers loyal to Soglo, apparently in an attempt to diminish Houngbédji's influence.

At the same time, **Kérékou**'s star was beginning to rise. He had managed to seem dignified in the way he accepted the results of the elections in 1991, and human in the way he conceded the failure of his rule. His post-leadership conversion to Catholicism was accompanied by speeches defending the poor and displaced. When he announced that he would run for the presidency in 1996, conventional wisdom was that he was the candidate Soglo needed to beat. When both Houngbédji and Assoum threw their party support behind Kérékou, it was enough to give the former president 52 percent of the vote.

Calling for national unity, Kérékou created the position of **prime minister** – the post was not stipulated in the constitution – to repay Houngbédji for his support. The fact that the two men had come together at all surprised many – in 1975, Kérékou had sentenced his new ally to death for plotting against the revolution. It was a measure of how much things had changed. Still remembered as a Marxist-Leninist, Kérékou included privatization as part of his economic revival plan and continued the **austerity measures** that Soglo had initiated.

International relations had improved in the aftermath of democratization, particularly with Western nations such as the US and France, and the goodwill continued following Kérékou's return to power. Cooperation also improved with neighbouring **Nigeria** as negotiations took place over the demarcation of their common border and measures aimed at curbing smuggling. In 1998, Kérékou was elected chair of the Conseil de l'Entente, and worked to consolidate relations among countries in the group, including Benin, Côte d'Ivoire, Togo, Burkina and Niger.

As he got deeper into his term, Kérékou, like Soglo before him, began to feel the pull between the agencies

12

that set up austerity programmes and the people who felt their sting. Some aspects of economic reforms were palatable, such as Kérékou's early **crackdown on corruption**. In 1997, he took his own cabinet to task for the mismanagement of funds allocated for development projects; later that year the heads of four large state-owned companies were sacked on charges of fraud and mismanagement. But the unveiling of the 1998 budget led to a series of **strikes** by civil servants who demanded an end to privatization, unpaid wage bonuses and the scrapping of the value added tax. As the strikes continued, Houngbédji resigned from his post as prime minister and withdrew the FARD's remaining ministers from the governing coalition.

That departure proved decisive in the legislative **elections of 1999**, when Houngbédji switched allegiance and aligned his Parti du Renouveau Démocratique (PRD) with those parties opposing Kérékou, including Soglo's RB. Once again providing the swing vote, Houngbédji gave a one-seat majority to the opposition and was elected president of the national assembly.

To the present

These same three key figures – Houngbédji, Soglo and Kérékou – faced each other in the **2001 presidential elections**. Alleged irregularities led to a boycott of the run-off poll by both the main opposition candidates – Soglo and Houngbédji suspected electoral fraud. However, Bruno Amoussou (now Kérékou's right-hand man) remained in the running to give a semblance of credibility to the election process. Kérékou retained the presidency.

Yet while parliament and the president came in for criticism, the **democratic ideal** in Benin remained intact. In December 2002, when voters went to the polls for the country's first municipal elections since the end of one-party rule in 1990, it was Kérékou's key opponents from the presidential election who were triumphant. Nicéphore Soglo emerged as mayor of Cotonou, and Adrien Houngbédji took the same title in the administrative capital, Porto Novo.

In **financial terms**, Kérékou continues to struggle to balance the demands of international creditor organizations against the need to protect those affected by the stringent economic measures they impose. The European Commission made a positive pledge to Benin in August 2002, promising €275million between then and 2007 as part of a programme to reduce **poverty** through sustainable economic and social development.

On the **international stage** Benin is also blossoming. In contrast to the socialist doctrine he once espoused, Kérékou is now cementing firmer links with France and the USA, who are keen to take advantage of the country's trend towards privatization. Benin also hosted a meeting for Nepad (the New Partnership for Africa's Development) in October 2002, and pledged troops for the peace-keeping force in Côte d'Ivoire.

With recent **cotton** crops some of the best in years, and inward **investment** growing, especially from a newly enthusiastic France, the immediate future for Benin looks relatively secure. The troubles in Côte d'Ivoire have shone a favourable light on Benin and Cotonou's status as a leading regional transit point has been enhanced. Presidential elections are due next in 2006, by which time both Soglo and Kérékou will be over 70 and constitutionally too old to stand. If that transition proceeds smoothly, the people of Benin could be in for a welcome era of peace and relative prosperity.

Music

Benin has diverse musical traditions. The music of the Fon played a crucial ceremonial role in the court at Abomey, capital of the country's major pre-colonial state Dan-Homey. The Gun people use a wide variety of instruments including a huge double log xylophone, percussion pots and raft zithers. The **modern music** of Benin mixes indigenous rhythms and melodies with Congolese styles. During the 1970s Benin's popular music scene was severely impeded by government curfews, but orchestras carried on some-how, the most successful being **Orchestre Poly-Rythmo**, led by horn player **Ignace de Souza**, **Disc Afrique** and **Les Astronauts**. Undoubtedly the country's best-known musical export is the dynamic voice of **Angélique Kidjo**, but you should also listen out for the synthesizing skills of Wally Badarou.

Angélique Kidjo

A singer of extraordinary power and grace, Kidjo is the first female African musician since Miriam Makeba to achieve real international stardom. Brought up in an artistic household in Ouidah by parents who provided unusual support for her stage-struck ideas, she is an irrepressible figure who hates artistic ghettoization and purists who would curtail her freedom to record as she likes. For more information, see ⓦwww.angeliquekidjo.com.

Ayé (Island). Some of this powerful album was recorded at Prince's Paisley Park studio in Minneapolis. It includes, of course, the huge hit "Agolo", a dancefloor killer.

Oremi (Island). A remarkable disc for Kidjo, exploring the music of the African diaspora – and, in particular, American R&B. She covers Jimi Hendrix's "Voodoo Child", employs jazz saxophonist Branford Marsalis, and generally funks things up big-time. With South African backing vocals adding timbre and texture, her art has never been more mature and sweetly inspired.

Black Ivory Soul (Sony). Featuring international musicians from Africa, Brazil and the USA, this album explores the musical and cultural kinship between Benin and Brazil.

Fifa (Island). In 1995, Angélique and her husband, bass player Jean Hébrail, travelled through Benin recording some traditional music that inspired the songs on this album.

Nel Oliver

A renowned producer and performer, Nel Oliver was inspired by funk since his first 1976 recording in France with the American band Ice. The same sound still motivates his music in Cotonou, where he re-settled in 1987.

Démocratie (Africa Distributions). With its "Afro-akpala-funk", this 1997 production easily reaches international standards and gets you dancing instantly.

Stan Tohon and the Tchink System

With his wild stage act, Stan has led his Tchink System to popularity all over West Africa since the late 1970s.

Tchink Attack (Donna Wana). This may lack some of the spontaneous power of the Tchink System's stage performances, but it's a vibrant disc, nonetheless, with some very interesting rhythms on the hit song "Dévaluation".

Books

A limited range of literature is available on Benin, which includes work from Bruce Chatwin, who also contributed a memorable piece to *The Best of Granta Travel* on the coup that installed Kérékou. Books marked ⊡ are especially recommended.

Stanley B. Alpern *Amazons of Black Sparta: The Women Warriors of Dahomey*. Alpern's fascinating book has rekindled interest in the all-female regiments of the Dahomey Amazons. It makes for a good read – not overwhelmingly technical, despite the thorough discussion of the methods of training and the tactics of battle.

Suzanne Preston Blier *African Vodun: Art, Psychology, and Power* (University of Chicago Press). Detailed academic study of the voodoo art of Benin and Togo – and related Haitian and New Orleans traditions.

⊡ **Annie Caulfield** *Show Me the Magic: Travels around Benin by Taxi*. Caulfield describes her hectic trip around the country from the back of a battered Peugeot taxi, with her control-freak driver Isidore. Funny, astute, revealing.

⊡ **Bruce Chatwin** *The Viceroy of Ouidah*. Without a doubt the first book to read on Benin – gripping, in Chatwin's inimitable style, from the prologue on, in its fictionalized account of the life of the Brazilian slave-trader Francisco Felix de Souza (see p.924).

Christophe Henning and Hans Oberlander *Voodoo: Secret Power in Africa* (Taschen). A sumptuous coffee-table book of strong images, with anecdote-based text from the author/photographers who travelled the country.

Patrick Manning *Slavery, Colonialism and Economic Growth in Dahomey 1640–1960*. Heavy scholarship, but well done, showing how Dahomey's economy continued to prosper through the slave trade until the eve of colonialism.

Francesca Pique, Leslie H. Rainer *Palace Sculptures of Abomey: History Told on Walls*. Exploring Fon culture, history and the kingship system, and the role of the royal palaces in Abomey, this also gives a fascinating insight into the significance of the bas-reliefs on the palace walls, as well as current conservation efforts.

Fiction

Olympe Bhêly-Quénum *Snares Without End*. An intriguing novel of village life, by the only Béninois writer to have been translated into English.

Paul Hazoumé *Doguicimi*. The essence of the Dan-Homey kingdom is captured in this carefully documented work of realist-romantic fiction.

Languages

Benin's official language is **French**, which is widely spoken. The fifty or so Béninois ethnic communities speak about as many different languages or distinct dialects, though some languages have become regional lingua francas. In the south, **Adja** and **Fon** – closely related to Ewe and Mina under the "Ewe group" umbrella – are widely spoken and probably the most useful if you want to learn a few phrases (see p.838 for some Mina). In the centre and east, **Yoruba** (see p.1034) takes over. **Bariba**, a Voltaic tongue, is the common language of Parakou and the northeast, while the old Songhaic language, **Dendi**, is spoken in the extreme north near the banks of the Niger.

Hausa and **Fula** are also widely used in the north.

Because of the proximity and influence of Nigeria and the importance of commerce, some Béninois speak a kind of trading English, though English is not likely to get you very far, even in Cotonou.

Glossary

Amazon The name given to female Fon soldiers by visiting Europeans. In Greek mythology, it referred to a race of Scythian female warriors who supposedly underwent mastectomies to facilitate use of their longbows; the word probably derives from the Greek for "without a breast"; see p.924.

Féticheur Traditional religious leader.

Tata Fortresslike houses built by the Somba in the region of Natitingou.

Vaudou/Vodu "Divinity" or "Other" (Fon). The belief system of the coast (based around these divinities), spread from these parts to Haiti with the slaves.

Yovo "White" or "European" (Fon).

12.1

Cotonou and the coast

On the basis of physical appearances, **COTONOU** is one of West Africa's least enticing cities. Though the population is under a million, it spreads over a considerable reach of monotonously flat landscape, dotted with lakes and clogged with residential, commercial and administrative *quartiers* that run chaotically into one another. At rush hour, the cratered, grubby grid of streets becomes a seemingly endless tide of rattling *mobylettes* kicking up clouds of dust and exhaust fumes. You might expect the **waterfront** to add a picturesque backdrop to this bleak environment, but the harbour view is unfortunately blocked by the **modern port** – located right in the heart of the city and redolent of export produce that's waited too long in the sun. To cap it all, with not a hill or geographical landmark in the whole of Cotonou, it's difficult to get your bearings on first arriving in the smoggy clamour.

But the city is something of an African melting pot, with a still-intact intellectual reputation that has only grown more visible with the government's liberalization over the last decade. Commercially, it has gained considerable importance due to the frequent closures of Lomé's duty-free port – most hotels here are more geared to regional traders than to tourists. Cotonou's saving grace is its fantastic **markets**. For want of other things to do by day, you could spend a good deal of your time in town shopping and browsing. Cotonou **nights** are thoroughly enjoyable by any standards, buzzing with people out to enjoy the cool air, and vendors crowding through the streets.

Three of the country's best-known attractions are each less than an hour out of the city. The stilt village of **Ganvié** is a thorough rip-off – though no less striking for that – but the official capital of Benin, **Porto Novo**, has a proud gravity that no amount of superficial exploitation could conceal, and **Ouidah** has an intrinsic appeal beyond its over-baked "fetish tourism". If you're heading west to Lomé, or arriving from that direction, you might stop a night at the virtually derelict old trading town of **Grand Popo**, whose magnificently picturesque lagoons and coconut groves provide the backdrop for a lethargic day or two sunning on the beach.

Ethnically, the coast is dominated by various Ewe-speaking peoples including the **Adja**, one of the earliest groups to arrive, formerly a community of renowned warriors who settled near the Togolese border town of Tado. Over time, the group fragmented and dispersed to form the **Xwala** and the **Xuéda** (Ouidah) along the coast and the **Gun** a little inland around Porto Novo.

Cotonou

The diamond-shaped **centre** of Cotonou is defined by three main thoroughfares – **Boulevard Saint Michel** in the northwest, **Boulevard Steinmetz** in the northeast and **Avenue Clozel** to the southeast. The **port** forms a natural barrier to the southwest, marking the centre's fourth boundary. Many of the hotels and restaurants listed below are within the confines of these streets, as are the major **businesses**, the **post office** and the **banks**.

East of the centre, Boulevard Saint Michel extends to the Nouveau Pont, and crosses the **lagoon** that cuts Cotonou in two, linking the downtown districts with the **Akpakpa district** on the east side of the city. At the bridge's western foot spreads the vast **Dantokpa Market**, one of the largest along the West African coast. About 1500m down the lagoon towards the ocean, Avenue Clozel extends over the **Ancien Pont** and continues east to join the road to Porto Novo.

West of the centre, Boulevard de France becomes Boulevard de la Marina and follows the coast. Running parallel, Avenue Pape Jean Paul II leads to the high-rent **Cocotiers** and **Haie Vive** districts near the airport. Along the way, it passes near the French and American embassies and the imposing Presidential Palace, or **Présidence**, a modern pile encircled by a seriously large fence with security cameras peering from every corner.

On the **north side of town**, Avenue de la République leads west from the Nouveau Pont up to the **Place de l'Etoile Rouge** – a monumental square (complete with torch-bearing cast-iron statue rising up from the giant red star at its centre) commemorating the country's now lapsed revolution.

Arrival, information and city transport

The **airport** is located 5km west of the centre along route de l'Aéroport. It has a small **exchange bureau** that opens for the day's few incoming flights, a branch of the Financial Bank (Mon–Fri 8am–10pm) that changes cash and traveller's cheques, and a Hertz car rental office. You'll need to take a taxi to get into town; there's an official list of prices in the arrivals section, with various fares for day- and nighttime journeys (CFA3000–6000). If you don't have much luggage, you could consider one of the **zemidjans** who wait in front of the airport and will take you to the centre for around CFA300–400, though be prepared to bargain strenuously.

Arriving by **bush taxi**, you're most likely to be let off in the city centre. Destinations in Benin have their own *autogares*, conveniently situated on or near one of the three main streets marking the centre. Arriving from Lomé or from the west, you end up at the **Gare de Jonquet** right in the heart of the downtown district, just off rue des Cheminots. From Parakou and northern towns, you'll arrive just southeast of here at **Gare d'Itajara**, while bush taxis from Porto Novo and Lagos arrive either at the **Gare de Dantokpa** at the corner of Avenue de la Paix and Boulevard St Michel, or at the **Gare de l'Ancien Pont**, near the bridge of the same name. **Abomey** is served by a separate *gare* located on rue de Dahomey, between Boulevard Steinmetz and the lagoon. The **train station** is also centrally located, just off Avenue Clozel. **Africalines** buses use a station in the far west of town on the route de l'Aéroport.

The Direction du Tourisme et de l'Hôtellerie (☎32.68.24, ☏32.68.23, ✉tourisme@elodia.intnet.bj), 2.5km out of town off the *Place de l'Etoile Rouge*, is

---

Moving on from Cotonou

The main international station for travel along the coast on the **Cotonou–Lomé axis** is the **Gare de Jonquet**. Vehicles depart regularly from here for Ouidah, Grand Popo, Porto Novo, Lagos and Lomé. The **Gare d'Itajara** is the place to get vehicles for **Parakou and the north**. For **Porto Novo, Lagos** and **Abidjan**, head to the **Gare de l'Ancien Pont**. Vehicles for Lagos also leave from the **Gare de Dantokpa**, as do cars to Porto Novo, Abomey-Calavi (for Ganvié) and Parakou. **Abomey** transport leaves from the *gare* near the Ciné Vog.

Africalines buses to Savalou, Parakou, Natitingou and Malanville depart from their station on route de l'Aéroport near Air France. It's best to book tickets in advance as services fill up quickly; see p.886 for fares and contact details for their head office.

For details of **trains** to Parakou, see p.886.

happy to hand out a slew of brochures and maps. Otherwise, they won't be able to do much for you. To find out about renting a car or joining an organized excursion to somewhere like Ganvié or the Pendjari National Park, you're better off going to a travel agent (see "Listings", p.910).

Within the city centre, **taxis** are shared and cost CFA250–350 for most destinations, though they are not as widely available as *zemidjans* – by far the most frequent form of transport in the centre. These should only cost you CFA150–300, even for quite long rides in town, but make sure to agree a price before setting off. There are no town buses.

Accommodation

From dirt-cheap *chambres de passage* to luxury money-temples, Cotonou has **accommodation** for everyone. Unless you're penniless, though, avoid the low-budget places where levels of hygiene are about as low as the prices: there's a number of very decent mid-range lodgings which aren't expensive. Most of the less expensive hotels are in or near the centre, while the more upmarket places are found east across the Ancien Pont, in Akpakpa, or west towards Cocotiers, with the odd more central exception.

Campers are provided for at the rustic but friendly *Motel le Verdict* (CFA1000 per person to camp, or ❶ for grubby, basic s/c doubles), 12km west of the centre on the route de Lomé. Pitching your tent in an isolated spot along the beach, on the other hand, is unsafe.

Central Cotonou

Alex's One street south of rue des Cheminots, ☎31.25.08, ✉ alexshotel@firstnet.bj. A new and well-regarded choice. Rooms are appealing and good value, with a/c, phone, fridge and TV; an attractive restaurant and popular nightclub are attached. ❼

Babo rue Agbeto Amadore ☎31.25.02, ☎31.46.07. A towering building visible from hd St Michel, with accommodation to suit a range of budgets. There are basic, tolerable, non-s/c rooms on the fourth and fifth floors, some with balconies; the lower floors have more appealing, s/c rooms with tasteful, cheery decor. ❶

Benin Vickenfel Off bd Steinmetz, near the Ciné Vog ☎31.38.14, ✉ vkfhotel@intnet.bj. Smallish rooms, all with a/c. Excellent location and great views from the top-floor restaurant. ❺

Concorde bd Steinmetz, near Ciné Vog ☎31.55.70, ☎31.13.68. Carpeted a/c rooms with hot water in the private bathroom, or spacious s/c rooms with fan and cold water. An attractive, central option, the chief drawback being the noise from the busy main road. ❶

Le Crillon Off bd Steinmetz near Ciné Vog ☎31.51.58. The most central of the inexpensive hotels. Rooms are well kept though small; all are s/c and have fan or a/c. Great ice cream is served at the *Trait d'Union* next door. ❷

Crystal bd Steinmetz, opposite Ciné Vog ☎31.22.08. First-floor hotel reached by a spiral staircase. Exceptionally clean rooms with attractive wooden panelling and fan or a/c, and relatively quiet for the location on the busy main street. ❸

Hôtel de la Plage Near the main post office ☎31.25.61 or 31.34.67, ☎31.25.60. Central, colonial-style place, nicely furnished and boasting a good deal of old-time charm, plus a pool and a private beach. All rooms have a/c; rates include breakfast. ❺

Pension de l'Amitié Off av Proche ☎31.42.01. Good budget option with clean airy rooms and tiled floors throughout. ❷

Pension des Familles l'Amazone av Proche ☎31.51.25. This central place has friendly staff and simple, clean rooms, with fan. ❶

Outside the centre

Alédjo On the east side of town, 4km from the centre ☎33.05.61/2, ☎33.15.74. A dull and decaying, though perfectly comfortable, hotel in a large tropical park, the *Alédjo* has a place in history as the venue of the March 1990 democracy conference. There's a pool, and the hotel is right next to a sheltered ocean bay ("La Crique"). ❻

Auberge La Pirogue (formerly the *Alises*) rte de Fidjrosse, 9km from the centre at Jacquot Plage ☎40.63.66. Set on a pleasant beach, six stylish and comfortable rooms in attractive thatched huts on the sand. There's also a great, though pricey, seafood restaurant. ❷

Benin Marina Hôtel bd de la Marina, 4km from the centre near the airport ☎30.01.00, ☎30.11.55. Two hundred luxury rooms (a double

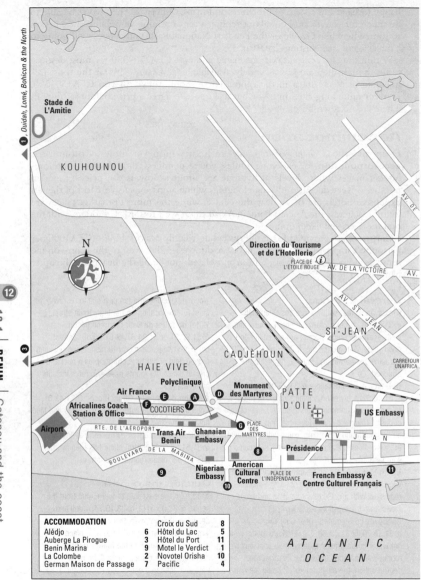

Stade de
L'Amitié

KOUHOUNOU

N

Direction du Tourisme
et de L'Hotellerie

PLACE DE
L'ÉTOILE ROUGE   AV. DE LA VICTOIRE   AV.

AV. DE

AV. ST - JEAN

ST-JEAN

CADJÈHOUN

CARREFOUR
UNAFRICA

HAIE VIVE

PATTE
D'OIE

Polyclinique

Air France   Monument
des Martyres

Africalines Coach   COCOTIERS
Station & Office   PLACE
DES
MARTYRES   US Embassy

Airport   RTE. DE L'AÉROPORT
Trans Air   Ghanaian   AV   J E A N
Benin   Embassy
BOULEVARD   DE LA MARINA   Présidence

American
Nigerian   Cultural
Embassy   Centre   PLACE DE   French Embassy &
L'INDÉPENDANCE   Centre Culturel Français

A T L A N T I C
O C E A N

ACCOMMODATION		Croix du Sud	8
Alédjo	6	Hôtel du Lac	5
Auberge La Pirogue	3	Hôtel du Port	11
Benin Marina	9	Motel le Verdict	1
La Colombe	2	Novotel Orisha	10
German Maison de Passage	7	Pacific	4

costs at least £100/$160 a night) and bungalows
(some with hazy ocean views), all fitted out with
colour TV, video and phone. The hotel is right on
the beach with a popular poolside bar and a
flourish of restaurants, including one with first-
class breakfast buffets. There's also a disco,

sauna, crafts shop, travel agency and bank.
Generically international and sterile, though. ⑧
La Colombe PK 5, rte de Porto Novo ☎ 33.32.02,
℻ 33.55.88. An obliging place 5km from the
centre; they're happy to negotiate on price and will
pick up free from the airport if you've a

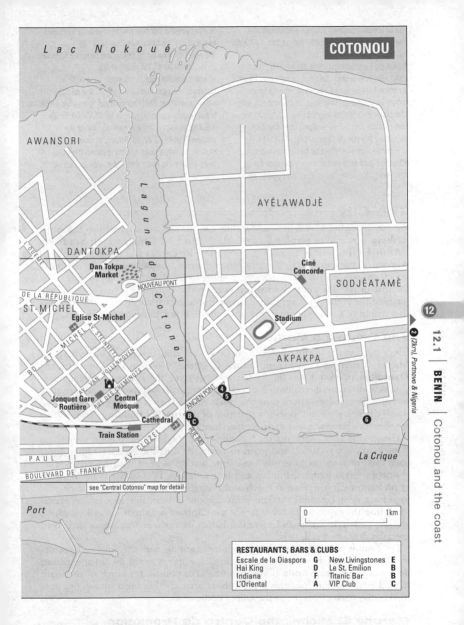

RESTAURANTS, BARS & CLUBS

Escale de la Diaspora	G	New Livingstones	E
Hai King	D	Le St. Emilion	B
Indiana	F	Titanic Bar	B
L'Oriental	A	VIP Club	C

reservation. Shared taxis into town cost CFA200. Some s/c rooms, with fan or a/c. **2**

Croix du Sud Off rte de l'Aéroport ☎ 30.09.54/55. Rooms are divided between a main block and a complex of attractive thatched bungalows clustered round a 25-metre pool – though note

that everything is in need of a lick of paint. **6**

German Maison de Passage Haie-Vive, 200m east of New Livingstones ☎ 30.45.76. Priority at this well-kept house is given to German development workers, but spare rooms are let to visitors at a bargain price, considering you have use of a well-equipped kitchen and communal lounge/dining area. CFA 5000 per person, CFA3000 for NGO volunteers.

Hôtel du Lac Akpakpa, near the Ancien Pont ☎33.19.19, ✆www.hoteldulac-benin.com. There's a choice here between attractive, comfortable rooms or luxurious bungalows at the water's edge. The place also boasts a great pool (CFA2500 for non-guests) and fabulous views over the river. ❻

Hôtel du Port bd de France ☎31.44.43/44, ✉w.demedeiros@firstnet.bj. Not in the most attractive part of town but hugely popular for its spacious, a/c rooms, bungalows and apartments.

Rooms around the courtyard come with balconies overlooking the attractive 25m pool. ❼

Novotel Orisha bd de la Marina, near the Nigerian embassy ☎30.41.77, ✆30.41.88, ✆www.novotel.com. A relatively rare sight in Cotonou – a new hotel with a pool and all the usual amenities. There's horse riding nearby which hotel guests can take part in for CFA7000/hr. ❽

Pacific av Clozel, on the eastern side of the Ancien Pont ☎33.22.35. Rooms of various standards, most quite spacious (avoid the noisy ones facing the road) and some with lagoon views. ❷

The City

By way of **sights**, Cotonou is unexciting. On the western approach to the city, a striking example of revolutionary architecture, the Chinese-built **Stade de l'Amitié** ("Friendship Stadium"), dominates the district and flaunts an atypical **pagoda** at the entrance. In the city centre, there's a **cathedral** built in an Italian neo-Renaissance style. Making a special effort to see these buildings, however – or for that matter, the **central mosque** over by the Gare de Jonquet – seems like scraping the bottom of a very small barrel. In the end, it's really only the **markets** that will leave a lasting impression, and Cotonou boasts some very good ones.

The Dantokpa Market

Every day, a steady stream of people can be seen skirting down the Boulevard Saint Michel or over the Pont Martin Luther King (the "Nouveau Pont") towards the **Dantokpa market**. From the bridge, you can sense the energy of commerce as you look down on the confusion of taxis, traders, stalls and merchandise spreading out in a thousand directions near the banks of the lagoon. In the middle of it all stands the heavy cement shoe-box structure of the **market building**, inside which are the cloth boutiques and stands of merchants.

The ground level of the market building is the food hall, devoted to everything from locally grown tubers and grain to boxes of Milo and Nescafé. Other floors have their own ranges of goods. One large section is filled with Nigerian-made cosmetics – skin lotion, shampoos and hair softeners. Piles of Savon de Marseille crush against Chinese enamel bowls and Nigerian plastics. **Cloth** is an especially important item; colourful Parakou prints are quite reasonable, though less prestigious than the expensive Dutch wax designs. **Clothes** and **shoes** – flip-flops, plastic sandals, Bata-style loafers and imitation Italian dress shoes – also have their own specialist domains and dealers.

The Dantokpa **Fetish Market** is worth investigating, with the usual wide assortment of animal body parts and whole dried specimens – and the usual excessive demands for cash are made if you want to take photos. It's north of the main market building, up along the lagoon shore after the big open square, the pole market, the wicker market and the empty bottle market.

Marché St Michel, the Centre de Promotion l'Artisanal and Marché Ganhi

The **Marché St Michel**, on Avenue de la Republic west of Gare de Dantokpa, is a small, pleasant area, on the edge of which you'll find people selling books – in English as well as French. To the southwest, the **Centre de Promotion l'Artisanal** (crafts market) on Boulevard St Michel provides the best location in town to shop for Béninois handicrafts. A series of hut-like shops contain familiar specimens of traditional national art – for example, the colourful **patchwork cloths** originating from Abomey that were once used as the banners of that city's kings. Wooden carvings and **masks** from the various regions are also common, as are different varieties of drums – though the ones sold here are mainly decorative. The good collection of jewellery makes for easily portable gifts.

Marché Ganhi is a small produce market down near the port, essentially these days aimed at and used by expats and wealthy Béninois. There's a general selection of produce here, but it's also a good place to score cheap cassettes or CDs of the latest sounds.

Eating and drinking

Cotonou never used to have much of a high culinary reputation as far as European and Asian cuisine goes, but new places are opening up and old ones are changing hands – so options are rapidly improving. Local food is quite decent, and the Béninois have a flair for tasty sauces made with plenty of vegetables and seafood or meat. For **street food**, try around the markets and *gares*, and also beside the rail tracks just off av Clozel, around the corner from the *Gerbe d'Or*.

Central Cotonou

Inexpensive

Chala-Ogoi av St Jean, just north of the intersection with bd St Michel. One of the city's best open-air restaurants, serving home cooking in cauldronlike pots; try the *purée d'igname* with *pied de boeuf*. Good salads too.

Chez Maman Bénin Near Ciné Bénin. A great selection of fish, chicken, beef and an array of tasty sauces are on offer at this well-established, popular haunt. The upstairs restaurant is more upmarket, with prices to match. Mon–Sat 9am–midnight.

Maquis le Lagon bd Steinmetz. Excellent grilled chicken and chips, served evenings only at tables on the pavement – a lively atmosphere is guaranteed. Around CFA2000 per person.

Mic-Mac av Clozel. One of the city's few fast-food joints. The *chawarmas* are a better bet than the burgers; the fries and salads are pretty good.

Restaurant Awa Seck av Proche. Senegalese-run establishment with *poulet yassa* and other filling dishes (there's more choice if you order in advance) in a small, pleasant setting. Around CFA1000 a meal.

Restaurant Fairouz bd Steinmetz. Great for *chawarmas* (CFA1500–2000) and sandwiches at lunchtime, with kebabs roasting out front to entice you in.

Moderate and expensive

After bd St Michel, 50m east of Ciné Bénin. Upstairs restaurant, red velvet upholstery and a pleasant terrace, serving tasty and reasonably priced European, African and some Middle Eastern dishes at moderate prices.

Costa Rica In the grounds of the Centre de Promotion l'Artisanal. Long an incredibly popular spot with expats, serving pricey pasta dishes and pizzas under a large thatched roof.

Le Festival des Glaces bd Steinmetz. New, popular "salon de thé, patisserie and pizzeria". Particularly noteworthy is its ice cream selection, one of the best in the city, though portions are a bit stingy.

La Gerbe d'Or av Clozel. The best pastries in town since way back – rum babas, eclairs and custard slices for around CFA500. Also serves croissants and wholewheat sandwiches. You can order all this at their upstairs restaurant, where you can also sample the great burgers, salads and ice cream.

Maquis Dunya av Proche, near Église St Michel. Intriguing Malian-themed place with some fantastic African specialities including *poulet yassa*; generous servings too.

Maquis le Mandingue Signposted off av Proche. Great little place with funky decor, including a range of petite wall hangings, and a predominately African menu at moderate prices.

Le Phenicien av Clozel, near the PTT. A surprising refuge on this busy street, this attractive restaurant serves a selection of European dishes throughout the day, with tempting crepes and beer on draught. Daily 6am–midnight.

Le Repaire de Bacchus rue Immeuble Natalys, off the southern end of av Proche. Newish, popular though pricey restaurant with a Western feel, beer on tap, a vast selection of wines and cocktails, and moderately priced European food. Happy hour daily 6–7pm.

Le Sorrento bd St Michel behind Hall des Arts ☏30.37.79. Benin's best Italian restaurant, and

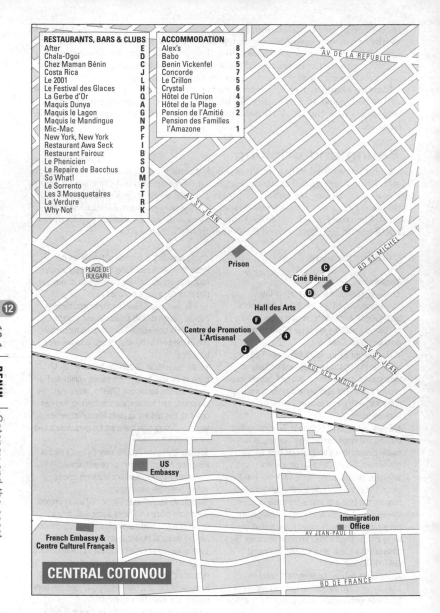

RESTAURANTS, BARS & CLUBS

After	E
Chala-Ogoi	D
Chez Maman Bénin	C
Costa Rica	J
Le 2001	L
Le Festival des Glaces	H
La Gerbe d'Or	Q
Maquis Dunya	A
Maquis le Lagon	G
Maquis le Mandingue	N
Mic-Mac	P
New York, New York	F
Restaurant Awa Seck	I
Restaurant Fairouz	B
Le Phenicien	S
Le Repaire de Bacchus	O
So What!	M
Le Sorrento	F
Les 3 Mousquetaires	T
La Verdure	R
Why Not	K

ACCOMMODATION

Alex's	8
Babo	3
Benin Vickenfel	5
Concorde	7
Le Crillon	5
Crystal	6
Hôtel de l'Union	4
Hôtel de la Plage	9
Pension de l'Amitié	2
Pension des Familles	
l'Amazone	1

AV DE LA REPUBLIC

PLACE DE BULGARIE

Prison

BD ST MICHEL

Ciné Bénin

C

D E

AV ST JEAN

Hall des Arts

F

Centre de Promotion L'Artisanal

J 4

AV ST JEAN

RUE DES AMOUREUX

US Embassy

Immigration Office

AV JEAN-PAUL II

French Embassy & Centre Culturel Français

CENTRAL COTONOU

BD DE FRANCE

extremely popular with the smarter set. Excellent pizza and unusual pasta dishes.

Les 3 Mousquetaires Off av Clozel ☎31.61.22. For the well-heeled Béninois or tourists with CFA to burn – tantalizing French cuisine in an attractive setting. Main courses CFA6500–15,000. Closed Sun.

La Verdure Off av Clozel ☎31.31.75. Casual bar-restaurant serving reasonably priced lobster and seafood specialities, and with an attractive courtyard at the back, plus pinball and a small pool table. Something of a social focus point for expats and young people.

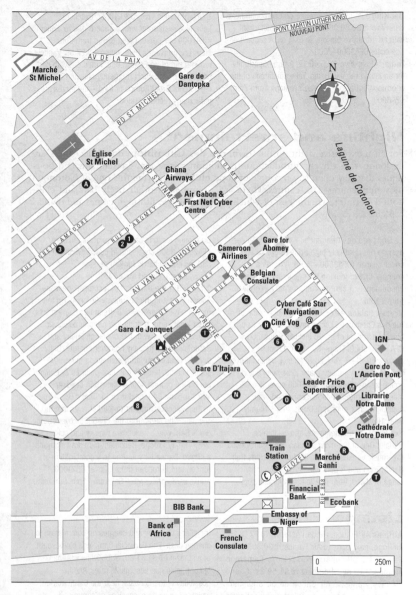

Out from the centre

Escale de la Diaspora Place de Martyrs.
Affectionally known as "the van" among resident
Peace Corps volunteers, a mobile kitchen with
plastic tables and chairs beside, serving great
snacks including burgers and chips at inexpensive
prices. Daily noon–midnight.

Hôtel du Lac Akpakpa, near the Ancien Pont
☎33.19.19. A great terrace for a drink and a meal,
looking out across the lagoon as the sun goes down.
Delicious cuisine covering a range of European
dishes, including some seafood specialities.

Hai King Just off the Carrefour de Cadjehoun near Haie-Vive ☎ 30.60.08. Great Chinese restaurant with an attractive balcony to dine on. A sauce with rice costs CFA3500–7000.

Indiana Haie-Vive ☎ 95.46.12. A rare opportunity for an Indian meal in Benin. Take advantage of the enormous buffets on Sunday evenings (from 7pm; CFA6000).

L'Oriental Haie Vive ☎ 30.18.27. Excellent Lebanese restaurant with a superb *mezze* dinner (CFA7000 per person) Wed & Sun from 8pm.

New Livingstones Haie-Vive ☎ 30.27.58. Vaguely reminiscent of an English pub, kitted out with dart boards and with sport frequently showing on the big screen. Great European food – the pizzas are particularly recommended.

Nightlife and entertainment

For an inexpensive night on the town, **rue des Cheminots**, down near the Gare de Jonquet, is a lively introduction. In addition to the many restaurants and boutiques that stay open late, a couple of good **clubs** have made this one of Cotonou's most active after-dark centres. There are a number of other lively bars and clubs dotted around town, the best of which are listed below, although names and owners can change rapidly.

Le 2001 rue des Cheminots. Extremely popular despite the relatively high price of drinks and the cover charge (CFA3500–4500). Attracts a younger crowd looking for music and romantic encounters – it can get rather sleazy. Nightly from 11pm.

Crystal Palace *Alex's Hôtel*, one block south of rue des Cheminots. Locals rave about this club, playing a variety of music including salsa. Cover CFA3000–5000. Thurs–Sun from 11pm.

New York, New York bd St Michel, behind the Hall des Arts. A popular place to be seen among young trendsetters. The CFA5000 cover is a bit steep, but it offers a dependably good time, especially after midnight. Dress smart. Nightly from 10pm.

So What! Off bd Steinmetz, above Librairie Buffalo. One of the most popular, consistently good live-music venues, playing host to musicians from Benin, Togo and Nigeria, and an extraordinary range of styles, from jazz to urban African pop.

Drumming lessons can also be arranged here. CFA2000–3000 cover on big concert nights (Fri & Sat), no entry charge for jam sessions (Tues–Thurs); closed Mon.

Titanic Bar rue 840, part of a complex near the Ancien Pont and the Lagune de Cotonou. On the roof of a garish yellow and green building – a great location for a drink and panoramic views across the city – with live bands on Friday and Saturday nights (usually no cover charge). Daily 6pm till late. If you fancy something more sophisticated, head to the ultra-posh *Le St Emilion* bar on the ground floor of the same building.

VIP Club rue 840, next door to *Titanic Bar*. As the name suggests, a rather upmarket nightspot for clientele who can afford the CFA6000 cover charge (Fri & Sat), which includes a whisky and coke.

Why Not av Proche. Basement club drawing quite a crowd. Dance till you drop to a combination of African and European music. Cover CFA4000, drinks same price. Mon–Sat from 11pm, Sun 8pm.

Listings

Airlines Air France, rte de l'Aéroport ☎ 30.18.15; Air Togo, next door to Air France ☎ 30.30.60; Air Gabon, bd Steinmetz ☎ 31.21.87; Cameroon Airlines, 119 av Steinmetz ☎ 31.59.37; Ghana Airways, opposite Air Gabon on bd Steinmetz ☎ 31.42.83; ✉ ghaircoo@firstnet.bj; Nigeria Airways, av du Gouveneur Ballot ☎ 31.58.24; Point-Afrique ☎ 08.27.88; Trans Air Benin, av Jean Paul II, next to the Ghanaian embassy ☎ 30.61.65, ✉ transairbenin@firstnet.bj.

Banks and exchange In the centre, the Bank of Africa on av Jean Paul II (Mon–Fri 8–11.30am & 3–5.30pm; ☎ 31.32.28) has good rates for

traveller's cheques and charges no commission to change cash. The Financial Bank, one block south of av Clozel (☎ 31.31.00, ✉ fbb@financial-bank-bj.com), also has acceptable rates. Another possibility is the Ecobank near the Ganhi market, which charges an excessive flat-commission rate of CFA5500 for traveller's cheques.

Beaches Most of those around the city are filthy and often have a dangerous undertow. The best strands are in front of the hotels, notably the *Benin Marina Hotel* and *Croix du Sud*, which are cleaner than that of the *Hôtel du Port*. Near the *Alédjo*, the sheltered cove known as La Crique is popular among expats and townspeople, since swimming is relatively safe. Or try west of the city at Jacquot Plage, a drive of about 9km. Don't take valuables on to any beach – La Crique, especially, is notorious for grab-and-runs.

Books and magazines SONAEC, almost next door to the *Gerbe d'Or* on av Clozel (☎31.22.42) has all the national papers as well as the best international selection, along with books in French – African and French literature, travel guides and so forth, and even a few novels in English. Alternatively, try the well-equipped Librairie Notre Dame, near the BSS supermarket on av Clozel, beside the cathedral; or the Librairie Buffalo off bd Steinmetz, beneath the *So What!* club.

Car rental Hertz has a branch at the airport which only opens up for incoming flights. They are also represented in Akpakpa (☎33.96.81, ℱ33.96.82). The *Benin Marina* operates its own car rental service (☎30.01.00).

Cinemas It's generally hard to see a decent film except on a small video screen or at the American or French cultural centres. Ciné Bénin shows a range of films (two or three a night), mostly action movies in French, as does the Ciné Concorde across the Nouveau Pont in Akpakpa.

Cultural centres The dynamic Centre Culturel Français is on rte de l'Aéroport (☎30.08.56, ℱ30.11.51), near to the French embassy. Besides a library (Tues, Fri & Sat 9.30am–noon & 3–7pm, Wed 9.30am–7pm, Thurs 3–7pm) and a café, they have regular art exhibitions and theatrical performances by local artists – you can pick up a schedule of events here. The American Cultural Centre, off the bd de la Marina (☎30.03.12), is also pretty lively and regularly shows films.

Embassies and consulates France, rte de l'Aéroport, Cocotiers ☎30.02.25/26, ℱ30.15.47, with a consulate on av du Général de Gaulle, near the Niger embassy ☎31.26.80 or 31.26.38 (Mon–Fri 8–11am); Ghana, rte de l'Aéroport ☎30.07.46 (Mon–Fri 8am–2pm); Niger, one block behind the main PTT ☎31.56.65; Nigeria, Lot 21, Patte d'Oie district ☎30.11.42; USA, rue Caporal Anani Bernard ☎30.06.50, ﷼cotonou.us embassy.gov. Note that visas for Nigeria are only issued to residents of Benin. The French consulate may be able to help with visas for Burkina Faso and Togo – although officially they can only issue visas to residents of Benin.

Hospitals The privately run Polyclinique les Cocotiers (general consultations Mon–Fri 8am–12.30pm & 4–7pm; ☎30.14.20) has the best reputation, though the most obvious place to head for treatment is the Centre National Hospitalier et Universitaire in the Patte d'Oie district (☎30.01.55).

For an ambulance, call ☎30.06.56.

Internet access Across from *Le Crillon*, Cyber Café Star Navigation offers a cheap but slow service (CFA500/hr). The PTT cybercafé in the telephone office on av Clozel charges the same price. Also worth trying is the First Net Cyber Centre adjacent to Air Gabon on bd Steinmetz, and Cyber Centre Planète Blue, in the same complex as *Titanic Bar* on rue 840.

Maps The Institut National de Cartographie, on rue des Libanais opposite Cash Supermarché (☎31.24.41; take the road opposite the Librairie Notre Dame) has reasonable survey maps of the country in 1:50,000 and 1:200,000 series, and city maps for Cotonou, Parakou, Porto Novo and Djougou (CFA3500–9800).

Pharmacies Pharmacie Jonquet, rue des Cheminots ☎31.20.80 (24hr); Pharmacie Notre Dame, av Clozel (☎31.23.14); Pharmacie Camp Ghezo, bd St Michel (☎31.55.52).

Photography Passport photos are done quickly at Photo Minute, opposite *Le Phenicien* on av Clozel and Photo Jardin, opposite the telephone office. The price is around CFA2000, depending on how quickly you want the pictures turned round. Photo Minute also does film development. Royal Photo, next to SONAEC on av Clozel, also does a good job at CFA2000 for the express passport-photo service.

Post and phones The main PTT is off av Clozel, near the port. International calls can be made easily from the telephone office on av Clozel (collect calls can be made only to France). Phonecards are on sale here (though there are few phones elsewhere which accept them), or there are booths here which run on a meter.

Supermarkets The three largest are all near the intersection of av Clozel and bd Steinmetz. La Pointe and Codiprix (both owned by the same people; daily 9am–1pm & 4–8pm, Sun am only) are the best for imported European products. Leader Price on bd Steinmetz offers more of the same. BSS (Benin-Self-Service; same hours), next to *Mic-Mac*, is pretty similar but doesn't carry as good a selection.

Swimming pools The cheapest and most central pool is at the *Hôtel du Port*, which non-guests can use for CFA1500 weekdays and CFA2000 at weekends. Though much nicer, the *Benin Marina*'s pool costs a steep CFA3500 weekdays, CFA4500 at weekends (and it's circular, so hopeless for serious length-swimming). The *Alédjo* has a smaller and cheaper alternative (CFA2000). The 25-metre pool at *Hôtel du Lac* is better value for CFA2500, and has several diving boards.

Travel agents One of the best organized is

Savana Tours, on bd St Michel (☎31.46.26), which runs trips to national attractions like Ganvié and Pendjari. Also reputable are C & C Voyages, on av Clozel near the Ancien Pont (☎31.31.70 or 31.31.78) and Phimex Voyages, bd Steinmetz (☎31.57.13 or 31.21.37). CBM Voyages, bd de France (☎31.49.02, ☎31.05.28), by the *Hôtel du Port*, has English-speaking staff and is extremely helpful; and finally, Benin Gulf Tour (☎30.04.04) in the grounds of the Centre de Promotion l'Artisanal.

Visa extensions From the Immigration Office, av Jean-Paul II (Mon–Fri 8–11am & 3–5pm; ☎31.41.13). Extensions for a month cost CFA12,000. One photo is required and the process takes about 48hr; visas can only be collected during the afternoon session.

Ganvié

GANVIÉ, said to be Africa's largest **lake village**, is an extraordinary sight. The entire settlement spreads across the shallow, grey-green waters on the northwest side of **Lac Nokoué**, opposite Cotonou, with wood and thatch houses built on tall stilts rising above the rippling surface. The village is only accessible by boat; even the market is held on the water, women selling wares from their canoes. The lake is "grooved", as the tourist leaflet puts it, "not by gondolas like in Venice but by graceful *pirogues* or heavy boats loaded to the boards". Not altogether surprisingly, the village is overrun with tourists whose presence has encouraged a commercial free-for-all in the little town, destroying the initial impressions of a tranquil aquatic idyll. If you have a low tolerance for this sort of thing, it's best to avoid Ganvié altogether and make your way to the less-commercialized places around Porto Novo (see p.919).

As the **slave trade** expanded after the Portuguese arrival on the coast in the sixteenth century, armies of the Dan-Homey king swept the surrounding countryside, rounding up people to trade with the Europeans for exotic goods such as cloth, gin and guns. Insecurity led to the widespread migration of weaker communities, and it was in this manner that the ancestors of the **Tofinu people**, who now inhabit Ganvié, came to settle in the area around Lake Nokoué. The earliest may have arrived in the sixteenth century, although at the end of the seventeenth century, an exodus of peoples from Tado near the Togolese border is known to have settled at the site of the present village, where they found sufficient space for grazing and farming. More importantly, the people were safe from invasion since, for religious reasons, the Dan-Homey were forbidden to extend their attacks over water. The name Ganvié probably derives from the Tofinu words *gan*, meaning "we are saved", and *vié*, "community". Today the stilt village is home to over twenty thousand people who make their living primarily from **fishing**, planting branches in the shallow waters to form a network of underwater fences known as *akadja*. Fish trapped in this way can be eaten, sold or kept for breeding.

Practicalities

The departure point for Ganvié is **Abomey-Calavi** (often shortened to simply Calavi), 18km northwest of Cotonou. From the Gare de Dantokpa in Cotonou, take one of the frequent shared **taxis** (around CFA300), which will drop you at the station in Calavi. From here it's a ten-minute walk (or CFA50 on a *zemidjan*) to the jetty where there's an official price-list for the tour of Ganvié. If you're on your own, it's an expensive CFA6050 for a two-hour *pirogue* ride or CFA7050 for a faster, motorized *pirogue*. The price decreases for groups: for an ordinary *pirogue* it's CFA4050 per person for groups of two to four, CFA3050 for larger groups, with a surcharge of CFA1000 or so if you want a motorized vessel. If, instead of stopping at Abomey-Calavi, you continue 5km up the northern highway to **Akassato**, you can approach Ganvié from behind and at slightly less cost, avoiding the worst tourist excesses. *Pirogues* punt you south 4km or so through the creeks and marshes to the edge of the lake and the stilt village.

You can **stay** the night by the jetty in Calavi at the *Auberge du Lac* (☎36.03.44; ❷), which, if renovations are complete by the time you read this, promises rooms with a/c or fan and a bar-restaurant with Western-style food. Alternatively there are several options in Ganvié itself. The brightly painted *Expotel Ganvié* (aka *Chez Raphael*) offers cold drinks and four basic rooms with bucket showers (☎49.75.99; ❷) – you can't miss the pink structure as you approach the village from Calavi. A step up, and worth the extra cost, *Auberge Carrefour Ganvié* (aka *Chez M*) has comfortable doubles with mosquito nets and clean communal showers and toilet (☎42.04.68; ❷). They also offer complimentary transport back to Calavi.

Ouidah

Hauntingly quiet after centuries of dynamic history, **OUIDAH**, 40km west of Cotonou, works a wonderful spell. This is a **voodoo** stronghold and the religion's influence penetrates as deeply as the salt air blowing off the ocean, its power outliving that of the **Portuguese fort** (now a museum). There are streets of French **colonial architecture** – all cracked facades and sagging wooden porches and shutters, and now dwelt in by poor families. The **python temple** adds a kitsch touch, but the use of snakes is part of authentic fetish practice – never mind the fact that they get rather more of a workout than they did in the days before tourism. There are plenty of other altars and temples scattered about the town, keeping the faith alive without the touristic overtones.

Back in the days when the shore of the Gulf of Benin was known as the **Slave Coast**, some of the largest trading posts and slave markets were sited here. Grand Popo, Porto Novo and Ouidah were synonymous with the trade and thus have infamous origins. Ouidah was captured by the "Amazon" warriors of King Agadja of Abomey in the early eighteenth century (see p.924) and, in the following years, the town grew into one of the foremost trading posts between Europe and the Dan-Homey empire. The **Portuguese**, who arrived at the spot, then known as Ajuda ("Help"), in 1580, waited over a century to build the fort of **São João Batista**. Part of their story is told in Bruce Chatwin's *The Viceroy of Ouidah* (see "Books" on p.899) and another version in Werner Herzog's quirky film *Cobra Verde*. Nearby, the **Danes**, **English** and **French** also built forts as they tried to gain their share of the growing trade with Africa. The last Portuguese slave ship left for Brazil in 1885. The Danish and English bastions today house businesses, while the Place du Fort Français now features a small outdoor theatre. Ouidah remained an important coastal city while under French dominion, but in the early twentieth century the colonists built a new and larger port at Cotonou. From then on, the old town went into a slow decline.

The Town

The **Ouidah Museum of History** (Mon–Fri 8am–noon & 3–6pm, weekends 9am–6pm; CFA1000), just east of the market and on rue du General Dodd, is housed in the Portuguese fort of **São João Batista**, built in 1721. Remarkably enough, a Portuguese flag waved symbolically over the building until the eve of Dahomey's independence in 1960, although the rest of the town was in French hands. The present museum traces the history of European exploration and exploitation of the Slave Coast region, and follows the dispersal of its people to the Caribbean and Brazil. The documentation includes displays of enlarged maps juxtaposed with period photographs and engravings. Many of the exhibits concentrate on the spread of the **voodoo religion** to Haiti, Cuba and Brazil, with examples of religious fetishes and pictures of rituals.

The **Maison du Brésil** (daily 7am–7pm; CFA1000), on the western side of town on Avenue de France, is a noteworthy Afro-Brazilian building from the turn of the

"**Voodoo**", also spelt *vodu*, *vodun*, *voudou* or *vudu*, is a confusing term. It does not signify a religion, at least not in Africa, but is a word used by the peoples of Togo and Benin for a spirit, demigod or intermediary. *Vodu* "priests", male and female, are individuals who are particularly susceptible to *vodu* influence, easily "possessed" or "mounted" by the *vodu*, who can thus display its emotions through a human channel. A **fetish** is an ordinary object imbued with some of this sacred power – a *vodu* charm available at any market.

The **Ewe** and other people of the coast – as well as the Fon around Abomey in Benin – believe in a supreme God, **Mawu**. Their religious stories link him (in some societies, Mawu is a woman, or even a couple, Mawu-Lisa) with creation. Shrines are rarely built for Mawu, however, but for the *vodu*, many of whom are associated with **natural forces** or with **ancestors**. The benevolence of *vodu* is sought by offerings; communities often pay homage to a specific *vodu* who becomes their main spiritual protector. In the Benin town of Ouidah, for example, **Dangbe** has a special place. Represented by the snake and sometimes by rainbows, curling smoke, running water or waving grass, Dangbe is associated with life and movement. In Abomey, he is known as **Da** and is shown on the bas-reliefs of the royal palace as a snake swallowing its tail – a symbol of eternity.

Throughout Togo and Benin, people honor **Buku** – a *vodu* associated with the sky. At Dassa Zoumé in Benin, townspeople dedicate one of their oldest temples to her. Renowned as an oracle, Buku's name is evoked in proverbs, blessings and curses, and people travel long distances to her shrines to pray, give offerings or make sacrifices. **So** (Hebiosso in Fon) is the *vodu* of thunder, with the power to strike down the impious. He is depicted at the Abomey palace as a red ram with lightning shooting from his mouth and two axes at his side. **Gu**, the guardian of smithing and war, also has associations with the sky.

Sapata is more closely identified with the earth and shrines dedicated to this *vodu* are usually seen outside villages near the fields. Linked to disease, he is respected and feared. Priests devoted to Sapata are known for their ability to treat illness and for their understanding of medicinal plants. **Hu** is connected with the ocean and water.

last century. It houses an exhibition of contemporary art that incorporates voodoo symbols into modern forms of expression. Sculptures made from the transformed carcasses of rusty *mobylettes* are the highlight of a collection that also includes less memorable paintings and collages, though some of the old photos on the upper floor are remarkable. Many of the works pay tribute to Africans in the diaspora in recognizing the cultural connection between Africa and the Americas. Closed for renovations at the time of research, the exhibition is currently on display in a nearby building (ask directions at the main building), but will return on completion of the work.

Ouidah's **basilica**, in the centre, is a formidable monument that was upgraded to its present status during the 1989 visit of Pope John Paul II, who also consecrated the new altar. Dating from the start of the twentieth century, it's recently been restored and fitted with new stained-glass windows.

The cathedral attracts nowhere near as many visitors as the nearby **python temple** (CFA1000, plus CFA2000 for cameras, CFA5000 for video), however, which guards the secrets of Ouidah's snake cult. Visitors get a brief tour of the temple and various fetishes before seeing and posing with the tame pythons – wrap-around snakes believed to give vitality and protection over your person. The whole performance is rather graceless, and on days when the reptiles are, understandably, tired, you may get no more than a peek into the room where they're kept.

His daughter, **Avlekete**, is honoured at the port of Cotonou and in nearby villages. **Legba**, the trickster, whose image is distinguished by an exaggerated phallus, contains elements of good and evil. Though Legba can bring bad luck on a house, he can also chase it away. His shrines can be seen everywhere – guarding the entrance to a community or compound, in a market, in fields, or at a crossroads.

Countless other *vodu* exist, and many occupy natural niches. **Iroko** trees, for example, are often believed inhabited by *vodu*. They are associated with fertility or new life, and you will often see sacrifices among their roots. The creation stories of some societies in the region tell of men and women descending to earth from the branches of an *iroko*.

There are many parallels between the *vodu* and the *orisa* of Yoruba religion in Nigeria, and also between *vodu* and elements of Akan religion further to the west in Ghana and Côte d'Ivoire – all the result of migrations and the wax and wane of empires. A further complexity was introduced by the return of Brazilians between the seventeenth and nineteenth centuries to the land of their (partial) ancestry. They reintroduced elements of Yoruba custom when they settled on this part of the coast.

Slaves sold across the Atlantic took their religious systems to North and South **America** and the Caribbean. Even metropolitan areas carry reminders: Legba statuaries made in the last fifty years can be found in New York City and Miami. But West African religions are more often identified with Brazil, Cuba and **Haiti**. Many Haitian slaves came from the Dahomey (Benin) coast and to this day their names for numerous *vodu* are virtually unchanged: Legba is known as Papa Legba, Sapata as Sabata, Avlekete as Aizan-Velekete. The *iroko* tree, known as *loko* in Fon, became Papa Loko. Only the supreme god Mawu was given a completely new, French, name – Bondieu.

In the Americas, **Catholicism** and the *vodu* system were soon melded together. But even in West Africa, many elements of Catholic teaching found fertile soil in the local belief system: the pantheon of a supreme God, the Virgin Mary and saints who could be called upon for help was a similar enough structure to Mawa and the *vodu*. St Patrick, not surprisingly, was identified with the snake *vodu* Dangbe, while St Peter was considered to be the Catholic incarnation of Legba.

An interesting walk through residential streets to the northeast of the centre leads to the **sacred forest of Kpasse** (daily 9am–6pm; CFA1000), just off rue de la Roncière. Tradition holds this site to be where Kpasse, a fourteenth-century chief, transformed himself into a tree in order to hide from his enemies. The ancient *iroko* tree still marks the spot and believers leave offerings by its roots. Modernist bronze statues depicting voodoo divinities are scattered about the woods and are explained during a guided tour – photography is permitted. While not an extraordinary adventure, a visit here is a pleasant pretext for a tramp through some pretty woods.

A final possible excursion is along the **Route des Esclaves**, the four-kilometre sandy track walked by slaves from their holding points in town to the beach. Starting in the Place Chaca (La Place des Enchères), the route runs down rue Don Francisco de Souza, past the old train station, before continuing through attractive, lush scenery. Dotted along the route are vivid green statues, the royal emblems of the various chiefs of Abomey, including Ghezzo and Benhanzin (see p.924). Various other monuments line the route, reminders of the scale and savagery of the slave trade. You'll pass a statue marking the tree of forgetfulness, where slaves were forced to circle the tree to forget their previous life, religion and culture, "to become a people with no will to react or rebel". Further along, just before the village of Zoungbodji, the **Monument of Repentance** is a colourful memorial, with bas-relief art depicting scenes of slavery. Continuing past other monuments, you'll eventually reach the beach and the **Door of No Return**, a vast and imposing arch also

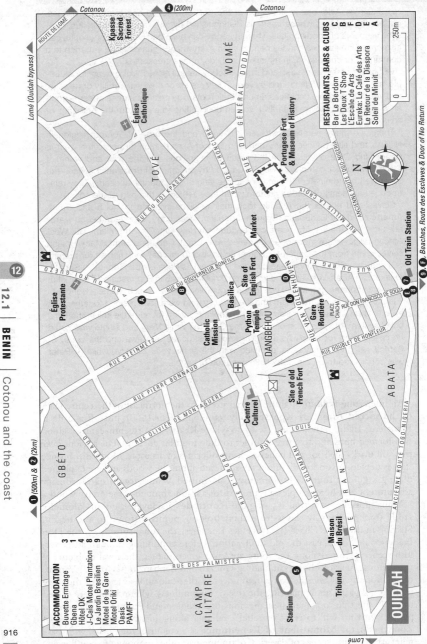

OUIDAH

ACCOMMODATION
Buvette Ermitage	3
Gbena	1
Hôtel DK	4
J-Cais Motel Plantation	8
Le Jardin Bresilien	9
Motel de la Gare	7
Motel Oriki	5
Oasis	6
PAMFF	2

RESTAURANTS, BARS & CLUBS
Bar Le Berdom	C
Les Deux T Shop	B
L'Escale de Arts	F
Eureka: Le Café des Arts	D
Le Retour de la Diaspora	E
Soleil de Minuit	A

Lomé (Ouidah bypass)

ROUTE DE LOMÉ

Cotonou

(200m)

Cotonou

Kpasse Sacred Forest

WOMÉ

RUE DU GÉNÉRAL DODD

Église Catholique

TOVÉ

RUE DU ROI KPASSE

RUE DE LA RONCIÈRE

Portuguese Fort & Museum of History

ANCIENNE ROUTE TOGO-NIGERIA

RUE MILLIS LA CROIX

N

250m

Beaches, Route des Esclaves & Door of No Return

Old Train Station

RUE DU RPG KITI

RUE VAN VOLLENHOVEN

Gare Routière

PLACE CHACHA

RUE DON FRANCISCO DE SOUZA

RUE DOUBLET DE HONFLEUR

ABATA

ANCIENNE ROUTE TOGO-NIGERIA

RUE DU ROI GUÉZO

Église Protestante

RUE DU GOUVERNEUR BONFILS

Basilica

Site of English Fort

Market

Catholic Mission

Python Temple

DANGBÉHOU

RUE STEINMEIZ

RUE PIERRE BONNAUD

Site of old French Fort

Centre Culturel

RUE OLIVIER DE MONTAGUERE

RUE ST. LOUIS

GBÉTO

RUE DES FRÈRES BRAUD

RUE D'ORGRE

RUE F COLOMBANI

AVENUE DE FRANCE

Maison du Brésil

RUE DES PALMISTES

CAMP MILITAIRE

Stadium

Tribunal

Lomé

decorated with bas-relief images and metal sculptures of slaves in shackles. The experience is marred only by the taxis and mopeds which hurry past.

Practicalities

Ouidah is easy to get to, with regular bush taxis heading here from the Gare de Jonquet in Cotonou. The **gare routière** is in the centre of town, but vehicles passing through are increasingly dropping passengers on the main highway, by the *Hôtel Gbena*, from where it's easy to catch a *zemidjan* for a ten-minute ride to the centre. The *gare routière* has irregular transport for Cotonou only; for Grand Popo and the west it's better to go to the main route de Lomé, where you can pick up transport from near the *Gbena* hotel.

Accommodation

Inexpensive accommodation can be found at any of the town's *bar-dancings*, including *Buvette Ermitage* northwest of the town (☎34.13.89; ❶), *J-Cais Motel Plantation* on the route des Esclaves (☎34.12.78; ❷), or the *Motel de la Gare* next to the old train station (☎34.10.47; ❶). They all provide no-frills s/c accommodation with fan.

Gbena rte de Lomé, 2km northwest of the centre ☎34.12.15, ☏34.12.03. For a long time the only place to stay in town, but the now dated decor reinforces the soulless atmosphere. Rooms have decent amenities, but ask for one away from the noisy main road. The restaurant serves okay food. ❹

Hôtel DK rte de Lomé, 1500m northeast of the centre ☎34.11.97. Newest and plushest accommodation available, with a decent pool and comfortable rooms featuring a/c, TV and phone. ❹

Oasis Across from the *gare routière* ☎34.10.91. Good value for money, and well located in the heart of town. ❸

Le Jardin Bresilien (aka *Auberge de la Diaspora*) 4km south of the centre and 200m east of the

Door of No Return ☎34.11.10, ✉dyasporah@yahoo.fr. Attractive thatched bungalows set among the palm trees by the beach, or less appealing budget accommodation behind. There's also a good restaurant, but it's not easy to find transport to take you back into the centre. ❷

Motel Oriki rue des Palmistes ☎34.10.04. Very presentable, s/c rooms set in a quiet area. Clean and spacious, but overpriced considering there's no a/c. ❸

PAMFF 2.5km northwest of the centre, signposted off the rte de Lomé ☎34.10.30, ☏34.10.81. Popular 26-room hotel with clean, comfy rooms arranged around a courtyard, and an attractive restaurant. ❷

Eating and drinking

For **food**, the friendly *Eureka: Le Café des Arts*, near the *Oasis*, is good for breakfasts and coffee; or *Les Deux T Shop* on rue du Gouverneur Bonfils, is a patisserie serving cakes, croissants and yoghurt. For something slightly more formal, *L'Escale de Arts* in the Village Artisanal de Ouidah serves limited filling meals, or try one of the hotel restaurants or the thatched terrace at *Le Retour de la Diaspora* on the road to the beach, which again has little variety but is good value. *Bar le Berdom* opposite the market is a lively **drinking** spot, while *Soleil de Minuit* on rue du Roi Guezo is the best **club** in town, with glitzy mirrors and a sleazy feel.

Grand Popo and around

At the height of the slave trade, **GRAND POPO**, some 70km west of Cotonou, rivalled Porto Novo, Ouidah and Aného (in Togo) as a major port. With the demise of the trade, however, its importance declined more dramatically than the other towns and, today, even vestiges of the more recent colonial past have literally been washed away by the advancing ocean. Locals remember the large church, commercial depots, administrative buildings and colonial mansions that disappeared into the water as recently as the 1960s, and though a few **antiquated buildings** still dot the road that leads to the old village from the main highway, most of the old quarter is entirely submerged.

As a result, Grand Popo looks very much like any of the other small fishing villages that stretch between Lomé and Cotonou, tucked between the lagoon and the ocean and lost in a sea of coconut trees. Though **voodoo** thrives here, few visitors even notice the snake pit, fetishes or temples, and most confine themselves mainly to the idyllic **beach**. If you do manage to drag yourself from the sand, look out for the *Villa Karo* (☎43.03.58, ✉karo@intnet.bj), a Finnish-African cultural centre which hosts a film night every Friday, a free concert on the first Saturday of the month, and a museum exhibiting art from all over West Africa.

Lac Ahémè provides the possibility for excursions (small boys will try to recruit you from the moment you arrive), and fishermen are happy to supplement their incomes by ferrying visitors in *pirogues*. The most popular destination is the **Bouche du Roy** – a vast expanse of water where the Mono River empties into the ocean. Along the way, you pass through scenic island villages.

Practicalities

Taxis from Cotonou depart from the Gare de Jonquet, and as with transport from Lomé, let you off at the junction on the main highway. It's 4km down the sandy track, through the old village to the town's most exclusive **accommodation**, the French-run *Auberge de Grand-Popo* (☎43.00.47; ❹). Housed in refurbished colonial buildings, the lodgings offer a refreshing combination of nostalgia and comfort; all rooms have private baths and fans, or you can camp for CFA1500 per head near the uninviting pool. The hotel's **restaurant** terrace sits right on the waterfront – spectacular scenery for European dishes (around CFA4000 for a meal). Back at the junction, *Hôtel Etoile de Mer* (☎43.04.83; ❷) is conveniently located on the main road, and has spotless rooms, some with a/c, though the highlight is the attractive restaurant set in a garden. On the western side of town, 2km from the junction near **Ewé Condji**, the excellent *Awalé Plage* (☎43.01.17, ✉awaleplage@yahoo.fr; ❹) has homely s/c chalets set in a large attractive compound. Camping is possible (CFA2000 per tent) down on the golden beach, and there's a rustic bar serving cold beers and juices. Try to time your stay with their extravagant fortnightly full-moon and "black-moon" (new-moon) beach parties. There are a couple of cheaper places to stay out on the road to the *Auberge*, namely *Plage Coin des Amis* (☎43.03.98; ❷) and *Doue Plage* (☎43.02.42; ❷), virtually next door, both offering basic fanless rooms with mosquito nets; the latter place is more established and comfortable. They both also allow camping for CFA1500 per person.

Among several eating options, *Farafina*, some 400m east of the *Auberge*, is popular with tourists and serves European cuisine for around CFA3000 a meal, plus a selection of cocktails; *Pizzeria Chez Marcel* just down the road is a cheaper alternative.

Lac Ahémè

A highly picturesque area to visit, **Lac Ahémè** is the lagoon that extends 30km inland from Grand Popo. There's a pleasant **hotel-restaurant** on the west shore, *Village-Club Ahémé* (☎43.00.29, ☎43.02.23; ❹) – a place for lazing away a few days, with plain, comfortable s/c, a/c rooms and optional excursions on the lake and around the district. **Possotomè**, 87km from Cotonou, is the nearest village. To reach the area, either charter a taxi and head north from Comè on a bad dirt road direct to Possotomè, or alternatively from Comè or Cotonou, take a shared taxi to Zoungbonou and then a *zemidjan* to Bopa or Possotomè on the lagoon itself.

Porto Novo and around

Capital of Benin, **PORTO NOVO** has two attributes Cotonou lacks – a geographical setting of some presence and a place in **history**. Sprawling over the hills surrounding the sizeable lagoon of Lac Nokoué, the town was formerly the centre of a large kingdom of the Gun people, whose **palace** has now been restored. More recently it served as capital of the French colony of Dahomey – the **colonial buildings** are reminders of this period – and the town was, and remains, the centre of the country's intellectual life and something of a barometer of political opinion in Benin.

Despite a population of around 225,000, Porto Novo seems much smaller. Perhaps this is because of its coherent layout, but the narrow streets and absence of modern structures also add to the provincial, passed-by feeling: most of the architecture in town harks back to the colonial and pre-colonial periods. For visitors, it's one of Benin's most interesting towns, with a strikingly good ethnographic museum, and is easily accessible, only 30km northeast of Cotonou, to which it's connected by good roads.

The Town

Porto Novo consists of four main parts. The **old town** in the centre is characterized by narrow dirt roads and *banco*-built houses. The old town runs into the **commercial centre** along Avenue Vicot Ballot, with the **Grand Marché** and surrounding businesses that stretch down to the lagoon on the southwestern flanks of the town. To the east, the **administrative district** is the location of the Présidence – the former **Governor's Palace** – and a couple of ministries and office buildings. Scattered around the margins, the zone of new **residential quarters** is inhabited by those who've moved to the city in recent years. Your most likely arrival point is at the *gare routière* on the northern side of the bridge, from where you can walk to most of the town's hotels, or easily take a one of the waiting *zemidjans*.

Porto Novo's superb **museum of ethnography** (Mon–Fri 8.30am–6pm, Sat & Sun 9am–6pm; ☎21.25.54; CFA1000) on Avenue no. 6 contains a wealth of well-presented artefacts from all Benin's peoples, each item accompanied by explanations and background. The visit kicks off at the entrance with a pair of beautifully **carved doors** from the palace of the king of Kétou, 100km north of Porto Novo. Impressive murals adorn the walls of the courtyard inside and on the ground floor of the museum you'll find a selection of voodoo masks, each with their own unique meaning and significance; there's also a small collection of musical instruments on display. Upstairs the exhibition explores "Birth, life and death in Benin" – for example, a blacksmith passing his trade to his son illustrates the cycle of life, family trades being passed from one generation to the next. Periodically there's a photo exhibition entitled "Slaves and Masters", and the content of the exhibitions can vary too, as items are brought out of or put back into storage. The guided tour, included in the entrance fee, really brings the items alive – the guides speak French and English.

Porto Novo's **Grand Marché** is on Avenue Victor Ballot. Held every four days in keeping with the traditional calendar, the market is a colourful affair that spreads over a large central square, with stalls selling agricultural goods from the surrounding countryside and fish from the nearby lagoon. The curious Brazilian-style building painted in muted pastel colours was built in the nineteenth century as a church, but is today the central mosque, dominating the scene.

Just southwest of the market, the **Musée Honmè de Porto Novo** (daily 9am–5.30pm; ☎21.35.66) has been restored and costs CFA1000 for the obligatory guided tour. It's an impressive maze of baked mud and thatch divided between the private residences of **King Toffa** and his entourage and the public assembly halls, but rather empty, except for a few rare mementos of the local kings. You have to

PORTO NOVO

N

Lagos (via Ikeja & Adjarra)

Mereídiondou

Financial Bank
Ciné Ire Akari
Château d'Eau

BOULEVARD EXTERIEUR (RUE 40)

BOULEVARD EXTERIEUR

RUE 110

Lycée Behanzin
Stadium
Musée Ethnographique
Gendarmerie
AVENUE NO 6
BIB Bank
PLACE KOKOYE
AVENUE NO 6
Présidence
OLD TOWN
Assemblée Nationale
RUE DE L'INSPECTION
PLACE BAYOL
Cathedral
Grand Marché
AVENUE VICTOR BALLOT
Bank of Africa
Musée Honmè de Porto Novo
BOULEVARD LAGUNAIRE
AV. WILLIAM PONTY
Gare Routière

ACCOMMODATION
Auberge Copacabana	6
Auberge Malabo	5
Beaurivage	4
Casa Danza	3
Le Centre Songhai	1
La Détente	7
Dona	2

Lagoon

0   500m

RESTAURANTS, BARS & CLUBS
Akango II	F
Aux Vente de Lac	H
Feelings	B
Java Promo	D
JPN	G
La Peniche Patisserie	A
La President	E
Super Bar Mahi	C

▼ Cotonou & Lagos (via Badagri)

rely on your imagination to bring to life the guide's detailed explanations of local history and court life.

Practicalities

Although Porto Novo is Benin's capital, Cotonou is the centre of business and government; Porto Novo doesn't even benefit greatly from Lagos traffic and trade, as it's off the main coastal highway. There is a post office, a **hospital** (☎21.35.90) and some pharmacies, but for banking (the three banks in town will only change cash euros) and just about every other facility, you'll find Porto Novo very limited indeed. **Internet** access is available at the office of the Jardin des Plantes et de la Nature (JPN; ☎21.38.66) near the Assemblée Nationale. For an evening film, head to Ciné Ire Akari (☎22.48.73) next to *Hôtel Dona*. Taxis and minibuses run frequently to both Cotonou and Lagos from the **gare routière** near the bridge.

Accommodation

Porto Novo has an unexceptional range of hotels for a town of its size.

Auberge Copacabana Lokpodji, 7km to the east of town on the lakeshore ☎93.65.04. It's a long, bumpy *zemidjan* ride along a rough track to get here, the reward being an appealing, tranquil location among the palms, basic but comfortable s/c rooms, and a restaurant serving excellent fish. ❶

Auberge Malabo bd Lagunaire ☎21.34.04. Has a seedy side thanks to its lively bar-restaurant, but it's near the lagoon and has decent s/c rooms and pleasant views. ❷

Beaurivage bd Lagunaire ☎21.23.99. Venerable, well-maintained hotel with a nicely planted terrace

overlooking the lagoon. Comfortable s/c, a/c rooms, but the staff and food are variable. ❹
Casa Danza Near the Assemblée Nationale ☎21.48.12. A once-popular restaurant now offering mediocre food, though it also has the town's most central accommodation. Rooms are s/c and come with choice of fan or a/c; some also have attractive tiled floors or balconies. ❷
Le Centre Songhai 3km north of town on the road to Pobé ☎22.50.92, ℻22.20.50. In a vast, beautifully wooded site, this is actually a voluntary organization established by a Nigerian academic from California, hosting students who study topics

such as fishing, agriculture and "sustainable socioeconomic entrepreneurship". There's spotless accommodation (a/c or fan) with shared facilities – an excellent deal. ❷
La Détente Off bd Lagunaire. Well located, offering a panorama of the lagoon and within walking distance of the palace and market. Rooms are homely enough, with comfortable furniture. ❷
Dona bd Extérieur, near Ciné Ire Akari ☎21.30.52, ℻21.25.25. Modern hotel with twenty nicely furnished s/c, a/c rooms, a bar-restaurant and a nightclub. ❹

Eating and nightlife

In addition to the street food in the markets and *gare routière*, and the pricey hotel **restaurants** at the *Dona* and *Beaurivage*, Porto Novo has quite a number of places to eat. For **European fare** specifically, the moderately priced restaurant under a pleasant thatched roof at the JPN (across from the Assemblée Nationale) is popular at lunchtimes. There's also the stylish *Akango II* on rue de l'Inspection, or the bustling *Java Promo* on Avenue Victor Ballot, or *La Président* (☎21.44.21) in place Bayol, the most upmarket of Porto Novo's restaurants, with a selection of wines. For decent West African cuisine, check out *Super Bar Mahi* off Avenue no. 6. Serving oodles of yam and *pâte*, it's open lunchtimes only (closed Sun) and crammed full of locals. Finally, *Aux Vente de Lac*, off Boulevard Lagunaire a little north of the *Beaurivage*, has a limited menu of European and local dishes, but boasts a great little courtyard at the back to sit in.

For **pastries and cakes**, *La Peniche Pâtisserie* (on bd Extérieur) has excellent *pain au chocolat*, croissants and yoghurts. *Feelings Night Club*, 500m beyond *Hôtel Beaurivage*, is where the well-to-do of the town **dance** the night away to African, *zouk* and American music (Wed & Fri–Sun 10pm till late; CFA3000 cover).

Around Porto Novo

Just 8km northeast of Porto Novo is the lively market centre of **ADJARRA**, where an important market takes place every fourth day. This small village has a reputation for its **drum-makers** and produces over fifty different types of *tam-tams* varying in construction, material (wood or clay) and colour. Their quality attracts many buyers from Nigeria. Alongside fruit and vegetables, the market also sells a selection of useful fetishes, medicinal herbs and *gris-gris* (lucky charms), as well as locally made pottery and hand-woven cloth. Frequent taxis, especially on market day, leave from the *gare routière* in Porto Novo, or alternatively, hire a *zemidjan* for the journey.

The stilt villages

Porto Novo's surrounding lagoon contains a number of stilt villages not unlike Ganvié, but until recently travellers seldom ventured to them. The closest and easiest to reach is **Aguégué**, 12km through the creeks (about 4hr by *pirogue*). There's no accommodation in the village, but just gliding through and having a gander makes for an interesting excursion. You may be asked to pay if you want to take pictures. *Piroguiers* near the bridge in Porto Novo can easily be found to take you there; alternatively, enquire after Hilaire, a very helpful tour guide who lives in the stilt houses behind *Hôtel La Détente* – his agency Iroko Tours offers visits to Aguégué and other stilt villages at competitive prices (CFA7000 per person by *pirogue*, CFA20,000 for a group in a motorboat). The *Hôtel Beaurivage* in Porto Novo also organizes trips to the villages (CFA12,000 for two people by *pirogue*; CFA20,000 for a larger group by motorboat).

12.2

Central Benin

B enin's interior is a relatively homogeneous series of **plains** dominated by low, sloping hills. This was the site of early kingdoms, most notably that of the **Fon** founded at **Abomey**. The Fon were formed by the arrival and intermarriage of the Ajda from the coast with local inhabitants, and today are one of Benin's biggest ethnic groups. The **Yoruba**, who share some cultural affinities with the Fon, also established a number of chiefdoms in the area. They came in a series of vague movements, setting out on family and community migrations from Oyo and Ife in present-day Nigeria in the twelfth century, and often ended up dominating the commercial activities of the interior. Further north, the **Bariba** carved out a small territory – the **Borgou country** – in the region of **Parakou**. These are still the main peoples of central Benin, an area of intensive agricultural production and small industries. The road **north from Cotonou** to Abomey passes through the **Lama depression**, a low-lying swampy region of clay soils, patches of rainforest and a designated forest reserve, the **Forêt de Ko (Lama)**.

Abomey and Bohicon

Capital of one of the great West African kingdoms in pre-colonial times, **ABOMEY** boasts a fascinating history and counts as one of Benin's greatest attractions. Commercially the town is overshadowed by **BOHICON**, 9km to the east, of which Abomey is essentially the ancient precursor, and which has benefited from its position on the rail line and main north–south highway (the French deliberately laid the railway to the east of Abomey to reduce the commercial power of the Abomey royal dynasties). Despite Bohicon's immense **market**, however, the town is a chaotic sprawl with little that could tempt you to stay, and most people skip Bohicon altogether and head straight out to Abomey, which is more manageable and, with the **royal palace and museum**, infinitely more interesting. Regular taxis connect the two towns, or by *zemidjan* it's a fifteen-minute ride for around CFA400.

If you want to **stay in Bohicon**, you've the choice of the friendly *Hôtel Relais Sinnoutin* (aka *3 Paillotes*), on the main road at the southern end of town (☎51.00.88; ②), with clean s/c rooms and a decent restaurant. You'll also need to visit Bohicon if you need to **change money**; the Bank of Africa in the centre changes both cash and traveller's cheques. From the **train station** right in the centre of Bohicon (☎51.02.10), there's a daily 3pm service to Cotonou (at least 3hr) and an 11.19am train to Parakou (6hr). In addition there is a sleeper train on Tuesday and Thursday nights.

Abomey

Abomey is fascinating to wander through, any path off the main roads leading through twisted alleyways with *banco* houses and colourfully painted **fetish temples**. Between the **royal palace** and the *préfecture*, overgrown plots with weather-worn mud ruins are vestiges of former royal palaces. It's also an excellent place to shop for local **crafts**.

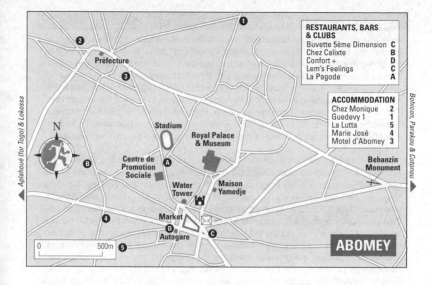

The royal palace and museum

In the three hundred years of the Dan-Homey empire, the kings gradually constructed a magnificent palace in the centre of Abomey. In fact, it was a vast complex of many palaces, since the sovereign never occupied the residence of his predecessor, but built a new one next to the old. By the time the French attacked the city in 1892, there was thus a honeycomb of twelve adjoining palaces, ten of which were soon destroyed by the invading army. Today, only two – those belonging to Ghezo and his successor Glele – remain intact, but even these have suffered badly from the effects, ultimately no less brutal, of the climate. Ongoing work has taken place with the help of funds from, among others, UNESCO, and several buildings have had their corrugated-iron roofs replaced with traditional thatch. In addition Japan is paying for the restoration of the walls circling the Palace of Behanzin, but plans to rebuild the other nine ruined palaces, which would require decades of work, have been ruled out. Nevertheless, the palaces magnificently recall the pomp and grandeur of the royal court, and have been designated as a World Heritage Site (CFA1500 entrance fee with compulsory guided tour).

The numerous artefacts on display are frequently changed and moved, but look out for the throne and banner of King Ghezo, currently housed in the palace of King Glele. The throne is built on top of four human skulls, symbolizing the king's conquests and domination over weaker peoples. The banners, which are known as the **royal tapestries**, are remarkable, vivid patchworks, woven with symbols and emblems relating the qualities of the various kings. The Palace of King Ghezo houses a display on the daily routine within the palace.

The massive walls of the complex are clad in brilliantly coloured bas-reliefs (the designs were re-created by American specialists and some of the originals are now stored inside) and as you walk round, the history of this powerful, energetic and brutal society comes alive. The **House of Pearls** is an animist temple, built by Glele so that his father's spirit could rest here after he was killed in battle with the Oyo kingdom. The walls incorporate the blood of 41 Oyo slaves (41 being a sacred number) and animal sacrifices are still performed here. After removing your shoes, you can also visit the **tomb of King Glele**, containing 41 wives selected to be buried with him (out of his supposed three thousand spouses), in addition to much of his treasure.

From as early as the sixteenth century, much of the present territory of Benin was coalescing into small, socially stratified **states** – a string of them along the coast (including Grand Popo and Ouidah) and a cluster of less clearly defined smaller states inland. A more powerful (though still very small) city-state had developed around the town of **Allada**, just 40km from the coast, which was renowned for its slave trading. At the end of the sixteenth century, three princes were in dispute over the rule of this little empire. The first, Meidji, eventually wrested power from his father. Of his two brothers, Zozerigbe headed south to Porto Novo where he founded the **Hogbonou** kingdom, while Do Aklin went north, where he founded the kingdom at **Abomey** in the early seventeenth century.

In 1654, one of the descendants of Do Aklin, **Ouegbaja**, killed the sovereign of Abomey, a king named **Dan**. Ouegbaja then built his palace over the body of the deceased monarch and his kingdom came to be known as **Dan-Homey**, meaning "from the belly of Dan". In the succession of kings, one of the greatest was **Agadja**, who ruled from 1708 to 1740. He conquered the surrounding mini-states of Allada, Savi and Ouidah and, in expanding his empire to the coast, earned the title Dé Houito, or "man of the sea". Having gained a gateway to the Atlantic, the empire embarked on a period of direct trade with Europe, a trade dependent above all on slaves. Meanwhile, however, the powerful Yoruba state of **Oyo** (to the east, in present-day Nigeria) was increasingly bent on retaining as much as possible of the trade for its own benefit. Through the middle of the eighteenth century, it repeatedly intimidated and attacked Dan-Homey, which, after 1748, formally became a vassal state of Oyo.

The Dan-Homey state became a dictatorship under the reign of **Ghezo**, who overthrew the previous king in 1818 and ruled bloodily for forty years. He ceded his monopoly rights in the slave trade to his right-hand man in Ouidah – the Brazilian **Francisco Felix de Souza** (the "viceroy" depicted in Bruce Chatwin's biographical novella and by Klaus Kinski in Werner Herzog's movie *Cobra Verde*) – and increasingly preyed on his own subject peoples. His autonomy was only limited by the duty he owed to Oyo. He reorganized the army into a powerful unit comprising 10,000 soldiers and 6000 female **"Amazon"** warriors, who were better armed than their male counterparts. Trained to use rifles as well as bows, they were reputed to cut off one of their breasts if it impaired their ability to shoot – an apocryphal story that probably sprang from the reactions of European visitors to the sight of well-drilled women soldiers.

The Dan-Homey kings amassed a stockpile of weapons through trade with the Europeans. By the end of the nineteenth century, the royal arsenal was full of modern weaponry and the stage was set for an intense conflict as the French started out in conquest of the interior. Hostilities were intense and fighting had already broken out between the French and the Fon when **King Behanzin** led an attack against the forces of **Colonel Dodds** as they advanced on Abomey. Behanzin lost the battle, and the capital of the Dan-Homey kingdom fell to the French on November 16, 1892. Abomey was already in flames as the colonial army marched into the city.

Crafts outlets

Attached to the palace, the **centre artisanal** is an effort to keep alive the craftsmanship that was the pride of the Abomey kings. The artisans were formerly constrained to produce their works for the royal court only. Crafts that were popular with the kings – brightly decorated tapestries, bronze statues made by the *cire perdue* (lost wax) method and jewellery – are still churned out, although the quality required by tourists is rather less than that demanded by royalty. This centre is the most obvious place to shop for crafts – although it may seem expensive, prices are wide open for negotiation.

Along the road running in front of the palace, the house with the lion and inscription on the front is the residence of the **Yamedje family** – the traditional embroiderers for the king. Members of the family still weave the tapestries, their works strewn over the ground, all for sale. Near to *Motel d'Abomey* there's a small but well-stocked craft outlet, the *Black Hand*, where weavers sell reasonably priced cloth.

Practicalities

Arriving in Abomey, you'll be let off somewhere around the market square or in the small **autogare**. Most of the hotels are a little too far away to walk, but there are plenty of *zemidjans* around. The *autogare* has vehicles to surrounding villages, while bush taxis for Cotonou fill up around the market. For road transport to most other destinations, it's faster to take a *zemidjan* or taxi to Bohicon for onward connections. Despite its importance as a tourist centre, Abomey has few services beyond the town's **post office**, which offers fast Internet connections.

Accommodation

Chez Monique On a dirt side-street, 200m west of the *préfecture* ☏ 50.01.68. Immensely popular with overlanders, *Monique*'s is an exotic spread, with pet monkeys and antelopes in the sprawling yard. The simple, clean s/c rooms have a fan and are quite comfortable, or you could camp for CFA2000 per person. ❷

Guedevy 1 2km north of the centre ☏ 50.03.04, ☏ 50.08.42. A vast complex – a main block with mock bas-reliefs on the entrance walls, and newer, more attractive thatched bungalows behind. They have s/c rooms with fan or a/c, plus a plain, inexpensive restaurant. ❷

La Lutta On a dirt track 500m west of the centre ☏ 04.61.77. Abomey's most central lodgings, and a great find for budget travellers. The double rooms are bearable if slightly dingy, and have fan and shower. The very friendly management can arrange inexpensive guided tours of the town. Food can be prepared to order. ❶

Marie José Just off the Lokassa road ☏ 50.02.89. Homely, welcoming set-up with a pleasant, quiet garden and spotless s/c rooms – an excellent retreat. ❷

Motel d'Abomey 200m from the *préfecture* ☏ 50.00.75, ☏ 50.00.93. The town's best hotel, boasting well-furnished private bungalows with TV, video and phone, plus s/c, a/c rooms, although everything is a little frayed around the edges. As a bonus, the restaurant is one of the town's best, and the *Prestige Nightclub* (CFA2000 entrance) is an added draw. ❸

Eating and drinking

Apart from the hotel restaurants, there's a surprising dearth of formal places to eat in town. Inexpensive **street food** is available around the market, or for a broader range of West African dishes, try *Chez Calixte* to the west of town. Just south of the stadium, the tiny, tidy *La Pagode* is a good place for a breakfast of omelette with coffee, or a lunch of rice and fish. Near the market, the *Buvette 5ème Dimension* is not only the liveliest **bar** in town but also offers simple **European meals** for around CFA1500. Another busy bar is the *Confort +* near the *autogare*. *Lem's Feelings Nightclub*, next door to *5ème Dimension* (with which it shares management), is the town's happening **club**, with European and African music pumping out at the weekends (CFA2500 entrance).

Dassa and rough routes in the west

The most straightforward way north from Cotonou is via the **trans-Benin high-way** to Parakou. Alternatively you could fork left at Dassa to follow the western *piste* leading directly to **Djougou** (see p.931), though public transport is slow and irregular. **The west** is an agricultural region hemmed in by the forests of Mont Kouffé and Mont Agoua, and was the location of an early **Yoruba** kingdom, conquered in the eighteenth century by the **Maxi** (related to the Fon). These are still the main peoples of the area, although numerous smaller groups result in a variety of regional building styles and customs. Despite the relative difficulties in getting about along this stretch it can be rewarding to travel off the beaten track, and you're likely to find contacts with people warm and immediate.

DASSA (or Dassa-Zoumé), 203km north of Cotonou, is a village tucked into a stunning landscape of heavy boulder formations and thick greenery. Aside from its aesthetic appeal, there's nothing of essential interest, with the possible exception of the **La Grotte Marial Notre Dame d'Arigbo** – a cave in which the Virgin Mary is said to have appeared, and which has become a pilgrimage site for Christians from across Africa and even Europe, who visit during August. An impressive **basilica** has been constructed in front of the cave, from where you can see the small statue of Mary and the shrine built into the rock face. Behind, a path marks the *marchez à genoux*, leading you past thirteen shrines. If you want to explore more of the surrounding countryside, you can **stay** at the *Auberge de Dassa-Zoumé*, just by the main roundabout on the highway (℡53.00.98; ❸). It's over-priced and feels frayed around the edges, but the rooms with fan or a/c are the best in town, and there's excellent food in the restaurant – and deer and monkeys lurking in the gardens. In town, there's the *Auberge St Augustin*, a friendly, family-run place with comfortable s/c doubles (℡53.02.50; ❷). Out of town, about 700m out on the route de Savalou, *Auberge Le Paradis* (℡53.02.07; ❷) has clean but cramped s/c rooms, some with TV, and a lively bar next door. Finally, *Auberge Le Cachette* on the road to the hospital offers good-value, no-frills rooms and has an attractive bar/restaurant – worth the trip for a drink even if you don't stay here (℡53.02.11; ❶).

The western route beyond **Savalou**, 30km north of Dassa, is little travelled, and involves longer waits for transport. It's difficult going, too, especially the stretch of washboard-surface up to **BASSILA**, 173km from Dassa, which is the first town along the way where you'll find **accommodation** and, perhaps more importantly, a *buvette* with the possibility of cold drinks. There's a small *chambre de passage* (❶) next to the filling station, run by a very friendly family.

12.3

The northern uplands and parks

Parakou is the northernmost large town on the main road. Beyond it, in the **northeast**, the only main centres of activity are **Kandi** and **Malanville**, small towns bolstered by agriculture and trade. The **northwest**, though harder to travel through, is a region of striking natural beauty dominated by the country's only serious highlands, the **Atakora Range**, and populated by a relatively ancient people, the **Somba**. Two towns of some size, **Natitingou** and **Djougou**, are the bases for discovering this outback region.

Northern Benin has some of West Africa's best faunal areas in the **Pendjari National Park** and, in the extreme north, the **"W" du Niger National Park**, which spreads across the frontiers of Niger and Burkina Faso. Access to Pendjari is relatively straightforward and there are several places to stay, but the Benin sector of the "W" park is extremely inaccessible (the most promising access is via Kandi) and has abundant wildlife – probably as a result.

Parakou

Formerly a station on the caravan routes, **PARAKOU**, with a population of nearly 200,000, is now the undisputed commercial centre of the interior. Its importance still derives from its position on the major roads and on the **railway** which terminates its snaillike trail here. The brewery and peanut-oil mill have brought about rapid growth in the last couple of decades, but Parakou is a town of little enduring interest, though abuzz with the activity of hundreds of small businesses, bars and passing traders.

Practicalities

Coming by bush taxi, you'll arrive in Parakou at the busy **gare routière**, located next to the main market and across from the post office. Africalines buses stop at *Bar 123* on the route de l'Aviation, 100m from the Financial Bank. The **train station** is on the western side of town. With the burgeoning business activity, there are branches of all the major **banks**; Eco-Bank gives the best rates for cash although they only change euros and dollars, while Financial Bank is the best for changing

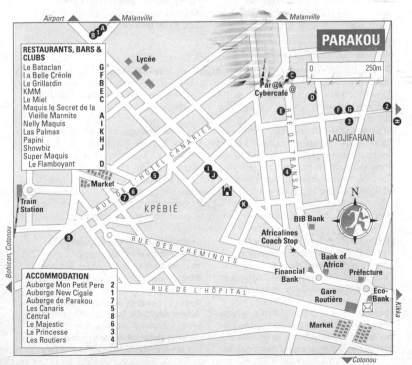

traveller's cheques. You can get **online** at Par@k Cyber-Café on route de Transa, near *Le Miel*.

Accommodation

Parakou has nothing in the way of world-class **accommodation**, but there are plenty of small, comfortable hotels that border on fancy, and one or two cheaper alternatives.

Auberge Mon Petit Pere 200m past *La Princesse*
℡ 61.10.57. Offering a real homely feel and large, spotless non-s/c rooms with mosquito nets. The garden contains a colourful outdoor bar/restaurant. ➊

Auberge New Cigale On the Malanville road, off rte de l'Aviation. Friendly French-run establishment. Rooms have fans and mosquito nets. There's also an excellent bar and a restaurant with Moroccan, French and Mexican food. ➋

Auberge de Parakou rue de l'Hôtel les Canaris ℡ 61.03.50, ✉ voyageur@intnet.bj. A member of the French-run chain, this is a cosy set-up with seven attractively furnished rooms with minimalist decor, some with a/c. ➌

Les Canaris rue de l'Hôtel les Canaris ℡ 61.11.69. Two shady courtyards provide a pleasant backdrop for various rooms ranging from non-s/c, low-comfort quarters (among the cheapest in town) to fully furnished a/c, s/c accommodation with private bath. ➋

Central rue de l'Hôtel les Canaris ℡ 61.01.24, ℻ 61.38.51. Actually west of the centre, in an imposing building hidden behind a walled garden, where you'll find their bar and restaurant. Slightly dated s/c rooms have a/c, TV and phone; some rooms have hot water. ➍

Le Majestic rue de l'Hôtel les Canaris ℡ 61.34.85. Smart, new three-storey hotel. Rooms have TV and en suite with hot water, and some feature balconies overlooking the lawn. ➍

La Princesse qtr Ladjifarani, off rte de Transa ℡ 61.04.16, ℻ 61.01.32. Set around a courtyard, the comfortable rooms offer phone, TV and video, and the town's best nightclub is attached. French and African food served in the *Nafi* restaurant, snacks in the *Plantation* bar. ➎

Les Routiers rte de Transa ℡ 61.21.27. Centrally located, swish accommodation, popular with expats. There's satellite TV in the stylishly decorated, a/c rooms, plus a lush garden and small pool at the back. ➎

Eating and nightlife

Despite Parakou's status as second city, **nights** are low-key; kerosene lamps light the darkness, indicating the stands of hundreds of nighttime vendors. It's safe and satisfying to wander around the route de l'Aviation, stopping for **street food** or a drink at one of the many *buvettes* – *Nelly Maquis*, *Show-Biz* and *Las Palmas* and are all recommended.

For **nightlife**, the hottest club in town is *Le Bataclan* opposite (and linked to) *La Princesse*, which plays African and European music (Thurs–Sun from 10pm). *KMM* is a cheaper, less pretentious alternative, which draws a large crowd to its disco and lively outdoor *buvette*, tucked in a clump of teak trees on route de Transa. Finally, the funky bar at *Auberge New Cigale* on the road to Malanville offers draught beer, table football, occasional live music at the weekend, and no shortage of atmosphere.

The prospects for good **eating** are actually better than the town's initial impression suggests, and you'll find a wide range of good African and European cuisine.

La Belle Créole qtr Ladjifarani, near *La Princesse* ℡ 61.10.25. One of the best in town, with an extensive menu of French, Italian and other European cuisine at moderate prices. Tables under a *paillote* with unmistakable lion statues at the garden entrance.

Hôtel/Restaurant Le Grillardin Next to *Auberge New Cigale* ℡ 61.27.81. Tatty accommodation, but they do have a plush restaurant, under a beautiful thatched roof, offering a range of French cuisine.

Le Miel (aka *Patisserie La Borgoise*) rte de Transa. Patisserie serving fantastic pastries, sandwiches, salads and ice cream, or a more filling *menu du jour*. Eat in the laid-back *salon de thé* upstairs.

Maquis le Secret de la Vieille Marmite Next to *Auberge New Cigale*. Delicious African sauces served from several giant pots, with either rice or *pâte*. Very cheap and incredibly popular.

Papini 600m beyond *Auberge Mon Petit Pere*

ⓣ61.04.26. Another hotel restaurant, quite an upmarket affair set around a tranquil courtyard, and serving pizzas cooked at an open oven and excellent steaks. If you can't find a *zemidjan*, it's actually a pleasant walk back to town.

Super Maquis Le Flamboyant qtr Ladjifarani, near *La Princesse*. The usual rice with fish, or couscous with chicken, plus Ivoirian specials, including chicken *kedjenou*. Attractive gardens and friendly service.

The northeast

The **northeast** is characterized by woodland and savanna scenery, broken by a series of small rivers (the Mékrou, Alibori and Sota) that descend gradually to join the Niger. It's the least densely populated region of the country, and ethnically very diverse. The **Dendi**, for example, are migrants from Mali's Songhai empire, who migrated south from the Niger River in the sixteenth century to the savanna districts around Kandi, Malanville and Djougou. **Fula** cattle herders crossed the Niger River at around the same time and still make up a sizeable proportion of the northern population. The **Bariba**, whose ethnic and linguistic affiliations are obscure, arrived before the fifteenth century from the northwest Nigeria region. They first settled around Nikki, but population pressure soon spread their communities to the districts of Parakou, Kandi and Kouande. Here they came to dominate predecessors like the **Bussa**, speakers of another obscure language (probably a Mande relict), who had also migrated west from northern Nigeria. Despite the important highway running through the region, linking Cotonou with Niamey, the Niger Basin remains economically undeveloped. Cotton is a big cash crop, but industrialization hasn't penetrated much beyond a cotton-seed plant in Kandi and a rice-husking factory in Malanville.

Kandi and around

Like Parakou, **KANDI** was formerly a stopping point on the caravan routes and grew to become a sizeable chiefdom – a vassal state of Bariba rulers in Nikki, to the southeast. Located 213km north of Parakou, it's a small town, and relies heavily on farming, a livelihood with which young people are becoming increasingly disenchanted. They've been deserting the countryside in numbers that are unsettling to the local economy, and heading east to Nigeria, which is linked to Kandi by a well-travelled *piste* that heads through Ségbana. You may question the attractions of a place from which even the townspeople are engaged in a mass exodus and, true enough, there's not a lot of note. Still, it's a convenient highway stopover and, with its dusty mango-shaded streets, not entirely charmless.

In the dry season, you can make simple arrangements at **Alfa Kouara**, about 40km north of Kandi, to walk to a nearby **waterhole**, where **wildlife** gathers; with luck, you'll even see elephants.

Practicalities

As district headquarters, Kandi has a post office and a bank – though note that the latter, which changes cash and traveller's cheques, is only open two Mondays a month. There are several good options for **accommodation** in town. *Auberge de Kandi* (ⓣ63.02.43; ❷), some 1500m from town on the road to Malanville, has an attractive spacious courtyard, well-kept rooms and a pricey restaurant. As you head in to town from here you'll pass the *Motel de Kandi* on the left (ⓣ63.03.03; ❷), where there are good-value, tidy s/c rooms, though the compound is quite scruffy. More centrally located near the *autogare*, the *Auberge La Rencontre* (ⓣ63.01.76; ❷) has a friendlier feel, with spotless s/c doubles with fan, some with a/c, and a great rooftop bar-restaurant.

Cheap *buvettes* for **eating and drinking** are scattered around the marketplace. More formal meals can be had at *Restaurant La Gargoterie*, which serves up the usual rice and sauce dishes. *Tropicana Nightclub* next to the cotton factory is a popular haunt with the locals (Fri–Sun from 11.30pm; CFA2000; ladies' night on Sun).

Malanville

Tucked in the northeast corner near the Nigerian and Niger borders and 733km from Cotonou, **MALANVILLE** is a trading town *par excellence* where you can run into people from all over West Africa. The **market**, held from Friday to Sunday, is Benin's largest after Cotonou, and large-scale regional rice-planting attracts wage-hungry labourers from as far afield as Mali. The presence of many foreigners, mixed with the Fula- and Songhai-speaking **Dendi** locals who form the majority of the town, makes for an upbeat atmosphere, and the lorries that line the main street add to the border-town feel. However, unless you time your visit with the huge market, the lack of notable sights means you're not likely to want to make an extended stay. Note that the Kandi–Malanville road was closed at night for several months in 2002 due to a spate of armed robberies, so check the current situation and plan your journeys accordingly.

Practicalities

Numerous bush taxis wait for passengers in the central *autogare*, mainly heading south to Kandi or Parakou. Alternatively Africalines have three buses a week to Cotonou via Kandi and Parakou, departing on Wednesdays, Fridays and Sundays at 10am. If you're heading north to **Niamey**, it's quicker and cheaper to catch a taxi to Gaya (CFA500), on the other side of the river, and to find another vehicle there.

On the southern edge of town, about 1500m from the *autogare*, a variety of rooms are available at the French-run *Rose des Sables* (📞67.01.25; ❷), with comfy but slightly overpriced s/c bungalows, or simpler rooms in a small "tower block" – there's also a restaurant attached (*menu du jour* CFA6000). In town, 1500m west of the *autogare*, *Motel Issifou* is clean enough and has a nice area up on the roof to sit on; the restaurant serves basic fare such as chicken and chips. Numerous **street food** stands line the paved road near the *autogare*, and you'll find a host of *buvettes* with cold drinks.

Parc National du "W" du Niger

The **"W" du Niger National Park** (open early Dec to late May) spreads over 10,000 square kilometres of wild bush in Niger, Burkina Faso and Benin – an area virtually without human habitation. The "W" (pronounced *double-vé* in French) refers to the double U-bend in the course of the Niger River at the point where the three countries meet. Though nearly half the park is in Benin, the only real viewing trails, and all the park lodgings and *campements*, are in Niger (see p.973) and Burkina.

Most of the big plains game is here, however, if you can find a way in. Although the **buffalo** herds are thinning out, **elephants** can still be spotted in the Béninois sector – notably in the Mékrou valley – while in the Mékrou's waters, unmistakeable herds of snorting **hippos** are fairly plentiful. All the cats are found in the "W" as well – **serval**, **caracal**, **leopard**, **cheetah** and **lion** – but you can visit repeatedly and never see a single specimen. Most commonly encountered are a good number of **antelope** species – bushbuck (*guibs harnachés* in French), cobs or waterbucks (*cob de buffon*, *cob defassa*), reedbuck (*redunca*) and the red-fronted gazelle – and, of course, **warthogs** (*phacochères*) and **baboons** (*babouins*). Aardvarks (*oryctéropes*) are around, too, but their nocturnal habits ensure they're rarely spotted.

Practicalities

You need your own 4WD vehicle to visit this park, at least on the Benin side. Even with one, there are no reliably motorable *pistes* until you cross the borders. The most common way to get to the park is up from Kandi to **Banikoara** (69km from Kandi), a small town where you'll find the last **accommodation** (a small *campement*; ●) before entering the reserve. From here, it's a short, 17-kilometre drive to **Kérémou** – one of the main gateways to the park in Benin.

The only area that's normally visited is the 400-square-kilometre triangle formed by the Kérémou–Diapaga road, the Mékrou River (which the road crosses) and the Benin–Burkina Faso border. There's a *piste* along the left bank of the Mékrou that leads up to the **Koudou Falls**. A plan is under consideration to build a bridge across the Mékrou at this point and to develop tracks that would follow the Benin side of the river all the way to Pekinga near the confluence with the Niger. In the meantime, you have to cross over to Burkina Faso near the falls to keep on motorable tracks.

The Somba country

The **northwest** is home to some of the oldest **civilizations** to migrate to Benin – a number of which lived for long periods with virtually no interaction. The best known are the **Somba** (more accurately the Otammari, or Betammaribe), famous for the fortresslike houses known as **Tatas-Somba** that they built to protect themselves from the slave raids of Dan-Homey warriors. They still live in largely isolated villages scattered along the base of the **Atakora Mountains**, though the young people are increasingly inclined to migrate to urban centres such as **Natitingou**, the Atakora provincial capital. Further south, Somba give way to the Yowa, part of the same cluster of Voltaic-speaking peoples, and the Songhai-speaking Dendi who live in the region of **Djougou**, a large commercial town on the main road to Togo.

Djougou

With a population of some 170,000, **DJOUGOU** is a large and busy town, located 134km from Parakou and easily accessible by paved road. Its importance as a major regional market has been assured by its position on the main roads linking Natitingou to Savalou, and Parakou to the Togolese border and through to Kara.

Djougou's large **autogare** adjoins the market and you shouldn't have any problem finding transport to Natitingou and Parakou. Many vehicles also head to **Kara** in Togo, via the border post at Kétao. Africalines buses stop in front of the Maison des Jeunes in the centre of town, and depart daily for Cotonou (8am) and Natitingou (4pm).

Accommodation options are very limited. The *Motel du Djougou* on the road to Parakou (☎80.00.69; ●) is reliable, with attractive thatched bungalows in a large compound, some with a/c. *Campement la Cachette*, up a dirt track off the Savalou road, has simpler rooms, all non-s/c (●). Both of these serve food. Opposite the *Motel du Djougou*, *Le Quasar* is a smarter dining option under a thatched roof, with a diverse range of local and foreign dishes for around CFA2000. To while away the night, try *New Jack's Night Club* out on the road to Savalou (Fri & Sat; CFA2000), or Ciné Sabari, not far from the *autogare*.

Natitingou

Home town of President Mathieu Kérékou, **NATITINGOU** has never received the degree of patronage extended to Yamoussoukro in Côte d'Ivoire or Kara in Togo, but even if Kérékou hasn't gone so far as to turn his birthplace into the national capital, he hasn't forgotten it either. Though only a small centre, Natitingou has the beginnings of an industrial base with the siting here of a SONAFEL juice factory and peanut-husking factories. You're more likely to notice other manifestations of the president's munificence in the town's modern Financial Bank on the main street and the beautiful luxury hotel. But despite these surprise perks, the real draw of the town lies in the countryside that surrounds it, a magnificent region of hills dotted with the Tata-Somba homes that have become as famous as anything in Benin. The **Musée Régionale de Natitingou**, near *Hôtel Bourgogne*, is worth a brief visit (CFA1000), exploring the music, clothing, housing and history of the region.

Practicalities

If you've entered the country from Burkina Faso and only have the 48-hour visa issued on the border, visit the Police Nationale Commissariat (on the left as you approach from Tanguiéta) for your visa extension. **Internet access** is available at Cyber Centre du Boulevard near the centre of town. Bush taxis leave sporadically for Boukoumbé, Tanguiéta (for Pendjari), Djougou and Parakou from the **gare routière** in the centre of town; just across the street, Africalines buses depart daily for Cotonou at 7am (CFA8500).

Accommodation

Natitingou has a surprisingly good range of accommodation, from budget to business class, and you can often bargain rates down.

Auberge la Montagne Up a dirt track beside Ciné Atacora. Spacious, spotless s/c rooms, and a homely set-up. Good value. ❷

Auberge Tanekas On the rte de Djougou, at the exit from town ☎82.15.52. Good location in a spacious leafy courtyard, but choose your room carefully – some rooms are small, dark and definitely showing their age. There are also attractive s/c bungalows available. ❷

Auberge le Vieux Cavalier Signposted up a track beside Ciné Atacora, 300m after *La Montagne* ☎82.13.24. Pretty much the cheapest in town and excellent value. Rooms with fan or a/c are set around a leafy courtyard, dotted with traditional-style bas-relief sculptures. They also have 4WD vehicles for rent. ❷

Bellevue Signposted up a dirt track about 200m north of Ciné Atacora ☎82.13.36, ✉belvu@intnet.bj. Good location on top of a hill, and with a very helpful manager, though the s/c rooms, some with a/c, are a tad overpriced. There's a good *menu* at CFA6000 for three courses. ❸

Bourgogne On the main road across from *Le Gourmet* ☎82.22.40, ☎82.24.40. A step above the budget hotels – simple, clean and comfortable accommodation, all a/c, in a convenient location. ❷

Kantaborifa Off the rte de Djougou on a dirt track just before *Auberge Tanekas* ☎82.11.66. Friendly place, with very presentable rooms, some with a/c, ranged around an attractive *paillote*. ❷

Tata Somba 1km west of the centre ☎82.11.24 or 82.20.99. A classy hotel in the Groupe Accor chain, with a swimming pool (CFA1500 for non-guests), the town's swankiest restaurant, and dated a/c rooms. The same chain manages the *campements* in the Pendjari National Park, so this is the best place for information on accommodation and vehicle rental if you're heading there. ❺

Eating and nightlife

In addition to the hotel **restaurants** and the market, *Le Gourmet* opposite *Hôtel Bourgogne* offers simple but tasty meals at reasonable prices. It's also a place to meet people from the region and possibly arrange to visit some of the Somba countryside. Another possibility is *Chez Antony*, on the route de Tanguiéta, where they serve up well-prepared and relatively inexpensive African dishes or the likes of chicken and chips; it's also a popular local drinking spot. *Le Basilic*, located 200m further up the same track as *Hôtel Kantaborifa*, has a diverse menu including pizza, and highly recommended home-made ice cream.

You'll find a couple of **discos** in town, including the open-air *Le Village*, located to the west of town out on the road to *Hôtel Tata Somba* – it's not too expensive and very local in flavour. Ciné Atacora, on the left if you're heading out of town towards Djougou, shows fairly recent American and French films nightly.

Around Natitingou

The **Betammaribe** were one of the first peoples to arrive in Benin, settling near the Atakora range at an unknown date a thousand years or more ago. Living in rela tive isolation, these people, commonly known as the **Somba**, resisted changes inflicted by the spread of Islam and the French invasion. Until quite recently, they lived in the seclusion of their fortified *tatas* and farmed their lands, wearing no more than the traditional *cache sexe* (pubic covering) of their ancestors. Although their subsistence way of life had been ignored for centuries, in the 1970s they were exposed to the raw glare of the French press – delighted to have located a rare example of "real Africa". Stung by the sensational reports of naked tribesmen, Kérékou's government ran a campaign to force the Somba to wear clothes. As a result of this humiliation and other insensitivities, the Somba remain a very private, reserved people, and outside of the main towns, such as Natitingou – where traditional ways are fast breaking down – it's difficult, and perhaps from no one's point of view very desirable, to penetrate their tight-knit communities.

Rather than forming large communities, the Somba built their homes about 500m apart from one another – the distance a man could throw a spear, you'll be told, which would surprise the holder of the world javelin record (under 100m). Whatever the brawn of their throwing arms (it seems more likely that 500m is the maximum dangerous range of an eighteenth-century musket), this defensive safeguard was adopted during slave-raiding days and the custom has carried over. Houses are still built like fortresses with round turrets for grain storage and internal animal pens. During slave raids, families could hole up in these houses for days on end until the marauding Dan-Homey armies went off in search of easier prey (see the section in the Togo chapter on the **Tamberma**, a people closely related to the Somba, for more information about this regional architecture; p.875). With your own vehicle, you could cross the nearby border and drive the *piste* that leads through the region of the Tamberma, arriving at **Kandé** in Togo. Though difficult, it's one of the most beautiful drives in this part of West Africa.

The **Tata-Somba** still dot the countryside around the Atakora region and it's worth a trip through these parts to take in the unusual architecture. The more accessible communities are generally friendly and not too camera-shy, provided you ask permission. Coming in by bush taxi from Djougou, you'll see some of the architecture from the roadside, notably along the stretch between Perma (56km from Djougou) and Natitingou.

One of the highest concentrations of Tata-Somba is found further west, however, along the road from Natitingou to **BOUKOUMBÉ**, 43km west of Natitingou, near the Togolese border. It's easiest to reach on market day – a four-day cycle – which is always the day before Natitingou's, but you should be able to get there by *zemidjan* most days (CFA5000 return journey). There are a couple of simple but decent **hotels**, including *Auberge Dinaba* (aka *Auberge Villageoise de Tourisme*; ❶) – ask around for directions in the vicinity of the Catholic mission, where you can have food prepared. Alternatively, *Chez Pascaline*, in the Zongo district not far from the roundabout at the exit of town, serves up couscous, rice and sauce.

Parc National de la Pendjari

The **Pendjari National Park**, one of the best game reserves in West Africa, spreads over 2750 square kilometres of woody savanna north of the Atakora range, up against the Pendjari River, which runs along the Burkinabe border. Unlike the "W" National Park, access to Pendjari is relatively straightforward.

From Natitingou, the usual route winds through the Atakora Mountains for 45km through to **TANGUIÉTA**, a village at the edge of the reserve, with a lively market on Mondays. There are several options for **accommodation**. The friendly and central *APP Bar-Dancing* (☎83.01.73; ❶) has grubby rooms with mosquito nets and fans, and there are video nights on Fridays and noisy dancing on Saturdays. *Le Baobab* (☎83.02.25; ❷), about 2km northwest of town on the route de Porga, has comfortable s/c rooms and an attractive garden.

There are two **waterfalls** in the area, the first – the **cascade de Tanguiéta** – about 1500m south on the road to Natitingou, and the second, larger, **cascades de Tanougou** near the village of the same name, 33km northeast of Tanguiéta on the road to Batia. Swimming at the latter, with the falls pounding your back, is a memorable experience. *Le Relais de Tanougou* (❷), by the waterfall, has six rooms you can book through the *Hôtel Tata Somba* in Natitingou.

At Tanguiéta, the road divides. You can aim northeast to **Batia**, where there's a park entrance, though no accommodation. However, most people continue north-west to the town of **PORGA**, 61km from Tanguiéta on the Burkina border, which has **lodgings** and the main park entrance gate. The *Hôtel Campement de Porga* (☎82.20.39, ❹) has bungalows and rooms, some air-conditioned. If you've made it this far without your own transport, you might hope to tag along with tourists heading into the park at Porga, though your chances would be just as good if you looked for a lift at the *Hôtel Tata Somba* in Natitingou. The south and northeast of the park are called **Zones Cynégétiques**, and are hunting blocks which can be traversed even when the park is closed.

Lions still stalk these parts and your chances of seeing them are relatively good. Other large mammals you have a good chance of spotting include **elephants** (notably in the south of the park) and **buffalo**, which roam in large herds. **Hippos** and **crocodiles** (*caïmans* in colloquial French) are widespread in the Pendjari River, while the same species of **antelope** as are found in the "W" park, plus **warthogs** and **monkeys**, are pretty sure bets. As usual, however, all the animals are most easily and abundantly seen at the end of the dry season, when their movements are restricted by the need to stay close to water.

Park practicalities

The park is only **open** from mid-December to mid-May. **Permits** to visit (CFA5000 per person admission for 15 days; guide fee CFA5000 per day) can be obtained from the *postes forestiers* in Porga, Batia and Banikoara, but for complete information, contact the Direction du Tourisme et de l'Hôtellerie in Cotonou (see p.902) or the *Hôtel Tata Somba* in Natitingou.

Inside the park, **accommodation** can be found at the remote *Hôtel Campement de la Pendjari*, located in the north of the park near the Burkina border and the Pendjari River (☎82.11.24, ❸). They have smart bungalows and twin rooms, plus a restaurant, bar and, miraculously, a swimming pool. If it's full, it's possible to **camp** for CFA3000 per person. Camping, under the supervision of rangers, is also per-mitted at the **Mare Yangouali** and the **Pont d'Arli**, where you can cross the Pendjari River into Burkina Faso and the Pendjari's extension there – **Arli National Park**.

Niger

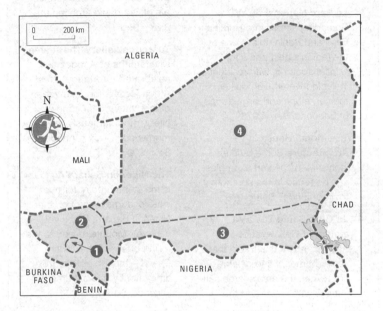

Niger highlights

* **Musée National, Niamey** One of West Africa's finest museums, home to a zoo, crafts centre and exhibition halls featuring everything from dinosaur skeletons to full-size examples of Nigérien houses. See p.964

* **Le Parc National du "W"** Spreading across into Burkina Faso and Benin, this is one of the region's best parks for wildlife spotting, with residents including waterbuck, duiker, roan antelope and large troops of baboons. See p.973

* **Traditional Hausa Architecture** Some outstandingly well-preserved examples can be found in the southern town of Zinder. See p.978

* **La Cure Salée** The area around In-Gall, west of Agadez, hosts this traditional yearly homecoming celebration, when the area's large salt flats fill with water and the nomadic herders return to feast, fatten their animals and look for wives. See p.984

* **The Grande Mosquée, Agadez** Its minaret towering over the town's low rooflines, the mosque is a classic example of Soudanic architecture, See p.985

* **Tuareg jewellery** The Tuareg silversmiths of Agadez are celebrated throughout West Africa for fashioning a variety of innovative, refined jewellery, most famously the renowned "Croix d'Agadez". See p.987

* **The Nigérien Sahara** Agadez is the starting point for two classic journeys through the Nigérien Sahara: to the volcanic Aïr Mountains and to the rolling dunes of the Ténéré Desert – though both require time, money and extreme persistence. See p.990

Introduction and Basics

Even by West African standards, Niger is a tantalizingly remote and little-visited destination. Most of the country comprises a vast expanse of largely uninhabited Sahelian desert, with the only areas of significant population concentrated in a small ribbon of cultivated land at its southern edge along the Niger River. Although the country formerly saw a steady trickle of trans-Saharan travellers arriving from the north, the troubles in Algeria effectively closed that route to Westerners and left Niger more isolated than ever.

Niger is drought-afflicted and desperately poor, but there's little obvious sense of destitution. The country exudes a feeling of orderliness and composure, as well as a new-found sense of optimism following the return to democracy after a period of military rule and the resolution of the **Tuareg conflict** which threw much of the country into turmoil during the 1990s. Deserted hotels across the country now stand hopefully open, waiting for the tourists to return.

There's plenty to go back for. The **Sahelian landscapes** of the north are among West Africa's most remarkable, while in **Agadez** the country has a desert city to rival – or even surpass – Timbuktu. Niger is also one of West Africa's most hassle-free countries, while well-maintained roads and good buses make getting around unusually straightforward.

People

Nearly half the population of Niger are **Hausa**-speaking. Engaged principally in agriculture and commerce, the Hausa have been long settled in the south, where they established large urban centres such as Maradi and Zinder. The overwhelming majority of Hausa are Muslim, but small splinter groups have retained traditional religious beliefs, notably in the Birnin-Konni district. If you don't have a chance to get further south to the original Hausa city-states in Nigeria, you can still see the brilliant **durbar festivals** – cavalry charges, clashing costumes and all – in Zinder, which retains its sultanate and beautiful quarters of traditional architecture.

The **Djerma** and **Songhai** speak the same language and probably have common origins. Numbering about one and a half million, they're the second largest group in Niger and have been politically dominant in the country for generations. Today's are descendants of those who fled the collapse of Gao's great Songhai empire, and live mostly along the banks of the Niger as far downstream as Tillabéri, retaining the essential class structure – nobles, commoners, slaves and craftspeople – of the old empire.

Fact file

The **République du Niger** has a confusing name for English-speakers. Pronouncing it like an unfinished "Nigeria" means nothing to Nigériens – the people of the country – who pronounce it "Nee-zhé". It's a vast country on the map, spreading over 1,270,000 square kilometres – twice the size of Texas and five times as big as Britain. In reality, however, the Sahara covers most of the northern region, making a large proportion of the country uninhabitable. A population of some ten million people is concentrated at fairly high density, mainly along the borders with Nigeria, Mali and Benin. Nearly one million people are reckoned to live in Niamey.

Niger faces a bleak economic prospect. The country's foreign debt amounts to some £1 billion ($1.6 billion), equivalent to nearly six times the value of its annual goods and services exports. Ninety-eight percent of the population is employed in agriculture, livestock and informal trade; and mining and manufacturing continue to slump due to the unstable price of Niger's unhealthy principal export resource – **uranium**.

The Djerma live further south in the regions of Niamey and Dosso.

Another large group, the **Fula** (Peul or Peulh in French), make up some ten percent of the population. Centuries ago they founded large kingdoms in what are now Senegal and Guinea, before spreading east. By the end of the nineteenth century, a group of town Fula (as opposed to nomads), led by Uthman Dan Fodio, had established a huge Islamic theocracy centred on Sokoto in Nigeria. In Niger today, the Fula are still divided into Muslim townspeople (Fulani) and nomadic herders, commonly called **Bororo** or **Wodaabé**, who largely follow traditional beliefs and maintain a colourful culture of dance and life-cycle ritual.

The **Tuareg** represent less than a tenth of Niger's population. Of Berber origin, they migrated to the desert regions of the Aïr around the seventh century, when they came to control long stretches of the Saharan routes, either pillaging passing caravans, offering protection to them, or both. Some Tuareg still take camel caravans to the Bilma salt mines, but an increasing number have been forced to seek jobs in the towns by the recent droughts and the rebellion. The Tuareg have a rather exaggerated reputation as sharp operators: they often work as guides and also produce some of Niger's finest crafts – especially leather- and silverwork.

In the region of Lake Chad, the **Kanouri** are one of Niger's smaller groups. These people are part of the legacy of the great neighbouring empires of **Kanem** and **Bornu**, which reached a peak in the sixteenth century. With the advent of colonialism, their territory was divided between Chad, Nigeria, Niger and Cameroon. Today, they're principally farmers and fishers, and in towns like Zinder they have mixed significantly with the Hausa. Descendants of marriages between the two groups are known as **Beriberi**.

Where to go

Vast expanses of Niger's million-plus square kilometres are desert. But most visitors see only the south, where thriving commerce and relative prosperity characterize the towns and agricultural districts. The **Niger** River, flowing for over five hundred kilometres through the southwest, is one of the country's few bodies of water – an attraction in itself. The cosmopolitan capital, **Niamey**, straddling the banks of "Le Fleuve", draws a mix of local and regional traders and international aid and business visitors. Air-conditioned hotels and restaurants provide welcome relief from the Sahelian bush, but the city's modern high-rises coexist uneasily with its sprawling markets and slum neighbourhoods of mud-brick homes.

From the capital, you can travel by road along the east bank of the Niger towards the Malian border, visiting Songhai villages and the commercial centres of **Tillabéri** and **Ayorou**, which has a spectacular market that unites all the peoples of the region. South of Niamey, the Niger is navigable only in short sections as it closes in on the game reserve named after the bends in the river – the **Parc National du "W" du Niger**.

A second main line of travel lies along the southern border with Nigeria and the **Hausa** towns of **Birnin-Konni**, **Maradi** and **Zinder**. These historic centres lie in the country's green belt and have been bolstered by agriculture – the region's dominant feature. The road from Zinder is paved all the way to **Nguigmi**, a Kanouri settlement near **Lake Chad**.

The vast desert regions of the **north** are now beginning to open up to visitors again following the end of the Tuareg rebellion. The region's main town, **Agadez**, is an ancient desert metropolis and seat of a powerful sultanate, and one of the most important centres in the southern Sahara. For determined travellers, it is also the starting point for visits to isolated oases in the **Ténéré** and **Bilma** regions and to the historic villages of the less remote **Aïr mountain region**, such as Timia, Iferouâne and Assodé. Getting to any of these places requires specialized preparations for desert travel, and whether you sign up for some kind of tour or take a guide in your own vehicle, the whole expedition is likely to cost a small fortune.

When to go

Most of Niger is scorching hot all year round. The heat is least oppressive from about

Average temperature and rainfall

Niamey

	Jan	Feb	Mar	Apr	May	June	July	Aug	Sept	Oct	Nov	Dec
Temperatures °C												
Min (night)	14	18	22	26	27	25	24	22	23	23	19	15
Max (day)	34	37	41	42	41	38	34	32	34	38	38	34
Rainfall mm	0	0	5	8	33	81	132	188	94	13	0	0
Days with rainfall	0	0	0	1	4	6	9	12	7	1	0	0

Agadez

	Jan	Feb	Mar	Apr	May	June	July	Aug	Sept	Oct	Nov	Dec
Temperatures °C												
Min (night)	10	13	17	21	25	24	24	23	23	20	15	12
Max (day)	29	33	38	41	44	43	41	38	40	39	35	32

Bilma

	Jan	Feb	Mar	Apr	May	June	July	Aug	Sept	Oct	Nov	Dec
Temperatures °C												
Min (night)	6	8	13	17	31	22	23	24	21	16	11	8
Max (day)	26	29	35	40	43	44	42	40	41	39	33	28

October or November through to March. If you're travelling on the rough overland route from Gao in Mali to Niamey, it's also worth trying to avoid the **rainy season**, which falls roughly between July and September, when heavy storms can knock out the *pistes* for days. In contrast, when the harmattan wind blows down from the north in November, it can kick up blinding clouds of dust and sometimes cause morning temperatures to tumble near to freezing point, especially in the north around Agadez, and in the Aïr mountains.

Getting there from the rest of Africa

Niger was formerly West Africa's main **overland** entry point (from Algeria across the Sahara), but the dire security situation in Algeria has now placed Niger on the extreme fringe of West African travel routes.

For important practical information applying to all West African countries, covering health, transport, cultural hints and more, plus details on getting to the region from beyond Africa, see Basics, pp.9–87.

Meanwhile, **flight** connections with the rest of the region remain barely adequate, though they are are slowly improving.

Flights

Within **West Africa**, direct flights to Niamey are nearly all from **Abidjan**, with Air Niger International (4 weekly) and Air Ivoire (2 weekly) providing most services. Air Niger International also flies from **Dakar** via **Bamako** once weekly, while Air Sénégal flies the same route twice weekly. From **Ouagadougou**, Air Burkina and Air Niger International both have twice-weekly connections. Air Niger International services fly via Abidjan, **Lomé** and **Cotonou**.

From **Lagos** you'll have to go to Abidjan with Nigeria Airways or Cameroon Airlines and pick up a flight from there (unless you fancy flying on a Nigerian domestic carrier to Sokoto and then taking a taxi for the last 500km). There are no direct flights from **west coast cities** (Nouakchott, Banjul, Bissau), nor from Accra, but there are reasonable connections with Air Ivoire from **Conakry**, Dakar, Bamako, Ougagdougou, Cotonou, Lomé and **Douala** via Abidjan.

From **the rest of Africa**, Abidjan is the obvious hub. There are weekly flights to Niamey from **Algiers** with Air Algérie and from **Casablanca** on Royal Air Maroc.

NIGER | Basics

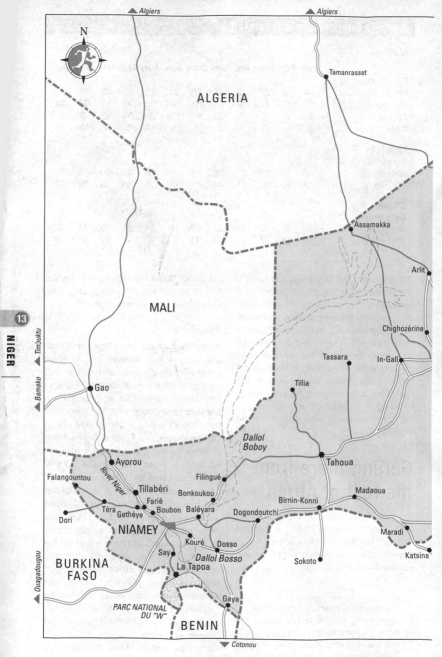

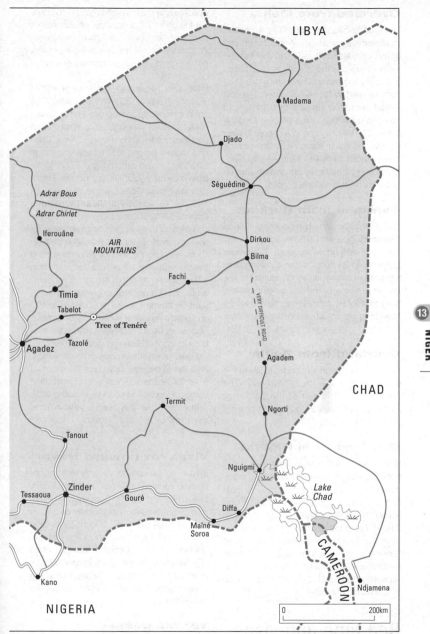

LIBYA

Madama

Djado

Séguédine

Adrar Bous

Adrar Chirlet

Iferouâne

AIR
MOUNTAINS

Dirkou

Bilma

Fachi

Timia

Tabelot

Tree of Ténéré

VERY DIFFICULT ROAD

Agadez

Tazolé

Agadem

CHAD

Termit

Ngorti

Tanout

Nguigmi

Lake
Chad

Zinder

Tessaoua

Gouré

Diffa

Maïné
Soroa

CAMEROON

Kano

Ndjamena

NIGERIA

0   200km

Overland from Mali

The road follows the Niger River from **Gao to Niamey**. It's a difficult stretch for drivers, awash with deep soft sand and the dreaded thorn trees (resulting in endless punctures), but motoring frustrations are more than compensated by Sahelian scenery at its best – dust-shrouded sunsets over the broad river and numerous fishing villages along the banks. SNTV in Niger, and Airfagosse, Ham Kouma and Askia Transport in Mali provide bus services between Niamey and Gao. Alternatively, bush taxis are available as far as the respective national borders.

Overland from Burkina

The 500-kilometre paved road linking **Ouagadougou** with Niamey is a relatively busy and straightforward route. The border is now open 24 hours a day, and formalities are pretty routine, although police at the border or some of the checkpoints before Niamey may try to make some money by requesting all sorts of vaccination certificates (meningitis, measles and so on).

Overland from Benin

The 1030-kilometre road **from Benin** is paved all the way from Cotonou. The offices on both sides of the border at Malanville are open 24 hours and present no special problems.

Overland from Nigeria

Numerous paved roads feed into Niger **from Nigeria**, retaining a Hausa-land commercial unity despite the frontier. The main entry routes are from Sokoto to Birnin-Konni, Katsina to Maradi, and Kano to Zinder. From the south, the best route is direct to Sokoto, then to the border at Birnin-Konni. If you're setting off from Kaduna or Kano, the best surfaced route is via Katsina to Maradi. Border crossings provide no unusual problems.

Red tape and visas

Niger cultivates one of the most irksome bureaucracies in the world. Although Nigériens are subject to much more scrutiny

at police and customs checkpoints throughout the country than tourists, officials have a reputation for being painfully no-nonsense. Though the situation seems to be improving, don't expect jocular exchanges or upbeat conversation.

Visas for Niger are required by all visitors except citizens of ECOWAS countries. They are not issued at the border, and are most easily obtained in neighbouring West African countries: Benin, Côte d'Ivoire, Ghana, Chad and Nigeria (Lagos and Kano). Visas cost £20/$30 for two months and £35/$50 for three months; if your itinerary includes Benin, Burkina Faso, Côte d'Ivoire or Togo, it's cheaper to acquire a **Visa Touristique Entente** (CFA25,000), which covers these five countries for three months. You can easily get hold of one at any of the embassies of these countries. Note that French embassies don't handle visas for Niger, but some Ivoirian embassies do; and that Niger has no representation in Bamako (although Mali has a consulate in Niamey). If you're arriving from Mali and need a visa, plan ahead. In general, Niger officials are literate and well-versed in the rules and regulations. Bluffing is rarely effective.

If you apply for a visa outside Africa, Nigérien embassies may ask for a return air ticket or, at the very least, the registration details of the vehicle you'll be travelling with.

To enter Niger you need a **yellow fever certificate** (except infants under 12 months).

Visas for onward travel

In Niamey, you can get visas for most neighbouring countries with little problem. Benin, Mali, Chad and Guinée-Conakry have diplomatic representation in Niamey and issue visas relatively painlessly. Burkina Faso, Côte d'Ivoire and Togo have no representation, but the French consulate handles their visas. Nigerian visas, however, are in principle only granted to residents of Niger, but if you make a good case for yourself, exceptions can be made.

Vehicle passes

If you're driving, you'll need a **carnet**. If you don't have one, the police will issue you with a Temporary Importation Document. You'll also be issued with a *laissez-passer*, a visa for your vehicle, with the same details as your Vehicle Registration Document (V5) or *carte grise*, to be surrendered on exit. There's no charge.

Third-party **insurance** is compulsory, and the police like to check it. It's not available at frontier posts, but the police allow travel without it to the nearest town. The large and efficient Société Nigérienne d'Assurances et de Réassurances, av de la Mairie, Niamey (☎73.55.26), has branches throughout the country and charges about CFA2000 a day.

If you wish to travel by car in the northern desert region – apart from on the main road between Assamakka and Agadez – you're required to submit a **feuille de route** (details of your journey plans) to the police for security reasons. The easiest way to get hold of these is through a Nigérien travel agency.

Information, websites and maps

Tourist **information** on Niger is virtually non-existent outside the country: there are no tourist offices abroad and no particularly informative **websites** apart from the French-language Ⓦwww.niger-gouv.ne – the official government site, which has general background information about the country.

In Niamey, the tourist office has a good, up-to-date plan of the capital, with many of the city's restaurants and hotels marked. The IGN publishes **maps** in scales of 1:2,500,000, 1:1,000,000, 1:500,000, 1:200,000 and 1:50,000. In Niamey, maps are available at the Direction de la Topographie (see p.968).

Health

In Niamey and other large towns, **tap water** is usually safe to drink; the borehole water of Arlit and Agadez is noted for its purity. **Cholera** epidemics, however, occur frequently along the Niger, and in the bush you should use purifying tablets or boil water. In case of an epidemic, even town water is suspect.

Health-care facilities are very limited. For minor ailments you can be treated at

Niamey's **hospital**. If you have a medical problem, embassies will always recommend a **private clinic**. For anything serious – surgery for example – they're sure to suggest repatriation.

Costs, money and banks

Niger is part of the **CFA zone**. At the time of writing, **exchange rates** were roughly CFA930 to £1, and CFA600 to US$1. It's essential, arriving either by air or from Nigeria, to have some US dollars or (preferably) euros in cash to tide you over until you reach a bank where you can change traveller's cheques. Money is frequently counted in multiples of CFA5 (*dela*) – see p.957.

The two main **banks** in Niger are the BIA and the SONI Bank. Outside Niamey, one or the other has branches in Zinder, Tahoua, Gaya, Maradi, Agadez and Arlit. SONI often charge three percent commission even for changing cash, but often gives a better rate for US dollars. The BIA doesn't generally charge to change cash and their commission is lower for traveller's cheques.

Credit cards can only really be used in Niamey, and even then only for major expenses such as car rental, luxury hotels and a handful of upmarket restaurants. Major ones that are accepted are American Express, Diner's Club, Visa and MasterCard. BIA give cash advances on credit cards (Visa and MasterCard). In Niamey, they also act as agents for Western Union if you need to **wire money**.

As far as **costs** are concerned, Niger is **expensive** relative to other CFA countries, though still fairly cheap in real terms. You can always find cheap street food and a basic room for the night, even if the choice is often limited. If your budget is less restricted, the biggest expenses are likely to be hotels and car rental, both of which can eat deeply into your pocket.

Getting around

Niger has a decent bus service, and it's possible to hitch a lift at some checkpoints.

Three main **surfaced routes** cover the western parts of Niger: Niamey to Gaya, Niamey to Zinder and Birnin-Konni to Agadez. The Route de l'Uranium (from Niamey to Agadez and Arlit) and the Route de l'Unité (connecting Maradi, Zinder and Lake Chad in the southeast) are also in reasonably good condition. In the southwest of the country there are also limited opportunities to travel by boat along the Niger River.

There are no scheduled domestic flights. If you must travel by plane, your only recourse is to hire a light aircraft with a pilot from Nigeravia, opposite the Tourist Office on rue Luebke in Niamey (☎73.30.64, ⓦwww.nigeravia.com). They rent out six- and ten-seater planes for CFA500,000 and CFA1,000,000 an hour respectively.

Buses, bush taxis and trucks

The former state-run Société Nationale des Transports Voyageurs (SNTV) operates a scheduled **bus network** between major towns. Because of the popularity of the service, it's imperative to book a seat in advance at the local SNTV office. The main competitor, EHGM, runs reliable services between Niamey and Zinder, Agadez and Diffa; they're about ten percent cheaper than SNTV. Other private bus companies are less expensive but best avoided, as they're slow, uncomfortable and unreliable, and take forever to fill up. **Fares** on main routes are about CFA13–14 per kilometre with SNTV.

Cheap but always overcrowded **taxis brousse** soak up the excess SNTV and EHGM passengers. **Trucks** also run between certain centres and often take travellers for a fee – a useful option for remote areas where transport is scarce.

Driving your own vehicle

Driving along the main tarmac roads is fast and straightforward: visibility is excellent and all bends and hazards are clearly marked well in advance. Driving **off the paved roads** is still subject to police jurisdiction, though in practice they're rarely fussed about it. For details of red tape drivers need to bear in mind, see p.20.

Petrol (gasoline) and diesel are generally plentiful, but supplies can be far apart. Fuel can be bought from either a filling station – dependent on electricity – or from an entrepreneur with half a dozen fifty-gallon drums at the roadside. Maps aren't generally a good guide to fuel supplies, so ask regularly. Fuel is generally expensive, except along the southern border between Birnin-Konni and Zinder, where there's a thriving black market in Nigerian petrol. North of Zinder, lubrication oils and transmission fluids can be hard to come by.

Hitching

Roadblocks and police checks at the entrance to every large town help to make **hitching** a possible alternative. Cars are obliged to stop at these controls and while the *gendarmes* are checking the papers you can ask drivers if they're headed your way. The police may help. Foreign aid workers often take hitchers for free; Nigérien drivers will almost invariably ask for money, in which case it pays to have an idea of the corresponding public transport fare, as drivers may try to overcharge you.

Hitching is fast. On the three main highways you can expect a vehicle going to one of the big towns or a neighbouring country at least once an hour, and most vehicles will stop. Lorry drivers sometimes turn off en route, so check the final destination and any detours to be made.

A hitch on a lorry usually means standing in the back for several hours under the blazing sun; hats and/or *cheches* are essential, plus some drinking water. Lifts in the cab can be noisy and very hot, and get exhausting if you're also trying to make conversation in French.

Boats

Large steamers don't ply the Niger below Gao, in Mali, but motorized **pirogues** venture along the river between Ayorou (near Mali) and Gaya (near Benin). However, they operate only during and after the rainy season when the water level is high enough. Deals have to be struck on your own in the river towns. Between March and September, it may also be possible to canoe-hop downstream from Gaya to Port Harcourt in southern Nigeria, but rapids and artificial barriers block the way at numerous points and prevent a continuous journey in the same vessel.

Accommodation

Hotels tend to be relatively expensive in Niger, but at least you'll find comfortable places with toilets and air conditioning in all the major towns. Budget accommodation seems especially bad value: you'll often have to pay upwards of CFA4000, even for a room with just a fan and shared facilities.

Camping sites are an idea that's caught on in Niger and you'll find them scattered lightly throughout the country. They usually cost around CFA2000 per person, plus a fee for each vehicle. There's no law against camping in the wild – the only restriction is that you must camp more than 20km from any village. **Staying with people** is now officially sanctioned.

Eating and drinking

Though Niger has concentrated heavily on improving its agriculture, food shortages occur in years of bad harvests or drought. Staples tend to be less varied than in countries to the south, meals being usually based around **millet**, **rice** or **niebé** – a type of bean that has become an important crop. Along the river, these are usually eaten with sauces and fresh or smoked fish. Another traditional food, **foura**, is one of Niger's most common dishes, and is eaten throughout the country. It consists of small balls of ground and slightly fermented millet, crushed in a calabash with milk, sugar and spices added.

Brochettes are sold everywhere on the streets: stuffed into a *demi-baguette* and doused with a bit of Maggi sauce, they make a quick, satisfying meal.

The Songhai often make a cornmeal stodge, or **pâte**, which is eaten with a baobab-leaf sauce perked up with fish or meat. Beef and mutton are common in the Hausa country and the nomadic regions of the north.

Niamey has a reasonable selection of **foreign restaurants**, but outside the capital, eating places tend to be much more modest, the selection of dishes usually being limited to things like grilled chicken or *steak-frites*. **Street food** is common, with vendors selling omelettes, salads, *riz gras* and a variety of other cheap meals.

Drinking

Niger's great beverage – in common with other Sahel countries – is **tea**, drunk on most occasions, especially on the road whenever a little time is available to fix up a fire. You'll also find **beer** in most towns, though it's rather expensive.

Communications

Niamey's **PTT** is quite modern and efficient, with a reliable poste restante. Making IDD **international phone calls** is straightforward from telecentres, found in all major towns. If you want to make a reverse-charge (collect) call, dialling ☎16 from a payphone puts you through to the foreign operator, who should be able to connect a reverse-charge (collect) call anywhere. Persistence may be needed. At the time of

⑬

NIGER | Basics

Accommodation price codes

All accommodation prices in this chapter are coded according to the following scale, whose equivalent in pounds sterling/US dollars is used throughout the book. Prices refer to the rate you can expect to pay for a room with two beds, including taxes. Single rooms, or single occupancy, will normally cost at least two-thirds of the twin-occupancy rate. For further details, see p.51.

❶ Under CFA4700 (under £5/$8).
❷ CFA4700–9000 (£5–10/$8–16).
❸ CFA9000–14,000 (£10–15/$16–24).
❹ CFA14,000–19,000 (£15–20/$24–32).

❺ CFA19,000–28,000 (£20–30/$32–48).
❻ CFA28,000–37,000 (£30–40/$48–64).
❼ CFA37,000–47,000 (£40–50/$64–80).
❽ Over CFA47,000 (over £50/$80).

writing, there was very little mobile-phone coverage in Niger.

Internet cafés haven't made much progress yet, and are only found in Niamey and a few bigger towns. Connections are often murderously slow; rates range between CFA1000 and CFA1600 an hour, but there's no guarantee that connections will be better at more expensive places.

The media

There's nothing much in the way of **newspapers** in Niger: *Le Sahel*, a government-owned news sheet, is published daily in Niamey, but has a very small circulation and holds little of any interest. There are also various independent news magazines, including *Kakaki*, *Alternative*, *Haske*, *Kakaki*, *La Tribune du Peuple*, *Le Démocrate* and *Le Républicain*. You can find French papers and news magazines in some of the bigger Niamey hotels and news and book stores, but little or nothing in English.

Nigérien **radio**, La Voix du Sahel, broadcasts in French, Hausa, Songhai-Djerma, Kanouri, Fulfuldé (Fula), Tamashek, Toubou, Gourmantché and Arabic. Private radio stations have also started to flourish in Niamey; Tenéré FM and Horizon FM are the most popular music stations and play traditional as well as modern music. The **TV service**, Télé-Sahel, comes on air each evening for a few hours, showing 1970s American movies dubbed into French, comedy programs and news. Many hotels and restaurants now have **satellite TV**, but generally only subscribe to French-language channels.

Entertainment

Wrestling and one-armed boxing (fist wrapped in cloth) attract big crowds, but there's not a great deal going on in terms of national "culture" in Niger – no theatre except the odd event in Niamey, and little happening musically. The film tradition, brief as it is, shows more promise.

Cinema

Nigérien comedy **cinema** has been dominated by three film-makers. **Oumarou Ganda** began his career as an actor in Jean Rouch's *Moi, un Noir*, after he was discovered by the noted French cinéaste on the docks at Abidjan. After appearing in other Rouch films, notably *La Pyramide Humaine*, he went on to become a film-maker in his own right and one of the great cultural archivists of African cinema, with works such as the autobiographical *Cabascabo* (1968), *Wazzou polygame* (1971) – the winner of the "Etalon-prize" at Burkina's FESPACO in 1972, *Saitane* (1973) – which looks critically at the authority of the Muslim marabouts – and *L'Exilé*. He died unexpectedly at the age of 46 in 1981, while filming *Gani Kouré, Le Vainqueur de Gourma*. Reflecting a distribution problem faced by most contemporary African film-makers, you're more likely to see his works abroad, or possibly at Niamey's Franco-Nigérien Cultural Centre, than in any ordinary Nigérien movie theatre.

Jean Rouch also inspired another relatively well-known film-maker, **Moustapha Alassane**. After studying at the Institut Nigérien de Recherche en Sciences Humaines, Alassane made a number of shorts, including *Aouré* (1962) and *La Bague du Roi Koda* (1963). One of his most famous feature films is *Femme, Villa, Voiture, Argent* (1972), a popular comedy dealing with the issue of cultural identity.

The third director to gain international acclaim is **Djingary Maïga**, producer of *L'Etoile Noire*, in which he also starred. Like many early African film-makers, Djingary's movies deal with the clash between Western values and traditional wisdom.

Music

Not much is heard in Europe about music from Niger. A few records of traditional music are available, but little of its modern music travels far.

In the realm of **music**, Niger remains rooted in tradition, and the country has produced no international stars. In Niamey, look out for performances of the national music and dance troupe **Karaka**. You might also catch a less worthy, mimed show that goes out on Télé-Sahel TV. For a taste of Nigérien music, the Agence de Cooperation Culturelle et Technique has put out two volumes of a record entitled *Festival de la Jeunesse Nigérienne*.

Pop artists you may well hear include Hausa singers **Mahaman Garba** and **Yan Ouwa** and the reggae of **Amadou Hamza**. In Niamey, listen out for the female singer, **Madelle Iddari**, as well as **Saadou Bori** and **Moussa Poussy**. Bori and Poussy's collaborative CD, *Niamey Twice* (Stern's), which helped put Niger on the musical map, features six original compositions from each singer which swing happily along. Bori's music is the more interesting thanks to its rare presentation of Hausa influences, and on the more offbeat tracks, like "Dango" and "Bori", the polyrhythms bubble through frenetically.

Inspired by Fula, Hausa, Songhai and Djerma traditional music, **Mamar Kassey** is the first group from Niger to take their music to an international audience and they can now compete with the best from Mali. Their album *Denké-Denké* (Daqui) features flute, lute, percussion, electric guitars and vocals leading you through old legends and tales from the sixteenth century, when the Songhai empire was the leading power in West Africa.

Directory

Airport departure tax for travel outside West Africa is CFA9000 (if not included in ticket). Airport tax for travel within West Africa is CFA2500.

Crafts and markets Niger has a wealth of mostly inexpensive and portable crafts. Agadez is well known for its silversmiths, who turn out some fine jewellery: popular items are the pendants known as "desert crosses", particularly the Croix d'Agadez. The Hausa towns, notably Zinder, specialize in leather goods, including sandals, bags and boxes. Fula weavers (*tisserands*) are noted for their geometrically patterned blankets. To get a good overview of the nation's

crafts, the National Museum in Niamey shows a wide range of the country's artisanal output. The best buys are in local markets, though for guaranteed quality and variety it's also worth checking out the official centres artisanales in Niamey.

Opening hours Due to the heat, business starts early in the morning and generally closes down for at least three hours in the afternoon. Banking hours vary from one institution to the next, but they're usually roughly Monday to Friday 7.30–11.30am and 3.30–5.30pm. Government offices are open Monday to Friday 7.30am–12.30pm and 3.30–6.30pm. Most businesses are open Monday to Friday 8am–12.30pm and 3–6.30pm, plus Saturday mornings.

Public holidays As 85 percent of Niger's population is Muslim, Islamic holidays (see p.61) are of great importance. The best place to be during festivities is Zinder. Other national holidays are: January 1, April 15 (Anniversary of the 1974 coup), August 3 (Independence Day) and December 18 (Proclamation of the Republic). Christmas and Easter are also office holidays.

Wildlife and national parks Niger's harsh climate and terrain have preserved some rare species from the vicissitudes of habitat spoliation and hunting (which was outlawed in 1964). Even in the south, hippos can nearly always be seen in the Niger River, and several herds of giraffe live in the vicinity of Tillabéri, Baleyara and Dosso (to the north, east and south of Niamey), where they're often to be seen from the road. The Parc National du "W" du Niger (which crosses borders into Burkina and Benin) has a good cross-section of savanna fauna, including several hundred elephants. Niger's portion of the park has the best visitor facilities.

Women travellers Though Niger is a Muslim country, women don't wear the veil and their presence is strongly felt in public. Women travellers generally have few problems, and female Western volunteers, for example, feel comfortable making trips across the country unaccompanied. Advances tend to be frequent but harmless and easily rebuffed.

13

NIGER | Basics

A brief history of Niger

After the demise of the Songhai empire, whose territory spread into western Niger, two spheres of influence predominated in the region. In the twelfth century, the Tuareg settled in the north around Agadez, and soon controlled regional trade. The Hausa spread from the original seven city-states founded in Nigeria in the tenth century to settle southern towns like Zinder and Maradi. Unlike the western Sudan, where trans-Saharan trade focused mainly on gold, slavery was the mainstay of the eastern routes and the basis of local economies.

Explorers on the Niger River

For centuries, news of cities like Timbuktu, Gao and Djenné (all in present-day Mali) had circulated in Europe, but although the Portuguese had been trading along the West African coast since the fifteenth century, no Western power had penetrated the interior. It wasn't until the eighteenth century that expeditions were launched into a region notorious for its hostility to Christians. In 1796, **Mungo Park** reached the Niger near Ségou (again, in present-day Mali) and described its eastern course. Until that time, Europeans believed the river flowed west – as documented by Leo Africanus in the sixteenth century – or that it was a branch of the Nile.

It was another thirty years before the Europeans saw Timbuktu. In 1826, **Gordon Laing** became the first white man to reach it, though he didn't return from the legendary city alive. In 1850, **Heinrich Barth** led a new expedition into the interior, his route from Tripoli, in Libya, taking him south through Agadez, Zinder and the Hausa country as far as Kano. He thus became the first European to explore the region of present-day Niger – and to return to Europe.

Colonial conquest

The information gleaned by these expeditions opened the doors to colonial conquests. France, anxious to link colonial settlements in West and Central Africa, was the most ambitious usurper of Sahelian territories. In 1854, General Louis Faidherbe became governor of Senegal and plotted the eastward expansion of France's West African empire. He sent troops up the Senegal River and east to the Niger. Following its course, they broke the resistance of such formidable adversaries as **Samory Touré** and **El Hadj Omar Tall**, who had founded the Tukulor empire of Ségou. By the end of the nineteenth century, the French had established a military presence at **Niamey**, which they quickly turned into the most important army post east of Bamako.

In 1898, spheres of influence were established between France and the United Kingdom, the principal powers vying for control of the Niger. The following year, the French sent an expedition to Lake Chad to demarcate borders between Niger and Nigeria. Led by two generals, **Voulet** and **Chanoine**, it was to be one of the bloodiest of the colonial missions. As the two soldiers pushed east with troops of Senegalese infantry, they embarked on a series of massacres, torching villages in their path and slaughtering the people. Birnin-Konni was virtually razed to the ground. Reports of the brutality reached France and the government sent an expedition led by Colonel Klobb to investigate. Infuriated that their tactics should be questioned, the generals went over the edge, murdered Klobb, broke with France and apparently set about conquering the territories for themselves. Their madness was only stopped when they were killed by their own infantry-men. Replacements were sent out and Lake Chad was finally reached in 1900.

French rule

With the territory's southern borders established, Niger became part of French West Africa in the following year. But the nature of this territory differed from that of its West African neighbours: officially, it was an **autonomous military territory**, and its importance was strategic, rather than commercial. Outside the army, the French presence was minimal: there was no French settlement and development was barely considered.

"Pacification" was a difficult process in Niger, as resistance sprouted in pockets across the country. One of the most serious **uprisings** was that of the **Kel Gress Tuareg**, who occupied Agadez from 1916 to 1917 and controlled most of the Aïr highlands. In 1919, a rebellion broke out in the region of Tahoua, which was only quelled in 1921, the same year that Niger was finally upgraded to the status of a **colony**.

World War II was a turning point in West African politics, and following the Brazzaville Conference of 1944, reforms were enacted which provided African representation in the national assembly, the senate and the assembly of the French Union. In 1956, the famous **Loi Cadre** was passed, establishing local government for the French colonies.

In the wake of these reforms, two political movements developed in Niger, the more radical of which was embodied in the Union Nigérienne Démocratique – also known as **Sawaba** – which dominated political life in the 1950s. Led by **Djibo Bakary**, the party fought vigorously against close ties with France and de Gaulle's proposed constitution, the main provision of which was for a Franco-African Community with limited autonomy for individual colonies, but continued economic dependence on Paris. For a while, it seemed probable that Niger would join Guinea in saying "no" to de Gaulle's proposal and in opting for immediate independence "with all its consequences".

In the event, the new constitution was approved in the landmark **1958 referendum** – a victory for the Parti Progressiste Nigérien (**PPN**) of **Hamani Diori**, who had advocated the alternative of close links with France. It's generally believed the election results were falsified. According to the official count, 370,000 people voted for the union compared to 100,000 who voted against, leaving 750,000 people who ostensibly didn't exercise their voting rights.

Despite its wide support, the Sawaba party was banned in 1959, and Bakary forced into exile. With the implicit backing of the French, the PPN was thus poised to dominate post-independence politics and Diori was assured the presidency of the new nation, formed in 1960.

Niger under Diori

Conservative politics prevailed in the days after independence, as Diori aligned his country with France and developed close ties with moderate neighbours, notably Côte d'Ivoire. Diori ruled with a small Council of Ministers, carefully selected to maintain the status quo. Sawaba tried to operate from abroad (its foreign backers included Algeria, Ghana and China), but opposition to government policies was rigorously suppressed. Various plots to overthrow Diori's regime in the early 1960s led to mass arrests and violence. When Sawaba was accused of leading a series of guerilla attacks near the Nigerian border in 1964, seven of the presumed assailants were publicly executed in Niamey.

By the late 1960s, the PPN – by then the only political party – was in a state of disarray and the target of mounting criticism. Diori made an effort to reorganize it, but was careful to stack the party leadership with faithful pre-independence politicians – and ensured that it remained ineffective as a forum for the discussion of opposing views. Despite his tight control over the political reins, however, he began to lose his grip on power as the economic situation deteriorated drastically in the late 1960s.

Diori was given a political reprieve when the mining of **uranium**, discovered in 1968, gave new financial hope to a nation that had previously gained seventy percent of its export earnings from groundnuts. Eager to take advantage of the new source of revenue, Diori accepted a minimal seventeen percent share for the national mining company, Société des Mines de l'Aïr (SOMAÏR), which was controlled by the French Atomic Energy Commission. However, 1968 also saw the start of the first great **Sahel drought**. Lasting until 1974, the natural catastrophe brought Niger to its knees.

By the early 1970s, over a million head of livestock (nearly two-thirds of the national herd) had died, and the pasturelands of the northern nomads had disappeared. International organizations helped establish emergency refugee camps and sent food supplies, but rumours began circulating that government officials were hoarding food and selling it off at hefty profits, rather than distributing it to those facing starvation. These were quickly confirmed by the discovery of **emergency food aid** stockpiled in the homes of several of Diori's ministers.

Kountché's coup

Disillusion with the government turned to anger. When Lieutenant-Colonel **Seyni Kountché** overthrew Diori in April 1974, there was widespread satisfaction, and even the French conceded they could do business with the new order. Kountché established a Conseil Militaire Suprême (CMS), which made a priority of dealing with corruption and reinvesting the government with credibility. In a conciliatory move, hundreds of political prisoners were released and Djibo Bakary returned home from exile.

In 1975, Kountché managed to renegotiate the terms under which uranium was mined, raising SOMAÏR's share to 33 percent and making the national company the biggest single partner. Fuelled by uranium revenues (prices for which soared following the oil crisis of the 1970s) and aided by the end of the drought, the economy began to pick up. Government workers received wage increases, roads were improved and prestigious building projects undertaken in Niamey. Even the agricultural sector improved dramatically. Niger, one of the countries hardest hit by the drought, was also one of the quickest to recover, and by the end of the decade, it could boast self-sufficiency in food production – no mean feat.

Niger had become something of an **economic oasis** in the middle of a poverty-stricken region, and that alone was enough to lend stability to Kountché's military regime. But policy and personality conflicts within the CMS threatened his authority, and he repeatedly reshuffled the ruling council and expelled critics. Following a new outbreak of political activity, Bakary was rearrested in 1975. A coup attempt the following year led to the execution of its alleged protagonists.

Even as he tightened the screws, however, Kountché made a number of goodwill gestures. In 1980, Diori and Bakary were granted a degree of freedom, along with many of their supporters. And by 1982, the president appeared to be making plans for a return to a constitutional government.

Setbacks in the 1980s

A Conseil National de Développement was established in 1983 as a means of granting greater participation on a local level. But the CND had barely started functioning when another coup attempt, this time led by some of Kountché's closest aides, nearly toppled the government while he was abroad.

Reforms thereafter proceeded at a slower pace, though the president eventually announced that a **National**

Charter, or draft constitution, would be drawn up and submitted to a referendum. The charter was submitted to voters in May 1987 – the first time elections had been held in the country since independence – and received overwhelming approval.

But even as Kountché was setting about reorganizing the government, the **economy** took an unexpected dive. Already in 1980, a combination of the world recession and cuts in nuclear power programmes had led to a drop in the price of uranium. Hopes that Niger would become one of the world's leading uranium producers faded rapidly. And as revenues dwindled and the national debt grew, another **drought** struck the country in the early 1980s. By 1984, the number of livestock had dropped by a half and, as cereal shortages climbed to nearly 500,000 tons, the country again found itself importing vast quantities of food, depending much on the USA. At about the same time, Nigeria closed its land borders and cut off some of Niger's important markets.

The downswing was accompanied by tensions with Niger's northern neighbour, **Libya**, which claims some 300 square kilometres of territory in northern Niger, an area with certified uranium deposits. After the Libyan army occupied northern Chad in 1980, Kountché's government had become wary of possible destabilization – with some justification after Gaddafi told reporters "We consider Niger second in line". Many observers suspected Gaddafi of behind-the-scenes support for the 1983 coup attempt. Gaddafi accused the Niger government of persecuting its **Tuareg** population – an issue about which Niamey is acutely sensitive – and may have encouraged dissent among the nomads, who have generally been sold short since independence.

Relations with other Maghreb countries – Morocco, Algeria and Tunisia – were strengthened over this period, however, and Niger has developed close ties with Saudi Arabia, Kuwait and other Arab states in the Gulf, Muslim *confrères* who have proved reliable sources of aid.

Colonel Ali Saïbou

In 1986, Kountché travelled abroad to countries that had been traditional sources of political and financial support. He made his first official trip to France, during which he suffered a brain haemorrhage and subsequently died, in November 1987.

Kountché's chosen successor as head of state, **Colonel Ali Saïbou**, the military Chief of Staff and a long-time supporter, followed the same orientation as his predecessor. In mid-1988 Saïbou announced the creation of a one-party state (the PPN and all the other parties having been disbanded when Kountché came to power), a move which was generally perceived as a step to further reforms started in the early 1980s. In 1989, the first congress was held of the military council's **National Movement for a Society of Development** (MNSD), a supra-political organization which promised great things, but within a party-state order that threatened to be elitist and almost exclusively urban-based. The government's fear of ethnic divisions in the country was so great that even acknowledging plurality was viewed as a danger.

The IMF-ordered economy forced in austerity measures which hit poor urban dwellers very hard. Students, too, felt the full impact of rising prices and reductions in already strapped services. In 1990 the university in Niamey was the scene of large-scale **student demonstrations** that ended in a violent clash with security forces. A week later a mass protest rally swept through the streets of the capital, while the Lagos-based opposition, the **Niger Movement of Revolutionary Committees** (MOUNCORE), issued statements demanding a popular uprising in Niger and the overthrow of the Saïbou clique.

Niger was put under the spotlight in June 1990, after *Le Monde* reported a **massacre** of about two hundred Tuareg civilians in reprisal for a Tuareg raid on Tchin-Tabaradene, near Tahoua. Amnesty International reported other atrocities near Tchin-Tabaradene and at In-Gal, in which dozens of people were summarily executed.

"Democracy" and Tuareg rebellion

As the national crisis deepened, Saïbou was compelled to speed up reforms. By the end of 1990, he had legalized opposition parties and formed a **national conference** to plot the country's future. Within a year, conference delegates had reduced the president's role to a ceremonial level and voted to suspend austerity measures imposed by the IMF and World Bank, an act which effectively made the country an outcast from the international financial community.

Despite two military mutinies (during which the army not only took over state broadcasting, but also detained Saïbou's prime minister before returning to the barracks when the government agreed to pay back-wages), plans for **elections** pressed on. A majority of seats in the national assembly was ultimately won by a new group of opposition parties – the Alliance des Forces du Changement (**AFC**) – whose candidate for president, **Mahamane Ousmane**, won the title in the presidential elections in March 1993. A Muslim and the first Hausa head of state in a traditionally Djerma political culture, the new leader of "democratic" Niger pledged to address the country's economic and social crises. He appointed another presidential contender, **Mahamadou Issoufou**, prime minister.

But student and labour unrest continued through 1992–93, and **Tuareg resistance** in the wake of Tchin-Tabaradene grew into a full-blown rebellion headed by the Front de Libération de l'Aïr et l'Azaouad (**FLAA**). Martial law was imposed across the entire north as security forces launched a major offensive against the rebels. Secret negotiations in France in 1993 led to a precarious truce whereby the north was to be demilitarized and talks were to open on the principal **Tuareg demands**: greater political autonomy, assistance for the return of refugees from Algeria and a commitment to regional development. Though the truce held into 1994, the FLAA began to splinter into more militant groups that refused to support any agreement that didn't specifically address demands for a federal system of government.

Meanwhile, President Mahamane tried to rekindle talks with Western creditors in the hopes of securing new loans and much-needed debt relief. During a 1993 visit to France, he received emergency financial assistance which allowed him to settle some pay arrears to public-sector employees, but when he conceded the government could not afford the back-pay accumulated under the transitional administration, new **strikes and mutinies** broke out in Maradi, Agadez, Tahoua and Zinder. Though the government found the funds to pay an extra month's arrears, the weakened economy continued to make the situation extremely volatile.

By mid-1994, the country was in a state of continual upheaval. A campaign of civil disobedience seeking proportional representation was mounted by key opposition leader **Tandja Mamadou**, of the National Movement for the Society of Development–Nassara (MNSD–Nassara, which had been the sole party between 1988 and 1990). Meanwhile, trade union leaders called an indefinite strike over demands for back-pay. Although the strike soon withered, Prime Minister Issoufou resigned in September for party political reasons; then his successor **Souley Abdoulaye** was voted out of office on a no-confidence ballot. President Mahamane shied away from nominating a third prime minister, instead calling a general election and announcing the dissolution of the national assembly.

The election, held in January 1995, gave a majority to the opposition parties grouped under the banner of the MNSD, whose candidate for prime minister was **Hama Amadou**. Hama's cabinet was chosen entirely from the ranks of the opposition. Two women were among them – a new departure in Niger – but no associates of President Mahamane. The political climate had come full circle.

Niger in 1995 seemed ready for **reconciliation**. The new government came to a back-pay agreement with the unions, and repealed anti-strike legislation. Most significantly, in Ouagadougou on April 15, the new government and the Tuareg rebels signed what was billed as a definitive and lasting peace accord – with Algerian, Burkinabe and French mediation (to many Nigériens the French are the least attractive partners in this, as they have long been suspected of promoting Tuareg nationalist ideals with the aim of creating a Francophile Saharan state).

After a brief period of goodwill, however, political cohabitation in Niger turned sour, and the constitution – which hadn't anticipated that the president and prime minister would come from different parties – was vague on power sharing. Frequent disputes arose between Mahamane and Hama, who wrangled over everything. The rift wasn't helped by the fact that Mahamane was a Hausa and Hama a Djerma; new government appointees, therefore, represented an ethnic as well as a political shift in power. Mahamane frequently refused to convene the Council of Ministers or to sign legislation and the wheels of government were just barely turning by the end of 1995. In the midst of the deadlock, the USTN once again renewed strike actions to demand payment of arrears to civil servants. They were soon joined by miners and students, who formed a campaign of disobedience.

The Maïnassara coup

In January 1996, the military intervened through a **coup d'état** led by **Ibrahim Baré Maïnassara**. He formed a ruling military body, the Conseil de Salut National (**CSN**), suspended the constitution, placed Hama and Mahamane under house arrest and declared a state of emergency. Western nations viewed it as an assault to democracy, and the IMF broke off loan negotiations. Maïnassara, however, seemed sincere in his desire to turn power back to the people, and within a few months set up a committee to draft a new constitution and scheduled elections for July. Apparently the taste of being on top agreed with him, since he also soon announced his intention to run for the presidency as a civilian.

Mahamane, Hama and the last elected head of the assembly, Issoufou, all threw their hats in the ring as well. The polling took place in July, but candidates outside the CSN were not reassured when the electoral commission overseeing the voting was dissolved before the polls had closed, nor by the fact that the government put them all under house arrest on the day of the election. Under these dubious circumstances, Maïnassara claimed an outright majority, with 52 percent of the vote.

The Fourth Republic

In his inaugural address as first president of the **Fourth Republic**, Maïnassara called for national unity as a means of creating social and economic stability. But in its outrage against the manipulation of the presidential elections, the opposition was hardly in the mood to be charitable. As the legislative elections approached, major opposition parties grouped to form the Front pour la Restauration et la Défense de la Démocratie (**FRDD**), which demanded that the presidential election results be annulled and that an unbiased election committee be re-established as conditions for participation. They must have known there was no chance of either happening and were cornered into boycotting the elections. Pro-Maïnassara parties swept the seats in the national assembly.

Future attempts to form a government of "national unity" met with equal resistance, so Maïnassara set out to further exclude and silence the opposition. **Human rights** organizations bemoaned the worsening situation in the country, citing increased arrests and deportation to northern cities, the intimidation of journalists, and the harassment of opposition activists. On the anniversary of the coup, the FRDD organized a demonstration in Niamey, which degenerated into violence. Among those arrested (yet again) were Mahamane, Hama and Issoufou. It was only a precursor of protests that would continue throughout 1997–98, most notably in politically sensitive Maradi and Zinder.

The government enjoyed more co-operation from the unions, but the privatization programme Maïnassara had committed the country to seemed to put him on a collision course with state workers too. Faced with a very narrow political base, Maïnassara based his presidency on the support of the military. In the regional and municipal elections of February 1999, the opposition swept polls throughout the country – excluding the government strongholds of Dosso and Agadez – but the results were annulled in their most powerful pockets of support, including Tillabéri, Tahoua, Maradi, Zinder and Diffa. Once again, the democratic process had been railroaded and the threat of unrest seemed imminent. Although that prospect didn't bode well for the president, worse were rumblings that Maïnassara planned to reshuffle the military to exclude members who increasingly disapproved of his means.

Before he got the chance, however, Maïnassara was **gunned down**, in April 1999, as he prepared to board the presidential helicopter. Although his body had nearly been severed in two by the blast of gunfire that came from his own presidential guard, the military played down the incident as "an unfortunate accident". Junior officers seized power and quickly formed the Conseil de Reconciliation Nationale (**CRN**), headed by Major **Daouda Malam Wanké**, who dissolved the assembly and the supreme court and sacked all senior members of the army and the police. On a more positive note, he immediately held closed-door meetings with the leaders of Niger's five largest political parties to set up guidelines for an interim government and a possible calendar for the restoration of democracy.

Although the country remained remarkably calm following the putsch, **international opinion** came down hard on the new regime. West African leaders condemned the assassination. The EU suspended aid to the country, followed by the Organisation de la Francophonie, whose thirtieth-year anniversary was scheduled to be marked in Niamey in 1999.

To the present

In October and November 1999 the promised legislative and presidential elections took place. The presidency was won by **Mamadou Tandja**, a retired lieutenant-colonel who had been unsuccessful in the elections of 1993 and 1996. The MNSD, the party he stood for, won the majority of seats in the parliament. Interestingly, Tandja retained former Tuareg rebel leader **Mohammed Anako** as a special advisor and minister without portfolio in the government, a gesture widely seen as a move to appease Tuaregs, who remained frustrated throughout the Maïnassara era at the slow pace of their reintegration into Niger society following the peace accords. Since then, more Tuaregs have gained posts in the government, among them the Minister of Tourism.

Early on, President Tandja committed to upholding the Enhanced Structural Adjustment Programme that his predecessor had worked out with the IMF and World Bank. But economically, Niger remains a classic case of a country over-dependent on a **single resource** – uranium – and thus hostage to commodity-price fluctuations. (Ironically, it was uranium that brought Niger its most recent spell in the world spotlight at the time of writing, US President George Bush having claimed in the run-up to US intervention in Iraq that Niger had sold uranium to the Iraqis. The CIA itself now regards these claims as unsubstantiated, and the decision to mention them in Bush's 2003 State of the Union address a mistake.) Improving agriculture is critical to Niger, as only three percent of the land is arable. Vast **irrigation projects** have been undertaken in the regions around Tillabéri, Birnin-Konni and Dosso, and there has been a positive trend towards smaller-scale projects involving co-operatives. But with its huge **public debt** and limited possibilities for further credit, the government will have to look increasingly to Niger's untapped potential to underwrite both future development and stability.

Books

Published material in English on Niger is really limited: if you want more than the handful of volumes devoted to the country, you'll need to read French. The late **Boubou Hama** was one of Niger's most prolific writers, publishing numerous historical works on the empires of Gao, Gobir and Songhai. A former president of the National Assembly, he also wrote works on politics, philosophy and folklore.

Carol Beckwith and Mario Van Offelen *Nomads of Niger*. Superbly illustrated essay on the Wodaabé Bororo and the Cure Salée.

Robert B. Charlick *Niger: Personal Rule and Survival in the Sahel* (o/p). Profile of the nation.

Peter Chilson *Riding the Demon: On the Road in West Africa*. Account of a year spent crisscrossing Niger by *taxi brousse*, getting inside the lives of drivers and passengers – recommended preparatory reading for serious budget travellers.

Paul Stoller *Fusion of the Worlds: an Ethnography of Possession among the Songhay of Niger*, and **Paul Stoller**

and **Cheryl Olkes** *In Sorcery's Shadow: a Memoir of Apprenticeship among the Songhay*. Stoller is a kind of Nigérien answer to Carlos Castaneda – apprenticed to a sorcerer, taking drugs. All interesting stuff.

Fiction

Kathlin Hill *Still Water in Niger*. In this novel, the unnamed narrator returns to Zinder after seventeen years.

Ibrahim Issa *Grandes Eaux Noires*. The first Nigérien novel to be published (before independence), this humorously manages to describe the travails of second-century BC Mediterranean explorers south of the Sahara.

Language

Surpassing even French and English, **Hausa** is the most international language in West Africa, estimated to be spoken by between 25 million and 100 million people. In terms of the area over which it's spoken, Hausa is today second only to Swahili in sub-Saharan Africa. The language developed into a regional lingua franca in the fifteenth century, when Hausa traders led caravans to North Africa, and it was through such commercial liaisons that Hausa became a trade language throughout northwest Africa.

Though there are many dialects of Hausa, the two most important are **Kano** and **Sokoto**. Differences are primarily phonetic and discrepancies don't prevent speakers of different dialects from understanding each other. The following words and phrases are based on the Kano dialect, which is generally considered to be "classical" Hausa.

Greetings

If the following list seems long and trivial, it barely gives a taste of the extended formal exchange that's so important in Hausa, as in most African languages.

All purpose greeting (men)	Salamu alaikum
(Response)	Alaika salamu
Greetings	Sanu
(Response)	Yauwa, sanu kadai
Are you in good health?	Kazo lafiya?
(Response)	Lafiya lau
How's the household /your family?	Ina gida?
Good morning (how was the night)?	Ina kwana?
How are your children?	Yaya yara?
Fine (general response)	Lafiya lau
Are you tired? (how's the tiredness)	Ina gajiya?
No, I'm not tired	Ba gajiya
What's the news?	Ina labari?
Everything's fine	Labari sai alheri
Good afternoon	Barka da yamma
(Response)	Barka kadai
See you tomorrow	Sai gobe
Okay, see you tomorrow	To, sai gobe
See you later	Sai an juma
Okay, see you later	To, sai an juma

Shopping

How much?	Nawa nawa ne?
Do you have oranges?	Akwai lemo?
Yes I do/no I don't have them	I, akwai/ah ah babu
How much are your oranges?	Lemo, nawa nawa ne?
They're expensive!	Kai, suna da tsada!
I'll give you CFA100	Zan biya ka dela ashirin
No deal (seller refusing)	Albarka
Give the money (offer accepted)	Kawo kudi

Numbers

1	daya
2	biyu
3	uku
4	hudu
5	biyar
6	shida
7	bakwai
8	takwas
9	tara
10	goma
11	goma sha daya
12	goma sha biyu
20	ashirin
25	ashirin da biyar
30	talatin
40	arba'in
50	hamsin
60	sittin
70	saba'in
75	saba'in da biyar
80	tamanin
90	casa'in (or tamanin da goma)
100	dari
200	dari biyu

250	dari biyu da hamsin	CFA100	dela ashirin
1000	dubu	CFA150	dela talatin
		CFA200	dela arba'in
		CFA450	dela tamanin
			da goma
		CFA500	dela dar
		CFA1000	jikai

In Niger, money is commonly counted in multiples of CFA5 (*dela*) – which can be difficult to calculate even if you're thinking in English.

Glossary

Azalai Camel caravans.

Baba Old man; a term of respect.

Birni Hausa word meaning a formerly fortified town.

Boro Bi Black person or people.

Canaris Large clay pots for storing water.

Dela CFA5, used as a basic unit for enumerating prices; thus CFA100 is expressed as twenty delas.

Djoliba Malinké name for the Niger. Literally "River of Blood", since the body of water was as vital to life as blood flowing in the veins.

Erg Shifting sand dunes common in the Ténéré.

Fech-fech Soft sand hidden beneath a hard crust.

Gravures Rupestres Rock paintings, common in the Aïr and Djado regions.

Kaya-kaya Wandering salesmen.

Kori Seasonal river course, or wadi (Hausa).

Razzia Slave raid.

Reg Stony wastes.

Wonki-wonki Launderers, common along the banks of the Niger in Niamey.

Zongo Section of a town or village where newly arrived strangers live.

NIGER | Basics

13.1

Niamey

As uranium money showered on Niger in the 1970s, **NIAMEY** changed almost overnight. Many of its dusty roads were paved, and a Voie Triomphale was traced through town, its bright streetlights blotting the Sahelian nights from memory. Avant-garde buildings such as the Palais des Congrès and, fittingly, the Office National de Recherches Minières were built, to be joined by futuristic hotels, banks and offices.

This development, however, was nowhere near as dramatic as in Abidjan or Lagos, and the juxtaposition of modernity and tradition – and between city and country – works remarkably well here. The sight of camel caravans crossing the Niger River on the Kennedy Bridge hardly seems incongruous, and neither does the spectacle of Fula, Hausa, Tuareg and Djerma traders gathering at the Petit Marché under the shadow of high-rise office blocks.

Over the past decade, however, tourists have largely shunned the city. Ten years ago Niamey was one of the most pleasant and low-key watering holes on the trans-Saharan route. But the combination of troubles in Algeria and Tuareg rebellions in northern Niger and Mali put an end to the steady flow of travellers, and Niamey's tourist industry ground to an almost complete halt – though with peace restored in the north and the border with Algeria reopened, visitors may start returning. Until then, the lack of tourists makes for an agreeably low-key atmosphere, while the city also offers an outstanding museum, good markets and some pleasant excursions within a short drive of the city.

Some history

Before the colonial era, Niamey was no more than a small village whose origins probably didn't predate the eighteenth century. When French troops swarmed into the desert in the 1890s, they recognized the strategic importance of this spot on the river and dug in their heels. By 1902, Niamey had grown into one of the most important military and administrative posts east of Bamako. When Niger officially became a colony, the larger urban centre at Zinder was chosen as the new capital, but the French administrators preferred Niamey's climate, and in 1926 they transferred the capital back again.

Throughout the colonial era, Niamey never developed much beyond the **European quarter** built in the plateau district. The population in the 1930s was under two thousand, though by independence it had increased to around thirty thousand. Real growth only occurred in the 1970s, with the population surging to over a quarter of a million by 1980. A great deal of the influx was caused by the **drought** of the mid-1970s, which sparked a rural exodus of biblical proportions. Niamey, fattened on uranium income, flourished as immigrants from the devastated provinces poured into the city to find food, housing and work. A second drought in the mid-1980s led to a new wave of immigration, further increasing the city's population. Today, it's estimated that nearly 800,000 people live in Niamey, and virtually every ethnic group in the country is represented here. This rapid growth, combined with the recent fall in the world price of uranium, has put huge strains on the city. Though Niamey provides comforts for travellers and expats with cash in their pockets, the benefits of modernization are now tempered by the spectre of shanty towns, mass unemployment and urban blight.

Arrival, city transport and information

Niamey spreads along 7km of the Niger's left (north) bank, and has now expanded to the other side of the river. The size of the city makes it difficult to get an immediate grip on its layout – a problem compounded by the French-style planning, with numerous roundabouts and streets that rarely run parallel.

You'll spend virtually your whole time on the left bank. To define a centre, use the **Pont Kennedy** as a landmark. To the north of the bridge, rue de Gaweye leads straight up to the **Grand Marché**, bordered by Boulevard de la Liberté. The entire **commercial centre** lies between this new market and the river, and this is where you'll come to shop, eat, change money and visit sights such as the **Musée National**. A bank and a number of airline offices are located in two important commercial buildings along rue de Gaweye: **Immeuble Sonara II** and **Immeuble El Nasr**. Northeast of the Grand Marché, rue du Sénégal leads to the residential neighbourhoods of **Abidjan** and **Kalleye**, and the **Grande Mosquée**.

To the **west of Pont Kennedy**, Avenue F. Mitterrand runs past the impressive *Hôtel Gaweye* as it heads towards the tree-lined avenues of the **Plateau district**. This colonial-looking neighbourhood is where most government ministries are located, along with the Palais du Président and many of the embassies. Continuing

---

Moving on from Niamey

Peugeot 504s and Japanese minibuses head from the main **Wadata gare routière** north to Tillabéri, south to Dosso and Gaya, east to Birnin-Konni, Maradi and Zinder, and northeast to Tahoua and Agadez. EHGM buses (☏74.37.16) to Zinder via Maradi, Arlit via Tahoua and Agadez, and non-stop to Diffa, also leave from here, as do taxis for most **international destinations**, including Lomé, Kano or Cotonou.

Taxis to Burkina leave from the Rive Droite – across the river from town, near the Douane. This is also where you can catch a *taxi brousse* to Say (and possibly on to Tamou for the Parc National du "W"). To leave quickly, it's best to break up the trip, paying for a seat for anything heading in the direction of Kantchari, the Burkinabe border town. From here, you can catch another bush taxi or, if you're lucky, the more comfortable Burkinabe Sans Frontières bus that leaves daily for Ouagadougou. Arrive early in the morning as traffic on this stretch is sparse – after midday, you could wait hours for a vehicle.

SNTV buses

There are two SNTV buses a week for Ouagadougou (Mon & Wed) and two for Gao (Mon & Thurs). Buses for Arlit – calling at Tahoua and Agadez – leave Monday, Saturday and Sunday. A further service heads to Zinder, with stops in Birnin-Konni and Maradi, on Monday, Thursday and Sunday. All buses are scheduled to leave at 7am, but check with SNTV as schedules may vary and delays are not uncommon. You'll need to buy tickets in advance to be sure of a seat (the ticket office is open Mon–Fri 8.30am–noon and Sat & Sun at 3.30pm for travel the following day). (Note that three other companies also run to Gao – Askia Transport, Airfagosse and Ham Kouma; all have ticket offices next to the Grand Marché. All three are very unreliable, using dodgy vehicles and suffering long delays at control points since they take passengers without identification papers. Unless SNTV is fully booked and you're desperate to travel on a specific date, they're really not worth the hassle.)

Flights

You can often get good deals on **flights to Europe** from Niamey, notably with Air Algérie, Royal Air Maroc and Point-Afrique. For up-to-date information, contact the airlines direct. There are no **domestic flights** in Niger, though you could hire an aircraft and pilot from Nigeravia (see p.944).

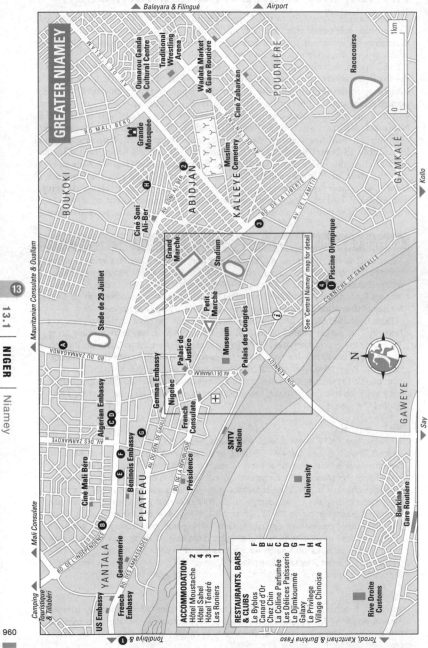

GREATER NIAMEY

▲ Baleyara & Filingué ▲ Airport

Oumarou Ganda
Cultural Centre
Traditional
Wrestling
Arena

Wadata Market
& Gare Routière

Cité Zabarkan

BD MALI BÉRO

Grande
Mosquée

Muslim
Cemetery

POUDRIÈRE

Racecourse

BOUKOKI

Ciné Soni
Ali-Ber

H

AV SONI ALI BER

2

ABIDJAN

3

BD DE LA LIBERTÉ

AV DE L'AMITIÉ

GAMKALÉ

▼ Kollo

Grand
Marché

Stadium

Petit
Marché

See Central Niamey map for detail

4 Piscine Olympique

CORNICHE DE GAMKALLE

Mauritanian Consulate & Ouallam

Stade de 29 Juillet

A

BD DU ZARMAGANDA

Palais de
Justice

Nigelec

German Embassy

French
Consulate

AV DE L'URANIUM

Museum

Palais des Congrès

i

PON KENNEDY

GAWEYE

▼ Say

Mali Consulate

Camping
Touristique
& Tillabéri

US Embassy

French
Embassy

YANTALA

BD DE L'INDÉPENDANCE

Ciné Mali Béro

B

Gendarmerie

BD DES AMBASSADES

Algerian Embassy

C D

AV DES ZARMAKOYE

Béninois Embassy

G

E F

AV DU GÉN DE GAULLE

BD DE LA RÉPUBLIQUE

Présidence

PLATEAU

SNTV
Station

University

Burkina
Gare
Routière

Rive Droite
Customs

▼ Torodi, Kantchari & Burkina Faso

Tondibiya & ①

N

0   1km

ACCOMMODATION
Hôtel Moustache   2
Hôtel Sahel   4
Hôtel Ténéré   3
Les Roniers   1

RESTAURANTS, BARS
& CLUBS
Le Byblos   F
Canard d'Or   B
Chez Chin   E
La Colline Parfumée   C
Les Délices Patisserie D
Le Djimkoummé   G
Galaxy   I
Le Privilège   H
Village Chinoise   A

13

west, you come to the bustling **Yantala districts** (confusingly, Yantala Haut is south of bd de l'Indépendance, while Yantala Bas is to the north), which you'll become familiar with if you stay at the *camping* near the entrance to town on the Tillabéri road.

East of the bridge, the rue du Sahel leads to the comfortably shaded residential streets of **Niamey Bas** district, where you'll find a good number of hotels and restaurants. Further east, Niamey Bas gives onto the **Gamkalé district** and then to the capital's **industrial zone**.

Niamey's **Diori Hamani airport** (℡73.47.25) is 14km southeast of the city centre on the Boulevard de l'Amitié (which becomes the Boulevard du 15 Avril). There are no buses from here into the centre, so you'll have to take a cab (around CFA3000). Arriving by *taxi brousse*, you're most likely to be dropped off at the **gare routière** in the Wadata district, about 4km from the centre. Large EHGM coaches stop at the **EHGM terminal** nearby. SNTV coaches arrive at the **SNTV station** on Corniche Yantala (℡72.30.20), west of the *Hôtel Gaweye*; late SNTV arrivals and Airfagosse and Ham Kouma arrivals from Gao stop at the Grand Marché.

City transport and information

It's easy to get a taxi into town from the *gare routière* and other road-transport arrival points: **collective taxis** cost around CFA200 (around twice that after midnight). If you hire the whole cab it will cost around CFA800 per short trip. **City buses** (daylight hours only) work out a little cheaper than shared taxis, but there are no printed schedules or map routes and they're very infrequent.

Although staff at the **tourist office**, on rue Luebke (Mon–Fri 8am–noon & 3.30–6pm; ℡73.24.47), aren't much help with questions about Niamey itself, they may be useful for organizing excursions to places like the Parc National du "W" du Niger, and their prices compare favourably with those of travel agents. More often than not, however, they'll simply refer you to Nigercar travel agent (see p.968).

Accommodation

Although Niamey has a number of mid-range and expensive **hotels**, there are few budget options, though some relief is provided by the **campground** out of town.

Budget accommodation and camping

Camping Touristique rte de Tillabéri, Yantala district. Set in a spacious site with good showers and toilets, plus two bar-restaurants. It's ideal if you have a car, but a little out of the way

otherwise (CFA200 by shared taxi from the centre). CFA3000 per person.

Hôtel Moustache av Soni Ali Ber, north of bd de la Liberté, Abidjan district ℡73.33.78. The best budget option near the centre, offering basic self-contained rooms (a/c or fan) and a lively

Security

Niamey has gone through a rough period in recent years, and the increase in crime is mainly the result of Niger's dismal economy. **Petty theft** is commonplace. The principal area to avoid is the **river bank on the north side**, especially the stretch along the Corniche between the *Grand Hôtel* in the east, past the Pont Kennedy, to the SNTV bus station in the west. The area around the **Petit Marché** can also seem tense, though given the volume of people, the greatest danger here – and incidentally, in front of the banks – is posed by pickpockets. Apart from these areas, the town still feels quite safe, even at night, and by taking precautions (like leaving all bags at your hotel) you're unlikely to feel – or be – threatened.

▲ Plateau District

◀ Plateau & Embassies

◀ SNTV Bus Station

AV. DU GÉNÉRAL DE GAULLE

American
Cultural
Centre

RUE DE LA TAPCA

Nigelec

Palais de
Justice

IGN

PLACE DE LA
REPUBLIC

BCEAO

AV. DES MINISTÈRES

BO. DE LA RÉPUBLIQUE

French
Consulate

Soni Bank

AV. F. MITTERAND

AV. DE L'URANIUM

AV. DE LA MAIRIE

Centre Culturel
Franco-Nigérien

Phamacie

CORNICHE DE YANTALA

Musée
Nationale

ACCOMMODATION

Gaweye Sofitel	3
Grand Hôtel	4
Maourey	1
Sahel	6
Ténéré	2
Terminus	5

Palais des
Congrès

3

RUE DE GAWEYE

T Immeuble
Sonara I

PLACE DES
MARTYRS

**RESTAURANTS, BARS
& CLUBS**

Le 61	G
2005	M
Caramel	H
La Cascade	D
Chocolat	F
La Cloche	J
Le Croissant d'Or	N
Damsi	T
Le Dragon d'Or	V
L'Extase	S
Hi-Fi	L
The Hilly	C
Jet-7	I
Le Koudou	U
Maquis 2000	O
Maquis Bleu	R
Le Méridien Fast Food	K
La Pizzeria	L
La Poêle Bleue	A
Restaurant Bamba	E
Restaurant Baobab	B
Restaurant de Dé	P
Teranga Bar	Q
L'Union	W

Niger River

PONT KENNEDY

CORNICHE DE

N

▼ Burkina, Gare Routière & Kantchari

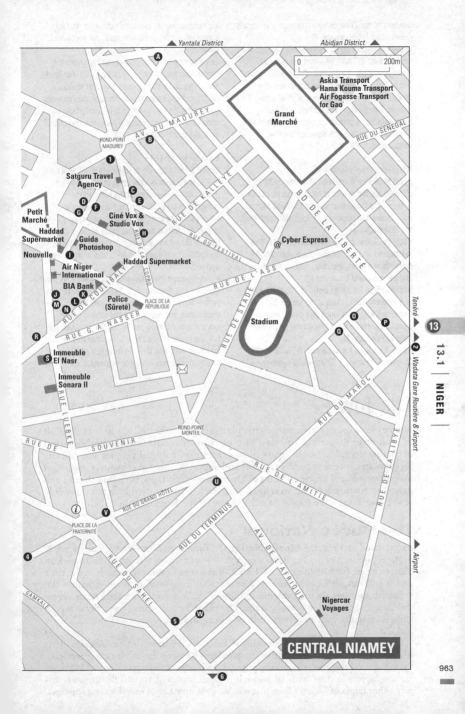

0   200m

Askia Transport
Hama Kouma Transport
Air Fogasse Transport
for Gao

Ⓐ

AV DU MAOUREY

ROND-POINT
MAOUREY

Grand
Marché

RUE DU SENEGAL

Ⓑ

❶

Satguru Travel
Agency

Ⓒ

Ⓔ

RUE DE KALLEYE

BD DE LA LIBERTÉ

Petit
Marché

Ⓓ

Ⓕ

Ⓖ

Ciné Vox &
Studio Vox

Ⓗ

RUE DU FESTIVAL

Haddad
Supermarket

RUE LA COPRO

@ Cyber Express

Nouvelle

Ⓘ

Guida
Photoshop

Haddad Supermarket

RUE DE L'ASS

Air Niger
International

BIA Bank

Ⓙ

Ⓚ

Ⓛ

RUE DE COULIBALY

Police
(Sûreté)

PLACE DE LA
RÉPUBLIQUE

RUE DE STADE

Ⓜ

Ⓝ

Stadium

Ⓞ

Ⓟ

Ⓡ

RUE G. A. NASSER

Ⓠ

Immeuble
El Nasr

Ⓢ

Immeuble
Sonara II

RUE UEBKE

✉

RUE DE
SOUVENIR

ROND-POINT
MONTEIL

RUE DU MAROC

RUE DE LA LIBE

RUE DE L'AMITIÉ

Ⓤ

ⓘ

Ⓥ

RUE DU GRAND HÔTEL

PLACE DE LA
FRATERNITÉ

RUE DU TERMINUS

AV DE L'AFRIQUE

▲ Airport

❹

RUE DU SAHEL

GAMKALE

Nigercar
Voyages

❺

Ⓦ

CENTRAL NIAMEY

▼❻

downstairs bar. Cheaper accommodation is usually reserved for hourly guests. ❸

Village Chinoise bd du Zarmaganda, next to the new stadium ☎72.33.98. Great-value basic accommodation. The functional and clean rooms (a/c or fan) all come with one single and one double bed; two rooms share one toilet and shower. There's also safe parking, a cheap restaurant and a pleasant outdoor bar where you can fill up on grilled fish. Advance booking recommended. ❷

Mid-range hotels

Hôtel Maourey Rond-Point Maourey ☎73.28.50, Ⓕ73.35.69. Set in a good location about halfway between the Grand Marché and the Petit Marché, with decent and reasonably priced self-contained a/c rooms. ❹

Hôtel du Sahel rue du Sahel ☎73.24.31. Well-maintained and comfortable place, with 35 a/c rooms (some facing the river), restaurant, disco and various crafts boutiques. ❺

Hôtel Ténéré bd de la Liberté ☎73.20.20. West of the centre, with spacious a/c rooms, a restaurant with a set lunch and dinner menu, and a popular poolside bar – though the pool itself is none too inviting. ❻

Hôtel Terminus rue du Sahel ☎73.26.92/93, Ⓔhotermi@intnet.ne. Thirty-eight good-value

a/c bungalows set around a well-kept garden, plus a swimming pool, gym, bar and restaurant. ❻

Les Roniers Tondibia road, about 7km from the centre past the US embassy ☎72.31.38. Far from the centre and suffering from a lack of visitors, which perhaps explains why it's such exceptionally good value. Accommodation is in comfortable bungalows grouped around a park with swimming pool and tennis court. ❺

Luxury hotels

Grand Hôtel Place de la Fraternité ☎73.26.41, Ⓕ73.26.43. With its easygoing atmosphere, this hotel holds its own against the more modern competitors on either side, and once ongoing renovations are completed it will undoubtedly regain its position as the top place in town. Choose between comfortable rooms or slightly bigger bungalows (same price); there's also a great pool and restaurant. ❼

Hôtel Gaweye Place Kennedy, near the Palais des Congrès and the river ☎72.34.00, Ⓔgaweye@int net.ne. Niamey's most luxurious hotel, but impersonal, and standards have slipped badly since it ceased being part of the *Sofitel* chain. The fully equipped rooms come with either river or museum view, and facilities include a pool, tennis courts, restaurants, bars and nightclubs. ❽

The Town

Niamey isn't exactly brimming with pleasures and pastimes, but it's not difficult to find ways of passing the day. The obvious place to start is the **National Museum** complex, which, apart from exhibits on national peoples and culture, incorporates extensive gardens, a zoo and shops. Niamey also boasts a couple of innovative cultural centres that regularly feature exhibitions, films, and theatre and dance performances. The **markets**, too, each with its own character, provide active diversions – the Grand Marché is one of the biggest in the Sahel.

The Musée National

Inaugurated in 1959, the **Musée National** (Tues–Sun: Nov–March 9am–noon & 3.30–5.30pm; April–Oct 9am–noon & 4–6pm; museum grounds Tues–Sun 8am–6.30pm; CFA1000, camera CFA5000) was a radical breakthrough at the time and is still out on its own among West African museums. Contained within the extensive grounds are the museum exhibition halls, a zoo, a working crafts centre and samples of Nigérien housing styles. The place feels alive and, especially at weekends, is crowded with an eclectic mix of young and old, foreign and local, scholarly and illiterate.

The main entrance to the grounds is from a side-street off the Avenue de la Mairie. Before heading into one of the pavilions housing the exhibition spaces, take a stroll around the **zoo** – especially popular with young kids from town. A big draw are the hippos in their artificial pond, but cages scattered around the grounds display other fauna of Niger – lions, hyenas, various monkeys, crocodiles and tortoises, all in a reasonable state of health. Aviaries contain vultures and a variety of more colourful birds.

Each of the museum pavilions – constructed in a stylized Hausa architectural design – is dedicated to a particular theme, such as costumes and jewellery, weapons, handicrafts and musical instruments. The paleontology and botany pavilion contains **dinosaur skeletons** from Gadoufaoua, in the Agadez region. Discovered accidentally by geologists prospecting for uranium, these skeletons are around 100 million years old, and the remote district is today one of the world's most renowned dinosaur sites outside the western USA. Outside the same pavilion are two dry branches, set in concrete, of the famous **Arbre du Ténéré**, a tree that once stood alone in the Ténéré desert and became a famous overlanders' landmark until it was knocked over by a truck driver. Formerly the only living thing for hundreds of miles around – and still marked on the Michelin map – the tree was transported to the museum and a sturdy steel replacement erected in the desert.

One section of the park is home to various examples of traditional Nigérien housing – a good opportunity to compare Fula thatched cones, Hausa mud-brick and plaster, Tuareg tents and other styles. The park also houses a *buvette* (bar) serving cold drinks and tasty *brochettes*. In addition, be sure to check out the **Centre Artisanale**. Goods sold here are usually more expensive than on the streets (in certain cases, substantially so), but part of the profits subsidizes the museum. Quality is controlled, so your silver jewellery won't turn green hours after you buy it or the camel-hide bag smell suspiciously of goat when it gets wet.

Cultural centres

Across from the museum's main entrance, the **Centre Culturel Franco-Nigérien** (℡73.48.34, ⓦwww.ccfn.ne) has a busy schedule that includes exhibits by local artists and craftsmen, dance and theatre performances, and regular outdoor film screenings (CFA500). You can stop by and pick up their events programme, or check the pages of *Le Sahel*. There's also a library and Internet café here.

Right across on the other side of town on Boulevard Mali Béro, near the Grande Mosquée, is the **Centre Culturel Oumarou-Ganda**, named after the late, great Nigérien film-maker. The centre's open-air amphitheatre hosts performances of traditional music, ballet and theatre, and there's also an open-air cinema. Check the paper for details of upcoming events.

The **Centre Culturel Americain** (Mon 9am–noon & 3–6pm, Wed, Fri & Sat 9am–noon; ℡73.31.69) also sponsors events and screens American news programmes and movies (Wed & Fri at 4.30pm; free). It's located off Avenue du Général de Gaulle near Nigelec, the state electricity supplier; ask a taxi to drop you there, and then follow the dirt side-street behind the Elf station.

The markets

Niamey's **Grand Marché** (daily until sunset) – also called the Nouveau Marché – makes a decidedly modern statement, with monumental entrance gates and a fountain or two for show, although the smooth lines and earth tones respect the more traditional styles of the Sahel. Inside, paved alleys lead through a maze of stalls grouped according to wares – clothing and fabrics; soaps, cosmetics and pharmaceuticals; hardware; ironmongery and utensils; and so forth. Along with the main market in Ouagadougou, this is one of West Africa's finest.

Further south in the **Zongo district**, where rue du Président Luebke and Avenue de la Mairie intersect, the **Petit Marché** has a more casual flavour. Merchants who can't secure a space in one of the Grand Marché stalls simply clear space on the ground and set up shop here. It's primarily a **food** market, and you'll find a good selection of fruits and vegetables, meat, fish and grains. People from all over the country converge here to buy and sell – a wide mixture of Fula, Djerma,

Tuareg and Hausa. Nearby streets give way to **crafts** stands – reasonable places to pick up jewellery, leather goods or blankets, though dealers tend to be aggressive and bargaining can turn into a battle.

There's another small market, devoted entirely to **pottery**, across from the tall SONI Bank down Avenue de la Mairie – look out for the beautiful hand-painted water pots produced in the village of Tondibia, just outside Niamey.

Eating and drinking

Niamey has a number of upmarket restaurants, and **street vendors** are very common. In the mornings there's a *caféman* on every busy corner, while evening stalls sell *fufu*, rice, macaroni or *tô* (cornmeal dough).

Inexpensive

During the day, you can get really cheap food at the Petit Marché, the Grand Marché or the *gare routière*. For street food after dark – notably beef *brochettes* or fried omelettes with onions, tomatoes and Maggi sauce – head for the places around rue de Kabekoira, especially in the general vicinity of the Ciné Vox. You can eat at all the places listed below for under CFA1500.

Caramel (Chez Michel) rue de la Copro. Pastry shop with decent, affordable croissants, brioches and sandwiches on home-made bread.

La Fontaine Bleue Behind the PTT. Outdoor restaurant offering salads, meats and snacks.

Galaxy Behind the Piscine Olympique on rue du Sahel, near the *Hôtel du Sahel*. This popular restaurant is largely deserted by day, when it offers cheap beer and a view not to be missed (as good as that from any of the expensive hotel *terrasses*); at night it serves inexpensive grilled chicken and there's occasional music and dancing. Take a cab; it's a bit dodgy to walk here after dark.

The Hilly rue de la Copro, near *Hôtel Maourey*. Typical outdoor bar where the Béninois chef cooks up, among other things, some of the tenderest *brochettes* you'll ever taste. There's also good music, and things gets quite lively at night.

Le Méridien Fast Food rue Coulibaly, next to

BIAO bank. Popular fast-food stand serving burgers and *chawarma*.

La Poêle Bleue Place Liberté, a few blocks from the Grand Marché. Extensive menu including omelettes, steak sandwiches and freshly made yoghurt at very good prices.

Restaurant Baobab av du Maouri near the Grand Marché. Excellent place for a quick and filling cheap meal, with rice or spaghetti stews (CFA500–600) and cold yoghurts. Gets packed with local businessmen at lunchtimes.

Restaurant Bemba rue du Festival. Senegalese place excelling in tasty *riz gras*. Popular with local bank and government workers.

Snack Bar La Cloche Near the corner of rue Luebke and rue du Coulibaly. Expat haunt (and packed with prozzies) serving salads, sandwiches and *chawarma*.

L'Union Behind *Hotel Le Terminus*. A friendly, colourful place serving inexpensive, well-made food and cool beer in a small courtyard.

Moderate

From Italian pizza to Ivoirian *poisson braisé*, it's possible to treat yourself to something a little out of the ordinary without spending much more than CFA3500.

Chocolat Opposite the Cascade near the Petit Marché. Ice cream, sweet and savoury crepes, and the usual burger and chips fast-food menu served in a blue and white French Riviera–style restaurant. Try the Indian crepes (CFA800).

La Colline Parfumee bd de l'Indépendance, near the *Delices Patisserie*. Good-value Chinese cooking

served in an atmospheric garden illuminated by red lanterns. If you're not so hungry, try one of the flavour-packed soups (CFA1000).

Le Croissant d'Or rue de Coulibaly. Patisserie patronized by French expats – a good sign if you crave something sweet.

Damsi On the ground floor of Immeuble Sonara I.

Excellent French, African and Asian food served on a terrace.

Diamangou Corniche de Gamkalé ☎73.51.43. French and African dishes (try the *brochettes de capitain*), and served aboard a boat docked in the Niger – one of the town's more romantic venues, and often completely full. A fantastic spot for a sundowner over one of their great aperitifs.

Le Djinkoumé Behind the German embassy in

Plateau district. A new and popular place serving mouthwatering Togolese and Nigérien dishes.

Maquis 2000 Behind the old stadium near *Teranga Bar*. Slightly upmarket Ivoirian food, featuring shellfish and *grillades* served on a pleasant terrace.

La Pizzeria rue du Coulibaly, next to *HiFi*. Niamey's best pizza, using real mozzarella and fresh vegetables, as well as many other well-prepared Italian dishes.

Expensive

Niamey has a surprisingly good selection of upmarket places to eat, with the raw ingredients usually imported direct from France. You'll pay up to CFA10,000 – or even above.

Le Byblos bd de l'Indépendance, Plateau district. Classy Lebanese restaurant – choose between outdoor seating in a relaxing compound garden, or eating inside in what looks like a large sitting room.

La Cascade Near the Petit Marché ☎73.28.32. Formerly one of the best French restaurants in town, specializing in fish. It's currently being refurbished, and may reopen under a new name.

Chez Chin bd de l'Indépendance, Plateau district ☎72.25.28. New and popular Chinese restaurant with seating in an air-conditioned interior and on a pleasant outdoor terrace.

Le Dragon d'Or rue du Grand Hôtel ☎73.41.23. Very popular place serving a wide variety of Chinese food.

Le Koudou Opposite the police station near Rond-Point Monteil ☎73.40.50. Good-value African, French and Creole dishes, and good grilled meats.

Tabakady Near the PTT ☎73.58.18. Another well-known French restaurant whose traditional cooking – including delicacies like oysters and salmon – gets high marks from the French community. Count on around CFA15,000 for a meal. It's a small place, so book in advance.

Nightlife

At first glance, **Niamey nights** seem very low-key, but if you persevere there's a lot of fun to be had. The bigger hotels have **discos** – the *El Raï* at the *Gaweye* and the *Fofo* at the *Sahel* – with high covers and expensive drinks; the latter can be quite fun on weekends. **Downtown clubs** include:

Le 61 Around the corner from *Chocolat* (see opposite). Rastafarian-themed place geared more towards locals than Europeans, with a supremely well-stocked bar and a dancefloor that heaves at weekends (especially after pay day).

2005 Near *La Cloche*. One of the best clubs in the centre, drawing an enthusiastic crowd (Thursday night is free for ladies). Mainly Western music.

La Cloche rue du Coulibaly. European-oriented place (and clogged with prostitutes after dark), though if this doesn't put you off, it's actually quite fun, with a pool table and pinball machines, plus a great selection of Lebanese snacks.

L'Extase In the basement in front of the Immeuble El Nasr. Dark and heaving, with music pumping all night.

Hi-Fi rue du Coulibaly. Energetic – at weekends

anyway – and with a good mix of African and Western music.

The Hilly Near the *Hôtel Maourey*. This outdoor bar is a good place for a less European-oriented evening out – if you're lucky, there'll be a spontaneous outbreak of dancing (most likely Friday and Saturday).

Ize-Gani Corniche de Gamkalé. Glitzy and exotic place which is popular with expats and gets especially crowded at weekends, when you can dance under the stars until the wee hours. For safety's sake, take a cab there and back.

Jet-7 By the Haddad supermarket. Good music and an informal atmosphere at a reasonable price.

Niamey Club rue du Coulibaly, near the *2005*. Good music and occasional live bands (entrance CFA500).

Le Privillege Near *Hôtel Mustache*. Lively

neighbourhood bar that also does cheap eats.
Teranga Bar Next to the old stadium, one block
north of rue du Maroc and two blocks south of bd

de la Liberté. Well-stocked bar set in a
meticulously maintained garden with flowering
bougainvillea. Popular with prostitutes.

Listings

Airlines Air Algérie, Immeuble Rivoli ☎73.38.98;
Air Burkina, c/o Air France ☎73.69.31; Air France,
Immeuble Sonara I ☎73.31.21, ☎73.29.15; Air
Ivoire, c/o Air France; Air Niger International, 3–5
rue Luebke ☎73.41.80, ☎73.41.79; Air Sénégal,
c/o Royal Air Maroc; Point-Afrique, opposite *Hôtel
Terminus* ☎73.4026; Royal Air Maroc, Immeuble
El-Nasr ☎73.28.85. Most of these offices are in
the area of the Petit Marché.

Banks Most are on, or near, av de la Mairie; the
most convenient are the BIA, SONI Bank and the
BCEAO Bank. There's also a Bank of Africa in
Immeuble Sonara II.

Books, newspapers and magazines Guida
Photoshop, around the corner from Haddad
Supermarket on av de la Mairie, is well stocked
with French newspapers, international magazines
(mostly in French), photographic books, Michelin
maps and a wide selection of guide books. For
browsing, there's also the library at the American
Cultural Centre.

Car rental Nigercar Voyages, av de l'Afrique
(☎72.23.31, ✉nicarvoy@intnet.ne), is the most
professional outfit in town, with a wide range of
vehicles available. The tourist office (see p.961)
may also be able to set you up with less formal
rental agencies.

Cinemas The Studio has a/c and the town's
newest films; Vox is an outdoor theatre which
often shows old action films. Both are downtown
near the Petit Marché. You could also try the
Cinéma Soni Ali-Ber, in Haut Niamey, and the
Cinéma Zarbakan, off the av de l'Entente in
Poudrière. Otherwise, check out what's on at the
two cultural centres (see p.965).

Embassies and consulates Algeria, off av de
l'Imazer, Plateau district ☎72.35.83, ☎72.35.93;
Benin, Plateau district ☎72.28.60; Canada, off bd
Mali Bero near the junction to av des Zarmakoye
☎75.36.86, ☎75.31.07; Chad, av du Général de
Gaulle, Plateau district ☎75.27.86, ☎72.43.61;
France: French Embassy, bd des Ambassades,
Yantala district ☎72.24.31, ☎72.25.18; French
Consulate, av des Ministères, by the hospital
roundabout ☎72.27.23, ☎73.40.12 (issues visas
for Côte d'Ivoire, Togo and Burkina Faso); Mali, just
off bd de la Liberté, next to the Grand Marché
☎75.24.10; Guinée ☎74.25.22; Mali, off bd de

l'Indépendance next to the Appeal Court
☎75.42.90, ☎75.42.90; Mauritania, off bd Mali
Béro, Yantala district ☎ & ☎72.38.43; Morocco,
rue Luebke ☎73.40.84, ☎73.14.27; Nigeria, bd
des Ambassades, 400m west of the US embassy
☎73.24.10; UK, Honorary Vice Consulate
☎73.20.15 or 73.25.39, ☎73.36.92; USA, bd des
Ambassades, Yantala district ☎72.26.61,
☎73.31.67.

Internet access Internet facilities are relatively thin
on the ground in Niamey. Cyber Express
(☎73.64.63; CFA1000 per hour), off rue de la
Copro, is a small and well-run outfit; Cyberspace, at
the French Cultural Centre across from the National
Museum (Tues–Sat 9am–12.30pm & 3.30–6.30pm;
☎73.48.34; CFA1500 per hour) has slow but
generally functioning connections; Intelcom, on the
ground floor in Immeuble El-Nasr (Mon–Sat
8am–1pm & 3.30–8pm; ☎73.59.94; CFA1600 per
hour), is more expensive but has student discounts.
Wherever you decide to go, it's a good idea to call in
advance and make sure they're up and running.

Maps The Direction de la Topographie
(☎72.33.23 or 72.24.67), off bd de la République
in Yantala near the French embassy, has 1:50,000
and 1:2,500,000 coverage of the country, and
1:20,000 maps of Niamey. Although there are
restrictions on the availability of all survey maps,
these are not always applied.

Pharmacies Almost every *quartier* has a small
neighbourhood pharmacy. Two of the most central
and best stocked are Pharmacie Kaocen, on the
rue du Coulibaly (☎73.54.54), and Pharmacie
Nouvelle, on rue Luebke (☎74.14.81).

Post and phones The PTT is on rue de Kabekoira,
down from the Sûreté National, with an efficient
poste restante (CFA200 per item collected) and
phone services.

Supermarkets The best of the European-style
supermarkets are the two branches of Haddad
Supermarket on av de la Mairie and rue de
Coulibaly. They're completely a/c and a carbon
copy of a Parisian *supermarché* – from the
shopping trolleys down to the boxed Camembert.
Vegetables and fruit are flown in directly from
France – for which you'll pay prices two to three
times higher than at source. Next door to the
branch on av de la Mairie, Peyrissac is somewhere

between a department store and discount hardware store. They may have hard-to-find camping supplies.

Swimming pools Non-guests can use the pools at the three major hotels – the *Terminus*, the *Grand* and the *Gaweye* – for CFA2000–2500. The last is the nicest, most central and priciest. Less expensive than any of the above is the Piscine Olympique on rue du Sahel, near the *Hôtel du Sahel*, and most days you'll have the whole place to yourself.

Travel agents The IATA-registered Satguru Travel Agency, next to *Hôtel Maourey* on rue de la Copro (℡73.69.31, ℯstts-nim@intnet.ne), handles tickets for all airlines flying to and from Niamey.

Nigercar Voyages, av de l'Afrique (℡72.23.31, ℱ73.64.83, ℯenicarvoy@intnet.ne), is reliable and offers a comprehensive set of trips through Niger – specializing in trips to the Parc National du "W" du Niger (see p.973) – and surrounding countries. Other travel agents tend to go in and out of business unpredictably.

Visa extensions You can get your visa extended at the Sûreté, on the corner of rue Nasser and av de la Mairie.

Wrestling Just down from the Centre Culturel Oumarou-Ganda, on bd Mali Bero, the Arène des Jeux Traditionels is a good place to check out a *lutte traditionelle*, at which Niger excels. Check the paper for announcements.

13.2

Southwest Niger

Southwest Niger is the greenest and most densely populated part of the country. As well as being an important crossroads for travel between Nigeria, Benin and Burkina, there are some worthwhile destinations in the region, just a few hours' travel out of Niamey, including superb markets to the northeast, and pleasant riverside excursion areas just north of the city.

North of Niamey, the scenic road to Gao in Mali, via **Tillabéri** and **Ayorou** (at the end of the tarmac), hugs the river most of the way. A paved road runs the whole way **south** to the Niger–Nigeria–Benin border at **Gaya**, but it's less interesting scenically than the route north of Niamey. A second southbound route traces the west bank of the river on tarmac to **Say**, before reverting to *piste* en route to Niger's only game reserve, the **Parc National du "W" du Niger**.

Northeast of Niamey

For a change of pace and a taste of Nigérien rural life, make a trip a few hours out of the city to the northeast. Taxis head daily from Niamey along the scenic route to **Filingué**, passing through the market towns of **Baleyara** – itself worth a day-trip from the capital – and **Bonkoukou**. There's considerable regional commerce here in crop and livestock production, and the paved road runs along a water-worn valley – a vestige of a river that once flowed south from the Sahara into the Niger. It's inspiring scenery, with rugged cliffs and hills for the whole 179km to Filingué. If you're heading for Tahoua and Agadez, this route provides an alternative to the main highway via Birnin-Konni.

Baleyara

Although the name **BALEYARA** (96km from Niamey) roughly translates as "where Bellah come together", it's primarily a Djerma settlement, where Tuareg, Hausa and Fula people congregate to trade at the gigantic **Sunday market**. The animal market is well known throughout western Niger, and for days before the market caravans can be seen wending their way towards the village. This is also one of the best places to find hand-woven Fula and Djerma blankets, leather goods, and intricately carved calabashes. There's really nowhere to stay in Baleyara, but there are several bars and no shortage of street food.

Bonkoukou and Filingué

Beyond Baleyara, the road southwards follows the **Dallol Bosso** – a rich valley cut out centuries ago by run-off waters from the Aïr Mountains feeding (when running) into the Niger River. To the north, this depression is known as the **Dallol Boboy**, which extends past **BONKOUKOU** – a town of semi-sedentary Tuareg which is home to an impressive Saturday market. You have to work hard to find crafts at Bonkoukou, but they are here.

A Hausa settlement and administrative town, with characteristic architecture (note the *chef du canton*'s house), **FILINGUÉ** boasts another important regional market, though it's less impressive than the two described above. On Sundays, the town snaps into life as traders make their way from the countryside and converge on the market square. Herds of livestock file in and are sold beside millet and other regional produce; you'll also find good buys of crafts ranging from pottery to woven blankets and mats. Filingué is the only town along the route with **accommodation** – *La Villa Verte* (❶), a substandard *campement* with bucket showers and kerosene lamps. There's a filling station in town, and a pharmacy, though little else in terms of services apart from a couple of small stores selling canned goods.

Transport to **Tahoua**, 225km beyond Filingué, depends on the demand created by local market days; you may have to wait several hours – or sometimes even days. The main route – which can get washed out during the rains – passes through **Talcho** (where the tarred surface ends) then veers eastward through an agricultural region dotted with Hausa villages, the largest of which are **Sanam** (market on Tuesday), **Chéguénaron** and **Tébaram**.

Northwest of Niamey

A small village on the banks of the Niger, **BOUBON** has become a popular weekend rural getaway for Niamey's expatriates. The town is some 25km northwest of the capital, approached by a small *piste* leading southwest from the main paved road; **taxis from Niamey** leave from in front of the Petit Marché. The village is especially known for its handmade pottery, sold at its Wednesday market and in vast quantities in Niamey's markets; it's also good for bird-watching. There's a *campement* (☎68.02.82; ❷) on **Boubon Island**, reached by *pirogue* from the mainland, with eight beautifully renovated thatched chalets, a good restaurant and a pool.

Midway between Niamey and Tillabéri, the town of **FARIÉ** used to be an important crossroads, as the only point between Gao and Gaya where cars could cross the river. A **ferry** still links the Niger's banks, and at the end of the dry season there's usually a passable ford, but the Kennedy Bridge in Niamey has removed the crossing's importance. Although there's nothing of specific interest here, Farié makes a base for scenic riverside meanderings.

The route to Burkina: Gothèye and Téra

A viable, if slow, alternative to the direct Niamey–Ouagadougou route is to cross

A walk along the Niger

If you've missed out on seeing riverside village life from a *pirogue*, a viable – albeit arduous – alternative is to make the four-hour **hike from Farié to Gothèye**. The path takes you close to the Niger through a series of small villages surrounded by vegetable gardens and mango orchards. After the rains, rice is grown in the shallows, but a short distance inland, the verdure soon gives way to Sahelian savanna with cattle and goats foraging for meagre nourishment from the gleanings of the harvest. Occasional waterholes provide some good **bird-watching** opportunities: golden orioles are common.

The Djerma-speakers who inhabit the villages are unused to tourists, especially those on foot, and are keen to talk – even if "Ça va?" is about the limit of the conversation. The general greeting in Djerma, *Fofo* (literally "Thank you"), goes a long way in breaking the ice.

There are plenty of opportunities to **camp** along the riverbank, but you'll need to bring everything with you. Supplies in the whole region are sparse. From the Niamey–Tillabéri road, it's 2km down to the vehicle ferry at Farié, which crosses every hour during the day (10min). A **path** then leads upstream from the tiny market on the far side, running roughly parallel to the road.

the river at Farié and continue 10km north towards **Gothèye**, which has basic food supplies and a bar-restaurant, but no fuel. The Sunday market boosts the otherwise limited traffic flow. Here, the road – paved all the way to Téra – veers "inland", away from the river towards northern Burkina Faso. The route passes through occasional villages among the millet stubble and acacia, with larger trees and more intensive cultivation taking over as the road climbs away from the river. Some 40km further, **Dargol** only comes to life for the Friday market. The next stop along the route, **Bandio**, has a small Saturday market, but otherwise no facilities.

The largest town in the region, **TÉRA** is backed by an earth dam that forms a reservoir after the rains (July–Dec). Built in the early 1980s to irrigate rice and bean fields, the reservoir and the pools below are now the focus of village life. The only **accommodation** is in the rudimentary *campement* (❶; no water or electricity), whose bar-restaurant is the only place to eat apart from the town's streetside stalls.

Minibuses leave Niamey for Téra from the Wadata *gare routière*. If you're heading to Burkina Faso, leave your passport at the police checkpoint over the bridge on the way into town. They'll hold it until you leave, and stamp you out of Niger, as this doubles as the border control. The *gare routière* and two filling stations are near the market on the opposite side of town to the *campement*.

Tillabéri

A Djerma town, and an important agricultural centre surrounded by fields of rice and millet, **TILLABÉRI** was never very lively even in the days when it saw a steady stream of overlanders grateful for the paved road after enduring hundreds of miles of thundering desert *piste*. Moreover, since the drought of the 1980s, the **giraffe herds** that once roamed the wooded savannas and provided a tourist attraction have migrated further south, and there's little to do in town besides take in the **market** – notably on the big trading days, Sunday and Wednesday. Tillabéri is a good place for a roadside stop, however, as it has a number of small **restaurants** and **bars**, some with fridges. There are modest and affordable **rooms** at the *Relais Touristique* (❶), which tries to bolster tourism by offering *pirogue* rides.

Ayorou

AYOROU, 88km north of Tillabéri, is a quiet Songhai fishing village on weekdays.

But on Sundays the population is swelled by diverse Sahelian peoples who, having crossed the river by *pirogue* or the savanna by mule, camel or on foot, converge for the weekly **market**. Famous throughout West Africa, it's an event well worth catching. An important element is the **animal market**, the main draw for nomads – Fula cattle herders, Tuareg with their camels, and Bella with mules. Songhai, Djerma and Sorko people bring fruits and vegetables, various grains, fish, goats and chickens, while Moorish (Mauritanian) merchants, in distinctive light blue robes and white headscarves, run their typical general stores. Traders also sell traditional medicine and a variety of **regional crafts**, especially jewellery and leatherwork.

Though most of Ayorou crouches along the eastern bank of the river, the oldest part of town, with traditional *banco* houses, spreads over the island of **Ayorou Goungou**. You can rent a *pirogue* to visit it, or one of the surrounding islands, at the mooring point near the market square. Your chances of seeing **hippopotamus** along this stretch of the river are good, and exotic **birds** are common, especially near the island of **Firgoun**, 12km north of town. If you have time for a jaunt downstream, you could take a *pirogue* from Ayorou to **Tillabéri** after the market closes – a one-day voyage, setting off Sunday evening or Monday morning. The trip involves plenty of weaving between the rapids and manoeuvring down narrow channels; there are some particularly exciting rapids just before you enter Tillabéri. There's no fixed price. During or shortly after the rainy season – when the river is high enough – you may even be able to rent a *pirogue* to take you as far as Niamey.

Ayorou's sole **hotel** is the once four-star *Hôtel Amenokal* (☎65.02.06, ✉hotelamenokal.yahoo.com; ❸), which serves primarily as a hunters' hangout; it tends to close and re-open quite frequently; ring in advance to check the latest situation.

South of Niamey

South of Niamey, towards the Benin border, the main road and river separate, joining up again only at Gaya. Near the town of **Kouré**, 60km down the road from the capital, the **giraffe herds** that were once the pride of Tillabéri have found refuge from drought and poaching in the surrounding countryside. In the rainy season, a day's giraffe-spotting here is easily arranged from Niamey: taxis to Kouré are no problem, and there's no shortage of local kids eager to take you to the giraffes. Expect to be mobbed, but choose a guide nonetheless (about CFA2000 per person), as they know where the herds are located. With luck, you may walk no more than a couple of kilometres before spotting these extraordinary animals sailing by in their slow-motion canter; however, a ten-kilometre trek is not uncommon. In either case the experience is well worth it, even more so given that these are some of the last giraffes left in West Africa. In the dry season the herds migrate again, well out of walking distance from the town.

Further south, the road passes through the important trading town of **DOSSO**, which occupies a crossroads position between Niamey, Benin, Maradi and Zinder. The *gare routière* here is frenetic, and there's a large market (though no bank). Dosso still has its traditional Djerma chief who lives in the *Djermakoye* – a compound built in the Sudanic style. With his permission you should be able to have a look inside. There's a limited range of **accommodation**. The motel-like *Hôtel Djerma* (☎65.02.06; ❹), near the *gare routière*, has spacious self-contained a/c rooms and a good, inexpensive bar-restaurant. The more basic *Auberge du Carrefour* (❸) on the Route de Niamey, a good fifteen-minute walk from the *gare routière*, has simple rooms (a/c or fan) with private showers but shared toilets. *Bar Koubeyni* (❶), just around the corner, is the cheapest place in town, with very simple rooms and outside toilets. The town teems with **places to eat and drink**: best is the *Restaurant des Artes*, at the new *Complex Artisanal de Dosso*, where a regional museum also is in the process of being established.

GAYA is the last town in Niger before crossing the river into Benin; the border post is now open 24 hours. If you decide to stay, **accommodation** is limited to the basic *Hôtel Dendi* (☏51.07.42; ❶), right by the *autogare*, offering simple, clean rooms with fan, water and electricity. You may notice people in your taxi heading to a house near the *gare routière*, where they get mats to sleep on the earth floor inside. People pay next to nothing for this privilege and there's no reason not to join them, though you'll elicit some embarrassed laughter.

Parc National du "W" du Niger

Part of the vast reserve that spreads across into Burkina Faso and Benin, the **Parc National du "W" du Niger** (pronounced *double-vé* and named after the double U-bend in the Niger River) covers 2200 square kilometres in Niger alone. It's one of West Africa's better game parks and relatively good for animal-watching, with herds of **elephant** concentrated in the Tapoa valley and **buffalo** (*buffle*) on the wooded savannas. Reports still come in of **lions** and **leopards** roaming the park, but they stay very well hidden. Easier to spot are antelope – waterbuck (*cob de buffon* or *cob defassa*) and **duiker** especially, as well as the big roan antelope (*hippotrague*) and hartebeest (*bubale*) – and large troops of **baboons** (*babouins*) scampering through the bush, often near the camp. **Warthogs** (*phacochères*) and **hippos** are also quite common. The park counts some 300 species of **birds**, with good showings of storks, herons and ibis. When the rainy season begins in June the park closes down, and doesn't usually reopen until early December, after the 400-odd kilometres of *piste* have been groomed.

The park entrance is 150km south of Niamey, via **Say** and **Tamou**. For the last 40 kilometres, after turning south at Tamou, the route runs through the **Réserve Totale de Faune de Tamou**, an appendage of the main park. If you're not driving or on an organized tour (and a visit to the park is hard to arrange otherwise), public transport from Niamey will get you as far as Say, where you may have to change to

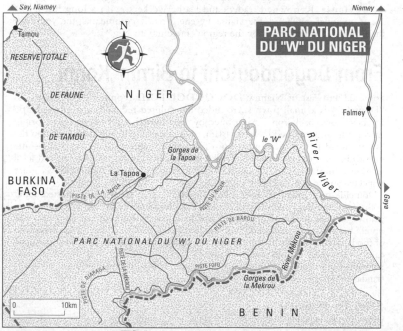

head on to Tamou. You're not likely to get down to La Tapoa without a lift from a park administration vehicle or from fellow travellers. At the park entrance you pay for a visitor's permit valid for the duration of your stay (☎78.41.12; CFA3500 per person per day plus CFA2500 if you want to stay inside the park overnight). You can also pick up a quite detailed and useful road map, though you're obliged to go with a **guide**. The main park **accommodation** is at the *Hôtel de la Tapoa* (☎68.03.40; ❺ including lunch or dinner; reservations in Niamey at the tourist office, or through any travel agent). The hotel is situated in the village of **La Tapoa** on the edge of the reserve and has comfortable bungalows and a/c rooms grouped around a swimming pool. Nigercar Voyages (see p.969) have set up a fantastic, fully equipped safari-style *campement* (CFA5500 per person plus CFA3500 to hire a tent), about 40km east of *Hôtel Tapoa* on the banks of the Mekrou river.

13.3

Southern Niger

Southern Niger is the nation's richest agricultural belt, and also contains the bulk of the country's population and is home to its biggest ethnic group, the **Hausa**. Renowned traders and leatherworkers, with a long history of regional statehood, the Hausa are energetically commercial, the vigour of their towns enhanced today by the region's proximity to Nigeria.

From Dogondoutchi to Birnin-Konni

Some 230km east of Niamey, **DOGONDOUTCHI** (commonly shortened to "Doutchi") is a small town surrounded by sculpted red cliffs reminiscent of a cowboy-movie backdrop. It's inhabited by the **Maouri**, a people of Hausa origin who consistently refused to adopt Islam, even in the nineteenth century, when the Sokoto jihad led to the conversion of the entire region. Islam has made some inroads in recent years, but this is still a stronghold of traditional beliefs, and local fetishers – notably the old chief of the nearby village of Baoura Bawa – are respected and feared, and are even said to have control over the elements.

Doutchi's only **place to stay**, *Hôtel Magama* (☎282; ❶–❷), is signposted about 200m from the bus park and has a number of comfortable self-contained a/c bungalows, as well as some very cheap and basic rooms with shared facilities. The hotel's bar-restaurant is friendly enough, but overpriced, and they tend to run out of food early in the day. Better options for **eating** are *Horizon 2000*, near the *auto-gare*, which does filling, stodgy meals for next to nothing, and the glitzy new *Sarradounia*, in the centre of town on the main road, offering sandwiches and the standard chicken-and-chips menu at reasonable prices.

Birnin-Konni

BIRNIN-KONNI is a lively town with traditional *banco* houses and characteristic dome-shaped granaries in the older neighbourhoods around the market. The town owes its prosperity to its position on the border: some neighbourhoods actually spill over into Nigeria, and a paved road pushes through the town to Sokoto, only 93km south. There's a lot of **trafficking** going on in these parts – most notably of cheap Nigerian fuel, which (when the petrol workers aren't on strike in Nigeria) you can buy from jars on the streets for a fraction of the price you'd pay at the pumps. Birnin-Konni also lies in one of the country's most fertile regions – the main streets are shaded by towering trees planted during the colonial period, and the **market** has a range of goods and produce that are expensive and scarce further north (Wednesday is the main trading day). The rows of moneychangers at the *autogare* surrounded by piles of Nigerian naira and CFA francs attest to the amount of cross-border trade. In fact, the *autogare* is the only place where you can **change money** – and, of course, it's cash only. **Bush taxis** to Sokoto in Nigeria leave constantly from a corner of the *autogare*, but you'll have to bargain hard.

Accommodation

Birnin-Konni has a couple of comfortable and reasonably affordable **places to stay**. The *Relais Touristique* (❷), off the Doutchi road on the outskirts of town, has a handful of excellent self-contained rooms and spacious bungalows, plus camping facilities (CFA1500 per person to camp, plus CFA1000 per vehicle). The bar and restaurant here are also pretty good, and they sometimes pull the TV onto the terrace in the evenings – a chance to see Niger's tiny TV station (Télé-Sahel) at work. The more central *Kado Hôtel* (☎364; ❷) has some basic self-contained rooms with fan on the ground floor, and some better and more expensive a/c rooms upstairs with a good streetside view; the restaurant does appetizing continental breakfasts and *poulet frites* at night. If you're broke, head for the super-cheap *Hôtel Wadata* (❶), on the main road about 500m north of the *autogare*, which looks like an old caravanserai and is just as basic. There's a good **disco** opposite the *Kado*, while its leafy courtyard is a pleasant place to linger over a last couple of cold beers before heading into Nigeria and Sharia Law.

Maradi

Sometimes dubbed Niger's "groundnut capital", as over half the country's crop is grown in the surrounding region, **MARADI** – Niger's third largest town – lies in an area of nascent industrialization. Maradi was formerly a province of Katsina, one of the original seven Hausa city-states, which lies over the Nigerian border, just 90km south. After the nineteenth-century Sokoto jihad, Hausa refugees fled to Maradi and eventually overthrew the Fula here. Sokoto and Maradi remained at odds for years afterwards.

Maradi has lost much of its traditional flavour (an anonymous-looking grid of streets was laid out in the 1950s), but it isn't devoid of interest. Foremost among the sights is the **Place Dan Kasswa**, bordered by the **Grande Mosquée** and the **Chief's Palace** – a colourful and typically Hausa confection. The **marketplace** is also impressive, spreading over a couple of blocks along the main Katsina road. You'll find a vast array of produce grown in the region or imported from Nigeria at prices much lower than in Niamey (Monday and Friday are the main days). Over by the Hôtel de Ville there's a shady public garden, with gazebo-like bar at one side and a church nearby.

Practicalities

Maradi has three **banks**: the BIA, across from the Sûreté; the Bank of Africa (BOA), on Katsina road next to the market; and SONI Bank, across from the market. Next door to the Bank of Africa, there's relatively reliable **Internet** access at Sareli Internet.

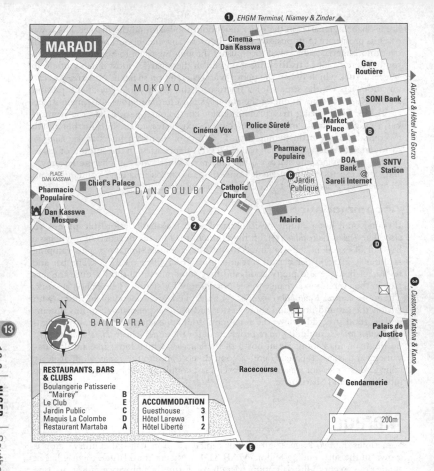

MARADI

MOKOYO

Cinema
Dan Kasswa

❹

Gare
Routière

SONI Bank

Cinéma Vox   Police Sûreté

Market
Place

❸

PLACE
DAN KASSWA

Chief's Palace

BIA Bank

Pharmacy
Populaire

BOA
Bank

SNTV
Station

@

Pharmacie
Populaire

DAN GOULBI

Catholic
Church

❸ Jardin
Publique

Sareli Internet

Dan Kasswa
Mosque

❷

Mairie

❹

BAMBARA

N

Palais de
Justice

Racecourse

Gendarmerie

0   200m

RESTAURANTS, BARS & CLUBS

Boulangerie Patisserie "Mairey"	B
Le Club	E
Jardin Public	C
Maquis La Colombe	D
Restaurant Martaba	A

ACCOMMODATION

Guesthouse	3
Hôtel Larewa	1
Hôtel Liberté	2

The **post office** is also on the Katsina road, near the Palais de Justice (CFA300 per poste restante letter). For medical needs, head to the Pharmacie Populaire, on place Dan Kasswa, or to the **hospital**, in the south of town.

Cheap **accommodation** options include *Hôtel Liberté* (☎41.03.80; ❷), halfway between the old town and the commercial centre, which has a range of rooms, most self-contained and some with a/c. A bit away from the centre, near the EHGM bus terminal, *Hôtel Larewa* (☎97.08.25 or 97.04.95; ❷) is another good inexpensive option, with basic self-contained rooms (fan or a/c) and a number of cheaper rooms with shared facilities. The hotel restaurant does a range of good inexpensive fare throughout the day. For a little luxury, the four-star *Hôtel Jan Gorzo* (☎41.01.40; ❹), on the Route de l'Aéroport, about 3km from town next to the watertower, has slightly run-down, self-contained a/c rooms, as well as a nightclub and one of the town's better restaurants. Even better is the *Guest House* (☎41.07.54; ❻), a real expat refuge, with six fully equipped and luxuriously furnished a/c rooms (another thirty less expensive rooms are planned) and an excellent European-style restaurant. It's next to the teachers' college in the expat residential area: follow the signs on the east side of the Katsina road, then turn right at the water tower

The area around the market is the place to look for inexpensive Nigérien **food**. *Martaba*, northeast of the *gare routière*, is a relaxing garden restaurant for rice with

Maradi's main **gare routière** is right next to the market on the Katsina road. Vehicles head off from here to all points, but note that you won't get into Nigeria without a visa and there are no issuing facilities at any of the border posts. **Taxis** generally stop at the border town of **Dan-Issa**, where you change vehicles for onward travel into Nigeria. There are twice-weekly SNTN **buses** for Niamey and Zinder. Private buses also service these towns.

beef scraps served in a soup and ice-cold fresh yoghurt. In the evenings, the Jardin Publique is a popular spot for grilled chicken cooked and served at outdoor stands or at the bar. The *Mairey* is the only bakery in town, and does good cakes and breads. *Le Club*, at the southern edge of town, has various facilities including a swimming pool, tennis courts, gym and video room, which you can use for CFA2500 per day, plus a reasonably priced bar-restaurant serving European dishes like crispy salads and freshly made hamburgers. *Maquis de Colombe*, on Katsina road, is currently the best place to head for **nightlife**, but bars and nightclubs in Maradi are constantly changing, so ask around.

Zinder

Formerly the largest town in Niger and briefly capital of the French colony, sleepy **ZINDER** has recently seen its influence slide. It's still Niger's second city, but much of the commerce with Nigeria – long the main source of its wealth – now passes through Maradi on the faster Kano–Niamey highway. But even in decline, Zinder remains a centre of trade, as a quick stroll through the impressive Grand Marché confirms. Nor has the town lost all its former glories, retaining some of the finest **traditional Hausa architecture** anywhere, and the old town of **Birni** is much better preserved than its Nigerian counterparts in Kano, Zaria and Katsina.

Some history

The sultanate of Zinder was founded by the **Kanouri**, descendants of the Kanem Bornu empire of the Lake Chad region. The Kanouri settled here after being chased out from northern territories by Tuareg invaders, and mixed with the Hausa population, which itself had fled the region of Sokoto under pressure from the Fulani. In the eighteenth and nineteenth centuries, the Kanouri and Hausa joined forces to found the powerful **Damagaram state**, of which Zinder was capital.

Zinder reached its apogee in the mid-nineteenth century under the reign of **Tamimoum**, who greatly enlarged the boundaries of Damagaram, introduced new crops and developed trade. Under his rule, a vast wall or *birni* was erected around the town. Originally ten metres high and fourteen deep, this wall has long since crumbled, though its remains can still be seen around the old town. According to legend, the structure's invincibility was ensured by incorporating into the walls a number of Korans and several virgin girls. Under subsequent rulers, however, Zinder's fortunes were tied more to those of the slave trade than to magic. By the 1890s, one of the Sahel region's biggest **slave markets** was regularly held here. To support his empire, the sultan led frequent raids on vassal villages and captives were sold in town, taken to Kano and then force-marched down to the coast. The **French** captured Zinder in 1899. With a population well in excess of 20,000, it was by far the region's biggest metropolis at the time and remained the effective capital of Niger until 1926.

The Town

Zinder comprises three separate districts, so distinct they're almost individual towns. To the north, **Zengou** was the original Hausa settlement, formerly a stopping point for camel caravans. **Birni** – the old fortified town and site of the sultan's palace and Grande Mosquée – lies about a kilometre to the southeast. Between the two is the **new town**, with administrative buildings laid out in characteristic French colonial style.

The most obvious attraction is the old quarter of **Birni**, reached from the new town by following Avenue de la République south beyond the old French fort (still used by the Nigérien military). This will take you past the **Grande Mosquée**, the front of which gives onto a large public square facing the **Sultan's Palace**, a two-storey *banco* building set apart by its size. There are tombs of the former sultans in the grounds, which you should be able to visit with authorization from the Mairie. Another noteworthy residence is that of the Fulani chief, just east of the mosque; the facade is decorated with colourful raised motifs, a common feature of Hausa architecture. All of Birni's buildings have been left in the traditional style, and walking through the narrow streets you get a real sense of what life was like in Zinder's heyday a century ago. A small new regional **museum** off av de la République has displays on Zinder's history, but it's seldom open.

Although **Zengou** has its fair share of modern cement buildings and corrugated-iron roofs – elements that are completely absent in Birni – the **traditional flavour**

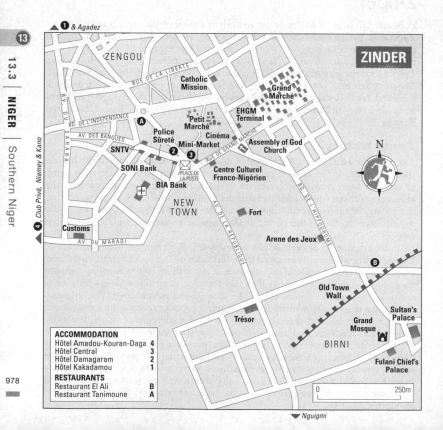

ZINDER

ACCOMMODATION
Hôtel Amadou-Kouran-Daga 4
Hôtel Central   3
Hôtel Damagaram   2
Hôtel Kakadamou   1

RESTAURANTS
Restaurant El Ali   B
Restaurant Tanimoune   A

is still strong. The oldest house in Zinder is in this quarter, and some of the town's showiest examples of Hausa architecture have been built here by the wealthier merchants. The pride in this style of decoration is by no means dead, and new, quite innovative, examples are commissioned all the time.

Zinder's **Grand Marché**, one of the country's biggest, has long been an important way-station between the Sahel and the regions to the south. Thursday is the main trading day. Salt pillars brought down from the Ténéré are sold next to the **animal market**, with its Tuareg, Fulani and Bousou traders. Hausa and other peoples from the south sell a variety of local and imported goods in and around the arcaded market building, which dates from the colonial period. This is perhaps the best place in the country to get low-price, quality **leather**, for which the Hausa have a long-standing reputation: sandals, bags, pouffes and pouches are sold around the market or by wandering merchants. Craftsmen also sell their wares direct from a number of workshops in the district.

Practicalities

Services are concentrated in the **new town**. They include the hotels and better restaurants, two **banks** (BIA and SONI), the **post office** and a couple of small **supermarkets**. There's also a cinema.

For such a large town, Zinder doesn't have an overabundance of **hotels**. The two main ones are both located off the central Place de la Poste. The *Hôtel Central* (❷) is the cheaper option, a run-down colonial-style pile offering dingy rooms with shower plus fan or noisy a/c (though it's now under new management, and may soon improve). It's also possible to camp on a rubble parking lot behind the hotel (CFA2000 per person). The outdoor bar is a popular but low-key place to hang out in the evening. Across the street, the *Hôtel Damagaram* (☏51.00.69; ❺) is bigger, nicer and correspondingly more expensive, but suffers from a similar lack of maintenance problems, though (again) new management might mean an improvement; the hotel's restaurant and nightclub are scheduled to reopen soon, and the lively outdoor bar is still going strong.

For **budget accommodation**, there are a number of small hotel-bar-restaurants clustered in Zengou, about twenty minutes' walk past the *Central* in the direction of Agadez. The *Hôtel Mallam Kakadamou* (☏51.05.68; ❶) is the best of the cheapies, with fanned rooms with shower (some with shared toilets) in a friendly family compound. There's a safe parking area, where you can also camp. Heading out of the centre the other way, the Kano road leads past the customs building (where, if you're driving, you may or may not be stopped), on to Zinder's best accommodation option, the *Hôtel Amadou Kourandaga* (☏51.07.42; ❹), with spacious a/c rooms surrounding a courtyard and hot water on tap. There are also a couple of cheaper rooms with fan. This is a popular expat hangout, and where Zinder's middle classes go for a quiet drink, so you might end up having a beer with the chief of police or the mayor. The restaurant does excellent meals at very reasonable prices, with mouthwatering Tunisian couscous a speciality. The hotel also has a well-stocked souvenir shop and safe parking. **Street food** is easy to find in town, especially in the Place de la Poste, across from the *Hôtel Central*. For something a little upmarket, try *El Ali*, behind Nigelec, which serves good chicken and *steak-frites* (but no alcohol) in a small garden. The a/c *Tanimoune* restaurant, near the main roundabout, has good European food. Watch hygiene everywhere: Zinder's **water** is considered suspect and usually needs purifying.

Zinder **nightlife** has recently gone from quiet to quieter, and options are limited. Both the *Damagaram* and the *Central* hotels have bars, and *Damagaram*'s nightclub is scheduled to re-open sometime soon. If you're feeling homesick or decadent, try the *Club Privé*, which has a swimming pool, sports facilities and a classy bar (open until 2am on weekdays, and 24hr at weekends). Officially, you need to be introduced by a member, so some smooth talking may be called for. For **live music**,

Moving on from Zinder

SNTV buses (☎51.04.68) have departures three times weekly from Zinder to **Niamey** via Maradi, Birnin-Konni, Dogondoutchi and Dosso (departing Mon, Tues & Fri at dawn), **Nguigmi** via Diffa (Mon and Fri) and **Agadez** (Sat). The *gare SNTV* is on av de la République near the *Hôtel Damagaram*. EHGM buses (☎51.04.49) have four weekly 6am departures from their terminal to Niamey (Mon, Tues, Thurs & Sat) from the terminal near the cinema. Unfortunately, their Niamey to Diffa buses don't stop in Zinder, so you'll have to return to Maradi to make that connection. **Private buses** and **bush taxis** leave from the **gare routière**, near the Petit Marché, and connect with all major towns. **Taxis** also head regularly to Kano in Nigeria along a good road; it works out a little cheaper to take a vehicle to the border, where you can easily find a taxi on to Kano.

check out what's on offer at the *Centre Culturel Franco-Nigérien*; they also have a reasonable (if pricey) bar-restaurant. The newly opened **cinema** has daily screenings of American films dubbed into French (CFA500).

Zinder to Agadez

The journey north **from Zinder to Agadez** (see p.982) can be accomplished comfortably in a day. If you're driving, it's worth taking your time on this stretch, as it's a relatively narrow band of the Sahel, with sights you won't get elsewhere. The **Kel Gress Tuareg** live in the region in their huts of fibre matting. There are tall Sodom apple trees, as well as many smaller, sometimes colourful plants, and you might see an ostrich or two. Be careful walking in what appear to be tufts of grass – the seeds have a casing like a small horse chestnut, the spikes of which draw blood.

The small town of **Tanout**, 140km north of Zinder, is a good stopping point for a cold drink or some dry Fulani cheese, and sometimes has petrol. Several wells beyond Tanout contain water – though you'll need a forty-metre rope. At the little village of **Aderbissinat**, there's sometimes a cursory police check, and foreigners stopping here are regarded with interest and curiosity by traders in the market (leather, sweets and basic food). The road then passes near the **Falaise de Tiguidit**, an escarpment with a wonderful view back across the plain.

On to Lake Chad

This infrequently travelled route heads through a region that was part of the Kanem Bornu empire up to the nineteenth century, and is now peopled by Hausa, Kanouri, Dangara and Manga. The road is sealed all the way, albeit with numerous potholes, particularly around Gouré, occasional sand-drifts around Maïné-Soroa and the usual hazards of animals and large birds in your path. Just 22km east of Zinder you arrive at **Miria**, the first oasis in these arid parts. The gardens here harbour date palms and groves of mango and guava. Sunday is the main **market day**; look out for local pottery.

A further 144km brings you to the small *sous-préfecture* of **Gouré**. It's another 330km to **Maïné-Soroa**, the next place of any size, where the people make a living drawing salt from the earth. The desert looms close to the east of town, and you can see large dunes from the roadside. **DIFFA**, an administrative town on the banks of the **Komadougou River** – which sometimes flows into Lake Chad – is 75km further on and has the last reliable filling station for eastbound drivers. The *Hôtel Kanady* (☎54.03.32; ❷), in front of the filling station, is the best accommodation in Diffa, with cleanish self-contained rooms (a/c or fan) and a reasonable bar-restaurant. For a drink, head to *Le Jardin*, a popular hangout with government workers and expats.

At the end of the road, **NGUIGMI** is nearly 600km from Zinder and a full 1500km from Niamey. An important town during the days of the Kanem Bornu empire, when it was home to the semi-nomadic Kanouri princes, Nguigmi became wealthy from its position on the trade routes to the **Kaourar oasis** (whence salt was brought by caravans) and, of course, from its site on the shores of **Lake Chad**. Today, access to the lakeshore is difficult: it has shrunk much farther south and virtually disappears in periods of drought – at times, the closest standing water to the town is 100km to the south. Nguigmi is devoid of basic facilities (including filling stations), so stock up in Diffa. You can ask the local churches to put you up for the night, or head for the basic *campement* (**❶**). *Restaurant Le Tal* is the best option for food. An SNTV bus leaves for Zinder (Wed & Sun); depending on the state of the road, you may end up spending the night under the stars. An even more arduous *piste* leads north of here to **Bilma**, a trip that takes between two and three days. The actual *piste* only goes as far as **N'gourti** (145km north of Nguigmi), after which it's 450km of desert with more than a hundred sand dunes to cross; a guide is a definite must. If you're heading **into Chad**, Nguigmi is where you take your official leave of Niger and drive, or find a ride, east, then south, around the lake to Ndjamena.

13.4

The Nigérien Sahara

To travel through the north of Niger takes some determination. It's a region with a stifling climate, great expanses of emptiness and very little water. From Niamey, a paved road leads the whole way to the boomtown of **Arlit** – the northernmost major settlement – passing through the commercial centre of **Tahoua** and the historic Tuareg stronghold of **Agadez**. Other interesting sites are difficult to reach and require preparation and a good guide.

The effort and expense is rewarded by beautiful **desert oases**, whose inhabitants eke out a living from the **salt trade**, transported by camel caravans which still cross the region. Trips through the volcanic moonscapes of the **Aïr region** or the awesome dunes of the **Ténéré desert** also provide opportunities to visit a wealth of **prehistoric sites** – including the rock paintings near **Iferouâne** – and a number of **springs and waterfalls**.

Tahoua

Niger's fifth largest town, **TAHOUA** is a major stopping point on the main road between Niamey and Agadez. Despite a population of over 60,000 and a wide mix of peoples, the town hasn't really warmed up to travellers – indeed it was expressly closed to them until the mid-1980s. There's little to detain you here, and even the pretty rosy dunes that have settled permanently on the edge of town have now been turned into a motorcross circuit and are only worth a special detour if you're into sand-dune racing. That said, the mountainous area east of Tahoua around the town of **Bouza** is dotted with tiny, picturesque villages and offers some interesting hiking opportunities. For advice and help, contact Moustafa Alassane, the owner of the *Hôtel de l'Amitié* (see below), and also a respected Nigérien film director.

Tahoua is primarily a commercial centre and boasts an animated **market** – the building is itself an attractive example of Sahel-inspired architecture. It's one of those places where everyone in Niger – Djerma, Hausa, Bororo, Fula, Tuareg, the odd tourist – comes together, notably on Sunday, the main trading day. The nomads bring salt pillars, dates, livestock and leather, which they sell to regional farmers who provide grain, cotton, spices, peanuts, tobacco and locally made indigo fabrics. Look out for the intermediaries called *dillali*, who bring together traders, help them strike a deal and even serve as translators. You could also check out the new **Centre Artisanal**, at the northwestern edge of town, whose workshops are busy with Tuareg craftsmen making jewellery and leatherware. Bargain hard if you decide to buy anything.

Practicalities

Tahoua's most useful facilities are the two **banks** in the town centre: SONI Bank (which changes cash euros only), and BIA (which changes traveller's cheques as well as cash). There's also an **Internet** café next to BIA, though it's only erratically open. **Accommodation** in Tahoua is limited. If you're on a budget, head for the shady *camping* (CFA1100 per person), about 2km west of town next to the Arènes des Jeux Traditionels (wrestling arenas). In town, *Hôtel les Bungalows* (☎61.05.53; ❷), across from the town hall and a short walk from the *gare routière*, is surrounded by pleasant gardens and has a few bungalows, the cheaper ones with fan only, the more expensive and comfortable ones with a/c. More expensive is the a/c *Hôtel de l'Amitié* (☎61.04.83; ❸), about 1km from the centre on the Birnin-Konni road, which is also home to a popular bar, a good restaurant, and a large car park where overland trucks used to park in days gone by, and which overland travellers are slowly beginning to find again.

The town's two best **restaurants** are *Les Délices*, down the road from *Hôtel les Bungalows* in the Jardin Public, which does excellent steak and chips, and the *Restaurant de la Paix*, a short walk from *Bungalows* towards the wrestling arenas, which offers fantastic Italian fare, including authentic dishes like *gnocchi*. The Jardin Public also houses a starlit **bar** that draws in the crowds most nights (and also does basic bar food). Tahoua's only **nightclub**, *Galaxy* (Fri & Sat only), is next door to *Hôtel de l'Amitié*.

Agadez

AGADEZ has been a major stopping point on the trans-Saharan routes for hundreds of years. You can read its history through buildings like the **Grande Mosquée** – a monument known throughout West Africa – or the more prosaic **camel market**, which has been attracting the peoples of the Sahel here for generations. Following the uprisings of the early 1990s and the troubles in Algeria, once-common visitors – who formerly included everyone from Bilma salt caravans to trans-Sahara tour groups and film crews – tapered off, while even the discovery of uranium to the north and the construction of new roads to Niamey and Zinder failed to lift the town out of its dusty isolation. Then, with the **Tuareg peace settlement** in 1998 (and the subsequent appointment of a Tuareg rebel leader as the Minister of Tourism), tourists gradually started returning, and Agadez is now well on the road to recovery, with new hotels and restaurants opening up and plenty of travel agents offering desert tours.

Some history

In the fourteenth century, Agadez was a small but flourishing commercial centre where Arabs from Tripoli traded with Hausa from Nigeria and Songhai from Gao. By the fifteenth century it was on its way to becoming the **capital of the Tuareg** – in so as far the nomads had such a thing – and in 1449, a **sultanate** was established under the leadership of **Ilissaouane**. Fifty years later, the town came to be controlled by the Songhai, and throughout the sixteenth century, Agadez marked the northernmost point of their great empire, with a huge population, for the time, of perhaps 30,000.

After the Songhai were defeated by the Moroccans, the Tuareg regained control of the town, but like other trading posts in the region it was already entering a period of long decline. Agadez fared better than most, however, thanks in large measure to its location near the salt mines of Bilma; trade continued, especially with Hausaland to the south. Nonetheless, by the time the German explorer **Heinrich Barth** arrived in 1850, the population had dwindled to about 7000, and many of the old buildings were in ruins.

Early in the twentieth century, Agadez was incorporated into French territory, though not without resistance. One of the most serious threats to colonial rule was led by the Tuareg reformer **Kaocen Ag Mohammed**, who swooped down from Djanet to take Agadez in 1916, aiming to reunite all Muslims of the region and to terminate foreign domination. Supported in his efforts by the Germans and the Turks, Kaocen held the town for three months before being ousted by the French, who sent up emergency reinforcements from Zinder. The rebellion having been quelled, the colonials killed over 300 suspected conspirators and guillotined many of the town's marabouts.

Since independence, the population of Agadez has rapidly increased, in part because of the discovery of **uranium** in Arlit, which provided an economic boost to the entire north, and partly due to the **droughts** of the 1970s and 1980s, which resulted in tens of thousands of Tuareg and Wodaabé herders converging on the town for food and water.

Arrival and information

As the main administrative town in the north, Agadez has plenty of facilities: **service stations**, a **hospital** and a small **airport**, plus a **PTT** with poste restante (Mon–Fri 7.30am–12.30pm & 3–5.30pm; CFA180 per letter). The Bank of Africa and BIA, both just off the Grand Marché, change euro cash and traveller's cheques. The government-run **tourist office** (Mon–Fri 7.30am–12.30pm & 3–6pm; no phone), north of the Grand Mosquée, can set you up with tours of the town and to the Cure Salée – if you're lucky – but not much else. Now that tourists have started reappearing, **travel agents** are popping up left, right and centre – at the time of writing there were over thirty in town, some of them a lot more professionally set up than others. For travel to the Ténéré Desert and Aïr Mountains, the most reliable are Agadez Expeditions (☏44.01.70), Dunes Voyages (☏44.03.72, ℻44.02.73), Expédition Ténéré Voyages (☏44.01.54, ⓦwww.tenere.fr.fm), Adrar Madet Voyages (☏44.03.37, ⓦwww.madet.online.fr) and Tidene Expeditions (☏44.05.68, ℻44.05.78). Guides must have a professional guide card: check it. Expect to pay around CFA20,000 per day per person for guide, 4WD transportation, food and somewhere to sleep in the desert. For tours within town the rate is between CFA5000 and CFA10,000 per person per day, although you shouldn't pay more than CFA500 just to be shown the way to Heinrich Barth's house or the Maison du Boulanger.

Accommodation

The number of **places to stay** in Agadez has increased steadily over the past few years, as have the prices, though there are still only a couple of budget places. If

Festivals in the Agadez region

The town of Agadez celebrates the Muslim holidays in style, especially the end of **Ramadan**, **Tabaski** and the **Prophet's Birthday**. Festivities marking these events begin with a morning prayer led by the *imam*, who then kills a lamb. Families return to their homes for a feast, after which the entire town reassembles along the streets between the mosque and the sultan's palace, as drummers announce the recommencement of festivities. Men gather on horseback, among them the red-turbanned sultan's guards, ready for the **cavalcades**, the highlight of the celebrations that last until sundown and then pick up again the next day. When the signal is given, the riders race their horses at a frenzied pace, kicking up clouds of dust. Men, women and children all strain for a better look, pressing dangerously close to the horsemen, who halt their charge in front of the palace, where the sultan and dignitaries are gathered.

A week after Tabaski, the week-long **Bianou** festival is also a feast for the senses, with colourful music and costumes and a carnival atmosphere. The town is divided into two sections (east and west), who compete against one another through dancing. Young musicians from each section dress up with dangling hats that look like floppy roosters' combs, which they shake back and forth while dancing and playing various instruments. It's an all-day, all-night celebration, especially lively when the two groups meet and try to out-do one another.

The Cure Salée

Along with the Muslim festivals, one of the more interesting celebrations of the nomadic Fula and Tuareg is the **Cure Salée**, a traditional homecoming that takes place some time after the rains, between July and September. Herders who have migrated to the far south in the dry season return to the region around **In-Gall**, west of Agadez, when the large salt flats fill with water. During this period, animals are fattened and given the "salt cure", punctuated by festivities including music, dancing, and camel and horse races.

During the first half of September, the **Wodaabé** – a nomadic Fula people known as the Bororo by Tuareg and sedentary Fula – stage a remarkable ceremony called

money is no object, however, you'll find some of West Africa's most outstanding accommodation here.

Auberge d'Azel Rte de Bilma, near the junction with Route de l'Aéroport ☎40.01.70, ⓦwww.agadez-tourisme.com. Fabulous small hotel with nine individual and beautiful rooms with brick vaulted ceilings, all sparkling clean and with every luxury you can imagine, including a well-stocked bar, a French restaurant, and a fantastic rooftop terrace with a beautiful view over downtown Agadez. The helpful French-Tuareg couple who run the place also run Agadez Expeditions (see above) and can advise on trips in the region. It's often full, so booking is recommended. ❻

Hôtel Agriboun Town centre, not far from the *gare routière* ☎44.03.07. A peaceful and inexpensive place, with simple self-contained rooms with fans and outside toilets. You can park inside the fenced courtyard. ❶

Hôtel de l'Aïr Town centre, near the Grand Mosquée ☎44.02.47. Formerly the sultan's palace and still wonderfully quiet, cool and dignified (apart from the bar, which has a wide selection of booze and customers). Despite the architectural grandeur, the rooms aren't fancy, though some have a/c. ❸

Hôtel Sahara West of the Grand Marché ☎44.01.97. Conveniently located, but very shoddy and only really worth staying at if everywhere else is full. It's currently under Nigerian management, and is usually full of Nigerians en route to Europe. Rooms are self-contained but grimy, and lack mosquito nets. ❷

Hotel Tchintoulous Rte de l'Aéroport, in front of the Grand Marché ☎ & ⓕ44.04.59. Another new place geared mainly towards backpackers and tour groups with a range of rooms suiting most tastes, some fully self-contained with a/c, others with fans and shared facilities. There's also a four-bed dorm (CFA5000 per person), and you can sleep on the terrace for CFA3500. The place feels a bit like a caravanserai, maybe because of the gravel floor in all the rooms. ❹ the **Gerewol**. Often likened to a beauty pageant, this is a party for unmarried men, who spend hours adorning themselves with jewellery and putting on make-up – red ochre on the face, white outlines for features like the nose and mouth, black on the lips and round the eyes. Elaborate hairpieces are also concocted using scarves, beads, braids and feathers. Having prepared themselves to emphasize Wodaabé ideals of male beauty – long slender bodies, bright white teeth and eyes, and straight hair – the bachelors line up in the festival arena to dance, roll their white eyes, flash their broad smiles and chant a droning melody. The young women, who also spend a considerable amount of time beautifying themselves, look on, and one by one come forward and take their choice of the most handsome man. According to custom, if a girl doesn't like the husband proposed for her by her parents, she can marry the man she desires, chosen at the *Gerewol*. A man who isn't happy with his new partner has some difficulty getting out of the social obligation to spend a night with her, but numerous weddings do take place over the course of the *Cure Salée*. Another Wodaabé *Cure Salée* event is the virility test known as the **Soro**. Here men stand in front of their girlfriends and allow other men to strike them several times across the chest. To show their courage to their loved one, they're expected to smile as they're beaten.

These elaborate demonstrations of manliness are part of an extensive and complex **codified social life**, which characterizes many pastoral peoples – it's similar in many respects, for example, to that of the Maasai, Samburu and Dinka in East Africa – and which finds expression in a mesh of taboos and ritual behaviour maintaining extraordinary social cohesion and group identity.

Although the events at the *Cure Salée* have been filmed and photographed often enough to make them relatively familiar images, you have to remember that the occasion is not a tourist spectacle. That said, more and more tourists seem to make it here, and it's no longer as difficult to get to as it used to be. The easiest way to visit is to go with a travel agent in Agadez; otherwise enquire at the tourist office.

Hôtel Telwa Bungalow Off the Tahoua road, northwest of the Grand Marché ℡44.02.64. Newly renovated motellike place, with comfortable, self-contained a/c rooms, a bar and a restaurant (with excellent pizza and pasta, as well as a few select Tuareg dishes). ❹

Hôtel Tidène Not far from the mosque by the Mobil station on rte de l'Aéroport ℡44.00.06, ℻44.05.78. A *banco*-style building with a pleasant garden, clean rooms with fan and a good-value restaurant. The manager speaks English, and breakfast – with fruit juice – is included. You can sleep on the roof for next to nothing. ❹

Pension Tellit Across from *Hôtel de l'Aïr* ℡44.02.31. Luxurious Italian-run place with a handful of attractively decorated and clean self-contained a/c rooms. The owner also has a second, equally tasteful place in Iferouâne. ❺

The Town

Agadez is a sprawling town, so taking up the offers of a young guide may be invaluable. You might find yourself invited into houses (men should avoid looking at the women within the courtyard), and you'll see all the sights you ask about.

The Grande Mosquée and around

Spiring through the one-storey skyline to a height of 27 metres, the tower of the **Grande Mosquée** is a landmark whose fame has spread beyond West Africa. Built in 1515, the mosque is a classic example of medieval Sudanic, with the wooden support beams protruding from the minaret like quills from a porcupine. Over the years the structure has been much renovated and was completely rebuilt in 1844, following the original style. In former days, the tower doubled as a sentry post, and it's worth climbing for views of the town and surrounding countryside. Though the

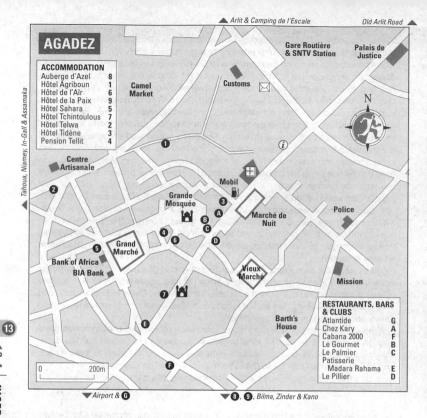

AGADEZ

ACCOMMODATION

Auberge d'Azel	8
Hôtel Agriboun	1
Hôtel de l'Aïr	6
Hôtel de la Paix	9
Hôtel Sahara	5
Hôtel Tchintoulous	7
Hôtel Telwa	2
Hôtel Tidène	3
Pension Tellit	4

RESTAURANTS, BARS & CLUBS

Atlantide	G
Chez Kary	A
Cabana 2000	F
Le Gourmet	B
Le Palmier	C
Patisserie Madara Rahama	E
Le Pillier	D

Map labels: Arlit & Camping de l'Escale · Old Arlit Road · Gare Routière & SNTV Station · Palais de Justice · Customs · Camel Market · Centre Artisanale · Grande Mosquée · Mobil · Marché de Nuit · Police · Grand Marché · Bank of Africa · BIA Bank · Vieux Marché · Mission · Barth's House · Tahoua, Niamey, In-Gall & Assamaka · Airport & · Bilma, Zinder & Kano · 200m

mosque is normally off limits to non-Muslims, there's a guardian who, in exchange for a *cadeau*, will lead you to the top, providing you don't arrive at prayer time. He's recently become accustomed to hefty *cadeaux* from wealthy tourists, and you may not be let in for less than several thousand CFA francs.

The nearby *Hôtel de l'Aïr* served as the **Kaocen Palace** early this century. It's a beautiful building, and even if you don't stay here you should stop by for a look. The large dining hall is where the sultan formerly received his audiences and, it's said, where subversives were hanged after the 1916 Tuareg uprising. You can go upstairs to the rooftop terrace bar for an interesting perspective on the mosque and town.

Also in the centre, the massive *banco* structure of the **Sultan's Palace** is the current residence of the traditional city ruler. The Nigérien government has left the basic structure of the sultanate intact, but although he's often called upon to mediate in local disputes, the sultan has no more than modest powers at state level. Agadez's main festivals always culminate at the informal public square in front of the palace.

About ten minutes' walk east of the mosque, the **Maison du Boulanger** is a beautifully decorated baker's house, with the old oven and other tools of trade still in place, not to mention the Sudanic splendour of the building itself. Nearby (ask a kid to show you the way) through some narrow dusty alleyways, the house that explorer **Heinrich Barth** stayed in when passing through Agadez in 1850 has been opened up as a small museum (CFA500). The house itself is quite unimpressive but inside – in one of the rooms – you'll see a small collection of Barth's belongings.

Silversmiths and saddlemakers in Agadez

The refined craftsmanship of the Agadez **silversmiths** has become a byword in West Africa and even in some international circles. Though these artists make a variety of innovative jewellery and other objects from precious metals, they're best known for the **desert cross** pendants, especially the renowned "Croix d'Agadez". Other towns with their own unique crosses include Bilma, In-Gall, Iferouâne, Tahoua and Zinder.

The smiths still work out of small *ateliers*, which you won't have to seek out, as young boys make it a point to propose a **tour** of the workshops to every tourist passing through. They say there's no obligation to buy, but once you're in the shops, the pressure to do so is intense. If you're fairly certain you're not interested in making a purchase, perhaps you should decline the whole show. That said, watching the *forgerons* producing jewellery by the time-honoured **lost-wax process** is genuinely interesting. A wax shape of the intended object is used to make a clay mould, which is then baked in a charcoal fire until all the wax has trickled out of the holes made for that purpose; liquid silver is poured into the mould, which after cooling is broken to free the hardened metal. Detailed carving and polishing can then take place. The craftsmen are known not only for the quality of their work, but also for the honesty of their materials. Unlike the market vendors, they have a reputation for straight dealing – when they say something is pure silver, it usually is.

Other artisans specialize in the **leatherwork** for which Agadez is also famous. The workshops still produce *rahlas* (camel saddles), covering the wooden frames with treated hides that are then decorated. They also make colourful sandals, with red and green leather in the design, and Tuareg "wallets" – stylized pouches worn round the neck with compartments for money, tobacco and other necessities.

The markets

Not far from the mosque, the **Grand Marché**, often called the Marché Moderne, is the town's main commercial venue. Tumbledown corrugated-iron sheds offer a variety of goods, loosely divided into food sections (expensive, as most fruit and vegetables have to be trucked in from the south), tools, fabrics and so on. Many traders sell **crafts** aimed at the tourist trade, and this is one of the cheapest places to get Tuareg and Fula **jewellery**. Quality is often wanting, however, since the shiny trinkets are often made from melted-down Algerian dinars or other alloys that quickly acquire a dull green patina. Leather goods – sandals, pouches and bags – also abound.

On the eastern side of the main north–south road that splits the town in two, the **Vieux Marché** is much less hectic, but worth visiting, since it lies in one of the town's oldest quarters. The dusty streets surrounding the market are tightly hemmed in by *banco* houses bearing the stamp of Sudanic and Hausa influence, with their smooth lines and decorated facades.

Most interesting, though, is the **camel market**, on the town's northwestern outskirts. In the mornings, camels, donkeys, sheep and goats are bought and sold in an open field bordered by stalls featuring nomadic goods – mostly salt pillars, rope, water containers and mats. If you've never sat on a camel, you can do so here by approaching one of the Tuareg traders. In exchange for a small tip, he'll help you into the saddle and let you circle the area – not exactly an adventure, but it gives you a taste.

Eating and nightlife

In addition to the hotel **restaurants**, Agadez has several small places dishing up inexpensive meals. At the cheapest end of the scale, the Marché de Nuit, opposite *Hôtel Tidène* on Route de l'Aéroport, consists of rows of stalls selling a vast range of stews and grilled meats, all freshly made. For **picnic supplies**, you can find

△ Grande Mosquée, Agadez

The **gare routière** is on the asphalt road to Arlit (the old *piste* to Arlit isn't used any longer), across from Customs. Most of the *taxis brousse* from here seem to be heading to Niamey via Tahoua, though with patience you can also find transport in other directions including the 450km scenic route to Zinder via Tanout, and Assamakka on the border to Algeria. Niamey in a day is just about possible on *taxis brousse*, with an early start and no delays – it's a little over 900km. The journey to Zinder can also be done in a day, if the minibus fills up early and there are no breakdowns. (At the *gare routière*, you'll see trucks getting ready to cross the desert into Libya, packed with potential illegal emigrants into Europe, if they ever make it that far. They pay a small fortune to cross the Sahara, and stories about how they're abandoned halfway across are not uncommon. It's a sad sight.)

SNTV **buses** leave from the terminal nearby and can get you to Arlit (five times a week – when the bus arrives from Niamey), Zinder (early Tuesday morning), and Tahoua, Maradi and Niamey (five times a week, also early in the morning).

The landing strip at Agadez airport is in the process of being repaired. Once it's fixed, Point Afrique (ⓦwww.point-afrique.com) plans to resume its **flights** between Agadez and Marseilles/Paris.

European canned and dry goods plus a selection of wine at the Mini Prix on the Route de l'Aéroport. They sell French cheese, British biscuits, Italian pasta and Mars bars – and it's not that expensive. Incidentally, the **water** in Agadez is perfectly drinkable straight from the tap.

Atlantide rte de l'Aéroport, past the Bilma road junction ☎44.05.90. Popular new restaurant serving European food as well as a few local specialities such as *alfitate* (wheat pancakes), either indoors or on a tranquil sandy terrace.

Chez Kary Next to the Mobil garage. Streetside shack with ice-cold drinks and a good selection of food such as steak and chips, omelette and potato salad at very reasonable prices.

Patisserie Madara Rahama rte de l'Aéroport, across from the small mosque. Good cold yoghurt and fresh pastries.

Le Pillier Near the Grand Mosquée ☎44.03.31. Run by the owner of the *Pension Tellit*, with outstanding – if pricey – Italian specialities, plus traditional Sahelian food.

Restaurant Gourmande Near the mosque. Copious helpings of Togolese dishes, as well as salads and tasty stews; it's almost always open, although they do sometimes run out of food.

Restaurant Palmier rte de l'Aéroport. New restaurant serving Tunisian couscous specialities as well as real Arab coffee on the street-facing terrace; waterpipes available on request.

Arlit

Overland routes from Algeria, closed since 1993 due to instability in Algeria and the Tuareg rebellion in northern Niger, have finally been reopened, and travellers can once again enjoy the spectacle of approaching **ARLIT** from the Algerian Hoggar and seeing the town appear from nowhere, like a vast aberration on the fringes of the Sahara. As little as forty years ago there was virtually nothing here, but after the discovery of uranium in the mid-1960s, a town burgeoned beside the vast complex built for the SOMAÏR company. Despite its recent origins, Arlit's prosperity has drawn a wide mix of people that makes it an attractive stopping point for desert-crossers, though it can't compare for interest with the diverse commercial centres of the south.

Arlit is really **two towns**. The first, built entirely for the mining company and its employees, is well planned and exclusive, with villas for engineers and executives, supermarkets stocked directly from France, a well-equipped hospital, and the town's best restaurants. The obvious divisions between the African and European workers – unequal housing, salaries and living standards – make this a disturbing sight, and you won't really have access to the facilities unless you know or befriend someone working here. A more **traditional town** has grown up in chaotic fashion alongside the mining complex. The large **market** – a maze of tiny stalls covered by mats and corrugated iron – sells vegetables, fresh meat (cut before your eyes in the open-air abattoir), and household items like decorated calabashes, pottery and basketware.

Practicalities

There's a BIA **bank** in town. The two best **places to stay** are the *Auberge la Caravane* (☎45.22.78; ❷), in the town centre, which has a choice of fanned or more expensive a/c rooms; and the grubbier *Tamesna* (☎45.23.32; ❷), on the main street near the market, which has a few noisy rooms behind the bar (you can also sleep on the terrace). The town's two **campsites** have suffered badly from the dearth of overland traffic, and can't be relied upon. The first is about 3km out of town along the road to Agadez, and is in rather bad shape, with facilities which don't go much beyond showers. The second, some 3km north of town, is an equally basic set-up and is "temporarily" closed.

The **restaurant** at the *Tamesna* does reasonable European-style meals such as *poulet frites* with canned peas, while the **bar and nightclub** here is a popular place to hide from the heat with a cold beer or soda with ice cubes – Arlit's water is perfectly pure – and the tables spill over into the shaded interior courtyard. At night this is the centre of the town's activity. Down the street the popular *Sahel* is good for inexpensive meals – *steak-frites*, rice and sauce – and has a lively bar at night. Also on the main drag, the *Restaurant N'Wana* prepares good couscous and salads that go down well with a cold beer on the patio.

SNTV **buses** (☎45.20.13) leave for Niamey five times weekly (Mon, Wed, Thurs, Fri & Sun) and involve an overnight stop in Agadez.

The Aïr Mountains and Ténéré Desert

Two classic journeys from Agadez lead through the volcanic **Aïr Mountains** and the rolling dunes of the **Ténéré Desert**. *Pistes* wend through both areas, but most of them are extremely demanding, and they often get washed away during the rainy season or obliterated from sight when unheralded winds kick up a desert sandstorm. Travel in this area requires experience, a good guide (a guide is mandatory throughout northern Niger apart from on the main Agadez to Assamakka road), and equipment, none of which comes cheap. It's also recommended that you drive two vehicles together in case of breakdowns or any other emergencies.

The road north from Arlit to Assamakka

The 200-kilometre drive from Arlit to Assamakka on the Algerian border takes three to six hours, depending on your vehicle and desert-driving experience. From Arlit, the main *piste* runs – within a distance of, at most, 3km – parallel to the line of *balises* (marker drums) which have in many cases been replaced with piles of tyres or rocks. The Assamakka customs post closes at 6pm and it's forbidden to enter Assamakka after dusk. If you have to camp en route, choose a mound or a gully well off the *piste* – where you won't be hit by a night-driving smuggler's lorry. You have to provide *une feuille de route* (details of your journey plans) to the police for security reasons before leaving Arlit. This is a precaution taken throughout the desert region of Niger.

Minibuses leave infrequently to the border from Arlit's *gare routière*, so you'll have a better chance of finding transport to the border in Agadez.

The Route de l'Aïr

The **Route de l'Aïr**, accessible from the old, unsurfaced Arlit road northeast from Agadez, is relatively good *piste* apart from the washboard surface and one or two other unexpected hazards. The road forks at Téloua (take a left); about 15km further on you can make a diversion left to **Tafadek**, a deep spring that's great for swimming and which is believed to possess curative properties. Back on the main *piste*, 77km out of Agadez, you branch off to the right from the Arlit road and follow the sign to **Elméki**, 125km from Agadez.

Just outside Elméki, you'll notice a number of tracks leading off the main route – they head to the mines and nowhere else. Follow instead the large *piste* to the village of **Kreb Kreb**, 72km from Elméki. (About 15km before Kreb Kreb, an alternative route leads directly north to Assodé, a shortcut that bypasses Timia.) Just after Kreb Kreb, the tracks lead through the beautiful **Agalak Range** – difficult driving, as the route crosses dry riverbeds (*kori*) and hidden stretches of sand.

Timia to Iferouâne

Roughly 220km from Arlit and a little more from Agadez is **TIMIA**, a large Tuareg-controlled village nestled between the Agalak Mountains and a wide desert *kori*. The town itself is one of the most beautiful oases in the Aïr, with extensive gardens and palms. Away from the boxlike *banco* houses that spread over the valley, well-maintained **Fort Timia**, also known as Fort Massu, was built by the French in the 1950s. You can stay here for a small fee and enjoy the striking view of the In-Sarek *oued* (riverbed) and mountains. On the outskirts of town, the **Cascade de Timia** grows from a trickling waterfall into something quite spectacular during the rains.

North of Timia, the road continues some 30km to the **ruins** of **ASSODÉ**. Founded as long as 1000 years ago, Assodé preceded Agadez as **capital of the Tuareg** and was once the most important town in the Aïr. As trans-Saharan trade declined, so did its fortunes, and Kaocen dealt the final blow when he sacked it in 1917. Today the site is a ghost town – its ruins lie east of the *piste* and you'll need sharp eyes to spot them. A maze of empty streets winds through abandoned houses and squares, though many of the larger buildings – including the **grande mosquée** – are remarkably well preserved.

Beyond Assodé, the tracks become progressively easier. After 90km, they lead to Niger's northernmost settlement of any size, **IFEROUÂNE**, a marvellous oasis on the fringes of the striking **Tamgak Mountains**. The *kori* running through town breathes life into some of the most beautiful **gardens** in the Aïr. When it comes to **accommodation**, choices are limited to the new *Pension Tellit* (☏44.02.31; ❹), run by the Italian owners of the *Pension Tellit* in Agadez. It's a beautiful *banco* building with five comfortable, fanned rooms with shared facilities and a good small restaurant with expensive beer.

Iferouâne is also the starting point for visiting the Aïr region's wealth of **prehistoric sites**. Just north of the town along the Zeline *kori*, neolithic rock paintings of giraffes, cattle and antelopes can be seen on a distinctive boulder outcrop. There are more such paintings in the valley of the Aouderer *kori* near Tezirek, 90km from Iferouâne.

The Ténéré

The route east from Agadez to Bilma leads through what's often described as the most beautiful desert in the Sahara: the **Ténéré**. This is strictly for the well-equipped: an arduous, 620-kilometre journey, with a great deal of very soft sand and hardly any supplies or water along the way. You must have a guide, and usually be in convoy, before the police will let you go. Markers along the route include the graves of victims of the crossing.

Leaving Agadez, take the Zinder road and, after a couple of kilometres, follow the eastern branch towards Bilma. The first 200-odd kilometres run through the southern Aïr, with alternating stretches of sand- and rock-strewn *piste*. After 270km, you arrive at the site of the **Arbre du Ténéré**, formerly the only tree growing in a region the size of France. For over a century it served as a landmark for desert crossers, until it was knocked over by a truck driver in 1973. A scrap-metal sculpture now marks the spot, while the remains of the real tree are exhibited in Niamey's National Museum.

After 500km, you arrive at **Fachi**, a small Toubou and Kanouri village with a few hundred inhabitants and cool groves of date palms. In the centre, the fortified palace (*ksar*) is built of salt blocks; you can also visit the **salt mines** on the eastern outskirts of town. The road covering the remaining 110km to Bilma is the one used by the *azalai*, or camel caravans, that still ply the region. It's full of long stretches of soft sand, and can be tough going.

Bilma

With around a thousand Kanouri, Tuareg and Toubou inhabitants, the small fortified town of **BILMA** seems nearly a miracle out here in the middle of nowhere. Set against the backdrop of the **Kaouar Cliffs** – and as picturesque and hospitable as you could wish – Bilma owes its existence to natural water sources, which support a sizeable *palmeraie* and gardens. People in Bilma often refer to themselves, distinctively, as **Beriberi** (or *Blibli*), a term which has various interpretations but usually implies Hausa-Kanouri. Many Beriberi are Hausa in all but name, and some speak Hausa as their first language.

Bilma is best known for its **salt manufacture** (for animal, rather than human, consumption) which just about maintains the viability of one of the desert's last camel caravan routes. Around twenty to forty caravans a year make the trek from Agadez, with up to a thousand camels in each one – although in living memory the figure was sometimes 50,000 or more. In recent years, the demand for Bilma's commodity has slackened in the traditional Hausa markets of southern Niger and Nigeria, where drought has depleted so much livestock. Meanwhile, Bilma is filled with unsold sixty-centimetre pillars of dirty brown, rock-hard salt, and the locals continue to make them in moulds of saline mud, piling up vast reserves for a fatter future. If you want **to stay** in Bilma, there's basic accommodation and a restaurant at *Le Camping Touristique de l'AKFO*. They can also help with well-informed guides to the region.

Nigeria

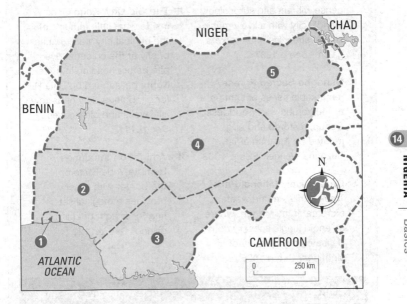

Nigeria highlights

* **Pepper soup** A fiery concoction of meat and chilli that will leave you bathed in sweat and breathing fire. **See p.1007**

* **Lagos** West Africa's biggest and wildest metropolis, a dense, vibrant and surprisingly friendly city with a lively music scene, street life and markets galore. **See p.1037**

* **Oshogbo Sacred Forest** A remarkable series of shrines to the Yoruba water goddess Oshun, restored and augmented by Austrian artist Suzanne Wenger. **See p.1063**

* **Cross River National Park** Track gorillas at the western extreme of their range, where splendid jungle scenery compensates for the rarity of sightings. **See p.1085**

* **Wikki Warm Springs** A true West African highlight, where crystal-clear waters bubble up over silver sand in the remote confines of Yankari National Park. **See p.1102**

* **The Old City, Kano** Once inside what little remains of the original city walls, pause briefly at the colourful dye pits before heading into the Kurmi bazaar and up Dala Hill for a fabulous view of narrow alleyways and old houses. **See p.1117**

* **A night on the dunes** Remote Yobe State on the border with Niger provides a magical setting for a night of star gazing. **See p.1122**

Introduction and Basics

Listen to Nigerian leaders and you will frequently hear the phrase *this great country of ours*. Nigeria is *not* a great country. It is one of the most disorderly nations in the world. It is one of the most corrupt, insensitive, inefficient places under the sun. It is dirty, callous, noisy, ostentatious, dishonest and vulgar. In short it is among the most unpleasant places on earth.

Chinua Achebe, *The Trouble With Nigeria*

Nigeria is a country many people feel needs no introduction: corruption, military coups and urban violence seem to be its very definition. And if Chinua Achebe – one of the country's most humane and respected writer-philosphers – can describe Nigeria thus, then seeking to defend it may seem perverse.

But Achebe wrote the above passage two decades ago, and, by way of contrast, consider the words of another Nigerian writer-philosopher, **Wole Soyinka**, speaking on the BBC in 1998: "Despite despots, in spite of the poverty and creeping dehumanization that we experience every day, I think that Nigerian society is more civilized than the United States."

In truth, Nigeria's notoriety is unduly influenced by its *de facto* capital, **Lagos** – a city of incalculable population and urban distress – and even Lagos, for all that its poorer districts may be terrible to live in, can be dynamic, exhilarating and surprisingly friendly, with a nightlife unrivalled in West Africa, and indeed most of the world. But if the unforgiving tempo of Lagos is too much, then leave the city – for **Oyo**, **Oshogbo**, **Ife**, **Benin**, or even giant **Ibadan** – and Lagos soon seems an anomaly: other cities certainly have their share of blight and bluster, but none really compares. These hinterland towns, where growth has been less dizzying and local traditions not yet bulldozed into oblivion, still show you hints of the greatness of the old Yoruba and Benin kingdoms in their palaces and museums, festivals and sacred sites.

To the **east** – beyond the geographical and cultural dividing line of the **Niger River** – the forests and plantations of the **Igbo country** stretch out behind the vast fan of the **river delta**. This region has made a remarkable recovery since the civil war of the late 1960s, caused by its attempted secession, and its creek and waterfront towns – **Onitsha**, **Warri**, **Port Harcourt** – have gained a new prosperity with their oil reserves. They're mostly busy, self-interested cities and faintly anonymous until you root around a little, but the engaging old trading base of **Calabar** is immediately attractive and probably the country's most easy-going city. There's a conservation focus, too, in this corner of the country, since the rediscovery in 1987 of **gorillas**, long thought to have been extinct, now protected in the wilds of the **Cross River National Park**.

Central Nigeria is a region of lower population, higher ground and some inspiring scenery, dotted with outcrops and massive stone inselbergs. It is one of the best parts of the country to travel around and its main city, **Jos**, is an old hill station with a rare line in museums. Two other **national parks** – **Kainji Lake** in the northwest, and the long-established **Yankari** with its remarkable natural swimming pool – are located in this central region. And the **eastern highlands** are some of the most beautiful and unexplored mountains in Africa, abutting Cameroon's much better known Rhumsiki region.

The north of the country is **Hausa–Fulani** territory, predominantly Islamic, like the neighbouring regions of the French-speaking Sahel. There's a more comfortable climate at these latitudes and the cities are manageable, but it's the region's history – embodied in the **walled old city** quarters of Zaria, Katsina and the big metropolis of Kano – that gives northern Nigeria a special slant. While they can't compare for flavour and historical atmosphere with the old cities of North Africa or the Middle East, these emirates (they were once independent under the

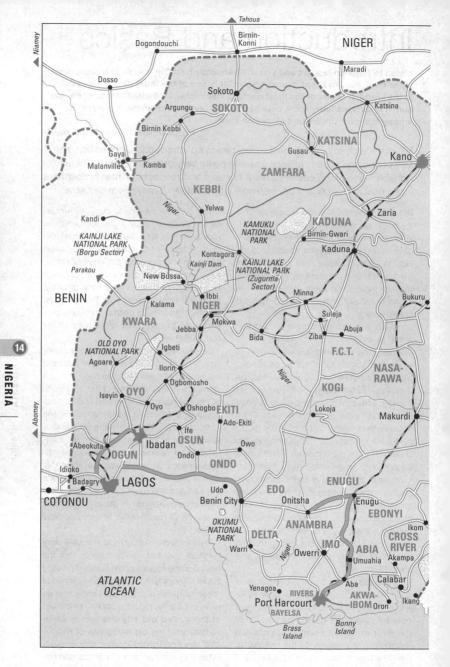

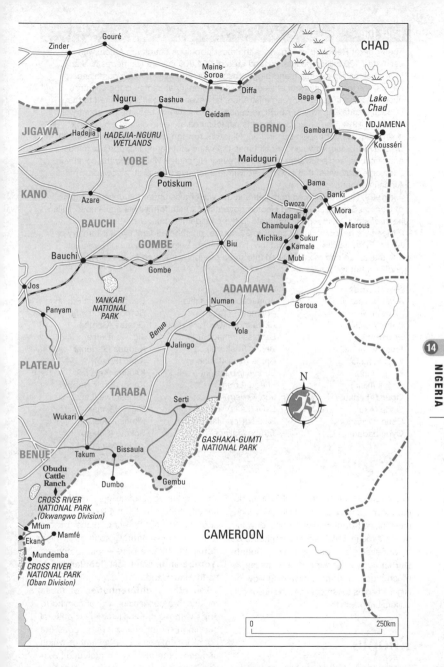

The **Federal Republic of Nigeria** is the most populous country in Africa, with an estimated 120 million people; its land area of 924,000 square kilometres is nearly four times as big as Britain and bigger than Texas and New Mexico combined. **Lagos**, the largest city (with at least thirteen million inhabitants), is the country's economic and cultural hub; administration, however, has been transferred to the Federal Capital Territory of **Abuja**, in central Nigeria, which became the country's capital in 1991. The principal **export** is oil, followed at some distance by cocoa, palm products, rubber, timber and tin. Nigeria's **foreign debt** is in the order of £20 billion ($33 billion) – two and a half times the value of its annual exports of goods and services, and equivalent to $275 for every Nigerian – which puts the country in a major league when that's compared with the relatively small sums owed by most African nations.

In 1999, Nigeria returned from years in the wilderness under the despotic regime of General Sani Abacha to an elected government, with former general – now civilian head of state – **Olusegun Obasanjo** in the presidential palace in Abuja.

Nigeria is a federation divided into **37 states**, plus the Federal Capital Territory of Abuja. Each has its own **capital** (given in brackets below) and state government. The states are commonly divided into three groups, separated by the Niger River and its tributary, the Benue.

Southwest	Southeast	North
Anambra (capital Awka)	Abia (capital Umuahia)	Bauchi (capital Bauchi)
Delta (Asaba)	Adamawa (Yola)	Borno (Maiduguri)
Edo (Benin City)	Akwa Ibom (Uyo)	Gombe (Gombe)
Ekiti (Ado-Ekiti)	Bayelsa (Yenagoa)	Jigawa (Dutse)
Kogi (Lokoja)	Benue (Makurdi)	Kaduna (Kaduna)
Kwara (Ilorin)	Cross River (Calabar)	Kano (Kano)
Lagos (Ikeja)	Ebonyi (Abakaliki)	Katsina (Katsina)
Ogun (Abeokuta)	Enugu (Enugu)	Kebbi (Birnin Kebbi)
Ondo (Akure)	Imo (Owerri)	Nassarawa (Lafia)
Osun (Oshogbo)	Lafia (Lafia)	Niger (Minna)
Oyo (Ibadan)	Rivers (Port Harcourt)	Plateau (Jos)
	Taraba (Jalingo)	Sokoto (Sokoto)
		Yobe (Damaturu)
		Zamfara (Gusau)

rule of emirs, now ceremonial figures) do have their special character. In the afternoon crush of the **Kurmi market** in Kano, or wandering through Zaria's striking **architecture**, or witnessing any of the amazing **Sallah Durbar** festivals at the end of Ramadan, a much bigger and more rewarding view of Nigeria begins to emerge than the one most visitors bring with them.

People

Geographically, Nigeria has been profoundly shaped by its two great rivers – the **Niger** and the **Benue** – which flow together in a Y-shape at the town of Lokoja. This isn't the centre of the country, but it exactly corresponds to the meeting place of the three great cultural spheres which dominate Nigerian life – the southwest (**Yorubaland**), southeast (**Igboland**) and north (**Hausaland**).

The **ethnic differentiation** of these regions is a convenient way of coming to grips with exceptionally complex cultural and linguistic groupings, but it does the country's "minorities" – several of which number in the millions – a profound injustice. Nigeria in fact has no fewer than 250 peoples, speaking nearly as many languages in perhaps 400 dialects, making it linguistically one of the world's most complex regions.

In the central part of the **southwest**, the Nupe are a major group and are culturally somewhat assimilated to the Yoruba. Other non-Yoruba-speakers include the **Edo**, **Urhobo**, **Itsekeri** and **Ijo**.

In the **southeast**, the Igbo (formerly spelt Ibo) have cultural affiliations with the **Tiv** and **Jukun**. They are almost matched in numbers by the cluster of minority peoples who speak **Ibibio**, **Efik**, **Ekoi**, **Kalabari** and **Ogoni** – among dozens of other languages.

In the **north**, the great Hausa–Fulani configuration has tended to obscure groups such as the **Gwari**, as well as the **Bauchi area** languages. In the northeast the picture is very fragmented and, in the many mountain districts where languages of the **Adamawa** and **Chadic groups** are spoken, who speaks what and who claims common ancestry with whom are questions still largely unanswered. In the far northeast people speak mainly **Kanuri** – a Saharan language that is the legacy of an independent imperial past.

When to go

There's a clear climatic division between north and south and many variations within the two major zones. The most comfortable time to be in Lagos is December and January; on the Plateau, November to February; in Kano, November and December; and in Calabar, December.

Rains in **the north** fall during a single season, roughly between May and September. Usually this amounts to no more than 500mm, most of it falling in the months of July and August. Typically the hottest months are March and April, when the harmattan winds have run their course and the rains not yet begun; at this time, midday temperatures often rise above 45°C (113°F) in the shade.

In the **southwest**, the long rains bucket down from March to July, with the wettest months usually May and June. There's a short lull, usually sometime in August (the "little dry"), then further heavy rain from September to October. The yearly rainfall in the southwest averages around 1800mm.

14

NIGERIA | Basics

Average temperatures and rainfall

Lagos

	Jan	Feb	Mar	Apr	May	June	July	Aug	Sept	Oct	Nov	Dec
Temperatures °C												
Min (night)	23	25	26	25	24	23	23	23	23	23	24	24
Max (day)	31	32	32	32	32	29	28	28	28	29	31	31
Rainfall mm	28	46	102	150	269	460	279	64	140	206	60	25
Days with rainfall	2	3	7	10	16	20	16	10	14	16	7	2

Kano

	Jan	Feb	Mar	Apr	May	June	July	Aug	Sept	Oct	Nov	Dec
Temperatures °C												
Min (night)	13	15	19	24	24	23	22	21	21	19	16	13
Max(day)	30	33	37	38	37	34	31	29	31	34	33	31
Rainfall mm	0	0	3	10	69	117	206	310	142	13	0	0
Days with rainfall	0	0	0	1	8	8	14	19	12	1	0	0

Jos

	Jan	Feb	Mar	Apr	May	June	July	Aug	Sept	Oct	Nov	Dec
Temperatures °C												
Min (night)	11	12	15	17	17	16	16	16	16	16	13	11
Max (day)	31	33	34	34	33	30	28	28	29	31	31	31
Rainfall mm	3	3	27	85	205	226	330	292	213	41	2	3

Calabar

	Jan	Feb	Mar	Apr	May	June	July	Aug	Sept	Oct	Nov	Dec
Temperatures °C												
Min (night)	23	23	23	23	23	22	22	22	22	22	23	23
Max (day)	30	32	32	31	30	30	28	28	29	29	30	30
Rainfall mm	43	76	153	213	312	406	450	405	427	310	191	43

In the **southeast**, the total annual rainfall can exceed 4000mm (about five times the annual average of London or Minneapolis) and there is a continuous and somewhat depressing rainy season from April to October, with a brief drying-off period in the middle which is not guaranteed every year. Temperatures in the south tend to be lower than in the north despite the region's proximity to the equator, but the humidity can be really oppressive.

Getting there from the rest of Africa

Air links within **West Africa** have one or two gaps: there are currently no direct flights, for example, from Bissau, Nouakchott or Ouagadougou. Flights from most other parts of West Africa arrive in Lagos, with just a couple to Kano.

One of the connections to Kano is Ethiopian Airlines' weekly flight from **Accra**. Apart from that, the Ghanaian capital has one or two services every day to Lagos on Ghana Airways, and four a week on Ethiopian. Bellview is the only airline currently running scheduled flights from the rest of English-speaking West Africa, with one or two services a week into Lagos from **Banjul**, **Freetown** and **Monrovia**.

From **Abidjan**, there's at least one flight a day. Nigeria Airways, Cameroon Airlines and Bellview are among the companies plying the route, supplemented by Air Gabon, EgyptAir and the Lebanese airline MEA.

Dakar has four flights a week to Lagos on Cameroon Airlines, and three on Air Gabon, while **Bamako** has a twice-weekly service to Lagos on Cameroon Airlines, supplemented by Ethiopian, who run one flight a week to Lagos and two to Kano. From **Conakry** there are two weekly flights to Lagos on

Bellview. Of nearby capitals, **Lomé** has two flights a week to Lagos, operated by Ethiopian Airlines, **Niamey** has one a week run by Sudan Airways, and **Douala** has four a week with Cameroon Airlines.

Lastly, there's a weekly flight from **Cotonou** on Cameroon Airlines, though given that it's only 120km from Lagos, and taking into account flight delays and formalities, plus getting to and from the airport, the land route is probably quicker.

Ethiopian Airlines fly twice a week to Kano from the Chadian capital, **Ndjamena**. From elsewhere in **Central Africa** there's one direct flight each week to Lagos from Kinshasa (on Congolese Airlines), and three from Libreville (on Air Gabon). There are currently no flights from Malabo, Equatorial Guinea.

From **East Africa**, Ethiopian Airlines flies daily to Lagos from Addis Ababa, while Kenya Airways has four weekly direct flights from Nairobi. Further north, Sudan Airways fly twice weekly from **Khartoum** to Kano, and EgyptAir fly weekly from **Cairo** to Lagos.

From **southern Africa**, South African Airways operates two direct flights a week to Lagos from Johannesburg.

Overland from Cameroon and Chad

The main frontier crossing from Cameroon is **Mamfé to Ikom**, over the Cross River bridge. Customs and immigration for Cameroon are in **Ekok**, on the east bank of the Cross (border open 24/7), whence you walk over the bridge to **Mfum**, the Nigerian post; for further details, see p.1087. From Mfum, you can catch a taxi to **Ikom** and onwards to **Calabar** or **Enugu**. There's a less often used route from **Mamfé** to Calabar, turning off south (left) from the "main" Ikom road at **Eyumajok**, 48km west of Mamfé. Note that the Mamfe–Ikom road is frequently impassable on the Cameroonian side during the rainy season. Incidentally, you might be able to hitch a ride on the occasional boats from **Limbé** or **Idenau** to Calabar (see p.1180).

Further north, out of the Bamenda Highlands, you can cross on foot from **Dumbo to Bissaula** (see p.1135), and there are minor crossings all the way along the

For important practical information applying to all West African countries, covering health, transport, cultural hints and more, plus details on getting to the region from beyond Africa, see Basics, pp.9–87.

mountainous border, though few see much traffic. The rough route from Garoua to **Yola** is a little busier, as is the northern route from Mora to **Banki** – a village straddling the border. Customs and immigration at Banki are generally low-key, and this is generally considered to be the easiest border crossing between Cameroon and Nigeria. Taxis are generally no problem from here to Maiduguri.

Finally, there's the northernmost crossing from **Kousseri** to **Fotokol** (Cameroon formalities) and **Gambaru** (Nigerian post). This is your likely way into Nigeria coming from **Ndjamena** in Chad. If you're transiting Cameroon like this and have a Nigerian visa, the Cameroon customs will issue you with a free one-day transit visa at the immigration post in Kousseri.

Overland from Niger

From Niger, two main routes aim for **Kano**: one from **Maradi**, which would allow you to take in the old Nigerian emirate of **Katsina**; the other from **Zinder**, a beautiful Hausa town. You can also cross from **Birnin-Konni to Sokoto**, or, further west, from **Gaya to Kamba**, from where you can connect to Sokoto. All four routes have good bush-taxi transport.

Overland from Ghana, Togo and Benin

The **coastal route** from **Accra** (476km) and **Lomé** (275km) to **Lagos** takes in some picturesque coastal scenery of palms, creeks and beaches. By private car, the trip takes about eight hours; it may take half as long again or more if you're travelling by public transport, as the vehicle is repeatedly unloaded and reloaded at the three borders, each with customs and immigration posts on both sides.

You can get taxis direct to Lagos from Accra, Lomé or Cotonou. They're relatively cheap these days, but you can further cut costs by taking the taxi to the frontier post at the village of **Kraké**, on the Benin border, and finding another vehicle on from there.

If you're intent on avoiding Lagos altogether, get yourself to **Porto Novo** in Benin, from where you can enter Nigeria 30km

north at the Idioko frontier post, continuing from here on the A5-1 to meet the main A5 Lagos–Abeokuta road 10km north of Ikeja. On public transport, you'll end up at the Oshodi motor park in northern Lagos, where you can get onward transport without going into the city centre.

Red tape and visas

Visas are required by all except ECOWAS nationals. Most Nigerian embassies or high commissions will only issue visas to nationals (or long-term residents) of the country where they are located. Thus it's better to obtain a visa in your country of residence before travelling abroad, since it is much easier for embassies to renew expired visas than issue new ones.

You may be asked to pay **customs duty** on some of your personal belongings – it's up to you to prove as cheerfully as possible that they are your personal belongings, and not dutiable merchandise. It's illegal to export antique works of art, and there's full scope for anything that looks old to be confiscated when you come to leave, unless you have obtained a **certificate of export** from the National Museum in Lagos. Barring that, anything you buy that looks like art or an antique is best sent home through an air- or sea-freight agency.

Information, websites and maps

Tourist offices and local branches of the Ministry of Information can be found throughout the country, and are listed in this chapter, but they are rarely very helpful. There are now local tourism boards in most states, as well as six federal tourism boards.

For a **map** of Nigeria alone, International Travel Maps publish a very good, up-to-date 1:900,000 road map that also shows physical geography, though there are errors in the spellings of some town names. In Nigeria you'll find **road maps** published by Spectrum, Peugeot and the Nigeria Mapping Company – all at 1:1,500,000. Spectrum's is the most up-to-date and the most widely available. Recently published **street plans** of Lagos and Abuja are available in some bookshops and stationery stores.

Websites

Nigeria Tourism Development Corporation ⓦ www.nigeriatourism.net. Among its features are listings of upmarket hotels and information on each of the country's national parks.
E-Nigeria ⓦ www.e-nigeria.info. Information and travel tips for visitors to Nigeria, covering topics from sport to society and business to beaches.
Nigerian government ⓦ www.nigeria.gov.ng. Includes a section on culture and tourism, a current list of Nigerian embassies abroad, and links to the websites of all the country's main daily newspapers.
NigeriaWorld ⓦ nigeriaworld.com. The latest news from Nigeria – headline stories and features.
Pidgin English Dictionary ⓦ www.ngex.com /personalities/babawilly/dictionary. A comprehensive glossary of all the *essenco* you need to *sabi* local pidgin English like a Naija.
Nigeria Arts ⓦ www.nigeria-arts.net. An excellent database of Nigerian arts and artists.
Odili.net ⓦ www.odili.net. Business- and consumer-oriented Nigerian portal, good for news and trends.

Health

Vaccination certificates for **yellow fever** are mandatory; immigration officials sometimes also demand cholera vaccination certificates. **Malaria**, however, should be your main health concern (see p.32).

Water is good and drinkable from taps in most towns across the country. In isolated rural areas, it requires boiling (one-cup immersion heaters are widely available), filtering or purification tablets. In the dry season, rural areas are often short of water and people have to make great efforts to keep supplied, so if you're travelling in rural areas in March or April, don't be surprised if there's a certain reluctance to fill your water bottles, at least for free.

Hospitals are reasonably well equipped in comparison to neighbouring countries. In Lagos, the **Eko Hospital** is one of the better places to go for treatment (see p.1051). Also recommended is the **Sacred Heart Hospital** in Abeokuta, 100km north of

Lagos. In a case of serious illness, contact your embassy. All major towns have **pharmacies**, though some aren't particularly well stocked.

Costs, money and banks

Nigeria's currency is the **naira** (₦), divided into 100 **kobo**. There are coins of 50 kobo and ₦1 (though you rarely see coins in use), and notes of ₦5, ₦10, ₦20, ₦50, ₦100, ₦200 and ₦500. The naira has fluctuated substantially over the last few years; currently, the approximate **rate of exchange** is US\$1 = ₦135, £1 = ₦200. Export and import of naira is prohibited.

You should generally find **costs** reasonable – even quite decent hotels can usually be found for under £10/\$16 a night, and eat well for £6/\$10 a day. Long-distance travel can be a real bargain.

If you're **wiring funds** through **Western Union**, you'll find that their main representatives in Nigeria are the First Bank of Nigeria. In principle they pay out in naira only, but money may be paid out in dollars at certain branches so long as it is wired in dollars.

Changing money

For changing money, **banks** are very much a last resort. Some may grudgingly agree to change cash US dollars, or occasionally sterling, at a very low rate, and take all day about it. You're much better off using privately operated **forex bureaux** (bureaux de change), present in most large towns – sometimes attached to upmarket hotels – and offering much the same rate as the **black market**. If using the latter, be wary of changing on the street – go to an office or shop if possible, always count out your naira and have them in your hand before handing over your hard currency, and abort the transaction if the dealer tries to hurry or distract you; private arrangements with expats or businesspeople are best. Dollars are the preferred currency, sterling second; euros are still unfamiliar to many people, but most forex bureaux will accept them, and (usually) CFAs.

Traveller's cheques are pretty much unusable in Nigeria, even though some Nigerian embassies demand them as proof of funds when you apply for a visa. If you do make the mistake of bringing them, your best bet is to go to the issuer's local representative and hope for the best. At the very least you'll need to have your purchase receipts. Credit cards aren't much use in Nigeria: you can't use them in ATMs, and only the most expensive hotels accept them.

Getting around

Nigeria has some 70,000km of paved roads, a remarkable figure for this part of the world. A rail network connects the northern and southern extremities of the country. Domestic air services are relatively good and reasonably priced. River travel on the Niger and Benue isn't developed commercially, most boats being for the benefit of bulk goods traffic rather than passengers.

Hitching in Nigeria isn't especially difficult – but you need to be confident of your abilities to tell a bad driver from a fast driver, and to act decisively on your conclusion – it's much better to be stranded on the highway than spread over it. Truck drivers are your best bet, and they'll often want payment.

Motors and buses

Road transport in Nigeria is easily the fastest in West Africa – often dangerously so. Bush taxis (called motors in Nigeria) are quick and comfortable, though any concerns you may have about speeding are justified: be prepared to shout at the driver to slow down if you fear for your life. Fortunately, overcrowding is the exception rather than the rule. There's usually a choice between a Peugeot 504 (estate or saloon, referred to as a "wagon") or a 16-seat Japanese minibus (known graphically as a "mauler"). There's rarely a long wait in the motor parks of major cities. Full-size buses ("luxury buses" as the operators like to call them, though they offer few comforts apart from a little more legroom than you might expect) also link major cities and usually run to fixed schedules. There are innumerable small bus companies but, surprisingly, no major firms covering the majority of the country.

As a rough indication of fares, the overnight Lagos–Sokoto trip costs ₦2000, only slightly more than the much shorter Lagos–Abuja journey, while the four-hour ride from Abuja to Jos costs ₦500.

Trains

The Nigeria Railway Corporation (NRC) operate services from Lagos to Kano (via Ibadan, Kaduna and Zaria), from Port Harcourt to Kano (via Enugu), and from Port Harcourt to Maiduguri (via Enugu and Bauchi). Services are erratic however – their schedules in Thomas Cook's International Train Timetables are published with the legend: "All services liable to suspension" – and you should check the latest situation with the NRC headquarters in Abuja (℡09/523 7498 or 523 1912). Even when running, and even if on time rather than hours late, trains are painfully slow. Fares are a little lower than on buses.

Flights

Nigeria Airways links Lagos with Calabar and Kano. Private airlines – including ADC (currently one of the largest), Albarka, Bellview, Chanchangi, Skyline, Sosoliso and TransSaharan – serve other cities including Abuja, Enugu, Jos, Kaduna, Maiduguri, Makurdi, Port Harcourt, Sokoto and Yola. Tickets aren't expensive (expect to pay ₦11,000 for Lagos–Kano one-way on Nigeria Airways) and on some routes there are several flights a day to and from Lagos. Reservations normally aren't taken, so get to the airport early even though your plane is likely to leave late. Flying can often be a lot more convenient (and safer) than travelling by road, but airports can be a long way from the towns they serve – this is especially true of Abuja, whose airport is some 40km out of town. Schedules and contact details for domestic airlines can be found online at ⓦwww.e-nigeria.info/tips4.htm.

Driving and cycling

Nigeria requires a carnet (see p.20) if you want to enter the country in your own vehicle. Be sure to get one before arriving here as the alternative is to pay 250 percent of the value of the car in hard currency at the border and receive it back in naira when you leave. When leaving the country, be wary of giving up your carnet, as the authorities may neglect to return their copy of the document to your national motorists' association as required, thereby holding up the release of your funds from bond.

Local Nigerian **insurance** doesn't cost much at the frontier, so it seems foolhardy not to buy it. If you have already bought a *carte brune* (see p.20), note that it is valid in Nigeria.

Fuel is inexpensive in Nigeria at ₦34 per litre. The problems of unavailability and long queues at filling stations are now largely a thing of the past, though they still occur sporadically. For the benefit of those who can't be bothered to find a filling station, fuel is still sometimes sold by the roadside.

If you're taking in Nigeria as part of a wider overland trip, it's worth **stocking up** with as much fuel in jerry cans as you can transport. You won't be taxed on this at the border, and fuel will be four times as expensive in the surrounding CFA countries (and possibly unavailable for days or weeks in the Sahel). Beware of taking large quantities of fuel into Cameroon, however: you don't want to be accused of being part of the major trade there in smuggled Nigerian petrol.

If you have your own vehicle, be careful where you leave it. Overlanders will encounter no special problems in northern Nigeria, but in the south some take a lesson from residents who carve their licence numbers on all windows and use crook locks. Never park in an unguarded area and leave nothing of value in your car at any time.

Car rental

The cost of **car rental** has gone down in recent years, but it's still quite pricey, as you're often obliged to hire a **driver** as well. Many Lagos outlets insist on this – and it's preferable if you're new to the city; elsewhere you may be able to drive yourself. The distinction between chauffeur-driven car rental and taking a taxi is blurred; make it clear who will pay for fuel.

Roads

Most Nigerian **main roads** were superb until the early 1990s, by which time they were beginning to need more maintenance than they were getting. Since then, the neglect of the network has become an increasing problem, causing serious accidents and millions of dollars' worth of damage in a society by now very mobile. In theory, collapsed sections of road are flagged by signs with a skull and crossbones followed at 100m intervals by 60, 50, 40 and 30 "Slow Down" signs. But hundreds of kilometres of road surface are now in a very bad state and the warning system is becoming redundant, so drive with caution. The worst roads are found in the southeast.

Few traffic signs are posted along the roads outside the major cities, except for regular roadside **marker stones** marked with the first three letters of the name of the next and previous major towns, and the distance in kilometres.

There are few **roadblocks** in central Nigeria, but they appear with increasing frequency towards the borders. Although often privately on the make, the officials are there to maintain law and order. Usually, they'll wave you through, but it's always advisable to slow down to be sure. If stopped, remain inside until told what to do, as half the officials will want you to stay put and the other half will want you to assemble outside: it's impossible to predict which. Often they'll be after a dash (₦20 is often enough), but it's wise to wait until that is clearly hinted at before offering one. The amount expected is usually small. They may also be waiting for a lift, and the minor inconvenience of an extra passenger is far outweighed by the ease with which one passes through subsequent roadblocks. Sometimes they may like to have a joke at your expense (such as storming up to shout about some minor misdemeanour, only to grin and give you a hearty thump on the back when you've been adequately terrified). It is wise to accept such jokes with good grace.

Lastly, it's not unknown for enterprising traders, or even highway **bandits**, to pose as a roadblock by setting up their wares on a couple of oil drums. Their ingenious exploits are faithfully reported in all the tabloid newspapers – but the number of robberies, as a proportion of the number of journeys made, is negligible. Nigerian officials are sometimes in plain clothes, but they usually show their ID as soon as you pull up, or on request. The more you talk to locals, the more you'll hear, and the safer you'll be. Incidents are reported close to the Niger border, on long-haul routes between the north and the south, and in and around cities during "go-slows".

Cycling

The perspective you get on the country from a **bicycle** saddle is unlike any other. Everyone you meet will think you're mad, but the rewards of cycling in Nigeria are as big as the country itself, and the supposed dangers fade to a manageable scale. You will never be ignored on the road, so the chance of being hit is diminished. Nevertheless, you should keep off the main highways as much as possible.

City transport

Every Nigerian town has countless bust-up old **taxis** making the rounds. The usual distinction applies between those vehicles (known as **drops**) which are driving fixed routes and piling customers in for very modest fees per sector, and those which hire out as private cabs and cost appreciably more for pre-agreed journeys. Whichever you choose, your progress in big cities may be slow during rush hours. To overcome the "go-slows" (traffic jams), a very cheap, common alternative in most cities are motorcycle taxis – called **okadas** in the south

(after a defunct airline), **achabas** in the north – which you hail at the roadside. They're mostly very competent, will usually find a way to take your luggage if you don't have too much, and can be hired in pairs or groups if you are travelling in company.

Accommodation

Although multinational hotel chains are represented, some of the newer hotels, notably in the Arewa chain, are Nigerian-owned and operated; these are inexpensive by the standards of neighbouring countries, and very comfortable. Two important, general points to note: all hotels levy a fifteen percent tax and some require a deposit, often equal to a night's lodging.

In towns of any size, rooms without electricity are rare, though cheap places with no generator may be subject to power cuts. Not everywhere has running water however, and even places with self-contained rooms may only be able to supply water in a bucket at some or all times of day.

Upmarket hotels (⑥–⑧) have every mod-con in the rooms and some also have tennis courts and pools. However, water and electricity can shut down frequently and unpredictably, but all bar the cheapest places will have generators to cope. Most hotels of standing have rates for residents and non-residents, the latter being substantially higher and often payable in foreign currency, but not always charged. **Mid-range** hotels (④ & ⑤) tend to be comfortable, with conveniences like satellite TV and air conditioning as standard.

Accommodation price codes

Accommodation prices in this chapter are coded according to the following scale, whose equivalent in pounds sterling/US dollars is used throughout the book. The price codes are based on the cost of a room with two beds, including tax. The term **"single"**, incidentally, refers to a room with one bed, which may in fact be a double bed. Single occupancy will normally cost at least two-thirds of the twin-occupancy rate. For further details, see p.51.

① Under ₦1000 (under £5/$8).
② ₦1000–2000 (£5–10/$8–16).
③ ₦2000–3000 (£10–15/$16–24).
④ ₦3000–4000 (£15–20/$24–32).

⑤ ₦4000–6000 (£20–30/$32–48).
⑥ ₦6000–8000 (£30–40/$48–64).
⑦ ₦8000–10,000 (£40–50/$64–80).
⑧ Over ₦10,000 (over £50/$80).

Rooms in **budget hotels** (❶–❸) may range from a bed and four walls to gadget-filled abodes cluttered with TV, rattling air-conditioning units and leaking fridges, but what you really want to check is whether there's a working shower and constant running water. Note that some hotels, particularly the cheaper ones, double as brothels.

The Evangelical Church of West Africa (**ECWA**) runs a series of **mission guest-houses** throughout the country, often in association with the Sudan Inland Mission (**SIM**). They're very inexpensive – and VSO and other volunteers get a discount. Rooms are generally tidy and spartan, but come quite well equipped in the better places.

If you're **driving**, it's essential to find a hotel with a **compound**, where the gates are locked and usually guarded through the night. There's usually no extra charge for parking in the compound.

Camping

If you have your own transport, **camping** can be a good option – but the further off the beaten track the better. You should be very wary of camping within 50km of the urban centres and it's wise to stay right away from the more congested parts of the south. Don't camp anywhere near busy roads with a car or other large vehicle, as the attention you'll attract spreads rapidly and isn't always welcome.

Eating and drinking

Food is not one of Nigeria's highlights, but European, Lebanese and Asian restaurants are found in large towns, and most hotels have their own restaurants for either Nigerian or **"continental"** (usually meaning British) meals, often with separate menus for the two. Many hotels also serve English break-fasts of eggs, toast, marmalade, tea and juice. Beware: Nigerian food in the south is usually fiery hot.

There's a wide range of foods and dishes in **chop houses** (*buka* in Yoruba) and local restaurants. In addition, chicken and chips and omelette and chips are universally available; in cheaper places the price of an omelette includes bread and "Lipton's" (tea-bag tea).

Vegetarians have a moderately difficult time in restaurants, as many apparently (even explicitly) "vegetarian" items on menus should be understood as "plus a bit of meat" – usually goat. But salad vegetables are often crisp and fresh, and delicious once you overcome any worries about them having been washed in unsterilized water. Good transport helps to provide fresh fruit and vegetables even to dry regions and parts of the country where they would otherwise be out of season.

If you're travelling cheaply it's easy enough to live on the basics. Bread (sweet, brick-shaped and often coloured yellow or pink), hard-boiled eggs, portions of deep-fried fish (with or without scalding chilli sauce), bananas, oranges and salted roast peanuts make for a reasonably balanced diet that's obtainable in the remotest parts of the country.

Drinking

Nigerians are great **beer** drinkers. Every state has its own breweries and their advertising hoardings are one of the countries' most per-vasive symbols. The most widely available brands are **Star** and **Gulder**, both equally alcoholic, though Star has a lighter flavour than Gulder. Among the other dozen-odd brands, Rock, Harp and 33 are probably the most popular. Be cautious with Nigerian **Guinness** – an impressive eight percent alcohol by volume – and with cheaper brands, which tend to provoke treacherous hangovers and, some maintain, diarrhoea.

As for Western-style **wine**, it's only in the poshest restaurants that you'll find any available. **Palm wine**, tapped from oil palms, is drunk in the south. Pasteurized bottled ver-sions are available, although their taste is a far cry from the frothy sweetness of the bush brews. Distilled, the wine becomes potent *ogogoro*, also common but usually more discreetly sold.

Tea and coffee are never great, but tea-bag tea, instant coffee, and chocolate drinks such as Bournvita can often be found during the morning at street breakfast stalls, which usually also rustle up bread and omelettes, sometimes even rice and beans.

Staples

Apu	Pounded cassava, mostly eaten in the southeast.
Àmàlà	Yams ground before boiling – the finished product has a brown colour of little initial appeal. Mostly eaten in the southwest.
Eba	Moist ball of steamy *gari* (cassava flour), overwhelmingly the favourite national dish.
Fufu	Fermented pounded cassava, most common in the southwest.
Pounded yam	Boiled yam that's been pounded to a wonderful, glazey, aerated blob.
Tuo	Cornflour mass, mainly eaten in the north.

Main dishes

Àkàrà	Fritter made from ground black-eyed beans (also called cow peas or *ogbono*) and chilli, usually sold from street stalls.
Begiri	Yoruba bean soup.
Bitter leaf	Not distant from spinach.
Bush meat	Any kind of game, often porcupine or grasscutter (aka cutting-grass or bush rat)
Cowleg	Prosaic local term for shin of beef, usually served with the foot, and with the skin on.
Dodo	Fried plantains.
Draw Soup	Slimy soup made from ground *ogbono* seeds which "draws" (ie it's viscous).
Egusi	Oily "soup" based on pounded melon seeds, usually containing stockfish or meat, and green leaves (bitter leaf or pumpkin leaf).
Eja gbigbe	Yoruba smoked fish on a stick.
Ìgbín	Large forest snails; rubbery in texture.
Jollof rice	Rice cooked with palm oil, and sometimes with vegetables and meat.
Moin-moin	A delicious steamed bean-cake snack with a slightly gelatinous texture, usually wrapped in a banana leaf, and found mainly in the south. *Kause* are the fried variety.
Okro	Gumbo, okra, ladies' fingers.
Pepper soup	A scorching chilli soup with meat (sometimes goat's head or cowleg) that will make your eyes water and your nose stream.
Soup	Any stew, often thick, fiery and palm-oil-based, with meat or smoked fish; eaten with rice or any of the starchy staples.
Stockfish	Air-dried fish, usually cod (from Iceland, Norway or Portugal) that's soaked and cooked.
Suya	The most common street food: grilled kebabs, usually of beef or goat, sold everywhere but especially in the north.

14

NIGERIA | Basics

Bottled **water** is widely available, as is the much cheaper "pure water" sold in plastic bags, and supposedly filtered, though not everybody trusts it. The usual international brands of fizzy sugar-and-chemical **sodas** ("minerals") are sold cold from fridges – at a filling station if nowhere else – all over the country. The same outlets also usually sell non-alcoholic malt sodas, often made by beer companies, which cost about twice the price. Fruit juice is imported and relatively expensive.

Communications

Mail is unpredictable: letters to and from Europe and North America can take anything from a couple of days to two weeks or more to arrive. Packages sent by post are quite likely to go astray. The poste restantes in Lagos, Kano and Kaduna, however, work well enough. To send mail out, the post office's EMS Speedpost is quick, inexpensive and reliable. Courier services are easily available – both DHL (☻www.dhl.com.ng) and UPS (☻www.ups.com) have offices in major cities and towns.

To **phone** abroad, you can dial directly from all cities and most towns. The access code for international calls is ☎009. To make a **reverse-charge** (collect) call to an overseas number, dial the international operator on ☎191. Phone connections are usually good, but you may be cut off in the middle of a conversation for no apparent reason. The cheapest way is via the Internet, a service provided by most cybercafés, though the line is echoey, with a time delay, and you cannot speak and listen at the same time. Street stands offering GSM calls on **cellphone** handsets (note that mobile coverage is limited to the major cities and towns) are pricier but, in large towns at least, more ubiquitous. Slightly more expensive still, but usually with a much better line, is to buy a **phonecard** from the offices of the Nigerian phone company, **NITEL**. Be aware however that only certain cardphones allow international calls, though you should always find at least one phone for international calls at any NITEL office. The most expensive way to call abroad is to use the services of touts who hang around NITEL offices, often having bought up all the phonecards, and charge outrageous rates for using them.

Internet connections are available in even the smallest towns. In big cities, you can even find offices open round the clock. Connection speeds vary but are generally on a par with ordinary dial-up connections at home. Prices are typically in the region of ₦200–300 per hour (some places charge by the minute). Usually you have to prepay for a specific time, getting cut off when you've used it up, but you don't have to use it all in one sitting.

The media

Nigeria is a country where it's fun to read the **newspapers**, and some fifteen percent of the population does so regularly. Most of the hundred or more titles are privately owned, outspoken and informative, and there's a wide range of styles and opinions. Nine national dailies dominate – the *Daily Times* (government owned, with a circulation of around 400,000), the *Guardian*, the *Punch*, *This Day*, the *Nigerian Observer*, the *Nigerian Tribune*, the *Nigerian Standard*, *New Nigerian* and the *Democrat*. Of these, the *Guardian* provides the most complete economic and political analysis, while the *Punch* and *This Day* are the most outspoken, but none of the papers is very strong on international news. The *Sunday Times* has a huge readership, and there are some twenty weekly news magazines.

Television

The first private **television** stations were licensed in 1993, when the government gave up its monopoly, and there are now more than thirty stations broadcasting to some five million TV sets. Programmes are in English and the national languages (Igbo, Yoruba, Hausa). Satellite dishes pick up most international stations, and in many hotels, even a lot of pretty cheap ones, you can watch CNN, the BBC, or English premiership football in the comfort of your room.

Radio

Radio is organized under the **FRCN** (Federal Radio Corporation of Nigeria), which broadcasts three short-wave programmes in English and national languages nationwide. Individual stations for the different states also broadcast their own medium-wave programmes. In Lagos particularly, a number of privately run FM stations have emerged. Music on Nigerian radio can be extremely good, and covers a wide spectrum of African styles, as well as gospel, soul, reggae and hip-hop, both imported and home-grown. BBC World Service is relayed locally by the Ray Power network on 106.5FM in Lagos, Abuja and Kano.

Opening hours, public holidays and festivals

Banks are open from Monday to Thursday between 8am and 3pm, and on Friday from 8am to 1pm. Shops are usually open daily except Sunday from 8am to 5pm. Some goods – drinks, cigarettes, etc – are available almost 24 hours.

Nigeria's official **public holidays** include the major Christian and Muslim celebrations plus New Year's Day, May Day and Independence Day (October 1). Muslim holidays marking the end of Ramadan (Sallah), Abraham's sacrificing of the sheep (Tabaski) and Muhammad's birthday are based on the lunar calendar (see p.61 for dates). In the north, notably in Kano and Katsina, these occasions often climax with spectacular "durbar" cavalry displays.

Traditional festivals

Ekpe festival (three days in Jan). Harvest festival and general thanksgiving for surviving the year; it's a ritualistic occasion celebrated among the Oboros in the area between Umuahia and Ikot Ekpene.

Fishing festival (Feb). Argungu, near Sokoto – unfortunately this has been cancelled for the last few years, though there's a smaller one in Gorgoram, which is less subject to cancellation.

Pategi Regatta (Feb & March). A regatta held every other year at Pategi, the big crossing point on the Niger, 100km downstream from Jebba (70km from Ilorin). This is one of the country's best-known events, and includes horse racing, swimming, dancing and music.

Egungun (usually April). A whole host of Yoruba ancestor festivals. Those at Ibadan, Badagry (near Lagos) and Okene (on the A2 between Benin City and Lokoja) draw huge crowds. There are masquerades and sporting events accompanied by exhilarating dancing and drumming.

Ikeji Izuogu (usually April). A five-day yam festival celebrated by the Arondizuogu people in parts of Imo State, for religious worship, thanksgiving, census and family reunion.

Ogun (June–Aug). Yoruba festival in honour of the god of iron, with singing, dancing and drumming. Held in numerous towns of the region.

Oshun (Aug/Sept). Festival in honour of the river goddess and guardian spirit of the people of Oshogbo. Another well-known celebration, but much of the week-long event is considered too sacred to be shared with visitors.

Sekiapu (Oct). Masquerades, regattas and a great deal of merriment in River and Cross River states.

Igue (Dec). Procession of the Oba of Benin. The ensuing celebration lasts several days and includes traditional dancing and a lot of drinking and eating.

Ofala (Dec). Festival in Onitsha and other towns along the Niger to honour the traditional ruler, who appears before his people.

Entertainment and sport

Nigeria has a thriving and complex cultural scene. Music, of course, is a massive industry, but cinema is blighted by financial incapacity, despite a plethora of straight-to-video releases. Theatre is lively and inventive and now benefiting from cross-fertilization with TV. In sports, soccer and athletics are the big crowd-pullers.

Music

Nigeria is one of the two or three big hubs of African music. The industry is well developed here, with numerous recording studios and pressing plants and, in spite of recession and poverty, a huge home market. The country also has a large enough population to sustain artists who sing in regional languages and experiment with indigenous styles. Three main **styles** of modern music have developed, *juju*, highlife and *fuji*, drawing from traditional sources and outside influences. Both *juju* and *fuji* are almost entirely sung in local languages, principally Yoruba. For more on Nigerian musical styles, and recommended CDs, see p.1026.

In Lagos, you can hear all the styles and stand a good chance of seeing international stars – Femi Kuti (son of Fela Kuti), King Sunny Ade, Victor Uwaifo, Sonny Okosun, Victor Olaiya – at any of three dozen or so clubs and hotel dancefloors. You can also be lucky enough to catch a big-name act in other cities around the country, especially in the south (Ibadan, Benin, Enugu, Port Harcourt or Calabar).

Cinema

Nigeria's first feature film was *Kongi's Harvest* (1970), directed by **Francis Oladele**. His next production, *Bullfrog in the Sun* (1972), was adapted from Chinua Achebe's novels *Things Fall Apart* and *No Longer at Ease*, and never properly distributed in Nigeria because of its politically sensitive subject matter. Such troubles have hit other films too. **Eddie Ugbomah** had great success with *The Rise and Fall of Dr Oyenusi* (1977), the true story of a Lagos gangster, and *The Mask* (1979), about a Nigerian secret agent sent to Britain to get back a stolen Benin mask. He even got away with *The Death of a Black President* (1983), covering events leading up to Murtala Muhammed's assassination, but his *Great Attempt* (1990) and *Ha, Yoruba* (1995) were both banned for political reasons.

West Africa's most prolific film-maker is **Ola Balogun**. He was behind the first Yoruba feature film, *Ajani Ogun*, in 1976, with stage actor Ade Folayan. Balogun secured his reputation abroad with films like *Cry Freedom* (1981) and *Money Power* (1982). Other important Nigerian directors include the late **Hubert Ogunde**, whose films, such as *Aiye* (1980; with Ola Balogun) and its sequel *Jaiyesinmi* (1983), often dealt with witchcraft and tradition.

Today, however, cinemas in Nigeria are in retreat – in Lagos most have been converted into charismatic churches. But if cinemagoing has dwindled, the film industry is more prolific than ever. The reason is the shift to video **"home movies"** largely sparked off by the success of **Christian Onu**'s 1992 Igbo-language witchcraft flick, *Living in Bondage*. As in Ghana, films shot and released on video for home viewing are now the norm in Nigeria, and hundreds are made every year, especially in the Lagos suburb of Surulere – dubbed "Nollywood". The majority are very low-budget and shot in Yoruba – Igbo and English releases tend to be higher-budget and aim for exportability. Among the new breed of directors, **Chico Ejiro** is Nigeria's "Mr Prolific", with over eighty video movies to his name, including the 2000 hit *Outkast* and its sequel *Outkast 2*, both among a slew of flicks that have been in hot water with Nigeria's board of censors for allegedly promoting "immorality".

Theatre

Nigeria has a 400-year-old theatrical tradition, with the **Yoruba language** as its outstanding vehicle. **Alarinjo Theatre**, originally the court entertainment of sixteenth-century Oyo, spread from city to city once the rulers allowed it to become a popular art form. By the nineteenth century, it was a major cultural influence, but waned with the penetration of Christianity, only to resurge again in the 1940s, when players performed biblical scenes before church congregations.

The most famous names in the travelling theatre genre were **Duro Lapido**, **Kola Ogunmola** and **Hubert Ogunde**; they gave voice to the changing social and cultural scene in southern Nigeria, right through the pre-independence era and successive federal governments since. You may be lucky and catch one of the noisy, half-improvised productions, though these days many groups are more involved with making their own films, which are popular well beyond southwest Nigeria.

English-language drama groups are mostly attached to the universities, don't attract any state or federal support and inevitably don't have a mass audience. **Wole Soyinka**, **John Pepper Clark**, **Femi Osofisan**, **Ola Rotimi** and **Bode Osanyin** are some of Nigeria's best-known playwrights. In Lagos, the **PEC Repertory Theatre** in George V Street (round the corner from the Onikan National Museum) is home to Nigeria's first full-time professional rep group, established by John Pepper Clark in 1992.

Football

Nigeria's soccer skills are highly respected in Africa. The national side – nicknamed **Super Eagles** – have now qualified for the finals of two World Cups in succession, getting through to the second round in 1998, though in 2002 they failed to make it past the group stage. The Super Eagles last won the African Cup of Nations in 1994, losing the final on penalties to Cameroon in 2000, when it was played in Nigeria.

At the time of writing, several of the Eagles' star players boot the ball for English clubs: striker **Nwankwo Kanu** for Arsenal, left back **Celestine Babayaro** for Chelsea, centre back **Joseph Yobo** for Everton and winger **Finidi George** for Ipswich. Other stars include the maverick midfielder **Augustine "Jay Jay" Okocha**, who plays for the French club Paris St Germain, and **Okechukwu Alozie Uche**, nicknamed the "Gentle Giant", a defender with Poland's Wisla Krakow.

Clubs currently in the ascendant in the Nigerian league include **Enugu Rangers**, and **Enyiba** of Aba, whose matches are often attended by enormous crowds. Nigeria's female team won the African Championship in 1998. Other top clubs are named after the companies that sponsor them: Lagos's main club, for example, after construction firm Julius Berger, and Benin City's after Bendel Insurance.

Crime and personal safety

Nigeria's dreadful reputation for trouble is exaggerated, but security is not something to take lightly in Lagos and other large cities. Lagos gangs are active and well organized. Even more disturbing is the huge number of handguns and other weapons in private possession and the implication of some police in criminal activities. Despite mandatory death sentences for armed robbery, burglaries are extremely common and night-watchmen are often killed.

But visitors, even long-term ones, are rarely at risk. Though outlaws may "control" entire neighbourhoods, you're most unlikely ever to see one, or anyone out of uniform carrying a gun. Leave valuables behind when you go out, and you're likely to be fine. Be alert, not paranoid.

You're unlikely to get yourself into real trouble in Nigeria unless you cross someone with serious influence. There are a lot of **drugs** floating around Lagos, however, and if you become involved you could easily find yourself in deep water. **Marijuana** (*igbo* or "wee-wee") is cultivated in the south – especially Delta State – and commonly smoked.

It became popular in the army during the civil war but its use is officially considered a serious offence. The Indian Hemp Decree of 1966 provides for ten-year jail sentences for smokers and the death sentence for cultivation or import. Lorry drivers have long used amphetamines, but Lagos's pivotal position in the worldwide transport of **hard drugs** in the 1980s and 1990s brought heroin and cocaine, plus accompanying misery and violence, onto the domestic market. Stay well clear.

In the north, sectarian conflict between Christians and Muslims rarely entangles foreigners, but it's always worth keeping an ear to the ground for troublespots and avoiding them. Ethnic conflict between Tivs and Jukuns in Plateau State occasionally erupts into violence too, but the main flashpoint currently is in the **Delta area** (Delta, Rivers and Bayelsa states – see p.1078), where resentment of multinational oil companies may be directed at foreigners if they are mistaken for company employees.

Women's issues

Flirtatious sexual harassment may occur in clubs and at parties, but not on the street. In the north of the country, it is a good idea to **dress "modestly"** (covering arms and legs for example, and wearing baggy rather than tight clothing).

In a country where the change from traditional to urban-industrial values is taking place remarkably quickly, women have achieved larger real gains here than elsewhere in West Africa. But while they occupy positions in business, government and increasingly in the universities, there's still a lot of ground to cover. Two groups – the National Committee for Women and Development, formed in the early 1980s, and the National Council of Women Societies, twenty years older (PO Box 3063, Tafawa Balewa Square Complex, Lagos; ☎01/263 1637) – aim to fight for more equitable integration in all spheres. A radical alternative to NCWS, Women in Nigeria (WIN), was founded in 1985 in the male bastion of Zaria, and now has groups nationwide. Finally, the Federation of Muslim

Women (FOMWAN; @www.ifh.org.uk/fomwan.html) is a non-political grouping of local associations working for the welfare of Muslim women, particularly in the field of sex- and childbirth-related healthcare.

Directory

Airport departure tax None.

Crafts Nigeria has a fantastic wealth of things worth acquiring, both utilitarian and aesthetic. Jewellery (including the antique, multicoloured glass trading beads that are now getting expensive), leatherware, carved calabashes, bronze figures made with the lost-wax method, hand-woven cloth and woodcarvings are the most obvious. Regrettably, you're likely to be offered ivory from time to time and various other animal products, including lizard-, snake- and crocodile-skin bags and belts. Possibly the best value and longest-lasting interest is to be had from musical instruments, which you'll find if you look beyond the souvenir stands at the big hotels. Talking drums – the expressive *iyaalu* tension drums which so unerringly imitate the Yoruba voice – are particularly worth looking out for.

Electricity Nigeria mainly uses three-square-pin plugs and sockets like Britain and Ireland. Adaptors that will take other plugs are widely available.

Emergencies The police emergency number is ☎199, but help doesn't always come in a hurry if you run into trouble.

Gay life Being gay in Nigeria is not easy, but there is a community, with its own advocacy group, Gentlemen Alliance, that is attempting to overturn centuries of ignorance about gay issues. AIDS awareness campaigning is important, but their priority is to educate the public at large about the existence of gays in every walk of life in Nigeria, and to overcome the view that homosexuality is an imported phenomenon.

Photography Although no permit is required, photography is something the military, the police and security agents are extremely touchy about. Be particularly careful around public buildings, including mosques, palaces, offices and railway stations. Photographing people in traditional costume, at country markets and the like, is likely to incur wrath among interfering types who may report you. On the other hand, many Nigerians are flattered if they attract the attention of your lens – although some may expect a small reward for their cooperation. On departure at land borders, you may be quizzed by the police about photographs, although they may accept your word that you haven't taken any. Remove film from your camera, and repack it, as a precaution, before the border. If you fly out, there's no problem.

Universities Nigeria has far more universities and colleges than all the other countries in West Africa put together, including the University of Lagos (UNILAG) and the University of Ibadan (UI), the nation's first, founded in 1948. There are still some expat visiting scholars and teachers, but you'll more often find Nigerian "profs" who have spent some time abroad. Nigeria also has a number of research institutes, some of which have a worldwide reputation.

Wildlife There's still a fair bit of wildlife to be seen in Nigeria, though little in the big-game league. The northern Yankari and Kainji Lake national parks contain elephants, hippos and larger antelopes, and there's the remote possibility of glimpsing lions or other big cats. There are gorillas in the thick forests of the southeast, but you're most unlikely to see them. The Gashaka-Gumpti National Park covers a huge area with terrain that varies from savanna grasslands to mountain forests. There are no elephants left here, but a variety of other wildlife, including chimpanzees. The Nigerian Conservation Foundation (NCF), PO Box 74638, Victoria Island, Lagos (☎01/264 2498 ext 7903, @www.ncf-nigeria.org), is making valiant efforts to rouse Nigerians from a complacent attitude to the wildlife heritage. One positive sign is the creation – following lobbying by environmental groups – of the Cross River National Park, comprising rainforest and mountain forest reserves.

A brief history of Nigeria

Nigerian history is the most complex and also one of the most ancient in West Africa. The earliest indications of the use of iron in the region come from the **Nok culture** (named after the Jos plateau village where much of the evidence was found) and date back to 300 BC. For reasons unknown, this civilization faded, and the next discoveries date from over a millennium later. The development, by the ninth century, of mineral wealth in the Yoruba and Igbo regions of the south, led to long-lasting and sophisticated political structures. In the north, kingdoms arose at much the same time – first the **Bornu empire** in the ninth century, then, not long afterwards, the **Hausa city-states** – and they became powerful stations on the trans-Saharan caravan routes, supplying many of the exotic requirements of medieval Europe.

The **slave trade** and, much later, **colonial invasion**, wreaked havoc on these indigenous states, as well as on the weaker, stateless communities living among them. Detailed coverage of pre-colonial history is included on a regional basis throughout the main guide section of this chapter.

Since the end of the nineteenth century, the **colonial protectorates**, and then the **federation** of modern Nigerian states, have been the setting for a panoply of events and characters set against a background of poverty, booming population and almost continual crisis. A substantial and expanding literature exists on the history, sociology and political science of Nigeria (see p.1030); the following summary is only the simplest historical framework, picking out the most salient features of Nigeria's history.

The arrival of Europeans

The **Portuguese** were the first Europeans to reach the Benin Gulf, in 1472, and within a short time they had made contact with the kingdom of **Benin**. Trade soon began, initially centred on pepper, ivory and other exotic goods. It was not until the second half of the seventeenth century, when the Americas had been widely colonized and plantations needed increasing supplies of labour, that the focus shifted to slaves.

The early Europeans had few permanent forts or settlements, basing themselves instead on offshore "hulks" near the ports. By the 1660s, these permanently moored ships were highly developed, sparking off an explosion of competitive slave-trading at ports like **Lagos**, **Warri**, **Calabar** and **Bonny**. Much of the driving force behind the trade, which was exploited by local chiefs, came from the insecurity of a West African arms race for the latest European muskets and cannon. In exchange for weaponry, the French and British, who had supplanted the Portuguese and Brazilians by the eighteenth century, were scarcely interested in buying anything except slaves.

The colonial carve-up

At the beginning of the nineteenth century, things appeared to change, as the newly republican **French** sent warships to the southeast Nigerian coast to break up the slave trade. To French cries of *"Liberté, Egalité, Fraternité"*, the British added their own hollow "Christianity, Commerce and Civilization". In fact, slaves no longer made economic sense; instead, in the wake of the European industrial revolution, **markets** were needed for manufactured goods and there was a massive demand for supplies of raw materials – cotton, sugar and the rest.

In 1851, the British shelled Lagos, ostensibly to quicken the demise of the slave trade, in practice to impose a puppet regime and improve the newly important palm-oil trade. The slave trade went underground, and slavers hid out in the lagoons around Lagos from where they would sneak out their cargo to Brazil, which was still an importer. Meanwhile the British seized Lagos Island in 1861 – which then became Lagos Colony, the first particle of Nigeria.

After the European Powers' **Berlin Conference** of 1885, the London-based **Royal Niger Company** was granted exclusive trading rights in the Niger River basin. With the Germans expanding to the east, and the French to the north and west, the British government took over the RNC in 1899 and began pushing it in all directions.

By 1900, they'd succeeded in drawing borders around a vast region of diverse peoples, who found themselves under the ultimate authority of northern and southern protectorates. In 1914 a federation was formed – in preference to a united colony – and named **Nigeria**, a term coined by Flora Shaw, *Times* correspondent and wife of the British colonial commander Lord Lugard.

Indirect rule

From the beginning, Nigeria was an ill-matched association and it was clear that conflict would arise between the conservative, largely Muslim and feudal **north**, and the more outward-looking **south**, with its Christian missions and, in the southeast, lack of rigid social hierarchies. At the very least, problems would be caused by the new territory's southward-looking orientation, away from the old Saharan routes and towards the ports and European trade.

The British, however, pressed ahead with their system of **"indirect rule"**, which in the **north** worked easily enough, to the benefit of both the Hausa–Fulani emirs (who carried on much as before) and the British administration. Lord Lugard simply took over the role of regional overlord from the Sultan of Sokoto, whose functions were perforce purely religious and ceremonial.

But indirect rule was a disaster in the **southeast**, where decisions and judicial processes were traditionally applied by consent among groups of senior men. In **Igboland**, the "Warrant Chiefs" commissioned by the British had no mandate for their authority, and on the contrary were usually independent-minded status-seekers who had acquired a mission education.

In **Yorubaland**, another variation was imposed. The British held Yoruba traditional rulers, with British "advisors", accountable for their decisions. But the British had failed to understand the fabric of Yoruba politics and perceived in their centralized **government of obas** and the traditional ceremonial-executive titles of the **Alafin of Oyo** and the **Oni of Ife**, simple dictatorships somewhat akin to the emirates of the north. Disregarding the fact that the Yoruba offices were posts given to selected senior men by others of high rank, Lugard tried to control the selection of pliant chiefs by men who, again, had no mandate to enforce his requirements. And he actively connived to empower those Yoruba elements who posed least threat to white prestige, to turn the clock back, as far as possible, to his own avowedly racist vision of an Africa untainted by progress.

While British rule led to internal schisms in Yorubaland, the region benefited from the fastest input of technology and **modern infrastructure**. There was electricity in Lagos by 1898, bridges between the islands and a rail link with Ibadan by 1900, all of which was to prove another source of division for north and south to deal with after independence.

The road to independence

Nigerians became involved in the political process relatively early, by the standards of other African colonies. In 1923, the first Africans, led by **Herbert Macaulay** – whose father, born in

Sierra Leone, was an *aku* (a Yoruba descended from freed slaves) – were elected to a legislative advisory council in Lagos. But local parties really only developed after the experience of World War II, when Nigerians returned from fighting for European ideals like "self-determination" and "liberty".

In 1944, the **National Council for Nigeria and the Cameroons** was formed by Herbert Macaulay and **Dr Nnamdi Azikwe**, an Igbo. Four years later, **Chief Obafemi Awolowo**, a Yoruba, founded a second party, the **Action Group**. By the end of the decade, the northerners also had their own party, the **Northern People's Congress**, with **Tafawa Balewa** at its head.

Predictably, these three parties came to represent **regional interests** – the NPC for the north, the NCNC for the east, and the AG for the west. As they jockeyed for position to rule an independent nation, the parties agreed on nothing, delaying reform in the process. In a dispute over the date for self-rule, suspicious northerners walked out of the colonial assembly in 1953, and bloody **riots in Kano** followed. Members from each region felt sure the other two were conspiring to dominate, and there was talk of dividing the country into several smaller political units in an effort to relieve the tension. The British argued such a measure would only stall independence further, an argument in which they were supported by the northern region, which had to have a friendly route to the sea.

Finally, in 1957, it was decided the nation would be formed of the three rival regions. **Tafawa Balewa** became the head of the new central government and Nigeria gained independence on October 1, 1960.

Independence: the early years

The early 1960s were characterized by an **uneasy coalition** between the north and the **southeast** against the powerful **southwest** region dominated by the Yoruba. The latter thus saw its worst fears realized and its leaders panicked when a bogus census in 1963 suggested the north had four million more inhabitants than the rest of the nation combined. The threat of Muslim domination in the political arena now seemed very real.

The southeast eventually slipped out of the coalition and Chief Awolowo raised angry cries against government tinkering with the country's structure. He was tried for treason and jailed. **Early chaos** seemed to be gaining momentum and in January 1966 the army toppled the government – killing Tafawa Balewa in the process – and set about trying to restore order.

Military rule

The new **military government** was headed by **General J. Aguiyi-Ironsi**, an Igbo. Northerners rioted in reaction to the radical early reforms that abolished the federation and imposed a unitary government dominated by Igbos. Fighting broke out within the army and, after only six months, Ironsi was killed in another **coup**, this time led by northern officers. As many as 7000 Igbos living in the north were massacred in the aftermath and up to half a million fled to the east.

But the military's new leader was different from his predecessors. **Yakubu Gowon** was a Christian northerner, a young and charismatic figure, who restored the tripartite federation and released Awolowo and other Action Group leaders of the west. But the southeast region, led by the military governor, **Lieutenant-Colonel C. Odumegwu-Ojukwu**, who rejected Gowon's leadership, pushed instead for a loose confederation.

In September 1966, elements of the northern army began the systematic **killing of Igbos** who had remained in the north. Official reports placed the deaths at 5000, though Igbos claimed that as many as 30,000 were massacred.

The pogrom was a decisive blow to the shaky federation. High-ranking Igbo civil servants began returning from Lagos to the regional capital at Enugu and pressuring Ojukwu to secede.

National politics in the early part of 1967 were completely dominated by the question of the future of the Federal Republic. The Ghanaian government attempted to mediate between the sides and, in January 1967, leaders of the federal government met with Ojukwu in Aburi. The meetings produced no acceptable compromise; nor did subsequent government moves to appease the east with conciliatory measures and guarantees.

At the last minute, Gowon announced the **division of the federation** into twelve separate states in an attempt to undermine the overweening north and disarm his critics from the ethnic minorities, especially in the southeast, who had long sought greater autonomy. It was too late. Fearing the Igbo constituency would be pushed permanently into the margins of national politics, Ojukwu unilaterally withdrew the Eastern Region from the federation and declared the independent **Republic of Biafra** on May 30, 1967.

The Biafran War

In July 1967, Biafran troops marched into the Western Region in an attempt to surround Lagos. Federal troops responded by blockading eastern ports and by attacking Biafra from the north and west. Despite a lack of manpower and resources, Biafra scored a number of military successes in the early days of the war, but by the end of 1967, the conflict had degenerated into a brutal **war of attrition**. Fighting was vicious and confused. Most of the major towns changed hands several times. Federal forces captured a number of coastal towns, reducing Biafra to an enclave in the Igbo heartland. Federal military atrocities, of which many were reported, further convinced the Igbos that they were engaged in an all-out war for survival.

Biafra gained considerable sympathy in the international press: for the first time, public opinion in the rich world was mobilized against Third World poverty. Yet few countries gave official recognition to Biafra, and French military and technical aid seemed suspiciously self-interested. The war dragged on for three years, claiming the lives of at least 100,000 soldiers, but many more Igbo civilians, of whom between half a million and two million are estimated to have perished as a result of the government's policy of **blockade and starvation**. Supported by British aid and Soviet arms, the Federal government finally captured the last rebel-held town of Owerri and quelled the rebellion in December 1969. Much of the southeast was ravaged.

Reconstruction

The gaping wounds of the war appeared to heal with remarkable speed. Gowon, who was still in power after four years, was careful not to humiliate the defeated and bereaved easterners or exclude them from the new federation. In fact, he offered an **amnesty** to all who had fought on the Biafran side, and vowed to rebuild the east while furthering the economic development of the entire country.

Reconstruction didn't take place overnight, but it is remarkable today how little evidence of the war remains, even in cities that were virtually destroyed. Gowon was aided in the early days of reconciliation by **oil revenues** that flooded into the coffers in the early 1970s, as Nigeria became one of the world's ten largest producers. But as blatant corruption became a national issue, and Gowon began dragging his feet on promises of a return to civilian rule and devoting most of his energies to international image-building, he was ousted, after nine years in power, in a bloodless coup led by **General Murtala Muhammed** in July 1975.

Murtala Muhammed

Of all Nigeria's leaders, Murtala Muhammed has been without doubt the most popular. Even today, his name is referred to with a reverence not normally reserved for politicians. Another northerner with considerable charisma, he structured all his policies around the return of power to an elected leadership and devoted himself to wiping out corruption.

Shortly after coming to power, Muhammed instigated **"Operation Deadwoods"** – a policy of forced dismissal or retirement of public officials on a whole range of charges from corruption to "infirmity". In all, more than 10,000 civil servants – police officials, senior diplomats, university professors, even military officers – were relieved of their posts. Swift action was taken against embezzlement of public funds. Assets were confiscated. Appointees were sacked for reasons as simple as a conflict of interests. It was a breath of fresh air in a stagnating and counterproductive bureaucracy and brought the government huge popularity.

By the end of 1975, Muhammed had concluded the purge and announced a four-year countdown to return the country to civilian rule. He had come to be regarded as a politician who made promises and kept them, and drew attention to the future and away from the divisive tragedy of the past. Nigerians felt they were leaders in a liberalizing movement that would sweep the continent and break the cycle of totalitarianism in Africa.

It's difficult to know if posterity would have been so kind to Muhammed had he lived to see his programmes carried out. After only six months of reshaping the country he was assassinated by disgruntled members of the military, shot while his car was in a Lagos traffic jam.

The Second Republic

The counter-coup was effective only in eliminating Muhammed, for the plotters were rounded up and with the help of Major General Ibrahim Babangida, was smoothly transferred to Muhammed's chief of staff, **Olusegun Obasanjo**, a Christian Yoruba. Obasanjo pledged to adhere to Muhammed's schedule for the return to civilian government and continued reshaping the civil service. A new constitution, based on that of the USA, was drawn up, and political parties were legalized in September 1978.

Five **political parties** were finally approved, but four were headed by familiar old names, had vague right-of-centre programmes and seemed to indicate the persistence of regional divisions. **Awolowo** and **Azikwe** (by then in their 70s) headed parties largely representing the west and the east respectively, or at least their personal power bases in those regions – the Unity Party of Nigeria and the Greater National People's Party. The National People's Party, from which the GNPP was a breakaway group, was led by a northern businessman, **Alhaji Waziri Ibrahim**. The National Party of Nigeria, based in Kaduna and led by **Alhaji Shehu Shagari**, claimed to cut across regional loyalties but was essentially the old NPC northern party, controlled as ever by the Fulani oligarchy. Shagari, himself a Fulani from a leading northern family, had been a member of the first civilian government and had served under Gowon's military regime. Lastly, in opposition to the NPN, another northern party had also been formed – the People's Redemption Party. Led by **Alhaji Aminu Kano**, it had radical socialist leanings and was explicitly committed to the cause of inter-ethnic co-operation.

In the complicated elections that spread over six weeks in 1979, all the parties achieved some representation, but Shagari won the all-important **presidential election**. He rode out his first term in Nigeria's new "Second Republic" on a wave of genuine popularity and public relief that the long period of military rule was over. But the new president didn't survive long untarnished. **Crackdowns on the press** – which had begun reporting government corruption, and even daring to point fingers at Shagari and his Kaduna clique – clearly signalled his insecurity, and he faced serious challenges from other northern parties and eastern allies in his unstable coalition.

The **economy**, too, was slipping badly. The oil boom had peaked in 1980. In December of that year serious **riots** broke out in Kano, prompted by the popular "jihadist" teachings and calls for social justice of Mai Tatsine. As foreign currency reserves dwindled and the external debt skyrocketed, the standard of living for most Nigerians rapidly declined, while government officials, cabinet ministers and the president himself made fortunes, indulging in what came to be known as "squandermania". Further, serious **riots in Maiduguri**, in October 1982, were dismissed by Shagari as "religious agitation" and, in February 1983, some two million immigrant workers – from Ghana, Cameroon, Chad and Niger – were expelled as economic scapegoats.

Despite these various obstacles, Shagari managed to get elected to a second term in October 1983, a sounder win, in fact, than his first, though achieved with less than sound methods.

Another coup: a new military regime

The inevitable happened barely three months after the 1983 elections, when another northerner – **Major-General Mohammed Buhari** – staged a bloodless takeover of power and suspended the 1979 constitution. Explaining his actions, the new leader announced shortly after the takeover: "The economic mess, the corruption and unacceptable level of unemployment could not be excused on the grounds that Nigeria was a practising democracy."

Buhari announced the "voluntary retirement" of high-ranking military officers and the inspector general of the police, all of whom were implicated in financial mismanagement and corrupt practices on a gigantic scale. Prominent members of Shagari's party were arrested, as was the president. Through such moves, Buhari sought to associate his regime with the purist popularity of Murtala Muhammed. Important elder statesmen from the martyred president's administration were brought into the new government, including former head of state Obasanjo.

The attack on graft – the **"War Against Indiscipline"** – even crossed international borders. One of the most wanted offenders was the former transport minister **Alhaji Umaru Dikko**, who was living in luxurious exile in London, from where he openly criticized the new government. In one of the more bizarre instances of abuse of diplomatic privilege, Dikko was kidnapped, drugged and bundled into a crate, ready to be shipped off as diplomatic baggage from Gatwick airport. The plot was only aborted when British customs officials queried the contents of the crate. Buhari's government quickly denied any responsibility, although the Nigerian High Commission was strongly implicated in the abduction. Diplomatic relations between the UK and Nigeria nearly broke over the incident.

Buhari, however, seemed serious in his efforts to wipe out corruption, and as a result was initially quite popular with people fed up with government abuse. But it soon became apparent that members of Shagari's Kaduna clique were not prominent among those convicted on corruption charges. In addition to the accusation of partiality, it was not long before Buhari himself was gaining a reputation as an unbending **autocrat**. As those accused of corruption were given sentences as long as 72 years, Buhari arrested many of his regime's critics and suppressed the Nigerian media in ways Shagari had not dared. On the discovery of an alleged coup plot in 1984, he swiftly executed a group of some forty soldiers. And two government decrees, reflecting the new hard line, proved extremely unpopular with the masses. The first, known as Decree 2, allowed for detention without trial of citizens regarded as a threat to the state. Decree 4 imposed press controls by insisting journalists verify the "truth" of their reporting.

Even more unpopular were **austerity measures** adopted by Buhari in 1984 as he sought to remedy the country's growing economic problems. Strong opposition to his rule grew as resulting price increases and shortages of consumer goods jolted the nation – especially its poorer citizens. Buhari tried to deflect criticism, as Shagari had done, by blaming the country's economic woes on foreign workers robbing Nigerians of jobs. **Mass expulsions of immigrants** were instigated and, in May 1985, up to a million foreigners – again many of them Ghanaian – were shipped out in chaotic conditions.

None of Buhari's drastic measures worked, partly because there was virtually no popular support for the man behind them and principally because the naira was overvalued and worthless. A new coup was orchestrated, in August 1985, by close associates of Buhari in the Supreme Military Council, led by army chief of staff **Major-General Ibrahim Babangida**, born in Minna in Niger State, but brought up in Kano.

The "period of transition": Ibrahim Babangida

Within a short time of taking office, **Babangida** and his new Armed Forces Ruling Council had released many of the political prisoners from Nigerian jails and a new sense of freedom began to be felt. Babangida began preparing the country once again for national elections. Such political moves went down well at home, though his economic policies were tough and unyielding. Shortly after taking power, he

declared an **economic state of emergency** and, in 1985, broke off loan negotiations with the IMF – a move that met with popular nationalistic support. But enthusiasm waned when the president imposed austerity measures of his own. He devalued the naira fourfold in the hope of attracting investors, and began privatizing unprofitable public enterprises and lifting government subsidies, notably on petrol.

Periodic **demonstrations and strikes** resulted, and, although conflict tended to be sparked by economic policies, **ethnic and religious tensions** were never far away. In 1986, Babangida announced that Nigeria had joined the Organization of the Islamic Conference. Despite stressing this had been done for cultural and religious reasons – and not political ones – non-Muslim southerners feared that the government and its northern power base were trying to impose Islamic rule on the whole country. There were campus protests and a number of deaths in northern universities in 1986 and, in 1987, **religious riots** broke out between Muslims and Christians in Kaduna State, leading to the deaths of dozens of people, the arrest of over a thousand and the banning of religious organizations at schools and universities.

Adding to the political frustration, Babangida thrice **postponed elections** between 1990 and 1992, leaving many to question if he ever intended to step down. In April 1990, a group of junior, Christian, officers attempted a coup, which was quickly put down but resulted in 300 deaths. Over the next two years, ethnic-religious clashes intensified. In April 1991, Muslim demonstrations erupted in Katsina, leading to violence and many deaths. In Bauchi, 130 people were killed when Christians slaughtered pigs in a market shared by Muslims. Later in the year, 300 people died in Kano, following demonstrations provoked by a touring Christian preacher.

Babangida's solution to the regional problem was to create **nine new states** in 1991, arguing they would stimulate stability and development while ensuring more equitable representation of ethnic minorities. Despite the measures, it seemed ethnic enmities remained the driving force of Nigerian politics. In February 1992, fighting broke out in Kaduna State between Hausa Muslims and Kataf Christians. In the east, a land dispute between the Tiv and Jukun peoples resulted in an estimated 5000 deaths.

The deteriorating economy put a further strain on Babangida's government. By mid-1992, **inflation** was already soaring at 50 percent and widespread rioting broke out in Lagos over a sharp increase in transport fares. There were a number of reported deaths as demonstrators, who demanded the government resign, were brutally dispersed by security forces. More protests ensued after prominent human-rights activists, including Dr Beko Ransome-Kuti (brother of musician Fela Kuti) and Chief Fani Fawehinmi were arrested for accusing the government of instigating the riots so as to delay elections. In June, the Academic Staff of Nigerian Universities called a nationwide strike in a wage dispute. Despite his stated commitment to collective bargaining, Babangida banned the union and, with it, the National Association of Nigerian Students. Most of the nation's thirty universities closed as a result.

The mood of the country was therefore downbeat as Nigerians prepared for **National Assembly elections** in July 1992. Despite the vast sums of money spent on the campaign, the election sparked little excitement among voters. Babangida had insisted on a **two-party system** and created the Social Democratic Party and the National Republican Convention in order to prevent the rise of regional, ethnic or religious interest groups. But Nigerian commentators liked to call them the "Yes" party and the "Yes Sir" party. The fact that the increasingly unpopular military regime had created, funded and written the platforms of both SDP and NRC led to widespread **voter apathy**. Despite slick, state-financed media blitzes, neither party challenged the government's handling of issues such as inflation or ethnic tension. Serious opposition seemed only to come from the nation's human-rights organizations, students and lawyers.

Although the SDP won majorities in both the House of Representatives and the Senate, the Armed Forces Ruling Council decided in mid-July that the legislature would not be inaugurated until after a new civilian president was sworn in.

Failed elections

When the **presidential elections** finally rolled around in June 1993, there were few signs of voter enthusiasm. The two candidates that emerged – **Moshood Abiola** of the SDP and **Bashir Tofa** of the NRC – stood out more for their abilities to amass huge fortunes than for any record of public service. Cynicism ran high among voters who found it hard to digest promises of prosperity in a country where annual per capita income had fallen from $1000 to $290 in the ten years preceding the elections.

The results, however, surprised observers. Abiola – a Muslim from the mainly Christian Yoruba country of the southwest – won an apparently clear victory with 58 percent of the vote. Winning in several northern states, he appeared to seal a mandate that cut across ethnic lines. Marring this triumph was a deadlock created by legal wrangling over the election results. The judiciary's partisan colouration in giving judgements on the elections created an atmosphere of suspicion between the north and south. On June 23, Babangida stepped in and annulled the elections.

Human-rights organizations immediately called for a campaign of civil disobedience. Mass **pro-democracy demonstrations** led to more violence and brought Lagos and much of the southwest to a standstill. Abiola declared himself winner on June 24, stating in a national broadcast, "From now on, the struggle in Nigeria is between the people and a small clique in the military determined to cling to power." But the standoff between civilians and the military also aroused old regional divisions: southerners remained convinced the military would never accept a southern president.

Babangida, who had started his presidential career as a liberal reformer, seemed, after the elections, ominously entrenched and intolerant of dissent. As troops put down anti-government riots in Lagos, the military threatened the death sentence for anyone whose words or deeds might undermine "the fabric of the nation" and shut down critical newspapers. Abiola fled the country.

Babangida steps down

But in August 1993, Babangida unexpectedly stepped aside as president and commander-in-chief of the armed forces. He insisted, however, that an **interim government** backed by decree would be the most favourable alternative to military rule and appointed **Ernest Shonekan** – former chairman of the United African Company, Nigeria's largest conglomerate – to lead the country until the next elections were held.

Abiola promptly returned from abroad, where he had been trying to rally foreign support for his claims to the presidency. But within weeks of taking over as head of state, Shonekan seemed to have swung public opinion behind himself. Former presidents **Nnamdi Azikwe** and **Olusegun Obasanjo** supported the interim government and the unions called off strikes. Meanwhile, Abiola isolated himself from the masses with his calls for an "economic blockade" of Nigeria and warnings of "a bloodbath" were he not sworn in. Preferring to stay in Lagos rather than tour the country to rally support, he increasingly became associated with a Yoruba, rather than a national cause.

But neither was Shonekan a credible figure. Ardent democrats labelled him a puppet of the military. Shonekan's ultimate downfall, however, was provoked when he tried to cut fuel subsidies in late 1993. As the price of petrol increased sixfold, rioting again broke out in Lagos and a general strike threatened economic devastation.

Military rule: the Abacha government

In November 1993, **General Sani Abacha**, who had been instrumental in the coups that toppled Shagari and Buhari, seized power – once again, the military stepped in "to save the nation from chaos". Abacha quickly set about purging the military of former Babangida loyalists, and dissolved all political parties and elected institutions. By then, politically numbed Nigerians didn't seem much worried that elected governors were replaced by military appointees and that the National Assembly ceded authority to a mainly military legislative council.

By mid-1994, Abacha was already being attacked from all sides. Civil-liberties groups, students and unions, with the support of retired generals like Olusegun Obasanjo, publicly urged him to step down. Although political parties were banned, **political organizations** were formed and began turning up the heat. Abacha could count only on northerners for support, and even there he was losing ground. The Sultan of Sokoto and other powerbrokers, from Katsina and Maiduguri, criticized the military's policy, leaving the **Emir of Kano** as Abacha's only ardent supporter.

The **Campaign for Democracy** became influential, having gained credibility by organizing many of the demonstrations that led to Babangida's downfall. Meanwhile, the **National Democratic Coalition** (Nadeco) campaigned for a return to a civilian government headed by Abiola, and grew into a broad-based movement with support in the north as well as the south. On the first anniversary of the elections, Abiola was persuaded to declare himself president. He was promptly arrested.

Abacha never fared well in terms of **international relations**; Nigeria effectively was a pariah state throughout his rule. Western nations deplored the banning of parties, arbitrary detention of opposition members and tight controls on the press. Officially, it was these policies that provoked **economic sanctions** against Nigeria, although the West was equally displeased with Abacha's resistance to IMF pressure to impose a tougher economic policy, the country's continued refusal to address the question of its massive debt and the new administration's tougher terms for drilling rights to Nigeria's oil reserves. The Commonwealth suspended Nigeria's membership, the US government "decertified" Nigeria, making the country ineligible for aid or for US support credits from the IMF, and Canada withdrew its diplomatic representation in Lagos. Some leaders – Nelson Mandela in particular – pushed for harder sanctions, including an oil blockade.

Amid the political turmoil, the economy provided no good news for Abacha. A crisis in the oil industry had been triggered by a fall in world market prices, by repeated strikes and by gross corruption. Billions of dollars were stolen from the country's oil earnings between 1995 and 1998. Nigerians had few illusions about the level of **government theft**, but seemed more angered than during past regimes, when grand building projects and government spending at least had a trickle-down effect.

The Ogoni affair (see box, p.1078) did not encourage **foreign investors** and led to European Union sanctions. During Abacha's tenure Nigeria was ranked the world's third riskiest location for business investment, after Iraq and Russia, with (to add to its unenviable human-rights record) a well-established reputation for perpetrating fraud against unwary foreign investors.

Throughout Abacha's tenure, revelations of coup plots and reports of bombings near the army barracks in Abuja led to the arrest of numerous officers, including high-ranking generals whom Abacha had considered loyal. Hundreds of dissenters languished in jail – including the 24 men convicted of a supposed coup attempt in March 1995, one of whom was former head of state Olusegun **Obasanjo**. Former secretary to Ibrahim Babangida, **Olu Falae**, joined him in jail two years later on charges of "conspiring to cause explosions".

In June 1995, the exiled Nobel laureate **Wole Soyinka** and others announced the formation of a **National Liberation Council** (NLC) of seventeen prominent opposition leaders. The NLC aimed to form a government-in-exile to campaign for the removal of the Abacha regime. Like many before him, Soyinka was charged *in absentia* for treason and, more than ever, was forced to militate in exile. Shortly thereafter, **Kudirat Abiola**, the wife of the imprisoned victor of the last presidential election and an outspoken critic of the administration, was murdered by unidentified assailants. The nation saw the hand of the government behind the assault and rioting broke out, above all in Abiola's Yoruba homeland. Students were especially vociferous and the University of Ibadan was closed by government troops.

Unrest was not limited to the south. In late 1996, the arrest of the local leader of Kaduna led to Muslim demonstrations that were violently quelled by the army. A year later, **Shehu Musa Yar Adua**, a respected northern politician who had been deputy head of state under Obasanjo, died mysteriously in jail, provoking thousands of supporters to riot in Katsina, calling for Abacha to step down. In the Delta Region, early 1997 saw an escalation of violence between the Ijo and Itsekiri.

Disruption in petroleum production, along with gross mismanagement and the siphoning of billions of dollars into the pockets of the generals, led to a national **fuel shortage** that, by 1998, effectively suspended the transport system in much of the country. To stave off a deepening crisis, Abacha, as head of the world's sixth largest crude-oil producer, was forced to begin importing oil. As if that wasn't embarrassment enough, the country's poverty soared to its highest level since independence.

In 1996, Abacha made some gestures at **reform**, when he announced the creation of five new parties and a calendar for the return to civil rule by 1998. But most of the country's civilian opposition was already in jail, and the parties that had been granted official status by the national electoral commission were all seen as being loyal to Abacha. At the same time, the government talked of sweeping economic reforms that included the sale of state assets, even in the oil and gas sector, the elimination of the preferential exchange rate for government ministries and a campaign against corruption. These plans, intended for the ears of the IMF, the World Bank and foreign investors, were shot down by the military Provisional Ruling Council, who feared a short-term hike in unemployment and a long-term setback to their system of political patronage.

Just months before the scheduled elections, in June 1998, Abacha died of a **heart attack**. When Nigeria radio announced the general's passing, critics and opponents of the regime poured into the streets of Lagos to celebrate.

Return to civilian rule

Following Abacha's death, a **transitional government** under **Abdulsalaam Abubakar** took office, promised elections the following year and released hundreds of political pris-

oners, including Obasanjo. But just days later, Nigerians were shocked and sceptical when Moshood Abiola died of an apparent heart attack in his jail cell after four years of solitary confinement, and just one day before his scheduled release. Foul play was immediately suspected and news of the death brought hundreds of youths onto the streets of Lagos where they clashed with police.

Accompanying preparations for a return to **civilian rule**, Abubakar began seeking economic reform to lift the country out of crisis. Negotiations began with the IMF for the implementation of a structural adjustment programme that included privatization and accountability – two essential ingredients for restoring the faith of creditors. In December 1998, three out of nine political parties contesting nationwide local elections gained more than five percent of the vote in 24 states, entitling them to official status and the right to present candidates in the upcoming presidential elections. They were the **People's Democratic Party** (PDP), the Alliance for Democracy (AD) and the All People's Party (APP).

The PDP – which had won 60 percent of the vote in the local elections – chose **Obasanjo** for its presidential candidate. Remembered for being the only military leader ever to hand power back to civilians, and for governing during a time of economic prosperity, Obasanjo was the frontrunner from the start (people joked that PDP stood for "Pre-Determined President"), and enjoyed broad support throughout the country. In fact, northerners were more enthusiastic about his candidacy than his fellow Yorubas, and his choice of a northern running mate gave him extra impetus in the region. **Chief Olu Falae**, an economist who represented a combined AD/APP ticket, struggled to keep pace with the PDP's campaign machine. Also a Yoruba with a northern running mate, Falae had less money and only patchy support outside his southwest stronghold. When polling took place in

March 1999, Obasanjo captured nearly two-thirds of the votes.

The president-elect didn't squander the foreign interest the elections had engendered. One of his first visits after being elected was to Sierra Leone president Ahmad Tejan Kabbah, who asked for continued Nigerian backing (Nigerian soldiers formed the backbone of the ECOMOG peacekeeping force and stayed on in Liberia until October 1999, and in Sierra Leone until April 2000). In the interval before being sworn in, Obasanjo made a global trip that covered Asia, Europe, the United States and Africa, from the Cape to Kenya. Overnight, Nigeria was an international player again.

Nigeria under Obasanjo

Abubakar dutifully turned power over to the **elected government** in May 1999, and in his last official act, banned Decree 2, the detention-without-trial law that had come to symbolize the tyranny and terror of successive military governments.

Sharia law in the northern states

Islamic religious law – known as **sharia**, Arabic for "the way" – is based on the Koran, the sayings of Muhammad, and the interpretations put on these over the centuries by Islamic jurists. Unlike Christian canonical law, it covers all aspects of life.

In the north, Muslims have long been able to settle family and civil disputes in *sharia* courts if they so wish, though criminal law was secular. In January 2000 however, the state of **Zamfara** made every Muslim who commits an offence against Islamic law within the state liable to punishment under *sharia*. Among other things, this involves amputation for theft, flogging and imprisonment for extramarital sex, and stoning to death for adultery. Gambling and alcohol are banned, and possession of a *juju* charm is a capital offence, as is worship of any god but Allah. In theory apostasy (renouncing Islam) is also punishable by death under *sharia*. The law was supported by most of Zamfara's population, well over ninety percent of whom are Muslim.

Seeing its popularity, other northern states were not far behind in implementing similar laws, and Zamfara was followed by Kano and then Kaduna, where demonstrations against the new law by members of the state's large Christian minority led to sectarian riots in which over 300 people were killed. Since then, every state north of the Niger and Benue bar Plateau State and the F.C.T. – twelve states in all – have introduced *sharia* penal codes. The first **amputation** was carried out in Zamfara in July 2000, and the following month two okada drivers were flogged for carrying female passengers – Zamfara has legislated for female-only transport, and women are not allowed to use anything else. As the state does not trust the federal police, vigilante groups have been empowered to enforce *sharia*.

In October 2001, a woman in Sokoto was sentenced to **death by stoning** for adultery. Amid a hail of worldwide condemnation, the appeal court backed down and acquitted her on a technicality. But in March 2002, a Zamfara court sentenced the then 30-year-old **Amina Lawal** to death by stoning for bearing a child out of wedlock, a sentence due to be carried out as soon as the daughter she had is weaned. President Obasanjo has stated that the sentence will not be carried out, but the court has refused to back down, and further sentences of stoning for adultery have since been passed. What the federal government will do to stop these executions remains to be seen.

Critics of the laws claim they are being used selectively to oppress women and the poor. But as Zamfara's state governor told the Lagos *Guardian*, "To be good Muslims, we have to have *sharia* to govern our lives," and most of the north's population apparently agrees with him.

In his inaugural address, Obasanjo declared his determination to "make significant changes within a year", and certainly the most extreme excesses of the military regime have been curbed. However, the tensions between north and south, and resentment of the foreign oil companies' activities in the Delta region, have both resurfaced in new forms.

In addition to the introduction of **sharia law** in some states (see opposite), **ethnic tensions** elsewhere in the country were simmering and sometimes boiling over. June 1999 saw over a hundred dead in clashes between Yorubas and Hausas in Shagamu near Lagos, followed in November by clashes leaving some fifty dead in Lagos itself, and blamed by the government on the Yoruba nationalist Oodua People's Congress (OPC). In Central Nigeria, an unrelated dispute between Tivs and Hausa-speaking Jukuns in Nassarawa State left a hundred dead. When Tivs kidnapped nineteen soldiers sent to restore order following rioting in Benue State, the army retaliated by going in mob-handed and killing some two hundred of them.

The 9/11 attacks in the USA and the subsequent American invasion of Afghanistan predictably sparked off fresh rioting between northern Muslims and Christians. In Jos, where tension between the two communities was already high, Muslim protests against the US Afghan campaign renewed intercommunal riots that had only been quelled the previous month.

The planned staging of the 2002 **Miss World** beauty pageant in Abuja caused further ructions. Various contestants pulled out in protest when a Sokoto *sharia* court passed sentence of death on 30-year-old divorcee Amina Lawal for adultery (a "crime" proven by her pregnancy), and when columnist Isioma Daniel joked in the popular daily *This Day* that the Prophet Muhammad himself would have enjoyed watching the show and probably chosen a wife from among its contestants, outraged young Muslims in Kaduna burnt down the paper's offices. They then went on a rampage against Christians that left two hundred dead and forced the pageant to relocate to London.

April 2003 saw fresh presidential elections and a number of registered political parties (far more than ever before) to contest them, most with no particular ideology or programme. On a 69 percent turnout, Obasanjo retained the presidency with 62 percent of the vote against 32 percent for his nearest rival, former military dictator Muhammad Buhari. Buhari immediately called the result "fraudulent", and certainly blatant ballot stuffing took place, though Commonwealth observers still felt the result represented the will of the voters.

The federal government and PDP state governors, many of whom are unpopular in their home states (which comprise the whole country with the exception of seven northern ANPP states), now have their work cut out for them to convince Nigerians that life is improving. **National strikes** in June 2003 were called off only after planned fifty-percent fuel price increases were cut back by the government. Meanwhile, the Independent Corrupt Practices and Related Offences Commission has been slowly looking into past misdeeds and is achieving some successes, but new corruption continues apace. And on the streets, the police seem powerless to deal with local ethnically-based **vigilante groups** which have sprung up all over in the face of lawlessness, but which frequently engage in bouts of mob-violence against other groups.

Any solution to the problems besetting Nigeria seems as remote as ever. Southerners – Yorubas nowadays as much as Igbos – increasingly feel that Nigeria should divide into its three constituent parts, an idea generally opposed by people in the north, which has a lot less in the way of natural resources and would be left economically marooned between the coast and the desert. Some have suggested that radical **decentralization** of power to the states could ease the tensions tearing the country apart, but the fact is that, great though its problems may be, Nigeria has managed to live with them for forty years so far, and can probably continue to do so for the foreseeable future.

Music

The Nigerian musical heritage extends from stately court drumming and trumpeting in the northern emirates to the work of the late **Fela Kuti** to drum out the military dictators, with LPs like *Vagabonds for Power* and *Coffin for Head of State*, to today's new wave of Christian rappers. Even if few Nigerian stars have forged successful overseas careers, and the last international label gave up trying to make money here in 1989 and quit the country, Nigeria has a well-developed music industry with numerous recording studios, and a huge market in pirated cassettes and CDs. For a quick overview of Nigerian music, try the *Rough Guide to the Music of Nigeria and Ghana* CD (World Music Network), which includes fine tracks from I.K. Dairo, Sunny Ade, Adewale Ayuba, Sir Victor Uwaifo and Chief Stephen Osita Osadebe among others.

The emirates of **Katsina** and **Kano** together with the sultanate of **Sokoto**, and to a lesser extent **Zaria** and **Bauchi**, are the major creative centres for **Hausa music**, which is surveyed on p.1119. The south of the country, however, and in particular the southwest, has by far the most musical energy, and the greatest profusion of artists and styles.

Igbo music

The Igbos have always been receptive to cultural change. This ease is reflected in their music and in the incredible variety of instruments played in Igboland. No local occasion would be complete without musicians and you should find them at any event associated with the *obi* (chief). The other major occasions are seasonal festivals, wrestling matches, a visit by a high-ranking official or the funeral of a prominent citizen.

In more traditional communities, royal music is played every day, when the **ufie** slit drum is used to wake the chief and to tell him when meals are ready. A group, known as **egwu ota**, which consists of slit-drums, drums and bells, performs when the *obi* is leaving the palace and again when he returns.

One of the most pleasing Igbo instruments is the **obo**, a thirteen-stringed raft zither, which can be heard at many a nostalgic palm-wine drinking session.

Yoruba music

Yoruba instrumental traditions are mostly based on drumming. The most popular form of traditional music today is **dundun**, played on hourglass tension drums of the same name. The usual *dundun* ensemble consists of tension drums of various sizes together with small kettledrums called **gudugudu**. The leading drum of the group is the *iyaalu* ("mother of the drums"), which talks by imitating the tone patterns of Yoruba speech. It's used to play out praise poetry, proverbs and other oral texts. Another important part of Yoruba musical life is **music theatre**, which mixes traditional music with storytelling or live drama.

Juju

The **origins** of *juju* music are not very clear, but it seems to have emerged as a Lagosian variation of Ghana's palm-wine music (see p.748). The word *juju* is thought to be a corruption of the Yoruba term *jo jo*, meaning "dance" – or may just be a dismissive epithet coined by colonial officers and retained, defensively, by its exponents.

The first records in this style started coming out in the early 1930s but it really took off just after World War II with the introduction of amplified sound. The major stars of the prewar period were **Irewolede Denge** ("grandfather of *juju*") and **Tunde King**; and after the war, **Ayinde Bakara** and the **Jolly Orchestra**.

The **1960s** saw the emergence of a great number of new *juju* singers and bands. Three came to dominate the scene; **I.K. Dairo**, **Ebenezer Obey** and, in the later 1960s, **Sunny Ade**. During and after the Nigerian civil war (1967–70) *juju* thrived at home as high-life artists from the eastern region either went to Biafra or fled abroad, and high-life as a whole lost its popularity.

Juju Roots, 1930s–1950s (Rounder, US). Excellent introduction to the early *juju* years, with comprehensive sleeve notes, featuring Irewolede Denge, Tunde King and Ojoge Daniel.

I.K. Dairo

Dairo had been playing in bands for a good part of his life when he formed the Morning Star Orchestra in 1957. By 1961, he had set up the popular Blue Spots and subsequently rose to become the best-known *juju* exponent in Nigeria.

Juju Master (Original Music). Singer, composer and band leader, Dairo was responsible for the consolidation of *juju* music among the Yoruba and introduced the accordion to the style. A classic round-up of Decca West Africa 45s.

Ebenezer Obey

Obey formed his first group, The International Brothers, in 1964. The success of his blend of talking drums, percussion and guitar had already caught on by the time he renamed his group The InterReformers in 1970. With a vast number of albums to his credit and enjoying a new lease of life in his old age, Obey maintains an immensely loyal following for his infectious, danceable *juju*.

Ju Ju Jubilation (Hemisphere/EMI). Satisfyingly bluesy, slightly offbeat *juju* compilation, from a musician whose expansive features and rather right-wing, Christian image are in contrast to rival *juju* artist Sunny Ade.

King Sunny Ade

Ade started his musical career playing with highlife bands in Lagos before making the transition to *juju*. He formed The Green Spots in 1966, changing the name of the group to the African Beats in 1974. By the end of the decade, Ade was one of the most popular musicians in the country, and in the 1980s he broke into the international scene, making three albums for Island Records.

Juju Music (Universal). The record that launched a million passions for African sounds. Still wonderful after all these years, *Juju Music* includes many of Ade's best songs, among them the sweet "365 is My Number".

On Bobby (Sunny Alade). This Nigerian release is probably the best *juju* album of all time – Ade runs through all the classic riffs in a flowing 1983 tribute to legendary band leader Bobby Benson.

Apala and fuji

Though never achieving the international success of *juju* and highlife, the wall-of-percussion sound of *fuji* has been popular in Nigeria since the 1970s. It has its roots in the Yoruba styles of *apala* and *sakara*, themselves products of Muslim influence on older musical forms in northern Yorubaland.

Haruna Ishola, one of Nigeria's greatest *apala* performers, helped pave the way for *fuji*. Before he died in 1983, he had produced some 25 LPs and opened his own recording studio. It's still relatively easy to find many of his later records like *Apala Songs*.

Today's *fuji* stars of Lagos are heroes of the slums – King Wasiu Ayinde Marshall I, Pasuma Wonder and Adewale Ayube.

Sikiru Ayinde "Barrister"

The leading Yoruba *fuji* singer, Barrister started singing *were* – the songs performed for early breakfast and prayers during Ramadan – at the age of 10. After a brief army career, he turned back to music and, in the early 1970s, formed the Supreme Fuji Commander, a 25-piece outfit. They soon became one of Nigeria's top bands, firing off a battery of hit records.

New Fuji Garbage (Globestyle). A recording which is likely to define *fuji* for Western ears for years to come. Barrister's voice here is slightly mellower than usual and the band surround it with a pounding panoply.

Ayinla Kollington

Fuji's "man of the people", Kollington is the source of social commentary in the Yoruba Muslim music scene. He was at one time a rival of Barrister, but the two now peacefully coexist in a market big enough for both.

Ijoba Ti Tun (KRLPS). Challenging lyrics, driving percussion and a touch of Hawaiian guitar on this Nigerian release.

Nigerian highlife

Highlife came to Nigeria from Ghana in the 1950s (see p.748 for more on Ghanaian highlife), and was quickly moulded by indigenous styles and influences from Cameroon and the Congo that give it a distinctively Nigerian flavour. Extra polish, and Western instruments – brass sections, electric keyboards and guitars – were added to home-grown rhythms and, by the 1960s, highlife was in the forefront of popular urban music. It lost its universal appeal during the civil war, when it retained mass popularity only in Igboland, quite quickly losing ground to *juju* among the Yorubas.

Old albums from the early highlife stars are rarities these days, although it is still possible to lay your hands on 1970s and 1980s material by the fabulous **Oriental Brothers** (and offshoots Dr Sir Warrior and Kabaka). Meanwhile a steady trickle of rereleases continues to refresh the style.

Oriental Brothers

Originally formed by three virtuoso brothers, Dan Satch, Godwin and Warrior, the Orientals then spawned three of the finest highlife bands ever, dominating the 1970s with hit after hit.

Heavy on the Highlife (Original Music). Wonderful burn-up of a guitar-highlife album – relentless, sexy grooves.

Prince Nico Mbarga and Rocafil Jazz

The late Prince Nico will forever *be* Igbo highlife – it's reckoned he sold some thirteen million copies of "Sweet Mother", making it the biggest-selling African song of all time. Hundreds of bands copied it; radio stations played it incessantly; vinyl copies could only be had at twenty times the normal price.

Aki Special (Rounder). Includes "Sweet Mother" – which makes as good a starting point as any for a collection of Nigerian music.

Afro-beat

Afro-beat was almost solely the creation of one extraordinary musician, **Fela Anikulapo-Kuti** (1938–97). The style has its own distinctive beats and rhythms which provided a flexible vehicle for Fela's political lyrics and call-and-response vocal style. He chose to sing in the lingua franca of pidgin English to avoid limiting his audience, and his eruptive performances and defiant lifestyle found him a huge following and brought him into constant conflict with the Nigerian authorities. A steady stream of hit albums included *Black President*, *Perambulator*, *Coffin for Head of State* and *Expensive Shit*.

Especially if you're a vinyl devotee, you'll find that Barclay's Fela boxed sets of classic original vinyl discs take Afrobeat appreciation to a higher level, pulling together key releases from the 1970s, his purplest period. In Nigeria, one of the best places to go hunting for Fela CDs is Obalende market in Lagos.

69 Los Angeles Sessions (Stern's). Some vintage numbers from Black Panther days – and ten tracks all under seven minutes make it unique in the Fela oeuvre.

Shakara/Fela's London Scene (Wrasse). The first of these is an all-time classic, paired here with a very early release.

The Best Of Fela Kuti/ The Black President (Barclay/Talking Loud in the UK; MCA in the US). Twin-CD compilation packed with immortal material.

Femi Kuti

Fela Kuti's son has had an independent career since the late 1980s with his group, the Positive Force. But only since his father's death in 1997 has his stock really risen.

Shoki Shoki (Barclay in the UK; MCA in the US) and **Fight To Win** (Wrasse; MCA). Femi is recognizably a Kuti, both in his voice and in the subject matter and lyrics of the songs with their muscular arrangements, but these albums are infused with a fresh dance-floor sensibility which old man Kuti's stoned diatribes never aimed to deliver.

Lagbaja!

Lagbaja! is the new prince of Afro-beat, wearing a mask when he performs, so as to empathize with the faceless masses and remind Yoruba fans of their roots. He has released three CDs in Nigeria, *We, Me* and *abami*, and won "Artist of the Year" in 2001 despite his harsh criticism of Obasanjo.

Ragga, galala and hip-hop

By 2003, after Obasanjo's re-election, a little confidence was returning to the nightlife scene in the south, though *sharia* law (see box on p.1024) had all but destroyed live music in the north. Local **ragga** is perennially popular (Tupac Shakur is a major youth icon) and the likes of Arthur Pepple, Blakky and Lt. Shotgun attract big audiences, but their songs, when recorded, are often banned from the radio.

Galala – a broadly reggae-style "healing" mix of Nigerian, Jamaican and African-American influences devised, or at least fostered, by born-again Christian toaster and owner of Lagos's Jahoha Studios, John Oboh (**Mighty Mouse**) – is currently the biggest sound in the poor quarters of the city and **Daddy Showkey** its big star.

Lastly, the hugely successful gospel-inflected hip-hop threesome of the 1990s, **The Remedies**, split up in 1999 and spawned new bands and recording careers, including Tony Tetuola, who had a massive hit in 2002 with "My Car", and the Plantashun Boyz. This Afro-hip-hop is clubby, non-threatening stuff that appeals to a more upmarket fan base than *galala*.

You'll have no trouble finding cassettes and CDs of this music, invariably pirated, in any Nigerian town, but none of this is easily available outside Nigeria.

Books

There's a vast body of books on and from Nigeria in print – and more being published all the time. Nigeria's post-colonial **literature** has been the continent's most prolific and most outspoken, its writers enjoying a greater liberty than most of their African counterparts. One of the greatest impetuses to national writing was Onitsha Market Literature, which emerged between 1947 and 1966. At the time, Onitsha was one of Nigeria's most important commercial centres, with a long history of mission education and cosmopolitan influence. Dozens of spare-time writers – teachers, office clerks and journalists – turned out some 200 books that were printed in the market itself.

There's a clutch of great Nigerian writers, including Nobel Prize–winner Wole Soyinka (who spends much time in the USA) and the renowned and more accessible author and opinion-moulder Chinua Achebe (who's often in Britain). There's also a new generation of writers who live abroad, the most well known being Ben Okri and Adewale Maja-Pearce.

In the reviews below, ◨ denotes a book that's especially recommended, while o/p denotes a title that is likely to be out of print in the West (though it may be available in Nigeria); we've indicated explicitly where a book is in fact a Nigerian publication. Many books listed are available in Nigeria at prices far lower than you would pay outside the country. University bookshops are often the best places to find Nigerian books, although there are decent bookstores in large cities, especially Lagos, that will have a substantially different selection from those you'd find on campus.

Country and state

Nigeria, the Land, Its Art and Its People (o/p). A brief, good-value anthology of prose, with photographs.

Chinua Achebe *The Trouble with Nigeria*. Two decades after its first publication, this remains an immensely useful insight into the complexity of Nigerian society and politics.

Claude Ake (ed) *The Political Economy of Nigeria*. A classic, uncompromising in its critique of political and economic conditions and the stranglehold on Nigeria of structures beyond its grasp. This book made the late Ake's reputation as one of Nigeria's most outspoken academics. With his later works, like *How Politics Underdevelops Africa* and *Democratization of Disempowerment*, he became one of the most brilliant observers of what went wrong.

William D. Graf *Nigerian State: Political Economy, State, Class and Political System in the Post-Colonial Era*. An overview analyzing political, social and economic shifts over the last 25 years.

◨ **Peter Holmes** *Nigeria: Giant of Africa* (o/p). Coffee-table format with nearly 200 photos. Detailed and interesting notes; nothing else on Nigeria of this type compares.

◨ **Karl Maier** *This House Has Fallen: Nigeria in Crisis*. An incisive survey by the London *Independent*'s former Africa correspondent of the political problems besetting modern Nigeria. Maier explains the issues thoroughly, and without ever taking sides, though he never shirks from criticism where it's due.

Egohosa E. Osaghae *The Crippled Giant*. The pessimism in the title and the analysis relates to the book's publication during the crisis of the Abacha regime. Overall, a concise introduction to four decades of Nigerian political history.

Ken Saro-Wiwa *A Month and a Day, A Detention Diary*. A living testimony from the leader of MOSOP (executed by the Abacha regime in 1995) against the atrocities meted out to the Ogoni people in Cross River State.

Wole Soyinka *The Open Sore of a Continent: A Personal Narrative of the Nigerian Crisis*. Accessible diagnosis of one of Africa's biggest wounds from one of its most admired writers.

Art and people

Omofolabo S. Ajayi *Yoruba Dance: The Semiotics of Movement and Body Attitude in a Nigerian Culture*. An insightful introduction to themes of Yoruba dance and the philosophical, aesthetic and religious underpinnings of movement as a means of communication.

J.S. Boston *Ikenga* (o/p). Explores the symbolism of carvings amongst varied peoples of Nigeria.

T.J.H. Chappel *Decorated Gourds in North Eastern Nigeria* (o/p). A substantial survey of their use, decoration and symbolism.

Henry J. Drewal and John Pemberton III *Yoruba: Nine Centuries of African Art and Thought*. Sumptuous and terribly expensive – a majestic, detailed photo and essay documentary on various Yoruba states and their individual artistic traditions.

Edward Fox *Obscure Kingdoms*. Excitingly written and brilliantly evocative accounts of journeys to the world's remoter royal corners, including a sizeable chapter on meetings in Nigeria with various *onis*, *obas* and *emirs*.

Berkare Gbadamosi and Ulli Beier *Not Even God Is Ripe Enough*. Full of amusing Yoruba folk tales.

Paula Girshick Ben-Amos *The Art of Benin*. Plenty of photos of bronzes and more.

Barry Hallen and J.O. Sodipo *Knowledge, Belief and Witchcraft*. A survey of Yoruba philosophical ideas.

G.I. Jones *Ibo Art*. Well-illustrated survey of arts and their role in Igbo society.

★ **A.D. Nzemeke and E.O. Erhage** (eds) *Nigerian Peoples and Culture* (United City Press, Nigeria). A cultural history of Nigeria's ethnic groups. Highly recommended in-depth study of the history of Nigerian society.

Robert S. Smith *Kingdoms of the Yoruba*. The classic historical work on pre-colonial Yoruba civilization.

Fiction and poetry

★ **Chinua Achebe** *Things Fall Apart*; *No Longer at Ease*; *Arrow of God*; *A Man of the People*; *Anthills of the Savannah*. One of Africa's best-known novelists, Achebe gained international fame with his classic first novel *Things Fall Apart* (1958), which deals with the encounter, at the turn of the last century, of missionaries, colonial officers and an Igbo village. Okwonkwo, a self-made man, rises to respected seniority, then falls, inexorably and tragically. It's a brilliant, moving book – universal in what it says on pride, and on fathers and sons. With it, the three following novels form part of a loose quartet: in *No Longer at Ease*, Okwonkwo's grandson, Obi, is a corrupt Lagos civil servant, trapped in his head between home and ambition; in *Arrow of God*, set in the 1920s, there's direct confrontation between an Igbo priest and a colonial officer; and in *A Man of the People*, Achebe adopts a more satirical approach, setting up an idealist against a rogue and showing how close their paths run. Achebe's characters bend and sweat with life and develop unexpected traits just as you thought you had the measure of them. His 1995 novel, a humanist fable, *Anthills of the Savannah*, was shortlisted for the Booker Prize.

Zainab Alkali *A Virtuous Woman, The Stillborn* (o/p). Alkali is unusual in being a woman writer from the conservative north of the country. "I see myself as a typical Nigerian woman who wants to get married, raise a family and live according to the expected norms of the society. . . A woman can never be anything else but a woman."

T.M. Aluko *One Man, One Wife* (o/p). Entertaining tale of Yoruba villagers' disillusionment with the missionaries' God and their return to traditional worship. *One Man, One Matchet* (o/p) is written in a similarly crafted and satirical style as it portrays conflict in a Western cocoa community. *Chief the Honourable Minister* (o/p) is the less amusing story of a schoolmaster appointed minister in a corrupt government.

Tafawa Balewa *Shaihu Umar.* Portrayal of a Hausa family at the beginning of the twentieth century, by Nigeria's first prime minister.

Simi Bedford *Yoruba Girl Dancing.* A British Nigerian's depiction of early life in Nigeria, adjustment to the UK, and the getting of wisdom.

John Pepper Clark *A Reed in the Tide* (o/p), *Casualties* and *A Decade of Tongues* (o/p) are poetry collections with which Clark first gained recognition. He is now better known as a playwright: for *Ozidi*, a play based on an Ijo saga; *State of the Nation*, a piece of social criticism (o/p); and *America, Their America* (o/p), a biting indictment of values in the United States where he studied in the early 1960s.

★ **Iheanyichukwu Duruoha** *Eaters of Dust* (Longman, Nigeria). As Biafra collapses, a teenage boy in its disintegrating army witnesses a war crime. Poignant, highly readable, and easily one of the best among a multitude of civil war novels.

T. Obinkaram Echewa *I Saw the Sky Catch Fire.* Fictional accounts of the effects of war, especially as it touches the lives of women. Powerful and moving, from a Nigerian-American author best known for his novel *The Land's Lord* about a French missionary in Africa.

Cyprian Ekwensi *Jagua Nana.* Superbly captures the life and rhythm of 1950s Lagos using a style resembling that of the traditional storyteller. *Burning Grass* is set in the north among Fula herders (an unusual setting for Ekwensi).

Buchi Emecheta *Slave Girl; Second Class Citizen; In the Ditch; Head above Water; Joys of Motherhood; Double Yoke; The Bride Price; Destination Biafra; Gwendolen* and *Rape of Shavi.* Emecheta writes, with a humour that refuses to be submerged, about the struggle to be a Nigerian woman and an independent person – in Nigeria and the UK.

Helon Habila *Waiting for an Angel.* A much acclaimed debut novel about the precarious life of a journalist under Abacha's military regime.

Festus Iyayi *Violence* (o/p); *Heroes.* A committed political writer, Iyayi was detained in 1988 for protesting against the government's human-rights abuses. *Violence* is a howl of anguish at the inhumanity of urban survival in Africa. *Heroes* is set in the dark backyard of Nigeria's soul, the civil war of 1967–69.

(Vincent) Chukwuemeka Ike *Toads for Supper; The Naked Gods; The Chicken Chasers; The Children are Coming; The Potter's Wheel* and *Sunset at Dawn.* A series of entertaining, critical novels by a brilliant comic writer. They have been republished by the University of Ibadan Press and are easily available in Nigeria, though less so abroad.

Eddie Iroh *Forty Eight Guns for the General* (o/p); *Toads of War* and *The Sirens in the Night* (o/p). Three thrillers that rode in on the wave of writing following the Biafran War.

Karen King-Aribasala *Kicking Tongues.* A wonderful collection of perspectives shared by travel companions who meet up at the *Eko Holiday Inn* in Lagos before embarking on a trip to Abuja. The characters, who range from a prostitute to village chief, seem to have little in common but are united in their disaffection with corruption and other facets of Nigerian politics.

Adewale Maja Pearce *Loyalties* (o/p). Evocative short stories and vignettes set in a Nigerian society always on the brink of chaos by a writer based in Britain.

Flora Nwapa *Efuru.* As in the later *Idu* (o/p), Nwapa, the first African woman to publish a novel, looks at women's roles – not always in a traditional way – in a society precariously balanced between the traditional and the new. *This is Lagos* is Nwapa's follow-up to her novels portraying women at odds with society – a collection of effective short stories on life in the metropolis. Flora Nwapa died in 1993.

⭐ **Ben Okri** *Flowers and Shadows* (o/p). Okri's excellent first novel was published when he was only 20. The angry, hallucinatory short story collections, *Incidents at the Shrine* and *Stars of the New Curfew*, propelled Nigerian literature into a new wide audience. Okri, based in Britain, provides razor-sharp dialogue and settings, fine evocations of character and an angular wit. With his Booker Prize–winning *The Famished Road*, he comes home to the themes of tradition and of Yoruba mythology. It was followed by a sequel, *Songs of Enchantment*, then by *Astonishing the Gods*, *Dangerous Love*, *Infinite Riches* and *In Arcadia*.

Niyi Osundare *Moonsongs*; *Songs of the Season*; *Waiting Laughters*; *Midlife*. One of Africa's best-known poets, committed to performance of poetry together with drumming and dancing, Osundare is a Commonwealth Prize–winner, who received the NOMA Award in 1991 for *Waiting Laughters*. His most easily obtained collection is *Selected Poems*.

Ken Saro-Wiwa *Sozaboy*; *A Forest of Flowers*; *Basi & Company: A Modern African Folktale*; *The Prisoner of Jebs*; *Pita Dumbrok's Prison*. Saro-Wiwa was a major figure on the Nigerian literary and political scene who was executed by the Abacha regime for his campaigning work on behalf of his people, the Ogoni.

Wole Soyinka *Ake*, *Isara* and other works. Known primarily as a playwright, Soyinka won the Nobel Prize for Literature in 1986, gaining international recognition not only for himself (becoming the first African to be so honoured), but for the writers of his continent. Soyinka's work is denser and less easy-going than Achebe's. He is also politically more outspoken, and during the Abacha regime, helped organize a major opposition group in exile. His early works include *The Lion and the Jewel*, *A Dance of the Forests* – an exercise in demythologizing Africa's historic idyll – and *Kongi's Harvest*. He later published poetry, sketching beautiful images in *Idanre, and Other Poems*. He has also worked substantially as a novelist with *The Interpreters* – in which a group of young intellectuals living in Lagos attempts to "interpret" their role in traditional and modern Nigeria – and the luminous, dream-like *Ake*, an autobiographical account of his childhood in Abeokuta. *Isara* is a biographical account of Nigeria in the times of his father, the memorable schoolmaster "Essay" from *Ake*. The sequel to *Isara*, *Ibadan: the Penkelmes Years*, focuses on his fight against the everyday repression of early post-independence Nigeria.

Amos Tutuola *Palm Wine Drinkard.* Heavily under the spell of Yoruba oral tradition, this recounts a journey into the "Dead Towns" of the supernatural. It was followed by *My Life in the Bush of Ghosts*.

Language

Nigeria's official **language** is English and in the larger cities – especially those with universities – it's spoken widely and with accents you'll adapt to easily. Pidgin English, however, which is spoken as a lingua franca everywhere, especially in the smaller towns and rural areas, will initially throw you. Keep trying, though; ask people to repeat phrases, and before long most visitors find their own speech punctuated with pidgin expressions.

The three most widely spoken ethnic languages are **Hausa** (see p.956), **Yoruba** and **Igbo**. Next to these, are some four hundred separate dialects representing twelve language families. The linguistic situation in central and southeast Nigeria is one of the most complicated in the world – on the islands of the Delta Region there are villages a few kilometres apart with mutually incomprehensible tongues.

Yoruba

Yoruba is the name given to a cluster of close dialects in the **Kwa** grouping, and as a tonal language, it can be difficult for foreigners to master even the basics. Because tone carries so much meaning, it's possible to communicate with little or no vocalization: talking drums were (and still are) able to transmit messages, and you don't have to listen to much of Sunny Ade's music to realize how easily this is accomplished. The diacritics in the following words and phrases are not accents but indicate the tone of the sound – either rising (´), or falling (`). **E** is pronounced "eh" or "ey" and **O** is pronounced "or" or "oh". The prefix "E" indicates a plural or formal construction: a younger person greets an older person first and uses a respectful "E" at the beginning of a greeting, which may be dropped when talking to someone of the same social standing and the same age or younger.

Greetings

Good morning (and response)	E káàárò
Good afternoon (and response)	E káàsán
Good evening (and response)	E káalé
On entering a house	E kúulé
Response	E káàbò
Greeting someone who is working	E kúushé
How are you?, How's life?	Shé alaáfíà ni
Response to (lit. thank you)	E kúushé and Shé alaáfíà ni Adúpé
Goodbye	Ó dàbò

Basic chat

I want	Mo féé
I don't want	Mi ò féé
Which one?	È wo?
This is the one	Eléyìí
Take (it)	E gbà
Water	Omi
Meat	Eran
Palm wine	Emu
Thank you (on receiving it)	E sheé
How much is (it)?	Èló ní?
It's ten naira	Naira mewa ni
To pay	Sanwó
Money	Owó
Please, reduce the price	E dín owó lori e
Give me	E fún mi
All right. OK	Ó dáa
Please	E jòó
Don't be annoyed	E má bínú
What's your name?	Kini oruko ré?
My name is Dayo	Dayo ni oruko mi
Greetings/ commiserations	Pèlé
I don't understand	Mi ò gbo
No, (not) at all	Rárá
My friend	Òré mi

Numbers

1	ookan

2	méjì
3	méta
4	merin
5	marun
6	mefa
7	meje
8	mejo
9	mesan
10	mewa
11	mokanla
12	mejila
13	metala
14	merinla
15	mèedogun
16	meridlogun
17	metadinlogun
18	mejidinlogun
19	mokondinlogun
20	ogun
21	mokan le logun
22	meji le logun
25	mèd ogbon
26	meridin logbon
30	ogbon
40	ogoji
50	adota
60	ogota
70	aadorin
80	ogorin
90	adorun
100	ogorun

Igbo

Igbo is also a tonal language and part of the great Kwa grouping – but it is not intelligible to Yoruba-speakers. Again, be prepared to squeeze your mouth a little to get an intelligible vowel sound.

Greetings

Hi/How are you?	Kèdú/Kèdú ka í mère?
How are the children?	Kèdú maka umú-àka?
I'm fine	Ó dì nma
Good morning?	Ututu òma?
Good night	Ka chíí fò
Welcome (to one who has arrived)	Nnòo
Keep up the good work/well done	Jisie ike
Thank you	Daalu/Imèela

Good bye	Ka e mesia

Basic chat

Please	Bìkó
Sorry (commiserations)	Ndó
What's your name?	Kèdú àha gí?
My name is Theodora	Áhà m bu Theodora
Where are you from?	E béè ka ísì?
I'm from Scotland	E sim Scotland
Where are you going?	E béè ka í na-ijè?
I'm going to Enugu	Á na m èje Enugu
I want	Á chorò m
I want to go to the market	Á chorò m ije ahia
I want to buy	Á chorò m ego
This one	Nke á
How much is this?	Nka á bù olé?
How much?/How much money?	Olé?/Egó olé?
Give	Nyé
Give me	Nyé m
Come	Byá
Go	Jé
Come in	Bhàta
Good	Ézí
This soup's tasty	Ófé tòrò èto
It's good	Ó dè úmá
Meat	Áné
Pepper	Ose
Water	Mmírí

Numbers

1	ótu
2	abúo
3	àtó
4	ànó
5	ìsé
6	ìsí
7	asáà
8	asáto
9	itenanì
10	irí
11	irí na ótu
12	irí na abúo
13	irí na àtó
14	irí na ànó
15	irí na ìsé
16	irí na ìsí
17	irí na asáà
18	irí na asáto
19	irí na itenanì

20	irí abúo	60		irí ìsí
21	irí abúo na ótu	70		irí asáà
22	irí abúo na abúo	80		irí asáto
30	irí àtó	90		irí itenanì
40	irí ànó	100		nari
50	irí ìsé	1000		puku

Glossary

Abule Hamlet or small village (Yoruba).

Agbada Yoruba cloak for men.

Alhaji One who has been to Mecca.

Amingo White person (from Portuguese).

Area boys Local hoodlums; in Lagos they're partly organized into a banned vigilante group called the Odua People's Congress, or OPC, who assert Yoruba supremacy at every opportunity.

Ariya Enjoyment, having a good time (Yoruba).

Babanriga Long Hausa tunic.

Bakassi Boys A banned, Aba-based Igbo vigilante group, the equivalent of Lagos's OPC, whose avowed aim is a separate southeastern state.

Batouri White person (Hausa).

Buba Yoruba shirt.

Buka Chop house (Yoruba).

Chiroma Traditional title of the far northeast.

Chop A verb meaning "to eat", though it can also be used to mean "food".

Dash Bribe or payment for service rendered or simply a gift (verb and noun).

Drop Can mean a shared taxi, a journey in one, or to disembark from a taxi or bus.

Durbar Staged horse gallops in which senior men pay homage to an emir in the Muslim regions.

F.C.T. Federal Capital Territory (Abuja).

Galadima Traditional title of the far northeast.

Go-slow Traffic jam.

GRA Government Reserved Area, civil servants' housing district.

Hisba Young Islamist vigilante (Hausa).

Ile Old (as in, for example, Ile-Ife).

Ileto Village (Yoruba).

Ilu Alade Big town (Yoruba).

Ilu Oloja Small market town (Yoruba).

Kabu kabu Commercial transport (Hausa).

Lappa Casual loin cloth (men and women).

Mai Traditional Kanuri ruler.

Moto Any car – a term you'll hear a lot if travelling by bush taxi.

Oba Traditional Yoruba king. The Nigerian government has allowed traditional rulers to keep their titles and in some cases has even supported regional monarchies. Although the obas have less *de jure* power than they once did, they still enjoy considerable prestige and often mediate in local disputes. In some cases, they've taken on official government functions to complement traditional roles.

Off To turn/switch something off.

Okada Motorcycle taxi.

On To turn/switch something on.

Onyeocha White person (Igbo).

Oyibo White person (Yoruba).

Sabi To know (pidgin, from Portuguese).

Sabon Gari Also spelt Sabongari, this is Hausa for "foreigners' town", meaning the Igbo and Yoruba quarter of a northern city.

SAP Economic Structural Adjustment Programme.

Shehu Chief, big man (Hausa).

Sokoto Yoruba trousers.

Yandabas Hausa vigilantes, the equivalent of Lagos's area boys.

NIGERIA | Basics

14.1

Lagos

f you're reading nervously, you wouldn't be the first traveller to approach **Lagos** with a sinking feeling of despair and trepidation, convinced you're going to hate the place – should you live through it. A city with somewhere above thirteen million inhabitants, Lagos has grown too big too fast. Long ago, the city overflowed from the **islands** at its heart, and the urban sprawl on the mainland has mushroomed alarmingly. Of the infrastructure – housing, roads, public transport, water, electricity and sewerage – only the new expressways show any sign of keeping up. Pollution, squalid overcrowding, violent crime and a 24-hour din are the inevitable results of the shortfall. Although the crime rate has decreased over the last years because of tightened security, the underlying social problems have not been solved.

But you might just be surprised. The **international airport** that was largely to blame for many travellers' terrible first impressions has been cleared of the touts who made life hell for newly arrived first-timers, and the once-predatory customs officials have also cleaned up their act. On approaching the city itself, you may find rather less chaos – and more to excite. For West Africa's foremost metropolis is, at the very least, a city of intense, voluble personality and breathtaking dynamism. Ships from around the globe berth at its **ports** of Apapa and Tin Can Island, and the **skyscrapers** that spike Lagos Island house a swarm of international firms. A more immediate sign of "success" is the commuter traffic packing the **flyovers**, regularly grinding to a halt in rush hour "go-slow" traffic jams, to be exploited by thousands of irrepressible **street vendors** trying to sell anything from imported apples to bathroom scales. And beyond the nonstop, unrestrained commercialism on the streets, universities, museums, galleries and the national theatre all attest to a thriving **intellectual and cultural life**.

While it would definitely be misleading to downplay its problems, Lagos is no more of a hell hole than any other seething, impoverished city. The risks of mugging and pickpocketing are real, but most people get through their stays safely, and find the city a friendly rather than a dangerous place. Travel with confidence, take elementary precautions, get into the rhythm, and you will almost certainly enjoy your visit.

Some history

The swampy mangrove zone around Lagos was originally inhabited by small hunting and fishing communities, but rainforest and marshes probably prevented large-scale settlement. **Portuguese mariners** first arrived at the islands around Lagos in 1472 and named the place *Lago de Curamo*, but it wasn't until much later that the area became an important port of trade. In the sixteenth century, **Yoruba settlers** came to Iddo and later moved onto Lagos Island and beyond. The settlement was eventually incorporated into the **Benin kingdom** – which at the time extended all the way to the area of Cotonou – and renamed Eko, the Benin name for camp or war camp. In the early eighteenth century, the ruling Oba granted a trade monopoly to the Portuguese whose main export was, by then, **slaves**. A hundred years later, the French and British governments began sending warships to break up the slave trade, as Lagos was used as a hideout by profiteers who took advantage of the many creeks and rivers to conceal their human cargo. In 1851, the **British** shelled Lagos and eventually forced the Oba to abandon the slave trade. Soon after, they captured the islands and formed Lagos Colony.

Early in the twentieth century, Lagos grew into an important commercial centre thanks to the port and the **railway line**, begun in 1896 and opened through to Kano in 1912. It became the capital of the southern Nigerian protectorate and later of the entire federation, when north and south were merged. After independence, Lagos maintained its role as capital until 1991, when the seat of government moved to Abuja. The city is still the country's undisputed commercial, industrial, cultural and diplomatic centre, although more and more countries are moving their main embassies to the new capital.

Arrival, information and city transport

Lagos spreads over some 200 square kilometres and comprises myriad **neighbour-hoods**. But the heart of the city, where you're likely to spend most of your time, is tucked onto **Lagos and Ikoyi islands** – now merged – and **Victoria Island**, to the south. If your stay is going to be any longer than a day or two, it's worth getting hold of a map or street atlas before you arrive, or as soon as possible afterwards.

By whatever means you come to Lagos, the **mainland** is your point of entry. Although there are bland neighbourhoods here (such as the administrative district of **Ikeja**), most districts are populated by the city's working class and poor – and they can feel distinctly threatening. This is where many Lagos horror stories have their origins, but that's largely because most of the city's rich don't live there. As a temporary visitor you're no more likely to run into serious, violent trouble on the mainland than anywhere else in Lagos (perhaps, in truth, less).

Arrival and information

Flying into Lagos from abroad, you'll land at **Murtala Muhammed Airport**, 8km north of Lagos Island as the crow flies. Note that if you're arriving on a domestic flight, you'll be using the separate domestic terminal off Agege Motor Road. Only limited numbers of **taxis** are licensed to trade at the airport (if in doubt, ask to see the driver's ID card), and there are no buses out here. Taxi fares into town are fixed (currently ₦3000 to the islands), and you should pre-pay, getting a receipt, at a desk by the exit from the arrivals hall, where you will be shown to a cab. Make sure that the driver knows the way to your destination, especially if it's after dark. If you're flying in during daylight hours, you could, alternatively, walk down the airport road about 2km and pick up a minibus to Obalende or Lagos Island. The best option of all is to arrange to be **met at the airport** – all of the travel agents detailed on p.1052 offer this service, as do all but the cheapest hotels.

By **minibus or long-distance taxi**, you'll arrive at one of several points on the mainland – Mile Two, Yaba, Ojota, Iddo, Oju Elegba or Ebute Ero. From these places, battered yellow private buses drop you at Lagos Island or Obalende, where you can get a cheap taxi to a hotel.

The **train station** is on Murtala Muhammed Way, near the Carter Bridge in Iddo, from where there are taxis and okadas to get you into the centre. These days it's unusual to arrive by **ship**, though a number of cargo lines still offer berths. Ships dock at Apapa, opposite Lagos Island and connected to it by ferry.

Information

The Nigerian Tourism Development Corporation's **tourist office**, the Tourism Information Centre, is on the mainland on the second floor of the Hanco Plaza Building, 113 Ikorodu Road, by the Fadeyi bus stop (Mon–Fri 8am–5pm;

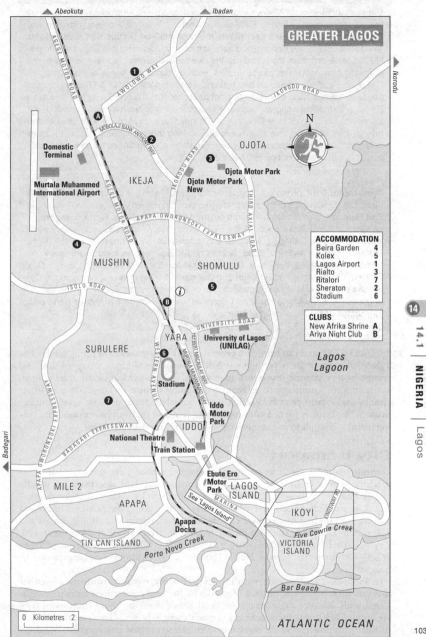

Abeokuta

Ibadan

Ikorodu

AGGE MOTOR ROAD

AWOLOWO WAY

IKORODU ROAD

A

1

MOBOLAJI BANK ANTHONY WAY

2

IKORODU ROAD

OJOTA

3

Ojota Motor Park

Ojota Motor Park New

N

Domestic Terminal

IKEJA

Murtala Muhammed International Airport

APAPA OWORONSOKI EXPRESSWAY

THIRD AXIAL ROAD

4

MUSHIN

SHOMULU

ISOLO ROAD

i

5

B

ACCOMMODATION
Beira Garden	4
Kolex	5
Lagos Airport	1
Rialto	3
Ritalori	7
Sheraton	2
Stadium	6

CLUBS
New Afrika Shrine	A
Ariya Night Club	B

UNIVERSITY ROAD

YABA

HERBERT MACAULAY WAY

MURTALA MUHAMMAD WAY

University of Lagos (UNILAG)

Lagos Lagoon

SURULERE

WESTERN AVENUE

6

Stadium

7

BADAGARI EXPRESSWAY

Iddo Motor Park

IDDO

National Theatre

Train Station

APAPA OWORONSOKI EXPRESSWAY

Ebute Ero Motor Park

LAGOS ISLAND

IKOYI

KINGSWAY RD

MILE 2

MARINA

See "Lagos Island"

Apapa Docks

APAPA

Five Cowrie Creek

VICTORIA ISLAND

TIN CAN ISLAND

Porto Novo Creek

Bar Beach

Badagari

ATLANTIC OCEAN

0 Kilometres 2

14

14.1 | **NIGERIA** | Lagos

Between them, Nigeria Airways and several private airlines – including ADC (currently one of the largest), Albarka, Bellview, Chachangi, Overland Airways, Sosoliso and TransSaharan – run several daily **flights** to Abuja and Port Harcourt, plus daily flights to Calabar, Enugu and Kaduna, and several weekly to Kano and Ibadan. Expect to pay ₦3000 for a taxi from the islands to the international airport, somewhat less to the domestic terminal (which you could also reach by bus along Agege Motor Road).

In principle, there should be two **trains** a week (departing Wed & Fri at noon) from Lagos to Kano, calling at Ibadan, Oshogbo, Jebba, Kaduna and Zaria, plus two more (Thurs & Sat) terminating at Kaduna. Even according to the timetable however, the journey to Kano takes over thirty hours – in practice a lot longer – with services frequently cancelled and invariably hours late, making this an option for rail enthusiasts only. For further information, call the Nigerian Railway Corporation's Lagos headquarters at Ebute-Metta junction (℡01/833 377).

By road

Ojota motor park, on Ikorodu Road near the junction with the airport road in the Ojota district, is for transport to the east of Nigeria, including Benin City, Onitsha, Enugu and Port Harcourt, plus Ibadan and some southwestern destinations. **Ojota new garage**, on Ikorodu Road 300m south of the main Ojota motor park, serves the southwest, including Ibadan, Oshogbo, Ilorin, Ife and other towns in Yorubaland. For the north, including Kaduna and Jos, Zaria, Sokoto and Kano, head to **Iddo motor park**, on Murtala Muhammed Way near the train station. The east, including Benin City, Onitsha, Enugu, Aba, Port Harcourt and Calabar, is served by transport using the **Oju Elegba motor park**, at Oju Elegba junction in Surulere district. Finally, for international destinations, including Lomé and Cotonou, use the **Ebute Ero motor park**, near Eko Bridge at the western tip of Lagos Island.

℡01/493 0220), and can help with general tourist information and hiring guides. For a detailed **map** of the city, there's WABP's *Street Map of Lagos*, an up-to-date and comprehensive volume. If you plan an extended stay, the guidebook *Lagos Easy Access*, available from Quintessence at Falomo Shopping Centre in Ikoyi (see p.1046), is chunky and expensive at ₦2500, but is an invaluable source of more detailed information. The book is packed with some three hundred pages of information (including maps) – enough to manage several years in the commercial capital.

City transport

Getting around Lagos can be a nightmare unless you have unlimited time or patience – or your own car and driver, like many expats. Lagos **taxis** are usually yellow Peugeot 504s with black stripes. You hail them by yelling out your destination. Use some discretion over where you say you're going (be prepared to get out and walk a hundred metres) as it can affect the fare, which you should discuss and agree on first. Stand in the door till you're sure the driver knows the price is agreed. Try also to have the notes ready, as change is a rare thing. Fares vary from ₦200–400 for short hops to ₦500–1500 for cross-city journeys; be prepared to haggle.

In addition, Lagos swarms with motley **privately owned minibuses** – either VWs or Japanese *kombis*, or local Mercedes or Bedford conversions known as *molue* (large, with aisles) or *danfo* (small, seat only). While these are cheap (maximum fares are around ₦30), the discomfort and – when traffic is heavy – hair-pulling slowness of them can undermine the resolve of even the staunchest city survivor. For short journeys, especially within the islands, **okadas** (motorcycle taxis) are the easiest way to get around. The drivers have a reputation for knowing the city well, but usually balk at trips far afield. Expect to pay anything from ₦20 to ₦100, depending on the length of your journey. As with taxis, you should agree the price before getting aboard.

A hundred-seater **ferry** runs across Lagos Harbour, from the south of Lagos Island (midway along Apongbon Street) to Apapa, then on to Mile Two using a canal west of the Apapa–Orowonsoki Expressway. Ferries also run from Victoria Island to the beaches (see p.1048).

Accommodation

There's no shortage of **hotels** in Lagos, most of them on the mainland, which is on the whole less convenient than the islands. Although parts of the mainland have a reputation as dangerous areas, those who enjoy Lagos's teeming streets and vibrant nightlife won't be intimidated – most of the music clubs are there for example. Upmarket hotels are expensive if you're paying the non-resident tariff (which some will insist on if you are a foreigner), but mid-range places with TV are good value. Budget travellers won't be disappointed, as plenty of cheap hotels and hostels are available. In general, even the cheapest places have air conditioning, virtually a necessity in Lagos's sweltering climate.

Lagos Island

The places reviewed here are shown on the map on pp.1044–1045.

Bristol 8 Martins St ☎01/266 1204 or 266 1207. A once-grand hotel, now much the worse for wear, though it offers good value at the lower end of the scale, with large if tatty s/c rooms. ❸

Ritz 41 King George V St (aka Yoruba Tennis Club Rd), Onikan ☎01/263 0481. A battered and grubby but secure and friendly hotel, with s/c rooms in a lively part of town, very handy for Obalende motor park and nearby chop houses. ❷

Wayfarers 52 Campbell St ☎01/263 0113. By Lagos Island Maternity Hospital, this has simple and safe s/c, a/c rooms. Good value, with a small restaurant and friendly management. Book ahead. ❾

Zeina 11 Smith St ☎01/263 3254. Moderately priced hotel, with a folksy feel and comfortable a/c rooms. Book in advance as space is limited. ❸

Ikoyi and Victoria Island

For locations of the accommodation here, see the map on p.1046.

B-Jay's 24 Samuel Manuwa St, Victoria Island ☎01/262 3706–8, or 774 6900/1, ☏ 262 2903, ✉bjays@alpha.linkserve.com. Excellent small hotel located in a safe residential neighbourhood. The large, spotless s/c rooms and suites have king-size beds and satellite TV. Friendly service-minded staff. Continental breakfast included. Rooms from $140. ❽

Eko Kuramo Waters, Victoria Island ☎01/262 4600–19, ⓦwww.lemeridien-eko.com. The sparkling white tower – rising a short distance from the open Atlantic – is one of the best, most expensive (rooms from $290) hotels in Lagos. Complete comfort in all departments, including a crystal-clear pool. ❽

Federal Palace Ahmadu Bello Rd, Victoria Island ☎01/262 3116–25, ☏ 262 3912. From the first

flush of independence, this has been one of the top hotels in Lagos. The lagoon-side bar offers spectacular views of the Lagos Island skyline and the ships nosing into harbour. At weekends, there's poolside dancing to live music. Rooms from $230. ❽

Ikoyi Kingsway Rd, Ikoyi ☎01/269 0148–57 or 269 1539–48. Once a colonial institution and top-notch hotel, now somewhat frayed at the edges, although renovation is planned. It's still reasonably good value and the amenities are all there – including a pleasant pool. ❽

Victoria Lodge 5 Ologun Agbaje St, Victoria Island ☎01/262 0885 or 261 7177, ☏01/261 3318. Very pleasant, homely and clean, with a/c bar and restaurant, and satellite TV in all rooms. ❽

YMCA 77 Awolowo Rd, Ikoyi ☎01/773 3599.

Recently rebuilt, this is one of the best budget options, with spanking new a/c family suites, non-a/c single rooms, and men-only four-bed dorms. Nigerians and other Africans board here and can be a big help showing you around the city. It's sometimes full so worth booking ahead; stays are limited to seven days. Dorm beds ₦300, ③

Mainland

Beira Garden Residential Ayao Estate, Plot 41 Olakunle Selesi Crescent, off Airport Rd, Ikeja ☎01/523 858 or 470 1744. A well-kept hotel with all conveniences, good management, and a pleasant atmosphere. Conveniently near the airport. ⑤

Rialto 6 Alhaji Amoo St, Ojota ☎01/493 5346. Off the beaten track in a working-class neighbourhood in the far north of the city (300m down Ogudu Rd by the Texaco station at Ojota motor park, then left), but handy for Ojota motor park. Very pleasant, clean and well run, with s/c lodgings, TV, small restaurant, bar, nightclub and friendly staff. ③

Kolex 3 Olufeko Close, off Femi Adebule St, Fola Agoro, Yaba ☎01/820 174 or 820 130 or 820 262, ⓕ822 451. Small, quiet and comfortable, with friendly staff, plus nightclub, restaurant and snooker bar. Located in a quiet neighbourhood. ④

Lagos Airport Hotel 111 Obafemi Awolowo Way, Ikeja ☎01/497 8670–9, ⓔlaph@rcl.nig.com. Exclusive hotel with a lovely garden and all the facilities, including a swimming pool. ⑧

Ritalori Animashawun St, off Eric Moore Rd, Surulere ☎01/288 5136. Decent hotel in a lively area, with a clean pool, though it's become rather shabby. ③

Sheraton Lagos 30 Mobolaji Bank, Anthony Way, Ikeja ☎01/497 8660–9, ⓦwww.sheraton .com/lagos. Lagos's smartest hotel, right by the airport, catering for businesspeople with no need to go into the city. All the usual five-star facilities, and there are booking desks for BA and Virgin. ⑧

Stadium Hotel 27–33 Iyun St, just west of the National Stadium, Surulere ☎01/833 593/4. Popular hotel with a/c rooms and an exciting disco with live music performances; always animated. ④

The City and the beaches

The effort of **getting around** the city is the only thing that really detracts from its worthwhile sites. It can literally take hours to accomplish journeys by car that could probably have been walked more quickly. Don't be afraid of venturing out on foot during the day, but be aware that many parts of town are dangerous at night, when mugging is common. In particular you should steer clear of the western half of Lagos Island and the poorer districts on the mainland after nightfall. Don't carry anything of value around with you if you can avoid it.

Lagos is almost alone among West African cities in having more than a single museum. The **Onikan National Museum** is highly recommended and, if you have time, make an effort to visit the **National Theatre** and see what's on view at its cultural centre and galleries; the local press will have details. **Lagos Island**, the oldest part of the city, preserves a number of dilapidated **Brazilian-style buildings** in the area around Campos Square and Campbell Street, and some colonial buildings along Broad Street.

Lagos Island

Lagos Island is the commercial centre and site of the towers that provide the city's striking skyline. Many of these high-rises – including most of the bank headquarters and **NITEL House**, Africa's tallest skyscraper – are on the south side of the island behind **Marina Street** (usually known simply as Marina), which used to run along the waterfront. Today, Marina is several hundred metres back from the water, shadowed by the zooming split-level expressway of **Apongbon Street**. But it retains some buildings of note, including the former **State House** (residence of the British governors); the headquarters of the famously inefficient **NEPA** (the electricity corporation), with the bronze statue of Sango the thunder god before it; Lagos's **General Post Office**; and the eighteenth-century **Anglican church**.

Broad Street, which runs parallel to Marina, is another well-known thoroughfare with more banks and markets and some fairly upmarket shops. Buildings of interest include the 1925 colonial **courthouse** on the corner of Kakawa Street, and the **tomb of Chief Daniel Conrad Taiwo**, who died in 1901 at the ripe old age of 120. The tomb stands 100m west of **Tinubu Square**, a landscaped roundabout with a perpetually defunct fountain (originally donated to the city by its Lebanese community in 1960 to celebrate Nigeria's independence), in one of the busiest parts of town. To the northwest, the **markets** of **Jankara**, **Isale Eko**, **Ebute Ero** and **Balogun** fill this part of the island with frenetic small-scale commerce.

Between the high-rises and the market stalls, and the exhaust emissions and the rains, a few Brazilian-style buildings have survived in the **Brazilian Quarter**, founded by returned former slaves. They're falling apart however, and jealously guarded against photographers. **The Palace of the Oba**, on the northern tip of the island on Upper King Street, is particularly unimpressive. Still, if you're keen on a hunt, the following, all on Lagos Island, may still be worthwhile: **Chief's House**, Ado Street; **Ebun House**, 85 Odunfa Street (300m east of Tinubu Square), a great pile of a place dating from 1914; **Brazilian House**, 29 Kakawa Street, off Broad Street; **Water House**, 12 Kakawa Street, built in the 1860s and one of the oldest houses in Lagos; **Cuban Lodge**, 40 Odunlami Street (adjacent to Kakawa Street), styled on an English cottage but with Brazilian features; **Da Silva House**, Odufege Street; and the comely **Shitta Mosque** on Martins Street, with its Brazilian tilework, built in 1894.

The eastern end of Marina is dominated by the enclosed open area called **Tafawa Balewa Square**, with its monumental equine statues rearing up at the entrance on the south side, in memory of the old racetrack that used to be here. The north side of the square was where many of the major airlines and travel agencies had their offices, though many have now relocated to Victoria Island; the south side is a bus and taxi park.

The Onikan National Museum

Just east of Tafawa Balewa Square, the **National Museum** (daily 9am–5pm; ₦30) is Nigeria's foremost, and a required visit, especially if the travelling exhibition "Treasures of Ancient Nigeria" happens to be home for a rest from world touring. The **"Treasures"** exhibition traces 2800 years of Nigerian art from the earliest terracotta figures from **Nok** in the Jos Plateau, through extraordinarily intricate and sophisticated **Igbo Ukwe** bronze castings from southeast Nigeria, to the almost Hellenic realism of the later **Ife and Owo** brass and terracotta busts – which provide a glimpse into Yoruba court life from the twelfth to the fifteenth century. The famous **Benin bronzes** were made exclusively for the Oba by master craftsmen working for the court, and represent some of the greatest masterpieces of West African art.

In the permanent collection, the **Symbols of Power and Authority Gallery** is designed to give an overview of the regal insignia of Nigeria's diverse ethnic groups. The display of **masquerades**, common to a range of peoples, shows off one of the oldest forms of cultural and artistic expression. In Nigeria, masquerades not only served to provide a link with the realm of the dead but were important in instigating other art forms like music, dance and drama. Other exhibits range from decorated pottery and calabashes from the different regions to shrines and household gods reflecting the importance of the supernatural in people's lives.

The **Benin Gallery** contains a selection of bronzes and ivory carvings, including the well-known waist mask that appears on the naira note and was symbol of the 1977 FESTAC festival (see p.1047). Unfortunately, many masterpieces of Benin art are still held abroad, despite numerous requests for their return from the Nigerian

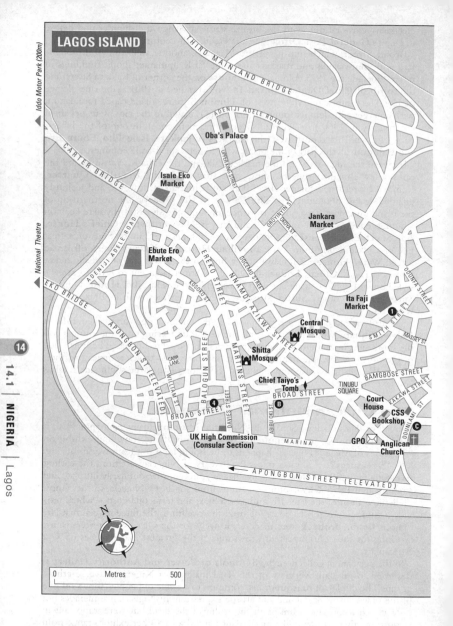

government. An additional permanent exhibition, **"Nigerian Governments: Yesterday and Today"**, traces the political history of the country from the slave trade to the present, though the only really impressive exhibit here is President Murtala Muhammed's bullet-holed car, which pays menacing homage to one of Nigeria's most popular leaders, assassinated in February 1976.

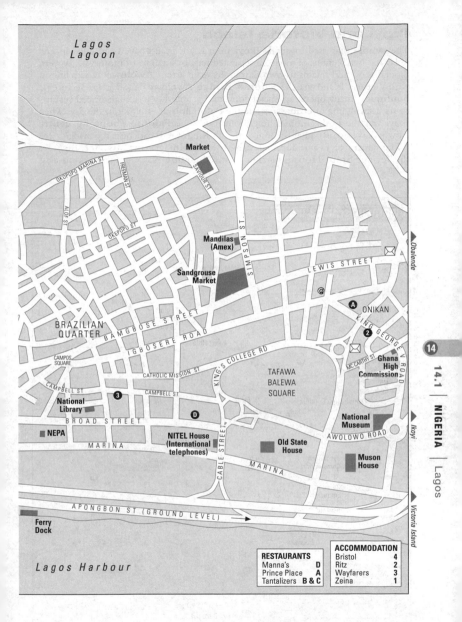

Lagos Lagoon

Market

Mandilas
(Amex)

Sandgrouse
Market

OKOPOPO MARINA ST

FREEMAN ST

ALOF ST

OKEPOPO ST

SAVIOUR ST

SIMPSON ST

LEWIS STREET

ONIKAN

A

2

KING GEORGE V ROAD

BRAZILIAN
QUARTER

BAMGBOSE STREET

IGBOSERE ROAD

CAMPOS
SQUARE

CATHOLIC MISSION ST

KING'S COLLEGE RD

McCARTHY ST

Ghana
High
Commission

TAFAWA
BALEWA
SQUARE

CAMPBELL ST

CAMPBELL ST

3

National
Library

D

BROAD STREET

NEPA

MARINA

NITEL House
(International
telephones)

CABLE STREET

Old State
House

National
Museum

AWOLOWO ROAD

Muson
House

MARINA

APONGBON ST (GROUND LEVEL)

Ferry
Dock

Lagos Harbour

▲ Obalende

▲ Ikoyi

▲ Victoria Island

14

14.1 | **NIGERIA** | Lagos

RESTAURANTS	
Manna's	**D**
Prince Place	**A**
Tantalizers	**B & C**

ACCOMMODATION	
Bristol	4
Ritz	2
Wayfarers	3
Zeina	1

If you're looking to buy woodcarvings, check out the museum's **craft village**, at least for an idea of how much you can expect to pay for works in Lagos – prices here are fixed. In fact, the chances are you won't find prices any cheaper outside the big hotels, where all the gear is often laid out. Lastly, you can take a break from all the culture in the very good **Museum Kitchen** (see p.1049).

Ikoyi and Victoria Island

The swamps that used to divide **Ikoyi** from Lagos Island have been filled in, and today the two sections of town are separated only by a tangle of motorway flyovers, though Ikoyi still retains its own flavour. Its main artery, **Awolowo Road**, links it with Victoria Island via the **Falomo Bridge**. Awolowo Road is home to chic **boutiques** (many operating out of converted private homes), high-priced **restaurants**, a sprinkling of **embassies** and the **Polo Club**, a reminder of the days when Ikoyi was the posh colonial neighbourhood. The **Falomo shopping centre** crowns Awolowo Road at the junction with Kingsway Road, near the bridge.

The centre of Ikoyi, dominated by the **administrative district**, includes the former **State House**. Further west, **Obalende** is a vibrant working-class

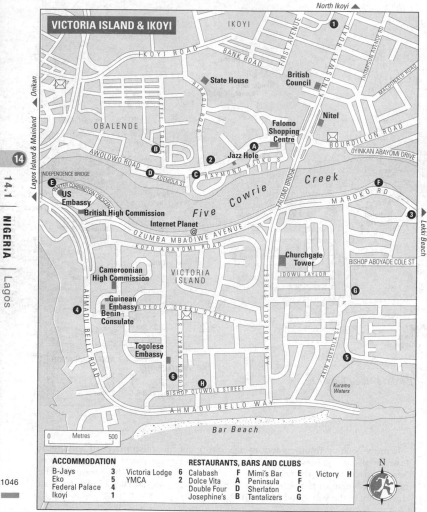

VICTORIA ISLAND & IKOYI

IKOYI

FIRST AVENUE

KINGSWAY ROAD

THOMPSON AVENUE

MACDONALL ROAD

IKOYI ROAD

BANK ROAD

◀ Onikan

◀ State House

British Council

RIBADU ROAD

EFFEL STREET

OBALENDE

Falomo Shopping Centre

Nitel

BOURDILLON ROAD

◀ Lagos Island & Mainland

AWOLOWO ROAD

Ⓑ

②

Ⓐ Jazz Hole

RAYMOND NJOKU ST

OYINKAN ABAYOMI DRIVE

INDEPENDENCE BRIDGE

Ⓓ ADEMOLA ST

Ⓒ

FALOMO BRIDGE

Cowrie

Creek

Ⓔ WALTER CARRINGTON CRESCENT

US Embassy

British High Commission

Internet Planet @

Five

MAROKO RD

Ⓕ

③

▶ Lekki Beach

OZUMBA MBADIWE AVENUE

KOFO ABAYOMI ROAD

Churchgate Tower

BISHOP ABOYADE COLE ST

Cameroonian High Commission

VICTORIA ISLAND

IDOWU TAYLOR

Ⓖ

④

Guinean Embassy

Benin Consulate

ADEOLA ODEKU STREET

AKIN ADESOLA STREET

AKIN ADESOLA ST

Togolese Embassy

IDUGUN AGBALE S

⑤

Kuramo Waters

Ⓗ BISHOP OLUWOLE STREET

AHMADU BELLO ROAD

AHMADU BELLO WAY

Bar Beach

0   Metres   500

N

14.1 | NIGERIA | Lagos

⑭

ACCOMMODATION				RESTAURANTS, BARS AND CLUBS			
B-Jays	3	Victoria Lodge	6	Calabash	F	Mimi's Bar	E	Victory	H
Eko	5	YMCA	2	Dolce Vita	A	Peninsula	F
Federal Palace	4			Double Four	D	Sherlaton	C
Ikoyi	1			Josephine's	B	Tantalizers	G

neighbourhood with a large market, numerous chop bars (good places for authentic pepper soup or *suya*) and watering holes where locals come to drink and dance.

The principal modern residential area of Lagos, **Victoria Island** (sometimes referred to as V.I.) is divided into thousands of expensive plots, many of them taken up by foreign **embassies** and expatriate residences. Near the **Independence Bridge** to Lagos Island, **Walter Carrington Crescent** (occasionally known by its former name, Eleke Crescent) has the highest concentration of diplomatic missions, including those of the UK and the USA. **Bar Beach**, the city's closest strand, runs along the island's southern flank.

The mainland

A vast reach of working-class districts, industrial zones and shanty towns heaves over the mainland for miles. Other than getting to and from the international airport, railway station or motor parks, there's little reason for visitors to spend much time here, although the residential **Surulere** district, 10km from Victoria Island, is home to the **National Stadium** and a vibrant **nightlife** quarter, and **Ebute Metta**, just short of Lagos Island, is the site of the **National Theatre** complex.

The National Theatre complex

Rising out of the low-rent district of Ebute Metta above the creeks, the **National Theatre**'s characteristic concave roof soon appears on your left-hand side if you take the Eko Bridge from Lagos Island to the mainland. Built for the second pan-African Festival of Arts and Culture (FESTAC), which Lagos hosted in 1977 at incredible cost (other legacies from the event include the Festac Town housing project), the theatre is a classic example of high-prestige, low-reward development. It's more a cultural complex than simply a theatrical venue, which is actually a role it rarely has the chance to play. The main ancillary site is the **Centre for Black and African Arts and Civilization** (downstairs from Entrance B; Mon–Sat 8am–5pm), which contains archives, a library and a museum with periodically

---

Lagos markets

Wherever you fetch up in Lagos, you'll find a market close by: there are literally dozens on the mainland, notably Tejuoso in Surulere, and the market in Apapa, which is also close to a good range of ordinary shops and supermarkets. On Lagos Island, **Jankara** market is the prime site and one of the cheapest places for new clothes or secondhand garments, general hardware, traditional musical instruments, cassettes, jewellery and trading beads, magical materials (*jujus*, skins, powders) and *aso-oke*, beautiful woven cloth which is used on special occasions. Northwest of Jankara, between Adeniji Adele Road and Ebute Ero Street, **Isale Eko market** specializes in food, crocks and baskets, and there are some ready-made clothes here too. In the same area, near the old Carter Bridge, is an **Ogogoro market** with scorching (and dangerous) local spirit for sale.

Focusing around the street of the same name on Lagos Island, **Balogun** market is the best place for **cloth**. In the rambling maze of alleys you'll find mostly imported material, including damasks, plus a wide range of African prints. A little to the east, around Nnamdi Azikiwe Street, you can find batiks and ready-made clothes, plus records and cassettes.

Between Lewis and Simpson streets at the eastern end of Lagos Island, **Sandgrouse** market is the best bet for **food** – fresh fish, shrimps and huge snails, as well as more conventional provisions.

Another food market, **Bar Beach market**, can be found towards the end of Ahmadu Bello Road on Victoria Island. In view of all the money and expats on the island, it's no surprise to find some **crafts** here too – including basketry, batiks and even Tuareg leather chests.

changing exhibits. The original FESTAC 1977 exhibits should still be on show. The **National Gallery of Modern Art**, at Entrance B of the theatre complex (Tues–Fri 10am–5pm, Sat & Sun noon–4pm; ₦20), is an exhibition space for the work of young Nigerian talents. Entrance C leads to a bar (with food Mon–Fri 1–5pm) and two cinema halls.

Across the street northwest of the theatre complex, the red-brick **National Gallery of Crafts and Design** displays and sells traditional Nigerian handicrafts (Mon–Sat 9am–5pm). The drinks stalls nearby are a great place to hang out in the early evening with a cheap beer and a meat pie or *moin-moin*.

Beaches

There are a number of beaches in and around Lagos, although the best of them are further out of town and you'll need transport to reach them. Many of the beaches conceal dangerous undersea currents; ask locals about possible risks, and never bathe alone.

Bar Beach, on Victoria Island, has always been unattractive and shadeless, but it's the closest spot to swim in the sea (and a meeting place for Christian sects). Since exceptional spring tides in 1990 and 1994 swept most of the sand away, the beach has been steeper and less enticing than ever. Still, people continue to come here because of the location – just off Ahmadu Bello Way, within walking distance of the homes on Victoria Island.

The most attractive beach near the city centre is 6km east at **Tarkwa Bay**, sheltered within the harbour and safe for swimming. **Lighthouse Beach** is beyond Tarkwa, and also attractive, but dangerous because of its strong currents.

Lekki Beach, 10km east of town, off the New Epe expressway (a continuation of Ozumba Mbadiwe Avenue) and along the Lekki Peninsula, is lined with coconut palms. Take a taxi to Gbara village and walk 2km down the sand road leading from the expressway to the beach, or arrange to be dropped directly at the beach. You can ride horses quite cheaply here, and food and drink are on sale. The Nigerian Conservation Foundation (NCF) has a fine **nature trail** at Lekki, with a well-marked route. It's a peaceful haven out of the city, where monkeys and small crocodiles can be spotted. The **market** at Lekki is a good place for a wander, with a range of beads, cloth and crafts, and the usual fruit, herbs and commodities, and Lekki Beach also hosts the Nigerian version of Jamaica's famous **Sunsplash** music festival, held here every year on Boxing Day (Dec 26). If you have your own transport, try the much quieter **Eleko beach**, 50km further east on the Epe expressway. Many expats rent beach huts on a long-term basis, but empty ones can usually be rented by the hour.

In the other direction, **Badagry**, 55km west of Lagos along the highway towards Benin, also has a lovely beach, but it belies a terrible history. For the estimated half a million-plus slaves between the sixteenth and eighteenth centuries who were packed here into horrific floating prisons for shipping abroad, this was the last place in Africa they ever saw. Today a **Slave Museum** has been set up in a building where captives were held awaiting transportation, and you can see the chains and shackles, whips and dungeons used to keep them under control. You can also see the port from which they embarked on a journey that many never survived, and the market at which they were bought and sold as goods. Should you wish to stay in Badagry, upmarket accommodation is available in the *Whispering Palms Resort* (☎01/585 1597 or 774 1279; ❺).

Ferries run from Victoria Island to **Tarkwa Bay** and other local beaches; Tarzan Boats, for example, operate a service from Walter Carrington Crescent.

Eating, drinking and nightlife

Lagos has thousands of cheap eating places, but is also geared up for splashing out: flashy restaurants, bars, clubs and discos abound, as do more tacky establishments.

None of these, however, will burn a big hole in your pocket. If you think you might go out on the town late in the evening, leave all but the necessary minimum of possessions in your hotel.

Street food and cafeterias

On **Lagos Island**, the supermarkets along Marina Street on Lagos Island all have cafeterias for reasonable lunches, and there's a cheap *Luncheonette Diner* serving tasty Nigerian meals in the yard to the southwest of Tafawa Balewa Square on Broad Street. McCarthy Street, by the Ghanaian High Commission in Onikan, also has a few good chop houses. *Prince Place*, 40 Lawson St, Onikan, is a small shack serving excellent, inexpensive barbecued fish with chips in the evenings from 6.30pm.

The **Obalende** area, on the west side of Ikoyi, is full of inexpensive restaurants and outdoor stands where you can buy fish, *suya* (kebabs), rice and so on. Don't miss the pepper soup, a speciality of this quarter, and the wonderfully flavoured chicken, charcoal grilled to order. On **Victoria Island**, street food is available from a small side-street directly opposite the *Eko Hotel*: boiled yams, beans and rice, *fufu* with meat or fried fish. Eat here and then have a drink in the *Eko* for rapid culture contrast.

One local fast-food chain worth trying is *Tantalizers*, at 19 and 91 Broad St on Lagos Island, and 39 Adetokumbo Ademola Rd, Victoria Island; they serve up reasonable chicken and rice, plus burgers, and pizza of sorts, at moderate prices. The ice cream, however, is worth avoiding.

Restaurants

Most of the pricier restaurants are on Lagos Island, Ikoyi and Victoria Island. A number of these are quite formal, and you'd do well to dress smartly and book ahead. On the **mainland** you're best off in the upmarket hotels, all of which have restaurants of a reliable standard.

Lagos Island

Manna's Restaurant Western House, first floor, 8/10 Broad St. Highly recommended bar-restaurant, serving Nigerian and international cuisine at moderate prices. Closed Sun.

Museum Kitchen National Museum. Extensive and excellent selection of reasonably priced stand-bys – *eba, moin-moin, fufu, dodo, egusi, ogbono* – plus a daily regional speciality dish. Closed at weekends.

La Scala Restaurant Muson House, 8/9 Marina ☏01/264 6885. Exclusive, expensive restaurant in a shopping centre, with French and Italian dishes and wines. Mon–Sat noon–2.30pm & 7–10.30pm.

Ikoyi and Victoria Island

Calabash Next door to the *Peninsula*, Plot 8, Ozumba Mbadiwe Ave. Very pleasant waterside place facing the 1004 Apartments development, with Nigerian dishes and live music some nights.

Dolce Vita 184 Awolowo Rd. Smart Italian restaurant with a comprehensive menu, plus a bar and nightclub.

Double Four 44 Awolowo Rd. Pizzas, Lebanese meze and a good range of other dishes. Tends to be crowded, with the TV blaring, but the food is tasty and not overpriced.

Josephine's Restaurant Keffi St. Reasonable fish-and-rice type meals at rock-bottom prices.

The Light House 14th floor, *Federal Palace Hotel*, Ahmadu Bello Rd ☏01/262 3116 ext 728. The city's top restaurant, serving European fare except on Wednesday evening, when a Chinese menu is on offer.

Peninsula 8 Ozumba Mbadiwe Ave. Terrace restaurant right on the lagoon, serving good Chinese meals. Even if you're not hungry, you can come for a drink and the view. Daily 11am–11.30pm.

The Sherlaton 108 Awolowo Rd. One of Lagos's best Indian restaurants and neither overpriced nor ostentatious. Daily noon–3.30pm (Sun until 5pm) & 7–11.30pm.

Victory Restaurant 31B Bishop Oluwole St. An extremely good-value restaurant, serving Nigerian dishes (including pepper soup, land snails and sometimes bush meat such as grasscutter) at very low prices.

Drinking and nightlife

Lagos is famous as a **music** centre, and the styles that have originated and evolved here – **highlife**, **juju**, **fuji** and **Afro-beat** – are as legendary and international as any in Africa. Lagosians are proud of this and prefer listening to their own music than to the anodyne Euro-American pop that's current over so much of West Africa. The daily *Evening Times* normally has details of what's on across a span of forty or fifty venues where you can dance till dawn and often see live performances. Several restaurants turn into nightclubs as the clock turns 11pm, while other nightclubs are just "gigs", used purely as music venues. The clubs listed here (mainly selected for their live pedigrees) are mostly on the mainland. Don't be intimidated. Get a taxi and get on down.

Ariya Night Club 12 Ikorodu Rd, at Jibowu St, Yaba. *Juju* club belonging to maestro King Sunny Ade, who used to play here quite often, though he rarely does nowadays.

Avondale (Thistle Bar) 36 Marine Rd, Apapa. Restaurant and bar with live music at weekends.

Faslak Nightclub Opposite NNPC, Apapa. Orlando "Dr Ganjah" Owoh, rebel granddad inventor of the *juju*-highlife hybrid he calls "toye", plays here every Thursday.

Jazzville 21 Majaro St, Onike, near Yaba. Bar-restaurant serving local dishes with fish-and-chips (noon–10pm) and with live jazz every Fri from midnight till dawn. Friendly management and lively clientele.

Mimi's Bar 3 Walter Carrington Crescent, within the NAPEX Complex, Victoria Island. A 24hr bar, popular with both expats and locals.

Motherlan' 64 Opebi Rd, Ikeja. Popular club in an outdoor amphitheatre, run by the equally popular

musician Lagbaja!, who plays here on the last Fri of the month.

Neighbours By the *Stadium Hotel*, Surulere. The place for weekend makossa sounds.

New Afrika Shrine Pepple St, Ikeja. Not Fela's original *Shrine*, but a remake by his son Femi, who also plays here on occasion. Fri & Sun are the big nights.

Niteshift 34 Salvation Rd, off Opebi Rd, Ikeja. Former Lagos celebrity hangout, now relocated to a domelike building called the Coliseum, less than a 10min drive from the *Sheraton* and *Airport Hotel*.

Pinto's 5 Allen Ave, Ikeja. Expensive but still very popular, this is one of the best international-style clubs, with a resident jazz band accompanying different singers. Open all night at weekends.

Stadium Hotel 27 Iyun Rd, just west of the National Stadium, Surulere ☎01/833 593. Home of highlife supremo Victor Olaiya and boasting a fantastic floorshow with dancers and contortionists.

Listings

Airlines Most airlines have their offices on Victoria Island (here denoted V.I.) and their opening hours are roughly Mon–Fri 8am–4pm: ADC Airlines, 84 Opebi Rd, Ikeja ☎01/493 6221 or 496 2230; AeroContractors, at the airport's domestic terminal ☎01/496 1340 or 2570, ✆reservations.los @acn.aero; Air France, Plot 9999F Idejo Dammol St, off Adeola Adeku St, V.I. ☎01/262 1455–9, plus a desk at *Eko Hotel*; Air Gabon, Plot 1661, Jolayemi St, V.I. ☎01/262 4902; Albarka, at the airport's domestic terminal ☎01/470 4100, ✆albarkaair@skannet.com, plus desk at *Ikoyi Hotel*; Associated Aviation, 56 Moshood Abiola Crescent, Ikeja ☎01/266 6185 or 493 3700; Bellview, 66B Opebi St, Ikeja ☎01/493 1731–5, and at Bellview Travels, Waterfront Plaza, Plot 270 Ozumba Mbadiwe Av, V.I. ☎/01/261 5098; British Airways, C&C Towers, Plot 1684 Sanusi Fafunwa

St, V.I. (☎01/262 1225–8), plus desk at *Sheraton Hotel*; Cameroon Airlines, 16A Oko-Awo Close, off Karimu Kotun St, V.I. ☎01/261 6270 or 4993; Chanchangi, at the airport's domestic terminal ☎01/774 4660 or 493 9744, ✆calagx@nigol.net.ng; EgyptAir, 22B Idowu Taylor St, V.I. ☎01/261 9233; Ethiopian Airlines, 4 Idowu St, V.I. ☎01/263 1125; Ghana Airways, 130 Awolowo Rd, S.W. Ikoyi ☎686 122 or 269 2658; Kenya Airways/KLM, Plot PC30, Churchgate Building, Afribank St, V.I. ☎01/261 9336 or 261 9420; Lufthansa, 150 Broad St at Martins St ☎01/266 4227 or 4326; Nigeria Airways, 14 Tafawa Balewa Square, Lagos Island ☎01/493 8491 or 773 9874; Overland Airways, 17 Simbiat Abiola Rd, Ikeja ☎01/497 6599; Skyline, 28 Creek Rd, Apapa ☎01/587 4434 or 4658; South African Airways, 28C Adetokunbo Ademola St, V.I.

☎01/262 0607–9; Sosoliso, 44 Ajanaku St, Opebi ☎01/497 1491–2, ✉fly@sosolisoairline.com; Swiss, Chuchgate Bldg, 4th floor, Plot PC 30, Afribank St, V.I. ☎01/261 9700 or 261 8480; Virgin Atlantic, *Sheraton Hotel*, Ikeji ☎01/497 8660–9 ext 053, ✉lagos.reservation.request@sly.virgin.com).

American Express Mandilas Travel Ltd, 33 Simpson St, Lagos Island ☎01/636 887.

Banks and exchange The *Federal Palace* and *Ikoyi* hotels both have forex bureaux, or try Consolidated Bureau de Change, 94A Bode Thomas St, Surulere ☎01/585 1595. Black-market changers usually hang out around the *Bristol Hotel* on Martins St, along Broad St on both sides of Tinubu Square, on Marina outside the post office, and on Victoria Island opposite the *Federal Palace* and *Eko* hotels. There are several banks along Broad St and Marina which will change cash dollars and occasionally sterling. Western Union agents First Bank of Nigeria are at 35 Marina (☎01/266 5900–20).

Bookshops Lagos has the best English-language bookshops in West Africa, and the best of these are both in Ikeja: Quintessence in the Falomo Shopping Centre (where you'll also find Glendora and The Bestseller), and the Jazz Hole at 168 Awolowo Rd. It's worth comparing prices before buying. On Lagos Island, there's CSS Bookshop at 50/52 Broad St, and secondhand books can be found at Affordable Books opposite 29 Marina St.

Car rental There are many agencies in Lagos, nearly all of whom insist on supplying a driver with the vehicle: Avis is at the airport (☎01/497 4420) and c/o Holt Leasing, 25 Creek Rd, Apapa (☎01/587 1531). Hertz is at 12 Keffi St, Obalende (☎01/269 3978–80), and at the airport. Cars can also be rented at the *Eko Hotel* (☎01/269 2194) and from Planet Rent-a-Car at the *Sheraton* (☎01/497 8600–9 ext 8049 or 8050).

Couriers DHL has offices at 32 Awolowo Rd, Ikoyi (☎01/269 2176–80); in the Lufthansa Building, 150 Broad St, Lagos Island (☎01/264 0013); and has other premises citywide. FedEx is at Okoi Arikpo House, 5 Idowu Taylor St, Victoria Island (☎01/261 0586 or 470 5074). UPS is at 12 Idowu Taylor St, Victoria Island (☎01/545 1883), and has other offices citywide.

Cultural centres and libraries Alliance Française, 2 Aromire Rd, off Kingsway Rd, opposite *Ikoyi Hotel* ☎01/269 2035 or 2365, ⊛www.maisondefrance-ng.com; The British Council, 11 Kingsway Rd (now officially Alfred Rewane Rd), Ikoyi ☎01/269 2188–92. The National Library, 4 Wesley St (Mon–Fri 7.30am–3.30pm; ☎01/265 6590), is a good reference library with books and periodicals.

Embassies and consulates Most are on Victoria Island (V.I.) and are open Mon–Fri. They include: Australia, 2 Ozumba Mbadiwe Ave, V.I. ☎01/261 8875 or 3124; Benin, 4 Abudu Smith St, V.I. ☎01/261 4385 or 4111; Burkina Faso, 15 Norman Williams St, Ikoyi ☎01/681 001; Cameroon, 5 Elsie Femi Pearse St, V.I. ☎01/261 2226 or 4386; Canada, 4 Idowu Taylor St, V.I. ☎01/262 2516; Central African Republic, Plot 137, Ajao Estate, New Airport, Oshodi ☎01/682 820; Chad, 2 Goriola St, V.I. ☎01/613116; Côte d'Ivoire, 3 Abudu Smith St, V.I. ☎01/261 0936; Equatorial Guinea, 7 Murtala Muhammed Drive, Ikoyi ☎01/268 3717 or 2013; France, 1 Oyinkan Abayomi Drive, Ikoyi ☎01/269 3427–30; Gabon, 8 Norman Williams St, Ikoyi ☎01/684 566 or 673; The Gambia, 162 Awolowo Rd, Ikoyi ☎01/682 192; Ghana, 21/23 King George V St, Onikan, Lagos Island ☎01/263 0015 or 0493; Guinea, 8 Abudu Smith St, V.I. ☎01/261 6961; Ireland, 35 Sinari Daranijo St, V.I. ☎01/262 4820; Liberia, 3 Idejo St, off Adeola Odeku St, V.I. ☎01/261 8899 or 1294; Mauritania, 1A Karimu Giwa Close, SW Ikoyi ☎01/268 2971; New Zealand, c/o the High Commission in London ☎+44 20 7930 8422, ✉nzhc.consular@freeuk.com; Niger, 15 Adeola Odeku St, V.I. ☎01/261 2300 or 2330; Senegal, 14 Kofo Abayomi Rd, V.I. ☎01/261 1722; Sierra Leone, 31 Alhaji Waziri Ibrahim St, V.I. ☎01/261 4666; South Africa, 4 Maduike St, off Raymond Njoku St, SW Ikoyi ☎01/269 3842; Togo, 96 Awolowo Rd, Ikoyi ☎01/268 1337; UK, 11 Walter Carrington Crescent, V.I. ☎01/261 9537; USA, 2 Walter Carrington Crescent, V.I. ☎01/261 0139 or 0097.

Hospitals and clinics The best hospital is undoubtedly the Eko Hospital in Mobalaji Bank Anthony Way, Ikeja, near the *Sheraton* (☎01/497 8800–2). St Nicholas Hospital at 57 Campbell St (☎01/260 0070–9), near the National Library on Lagos Island, is more central, with a 24hr casualty service. Recommended general practitioners include Dr M. Semaan and Dr D. Semaan, St Francis Clinic, Keffi St, Ikoyi (☎01/269 2305); for dental treatment try Dr Bode Karunwi, Schubbs Dental Clinic, 5 Douala Rd, Apapa (☎01/545 2228).

Internet access Cybercafés spring up and disappear with gay abandon, and prices are currently falling from a once-standard ₦10/min to ₦200/hr or even less. One of the most comfortable places, with fast connections, is Internet Planet, in the Mr Biggs building at 82 Ozumba Mbadiwe St, Victoria Island (Mon–Sat 9am–7pm). On Lagos Island, e-world, on the first floor of Lapal House, on the corner of Igbosere and Strachca sts in

Onikan, is open 24hr most of the week, though closed Sat 8pm–Sun 2pm.

Mail and telephones The GPO is on Marina St, Lagos Island (Mon–Fri 8am–noon & 2–4pm, Sat 8am–noon), with main branches on Awolowo Rd (at the junction with Kingsway Rd), Ikoyi, and Adeola Odeku St, Victoria Island. Both branches are closed Sat. NITEL is on Cable St, Lagos Island (daily 24hr).

Pharmacies Chyzob, 168 Awolowo Rd, Ikoyi ℡01/269 4545; Medicine Plus, 2nd floor, Mega Plaza, 14 Idowu Martins St, Victoria Island; Nigerian Medicine Stores Ltd, 4 Tinubu Square, Lagos Island ℡01/263 2546.

Supermarkets On Victoria Island, try La Pointe Supermarket, 74B Adetokunbo Ademola St or Park 'N' Shop at Guru Plaza, 47B Adeola Odeku St. In Ikoyi, there's Goodies Supermarket at 195 Awolowo Rd, and on the mainland in Ikeja you'll find Park 'N' Shop at 16 Mobolaji Bank Anthony Way.

Swimming pools The big hotels have pools, but those at the *Ikoyi* and *Federal Palace* (in theory open for a fee to non-guests) usually don't have water. The *Eko Hotel*'s pool has the cleanest water, but is reserved for residents only.

Travel agents and tour operators Many agencies are grouped around the north side of Tafafa Balewa Square. Others include: Bitts Travels & Tours, E7 Falomo Shopping Centre, V.I. (℡01/269 6095, ℻269 1337), which organizes excursions for groups to various tourist destinations; Transcap Travel, CFAO Building, 1 Davies St (between Balogun and Martins streets), Lagos Island (℡01/266 0321 or 266 5063); and Jemi-Alade Tours, 5 Olaide Tomori St, Ikeja (℡ & ℻01/496 0297), running upmarket slave-route tours covering southwestern Nigeria and the Benin republic.

14.2

The southwest

The towns and rural parts of the southwest, often referred to as **Yorubaland**, have an exceptional wealth of cultural interest and natural beauty. In pre-colonial times, the **Yoruba** created one of the most powerful empires in West Africa – and the area is still charged with reminders. Most of the larger towns, for example, still have ruling **obas**, or kings, who wield a good deal of political clout despite limitations imposed on them by the federal government system. The obas continue to live in **royal palaces**, many of which can be visited, like the palace at **Oyo**, former capital of the Yoruba kingdom of the same name.

Some of what is now known about the area's more distant past is the result of excavations carried out in **Ife**. The brass and terracotta statues found here drew international attention and suggest a sophisticated civilization dating back to at least the ninth century. According to Yoruba legend, however, Ife is even older – the first place in the world to be created. It has naturally enjoyed a position as the holiest place in the Yoruba realm, a sort of Mecca of Yoruba religion. Here and throughout the region, the living wood of the **old religion** still breathes beneath a thick layer of Christian or occasionally Islamic belief. You'll see shrines and temples in almost all the towns. At **Oshogbo**, a whole **Sacred Forest** has been set aside as a reserve for worshippers, or "fetishers": the shrines here are vast and amazing and the wor-shippers only too eager to show visitors around – definitely a Nigerian highlight.

Once you cross over into **Edo State**, it's a short distance to **Benin City**, once a formidable kingdom, though already in decline by the time the British arrived. Faced with the modern town of the same name, you may be hard pressed to conjure up images of the former empire, but there are vestiges of the past, including ruins of the **great wall** that surrounded the city, and numerous bronze and ivory **sculptures** housed in the city's renowned museum. Some traditional skills have been preserved in the numerous workshops and galleries around town – excellent places to buy art and crafts, particularly in brass and bronze.

Abeokuta

ABEOKUTA, 100km north of Lagos, on the old road to Ibadan (1hr by minibus from Ojota new garage), is "Ake" in Wole Soyinka's novel of the same name (the name of the royal district of the town where he grew up), and birthplace of not only Soyinka but also musician Fela Kuti and President Olusegun Obasanjo. The capital of Ogun State, Abeokuta was founded in the early 1800s as a site for freed Yoruba slaves, some of whom were liberated by the British Royal Navy, and some of whom had made their own way back to their homeland from Freetown and elsewhere. It's an attractive town, with a spectacular, and easily climbable, outcrop of gigantic granite boulders overlooking it – Abeokuta means "under the rock". The rock can be visited and climbed (daily 7am–6pm; ₦50, plus ₦150 to bring a camera, ₦250 camcorder), and guides are on hand to show you the old war hide-outs, and the main shrine where the chief oba makes a public sacrifice to the gods every August 5 for the peace and tranquillity of the town. In bygone times the sacrifice was human, a curfew having been declared some days before, and anyone unwittingly in breach of it (invariably a stranger in town) was arrested to be the victim. At the base of the rock, the **Oluma Art Movement** has set up workshops and a gallery for traditional and modern art.

The centre of the town is dominated by the **chief oba's palace** (Abeokuta also has four lesser obas) and adjacent **Anglican church**, the oldest church building in Nigeria. Vehicles from Lagos use the **Kuto garage**. The town's top **hotel** is the *Gateway Hotel*, on Ibrahim Babangida Boulevard conveniently near Kuto garage (☏039/241 904 to 5 ℻241 716; ❸); it has air conditioning, satellite TV, a Chinese restaurant and an Olympic-size pool. A cheaper option is the hotel's annexe, run as a separate establishment, not far away on Ademola Road (☏039/240 004; ❸). A relaxing retreat set among slightly scruffy gardens, it has a good restaurant and very helpful management. Other budget options are the *Alafia Guest House*, in Oke Ilewo district (☏039/240 788; ❸), and the *Front Line*, on Oluwo Road, Onikolobo Ibara (no phone; ❷).

Ibadan

The south's second city and the modern capital of Oyo State, **IBADAN** (pronounced with the stress on the first "a") is a vast metropolis that sprawls so far you think it's never going to stop. The city's horizons are marked by few Lagos-style high-rises but instead by a plethora of two-storey, corrugated-iron-roofed houses, spreading like an urban fungus over the low hills. People here still assert Ibadan has the biggest population of any city in Africa, though this hasn't been true since the 1960s; the current population is probably around five million.

Founded by Yoruba renegades at the end of the eighteenth century, Ibadan occupies a strategic position between the forest and the plains, its name deriving from *eba odan*, meaning "field between the woods and the savanna". The settlement began to grow after 1829, when it became an important Yoruba military headquarters and a refuge for people dispossessed in Fulani raids on northern Oyo. By the time the British forced it into a treaty of protection in 1893, it was already extraordinarily large for its time, with an estimated population of 120,000. In colonial times, Ibadan went on to become an important trading centre, which it remains. It is also a major academic city: the **University of Ibadan**, founded in 1948, was the first in the country and is still considered one of West Africa's best.

Arrival and transport

Arriving **by road**, you're likely to be dropped off on the edge of town, at Iwo Road or Agodi Gate motor park ("Gate") in the east, or New Garage in the southeast. The places you'll probably want to make for are **Dugbe**, around the western end of Dugbe Road in the centre of town; or **Mokola**, around Mokola Roundabout 1km north of Dugbe and near the main area of cheap hotels. A useful minibus service connects Agodi Gate motor park with Mokola and Dugbe; another connects it with Iwo Road. There are a couple of centrally located arrival points – Sango motor park south of Dugbe, and Bere Square a couple of kilometres east of here. The **train station** is centrally located just west of Magazine Road. Ibadan's **airport** is 12km southeast of town.

Public transport consists of minibuses, taxis (which look exactly like ordinary cars), and okadas (motorcycle taxis). Shared taxis function like buses, using the same stops (which are often unmarked, so ask), and charging the same fares. You'll find **banks** in the area around Cocoa House, south of Dugbe Road, and, of more relevance if you're changing money, several **bureaux de change**. Leventis and UTC **supermarkets** are located nearby. The post office (Mon–Fri 8am–5pm, Sat 9am–1pm) is just west of here on Dugbe Road. There are a couple of **Internet** places in Center Point Plaza, Dugbe.

Accommodation

Ibadan has dozens of hotels and lodging houses, but they tend to be a little pricey for what you get.

Alma Guest House 19 Oyo-Ibadan Ave, Bodija ☎02/810 0657. Signposted off Bodija Rd 200m north of the customs post, this is small, quiet and clean, with a restaurant serving Nigerian and continental dishes. All rooms are s/c with satellite TV. ❸

Dick Hotel N6/328 Ago-Tapa, off Oyo Rd, Mokola ☎02/241 1263. Nothing special, but adequate for the price, with no a/c but good ceiling fans. ❷

Edu Guest House 37 Onireke Layout, off Onireke Rd ☎02/241 4327. A pleasant establishment with large a/c rooms in a quiet neighbourhood. ❷

Green Springs Hotel Old Ife Rd ☎02/810 5198. An older hotel resembling a miniature housing estate in leafy surroundings, with both a/c, s/c bungalow-style rooms, and s/c suites with a/c and satellite TV. There's a good bar and a restaurant with live highlife and *juju* music every Sun evening. ❹

Moving on from Ibadan

Vehicles for Ife and the southeast mostly leave from Gate motor park. Minibuses for Gate leave from Queens Cinema on Dugbe Rd, by the footbridge 300m north of Dugbe centre. For Oyo and points north (Abuja, Kaduna, Kano), transport mostly leaves from Iwo Road (accessible by bus from Gate), though a few still use Sango motor park. Vehicles for Lagos leave from New Garage, but there are also Lagos vehicles from Iwo Road, from Bere Square, and even direct from Dugbe.

Trains leave for Lagos via Abeokuta, and Kano via Kaduna. Check at the station to get the latest schedules, or call NRC's Kaduna office (☎062/231 880 or 791). There are **flights** to Lagos, Abuja and Ilorin with Skyline from Ibadan's domestic airport. Nigeria Airways has offices at 9 Liberty Road, southwest of town (☎02/231 5122), but no scheduled flights out of Ibadan. A number of **travel agents** act for the international airlines; Tess Travels, F3 Centre Point Plaza, opposite AfriBank in Dugbe (☎0802/350 9261), is an excellent place to make travel arrangements in Nigeria and beyond.

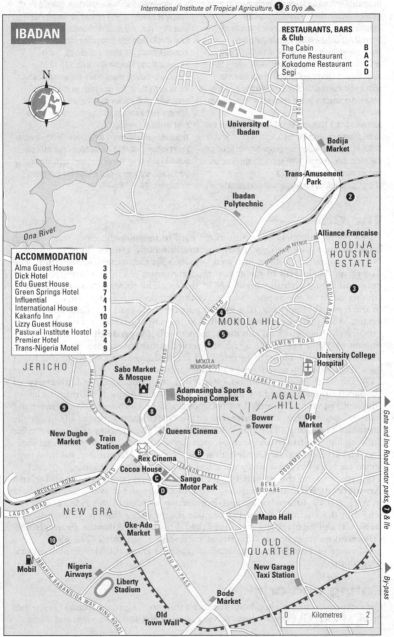

IBADAN

RESTAURANTS, BARS & Club

The Cabin	**B**
Fortune Restaurant	**A**
Kokodome Restaurant	**C**
Segi	**D**

University of Ibadan

Bodija Market

Trans-Amusement Park

❷

Ibadan Polytechnic

Alliance Francaise

BODIJA HOUSING ESTATE

Ona River

ACCOMMODATION

Alma Guest House	**3**
Dick Hotel	**6**
Edu Guest House	**8**
Green Springs Hotel	**7**
Influential	**4**
International House	**1**
Kakanfo Inn	**10**
Lizzy Guest House	**5**
Pastoral Institute Hostel	**2**
Premier Hotel	**4**
Trans-Nigeria Motel	**9**

❸

❹ MOKOLA HILL

❺

University College Hospital

JERICHO

Sabo Market & Mosque

Adamasingba Sports & Shopping Complex

AGALA HILL

Bower Tower

Oje Market

New Dugbe Market

Train Station

Queens Cinema

Rex Cinema

Cocoa House

Sango Motor Park

BERE SQUARE

NEW GRA

Oke-Ado Market

Mapo Hall

OLD QUARTER

Mobil

Nigeria Airways

Liberty Stadium

Bode Market

New Garage Taxi Station

Old Town Wall

0 Kilometres 2

14

14.2 | NIGERIA

Gate and Ino Road motor parks ❶ & Ife ▶

By-pass ▶

Abeokuta ▲

Lagos Road

Abeokuta Road

Ibrahim Babangida Way (Ring Road)

Lagos (E1 Expressway) ▼

Hotel Influential On Mokola Hill ☎02/241 4894. Reasonably priced and recently renovated, in a handy location next to *Premier Hotel*. ❹

International House International Institute of Tropical Agriculture (IITA), 5km beyond the University of Ibadan on Oyo Rd ☎02/241 2626, ✉iita@cgnet.com. Private guesthouse within the beautiful and secure compound of the institute, with a vast range of facilities – including a sports centre, bar, snack bar and cafeteria – and rates to match. ❽

Kakanfo Inn 1 Nihinlola St, off Adebiji St, near the Mobil Station on Ring Rd ☎02/231 1471–3 or 231 8603–10, ⊛www.kakanfoinn.com. Stylish hotel on the south side of town, with spacious a/c doubles and an excellent restaurant. ❻

Lizzy Guest House 40 Adenle Ave, signposted from

Oyo Rd ☎02/241 3350. Comfortable guesthouse with inexpensive s/c, a/c rooms with satellite TV. ❹

Pastoral Institute (PI) Hostel UI-Secretariat Rd, near the university ☎02/810 3928. Clean s/c rooms with fans and mosquito nets; breakfast included. Strict 10.30pm curfew. ❸

Premier Hotel Mokola Hill ☎02/241 1234. Expensive-looking place that's not unreasonable for what it offers. You can relax in relative style here, with all the amenities, including a pool and Chinese restaurant, not to mention some of the best views in town. ❺

Trans-Nigeria Motel 1 Bale Oyewole Rd, Jericho Reservation ☎02/241 4680. Nice colonial-style building in a quiet neighbourhood, with reasonably priced a/c, s/c rooms and a Nigerian-European restaurant. ❸

The City

Given Ibadan's unwieldy dimensions, it's hard to pinpoint the city's heart, though by default you'd have to say it beats around the **New Dugbe Market** – one of Nigeria's largest. Should you lose your way, look for the strange **Bower Memorial Tower** on **Agala Hill** to the east, a good viewpoint to climb and a visible reference point from virtually anywhere in the city. The tower of **Cocoa House** is another guide for the disoriented. One of the few skyscrapers in town, it's evidence of the regional importance of a vital export crop and marks Ibadan's commercial centre. More good views are to be had in the **Old Quarter**, where the British established themselves on the city's highest hill. **Mapo Hall** was built on the summit of Mapo Hill in the 1920s and served as the colonial government house. Today, the stylish building is mostly used for wedding receptions, and if it hasn't been rented out, you're welcome to wander around.

On the north side of town, on Oyo Road, the campus of the **University of Ibadan** (UI) was designed for the most part by the distinguished British architect, Maxwell Fry, who also worked with Gropius and Le Corbusier. You can meet and mix with people here at the **cafeteria** or the **coffee shop** (open to all), or use the university **bookshop** (Mon–Fri 7.30am–4.30pm). The Institute of African Studies building houses a **museum** (open by special request) with bronze statues and carvings. The UI **Zoological Garden**, near the Zoological Department, has been neglected for years, but has recently got a face lift and some new animals.

On your way to the university, you'll pass the huge new **Transwonderland Amusement Park**, an attraction as close to Disneyland as you'll find anywhere in Africa. It's a somewhat surreal experience to sample the rides and Ferris wheel in the environment of Ibadan, but it's proving a big hit in the city – at weekends and holidays, the place is packed. Nearby, the **Alliance Française**, 45 Oshumtokun Avenue, on the corner of Bodija Road (☎02/241 4937), has a good range of French-language reading material and a full artistic and cultural programme.

Eating and drinking

For inexpensive dining, chop houses are a bit thin on the ground around Dugbe, but up on Mokola Hill, there are *bukas* serving *begiri* (traditional bean soup) and *àmàlà*.

Bisi *Kakanfo Inn*, 1 Nihinlola St ☎022/311 471. This upmarket hotel also features one of the

town's best Indian restaurants, with a varied menu and friendly service.

Ibadan area markets

Some of Ibadan's **markets** work on an eight-day cycle, which is fine as long as you know where you are in it: check local papers such as the weekly *Irohin Yoruba* for details.

Bode Near Molete bridge, and specializing in beads.

Mokola 3km north of Cocoa House. Food, pots and baskets. Daily.

New Dugbe Near the train station. A massive general market. Daily.

Oje Near Mapo Hall, east of Bere Road, this is one of the biggest cloth markets in Africa, with over three million yards sold annually (watch out for the *aso-oke* strip cloth made in Iseyin and locally produced tie-dyes), plus trade beads. Every sixteen days.

Ojoo 2km north of the university, west of the Oyo road. Every eight days.

Onidundu 14km north of IITA, west of the Oyo road, specializing in spices, herbs, mats and baskets. Every eight days.

Sabo Near the Friday mosque. The big food and domestic market; this is *the* place to get a good food pestle. Daily.

University market University of Ibadan. A souvenir market. Daily.

The Cabin Ogupa Oyo Rd, off Lebanon St. Lebanese and European specialities, including great steaks and ice cream.

Fortune Restaurant 27 Kudeti Ave, off Onireke Rd. A long and rather good Chinese menu. Mon–Fri 12.30–3.30pm & 7.30–10.30pm, Sun 7.30–10.30pm.

Kokodome Restaurant By Cocoa House. Lebanese, European and American food, including cheeseburgers and fries. For a small fee, you can spend the day at the pool and have food brought to your patio table; sit-down eating is upstairs. There's a good disco here on Fridays (*Legend Nightclub*) with no cover charge, though you have to dine at the restaurant to get in.

Segi Femi Johnson House (aka the Glass House), 1 Alhaji Jimoh Odutola Rd ☎02/241 4838. An upmarket, but far from outrageously priced, mainly Lebanese restaurant with excellent food and formal service.

Oyo and around

OYO is a relatively small town by Nigerian standards, with only a quarter of a million inhabitants, and its characteristic rust-stained roofscape looks like an Ibadan that never quite took off. On its earlier site to the north, the town was the capital of a Yoruba-speaking empire that stretched as far as present-day Togo (including such important vassal states as Dan-Homey; see p.924). At its apogee around 1700, Oyo was probably the most powerful state in West Africa.

Oyo was founded on the northern Yoruba savanna some time between the eleventh and thirteenth centuries, according to legend by **Oranmiyan**, the youngest of the Ife princes (sons of Oduduwa). It was strategically located in a part of the savanna relatively free from tsetse flies, and so could use **horses** for transport and war. From its old capital in **Oyo-Ile**, in the present-day **Oyo-Ile National Park**, Oyo began to expand southwards in the sixteenth century, using both its highly efficient cavalry and its infantry to extend its power to the coast. Until the end of the eighteenth century, most of its wealth came from control of the trade routes between the coast and the north. By the late eighteenth century, however, the courts of Lisbon and Oyo were increasingly involved as partners in the slave trade. The name "Yoruba" is a corruption of "Yooba", meaning "the dialect of the Oyo people". The fact that missionaries applied the term to all the peoples of the region attests to the city's far-reaching power, but revolt by its vassals and war with the Muslim jihadists from the north spelt the end of the empire in the nineteenth century.

The present town of Oyo was founded in the 1820s, when Oyo-Ile fell to Muslim raiders. The Alafin (the local name for the traditional ruler) attempted to re-establish the grandeur of the old capital at **Ago**, a market town south of Oyo-Ile, which he named Oyo. Although the only hint of its grand past is a sign welcoming visitors to "The City of Warriors", Oyo is an excellent place to buy crafts (carved calabashes, talking drums and so forth) and a good base for visiting Old Oyo National Park.

The Town

Although, transport-wise, your main point of reference will probably be **Owode**, where Antiba Street and Iseyin Road meet the main Ibadan–Ilorin highway, the town of Oyo really centres around **Abiodun Atiba Hall** (also called Town Hall), perched high on a hilltop. If you're walking up from the highway, you can see this monumental building from a kilometre away. When you arrive at the hall, you'll see the market spreading out before you on Palace Road.

Oyo's main point of interest is the **Alafin's Palace**, situated on Palace Road beyond the market. Townspeople will tell you that the present ruler is still head of all the obas of Yorubaland, although the Oni of Ife is also considered to hold the title. In fact a raging dispute – going back to colonial times when the practice of rotating the Chair of the Council of Obas was upset – has occupied attention for years and the two leaders are effectively at daggers drawn. The Oni of Ife, as the descendant of Oduduwa, is more a spiritual leader, however, and in theory should not be open to challenge by earthly office-holders. Whatever disputes there may be, the Alafin of Oyo is one of the nation's most influential traditional rulers. His residence is a curious compound – statues and carvings line the grounds, and there are numerous low buildings, some decorated with traditional symbols and all roofed in the ubiquitous rusty corrugated iron. You'll have to get a guide at the gate before visiting the grounds – money is never discussed, but at the end of the tour you're expected to dash something. Put all thoughts of seeing inside the palace out of your head.

Back at the **market**, besides the usual provisions and various household goods, you can find wonderful leatherwork and intricately carved **calabashes** – a local speciality, carved at the market in small *ateliers*. Another speciality are "talking drums" (*dundun*), these too made and sold in market workshops. Although shops on the highway sell those wares to passing travellers (LSA at 19 Owode Commercial Rd, 200m east of Owode junction, is a good place for drums), you'll get a better deal and more choice, certainly for calabashes, in the market itself, where you can also see them being made. The Akesan Oyo Co-operative Calabash Carvers Society, just 20m on the left down the street opposite the post office, is an excellent place where you can even choose your calabash and have it carved to order.

Practicalities

Vehicles for Lagos and Ibadan arrive and leave from Owode junction. For Ilorin and the north, they leave from across the main road, 200m east. Vehicles for Oshogbo leave from Awe, 2km east of Owode.

The **post office** is directly opposite the market. There are branches of First and National **banks** on Atiba Street, and moneychangers hang out by the town hall, but in view of the lack of forex bureaux, you're best advised to change money before arriving. If you're planning to visit Old Oyo National Park, contact the **park headquarters** off Iseyin Road, Isokun (☎038/240 125, ☏038/240 699; Mon–Fri 8am–4pm), before leaving Oyo.

The two best-known **hotels**, both mid-range, are located at the entrance to town as you arrive from Ibadan. The *Labamba Hotel* on Ibadan Road, 3km west of Owode (☎038/230 443–4; ➌), with groovy 1960s science-fiction-style chalets in well-kept grounds, is the more charming and expensive of the two, but the *Adeshakin International Hotel*, Asaba, on Iwo Road near Awe (2km east of Owode; ☏038/241 907 or 240 107; ➋) is good value, with doubles that are more like suites, a bar and a restaurant serving Nigerian dishes. The *Oyo Merry Time* at Owode junction (☏038/230 344; ➊) has reasonably clean s/c rooms at the back of the New Covenant Church.

For cheap **eating** in Oyo, you can eat at the chop bars in Owode, and wash down the meal with frothy palm wine (ask around in the market – you'll soon locate a place that sells it). Don't leave town without sampling *begiri* and *wara* (curd cheese), which you can buy in **Akesan market**.

Around Oyo

Heading **north from Oyo** towards Jebba (see p.1089), you pass through **Ogbomosho**, a large and unpleasant industrial centre, and **Ilorin**, the capital of Kwara State, a workaday trading town with a strong Muslim flavour. Neither offer much to entice visitors, though accommodation can be found at both and Ogbomosho has an excellent Baptist hospital. If you're driving, note that the road between the two towns is a notorious accident blackspot. Some 50km southeast of Ilorin, on the Lokoja road, turn off at the small town of **Oro** to the fascinating vil-lage of **Esie**, where over eight hundred carved soapstone images of humans and animals date from the twelfth century. Their origin is difficult to trace, but some features resemble findings from the Nok culture.

West of Oyo, though best reached on the new highway from Ibadan, the small town of **ISEYIN** is famous locally for its wonderful **night market** and cashew trees. It's also one of the main centres for **aso-oke** strip cloth – most of its weaves come from here. If you're staying, try the *Trans-Nigeria Hotels Resthouse*, on the way into Iseyin from the south. A good day-trip from Iseyin is to the **Ikere Gorge Dam**, where you can go fishing or boating on the lake.

Between Iseyin and the border of Benin, there's a wealth of beautiful countryside dotted with old Yoruba **hill forts**. If you've got your own transport, visit **Ado-Awaiye**, 26km south of Iseyin, and **Shaki** and **Ogboro**, respectively 87km and 105km to the north of Iseyin, both off the Agoare–Kaiama road that leads north through the Oyo and Kwara backcountry to Borgu Game Reserve (see p.1089).

North of Iseyin is **Old Oyo National Park** (Dec–April; ₦50). The park is not only important for its animals (including elephants, buffaloes, antelope, hartebeast and duikers), but also archeologically, as the northern part is the site of the ruined city of Oyo-Ile, the original site of Oyo. The main entrance for wildlife viewing is at **Sepeteri** (accessible by direct public transport from Iseyin; from Oyo, you'll need to take a vehicle to Shaki, then another to Sepeteri), where you'll find park rangers, guides and chalet accommodation (➊). For the Oyo-Ile archeological site, however, the best point of entry is at **Igbeti**, also staffed by rangers and with chalet accom-modation (➊). Igbeti is connected by public transport with Sepeteri and with Ogbomosho, which is the best way to get to it from Oyo.

Ife

According to Yoruba legend, **IFE** (also known as **Ile-Ife**), was the first Yoruba city, and indeed, the first city in creation. Custom says it was at this spot that the supreme God **Olodumare** threw an iron chain from the heavens into the waters below. He then instructed his son **Oduduwa** to climb down the chain, carrying with him a calabash full of sand, a chicken and an oil-palm nut. Oduduwa dumped the sand on the water and let the chicken loose. The bird began scratching in the sand, causing dry earth to appear, and meanwhile the palm nut produced a tree. The sixteen fronds of the palm tree represented the sixteen crowned rulers of

Yorubaland and its sixteen cities. More prosaically, **excavations** indicate that Ife was probably founded as a Yoruba city in the ninth century. They have also revealed much about the lifestyle of the royal court: many of the brass and terracotta sculptures from the digs are today on display in the **Ife museum**.

Although Ife was already in political and economic decline by the early 1500s, the town remained a spiritual focus and is still an important symbol of Yoruba nationhood. In addition, it has had a post-independence renaissance as a modern cultural centre with Nigeria's most extensive university campus – the **Obafemi Awolowo University**. The thousands of students add energy to what would otherwise be a sleepy town and provide the opportunity for animated conversation.

Arrival and accommodation

Coming into Ife, you will almost certainly arrive from the west, on the Ibadan Road. At the beginning of town this forks, with the Ondo Road heading south toward the Oba's palace and museum, while the Ibadan Road continues into the commercial centre, where a right turn down Aderemi Road will take you down to the palace and museum.

All of the **places to stay** reviewed are west of the town centre. The *Mayfair* and *Central Olympic* (both near the junction of Ibadan Road with Ondo Road) are closest to town.

Central Olympic Motel Ondo Rd ⌕036/231 591. Ife's budget option, with s/c single and double rooms, and some non-s/c single rooms. ❶
Hotel Diganga Ibadan Rd, 300m past the campus gate ⌕036/233 200 or 231 791. Good-value, clean and friendly, with a spanking new annexe. Most rooms are s/c with a/c, fans and satellite TV, but there are some ultra-cheap non-s/c "ecco singles" in the annexe. The bar-restaurant fills with students in the evening. Buses run here till 9 or 10pm. ❷

Mayfair Hotel 22/26 Ibadan Rd, about 1km from the junction with Aderemi Rd ⌕036/233 254 or 232 102. A good hotel with comfortable a/c rooms. ❷
University Conference Centre On campus ⌕036/230 809; ⊕230 705, ✉ccgh@oauife .edu.ng., Rooms with TV and a/c, plus bar and large restaurant, though the pool and tennis courts belong to the staff club and aren't available to guests. Good value, and not too far from the centre of the campus. ❷

The Town

Although you won't be able to visit the residence at the **Oni's** (Oba's) **Palace** in the Enuwa area of Ife, it's easy enough to walk around the courtyard, with its statues and dignitaries milling about. One of the oba's messengers will take you around (with a translator) to show you the **meeting hall** where local criminal cases are tried under the Yoruba penal code, and the **shrine to Ogun**, where a dog or goat is sacrificed each September.

Adjacent to the royal palace, and not to be missed, is the **National Museum** (daily 8am–6pm; ₦10). As much as a millennium ago, the Oni of Ife wielded great political and spiritual powers. He commanded a whole army of servants, including indentured artists who made brass castings for him and his retinue – staffs, chest ornaments, and miniature pieces in abstract designs or animal shapes. The museum also contains terracotta works dating from the tenth to the thirteenth centuries and more recent wooden carvings. But the most precious treasures are the magnificent **brass and bronze heads** of the Oni and other senior royal figures, made by the lost-wax method (some of the best examples are in the National Museum in Lagos). The sculptors of the heads worked pure copper and copper alloys of various composition – either with more tin (to make bronze) or more zinc (to make brass) – in a realistic mode of expression that is relatively uncommon in African art. They were clearly technical virtuosos of enormous skill, producing heads of rare grace, scored with the fine lines of scarification indicating royal rank. But there is an imperious remote vanity about these heads, and a sense of duty and proscribed creativity, indicating the sculptors' obsession with formal ways of doing things.

In an unmarked garden not far from the museum, the **Oranmiyan Staff** – a carved and decorated stone monolith about five metres high – symbolizes the sword of the first Alaafin of Oyo.

Ife also has a small **Pottery Museum**, two floors of dusty pottery works including musical jars (like skinless drums), coolers and cooking jugs. It's located on More Road (daily 8am–6pm; free though donations are encouraged), a couple of kilometres east of the National Museum.

The university

Obafemi Awolowo University, west of town, was established in the 1960s, and renamed after the first premier of the Western Region when he died in 1987 – a name tag that didn't meet with unanimous approval. Oduduwa Hall, opposite the students' union cafeteria, but best seen from the other side, is an amazing piece of 1960s architecture, and the scope of the grounds and facilities (this is the third largest university campus in the world) is an impressive indication of the stress laid on higher education by the governments of the early independence era.

The university has its own **Museum of Natural History** (Mon–Fri 8am–3.30pm; free) on the top floor of the agriculture faculty, 200m from the university hall. The nearby trees are full of bats, whose wheeling swarms make something of a spectacle, and also nearby is a rather unspectacular **zoo** (daily 10am–4pm; ₦5). There's also an excellent bookshop by the university hall, with a wide selection of Nigerian literature at very low prices. To get there, take one of the frequent minibuses from the town centre to "Campus" which drops you in the heart of things. If the driver lets you down at the **campus gate**, you're only halfway to the university and must catch another bus or flag down students driving into college.

Eating and drinking

For **cheap eating**, the *Momo Ade Food Centre* at 14 Aderemi Rd (behind *Prof. Ojulari's Pool Agency*) is one of several basic chop houses on Aderemi Road near the junction with Ibadan Road serving *eba* and pounded yam with soup. *Ogbe Restaurant*, on Ondo Road by the junction with Ibadan Road, also has cheap and filling Nigerian food, and cold beer.

There's a host of eating places on or around the **campus**. Apart from whole areas of *bukas* doing hot food all day, the student union cafeteria offers a pretty good and inexpensive selection, with further choices in the adjoining New Buka concrete yard, two rows of largely African mini-restaurants.

Oshogbo

Despite a population close on half a million and an important modern sheet-metal plant, **OSHOGBO** seems somehow smaller and more traditional than either Ife or Oyo. **Traditional religion** is perhaps no more prevalent here than in other Yoruba towns, but it's more obvious, especially in the **Sacred Forest**, with its sculptures and temples. Ironically, the renaissance of the religion and art of the town was in part due to an influx of European artists and philosophers who moved here in the 1950s, the most notable of whom was **Suzanne Wenger**, an Austrian painter and sculptor. In 1991, Oshogbo became capital of the then newly created Osun State, a status which has brought a flurry of activity and pushed up rents, but doesn't yet seem to have translated into increased prosperity for the townspeople.

A glossary of Yoruba religion

Aje The malevolent and destructive aspects of womanhood.

Efe Male masks.

Egungun Masks to honour family ancestors, worn during the annual festival of the secret, male society of the same name. Some *egungun* are put on just for entertainment, to mock police, prostitutes, avaricious traders, people with deformities or anyone who unsettles the community. Many come from Abeokuta, and reflect that town's links with Sierra Leone.

Ekiti masks These come from the eastern (*ekiti*) Yoruba kingdoms. Best known is the *ekiti epa* mask, a wooden helmet surmounted by a carved figure.

Eshu Messenger of the *orisha* (gods) and the divine trickster responsible for everything that goes wrong in the world. Every marketplace has a shrine to him, often a simple pillar of sun-baked mud, over which the priests pour daily libations to preserve harmony in the market and community. Devotees of Eshu keep wooden sculptures of him in their houses.

Gelede The Gelede society is found only in some of the western Yoruba kingdoms. Its job is to appease female witches by entertaining them.

Ibeji Twins. If a twin dies, an image is carved of the dead child.

Ifa (also known as Orunmila) A powerful and respected oracle, consulted by those afflicted by disease or madness, or by anyone with a problem to solve. A series of sacred texts – poetic sayings – are interpreted by the *babalawo* or "father of secrets" using the Ifa board and cowries, seeds or stones thrown in a pattern.

Ijebu masks The Ijebu kingdoms of southern Yoruba have imported some of the Delta region's religious societies (like Ekine) from the Ijo. Their masks tend toward the formalistic cubism of Ijo sculpture, quite distinct from the naturalistic lines of northern Yoruba sculpture.

Iyamapo Goddess of women's crafts, including weaving and dyeing.

Nanabuku Controller of the wind.

Obatala (or Orishanla) Responsible for the creation of each individual human form, to which Olodumare gives life and destiny. Obatala's devotees wear white beads and on ceremonial occasions dress in white cloth.

Ogboni The Ogboni society, to which all Yoruba chiefs, priests and senior men belong, is the cult of the earth. It also has a judicial role, being responsible for all cases of human bloodshed – which is an offence against the earth – and a political one, in providing a forum for discussion free of outside interference. Meetings take place in a cult house, where the society's rites and discussions are kept secret from non-members.

Ogun God of war and iron, traditionally worshipped at times of war to seek success in battle, and by hunters seeking successful hunting. More modern devotees include all those who use iron or steel to make a living, or who drive on roads or fly planes.

Olodumare (also known as Olorun) The Yoruba supreme deity and creator god.

Orisha Oko God of the farm.

Osanyin God of medicine, responsible for the magical therapeutic action of leaves, herbs and other ingredients. There's a fundamental relationship between Osanyin and all other cults: devotees use appropriate medicines in order to enter into a close relationship with their chosen *orisha* during their initiation and subsequent life in the cult.

Oshun (or Oya) Goddess of the river which flows through Oshogbo, the patron deity of the town and bringer of fertility to women.

Shango God of thunder and lightning, identified with one of the very earliest kings of Oyo. Has now been co-opted by NEPA, the national electricity company.

The Town

The normal way to get around Oshogbo is by shared taxi. In town, try to visit the **Oba's Palace**, on the junction of Catholic Mission and Osun Shrine roads. Besides the old and new palace buildings, the grounds contain a temple to Oshun (see opposite) with traditional wall paintings and sculpted wooden pillars. Aged priestesses guard the inside of the temple and will say prayers for you in exchange for an offering. Directly across from the palace is the **market shrine**, the meeting place for elders and "King Makers", decorated with carved wooden totems and abstract paintings at the front, and with a tree growing out of the back. Flamboyant **Brazilian houses** with wild ornamentation and bright colours line the whole length of Catholic Mission Street to the northwest.

King's Market spreads out opposite the palace. Besides the wide selection of fruit and vegetables, which grow easily in this fertile part of the country, you'll notice a lot of *juju*, sacred pots and other ritual articles. **Suzanne Wenger's house** is nearby on Ibokun Street and it's worth having a look at from the outside for the imaginative architecture and the ornamentation replete with traditional imagery and symbolism. If Adunni (Wenger's Yoruba name) is in, you may be able to meet her; she has a shop with artefacts for sale, and will gladly sell you a copy of her book, *The Sacred Groves of Oshogbo*. For a deeper understanding of Yoruba religion, it makes interesting reading, and the photographs are beautiful.

The Sacred Forest

Suzanne Wenger was interested in the beliefs and language of the Yoruba as inspiration for her painting, but she soon became a follower of **Obatala** – the Yoruba God of Creation – and, as local women came to appreciate her charismatic "artistic power", became a priestess of the religion in the 1960s. She has been a prime mover in restoring Oshogbo's **Sacred Forest**, which is devoted to the female water deity **Oshun Goddess**. With the help of Nigerian artists, she set about rebuilding the broken-down shrines, places of worship and sculptures, using modern cement

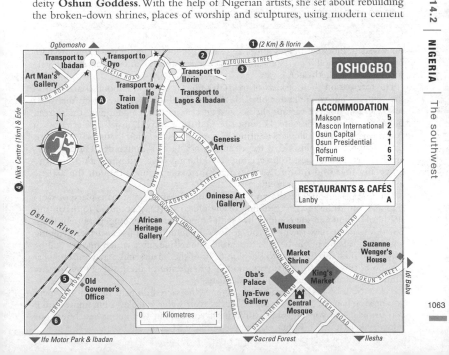

Oshogbo was the site of a famous **artists' workshop**, set up as an offshoot of Ibadan's Mbari Club in the 1960s by writer Ulli Beier (previously married to Suzanne Wenger) and artist Georgina Beier. They ran it for three years, attracting a collection of locals and performers involved in the Duro Ladipo Travelling Theatre. Nigerian artists such as Twins Seven Seven, Muraina Oyelami, Jimoh Buraimoh, Rufus Ogundele, Adebisi Fabunmi and others learnt new techniques from Georgina Beier. Some of these artists are now world famous, and rich and influential at home; Oshogbo remains a major centre of artistic activity, with a large number of galleries and studios.

You can meet the artists and buy their work (and batiks, a speciality of Oshogbo) at their open studios. **Twins Seven Seven (Art Man)** is a particularly entertaining, maverick character, who has determinedly made his art the most commercially successful (if you and he are talking money, talk hard). His gallery, where you can buy ceramics, metal sculptures and appliqué, is off Ede Road by the Boras filling station. **Jimoh Buraimoh** works with beaded collage, beads being traditionally a part of royal insignia on the Yoruba beaded crown, and his murals adorn public buildings all over Lagos. He and his sons run the African Heritage Gallery off Odi Olowo Road in Buraimoh Street.

Nike Davies (a former wife of Twins Seven Seven) has set up the **Nike Centre** for young artists, west on Iwo Road (take a taxi from the Oke Fia garage; if the driver doesn't know the centre, ask for the Dada estate and look out for the signpost). Recently renovated and enlarged, it's booming with creativity, and heavily into batik, painting, carving and even quilt making. Other galleries you might want to visit include Onirese Arts, 58 Station Road, for rather pricey engraved calabashes and batiks; Genesis Art, 138 Station Road, for paintings and wood and brass sculptures; and Iya-Ewe, 7 Osun Shrine Road, for paintings.

Ulli Beier's **museum**, at 27 Catholic Mission Road (daily 10am–5pm; free), contains a small collection of antiquities from around Nigeria, and some from Papua New Guinea.

on wooden and steel frames and a style that combined traditional elements with her own inspiration. The results are spectacular, mysterious and unique, though getting a little weatherbeaten now.

The forest is on the outskirts of town. It's not far to walk – about 2km south of the centre – but you're better off taking a taxi there the first time. From the roadside, you can observe various shrines and an elaborate fence confining the retreat, before arriving at the gate. During the **Oshun Festival**, usually celebrated in August, you'll find followers waiting by the road. The forest costs ₦100 to visit (₦10 for students), plus ₦250 for a camera, ₦500 for a camcorder. Guided tours are available, and it's best to be accompanied during your visit, since it's difficult to make any meaning out of the sites without explanation, although the artistic expression is impressive in itself.

The first place you'll be shown is the **Oshun Temple** – the main place of worship and said to be the first building of the old town (Oshogbo used to be on this site until Oshun said she couldn't live with human beings any longer and sent them off to found the new town). If you go into the temple, you'll see shrines dripping with palm oil and might be asked to make a **sacrifice**, after which prayers will be made. You may also be asked to kneel in front of the shrines and pray yourself: what you do at this point is up to you, though a rendering of the Lord's Prayer or any humble invocation would be quite adequate.

Next, you'll be taken down to the **river** – the sacred domain of Oshun, where you may be handed a calabash full of murky river water. It makes a big impression if you drink it and you probably won't die if you do, but you know best how your body is likely to react. Either way, you're unlikely to cause offence.

Walking through the forest, you'll be shown shrines depicting a myriad of deities (see box, p.1062), all of whom are represented by statues on the site of the market of the old town. The god of creation, **Obatala**, is portrayed riding on an elephant. Other temples in the forest include **Ohuntoto's Building**, a place of prayer to Ohuntoto, the son of Obatala. Designed by Wenger, the architecture forces you into the world of the fantastic – one of the rooms is in the shape of an ear so that those who pray will have their prayers heard.

Practicalities

The main **motor park** is Dugbe (old garage) on Okefia Road, with others nearby and spread around at the entrances to the town; for Ilesha, there's a motor park outside town on the Ilesha road. The **train station** is centrally located on Alhaji Sonmonu Hassan Road. The **post office** and NITEL telephone office are both on Station Road. To get **online**, the best place is Ladatex Links, opposite the *Osun Capital Hotel* on the Iwo–Ibadan Road. For good Nigerian or continental **food**, *Lanby Restaurant* at 3 Alekuwolo Road is the best in town, and will easily fill you up for less than ₦750 for two courses plus a soft drink. There are several **hotels**, the best of which are reviewed here.

Makson Woleola St, near the old governor's office ☎035/242 668. Clean a/c doubles and singles with fan, featuring satellite TV, plus a restaurant, bar, and nightclub on Fridays. ②

Mascon International Off Ajegunle St ☎035/240 246. Rather grubby and used by prostitutes, but dirt cheap, friendly and central, with a bar-restaurant on the first floor and a pool room in the basement. Rooms are poky but are s/c and come with a/c and fan. ①

Osun Capital Iwo–Ibadan Rd, Dada Estate ☎035/240 396. Slightly grimy accommodation featuring s/c single rooms with fan, and doubles with a/c, fan and TV; also has its own restaurant and bar. The water supply is sporadic. ②

Osun Presidential Old Ikirun Rd ☎035/242 399. Oshogbo's top hotel, with comfortable if slightly tatty a/c rooms, plus a cinema. ②

Rofson 51 Gbongan Rd ☎035/240 701. Good-value s/c rooms with a/c, fan and satellite TV, plus ultra-cheap s/c single rooms with fan. Restaurant, bar and VIP bar; Friday-night gig. ①

Terminus Ajegunle St ☎035/240 423. This has seen better days but is still reasonably comfortable and central, with s/c double rooms and a/c junior suites. ②

Benin City and around

Long before Europeans arrived on the West African coast, Benin, now the capital of Edo State, was capital of a powerful empire with a **divine king**. A direct descendant of this line, the **oba**, still reigns over his kingdom, though his duties are of course largely ceremonial nowadays. Today the city is as businesslike as any in Nigeria – feverish, dirty, noisy and crowded. It has no coast, and little in the way of open spaces to escape to, yet its remarkable history, traced in the **Benin National Museum**, has made the town into something of a cultural centre.

Some history

When you go into it you enter a great broad street, which . . . seems to be seven or eight times broader than the Warmoes street in Amsterdam . . . and thought to be four miles long . . . The houses in this town stand in good order, one close and evenly spaced with its neighbour . . . They have square rooms, sheltered by a roof that is open in the middle, where the rain, wind and light come in . . . The king's court is very great . . . built around many square shaped yards . . . I went into the court far enough to pass through four great yards . . . and yet wherever I looked I could still see gate after gate which opened into other yards.

From *Olfert Dapper's Description of Benin*
Recorded in 1602, published in Amsterdam in 1668

Benin is west of the Igbo country, and mainly peopled by the **Edo** or **Bini** (hence "Benin") who, according to their own oral history, migrated from the east – perhaps, some would dare say, Egypt. Whatever the case, the Edo settlement in West Africa was founded by **Ere**, a man credited with being the inventor of order and instigator of traditions.

Sometime in the late twelfth century or thereabouts, the chiefs impeached their king and for some years were governed by a democratically elected ruler. But this system also failed and the chiefs appealed to Ife to send over a capable monarch. The Yoruba prince **Oranmiyan** arrived and married a local woman. Their son **Eweka** became the first oba and the royal palace was built during his reign.

From Oranmiyan's time onward, **bronze** achieved an important symbolic status: the very notion of kingship seemed to reside in this alloy of tin, locally mined, and copper, which was imported at great expense. When an oba died, it was customary to send his head to Ife to have a portrait cast, but in the mid-fourteenth century, the Edo became bronze-workers themselves. This art form, however, was reserved strictly for the court. A smith foolish enough to waste his talent on anyone other than the oba was quickly executed.

The kingdom enjoyed its **golden era** between the fifteenth and the seventeenth centuries, its warrior kings conquering and ruling a huge empire reaching from Porto Novo in the West to beyond the Niger River in the east. One of the greatest rulers was **Oba Ewuare**, who ascended to the throne around 1440. He expanded the empire and brought new wealth – slaves, ivory, livestock – rolling into the city. Ewuare also greatly enlarged the capital, adding wide avenues and nine new gates, each manned by a tax collector. When the **Portuguese** first arrived here, in 1485, they encountered a vast capital – the heart of a capable kingdom.

Other Europeans – English, Dutch, Florentines – quickly followed the Portuguese to the Bight of Benin. Their requirements were slaves, ivory, pepper, leather and handmade cloth. The oba, **Ozula the Conqueror**, had plenty to offer from a string of fruitful conquests but refused to sell slaves after 1516, after only a few seasons of trade. He willingly exchanged his stocks of pepper and ivory, however, for metals, silk and velvet cloth, mirrors and European horses – most of which quickly succumbed to sleeping sickness. Ambassadors were exchanged with several European nations in the sixteenth century and the Oba's court acquired a Portuguese cultural veneer.

The oba became interested in **guns**, but the pope had forbidden traders to sell weapons to heathens. Oba Ozula sent a son to Portugal to be converted and promised to build churches in his kingdom. He never built any, but he got the guns: the Vatican looked the other way and trade flourished. Copper and copper alloys became plentiful and the oba could afford to commission unlimited metal plaques to line his palace walls. Heady from the booming business, the trade partners even fought side by side, as when Portuguese mercenaries aided the Edo in their war against the neighbouring kingdom of Idah to the northeast, at the end of the sixteenth century. The Portuguese did very well out of the trade, even though it was only in the eighteenth century that they only succeeded in overturning the sanction against slave-trading out of Benin's dominions. Even then, the obas placed strict limits on the numbers sold.

By the late nineteenth century, the **British Empire** had become the Benin kingdom's principal partner, and London was increasingly determined to develop new commodity sources and expand her markets for manufactured goods. The oba's council increasingly perceived the calculating Europeans as a threat, while the oba himself tried hard to find ways of negotiating a peaceful takeover that would allow him maximum power. His council sabotaged his plans and attacked and slaughtered a British negotiating team, though civil war was averted. Benin retreated behind the massive city walls to concentrate on metaphysical ways of dealing with the impending disaster of invasion.

Creating an image of savagery was in Britain's interest, since public opinion at home would accept relatively painless war and invasion as long as it was linked to a "civilizing mission". When the British Army launched a retaliatory "punitive expedition" to crush and seize Benin in 1897, they apparently found the oba had made one last desperate effort to save the city in the only way he knew, and had ordered human sacrifices on a massive scale. The British reported corpses lying everywhere and the pervasive stench of death in the town. The king himself had escaped, but was captured in the forest and sent into exile. His palace was pillaged. The great art treasures were sent to England – where they remain to this day, many in the British Museum in London. Others were sold to private collections.

The stories of sacrifice undoubtedly had some basis in fact – the oba's efforts to appease the spirits and ward off the encroaching white men were by no means extraordinary – but there was certainly sensationalist reporting too. Writing in the *Evening News* forty years after the event, Major James F. Ellison referred to a "14 hours running fight with the fleeing enemy" all around the city walls. Inside,

Benin ran with blood. Human sacrifices were everywhere. Some of the human beings who were in chains were still alive, speedily to be liberated. Around a huge tree in the centre of the city were erected poles on which were cross-pieces. On these were bodies, remains of those who had been sacrificed. In the Valley of the Skulls were hundreds of human heads and bones.

After the campaign, the British press referred to Benin as the "City of Blood and Crucifixions". Robert Home's *City of Blood Revisited: A New Look at the Benin Expedition of 1897*, published in the 1980s, reveals the fumbling lack of purpose behind British imperialism in West Africa.

Arrival and accommodation

Although Benin is a big city with probably over a million inhabitants, it's well laid-out and not especially difficult to get to grips with. Everything centres around **King's Square** (popularly known as **Ring Road**), a roundabout at the heart of town, with minibuses and shared taxis heading here from all the motor parks. The airport is 2km southwest of town, down Airport Road.

Just off Ring Road is the **Oba's Market**, once one of the largest and most animated in the region. It burned down in 1983, but rebuilding is now complete. **Moneychangers** hang out on the north side of Oba Market Street by Ibiwe

Moving on from Benin City

Vehicles to **Onitsha and the east** leave from the Agbor motor park on Ikpoba Slope, out at the end of Akpakpava Road to the northeast, 8km from Ring Road. To **Lagos** and the west, head to the Uselu motor park on Lagos Road. **Buses** – cheaper and slower than taxis – leave from a row of service stations on Urubi Street in the Iyaro neighbourhood. Departure times and destinations need careful advance checking.

If you're **driving** on the main road east out of the city (the A232), you'll find that the road goes to Onitsha, from where you branch either to Enugu by the new expressway link, or south on the A6 to Owerri and Port Harcourt. You'll hear dire warnings about this route, as it holds something of a record for accidents in Nigeria – and that says a lot. If you're going directly to **Port Harcourt**, you might want to consider the A2 rainforest route via Sapele and **Warri**. Look for palm-wine sellers along the roadside, but don't even inhale near the stuff if you're behind the wheel.

The only airline currently offering **flights** from Benin City is Associated Aviation, who fly daily to Lagos and Abuja.

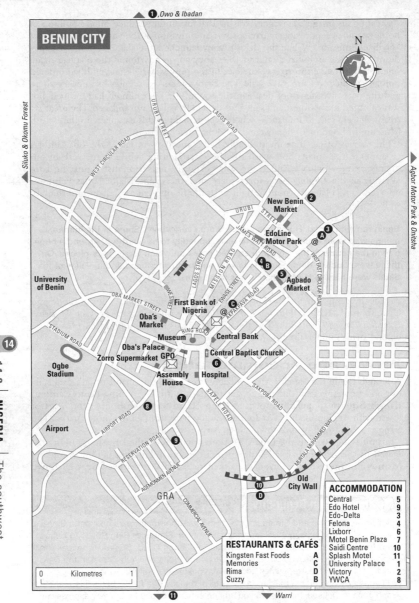

BENIN CITY

Owo & Ibadan

Siluko & Okomu Forest

Agbor Motor Park & Onitsha

Warri

New Benin Market

EdoLine Motor Park

University of Benin

Agbado Market

First Bank of Nigeria

Oba's Market

Oba's Palace

Museum

Zorro Supermarket

GPO

Central Bank

Central Baptist Church

Ogbe Stadium

Assembly House

Hospital

Airport

GRA

Old City Wall

ACCOMMODATION

Central	5
Edo Hotel	9
Edo-Delta	3
Felona	4
Lixborr	6
Motel Benin Plaza	7
Saidi Centre	10
Splash Motel	11
University Palace	1
Victory	2
YWCA	8

RESTAURANTS & CAFÉS

Kingsten Fast Foods	A
Memories	C
Rima	D
Suzzy	B

0   Kilometres   1

Street, with major **banks** nearby on Ring Road. The most central **post office** and **NITEL** call office are just off Ring Road, on Akpakpava Road, but the **GPO** is just south of it on Airport Road. A number of places offer **Internet access**, among them the Presok Cybercafé at 128 Akpakpava Road, which is open 24/7, and Vic Biz International, off Ring Road on the second floor at 7 Akpakpava Road (daily 7am–8.30pm); both places currently charge ₦100 an hour.

Accommodation

As you would expect in a big city, there are plenty of hotels to choose from in Benin, from basic sleazy dives to attempts at international reputation-building. Several are conveniently located near Ring Road.

Central Hotel 76 Akpakpava Rd ☎052/200 780. A little run-down, but perfectly acceptable s/c rooms with a/c, or cheaper ones with fans. Listen out for live-music performances in the popular courtyard bar. ②

Edo Hotel Okada Ave, GRA ☎052/258 984. Old-fashioned charm and competitive prices for s/c rooms with a/c and satellite TV. There's also a restaurant and pleasant garden with a bar. ②

Edo-Delta Hotel 134 Akpakpava Rd ☎052/252 722. Has s/c rooms ranging from cheap singles to moderate suites, with a TV in every room, laundry service, bar-restaurant and constant water supply. ②

Hotel Felona 6 Dawson Rd, off Akpakpava Rd ☎052/251 194. A new, very comfortable hotel with a/c rooms, satellite TV and a good restaurant. ⑤

Lixborr Hotel 4 Sakpoba Rd, Idubor Arts Gallery Building ☎052/256 699. Ideally situated near the museum and King's Square. Comfortable a/c accommodation with private bath. ③

Motel Benin Plaza 1 Reservation Rd ☎052/254 779 or 254 742, ℻052/259 125, ⓦwww.motelbeninplaza.com. In a quiet

neighbourhood, with chalets – with a/c and satellite TV – grouped around a swimming pool. There's a pleasant indoor bar and restaurant serving Nigerian and European dishes. ⑤

Saidi Centre 271 Murtala Muhammed Way, near Sapele Rd junction ☎052/252 125 or 250 460 or 252 047, ℻052/250 588, ℮saidihotelsltd @yahoo.com. Large, popular hotel with a/c rooms and suites with satellite TV. Good Chinese and European restaurant, swimming pool and bar. ⑤

Splash Motel 19 Uwangbo St, by Etete Rd, GRA, 3km south of Ring Rd. Small, fairly new motel with s/c, a/c rooms. ②

University Palace Hotel 4 Federal Government Girls College Rd, Ugbowo ☎052/600 361 or 602 095. The guest house of University of Benin, but located outside campus, some 5km north of town. Some rooms have a/c, and there's a restaurant with assorted continental and Nigerian dishes. ③

Victory Hotel 2 Victory Rd, off New Lagos Rd. Very basic rooms, but staff are friendly. Car park available. ①

YWCA 29 Airport Rd ☎052/252 186. Budget accommodation for women only. Central and friendly. ②

The City

King's Square, as its name (if not its various bronze statues) would suggest, is where you'll find the **Oba's Palace**. You may have to ask someone to point it out among the various buildings along the square, because the bland exterior doesn't shout to be noticed. The modest interior of the palace can be visited by prior arrangement (addressing your letter most respectfully to The Secretary to Oba, Oba's Palace, Benin City, Edo State), though you'll have to state the date you want to visit and provide a return address. The oba himself never makes public appearances except for festivals or important court or civil state occasions. By simply showing up at the palace, on the other hand, you're virtually guaranteed to find someone willing to recount the history and give a short tour of the grounds outside the palace.

The **Benin National Museum**, in the middle of Ring Road (daily 9am–4pm; ₦20) – when the traffic's heavy, it's a life-risking manoeuvre getting to it – contains many sacred royal treasures and some of the legendary artworks of the former empire. Most of the kingdom's treasures were stolen and taken abroad following the British invasion of 1897, so that today Benin can claim only the world's third largest collection of Benin art – after London and Berlin. It's an impressive collection nonetheless and very well displayed: there are examples of the **bronze plaques** that lined the palace interior together with masks, ivory works and a series of heads exemplifying the three distinct periods of an art form that spanned five centuries.

If you're interested in the vestiges of the **old city wall** – once a complex series of ramparts amounting to hundreds of kilometres of earthworks radiating out from the city, and the world's second largest man-made structure after China's Great Wall –

there's a small morsel of the inner wall on Ibiwe Street, northwest of Ring Road. Chief Orokhiri Norie-Eson House at 19 Ibiwe Street is one of the few buildings left which survived the 1897 British onslaught; it faces a nice old colonial building across the street at no. 14. A larger chunk of city wall can be seen to the southeast on Sakpoba Road, and on Sapele Road, 100m past the Agil station and immediately after the Oredo Primary Health Care Centre. Here too, you can clearly see the **moat**, a defensive ditch dug on its outside to supplement the wall and provide the earth to build it. Both the moat and the wall are now largely overgrown with vegetation.

The best place for buying **crafts**, naturally including replica bronze busts, is on Igun Street, although there are also workshops and galleries on Airport Road and Mission Road. **Bookshops** are concentrated on Ibiwe Street opposite the Oba's Market, and mostly sell school textbooks, but some have a good selection of secondhand non-fiction too, notably Newman Books at no. 11 and an unnamed shop two doors on from it.

Eating

One of the best markets for street food is **New Benin Market** northeast of the centre. You can get some of the town's best fruit here during the day and cheap finger-food (*suya* or grilled chicken, for example) at night, when this turns into a very active area and many shops and bars stay open late. A smaller market in a similar vein near Ring Road is the **Agbado Market**, on Akpakpava Road, just next to the *Central Hotel*.

For Nigerian **food**, the *Suzzy Restaurant* isn't at all bad, at 2 Hudson Lane, off Akpakpava Road by no. 95. Nearby, at 112 Akpakpava Road, by the corner of First East Circular Road, *Kingsben Fast Foods* is a good spot to stop for meat pie, *chin-chin* (crunchy fried pastry eaten as a savoury appetizer) or *moin-moin*, while over on Mutala Muhammed Way, just off Sapele Road, you can get decent, moderately priced Chinese food at *Rima Restaurant*, which also has a snack bar for a quick bite. Just across the street, the *Saidi Centre* hosts the city's best restaurant, with a Chinese, Lebanese and European menu, and the energetic owner always in the background. *Memories Restaurant*, on the first floor (above Karo Chemist's), at 29 Akpakpava Road, serves mainly Nigerian dishes, but also sandwiches and hamburgers.

Okumu National Park

The **Okumu National Park** is a patch of indigenous forest of the kind that blanketed southern Nigeria before the nineteenth-century European invasion and, as such, it's an important island of biodiversity (the endangered white-throated monkey is found only here). At 35km west of Benin City, near the small town of **Udo**, it makes an easy day-trip from Benin City. You might make it to Okumu by taxi, but most visitors drive themselves. It's possible to **stay** in the forest reserve, at the somewhat disconcertingly named *African Timber & Plywood Guest House* – actually a delightful old colonial cabin in a remote setting – but you'll need to bring your own food for the nature trail. Despite encroaching development, a herd of **forest elephants** is hanging on at Okumu, as well as scattered bushcows and yellow-backed duikers, plus various species of monkeys, an array of birdlife and the usual startling variety of reptiles and invertebrates. An observation platform in the forest canopy provides good viewing possibilities, and there's a river where you can swim.

14.3

The southeast

Most of the southeast is known as the **Igbo Country**, although numerous other peoples also live in the region. The whole southeastern area, from Enugu south to Port Harcourt, has also been called the "Taiwan" of Nigeria, due in part to its heavy industry and oil riches, but mostly because of its industries, capable of fixing and copying almost any product. There are a number of thriving commercial towns in the region which might provide a useful stopover on longer journeys, though none are worth going out of your way to see. The **Niger River** passes through one such town, **Onitsha**, which was heavily damaged in the Biafran War but has quickly regained its commercial buzz. **Enugu**, to the northeast, has survived the civil war largely unscathed, and is now a vital economic centre, home to many multinational firms.

As it approaches the coast, the Niger River fans out into the endless meandering channels of the **Delta Region**. The major town in the area, **Port Harcourt**, is another modern affair that has grown quickly since independence. You'll understand why when you see **oil flares** belching black smoke and flames on the seaward horizon: this is the heart of Nigeria's oil country, though it's also a good place for exploring **creek villages** and island towns like nearby **Bonny**. **Calabar**,

The Igbos

Igbo-speakers have played an important role in the history of Nigeria. Unlike the Yorubas of the southwest, or the city-states of the centre and north, the people of the southeast forest country have traditionally maintained much more clan-based societies with fewer social hierarchies, centred around the village and its all-male council. The lack of evolution of a central kingdom among the Igbos can partly be explained by the difficulties of communication in their rainforest.

Largely spurning slavery in their own culture, these communities fell easy prey when slavery was imposed from outside from the sixteenth to the nineteenth centuries. Later, having few cumbersome political structures to set up barriers, they quickly adapted to the new ideas of colonial society – its stress on personal achievement, on virtue earned through work and self-advancement, on business acumen and the creation of wealth. By the time World War II was over, Igbos were clearly dominating the roles allowed to native Nigerians by the colonial government. Their success was partly responsible for the bloody trauma of **Biafra** – the still-born Igbo republic declared in 1967 – which resulted in civil war and a federal blockade that brought widespread starvation. And their continued dynamism is still the source of frustration among other groups in Nigeria – in particular the Hausa and Fulani Muslims of the north. It has tended to earn southeast Nigerians a reputation as survivors – after all, they have the **oil**. But having relatively poor representation in the Federal Republic's formal political structures (and those representatives often corrupt and rarely called to account) has meant an acknowledged deficit of infrastructure and social services in the southeastern states. The Igbos' image in Nigeria is a cruelly contradictory one which has parallels with many commercially successful peoples around the world. Meanwhile, the dream of an independent Biafra is far from dead, and many Igbos believe that its realization is just a matter of time.

relaxing and scenic, spreads over a hill overlooking the Calabar River in the very far southeast. Once a big slave port and now devoted to the palm-oil trade, the town is one of Nigeria's most enjoyable. It's the natural base for visits to one of Nigeria's most exciting natural history sites, the **Cross River National Park**, separated into the Okwangwo and Oban divisions. As at the long-established **Obudu Cattle Ranch**, a little further north, there are gorillas in these protected hill forests, and basic facilities are in place for visitors to see them.

Enugu

In sharp contrast to Benin City, **ENUGU**, capital of the newly formed Enugu State and the effective capital of Igboland, is a town without a long history. It was founded in 1909 when **coal deposits** were discovered in the area. Some time later iron ore was also found, and when the railway came through in 1916, the town's economic future was sealed. It became capital of the Eastern Region in the 1930s (which dates most of the large government buildings) and later was the headquarters of the secessionist republic of Biafra. Although the town was all but deserted during the civil war, it has since rediscovered its old vitality. Industry has taken off and there's even a Mercedes assembly plant, which must be some crude indicator of local prosperity. Enugu displays a certain colonial charm and has the odd, shady open space, but its main interest is as putative capital of the Igbo region, a good place to hang out and meet people despite the lack of obvious sights.

Some 3km north of the centre, at 58 Abakaliki Road, the recently established **National Museum** (daily 8am–4pm; free) houses cultural artefacts from the area, including carvings and masquerade objects, costumes and fabrics, musical instruments and weapons. It doesn't get many visitors though, so you may have to wait around while they go off to find the key. A number of **parks** dot Enugu, including the Murtala Muhammed Park, west of the centre across from the bustling new market; jacaranda and other flowering trees make it a pleasant place to relax in the afternoon heat.

Practicalities

Most vehicles arrive at **Ogbete motor park**, slap-bang in the centre of town, but you may be dropped at **Garki motor park**, on Agbani Road 3km south of town, in which case you'll probably want to take a taxi into town. The **train station** is located in one of the town's main strips, Ogui Road. The **airport**, 5km north of town, is served by buses and taxis. The area around Okpara Avenue is where you'll find most of the banks and the **post office**, with **NITEL** next door. Enugu's vast **administrative district** straggles off behind. On Ogui Road you'll find a branch

---

Moving on from Enugu

Most vehicles leave from **Ogbete motor park**. There are two main yards, with southbound vehicles for Port Harcourt, Aba and Umuahia leaving from near the Holy Ghost Cathedral, while north- and westbound vehicles leave from Okpara Avenue opposite the prison. Others line Market Road and Okpara Avenue between the two yards. Other vehicles leave from **Garki motor Park**. There should in theory be **train services** north to Maiduguri (via Makurdi, Jos, Bauchi and Gombe) and south to Port Harcourt, but the railway is often out of action for one reason or another, and it's painfully slow even when running. Sosoliso (office at the airport ☏042/553 500; booking desk at the *Presidential Hotel*) run **flights** to Lagos, Port Harcourt and Owerri. Nigeria Airways do not fly from Enugu, but have an office at 23 Okpara Ave (☏042/332 881 or 914).

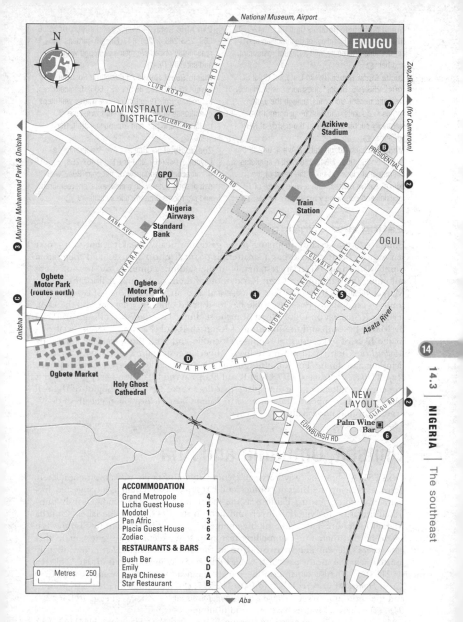

National Museum, Airport

ENUGU

Zoo, zIkom (for Cameroon)

GARDEN AVE

CLUB ROAD

ADMINSTRATIVE
DISTRICT
COLLIERY AVE

①

Azikiwe
Stadium

PRESIDENTIAL RD

Ⓐ

Ⓑ

②

STATION RD

GPO

Nigeria
Airways

Standard
Bank

BANK AVE

OKPARA AVE

Train
Station

OGUI ROAD

OGUNBIYI STREET

CARTER STREET

OKO STREET

OGUI

Murtala Muhammad Park & Onitsha

③

Ogbete Motor Park
(routes north)

Ⓒ

Onitsha

Ogbete
Motor Park
(routes south)

④

⑤

Asata River

MOOREHOUSE STREET

14

14.3 | NIGERIA | The southeast

Ogbete Market

Holy Ghost
Cathedral

Ⓓ

MARKET RD

NEW
LAYOUT

OLIAGU RD

②

Palm Wine
Bar

⑥

ZIK AVE

EDINBURGH RD

ACCOMMODATION
Grand Metropole	4
Lucha Guest House	5
Modotel	1
Pan Afric	3
Placia Guest House	6
Zodiac	2

RESTAURANTS & BARS
Bush Bar	C
Emily	D
Raya Chinese	A
Star Restaurant	B

0 — Metres — 250

Aba

post office, plus several **bureaux de change** – one cluster at the southern end, and
another in the row of shops adjoining the stadium.

Accommodation

There's a decent selection of mid-range **hotels** in Enugu, though inexpensive
places are thin on the ground.

Grand Metropole Hotel 19 Ogui Rd ☎042/251 971 or 252 235. Flamboyant decor, clean and comfortable a/c rooms, and a decent restaurant and bar. ❸

Lucha Guest House Nweko Lane, off Ogidi St ☎042/253 795. Budget guesthouse with friendly staff and decent s/c rooms, though the water comes in buckets, and with no generator the electricity supply is totally at the mercy of NEPA's vagaries. ❷

Modotel 2 Club Rd, off Garden Ave ☎042/258 780–1 or 258 000, ☎042/258 868. A sparkling international-class set-up in the heart of the administrative district, with a wide range of facilities and surprisingly reasonable prices. ❺

Pan Afric Hotel 24 Kingsway Rd, GRA ☎042/256 089, 255 248 or 251 844. Elegant gardens and reasonably priced s/c rooms equipped with a/c and satellite TV. ❸

Placia Guest House 25 Edinburgh Rd, Ogui New Layout (☎042/255 851 or 251 565). Choice of s/c, a/c rooms with TV and telephone in this well-kept guesthouse in the older part of town. Fine restaurant and bar, and exceptional staff. Good value. ❸

Zodiac Hotel 5/7 Rangers Ave, Independence Layout ☎042/457 900 or 911, ☎457 758, ✉zodiachotels.enugu@skannet.com. Busy, well-established hotel, with a pool, excellent restaurant and s/c rooms with a/c and satellite TV. ❺

Eating and drinking

Enugu is not a terribly inspiring place gastronomically speaking, but you won't starve here. Station Road has a smattering of small **chop houses**, and there are a number of cheap Nigerian restaurants in the stadium complex (the row of shops adjoining the stadium) on Ogui Road, most of them on the upper floor. *Emily* at 3 Market Road offers similar fare – rice, *eba* and so on, with a choice of two or three soups to accompany. For reasonable fast food (fried chicken, *jollof* rice and the like), try *Star Restaurant* on Ogui Road near the stadium. The *Bush Bar*, off Agbani Road by Mayor bus stop and the junction of Kenneth Road is a chop house specializing in the likes of grasscutter, porcupine, crocodile and wild pig. *Full Time Garden* by *Modotel* on Club Road is a more lively Nigerian restaurant and bar, with open-air drinking and dining. For something more international, try the pleasant but pricey *Raya Chinese Restaurant* at 77 Ogui Road. **Palm wine** isn't always very good, and is sometimes adulterated, but one place that does serve up a tasty mugful of the real McCoy is a bar opposite the entrance to *Placia Guest House*, which gets fresh deliveries in around noon daily.

Onitsha, Umuahia and Aba

ONITSHA, about halfway between Benin City and Enugu, was almost completely destroyed during the Biafran conflict, and has since been rebuilt as a congested, frenetic commercial centre. Famous as the location of the earliest indigenously published literature in Nigeria (novels and tracts from 1949, under the label "Onitsha Market Literature"), it's still a highly energetic place – though your first impression might be that there's no compelling reason to stay, except for a night stop. In that case, there's decent **accommodation** at the *Traveller's Palace Hotel*, conveniently located near the motor park at 8 Agbu Ogbuefi St, Woliwo Layout (☎046/211 013 or 211 025; ❷). Also worth considering are the nearby, excellent-value *People's Club Guest House*, off Owerri Road (☎046/212 717; ❷), with huge if rather tatty rooms; and the more upmarket *Bolingo Hotels and Towers*, at 74 Zik Ave, Fegge (☎046/210 948; ❸), where all rooms have air conditioning.

Midway along the expressway linking Enugu and Port Harcourt, **UMUAHIA**'s large central market and quiet tree-lined streets belie the days when this town served as a strategic military headquarters in the Biafran conflict. As a fitting memorial to that conflict, a **National War Museum** (Mon–Fri 9am–5.30pm, Sat & Sun 10am–5.30pm; ₦120) has been set up in the former Eastern Nigeria TV relay station from where the *Voice of Biafra* was transmitted. It's an interesting collection of memorabilia, with period photographs accompanying displays of guns, swords

14

14.3 | NIGERIA | The southeast

and uniforms. Outside you can wander among the "Red Devil" Biafran troop transporters, field guns and aircraft. Most striking among the latter is the tiny "Baby Biafran" bomber, adapted from a Swedish sports plane and utterly dwarfed by the Nigerian Air Force's Ilyushin, supplied by Egypt along with pilots, whose random bombings earned it the nickname "Genocide". Also in the grounds, a small **café** has been set up on board the NSS *Bonny*, a former naval vessel that was instrumental in the federal forces' capture of Bonny Island from the Biafrans. The museum is located on War Museum Road, which leads off the main Enugu road at the eastern end of Umuahia. Across town from the museum, you can also visit its annex, the private **bunker** at 15A Okpara Ave, GRA, from where Biafran leader, Colonel Ojukwu, commanded his troops (same times and prices as the museum). Adjoining the bunker is a guesthouse (no phone; ❷) offering cheap **accommodation** in functional, government-issue rooms. Nearby, the grandiose *Hotel Royal Dangrete* off Eze Akanu Ibaru Road (☎088/221 955 or 222 102, ℻223 787; ❼) offers deluxe rooms and an independent electricity supply. In the centre of town, reasonable budget accommodation in s/c rooms, some with a/c and/or TV, or ultra-cheap non-s/c singles, can be had at *Panadim Guest House*, 28 Warri Road (☎088/220 518; ❷). Around the corner on the same block, the *Lily Christus Standard Canteen* on Ibeku Road has good chop at very low prices indeed.

Continuing south from Umuahia, the road bangs into the unprepossessing outskirts of **ABA**, an ugly commercial town and the capital of Abia State, with its vast **Ariara Market** spilling onto the expressway. If you choose, or are obliged, to stop here, the **Museum of Colonial History** (daily 9am–5pm; ₦10) is only a two-minute walk from the chaos of the main motor park, on the A342 Ikot Ekpene Road (leading east out of town). The small, orderly collection, housed in a wooden British administrative building, traces the history of Nigeria through well-presented and informative exhibits of photos from pre-colonial times to the 1960s, but is too dark to see properly during power cuts. There's a cluster of crafts shops, chop bars and weaving huts in the museum compound. Among more inexpensive **hotels**, the *Ariss Plaza Hotel*, at 70B Ikot Ekpene Road (☎082/221 731, ✉gincov@phca .linkserve.com; ❷), and the newer *Lekota Springs Hotel* at 49 Ikot Ekpene Road (☎0803/341 2138; ❸) are central and fairly good value. Further from the town centre, and more upmarket, are the modern *Binez Hotel*, at 5/7 Nwogu St, Umungasi (☎082/440 030, ℻222 941; ❺), where all rooms are s/c and a/c; and the deluxe *Crystal Park Hotel*, Crystal Park Avenue, off Port Harcourt Road (☎082/221 588 or 221 742; ❼).

Port Harcourt and around

Capital of Rivers State, **PORT HARCOURT** ("Po-ta-ko" in Pidgin) promotes itself as the "**Garden City**" – though given its location in the rainforest, it would be remarkable if it wasn't green. Port Harcourt first came to prominence during World War I, as a result of military operations mounted from here against German Kamerun. But the fortunes of the modern city are thanks primarily to the **oil wells** that have sprouted throughout the region since 1956, when commercial quantities were discovered in **Oloibiri**. The first shipload of Nigerian crude was exported from Port Harcourt in 1958 and the country was launched on a new economic course that promised rapid industrial development and prosperity. As a side benefit, Port Harcourt has acquired a strikingly modern aspect, with wide avenues, flyovers and high-rise blocks easily outshooting the last of the giant forest trees left standing in the city limits. Yet the "**Old Township**" (founded in 1913) has survived the rapid growth and if you were to limit your time to this corner of the city, you could come away believing that Port Harcourt is still a small town with a good deal of charm. This part of town is also the departure point for ferries to the rustic islands of **Brass** and **Bonny**.

Orientation, arrival and information

Port Harcourt is divided by the **flyover** – a freeway overpass that's something of a symbol of the town's modernity – into two distinct zones, the new town to the north and the old town to the south. The **Aba Road**, also called the **Expressway**, runs clean through the new part of town, from the air force base in the northern suburbs down to the flyover. "Expressway" is no exaggeration, since cars seem to be out to break speed records as they scream down it; pedestrian overpasses are few and far between. Banks and various governmental buildings line the Aba Road, while **Azikiwe Road**, south of the flyover, is effectively the city centre, where you'll see the towering state headquarters of several banks.

The **airport** is 40km northwest of town (a 45min ride into the centre by taxi), while the **train station** is on Odual Road in the Old Township. If you're using road transport, you're likely to be dropped at either the **Abali motor park** (also known as **Leventis motor park**), located on Aba Road by the flyover, or at the **Diobu Mile 3 motor park** at Owerri Road, which is a good 5km north of the old town. Fortunately, public transport connections are good, with plenty of minibuses, drops and okadas connecting Abali ("Park" or "Flyover") and Mile 3 with most parts of town; the Mile 3 motor park actually caters mostly for intra-city buses, taxis and shared taxis. A minibus service connects Abali motor park with Lagos Road bus station ("Lagos") opposite the Old Market, while another runs south, to Creek Road, then Churchill Road and Harold Wilson Drive.

Moneychangers hang out in front of the *Presidential Hotel* in the new town, and in the Old Township on the four westernmost blocks of Victoria Street (parallel with Aggrey Street, a block to its south). There's also a legitimate bureau de change operated by Emerald Tours on Aba Road a short walk south of Garrison junction. The **GPO** is on Station Road, north of the Old Township, with **NITEL** directly behind it. The offices of the helpful **Rivers State Tourism Board** are at 35/37 Aba Road (☎084/334 901). There's an **Internet** place at 71 Niger Street in the Old Township.

Accommodation

Port Harcourt has a good cross-section of places to stay, though some are a fair distance from the central area – this town is built for drivers.

Moving on from Port Harcourt

Port Harcourt has vehicles to almost everywhere – it's literally at the end of the road, or at least the Old Township is – and transport isn't hard to find. There's transport to the nearer towns (Owerri and Onitsha), and to Ibadan and the Borikiri terminal in Lagos, from **Mile 3 motor park**, though for services to Calabar, Benin City and just about everywhere else, head to **Abali park**. To get a seat on the cheapest luxury buses, you'll need to book a day in advance, or start very early.

As for **trains**, there should be a service to Maiduguri via Enugu, Makurdi, Jos, Bauchi and Gombe, but services are erratic. Ask at the station or at the local NRC office on Old Market Road (☎084/301 060) to get the latest timetable.

There are plenty of flights to **Lagos** – on Nigeria Airways, Bellview, AeroContractors and Chanchangi, among others – plus five flights a week to **Abuja** on Overland Airways, and international services to London (on Virgin) and Paris (on Air France). There are plenty of **airline offices**: Bellview (☎084/230 518–9), Air France (☎084/238 106) and KLM (☎084/235 468) all have offices above the *Eastern Garden* restaurant at 47 Aba Road; AeroContractors (☎084/230 006, ✉reservations.phc@acn.aero) is at the airport; British Airways is at the State Tourist Hotel Corporation Building on Aba Road (☎084/238 351 or 233 011); Nigeria Airways is at 6 Bank Rd (☎084/332 931 or 941); and Swiss Airlines is represented by Panalpina, Plot 463/4, Trans-Amadi Layout (☎084/238 679–80).

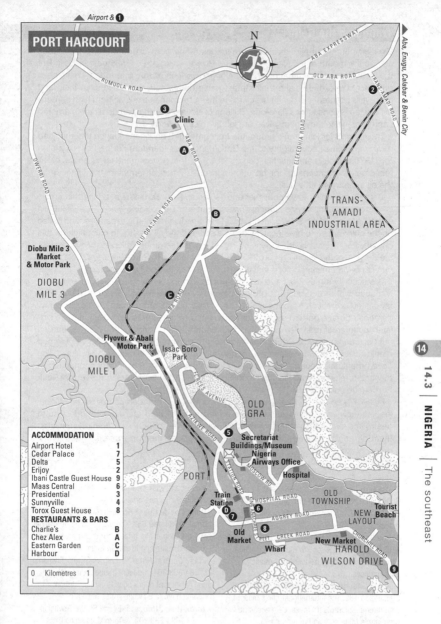

PORT HARCOURT

Airport & ❶

TRANS-
AMADI
INDUSTRIAL
AREA

Diobu Mile 3
Market
& Motor Park

DIOBU
MILE 3

Flyover & Abali
Motor Park

DIOBU
MILE 1

Issac Boro
Park

OLD
GRA

Secretariat
Buildings/Museum
Nigeria
Airways Office

Hospital

PORT

Train
Station

OLD
TOWNSHIP

NEW
LAYOUT

Tourist
Beach

Old
Market

New Market

Wharf

HAROLD
WILSON DRIVE

Clinic

ACCOMMODATION
Airport Hotel	1
Cedar Palace	7
Delta	5
Erijoy	2
Ibani Castle Guest House	9
Maas Central	6
Presidential	3
Sunnyville	4
Torox Guest House	8

RESTAURANTS & BARS
Charlie's	B
Chez Alex	A
Eastern Garden	C
Harbour	D

0   Kilometres   1

Airport Hotel Owerri Rd, 40min from the centre ☎084/233 506 or 524 or 530, ☏234 084, ✉phc_airporthotel@phca.linkserve.com.ng. Surrounded by countryside and mostly used by passengers arriving at or leaving from the airport (5km distant), this is Port Harcourt's premier hotel.

The decor is a little tatty by international standards, but the place has all the facilities you might want, including a golf course. ❼
Cedar Palace Hotel 11 Harbour Rd ☎084/333 877. Near the train station and port, with a/c rooms. ❸

Trouble in the Delta

Over 90 percent of Nigeria's export earnings come from **crude oil**, and two states astride the mouth of the Niger – Delta and Rivers – produce over 85 percent of it. But the local population – most of whom belong to various **ethnic minorities** – have seen precious little of the wealth their states generate. Instead, they have seen their land and rivers polluted and health problems in their communities arising from high carbon-dioxide emissions at gas flare-offs. Billions of dollars' worth of crude oil are extracted each year, while they themselves are left in abject poverty.

The region's largest ethnic group, the **Ijo**, contended on independence that they had never ceded their sovereignty to the British and were therefore not part of Nigeria. In the 1970s, local communities began lobbying the government for a share of oil resources to compensate for pollution and destruction of farmland and fisheries by the oil industry, to little avail.

In 1990, the well-known publisher and TV writer, **Ken Saro-Wiwa**, penned an article in the government-owned *Sunday Times*, entitled "The coming war in the Delta", in which he accused the Shell oil company of racism towards the Delta peoples, and called on the government to give local residents a share of the oil wealth. To campaign for this on behalf of his people, the Ogoni, he set up a pressure group called the Movement for the Survival of the Ogoni People (**MOSOP**) which, thanks to Saro-Wiwa, was able to link up with environmental groups in the West and generate worldwide publicity.

The security forces began to combat opposition to the oil companies, often brutal-ly. Faced with a demonstration by villagers from Umuechem in October 1990, Shell requested protection from the police, who broke up the protest and shot dead eighty demonstrators, a pattern subsequently repeated elsewhere. In July 1993, a more sin-ister tactic emerged: members of a neighbouring ethnic group, the Andonis, carried out two **massacres** of Ogonis for no apparent reason. Government sources blamed ethnic rivalry, but witnesses saw men in military uniforms directing operations. The government also began a campaign of harassment against Saro-Wiwa, banned unau-thorized foreigners from visiting Ogoniland and set up a brutal **Internal Security Task Force** (subsidized by Shell).

MOSOP also had its thugs, unemployed youths who branded as traitors any Ogoni leaders inclined to conciliation. When a mob of them beat four Ogoni moderates to death, the authorities arrested Saro-Wiwa and the MOSOP leadership, convicted them of the murders and, in November 1995, hanged them, despite an international outcry.

Delta Hotel 1–3 Harley St ☎084/300 191. Good-value twin rooms, a bar, and a restaurant serving Nigerian and Continental dishes. ❸

Erijoy Hotel Plot 5 Trans-Amadi Industrial Layout ☎084/232 750. Spotless a/c rooms, a pool and gym, and plays host to frequent live-music performances. ❻

Hotel Presidential Aba Expressway ☎084/239 505, ℗234 165. The international-class hideout, with three restaurants (Chinese, Lebanese and Nigerian), a huge pool and a gym. ❽

Hotel Sunnyville 68 Olu Obasanjo Rd ☎084/333 169 or 238 286. Clean a/c affair near the Mile 3

motor park, with s/c rooms and its own nightclub. Rate includes one breakfast. ❸

Ibani Castle Guest House 31/33 Harold Wilson Drive ☎084/480 657. The rooms could be cleaner and the food is overpriced, but this is pretty much the cheapest place to stay in town. ❷

Maas Central Hotel 3 Freetown St, Old Township ☎084/333 304. A decent budget hotel with a bar and restaurant near Lagos Road bus station. Rooms have fans, while suites have a/c. ❸

Torox Guest House 29 Bende St, Old Township ☎ & ℗084/233 102, ✉Torox@yahoo.co.uk. A clean, well-kept little establishment in the most vibrant part of the Old Township. ❹

The Town

Aggrey Road runs through the heart of the **Old Township** and constitutes the

The Internal Security Task Force now started terrorizing communities other than the Ogoni, and the **violence escalated**. In December 1997, a gathering of Ijo community representatives demanded the companies suspend all operations "pending the resolution of the issue of resource ownership and control in the Ijo area". When Ijo youths protested in support of this in Yenagoa, security forces opened fire on them, killing dozens. This was taken as a declaration of war, and youths began sabotaging pipelines, occupying company premises and kidnapping oil workers. The oil companies started employing people from certain communities to guard installations against others, sparking off **intercommunal feuds**. This added to tensions already existing between some ethnic groups, notably between Ijos, Itsekiris and Urhobos in Warri, which erupted in June 1999 into riots resulting in the deaths of some 200 people.

Late 1999 saw a series of horrific incidents. In October, in Choba, Rivers State, following attacks by local youths on the American pipeline-laying firm Wilbros, police and troops took over the village and raped 67 women, including girls as young as 12, atrocities that shocked the nation. Even worse was to follow in November, when a gang of young thugs formerly employed by the Bayelsa State governor in his election campaign, took over part of Odi, the state's second-biggest town, and abducted and killed twelve police sent to arrest them. The government responded by **sending in troops** who razed the town completely, killing several hundred people and evicting thousands more. The massacre was followed by police and army attacks on Ijo communities throughout Bayelsa, Delta and Rivers states. Since then, local people have on occasion occupied oil installations and taken expat workers hostage, as a form of protest.

Nigeria's **Allocation of Revenue Act** of 2002, sponsored by the President, reconfirmed a stipulation in the 1999 Constitution that thirteen percent of oil revenue is supposed to remain in the states that produce it. The act, passed to reverse a Supreme Court ruling exempting revenue from offshore reserves from this requirement, was widely seen as a move towards reconciliation between the government and local communities, though cynics branded it a ploy to win votes in the 2003 election. Whether the 2002 act can ease the situation in the Delta and help end the violence remains to be seen. Meanwhile Shell, the biggest player in the Delta, has acknowledged it needs to clean up its act, and has recently opened its books to disclose "levies" paid to the Nigerian government of around $1 billion per year.

high street. From here, in the crowded southern quarter of the city, you get striking views of the distant oil flares as you take in a wide variety of stalls, restaurants and shops lining the street. On the southern side of the township, down near the creek, you'll find two of Port Harcourt's main markets – the wonderfully chaotic **Creek Road Market**, excellent for fish, and **New Layout Market**. To the east, a **"tourist beach"** was recently set aside down by Ndoki Street, and though the surrounding parks are quite pleasant, the site hasn't yet sparked much interest.

The Secretariat Complex at the bottom of Azikiwe Road houses the small **State Museum** (Mon–Fri 7am–4pm; free). Its examples of regional art include outstanding examples of the colourful, often bizarre local **masks**, plus a few domestic utensils from major ethnic groups in the area – Ijo, Ikwerre, Etche, Ogoni, Ekpeye and Ogba. Round the corner at 2 Harley Street, a branch of the **National Museum** is due to open, with bronzes and sculptures from around the country.

Just off the Aba Road, the **Kaduna Street Public Market** is a good place for produce, including the fresh fish which is so plentiful around here. Other markets are in **Diobu neighbourhood** at Mile 1 and Mile 3. Azikwe Road has a fine showing of **supermarkets**.

In keeping with Port Harcourt's image as a garden city, the **Isaac Boro Park**, near the flyover, adds a bit of extra green to the city centre. The park is dedicated to Major Isaac Adaka Boro, a champion of the minority peoples of the southeast, who, in defending his cause against Governor Ojukwu's Igbo domination, was killed in 1968 fighting for the federal forces during the civil war.

Eating, drinking and nightlife

For **inexpensive eating** head to "Suya Street" – the expats' name for Ogu Street, two blocks east of King Amachree Street in the Old Township, an atmospheric road lined with food stalls and glowing with the warm light of wood fires in the evening. Cheap eating-houses and bars can be found nearby on Victoria Street, and there's also a slew of chop houses on the west side of Station Road between the station and the GPO. *Harbour Restaurant* on Harbour Road near the *Cedar Palace Hotel* is a slightly less downmarket venue for Nigerian dishes at moderate prices. For **foreign cuisine**, the *Eastern Garden Chinese Restaurant* at 47 Aba Road is easily the best Chinese restaurant in town; for Lebanese food, the *Hotel Presidential* hosts the excellent *Why Not Restaurant*. More upmarket, *Charlie's Restaurant*, at 214 Aba Road, has a wide range of dishes, including salads and desserts, and plays live jazz on Wednesday and Sunday, while at 175B Aba Road, *Chez Alex Restaurant* has a menu of Lebanese, Chinese, Nigerian and continental dishes, and serves wine.

As you would expect in a town the size of Port Harcourt, there are numerous **nightclubs** catering to all (male) tastes, although the scene changes rapidly. Ask around to find out which place is currently popular or is likely to have a live band; the big nights are Thursday to Saturday. In the old part of town, have a look at the *Ibani Castle Hotel*'s in-house *Orupolo Night Club* at 31 Harold Wilson Drive, or the *Tropicana* in the *Cedar Palace Hotel*. Of the numerous **cinemas** around town, the one in the *Hotel Presidential* is best.

Bonny and Brass islands

Bonny and Brass islands, both separated from the mainland by channels of the Niger delta, were the first fifteenth-century Portuguese toeholds in Nigeria, and later became missionary gateways (St Stephen's on Bonny is one of the oldest Anglican churches in the country), but are now devoted to the oil industry. The islands still hold some wonderfully ornate Victorian tombstones and monuments and some great old houses. Local chiefs tend to wear Edwardian shirts with tucked fronts and top hats.

You can travel by public ferry to the islands (3hr to Bonny, 6hr to Brass), or alternatively charter a speedboat, which is faster but more expensive. The boats depart from the wharf south of Creek Road and head to numerous destinations besides these two islands (Ke, Bekingkiri, etc). There are sheds for booking the ferries, but for the small boats just go to the jetty where people and cargo are loading. Expect to bargain hard to get the regular price.

Accommodation can be found at a number of hotels on Bonny. The least expensive is the *Beach Hotel*, with shabby rooms with shared facilities that still cost more than anything on the mainland. The other town hotels are considerably more comfortable. Beware of zealous immigration officials, and be fully armed with your paperwork.

Calabar and around

It's not just its position perched high on the hills overlooking the river that makes **CALABAR** such a pleasant town to visit. There's a general good ambience created by its compact size and the outgoing nature of the Efik, Ibibio and Kalabari residents. Calabar offers a fine introduction to the nicer facets of Nigerian life and, if you're heading east, it's a good place to prepare for in-your-face Cameroon and the rigours of Central Africa. The waterfront sums up its elegantly run-down, colonial feel: apart from Lagos, Calabar is the only Nigerian city near the coast, and the tension that crackles in so many other large towns is absent, as if whisked away on the ocean breeze. Calabar also has the best **culinary reputation** in the country, with lots of varied, traditional cooking. Nigerians say that if a Calabar woman cooks for you, you'll never leave the town.

If you've any choice about when you visit, opt for October, **masquerade month** in Calabar, the time when cultural values and traditional beliefs are most in evidence. The masquerades – **Sekiapu** – include not only continuous drumming and dancing, sculpted masks and elaborate and dazzlingly costumed performers, but regattas of huge, fabulously decked, competitive team canoes.

Some history

The **Qua** (or Ekoi), who came from the northern woodlands and were principally hunters and farmers, were the first people to settle in the Calabar area. Later migration brought the **Efik** and **Efut** – predominantly fishers and subsistence farmers. The Portuguese arrived in the closing years of the fifteenth century and the economic orientation of the local people slowly shifted to **trading**. By the seventeenth century, the Efik were in control of the lucrative export of **slaves**. Efik settlements on the estuary of the Calabar River developed into trading **city-states** that dealt with the Portuguese, Dutch, French, German and English. Rich and powerful, the rulers took European names to emphasize their importance – the Dukes, the Jameses, the Henshaws – and welcomed **missionaries**, despite their opposition to the slave trade. Calabar thus became a centre of education and religion, and local rulers gained further advantages with the European trading partners, as the Efik forbade missionaries to come into contact with ethnic groups in the hinterland. With their understanding of the ways of the West, the Efik made the transition as smoothly as anyone could have expected when trade shifted from slaves to **palm oil** and, later, when Nigeria became a colony and the Efik were ruled "indirectly", through their chiefs. At the end of the nineteenth century, Calabar became the capital of Southern Nigeria. During the **Biafran War**, the town was recaptured from the secessionists and served as an important federal forces naval base.

Arrival, city transport and information

At the centre of Calabar is **Watt Market**. The busiest streets in town are the long-established and central **Calabar Road**, which runs through the middle of the market, dividing foodstuffs on one side from cloth and household goods on the other, and the newer commercial street called **Ndidem Nsang Iso Road**. Calabar Road is where you'll find the **motor park**, where you're likely to arrive, northeast of Watt Market. The **airport** is 1.5km east of town.

Calabar is an easy town to get around. **Taxis**, together with even cheaper buses and motorcycle taxis, provide nearly 24-hour mobility. City buses run on set routes and will usually stop wherever you wave them down. **Motorcycle taxis** usually cost the same as a shared taxi for a short hop, though it may be double this for long transits across town. Like taxi fares, prices double after dark, though you may be able to negotiate a good price for two up on the bike.

The **tourist office** (Mon–Fri 9am–4pm; ☎087/235 606) is in the Cultural Centre on Mary Slessor Avenue. Calabar Road is home to the **post office** and major **banks**, between the market roundabout and the *Metropolitan Hotel*. The **NITEL** call office is up towards the huge Calabar Stadium, at 2 Club Road. You can get **online** at Glorious Technologies on Ndidem Nsang Iso Road (Mon–Sat 8am–10pm, Sun 6–10pm).

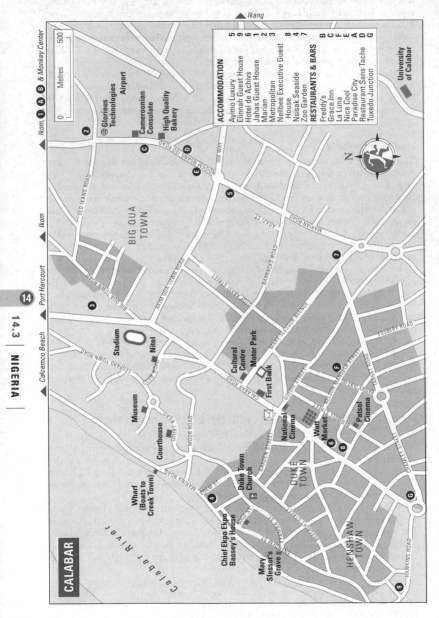

CALABAR

Calabar River

Ikang ▲

Ikom, **1** **A** **B** & Monkey Center ◀   Ikom ◀   Port Courcourt ◀   Calcemco Beach ◀

14.3 | **NIGERIA**

14

1082

Wharf (Boats to Creek Town)

Chief Ekpo Ekpo Bassey's House

Mary Slessor's Grave

Museum

Courthouse

Stadium

Nitel

Cultural Centre
Motor Park

First Bank

National Cinema

Duke Town Church

Wall Market

Patsol Cinema

DUKE TOWN

HENSHAW TOWN

BIG QUA TOWN

@ Glorious Technologies
Airport

Cameroonian Consulate

High Quality Bakery

University of Calabar

Metres 0 — 500

N

ACCOMMODATION
Ayimo Luxury   5
Elinnah Guest House   9
Hotel de Achivs   6
Jahas Guest House   1
Marian   2
Metropolitan   3
Neilbee Executive Guest
  House   8
Nsisak Seaside   4
Zoo Garden   7

RESTAURANTS & BARS
Freddy's   B
Grace Inn   C
La Luna   F
Nice Cool   E
Paradise City   A
Restaurant Sans Tache   D
Tuxedo Junction   G

Most vehicles go from the **Watt Market motor park**, from where there's regular transport west to **Port Harcourt**, north to **Ekang** (the route you need for Oban Rainforest Reserve and Cameroon) and north to **Ikom** (for Cameroon and northern Cross River State). Crosslines has its own garage in Calabar Road, north of the *Metropolitan Hotel* and runs a daily bus to **Jos** (12–14hr), plus services north to **Ekang** (via Oban village) and **Obudu** (via Ikom), and west to **Aba**. There's also a motor park for **Oban** at the junctions of Akim Qua Town Road and Ndidem Nsang Iso Road.

Chanchangi and ADC **fly** daily to Lagos from Calabar's **airport**. Nigeria Airways do not fly to Calabar, but have an office at 45 Bedwell St (℡087/232 488 or 230 194).

Into Cameroon

Details on crossing into Cameroon by **land** from Ikom are given on p.1087, but the most direct crossing into Cameroon from Calabar is 120km to the northeast, between **Ekang** and **Otu**, at the end of the Oban Division road. For **sea crossings**, there is a regular ferry service direct from Calabar to Limbé (3 or 4 weekly) from Calcemco Beach, on the river just north of town; alternatively, boats depart from Oron (see p.1085), 25km away from Calabar, to the Cameroonian town of Idenao, 48km north of Limbé. Ferries from Calabar to Oron leave from near the *Nsikak Hotel*. It's also possible to cross by boat from the seaside border town of **Ikang** over to **Ekondo beach** and **Bulo beach** in Cameroon, near the town of Mundemba, from where you can get transport through Ekondo Titi to Kumba (see p.1188).

Tourist **visas** are usually issued with no fuss at the Cameroonian Consulate, 21 Ndidem Nsang Iso Rd (℡087/222 782), costing CFA30,000 for single entry (CFA60,000 multiple entry), plus CFA1000 for a stamp, and three passport photos. In principle, visas take two working days to issue, but you may be able to get one the same day if you come early.

Accommodation

There's a host of pleasant, small, family-run hotels, many of which have air conditioning and TV at affordable prices.

Ayimo Luxury Hotel 74 Ndidem Nsang Iso Rd ℡087/221 770. An older place which has worn well. Their double rooms are quite reasonable for two, but slightly pricey if you're on your own. ❷

Elinnah Guest House 25 Hawkins Rd ℡087/233 151 or 235 727. Pleasant affair near the river, with clean s/c, a/c rooms. ❷

Hotel de Achivs 3 Clifford Lane, the unpaved alley by 83 Calabar Rd, near the market. Non-s/c singles or s/c double rooms with fans. The staff are pleasant and they have a bar/TV room with snacks – try the snail kebabs, a local delicacy. ❶

Jahas Guest House 107 Marian Road Extension, the continuation of Ndidem Nsang Iso Rd ℡087/233 785. Large, comfortable s/c rooms with a/c, near the Drill Monkey sanctuary but not conveniently located for the town centre. ❸

Marian Hotel 125 Old Ikang Rd ℡087/230 233. Modern, comfortable a/c chalets in a quiet area away from the centre, with a garden. There's also an excellent Nigerian and continental restaurant, plus parking space for cars. ❹

Metropolitan Hotel Calabar Rd ℡087/230 911, ℡087/230 914, ✉metrocal@skannet.com. Calabar's large, international-class place, with a pool and car park. All rooms have satellite TV and a/c, and the restaurant, cocktail bar and nightclub are highly rated. ❺

Nelbee Executive Guest House 5 Dan Achibong St, off Calabar Rd ℡087/232 684. Inexpensive lodging in s/c rooms with a/c and running water, and a good restaurant featuring garlic steak and fish pepper soup. ❸

Nsikak Seaside Hotel 23 Edem St ℡087/228 443. The modern-looking facade on the waterfront belies a faded interior with scruffy non-s/c, non-a/c rooms. The top-floor bar is enclosed by huge bay windows for a beautiful view of the river and town. ❶

Zoo Garden Hotel Mary Slessor Ave, opposite Target St ℡087/234 673. Good-value s/c double rooms with a/c and satellite TV. ❹

The Town

There's still a good deal of **colonial architecture** in the older parts of Calabar, especially around the Henshaw Town, Duke Town and waterfront districts. The **courthouse**, not far from the Calabar Museum and the river, is a characteristic piece of period design and many other buildings are still inhabited or in use despite their dilapidated condition. Another good example is the nineteenth-century **house of Chief Ekpo Ekpo Bassey** at 19 Boco Street, now falling into extravagant disrepair. Nearby, the **Duke Town church** is one of the oldest in Nigeria, established in the nineteenth century by Presbyterian missionaries. Continuing uphill on Eyamba Street past the church takes you to the **old cemetery** – an enchanting, if neglected, spot, with stunning views over the town and river. The tomb of one of southern Nigeria's most influential missionaries, **Mary Slessor**, from Dundee, near Edinburgh, lies here, marked by a plaque.

Calabar Museum

On the hill overlooking the waterfront, **Calabar Museum** (daily 9am–6pm; ₦10) is housed in the **Old Government House**, the former residence of the colonial governor. The building, designed and built in Glasgow and shipped over in pieces, has been beautifully restored. As a museum, it has few, if any, equals in the country.

The museum concentrates on the **history** of old Calabar, rather than on ethnography or art, and the collections are clearly documented and displayed. In fact, there's almost too much to contemplate here in one visit, with a mass of details on trading, missionary activities and colonial administration. It's a remarkable collection spanning pre-colonial days, the slave and palm-oil eras, British invasion and anticolonial resistance, ending with the path to independence. The museum also contains a **craft village** and shop, and there's a good outdoor bar with wonderful views over the town. The small **bookshop** has interesting material on the history and culture of the region.

The Drill Monkey Rehab Center

Northeast of town, off Ndidem Nsang Iso Road and behind the *Jahas Guest House*, the Oregon-based wildlife conservation group Pandrillus have set up a **Drill Monkey Rehab Center**, where they take in orphaned drill monkeys and prepare them for release into the wild. The drill monkey – native only to Cross River State in Nigeria, the southwest of Cameroon and the island of Bioko in Equatorial Guinea – is one of Africa's most endangered primates, and its biggest threat comes from poachers who hunt it for bush meat. Often, having killed a nursing mother, the poachers will sell the babies as pets – something they become increasingly unsuited for as they grow – and it is these infants, seized by the authorities or given in by members of the public, that are rehabilitated in the centre, which also takes in chimpanzees in similar circumstances. The centre can be visited (daily 9am–5pm; no charge but donations appreciated) and there's usually someone on hand to show you around. It is also possible to visit the **Afi Mountain Drill Ranch** near Katabang in the north of Cross River State (see p.1087).

Eating, drinking and nightlife

For **food**, try the nationally famous Calabar soup containing periwinkles. A number of zesty **clubs** enliven Calabar nights: *La Luna*, on Nelson Mandela Street, has regular live music at weekends; *Paradise City*, at 87 Atekong Drive, off Ndidem Nsang Iso Road, is currently one of Calabar's flashiest and most popular clubs, with live music (reggae or highlife) from Wednesday to Saturday; and *Tuxedo Junction*, at 39 Chamley St – doors open around 8pm, but the real excitement is after midnight.

Restaurants

Freddy's Restaurant 90 Atekong Drive ☎ 087/232 821. Upmarket restaurant with continental and Lebanese dishes, and specialities like hummus, pepper steak and avocados stuffed with shrimp. Good but pricey – a popular choice among expats.

Grace Inn 29 Ndidem Nsang Iso Rd. A small place specializing in bush meat, usually porcupine served with plantain and accompanied by cold beer.

High Quality Bakery 102 Ndidem Nsang Iso Rd. Fresh bread and cakes, superb meat pies, and sometimes pizza. Good ice cream too. Daily 6am–6pm.

Nice Cool Restaurant 9 Ndidem Nsang Iso Rd. Simple Nigerian dishes like chicken, rice, *gari* and pounded yam for around ₦200.

Restaurant Sans Tache 19 Ndidem Nsang Iso Rd. Inexpensive place where you can try Efik specialities.

Creek Town

From the waterfront (Marina Road), you can catch a "fly boat" (motor boat) or a rowing boat to nearby **Creek Town** (also spelt Greek Town: even residents seem to have lost track of the correct name), a one-hour ride down the Calabar River, with dense mangrove greenery reminiscent of scenes from *The African Queen*. On arrival, there's little specifically to visit, but you can wander around and absorb the intimate creekside village atmosphere. The people here are very proud of the **Creek Town church**, which is, indeed, a fine piece of colonial architecture, one they claim to be older than that in Duke Town. Some of the houses still have small "factories" where they produce **palm oil** using antiquated nineteenth-century mills from Britain. If you express interest, people will be happy to show you their production methods. The town has a small **market** and numerous **palm-wine bars** – look for the tell-tale phallic gourds that serve as cups, hung in front of the bars – where you'll find the beverage much fresher, and therefore much less alcoholic and more quaffable, than in Calabar town itself. At one time it was commonly served with grilled **monkey meat**, but the killing of monkeys for bush meat is now illegal as it is endangering rare species.

Oron

Across the creek from Calabar, **ORON** is a departure point for **boats to Cameroon**. Boats ply regularly from Oron to the Cameroonian town of **Idenao**, 48km north of **Limbé** (Victoria). Motor boats are the quickest option (3–4hr) for the 150-kilometre sea voyage around the creeks and mangroves, though substantially more expensive than the fishing boats that take up to two days. The latter are commonly taken by local people, but you may be dropped on the coast almost anywhere and then run the risk of missing official entry procedures to Cameroon. Make sure your passport is stamped as soon as possible after arrival.

It's likely you'll have to spend the night in Oron in order to get an early boat to Cameroon, in which case, decent and affordable **accommodation** can be found at the *Maycom Guest House* (❷). You'll find a brilliant collection of regional artwork at Oron's **National Museum**, located right next to the ferry dock and easily visited while waiting for a boat. The Oron region is famous for its woodcarvings, especially the Ekpo figures, used in ceremonies for communication with ancestors. There are some fine examples on display in the museum which is quite extensive, despite being greatly damaged in the Biafran conflict. You can pick up a copy of the *Guide to the Oron National Museum* which is full of information about the musical instruments, bronzes, pottery and carvings on display.

Cross River National Park and around

The natural vegetation of **Cross River State** is almost entirely **rainforest**, though large reaches have been cleared for oil-palm plantations since the early twentieth century. Some of the most exciting wildlife and conservation projects in Africa are currently under development in the two areas of the **Cross River National Park**: the **Oban Division** between Calabar and Ikom, and the **Okwangwo Division** north of Ikom – the latter with its rediscovered **gorilla** denizens. It was thought the gorilla had disappeared from most of West Africa in the nineteenth century, and from Nigeria and western Cameroon several decades ago, but the WWF has located at least four separate gorilla populations, mostly around Mbe Mountain in the Okwangwo Division. It's thought there may be around a hundred individuals in the park. The park is one of the richest reserves in rainforest plant species in the whole of Africa, and also features some 1500 species of animals, including forest elephants (about 400, all in the Oban Division), duikers, antelope and chimpanzees, but visiting is difficult and you are unlikely to see any apes or elephants in any case.

Oban Division

Because the main purpose of the park is to conserve wildlife rather than to be a tourist attraction, there is little infrastructure and few facilities, and the Oban Division can really only be visited if you have your own transport. From Calabar, you can **rent a vehicle** and obligatory driver at the *Metropolitan Hotel* (see p.1083). Having transport allows you the flexibility to turn off the road near the village of **Aningeje** (about fifty minutes from Calabar: look for the sign indicating the Kwa Falls oil-palm plantation) and have a wander around the dramatic **Kwa Falls**. The entire stretch to Oban is a rough one, though once you reach the village, the road improves towards the Cameroon border. Just outside Oban village, **accommodation** can be found at the *Jungle Club* (➊), with simple s/c rooms.

Each village between Oban and the border has a Village Liaison Assistant (VLA), a resident employee of the Nigeria National Parks, easily tracked down by asking around town on arrival. Besides providing up-to-date information on the state of the conservation project and how it affects their local communities, VLAs can also arrange **guided treks** in the forest for a reasonable fee. The forest trail at **Mfaminyen** (the last village before the border) is the best organized.

You could also drive straight to the park's headquarters at **Akamkpa**, a 45-minute drive north from Calabar along the highway to Ikom, where there's an **Information Centre** (➘087/222 261 or 221 694, ➘221 695) with s/c rooms and good food available nearby at the *Motel de Conscience* (➊).

Ikom and around

The border town of **IKOM** is hardly a Cross River attraction, but it's busy and tolerable enough. The surrounding countryside is famous for the **Ikom Monoliths**, curious stone steles intricately carved with abstract human figures. There are some three hundred of these statues spread throughout the area, but the easiest to reach are near the village of **Alok**, just off the A4, 50km north of Ikom. You can find a guide in the village. Though early estimates traced the monoliths to the sixteenth century, they are now believed to date as far back as 200 AD. Their origins and significance are unclear.

If you need to stay, the *Lisbon Hotel* at 70 Calabar Road (➊) is clean and has friendly staff and reasonable food. The town has a number of shops and the usual services. Moneychangers in the market will buy and sell Central African CFA and naira. If you are making for Cameroon, there are regular taxis during the day and early evening to the border post at Mfum, 26km away.

Okwangwo Division

Hidden in the bush between Ikom and Obudu, the **Okwangwo Division** consists of a breathtaking expanse of cloud-drenched mountain forest, home to a number of rare primates, including gorillas, chimpanzees and drills, as well as duikers, mountain

Cross River State's main crossing point into Cameroon is from **Mfum** to Ekok, southeast of Ikom and northeast of Ekang. Taxis from Ikom will take you to the Nigerian customs and immigration post at Mfum, where you complete border formalities before crossing the bridge into Cameroon (see p.1144). Early in the day, shared vehicles are hard to come by and you may need to charter a taxi or okada. **Ekok** is a lively place to stay the night, with something of a Wild West feel about it. There are four basic hotels, several bars and plenty of loud music, but no bank, though moneychangers will sell Central African CFAs for naira, and will also change dollars or euros, though not at a good rate. Naira are acceptable currency for the short journey to **Mamfé** (see p.1190), which has banks, but the price will be a lot more than you're officially allowed to export from Nigeria. There are also direct vehicles from Ekok to **Bamenda**.

foxes and porcupines. A trek along its trails (allow a couple of days at least) will see you crawling through thickets, fording streams and grabbing at branches as you slip on mossy boulders. Expect to come out bruised, battered and blistered – and to have a brilliant time. There are two forest camps at the park, with **tents for hire** and camp catering facilities, but no electricity; bring your own provisions and sleeping gear.

One camp is situated near the small town of **Kanyang**, some 45 minutes from Ikom. If you're relying on public transport, ask to be dropped at Kanyang and follow the signs to the Kanyang forest camp. You may be able to get a local guide here to take you off through the forest to places with evocative names like **Gorilla Rock** and **Swimming Pool Camp** (a large splash pool formed by a waterfall cascading into a limestone gully). You camp out along the way, and you should be prepared for dampness and cold. Don't forget provisions and something to start a fire.

Half an hour further north is **Buatong**, where you'll find the **park headquarters** for the Okwangwo Division (4km off the main road), where there's accommodation (take your own provisions). Numerous trails for trekking and a botanical garden are available, as well as guided treks into the heart of the spectacular beauty of the area. To get to Buatong from Calabar by public transport, you'll need to start out early and change at Ikom.

The Afi Mountain Drill Ranch

About 4km south of Kanyang, a track leads 6km west to **Katabang**, which can be reached by shared taxi and produces some excellent palm wine (visitors to the village traditionally pay a visit first to the chief and bring a courtesy gift, usually a bottle of spirits, though this is not expected if you're just passing through). Some 6km north of Katabang is the **Afi Mountain Drill Ranch**, part of the Afi Mountain Wildlife Sanctuary. Dedicated to the rehabilitation of drill monkeys, the ranch is run, like the centre in Calabar (see p.1084), by the American wildlife charity Pandrillus. As well as rescued and rehabilitated drill monkeys and chimpanzees, the area has a population of rare Cross River gorillas, though you would be extremely lucky to see any. It also offers excellent bird-watching, with a large migratory swallow roost.

Visitors are welcome, and low-priced accommodation is available – it can be arranged in Calabar (✆087/234 310, ✉drill@infoweb.abs.net) – but you should take your own food, and preferably drinking water (or a water purification kit). There is a small access fee to the Wildlife Sanctuary (₦500 per night, ₦350 for day visits, ₦500 per car), and the ranch also levies a small fee for community development (₦100) as part of its commitment to working with, and for the benefit of, local residents. For those who want to explore the area, wildlife rangers are on hand to act as guides. The Drill Center produce an information sheet for visitors, which is available from them by email.

14

14.3 | **NIGERIA** | The southeast

Obudu Cattle Ranch

The best-known attraction in Cross River is **Obudu Cattle Ranch**, in the north of the state. This hill resort-cum-cattle station is spread across the north-facing slopes of Oshie Ridge in the folds of the beautiful **Sonkwala Mountains** (1500–1900m above sea level). Obudu Ranch used to be a fashionable place for oil-industry expats to escape the rough climate of the delta oilfields, as it offers a virtually temperate climate and exotic fresh garden produce like strawberries and cauliflowers. Today, the *Ranch Hotel* (PO Box 87, Obudu, Cross River State; ⑥) still offers chalet **accommodation** ranging from moderate singles to executive suites, or you can rent a private lodge. Basic provisions are available at the workers' village, or at the on-site shop, where there's a bar.

More interesting than the putting green or table tennis are the **hiking** opportunities in the district. The best time to visit is just after the rainy season, when the air is clean and fresh, the views are fantastic and the nights almost cold. A path leads from the hotel to a striking waterfall about 7km away. Also in the area is a natural spring – "the grotto" – but most interesting is the **Gorilla Camp**, a thirteen-kilometre trek through dense bush, involving some arduous climbing over hills and valleys. A guide is necessary and even though you're unlikely to see gorillas, the lush mountain scenery is reward in itself.

The easiest way up here from Calabar is to head to Ikom (take the A4 if driving, not the A4-2). There are usually direct vehicles from Ikom to **Obudu village** (along the N40), or you can find transport from Enugu or Ikom to **Ogoja**, whence it's 66km to Obudu. In the village, you can rent a taxi or motorbike to the ranch. The road is good all the way and still improving; the final stretch – beset with hairpins as it snakes up to the ranch – is a wonderful climax to the trip. Getting away depends on the vagaries of taxis returning to Obudu after dropping other guests, or lorries heading into town. From Obudu there are occasional vehicles to Ikom, Ogoja or Calabar, but you may have a long wait. The ranch gets busy during holidays and **advance bookings** are advisable: they can be made by post, or at the Cross River State House in Lagos. Alternatively, local travel agents can usually help.

14.4

Central Nigeria

The huge area that is **"Central Nigeria"** is an artificial division, and really consists of the middle margins of the country's more natural divisions into southwest, southeast and north. However, the centre has quite a concentration of places of interest. If the federal capital of **Abuja** has little to offer, the same cannot be said of one of the country's most favoured towns, **Jos**, on its fine, high plateau of almost Mediterranean climate. **Bauchi** is less attractive, though pleasantly spacious, while **Yankari National Park**, not far away, is the country's best-organized park and its **Wikki Warm Springs** a pristine attraction in their own right. The **Kainji Lake National Park** is also worth striking out to, though this is quite involved without your own transport.

Kainji Lake National Park and around

Scenically and climatically, the **Kainji Lake National Park** feels more like a part of northern Nigeria, but it's remote and far to the west, and most commonly and easily approached from the south. Open from December to June, the park is split into two sectors, **Borgu**, mainly savanna and indeed the only one equipped for wildlife spotting; and **Zugurma**, more forested and inhabited by colobus monkeys. The best time to visit is in the dry season, after the grass is burned, when you've a better chance of seeing the animals – waterbucks, lions, leopards, baboons, green and patas monkeys, crocodiles, warthogs and hippos. For **information** about the park and its accommodation, contact the park offices in New Bussa (℡031/670 424 or 670 315) or Abuja (℡09/530 0429).

Jebba and Zugurma

North of Ilorin (see p.1059) you leave Yorubaland and enter a drier and less monoethnic environment, populated by a mix of Nupe, Bussa, Borgu, Kamberi, Fulani and Hausa communities. After some 70km you reach **JEBBA** (off the road to the east) before crossing the Niger on a fine, low bridge. The bridge passes over an island in the river where, just to its west, a monument marks the last resting place of Scottish explorer **Mungo Park**, killed near today's Kainji Dam in 1805 by people who apparently thought he and his expedition were a party of raiding Fulani jihadists. His boat is preserved at Jebba train station. There are several reasonable **places to stay** should you decide to break your journey at Jebba. One option is the excellent-value *Nigerian Paper Mill Guest House* (℡031/400 007; ❷), a kilometre up the hillside to the west of the highway (turn off 300m south of the bridge); rooms here have a/c, fridge and TV. On the other side of the highway, decent singles and doubles, some with a/c, are available at the very inexpensive, friendly *Goodwill Guest House and Canteen* at 2 Elder Etim St (℡031/400 114; ❶), 500m up Paper Mill Road, the main street through the centre of town.

From **Mokwa**, 38km north of Jebba (if heading to Kainji on public transport, ask to be dropped off here at Kainji junction), a good road sweeps off northwest to New Bussa and the national park. There are few towns up here amid the wild bush and dry patchy farmlands. **Zugurma** (24km from Mokwa) is a pretty halt, however, with a fine, jungly stream running past and, beyond, you're sure to see some wildlife – monkeys at least. Some 18km further up the road towards Kainji Dam, **Ibbi**, the gateway to the smaller **Zugurma sector** of the national park, has spacious, cool, comfy **rooms** with a/c, TV, fridge and running water at the *Ibbi Tourist Camp* (❷). A small museum houses arms and skins seized from poachers.

Kainji Dam and New Bussa

Kainji Dam is impressive, though you probably won't be allowed to go onto it – the road runs past it, below. It was just north of here, at Old Bussa, which has now been submerged by the artificial Kainji Lake, that the Scottish explorer Mungo Park was killed (see above). You can take a boat cruise on the lake, and even tour the hydro-electric complex.

The local town, **NEW BUSSA**, around 100km from Mokwa, is dull and scruffy with little of interest, but an excellent first base for the national park's Borgu sector, just 20km to the west. The park office 7km south of town does not sell tickets or arrange transport – for that you'll have to continue to Wawa (see below). New Bussa has two good places to **stay**: *Hotel Holy Year '75* on the Wawa Road (℡031/670 709; ❷), and *Hotel Brahmatola* at 199 Ibadan Way (℡031/670 027; ❶), both with inexpensive a/c doubles and even cheaper non-a/c singles. The *White House Guest Inn* (no phone; ❶), 50m from the *Holy Year '75*, also has very cheap, non-a/c rooms. A pleasant alternative, 3km out of town and popular with expats, are the chalet rooms and safari atmosphere at the *Kainji Motel* on Niger Crescent (☎031/670 032; ❷). Run by NEPA, accommodation here has air conditioning, hot and cold running water and satellite TV, and there's a **restaurant** too. Niger Crescent is at the end of Murtala Muhammed Road, where a left or a right will take you to the motel.

Borgu sector

Though it's the only part open for wildlife viewing, the **Borgu sector** of Kainji Lake National Park (Dec–June) doesn't get a lot of visitors, and it's doubtful if it has a lot of big game wildlife – in fact it looks certain that much has been poached out. However it's uninhabited by humans, and its 4000-odd square kilometres do contain plentiful numbers of various **antelope** species, monkeys and warthogs, plus several families of **hippos** in the pools of the somewhat seasonal Oli River which flows through the reserve. Lions may still roam the bush too, but elephants have not been seen for years. The smaller animals are surely there, but harder to spot.

The roads through Borgu tend to be well maintained. Vehicles can be rented and rangers hired as compulsory companions to your game drive; they are to be found up at the guard post and headquarters at Kaiama Road, **Wawa**. This is where you pay your fees (entrance ₦200 per person plus ₦400 per car; viewing fee ₦200; guided tour ₦400 per person plus ₦2000 for a camera or ₦4000 for a camcorder), and where you'll find a small museum, as at Zugurma, of guns and animal remains seized from poachers. **Rooms** are available here at the *Hotel Annex* (❷) or, for students only, the *Student Hostel* (₦200 per person). Alternatively, you can stay inside the park at the *Oli River Tourist Camp* (four-person chalet ₦2000, rooms ❷), 72km from Wawa, on the banks of the Oli River, with chalets and hotel accommodation, and full catering facilities.

Bida

Heading east towards Abuja from Kainji Dam, you'll pass through the old Nupe capital of **BIDA**. Nupe was an early kingdom, contemporaneous with the Hausa emirates, that lasted from around 1400 until its submission to Fulani rule after the nineteenth-century jihads. The Nupe people (who speak a Kwa language related to Yoruba) are still renowned **crafts experts**, and Bida has a reputation as a place to buy locally made metal jewellery, as well as cylindrical coloured-glass trading beads whose style is supposed to have originally derived from the markets of medieval Venice.

Neither of the town markets particularly reflects Bida's reputation for crafts, but a quick walk along the **Sotamaku Road** brings you to a host of **metal workshops** heralded by a glittering array of brass and aluminium plates, bowls and ornaments. Inside, school-age boys pump away at goatskin bellows while their elder brothers reshape old pans and scrap metal using gearbox housings, crankcases and steel rods as anvils. The same sweatshop approach is used in the **Masaga** area where **glass beads** are made from melted-down beer and minerals bottles, which lend an opaque lustre quite different from the trading beads found elsewhere. Steel rods are dipped into the glass and a single bead is formed as the rod is spun over a furnace. The panoply of patterned beads so formed is then strung on to necklaces or sold singly on roadside stands.

Harder to locate are the traditional Nupe **ten-legged stools** carved from a single piece of wood. Apart from their intricately patterned tops and unsurpassed stability, they're unusual because the seat is cut along the grain of the wood rather than across. The stools can still be bought in local villages, but dealers rapidly snap them up to sell in Lagos, where they fetch high prices. If you're keen to buy, start asking around a hundred metres south of the Total petrol station, and hopefully someone can lead you to an artisan with some unclaimed stock.

Practicalities

Arriving in Bida, you're likely to be dropped at the motor park on the Abuja–Ilorin road. Most points of interest are within walking distance of here, but you may want a taxi to the **hotels**, which are mostly on the outskirts of town. The closest to the centre, but with little else to recommend it, is the *Nasara Guest Inn*, on Kontagora Road (☎066/462 256; ❶), with singles and doubles, some with a/c. The Niger State Tourism Corporation's rather run-down *Niger Motel* in the GRA (☎066/641 025; ❷) has good-value s/c rooms with a/c. However the best-value hotel in town – and also the best, if far from deluxe – is the *Dhiyafah Satellite Motel* (☎066/462 179; ❶). Opposite the Emir's Palace in the centre of town, at Niger Street, it has largish a/c rooms set around a sunny courtyard, and friendly staff. There's a reasonable **restaurant** here too, though you'll need to order meals in advance. Otherwise, the scope for eating isn't great – ordinary street food is on offer around the Total station junction.

Abuja

Work on the capital at **ABUJA** began in 1981 and, almost overnight, the peaceful setting of this hitherto sparsely populated corner of the Niger State was transformed into Africa's biggest construction site. The federal government's decision to create a new capital dates from 1976, when the experience of the civil war made it clear that Lagos, with a seventy-five percent Yoruba population, was not conducive to relieving ethnic tensions – besides, Lagos had already outgrown its capacities. However, the enormous cost of creating a city from scratch, especially one with such ambitious designs and such opportunities for misappropriation, led to serious economic difficulties for the civilian presidency of Shehu Shagari. After the 1983 coup which deposed him, the project came to an abrupt standstill and it wasn't until 1991 that the capital was officially transferred from Lagos. A distinctive Abuja pulse is only now beginning to emerge, and the city is developing into a real political capital with increasing numbers of foreign **embassies** based here, but you'd have to be especially interested in urban planning or golf – Abuja has possibly the best course in Africa – to find any reason to want to stay, especially since pretty much everything in Abuja is at least half as expensive again as elsewhere in the country.

Moving on from Abuja

Most vehicles leave from **Area 1 motor park**. If you can't find a direct vehicle to your destination, try the regular service to **Suleja**, one of the original settlements now swamped by the Federal Capital Territory, which has a much more active motor park. One thing to look out for if heading to or through Suleja is **Zuma Rock**, a kilometre-long inselberg 55km west of Abuja and east of the main road between Ziba and Suleja, that's Nigeria's answer to Ayers Rock. It can't be climbed without special equipment, so it isn't really worth a visit in its own right, but it's an impressive landmark and highly photogenic.

There's no **railway** line through Abuja, although a high-speed train is planned to Kaduna. Abuja nonetheless has the headquarters of the Nigeria Railway Corporation, at Plot 739, Zone A6, Panama St, off IBB Way, Maitama (☎09/523 7498–99 or 1912–13).

There are numerous **flights** to Lagos (1hr) on various airlines (of which Bellview is the most reliable), and a weekday service to Port Harcourt on Overland Airways. There are also regular flights to Maiduguri, Enugu and Benin City. Airline offices are detailed in "Listings", p.1094.

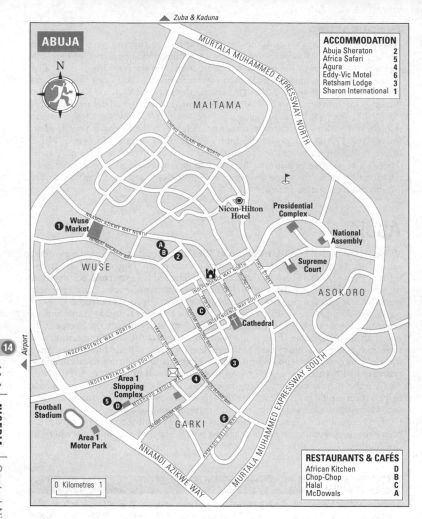

ABUJA

▲ Zuba & Kaduna

ACCOMMODATION

Abuja Sheraton	2
Africa Safari	5
Agura	4
Eddy-Vic Motel	6
Retsham Lodge	3
Sharon International	1

MAITAMA

MURTALA MUHAMMED EXPRESSWAY NORTH

SHEHU SHAGARI WAY NORTH

Nicon-Hilton Hotel

Presidential Complex

National Assembly

NNAMDI AZIKWE WAY NORTH

Wuse Market

HERBERT MACAULAY WAY

WUSE

INDEPENDENCE WAY NORTH

Supreme Court

ASOKORO

THIRD STREET

SECOND ST.

FIRST ST.

INDEPENDENCE WAY SOUTH

Cathedral

Airport ◀

INDEPENDENCE WAY NORTH

YAKUBU GOWON WAY

USUMA NYANYA WAY

Area 1 Shopping Complex

Football Stadium

MOSHOOD ABIOLA WAY

TAFAWA BALEWA WAY

GARKI

AHMADU BELLO WAY

MURTALA MUHAMMED EXPRESSWAY SOUTH

Area 1 Motor Park

NNAMDI AZIKWE WAY

0 Kilometres 1

RESTAURANTS & CAFÉS

African Kitchen	D
Chop-Chop	B
Halal	C
McDowals	A

Arrival and information

The only way into town from the **airport**, 37km distant, is by taxi; expect to pay ₦1500–2000. Most people arrive in Abuja by minibus at the **Area 1 motor park** in the Garki area of town, by the junction of the city's orbital ring road (Nnamdi Azikwe Way) with Moshood Abiola Road (aka Festival Road). Thanks to the motor park and nearby market (or "shopping complex"), this is one of the few pockets of life in a town that's mostly pretty placid. Private bus companies may leave you at Julius Berger Junction, further north up the ring road at its junction with Herbert Macaulay Way in Wuse. Unfortunately the city, designed for motor transport, is too large to manage on foot, and it can be a challenge to find the rare buses and shared taxis, even okadas. For **tourist information**, the Nigeria Tourism Development Corporation have their HQ at the Old Secretariat in Garki Area 1 (☎09/234 2764, ✆ntdc@metrong.com).

Accommodation

Really inexpensive lodging doesn't exist in Abuja, though good-value weekend deals can be found at the international hotels. Many hotels are found in **Garki**, the southern district of Abuja, with another cluster in **Wuse**, west of the market.

Abuja Sheraton Hotel & Towers Ladi Kwali St ☎09/523 0225–44, ☏523 1570–1, ✉sales_abuja@sheraton.com. Over six hundred rooms, four restaurants, a nightclub and casino, pool and garden bar, health club, travel agency, business centre and banquet hall – this hotel has it all. **8**

Africa Safari Hotel (aka Sunny Guest Inn) Plot 11 Benue Crescent, Area 1, Section 1, Garki ☎09/523 1881 or 1365, ☏523 1365. Relatively inexpensive high-quality hotel with clean and pleasant a/c rooms, and a couple of poky non-a/c singles. A big advantage of this place is the location, just a 10min walk from Area 1 motor park (down Moshood Abiola Rd, first left into Funtua St, then left at the end and follow the signs). **4**

Agura Hotel Corner of Muhammadu Buhari Way and Moshood Abiola Way ☎09/234 1753–60,

☏09/234 2115. All the perks and facilities of the big hotels, but much cheaper and less pretentious. **7**

Eddy-Vic Motel Plot 466 Ahmadu Bello Way, Garki II ☎09/234 5576 or 670 6749. Relatively cheap lodge with s/c, a/c rooms, plus a restaurant and bar. **5**

Retsham Lodge Plot 808 Uyo Crescent, Area 11, Garki ☎09/234 0805, ☏09/234 0806. Good-value lodging, with s/c rooms with a/c, TV and fridge, as well as a laundry service and restaurant. To find it, take Warri St off Tafawa Balewa Way, turn left at the end, then first right. There's a 25 percent discount at weekends. **5**

Sharon International Plot 220, Wuse Zone 6 ☎09/523 3444–5, ☏09/523 3447. Moderately priced hotel with cosy rooms, all with a/c, fan, fridge, satellite TV, plus a restaurant (but no alcohol). **4**

The City

Abuja was designed with a population of three million in mind; at the current rate of growth, the city could soon be too small. That said, don't expect to meet an "Abuja local". The indigenous **Gwari**, a semi-nomadic people, were unceremoniously evicted from their ancestral lands, and the capital is now populated by people from all parts of the country. Today, the Gwari have nearly disappeared as a distinct ethnic and linguistic (Kwa-speaking) community.

The city has a beautiful setting, with a backdrop of stunning stone inselbergs and a good deal of greenery, but the landscaped boulevards with wonderful views across the savanna are gradually being filled with international hotels and office buildings. The magnificent **Central Mosque**, with its large golden dome and fairytale minarets, remains a definite landmark. There's a **market** on Kashim Ibrahim Way, in Wuse Zone 4, a small zoo in **Julie Useni Park** in Garki Area 1, and the celebrated **golf course** in Asokoro, not far from the Presidential Complex, but in the continued absence of the projected National Museum, or any other worthy distraction, many travellers resign themselves to one of the air-conditioned cocktail lounges at the *Nicon Hilton* – West Africa's largest hotel, on Shehu Shagari Way North – or the *Sheraton*.

Eating and nightlife

All the hotels have **restaurants**, most of which are fairly good and open to the public. The major hotels also have more or less functioning **nightclubs**: those at the *Agura*, *Hilton* and *Sheraton* hotels are among the best.

Elsewhere in the city, there are two main areas for eating. One is the market by Area 1 motor park in Garki, alive in the evenings with *suya* stalls and chop houses. The outdoor *African Kitchen* here (take Funtua Street, the first left off Moshood Abiola Road coming from the motor park, and the entrance is in the first yard on the right) is the place to get stuff like pounded yam and *egusi*. The other main food area is a small street signposted "Zone 4 Cornershops" off Lady Kwali Street in

Wuse Zone 4 near the *Sheraton*, and the adjoining Addis Ababa Crescent. Here, the *Chop-Chop* on the corner of Lady Kwali Street and Zone 4 Cornershops offers meat or chicken with a choice of rice, chips, *amala*, *eba* and even *jollof* spaghetti, while *McDowals Restaurant*, 6 Addis Ababa Crescent, Wuse Zone 4, is popular among Abuja's expats for its delicious and affordable food, but doesn't serve alcohol. In the central area, the affordable *Halal Restaurant*, at the National Centre for Women Development on Fifth Street, serves Nigerian, continental and Lebanese dishes.

Listings

Airlines AeroContractors, at the airport ☎09/810 0197, plus a desk at the *Nicon Hilton* hotel; Albarka, 8A Udi St, off Aso Drive, Maitama ☎09/523 3554, plus a desk at the *Agura Hotel*; Bellview, at the airport ☎09/810 0089, plus desks at the *Agura*, *Sheraton* and *Nicon-Hilton* hotels; British Airways, at the airport ☎09/810 0021–2, plus a desk at the *Nicon-Hilton Hotel* ☎09/413 9608 or 9610; KLM, *Sheraton Hotel* ☎09/523 9965–6; Nigeria Airways, UTC Building, by Luzumba Commercial Complex, off Moshood Abiola Rd, Garki ☎09/234 1737; Swiss, c/o Panalpina, Plot 285, Samuel Akintola Ladoke Blvd, off Ahmadu Bello Way, Garki II ☎09/523 9311–3. In addition to those listed, Chanchangi, IRS, Skyline and TransSaharan all have booking desks at the *Agura Hotel*.

Banks and exchange Bureaux de change can be found at the Luzumba Commercial Complex off Moshood Abiola Rd in Garki, among the Zone 4 Cornershops adjoining Addis Ababa Crescent and Lady Kwali St near the *Sheraton Hotel* in Wuse Zone 4, and in Garki Area 1 shopping complex on Moshood Abiola Rd, near Area 1 motor park. Moneychangers hang out near the *Sheraton* on Lady Kwali St. Among the various banks in town, Western Union's representative, First Bank of Nigeria, has its main branch at Plot 777, Muhammadu Buhari Way (☎09/234 6833–5).

Couriers DHL, Plot 609, Dambata Close, off Tafawa Balewa Way, Garki Area 7 ☎09/234 6557–8; UPS, Plot 781, Obafemi Awolowo St, Area 2, Garki ☎09/234 7979.

Cultural Centres British Council, Plot 2935, IBB Way, Maitama ☎09/413 7870–7; Alliance Française, 32 Udi St, off Aso Drive, Maitama ☎09/523 50 88.

Embassies Australia, Arizona Building, opposite Maitama Hospital, Maitama ☎09/314 3778; Benin, Plot 2858A, Danube St, off IBB Way, Maitama ☎09/523 8424; Canada, 3A Bobo St, off Gana St, Maitama ☎09/413 9910–1; Chad, 10 Mississippi St, Plot 152, Maitama ☎09/413 0751; Gambia, Plot 25, Ontario Crescent, off Mississippi St, Maitama ☎09/413 8545; Ghana, Plot 301, Olusegun Obasanjo Way, Area 10, Garki ☎09/234 5192–3; Guinea, Plot 679, Agadez Crescent, off Amino Kano Crescent, Wuse II; European Union (also representing several member states), Europe House, 63 Usuma St, Maitama ☎09/413 3146–8; Ireland, Plot 415, Negro Crescent, Maitama ☎09/413 1751; Mali, Plot 465, Nouakchott St, Zone 1, Wuse ☎09/523 0494; Niger, 7 Sangha St, off Mississippi St, Maitama ☎09/413 5434–6; South Africa, Plot 676, Vaal St, off Rhine St, off IBB Way, Maitama ☎09/413 3776; Togo, Plot 664, Usuma St, Maitama ☎09/413 9833; UK, Plot 364, Dangote House, Aguyi Ironsi St, Maitama ☎09/413 4561–5; USA, 9 Mambilla St, off Aso Drive, Maitama ☎09/523 5857 or 0960–6.

Internet access Cybercafés can be found in Garki Area 1 shopping complex, in Luzumba Commercial Complex off Moshood Abiola Rd in Garki, at Metro Plaza in the Central Area, in Zone 4 Cornershops off Addis Ababa Crescent in Wuse Zone 4, and in Wuse Shopping Plaza on Herbert Macaulay Way in Wuse Zone 3.

Post office The GPO (Mon–Fri 8am–4pm) is on Moshood Abiola Rd, Garki Area 10. There's a branch office in Garki Area 1 shopping complex.

Travel agents Try Emerald Tours, Ali Akilu Crescent, off Usman dan Fodio Crescent, Asokoro; they can arrange trips to Yankari, Obudu Cattle Ranch, Kano and Katsina.

Jos and around

Set 1200m above sea level, **JOS** enjoys a mild climate that has long attracted Europeans weary of the coastal humidity or the northern heat and dust. Laid out in a beautiful, rocky landscape, the hill resort grew up around **tin mines** exploited by the British at the beginning of the twentieth century — and still partly managed by expatriates. Jos's history, though, can be traced back much further to the **Nok culture** (named after the Jos plateau village of the same name) which spread throughout central Nigeria between 2800 and 1800 years ago. Terracotta artefacts left behind by this civilization were discovered quite accidentally in the mines and are today housed in the **Jos Museum**.

This is only one of many sights around a town that seems to have been intentionally designed for visitors. Other diversions include the **zoo** (now slightly depressing) and the **Museum of Traditional Nigerian Architecture**, where life-size replica buildings from Zaria, Kano, Katsina and other cities have been constructed. Here you can visit the gems of traditional architecture which have largely fallen into disrepair or disappeared altogether in their native cities.

Orientation, arrival and information

The **main market** is an unmistakeable landmark, covering a large area in the middle of town. It's a massive modern structure with a wild, colourful design, and well stocked to boot. From the market, **Ahmadu Bello Road**, one of the town's main thoroughfares, runs down towards the **post office**.

The **airport** is 29km south of town, and served by taxis. The **train station** is quite centrally located off Bauchi Road, east of Ahmadu Bello Road. A pedestrian bridge to the south leads over the tracks (though most people just walk across them) from **Beach Road** ("The Beach") to **Murtala Muhammed Way**, another major thoroughfare. Arriving by road transport from the north, you'll probably be dropped at **Bauchi Road motor park**, 3km north of the centre. A similar distance northwest of the centre is the **Zaria Road motor park**, where you might well end up if arriving from the south. If you arrive by Peugeot or minibus, you'll probably be dropped at Plateau Riders motor park, on Tafewa Balewa Street in the centre.

Along Ahmadu Bello Road are a number of **supermarkets** and several **banks**, although the major ones are behind the post office around Bank Street. **Bureaux de change** are plentiful in Jos, with one on Museum Street, several at the southern end of Beach Road, and a good one at 15 Beach Road, on the corner of Fidelis N. Tapgun Road, which claims to change "any currency" – they certainly take dollars, pounds, euros and CFAs. For international **telephone calls**, Grakol, at 10 Ahmadu Bello Road, is half the price of NITEL, on Museum Street. The **tourist office** (Mon–Fri 8am–4pm) is at 31 Yakubu Gowon Way (☎073/465 747, ☎073/463 040, ✉platstate@tourism.hisen.org), and can rent out vehicles; it also maintains information desks at the *Hill Station* and *Plateau* hotels (Mon–Sat 8am–2pm).

14

14.4 | **NIGERIA** | Central Nigeria

Moving on from Jos

The main motor park for the **north** is the **Bauchi Road motor park**, serving Bauchi, Kano, Kaduna, Maiduguri, Sokoto and all points north. Daily morning bus services to Calabar and Port Harcourt are operated by Crosslines from their office on Bauchi Road by the motor park. The main motor park for the **south**, including Lagos, Ibadan and Abuja is the **Zaria Road motor park**. Overnight **luxury bus** services to Lagos and Ibadan are operated by a handful of firms with offices around the junction of Zaria By-Pass and Tafewa Balewa Street. Fast Peugeots and minibuses, pre-bookable and mostly leaving mornings, go from **Plateau Riders motor park**, serving Abuja, Kano, Benin City and other long-distance destinations.

There should be a very slow weekly **train** service to Port Harcourt, leaving at noon on Thursday and taking at least two days, but it's often out of action for weeks on end. ADC **fly** five times weekly to Lagos and Abuja. Nigeria Airways have an office at 6 Bank Street (☎073/452 298–9), though they don't fly from Jos.

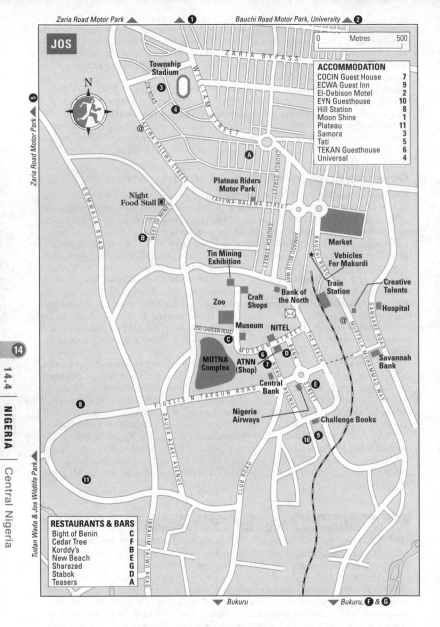

Accommodation

Jos has a variety of places to stay, including several good mission-type guesthouses.

COCIN Guest House 5 Noad Ave, behind Central Bank ☏073/452 286. One of the town's many mission-oriented places with clean and comfortable s/c rooms and dorms; they'll put you up if they have space. Dorm beds ₦250. ❶

ECWA Guest Inn Off Kano Rd and behind

Challenge Books ☎073/450 572. Clean, inexpensive and safe, this is often used by travellers; rooms (including dorms) come at various prices, some s/c with hot water. The restaurant serves solid helpings of meals like "Irish stew and two veg" and there's a pleasant living room with satellite TV. Dorm beds ₦450, ②

El-Debison Motel Forest Camp, behind University Staff Qtrs, off Bauchi Rd ☎073/610 519. Small, charming and spotless guesthouse in a quiet neighbourhood north of the centre, near Bauchi Rd motor park. All rooms are s/c, with fans or a/c, and satellite TV. ②

EYN Guesthouse Opposite ECWA Guest Inn, off Kano Rd ☎073/452 056. Good-value budget accommodation with cooking facilities in the rooms (no meals are served). Dorm beds ₦450, ②

Hill Station Hotel Tudun Wada Rd ☎073/455 300 or 454 817, ☎073/455 399. An attractive building looking out on the hills and still the best hotel in town, though it's beginning to feel a little run-down. The rooms have a/c and satellite TV, and there's a pool (₦150 for non-residents) ⑥

Moon Shine Hotel 18 Igbo-Ukwe St, 500m north of the Township Stadium ☎073/611 116 or 610 361. Good value with comfortable s/c rooms and a decent restaurant. The annexe across the street is slightly posher. ②

Plateau Hotel Resthouse Rd, Tudun Wada ☎073/455 741. Slightly expensive, but well kept and good value. Pleasant swimming pool (₦200 for non-residents), restaurant and bar with occasional live music. ④

Samora Hotel 18 Pankshin St ☎073/455 516. A friendly and good-value hotel opposite the Township Stadium, with clean s/c rooms and a cheap restaurant. ②

Tati Hotel Zaria Rd, next to Zaria motor park ☎073/455 897. In a pricier league than the mission guesthouses, but good value, with extras like a/c, fan and phones, and a popular weekend nightclub. The comforts come with friendly service, but running water is sporadic. ②

TEKAN Guest House 6 Noad Ave ☎073/453 036. Friendly and clean missionary centre with inexpensive rooms, some s/c, and even less expensive beds in the dorm. Dorm beds ₦300, ①

Universal Hotel 9–11 Pankshin St ☎073/450 338. Cheap and cheerful with s/c singles and doubles (though water comes in a bucket), and even cheaper non-s/c singles. ①

The Town and around

Jos's tourist attractions are concentrated in a small area around the museum, best accessed by taking Museum Street off Ahmadu Bello Way by the post office. Sightseeing aside, Jos is a good place to buy **crafts**, especially leather and basket-work. Craft shops can be found by the Tin Mining Exhibition near the museum, on Noad Avenue opposite the *TEKAN Guest House*, and at the southern end of Beach Road. There is also an upmarket craft shop called Creative Talents on Murtala Muhammed Way near the station, and a fair-trade craft shop run by the Alternative Trade Network of Nigeria (ATNN) at 1 Museum Street, opposite NITEL.

Jos National Museum

Jos National Museum (daily 8am–5.30pm; ₦20) was created in 1952 to house **Nok terracotta figures** first found in the tin mines near Nok in the 1920s. These pieces are complemented by exhibits showing aspects of the art and culture – masks, weaving, medicine, ceremonies – of central Nigerian peoples. The collections are extremely well presented and the brief explanations are helpful. At the end of the museum (notice, as you're leaving, the massive gate taken from the ancient wall around Bauchi), an extensive **pottery collection** is displayed in a cool court-yard with ponds and trees.

The zoo and Tin Mining Exhibition

Set in a park opposite the Jos National Museum, the **zoo** (daily 8am–6pm; ₦20) has recovered from former neglect, but it is still less interesting than the wildlife park (see overleaf). Near the zoo, several old locomotives and carriages plus track from the **Bauchi Light Railway** (which closed in 1959) are on display, along with other vehicles from the early twentieth century. Also nearby, the **Tin Mining**

Exhibition (Mon–Sat 9am–4pm; ₦20) is a tiny one-room museum dedicated to the history and technology of mining in the area.

Museum of Traditional Nigerian Architecture

Probably the most unusual museum, and one well worth spending some time to discover, is the **Museum of Traditional Nigerian Architecture (MOTNA)**, which covers a vast area opposite the zoo. Full-scale reproductions of the country's most impressive monuments have been built on the site. You get a better idea of the magnitude of the **Kano Wall** here than you do in its city of origin, especially if you climb the narrow staircase leading to the top. The **Zaria Friday Mosque** with its impressive vaulting reveals the highly sophisticated technical skills of the Hausa. There are also smaller copies of the **Katsina Palace** and the **Ilorin mosque**. Entry is free, but guides show you round for a fee that goes to the upkeep of MOTNA.

Jos Wildlife Park

Not to be confused with the zoo, the **Jos Wildlife Park** (daily 10am–dusk; ₦50), southwest of town, off the Jos–Bukuru road (Yakubu Gowon Way), is a more worthwhile encounter. The drive-through park, covering an area of about eight square kilometres, contains a large variety of animals, including antelopes and monkeys, lions in a large enclosure, some elephants, buffaloes and hippos, and various other species, some of which are in ordinary cages near the entrance, or in semi-natural large enclosures. If you're in a 4WD vehicle, you should be able to make it to the observation tower at the highest point in the park, where there's a good view of Jos and the plateau. Otherwise, rent a taxi in Jos for a three-hour visit, or take Bukuru-bound public transport, which can drop you at the junction for the road to Miango to the west. The park entrance is 4km down this road: if it's a weekend, you might get a lift with other visitors.

Jos Plateau

If you want to get into the **Jos Plateau** countryside, take a taxi or minibus out to **Bukuru** from the end of Tafewa Balewa Street, near the market. You can stay in the very nice *Yelwa Club* (the former Tin Miners' Club) in Bukuru, which has a pool and is surprisingly cheap. For **camping**, the Vom area to the southwest of Jos is pretty, with plenty of good grassy spots amid boulders and groves of gum trees. At **Assop Falls**, 64km south of Jos on the Abuja Road (A3), you can scramble across rocks and get quite close to the falls (₦200 entry), which are at their most impressive in the rainy season (July–Sept).

Eating

For a town of its size, Jos has one of the widest choices of eating places in Nigeria, with some good Nigerian restaurants and a couple of excellent Lebanese ones for good measure.

Bight of Benin Zoo Garden Rd, near the museum. Good cooking, in a replicated Benin noble's house. A cool place to take a break, with a limited menu of national specialities at reasonable prices.

Cedar Tree 17 Yakubu Gowon Way, 500m beyond the *Sharazad*, on the right as you head out of town ☎073/464 890. Excellent and far from outrageously priced Lebanese restaurant, well worth the splurge and the effort of getting to.

Elysan Restaurant *Hill Station Hotel*. Jos's only Chinese restaurant – not the most authentic oriental cooking, but it may be a pleasant change from Nigerian fare.

Korddy's Off West of Mines. A very popular restaurant where the specialities include goat head and fish pepper soup.

New Beach Restaurant 5 Bank St. Moderately priced English and Nigerian dishes, the former including mushroom soup and curry beef.

Sharazad Yakubu Gowon Way, 2km out of the

centre towards Bukuru ☏073/462 281. A range of good, well-prepared Lebanese, European and Chinese dishes at reasonable prices (although it's one of the more expensive places in town). Popular with expats.

Stabok Bank St. Toasted sandwiches and fish-

and-chips-type meals complement Nigerian specialities in this popular local bar-restaurant.

Teasers 2 Niger Ave. A bar-restaurant serving good, solid Nigerian chop at very reasonable prices. The *jollof* rice is fiery, and particularly recommended.

South from Jos

South of Jos, beyond the plateau, the topography is complex and travel delightful. Forests of gum trees spread around **Panyam** and from here on the road (surfaced, whatever the maps may say) drops down a breathtaking escarpment through coniferous woods and Mediterranean landscapes to **Shendam** and **Yelwa**. It's fine cycling country; otherwise, apart from one or two exhausting through-bus services to big cities in the southeast, travelling by road becomes chancy as you get into this eastern part of Central Nigeria. If you're travelling south on this road into **Taraba State**, you're in a position to make an unusual entry into the Northwest Province of Cameroon at **Dumbo** (see p.1135). The more direct route south from the Jos Plateau follows the A3 and A4 into **southern Cameroon** via Ikom and Ekok (see p.1087).

Located in the fertile middle belt, where the forests of the south gradually turn into the savanna of the north, **Benue State** has been called "the food basket of Nigeria". **MAKURDI**, its capital, has become a major agricultural trading centre and is one of the original homelands of the farming Tiv people, while also on the fringes of Igboland. Lying roughly midway between Jos and Cameroon, on the south bank of the Benue River, Makurdi is a fair-sized town with several small and medium **hotels**: the *Dolphin* – part of a complex of cinemas, restaurants and lodgings in Secretariat Road to the north of town – is clean, welcoming and inexpensive. An unreliable passenger service runs through on the **rail** line between Maiduguri and Port Harcourt; check at the train station for schedules.

Bauchi, Yankari and around

Northeast from Jos, the road drops down from the plateau in a spectacular curve, turns east and then runs across featureless plains to **BAUCHI**, capital of the state of the same name. The town gives a more exotic first impression from the north down the A3 Kano–Maiduguri route, an approach which lines up a grand assembly of inselbergs known as the **Belo Hills** shortly before you arrive. Bauchi is the nearest big centre to **Yankari National Park** and if you don't have your own transport you'll very likely have to spend a night here before getting to the reserve.

After the Fulani jihad, in the 1840s, an emirate was established at Bauchi, but despite the **Emir's palace**, the **old mosque**, and some remnants of its **city wall**, the town – which radiates in several directions from the roundabout by its **Central Market** – is a large, seemingly impersonal place with little of enduring interest. If you're stuck here waiting for transport, you could spend an interesting half-hour at the **Mausoleum of Tafawa Balewa** (daily 7am–6pm; free), 300m north of the Central Market roundabout on Ran Road. Balewa was Nigeria's first prime minister, and on weekdays you may be able to see a video of his independence speech. A tour of the complex takes you up a ramp through regions of dark and light – symbolizing colonial repression and the hope of independence – and leads to the roofless mausoleum. The concrete and stone are austere, but the site remains a powerful monument to the fight for self-determination.

Bauchi practicalities

Bauchi's main **motor park** is on Ran Road, north of Ran Gate in the old city wall and 1km north of the Central Market. There's no airport here (the closest is at Jos), though Nigeria Airways maintain a Bauchi office at 40 Kobi St (℡077/542 800). The **train station** is some way east of town on the Gomba road.

There are a dozen or more **inexpensive** hotels in Bauchi. The best of them are the *CFA Hotel*, 800m east of Central Market on Gombe Road, just outside Wambai Gate (℡077/543 563 or 643; ❷) and conveniently located if you're planning to catch an early taxi to the national park; and the *Sogiji Hotel*, 1km north of the Central Market on Ran Road, just outside Ran Gate (℡077/543 454; ❶), slightly run-down but still good value and handy for the nearby motor park. Of the more **upmarket** places, the *Zaranda Hotel*, 3km west of town on the Jos Road (℡077/543 814–20, ℻543 640; ❺), is the poshest looking and the priciest, with a booking office (℡077/542 174) for Yankari National Park and its lodge, and car rental facilities, but the water supply is erratic and the food awful. A far better place is the *Awalah Hotel* on the Kano Road (℡077/542 344 or 377; ❷), with friendly service, comfortable rooms and a good-sized pool (₦150 for non-residents).

Yankari National Park

Covering over 2200 square kilometres of protected bush, **Yankari National Park** was the first game reserve in Nigeria and it remains the most popular (entry ₦200, park viewing fee ₦200, camera ₦100, digital camera ₦1000, camcorder ₦1500, car ₦100). However, despite the authorities' best efforts, poaching is still widespread and has taken its toll on the once abundant wildlife. You're likely to see herds of **gazelle** and **antelope**, and **elephants** with a little luck, but **lions**, which still hunt in the park (together with leopards), are getting increasingly shy and elusive. Other animals include warthogs, hippos, waterbuck, buffaloes, several species of duiker, hartebeest, various monkeys and crocodiles. Although the park is open all year, the best time to see animals is during the dry season (Feb–April), when they are driven closer to the lodge. In addition to the animals, **Wikki Warm Springs** is reason to come to the park in itself. If you have any difficulty organizing game-viewing trips at the lodge, you probably won't be unhappy spending your time in its crystal-clear waters.

Reaching the park

There is no regular transport from Bauchi east to *Wikki Warm Springs Lodge*, the main focus in Yankari. If you don't have a car you can take a **shared taxi** from the Gombe station on the east side of Bauchi. These vehicles can drop you at **Dindima** on the highway, where the Yankari road splits off south – or they sometimes go to villages along the latter road and will let you off right in front of the park gate en route. Either way, you still have to get a lift for the rest of the journey with incoming visitors (if you inform the guards at the gate you're looking for a ride into the park, they're usually pretty good about asking the cars on their way in). Note that in the middle of the week and on certain quiet weekends, the park may be devoid of visitors, in which case you could be really stuck. For that reason, avoid setting off from Bauchi in the late afternoon.

Another way of getting to the camp is to **charter a taxi** in Bauchi and arrange a price with the driver – you'd pay around ₦8000. If you're **cycling**, the road from Bauchi highway to Wikki is a fine and exciting day's ride in the park, with no serious worries about animals.

Park accommodation and eating

A range of accommodation is available at the **lodge**, where there's even a small **natural history museum** (free) – well laid out and full of local tales. The chalets

△ Dye pits, Kano

or *rondavels* (❶) have become rather run-down, and water and electricity are frequently off during the day (and routinely go off at a set time late each evening). Luxury and executive suites are better (❺ & ❻ respectively). Camping is possible as an alternative (₦300 per person), and there is also a cheap hostel with dorm accommodation for students (₦100). If you're visiting the park on a weekend or any major holiday, it's a good idea to make advance **reservations** – the lodge gets very full, particularly at Easter. In theory you can book at the *Zaranda Hotel* in Bauchi, at the park office on Maiduguri Bypass in Bauchi (☎077/543 674), or by fixing things up several days beforehand with any local travel agency, but in practice, bookings do not seem to get through to the park itself.

The **restaurant** near the lodge serves European meals at reasonable prices – to save money, bring provisions from Bauchi and do your own cooking. A pleasant **outdoor bar** here overlooks the savanna.

Game-viewing

Morning and afternoon **game-runs** are organized at the lodge. If you don't have your own car, you can go on one of the camp vehicles – a lorry with benches in the back – for a fee, provided they get enough people together to form a worthwhile group. If you have your own vehicle, you must take one of the rangers – which isn't a bad idea anyway, as they're most likely to know where to see animals and can direct you to other sites like the **Marshall Caves**, believed to have once been inhabited, or the **Borkono Falls** (at their most spectacular in September). On any drive – assuming you go early in the morning, which is best, or late afternoon – you'll see antelope and gazelles of various species, and there's every likelihood you will see elephants. To see any predators at all, however, you'd need to be very lucky.

Wikki Warm Springs

Below the restaurant, a steep path leads down to **Wikki Warm Springs** (₦150). It's hard to think of any site in West Africa more completely satisfying from a hedonistic point of view. Twelve million litres a day of perfectly clear, clean water at a steady ideal temperature of 31°C come bubbling up from a dark hole at the bottom of a deep pool, at the base of a steep, sheltering cliff. Nothing, save perhaps the persistent hassles of monkeys and baboons, detracts from the site's beauty. From its source, the water flows out for a hundred metres or more past steep banks of overhanging foliage, over a bed of glistening sand. It's almost too pretty, especially at night when it's lit by floodlamps – like an elaborate bit of New Age interior design.

The access side of the stream is concreted over, which keeps it clean, and there are parts shallow enough for toddlers to enjoy, and deeper areas for bigger swimmers. Downstream, camp staff wash clothes and bathe. Access is free if you're staying at the camp but there's a charge if you're just here for the day – as rather a lot of people are at weekends. If you take food or valuables down there, watch out for those monkeys.

Gombe to Numan

Beyond Yankari, in Gombe State, the terrain between **Gombe** and **Numan** (on the edge of Adamawa State) is a superb stretch of scenery and, if you've got your own transport, you can attempt some fantastic **hikes and climbs** in the Mouri mountains. **Tangale Hill** near Kaltungo is a steep and stunning volcanic plug and a brisk three-hour climb, but you'll need permission from the emir of the little town and help from local men in guiding you up. Don't count on staying in Numan, a shabby town with two dreadful hotels, that was caught up in Muslim–Christian violence in 2003.

14.5

The north and northeast

ormerly a conglomeration of disunited and often warring emirates, the **Hausa country** spreads over the arid savanna of the northern plateaux and comprises the largest geographical entity in Nigeria. In this vast region, Hausa makes sense as a linguistic rather than an ethnic grouping, since there are many different northern peoples. The religious (and in many respects political) head of all the Hausa peoples is in fact a Fulani – the **Sultan of Sokoto** – and has been for nearly 200 years. Thanks to the common faith of **Islam** and the lingua franca of Hausa, however, a bond has been created among northerners that puts them politically at an advantage over the south. In recent years, the introduction of *sharia* law (see box, p.1024), although interpreted differently from state to state, has widened the north–south divide even further.

The area near **Lake Chad** in the northeast of the country is peopled by the **Kanuri**, who, in around the ninth century, migrated from the northern, desert regions of Kanem to form the new empire of Bornu which grew rich on **trans-Saharan trade**. In the context of the current Federal Republic, this kingdom translates roughly into the thinly populated **Yobe** and **Borno** states, the latter with its capital in **Maiduguri**, the only major town in the rather isolated northeast. Further west, the Hausa city-states (the **Hausa Bakwai**: Gobir, Katsina, Kano, Zaria, Daura, Rano and Biram) developed into powerful emirates from around the eleventh century and had partially converted to Islam by 1400. Old walled cities from this era still exist in **Katsina**, **Zaria** and **Kano**. Kano today is a major urban centre, with an international airport and diverse industries. Development has come

The origin of the seven Hausa states

The Hausa have a rich oral literature outside the influence of more recent Islamic tales. In folk history, the origin of their states, the Hausa Bakwai, is traced to **Bayajida**, son of the king of Baghdad, who fled his homeland after a bitter dispute with his father. After years of wandering, he arrived in Bornu and was recognized as a natural leader by the *mai* or king, who gave one of his daughters in marriage to the boy. Bayajida fell out with his father-in-law, and fled again, with his pregnant wife, to a place called Garun Gabas. He left his Bornu wife here, where she gave birth to a son, **Biram**, who later established the first of the Hausa Bakwai, named after him, in the area to the east of Kano. Meanwhile Bayajida had taken off again for the west and, in the middle of the night, fetched up at Daura, a place east of Katsina that was ruled at the time by a dynasty of queens. He stopped an old woman, Ayana, to ask for water and was told it was the wrong day of the week: the snake who owned the well only allowed people to draw water on a Friday. Nobody had been able to kill the snake. Bayajida, of course, went straight to the well, woke up the snake and chopped its head off. Then he drank his fill, pocketed the head and moved on. The next day was Friday and the queen wanted to know who had killed the snake. Ayana told her about the stranger and the queen sent messengers to catch up with the restless Bayajida, who agreed to return – and then asked her to marry him as a reward. They had a son, **Bawo**. Following the death of Bayajida, Bawo's own six sons went on to found the remaining towns of the Hausa Bakwai – Daura, Katsina, Kano, Rano, Gobir and Zaria.

more slowly to the conservative Islamic stronghold of **Sokoto**, the spiritual capital of the north, while **Kaduna** (further south and regarded by many as part of Central Nigeria) is a much more anonymous, modern town neatly laid out by the British colonials as an uncontroversial administrative capital. Unfortunately, Kaduna's halfway-house position and mixed Muslim/Christian population has played an unhappy role in recurring religious riots.

This section also includes the remote eastern reaches of Nigeria – the states of **Adamawa** and **Taraba** – where the mountain forests remain poorly mapped and very little travelled. Here, there are some fine opportunities for hiking and some unusual options for routes into Cameroon.

The introduction of Islamic **sharia** law in the northern and northeastern states naturally has implications for travel in the region, though the impact on travellers isn't as wide-ranging as you might expect. It's true that *sharia* has led to a palpable decline in drinking and nightlife options in the cities, and as for **accommodation**, the only places that serve alcohol on the premises are the priciest hotels, plus those owned by the federal government or military, or located in predominantly Christian neighborhoods. It's certainly not taboo to ask if alcohol is allowed on the premises when choosing a place to stay; staff will readily suggest alternative accommodation if they can't oblige. Hotel **swimming pools** haven't escaped *sharia*: many pools in the stricter states – Sokoto, Katsina and Zamfara – have been emptied, and where pools remain in use you may find that men and women are allocated separate sessions. Women-only **bush taxis** have even been introduced in Zamfara State, though in most cases foreign women will be treated as honorary men and allowed to ride in whichever taxi they wish. Ultimately, however, foreigners aren't expected to know or be able to adhere to the same codes of behaviour that local people observe – it would be very unlikely, for example, for an unmarried foreign couple to be prevented from sharing accommodation. The usual, commonsense codes regarding **appropriate dress** are all you really need to bear in mind: shorts and sleeveless tops on men or women don't go down well with the more conservative locals (for more on appropriate clothing for women, see p.71).

Kaduna

KADUNA is usually looked on as the first town of the north. This is a slightly misleading assumption since it doesn't have much in common with the other towns in this section. It's a place, however, that on any major travels through Nigeria, you're unlikely to avoid. With no palace (the town was formerly a fief of the Zaria Emirate), no city wall and no ancient mosque, Kaduna is essentially a modern town with broad avenues and a bustling business environment. It's not the kind of place you'd want to spend weeks or even days discovering (indeed there's not much to find), but hitting upon this kind of cosmopolitan atmosphere, second only to Kano in the north, is not completely disagreeable either, especially if you've just arrived from the remote rural areas of Niger or Nigeria.

Some history

Originally conceived as the capital of the Northern Region, and perhaps the entire federation, Kaduna represents one of the best examples of a town created to be the seat of government. The original **northern capital** was at Zungeru, on the Kaduna River 150km southwest of Kaduna, but when **Sir Frederick Lugard** became governor of the amalgamated colonial federation in 1912, he shifted the site to the small town of Kaduna, which had the advantage of being near a good water supply and on the line of the newly constructed railway. Within easy striking range of all the former emirates, the spot was also strategically important. The West

African Frontier Force moved here from Zaria in 1912, and in 1917 the civil administration was transferred from Zungeru.

Kaduna lost its role as capital of northern Nigeria when the states were created in 1967, but it has continued to thrive as a centre for the **army** (in 1965, 28 percent of the city's area was taken up by the armed forces) and **industry**. Near Nigeria's main cotton-growing region, Kaduna contains several textile mills, a vast oil refinery under constant repair, a Peugeot assembly plant and numerous other industries.

For a northern city, Kaduna has an unusually large Christian population made up primarily of southerners who arrived many decades ago to work in the city's factories. Ever since, there has been tension between the migrants and the large indigenous Muslim population, occasionally resulting in outbreaks of violence. However, after the introduction of the Islamic **sharia** legal code in 2000 (see box, p.1024) things went from bad to worse. In May 2000, following a weekend of gatherings, first by pro-*sharia* Muslims on the Friday, later by anti-*sharia* Christians on the Sunday, there were three days of **havoc**: businesses, properties and places of worship were burnt to the ground and the streets were flooded with the wounded and the homeless. Eventually the situation was brought under control by the army and the police (though there is still debate as to whether the soldiers were shooting into the crowds). The official death toll was over four hundred, though unofficial estimates put the figure in the thousands. A second set of riots broke out in 2002, sparked off by an article written in the Nigerian press concerning the **Miss World** beauty pageant due to be held in Abuja (see p.1025). This time more than two hundred people died and some 1500 were left injured or homeless.

The riots have left both physical and emotional scars. Southerners who have lived their entire lives here have started leaving, and people are edgy, concerned about possible new disturbances. The atmosphere in Kaduna is subdued, and willingness to talk about what happened is a highly individual matter, so don't prompt discussion. Needless to say, there's growing concern that the clashes will recur and both sides are said to be re-arming, so you might want to seek advice on the current situation before deciding whether to head to Kaduna.

Arrival, information and city transport

Kaduna is bypassed by the highway (A1/A125) between Lagos and the north, and the expressway linking Kano with Abuja. Shared taxis and minibuses arriving from Zaria, Sokoto or Kano stop at the **Kawo motor park** at the northern edge of town, at the top of Alli Akilu Road. Overnight buses arriving from Lagos stop at

---

Moving on from Kaduna

Kawa motor park is used by transport for **Zaria**, **Sokoto** and **Kano**, while overnight coaches to Lagos leave from Mado motor park. **Abuja** and **Jos** are served from the Kadung Yam motor park at Kachia Road. Kaduna State Transport has three scheduled buses daily to **Katsina**, the earliest leaving at 7am. Six-seater Peugeots heading broadly south – to Benin City, Ibadan, Enugu, Onitsha, Warri and so forth – leave from the Esan car park on Constitution Road; seats on these need to be booked in advance.

Kaduna grew up with the **railway** and is Nigeria's major railway town, with services to Kano, Port Harcourt and Lagos. Trains depart Mondays and Fridays to Lagos, leaving Kano in the morning. In view of the unreliable state of the service, check at the station for current times, or ring the NRC direct (☏062/231 880 or 791).

According to the (not altogether reliable) schedules, there are at least daily **flights** to Lagos on Nigeria Airways. In addition, there are flights to Lagos on IRS Airlines (Mon–Thurs at 11.30am via Abuja) and Changchangi Airlines (Mon–Fri at 7.30am & 12.30pm, Sat & Sun at 8am). See p.1109 for airline contact details.

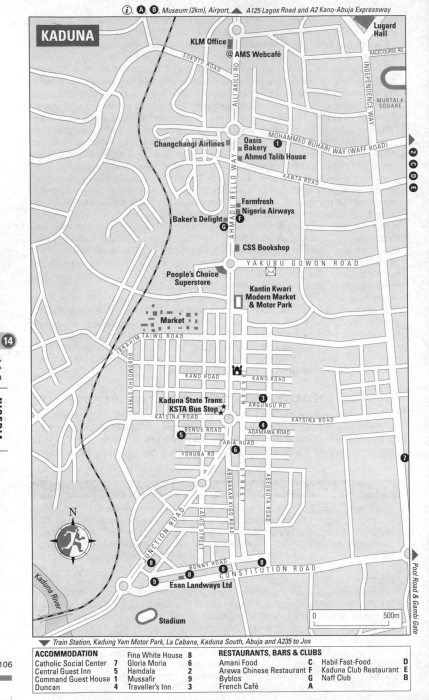

KADUNA

ⓘ, Ⓐ, Ⓑ, Museum (2km), Airport, ▲ A125 Lagos Road and A2 Kano-Abuja Expressway

Lugard Hall
RACECOURSE RD.
KLM Office
@ AMS Webcafé
SOKOTO ROAD
ALLI AKILU RD.
INDEPENDENCE WAY
MURTALA SQUARE

Changchangi Airlines
Oasis Bakery ❶
MOHAMMED BUHARI WAY (WAFF ROAD)
Ahmed Talib House
KANTA ROAD

Farmfresh
Nigeria Airways Ⓕ
Baker's Delight Ⓖ
AHMADU BELLO WAY

CSS Bookshop

YAKUBU GOWON ROAD
People's Choice Superstore
Kantin Kwari Modern Market & Motor Park

BRAHIM TAIWO ROAD
OGOMOSHO STREET
Market

KANO ROAD
KANO ROAD
IBADAN STREET
Kaduna State Trans KSTA Bus Stop ★
❸ ARGUNGU RD.
KATSINA ROAD
KATSINA ROAD
❺ BENUE ROAD
❹ ADAMAWA ROAD
ZARIA ROAD
❻
YORUBA RD
ABUBAKAR KIGO ROAD
ABEOKUTA ROAD
❼

N

JUNCTION ROAD
LAGOS STREET
❽
❾ Esan Landways Ltd
BONNY ROAD
❽
CONSTITUTION ROAD
❽

Pool Road & Gambi Gate

Kaduna River

Stadium

0   500m

▼ Train Station, Kadung Yam Motor Park, La Cabana, Kaduna South, Abuja and A235 to Jos

ACCOMMODATION			
Catholic Social Center	7	Fina White House	8
Central Guest Inn	5	Gloria Moria	6
Command Guest House	1	Hamdala	2
Duncan	4	Mussafir	9
		Traveller's Inn	3

RESTAURANTS, BARS & CLUBS			
Amani Food	C	Habil Fast-Food	D
Arewa Chinese Restaurant	F	Kaduna Club Restaurant	E
Byblos	G	Naff Club	B
French Café	A		

the **Mado motor park** nearby, a short distance down Western Bypass. If arriving from Abuja or Jos by shared taxi, chances are you will be dropped off at **Kadung Yam motor park** on Kachia Road, about 2km south of the river. Kaduna State Transport buses use their terminal in the centre of town on the Katsina Road roundabout. The Esan travel company on Constitution Road has six-seater Peugeots arriving here from southern Nigeria. The **train station** is just south of the river, 1km from Constitution Road. Transport into the centre from the outlying arrival points is easy, with minibuses plying the main arteries nonstop; a drop costs ₦30. The **airport** is roughly 40km to the north, from where a taxi into town costs around ₦1500.

There's a **Tourist Information Centre** (no phone) on Wurno Road at the northern end of town, off Alli Akilu Road and near the KSBC transmitter, but they have little of practical value to offer.

Accommodation

Kaduna has a good range of **hotels** for all budgets. Most of the better hotels are located along Mohammed Buhari Way (aka WAFF Rd). Two cheaper groupings of lodgings are on and around Constitution Road and in the Katsina Road neighbourhood.

Catholic Social Center Independence Way next to the easily spotted new, red tin-roofed chapel. A large compound with three buildings containing tidy, comfortable and clean s/c fanned or a/c rooms. There's also a good-value restaurant serving set meals throughout the day. **②**

Central Guest Inn Benue Rd. One of the centre's cheapest options with a few basic fanned rooms with shared facilities. The courtyard is often used for celebrations, so it can get noisy (but fun). No alcohol. **①**

Command Guest House Mohammed Buhari Way ☎062/242 918, ℮commandguesthouse @yahoo.com. The most exclusive place in town, within an ex-military compound. Soldiers still maintain security during times of trouble. The luxurious s/c, a/c rooms all come with TV and a constant supply of hot water. There's also a classy indoor restaurant, a snooker room, and a relaxed garden bar doing sublime grilled fish. The tennis and squash courts are open to non-residents for ₦100 a day. **❼**

Duncan X6 Katsina Rd ☎062/240 947. Friendly and good-value hotel offering s/c rooms, some with fan, others with a/c and TV, some also with a balcony. There's a good upstairs restaurant. No alcohol. **②**

Fina White House Hotels NE20 Bonny Rd

☎062/218 143. Actually four establishments near each other, with a variety of rooms and prices. The cheapest is on Junction Road with a few small, non-s/c rooms with fan around a courtyard, whereas the most expensive one, on Bonny Road, has s/c, a/c rooms, complete with fridge and TV. All four hotels have restaurants and lively bars, popular with visiting football teams (the stadium is just across Constitution Rd). **①–❸**

Gloria Moria Ahmadu Bello Way ☎062/240 222. A large, seedy place; rooms are s/c, with a/c and TV; its main selling point is the central location. **❸**

Hamdala 20 Mohammed Buhari Way ☎062/235 440. The s/c, a/c rooms are somewhat run-down, but it does have a bar serving cool beer, and an inviting, well-maintained swimming pool (open to non-residents for ₦200). **❺**

Mussafir 15 Constitution Rd ☎062/240 470. Clean and comfy a/c rooms all with TV. The rooms are a bit on the small side, but the restaurant does decent food – and there's room service. **②**

Traveller's Inn Guest House Argungu Road, across from the lively *Safari Hotel* bar ☎062/217 912. A good-value, central, three-storey hotel offering a range of large s/c rooms, some with a/c. The brilliant hotel restaurant serves local fare at very reasonable prices. **②**

The Town

Kaduna's vast and purposeful layout reflects its former function as seat of government. One of the principal tree-lined avenues, Independence Way, is lined with **administrative buildings**, including, at the northern end, the monumental **Lugard Hall** with its impressive dome. The golf course and racecourse are nearby.

The main commercial axis, **Ahmadu Bello Way**, runs north–south parallel to Independence Way. The major offices and businesses are along this street, as are most of the banks, restaurants and some hotels. In the far north of town, Ahmadu Bello Way becomes Alli Akilu Road.

Past the State House on Alli Akilu Road, the **Kaduna National Museum** (daily 9am–5pm; ₦20) houses a small collection of masks, musical instruments, leather- and brasswork and miscellaneous ethnographia. Its **Gallery of Nigerian Prehistory** traces the country's past back to Neolithic times (the New Stone Age ended in parts of Nigeria, as in many other parts of West Africa, within the last one thousand years), and exhibits Nok bronzes and terracotta work from Ife and Benin. It doesn't take very long to look round the museum, but the exhibits are well presented and documented. Behind, a **Hausa village** has been re-created, and **traditional crafts** – weaving, forging, leatherwork – are carried out in the different buildings. Just north of the museum, the **Arewa House** on Rabah Road, off Alli Akilu Road, was the residence of Sir Ahmadu Bello, the Sardauna of Sokoto, when he served as Regional Premier of Northern Nigeria. It now contains a well-stocked library with archives, pleasant gardens, and a large historic conference hall used when northern rulers get together to discuss.

Kaduna's large **market** is off Ahmadu Bello Way, in the centre of the commercial area. As in many northern cities, it's a good place to get leather goods and cloth, although most of the area is dedicated to plasticware, factory clothes and other modern goods. There's a good food section at the back of the market with a range of fruit and vegetables. Further south, Ahmadu Bello Way becomes Junction Road, then crosses the bridge spanning the **Kaduna River** to **Kaduna South** – the industrial side of town.

If you fancy getting out of town a little, the **riverbank** on the southeast side of town is a recommended area, though somewhat difficult to get to. Get a town taxi and ask for Malali, and get out near Malali "GTC" on Rabah Road. A walk parallel to the school, then over the hill through a housing estate, brings you down to the river. You can watch fishermen and lounge around on the rocks in relative peace and quiet; *kaduna* means crocodile in Hausa, but you're very unlikely to see one. There's a pleasant but modest restaurant, *Lesbora*, on Rabah Road on the way back. Another relaxing riverside outing is to a small park running alongside the river by Gambi Gate off Pool Road (the continuation of Constitution Road).

Eating and nightlife

There's good **suya** to be had from street food stalls, and a number of good **bakeries** are to be found on Ahmadu Bello Way; try the Oasis Bakery near the junction with Kanta Road, or Farm Fresh next to Nigerian Airways, both selling yoghurt, cakes and delicious pies. The *French Café* has a great bakery as well.

Since the riots in 2000 and 2002 people have become less inclined to go out at night, and Kaduna's already sedate nightlife has become even quieter.

Restaurants

Amani Food Alkali Road. Undoubtedly Kaduna's best Lebanese restaurant, serving mouth-watering *fattoush* – a herby salad containing toasted flat bread – and grills, all at moderate prices.

Arewa Chinese Restaurant 28 Ahmadu Bello Way. A decent Chinese restaurant in pleasant airy surroundings.

Byblos Restaurant D80 Ahmadu Bello Way. Pleasant a/c place serving Chinese and Nigerian food.

French Café 2 Alli Akilu Road. An excellent new place serving fantastic pizzas, burgers, salads and other Western dishes. The in-house bakery sells a huge selection of tasty pastry and bread. Steer clear of the disappointing ice cream, though. Take-away available.

Habil Fast-Food Mohammed Buhari Way. Kaduna's best hamburger joint, offering an agreeable combination of fast food, a/c and music videos.

Kaduna Club Restaurant Mohammed Buhari Way, opposite *Hamdala* hotel. Popular place that, besides showing CNN, serves reasonably priced,

well-prepared Nigerian and continental dishes.
Naff Club Air Force compound, Rabah Rd
☎064/242 253. A posh indoor restaurant and bar,
serving so-so European fare. The main attraction,

however, is the spacious outdoor terrace offering
local meals, salads, and very good meat pies. Live
gigs most weekends fill up the place until dawn.
Popular with expats and locals alike.

Listings

Airlines Changchangi Airlines, Ahmadu Bello Way
☎062/249 949; IRS Airlines, at the *Hamdala* hotel
☎0803/7879 316; KLM, Philips House, 4 Alli Akilu
Rd ☎062/241 133, ⊕246 419; Nigeria Airlines, 26
Ahmadu Bello Way ☎062/245 632 (Mon–Fri
8am–5pm & Sat 8am–1pm). The Eminence Travel
Agency, Ahmed Talib House, 18/19 Ahmadu Bello
Way (☎062/210 034 or 235 432), represents a
number of international airlines.
Banks and exchange The main branches of the
major banks cluster around the intersection of
Ahmadu Bello Way and Yakubu Gowon Rd. For
foreign exchange, try Al-Ameen Bureau de Change
at the *Hamdala* hotel (☎062/238 474).
Consulates British High Commission Liaison
Office, 3 Independence Way ☎062/233 380/1,
⊕062/237 267, ✉bhc.kad@skannet.com.
Internet access Inet, on the junction of Issa Keita

and Sultan roads, and AMS webcafé, on Alli Akilu
Road, are both fast and reliable, and there are
plenty of other places scattered around town
where you can get online.
Pharmacies The two pharmacies in front of the
Hamdala hotel are well stocked.
Phones The NITEL call office is on Golf Course Rd,
with additional offices at Lafia Rd, GRA, and in
Kaduna South.
Post office The GPO is on Yakubu Gowon Rd in
the heart of the banking district. Poste restante
here is reasonably reliable. Branches can be found
across from the train station and at Bank
Roundabout, Kaduna North.
Supermarkets There's a large People's Choice
Superstore and a Baker's Delight on Ahmadu Bello
Way near the intersection with Yakubu Gowon Rd,
both well stocked with foreign goods.

Around Kaduna

About 120km west of Kaduna on the A125, the town of **Birnin Gwari** is where a
dirt road a few kilometres south of the centre leads off to the north to a village
called **Dagara**. Head up this road and after anything between one and three hours
(depending on recent weather and the condition of the road), you'll arrive at the
entrance to **Kamuku National Park** (₦200, plus ₦100 for a camera), home to a
small herd of elephants and other savanna species, along with a mass of birdlife.
You'll need a guide to trek into the reserve, something the park HQ in Birnin
Gwari or people in Dagara should be able to help with. There's basic **accommodation** at *Winners Guesthouse* (❶) across the road from the park HQ.

Zaria

One of the seven Hausa Bakwai, the old town of **ZARIA** has withstood the tests
of time rather better than most of the other emirates. The **ancient wall**, built by
Queen Amina some 950 years ago, has largely crumbled away, but some of the old
gates have been restored and are very impressive. The **Emir's Palace** is a beautiful
example of traditional architecture. Almost all the homes in old Zaria are built in
the traditional style, and many display the detailed exterior decoration for which
the town is famous. It's quite possible to arrive in Zaria, 80km north of Kaduna, in
the morning, take a look around, and then head out before evening.

Zaria is also noted for the radical student life of **Ahmadu Bello University**, to
the north of the centre, which has been the scene of some violent clashes with
security forces in the past, though things calmed down after the vice chancellor, a
former army major, left office. However, during the 2000 and 2002 clashes in
Kaduna, Zaria experienced a resurgence of tension, and the university was once
again the scene of violent disturbances. It's worth keeping your ear to the ground

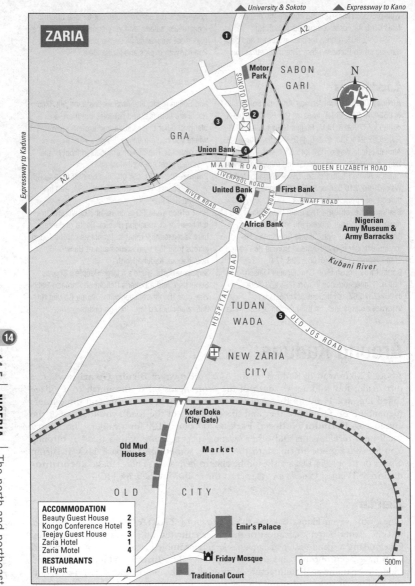

ZARIA

▲ University & Sokoto   ▲ Expressway to Kano

A2

SABON
GARI

Motor
Park

◀ Expressway to Kaduna

GRA

SOKOTO ROAD

Union Bank

MAIN ROAD   QUEEN ELIZABETH ROAD
LIVERPOOL ROAD

United Bank

First Bank

RIVER ROAD   PARK ROAD   RWAFF ROAD

@

Africa Bank

Nigerian
Army Museum &
Army Barracks

Kubani River

HOSPITAL ROAD

TUDAN

WADA

OLD JOS ROAD

NEW ZARIA
CITY

Kofar Doka
(City Gate)

Old Mud
Houses

Market

OLD   CITY

Emir's Palace

Friday Mosque

Traditional Court

N

ACCOMMODATION
Beauty Guest House 2
Kongo Conference Hotel 5
Teejay Guest House 3
Zaria Hotel 1
Zaria Motel 4
RESTAURANTS
El Hyatt A

0   500m

before deciding on a visit to Zaria, though frankly you're unlikely to encounter any problems in the town itself.

The Town

To explore the **old town**, the best plan is to rent a taxi with a clued-up driver for half a day or – failing that – to rent a taxi and find a guide at the same time. To visit the Emir's Palace you have to make a request at the secretary's office next door – normally granted if the Emir is at home.

The main centers of activity in the old town are the **Emir's Palace** (Gidan Sarki) and the **market**. Scattered around the latter are the houses and stores of traders and the craftsmen's workshops (including leatherworkers, tailors and dye pits), many of which can be visited. The palace, with its elaborately decorated facade, is to the south of the market (as in other northern cities, palace and market are set well apart from one another) and is surrounded by a high-walled enclosure. The main entrance, the **Kofar Fada**, faces a large square where ceremonies are held, including the annual **durbar** cavalry charges.

Nearby, the **Friday Mosque** was formerly one of the most magnificent in the region, though it's now enclosed by a plain-looking modern structure. It dominates one side of the square, surrounded by the offices of court counsellors and the homes of leading citizens. According to the story (tales of this ilk are common in Nigeria, told in relation to other magnificent buildings), the architect who designed it in 1834, Babban Gwani Mallam Mikaila, was later commissioned to build a mosque for the Emir of Birnin Gwari. Immediately after it was completed, this Emir seized him and had him put to death so he would never create a more beautiful building elsewhere. The architecture is outstanding, especially the inside vaulting, though the replica of the mosque in Jos gives a better idea of what the building actually looks like.

The new town

After the British arrived, a new town – **Sabon Gari** – was built some 3km north of the walled city, across the **Kubani River**, with a Government Residential Area (GRA) with beautiful, old colonial villas west of Sokoto Road, the town's main artery that becomes Hospital Road at the junction with Main Road. It was in this part of town, now home to the main market, that Yoruba and Igbo traders settled near the rail tracks early last century. The flowery, shaded streets are perfect for a walk. Hospital Road leads south across the bridge to the **Tudan Wada** neighbourhood where most of the infrastructure is located – the hospital, schools and teacher training colleges.

East of Hospital Road, the Chindit army barracks – Zaria's second most important employer after the University – house the **Nigerian Army Museum**, a small exhibition tracing the history of the Nigerian armed forces through displays of weaponry and other assorted memorabilia (uniforms, medals, maps and period photographs). The eras of military government are covered with a degree of comradely back-slapping, but the sections on the Biafran War and the Burma Campaign during World War II make a visit worthwhile. To get there, follow the signs along RWAFF Road, or take a motorbike from Sabon Gari (it's a long walk). You need a visitor's pass from the guards at the gate to enter the compound; a dash usually helps.

Practicalities

On public transport, you'll arrive at the **main motor park** by the Kano expressway junction at the northern end of town, from where there are plenty of **minibuses** and **taxis** into town. **Banks** can be found in the vicinity of the market in the new town. There's an **Internet** café on Hospital Road, near *El Hyatt* **restaurant** on Hospital Road, which is actually a good place to eat (Mon–Fri 8am–10pm): it's a large, glitzy establishment serving snacks (meat pies, Scotch eggs etc), nice salads, and chicken and chips. *El Hyatt* aside, there's reasonable food to be had at the town's hotel restaurants.

Due to the strict interpretation of *sharia* law in Zaria, the only places you'll find beer are at a few federal government–run accommodations (such as the *Zaria Motel*). Don't expect a refreshing swim either, as all the hotels' swimming pools have been emptied due to *sharia* law.

Accommodation

Zaria has a number of pleasant and moderately priced **hotels**.

Beauty Guest House Sokoto Road ☎069/334 038 or 331 688. Decent s/c rooms with fan. There's also a plain little restaurant serving Nigerian food, and a very easy-going atmosphere. ❷

Kongo Conference Hotel Old Jos Rd ☎069/332 872, ℗332 875. Part of the Arewa chain, this is the town's nicest hotel. Rooms are equipped with a/c, fridge and TV. Completing the picture are a spacious restaurant and a very Seventies terrace-bar – one of the few places in Zaria with cold beer, even during Ramadan. ❹

Teejay Guest House 6 Western Way Close, in the GRA, signed from Sokoto Rd ☎069/333 303. A clutch of white modern buildings in a walled compound. The rooms are s/c and a/c, and of a high standard. HB ❸

Zaria Hotel Sokoto Road ☎069/332 820 or 332 829. One of the slickest places in town, with a/c rooms, a restaurant, a bar serving alcohol, and a good bookshop. Frequent minibuses to the centre stop in front of the hotel. ❸

Zaria Motel Behind Union Bank, in the GRA ☎069/332 451. Central and friendly government-run guesthouse set in a spacious, leafy garden with large a/c bungalows equipped with showers and TV. The bar serves cool beer and snacks. Advance bookings recommended. ❷

Kano

The largest town in the north, and effectively Nigeria's second city (despite being smaller than Ibadan), the 1000-year-old Hausa metropolis of **KANO**, capital of the state of the same name, is a strange mixture of modern and traditional, with the former gaining ground and invading the latter every year. The city currently has a population of two and a half million, and continues to spread, apparently unchecked, over the dusty savanna, growing industrialization in the region drawing people from the countryside. Its vehicle pollution, especially at the close of the dry season in April or May, has to be breathed to be believed. Like Lagos, Kano combines its commercialism with being an important academic centre.

The other side of Kano is its history. The **Gidan Makama Museum** is a beautiful effort to protect its heritage, housing historical exhibits of the city and its environs in a former Makama chief's palace, restored to show off the intricacy and technical excellence of the ancient architecture – qualities which can also be admired at the **Emir's Palace** and the **Central Mosque** nearby. Other reminders of the past include the **old market** and the **dye pits** where, beside a busy multi-laned avenue, cloth is still soaked in indigo in the gloriously messy way it's been done for centuries. Yet everywhere there's a distinct feeling that much more could be done to preserve the ties with Kano's past, especially upkeep of the **old city wall**, which resisted British colonial invaders with greater success than it has the elements in recent years. Although a few of the great **gates** that once protected the emirate still stand, much of the wall has now become huge lumps of rain-smoothed mud, and people still dig away at it to make bricks for new homes.

Some history

Kano's history (its courtly history at any rate) has been preserved in the **Kano Chronicles**, which give the most detailed account of any Sudanic nation with the exception of Songhai. A compilation of brief histories of the region, the chronicles originated in the mid-seventh century, shortly after the introduction of Arabic. The first settlement of Kano was founded on **Dala Hill**, where archeologists have uncovered furnaces and slag heaps indicating iron-working from as early as the sixth century; this settlement was later conquered by the descendants of **Bagauda** – one of the six sons of **Bawo** who founded the Hausa Bakwai – the seven legitimate Hausa states (see p.1103).

Kano was fortified at the beginning of the twelfth century during the reign of **Gijimasu**. Later, under **Yaji** (1359–85), it developed a powerful army that used new technology – quilted armour, iron helmets and chainmail – to overthrow its adversaries. The city became independent of its neighbours and gained control of the trans-Saharan trade in gold and salt. It thus acquired wealth and power to rival Timbuktu and Gao. Additions to the walled city were made in the fifteenth century under **Muhammed Rumfa**, who had converted to Islam and who transformed Kano from a local military chiefdom to an Islamic sultanate with close links across the Sahara and to Arabia.

Contact with Europe came in the mid-sixteenth century. **Portuguese** attempts to establish a trading centre were thwarted, but settlers from Ragusa (now Dubrovnik in Croatia) maintained a presence in Kano throughout the 1560s and 1570s, under the protection of the North African–based Turkish Ottoman sultan.

Over the next two centuries, Kano warred continuously with the neighbouring states of Bornu and Katsina. At the same time, European maritime powers on the coast slowly undermined the trans-Saharan routes that were the basis of Kano's power and autonomy. Although the textile and leather **industries** kept the economy going (indigo-dyed cloth and soft red leather, known as "Moroccan", were exported as far afield as Europe), the state's political structure was fragile. When the Fulani, led by Usman dan Fodio, waged their religious war, or **jihad**, Kano was unable to resist; the city fell in 1807. A new era of hostilities followed, and it was during this period that **European explorers** reached Kano – Clapperton in 1824, Barth in 1853 and Monteil in 1891. By the end of the nineteenth century, **British imperial designs** posed a direct threat to the emirate. Kano refortified its walls and prepared to resist, but in 1903 the city fell to British troops.

Kano effectively became a laboratory for testing the theories of colonial rule. The British appointed a compliant emir in order to try out a system of **indirect rule** – successful in colonial terms, but a disastrous precursor to independence. The railway was opened in 1911, the airport in 1937, and Kano's future as the dominant city of northern Nigeria, and the biggest in the Sahel, was sealed. After World War II, Kano became the centre of a renewed **Islamic nationalism** in Nigeria, intent on resisting the power of the southern regions of the country as much as, if not more than, the British, who were clearly intent on pulling out. The rift with southern Nigeria, especially with the Igbo community in the southeast, continued after independence, through the Biafran War and into recent years. In 1980, a mad Kano prophet, **Maitatsine**, whipped up a frenzy among landless peasants and unemployed townspeople against Nigerian armed forces in the city, in an uprising that left dozens of casualties. And almost every year sees at least one major disturbance arising from ethnic tensions, usually an ordinary urban murder that leads to an ethnic riot. Seen in this light, it seems quite surprising that the introduction of *sharia* law (see box, p.1024) hasn't had the same violent repercussions here as it has in Kaduna. But not only is the *sharia* not interpreted as strictly here as it is in the neighbouring Katsina and Kaduna states, there also appears to be more tolerance of people of different religious backgrounds.

Arrival, transport and information

Kano, with its international airport, is a good place to start West African travels – reasonably lively but not so intolerably frenetic and intimidating as to put you right off – and well placed for Niger and Mali. **Aminu Kano Airport** is only 8km from the central Sabon Gari quarter of the city, an inexpensive taxi ride (₦300). The Tourist Information Centre (open when flights arrive) in the arrival hall has similar materials to the Kano State tourist office in town (see p.1116). The main **motor parks** are all off the main roads leading into town. Vehicles arriving from Katsina and Niger stop at the **Kofar Ruwa motor park**, off Katsina Road north of the old city. Long-distance taxis and minibuses coming in on the Kaduna Expressway

KANO

N

Kofar
Mazugai

DALA HILL

FAGGE

OLD CITY

Kofar
Wambai

Orion
Cinema

KOFAR WAMBAI ROAD

Kurmi
Market

Kofar
Mata

Cloth
Market

Dye Pits

KOFAR MATA ROAD

Festival
Stadium

ACCOMMODATION

Baptist Guest House	6
Central	12
Criss Cross Hotel	3
ECWA Guest House	2
Hotel De France	9
Kano Tourist Camp	10
Le Mirage	1
Ni'mah Guest Palace	7
Prince Hotel	13
Royal Tropicana	11
Skyworld	4
Tahir Guest Palace	8
TYC	5

RIMI MARKET ROAD

Central
Mosque

Kofar
Nassarawa

**RESTAURANTS, BARS
& CLUBS**

Arabian Sweets	G
Bakers Delight	F
De Recipee	A
Domo	B
Empire Peking	E
Halal Meat Restaurant	H
Hongfu	J
La Locanda	D
Mr Bigs	C
Smart Tandoor	E
Torona	I

Emir's
Palace

British Council
Library

EMIR'S PALACE ROAD

Gidan Makama
Museum

Kofar
Sabwar

B.U.K. ROAD

Old City Wall Alignment

Kofar
Na Isa

Kofar
Dan Agundi

14

14.5 | NIGERIA | The north and northeast

◀ University Guest House & University

and from the east arrive at the **Nai Bawa motor park** off Zaria Road, about 5km south of the centre. The smaller **Gashua motor park** off Hadejia Road in the east is used by vehicles arriving from Hadejia, Nguru and Gashua. Overnight buses arriving from Lagos and Port Harcourt stop in New Road in Sabon Gari, next to the old Eldorado cinema. The **train station** is on Fagge Road just south of the centre.

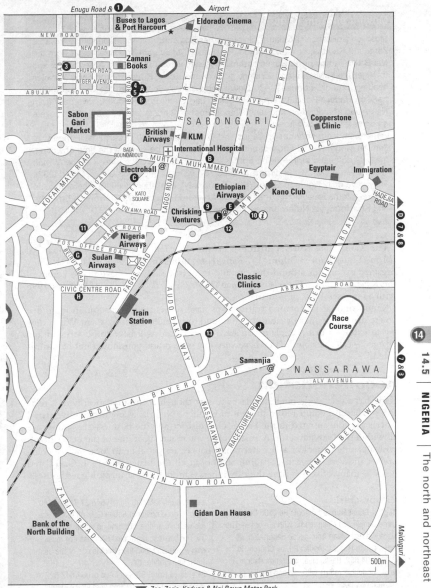

Transport within the city takes the form of taxis, minibuses and achabas. A shared-taxi ride into the centre, from any of the motor parks on the outskirts, costs ₦100–200. A drop in a minibus is ₦10. Travelling by achaba within the centre, at ₦20 a drop, is quick and easy, but to head into the centre from the outer motor parks it's best to get a taxi or minibus as the traffic is notoriously chaotic.

Most long-distance taxis and minibuses heading south on the expressway towards Zaria and Kaduna, or east towards Jos, Bauchi, Maiduguri and Yola, leave from the **Nai Bawa motor park**. Buses and minibuses towards Katsina, the Niger border and to Niger itself (Maradi and Zinder), go from the **Kofar Ruwa motor park**. Vehicles heading, broadly, northeast – to Nguru and Gashua – leave from the **Gashua motor park** on Hadejia Road. Overnight buses to Lagos and Port Harcourt leave daily from New Road at around 5pm to reach Lagos around 12 hours later (₦1600–1800; tickets go on sale on the day itself).

There are **train services** to Lagos and Port Harcourt, with departures, in theory, at 8am on Mondays and Fridays; check at the station to be sure. At the time of writing, the only domestic **airline** flying from Kano was IRS, who have a desk at the *Ni'mah Guest Palace* and at the airport (℡0803/787 9316 or 346 8468 or 0804/412 1232). They have daily flights to Lagos (₦9000 one way), and Abuja (₦6000). There are also several international flights from here: to **Amsterdam** with KLM, **Cairo** with EgyptAir, and **Khartoum** via **Ndjamena** and **Niamey** with Sudan Airways.

The Kano State **tourist office** is at the *Kano Tourist Camp*, 11A Bompai Rd (Mon–Thurs 8am–3.30pm, Fri 8am–1pm; ℡064/633 105 or 631 541). They organize excursions around the city and to nearby sites, and have maps, copies of the *Kano State Hotel Guide*, and a *Kano Tourist Guide Book* – a pamphlet from 1998 with a few useful bits of information.

Kano's orange-uniformed traffic cops have something of a reputation, and if you're driving, sooner or later you're bound to be pulled over by them. When they try to extract a bribe, explain you have no cash and will have to be arrested and charged – call their bluff. They have very few powers and you should not be intimidated.

Accommodation

Kano has a very wide range of places to stay, though accommodation here is relatively expensive compared to the rest of northern Nigeria. Many inexpensive **small hotels** are concentrated in the Sabon Gari district, and the business-class hotels are all within the Nassarawa GRA area. Unless you're staying at one of the better hotels with a private generator and water tank, chances are you'll be in for a spell of cold-bucket showers. You can consume alcohol at all the places in Sabon Gari listed below – many of which have their own bars – though not at mission guesthouses.

Sabon Gari

Baptist Guest House 58 Abuja Rd ℡064/648 113. Large, simple and clean rooms with a/c or fan. The place is a real haven from hectic Sabon Gari. ❶

Criss Cross Hotel 2 Ibadan Rd, by Church Rd ℡064/634 652. Basic, clean accommodation in single or double rooms with fan and bucket shower. Very good value. ❶

ECWA Guest House Mission Compound, between Mission Rd and Zaria Ave ℡064/631 410. Large leafy compound with spacious rooms (some with a/c, and there are a few singles) and friendly staff. It's a homely place but you have to be on your mettle in one respect – smoking is not allowed on the premises. Fills up quickly, so it's a good idea to book in advance. ❶

Le Mirage 27 Enugu Rd ℡064/637 788 or 640 037. A good option in Sabon Gari. All rooms are s/c with a/c, fridge, hot running water and satellite TV. The bar-restaurant next door has live music every weekend, and the street is one of the best in town for nightlife. ❷

Skyworld Hotel 95 Niger Ave ℡064/647 622. A mishmash of rooms packed with kitsch, gaudy decor. All come with a/c, TV and bucket shower. The restaurant serves African and continental dishes, and there's a disco some weekends. ❷–❸

TYC Hotel 44 Abuja Rd ℡064/647 491. Rooms here range from singles to elaborate suites with colour TV and fridge, all with a/c and bucket showers. The previously popular roof-terrace bar is no more – bits of it collapsed during a storm – but you can still take your drinks up and survey the lights of Sabon Gari at night. Good value and very friendly. **❷**

Elsewhere in Kano

Central Bompai Rd ☏ 064/630 000–9, ℻ 630 628 or 633 841. Once the most popular international-class hotel in Kano, now in dire need of a complete overhaul, the a/c rooms somewhat grubby. But it does have a good location, and the bar serves cold beer. **❹**

Hotel De France 54 Tafawa Balewa Rd ☏ 064/646 416. One of the longest-established hotels in Kano, still very pleasant and breezy with cool tiled floors and a/c rooms with satellite TV. There's a bright and welcoming restaurant serving well-prepared, reasonably priced Nigerian and European dishes. **❹**

Kano Tourist Camp 11A Bompai Rd ☏ 064/642 017. Close to lots of shops and good places to eat, and with the Kano State Tourist Board on site, this has a range of rooms, most of which are s/c, some with a/c, all at reasonable rates. There are also dorms, space to camp, and free secure parking. Dorm beds/camping ₦300, **❷**

Ni'mah Guest Palace 8B Sulaiman Crescent ☏ 064/642 946 or 644 557, ℻ 647 616. More laid-back than the nearby *Tahir*, this has comfortable rooms with all the usual mod-cons, an Internet café, a pleasant restaurant, a small pool and its own mosque. **❻**

Prince Hotel Tamandu Rd, off Audu Bako Way ☏ 064/639 402 or 633 393, ℻ 635 944. Top-notch place with fully equipped s/c rooms (a/c, satellite TV, fridge and hot water) as well as a pleasant patio-bar serving alcohol, a pool, and a pricey but highly recommended restaurant. All efficiently run and very popular with expats. Advance booking recommended. **❼**

Royal Tropicana 17/19 Niger St ☏ 064/639 352 or 647 496, ℻ 639 358. A huge business-class place, with characterless a/c rooms conveniently provided with satellite TV, fridge, and a nice view of downtown Kano from the upper floors. It used to have three bars, now reduced to a dark basement bar – with beer available – hidden at the back. There's also a pricey restaurant. **❺**

Tahir Guest Palace 4 Ibrahim Natsugune Rd ☏ 064/646 988, 638 912 or 632 057, ℻ 646 284, ✉ tahir@ecnx.net. Substantial, marble-clad place with its own mosque, four generators and a private water tower. Apart from the usual luxuries (a/c, hot water, satellite TV), the spacious rooms come with gigantic double beds. There's also a small pool (enquire about the strictly single-sex swimming times at reception) and a restaurant serving both Nigerian and European food. **❼**

The Old City

Most of Kano's special appeal lies in the **old city**, down Kofar Mata Road from the modern centre. The fortified **town wall** has all but disappeared, but some of the original **city gates** (*kofar*) have been restored and are worth a look. The best-preserved gates are both on B.U.K. Road – Kofar Na Isa (literally, "I have arrived") and Kofar Dan Agundi.

As you walk round the old city, be on the lookout for examples of traditional **Hausa exterior decorations**. Particularly beautiful is the "masque" style of house facade – there's a fine example just past the dye pits, on the left as you head into the old city by the modern Kofar Mata gate. However, the Kano houses are grubbier than similar buildings in, say, Zinder in Niger, where the toll of rain, exhaust fumes and industrial pollution is that much less.

The dye pits

Inside Kofar Mata (small hillocks indicate where the wall used to be), you'll see the **dye pits** on the right. They soak cloth here in natural indigo using great basins of dye buried in the hard ground. Kano fabrics once clothed most of the people in the Sahara region and were highly valued. You can buy material or ready-made clothes from the several small stalls nearby, or even have some of your own clothes dyed. But beware: if you take a picture, you'll be asked for a dash (the demanding upturned palms are plain to see on most snaps of the dye pits). More spectacular than Kano's dye pits are those in **Kura**, a small town 30km south of Kano, just off the expressway to Zaria, in the heart of a major cloth-dyeing area.

14

14.5 | **NIGERIA** | The north and northeast
1117

Id al-Fitr in Kano

In the cities of the north, the festival of **Id al-Fitr**, at the end of Ramadan (for dates, see p.61), is an important social as well as a religious occasion, allowing the emirs, their officers and their people to meet and reaffirm their mutual positions in society. Some festivals, particularly those in Kano and Katsina, draw sizeable crowds of visitors to see the annual **durbars**, or cavalry parades.

Kano's Id al-Fitr festivities begin at 7.30am, when the emir leaves his palace on foot through the compound's northeastern Fatalwa gate, and appears at the *id* ground east of the Kofar Mata, where, after a prayer, the chief imam of Kano slaughters the emir's ram, followed by other sacrifices. The emir leaves, reappearing at the palace's Kwaru Gate at around 9.30am to address the crowds.

The following day, the **Hawan Daushe Durbar**, is the most dramatic, when no fewer than 5000 heavily decorated riders parade through the streets of the old city to salute the emir. The durbar sets out from Kofar Arewa at 4pm and ends when the emir returns to his palace at around 6.30pm.

The third day of Id al-Fitr dates back to the colonial days when the emir used to pay homage to the resident administrator, followed by an exchange of addresses. This tradition (**Hawan Nassarawa**) is maintained, only with the colonial governor replaced by the head of the state government. On the fourth day, known as **Hawan Fanisau**, or the Dorayi Durbar, the emir treats his district, village and ward heads to lunch at his palaces of Fanisau or Dorayi.

The Central Mosque and Emir's Palace

Further down Kofar Mata Road, the **Central Mosque** is imposing, though not the most noteworthy building architecturally. It has, however, been of enormous importance as a focus for the Islamic nationalism that has so bedevilled successive federal governments. The best time to visit is before or after Friday prayers when worshippers in the tens of thousands turn up, an impressive sight. With proper authorization you can climb one of its two minarets for fine views over the city (enquire at the secretary's office at the entrance to the Emir's Palace or at the tourist office).

Behind the mosque, the **Emir's Palace** spreads out over a huge acreage. Its traditional architecture blends easily with the buildings of the old city, albeit on a rather larger and more stately scale. The front is far more modern and obviously palatial. The tourist office will arrange a visit for a steep ₦1000 per person, not really worth it unless you've a fetish for palaces. The emir and his family still live in a section of the palace that you won't see, and the remainder is a collection of administrative buildings that don't have much regal atmosphere to them.

Kurmi market and Dala Hill

North of the Central Mosque and Emir's Palace, the ancient **Kurmi market** (also known as the **city market**) forms an almost impossibly tight maze of alleys and stalls. They're pressed together to exclude the heat, but there are so many people milling about that it gets claustrophobic and sweaty anyway. The busiest and best time to visit is the afternoon, any day except Friday. The market retains a strong traditional flavour, although certain sellers with an eye on tourist bucks turn out shoddy and not very traditional junk. As always, you have to confront the question of the "authenticity" of the goods you're buying, but it's not yet too common a dilemma, and **leather**, **textiles**, **brass**, **silver** and **ironwork**, **pottery**, **calabash carving** and **beads** will continue to be made whether tourists buy them or not – and are good value. Be sure to stop at the section for local riding tack, housed in the market's oldest structure, dating from the nineteenth century.

Hausa communities are concentrated in the cities of northern Nigeria and Niger, but they have spread right across West and Central Africa, setting up shops in the smallest towns, content to live among strangers. The Hausa have long been famous for their art and music which has flourished since the sixteenth century and the fall of the Songhai empire, with whose music Hausa music has many parallels.

Hausa music splits into **urban music** of the court and state, and **rural music**. Ceremonial state music – *rokon fada* – still plays a great part (though to western ears not a very tuneful one) in Hausa traditions, while court praise singers still play for the amusement of emirs and sultans, usually in private. The emirates of **Katsina** and **Kano** together with the sultanate of **Sokoto**, and to a lesser extent **Zaria** and **Bauchi**, are the major creative centres.

The instruments of **ceremonial music** are largely seen as prestige symbols of authority, and ceremonial musicians tend to be chosen for their family connections rather than any musical ability. **Court musicians**, on the other hand, are always chosen for their musical skills. It's hardly surprising that the most talented players are rarely seen in public, as each is exclusively dependent on a single wealthy patron. The greatest praise singer was **Narambad**, who lived and worked in Sokoto. He died in 1960 and it's doubtful you can still get his recordings.

The most impressive of the state **instruments** is the elongated trumpet called *kakakai*, which was originally used by the Songhai cavalry and was taken up by the rising Hausa states as a symbol of military power. *Kakakai* are usually accompanied by *tambura*, large state drums. Lesser instruments include the *farai*, a small double-reed woodwind instrument, the *kafo*, an animal horn, and the *ganga*, a small snare drum. Ceremonial music can always be heard at the *sara*, the weekly statement of authority which takes place outside the emir's palace on a Thursday evening. The principal instruments accompanying **praise songs** are percussive – small kettle-drums, called *banga* and *tabshi*, and talking drums, *jauje* and *kotso*.

Traditional **rural music** appears to be dying out in favour of modern pop, drawing inspiration from traditional roots. The last expressions of rural music are to be found in traditional dances like the *asauwara*, for young girls, and the **bori**, the dance of the spirit possession cult, which dates back to a time before Islam became the accepted religion and continues to thrive alongside the teachings of the Koran, especially in Zaria.

Popular music thrives in town and countryside and musicians can still make a good living satisfying local needs and, as ever, expressing, and sometimes moulding, public opinion. The leading Hausa singer, **Muhamman Shasta**, is always accompanied by a troupe of virtuoso drummers who play *kalangu*, small talking drums. There's a fair number of other worthy artists such as **Dan Maraya Jos**, leading exponent on the *kontigi* one-stringed lute; **Audo Yaron Goje** who plays the *goje* or fiddle; and **Ibrahim Na Habu**, who popularized a type of small fiddle called the *kukkuma*. All such musicians are threatened by the north's widespread adoption of *sharia* law. Catch them while you still can.

The market swarms with petty hustlers and **"guides"**. A guide can be instructive and helpful, once you and he have got to know each other, as his presence saves you from the onslaught of other would-be assistants. Come to terms with just one, accept you'll have to pay him something and be prepared for a little transparent salesmanship at certain stalls of his acquaintance.

Dala Hill, site of the original settlement in Kano, rises up to the north of the Kurmi market, pretty well in the centre of the old city. You can walk up – it involves finding your way through narrow alleys and backstreets – and can usually find a kid to take you for a dash, but remember to agree the price first. Early morning visits are the most rewarding, the cocktail of cool air and the sun rising over Kano truly magical.

Gidan Makama National Museum

The grandiose building across the square in front of the Emir's Palace is the **Gidan Makama National Museum** (daily 8am–5pm; ₦50). Formerly a palace itself, the building is as interesting for its fifteenth-century Sudanic architecture (sadly beginning to show signs of disrepair) as for the exhibits inside. Fittingly, the displays in the first room explain the technological and decorative aspects of traditional Hausa building styles. Rooms two to six trace the history of Kano and the other Hausa states through drawings, photographs, documents and reconstructions spanning a thousand years – a dense and informative chronology, not for the faint-hearted. The seventh room focuses explicitly on the colonial era, while room eight is devoted to the arrival of Islam and the Muslim tenets. Finally, rooms nine and ten are dedicated to a less demanding selection of **traditional arts** – music, weaving, brasswork and so on. Set aside a couple of hours to visit, as it's well worth the time. The museum courtyard is also interesting, with the replica of a Madobi hut (a woman's hut), full of the bits and bobs she needs to collect in preparation of marriage. There's also a poorly stocked craft shop and a small arena used for cultural events.

The Kano State History and Culture Bureau

The **Gidan Dan Hausa** in the old colonial residential quarter – the Nassarawa area – is another impressive Hausa structure worth visiting. Built in 1909, it was the first British colonial residence in Kano. Today it houses the Kano State History and Culture Bureau (Mon–Fri 8am–5pm; free), whose "hall of fame" photo gallery, with portraits of administrators and rulers in the history of Kano State, is curiously informative.

The New City

The intersection of Murtala Muhammed Way and Lagos/Airport Road is the centre of modern Kano, the heart of its main commercial district, at any rate. Continuing south on Lagos Road brings you to Post Office Road and the **GPO**. Vendors on Bompai Road sell various **crafts** of reasonable quality, though the old city is a better place to shop for these.

North of Murtala Muhammed Way, the **Sabon Gari** ("New Town") neighbourhood is home to mainly Igbo and Yoruba workers and has a distinct southern Nigerian flavour, with a large number of Kano's churches and missions, and plenty of cheap hotels and energetic bars. It's particularly animated after dark and something of a relief after the more austere "dry" areas of the old city. The recently rebuilt **Sabon Gari Market** always draws the crowds; get provisions and other odds and ends here.

Slightly out of town on the Zaria road, the **Audo Bako Zoo** is in reality more of a botanical garden, with very few animals left. It's nothing to go out of your way for, but a good excuse for a late afternoon stroll if you've little else to do.

Eating, drinking and nightlife

If your travels have featured Kano as a significant goal for any length of time, you won't be disappointed with the variety of edible treats on offer. The whole gamut of West African food is available here, together with a full variety of imports in the shops and supermarkets. If you fancy a beer together with some southern delicacies, head for one of the many outdoor bars lining Enugu Road, in the north of Sabon Gari, where you can also try a bowl of their speciality, *isi iwu* (goat's head pepper soup – mind the eyeballs).

The only area of town to retain something approaching the pre-*sharia* level of **nightlife** is **Sabon Gari**. Down Enugu Road, you'll find a line of terraced bars where the party continues until the wee hours of the morning, as well as *Le Mirage* bar-restaurant with live music every weekend. On some weekends the conference hall at the *Skyworld* hotel turns into a bar/disco with its own DJ. The rest of the city is pretty quiet in the evening, with the notable exception of the quite animated bar at the *Central* hotel.

Restaurants and cafés

Arabian Sweets 4 Beirut Rd. Inexpensive Lebanese pastry shop with deliciously sticky Middle Eastern sweets, Italian ice cream, and a burger-bar extension at the front.

Bakers Delight 3 Bompai Rd. Freshly made bread and cakes, as well as meat pies and breakfast foods.

Calypso At the *Prince Hotel*, Tamandu Rd ☎064/639 402. High-quality, pricey Lebanese cuisine, arguably the best in town. It's a popular expat hang-out with a well-stocked bar.

De Recipee Kitchen 58 Abuja Rd, Sabon Gari, on the first floor of the Baptist church compound overlooking the street. Filling breakfasts, salads and sandwiches for lunch, and Nigerian and European dishes for dinner, accompanied by soft drinks.

Domo Murtala Muhammed Way, a short stroll from *Tourist Camp*. Inexpensive place which does a fine omelette and chips for breakfast, and dishes like rice with chicken or beef stew later in the day.

Empire Peking 3 Bompai Rd. Popular Chinese restaurant which does mouthwatering Chinese fare at very reasonable prices.

Halal Meat Restaurant 101 Inuwa Wada Lane, opposite Beirut Rd. A Lebanese butcher-cum-restaurant dishing up good salads and sandwiches, as well as more filling European and African meals, at reasonable prices.

Hongfu Restaurant Directly opposite Nassarawa Hospital, Hospital Rd. Authentically Chinese establishment with a huge variety of dishes.

La Locanda 40 Sultan Rd, off Ahmadu Bello Way. Among the absolute top places in town, where you can splash out on superb Italian food. Pizzas can be ordered to take away. Beer, wine and cocktails available from the bar.

Mr Bigs Niger St. Fast-food joint also serving more substantial meals (*jollof* rice, spaghetti, chicken). Eat in or take away.

Smart Tandoor 3 Bompai Rd ☎064/645 089 or 647 879. A superb Indian restaurant with fabulous chicken *tikka masala* and Indian sweetmeats for dessert. Reasonable prices.

Torona Off Audu Bako Way, near the *Prince Hotel*. Another excellent Lebanese place which also does a few European dishes and serves alcohol.

Listings

Airlines British Airways, African Alliance House, F1 Airport Rd ☎064/637 310, 637 320 or 637 330, ☏064/ 639 425; EgyptAir, 14C Murtala Muhammed Way ☎064/630 759; Ethiopian Airlines, 7 Bompai Rd ☎064/634 128, 634 090 or 637 498; IRS, at the airport ☎0803/787 9316 or 346 8468 or 0804/412 1232; KLM, 17 Airport Rd ☎064/630 061 or 630 063, ☏644 325, ✉klm@ecnx.net; Nigeria Airways, 3 Bank Rd ☎064/647 314 and at the airport ☎064/637 801; Sudan Airways, Post Office Rd ☎064/644 758 or 648 026.

Banks and exchange Most banks are located around the intersection of Lagos and Bank roads. There are good forex bureaux at the *Central* hotel parking lot (to the right of the hotel's entrance) and at the *Tourist Camp*.

Books Zamani Books, at 84 Church Rd, Sabon Gari (Mon–Fri 8am–12.30pm & 2–5.30pm, Sat 8am–2.30pm), has a broad spectrum of books, including novels by African writers, and a *Kano Street Guide*.

Consulates Niger, 52 Sultan Rd, Nassarawa GRA ☎064/632 986; UK, honorary consul at 2 Tsauna Close, off Amadu Bello Way ☎064/631 686, ☏632

590, ✉bhc.kan@skannet.com.

Cultural centres British Council has a library at 10 Emir Palace Road (Mon–Fri 9am–6pm, Sat 9am–2pm; ☎064/646 652 or 643 489). They have English books and newspapers, BBC World on TV, and Internet access. Membership is only open to Kano residents but visitors may be allowed to use their resources on request. Once in a blue moon they stage cultural performances at the small theatre behind.

Hospitals and clinics Classic Clinics on Abbas Road, just off Hospital Road in Nassarawa GRA is the best place for emergencies. International Hospital on the corner of Niger St and Airport Rd is open 24hr (☎064/649 533 or 643 093, ☏639 948, ✉interclinicshospital@yahoo.com). Their dentist is available daily except Sun 2–7pm. Otherwise try the Copperstone Hospital, 5 Court House Close, off Miller Road (☎064/634 620).

Internet access Electrohall, Murtala Muhammed Way at the junction to Niger St; Chrisking Ventures, opposite *Central* hotel (Mon–Fri 8am–7pm, Sat 9am–6pm); Samanja, Race Course Rd, Nassarawa GRA between the two Hospital Rd roundabouts.

There are many more Internet places in the Niger St/Beirut Rd area, but at the time of writing many of these had slow connections and were relatively expensive.

Pharmacies Well Care Pharmacy, Hadejia Rd, is well stocked.

Phones The new NITEL office at the end of Zoo Rd has better long-distance connections than the Lagos Rd premises (near the corner of Ibrahim Taiwa Rd). They both have fax and card-phone services. Otherwise, there are telecentres on almost every street corner.

Post The GPO is on Post Office Rd (Mon–Fri 8am–5pm & Sat 9am–1pm). The poste restante service is free and reliable.

Supermarkets Well Care pharmacy and supermarket, on Hadejia Rd, has the widest range of imports, but the row of shops in front of the *Central* hotel are also well supplied.

Travel agents Most travel agents are found in the Civic Centre, Beirut, and Post Office roads area. One of the more established is Habis Travels Ltd, 15/16B Post Office Rd (☏064/631 258).

North from Kano: Nguru and Katsina

Three hours' drive northeast of Kano is **NGURU**, the gateway to the **Hadejia-Nguru Wetlands Conservation Project**, where there are excellent opportunities for **bird-watching**. The wetlands are unique both in their extent – encompassing eastern parts of Jigawa State and western parts of Yobe State – and in their location in a region that is otherwise attractively desertlike, with scattered camel caravans and several oases. The project was started in the 1980s, to manage water resources sustainably by preserving the wetlands for agricultural purposes while creating a sanctuary for migrating birds seeking refuge in Africa during the cold European winter – thousands seek shelter here during the dry harmattan season.

The project has its headquarters in Nguru, where they have a comfortable **guesthouse** (❷). Staff can help you rent a canoe to get out to the **Dagona Wildfowl Sanctuary**, situated on a small island; it's one of the best spots to view the birdlife, including ibis, duck, geese, waders and pelicans. If you're here in February, it's worth checking whether the **Gorgoram Fishing Festival**, cancelled in recent years, is taking place again. It's similar to the Argungu festival (see p.1128), at which fishermen gather to compete and show their skills, but on a much smaller scale.

From here, it's possible to spend a night under the stars on the sand **dunes** of the far north, near the border with Niger. This fascinating trip takes you past some of the most isolated villages you are likely to come across in Nigeria, as well as numerous nomadic **Fulani settlements**, before reaching the perfectly shaped, incredibly photogenic dunes of the north. You'll need to hire a vehicle and driver (or a guide if you have your own transport) through the Wetlands Conservation Project, or in **Gashua**, 65km east of Nguru, through a development project called NEAZDP (☏076/700 044).

Katsina

KATSINA is tucked away in the extreme north, floundering in the dry Sahelian badlands. During the harmattan season, from December to May, it's easy to appreciate the value of the traditional clothing, protecting everything except the eyes from the blowing sand. Efforts to pump some modern development into the region, notably through the installation of a steel rolling plant in 1982, have so far brought few noticeable signs of change, other than the dual-laned highways that wrap around the outskirts of town.

Vestiges of the once-powerful **Katsina Emirate** – one of the oldest of the seven Hausa states – have hardly fared better. One or two of the original city gates still stand in varying states of ruin, but the fortifications that once surrounded the town have been all but flattened. Reminders of the past remain in the **Emir's Palace** and the **Gobarau Tower** that once served as a sentry post. You can visit these, but the real pleasure of Katsina perhaps lies more in simply wandering the dusty streets, absorbing the atmosphere of a traditional Hausa city that shows few signs of modernity.

Katsina is strategically located along the highway linking Kano with Niamey, the capital of Niger. Besides the long-haul transport passing through, there's an important short-distance trade across the border, making for lively **markets** in both Katsina and nearby Maradi.

Unhappily, Katsina State has made a name for itself in recent years, following the death by stoning sentence passed in 2002 by the *sharia* court on one of its residents, Amina Lawal, whose misfortune was to bear a child out of wedlock. The world media has kept a watchful eye on Katsina, monitoring appeal upon appeal on Amina's behalf, and the sentence hadn't been carried out at the time of writing – indeed no such punishment has actually been meted out in modern Nigeria.

The Town

"Downtown" Katsina spreads along Ibrahim Babangida (IBB) Way between the **Kofar Kaura**, a recent stone gate built to replace an older mud-brick one, and the **Central Mosque** with its onion domes. Just beyond the mosque, the road veers left and continues to the **Emir's Palace**. The entrance to this building looks more recent than you might expect, but this is in part because it's one of the few buildings that is well maintained. Inside, the large compound is a hodgepodge of old mud-brick and new concrete buildings. To visit the palace, you'll need to enquire at the Ministry of Information building on IBB Way.

The huge **Kangiwa Square**, in front of the palace, is filled every Friday with the overspill from **Katsina Central Mosque**, just to the south. The square is the site of the annual **Sallah Durbar**, the high point of the Id al-Fitr celebrations. The celebrations begin in the early morning with prayers outside the town wall, following which horsemen, decked in their finest regalia parading through town, stage a durbar in front of the Emir's Palace, while women perform traditional dances.

Follow the paved road to the west to reach the **Central Market**, a short way from the palace. You'll find a few fruits and vegetables here (mangos in season, oranges, tomatoes, onions and okra), decorated calabashes and pottery with a bronzey glaze, cereals (corn and different kinds of millet) and livestock including the occasional camel. Note the Fulani women selling milk and *nono*, home-made yoghurt, from calabashes.

The **Gobarau Tower** can be made out to the north of the market. To reach the minaret, follow the unmarked street (actually Gobarau Road) on the eastern edge of the market. Built in the seventeenth century as a lookout post, the tower later served as the muezzin's platform in pre-loudspeaker days. A guide will take you to the top and explain the history for a small dash. From the minaret, Hospital Road leads past a walled cemetery to the **Kofar Uku**. This gate "of the three doors", built in the seventeenth century according to locals, was formerly attached to Katsina Teacher Training College, the first institute of higher learning in town, and alma mater to Ahmadu Bello (the first premier of Northern Nigeria), Abubakar Tafawa Balewa (Nigeria's first prime minister), Alhaji Shehu Shagari (the first president) and General Yakubu Gowon, the former military head of state. Other gates of note include the **Kofar Guga** and, at the end of Nagogo Street, the **Kofar Durbi**, where you can still see part of the ancient wall called **Ganuwar Aminu**, supposed to originate from the reign of King Marabu about 900 years ago. Nowadays the old Katsina College has become the mildly interesting **Katsina Museum**.

Practicalities

From the **motor park** on the outskirts of town on Kano Road, you can get a taxi or an achaba into the centre. IBB Way has the major **banks**, the **post office** and the big trading stores, as well as most of the central **hotels**, clustered outside the Kofar

Kaura. The *Abuja Guest Inn*, off IBB Way (☎065/304 412; ❸), has s/c rooms with a/c and fan. The serenely located *Katsina Motel*, 1 Mohammed Bashir Road (no phone; ❸), has comfortable s/c, a/c rooms. For a spot of luxury, *Liyafa Palace Hotel* off Kano Road (☎065/431 165, ℻065/432 690; ❹) is the biggest and best in town, although some distance outside the centre towards Kano. As for **eating**, *Katsina City Restaurant*, at 115 IBB Way, serves local and European dishes, but no alcohol.

Sokoto and around

Until the beginning of the nineteenth century, **SOKOTO** was a small town of little significance, surrounded by the Hausa city-states. It only gained its present status as **religious capital** of the north after Usman dan Fodio's jihad led to the creation of the **Sokoto Khalifate** in 1807. The present emir is leader of all other Hausa emirates to this day, and effective spiritual leader of Muslim Nigeria. Modernization came slowly to this region as development goals conflicted with the khalif's own ideas about what "civilization" should entail. Thus, at the wish of the khalif, the railway line that pushed northwards as far as Kaura Namoda, in the 1920s, was never extended to Sokoto. The town's isolation from corrupting outside influences was thus preserved.

Some history

The **Fulani** of Sokoto are thought to have migrated from Mali in the thirteenth century and to have settled in **Gobir**, then a powerful ancient kingdom. Known as *fulani gidan* (town Fulani as opposed to pastoral nomads), they were mainly traders and highly regarded Muslims. The most learned were welcomed into the Hausa emirs' courts as advisors, where some succumbed to lives of indolence; others kept on the move and preferred a more ascetic lifestyle, teaching and speaking on behalf of the poor.

Usman dan Fodio, from Gobir, was of the latter mould, preaching energetically against the corrupt influence of high office and the lax ways of the traditional non-Muslim (or quasi-Muslim) Hausa emirs. There was much support for his stand, which called for the widely ignored or circumvented *sharia* legal code to be respected. Naturally, there was also plenty of resentment of his politicking piety from traditionalists with an interest in maintaining the status quo. By 1804, the tension had led to the birth of a radical reform movement and to civil war in Gobir, where the traditionalist emir first used arms against the reformers. Dan Fodio was a reluctant warrior and, while he agreed to be appointed Amir al-Muminin (Commander of the Faithful), the military leadership of the jihad was handled by his brother Abdullah and son Muhammedu Bello.

Weakened from centuries of warring, the Hausa emirates fell quickly and, over the space of four years, with growing popular support, dan Fodio became the uncontested ruler of the entire north. Although often characterized as a war of pious Muslim Fulani against corrupt Hausa, the reality was considerably more complicated and very much determined by people's economic position – the jihad promised a more equitable distribution of wealth and the reduction of taxes and levies. In 1809, dan Fodio's son, **Bello**, who later became the first sultan, established Sokoto as the *sarkin musulmi*, the spiritual and political capital of the empire. By the time of Bello's death in 1835, Sokoto was effectively the capital of Islam for the whole of West Africa.

The **social consequences** of the jihad were many. Dan Fodio had created, for the first time in the region, a single state with a central government controlling the entire north (with the exception of Bornu) and extending deep into present-day Cameroon and south into the Yoruba country which up to then had resisted Islam. As a result, trade was facilitated throughout the region and the Arabic language and writing spread with the teachings of the Koran. When the **British** conquered Sokoto in 1903, they took advantage of the highly stratified and unified government system to implement their policy of indirect rule.

The Town

Despite Sokoto's rich history, there's little in the way of sightseeing unless you regard the city, with its calm self-esteem and well-structured pattern of wide streets, as an attraction in its own right. The city's core is the **Sultan's Palace**, the nearby **Masallachin Shehu** (Shehu Mosque), and Bello Mosque, on Sultan Bello Road. The mosques, with their Sudanic aura, are pleasant enough to look at, but non-Muslims aren't allowed in. As for the palace, there's not much of a Sudanic aura left as the place was completely renovated in the 1970s in marble and glass. On Thursday mornings, a group of colourfully clad Hausa musicians play in front of the main palace gate and are worth waiting around for.

Just before the Shehu Mosque, if you take Sultan Bello Road from the palace, a dirt road leads off to the left towards **Hubbare**, the former home of Shehu Usman dan Fodio (a small signboard on the centre strip of Sultan Bello Road indicates the way). Follow it until you reach a small square, where you'll have to ask around to be pointed towards the otherwise unremarkable house. Inside it is the **Shehu's Tomb**, where dan Fodio is buried alongside with eight family members including his mother, his companions and his imam. On Thursdays and Fridays, people from throughout the region still make pilgrimages to this spot to pay homage. Christians are not welcome inside, and Muslim women can only visit the house after nightfall, when the men have finished.

The **Sokoto Museum**, now known as the **Waziri Junaidu History and Culture Bureau**, on Ali Akilu Road (Mon–Fri 9.30am–4pm; ₦200), is a surprisingly interesting museum and archive devoted to the region's history. On the ground floor, one room is dedicated to the pre-jihad Hausa state as well as the jihad period, both well documented and richly illustrated with maps, weapons and tools. A second room looks at the colonial era: letters, photos, weapons and furniture, including a wooden throne with a naked boy carved into its back given to the Sultan of Sokoto by a culturally insensitive Queen Elizabeth. The boy's head had to be removed before the Sultan could sit in it. Two other rooms contain musical instruments, Sokoto's old city gates, and various ancient farming implements, as well as a photo exhibit of the various administrations – military and civilian – that have ruled Sokoto State since independence; note the very gradual arrival of women into power. Upstairs, the archives contain original religious scripts by Usman dan Fodio and his brother Abdullah. Well-informed guides are happy to show you around and give you their take on recent politics.

You won't be disappointed by Sokoto's **Central Market** either, adjacent to the central motor park. It's one of the biggest and best stocked in the entire Sahel Region – an amazingly well-planned, clean, modern site with a startling abundance of flowering plants and trees. And for what seems like such an isolated city there's a remarkable variety of stuff here – produce ranges from pineapples, coconuts and mangos to millet, sorghum, a mass of vegetables and all the usual proliferation of spices and condiments. There's a large **cloth emporium** with busy tailors; prices, especially for cloth, are cheap when compared with elsewhere in Nigeria and mostly fixed – there's little or no haggling here. A pleasant and inexpensive **outdoor restaurant** has been set up round the large, green-and-white tower that dominates the whole area.

Practicalities

The main **motor park** is north of the centre, near the central market. If you arrive on one of the overnight buses from **Lagos** operated by the Young Shall Grow company, you'll end up at their terminal off Abdulahi Fodio Road, in front of *Ibro*

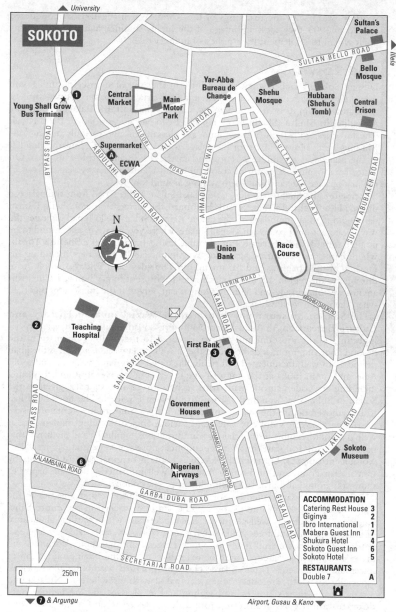

SOKOTO

University

Young Shall Grow
Bus Terminal

Central
Market

Main
Motor
Park

Yar-Abba
Bureau de
Change

Shehu
Mosque

Sultan's
Palace

SULTAN BELLO ROAD

Bello
Mosque

Hubbare
(Shehu's
Tomb)

Central
Prison

Illela

BYPASS ROAD

ABDULAHI

Supermarket

ECWA

KILGORI ROAD

ALIYU JEDI ROAD

AHMADU BELLO WAY

ROAD

FODIO ROAD

N

SULTAN ATIKU ROAD

SULTAN ABUBAKER ROAD

Union
Bank

Race
Course

ILORIN ROAD

KANO ROAD

IBRAHIM DASUKI RD

Teaching
Hospital

SANI ABACHA WAY

First Bank

3   4
5

BYPASS ROAD

Government
House

MUHAMMED GADO NASKO ROAD

ALI AKILU ROAD

Sokoto
Museum

KALAMBAINA ROAD

Nigerian
Airways

GUSAU ROAD

GARBA DUBA ROAD

SECRETARIAT ROAD

0   250m

ACCOMMODATION
Catering Rest House   3
Giginya   2
Ibro International   1
Mabera Guest Inn   7
Shukura Hotel   4
Sokoto Guest Inn   6
Sokoto Hotel   5
RESTAURANTS
Double 7   A

7 & Argungu

Airport, Gusau & Kano

International Hotel, not far from the main motor park. The **airport** is 9km south of
the city. **Public transport** in Sokoto is based almost entirely on motorcycles
(*kabuski* or *kabukabu*) and taxis. An average motorcycle drop is ₦20, while taxis cost
a little more.

Sokoto's main commercial district lies along Kano Road, where you'll find the
major **banks** and hotels. The **GPO** is on Sani Abacha Way, not far away. The Yar-Abba

Moving on from Sokoto

The main **motor park** in the north of the city handles transport leaving regularly for **Kano**, **Zaria**, **Kaduna** and **Illela**, the border town facing **Birnin-Konni** in Niger. Note that the quickest way from Sokoto to Katsina is to head into Niger and follow the Niamey–Kano highway from Birnin-Konni through **Maradi** and head back into Nigeria, although this requires a visa for Niger and a multi-entry visa for Nigeria. The route is used by some public transport – expect to have to change vehicles in Maradi or Birnin-Konni. Vehicles to **Argungu** (and on to the Nigeria–Niger–Benin border at Gaya/Malanville) are less frequent, as are vehicles heading south down the A1 to **Yelwa** and **Kontagora**. Young Shall Grow overnight buses to Lagos leave from their terminal daily at 3.30pm (₦2000), arriving in Lagos during the early hours of the morning.

Nigeria Airways, on 2 Sultan Ibrahim Dasuki Rd (☏060/232 252), is the only airline flying out of Sokoto, to Lagos via Kano (Sun 11am; ₦7000).

---

exchange bureau on Aliyu Jedi Road, north of the centre, changes most Western currencies. **Internet cafés** were thin on the ground at the time of writing, but the university was in the process of setting one up that should be running by the time you read this; minibuses to the campus leave from the *Ibro International* roundabout throughout the day.

Accommodation and eating

Most of the hotels are located on and around Kano Road, near the teaching hospital, but a few good places can also be found near the main motor park. However, it's disappointing that in such a baking-hot place, all the hotel pools have been emptied, thanks to the local implementation of *sharia*.

Sokoto doesn't abound with **restaurants**. The Lebanese-run *Double 7* on Abdulahi Fodio Road, next to a well-stocked (for Sokoto) supermarket of the same name, serves tasty Middle Eastern meals, including good salads. The restaurant at the Young Shall Grow bus terminal does excellent Nigerian fare at keen prices.

Hotels
Catering Rest House Shinkafa Rd ☏060/232 463. There are two entrances, one via the *Shukura Hotel* (continue right past the hotel), the other off Shinkafa Rd. All rooms are s/c and most have a/c, though there are some spartan doubles with fan which are only really worth staying in if the *Ibro* is full. ❶
Giginya Hotel Bypass Rd ☏060/231 262 or 231 265, ☏231 671. Sizeable business-class hotel with spacious doubles equipped with a/c and satellite TV. There's a good restaurant too. ❺
Ibro International Abdullahi Fodio Rd ☏060/232 510. Well located, this is a tad run-down but is gradually being refurbished.

Their s/c rooms, with fan, are the best bargain in town. ❶
Mabera Guest Inn 15 Darge Rd ☏060/232 178. Smallish s/c, a/c rooms, a 10min achaba ride from the centre. No restaurant. ❶
Shukura Hotel ☏060/230 006 or 230 007, ☏234 648. A comfortable choice, pretty much of the same standard as the *Giginya*. ❺
Sokoto Guest Inn Kalaimbaina Rd ☏060/232 672. Good-value accommodation with well-kept doubles and a good restaurant. ❷
Sokoto Hotel Kano Rd ☏060/232 126. Somewhat on the decline now that the once popular bar and swimming pool have closed. Rooms are a/c and s/c, though some have bucket showers. ❹

Argungu

Ninety-nine kilometers southwest of Sokoto by good paved roads, **ARGUNGU** makes for an interesting excursion, particularly when the annual fishing festival takes place in February/March. Sadly this well-known event has been in abeyance since the riots in Kaduna in 2000, when both participants and spectators became apprehensive about travelling, but may resume in the near future. The town also houses the **Kanta Museum** with historical relics and traditional artefacts, and a noticeable **Emir's Palace**.

Argungu has an illustrious place in the annals of West African history. The **Kingdom of Kebbi**, which had formerly been an outlying province of the **Songhai Empire**, was founded near here in the early sixteenth century by **Muhammedu Kanta**, a general in the army of the Songhai emperor Askia Muhammed. When the Songhai invaded the Hausa states between 1512 and 1517, Kanta revolted against his overlords, and established himself as an independent ruler of the area between the Niger and Sokoto rivers. The capital of his kingdom was Argungu or "Birnin Lelaba Dan Badan" as it was named at that time.

Later, Argungu was one of the pockets of traditionalist resistance to Usman dan Fodio's Fulani jihad, and was never successfully conquered by Sokoto. An apocryphal account even derives the town's name from the Fulani moan *Ar sunyi gungu* (Oh dear, they've regrouped), since their invasions were repeatedly repulsed. Another theory has it that the original name of the town was changed to Argungu from the Kebbi saying *Ar! Mu yi gungu*, a fishing expression meaning "Let us get together in one place". The Kebbi emirate fell to the British at the beginning of the twentieth century and became part of the Northern Nigeria protectorate.

The fishing festival

Although historians date the **fishing festival** back to the era of the great Kunta in the sixteenth century, the festival as it exists today dates from 1934, when the Sultan of Sokoto made his first peaceful visit to Argungu. The festival takes place in February or March on a stretch of the **Sokoto River** (the **Rima** to people who live here) known as Matan Fada, where it braids into a multitude of channels. Here, thousands of huge *giwan ruwa* fish (some weighing as much as 100kg) are penned in a confined, shallow lake. On the chosen day, the signal is given and hundreds of fishermen plunge into the waters watched by thousands of onlookers. Using only hand-held "butterfly" or clap nets called *homa*, and hollowed calabashes with an opening at the top, they thrash around among their prey. Fishing is banned for the rest of the year in this part of the river, and rituals are performed to try to ensure the biggest possible catches.

The fishing show, however, is only the climax of a festival that spreads over three days, and includes a long list of other sporting activities and competitions (boxing, archery, camel and donkey races), punctuated with endless speeches by local leaders and sponsors. In Mala, downstream from Argungu, the **Kabanci displays** are another side show, with canoe races and swimming and diving contests.

You can get details of the festival dates (and whether it's happening or not) from Kebbi State Liaison offices in the government administrative districts of state capitals throughout the country. To visit at festival time, it's imperative to make room reservations in advance; you can **stay** at the *Grand Fishing Hotel* (☎060/550 547; ❶) or at one of several guesthouses in nearby Birnin Kebbi, the state capital.

Maiduguri

The northeast's closest major town to the Cameroon border, **MAIDUGURI** is the first (or last) stop in Nigeria for many overlanders. The town is incredibly flat and hot, and has that quiet, nothing-happening feeling characteristic of so many places in the arid Sahel. If it wasn't for the **neem trees** lining the neatly laid-out avenues and providing a bit of respite from the merciless sun, you might find it unbearable. But as capital of the **Borno State**, Maiduguri has good infrastructure and makes a reasonable resting point for further travels in the arid north.

The people of Borno are largely **Kanuri**; women, especially, are elegant dressers and hairstylists and often wear nose rings. If you spend a night here, you may come to appreciate a second level of life in Maiduguri, as experienced by the many students from all over Nigeria, who live on the university campus and probably feel almost as much strangers in this northwestern outpost as you do.

The Town

Thanks to its fairly modern origins, Maiduguri is a well-planned city and easy to get around. Its characteristic landmarks are the **roundabouts** which have come almost to designate neighbourhoods and are thus convenient markers for orientation. The major ones include "**West End**", with three large cast-iron fish in the middle, "**Banks**", a large spikey phallic symbol, "**Welcome**", a green-and-white concrete statue, "**Post Office**" near the GPO, "**NEPA**" near the market, "**Customs**" near the museum, and "**Eagle**", with a large eagle statue in the south of town.

Maiduguri doesn't have much in the way of sights, and any exploring, at almost any time of year, should be done in the early hours before the town gets intolerably hot. An obvious place to start is at the **Shehu's Palace**. A colonial-style building with a clock tower, the palace doesn't officially allow visits, but the guards at front will try to arrange for you to look around if you express an interest. Inside, the

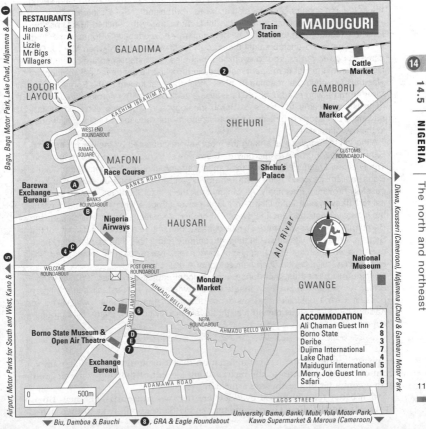

The Kanem-Bornu empire

The rise of the **Kanem-Bornu empire** was a consequence of the spreading Sahara and the subsequent migration of nomadic peoples who concentrated in the **Lake Chad** basin, in districts that had been covered in lake water in earlier times. Conflicts flared between the newcomers and established communities. The **Kanuri** (a people of distinctively Saharan origins, with a language quite unrelated to Hausa, whose distant ancestors are presumed to have farmed and hunted in the era of Saharan fertility) eventually gained the upper hand in the struggles, out of which arose the **Sefawa dynasty** which ruled over **Kanem** – the concretion of mini-states northeast of Lake Chad – from about 850 AD.

Oral history claims that the founder of the dynasty was **Sayf Dhi Yazam**, and that he was of Arab origin, though it is more likely that the first dynastic family had Berber connections. Whatever the truth, the authority of the *mai* (as the kings of the dynasty were known – they converted to Islam in the eleventh century) gradually spread over nomadic peoples, and the *mai* came to be accepted as a divine ruler. In Mecca, a special guesthouse was built for Kanem pilgrims and in Spain, the court of El Mansur (1190–1214) in Seville numbered renowned Kanem poets among the courtiers.

The Bornu empire functioned as a channel for trade and the **exchange of ideas** across the Sahara, connecting the three major camel caravan routes from Tripoli, Egypt and Sudan. It was through Bornu power that Islam entered Nigeria from the twelfth century onwards, spreading peacefully across the northern Hausaland during the fourteenth century, and reaching as far as Yorubaland in the same period.

A new series of conflicts arose in the thirteenth century that incited **Mai Umar bin Idris** to emigrate west to Bornu. The new empire – now effectively Bornu, rather than Kanem – remained unstable until the end of the fifteenth century when **Mai Ali Gaji** came to power, put an end to dynastic squabbles and established a new capital at Ngarzagamo, the first permanent residence in more than a century. A new golden era was thus launched that reached its peak under the best known of the Bornu rulers – **Idris Aloma** – who ruled until 1603. He was a zealous Muslim reformer under whose reign Islam became the basis of Bornu ideology and who also achieved military advances by importing Turkish mercenaries and military advisors to instruct his troops in the use of muskets.

Although the empire was among the most severely affected by the decline in trans-Saharan trade, Bornu was the only northern power to repulse dan Fodio's invasion. The Fulani did manage to attack the capital city and sent the king into retreat, but a Bornu *malam* (teacher) named **Al-Kanemi** organized a counter-offensive that successfully drove out the enemy. Al-Kanemi took the title of Shehu and moved the capital to **Kukawa**, near Lake Chad. In a later power struggle with the Sefawa dynasty, the *mais* were defeated and the dynasty abolished. As a result, Al-Kanemi became the Bornu ruler and his sons started a new dynasty, bringing to a close the dynasty of the Sefawa, which, with its origins in the ninth century and a final date of 1846, may have been the world's most enduring line of royal rulers. Kukawa, on the other hand, still exists today, ruled by the Shehu ancestors of Al-Kanemi.

Maiduguri gained its importance as a regional capital only after 1907 when the British reinstated the Shehu in the new town where they had established a military base. It wasn't until after independence, however, that the town was linked to Kaduna by rail and thus gained a slight advantage for its beef, leather and groundnut exports.

emphasis is more on modern administration than Bornu history: a guide trails you from one scorching patio to the next, making a point of showing you every room with a computer or a leatherette armchair.

Much better for a historical overview are the two **museums**. The new **Borno State Museum** (Mon–Thurs 8am–4pm & Fri 8am–noon), next to the open-air theatre and off Shehu Lamido Way, gives a historical introduction to the people of Borno State, and displays fishing, farming and hunting tools in one room. The other room focuses on typical Borno kitchenware, traditional pottery, blacksmithing, weaving and a display of local jewellery, all accompanied by informative plaques. Not quite as good is the **National Museum** (Mon–Fri 8am–4pm) south of Customs Roundabout on Bama Road, where there is a similar display, plus an interesting replica of the **Dufuna canoe**, known to be the oldest boat ever found in Africa (8000–6000 BC); the original is in Damaturu, Yobe State, undergoing conservation. In the courtyard there is a reproduction of a Shuwa hut (the Shuwa are nomadic people from northern Borno and Yobe states), and a traditional mud house furnished with cooking utensils and calabashes. Neither museum has a set entry fee but a ₦20 donation is appreciated.

The **zoo**, located across from the *Safari Hotel* at the end of Shehu Lamido Way (daily 9am–5.30pm; ₦20), is actually not bad, whatever your feelings about zoos. Many of the animals are captives without cages, and are kept in place by large ditches surrounding reproductions of their habitats. Shaded in a spacious forest of neem trees, the zoo and park are excellent places for a picnic, and it's a popular Sunday destination.

Maiduguri's colourful **Monday Market** takes place in a covered cement building in the commercial centre of town. The **New Market** sprouted a few years back in the Gamboru district near Customs Roundabout and, apart from all the usual gear, is well known locally for its attractive hand-woven **mats** made of reeds from Lake Chad.

When the afternoon sun begins to drum down, head to one of the town's **swimming pools**. The best is at *Deribe Hotel* (₦150), which has crystal-clear water, but unfortunately it's only filled between March and July (post-harmattan and pre-rains). It's uncertain whether the new Arewa management will keep the pool at the *Lake Chad Hotel* going (₦100). The *Maiduguri International Hotel* has a large pool (₦100) with poolside bar (soft drinks only), as well as good *suya*.

Practicalities

Shared taxis from **Kano**, **Gashua** and **Bauchi** arrive at the motor park outside the town gate, along Airport Road. Arrivals from **Baga** stop at the motor park north of the West End, past the railway tracks. Vehicles arriving from **Dikwa** and **Ndjamena** in Chad via **Kousseri** in Cameroon arrive at the Gambaru motor park on Dikwa Road, east of Customs Roundabout. Coming from **Yola** or **Banki**, the border town with Cameroon, you'll be dropped at the motor park on Bama Road. The **airport** is 6km west of town. The easiest way to get around town is by **collective taxi** to any of the roundabouts (₦20 a drop), and walking from there to your destination. Alternatively, an achaba will take you straight to your destination for between ₦20 and ₦100.

Maiduguri's **banks** are all centred around Banks Roundabout. The city's two main **forex bureaux** are Barewa Exchange, next to the racecourse, and Exchange Bureau across from *Dujima International Hotel*, both quick, efficient and able to change both types of CFA.

Accommodation

Maiduguri accommodation ranges from cheap lodgings to international-standard hotels. Although many of these are run by Christian southerners, none serves alcohol.

Ali Chaman Guest Inn Near the train station ☎ & ℗ 076/236 939. Comfortable rooms, some with a/c and TV, all s/c with cold water (hot water supplied by the bucket on demand). There's also a restaurant serving cheap Nigerian food. ❷
Borno State Hotel 1 Talba Rd, Old GRA

☎ 076/232 333. To get here, turn right at the Eagle roundabout on the way out of town. Rooms are s/c and some have a/c. At the time of writing, the hotel was undergoing a complete refurbishment and prices may have climbed by the time you read this. ❶

There are several **motor parks** in Maiduguri. For **Kano**, **Gashua** and **Bauchi** (the northern route via Damaturu), the motor park is just outside the town gates along Airport Road. For **Baga** and **Lake Chad**, the park is just up from the West End, past the railway tracks. For **Bama**, **Yola** and **Cameroon**, the motor park is on Bama Road. For **Dikwa**, and on to Ndjamena via Kousseri in Cameroon (see below), the Gambaru motor park is on Dikwa Road, east of Customs Roundabout.

Trains should in principle run to Port Harcourt (change at Kafanchan junction for Lagos), but at the time of writing, the train only went as far as Bajoga, Gombe State (4 weekly) and was always late. A one-way to Lagos costs ₦3000 in first class, ₦1500 in second class and takes anywhere between 24 hours and one week. Check latest developments at the station.

Only Albarka Airways (☎076/230 121) **fly** from Maiduguri, with departures to Lagos (Mon–Fri at 7am, Sun 8.30am; ₦15,000) via Abuja (₦8500). At their airport office (Mon–Fri & Sun 5.30am–7pm), you can buy tickets up until the morning of the day you want to travel. *Lake Chad Hotel* and *Maiduguri International Hotel* both have Albarka ticket desks (Mon–Thurs & Sat 10am–5pm) where you can make advance bookings.

To Cameroon and Chad

If you're making the short crossing of Cameroon to **Ndjamena**, Chad, start by taking a vehicle from the **Gamburu motor park** on the northeast side of Maiduguri (you need a visa for Chad, but you won't need a Cameroon visa if you're simply passing through this narrow neck of the country en route to Chad). Four- and six-seater taxis shuttle to the village of Gamburu. From **Fotokol** on the Cameroonian side (where you'll have to seek out the *douaniers* and *gendarmes*, 1km away, for your transit stamp) you take a much more expensive ride to **Kousseri**, 100km away. For Kousseri and onward into **Chad**, see p.1251.

The main northern route into Cameroon via the border town of Banki is on a good tarred road that leads past Bama straight to the border (minibuses from the **Bama motor park** leave continually throughout the day). Once in Banki, achabas will be waiting to take you to customs, but unless you're heavily laden you might as well do the short distance by foot. Border formalities are surprisingly painless, which may explain why many southern Nigerians choose to use this crossing rather than the more convenient crossing at Ikom. Vehicles for Mora and Maroua wait outside the Cameroon immigration office, as do moneychangers ready to swap your naira for CFA.

Deribe Deribe St, off Kashim Ibrahim Rd ☎076/232 663, ℻232 662. Modern, pleasant rooms equipped with a/c and TV, and the town's best pool (filled March–July). Among the nicest of the hotels in this price bracket. ❹

Dujima International Shehu Laminu Way, opposite the open-air theatre, in the old GRA ☎076/233 297 or 233 231. Typical business-traveller hotel with large s/c singles and doubles, all with a/c and TV. The only drawback is the cold-water bucket showers. ❸

Lake Chad Kashim Ibrahim Rd ☎076/232 400 or 232 453, ℻232 041. Once the city's top hotel, now a worn-looking member of the Arewa chain. The a/c rooms all have cold showers and TV, and there's a swimming pool, occasionally filled. ❺

Maiduguri International Stadium Rd, turn right after the Kano motor park junction ☎076/235 979 or 235 984, ℻235 871. Huge, verging-on-five-star hotel opened by the state government in the late 1990s but still encountering teething problems – hence the very good rates. The s/c rooms are all fully equipped with hot water, TV, fridge, and great views. There's also a swimming pool, tennis courts and two restaurants. The main drawback is the distance to the centre (₦50 by achaba). ❸

Merry Joe Guest Inn Bolori Layout ☎076/231 261. Small, friendly place in the residential northern part of town. With fans and sometimes TV, rooms are basic s/c affairs, and there's a good inexpensive restaurant. ❶

Safari Across from the zoo, at 21 Shehu Laminu Way ☎076/234 692. Gloomy and run-down s/c fanned rooms with water supplied by the bucket, but very friendly and very central. ❶

Eating, drinking and nightlife

Most hotels in Maiduguri have in-house **restaurants** but they often charge outrageous prices for simple meals; better-value options are easily found around town. In between the *Dujima* and *Safari* hotels, along Shehu Laminu Way, you'll find the shack-like *Hanna's Restaurant* serving assorted African dishes as well as good salads at very reasonable prices. Next door, *Villagers Restaurant* serves similar good-value food. *Jil Restaurant* (daily except Sun) is a popular place halfway between West End and Banks roundabouts, and dishes up a wide range of English and African meals, and fresh juices. They have a generator, which means there's always light, and a TV showing CNN. *Mr Bigs* fast-food joint is popular with well-off locals during weekends. Easily spotted at Bank Roundabout, it does the usual array of burgers and sausage rolls as well as more filling *jollof* rice and roast chicken meals. Finally, the welcoming *Lizzie Restaurant* next to *Lake Chad* hotel (daily except Sun) does an array of well-made local and European dishes.

With the introduction of *sharia* law, the already tranquil Maiduguri nights have become even quieter. However, there is always **beer** to be had at two places – both on military premises south of the centre: the Mamy Market at the army barracks, and the Air Force Officers' Mess next to Nipost (off Shehu Lamido Way). Officially, you have to be a member to get in, but guests are usually welcome.

The far east

Although Maiduguri feels like the end of the road – and certainly most Nigerians consider the town is already at the back of beyond – it is 100km further to the borders of Niger, Chad or Cameroon. Getting to **Lake Chad** is somewhat difficult, and police are suspicious of people heading there, whether they've on public transport or driving. An additional problem is the total retreat of the lake itself from Nigerian territory over the last few years. The place to go if you want to check out the situation is **Baga**, connected to Maiduguri by shared taxi. When you get into town, check in with the police, who won't take long anyhow to discover your arrival. There's a customs and immigration post at Baga and, if the water is high, foot passengers may be able to get a boat across into Chad: the village of Baga Sola is 76km away to the northwest, about three days by pole and paddle or a full day by outboard. If there's no water (and chances are there won't be), you can put up at the *Baga State* **hotel** (❶).

Adamawa State

The wedge of **Adamawa State** spreads from the Sahel near Maiduguri south along the mountainous Cameroon borderlands to Taraba State. It's a huge, little-visited region but, if you can devote the necessary time, offers some of Nigeria's best rewards in terms of landscapes and traditional rural communities. *Sharia* law is interpreted less strictly here than in other northern states and the largely endemic conflicts are more to do with competition over limited resources – between cattle-herding Fulani and settled farmers – than religion. That said, chances that you'll witness a clash are minimal; they mostly happen in remote rural areas, at night.

If you enter the state south of Gwoza, the scenery starts to become spectacularly spiky and volcanic. There are terrific hikes up into the **Mandara Mountains** east of the A13 Madagli–Mubi road. One route starts off from **Chambula**, about 12km southwest of Madagli, and goes some 10km southeast to **Mildo Market**. About 5km further you reach a school (keep asking, young people generally speak English and there's even hope of flagging down transport, especially during the market on Tuesday) from where you can expect (or hope) to be taken around the region.

The payoff for such remote meanderings is **SUKUR**, the seat of a once powerful mountain kingdom, and now a UNESCO World Heritage site. There's a remarkable stone causeway – product of ancient civil engineering – from the school up to this village. Few travellers make it this far and the people are refreshingly welcoming. They've set up a small "**guesthouse**", a traditional round hut with straw mats to sleep on, and have started a regional artefacts museum. Neither is exactly a reason for coming here, but the village itself is and people are more than willing to share their guinea corn and green leaf soup and show you around their unusually constructed compounds – round huts held together with stone, mud and thatch and surrounded by a protective wall. You can visit the **king** (*heedi*); slow clapping to greet him meets with enthusiastic approval. He's remarkably hospitable, and seems eager to recount the history of Sukur, from the early slave raids to the period when this village was part of Cameroon. People don't expect payment, even, as yet, for staying in the guesthouse, but given the level of generosity, you'll find it hard not to reciprocate with a gift (food does fine – it's a long way to the market).

Further south along the A13, **Kamale** is a village with an amazing **volcanic plug** nearby – accessible from Michika, 20km south of Chambula. This whole area has everything in common with its Cameroonian counterpart (see p.1248) and mountain people don't generally draw much of a boundary line. But, whereas the Cameroonian side is geared towards tourism (in some villages to an almost grotesque degree, with postcard sellers and potential guides throwing themselves at you when you arrive) the Nigerian experience is a lot more challenging, but also much more authentic.

Yola and Jimeta

The Adamawa State capital is **YOLA**, an unexceptional, flat, spacious town near the banks of the Benue. **Jimeta**, the administrative side of Yola, is 5km north of the city centre, and where all the hotels and the main **motor park** on Galadima Aminu Way are located. There are shared-taxi departures to Maiduguri, Gombe, Bauchi, Jos, Kano and local destinations throughout the day. The **mass transit motor park**, Atiku Bubakar Way, next to Jimeta's main shopping complex, is where long-distance buses leave, with daily 7am departures to Abuja, Jos, Kano, Lagos, Kaduna and Maiduguri. Fares with long-distance buses are slightly cheaper than shared taxis. The **airport** is 9km from town; Albarka Airlines (☎075/626 145) have a Monday to Friday (8am) flight to Lagos via Maiduguri and Abuja.

Jimeta's only **Internet** place is Micoh Cybercafé at 10 Hospital Road (Mon–Fri 7.30am–6.30pm & Sat 7.30am–4pm; ☎ & ℻075/626 111), in front of Eyn Church. The Gashaka-Gumti National Park office is on Mubi Road (Mon–Fri 8am–5pm; ☎075/626 069, ℻626 118), which runs behind Micoh Cybercafé.

The *Bekaji Guest Inn*, 21 Galedima Aminu Way (☎075/624 724; ❶), is centrally located, next to Lamido Cinema (showing evening movies) and about 1km from the motor park. It has very basic s/c (bucket shower) rooms and friendly staff. Behind the central motor park, on the market side, the spacious compound of *Bagale Motels* at 3 Babale Street (☎075/624 684; ❸) offers decent s/c a/c two-room chalets with hot showers. For something even more upmarket, try the *Yola International Hotel* on Kashim Ibrahim Road (☎075/624 366, ℻624 538; ❹), part of the Arewa chain. It has seen better days, but the standard is still high for Yola, with s/c, rooms all equipped with satellite TV, a/c and fridge. The restaurant serves both Nigerian and European dishes, and there's a bar selling cold beer. Make sure not to miss the great view of the Benue and the surrounding hills from the garden terrace.

The best place to **eat** and drink is the *Pool Bar Restaurant* (daily 5–11.30pm) on Garkida Road, at the northern edge of Jimeta. They have a wide selection of African and European dishes including roast beef (if ordered in advance), and there's cold beer served either in the restaurant or out in a pretty garden. Also good is the *Dreams Restaurant and Snack*, 13 Atiku Abubakar Road (daily 6.30am–10pm), next to the police roundabout. They serve hamburgers, chicken-and-chips and the like, but no alcohol.

Gashaka-Gumpti and Gembu

Dramatic highland regions span Adamawa and **Taraba** states – to the southeast of Yola the **Atlantika Mountain Range**, to the southwest the **Shebshi Mountains** (with 2042-metre Vogel Peak), and, in the far south, in the corner of Nigeria tucked into western Cameroon, the verdant **Mambila Plateau** with Nigeria's highest peak, the Chappel Waddi (Mountain of Death; 2418m). Although the region – a high grassland plateau with a pleasant climate and sparse cattle ranches and tea plantations – is similar to Obudu (see p.1088), it wasn't until recently that travellers began visiting this remote region.

An area of 6670 square kilometres of mountain forests and savanna abutting the border is now protected as the **Gashaka-Gumpti National Park**. This is the site of a major World Wildlife Fund project, in collaboration with the Adamawa and Taraba state governments, who are responsible for the Gumti and Gashaka parts of the park respectively. The area harbours a sizeable **chimpanzee** population and, after an absence of several decades, **elephants**; it is thought that the park also harbours such rare species as leopards and lions, as well as giant forest hogs and hartebeests.

Efforts to gear up the park for visitors are in progress at the park office in **SERTI**, a village on the "main" Yola–Gembu road, where there is simple **accommodation** (●) but no electricity or running water. The park entrance is 15km to the southeast, and rangers will gladly give you a lift if they need to venture into the park, but it's unpredictable as to whether you come across one. If you want to visit the park under your own steam, you can rent a vehicle from the rangers, and one of them will accompany you as your driver and guide (₦2000–3000 per day).

Gembu

In **GEMBU**, the main town of the region, 137km south of Serti and 430km south of Yola (very hard and slow travel by occasional bush taxi or land rover), there's the *Daula Hotel*, with basic fanned rooms and sporadic electricity and water (●). An hour's trek towards Cameroon from Gembu takes you to the red-clay valley of the **Donga River**, a superb sight as it snakes through the jungle. You can cross by canoe or raft, and climb a towering rocky peak on the other side for magnificent views (two hikes or 4WD routes lead up into Cameroon near here, but ask local people about current conditions and the viability of driving). Another excursion from Gembu takes you to the **Highland Tea Plantation** and factory, beyond **Kakara** (a village 30km northwest of Gembu). You'll probably be the first traveller the management here has seen in a while, and they'll not only give you a tour of the place but let you stay in the club for a small fee, watch TV and videos, feed you and ply you with beer, before sending you off with a kilo of produce.

Wukari to Cameroon – the Dumbo Trek

The bustling market town of **WUKARI** has a number of lodging options: try the good-value *Hospitality Hotel*, IBB Road (●), or the central and very inexpensive *Ishaku Hotel* (●), at the junction of Takum and Rafia roads. From here, head for **TAKUM**, where the highlands ahead begin to make their presence felt (the *Dadin Kowa Guest Inn*, on the Yola road, is a reasonable place to stay; ●). Takum is at the southern end of the paved road and beyond it, looping into the green hills, with bananas and fleshy jungle plants increasingly conspicuous, there is just an earth track, mostly in reasonable condition, passing over innumerable frog-filled streams up to the village of **Bissaula** (also spelt Bissuala). You'll be able to get transport as far as here, though don't miss any vehicles that are going, as they're not numerous.

The Michelin map used to mark as a "recognized track" the route that snakes from Bissaula to **Dumbo** on the Bamenda Highlands Ring Road in Cameroon: an optimistic gesture, as it consists only of a rough footpath inaccessible to any vehicle.

If you are keen to do some **trekking**, though, it's a winner: a moderately tough two-day hike (about 40km) that takes in towering trees, squealing parrots, leaping monkeys, thatched-hut hamlets in smoky forest clearings, and lines of porters (mostly portering on their own accounts, beer, cigarettes and cloth). When you reach the top, it seems half of southern Nigeria is spread out below.

You shouldn't set off trekking on your own as orientation here is very difficult. For about ₦3000 (CFA15,000) you can hire the services of a **porter** to walk up to Dumbo with your luggage (the Nigerian immigration post will stamp you out and write "Footing" in your passport). If you opt to carry your own luggage, you should join a group for the initial stages of the trek. You walk for about two hours through lush forest and farm plots, then start climbing the steep scarp, which takes a couple of hours to the top. People generally leave Bissaula late afternoon, and either spend the night in a village at the foot of the scarp and then set off at 4am, or reach the top of the scarp after dark and spend the night in the village there. With an early start on day two you can be in Dumbo (see p.1208) by evening, but it's less exhausting to arrive mid-morning on day three. You should be aware of the fact that the Cameroonian immigration and customs post at Dumbo isn't frequently blessed with tourists and may try to extract presents from you. If you take photos on the trek, try to be discreet, this being a border area.

Cameroon

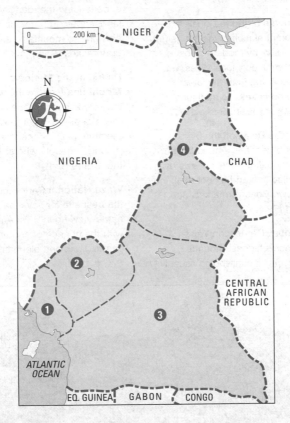

Cameroon highlights

✳ **Cameroonian music** One of West Africa's most varied musical feasts – from sexy urban *makossa* and *bikutsi* to the strange music and instruments of the forest-dwelling Baka. See p.1161

✳ **Douala nightlife** Douala's vibrant nightlife runs the gamut from flashy modern clubs to determinedly local dives, with everything from the latest European hits to traditional *balafon* music. See p.1177

✳ **Limbé** Relax on the black-sand beaches around Limbé and soak up ocean views over grilled fish and a cool drink in Down Beach's market. See p.1179

✳ **Mount Cameroon** West Africa's highest mountain, offering a challenging ascent and a memorable range of landscapes and views en route. See p.1185

✳ **Biking around the Ring Road** A classic Cameroonian adventure and an excellent way of experiencing the road's varied landscapes, from forest and savanna to mountains and crater lakes. See p.1205

✳ **Hiking in the Mandara Mountains** Explore the haunting volcanic landscapes of these peaks and get to know the staunchly independent mountain people who still live there. See p.1248

✳ **Waza National Park** Probably the best site for savanna game-viewing in West Africa, with the chance of spotting giraffe, lions and elephants. See p.1251

Introduction and Basics

The **landscapes of Cameroon** are exceptional. The country stretches from the fringes of the Sahara in the north to the borders of Congo and Gabon in the south and takes in every African variation in between: from equatorial rainforest (some of the continent's most unexploited tracts) to moist, tree-scattered savanna; from dry grassy plains to bucking volcanic ranges flecked with crater lakes; from gaunt rocky massifs to the hot basin of Lake Chad; and, to cap it all, the highest mountain on this side of the continent – the 4095 metres of Mount Cameroon – rising direct from the ocean shore to an impressive cloud-wreathed summit. For good measure, the country also has some entrancing beaches and several large parks, with rewarding quantities of wildlife, including species found nowhere else in the region. At the simple level of tourism, it's hard to oversell Cameroon – it's simply the most dramatic country in West Africa.

There's another side to Cameroon in its hugely stimulating cultural make-up, which exhibits some striking **ethnic distinctions**: the Muslim sultanates of the north are reminiscent of northern Nigeria, and also have strong Arab connections, but exist alongside the avowedly non-Muslim people of the mountainous Rhumsiki district; in the forests of the far south, the so-called "Pygmies" – the region's original inhabitants – still live a life of hunting and gathering largely untroubled by the modern nation state; and in the mountains and pasturelands of the country's western "bulge", a remarkable complex of kingdoms has developed over the last four hundred years, speaking dozens of Bantoid languages (closely related to Bantu). This is the only country in West Africa with a large **Bantu-speaking** population (the Bantu languages, including Swahili and Zulu, are some of the most important in Africa), which gives the south much in common with the Central African region. Coupled with its natural diversity, it's a country that can claim to embody cultural elements of the entire continent.

Cameroon has a colonial past of German, French and British occupation. With the current division between Francophone and Anglophone affecting every aspect of national life, impressions of contrast and fragmentation are never far away. Recurring outbursts – sometimes fierce – of old Anglo–Francophone tensions have led repeatedly to calls for secession in the west.

And, since the economy began faltering in the 1990s, opposition has become more vocal in the northern regions as well.

The increasing importance of **tourism** as a source of foreign exchange has led to some improvement in official attitudes to foreign visitors. The searches and controls that once dogged visitors from the moment of arrival are no longer so aggressive. There are, however, still numerous roadblocks – little havens where police and customs officials extract "dash money" (bribes) – throughout the country. The tourist industry also still has upmarket expectations: backpackers who sleep in D-class hotels and cram into bush taxis are still prone to be put down as *pauvres blancs*, and may experience the disdain of local law officers.

People

The oldest group of people to have lived in Cameroon are the **"Pygmies"** of the south and southeast forests. Although forced onto the defensive by the expansion of the various Bantu-speaking groups, and with their livelihood threatened by extensive logging, many have today settled in small villages. However, most still opt for the traditional independence of the few remaining impenetrable areas of the rainforest, where they continue to live by hunting and gathering.

Bantu-speaking populations have spread gradually southeast through the Cameroon region into central Africa over the past two

The **Republic of Cameroon** (or République du Cameroun to Francophones) covers 475,000 square kilometres, an area twice the size of Britain and somewhat larger than California, with a population estimated at more than sixteen million. The name derives from *camarões*, the Portuguese for prawns, which the first European visitors found in large quantities in the Wouri River. The common reference to **"Cameroons"** is a legacy of the colonial division into two Cameroons – French and British – a dual heritage preserved in the official bilingualism (easily dominated by French). The country has been ruled since 1982 by **Paul Biya**, long the head of the Rassemblement Démocratique du Peuple Camerounais (RDPC), the country's sole political party until opposition parties were legalized in 1990. The country's foreign debt of $6.6 billion is more than two times the value of its annual exports of goods and services – a huge figure for the country's relatively small population, equivalent to $412 for every Cameroonian, a sum few could expect to earn in a year.

Cameroon is divided into ten administrative **provinces**, with governors appointed by the president. You may find their names confusing at first, especially in western Cameroon in that, for example, South West Province extends further north and west than West Province. The provinces and their capitals are:

Centre/Centre (Yaoundé)
South/Sud (Ebolowa)
East/Est (Bertoua)
Littoral/Littoral (Douala)
South West/Sud Ouest (Buéa)
West/Ouest (Bafoussam)

North West/Nord Ouest (Bamenda)
Adamawa/Adamaoua (Ngaoundéré)
North/Nord (Garoua)
Extreme North/Extrême Nord (Maroua)

thousand years, migrating in strength from the Adamawa range and settling along the coast from about the fifteenth century. The first to migrate were the **Bassa** and **Bakoko**, followed by the **Douala**. In the nineteenth century, pushed along in a chain reaction by migrations engendered after the Fulani Sokoto invasions in Nigeria, the **Fang**, **Ewondo** and **Eton** came from the plateaux in the east to settle in the central southern region around Yaoundé.

In the west of the country, waves of northern immigration between the sixteenth and nineteenth centuries saw the installation of **"Semi-Bantu"** peoples. The first to arrive were the **Tikar**, who probably came from the area near Ngaoundéré and who today live in semiautonomous chiefdoms throughout the Grassfields. In the eighteenth century a splinter group broke away from the Tikar country to form the powerful **Bamoun** empire a little to the east. The **Bamiléké** – a fusion of peoples from the north, east and southwest, whose arrival spread over three centuries – settled in the plateau region south of the Noun River. Now the country's largest single ethnic group, the Bamiléké are also numer-

ous in Douala where they have come to control a good deal of the national economy.

The predominant group in the north is the **Fula** (also known as Fulani, Foulbé or Peul), who settled in principalities (*lamidats*) around the early nineteenth century, bringing Islam with them. The Mandara Mountains of the far northwest are inhabited by staunchly non-Muslim groups known collectively as **Kirdi** – which just means "infidels". Pushed to these desolate extremities by the Muslim invasions of dan Fodio, an early nineteenth-century Islamic leader from Nigeria, they comprise numerous Adamawa- and Chadic-speaking peoples: the **Podoko**, **Fali**, **Kapsiki**, **Mafa** and **Bata**. Principally farmers, they grow millet and sorghum in terraced gardens on the rocky slopes of the mountains.

The northern plains near Lake Chad are home to the **Choa**, seminomadic peoples of Arab origin who share these open spaces with the **Kotoko** – descendants of the ancient Sao culture – who live from fishing and growing a few cereals. Near the Logone River live the **Toupouri**, **Massa** and **Mousgoum**, people of pre-Islamic belief who are increasingly becoming Islamicized.

Where to go

Cameroon's main city, **Douala**, is a seething, sweltering metropolis that wins few accolades. Fortunately, an hour's drive from Douala, the black-sand beaches of **Limbé**, in South West Province, are a good, quick getaway. Between the strands, in the rich soil beneath Mount Cameroon, the dense vegetation pushes right to the water's edge, although it has increasingly been cleared to create plantations of tea, bananas, rubber

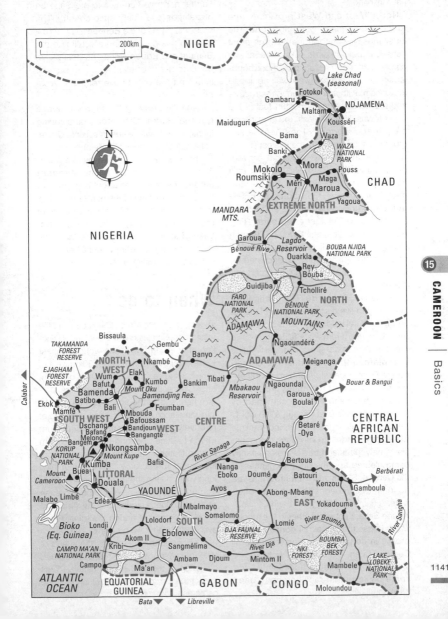

trees and oil palms. The trek up **Mount Cameroon**, a still active volcano, is a challenging but perfectly feasible ascent. To the north of the mountain, the country drops towards the Nigerian border and the **Korup rainforest**, now a fairly easily accessible national park.

North West and **West** provinces (the former predominantly Anglophone, the latter mostly Francophone) are the most densely populated parts of Cameroon, and contain some of the country's most popular sites. Both are relatively well equipped for tourism, with a developed infrastructure and even a quite cosmopolitan feel in the larger towns. Nevertheless, the landscapes are often rugged. Together, these provinces form probably the easiest part of Cameroon in which to strike out on your own; visiting the Bamiléké district and **Foumban**, with its Sultan's Palace and major crafts market; the **traditional chiefdoms** of the Bamoun, Tikar and others around the 400-kilometre red-earth **Ring Road**; and the beautiful **Grassfields** area through which the Ring Road circles. The whole of this upland region is renowned for its thatched architecture and animated traditional life.

The capital, **Yaoundé**, is climatically a better city to live and work in than Douala, and a more relaxed place to rest up from travels, though it remains a fairly aggressive metropolis with its share of tension. The vast **plateau** that stretches to the east, covered with huge tracts of hardwood rainforest – sapele, mahogany, iroko and obiche – has been severely damaged by logging during the past decade. With eighty percent of all Cameroon's indigenous forests now divided up into logging concessions, new roads and tracks are constantly being cleared and the great expanses of the **Central**, **South** and **East** provinces are no longer as impenetrable as they once were. A number of **"Pygmy"** bands, including the Baka, hunt and gather in the jungle, which is also the domain of **gorillas** – quite prolific in certain areas. The reserves of Campo Ma'an, Dja and Lake Lobéké are slowly becoming more accessible, and some basic tourist facilities have been developed.

North of Yaoundé, the northern sectors of Central and Eastern provinces comprise an immense, empty savanna, patched with forest. Together with the gaunt **Adamawa range**, they effectively cut the country in two and hinder north–south overland travel. Further north you come into pre-Sahelian grasslands and dusty bush country. The upper tributaries of the **Bénoué** (Benue) flow through this region, where you'll find the **Bénoué** and **Bouba Ndjida** national parks, home to herds of elephants and buffalo, lions and the only native rhinos in West Africa.

In the flat plains of the far north, **Waza National Park** is Cameroon's outstanding faunal reserve, with elephants, lions, giraffe, ostriches and a host of antelope species. To the west, a few hours away, the otherworldly volcanic plugs of the **Mandara Mountains** offer a beautiful backdrop to the stony homeland of the non-Muslim Kirdi "mountain people". The northernmost tip of the country, leading up to what's left of **Lake Chad**, is usually dry, but floods under the waters of the **Logone** and **Chari** rivers during the brief annual rains.

When to go

The region around Mount Cameroon and the western mountains has the dubious distinction of boasting one of the world's highest levels of **rainfall**: Debundscha, 30km west of Limbé, is the second wettest place on earth, after Cherrapungi in India. The general pattern here and in **the south** can be divided into three approximate seasons: a period of relatively light but persistent rains from March to June; the long rainy period from July to October; and the dry season from November to February. Travel can involve long waits during the rains, especially to or from towns accessible only by track, such as Mamfé. Roads around the Grassfields are often unmotorable during the rains, when even 4WDs can have problems. The savannas further north choke towards the end of the dry season with fine red laterite dust, blown up by the northerly harmattan. Plants and crops turn rusty red, while lungs – and cameras – seize up.

Average temperatures and rainfall

Yaoundé

	Jan	Feb	Mar	Apr	May	June	July	Aug	Sept	Oct	Nov	Dec
Temperatures °C												
Min (night)	19	19	19	19	19	19	19	18	19	18	19	19
Max (day)	29	29	30	29	28	28	26	26	27	28	28	29
Rainfall mm	23	66	147	170	196	152	74	79	213	295	117	23
Days with rainfall	3	5	13	15	18	17	11	10	20	24	14	4

Douala

	Jan	Feb	Mar	Apr	May	June	July	Aug	Sept	Oct	Nov	Dec
Temperatures °C												
Min (night)	23	23	23	23	23	23	22	22	23	22	23	23
Max (day)	31	32	32	32	31	29	27	27	29	30	30	31
Rainfall mm	46	94	203	231	300	539	742	693	531	429	155	64
Days with rainfall	4	6	12	12	16	19	24	24	21	20	10	6

Kousséri

	Jan	Feb	Mar	Apr	May	June	July	Aug	Sept	Oct	Nov	Dec
Temperatures °C												
Min (night)	14	16	21	23	25	24	22	22	22	21	17	14
Max (day)	34	37	40	42	40	38	33	31	33	36	36	33
Rainfall mm	0	0	0	3	31	66	170	320	119	36	0	0
Days with rainfall	0	0	0	1	6	10	15	22	13	4	0	0

Northern Cameroon, north of the Adamawa Plateau, has a different weather pattern, characterized by a long rainy season from May to October. Although travel in the north doesn't present any special problem during this period, note that many national parks are closed, depending on the rains, roughly between May and December. Overall, the **ideal time to visit**, taking into account the different regional patterns, is December and January.

Getting there from the rest of Africa

Getting to Cameroon is made easy by the fact that the national carrier, Cameroon Airlines, is one of Africa's best. Flying in, however, means that you'll arrive in the rather

For important practical information applying to all West African countries, covering health, transport, cultural hints and more, plus details on getting to the region from beyond Africa, see Basics, pp.9–87.

heavy city of Douala (unless you catch one of the few direct flights to Yaoundé or Garoua). Arriving overland from the east, Cameroon feels like the threshold of a new region, which it is, as you leave the confines of the Central African rainforest and enter West Africa.

Flights

Cameroon has **international airports** at Yaoundé and Garoua, but most foreign flights still arrive in Douala. Cameroon Airlines (@ www.iccnet.cm/camair) have flights to Douala from **Dakar** via **Bamako**, **Abidjan** and **Lagos** (twice weekly); from Dakar via Abidjan and Lagos (weekly); from Dakar via Lagos and **Cotonou** (weekly); from Abidjan via Cotonou (weekly); and nonstop from Cotonou (weekly).

Elsewhere within West Africa, Nigeria Airways fly weekly from **Lagos** via **Port Harcourt** (weekly). There are also connections three times weekly from Lomé with Air Gabon. From the Sahel capitals of **Ouagadougou** and **Niamey**, the easiest connections to Douala are via Abidjan with Air Niger from Niamey, Air Burkina from Ouagadougou, or Air Ivoire from both, and then on to Douala with Cameroon Airways (five weekly).

Cameroon has good air links with **Central Africa**. Cameroon Airlines have direct flights to Douala from **Bangui** (four weekly; one via **Ndjamena** in Chad; one via Yaoundé); **Point Noire** in Congo-Brazzaville (twice weekly); **Brazzaville** (four times weekly; one via **Kinshasa**); Libreville (daily; there are also daily services with Air Gabon); and Kinshasa (3 weekly; one via Brazzaville). There are also six flights weekly with Cameroon Airlines to Douala from Ndjamena (either nonstop or via Bangui and Yaoundé or Garoua and Yaoundé) and three flights weekly from **Malabo** in Equatorial Guinea with Air Gabon and daily with Cameroon Airlines.

Kenya Airways have twice-weekly nonstop connections from **Nairobi** to Douala via Yaoundé. From southern Africa, there are twice weekly nonstop flights with Cameroon Airlines to Douala from **Johannesburg**.

Overland from Nigeria

The two main overland routes from Nigeria go to **Mamfé** in the west of Cameroon and **Mora** in the north. You'll need to already have a visa to use the Mora crossing (see p.1132). The straightforward western route involves getting a bush taxi from **Calabar to Ikom**, from where taxis leave regularly for the busy border. After completing the often protracted Nigerian customs and immigration formalities, you walk over the bridge spanning the Cross River and up the hill to the Cameroonian post at **Ekok**. Taxis from Ekok to Mamfé rattle along bumpy tracks through a beautiful but tortuous mountain region. A couple of variations on this route involve travelling by *pirogue*: one leads from Ekok down the Cross River to Mamfé, the other passes through the creeks from Calabar via the Oban Rainforest National Park. You can also take the **irregular ferry** from Calabar to Idenau (see p.1083) although this may not be advisable while the border dispute over the Bakassi peninsula is still ongoing.

The main northern route (which involves less border hassle than the western route) leads from **Maiduguri** via **Bama** over a good, flat paved road to the border post at Banki. Customs and immigration formalities are delt with swiftly and black-market money traders are ready and waiting once you're done. From here it's easy to find transport at the Banki motor park next to immigration, from where it's a bumpy two-hour journey on rough tracks across the plains (look out for antelope) to **Mora** and on to Maroua or up to Waza National Park.

Overland from Central African Republic

A reasonable graded road runs from **Bouar**, in the west of Central African Republic, to the Cameroonian border post at **Garoua-Boulai**. Once you've crossed the border, a fast new paved road (courtesy of the new Chad–Cameroon oil pipeline) connects Garoua-Boulai with Meiganga, 100km to the north, where you can find onward transport to Ngaoundal (273km from Garoua-Boulai) and a **train** either southwest to **Yaoundé** or north to **Ngaoundéré**. The paved road also continues 260km south from Garoua-Boulai to **Bertoua**, from where it's a 45-minute journey to the train station at **Bélabo**. For schedule details, see the relevant "Moving on" sections. A rougher route leads from **Bebérati** in Central African Republic to **Batouri**, 90km from Bertoua.

Overland from Equatorial Guinea and Gabon

The main road from **Bata** in **Equatorial Guinea** heads far inland to **Ebebiyin**, at the point where Gabon, Cameroon and Equatorial Guinea all meet. From here, the route goes via **Ambam** to **Ebolowa** where there's the choice of heading either direct to Yaoundé on a fast paved road or taking the slower but more scenic coastal route via **Kribi**. From Bata there's also the option of travelling straight north on the *piste* to the border town of **Yengue** on the **Ntem River**, where you can pick up motorized *pirogues* travelling downriver to the beach a few kilometres south of **Campo**. From Campo there are shared taxis to Kribi.

You'll also use the Ambam arrival point if you come from **Gabon**. This is reached from **Libreville** via **Oyem**, where you can pick up transport to Ambam.

Overland from Chad

There is now a bridge between **Ndjamena** – the capital of Chad – and **Kousséri** in Cameroon. Details of this border crossing are given on p.1252.

Red tape and visas

All passport holders (other than certain African nationals) need a visa to enter Cameroon. At the time of writing it was also possible to obtain visas at **Douala and Yaoundé airports** for CFA30,000, but don't count on it. Contact your nearest embassy or Cameroon Airlines beforehand if you want to use this option. There are no embassies or consulates in the Sahel states.

Visas cost about £30/$50, are valid for one month and must be activated within three months of issue. You'll usually need to show either a return air ticket, a letter of invitation from a Cameroonian resident, or proof of your intended onward route – including any other relevant visas. It's not hard to extend your stay in any of the provincial capitals, but it's just as pricey as getting a visa.

If you are travelling from Central or East Africa, Cameroonian embassies and consulates can be found in **Central African Republic** (Bangui; ☎61.16.87, ℻61.18.57); **Chad** (Ndjamena; ☎52.28.94); **Equatorial Guinea** (Malabo; ☎24.64 or 26.63, ℻22.63); **Congo-Brazzaville** (Brazzaville; ☎83.34.84 or 83.55.10, ℻83.67.99); **Democratic Republic of Congo** (Kinshasa; ☎32.232 or 32.267); and **Ethiopia** (Addis Ababa; ☎44.81.16 or 51.48.44, ℻51.03.50).

When you arrive in Cameroon – especially if you come in overland – immigration officers may well want to check that you have what they consider to be **sufficient funds** to stay in the country. A credit card usually does the trick. **Health certificates** are rarely checked on the road, but may be asked for at the border. A certificate for yellow fever is obligatory, and also for cholera when there are epidemics in Cameroon or neighbouring countries. It's a good idea to have this latter certificate, though the jab itself isn't considered effective.

Information, websites and maps

In the UK, tourist leaflets and information are available at the Cameroon Airlines office in London (84 Holland Park, London W11 3RB ☎020/7727 9311). The embassies (see p.22) may also have some information, though it's probably the same stuff.

It's well worth getting hold of some **maps** before arriving in Cameroon. Much the best-looking is the Macmillan road map of Cameroon, which has excellent city maps for Douala and Yaoundé, though it's now rather out of date (1988). The 1994 Institut Géographique National map has more up-to-date information about recently surfaced roads, but is inaccurate when it comes to showing the year-round viability of many others, and is less clearly designed. Both maps are at a scale of 1cm=15km. The Michelin 741 is good, though you need Michelin 746 as well if you want coverage of the southernmost hundred kilometres of the country. Good **city maps** of Yaoundé and Douala and a few less-detailed country maps are sold on the street and in bigger bookshops in Cameroon itself.

Websites

The best Cameroon-related **websites** are:

ⓦ **www.camnet.cm/mintour/tourisme** The Ministry of Tourism's official website in French.

ⓦ **www.cameroonnews.com** Current Cameroonian news and sport updates.

ⓦ **www.bakwerilands.org** Official homepage of the Bakweri people in South West Province.

ⓦ **www.southerncameroons.org** Official website of the Federal Republic of Southern Cameroons, the two Anglophone provinces that call for secession.

ⓦ **www.cameroun-plus.com** French portal, with loads of practical information including hotels, banks and travel agencies.

Health

Malaria prophylaxis is essential throughout the country (see p.32). A serious new health risk in the southeast is usually fatal **Ebola fever**: this may cross over from Congo or Gabon, where it is widespread among chimpanzees and gorillas and transmitted through consumption of their meat. It's not recommended to drink the **tap water** in major towns; you can find bottled water everywhere except in small villages, though it becomes increasingly expensive the further you get from urban centres. Cameroon, like most countries in West Africa, has a serious **schistosomiasis** (bilharzia) problem, though it's usually safe enough to use free-flowing stream water in the highlands, especially after rain.

Most **pharmacies** have a reasonable stock of medicines and **hospital care** is good in the capital, although the "polyclinics" in the rest of the country are generally poorly stocked and often dirty.

Costs, money and banks

Cameroon is part of the Central African economic zone and uses the **Central African Franc** (CFA; approximately CFA930 to £1, and CFA600 to US$1). Although Central African CFA are exactly equivalent in value to West African CFA, the bills for the two regions are different and cannot be used on the street.

The best way to carry your money is in **euros**, ideally in cash, though banks are more likely to accept euro traveller's cheques, and commission fees are lower than for other currencies. Only banks in major towns change **sterling** and **dollars** cash or traveller's cheques. Banks that change sterling are Standard Chartered, Amity and the main branches of BICEC (Banque Internationale du Cameroun pour l'Épargne et le Crédit). Citi Bank, CBC (Commercial Bank of Cameroon) and the main branches of Crédit Lyonnais Cameroun also change dollars but not sterling. It's worth nothing that outside the major cities, banks frequently run out of money, especially around payday (at the end of the month).

Credit cards (most often Visa) can be used in big-city hotels and some shops and restaurants. You can only use them to get **cash advances** in hotels where you're actually staying. The main branches of SGBC (Société Générale de Banques au Cameroun) in Douala, Yaoundé and Garoua

have ATM machines which accept Visa and Plus cards. SGBC and BICEC are also linked up with **Western Union**, and it's possible to have money transferred to Cameroon at no cost to the recipient.

You can also change money on the **black market**, where you may be able to get up to twenty percent over for your cash. It shouldn't be too hard to find a businessman who needs foreign currency – try asking in your hotel. A few **exchange bureaus** have opened, with the same rates as banks.

Costs

Cameroon is one of the more expensive countries in West Africa. A cheap night's **accommodation** costs around CFA3000–6000 (or around CFA5000–8000 for two people sharing a room); Douala is significantly more expensive. The country's most expensive **luxury hotels** charge up to CFA150,000 per night.

The cost of **public road transport** varies widely, depending on the remoteness of the route and the condition of the road. As a general guideline, count on CFA1000 for an hour's travel on good roads; in the rainy season, or where the roads are bad, you'll pay more to cover the same distance.

Getting around

Cameroon's **roads** can be OK, though the good-quality paved sections are often separated by many kilometres of rough dirt track. The country's **trains** only cover certain very limited routes – barely venturing into the north or west, for example. As for **flying**, Cameroon Airlines serve a good deal of the country, though at a price.

By road

Although 35,000km of roads crisscross Cameroon, only a fraction of this network is paved, and even this is often in disrepair, with sections washed out by floods or pitted with potholes. Less-used dirt roads in particular can be blocked for days by overturned vehicles or collapsed bridges.

That said, the roads around and between **Douala** and **Yaoundé** are always reliable, as are those from Douala and Yaoundé to

Bamenda or **Foumban** via Bafoussam (though not via **Mamfé**, which some maps show as the main road).

Western Cameroon has a reasonable road network, while the north is well served by the highway between **Ngaoundéré** and **Kousséri**.

The entire **centre** of the country, however, lacks a good system, the **Adamawa Plateau** providing a formidable obstacle. Between **Yaoundé** and **Ngaoundéré**, where the dirt roads are quite appalling, you'd be wiser taking the train – in fact, you can even take a car on the train, though that option has become quite expensive (CFA100,000) and is sometimes unsafe for the car. In the east of the country, the dense forest is another barrier to overland travel, and there is only one good paved road, linking Bertoua with Meiganga in the centre. **South of Yaoundé** there are good paved roads to Ambam and the border of Gabon and Equatorial Guinea via Ebolowa, Sangmélima and Kribi. The rest of the south is held together by dirt roads and tracks through the forest.

There are a few problems and potential dangers peculiar to road travel in Cameroon. Firstly, the speeds at which many drivers travel on the country's few smooth highways can be hair-raising, and horrendous **accidents** are not uncommon. Be extra vigilant when driving on these fast roads, and expect the unexpected from on-coming traffic. Secondly, the law that forbids motorists involved in an accident to move their cars until the police have inspected the site – meaning that all traffic may be held up for a couple of hours. Thirdly, the behaviour of Cameroonian **hitchhikers**, who often attempt to stop cars by standing in the middle of the road with both arms outstretched. Stopping is an implicit offer of a lift, so they tend to stand just round a blind corner where cars will be forced to screech to a halt to avoid killing them.

Recent years have also seen an increasing number of **highway robberies**, especially in Adamawa Province and further north near the Chadian border. Bandits tend to operate in large gangs, are often armed and can turn nasty if they encounter resistance.

Taxis and buses

Most Cameroonians rely on share taxis, *clandos* or *agences de voyage* to get around. **Agences de voyage** provide fixed-priced – and often timetabled – transport between most towns. Each agency runs certain routes, and finding out who goes where can be very time-consuming, especially as both *agences* and routes change

Roadblocks

The one hazard even the most careful driver can't avoid in Cameroon is **police roadblocks**. These are usually on the outskirts of towns, often outside a bar or café. They're not easy to spot, as they may consist of no more than a policeman fast asleep in camouflage fatigues and a piece of string stretched across the road (or, more worryingly, the occasional nail-studded board). Cameroonian police are less troublesome to foreigners than they were a few years ago, but can still be drunk, abusive, surly, and alarmingly casual about pointing a gun at your stomach. The best precaution is always to travel with a full clutch of **documents**, whatever current regulations may say – it's easier to show an International Medical Certificate ("carte jaune") than to insist that you aren't required to carry it.

As a foreigner, you're permitted to move about with a certified photocopy of your passport, which avoids the fear of having it confiscated at a police check. Take the original and copies of the first five pages (as well as your visa) with a CFA500 fiscal stamp (available from the Ministry of Finance) to any main police station, where it will be stamped and signed.

A more worrying development, which has become increasingly common in recent years, are the **fake roadblocks**, set up by armed bandits and usually appearing at night. Local drivers usually know which roadblocks are fake, so if your vehicle suddenly starts speeding up to pass one, you'll know why.

constantly. Even more confusingly, the agencies don't use official motor parks, but instead fill their vehicles outside their own ticket offices. Fortunately, booking offices for agencies going in the same general direction are often found in the same neighbourhood. Most agency vehicles are minibuses, but for connections between major towns and cities they run more comfortable buses. Both tend to pass police checkpoints with less trouble than share taxis and *clandos*.

Share taxis are government-registered minibuses or saloon cars travelling from motor park to motor park at a fixed rate, though they often pile in extra passengers after leaving the motor park control. **Clandos** are ramshackle vehicles retired from government service and operate as unregistered unofficial competition to the *agences* and share taxis. They tend to run on routes that none of the others cover, or snatch passengers from the share taxis outside the motor parks, piling people on top of each other and charging similar prices. They also tend to break down constantly, so take plenty of water with you.

Within cities, **yellow taxis** are also shared and cost CFA150 for most short distances (a "drop" in English, *ramassage* in French) – one of the few real bargains in Cameroon. Taxi drivers generally don't attempt to overcharge – it's hard to imagine why not – but be sure to agree on a fare before you get in. In all smaller towns and most of the north – from Ngaoundéré and northwards – **motos** provide the easiest form of transport. For CFA100 these small motorcycles will take you anywhere you choose within the city limits and, for a bit more, outside the limits too.

Car rental

You'll find **car rental** agencies only in the larger towns (Douala, Yaoundé, Garoua, Maroua, Bafoussam and Ngaoundéré); we've given addresses in the relevant "Listings" or "Moving on" sections of the *Guide*. Car **rental rates** are extremely high, especially with the main operators such as **Europcar** and **Avis** – although they at least back up their high prices with reliable cars. If you rent on a daily basis, expect to pay about CFA46,000 per day for a small

European or Japanese car, made up of a basic rate of around CFA21,000 per day, plus CFA200 per kilometre and extra charges for taxes and insurance. For a 4WD, expect to pay around CFA50,000, plus CFA300 per kilometre and other charges. A hefty deposit of CFA500,000 is usually required on all vehicles. Rental charges are largely the same throughout the country, although you'll be charged extra for any *piste* driving.

By rail

There are two main railway routes. The first is the 93-kilometre western line from **Douala to Kumba**, which can take up to six hours – it's quicker to do this journey by road. The branch to **Kumba** from Mbanga can be useful, however, as the road can be very difficult, especially in the wet season.

The substantially longer **Transcamerounais line** links Douala and Yaoundé with **Ngaoundéré** in the north. **Transcam I** covers the 308-kilometre stretch from **Douala to Yaoundé** with two services a day in each direction (CFA4000 first class), leaving Douala at 7.15am and 1.40pm, and Yaoundé at 7.15am and 1.30pm. The journey takes over three hours, meaning that it's often easier to do the trip by road. **Transcam II** forges on for 620km from **Yaoundé to Ngaoundéré**, with a daily overnight service in each direction (CFA15,000 in first class). This is a fairly quick trip – roughly twelve hours, assuming there are no delays – and just as quick as going by road.

Carriages are relatively comfortable, with couchettes (linen, blankets and pillows are provided), plus fans and washing facilities in first class. Second class (roughly two-thirds of the first-class fare) has seats only and is often crowded. Food is available from vendors in the stations, but take your own water.

The railway authorities are extremely sensitive about foreigners taking **photographs**, and it would be wise to pack your camera deep inside your bag during the journey. Due to the increased risk of **theft** it's also advisable to keep your bags far away from windows. Thieves tend to sit on the roof of the train and poke their arms in through the windows to grab whatever they can get –

personal stereos, sunglasses and shoes have all been seen leaving the carriage in this fashion.

By air

Cameroon Airlines operate a reasonably efficient domestic service connecting **Douala** and **Yaoundé** with each other and with **Bertoua**, **Bafoussam**, **Garoua**, **Maroua** and **Ngaoundéré**. Details are given in the relevant town sections in the guide. The northern towns are usually linked in series, which makes the flight up to (or back from) Maroua very long. Note that Cameroon Airlines offer **student reductions** and often have other discounted fares such as weekend excursions (available to all; out Friday or Saturday, back Sunday or Monday).

One to two daily flights connect Yaoundé and Douala. Most other links have services varying from three to six times a week. Note that flights are often either cancelled or overbooked; arrive early and hope for the best.

To reach more inaccessible areas, such as isolated national parks and game reserves, it's possible to charter small planes through Air Affaire Afrique, but you'll need deep pockets.

Accommodation

International-standard hotels in Cameroon are officially graded from one to five stars, and although it's hard to work out exactly how this system works, if a hotel has a star, it should guarantee some degree of international-standard comfort.

The majority of hotels and *auberges*, however, are **"unclassified"**. This doesn't necessarily mean that the place isn't worth staying at – indeed you tend to get more for your money in the unclassified category. **Room rates** tend to be negotiable in all categories; more expensive places in particular are often prepared to reduce their rates if you can give them a good reason – like staying more than one night or threatening to move to the hotel across the road.

Camping and missions

If you have your own transport, **camping** away from the major urban centres is a fine alternative to hotel living. The game parks and natural reserves are sometimes restricted, but elsewhere, there are tens of thousands of square kilometres of wild country which you can freely pitch a tent in. See p.51 for general advice.

The **missions** scattered throughout Cameroon may put up travellers, but they don't have to – and don't always want to. In Douala and Yaoundé, the religious institutions are a real godsend if you're travelling on your own and don't want to pay for a double room in a hotel. In the face of the ever-increasing demand, however, many missions have started putting up their prices and are starting to turn away all who are not visiting on church business. In recent years the government has tried to enforce this policy by decree.

Staying with people

There's a large Western presence in Cameroon, so you won't be considered special or exotic, and you're unlikely to receive many offers to **stay with people**. You may find exceptions in the north, however, where

---

Accommodation price codes

All accommodation prices in this chapter are coded according to the following scale, whose equivalent in pounds sterling/US dollars is used throughout the book. Prices refer to the rate you can expect to pay for a room with two beds, including taxes. Single rooms, or single occupancy, will normally cost at least two-thirds of the twin-occupancy rate. For further details, see p.51.

❶ Under CFA4700 (under £5/$8).
❷ CFA4700–9000 (£5–10/$8–16).
❸ CFA9000–14,000 (£10–15/$16–24).
❹ CFA14,000–19,000 (£15–20/$24–32).

❺ CFA19,000–28,000 (£20–30/$32–48).
❻ CFA28,000–37,000 (£30–40/$48–64).
❼ CFA37,000–47,000 (£40–50/$64–80).
❽ Over CFA47,000 (over £50/$80).

the rocketing price of accommodation in out-of-the-way villages such as Mokolo has given enterprising young people the idea of "inviting" travellers to spend the night in their homes. If you stay a couple of days, they can earn a month's income, even for a contribution that is negligible compared to what you'd pay in a hotel. You might find this blend of commerce and camaraderie a little difficult to handle, but it's a solution that benefits both parties. Be clear about prices before agreeing to any such arrangements.

Eating and drinking

Cameroon has a rich and varied cuisine, with a heavy emphasis in the north on maize, millet and groundnuts, and in the south on cassava, yams and plantains. These staples can be boiled, pounded or even grilled, but invariably turn out bland – a characteristic which may put you off at first, though it complements the fiercely peppered sauces quite nicely.

Fruit and vegetables in Cameroon are probably the best in the whole of West Africa, and the variations in climate and altitude mean you can get nearly everything all year round – except the luscious and varied types of **mangos** in which Cameroon excels, which are in season from February to May. There's a healthy demand for **salads** in Cameroon.

For cheap, freshly made food, you can't beat the **streetside stands**, usually rickety wooden counters lined by benches and with an array of delicacies on offer ranging from spicy bean stew to avocado salad and the unique spaghetti omelette, all served with – or in – a fresh baguette. Streetside stands tend to run out of food by early afternoon, after which grills take over. In the south especially, **grilled fish** is a popular evening meal, served with beer and *miondo* (fried plaintain). In the north, you'll find tasty little snack kebabs known as **soya** (exactly like the *suya* of Nigeria), which make a good meal with some chopped raw onion and French bread.

In common with much of Francophone West Africa, **French cuisine** dominates in the big hotels and expensive **restaurants**,

where you can pay CFA10,000–20,000 per head – though all the glitter is no guarantee of good food. Restaurants in Yaoundé also serve a wide variety of **Cameroonian dishes** (although you're unlikely to find such specialized regional treats as fried termites, grasshoppers, dog, snake or cat). Beware, however, of upmarket restaurants serving **plats typiques** — they may simply be charging the earth for ordinary Cameroonian dishes.

Dishes and staples

Bongo tchobi is a striking fish or meat dish, cooked in a black sauce made from various forest seeds and bark. **Bobolo**, from the south and central provinces, is a heavy, nearly translucent, fermented cassava preparation served in a miniature baguette shape. **Miondo**, from Littoral province, is practically the same thing, but made with smaller strips of cassava wrapped in banana leaves. The most widely eaten southern dish is **ndolé**, made from a boiled and finely shredded bitter leaf plus groundnuts or *agussi* (melon seeds). It's seasoned with hot oil and spices, cooked with fish or meat and eaten with one of the many starchy staples. The similar **kwem** is made from pounded cassava leaves and groundnuts cooked in a red palm-oil sauce. Such meals are served throughout the south in small restaurants known as **chantiers** ("worksites"), run by *veuves joyeuses* ("merry widows") or *tantes* ("aunties").

Buying your own food

A wide range of foods is available in the markets, and basic vegetables like potatoes, cereals, onions, tomatoes and yams are roughly the same price throughout the country, with reductions near the place of cultivation. Fruit and vegetables for export, such as pineapples, avocados and mangos, vary enormously in price depending on area and season. At harvest time in a growing area you can buy a sack of ten pineapples for CFA1500.

Good **bread and pastries** are available throughout the country at fixed prices, and there's a good selection of **supermarkets** in most major towns. One final bargain, wherever you might be in Cameroon, are the locally produced **chocolate bars**.

Drinking

Brewing is the country's second biggest industry, something that is evident in the vast selection of **beer** (the largest in Africa) on sale pretty much everywhere. Even in the most remote corners where public transport is sparse – you can be certain that, even if everything else fails on the rough road, the beer truck will get through. Brasseries du Cameroun produces the most popular brands: **La 33 Export** and **Castel**, while Guinness Cameroon produce a dark and bitter **Guinness FES** – stronger than its Irish counterpart, enjoyed in the north with kola nut to enhance its sweetness. They also brew the more expensive **Gold Harp**, considered the most prestigious of Cameroon's beers (hence the acronym: "**G**overnment **O**fficers **L**ike **D**rinking **H**eavily **A**fter **R**eceiving **P**ayment").

You can also find the usual international **soft drinks** everywhere, as well as plenty of local, sweet, brightly coloured carbonates. Pamplemousse (grapefruit) and Djino Cocktail (mixed fruits) are tasty carbonated fruit juices. **Bottled water** can be had almost everywhere that sells drinks, and from most grocery stores.

Of **traditional alcoholic** drinks, palm wine (white *mimbo*, *matango* or *mbu*) is available throughout the south and west, hence the many names. Try to buy any wine as close to source as possible and make local enquiries to be sure that it hasn't been diluted with bad water, or artificially sweetened with saccharin. The **distilled spirit** from palm wine is generally known as *afofo* (*arki* in Francophone areas) – this "African Gin" mixes well with a tonic. Other indigenous drinks include the millet beer of the north (*bilibili*) and *kwatcha* (or *sha*), a thick, opaque corn beer.

Communications

Cameroon has a real mixture of communication facilities, ranging from sophisticated telecom systems in the metropolitan areas to virtually no communications, apart from

> Cameroon's IDD code is ☎237.

post, in remote parts of the centre and far south.

Post offices are open Monday to Friday 8am–3.30pm and Sat 8am–1pm. Letters to Europe take a week to fourteen days. The **poste restante** service operates well enough in Yaoundé and Douala, and costs CFA125 per letter.

Douala and Yaoundé have a sophisticated, generally reliable **telephone** system, with IDD to Europe and America. Connections within and between the two cities are good, though phoning upcountry is considerably less reliable. Most towns have a multitude of fax/phone shops which can tell you the best times of day for connections to different areas. Streetside **mobile phone** (cellphone) **booths** are becoming an increasingly popular alternative to using fax/phone shops. If you want to use your own mobile phone, Orange Cameroon has roaming agreements with Orange UK and Orange South Africa, as well as O$_2$ UK and Vodafone UK. MTN Cameroon has no roaming agreements yet.

Internet access is gradually spreading throughout the country; prices vary wildly – from CFA500 per hour to CFA400 per minute – depending on whether landlines or mobile phone lines are being used. Most towns are fairly well provided with cybercafés offering fast and efficient connections, though in a few towns which still suffer from unreliable landlines, Internet access tends either to be nonexistent or very expensive.

The media

Cameroon's journalists have endured well-documented harassment, despite the liberalization of the press laws in the 1990s, and as a result the press is quite limited, especially in comparison to print-mad Nigeria. The country's only daily **newspaper**, *The Cameroon Tribune* (Ⓦwww.cameroon-trib-une.cm), is published in French and English editions and presents the (laconic) voice of the government – with so few lines to read between it's hard keeping informed. The independent press mushroomed in the early

1990s but has been the target of severe government harassment since. *The Herald* is the thrice-weekly Anglophone opposition party organ, though it's almost as uninformative as *The Cameroon Tribune*. The Francophone opposition paper *Le Messager* (Ⓦ *www.wagne.net/messager*) and the *Cameroon Post* are the two most widely read weekly opposition papers and the best of the domestic press; they may or may not survive.

Cameroon Radio and Television Centre in Yaoundé broadcasts on one **television** channel across the country. The programme quality isn't bad, and there are some English-language broadcasts, but **satellite** is becoming more and more common – hotel bars are more likely to show CNN (or TV5 in Francophone areas).

CRTV also run a national **radio** station in both English and French. Local news, often in local languages, is broadcast from its ten provincial stations between programmes of African music. There is no BBC FM relay in Cameroon, though you can pick up the BBC via local stations which have broadcasting contracts near the borders of Central African Republic and Nigeria.

Directory

Airport departure tax International flights CFA10,000; domestic flights CFA500.

Arts and crafts The most famous region for art is the Bamoun–Bamiléké district of West and North West provinces, known for carved statues, masks and bas-reliefs. The long tobacco pipes used by the Tikar and other people of the region have become popular tourist items and are widely available. Northern Cameroon is more renowned for leather and jewellery, fashioned primarily by the Fulani. Samples from all the regions can be found at the Marché Artisinale in Yaoundé.

It's illegal to take antiques and certain works of art out of the country without government authorization. Many antiques are smuggled down the Gamana and Donga rivers from Nigeria, which has strict views about the export of its heritage, and harsh penalties for smugglers. If you are continuing north from Cameroon, don't buy anything that even looks old; it will almost certainly be confiscated by Nigerian customs officers, whether antique or not. There's not likely to be a problem exporting artworks through Douala airport, as export rules are loosely observed. If you want to check, contact the Délégation Provinciale du Tourisme in Douala (☎342.14.22 or 342.11.91) or Yaoundé (☎222.44.11) and they will direct you to the appropriate ministry, depending on the material the artefact is made of.

Crime Douala and, increasingly, Yaoundé are especially dangerous after dark; stabbings are common, with money the main motive. It's safest not to carry anything of value in the street – preferably not even a bag – and to follow carefully local advice about which areas are dangerous. Always try to look as if you know where you are going. Cameroonian justice is rough: the death penalty exists even for minor thefts, though few get as far as the courts. They may be dealt with by a roughing-up behind the police station or, if the cry of "*voleur!*" heard, by a beating from an angry crowd.

Dress and appearance Cameroonians are easy-going when it comes to dress code, and unless you're on official business, you can basically wear what you want. Having said that, a strong streak of puritanism runs through Cameroon's official psyche, especially in the Anglophone regions, and Western men will attract the disdain of officials if they go bare-chested, wear earrings or have long hair – especially in dreadlocks. Non-officials, however, tend to be a lot more open-minded. Shorts are acceptable if you are engaged in some kind of sporting activity, like hiking or biking, or if it's obvious that you're on holiday. In the Muslim areas of the north the dress code is not nearly as strict as in neighbouring Nigeria, and although it's recommended that women should cover up knees and shoulders (especially when visiting mosques), it's not obligatory, and certainly not in Kirdi areas, where traditional religion often encourages walking around stark naked (dressed in only a few nose spikes and a string around the waist).

Education Cameroon performs relatively well in terms of education compared to many of its neighbours. In 1994, the last time a survey was carried out, nearly ninety percent of children were receiving primary education and, in 1995, UNESCO estimated the adult literacy rate at over sixty percent. The University of Yaoundé now has 50,000 students, and in the early 1990s, the specialist faculties at Douala, Dschang, Buea and Ngaoundéré were upgraded to university campuses. Students from South West and North West provinces commonly head to Nigeria to pursue higher education.

Emergencies Police ☏ 17; fire ☏ 18.

Football Soccer, always a wildly popular sport in Cameroon, had its status lifted almost to that of a religion by the Indomitable Lions' mighty result in the 1990 World Cup (they reached the quarter-finals at odds of 100:1). Two contentious disallowed goals in the 1998 World Cup match against Chile lost Cameroon the game and took them out of the competition, leaving the nation feeling cheated. Things were even worse during the 2002 World Cup, when the team failed to progress beyond the first round, having lost to a ten-man German side and conceded a late draw to the Republic of Ireland – especially disappointing given that Cameroon had just won the African Cup of Nations in 2001 and the Olympic championship in 2000. Cameroon certainly has some of Africa's, and the world's, finest players, though regrettably for home games, many have given their careers to European clubs. The big teams are Canon of Yaoundé, Bamboutos of Mbouda, PWD of Bamenda and Cottonsport of Garoua. The death in 2003 during an international game of Marc-Vivien Foe paralysed the nation for days.

Holidays and festivals Shops and administrative services all shut down for the major Muslim and Christian holidays. The most important of the official holidays, the Fête Nationale, takes place every May 20. On this day, parades and speeches commemorate the 1972 approval of the referendum for a united Cameroon. Other national holidays include Labour Day (May 1) and Youth Day (February 11). Local festivals take place too, the most well-known of which are the Lela festival in Bali (mid-Dec); the grass-gathering ceremony in Bafut (end of April); and the End-of-Year festival, also in Bafut (late Dec); the Ngoun festival in Foumban

(Dec); and the harvest festivals in the north (Jan–March).

Opening hours Most businesses, banks and offices follow the practice of continuous weekday opening (Mon–Fri 7.30/8am–3pm, Sat 8am–1pm), but the old opening hours (Mon–Fri 8am–noon & 2.30–5.30pm) are also common. As a general rule, the further north you go, the higher the chances are that shops and businesses will be shut during the hot lunchtime hours.

Photography Taking photographs is hedged about with restrictions. These go beyond the usual military and "national security" taboos to include anywhere the president is likely to stay when travelling, parades, festivals and anything "likely to cause a decline in morality and damage the country's reputation". The interpretation of this law is left to the person who decides to take you to task for breaking it. Taking pictures in Yaoundé, Douala and anywhere in the forest zone is likely to lead to trouble unless you're very discreet or very charming.

Religion About half the population follows traditionalist belief, while around a third are Christian and a sixth Muslim. About half of Christians are Catholics and the other half affiliated with Protestant denominations. The Northwestern and Southwestern Anglophone provinces are largely Protestant; the Francophone provinces of the southern and western regions largely Catholic. Muslims are concentrated mainly in the northern provinces, and the Bamoun people of West Province are also predominantly Muslim. Cameroon's large population practising traditional African religions is mostly found in the rural areas, rarely in the cities.

Wildlife and national parks Cameroon is blessed with a wonderful natural heritage, as Gerald Durrell discovered in the 1950s. The country's national parks offer the closest thing to an East African safari to be found on this side of the continent, and there are greater opportunities for walking too. Cameroon has the last – dwindling – population of rhinos in West Africa, along with most other African big game, including large numbers of elephants. Fortunately, the government seems fairly committed to saving some of its wildlife – even at the expense of lucrative logging contracts and difficult decisions

CAMEROON | Basics

over local development. The latest initiative, in league with the influential Worldwide Fund for Nature, is taking place in the extremely remote southeastern corner of the country, south of Yokadouma. Of the three areas of wildlife-rich rainforest in this area, Lake Lobéké Forest is now a national park and will be managed by the World Wildlife Fund. It's hoped that the other two reserves, Nki and Boumba Bek soon will follow suit. The country actively encourages paid-up hunting, as part of its conservation strategy.

A brief history of Cameroon

The first **Bantoid-speaking peoples** moved to the southern half of the Cameroon region from the Nigerian plateau by 200–100 BC, displacing the original inhabitants, the so-called "Pygmies", and pushing them deep into the forests. But the earliest clearly defined presence in Cameroon is that of the materially advanced **Sao culture**, which developed around Lake Chad and left archeological evidence in the form of bronze and terracotta human and animal figures, coins, dishes, jewellery and funeral jars. From the eighth century, the Sao evidently began mixing with peoples who had been pushed south by the powerful empire then forming in Kanem (the Kotoko who live along the banks of Lake Chad and the Logone River are thought to be their descendants).

Today, Cameroon is a complicated mixture of peoples, none of them really predominant. As an archetypal example of an artificial state, its present configuration derives in large part from the imposed colonial history of the last hundred years, a legacy from which it is still struggling to break free.

The arrival of the Portuguese

In 1472, the Portuguese navigator **Fernando Po** led an expedition around the Bay of Biafra, becoming the first European to penetrate the estuary of the **Wouri River**, which he called Río dos Camarões ("Prawn River"). From this time on, the coastal region gained influence, taking over from such northern powers as the **Bornu Empire** (which extended down to the Benoué in the sixteenth century). The centre of trade shifted to the regions around Douala, Limbé and Bonaberi, where local chiefs signed consecutive trade agreements with the Portuguese, Dutch, English, French and Germans. These chiefs rounded up slaves and ivory which they traded for cloth, metal and other European products.

Although commerce flourished over the ensuing four centuries, the Europeans didn't settle on the Cameroonian coast until the nineteenth century, when British missionaries began to protest against the **slave trade**. In 1845, an English pastor, **Alfred Saker**, founded the first European settlement in Cameroon at Douala. Although he set up churches and schools Saker was hardly a liberator. He recognized early on the strategic importance of **Douala** and **Victoria** and pushed for them to become crown colonies.

With the arrival of British, German and French **commercial houses**, trade shifted to "legitimate" exports of palm oil, ivory and gold. But the **Douala chiefs** became increasingly worried they would lose their role as middlemen between interior peoples and the Europeans and sought British guarantees that would have led to a protectorate. Queen Victoria hesitated. By the time she finally sent an envoy to make an arrangement, the Germans had beaten her to it. On July 12, 1884, **Gustav Nachtigal** signed a treaty with the Douala chiefs **Bell**, **Deïdo** and **Akwa**, who willingly ceded their sovereignty to Kaiser Wilhelm in exchange for trade advantages.

The German, French and British occupations

In 1885, Baron von Soden became the first governor of Kamerun, and spent the next ten years trying to quell **rebellions** in the interior. He was replaced by **von Puttkamer**, who relied on forced labour and brutality to carve out the colony's first **railway line** in 1907. But the promising economic results of the German activities, which included building some roads, hospitals and schools, came to an abrupt halt with the outbreak of **World War I**. In 1916, after a long, arduous and bloody campaign, the Allies wrested control of the territory from Germany. In 1922 it was officially placed under French and British mandates – though only about one-fifth of the area was ceded to Britain.

The **British Cameroons** were joined to Nigeria in an administrative union, but lay outside the framework of development plans for Nigeria, and received only minimal funding. Ironically, much of the growth in the region after World War I was spurred by the **Germans**, who returned as private citizens to develop the plantations around the Victoria plains. (When, in the 1930s, many of them rallied to the call of Nazism, they were expelled and their private development efforts consolidated into the Cameroon Development Corporation, today the country's second biggest employer.) The **French** were more active in developing the infrastructure. Cultivation of the main export commodities of cocoa, palm oil and timber increased dramatically. French plans, however, relied heavily on exacting taxes or forced labour (in lieu of tax) to extend the road network, enlarge Douala's port and build up the vast plantations – activities which led to well-founded grievances against French rule.

The beginnings of nationalism

After World War II, the United Nations renewed the French and British mandates. The **British sector** continued – essentially – to be ruled from Nigeria. On the eve of independence, two camps emerged; the first pushing to become a state within the Nigerian federation; the second calling for reunification with "the other" Cameroon.

In the **French territory** the call for reunification was also voiced. Political parties began to form, including the **Union des Populations Camerounaises** (UPC) and the less radical Bloc Démocratique Camerounais of northerner **Ahmadou Ahidjo**.

The UPC was the first party to call both for unification of the two separate Cameroons and for **independence from France**. Prevented by force of opposition from attaining these demands legally, it organized a **revolt** in the larger towns of the French colony in 1955. The uprising was put down, but at the cost of hundreds of lives and huge economic waste and destruction. The UPC, using increasingly extreme and violent liberation tactics, was banned in 1956 by the French government, but its influence barely diminished, especially in the Bamiléké country and Sanaga region, where rebellion continued to foment and was brutally suppressed.

The UPC's actions acted as a catalyst to Cameroonian nationalism and focused the attention of more conservative parties on developing specific policy. Its influence was felt by leaders such as Ahidjo, who was still working within the political mechanism put in place by the French. In 1958 he founded a new party, **l'Union Camerounaise**, and became the prime minister of the Assemblée Legislative du Cameroun. His platform called for reunification, total independence and national reconciliation.

Independence

Ahidjo met his first aim when he proclaimed **independence** on January 1, 1960. The following year, his goal of reunification was also partly satisfied. Following a United Nations plebiscite, the northern half of the former British territory voted to join Nigeria, while the southern British Cameroons voted to join the Francophone territory. But national reconciliation proved more difficult as the UPC problem dragged on and it took a further twelve years before Ahidjo (with continued French assistance) prevailed over the rebels, when their last members were executed. In a remarkably astute piece of political manoeuvring, he then neutralized much of the internal opposition by integrating it into his government and the enlarged party, **l'Union Nationale Camerounaise**.

As the political wrinkles were being ironed out – symbolized by the adoption of a new constitution, the dissolution of the federal system and the formation of the **United Republic of Cameroon** in 1972 – progress was also being made on the economic front. Like Houphouët-Boigny in Côte d'Ivoire, Ahidjo focused first on developing agriculture and then moved on to basic industry. Thanks in part to the discovery of oil, the country's GNP nearly doubled in the first twenty years of independence. By the end of the 1970s, Cameroon was thus shaping up

as one of the rare stable countries in the region. If reports of political prisoners and repression trickled out of the country, and Anglophone students (to single out just one obvious group) were supremely dissatisfied with the way Cameroon was going, the West turned a blind eye to the autocratic excesses of a reliable friend.

A change of regime

Yet, as the years dragged on, it looked as though Ahidjo was settling into a pattern all too familiar in post-independence Africa – that of the powerful political leader who refuses to relinquish power or look to the future. He had been president for 22 years when he rather unexpectedly stepped down in 1982, citing ill-health as his reason. Just as Senghor had done in Senegal, he passed the sceptre to a young prime minister of his own grooming, though from a different background – the 49-year-old bilingual southerner, **Paul Biya**. Despite being recognized for his honesty and competence, Biya had barely been in office a year when his reputation, and that of Cameroon, took a beating in the international press.

Trouble started in 1983 when Biya fired the prime minister and several members of his cabinet, on the grounds that he had uncovered a **treasonous plot**. Ahidjo resigned as UNC party boss and, from his residence on the French Riviera, openly criticized his heir, claiming that Biya was turning Cameroon into a police state, and asserting that he had been tricked into relinquishing power by faked health reports (it seems the former president was resentful that Biya would not allow him to transfer his vast fortune out of Cameroon, and was sensitive to Muslim worries that the balance of power had shifted to southern Christians). The showdown had begun, but Biya seemed to have all the cards, and Ahidjo was sentenced to death in absentia.

Although Biya then pardoned his predecessor, things went from bad to worse in 1984, when units of the presidential guard formed by Ahidjo (and still loyal to the ex-president) revolted in Yaoundé. They were only put down by the army after three days of street fighting in the capital and an unknown death toll that has been estimated at as many as 1000. Ahidjo denied any involvement, but Biya cracked down on dissidents, and dozens of guard members were secretly tried and executed. Calm returned and Biya consolidated his position, but the incident showed the world that, even in Cameroon, stability is fragile.

Consolidation of power

For months after the coup attempt, Biya rarely left the presidential palace. Indeed, many observers expected a further attempt to overthrow him, and it was widely believed that an irreparable rift between the north and the rest of the country had been opened. But after a series of purges within the government, military and public sector, the president seemed to gain confidence.

As the nation prepared for the five-year congress of the UNC, in 1985, expectations ran high that Biya would announce sweeping reforms, including the revival of a multiparty system. Such hopes were disappointed when the president directed that no legal opposition to the ruling party would be allowed. Furthermore, he announced he was changing the UNC's name to the Rassemblement Démocratique du Peuple Camerounais (RDPC), apparently a move to distance the political body from its association with Ahidjo. At the same time, he moved towards a **cautious democratization** within the party, and in 1986 elections were held for members of RDPC bodies from the village level up to the *départements*, which saw the emergence of a number of new faces.

At the **international level**, relations improved with the West, and in 1985 Biya made a much-publicized official visit to France. This was viewed as a conciliatory move, as the two countries had been on bad terms due to the widely believed suspicion of French complicity in the attempted coup of 1984. In 1986, Cameroon became the fourth African nation, after Zaire (Democratic Republic of Congo), Liberia and Côte d'Ivoire, to restore diplomatic relations with Israel, partly in response to the wishes of the American government, with whom Biya was seeking closer ties after the cooling of relations with France.

These events, however, were largely overshadowed by the worst natural disaster in the nation's history. In late 1986, an eruption of underwater volcanic gases escaped at **Lake Nyos**, a crater lake in the grassfields of North West Province. A cloud of deadly chemicals leaked into the atmosphere, suffocating as many as 3000 people almost instantly and killing thousands of livestock. The catastrophe caused great insecurity among local people, who still depend heavily on the crater lakes for fish and drinking water, and even some of the country's Anglophone intelligentsia persisted in the belief that a crude American or Israeli experiment in chemical warfare had been carried out at the lake site. Rumour aside, Lake Nyos served to bring Cameroon under the international spotlight once again.

At the end of 1986, Biya announced that **elections**, scheduled for early 1989, would be brought forward to April 1988. The sole presidential candidate, he was "elected" to a new term by 98.75 percent of the votes – albeit a bit of a dip compared to his 99.98 percent win in 1984.

The 1990s

At the end of the 1980s, Biya's great strength – apart from skill at political manoeuvring – lay in the relative stability of the economy. Cameroon moved to the middle-bracket status of underdeveloped nations, with a gross national product per person considerably above West Africa's average. When coffee and cocoa prices dropped in the early 1980s, Cameroon was able to fall back on its rapidly growing oil exports, which actually pushed foreign trade into a surplus. But as the country entered its fourth decade of independence, economic and political stability were about to undergo serious challenges.

Not that the decade didn't start without optimism. In 1990, Biya indicated a willingness to go down the road to a multiparty system. However, Amnesty International's much publicized concern about **political detentions and torture** and steady pressure from Paris on reforms, explicitly tied to **debt relief**, made this announcement of measures to liberalize politics look like a response to unexpected events, rather than a planned programme of reform. Nonetheless, in anticipation of the changes, the newly formed, but unlicensed **Social Democratic Front** – the vanguard of the pro-democracy movement – proceeded, despite a government ban, with its inaugural rally in Bamenda in May 1990. The organizers managed to get over 30,000 people onto the streets. After a peaceful demonstration, attempts to disperse the crowd met with stone-throwing and, in the ensuing rout, troops shot into fleeing marchers, killing six people and injuring dozens more. On the same day in Yaoundé, the university campus was the scene of brutal attacks on students supporting the rally.

Leaders of the SDF, not all of them from the Anglophone region, claimed that the Anglophone districts were being treated like a colony by the Francophone areas. As support withered for the government in North West and South West provinces, the Bamiléké of West Province – powerful in Cameroonian commerce – also lost enthusiasm after the slaying of a senior lawyer, **Pierre Bouobda**, at a Bafoussam roadblock. The ill will from the west, added to continued resentment from the north about the treatment of Ahidjo and his barons, contributed to a heavy show of support for the opposition.

As pressure mounted, the national assembly adopted a draft law in December 1990 for the introduction of a multiparty political system. By early 1991, over twenty opposition parties had registered and – under the banner of the **National Coordination Committee of Opposition Parties** (NCCOP) – collectively began calling for a national conference to outline the country's political future.

Biya flatly refused, and seemed taken aback that the opposition, with its disparate regional, ethnic, religious and political elements, had united so quickly against him. He placed seven of Cameroon's ten provinces under military rule, lashed out at the mushrooming **independent press**, and prohibited opposition gatherings. As security forces became increasingly violent in their crackdown on opposition rallies, the NCCOP tried a tougher tactic – a nationwide campaign of civil disobedience. **Operation Ghost Town** began in July 1991 as a highly effective strike that closed the ports and brought business and transport to a halt from Monday to Friday. The economic effect was crippling for the big towns and industries. Even in Douala, business slammed to a standstill.

The strikes dragged on through November 1991, when the government, opposition and civilian organizations agreed on the formation of a constitutional committee. Biya finally consented to release all political prisoners, lifted the ban on opposition meetings and set legislative elections for February 1992. Not everyone was happy, however. As Biya began tailoring the process to suit RDPC aims (he insisted on a single round of voting and forbade coalitions from participating), many opposition elements – including two of the four principal parties, the SDF and the Union Démocratique Camerounaise – called for an **election boycott**. The RDPC won 88 of 190 seats.

Biya's political support was clearly flagging, and a secret committee, set up to control every aspect of the poll, made a shameless attempt to influence the National Vote Counting Commission and skew the voter register. The domestic media were tightly controlled, and the Douala-based printing house which published most of the independent newspapers was surrounded and closed.

But the principal opposition contender – the SDF's **John Fru Ndi**, an Anglophone bookseller from Bamenda – was better organized than Biya expected and gathered widespread support throughout the country. Internationally, he scored high marks as he travelled to Germany, Britain and the US, and Nigeria openly backed his candidacy.

The opposition's momentum, however, was no match for Biya's tight control over the election process. After the polls of October 11, 1992, the president claimed 39.9 percent of the vote to Fru Ndi's 35.9 percent. The United States' National Democratic Institute, which had monitored the elections, wrote a scathing report of wilful fraud and widespread irregularities. Predictably, demonstrations broke out. Amnesty International reported mass arrests and related deaths as a **state of emergency** was declared in western Cameroon. Fru Ndi and other prominent leaders were placed under house arrest. Journalists were detained and tortured.

The bad press refocused international attention on Cameroon. South Africa's Nobel Prize–winning peacemaker **Desmond Tutu** tried to negotiate a settlement, but the government and opposition were too far apart to consider his proposals for a unity government. After his release, Fru Ndi flew to Washington, where President Clinton quickly imposed economic sanctions on the Biya government. For his part Biya flew to Paris and negotiated a loan of $115 million to help stave off IMF pressure to resolve the growing **national debt crisis**.

Biya's recovery

Biya, who had spent years cultivating the image of a humane and stable leader, came out of the fight bruised and battered, with international papers describing him as a degenerate autocrat. Nonetheless, Biya slowly gathered hesitant support from the international community. His first major breakthrough came at the end of 1995 when, after protracted discussions, Cameroon was admitted into the **Commonwealth**, despite opposition objections that the country did not respect stipulated standards of human rights and democracy. Improved ties with Britain piqued French interest in Biya, as did the fact that by the end of the 1990s, Cameroon was one of the few Central African countries that was not in complete crisis. Given the regional instability, foreign governments were reluctant to stir up divisions within Cameroon and resigned themselves to the status quo.

At home, the president was effective in dividing the opposition. Western Cameroonians increasingly called for a return to a federal system of government, while more radical members advocated **secession**. In 1995, the **Southern Cameroons National Council** (SCNC) emerged and called for an autonomous state. English-speaking representatives in the government criticized the demands, which also alienated Bamiléké support within the SDF. By focusing on regional rather than national issues, the movement estranged northerners from an opposition coalition; their principal party, the Union Nationale pour la Démocratie et le Progrès (UNDP) had participated in the legislative elections and could therefore pursue regional aims in parliament.

By the time of legislative elections in 1997, there was little cohesion left within the opposition, but Biya took no chances of an upset, exercising a tight control over the proceedings and refusing once again to create an independent electoral commission. International observers substantiated opposition accusations of vote

15

CAMEROON | Basics

rigging and fraud, though there was little they could do about it. The RDPC claimed 109 of the 180 national assembly seats, the SDF took 43, and the UNDP saw its representation sink to 13 seats.

Despite the setback, the opposition failed to unite behind a single candidate for the presidential elections later that year, deciding instead to call a boycott, citing the country's history of corrupt elections and the lack of any meaningful reform. Criticism by the United States and France of the boycott as "undemocratic" signalled the fact that Western countries had abandoned supporting change in Cameroon in favour of seven more years of Biya.

Only the **threat of war** shifted the focus from domestic politics. Throughout much of the 1990s and into the new millennium, hostilities with Nigeria flared over the long-disputed border at the Bakassi Peninsula. Though the conflict was originally limited to localized incidents, the military posturing on both sides led to clashes in 1996. Tensions eased in 1998, following an exchange of more than two hundred prisoners of war, but the 2002 ruling by the International Court of Justice in The Hague that sovereignty should be given to Cameroon caused tensions to rise again. Nigeria promptly rejected the ruling, and troops were re-posted on both sides of the border, while a joint commission was set up by the UN to negotiate a new settlement acceptable to both parties.

At home, addressing the **economy** and keeping relations as smooth as possible with foreign creditors continued to be Biya's biggest task. By 1999, the IMF was financing its fifth structural adjustment agreement with Cameroon and, in a notable turnaround from ten years earlier, was lauding the country for its effective implementation of the programme. As 2000 approached, economic growth was above 5.5 percent, with inflation held at 3 percent. But despite the good news, the German-based non-governmental organization Transparency International ranked Cameroon as the **world's most corrupt country** in 1998. Biya downplayed the report, but still promised to crack down on those "who are well versed in cheating, fraud and even swindling". Though a few prominent managers of state-owned companies were sacked after the report, there still remains substantial room for improvement.

Despite the economic upswing, members of Biya's own cabinet acknowledged that the country's positive economic growth had not brought much in the way of improved development to the country. One hope of reversing this trend was the building of a thousand-kilometre **pipeline** from the oilfields of southern Chad through Cameroon to the port at Kribi. Despite objections by powerful international environmental lobbyists, the project was begun in 2000 and the country now stands to gain $20 million annually when oil starts flowing (currently expected to start by late 2003). The timing is fortuitous since Cameroon's own oil industry has declined and the country will soon be a net oil importer. The new pipeline-funded road linking Bertoua to Meiganga via Garoua-Boulai was another tangible benefit.

Despite economic and social problems – unpaid back-salaries, unemployment, poor health and education services and rampant corruption – Biya's RDPC once again triumphed easily in the parliamentary and municipal **elections** of July 2002, taking 286 of the country's 336 town councils (compared to 219 in 1997), while Fru Ndi's SDF lost heavily (taking just 21 seats compared to 43 in 1997). As usual, these elections were accompanied by widespread claims of fraud and vote-rigging – in many Anglophone areas election ballots simply never arrived. Biya has still to decide whether to stand for yet another seven-year term at the presidential elections scheduled for 2004. Judging by the pomp which attended celebrations marking his first 25 years in power in 2002, however, it looks doubtful whether he is ready to hand over the reins just yet.

Music

Of all Cameroon's artists, it's been musicians who have most successfully put the country on the map for a world audience. **Francis Bebey**, who died in May 2001, was Cameroon's honorary cultural ambassador to the world – a multitalented artist in the broadest sense. More familiar in the record shops is the tireless saxophonist, singer, pianist and arranger **Manu Dibango**, who helped popularize the *makossa* style. *Makossa* – the name derives from *kosa*, to strip off – is Cameroon's biggest dance music, a sexy, fast-paced rhythm, now increasingly underscored by thunderous bass and, with the influence of Paris, only a squeeze away from *zouk*. Of the hundreds of musicians, **Sam Fan Thomas** and **Moni Bile** are the two other best-known exponents.

Less enduring stars of recent years were **Les Têtes Brulées**, who became internationally famous in 1989 with an album of the same name. Their music and wild cross-cultural appearance (day-glo "tribal paint", shaved and sculpted hair and the clumpiest trainers they could find) stirred up a whirlwind of excitement abroad, and confusion and controversy at home. If their success has now burnt itself out, their fast-paced musical style, **bikutsi**, is still very popular, especially in Yaoundé.

Folk music

There are hundreds of ethnic groups in Cameroon, many of them possessing a distinctive musical culture and dances. More than two hundred different dances are still performed on a whole range of occasions, the majority accompanied by instrumental ensembles.

In the south, the **Bakweri**, **Bamiléké**, **Bamoun** and **Beti** have mostly xylophone or drum ensembles and their masked dance dramas are well worth seeing. The Sultan of Bamoun's Musical Theatre (see p.1212) is a remarkable institution. Also in the south, the **Bulu**, **Fang**, **Eton** and **Mvele**, who play a wide diversity of musical instruments including the **ngkul**, a slit drum formerly used to convey messages but now only used to accompany the **ozila** or initiation dance; the **mendzan**, a small xylophone; and the **mvet**, a long stick-zither (*mvet* refers not only to the instrument but also the pantomime and dances associated with it). The **Baka** forest people have a range of fascinating instruments, including the earth bow, which uses the forest floor as a resonator.

The Baka Forest People *Heart of the Forest* (Hannibal). Showcase for the Baka pygmies' extraordinary singing, and their various instruments – inspiration for the group Baka Beyond (whose Martin Cradick recorded this). Seamlessly stringing together trancey instrumental grooves, sploshing water drum sessions, kids' campfire rhymes and, best of all, *yelli* songs that draw you deep into the forest, the selection gives a generous overview of the Bakas' music without descending into ethnomusicology – and everyone on it gets a cut of the royalties. Check out their website Ⓦwww.baka.co.uk, which also includes a full list of albums produced by Baka Beyond, the more recent ones with a strong Celtic influence.

Francis Bebey

Africa's "Renaissance man", Bebey worked his way through jazz and most of his country's roots music. A multi-instrumentalist and musicologist, amongst other things, he defied categorization, singing in English, French and Douala, experimenting with styles ranging from classical guitar and traditional rhythms to *makossa* and regular pop. He released some twenty albums, and you never know what you'll find on any of them.

Nandolo/With Love – Works 1963–1994 (Original Music). A fine sampling of Bebey's talents, from bamboo flute to wonderful guitar and thumb-piano pieces.

Travail au noir (Ozileka/Sonodisc). From melodic guitar to traditional Bantou Lullaby, the texts are powerful and the music enchanting.

Dibiye (Pee Wee). The master's last album. Most of the tracks are sung in Douala and offer a nostalgic tribute to his African roots.

Makossa and other pop music

Makossa, the pop music of Cameroon, was created in the 1950s but has its roots in the 1930s. Mission schools created their own bands to usher the pupils into assembly, using xylophones and percussion instruments. These bands performed at dances outside school hours, playing a mixture of Western and local styles. Guitars were introduced before the war and guitarists would perform accompanied by a bottle player. There were three main dance styles at the time: *asiko* – percussion and xylophone music; *ambasse bey* – a guitar-based dance with much faster rhythms; and the fledgling *makossa*, a popular folk dance, named after the word for "to strip off".

Although *makossa* endures, other styles are more ephemeral. The huge publicity given to **bikutsi** – the war rhythm of the Beti people zapped up for amps and guitars – in the early 1990s was at least partly due to the ethnic provenance of the president. Although still very much alive locally, it looked for a few months in 1994 as if **Les Têtes Brulées** would make it big on the world stage.

Bend-skin is a kind of percussion-led folk music, of which Kouchoum

Mbada are the main protagonists. Recently, a new wave of female singers such as **Sally Nyolo** and **Coco Mbassi** have risen to international prominence. A far cry from *makossa* and other energetic dance beats, their music is based on an adherence to simple melodies enhanced by searching lyrics.

Moni Bilé

Suave but exciting, Bilé is one of the best *makossa* musicians and was the most influential artist of the 1980s – his high-tech productions outsold all others.

10th Anniversary: Best of Moni Bilé (MAD Productions/Sonodisc). Enjoy the mellow growl and revisit those great dancefloor stirrers, "Bijou" and "O Si Tapa Lambo Lam".

Amour & Espérance (JPS). Mellow love lyrics, although still with an underlying *makossa* dance feel.

Manu Dibango

Sax-player, composer, singer, pianist and arranger, Dibango's inspirations are diverse. He has lived and recorded in Brussels, Paris, Zaire, the United States, Jamaica and Côte d'Ivoire. He started a whole wave of urban popular music with the release of his album *Soul makossa* in 1973 (somewhat confusingly named, as it contains nothing that a Cameroonian musician would recognise as *makossa*). This record paved the way for a new generation of artists who now rely on a combination of traditional inspiration and high-tech recording facilities to produce the highly exportable dance music that has turned Douala into one of the dynamos of African music. Now in the superstar class – more than thirty years after his first single – Manu Dibango is one of the few African artists guaranteed to draw a full house anywhere in the world.

Live '91 (Stern's). The catalogue of Africa's foremost jazz sax-player is so vast, it's hard to know where to begin. If you find nothing to enjoy amongst the eclectic set on this old but representative CD, then you probably don't like him.

Homemade (Celluloid/Melodie). Classic cuts from the 1970s when Manu was really blowing up his own kind of Afrofusion into a massive sound. Includes the often reprised "Ah Freak son fric".

CubAfrica (Celluloid/Melodie). Mellow versions of Cuban classics, accompanied on acoustic instruments by Cuarteto Patria and Manu's eternal guitar partner, Jerry Malekani.

Sax & Spiritual (Soul Paris). One of his more jazzy albums, made in faultless collaboration with Guinean pianist Lamabastani.

Anthology (Eagle Records). Triple CD covering Manu's best tracks and offering an excellent introduction to his unique range of styles.

Kamer Feeling (JPS). Recent album where the sax once again takes centre stage in a world of afro-soul-jazz.

Lapiro de Mbanga

Master of Cameroonian rap – Mbanga's music offers a tough blend of politics, rhythm and language couched in a range of styles from *makossa* to Congolese *soukous*.

Ndinga Man Contre-Attaque: na wou go pay? (JPS). Featuring a tough mix of *makossa*, *zouk*, *soukous* and Afrobeat, Lapiro rebuts the criticism that he sold out to the powers that be.

Coco Mbassi

Young and talented female artist who was nominated as best newcomer by BBC Radio 3 in 2003. Before starting her solo career, Mbassi worked as a vocalist for Salif Keita, Touré Kunda, Oumou Sangaré and Dee Dee Bridgewater (to name a few). Her music has gospel and jazzy tones to it, as well as deep African roots.

Sepia (Tropical). Promising first album, with light drums and soft rhythms accompanying Mbassi's suave and multi-nuanced, gripping voice.

Sally Nyolo

A former singer in the all-female a capella band Zap Mama, Sally released *Tribu*, her first solo album in 1996, and promptly received the Prix Découverte by Radio Française Internationale. Since then she has released three more albums showing a consistent stylistic development, with increasingly thoughtful lyrics and music which attempt to find a link between her Cameroonian roots and western influences.

Tribu (Lusafrica). A strongly melodic album, with Nyolo's strong voice accompanied by hypnotic drums and guitars.

Multiculti (Lusafrica). Sally's thoughtful second album explores her own experience of the cultural contrast between the forests of Central Africa and the boulevards of Paris.

Béti (Lusafrica). Inspired by a trip back home, this album is an homage to the women of the Beti ethnic group and shows unmistakeable *bikutsi* influences, but also uses traditional instruments such as the *kora*.

Zaione (Lusafrica). Nyolo's most recent album, this cocktail of *bikutsi* and reggae is another example of how Nyolo has developed a personal style by mixing different types of music and penning lyrics drawing heavily on her own experiences.

Anne-Marie Nzie

"La voix d'or du Cameroun", Anne-Marie Nzie started singing at the age of eight and was a national star by the 1950s. Though no longer a chart-topper, she remains one of the most respected and popular female singers in the country, still pumping out robust music with her quavering, Piaf-like voice. Her semi-acoustic amalgam of traditional and modern instrumentation, and the variety of rhythms and moods make a welcome change from *makossa*.

Beza Ba Dzo (Indigo). Anne-Marie's second album projects her folklore-based material with power and energy.

Petit-Pays

Initially fronted by the unmistakeable voice of Sammy Diko, Petit-Pays became the best-known *makossa* band in the country. Diko left the band to pursue a solo career in the late 1990s and the band's fortunes took a bit of a dive before a new lead singer, Phillip Guy, brought them back into the limelight (albeit with mostly the same repertoire of songs). Hardly a day passes now when you don't hear one of their songs played somewhere, while their best-known track, "Merci Merci", has an irritating habit of popping into your head every time you hear someone say thank you.

Coup d'état (JPS). Singalong party music, with electric guitars and a drum kit that gives the music a feverish pace.

Les Têtes Brulées

Les Têtes Brulées came to Europe on a high note, just when the national football team was showing promise in the 1994 World Cup (early shows had them playing football on stage).

Les Têtes Brulées (Bleu Caraibes). The CD which broke *bikutsi* to the world, with lots of energy but little depth.

Sam Fan Thomas

Thomas recorded several albums with minor hits, but had to wait until 1984 and the release of *Makassi* to achieve a wider reputation. The album's single, "African Typic Collection", ignited his reputation when it became an international dance hit.

The Best of Sam Fan Thomas (TJR). Thomas ran out a string of soundalike records following that first big hit and tried to trademark the *makassi* style. Here we have an hour and a quarter of bright, perky, singalong tunes.

African Typic Collection (Virgin Earthworks). Four Cameroonian songs (and one stray Cape Verdean number) packaged around the mega-hit title song. With Charlotte Mbango.

No Satisfaction (JPS). Thomas's most recent and readily available album, with a wild tempo enhanced by powerful drums and bass.

Cinema

Many Cameroonian films deal with the conflict between living in a modern world and keeping old traditions alive. The profile of the country's cinema has been boosted by internationally recognized directors such as Jean-Marie Teno and Bassek ba Kobhio. **Jean-Paul Ngassa** was one of the pioneers of Cameroonian cinema with his production of *Aventures en France* in 1962, followed by *La Grand Case Bamilékée* in 1965. After *Une Nation est Née*, in 1970, Cameroonian production went into a lull until **Daniel Kamwa** brought a new spark with his 1972 prize-winning short *Boubou Cravatte*. The 1977 production of *Pousse Pousse* – a comical look at the conflict between traditional customs and modern urban lifestyles as expressed through the issue of bride price – established him as a producer with wide public appeal, even if the movie got a mediocre reception in Europe. *Pousse Pousse* was seen by some 700,000 moviegoers, making it one of the most popular African films of the period. The success was followed by *Notre Fille* in 1980.

During the same period **Jean Pierre Dikongue-Pipa** began making waves. *Muno Moto*, made in 1975, won encouraging reviews in France, although it was hardly as popular at home as *Pousse Pousse*. Pipa's other productions include *Prix de la Liberté* (1978), *Badiaga* (1983) and *Music Music* (1983).

Although Kamwa and Dikongue-Pipa are still the best-known Cameroonian producer-directors, a new generation began to emerge in the early and mid-1980s. After studying at the École Supérieure d'Études Cinématographiques in Paris, **Louis Balthazar Amadangoleda** made his first full-length film, *Les trois petits cireurs*, in 1985. Based on the novel of the same name by Francis Bebey, it looks at delinquency and its consequences.

A former professor of literature, **Arthur Si Bita** turned to film in 1978 and made a couple of shorts, including *No Time to Say Goodbye*, shot in Ouagadougou. His first feature-length film, *Les Cooperants*, traces the adventures of six youths from the city who decide to return to the village.

With his first feature-length film, *L'Appat du Gain* (1982), **Jules Takam** breaks away from common themes of bride price, marriage and traditional custom and offers instead a fast-paced political intrigue based in Paris.

Jean-Claude Tchuilen came out with a promising first feature film in 1984 – *Suicides* – a well-paced psychodrama, also set in Paris. It was banned for being inflammatory when first released in Cameroon and never bounced back commercially after the ban was lifted.

Of the new generation, **Jean-Marie Teno** has emerged as the most internationally recognized. Early shorts – *Schubbah* (1984), *Hommage* (1985) and *La Caresse et la Gifle* (1987) – earned him acclaim, but his feature, *Afrique, Je te Plummerai* (1991), thrust him into the spotlight. His follow-up to that documentary on the abuses of the Biya government, *Clando* (1996), treats similar themes of corruption and chaos in modern Africa through the story of a black-market cab driver whose scrapes with the law lead him on a journey to Germany and back. The past few years have seen the prolific Teno produce *With Chef!* (1999), exploring the failure of democracy and the exploitation of women in contemporary Cameroon; *Vacances au Pays* (1999), a personal documentary about his return to Bandjoun (West Province) after thirty years; and *Le Marriage d'Alex* (2002), a subtle but comic look at polygamy in Cameroon.

Also well known is **Bassek ba Kobhio**, whose *Sango Malo* (1991) examines a rural teacher's struggle to replace a strict and inappropriate European curriculum with education that the villagers can use to build a self-reliant community and shape their own future. He takes a revisionist view of Albert Schweitzer in *Le Grand Blanc de Lambarene* (1995), shot on location in Gabon, the site of the doctor's hospital. *Le Silence de la Forêt* (2002), inspired by a novel by Central African Republic writer Etienne Goyemide, tells the story of a teacher who meets a "pygmy" asking for food at a village party and finds himself embarking on a journey into the forest.

Finally, **Jean-Pierre Bekolo** directed his first feature, *Quartier Mozart* (1992), at the age of 25. This imaginative story features a young girl with magical gifts who transforms herself into a virile male, Mister Guy, and has a lot of fun with gender roles in the process.

Books

There's a fair number of books about Cameroon, and the country has the advantage of a dual linguistic heritage which has inspired a relatively rich literature, though predominantly in French. Books marked ⊡ are especially recommended.

General accounts and travelogues

Nigel Barley *Innocent Anthropologist: Notes from a Mud Hut* and *A Plague of Caterpillars*. The two books that did for anthropology what Durrell did for animal collecting – and infuriated anthropologists.

⊡ **Gerald Durrell** *The Overloaded Ark*, *The Bafut Beagles* and *A Zoo in My Luggage*. Durrell's animal-collecting exploits in the British Cameroons – first freelance, and then for his Jersey Conservation Trust Zoo – are delightfully recounted and still funny, apart from an unexceptionally colonial attitude to quaint native behaviour. But it's hard indeed to recognize the present town of Mamfé – even less Bafut – in his misty pictures.

Dervla Murphy *In Cameroon with Egbert*. Entertaining light read describing the picaresque adventures of Murphy and daughter on horseback in Cameroon.

History, politics, art and society

Mark DeLancey *Cameroon: Dependence and Independence*. Survey of history, economics and politics.

Philippe Gaillard *Le Cameroun* (two volumes). General political and economic survey in French from colonial times to the late 1980s.

Albert Mukong *Prisoner without a Crime*. The darker side of political life under Biya, this tells the story of six years of imprisonment with graphic details of arbitrary justice, brutality and torture. Leave at home.

Claude Njiké-Bergeret *La Sagesse de mon Village*. Cultural study of Bangangté in West Province. The author describes the difficulty of being part of two very different cultures, French and Cameroonian, and does an in-depth analysis of his Cameroonian roots.

Tamara Northern *Art of Cameroon*. Large-format, colour-illustrated survey of regions and their art.

Joseph Sheppherd *Leaf of Honey*. An American anthropologist's study of the Ntuumu people of Cameroon, laced with their proverbs and their views about life.

Colin Turnbull *The Forest People*. An account of the Ituri forest Bambuti ("Pygmies") in Congo; the best writing in English on the oldest African people. Essential, delightful reading for forest stays in Cameroon.

Fiction

Léon-Marie Ayissi *Contes et Berceuses Béti*. Satisfying collection of Beti folktales.

Francis Bebey *Agatha Moudio's Son* (translated from *Le Fils d'Agatha Moudio*). By someone better known as a musician (see p.1161), this debut novel is a tragicomic study of human relations in a traditional village society.

⊡ **Mongo Beti** *The Poor Christ of Bomba*. One of the senior figures of African literature – living in exile since 1959 – Beti's novels combine political satire with more basic human conflict. *Poor Christ*, the most cynical of his novels, deals with the perverse efforts of a French priest to convert the whole village, with disastrously ironic consequences. Later works, *Mission to Kala* and *King Lazarus* established his mastery of social satire. After independence, Beti embarked on a long period of silence until the publication of his critique of the Ahidjo regime – *Main basse sur le Cameroon*, which he followed with *Remember Ruben* and *Perpetua and the Habit of Unhappiness*.

Calixthe Beyala *Your Name Shall be Tanga* and *The Sun Hath Looked Upon Me*. An emerging name in West African fiction, Beyala's heroes are women forced to act against poverty and the injustices of male-based societies.

Benjamin Matip *Afrique nous t'ignorons*. Matip contemplates the past from a young African's perspective – separated from tradition by Western education and World War II. The novel also hits out at the exploitation of Cameroonian planters: it contributed to an outpouring of anticolonial literature in the 1950s. Matip's *A la Belle Etoile: Contes et Nouvelles d'Afrique* is a classic collection of folktales.

Ndeley Mokoso *Man Pass Man!* A string of darkly funny short stories. The subject of the title tale – maraboutic meddling on the football pitch – was rumoured as an explanation for Cameroon's success in the 1990 World Cup.

Jacques Mariel Nzouankeu *Le Souffle des Ancêtres*. Tales that illustrate the conflict between humans and the metaphysical forces that are believed to dominate their destinies.

Ferdinand Oyono *Houseboy* (translated from *Une Vie de Boy*). Oyono was one of the first satirical writers of the anticolonial period to break from an autobiographical form in this scathing satire about colonialism. *The Old Man and the Medal* (translated from *Le Vieux Négre et la Médaille*) is less caustic, but equally effective, both in its criticism of colonial insensitivity, and of blind adherence to tradition.

Guillaume Oyônô-Mbia *Three Suitors, One Husband* and *Until Further Notice*. Written in English, these three plays are comic masterpieces. His later play in French, *Notre Fille ne se mariera pas*, like *Three Suitors*, deals with the familiar theme of the bride price in a changing African society. It was made into the 1980 film *Notre Fille* by Daniel Kamwa.

René Philombe *Lettres de ma Cambuse*. Life in the urban slums described – even on the basis of personal experience – with humour. Subsequent work includes an inspired collection of short stories, *Histoires queue de chat: quelques scènes de la vie camerounaise* (also published in France).

Languages

Uniquely in Africa, Cameroon has **two official languages**, French and English, and a demanding but worthy policy of bilingualism in education and the civil service. In practice, French has always had the upper hand, as English is spoken only in the North West and South West provinces, which are inhabited by 22 percent of the population. People tend to identify strongly with their Anglophone or Francophone heritage, and it's not uncommon for tempers to rise when a person from the Anglophone regions insists on speaking English to a taxi driver in Yaoundé, or vice versa. In North West and South West provinces, people in major towns usually speak **Pidgin English**, which is a different language, and doesn't come easily to an outsider, though you'll recognize a few words. In the south, **Douala** and **Bassa** are often used as trading languages, while in the north, **Fulani** has taken on that role.

Glossary

Auberge Cheap hotel or *maison de passage*, usually with shared facilities.

Ba- Means "people of" in the Bantu and Semi-Bantu languages, widely extended (by European geographers) to indicate their towns and villages. Place names are a good deal easier to remember if this prefix is mentally dropped.

Boukarou In hotel jargon, bungalow-like huts with thatched roofs.

Chantier Literally a construction site. In Yaoundé's popular jargon "street food stands".

Circuit Northern appellation for *chantier*.

Dash Present, gift or bribe.

Gare routière Motor park.

Fon In western Cameroon, a chief or king.

Kirdi Collective name for the mountain people of the Mandara range. It means pagan, since most of these people are non-Muslim and non-Christian.

Lamidat In the north, equivalent to a sultanate. The sultan is the Lamido.

Mayo In the north, a river or dried riverbed.

Ramassage "Collection" or "pick up". You take a taxi *en ramassage*, meaning you share it (and the fare) rather than rent it individually.

Saré Sudan-style huts common in the north.

Sauvetteurs Wandering vendors, hawkers.

15.1

Douala and South West Province

he **economic capital** of Cameroon, **DOUALA** is a vast and energetic city. The driving force behind its growth has been the **port**, which handles most of the nation's maritime traffic and has stimulated regional development in trade and industry. But despite Douala's activity and relative prosperity, the cityscape is a relentless urban jungle distinguished neither by traditional flavour nor modern flashiness. Urban planners have concentrated their efforts on Yaoundé in the interior, with the result that Douala suffers from overpopulation and a worn-down and inadequate infrastructure. For **nightlife**, however, Douala cannot be beaten: its multitude of **restaurants** include some of the best in West Africa, whilst **live music** is always to be found somewhere around the corner.

There are a wide variety of natural highlights within easy reach of the metropolis. For simple rest and recuperation, you can't beat the black-sand beaches around **Limbé**, a small town with a distinctly colonial flavour at the foot of **Mount Cameroon** – West Africa's highest peak. The colonial town of **Buea** is only 70km away, 1000m up the slopes of the mountain, and makes a good base for climbing expeditions. Continuing north, **Kumba**, a vibrant commercial town located near beautiful **Lake Barombi Mbo**, makes a good stopover on the way to **Korup National Park** and Nigeria. East of Kumba, and still only a few hours' drive from Douala, **Mount Kupe** and the **Manengouba twin crater lakes** provide enjoyable hiking.

Douala

Despite its status as the nation's largest and wealthiest city, **DOUALA** is not its most attractive. The dreary architecture, relentless bustle and oppressive heat and humidity can be overwhelming, but if you can muster the energy to explore, the **market area** around the Lagos neighbourhood is the liveliest in Cameroon, while the Deido, Akwa and Bonapriso quarters offer some of the best **nightlife** in West Africa. Douala's many different facets are apparent in its many quarters, and with a population that has skyrocketed in recent years to well over a million, it has undergone some rapid changes. Although most of the city is fairly safe, crime is rampant in other areas, especially the area around the port – don't walk around with anything visibly valuable and try to look as if you know where you are going.

Some history

Like so many settlements on the West African coast, the Douala area was once home to small fishing communities who first encountered Europeans when the **Portuguese** made contact at the end of the fifteenth century. Although trade – especially in slaves – between local rulers and seafarers continued, Europeans only settled on the banks of the Wouri (or Cameroons) River in the nineteenth century. The first of these were **English missionaries** led by **Alfred Saker** who, in 1845, founded a small community at the site where the Église du Centenaire stands today. By that time, the **Douala people** (who probably arrived in the estuary at the beginning of the seventeenth century) were established in two groups united around the **Bell** and **Akwa** families.

German trading companies followed in the footsteps of the missionaries and quickly persuaded Bismarck to protect their interests in the region. The German chancellor thus sent **Gustav Nachtigal** to claim the lands in the name of the Kaiser. In July 1884, Nachtigal signed treaties with the chiefs Bell, Akwa and Deïdo. With a flick of a pen, British designs in the region were wiped out, while the Douala chiefs had ceded legal rights to the territory (at least according to German law). In 1885, a German governor was appointed and **Kamerunstadt** became the capital. The name stuck until 1907, when it was changed to Douala.

After World War I, Douala became part of the French protectorate. Although it was no longer capital of the territory, the French began large-scale urban construction, and enlargement of the port. Industry followed, and Douala forged ahead to become the economic engine of the whole country.

Arrival, information and city transport

The **airport** at Douala, a stone's throw southwest of the Bonapriso neighbourhood, handles the majority of **international** flights to Cameroon, though it's showing signs of age and is surprisingly small. It costs CFA2000 to hire a **yellow taxi** into the centre.

Moving on from Douala

By road

Almost all of Douala's *agences de voyage* with services to **Yaoundé**, **Kribi and the east** are based around the junction of bd Ahidjo and av Jamot. The main companies for Yaoundé are Central Voyages (☏342.03.16 or 342.26.69), Confort Voyages (☏983.95.27) and Garanti Express (☏342.61.91). *Agences* for **Ebolowa and the south** include Buca Voyage (☏342.29.35) and Jet Voyage. *Agences de voyage* for **Bamenda, Bafoussam and the southwest** all have offices in the Bonaberi area. Garanti Express has a second outlet here. Other agencies include Vatikan Express (☏783.95.27), for Bamenda; Jeannot Express, for Buea; and Tchatcho Voyages (☏342.02.10), for Kumba; Jeannot and Tchatcho services stop en route in **Mutengene**, where it's easy to find share taxis to **Limbé**. **Share taxis** to Limbé, Buea, Mbanga and Kumba leave from the Bonaberi motor park.

By train

Enquiries should be made in advance to Camrail (☏340.24.13 or 340.14.22), since schedules change frequently. You can buy tickets to Yaoundé and Kumba. There are two daily trains to **Yaoundé** (at 7am and 1.30pm; 4hr; CFA4000 first class, CFA2250 second). Trains to **Kumba** leave daily but are extremely slow – it's better, especially in the wet season, when the roads are bad, to take a share taxi on the good road to Mbanga and catch a train to Kumba (4 daily; 2–3hr) from there.

By air

Cameroon Airlines, 3 av de Gaulle (☏342.32.22 or 342.25.25) have flights to **Maroua** (Mon, Wed & Fri–Sun; CFA98,300 one way); **Garoua** (Tues & Thurs–Sat; CFA77,600 one way); **Ngaoundéré** (Mon, Wed, Fri & Sun; CFA60.200 one way); **Bertoua** (Mon, Wed & Fri; CFA50,050 one way); and **Yaoundé** (daily; CFA29,700 one way). Domestic airport tax is CFA500.

If you arrive **by train** from Yaoundé you'll come in at the **Gare de Bessenge**, just off Boulevard de la République in the northeastern part of the city centre. The quickest way into town from here (and the best way of getting around in general) is to catch a yellow taxi. The standard fare for a "drop" (a journey within the city limits in a share taxi) is CFA150.

Coming into central Douala **by bus** or **minibus** with an *agence de voyage* you usually end up at the company's booking office, although you can ask to be dropped off along the way. Most of the *agences de voyage* are based around the junction of Boulevard Ahmadou Ahidjo and Avenue du Docteur Jamot, less than a kilometre from the centre. *Agences* arriving from West, North West and South West provinces are based around **Bonabéri**, about 6km north of the centre across the Wouri River. You can catch share taxis from here to Rond-point Deïdo (or simply "Rond-point"), 2km to the north of the centre (CFA200), from where a second drop will take you further into the centre. The entire journey in a hired cab costs CFA1500. Long-distance drivers sometimes continue all the way into the centre. If this happens, ask to be dropped at the Wouri Cinema, which is central and within walking distance of several moderately priced hotels.

The **Délégation Provinciale du Tourisme** (☎342.14.22 or 342.14.10) is located on Avenue de Gaulle beyond the tennis club. They usually have **city maps** and information about travel in and around Douala, including an extensive list of recommended hotels in all price ranges. Some bookshops and street vendors sell street maps of Douala for CFA2000, but many streets are unnamed both on the map and on the ground. Locals and taxi drivers give directions by landmarks – hotels, nightclubs, water towers – rather than by street names.

Accommodation

Cheap accommodation doesn't really exist in Douala – even the missions charge premium rent on rooms. Although there are a number of decent places in the moderate category, the city seems to belong to the international hotels.

Inexpensive to moderate

La Côte av King Akwa ☎342.46.43. Small, box-like self-contained rooms (some with a/c), often rented out by the hour. There's also a good-value restaurant and a bar with TV. **❷**

Foyer du Marin rue Galliéni, off bd de la Liberté ☎342.27.94, ℮ doula@seemannsmission.org. One of the city's best-value mid-range places (although in theory it's reserved for the use of seamen), with clean self-contained a/c rooms, as well as a swimming pool. Popular with expats, perhaps due to the draught beer and grilled sausages. Book in advance, as it's often full. **❹**

Hila bd de l'Unité, near the Marché Central ☎342.15.86, ℱ342.33.27. Conveniently located for agency transport to Yaoundé, with well-managed, clean, self-contained rooms with a/c, plus a good-value restaurant and bar. **❸**

Lido rue Joffre, near the *Foyer du Marin* ☎342.40.86. In a quiet and therefore slightly dodgy area, with self-contained a/c rooms, plus a bar and restaurant. **❷**

Littoral 38 av Douala Manga Bell, Bali ☎342.58.05. Not the classiest place in town – it's slightly grubby – but decent value, and near the

Marché Central and the busy *Phaco* club. **❷**

Le Ndé bd de la Liberté ☎342.70.34, ℱ342.76.04. Clean mid-range place with comfortable – but ageing – a/c rooms, plus a small uninviting swimming pool and a bar-restaurant. **❹**

Procure Générale des Missions Catholiques rue Franqueville, Akwa ☎342.27.97. Very comfortable and reasonably priced establishment, with a/c and a swimming pool, but missionaries get first priority, and it's often full. **❸**

Solidarité Near *Pasta Della Mama*, Bali ☎343.13.46. Tiny and basic self-contained a/c rooms, but it's clean, cheap and it has a very affordable bar-restaurant. **❶**

Sportif av des Palmiers, Bonapriso ☎ & ℱ342.67.55. A range of self-contained rooms of varying standards, some with a/c and TV. Within walking distance of Bonapriso's nightlife, and *en route* to the airport. **❷**

Expensive

Akwa Palace bd de la Liberté, Akwa ☎342.26.01, ℮ akwa.palace@ifrance.com. The oldest of the international hotels, still boasting an older wing in all

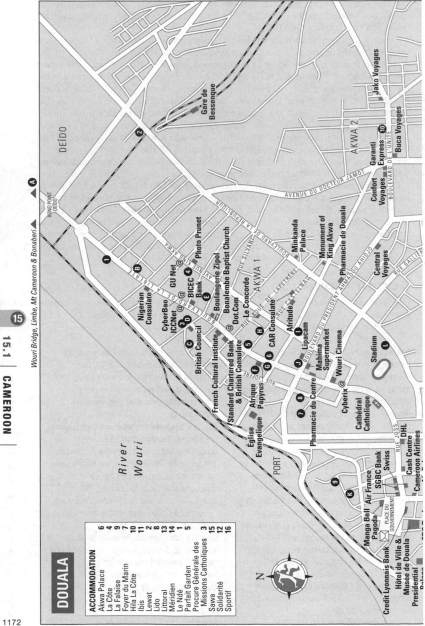

Wouri Bridge, Limbe, Mt Cameroon & Bonaberi ▲

DOUALA

ACCOMMODATION
Akwa Palace	6
La Côte	4
La Falaise	9
Foyer du Marin	7
Hila La Côte	10
Ibis	11
Lewat	2
Lido	8
Littoral	13
Méridien	14
Le Ndé	1
Parfait Garden	5
Procure Générale des Missions Catholiques	3
Sawa	15
Solidarité	12
Sportif	16

DEÏDO

ROND POINT DEÏDO ▲ Ⓐ

Gare de Bessengue

River Wouri

Nigerian Consulate

CyberBao ICCNet @ GU Net @

BICEC ④ Photo Prunet @

Boulangerie Zipol

Dot.Com @ Bonalembe Baptist Church

British Council

French Cultural Institute

Standard Chartered Bank & British Consulate

Église Evangelique

Afrique Papyrus

Le Concorde

CAR Consulate

Afritude

Lipacam

Mahima Supermarket

Wouri Cinema

Cyberix @

Cathédral Catholique

Pharmacie du Centre

PORT

RUE SYLVANI

BOULEVARD DE LA RÉPUBLIQUE

AVENUE DU GÉNÉRAL DE GAULLE

BOULEVARD DE LA LIBERTÉ

AKWA 1

AKWA 2

Minkanda Palace

Monument of King Akwa

Pharmacie de Douala

Central Voyages

Confort Voyages

Garanti Express

Buca Voyages

Jako Voyages

BOULEVARD DE L'UNITÉ

AVENUE DU DOCTEUR JAMOT

BOULEVARD DU PRÉSIDENT AHMADOU AHIDJO

RUE GALLIENI

Stadium

Manga Bell Pagoda

Air France

SGBC Bank

Swiss

Cash Centre

DHL

Cameroon Airlines

Credit Lyonnais Bank

Hôtel de Ville & Musée de Douala

Presidential Palace

PLACE DU GOUVERNEMENT

RUE JOSS

RUE KITCHENER

N

15

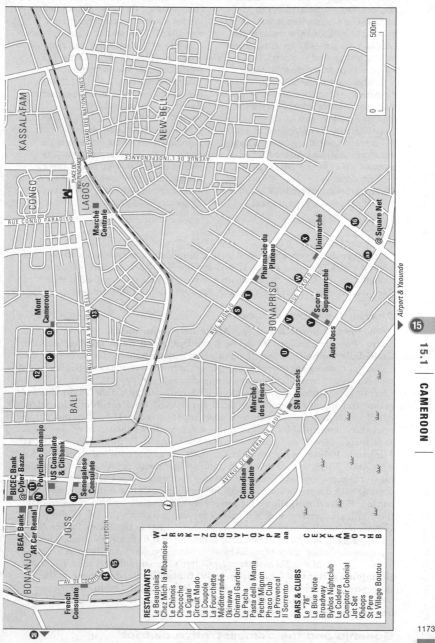

RESTAURANTS
Le Beaujolais	W
Chez Mich la Mbamoise	L
Le Chinois	R
Chococho	S
La Cigale	K
Circuit Mado	I
La Coupole	N
La Fourchette	D
Méditerranée	G
Okinawa	U
Oriental Garden	V
Le Pacha	T
Pasta della Mama	Q
Peche Mignon	Y
Phaco Club	P
Le Provencal	N
Il Sorrento	aa

BARS & CLUBS
Le "78"	C
Le Blue Note	E
Broadway	X
Byblos Nightclub	F
Le Coldera	A
Comptoir Colonial	M
Jet Set	O
Khéops	J
St Pere	H
Le Village Boutou	B

BONANJO

JOSS

BALI

BONAPRISO

NEW-BELL

KASSALAFAM

CONGO

BEAC Bank
AR Car Rental

BICEC Bank
@ Cyber Bazar

Polyclinic Bonanjo

US Consulate
& Citibank

Senegalese
Consulate

French Consulate

Canadian Consulate

Mont Cameroon

Marché Centrale

Pharmacie du Plateau

Unimarché

@ Square Net

Score Supermarché

Auto Joss

SN Brussels

Marché des Fleurs

RUE CONGO PARADISO

RUE CONGO

BOULEVARD DES NATIONS UNIES

AVENUE DE L'INDEPENDANCE

AVENUE DOUALA MANGA BELL

AVENUE DE GENERAL DE GAULLE

RUE NJONJO

RUE TOKOTO

RUE VERDUN

AV. DE COCOTIERS

PLACE DU LAGOS

INDEPENDANCE

▼ Airport & Yaounde

0   500m

15

15.1 | CAMEROON

1173

its colonial pomp. There's a pleasant pool and gardens, plus a casino and an excellent restaurant. Visa, MasterCard and Diners Club only. ⑤

La Falaise rue Kitchener, Bonanjo ☎ 342.46.46, Ⓕ 342.68.91. Perched on a hill overlooking the Wouri River, this long-established and good-value hotel has a/c rooms and a restaurant. ④

Ibis Off av de Gaulle, Bonanjo ☎ 342.58.00, Ⓦ www.ibishotel.com. Affordable luxury – though the rooms are a bit small – abuzz with the activity of the poolside terrace, restaurants and shops. Major credit cards accepted. ⑦

Lewat 2699 bd de la République, not far from the railway station ☎ 340.00.24, Ⓦ www.lewathotel .ht.st. Comfortable rooms, dedicated staff and a restaurant with a good cook who also prepares vegetarian dishes. ⑤

Méridien av des Cocotiers ☎ 343.50.00, Ⓦ www.lemeridien-hotels.com. The most

expensive and classy hotel in town, with numerous restaurants, a casino, swimming pool, tennis courts, travel agent and a well-stocked bookshop, plus free admission to a health club and gymnasium 3km from the hotel. Major credit cards accepted – which is just as well, given room rates of over CFA100,000. ⑧ (deposit CFA200,000).

Parfait Garden bd de la Liberté near *Hôtel Akwa Palace*, Akwa ☎ 342.63.57, Ⓕ 343.02.65. All the facilities of a luxury hotel, but lacking in charm. Visa only. ⑥ (deposit CFA65,000).

Sawa av de Verdun, off av de Gaulle, Bonanjo ☎ 342.08.66, Ⓔ hotelsawa@camnet.cm. Beginning to show signs of wear and tear. The main plus is the large clean pool and in-house massage service (CFA10,000 an hour). Crafts, curios and some good jewellery are sold in the foyer. MasterCard, American Express and Visa only. ⑧ (deposit CFA100,000).

The City

Douala sprawls in every direction. Much of its industry and many of its workers are housed on the far side of the Wouri Bridge, on the west bank of the river. Nonetheless, the various distinct quarters into which the town is divided – most of them named after local ruling families – aren't too difficult to work out.

Akwa: the modern centre

As the main commercial area, the **Akwa neighbourhood** is more or less the centre of the modern city. Its lifeline is the **Boulevard de la Liberté**, with the **Cathédrale Catholique** something of a landmark at its southern end. Built in the 1930s, this is one of the few attractive edifices in town, even if its neo-Romanesque style is a bit incongruous in this sweltering climate.

Continuing north, you pass the Akwa PTT (post office) and the Wouri Cinema before arriving at the wide tree-lined **Boulevard du Président Ahmadou Ahidjo**. Here, numerous department stores, supermarkets and boutiques provide an upmarket commercial backdrop for the street vendors selling clothes, shoes and accessories. North of here, along Boulevard de la République, stands the **Minkanda Palace**, an interesting palace built in a curious mish-mash of styles for King Akwa XII, who died in 1976. A statue of him stands outside the palace, while his tomb-cum-monument can be found a few hundred metres south of here. Turning back down Boulevard Ahidjo and heading east, towards the river, takes you past the **Église Évangelique** (or Temple du Centenaire), built to commemorate the 100th anniversary of Alfred Saker's arrival, and down the hill to the **port**. Continuing north along Boulevard de la Liberté leads to the **Akwa Palace** (now the *Hôtel Akwa Palace*), an old colonial hotel that was Cameroon's ultimate luxury accommodation for many years, and still retains a certain charm. Beyond the hotel on the corner of rue Silvani stands another German colonial relic, the small **Bonalembe Baptist Church** of 1899. Businesses become more sparse on Boulevard de la Liberté as it heads towards **Rond-point Deïdo**, where it turns west towards the **Wouri Bridge** and over to the industrial **Bonabéri** neighbourhood on the west bank of the Wouri River.

Bonanjo and the administrative district

Heading south from the Cathédral Catholique, Boulevard de la Liberté curves west and crosses a bridge, changing its name to rue Joss before continuing downhill to **Place du Gouvernement** and Avenue de Gaulle. This is the heart of the administrative quarter and the **Bonanjo** district. The **Poste Centrale**, with a large monument commemorating the fallen of World War I, dominates the square. On one corner, you'll see the pagoda-shaped colonial house which was once the **palace** of Prince Rudolf Manga Bell. The grandson of a Douala signatory of the German treaty, the prince was later executed by the Germans for treason. The pagoda is still owned by the Manga Bell family and now houses a travel agency, a fancy French café and the **Musée Doual'art**, home to a small collection of modern African art. Southwest of the square, the impressive **Presidential Palace**, also from the German colonial era, is out of bounds, especially if you've got a camera – stories of innocent tourists being beaten up by the security police are not unheard of.

Continuing south along Avenue de Gaulle brings you to the **Joss** neighbourhood, with its old **German colonial buildings**. North of the *Hôtel Méridien*, **Avenue des Cocotiers** gives a good impression of German colonial architecture and city planning.

The national museum

The rather forlorn **Musée de Douala** (Mon–Fri 9am–4pm; CFA1000 with a guide, CFA500 without) is housed in the **Hôtel de Ville** behind Place du Gouvernement. It's not signed anywhere; just walk into the City Hall and head upstairs and you'll find the museum on the first floor. As with all other government-run museums in Cameroon, the place lacks funding and is in a constant state of disarray. The collection consists of a dusty selection of poorly presented and inadequately explained national treasures, but gives a generous overview of regional art, and has one or two rare pieces – potentially interesting, if you're going to be travelling around the country.

Visits start in a sort of **entrance hall**, framed by posts from the famous **Bandjoun chiefdom**. Here the whole history of the nation, from the Paleolithic Age to the colonial era is embodied in a somewhat haphazard assortment of artefacts. Standing out from the clutter are some clay **Bamoun statues** and one beautiful bronze cast. The museum's two other rooms aren't much more coherent (and are currently being reorganized). If you look around, you'll find art from the forests of southern Cameroon, such as **Fang statues**, along with colourful sculpted Douala decorations for the bows of *pirogues*. A Basso cloak made of hammered tree bark is especially striking, as are various musical instruments and games. There's also a suit of mail together with spears, saddles and harnesses, and numerous sculptures, including a magnificent **bas-relief** depicting the Sultan Njoya returning from war. Last come a few thrones, and statues representing chiefs and servants. Notice the sculpted wooden posts – a traditional part of Bamiléké architecture used to decorate the house of a chief.

Markets

The districts of Lagos and Kassalafam are two of the liveliest neighbourhoods in town, and well worth visiting even if you don't want to buy anything from their bustling markets. From Bonanjo, Avenue Douala Manga Bell leads east through the Bali quarter and on to the **Lagos** quarter, where you'll find the **Marché Central** – the biggest market in the country. It spreads south of Avenue Douala Manga Bell and is hemmed in by the rue Congo Paraiso to the west. The northeast corner is marked by the busy Place de l'Indépendance and the adjacent **mosque**, in front of which assorted barks, seeds and powders – the essential ingredients of the African pharmacy – are sold. Nearby, on rue Congo Paraiso, the **Marché Congo** specializes in African and imported fabrics. The market area continues past Place de l'Indépendance up Boulevard des Nations Unies, where it merges with the **Marché de Kassalafam**, primarily a fruit and vegetable market.

Arts and crafts are sold at the **Marché des Fleurs**, off Avenue de Gaulle in the Bonapriso quarter. Foumban (see p.1212) has a reputation for being the best place in Cameroon to buy authentic artefacts (and high-quality reproductions), but this market rates a good second. They also sell good-quality jewellery as well as both real and fake antiques. The masks, both new and old (and it's pretty hard to tell which is which), are imported from all over West Africa, and are the same as those on sale in London or Paris at ten to twenty times the price.

Eating and drinking

Eating in Douala can be very expensive. Many of the upmarket restaurants are grouped in the **Bonapriso** quarter, the town's prime residential area. The town also flaunts a number of Parisian-style **cafés**, where shoppers retire for a break and businesspeople do deals. You can relax in their air-conditioned comfort for as long as you like for the price of a coffee (about CFA1000). *Akwa Palace*, *Le Délice* and *Glacier Modern* take turns at being the in place of the moment and do superb pastries for CFA1500. There's a large array of **street food** in the **Akwa** quarter near *Hotel Beausejour*, including crispy salads, spicy beans with fresh bread, and surprisingly tasty spaghetti omelettes, though the food usually runs out by about 4pm.

Cheap to moderate

You'll pay no more than CFA6000 a head (without drinks) to eat at the following restaurants and bars, and considerably less at some of them.

Chez Mich la Mbamoise bd de la République, Bali. An outdoor restaurant with a lively atmosphere, friendly staff and reasonably priced Cameroonian dishes. Count on CFA5000 per head.

Le Chinois av de Gaulle, Bonanjo ☎342.33.10. The oldest Chinese restaurant in town, and very affordable, except for the expensive Sunday buffet (CFA9000).

Chococho rue Njo-njo, Bonapriso. This popular local bakery produces the best chocolate croissants in Douala, as well as pizzas and sandwiches.

Circuit Mado Akwa, near the *Hôtel Akwa Palace*. Lively place serving homely Cameroonian cooking, featuring freshly grilled sole or *Poulet DG* – a mixture of chicken and plantains in a spicy sauce. Expect to pay CFA4000 per head.

La Coupole 105 av de Gaulle, Bonapriso ☎342.29.60. Good-value Italian-style food (including pizzas) as well as some Lebanese specialities. Expect to pay between CFA4000 and 6000 per person.

Foyer du Marin At the *Foyer du Marin*, Akwa. Tasty German sausages (CFA1500 each) and cool draught beer served in a relaxing poolside atmosphere.

Méditerranée bd de la Liberté, Akwa. Outdoor restaurant on one of the busiest streets in Douala serving Greek dishes at reasonable prices – CFA3000 for moussaka. Popular with prostitutes.

Le Pacha rue Njo-njo between the church and the pharmacy, Bonapriso. Lebanese restaurant with salads and snacks like *chawarmas* (CFA1500), plus more filling meals.

Pasta della Mama rue de l'Union Française, Bali ☎953.26.08. Italian-style food with a good-value *menu du jour* for CFA3500.

Le Provencal av de Gaulle, Bonanjo ☎342.70.17. Good-value French fare in a popular lunchtime restaurant. Weekdays only.

Il Sorrento av de Gaulle, Bonanjo. Lively pizza place with music at weekends. Count on around CFA5000 per head without drinks. They also do take-aways. Open evenings only.

Expensive

Le Beaujolais rue Tokoto, Bonapriso ☎342.70.11. Posh European cuisine, plus a small bar and a pool table.

Le Café des Arts Manga Bell historical pagoda ☎981.10.87. Upmarket rustic French restaurant with soothing (mostly classical) music. There's also a pleasant garden, excellent for unwinding with a

cool drink. Allow around CFA8000 per head without drinks.

La Cigale rue Kitchener, Joss, near *Hôtel La Falaise*. French-Lebanese place offering pizza and live music at weekends. There's also a good bar here.

La Fourchette rue Franqueville, Akwa

$\mathcal{T}$ 342.14.88. One of the few good French restaurants in Akwa – comfortable but expensive.
Okinawa rue de la Boucherie Nourry, Bonapriso $\mathcal{T}$ 342.69.10. High-quality Japanese sushi, as well as kebabs.
Oriental Garden, 10 rue Afcodi, Bonapriso $\mathcal{T}$ 342.69.38. Excellent Chinese restaurant with chefs from China. Allow CFA15,000 per head.
Peche Mignon Opposite Score supermarket, Bonapriso. Excellent French food in cosy surroundings.

Phaco Club Just off av Douala Manga Bell, near the Sonel building $\mathcal{T}$ 955.30.08. As rumbustious as the warthog it's named after – but much friendlier. Tasty African food, including chicken wrapped in banana leaves and exotic bush meats, and dancers or musicians perform nightly. Allow CFA8000 per person, without drinks.
Le Tournebroche At the *Hôtel Akwa Palace* $\mathcal{T}$ 342.05.40. Top-class French restaurant; allow CFA15,000 per person without drinks.

Nightlife

Douala's **clubs** open, close down and change hands quite frequently, but even if the name of a place changes it generally remains a club, and the taxi drivers tend to know both past and present names. Clubs usually open around 11pm or midnight and close when they get quiet, sometime between 3am and 5am. Entry **prices** vary enormously for foreigners, locals, men and women, but, once in, you rarely come under pressure to spend. Drinks cost anything from CFA3000–8000, or you can buy a bottle of whisky for about CFA25,000 to be kept for you behind the bar.

Le "78" rue Sylvani, Akwa. Popular venue for expats and prostitutes, with modern light and sound systems and the latest Western music (most of the time, anyway).
Le Blue Note Near *Glacier Moderne*, Akwa. One of the best clubs in town at the moment, playing a good mix of European and Cameroonian music and attracting a large crowd at weekends.
Broadway rue Toyota, Bonapriso. The Cameroonian version of a *Hard Rock Café*, with lots of dancing and different performers every night.
Byblos Nightclub Across from *Hôtel Beausejour*, Akwa. Upmarket local club featuring mostly African music. Cheap entrance (CFA3000).
Le Coldera rue de la Joie, Deïdo. A popular locals' nightclub – you're likely to be the only foreigner here.
Comptoir Colonial Youpewe Naval Base Douala Port, Joss. Beautiful and trendy portside bar-

restaurant made of wood and bamboo. On clear days you can see Mount Cameroon from the terrace.
Jet Set av de Gaulle, near Cameroon Airlines. Attracts a mainly young Cameroonian crowd with its good mix of African and Western music.
Khéops bd de Ahmadu Ahidjo, near bd de la Liberté junction. Flashy new nightclub which is currently flavour of the month, churning out Western and Cameroonian dance tunes.
St Pere rue Castelnau, behind *Hôtel Parfait Garden*. Popular among expats as a place to begin the night, with western pop; most head off to *Le "78"* later on.
Le Village Boutou rue Kotto Deo near *Hôtel Ndé*. Traditional *balafon* music from the Bertoua area in a simple bar room with cheap beer and local food. Free entrance; the music starts at 10pm. Closed Monday and Tuesday.

Listings

Airfreight Parcels, valuables and express items can be sent and received through DHL, 224 rue Joss, Bonanjo $\mathcal{T}$ 342.36.36.
Airlines Most airline offices are in the Bonanjo neighbourhood or in Akwa along bd de la Liberté. They include: Air France, 1 Place du Gouvernement $\mathcal{T}$ 342.15.55 $\mathcal{F}$ 342.99.52; Air Gabon, near the *Ibis* hotel off av de Gaulle $\mathcal{T}$ 342.49.43; Cameroon Airlines, 3 av de Gaulle $\mathcal{T}$ 342.25.25 or 342.32.22, $\mathcal{F}$ 342.49.49, and at the *Hôtel Akwa Palace* $\mathcal{T}$ 342.26.01; Kenya Airways, at Saga Voyages, rue

de Trieste $\mathcal{T}$ 342.96.91, $\mathcal{F}$ 342.05.18; Nigeria Airways, 17 bd de la Liberté $\mathcal{T}$ 342.73.21; SN Brussels Airlines, av de Gaulle $\mathcal{T}$ 342.05.15, $\mathcal{F}$ 342.60.74.
Banks Major branches in the Bonanjo neighbourhood include: Banque Internationale du Cameroon pour l'Épargne et le Crédit (BICEC), av de Gaulle; Société Général de Banques au Cameroon (SGBC), rue Joss (which represents Thomas Cook); Société Crédit Lyonnais (SCL), rue Joss; Comercial Bank of Cameroon (CBC), av de

Gaulle; and Citi Bank in the American Consulate building. All of these – apart from Citi Bank – also have branches in Akwa, where you'll find the head office of Standard Chartered Bank Cameroon, 57 bd de la Liberté. All change cash US dollars and euros; Standard Chartered also change pounds sterling. There's an ATM at SGBC. There are lots of black-market traders in front of the *Hôtel Akwa Palace* (usually offering better rates for US dollars than the banks, as well as a quicker service).

Books Afrique Papyrus, bd de la Liberté, and the bookshop at *Hôtel Méridien* sell international magazines and books in English. Lipacam, 27 av Ahidjo, sells mainly educational books, but also has some fiction in French and a few maps. You can also usually find IGN or Macmillan maps at these places.

Car rental Avis, at *Hôtel Akwa Palace* (☎342.03.47 or 342.70.56, ℉342.70.56) and at Douala Airport (☎330.02.01); Auto Joss, rue Monoprix near the Score supermarket ☎ & ℉342.86.19; Business H Center, at *Hôtel Méridien* ☎343.27.05, ℉343.27.06; Europcar, rue Njo Njo ☎343.21.26, ℉343.21.24.

Cinemas The two big air-conditioned cinemas are Le Concorde, on rue Lapeyrère, and Le Wouri, on bd de la Liberté. The Centre Culturel Français shows French films.

Consulates Most main embassies are in Yaoundé, but a number of countries maintain consulates in Douala, including: Benin, Bepanda Collège Maturité ☎ & ℉340.21.53; Canada, 1726 av de Gaulle ☎343.31.03, ℉342.31.09; Central African Republic, next to King Akwa College, rue Castelnau ☎ & ℉343.45.47; Democratic Republic of Congo, 70 rue Sylvanie ☎343.20.29, ℉343.19.69; Equatorial Guinea, rue Tokoto, Bonapriso ☎993.84.24 or 342.96.09; France, av des Cocotiers ☎342.62.50, ℉343.31.05; Niger, next to the central mosque ☎342.63.69; Nigeria, bd de la Liberté ☎343.21.68, ℉343.07.66; Senegal, Galerie MAM, Bonanjo ☎342.28.63, ℉342.22.73; Togo, 490 rue Dicka Mpondo, Akwa ☎342.11.87; UK, 3rd Floor, Standard Chartered Building, bd de la Liberté ☎342.21.77, ℉342.88.96; USA, 3rd Floor, Flatters Building, off av de Gaulle ☎342.03.03, ℉342.77.90.

Cultural centres British Council, rue Joffre, Akwa ☎342.51.45; Centre Culturel Français, bd de la Liberté ☎342.69.96, ⓦwww.francophone.net /ccfdouala; Centre Culturel Africain, in the Collège Liberman, rue des Écoles ☎342.28.90. The latter runs courses in African languages.

Doctors For emergencies, go to Polyclinic

Bonanjo, av de Gaulle next to the *Ibis* hotel (☎343.99.10 or ☎342.17.80), or contact your consulate for advice.

Internet Cyber Bazaar, av de Gaulle across from the *Ibis* hotel ☎342.60.36 (Mon–Sat 8am–11pm, Sun 2–11pm; CFA500/hr); CyberC@fé, bd de la Liberté (CFA600/hr); Cyberix, bd de la Liberté, near Akwa post office (Mon–Fri 8am–8pm, Sun 10am–5pm; CFA1000/hr); Dot.com, bd de la Liberté (daily 8am–11.30pm; CFA800/hr); GU.net, bd de la Liberté (Mon–Fri 8am–noon & 2.30–6.30pm; CFA500/hr); Square Net, av de Gaulle, near *Hôtel Sportif* (Mon–Sat 8am–midnight, Sun noon–9pm; CFA800/hr).

Pharmacies Among the main 24hr pharmacies are Pharmacie du Centre, 38 bd de la Liberté; and Pharmacie de Douala, bd Ahidjo.

Photo processing Laboratorie Photo Prunet, 545 rue Pau, does high-quality but expensive processing; they also sell old photos of Douala.

Post office The Poste Centrale is on Place du Gouvernement in Bonanjo. Branches include: Poste d'Akwa, bd de la Liberté; Poste de New Bell, av Douala Manga Bell; and Poste de Deïdo, rue Dibombé.

Supermarkets Score and Unimarché, both in Bonapriso, stock French delicacies flown in from Paris – lobsters, caviar, champagne, pastries and fresh European vegetables, all available at something less than twice the Champs Élysées price. Mahima supermarket on bd Ahidjo and Cash Center on rue Joss are much cheaper, and sometimes have American goodies.

Swimming pools Non-guests can use the pools at the *Akwa Palace* (CFA2000), *Sawa* (CFA4000) and *Méridien* (CFA5000). They're all expensive, but worth it when the humidity gets too much. Alternatively, try the smaller pool at the *Foyer du Marin* (CFA1000).

Travel agencies Most travel agents offer a small selection of tours within the country; they tend to be expensive (around CFA800,000 for a ten-day round trip, including domestic flights) but are generally well organized. Agencies in Akwa include Jully Voyages, rue Boué de Lapeyrère behind Standard Chartered Bank ☎342.32.09, ℉342.84.38; and Jet Cam Tour, on the corner of bd de la Liberté and rue Galliéni ☎343.30.78, ℉343.27.57. Agencies in Bonanjo include Cameroun Horizon, behind the Pagoda Manga Bell ☎342.94.24, ⓔcamhoriz @camnet.cm; Ebene Voyages ☎342.29.85, ⓔebene.voyages@camnet.cm (for tours with an ecotourist twist); and Delmas Voyages, rue Kitchener ☎342.11.84.

Limbé

LIMBÉ is everything Douala isn't – small, scenic and restful – with the mass of Mount Cameroon looming to the north. This is the nearest town to Douala on the open ocean, and it owes its popularity primarily to the surrounding beaches along the shore of **Ambas Bay**. There's a holiday feel to the place, with historical touches added in its well-preserved German and British **colonial buildings** and its shady **botanic garden**. Yet despite the influx of holidaying expats and weekenders, Limbé is not the expensive and overdone resort town you might expect, and there's enough economic life in the old **port** and the market, plus the nearby oil refinery and various agricultural projects, for the town not to rely wholly on its tourist industry.

In light of the unresolved **Bakassi border dispute** with Nigeria (see p.1160) there's currently also a strong navy presence in Limbé, something that's felt most noticeably in the town's nightlife, with lots of drunken sailors getting into fights.

Some history

Limbé (called **Victoria** until 1983) was created by the London Baptist Missionary Society, after they were chased from Fernando Po by the Spanish in the mid-1850s. The missionaries turned to **Alfred Saker** – a former navy engineer converted to missionary work – and asked him to secure them a foothold on the mainland. Saker bought the lands around the **Ambas Bay** from the Isubu king, William of Bimbia, and, in 1858, founded Victoria.

At first, Victoria was effectively an African Christian colony. The first inhabitants of the town were mostly **freed slaves** from Jamaica, Ghana and Liberia, and converted Bakweri and Bimbia (indigenous peoples related to the Douala). From 1859, these townspeople were governed by their own tribunal, headed first by a Jamaican and then by a Sierra Leonean recaptive. At first, the town centred around the church, the school (established in 1860), and the missionary residences. But by the 1870s, English and German **commercial enterprises** – John Holt, the Ambas Bay Trading Co. and the Woermann Co. – had established their own businesses alongside the church. Contrary to Saker's wishes, the site was neither turned into a British naval base nor declared a British colony, but was left to the Baptists to administer.

British holdings in Cameroon were ceded to the Germans on May 7, 1875. Victoria posed a special problem, however, as it belonged technically to the missionaries and not the crown. The problem was solved in 1887 when Presbyterian missionaries from Basel purchased the land, and incorporated it into the Kaiser's colony. The town then became an important urban centre surrounded by the commercial plantations of the **West Afrikanische Pflanzung Victoria**. By the beginning of the twentieth century, the Victoria–Buea–Douala triangle had become the political and economic nerve centre of German Kamerun, and Victoria grew to become the colony's second port, exporting large quantities of cocoa and other agricultural products. Although the Victoria territory became part of the British protectorate in 1915, German companies swiftly regained economic control of the district by buying back their old concessions.

With the outbreak of World War II, the Germans' lands were once again confiscated. In 1947, the British founded the **Cameroon Development Corporation** (CDC), and the vast regional plantations – dense stands of cocoa, bananas, oil palms and rubber trees which can still be seen as you drive through the region – spurred Victoria into a new period of expansion. After independence, the CDC was taken over by the government, and although it has since been partially privatized, it remains the district's biggest employer. In recent years, Limbé has become an opposition stronghold and a focus of Anglophone resentment at being treated in a colonial fashion by Yaoundé.

Arrival and accommodation

The motor park used by vehicles to and from **Douala**, **Buea** and **Kumba** is at **Mile 4**, on the Douala road. Most **hotels** cater to affluent Douala weekenders. However, given the standards of accommodation, prices seem reasonable if you've just come from that city.

Atlantic Beach At the town end of the Botanic Garden ⊕ 333.23.32, ⓕ 333.23.33. Originally the research laboratory for the Botanic Garden, this is now Limbé's most luxurious hotel, with a/c rooms equipped with satellite TV and hot running water. The seaview restaurant is popular, as is the swimming pool (CFA1000 for non-guests). Euros, dollars and pounds accepted. ❹

Bay Near the main roundabout ⊕ 333.23.32, ⓕ 333.23.33. Clean self-contained rooms with fans in a restored colonial building with a fabulous view of Ambas Bay. This place is co-managed by the *Atlantic Beach*, though it's not nearly as luxurious, and is a bit run-down. Guests can use the *Atlantic Beach* swimming pool for free. ❸

Botanic Garden Guest House ⊕ 333.26.20. Scenically located guesthouse with a small dorm (CFA3000 per person) plus cooking facilities and a garden with access to the sea and space to pitch a tent (CFA1000 per person). Pay at the Botanic Garden Visitors' Centre.

Bevista Just past the *gendarmerie*, 1.5km west of the centre ⊕ 333.26.35. Basic but good-sized self-contained rooms with fans or a/c; some also have TV. ❷

Holiday Inn Resort Off Church St at the end of the road ⊕ 333.22.90, ⓔ hiresort@yahoo.co.uk.

Rapidly expanding establishment with a range of spotless self-contained a/c rooms with hot water. The restaurant does good, albeit expensive, fare, and there also a business centre with Internet access (CFA1000 per hour) and a beer garden out the back. ❸

King William Square Off the main roundabout ⊕ 774.72.11, ⓔ greenturcm@yahoo.com. Centrally located, with simple but clean a/c rooms. The manager also runs Green Tours Cameroon, which arranges treks and excursions in the area. ❸

Metropolitan Visitors Lodge Church Rd, near the *T-Complex* bar ⊕ 997.20.12. New and inexpensive place with smallish self-contained rooms with fan, a good-value restaurant and safe parking. ❷

Miramare 2km west of the centre ⊕ 333.23.32, ⓕ 333.23.33. Co-managed by the *Atlantic Beach*, but much cheaper, and with beautiful views of Ambas Bay from its seaside position. Basic but clean *boukarous*, some with a/c, and a pool (though it's sometimes infested with algae). ❸

Victoria Guest House Next to the *Bay Hotel* ⊕ 333.24.46. Friendly and homely place with a mixed bag of rooms with or without a/c, most of them self-contained, and always clean. ❸

The Town

The beachfront is the obvious place to start a visit. A main thoroughfare runs along the shoreline from **Down Beach**, the nearby **fish market** and German

Moving on from Limbé

The main *agences de voyage* in Limbé are Guarantee Express at Mile 2 (for **Bamenda**, **Bafoussam**, Douala and **Yaoundé**), and Patience Express (opposite the hospital, for Bamenda, Bafoussam, Yaoundé and Douala).

It's possible to take a share taxi 48km up the coast to **Idenao** and continue to Nigeria by boat from there (CFA10,000). Avoid the cheaper cargo vessels, which are laden with smuggled goods and apt to sink (as in June 1995, for example, when 100 people drowned), as well as tending to make clandestine entries in remote areas, leaving you with the problem of finding further onward transport. You'll also lack an official stamp in your passport, which will inevitably create serious problems with immigration officials somewhere down the road. Finally, you'll be passing through waters which are at the centre of the heated border dispute between Cameroon and Nigeria. Navy boats patrol the area and the frontiers have closed for brief periods. Check out the latest situation in Limbé before heading out this way.

15

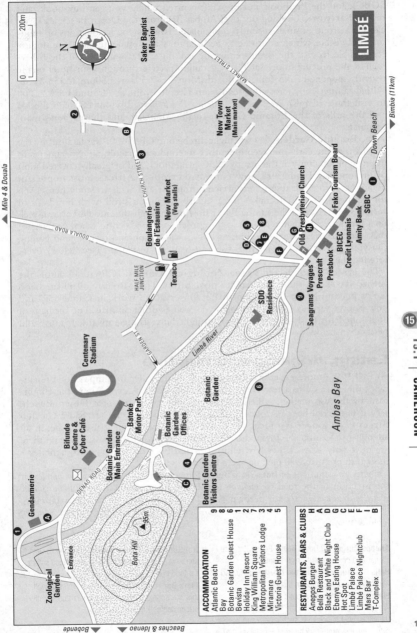

ACCOMMODATION
Atlantic Beach	9
Bay	8
Botanic Garden Guest House	6
Bevista	1
Holiday Inn Resort	2
King William Square	7
Metropolitan Visitors Lodge	3
Miramare	4
Victoria Guest House	5

RESTAURANTS, BARS & CLUBS
Aneps Burger	H
Bella Restaurant	A
Black and White Night Club	D
Ebenye Eating House	G
Hot Spot	C
Limbé Palace	E
Limbé Palace Nightclub	F
Mars Bar	I
T-Complex	B

LIMBÉ

colonial-era **government school**, over to the *Atlantic Beach Hotel*. In between are most of the town's major **banks** (BICEC, Crédit Lyonnais, Amity and SGBC), and the Presbook and Prescraft centres, where you can buy books and regional **artwork**. Looking out over Ambas Bay from the Down Beach area, you can see a group of small, recently depopulated **islands**, the foundations of buildings still visible, which continue to be used for traditional rites and ceremonies. It's possible to visit the islands either by striking a deal with one of the fishermen at the port or (more safely) by arranging a trip through your hotel or the recently reopened Fako Tourism Board (Mon–Fri 7.30am–3.30pm; ☎333.25.36, ✉ftb@camnet.cm), across the road from Crédit Lyonnais (around CFA25,000 to visit three islands). West of the *Atlantic Beach*, a road winds between the sea and the hills of the Botanic Garden to the *Miramare* and the garden's main entrance.

The **Botanic Garden** (🌐www.mcbcclimbe.org; CFA1000) was laid out by the Germans in the early nineteenth century to conduct agricultural experiments to improve productivity at the nearby CDC plantations, and originally covered most of present-day Limbé. It's now considered tropical Africa's most important botanic garden, with researchers arriving from far and wide to study here. Even for the non-specialist it makes for a superb afternoon stroll, with hundreds of varieties of trees, and the Limbé River flowing through the middle. You can pick up a brochure of suggested trails at the garden's visitors' centre when you arrive; they can also give advice on things to do in the region and recommend guides. On your way around, don't miss the *Hot Spot* bar-restaurant (see below) overlooking the bay.

The garden is connected to the **Zoological Garden** (CFA1000) across the Idenao Road past the oddly remote **post office**. This formerly dilapidated zoo is fast becoming the focus of primate conservation work in Cameroon, and now houses various species of monkey as well as other animals. The orphans of apes killed for bush meat are often brought here, as are unwanted household pets.

Eating, drinking and nightlife

As well as the more expensive **European food** on offer in Limbé's hotel restaurants, there are quite a few good inexpensive places in town. Along the Bimbia road, by the fish market, grilled fresh fish is prepared *en masse* at **Down Beach**, served with cool beer in concrete rondavels overlooking the sea. Sadly, **Garden Street** is no longer the focus for food and entertainment it used to be: in an attempt to clean up the town, the council has torn down all the shacks, and there are now only a few ladies left selling fish and beer on solitary park benches – though things may well pick up again before too long.

There are a number of **bars** on Church Street, such as the popular *T-Complex*, at the junction of the road to *Holiday Inn*. *Limbé Palace*, under *King William Square Hotel*, is the classiest a/c bar in town, with a games room in the back. For **dancing**, choose between the *Black and White Night Club* and the new *Limbé Palace Nightclub*, a block away.

Anepps Burger Off Down Beach Road. Standard burger and chicken-and-chips menu.

Bella Restaurant Behind the zoo. Well-prepared Cameroonian and European dishes.

Ebenye Eating House Around the corner from *Anepps Burger* and behind the Nigerian Union. Delicious local specialities such as *eru* and water *fufu* – *eru* is a protein-rich forest vegetable; *fufu* is pounded cassava.

Hot Spot In the Botanic Garden. The town's best sea view, plus good and reasonably priced salads, seafood and other Western dishes.

Mars Bar Perched precariously on the sea wall, this is a scenic spot for sundowners and slightly pricey seafood meals.

Around Limbé

West of Limbé, a string of **beaches** awaits, all with fine black sand (actually, a deep, bitter-chocolate colour), a result of the ocean's grinding of ancient lava flows from Mount Cameroon. The combination of lush tropical vegetation with the sea and the mountain produces a paradisiacal landscape, often enriched by the brooding purple and yellow of an impending storm or the green-and-gold sheen left behind by a recent downpour. Furthermore, the waters around here are perfect for swimming – unlike most places along the West African coast. You can get **transport to the beaches** from the Batoké motor park in front of the **stadium**. Either hire a cab direct to your destination, or take a shared taxi heading along the coast.

In recent years a number of new **seafront hotels** have sprung up in the area around **BOBENDE**, just north of Limbé past the CDC junction on Sonara road. The oldest is *FINI* (℡333.26.97, ✉dgi.pise@camnet.cm; ❹), which has an excellent restaurant and good-value rooms. The more polished *Costal Beach Hotel* (℡ & ℻333.29.27; ❹) has immaculate self-contained a/c rooms with satellite TV (some also have sea view). A few hundred metres further north is the new *Costa Marina* (℡774.72.11; ❹), with accommodation in comfortable rondavels, plus a tennis court and pool. Unfortunately, none of these hotels have particularly attractive beaches.

To get to the most popular beach, where you can also **camp**, ask to be dropped at **Mile 6**; a signboard points through 500m of palm groves to the sea. Mile 6 is a public beach with a guardian, so you have to pay CFA500 to use it, and more to camp. The nearby oil refinery isn't nearly as distracting as might be expected.

If you'd rather be watching fishing boats, head two miles further on to **BATOKÉ**, a fishing village with a stunning (free) beach surrounded by mountains that drip with vegetation. A sign on the main road leads down to *Etisah Beach* (℡997.49.98, ✉etisahbeach@yahoo.fr; ❸), a small hotel 300m from the beach on the outskirts of Batoké which offers basic rooms (fan or a/c), and a restaurant serving exotic bush-meat meals. Further along the coast, the road makes a small diversion around the tip of the massive 1999 **lava flow** before reaching **Mile 11 beach** and the luxurious *Seme New Beach Resort* (℡333.27.69, ✉camrevtour@camnet.cm; ❹), where you can use the guarded beach (CFA1000 including a soft drink) and eat at a slightly overpriced restaurant.

Beyond Mile 11, the paved road continues all the way to Idenao, passing numerous other unspoiled beaches, as well as the second wettest place on earth, **DEBUND-SCHA**, 28km from Limbé (Mile 17). There's a **crater lake** at Cape Debundscha which is well worth exploring, while from **IDENAO** you can trek through the dense forest to the **Bomana falls**. If you want to visit **Korup National Park** (see p.1191) it's possible to reach Mundemba – the village at the main entrance – by boat from Idenao; this costs around CFA60,000 per day for a six-person boat (the trip only takes a few hours but departure times depend on the tides) – it's the same boat that plies between Idenao and Nigeria, plying through creeks and up the Ndian River through an area prolific with birds and monkeys.

Heading **south from Limbé**, after 10km you pass the army camp at Man O' War Bay (no photography) before reaching the small village of **BIMBIA**, the site of the original **Camp Saker**, where the missionary first landed – relics from the slave trade can still be seen here. Today, Bimbia consists of a Baptist Church and a small holiday camping and chalet set-up overlooking the ocean (❷; bookings in Limbé through the Saker Baptist Mission just north of Market Street; ℡333.23.23), which also arranges transport quicker than having to wait for share taxis from the fish market to fill up. Two kilometres past Bimbia you'll find the start of the **Bimbia-Bonadikombo Nature Trail**, a two-hour hike which follows a river through mangroves and a variety of lowland forest types to **Bonadikombo**, from where you can catch a share taxi back to Limbé (CFA150). Community Forest Guides from Bimbia will take you around for CFA2500 per person.

North of Limbé, heading inland from Bota, an enjoyable 5km trek uphill to **BONJONGO**, following the Bonjongo road, leads to the impressive old German Palatine Mission Church and a great view of Ambas Bay. Bonjongo is one of three possible departure points for the walk up the 1713m **Small Mount Cameroon** (also known as Etinde). The other starting points are **Etomé**, just north of Batoké on the coast, and **Ekonjo**, a little closer to the top. Wherever you start from it's a hard day's trek up the steep slope, but you'll get a good impression of the montane forest. **Guides** for the climb (and other excursions in the area) can be found through the Botanic Garden Visitors' Centre (see p.1182); through Green Tours Cameroon at the *King William Square Hotel* (☎774.72.11, @greenturcm @yahoo.com); or through Cameroon Rev'Tours (☎342.10.05, @camrevtous @camnet.cm) at *Seme New Beach*. The tourist office in Limbé may also be able to help. Expect to pay a guide CFA5000–10,000 a day, plus extra fees such as the "village tax" (CFA10,000) which is paid to the village you set off from, as well as a bottle of whisky for the village chief and another bottle to appease the mountain spirits if you make it to the top.

Buea and Mount Cameroon

Briefly the capital of German Kamerun, **BUEA** is located on the slopes of **Mount Cameroon**, some 70km west of Douala. Perched more than 1000m above the ocean, the town breathes in a relatively cool climate – something the Germans were always keen to seek out during their colonial days. Buea's principal attraction for visitors is as a base from which to climb Mount Cameroon; apart from this, the town doesn't have a lot to offer.

The Germans began establishing military outposts in their new protectorate in 1895, with the arrival of colonial governor **Jesco von Puttkamer**. Buea was one such spot, and was made capital in place of Douala from 1901 until 1909. It still retains many reminders of its **colonial past**, including administrative buildings, an old school, numerous villas built on piles and a magnificent **palace** built as von Puttkamer's residence. Today, this German *schloss* is used by the prime minister – meaning that you could be arrested for taking pictures.

During British rule, Buea was placed under the authority of the Lieutenant Governor of the Southern Provinces of Nigeria. On the eve of independence, the town had dwindled to 3000 inhabitants and was primarily a colonial resort. But Buea reacquired its prestige as an administrative centre when it became capital of the English-speaking West Cameroon, in the post-independence federation. Over the next ten years, it received substantial public investment in the form of government buildings – including a university – and the population grew rapidly. Since then, Buea has been demoted to capital of South West Province only, and expansion has once more given way to calm stagnation.

Practicalities

All public transport to Buea stops in the area around the **Mile 17 motor park** near the university and 5km from the centre. It's CFA300 for a share taxi from here to the centre. If you're heading on to Nigeria, there's a **Nigerian consulate** in town (☎332.25.28), where, with persistence, you should be able to get a visa for about CFA30,000 (depending on your nationality). To find the consulate, turn left at the police station roundabout as you're coming into town from Limbé, from where it's around 200m past the *Mountain Hotel* on the left. The **tourist office**, on the main drag (Mon–Fri 8am–3.30pm, but best before 2.00pm; ☎332.25.34, ⓕ332.26.56), organizes guided ascents of the mountain (although it's better to organize your ascent through the Inter-Communal Eco Tourism Board – see opposite). However you choose to do it, arranging practical matters for the climb invariably requires you to spend the night in Buea; there are several reasonably comfortable places **to stay**:

Mermoz Long St (the old Limbé Rd) ☎ 332.23.49, ⓕ 332.21.00. Perhaps the best place to stay in town, with clean and comfortable self-contained rooms with hot water and TV. Also has a good-value restaurant and bar. **②**

Mountain 400m south of the police station roundabout, a bit past *Parliamentarian Flats* ☎ 332.22.35, ⓔ mt_hotel@yahoo.com. This cosily nostalgic place is reminiscent of an old hunting lodge, with a fireplace in the trophied lobby, plus a pool (CFA1000 for non-guests) and a slightly overpriced restaurant. Although it's now slightly run-down, the rooms are self-contained and spacious, and come with hot water and balconies (facing either Mount Cameroon or a flowery garden). The in-house *Xtasy Nite Club* (Fri & Sat from 10pm; CFA1500) is very popular. **④**

O.I.C. (Opportunity Industrialization Centre) Next to Soppo market on the main road into the centre ☎ & ⓕ 332.25.86. Large, good-value rooms, all with hot showers and TV, and a popular restaurant (mains CFA2500), though the more expensive new section isn't worth the extra cost. **③**

Parliamentarian Flats 250m south of the police station roundabout ☎ 332.24.59. Government-owned hotel overlooking the slopes of Mount Cameroon with clean self-contained rooms with hot water; being slowly renovated at the time of writing. **②**

Presbyterian Guest House Past the police station roundabout up the hill towards Upper Farm ☎ 332.23.36, ⓔ pcc.modoffice@camnet.cm. Sparklingly clean basic double rooms, a few self-contained, plus use of a well-equipped kitchen (CFA500). Great views but no hot showers. **②**, or CFA1000 to camp.

Mount Cameroon

Buea is the usual starting point for the ascent of the occasionally active volcano **Mount Cameroon** (the most recent **eruption**, in May 2000, lasted roughly three weeks; nobody was hurt). At 4095m high, and rising directly from sea level, Mount Cameroon is easily the tallest mountain in West and Central Africa, on a par with the higher peaks in the Alps and just lower than Mount Whitney in California. Despite the equatorial latitude, the highest slopes get freezing rain and occasional snow mixed in with unusually high winds, and the climate at the summit is alpine – conditions which, in conjunction with the very steep, stony slopes, can make it an arduous climb. You'll need a guide.

Determination, however, rather than superfitness or technique, is the attribute that will get you to the top – as most people do. Ideally you should go during the "dry" season (roughly mid-Nov to the end of April). The traditional route up the mountain – the direct and steep old **Guinness Track** – has now been supplemented by a number of other tracks. All these trails are up the mountain's southeast face, avoiding the extremely heavy rainfall which afflicts the western slopes and the thunderstorms of the eastern and northern slopes. A new descending trails follows an old elephant track on the northwestern slope.

The tourist office in Buea only organizes climbs up the Guinness Track (CFA9000 per person per day), but this has not been well maintained in recent years, and gives only a limited impression of the mountain. If you wish to help conserve the mountain's unique biodiversity, you should arrange your climb through the **Inter-Communal Eco Tourism Board** (Mon–Fri 8am–5pm, Sat & Sun 7am–noon; ☎ 332.20.38, ⓔ mountceo@iccnet2000.com), based near the *Presbyterian Guest House* under the Buea Local Council Office and opposite the town market. They arrange tours following old hunters' trails up the mountain and using local guides (often ex-hunters themselves).

Every climber with the Eco Tourism Board pays CFA3000 per day towards a fund, a major proportion of which goes into village development projects. Every group must have a guide (CFA6000 per day) and porters (CFA5000 per day). For trips of two or more days you'll need at least one porter to every climber, especially if you're climbing to the summit, when they have to carry sufficient water for one and a half days of drinking and cooking.

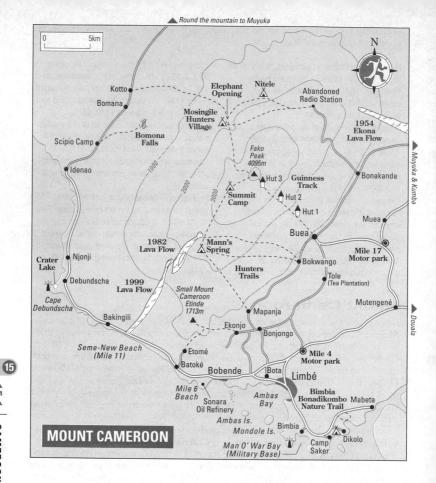

MOUNT CAMEROON

Depending on which trail you choose, the climb to the summit and down again can be done in between two and five days. It's possible, if you're very fit, to do the trek in a single day, making a pre-dawn start to be on the summit by mid-afternoon, and back down in Buea shortly after dark, but obviously you won't have much time to absorb the mountain's moods and images.

Equipment requirements need not be daunting. Footwear is the most important item: ideally you should wear waterproof hiking boots with ankle support. Plenty of people tackle the mountain in running shoes, but only the sturdiest will cushion your feet from jabbing rocks. Good sleeping bags and warm, waterproof clothes are necessary if you're staying a night on the mountain, and you'll also need to bring a tent if you're camping – you might be able to hire one in Buea (along with a few other items), but don't count on it. Depending on the arrangements you make with the guide and porters, you either bring a stove and cook your own **food**, or eat together with them by paying for the supplies. Take plenty of dried foods (nuts, raisins and chocolate are recommended), and water, which is only available at Hut 1 and Mann's Spring on the way up, and at the Elephant Opening on your way down.

The Race of Hope

Since its inception in 1973, the annual **Race of Hope** (formerly known as the Guinness Mountain Marathon, and still often referred to by that name) has achieved a reputation as one of the toughest athletic events in the world. On the last weekend in January or first of February, a field of about 350 runners slog 37km over tortuous terrain from the Buea sports stadium up the Guinness Track's jungly lower slopes to the chilly summit of Mount Cameroon and back. Although Cameroonians dominate the competition, they have been joined by an international array of athletes, including Europeans and representatives of most African countries. Fifty thousand spectators watch the proceedings, with the men's winner usually completing the event in around four and a half hours and the women's winner in about five hours. If you want to take part, you'll have to be nominated by a sports club and complete the qualifying races. For more information contact the Athletics Federation (☎222.47.44) in Yaoundé.

The climb

You can start the climb from several points – depending on how much time you have. The so-called **Guinness Track** takes a straight line from Buea to the summit, along which there are three basic (and rat-infested) **mountain huts**, with a bare minimum of furnishings.

Most people prefer to ascend by one of the old **hunters' trails**, where there are basic **campsites**. From **Bokwango** or **Mapanja**, you ascend through farmland and village plantations and then into montane forest before emerging into open savanna after about four hours. On clear days there are wonderful views of Small Mount Cameroon (Etinde), the ocean and Malabo Island, the sister volcano to Mount Cameroon. The first camp is on the forest/savanna margin next to **Mann's Spring** (after German geographer Gustav Mann), which is also the destination of a shorter one day trek up the mountain. If you're lucky you might find antelopes drinking at the spring. The ascent to the summit continues past the lava flow from the 1999 eruption. From here, the climbing gets steeper as you move through colder **grasslands** to the Summit Camp, about 450m from the top. By now you're likely to be noticing minor altitude effects – shortness of breath and lassitude. Before sunrise on the third day you make the final ascent to **Fako peak** at 4095m, where you can sign the book to mark your triumph. Disappointingly, whatever the time of year or day it's rare to get a clear view from Fako, but early morning is the best bet.

The **descent** can be made into Buea down the Guinness Track in just five leg-dissolving hours – with occasional encouragement from a "Guinness Is Good For You" sign. With more time available you can descend on the opposite side of the mountain through a completely different microclimate. This descent starts down a deep lava valley into a savanna region where you may see antelopes. Close to the Bonakanda hunters' village you come across **Bat Cave** and, a little further on, the camp for the third night close to the Mosingile hunters' village.

Heading northwest from Mosingile takes you through forest towards Kotto, past the **elephant opening**, a clearing ploughed by forest elephants where they congregate to eat, drink and bathe. Forest elephants are extremely elusive, so it's very unlikely that you'll see the beasts themselves, though you may see their spoor. This route continues west to meet the mountain ring road in Kotto, where you can arrange to be collected by vehicle or walk east to Nitele hunters' village. From Nitele it's a steep climb of four or five hours to an abandoned British Post and Telecommunications Radio Station, now classified as an **industrial monument**. If the road has been repaired, you might be able to arrange for a good 4WD vehicle to collect you here, or camp again and trek back to Buea over a remarkable plateau and down a motorable road from Bonakanda. An **alternative route** from

Mosingile hunters' village follows the contours east direct to the radio station, avoiding the climb but also missing the elephant opening.

Kumba and around

The first of the major towns of western Cameroon that you come to heading north from Buea or Douala is the agricultural and commercial centre of **KUMBA**. Although the town itself is large and uninspiring, with a population approaching 130,000, it's in the heart of a beautiful region, while **Lake Barombi Mbo** – a picturesque crater lake just 5km out of town – is like another world.

Kumba's layout is disorienting: the town has no real centre – or rather it has too many – and single-storey wooden-plank houses spread in all directions. There's a very big **market** here, specializing in goods imported from Nigeria (there's a large Igbo immigrant community in Kumba), and even if, like most travellers, you're just passing through, it's worth a look. North and east of the market you'll find the **post office**, **banks** (BICEC and Crédit Lyonnais) and **agences de voyage**, all of which have connections to Douala and Bamenda; Garanti Express also has services to Mamfé (sometimes continuing onto Onitsha in Nigeria). The main **administrative quarter** is located a good 4km northwest of the market and yet another centre has grown up around the old **train station**.

For **share taxis** to Tombel, Bafoussam and Bamenda, the **Three Corners motor park** is 3km northeast of the stadium. The **Buea motor park**, on the Buea road, has share taxis to Limbé, Douala and Buea, while the **Mbonge road motor park**, west of the town centre on the Ekondo Titi road, has share taxis to Ekondo Titi and Mundemba (for Korup National Park).

Accommodation and eating

As you'd expect in a busy market centre such as this, there's a host of reasonably cheap hotels, most with reasonable **restaurants**. *Classy Burger* serves decent fast food and beer.

Azi Motel Buea Rd ☎ 335.42.91. Conveniently located if you're arriving by public transport from the south, this good-value and friendly hotel has clean self-contained rooms with fans or a/c, all with hot showers and mosquito netting. There's a bar, restaurant and business centre with Internet access and Kumba's most reliable long-distance telephone. ❷
Bridge Inn Mundemba Rd, on the outskirts of town. Simple self-contained rooms with a/c or fans, and a bar. You can camp in the grounds for CFA2000 per person. ❶
Kanton Kramer Ave, near Tavern Junction ☎ 335.43.82. New hotel with an array of spacious and clean self-contained rooms (a/c or fan). There's

also a downstairs restaurant and safe parking. ❷
Metropole Off the Mundemba Rd ☎ 335.40.64. A relatively new hotel featuring comfortable self-contained rooms – some with hot water and TV – with a/c or fan. Often full. ❷
Shamrock A short walk east of the Buea Rd off Tavern Junction ☎ 335.42.44. A glitzy new place, owned by Tchatcho Voyages, featuring a range of tiled self-contained rooms, some with TV and a/c. ❸
Tavern Cross Junction On the Buea Rd, near the town centre ☎ 335.43.39. Simple, excellent-value self-contained rooms with fans or a/c. Inexpensive Cameroonian food is served in the restaurant and there's also a lively street-front bar. ❶–❷

Lake Barombi Mbo

You can walk from Kumba to **Lake Barombi Mbo** in about ninety minutes; in the dry season after the road has been graded it's also possible to reach the lakeshore by taxi (CFA500). Follow Lake Road (clearly signposted) which turns off to the left just after the SDO's (Senior Divisional Officer's) office about 3km from the town centre past the German colonial administration buildings. Alternatively, take a

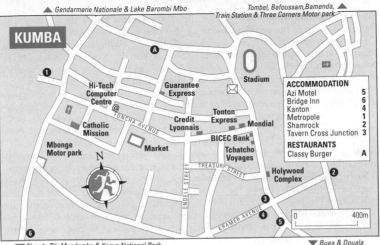

KUMBA

Hi-Tech Computer Centre

Guarantee Express

Stadium

Catholic Mission

Tonton Express

Credit Lyonnais

Mondial

BICEC Bank

Mbonge Motor park

Market

Tchatcho Voyages

TREASURY STREET

Holywood Complex

ENDELE STREET

KRAMER AVENUE

FONCHA AVENUE

ACCOMMODATION
Azi Motel — 5
Bridge Inn — 6
Kanton — 4
Metropole — 1
Shamrock — 2
Tavern Cross Junction — 3

RESTAURANTS
Classy Burger — A

0 — 400m

taxi to the Lake Road junction (CFA150) from where it's a pleasant 2km walk to the lake. The area's dense forest crowds right down the inside of the crater to the lakeshore, providing an unbelievable green backdrop. The lake – 2.5km across and 110m deep – is crystal clear and perfect for swimming. You'll see a couple of fishing boats when you arrive, and if their owners are around, they'll paddle you around the lake, or take you across it to the small village of Barombi on the other side. The price of the trip is negotiable (around CFA1000). Although the lake is basically safe for swimming, stay out of the water immediately around the village, as bilharzia is quite prevalent there.

The Mamfé Depression

The **Mamfé Depression** is a low-lying, thickly forested area bounded to the north, south and east by a semicircular range of mountains. **Mount Kupe**, with its unique flora and fauna, lies in the southeast of this range, approximately 45km northeast of Kumba. Following the volcanic rift north, taking the Bangem road, is

The ecology of Barombi Mbo

The **Barombi** people of the lakeshores are completely dependent on the lake and seem to have lived in a harmonious symbiosis with it for hundreds of years. The **fish** they catch are an obscure series of small cichlid species (mouth-breeding fish) called *pundu*, *kululu*, *dikume* and *pingu* – and a single type of catfish. All of them live only here, some at depths scientists haven't been able to account for in terms of normal fishy physiology. Traditional hand-woven gill-nets and basket traps select only larger fish, ensuring their continued survival. Traditionally, the Barombi took further care to guarantee their livelihood by actively appeasing the lake at their Ndengo cult grove. More and more young people, though, are installing themselves down in Kumba or further afield and leaving the old ways behind. Kumba itself is now drawing not just people but the lake's very water, which is piped to the town system. The surrounding forest is also under increasing pressure as areas are cleared for farming and the wood taken for fuel. It now remains to be seen if the road will improve the local economy or accelerate the destruction of the resource that locals have always depended upon.

the **Manengouba Massif** and the beautiful **Twin Crater Lakes**. Passing through the depression is the southernmost of the two main overland routes from Cameroon to Nigeria, which runs through the somewhat isolated enclave of **Mamfé**, in the middle of dense forest about 65km short of the border. Only Nigeria-bound travellers are likely to visit Mamfé, and even then only in the dry season, since during the rains the *piste* leading to Mamfé can become very difficult, even for 4WDs. Despite the many extra kilometres, Banki in the north is the preferred crossing point into Nigeria (see p.1250) – this border crossing is also far less of a hassle to negotiate, and the risk of having to bribe your way through is smaller.

If you can cope with its difficulties, however, the direct route from Kumba to Mamfé is quite a trip. The road passes through dense rainforest, and occasionally yields spectacular views as it detours around mountains. This region has its own unique flora and fauna, and contains many forest reserves and protected areas such as **Korup National Park**. From **Mundemba**, at the entrance to the park, it's relatively straightforward – depending on the status of the border dispute over the oil-rich Bakassi Peninsula – to continue by boat via the creeks to Ikang and Calabar in Nigeria, although at the time of writing these boats were not in service. However, you can still travel as far as Idenau by boat, where it's possible to find coastal boats to Calabar.

Mount Kupe

Mount Kupe (2050m), revered by the local people as the home of their ancestral and forest spirits, is approached from the small Bakossi village of **NYASOSO**, about 10km north of Tombel. Regular share taxis connect through from Kumba. The mountain is shrouded in a unique cloud forest which supports rich biodiversity, much of it endemic to the area. **Chimpanzees** and several species of globally threatened primates live on the mountain, but it's the diverse **birdlife** that has given the mountain its international reputation – over 320 species have been recorded to date.

The Mount Kupe Forest Project office is in Nyasoso; they can arrange **accommodation** in private homes in the village at a fixed rate of CFA3000 per person. The project also has information about the mountain's unique ecology, and they may provide you with a species list if you're a keen bird-watcher. To climb the mountain you'll have to pay a Community Forest Fee of CFA2000 per person and take a guide at CFA3500 for the day. Optional porters cost CFA2500 per day.

The **climb** to the summit is steep, and slippery when wet, but can be done in six hours if you are reasonably fit. There are two marked routes up to the summit, known as **Max's Trail** and **Shrike Trail**, which can be used to make a round trip. The trail leads through a fascinating forest, with fruits, flowers, soft green mosses, lichens and other epiphytes dangling from the trees. Once you have pushed your way up and out of the thicket onto the summit, you are rewarded with a spectacular view – if the weather is clear – and you may be lucky enough to hear chimpanzees calling in the misty forest below. You can also go out **at night**, and with the aid of a guide and a good torch, there are good chances of spotting several species of bushbaby and loris. It's also possible to camp for free on the mountain, whilst arranging for a porter to bring up food from the village – prices are fixed: CFA2500 for lunch and dinner, CFA1000 for breakfast.

As an alternative to the demanding climb, the project has created an informative 2km self-guided **nature trail**. With luck you may be able to get a free printed guide at the project office.

Manengouba twin crater lakes

BANGEM, approximately 40km north of Nyasoso, is a good base for some rewarding day-treks in the area, including the spectacular **twin crater lakes** nestled in the huge grassy bowl of the Manengouba caldera. These sacred lakes, called **Man**

Lake and **Woman Lake**, are curiously different in colour – the larger "female" lake is blue and the smaller "male" lake is vivid green from algal growth.

Bangem, a small administrative centre, has several basic **accommodation** options. In the town square, *Prestige Inn* (❶) has rooms with a shared toilet and bucket shower. Heading out of town on the Melong road, the government guesthouse (CPDM *Party House*; ❶) on the right-hand side, is slightly more expensive and has tidy rooms. The *Catholic Mission* (❶), close to the town square, generally only accommodates missionaries.

The **walk to the lakes** is straightforward and can be done without a guide, but you must register and pay a fee of CFA1000 per person to the council clerk at the police station by the CPDM *Party House*. Buy provisions and drinking water in the town, as there are no shops on the way. To reach the lakes, head southeast out of town along 2nd Street and stick to the main track. The walk takes about three hours and is a steady climb until the final approach to the summit, where the track switchbacks up the steep crater rim, with the flat expanse of the caldera floor coming into view ahead. The track continues into and across the crater but soon becomes indiscernible among the cattle tracks and grasses. Carry on in the same direction towards the peaks on the far side and the larger Woman Lake reveals itself. Man Lake is a short climb to the right around a distinctive small steep hill. You can **camp** by – and fish and swim in – Woman Lake, but swimming is forbidden in Man Lake (and attempts to do so would be pretty foolhardy anyway, as the lake is surrounded by treacherously steep forested slopes).

Korup National Park

The **Korup National Park**, which adjoins Nigeria's Cross River National Park (see p.1086), contains Africa's oldest and most diverse rainforest, and is one of the continent's most important conservation sites, with a remarkably high number of **endemic species**. The park consists of 1260 square kilometres of ancient, mainly lowland, **tropical rainforest**, the southern part of which is almost certainly primary. As a result of its inaccessibility, the infertility of its soils and the low density of commercially valuable tree species in it, the park has suffered very little disturbance either in historic or prehistoric times. While other forests in the region have been affected by shifting cultivation and logging, Korup has remained largely untouched, and now boasts 410 different species of birds, 101 mammals, 92 amphibians, 82 reptiles, 130 fishes, 950 butterflies, 620 trees and shrubs, and 480 herbs and climbers, making it a hotspot of biodiversity.

As home to a quarter of all African **primates**, Korup is a critically important site for the conservation of species including chimpanzees and **drills**, the rarest and most endangered primate in Africa. The park also boasts more **bird species** than any other site in Africa, including a number of rare and endangered species such as the red-headed rockfowl, whilst its fast-flowing rivers are home to many varieties of **fish** previously unknown to zoologists – including a freshwater "flying-fish" and a venomous sand-burrowing catfish. In addition, new natural pharmacological products are being discovered all the time.

Access

The *piste* leading from Kumba to the village of **Mundemba**, at the main entrance to the park, is reasonable and **share taxis** run regularly between the two towns, although much more frequently in the dry season. Count on a full day's travel from Douala to the park, via Kumba and Ekondo Titi. You can reach Mundemba **by boat** from Idenao, a two- to three-hour trip along the Ndian River which brings you to Bulu Beach near Mundemba. Coming overland **from Mamfé**, the northernmost entrance to Korup is at **Baro**, which you reach via **Nguti** on the Mamfé–Kumba road. Public transport is hard to find for the 30km from Nguti to Baro, but there are occasional share taxis. If you want to spend a night in Nguti, the

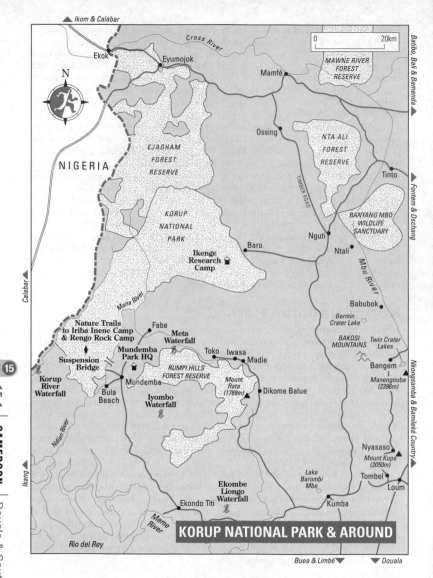

KORUP NATIONAL PARK & AROUND

Buea & Limbé ▼   ▼ Douala

Saint John of God Hospital Guesthouse (●) has self-contained rooms, running water and electricity in the evenings, while *Green Castle* (●) also has self-contained rooms and a common room where you can buy drinks and order food.

Mundemba

Arriving in **MUNDEMBA**, you'll see the unmissable **Korup Tourist Information Centre** (June–Oct: Mon–Fri 7.30am–3.30pm, Sat & Sun 7.30–8.30am & 4.30–5.30pm; Nov–May: daily 7am–5pm; ⓔkorup@wwf.cm) on the right-hand side of the road as you reach the middle of town. They collect a

CFA5000 **park entrance fee** per day and assign an obligatory guide (CFA4000 per day, plus CFA2000 per day per porter as needed; with CFA1000 on top for overnight stays). An additional CFA3000 is collected per person for each night of camping. The guides are excellent company and, since they live in the forest, know the terrain well and are enthusiastic leaders. Note that visiting the park without a guide is illegal. Formalities out of the way, it's 8km from the Tourist Centre to the park entrance; a vehicle is available for hire (CFA8000 return for up to eight passengers including guide and porters).

There's modest **accommodation** at the popular *Iyas Hotel* (❷), which has clean self-contained twin rooms with fans, or the similar *Korup Park Hotel* (❷) with a bar-restaurant. The more basic *Vista Palace* (❶) has neat and reasonably priced rooms, some with shared facilities, and a good restaurant. If you want to make guide or accommodation arrangements before arriving at Korup, contact the conservator on Ⓔ korup@wwf.cm or the WWF representatives in Yaoundé (☎221.62.67, Ⓦ www.wwfcameroon.org).

The park

At the park entrance, an impressive **suspension bridge** spans the Mana River, allowing year-round access to the park. If you only have time for a **day-trip**, follow the nature trail marked with posts which point out the forest's interesting features – everything from termite mounds to an endless variety of plants and trees.

For longer visits, several **tourist camps** have been set up inside the park, with accommodation in insect-screened huts. The closest, *Iriba Inene Camp*, is only 1.5km from the park entrance on the nature trail. Each camp has a kitchen with firewood, water for drinking, natural bathing points and latrine-type toilets. You need to bring your own camping mattress, and insect repellent is a good idea as tiny sweat bees sometimes swarm the camps during the day, and swimming in rivers during your hikes is likely to attract blackflies, known in French as *mout-mout* – nasty creatures with a stinging, itchy bite. Beware too of driver ants.

The possibilities for exploring are pretty well unlimited, and two or three days of hiking is not unreasonable. In the southern sector of the park, trails lead to the **Mana River Waterfall**, to the **Rengo Rock** camp (cave explorations in the area), and up to **Mount Yuhan** (1079m). The most attractive camp is **Chimpanzee camp**, 10km from the entrance. Hiking in the opposite direction (out of the park) leads to the **Meta Waterfall**, on the headwaters of the Mana River (half a day's trek from Mundemba) and on to the **Iyombo Waterfall**. Further east, **Mount Rata** rises to an elevation of 1769m, the highest peak in the **Rumpi Hills**. Despite the wealth of wildlife, your chances of seeing large animals are slim, though most people at least spot monkeys scampering through the canopy, and elusive duiker antelope in the undergrowth.

You can go into the park's northern sector via **BARO**. The park staff here are welcoming, and you can hire porters, but no guides; in addition, although there's a building to sleep in, you'll need your own sleeping and cooking gear. All things considered, visiting the park from the southern sector is definitely preferable.

Mamfé and around

MAMFÉ is basically a stopover point for travellers or traders, many of whom use the town as a base to unload goods they have smuggled from Nigeria on small boats up the **Cross River**. The constant comings and goings add energy to the otherwise sleepy town, but make it rather anonymous as well: it could be almost anywhere in West Africa. Today the administrative headquarters of the Manyu district of South West Province, Mamfé (the name is a corruption of Mansfield, the settlement's first German district officer) was later part of the British Cameroons and subject to the policy of **"indirect rule"** expressed through the creation of Native Authorities. In 1959, the town hosted the **Mamfé Conference**, which tried

Regular share taxis and minibuses to **Ekok**, **Bamenda** and **Kumba** leave from the main motor park in the centre of town. Garantee Express, Tonton Voyages and Tchatcho Voyages are the only *agences de voyage* with regular connections to Kumba (and occasionally Onitsha in Nigeria); their offices are near the motor park. There are no agencies connecting Mamfé with Bamenda. During the wet season the road in both directions can be very bad, and you should estimate for a full day of strenuous driving. Motorized *pirogues* heading up the **Cross River** to Ekok can be caught by the old German Bridge. To get to **Korup National Park** (see p.1191), take a taxi as far as Nguti for the northern entrance, or proceed to Kumba and change there for Mundemba, the main entrance.

The mountain road to **Dschang** is difficult at any time of year, and generally impassable during the rains. Enquire at the motor park to see if any transport is headed along the road and prepare to be terrified for much of the trip – wrecked vehicles strewn down the cliffsides attest to the danger of the route. Going through this beautiful scenery by mountain bike, in the other direction – downhill – is a much better option.

(unsuccessfully) to establish voting rules for the upcoming UN plebiscite. In 1961 its inhabitants voted for unification with the Cameroon Republic, since when its status has declined.

Practicalities

Considering its remoteness, Mamfé has a reasonable infrastructure – district buildings, hospital, filling station and missions. If you've just arrived from Nigeria, and have made it this far without CFA francs, you may be relieved to discover that there's a BICEC **bank** here. In principle they should change traveller's cheques and cash, but as they usually don't have the current rates, you can only be certain of changing euros. There's also an active black market in Mamfé for changing naira, but the rate is better at the border.

If you've just arrived from Nigeria, Cameroonian prices are rather a shock. But **accommodation** seems pretty expensive in Mamfé even if you've come from the other direction, especially once you see what you actually get for your money.

Data Guest House 1km north of the town centre ☏ 334.13.99. The best-value hotel in town, with friendly staff, good food and a range of clean self-contained rooms (fan or a/c), all with TV, and a striking view over the Cross River. ❷

Great Aim Hotel North of the motor park. Good bar-restaurant and basic rooms with shared facilities and fans. ❶

Heritage Hotel Opposite the government high school on the Nguti road. One of the better places in town with a range of clean rooms with varying degrees of facilities, but you'll have to order food a day in advance. ❷

Ekok: the Nigerian border

Sixty-three kilometres west of Mamfé is the tiny border town of **EKOK**. In the dry season it's possible to cover this stretch in two to three hours; in the wet season the road is practically impassable, and often the only viable alternative is to reach Ekok by motorized *pirogue*. The border is open 24/7, so there's no need **to stay** here. If you do, several basic and cheap places (all ❶) survive from the times when the border shut every evening. There's no **bank** in Ekok, but plenty of money-changers who give a better rate for naira than on the Nigerian side of the border.

15.2

The central highlands

The landscapes of Cameroon's mountainous west – the Central Highlands – are overwhelmingly beautiful, ranging from the **volcanic hills** of the **Grassfields** to sheer cliffs with **waterfalls** and **crater lakes** hidden behind dense vegetation. The area is also interesting from a cultural point of view, with many of its old chiefdoms surviving into an era when increasing agricultural prosperity has brought one of the fastest rates of development in the country. There's a wealth of sights and towns which you could spend weeks or months exploring.

The area divides up fairly clearly into the **Bamiléké country** in the south, the **Bamenda Grassfields** in the north and the **Bamoun country** in the east. The main town in Bamiléké country – and the capital of West Province – is the rapidly growing centre of **Bafoussam**. Its wealth was formerly based on coffee production, but recent industrialization means that it's no longer a very soulful place, though it does make a convenient springboard for visiting other, more characterful regional towns. These include **Bandjoun**, which retains the traditional flavour of its old chiefdom and boasts the region's best-preserved **palace**; and the old German colonial resort of **Dschang**, situated in the mountains at an altitude of 1400m, which has a mild, almost European climate.

Bamenda is the capital of North West Province. In the past this has been the starting point for the difficult **Ring Road**, which dips and bends through the mountainous **Grassfields**, a district of hilly, moist savanna, passing through a number of **Tikar chiefdoms** and Fulani settlements along the route. Collapsed bridges and impassable roads mean that it's currently impossible to do this trip, though with luck this will soon change.

In Bamoun country, the cultural and historical highpoint is **Foumban**, a town with a remarkable turn-of-the-century palace, notable museums and a thriving crafts industry. For all its rich past, however, Foumban takes an economic backseat to Bamenda.

Bafoussam

The **administrative capital** of the West Province, **BAFOUSSAM** is a noisy and vibrant centre of commercial hyperactivity whose population has mushroomed to over 200,000 in the last two decades – if you enjoy Third World hustle and bustle, Bafoussam will have a strong appeal. Situated on the edge of the Francophone zone, the Gallic influence is fairly unmistakeable too, especially if you've just arrived from "Anglo" Bamenda. The Bamiléké, who dominate the city, are famous for their commercial energy and are renowned as traders throughout the country. However, they never sell their land, so newcomers rarely integrate and the city is culturally very homogenous. The traditional **chefferie** (chief's compound) – to the southeast, off the route de Douala, may be worth a visit if you don't have time to visit the more impressive *chefferie* of Bandjoun, but in true Bamiléké style they tend to demand an extortionate entrance fee, and you'll have to haggle hard to be allowed in for the standard CFA1000 per head and CFA1500 for a camera.

Bafoussam owes its prosperity largely to **Arabica coffee**, which flourishes in the surrounding hills. **Industry**, spurred on by earnings from the coffee crop, has also made deep inroads in recent years. The Union des Coopératives du Café de l'Ouest (UCCAO) set up a coffee-processing plant in the 1970s, and a Brasseries du Cameroun brewery, a cigarette factory and a printing press have all started operations since then.

Accommodation

Bafoussam has a surprising lack of inexpensive **accommodation** for a town of its size.

Le Continental av de la République ☎344.14.58. Slightly run-down but quite comfortable, with spacious self-contained rooms with balcony, hot water and TV, though the once busy restaurant and bar are now very quiet. ❷

Fédéral 87 rue Joumou ☎344.13.09. Good-value hotel with sparklingly clean self-contained rooms

with hot water and TV, and some cheap and newly done-up apartments. There's also a good restaurant and a classy bar. ❷

Nicotel Off *Place de l'Indépendance*, behind the post office ☎344.24.18. A friendly new hotel offering immaculate large self-contained rooms, all with hot water and TV, and a few with balcony.

15.2 | CAMEROON | The central highlands

There's also a cosy small indoor bar-restaurant. **②** **Le Président** rue Nguetti Michel, near the BICEC bank ☏ 344.11.36. Once Bafoussam's grandest hotel, and though it's no longer very luxurious, the dark a/c rooms are very reasonably priced. **②** **Ramada** Off the *Carrefour Total* ☏ 999.43.33 or 795.54.87. Simple self-contained rooms with cold water and a comfortable TV bar. **②** **Résidence Saré** On the outskirts of town off route

de Bamenda ☏ 344.25.99. Slightly run-down chalets, with hot showers, fridge, satellite TV and a/c. **④** **Talotel** Off the Marché *rond-point* ☏ 776.95.15 or 999.49.60, ✉ talotel@yahoo.fr. The most luxurious hotel in town, centrally located and with tastefully decorated self-contained rooms with satellite TV. There's also a high-quality restaurant and a lively outdoor bar, and a car rental service is planned. **⑤**

The Town

Bafoussam's dual administrative and commercial functions are reflected in its layout. The broad avenues of the administrative quarter, where you'll find the Résidence du Gouverneur, Préfecture and Mairie, are neatly gathered on a hill in the **Tamdja neighbourhood**. From the roundabout where the Palais de Justice stands, the main **Avenue Wanko** heads downhill to the north towards the **market**. You'll find the major **banks**, including CBC and BICEC, either on or around Avenue Wanko; Crédit Lyonnais at the Carrefour Total near the Foumban road. The **Ministère du Tourisme** (☏ 344.77.82), behind the Palais de Justice, may be able to help with a few leaflets and advice. Bafoussam's **market**, held every four days, is in the middle of the older commercial neighbourhoods of Djeleng and Famla and has a wide range of **crafts**. For **Internet** access, try L'Excellence.net, off rue du Marché near the market, or Cybercafé le Prestige, on the Foumban road next to *La Bauxite* (both CFA1000 per hour; daily 9am–8pm).

Eating, drinking and nightlife

There are a number of good, cheap **eating places** on the Foumban road near Carrefour Total. Try *Le Refuge* for excellent African dishes, or *La Bauxite*, a snack bar selling salads and simple meals. Next to *La Bauxite*, the *Patisserie de la Paix* makes a good place to stop for fresh baked bread and pastries. *La Bouff à Baf*, further along the same road, serves filling breakfasts and healthy portions of rice, beans and vegetables during the day. There's also good chop at the *Express Café*, while further out along the Bamenda road (turn right after the Shell Station) there's a whole line of street stalls selling cheap, freshly made omelettes and salad. Quality coffee can be had at any of the hexagonal UCCAO stands spread throughout town, including on rue du Marché and just before the Dschang *gare routière*. An excellent **bar** from which to watch the hectic street life is the *Rubis Club*, on rue du Marché. Food

Moving on from Bafoussam

Several agencies on Foumban road, such as Moungo Voyages and Jojo Voyages, have daily departures for **Foumban**. Alternatively, share taxis or *clandos* to Foumban and Foumbot can be found around Carrefour Total, opposite Crédit Lyonnais. If you're heading north, Jeannot Express, on the Bamenda road two kilometres northwest of the centre, has regular departures to **Bamenda** and **Dschang**. Nearby, Unity Express and Mazi Group Express also have departures for Bamenda. If you are heading south, you'll find a good number of agencies based on the southern end of town, beyond Place de l'Indépendance on the road to Bandjoun. Garanti Voyages, Confort Voyages, Central Voyage and Binam Voyages all have regular daily departures to **Douala** and **Yaoundé**. This stretch of road south of Place de l'Indépendance is also the best place to catch share taxis to **Bandjoun** (CFA300). Alternatively, the small *gare routière* in front of *Hotel La Délicieuse* in the centre of town has *clandos* leaving for local trips when full. To rent a car, your best bet is to ask at *Talotel*.

vendors pass by in a steady stream here selling delicacies such as filled intestines and sausages; alternatively, try whatever is on the day's menu from the nearby streetside chop shops.

For **nightlife**, the *Arcade de L'Ouest,* off Avenue de la République across from the market, has live music every Wednesday, and jazz bands playing most weekends. *Le Ritz Palace* nightclub, in front of *Talotel,* is the place to go to dance, along with *Le Byblos,* a bit further along on the same road.

The Bamiléké country

The **Bamiléké country** is roughly a triangle, delineated by the Noun River to the northeast and the Bamboutous mountains to the west. The main roads in the area (all paved) pass through **Bafoussam**, **Bandjoun**, **Bangangté**, **Bafang**, **Dschang** and **Mbouda**, all accessible by public transport. The area has numerous **chefferies** (chiefdoms) and natural attractions including **crater lakes** and **waterfalls**.

Bandjoun

Twenty kilometres south of Bafoussam, **BANDJOUN** is the largest and best preserved of the Bamiléké chiefdoms. The **chefferie** (chief's compound) is situated 3km south of Bandjoun on the route de Bangangté and you can reach it by catching a share taxi from the *gare routière.* Bandjoun is the ideal place to admire traditional Bamiléké architecture at its best (see box, opposite). Traditionally, the chief's compound was the largest in town, incorporating several huts encircled by a bamboo fence. Inside were rooms and granaries for the chief and each of his wives, who could be quite numerous. Larger public buildings used for assemblies, judicial gatherings and dispute settlements or meetings of secret societies also figured in the compound. Commonly, a large square preceded the entrance-way to the "palace" and served as a **market** (market day in the Bamiléké country traditionally falls every eight days).

The Bandjoun chieftaincy follows this basic pattern more faithfully than others in the region, where cement and corrugated metal sheeting are replacing traditional building materials, though even here the chief lives in a modern palace of 1994. Opposite, another colonial-style palace houses the **treasury** – the chief's collection of carved thrones, arms, pipes and other memorabilia. You have to pay an **entrance fee** of CFA1000 to visit the grounds, and there's a further charge of CFA1500 to take photos. A visit to the treasury museum is included in the price.

When it comes to **accommodation**, Bandjoun hasn't got many options. The central and friendly *Koung Khi* (☎757.11.01; ❷), five minutes' walk from the *gare routière,* has a range of basic but clean self-contained rooms, plus a bar and a nightclub (Fri–Sun; CFA500). Alternatively, the pricey *Centre Climatique de Bandjoun* (☎344.67.50, ✉ccbandjoun@camnet.cm; ❺), one kilometre outside town on the Bafoussam road, offers spacious self-contained rooms with TV and hot water, and a restaurant packed with local Bamiléké businessmen. Restaurants in Bandjoun are thin on the ground, but there are plenty of good food stalls in and around the *gare routière.*

From Bangangté to Bafang

There is a direct road from Bafoussam to Bafang, but the scenery along the road that heads south from Bandjoun via Bangangté (towards Yaoundé) to Bafang makes a good detour, since it passes through one of the Bamiléké country's most spectacular stretches. West of Bangangté, the **Col de Bana** (the Bana Pass) offers grand panoramic views.

BANGANGTÉ is a fairly large town, with its share of administrative buildings and a wide avenue that leads from the Préfecture down to the modern Maison du Parti. When the **chefferie** here was renovated, modern buildings were replaced with traditional Bamiléké structures, and the complex may eventually rival that of Bandjoun. There are several places to **stay**. The *Paysan* (☎348.41.88; ❷), conveniently located next to the *gare routière*, has nice self-contained rooms and a busy restaurant; while the *Bazar* (☎348.44.38; ❷), 200m up the main street east of the *gare*, has clean self-contained rooms and a large street-facing balcony which provides a great vantage point. A few hundred metres west of the *gare* on the main road, the new and upmarket *Foua Ndigong Cristal* (☎348.91.16; ❹) offers sparklingly clean self-contained rooms with hot water – a few with TV – and a bar-restaurant. Good inexpensive food can be had in chop houses across from the *gare*. The town also has a **post office**.

The road from Bangangté to Bafang is good (share taxis ply regularly between the two towns) and passes by another traditional chiefdom, the **Chefferie de Bana**, located off the main road.

Bafang

A line of small businesses at a major intersection on the Bamenda and Foumban–Douala road marks the centre of **BAFANG**. There's no exceptional reason to spend long here, and **accommodation** is limited and generally expensive. The overpriced *La Falaise* (☎348.63.13; ❸), across from the Palais de Justice, has self-contained a/c rooms, most with hot water, and a bar-restaurant. Better value is the large *Grand Luxe* (☎348.61.58; ❷), next to the Palais de Justice, with clean self-contained rooms, a fabulous view of the surrounding hills from its balconies and a café-bar that does breakfasts. The least expensive option is *Le Samaritain* (☎348.71.55; ❷), with basic but clean and good-sized self-contained rooms.

The paved road continues directly south from Bafang to Douala and Kumba, north to Bamenda and Foumban via Bafoussam, and southeast to Yaoundé via Bangangté. The main road is lined by numerous *agences de voyage* heading in either direction. Central Voyages connect Douala, Yaoundé and Bamenda; Ton Ton, Amour Mezan and Garanti Express stop here en route between Douala, Kumba and Bamenda, Papa Gassi goes to Douala and Gala Voyages to Yaoundé. There's no direct service to Foumban; you'll have to go to Bafoussam and change there.

Around Bafang

The scenery around Bafang is striking, with numerous **waterfalls**. One of these, the **Chute de la Mouenkeu**, is only a kilometre outside the town (on the Nkongsamba road). A sign points to the falls, a short walk into the woods.

More spectacular (and famous) are the **Chutes d'Ekom**, 30km further down the Nkongsamba road. If you have your own car, turn off the main road onto a dirt road heading southeast at a red sign indicating the *Chefferie de Bayong* and – in smaller writing – the *Chutes*. From here, it's about 10km to the falls, though you

---

Bamiléké architecture

Characteristic Bamiléké houses consist of a square room topped with a conical roof covered with a thick layer of thatch. Although the principle seems simple enough, an elaborate framework is necessary to make the conical roof sit on square walls. The walls are built of palm fronds or bamboo filled in with mud, and a circular platform is then set on top of the walls. Finally, a pyramid-shaped frame is constructed on top of the platform and the thatch is added (though in recent years the trend has been to replace thatch with shiny corrugated-iron sheets). The exteriors of the buildings are often decorated with bamboo and intricately carved wooden boards.

have to walk the last few kilometres. At weekends, there are plenty of villagers from Ekom Nkam around who will be keen to give you directions for a small fee; they'll know what you're looking for even before you tell them. In a beautiful forest setting, the **Nkam River** plunges eighty dramatic metres from the clifftop to the valley below. Unfortunately, the dirt road is almost impassable in the rainy season – ask about the status of the road before you head off.

Dschang and around

Three routes lead to the pleasant university town of **DSCHANG**: the paved road linked to the main Bafoussam–Bamenda road (less than an hour from Bafoussam and three hours from Bamenda along a road which passes the Bamboutous Mountains); the steep and, in sections, terrifying back road to Mamfé; and the German-built **route des Mbo**, a scenic but slow *piste* that starts in Melong and winds its way through coffee and cocoa plantations, currently impassable all the way to Melong as a number of bridges have collapsed along the route.

Dschang was founded by the Germans in 1903. During the 1940s, Europeans forced by the war to stay in Africa all year round built a **vacation colony** here, attracted by the mild climate. The resulting complex, the *Centre Climatique* (☎345.10.58, ✉centreclimatique@hotmail.com; ❸), still attracts numerous tourists with its landscaped gardens, first-class restaurant, swimming pool (CFA1000 for non-residents) and horseback riding in the gardens. The centre offers some of the best – although these days slightly run-down – accommodation in the region, with various types of bungalows, some luxurious, with a fireplace and large veranda, and others more basic, with shared toilet facilities. The centre is a short distance outside town, next to the Agricultural University.

Dschang is proud home to Cameroon's only **tourist office** (Mon–Fri 8am–3pm; ☎345.21.25), somewhat of a paradox as it doesn't have much to offer apart from its colourful **market**, one of the biggest in the area, and the **arts and crafts shops** at the university entrance and at the entrance to the market. The surrounding countryside, however, is well worth exploring if you have a car. From Place de l'Indépendance, the route to Fongo-Tongo (towards Mamfé) leads through a series of hills and valleys, passing two waterfalls. The first, the **Cascade de Lingam**, 10km from Dschang, is signposted. The more impressive **Chute de la Mamy Wata** is roughly 10km past Fongo-Tongo and reached by a small side-road that ends at the top of the falls. Towards the end of the dry season, however, both waterfalls are fairly unimpressive. Another excursion is to the **tea plantation** at **Dsjutittsa**, a beautiful and tranquil place 20km north of Dschang, where it's also sometimes possible to stay at the plantation lodge.

Practicalities

If you don't want to stay at the *Centre Climatique* (see above), the town also has some reasonable-value smaller **hotels**. A good choice is the *Constellation* (☎345.10.61; ❷), near the Bafoussam *clando* minibus stop, with a range of clean self-contained rooms, some with hot water. Two other reasonable options are the *Cendrillon* (☎345.18.98; ❷), behind the university administration building, with hot showers and a good restaurant; and the *Kemtsop* (☎234.14.95; ❷), near the rural council on the Bafoussam road, with basic rooms and a bar.

A good place **to eat** is the *Phenix Restaurant*, which does filling breakfasts, sandwiches and tasty local dishes such as rabbit stew. Of the town's **bars**, *La Maison Combatant* is a popular place and offers an unusual array of grilled meat (from elephant to rat) to accompany your beer. After dark, *Virgin* and *Conclusion* are the nightclubs to head for.

Moving on from Dschang, there are plenty of public-transport options. *Clando* minibuses heading for **Bafoussam** pick up passengers on the main road on the way. There are frequent buses to **Douala** and **Yaoundé** with various *agences de voyage* including Azinmeda (℡756.12.15), Tabo Express (℡793.17.55) and Kani Express (℡759.60.84; by large coach). Unity Express (℡792.73.16) and Mazi Group (℡436.37.41) link Dschang with **Bamenda** via **Mbouda**.

Bamenda and around

Apart from the glorious pines-and-bananas setting of the town, **BAMENDA** stands out as being at the centre of Cameroon's opposition movement. Home of the presidential candidate, bookseller **John Fru Ndi**, it was here that the initial riots leading to multipartyism took place after police opened fire on the inaugural rally of the Social Democratic Front. Following the elections, security forces arrived en masse in the town, surrounding Fru Ndi's compound and arresting prominent party leaders. In 1995, members of the newly emerged Anglophone organization, the Southern Cameroon National Council (SCNC), demanded the establishment of an **Anglophone republic** – Southern Cameroon – and throughout the early and mid-1990s Bamenda was the site of numerous violent confrontations, driving local businesses to despair. This is not to say that Bamenda is dangerous, although it bubbles with political enthusiasm and discussions.

There are good excursions from Bamenda to the nearby Fondom of **Bali**, a major crafts centre, and to the swimmable **Awing Crater Lake**, near **Mount Lefo**.

The Town

Capital of North West Province and the heart of Anglophone Cameroon, Bamenda is really two towns – one administrative and the other commercial – separated by a steep scarp. The **government buildings** perch high on the clifftop in a neighbourhood known as **Up Station** (or Supply Station). With its sweeping views and cooler air, this spot used to be favoured by the wealthy Germans and British, and remains a high-class **residential area**, the stomping ground of expats, civil servants and the local business elite. Arriving from the cities of the south to this part of town, Bamenda seems to be nodding off, almost suburban. From Up Station, a tortuous road (it has the hideous honour of being Cameroon's most accident-prone highway) was carved out by the Germans at the beginning of the century, and snakes its reluctant way down to the hot valley and the Nkwen motor park, 300m below.

Downtown Bamenda is a vast conglomeration of small businesses and working neighbourhoods. A mid-morning stroll down Commercial Avenue, with its dual carriageway of workshops and pounding stereos, is fit introduction to the real heart of town. **Local crafts** are sold at the Prescraft Centre, next to the British Council Library (see below), where you'll find a good selection of fixed-price bronzes, carvings and basketwork. Another crafts centre well worth visiting is the Handicraft Cooperative, located at the eastern end of town, along the road that climbs to Up Station. Here you'll find an even larger stock of crafts – from extravagant masks and life-size tribal warriors, to woven baskets and dinkey bottle-openers – sold at fixed prices. The **Main Market**, behind *Ideal Park Hotel*, is one of the biggest in the west, and offers cheap deals on goods smuggled in from Nigeria, and on local crafts.

Practicalities

The **Ministry of Tourism** (℡794.99.93), 250m west of City Chemist roundabout on Commercial Avenue, has expensive and blurry blueprint maps of the town and North West Province. Two **travel agencies**: Highlands Tourism Group (℡336.18.35, ✉akwohnkooh@yahoo.com), next to the Ministry, and ECO Travels & Tourism (℡774.09.66, ✉nkembengsitepecot@hotmail.com), at Up Station close

Bamenda has excellent onward connections, with numerous *agences de voyage* going in all directions. Before deciding which company to travel with it's a good idea to ask around; services with the most popular company will fill up fastest. Most agencies have connections to **Douala** – the biggest two are Garanti Express (T336.25.27) and Vatikan Express (T336.20.86), next to each other on Sonac road. Both also have frequent departures to **Yaoundé** and destinations in North West Province; Garanti has services to **Wum, Fundong, Nkambé, Ndu** and **Kumbo**. Symbol of Unity Express also has daily buses to Wum. Minibuses for **Bafoussam** and **Dschang** are run by Jeannot Express (T336.10.42), on Hotel Ayaba Road, Unity Express (T957.10.66) and Mazi Group Express (T336.23.35), both near Hospital roundabout. Tchatcho Voyages have buses to **Kumba**. Although many companies advertise connections to **Limbé** and **Buea**, you'll generally have to change bus along the way to another vehicle from the same agency. Patience Express may be your best bet for a direct connection. There are no direct services to **Foumban**; you'll have to go via Bafoussam.

Share taxis and rackety old minibuses leave from Bamenda's three motor parks: **Nkwen park** (for Bamessing, Ndop and Kumbo); **Ntarikon park**, in the north of town (for Mankon, Bafut and Wum on the Ring Road); and **Bali park** (for Bali, Batibo and Mamfé).

to Government junction, do tours around North West Province and can also help with 4WD hire (CFA50,000 per day). All the major **banks** – Amity, BICEC and SGBC – are on Commercial Avenue; in principle all change traveller's cheques and cash. Alternatively, one of the two well-stocked supermarkets – Tower and Vatikan – might be able to change cash. At the southern end of Commercial Avenue is the **British Council Library** (Mon–Fri 9.30am–4.30pm, Sat 9.30–noon). Access is officially restricted to members, but they'll usually let you skim through their good range of periodicals and newspapers, all about two weeks out of date; they also show BBC World Service television throughout the day. There are numerous **Internet** cafés in Bamenda: the fastest and most reliable is CamGis (Mon–Fri 10am–8pm, Sat 8am–9.30pm, Sun 2–9.30pm; CFA800–1000 per hour), on the third floor of the Tower building (owned by Fru Ndi) on Commercial Avenue.

Accommodation

Bamenda offers **accommodation** of almost every imaginable description, from mission dorms and cheery brothels to comfortable hotels, so it's a good base for trips out to nearby districts.

Ayaba Hotel Ayaba Rd T336.15.36, F336.35.75. Bamenda's most luxurious hotel, though now looking a little worn. Facilities include a tennis court and a swimming pool (non-guests CFA1500). **6**

Baptist Mission At the foot of the road to Up Station, near Nkwen motor park T336.12.85. A quiet, clean and friendly place, with simple twin-bed rooms with shared facilities, including hot showers. The clinic across the road does good breakfasts. **1**

Donga Palace Hotel Ayaba Rd, near the southern end of Commercial Ave. Inexpensive but rather dingy self-contained rooms, and the whole hotel bears a distinct resemblance to a cheap brothel,

though there's a friendly bar to hang out in. **1**

Ex-Serviceman's Guesthouse Off Hotel Ayaba Rd, up a small hill. The best of the town's cheap, brothel-type places, with a few spacious self-contained rooms and a bar. **1**

Ideal Park Off Commercial Ave, across from the Congress hall T336.11.66. The oldest hotel in town and one of the best-value places to stay, with clean self-contained rooms (the cheapest only with cold water) and an excellent bar and restaurant. For safety reasons, take a taxi to and from the hotel after dark. **1**

International International St, behind Commercial Ave, opposite the police station T336.25.27. Centrally located, with spacious self-contained

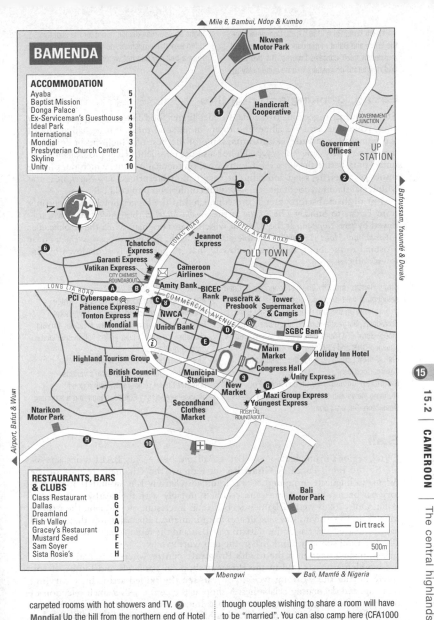

BAMENDA

ACCOMMODATION

Ayaba	5
Baptist Mission	1
Donga Palace	7
Ex-Serviceman's Guesthouse	4
Ideal Park	9
International	8
Mondial	3
Presbyterian Church Center	6
Skyline	2
Unity	10

Mile 6, Bambui, Ndop & Kumbo

Nkwen
Motor Park

Handicraft
Cooperative

GOVERNMENT
JUNCTION

Government
Offices

UP
STATION

Bafoussam, Yaoundé & Douala

HOTEL AYABA ROAD

OLD TOWN

SONAC ROAD

Jeannot
Express

Tchatcho
Express

Garanti Express
Vatikan Express

CITY CHEMIST
ROUNDABOUT

Cameroon
Airlines

LONG LIA ROAD

Amity Bank

BICEC
Bank

COMMERCIAL AVENUE

PCI Cyberspace @

Prescraft &
Presbook

Tower
Supermarket
& Camgis

SGBC Bank

Patience Express
Tonton Express
Mondial

NWCA

Union Bank

Holiday Inn Hotel

Highland Tourism Group

Main
Market

British Council
Library

Municipal
Stadium

Congress Hall

Unity Express

New
Market

Mazi Group Express
Youngest Express

Ntarikon
Motor Park

Airport, Bafut & Wum

Secondhand
Clothes
Market

HOSPITAL
ROUNDABOUT

Bali
Motor Park

RESTAURANTS, BARS & CLUBS

Class Restaurant	B
Dallas	G
Dreamland	C
Fish Valley	A
Gracey's Restaurant	D
Mustard Seed	F
Sam Soyer	E
Sista Rosie's	H

Dirt track

0   500m

Mbengwi

Bali, Mamfé & Nigeria

carpeted rooms with hot showers and TV. ❷
Mondial Up the hill from the northern end of Hotel Ayaba Rd ☏336.18.32, ⓕ336.28.84. Clean and large self-contained rooms (some with TV) with peaceful balconies overlooking town. ❷
Presbyterian Church Centre 1km north from Commercial Ave ☏336.40.70. A bit far from the town centre, but well signposted, offering dorm beds (CFA2000) and tidy rooms with clean sheets,

though couples wishing to share a room will have to be "married". You can also camp here (CFA1000 per tent). ❶
Skyline Up Station ☏336.12.89. Set on a tremendous cliff-edge perch, this grand old hotel overlooks downtown Bamenda and has comfortable self-contained rooms all with balconies. There's also a pool and restaurant; the only drawback is the distance to the centre. ❹

Unity Off Wum Rd ⓣ 336.37.82. Convenient for the Wum and Bafut motor parks, with a range of inexpensive self-contained rooms. The lively bar and restaurant downstairs can be quite noisy at night, so you may decide to opt for the slightly more expensive upstairs rooms, which also benefit from a balcony and hot water. ❶

Eating, drinking and nightlife

Street eating is good in Bamenda. Besides finger food like *soya* and grilled corn cobs, which are available all around town, more solid meals can be had at any of the numerous **roadside restaurants**, some of the best of which can be found by the town's many *agences de voyage*. There's also the excellent *Gracey's Restaurant* (daily until 7pm), beside the Prescraft Centre on Commercial Avenue, which does filling dishes of omelette, salad and chips at very reasonable prices. *Sam Soyer*, near the Municipal stadium, does fantastic *soya* with condiments and cold beer.

Most **nightclubs** in Bamenda are connected to the bigger hotels; all open only from Friday to Sunday. The *Njang* at the *Ayaba Hotel* is the classiest in town, followed by the *Tropicana* at the *Mondial* which is also popular, while the *Marakana* at *International Hotel* is more affordable and very lively, but not as busy as *Dallas*, near Hospital roundabout, which is so rowdy that it's periodically shut down by the town's officials.

Class Restaurant City Chemist roundabout. Good selection of well-prepared local dishes.
Dreamland On the first floor above Amity Bank. Breakfasts, burgers and filling lunchtime buffets (noon–3pm; CFA1500), plus a huge widescreen TV showing CNN and BBC.
Fish Valley Longla Rd, near the Presbyterian Centre. Good fish.
Handicraft Cooperative Station Road. For stunning views and tasty chicken DG and salads. Open Mon–Sat until 5pm.

Mustard Seed Commercial Avenue. Western and African fare and a popular streetside terrace.
Sista Rosie's Wum Rd, near the *Unity* hotel. Legendary venue (now in a new location) serving probably the town's best grilled fish in spacious garden *boukarous*.
Skyline Hotel Up Station, a taxi ride from downtown. The best of the town's various upmarket hotel restaurants, with a good atmosphere, classy European food and a stunning view.

Bali

Of the region's main chiefdoms – Bafut, Bali and Nso – only **BALI** is not accessible by the Ring Road. A **Chamba** settlement (the Chamba are part of the Adamawa linguistic grouping), it was founded relatively late, around 1830. Its history has been a series of wars and conflicts, notably with the nearby kingdom of Bafut. Only 20km west of Bamenda, Bali is an interesting stopover on the road to Mamfé, and a satisfying day's excursion from Bamenda, especially now that the road has been paved as far as Batibo (20km past Bali and the region's palm-wine capital). The beautiful **scenery** alone makes the trip worthwhile.

Bali's main attraction is the town's **Prescraft centre** where they make most of the wooden artefacts sold in the Prescraft shops in Bamenda and Limbé. If you arrive during the working week, you can see the skilled artists busy carving, weaving, and decorating calabashes. A shop at the centre sells a small selection of the results. Another good reason to stop is for the **Fon's palace**, not so much to see the modern palace (though that does have an interesting small exhibition), but more in the hope of having an audience with the Fon (chief) himself, a German-educated philosopher who is always keen to meet visitors to his Fondom. If you're lucky he might even pull out some of his palm wine – reputedly the best in the area. The palace is also the place to get information and a guide for day-trips in the area, such as to the sacred cave where you'll see the skulls of Bali's many warrior enemies. Also recommended is **Forthung's Tower of Babel**, an incomplete 72-room building, which would have outdone the Fon's palace, had witchcraft not been used to prevent this grand treason from happening. Forthung died before it was completed.

With the completion of the new paved road, there's really no reason to **stay overnight** in Bali. If you do, the *Prescraft Centre* has two rooms (❷) with a fully equipped kitchen in an old mission house. Book at Prescraft in Bamenda (☎336.12.81); the price is reduced if you bring your own bedding.

Awing crater lake and Mount Lefo

Another possible excursion from Bamenda is to the tranquil **Awing crater lake,** just north of Santa on the Douala–Yaoundé road. A signpost points to a road leading east to the Bafut Ngemba Forestry Reserve; the lake is just beyond the reserve. Many Bamenda expats come here to swim at weekends, and Cameroonians to fish, although for superstitious reasons many prefer to steer clear of it altogether. If you ask the Fon of Awing for permission (a few kilometres further down the road) you can **camp** in the beautiful hills surrounding the lake. A major **tourist resort** is planned for the area – but may not take off for many years yet.

Mount Lefo (2250m), the fourth highest mountain in Cameroon – and West Africa – is a day's demanding climb from Lake Awing; the Fon of Awing will provide you with a guide (around CFA3000). On the lower slopes the climbing is easy, but the last few hundred metres to the peak are very steep. There are wonderful views of the Bamenda plateau from the summit, and of crater lakes in various stages of geological formation.

The Ring Road

The **Ring Road** comprises 360km of difficult red-earth road interspersed by a few paved sections. Despite the demanding road conditions, this is a highly recommended route, bucking and swerving through some of the finest scenery in Africa, the verdant pasturelands of the **Grassfields**. But don't expect rolling savanna – for the most part the Grassfields are hilly meadows of rank herbage between stands of hardwood forest and patches of shifting agriculture. Natural sites in the region include the thundering **Menchum Falls**, a number of volcanoes such as **Mount Oku** (3011m), and nearly forty clear **crater lakes**, many of them sacred, and at least one of them (Nyos) potentially dangerous. Terraced farmlands defy the steep slopes; the mountain soils, ploughed along the contours, sustain crops like cocoyams, maize and plantains. Cash crops, such as coffee, grow at higher altitudes, and **Fulani herders** roam the pastures to graze their cattle.

The best way to tour the Ring Road is by **car**, which allows you the freedom to stop between the route's main centres, **Bamenda**, **Wum**, **Nkambé** and **Kumbo**. Unfortunately, at the time of writing, the northern stretch of the road – between Nkambé and Wum – has become completely **impassable** to vehicles since the bridges at Nyos and Weh collapsed. With persistence it should be possible to complete the route in a 4WD vehicle, avoiding the collapsed bridges and crossing the rivers elsewhere. Otherwise, until the bridges along the northern stretch are repaired, the choice is between doing the Ring Road as a "U" or following an increasingly popular alternative route – **the small ring road** – via Bamenda, Wum, Weh, Fundong, Belo and Bambui. The Bamenda tourist office (☎794.99.93) can update you on road conditions. With a good 4WD vehicle, and provided the bridges have been repaired, you could rush round the entire Ring Road in two days (the small ring road can be done in a day).

All larger towns on the two routes are accessible by **public transport** and offer basic accommodation. However, many of the most interesting sites described below are off the main road, and you'll have to forgo them if you don't have your own transport unless you're willing to trek. Travelling by public transport also means it's very difficult to camp as you travel, and camping in the countryside – when you can find a flat space – is one of the Ring Road's greatest pleasures. Should you choose to **cycle** some or all of the way round, beware that any rain will stop your machine dead in its tracks, horribly clogged with mud. In dry conditions, though, this is outstanding mountain-bike territory; allow around a week for the circuit. Whichever way you go, try to have a larger-scale **map** than the Michelin (try the tourist office in Bamenda); there's a certain frustration in trying to follow a twisting, village-spotted route at 40km to 1cm. It's also a good idea to bring some local whisky, available in most larger towns, to present to the Fons (chiefs), if you visit any of the palaces in the various chiefdoms.

Bafut

The first stop along the Ring Road, heading in a clockwise direction from Bamenda, is the chiefdom of **BAFUT**, which acquired international fame in the 1950s and 1960s as the site of two animal-collecting trips by the naturalist Gerald Durrell. His account of the first, *The Bafut Beagles* (a reference to the team of hunters he assembled), makes amusing reading, though Bafut today feels a far cry from those slightly mythologized days of assistant district commissioners and pink gin.

Bafut is a **Tikar** community – people who migrated to Bafut from the northern regions of Lake Chad – and the most powerful of the traditional kingdoms in the Grassfields, divided into 26 **wards** in a ten-kilometre stretch of the Ring Road that trails along a ridge above the Menchum valley. The current Fon of Bafut – **Abumbi II** – is a Paramount Fon, titular overlord of a large number of lesser Fons in the region, and son of the Fon featured in Gerald Durell's book. Still quite young (he still has only 52 wives, compared to the previous Fon's 152), Abumbi was chosen in his father's 100-odd offspring to ascend to the throne when the aged Fon died in 1971. Although he was educated in Yaoundé, he was allowed to succeed his father – in theory, upon pain of death if he broke local tradition. In **religion**, although the Tikar have long been dominated by Fulani Muslims, and thus heavily Islamicized themselves, they've also (perhaps not coincidentally) been the subjects of intense Presbyterian missionary work, so you'll meet a fair few Christians too.

Taxis ply the 20-kilometre paved stretch between Bamenda and Bafut continuously. For **accommodation**, Gerald Durell's old residence overlooking the palace grounds – built by the Germans for the Fon to reside in – is currently being refurbished as a guesthouse (③). You can book rooms through the palace (☎796.83.05; call late evening). Alternatively, the *Savanna Botanic Gardens* (②), 5km down the Bamenda road, is beautifully situated in parklike grounds and has a few spacious self-contained rooms – but also a persistent water problem, hence the low price. You can also **camp** here, and there's an excellent but pricey **bar-restaurant**.

The Town

The main attraction in Bafut is the **Fon's Palace**, a large complex laid out in a quiet pattern of dark interiors and bright courtyards. The most sacred building in the complex is the **Achum**, the previous Fon's palace, with its striking, pyramidal thatched roof. Dedicated to the ancestors, only the Fon and other notables are allowed to enter this shrine. A visit to the royal compound and grounds costs CFA1000 per person and CFA1500 for a camera. The Fon's wives act as guides, and sell home-made souvenirs within the compound. There's also a small and disorganized museum (CFA2000) filled with the Fon's knick-knacks; it's not really worth a visit at present, but may improve when it's moved to the guesthouse in the near future. Bafut's **market** takes place every eight days and is very lively. People come from all over the region for its selection of fruits, vegetables, spices, meat and animals.

The yearly **grass-cutting ceremony** is still performed much as it was in the 1950s when described by Durrell. The entire community goes into the grasslands at the end of the dry season (usually late April) to collect bundles for rethatching the Achum and other important buildings, trooping in front of the Fon with their offerings. It's a confirmation of community spirit and always ends up with tremendous feasting and the consumption of huge quantities of palm wine. A second annual **festival** takes place a week or so before Christmas, with formal, dressy presentations and much discharging of old guns, followed by a noisy series of dances and musical shows.

Wum and around

Travelling towards **Wum**, the last important town along the west side of the Ring Road from Bafut, the vegetation grows increasingly dense as the road follows the course of the **Menchum**. This stretch of road has deteriorated drastically during the past years and is virtually impassable in the wet season. About 20km short of Wum, the **Menchum Falls** plunge spectacularly down a rocky cliffside, but they're set slightly off the road (on the west side) and you could easily pass right by without noticing them. If you have your own car, start looking out about 30km north of Bafut and listen for the thundering sound of falling water. At the exact spot, you'll probably see tyre marks where cars have pulled off the road. If you ask your taxi driver to pull off for a moment here, he's likely to oblige. There are no facilities of any kind here, nor anything to stop you boulder-hopping across the river in the dry season – except common sense; a French woman was swept over the edge in the 1990s doing just this.

WUM is effectively a roadhead: beyond the town, public transport more or less fades out except on market days. The best **hotels** in town are the *Morning Star Hotel* (℡336.26.34; ❶), off the Bamenda road, which has a few self-contained rooms, a top-floor veranda with a stunning view of the surrounding hills, and a bar; and *Lake Nyos City Hotel* (❶), near the motor park, which also has self-contained rooms with great views from upstairs. Unless you arrange to have **food** prepared at the hotels, your best bet is to head for the motor park. Try the *Prisma* near Symbol of Unity Express, or *New Deal* near Pressbook, a popular "off-licence" where you can also buy food. For grilled fish, *Patience* near the market is the place to head for.

Three kilometres northwest of the town centre, **Lake Wum** is a beautiful crater lake nestled in the patchily cultivated hills. Fulani herders graze their cattle in the open fields and bring them down to the lake to drink. You can swim here (although the banks are a bit muddy) – the cool, green waters are immensely deep. If you're equipped to **camp**, contact the SDO (Senior Divisional Officer) in Wum for permission. Be aware of the justified paranoia of some locals about their crater lakes; see the advice about Lake Nyos on p.1208.

It's impossible to **move on** from Wum to Nkambé by collective transport now that the bridges have collapsed at Weh and Nyos. If these are repaired, you might find extremely infrequent (around once a week) transport to Nkambé, although even this won't run when the rains start in April. You may be able to rent a truck and driver at the motor park for a steep CFA40,000 to take you to Nkambé. When you see the condition of the road – it's not much more than a cattle track – you'll understand why the price is so high. Get ready for a very rough ride.

Wum to Bambui: the small ring road

Northeast of Wum, the Ring Road branches at **Weh**. If you head right (south), you get back to Bamenda via the **small ring road** (infrequent public transport) and the town of Fundong. Alternatively you can hire a motorbike with driver in Wum (CFA5000) and do the three-hour bumpy journey across magnificent highland savanna straight to Fundong, cutting out Weh in the process. En route you'll probably pass numerous Fulani herders on horseback (many with mobile phones clipped onto their belts) and see some amazing birdlife. In **FUNDONG** you'll find the

Chimney waterfalls and good basic **accommodation** at the *Tourist Home Hotel* (❶) and *Millennium Summer Hotel* (☎777.03.40; ❶). From here, there's daily Garanti Express transport back to Bamenda along a faultlessly paved new road. Further along this road is **BELO** village, two hours from Bamenda and the starting point for a beautiful three-hour hike into the **Ijim Forest** – bordering the Kilum Forest and Mount Oku.

Wum to Nkambé

Continuing east on the main Ring Road, Weh offers the last chance until Nkambé of pumped water, market produce and chop-house food. After Weh, the road becomes wilder and switchbacks into a broad valley where a **collapsed bridge** abruptly stops all further traffic. Beyond here, the population diminishes drastically and the **landscapes** become astonishingly beautiful, at their pristine best – and most startlingly colourful – after the **rains** have started in April.

It's easy to understand why the area has acquired the name **Grassfields**. Frequent burning on the slopes favours the growth of grass over shrubs and bushes, making for excellent grazing – you're likely to see Fulani and their cattle along this stretch.

Lake Nyos

The dead village of **Nyos** is on the Ring Road about 30km from Weh (not, as marked on some maps, south of it). The notorious **Lake Nyos** is a couple of kilometres to the south. The deep crater lake was the site of a mysterious natural **gas eruption** in 1986 which killed up to 3000 people when a cloud of suffocating gas, mainly carbon dioxide, billowed off its surface and rolled northwards down the valley towards Su-bum. Scientists believe that a reaction between the warmer surface waters and the cold carbon-dioxide-saturated waters of the lake depths caused the huge release of gas – something which could happen again at any of the deep lakes in the region. As a preventative measure scientists have begun venting a number of lakes to decrease gas pressures at the bottom. The crater lakes are supposed to be the homes of the spirits of the Fons, and many locals still believe that Western scientific experimenting caused the event – foreigners are regarded suspiciously by some locals, who you may have to convince of your harmless intentions.

Su-Bum (Soumbon) – a scattering of houses and smoke-stained compounds looped along the valley about 30km from Weh – is now the only settlement of any size in the Nyos area. It too suffered a number of casualties from the gas disaster. More happily it boasts quite spectacular avocados. Camping or staying with people are the only options there.

Kimbi River Game Reserve

Some 50km from Weh, but currently only accessible from Nkambé in the east (2–3hr; only accessible by 4WD in the rainy season), lies the **Kimbi River Game Reserve**. The most abundant animals here are thought to be **waterbuck and buffalo**, though they're suffering severely from poaching. There's a **resthouse** (❶) of doubtful standard in the reserve – ask at the tourist office in Bamenda (☎794.99.93). You'll need your own 4WD transport to explore the park; there are no vehicles available for hire.

Dumbo: trekking into Nigeria

Seventy-four kilometres from Weh (and 21km from Nkambé) at **Misanje**, a pleasant market village with a small **auberge** (❶), a branch road heads north to **DUMBO** (17km) and the start of an exceptional trekking route – strictly foot traffic only – into Nigeria. Customs and immigration are in Dumbo. Officials are generally friendly here, and may even help you find a guide-cum-porter to continue to Nigeria (about CFA5000). There's **accommodation** at *The Greenland* (❶).

The first quarter of the 40-kilometre trek is a gentle climb, which levels out for a few kilometres before reaching the edge of the escarpment and the steep, beautiful descent into Nigeria. The first small town you reach is **Bissaula** (see p.1135), where customs and immigration officials will be waiting. With an early start, the trek can even be done in one day, but there's no accommodation in Bissaula, so you may choose to spend a night in a mountain village before catching early-morning transport out of Bissaula

Nkambé to Kumbo

NKAMBÉ, on the northeast side of the Ring Road, is a large town by Grassfields standards, signalling your return from remote regions with filling stations, numerous eating and drinking houses, and a few hotels – the best are the inexpensive *Divisional Hotel* (☎336.13.24; ❶) and the more comfortable *Millennium Star Hotel* (☎751.68.70; ❷).

From Nkambé, you can catch a share taxi heading north to **Ako** and the Nigerian border. To the south, the route continues at an altitude of between 1500m and 2000m, soon becoming more densely populated and passing through the chiefdom of **Mbot**, which has its own Fon and palace. **NDU**, a couple of kilometres further, is the site of Cameroon's largest tea plantation, an enterprise begun by the British in the 1950s. In Ndu, *Dallas Hotel* (❶) is a clean and convenient stopover, with bucket showers (there is no running water in Ndu) and electricity. A road leads east from Ndu to **Sabongari**, where a motorable track connects with Gembu in Nigeria. South to Kumbo, about 10km before you reach the town, the region's largest cattle market takes place every Friday in the small village of **Takija**.

Kumbo

KUMBO stands on a plateau 2000m above sea level. One of the biggest towns in the Grassfields, it has plenty of accommodation, banks and other facilities, including two of the best hospitals in the region. It's also the seat of another powerful **chiefdom** – as important as those of Bali and Bafut – that of the **Nso** linguistic group (the Banso). The Fon lives here in a **palace** with both old and new sections (the latter with a decidedly Islamic flavour, as the last Fon was from the Muslim side of the family lineage). Though now predominantly a Catholic community, the Banso are traditionalists. Don't offer traditional office-holders your hand when greeting, nor cross your legs while seated, nor drink in their presence, nor pass the traditional policeman (the *Ngwerong*) on his left. The Banso were defeated by the Germans in 1906, and their Fon executed in Bamenda – bitter history to which they have never been completely reconciled.

There's a large **market** in Kumbo every eight days, while once every year a spectacular **horse race** is held at the Tobin Stadium. Fulani and Banso people from throughout the region assemble here for the event, which usually takes place in November. If you can plan it right, it's exhilarating to watch their daredevil bareback riding; for more information, contact the tourist office in Bamenda (☎794.99.93). On a slightly more offbeat note, there's a **cave** about half a kilometre east of Kumbo which is the resting place of a number of old skulls from long-ago traditional feuds. Find someone to take you.

As for **accommodation**, the bottom line is the *Central Inn Hotel* (☎348.10.15; ❶), overlooking the central motor park. *Merry Land* (☎348.10.77; ❶) is better and has a good range of rooms, but the most comfortable and best-value hotel in town is the *Fomo 92* (☎348.16.16, 🖷348.16.61; ❷), off the Nkambé road just north of town. For **food**, the *Casablanca 2000* serves excellent chicken DG and cold beer at very reasonable prices. The *Samba* **nightclub** is a good place to shake off the Ring Road dust.

Elak

From Kumbo, you can detour off the Ring Road to **ELAK**, the principal village of the Oku Fondom. The Oku people are renowned for their black magic and traditional medicines as well as their rich culture. The Oku cultural week, held at the **Fon's palace** around Easter, is a good opportunity to witness Oku masked dancing.

Elak is situated high on the northern slopes of **Mount Oku** – at 3011m, the second highest point in West Africa after Mount Cameroon. It's a pleasant climb to the summit, passing first through steep farmland and then into the **Kilum Forest** which, together with the neighbouring **Ijim Forest**, constitutes the largest remaining fragment of the montane forest that once covered much of the highlands. The forest is home to diverse birdlife: you may see the very localized and unmistakeably red-headed **Bannerman's turaco** and the rare **banded wattle-eye**. At 2800m the forest gives way to sub-alpine grassland. From these cool heights you can reputedly see Mount Cameroon on exceptionally clear days. For more information about the ecology of the forests contact the **Kilum Mountain Forest Project** in Elak or call the project manager in Bamenda on ☏336.32.93.

On the western slopes of the mountain, at 2200m, is **Lake Oku**, a spectacular deep green crater lake encircled by a splendid dark forest. Lake Oku is sacred and tradition forbids fishing and swimming, though exceptions are sometimes made for foreigners. However, for the sake of protocol, you should ask the Fon for permission before setting out to the lake or up the mountain. To do so, go to the **Fon's palace** at the far end of town equipped with the customary gift of a bottle of wine or local whisky. Here you will be given permission to climb the mountain or see the lake and someone will be assigned as your guide. Agree a price before setting off (around CFA5000).

The basic *Touristic Hotel* (**❶**), just below the marketplace, has friendly service and a bar – usually playing loud music. There are also several private houses in Elak with rooms available to rent. While in Oku, don't miss the extremely tasty local **honey**.

Kumbo to Bamenda

The leg from Kumbo to Bamenda is the most populous stretch of the Ring Road. South to **JAKIRI** it affords panoramic views of the **Ndop Plains** stretching out to the east and forming a bed for the vast waters of the **Lake Bamendjing** reservoir. Jakiri was the headquarters of British troops from 1958 to 1961 when Southern Cameroon was on the verge of independence. A spectacular range of hills rears up near the town. If you decide to **stay** in Jakiri, there's the basic *Hotel Trans Afrique* (**❶**).

From Jakiri, you can branch off on a direct road to Foumban, 75km to the southeast. The main Ring Road continues on through ravishing scenery to **NDOP** and Bambui, whence it's a twelve-kilometre hop to Bamenda.

Foumban

Capital of the Bamoun people and seat of their **sultan**, the town of **FOUMBAN** is charged with history and culture. You're reminded of it at every turn as you pass monuments like the outstanding **Royal Palace**, built at the beginning of the century, the **Musée des Arts et des Traditions Bamoun** or the *ateliers* of the talented **craftsmen** who churn out works in bronze, ebony and a host of other materials. These elements have given Foumban the most touristy feel of any town in the west, and you'll be the target of endless children who want to be your guide, shouting claims to be "sons of the sultan" (with such a prolific ruler, there may be an element of truth to many of them). There's definitely an unusual pressure to

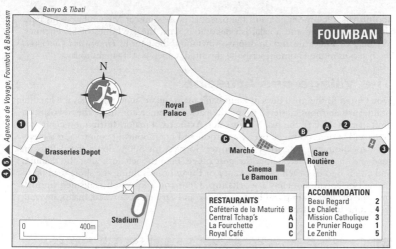

FOUMBAN

N

Royal Palace

① ② Agences de Voyage, Foumbot & Bafoussam ④ ⑤

Brasseries Depot

⓪

C Marché

B **A** ②

3

Gare Routière

Cinema Le Bamoun

Stadium

0   400m

RESTAURANTS	
Caféteria de la Maturité	B
Central Tchap's	A
La Fourchette	D
Royal Café	C

ACCOMMODATION	
Beau Regard	2
Le Chalet	4
Mission Catholique	3
Le Prunier Rouge	1
Le Zenith	5

▼ Village des Artisans & Musée des Arts et Traditions Bamoun

spend money at every turn – "come in to my shop, just for the pleasure of your eyes". Such an atmosphere, however, shouldn't deter you from visiting Foumban. Delving into its history and culture is a rewarding step towards an understanding of the whole region.

The Town

While the **administrative quarter** – with the town hall, post office, hospital and *préfecture* – clusters on the west of town, the sites more likely to draw your attention are all in the centre, within walking distance of the **Royal Palace**. Built in 1917 by King Njoya, the old palace (the present sultan lives in a new one) is a notable architectural achievement, unique in Africa. The townspeople may tell you the king conceived his design in a dream, but he must have done some studying to enable him to combine assorted elements of German Baroque with such pure Romanesque forms – he was greatly influenced by a visit to the German castle at Buea.

The Palace and Sultan's Museum

You approach the palace by means of a vast **courtyard** lined with *rônier* palms, tempering its blue tones with long shadows. Constructed entirely of locally made bricks, the mass is supported by strong pillars, the walls are carried by arcades and the structure embellished with balconies worked with intricately carved wood. As you enter the building, you can't help but be impressed by the grandeur of the entrance hall, the armoury and the reception hall with its ceiling supported by four majestic columns. In the morning you can pass by to watch as the sultan holds court in the palace foyer. After prayers on Fridays, starting at around 1.30pm, you can also witness a colourful and deeply traditional event take place, as court musicians play for the sultan while brilliantly dressed subjects pay their respects and seek the sultan's advice and good offices.

Tickets are sold in the reception hall (CFA2000) for the **Sultan's Museum** upstairs, one of the most interesting museums in Cameroon; you'll be shown around by very knowledgeable bilingual guides. A private collection of memorabilia from the long line of kings gives a very personal overview of Bamoun history. Among the eclectic assortment of objects are thrones decorated with beadwork, masks, shields and weapons made from hides and woven raffia palms, and a large collection of

sculptures. One room contains the personal possessions of Mbuémbué – his pipe, shields and dagger, and a calabash decorated with the jawbones of his enemies. Writings by Njoya are also on display – including the famous *History and Customs of the Bamouns* in the Shumom script he invented, which is still taught today.

The Village des Artisans

Don't listen to the small boys in Foumban's main square, who insist that the handful of little artisan shops clustered round the palace entrance constitute the town's main craft market. In fact, the real **Village des Artisans**, a major distribution centre for crafts and antiques from all over Cameroon and neighbouring countries, is a pleasant two-kilometre walk from the centre. Go west for 500m down the Bafoussam road and then turn left before the post office. Take the left fork after the stadium, and you'll find that each of the twenty or thirty houses lining the short road up to the village square contains a **workshop**. Here you can watch craftsmen from all over the country casting and beating metals, and carving kola wood, mahogany and, from time to time, ivory.

The Bamoun Empire

The Bamoun Empire dates from the fourteenth century and was founded by **Nshare Yen**, the first of seventeen kings in the present dynasty. Son of a Tikar chief, Nshare led a faction of rebels away from the main territory and settled in the eastern country known as Pa-Mben. Here he consolidated his power and proclaimed himself king, establishing **Mfom-Ben** (whence Foumban) as his capital. The subsequent history has been carefully recorded, and today the accomplishments of all Nshare's successors are known in detail.

One of the most remarkable was **Mbuémbué**, a giant of a leader (he is said to have been 2.6m tall) whose first words were, "I will make the borders of the kingdom with blood and black iron; borders made with words are inevitably erased." Speaking at a normal level, his voice carried 2km (when he shouted, he could be heard for 15km). Not surprisingly, people listened. He fortified his capital (ruins of the old walls can be seen today), withstood Fulbe (Fulani) invasions and pushed back his Tikar and Bamiléké rivals, thus expanding the empire.

Of all the kings, however, the greatest was the sixteenth in the dynasty, **Ibrahim Njoya** (reigned 1895–1924), under whose rule Bamoun culture experienced a golden age. A remarkable figure, he masterminded numerous inventions, not least of which was the **Bamoun alphabet** (one of only two in the whole West African region; the other was the Vai script in Liberia). Shumom, the language of the Bamoun, consists largely of monosyllabic roots, so Njoya's 510 original signs were easily converted, in 1909, into a syllabary and later refined into a true alphabet.

Once the alphabet was created, Njoya founded schools throughout the kingdom to teach the new writing. He also tried, less successfully, to design a printing press, and set about recording Bamoun tradition. It is thanks to his *History and Customs of the Bamouns* that so much is known about the empire (or, to be accurate, about his account of it, as related through oral tradition). Njoya also drew up a map of his kingdom, invented an electric mill and designed the outstanding **Royal Palace**.

Having converted to Islam he was proclaimed Sultan of Bamoun, but with the arrival of Christian missionaries, he attempted to create a **new religion** that fused Islam, Christianity and traditional beliefs. The secular state (first colonial, later independent) tended to restrain this development, but Bamoun **court music and theatre** still reflect it and Islam, especially, is a strong influence on Bamoun sculpture. Njoya was deposed by the French in 1924, and eventually exiled to Yaoundé where he died in 1933, his pro-German views still mistrusted by the French. The present sultan is Mboumbou Njoya Ibrahim.

15

Agences de voyage headed for Douala and Youndé via Bafoussam are all located outside town, past the town gate and hospital. Moungo Voyages (☎348.26.04) and Butsi Voyages have a few daily connections to **Douala** and **Yaoundé**, and regular daily departures to **Bafoussam**. Alliance, Narral and Mayo-Banyo Voyages, located in the same area, have a few weekly minibuses to **Ngaoundéré** via **Tibati** and **Banyo**, but note that this route is notoriously difficult; the *agences* advertise ten to twelve hours to get to Ngaoundéré, but in reality it can take several days, depending on the state of the road, and it's only possible during the dry season. An option is to stop in **Banyo**, where you can spend the night at one of the inexpensive hostels (❶) near the market. From here to **Tibati** takes half a day, and you can then get another taxi (along paved road) to **Ngaoundal** (1hr 30min) or directly to **Ngaoundéré** (around half a day).

The **gare routière**, in the town centre next to the market, has share taxis for short distances like Foumbot, but only rarely for longer distances. Minibuses and *clandos*, for longer distances, can be found near the agencies outside town and will take you to Kumbo via Jakiri, Nkongsamba, Bafoussam and Bamenda, leaving when full.

Some of the finished artefacts are bright and new-looking, while some are tarnished to suit European tastes for elusive "authenticity", but there's little attempt to fool you that you are buying a valuable antique when you can see identical items being manufactured alongside. Nevertheless, some shops also sell genuine antiques, mainly smuggled from Nigeria – you'll need some expertise to tell the difference.

Musée des Arts et des Traditions Bamoun

On the square above the Village des Artisans is the **Musée des Arts et des Traditions Bamoun** (Mon–Sat 8am–4pm). You enter through two ornate carved doors, and begin your visit in the **Salle Mosé Yeyap** (Mosé Yeyap was a patron of the arts at the time of Sultan Njoya, and this museum started off as his private collection). Along the walls, a series of intricately carved wooden plaques portray important events in Bamoun history. Beside these are jugs for heating palm wine, clay masks, and samples of naturally dyed cloth. Notice the collection of clay and bronze pipes (some up to 2m long) used by dignitaries in traditional ceremonies, as well as the engraved gongs that the sultan would present to military heroes.

The **Salle du Guerrier** contains military relics recalling the many clashes between the Bamoun and their Bamiléké, Tikar and Fulani neighbours. You'll see spears, *coupe-coupes* (engraved cups), protective charms and a calabash decorated with a skull and jawbones that was used in victory celebrations. In the **Salle du Notable**, a carved bed and table, weapons for fighting and hunting, and riding gear evoke the lifestyle of the Bamoun elite. The **Salle du Danseur** is dedicated to music and dance, with costumes and unusual instruments including a xylophone with carved snake heads. The Sultan's **court orchestra** still play these instruments to accompany elaborate set theatrical pieces, and have toured abroad. The final room, the **Salle de la Cuisine Bamoun**, contains cooking utensils – pottery, baskets for smoking meat and mortars – used by Bamoun women.

The attendants are welcoming and helpful, not importunate but always ready to answer any questions; a donation is expected, around CFA1000. Don't forget to ask before taking pictures: permission is usually granted, but not as a rule, as they fear people will make postcards out of the photos.

Practicalities

There's nowhere official to **change money** in Foumban, though you can usually change cash dollars and euros at a few shops around the market. For **food**, apart from the few hotel restaurants, you might try the *Caféteria de la Maturité* close to the *gare routière* in the centre, which serves fresh salad and good helpings of rice, beans and meat for about CFA500. The *Royal Café*, across from the mosque, sells well-prepared though somewhat expensive Cameroonian dishes; there's a great view of the Foumban valley from the terrace. *Central Tchap's*, near hotel *Beau Regard* on the main road, is a great place to sit and enjoy a drink or try the freshly grilled fish prepared every evening by women in front of the bar. *La Fourchette*, further along the Bafoussam road, has hamburgers and pizza.

Due to a heavy tourist presence, Foumban's **hotels** tend to be poor value. The best hotels are on the outskirt of town.

Beau Regard On the main commercial street ☎ 348.21.83. Centrally located, but quite run-down, though the (mainly self-contained) rooms are clean. ❶

Le Chalet Off rte de Bafoussam ☎ 348.24.12. Airy rooms in a quiet setting – comfortable and good value despite the distance from the centre. For safety, take a taxi home at night. ❷

Mission Catholique On the main street next to the church. Two dorms with a few beds and shared facilities. Very basic, but central. CFA2500 per person.

Le Prunier Rouge Near the Brasseries depot, within walking distance of the centre ☎ 348.23.52. An older place with some charm (though the namesake plum tree that grew through the roof of the restaurant is gone). Rooms are very basic, but there's a picturesque view from upstairs. ❶

Le Zenith Off the rte de Bafoussam at the edge of town ☎ 348.24.25. Newly repainted hotel, with small but clean self-contained rooms, and hot water if you're lucky. ❷

15.3

Yaoundé and the south

As the capital of Cameroon, Yaoundé has been consciously developed as a showcase, but remains essentially a large town interspersed with prestige buildings, not all of them finished. Still, you'll find most of the facilities you need, many good restaurants, and a city that is relatively easy to get around.

Only a few hours away to the southwest, spectacular **beaches** dot the Atlantic coastline between the fishing village of **Londji** and **Campo**, on the border of Equatorial Guinea. In between, the nation's second port, **Kribi**, has become something of a holiday centre where Yaoundé's well-to-do head for the weekend. When you've had enough beach life, **Campo Ma'an National Park**, east of Campo, makes a satisfying day-trip into the rainforest. Elsewhere, the thick forest which covers the interior of the south makes travel difficult. With determination and time, you could explore these forests from towns like **Ebolowa** or **Mbalmayo** as bases.

Yaoundé

Comparisons between the rival cities of **YAOUNDÉ** and Douala are inevitable – but most visitors prefer the capital. Set at an altitude of some 700m, Yaoundé enjoys a cooler climate and lies amid magnificent natural surroundings, heavy with green vegetation, and with a range of peaks, including **Mont Fébé**, as a backdrop. The city's architecture adds to the positive impression, and new buildings, especially in the administrative quarter, give the city at least a superficial feeling of progressiveness lacking in Douala. But what Yaoundé has gained in credibility, it has perhaps lost in colour and spontaneity; somehow it all seems a bit stiff.

Some history

The name **Yaoundé** is a corruption of **Ewondo**, the name of the ethnic group living in the area when the Germans arrived, who, incidentally, still use the area's original name: *Ongola*. The Ewondo's history has them crossing the **Sanaga River** on the back of a giant snake before settling on the hilltops of the site of present-day Yaoundé. When the **Germans** crisscrossed the country at the end of the nineteenth century, setting up military posts to affirm their influence in the new protectorate, they established a small presence here; their first commercial enterprises followed in 1907. After World War I, the French chose the budding settlement as capital of their newly acquired territory; the British had claims to the former capital, Buea, so Yaoundé became the administrative centre more or less by default. It has continued in that role ever since (except for a brief period during World War II), although its population and industry lag far behind Douala's.

Arrival, information and city transport

Travelling to Yaoundé with an *agence de voyage*, you're most likely to arrive at the office of whichever company you're travelling with; most are based in **Mvan** neighbourhood, about 3km south of Place Ahmadou Ahidjo (better known as the Score roundabout). You can catch a **yellow share taxi** into town (CFA200). If you arrive from West or North West province – Bafoussam, Foumban and Bamenda – you'll be dropped off at one of the company offices near the *gare routière* in **Etoudi**, about 4km north of the centre. This is also where you may find yourself if you're arriving from the east by either *agence* or by share taxi. Otherwise, Carrefour Obili, west of the city near the University of Earth Sciences, is where you'll arrive if you come by share taxi from Bamenda or the southwest. There are a few *agences* based here as well.

Nsimalen International **airport** is roughly 18km south of place Ahmadou Ahidjo down Boulevard de l'OCAM; a taxi into town costs CFA1700 (CFA3500 private hire). By train, you'll arrive at the **railway station** just off place Elig-Essono, about a kilometre north of place Ahmadou Ahidjo. Several of the cheaper accommodation options are located north of the station, away from the centre.

With its undulating hills spreading over an area of some forty square kilometres, and with few straight streets, orientation can be difficult. Unless you have your own transport or a healthy budget, you'll probably find yourself dependent on the omnipresent yellow **share taxis**. A drop within town officially costs CFA150 (more for longer distances or late at night), but as demand is quite high, you may often have to up the ante to get a ride. Do like everyone else, shout out your destination and follow it by how much you're willing to pay: if they accept, they'll stop.

The **Ministère du Tourisme**, off Boulevard Rudolf Manga Bell (Mon–Fri 9am–noon & 1–5pm; ☎222.44.1, Ⓦwww.camnet.cm/mintour/tourisme), should be able to help with a few leaflets and basic advice, although – as it's a ministry and not a tourist office – finding someone to talk to can sometimes be a problem. They also find the concept of travelling on a budget a bit odd, though they're slowly adapting.

Accommodation

While Yaoundé has the luxury hotels you'd expect of a capital city, it also possesses a reasonable network of moderately priced accommodation. Small hotels here are less

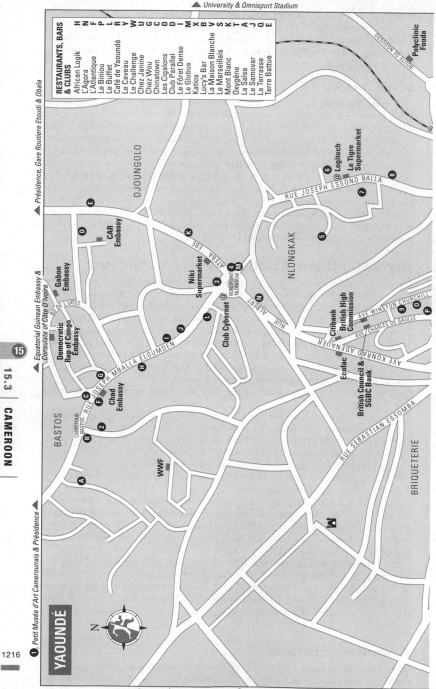

YAOUNDÉ

RESTAURANTS, BARS & CLUBS

African Logik	H
L'Agora	N
L'Atlantique	F
Le Biniou	P
Le Buffet	L
Café de Yaoundé	R
Le Caveau	Y
Le Challenge	W
Chez Janine	U
Chez Wou	G
Chinatown	C
Les Cigalons	O
Club Parallel	D
Le Fôret Dense	I
Le Globus	M
Katios	X
Lucy's Bar	B
La Maison Blanche	V
Le Marseillais	S
Mont Blanc	K
Oxygène	T
La Salsa	A
Le Samovar	J
La Terrasse	Q
Terre Battue	E

▲ University & Omnisport Stadium

▲ Présidence, Gare Routière Etoudi & Obala

▲ Equatorial Guinean Embassy & Consulate of Côte D'Ivoire

▲ Petit Musée d'Art Camerounais & Présidence

● Edea, ▲ Douala, the West & Nigeria

Palais des Congrès & New Grand Mosque (0.2 km)

DJOUNGOLO

BASTOS

NLONGKAK

BRIQUETERIE

Polyclinic Fouda

ROUTE DE NGOUSSO

RUE JOSEPH ESSONO BALLA

Le Tigre Supermarket

Logitech

CAR Embassy

Gabon Embassy

BD DE L'URSS

Democratic Rep of Congo Embassy

Chad Embassy

CARREFOUR BASTOS

RUE JOSEPH MBALLA ELOUMDEN

WWF

Niki Supermarket

ATEBA EBE

RONDPOINT NLONGKAK

Club Cybernet

RUE ALBERT

Citibank

British High Commission

Ecofac

British Council & SGBC Bank

AVE KONRAD ADENAUER

AVE CHARLES DE GAULLE

AVE WINSTON CHURCHILL

RUE SEBASTIAN ESSOMBA

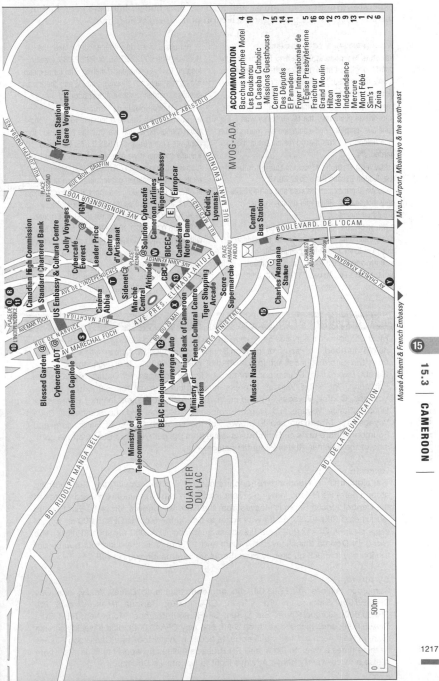

ACCOMMODATION
Bacchus Morphee Motel	4
Les Boukarou	10
La Caseba Catholic Missions Guesthouse	7
Central	15
Des Députés	14
El Panaden	11
Foyer Internationale de l'Église Presbytérienne	5
Fraicheur	16
Grand Moulin	8
Hilton	12
Idéal	3
Independance	9
Mercure	13
Mont Fébé	1
Sim's	2
Zeina	6

▼ Mvan, Airport, Mbalmayo & the south-east

Museé Athemi & French Embassy ▼

15.3 | CAMEROON

15

1217

▼ Quartier Ndjong-Melen

expensive than those in Douala, and if you're on a budget but can't get a bed in a mission, there's still a pretty good selection of inexpensive lodgings.

Inexpensive to moderate

Bacchus Morphée Motel Behind Texaco by *rond-point* Nlongkak. Cheap, boxlike self-contained rooms in a central location, halfway between the centre and Bastos. ❷

Les Boukarou rue Narvick ☏233.39.06. Newly refurbished place near the US embassy with spacious, carpeted self-contained a/c rooms and a nice balcony. There's a good restaurant in the garden. ❸

La Caseba Catholic Missions Guesthouse Off rue Joseph Essono Balla ☏21.30.13, ✉casba@rctmail.net. Relaxed and comfortable guesthouse with single and double rooms. Breakfast included. ❷

Central Off rue Jezouin ☏222.65.98, ✉centralhotel@yahoo.com. One of the oldest places in town, with large, comfortable and recently refurbished rooms, all self-contained with bathtub, plus TV and desk. There's an outstanding but pricey hotel restaurant. ❺

El Panaden place de l'Indépendance, near the Hôtel de Ville ☏222.27.65, ℻222.27.86. Ideally located for the commercial district. The large clean a/c rooms have hot showers and TV, and there's an excellent garden restaurant next door. ❸

Foyer Internationale de l'Église Presbytérienne Off rue Onembele Nkou by *rond-point* Nlongkak, a short walk up the hill behind the concrete water towers ☏985.23.76. Clean and friendly colonial-style guesthouse with single rooms and dorm beds (CFA2000) with shared facilities. Missionaries get first crack, so the place is often full. If you do get a room, it's wise to take a taxi back at night as the path is very dark. ❷

Fraicheur On the road parallel to bd de l'OCAM ☏222.86.02, ℻223.38.15. Excellent-value hotel with everything you need: friendly staff, clean self-contained rooms, a good restaurant, and a pleasant rooftop bar. ❷

Grand Moulin rue Joseph Essono Balla ☏220.68.19, ℻220.68.20. Friendly place with

---

Moving on from Yaoundé

Most of Yaoundé's *agences de voyage* are on the main road leading south to the **Mvan** neighbourhood, 3km south of town on Boulevard de l'OCAM. A drop with a yellow taxi from the Score roundabout (place Ahidjo) costs CFA200. The main *agences* are: Garanti Express for Douala and Bamenda; Central Voyages, for Douala and Kribi; La Kribienne, for Kribi; Vatikan Express and Amour Mezan for Bamenda; Central Voyages, Confort Voyages and Binam Voyages for Bafoussam; Jeannot Express for Buea; Alliance Voyage and Narral Voyages for Bertoua and the southeast; Buca Voyages for Mbalmayo and Ebolowa. For the **western towns** of Bafoussam and Foumban, **share taxis** and **minibuses** leave from the *gare routière* Etoudi on the north side of the city, near the presidential palace.

By train

The night train to **Ngaoundéré** (departs daily at 6.10pm, arriving the next morning around 6am) via Belabo (arriving around midnight) and Ngaoundal (for road routes to the Central African Republic) leaves from the **Gare Voyageurs**, off place Elig-Essono (enquiries ☏223.40.03). A one-way ticket to Ngaoundéré costs CFA15,000 for a first-class sleeper, CFA12,000 for a first-class seat, and CFA9000 for second class. The two daily **Douala** trains leave at 7.40am and 1.30pm (taking around four hours), but the journey is much quicker by road. For more information see p.1148.

By plane

Cameroon Airlines (☏223.03.04) run **domestic** flights to Douala (daily; one way CFA29,700); Bafoussam (Fri & Sun; CFA21,000); Bertoua (Mon, Wed & Fri; CFA30,000); Garoua (Thurs, Sat & Sun; CFA67,000); Maroua (Mon, Wed, Fri & Sun; CFA85,000); and Ngaoundéré (Mon & Fri; one way CFA46,000), plus a weekly service (Sun) to Ndjamena in Chad via Garoua. In addition, Air France and Cameroon Airlines fly three times a week to Paris, and SN Brussels Airlines fly weekly to Brussels. There is also a twice-weekly Kenya Airways flight to Nairobi via Douala.

large, self-contained rooms a fifteen-minute walk from the Gare Voyageurs. **③**

Idéal By *rond-point* Nlongkak ☎ 220.98.52, ℻ 220.98.52. Popular and good-value hotel conveniently located for Bastos and the city centre. The self-contained rooms are clean, but there's cold water only and no a/c. Often full, so it's a good idea to book in advance. **②**

Indépendance av Winston Churchill ☎ 23.47.71, ℻ 222.87.26. This once luxurious but now faded hotel has become very affordable, with run-down a/c rooms with hot water. There's a lively nightclub, *Le Rramdam "O" Black*, in the basement. **④**

Sim's 1 Off rue Joseph Mballa Eloumden, Bastos ☎ 220.53.75, ℻ 220.53.76. Small but clean self-contained a/c rooms with TV; lacking in charm but convenient for the Bastos nightlife. **③**

Zeina Off rue Joseph Essono Balla ☎ 221.22.35, ℻ 222.48.33. New and friendly hotel with tidy self-contained rooms (fan or a/c) and an affable restaurant. **③**

Expensive

Des Députés In the administrative quarter near the lake ☎ 223.15.55 or 222.40.77, ℻ 223.37.10. Bland modern hotel with a/c rooms, pool (CFA2500 for non-guests), tennis courts, a bar-restaurant overlooking the lake, and a nightclub. Major credit cards accepted. **⑦**

Hilton bd du 20 Mai ☎ 223.36.46, ⓦ www.yaounde.hilton.com. This swanky hotel far outranks Yaoundé's other upmarket establishments, both in style and price. Facilities include lavish gardens with pool, fitness club, shops, a total of seven bars and restaurants, tennis court, nightclub and casino. Major credit cards accepted; prices may be negotiable. **⑧**

Mercure av Ahidjio ☎ 222.21.31, ⓦ www.accor-hotels.com. Smallish but well-equipped and immaculate rooms, plus a posh restaurant. **⑥**

Mont Fébé Mont Fébé ☎ 221.40.02, ℻ 221.60.70. A short taxi ride from the centre (CFA1000), the main attraction at this international-standard hotel is the fabulous view – choose between a room with a view of the mountain or the golf course. There's a pleasant pool, tennis court, nightclub, casino and three restaurants. **⑧**

The City

There aren't that many specific targets to aim for in Yaoundé, beyond the usual pleasures of sampling some good restaurants and visiting the main market, although the **Musée National** is worth a visit for its small permanent exhibition. The city's two other collections are a taxi ride away: the immaculately presented **Petit Musée d'Art Camerounais**, one of West Africa's most worthwhile museums, and the new **Musée Afhemi**, housing the vast private collection of a Bamiléké notable from West province.

The commercial centre

Despite the confusion caused by its asymmetrical layout, Yaoundé does have a walkable centre, with its heart at **place Ahmadou Ahidjo** – better known as **Score roundabout**. The most startling of the many buildings grouped around this square is the very 1950s **Cathedral Notre Dame**, with a sloping roof that seems to go on forever. The city's main arteries shoot out from place Ahidjo. To the east, Avenue Monseigneur Vogt runs uphill past many of the city's major banks. Avenue du Président El Hadj Ahidjo leads northwest of place Ahidjo up to the colourful **Marché Central** – a building sprawling with innovative thieves, so be cautious – while Avenue Kennedy, off Avenue Ahidjo, is one of the city's classier streets, flaunting a distinctly French flavour with its upmarket shops and a few fine lunchtime spots. This street ends in place Kennedy, where you'll find the **Centre d'Artisanat**, the town's biggest crafts depot and well worth checking out. Avenue de l'Indépendance leads from place Kennedy to place de l'Indépendance, dominated by the futuristic **Hôtel de Ville** (town hall).

The Lake Quarter and Melen

Most of the administrative buildings in town congregate to the west of place Ahidjo, between Boulevard du 20 Mai and the town lake. Known as the **Quartier du Lac**, this tranquil neighbourhood, divided by imposing avenues, has long been a construction site for experiments in modern architecture, and buildings such as the Ministry of Telecommunications **Ministère des Postes et Télécommunications** or the imaginative headquarters of the **Banque des États de l'Afrique Centrale** have gone a long way towards changing Yaoundé's image in recent years. On Boulevard Rudolph Manga Bell, next to the High Court, the **Musée National** is housed in an impressively restored colonial building and former presidential palace. On Boulevard de la Réunification, which marks the southern fringe of this *quartier*, the **Monument de la Réunification** rises up in a helter-skelter spiral commemorating the coming together of Cameroon's French- and English-speaking components. In the middle of the neighbourhood, the *lake* itself hardly provides the serene natural backdrop you might imagine. It's more like a stagnant pond – and a perfect mosquito breeding ground.

Petit Musée d'Art Camerounais

Situated in a Benedictine monastery above *Hôtel Mont Fébé*, the **Petit Musée d'Art Camerounais** (Thurs, Sat & Sun 3–6pm; donation) is way out of the centre up the Mont Fébé hill, offering a fantastic panoramic view of the city. The museum is only accessible by taxi; expect to pay CFA2000 each way. A narrow flight of steps takes you up to the museum from the main road that continues to the hotel. When you arrive, go upstairs to the second-floor reception and a monk will lead you to the exhibition. If you arrive outside museum hours and reception is open, they'll let you in for CFA1000.

The museum's stark interior is like a monument to minimalism, with clean whitewashed walls to focus attention on the displays. Although the collection is small, it contains many masterpieces, notably from the West provinces. First of all is a display of pipes (in ivory, wood and terracotta) including some amazing **Bamoun bronze pipes**. Another room features **masks**, mainly from the Grassfields, and a fantastic wooden **bas-relief** depicting a market scene. Notice, too, a king's carved wooden bed, and intricate wooden panels showing scenes from a hunt. A third room contains **Tikar bronzes** and includes pipes, bells used to call the ancestors, and a king's throne. Look out for some unusual **dice** made of fruit kernels, used by forest people of southern Cameroon as lucky charms.

Musée National

In the ministerial area, off Avenue des Ministères, the impressive and well-kept old presidential palace is now home to the **Musée National** (Mon–Sat 9am–4pm; CFA1000), its entrance highlighted by two impressive Bamoun masks. The ground floor consists of three rooms. That on the left houses changing art exhibitions, while the room next door is packed with masks, musical instruments, seats and thrones, hunting and fishing tools, weaving and smithing tools, and a good selection of Fang sculptures, all on loan from private collections – all rather disorganized, and with minimal labelling. The museum's highlight, in the room to the right of the entrance, is a very interactive exhibition devoted to Cameroon's regional culture, architecture and decorative arts, including body art, traditional rituals and society, and how to build a *pirogue*.

Musée Afhemi

Tucked away about 2km south of the centre in the Nsimeyong residential area is one of Cameroon's finest museums, the privately run Musée Afhemi (Tues–Sun 9am–7pm; CFA3000). Housed in a converted villa, the museum contains over two thousand traditional art objects, artefacts, antiquities and paintings, some more than nine hundred years old and made of wood, bronze, copper, silver, brass and fired clay – the collection is extremely rich in traditional hand-woven fabric, hand-embroidered cloth, mud cloth, tie-dyed fabric, batik and beaded objects. The front porch has been made into an art gallery, and it's possible to have lunch here (CFA3000; book in advance on ☎231.90.38).

The exhibits are spread over five rooms, each with a distinct theme. The central room contains twenty or so dummies wearing traditional dress with ritual or ceremonial masks covering their heads. The second room is devoted to charms and *ju-jus*, with a jumble of healing art works and power mediums, vectors of good omens, and repellants of dangerous charms – powerful stuff. Room number three focuses on Baliléké women, with dummies dressed in traditional women's clothing and masks. The fourth room has an array of traditional musical instruments, while the fifth is packed with pottery.

Mass at Ndjong-Melen and Mvog-Betsi Zoo

The animated **mass** at Ndjong-Melen is a famous outing, though it isn't staged for tourists. Every Sunday from 9.30am to noon the congregation in the **Catholic church** in the quarter of Ndjong-Melen works itself into a state of high excitement during the Ewondo-language service. There's wonderful music, dancing and high-energy drumming, and everyone wears their most colourful outfits.

For something equally audible, also in the Melen quarter (but otherwise a completely different kettle of fish), the newly renovated **Mvog-Betsi Zoo** (daily 9am–6pm; CFA2000, camera CFA5000, video CDA10,000) is no longer a place to avoid with horror and disgust, and actually makes for quite a pleasurable afternoon. Concerned mainly with primate protection and conservation, the zoo now houses relatively content-looking native primates including mandrills, mangabeys, guenons and a group of highly endangered drills, along with the inevitable lion, hyenas, snakes and other reptiles.

The zoo also manages a second site at **Mfou National Park**, on the southern outskirts of Yaoundé. The spacious enclosures here are home to orphaned native primates, including gorillas and chimps, whose parents were slaughtered as a result of the illegal bush-meat trade, the most serious threat to Cameroon's wildlife today. To visit the enclosures either ask at the zoo or call ☎221.90.44 or 969.01.81.

The northern suburbs

Yaoundé's poor and working-class districts are mostly tucked away in valleys, hidden from sight by the hilltops. Such neighbourhoods include the **Briqueterie**, just northwest of town, site of the town's former **Grande Mosquée**, and **Messa**, also in the northwest, which houses **Marché Mokolo**, the liveliest and most approachable market in Yaoundé, where you can find fabrics, clothes and foodstuffs. The prestigious **Palais des Congrès** and the new **Grande Mosquée** are further north towards Mont Fébé. In the extreme north of town, the **Bastos** neighbourhood is the most exclusive residential area. Site of the nation's first factory (making the Bastos cigarettes which gave it its name), this quarter is now better known for its many embassies and the modern, and grandiose, **Présidence** – the presidential palace.

Eating, drinking and nightlife

The surest way of guaranteeing yourself **cheap eating** is to seek out Yaoundé's streetside food stalls. During working hours, there are lots of these around the administrative Lake Quarter, catering for government employees. If you're staying at the *Presbyterian Mission* or *Hôtel Idéal*, there are numerous **small eateries** nearby on and around rue Ateba Ebé which serve good omelettes and Nescafé breakfasts, and filling rice and bean dishes later in the day. For luscious fresh pastry, croissants and *pain au chocolat*, as well as ice cream, head for *Boulangerie Calfatas*, on rue Nachtigal, just south of place de l'Indépendance.

Restaurants: inexpensive to moderate

Cheaper places are easy to stumble upon in the residential districts of Bastos, Messa and especially Briqueterie, though they are noticeably rarer in the centre. Many of these places also double as live-music venues.

African Logik rte de Bastos. Open-air restaurant (it's behind a designer-clothes boutique) offering grilled fish and chips accompanied by cool beer, plus live music a couple of nights a week.

L'Atlantique rue Eloumden, Bastos ☎221.43.44. Good starters and excellent pizzas served in a pleasant courtyard. Reasonable prices (CFA3000–5000).

Le Biniou rue de Gaulle, next door to *La Terrasse*. New Breton restaurant serving crêpes with every imaginable topping (CFA1200–4500), plus standard French fare and fine French wines and cider.

Le Buffet rue Eloumden, just up from *rond-point* Nlongkak. Good but inexpensive counter meals (mains CFA1500). Very busy in the evenings.

Le Challenge av Kennedy. Self-service snack bar offering well-prepared lunches of chicken, steak or stew (mains CFA2500).

Chinatown rue Eloumden, across from *L'Atlantique*, Bastos ☎221.45.14. Chinese fare served on a large veranda. Does a popular all-you-can-eat buffet (CFA8000) on Sundays.

Le Globus Above *rond-point* Nlongkak. Watch the city's bustle while tucking into well-made and reasonably priced fish or meat dishes (CFA2500).

La Maison Blanche rue Rudolphe Abessolo. Lively outdoor nightspot with excellent grilled fish and streetlife.

Le Marseillais av Foch. Very good value for the centre, with fab breakfasts and snacks. There are other branches around the city, including one opposite the Abbia Cinema.

Mont Blanc Off *rond-point* Nlongkak, on the Ateba Ebé road. Popular mid-range restaurant with an affordable French menu and a few Cameroonian specialities (CFA2000–4000).

La Terrasse Next door to hotel *El Panaden* by place de l'Indépendance. Garden restaurant serving mainly Italian food, including pizzas (CFA2500–5400), plus some Cameroonian dishes. Live Cameroonian or European music in the evening.

Terre Battue Off rte de Obala (rue Ebé). One of the best live-music spots in Yaoundé, and also has good grilled food after 9pm, though the beer's expensive.

Restaurants: expensive

As in Douala, upmarket restaurants can be extremely expensive – up to CFA30,000 for a full meal.

L'Agora rue Ateba Ebé, south of *rond-point* Nlongkak up a small hill ☎222.35.96. Upmarket Cameroonian cuisine with unusual main dishes including crocodile, pangolin and porcupine (usually only one or two of these is actually available at any one time). Less adventurous tastebuds will be tempted by the excellent fish and chicken dishes.

Café de Yaoundé av Winston Churchill ☎222.85.94. Superior Italian fare (including pizza) served on an upper level with a fine view of the neighbourhood..

Chez Wou rue Eloumden, Bastos ☎220.46.79. Authentic-looking Chinese restaurant with excellent but expensive food.

Les Cigalons av Winston Churchill ☎223.41.25. Classy French and Mediterranean food (mains around CFA7000). They also do a three-course Saturday lunch for CFA9500.

Le Fôret Dense rue Eloumden, Bastos ☎220.53.08. Excellent Cameroonian food like *ndole* and *folong*, as well as tasty porcupine *ndombas* and other exotic dishes, served indoors or in pleasant outdoor *boukarous*.

La Salsa Off rue Eloumden behind the Nigerian ambassador's residence, Bastos ☎767.46.12. New restaurant with a great selection of seafood dishes and high-quality French and Italian fare, plus a good selection of fine wines.

Le Samovar rue Eloumden ☎221.55.28. Authentic dishes from Russia and some not-so-traditional pizza fired up in the outdoor oven.

Le Sommet At the *Hôtel Mont Fébé* ☎222.42.24. One of the best restaurants in town, with fabulous views and an especially popular Sunday-morning brunch. There is also a cheaper snack bar in the hotel and a poolside bar.

Nightlife

Yaoundé has little of Douala's after-dark energy. Some restaurants double as music venues, while there are also hotel discos and a few well-known clubs, but, apart from these, a number of bars and a few small places in Briqueterie and Messa are about all the city can offer. It's also dangerous to wander around after dark – take a taxi. The places listed below are geared towards dancing.

Le Caveau South of place Ahidjo. Posh *boîte* popular with rich Cameroonians and expats that throbs with the latest Central African hits. Occasional live bands playing the local *bikutsi* music.

Chez Jeanine Near *Maison Blanche* (see opposite). *Bassa* music played every weekend to raucous crowds – dress down rather than up.

Club Parallel Near *Terre Battue* (see opposite). Inexpensive cabaret with live Afro-pop, Western or traditional music every weekend. There's also great grilled chicken and a quieter outdoor area for talking.

Katios av Ahidjo at rue Goker. One of the most expensive places in town – and a bit of a meat market – with pulsating lights, good music and several dance areas.

Lucy's Bar rue Eloumden, near *Sim's 1 Hotel*, Bastos. Popular new bar with a glitzy Western atmosphere.

Oxygène Next to *Hôtel Royale*, off av de l'Indépendance. Laid-back club, with Western and African sounds and a middle-class clientele that includes a good number of expats.

Listings

Air freight DHL ☎ 223.13.58.

Airlines Air France, 528 rue Nachtigal ☎ 223.43.78, ⓕ 222.12.92; Cameroon Airlines, av Monseigneur Vogt ☎ 223.03.04 or 223.40.01; SN Brussels, av Foch in front of police station ☎ 223.47.29, ⓕ 223.47.40; Swiss, av Foch ☎ 222.97.37, ⓕ 222.63.29. For additional flight information, including international carriers, call the airport on ☎ 223.17.44.

Banks The main banks are near place Ahidjo: BICEC, Union Bank of Cameroon, SGBC (agent for Thomas Cook), Crédit Lyonnais, Commerical Bank of Cameroon (CDC). Standard Chartered is just south of place de l'Indépendance. Citibank and SGBC are both on av de Gaulle. Yaoundé's only working ATM. Street traders can be found on av Kennedy near the av Ahidjo junction.

Bookshops A limited selection of books can be found in the street stalls by place Ahidjo. The little bookshop at the back of Tigre Arcade, on avenue John Kennedy, has classic novels, books about Cameroon and Africa (mainly in French, though a few are in English), plus maps of Yaoundé and Douala.

Car rental The following are reliable but expensive: Avis, *Hilton Hotel* ☎ 223.36.46, ⓕ 230.30.10 and rte de Douala ☎ 230.22.85 or 230.20.88; Auvergne Auto, next to the *Hilton* ☎ 222.57.06; Eurovoyages, rue Narvick ☎ 222.66.10; and Europcar, off av Vogt ☎ 223.08.11, ⓕ 222.39.81.

Cinemas The best cinemas with the most up-to-date films are Le Capitole, av Maréchal Foch, and l'Abbia, rue Nachtigal. There's also a cinema at the French Cultural Centre.

Cultural centres British Council, av Charles de Gaulle ☎ 221.16.96 or 220.31.72; Centre Culturel Français, av Ahidjo ☎ 222.09.44 or 223.58.51; American Cultural Centre, rue Narvick ☎ 223.14.37; Goethe Institute (German cultural centre), av Kennedy ☎ 222.35.77.

Dentists Adventist Clinic ☎ 222.11.10 and Polyclinic Fouda ☎ 222.66.12, rte de Ngousso, east of the railway tracks.

Doctors Polyclinic Fouda (see above); General Hospital ☎ 220.28.02 or 220.11.22; Cabinet Médical International ☎ 223.98.51.

Embassies and consulates Canada, Imm. Stamatiades, av de l'Indépendance ☎ 223.02.03 or ☎ 223.23.11; Central African Republic, off rue Albert Ateba Ebé ☎ & ⓕ 220.51.55; Chad, rue Joseph Mballa Eloumden, Bastos ☎ & ⓕ 221.06.24; Congo-Brazzaville, rue Restaurant la Riviera, Bastos ☎ & ⓕ 221.24.58; Côte d'Ivoire, Bastos ☎ & ⓕ 221.74.59; Democratic Republic of Congo, bd de l'URSS, Bastos ☎ 220.51.03; Equatorial Guinea, Bastos ☎ 221.08.04; France, Plateau Atémengué ☎ 223.40.13 or 222.17.76, ⓕ 223.50.43; Gabon, off bd de l'URSS, Bastos Ekoudou ☎ & ⓕ 221.02.24; Nigeria, off av Monseigneur Vogt ☎ 222.34.55, ⓕ 223.55.51; UK, av Winston Churchill ☎ 222.07.96 or 222.05.45, ⓕ 222.01.48; USA, rue de Nachtigal ☎ 223.40.14 or 223.05.12, ⓕ 223.07.53.

Internet Blessed Garden, rue de Narvick (Mon–Sat 8am–11pm; CFA600 per hour); Club Cybernet, *rond-point* Nlongkak (Mon–Sat 8am–9pm, Sun noon–5pm; CFA500 per hour); Cyber Espace, in front of African Logik, rue Eloumden, Bastos

(Mon–Sat 8am–8.30pm; CFA600 per hour); Solution Cyber Café, av Kennedy (Mon–Fri 8am–9pm; CFA500 per hour); Logitech, rue Joseph Essono Balla (daily 9am–10pm; CFA800 for 90min); Sidenet, av de l'Indépendance (Mon–Sat 8am–11pm, Sun 3pm–8pm; CFA500 per hour); Cybercafé Everest, off place Elig-Essono (daily 8am–8pm; CFA500 per hour).

Maps The Centre Géographique National, av Monseigneur Vogt (☎222.29.21), has city, regional and national maps, but you'll probably have to order what you want since they don't have much stock. For basic city maps of Yaoundé and Douala, Tigre Arcade, on avenue John Kennedy, has a stock of 1:15000 and 1:20000 sheets.

National parks For information about Waza and Korup national parks and the protected areas around Yokadouma, contact the new WWF head office behind the BAT cigarette factory in Bastos

(☎221.62.67, ⓦwww.wwfcameroon.org). Ecofac on av Adenauer (☎222.42.71, ⓦwww.ecofac.org) can help with information about Dja Reserve.

Pharmacies Among the best stocked are the Pharmacie Française (☎222.14.76), on the corner of av Kennedy and av Ahidjo, and Provinciale, av Adenauer (☎220.94.93).

Post offices The main post office (Mon–Fri 7.30am–3.30pm, Sat & Sun 7.30am–noon) is on place Ahidjo and has an international (only) phone and fax service. Poste restante costs CFA200, but they don't hold letters very long.

Supermarkets The Niki chain is one of the cheapest; their three stores are in Mvog-bi (south of the Score roundabout), Messa (western qtr) and Nlongkak. Score, on place Ahmadou Ahidjo is well stocked, while Tigre, in the north of town on rue Essono Bella, is the best place for one-stop shopping. For more exclusive Western food head for Pavillion Vert on rue Eloumden.

The Province du Sud

As an escape from Douala or Yaoundé, or from the rigours of overlanding, **Kribi** and the white-sand **beaches** of the "south coast" are hard to beat. The quickest route to Kribi from Yaoundé is via **EDEA**, an attractive town at the southernmost bridge over the broad **Sanaga River**. If you want to stay here, try the upmarket *La Sanaga* (☎346.49.62, ⓕ346.48.86; ➎), which overlooks the river and the impressive Sanaga hydro-electric plant. The town has a market, a post office and banks, and makes a good living from the passing Douala–Yaoundé–Kribi trade. Three alternative routes from Yaoundé to Kribi run through the forests along tracks which, in the dry season at any rate, are usually passable in normal cars; two of these routes go first to **Ebolowa**, then on either via **Lolodorf** or **Akom II**. The third goes by paved road to Eséka (37km south of the Yaoundé–Edea road) and on to Lolodorf on a rugged *piste*. Travel can be painfully slow along these stretches, but the roads take in lush scenery punctuated with the occasional waterfall, and skirt a number of "Pygmy" villages.

Mbalmayo and Sangmélima

Heading south through rich forests broken by plantations of coffee and cocoa, the N2 highway links the capital to Ebolowa, then continues to the borders of Gabon and Equatorial Guinea. The first major stop along the way is **MBALMAYO**, a prosperous town with a bank, post office and accommodation, though there's no real reason to stay here. If you do, the best option is about 10km out of town, on the Ebolowa road, at the *Ebogo Tourist Site* (➋), located on the western edge of the Mbalmayo Forest Reserve, which arranges day-trips up the **Nyong River** by *pirogue*. You can actually get as far as Mbalmayo by train, but the road is so good (and so frequently served by share taxis and minibuses, as well as a regular service run by Buca Voyages to Yaoundé via Mbalmayo) that there's little point.

From Mbalmayo, the N9 branches southeastward to **SANGMÉLIMA**, another large town in the forest region, centre of the president's Beti ethnic group. There's modest **accommodation** in Sangmélima at the *Hôtel Bel Air* (☎228.81.42; ➋) with simple self-contained rooms, a bar and a restaurant. The slightly more upmarket *Hôtel Afamba* (☎228.84.27; ➋) has rooms with a/c and TV; but for atmosphere, you can't beat the *Jardin des Tropiques* on the route de Mbalmayo (℡228.86.91; ❸), whose a/c bungalows press right up to the forest's edge. The **Gabonese border** at **Nsak** is 150km away to the south, and if you follow the road eastwards you'll reach a less used access point to **Dja Reserve** (see p.1231) at **Djoum**; there's basic accommodation here at the *Hôtel Jeannette* (❶), and you can arrange trips into the reserve at the Ecofac forest post – contact Ecofac Yaoundé (℡220.42.71, ⓦwww .ecofac.org) for further information.

Ebolowa and around

To get to the coast or the borders, take the road that leads from Mbalmayo via Ngoulémakong to **EBOLOWA**, a lively provincial capital and important cocoa marketing centre. While there's not much in the way of sights – though you could stop by the **Hôpital Enongal** to contemplate the dentist's chair where Albert Schweitzer sat while having his teeth done – it's a pleasant stopping point in the forest region, with a large market that spreads out near the town's artificial **lake**. With over 40,000 inhabitants, Ebolowa also has good services, including a **bank** (Crédit Lyonnais), a **post office**, pharmacies and even a small supermarket.

There are several small **hotels**, the best of which are reviewed below. Most have **restaurants** and **bar/dancings** that make for rather wild nights in the jungle. Water supplies are irregular in town, and even the best hotel can't guarantee enough pressure for a decent bath.

La Cabane Bambou Near the town centre and market ℡788.88.85. Inexpensive *auberge* with basic rooms, some self-contained. ❶

Les Forestiers Past the lake in the Angolé quarter ℡953.69.40. Converted villa owned by a local forester with a range of rooms, some self-contained, and a restaurant serving local delicacies such as pangolin. A good place to stay if you want to explore the forest – the loggers who often stay here are happy to help with suggestions. ❷

Mvila On the Ambam road, within walking distance of the Kribi and Ambam motor parks ℡ & ℻228.43.34. Smart new hotel with clean, self-contained rooms, some with TV and hot water. Also has a first-rate restaurant with a good selection of wines. ❷

Porte Jaune Off the Yaoundé road about 1km from the centre ℡228.39.29 or 228.49.39. The best hotel in town with a choice of self-contained rooms with a/c or fan, plus safe parking and a good restaurant. ❷

Le Ranch At the foot of Mount Ebolowa, 1km southwest of the centre ℡228.40.37 or 220.35.32. Formerly the best in town, though now a somewhat dilapidated place – the main attraction nowadays is the peaceful rural setting. The self-contained rooms all come with cold showers and some have fans. There's also a restaurant and a bar. ❷

Sotha Ane Rouge Off the town's main roundabout ℡228.34.38. An easy walk from the main *agences de voyage* and *gare routière*, with very basic rooms (only a few self-contained), though the central location and a great first-floor terrace compensate. ❶

Moving on from Ebolowa

Ebolowa's few **agences de voyage** are on the Yaoundé road, with frequent daily departures to Yaoundé via Mbalmayo. The most reliable are Buca Voyages and Jet Voyages. From the main *gare routière*, there are also frequent **share taxis** to Yaoundé. **Minibuses** to Kribi are less frequent and depend very much on the state of the roads, but **clandos** can usually be found at the Kribi *gare routière* to the south of Ebolowa on the route d'Ambam. During the rainy season the journey may take a couple of days, stopping overnight on the way in Akom II or Lolodorf, depending on which road is better.

If you're continuing to **Gabon** or **Equatorial Guinea**, you need to get to Ambam (see p.1226). Frequent minibuses leave daily from the Ambam *gare routière* just next to the Kribi motor park.

Ambam and on to Gabon and Equatorial Guinea

A good paved road continues south from Ebolowa all the way through dense forest to **AMBAM**, the last major town before the borders of Equatorial Guinea and Gabon. There's a large market here with an international array of traders, and **accommodation** at rudimentary *auberges* or the slightly better *Ambam Sejour* (❶). But this is essentially a transit town, and your main objective will be to move on to somewhere else.

Share taxis **to Gabon** leave from Ambam's market and take little more than an hour to reach the border. On Saturdays, they stop at **Aban Minkoo** for the eventful weekly market. Once at the border, you can take a car ferry across the Ntem River or hire a *pirogue*. The car ferry – soon to be replaced by a new bridge – stops running promptly at 5pm every day. Taxis on the other side assure regular transport to **Bitam**. Share taxis **to Equatorial Guinea** leave from the motor park, across from the post office. Halfway to the border, your vehicle crosses the Ntem River on a regular ferry and then pushes on to the frontier town of **Ebebiyin**. You'll be dropped on Cameroonian territory, some 2km before reaching the town. After walking through customs, you can continue in a waiting taxi.

Lolodorf and Akom II

From Ebolowa, it's 73km by a seasonal *piste* to **LOLODORF** (its name – "Lolo's village" – is about the only reminder of the German presence in the area, as most towns were renamed by the French). You can find fuel here, along with accommodation in a few cheap *auberges* (❶); a brand new hotel is currently under construction. Only 110km separate Lolodorf from Kribi, but the rough tracks that wind through the hilly tropical forest make for a long trip. As a payoff, however, this route does pass by numerous "Pygmy" villages where, unlike in the extreme east of the country, the people have adopted a sedentary lifestyle. After 34km you reach the village of **Bidjoka**, from where you can walk to the **Bidjoka Falls**.

If the road via Lolodorf isn't passable, an alternative, more southern route runs to Kribi via **AKOM II**, on the border of the **Campo Ma'an National Park** (see p.1230). Trekking into the reserve from here is difficult but very rewarding. There's basic accommodation at *Auberge Jacquie-Voyages* (❶); they may also be able to help find a guide.

Kribi

Colonial reminders abound in **KRIBI**, creating a quiet, nostalgic feeling. The home-town of the Bassa, Kribi was a noted hotbed of UPC radicalism in the 1950s. The **port** at the centre of town was built by the Germans and is today too shallow for larger vessels to enter the harbour: from the nearby hillside, crowned with its colonial **cathedral**, you can see ships anchored a few kilometres offshore as their cargo is docked by lighter. The former **German administrative buildings** lining the beachfront in the northwest of town now house government offices such as the *préfecture* and the **tourist office** (☎346.10.80). Kribi's only **bank** (BICEC) is on the Lolodorf road. On the same road is the town's best **Internet** place, *Club Internet* (daily 8am–8pm; CFA1000 per hour).

Kribi is Cameroon's second-largest port, and in recent years the region has experienced an economic boom with the completion of the (environmentally questionable) Chad–Cameroon oil pipeline which terminates just south of here. A fast highway linking the town to Yaoundé and Douala, opened in 1991, slashed travelling time from Douala from nine hours to less than three and opened the tourism floodgates. However, there are fortunately still numerous remote corners where you can escape from the weekend sunseekers.

Kribi's name is said to come from the word *kiridi*, which, roughly translated, means "short men" – a reminder that you're in **"Pygmy"** country. The "Pygmies" were the original inhabitants of the district, although nowadays Bantu-speakers like the **Batanga** and **Bakoko** predominate, and you might not see a single convincing "Pygmy". The "Pygmies", of course, don't call themselves by that term and every community is part of a small cluster of bands. Traditionally nomadic, they are now increasingly sedentary, and more and more dependent on the larger economy of Cameroon beyond the forest. All Africa's people of small stature have completely lost their original languages and now speak the local language of the dominant people – in this area Bassa.

Accommodation

Because of the relatively heavy tourist presence, **accommodation** tends to be relatively expensive in Kribi, especially the beachside resorts. If you're on a tight budget, town hotels are a lot cheaper (although still expensive in Cameroon terms). Staying in town also makes it easier to enjoy inexpensive food and Kribi's buzzing nightlife. In the beachside hotels' off season, on weekdays or if you're staying for an extended period, bargaining can knock ten to thirty percent off the regular room rate.

Auberge de Kribi On Lolodorf road, near Syd Voyage ☎ & ℻ 346.15.41. Clean and simple but superb-value rooms with fans and shared facilities including hot showers. ❶

Auberge du Phare Just south of the bridge ☎ 346.11.08, ℻ 346.13.38. Clean and well-managed rooms (mostly a/c) along with breezy beachfront vistas from the popular restaurant. ❸

Coco Beach On the beach south of the bridge ☎ 346.15.84, ℻ 346.18.19. Luxurious a/c rooms with showers and hot water. Often full, so book ahead. ❺

Framotel North of town off the Edéa road ☎ 346.16.40, ✉ equateur.evasion@camnet.cm. One of Kribi's most child-friendly hotels, with a playground and large lawns dotted with fully equipped a/c bungalows. Although not on the seafront, the hotel has its own private beach, 200m down the road, with beach beds, a bar-grill and two guards. ❹

Gael Opposite Central Voyages ☎ 246.21.26, ℻ 246.16.20. Popular place within walking distance of the lively route de la Poste, with smallish self-contained rooms and a good-value bar-restaurant. ❸

Manapani le Nema 1.5km south of the bridge ☎ 346.17.79, ✉ hotelmanapanilenema

@hotmail.com. Unpretentious and friendly hotel by the beach with a good range of clean self-contained rooms (a/c or fan) and a little restaurant facing the sea. ❹

Maribell Beach At the edge of the administrative quarter near *La Paix* ☎ 346.15.15, ℻ 346.19.90. Glitzy new place with fully equipped a/c rooms and an equally plush bar-restaurant. Kribi's beach park is 300m to the north. ❹

L'Ocean 600m south of the bridge ☎ 346.13.35 or ☎ 990.01.69. Pleasant self-contained bungalows facing the sea, and a first-class restaurant. ❺

La Paix Near the tourist office in Kribi's quiet administrative quarter ☎ 997.75.18. Inexpensive hotel with clean self-contained rooms and friendly, informative staff. The beach is 500m to the north. ❷

Résidence Jully North of Kribi by the seafront off the Edéa road ☎ 346.19.62, ✉ resjully@yahoo.fr. Luxurious a/c rooms with sports facilities, Chinese massage, and two beachfront restaurants. Breakfast included. ❺

Thy Breiz South of the bridge, 1km from the centre ☎ 346.14.99. Set in an ideal beachfront location with a couple of cheaper self-contained rooms with fan and some much more expensive, but very comfortable, a/c rooms. ❸–❺

Eating, drinking and nightlife

For moderate-to-expensive **dining**, you can hardly beat the beachfront seafood restaurants of the hotels, many of which are so busy at weekends that they run out of food midway through the dinner hour. Of the restaurants in town, *Le Cigare*

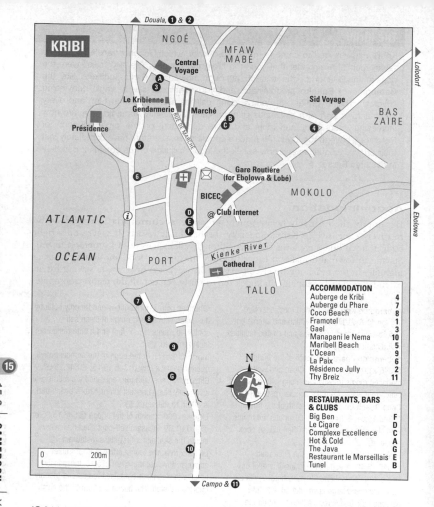

▲ Douala, **1** & **2**

KRIBI

NGOÉ

MFAW MABÉ

Central Voyage

Le Kribienne
Gendarmerie   Marché

Présidence

Sid Voyage

BAS ZAIRE

Lolodorf

A **3**

RUE DE MARCHÉ

B
C

4

5

6

ATLANTIC

OCEAN

Gare Routiére
(for Ebolowa & Lobé)

BICEC

@ Club Internet

D
E
F

MOKOLO

Ebolowa

(i)

Kienke River

PORT

Cathedral

TALLO

7

8

9

G

N

10

0   200m

▼ Campo & **11**

ACCOMMODATION	
Auberge de Kribi	4
Auberge du Phare	7
Coco Beach	8
Framotel	1
Gael	3
Manapani le Nema	10
Maribell Beach	5
L'Ocean	9
La Paix	6
Résidence Jully	2
Thy Breiz	11

RESTAURANTS, BARS & CLUBS	
Big Ben	F
Le Cigare	D
Complexe Excellence	C
Hot & Cold	A
The Java	G
Restaurant le Marseillais	E
Tunel	B

(☎346.19.28) and *Restaurant le Marseillais* (☎346.18.63), both on route de la Poste, are well known for their seafood and draft beer. Further along the same road you'll find more affordable grilled fish prepared at one of the numerous fish stands and served at the many bars, such as the popular *Tunel*. *Hot & Cold*, in front of hotel *Gael* and across the road from Central Voyages, is Kribi's best sandwich spot, and also does fresh fruit juice and ice cream.

Kribi has a number of good **clubs** that keep going late into the night at weekends. *Big Ben*, near the bridge, is the town's golden oldie. *The Java*, at *Hotel Palm Beach Plus*, is the upmarket place to go (CFA5000 entry fee), with a mix of African and European hits. The seafront bar gets lively at the weekend, with a DJ playing until midnight. At the more lively end of route de la Poste, a number of bars double up as dance venues, such as the packed *Complexe Excellence* near the *Tunel*.

The coast around Kribi

With their wild vegetation, white sand and calm waters, the beaches along the coast

There are frequent *agences de voyage* departures to **Yaoundé** and **Douala** with Kribi's two main companies, Central Voyages and La Kribienne. Syd Voyages, east of the centre, has regular transport to **Ebolowa** via **Lolodorf** and **Bipindi**. For Ebolowa via **Akom II**, **Grand Batanga** and further south to **Campo**, go the *gare routière* next to BICEC. As usual, most *gare routière* departures are in the early hours of the morning.

north and south of Kribi are among the most beautiful anywhere in Africa. They stretch over 100km, from the small village at **Londji** to the town of **Campo** on the border of Equatorial Guinea. Beach bums will be in their element, though the paradise is no longer a well-kept secret, and tourist facilities are gradually making their mark. If you have transport, the **Campo Ma'an National Park**, east of Campo, is well worth exploring, protecting stretches of forest which are among the globe's most important sites of biodiversity.

Londji and the beaches to the north

North of Kribi, the road to Edéa hugs the coastline as it skirts some of the area's most picturesque strands, first passing the village of Mpalla and then, after 15km, **Cocotier Plage** (a beautiful beach where there are rudimentary bungalows for rent) before arriving at **LONDJI**. Some 25km from Kribi – and 500m before the Kribi tollgate – this small fishing village spreads round a large bay with calm, warm water, white sands and coconut trees. The *Auberge Jardinière* (☎991.72.69; ❸) nestles on the beach and offers the best **accommodation** in the village (despite being rather run-down) and excellent seafood. It can get crowded with expats at weekends, though on other days you'll have the place and the beach to yourself. If you're on a budget, there are humbler *boukarous* (❷) for rent along the beach. **Camping** is also possible on the two beaches, Paris Plage and London Beach, for around CFA2500 per person, payable to the village chief, who has employed guards to keep thieves at bay. You can order fresh fish from the guards, or fill up in town on fish, snail kebabs and rice. A couple of local bars sell beer, minerals and freshly tapped palm wine.

After midnight, **fishermen** set out in wooden canoes across the bay, stirring up phosphorescence in the water as they paddle towards the deeper ocean. You can arrange with the beach guards to be taken along – for a price – though it's not always an eventful experience. If you're missing nightlife and restaurants, there are share taxis to and from Kribi during most of the day. They stop running in the early evening, however, and it costs CFA2000–3000 to hire a taxi back to Londji.

The southern beaches to Campo

Another *piste* follows the coastline southwards from Kribi to the Ecuato-Guinean border, passing still more beaches, all exotically named – Marseilles, Océan Amérique, Azure. Seven kilometres from town, just before **Grand Batanga**, a small signpost points down to the **Chutes de la Lobé**, where the river of the same name comes thrashing over a rocky descent as it plunges directly into the ocean. The force of these rapids stirs up an unappealing brownish foam in the bay, but the surrounding beaches are clean and have excellent swimming.

There are a couple of **eating** places at the foot of the falls selling grilled shrimp and fish. If you want to stay, there are several good places close by. *Tara Plage* (☎346.20.83; ❸;), about 2km before the waterfalls and 4km south of the bridge in Kribi, is the best budget hotel on the beachfront, with friendly staff and basic but comfortable self-contained fanned rooms. It also has spacious four-person villas (CFA20,000), as well as tents for rent (CFA4000) if you want to camp. The only drawback is the pricey restaurant and the distance to town. The more luxurious and idyllically located *Hotel Ilomba* (☎991.29.23 or 991.32.36; ❺) is about 500m from the falls and has deluxe *boukarous* and a good but expensive restaurant. You can walk to the *chutes* from Kribi, but be aware that thieves reputedly try their luck along this stretch of the beach. You'll also get numerous offers for **pirogue trips** up the Lobé River, though these tend to be expensive and disappointing (three hours for CFA10,000). While paddling upstream is both picturesque and very peaceful, the "Pygmy" villages you've ostensibly come to visit are completely inauthentic and the "traditional" hunting trips – with people taller than you – really seem like something out of a second-rate theme park.

The beaches between Grand Batanga and the fishing village of **Eboundja**, 20km south of Kribi, are amongst the most beautiful and isolated in the region. The local chief at Eboundja authorizes camping on the beach and can help arrange meals and fishing-boat excursions. There's nowhere to stay, unless you're lucky enough to bag a room at the Catholic Mission, though the upmarket French-owned *Mimado* restaurant (☎997.79.17) in Eboundja plans to have rooms in the future, and in the meantime is a very good place **to eat**.

Some 25km further south, a rocky land formation, the **Rocher du Loup**, rises in a dramatic – but not very wolflike – fashion from the water. South of here, you're getting into very remote districts as the road reaches yet another fishing village, **Ebodjé**, site of a successful sea-turtle conservation and eco-tourism initiative. Between November and January hundreds of sea turtles come ashore to lay their eggs. You can stay in private homes (❶) and have food prepared for you at the town's only restaurant (CFA2000 per meal).

Campo Ma'an National Park

The southbound *piste* finally peters out at the two-bit border town of **CAMPO**, starting point for visits to the newly created, 2640-square-kilometre **Campo Ma'an National Park** (daily 8am–6pm). This is one of the world's most important biodiversity sites, protecting various types of rainforest ranging in altitude from sea level to 800m. Access to the area is still agonizingly difficult (you'll need your own transport), and, once inside, the dense forest makes it almost impossible to see anything. But the sparse infrastructure is improving, and with the rehabilitation of an old German road connecting Campo with Ma'am you can now spend a full day driving through the park with at least a theoretical chance of seeing buffalo and elephant if you make an early start. You can pick up the obligatory **guide** (CFA3000) in either Nkoélon, west of the park, or Ebianemayong, to the east; they can also take you on short treks into clearings where there's a good chance you'll spot some of the eighty different monkey species living in the park, and maybe some unusual birdlife – you might even see the world's rarest bird, the colourful small bald *picatharte* or rockfowl. Park fees (CFA5000) should be paid at the Forest Office in Campo, but are seldom asked for.

Accommodation in Campo is limited to a simple *auberge* (❷). You can expect customs and immigration checks in the vicinity of the town, whether or not you're crossing into Equatorial Guinea. The town's beach stretches south to the mouth of the **Ntem River**, which marks the border with Equatorial Guinea. From the beach you can negotiate with a *piroguier* to take you 10km up the Ntem River to **Yengue** in Equatorial Guinea. There's a frontier post here (make sure to get your passport stamped before continuing), and tracks leading to the road to **Bata**.

The Province de l'Est

Three hundred kilometres of partially paved road separate Yaoundé from **Bertoua**, the capital of East Province – a region which has changed dramatically due to gold prospecting and virtually unrestricted logging of the rainforest. Not long ago, places like **Yokadouma** and **Lomié** were isolated villages surrounded by undisturbed forest havens. Now, they have a boom-town atmosphere, with a multitude of colourful bars, brothels and *auberges*.

The roads heading east from Yaoundé are largely maintained by the logging companies, but the heavy trucks often corrugate the roads badly and from time to time they become impassable to ordinary vehicles. Formerly, the main route to Bertoua followed the **Sanaga River** to **Nanga-Eboko**, though a second road following the course of the **Nyong River** via **Abong Mbang** is now more frequently used, since it's paved as far as **Ayos** (145km from Yaoundé). Past Ayos, and if you can distract your attention from the hundreds of logging trucks, these routes provide a sense of being away from it all. Both **Somalomo**, 75km south of Ayos, and **Lomié**, 127km south of Abong Mbang, are good bases for treks in to the **Dja Faunal Reserve**, a large swathe of pristine rainforest to the west.

Most travellers press eastwards towards **Bertoua**, passing through **Doumé**, formerly the capital of the eastern region and site of some remarkable colonial vestiges, including a German cathedral and an imposing German fortress. Moving on from Bertoua to the **Central African Republic**, a newly paved road slides northeast to **Garoua-Boulai**, a long journey through a great swathe of jungle and grassland to a busy crossing point and marketplace on the savanna fringes of central Cameroon.

Heading directly east from Bertoua you reach **Batouri**, a busy town en route to Berbérati in the Central African Republic, and to **Yokadouma**, the gateway to the southeastern corner of the country. The three **forest reserves** in this area – Lake Lobéké, Boumba Bek and Nki – are gradually becoming more accessible to visitors and offer some of the most satisfying game viewing in West Africa.

Dja Faunal Reserve

The **Dja Faunal Reserve**, bounded on three sides by the Dja River, is the largest intact area of primary rainforest in Cameroon. After many years of relative obscurity it was made a Unesco World Heritage site in 1987 and is now one of the most visited protected areas in southern Cameroon – although numbers are still minimal. The reserve has been managed by Ecofac (Ecosystèmes Forestiers d'Afrique Centrale) since 1992, and a number of tourist facilities have begun appearing – it's now possible to arrange visits into the reserve from three different starting points. Beginning your trip from **SOMALOMO**, 260km from Yaoundé, is easiest and most rewarding. You can stay at one of Somalomo's cheap hotels (❷) or at Ecofac's training centre (❸), where staff can also help with guides (CFA3000 per day), porters (CFA2000/day) and planning your trip. With time to spare, visit the town's amazing orchid *ombrière* – in flower mostly between July and September. From Somalomo it's a long 36km hike to the Ecofac camp at **Bouamir**, a forest clearing were you can set up camp while exploring the area on shorter day-trips. You can also enter the reserve from **Lomié** or from the southern town of **Djoum** (see p.1225), but there's little infrastructure here and merely reaching the reserve involves a long hike. Guides and porters can be found through the village's Ecofac forest post.

The reserve's **wildlife** includes a large population of lowland gorillas, chimpanzee, mandrill, forest elephants, sitatunga and buffalo, though it's very difficult to see. This is partly due to the nature of the forest (it's difficult to see more than a few metres), but is also as a result of intense hunting, though this is fortunately less of a problem in the area around Bouamir. **Bird-watching**, however, can be extremely rewarding throughout the reserve, the northwest being especially good for hornbills and a certain area around Bouamir for the rare picatharte. The eastern part of the reserve is home to **Baka pygmies**, or *gens du forêt*, who live along the boundary in relatively traditional camps. From Lomié, you can arrange to trek into the forest with Baka guides – easiest to find at the Ecofac post – and stay in their villages.

△ Lowland gorilla

The best place to **stay** in Lomié itself is the *Auberge de Raphia*, 2km out of the town (●), which is clean and helpful, and has a decent bar-restaurant. It's a good idea to stock up with supplies before entering the reserve. If you have the choice, try to visit between November and March, when visibility is best. Reserve fees are CFA5000 per day and CFA2000 per camera. For **information**, contact Ecofac in Yaoundé (☎220.42.71, ⊕www.ecofac.org).

Bertoua

Situated on the border of the savanna and the forest, Bertoua has grown rapidly in recent years to become the country's tenth largest town, with a population of some 140,000. Growth has been largely thanks to logging and gold mining, and there's a lively sense of commerce too, but the town is above all an **administrative centre**, seat of the East Province and of the Lom and Djérem *département*. It's an uninspiring place to visit, however, and for overland travellers, the most salient feature is likely to be its well-stocked provisions shops (handy for changing money) and a good selection of **accommodation**, which makes Bertoua an obvious stopping point on the roads to and from the Eastern Province and Central Africa.

The main **agences de voyage** are located near the market and town centre. Narral Voyages and Alliance Voyages have daily departures for **Yaoundé**, **Batouri** and along the fast new road to **Garoua-Boulai**. Alliance also has daily connections to **Yokadouma** (a full day, leaving early morning). Rackety minibuses run by Haut Ngyong Voyage travel to remote destinations such as the CAR border town of **Gamboula**, **Lomié**, and **Belabo**, the closest town on the **Transcam railway** line. Unfortunately, trains heading both north and south reach Belabo late at night, and as trains are more often delayed than on time, you may end up with a long wait. What's more, the train station in Belabo has a reputation for being very unsafe, so if you choose this route, keep alert for hands exploring your luggage.

Accommodation

Ambience Behind the market and near the *agences de voyage* offices. A good budget choice with very inexpensive rooms; private bath optional. ●

De l'Est At the *rond-point* Poste Central behind Espace Nkam Palace restaurant-nightclub ☎951.58.93. Formerly ramshackle place now under promising new management. Rooms come self-contained or with shared facilities. ●

Mansa North of the centre ☎224.60.50, ⑥224.15.88. A symbol of recent economic expansion and far and away the town's top hotel, with a/c rooms, an artificial lake, tennis court and an inviting pool (CFA2000 for non-guests). ●

Paris Behind the market in quartier Elevage ☎224.20.46. Sparkling new place with a range of self-contained rooms, some with a/c and TV. ●

Phenix Palace Up the road from the main *agences de voyage* offices ☎224.27.29. Friendly and good-value hotel with a range of clean self-contained rooms and a good bar-restaurant. ●

Garoua-Boulai

The brand new tarred road leading north of Bertoua to **GAROUA-BOULAI** is one of the most tangible benefits of the Chad–Cameroon oil pipeline, and takes in some fine mountain scenery near Ndokayo, with panoramic views over the valley of the **Lom River**. The Adamawa Mountains are not far to the north, and many Fulani herders pass through Garoua-Boulai. There's inexpensive **accommodation at Garoua-Boulai**, including two places at the main junction: *La Forestière* (●) and the slightly better *Mission Catholique* (●). Another option is to stay with the Sisters at the mission off the road to Meiganga; they have clean rooms (●) as well as dormitory space.

Crossing the border into the **Central African Republic** is relatively uncomplicated on either side. After dealing with customs in **Béloko**, the frontier post in

Central African Republic, it's another 160km to Bouar on the main road to Bangui. If you're continuing to **northern Cameroon**, the town's three *agences*, Narral, Alliance and Kawtal, all have daily connections to **Ngaoundéré** on the fast road as far as **Maiganga**, where you can branch westwards to catch the train at **Ngaoundal**. Narral Voyages and Alliance Voyages also have regular daily connections to **Bertoua**.

Batouri

East of Bertoua, the forest yields to hilly savanna broken by rivers and woodlands. Travel is difficult along the poorly maintained *piste* leading to **BATOURI**, the last main town before the border with the Central African Republic. You can **stay** at the basic but pleasant *Hôtel Cooperant* (☎226.23.00; ❶) a hundred metres up the hill from the *agences de voyage* in the centre of town. There's also the new *Hôtel Belle Etoile* (☎226.25.18; ❷), south of the centre, with comfortable self-contained rooms, a good restaurant, and traditional Kako music every evening. A CFA150 *moto* ride away from the centre, the *Hôtel Mont Pandi* (☎226.25.77; ❷) has run-down self-contained rooms, compensated for by the beautiful setting and the excellent bar-restaurant serving tasty specialities such as porcupine. The most relaxing place to stay is with the welcoming sisters at the Catholic *Collège Bari* on top of the hill at the entrance of town arriving from Bertoua (leave a donation).

With **Mount Pandi** flanking the town, Batouri is base for some interesting expeditions. The east is famous for its **gold mines**, which still attract prospectors from many parts of West and Central Africa; find a guide to take you to **Kambele**, a makeshift mining village 6km from town. Seeing the river panners and the gold scales in the market (dominated by Hausa speculators), it's hard to avoid Wild West comparisons, but behind these images lies the real danger inherent in digging.

The town's two *agences de voyage*, Narral and Alliance, both leave before dawn to tackle the 102km of tortuous track to the frontier town of **Kentzou**. Border formalities are dealt with efficiently and connections by share taxi to **Berbérati**, 100km into the Central African Republic, are usually quick. Narral and Alliance also run services throughout the day to **Bertoua**, while Alliance despatches vehicles along the long, slow road to **Yokadouma**.

Yokadouma and around

YOKADOUMA is one of the fastest growing towns in Cameroon, abuzz with the activities of opportunist gold diggers, game hunters, loggers and environmentalists, who have assembled here from all over West and Central Africa. Reaching Yokadouma, however, can be a trying experience. The 200km *piste* from Batouri is maintained regularly by the logging companies, but it's wrecked as rapidly as it's repaired. Bridges often collapse and traffic jams of hundreds of trucks are not uncommon. Before you travel, ask in the motor park in Batouri or Bertoua about the state of the road.

There's a range of **places to stay** in Yokadouma to suit most budgets. In the centre of town are *La Cachette* (☎224.28.63; ❷), with clean, self-contained rooms and a potentially noisy bar-restaurant-nightclub; and *Libeta* (❶), with slightly dingier, but a lot quieter, self-contained rooms. Best in town, however, is the popular *L'Elephant* (☎224.20.77; ❷), with clean, self-contained a/c rooms with hot water and a popular bar-restaurant. It's a five-minute walk from the centre, clearly signposted from the main roundabout. For **food**, most of the hotels are good bets, although you can't beat the atmosphere at *La Falaise* across from the WWF office. Inexpensive chop shops are mostly found in the area around the main roundabout.

If you're in Yokadouma to visit the forest reserves to the south, your first stop should be the WWF office in the administrative quarter north of the centre. Together with the Ministry of Environment and Forests (MINEF; ☎224.28.99) they assist in arranging trips into the reserves and can help with transportation. WWF are in radio contact with their various forest posts and are happy to radio ahead to arrange for a guide to take you into the forest.

Yokadouma's only **agence de voyage** is Alliance Voyages, near the main roundabout. They have regular departures for Batouri and Bertoua, as well as to the southern border town of Moloundou. Most departures are early in the morning.

The southeastern rainforests

The southeastern corner of Cameroon is covered by 27,000 square kilometres of dense, humid Congo Basin rainforest – the second richest forest region in the world, only surpassed by the Amazon in Brazil. Of this enormous area, 7000 square kilometres are protected within three reserves – Lobéké National Park, Boumba Bek and Nki forest reserves – managed jointly by WWF and MINEF as the Jengi Forest Project; Jengi meaning "spirit of the forest" in Baka. The remaining area is divided into logging and professional hunting concessions, community hunting areas and village areas. People here depend entirely on the forest for survival, and the area supports a rich variety of **wildlife**, including forest elephants, buffalo, bongo, chimpanzees, gorillas, duiker and a multitude of monkeys, though to experience just a fraction of it you'll need lots of patience.

Most accessible is **Lobéké National Park** – contiguous with Dranga-Sangha in Central African Republic and Nouabale-Ndoki in Congo-Brazzaville, which forms the tri-national Sangha Conservation Area, the largest area of protected rainforest in Africa. Its rich fauna can be viewed from stilted platforms (miradors) constructed in forest clearings by the WWF for research purposes, and staying in one overnight is a truly magical experience, with amazing birdlife flitting around and large mammals walking past underneath. To reach one of the park's four miradors involves hiking. The most popular and easiest to get to is the *Petit Savanne*, a six-hour hike from the main road heading southeast from the WWF camp at Mambele (halfway to Moloundou on the Congo-Brazzaville border). You can stay at the camp before setting off (CFA5000 per person) and, unless you have already arranged things with WWF in Yaoundé, camp staff will help find you a Baka guide to take you into the forest (CFA3000 per day). With a good guide (and most of them are) the trek itself is out of this world. The guide moves noiselessly and rapidly through the dense forest, alert to every sound, pointing out easily missed highlights every few minutes. It's not unusual to come across a gorilla on your path. But beware, they can be dangerous, so do exactly as your guide tells you.

The contiguous **Boumba Bek** and **Nki forests** are pristine, and protected by rivers. The westernmost reserve, Nki, is only accessible by boat up the Dja River (arrange through the WWF in Moloundu, on the Congo-Brazzaville border) or by road to Ndongo (west of Moloundou) followed by a four-hour trek to Nki falls. It takes two days of strenuous hiking to reach the miradors in Boumba Bek (arrange with the WWF post in Ngato, 30km south of Yokadouma). Needless to say, trips into any of these areas require full self-sufficiency: water, food, insect repellant and sturdy boots an absolute must. If possible, make pre-arrangements with WWF in Yaoundé (☏221.70.83 or 221.62.67, ✉jengi@wwf.cm).

15.4

Northern Cameroon

N orthern Cameroon is separated from the rest of the country by a vast, almost trackless region in the centre. This huge expanse of rolling savanna and forests – as big as Scotland or Maine – is thinly populated and crossed by just three *pistes* and the railway. On its northern edge, the **Adamawa Mountains** cut across the centre of Cameroon, effectively dividing the country into two quite distinct parts. Beyond here, a flat plateau stretches over much of the north, with light forests and grasslands replacing the south's thick vegetation, indicating that the climate is harsher and nature less generous. It's a tough journey by road from Yaoundé, Bertoua or Bamenda to the first town of northern Cameroon, **Ngaoundéré** – good enough reason to use the train – though once you've made it this far, the mostly flat and sealed highway which runs from Ngaoundéré all the way to **Kousséri** makes the north one of the easiest regions to travel through. There are no less than six **game parks** in the north, ranging from the hilly **Bouba Ndjida National Park**, home to the almost extinct West African **black rhinoceros**, to the popular **Waza National Park**, whose flat savanna is ideal for spotting herds of giraffe and elephant, as well as lions and numerous other species.

In the extreme northwest, the volcanic **Mandara Mountains** have been scoured by thousands of years of harmattan winds, and the people of the region squeeze their livelihood out of the dry rocky slopes. Although this region has been discovered by travel operators, you can, if you're determined enough, work your way off the more beaten tracks and away from such overrun sites as **Roumsiki** to villages which may not be any more authentic but are at least less tainted by organized tourism.

While the mountain people of the northwest have retained traditional religious beliefs, the rest of the region bears the stamp of **Islam**, brought by Fulani migrants, who established principalities called **lamidats** in the eighteenth century. The Muslim influence is especially noticeable in towns such as **Garoua** and **Maroua**, which seem unusually large and dynamic in a region where you might expect climate and geography to reduce energy to a minimum.

Ngaoundéré and around

Coming from the south, **NGAOUNDÉRÉ**, with its mango-shaded streets and mild climate (the result of its location at an elevation of 1400m), proves a satisfying introduction to the north. Though rapidly growing, the old Fulani settlement still thrives in the neighbourhood around the Lamido's Palace, and the local dress and architecture bear witness to a Sudanic tradition that is very much alive.

The first people to settle around Ngaoundéré – which means "mountain with a navel" in their language – were the **Mboum**, whose claims to the area were lost to the **Fulani** after a military siege in the early 1830s. By 1835, **Ardo Ndjobdji** had established the Muslim **lamidat** and the Mboum became Fulani vassals. The city was surrounded by a protective wall in 1865 and extended its influence over a vast territory to the south and east; by the end of the nineteenth century, the town's population had grown to 10,000. Ngaoundéré changed little during the colonial period, and it wasn't until the **Trans-Cameroonian Railroad** was extended here in 1974 that a real boom occurred; by 1983 the population had rocketed to nearly 60,000, and it may be close to 180,000 by now. New *quartiers* have grown up around the old centre, adding a sense of vitality to the traditional core, while growing economic activity now includes an industrial slaughterhouse (livestock is a regional mainstay), a dairy and a tannery.

Accommodation

Auberge al Hilal rue de la Gare, next door to Touristique Express ☏ 225.19.97. Six simple self-contained rooms with hot water; very convenient for *agences de voyage* and the train station. No alcohol. ❷

Auberge du Château Off rue du Petit Marché ☏ 225.20.42. Grubby, no-frills rooms without fan or bath, but among the cheapest in the centre. ❶

Auberge de la Gare Near the train station ☏ 225.22.17. Friendly place with 24hr reception and well-maintained self-contained rooms set around a courtyard, where you can park safely. The restaurant serves good cheap food. ❷

Le Motel Marhaba entertainment complex, rue Ahidjo ☏ 225.18.93, ⓕ 225.16.71. A range of self-contained rooms with hot showers, and a convenient base for the *Marhaba* nightclub next door. ❷

Possada Style Off rue Ahidjo north of the cathedral ☏ 225.17.03. Small but clean self-contained rooms with hot water. The only drawback is that there's nowhere to eat nearby. ❷

Du Rail rte de Garoua, a 10min walk from the train station and *agences de voyage* if you're arriving from the north ☏ 225.10.13. The best mid-range hotel in town, with clean and spacious self-contained rooms, all with hot water, some with TV. The hotel restaurant does good-value basic meals, but alcohol isn't permitted. ❸

Le Relais Behind the now defunct Cinéma Le Nord ☏ 225.11.38. Spacious but slightly run-down self-contained rooms, convenient for the centre. ❷

Transcam Off the rte de Garoua-Boulai ☏ & ⓕ 225.12.52. Showy place with TV and other perks in a/c rooms and *boukarous*. Service is good, and there's a first-rate bar, restaurant and nightclub across the road. Amex and Visa accepted. Deposit CFA25,000. ❺

The Town

The **old town** centres around the **Lamido's Palace**, which is a *saré* – the Hausa word for this style of housing – made of *banco* huts with vast straw rooftops that swoop down nearly to the ground. A large wall surrounding the compound keeps the maze of courtyards, private dwellings and public rooms out of view from the street. For an **inside visit**, ask at the Lamido's Secretariat, housed in a new concrete building at the palace entrance, or preferably go to the **tourist office** on rue Ahidjo. The tourist office will make a booking for you (CFA2000, CFA1000 for a guide and another CFA1000 per camera). By far the best time to visit the palace is on Fridays in time for the **Friday prayer**. Dignitaries in brightly coloured *boubous* – magnificent accents of orange and red against the ochre tints of the town – come to pay their respects to the Lamido, who leads a procession to the mosque. Similar displays take place on Saturday and Sunday.

Ngaoundéré's **Grand Marché** is down the main avenue from the palace, and surrounded by an arcaded wall. Despite the name, however, the **Petit Marché**, on the road of the same name, is now the town's main market, and is far more interesting. The main avenue from both markets lead to the commercial centre, with its **banks** and **post office**.

The **Ministère du Tourisme** on rue Ahidjo (Mon–Fri 9am–noon & 1–5pm; ☏ 225.24.63) has enthusiastic staff and good regional travel tips. They can also recommend places to eat and sleep in town and aren't snooty about directing you to the cheaper *auberges* if you make it clear that you're on a budget. It's a good idea to also check the events calendar of the Alliance France-Camerounais Adamaoua at the tourist office – they arrange various musical and cultural events which it would be a shame to miss.

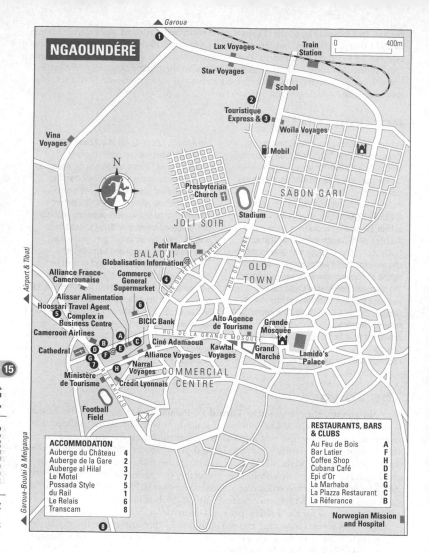

NGAOUNDÉRÉ

▲ *Garoua*

Lux Voyages

Train Station

0   400m

Star Voyages

School

Touristique
Express &

Woïla Voyages

Vina
Voyages

Mobil

SABON GARI

N

Presbyterian
Church

Stadium

JOLI SOIR

OLD
TOWN

Petit Marché

BALADJI

Globalisation Information@

Alliance France-
Camerounaise

Commerce
General
Supermarket

Alissar Alimentation

Hoossari Travel Agent

Complex in
Business Centre

BICIC Bank

Cameroon Airlines

Alto Agence
de Tourisme

Grande
Mosquée

Cathedral

Ciné Adamaoua

Alliance Voyages

Kawtal
Voyages

Grand
Marché

Lamido's
Palace

Narral
Voyages

COMMERCIAL
CENTRE

Ministère
de Tourisme

Crédit Lyonnais

RUE AHIDJO

RUE DE LA GRANDE MOSQUÉE

RUE DE LA GARE

RUE DU PETIT MARCHÉ

Football
Field

ACCOMMODATION

Auberge du Château	4
Auberge de la Gare	2
Auberge al Hilal	3
Le Motel	7
Possada Style	5
du Rail	1
Le Relais	6
Transcam	8

**RESTAURANTS, BARS
& CLUBS**

Au Feu de Bois	A
Bar Latier	F
Coffee Shop	H
Cubana Café	D
Epi d'Or	E
La Marhaba	G
La Plazza Restaurant	C
La Réferance	B

Norwegian Mission
and Hospital

Eating, drinking and nightlife

You'll find numerous cheap eating places around the *agences de voyage*. For something a little fancier, there are lots of places to choose between in the commercial centre. The only two **nightclubs** are at Marhaba (CFA1500) and Transcam (CFA3000). The Alliance France-Camerounais Adamaoua sometimes arranges live music events.

Au Feu de Bois Across from Alissar Alimentation in the commercial centre. Specializes in *ndolé*, but also serves the standard chicken-and-chips menu.

Bar Latier At the Marhaba end of the commercial centre's main street. Serves six varieties of locally produced yoghurt and milk, plus steaks, salads, and coffee and cake at reasonable prices.

Coffee Shop Near the BICEC bank. Fresh coffee, plus *steak-frites* and good-sized portions of salad.

Cubana Café Garden Court Square. Quick coffee and omelettes for early risers.

Epi d'Or Halfway down the commercial centre's main street. Cool beer and pizza or hamburgers served on a streetside terrace from where you can watch the occasional Lamido procession, as well as football matches on an outdoor TV. Gets crowded most weekends.

La Marhaba rue Ahidjo, next to *Le Motel*. A good bet for grilled fish and cold beer – and dancing at weekends.

La Plazza Restaurant Next to Alissar Alimentation in the commercial centre. Good French cuisine at European prices.

Listings

Banks BICEC is in the town centre halfway between Ciné Adamaoua and the tourist office, but first try Crédit Lyonnais (☎225.11.09) on av Ahidjo – this is the best (and sometimes only) place to change traveller's cheques. You may get a better rate for cash in one of the town's many hardware stores.

Car rental Car rental is very expensive after you figure in the daily rate, the insurance, the driver, the kilometre charge and of course fuel. Prices for more than a day are negotiable. Try Vina Voyages, on av Ahidjo, or Hoosari Travel Agent, next to Alissar Alimentation in the commercial centre.

Cinemas Ciné Adamaoua, in the centre of town.

Internet Internet access is outrageously expensive in Ngaoundéré, as connections go via mobile-phone networks to Yaoundé, though this is bound to change soon. Try Globalisation Information, on rue du Petit Marché (Mon–Sat 8am–9pm; a hefty CFA400 per minute), or Complex in Business Centre, in the commercial centre next to the Mobil garage (daily 7.30am–11pm), which is promising rates of CFA1500 per hour when fully operational.

Hospital Norwegian Mission hospital, southeast of town ☎225.11.95.

Supermarkets Wine, cheese and other imported goods are available at ETS Alissar Alimentation, close to *La Plazza Restaurant*, and at Commerce General, behind *Hôtel le Relais*.

Travel Agencies For excursions in and around Ngaoundéré, Alto Agence de Tourisme, in front of the *litahi* tree by the Grand Marché (☎ & ℱ225.11.29), offers some interesting day-trips on horseback or mountain bike.

Moving on from Ngaoundéré

Heading south to **Yaoundé**, your best bet is the **train**. The modern railway station (enquiries ☎225.12.71 or 225.92.30) is 1km north of the commercial centre. Couchette trains leave every evening at 6.20pm, arriving in Yaoundé between 7.30 and 10am the following morning (in theory, at least). If you're heading to **eastern Cameroon** or on to the **Central African Republic**, you can either take the Yaoundé train to Bélabo, arriving at a dodgy station between 10pm and midnight, or the slower Navette train, which leaves at 6.30am and arrives early in the evening. From Bélabo, Haut Nyong minibuses continue to Bertoua. Another option is to take a southbound service with one of the various *agences de voyage* – Narral, Kawtal and Alliance Voyages – on the slow *piste* to **Meiganga**, where a new pipeline-funded paved road continues to the border town of **Garoua-Boulai** and on to **Bertoua**. Narral, Alliance and Mayo-Banyo Voyages also run services westwards along the long and rugged road to **Foumban** via **Tibati**. Several *agences de voyage* also operate daily connections to the north. Woïla Voyages (☎985.54.87) has two daily departures to **Garoua** and **Maroua** (one in the morning, one early afternoon) in comfortable buses. Alternatively, Lux Voyage (☎954.36.44), Touristique Express (☎225.19.73) and Star Voyage (☎225.24.60) run several daily departures, stopping in Guidjiba en route, for connections to Tchollire and Benoue and Bouba Ndjida national parks.

Cameroon Airlines (☎225.12.95 or 980.09.30) have four **flights** weekly (Mon, Wed, Fri & Sun) to Yaoundé and Douala. You can check latest schedules by calling the airport on ☎225.12.84.

Around Ngaoundéré

If you have your own transport there are some easy side-trips in the environs of Ngaoundéré. The nearest site of scenic interest is **Lac Tison**, just 10km from town. Take the Meiganga road south and after 6km a signpost points east to the crater lake, deep in the woods 3km further on. It's a pleasant ride along a *piste* bordered by awkward boulder formations, but forget swimming when you get there, as bilharzia is a real risk. Back on the Meiganga road, 15km from town just past the village of Wakwa, the well-known waterfall, **Chute de la Vina**, tumbles 30m down onto a table of rock.

A popular weekend getaway (though it's currently shut following a change of management) is the **Ngaoundaba Ranch** (bookings via Alissar Alimentation, Ngaoundéré ☎225.24.69; ❸), 40km towards Meiganga turning left on a well sign-posted dry-season road. Perched in the mountains by a beautiful **crater lake**, the main lodge recalls a Hemingwayesque vision of Africa, from where the now-deceased founder once led guests on hunting safaris. The image lives on as visitors gather for meals at a long trestle table with animal trophies on the heavy stone and wood-beam walls. Most of the bougainvillea-bedecked *boukarous* have panoramic views of the area, which is great for **bird-watching**. Other diversions include swimming, fishing and boat trips on the lake.

Bénoué and Bouba Ndjida national parks

Although overshadowed by the superb Waza National Park further north (see p.1251), there's rewarding **game viewing** at the **Bénoué** and **Bouba Ndjida national parks**, off the Ngaoundéré–Garoua road and the Bénoué buffer zone to the north. The once-prolific wildlife of **Faro National Park** has been severely depleted by poaching, so unless you're interested in seeing the landscape (a mountain-dotted slab of bush) there is really no reason to visit. Unfortunately, you can't get around the parks without your own transport, so if you don't have a vehicle you're left with the painfully expensive option of **renting a car** in one of the main towns (Ngaoundéré, Garoua or Maroua), or the uncertain option of hitching a lift in with mobile tourists.

The tranquil **campements** in these areas provide a relaxing break away from it all; you should reserve in advance, especially for weekends or holidays (contact the individual camp or the Délégation Provincial du Tourisme pour le Nord, Garoua (☎227.22.90, ☏227.13.64). Note that Cameroonian conservation policy makes special provision for big-game hunting, with macabre head prices on every species, from elephants down to monkeys. Hunting blocks are well defined, and the paths of camera- and gun-users don't cross.

North of Bénoué, within the Bénoué National Park buffer zone, is the privately run **Campement des Eléphants** (☎986.08.00, satellite ☎872.761.274.548, ✉peraarhaug@yahoo.fr; ❹), a unique research camp offering unusual wildlife experiences. Beautifully positioned on a rise overlooking a dry-season watering point on the Mayo Farda river delta – a tributary to Lake Lagdo – the camp arranges enjoyable and educational treks and river trips into the fauna-rich surrounding area, which is also home to a large population of elephants. Excursions are expensive (around CFA50,000 per person per day), but well organized and worth every penny. Book well in advance.

Rey Bouba, west of Bouba Ndjida National Park, is one of the most influential and traditional of the Fulani *lamidats*. It's a worthwhile excursion to the village, where you can stay on the floor of a traditional resthouse (around CFA5000), but you may have to wait days for an audience with the Lamido himself. Agencies plying the road between Ngaoundéré and Garoua stop in Guidjiba, where you can catch share taxis to Tchollíré, but you'll have to find a vehicle going north for the remaining 35km to Rey Bouba; your best chance is Friday – market day.

Bénoué National Park

Coming north from Ngaoundéré, you can enter the **Bénoué National Park** (Dec–May; entrance fee CFA5000, obligatory guide CFA3000 per day, vehicle CFA2000 per day) either at Mayo Alim or Banda. From both these towns, tracks lead through the park to the *Campement du Buffle Noir* (☎227.32.75, or reservations through the Délégation Provincial du Tourisme pour le Nord in Garoua ☎227.22.90, ℻227.13.64; ❹). Situated on the banks of the Bénoué River, this camp has self-contained a/c **rooms** grouped in simple and comfortable *boukarous*. With prior permission you may be able to camp in the grounds. Meals at the restaurant cost CFA5000–8000.

Antelopes such as kob, waterbuck and hartebeest predominate in the park, but you may also see **buffalo** and Africa's largest antelope, the rare **Derby eland** – this is the only place in Africa where you have a realistic chance of seeing it. **Elephants** and **lions** are not as prolific as at Waza, but **hippos** and **crocodiles** are common in the river. Fishing is possible in the park (CFA5000 per day), but you need to go with someone who has a fishing permit, or buy an expensive permit yourself (CFA70,000; valid for a year). A popular spot for fishing is at the *Campement du Grand Capitaine* (c/o the Garoua tourist office on ☎227.22.90, ❹), the park's second resthouse, which lies on the main road leading from Guidjiba to Tchollíré; this *campement* is more like a private club for hunters and fishermen, however, and they may refuse to give you a room even if they're not full – ring ahead to check.

Bouba Ndjida National Park

The **Bouba Ndjida National Park** (Nov–May; entrance fee CFA5000, obligatory guide CFA3000 per day) was created in 1968 to protect the now nearly extinct **black rhinoceros** and the increasingly rare **Derby eland** (though this is now more prevalent in Bénoué). The main access is via Koum, 40km east of Tchollíré, where fees are paid and vehicles arranged into the park. The rugged landscape, with rivers and relatively thick vegetation, makes this one of the country's most beautiful parks, but the vast space (2200 square kilometres and 450km of track) and thick bush means that the animals are more dispersed and not as visible as in Waza, for example. Its isolation and proximity to the Chadian border also means that the risk of armed robbers is very real. A salt lick was created to attract the rhinos, but it's still almost impossible to spot them. There's more chance of seeing **elephants** and **buffaloes**, and, with luck, **lions** (which sometimes approach the resthouse) and **leopards**. The rustic *Bouba Ndjida camp* (reservations via the Garoua tourist office on ☎227.22.90; ❹; meals CFA6000) is 40km inside the park and overlooks the Mayo Lidi river.

Garoua

The capital of Northern Province, **GAROUA** has grown rapidly since independence and now has a population nearing 380,000. Surprisingly, for a town situated so far into the interior, it has the country's fourth largest port, on the banks of the **Bénoué (Benue) River**. This has helped smooth the way for local industrialization – though being former president Ahidjo's birthplace was no hindrance: he was always ready to invest in his home town. As the principal administrative and economic focus of the north, Garoua's more traditional aspects have been eclipsed to a large extent by its heterogeneous blend of northern Cameroonians, Nigerians and

Chadians. Traditional *saré* buildings – quite common up to the 1960s – have given way to cement homes with tin roofs, and the centre of town is dotted with modern blocks. Growth has brought increased facilities – banks, hotels and tourist information – making Garoua a convenient springboard for the next destination.

Some history

Fali and Bata people were the first to settle along the banks of the Bénoué, in the eighteenth century. They were followed by **Kilba Fulani** – herders who came in the early nineteenth century. After dan Fodio's jihad (see p.1124), the Fulani built a fortification (*ribadou*) around the town they called Ribadou-Garoua, to stave off Fali invasions. Other Muslims – Hausa, Bornu and Shua Arabs – arrived in the second half of the nineteenth century, lending an early urbanism to the settlement. The present **lamidat** dates from 1839.

The **Germans** colonized Garoua in 1901 and set up a small port (British steamers from the Niger Company had been trading in ivory, salt and cloth since 1890). Enlarged in 1930, the port served as a vital link between Cameroon, Chad and Nigeria, even though it has only ever been able to function during the rainy season from mid-July to mid-October. As a result, Garoua became an important focus of international attention in Cameroon, and has always had a large expatriate community. After independence, the roads were improved, and investment increased in cotton, the regional cash crop, and its related industries. In time, these were joined by a brewery and soapworks.

Accommodation

For a town the size of Garoua, there are surprisingly few hotels, but there is some accommodation in all price ranges, including a couple of very comfortable places in the international class.

Ahlan Wassalan rue de la Gendarmerie, in the heart of the commercial centre across from the Total station ☏ 227.23.87. Run by two friendly sisters, this small new *auberge* has a few hot, self-contained boxlike rooms. **①**

La Bénoué On the northern edge of the commercial centre, after *Relais St Hubert* ☏ 227.15.58, ⒻⒶ⒳ 227.15.53. Aging but OK, in shaded surroundings with a pool, tennis courts, good restaurant and a nightclub. **④**

Centrale rue Adamou Amar. Basic but central *auberge*, just behind the Marché Central and across the road from *Mille Glaces* ice-cream parlour, rooms with fan or a/c, some self-contained. **②**

La Cité rue du Petit Marché ☏ 227.24.93. Friendly *auberge* (although it's now falling into decline) in a lively neighbourhood, with self-contained rooms, some with a/c, and a reasonable restaurant. **②**

Hiala Village rue Boumaré in front of Cinéma Le Bénoué (formerly the Cinéma Étoile) ☏ 227.24.07. Centrally located near the port, this friendly and newly renovated *auberge* has small but clean self-contained rooms (a/c or fan), some with TV, and a decent bar-restaurant. **②**

Relais Saint Hubert On the northern edge of the commercial centre ☏ & ⒻⒶ⒳ 227.30.33. Set in an attractive garden with a pleasant swimming pool and a decent restaurant and bar, though the once luxurious a/c *boukarous* or more expensive rooms in a new block are already showing signs of disrepair. **④**

Le Salam Near the main *agences de voyage* and close to the Marché Central ☏ 227.24.26, ⒻⒶ⒳ 227.20.14. A range of simple rooms with fan, some self-contained – good for small budgets. The outdoor showers are perfect for the hot climate. Often full. **①**

Tourist Motel bd 20 Mai ☏ 997.92.41, ⒻⒶ⒳ 227.31.62. Well-kept hotel with comfortable a/c rooms, a good restaurant and a very nice swimming pool (CFA1000 for non-guests). It's a bit far from the centre of town, but conveniently located for the airport. **⑤**

The Town

Aside from the monumental **Grande Mosquée** on the route de Maroua – one of Cameroon's largest, but closed to non-Muslims – there's nothing around town worth going out of your way for, apart from the huge **Marché Central**, best at

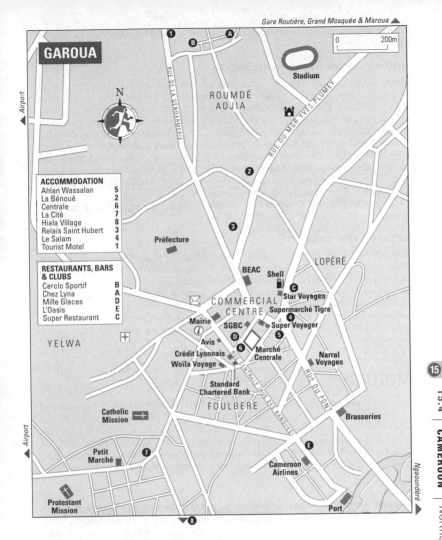

weekends. Here you'll also find the **Centre Artisanal**, with masks and statuettes (though they tend towards airport-art anonymity) along with some tempting leatherwork. Be prepared to bargain vigorously. Just north of the market, traditional medicine sellers spread out their wares under the neem trees, while across the street, bookings for game-park lodgings can be made at the **tourist office** (Délégation Provinciale du Tourisme pour le Nord; Mon–Fri 8am–3.30pm; ☎227.22.90, ℻227.13.64).

The commercial centre encompasses **banks**, including BICEC, SGBC (which has the only working ATM in the north), Crédit Lyonnais and Standard Chartered, all within 100m of the **post office**, and administrative buildings such as the Mairie, with the obligatory fountain in front. It's more interesting to wander through the **Yelwa** district, where the **Petit Marché** keeps things lively and where there's a good concentration of bars and *circuits* (the northern name for a small eatery). The energy, which continues **after dark**, makes it a likeable place to seek out an evening's entertainment.

Eating, drinking and nightlife

There are a number of cheap restaurants grouped around the central cluster of *agences de voyage*, all serving omelette breakfasts, rice, plantains, yams or macaroni with beef sauce. The *Super Restaurant,* opposite the Shell garage, serves the same sort of hunger-stoppers with freshly blended fruit juices. Popular bar-restaurants include the *Cercle Sportif* and *Chez Lyna*, at the northern end of Roumdé Adjia *quartier*. The beer is very reasonably priced, and both serve decent food for about CFA2000 a plate. There are cheap snacks aplenty in the *circuits* and food stalls around the animated Petit Marché. For something a bit more upmarket, *L'Oasis*, near the port, does excellent sea food and steak. Imported foods are sold at the Supermarché Tigre near the Marché Central.

If you're looking for somewhere to **dance**, head for the nightclub at the *Hôtel Bénoué*.

Around Garoua

About 50km south of Garoua at the town of **Ngong** is the German-run **Lagon Blue** resort (☎953.53.53 or contact the CDG supermarket in Maroua; ❺), set on the beautiful Lagdo Lake. This is one of the most tranquil hotels in Cameroon, with the choice of *boukarous* (fan or a/c), all with terraces overlooking the picturesque lake and colourful flower garden. The lakeside beach is delightful, although there's no guarantee that the waters are completely bilharzia free. There's also a good bar-restaurant, and if you come during the week, chances are you'll have the entire place to yourself.

Maroua

One of Cameroon's few pre-colonial cities, **MAROUA** already had a population of some 25,000 when French administrators took their first census in 1916, and four times that number lived within 20km of the town. It's now the north's second-largest city, and has retained a much more traditional flavour than Garoua, with old neighbourhoods spread out on both banks of the **Mayo Kaliao** (a dry expanse of sand for half of the year) and criss-crossed with streets shaded by sweet-smelling neem trees.

Moving on from Garoua

Transport out of Garoua is straightforward. The main *agences de voyage* are clustered close to the Marché Central; all run a service north to **Maroua** and south to **Ngaoundéré**. The larger agencies include Lux Voyages (☎227.52.98), Narral Voyages (☎227.11.16), Super Voyages (☎227.12.03), Star Voyages (☎227.14.85) and Woïla Voyages ☎227.30.82); the last is considered the most comfortable, although they charge a little but more. For destinations such as Gaschiga (customs and immigration) and Demsa for Yola in **Nigeria** (a bad road), minibuses leave from the *gare routière*, 4km from the centre of town on the route de Maroua.

Cameroon Airlines **fly** to Douala (Tues, Thurs, Fri & Sat; CFA77,600 one way), Yaoundé (Thurs, Sat & Sun; CFA67,100 one way), and Ndjamena in Chad (Sun). Precise information and reservations are available by calling Cameroon Airlines (☎227.10.55 or 227.29.29) or the airport (☎227.14.81). You can **rent a car** at Avis, at Lasal, in the Commercial Centre (☎227.12.98), or at Norga Voyages, near Cameroon Airlines (☎227.26.17).

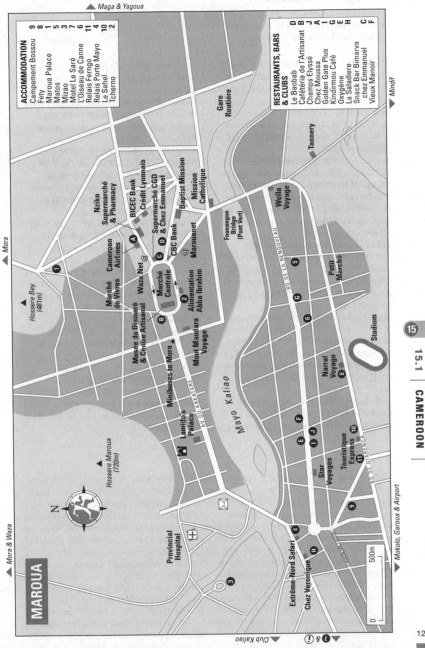

Accommodation

Maroua has a good selection of accommodation for all budgets. Most of the inexpensive **auberges** can be found on the south side of the river near the stadium. **Upmarket lodgings** are in the west, near the river and the Kaygama district.

Campement Bossou South of the river off bd de Diarenga. Clean, basic *boukarous* with fans and shared (cold) showers in a quiet location. Popular with budget travellers. **1**

Fety Next to Narral Voyages, bd de Diarenga ☏ 229.29.13. Bright, clean self-contained rooms with a/c and hot water, plus a small bar and good-value restaurant. **2**

Maroua Palace qtr Djoudandou ☏ 229.32.52, ☏ 229.15.25. International-class hotel rising from the base of the northern hills, a good kilometre from the centre. Rooms have a/c, TV and phone, and there's a pool (CFA1500 for non-guests) and a good restaurant. American Express and Visa accepted. **5**

Matos Off bd de la Renouveau, right after *Kindirmou Café* and opposite the Evangelical mission ☏ 990.19.01. Set in a peaceful garden, this converted villa has spacious a/c rooms with hot showers. No restaurant, but there is a bar selling beer. **2**

Mizao North of the river, behind the hospital ☏ 229.13.00, ☏ 229.13.04. Clean self-contained rooms, all with a 1970s retro look and a bit run-down, but still comfortable. The restaurant offers a *menu* at CFA6000, and there's a nightclub, tennis courts and swimming pool (CFA1500 for non-guests). **5**

Motel Le Saré South of the river towards the tourist office ☏ 229.12.94, ☏ 229.18.04. As spacious as the *Mizao*, but far more likeable, in a large shaded garden with its own pool. Currently under renovation, but scheduled to reopen in 2004.

L'Oiseau de Canne Near the stadium ☏ 986.12.21. A clean, tidy place run by the owner of *Cafétéria de l'Artisanat* in the centre, with a number of basic rooms (fan or a/c) set around a well-kept courtyard. **2**

Relais Ferngo South of the river, off bd de Diarenga ☏ 229.21.53. Budget satellite of the *Relais de la Porte Mayo*, with less classy self-contained a/c *boukarous* in a peaceful compound, plus a quiet bar and a campsite (CFA1000 per person) with shower and toilet. **2**

Relais Porte Mayo Near the river ☏ 229.26.92, ☏ 229.29.85. The town's best mid-range place, with comfortable a/c *boukarous* in a garden setting, plus a pleasant courtyard restaurant, shops and a steady stream of crafts vendors. It's a popular rendezvous for expats and a good place to seek information, hire vehicles or arrange tours (through Porte Mayo Voyages). **4**

Le Sahel 11 boulevard de Diarenga, next to Touristique Express ☏ 229.29.60, ☏ 229.30. Good-sized clean rooms with hot water and TV, friendly staff and a good restaurant. **3**

Tcherno Across from the Central Market, next to Alimentation Abba Ibrahim ☏ 229.23.64, ☏ 229.21.52. New pink multistorey hotel with self-contained rooms (fan or a/c), TV and hot showers, plus an inexpensive restaurant and bar with street-side terrace. **2**

The Town

The **Musée du Diamaré**, near the market (daily 8am–1.30pm & 2.30–6pm; donation), contains only a small collection of regional objects, but is worth checking out nonetheless. They don't get many visitors, so the caretaker is usually very eager to provide thoughtful explanations of the assortment of objects from the **Sao civilization**, and artefacts collected from the Toupouri, Massa and Mousgoum peoples. The **Fulani** are represented by carved calabashes, jewellery and clothing, including a beautifully crafted *boubou* (large gown) worn by a *lamido* for special occasions. Notice the shield made from a dried and shaped elephant ear.

The **centre artisanal**, in the same building as the museum, is a large craft market with innumerable stands. The emphasis is on the locally made **leather goods** for which Maroua is famous (sandals, bags, round floor cushions) but there are goods from throughout Central and West Africa as well. Jewellery and hand-woven cloth can be good value here, but bargain astutely and take your time choosing; there's a vast selection. If you can overcome the smell, the photogenic **tannery** (CFA1000 for an obligatory guide), to the southeast of town on the road to Mindif, is another interesting place to visit.

Maroua's large **market** spreads out behind the museum. Although it's held daily, the main market day is Monday, when **Kirdi** ("pagan") peoples come from all over the region to trade. Everything from car parts and Japanese electrical goods to locally made cloth and traditional medicines is sold here. Just north of the market, the **Marché de Vivres** sells fresh produce. From the main market, a broad avenue leads several hundred metres southeast to the Founangué Bridge (also known as Pont Vert), while Avenue du Kakataré stretches southwest nearly 2km past the Lamido's Palace to the very colonial **post office**. From the post office roundabout, the road heading uphill to the northwest leads to the **hospital**. The **Ministry of Tourism** (Mon–Fri 9am–noon & 2–5pm; ☏229.11.65 or 229.22.98) is reached by crossing the bridge and heading on a further 2km southwest, but you're probably better off making arrangements for trips in the area through one of the larger hotels or Fagus Voyages (☏986.18.71, ⊛www.fagusvoyages.com).

The main way of shuttling between sites is on the back of a **moto** (CFA100); they're quicker and easier to flag down than shared or private taxis.

Eating and drinking

Maroua offers a good range of **eating places**, from the inexpensive *circuits* to the more formal restaurants of the big hotels. **L'Avion Me Laisse**, a street close to the western end of Boulevard de la Renouveau, has a collection of small but lively bars where you can eat grilled fish. The street was named by the first woman who started a business there – after her German boyfriend had left her. A number of the cheap restaurants cluster around the Centre Artisanal. The greatest concentration of **bars** and **clubs** is along Boulevard de la Renouveau; the better ones include the *Golden Gate Plus*, *Champs Elysées*, *Vieux Manoir* and *Oxygène*, which has a smart little disco.

Le Baobab East of the market, across the street from the CBC Bank ☏756.64.50. Good Cameroonian dishes, like chicken in groundnut sauce (CFA2800), served in thatched *boukarous*.

Cafétéria de l'Artisanat Directly opposite the Centre Artisanal. Ice-cold yoghurt, and meals for around CFA1000 a plate.

Chez Moussa (also known as *Chez Kassariyel*) East of the market, by Cameroon Airlines. A likeable place where you can sit outside on mats in the peaceful courtyard whilst dining on fresh salads and well-made main courses (CFA2000–3000) washed down with the excellent fresh juice.

Kindirmou Café At the eastern end of bd de la Renouveau, near *Matos* hotel and auberge *L'Oiseau de Canne*. A great snack spot serving Fulani yoghurt (*kindirmou*) with fruit and omelette breakfasts.

Relais Porte Mayo At the *Relais Porte Mayo* hotel. Popular place with a good and varied menu, including Vietnamese specialities, which fills nightly with an expat crowd chatting noisily in French, English and German. Mains CFA4000–5000.

La Saladiere A stone's throw from *Relais Porte Mayo*. Well-prepared Cameroonian dishes (CFA1500) served in a stylish setting, with white tablecloths and raked sandy floors, indoors and out.

Snack Bar Bimarva Chez Emmanuel Next to the CDG supermarket, just east of the market. A very popular restaurant offering a good range of foods at moderate prices, as well as cold beer and satellite TV news.

Listings

Banks BICEC, CBC and Crédit Lyonnais, all near the market, change cash euros and US dollars, and euro traveller's cheques. To change US dollars cash head for Alimentation Abba Ibrahim (see below), which gives a better rate and a quicker service than the banks.
Car rental and tour organizers Maroua's most professional set-up by far is the Swiss-run Fagus Voyages (☏986.18.71, ⊛www.fagusvoyages.com), who offer reliable 4WDs plus driver at fair prices and some well-thought-out tours. Other options are the agency at *Relais Porte Mayo* (see opposite) and Extrême-Nord Safari (☏229.19.32, ⊜arkaint@tin.it), next door.
Hospitals CNPS Hospital ☏229.12.74 or 229.12.71; Hospital Meskine ☏229.25.79.
Internet The two best places are Waza.net, north of the market across from Nziko supermarket

The **gare routière** east of the Founangué Bridge has regular transport to destinations across the north all the way to **Kousséri**, where a bridge crosses over to **Njamena** in Chad (see p.1251). If you're heading south to **Garoua** and **Ngaoundéré**, use one of the *agences de voyage*: Woïla Voyages is best, with two morning departures in large comfortable coaches; alternatively, try Narral Voyages or Touristique Express; both are situated on Boulevard de Diarenga across from the stadium. Narral also has connections to **Moubi** in Nigeria and major towns between Maroua and Garoua, such as Guider and Fingil on the Chadian border. Star Voyages on bd de la Renouveau has regular services to Garoua as well as to Mora, Yagua, Kaele, Guidiguis and Toloum. Mont Mandara Voyages, just off av du Katare, has minibuses for **Mora** throughout the day, as well as regular connections to **Banki** on the Nigerian border and Kousséri up north by the Chadian border. On the corner, *clando* minibuses leave for Mora when full.

Cameroon Airlines **fly** to Yaoundé and Douala (Mon, Wed, Fri, Sat & Sun) and Ngaoundéré (Sat). Contact Cameroon Airlines (☎229.15.15) or call the airport (☎229.10.21) for flight information.

(Mon–Sat 9am–10pm, Sun 10am–6pm; CFA1200 per hour); and the faster Marouanet, on the first floor opposite the Mobil station (Mon–Sat 9am–8pm, Sun 10am–6pm; CFA1500 per hour).
National parks For information about Waza National Park, contact IUCN, qtr Kaygama (☎229.22.71) or Fagus Voyages (see above).
Supermarkets CGD Supermarché, east of the market, is large and well-stocked, but Nziko,

opposite Cameroon Airlines, and Alimentation Abba Ibrahim are better value. The latter may also change money.
Swimming pools Best value is the swimming pool at *Club Kaliao* (CFA1000). The pool at *Hôtel Mizao* (CFA1500) is closest to the centre, though the one at *Le Saré* (CFA1500) has a nicer setting. *Maroua Palace*'s pool (CFA1500) is overlooked by the hotel and not very private.

Mokolo, Mora and the Mandara Mountains

Beautiful and haunting, the denuded volcanic plugs of the **Mandara Mountains** rise up to the west of Maroua like stony brown fingers. They form the backdrop to some of the country's most fascinating and desolate scenery, and are home to communities who have come to be known as the "mountain people" – staunch non-Muslims who were pushed to the extremities of the inhabitable areas during the Muslim wars of the nineteenth century. Today, the region highlights Cameroon's most striking contrasts in the cultural clash of Kirdi, Fulani and Shua Arabs from the far north. In its ethnolinguistic complexity, highland setting and stone buildings – as well as the rise of organized adventure tourism – the Mokolo district bears superficial similarities to the Dogon country in Mali.

There is **no bank** in Mokolo nor in any of these villages and towns, so change money in Maroua. **Fuel** is only sold at stations in Mokolo and Mora.

Mokolo and around

The main point of entry to the region, **MOKOLO** is the capital of the **Mafa** people (also called Matakam by the Fulani) – one of the most populous groups in the mountains. Mokolo, however, is a quiet town (perhaps "village" is more accurate), with round houses of stone with thatched roofs, a market (on Wednesdays), a motor park and not much else. You can **stay** at the expensive *Campement du Flamboyant* (☎229.51.16; ❹), which has a/c *boukarous*, a restaurant and bar; you may be able to camp in the compound. There are cheaper but grimy rooms at the *Mecheme Bar* (**❷**) around the corner. A better option is to stay with people in town – ask around, and expect to pay around CFA2000 per person. The **Centre Artisanal** in the village of **Djingliya**, 15km from Mokolo, also has a few rooms (**❷**) and a restaurant and bar. They sell excellent basketwork at rock-bottom – and fixed – prices.

There are numerous villages in the mountains where you can arrange to stay in people's homes for a small fee. Payment in cash isn't necessarily appreciated, so discuss appropriate alternatives with your guide before leaving. A guide should cost about CFA5000 a day, and you can hire a donkey with driver to carry your luggage for another CFA5000. If you're here on a Thursday, head for the isolated mountain village of **Tourou** – a few hours by *moto* – and witness the unusual red calabash hat-clad women milling around the market selling traditional beer from clay pots. As elsewhere in the region, they're used to tourists, so be prepared to pay to take photos. It's also possible to explore the area on **horseback**; Fagus Voyages in Maroua (see p.1247) run good tours. On the highest paths you can cross undetected and unmolested into Nigerian territory (see p.1134), but you should be wary of going further into Nigeria without making a formal exit from Cameroon.

If you're heading on to Roumsiki, trucks from the **motor park** depart early in the morning. During the rest of the day, vehicles leave when full from the western edge of town, where the paved road towards Roumsiki ends and becomes a bumpy *piste*. Travelling to Roumsiki by *moto* will set you back CFA3500.

Roumsiki

A brief visit to **ROUMSIKI**, 50km from Mokolo, is very much a standard item on Cameroon's tourist circuit. It's a small and fairly ordinary village in itself, but wherever you look, the scenery is breathtaking. Roumsiki lies deep in the mountains, surrounded by magnificent time-worn peaks, the highest of which is muchphotographed **Zivi**. Houses built of local stone in the traditional style blend in with the gothic backdrop, changing shades of ochre and orange to umber and russet as the sun moves over the horizon.

The appeal of the visit is largely to get a taste of the "real" Cameroon, and the built-in flaw is that the more people come, the more distorted and unreal life in the village becomes. You have no option when arriving at Roumsiki other than to allow the little kids who greet you to act as your guides (unless you brought a paid companion with you or head straight for one of the hotels, all of which arrange guided trips in the area). They follow their own rigid programme in showing you what they imagine every tourist wants to see. There's no point resisting their help and trying to explore the village on your own; you'll just be made to feel like an unwelcome voyeur. So let the boys show you the **féticheur**, who tells your future by watching the way a river crab moves pieces of wood; the **weavers**, who make cloth by hand; the **potters** and the **blacksmiths**. They also explain how the huts are made and tell you about local customs and history. The people of Roumsiki are called **Margui**, or **Kapsikis** – "those who have grown tall". In the evening, your guides even accompany you to a nearby peak to get a better view of the sunset. Your every question, in fact, is answered before you ask it. It's quite interesting on a superficial level, but it's about as personal as watching a television documentary. The bottom line is definitely money, and you'll just have to accept that (bring lots of small change). For **longer treks** into the mountains – up to a couple of days – your best bet is to head for one of the hotels. All offer pre-planned tours at a cost of anything between CFA7500 and CFA12,500 per day, all inclusive. Travelling by horseback costs around CFA3000 per hour.

You can **stay** in the village at the new *Tour d'Argent* (**☎**986.19.80; **❶**), which is primarily a good restaurant, but also has a few inexpensive *boukarous* out back. *Campement de Rhumsiki* across the road (BP 27, Mokolo; CFA15.500) is no longer up to its former high standards but still the best bet in town if you want hot showers. They have a/c *boukarous* – the more expensive with beautiful mountain views – and the promise of a swimming pool in the future. Less expensive is *Maison de l'Amitié* (call Lara Voyages in Maroua for booking ☎229.21.13) with stylish and spacious self-contained a/c or fanned *boukarous* (CFA9500) and an outdoor restaurant. Cheaper still is the *Auberge Le Kapsiki* (☎229.33.56 or ☎990.18.78; CFA5000), with fans and shared facilities, plus a bar and restaurant, run by a friendly English-speaking proprietor who started his career in tourism guiding overlanders through the Dogon country in Mali. Alternatively you can arrange to sleep in people's homes. Ask the little kids, but do so before the last taxi heads back to Mokolo. Once they know you can't escape, prices rise. It's possible to find direct transport to and from Maroua on Sundays – Roumsiki's market day.

Mora and around

On market days (Wednesday for Mokolo and Sunday for Mora) you can get a share taxi from Mokolo to **MORA** via **Koza** – a picturesque track road that cuts through the heart of the **Mafa country**. Even on these days, you will have to leave Mora very early in the afternoon to get back to Mokolo with the last taxi. On other days, you'll probably have to go by the less scenic but fast route that passes through Maroua. Mora is last stop en route to **Banki** on the border to Nigeria, and an excellent spot to have your last cold beer before facing *sharia* rule next door.

Capital of the **Wandala** (also called Mandara) – a people who accepted Islam in the late seventeenth century after their contact with the Bornu Empire – Mora is especially known for a **market** which attracts a wide range of peoples from throughout the region. Muslim Fulani, Wandala and Shua women sell their goods alongside the traditionalist mountain people – **Podoko**, **Guizica** and **Mofou** – who retain their own firm views on suitable dress and headgear. It's a colourful mixture of cultures, and the market produce ranges from goat's milk to mangos and millet. Donkeys and goats are sold in the **animal market**, and you'll also find jewellery and carved calabashes.

The best option for budget **accommodation** is the *Auberge Mora Massif* (❶), located in a tranquil part of town, clearly signposted a few blocks east of the motor park; turn right at the communal water pump. The self-contained fanned rooms here are kept clean by attentive staff, and the bar-restaurant serves meals (if you order well in advance) and cold drinks. The slightly more expensive *Hôtel Sange de Podoko* (❷), off the main road to Maroua, offers self-contained *boukarous* with fans or a/c and a good bar-restaurant (again, order food well in advance). A good ultra-cheap option is the *Auberge Oudjila* (❶), around the corner, with basic, small self-contained *boukarous* and a lively all-day bar.

Oudjilla

Mora is the departure point for the eleven-kilometre trip to the village of **OUD-JILLA** in the mountains, a spot which, like Roumsiki, has become a magnet for tourism. You can barely set foot in Mora without a posse of gushing teenagers racing up to you on motorbikes and asking, "Mistah, tu vas où, à Oudjilla?"

Oudjilla is an authentic **Podoko village**, though once again your experience there may seem a bit contrived. You're led on arrival to the *saré* of the chief, who lives in a walled compound encompassing a maze of roofed passageways which connect the many huts housing his fifty-plus wives and countless children. For a negotiable price, you get to visit the chief's compound and see the hut that serves for public deliberations; another where the chief's father is buried and where jugs of millet beer are stored; and the sacrificial pen where the chosen cow awaits slaughter during the harvest festival. You're taken into the hut of one of the wives to see the kitchen and the utensils used for pounding millet, storing water and so on.

At the end, you're "invited" to take pictures of the chief and some of his wives with shaved heads and bare chests. For just a little more money, the wives might even do a harvest dance. It makes for the kind of photographs that put postcards to shame, but, at the same time, is liable to leave you feeling rather empty. To get beyond the performance, however, would take more time and dedication than most people have. There's nothing to stop you putting your feelings back in balance by exploring some of the other roads in this region; or by trying, "Non, merci, Oudjilla ne m'intéresse pas, mais pourrais-tu me diriger à…?" (then picking a small name from the map).

Waza National Park

With a minimum of vegetation, **Waza National Park** (mid-Nov to mid-June; fees per day: entrance CFA5000; obligatory guide CFA3000; camera CFA2000; vehicle CFA2000) spreads over 1700 square – and flat – kilometres and is probably the best site for savanna game-viewing in West Africa. The main park entrance, just outside the small town of **Waza**, is marked by two Mousgoum huts. Pay your fee here, before heading to the nearby *Campement de Waza* (☎229.16.46 or 765.77.17; ❸), which you should book in advance. Set on a hill, this excellent camp offers a choice of *boukarous* (fan or a/c) equipped with running water and electricity and grouped around a clean swimming pool (CFA1000 for non-guests). Expect to pay about CFA6000 for meals at the restaurant, which affords a splendid panorama of the surrounding park. If this is out of your range, the grubby *Centre d'Accueil* (☎229.22.07; ❷) near the park entrance has *boukarous* with mosquito nets and shared facilities. You can also camp here for CFA2500 a tent, and there's a restaurant which prepares Cameroonian and standard tourist food (CFA2500). In Waza village itself, *Chez Madame Bamenda*, a bar-restaurant, has a limited number of boxlike rooms (❶).

Since Waza is the most popular of the game parks, it's also the one you have the best chance of hitching into. Your only other option, if you don't have your own transport, is to hire a 4WD in Maroua. Try Fagus Voyages (☎986.18.71, ⓦwww.fagusvoyages.com), who have reliable vehicles and experienced drivers at reasonable prices.

Giraffe are quite plentiful here, and congregate near the gate. There's a substantial **elephant** population too, which, with luck, you should have no problem seeing. Your chances of finding **lions** are also pretty good. **Ostriches** tend to be shy, but **antelopes** such as waterbuck and roan are often spotted. Waza is especially good for **bird-watching**.

Kousséri and the northern extremity

At the confluence of the **Logone** and **Chari** rivers, **KOUSSÉRI** lies directly opposite the capital of Chad – **Ndjamena**. The bridge and *pirogues* that link them are the main *raison d'être* for a town that would otherwise be right off the beaten track. Principal sites in town include the **port** and **market** where, not surprisingly, fish is the mainstay (market day is Thursday). There are very few **places to stay** in Kousséri. *La Terrasse* (❷), in front of the Elf petrol station, is the best option, with clean self-contained rooms (fan or a/c) and a pretty terraced restaurant. There's also a run-down *auberge* nearby with fanned rooms (❶). There are **no banks** in Kousséri. A potholed tar road links Kousséri to the south via Maroua, it's especially bad between Mora and Maroua. Boats still provide an important link with **Ndjamena**, but the bridge downstream from the centre of Kousséri offers an easier crossing.

From Kousséri, you can enter **Chad** – directly into its capital, Ndjamena – across the new bridge (which closes promptly at 5pm every day). Taxis across are cheap and frequent. Since the situation in Chad has calmed down, there's no more than the routine drama of border formalities you'd expect to encounter anywhere.

If you're continuing into **Nigeria**, Fotokol is your last destination in Cameroon: Gamboru, over the border in Nigeria, is 140km short of Maiduguri (see p.1128). If you happen to be travelling **direct from Ndjamena to Maiduguri** in Nigeria, you need a *visa de passage* to cross the 100km or so of Cameroonian territory from Kousséri to Fotokol.

Making for **Niger** circumventing Nigeria, you can cross the border into Chad at a number of places for the detour around the lake to **Nguigmi** (see p.981). If you're in Kousséri, cross here to Ndjamena rather than risk going further north and finding yourself in a difficult position with nobody authorized to process your entry. If you're driving and intending heading the same way, Ndjamena is your most northerly reliable crossing point in any case.

Lake Chad and the Kalamaloué National Park

Accommodation facilities don't exist **north of Kousséri**. In the towns along the route to **Lake Chad**, you're therefore at the mercy of the local authorities (police or *lamidos* – it's usually possible to camp with permission more or less wherever you want for a negotiable fee). Problems you may have getting to the lake, however, generally have less to do with police than with the fact that the elusive waters have receded well to the north of the bigger towns.

From Kousséri, take a share taxi to **Makari**, which has a market on Wednesdays, when transport is easiest to arrange. It's a scenic route that hugs the banks of the **Chari River**, then veers westward through desert landscapes to **Maltam**, before heading north. In Makari, you can get a share taxi on to **Blangoua** on the river. Between July and October, the only months when the river isn't dry, you can charter a motorized *pirogue* for the hour-long journey to Lake Chad (around CFA5000). An alternative is to charter a taxi at great cost.

Just outside Kousséri you'll pass through the smallest and most recently created of Cameroon's northern reserves, the **Kalamaloué National Park**, which stretches along the road from Kousséri to Maltam. To visit, you'll need permission from the Délégué du Ministère de l'Environnement in Kousséri, as there's no ranger based in the park. The park's *campement* was closed at the time of writing, so there's no accommodation inside the park (the closest accommodation is in Kousséri and Waza). It's not much of a park, with very few animals remaining, but you can take guided **walking tours** to see crocodiles, elephants and hippos in the Chari River that borders the park and separates it from the outskirts of Ndjamena on the opposite bank.

Index

and small print

Index

Map entries are in colour.

A

B

L

N

A rough guide to Rough Guides

In the summer of 1981, Mark Ellingham, a recent graduate from Bristol University, was travelling round Greece and couldn't find a guidebook that really met his needs. On the one hand there were the student guides, insistent on saving every last cent, and on the other the heavyweight cultural tomes whose authors seemed to have spent more time in a research library than lounging away the afternoon at a taverna or on the beach.

In a bid to avoid getting a job, Mark and a small group of writers set about creating their own guidebook. It was a guide to Greece that aimed to combine a journalistic approach to description with a thoroughly practical approach to travellers' needs – a guide that would incorporate culture, history and contemporary insights with a critical edge, together with up-to-date, value-for-money listings. Back in London, Mark and the team finished their Rough Guide, as they called it, and talked Routledge into publishing the book.

That first *Rough Guide to Greece*, published in 1982, was a student scheme that became a publishing phenomenon. The immediate success of the book – with numerous reprints and a Thomas Cook Prize shortlisting – spawned a series that rapidly covered dozens of destinations. Rough Guides had a ready market among low-budget backpackers, but soon also acquired a much broader and older readership that relished Rough Guides' wit and inquisitiveness as much as their enthusiastic, critical approach. Everyone wants value for money, but not at any price.

Rough Guides soon began supplementing the "rougher" information about hostels and low-budget listings with the kind of detail on restaurants and quality hotels that independent-minded visitors on any budget might expect, whether on business in New York or trekking in Thailand.

These days the guides – distributed worldwide by the Penguin Group – offer recommendations from shoestring to luxury and cover more than 200 destinations around the globe, including almost every country in the Americas and Europe, more than half of Africa, and most of Asia and Australasia. Our ever-growing team of authors and photographers is spread all over the world, particularly in Europe, the USA and Australia.

In 1994, we published the *Rough Guide to World Music* and *Rough Guide to Classical Music*, and a year later the *Rough Guide to the Internet*. All three books have become benchmark titles in their fields – which encouraged us to expand into other areas of publishing, mainly around popular culture. Rough Guides now publish:

- Travel guides to more than 200 destinations worldwide
- Dictionary phrasebooks to 22 major languages
- History guides ranging from Ireland to Islam
- Maps printed on rip-proof and waterproof Polyart™ paper
- Music guides running the gamut from Opera to Elvis
- Restaurant guides to London, New York and San Francisco
- Reference books on topics as diverse as the Weather and Shakespeare
- Sports guides from Formula 1 to Man Utd
- Pop culture books from Lord of the Rings to Cult TV
- World Music CDs in association with World Music Network.

Visit **www.roughguides.com** to see our latest publications.

Rough Guide credits

Text editors: Richard Lim and Gavin Thomas
Managing director: Kevin Fitzgerald
Series editor: Mark Ellingham
Editorial: Martin Dunford, Kate Berens,
Ann-Marie Shaw, Helena Smith, Olivia Swift,
Ruth Blackmore, Geoff Howard, Claire
Saunders, Alexander Mark Rogers, Polly
Thomas, Joe Staines, Duncan Clark, Peter
Buckley, Lucy Ratcliffe, Clifton Wilkinson,
Alison Murchie, Fran Sandham, Sally
Schafer, Matthew Milton, Andy Turner,
Karoline Densley (UK); Andrew Rosenberg,
Yuki Takagaki, Richard Koss, Hunter
Slaton (US)
Design & Layout: Helen Prior, Julia Bovis,
Dan May, John McKay, Sophie Hewat (UK);
Madhulita Mohapatra, Umesh Aggarwal,
Sunil Sharma (India)

Cartography: Maxine Repath, Ed Wright,
Katie Lloyd-Jones (UK); Manish Chandra,
Rajesh Chhibber, Jai Prakash Mishra (India)
Cover art direction: Louise Boulton
Picture research: Sharon Martins, Mark
Thomas, Jj Luck
Online: Kelly Martinez, Anja Mutic-Blessing,
Jennifer Gold, Audra Epstein, Suzanne
Welles, Cree Lawson (US); Manik Chauhan,
Amarjyoti Dutta, Narender Kumar (India)
Finance: Gary Singh
Marketing & Publicity: Richard Trillo, Niki
Smith, David Wearn, Chloë Roberts, Demelza
Dallow, Geoff Colquitt, David Wechsler,
Megan Kennedy (US)
Administration: Julie Sanderson
RG India: Punita Singh

Publishing information

This fourth edition published November 2003 by
Rough Guides Ltd,
80 Strand, London WC2R 0RL.
345 Hudson St, 4th Floor,
New York, NY 10014, USA.
Distributed by the Penguin Group
Penguin Books Ltd,
80 Strand, London WC2R 0RL
Penguin Putnam, Inc.
375 Hudson Street, NY 10014, USA
Penguin Books Australia Ltd,
487 Maroondah Highway, PO Box 257,
Ringwood, Victoria 3134, Australia
Penguin Books Canada Ltd,
10 Alcorn Avenue, Toronto, Ontario,
Canada M4V 1E4
Penguin Books (NZ) Ltd,
182–190 Wairau Road, Auckland 10,
New Zealand
Typeset in Bembo and Helvetica to an original
design by Henry Iles.
Printed in Italy by LegoPrint S.p.A

© Jim Hudgens and Richard Trillo

No part of this book may be reproduced in any
form without permission from the publisher
except for the quotation of brief passages in
reviews.

1296pp includes index
A catalogue record for this book is available from
the British Library

ISBN 1-85828-118-6

The publishers and authors have done their best
to ensure the accuracy and currency of all the
information in **The Rough Guide to West Africa**,
however, they can accept no responsibility for
any loss, injury, or inconvenience sustained by
any traveller as a result of information or advice
contained in the guide.

1 3 5 7 9 8 6 4 2

Help us update

We've gone to a lot of effort to ensure that the
fourth edition of **The Rough Guide to West
Africa** is accurate and up-to-date. However,
things change – places get "discovered",
opening hours are notoriously fickle,
restaurants and rooms raise prices or lower
standards. If you feel we've got it wrong or left
something out, we'd like to know, and if you
can remember the address, the price, the
time, the phone number, so much the better.

We'll credit all contributions, and send a
copy of the next edition (or any other Rough

Guide if you prefer) for the best letters.
Everyone who writes to us and isn't already a
subscriber will receive a copy of our full-colour
thrice-yearly newsletter. Please mark letters:
"Rough Guide West Africa Update" and
send to: Rough Guides, 80 Strand, London
WC2R 0RL, or Rough Guides, 4th Floor, 345
Hudson St, New York, NY 10014. Or send an
email to **mail@roughguides.com**

Have your questions answered and tell
others about your trip at
www.roughguides.atinfopop.com

Acknowledgements

The **authors** jointly want to thank: all our contributors for tireless research; Jo Mead for a fine new index; Diane Margolis for proofreading; Umesh, Madhu and Sunil for typesetting; Mark Thomas for picture research; Ed, Jai, Katie, Manish, Maxine, Rajesh and Stratigraphics for the maps; Louise Boulton for the beautiful cover; Julia Bovis for production; and our kind editors Richard Lim and Gavin Thomas for skilfully keeping this guide on the rails for so many months and getting it to its destination in infinitely better shape than when we set off. Mille mercis.

James thanks Apou Gata Djima, Lisa Washington, Kairn Kleiman, Vijitha and Ndede Eyango, Anthony Mainer, Julia Bromhead, Gotzon Zaratiegi, Conerly Casey, Kendahl Radcliffe, Shirley Radcliffe, Luc and Fati Denesle, Belinda Sunnu and Elvis Nya Ndjenou.

Richard Trillo thanks Tom Bullough for updates; Daouda Dicko for a fine hike; Chris Frean for news; Paul Everett for Salone (next time!); Rachel and Jeremy Nash and family for kind hospitality in Burkina Faso; Ron Hughes and Vicky Parnaby of Cape Verde Travel for assistance; and most of all Teresa, Alex, David and Phoebe for once again putting up with my absence while I was actually at home – and especially, this time, to David who came with me to Mali and Burkina and helped so enthusiastically to answer the ça vas? and shake all the hands.

Adam and Katrine would like to thank: in Ghana, Mrs E Asiedu and Alex Wilson in Accra, Prince Abdal in Bolga, and Daisy Okojie in Kumasi, and Joshua Middleman in Boabeng-Fiema; in Burkina Faso, Francoise, Jean Louis and Sally Gallois in Diébougou – keep up the good work; in Benin, Charles Leeuwen from KIT, Iain and Carrie Steele and Mick McMillan; and in Togo, Albert Toose and Margeret Benians in Lomé, and Birgit Kerstens in Glidji. And in the UK, thanks to Tom McCaskie, Lynne Brydon and Stuart Barnes from CWAS, Clive Charlton, and Richard Trillo for all their patience and advice.

Thanks from **Brendon** to Ron and Vicki at Cape Verde Travel, Richard Trillo for maps and encouragement, Robert Griffin and Keith Munro for making the effort, Julie and Daniel Pereira, John Fernandes and Jose the barman on Brava, Ivan Brito and Odilio in Cidade Velha, Francisco and Patrick on Fogo, Mani in Mindelo, Sebastian Tul and Atila Amara in Sal Rei, Manuel Conceição in Ribeira Brava, Leonor Santos at TACV Praia, Blaise and Sandre on Santo Antão, Nauts Roman and Alan. Thanks also to all the Senegalese, not least Abdoulaye and Samba.

Chris thanks his faithful travel companion Maureen for everything; Phil and Mari Manning for a memorable trip to Diawling; Tim and Debbie Johnson and Don Jones for helping find the crocodiles of Matmata; Joel, Tim and Fleur for hospitality in Nouadhibou; His Excellency Dr Youssouf Diagana and Mr Waana Saada for obtaining official permission; SNIM and MKT for help with transport and accommodation; Philip Clarke and Susanna Clarke for useful comments on the script; Leslie Abramson, Sebastian Cooke, Stan and Beth Doerr, Jackie Hutchinson, Elias Mendes-Gomes, Betty Miller, Grant Smith, Richard Trillo, Andy and Nancy Wagler, and Dean Young for their useful information; and Matthew Teller and Martin Varley who inspired me to be a writer.

From **Daniel**, thanks to Abigale Davies, Michael Modebelu and J.A.A. Jinadu for their help in Nigeria, to Tayo Situ for Yoruba language assistance, and to Lone.

Thanks from **Emma** to the following for their generous assistance in The Gambia: Simon & Nicole Angling; Adama Bah; John Baldwin; Clive Barlow; Ablay Bayo; Farid and Fouzia Bensouda of Coconut Residence; Debbie Burns; Baba Ceesay; David Clamp; Nick Clark; Ebrima Colley; Famara Drammeh; Ludovic Dumont; Patrick Dyke; Modou Lamin Faye; George Foster; Charbel Hobeika; Karen Hobbs; Modou Gaye; Francis Glynn, May Rooney, Aimee and everyone at GTS; Harold Goodwin; Sallie Grayson; Marianne Harstad; Derek & Jenny Hewitt; Dan, Mandy and Manuel Huertas; Baba Ishangi; Joe & Nina; Ous Jagne; Mawdo Jallow; Khadija Jammeh; Jette Jarra; Malick Jeng and his colleagues at Gambia Tourism Authority and the Ministry of Tourism; Amadou Johnson; David Llewellyn-Griffiths; Monika Kili-Cole and her team at Gambia River Excursions and Janjang Bureh Camp; Nigel Killikelly; Will Knowles; Alagi Mbye; Evamaria Minuth; Geri Mitchell, Maurice Phillips, Abi and everyone at Safari Garden; Sarah McLaughlin & Simon;

Hu Morris; Suelle Nachif; Farma Njie; The Professor of Fajara; RM Tours; Lamin Sanyang; Angie Silva; Ann Slind; Kawsu Sillah; Sulayman Sonko; Patrick Sothern and his team at West African Tours especially Ibrahim, Kalifa, Numo, Alhaji and Ben; Martine Stone; Helen Stott; Mark Stratton; Foday Suso; Tony Tabbal; Mark Thompson and everyone at Bird Safari Camp; Foday Trawally and Ann Rivington at Madiyana Lodge; Lawrence Williams and James English of Makasutu. Thanks to The Gambia Experience for travel arrangements and to Sony UK. Very special thanks also go to Max Adam, Piers Northam and Nathan Pope.

Katharina sends thanks to Ibrahima Dieng, Salimatou Diallo, Sarata Diallo, Moustapha Diallo at the Office de Tourisme in Conakry, the Ministry of Tourism, the British Consulate, the German embassy, the Parisienne office in Kankan, Lamine Bah Freetown, the GTZ in Sierra Leone, Dr Belco in Bissau, Telivel Diallo, Daimou Diallo in Dalaba, and everyone else who helped with information, accomodation or in any other way.

In Mali, **Lone and Nathalie** would like to thank Jutta Ratschinske (Mankan Te) for her help in the Mopti region, Gaoussou Dembele, and Sekou and Birgitte Bülow for their assistance in the Dogon country, and Alida Jay Boye for help with Timbuktu. In Niger, thank you to Moussa Labaty Maiga, to Rémi Hallegouet and Titi in Agadez, as well as Eric Van Sprundel in Zinder. In Nigeria, we thank the staff at the Kano Tourist Office, and also Steven Frasier, Christophe Carillon and Dominic Okutue. In Cameroon, thanks to François and Gina Favarger for taking us to fantastic places in the north, the girls at the British Council in Yaoundé, Martin Smith, Anatole Moayika from the Douala Tourist Board, David Hoyle for help with Nguti, Jacqui Sunderland-Groves for news about gorillas in Takamanda, Andrew Dunn and Linda Kamga with latest developments in Korup National Park and lastly Elias Ndive for taking us up Mount Etinde. Lone would also like to thank Mette, Henrik and Nina. Nathalie sends a special thank you to Helen Tunnicliffe. Lastly we would like to thank all the VSO and Peace Corps volunteers we came across.

Thanks from **Sam** to Oumar Baldé in Joal; Ibou Ba in Dakar; Balaye Sanokho at Dar Salam; Tekheye Faye, Abdoul Mbaye and Abdoulaye Dia in Ziguinchor; Ibrahima Ndiaye in Elinkine, and to Katy Tuthill.

Readers' letters

Thanks to all the following who took the trouble to write in with their comments and suggestions (and apologies to anyone whose name we've inadvertently misspelt or omitted):

O.S. Akosile, Victor Awasung, Hans-Jochen Baethge, Monika and Jerry Baker, Jerry van Beers, Kate Blacker, Russel Blackwell, Chris Bramley, Lisa Brooks, Jane Broughton, Anna Brown, Steve Bryant, Mary Buchalter, Simon Bush, Adrian Carr, Sarah Castle, Tony Chafer, Margaret and Jim Clark, Brad Clinehens, Andrew Connor, Peter Conteh, Floreme Crovato, Hillary Dennison, Kathinka Devold Kjellsen, Frederick Dove, Ludovic Dumont, Marie-Louise Dungworth, Jeroen Eggermont, Assou Faradjiti, Ferdinand Fellinger, Andrew Gilmour, Abdoulaye Goudiaby, Robin Graham, Jeri Gray, Toby Green, F. Greenaway, Alice Guegen, Morten Hagen, David Hapgood, Ruth and James Harvey, Simon Heap, James Korede, Margarete Kuderna, Monica Kearns, Evanthia Karpouzli, Pratul Kumar, Keith A. Law, Joy Lawson, Wendy Lubin, T.C. Luce, Richard Lucy, Mariama Ludovic de Lys, Eben Mensah, Erika Maag, Jim Mann Taylor, Kristy Manuliak, Andy Morgan, Angus Neil, Graham Nelson, Dr Paul Nugent, Okigbo Ojukwu, Moussa Ouattara, Sasa Pöllmann, Nick Pretzlik, Melissa Racouillat, Andrew Rodrigues, Lily Ryan-Collins, Anderson Sarpong, Bryan Savage, Johan Schepkens, Rahel Schupbach, Chris Scott, Laura Seay, Julie Sherman, Ezra Simon, Christopher K. Starr, Rev Joseph Sullivan, Kendall Sumner, Clare Sutton, Sharon Swyer, Robin Syred, Susan Towler, Phil Twomey, Anne-Marie Vieira, Philip Wilkinson, Alison Wilson, F. Wolfart, Alan R. Wood.

SMALL PRINT

Photo credits

Cover

Main front picture Friday mosque, Djenné
© Axiom
Small top front picture Dogon dancer
© Getty
Small lower front picture Bus Emma © Gregg
Back top picture Dabola © Emma
Gregg/James McCormick
Back lower picture Dogon Country
© Emma Gregg

Colour introduction

Hombori, Mali © Richard Trillo
Stack of cooking pots, chief's house in
Tiébélé, Burkina Faso © Adam
Musgrave/Katrine Green
Melons and limes, Cameroon
© François Favarger
Replacing a roof, Wukari, Nigeria
© Richard Trillo
Djenné weekly market © Emma Gregg
Niger River, South of Gao © Richard Trillo
Women pounding millet © Emma Greg
Children playing near slave fort, Ghana
© Adam Musgrave/Katrine Green
Central market, Kumasi
© Adam Musgrave/Katrine Green
Peanuts © Emma Gregg
Female fertility shrine, Togoville, Togo
© Adam Musgrave/Katrine Green
Orange seller at bush taxi stop © Emma
Gregg
Overlanders' convoy © Jack Barker
Crafts for sale, Youga-Na Mali © Richard
Trillo
Boys playing warri, northern Ghana
© Adam Musgrave/Katrine Green
Kora player © Emma Gregg
Colithrix monkey © Emma Gregg
Beach near Cape Coast, Ghana
© M. Jelliffe/Trip

Black and whites

Mauritanian reception where a newborn
child is named © Jonathan Shadid (p.92)
Baobab in Senegal © Sam Thorne (p.146)
Palais de Justice, St-Louis © Sam Thorne
(p.219)

Jola drumming and dancing session
© Emma Gregg (p.248)
An elders' meeting house or togu-na
© Adam Musgrave/Katrine Green (p.306)
Tellem architecture, Youga-Dogourou, Dogon
escarpment © Richard Trillo (p.372))
Shipwreck at São Vicente, Cape Verde
© Richard Trillo (p.408)
Cha das Caldeiras, Fogo © Richard Trillo
(p.458)
Bijagós children © Emma Gregg (p.486)
Bus in the Fouta Djalon (p.530) © James
McCormick
Kouroussa children © James McCormick
(p.571)
Fula meeting house, Dalaba © Richard Trillo
(p.581)
Moa River, Tiwai Island Nature Reserve
© Richard Trillo (p.598)
Rooftops, Tiébélé © Adam Musgrave/Katrine
Green (p.650)
Cabaret, Gaoua © Adam Musgrave/Katrine
Green (p.693)
Elmina Castle © Adam Musgrave/Katrine
Green (p.722)
Wli Falls © Adam Musgrave/Katrine Green
(p.773)
Voodoo dolls and fetishes, Lomé, © Caroline
Penn/Corbis (p.818)
Tamberma Country © Adam Musgrave/
Katrine Green (p.863)
Pirogue, Ganvié © Adam Musgrave/Katrine
Green (p.880)
Gerewol Festival © Tiziana & Gianni
Baldizzone/Corbis (p.936)
Grande Mosquée, Agadez © Robert Harding
(p.988)
Wiki Warm Springs Yankari National Park
© Gary Cook/Alamy (p.994)
Dye pits, Kano, Nigeria © Financial
Times/Robert Harding (p.1101)
Northern Cameroon © Sylvain Grandadam/
Robert Harding (p.1138)
Lowland gorilla © Martin Harvey/Gallo
Images/Corbis (p.1232)

stay in touch

roughnews

Rough Guides' FREE full-colour newsletter

News, travel issues, music reviews, readers' letters and the latest dispatches from authors on the road

If you would like to receive roughnews, please send us your name and address:

62-70 Shorts Gardens
London, WC2H 9AH, UK

4th Floor, 345 Hudson St,
New York NY10014, USA

newslettersubs@roughguides.co.uk

Visit us online
roughguides.com

Information on over 25,000 destinations around the world

- **Read** Rough Guides' trusted travel info
- **Share** journals, photos and travel advice with other readers
- Get exclusive Rough Guide **discounts** and travel **deals**
- Earn membership points every time you contribute to the
  Rough Guide **community** and get **free** books, flights and trips
- Browse thousands of CD reviews and artists in our **music** area

"The Rough Guides are near-perfect reference works"
Philadelphia Inquirer

Music Reference Guides

Classical music
Country music
Jazz
Opera
Rock
Reggae music
World Music — Africa, Europe and the Middle East
World Music — Latin and North America, Caribbean, India, Asia and Pacific
Music USA

Pocket Guides

Cult Pop
THE BEATLES
Elvis
Cuban Music
Drum n Bass
Techno
House
Irish Music

Rough Guide Music Guides

Available from high street bookstores or online at www.roughguides.com

Rough Guides travel

key: 🌐 map   ▣ phrasebook   ⊙ cd

Rough Guides publishes new books every month:

NOTES

NORTH SOUTH TRAVEL
Great discounts

North South Travel is a small travel agent offering excellent personal service. Like other air ticket retailers, we offer discount fares worldwide. But unlike others, all available profits contribute to grassroots projects in the South through the NST Development Trust Registered Charity No. 1040656.

For **quotes** or queries, contact Brenda Skinner or Bridget Christopher, Tel/Fax 01245 608 291. Recent **donations** made from the NST Development Trust include support to Djoliba Trust, providing micro-credit to onion growers in the Dogon country in Mali; assistance to displaced people and rural communities in eastern Congo; a grant to Wells For India, which works for clean water in Rajasthan; support to the charity Children of the Andes, working for poverty relief in Colombia; and a grant to the Omari Project which works with drug-dependent young people in Watamu, Kenya.

Great difference

Email brenda@nstravel.demon.co.uk
Website www.nstravel.demon.co.uk

ATOL 75401

North South Travel, Moulsham Mill, Parkway, Chelmsford, Essex, CM2 7PX, UK

The ideas expressed in this code were developed by and for independent travellers.

Learn About The Country You're Visiting

Start enjoying your travels before you leave by tapping into as many sources of information as you can.

The Cost Of Your Holiday

Think about where your money goes - be fair and realistic about how cheaply you travel. Try and put money into local peoples' hands; drink local beer or fruit juice rather than imported brands and stay in locally owned accommodation. Haggle with humour and not aggressively. Pay what something is worth to you and remember how wealthy you are compared to local people.

Embrace The Local Culture

Open your mind to new cultures and traditions - it will transform your experience. Think carefully about what's appropriate in terms of your clothes and the way you behave. You'll earn respect and be more readily welcomed by local people. Respect local laws and attitudes towards drugs and alcohol that vary in different countries and communities. Think about the impact you could have on them.

Exploring The World – The Travellers' Code

Being sensitive to these ideas means getting more out of your travels - and giving more back to the people you meet and the places you visit.

Minimise Your Environmental Impact

Think about what happens to your rubbish - take biodegradable products and a water filter bottle. Be sensitive to limited resources like water, fuel and electricity. Help preserve local wildlife and habitats by respecting local rules and regulations, such as sticking to footpaths and not standing on coral.

Don't Rely On Guidebooks

Use your guidebook as a starting point, not the only source of information. Talk to local people, then discover your own adventure!

Be Discreet With Photography

Don't treat people as part of the landscape, they may not want their picture taken. Ask first and respect their wishes.

We work with people the world over to promote tourism that benefits their communities, but we can only carry on our work with the support of people like you. For membership details or to find out how to make your travels work for local people and the environment, visit our website.

www.tourismconcern.org.uk

TourismConcern
Campaigning for Ethical and Fairly Traded Tour

MUSIC ROUGH GUIDE

Rough Guides To A World Of Music

'stick to the reliable Rough Guide series'
The Guardian (UK)

'Over the past few years the Rough Guide CDs, with
their stylish covers, have distinguished themselves
as approachable and well-chosen introductions to
the music of the countries concerned. They have
been consistently well-reviewed and, like the
guidebooks themselves, stand out as an obvious
first choice for journeys in world music'
Simon Broughton, Editor Songlines

Hear sound samples at
WWW.WORLDMusic.NET

Available from book and record shops worldwide
or order direct from

World Music Network
6 Abbeville Mews
88 Clapham Park Road
London SW4 7BX
UK

T 020 7498 5252   F 020 7498 5353
E post@worldmusic.net

CAPE VERDE TRAVEL
and Eastgate Travel
14 Market Place
Hornsea
East Yorkshire
HU18 1AW, England
Proprietor : Ron Hughes P.Q.R.C

ATOL 3639

ABTA V9926

DISCOVER THE CAPE VERDE ISLANDS

Let us coordinate your leisure and business arrangements, conventions and festivals.

We have a practical, working knowledge of all islands. Resources being tried and tested. Opportunities are plentiful.

Appreciate the variety, contrast and culture of these Atlantic islands. The sunshine, music, people and food.

Air travel, ground arrangements, hotels and transport. We can provide our services to visitors from all over the World. So from wherever you are you can use our reservation services. Contact us and let your discovery begin.

Tel: 00 44(0)1964 536191
Fax: 00 44(0)1964 536192
Email: sales@capeverdetravel.com
Website: www.capeverdetravel.com

CALL 1617 338 0111

Africa

CULTURAL ADVENTURE TOURS & SAFARIS

BENIN, BOTSWANA, BURKINA FASO, CAMEROON, ETHIOPIA, GHANA,
GUINEA, KENYA, MALI, MAURITANIA, MOZAMBIQUE, NAMIBIA, NIGER,
SENEGAL, SOUITH AFRICA, TANZANIA, THE GAMBIA,
TOGO, UGANDA, ZAMBIA

Air Fares

Destination:		Round trips from:	
Abidjan, Côte d'Ivoire	$1014	Douala, Cameroon	$1274
Accra, Ghana	$1014	Harare, Zimbabwe	$1190
Bamako, Mali	$1014	Johannesburg, S.A.	$1050
Banjul, The Gambia	$824	Lagos, Nigeria	$1024
Capetown, S.A.	$1050	Lome, Togo	$1024
Conakry, Guinea	$1014	Nairobi, Kenya	$1200
Cotonou, Benin	$1024	Niamey, Niger	$1024
Dakar, Senegal	$791	Ouagadougou, B.F.	$1024

New York departures + tax. Group departures on request. Ask for other destinations & tour packages.
Rates are subject to change

SPECTOR TRAVEL OF BOSTON, INC.
EST. 1989
AFRICA TOURISM CONSULTANTS
TEL: 800 TRY AFRICA or 617 338 0111
FAX: 617 338 0110 www.spectortravel.com
africa@spectortravel.com

CALL 1617 338 0111

CALL 1800 TRY AFRICA

CALL 1800 TRY AFRICA

THE GATEWAY TO WEST AFRICA
WITH
THE GAMBIA EXPERIENCE

Friendly people

Interesting African culture

Unspoilt and uncommercialised

Value for money

THE UK'S ONLY SPECIALIST

Over 17 years experience travelling to The Gambia

Expert reservations - all UK staff have been to The Gambia

AITO 3 star responsible tourism award winners

RANGE OF FLIGHTS

Direct from Manchester, Bristol & Gatwick plus Glasgow departures

All year round - 6 flights a week in winter

Premium Class - Exclusive upgraded flight service

BEST CHOICE

Widest range of accommodation - 2 grade to deluxe eco-lodges

Birdwatching, Fishing, Upriver & Cultural holidays

Competitive prices

Tailor-made itineraries

For a brochure call:
02380 730 888
or visit: www.gambia.co.uk

The Gambia Experience, Kingfisher House, Rownhams Lane, North Baddesley, Hampshire SO52 9LP

take the hassle
out of kitting out...

....click here

home   online shop   travel health zone   customer service   links   product search   search →

nomad
travel store   www.nomadtravel.co.uk
                                                    request a catalogue   contact us

new store now open
VICTORIA, LONDON SW 1

also at:

52 Grosv enor Gdns, Victoria, London   SW1   020 78 23 58 23
3-4 Wellington Terra   ce, Turnpike La   ne, London   N8   020 88 89 70 14
40 Ber nard Stree t, Russ ell Square, London WC1   020 78 33 41 14
43 Que ens Road, Clifto   n, Bristol BS 8   0117 9 22 65 67

catalo gue : Tel: 020 8889 7014

clothing   equipment   vaccinations
anti-m alarials yellow fever

N⬥ TIME TO PA⬥K?

When disaster or war strike, there is no time to pack your bags.

Every year hundreds of thousands of people in Africa are forced to flee their homes and literally run for their lives.

MEDAIR, specialising in emergency humanitarian aid, provides life-saving care to over 3 million victims of disaster and conflict worldwide, regardless of race, sex, religion or age.

But with MEDAIR it's life that counts, not statistics.

We're committed to making our assistance as personal as possible. That's why our programmes are made to suit individual needs, from healthcare, health education and trauma counselling, to reconstruction, food-distribution and improving water supplies.

*Join us on the frontline
and see how you can help
by visiting www.MEDAIR.org
or e-mailing info@MEDAIR.org.uk*

With thanks to Rough Guides for sponsoring this advertisement.

AFRICA CONFIDENTIAL

Edited by PATRICK SMITH

Highly readable, exciting and challenging, offering you the unique *Africa Confidential* insight and evaluation.

Africa Confidential keeps you up-to-date on current affairs in Africa. Every edition deals with the critical subjects of the day and - when the news demands it – special supplements provide extended coverage of important people, events and areas.

BLACKWELL PUBLISHING
E-MAIL UPDATES

Advance notification of the latest articles in *Africa Confidential* e-mailed directly to your desktop. Join our free e-mail alerting service, and we'll send you journal tables of contents (with links to abstracts) and news of the latest books in your field.

SIGNING UP IS EASY. Simply visit:
www.blackwellpublishing.com/ealerts

◎ Choose which discipline interests you, and we'll send you a message every two weeks

◎ OR select exactly which books and journals you'd like to hear about, and when you'd like to receive your messages.

E-mail alerts are also available for some journals through Blackwell Synergy. For further details, visit: www.blackwell-synergy.com

"Know a crocodile from a piece of wood"
African Proverb

WWW.BLACKWELLPUBLISHING.COM/JOURNALS/AFCO

Journal Customer Services, Blackwell Publishing,
PO Box 1354, 9600 Garsington Road, Oxford, OX4 2XG, UK. Tel: +44 (0) 1865 778315
customerservices@oxon.blackwellpublishing.com

visit our website for contents listings, abstracts, samples, and to subscribe
blackwellpublishing.com

Blackwell
Publishing

Discover **THE GAMBIA**

WITH WEST AFRICAN TOURS

With over 15 years of experience in the provision of tour programs for individuals and groups – why not let West African Tours help you get the most from your visit to The Gambia?

WILDLIFE – CULTURE – FISHING HISTORY – ADVENTURE RIVER CRUISING & MORE!

CALL ANGELA ANDREWS OR PATRICK SOTHERN

TEL: +220 495258/495532
FAX: +220 496118

EMAIL: WATOURS@GAMTEL.GM
WWW.WESTAFRICANTOURS.COM

WEST AFRICAN TOURS